The
Four Translation
New Testament

The Four Translation New Testament

KING JAMES

NEW AMERICAN STANDARD BIBLE

WILLIAMS—IN THE LANGUAGE OF THE PEOPLE

BECK—IN THE LANGUAGE OF TODAY

Printed for
DECISION MAGAZINE
by
WORLD WIDE PUBLICATIONS
1313 Hennepin Avenue
Minneapolis, Minnesota 55403

225.32
I93
1966

PRINTED IN U.S.A.

LIBRARY OF CONGRESS CATALOG CARD NUMBER: 66-15920

Contents

Foreword

There has never been a time when we need to study the Bible more in the light of current events. It was Dwight L. Moody who said, "It is amazing how much light the Scriptures throw on the commentaries!" These new translations, in modern, easy reading, have been prepared by scholars in America who believe that the entire Bible is the Word of God. While the Word of God never changes, with each generation a new language with new words is to be found in our modern day dictionaries. This is why Tyndale, Coverdale and other translators came forth with translations several centuries ago. Many translations have been presented through the years.

Therefore, new translations in the idiom of the day are both desirable and helpful in understanding and presenting the Word of God with clarity in our modern day language.

While the King James Version of the Scriptures has never been surpassed in majestic language, yet we believe that much good can come from studying these other three translations and comparing them with the King James.

We are therefore making available for the first time to our DECISION readers, in addition to the King James, three additional American language translations: THE NEW AMERICAN STANDARD, THE NEW TESTAMENT IN THE LANGUAGE OF THE PEOPLE, and THE NEW TESTAMENT IN THE LANGUAGE OF TODAY. You will be able to study four translations in columns, side by side. This will make a good private study for the Bible student, some interesting reading for family devotions, and will give a new light to the meaning of the original text. It will be easy to make comparative studies since the texts are printed side by side on facing pages.

The modern day translators' preface introduces each of the versions that are presented. We are therefore happy to present to the readers of DECISION Magazine this copy of THE FOUR TRANSLATION NEW TESTAMENT: KING JAMES; NEW AMERICAN STANDARD; WILLIAMS—NEW TESTAMENT IN THE LANGUAGE OF THE PEOPLE; BECK—NEW TESTAMENT IN THE LANGUAGE OF TODAY.

GEO. M. WILSON

The New Testament

OF OUR LORD AND SAVIOUR
JESUS CHRIST

Translated out of the original Greek and with the former
translations diligently compared and revised

Set forth in 1611
And commonly known as the

KING JAMES VERSION

The Epistle Dedicatory

TO THE MOST HIGH *and* MIGHTY PRINCE JAMES *by the Grace of God* KING OF GREAT BRITAIN, FRANCE, *and* IRELAND, DEFENDER OF THE FAITH, &C. *The Translators of this Bible wish Grace, Mercy, and Peace, through* JESUS CHRIST *our Lord*

Great and manifold were the blessings, most dread Sovereign, which Almighty God, the Father of all mercies, bestowed upon us the people of England, when first he sent Your Majesty's Royal Person to rule and reign over us. For whereas it was the expectation of many, who wished not well unto our Sion, that upon the setting of that bright Occidental Star, Queen Elizabeth of most happy memory, some thick and palpable clouds of darkness would so have overshadowed this Land, that men should have been in doubt which way they were to walk; and that it should hardly be known, who was to direct the unsettled State; the appearance of Your Majesty, as of the Sun in his strength, instantly dispelled those supposed and surmised mists, and gave unto all that were well affected exceeding cause of comfort; especially when we beheld the Government established in Your Highness, and Your hopeful Seed, by an undoubted Title, and this also accompanied with peace and tranquillity at home and abroad.

But among all our joys, there was no one that more filled our hearts, than the blessed continuance of the preaching of God's sacred Word among us; which is that inestimable treasure, which excelleth all the riches of the earth; because the fruit thereof extendeth itself, not only to the time spent in this transitory world, but directeth and disposeth men unto that eternal happiness which is above in heaven.

Then not to suffer this to fall to the ground, but rather to take it up, and to continue it in that state, wherein the famous Predecessor of Your Highness did leave it: nay, to go forward with the confidence and resolution of a Man in maintaining the truth of Christ, and propagating it far and near, is that which hath so bound and firmly knit the hearts of all Your Majesty's loyal and religious people unto You, that Your very name is precious among them: their eye doth behold You with comfort, and they bless You in their hearts, as that sanctified Person, who, under God, is the immediate Author of their true happiness. And this their contentment doth not diminish or decay, but every day increaseth and taketh strength, when they observe, that the zeal of Your Majesty toward the house of God doth not slack or go backward, but. is more and more kindled, manifesting itself abroad in the farthest parts of Christendom, by writing in defence of the Truth, (which hath given such a blow unto that man of sin, as will not be healed,) and every day at home, by religious and learned discourse, by frequenting the house of God, by hearing the Word preached, by cherishing the Teachers thereof, by caring for the Church, as a most tender and loving nursing Father.

There are infinite arguments of this right Christian and religious affection in Your Majesty; but none is more forcible to declare it to others than the vehement and perpetuated desire of accomplishing and publishing of this work, which now with all humility we present unto Your Majesty. For when Your Highness had once out of deep judgment apprehended how convenient it was, that out of the Original Sacred Tongues, together with comparing of the labours, both in our own, and other foreign Languages, of many worthy men who went before us, there should be one more exact Translation of the Holy Scriptures into the English Tongue; Your Majesty did never desist to urge and to excite those to whom it was commended, that the work might be hastened, and that the business might be expedited in so decent a manner, as a matter of such importance might justly require.

And now at last, by the mercy of God, and the continuance of our labours, it being brought unto such a conclusion, as that we have great hopes that the Church of England shall reap good fruit thereby; we hold it our duty to offer it to Your Majesty, not only as to our King and Sovereign, but as to the principal Mover and Author of the work: humbly craving of Your most Sacred Majesty, that since things of this quality have ever been subject to the censures of illmeaning and discontented persons, it may receive approbation and patronage from so learned and judicious a Prince as Your Highness is, whose allowance and acceptance of our labours shall more honour and encourage us, than all the calumniations and hard interpretations of other men shall dismay us. So that if, on the one side, we shall be traduced by Popish Persons at home or abroad, who therefore will malign us, because we are poor instruments to make God's holy Truth to be yet more and more known unto the people, whom they desire still to keep in ignorance and darkness; or if, on the other side, we shall be maligned by selfconceited Brethren, who run their own ways, and give liking unto nothing, but what is framed by themselves, and hammered on their anvil; we may rest secure, supported within by the truth and innocency of a good conscience, having walked the ways of simplicity and integrity, as before the Lord; and sustained without by the powerful protection of Your Majesty's grace and favour, which will ever give countenance to honest and Christian endeavours against bitter censures and uncharitable imputations.

The Lord of heaven and earth bless Your Majesty with many and happy days, that, as his heavenly hand hath enriched Your Highness with many singular and extraordinary graces, so You may be the wonder of the world in this latter age for happiness and true felicity, to the honour of that great GOD, and the good of his Church, through Jesus Christ our Lord and only Saviour.

New American Standard Bible New Testament

TEXT EDITION

Scriptural Promise

"The grass withers, the flower fades, but the Word of our God shall stand forever." Isaiah 40:8

Foreword

The New American Standard Bible has been produced with the conviction that the words of Scripture as originally penned in the Hebrew and Greek were inspired by God. Being the eternal Word of God, the Holy Scriptures speak with fresh power to each generation, to give us wisdom that leads to salvation, that we may serve to the glory of Christ.

It has been the purpose of the Editorial Board to present to the modern reader a revision of the American Standard Version in clear and contemporary language. The attempt has been made to adhere to the original languages of the Holy Scriptures as closely as possible and at the same time to obtain a fluent and readable style according to current English usage.

Four-fold Aim

OF

THE LOCKMAN FOUNDATION PUBLICATIONS

1. These publications shall be true to the original Greek.

2. They shall be grammatically correct.

3. They shall be understandable to the masses.

4. They shall give the Lord Jesus Christ His proper place, the place which the Word gives Him, and no work will ever be personalized.

Preface to
The New American Standard Bible
A. D. 1963

The producers of this translation were imbued with the conviction that interest in the American Standard Version should be renewed and increased. They have labored with prayerful seriousness to this end. This great responsibility was assumed only after the need was thoroughly established in the minds of many. That which is forever settled in heaven (Psa. 119:89) must ever be available on earth. Such availability is contingent upon (1) clarity of language in its current understanding and (2) the most appealing form of presentation contemporary facilities afford.

All that exists has a cause from which it springs, and this important undertaking was born of no light impulses. It was inspired and encouraged by wholesome and meaningful reasons. The chief inducement, of course, was the recognized value of the version of 1901 which deserves and demands perpetuation. The following observations are advanced as justifiable encouragement:

1. The American Standard Version of 1901 has been in a very real sense the standard for many translations.
2. It is a monumental product of applied scholarship, assiduous labor and thorough procedure.
3. It has enjoyed universal endorsement as a trustworthy translation of the original text.
4. The British and American organizations were governed by rules of procedure which assured accuracy in the completed work.
5. The American Standard Version, itself a revision of the 1881-1885 edition, is the product of international collaboration, invaluable for perspective, accuracy and finesse.
6. Unlike many modern translations of the Scriptures, the American Standard Version retains its acceptability for pulpit reading and for personal memorization.

Perhaps the most weighty impetus for this undertaking can be attributed to a disturbing awareness that the American Standard Version of 1901 was fast disappearing from the scene. As a generation which knew not Joseph was born, even so a generation unacquainted with this great and important work has come into being. Recognizing a responsibility to posterity, THE LOCKMAN FOUNDATION felt an urgency to rescue this noble achievement from an inevitable demise, to preserve it as a heritage for coming generations, and to do so in such a form as the demands of passing time dictate.

THE FOUNDATION, a corporation not for profit in the State of California, took the initiative in the work of revision, engaging consultants to lay the groundwork for text arrangement, textual revision, linguistic accuracy and editorial finalizing.

1. TEXT ARRANGEMENT: This initial step was taken with caution and concern. Page construction registers the first impression when attention is given to a volume. But appearance is not the only consideration in designing a format of the printed page; utility is a major factor! Whatever tends to make the reading easier and more enjoyable is the desirable design.

2. TEXTUAL REVISION: Words are the vehicle of thought, and most languages, especially the English, have a flexibility which economic and cultural progress utilizes. Passing time with myriads of inventions and innovations automatically renders obsolete and inexpressive words that once were in acceptable usage. The ever-present danger of stripping divine Truth of its dignity and original intent was prominently before the minds of the producers at all times. An editorial board composed of linguists, Greek scholars and pastors undertook the responsibilities of translation and revision.

Principles of Revision

Greek Text: In revising the ASV, consideration was given to the latest available manuscripts with a view to determining the best Greek text. In most instances the 23rd edition of the Nestle Greek New Testament was followed.

Modern English Usage: The attempt has been made to render the grammar and terminology of the ASV in contemporary English. When it was felt that the word-for-word literalness of the ASV was unacceptable to the modern reader, a change was made in the direction of a more current English idiom.

The Appendix to the Old Testament of the 1901 edition listed the particulars in which the 1885 revision differed. The Appendix to the New Testament of the 1901 edition revealed the readings and renderings which appeared in the Revised New Testament of 1881 in place of those preferred by the American New Testament Revision Company.

There has been no attempt in this preface to present illustrations of changes made in the text. This would not only become a rather cumbersome undertaking, but its value would be obviated in that most discerning people have their own favorite proof texts by which they measure the merits and accuracy of new translations.

It is enthusiastically anticipated that the general public will be grateful to learn of the availability, value and need of the New American Standard Bible. It is released with the strong confidence that those who seek a knowledge of the Scriptures will find herein a source of genuine satisfaction for a clear and accurate rendering of divinely-revealed truth.

Editorial Board

The Lockman Foundation

Notes on the Translation of Greek Tenses

1. A careful distinction has been made in the treatment of the Greek aorist tense (usually translated as the English past, "He did") and the Greek imperfect tense (rendered either as English past progressive, "He was doing"; or, if inceptive, as "He *began* to do" or "He started to do"); or else if customary past, as "He used to do." "Began" is italicized if it renders an imperfect tense, in order to distinguish it from the Greek verb for "begin."

2. On the other hand, not all aorists have been rendered as English pasts ("He did"), for some of them are clearly to be rendered as English perfects ("He has done"), or even as past perfects ("He had done"), judging from the context in which they occur. Such aorists have been rendered as perfects or past perfects in this version.

3. As for the distinction between aorist and present imperatives, the Board has usually rendered these imperatives in the customary manner, rather than attempting any such fine distinction as "Begin to do!" (for the aorist imperative) or, "Continually do!" (for the present imperative).

4. As for sequence of tenses, the Board took care to follow English rules rather than Greek in translating Greek presents, imperfects and

aorists. Thus, where English says, "We knew that he was doing," Greek puts it, "We knew that he does"; similarly, "We knew that he had done," is the Greek, "We knew that he did." Likewise, the English, "When he had come, they met him," is represented in Greek by: "When he came, they met him." In all cases a consistent transfer has been made from the Greek tense in the subordinate clause to the appropriate tense in English.

5. In the rendering of negative questions introduced by the particle mē (which always expects the answer, "No") the wording has been altered from a mere, "Will he not do this?" to a more accurate, "He will not do this, will he?"

6. In regard to the use of historical present, the Board recognized that in some contexts the present tense seems more unexpected and unjustified to the English reader than a past tense would have been. But Greek authors frequently used the present tense for the sake of heightened vividness, thereby transporting their readers in imagination to the actual scene at the time of occurrence. However, the Board felt that it would be wise to change these historical presents into English past tenses. Therefore verbs marked with an asterisk (*) represent historical presents in the Greek which have been translated with an English past tense in order to conform to modern usage. (e.g., John 1:38—"Jesus . . . beheld . . . and says" has been changed to "Jesus . . . beheld . . . and *said.")

Explanation of General Format

MARGINAL NOTES AND CROSS REFERENCES have been deleted from this edition. Footnotes are used only where the text requires them for clarification.

QUOTATION MARKS are used in the text in accordance with modern English usage.

PUNCTUATION CHANGES have been made in order to conform with modern practice.

"THOU, THY AND THEE" are changed to "you" except in the language of prayer when addressing Deity.

PERSONAL PRONOUNS are capitalized when pertaining to Deity.

ITALICS are used in the text to indicate words which are not found in the original Greek but implied by it.

SMALL CAPS are used in the text to indicate Old Testament quotes.

SECOND PERSON PRONOUNS are marked "you^s" or "you^pl" when it cannot be determined from the context whether they are singular or plural.

ASTERISK—In regard to the use of historical present, the Board recognized that in some contexts the present tense seems more unexpected and unjustified to the English reader than a past tense would have been. But Greek authors frequently used the present tense for the sake of heightened vividness, thereby transporting their readers in imagination to the actual scene at the time of occurrence. However, the Board felt that it would be wise to change these historical presents into English past tenses. Therefore verbs marked with an asterisk (*) represent historical presents in the Greek which have been translated with an English past tense in order to conform to modern usage. (e.g., John 1:38—"Jesus . . . beheld . . . and says" has been changed to "Jesus . . . beheld . . . and *said.")

The New Testament

IN THE LANGUAGE
OF THE PEOPLE

By

CHARLES B. WILLIAMS

CHICAGO

MOODY PRESS

1963

Publishers' Preface

In the minds of many exacting Greek scholars this is the best translation of the New Testament existing in the English language today. Yet, it is not scholarly at the expense of readability. Instead, it will be found to be especially useful for devotional reading in the family circle as well as for private Bible study. This translation is so lucid that anyone can understand the message, and yet it manifests such genuine scholarship that the most exacting scholar can revel in it. It is unique in its copious and illuminating notes on problem passages.

Many evangelical Christians have wished for a modern, easy-reading translation prepared by a scholar who believes, as they do, that the entire Bible is the Word of God. The publishers are happy to be able to present this volume in answer to that long-felt need. Although there is undoubtedly value in any translation by a competent scholar, there is special value in the reader's knowing that the author is thoroughly acquainted both with the text and also with the spirit of the text.

We find two extremes among private translators. Some have been exactly literal, translating the Greek almost word for word, by-passing the thought that translation is a carrying over of ideas rather than words. As Arthur Way points out in giving his translation of Paul's Epistles and Hebrews, the Authorized and Revised Versions have done just that, thereby serving not one age, but succeeding ages in avoiding paraphrases and explanatory notes that would be limited to a certain time or people. Highest praise is given to both versions for that ageless service. Others have been excessively idiomatic, or unduly free with their use of paraphrase, even to the extent of adding words, phrases, and sentences to aid in clarifying the meaning of the text. In the present volume the translator seeks to avoid these extremes. He adheres faithfully to the sense of the Greek, as well as rendering it into language easily understood by the average reader.

But the most significant contribution in this translation, and the sphere in which it surpasses the majority of others, is in its bringing out the revealing tense distinctions in the Greek verbs. A good example of this is the translation of the future perfect passive tense in Matthew 16:19 and 18:18. Dr. Williams has rendered these verbs correctly, "Whatever you forbid on earth must be what is already forbidden in heaven."

Attempting to convey accurately the thought of the Greek, rather than to translate its single words, Dr. Williams has added explanatory notes at the beginning of each book, and footnotes, to further clarify the meaning.

Although the publishers do not concur with every rendering in this translation, they are grateful for the opportunity of presenting it to fellow Christians around the world.

Foreword

Recently we celebrated the four-hundredth anniversary of the publication of the entire English Bible by Miles Coverdale, the Oxford scholar who first translated the whole Bible into English. The year 1936 was the four-hundredth anniversary of the strangling and burning of William Tyndale, who was condemned to death for translating the New Testament into English and for seeking to put it into the hands of the plain people. In these four centuries scores of other translations have been made. Then why make another? someone asks. A distinguished Bible scholar answers, "Language is a fluid thing. It does not remain fixed for a day. There is therefore constant need of retranslation."

Our aim in publishing this new translation is that of Tyndale, "to cause the plowboy to know the Scriptures." Our aim is to make this greatest book in the world readable and understandable by the plain people. Only three books in the New Testament are written in anything like good literary Greek—Luke, the Acts, and Hebrews. In our translation of these books we have tried to use good, smooth English. Elsewhere we use simple everyday English which reproduces the everyday Greek which the writers used. In accord with this aim we have used practical everyday words to replace many technical religious and theological terms. In other words, we have tried to use the words and phrases that are understandable by the farmer and the fisherman, by the carpenter and the cowboy, by the cobbler and the cab-driver, by the merchant and the miner, by the milkmaid and the house-mistress, by the woodcutter and the trucker. If these can understand it, it is certain that the scholar, the teacher, the minister, the lawyer, the doctor, and all others can.

This is not a word-for-word translation, like an interlinear. It is rather a translation of the thought of the writers with a reproduction of their diction and style. Greek idioms are not brought over into our translation, but are expressed in corresponding English idioms which express the same thoughts as the Greek idioms. It is the thoughts of our New Testament, not its single words, that we have tried to translate.

Our translation is based on the Westcott and Hort Greek text, recognized as the authoritative text throughout the English speaking world. When there are conflicting variations in the Greek Manuscripts, we have generally followed the Vatican Manuscript, which is the oldest and usually conceded the best.

May the face of the Christ, who is the Theme of this book and the Light of the world, shine into the heart and upon the life of everyone who reads it!

CHARLES B. WILLIAMS

The New Testament

IN THE LANGUAGE
OF TODAY

by
WILLIAM F. BECK
(B. A., B. D., M. S. T., Th. D.)

Fifth Printing 1964
Slightly Revised
Concordia Publishing House, St. Louis, Missouri
Concordia Publishing House Ltd., London, W. C. 1
© 1963 Concordia Publishing House
Library of Congress Catalog Card No. 63-8909

Preface

The preservation of our New Testament is a marvel of God's wisdom. It came through fire and sword.

In the persecution of A. D. 303 Emperor Diocletian ordered a systematic search that swept away the Biblical manuscripts from Asia Minor and Syria. The sacred writings were shoveled into carts and hauled to the market places to be burned. The goal was to wipe out Christianity. Later the Goths, Vandals, Moslems, and Mongols did their worst to destroy the Christian faith.

But Jesus had promised, "Heaven and earth will pass away, but what I say will not pass away" (Luke 21:33). How was it done? Not by keeping one original copy in an ark of the covenant which men could destroy but by sending out thousands of manuscripts all over the earth. We have almost 5,000 Greek manuscripts of the New Testament or parts of it plus many thousands of the Latin, Syriac, and other translations. Every manuscript and fragment is a flame of the Spirit's fire appearing in such an inextinguishable quantity everywhere in the world no organized hostility of men can ever put it out.

To match this vast evidence for the truth, God wants us to have a passion for it, to use all the best evidence from the manuscripts, dictionaries, and grammars as light on the text, and to search with burning hearts for its exact meaning.

In recent years two very important papyri, called P[66] and P[75], both from about A. D. 200, have been published. These papyri now provide us with the finest evidence for the following readings:

Luke 22:19-20: "Jesus took bread, gave thanks, broke it, and gave it to them, saying, 'This is My body, which is given for you. Do this to remember Me.' He did the same with the cup when the supper was over, saying, 'This cup is the new covenant in My blood, poured out for you.' "

24:6: "He is not here; He has risen."

40: "He showed them His hands and His feet."

51: "While He was blessing them, He parted from them and was taken up to heaven."

John 1:18: "the only Son who is God"

8:57: "Abraham has seen You?"

Every word in these and other fine manuscripts was carefully checked to make this an accurate New Testament.

And what is the language of the papyri? When Matthew, John, Paul, and the others wrote the New Testament, which language did they use? Not the Hebrew of the Old Testament.

Not the classical Greek of Aristotle and Plato.

Not even the literary Greek of the first century.

But the *everyday Greek* of the people of Jesus' day.

The many papyri that were found are like a tape recording of what people said offguard, at their "coffee and doughnuts." This is the language of the New Testament.

If Jesus came into our home today, how would He talk? Just as we talk to one another. He would take the words out of our lives and put heaven's meaning into them.

This is the most winning way. We see it on Pentecost. Watch the people from many different countries, talking their own dialects, and see the sparkle in their eyes as they are stirred to say, "How does every one of us hear his own language in which he was born? . . . We hear them tell in our languages the wonderful things of God" (Acts 2:8, 11). This is Paul's way—"I would rather say five words that can be understood, in order to teach others, than ten thousand words in a language nobody understands." (1 Cor. 14:19)

Today our language carries a world responsibility. It is written, spoken, broadcast, and understood on every continent. 250 million people use English as their primary language, and 600 million people understand it. It is spreading at an accelerating speed.

Radio and television are bringing the world together, and the closer the world lives the more it will talk our language.

God wants to use our language to talk to the world—before the end! He means to reach every man, woman, and child everywhere. We hold in our hands the doorknob to millions of hearts.

And so this New Testament is in the living language of today and tomorrow. It uses "you" and "don't" and "12 o'clock" and "hurry" and "worry." It says, "Jesus looked at him and loved him." (Mark 10:21)

Let's not feel ashamed of our language. The Father's only Son CAME DOWN to be our flesh, was counted among criminals and considered too shameful to be crucified in the holy city. He did this to take away our sins and give us His glory. And just as He became flesh like ours, so He talked to people in a language that was flesh of their flesh. Today He would talk a language that is direct and forceful—like the prophets; that is fresh and simple—like His telling the lame man, "Get up and walk."

In His Word the Spirit of the living God is talking to us, and His book is the book of life. His vital touch is on every page, in every word. And when we let God speak the living language of today, a reader can instantly get into the spirit of the words to the point where the printed book seems to vanish and he hears the truth fresh from the lips of his God. He reads on and on, delighted with the meaning that shines to light up his way.

When we personally ground everything we believe in His Word, we have God so near, we will not go wrong. We will sharply distinguish what God says from what men say and will know what is true and false, what is right and wrong.

We need a spiritual missile. This is it—the sword of the Word in its unveiled power. As we find in the atom a kind of pure power of God, so we get in His unencumbered Word a pure power that cleanses and creates life.

Let His full power work on you and grip you, and you will feel secure, ready to stand your ground alone, like Jesus answering every challenge with the invincible "It is written."

And so you get the kind of faith with which you can stand strong and free, ready to face anything, a faith that makes you want to tell everybody about it, a certainty that will enable you to say yes even when all the world says no.

Starting with God in His Word, we have a striking power. "Publicly and vigorously Apollos proved the Jews were wrong as he showed them from the Bible Jesus is the promised Savior." (Acts 18:28)

That's the kind of man and woman God wants. That's what the church must have. That's what the world needs desperately.

Note. The New Testament quotes the Old Testament about 1,005 times. In this New Testament such words quoted from the Old Testament are in italics and numbered; see, for example, Matt. 1:23.

The
Four Translation
New Testament

THE GOSPEL
ACCORDING TO
SAINT MATTHEW

1 The book of the generation of Jesus Christ, the son of David, the son of Abraham. 2Abraham begat Isaac; and Isaac begat Jacob; and Jacob begat Judas and his brethren; 3And Judas begat Phares and Zara of Thamar; and Phares begat Esrom; and Esrom begat Aram; 4And Aram begat Aminadab; and Aminadab begat Naasson; and Naasson begat Salmon; 5And Salmon begat Booz of Rachab; and Booz begat Obed of Ruth; and Obed begat Jesse; 6And Jesse begat David the king; and David the king begat Solomon of her *that had been the wife* of Urias; 7And Solomon begat Roboam; and Roboam begat Abia; and Abia begat Asa; 8And Asa begat Josaphat; and Josaphat begat Joram; and Joram begat Ozias; 9And Ozias begat Joatham; and Joatham begat Achaz; and Achaz begat Ezekias; 10And Ezekias begat Manasses; and Manasses begat Amon; and Amon begat Josias; 11And Josias begat Jechonias and his brethren, about the time they were carried away to Babylon: 12And after they were brought to Babylon, Jechonias begat Salathiel; and Salathiel begat Zorobabel; 13And Zorobabel begat Abiud; and Abiud begat Eliakim; and Eliakim begat Azor; 14And Azor begat Sadoc; and Sadoc begat Achim; and Achim begat Eliud; 15And Eliud begat Eleazar; and Eleazar begat Matthan; and Matthan begat Jacob; 16And Jacob begat Joseph the husband of Mary, of whom was born Jesus, who is called Christ. 17 So all the generations from Abraham to David *are* fourteen generations; and from David until the carrying away into Babylon *are* fourteen generations; and from the carrying away into Babylon unto Christ *are* fourteen generations.

18 Now the birth of Jesus Christ was on this wise: When as his mother Mary was espoused to Joseph, before they came together, she was found with child of the Holy Ghost. 19 Then

THE GOSPEL
ACCORDING TO
MATTHEW

1 The book of the genealogy of Jesus Christ, the son of David, the son of Abraham.

2 To Abraham was born Isaac; and to Isaac, Jacob; and to Jacob, aJudah and his brothers; 3 and to Judah were born Perez and Zerah by Tamar; and to Perez was born Hezron; and to Hezron, Ram; 4 and to Ram was born Amminadab; and to Amminadab, Nahshon; and to Nahshon, Salmon; 5 and to Salmon was born Boaz by Rahab; and to Boaz was born Obed by Ruth; and to Obed, Jesse; 6 and to Jesse was born David the king.

And to David was born Solomon by her *who had been the wife* of Uriah; 7 and to Solomon was born Rehoboam; and to Rehoboam, Abijah; and to Abijah, Asa; 8 and to Asa was born Jehoshaphat; and to Jehoshaphat, Joram; and to Joram, Uzziah; 9 and to Uzziah was born Jotham; and to Jotham, Ahaz; and to Ahaz, Hezekiah; 10 and to Hezekiah was born Manasseh; and to Manasseh, Amon; and to Amon, Josiah; 11 and to Josiah were born Jeconiah and his brothers, at the time of the deportation to Babylon.

12 And after the deportation to Babylon, to Jeconiah was born Shealtiel; and to Shealtiel, Zerubbabel; 13 and to Zerubbabel was born Abiud; and to Abiud, Eliakim; and to Eliakim, Azor; 14 and to Azor was born Zadok; and to Zadok, Achim; and to Achim, Eliud; 15 and to Eliud was born Eleazar; and to Eleazar, Matthan; and to Matthan, Jacob; 16 and to Jacob was born Joseph the husband of Mary, by whom was born Jesus, who is called Christ.

17 Therefore all the generations from Abraham to David are fourteen generations; and from David to the deportation to Babylon fourteen generations; and from the deportation to Babylon to *the time of* Christ fourteen generations.

18 Now the birth of Jesus Christ was as follows. When His mother Mary had been betrothed to Joseph, before they came together she was found to be with child by the Holy Spirit. 19And Joseph her husband, being a

[a] Gr., *Judas*. Names of Old Testament characters will be given in their Old Testament form throughout this version.

THE GOOD NEWS
AS IT WAS TOLD BY

MATTHEW

MATTHEW

1 *Jesus' family tree, birth, and name*

The family tree of Jesus Christ, a descendant of David, a descendant of Abraham.

2 Abraham was the father of [a] Isaac, Isaac the father of Jacob, Jacob the father of Judah and his brothers, 3 Judah the father of Perez and Zerah, whose mother was Tamar; Perez the father of Hezron, Hezron the father of Abram, 4 Abram the father of Aminadab, Aminadab the father of Nahshon, Nahshon the father of Salmon, 5 Salmon the father of Boaz, whose mother was Rahab; Boaz the father of Obed, whose mother was Ruth; Obed the father of Jesse, 6 Jesse the father of King David.

David was the father of Solomon, whose mother had been Uriah's wife; 7 Solomon the father of Rehoboam, Rehoboam the father of Abijah, Abijah the father of Asa, 8 Asa the father of Jehoshaphat, Jehoshaphat the father of Joram, Joram the father of Uzziah, 9 Uzziah the father of Jotham, Jotham the father of Ahaz, Ahaz the father of Hezekiah, 10 Hezekiah the father of Manasseh, Manasseh the father of Amon, Amon the father of Josiah, 11 Josiah the father of Jechoniah and his brothers, at the time of the Babylonian Exile.[b]

12 After the Babylonian Exile Jechoniah became the father of Shealtiel, Shealtiel the father of Zerubbabel, 13 Zerubbabel the father of Abiud, Abiud the father of Eliakim, Eliakim the father of Azor, 14 Azor the father of Sadoc, Sadoc the father of Achim, Achim the father of Eliud, 15 Eliud the father of Eliazar, Eliazar the father of Matthan, Matthan the father of Jacob, 16 Jacob the father of Joseph, the husband of Mary, who was the mother of Jesus who is called the Christ.

17 So all the generations from Abraham to David are fourteen, from David to the Babylonian Exile fourteen, from the Babylonian Exile to Christ fourteen.

18 Now the birth of Christ Jesus occurred under these conditions: After His mother, Mary, was engaged to Joseph, but before they had lived together, she was found to be an expectant mother through the influence of the Holy Spirit.[c] 19 But her husband, Joseph, be-

1 This is a record showing how Jesus Christ was a descendant of David and of Abraham.

2 Abraham was the father of Isaac,
Isaac was the father of Jacob,
and Jacob was the father of Judah and his brothers.
3 Judah was the father of Perez and Zerah,
and Tamar was their mother.
Perez was the father of Hezron,
Hezron was the father of Ram,
4 Ram was the father of Aminadab,
Aminadab was the father of Nahshon,
Nahshon was the father of Salmon,
5 and Salmon was the father of Boaz, and Rahab was his mother.
Boaz was the father of Obed, and Ruth was his mother.
Obed was the father of Jesse,
6 and Jesse was the father of King David.
David was the father of Solomon,
and Uriah's wife was his mother.
7 Solomon was the father of Rehoboam,
Rehoboam was the father of Abijah,
Abijah was the father of Asa,
8 Asa was the father of Jehoshaphat,
Jehoshaphat was the father of Joram,
Joram was the father of Uzziah,
9 Uzziah was the father of Jotham,
Jotham was the father of Ahaz,
Ahaz was the father of Hezekiah,
10 Hezekiah was the father of Manasseh,
Manasseh was the father of Amon,
Amon was the father of Josiah,
11 and Josiah was the father of Jechoniah and his brothers when the people were taken away to Babylon. 12 After they had been taken away to Babylon,
Jechoniah was the father of Shealtiel,
Shealtiel was the father of Zerubbabel,
13 Zerubbabel was the father of Abiud,
Abiud was the father of Eliakim,
Eliakim was the father of Azor,
14 Azor was the father of Zadok,
Zadok was the father of Achim,
Achim was the father of Eliud,
15 Eliud was the father of Eleazar,
Eleazar was the father of Matthan,
Matthan was the father of Jacob,
16 and Jacob was the father of Joseph, the husband of Mary; she was the mother of Jesus, who is called Christ.
17 So there are, in all, fourteen generations from Abraham to David, fourteen from David to the Babylonian Captivity, and fourteen from the Babylonian Captivity to Christ.

An Angel Comes to Joseph

18 This is how Jesus Christ was born. His mother Mary had promised Joseph to be his wife. But before they lived together, it was found that she was going to have a child—by the Holy Spirit. 19 Joseph, her husband, was a

[a] Lit., *begot.* [b] Grk., *the removal to B.* [c] Lit., *from* or *out of.*

3

K.J.V.

Joseph her husband, being a just *man*, and not willing to make her a public example, was minded to put her away privily. 20 But while he thought on these things, behold, the angel of the Lord appeared unto him in a dream, saying, Joseph, thou son of David, fear not to take unto thee Mary thy wife: for that which is conceived in her is of the Holy Ghost. 21And she shall bring forth a son, and thou shalt call his name JESUS: for he shall save his people from their sins. 22 Now all this was done, that it might be fulfilled which was spoken of the Lord by the prophet, saying, 23 Behold, a virgin shall be with child, and shall bring forth a son, and they shall call his name Emmanuel, which being interpreted is, God with us. 24 Then Joseph being raised from sleep did as the angel of the Lord had bidden him, and took unto him his wife: 25And knew her not till she had brought forth her firstborn son: and he called his name JESUS.

2 Now when Jesus was born in Bethlehem of Judea in the days of Herod the king, behold, there came wise men from the east to Jerusalem, 2 Saying, Where is he that is born King of the Jews? for we have seen his star in the east, and are come to worship him. 3 When Herod the king had heard *these things*, he was troubled, and all Jerusalem with him. 4And when he had gathered all the chief priests and scribes of the people together, he demanded of them where Christ should be born. 5And they said unto him, In Bethlehem of Judea: for thus it is written by the prophet, 6And thou Bethlehem, *in* the land of Juda, art not the least among the princes of Juda: for out of thee shall come a Governor, that shall rule my people Israel. 7 Then Herod, when he had privily called the wise men, inquired of them diligently what time the star appeared. 8And he sent them to Bethlehem, and said, Go and search diligently for the young child; and when ye have found *him*, bring me word again, that I may come and worship him also. 9 When they had heard the king, they departed; and, lo, the star, which they saw in the east, went before them, till it came and stood over where the young child was. 10 When they saw the star, they rejoiced with exceeding great joy.

11 And when they were come into the house, they saw the young child with Mary his mother, and fell down, and worshipped him: and when they had opened their treasures, they presented unto him gifts; gold, and frankincense, and myrrh. 12And being warned of God in a dream that they should not return to Herod, they departed into their own country another way. 13And when they were departed, behold, the angel of the Lord appeareth to Joseph in a dream, saying, Arise, and take the young child and his mother, and flee into Egypt, and be thou there until I bring thee word: for Herod will seek the young child to destroy him. 14 When he arose, he took the young child and his mother

N.A.S.

righteous man, and not wanting to disgrace her, desired [a]to put her away secretly. 20 But when he had considered this, behold, an angel of the Lord appeared to him in a dream, saying, "Joseph, son of David, do not be afraid to take Mary as your wife; for that which has been [b]conceived in her is of the Holy Spirit. 21 "And she will bear a Son; and you shall call His name Jesus, for it is He who will save His people from their sins." 22 Now all this took place that what was spoken by the Lord through the prophet might be fulfilled, saying, 23 "BEHOLD, THE VIRGIN SHALL BE WITH CHILD, AND SHALL BEAR A SON, AND THEY SHALL CALL HIS NAME IMMANUEL;" which translated means, "GOD WITH US." 24And Joseph arose from his sleep, and did as the angel of the Lord commanded him, and [c]took *her* as his wife; 25 and [d]kept her a virgin until she gave birth to a Son; and he called His name Jesus.

2 Now after Jesus was born in Bethlehem of Judea in the days of Herod the king, behold, [e]magi from the East arrived in Jerusalem, saying, 2 "Where is He who has been born King of the Jews? For we saw His star in the East, and have come to worship Him." 3And when Herod the king heard it, he was troubled, and all Jerusalem with him. 4And gathering together all the chief priests and scribes of the people, he *began* to inquire of them where the Christ was to be born. 5And they said to him, "In Bethlehem of Judea; for so it has been written by the prophet,

6 'AND YOU, BETHLEHEM, LAND OF JUDAH,
   ARE BY NO MEANS LEAST AMONG THE LEADERS OF JUDAH;
   FOR OUT OF YOU SHALL COME FORTH A RULER,
   WHO WILL SHEPHERD MY PEOPLE ISRAEL.' "

7 Then Herod secretly called the magi, and ascertained from them the time the star appeared. 8And he sent them to Bethlehem, and said, "Go and make careful search for the Child; and when you have found *Him*, report to me, that I too may come and worship Him." 9And having heard the king, they went their way; and lo, the star, which they had seen in the East, went on before them, until it came and stood over where the Child was. 10And when they saw the star, they rejoiced exceedingly, with great joy. 11And they came into the house and saw the Child with Mary His mother; and they fell down and worshiped Him; and opening their treasures they presented to Him gifts of gold and frankincense and myrrh. 12And having been warned *by God* in a dream not to return to Herod, they departed for their own country by another way.

13 Now when they had departed, behold, an angel of the Lord *appeared to Joseph in a dream, saying, "Arise and take the Child and His mother, and flee to Egypt, and remain there until I tell you; for Herod is going to search for the Child to destroy Him." 14And he arose and took the Child and His mother by

[a] Or, *to divorce her.* [b] Gr., *begotten.* [c] Or, *took his wife to himself.* [d] Lit., *was not knowing her.* [e] Pronounced may-ji, a caste of wise-men specializing in astrology, medicine and natural science.

4

WILLIAMS

cause he was an upright man and did not want to disgrace her, decided to break the engagement by secretly divorcing her.

20 But just as this thought occurred to him, an angel of the Lord appeared to him in a dream, and said, "Joseph, descendant of David, do not fear to take Mary as your wife, for it is through the influence of the Holy Spirit that she has become an expectant mother. 21And she will have a son, and you must name Him Jesus, for it is He who is to save His people from their sins."

22 Now all this occurred to fulfill what the Lord had said through the prophet:

23 "The virgin will become pregnant and have a son,

And they will call Him Immanuel"—

which means "God with us." 24 So when Joseph awoke from his sleep, he did as the angel of the Lord directed him, and took her as his wife; 25 but he did not live with her as a husband until she had had a son; and he named Him Jesus.

2 *Stargazers come to worship the baby king; King Herod, disturbed, slaughters all the boy babies; Joseph flees to Egypt to save the baby Jesus; back at Nazareth*

Now when Jesus was born at Bethlehem in Judea in the days of King Herod, stargazers came from the East to Jerusalem 2 and asked, "Where is He that is born King of the Jews? We saw His star when it rose and have come to worship Him."

3 Now when King Herod heard of it, he was disturbed, and all Jerusalem with him. 4 So he called together all the high priests and scribes of the people, and anxiously asked them where the Christ was to be born. 5 They told him, "At Bethlehem in Judea, for this is what the prophet wrote:

6 'And you, Bethlehem in Judah's land,
You are not at all the least among the leading places of Judah;
For out of you will come a ruler,
Who will shepherd my people Israel.' "

7 Then Herod secretly sent for the stargazers, and found out from them exactly the time the star appeared. 8 So he sent them to Bethlehem with this order, "Go and carefully search for the child, and when you find Him, bring back word to me, that I too may come and do Him homage."

9 After listening to the king, they started on their journey, and the star which they had seen rise led them on until it came and stopped over the place where the child was. 10 When they saw the star, they were thrilled with ecstatic joy, 11 and went into the house and saw the child with His mother, Mary; and they fell at His feet and worshiped Him. They opened up their treasure sacks and presented Him with gifts of gold, frankincense, and myrrh. 12 Then, as they had been divinely warned in a dream not to return to Herod, they set out to their own country by another route.

13 After they had gone, an angel of the Lord appeared to Joseph in a dream and said, "Wake up! Tenderly take the child and His mother, and escape to Egypt; stay there until I further direct you, for Herod is going to search for the child to destroy Him."

14 Then he awoke and tenderly took the child and His mother by night and made their

BECK

good man and didn't want to disgrace her. So he decided to divorce her secretly.

20 After he thought about it, he in a dream saw the Lord's angel, who said, "Joseph, son of David, don't be afraid to take your wife Mary home with you; her Child is from the Holy Spirit. 21 She will have a Son, and you will call Him Jesus, because He will save His people from their sins. 22All this happened so that what the Lord said through the prophet would come true: 23 *The virgin will conceive and have a Son, and He will be called Immanuel,"* 1 which means God-with-us.

24 When Joseph awoke, he did what the Lord's angel had ordered him to do. He took his wife home with him 25 but didn't live with her as a husband till she had a Son. And he called Him Jesus.

The Wise Men

2 Jesus was born in Bethlehem in Judea when Herod was king. Then Wise Men came from the east to Jerusalem. 2 "Where is the Child who was born King of the Jews?" they asked. "We saw His star rise and have come to worship Him."

3 When King Herod heard about this, he became alarmed and all Jerusalem with him. 4 He called together all of the people's ruling priests and men trained in the Bible and tried to find out from them where the promised Savior was to be born.

5 "In Bethlehem, in Judea," they told him, "because the prophet has written: 6*And you, Bethlehem,* land of Judah, *are* not at all *the least among the leading towns of Judah, since from you will come a leader who will be the Shepherd of My people Israel."* 2

7 Then Herod secretly called the Wise Men and found out from them the exact time the star appeared. 8 Then he sent them to Bethlehem. "Go and search carefully for the little Child," he said. "And when you find Him, report to me, so that I too may go and bow down before Him."

9 After hearing the king, they started out. And there was the star they had seen when it rose! It led them on till it came to a stop over the place where the Child was. 10 They were extremely happy to see the star. 11 They went into the house and saw the little Child with His mother Mary. Kneeling, they worshiped Him. Then they opened their treasure chests and offered Him gifts: *gold, incense,*3 and myrrh.

12 But God warned them in a dream not to go back to Herod. So they went home to their country by another road.

To Egypt!

13 After the Wise Men left, Joseph in a dream saw the Lord's angel, who said, "Get up, take the little Child and His mother, and flee to Egypt. Stay there till I tell you. Herod is going to search for the Child to kill Him."

14 Joseph got up at night, took the little Child

[1] Is. 7:14; 8:8, 10
[2] Micah 5:2, 4; 2 Sam. 5:2
[3] Is. 60:6; Ps. 72:10, 15

5

K.J.V.

by night, and departed into Egypt: 15And was there until the death of Herod: that it might be fulfilled which was spoken of the Lord by the prophet, saying, Out of Egypt have I called my son.

16 Then Herod, when he saw that he was mocked of the wise men, was exceeding wroth, and sent forth, and slew all the children that were in Bethlehem, and in all the coasts thereof, from two years old and under, according to the time which he had diligently inquired of the wise men. 17 Then was fulfilled that which was spoken by Jeremy the prophet, saying, 18 In Rama was there a voice heard, lamentation, and weeping, and great mourning, Rachel weeping for her children, and would not be comforted, because they are not.

19 But when Herod was dead, behold, an angel of the Lord appeareth in a dream to Joseph in Egypt, 20 Saying, Arise, and take the young child and his mother, and go into the land of Israel: for they are dead which sought the young child's life. 21And he arose, and took the young child and his mother, and came into the land of Israel. 22 But when he heard that Archelaus did reign in Judea in the room of his father Herod, he was afraid to go thither: notwithstanding, being warned of God in a dream, he turned aside into the parts of Galilee: 23And he came and dwelt in a city called Nazareth: that it might be fulfilled which was spoken by the prophets, He shall be called a Nazarene.

3 In those days came John the Baptist, preaching in the wilderness of Judea, 2And saying, Repent ye: for the kingdom of heaven is at hand. 3 For this is he that was spoken of by the prophet Esaias, saying, The voice of one crying in the wilderness, Prepare ye the way of the Lord, make his paths straight. 4And the same John had his raiment of camel's hair, and a leathern girdle about his loins; and his meat was locusts and wild honey. 5 Then went out to him Jerusalem, and all Judea, and all the region round about Jordan, 6And were baptized of him in Jordan, confessing their sins.

7 But when he saw many of the Pharisees and Sadducees come to his baptism, he said unto them, O generation of vipers, who hath warned you to flee from the wrath to come? 8 Bring forth therefore fruits meet for repentance: 9And think not to say within yourselves, We have Abraham to our father: for I say unto you, that God is able of these stones to raise up children unto Abraham. 10And now also the axe is laid unto the root of the trees: therefore every tree which bringeth not forth good fruit is hewn down, and cast into the fire. 11 I indeed baptize you with water unto repentance: but he that cometh after me is mightier than I, whose shoes I am not worthy to bear: he shall baptize you with the Holy Ghost, and with fire: 12 Whose

N.A.S.

night, and departed for Egypt; 15 and was there until the death of Herod; that what was spoken by the Lord through the prophet might be fulfilled, saying, "OUT OF EGYPT DID I CALL MY SON."

16 Then when Herod saw that he had been tricked by the magi, he became very enraged, and sent and slew all the male children who were in Bethlehem and in all its environs, from two years old and under, according to the time which he had ascertained from the magi. 17 Then that which was spoken through Jeremiah the prophet was fulfilled, saying,

18 "A VOICE WAS HEARD IN RAMAH,
WEEPING AND GREAT MOURNING,
RACHEL WEEPING FOR HER CHILDREN;
AND SHE REFUSED TO BE COMFORTED,
BECAUSE THEY WERE NO MORE."

19 But when Herod was dead, behold, an angel of the Lord *appeared in a dream to Joseph in Egypt, saying, 20 "Arise and take the Child and His mother, and go into the land of Israel; for those who sought the Child's life are dead." 21And he arose and took the Child and His mother, and came into the land of Israel. 22 But when he heard that Archelaus was reigning over Judea in place of his father Herod, he was afraid to go there; and being warned by God in a dream, he departed for the regions of Galilee, 23 and came and resided in a city called Nazareth; that what was spoken through the prophets might be fulfilled, "He shall be called a Nazarene."

3 Now in those days John the Baptist *came, preaching in the wilderness of Judea, saying, 2 "Repent, for the kingdom of heaven is at hand." 3 For this is the one referred to by Isaiah the prophet, saying,
"THE VOICE OF ONE CRYING IN THE WILDERNESS,
'MAKE READY THE WAY OF THE LORD,
MAKE HIS PATHS STRAIGHT!' "
4 Now John himself had a garment of camel's hair, and a leather belt about his waist; and his food was locusts and wild honey. 5 Then Jerusalem was going out to him, and all Judea, and all the district around the Jordan; 6 and they were being baptized by him in the Jordan River, as they confessed their sins. 7 But when he saw many of the Pharisees and Sadducees coming for baptism, he said to them, "You brood of vipers, who warned you to flee from the wrath to come? 8 "Therefore bring forth fruit in keeping with your repentance; 9 and do not suppose that you can say to yourselves, 'We have Abraham for our father;' for I say to you, that God is able from these stones to raise up children to Abraham. 10 "And the axe is already laid at the root of the trees; every tree therefore that does not bear good fruit is cut down, and thrown into the fire. 11 "As for me, I baptize you [a]in water for repentance; but He who is coming after me is mightier than I, and I am not even fit to remove His sandals; He Himself will baptize you with the Holy Spirit and fire. 12 "And His winnowing fork is in His hand, and

[a] The Greek here can be translated in, with or by.

WILLIAMS

escape to Egypt; 15 he stayed there until Herod's death, so as to fulfill what the Lord had said by the prophet, "Out of Egypt I called my Son."

16 Then Herod, because he saw that a trick had been played on him by the stargazers, was very angry, and sent and slaughtered all the boy babies in Bethlehem and in all that neighborhood, from two years down, in accordance with the time which he had found out from the stargazers. 17 Then the saying was fulfilled which was spoken by the prophet Jeremiah:

18 "A sob was heard in Ramah,
Weeping and great wailing,
Rachel weeping for her children,
And she refused to be comforted, because
    they were gone."

19 But after Herod died, an angel of the Lord in a dream appeared to Joseph in Egypt, 20 and said, "Wake up, tenderly take the child and His mother, and make the trip to the land of Israel, for those who sought the child's life are dead."

21 Then he awoke, tenderly took the child and His mother, and made the trip to the land of Israel. 22 But because he heard that Archelaus was ruling over Judea in the place of his father, Herod, he was afraid to go there; and because he was divinely warned in a dream, he set out for the region of Galilee. 23 He went to a town called Nazareth and made his home there, so that the saying of the prophet was fulfilled:

"He shall be called a Nazarene."

3 *John preaches repentance and baptizes people who confess their sins; Jesus is baptized and heaven endorses Him as the Christ*

In those days John the Baptist appeared, and kept preaching in the desert of Judea, 2 and saying, "Repent! for the kingdom of heaven is near."

This is he who was mentioned by the prophet Isaiah, when he said:

"Here is a voice of one who shouts in the desert,
'Get the road ready for the Lord;
Make the paths straight for him.'"

4 This very John had his clothing made of camel's hair, and wore a leather belt around his waist; his food was dried locusts and wild honey.

5 Then Jerusalem and all Judea, even the whole Jordan district, continued to go out to him 6 and were baptized by him in the Jordan River, as one by one they continued to confess their sins. 7 But when he saw many of the Pharisees and Sadducees coming for baptism, he said to them, "You brood of vipers, who warned you to escape from the wrath that is coming? 8 Produce, then, fruit that is consistent with the repentance you profess, 9 and do not presume to say to yourselves, 'We have Abraham for our forefather!' for I tell you, God can raise up descendants for Abraham even out of these stones. 10 Now the axe is already lying at the roots of the trees. Every tree then that fails to bear good fruit is to be cut down and thrown into the fire. 11 I am baptizing you in water to picture your repentance. But He that is coming after me is stronger than I am, and I am not fit to carry His shoes. He will baptize you in the Holy Spirit and in fire; 12 His winnowing-fork

BECK

and His mother, and went to Egypt. 15 He stayed there till Herod died. In this way what the Lord said through the prophet was to come true: *I called My Son from Egypt.*[4]

16 When Herod saw that the Wise Men had tricked him, he got very angry and sent men to kill all the boys in Bethlehem and in all the country around it, up to two years old, according to the exact time he had found out from the Wise Men. 17 Then what the prophet Jeremiah said came true:

18 *A cry is heard in Rama!*
Weeping and bitter wailing:
Rachel crying over her children,
And refusing to be comforted
    Because they are gone.[5]

19 But when Herod died, the Lord's angel appeared to Joseph in Egypt in a dream 20 and told him, "Get up, take the little Child and His mother, and go to the land of Israel. Those who tried to kill the little Child are dead."

21 Joseph got up, took the little Child and His mother, and came to the land of Israel. 22 But when he heard, "Archelaus has succeeded his father Herod as king of Judea," he was afraid to go back there. And being warned in a dream, he went to Galilee. 23 He came and made his home in a town by the name of Nazareth. And so what the prophets said came true: Jesus was to be called a man from Nazareth.*

John Prepares the Way

3 The time came when John the Baptizer appeared in the wilderness of Judea and preached: 2 "Repent—the kingdom of heaven is near." 3 He was the one of whom the prophet Isaiah said:

Someone will be calling in the wilderness,
"Prepare the way for the Lord,
Make the paths straight for Him."[6]

4 John wore clothes of camel's hair and a leather belt around his waist. And he lived on grasshoppers and wild honey.

5 Then Jerusalem, all Judea, and the whole Jordan valley came out to him. 6 As they confessed their sins, he baptized them in the Jordan River.

7 He also saw many Pharisees and Sadducees coming for baptism. "Brood of snakes, who warned you to run away from the punishment waiting for you?" he asked them. 8 "Do the works that show you have repented. 9 Don't think you can tell yourselves, 'Abraham is our father.' I tell you, God can raise children for Abraham from these stones. 10 The ax is now ready to strike at the roots of the trees, and any tree that doesn't produce good fruit will be cut down and thrown into the fire. 11 I baptize you with water for a change of heart. But the One who is coming after me is mightier than I. I'm not good enough to carry away His shoes. He will baptize you with the Holy Spirit and fire. 12 He has the winnowing shovel in His hand

---

* According to Is. 11:1 the Savior would be a Nezer, a sprout, growing from the roots of the tree of David.
[4] Hos. 11:1
[5] Jer. 31:15
[6] Is. 40:3

K.J.V.

fan *is* in his hand, and he will thoroughly purge his floor, and gather his wheat into the garner; but he will burn up the chaff with unquenchable fire.

13 Then cometh Jesus from Galilee to Jordan unto John, to be baptized of him. 14 But John forbade him, saying, I have need to be baptized of thee, and comest thou to me? 15And Jesus answering said unto him, Suffer *it to be so* now: for thus it becometh us to fulfil all righteousness. Then he suffered him. 16And Jesus, when he was baptized, went up straightway out of the water: and, lo, the heavens were opened unto him, and he saw the Spirit of God descending like a dove, and lighting upon him: 17And lo a voice from heaven, saying, This is my beloved Son, in whom I am well pleased.

4 Then was Jesus led up of the Spirit into the wilderness to be tempted of the devil. 2And when he had fasted forty days and forty nights, he was afterward a hungered. 3And when the tempter came to him, he said, If thou be the Son of God, command that these stones be made bread. 4 But he answered and said, It is written, Man shall not live by bread alone, but by every word that proceedeth out of the mouth of God. 5 Then the devil taketh him up into the holy city, and setteth him on a pinnacle of the temple, 6And saith unto him, If thou be the Son of God, cast thyself down: for it is written, He shall give his angels charge concerning thee: and in *their* hands they shall bear thee up, lest at any time thou dash thy foot against a stone. 7 Jesus said unto him, It is written again, Thou shalt not tempt the Lord thy God. 8Again, the devil taketh him up into an exceeding high mountain, and sheweth him all the kingdoms of the world, and the glory of them; 9And saith unto him, All these things will I give thee, if thou wilt fall down and worship me. 10 Then saith Jesus unto him, Get thee hence, Satan: for it is written, Thou shalt worship the Lord thy God, and him only shalt thou serve. 11 Then the devil leaveth him, and, behold, angels came and ministered unto him.

12 Now when Jesus had heard that John was cast into prison, he departed into Galilee; 13And leaving Nazareth, he came and dwelt in Capernaum, which is upon the sea coast, in the borders of Zabulon and Nephthalim: 14That it might be fulfilled which was spoken by Esaias the prophet, saying, 15 The land of Zabulon, and the land of Nephthalim, *by* the way of the sea, beyond Jordan, Galilee of the Gentiles; 16 The people which sat in darkness saw great light; and to them which sat in the region and shadow of death light is sprung up.

17 From that time Jesus began to preach, and to say, Repent: for the kingdom of heaven is at hand.

N.A.S.

He will thoroughly clean His threshing-floor; and He will gather His wheat into the barn, but He will burn up the chaff with unquenchable fire."

13 Then Jesus *arrived from Galilee at the Jordan *coming* to John, to be baptized by him. 14 But John tried to prevent Him, saying, "I have need to be baptized by You, and do You come to me?" 15 But Jesus answering said to him, "Permit *it* at this time; for in this way it is fitting for us to fulfill all righteousness." Then he *permitted Him. 16And after being baptized, Jesus went up immediately from the water; and behold, the heavens were opened, and he saw the Spirit of God descending as a dove, *and* coming upon Him; 17 and behold, a voice out of the heavens, saying, "This is [a]My beloved Son, in whom I am well pleased."

4 Then Jesus was led up by the Spirit into the wilderness to be tempted by the devil. 2And after He had fasted forty days and forty nights, He [b]then became hungry. 3And the tempter came and said to Him, "If You are the Son of God, command that these stones become bread." 4 But He answered and said, "It is written, 'MAN SHALL NOT LIVE ON BREAD ALONE, BUT ON EVERY WORD THAT PROCEEDS OUT OF THE MOUTH OF GOD.'" 5 Then the devil *took Him into the holy city; and he stood Him on the pinnacle of the temple, 6 and *said to Him, "If You are the Son of God throw Yourself down; for it is written,

'HE WILL GIVE HIS ANGELS CHARGE CONCERN-
ING YOU;

AND ON THEIR HANDS THEY WILL BEAR YOU UP,
LEST YOU STRIKE YOUR FOOT AGAINST A
STONE.'"

7 Jesus said to him, "On the other hand, it is written, 'YOU SHALL NOT [c]TEMPT THE LORD YOUR GOD.'" 8Again, the devil *took Him to a very high mountain, and *showed Him all the kingdoms of the world, and their glory; 9 and he said to Him, "All these things will I give You, if You fall down and worship me." 10 Then Jesus *said to him, "Begone, Satan! For it is written, 'YOU SHALL WORSHIP THE LORD YOUR GOD, AND SERVE HIM ONLY.'" 11 Then the devil *left Him; and behold, angels came and *began* to minister to Him.

12 Now when He heard that John had been taken into custody, He withdrew into Galilee; 13 and leaving Nazareth, He came and settled in Capernaum, which is by the sea, in the region of Zebulun and Naphtali. 14 *This was* to fulfill what was spoken through Isaiah the prophet, saying,

15 "THE LAND OF ZEBULUN AND THE LAND OF
NAPHTALI,

BY THE WAY OF THE SEA, BEYOND THE JORDAN,
GALILEE OF THE [d]GENTILES.

16 "THE PEOPLE WHO WERE SITTING IN DARK-
NESS SAW A GREAT LIGHT,

AND TO THOSE WHO WERE SITTING IN THE
LAND AND SHADOW OF DEATH,

UPON THEM A LIGHT DAWNED."

17 From that time Jesus began to preach and say, "Repent; for the kingdom of heaven is at hand."

[a] Lit., *My son, the Beloved.* [b] Lit., *later, afterward.* [c] Or, *put to the test.* [d] Or, *nations.*

WILLIAMS

is in His hand, and He will clean out His threshing-floor and store His wheat in His barn, but He will burn up the chaff with fire that never can be put out."

13 Then Jesus came from Galilee to the Jordan to John to be baptized by him. 14 But John tried to prevent Him by saying, "I have need to be baptized by you, and you come to me!"

15 But Jesus answered him, "Let it be so now, for this is the fitting way for both of us to do our full duty to God." [a]

Then he yielded to Him. 16And as soon as Jesus was baptized, He at once went up out of the water, and look! the heavens opened, and John saw the Spirit of God coming down like a dove upon Him, 17 and a voice from heaven said, "This is my Son, my Beloved, in whom I am delighted!"

4 *Jesus tempted by the devil; makes Capernaum headquarters; calls four fishermen to His service*

Then Jesus was guided by the Spirit into the desert, to be tempted by the devil. 2After fasting forty days and forty nights, He at last felt hungry. 3And the tempter came up and said to Him, "If you are God's Son, order these stones to turn to bread."

4 But He answered, "The Scripture says, 'Not on bread alone can man live, but on every word that comes from the mouth of God.' "

5 Then the devil took Him into the holy city, and had Him stand on the tip-top turret of the temple, 6 and said to Him, "If you are God's Son, throw yourself down, for the Scripture says:

"'He will give His angels directions about you,
And they will bear you up on their hands,
So you will never strike your foot against a stone.' "

7 Jesus said to him, "Again the Scripture says, 'You must not try the Lord your God.' "

8 Again the devil took Him up on a very high mountain, and showed Him all the kingdoms of the world, and their splendor, 9 and said to Him, "Every bit of this I will give to you, if you will fall on your knees and worship me."

10 Then Jesus said to him, "Begone, Satan! For the Scripture says, 'You must worship the Lord your God, and serve Him alone.' "

11 Then the devil left Him, and angels came and continued to wait upon Him.

12 Now when Jesus heard that John had been arrested, He set out for Galilee. 13 But He left Nazareth and made His home in Capernaum, by the sea, in the district of Zebulon and Naphtali, 14 to fulfill what was spoken by the prophet Isaiah:

15 "Land of Zebulon and land of Naphtali
On the road to the sea, across the Jordan,
Galilee of the nations;
16 The people that were living in darkness
Have seen a great light,
And on those that were living in the land of the shadow of death
A light has dawned."

17 From that time Jesus continued to preach and say, "Repent! for the kingdom of heaven is near."

[a] Grk., *to fulfill all righteousness.*

BECK

and will clean up His threshing floor. His wheat He'll gather into His barn, but the chaff He'll burn in a fire that can't be put out."

John Baptizes Jesus

13 Then Jesus came from Galilee to John at the Jordan to be baptized by him. 14 John tried to stop Him. "I need to be baptized by You," he said, "and You come to me?"

15 "Let Me have My way now," Jesus answered him. "That is how we should accomplish every righteous purpose." Then John gave in to Him. 16As soon as Jesus was baptized, He stepped out of the water, and now heaven was opened, and He saw God's Spirit coming down on Him as a dove. 17And a voice from heaven said, "This is *My Son,* whom I love and *delight in.*" [7]

The Devil Tempts Jesus

4 Then the Spirit led Jesus into the wilderness to be tempted by the devil. 2 He didn't eat anything for forty days and then got hungry. 3 The tempter came to Him. "If You're God's Son," he said to Him, "tell these stones to become loaves of bread."

4 "It is written," Jesus answered, "*A man doesn't live on bread alone but on every word that God speaks.*" [8]

5 Then the devil took Him into the Holy City and had Him stand on the edge of the temple. 6 "If You're God's Son," he told Him, "jump down. It is written: *He will order His angels to help you. They will carry you in their hands and never let you stub your foot against a stone.*" [9]

7 "It is also written," Jesus answered him, "*Don't test the Lord your God.*" [10]

8 Then the devil took Him to a very high mountain and showed Him all the kingdoms in the world and their glory. 9 "All this I'll give You," the devil told Him, "if You'll bow down and worship me."

10 Then Jesus answered him, "Go away, devil! It is written: Worship *the Lord your God, and serve Him* [11] *only.*"

11 Then the devil left Him, and angels came and served Him.

At Home in Capernaum

12 When Jesus heard John had been put in prison, He went back to Galilee. 13 Leaving Nazareth, He went and made His home in Capernaum by the lake, in the area of Zebulun and Naphtali. 14And so what the prophet Isaiah said was to come true:

15 *Land of Zebulun and land of Naphtali,
The way to the sea, across the Jordan,
Galilee of the Gentiles!*
16 *The people sitting in the dark will see a great light.
For those sitting in the land of the shadow of death a light will rise.* [12]

17 Then Jesus began to preach: "Repent— the kingdom of heaven is here!"

[7] Ps. 2:7; Is. 42:1
[8] Deut. 8:3
[9] Ps. 91:11-12
[10] Deut. 6:16
[11] Deut. 6:13
[12] Is. 9:1-2

K.J.V.

18 And Jesus, walking by the sea of Galilee, saw two brethren, Simon called Peter, and Andrew his brother, casting a net into the sea: for they were fishers. 19And he saith unto them, Follow me, and I will make you fishers of men. 20And they straightway left *their* nets, and followed him. 21And going on from thence, he saw other two brethren, James *the son* of Zebedee, and John his brother, in a ship with Zebedee their father, mending their nets; and he called them. 22And they immediately left the ship and their father, and followed him.

23 And Jesus went about all Galilee, teaching in their synagogues, and preaching the gospel of the kingdom, and healing all manner of sickness and all manner of disease among the people. 24And his fame went throughout all Syria: and they brought unto him all sick people that were taken with divers diseases and torments, and those which were possessed with devils, and those which were lunatic, and those that had the palsy; and he healed them. 25And there followed him great multitudes of people from Galilee, and *from* Decapolis, and *from* Jerusalem, and *from* Judea, and *from* beyond Jordan.

5 And seeing the multitudes, he went up into a mountain: and when he was set, his disciples came unto him: 2And he opened his mouth, and taught them, saying, 3 Blessed *are* the poor in spirit: for theirs is the kingdom of heaven. 4 Blessed *are* they that mourn: for they shall be comforted. 5 Blessed *are* the meek: for they shall inherit the earth. 6 Blessed *are* they which do hunger and thirst after righteousness: for they shall be filled. 7 Blessed *are* the merciful: for they shall obtain mercy. 8 Blessed *are* the pure in heart: for they shall see God. 9 Blessed *are* the peacemakers: for they shall be called the children of God. 10 Blessed *are* they which are persecuted for righteousness' sake: for theirs is the kingdom of heaven. 11 Blessed are ye, when *men* shall revile you, and persecute *you*, and shall say all manner of evil against you falsely, for my sake. 12 Rejoice, and be exceeding glad: for great *is* your reward in heaven: for so persecuted they the prophets which were before you.

13 Ye are the salt of the earth: but if the salt have lost his savour, wherewith shall it be salted? It is thenceforth good for nothing, but to be cast out, and to be trodden under foot of men. 14 Ye are the light of the world. A city that is set on a hill cannot be hid. 15 Neither do men light a candle, and put it under a bushel, but on a candlestick; and it giveth light unto

N.A.S.

18 And walking by the sea of Galilee, He saw two brothers, Simon who was called Peter, and Andrew his brother, casting a net into the sea; for they were fishermen. 19And He *said to them, "Follow Me, and I will make you fishers of men." 20And they immediately left the nets, and followed Him. 21And going on from there He saw two other brothers, James the *son* of Zebedee, and John his brother, in the boat with Zebedee their father, mending their nets; and He called them. 22And they immediately left the boat and their father, and followed Him.

23 And *Jesus* was going about in all Galilee, teaching in their synagogues, and proclaiming the gospel of the kingdom, and healing every kind of disease and every kind of sickness among the people. 24And the news about Him went out into all Syria; and they brought to Him all who were ill, taken with various diseases and pains, demoniacs, epileptics, paralytics; and He healed them. 25And great multitudes followed Him from Galilee and Decapolis and Jerusalem and Judea and *from* beyond the Jordan.

5 And when He saw the multitudes, He went up on the mountain; and after He sat down, His disciples came to Him. 2And opening His mouth He *began* to teach them, saying,

3 "Blessed are the poor in spirit, for theirs is the kingdom of heaven.

4 "Blessed are those who mourn, for they shall be comforted.

5 "Blessed are the ᵃhumble, for they shall inherit the earth.

6 "Blessed are those who hunger and thirst for righteousness, for they shall be satisfied.

7 "Blessed are the merciful, for they shall receive mercy.

8 "Blessed are the pure in heart, for they shall see God.

9 "Blessed are the peacemakers, for they shall be called sons of God.

10 "Blessed are those who have been persecuted for the sake of righteousness, for theirs is the kingdom of heaven. 11 "Blessed are you when *men* revile you, and persecute you, and say all kinds of evil against you falsely, on account of Me. 12 "Rejoice, and be glad, for your reward in heaven is great, for so they persecuted the prophets who were before you. 13 "You are the salt of the earth; but if the salt has become tasteless, how will it be made salty *again*? It is good for nothing any more, except to be thrown out and trampled under foot by men. 14 "You are the light of the world. A city set on a hill cannot be hidden. 15 "Nor do *men* light a lamp, and put it under the peck-measure, but on the lampstand; and it gives light to all who are in

[a] Or, *gentle, meek.*

WILLIAMS

18 As He was walking by the shore of the sea of Galilee, He saw two brothers, Simon who was surnamed Peter, and his brother Andrew, casting a net into the sea, for they were fishermen. 19 He said to them, "Come! Follow me, and I will make you fishermen for catching men."

20 And at once they left the nets and followed Him. 21 And as He was going on from that point, He saw two others, brothers, James, the Son of Zebedee, and his brother John, in the boat with their father Zebedee, getting their nets in order; and He called them. 22 And at once they left the boat and their father, and followed Him.

23 Then He went all over Galilee, as He continued teaching in their synagogues, preaching the good news of the kingdom, and curing any disease or malady among the people. 24 So the news about Him spread all over Syria, and people brought to Him all who were sick with various diseases, especially those who were suffering with torturing diseases; and he cured them. 25 So great crowds followed Him, from Galilee and Decapolis, from Jerusalem and Judea, and from the other side of the Jordan.

5 *The Address on the Mount*

When He saw the crowds, He went up on the mountain. After He had taken His seat, His disciples came up to Him. 2 Then He opened His mouth and continued to teach them as follows:

3 "Blessed are those who feel poor in spiritual things, for the kingdom of heaven belongs to them.

4 "Blessed are the mourners, for they will be comforted.

5 "Blessed are the lowly in mind, for they will possess the land.

6 "Blessed are those who hunger and thirst for being and doing right, for they will be completely satisfied.

7 "Blessed are those who show mercy, for they will have mercy shown them.

8 "Blessed are the pure in heart, for they will see God.

9 "Blessed are the peacemakers, for they will be called God's sons.

10 "Blessed are those who suffer persecution for being and doing right, for the kingdom of heaven belongs to them.

11 "Blessed are you when people abuse you, and persecute you, and keep on falsely telling all sorts of evil against you for my sake. 12 Keep on rejoicing and leaping for ecstasy, for your reward will be rich in heaven; for this is the way they persecuted the prophets who lived before you.

13 "You are the salt of the earth. But if salt loses its strength, what can make it salt again? It is good for nothing but to be thrown away and trodden under foot. 14 You are the light of the world. A city that is built upon a hill cannot be hidden. 15 People do not light a lamp and put it under a peck-measure but on a lampstand, and it gives light to all that are in the

BECK

"Come with Me"

18 As He was walking along the shore of the Lake of Galilee, He saw two brothers, Simon, also called Peter, and his brother Andrew (who were fishermen), casting a net into the lake. 19 "Come, follow Me," Jesus told them, "and I will make you fishers of men." 20 Immediately they left their nets and followed Him.

21 He went on and saw two other brothers, James, Zebedee's son, and his brother John. They were in their boat with their father Zebedee, mending their nets. He called them, 22 and immediately they left the boat and their father and followed Him.

Preaching in Galilee

23 Then He went around everywhere in Galilee, teaching in their synagogs, preaching the good news of the Kingdom, and healing every kind of disease and sickness among the people.

24 The news about Him spread all over Syria. And the people brought to Him all who were suffering from various diseases and were in great pain, those who were plagued by devils, the epileptics, and the paralyzed, and He made them well. 25 Large crowds followed Him from Galilee, the Ten-Towns, Jerusalem, Judea, and the other side of the Jordan.

Happy People

5 When Jesus saw the crowds, He went up the hill. And when He sat down, His disciples came to Him. 2 Then He began to teach them:

3 "Happy are those who are *poor in spirit*[13]— they have the kingdom of heaven.

4 Happy are *those who mourn*— they will *be comforted*.[14]

5 Happy are *those who are gentle*— they *will own the land*.[15]

6 Happy are those who hunger and thirst to be righteous— they will be satisfied.

7 Happy are *those who are merciful*— *they will find mercy*.[16]

8 Happy are *those whose hearts are pure*[17]— they will see God.

9 Happy are those who make peace— they will be called God's sons.

10 Happy are those who are persecuted for doing right— they have the kingdom of heaven.

11 Happy are you when people insult you, persecute you, lie and tell only evil about you on account of Me. 12 Be happy and delighted because you have a great reward in heaven. That's how they persecuted the prophets who were before you."

A Salt and a Light

13 "You are the salt of the world. If salt loses its taste, how will it be made salty again? It's no longer good for anything but to be thrown out and trampled on by people.

14 "You are the light of the world. A town can't be hid when it's built on a hill. 15 And you don't light a lamp and put it under the peck measure but on the lampstand, where it gives

[13] Is. 57:15
[14] Is. 61:2
[15] Ps. 37:11
[16] 2 Sam. 22:26; Ps. 18:25
[17] Ps. 24:4; 51:10; 73:1

K.J.V.

all that are in the house. 16 Let your light so shine before men, that they may see your good works, and glorify your Father which is in heaven.

17 Think not that I am come to destroy the law, or the prophets: I am not come to destroy, but to fulfil. 18 For verily I say unto you, Till heaven and earth pass, one jot or one tittle shall in no wise pass from the law, till all be fulfilled. 19 Whosoever therefore shall break one of these least commandments, and shall teach men so, he shall be called the least in the kingdom of heaven: but whosoever shall do and teach *them*, the same shall be called great in the kingdom of heaven. 20 For I say unto you, That except your righteousness shall exceed *the righteousness* of the scribes and Pharisees, ye shall in no case enter into the kingdom of heaven.

21 Ye have heard that it was said by them of old time, Thou shalt not kill; and whosoever shall kill shall be in danger of the judgment: 22 But I say unto you, That whosoever is angry with his brother without a cause shall be in danger of the judgment: and whosoever shall say to his brother, Raca, shall be in danger of the council: but whosoever shall say, Thou fool, shall be in danger of hell fire. 23 Therefore if thou bring thy gift to the altar, and there rememberest that thy brother hath aught against thee; 24 Leave there thy gift before the altar, and go thy way; first be reconciled to thy brother, and then come and offer thy gift. 25 Agree with thine adversary quickly, while thou art in the way with him; lest at any time the adversary deliver thee to the judge, and the judge deliver thee to the officer, and thou be cast into prison. 26 Verily I say unto thee, Thou shalt by no means come out thence, till thou hast paid the uttermost farthing.

27 Ye have heard that it was said by them of old time, Thou shall not commit adultery: 28 But I say unto you, That whosoever looketh on a woman to lust after her hath committed adultery with her already in his heart. 29 And if thy right eye offend thee, pluck it out, and cast *it* from thee: for it is profitable for thee that one of thy members should perish, and not *that* thy whole body should be cast into hell. 30 And if thy right hand offend thee, cut it off, and cast *it* from thee: for it is profitable for thee that one of thy members should perish, and not *that* thy whole body should be cast into hell. 31 It hath been said, Whosoever shall put away his wife, let him give her a writing of divorcement: 32 But I say unto you, That whosoever shall put away his wife, saving for the cause of fornication, causeth her to commit adultery: and whosoever shall marry her that is divorced committeth adultery.

33 Again, ye have heard that it hath been said by them of old time, Thou shalt not forswear thyself, but shalt perform unto the Lord thine oaths: 34 But I say unto you, Swear not at all; neither by heaven; for it is God's throne: 35 Nor

N.A.S.

the house. 16 "Let your light shine before men in such a way that they may see your good works, and glorify your Father who is in heaven.

17 "Do not think that I came to abolish the Law or the Prophets; I did not come to abolish, but to fulfill. 18 "For truly I say to you, until heaven and earth pass away, not the smallest letter or stroke shall pass away from the Law, until all is accomplished. 19 "Whoever then annuls one of the least of these commandments, and so teaches others, shall be called least in the kingdom of heaven; but whoever keeps and teaches *them*, he shall be called great in the kingdom of heaven. 20 "For I say to you, that unless your righteousness surpasses *that* of the scribes and Pharisees, you shall not enter the kingdom of heaven.

21 "You have heard that the ancients were told, 'You shall not commit murder;' and 'Whoever commits murder shall be [a]liable to the court;' 22 but I say to you that every one who is angry with his brother[b] shall be guilty before the court; and whoever shall say to his brother, '[c]Raca,' shall be guilty before [d]the supreme court; and whoever shall say, 'You fool,' shall be guilty *enough to go* into the [e]hell of fire. 23 "If therefore you are presenting your offering at the altar, and there remember that your brother has something against you, 24 leave your offering there before the altar, and go your way, first be reconciled to your brother, and then come and present your offering. 25 "Make friends quickly with your opponent at law while you are with him on the way; in order that your opponent may not deliver you to the judge, and the judge to the officer, and you be thrown into prison. 26 "Truly I say to you, you shall not come out of there, until you have paid up the last [f]cent.

27 "You have heard that it was said, 'YOU SHALL NOT COMMIT ADULTERY;' 28 but I say to you, that every one who looks on a woman to lust for her has committed adultery with her already in his heart. 29 "And if your right eye makes you stumble, tear it out, and throw it from you; for it is better for you that one of the parts of your body perish, than for your whole body to be thrown into hell. 30 "And if your right hand makes you stumble, cut it off, and throw it from you; for it is better for you that one of the parts of your body perish, than for your whole body to go into hell. 31 "And it was said, 'WHOEVER DIVORCES HIS WIFE, LET HIM GIVE HER A CERTIFICATE OF DISMISSAL;' 32 but I say to you that every one who divorces his wife, except for *the* cause of unchastity, makes her commit adultery; and whoever marries a divorced woman commits adultery.

33 "Again, you have heard that the ancients were told, 'YOU SHALL NOT MAKE FALSE VOWS, BUT SHALL FULFILL YOUR VOWS TO THE LORD.' 34 "But I say to you, make no oath at all; either by heaven, for it is THE THRONE OF GOD; 35 or

---

[a] Or, *guilty before.* [b] Some mss. insert here: *without cause.* [c] Aramaic for *emptyhead* or, *good for nothing.* [d] Lit., *the Sanhedrin* [e] Gr., *Gehenna.* [f] Lit., *quadrans* (equaling two lepta or mites), I.e., 1/64 of a denarius.

WILLIAMS

house. 16 Let your light shine before people in such a way that they may see your good deeds, and praise your Father in heaven.

17 "Do not suppose that I have come to set aside the law or the prophets. 18 I have not come to set them aside but to fill them up to the brim. For I solemnly say to you, heaven and earth would sooner pass away than the dotting of an 'i' *a* or the crossing of a 't' *a* from the law, until it all becomes in force. 19 Whoever, therefore, breaks one of the least of these commands and teaches others so to do, will be ranked as least in the kingdom of heaven; but whoever practices them and teaches others so to do, will be ranked as great in the kingdom of heaven. 20 For I tell you that unless your righteousness far surpasses that of the scribes and Pharisees, you will never get into the kingdom of heaven at all.

21 "You have heard that it was said to the men of old, 'You must not murder,' and 'Whoever murders will have to answer to the court.' 22 But I say to you:

"Everyone who harbors malice against his brother, will have to answer to the court, and whoever speaks contemptuously to his brother, will have to answer to the supreme court; and whoever says to his brother, 'You cursed fool!' will have to pay the penalty in the pit of torture. 23 So if, in the very act of presenting your gift at the altar, you remember that your brother has something against you, 24 leave your gift right there at the altar, and first go and make peace with your brother, and then come back and present your gift. 25 Be quick to come to terms with your opponent while you are on the road to court with him, so that he may not turn you over to the judge, and the judge turn you over to the officer, and you be put in prison. 26 I solemnly say to you, you will never get out at all until you have paid the last penny.

27 "You have heard it was said, 'You must not commit adultery.' 28 But I tell you that anyone who looks at a woman so as to have an evil desire for her at once has already committed adultery with her in his heart. 29 So if your right eye causes you to do wrong, pluck it out of your way; for it is better to have one part of your body suffer loss than to have your whole body go down to the pit.*b* 30 And if your right hand causes you to do wrong, cut it off and put it out of your way, for it is better to have one part of your body suffer loss than to have your whole body go down to the pit.

31 "It was also said, 'Whoever divorces his wife must give her a certificate of divorce.' 32 But I tell you that whoever divorces his wife for any other ground than unfaithfulness,*c* causes her to commit adultery, and whoever marries a wife who is thus divorced commits adultery.

33 "Again, you have heard that it was said to the men of old, 'You must not swear falsely, but you must perform your oaths as a religious duty.'*d* 34 But I tell you not to swear at all, either by heaven, for it is God's throne, 35 or

---

BECK

light to everybody in the house. 16 So let your light shine before people that they may see the good you do and praise your Father in heaven."

Jesus Keeps the Law

17 "Don't think that I came to set aside the Law or the prophets. I didn't come to set them aside but to fulfill them. 18 I tell you the truth, till heaven and earth pass away, not an *i* or the dot of an *i* of the Law will pass away till everything is done. 19 Anyone, then, who sets aside one of the least of these commandments and teaches others to do the same will be called the least in the kingdom of heaven. But anyone who does and teaches what they say will be called great in the kingdom of heaven. 20 I tell you, unless your righteousness is much better than that of the Bible scholars and Pharisees, you will never get into the kingdom of heaven."

Don't Kill

21 "You have heard that long ago the people were told: 'Don't kill.'[18] Whoever kills must answer for it in court.'

22 "But I tell you, anyone who is angry with his brother must answer for it in court. Anyone who calls his brother an 'emptyhead' must go before the highest court. Anyone who calls him a 'fool' must go into hellfire.

23 "So if you're bringing your gift on the altar and remember there that your brother has something against you, 24 leave your gift there before the altar and go. First make up with your brother, and then come and offer your gift.

25 "If someone wants to sue you, be quick to make up with him while you are still on the way with him, or your accuser will hand you over to the judge, and the judge to the officer, and you will be put in prison. 26 I tell you the truth, you will never get out until you pay the last cent."

Don't Lust

27 "You have heard it was said: 'Don't commit adultery.'[19]

28 "But I tell you, anyone who looks at a woman to lust after her has already committed adultery with her in his heart.

29 "If your right eye causes you to sin, tear it out and throw it away. It is better for you to lose a part of your body than to have all of it thrown into hell. 30 And if your right hand causes you to sin, cut it off and throw it away. It is better for you to lose a part of your body than to have all of it go to hell.

31 "It was said: 'Anyone who divorces his wife *must give her a divorce paper*.'[20] 32 But I tell you, anyone who divorces his wife, except for her being sexually unfaithful, makes her a partner in adultery. And also the man who marries the divorced woman is living in adultery."

Don't Swear

33 "Again, you have heard that long ago the people were told: 'Don't swear to a lie.'[21] and: 'Give the Lord what you swear to give Him.'[22]

34 "But I tell you, don't swear at all, not by heaven—it *is* God's throne; 35 or by *the earth*—

---

[a] In Grk., the smallest letter of the Hebrew alphabet, or horn (curve) of a letter, equivalent to our dotting of an *i* or crossing of a *t*. [b] Grk., *Gehenna*, a valley or pit where refuse is thrown, here the pit of future punishment. [c] Grk., *fornication*, an expression of unfaithfulness. [d] Grk., *for the Lord*.

[18] Ex. 20:13; Deut. 5:17
[19] Ex. 20:14; Deut. 5:18
[20] Deut. 24:1
[21] Lev. 19:12
[22] Num. 30:2; Deut. 23:21; Ps. 50:14

K.J.V.

by the earth; for it is his footstool: neither by Jerusalem; for it is the city of the great King. 36 Neither shalt thou swear by thy head, because thou canst not make one hair white or black. 37 But let your communication be, Yea, yea; Nay, nay: for whatsoever is more than these cometh of evil.

38 Ye have heard that it hath been said, An eye for an eye, and a tooth for a tooth: 39 But I say unto you, That ye resist not evil: but whosoever shall smite thee on thy right cheek, turn to him the other also. 40And if any man will sue thee at the law, and take away thy coat, let him have thy cloak also. 41And whosoever shall compel thee to go a mile, go with him twain. 42 Give to him that asketh thee, and from him that would borrow of thee turn not thou away.

43 Ye have heard that it hath been said, Thou shalt love thy neighbour, and hate thine enemy. 44 But I say unto you, Love your enemies, bless them that curse you, do good to them that hate you, and pray for them which despitefully use you, and persecute you; 45 That ye may be the children of your Father which is in heaven: for he maketh his sun to rise on the evil and on the good, and sendeth rain on the just and on the unjust. 46 For if ye love them which love you, what reward have ye? do not even the publicans the same? 47And if ye salute your brethren only, what do ye more than others? do not even the publicans so? 48 Be ye therefore perfect, even as your Father which is in heaven is perfect.

6 Take heed that ye do not your alms before men, to be seen of them: otherwise ye have no reward of your Father which is in heaven. 2 Therefore when thou doest thine alms, do not sound a trumpet before thee, as the hypocrites do in the synagogues and in the streets, that they may have glory of men. Verily I say unto you, They have their reward. 3 But when thou doest alms, let not thy left hand know what thy right hand doeth: 4 That thine alms may be in secret: and thy Father which seeth in secret himself shall reward thee openly.

5 And when thou prayest, thou shalt not be as the hypocrites are: for they love to pray standing in the synagogues and in the corners of the streets, that they may be seen of men. Verily I say unto you, They have their reward. 6 But thou, when thou prayest enter into thy closet, and when thou hast shut thy door, pray to thy Father which is in secret and thy Father which seeth in secret shall reward thee openly. 7 But when ye pray, use not vain repetitions, as the heathen do: for they think that they shall be heard for their much speaking. 8 Be not ye therefore like unto them: for your Father knoweth what things ye have need of, before ye ask him. 9After this manner therefore pray ye: Our Father which art in heaven, Hallowed be thy name. 10 Thy kingdom come. Thy will be done in earth, as it is in heaven. 11 Give us this day our daily

N.A.S.

by the earth, for it is the footstool of His feet; or by Jerusalem, for it is THE CITY OF THE GREAT KING. 36 "Nor shall you make an oath by your head, for you cannot make one hair white or black. 37 "But let your statement be, 'Yes, yes' or 'No, no;' and anything beyond these is of evil.

38 "You have heard that it was said, 'AN EYE FOR AN EYE, AND A TOOTH FOR A TOOTH.' 39 "But I say to you, do not resist him who is evil; but whoever slaps you on your right cheek, turn to him the other also. 40 "And if any one wants to sue you, and take your ᵃshirt, let him have your ᵇcoat also. 41 "And whoever shall force you to go one mile, go with him two. 42 "Give to him who asks of you, and do not turn away from him who wants to borrow from you.

43 "You have heard that it was said, 'YOU SHALL LOVE YOUR NEIGHBOR, AND HATE YOUR ENEMY.' 44 "But I say to you, love your enemies, and pray for those who persecute you; 45 in order that you may be sons of your Father who is in heaven; for He causes His sun to rise on the evil and the good, and sends rain on the righteous and the unrighteous. 46 "For if you love those who love you, what reward have you? Do not even the tax gatherers do the same? 47 "And if you greet your brothers only, what do you do more than others? Do not even the Gentiles do the same? 48 "Therefore you are to be perfect, as your heavenly Father is perfect.

6 "Beware of practicing your righteousness before men to be noticed by them; otherwise you have no reward with your Father who is in heaven.
2 "When therefore you give alms, do not sound a trumpet before you, as the hypocrites do in the synagogues and in the streets, that they may be honored by men. Truly I say to you, they have their reward in full. 3 "But when you give alms, do not let your left hand know what your right hand is doing; 4 that your alms may be in secret; and your Father who sees in secret will repay you.
5 "And when you pray, you are not to be as the hypocrites; for they love to stand and pray in the synagogues and on the street corners, in order to be seen by men. Truly I say to you, they have their reward in full. 6 "But you, when you pray, GO INTO YOUR INNER ROOM, AND WHEN YOU HAVE SHUT YOUR DOOR, pray to your Father who is in secret, and your Father who sees in secret will repay you. 7 "And when you are praying, do not use meaningless repetition, as the Gentiles do, for they suppose that they will be heard for their many words. 8 "Therefore do not be like them; for your Father knows what you need, before you ask Him.
9 "Pray, then, in this way:
'Our Father who art in heaven,
Hallowed be Thy name.
10 'Thy kingdom come.
Thy will be done,
On earth as it is in heaven.
11 'Give us this day our daily bread.

[a] Tunic or garment worn next to the body. [b] Cloak or outer garment.

WILLIAMS

by the earth, for it is His footstool, or by Jerusalem, for it is the city of the Great King. 36 Never swear by your own head, for you cannot make a single hair white or black. 37 But your way of speaking must be a simple 'Yes' or 'No.' Anything beyond this comes from the evil one.

38 "You have heard that it was said, 'An eye for an eye and a tooth for a tooth.' 39 But I tell you not to resist the one who injures you; but if anyone slaps you on one cheek, turn him the other, too; 40 and if anyone wants to sue you for your shirt, let him have your coat, too. 41And if anyone forces you to go one mile, go with him two. 42 If anyone, whoever he may be, keeps on begging you, give to him; if anyone wants to borrow from you, do not turn him away.

43 "You have heard that it was said, 'You must love your neighbor and hate your enemy.' 44 But I tell you, practice loving your enemies and praying for your persecutors, 45 to prove that you are sons of your Father in heaven, for He makes His sun rise on bad as well as good people, and makes the rain come down on doers of right and of wrong alike. 46 For if you practice loving only those who love you, what reward will you get? Do not even the tax-collectors practice that? 47 And if you say 'Good morning' to your brothers only, what more than others are you doing? 48 So you, my followers, ought to be perfect, as your heavenly Father is."

6 *The Address on the Mount concluded*

"Take care not to do your good deeds in public, to attract the attention*a* of people; if you do,*b* you will get no reward from your Father in heaven. 2 So whenever you do your deeds of charity, never blow your own horn in public, as the hypocrites are in the habit of doing in the synagogues and on the street corners, to be praised by the people. I solemnly say to you, they already have their reward. 3 But whenever you, a follower of mine, do a deed of charity, never let your own left hand know what your right hand is doing, 4 so that your deed of charity may be secret, and your Father who sees what is secret will reward you.

5 "Also, whenever you pray, you must not be like the hypocrites, for they love to pray standing in the synagogues and on the street corners, to attract the attention of people. I solemnly say to you, they already have their reward. 6 But whenever you, follower of mine, pray, you must go to your most private place, shut the door, and pray to your Father in secret, and your Father who sees what is secret will reward you. 7And whenever you pray, you must not keep on repeating set phrases, as the heathen do, for they suppose that they will be heard in accordance with the length of their prayers. 8 So then you must not be like them, for your Father knows what you need before you ask Him. 9 So this is the way you must pray:

Our Father in heaven,
Your name be revered,
10 Your kingdom come,
Your will be done on earth as it is done in heaven.
11 Give us today our daily bread for the day,

[a] Grk., *to be seen by men.* [b] Grk., *otherwise.*

BECK

it *is His footstool,*[23] or by Jerusalem—*it is the city of the great King.*[24] 36 And don't swear by your head, because you can't make one hair white or black. 37 Just say, 'Yes, yes; no, no.' Anything more comes from the evil one."

Love Your Enemies

38 "You have heard it was said, *'An eye for an eye, and a tooth for a tooth.'*[25] 39 "But I tell you, don't oppose an evil man. If anyone slaps you on your right cheek, turn the other cheek to him. 40 If anyone wants to sue you for your shirt, let him have your coat too. 41 If anyone makes you go one mile, go two miles with him. 42 If anyone asks you for anything, give it to him, and when anyone wants to borrow from you, don't turn away.

43 "You have heard it was said, *'Love your neighbor,*[26] and hate your enemy.'

44 "But I tell you, Love your enemies, and pray for those who persecute you. 45 In this way you will show you are sons of your Father in heaven. He makes His sun rise on people whether they are bad or good and lets rain fall on them whether they do right or wrong.

46 "If you love those who love you, what's your reward? Don't tax collectors do that too? 47 If you treat only your brothers kindly, are you doing anything extraordinary? Don't the people of the world do that too? 48 *Be perfect*[27] as your Father in heaven is perfect."

Don't Blow Your Horn

6 "Be careful not to do your good works before people to be seen by them. If you do, your Father in heaven will not reward you. 2 So when you give to the poor, don't blow your horn, as hypocrites do in the synagogs and on the streets to be praised by people. I tell you, that's really all the reward they'll get. 3 When you give to the poor, don't let your left hand know what your right hand is doing, 4 that your giving may be secret. Then your Father, who sees what is secret, will reward you."

How to Pray

5 "When you pray, don't be like hypocrites, who like to stand praying in synagogs and on street corners in order to be seen by people. I tell you, that's really all the reward they'll get. 6 But when you pray, *go into your own room, shut your door, and pray*[28] to your Father, who is with you when you're alone, and your Father, who sees what is secret, will reward you.

7 "When you pray, don't say meaningless words, like pagans, who think they'll be heard if they talk a lot. 8 Don't be like them. Your Father knows what you need before you ask Him.

9 "This is how you should pray:

Our Father in heaven—
May Your name be kept holy,
10 Your kingdom come,
And Your will be done on earth as it is done in heaven.
11 Give us today our daily bread.

[23] Is. 66:1
[24] Ps. 48:2
[25] Ex. 21:24; Lev. 24:20; Deut. 19:21
[26] Lev. 19:18
[27] Deut. 18:13
[28] 2 Kings 4:33; Is. 26:20

K.J.V.

bread. 12And forgive us our debts, as we forgive our debtors. 13And lead us not into temptation, but deliver us from evil: For thine is the kingdom, and the power, and the glory, for ever. Amen. 14 For if ye forgive men their trespasses, your heavenly Father will also forgive you: 15 But if ye forgive not men their trespasses, neither will your Father forgive your trespasses.

16 Moreover when ye fast, be not, as the hypocrites, of a sad countenance: for they disfigure their faces, that they may appear unto men to fast. Verily I say unto you, They have their reward. 17 But thou, when thou fastest, anoint thine head, and wash thy face; 18 That thou appear not unto men to fast, but unto thy Father which is in secret: and thy Father which seeth in secret shall reward thee openly.

19 Lay not up for yourselves treasures upon earth, where moth and rust doth corrupt, and where thieves break through and steal: 20 But lay up for yourselves treasures in heaven, where neither moth nor rust doth corrupt, and where thieves do not break through nor steal: 21 For where your treasure is, there will your heart be also. 22 The light of the body is the eye: if therefore thine eye be single, thy whole body shall be full of light. 23 But if thine eye be evil, thy whole body shall be full of darkness. If therefore the light that is in thee be darkness, how great *is* that darkness!

24 No man can serve two masters: for either he will hate the one, and love the other; or else he will hold to the one, and despise the other. Ye cannot serve God and mammon. 25 Therefore I say unto you, Take no thought for your life, what ye shall eat, or what ye shall drink; nor yet for your body, what ye shall put on. Is not the life more than meat, and the body than raiment? 26 Behold the fowls of the air: for they sow not, neither do they reap, nor gather into barns; yet your heavenly Father feedeth them. Are ye not much better than they? 27 Which of you by taking thought can add one cubit unto his stature? 28And why take ye thought for raiment? Consider the lilies of the field, how they grow; they toil not, neither do they spin: 29And yet I say unto you, That even Solomon in all his glory was not arrayed like one of these. 30 Wherefore, if God so clothe the grass of the field, which to day is, and to morrow is cast into the oven, *shall he* not much more *clothe* you, O ye of little faith? 31 Therefore take no thought, saying, What shall we eat? or, What shall we drink? or, Wherewithal shall we be clothed? 32 (For after all these things do the Gentiles seek:) for your heavenly Father knoweth that ye have need of all these things. 33 But seek ye first the kingdom of God, and his righteousness; and all these things shall be added unto you. 34 Take therefore no thought for the morrow: for the morrow shall take thought for the things of itself. Sufficient unto the day *is* the evil thereof.

N.A.S.

12 'And forgive us our debts, as we also have forgiven our debtors.

13 'And do not lead us into temptation, but deliver us from evil. [For Thine is the kingdom, and the power, and the glory, forever. Amen].'

14 "For if you forgive men for their transgressions, your heavenly Father will also forgive you. 15 "But if you do not forgive men, then your Father will not forgive your transgressions.

16 "And whenever you fast, do not put on a gloomy face as the hypocrites *do;* for they neglect their appearance in order to be seen fasting by men. Truly I say to you, they have their reward in full. 17 "But you, when you fast, anoint your head, and wash your face; 18 so that you may not be seen fasting by men, but by your Father who is in secret; and your Father who sees in secret will repay you.

19 "Do not lay up for yourselves treasures upon earth, where moth and rust destroy, and where thieves break in and steal; 20 but lay up for yourselves treasures in heaven, where neither moth nor rust destroys, and where thieves do not break in or steal; 21 for where your treasure is, there will your heart be also. 22 "The lamp of the body is the eye; if therefore your eye is clear, your whole body will be full of light. 23 "But if your eye is bad, your whole body will be full of darkness. If therefore the light that is in you is darkness, how great is the darkness! 24 "No one can serve two masters; for either he will hate the one and love the other, or he will hold to one and despise the other. You cannot serve God and [a]Mammon. 25 "For this reason I say to you, do not be anxious for your life, *as to* what you shall eat, or what you shall drink; nor for your body, *as to* what you shall put on. Is not life more than food, and the body than clothing? 26 "Look at the birds of the air, that they do not sow, neither do they reap, nor gather into barns; and *yet* your heavenly Father feeds them. Are you not worth much more than they? 27 "And which of you by being anxious can add a *single* cubit to his life's span? 28 "And why are you anxious about clothing? Observe how the lilies of the field grow; they do not toil nor do they spin, 29 yet I say to you that even Solomon in all his glory did not clothe himself like one of these. 30 "But if God so arrays the grass of the field, which is *alive* today and tomorrow is thrown into the furnace, *will He* not much more *do so for* you, O men of little faith? 31 "Do not be anxious then, saying, 'What shall we eat?' or, 'What shall we drink?' or, 'With what shall we clothe ourselves?' 32 "For all these things the Gentiles eagerly seek; for your heavenly Father knows that you need all these things. 33 "But seek first His kingdom, and His righteousness; and all these things shall be added to you. 34 "Therefore do not be anxious for tomorrow; for tomorrow will care for itself. *Each* day has enough trouble of its own.

[a] Or, *riches.*

WILLIAMS

12 And forgive us our debts, as we have forgiven our debtors;

13 And do not let us be subjected *c* to temptation,
But save us from the evil one.

14 "For if you forgive others their shortcomings, your heavenly Father will forgive you, too. 15 But if you do not forgive others, your heavenly Father will not forgive your shortcomings either.

16 "Also whenever you fast, you must not look gloomy like the hypocrites, for they put on a gloomy countenance, to let people see them fasting. I solemnly say to you, they already have their reward. 17 But whenever you, follower of mine, fast, perfume your head and wash your face, 18 so that your fasting may be seen, not by men but by your Father who is unseen, and your Father who sees what is secret will reward you.

19 "Stop storing up your riches on earth where moths and rust make away with them, and where thieves break in and steal them. 20 But keep on storing up your riches in heaven where moths and rust do not make away with them and where thieves do not break in and steal them. 21 For wherever your treasure is, there too your heart will be.

22 "The eye is the very lamp of the body. If then your eye is sound, your whole body will be full of light. 23 But if your eye is unsound, your whole body will be full of darkness. If then the very source of light in you is darkness, how dense is that darkness! 24 No one can be a slave to two masters, for either he will hate one and love the other, or else he will be devoted to one and despise the other. You cannot be slaves of God and money. 25 So I tell you, stop worrying about your life, as to what you will have to eat or drink, or about your body, as to what you will have to wear. Is not life worth more than food and the body worth more than clothes? 26 Take a good look at the wild birds, for they do not sow or reap, or store up food in barns, and yet your heavenly Father keeps on feeding them. Are you not worth more than they? 27 But which of you by worrying can add a single minute to his life? 28 And why should you worry about clothes? Look at the wild lilies and learn how they grow. They do not toil or spin; 29 but I tell you, not even Solomon, in all his gorgeous splendor, was ever dressed up like a single one of these. 30 Now if God so gorgeously dresses the wild grass which today is green but tomorrow is tossed into the furnace, will He not much more surely clothe you, O you with little faith? 31 So never worry and say, 'What are we going to have to eat? What are we going to have to drink? What are we going to have to wear?' 32 For the heathen are greedily pursuing all such things; and surely your heavenly Father well knows that you need them all. 33 But as your first duty keep on looking for His standard of doing right,*d* and for His will,*e* and then all these things will be yours besides. 34 So never worry about tomorrow, for tomorrow will have worries of its own. Each day has evil enough of its own."

BECK

12 And forgive us our sins as we have forgiven those who sin against us.

13 And don't bring us into temptation,
But deliver us from evil.*

14 "If you forgive the sins of others, your Father in heaven will forgive you. 15 But if you don't forgive the sins of others, your Father will not forgive your sins."

Fasting

16 "When you fast, don't look sad like hypocrites. They disfigure their faces to show people they are fasting. I tell you, that's really all the reward they'll get. 17 But when you fast, anoint your head, and wash your face 18 so that nobody will see you fasting except your Father, who is with you when you're alone. And your Father, who sees what is secret, will reward you."

Treasures

19 "Don't store up for yourselves treasures on earth,
Where moth and rust destroy them
And thieves break in and steal.

20 "But store up for yourselves treasures in heaven,
Where no moth or rust destroys them
And no thieves break in and steal.

21 Where your treasure is, there your heart will be.

22 "The eye is the lamp of the body. If your eye is healthy, you have light for your whole body. 23 But if your eye is bad, your whole body will be dark. How dark it is when the light in you is dark!

24 "Nobody can serve two masters. Either he will hate the one and love the other or be loyal to the one and despise the other. You can't serve God and money."

Don't Worry!

25 "So I tell you, don't worry about what you'll eat or drink to keep alive or what you'll wear on your bodies. Isn't life more than food, and the body more than clothes?

26 "Look at the birds in the air. They don't sow or cut grain or gather anything into barns; but your Father in heaven feeds them. Aren't you worth more than they?

27 "Can any of you by worrying add anything to your life?

28 "And why worry about clothes? See how the flowers grow in the field, and learn from them. They don't work and they don't spin. 29 Yet, I tell you, even Solomon in all his glory didn't dress like one of these. 30 If that's how God dresses the grass in the field, which lives today and tomorrow is thrown into a stove, how much more certainly will He put clothes on you —who trust Him so little?

31 "Don't worry, then, and say, 'What are we going to eat?' or, 'What are we going to drink?' or, 'What are we going to wear?' 32 The people of the world run after all these things. Your Father in heaven knows you need them all. 33 First be eager to have God as your King and His righteousness, and you'll get all these other things too.

34 "So, don't worry about tomorrow. Tomorrow will take care of itself. Each day has enough trouble of its own."

---

[c] Greek, *do not bring*, etc. [d] Following the Vatican Ms. which omits the word *God* and transposes the nouns. [e] Greek, *His righteousness*—so *His way of doing right; His kingdom*—so *His will.*

* The doxology is found in later manuscripts: "You are the King who rules with power and glory forever. Amen."

K.J.V.

7 Judge not, that ye be not judged. 2 For with what judgment ye judge, ye shall be judged: and with what measure ye mete, it shall be measured to you again. 3 And why beholdest thou the mote that is in thy brother's eye, but considerest not the beam that is in thine own eye? 4 Or how wilt thou say to thy brother, Let me pull out the mote out of thine eye; and, behold, a beam is in thine own eye? 5 Thou hypocrite, first cast out the beam out of thine own eye; and then shalt thou see clearly to cast out the mote out of thy brother's eye.

6 Give not that which is holy unto the dogs, neither cast ye your pearls before swine, lest they trample them under their feet, and turn again and rend you.

7 Ask, and it shall be given you; seek, and ye shall find; knock, and it shall be opened unto you: 8 For every one that asketh receiveth; and he that seeketh findeth; and to him that knocketh it shall be opened. 9 Or what man is there of you, whom if his son ask bread, will he give him a stone? 10 Or if he ask a fish, will he give him a serpent? 11 If ye then, being evil, know how to give good gifts unto your children, how much more shall your Father which is in heaven give good things to them that ask him? 12 Therefore all things whatsoever ye would that men should do to you, do ye even so to them: for this is the law and the prophets.

13 Enter ye in at the strait gate: for wide is the gate, and broad is the way, that leadeth to destruction, and many there be which go in thereat: 14 Because strait is the gate, and narrow is the way, which leadeth unto life, and few there be that find it.

15 Beware of false prophets, which come to you in sheep's clothing, but inwardly they are ravening wolves. 16 Ye shall know them by their fruits. Do men gather grapes of thorns, or figs of thistles? 17 Even so every good tree bringeth forth good fruit; but a corrupt tree bringeth forth evil fruit. 18 A good tree cannot bring forth evil fruit, neither can a corrupt tree bring forth good fruit. 19 Every tree that bringeth not forth good fruit is hewn down, and cast into the fire. 20 Wherefore by their fruits ye shall know them.

21 Not every one that saith unto me, Lord, Lord, shall enter into the kingdom of heaven; but he that doeth the will of my Father which is in heaven. 22 Many will say to me in that day, Lord, Lord, have we not prophesied in thy name? and in thy name have cast out devils? and in thy name done many wonderful works? 23 And then will I profess unto them, I never knew you: depart from me, ye that work iniquity.

24 Therefore whosoever heareth these sayings of mine, and doeth them, I will liken him unto a wise man, which built his house upon a rock: 25 And the rain descended, and the floods came, and the winds blew, and beat upon that house;

N.A.S.

7 "Do not judge lest you be judged yourselves. 2 "For in the way you judge, you will be judged; and by your standard of measure, it shall be measured to you. 3 "And why do you look at the speck in your brother's eye, but do not notice the log that is in your own eye? 4 "Or how can you say to your brother, 'Let me take the speck out of your eye,' and behold, the log is in your own eye? 5 "You hypocrite, first take the log out of your own eye; and then you will see clearly enough to take the speck out of your brother's eye.

6 "Do not give what is holy to dogs, and do not throw your pearls before swine, lest they trample them under their feet, and turn and tear you to pieces.

7 "Ask, and it shall be given to you; seek, and you shall find; knock, and it shall be opened to you. 8 "For every one who asks receives; and he who seeks finds; and to him who knocks it shall be opened. 9 "Or what man is there among you, when his son shall ask him for a loaf, will give him a stone? 10 "Or if he shall ask for a fish, will not give him a snake, will he? 11 "If you then, being evil, know how to give good gifts to your children, how much more shall your Father who is in heaven give what is good to those who ask Him! 12 "Therefore whatever you want others to do for you, do so for them; for this is the Law and the Prophets.

13 "Enter by the narrow gate; for the gate is wide, and the way is broad that leads to destruction, and many are those who enter by it. 14 "For the gate is small, and the way is narrow that leads to life, and few are those who find it.

15 "Beware of the false prophets, who come to you in sheep's clothing, but inwardly are ravenous wolves. 16 "You will know them by their fruits. Grapes are not gathered from thornbushes, nor figs from thistles, are they? 17 "Even so every good tree bears good fruit; but the rotten tree bears bad fruit. 18 "A good tree cannot produce bad fruit, nor can a rotten tree produce good fruit. 19 "Every tree that does not bear good fruit is cut down, and thrown into the fire. 20 "So then, you will know them by their fruits. 21 "Not every one who says to Me, 'Lord, Lord,' will enter the kingdom of heaven; but he who does the will of My Father, who is in heaven. 22 "Many will say to Me on that day, 'Lord, Lord, did we not prophesy in Your name, and in Your name cast out demons, and in Your name perform many miracles?' 23 "And then I will declare to them, 'I never knew you; DEPART FROM ME, YOU WHO PRACTICE LAWLESSNESS.'

24 "Therefore every one who hears these words of Mine, and acts upon them, may be compared to a wise man, who built his house upon the rock; 25 and the rain descended, and the floods came, and the winds blew, and burst

WILLIAMS

BECK

7 *The Address on the Mount concluded*

"Stop criticizing others, so that you may not be criticized yourselves. 2 For exactly as you criticize others, you will be criticized, and in accordance with the measure that you give to others, it will be measured back to you. 3 Why do you keep watching the tiny speck in your brother's eye, but pay no attention to the girder in your own? 4 How can you say to your brother, 'Let me get that tiny speck out of your eye,' while all the time there is a girder in your own? 5 You hypocrite, first get the girder out of your own eye, and then you can see well enough to get the tiny speck out of your brother's eye.

6 "You must never give the things that are sacred to dogs, and you must never throw your pearls before hogs, for fear they might trample them under their feet and turn and tear you in pieces.

7 "Keep on asking, and the gift will be given you; keep on seeking, and you will find; keep on knocking, and the door will open to you. 8 For everyone who keeps on asking, receives, and everyone who keeps on seeking, finds, and to the one who keeps on knocking, the door will open. 9 What human father among you, when his son asks him for bread, will give him a stone? 10 Or if he asks for a fish, will he give him a snake? 11 So if you, in spite of your being bad, know how to give your children what is good, how much more surely will your heavenly Father give what is good to those who keep on asking Him? 12 Then you must practice dealing with others as you would like for them to deal with you; for this is the summing up of the law and the prophets.

13 "Go in by the narrow gate; for broad and roomy is the road that leads to destruction, and many are going in by it. 14 But narrow is the gate and hard is the road that leads to life, and few are they that find it.

15 "Look out for false prophets, who come to you under the guise[a] of sheep, but inside they are devouring wolves. 16 You must recognize them by their fruits. People do not pick grapes from thornbushes or figs from thistles, do they? 17 So any healthy tree bears good fruit and a sickly tree bears poor fruit. 18 A healthy tree cannot bear poor fruit, and a sickly tree cannot bear good fruit. 19 Any tree that does not bear good fruit is cut down and burned up. 20 So you must recognize them by their fruits. 21 Not everyone who says to me, 'Lord, Lord,' will get into the kingdom of heaven, but only those who practice doing the will of my Father in heaven. 22 Many will say to me on that day, 'Lord, Lord, was it not in your name that we prophesied, and in your name that we drove out demons, and in your name that we did many wonder-works?' 23 And then I will say to them openly, 'I never knew you at all. Go away from me, you who practiced doing wrong.' "

24 "So everyone who listens to my words and practices their teaching, will be like a prudent man who built his house on a rocky foundation. 25 And the rain fell, and the rivers rose, and the winds blew and beat against that house,

Criticize Yourself

7 "Don't judge, so that you will not be judged. 2 The way you judge others, you'll be judged, and the measure you measure with will be used for you.

3 "Why do you look at the speck in your brother's eye and don't notice the log in your own eye? 4 Or how can you say to your brother, 'Let me take the speck out of your eye,' when you have that log in your own eye? 5 You hypocrite, first throw the log out of your own eye. Then you'll see clearly enough to take the speck out of your brother's eye."

Pearls to Pigs

6 "Don't give anything holy to the dogs or throw your pearls to the pigs, or they'll trample them under their feet and then turn and tear you to pieces."

Pray

7 "Ask, and it will be given to you. Search, and you will find. Knock, and the door will be opened for you. 8 Anyone who asks receives; anyone who searches finds; and anyone who knocks, the door will be opened for him.

9 "If your son asks you for bread, will any of you give him a stone? 10 Or if he asks for a fish, will you give him a snake? 11 Now if you, bad as you are, know enough to give your children good gifts, how much more will your Father in heaven give good things to those who ask Him?"

The Golden Rule

12 "Do for others everything you want them to do for you. That is the Law and the prophets."

The Narrow Gate

13 "Go through the narrow gate. The gate is wide, and the way is broad that leads to destruction, and many are going that way. 14 But the gate is small, and the way is narrow, that leads to life, and only a few are finding it."

False Prophets

15 "Beware of false prophets. They come to you dressed like sheep, but in their hearts they're greedy wolves.

16 "You will know them by what they do. Can we pick grapes from thornbushes or figs from thistles? 17 No, every good tree bears good fruit, and a bad tree bad fruit. 18 A good tree cannot bear bad fruit, or a bad tree good fruit. 19 Any tree that doesn't bear good fruit is cut down and thrown into the fire. 20 So you will know them by what they do.

21 "Not everyone who calls Me Lord, Lord, will get into the kingdom of heaven, only he who does what My Father in heaven wants. 22 Many will say to Me on that Day, 'Lord, Lord, didn't we *prophesy in Your name,*[29] drive out devils in Your name, and do many miracles in Your name?' 23 Then I will tell them frankly, 'I never knew you. *Get away from Me, you who are so busy doing wrong.' "*[30]

Build on a Rock

24 "Anyone who hears and does what I say is like a man who had the sense to build his house on a rock. 25 The rain poured down, the torrents came, the winds blew, and they dashed

[29] Jer. 14:14; 27:15
[30] Ps. 6:8

[a] Grk., *in the clothes of*, etc.

K.J.V.

and it fell not: for it was founded upon a rock. 26And every one that heareth these sayings of mine, and doeth them not, shall be likened unto a foolish man, which built his house upon the sand: 27And the rain descended, and the floods came, and the winds blew, and beat upon that house; and it fell: and great was the fall of it. 28And it came to pass, when Jesus had ended these sayings, the people were astonished at his doctrine: 29 For he taught them as *one* having authority, and not as the scribes.

8 When he was come down from the mountain, great multitudes followed him. 2And, behold, there came a leper and worshipped him, saying, Lord, if thou wilt, thou canst make me clean. 3And Jesus put forth *his* hand, and touched him, saying, I will; be thou clean. And immediately his leprosy was cleansed. 4And Jesus saith unto him, See thou tell no man; but go thy way, shew thyself to the priest, and offer the gift that Moses commanded, for a testimony unto them.

5 And when Jesus was entered into Capernaum, there came unto him a centurion, beseeching him, 6And saying, Lord, my servant lieth at home sick of the palsy, grievously tormented. 7And Jesus saith unto him, I will come and heal him. 8 The centurion answered and said, Lord, I am not worthy that thou shouldest come under my roof: but speak the word only, and my servant shall be healed. 9 For I am a man under authority, having soldiers under me: and I say to this *man*, Go, and he goeth; and to another, Come, and he cometh; and to my servant, Do this, and he doeth *it*. 10 When Jesus heard *it*, he marvelled, and said to them that followed, Verily I say unto you, I have not found so great faith, no, not in Israel. 11And I say unto you, That many shall come from the east and west, and shall sit down with Abraham, and Isaac, and Jacob, in the kingdom of heaven: 12 But the children of the kingdom shall be cast out into outer darkness: there shall be weeping and gnashing of teeth. 13And Jesus said unto the centurion, Go thy way; and as thou hast believed, *so* be it done unto thee. And his servant was healed in the selfsame hour.

14 And when Jesus was come into Peter's house, he saw his wife's mother laid, and sick of a fever. 15And he touched her hand, and the fever left her: and she arose, and ministered unto them.

16 When the even was come, they brought unto him many that were possessed with devils: and he cast out the spirits with *his* word, and healed all that were sick: 17That it might be fulfilled which was spoken by Esaias the prophet, saying, Himself took our infirmities, and bare *our* sicknesses.

18 Now when Jesus saw great multitudes about him, he gave commandment to depart unto

N.A.S.

against that house; and *yet* it did not fall; for it had been founded upon the rock. 26 "And every one who hears these words of Mine, and does not act upon them, will be like a foolish man, who built his house upon the sand. 27 "And the rain descended, and the floods came, and the winds blew, and burst against that house; and it fell, and great was its fall."

28 The result was that when Jesus had finished these words, the multitudes were amazed at His teaching; 29 for He was teaching them as *one* having authority, and not as their scribes.

8 And when He had come down from the mountain, great multitudes followed Him. 2And behold, a leper came to Him, and bowed down to Him, saying, "Lord, if You are willing, You can make me clean." 3And stretching out His hand, He touched him, saying, "I am willing; be cleansed." And immediately his leprosy was cleansed. 4 And Jesus *said to him, "See that you tell no one; but go, SHOW YOURSELF TO THE PRIEST, and present the offering that Moses prescribed, for a testimony to them."

5 And when He had entered Capernaum, a centurion came to Him, entreating Him, 6 and saying, "Sir, my servant is lying paralyzed at home, suffering great pain." 7And He *said to him, "I will come and heal him." 8 But the centurion answered and said, "Lord, I am not qualified for You to come under my roof, but just say the word, and my servant will be healed. 9 "For I too am a man under authority, with soldiers under me; and I say to this one, 'Go!' and he goes, and to another, 'Come!' and he comes, and to my slave, 'Do this!' and he does *it*." 10 Now when Jesus heard *this*, He marveled, and said to those who were following, "Truly I say to you, I have not found such great faith with anyone in Israel. 11 "And I say to you, that many shall come from east and west, and *recline *at table* with Abraham, and Isaac, and Jacob, in the kingdom of heaven; 12 but the sons of the kingdom shall be cast out into the outer darkness; in that place there shall be weeping and gnashing of teeth." 13And Jesus said to the centurion, "Go your way; let it be done to you as you have believed." And the servant was healed that *very* hour.

14 And when Jesus had come to Peter's home, He saw his mother-in-law lying sick in bed with a fever. 15And He touched her hand, and the fever left her; and she arose, and began to wait on Him. 16And when evening had come, they brought to Him many who were demon-possessed; and He cast out the spirits with a word, and healed all who were ill; 17 in order that what was spoken through Isaiah the prophet might be fulfilled, saying, "HE HIMSELF TOOK OUR IN-FIRMITIES, AND CARRIED AWAY OUR DISEASES."

18 Now when Jesus saw a crowd around Him, He gave orders to depart to the other side.

[a] Or, *dine.*

WILLIAMS

BECK

WILLIAMS

but it did not fall, for its pillars had been laid on a rocky foundation. 26And anyone who listens to my words and does not practice their teaching, will be like an imprudent man who built his house on sand. 27And the rain fell, and the rivers rose, and the wind blew and beat against that house, and it collapsed, and the wreck of it was complete."

28 When Jesus had closed this address,[b] the result was that the crowds were dumfounded at His teaching, 29 for He was teaching them as one who had authority to teach, and not as their scribes did.

8 *A leper cured; a Roman captain's great faith incites Jesus' wonder; several sick people cured—Peter's mother-in-law, two insane men, and others*

When He came down from the mountain, great crowds followed Him. 2And a leper came up to Him, and prostrated himself before Him, and said, "Lord, if you choose to, you can cure me."

3 Then He put out His hand and touched him, and said, "I do choose to; be cured." And at once his leprosy was cured. 4 Then Jesus said to him, "See that you tell nobody, but go, show yourself to the priest, and, to testify[a] to the people, make the offering that Moses prescribed."

5 When He got back to Capernaum, a Roman military captain came up to Him and kept begging Him, 6"Lord, my servant-boy is at home bed-ridden with paralysis and suffering terrible tortures!"

7 He said to him, "I will come and cure him."

8 But the captain answered, "I am not fit for you to come under my roof, but simply speak the word, and my servant-boy will be cured. 9 For I, too, am under authority of others, and have soldiers under me, and I order this one to go, and he goes, another to come, and he comes, my slave-boy to do this, and he does it."

10 When Jesus heard it, He was astounded, and said to His followers, "I solemnly say to you, I have not found, in a single case among the Jews, so great faith as this. 11 I tell you, many will come from the east and from the west and take their seats at the feast with Abraham and Isaac and Jacob, in the kingdom of heaven, 12 while the heirs of the kingdom will be turned out into the darkness outside, where they will be weeping and grinding their teeth."

13 Then Jesus said to the captain, "Go; it must be done for you as you have believed." And his servant-boy was cured that very hour.

14 When He went into Peter's house, He saw his mother-in-law lying in bed sick with fever. 15 He touched her hand, the fever left her, and she got up and began to wait on Him.

16 When evening had come, they brought to Him many who were under the power of demons, and at a mere word He drove the spirits out, and cured all who were sick, 17 and so fulfilled what was spoken by Isaiah the prophet, "He took our sicknesses and bore away our diseases."

18 Now Jesus, because He saw a crowd about Him, gave orders to cross to the other side.

BECK

against that house. But it didn't go down, because its foundation was on the rock.

26 "Everyone who hears what I say but doesn't do it is like a man who was so foolish he built his house on sand. 27 The rains poured down, the torrents came, the winds blew, and they dashed against that house. And it went down with a big crash."

28 When Jesus finished speaking, the crowds were amazed at His teaching. 29 He taught them with authority and not like their Bible scholars.

8 He went down the hill, and large crowds followed Him.

Jesus Heals a Leper

2 There was a leper, who went to Him and bowed down to the ground before Him. "Lord, if You want to," he said, "You can make me clean."

3 Jesus stretched out His hand and touched him. "I want to," He said. "Be clean!" Immediately the leprosy left him, and he was clean.

4 "Be careful not to tell anyone," Jesus said to him, "but go, *let the priest examine*[31] you, and offer the sacrifice Moses ordered, to show them you're well."

A Believing Captain

5 He went to Capernaum. There a captain came to Him and begged Him: 6 "Lord, my slave is lying paralyzed at home. He's suffering terribly."

7 "I will go and make him well," Jesus said.

8 "Lord," the captain answered, "I'm not good enough for you to come under my roof. But just say a word, and my slave will be made well. 9 I'm only a man who has to obey others, but I have soldiers under me. I tell one of them, Go, and he goes. And another, Come, and he comes. And my slave, Do this, and he does it."

10 Surprised to hear this, Jesus said to the people who were following Him, "I tell you the truth, not even in Israel have I found such faith. 11 I also tell you, many will come *from the east and the west*[32] and will eat with Abraham, Isaac, and Jacob in the kingdom of heaven, 12 but those who were born to be the heirs of the kingdom will be thrown out into the dark. There they will cry and grind their teeth."

13 "Go," Jesus told the captain. "Let it be as you believed." And the slave was made well in that hour.

Peter's Mother-in-Law

14 Jesus went into Peter's home, and there He saw his mother-in-law down in bed with a fever. 15 He touched her hand, and the fever left her. She got up and waited on Him.

16 In the evening the people brought Him many who were plagued by devils. He drove out the spirits by talking to them, and all who were sick He made well. 17 In this way what the prophet Isaiah said was to come true, *He took away our sicknesses and carried our diseases.*[33]

18 When Jesus saw a crowd around Him, He gave orders to cross to the other side.

[31] Lev. 13:7, 49
[32] Mal. 1:11
[33] Is. 53:4

[b] Grk., *these words.* [a] Grk., *for a testimony.*

K.J.V.

the other side. 19And a certain scribe came, and said unto him, Master, I will follow thee whithersoever thou goest. 20And Jesus saith unto him, The foxes have holes, and the birds of the air *have* nests; but the Son of man hath not where to lay *his* head. 21And another of his disciples said unto him, Lord, suffer me first to go and bury my father. 22 But Jesus said unto him, Follow me; and let the dead bury their dead.

23 And when he was entered into a ship, his disciples followed him. 24And, behold, there arose a great tempest in the sea, insomuch that the ship was covered with the waves: but he was asleep. 25And his disciples came to *him*, and awoke him, saying, Lord, save us: we perish. 26And he saith unto them, Why are ye fearful, O ye of little faith? Then he arose, and rebuked the winds and the sea; and there was a great calm. 27 But the men marvelled, saying, What manner of man is this, that even the winds and the sea obey him!

28 And when he was come to the other side into the country of the Gergesenes, there met him two possessed with devils, coming out of the tombs, exceeding fierce, so that no man might pass by that way. 29And behold, they cried out, saying, What have we to do with thee, Jesus, thou Son of God? art thou come hither to torment us before the time? 30And there was a good way off from them a herd of many swine feeding. 31 So the devils besought him, saying, If thou cast us out, suffer us to go away into the herd of swine. 32And he said unto them, Go. And when they were come out, they went into the herd of swine: and, behold, the whole herd of swine ran violently down a steep place into the sea, and perished in the waters. 33And they that kept them fled, and went their ways into the city, and told every thing, and what was befallen to the possessed of the devils. 34And, behold, the whole city came out to meet Jesus: and when they saw him, they besought *him* that he would depart out of their coasts.

N.A.S.

19And a certain scribe came and said to Him, "Teacher, I will follow You wherever You go." 20And Jesus *said to him, "The foxes have holes, and the birds of the air *have* nests; but the Son of Man has nowhere to lay His head." 21And another of the disciples said to Him, "Lord, permit me first to go and bury my father." 22 But Jesus *said to him, "Follow Me; and allow the dead to bury their own dead."

23 And when He got into the boat, His disciples followed Him. 24And behold, there arose a great storm in the sea, so that the boat was covered with the waves; but He Himself was asleep. 25And they came to *Him*, and awoke Him, saying, "Save *us*, Lord; we are perishing!" 26And He *said to them, "Why are you timid, you men of little faith?" Then He arose, and rebuked the winds and the sea; and it became perfectly calm. 27And the men marveled, saying, "What kind of a man is this, that even the winds and the sea obey Him?"

28 And when He had come to the other side into the country of the Gadarenes, two men who were demon-possessed met Him as they were coming out of the tombs; *they were* so exceedingly violent that no one could pass by that road. 29And behold, they cried out, saying, "What do we have to do with You, Son of God? Have You come here to torment us before the time?" 30 Now there was at a distance from them a herd of many swine feeding. 31And the demons *began* to entreat Him, saying, "If You are *going to* cast us out, send us into the herd of swine." 32And He said to them, "Begone!" And they came out, and went into the swine; and behold, the whole herd rushed down the steep bank into the sea, and perished in the waters. 33And the herdsmen fled, and went away to the city, and reported everything, including the *incident* of the demoniacs. 34And behold, the whole city came out to meet Jesus; and when they saw Him, they entreated *Him* to depart from their region.

9 And he entered into a ship, and passed over, and came into his own city. 2And, behold, they brought to him a man sick of the palsy, lying on a bed: and Jesus seeing their faith said unto the sick of the palsy; Son, be of good cheer; thy sins be forgiven thee. 3And, behold, certain of the scribes said within themselves, This *man* blasphemeth. 4And Jesus knowing their thoughts said, Wherefore think ye evil in your hearts? 5 For whether is easier, to say, *Thy* sins be forgiven thee; or to say, Arise, and walk? 6 But that ye may know that the Son of man

9 And getting into a boat, He crossed over, and came to His own city. 2And behold, they were bringing to Him a paralytic, lying on a bed; and Jesus seeing their faith said to the paralytic, "Take courage, *My* son, your sins are forgiven." 3And behold, some of the scribes said to themselves, "This *fellow* blasphemes." 4And Jesus knowing their thoughts said, "Why are you thinking evil in your hearts? 5 "For which is easier, to say, 'Your sins are forgiven,' or to say, 'Rise, and walk'? 6 "But in order that

WILLIAMS

19And a scribe came up and said to Him, "Teacher, I will follow you wherever you may go."

20 And Jesus said to him, "Foxes have holes, even wild birds have roosts, but the Son of Man has nowhere to lay His head."

21 Another of His disciples said to Him, "Lord, let me first go back and bury my father."

22 And Jesus said to him, "Follow me, and leave the dead to bury their own dead."

23 And He got into a boat, and His disciples went with Him. 24And suddenly a furious storm came up, so that the boat was being covered over by the bursting billows, but He kept on sleeping. 25 So they went to Him and woke Him up, and said, "Lord, save us; we are going down!"

26 And He said to them, "Why are you afraid, O you with little faith?"

Then He got up and rebuked the winds and the sea, and there was a great calm. 27And the men were dumfounded, and said, "What sort of man is this, for even the winds and the sea obey Him!"

28 When He reached the other side, in the district of Gadara, there faced Him two men, who were under the power of demons, who were just coming out from the tombs. They were such terrors that nobody could pass that way. 29And they suddenly screamed, "What do you want of us, you Son of God? Have you come here before the appointed time to torture us?"

30 Now there was not far from there a large drove of hogs feeding. 31And the demons kept begging Him and saying, "If you are going to drive us out, send us into the drove of hogs."

32 And He said to them, "Begone!"

And they went out of the men and got into the hogs, and suddenly the whole drove, in a stampede, rushed over the cliff into the sea, and died in the water. 33And the men who fed them fled, and went off to the town, and told it all, and what occurred to the two men who were under the power of demons. 34And suddenly all the town turned out to meet Jesus, and as soon as they saw Him, they begged Him to move on and leave their neighborhood.

9 *A paralyzed man cured; Matthew the tax-collector, converted, gives Jesus a banquet; two short stories about fasting; a woman with a hemorrhage cured; Jairus' daughter raised to life; two blind men cured*

And He got into a boat and crossed to the other side, and went into His home[a] town. 2And all at once some men were bringing to Him a paralyzed man, lying on a couch. And because He saw their faith, Jesus said to the paralyzed man, "Cheer up, my child, your sins are forgiven."

3 Then some of the scribes said to themselves, "He is a blasphemer."

4 And Jesus knew their thoughts, and said, "Why do you have such wicked thoughts in your hearts? 5 For which is easier, to say 'Your sins are forgiven,' or, to say 'Get up and go to walking'? 6 But to show[b] you that the Son

[a] Grk., *His own town;* i.e., Capernaum. [b] Grk., *that you may know.*

BECK

"I Will Follow You, but—"

19 A man trained in the Bible came to Him and said, "Teacher, I will follow You anywhere You go."

20 "Foxes have holes," Jesus told him, "and birds in the air have nests, but the Son of Man doesn't have a place to lay His head."

21 "Lord," another disciple said to Him, "first let me go and bury my father."

22 But Jesus told him, "Follow Me and let the dead bury their dead."

23 Jesus stepped into a boat, and His disciples went with Him. 24 Suddenly a big storm stirred the lake so that the waves were covering the boat. But He was sleeping.

25 So they went and woke Him up. "Lord, save us!" they said. "We're drowning!"

26 "Why are you afraid?" He asked them. "You trust Me so little!" Then He got up and ordered the winds and the lake to be quiet, and they became very calm.

27 The men were amazed and said, "What kind of man is He? Even the winds and the lake obey Him!"

The Gadarenes

28 He went to the country of the Gadarenes on the other side of the lake. There two men with devils in them came out of the burial places and met Him. They were so savage nobody could go along that road.

29 "Let us alone, Son of God!" they shouted. "Did you come here to torture us before it is time?"

30 Far away a herd of many hogs was feeding. 31 "If you mean to drive us out," the devils were begging Jesus, "send us into that herd of hogs."

32 "Go," He told them. They came out and went into the hogs. Then the whole herd stampeded down the cliff into the lake and died in the water.

33 Those who had taken care of the hogs ran away and went into the town, where they told everything, especially about the men plagued by devils. 34 Then the whole town came out to meet Jesus. When they saw Him, they begged Him to leave their country.

9 He got into a boat and crossed over.

Jesus Forgives Sins

1 Jesus came to His own town. 2 There people brought Him a paralyzed man, lying on a bed.

When Jesus saw their faith, He said to the paralytic, "Courage, son! Your sins are forgiven."

3 Then some of the Bible scholars said to themselves, "He's blaspheming."

4 Jesus knew what they were thinking. "Why do you think evil in your hearts?" He asked them. 5 "Is it easier to say, 'Your sins are forgiven,' or to say, 'Get up and walk'? 6 I want

K.J.V.

hath power on earth to forgive sins, (then saith he to the sick of the palsy,) Arise, take up thy bed, and go unto thine house. 7 And he arose, and departed to his house. 8 But when the multitudes saw *it*, they marvelled, and glorified God, which had given such power unto men.

9 And as Jesus passed forth from thence, he saw a man, named Matthew, sitting at the receipt of custom: and he saith unto him, Follow me. And he arose, and followed him.

10 And it came to pass, as Jesus sat at meat in the house, behold, many publicans and sinners came and sat down with him and his disciples. 11 And when the Pharisees saw *it*, they said unto his disciples, Why eateth your master with publicans and sinners? 12 But when Jesus heard *that*, he said unto them, They that be whole need not a physician, but they that are sick. 13 But go ye and learn what *that* meaneth, I will have mercy, and not sacrifice: for I am not come to call the righteous, but sinners to repentance.

14 Then came to him the disciples of John, saying, Why do we and the Pharisees fast oft, but thy disciples fast not? 15 And Jesus said unto them, Can the children of the bridechamber mourn, as long as the bridegroom is with them? but the days will come, when the bridegroom shall be taken from them, and then shall they fast. 16 No man putteth a piece of new cloth unto an old garment; for that which is put in to fill it up taketh from the garment, and the rent is made worse. 17 Neither do men put new wine into old bottles: else the bottles break, and the wine runneth out, and the bottles perish: but they put new wine into new bottles, and both are preserved.

18 While he spake these things unto them, behold, there came a certain ruler, and worshipped him, saying, My daughter is even now dead: but come and lay thy hand upon her, and she shall live. 19 And Jesus arose, and followed him, and *so did* his disciples.

20 And, behold, a woman, which was diseased with an issue of blood twelve years, came behind *him*, and touched the hem of his garment: 21 For she said within herself, If I may but touch his garment, I shall be whole. 22 But Jesus turned him about, and when he saw her, he said, Daughter, be of good comfort; thy faith hath made thee whole. And the woman was made whole from that hour. 23 And when Jesus came into the ruler's house, and saw the minstrels and the people making a noise, 24 He said unto them, Give place: for the maid is not dead, but sleepeth. And they laughed him to scorn. 25 But when the people were put forth, he went in, and took her by the hand, and the maid arose. 26 And the fame hereof went abroad into all that land.

27 And when Jesus departed thence, two blind men followed him, crying, and saying, *Thou* Son of David, have mercy on us. 28 And when

N.A.S.

you may know that the Son of Man has authority on earth to forgive sins"—then He *said to the paralytic, "Rise, take up your bed, and go home." 7 And he rose, and went to his home. 8 But when the multitudes saw *this*, they were filled with awe, and glorified God, who had given such authority to men.

9 And as Jesus passed on from there, He saw a man, called Matthew, sitting in the tax office; and He *said to him, "Follow Me!" And he rose, and followed Him.

10 And it happened that as He was reclining *at table* in the house, behold many tax-gatherers and sinners came and joined Jesus and His disciples *at the table*. 11 And when the Pharisees saw *this*, they said to His disciples, "Why does your Teacher eat with the tax-gatherers and sinners?" 12 But when He heard this, He said, "*It is* not those who are healthy who need a physician, but those who are ill. 13 "But go and learn what *this* means, 'I DESIRE COMPASSION, ªAND NOT SACRIFICE;' for I did not come to call *the* righteous, but sinners."

14 Then the disciples of John *came to Him, saying, "Why do we and the Pharisees fast, but Your disciples do not fast?" 15 And Jesus said to them, "The attendants of the bridegroom cannot mourn, as long as the bridegroom is with them, can they? But the days will come when the bridegroom is taken away from them, and then they will fast. 16 "But no one puts a patch of unshrunk cloth on an old garment; for the patch pulls away from the garment, and a worse tear results. 17 "Nor do *men* put new wine into old wine-skins; otherwise the wine-skins burst, and the wine pours out, and the wine-skins are ruined; but they put new wine into fresh wine-skins, and both are preserved."

18 While He was saying these things to them, behold, there came a synagogue official, and bowed down before Him, saying, "My daughter has just died; but come and lay Your hand on her, and she will live." 19 And Jesus rose and *began* to follow him, and *so did* His disciples. 20 And behold, a woman who had been suffering from a hemorrhage for twelve years, came up behind Him and touched the fringe of His cloak; 21 for she was saying to herself, "If I only touch His garment, I shall get well." 22 But Jesus turning and seeing her said, "Daughter, take courage; your faith has made you well." And at once the woman was made well. 23 And when Jesus came into the official's house, and saw the flute-players, and the crowd in noisy disorder, 24 He *began* to say, "Depart; for the girl is not dead, but is asleep." And they were laughing at Him. 25 But when the crowd had been put out, He entered and took her by the hand; and the girl arose. 26 And this news went out into all that land.

27 And as Jesus passed on from there, two blind men followed Him, crying out, and saying, "Have mercy on us, Son of David!" 28 And

[a] I.e., more than.

24

WILLIAMS

of Man has authority to forgive sins on earth"
—turning to the paralyzed man, He said to
him—"Get up, pick up your bed, and go
home."

7 And he got up and went home. 8And the
crowds saw it, and were stricken with awe, and
gave praise to God for giving such power to
men.

9 And as He was passing along from there,
He saw a man named Matthew in his seat at
the tax-collector's desk, and He said to him,
"Follow me." And he got up and followed
Him.

10 While He was at table in the house many
tax-collectors and notorious sinners came in
and took their seats at table with Jesus and His
disciples. 11And when the Pharisees saw this,
they said to His disciples, "Why does your
Teacher eat with tax-collectors and notorious
sinners?"

12 And when He heard it, He said, "It is
not well, but sick people that have to send for
a doctor. 13 Go, learn what this means, 'It is
mercy and not sacrifice that I want.' It is not
upright but sinful people that I have come to
invite."

14 Then John's disciples went up to Him,
and said, "Why do we and the Pharisees practice fasting, but your disciples do not?"

15 Jesus said to them, "The wedding guests
cannot mourn, can they, as long as they have
the bridegroom with them? But a time will
come when the bridegroom will be taken away
from them, and then they will fast. 16 Nobody
sews a patch of brand-new* goods on an old
coat, for such a patch would tear away from the
coat, and the hole would be bigger than ever.
17 Nobody pours new wine into old wine-bottles;
or, if they do, the bottles burst, the wine runs
out, and the bottles are ruined. But people
pour new wine into new wine-bottles, and so
both are preserved."

18 And just as He was saying these things to
them, an official came up and fell on his knees
before Him, and said, "My daughter has just
died, but come and lay your hand upon her
and she will come to life."

19 And Jesus got up and followed him; and
His disciples, too. 20And a woman who had
had a hemorrhage for twelve years came up
and touched the tassel on His coat.d 21 For she
kept saying to herself, "If I can only touch
His coat, I will get well."

22 And Jesus, on turning and seeing her,
said, "Cheer up, my daughter! Your faith has
cured you." And from that moment the woman
was well.

23 And Jesus, on coming to the house of the
official, and on seeing the flute-players and the
wailing crowd, 24 said, "Go away, for the girl
is not dead, but is sleeping." And they began
to laugh in His face. 25 But when the crowd
had been driven out, He went in and took hold
of her hand, and the girl got up. 26And the
news about her spread all over that country.

27 As Jesus was passing along from there,
two blind men followed Him, shouting, "Do
pity us, O Son of David!"

28 After He had gone into the house, and

BECK

you to know the Son of Man has power on
earth to forgive sins." Then He said to the paralyzed man, "Get up, take your bed, and go
home."

7 He got up and went home. 8 When the
crowd saw this, they were frightened, and they
praised God for giving such power to men.

Matthew

9 When Jesus left that place, He saw a man
by the name of Matthew sitting in the tax
office. "Come with Me," He told him. He got
up and went with Him.

10 As Jesus was lying down to eat at his
home, many tax collectors and sinners came and
ate with Jesus and His disciples. 11 When the
Pharisees saw this, they asked His disciples,
"Why does your Teacher eat with tax collectors
and sinners?"

12 Jesus heard them and said, "Those who
are healthy don't need a doctor, but the sick.
13 Go and learn what this means: *I like mercy
and not* mere *sacrifice.*84 I didn't come to call
righteous people but sinners."

The Bridegroom

14 Then John's disciples came to Jesus. "We
and the Pharisees fast," they said. "Why don't
Your disciples fast?"

15 Jesus asked them, "Can the bridegroom's
friends mourn while the bridegroom is with
them? The time will come when the bridegroom
will be taken away from them; then they'll fast.
16 "Nobody sews a piece of new cloth on an
old garment. The patch will tear away some of
the garment, and the hole will get worse. 17 Nobody pours new wine into old wineskins. If you
do, the skins burst, the wine runs out, and the
skins are ruined. No, you pour new wine into
fresh skins; then both are preserved."

The Daughter of Jairus

18 While He was talking to the people, a
leader came to Him and bowed down to the
ground before Him. "My daughter just died,"
he said, "but come, lay your hand on her, and
she will live."

19 Jesus and His disciples got up and followed him.

20 Now there was a woman who had a flow
of blood for twelve years. She came to Him
from behind and touched the tassel of His garment. 21 "If I only touch His garment," she said
to herself, "I'll get well."

22 Jesus turned and saw her. "Cheer up,
daughter," He said, "your faith made you well."
After that the woman was well.

23 When Jesus came to the leader's home, He
saw the flute players and the noisy crowd.
24 "Go away," He said. "The little girl isn't
dead; she's sleeping." But they laughed at Him.

25 When the crowd had been put outside, He
went in and took her hand, and the little girl
got up.

26 The news about this spread all over that
part of the country.

Two Blind Men

27 When Jesus left that place, two blind men
followed Him and called, "Have pity on us,
Son of David."

28 He went into a house, and there the blind

---

[c] Grk., *unshrunken*. [d] Really *a tunic*, but our
word, *coat*, modernizes it.

[34] Hos. 6:6

K.J.V.

he was come into the house, the blind men came to him: and Jesus saith unto them, Believe ye that I am able to do this? They said unto him, Yea, Lord. 29 Then touched he their eyes, saying, According to your faith be it unto you. 30And their eyes were opened; and Jesus straitly charged them, saying, See *that* no man know *it*. 31 But they, when they were departed, spread abroad his fame in all that country.

32 As they went out, behold, they brought to him a dumb man possessed with a devil. 33And when the devil was cast out, the dumb spake: and the multitudes marvelled, saying, It was never so seen in Israel. 34 But the Pharisees said, He casteth out devils through the prince of the devils. 35And Jesus went about all the cities and villages, teaching in their synagogues, and preaching the gospel of the kingdom, and healing every sickness and every disease among the people.

36 But when he saw the multitudes, he was moved with compassion on them, because they fainted, and were scattered abroad, as sheep having no shepherd. 37 Then saith he unto his disciples, The harvest truly *is* plenteous, but the labourers *are* few; 38 Pray ye therefore the Lord of the harvest, that he will send forth labourers into his harvest.

N.A.S.

after He had come into the house, the blind men came up to Him, and Jesus *said to them, "Do you believe that I am able to do this?" They *said to Him, "Yes, Lord." 29 Then He touched their eyes, saying, "Be it done to you according to your faith." 30And their eyes were opened. And Jesus sternly warned them, saying, "See *here*, let no one know *about this!*" 31 But they went out, and spread the news about Him in all that land.

32 And as they were going out, behold, a dumb man demon-possessed was brought to Him. 33And after the demon was cast out, the dumb man spoke; and the multitudes marveled, saying, "Nothing like this was ever seen in Israel." 34 But the Pharisees were saying, "He casts out the demons by the ruler of the demons."

35 And Jesus was going about all the cities and the villages, teaching in their synagogues, and proclaiming the gospel of the kingdom, and healing every kind of disease and every kind of sickness. 36And seeing the multitudes, He felt compassion for them, because they were distressed and downcast like sheep without a shepherd. 37 Then He *said to His disciples, "The harvest is plentiful, but the workers are few. 38 "Therefore beseech the Lord of the harvest to send out workers into His harvest."

10 And when he had called unto *him* his twelve disciples, he gave them power *against* unclean spirits, to cast them out, and to heal all manner of sickness and all manner of disease. 2 Now the names of the twelve apostles are these; The first, Simon, who is called Peter, and Andrew his brother; James *the son* of Zebedee, and John his brother; 3 Philip, and Bartholomew; Thomas, and Matthew the publican; James *the son* of Alpheus, and Lebbeus, whose surname was Thaddeus; 4 Simon the Canaanite, and Judas Iscariot, who also betrayed him. 5 These twelve Jesus sent forth, and commanded them, saying, Go not into the way of the Gentiles, and into *any* city of the Samaritans enter ye not: 6 But go rather to the lost sheep of the house of Israel. 7And as ye go, preach, saying, The kingdom of heaven is at hand. 8 Heal the sick, cleanse the lepers, raise the dead, cast out devils: freely ye have received, freely give. 9 Provide neither gold, nor silver, nor brass in your purses; 10 Nor scrip for *your* journey, neither two coats, neither shoes, nor yet staves: for the workman is worthy of his meat. 11And into whatsoever city or town ye shall enter, inquire who in it is worthy; and there abide till ye go thence. 12And when ye come into a house, salute it. 13And if the house be worthy, let your peace come upon it: but if it be not worthy, let your peace return to you. 14And whosoever

10 And having summoned His twelve disciples, He gave them authority over unclean spirits, to cast them out, and to heal every kind of disease and every kind of sickness. 2 Now the names of the twelve apostles are these: The first, Simon, who is called Peter, and Andrew his brother; and James the *son* of Zebedee, and John his brother; 3 Philip and Bartholomew; Thomas and Matthew the tax-gatherer; James the *son* of Alphaeus, and Thaddaeus; 4 Simon the Cananaean, and Judas Iscariot, the one who betrayed Him. 5 These twelve Jesus sent out after instructing them, saying, "Do not go in *the* way of *the* Gentiles, and do not enter *any* city of the Samaritans; 6 but rather go to the lost sheep of the house of Israel. 7 "And as you go, preach, saying, 'The kingdom of heaven is at hand.' 8 "Heal *the* sick, raise *the* dead, cleanse *the* lepers, cast out demons; freely you received, freely give. 9 "Do not acquire gold, or silver, or copper for your money belts; 10 or a bag for *your* journey, or even two tunics, or sandals, or a staff; for the worker is worthy of his support. 11 "And into whatever city or village you enter, inquire who is worthy in it; and abide there until you go away. 12 "And as you enter the house, give it your greeting. 13 "And if the house is worthy, let your *greeting of* peace come upon it; but if it is not worthy, let your *greeting of* peace return to you. 14 "And who-

WILLIAMS

the blind men had gone up to Him, Jesus said to them, "Do you really believe that I can do this?"

They said to Him, "Yes, Lord."

29 Then He touched their eyes, and said, "In accordance with your faith it must be done for you." 30And their eyes received strength to see.[e] Then Jesus sternly charged them, "See that nobody knows it." 31 But they went out and spread the news about Him all over that country.

32 But at the very time they were going out, some people brought to Him a dumb man, who was under the power of a demon, 33 and after the demon had been driven out, the dumb man could talk. So the crowds were dumfounded, saying, "Never before among the Jews was anything like this!"

34 But the Pharisees kept on saying, "It is by the help of the prince of the demons that He drives them out."

35 Jesus kept visiting all the towns and villages, teaching in their synagogues, preaching the good news of the kingdom, and curing every sort of sickness and ailment.

36 When He saw the crowds, His heart was moved with pity for them, because they were tired and scattered like sheep without a shepherd. 37 Then He said to His disciples, "The harvest is plentiful, but the reapers are scarce. 38 So pray the Lord of the harvest to send out reapers to His harvest field."

BECK

men came to Him. "Do you believe I can do this?" Jesus asked them.

"Yes, Lord," they told Him.

29 Then He touched their eyes and said, "As you believed, so it must be done to you!" 30 Then they could see again.

"See that nobody finds out about this!" He sternly ordered them. 31 But they went out and spread the news about Him all over that part of the country.

A Dumb Man

32 As they were going out, a dumb man with a devil in him was brought to Him. 33 But as soon as the devil was put out, the dumb man spoke.

The crowds were amazed and said, "We've never seen anything like this in Israel."

34 But the Pharisees declared, "The ruler of the devils helps Him drive out the devils."

Pray for Workers

35 Then Jesus traveled through all the towns and villages, teaching in their synagogs, preaching the good news of the Kingdom, and healing every disease and sickness.

36 As He saw the crowds, He felt sorry for them, because they were troubled and helpless *like sheep without a shepherd.*[35] 37 Then He said to His disciples, "There's much grain to be harvested, but there are only a few workers. 38 Ask the Owner of the crop to send out workers to bring in His grain."

---

10 *The twelve appointed and sent out; warned against persecutors; rewards promised for service to others*

Then He called His twelve disciples to Him, and gave them authority over foul spirits, so that they could drive them out, and so that they could cure any disease or ailment.

2 Here are the names of the twelve apostles: first, Simon, who was named Peter, and his brother Andrew, James the son of Zebedee and his brother John, 3 Philip and Bartholomew, Thomas and Matthew the tax-collector, James the son of Alpheus, and Thaddeus, 4 Simon the zealot, and Judas Iscariot, who afterward betrayed Him.

5 Jesus sent these twelve out, after giving them the following charge:

"Do not go to the heathen, or to any Samaritan town, 6 but rather to the lost sheep of Israel's house. 7And as you go continue to preach, 'The kingdom of heaven is near.' 8 Keep on curing the sick, raising the dead, healing lepers, and driving out demons. You received and gave no pay; you must give and take none. 9 Do not accept gold or silver or even copper money for your purse, 10 and do not take a bag for your journey, nor two shirts, nor any shoes, nor a staff, for the workman deserves his support. 11 Into whatever town or village you go, inquire for some deserving person, and stay at his house until you leave the place. 12As you go into his house, wish it well, 13 and if the house should prove deserving, may your good wish for peace upon it come true; but if not, may your good wish bring peace to yourselves. 14And whoever will not welcome you, or

Jesus Sends Out the Twelve

10 Jesus called His twelve disciples and gave them authority to drive out unclean spirits and heal every disease and sickness.

2 These are the names of the twelve apostles: first, Simon, called Peter, and his brother Andrew; James, Zebedee's son, and his brother John; 3 Philip and Bartholomew, Thomas and Matthew, the tax collector; James, the son of Alphaeus, and Thaddaeus; 4 Simon the Zealot, and Judas, the man from Kerioth, who betrayed Him.

5 Jesus sent these twelve out with the following instructions: "Don't go among the Gentiles or into any town of the Samaritans. 6 But go to the lost sheep of Israel. 7As you go, preach, 'The kingdom of heaven is here.' 8 Heal the sick, raise the dead, cleanse lepers, drive out devils. Give these things as you received them—without pay.

9 "Don't take any gold, silver, or copper money along in your pockets, 10 and no bag for the way. Don't take two tunics, or shoes, or a stick—a worker earns his keep.

11 "When you go into any town or village, look for a person there who is deserving, and stay with him till you leave. 12 When you go into a home, greet it. 13 If the home is deserving, let your peace come on it. But if it's unworthy, let your peace come back to you. 14 If

---

[e] Grk., *were opened.*   [35] Num. 27:17; 1 Kings 22:17; Ezek. 34:5

shall not receive you, nor hear your words, when ye depart out of that house or city, shake off the dust of your feet. 15 Verily I say unto you, It shall be more tolerable for the land of Sodom and Gomorrah in the day of judgment, than for that city.

16 Behold, I send you forth as sheep in the midst of wolves: be ye therefore wise as serpents, and harmless as doves. 17 But beware of men: for they will deliver you up to the councils, and they will scourge you in their synagogues; 18And ye shall be brought before governors and kings for my sake, for a testimony against them and the Gentiles. 19 But when they deliver you up, take no thought how or what ye shall speak: for it shall be given you in that same hour what ye shall speak. 20 For it is not ye that speak, but the Spirit of your Father which speaketh in you. 21And the brother shall deliver up the brother to death, and the father the child: and the children shall rise up against their parents, and cause them to be put to death. 22 And he shall be hated of all men for my name's sake: but he that endureth to the end shall be saved. 23 But when they persecute you in this city, flee ye into another: for verily I say unto you, Ye shall not have gone over the cities of Israel, till the Son of man be come. 24 The disciple is not above his master, nor the servant above his lord. 25 It is enough for the disciple that he be as his master, and the servant as his lord. If they have called the master of the house Beelzebub, how much more shall they call them of his household? 26 Fear them not therefore: for there is nothing covered, that shall not be revealed; and hid, that shall not be known. 27 What I tell you in darkness, that speak ye in light: and what ye hear in the ear, that preach ye upon the housetops. 28And fear not them which kill the body, but are not able to kill the soul: but rather fear him which is able to destroy both soul and body in hell. 29Are not two sparrows sold for a farthing? and one of them shall not fall on the ground without your Father. 30 But the very hairs of your head are all numbered. 31 Fear ye not therefore, ye are of more value than many sparrows. 32 Whosoever therefore shall confess me before men, him will I confess also before my Father which is in heaven. 33 But whosoever shall deny me before men, him will I also deny before my Father which is in heaven. 34 Think not that I am come to send peace on earth: I came not to send peace, but a sword. 35 For I am come to set a man at variance against his father, and the daughter against her mother, and the daughter in law against her mother in law. 36And a man's foes shall be they of his own household. 37 He that loveth father or mother more than me is not worthy of me: and he that loveth son or daughter more than me is not worthy of me. 38 And he that taketh not his cross, and followeth after me, is not worthy of me. 39 He that findeth his life shall lose it: and he that loseth his life for my sake shall find it.

40 He that receiveth you receiveth me; and he that receiveth me receiveth him that sent me. 41 He that receiveth a prophet in the name of a prophet shall receive a prophet's reward; and he that receiveth a righteous man in the name of a righteous man shall receive a righteous man's reward. 42And whosoever shall give to drink unto one of these little ones a cup of cold water only in the name of a disciple, verily I

ever does not receive you, nor heed your words, as you go out of that house or that city, shake off the dust of your feet. 15 "Truly I say to you, it will be more tolerable for the land of Sodom and Gomorrah in the day of judgment, than for that city.

16 "Behold, I send you out as sheep in the midst of wolves; therefore be shrewd as serpents, and innocent as doves. 17 "But beware of men; for they will deliver you up to the courts, and scourge you in their synagogues; 18 and you shall even be brought before governors and kings for My sake, as a testimony to them and to the Gentiles. 19 "But when they deliver you up, do not become anxious about how or what you will speak; for it shall be given you in that hour what you are to speak. 20 "For it is not you who speak, but it is the Spirit of your Father who speaks in you. 21 "And brother will deliver up brother to death, and a father his child; and CHILDREN WILL RISE UP AGAINST PARENTS, and cause them to be put to death. 22 "And you will be hated by all on account of My name, but it is the one who has endured to the end who will be saved. 23 "But whenever they persecute you in this city, flee to the next; for truly I say to you, you shall not finish going through the cities of Israel, until the Son of Man comes.

24 "A disciple is not above his teacher, nor a slave above his master. 25 "It is enough for the disciple that he become as his teacher, and the slave as his master. If they have called the head of the house Beelzebul, how much more the members of his household! 26 "Therefore do not fear them, for there is nothing covered that will not be revealed, and hidden that will not be known. 27 "What I tell you in the darkness, speak in the light; and what you hear whispered in your ear, proclaim upon the housetops. 28 "And do not fear those who kill the body, but are unable to kill the soul; but rather fear Him who is able to destroy both soul and body in hell. 29 "Are not two sparrows sold for a ᵃcent? And yet not one of them will fall to the ground apart from your Father. 30 "But the very hairs of your head are all numbered. 31 "Therefore do not fear; you are of more value than many sparrows. 32 "Every one therefore who shall confess Me before men, I will also confess him before My Father who is in heaven. 33 "But whoever shall deny Me before men, I will also deny him before My Father who is in heaven.

34 "Do not think that I came to bring peace on the earth; I did not come to bring peace, but a sword. 35 "For I came to SET A MAN AGAINST HIS FATHER, AND A DAUGHTER AGAINST HER MOTHER, AND A DAUGHTER-IN-LAW AGAINST HER MOTHER-IN-LAW; 36 and A MAN'S ENEMIES WILL BE THE MEMBERS OF HIS HOUSEHOLD. 37 "He who loves father or mother more than Me is not worthy of Me; and he who loves son or daughter more than Me is not worthy of Me. 38 "And he who does not take his cross and follow after Me is not worthy of Me. 39 "He who has found his life shall lose it, and he who has lost his life for My sake shall find it.

40 "He who receives you receives Me, and he who receives Me receives Him who sent Me. 41 "He who receives a prophet in the name of a prophet shall receive a prophet's reward; and he who receives a righteous man in the name of a righteous man shall receive a righteous man's reward. 42 "And whoever in the name of a disciple gives to one of these little ones even a cup of

[a] Gr., assarion, the smallest copper coin.

WILLIAMS

listen to your words, on leaving that place shake off from your feet its very dust. 15 I tell you, the punishment on the day of judgment will be lighter for the land of Sodom and Gomorrah than for that town.

16 "Listen! I am sending you out as sheep surrounded by wolves. So you must be sensible like serpents and guileless like doves. 17 Be on your guard against men, for they will turn you over to the courts and will flog you in their synagogues, 18 and you will be brought before governors and kings for my sake, to bear witness to them and the heathen. 19 But when they turn you over to the courts, you must not worry at all about how or what you ought to speak, for it will be given you at that hour what you ought to speak. 20 For it is not you who are speaking, but the Spirit of your Father that is speaking through you. 21 One brother will turn another over to death, and a father his child, and children will take a stand against their parents, and will have them put to death.ᵃ 22And you will be hated by all men, because you bear my name; but whoever bears up to the end will be saved. 23 But whenever they persecute you in one town, flee to a different one. For I solemnly say to you, you will not cover all the towns of Israel before the Son of Man returns. 24 No pupil is better than his teacher, and no slave is better than his master. 25 The pupil should be satisfied to become like his teacher, and the slave should be satisfied to become like his master. If men have called the Head of the house Beelzebub, how much worse names will they heap upon the members of His family! 26 So you must never be afraid of them; for there is nothing covered that will not be uncovered, nor a secret that will not be known. 27 What I speak to you in the dark, tell in the light, and what you hear whispered in your ears, you must proclaim from housetops. 28 You must never be afraid of those who kill the body, but cannot kill the soul. But rather you must keep on fearing Him who can destroy both soul and body in the pit.ᵇ 29 Do not sparrows sell for a cent apiece? And yet not one of them can fall to the ground without your Father's notice. 30 Even the very hairs on your head have all been counted by God. 31 So stop being afraid; you are worth more than many sparrows. 32 Therefore, everyone who will own me before men I will own before my Father in heaven, 33 but anyone who disowns me before men I will disown before my Father in heaven.

34 "Do not suppose that I have come to bring peace to the earth. I have not come to bring peace but a sword. 35 For I have come to set a man against his father, and a daughter against her mother, and a daughter-in-law against her mother-in-law, 36 and a man's enemies will be members of his own family. 37Anybody who loves father or mother more than he loves me is not worthy of me, 38 and nobody is worthy of me who does not take up his cross and follow me. 39Anybody who gains his lower life will lose the higher life, and anybody who loses his lower life for my sake will gain the higher life.

40 "Whoever welcomes you welcomes me, and whoever welcomes me welcomes Him who sent me. 41 Whoever welcomes a prophet as a prophet will receive the same reward as a prophet, and whoever welcomes an upright man as such will receive the same reward as the upright man. 42And I solemnly say to you, no one who gives a cup of cold water to one of

[a] Grk., *will put them to death*. [b] Grk., *Gehenna*, almost equivalent to our word *pit*.

BECK

anyone doesn't welcome you or listen to what you say, leave that house or town, and shake the dust off your feet. 15 I tell you the truth, on Judgment Day it will be easier for the land of Sodom and Gomorrah than for that town.

16 "You see, I'm sending you like sheep among wolves. So be shrewd as snakes and innocent as doves. 17 Be on your guard against men, because they'll hand you over to their courts and whip you in their places of worship. 18 On My account you'll be dragged before governors and kings to testify to them and to the nations. 19 But when they hand you over to the authorities, don't worry how you'll speak or what you'll say. When the time comes, you'll be told what to say. 20 It isn't you speaking but your Father's Spirit speaking through you.

21 "A brother will betray his brother to death, and a father his child. Children will *turn against*ᵃᵃ their parents and kill them. 22 Everybody will hate you because of My name. But be faithful to the end, and you will be saved. 23 When they hunt you in one town, flee to another. Let me assure you, before you have gone through all the towns of Israel, the Son of Man will come.

24 "A pupil isn't above his teacher, or a slave above his master. 25A pupil should be satisfied to share his teacher's lot and a slave to share his master's. If the master of the house was called Beelzebul, how much more certainly the members of his household! 26 So, don't be afraid of them.

"All that's covered will be uncovered, and all that's hidden will be known. 27 What I say to you in the dark, tell in the daylight; and what you hear whispered in your ear, preach from the housetops. 28 Don't be afraid of those who kill the body and can't kill the soul, but fear Him who can destroy soul and body in hell. 29Aren't two sparrows sold for a cent? And not one of them will fall to the ground without your Father's permission. 30As for you, even the hairs on your head are all counted. 31 So don't be afraid. You're worth more than many sparrows. 32 Whoever will confess Me before other people, him will I confess before My Father in heaven. 33 Whoever will deny Me before others, him will I deny before My Father in heaven.

34 "Don't think that I came to bring peace to the earth. I didn't come to bring peace but a sword. 35 I came to set *a man against his father, a daughter against her mother, a daughter-in-law against her mother-in-law. 36A man's enemies will be those in his own home.*ᵃᵇ 37 If you love father or mother more than Me, you're not worthy of Me; and if you love son or daughter more than Me, you're not worthy of Me. 38 If you don't take your cross and follow Me, you're not worthy of Me. 39 If you find your life, you'll lose it, but if you lose your life for Me, you'll find it.

40 "Anyone who welcomes you welcomes Me; and anyone who welcomes Me welcomes Him who sent Me. 41Anyone who welcomes a prophet because he is a prophet will get a prophet's reward. Anyone who welcomes a righteous man because he is righteous will get a righteous man's reward. 42Anyone who will give one of these little ones just a cup of cold

[36] Micah 7:6

say unto you, he shall in no wise lose his reward.

cold water to drink, truly I say to you he shall not lose his reward."

11 And it came to pass, when Jesus had made an end of commanding his twelve disciples, he departed thence to teach and to preach in their cities. 2 Now when John had heard in the prison the works of Christ, he sent two of his disciples, 3And said unto him, Art thou he that should come, or do we look for another? 4 Jesus answered and said unto them, Go and shew John again those things which ye do hear and see: 5 The blind receive their sight, and the lame walk, the lepers are cleansed, and the deaf hear, the dead are raised up, and the poor have the gospel preached to them. 6And blessed is he, whosoever shall not be offended in me.

7 And as they departed, Jesus began to say unto the multitudes concerning John, What went ye out into the wilderness to see? A reed shaken with the wind? 8 But what went ye out for to see? A man clothed in soft raiment? behold, they that wear soft *clothing* are in kings' houses. 9 But what went ye out for to see? A prophet? yea, I say unto you, and more than a prophet. 10 For this is *he*, of whom it is written, Behold, I send my messenger before thy face, which shall prepare thy way before thee. 11 Verily I say unto you, Among them that are born of women there hath not risen a greater than John the Baptist: notwithstanding, he that is least in the kingdom of heaven is greater than he. 12And from the days of John the Baptist until now the kingdom of heaven suffereth violence, and the violent take it by force. 13 For all the prophets and the law prophesied until John. 14And if ye will receive *it*, this is Elias, which was for to come. 15 He that hath ears to hear, let him hear.

16 But whereunto shall I liken this generation? It is like unto children sitting in the markets, and calling unto their fellows, 17And saying, We have piped unto you, and ye have not danced; we have mourned unto you, and ye have not lamented. 18 For John came neither eating nor drinking, and they say, He hath a devil. 19 The Son of man came eating and drinking, and they say, Behold a man gluttonous, and a winebibber, a friend of publicans and sinners. But wisdom is justified of her children.

20 Then began he to upbraid the cities wherein most of his mighty works were done, because they repented not: 21 Woe unto thee, Chorazin!

11 And it came about that when Jesus had finished giving instructions to His twelve disciples, He departed from there to teach and preach in their cities.

2 Now when John in prison heard of the works of Christ, he sent *word* by his disciples, 3 and said to Him, "Are You the Coming One, or shall we look for someone else?" 4And Jesus answered and said to them, "Go and report to John the things which you hear and see: 5 *the* BLIND RECEIVE SIGHT and *the* lame walk, *the* lepers are cleansed and *the* deaf hear, and *the* dead are raised up, and *the* POOR HAVE THE GOSPEL PREACHED to them. 6 "And blessed is he who keeps from stumbling over Me."

7 And as these were going *away*, Jesus began to say to the multitudes concerning John, "What did you go out into the wilderness to look at? A reed shaken by the wind? 8 "But what did you go out to see? A man dressed in soft *clothing*? Behold, those who wear soft *clothing* are in kings' palaces. 9 "But why did you go out? To see a prophet? Yes, I tell you, and one who is more than a prophet. 10 "This is the one about whom it was written,
'BEHOLD, I SEND MY MESSENGER BEFORE YOUR FACE,
WHO WILL PREPARE YOUR WAY BEFORE YOU.'
11 "Truly, I say to you, among those born of women there has not arisen *anyone* greater than John the Baptist; yet he who is least in the kingdom of heaven is greater than he. 12 "And from the days of John the Baptist until now the kingdom of heaven suffers violence, and violent men take it by force. 13 "For all the prophets and the Law prophesied until John. 14 "And if you care to accept *it*, he himself is Elijah, who was to come. 15 "He who has ears to hear, let him hear. 16 "But to what shall I compare this generation? It is like children sitting in the market places, who call out to the other *children*, 17 and say, 'We played the flute for you, and you did not dance; we sang a dirge, and you did not mourn.' 18 "For John came neither eating nor drinking, and they say, 'He has a demon!' 19 "The Son of Man came eating and drinking, and they say, 'Behold, a gluttonous man and a drunkard, a friend of tax-gatherers and sinners!' Yet wisdom is vindicated by her deeds."

20 Then He began to reproach the cities in which most of His miracles were done, because they did not repent. 21 "Woe to you,

WILLIAMS | BECK

WILLIAMS

the least of my disciples,ᶜ because he is a disciple, will ever fail to get his reward."

11 *John the Baptist, by a delegation, asks Jesus a question; John praised by Jesus; cities rejecting Jesus cursed; burden-bearers invited to Jesus for rest*

When Jesus had closed this charge to His disciples, He left there to teach and preach in their towns.

2 Now when John in prison heard of the doings of the Christ, he sent this message by his disciples: 3 "Are you the One who was to come, or should we keep on looking for a differentª one?"

4 And Jesus answered them, "Go and tell John what you hear and see: 5 the blind are seeing and the crippled are walking, the lepers are being healed and the deaf are hearing, the dead are being raised and the poor are having the good news preached to them. 6 And happy is the man who finds no cause for stumbling over me."

7 But as they were leaving, Jesus began to speak to the crowds about John: "What did you go out into the desert to gaze at? A reed that is tossed to and fro by the wind? 8 If not, what did you go out there to see? A man dressed in silks and satins?ᵇ No, people who dress in that way are found in the palaces of kings. 9 If not, why did you go out there? To see a prophet? 10 This is the man of whom the Scripture says,

" 'Attention! I am sending my messenger on before you;

He will prepare the road ahead of you.'

11 "I solemnly say to you, of all men born of women no one greater than John the Baptist has ever appeared; and yet the one who is least important in the kingdom of heaven is greater than he. 12 And from the days of John the Baptist until the present moment the kingdom of heaven has been continuously taken by storm, and those who take it by storm are seizing it as a precious prize. 13 For up to the days of John all the prophets, and even the law, prophesied about it, 14 and if you are willing to accept it, John himself is the Elijah who was to come. 15 Let him who has ears listen!

16 "But to what can I compare the leaders of this age? They are like little children sitting in the market places and calling to their fellows in the game,ᶜ

17 " 'We played the wedding march for you, but you did not dance;

We sang the funeral dirge, but you did not beat your breasts.'

18 For John came neither eating nor drinking with others, and yet they said, 'He has a demon.' 19 The Son of Man came eating and drinking with others, and they say, 'Just look at Him! A glutton and a wine-drinker, a chum of tax-collectors and notorious sinners!' And yet wisdom is vindicated by her doings!"

20 Then He began to censure the cities in which His many, many wonder-works had been done, because they did not repent. 21 "A curse

BECK

water because he is My disciple, I tell you, will certainly not lose his reward."

11 After Jesus finished giving His twelve disciples these instructions, He went on from there to teach and preach in their towns.

About John

2 When John, who was in prison, heard about the works of Christ, he sent his disciples 3 to ask Him, "Are You the One who is coming, or should we look for someone else?"

4 "Go," Jesus answered them, "tell John what you hear and see: 5 *The blind see,* the lame walk, lepers are made clean, the *deaf hear,* the dead are raised, and *the poor hear the good news,*³⁷ 6 and happy is anyone who doesn't turn against Me."

7 When they were leaving, Jesus talked to the crowds about John:

"What did you go out into the wilderness to see—a reed shaken by the wind? 8 What, then, did you go out to see—a man dressed in soft robes? Those who wear soft robes you'll find in the palaces of kings.

9 "What, then, did you go out for—to see a prophet? Let Me assure you, he's even more than a prophet. 10 This is the one of whom it is written, *'I will send My messenger ahead of You to prepare* Your *way before*³⁸ You.' 11 I tell you the truth, there never has appeared a woman's son greater than John the Baptizer. Yet the least in the kingdom of heaven is greater than John. 12 From the time of John the Baptizer till now the kingdom of heaven has been suffering violence, and violent men are trying to take it by force. 13 All the prophets and the Law prophesied up to the time of John, 14 but he (are you willing to accept it?) is the Elijah who has to come. 15 If you can hear, listen!

16 "How should I picture the people of this age? They're like little children sitting in the marketplaces and calling to others: 17 'We played a tune on the flute for you, but you didn't dance. We sang a funeral song, but you didn't beat your breasts.' 18 John the Baptizer has come; he doesn't eat or drink, and people say, 'There's a devil in him!' 19 The Son of Man has come; He eats and drinks, and people say, 'Look at the glutton and drunkard, the friend of tax collectors and sinners!' And yet what a wise person does proves he's right."

Woe!

20 Then He began to denounce the cities where He had done most of His miracles, because they had not repented: 21 "Woe to you,

[c] Grk., *least of these little ones; so disciples.*
[a] Grk. word means *another of different quality.*
[b] Not expressed but strongly implied; Grk., *soft clothing,* Eng. *silks and satins.* [c] A wedding or funeral game often played by little children who sometimes balked in the game. The Pharisees compared to them.

[37] Is. 29:18; 35:5; 61:1
[38] Ex. 23:20

K.J.V.

woe unto thee, Bethsaida! for if the mighty works, which were done in you, had been done in Tyre and Sidon, they would have repented long ago in sackcloth and ashes. 22 But I say unto you, It shall be more tolerable for Tyre and Sidon at the day of judgment, than for you. 23 And thou, Capernaum, which art exalted unto heaven, shalt be brought down to hell: for if the mighty works, which have been done in thee, had been done in Sodom, it would have remained until this day. 24 But I say unto you, That it shall be more tolerable for the land of Sodom in the day of judgment, than for thee.

25 At that time Jesus answered and said, I thank thee, O Father, Lord of heaven and earth, because thou hast hid these things from the wise and prudent, and hast revealed them unto babes. 26 Even so, Father; for so it seemed good in thy sight. 27 All things are delivered unto me of my Father: and no man knoweth the Son, but the Father; neither knoweth any man the Father, save the Son, and he to whomsoever the Son will reveal him.

28 Come unto me, all ye that labour and are heavy laden, and I will give you rest. 29 Take my yoke upon you, and learn of me; for I am meek and lowly in heart: and ye shall find rest unto your souls. 30 For my yoke is easy, and my burden is light.

12 At that time Jesus went on the sabbath day through the corn; and his disciples were a hungered, and began to pluck the ears of corn, and to eat. 2 But when the Pharisees saw it, they said unto him, Behold, thy disciples do that which is not lawful to do upon the sabbath day. 3 But he said unto them, Have ye not read what David did, when he was a hungered, and they that were with him; 4 How he entered into the house of God, and did eat the shewbread, which was not lawful for him to eat, neither for them which were with him, but only for the priests? 5 Or have ye not read in the law, how that on the sabbath days the priests in the temple profane the sabbath, and are blameless? 6 But I say unto you, That in this place is one greater than the temple. 7 But if ye had known what this meaneth, I will have mercy, and not sacrifice, ye would not have condemned the guiltless. 8 For the Son of man is Lord even of the sabbath day. 9 And when he was departed thence, he went into their synagogue:

10 And, behold, there was a man which had his hand withered. And they asked him, saying, Is it lawful to heal on the sabbath days? that they might accuse him. 11 And he said unto them, What man shall there be among you, that shall have one sheep, and if it fall into a pit on the sabbath day, will he not lay hold on it, and lift it out? 12 How much then is a man better than a sheep? Wherefore it is lawful to do well on the

N.A.S.

Chorazin! Woe to you, Bethsaida! For if the miracles had occurred in Tyre and Sidon which occurred in you, they would have repented long ago in sackcloth and ashes. 22 "Nevertheless I say to you, it shall be more tolerable for Tyre and Sidon in the day of judgment, than for you. 23 "And you, Capernaum, will not be EXALTED TO HEAVEN, will you? You shall DESCEND TO HADES; for if the miracles had occurred in Sodom which occurred in you, it would have remained to this day. 24 "Nevertheless I say to you that it shall be more tolerable for the land of Sodom in the day of judgment, than for you."

25 At that time Jesus answered and said, "I praise Thee, O Father, Lord of heaven and earth, that Thou didst hide these things from the wise and intelligent and didst reveal them to babes. 26 "Yes, Father, for thus it was well-pleasing in Thy sight. 27 "All things have been handed over to Me by My Father; and no one knows the Son, except the Father; nor does anyone know the Father, except the Son, and anyone to whom the Son wills to reveal Him. 28 "Come to Me, all who are weary and heavy laden, and I will give you rest. 29 "Take My yoke upon you, and learn from Me, for I am gentle and humble in heart; and YOU SHALL FIND REST FOR YOUR SOULS. 30 "For My yoke is easy, and My load is light."

12 At that time Jesus went on the Sabbath through the grainfields, and His disciples became hungry and began to pick the heads of grain and eat. 2 But when the Pharisees saw it, they said to Him, "Behold, Your disciples do what is not lawful to do on a Sabbath." 3 But He said to them, "Have you not read what David did, when he became hungry, he and his companions; 4 how he entered the house of God, and they ate the consecrated bread, which was not lawful for him to eat, nor for those with him, but for the priests alone? 5 "Or have you not read in the Law, that on the Sabbath the priests in the temple break the Sabbath, and are innocent? 6 "But I say to you, that something greater than the temple is here. 7 "But if you had known what this means, 'I DESIRE COMPASSION, AND NOT A SACRIFICE,' you would not have condemned the innocent. 8 "For the Son of Man is Lord of the Sabbath."

9 And departing from there, He went into their synagogue. 10 And behold, there was a man with a withered hand. And they questioned Him, saying, "Is it lawful to heal on the Sabbath?"— in order that they might accuse Him. 11 And He said to them, "What man shall there be among you, who shall have one sheep, and if it falls into a pit on the Sabbath, will he not take hold of it, and lift it out? 12 "Of how much more value then is a man than a sheep! So then, it is

WILLIAMS

on you, Chorazin! A curse on you, Bethsaida! For if the wonder-works done in you had been done in Tyre and Sidon, long ago they would have repented in sackcloth and ashes. 22 Moreover, I tell you, on the day of judgment the punishment will be lighter[d] for Tyre and Sidon than for you! 23 And you, Capernaum, are you to be exalted to heaven? No, you belong to the regions of the dead! [e] For if the wonder-works done in you had been done in Sodom, it would have continued until today. 24 But I tell you, on the day of judgment the punishment will be lighter for the land of Sodom than for you!"

25 At that time Jesus said, "I thank You, Father, Lord of heaven and earth, for concealing these matters from wise and learned men, and for revealing them to little children. 26 Yes, Father, I thank You that Your good pleasure made it so. 27 All things have been entrusted to me by my Father, and no one but the Father perfectly knows the Son, and no one but the Son perfectly knows the Father, and the one to whom the Son chooses to make Him known. 28 Come to me, all of you who toil and carry burdens, and I, yes, I, will lead you into rest. 29 Put on my yoke, and learn from me, for I am gentle and humble in heart, and you will find rest for your souls, 30 for the yoke I offer is easy to wear, and the load I ask is light to bear."

12 *His curing a withered hand on the sabbath incites his enemies to plot Jesus' death; the unforgivable sin described; a spectacular sign refused; real kinsmen of Jesus*

At that time Jesus walked one sabbath through the wheat fields, and His disciples became hungry, and began to pull the heads of wheat and eat them. 2 And when the Pharisees saw it, they said to Him, "Just look! Your disciples are doing something that it is against the law to do on the sabbath!"

3 But He said to them, "Did you never read what David did, when he and his soldiers became hungry? 4 How he went into the house of God, and they ate the sacred loaves, which it was against the law for him or his soldiers to eat, or for anyone except the priests? 5 Or, did you never read in the law that the priests in the temple break the sabbath, and yet are not guilty? 6 But I tell you, there is something greater than the temple here! 7 If you only knew what that saying means, 'It is mercy and not sacrifice that I want,' you would not have condemned men who are not guilty. 8 For the Son of Man is Lord of the sabbath."

9 And on leaving there He went into their synagogue. 10 Now there was a man there with one hand withered. And, to get a charge against Him, they asked Him, "Is it right to cure people on the sabbath?"

11 But He said to them, "What man is there among you, if he has only one sheep and it falls into a ditch on the sabbath, will not lay hold on it and lift it out? 12 And how much more a man is worth than a sheep! So it is

[d] Grk., *it will be more bearable.* [e] Grk., *Hades, land of the dead.*

BECK

Chorazin! Woe to you, Bethsaida! If the miracles done in you had been done in Tyre and Sidon, they would long ago have repented in sackcloth and ashes. 22 I tell you, on Judgment Day it will be easier for Tyre and Sidon than for you. 23 And you, Capernaum, will you be *lifted up to heaven? You will go down to hell!* [39] If the miracles that have been done in you had been done in Sodom, it would still be there today. 24 I tell you, on Judgment Day it will be easier for the country of Sodom than for you."

"Come to Me!"

25 At that time Jesus said, "I praise You, Father, Lord of heaven and earth, for hiding these things from wise and intelligent people and uncovering them for little children. 26 Yes, Father, I praise You for wanting it to be that way.

27 "My Father put everything in My hands. Only the Father knows the Son. And only the Son—and anyone to whom the Son wants to reveal Him—knows the Father.

28 "Come to Me, all you who are working hard and carrying a heavy load,
And I will give you rest.
29 Take My yoke on you and learn from Me—
I am gentle and humble-minded—
Then *you will find your rest.*[40]
30 My yoke is easy,
And My load is light."

Lord of the Sabbath

12 At that time Jesus walked through the grainfields on a Sabbath. His disciples were hungry and began to pick the heads of grain and eat them.

2 When the Pharisees saw this, they said to Him, "Look, Your disciples are doing something they shouldn't do on a day of rest."

3 "Haven't you read what David did," Jesus asked them, "when he and his men got hungry— 4 how he went into God's house and ate the *loaves laid before God,*[41] which he and his men had no right to eat, but only the priests? 5 Or haven't you read in the Law that the priests in the temple work on a Sabbath as on other days and yet do no wrong? 6 I tell you, here is something greater than the temple. 7 If you knew what this means, *I like mercy and not* mere *sacrifice,*[42] you would not have condemned the innocent. 8 The Son of Man is Lord of the Sabbath."

The Shriveled Hand

9 He went on to another place and went into their synagog, and there was a man with a shriveled hand.

10 "Is it right to heal on a Sabbath?" they asked Him. They wanted to accuse Him of something.

11 "If anyone of you has only one sheep," Jesus asked them, "and it falls into a hole on a Sabbath, won't you take hold of it and lift it out? Now, isn't a man much more valuable than a sheep? 12 It is right, then, to do good on a day of rest!"

[39] Is. 14:13, 15
[40] Jer. 6:16
[41] Lev. 24:5-8; 1 Sam. 21:6
[42] Hos. 6:6

K.J.V.

sabbath days. 13 Then saith he to the man, Stretch forth thine hand. And he stretched *it* forth; and it was restored whole, like as the other.

14 Then the Pharisees went out, and held a council against him, how they might destroy him. 15 But when Jesus knew *it*, he withdrew himself from thence: and great multitudes followed him, and he healed them all; 16And charged them that they should not make him known: 17 That it might be fulfilled which was spoken by Esaias the prophet, saying, 18 Behold my servant, whom I have chosen; my beloved, in whom my soul is well pleased: I will put my Spirit upon him, and he shall shew judgment to the Gentiles. 19 He shall not strive, nor cry; neither shall any man hear his voice in the streets. 20A bruised reed shall he not break, and smoking flax shall he not quench, till he send forth judgment unto victory. 21And in his name shall the Gentiles trust.

22 Then was brought unto him one possessed with a devil, blind, and dumb: and he healed him, insomuch that the blind and dumb both spake and saw. 23And all the people were amazed, and said, Is not this the Son of David? 24 But when the Pharisees heard *it,* they said, This *fellow* doth not cast out devils, but by Beelzebub the prince of the devils. 25And Jesus knew their thoughts, and said unto them, Every kingdom divided against itself is brought to desolation; and every city or house divided against itself shall not stand: 26And if Satan cast out Satan, he is divided against himself; how shall then his kingdom stand? 27And if I by Beelzebub cast out devils, by whom do your children cast *them* out? therefore they shall be your judges. 28 But if I cast out devils by the Spirit of God, then the kingdom of God is come unto you. 29 Or else, how can one enter into a strong man's house, and spoil his goods, except he first bind the strong man? and then he will spoil his house. 30 He that is not with me is against me; and he that gathereth not with me scattereth abroad.

31 Wherefore I say unto you, All manner of sin and blasphemy shall be forgiven unto men: but the blasphemy *against* the *Holy* Ghost shall not be forgiven unto men. 32And whosoever speaketh a word against the Son of man, it shall be forgiven him: but whosoever speaketh against the Holy Ghost, it shall not be forgiven him, neither in this world, neither in the *world* to come. 33 Either make the tree good, and his fruit good; or else make the tree corrupt, and his fruit corrupt: for the tree is known by *his* fruit. 34 O generation of vipers, how can ye, being evil, speak good things? for out of the abundance of the heart the mouth speaketh. 35A good man out of the good treasure of the heart bringeth forth good things: and an evil man out of the evil treasure bringeth forth evil things. 36 But I say unto you, That every idle word that men shall speak, they shall give account thereof in the day of judgment. 37 For by thy words thou shalt be justified, and by thy words thou shalt be condemned.

N.A.S.

lawful to do good on the Sabbath." 13 Then He *said to the man, "Stretch out your hand!" And he stretched it out, and it was restored to normal, like the other. 14 But the Pharisees went out, and counseled together against Him, *as to* how they might destroy Him.

15 But Jesus, aware of *this,* withdrew from there. And many followed Him, and He healed them all, 16 and warned them not to make Him known; 17 in order that what was spoken through Isaiah the prophet, might be fulfilled, saying,

18 "Behold, My Servant whom I have chosen;
My Beloved in whom My soul is well pleased;
I will put My Spirit upon Him,
And He shall proclaim justice to the Gentiles.
19 "He will not quarrel, nor cry out;
Nor will any one hear His voice in the streets.
20 "A battered reed He will not break off,
And a smoldering wick He will not put out,
Until He leads justice to victory.
21 "And in His name the Gentiles will hope."

22 Then there was brought to Him a demon-possessed man *who was* blind and dumb, and He healed him, so that the dumb man spoke and saw. 23And all the multitudes were amazed, and *began to* say, "This *man* cannot be the Son of David, can he?" 24 But when the Pharisees heard it, they said, "This man casts out demons only by Beelzebul the ruler of the demons." 25And knowing their thoughts He said to them, "Any kingdom divided against itself is laid waste; and any city or house divided against itself shall not stand. 26 "And if Satan casts out Satan, he is divided against himself; how then shall his kingdom stand? 27 "And if I by Beelzebul cast out demons, by whom do your sons cast them out? Consequently they shall be your judges. 28 "But if I cast out demons by the Spirit of God, then the kingdom of God has come upon you. 29 "Or how can anyone enter the strong man's house and carry off his property, unless he first binds the strong *man?* And then he will plunder his house. 30 "He who is not with Me is against Me; and he who does not gather with Me scatters. 31 "Therefore I say to you, any sin and blasphemy shall be forgiven men; but blasphemy against the Spirit shall not be forgiven. 32 "And whoever shall speak a word against the Son of Man, it shall be forgiven him; but whoever shall speak against the Holy Spirit, it shall not be forgiven him, either in this age, or in the *age* to come. 33 "Either make the tree good, and its fruit good; or make the tree rotten, and its fruit rotten; for the tree is known by its fruit. 34 "You brood of vipers, how can you, being evil, speak what is good? For the mouth speaks out of that which fills the heart. 35 "The good man out of *his* good treasure brings forth what is good; and the evil man out of *his* evil treasure brings forth what is evil. 36 "And I say to you, that every careless word that men shall speak, they shall render account for it in the day of judgment. 37 "For by your words you shall be justified, and by your words you shall be condemned."

WILLIAMS

right to do good on the sabbath." 13 Then He said to the man, "Hold out your hand." And he held it out, and it was cured so that it became like the other. 14 But the Pharisees went out and held a consultation against Him, to put Him to death.

15 But because Jesus knew it, He left there. And many people followed Him, and He cured them all, 16 and charged them not to publish Him, 17 and in this way fulfilled the saying spoken by the prophet Isaiah:

18 "Here is my Servant whom I have chosen,
My Beloved, in whom my soul delights itself.
I will endow Him with my Spirit,
And He will announce a judgment to the heathen.
19 He will not debate, nor challenge anyone;
His voice will no one hear in the streets;
20 A broken reed He will not break off;
A flickering wick He will not put out,
Until He brings His judgment to victory.
21 On His name the heathen will set their hopes."

22 At that time some people brought to Him a man under the power of demons, who was blind and dumb, and He cured him, so that the dumb man could talk and see. 23 And all the crowds of people were dumfounded, and began to say, "He is by no means the Son of David, is He?" 24 But when the Pharisees heard it, they said, "This man is not driving out demons except by the help of Beelzebub, the prince of the demons."

25 But because He knew their thoughts, He said to them, "Any kingdom that is not united is in the process of destruction, and any city or family that is not united cannot last. 26 Now if Satan is driving out Satan, he has become disunited; how then can his kingdom last? 27 And if I am driving out demons by the help of Beelzebub, by whose help are your sons driving them out? So they must be your judges. 28 But if I by the Spirit of God am driving the demons out, then the kingdom of God has come to you. 29 Or, how can anyone get into a giant's house and carry off his goods, unless he first binds the giant? After that he can make a clean sweep of his house. 30 Whoever is not in partnership with me is against me, and whoever does not gather in partnership with me scatters. 31 So I tell you, every sin and all abusive speech will be forgiven men, but abuse against the Spirit cannot be forgiven. 32 And whoever speaks a word against the Son of Man will be forgiven for it, but whoever speaks abusively against the Holy Spirit will not be forgiven for it, either in this world or in the world to come.

33 "You must either make the tree healthy and its fruits healthy or make the tree sickly and its fruits sickly, for a tree is judged by its fruit. 34 You brood of vipers! How can you, wicked as you are, say anything that is good? For the mouth talks about the things that fill the heart.[a] 35 The good man out of his good inner storehouse, brings out good things, the bad man, out of his bad one, bad things. 36 So I tell you, for every worthless word that men utter they will have to give account on the day of judgment; 37 for it is by your words that you will be acquitted and by your words that you will be condemned."

BECK

13 Then He told the man, "Stretch out your hand." He stretched it out and it was made healthy again like the other hand.

14 But the Pharisees left and plotted against Him to kill Him. 15 Jesus knew about this, and so He left.

The Servant

Many followed Him, and He healed them all, 16 but He ordered them not to tell people who He was. 17 In this way what the prophet Isaiah said was to come true:

18 *Here is My Servant whom I have chosen,*
Whom I love and delight in.
I will put My Spirit on Him,
And He will announce justice to the nations.
19 *He will not quarrel or shout.*
Nor will anyone hear His voice in the streets.
20 *He will not crush a bruised reed*
Or put out a smoking wick
Till He has made justice victorious.
21 *And His name will be the hope of the nations.*[43]

Power over the Devil

22 At that time some people brought to Jesus a man who had a devil and was blind and couldn't talk. Jesus healed him so that he could talk and see.

23 The people were all amazed. "Could this be the Son of David?" they asked. 24 When the Pharisees heard about it, they said, "He can drive out the devils only with the help of Beelzebul, who rules over the devils."

25 Knowing what they were thinking, Jesus said to them, "If one part of any kingdom fights another, it loses its people. And if one part of any town or home fights another, it will not stand. 26 If the devil drives out the devil, he's fighting against himself. How then will his kingdom stand? 27 Now if Beelzebul helps Me drive out the devils, who helps your sons drive them out? That's why they'll be your judges. 28 But if God's Spirit helps Me drive out the devils, then God's kingdom has come to you. 29 How can anyone go into a strong man's house and take away his goods without first tying the strong man up? After that he'll rob his house.

30 "Anyone who's not with Me is against Me, and anyone who doesn't help Me gather scatters. 31 So I tell you, any sin or slander will be forgiven, but slandering the Spirit will not be forgiven. 32 Anyone who talks against the Son of Man will be forgiven, but anyone who talks against the Holy Spirit will not be forgiven in this world or the next.

33 "Either the tree is good, and then its fruit is good. Or the tree is bad, and then its fruit is bad. You can tell a tree by its fruit. 34 Brood of snakes, how can you who are so evil say anything good? What you say flows from your hearts. 35 A good man produces good things from the good stored in him, but an evil man produces evil from the evil stored in him. 36 But I tell you, on Judgment Day people will have to give an account of every useless word they say. 37 By your words you'll be acquitted, and by your words you'll be condemned."

[a] Grk., *out of the fullness*, etc.

[43] Is. 41:8-9; 42:1-4; Hab. 1:4

K.J.V.

38 Then certain of the scribes and of the Pharisees answered, saying, Master, we would see a sign from thee. 39 But he answered and said unto them, An evil and adulterous generation seeketh after a sign; and there shall no sign be given to it, but the sign of the prophet Jonas: 40 For as Jonas was three days and three nights in the whale's belly; so shall the Son of man be three days and three nights in the heart of the earth. 41 The men of Nineveh shall rise in judgment with this generation, and shall condemn it: because they repented at the preaching of Jonas; and, behold, a greater than Jonas is here. 42 The queen of the south shall rise up in the judgment with this generation, and shall condemn it: for she came from the uttermost parts of the earth to hear the wisdom of Solomon; and, behold, a greater than Solomon is here. 43 When the unclean spirit is gone out of a man, he walketh through dry places, seeking rest, and findeth none. 44 Then he saith, I will return into my house from whence I came out; and when he is come, he findeth it empty, swept, and garnished. 45 Then goeth he, and taketh with himself seven other spirits more wicked than himself, and they enter in and dwell there: and the last state of that man is worse than the first. Even so shall it be also unto this wicked generation.

46 While he yet talked to the people, behold, his mother and his brethren stood without, desiring to speak with him. 47 Then one said unto him, Behold, thy mother and thy brethren stand without, desiring to speak with thee. 48 But he answered and said unto him that told him, Who is my mother? and who are my brethren? 49 And he stretched forth his hand toward his disciples, and said, Behold my mother and my brethren! 50 For whosoever shall do the will of my Father which is in heaven, the same is my brother, and sister, and mother.

13 The same day went Jesus out of the house, and sat by the sea side. 2 And great multitudes were gathered together unto him, so that he went into a ship, and sat; and the whole multitude stood on the shore. 3 And he spake many things unto them in parables, saying, Behold, a sower went forth to sow; 4 And when he sowed, some seeds fell by the way side, and the fowls came and devoured them up: 5 Some fell upon stony places, where they had not much earth: and forthwith they sprung up, because they had no deepness of earth: 6 And when the sun was up, they were scorched; and because they had no root, they withered away. 7 And some fell among thorns; and the thorns sprung up, and choked them: 8 But other fell into good ground, and brought forth fruit, some a hundredfold, some sixtyfold, some thirtyfold. 9 Who hath ears to hear, let him hear. 10 And the disciples came, and said unto him, Why speakest thou unto them in parables? 11 He answered and said unto them, Because it is given unto you to know the mysteries of the kingdom of heaven, but to them it is not given. 12 For whosoever hath, to

N.A.S.

38 Then some of the scribes and Pharisees answered Him, saying, "Teacher, we want to see a sign from You." 39 But He answered and said to them, "An evil and adulterous generation craves for a sign; and yet no sign shall be given to it but the sign of Jonah the prophet; 40 for just as JONAH WAS THREE DAYS AND THREE NIGHTS IN THE BELLY OF THE SEA-MONSTER; so shall the Son of Man be three days and three nights in the heart of the earth. 41 "The men of Nineveh shall stand up with this generation at the judgment, and shall condemn it because they repented at the preaching of Jonah; and behold, something greater than Jonah is here. 42 "The Queen of the South shall rise up with this generation at the judgment and shall condemn it; because she came from the ends of the earth to hear the wisdom of Solomon; and behold, something greater than Solomon is here. 43 "Now when the unclean spirit goes out of a man, it passes through waterless places, seeking rest, and does not find it. 44 "Then it says, 'I will return to my house from which I came;' and when it comes, it finds it unoccupied, swept, and put in order. 45 "Then it goes, and takes along with it seven other spirits more wicked than itself, and they go in and live there; and the last state of that man becomes worse than the first. That is the way it will also be with this evil generation."

46 While He was still speaking to the multitudes, behold, His mother and His brothers were standing outside, seeking to speak to Him. 47 And someone said to Him, "Behold, Your mother and Your brothers are standing outside seeking to speak to You." 48 But He answered the one who was telling Him and said, "Who is My mother and who are My brothers?" 49 And stretching out His hand toward His disciples, He said, "Behold, My mother and My brothers! 50 "For whoever shall do the will of My Father who is in heaven, he is My brother and sister and mother."

13 On that day Jesus went out of the house, and was sitting by the sea. 2 And great multitudes gathered about Him, so that He got into a boat and sat down, and the whole multitude was standing on the beach. 3 And He spoke many things to them in parables, saying, "Behold, the sower went out to sow; 4 and as he sowed, some seeds fell beside the road, and the birds came and devoured them. 5 "And others fell upon the rocky places, where they did not have much soil; and immediately they sprang up, because they had no depth of soil. 6 "But when the sun had risen, they were scorched; and because they had no root, they withered away. 7 "And others fell among the thorns, and the thorns came up and choked them out. 8 "And others fell on the good soil, and *yielded a crop, some a hundredfold, some sixty, and some thirty. 9 "He who has ears, let him hear."

10 And the disciples came and said to Him, "Why do You speak to them in parables?" 11 And He answered and said to them, "To you it has been granted to know the mysteries of the kingdom of heaven, but to them it has not been granted. 12 "For whoever has, to him

WILLIAMS

38 Then some of the scribes and Pharisees answered Him as follows: "Teacher, we would like to see a spectacular sign given by you."

39 But He answered, "Only a wicked and treacherous age is hankering for a spectacular sign, and no sign will be given it but the sign of the prophet Jonah. 40 For as Jonah was in the whale's stomach for three days and nights, the Son of Man will be three days and nights in the heart of the earth. 41 The men of Nineveh will rise with the leaders of this age at the judgment and condemn them, for they turned to the message preached by Jonah, and there is more than Jonah here! 42 The queen of the south will rise with the leaders of this age at the judgment and condemn them, for she came from the farthest limits of the earth to listen to Solomon's wisdom, and there is more than Solomon here!

43 "Whenever the foul spirit goes out of a man, it wanders about in deserts in search of rest, but cannot find it. 44 Then it says, 'I will go back to my house which I left,' and it finds it unoccupied, swept, and ready for use.

45 "Then it goes and gets seven other spirits more wicked than itself, and they go in and make their home there, and so the end of that man is worse than the beginning. This is the way it will be with the wicked leaders of this age."

46 While He was still speaking to the crowds, His mother and His brothers had taken their stand outside, trying hard to get to speak to Him. 48 But He answered the man who told Him, "Who is my mother, and who are my brothers?" 49 And with a gesture toward His disciples He said, "Here are my mother and my brothers. 50 For whoever does the will of my Father in heaven is my mother and sister and brother."

13 *Teaching by stories—the sower, the wild wheat, the mustard seed, the yeast, the buried pot of gold, the costly pearl, the dragnet*

That same day Jesus went out of His house and was sitting on the seashore. 2 And the crowds that gathered about Him were so great that He got into a boat and remained sitting in it, while all the crowd stood on the seashore. 3 And in stories, by way of comparison, He told them many things, as He continued to speak:

"A sower went out to sow, 4 and as he was sowing, some of the seed fell along the path, and the birds came and ate them up, 5 and some fell upon rocky ground where they did not have much soil, and at once they sprang up, because there was no depth of soil, 6 and when the sun was up they were scorched and dried up, because they had no root. 7 And some fell among the thorns, and the thorns grew up and choked them out. 8 And some fell in rich soil, and yielded a crop, some a hundred, some sixty, some thirty-fold. 9 Let him who has ears listen."

10 Then His disciples came up to Him and asked, "Why do you speak to them in stories?"

11 He answered: "It is you and not they who are granted the privilege of knowing the secrets of the kingdom of heaven. 12 For to anyone

BECK

The Sign of Jonah

38 Then some Bible scholars and Pharisees said, "Teacher, we want You to show us some wonderful proof."

39 "The wicked and unfaithful people of today are looking for a proof," He answered them, "but the only proof they'll get is the prophet Jonah. 40 As *Jonah was in the belly of the big fish three days,*[44] so the Son of Man will be in the bosom of the earth three days. 41 The men of Nineveh will rise up in the Judgment with these people and condemn them, because they repented when Jonah preached; and here you see more than Jonah. 42 The queen from the south will rise up in the Judgment with these people and condemn them, because she came from the ends of the earth to hear Solomon's wisdom; and here you see more than Solomon.

43 "When an unclean spirit comes out of a man, he goes through dry places looking for a place to rest but doesn't find any. 44 Then he says, 'I'll go back to the home I left.' He comes and finds it empty, swept, and decorated. 45 Then he goes and takes home with him seven other spirits worse than himself, and they go in and live there. In the end that man is worse than he was before. That's what will happen to the wicked people of today."

The Mother and Brothers of Jesus

46 He was still talking to the people when His mother and brothers were standing outside wanting to talk to Him. 47 "Your mother and Your brothers are standing outside," somebody told Him, "and want to talk to You."

48 "Who is My mother," He asked the man that told Him, "and who are My brothers?" 49 Pointing with His hand to His disciples, He said, "These are My mother and My brothers. 50 If you do what My Father in heaven wants, you are My brother and sister and mother."

The Sower

13 That same day Jesus left the house and sat down by the lake. 2 But so many people gathered around Him that He stepped into a boat and sat there while all the people stood on the shore. 3 Then He told them many things in parables.

"A sower went out to sow," He said. 4 "As he was sowing, some seed fell along the road, and the birds came and ate it. 5 Some seed fell on rocky ground, where it didn't have much soil. Because the soil wasn't deep, the seed came up quickly. 6 When the sun rose, it was scorched, and because it had not taken root, it withered. 7 Some seed fell on thorns, and the thorns grew up and choked it. 8 But some seed fell on good ground and produced grain, some a hundred, some sixty, and some thirty times as much as was sown. 9 You have ears to hear; then listen."

10 The disciples came to Him. "Why are you talking to them in parables?" they asked Him.

11 "You are given the privilege to know the secrets of the kingdom of heaven," He answered, "but it isn't given to the others. 12 If you have

[44] Jonah 1:17

37

K.J.V.

him shall be given, and he shall have more abundance: but whosoever hath not, from him shall be taken away even that he hath. 13 Therefore speak I to them in parables: because they seeing see not; and hearing they hear not, neither do they understand. 14 And in them is fulfilled the prophecy of Esaias, which saith, By hearing ye shall hear, and shall not understand; and seeing ye shall see, and shall not perceive: 15 For this people's heart is waxed gross, and *their* ears are dull of hearing, and their eyes they have closed; lest at any time they should see with *their* eyes, and hear with *their* ears, and should understand with *their* heart, and should be converted, and I should heal them. 16 But blessed *are* your eyes, for they see: and your ears, for they hear. 17 For verily I say unto you, That many prophets and righteous *men* have desired to see *those things* which ye see, and have not seen *them;* and to hear *those things* which ye hear, and have not heard *them*.

18 Hear ye therefore the parable of the sower. 19 When any one heareth the word of the kingdom, and understandeth *it* not, then cometh the wicked one, and catcheth away that which was sown in his heart. This is he which received seed by the way side. 20 But he that received the seed into stony places, the same is he that heareth the word, and anon with joy receiveth it; 21 Yet hath he not root in himself, but dureth for a while: for when tribulation or persecution ariseth because of the word, by and by he is offended. 22 He also that received seed among the thorns is he that heareth the word; and the care of this world, and the deceitfulness of riches, choke the word, and he becometh unfruitful. 23 But he that received seed into the good ground is he that heareth the word, and understandeth *it;* which also beareth fruit, and bringeth forth, some a hundredfold, some sixty, some thirty.

24 Another parable put he forth unto them, saying, The kingdom of heaven is likened unto a man which sowed good seed in his field: 25 But while men slept, his enemy came and sowed tares among the wheat, and went his way. 26 But when the blade was sprung up, and brought forth fruit, then appeared the tares also. 27 So the servants of the householder came and said unto him, Sir, didst not thou sow good seed in thy field? from whence then hath it tares? 28 He said unto them, An enemy hath done this. The servants said unto him, Wilt thou then that we go and gather them up? 29 But he said, Nay; lest while ye gather up the tares, ye root up also the wheat with them. 30 Let both grow together until the harvest: and in the time of harvest I will say to the reapers, Gather ye together first the tares, and bind them in bundles to burn them: but gather the wheat into my barn.

31 Another parable put he forth unto them, saying, The kingdom of heaven is like to a grain of mustard seed, which a man took, and sowed in his field: 32 Which indeed is the least of all seeds: but when it is grown, it is the greatest

N.A.S.

shall *more* be given, and he shall have an abundance; but whoever does not have, even what he has shall be taken away from him. 13 "Therefore I speak to them in parables; because while seeing they do not see, and while hearing they do not hear, nor do they understand. 14 "And in their case the prophecy of Isaiah is being fulfilled, which says,

'YOU WILL KEEP ON HEARING, BUT WILL NOT UNDERSTAND;
AND YOU WILL˙ KEEP ON SEEING, BUT WILL NOT PERCEIVE;
15 FOR THE HEART OF THIS PEOPLE HAS BECOME DULL,
AND WITH THEIR EARS THEY SCARCELY HEAR,
AND THEY CLOSED THEIR EYES;
LEST THEY SHOULD SEE WITH THEIR EYES,
AND HEAR WITH THEIR EARS,
AND UNDERSTAND WITH THEIR HEART AND TURN AGAIN,
AND I SHOULD HEAL THEM.'

16 "But blessed are your eyes, because they see; and your ears, because they hear. 17 "For truly I say to you, that many prophets and righteous men desired to see what you see, and did not see *it;* and to hear what you hear, and did not hear *it*. 18 "Hear then the parable of the sower. 19 "When any one hears the word of the kingdom, and does not understand it, the evil *one* comes and snatches away what has been sown in his heart. This is the one on whom seed was sown beside the road. 20 "And the one on whom seed was sown on the rocky places, this is the man who hears the word, and immediately receives it with joy; 21 yet he has no *firm* root in himself, but is *only* temporary, and when affliction or persecution arises because of the word, immediately he falls away. 22 "And the one on whom seed was sown among the thorns, this is the man who hears the word, and the worry of the world, and the deceitfulness of riches choke the word, and it becomes unfruitful. 23 "And the one on whom seed was sown on the good ground, this is the man who hears the word and understands it; who indeed bears fruit, and brings forth, some a hundredfold, some sixty, and some thirty."

24 He presented another parable to them, saying, "The kingdom of heaven may be compared to a man who sowed good seed in his field. 25 "But while men were sleeping, his enemy came and sowed ᵃtares also among the wheat, and went away. 26 "But when the wheat sprang up and bore grain, then the tares became evident also. 27 "And the slaves of the landowner came and said to him, 'Sir, did you not sow good seed in your field? How then does it have tares?' 28 "And he said to them, 'An enemy has done this!' And the slaves *said to him, 'Do you want us, then, to go and gather them up?' 29 "But he *said, 'No; lest while you are gathering up the tares, you may root up the wheat with them. 30 " 'Allow both to grow together until the harvest; and in the time of the harvest I will say to the reapers, "First gather up the tares; and bind them in bundles to burn them up; but gather the wheat into my barn." ' "

31 He presented another parable to them, saying, "The kingdom of heaven is like a mustard seed, which a man took and sowed in his field; 32 and this is smaller than all *other* seeds; but when it is full grown, it is larger

---

[a] Or, *darnel*, a weed resembling wheat.

WILLIAMS

who has, more will be given, and his supply will overflow, but from anyone who does not have, even what he has will be taken away. 13 This is why I am speaking to them in stories, because they look but do not see, they listen but do not really hear or understand. 14 So in them the prophecy of the prophet Isaiah is fulfilled, which says:

" 'You will listen and listen and not understand,
And you will look and look and never see at all,
15 For this people's soul has grown dull,
And with their ears they can scarcely hear,
And they have shut tight their eyes,
So that they will never see with their eyes,
And hear with their ears,
And understand with their hearts, and turn to me,
So that I may cure them!'

16 "But blessed are your eyes, for they are beginning to see, and your ears, for they are beginning to hear. 17 For I solemnly say to you, many prophets and upright men yearned to see what you are seeing, and did not see it, and to hear what you are hearing, and did not hear it.
18 "Now listen closely to the story of the sower. 19 When anyone hears the message of the kingdom and does not understand it, the wicked one comes and carries off the seed that was sown in his heart. This is what was sown along the path. 20And what was sown upon the thin rocky soil illustrates the man who hears the message and bubbling over with joy at once accepts it, 21 but it takes no real root in him, and he lasts only a little while, and just as soon as suffering and persecution come for the truth's sake, he at once[a] yields and falls. 22And what was sown among the thorns illustrates the man who hears the message, and the worries of the times and the pleasures of being rich choke the truth out, and he yields no fruit. 23And what was sown in rich soil illustrates the man who hears the message and understands it, and yields fruit, one a hundred, one sixty, another thirtyfold."
24 He told them another story, as follows: "The kingdom of heaven is like a man who sowed seed in his field. 25 But while the world was sleeping, his enemy came and sowed wild[b] wheat seed in the midst of the good seed, and went away. 26And when the wheat plants grew up and yielded their ripened grain, the wild wheat plants appeared too. 27And the farmer's slaves came up to him and said, 'Master, did you not sow good seed in your field? Then where did the wild wheat plants come from?' 28 He said to them, 'An enemy has done this.' Then they said to him, 'Do you want us, then, to go and gather them?' 29And he said, 'No, never, for while you are gathering the wild wheat plants you might root up the good ones with them. 30 Let them both grow together until harvest time, and at the harvest time I will order the reapers,

'Gather first the wild wheat plants and tie them into bundles to be burned up, but get the wheat into my barn.' "

31 He told them this story, as follows: "The kingdom of heaven may be compared to a mustard seed which a man took and sowed in his field. 32 It is the smallest of all seeds, but when it is grown it is the largest of plants; yea, it

BECK

something, you'll be given more, and so you'll get more and more. But if you don't have what you should have, even what you have will be taken away from you. 13 I talk to them in parables because they see and yet don't see, and hear and yet don't hear or understand. 14 In them more and more Isaiah's prophecy is coming true:

You will hear but never understand,
You will look but never see,
15 These people have become dull at heart and hard of hearing
And have shut their eyes
So that their eyes will never see, their ears never hear,
or their hearts understand,
And they will never turn to Me and let Me heal them.[45]

16 "Happy are your eyes because they see and your ears because they hear. 17 Let me assure you, many prophets and righteous people longed to see what you see and didn't see it, to hear what you hear and didn't hear it.
18 "Listen to what the parable of the sower means. 19 When anyone hears the message of the kingdom but doesn't understand it, the evil one comes and takes away what was sown in his heart. That is what was sown along the road. 20 In another the seed falls on rocky ground. He's one who welcomes the Word with joy as soon as he hears it, but it doesn't take root in him. 21 He believes for a while, but as soon as the Word brings him trouble or persecution, he falls away. 22 In another the seed is sown among thorns. He's one who hears the Word, but the worry of the world and the deceitful pleasure of riches choke the Word, and it can't produce anything. 23 But in another seed is sown on good ground. He's one who continues to hear and understand the Word and so goes on producing good things, one a hundred, another sixty, and another thirty times as much as was sown."

Weeds in the Wheat

24 Jesus pictured it to them another way: "The kingdom of heaven is like a man who sowed good seed in his field. 25 But while people were sleeping, his enemy came and sowed weeds among the wheat and went away. 26 When the wheat came up and formed kernels, then the weeds showed up too.
27 "The owner's slaves came to him and asked him, 'Master, didn't you sow good seed in your field? Where did the weeds come from?'
" 'An enemy did that,' he told them.
28 " 'Do you want us to go and pull them out?' the slaves asked him.
29 " 'No,' he said, 'if you pull out the weeds, you may pull up the wheat with them. 30 Let both grow together till the harvest. When the grain is cut, I will tell the reapers, "Gather the weeds first, and tie them in bundles to be burned, but bring the wheat into my barn." ' "

A Mustard Seed and Yeast

31 He pictured it to them another way: "The kingdom of heaven is like a mustard seed a man took and sowed in his field. 32 It's the smallest of all seeds, but when it has grown, it's the

---

[a] Grk., he is caused to stumble. [b] An odious weed, which looks like a stalk of wheat, was often called wild wheat.

[45] Is. 6:9-10

K.J.V.

among herbs, and becometh a tree, so that the birds of the air come and lodge in the branches thereof.

33 Another parable spake he unto them; The kingdom of heaven is like unto leaven, which a woman took, and hid in three measures of meal, till the whole was leavened. 34 All these things spake Jesus unto the multitude in parables; and without a parable spake he not unto them: 35 That it might be fulfilled which was spoken by the prophet, saying, I will open my mouth in parables; I will utter things which have been kept secret from the foundation of the world. 36 Then Jesus sent the multitude away, and went into the house: and his disciples came unto him, saying, Declare unto us the parable of the tares of the field. 37 He answered and said unto them, He that soweth the good seed is the Son of man; 38 The field is the world; the good seed are the children of the kingdom; but the tares are the children of the wicked one; 39 The enemy that sowed them is the devil; the harvest is the end of the world; and the reapers are the angels. 40 As therefore the tares are gathered and burned in the fire; so shall it be in the end of this world. 41 The Son of man shall send forth his angels, and they shall gather out of his kingdom all things that offend, and them which do iniquity; 42 And shall cast them into a furnace of fire: there shall be wailing and gnashing of teeth. 43 Then shall the righteous shine forth as the sun in the kingdom of their Father. Who hath ears to hear, let him hear.

44 Again, the kingdom of heaven is like unto treasure hid in a field; the which when a man hath found, he hideth, and for joy thereof goeth and selleth all that he hath, and buyeth that field.

45 Again, the kingdom of heaven is like unto a merchantman, seeking goodly pearls: 46 Who, when he had found one pearl of great price, went and sold all that he had, and bought it.

47 Again, the kingdom of heaven is like unto a net, that was cast into the sea, and gathered of every kind: 48 Which, when it was full, they drew to shore, and sat down, and gathered the good into vessels, but cast the bad away. 49 So shall it be at the end of the world: the angels shall come forth, and sever the wicked from among the just, 50 And shall cast them into the furnace of fire: there shall be wailing and gnashing of teeth. 51 Jesus saith unto them, Have ye understood all these things? They say unto him, Yea, Lord. 52 Then said he unto them, Therefore every scribe *which is* instructed unto the kingdom of heaven, is like unto a man *that is* a householder, which bringeth forth out of his treasure *things* new and old.

53 And it came to pass, *that* when Jesus had finished these parables, he departed thence. 54 And when he was come into his own country, he taught them in their synagogue, insomuch that they were astonished, and said, Whence hath this *man* this wisdom, and *these* mighty works? 55 Is not this the carpenter's son? is not

N.A.S.

than the garden plants, and becomes a tree, so that THE BIRDS OF THE AIR come and NEST IN ITS BRANCHES."

33 He spoke another parable to them; "The kingdom of heaven is like leaven, which a woman took, and hid in three pecks of meal, until it was all leavened."

34 All these things Jesus spoke to the multitudes in parables, and He was not talking to them without a parable, 35 so that what was spoken through the prophet might be fulfilled, saying,

"I WILL OPEN MY MOUTH IN PARABLES;
I WILL UTTER THINGS HIDDEN SINCE THE FOUNDATION OF THE WORLD."

36 Then He left the multitudes, and went into the house. And His disciples came to Him, saying, "Explain to us the parable of the tares of the field." 37 And He answered and said, "The one who sows the good seed is the Son of Man, 38 and the field is the world; and *as for* the good seed, these are the sons of the kingdom; and the tares are the sons of the evil *one;* 39 and the enemy who sowed them is the devil, and the harvest is the end of the age; and the reapers are angels. 40 "Therefore just as the tares are gathered up and burned with fire, so shall it be at the end of the age. 41 "The Son of Man will send forth His angels, and they will gather out of His kingdom all STUMBLING-BLOCKS, AND THOSE WHO COMMIT LAWLESSNESS, 42 and will cast them into the furnace of fire; in that place there shall be weeping and gnashing of teeth. 43 "Then THE RIGHTEOUS WILL SHINE FORTH AS THE SUN in the kingdom of their Father. He who has ears, let him hear.

44 "The kingdom of heaven is like a treasure hidden in the field; which a man found and hid; and from joy over it he goes and sells all that he has, and buys that field.

45 "Again, the kingdom of heaven is like a merchant seeking fine pearls, 46 and upon finding one pearl of great value, he went and sold all that he had, and bought it.

47 "Again, the kingdom of heaven is like a drag-net cast into the sea, and gathering *fish* of every kind; 48 and when it was filled, they drew it up on the beach; and they sat down, and gathered the good *fish* into containers, but the bad they threw away. 49 "So it will be at the end of the age; the angels shall come forth, and take out the wicked from among the righteous, 50 and will cast them into the furnace of fire; there shall be weeping and gnashing of teeth.

51 "Have you understood all these things?" They *said to Him, "Yes." 52 And he said to them, "Therefore every scribe who has become a disciple of the kingdom of heaven is like a head of a household, who brings forth out of his treasure things new and old."

53 And it came about that when Jesus had finished these parables, He departed from there. 54 And coming to His home town He *began* teaching them in their synagogue, so that they became astonished, and said, "Where *did* this man *get* this wisdom, and *these* miraculous powers? 55 "Is not this the carpenter's son? Is

WILLIAMS

grows into a tree, so that the wild birds come and roost in its branches."

33 He told another story: "The kingdom of heaven may be compared to yeast which a woman took and worked into a bushel of flour until it all had risen."

34 Jesus told the crowds all this in stories, and without a story He told them nothing, 35 to fulfill what was spoken by the prophet:

"I will open my mouth in stories,

I will utter truths concealed since creation."

36 Then He left the crowds and went into His house. And His disciples came up to Him and said, "Explain to us the story of the wild wheat in the field."

37 And He answered: "The sower of the good seed is the Son of Man; 38 the field is the world; the good seed are the members of the kingdom; the wild wheat seed are the followers of the wicked one. 39 The enemy who sowed them is the devil, the harvest is the close of the age, the reapers are angels. 40 Just as the wild wheat plants are gathered and burned up, so it will be at the close of the age. 41 The Son of Man will send out His angels, and they will gather out of His kingdom all those who cause wrongdoing, and the wrongdoers,ᶜ 42 and will throw them into the furnace of torturing punishment; there they will wail and grind their teeth. 43 Then the upright will shine out like the sun in the kingdom of their Father. Let him who has ears listen!

44 "The kingdom of heaven is like a pot of gold which was buried in a field, which a man found and buried again; and for joy over it he went and sold all he had and bought that field.

45 "Again, the kingdom of heaven is like a gem-dealer who was looking for beautiful pearls. 46 One day he found a very costly pearl, and he went and sold all he had and bought it.

47 "Again, the kingdom of heaven is like a dragnet that was let down into the sea, and gathered fish of every kind, 48 which, when it was full, the fishermen drew up on the shore, and sat down and picked out the good fish for their baskets and threw the bad away. 49 So it will be at the close of the age; the angels will go out and separate the wicked from the upright, 50 and will throw them into the furnace of torturing punishment. There they will wail and grind their teeth.

51 "Do you understand all these stories?" They answered Him, "Yes."

52 He said to them, "Every scribe who has become a disciple in the kingdom of heaven is like a householder who can bring out of his storeroom new furnishings as well as old."

53 When Jesus had finished these stories, He left there. 54 He went to His own home town, and kept teaching in their synagogue in such a way that they were dumfounded, and said, "Where did He get this wisdom and this power to do such wonder-works? 55 Is He not the car-

BECK

largest of the garden plants; it becomes a tree big enough for the *birds* to come and *nest in its branches.*" [46]

33 He pictured it to them another way: "The kingdom of heaven is like yeast a woman took and mixed into a bushel of flour till it was all fermented."

34 Jesus used parables to tell the crowds all these things. He wouldn't tell them anything without a parable, 35 so that what the prophet said would come true:

I will open My mouth to speak in parables,
I will tell what has been hidden since the
world was made. [47]

The Meaning of the Weeds in the Wheat

36 When Jesus had dismissed the people and gone into the house, His disciples came to Him and said, "Tell us what the parable of the weeds in the field means."

37 "The sower who sows the good seed," He answered, "is the Son of Man. 38 The field is the world. The good seed are the sons of the kingdom. The weeds are the sons of the evil one. 39 The enemy who sowed them is the devil. The harvest is the end of the world. The reapers are the angels. 40 As the weeds are gathered and burned, so it will be at the end of the world. 41 The Son of Man will send His angels, and they will take out of His kingdom *those who do wrong and all who lead others to do wrong,* [48] 42 and will throw them into the fiery furnace, where they will cry and grind their teeth. 43 Then *the righteous will shine like* [49] the sun in their Father's kingdom. If you have ears, listen!"

The Treasure, the Pearl, and the Fish

44 "The kingdom of heaven is like a treasure buried in a field. When a man found it, he buried it again and was so delighted with it he went and sold everything he had and bought that field.

45 "Here's another picture of the kingdom of heaven: A dealer was looking for fine pearls. 46 When he found a very expensive pearl, he went and sold everything he had and bought it.

47 "Again, the kingdom of heaven is like a net that was let down into the lake, and it gathered all kinds of fish. 48 When it was full they pulled it on the shore, sat down, and picked out the good fish and put them in containers but threw the bad ones away. 49 So it will be at the end of the world. The angels will go out and separate the wicked from the righteous 50 and throw them into the fiery furnace, where they will cry and grind their teeth.

51 "Did you understand all this?"

"Yes," they answered.

52 "And so every Bible student trained for the kingdom of heaven," He told them, "is like the owner of a house who brings out of his storeroom new things and old."

53 When Jesus had finished these parables, He left that place.

His Last Visit to Nazareth

54 He went to His home town and taught the people in their synagog in such a way they were amazed. "Where did He get this wisdom and the power to do these miracles?" they asked. 55 "Isn't He the carpenter's son? Isn't His

[46] Ps. 104:12; Ezek. 17:23; 31:6
[47] Ps. 78:2
[48] Zeph. 1:3; Job 12:16
[49] Dan. 12:3

[c] Lit., *all that cause others to stumble,* etc.

K.J.V.

his mother called Mary? and his brethren, James, and Joses, and Simon, and Judas? 56 And his sisters, are they not all with us? Whence then hath this *man* all these things? 57 And they were offended in him. But Jesus said unto them, A prophet is not without honour, save in his own country, and in his own house. 58 And he did not many mighty works there because of their unbelief.

14 At that time Herod the tetrarch heard of the fame of Jesus, 2 And said unto his servants, This is John the Baptist; he is risen from the dead; and therefore mighty works do shew forth themselves in him.

3 For Herod had laid hold on John, and bound him, and put *him* in prison for Herodias' sake, his brother Philip's wife. 4 For John said unto him, It is not lawful for thee to have her. 5 And when he would have put him to death, he feared the multitude, because they counted him as a prophet. 6 But when Herod's birthday was kept, the daughter of Herodias danced before them, and pleased Herod. 7 Whereupon he promised with an oath to give her whatsoever she would ask. 8 And she, being before instructed of her mother, said, Give me here John Baptist's head in a charger. 9 And the king was sorry: nevertheless for the oath's sake, and them which sat with him at meat, he commanded *it* to be given *her*. 10 And he sent, and beheaded John in the prison. 11 And his head was brought in a charger, and given to the damsel: and she brought *it* to her mother. 12 And his disciples came, and took up the body, and buried it, and went and told Jesus.

13 When Jesus heard *of it*, he departed thence by ship into a desert place apart: and when the people had heard *thereof*, they followed him on foot out of the cities. 14 And Jesus went forth, and saw a great multitude, and was moved with compassion toward them, and he healed their sick.

15 And when it was evening, his disciples came to him, saying, This is a desert place, and the time is now past; send the multitude away, that they may go into the villages, and buy themselves victuals. 16 But Jesus said unto them, They need not depart; give ye them to eat. 17 And they say unto him, We have here but five loaves, and two fishes. 18 He said, Bring them hither to me. 19 And he commanded the multitude to sit down on the grass, and took the five loaves, and the two fishes, and looking up to heaven, he blessed, and brake, and gave the loaves to *his* disciples, and the disciples to the multitude. 20 And they did all eat, and were filled: and they took up of the fragments that remained twelve baskets full. 21 And they that had eaten were about five thousand men, beside women and children.

N.A.S.

not His mother called Mary, and His brothers, James and Joseph and Simon and Judas? 56 "And His sisters, are they not all with us? Where then *did* this man *get* all these things?" 57 And they took offense at Him. But Jesus said to them, "A prophet is not without honor except in his home town, and in his *own* household." 58 And He did not do many miracles there because of their unbelief.

14 At that time Herod the tetrarch heard the news about Jesus, 2 and said to his servants, "This is John the Baptist; he has risen from the dead; and that is why miraculous powers are at work in him." 3 For Herod had seized John, and bound him, and put him in prison on account of Herodias, the wife of his brother Philip. 4 For John had been saying to him, "It is not lawful for you to have her." 5 And although he wanted to put him to death, he feared the multitude, because they regarded him as a prophet. 6 But when Herod's birthday came, the daughter of Herodias danced before *them* and pleased Herod. 7 Thereupon he promised with an oath to give her whatever she asked. 8 And having been prompted by her mother, she *said, "Give me here on a platter the head of John the Baptist." 9 And although he was grieved, the king commanded *it* to be given because of his oaths, and because of his dinner-guests. 10 And he sent and had John beheaded in the prison. 11 And his head was brought on a platter and given to the girl; and she brought *it* to her mother. 12 And his disciples came and took away the body and buried it; and they went and reported to Jesus.

13 Now when Jesus heard *it*, He withdrew from there in a boat, to a lonely place by Himself; and when the multitudes heard *of this*, they followed Him on foot from the cities. 14 And when He came out, He saw a great multitude, and felt compassion for them, and healed their sick. 15 And when it was evening, the disciples came to Him, saying, "The place is desolate, and the time is already past; so send the multitudes away, that they may go into the villages, and buy food for themselves." 16 But Jesus said to them, "They do not need to go away; you give them *something* to eat!" 17 And they *said to Him, "We have here only five loaves, and two fish." 18 And He said, "Bring them here to Me." 19 And ordering the multitudes to recline on the grass, He took the five loaves and the two fish, and looking up toward heaven, He blessed *the food*, and breaking the loaves He gave them to the disciples, and the disciples *gave* to the multitudes, 20 and they all ate, and were satisfied. And they picked up what was left over of the broken pieces, twelve full baskets. 21 And there were about five thousand men who ate, aside from women and children.

WILLIAMS

penter's son? Is not His mother's name Mary, are not His brothers James, Joseph, Simon and Judas? 56And are not His sisters all living here with us? Where then did He get all these things?" 57And so they found a cause for stumbling over Him.

But Jesus said to them, "A prophet never fails to be honored except in his native neighborhood and in his own home." And so 58 He did not do many wonder-works there, because of their lack of faith.

14 *Antipas, governor of Galilee, supposes Jesus is John the Baptist risen from the dead; Jesus feeds five thousand, walks on the sea, and cures many*

At that time Herod the governor heard the reports about Jesus, 2 and said to his attendants, "This is John the Baptist. He has risen from the dead, and that is why the powers are at work through him."

3 For Herod had arrested John and bound him and put him out of the way by putting him in prison, just to please Herodias,[a] his brother Philip's wife, 4 for John had said to him, "It is not right for you to have her as wife." 5 Although he wanted to have him killed, he was afraid of the people, for they regarded him as a prophet.

6 But when Herod's birthday came, Herodias' daughter danced before the guests. Herod was fascinated by her, 7 and so passionately[b] promised to give her anything she might ask for. 8And she, prompted by her mother, said, "Give me John the Baptist's head right here on a platter." 9And the king was sorry, but on account of his oath and his guests, he ordered it to be given her. 10And he sent and had John beheaded in prison. 11And his head was brought on a platter and given to the girl, and she took it to her mother. 12 Then John's disciples came and carried off his corpse, and buried him, and went and reported it to Jesus.

13 When Jesus heard it, He left there in a boat for a quiet place, to be alone. And when the crowds heard of it, they followed Him on foot from the towns. 14 So when He got out of the boat and saw a great crowd, His heart was moved with pity for them, and He cured their sick people. 15 But when it was evening, His disciples came to Him and said, "This is a destitute place, and the day is over; send the crowds off to the villages to buy themselves food."

16 But Jesus said to them, "They do not need to leave here; give them something to eat yourselves."

17 They said to Him, "We have nothing here but five loaves and two fish."

18 He said, "Bring them here to me." 19After ordering the crowds to sit down on the grass, He took the five loaves and two fish and looked up to heaven and blessed them; then He broke the loaves in pieces and gave them to the disciples, and they gave them to the people. 20And they all ate and had a plenty. Then they took up the pieces left over, which made twelve basketfuls. 21 The people fed numbered about five thousand men, besides women and children.

[a] Grk., *on account of, for the sake of,* H. [b] Grk., *with an oath he promised,* Ara. constr. for emph.

BECK

mother's name Mary, and aren't James, Joseph, Simon, and Judas His brothers? 56And aren't all His sisters here with us? Where did He get all this?" 57 So they turned against Him.

"A prophet is without honor only in his home town and in his family," Jesus told them. 58 Their unbelief kept Him from doing many great works there.

Herod Kills John

14 At that time Herod, the governor, heard the news about Jesus. 2 "This is John the Baptizer!" he told his servants. "He's risen from the dead, and that's why these powers are working in Him."

3 Herod had arrested John, bound him, and put him in prison on account of Herodias, the wife of his brother Philip, 4 because John was telling him, "It isn't right for you to have her." 5 Herod wanted to kill him but was afraid of the people because they considered John a prophet.

6 When Herod's birthday was celebrated, the daughter of Herodias danced before the guests. 7 Herod was so delighted with her he swore to give her anything she might ask for.

8 Urged on by her mother, she said, "Give me here on a platter the head of John the Baptizer."

9 Then the king felt sorry. But he had sworn to do it, and there were the guests—so he ordered it given to her. 10 He sent and had John's head cut off in prison. 11And his head was brought on a platter and given to the girl, who took it to her mother.

12 John's disciples came and took his body away and buried it. Then they went and told Jesus.

Jesus Feeds Five Thousand

13 When Jesus heard about John, He left in a boat and went to a deserted place to be alone. The people heard of it and followed Him on foot from the towns. 14 When Jesus stepped out of the boat, He saw a big crowd. He felt sorry for them and healed their sick.

15 In the evening the disciples came to Him. "This is a deserted place," they said, "and it's late. Send the crowds away to the villages to buy themselves some food."

16 "They don't need to go away," Jesus answered them. "You give them something to eat."

17 "All we have here is five loaves and two fish," they told Him.

18 "Let Me have them," He said.

19 He ordered the people to sit down on the grass. Then taking the five loaves and the two fish and looking up to heaven, He blessed them. Breaking the loaves, He gave them to the disciples, and they gave them to the people. 20All of them ate and had a hearty meal. They picked up the pieces that were left—twelve baskets full.

21 Some five thousand men had eaten, not counting women and children.

K.J.V.

22 And straightway Jesus constrained his disciples to get into a ship, and to go before him unto the other side, while he sent the multitudes away. 23And when he had sent the multitudes away, he went up into a mountain apart to pray: and when the evening was come, he was there alone. 24 But the ship was now in the midst of the sea, tossed with waves: for the wind was contrary. 25And in the fourth watch of the night Jesus went unto them, walking on the sea. 26And when the disciples saw him walking on the sea, they were troubled, saying, It is a spirit; and they cried out for fear. 27 But straightway Jesus spake unto them, saying, Be of good cheer; it is I; be not afraid. 28And Peter answered him and said, Lord, if it be thou, bid me come unto thee on the water. 29And he said, Come. And when Peter was come down out of the ship, he walked on the water, to go to Jesus. 30 But when he saw the wind boisterous, he was afraid; and beginning to sink, he cried, saying, Lord, save me. 31And immediately Jesus stretched forth *his* hand, and caught him, and said unto him, O thou of little faith, wherefore didst thou doubt? 32And when they were come into the ship, the wind ceased. 33 Then they that were in the ship came and worshipped him, saying, Of a truth thou art the Son of God.

34 And when they were gone over, they came into the land of Gennesaret. 35And when the men of that place had knowledge of him, they sent out into all that country round about, and brought unto him all that were diseased; 36And besought him that they might only touch the hem of his garment: and as many as touched were made perfectly whole.

15 Then came to Jesus scribes and Pharisees, which were of Jerusalem, saying, 2 Why do thy disciples transgress the tradition of the elders? for they wash not their hands when they eat bread. 3 But he answered and said unto them, Why do ye also transgress the commandment of God by your tradition? 4 For God commanded, saying, Honour thy father and mother: and, He that curseth father or mother, let him die the death. 5 But ye say, Whosoever shall say to *his* father or *his* mother, *It is* a gift, by whatsoever thou mightest be profited by me; 6And honour not his father or his mother, *he shall be free.* Thus have ye made the commandment of God of none effect by your tradition. 7 *Ye* hypocrites, well did Esaias prophesy of you, saying, 8 This people draweth nigh unto me with their mouth, and honoureth me with *their* lips; but their heart is far from me. 9 But in vain they do worship me, teaching *for* doctrines the commandments of men.

10 And he called the multitude, and said unto them, Hear, and understand: 11 Not that which goeth into the mouth defileth a man; but that which cometh out of the mouth, this defileth a

N.A.S.

22 And immediately He made the disciples get into the boat, and go ahead of Him to the other side, while He sent the multitudes away. 23And after He had sent the multitudes away, He went up to the mountain by Himself to pray; and when it was evening, He was there alone. 24 But the boat was already many *a*stadia away from the land, battered by the waves; for the wind was contrary. 25And in the *b*fourth watch of the night He came to them, walking upon the sea. 26And when the disciples saw Him walking on the sea, they were frightened, saying, "It is a ghost!" And they cried out for fear. 27 But immediately Jesus spoke to them, saying, "Take courage, it is I; do not be afraid." 28And Peter answered Him and said, "Lord, if it is You, command me to come to You on the water." 29And He said, "Come!" And Peter got out of the boat, and walked on the water and came toward Jesus. 30 But seeing the wind, he became afraid, and beginning to sink, he cried out, saying, "Lord, save me!" 31And immediately Jesus stretched out His hand and took hold of him, and *said to him, "O you of little faith, why did you doubt?" 32And when they got into the boat, the wind stopped. 33And those who were in the boat worshiped Him, saying, "You are certainly God's Son!"

34 And when they had crossed over, they came to land at Gennesaret. 35And when the men of that place recognized Him, they sent into all that surrounding district and brought to Him all who were ill; 36 and they *began* to entreat Him that they might just touch the fringe of His cloak; and as many as touched *it* were cured.

15 Then some Pharisees and scribes *came to Jesus from Jerusalem, saying, 2 "Why do Your disciples transgress the tradition of the elders? For they do not wash their hands when they eat bread." 3And He answered and said to them, "And why do you yourselves transgress the commandment of God for the sake of your tradition? 4 "For God said, 'HONOR YOUR FATHER AND MOTHER,' and, 'HE WHO SPEAKS EVIL OF FATHER OR MOTHER, LET HIM BE PUT TO DEATH.' 5 "But you say, 'Whoever shall say to *his* father or mother, "Anything of mine you might have helped by has been given to God," 6 he is not to honor his father *c*or his mother*d*.' And *thus* you invalidated the word of God for the sake of your tradition. 7 "You hypocrites, rightly did Isaiah prophesy of you, saying,

8 'THIS PEOPLE HONORS ME WITH THEIR LIPS, BUT THEIR HEART IS FAR AWAY FROM ME.

9 BUT IN VAIN DO THEY WORSHIP ME, TEACHING AS THEIR DOCTRINES THE PRECEPTS OF MEN.'"

10And He called to Himself the multitude, and said to them, "Hear, and understand. 11 "Not what enters into the mouth defiles the man, but what proceeds out of the mouth, this

---

[a] A stadion was about 600 feet. [b] I.e., 3-6 a.m. [c] Many mss. omit, *or his mother.* [d] I.e., *by supporting them with it.*

44

WILLIAMS

22 And He at once had the disciples get into the boat and cross to the other side ahead of Him, while He dismissed the crowds. 23After He had dismissed the crowds, He went up the hill alone to pray. And after the evening came on, He was there alone, 24 but the boat was already a long way from shore, and was being tossed by the waves, for the wind was against them. 25 Just before day° He went out to them, walking on the sea. 26And when the disciples saw Him walking on the sea, they were terrified, and said, "It is a ghost!" And they screamed with fright.

27 Then Jesus at once spoke to them, "Be men of courage! It is I; stop being afraid."

28 Peter answered Him, "Lord, if it is you, let ᵈ me come to you on the water."

29 And He said, "Come."

And Peter got down out of the boat and walked on the water, and he went toward Jesus. 30 But when he felt the wind, he was frightened, and as he began to go down, he cried out, "Lord, save me!"

31 Jesus at once put out His hand and caught hold of him, and said to him, "O you of little faith! Why did you waver so?"

32 And when they got into the boat, the wind lulled. 33And the men in the boat worshiped Him, and said, "You are certainly God's Son."

34 And they crossed over to the other side and came to Gennesaret. 35And the men of that place recognized Him, and sent into all the countryside and brought to Him all who were sick, 36 and they continued to beg Him to let them touch just the tassel on His coat, and all who barely touched it were completely cured.

15 *Real defilement described by Jesus; a heathen mother's daughter cured because of her wonderful faith; Jesus returns to Galilee and feeds four thousand*

Then some Pharisees and scribes from Jerusalem came to Jesus, and asked Him, 2 "Why do your disciples break the rules handed down by our forefathers? For they do not practice washing their hands when they take their meals."

3 But He answered, "Why do you too break God's command for the sake of the rules that have been handed down to you? 4 For God said, 'Honor your father and mother,' and 'Whoever curses his father or mother must certainly be put to death.' 5 But you say, 'Whoever tells his father or mother, "Everything I have that might be used for helping you, is devoted to God," 6 is under no obligation at all to help ᵉ his parent.' So you have set aside what God has said for the sake of what has been handed down to you. 7 You hypocrites! Isaiah prophesied beautifully about you, when he said:

8 " 'This people honor me with their lips,
But their hearts are far, far away from me;
9 Their worship of me is an empty show;
The things they teach are only men's precepts.' "

10 And He called the people to Him and said, "Listen to this and learn it! 11 It is not what goes into a man's mouth that makes him foul; no, it is what comes out of a man's mouth that makes him foul."

[c] Grk., *in the fourth watch*, 3-6 A.M. [d] Grk., *command me*, etc. [a] Grk., *honor*.

BECK

Jesus Walks on Water

22 Jesus quickly made the disciples get into the boat and go on ahead to the other side while He dismissed the people. 23After sending them away, He went up the hill to be alone and pray. When it got late, He was there alone.

24 The boat, now many hundred yards from the shore, was troubled by the waves because the wind was against them.

25 Toward morning He came to them, walking on the lake. 26 When the disciples saw Him walking on the lake, they were terrified. "It's a ghost," they said, and they cried out in terror.

27 Immediately He talked to them. "Have courage," He said. "It is I. Don't be afraid."

28 "Lord, if it's You," Peter answered Him, "order me to come to You on the water."

29 "Come," He said. So Peter got out of the boat, walked on the water, and went toward Jesus. 30 But when he saw the wind, he was frightened and started to sink. "Lord, save me!" he cried.

31 Quickly Jesus stretched out His hand and caught him. "How little you trust Me!" He said to him. "Why did you doubt?"

32 When they stepped into the boat, the wind stopped. 33And the men in the boat bowed down before Him and said, "You certainly are God's Son."

34 They crossed over and came to the shore at Gennesaret. 35 The men of that place recognized Jesus and sent messengers all around that country, and the people brought Him all the sick ones, 36 and they begged Him just to let them touch the tassel of His garment. All who touched it were made well.

Unclean Hands

15 Then some Pharisees and Bible scholars came to Him from Jerusalem. 2 "Why do your disciples sin against the rules handed down by our fathers?" they asked. "They don't wash their hands when they eat."

3 "Why do you sin against God's commandment for the sake of your rules?" He asked them. 4 "For example, God has said, *Honor father and mother,*⁵⁰ and, *Anyone who curses father or mother must die.*⁵¹ 5 But you say, 'Whoever tells his father or mother, "I'm giving God anything by which I might help you," doesn't have to honor his father.' 6 For the sake of your rules you have set aside what God has said. 7 Hypocrites, Isaiah was right when he prophesied about you: 8 *These people honor Me with their lips, but their hearts are far away from Me. 9 They worship Me in vain because they teach men's rules.*⁵²

10 Then he called the people and told them: "Listen to Me and understand this: 11 What comes into his mouth doesn't make a person unclean, but what goes out of his mouth makes him unclean."

[50] Ex. 20:12; Deut. 5:16
[51] Ex. 21:17; Lev. 20:9
[52] Is. 29:13

45

K.J.V.

man. 12 Then came his disciples, and said unto him, Knowest thou that the Pharisees were offended, after they heard this saying? 13 But he answered and said, Every plant, which my heavenly Father hath not planted, shall be rooted up. 14 Let them alone: they be blind leaders of the blind. And if the blind lead the blind, both shall fall into the ditch. 15 Then answered Peter and said unto him, Declare unto us this parable. 16And Jesus said, Are ye also yet without understanding? 17 Do not ye yet understand, that whatsoever entereth in at the mouth goeth into the belly, and is cast out into the draught? 18 But those things which proceed out of the mouth come forth from the heart; and they defile the man. 19 For out of the heart proceed evil thoughts, murders, adulteries, fornications, thefts, false witness, blasphemies: 20 These are *the things* which defile a man: but to eat with unwashen hands defileth not a man.

21 Then Jesus went thence, and departed into the coasts of Tyre and Sidon. 22And, behold, a woman of Canaan came out of the same coasts, and cried unto him, saying, Have mercy on me, O Lord, *thou* Son of David; my daughter is grievously vexed with a devil. 23 But he answered her not a word. And his disciples came and besought him, saying, Send her away; for she crieth after us. 24 But he answered and said, I am not sent but unto the lost sheep of the house of Israel. 25 Then came she and worshipped him, saying, Lord, help me. 26 But he answered and said, It is not meet to take the children's bread, and to cast *it* to dogs. 27And she said, Truth, Lord: yet the dogs eat of the crumbs which fall from their masters' table. 28 Then Jesus answered and said unto her, O woman, great *is* thy faith: be it unto thee even as thou wilt. And her daughter was made whole from that very hour. 29And Jesus departed from thence, and came nigh unto the sea of Galilee; and went up into a mountain, and sat down there. 30And great multitudes came unto him, having with them *those that were* lame, blind, dumb, maimed, and many others, and cast them down at Jesus' feet; and he healed them: 31 Insomuch that the multitude wondered, when they saw the dumb to speak, the maimed to be whole, the lame to walk, and the blind to see: and they glorified the God of Israel.

32 Then Jesus called his disciples *unto him,* and said, I have compassion on the multitude, because they continue with me now three days, and have nothing to eat: and I will not send them away fasting, lest they faint in the way. 33And his disciples say unto him, Whence should we have so much bread in the wilderness, as to fill so great a multitude? 34And Jesus saith unto them, How many loaves have ye? And they said, Seven, and a few little fishes. 35And he commanded the multitude to sit down on the ground. 36And he took the seven loaves and the fishes, and gave thanks, and brake *them,* and gave to his disciples, and the disciples to the multitude. 37And they did all eat, and were filled: and they took up of the broken

N.A.S.

defiles the man." 12 Then the disciples *came and *said to Him, "Do You know that the Pharisees were offended when they heard this statement?" 13 But He answered and said, "Every plant which My heavenly Father did not plant shall be rooted up. 14 "Let them alone; they are blind guides ᵃof the blind. And if a blind man guides a blind man, both will fall into a pit." 15And Peter answered and said to Him, "Explain the parable to us." 16And He said, "Are you also still without understanding? 17 "Do you not understand that everything that goes into the mouth passes into the stomach, and is eliminated? 18 "But the things that proceed out of the mouth come from the heart, and those defile the man. 19 "For out of the heart come evil thoughts, murders, adulteries, fornications, thefts, false witness, slanders. 20 "These are the things which defile the man; but to eat with unwashed hands does not defile the man."

21 And Jesus went away from there, and withdrew into the district of Tyre and Sidon. 22And behold, a Canaanite woman came out from that region, and *began* to cry out, saying, "Have mercy on me, O Lord, Son of David; my daughter is cruelly demon-possessed." 23 But He did not answer her a word. And His disciples came to *Him* and kept asking Him, saying, "Send her away, for she is shouting out after us." 24 But He answered and said, "I was sent only to the lost sheep of the house of Israel." 25 But she came and *began* to bow down before Him, saying, "Lord, help me!" 26And He answered and said, "It is not good to take the children's bread and throw *it* to the dogs." 27 But she said, "Yes, Lord; but even the dogs feed on the crumbs which fall from their masters' table." 28 Then Jesus answered and said to her, "O woman, your faith is great; be it done for you as you wish." And her daughter was healed at once.

29 And departing from there, Jesus went along by the sea of Galilee, and having gone up to the mountain, He was sitting there. 30And great multitudes came to Him, bringing with them *those who were* lame, crippled, blind, dumb, and many others, and they laid them down at His feet; and He healed them, 31 so that the multitude marveled as they saw the dumb speaking, the crippled restored, and the lame walking, and the blind seeing; and they glorified the God of Israel.

32 And Jesus summoned to Himself His disciples, and said, "I feel compassion for the multitude, because they have remained with Me now three days and have nothing to eat; and I do not wish to send them away hungry, lest they faint on the way." 33And the disciples *said to Him, "Where would we get so many loaves in a desert place to satisfy such a great multitude?" 34And Jesus *said to them, "How many loaves do you have?" And they said, "Seven, and a few small fish." 35And He directed the multitude to sit down on the ground; 36 and He took the seven loaves and the fish; and giving thanks, He broke *them* and started giving *them* to the disciples, and the disciples *in turn,* to the multitudes. 37And they all ate, and were satisfied, and they picked up what was left over of the broken pieces,

[a] Some mss. omit: *of the blind.*

46

WILLIAMS

12 Then His disciples came up to Him and asked, "Do you know that the Pharisees were knocked breathless [b] to hear what you have just said?"

13 He answered, "Every plant that my heavenly Father did not plant must be rooted up. 14 Let them alone. They are blind teachers! And if one blind man guides another, they will both fall into the ditch."

15 Then Peter said to Him, "Explain the maxim for us."

16 And He said, "Are you too, even yet, without understanding? 17 Do you not understand that whatever goes into the mouth passes into the stomach and afterwards into the waste? 18 But the things that come out of the mouth come from the heart, and they make the man foul. 19 For out of the heart come evil thoughts, murder, adultery, immorality, stealing, false witnessing, irreverent speech. 20 These are the things that make a man foul, but eating with unwashed hands does not make a man foul."

21 Then Jesus left there and slipped away to the neighborhood of Tyre and Sidon. 22 And a Canaanite woman of that district came out and pleaded, saying, "Do pity me, Lord, Son of David; my daughter is suffering horrors from a demon."

23 But He did not answer her a word. And His disciples came up and kept begging Him, "Send her away, for she keeps on screaming after us."

24 But He answered, "I have been sent only to the lost sheep of Israel's house."

25 But she came and bowed to Him, and kept praying, "Lord, help me!"

26 He answered, "It is not right to take the children's bread and throw it to the house dogs."

27 She said, "Yes, Lord, and yet the house dogs usually eat the crumbs that fall from their master's table."

28 Then Jesus answered her, "O woman, wonderful [c] is your faith! You must have what you want." And her daughter was cured at that very moment.

29 Then Jesus left there and went to the shore of the sea of Galilee. Then He went up the hill and kept sitting there, 30 and great crowds came up to Him bringing with them the lame, the crippled, the blind, the deaf, and many others. They laid them at His feet, and He cured them, 31 so that the crowd was astonished to see the dumb talking, the lame walking, and the blind seeing. So they praised the God of Israel.

32 Then Jesus called His disciples to Him, and said, "My heart is moved with pity for the crowd, for it is now three days they have been staying with me, and they have nothing at all left to eat, and I fear they might give out on the way home."

33 The disciples said to Him, "Where in this destitute place can we get bread enough to satisfy such a crowd?"

34 Then Jesus asked them, "How many loaves have you on hand?"

They answered, "Seven and a few small fish." 35 Then He ordered the crowd to sit down on the ground, 36 and He took the seven loaves and the fish and gave thanks; then He broke them in pieces, and kept giving the pieces to the disciples, and they to the crowds. 37 And they all ate and had a plenty, and they took up the pieces left over, which made seven

BECK

12 Then the disciples came to Him. "Do you know the Pharisees were offended when they heard You say that?" they asked Him.

13 "Any plant My Father in heaven didn't plant," He answered, "will be torn out by the roots. 14 Let them go; they are blind leaders. When one blind man leads another, both will fall into a ditch."

15 "Tell us what You mean by this illustration," Peter said to Him.

16 "Are you still as dull as the others?" He asked. 17 "Don't you know that everything that goes into the mouth goes into the stomach and so passes away? 18 But what goes out of the mouth comes from the heart, and that makes a person unclean. 19 Yes, out of the heart come evil thoughts, murders, adulteries, sexual sins, stealing, lies, slanders. These are the things that make a person unclean. 20 But eating without washing your hands doesn't make you unclean."

21 Leaving that place, Jesus went away to the neighborhood of Tyre and Sidon.

22 There was a Canaanite woman of that territory who came out and called, "Have pity on me, Lord, Son of David! A devil is making my daughter miserable."

23 But He didn't answer her a word. Then His disciples came to Him and urged Him, "Send her away. She's yelling after us."

24 "I was sent only to the lost sheep of Israel," He answered.

25 She came and bowed down before Him. "Lord, help me!" she said.

26 "It isn't good," He answered, "to take the children's bread and throw it to the puppies."

27 "You're right, Lord," she said, "but even the puppies eat some of the crumbs that drop from their masters' table."

28 Then Jesus answered her, "O woman, you have a great faith! Let it be done for you as you wish." At that moment her daughter was made well.

29 Jesus left that place and went along the shore of the Lake of Galilee. Then He went up a hill and sat there. 30 Many people came to Him, bringing the lame, blind, crippled, deaf, and many others and laid them at His feet. 31 He made them well, so that the people were surprised to find that the dumb talked, the cripples had sound limbs, the lame walked around, and the blind could see. And they praised the God of Israel.

Jesus Feeds Four Thousand

32 Jesus called His disciples. "I feel sorry for the people," He said. "They've been with Me three days now and have nothing to eat. I don't want to let them go without eating; they may get exhausted on the way."

33 "Where could we get enough bread in a wilderness to feed such a crowd?" His disciples asked Him.

34 "How many loaves do you have?" Jesus asked them.

"Seven," they said, "and a few small fish." 35 He ordered the people to sit down on the ground. 36 Then He took the seven loaves and the fish, gave thanks, broke them, and gave them to the disciples, and they gave them to the people. 37 All of them ate and had enough. They picked up the pieces that were left—seven bas-

[b] Grk., *caused to fall.* [c] Grk., *great.*

K.J.V.

meat that was left seven baskets full. 38And they that did eat were four thousand men, beside women and children. 39And he sent away the multitude, and took ship, and came into the coasts of Magdala.

16 The Pharisees also with the Sadducees came, and tempting desired him that he would shew them a sign from heaven. 2 He answered and said unto them, When it is evening, ye say, *It will be* fair weather: for the sky is red. 3And in the morning, *It will be* foul weather to day: for the sky is red and lowering. O *ye* hypocrites, ye can discern the face of the sky; but can ye not *discern* the signs of the times? 4A wicked and adulterous generation seeketh after a sign; and there shall no sign be given unto it, but the sign of the prophet Jonas. And he left them, and departed. 5And when his disciples were come to the other side, they had forgotten to take bread.

6 Then Jesus said unto them, Take heed and beware of the leaven of the Pharisees and of the Sadducees. 7And they reasoned among themselves, saying, *It is* because we have taken no bread. 8 *Which* when Jesus perceived, he said unto them, O ye of little faith, why reason ye among yourselves, because ye have brought no bread? 9 Do ye not yet understand, neither remember the five loaves of the five thousand, and how many baskets ye took up? 10 Neither the seven loaves of the four thousand, and how many baskets ye took up? 11 How is it that ye do not understand that I spake *it* not to you concerning bread, that ye should beware of the leaven of the Pharisees and of the Sadducees? 12 Then understood they how that he bade *them* not beware of the leaven of bread, but of the doctrine of the Pharisees and of the Sadducees.

13 When Jesus came into the coasts of Cesarea Philippi, he asked his disciples, saying, Whom do men say that I, the Son of man, am? 14And they said, Some *say that thou art* John the Baptist; some, Elias; and others, Jeremias, or one of the prophets. 15 He saith unto them, But whom say ye that I am? 16And Simon Peter answered and said, Thou art the Christ, the Son of the living God. 17And Jesus answered and said unto him, Blessed art thou, Simon Bar-jona: for flesh and blood hath not revealed *it* unto thee, but my Father which is in heaven. 18And I say also unto thee, That thou art Peter, and upon this rock I will build my church; and the gates of hell shall not prevail against it. 19And I will give unto thee the keys of the kingdom of heaven: and whatsoever thou shalt bind on earth shall be bound in heaven; and whatsoever thou shalt loose on earth shall be loosed in heaven. 20 Then charged he his disciples that they should tell no man that he was Jesus the Christ.

N.A.S.

seven full baskets. 38And those who ate were four thousand men, besides women and children. 39And dismissing the multitudes, He got into the boat, and came to the region of Magadan.

16 And the Pharisees and Sadducees came up, and testing Him asked Him to show them a sign from heaven. 2 But He answered and said to them, "When it is evening, you say, 'It will be fair weather, for the sky is red.' 3 "And in the morning, 'There will be a storm today, for the sky is red and threatening.' Do you know how to discern the appearance of the sky, but cannot *discern* the signs of the times? 4 "An evil and adulterous generation seeks after a sign; and a sign will not be given it, except the sign of Jonah." And He left them, and went away.

5 And the disciples came to the other side and had forgotten to take bread. 6And Jesus said to them, "Watch out and beware of the leaven of the Pharisees and Sadducees." 7And they began to discuss among themselves, saying, "It is because we took no bread." 8 But Jesus, aware of this, said, "You men of little faith, why do you discuss among yourselves because you have no bread? 9 "Do you not yet understand or remember the five loaves of the five thousand, and how many large baskets you took up? 10 "Or the seven loaves of the four thousand, and how many baskets you took up? 11 "How is it that you do not understand that I did not speak to you concerning bread? But beware of the leaven of the Pharisees and Sadducees." 12 Then they understood that He did not say to beware of the leaven of bread, but of the teaching of the Pharisees and Sadducees.

13 Now when Jesus came into the district of Caesarea Philippi, He *began* asking His disciples, saying, "Who do people say that the Son of Man is?" 14And they said, "Some *say* John the Baptist; some, Elijah; and others, Jeremiah, or one of the prophets." 15 He *said to them, "But who do you say that I am?" 16And Simon Peter answered and said, "Thou art the Christ, the Son of the living God." 17And Jesus answered and said to him, "Blessed are you, Simon Barjonas, because flesh and blood did not reveal *this* to you, but My Father who is in heaven. 18 "And I also say to you that you are Peter, and upon this rock I will build My church; and the gates of Hades shall not overpower it. 19 "I will give you the keys of the kingdom of heaven; and whatever you shall bind on earth shall have been bound in heaven, and whatever you shall loose on earth shall have been loosed in heaven." 20 Then He warned the disciples that they should tell no one that He was the Christ.

WILLIAMS

hamper[d] basketfuls. 38 Those fed numbered four thousand men, besides women and children.

39 Then He sent the crowds away, got into the boat, and went to the district of Magadan.

16 *A spectacular sign not to be given; warning against the teaching of the Pharisees and the Sadducees; Jesus foretells his death; the founding of the church*

The Pharisees and the Sadducees came up, and to test Him asked Him to show them a spectacular sign from heaven. 2 He answered,[a] 4 "It is a wicked and immoral [b] age that is hankering for a spectacular sign, so no sign will be given it but the sign of Jonah." Then He left them and went away.

5 When the disciples crossed the sea, they forgot to take any bread. 6 And Jesus said to them, "Look out, and keep on guarding yourselves against the yeast of the Pharisees and the Sadducees!"

7 Then they began to discuss it among themselves, and said, "It is because we did not take any bread."

8 Jesus knew it and said, "Why are you discussing among yourselves the fact that you have no bread? Have you so little faith? 9 Do you not understand yet? Do you not remember the five loaves for the five thousand and how many basketfuls you took up? 10 Nor the seven loaves for the four thousand and how many hamperbasketfuls you took up? 11 How is it that you do not understand that I did not speak to you about bread, when I said, keep on guarding yourselves against the yeast of the Pharisees and the Sadducees?" 12 Then they understood that He meant, guard yourselves not against yeast for bread,[c] but against the teaching of the Pharisees and the Sadducees.

13 When Jesus reached the district of Caesarea Philippi, He asked His disciples," "Who do people say that the Son of Man is?" 14 They answered, "Some say John the Baptist, some Elijah, and others Jeremiah or one of the prophets."

15 He said to them, "Who do you yourselves say that I am?"

16 Simon Peter answered, "You are the Christ, the Son of the living God."

17 Then Jesus answered him, "Blessed are you, Simon, son of Jonah, for it is not man[d] that made this known to you, but my Father in heaven. 18 And I, yes I, tell you, your name from now on is to be Peter, Rock, and on a massive rock like this[e] I will build my church, and the powers of the underworld [f] shall never overthrow it. 19 I will give you the keys of the kingdom of heaven, and whatever you forbid on earth must be what is already forbidden in heaven, and whatever you permit on earth must be what is already permitted in heaven." 20 Then He admonished the disciples not to tell anyone that He was the Christ.

[d] Very large baskets, so our *hampers.* [a] Best Mss. om. all from, *He ans.* to close of v. 3. [b] Grk., *adulterous.* [c] Fol. B, the oldest Ms. [d] Grk., *flesh and blood,* meaning man in his frailty. [e] A different word from the word trans. *Peter;* i. e., πέτρα, a massive rock, meaning *faith in the Christ, the Son of God.* [f] Grk., *hades, underworld.*

BECK

kets full. 38 Four thousand men had eaten, not counting women and children.

39 Then He dismissed the people.

A Proof from Heaven

39 He stepped into the boat and came into the neighborhood of Magadan.

16 The Pharisees and Sadducees came and, to test Him, asked Him to show them some wonderful proof from heaven.

2 He answered them, "In the evening you say, 'The weather will be fine, because the sky is red.' 3 And in the morning: 'There will be a storm today, because the sky is red and gloomy.' You know how to judge the appearance of the sky correctly but can't judge the signs of the times.*

4 "The wicked and unfaithful people of today demand a proof, and the only proof they'll get is that of Jonah."

Then He left them and went away.

The Yeast of the Pharisees

5 When the disciples started out for the other side, they forgot to take bread.

6 Jesus said to them, "Beware of the yeast of the Pharisees and Sadducees!"

7 As they were arguing about this, they mentioned, "We didn't take any bread."

8 Aware of what was going on, Jesus asked, "Why are you arguing about not having any bread? You have so little faith! 9 Don't you understand yet, and don't you remember the five loaves for the five thousand and how many baskets full you picked up? 10 Or the seven loaves for the four thousand and how many baskets full you picked up? 11 Why don't you see I wasn't talking to you about bread? But beware of the yeast of the Pharisees and Sadducees!"

12 Then they understood He didn't warn them against the yeast in bread but against the teaching of the Pharisees and Sadducees.

"You Are the Son of God"

13 When Jesus came to the neighborhood of Philip's Caesarea, He asked His disciples, "Who do people say the Son of Man is?

14 "Some say John the Baptizer," they answered, "others Elijah, still others Jeremiah, or one of the prophets."

15 "Who do you say I am?" He asked them.

16 "You are the promised Savior," Simon Peter answered, "the Son of the living God!"

17 "Happy are you, Simon, son of John," Jesus answered him, "because no flesh and blood, but My Father in heaven has revealed this to you. 18 I tell you, you are Peter, and on this rock I will build My church, and the forces of hell will not overpower it. 19 I will give you the keys of the kingdom of heaven. Anything you bind on earth will be bound in heaven, and anything you free on earth will be freed in heaven."

20 Then He warned the disciples not to tell anyone that He was the promised Savior.

* Jesus' words in verses 2-3 are omitted in some of our oldest manuscripts.

K.J.V.

21 From that time forth began Jesus to shew unto his disciples, how that he must go unto Jerusalem, and suffer many things of the elders and chief priests and scribes, and be killed, and be raised again the third day. 22 Then Peter took him, and began to rebuke him, saying, Be it far from thee, Lord: this shall not be unto thee. 23 But he turned, and said unto Peter, Get thee behind me, Satan: thou art an offence unto me: for thou savourest not the things that be of God, but those that be of men.

24 Then said Jesus unto his disciples, If any *man* will come after me, let him deny himself, and take up his cross, and follow me. 25 For whosoever will save his life shall lose it: and whosoever will lose his life for my sake shall find it. 26 For what is a man profited, if he shall gain the whole world, and lose his own soul? or what shall a man give in exchange for his soul? 27 For the Son of man shall come in the glory of his Father with his angels; and then he shall reward every man according to his works. 28 Verily I say unto you, There be some standing here, which shall not taste of death, till they see the Son of man coming in his kingdom.

N.A.S.

21 From that time Jesus Christ began to show His disciples that He must go to Jerusalem, and suffer many things from the elders and chief priests and scribes, and be killed, and be raised up on the third day. 22 And Peter took Him aside and began to rebuke Him, saying, "God forbid *it*, Lord! This shall never happen to You." 23 But He turned and said to Peter, "Get behind Me, Satan! You are a stumbling-block to Me; for you are not setting your mind on God's interests, but man's." 24 Then Jesus said to His disciples, "If any one wishes to come after Me, let him deny himself, and take up his cross, and follow Me. 25 "For whoever wishes to save his life shall lose it; but whoever loses his life for My sake shall find it. 26 "For what will a man be profited, if he gains the whole world, and forfeits his soul? Or what will a man give in exchange for his soul? 27 "For the Son of Man is going to come in the glory of His Father with His angels; and WILL THEN RECOMPENSE EVERY MAN ACCORDING TO HIS DEEDS. 28 "Truly I say to you, there are some of those who are standing here who shall not taste death until they see the Son of Man coming in His kingdom."

17 And after six days Jesus taketh Peter, James, and John his brother, and bringeth them up into a high mountain apart, 2 And was transfigured before them: and his face did shine as the sun, and his raiment was white as the light. 3 And, behold, there appeared unto them Moses and Elias talking with him. 4 Then answered Peter, and said unto Jesus, Lord, it is good for us to be here: if thou wilt, let us make here three tabernacles; one for thee, and one for Moses, and one for Elias. 5 While he yet spake, behold, a bright cloud overshadowed them: and behold a voice out of the cloud, which said, This is my beloved Son, in whom I am well pleased; hear ye him. 6 And when the disciples heard *it*, they fell on their face, and were sore afraid. 7 And Jesus came and touched them, and said, Arise, and be not afraid. 8 And when they had lifted up their eyes, they saw no man, save Jesus only. 9 And as they came down from the mountain, Jesus charged them, saying, Tell the vision to no man, until the Son of man be risen again from the dead. 10 And his disciples asked him, saying, Why then say the scribes that Elias must first come? 11 And Jesus answered and said unto them, Elias truly shall first come, and restore all things. 12 But I say unto you, That Elias is come already, and they knew him not, but have done unto him whatsoever they listed. Likewise shall also the Son of man suffer of them. 13 Then the disciples understood that he spake unto them of John the Baptist.

17 And six days later Jesus *took with him Peter and James and John his brother, and *brought them up to a high mountain by themselves. 2 And He was transfigured before them; and His face shone like the sun, and His garments became as white as light. 3 And behold, Moses and Elijah appeared to them, talking with Him. 4 And Peter answered and said to Jesus, "Lord, it is good for us to be here; if You wish, I will make three tabernacles here, one for You, and one for Moses, and one for Elijah." 5 While he was still speaking, behold, a bright cloud overshadowed them; and behold, a voice out of the cloud, saying, "This is My beloved Son, with whom I am well pleased; hear Him!" 6 And when the disciples heard *this*, they fell on their faces and were much afraid. 7 And Jesus came to *them* and touched them and said, "Arise, and do not be afraid." 8 And lifting up their eyes, they saw no one, except Jesus Himself alone.

9 And as they were coming down from the mountain, Jesus commanded them, saying, "Tell the vision to no one until the Son of Man has risen from the dead." 10 And His disciples asked Him, saying, "Why then do the scribes say that Elijah must come first?" 11 And He answered and said, "Elijah is coming, and will restore all things; 12 but I say to you, that Elijah already came, and they did not recognize him, but did to him whatever they wished. So also the Son of Man is going to suffer at their hands." 13 Then the disciples understood that He had spoken to them about John the Baptist.

| WILLIAMS | BECK |

"I Will Die and Rise Again"

21 It was just after that that Jesus Christ for the first time clearly taught His disciples that He had to go to Jerusalem and submit to many forms of suffering at the hands of the elders, high priests, and scribes, and be killed, but be raised to life on the third day. 22 And Peter took Him aside and began to chide Him, as he said, "Heaven shield you, my Lord! This must never be your lot!"

23 But he turned and said to Peter, "Get out of my way, you Satan! You are a hindrance[g] to me, for this view of yours is not from God but from men."

24 Then Jesus said to His disciples: "If anyone wants to be my disciple, he must say 'No' to self, put his cross on his shoulders, and keep on following me. 25 For whoever wants to save his higher life will have to give up the lower life, and whoever gives up his lower life for my sake will find the higher life. 26 For what benefit will it be to a man, if he gains the whole world and loses his higher life? What price would a man pay to buy back his life? 27 For the Son of Man is going to come in His Father's splendor, with His angels, and then He will pay back to everyone in accordance with what he has done. 28 I solemnly say to you, some of the people standing here will certainly live[h] to see the Son of Man coming in His kingdom."

21 After this, Jesus Christ kept pointing out to His disciples He had to go to Jerusalem, suffer much from the elders, ruling priests, and Bible scholars, be killed, and then on the third day rise.

22 But Peter took Him aside and started to correct Him, "God be merciful to You, Lord! This must never happen to You!"

23 Turning, He said to Peter, "Get behind Me, devil! You're tempting Me to sin, because you're not thinking what God thinks but what men think."

Take the Cross

24 Then Jesus said to His disciples, "If you want to follow Me, deny yourself, take up your cross, and come with Me. 25 If you want to save your life, you will lose it. But if you will lose your life for Me, you will find it. 26 What good will it do you to win the whole world and lose your life? Or what would you give to buy back your life? 27 The Son of Man is going to come with His angels in His Father's glory, and then *He will give each one according to what he has done.*[53] 28 Let Me assure you, there are some standing here who will never taste death till they see the Son of Man coming to rule as King."

Jesus Shows His Glory

17 Jesus transfigured; an epileptic boy cured; faith that removes mountains; temple tax paid by Jesus

Six days after this, Jesus took Peter and James and his brother John, and led them up on a high mountain, by themselves. 2 And in their presence His appearance was changed and His face shone like the sun, and His clothes turned as white as light. 3 Then Moses and Elijah appeared to them and kept talking with Him. 4 And Peter interrupted, and said to Jesus, "Lord, it is good for us to be here! If you consent, I will put up three tents here, one for you, one for Moses, and one for Elijah."

5 While he was still speaking, a bright cloud cast its shadow over them, and a voice from the cloud said, "This is my Son, my Beloved, in whom I am delighted. Keep on listening to Him!" 6 When the disciples heard it, they fell upon their faces, for they were terribly frightened.

7 Then Jesus came and touched them, and said, "Get up and do not be so afraid." 8 They looked up and saw no one but Jesus Himself.

9 And as they were going down the mountain, Jesus warned[a] them, saying, "Never mention to anyone what you have seen until the Son of Man is raised from the dead."

10 The disciples asked Him, "Why then do the scribes say that Elijah must come first?"

11 He answered, "Elijah does come and will get everything ready. 12 But I say to you, Elijah has already come, and they did not recognize him, but treated him as they pleased. Just so the Son of Man is going to suffer at their hands." 13 Then the disciples understood that He spoke to them about John the Baptist.

17 After five days Jesus took with Him Peter, James, and John, the brother of James, and led them up a high mountain to be alone with them.

2 He was changed before them, His face shone like the sun, and His clothes became as white as light. 3 And there Moses and Elijah appeared to them and were talking with Him.

4 "Lord," Peter said to Jesus, "it's good for us to be here. If You wish, I'll put up three shelters here, one for You, one for Moses, and one for Elijah."

5 He was still speaking when a bright cloud suddenly overshadowed them, and a voice came out of the cloud: "This is *My Son* whom I love and *delight in. Listen to Him.*"[54]

6 When the disciples heard this, they fell down with their faces on the ground; they were terrified. 7 But Jesus came and touched them. "Get up," He said, "and don't be afraid." 8 They looked up and saw no one but Jesus.

9 On their way down the mountain Jesus ordered them, "Don't tell anyone what you have seen till the Son of Man has risen from the dead."

10 So the disciples asked Him, "Why, then, do those who know the Bible say, 'First Elijah has to come'?"

11 *"Elijah* does come," He answered, "and *must put* everything *in order again.*[55] 12 But I tell you Elijah has already come, and people didn't know him, but treated him as they pleased. In the same way they're going to make the Son of Man suffer."

13 Then the disciples understood He was talking about John the Baptizer.

---

[g] Grk., *the stick that throws the trap to catch the prey;* so *hindrance.* [h] Grk., *will not at all die,* so *surely live.* [a] Grk., *ordered.*

[53] Ps. 62:12; Prov. 24:12
[54] Ps. 2:7; Is. 42:1; Deut. 18:15
[55] Mal. 4:5-6

K.J.V.

14 And when they were come to the multitude, there came to him a *certain* man, kneeling down to him, and saying, 15 Lord, have mercy on my son; for he is lunatic, and sore vexed: for ofttimes he falleth into the fire, and oft into the water. 16And I brought him to thy disciples, and they could not cure him. 17 Then Jesus answered and said, O faithless and perverse generation, how long shall I be with you? how long shall I suffer you? bring him hither to me. 18And Jesus rebuked the devil; and he departed out of him: and the child was cured from that very hour. 19 Then came the disciples to Jesus apart, and said, Why could not we cast him out? 20And Jesus said unto them, Because of your unbelief: for verily I say unto you, If ye have faith as a grain of mustard seed, ye shall say unto this mountain, Remove hence to yonder place; and it shall remove: and nothing shall be impossible unto you. 21 Howbeit this kind goeth not out but by prayer and fasting.

22 And while they abode in Galilee, Jesus said unto them, The Son of man shall be betrayed into the hands of men: 23And they shall kill him, and the third day he shall be raised again. And they were exceeding sorry.

24. And when they were come to Capernaum, they that received tribute *money* came to Peter, and said, Doth not your master pay tribute? 25 He saith, Yes. And when he was come into the house, Jesus prevented him, saying, What thinkest thou, Simon? of whom do the kings of the earth take custom or tribute? of their own children, or of strangers? 26 Peter saith unto him, Of strangers. Jesus saith unto him, Then are the children free. 27 Notwithstanding, lest we should offend them, go thou to the sea, and cast a hook, and take up the fish that first cometh up; and when thou hast opened his mouth, thou shalt find a piece of money: that take, and give unto them for me and thee.

N.A.S.

14 And when they came to the multitude, a man came up to Him, falling on his knees before Him, and saying, 15 "Lord, have mercy on my son; for he is an epileptic, and is very ill; for he often falls into the fire, and often into the water. 16 "And I brought him to Your disciples, and they could not cure him." 17And Jesus answered and said, "O unbelieving and perverted generation, how long shall I be with you? How long shall I put up with you? Bring him here to Me." 18And Jesus rebuked him, and the demon came out of him, and the boy was cured at once.

19 Then the disciples came to Jesus privately and said, "Why could we not cast it out?" 20And He *said to them, "Because of the littleness of your faith; for truly I say to you, if you have faith as a mustard seed, you shall say to this mountain, 'Move from here to there,' and it shall move; and nothing shall be impossible to you. 21 ["*But this kind does not go out except by prayer and fasting."]

22 And while they were gathering together in Galilee, Jesus said to them, "The Son of Man is going to be delivered into the hands of men; 23 and they will kill Him, and He will be raised again on the third day." And they were deeply grieved.

24 And when they had come to Capernaum, those who collected the *b*two-drachma *tax* came to Peter, and said, "Does your teacher not pay the *b*two-drachma *tax?*" 25 He *said, "Yes." And when he came into the house Jesus spoke to him first, saying, "What do you think, Simon? From whom do the kings of the earth collect customs or poll-tax, from their sons or from strangers?" 26And upon his saying, "From strangers," Jesus said to him, "Consequently the sons are exempt. 27 "But, lest we give them offense, go to the sea, and throw in a hook, and take the first fish that comes up; and when you open its mouth, you will find a *c*stater; take that and give to them for you and Me."

18 At the same time came the disciples unto Jesus, saying, Who is the greatest in the kingdom of heaven? 2And Jesus called a little child unto him, and set him in the midst of them, 3And said, Verily I say unto you, Except ye be converted, and become as little children, ye shall not enter into the kingdom of heaven. 4 Whosoever therefore shall humble himself as this little child, the same is greatest in the kingdom of heaven. 5And whoso shall receive one such little child in my name receiveth me. 6 But whoso shall offend one of these little ones which believe in me, it were better for him that a millstone were hanged about his neck, and *that* he were drowned in the depth of the sea.

18 At that time the disciples came to Jesus, saying, "Who then is greatest in the kingdom of heaven?" 2And He called a child to Himself and stood him in their midst, 3 and said, "Truly I say to you, unless you are converted and become like children, you shall not enter the kingdom of heaven. 4 "Whoever then humbles himself as this child, he is the greatest in the kingdom of heaven. 5 "And whoever receives one such child in My name receives Me; 6 but whoever causes one of these little ones who believe in Me to stumble, it is better for him that a heavy millstone be hung around his neck, and that he be drowned in the depth of the sea.

[a] Most ancient mss. omit this verse. [b] Equivalent to two denarii or two days wages paid as a temple tax. [c] Or, *shekel*, worth four drachmas.

WILLIAMS

14 When they reached the crowd, a man came up to him, kneeling before Him and saying, 15 "Lord, do pity my son, for he has epilepsy and suffers excruciating pain, and often falls into the fire or into the water. 16 I brought him to your disciples, and they could not cure him."

17 And Jesus answered, "O you unbelieving and perverted people of the times! How long can I put up with you? Bring him here to me!" 18 And Jesus reproved the demon, and it came out of him, and the boy was cured that very moment.

19 After that the disciples came to Jesus and privately asked, "Why is it we could not drive it out?"

20 He answered them, "Because you have so little faith! For I solemnly say to you, if you have the faith that is living like a grain of mustard, you can say to this mountain, 'Move over from here to yonder,' and it will move over, and nothing will be impossible for you to do." b

22 While they were going about in Galilee, Jesus said to them, "The Son of Man is going to be turned over into the hands of men, 23 and they will kill Him, but on the third day He will be raised again." And they were crushed with grief.

24 When they reached Capernaum, the collectors of the temple tax came to Peter and asked, "Does your Teacher pay the temple tax?"

25 He answered, "Yes."

When Jesus reached home—He got there ahead of Simon—He asked him, "What do you think about it, Simon? From whom do civil rulers collect duties or taxes, from their own citizens or from aliens?"

26 He answered, "From aliens."

Jesus said to him, "So their own citizens are exempt, 27 but still, that we may not influence them to do anything wrong, go down to the sea and throw over a hook. Pull in the first fish that bites, open its mouth and you will find in it a dollar. Take it and pay the tax for both of us."

18 *He tells three stories: being like children; the lost sheep found; the unforgiving slave; He also talks about united prayer, and how to settle private differences*

Just at that moment the disciples came up and asked Jesus, "Who then is greatest in the kingdom of heaven?"

2 And He called a little child to Him, and had him stand in the midst of them, 3 and said:

"I solemnly say to you, unless you turn and become like little children, you can never get into the kingdom of heaven at all. 4 So then, whoever becomes as lowly as this little child is the greatest in the kingdom of heaven, 5 and whoever welcomes one little child like this for my sake welcomes me. 6 But whoever leads one of these little ones, who believe in me, to do wrong, had better have a great millstone hung around his neck to sink him to the bottom of

[b] V. 21 not in the best manuscripts.

BECK

The Epileptic Boy

14 When they came to the people, a man came to Jesus and knelt before Him. 15 "Lord," he said, "have pity on my son. He's epileptic and very sick. Often he falls into fire or into water. 16 I brought him to Your disciples, but they couldn't make him well."

17 "O you unbelieving and perverted people!" Jesus answered. "How long must I be with you? How long must I put up with you? Bring him here to Me."

18 Jesus talked sharply to the devil, and he came out of the boy, and after that the boy was well.

19 Afterwards, when Jesus was alone, the disciples came to Him. "Why couldn't we drive out the spirit?" they asked.

20 "You have so little faith," He told them. "I tell you the truth, if you have faith no bigger than a mustard seed, you will say to this mountain, 'Move from here to there,' and it will move.* Then you can do anything."

"I Will Die and Rise Again"

22 While they were getting together as a group in Galilee, Jesus told them, "The Son of Man is going to be betrayed into the hands of men, 23 and they will kill Him, but on the third day He will rise." Then they felt very sad.

A Coin in a Fish's Mouth

24 When they came to Capernaum, the collectors of the temple tax came to Peter. "Doesn't your Teacher pay the temple tax?" they asked.

25 "Certainly," he answered.

Peter went into the house, but before he could speak, Jesus asked him, "What do you think, Simon? From whom do the kings of the world collect toll or tax—from their children or from other people?"

26 "From other people," he answered.

"Then the children are free," Jesus told him. 27 "But we don't want to give them a reason to think wrong of us. So go to the lake and throw in a hook. Take the first fish that comes up, open its mouth, and you will find a coin. Take that and give it to them for Me and you."

Who Is the Greatest?

18 At that time the disciples came to Jesus and asked, "Who is really the greatest in the kingdom of heaven?"

2 He called a little child and had him stand in front of them. 3 "I tell you the truth," He said to them, "if you don't change and become like little children, you will never get into the kingdom of heaven. 4 If you become humble like this little child, you are the greatest in the kingdom of heaven. 5 And if you welcome a child like this in My name, you welcome Me."

Do I Lead Others to Sin?

6 "If anyone leads into sin one of these little ones who believe in Me, it would be better for him to have a big millstone hung around his neck and be drowned in the lake where it's deep.

* Our two oldest manuscripts do not have v. 21: "This kind goes out only by prayer and fasting." See Mark 9:29.

K.J.V.

7 Woe unto the world because of offences! for it must needs be that offences come; but woe to that man by whom the offence cometh! 8 Wherefore if thy hand or thy foot offend thee, cut them off, and cast *them* from thee: it is better for thee to enter into life halt or maimed, rather than having two hands or two feet to be cast into everlasting fire. 9And if thine eye offend thee, pluck it out, and cast *it* from thee: it is better for thee to enter into life with one eye, rather than having two eyes to be cast into hell fire. 10 Take heed that ye despise not one of these little ones; for I say unto you, That in heaven their angels do always behold the face of my Father which is in heaven. 11 For the Son of man is come to save that which was lost. 12 How think ye? if a man have a hundred sheep, and one of them be gone astray, doth he not leave the ninety and nine, and goeth into the mountains, and seeketh that which is gone astray? 13And if so be that he find it, verily I say unto you, he rejoiceth more of that *sheep*, than of the ninety and nine which went not astray. 14 Even so it is not the will of your Father which is in heaven, that one of these little ones should perish.

15 Moreover if thy brother shall trespass against thee, go and tell him his fault between thee and him alone: if he shall hear thee, thou hast gained thy brother. 16 But if he will not hear *thee, then* take with thee the one or two more, that in the mouth of two or three witnesses every word may be established. 17And if he shall neglect to hear them, tell *it* unto the church: but if he neglect to hear the church, let him be unto thee as a heathen man and a publican. 18 Verily I say unto you, Whatsoever ye shall bind on earth shall be bound in heaven; and whatsoever ye shall loose on earth shall be loosed in heaven. 19Again I say unto you, That if two of you shall agree on earth as touching any thing that they shall ask, it shall be done for them of my Father which is in heaven. 20 For where two or three are gathered together in my name, there am I in the midst of them.

21 Then came Peter to him, and said, Lord, how oft shall my brother sin against me, and I forgive him? till seven times? 22 Jesus saith unto him, I say not unto thee, Until seven times: but, Until seventy times seven.

23 Therefore is the kingdom of heaven likened unto a certain king, which would take account of his servants. 24And when he had begun to reckon, one was brought unto him, which owed him ten thousand talents. 25 But forasmuch as he had not to pay, his lord commanded him to be sold, and his wife, and children, and all that he had, and payment to be made. 26 The servant therefore fell down, and worshipped him, saying, Lord, have patience with me, and I will pay thee all. 27 Then the lord of that servant was moved with compassion, and loosed him, and forgave him the debt. 28 But the same servant went out, and found one of his fellow servants, which owed him a hundred pence: and he laid hands on him, and took *him* by the throat, saying, Pay me that thou owest. 29And his fellow servant fell down at his feet, and besought him, saying, Have patience with me, and I will pay thee all. 30And he would not: but went and cast him into prison, till he should pay the debt.

N.A.S.

7 "Woe to the world because of *its* stumbling-blocks! For it is inevitable that stumbling-blocks come; but woe to that man through whom the stumbling-block comes! 8 "And if your hand or your foot causes you to stumble, cut it off and throw it from you; it is better for you to enter life crippled or lame, than having two hands or two feet, to be cast into the eternal fire. 9 "And if your eye causes you to stumble, pluck it out, and throw it from you. It is better for you to enter life with one eye, than having two eyes, to be cast into the hell of fire. 10 "See that you do not despise one of these little ones, for I say to you, that their angels in heaven continually behold the face of My Father who is in heaven. 11 ["*c*For the Son of Man has come to save that which was lost.] 12 "What do you think? If any man has a hundred sheep, and one of them has gone astray, does he not leave the ninety-nine on the mountains and go and search for the one that is straying? 13 "And if it turns out that he finds it, truly I say to you, he rejoices over it more than over the ninety-nine which have not gone astray. 14 "Thus it is not *the* will of your Father who is in heaven that one of these little ones perish.

15 "And if your brother sins*b*, go and reprove him in private; if he listens to you, you have won your brother. 16 "But if he does not listen *to you,* take one or two more with you, so that BY THE MOUTH OF TWO OR THREE WITNESSES EVERY FACT MAY BE CONFIRMED. 17 "And if he refuses to listen to them, tell it to the church; and if he refuses to listen even to the church, let him be to you as a Gentile and a tax-gatherer. 18 "Truly I say to you, whatever you shall bind on earth shall have been bound in heaven; and whatever you loose on earth shall have been loosed in heaven. 19 "Again I say to you, that if two of you agree on earth about anything that they may ask, it shall be done for them by My Father who is in heaven. 20 "For where two or three have gathered together in My name, there I am in their midst."

21 Then Peter came and said to Him, "Lord, how often shall my brother sin against me and I forgive him? Up to seven times?" 22 Jesus *said to him, "I do not say to you, up to seven times, but up to seventy times seven. 23 "For this reason the kingdom of heaven may be compared to a certain king who wished to settle accounts with his slaves. 24 "And when he had begun to settle *them,* there was brought to him one who owed him *c*ten thousand talents. 25 "But since he did not have *the means* to repay, his lord commanded him to be sold, along with his wife and children and all that he had, and repayment to be made. 26 "The slave therefore falling down, prostrated himself before him, saying, 'Have patience with me, and I will repay you everything.' 27 "And the lord of that slave felt compassion and released him and forgave him the debt. 28 "But that slave went out and found one of his fellow-slaves who owed him a hundred *d*denarii; and he seized him and *began* to choke *him,* saying, 'Pay back what you owe.' 29 "So his fellow-slave fell down and *began* to entreat him, saying, 'Have patience with me and I will repay you.' 30 "He was unwilling however, but went and threw him in prison until he should pay

[a] Most ancient mss. omit this verse. [b] Many mss. add here: *against you.* [c] About $10,000,000 in silver content but worth much more in buying power. [d] The denarius was worth 18 cents in silver, equivalent to a day's wage.

the sea. 7 A curse on the world for such influences to do wrong! For they must come, but a curse on the man from whom these influences come!

8 "And if your own hand or your own foot makes you do wrong, cut it off and put it out of your way. It is better for you to get into life maimed or crippled than to have both hands or both feet to be thrown into everlasting torture.ᵃ 9 And if your own eye makes you do wrong, pluck it out and put it out of your way. It is better for you to go into life with a single eye than to have both eyes to be thrown into the pit of torture.ᵇ

10 "Be careful not to look with scorn on a single one of these little children, for I tell you that in heaven their angels have uninterrupted access to my Father in heaven.ᶜ

12 "What do you think? If a man has a hundred sheep and one of them gets lost, will he not leave the ninety-nine on the hillsides, and go and search for the one that is lost? 13 And if he finds it, I solemnly say to you, he rejoices over it more than he does over the ninety-nine that did not get lost. 14 Just so it is not the will of my Father in heaven that a single one of these little ones be lost.

15 "Again, if your brother wrongs you, go and while alone with him show him the wrong. If he listens to you, you have won back your brother. 16 But if he does not listen to you, take along with you one or two others, so as to have every word confirmed by the testimony of two or three witnesses. If he refuses to listen to them, report it to the church. 17 And if he refuses to listen to the church, treat him as a heathen and as a tax-collector. 18 I solemnly say to you, whatever you forbid on earth must be already forbidden in heaven, and whatever you permit on earth must be already permitted in heaven.

19 "Again, I tell you, if only two of you on earth agree on what they pray for, they will get it from my Father in heaven. 20 For wherever two or three have met as my disciples, I am right there with them."

21 Then Peter came up to Him and asked, "Lord how many times may my brother wrong me and I have to forgive him? As many as seven?"

22 Jesus answered him: "I tell you, not as many as seven, but as many as seventy times seven! 23 So the kingdom of heaven may be compared to a king who decided to settle up his accounts with his slaves. 24 And when he began, a man was brought to him who owed him ten million dollars. 25 And because he could not pay it, his master ordered him to be sold, yea, even his wife and children and all he had, and payment to be made. 26 So the slave fell down at his feet and pleaded, 'Give me time, and I will pay you every cent of it.' 27 And his master's heart was moved with pity, and he let the slave go free with his debt cancelled.

28 "But that slave went out and found one of his fellow-slaves who owed him twenty dollars, and he caught him by the throat and began to choke him, demanding, 'Pay me what you owe me.'

29 "And his fellow-slave fell down before him and pleaded, 'Give me time, and I will pay you.' 30 But he refused and went out and had him put in jail until he should pay the debt.

7 Woe to the world because it tempts people to sin! Temptations to sin must come, but woe to that man who tempts others to sin!

8 "If your hand or your foot makes you sin, cut it off and throw it away. It is better for you to go into life without one hand or one foot than to have two hands or two feet and be thrown into the everlasting fire. 9 If your eye makes you sin, tear it out and throw it away. It is better for you to go into life with one eye than to have two eyes and be thrown into hellfire.

10 "Be careful not to despise one of these little ones. I tell you their angels in heaven always see the face of My Father in heaven.*

12 "What do you think? If a man has a hundred sheep and one of them gets lost, will he not leave the ninety-nine in the hills and go and look for the sheep that's wandering away? 13 And if he finds it, I tell you he's certainly more delighted with it than with the ninety-nine that didn't get lost. 14 So your Father in heaven doesn't want one of these little ones to be lost."

Tell Him His Fault

15 "If your brother sins against you, go, and when you're alone with him, show him how he is wrong. If he listens to you, you have won your brother. 16 But if he won't listen, take one or two with you so that *you have two or three witnesses for everything.*⁵⁶ 17 If he won't listen to them, tell it to the church. But if he won't even listen to the church, treat him like a pagan and a tax collector. 18 I tell you the truth: Whatever you don't forgive on earth will not be forgiven in heaven, and whatever you forgive on earth will be forgiven in heaven.

19 "Again I tell you: If two of you here on earth agree to ask for anything, My Father in heaven will certainly do it for you. 20 Where two or three have come together to be with Me, there I am among them."

Forgive!

21 Then Peter came to Jesus and asked Him, "Lord, how often do I have to forgive my brother who sins against me? Seven times?"

22 "I tell you," Jesus answered him, "not seven times but seventy times seven times.

23 "That is why the kingdom of heaven is like a king who wanted to settle accounts with his slaves. 24 When he began to do so, there was brought to him one who owed him ten thousand talents.** 25 But he couldn't pay it, and so the master ordered him, his wife, his children, and all he had to be sold to pay the debt. 26 Then the slave got down on his knees and, bowing low before him, begged: 'Be patient with me, and I'll pay you everything.'

27 "The master felt sorry for his slave, freed him, and canceled his debt. 28 But when that slave went away, he found one of his fellow slaves who owed him a hundred denarii.† He grabbed him and started to choke him. 'Pay what you owe,' he said.

29 "Then his fellow slave got down on his knees and begged him, 30 'Be patient with me, and I'll pay you.' But he refused and went and put him in prison till he would pay what he owed.

---

[a] Grk., *fire*, symbol of severe punishment. [b] Grk., *Gehenna of fire*, so *pit of torture*. [c] V. 11 omitted in best Mss.

* Our two oldest manuscripts do not have v. 11: "The Son of man came to save the lost." See Luke 19:10.
** One "talent" of silver weighed about as much as 1,500 silver dollars.
† One denarius was a day's pay.
[56] Deut. 19:15

K.J.V.

31 So when his fellow servants saw what was done, they were very sorry, and came and told unto their lord all that was done. 32 Then his lord, after that he had called him, said unto him, O thou wicked servant, I forgave thee all that debt, because thou desiredst me: 33 Shouldest not thou also have had compassion on thy fellow servant, even as I had pity on thee? 34And his lord was wroth, and delivered him to the tormentors, till he should pay all that was due unto him. 35 So likewise shall my heavenly Father do also unto you, if ye from your hearts forgive not every one his brother their trespasses.

19 And it came to pass, *that* when Jesus had finished these sayings, he departed from Galilee, and came into the coasts of Judea beyond Jordan; 2And great multitudes followed him; and he healed them there.

3 The Pharisees also came unto him, tempting him, and saying unto him, Is it lawful for a man to put away his wife for every cause? 4And he answered and said unto them, Have ye not read, that he which made *them* at the beginning made them male and female, 5And said, For this cause shall a man leave father and mother, and shall cleave to his wife: and they twain shall be one flesh? 6 Wherefore they are no more twain, but one flesh. What therefore God hath joined together, let not man put asunder. 7 They say unto him, Why did Moses then command to give a writing of divorcement, and to put her away? 8 He saith unto them, Moses because of the hardness of your hearts suffered you to put away your wives: but from the beginning it was not so. 9And I say unto you, Whosoever shall put away his wife, except *it be* for fornication, and shall marry another, committeth adultery: and whoso marrieth her which is put away doth commit adultery.

10 His disciples say unto him, If the case of the man be so with *his* wife, it is not good to marry. 11 But he said unto them, All *men* cannot receive this saying, save *they* to whom it is given. 12 For there are some eunuchs, which were so born from *their* mother's womb: and there are some eunuchs, which were made eunuchs of men: and there be eunuchs, which have made themselves eunuchs for the kingdom of heaven's sake. He that is able to receive *it,* let him receive *it.*

13 Then were there brought unto him little children, that he should put *his* hands on them, and pray: and the disciples rebuked them. 14 But Jesus said, Suffer little children, and forbid them not, to come unto me: for of such is the kingdom of heaven. 15And he laid *his* hands on them, and departed thence.

16 And, behold, one came and said unto him, Good Master, what good thing shall I do, that I may have eternal life? 17And he said unto him, Why callest thou me good? *there is* none good but one, *that is,* God: but if thou wilt enter into

N.A.S.

back what was owed. 31 "So when his fellow-slaves saw what had happened, they were deeply grieved and came and reported to their lord all that had happened. 32 "Then summoning him, his lord *said to him, 'You wicked slave, I forgave you all that debt because you entreated me. 33 'Should you not also have had mercy on your fellow-slave, even as I had mercy on you?' 34 "And his lord, moved with anger, handed him over to the torturers until he should repay all that was owed him. 35 "So shall My heavenly Father also do to you, if each of you does not forgive his brother from your heart."

19 And it came about that when Jesus had finished these words, He departed from Galilee, and came into the region of Judea beyond the Jordan; 2 and great multitudes followed Him, and He healed them there.

3 And *some* Pharisees came to Him, testing Him, and saying, "Is it lawful *for a man* to divorce his wife for any cause at all?" 4And He answered and said, "Have you not read, that He who created *them* from the beginning MADE THEM MALE AND FEMALE, 5 and said, 'FOR THIS CAUSE A MAN SHALL LEAVE HIS FATHER AND MOTHER, AND SHALL CLEAVE TO HIS WIFE; AND THE TWO SHALL BECOME ONE FLESH'? 6 "Consequently they are no more two, but one flesh. What therefore God has joined together, let no man separate." 7 They *said to Him, "Why then did Moses command to GIVE HER A CERTIFICATE AND DIVORCE HER"? 8 He *said to them, "Because of your hardness of heart, Moses permitted you to divorce your wives; but from the beginning it has not been this way. 9 "And I say to you, whoever divorces his wife, except for immorality, and marries another commits adultery." 10 The disciples *said to Him, "If the relationship of the man with his wife is like this, it is better not to marry." 11 But He said to them, "Not all men *can accept this statement, but *only* those to whom it has been given. 12 "For there are eunuchs who were born that way from their mother's womb; and there are eunuchs who were made eunuchs by men; and there are *also eunuchs who made themselves eunuchs for the sake of the kingdom of heaven. He who is able to accept *this,* let him accept *it.*"

13 Then *some children were brought to Him so that He might lay His hands on them and pray; and the disciples rebuked them. 14 But Jesus said, "Let the children alone, and do not hinder them from coming to Me; for the kingdom of heaven belongs to such as these." 15And after laying His hands on them, He departed from there.

16 And behold, one came to Him and said, "Teacher, what good thing shall I do that I may obtain eternal life?" 17And He said to him, "Why are you asking Me about what is good? There is *only* One who is good; but if you wish to enter into life, keep the command-

WILLIAMS

31 "When his fellow-slaves saw what had happened, they were greatly troubled, and went and reported all that happened to their master. 32 Then his master called him to him, and said, 'I cancelled all that huge debt of yours, because you pleaded with me to do so. 33 Ought you not to have shown mercy to your fellow-slave, as I too had done for you?' 34 And the master was enraged and turned him over to the official torturers, until he should pay the whole debt. 35 This is the way my heavenly Father too will deal with you, if you do not, each one, heartily forgive your brother."

19 *Jesus leaves Galilee; answers the question about divorce; blesses little children; tells of the perils of riches and the rewards of self-sacrifice*

When Jesus had finished this discourse, He left Galilee and went into the district of Judea that is on the other side of the Jordan. 2 And great crowds thronged after Him, and He cured them there.

3 And some Pharisees came up to Him, to try Him out with the question, "Is it right for a man to divorce his wife for any cause?"

4 And He answered, "Have you not read that the Creator at the beginning made them male and female, 5 and said, 'For this reason a man must leave his father and mother and be united to his wife, and the two of them must be one'? 6 So they are no longer two but one. Therefore, what God has joined together man must stop separating."

7 Then they asked Him, "Why did Moses command us to give a written divorce charge, and in this way to divorce a wife?"

8 He answered them, "It was because of your moral perversity that Moses allowed you to divorce your wives, but it was not so from the beginning. 9 I tell you, whoever divorces his wife for any other cause than her unfaithfulness, and marries another woman, commits adultery."

10 The disciples said to Him, "If that is a man's relation to his wife, there is no advantage in getting married."

11 He said to them, "It is not every man who has the capacity to carry out this saying, but it is for those to whom the capacity has been given. 12 For some are born incapable of marriage,*a* and some have been made so by men, and some have made themselves so for the sake of the kingdom of heaven. Let him accept it who can."

13 After that some little children were brought to Him, for Him to lay His hands on them and pray for them, but His disciples reproved those who brought them. 14 But Jesus said, "Let the little children alone, and stop preventing them from coming to me, for to such as these the kingdom of heaven belongs." 15 And He laid His hands on them and left there.

16 And a man came up to Him and asked, "What is there good that I can do to possess eternal life?"

17 And He answered him, "Why do you ask me about what is good? There is only One who is perfectly good. But if you want to get into that life, you must practice keeping the commandments."

[a] Grk., *some are eunuchs who,* etc.

BECK

31 "When his fellow slaves saw what had happened, they felt very sad and went and told their master the whole story.

32 "Then his master sent for him. 'You wicked slave!' he said to him. 'I canceled all you owed me, because you begged me. 33 Shouldn't you also have treated your fellow slave as mercifully as I treated you?' 34 His master was so angry he handed him over to the torturers till he would pay all he owed him.

35 "That is what My Father in heaven will do to you if each of you will not heartily forgive his brother."

Husband and Wife

19 When Jesus finished saying this, He left Galilee and went to the part of Judea on the other side of the Jordan. 2 Large crowds followed Him, and He made them well there.

3 Some Pharisees, coming to Him to test Him, asked Him, "Is it right for a man to divorce his wife for any reason?"

4 "Haven't you read," He asked them, "He who created them from the beginning *made them a male and a female?"* [57] 5 And He added: *"That is why a man will leave his father and mother and live with his wife, and the two will be one flesh."* [58] 6 And so they are no more two but one flesh. Now, what God has joined together man must not separate."

7 "Why, then, did Moses order a man *to make out a divorce paper and divorce his wife?"* [59] they asked Him.

8 He answered them, "Because your minds are closed, Moses let you divorce your wives, but originally there was no such thing. 9 I tell you, if anyone divorces his wife, except for adultery, and marries another, he's living in adultery."

10 "If a man has to have such grounds in dealing with his wife," the disciples told him, "it's better not to marry."

11 "Not all can do this," He told them, "only those to whom it has been given. 12 Some can't marry because they were born that way. Others, because they have been mutilated by men. And still others have decided to do without marriage for the kingdom of heaven. If anyone can do it, let him do it."

Jesus Loves Children

13 Then some people brought little children to Jesus to have Him lay His hands on them and pray. But the disciples sternly told them not to do it.

14 "Let the little children come to Me," Jesus said, "and don't keep them away. The kingdom of heaven belongs to such as these." 15 He laid His hands on them and then went away.

The Rich Young Leader

16 There was one who came and asked Him, "Teacher, what good thing should I do to get everlasting life?"

17 "Why do you ask Me about something good? Only One is good. If you want to go into life, keep the commandments."

[57] Gen. 1:27; 5:2
[58] Gen. 2:24
[59] Deut. 24:1

K.J.V.

life, keep the commandments. 18 He saith unto him, Which? Jesus said, Thou shalt do no murder, Thou shalt not commit adultery, Thou shalt not steal, Thou shalt not bear false witness, 19 Honour thy father and *thy* mother: and, Thou shalt love thy neighbour as thyself. 20 The young man saith unto him, All these things have I kept from my youth up: what lack I yet? 21 Jesus said unto him, If thou wilt be perfect, go *and* sell that thou hast, and give to the poor, and thou shalt have treasure in heaven: and come *and* follow me. 22 But when the young man heard that saying, he went away sorrowful: for he had great possessions.

23 Then said Jesus unto his disciples, Verily I say unto you, That a rich man shall hardly enter into the kingdom of heaven. 24And again I say unto you, It is easier for a camel to go through the eye of a needle, than for a rich man to enter into the kingdom of God. 25 When his disciples heard *it*, they were exceedingly amazed, saying, Who then can be saved? 26 But Jesus beheld *them*, and said unto them, With men this is impossible; but with God all things are possible.

27 Then answered Peter and said unto him, Behold, we have forsaken all, and followed thee; what shall we have therefore? 28 And Jesus said unto them, Verily I say unto you, That ye which have followed me, in the regeneration when the Son of man shall sit in the throne of his glory, ye also shall sit upon twelve thrones, judging the twelve tribes of Israel. 29And every one that hath forsaken houses, or brethren, or sisters, or father, or mother, or wife, or children, or lands, for my name's sake, shall receive a hundredfold, and shall inherit everlasting life. 30 But many *that are* first shall be last; and the last *shall be* first.

20 For the kingdom of heaven is like unto a man *that is* a householder, which went out early in the morning to hire labourers into his vineyard. 2And when he had agreed with the labourers for a penny a day, he sent them into his vineyard. 3And he went out about the third hour, and saw others standing idle in the marketplace, 4And said unto them; Go ye also into the vineyard, and whatsoever is right I will give you. And they went their way. 5Again he went out about the sixth and ninth hour, and did likewise. 6And about the eleventh hour he went out, and found others standing idle, and saith unto them, Why stand ye here all the day idle? 7 They say unto him, Because no man hath hired us. He saith unto them, Go ye also into the vineyard; and whatsover is right, *that* shall ye receive. 8 So when even was come, the lord of the vineyard saith unto his steward, Call the labourers, and give them *their* hire, beginning from the last unto the first. 9And when they came that *were hired* about the eleventh hour, they received every man a penny. 10 But when the first came,

N.A.S.

ments." 18 He *said to Him, "Which ones?" And Jesus said, "YOU SHALL NOT COMMIT MURDER; YOU SHALL NOT COMMIT ADULTERY; YOU SHALL NOT STEAL; YOU SHALL NOT BEAR FALSE WITNESS; 19 HONOR YOUR FATHER AND MOTHER; and YOU SHALL LOVE YOUR NEIGHBOR AS YOURSELF." 20 The young man *said to Him, "All these things I have kept; what am I still lacking?" 21 Jesus said to him, "If you wish to be complete, go *and* sell your possessions and give to *the* poor, and you shall have treasure in heaven; and come, follow Me." 22 But when the young man heard this statement, he went away grieved; for he was one who owned much property.

23 And Jesus said to His disciples, "Truly I say to you, it is hard for a rich man to enter the kingdom of heaven. 24 "And again I say to you, it is easier for a camel to go through the eye of a needle, than for a rich man to enter the kingdom of God." 25And when the disciples heard *this*, they were very astonished and said, "Then who can be saved?" 26And looking upon *them* Jesus said to them, "With men this is impossible, but with God all things are possible." 27 Then Peter answered and said to Him, "Behold, we have left everything and followed You; what then will there be for us?" 28And Jesus said to them, "Truly I say to you, that you who have followed Me, in the regeneration when the Son of Man will sit on His glorious throne, you also shall sit upon twelve thrones, judging the twelve tribes of Israel. 29 "And everyone who has left houses or brothers or sisters or father or mother[a] or children or farms for My name's sake, shall receive many times as much, and shall inherit eternal life. 30 "But many *who are* first will be last; and *the* last, first.

20 "For the kingdom of heaven is like a landowner who went out early in the morning to hire laborers for his vineyard. 2 "And when he had agreed with the laborers for a [b]denarius for the day, he sent them into his vineyard. 3 "And he went out about the [c]third hour and saw others standing idle in the market place; 4 and to those he said, 'You too go into the vineyard, and whatever is right I will give you.' And *so* they went. 5 "Again he went out about the [d]sixth and ninth hour, and did the same thing. 6 "And about the [e]eleventh *hour* he went out, and found others standing; and he *said to them, 'Why have you been standing here idle all day long?' 7 "They *said to him, 'Because no one hired us.' He *said to them, 'You too go into the vineyard.' 8 "And when evening had come, the owner of the vineyard *said to his foreman, 'Call the laborers and pay them their wages, beginning with the last *group* to the first.' 9 "And when those *hired* about the eleventh hour came, each one received a [b]denarius. 10 "And when those *hired* first came, they thought that they would

[a] Many mss. add here: *or wife.* [b] The denarius was worth 18 cents in silver, equivalent to one day's wage. [c] I.e., 9 a.m. [d] I.e., Noon and 3 p.m. [e] I.e., 5 p.m.

WILLIAMS	BECK

WILLIAMS

18 He asked Him, "What sort of commandments?"

Jesus answered, "You must not murder, You must not commit adultery, You must not steal, You must not lie, 19 You must practice honoring your father and mother, and you must love your neighbor as you do yourself."

20 The young man said, "I have kept all these commandments; what more do I lack?"

21 Jesus said to him, "If you want to be perfect, go and sell everything you have and give the money to the poor, and you will have riches in heaven; then come back here and follow me." 22 And when the young man heard that, he went away in deep distress, for he owned a great deal of property.

23 Jesus said to His disciples, "I solemnly say to you, it will be hard for a rich man to get into the kingdom of heaven. 24 Again, I tell you, it is easier for a camel to go through a needle's eye than for a rich man to get into the kingdom of heaven."

25 But when the disciples heard this, they were dumfounded, and asked, "Who then can be saved!"

26 But Jesus looked at them and said, "This is impossible for men, but anything is possible for God."

27 Then Peter answered Him, "We have left everything we had and followed you. What then are we to get?"

28 Jesus said to them: "I solemnly say to you, in the new order of life,[b] when the Son of Man shall take His seat on His glorious throne, you too, who have followed me, will sit on twelve thrones, and judge the twelve tribes of Israel. 29 And everyone who has given up home or brothers or sisters or father or mother or children or farms, for my sake, will receive many times as much, and in addition will be in possession of eternal life. 30 But many who are first now will be last then, and many who are last now will be first then.

20 *The story of the laborers; He again foretells His death; He rebukes a mother's ambition; cures two blind men*

"For the kingdom of heaven is like an owner of an estate who went out early in the morning to hire laborers for his vineyard. 2 When he had contracted with the laborers at twenty cents a day, he sent them off to his vineyard. 3 He went out again about nine o'clock and found others standing around doing nothing. 4 So he said to them, 'You too go out to my vineyard, and I will pay you what is right.' And they went. 5 Again he went out about twelve o'clock and three o'clock, and did as before. 6 About five he went out again and found still others standing around, and he said to them, 'Why have you been standing here all day doing nothing?' 7 They answered him, 'Because nobody has hired us.' He said to them, 'You too go out to my vineyard.'

8 "When evening came, the owner of the vineyard said to his manager, 'Call the laborers and pay them their wages, beginning with the last and ending with the first.' 9 And they who had been hired at five o'clock came and received twenty cents each. 10 And those who were hired first, when they came, supposed that

[b] Grk., *in the regeneration*, etc.

BECK

18 "Which commandments?" he asked Him. Jesus said, *"Don't murder, don't commit adultery, don't steal, don't lie,* 19 *honor father and mother,*[60] *and love your neighbor like yourself."* [61]

20 "I've kept all these," the young man told Him. "What else do I need?"

21 "If you want to be perfect," Jesus told him, "go, sell what you have, give the money to the poor, and you'll have a treasure in heaven. Then come and follow Me."

22 When the young man heard this, he went away sad, because he was very rich.

23 "I tell you the truth," Jesus said to His disciples, "it is hard for a rich man to get into the kingdom of heaven. 24 Again I tell you it's easier for a camel to go through a needle's eye than for a rich man to get into God's kingdom."

25 The disciples, hearing this, were dumfounded. "Who, then, can be saved?" they asked.

26 "Men can't do this," Jesus said as He looked at them, "but *God can do anything."* [62]

27 Then Peter spoke up: "Look! We gave up everything and followed You. So what will we get?"

28 "Let Me assure you," Jesus said to them, "in the new life, when the Son of Man sits on His throne of glory, you who followed Me will also sit on twelve thrones and rule the twelve tribes of Israel. 29 And everyone who gave up homes, brothers or sisters, father, mother, or children, or fields for Me will get many times as much, and then everlasting life. 30 But many who are first will be last, and many who are last will be first."

"The Last Will Be First"

20 "The kingdom of heaven is like the owner of a place who went out early in the morning to hire men to work in his vineyard. 2 He agreed with the workers to pay them a denarius a day and sent them into his vineyard. 3 About nine o'clock he went out and saw others standing in the marketplace doing nothing. 4 'You go into the vineyard too,' he told them, 'and I'll pay you what's right.' So they went.

5 "He went out again about twelve o'clock and three o'clock and did the same thing. 6 About five o'clock he went out and found some others standing around. 'Why are you standing here all day long doing nothing?' he asked them.

7 " 'Nobody has hired us,' they answered him.

" 'You go into the vineyard too,' he told them.

8 "When evening came, the owner of the vineyard told his manager, 'Call the men and give them their pay. Start with the last and go on to the first.'

9 "Those who started working around five o'clock came, and each got a denarius. 10 When the first ones came, they expected to get more,

[60] Ex. 20:12-16; Deut. 5:16-20
[61] Lev. 19:18
[62] Gen. 18:14; Job 42:2; Zech. 8:6

K.J.V.

they supposed that they should have received more; and they likewise received every man a penny. 11And when they had received *it*, they murmured against the goodman of the house, 12 Saying, These last have wrought *but* one hour, and thou hast made them equal unto us, which have borne the burden and heat of the day. 13 But he answered one of them, and said, Friend, I do thee no wrong: didst not thou agree with me for a penny? 14 Take *that* thine *is*, and go thy way: I will give unto this last, even as unto thee. 15 Is it not lawful for me to do what I will with mine own? Is thine eye evil, because I am good? 16 So the last shall be first, and the first last: for many be called, but few chosen.

17 And Jesus going up to Jerusalem took the twelve disciples apart in the way, and said unto them, 18 Behold, we go up to Jerusalem; and the Son of man shall be betrayed unto the chief priests and unto the scribes, and they shall condemn him to death, 19And shall deliver him to the Gentiles to mock, and to scourge, and to crucify *him*: and the third day he shall rise again.

20 Then came to him the mother of Zebedee's children with her sons, worshipping *him*, and desiring a certain thing of him. 21And he said unto her, What wilt thou? She saith unto him, Grant that these my two sons may sit, the one on thy right hand, and the other on the left, in thy kingdom. 22 But Jesus answered and said, Ye know not what ye ask. Are ye able to drink of the cup that I shall drink of, and to be baptized with the baptism that I am baptized with? They say unto him, We are able. 23And he saith unto them, Ye shall drink indeed of my cup, and be baptized with the baptism that I am baptized with: but to sit on my right hand, and on my left, is not mine to give, but *it shall be given to them* for whom it is prepared of my Father. 24And when the ten heard *it*, they were moved with indignation against the two brethren. 25 But Jesus called them *unto him*, and said, Ye know that the princes of the Gentiles exercise dominion over them, and they that are great exercise authority upon them. 26 But it shall not be so among you: but whosoever will be great among you, let him be your minister; 27 And whosoever will be chief among you, let him be your servant: 28 Even as the Son of man came not to be ministered unto, but to minister, and to give his life a ransom for many. 29And as they departed from Jericho, a great multitude followed him.

30 And, behold, two blind men sitting by the way side, when they heard that Jesus passed by, cried out, saying, Have mercy on us, O Lord, *thou* Son of David. 31And the multitude rebuked them, because they should hold their peace: but they cried the more, saying, Have mercy on us, O Lord, *thou* Son of David. 32And Jesus stood still, and called them, and said, What will ye that I shall do unto you? 33 They say unto him, Lord, that our eyes may be opened. 34 So Jesus had compassion *on them*, and touched their eyes: and immediately their eyes received sight, and they followed him.

N.A.S.

receive more; and they also received each one a °denarius. 11 "And when they received *it*, they grumbled at the landowner, 12 saying, 'These last men have worked *only* one hour, and you have made them equal to us who have borne the burden and the scorching heat of the day.' 13 "But he answered and said to one of them, 'Friend, I am doing you no wrong; did you not agree with me for a °denarius? 14 'Take what is yours and go your way, but I wish to give to this last man the same as to you. 15 'Is it not lawful for me to do what I wish with what is my own? Or is your eye envious because I am generous?' 16 "Thus the last shall be first, and the first last."

17 And as Jesus was about to go up to Jerusalem, He took the twelve *disciples* aside by themselves, and on the way He said to them, 18 "Behold, we are going up to Jerusalem; and the Son of Man will be delivered up to the chief priests and scribes, and they will condemn Him to death, 19 and will deliver Him up to the Gentiles to mock and scourge and crucify *Him*, and on the third day He will be raised up."

20 Then the mother of the sons of Zebedee came to Him with her sons, bowing down, and making a request of Him. 21And He said to her, "What do you wish?" She *said to Him, "Command that in Your kingdom these two sons of mine may sit, one on Your right and one on Your left." 22 But Jesus answered and said, "You do not know what you are asking for. Are you able to drink the cup that I am about to drink?" They *said to Him, "We are able." 23 He *said to them, "My cup you shall drink; but to sit on My right and on *My* left, this is not Mine to give; but *it is* for those for whom it has been prepared by My Father." 24And hearing *this*, the ten became indignant at the two brothers. 25 But Jesus called them to Himself, and said, "You know that the rulers of the Gentiles lord it over them, and *their* great men exercise authority over them. 26 "It is not so among you, but whoever wishes to become great among you shall be your servant, 27 and whoever wishes to be first among you shall be your slave; 28 just as the Son of Man did not come to be served, but to serve, and to give His life a ransom for many."

29 And as they were going out from Jericho, a great multitude followed Him. 30And behold, two blind men sitting by the road, hearing that Jesus was passing by, cried out, saying, "Lord, have mercy on us, Son of David!" 31And the multitude sternly told them to be quiet; but they cried out all the more, saying, "Lord, have mercy on us, Son of David!" 32And Jesus stopped and called them, and said, "What do you wish Me to do for you?" 33 They *said to Him, "Lord, we want our eyes to be opened." 34And moved with compassion, Jesus touched their eyes; and immediately they received their sight, and followed Him.

[a] The denarius was worth 18 cents in silver, equivalent to one day's wage.

WILLIAMS

they would receive more; but they too received twenty cents each. 11 And as they received it, they began to grumble against the owner of the estate, 12 and say, 'These last worked only one hour, and yet you have put them on the same footing with us who have borne the heavy burdens and scorching heat of the day.' 13 But he answered one of them, 'Friend, I am doing you no injustice. Did you not contract with me at twenty cents? 14 Take what belongs to you and go. I want to give this man hired last as much as I do you. 15 Have I not the right to do what I please with my own money? Or, is your eye causing you to be covetous,*ᵃ* because I am generous?' 16 So those who are last now will be first then, and those first will be last."

17 And as Jesus was about to go up to Jerusalem, He took the twelve disciples aside, and said to them while on the road, 18 "Listen! We are going up to Jerusalem, and the Son of Man will be turned over to the high priests and the scribes, and they will sentence Him to death, 19 and turn Him over to the heathen to mock and flog and crucify, but on the third day He will rise again."

20 Then the mother of Zebedee's sons came up to Him with her sons, kneeling to Him and asking a favor of Him. 21 And He asked her, "What do you want?"

She answered Him, "Give orders that these two sons of mine may sit one at your right and one at your left in your kingdom."

22 But Jesus answered, "You do not realize what you are asking for. Can you drink the cup that I am about to drink?"

They answered, "Yes, we can."

23 He said to them, "You will drink the cup that I am to drink, but seats at my right and at my left are not mine to give, but they will be given to those for whom they have been prepared by my Father."

24 When the other ten heard of it, they were indignant at the two brothers. 25 But Jesus called them to him and said, "You know that the rulers of the heathen lord it over them, and their great men rule as despots over them. 26 It is not to be so among you, but whoever wants to be great among you must be your servant, 27 and whoever wants to hold first position among you must be your slave, 28 just as the Son of Man has come, not to be served but to serve, and to give His life a ransom price to set many free."*ᵇ*

29 As they were leaving Jericho, a great crowd followed Him. 30And two blind men sitting by the roadside heard that Jesus was passing and cried out, "Do pity us, Lord, you Son of David!" 31 The crowd reproved them and urged them to keep quiet, but they cried out all the louder, "Do pity us, Lord, you Son of David!"

32 And Jesus stopped and called them, and asked, "What do you want me to do for you?"

33 They answered Him, "Lord, we want our eyes opened!" 34 Then Jesus' heart was moved with pity, and He touched their blinded eyes, and at once they could see again, and followed Him.

BECK

but each of them, too, got a denarius. 11 They took it, but they grumbled against the owner: 12 'These last men worked only one hour, and you've treated them exactly like us who have worked hard all day in the blazing sun.'

13 " 'Friend, I'm doing you no wrong,' he answered one of them. 14 'You agreed with me on a denarius, didn't you? Take your money and go. I want to give this last man as much as I give you. 15 Don't I have the right to do as I please with what is mine? Or are you jealous because I'm generous?'

16 "In this way the last will be first and the first last."

17 When Jesus was going up to Jerusalem, He took the twelve by themselves and said to them on the way: 18 "Look, we're going up to Jerusalem, and the Son of Man will be betrayed to the ruling priests and Bible scholars, 19 who will condemn Him to die and hand Him over to the Gentiles to be mocked, scourged, and crucified, but on the third day He will rise."

20 Then the mother of Zebedee's sons came to Jesus with her sons and bowed before Him to ask Him for something.

21 "What do you want?" He asked her.

She told Him, "Promise that one of my two sons will sit at Your right and the other at Your left in Your kingdom."

22 "You don't know what you're asking," Jesus answered. "Can you drink the cup I'm going to drink?"

"We can," they told him.

23 "You'll drink My cup," He told them. "But sitting at My right and left is something I can give only to those for whom My Father prepared it."

24 When the other ten heard about it, they got angry with James and John. 25 Jesus called them and said, "You know the rulers of the nations are lords over them, and their great men are tyrants over them. 26 But among you it's different. Anyone who wants to become great among you must be your servant, 27 and anyone who wants to be first among you must be your slave, 28 just as the Son of Man did not come to be served but to serve and give His life as a ransom for all people."

Two Blind Men

29 As they were leaving Jericho, a large crowd followed Him. 30And there were two blind men sitting by the road. When they heard, "Jesus is passing by," they called, "Lord, have pity on us, Son of David!"

31 The crowd urged them to be quiet. But they called all the louder, "Lord, have pity on us, Son of David!"

32 Jesus stopped and called them. "What do you want Me to do for you?" He asked.

33 "Lord, we want to see," they told Him.

34 Jesus felt sorry for them and touched their eyes, and immediately they could see. And they followed Him.

[a] Grk., *wicked.* [b] Grk., *a ransom for many;* i.e., a price paid to set many free.

21 And when they drew nigh unto Jerusalem, and were come to Bethphage, unto the mount of Olives, then sent Jesus two disciples, 2 Saying unto them, Go into the village over against you, and straightway ye shall find an ass tied, and a colt with her: loose *them,* and bring *them* unto me. 3 And if any *man* say aught unto you, ye shall say, The Lord hath need of them; and straightway he will send them. 4All this was done, that it might be fulfilled which was spoken by the prophet, saying, 5 Tell ye the daughter of Sion, Behold, thy King cometh unto thee, meek, and sitting upon an ass, and a colt the foal of an ass. 6And the disciples went, and did as Jesus commanded them, 7And brought the ass, and the colt, and put on them their clothes, and they set *him* thereon. 8And a very great multitude spread their garments in the way; others cut down branches from the trees and strewed *them* in the way. 9And the multitudes that went before, and that followed, cried, saying, Hosanna to the Son of David: Blessed *is* he that cometh in the name of the Lord; Hosanna in the highest. 10And when he was come into Jerusalem, all the city was moved, saying, Who is this? 11And the multitude said, This is Jesus the prophet of Nazareth of Galilee.

12 And Jesus went into the temple of God, and cast out all them that sold and bought in the temple, and overthrew the tables of the money changers, and the seats of them that sold doves, 13And said unto them, It is written, My house shall be called the house of prayer; but ye have made it a den of thieves. 14And the blind and the lame came to him in the temple; and he healed them. 15And when the chief priests and scribes saw the wonderful things that he did, and the children crying in the temple, and saying, Hosanna to the Son of David; they were sore displeased, 16And said unto him, Hearest thou what these say? And Jesus saith unto them, Yea; have ye never read, Out of the mouth of babes and sucklings thou hast perfected praise?

17 And he left them, and went out of the city into Bethany; and he lodged there. 18 Now in the morning, as he returned into the city, he hungered. 19And when he saw a fig tree in the way, he came to it, and found nothing thereon, but leaves only, and said unto it, Let no fruit grow on thee henceforward for ever. And presently the fig tree withered away. 20And when the disciples saw *it,* they marvelled, saying, How soon is the fig tree withered away! 21 Jesus answered and said unto them, Verily I say unto you, If ye have faith, and doubt not, ye shall not only do this *which is done* to the fig tree, but also if ye shall say unto this mountain, Be thou removed, and be thou cast into the sea; it

21 And when they had approached Jerusalem and had come to Bethphage, to the Mount of Olives, then Jesus sent two disciples, 2 saying to them, "Go into the village opposite you, and immediately you will find a donkey tied *there* and a colt with her; untie *them,* and bring *them* to Me. 3 "And if anyone says something to you, you shall say, 'The Lord has need of them;' and immediately he will send them." 4 Now this took place that what was spoken through the prophet might be fulfilled, saying,
5 "SAY TO THE DAUGHTER OF ZION,
'BEHOLD YOUR KING IS COMING TO YOU,
GENTLE AND MOUNTED UPON A DONKEY,
EVEN UPON A COLT, THE FOAL OF A BEAST OF BURDEN.' "
6And the disciples went and did just as Jesus had directed them, 7 and brought the donkey and the colt, and laid on them their garments; on which He sat. 8And most of the multitude spread their garments in the road, and others were cutting branches from the trees, and spreading them in the road. 9And the multitudes going before Him, and those who followed after were crying out, saying,
"HOSANNA to the Son of David;
BLESSED IS HE WHO COMES IN THE NAME OF THE LORD;
HOSANNA in the highest!"
10And when He had entered Jerusalem, all the city was stirred, saying, "Who is this?" 11And the multitudes were saying, "This is the prophet Jesus, from Nazareth in Galilee."

12 And Jesus entered the temple and cast out all those who were buying and selling in the temple, and overturned the tables of the money-changers and the seats of those who were selling doves. 13And He *said to them, "It is written, 'MY HOUSE SHALL BE CALLED A HOUSE OF PRAYER;' but you are making it a robbers' den." 14And *the* blind and *the* lame came to Him in the temple, and He healed them. 15 But when the chief priests and the scribes saw the wonderful things that He had done, and the children who were crying out in the temple and saying, "Hosanna to the Son of David," they became indignant, 16 and said to Him, "Do You hear what these are saying?" And Jesus *said to them, "Yes; have you never read, 'OUT OF THE MOUTH OF INFANTS AND NURSING BABES THOU HAST PREPARED PRAISE FOR THYSELF'?" 17And He left them and went out of the city to Bethany, and lodged there.

18 Now in the morning, when He returned to the city, He became hungry. 19And seeing a lone fig tree by the road, He came to it, and found nothing on it except leaves only; and He *said to it, "No longer shall there ever be *any* fruit from you." And at once the fig tree withered. 20And seeing *this,* the disciples marveled, saying, "How did the fig tree wither at once?" 21And Jesus answered and said to them, "Truly I say to you, if you have faith, and do not doubt, you shall not only do what was done to the fig tree, but even if you say to this mountain, 'Be taken up and cast into the sea,'

WILLIAMS

21 *Jesus rides as King into Jerusalem; drives the traders out of the temple; tells two stories: the two sons; the villainous tenants*

When they were near Jerusalem and had come to Bethphage and the Mount of Olives, Jesus sent two disciples on ahead, 2 and ordered them, "Go into the village that is ahead of you, and at once you will find a donkey tied there, and a colt with her. Untie her and bring them to me. 3 If anyone says anything to you, you will say, 'The Lord needs them,' and he at once will send them."

4 Now this occurred to fufill what was spoken by the prophet:

5 "Tell the daughter of Zion
Your King is now coming to you,
Gentle, and riding on a donkey,
Yea, on the colt of a beast of burden."

6 So the disciples went and did as Jesus had directed them. 7 They brought the donkey and the colt and laid their coats upon them, and Jesus took His seat on them. 8 And most of the crowd spread their coats along the road, but some were cutting branches from the trees and spreading them along the road. 9 And the crowds that went in front of Him and followed Him shouted:

"Welcome the Son of David!
Blessed be He who comes in the name of the Lord;
Welcome Him from on high!"

10 When He came into Jerusalem, the whole city was trembling with excitement, and asking, "Who is He?" 11 And the crowds kept saying, "He is the prophet Jesus of Nazareth in Galilee."

12 And Jesus went into the temple and drove out all the buyers and sellers, and turned the money-changers' tables and the dove-dealers' seats upside down, 13 and said to them, "The Scripture says, 'My house must be called a house of prayer,' but you have made it a cave for robbers."

14 Then blind and crippled people came to Him, and He cured them. 15 But because the high priests and scribes saw the wonders that He did and the children shouting in the temple, "Welcome the Son of David," they were indignant 16 and asked Him, "Do you hear what they are saying?"

Jesus answered them, "Yes. Did you never read this, 'Out of the mouths of little children, yea, of infants, you have perfect praise'?"

17 And He left and went out of the city to Bethany, and spent the night there.

18 Early next morning when He returned to the city, He felt hungry. 19 As He saw a fig tree by the roadside, He came to it but found on it nothing but leaves, and said to it, "Never again shall a fig grow on you!" And the fig tree at once withered up.

20 When the disciples saw it, they were dumfounded, and asked, "How is it that the fig tree withered up all at once?"

21 And Jesus answered them, "I solemnly say to you, if you have faith and do not doubt at all, you will not only do the sort of wonder done to the fig tree, but even if you say to this mountain, 'Get up and throw yourself into the

BECK

The King Comes to Jerusalem

21 When they came near Jerusalem and had reached Bethphage and the Mount of Olives, Jesus sent two disciples. 2 "Go into the village ahead of you," He told them, "and without any trouble you'll find a donkey tied up and a colt with her. Untie them and bring them to Me. 3 If anybody says anything to you, say, 'The Lord needs them,' and immediately he will send them."

4 This happened so that what the prophet said would come true:

5 *Tell the daughter of Zion,*
"Look! Your King is coming to you,
Gentle, riding on a donkey and on a colt
of a donkey." [63]

6 The disciples went and did as Jesus had directed them. 7 They brought the donkey and the colt and laid their garments on them; and Jesus sat on them. 8 Most of the people spread their garments on the road. Others cut branches from the trees and spread them on the road. 9 The people who went ahead of Him and followed Him were shouting:

"Our Savior, the Son of David!
Blessed is He who is coming in the Lord's
name! [64]
Our Savior—in the highest heavens!"

10 When He came into Jerusalem, the whole city was excited, asking, "Who is this?" 11 The crowds answered, "This is the Prophet Jesus from Nazareth in Galilee."

In the Temple

12 Jesus went into the temple and put out all who were selling and buying in the temple and upset the tables of the money changers and the chairs of those who sold pigeons. 13 "It is written," He told them, *"My house should be called a house of prayer,* [65] but you're making it a den of robbers!"* [66]

14 Blind and lame persons came to Him in the temple, and He made them well.

15 When the ruling priests and the Bible scholars saw the wonderful things He did, and the children shouting in the temple, *"Our Savior,* [64] the Son of David!" they didn't like it at all. 16 "Do You hear what they're saying?" they asked Him.

"Yes," Jesus answered them. "Haven't you ever read, *You have made children and babies at the breast praise You?"* [67]

17 He left them and went out of the city to Bethany and spent the night there.

Nothing but Leaves

18 In the morning as He went back to the city, Jesus was hungry, 19 and seeing a fig tree by the road, He went up to it and found nothing on it but leaves. "May no fruit ever grow on you again!" Jesus said to it. And immediately the fig tree dried up.

20 The disciples were surprised to see this. "How did the fig tree dry up so quickly?" they asked.

21 "I tell you the truth," Jesus answered them: "If you believe and don't doubt, you will not only do what I did to the fig tree, but if you will say to this mount,* 'Be lifted up and be

* The Mount of Olives.
[63] Is. 62:11; Zech. 9:9
[64] Ps. 118:25-26
[65] Is. 56:7
[66] Jer. 7:11
[67] Ps. 8:2

K.J.V.

shall be done. 22And all things, whatsoever ye shall ask in prayer, believing, ye shall receive.

23 And when he was come into the temple, the chief priests and the elders of the people came unto him as he was teaching, and said, By what authority doest thou these things? and who gave thee this authority? 24And Jesus answered and said unto them, I also will ask you one thing, which if ye tell me, I in like wise will tell you by what authority I do these things. 25 The baptism of John, whence was it? from heaven, or of men? And they reasoned with themselves, saying, If we shall say, From heaven; he will say unto us, Why did ye not then believe him? 26 But if we shall say, Of men; we fear the people; for all hold John as a prophet. 27And they answered Jesus, and said, We cannot tell. And he said unto them, Neither tell I you by what authority I do these things.

28 But what think ye? A *certain* man had two sons; and he came to the first, and said, Son, go work to day in my vineyard. 29 He answered and said, I will not; but afterward he repented, and went. 30And he came to the second, and said likewise. And he answered and said, I *go*, sir; and went not. 31 Whether of them twain did the will of *his* father? They say unto him, The first. Jesus saith unto them, Verily I say unto you, That the publicans and the harlots go into the kingdom of God before you. 32 For John came unto you in the way of righteousness, and ye believed him not; but the publicans and the harlots believed him: and ye, when ye had seen *it*, repented not afterward, that ye might believe him.

33 Hear another parable: There was a certain householder, which planted a vineyard, and hedged it round about, and digged a winepress in it, and built a tower, and let it out to husbandmen, and went into a far country: 34And when the time of the fruit drew near, he sent his servants to the husbandmen, that they might receive the fruits of it. 35And the husbandmen took his servants, and beat one, and killed another, and stoned another. 36Again, he sent other servants more than the first: and they did unto them likewise. 37 But last of all he sent unto them his son, saying, They will reverence my son. 38 But when the husbandmen saw the son, they said among themselves, This is the heir; come, let us kill him, and let us seize on his inheritance. 39And they caught him, and cast *him* out of the vineyard, and slew *him*. 40 When the lord therefore of the vineyard cometh, what will he do unto those husbandmen? 41 They say unto him, He will miserably destroy those wicked men, and will let out *his* vineyard unto other husbandmen, which shall render him the fruits in their seasons. 42 Jesus saith unto them, Did ye never read in the Scriptures, The stone which the builders rejected, the same is become the head of the corner: this is the Lord's doing, and it is marvellous in our eyes? 43 Therefore say I

N.A.S.

it shall happen. 22 "And everything you ask in prayer, believing, you shall receive."

23 And when He had come into the temple, the chief priests and the elders of the people came to Him as He was teaching, and said, "By what authority are You doing these things, and who gave You this authority?" 24 But Jesus answered and said to them, "I will ask you one thing too, which if you tell Me, I will also tell you by what authority I do these things. 25 "The baptism of John was from what *source*, from heaven or from men?" And they *began* reasoning among themselves, saying, "If we say, 'From heaven,' He will say to us, 'Then why did you not believe him?' 26 "But if we say, 'From men,' we fear the multitude; for they all hold John to be a prophet." 27And they answered Jesus and said, "We do not know." He also said to them, "Neither will I tell you by what authority I do these things. 28 "But what do you think? A man had two sons, and he came to the first and said, 'Son, go work today in the vineyard.' 29 "And he answered and said, 'I will, sir;' and he did not go. 30 "And he came to the second and said the same thing. But he answered and said, 'I will not;' *yet* he afterward regretted *it* and went. 31 "Which of the two did the will of his father?" They say, "The latter." Jesus *said to them, "Truly I say to you that the tax-gatherers and harlots will get into the kingdom of God before you. 32 "For John came to you in the way of righteousness and you did not believe him; but the tax-gatherers and harlots did believe him; and you, seeing this, did not even feel remorse afterward so as to believe him.

33 "Listen to another parable. There was a landowner who PLANTED A VINEYARD AND PUT A WALL AROUND IT AND DUG A WINEPRESS IN IT, AND BUILT A TOWER, and rented it out to vine-growers, and went on a journey. 34 "And when the harvest time approached, he sent his slaves to the vine-growers to receive his produce. 35 "And the vine-growers took his slaves and beat one, and killed another, and stoned a third. 36 "Again he sent another group of slaves larger than the first; and they did the same thing to them. 37 "But afterward he sent his son to them, saying, 'They will respect my son.' 38 "But when the vine-growers saw the son, they said among themselves, 'This is the heir; come, let us kill him, and seize his inheritance.' 39 "And they took him, and cast him out of the vineyard, and killed *him*. 40 "Therefore when the owner of the vineyard comes, what will he do to those vine-growers?" 41 They *said to Him, "He will bring those wretches to a wretched end, and will rent out the vineyard to other vine-growers, who will pay him the proceeds at the *proper* seasons." 42 Jesus *said to them, "Did you never read in the Scriptures,

'THE STONE WHICH THE BUILDERS REJECTED,
THIS BECAME THE CHIEF CORNER *stone*;
THIS CAME ABOUT FROM THE LORD,
AND IT IS MARVELOUS IN OUR EYES'?
43 "Therefore I say to you, the kingdom of

WILLIAMS

sea,' it will be done. 22 And whatever you ask for in prayer, if you believe it, you will get it."

23 And when He had come into the temple, the high priests and elders of the people came up to Him while He was teaching, and asked, "What sort of authority have you for doing these things, and who gave you this authority?" 24 Jesus answered them, "Let me too ask you just one question, and if you answer it, I will tell you what sort of authority I have for doing as I do. 25 Where did John's baptism come from? From heaven, or from men?" They argued it out among themselves in this way, "If we say, 'From heaven,' He will say to us, 'Then why did you not believe him?' 26 But if we say, 'From men,' we are afraid of the people, for they all consider John a prophet." 27 So they answered Jesus, "We do not know."

He also answered them, "Nor am I going to tell you what sort of authority I have for doing as I do.

28 "But what do you think? There was a man who had two sons. He came to the first and said, 'Son, go and work in my vineyard today.' 29 And he answered, 'I will, sir,' but he did not go. 30 Then he came to the second and said the same thing. And he answered, 'I will not.' But afterward he changed his mind and went. 31 Which of the two did what his father wanted?"

They answered, "The second one."

Jesus said to them, "I solemnly say to you, the tax-collectors and prostitutes will get into the kingdom of heaven ahead of you. 32 For John came to you walking in the way of uprightness, and yet you did not believe him. The tax-collectors and prostitutes did believe him; but you, even though you saw that, would not change your minds afterward and believe him.

33 "Listen to another story. There was once an owner of an estate who planted a vineyard and built a fence around it, and hewed out a wine-vat in it, and built a tower, and rented it to tenant farmers,ᵃ and then went abroad. 34 But when the time for gathering grapes was near, he sent his slaves to the tenants to collect his rent. 35 But the tenants took his slaves and beat the first one, killed the second, and stoned the third. 36 Again he sent other slaves, and more than at first, and they treated them exactly the same way. 37 At last he sent his son to them, for he said to himself, 'They will surely respect my son.' 38 But when the tenants saw the son, they said among themselves, 'This is his heir, come on, let us kill him, and get all that is coming to him!' 39 So they took him and drove him out of the vineyard and murdered him. 40 Now when the owner of the estate comes back, what will he do to these tenants?"

41 They answered, "In vengeance he will put the scoundrels to death, and rent the vineyard to other tenants who will promptly pay him the rent."

42 Then Jesus said to them, "Did you never read in the Scriptures:

'That stone which the builders threw away
Has become the cornerstone;
This is the work of the Lord
And seems wonderful to us'?

43 "This, I tell you, is why the kingdom will

BECK

thrown into the sea,' * it will be done. 22 Anything you ask for in prayer, believe, and you will get it."

From Heaven

23 When He came to the temple and was teaching, the ruling priests and the elders of the people came to Him. "By what authority are You doing these things?" they asked. "And who gave You the right to do them?" 24 Jesus answered them, "I will ask you a question. And if you answer Me, I'll tell you by what authority I'm doing these things. 25 John's baptism—was it from heaven or from men?"

They argued among themselves, "If we say, 'From heaven,' He will ask us, 'Then why didn't you believe him?' 26 But if we say, 'From men,' we're afraid of the people; they all think John is a prophet." 27 So they answered Jesus, "We don't know."

Then Jesus also told them, "Neither will I tell you by what authority I'm doing these things."

Say and Do

28 "Now, what do you think of this? A man had two sons. He went to the first and said, 'Son, go and work in the vineyard today.' 29 " 'I won't,' he answered. Later he changed his mind and went. 30 "The father went to the other one and told him the same thing. He answered, 'I will, sir,' but didn't go. 31 "Which of the two did what the father wanted?"

They answered, "The first."

Jesus said to them, "I tell you the truth, tax collectors and prostitutes are going into God's kingdom ahead of you. 32 John came to you in a righteous way, but you didn't believe him; the tax collectors and prostitutes believed him. But even when you had seen that, you didn't change your minds and believe him."

God's Vineyard

33 "Listen to another story:

"A man who owned property *planted a vineyard.* He *put a wall around it, cut a winepress into the rock, and built a watchtower.*⁶⁸ Then he rented it out to workers and left home. 34 "When the grapes were getting ripe, he sent his slaves to the workers to get his share of the grapes. 35 The workers took his slaves and beat one, killed another, and stoned a third. 36 Then he sent other slaves, this time a larger number, and they treated these the same way. 37 "Finally he sent his son to them, saying, 'They will respect my son.' 38 "When the workers saw the son, they said to one another, 'This is the heir. Come, let's kill him and get his inheritance.' 39 So they took him, threw him out of the vineyard, and killed him. 40 "Now, when the owner of the vineyard comes, what will he do to those workers?" 41 He was told, "He will have those scoundrels die a miserable death and rent out the vineyard to other workers who will bring him the grapes when they're ripe." 42 Jesus asked them, "Haven't you ever read in your Bible, *The stone the builders rejected has become the cornerstone. The Lord has done it, and we think it is wonderful?* ⁶⁹ 43 That is

* The Dead Sea, which can be seen from the Mount of Olives.
[68] Is. 5:1-2
[69] Ps. 118:22-23

[a] Grk., *tillers of the earth.*

65

K.J.V.

unto you, The kingdom of God shall be taken from you, and given to a nation bringing forth the fruits thereof. 44And whosoever shall fall on this stone shall be broken: but on whomsoever it shall fall, it will grind him to powder. 45And when the chief priests and Pharisees had heard his parables, they perceived that he spake of them. 46But when they sought to lay hands on him, they feared the multitude, because they took him for a prophet.

22 And Jesus answered and spake unto them again by parables, and said, 2 The kingdom of heaven is like unto a certain king, which made a marriage for his son, 3And sent forth his servants to call them that were bidden to the wedding: and they would not come. 4Again, he sent forth other servants, saying, Tell them which are bidden, Behold, I have prepared my dinner: my oxen and *my* fatlings *are* killed, and all things *are* ready: come unto the marriage. 5 But they made light of *it,* and went their ways, one to his farm, another to his merchandise: 6And the remnant took his servants, and entreated *them* spitefully, and slew *them.* 7 But when the king heard *thereof,* he was wroth: and he sent forth his armies, and destroyed those murderers, and burned up their city. 8 Then saith he to his servants, The wedding is ready, but they which were bidden were not worthy. 9 Go ye therefore into the highways, and as many as ye shall find, bid to the marriage. 10 So those servants went out into the highways, and gathered together all as many as they found, both bad and good: and the wedding was furnished with guests.

11 And when the king came in to see the guests, he saw there a man which had not on a wedding garment: 12And he saith unto him, Friend, how camest thou in hither not having a wedding garment? And he was speechless. 13 Then said the king to the servants, Bind him hand and foot, and take him away, and cast *him* into outer darkness; there shall be weeping and gnashing of teeth. 14 For many are called, but few *are* chosen.

15 Then went the Pharisees, and took counsel how they might entangle him in *his* talk. 16And they sent out unto him their disciples with the Herodians, saying, Master, we know that thou art true, and teachest the way of God in truth, neither carest thou for any *man:* for thou regardest not the person of men. 17 Tell us therefore, What thinkest thou? Is it lawful to give tribute unto Cesar, or not? 18 But Jesus perceived their wickedness, and said, Why tempt ye me, *ye* hypocrites? 19 Shew me the tribute money. And they brought unto him a penny. 20And he saith unto them, Whose *is* this image and superscription? 21 They say unto him, Cesar's. Then saith he unto them, Render therefore unto Cesar the things which are Cesar's;

N.A.S.

God will be taken away from you, and be given to a nation producing the fruit of it. 44 "And he who falls on this stone will be broken to pieces; but on whomever it falls, it will scatter him like dust." 45And when the chief priests and the Pharisees heard His parables, they understood that He was speaking about them. 46And when they sought to seize Him, they became afraid of the multitudes, because they held Him to be a prophet.

22 And Jesus answered and spoke to them again in parables, saying, 2 "The kingdom of heaven may be compared to a king, who gave a wedding feast for his son. 3 "And he sent out his slaves to call those who had been invited to the wedding feast, and they were unwilling to come. 4 "Again he sent out other slaves saying, 'Tell those who have been invited, "Behold, I have prepared my dinner; my oxen and my fattened livestock are *all* butchered and everything is ready; come to the wedding feast." ' 5 "But they paid no attention and went their way, one to his own farm, another to his business, 6 and the rest seized his slaves and mistreated them and killed them. 7 "But the king was enraged and sent his armies, and destroyed those murderers, and set their city on fire. 8 "Then he *said to his slaves, 'The wedding is ready, but those who were invited were not worthy. 9 'Go therefore to the main highways, and as many as you find *there,* invite to the wedding feast.' 10 "And those slaves went out into the streets, and gathered together all they found, both evil and good; and the wedding hall was filled with dinner-guests. 11 "But when the king came in to look over the dinner-guests, he saw there a man not dressed in wedding clothes; 12 and he *said to him, 'Friend, how did you come in here without wedding clothes?' And he was speechless. 13 "Then the king said to the servants, 'Bind him hand and foot, and cast him into the outer darkness; in that place there shall be weeping and gnashing of teeth.' 14 "For many are called, but few *are* chosen."

15 Then the Pharisees went and counseled together how they might trap Him in what He said. 16And they *sent their disciples to Him, along with the Herodians, saying, "Teacher, we know that You are truthful and teach the way of God in truth, and defer to no one; for You are not partial to any. 17 "Tell us therefore, what do You think? Is it lawful to give a poll-tax to Caesar, or not?" 18 But Jesus perceived their malice, and said, "Why are you testing Me, you hypocrites? 19 "Show Me the coin *used* for the poll-tax." And they brought Him a denarius. 20And He *said to them, "Whose likeness and inscription is this?" 21 They *said to Him, "Caesar's." Then He *said to them, "Then render to Caesar the things that are Caesar's; and to God the things that are God's."

WILLIAMS

be taken away from you, and given to a people who will pay a fair rent for it. 44 Who ever falls upon that stone will be broken to pieces, but whom ever it falls upon will be crushed to powder."

45 When the high priests and the Pharisees heard His stories, they knew that He was speaking about them, 46 but although they were trying to have Him arrested, they were afraid of the people, for they considered Him a prophet.

22 Jesus tells the story of the king's wedding feast; enemies trying to trap him with three questions: is it right to pay taxes to Caesar? Is there a future life? Which is the first commandment?

Then Jesus again spoke to them in stories, and said:
2 "The kingdom of heaven is like a king, who gave a wedding reception for his son. 3 And he sent his slaves to summon those who had been invited to the wedding reception, but they refused to come. 4 A second time he sent other slaves, and said to them, 'Tell the invited guests that I have my reception all ready, my bullocks and fatlings are butchered, and everything is ready. Come to the wedding reception!' 5 But they paid no attention to it, but went off, one to his farm, another to his place of business, 6 and the rest seized his slaves, treated them with violence, and murdered them. 7 Then the king was enraged, and sent his soldiers to put those murderers to death and burned their city. 8 After that he said to his slaves, 'My wedding reception is ready, but those invited have proved unworthy. 9 So go out to the country crossroads and invite everybody you find to my wedding reception.' 10 And those slaves went out into the roads and gathered everybody they found, both good and bad, and the bridal-hall was packed with guests. 11 But when the king came in to take a look at the guests, he saw there a man who did not have on a wedding suit.ª 12 So he said to him, 'My friend, how is it that you came in here without a wedding suit on?' But his lips were sealed. 13 Then the king said to his attendants, 'Tie him hand and foot and throw him out into the darkness on the outside, where he will have to weep and grind his teeth.' 14 For many are invited, but few are selected.

15 Then the Pharisees went and made a plot to trap Him in argument. 16 So they sent to Him their disciples with the Herodians, to say to Him, "Teacher, we know that you are in the habit of telling the truthᵇ and of teaching the way of God in honesty, and you do not care what anyone says, for you are not partial. 17 So give us your opinion on the question: Is it right to pay Caesar the poll-tax, or not?"

18 But Jesus saw their malicious plot, and so asked, "Why are you testing me so, you hypocrites? 19 Show me a poll-tax coin."
20 And He asked them, "Whose likeness and title is this?"
21 They answered, "Caesar's."
Then He said to them, "Pay Caesar, therefore, what belongs to Caesar, and pay God

BECK

why I tell you, God's kingdom will be taken away from you and be given to a people who will do its works. 44 Anyone who falls on that Stone will be dashed in pieces, and if It falls on anyone, It will scatter him like dust."

45 When the ruling priests and Pharisees heard His stories, they knew He was talking about them. 46 They wanted to grab Him but were afraid because the people thought He was a prophet.

Come to the Wedding!

22 Again Jesus used stories in talking to them. He said:
2 "The kingdom of heaven is like a king who prepared a wedding for his son. 3 He sent his slaves to call those who had been invited to the wedding, but they refused to come. 4 Then he sent other slaves and said to them, 'Tell the people who are invited, "Look here! I prepared my dinner. My bulls and fattened calves are killed, and everything is ready. Come to the wedding." '

5 "But they paid no attention and went away, one to his farm, another to his business, 6 and the rest took his slaves, shamefully mistreated them, and murdered them.

7 "The king got angry. He sent his soldiers, and they killed those murderers and burned their city.

8 "Then he said to his slaves: 'The wedding is ready, but the people who were invited didn't deserve the honor. 9 Now go where the roads leave the city, and call everybody you find there to the wedding.' 10 Those slaves went out on the roads and brought in all the people they found, bad and good. And the wedding hall was filled with guests.

11 "When the king came in to look at the guests, he saw there a man without a wedding garment. 12 'Friend,' he asked him, 'how did you get in here without a wedding garment?'

13 "The man couldn't say a thing. Then the king told the servants, 'Tie him hand and foot, and throw him out into the dark. There he will cry and grind his teeth.'

14 "Many are invited, but few are chosen."

Taxes

15 Then the Pharisees went and plotted to trap Him with a question. 16 They sent their disciples with Herod's men to say to Him: "Teacher, we know You're honest and really teach God's way and don't care what others think, because You don't favor any special persons. 17 Now tell us: What do You think? Is it right to pay a tax to Caesar or not?"

18 Seeing through their wicked way, Jesus asked, "Why do you test Me, you hypocrites? 19 Show Me the coin with which the tax is paid."

20 They brought Him a denarius. "Whose head is this and whose inscription?" He asked them.

"Caesar's," they said.
21 "Give Caesar what is Caesar's," He told them, "and God what is God's."

[a] Modern term for ancient term, garment. [b] Grk., being true.

67

K.J.V.

and unto God the things that are God's. 22 When they had heard *these words,* they marvelled, and left him, and went their way.

23 The same day came to him the Sadducees, which say that there is no resurrection, and asked him, 24 Saying, Master, Moses said, If a man die, having no children, his brother shall marry his wife, and raise up seed unto his brother. 25 Now there were with us seven brethren: and the first, when he had married a wife, deceased, and, having no issue, left his wife unto his brother: 26 Likewise the second also, and the third, unto the seventh. 27 And last of all the woman died also. 28 Therefore in the resurrection, whose wife shall she be of the seven? for they all had her. 29 Jesus answered and said unto them, Ye do err, not knowing the Scriptures, nor the power of God. 30 For in the resurrection they neither marry, nor are given in marriage, but are as the angels of God in heaven. 31 But as touching the resurrection of the dead, have ye not read that which was spoken unto you by God, saying, 32 I am the God of Abraham, and the God of Isaac, and the God of Jacob? God is not the God of the dead, but of the living. 33 And when the multitude heard *this,* they were astonished at his doctrine.

34 But when the Pharisees had heard that he had put the Sadducees to silence, they were gathered together. 35 Then one of them, *which was* a lawyer, asked *him a question,* tempting him, and saying, 36 Master, which *is* the great commandment in the law? 37 Jesus said unto him, Thou shalt love the Lord thy God with all thy heart, and with all thy soul, and with all thy mind. 38 This is the first and great commandment. 39 And the second *is* like unto it, Thou shalt love thy neighbour as thyself. 40 On these two commandments hang all the law and the prophets.

41 While the Pharisees were gathered together, Jesus asked them, 42 Saying, What think ye of Christ? whose son is he? They say unto him, *The son* of David. 43 He saith unto them, How then doth David in spirit call him Lord, saying, 44 The Lord said unto my Lord, Sit thou on my right hand, till I make thine enemies thy footstool? 45 If David then call him Lord, how is he his son? 46 And no man was able to answer him a word, neither durst any *man* from that day forth ask him any more *questions.*

N.A.S.

22 And hearing *this,* they marveled, and leaving Him, they went away.

23 On that day *some* Sadducees (who say there is no resurrection) came to Him and questioned Him, 24 saying, "Teacher, Moses said, 'IF A MAN DIES, HAVING NO CHILDREN, HIS BROTHER AS NEXT OF KIN SHALL MARRY HIS WIFE, AND RAISE UP AN OFFSPRING TO HIS BROTHER.' 25 "Now there were seven brothers with us; and the first married and died, and having no offspring left his wife to his brother; 26 so also the second, and the third, down to the seventh. 27 "And last of all, the woman died. 28 "In the resurrection therefore whose wife of the seven shall she be? For they all had her." 29 But Jesus answered and said to them, "You are mistaken, not understanding the Scriptures, or the power of God. 30 "For in the resurrection they neither marry, nor are given in marriage, but are like angels in heaven. 31 "But regarding the resurrection of the dead, have you not read that which was spoken to you by God, saying, 32 'I AM THE GOD OF ABRAHAM, AND THE GOD OF ISAAC, AND THE GOD OF JACOB'? God is not *the* God of *the* dead but of *the* living." 33 And when the multitudes heard *this,* they were astonished at His teaching.

34 But when the Pharisees heard that He had put the Sadducees to silence, they gathered themselves together. 35 And one of them, [a] a lawyer, asked Him a question, testing Him, 36 "Teacher, which is the great commandment in the Law?" 37 And He said to him, " 'YOU SHALL LOVE THE LORD YOUR GOD WITH ALL YOUR HEART, AND WITH ALL YOUR SOUL, AND WITH ALL YOUR MIND.' 38 "This is the great and foremost commandment. 39 "And a second is like it, 'YOU SHALL LOVE YOUR NEIGHBOR AS YOURSELF.' 40 "On these two commandments depend the whole Law and the Prophets."

41 Now while the Pharisees were gathered together, Jesus asked them a question, 42 saying, "What do you think about the Christ, whose son is He?" They *said to Him, "The son* of David." 43 He *said to them, "Then how does David in the Spirit call Him 'Lord,' saying,

44 'THE LORD SAID TO MY LORD,
"SIT AT MY RIGHT HAND,
UNTIL I PUT THINE ENEMIES BENEATH THY FEET." '

45 "If David then calls Him 'Lord,' how is He his son?" 46 And no one was able to answer Him a word, nor did anyone dare from that day on to ask Him another question.

23 Then spake Jesus to the multitude, and to his disciples, 2 Saying, The scribes and the Pharisees sit in Moses' seat: 3 All therefore whatsoever they bid you observe, *that* observe and do; but do not ye after their works: for

23 Then Jesus spoke to the multitudes and to His disciples, 2 saying, "The scribes and the Pharisees have seated themselves in the chair of Moses; 3 therefore all that they tell you, do and observe, but do not do according to their deeds; for they say *things,* and do not

WILLIAMS

what belongs to God." 22And when they heard it, they were dumfounded; and they left Him and went away.

23 On the same day some Sadducees, who claim that there is no resurrection, came up to Him, and asked this question: 24 "Teacher, Moses said, 'If a man dies without children, his brother must marry his widow and raise up a family for him.' 25 Now there were seven brothers among us. The first married and died without children, and left his widow to his brother. 26 The second also died, and the third, and all down to the seventh. 27 Last of all the woman died, too. 28 Now at the resurrection which one's wife, of the seven, will she be? For they all married her."

29 Jesus answered them, "You are wrong in your views, because you do not understand the Scriptures nor the power of God, 30 for after the resurrection men do not marry and women are not married, but continue to live together as the angels do in heaven. 31 But did you never read, on the resurrection of the dead, what God said to you, 32 'I am the God of Abraham and the God of Isaac and the God of Jacob'? Now God is not the God of dead but of living men." 33And when the crowds heard this, they were dumfounded at His teaching.

34 Now the Pharisees heard that He had silenced the Sadducees, and so they had a meeting. 35And one of their number, an expert in the law, to tempt Him, asked, 36 "Teacher, what sort*c* of command is greatest in the law?"

37 And He answered him, "You must love the Lord your God with your whole heart, your whole soul, and your whole mind.' 38 This is the greatest command, and is first in importance. 39 The second is like it: 'You must love your neighbor as you do yourself.' 40 The essence of the whole law and the prophets is packed *d* into these two commands."

41 And when the Pharisees came together, Jesus asked them, 42 "What is your opinion of the Christ? Whose son is He?"

They answered Him, "He is David's son."

43 He asked them, "How then does David, under the guidance of the Spirit, call Him Lord, when he says:

44 "'The Lord has said to my Lord, Sit at my right hand,

Until I put your enemies under your feet'? 45 If David, then, calls Him Lord, how can He be his son?" 46And not one could answer Him a word, and from that day on no one ever dared to ask Him any more questions.

BECK

22 They were surprised to hear this. Then they let Him alone and went away.

The Dead Live

23 On that day some Sadducees, who say the dead don't rise, came to Him with this question: 24 "Teacher, Moses said, *If anyone dies childless, his brother should marry his widow and have children for his brother.*[70] 25 Now, there were seven brothers among us. The first married and died, and since he had no children, he left his widow to his brother. 26 The second brother did the same, and so did the third and the rest of the seven. 27 Last of all the woman died. 28 Now, when they rise from the dead, which of the seven will be her husband? You know they all married her."

29 "You're wrong," Jesus answered them. "You don't know your Bible or God's power. 30 When the dead rise, men and women don't marry but are like angels in heaven. 31About the dead rising—didn't you read what God told you: 32 *I am the God of Abraham, the God of Isaac, and the God of Jacob?*[71] He's not the God of the dead but of the living."

33 His teaching amazed the people who heard Him.

Love God and Your Neighbor

34 When the Pharisees heard He had silenced the Sadducees, they got together. 35 One of them, an expert in the Law, tested Him by asking Him, 36 "Teacher, which is the greatest commandment in the Law?"

37 Jesus answered him, "*Love the Lord your God with all your heart, with all your life, and with all your*[72] mind. 38 This is the greatest and most important commandment. 39 The next is like it: *Love your neighbor like yourself.*[61] 40All the Law and the prophets depend on these two commandments."

David's Son

41 While the Pharisees were still together, Jesus asked them, 42 "What do you think of the promised Savior? Whose Son is He?" "David's," they answered Him.

43 He asked them, "Then how can David by the Spirit call Him Lord? He says,

44 *The Lord said to my Lord, 'Sit at My right Till I put Your enemies under Your feet.'*[73]

45 Now, if David calls Him Lord, how can He be his Son?"

46 Nobody could answer Him, and after that nobody dared to ask Him another question.

Beware!

23 Then Jesus said to the crowd and to His disciples:

2 "The Bible scholars and the Pharisees sit in Moses' seat. 3 Do everything they tell you, and follow it; but don't do what they do, be-

---

23 *Jesus exposes the sins of the Pharisees; warns the people against them; pronounces seven woes against them; weeps over Jerusalem*

Then Jesus said to the crowds and to His disciples:

2 "The scribes and Pharisees have taken Moses' seat as teachers. 3 So everything they tell you, do and practice, but stop doing what they do, for they preach but do not practice.

[c] Quality emphasized. [d] Grk., *On these hang the weight,* etc.

[70] Gen. 38:8; Deut. 25:5-6
[71] Ex. 3:6
[72] Deut. 6:5
[73] Ps. 110:1

K.J.V.

they say, and do not. 4 For they bind heavy burdens and grievous to be borne, and lay *them* on men's shoulders; but they *themselves* will not move them with one of their fingers. 5 But all their works they do for to be seen of men: they make broad their phylacteries, and enlarge the borders of their garments, 6And love the uppermost rooms at feasts, and the chief seats in the synagogues, 7And greetings in the markets, and to be called of men, Rabbi, Rabbi. 8 But be not ye called Rabbi: for one is your Master, *even* Christ; and all ye are brethren. 9And call no *man* your father upon the earth: for one is your Father, which is in heaven. 10 Neither be ye called masters: for one is your Master, *even* Christ. 11 But he that is greatest among you shall be your servant. 12And whosoever shall exalt himself shall be abased; and he that shall humble himself shall be exalted.

13 But woe unto you, scribes and Pharisees, hypocrites! for ye shut up the kingdom of heaven against men: for ye neither go in *yourselves,* neither suffer ye them that are entering to go in. 14 Woe unto you, scribes and Pharisees, hypocrites! for ye devour widows' houses, and for a pretence make long prayer: therefore ye shall receive the greater damnation. 15 Woe unto you, scribes and Pharisees, hypocrites! for ye compass sea and land to make one proselyte; and when he is made, ye make him twofold more the child of hell than yourselves. 16 Woe unto you, *ye* blind guides, which say, Whosoever shall swear by the temple, it is nothing; but whosoever shall swear by the gold of the temple, he is a debtor! 17 *Ye* fools and blind: for whether is greater, the gold, or the temple that sanctifieth the gold? 18And, Whosoever shall swear by the altar, it is nothing; but whosoever sweareth by the gift that is upon it, he is guilty. 19 *Ye* fools and blind: for whether *is* greater, the gift, or the altar that sanctifieth the gift? 20 Whoso therefore shall swear by the altar, sweareth by it, and by all things thereon. 21And whoso shall swear by the temple, sweareth by it, and by him that dwelleth therein. 22And he that shall swear by heaven, sweareth by the throne of God, and by him that sitteth thereon. 23 Woe unto you, scribes and Pharisees, hypocrites! for ye pay tithe of mint and anise and cummin, and have omitted the weightier *matters* of the law, judgment, mercy, and faith: these ought ye to have done, and not to leave the other undone. 24 *Ye* blind guides, which strain at a gnat, and swallow a camel. 25 Woe unto you, scribes and Pharisees, hypocrites! for ye make clean the outside of the cup and of the platter, but within they are full of extortion and excess. 26 *Thou* blind Pharisee, cleanse first that *which is* within the cup and platter, that the outside of them may be clean also. 27 Woe unto you, scribes and Pharisees, hypocrites! for ye are like unto whited sepulchres, which indeed appear beautiful outward, but are within full of dead *men's* bones, and of all uncleanness. 28 Even so ye also out-

N.A.S.

do *them.* 4 "And they tie up heavy loads, and lay them on men's shoulders; but they themselves are unwilling to move them with *so much as* a finger. 5 "But they do all their deeds to be noticed by men; for they broaden their [a]phylacteries, and lengthen the tassels *of their garments.* 6 "And they love the place of honor at banquets, and the chief seats in the synagogues, 7 and respectful greetings in the market places, and being called by men, Rabbi. 8 "But do not be called Rabbi; for One is your Teacher, and you are all brothers. 9 "And do not call *anyone* on earth your father; for One is your Father, He who is in heaven. 10 "And do not be called leaders; for One is your Leader, *that is,* Christ. 11 "But the greatest among you shall be your servant. 12 "And whoever exalts himself shall be humbled; and whoever humbles himself shall be exalted.

13 "But woe to you, scribes and Pharisees, hypocrites, because you shut off the kingdom of heaven from men; for you do not enter in yourselves; nor do you allow those who are entering to go in. 14 ["[b]Woe to you, scribes and Pharisees, hypocrites, because you devour widows' houses, even while for a pretense you make long prayers; therefore you shall receive greater condemnation.]

15 "Woe to you, scribes and Pharisees, hypocrites, because you travel about on sea and land to make one proselyte; and when he becomes one, you make him twice as much a son of hell as yourselves.

16 "Woe to you, blind guides, who say, 'Whoever swears by the temple, that is nothing; but whoever swears by the gold of the temple, he is obligated.' 17 "You fools and blind men; which is more important, the gold, or the temple that sanctified the gold? 18 "And, 'Whoever swears by the altar, *that* is nothing, but whoever swears by the offering upon it, he is obligated.' 19 "You blind men, which is more important, the offering or the altar that sanctifies the offering? 20 "Therefore he who swears, swears *both* by the altar and by everything on it. 21 "And he who swears by the temple, swears *both* by the temple and by Him who dwells within it. 22 "And he who swears by heaven, swears *both* by the throne of God and by Him who sits upon it.

23 "Woe to you, scribes and Pharisees, hypocrites! For you tithe mint and dill and cummin, and have neglected the weightier provisions of the law: justice and mercy and faithfulness; but these are the things you should have done without neglecting the others. 24 "You blind guides, who strain out a gnat and swallow a camel!

25 "Woe to you, scribes and Pharisees, hypocrites! For you clean the outside of the cup and of the dish, but inside they are full of robbery and self-indulgence. 26 "You blind Pharisee, first clean the inside of the cup and of the dish, so that the outside of it may become clean also.

27 "Woe to you, scribes and Pharisees, hypocrites! For you are like whitewashed tombs which on the outside appear beautiful, but inside they are full of dead men's bones and all uncleanness. 28 "Even so you too outwardly ap-

[a] I.e., small boxes containing Scripture texts worn for religious purposes. [b] This verse not found in the earliest mss.

WILLIAMS

4 They tie up heavy burdens and fasten them on men's shoulders, but they refuse to lift a finger to help bear them. 5 They do what they do to attract people's attention. They wear on their coats Scripture texts in big letters, and they wear large tassels, 6 and they like the places of honor at feasts and the front seats in synagogues, 7 to be greeted with honor in public places, and to have men call them 'Teacher.' 8 But as for you, you must not seek for others to call you 'Teacher,' for you have but one who is 'Teacher,' and you are all brothers. 9 And you must not call anyone on earth 'father,' for the Heavenly One is your Father. 10 And you must not be called 'leaders,' for you have only one Leader, and that is Christ. 11 Whoever is greatest among you must be your servant. 12 Whoever exalts himself will be humbled, and whoever humbles himself will be exalted.ᵃ

13 "A curse on you, you hypocritical scribes and Pharisees! For you bolt the doors of the kingdom of heaven in men's faces, for you neither go in yourselves, nor do you let those who are trying to do so go in.ᵇ 15 A curse on you, you hypocritical scribes and Pharisees! For you scour land and sea to win a single convert, and when he is won you make him twice as fit for the pitᶜ as you are. 16 A curse on you, you blind leaders who say, 'Whoever swears by the sanctuary is not duty-bound, but whoever swears by the gold of the sanctuary is duty-bound.' 17 You blind fools! which is greater, the gold, or the sanctuary that makes the gold sacred? 18 You say, 'Whoever swears by the altar is not duty-bound, but whoever swears by the offering on the altar is duty-bound!' 19 You blind men! which is greater, the offering, or the altar that makes the offering sacred? 20 So whoever swears by the altar swears by everything on it; 21 whoever swears by the sanctuary swears by it and by Him who dwells in it; 22 whoever swears by heaven swears by the throne of God and by Him who sits on it.

23 "A curse on you, you hypocritical scribes and Pharisees! For you pay tithes on mint and dill and cummin, and yet leave out the more vital matters of the law, justice, love and fidelity. These latter especially you ought to have done, but ought not to have left out the former. 24 You blind leaders, who are straining out the gnat but gulping down the camel! 25 A curse on you, you hypocritical scribes and Pharisees, for you clean the outside of the cup and the dish, but inside they are full of your greed and self-indulgence. 26 You blind Pharisee! You must first clean the inside of the cup and the dish, so that the outside may be clean too.

27 "A curse on you, you hypocritical scribes and Pharisees, for you are like white-washed tombs, which look beautiful on the outside, but inside are full of dead people's bones and everything that is unclean! 28 So you, too, on the

BECK

cause they don't do what they say. 4 They tie together heavy loads that are hard to carry and lay them on the shoulders of others, but they won't raise a finger to move them.

5 "They do everything in order to be seen by others. They make their phylacteries broad and the tassels of their garments long.* 6 They like the places of honor at dinners and the front seats in synagogs, 7 to be greeted in the marketplaces and have people call them rabbi. 8 But don't you let them call you rabbi, because you have only one Teacher, and you are all brothers. 9 And don't call anyone on earth your father; you have only one Father, and He is in heaven. 10 Don't have others call you teachers; you have only one Teacher, and that is Christ. 11 The greatest among you will be one who serves you. 12 If you honor yourself, you will be humbled, but if you humble yourself, you will be honored."

Woe!

13 "Woe to you Bible scholars and Pharisees, you hypocrites! You lock people out of the kingdom of heaven. You won't come into it yourselves, and when others try to come in, you won't let them.**

15 "Woe to you Bible scholars and Pharisees, you hypocrites! You go around lake and land to convert a single person, and when he's converted, you make him twice as fit for hell as you are.

16 "Woe to you blind guides! You say, 'If anyone swears by the temple, that's nothing. But if anyone swears by the gold in the temple, he must keep his oath.' 17 Blind fools! Which is greater, the gold or the temple that made the gold holy? 18 Or again, 'If anyone swears by the altar, that's nothing. But if anyone swears by the gift that's on it, he must keep his oath.' 19 You blind men! Which is greater, the gift or the altar that makes the gift holy? 20 If you swear by the altar, you swear by it and by everything on it. 21 If you swear by the temple, you swear by it and by Him who lives there. 22 And if you swear by heaven, you swear by God's throne and by Him who is sitting on it.

23 "Woe to you Bible scholars and Pharisees, you hypocrites! You give a tenth of mint and dill and cummin but have neglected the more important things of the Law: to be just, merciful, and trustworthy. You should have done the one without neglecting the other. 24 Blind guides! You strain out the gnat but swallow the camel.

25 "Woe to you Bible scholars and Pharisees, you hypocrites! You clean the outside of a cup and of a dish, but inside they're full of greed and uncontrolled lust. 26 You blind Pharisee! First clean the inside of the cup and of the dish in order to make also the outside of it clean. 27 Woe to you Bible scholars and Pharisees, you hypocrites! You're like white-washed graves that look beautiful on the outside but inside are full of dead men's bones and every kind of decay. 28 So on the outside you look good to

* A phylactery was a small leather box fastened by a leather strap on the forehead or on the left arm. In the box were pieces of parchment on which were written the words of Ex. 13:1-10, 11-16; Deut. 6:4-9, 13-21.—An Israelite wore a tassel on each of the four corners of his outer garment. (Num. 15:38-40; Deut. 22:12)

** Our oldest manuscripts do not have v. 14: "Woe to you Bible scholars and Pharisees, you hypocrites! You swallow the widows' houses and then, to cover up, make long prayers. For this you'll be punished all the more." See Mark 12:40; Luke 20:47.

[a] Some authorities add here the words contained in vs. 14 of K. J. Version. [b] V. 14. Not in best manuscripts. [c] Grk., double son of Gehenna.

K.J.V.

wardly appear righteous unto men, but within ye are full of hypocrisy and iniquity. 29 Woe unto you, scribes and Pharisees, hypocrites! because ye build the tombs of the prophets, and garnish the sepulchres of the righteous, 30And say, If we had been in the days of our fathers, we would not have been partakers with them in the blood of the prophets. 31 Wherefore ye be witnesses unto yourselves, that ye are the children of them which killed the prophets. 32 Fill ye up then the measure of your fathers. 33 *Ye* serpents, *ye* generation of vipers, how can ye escape the damnation of hell?

34 Wherefore, behold, I send unto you prophets, and wise men, and scribes: and *some* of them ye shall kill and crucify; and *some* of them shall ye scourge in your synagogues, and persecute *them* from city to city: 35 That upon you may come all the righteous blood shed upon the earth, from the blood of righteous Abel unto the blood of Zacharias son of Barachias, whom ye slew between the temple and the altar. 36 Verily I say unto you, All these things shall come upon this generation. 37 O Jerusalem, Jerusalem, *thou* that killest the prophets, and stonest them which are sent unto thee, how often would I have gathered thy children together, even as a hen gathereth her chickens under *her* wings, and ye would not! 38 Behold, your house is left unto you desolate. 39 For I say unto you, Ye shall not see me henceforth, till ye shall say, Blessed *is* he that cometh in the name of the Lord.

24 And Jesus went out, and departed from the temple: and his disciples came to *him* for to shew him the buildings of the temple. 2And Jesus said unto them, See ye not all these things? verily I say unto you, There shall not be left here one stone upon another, that shall not be thrown down.

3 And as he sat upon the mount of Olives, the disciples came unto him privately, saying, Tell us, when shall these things be? and what *shall be* the sign of thy coming, and of the end of the world? 4And Jesus answered and said unto them, Take heed that no man deceive you. 5 For many shall come in my name, saying, I am Christ; and shall deceive many. 6And ye shall hear of wars and rumours of wars: see that ye be not troubled: for all *these things* must come to pass, but the end is not yet. 7 For nation shall rise against nation, and kingdom against kingdom: and there shall be famines, and pestilences, and earthquakes, in divers places. 8All these *are* the beginning of sorrows. 9 Then shall they deliver you up to be afflicted, and shall kill you: and ye shall be hated of all nations for my name's sake. 10And then shall many be offended, and shall betray one another, and shall hate one another. 11And many false prophets shall rise, and shall deceive many. 12And because iniquity shall abound, the love of many shall wax cold. 13 But he that shall endure unto the end, the same shall be saved. 14And this gospel of the

N.A.S.

pear righteous to men, but inwardly you are full of hypocrisy and lawlessness. 29 "Woe to you, scribes and Pharisees, hypocrites! For you build the tombs of the prophets and adorn the monuments of the righteous, 30 and say, 'If we had been *living* in the days of our fathers, we would not have been partners with them in *shedding* the blood of the prophets.' 31 "Consequently you bear witness against yourselves, that you are sons of those who murdered the prophets. 32 "Fill up then the measure *of the guilt* of your fathers. 33 "You serpents, you brood of vipers, how shall you escape the sentence of hell? 34 "Therefore, behold, I am sending you prophets and wise men and scribes; some of them you will kill and crucify, and some of them you will scourge in your synagogues, and persecute from city to city; 35 that upon you may fall *the guilt of* all the righteous blood shed on earth, from the blood of righteous Abel to the blood of Zechariah, the son of Berechiah, whom you murdered between the temple and the altar. 36 "Truly I say to you, all these things shall come upon this generation.

37 "O Jerusalem, Jerusalem, who kills the prophets and stones those who are sent to her! How often I wanted to gather your children together, the way a hen gathers her chicks under her wings, and you were unwilling. 38 "Behold, your house is being left to you desolate. 39 "For I say to you, from now on you shall not see Me until you say, 'BLESSED IS HE WHO COMES IN THE NAME OF THE LORD.' "

24 And Jesus came out from the temple and was going away when His disciples came up to point out the temple buildings to Him. 2And He answered and said to them, "Do you not see all these things? Truly I say to you, not one stone here shall be left upon another, which will not be torn down."

3 And as He was sitting on the Mount of Olives, the disciples came to Him privately, saying, "Tell us, when will these things be, and what *will be* the sign of Your coming, and of the end of the age?" 4And Jesus answered and said to them, "See to it that no one misleads you. 5 "For many will come in My name, saying, 'I am the Christ,' and will mislead many. 6 "And you will be hearing of wars and rumors of wars; see that you are not frightened, for *those things* must take place, but *that* is not yet the end. 7 "For nation will rise against nation, and kingdom against kingdom, and in various places there will be famines and earthquakes. 8 "But all these things are *merely* the beginning of birthpangs. 9 "Then they will deliver you up to tribulation, and will kill you, and you will be hated by all nations on account of My name. 10 "And at that time many will fall away and will betray one another and hate one another. 11 "And many false prophets will arise, and will mislead many. 12 "And because lawlessness is increased, most people's love will grow cold. 13 "But the one who endures to the end, it is he who shall be saved. 14 "And this gospel of the

WILLIAMS

outside seem to people to be upright, but inside you are full of hypocrisy and lawlessness.
29 "A curse on you, you hypocritical scribes and Pharisees, for you build tombs for the prophets, and decorate monuments for the upright, 30 and say, 'If we had lived in the days of our forefathers, we would not have been sharers with them in shedding the blood of the prophets.' 31 So you are witnessing against yourselves that you are the descendants of those who murdered the prophets. 32 Then fill up to the brim the cup of your forefathers' guilt! 33 You serpents! You brood of vipers! How can you escape a sentence to the pit? d 34 Therefore, I am going to send you prophets, wise men, and scribes, some of whom you will kill—even crucify—and some you will flog in your synagogues and chase from city to city, 35 so that on you will come all the righteous blood shed on the earth from the blood of upright Abel to the blood of Zechariah, Barachiah's son, whom you murdered between the sanctuary and the altar. 36 I solemnly say to you, all this will come upon this age!
37 "O Jerusalem, Jerusalem! the city that has kept on murdering the prophets, and stoning those who have been sent to her, how often I have yearned to gather your children around me, as a hen gathers her chickens under her wings, but you refused! 38 Now your house is abandoned by me! 39 For I tell you, you will never see me again until you say, 'Blessed be He who comes in the name of the Lord.' "

24 *Jesus tells of the doom of the city; the signs of His coming; the stories of the fig tree and of the faithful servants*

And Jesus left the temple, and was going away, when His disciples came up to Him, to show Him the temple buildings. 2 But He answered them, "Do you see all these things? I solemnly say to you, there shall not be left here one stone upon another that shall not be torn down."
3 While He was sitting on the Mount of Olives, the disciples came up to Him by themselves, and said, "Tell us when this is to take place, and what will be the sign of your coming and of the end of the age."
4 Jesus answered, "Look out that no one misleads you about it, 5 for many will come bearing the name of the Messiah, and saying, 'I am the Christ,' and will mislead many people. 6 You are going to hear of wars and rumors of wars; take care not to be scared out of your wits. They have to come, but that is not the end yet. 7 For nation will go to war with nation, and kingdom with kingdom, and there will be famines and earthquakes in many places. 8 But all this is but the beginning of the agonies. 9 At that time they will turn you over to torture, and will murder you, and you will be hated by all the heathen, because you bear my name. 10 Then many will fall by the way, and will betray one another and hate one another. 11 Many false prophets will appear and mislead many people; 12 and because of the increasing crime wave,a most people's love will grow cold. 13 But whoever bears up to the end will be saved. 14 And this good news of the kingdom must be

[d] Grk., *the judgment to Gehenna.* [a] Grk., *lawlessness.*

BECK

people, but inside you're full of hypocrisy and crime.
29 "Woe to you Bible scholars and Pharisees, you hypocrites! You build the tombs of the prophets and decorate the graves of the righteous 30 and say, 'If we had lived at the time of our fathers, we wouldn't have helped them murder the prophets.' 31 And so you testify against yourselves that you are the sons of those who murdered the prophets. 32 Go on, finish what your fathers started!
33 "You snakes! Brood of vipers! How can you escape being condemned to hell?
34 "That's why I'm sending you men to speak God's Word, men who are wise and know the Bible. Some of them you will kill and crucify. Others you will whip in your synagogs and hunt from town to town, 35 so that all the innocent blood poured on the ground will come on you, from the blood of righteous Abel to the blood of Zechariah, Barachiah's son, whom you murdered between the holy place and the altar. 36 I tell you, all this will certainly come on the people of today.
37 "Jerusalem, Jerusalem, you murder the prophets and stone those sent to you! How often I wanted to bring your children together as a hen gathers her chicks under her wings, but you didn't want to! 38 Now your *house will be left* to you *a deserted place.*74 39 I tell you, you will not see Me again till you say, *'Blessed is He who is coming in the Lord's name.' "* 64

Sorrow Ahead!

24 When Jesus walked out of the temple and was going away, His disciples came to show Him the buildings of the temple. 2 "You see all these things?" Jesus asked them. "I tell you the truth: Not a stone will be left on another here but will be torn down."
3 When He was sitting on the Mount of Olives, His disciples came to Him alone, saying, "Tell us, when will this be and how can we tell when You're coming back and the world will come to an end?"
4 "Be careful not to let anyone deceive you," Jesus answered them. 5 "Many will come using My name and saying, 'I am Christ' and will deceive many.
6 "You will hear of wars and rumors of wars. See that you don't get alarmed. It *must happen,*75 but that's not the end yet. 7 *Nation will fight against nation,* and *kingdom against kingdom,*76 and there will be famines and earthquakes in different places. 8 But all these are only the first pains.*
9 "Then they will hand you over to those who will make you suffer, and they will kill you, and all nations will hate you on account of My name. 10 Then *many will fall away*77 and betray one another and hate one another. 11 Many false prophets will arise and lead many people astray. 12 And because there will be more and more wickedness, the love of most people will turn cold. 13 But endure to the end, and you will be saved.
14 "This good news of the Kingdom must be

* As in childbirth, sharper pains will follow before the Savior comes in glory.
[74] Jer. 12:7; 22:5
[75] Dan. 2:28
[76] Is. 19:2; 2 Chron. 15:6
[77] Dan. 11:41

K.J.V.

kingdom shall be preached in all the world for a witness unto all nations; and then shall the end come. 15 When ye therefore shall see the abomination of desolation, spoken of by Daniel the prophet, stand in the holy place, (whoso readeth, let him understand,) 16 Then let them which be in Judea flee into the mountains: 17 Let him which is on the housetop not come down to take any thing out of his house: 18 Neither let him which is in the field return back to take his clothes. 19 And woe unto them that are with child, and to them that give suck in those days! 20 But pray ye that your flight be not in the winter, neither on the sabbath day: 21 For then shall be great tribulation, such as was not since the beginning of the world to this time, no, nor ever shall be. 22 And except those days should be shortened, there should no flesh be saved: but for the elect's sake those days shall be shortened. 23 Then if any man shall say unto you, Lo, here *is* Christ, or there; believe *it* not. 24 For there shall arise false Christs, and false prophets, and shall shew great signs and wonders; insomuch that, if *it were* possible, they shall deceive the very elect. 25 Behold, I have told you before. 26 Wherefore if they shall say unto you, Behold, he is in the desert; go not forth: behold, *he is* in the secret chambers; believe *it* not. 27 For as the lightning cometh out of the east, and shineth even unto the west; so shall also the coming of the Son of man be. 28 For wheresoever the carcass is, there will the eagles be gathered together.

29 Immediately after the tribulation of those days shall the sun be darkened, and the moon shall not give her light, and the stars shall fall from heaven, and the powers of the heavens shall be shaken: 30 And then shall appear the sign of the Son of man in heaven: and then shall all the tribes of the earth mourn, and they shall see the Son of man coming in the clouds of heaven with power and great glory. 31 And he shall send his angels with a great sound of a trumpet, and they shall gather together his elect from the four winds, from one end of heaven to the other. 32 Now learn a parable of the fig tree; When his branch is yet tender, and putteth forth leaves, ye know that summer *is* nigh: 33 So likewise ye, when ye shall see all these things, know that it is near, *even* at the doors. 34 Verily I say unto you, This generation shall not pass, till all these things be fulfilled. 35 Heaven and earth shall pass away, but my words shall not pass away.

36 But of that day and hour knoweth no *man*, no, not the angels of heaven, but my Father only. 37 But as the days of Noe *were*, so shall also the coming of the Son of man be. 38 For as in the days that were before the flood they were eating and drinking, marrying and giving in marriage, until the day that Noe entered into the ark, 39 And knew not until the flood came, and took them all away; so shall also the coming

N.A.S.

kingdom shall be preached in the whole world for a witness to all the nations, and then the end shall come.

15 "Therefore when you see the ABOMINATION OF DESOLATION which was spoken of through Daniel the prophet, standing IN THE HOLY PLACE (let the reader understand), 16 then let those who are in Judea flee to the mountains; 17 let him who is on the housetop not go down to get the things out that are in his house; 18 and let him who is in the field not turn back to get his cloak. 19 "But woe to those who are with child and to those who nurse babes in those days! 20 "But pray that your flight may not be in the winter, or on a Sabbath; 21 for then there will be a great tribulation, such as has not occurred since the beginning of the world until now, nor ever shall. 22 "And unless those days had been cut short, no life would have been saved; but for the sake of the elect those days shall be cut short. 23 "Then if any one says to you, 'Behold, here is the Christ,' or 'There *He is*,' do not believe *him*. 24 "For false Christs and false prophets will arise and will show great signs and wonders, so as to mislead, if possible, even the elect. 25 "Behold, I have told you in advance. 26 "If therefore they say to you, 'Behold, He is in the wilderness,' do not go forth, *or*, 'Behold, He is in the inner rooms,' do not believe *them*. 27 "For just as the lightning comes from the east, and flashes even to the west, so shall the coming of the Son of Man be. 28 "Wherever the corpse is, there the vultures will gather.

29 "But immediately after the tribulation of those days THE SUN WILL BE DARKENED, AND THE MOON WILL NOT GIVE ITS LIGHT, AND THE STARS WILL FALL from the sky, and the POWERS OF THE HEAVENS WILL BE shaken, 30 and then the sign of the Son of Man will appear in the sky, and then all the tribes of the earth will mourn, and they will see the SON OF MAN COMING ON THE CLOUDS OF THE SKY with power and great glory. 31 "And He will send forth His angels WITH A GREAT TRUMPET and THEY WILL GATHER TOGETHER His elect FROM THE FOUR WINDS, FROM ONE END OF THE SKY TO THE OTHER.

32 "Now learn the parable FROM THE FIG TREE: when its branch has already become tender, and puts forth its leaves, you know that summer is near; 33 even so you too, when you see all these things, recognize that He is near, *right* at the door. 34 "Truly I say to you, this generation will not pass away until all these things take place. 35 "Heaven and earth will pass away, but My words shall not pass away. 36 "But of that day and hour no one knows, not even the angels of heaven, nor the Son, but the Father alone. 37 "For the coming of the Son of Man will be just like the days of Noah. 38 "For as in those days which were before the flood they were eating and drinking, they were marrying and giving in marriage, until the day that NOAH ENTERED THE ARK, 39 and they did not understand until the flood came and took them

WILLIAMS

preached all over the inhabited world, for a testimony to all the heathen, and then the end will come.

15 "So when you see the destructive desecration, mentioned by the prophet Daniel, standing in the Holy Place"—let the reader take notice—[b] 16 "then let those who remain in Judea fly to the hills; 17 let him who is on the roof of his house not come down to get his household goods out; 18 let him who is in the field not turn back to get his coat. 19Alas for women who are expectant mothers and those who have nursing babies in those days! 20And pray for your flight not to be in winter or on the sabbath, 21 for there will be greater misery at that time than ever has been since the world began, or ever will be again. 22And if those days had not been cut short, nobody would have escaped, but for the sake of God's chosen people[c] those days will be cut short.

23 "If anyone at that time says to you, 'Here is the Christ!' or 'There He is!' do not believe it, 24 for false Christs and false prophets will announce themselves,[d] and they will show great signs and wonders to mislead, if possible, God's chosen people. 25 Remember, I have told you beforehand. 26 So if they say to you, 'Here He is in the desert,' do not go out to see, or 'Here He is in some secret place,' do not believe it. 27 For just as the lightning starts in the east and flashes clear to the west, so the coming of the Son of Man will be. 28 Wherever there is a carcass, there the vultures will flock.

29 "And immediately after the misery of those days, the sun will turn dark, the moon will not shed its light, the stars will fall from the sky, and the powers of the sky will be shaken. 30And then the sign of the Son of Man will appear in the sky, and then all the nations of the earth will mourn when they see the Son of Man coming on the clouds of the sky in overwhelming power and splendor. 31And He will send out His angels with a loud trumpet call, and they will gather His chosen people from the four points of the compass, from one end of the sky to the other.

32 "Now learn what the story of the fig tree means. Just as soon as its branches grow tender, and put forth leaves, you know that summer is near. 33 So when you see all these things, you will know that He is right at your door. 34 I solemnly say to you, the present age will not pass away before all this takes place. 35 Sky and earth will pass away but my words will never pass away. 36 But about that day or hour not a single one knows—not even the angels in heaven or the Son; not a single one but the Father alone. 37 For just as it was in the days of Noah, so it will be at the coming of the Son of Man. 38 For just as in the days before the Flood people went on eating and drinking, marrying and being married, until the very day Noah entered the ark, 39 and knew nothing about it until the Flood came and swept them

BECK

preached all over the world so that all nations hear the truth, and then the end will come."

Jerusalem Will Be Destroyed

15 "When you see what the prophet Daniel told about *the abomination laying waste the land* and standing *in the holy place*[78] (anyone who reads this should understand it), 16 then if you're in Judea, flee to the hills. 17 If you're on the roof, don't come down to get the things in your house. 18 If you're in the field, don't turn back to get your garment.

19 "Woe to the women who in those days are expecting babies or nursing them. 20 Pray that it may not be winter or a Sabbath when you flee. 21 It will be a time of great *misery such as hasn't been from the beginning* of the world *till now*[79] and never will be again. 22And if that time had not been cut short, nobody would be saved. 23 But that time will be cut short for the sake of those whom He has chosen."

Jesus Is Coming

23 "If anyone tells you then, 'Look, here is Christ!' or, 'There He is!' don't believe it, 24 because false Christs and false *prophets* will *come, and do* great *miracles and wonders*[80] to deceive if possible even those whom God has chosen. 25 You see, I've told you this before it happens. 26 So when you're told, 'There He is in the wilderness,' don't go out; or, 'Here He is in the inner rooms,' don't believe it. 27 The Son of Man will come like the lightning that flashes from the east to the west.— 28 Where the dead body is, there the vultures will gather.

29 "Right after the misery of that time *the sun will turn dark, the moon will stop shining, the stars will be falling from the sky,* and *the powers of heaven*[81] will be shaken. 30 Then the sign announcing the Son of Man will appear in the sky, and then *all the people on earth will mourn*[82] when they see *the Son of Man coming on the clouds in the sky*[83] with power and great glory. 31And *with a loud trumpet call*[84] He will send out His angels, and they *will gather* His chosen ones *from the north, south, east, and west, from one end of the sky to the other.*[85]

32 "Learn this lesson from a fig tree: When its branch gets tender and grows leaves, you know summer is near. 33 So also when you see all these things, you know that He is near, at your door.

34 "I tell you the truth: These people will not pass away till all this happens. 35 Heaven and earth will pass away, but what I say will not pass away."

Be Ready!

36 "No one knows about that day or hour, not the angels in heaven, not even the Son, but only the Father.

37 "When the Son of Man comes, it will be like the time of Noah. 38 In the days before the flood, they were eating and drinking, and men and women were marrying till the day *Noah went into the ark.* 39 They learned nothing till *the flood came*[86] and swept them all away.

[78] Dan 9:27; 11:31; 12:11
[79] Dan. 12:1
[80] Deut. 13:1
[81] Is. 13:10; 34:4
[82] Zech. 12:10, 12
[83] Dan. 7:13
[84] Is. 27:13
[85] Deut. 30:4; Zech. 2:6
[86] Gen. 7:6-7

[b] Grk., *understand.* [c] Grk., *the elect.* [d] Grk., *rise.*

K.J.V.

of the Son of man be. 40 Then shall two be in the field; the one shall be taken, and the other left. 41 Two *women shall be* grinding at the mill; the one shall be taken, and the other left.

42 Watch therefore; for ye know not what hour your Lord doth come. 43 But know this, that if the goodman of the house had known in what watch the thief would come, he would have watched, and would not have suffered his house to be broken up. 44 Therefore be ye also ready: for in such an hour as ye think not the Son of man cometh. 45 Who then is a faithful and wise servant, whom his lord hath made ruler over his household, to give them meat in due season? 46 Blessed *is* that servant, whom his lord when he cometh shall find so doing. 47 Verily I say unto you, That he shall make him ruler over all his goods. 48 But and if that evil servant shall say in his heart, My lord delayeth his coming; 49And shall begin to smite *his* fellow servants, and to eat and drink with the drunken; 50 The lord of that servant shall come in a day when he looketh not for *him,* and in an hour that he is not aware of, 51And shall cut him asunder, and appoint *him* his portion with the hypocrites: there shall be weeping and gnashing of teeth.

25 Then shall the kingdom of heaven be likened unto ten virgins, which took their lamps, and went forth to meet the bridegroom. 2And five of them were wise, and five *were* foolish. 3 They that *were* foolish took their lamps, and took no oil with them: 4 But the wise took oil in their vessels with their lamps. 5 While the bridegroom tarried, they all slumbered and slept. 6And at midnight there was a cry made, Behold, the bridegroom cometh; go ye out to meet him. 7 Then all those virgins arose, and trimmed their lamps. 8And the foolish said unto the wise, Give us of your oil; for our lamps are gone out. 9 But the wise answered, saying, *Not so;* lest there be not enough for us and you: but go ye rather to them that sell, and buy for yourselves. 10And while they went to buy, the bridegroom came; and they that were ready went in with him to the marriage: and the door was shut. 11Afterward came also the other virgins, saying, Lord, Lord, open to us. 12 But he answered and said, Verily I say unto you, I know you not. 13 Watch therefore; for ye know neither the day nor the hour wherein the Son of man cometh.

14 For *the kingdom of heaven is* as a man travelling into a far country, *who* called his own servants, and delivered unto them his goods. 15And unto one he gave five talents, to another two, and to another one; to every man according to his several ability; and straightway took his journey. 16 Then he that had received the five talents went and traded with the same, and made *them* other five talents. 17And likewise he that *had received* two, he also gained other two. 18 But he that had received one went and digged

N.A.S.

all away, so shall the coming of the Son of Man be. 40 "Then there shall be two men in the field; one will be taken, and one will be left. 41 "Two women *will be* grinding at the mill; one will be taken, and one will be left. 42 "Therefore be on the alert, for you do not know which day your Lord is coming. 43 "But be sure of this, that if the head of the house had known at what time of the night the thief was coming, he would have been on the alert and would not have allowed his house to be broken into. 44 "For this reason you be ready too; for the Son of Man is coming at an hour when you do not think *He will.*

45 "Who then is the faithful and sensible slave whom his master put in charge of his household to give them their food at the proper time? 46 "Blessed is that slave whom his master finds so doing when he comes. 47 "Truly I say to you, that he will put him in charge of all his possessions. 48 "But if that evil slave says in his heart, 'My master is not coming for a long time,' 49 and shall begin to beat his fellow-slaves and eat and drink with drunkards; 50 the master of that slave will come on a day when he does not expect *him* and at an hour which he does not know, 51 and shall cut him in pieces and assign him a place with the hypocrites; weeping shall be there and the gnashing of teeth.

25 "Then the kingdom of heaven will be comparable to ten virgins, who took their lamps, and went out to meet the bridegroom. 2 "And five of them were foolish, and five were prudent. 3 "For when the foolish took their lamps, they took no oil with them, 4 but the prudent took oil in flasks along with their lamps. 5 "Now while the bridegroom was delaying, they all got drowsy and *began* to sleep. 6 "But at midnight there was a shout, 'Behold, the bridegroom! Come out to meet *him.*' 7 "Then all those virgins arose, and trimmed their lamps. 8 "And the foolish said to the prudent, 'Give us some of your oil, for our lamps are going out.' 9 "But the prudent answered, saying, 'No, there will not be enough for us and you *too;* go instead to the dealers and buy *some* for yourselves.' 10 "And while they were going away to make the purchase, the bridegroom came, and those who were ready went in with him to the wedding feast; and the door was shut. 11 "And later the other virgins also came, saying, 'Lord, Lord, open up for us.' 12 "But he answered and said, 'Truly I say to you, I do not know you.' 13 "Be on the alert then, for you do not know the day nor the hour.

14 "For *it is* just like a man *about* to go on a journey, who called his own slaves, and entrusted his possessions to them. 15 "And to one he gave five talents, to another, two, and to another, one, each according to his own ability; and he went on his journey. 16 "Immediately the one who had received the five talents went and traded with them, and gained five more talents. 17 "In the same manner the one who had *received* the two *talents* gained two more. 18 "But he who received the one *talent* went

WILLIAMS

all away, so it will be at the coming of the Son of Man. 40 Two men will be in the field; one will be taken, one will be left. 41 Two women will be grinding with the handmill; one will be taken, one will be left. 42 So keep on watching, for you do not know on what day your Lord is coming. 43 But be sure of this, that if the master of the house had known in exactly what part of the night the thief would come, he would have been on guard and would not have let his house be broken into. 44 So you, too, must continue to be ready, for at an hour you are not expecting Him the Son of Man will come.

45 "Who then is the faithful and thoughtful slave, whom his master put in charge of his household, to deal out to the members of it their supplies at the proper time? 46 Blessed is that slave if, when his master comes back, he finds him so doing. 47 I solemnly say to you, he will put him in charge of all his property. 48 But if the slave is bad and says to himself, 'My master is going to be gone a long time,' 49 and begins to beat his fellow-slaves, and keeps on eating and drinking with those who get drunk, 50 the master of that slave will come on the very day he is not expecting him, 51 and will cut him in two, and give him his share with the hypocrites, where they will weep and grind their teeth."

25   *Jesus tells the story of the ten brides-maids; the story of the talents; the last judgment*

"Then the kingdom of heaven will be like ten bridesmaids who took their lamps and went out to meet the bridegroom. 2 Now five of them were thoughtless and five were thoughtful. 3 For the thoughtless ones took their lamps but took no oil with them. 4 But the thoughtful ones not only took their lamps but also extra oil in their oilcans. 5 While the bridegroom was delaying, they all got drowsy and dropped off to sleep. 6 But at midnight there was a shout, 'Here comes the bridegroom! Go out to meet him!' 7 Then all those bridesmaids awoke and trimmed their lampwicks. 8 And the thoughtless ones said to the thoughtful ones, 'Give us some of your oil, for our lamps are going out.' 9 But the thoughtful ones answered, 'No, no, there may not be enough for you and us. Go to the store[a] and buy your own oil.' 10 And while they were going to buy it, the bridegroom came, and the bridesmaids that were ready went in with him to the wedding reception; and the door was closed. 11 At last the rest of the bridesmaids came, and kept begging, 'Master, master, open the door for us!' 12 But he answered, 'I positively say to you, I do not know you.' 13 So you must keep on watching, for you do not know either the day or the hour.

14 "For it is just like a man who was going on a long journey from his homeland, who called to him his slaves and turned his property over to them. 15 He gave one five thousand dollars, another two thousand, another one thousand, to each in accordance with his ability. Then he started on his long journey. 16 The man who had received the five thousand dollars at once went out and invested it, and made five thousand more. 17 In the same way the man who had received the two thousand made two thousand more. 18 But the man who

[a] Grk., *the sellers.*

BECK

That's how it will be when the Son of Man comes.

40 "Then there will be two men in the field—one will be taken and the other left. 41 Two women will be grinding at a mill—one will be taken and the other left.

42 "Watch, then, because you don't know which day your Lord is coming. 43 You know if the owner of a house had known what time of the night the burglar was coming, he would have stayed awake and not let anyone break into his house. 44 You, too, get ready, because the Son of Man is coming when you don't expect Him.

45 "Now, who is the faithful and sensible slave whom the Master has put in charge of his servants to give them their food at the right time? 46 Happy is that slave whom his master finds doing this when he comes. 47 I tell you, he will certainly put him in charge of all his property. 48 But if that slave is wicked and says to himself, 'My master is staying a long time,' 49 and starts to beat his fellow slaves and eats and drinks with the drunkards, 50 the master of that slave will come one day when he's not expecting him and at a time he doesn't know and will cut him in pieces and put him with the hypocrites. 51 There they will cry and grind their teeth."

The Bridegroom Is Coming

25   "Then the kingdom of heaven will be like ten girls who took their lamps and went out to meet the bridegroom. 2 Five of them were foolish, and five were wise. 3 The foolish girls brought their lamps, but they took no extra oil. 4 The wise took flasks of oil with their lamps. 5 But the bridegroom delayed, and so they all dozed off to sleep.

6 "At midnight there was a shout, 'Here's the bridegroom! Come out and meet him!' 7 Then all those girls woke up and got their lamps ready.

8 "But the foolish asked the wise, 'Give us some of your oil. Our lamps are going out.'

9 "The wise girls answered, 'There will never be enough for us and for you. Better go to the dealers and buy some for yourselves.'

10 "While they were away buying it, the bridegroom came, and the girls who were ready went with him to the wedding, and the door was shut.

11 "Later the other girls also came and said, 'Lord, lord, open the door for us!'

12 "'I tell you the truth,' he answered them, 'I don't know you.'

13 "Keep awake, then, because you don't know the day or the hour."

Three Kinds of Workers

14 "It's like a man going on a trip. He called his slaves and put his money in their hands. 15 He gave one man $10,000,* another $4,000, and another $2,000, each according to his ability. Then he left.

16 "The one who got $10,000 immediately went and put it into business and made another $10,000. 17 The one who had $4,000 did the same and made another $4,000. 18 But the

* It is hard to estimate the real value of a "talent." It is here taken to be equal to $2,000.

K.J.V.

in the earth, and hid his lord's money. 19After a long time the lord of those servants cometh, and reckoneth with them. 20And so he that had received five talents came and brought other five talents, saying, Lord, thou deliveredst unto me five talents: behold, I have gained beside them five talents more. 21 His lord said unto him, Well done, *thou* good and faithful servant: thou hast been faithful over a few things, I will make thee ruler over many things: enter thou into the joy of thy lord. 22 He also that had received two talents came and said, Lord, thou deliveredst unto me two talents: behold, I have gained two other talents beside them. 23 His lord said unto him, Well done, good and faithful servant; thou hast been faithful over a few things, I will make thee ruler over many things: enter thou into the joy of thy lord. 24 Then he which had received the one talent came and said, Lord, I knew thee that thou art a hard man, reaping where thou hast not sown, and gathering where thou hast not strewed: 25And I was afraid, and went and hid thy talent in the earth: lo, *there* thou hast *that is* thine. 26 His lord answered and said unto him, *Thou* wicked and slothful servant, thou knewest that I reap where I sowed not, and gather where I have not strewed: 27 Thou oughtest therefore to have put my money to the exchangers, and *then* at my coming I should have received mine own with usury. 28 Take therefore the talent from him, and give *it* unto him which hath ten talents. 29 For unto every one that hath shall be given, and he shall have abundance: but from him that hath not shall be taken away even that which he hath. 30And cast ye the unprofitable servant into outer darkness: there shall be weeping and gnashing of teeth.

31 When the Son of man shall come in his glory, and all the holy angels with him, then shall he sit upon the throne of his glory: 32And before him shall be gathered all nations: and he shall separate them one from another, as a shepherd divideth *his* sheep from the goats: 33And he shall set the sheep on his right hand, but the goats on the left. 34 Then shall the King say unto them on his right hand, Come, ye blessed of my Father, inherit the kingdom prepared for you from the foundation of the world: 35 For I was a hungered, and ye gave me meat: I was thirsty, and ye gave me drink: I was a stranger, and ye took me in: 36 Naked, and ye clothed me: I was sick, and ye visited me: I was in prison, and ye came unto me. 37 Then shall the righteous answer him, saying, Lord, when saw we thee a hungered, and fed *thee?* or thirsty, and gave *thee* drink? 38 When saw we thee a stranger, and took *thee* in? or naked, and clothed *thee?* 39 Or when saw we thee sick, or in prison, and came unto thee? 40And the King shall answer and say unto them, Verily I say unto you, Inasmuch as ye have done *it* unto one of the least of these my brethren, ye have done *it* unto me. 41 Then shall he say also unto them on the left hand, Depart from me, ye cursed, into everlasting fire, prepared for the devil and his angels: 42 For I was a hungered, and ye gave me no meat: I was thirsty, and ye gave me no drink:

N.A.S.

away and dug in the ground, and hid his master's money. 19 "Now after a long time the master of those slaves *came and *settled accounts with them. 20 "And the one who had received the five talents came up and brought five more talents, saying, 'Master, you entrusted five talents to me; see, I have gained five more talents.' 21 "His master said to him, 'Well done, good and faithful slave; you were faithful with a few things, I will put you in charge of many things; enter into the joy of your master.' 22 "The one also who had *received* the two talents came up and said, 'Master, you entrusted to me two talents; see, I have gained two more talents.' 23 "His master said to him, 'Well done, good and faithful slave; you were faithful with a few things, I will put you in charge of many things; enter into the joy of your master.' 24 "And the one also who had received the one talent came up and said, 'Master, I knew you to be a hard man, reaping where you did not sow, and gathering where you scattered no *seed.* 25 'And I was afraid, and went away and hid your talent in the ground; see, you have what is yours.' 26 "But his master answered and said to him, 'You wicked, lazy slave, you knew that I reap where I did not sow, and gather where I scattered no *seed?* 27 'Then you ought to have put my money in the bank, and on my arrival I would have received my *money* back with interest. 28 'Therefore take away the talent from him, and give it to the one who has the ten talents.' 29 "For to everyone who has shall *more* be given, and he shall have an abundance; but from the one who does not have, even what he does have shall be taken away. 30 "And cast out the worthless slave into the outer darkness; in that place there shall be weeping and gnashing of teeth.

31 "But when the Son of Man comes in His glory, and all the angels with Him, then He will sit on His glorious throne. 32 "And all the nations will be gathered before Him; and He will separate them from one another, as the shepherd separates the sheep from the goats; 33 and He will put the sheep on His right, and the goats on the left. 34 "Then the King will say to those on His right, 'Come, you who are blessed of My Father, inherit the kingdom prepared for you from the foundation of the world. 35 'For I was hungry, and you gave Me *something* to eat; I was thirsty, and you gave Me drink; I was a stranger, and you invited Me in; 36 naked, and you clothed Me; I was sick, and you visited Me; I was in prison, and you came to Me.' 37 "Then the righteous will answer Him, saying, 'Lord, when did we see You hungry, and feed You, or thirsty, and give You drink? 38 'And when did we see You a stranger, and invite You in, or naked, and clothe You? 39 'And when did we see You sick, or in prison, and come to You?' 40 "And the King will answer and say to them, 'Truly I say to you, to the extent that you did it to one of these brothers of Mine, *even* the least *of them,* you did it to Me.' 41 "Then He will also say to those on His left, 'Depart from Me, accursed ones, into the eternal fire which has been prepared for the devil and his angels; 42 for I was hungry, and you gave Me *nothing* to eat; I was thirsty, and you gave Me nothing to drink;

WILLIAMS

had received the one thousand went off and dug a hole in the ground and buried his master's money. 19After a long time the master of those slaves came back and settled accounts with them. 20 The man who had received the five thousand dollars came up and brought him five thousand more, saying, 'You turned over to me five thousand dollars; here are five thousand more I made.' 21 His master said to him 'Well done, my good and faithful slave, you have been faithful in the use of a small amount; I will put you in charge of a larger one. Come, share your master's joy!' 22 Then the man who had received the two thousand came up and said, 'Master, you turned over to me two thousand dollars; here are two thousand more I made.' 23 His master said to him, 'Well done, my good and faithful slave, you have been faithful in the use of a small amount; I will put you in charge of a larger one. Come, share your master's joy!' 24 Then the man who had received the one thousand came up and said, 'Master, I knew you were a hard man, who reaped where you had not sown, who gathered where you had not threshed. 25 So I was afraid, and went off and buried your thousand dollars in the ground. Here is your money.' 26 His master answered him, 'You wicked, lazy slave, you knew that I reaped where I had not sown and gathered where I had not threshed. 27 So you ought to have deposited my money with the bankers, so that when I came back I could have collected my principal [b] with interest. 28 So take the thousand dollars away from him and give it to him who has ten thousand. 29 For the man who has will have more given to him, even till it overflows, but from the man who has nothing even what he has will be taken away. 30And throw the good-for-nothing slave out into the darkness on the outside, where he will weep and grind his teeth.'

31 "When the Son of Man comes in His splendor, and all the angels with Him, He will take His seat on His splendid throne, 32 and all the nations will be gathered before Him, and He will separate them from one another, just as a shepherd separates his sheep from his goats, 33 and He will put the sheep at His right hand and the goats at his left. 34 Then the King will say to those at His right, 'Come, you who are blessed by my Father, take possession of the kingdom prepared for you from the creation of the world. 35 For when I was hungry, you gave me something to eat, when I was thirsty you gave me something to drink, when I was a stranger you welcomed me to your homes,[c] 36 when I needed clothes you put them on me, when I was sick you looked after me, when I was in prison you came to see me.' 37 Then the upright will answer, 'Lord, when did we ever see you hungry and give you something to eat, or thirsty, and give you something to drink? 38 When did we ever see you a stranger and welcome you to our homes, or needing clothes, and put them on you? 39 When did we ever see you sick or in prison, and come to see you?' 40And the King will answer them, 'I solemnly say to you, every time you did a good deed to one of these most insignificant brothers of mine, you did a good deed to me.'

41 "Then the King will say to those at His left, 'Begone from me, you who are now cursed, to the everlasting fire prepared for the devil and his angels. 42 For when I was hungry you gave me nothing to eat, when I was thirsty you gave

BECK

one who got $2,000 went and dug a hole in the ground and hid his master's money.

19 "After a long time the master of those slaves came and had them give an account. 20 The one who got $10,000 came and brought another $10,000. 'Master,' he said, 'you let me have $10,000. See, I've made another $10,000.'

21 " 'Well done, good and faithful slave!' his master answered him. 'You proved you could be trusted with a little. I will put you in charge of something big. Come and be happy with your master.'

22 "The one who got $4,000 came and said, 'Master, you let me have $4,000. See, I've made another $4,000.'

23 " 'Well done, good and faithful slave!' his master answered him. 'You proved you could be trusted with a little. I will put you in charge of something big. Come and be happy with your master.'

24 "Then came also the one who got $2,000. 'Master' he said, 'I found out you're a hard man. You get grain where you didn't sow, and you gather where you didn't scatter. 25 I was afraid, so I went and hid your $2,000 in the ground. There's your money!'

26 " 'You wicked and lazy slave!' his master answered him. 'You knew I get grain where I didn't sow and gather where I didn't scatter? 27 Then you should have invested my money with the bankers, and when I came back, I could have gotten my money back with interest. 28 Take the $2,000 away from him, and give it to the one who has $10,000. 29 Whoever has anything will receive, and so he will have more and more. And from him who doesn't have what he should have, even what he has will be taken away. 30 Throw this good-for-nothing slave out into the dark where there will be crying and grinding of teeth.' "

Jesus Will Judge the World

31 "When the Son of man *comes* in His glory *and all the* angels *with Him*,[87] then He will sit on His throne of glory. 32And all nations will be gathered before Him, and He will separate them from one another, as a shepherd separates the sheep from the goats, 33 and He will have the sheep stand at His right but the goats at His left.

34 "Then the King will say to those at His right, 'Come, you whom My Father blessed, inherit the kingdom prepared for you from the time the world was made. 35 I was hungry, and you gave Me something to eat; I was thirsty, and you gave Me a drink; I was a stranger, and you took Me into your homes; 36 naked, and you gave Me something to wear; sick, and you looked after Me; in prison, and you visited Me.'

37 "Then the righteous will ask Him, 'Lord, when did we see You hungry and feed You, or thirsty and give You a drink? 38 When did we see You a stranger and take You into our homes, or naked and give you something to wear? 39 When did we see You sick or in prison and visit you?'

40 "And the King will answer them, 'Let Me assure you, anything you did for one of My brothers here, however humble, you did for Me.'

41 "Then He will say to those at His left, 'Go away from Me, you cursed ones, into the everlasting fire prepared for the devil and his angels. 42 I was hungry, and you gave Me nothing to eat; thirsty, and you didn't give Me a

[b] Grk., *property*. [c] Grk., *brought me together with yourselves*.

[87] Zech. 14:5

K.J.V.

43 I was a stranger, and ye took me not in: naked, and ye clothed me not: sick, and in prison, and ye visited me not. 44 Then shall they also answer him, saying, Lord, when saw we thee a hungered, or athirst, or a stranger, or naked, or sick, or in prison, and did not minister unto thee? 45 Then shall he answer them, saying, Verily I say unto you, Inasmuch as ye did *it* not to one of the least of these, ye did *it* not to me. 46And these shall go away into everlasting punishment: but the righteous into life eternal.

26 And it came to pass, when Jesus had finished all these sayings, he said unto his disciples, 2 Ye know that after two days is *the feast of* the passover, and the Son of man is betrayed to be crucified. 3 Then assembled together the chief priests, and the scribes, and the elders of the people, unto the palace of the high priest, who was called Caiaphas, 4And consulted that they might take Jesus by subtilty, and kill *him*. 5 But they said, Not on the feast *day,* lest there be an uproar among the people.

6 Now when Jesus was in Bethany, in the house of Simon the leper, 7 There came unto him a woman having an alabaster box of very precious ointment, and poured it on his head, as he sat at meat. 8 But when his disciples saw *it,* they had indignation, saying, To what purpose *is* this waste? 9 For this ointment might have been sold for much, and given to the poor. 10 When Jesus understood *it,* he said unto them, Why trouble ye the woman? for she hath wrought a good work upon me. 11 For ye have the poor always with you; but me ye have not always. 12 For in that she hath poured this ointment on my body, she did *it* for my burial. 13 Verily I say unto you, Wheresoever this gospel shall be preached in the whole world, *there* shall also this, that this woman hath done, be told for a memorial of her.

14 Then one of the twelve, called Judas Iscariot, went unto the chief priests, 15And said *unto them,* What will ye give me, and I will deliver him unto you? And they covenanted with him for thirty pieces of silver. 16And from that time he sought opportunity to betray him.

17 Now the first *day* of the *feast of* unleavened bread the disciples came to Jesus, saying unto him, Where wilt thou that we prepare for thee to eat the passover? 18And he said, Go into the city to such a man, and say unto him, The Master saith, My time is at hand; I will keep the passover at thy house with my disciples. 19And the disciples did as Jesus had appointed them; and they made ready the passover. 20 Now when the even was come, he sat

N.A.S.

43 I was a stranger, and you did not invite Me in; naked, and you did not clothe Me; sick, and in prison, and you did not visit Me.' 44 "Then they themselves also will answer, saying, 'Lord, when did we see You hungry, or thirsty, or a stranger, or naked, or sick, or in prison, and did not take care of You?' 45 "Then He will answer them, saying, 'Truly I say to you, to the extent that you did not do it to one of the least of these, you did not do it to Me.' 46 "And these will go away into eternal punishment, but the righteous into eternal life."

26 And it came about that when Jesus had finished all these words, He said to His disciples, 2 "You know that after two days the Passover is coming, and the Son of Man is *to be* delivered up for crucifixion." 3 Then the chief priests and the elders of the people were gathered together in the court of the high priest, named Caiaphas; 4 and they plotted together to seize Jesus by stealth, and kill *Him.* 5 But they were saying, "Not during the festival, lest a riot occur among the people."

6 Now when Jesus was in Bethany, at the home of Simon the leper, 7 a woman came to Him with an alabaster vial of very costly perfume, and she poured it upon His head as He reclined *at table.* 8 But the disciples were indignant when they saw *this,* and said, "What is the point of this waste? 9 "For this *perfume* might have been sold for a high price and *the money* given to the poor." 10 But Jesus, aware of this, said to them, "Why do you bother the woman? For she has done a good deed to Me. 11 "For the poor you have with you always; but you do not always have Me. 12 "For when she poured this perfume upon My body, she did it to prepare Me for burial. 13 "Truly I say to you, wherever this gospel is preached in the whole world, what this woman has done shall also be spoken of in memory of her."

14 Then one of the twelve, named Judas Iscariot, went to the chief priests, 15 and said, "What are you willing to give me to deliver Him up to you?" And they weighed out to him thirty pieces of silver. 16And from then on he *began* looking for a good opportunity to betray Him.

17 Now on the first *day* of the *Feast* of Unleavened Bread the disciples came to Jesus, saying, "Where do You want us to prepare for You to eat the Passover?" 18And He said, "Go into the city to a certain man, and say to him, 'The Teacher says, "My time is at hand; I am *to* keep the Passover at your house with My disciples." ' " 19And the disciples did as Jesus had directed them; and they prepared the Passover.

20 Now when evening had come, He was re-

WILLIAMS

me nothing to drink, 43 when I was a stranger you did not welcome me to your homes, when I needed clothes you did not put them on me, when I was sick and in prison, you did not look after me.' 44 Then they will answer, 'Lord, when did we ever see you hungry, or thirsty, or a stranger, or needing clothes, or sick, or in prison, and did not wait on you?' 45 Then He will answer, 'I solemnly say to you, every time you failed to do a good deed to one of these most insignificant people, you failed to do a good deed to me.' 46 Then these will go away to everlasting punishment, but the upright to everlasting life."

26 *They plot to kill Jesus; Judas pointed out as the betrayer; Jesus anointed by Mary; Judas bargains to betray Him; Jesus institutes the memorial supper; foretells that Peter will disown Him; after struggling in Gethsemane He is arrested as Judas betrays Him; tried in Jewish court; disowned by Peter*

When Jesus had ended this discourse, He said to His disciples, 2 "You know that in two days the Passover Feast will take place, and the Son of Man will be turned over to be crucified." 3 Then the high priests and the elders of the people met in the palace of the high priest, whose name was Caiaphas, 4 and plotted to arrest Jesus by stratagem and put Him to death. 5 But they kept saying, "It must not be at the feast, for^a a riot may break out among the people." 6 When Jesus came back to Bethany, to the home of Simon the leper, 7 a woman with an alabaster bottle of very costly perfume came up to Him while He was at table and poured it upon His head. 8 When the disciples saw it, they were very indignant, and said, "Why such waste? 9 Surely it could have been sold for a large sum and the money given to the poor." 10 But Jesus, because He understood them, said to them, "Why do you embarrass^b the woman? She has done a good deed to me, 11 for you always have the poor among you, but you will not always have me. 12 For in putting this perfume on my body she has done it to prepare me for my burial. 13 I solemnly say to you, all over the world wherever this good news is proclaimed, the good deed that she has done will be told, in memory of her." 14 Then one of the Twelve, whose name was Judas Iscariot, went to the high priests, 15 and said, "What will you give me to turn Him over to you?" Then they paid him thirty pieces of silver. 16 So from that time he kept looking for a good opportunity to turn Him over to them. 17 On the first day of the Passover Feast the disciples came to Jesus and said, "Where do you want us to get the Passover supper ready for you to eat?" 18 And He said, "Go into the city, to a certain man, and say to him, 'The Teacher says, "My time is near. I am going to keep the Passover at your house with my disciples."'" 19 So the disciples did as Jesus directed them, and got the Passover supper ready. 20 When evening came, He was sitting at

BECK

drink; 43 a stranger, and you didn't take Me into your homes; naked, and you didn't give Me anything to wear; sick and in prison, and you didn't look after Me.' 44 "Then they, too, will ask, 'Lord, when did we see You hungry or thirsty or a stranger or naked or sick or in prison and didn't help you?' 45 "Then He will answer them, 'I tell you the truth, anything you didn't do for one of these, however humble, you didn't do for Me.' 46 "Then *these* will go away *to everlasting* punishment, but the righteous *to everlasting life.*" [88]

The Plot

26 When Jesus finished saying all this, He told His disciples, 2 "You know that in two days the Passover will be celebrated, and the Son of Man will be handed over to be crucified." 3 Then the ruling priests and the elders of the people met in the palace of the high priest, whose name was Caiaphas. 4 They plotted by some trick to arrest Jesus and kill Him. 5 But they said, "Not in the festival crowd, or there may be a riot among the people."

Mary Anoints Jesus

6 Jesus came to Bethany and went into the home of Simon the leper. 7 There a woman came to Him with an alabaster jar of expensive perfume, and she poured it on His head while He was lying at the table. 8 The disciples saw it and didn't like it. "Why should there be such a waste?" they asked. 9 "This could have been sold for a big sum and the money given to the poor." 10 Knowing what was going on, Jesus asked them, "Why do you trouble the woman? She has done a beautiful thing to Me. 11 The poor you always have with you, but you will not always have Me. 12 She poured this perfume on My body to prepare Me for My burial. 13 I tell you, wherever this good news is preached in the whole world, certainly what she has done will also be told in memory of her."

Judas Plans to Betray Jesus

14 Then one of the twelve, called Judas, the man from Kerioth, went to the high priests. 15 "What will you give me?" he asked. "I will betray Him to you." 16 They *weighed out thirty shekels* of silver*[89] for him. And from then on he was looking for a chance to betray Him.

The Passover

17 On the first of the Passover days of bread without yeast the disciples came to Jesus. "Where do You want us to get things ready for You to eat the Passover?" they asked. 18 "Go into the city," He said, "to a certain man and tell him: 'The Teacher says, "My time is near. I'm going to celebrate the Passover with My disciples at your house."'" 19 The disciples did as Jesus directed them and got the Passover ready. 20 In the evening He lay down with the twelve for the supper.

* A silver shekel weighed as much as our half dollar.
[88] Dan. 12:2
[89] Zech. 11:12

[a] Grk., *lest*. [b] Grk., *trouble*.

K.J.V.

down with the twelve. 21And as they did eat, he said, Verily I say unto you, that one of you shall betray me. 22And they were exceeding sorrowful, and began every one of them to say unto him, Lord, is it I? 23And he answered and said, He that dippeth *his* hand with me in the dish, the same shall betray me. 24 The Son of man goeth as it is written of him: but woe unto that man by whom the Son of man is betrayed! it had been good for that man if he had not been born. 25 Then Judas, which betrayed him, answered and said, Master, is it I? He said unto him, Thou hast said.

26 And as they were eating, Jesus took bread, and blessed *it,* and brake it, *and* gave *it* to the disciples, and said, Take, eat; this is my body. 27And he took the cup, and gave thanks, and gave *it* to them, saying, Drink ye all of it; 28 For this is my blood of the new testament, which is shed for many for the remission of sins. 29 But I say unto you, I will not drink henceforth of this fruit of the vine, until that day when I drink it new with you in my Father's kingdom. 30And when they had sung a hymn, they went out into the mount of Olives. 31 Then saith Jesus unto them, All ye shall be offended because of me this night: for it is written, I will smite the Shepherd, and the sheep of the flock shall be scattered abroad. 32 But after I am risen again, I will go before you into Galilee. 33 Peter answered and said unto him, Though all *men* shall be offended because of thee, *yet* will I never be offended. 34 Jesus said unto him, Verily I say unto thee, That this night, before the cock crow, thou shalt deny me thrice. 35 Peter said unto him, Though I should die with thee, yet will I not deny thee. Likewise also said all the disciples.

36 Then cometh Jesus with them unto a place called Gethsemane, and saith unto the disciples, Sit ye here, while I go and pray yonder. 37And he took with him Peter and the two sons of Zebedee, and began to be sorrowful and very heavy. 38 Then saith he unto them, My soul is exceeding sorrowful, even unto death: tarry ye here, and watch with me. 39And he went a little further, and fell on his face, and prayed, saying, O my Father, if it be possible, let this cup pass from me: nevertheless, not as I will, but as thou *wilt.* 40And he cometh unto the disciples, and findeth them asleep, and saith unto Peter, What, could ye not watch with me one hour? 41 Watch and pray, that ye enter not into temptation: the spirit indeed *is* willing, but the flesh *is* weak. 42 He went away again the second time, and prayed, saying, O my Father, if this cup may not pass away from me, except I drink it, thy will be done. 43And he came and found them asleep

N.A.S.

clining *at table* with the twelve disciples. 21And as they were eating, He said, "Truly I say to you that one of you will betray Me." 22And being deeply grieved, they each one began to say to Him, "Surely not I, Lord?" 23And He answered and said, "He who dipped his hand with Me in the bowl is the one who will betray Me. 24 "The Son of Man *is to* go, just as it is written of Him; but woe to that man through whom the Son of Man is betrayed! It would have been good for that man if he had not been born." 25And Judas, who was betraying Him, answered and said, "Surely it is not I, Rabbi?" He *said to him, "You have said *it* yourself."

26 And while they were eating, Jesus took *some* bread, and after a blessing, He broke it and gave *it* to the disciples, and said, "Take, eat; this is My body." 27And He took a cup and gave thanks, and gave *it* to them, saying, "Drink from it, all of you; 28 for this is My blood of the covenant, which is *to be* shed on behalf of many for forgiveness of sins. 29 "But I say to you, I will not drink of this fruit of the vine from now on until that day when I drink it new with you in My Father's kingdom."

30 And after singing a hymn, they went out to the Mount of Olives.

31 Then Jesus *said to them, "You will all fall away because of Me this night, for it is written, 'I WILL STRIKE DOWN THE SHEPHERD, AND THE SHEEP OF THE FLOCK SHALL BE SCATTERED.' 32 "But after I have been raised, I will go before you to Galilee." 33 But Peter answered and said to Him, "*Even* though all may fall away because of You, I will never fall away." 34 Jesus said to him, "Truly I say to you that this *very* night, before a cock crows, you shall deny Me three times." 35 Peter *said to Him, "Even if I must die with You, I will not deny You." All the disciples said the same thing too.

36 Then Jesus *came with them to a place called Gethsemane, and *said to His disciples, "Sit here while I go over there and pray." 37And He took with Him Peter and the two sons of Zebedee, and began to be grieved and distressed. 38 Then He *said to them, "My soul is deeply grieved, to the point of death; remain here and keep watch with Me." 39And He went a little beyond *them,* and fell on His face and prayed, saying, "My Father, if it is possible, let this cup pass from Me; yet not as I will, but as Thou wilt." 40And He *came to the disciples and *found them sleeping, and *said to Peter, "So, you *men* could not keep watch with Me for one hour? 41 "Keep watching and praying, that you may not enter into temptation; the spirit is willing, but the flesh is weak." 42 He went away again a second time and prayed, saying, "My Father, if this cannot pass away unless I drink it, Thy will be done." 43And He came back and found them sleeping, for their

WILLIAMS

the table with the Twelve. 21And while they were eating, He said, "I solemnly say to you, one of you is going to betray me."

22 They were cut to the bottom of their hearts,c and began to ask one by one, "It cannot be I, can it, Lord?"

23 He answered, "The man who has just dipped his hand with me in the dish is the man who is going to betray me. 24 The Son of Man is going away as the Scriptures say of Him, but a curse will be on that man by whom He is betrayed. It would have been better for that man, if he had never been born!"

25 Then Judas, who afterward betrayed Him, answered by asking, "It cannot be I, can it, Rabbi?"

Jesus answered him, "Yes, you are the man."

26 While they were eating, Jesus took a loaf and blessed it; then He broke it in pieces and gave it to the disciples, and said, "Take this and eat it; this is my body." 27 He also took the cup of wine and gave thanks; then He gave it to them, saying, "All of you drink some of it, 28 for this is my blood which ratifies the covenant, the blood which is to be poured out for many for the forgiveness of their sins. 29 I tell you, I will never again drink the product of the vine till the day when I drink the new wine with you in my Father's kingdom."

30 After singing a hymn, they left the city, and went up the Mount of Olives.

31 Then Jesus said to them, "You will all stumble over me tonight, for the Scripture says, 'I will strike the shepherd, and the sheep of the flock will be scattered.' 32 But after I am raised from the dead, I will go back to Galilee to meet you."

33 Peter answered, "Though all the rest of them stumble over you, I will never do so."

34 Jesus said to him, "I solemnly say to you, this very night, before a cock crows, you will disown me three times."

35 Peter answered, "Even if I have to die with you, I will never disown you."

36 Then Jesus came with them to a place called Gethsemane, and He said to the disciples, "Sit down here while I go over yonder and pray." 37And He took Peter and Zebedee's two sons along with Him and He began to give way to His grief and distress of heart. 38 Then He said to them, "My heart is breaking, it almost kills me! You must stay here and keep watching with me."

39 Then He walked on a few steps and threw Himself upon His face, and in this attitude continued to pray, and say, "My Father, if it is possible, let this cup pass by me; and yet, I pray, not what I want but what you want."

40 Then He came back to the disciples and found them asleep. He said to Peter, "Could you not then watch with me a single hour? 41 You must all keep watching and praying that you may not be exposed to temptation. Man's spirit is willing but human natured is weak."

42 A second time He went away and prayed, "My Father, if it cannot pass by without my drinking it, your will be done." 43 He came back again and found them still sleeping, for their eyes were so heavy they could hardly hold

BECK

"Is It I?"

21 While they were eating, He said: "I tell you the truth: One of you is going to betray Me!"

22 Feeling deeply hurt, they asked Him one by one, "You don't mean me, Lord?"

23 "One who is dipping into the bowl with Me will betray Me!" He answered, 24 "The Son of Man is going away as it is written about Him, but woe to that man who betrays the Son of Man! It would be better for that man if he had never been born."

25 "You don't mean me, Master?" asked Judas, who was going to betray Him.

"I do!" He told him.

The Lord's Supper

26 While they were eating, Jesus took bread and blessed it. He broke it and gave it to the disciples, and said, "Take and eat. This is My body."

27 Then He took a cup and gave thanks. He gave it to them, saying, "Drink of it, all of you. 28 This is My blood of the covenant,90 poured out for all to forgive their sins.

29 "I tell you, I will not drink again of this product of the vine till that day when I drink it with you in a new way in My Father's kingdom."

30 Then they sang a hymn.*

"You Will Deny Me"

They started out for the Mount of Olives.

31 Then Jesus said to them, "Tonight you will all turn against Me. It is written: I will strike down the Shepherd, and the sheep of the flock will be scattered.91 32 But after I have risen, I will go ahead of you to Galilee."

33 "Even if they all turn against You," Peter answered Him, "I'll never turn against You."

34 "I tell you the truth," Jesus told him, "tonight, before the rooster crows, you will deny Me three times."

35 "Even if I have to die with You," Peter told Him, "I'll never deny You!" All the other disciples said the same thing.

Gethsemane

36 Then Jesus went with the disciples to a place called Gethsemane and told them, "Sit down here while I go over there and pray."

37 Taking Peter and Zebedee's two sons with Him, He started to feel sad and troubled. 38 Then He said to them, "I am so full of sorrow92 I am almost dying. Stay here and keep awake with Me."

39 Going ahead a little, He bowed down with His face on the ground and prayed, "My Father, if it is possible, let this cup pass away from Me. But let it not be as I want it but as You want it."

40 Coming to the disciples, He finds them asleep. He says to Peter, "So you couldn't keep awake with Me one hour! 41 Stay awake and pray that you may not be tempted. The spirit is willing, but the flesh is weak."

42 Then He went away a second time and prayed, "My Father, if this cannot pass by without My drinking it, Your will be done."

43 He came again and found them asleep. They couldn't keep their eyes open.

* Perhaps Psalms 115-118.
[90] Ex. 24:8; Jer. 31:32; Zech. 9:11
[91] Zech. 13:7
[92] Ps. 42:5; 43:5

[c] Grk., exceedingly grieved. [d] Grk., flesh.

K.J.V.

again: for their eyes were heavy. 44And he left them, and went away again, and prayed the third time, saying the same words. 45 Then cometh he to his disciples, and saith unto them, Sleep on now, and take *your* rest: behold, the hour is at hand, and the Son of man is betrayed into the hands of sinners. 46 Rise, let us be going: behold, he is at hand that doth betray me.

47 And while he yet spake, lo, Judas, one of the twelve, came, and with him a great multitude with swords and staves, from the chief priests and elders of the people. 48 Now he that betrayed him gave them a sign, saying, Whomsoever I shall kiss, that same is he; hold him fast. 49And forthwith he came to Jesus, and said, Hail, Master; and kissed him. 50And Jesus said unto him, Friend, wherefore art thou come? Then came they, and laid hands on Jesus, and took him. 51And, behold, one of them which were with Jesus stretched out *his* hand, and drew his sword, and struck a servant of the high priest, and smote off his ear. 52 Then said Jesus unto him, Put up again thy sword into his place: for all they that take the sword shall perish with the sword. 53 Thinkest thou that I cannot now pray to my Father, and he shall presently give me more than twelve legions of angels? 54 But how then should the Scriptures be fulfilled, that thus it must be? 55 In that same hour said Jesus to the multitudes, Are ye come out as against a thief with swords and staves for to take me? I sat daily with you teaching in the temple, and ye laid no hold on me. 56 But all this was done, that the Scriptures of the prophets might be fulfilled. Then all the disciples forsook him, and fled.

57 And they that had laid hold on Jesus led *him* away to Caiaphas the high priest, where the scribes and the elders were assembled. 58 But Peter followed him afar off unto the high priest's palace, and went in, and sat with the servants, to see the end. 59 Now the chief priests, and elders, and all the council, sought false witness against Jesus, to put him to death; 60 But found none: yea, though many false witnesses came, *yet* found they none. At the last came two false witnesses, 61And said, This *fellow* said, I am able to destroy the temple of God, and to build it in three days. 62And the high priest arose, and said unto him, Answerest thou nothing? what *is it which* these witness against thee? 63 But Jesus held his peace. And the high priest answered and said unto him, I adjure thee by the living God, that thou tell us whether thou be the Christ, the Son of God. 64 Jesus saith unto him, Thou hast said: nevertheless I say unto you, Hereafter shall ye see the Son of man sitting on the right hand of power, and coming in the clouds of heaven. 65 Then the high priest rent his clothes, saying, He hath spoken blasphemy; what further need have we of witnesses? behold, now ye have heard his blasphemy. 66 What think ye? They answered and said, He is guilty of death. 67 Then did they spit in his face, and buffeted him; and others smote *him* with the palms of their hands, 68 Saying, Prophesy unto us, thou Christ, Who is he that smote thee?

N.A.S.

eyes were heavy. 44And He left them again, and went away and prayed a third time, saying the same thing once more. 45 Then He *came to the disciples, and *said to them, "Are you still sleeping and taking your rest? Behold, the hour is at hand and the Son of Man is being betrayed into the hands of sinners. 46 "Arise, let us be going; behold, the one who betrays Me is at hand!"

47 And while He was still speaking, behold, Judas, one of the twelve, came up, accompanied by a great multitude with swords and clubs, from the chief priests and elders of the people. 48 Now he who was betraying Him gave them a sign, saying, "Whomever I shall kiss, He is the one; seize Him." 49And immediately he came to Jesus and said; "Hail, Rabbi;" and kissed Him. 50And Jesus said to him, "Friend, *do* what you have come for." Then they came and laid hands on Jesus and seized Him. 51And behold, one of those who were with Jesus reached and drew out his sword, and struck the slave of the high priest, and cut off his ear. 52 Then Jesus *said to him, "Put your sword back into its place; for all those who take up the sword shall perish by the sword. 53 "Or do you think that I cannot appeal to My Father, and He will at once put at My disposal more than twelve ° legions of angels? 54 "How then shall the Scriptures be fulfilled, that it must happen this way?" 55At that time Jesus said to the multitudes, "Have you come out with swords and clubs to arrest Me as though *I were* a robber? Every day I used to sit in the temple teaching and you did not seize Me. 56 "But all this has taken place that the Scriptures of the prophets may be fulfilled." Then all the disciples left Him and fled.

57 And those who had seized Jesus led Him away to Caiaphas, the high priest, where the scribes and the elders were gathered together. 58 But Peter also followed Him at a distance as far as the courtyard of the high priest, and entered in, and sat down with the officers to see the outcome. 59 Now the chief priests and the whole Council kept trying to obtain false testimony against Jesus, in order that they might put Him to death; 60 and they did not find it, even though many false witnesses came forward. But later on two came forward, 61 and said, "This man stated, 'I am able to destroy the temple of God and to rebuild it in three days.' " 62And the high priest stood up and said to Him, "Do You make no answer? What is it that these men are testifying against You?" 63 But Jesus kept silent. And the high priest said to Him, "I adjure You by the living God, that You tell us whether You are the Christ, the Son of God." 64 Jesus *said to him, "You have said it *yourself;* nevertheless I tell you, hereafter you shall see THE SON OF MAN SITTING AT THE RIGHT HAND OF POWER, *and* COMING ON THE CLOUDS OF HEAVEN." 65 Then the high priest tore his robes, saying, "He has blasphemed! What further need do we have of witnesses? Behold, you have now heard the blasphemy; 66 what do you think?" They answered and said, "He is deserving of death!" 67 Then they spat in His face and beat Him with their fists, and others slapped Him, 68 and said, "Prophesy to us, You Christ; who is the one who hit You?"

[a] A legion equaled 6,000 troops.

84

WILLIAMS

them open. 44 Then He left them again and prayed the third time, using the same words.[e] 45After that He came back to the disciples and said to them:

"Still sleeping! Still resting! See! The time has come for the Son of Man to be betrayed into the hands of sinful men! 46 Get up and let us be going. Look! Here comes my betrayer!"

47 Even while He was still speaking, here came Judas, one of the Twelve, and with him a crowd, with swords and clubs, from the high priests and the elders of the people. 48 Now His betrayer had given them a signal by saying, "The one I kiss is He. Seize Him!" 49And he went straight up to Jesus and said, "Good evening, Rabbi," and affectionately kissed Him.

50 Jesus said to him, "My friend, do what you came for."

Then they came up, laid hands on Jesus, and arrested Him. 51 One of the men with Jesus put out his hand and drew his sword, and with a thrust at the high priest's slave cut off his ear. 52 Then Jesus said to him, "Put your sword back where it belongs, for all who wield the sword will die by the sword. 53 Do you suppose that I am unable to appeal to my Father and have Him furnish me on the spot one hundred thousand angels? 54 How then could the Scriptures be fulfilled, for they say this is the way it must be?"

55 At that time Jesus said to the crowds: "Have you come out with swords and clubs to arrest me, as though I were a robber? Day after day I used to sit teaching in the temple, and you never laid hands on me. 56 But this has all taken place so that the writings of the prophets may be fulfilled." Then the disciples all forsook Him and made their escape.

57 The men who had laid hands on Jesus took Him away to Caiaphas, the high priest, at whose home the scribes and elders had met. 58And Peter followed Him at a distance as far as the courtyard of the high priest's home; he even went inside and was sitting among the attendants to see how it would end. 59 Now the high priests and the whole council were trying to get false testimony against Jesus, to have Him put to death; 60 but they could not, although many false witnesses came forward to testify.

At last two men came forward 61 and said, "This man said, 'I can tear down the temple of God, and build it again in three days.'"

62 Then the high priest arose and said to Him, "Have you no answer to make? What do you say to the evidence that they bring against you?" 63 But Jesus kept silent. So the high priest said to Him, "I charge you, on your oath, in the name of the living God, tell us whether you are the Christ, the Son of God."

64 Jesus answered him, "Yes, I am. But I tell you, you will all soon see the Son of Man seated at the right hand of the Almighty, and coming on the clouds of the sky."

65 Then the high priest tore his clothes, and said, "He has uttered blasphemy. What more evidence do we need? You have just heard His blasphemy. 66 What do you think now?"

Then they answered, "He deserves to die."

67 After that they spit in His face and hit Him with their fists, and others boxed His ears, 68 saying, "Play the prophet, you Christ, and tell us who struck you."

BECK

44 Leaving them again, He went and prayed the same prayer a third time. 45 Then He came to the disciples. "Are you going to sleep on now and rest?" He asked them. "Now the time has come, and the Son of Man will be betrayed into the hands of sinners. 46 Get up, let us go. Here comes the man to betray Me!"

The Arrest

47 While He was still talking, there came Judas, one of the twelve, and with him a large crowd with swords and clubs, from the ruling priests and elders of the people. 48 The traitor had given them a signal. "The One I kiss," he said, "is the man. Grab Him."

49 Then Judas quickly stepped up to Jesus and said, "Greetings, Master!" and kissed Him.

50 "Friend, what are you here for?" Jesus asked him. Then the others came forward, took hold of Jesus, and arrested Him. 51 One of the men with Jesus reached for his sword and drew it. He struck the high priest's slave and cut off his ear. 52 Then Jesus told him, "Put your sword back in its place. All who take the sword must die by the sword. 53 Or do you think I couldn't call on My Father to send, right now, more than seventy thousand angels to help Me? 54 How, then, could the Bible be true when it says this must happen?"

55 Then Jesus said to the crowd, "You came out to arrest Me with swords and clubs as if I were a robber! Day after day I sat and taught in the temple, and you didn't arrest Me. 56 But all this has happened so that what the prophets have written would come true."

Then all the disciples left Him and ran away.

The First Trial Before the Jewish Court

57 Those who arrested Jesus took Him to Caiaphas, the high priest, where the Bible scholars and the elders had been called together. 58 Peter followed Him at a distance till he came to the high priest's courtyard. Going inside, he sat with the attendants to see how this would end.

59 The ruling priests and the whole Jewish court tried to get false testimony against Jesus in order to kill Him 60 but didn't find any, although many came forward to give false testimony. At last two men came forward, 61 saying, "He said, 'I can tear down God's temple and build it in three days.'"

62 The high priest got up and asked Him, "Don't You have anything to say to this? What are these men testifying against You?"

But Jesus was silent.

63 Then the high priest said to Him, "Swear by the living God, and tell us, are You the promised Savior, the Son of God?"

64 "I am," Jesus answered him. "But I tell you, from now on you will all see *the Son of Man sitting at the right hand of* power and *coming on the clouds of heaven.*" [93]

65 Then the high priest tore his robes. "He has blasphemed!" he declared. "Why do we need any more witnesses? You just heard the blasphemy. 66 What's your verdict?"

"He must die!" they answered.

67 Then they spit in His face, struck Him with their fists, and some slapped Him, 68 saying, "Prophesy, You Christ, and tell us: Who hit You?"

---

[e] Grk., *saying the same word.*

[93] Ps. 110:1; Dan. 7:13

K.J.V.

69 Now Peter sat without in the palace: and a damsel came unto him, saying, Thou also wast with Jesus of Galilee. 70 But he denied before *them* all, saying, I know not what thou sayest. 71And when he was gone out into the porch, another *maid* saw him, and said unto them that were there, This *fellow* was also with Jesus of Nazareth. 72And again he denied with an oath, I do not know the man. 73And after a while came unto *him* they that stood by, and said to Peter, Surely thou also art *one* of them; for thy speech bewrayeth thee. 74 Then began he to curse and to swear, *saying,* I know not the man. And immediately the cock crew. 75And Peter remembered the word of Jesus, which said unto him, Before the cock crow, thou shalt deny me thrice. And he went out, and wept bitterly.

27 When the morning was come, all the chief priests and elders of the people took counsel against Jesus to put him to death: 2And when they had bound him, they led *him* away, and delivered him to Pontius Pilate the governor.

3 Then Judas, which had betrayed him, when he saw that he was condemned, repented himself, and brought again the thirty pieces of silver to the chief priests and elders, 4 Saying, I have sinned in that I have betrayed the innocent blood. And they said, What *is that* to us? see thou *to that.* 5And he cast down the pieces of silver in the temple, and departed, and went and hanged himself. 6And the chief priests took the silver pieces, and said, It is not lawful for to put them into the treasury, because it is the price of blood. 7And they took counsel, and bought with them the potter's field, to bury strangers in. 8 Wherefore that field was called, The field of blood, unto this day. 9 Then was fulfilled that which was spoken by Jeremy the prophet, saying, And they took the thirty pieces of silver, the price of him that was valued, whom they of the children of Israel did value; 10And gave them for the potter's field, as the Lord appointed me. 11And Jesus stood before the governor: and the governor asked him, saying, Art thou the King of the Jews? And Jesus said unto him, Thou sayest. 12And when he was accused of the chief priests and elders, he answered nothing. 13 Then said Pilate unto him, Hearest thou not how many things they witness against thee? 14And he answered him to never a word; insomuch that the governor marvelled greatly. 15 Now at *that* feast the governor was wont to release unto the people a prisoner, whom they would. 16And they had then a notable prisoner, called Barabbas. 17 Therefore when they were gathered together, Pilate said unto them, Whom will ye that I release unto you? Barabbas, or Je-

N.A.S.

69 Now Peter was sitting outside in the courtyard, and a certain servant-girl came to him and said, "You too were with Jesus the Galilean." 70 But he denied *it* before them all, saying, "I do not know what you are talking about." 71And when he had gone out to the gateway, another *servant-girl* saw him and *said to those who were there, "This man was with Jesus of Nazareth." 72And again he denied *it* with an oath, "I do not know the man." 73And a little later the bystanders came up and said to Peter, "Surely you too are *one* of them; for the way you talk gives you away." 74 Then he began to curse and swear, "I do not know the man!" And immediately a cock crowed. 75And Peter remembered the word which Jesus had said, "Before a cock crows, you will deny Me three times." And he went out and wept bitterly.

27 Now when morning had come, all the chief priests and the elders of the people took counsel against Jesus to put Him to death; 2 and they bound Him, and led Him away, and delivered Him up to Pilate the governor.

3 Then when Judas, who had betrayed Him, saw that He had been condemned, he felt remorse and returned the thirty pieces of silver to the chief priests and elders, 4 saying, "I have sinned by betraying innocent blood." But they said, "What is that to us? See *to that* yourself!" 5And he threw the pieces of silver into the sanctuary and departed; and he went away and hung himself. 6 And the chief priests took the pieces of silver and said, "It is not lawful to put them into the temple treasury, since it is the price of blood." 7And they counseled together and with the money bought the Potter's Field as a burial place for strangers. 8 For this reason that field has been called the Field of Blood to this day. 9 Then that which was spoken through Jeremiah the prophet was fulfilled, saying, "AND THEY TOOK THE THIRTY PIECES OF SILVER, THE PRICE OF THE ONE WHOSE PRICE HAD BEEN SET BY THE CHILDREN OF ISRAEL; 10 AND THEY GAVE THEM FOR THE POTTER'S FIELD, AS THE LORD DIRECTED ME."

11 Now Jesus stood before the governor, and the governor questioned Him, saying, "Are You the King of the Jews?" And Jesus said to him, "*It is as* you say." 12And while He was being accused by the chief priests and elders, He made no answer. 13 Then Pilate *said to Him, "Do You not hear how many things they testify against You?" 14And He did not answer him with regard to even a single charge, so that the governor was quite amazed. 15 Now at *the* feast the governor was accustomed to release for the multitude *any* one prisoner whom they wanted. 16And they were holding at that time a notorious prisoner, called Barabbas. 17 When therefore they were gathered together, Pilate said to them, "Whom do you want me to release for you? Barabbas, or Jesus who is

WILLIAMS

69 Now Peter was sitting outside in the court-yard, and a waiting-girl came up to him, and said, "You, too, were with Jesus the Galilean."
70 But he denied it before them all, and said, "I do not understand what you mean."
71 Then he went out into the gateway, and another waiting-girl saw him, and said to those there, "This fellow was with Jesus the Nazarene."
72 Again he denied it, and even swore, "I do not know the man!"
73 A few minutes afterward the bystanders came up to Peter and said, "You are surely one of them, too, for your accent gives you away."
74 Then he commenced cursing and swearing, "I do not know the man!" And at once a cock crowed. 75 Then Peter remembered Jesus' words, "Before a cock crows, you will disown me three times." And he went outside and wept bitterly.

27 *Jesus turned over to the Roman court; Judas commits suicide; Jesus tried in the Roman court; mocked; crucified; buried*

As soon as day broke, all the high priests and elders held a consultation against Jesus, to put Him to death. 2 So they bound Him, led Him away, and turned Him over to Pilate the governor.
3 Then Judas, who had betrayed Him, as he felt condemned, in remorse brought back the thirty pieces to the high priests and elders, 4 and said, "I did wrong in turning an inno-cent* man over to death."
But they said, "What is that to us? You must see to that yourself."
5 Then he tossed the money into the temple and left, and went off and hanged himself.
6 The high priests picked up the money and said, "It is not legal to put it into the conse-crated treasury, for it is blood-money." 7 So after consultation they bought with it the Pot-ter's Field as a burying-ground for strangers. 8 Now this piece of ground has ever since been called, "The Field of Blood." 9 In that way the words spoken by the prophet Jeremiah were fulfilled: "They took the thirty pieces of silver, the price of the one whose price had been fixed by some Israelites, 10 and gave them for the Potter's Field, as the Lord directed me."
11 Now Jesus stood before the governor, and the governor asked Him, "Are you the king of the Jews?"
Jesus answered, "Yes." 12 And while the charges were being made against Him by the high priests and elders, He made no answer.
13 Then Pilate said to Him, "Do you not hear how strong is the evidence they are bring-ing against you?" 14 But He did not answer him a single word, so that the governor was dumfounded beyond expression.
15 Now at the feast the governor was accus-tomed to set any prisoner free whom the people wanted. 16 At that time they had a notorious prisoner named Barabbas. 17 So when they met for this purpose, Pilate asked them, "Which one do you want me to set free, Barabbas, or

BECK

Peter Denies Jesus

69 Peter was sitting out in the courtyard. A maid came to him, saying, "You, too, were with Jesus, the Galilean."
70 But he denied it in front of all of them: "I don't know what you're talking about."
71 As he went out to the entrance, another maid saw him. "He was with Jesus from Naza-reth," she told those who were there.
72 Again Peter denied, and he swore, "I don't know the Man!"
73 After a little while the men who were standing there came and told Peter, "Sure, you're one of them. Anyone can tell by the way you talk."
74 Then he started to curse and swear, "I don't know the Man!" 75 Just then the rooster crowed, and Peter remembered Jesus saying, "Before the rooster crows, you will deny Me three times." And he went outside and cried bitterly.

The End of Judas

27 In the morning all the ruling priests and the elders of the people decided to kill Jesus. 2 They bound Him, led Him away, and handed Him over to Pilate, the governor.
3 When Judas, who betrayed Him, saw that Jesus was condemned, he felt sorry and brought the thirty shekels of silver back to the high priests and elders. 4 "I have sinned," he said. "I have betrayed innocent blood."
"What do we care about that?" they asked. "See to it yourself."
5 Then he threw the money into the temple and left. He went away and hanged himself.
6 The high priests took the money. "It isn't right to put this into the temple treasury," they said; "it's blood money." 7 So they decided to buy with it the potter's field for the burial of strangers. 8 That's why that field has ever since been called the Field of Blood. 9 Then what the prophet Jeremiah said came true: *I took the thirty shekels of silver, the price of Him on whom some men of Israel set a price, 10 and I gave them for the potter's field, as the Lord directed me.*[94]

Before Pilate

11 Jesus stood before the governor. "Are You the King of the Jews?" the governor asked Him. "Yes," Jesus answered.
12 While the ruling priests and elders were accusing Him, He said nothing. 13 Then Pilate asked Him, "Don't You hear how many accusa-tions they are bringing against You?"
14 But Jesus didn't answer him in regard to anything that was said, so that the governor was very much surprised.

Barabbas

15 Now, at every festival the governor used to free one prisoner whom the crowd wanted. 16 Just then there was a well-known robber by the name of Barabbas. 17 When the people had gathered, Pilate asked them, "Whom do you want me to set free for you, Barabbas or Jesus,

[a] Grk., *innocent blood.*

[94] Zech. 11:12-13; Jer. 32:6-9

K.J.V.

sus which is called Christ? 18 For he knew that for envy they had delivered him.

19 When he was set down on the judgment seat, his wife sent unto him, saying, Have thou nothing to do with that just man: for I have suffered many things this day in a dream because of him. 20 But the chief priests and elders persuaded the multitude that they should ask Barabbas, and destroy Jesus. 21 The governor answered and said unto them, Whether of the twain will ye that I release unto you? They said, Barabbas. 22 Pilate saith unto them, What shall I do then with Jesus which is called Christ? *They* all say unto him, Let him be crucified. 23 And the governor said, Why, what evil hath he done? But they cried out the more, saying, Let him be crucified.

24 When Pilate saw that he could prevail nothing, but *that* rather a tumult was made, he took water, and washed *his* hands before the multitude, saying, I am innocent of the blood of this just person: see ye *to it*. 25 Then answered all the people, and said, His blood *be* on us, and on our children.

26 Then released he Barabbas unto them: and when he had scourged Jesus, he delivered *him* to be crucified. 27 Then the soldiers of the governor took Jesus into the common hall, and gathered unto him the whole band *of soldiers*. 28 And they stripped him, and put on him a scarlet robe.

29 And when they had platted a crown of thorns, they put *it* upon his head, and a reed in his right hand: and they bowed the knee before him, and mocked him, saying, Hail, King of the Jews! 30 And they spit upon him, and took the reed, and smote him on the head. 31 And after that they had mocked him, they took the robe off from him, and put his own raiment on him, and led him away to crucify *him*. 32 And as they came out, they found a man of Cyrene, Simon by name: him they compelled to bear his cross. 33 And when they were come unto a place called Golgotha, that is to say, a place of a skull,

34 They gave him vinegar to drink mingled with gall: and when he had tasted *thereof*, he would not drink. 35 And they crucified him, and parted his garments, casting lots: that it might be fulfilled which was spoken by the prophet, They parted my garments among them, and upon my vesture did they cast lots. 36 And sitting down they watched him there; 37 And set up over his head his accusation written, THIS IS JESUS THE KING OF THE JEWS. 38 Then were there two thieves crucified with him; one on the right hand, and another on the left.

39 And they that passed by reviled him, wagging their heads, 40 And saying, Thou that destroyest the temple, and buildest *it* in three days, save thyself. If thou be the Son of God, come down from the cross. 41 Likewise also the chief priests mocking *him*, with the scribes and elders, said, 42 He saved others; himself he cannot save. If he be the King of Israel, let him now come down from the cross, and we will believe him. 43 He trusted in God; let him deliver him now, if he will have him: for he said, I am the Son

N.A.S.

called Christ?" 18 For he knew that because of envy they had delivered Him up. 19 And while he was sitting on the judgment-seat, his wife sent to him, saying, "Have nothing to do with that righteous Man; for last night I suffered greatly in a dream because of Him." 20 But the chief priests and the elders persuaded the multitudes to ask for Barabbas, and to put Jesus to death. 21 But the governor answered and said to them, "Which of the two do you want me to release for you?" And they said, "Barabbas." 22 Pilate *said to them, "What then shall I do with Jesus who is called Christ?" They all *said, "Let Him be crucified!" 23 And he said, "Why, what evil has He done?" But they kept shouting all the more, saying, "Let Him be crucified!" 24 And when Pilate saw that he was accomplishing nothing, but rather that a riot was starting, he took water and washed his hands in front of the multitude, saying, "I am innocent of this Man's blood; see *to that* yourselves." 25 And all the people answered and said, "His blood *be* on us and on our children!" 26 Then he released Barabbas for them; but Jesus he scourged and delivered over to be crucified.

27 Then the soldiers of the governor took Jesus into the Praetorium and gathered the whole *Roman* cohort around Him. 28 And they stripped Him, and put a scarlet robe on Him. 29 And after weaving a crown of thorns, they put it on His head, and a reed in His right hand; and they kneeled down before Him and mocked Him, saying, "Hail, King of the Jews!" 30 And they spat on Him, and took the reed and *began* to beat Him on the head. 31 And after they had mocked Him, they took His robe off and put His garments on Him, and led Him away to crucify *Him*.

32 And as they were coming out, they found a certain Cyrenian named Simon; this man they pressed into service to bear His cross.

33 And when they had come to a place called Golgotha, which means Place of a Skull, 34 THEY GAVE HIM WINE TO DRINK MINGLED WITH GALL; and after tasting *it*, He was unwilling to drink. 35 And when they had crucified Him, THEY DIVIDED UP HIS GARMENTS AMONG THEMSELVES, CASTING LOTS; 36 and sitting down, they *began* to keep watch over Him there. 37 And they put up above His head the charge against Him which read, "THIS IS JESUS THE KING OF THE JEWS." 38 At that time two robbers *were crucified with Him, one on the right and one on the left. 39 And those who were passing by were hurling abuse at Him, WAGGING THEIR HEADS, 40 and saying, "You who destroy the temple and rebuild it in three days, save Yourself! If You are the Son of God, come down from the cross." 41 In the same way the chief priests, along with the scribes and elders, were mocking *Him*, and saying, 42 "He saved others; He cannot save Himself. He is the King of Israel; let Him now come down from the cross, and we shall believe in Him. 43 HE TRUSTS IN GOD; LET HIM DELIVER *Him* now, IF HE TAKES PLEASURE IN HIM; for He

WILLIAMS

Jesus, the so-called Christ?" 18 For he knew that they had turned Him over to the court out of envy.

19 Now while he was on the bench, his wife sent him this word, "Do not have anything to do with that righteous man, for I have this morning suffered excruciating pain in a dream caused by Him."

20 But the high priests and the elders lined up the crowds to ask for Barabbas, and to have Jesus put to death. 21 Still the governor answered, "Which of the two do you want me to set free for you?"

And they said, "Barabbas."

22 Pilate asked them, "What then shall I do with Jesus, the so-called Christ?"

They all answered, "Have Him crucified!"

23 He asked, "Why, what has He done that is wrong?"

But they kept on shouting louder and louder, "Have Him crucified!"

24 So Pilate, since he saw that he was making no headway with them, but that a riot was about to break out instead, took some water and washed his hands before the crowd, and said, "I am not responsible for this man's death; you must see to it yourselves."

25 And all the people answered, "His blood be on us and on our children!" 26 Then he set Barabbas free for them, but had Jesus flogged and turned over to be crucified.

27 Then the governor's soldiers took Jesus into the barracks, and gathered about Him the whole battalion. 28 Then they stripped Him, and put a purple cloak on Him, 29 and made a crown of thorns and set it on His head, and they put a stick in His hand, and kneeling before Him they made sport of Him, saying, "All hail, you king of the Jews!" 30 And they spit on Him, and took the stick and kept hitting Him on the head. 31And when they had finished making sport of Him, they took off the cloak, and put His own clothes back on Him, and led Him away to be crucified.

32 As they were going out of the city, they found a Cyrenian named Simon, and they forced him to carry Jesus' cross. 33 When they came to a place called Golgotha, which means the Place of the Skull, 34 they gave Him some wine mixed with gall, but when He tasted it, He would not drink it. 35 Then they crucified Him and divided among them His clothes by drawing lots, 36 and sitting down they kept watch of Him there. 37 They put above His head the charge against Him, which read:

THIS IS JESUS, THE KING OF THE JEWS."

38 At the same time two robbers were crucified with Him, one at His right and one at His left. 39And the passers-by kept hissing at Him, shaking their heads 40 and saying, "You who would tear down the temple and build another in three days, save yourself! If you are really the Son of God, come down from the cross."

41 And the high priests, too, made sport of Him, with the scribes and elders, and said, 42 "He saved others but He cannot save Himself. He is the king of Israel, is He? Well, let Him come down from the cross, and we will believe in Him. 43 He has put His trust in God; let God deliver Him now, if He cares for Him,

BECK

who is called Christ?" 18 He knew they had handed Jesus over to him because they were jealous.

19 While he was sitting on the judge's seat, his wife sent someone to tell him, "Let that righteous Man alone. I suffered much in a dream last night on account of Him."

20 But the ruling priests and elders persuaded the people to ask for Barabbas and kill Jesus. 21 "Which of the two," the governor asked them, "do you want me to set free for you?" They said, "Barabbas."

22 "Then what should I do with Jesus, who is called Christ?" Pilate asked them.

"He must be crucified!" all of them said.

23 "Why, what wrong has He done?" he asked.

But they kept yelling all the louder, "He must be crucified!"

24 When he saw he wasn't getting anywhere, but a riot was breaking out instead, Pilate took water and washed his hands before the crowd. "I am innocent of this One's blood," he said. "See to it yourselves!"

25 And all the people answered, "His blood be on us and on our children."

26 Then he freed Barabbas for them, but Jesus he scourged and handed over to be crucified.

"Hail, King!"

27 Then the governor's soldiers took Jesus into the governor's palace and gathered the whole troop of soldiers around Him. 28 They took off His clothes and put a scarlet cloak on Him. 29 They twisted some thorns into a crown, placed it on His head, and put a stick in His right hand. Then they knelt before Him and mocked Him, saying, "Hail, King of the Jews!" 30 They spit on Him, took the stick, and hit Him on the head.

"They Crucified Him"

31 After mocking Him, they took off the cloak and put His own clothes on Him. Then they took Him away to crucify Him.

32 Going out, they found a man from Cyrene by the name of Simon. They forced him to carry His cross.

33 They came to a place called Golgotha, which means Skull Place. 34 *They offered Him a drink* of wine, mixed with *gall*,[95] but when He tasted it, He refused to drink it. 35 They crucified Him. And *they divided His clothes among them by throwing lots.*[96] 36 Then they sat down there and kept watch over Him. 37 They put above His head a notice stating why He was being punished. It read: THIS IS JESUS, THE KING OF THE JEWS. 38 Then they crucified two robbers with Him, one at His right and the other at His left.

39 Those who passed by abused Him, *shaking their heads*[97] 40 and saying, "You tear down the temple and build it in three days—save Yourself, if You are God's Son, and come down from the cross." 41 The ruling priests, with the Bible scholars and elders, mocked Him in the same way, saying, "He saved others—but He cannot save Himself. 42 He's King of Israel— He should come down from the cross now, and we'll believe Him. 43 *He trusts God—God deliver Him now seeing He delights in Him.*[98] He

[95] Ps. 69:21
[96] Ps. 22:18
[97] Ps. 109:25
[98] Ps. 22:8

K.J.V.

of God. 44 The thieves also, which were crucified with him, cast the same in his teeth. 45 Now from the sixth hour there was darkness over all the land unto the ninth hour. 46And about the ninth hour Jesus cried with a loud voice, saying, Eli, Eli, lama sabachthani? that is to say, My God, my God, why hast thou forsaken me? 47 Some of them that stood there, when they heard *that*, said, This *man* calleth for Elias. 48And straightway one of them ran, and took a sponge, and filled *it* with vinegar, and put *it* on a reed, and gave him to drink. 49 The rest said, Let be, let us see whether Elias will come to save him.

50 Jesus, when he had cried again with a loud voice, yielded up the ghost. 51And, behold, the vail of the temple was rent in twain from the top to the bottom; and the earth did quake, and the rocks rent; 52And the graves were opened; and many bodies of the saints which slept arose, 53And came out of the graves after his resurrection, and went into the holy city, and appeared unto many. 54 Now when the centurion, and they that were with him, watching Jesus, saw the earthquake, and those things that were done, they feared greatly, saying, Truly this was the Son of God. 55And many women were there beholding afar off, which followed Jesus from Galilee, ministering unto him: 56Among which was Mary Magdalene, and Mary the mother of James and Joses, and the mother of Zebedee's children. 57 When the even was come, there came a rich man of Arimathea, named Joseph, who also himself was Jesus' disciple: 58 He went to Pilate, and begged the body of Jesus. Then Pilate commanded the body to be delivered. 59And when Joseph had taken the body, he wrapped it in a clean linen cloth, 60And laid it in his own new tomb, which he had hewn out in the rock: and he rolled a great stone to the door of the sepulchre, and departed. 61And there was Mary Magdalene, and the other Mary, sitting over against the sepulchre.

62 Now the next day, that followed the day of the preparation, the chief priests and Pharisees came together unto Pilate, 63 Saying, Sir, we remember that that deceiver said, while he was yet alive, After three days I will rise again. 64 Command therefore that the sepulchre be made sure until the third day, lest his disciples come by night, and steal him away, and say unto the people, He is risen from the dead: so the last error shall be worse than the first. 65 Pilate said unto them, Ye have a watch: go your way, make *it* as sure as ye can. 66 So they went, and made the sepulchre sure, sealing the stone, and setting a watch.

N.A.S.

said, 'I am the Son of God.'" 44And the robbers also who had been crucified with Him were casting the same insult at Him.

45 Now from the [a]sixth hour darkness fell upon all the land until the [b]ninth hour. 46 And about the ninth hour Jesus cried out with a loud voice, saying, "ELI, ELI LAMA SABACH-THANI?" that is, "MY GOD, MY GOD, WHY HAST THOU FORSAKEN ME?" 47And some of those who were standing there, when they heard it, *began* saying, "This man is calling for Elijah." 48And immediately one of them ran, and taking a sponge, he filled it with sour wine, and put it on a reed, and gave Him a drink. 49 But the rest *of them* said, "Let us see whether Elijah will come to save Him."[c] 50And Jesus cried out again with a loud voice, and yielded up *His* spirit. 51And behold, the curtain of the temple was torn in two from top to bottom, and the earth shook; and the rocks were split, 52 and the tombs were opened; and many bodies of the saints who had fallen asleep were raised; 53 and coming out of the tombs after His resurrection they entered the holy city and appeared to many. 54 Now the centurion, and those who were with him keeping guard over Jesus, when they saw the earthquake and the things that were happening, became very frightened and said, "Truly this was a son of God!" 55And many women were there looking on from a distance, who had followed Jesus from Galilee, ministering to Him; 56 among whom was Mary Magdalene, *along with* Mary the mother of James and Joseph, and the mother of the sons of Zebedee.

57 And when it was evening, there came a rich man from Arimathea, named Joseph, who himself had also become a disciple of Jesus. 58 This man came to Pilate and asked for the body of Jesus. Then Pilate ordered *it* to be given over *to him*. 59And Joseph took the body and wrapped it in a clean linen cloth, 60 and laid it in his own new tomb, which he had hewn out in the rock; and he rolled a large stone against the entrance of the tomb and went away. 61And Mary Magdalene was there, and the other Mary, sitting opposite the grave.

62 Now on the next day, which is *the one* after [d]the preparation, the chief priests and the Pharisees gathered together with Pilate, 63 and said, "Sir, we remember that when he was still alive that deceiver said, 'After three days I *am to* rise again.' 64 "Therefore, give orders for the grave to be made secure until the third day, lest the disciples come and steal Him away and say to the people, 'He has risen from the dead,' and the last deception will be worse than the first." 65 Pilate said to them, "You have a guard; go, make it *as* secure as you know how." 66And they went and made the grave secure, and along with the guard they set a seal on the stone.

[a] I.e., noon. [b] I.e., 3 p.m. [c] Some early mss. add: *And another took a spear and pierced His side, and there came out water and blood.* (cf. John 19:34). [d] Or, *Friday.*

WILLIAMS

for He said, 'I am the Son of God.' " 44 Even the robbers who were crucified with Him made sport of Him in the same way.

45 Now from twelve o'clock till three, darkness covered the whole land. 46About three Jesus cried out with a loud voice, *"Eloi, Eloi, lama sabachthani?"* which means, "My God! My God! why have you forsaken me?"

47 Some of the bystanders, when they heard it, said, "He is calling for Elijah." 48 So one of them at once ran off and took a sponge and soaked it in vinegar, put it on a stick and held it up to Him to drink.

49 But the others said, "Wait; let us see if Elijah does come to deliver Him."

50 But Jesus cried out again with a loud voice, and gave up His spirit. 51And at once the curtain of the sanctuary was torn from top to bottom, the earth shook, the rocks were split, 52 the tombs were opened, and many bodies of saints then sleeping in death[b] rose 53 and left their tombs, and after His resurrection went into the holy city and appeared to many people.

54 And the army captain and his men, who were keeping guard over Jesus, who felt the earthquake and saw all that was taking place, were terribly frightened, and said, "Surely this was God's Son."

55 Now several women were there looking on from a distance, who accompanied Jesus from Galilee to care for Him, 56 among them Mary of Magdala, Mary the mother of James and Joseph, and the mother of Zebedee's sons.

57 Although it was now evening, a rich man named Joseph, from Arimathea, who was himself a disciple of Jesus, 58 came to Pilate and asked for Jesus' body. Then Pilate ordered it to be given to him. 59 So Joseph took the body and wrapped it in clean linen, 60 and laid it in a tomb of his, which he had cut out of the rock, and he rolled a big boulder over the doorway of the tomb, and went away. 61And Mary of Magdala and the other Mary kept sitting there in front of the tomb.

62 On the next day, which is the day after the Preparation Day, the high priests and Pharisees met and went in a body to Pilate, 63 and said, "Sir, we remember that that pretender said while He was living, 'After three days I will rise again.' 64 Issue an order then to have the tomb closely guarded, so that His disciples cannot come and steal Him and tell the people that He rose from the dead, and the last deception be worse than the first."

65 Pilate said to them, "Take the military guard and go and make it as secure as you can." 66 So off they went and made the tomb secure by sealing the boulder and setting a guard.

BECK

said, 'I am God's Son.' " 44 In the same way also the robbers crucified with Him insulted Him.

Jesus Dies

45 At twelve o'clock darkness came over the whole country and lasted until three in the afternoon. 46About three o'clock Jesus called out loud, *"Eli, Eli, lema, sabachthani?"* [99] which means, "My God, My God, why did You forsake Me?" 47 Hearing Him some of those standing there said, "He's calling Elijah." 48And just then one of the men ran, took a sponge, soaked it in *sour wine*, put it on a stick, and *gave Him a drink.* [95] 49 The others said, "Let's see if Elijah comes to save Him."

50 But Jesus called out loud again and gave up His spirit. 51 Just then the curtain in the temple was torn in two from top to bottom, the earth was shaken, the rocks were split, 52 the graves were opened, and many bodies of the holy people asleep in death were brought back to life; 53 they came out of the graves and after He had risen went into the holy city, where many saw them. 54 Now, when the captain and those watching Jesus with him saw the earthquake and the other things happening, they were terrified. "He certainly was the Son of God," they said.

55 There were many women watching *from a distance.* [100] They had followed Jesus from Galilee to help Him. 56Among them were Mary from Magdala and Mary, the mother of James and Joseph, and the mother of Zebedee's sons.

Jesus Is Buried

57 In the evening there came a rich man from Arimathea by the name of Joseph, who had also become a disciple of Jesus. 58 He went to Pilate and asked for Jesus' body. Then Pilate ordered it given to him.

59 Joseph took the body, wrapped it in some clean linen cloth, 60 and laid it in his own unused grave that he had cut in the rock. After rolling a big stone against the door of the grave, he went away. 61 Mary from Magdala and the other Mary were there, sitting opposite the grave.

The Guard

62 The next day—the Saturday after the day of preparation—the ruling priests and Pharisees met with Pilate. 63 "Sir," they said, "we remember how that deceiver said while He was still alive, 'On the third day I will rise.' 64 Now, order the grave to be made secure till the third day, or His disciples may come and steal Him and tell the people, 'He rose from the dead.' Then the last deception will be worse than the first."

65 "Take a guard," Pilate told them; "go and make it as secure as you know how."

66 So they went and secured the grave by sealing the stone and setting the guard.

[b] Grk., *sleeping.*

[99] Ps. 22:1
[100] Ps. 38:11

K.J.V.

28 In the end of the sabbath, as it began to dawn toward the first *day* of the week, came Mary Magdalene and the other Mary to see the sepulchre. 2And, behold, there was a great earthquake: for the angel of the Lord descended from heaven, and came and rolled back the stone from the door, and sat upon it. 3 His countenance was like lightning, and his raiment white as snow: 4And for fear of him the keepers did shake, and became as dead *men*. 5And the angel answered and said unto the women, Fear not ye: for I know that ye seek Jesus, which was crucified. 6 He is not here: for he is risen, as he said. Come, see the place where the Lord lay. 7And go quickly, and tell his disciples that he is risen from the dead; and, behold, he goeth before you into Galilee; there shall ye see him: lo, I have told you. 8And they departed quickly from the sepulchre with fear and great joy; and did run to bring his disciples word.

9 And as they went to tell his disciples, behold, Jesus met them, saying, All hail. And they came and held him by the feet, and worshipped him. 10 Then said Jesus unto them, Be not afraid: go tell my brethren that they go into Galilee, and there shall they see me.

11 Now when they were going, behold, some of the watch came into the city, and shewed unto the chief priests all the things that were done. 12And when they were assembled with the elders, and had taken counsel, they gave large money unto the soldiers, 13 Saying, Say ye, His disciples came by night, and stole him *away* while we slept. 14And if this come to the governor's ears, we will persuade him, and secure you. 15 So they took the money, and did as they were taught: and this saying is commonly reported among the Jews until this day.

16 Then the eleven disciples went away into Galilee, into a mountain where Jesus had appointed them. 17And when they saw him, they worshipped him: but some doubted. 18And Jesus came and spake unto them, saying, All power is given unto me in heaven and in earth.

19 Go ye therefore, and teach all nations, baptizing them in the name of the Father, and of the Son, and of the Holy Ghost: 20 Teaching them to observe all things whatsoever I have commanded you: and, lo, I am with you alway, *even* unto the end of the world. Amen.

N.A.S.

28 Now late on the Sabbath, as it began to dawn toward the first *day* of the week, Mary Magdalene and the other Mary came to look at the grave. 2And behold, a severe earthquake had occurred, for an angel of the Lord descended from heaven and came and rolled away the stone and sat upon it. 3And his appearance was like lightning, and his garment as white as snow; 4 and the guards shook for fear of him, and became like dead men. 5And the angel answered and said to the women, "Do not be afraid; for I know that you are looking for Jesus who has been crucified. 6 "He is not here, for He has risen, just as He said. Come, see the place where He was lying. 7 "And go quickly and tell His disciples that He has risen from the dead; and behold, He is going before you into Galilee, there you will see Him; behold, I have told you." 8And they departed quickly from the tomb with fear and great joy and ran to report it to His disciples. 9And behold, Jesus met them and greeted them. And they came up and took hold of His feet and worshiped Him. 10 Then Jesus *said to them, "Do not be afraid; go and take word to My brethren to leave for Galilee, and there they shall see Me."

11 Now while they were on their way, behold, some of the guard came into the city and reported to the chief priests all that had happened. 12And when they had assembled with the elders and counseled together, they gave a large sum of money to the soldiers, 13 and said, "You are to say, 'His disciples came by night and stole Him away while we were asleep.' 14 "And if this should come to the governor's ears, we will win him over and keep you out of trouble." 15And they took the money and did as they had been instructed; and this story was widely spread among the Jews, *and is* to this day.

16 But the eleven disciples proceeded to Galilee, to the mountain which Jesus had designated. 17And when they saw Him, they worshiped *Him;* but some were doubtful. 18And Jesus came up and spoke to them, saying, "All authority has been given to Me in heaven and on earth. 19 "Go therefore and make disciples of all the nations, baptizing them in the name of the Father and the Son and the Holy Spirit, 20 teaching them to observe all that I commanded you; and lo, I am with you always, even to the end of the age."

WILLIAMS
BECK

WILLIAMS

28 *The two Marys see the empty tomb; the Jewish court persuades the guard to deceive the people; Jesus meets His disciples and gives them His last directions*

After the sabbath, as the first day of the week was dawning, Mary of Magdala and the other Mary went to get a look at the tomb. 2 Now there had been a great earthquake. For an angel of the Lord came down from heaven and went and rolled the boulder back and remained sitting upon it. 3 His appearance was as bright as lightning and his clothes as white as snow. 4 The men on guard trembled in awe of him, and became like dead men. 5 And the angel said to the women, "Do not be afraid, for I know that you are looking for Jesus who was crucified. 6 He is not here; He has risen, as He said He would do. Come, get a look at the place where He was lying. 7 Then run and tell His disciples, 'He has risen from the dead, and is going back to Galilee ahead of you; you will see Him there.' This is my message to you." 8 So off they, hurried from the tomb, frightened and yet in ecstasy, and ran to break the news to His disciples.

9 Then Jesus met them Himself, and said, "Good morning!" And they went up to Him and clasped His feet, and worshiped Him. 10 Then Jesus said to them, "Do not be afraid. Go, tell my brothers to go back to Galilee, and there they will see me."

11 While they were on their way, some members of the guard went into the city and told the high priests everything that had taken place. 12 So they met and held a consultation with the elders, and bribed the soldiers with a large sum of money, 13 and said to them, "Tell the people that His disciples came by night, while we were sleeping, and stole Him away. 14 And if news of it gets to the governor's ears, we will make it all right with him, and keep you out of trouble." 15 So they took the money and did as they were told. And this story has been told among the Jews down to the present time.

16 The eleven disciples went to Galilee to the mountain to which Jesus had directed them, 17 and as soon as they saw Him, they fell down and worshiped Him, though some were in doubt about it. 18 Then Jesus came up to them, and said, "Full *a* authority in heaven and on earth has been given to me. 19 Go then and make disciples of all the nations, baptize them into the name of the Father, the Son, and the Holy Spirit, 20 and teach them to practice all the commands that I have given you. And I myself will surely be with you all the days, down to the very close of the age."

BECK

Jesus Rises

28 After the Sabbath, as the first day of the week was dawning, Mary from Magdala and the other Mary went to look at the grave.

2 There was a great earthquake. The Lord's angel came down from heaven, went and rolled the stone away and sat on it. 3 He was as bright as lightning, and his clothes were as white as snow. 4 The guards were so afraid of him they shook and became like dead men.

5 "Don't be afraid," the angel said to the women. "I know you're looking for Jesus, who was crucified. 6 He is not here. He has risen as He said. Come, see the place where He was lying. 7 And go quickly, tell His disciples, 'He has risen from the dead. You know, He is going ahead of you to Galilee. There you will see Him.' Now, I have told you."

8 They hurried away from the grave with fear and great joy and ran to tell His disciples.

9 And there—Jesus met them and said, "Good morning!" They went up to Him, took hold of His feet, and worshiped Him.

10 Then Jesus said to them, "Don't be afraid. Go, tell My brothers to go to Galilee, and there they will see Mo."

The Guards

11 While the women were on their way, some of the guards went into the city and told the high priests everything that happened.

12 These met with the elders and agreed on a plan. They gave the soldiers a large sum of money 13 and told them, "Say, 'His disciples came at night and stole Him while we were sleeping.' 14 And if this comes to a hearing before the governor, we'll persuade him and see that you have nothing to worry about."

15 They took the money and did as they were told. And that story has been spread among the Jews to this day.

"Go!"

16 The eleven disciples went to the mountain in Galilee where Jesus had told them to go. 17 When they saw Him, they worshiped Him, but some doubted.

18 Coming nearer, Jesus spoke to them. "I have been given all power in heaven and on earth," He said.

19 "Go and make disciples of all people: Baptize them into the name of the Father, the Son, and the Holy Spirit, 20 and teach them to do everything I have commanded you. And remember, I am with you always till the end of the world."

[a] Modern greeting for ancient.

K.J.V.

THE GOSPEL
ACCORDING TO
SAINT MARK

1 The beginning of the gospel of Jesus Christ, the Son of God; 2As it is written in the prophets, Behold, I send my messenger before thy face, which shall prepare thy way before thee. 3 The voice of one crying in the wilderness, Prepare ye the way of the Lord, make his paths straight. 4 John did baptize in the wilderness, and preach the baptism of repentance for the remission of sins. 5And there went out unto him all the land of Judea, and they of Jerusalem, and were all baptized of him in the river of Jordan, confessing their sins. 6And John was clothed with camel's hair, and with a girdle of a skin about his loins; and he did eat locusts and wild honey; 7And preached, saying, There cometh one mightier than I after me, the latchet of whose shoes I am not worthy to stoop down and unloose. 8 I indeed have baptized you with water: but he shall baptize you with the Holy Ghost. 9And it came to pass in those days, that Jesus came from Nazareth of Galilee, and was baptized of John in Jordan. 10And straightway coming up out of the water, he saw the heavens opened, and the Spirit like a dove descending upon him: 11And there came a voice from heaven, *saying,* Thou art my beloved Son, in whom I am well pleased. 12And immediately the Spirit driveth him into the wilderness. 13And he was there in the wilderness forty days tempted of Satan; and was with the wild beasts; and the angels ministered unto him. 14 Now after that John was put in prison, Jesus came into Galilee, preaching the gospel of the kingdom of God, 15And saying, The time is fulfilled, and the kingdom of God is at hand: repent ye, and believe the gospel. 16 Now as he walked by the sea of Galilee, he saw Simon and Andrew his brother casting a net into the sea: for they were fishers. 17And Jesus said unto them, Come ye after me, and I will make you to become fishers of men. 18And straightway they forsook their nets, and followed him. 19And when he had gone a little further thence, he saw James the *son* of Zebedee, and John his brother, who also were in the ship mending their nets. 20And straightway he called them: and they left their father Zebedee in the ship with the hired servants, and went

N.A.S.

THE GOSPEL
ACCORDING TO
MARK

1 The beginning of the gospel of Jesus Christ, ᵃthe Son of God.
2 As it is written in Isaiah the prophet,
"BEHOLD, I SEND MY MESSENGER BEFORE YOUR FACE,
WHO WILL PREPARE YOUR WAY;
3 "THE VOICE OF ONE CRYING IN THE WILDERNESS,
'MAKE READY THE WAY OF THE LORD,
MAKE HIS PATHS STRAIGHT.' "
4 John the Baptist appeared in the wilderness ᵇpreaching a baptism of repentance for the forgiveness of sins. 5And all the country of Judea was going out to him, and all the people of Jerusalem; and they were being baptized by him in the Jordan River, confessing their sins. 6And John was clothed with camel's hair and, *wore* a leather belt around his waist, and his diet was locusts and wild honey. 7And he was preaching, and saying, "After me comes One who is mightier than I, and I am not *even* fit to stoop down and untie the thong of His sandals. 8 "I baptized you ᶜwith water; but He will baptize you ᶜwith the Holy Spirit."
9 And it came about in those days that Jesus came from Nazareth in Galilee, and was baptized by John in the Jordan. 10And immediately coming up out of the water, he saw the heavens opening, and the Spirit like a dove descending upon Him; 11 and a voice came out of the heavens: "Thou art My Beloved Son, in Thee I am well pleased."
12 And immediately the Spirit *impelled Him to go* out into the wilderness. 13And He was in the wilderness forty days being tempted by Satan; and He was with the wild beasts, and the angels were ministering to Him.
14 And after John had been taken into custody, Jesus came into Galilee, preaching the gospel of God, 15 and saying, "The time is fulfilled, and the kingdom of God is at hand; repent and believe in the gospel."
16 And as He was going along by the sea of Galilee, He saw Simon and Andrew, the brother of Simon, casting a net in the sea; for they were fishermen. 17And Jesus said to them, "Follow Me, and I will make you become fishers of men." 18And they immediately left the nets and followed Him. 19And going on a little farther, He saw James the *son* of Zebedee, and John his brother, who were also in the boat mending the nets. 20And immediately He called them; and they left their father Zebedee in the boat with the hired servants, and went away to follow Him.

[a] Many mss. omit, *the Son of God.* [b] Or, *proclaiming.* [c] The Greek here can be translated *in, with* or *by.*

WILLIAMS

MARK

1 *John the Baptist preaching and baptizing; Jesus is baptized; He is tempted; He begins preaching in Galilee; He cures many people sick with fever, leprosy, etc.*

The beginning of the good news of Jesus Christ. 2As it is written in the prophet Isaiah: "Here I send my messenger ahead of you; He will prepare your way;
3 He is a voice of one who shouts in the desert,
'Get the road ready for the Lord,
Make the paths straight for Him' ";
4 John the Baptizer appeared in the desert and was preaching a baptism conditioned on repentance to obtain the forgiveness of sins. 5And people from all over Judea and everybody in Jerusalem kept on going out to him and being baptized by him in the Jordan River, confessing their sins. 6 Now John wore clothing made of camel's hair, with a leather belt around his waist, and he used to live on dried locusts and wild honey.
7 He kept preaching the following message, "After me there is coming One who is stronger than I am, whose shoes I am not fit to stoop down and untie. 8 I have baptized you in water, but He will baptize you in the Holy Spirit."
9 Now in those days Jesus came from Nazareth in Galilee, and was baptized by John in the Jordan. 10And just as soon as He started to come up out of the water, He saw the heavens split open and the Spirit coming down like a dove to enter Him. 11And out of the heavens came a voice, "You are my Son, my Beloved! In you I am delighted!"
12 Then the Spirit at once drove Him out into the desert. 13And He stayed in the desert forty days, while He was being tempted by Satan; yea, He was with the wild beasts, but the angels continued to wait upon Him.
14 Now after John was arrested, Jesus went into Galilee, proclaiming the good news of God:
15 "The time is ripe and the kingdom of God is near; repent and believe in the good news."
16 As He was walking along the shore of the sea of Galilee, He saw Simon and his brother Andrew casting their nets in the sea, for they were fishermen. 17 So Jesus said to them, "Come, follow me, and I will make you fishermen for catching men." 18And at once they forsook their nets and followed Him. 19 He walked on a little farther and saw James, the son of Zebedee, and his brother John; they too were in their boats getting their nets in order. 20 He at once called them. They left their father Zebedee in the boat with the hired men, and went after Him.

1 Beginning the good news about Jesus Christ, God's Son:
2 It is written in the prophet Isaiah:

I will send My messenger ahead of You to prepare the way[1] *for You.*
3 *Someone will be calling in the wilderness:*
"Prepare the way for the Lord,
Make the paths straight for Him." [2]

4 So John the Baptizer came into the wilderness, preaching that people repent and be baptized to have their sins forgiven. 5All Judea and all the people of Jerusalem were coming out to him. As they confessed their sins, he baptized them in the Jordan River.
6 John was dressed in camel's hair with a leather belt around his waist. And he lived on grasshoppers and wild honey.
7 He preached: "The One who is mightier than I is coming after me. I'm not good enough to bend down and untie His shoe straps. 8 I have baptized you with water. He will baptize you with the Holy Spirit."

John Baptizes Jesus

9 It was in those days that Jesus came from Nazareth in Galilee and was baptized by John in the Jordan. 10 Just as He stepped out of the water, He saw heaven torn open and the Spirit coming down as a dove on Him. 11And a voice from heaven said, "You are *My Son* whom I love. *I am delighted*[3] with You."

The Devil Tempts Jesus

12 Then the Spirit drove Him out into the wilderness, 13 and He was in the wilderness for forty days while the devil tempted Him. He was there with the wild animals. And the angels served Him.

"Come with Me"

14 After John had been put in prison, Jesus went to Galilee and preached God's good news: 15 "The time has come, and God's kingdom is here. Repent, and believe the good news."
16 As He was walking along the Lake of Galilee, He saw Simon and Simon's brother Andrew (who were fishermen) casting a net into the lake. 17 "Come, follow Me," Jesus told them, "and I will make you fishers of men." 18 Immediately they left their nets and went with Him.
19 Going on a little farther, He saw James, Zebedee's son, and his brother John in their boat mending the nets. 20 Then He called them, and they left their father Zebedee with the hired men in the boat and followed Him.

[1] Mal. 3:1
[2] Is. 40:3
[3] Ps. 2:7; Is. 42:1

K.J.V.

after him. 21And they went into Capernaum; and straightway on the sabbath day he entered into the synagogue, and taught. 22And they were astonished at his doctrine: for he taught them as one that had authority, and not as the scribes. 23And there was in their synagogue a man with an unclean spirit; and he cried out, 24 Saying, Let us alone; what have we to do with thee, thou Jesus of Nazareth? art thou come to destroy us? I know thee who thou art, the Holy One of God. 25And Jesus rebuked him, saying, Hold thy peace, and come out of him. 26And when the unclean spirit had torn him, and cried with a loud voice, he came out of him. 27And they were all amazed, insomuch that they questioned among themselves, saying, What thing is this? what new doctrine is this? for with authority commandeth he even the unclean spirits, and they do obey him. 28And immediately his fame spread abroad throughout all the region round about Galilee. 29And forthwith, when they were come out of the synagogue, they entered into the house of Simon and Andrew, with James and John. 30 But Simon's wife's mother lay sick of a fever; and anon they tell him of her. 31And he came and took her by the hand, and lifted her up; and immediately the fever left her, and she ministered unto them. 32And at even, when the sun did set, they brought unto him all that were diseased, and them that were possessed with devils. 33And all the city was gathered together at the door. 34And he healed many that were sick of divers diseases, and cast out many devils; and suffered not the devils to speak, because they knew him. 35And in the morning, rising up a great while before day, he went out, and departed into a solitary place, and there prayed. 36And Simon and they that were with him followed after him. 37And when they had found him, they said unto him, All men seek for thee. 38And he said unto them, Let us go into the next towns, that I may preach there also: for therefore came I forth. 39And he preached in their synagogues throughout all Galilee, and cast out devils. 40And there came a leper to him, beseeching him, and kneeling down to him, and saying unto him, If thou wilt, thou canst make me clean. 41And Jesus, moved with compassion, put forth his hand, and touched him, and saith unto him, I will; be thou clean. 42And as soon as he had spoken, immediately the leprosy departed from him, and he was cleansed. 43And he straitly charged him, and forthwith sent him away; 44And saith unto him, See thou say nothing to any man: but go thy way, shew thyself to the priest, and offer for thy cleansing those things which Moses commanded, for a testimony unto them. 45 But he went out, and began to publish it much, and to blaze abroad the matter, insomuch that Jesus could no more openly enter into the city, but was without in desert places: and they came to him from every quarter.

N.A.S.

21 And they *went into Capernaum; and immediately on the Sabbath He entered the synagogue and began to teach. 22And they were amazed at His teaching; for He was teaching them as one having authority, and not as the scribes. 23And just then there was in their synagogue a man with an unclean spirit; and he cried out, 24saying, "What do we have to do with You, Jesus of ªNazareth? Have You come to destroy us? I know who You are— the Holy One of God!" 25And Jesus rebuked him, saying, "Be quiet, and come out of him!" 26 And throwing him into convulsions, the unclean spirit cried out with a loud voice, and came out of him. 27 And they were all amazed, so that they debated among themselves, "What is this? A new teaching with authority! He commands even the unclean spirits, and they obey Him." 28 And immediately the news about Him went out everywhere into all the surrounding district of Galilee.

29 And immediately after they had come out of the synagogue, they came into the house of Simon and Andrew, with James and John. 30 Now Simon's mother-in-law was lying sick with a fever; and immediately they *spoke to Him about her. 31And He came to her and raised her up, taking her by the hand, and the fever left her, and she began to ᵇwait on them.

32 And when evening had come, after the sun had set, they began bringing to Him all who were ill and those who were demon-possessed. 33And the whole city had gathered at the door. 34And He healed many who were ill with various diseases, and cast out many demons; and He was not permitting the demons to speak, because they ᶜknew who He was.

35 And in the early morning, while it was still dark, He arose and went out and departed to a lonely place, and was praying there. 36And Simon and his companions hunted for Him; 37 and they found Him, and *said to Him, "Everyone is looking for You." 38And He *said to them, "Let us go somewhere else to the towns nearby, in order that I may preach there also; for that is what I came out for." 39And He went into their synagogues throughout all Galilee, preaching and casting out the demons.

40 And a leper *came to Him, beseeching Him and falling on his knees before Him, and saying to Him, "If You are willing, You can make me clean." 41And moved with compassion, He stretched out His hand and touched him, and *said to him, "I am willing; be cleansed." 42And immediately the leprosy left him and he was cleansed. 43And He sternly warned him and immediately sent him away, 44 and He *said to him, "See that you say nothing to anyone; but go, show yourself to the priest and offer for your cleansing what Moses commanded, for a testimony to them." 45 But he went out and began to proclaim it freely and to spread the news about, to such an extent that Jesus could no longer publicly enter a city, but ᵈstayed out in unpopulated areas; and they were coming to Him from everywhere.

[a] Lit., Nazarene. [b] Or, serve. [c] Some mss. read: knew Him to be Christ. [d] Lit., was.

WILLIAMS

21 They went into Capernaum, and as soon as the first sabbath came, He went into the synagogue and began to teach. 22And they were dumfounded at His teaching, for He was teaching them like one who had authority to teach, and not like the scribes. 23 Just at that moment there was a man in their synagogue who was under the spell of a foul spirit, and so he screamed, 24 "What do you want of us, Jesus, you Nazarene! Have you come to destroy us? I know who you are, God's Holy One!" 25 Jesus reproved him, saying, "Hush up, get out of him!" 26 Then the foul spirit convulsed him and with a deafening shriek got out of him. 27 They were all so dumfounded that they kept discussing it among themselves, and asking, "What does this mean? It is a new teaching. He gives orders with authority even to foul spirits, and they obey Him." 28And His fame at once spread in all directions all over that part of Galilee.

29 As soon as they left the synagogue, they went home with Simon and Andrew, in company with James and John. 30And Simon's mother-in-law was confined to her bed with a fever. So they at once tell Him about her. 31 Then He went up to her, grasped her hand, and had her get up.[a] The fever left her, and she began to wait upon them.

32 In the evening, when the sun had gone down, they kept on bringing to Him all the people who were sick or under the power of demons, 33 and the whole town gathered at the door. 34And He cured many who were sick with various diseases, and drove out many demons, and would not let the demons speak a word, because they knew who He was.

35 Early in the morning, long before daybreak, He got up and went out to a lonely spot, and stayed praying there. 36And Simon and his companions diligently searched for Him 37 and found Him, and said to Him, "Everybody is looking for you."

38 And He said to them, "Let us go somewhere else, to the neighboring towns, to preach in them, too, for that is why I came out here." 39 So He went all over Galilee, preaching in their synagogues and driving out demons.

40 There came to Him a leper, begging Him on his knees, saying to Him, "If you want to, you can cure me."

41 And His heart was moved with pity for him, so He stretched out His hand and touched him, and said, "I do want to! Be cured!" 42And the leprosy at once left him, and he was cured. 43 But Jesus at once drove him out of their presence, and gave him this stringent charge, 44 "See that you tell nobody a single word about it. Begone; show yourself to the priest, and to prove it to the people, make the offering for your purification which Moses prescribed." 45 But he went out and began to publish it so much and to spread the story so far, that Jesus could not any more go into any town openly, but had to stay out in thinly settled places. But the people kept coming to Him from every quarter.

BECK

Jesus Drives Out a Devil

21 Then they went to Capernaum. The next Sabbath Jesus went into the synagog and began to teach. 22 His teaching amazed the people because He taught them as one who had authority and not like the Bible scholars.

23 There was in their synagog just then a man with an unclean spirit. 24And he screamed, "Leave us alone, Jesus from Nazareth! You've come to destroy us! I know who You are— God's Holy One."

25 Jesus talked sharply to him: "Be quiet, and come out of him." 26 The unclean spirit threw the man into convulsions and with a loud shriek came out of him.

27 They were all so amazed they argued with one another: "What is this? A new teaching! With authority! He gives orders to the unclean spirits, and they obey Him!"

28 The news about Him quickly spread everywhere in all the surrounding country of Galilee.

Peter's Mother-in-Law

29 Right after leaving the synagog, they went into the home of Simon and Andrew. James and John went with them. 30 Simon's mother-in-law was down in bed with a fever, and so the first thing they did was to tell Him about her. 31 He went to her, took her hand, and helped her get up. The fever left her, and she waited on them.

32 In the evening when the sun had gone down, the people brought to Him all the sick and those plagued by devils. 33 The whole town had gathered at His door. 34 He healed many who were suffering from various sicknesses and drove out many devils and wouldn't let the devils talk, because they knew Him.

Preaching in Galilee

35 In the morning, long before daylight, Jesus got up and went out to a lonely place, and there He prayed. 36 Simon and those who were with him searched for Jesus. 37 When they found Him, they told Him, "Everybody's looking for You."

38 "Let us go somewhere else," He told them, "to the small towns that are near, so that I may preach there too. That's why I've come."

39 He went and preached in their synagogs everywhere in Galilee and drove out the devils.

Jesus Heals a Leper

40 A leper came to Him and begged Him on his knees, "If You want to, You can make me clean."

41 Jesus felt sorry for him, stretched out His hand, and touched him. "I want to," He said. "Be clean!" 42 Immediately the leprosy left him, and he was made clean.

43 Jesus sent him away with a stern warning: 44 "Be careful not to say anything to anyone, but go, *let the priest examine*[4] you, and for your cleansing offer the sacrifices Moses ordered, to show them you're well."

45 But when he had left, he talked so much and spread the news till Jesus could no longer openly go into a town. He stayed out in lonely places, and still the people kept coming to Him from everywhere.

[a] Grk., *raised her.*   [4] Lev. 13:7, 49

K.J.V.

2 And again he entered into Capernaum after some days; and it was noised that he was in the house. 2And straightway many were gathered together, insomuch that there was no room to receive them, no, not so much as about the door: and he preached the word unto them. 3And they come unto him, bringing one sick of the palsy, which was borne of four. 4And when they could not come nigh unto him for the press, they uncovered the roof where he was: and when they had broken it up, they let down the bed wherein the sick of the palsy lay. 5When Jesus saw their faith, he said unto the sick of the palsy, Son, thy sins be forgiven thee. 6 But there were certain of the scribes sitting there, and reasoning in their hearts, 7 Why doth this man thus speak blasphemies? who can forgive sins but God only? 8And immediately, when Jesus perceived in his spirit that they so reasoned within themselves, he said unto them, Why reason ye these things in your hearts? 9 Whether is it easier to say to the sick of the palsy, Thy sins be forgiven thee; or to say, Arise, and take up thy bed, and walk? 10 But that ye may know that the Son of man hath power on earth to forgive sins, (he saith to the sick of the palsy,) 11 I say unto thee, Arise, and take up thy bed, and go thy way into thine house. 12And immediately he arose, took up the bed, and went forth before them all; insomuch that they were all amazed, and glorified God, saying, We never saw it on this fashion. 13And he went forth again by the sea side; and all the multitude resorted unto him, and he taught them. 14And as he passed by, he saw Levi the son of Alpheus sitting at the receipt of custom, and said unto him, Follow me. And he arose and followed him. 15And it came to pass, that, as Jesus sat at meat in his house, many publicans and sinners sat also together with Jesus and his disciples; for there were many, and they followed him. 16And when the scribes and Pharisees saw him eat with publicans and sinners, they said unto his disciples, How is it that he eateth and drinketh with publicans and sinners? 17 When Jesus heard it, he saith unto them, They that are whole have no need of the physician, but they that are sick: I came not to call the righteous, but sinners to repentance. 18And the disciples of John and of the Pharisees used to fast: and they come and say unto him, Why do the disciples of John and of the Pharisees fast, but thy disciples fast not? 19And Jesus said unto them, Can the children of the bridechamber fast, while the bridegroom is with them? as long as they have the bridegroom with them, they cannot fast. 20 But the days will come, when the bridegroom shall be taken away from them, and then shall they fast in those days. 21 No man also seweth a piece of new cloth on an old garment; else the new piece that filled it up taketh away from the old, and the rent is made worse. 22And no man putteth new wine into old bottles; else the new wine doth burst the bottles, and the wine is spilled, and the bottles will be marred: but new wine must

N.A.S.

2 And when He had come back to Capernaum several days afterward, it was heard that He was at home. 2And many were gathered together, so that there was no longer room, even near the door; and He was speaking the word to them. 3And they *came, bringing to Him a paralytic, carried by four men. 4And being unable to get to Him on account of the crowd, they removed the roof above Him; and when they had dug an opening, they let down the pallet on which the paralytic was lying. 5And Jesus seeing their faith *said to the paralytic, "My [a]son, your sins are forgiven." 6 But there were some of the scribes sitting there and reasoning in their hearts, 7 "Why does this man speak that way? He is blaspheming; who can forgive sins but God alone?" 8And immediately Jesus, perceiving in His spirit that they were reasoning that way within themselves, *said to them, "Why are you reasoning about these things in your hearts? 9 "Which is easier, to say to the paralytic, 'Your sins are forgiven;' or to say, 'Arise, and take up your pallet and walk'? 10 "But in order that you may know that the Son of Man has authority on earth to forgive sins"—He *said to the paralytic, 11 "I say to you, rise, take up your pallet and go home." 12And he rose and immediately took up the pallet and went out in the sight of all; so that they were all amazed and were glorifying God, saying, "We have never seen anything like this."

13 And He went out again by the seashore; and all the multitude were coming to Him, and He was teaching them. 14And as He passed by, He saw Levi the son of Alpheus sitting in the tax office, and He *said to him, "Follow Me!" And he rose and followed Him.

15 And it came about that He was reclining at table in his house, and many tax-gatherers and sinners were dining with Jesus and His disciples; for there were many of them, and they were following Him. 16And when the scribes of the Pharisees saw that He was eating with the sinners and tax-gatherers, they began saying to His disciples, "Why is He eating and drinking with tax-gatherers and sinners?" 17And hearing this, Jesus *said to them, "It is not those who are healthy who need a physician, but those who are sick; I did not come to call the righteous, but sinners."

18 And John's disciples and the Pharisees were fasting; and they *came and *said to Him, "Why do John's disciples and the disciples of the Pharisees fast, but Your disciples do not fast?" 19And Jesus said to them, "While the bridegroom is with them, the attendants of the bridegroom do not fast, do they? So long as they have the bridegroom with them, they cannot fast. 20 "But the days will come when the bridegroom is taken away from them, and then they will fast in that day. 21 "No one sews a patch of unshrunk cloth on an old garment; otherwise the patch pulls away from it, the new from the old, and a worse tear results. 22 "And no one puts new wine into old wineskins; otherwise the wine will burst the skins, and the wine is lost, and the skins as well; but one puts new wine into fresh wine-skins."

[a] Lit., child.

WILLIAMS | BECK

Jesus Forgives Sins

WILLIAMS

2 *Jesus cures a paralyzed man; calls Levi; tells three stories about fasting; claims to be Lord of the sabbath*

After some days He came back to Capernaum, and it was reported that He was at home, 2 and so many people gathered there that there was no longer any room even around the door. He was telling them His message. 3 Then four men came bringing to Him a paralyzed man. 4 And as they could not get him near to Jesus, on account of the crowd, they dug through the roof over the spot where He was standing and let the pallet down that the paralyzed man was lying on.

5 When Jesus saw their faith, He said to the paralyzed man, "My son, your sins are forgiven."

6 Some scribes were sitting there arguing and saying to themselves, 7 "Why is He talking this way? He is blaspheming. Who can forgive sins but God alone?" 8 Now Jesus at once felt in His spirit that they were arguing about this, and said, "Why are you arguing to yourselves about this? 9 Which is easier, to say to the paralyzed man, 'Your sins are forgiven,' or to say to him, 'Get up, pick up your pallet and start walking'? 10 But to show you that the Son of Man has authority to forgive sins on earth," turning to the paralyzed man He said, 11 "I tell you, get up, pick up your pallet, and go home." 12 Then he got up and at once picked up his pallet, and went out before them all.

The result was that they were all dumfounded and began to praise God and say, "We have never seen anything like this before."

13 He went out of the town again and along the seashore, and all the people kept coming to Him and He kept teaching them. 14 And as He was passing by, He saw Levi, the son of Alpheus, sitting in the tax-collector's office, and He said to him, "Follow me." Then he got up and followed Him.

15 Levi was at table in his house, and he had many tax-collectors and notorious sinners as guests, along with Jesus and His disciples, for there were many of them, and they began to follow Him. 16 And when the scribes who belonged to the Pharisees' party saw that He was eating with notorious sinners and tax-collectors, they said to His disciples, "Why does He eat with tax-collectors and notorious sinners?"

17 Jesus heard it, and said to them, "Not well but sick people have to send for the doctor. It is not upright but sinful people that I have come to invite."

18 Now John's disciples and the Pharisees were keeping a fast. So some people came and asked Him, "Why do John's disciples and the Pharisees' disciples practice fasting, but yours never do?"

19 Jesus answered them, "The wedding guests cannot fast, can they, while the bridegroom is with them? As long as they have the bridegroom with them they cannot fast. 20 But a time is coming when the bridegroom will be taken away from them, and then they will fast. 21 No one sews a patch of brand-new goods on an old coat; or, if he does, the patch tears away, the new from the old, and the hole becomes bigger than ever. 22 No one puts new wine into old wine-bottles; or, if he does, the wine will break the bottles, and the wine is lost, and the bottles too. New wine is to be put up in new bottles."

BECK

2 Some days later Jesus came again to Capernaum, and people heard, "He's home." 2 So many gathered that there was no room even in front of the door. He was speaking the Word to them.

3 Then some people came and brought Him a paralyzed man, carried by four men. 4 But when they couldn't bring him to Jesus on account of the crowd, they opened up the roof over the place where Jesus was. Through the opening they had dug they let down the bed on which the paralytic was lying.

5 Seeing their faith, Jesus said to the paralytic, "Son, your sins are forgiven."

6 There were some Bible scholars sitting there, and they questioned within themselves: 7 "Why does He say this? He's blaspheming. Who but God alone can forgive sins?"

8 Immediately Jesus knew in His Spirit what they were thinking. "Why do you have these thoughts in your hearts?" He asked them. 9 "Is it easier to say to this paralyzed man, 'Your sins are forgiven,' or to say, 'Get up, take your bed, and walk'? 10 I want you to know the Son of Man has power on earth to forgive sins"— then He said to the paralyzed man, 11 "I tell you, get up, take your bed, and go home."

12 The man got up, immediately took his bed, and walked out before all of them, so that all were amazed and praised God. "Never have we seen anything like this," they said.

Matthew

13 Again Jesus went out along the lake. All the people were coming to Him, and He taught them.

14 As He passed by, He saw Levi, the son of Alphaeus, sitting in the tax office. "Come with Me," He told him. He got up and went with Him.

15 As Jesus was lying down to eat at his home, many tax collectors and sinners were eating with Jesus and His disciples, because there were many who followed Him. 16 When the Bible scholars, who were Pharisees, saw Him eating with sinners and tax collectors, they asked His disciples, "Why does He eat with tax collectors and sinners?"

17 Jesus heard them and answered them: "Those who are healthy don't need a doctor, but the sick. I didn't come to call righteous people but sinners."

The Bridegroom

18 John's disciples and the Pharisees, who were fasting, came to Jesus. "John's disciples and the disciples of the Pharisees fast," they told Him. "Why don't Your disciples fast?"

19 Jesus asked them, "Can the bridegroom's friends fast while the bridegroom is with them? As long as they have the bridegroom with them, they can't fast. 20 The time will come when the bridegroom will be taken away from them, and on that day they'll fast.

21 "Nobody sews a piece of new cloth on an old garment. If you do, the new patch will tear away some of the old cloth, and the hole will get worse. 22 Nobody pours new wine into old wineskins. If you do, the wine will burst the skins, and the wine and the skins will be lost. Yes, new wine has to be poured into fresh skins."

K.J.V.

be put into new bottles. 23And it came to pass, that he went through the corn fields on the sabbath day; and his disciples began, as they went, to pluck the ears of corn. 24And the Pharisees said unto him, Behold, why do they on the sabbath day that which is not lawful? 25And he said unto them, Have ye never read what David did, when he had need, and was a hungered, he, and they that were with him? 26 How he went into the house of God in the days of Abiathar the high priest, and did eat the shewbread, which is not lawful to eat but for the priests, and gave also to them which were with him? 27And he said unto them, The sabbath was made for man, and not man for the sabbath: 28 Therefore the Son of man is Lord also of the sabbath.

3 And he entered again into the synagogue; and there was a man there which had a withered hand. 2And they watched him, whether he would heal him on the sabbath day; that they might accuse him. 3And he saith unto the man which had the withered hand, Stand forth. 4And he saith unto them, Is it lawful to do good on the sabbath days, or to do evil? to save life, or to kill? But they held their peace. 5And when he had looked round about on them with anger, being grieved for the hardness of their hearts, he saith unto the man, Stretch forth thine hand. And he stretched it out: and his hand was restored whole as the other. 6And the Pharisees went forth, and straightway took counsel with the Herodians against him, how they might destroy him. 7 But Jesus withdrew himself with his disciples to the sea: and a great multitude from Galilee followed him, and from Judea, 8And from Idumea, and from Jerusalem, and from Idumea, and from beyond Jordan; and they about Tyre and Sidon, a great multitude, when they had heard what great things he did, came unto him. 9And he spake to his disciples, that a small ship should wait on him because of the multitude, lest they should throng him. 10 For he had healed many; insomuch that they pressed upon him for to touch him, as many as had plagues. 11And unclean spirits, when they saw him, fell down before him, and cried, saying, Thou art the Son of God. 12And he straitly charged them that they should not make him known. 13And he goeth up into a mountain, and called unto him whom he would: and they came unto him. 14And he ordained twelve, that they should be with him, and that he might send them forth to preach, 15And to have power to heal sicknesses, and to cast out devils: 16And Simon he surnamed Peter; 17And James the son of Zebedee, and John the brother of James; and he surnamed them Boanerges, which is, The sons of thunder: 18And Andrew, and Philip, and Bartholomew, and Matthew, and Thomas, and James the son of Alpheus, and

N.A.S.

23 And it came about that He was passing through the grainfields on the Sabbath, and His disciples began to make their way along while picking the heads *of grain.* 24And the Pharisees were saying to Him, "See here, why are they doing what is not lawful on the Sabbath?" 25And He *said to them, "Have you never read what David did when he was in need and became hungry, he and his companions: 26 "How he entered into the house of God in the time of Abiathar *the* high priest, and ate the consecrated bread, which is not lawful for *anyone* to eat except the priests, and he gave *it* also to those who were with him?" 27And He was saying to them, "The Sabbath was made for man, and not man for the Sabbath. 28 "Consequently, the Son of Man is Lord even of the Sabbath."

3 And he entered again into a synagogue; and a man was there with a withered hand. 2And they were watching Him *to see* if He would heal him on the Sabbath, in order that they might accuse Him. 3And He *said to the man with the withered hand, "Rise and *come forward!*" 4And He *said to them, "Is it lawful on the Sabbath to do good or to do harm, to save a life or to kill?" But they kept silent. 5And after looking around at them with anger, grieved at their hardness of heart, He *said to the man, "Stretch out your hand." And he stretched it out, and his hand was restored. 6And the Pharisees went out and immediately *began* taking counsel with the Herodians against Him, *as to* how they might destroy Him. 7 And Jesus withdrew to the sea with His disciples; and a great multitude from Galilee followed; and *also* from Judea, 8 and from Jerusalem, and from Idumea, and beyond the Jordan, and the vicinity of Tyre and Sidon, a great multitude heard of all that He was doing and came to Him. 9And He told His disciples that a boat should stand ready for Him because of the multitude, in order that they might not crowd Him; 10 for He had healed many, with the result that all those who had afflictions pressed about Him in order to touch Him. 11And whenever the unclean spirits beheld Him, they would fall down before Him and cry out, saying, "You are the Son of God!" 12And He earnestly warned them not to reveal His identity.

13 And He *went up to the mountain and *summoned those whom He Himself wanted, and they came to Him. 14And He appointed twelve[a], that they might be with Him, and that He might send them out to preach, 15 and to have authority to cast out the demons. 16And He appointed the twelve: Simon (to whom He gave the name Peter), 17 and James, the *son* of Zebedee, and John the brother of James (to them He gave the name Boanerges, which means, "Sons of thunder"); 18 and Andrew, and Philip, and Bartholomew, and Matthew, and Thomas, and James the *son* of Alphaeus, and Thaddaeus, and Simon the Cananaean;

[a] Some early mss. add: *whom He named apostles.*

WILLIAMS

23 On the sabbath He was passing through the wheat fields, and His disciples started to make a path by pulling off the wheat heads. 24 So the Pharisees were saying to Him, "Just look! Why are they doing on the sabbath what it is against the law to do?"

25 He answered them, "Have you never read what David did when he and his soldiers were in need and hungry? 26 How is it that he went into the house of God, when Abiathar was high priest, and ate the sacred loaves, which it is against the law for anyone except the priests to eat, and gave part of them to his soldiers, too?" 27 Then He said to them, "The sabbath was made to serve man and not man to keep the sabbath. 28 So the Son of Man is Lord even of the sabbath."

3 *Jesus cures the man with a withered hand, and many others; selects the twelve; answers the charge that he is in league with demons; tells of the unforgiveable sin*

Then He went into a synagogue again, and a man was there who had a withered hand. 2 And they kept closely watching Him, to see whether He would cure him on the sabbath, to get a charge to bring against Him. 3 But He said to the man with the withered hand, "Get up in the crowd."

4 Then He asked them, "Is it right to do people good on the sabbath, or to do them evil, to save life or to take it?" But they had nothing to say. 5 So Jesus looked around at them in anger, because He was pained over their stubbornness of mind,[a] and said to the man, "Hold out your hand." And he held it out, and his hand was cured.

6 Then the Pharisees went out and held a consultation with the Herodians against Him, to put Him to death.

7 So Jesus retired with His disciples to the sea, and a vast throng of people followed Him from Galilee, and from Judea, 8 and from Jerusalem, and from Idumea, and from the other side of the Jordan, and from the neighborhood of Tyre and Sidon—yes, a vast throng of people, as they kept hearing of the great things that He was doing, came to Him. 9 So He told His disciples to keep a little boat ready for Him all the time, to prevent the crowds from crushing Him. 10 For He cured so many people that all who had ailments kept crowding up against Him to touch Him. 11 And whenever the foul spirits saw Him, they fell down before Him and screamed, "You are the Son of God." 12 But He charged them time after time not to tell who He was.

13 Then He went up on the hillside and summoned to Him those whom He wanted, and they went to Him. 14 And He appointed the Twelve, to whom He gave the title, apostles, to be with Him, to send them forth to preach, 15 and to have the right to drive out the demons. 16 The Twelve whom He appointed were: Peter, the name which He gave to Simon, 17 James the son of Zebedee, and John, James's brother (He named them Boanerges, which means, Sons of Thunder), 18 Andrew, Philip, Bartholomew, Matthew, Thomas, James the son

BECK

Lord of the Sabbath

23 Jesus was going through the grainfields on a Sabbath. As the disciples walked along, they were picking the heads of grain.

24 The Pharisees asked Him, "Look, why are they doing something they shouldn't do on a day of rest?"

25 "Haven't you ever read what David did," Jesus asked them, "when he and his men were in need and got hungry—26 how he went into God's house when Abiathar was high priest, and he ate the *loaves laid before God,*[5] which only the priests had the right to eat? And he gave his men some too."

27 Then He added, "The Sabbath was made for a man, not man for the Sabbath. 28 The Son of Man is Lord also of the Sabbath."

The Shriveled Hand

3 He went again into a synagog, and there was a man with a shriveled hand. 2 Some men were watching Jesus to see if He would heal him on a Sabbath; they wanted to accuse Him of something.

3 "Get up," He told the man with the shriveled hand, "and come forward." 4 Then He asked them, "Is it right on a day of rest to do good or to do evil, to save a life or to kill?"

But they were silent. 5 Looking around at them, He felt angry as well as sorry because their minds were closed. Then He told the man, "Stretch out your hand." He stretched it out, and his hand was made healthy again.

6 But the Pharisees left and immediately started plotting with Herod's men how to kill Him.

Many Are Healed

7 Jesus went away with His disciples to the lake. A big crowd from Galilee followed Him; 8 and also from Judea, Jerusalem, Idumea, the other side of the Jordan, and the neighborhood of Tyre and Sidon there were many people who heard about everything He was doing and came to Him. 9 To keep the crowd from crushing Him He told His disciples to have a small boat ready for Him. 10 He healed many so that all who had diseases rushed up to Him in order to touch Him. 11 Whenever the unclean spirits saw Him, they would fall down before Him and yell, "You're God's Son!" 12 But He strictly ordered them not to tell who He was.

Twelve Apostles

13 He went up the hill and called those whom He wanted, and they came to Him. 14 He appointed twelve to be with Him and be sent out by Him to preach 15 and have power to drive out devils.

16 He appointed the twelve and gave Simon the name Peter; 17 James, Zebedee's son, and John, the brother of James—He also gave these the name Boanerges, which means "thunderbolts"; 18 Andrew, Philip, Bartholomew, Matthew, and Thomas; James, the son of Alphaeus, and Thaddaeus; Simon the Zealot;

[a] Grk., *hardness of heart.*

[5] Lev. 24:5-8; 1 Sam. 21:6

K.J.V.

Thaddeus, and Simon the Canaanite, 19And Judas Iscariot, which also betrayed him: and they went into a house. 20And the multitude cometh together again, so that they could not so much as eat bread. 21And when his friends heard *of it,* they went out to lay hold on him: for they said, He is beside himself.

22 And the scribes which came down from Jerusalem said, He hath Beelzebub, and by the prince of the devils casteth he out devils. 23And he called them *unto him,* and said unto them in parables, How can Satan cast out Satan? 24And if a kingdom be divided against itself, that kingdom cannot stand. 25And if a house be divided against itself, that house cannot stand. 26And if Satan rise up against himself, and be divided, he cannot stand, but hath an end. 27 No man can enter into a strong man's house, and spoil his goods, except he will first bind the strong man; and then he will spoil his house. 28 Verily I say unto you, All sins shall be forgiven unto the sons of men, and blasphemies wherewith soever they shall blaspheme: 29 But he that shall blaspheme against the Holy Ghost hath never forgiveness, but is in danger of eternal damnation: 30 Because they said, He hath an unclean spirit.

31 There came then his brethren and his mother, and, standing without, sent unto him, calling him. 32And the multitude sat about him, and they said unto him, Behold, thy mother and thy brethren without seek for thee. 33And he answered them, saying, Who is my mother, or my brethren? 34And he looked round about on them which sat about him, and said, Behold my mother and my brethren! 35 For whosoever shall do the will of God, the same is my brother, and my sister, and mother.

N.A.S.

19 and Judas Iscariot, who also betrayed Him. 20 And He *came ᵃhome, and the multitude *gathered again, to such an extent that they could not even eat a meal. 21And when His own ᵇpeople heard *of this,* they went out to take custody of Him; for they were saying, "He has lost His senses." 22And the scribes who came down from Jerusalem were saying, "He is possessed by Beelzebul," and "He casts out the demons by the ruler of the demons." 23And He called them to Himself and began speaking to them in parables, "How can Satan cast out Satan? 24 "And if a kingdom is divided against itself, that kingdom cannot stand. 25 "And if a house is divided against itself, that house will not be able to stand. 26 "And if Satan has risen up against himself and is divided, he cannot stand, but is finished! 27 "But no one can enter the strong man's house and plunder his property unless he first binds the strong man, and then he will plunder his house. 28 "Truly I say to you, all sins shall be forgiven the sons of men, and whatever blasphemies they utter; 29 but whoever blasphemes against the Holy Spirit never has forgiveness, but is guilty of an eternal sin;"— 30 because they were saying, "He has an unclean spirit."

31 And His mother and His brothers *arrived, and standing outside they sent *word* to Him, and called Him. 32And a multitude was sitting around Him, and they *said to Him, "Behold, Your mother and Your brothersᶜ are outside looking for You." 33And answering them, He *said, "Who are My mother and My brothers?" 34And looking about on those who were sitting around Him, He *said, "Behold, My mother and My brothers! 35 "For whoever does the will of God, he is My brother and sister and mother."

4 And he began again to teach by the sea side: and there was gathered unto him a great multitude, so that he entered into a ship, and sat in the sea; and the whole multitude was by the sea on the land. 2And he taught them many things by parables, and said unto them in his doctrine, 3 Hearken; Behold, there went out a sower to sow: 4And it came to pass, as he sowed, some fell by the way side, and the fowls of the air came and devoured it up. 5And some fell on stony ground, where it had not much earth; and immediately it sprang up, because it had no depth of earth: 6 But when the sun was up, it was scorched; and because it had no root, it withered away. 7And some fell among thorns, and the thorns grew up, and choked it, and it yielded no fruit. 8And other fell on good ground, and did yield fruit that sprang up and increased, and brought forth, some thirty, and some sixty, and some a hundred. 9And he said unto them,

4 And He began to teach again by the seashore. And such a very great multitude gathered before Him that He got into a boat in the sea and sat down; and all the multitude were by the seashore on the land. 2And He was teaching them many things in parables, and was saying to them in His teaching, 3 "Listen *to this!* Behold, the sower went out to sow; 4 and it came about that as he was sowing, some *seed* fell beside the road, and the birds came and ate it up. 5 "And other *seed* fell on the rocky *ground* where it did not have much soil; and immediately it sprang up because it had no depth of soil. 6 "And after the sun had risen, it was scorched; and because it had no root, it withered away. 7 "And other *seed* fell among the thorns, and the thorns grew up and choked it, and it yielded no crop. 8 "And other *seeds* fell into the good soil and as they grew up and increased, they were yielding a crop and were producing thirty, sixty, and a hundredfold." 9And He was saying, "He who has ears to hear, let him hear."

[a] Lit., *into a house.* [b] Or, *kinsmen.* [c] Later mss. add: *and Your sisters.*

WILLIAMS

of Alpheus, Thaddeus, Simon the Zealot, 19 and Judas Iscariot, who betrayed Him.

Then He went home. 20And again the crowds gathered so that it was not possible for them even to take their meals. 21 His kinsmen heard of it and came over to get hold of Him, for they kept saying, "He has gone crazy."

22 And the scribes who had come down from Jerusalem kept saying, "He is under the spell of Beelzebub and by the help of the prince of the demons He drives out the demons."

23 So He called them to Him, and continued speaking to them in short stories, as follows: "How can Satan drive out Satan? 24 If a kingdom is disunited, that kingdom cannot last. 25And if a household is disunited, that household cannot last. 26And if Satan has made an insurrection against himself and become disunited, he cannot last but is surely coming to an end. 27 But no one can get into a giant's house and carry off his goods, unless he first binds the giant; after that he can make a clean sweep of his house. 28 I solemnly say to you, men will be forgiven for all their sins and all the abusive things they say. 29 But whoever speaks abusively against[b] the Holy Spirit can never get forgiveness, but is guilty of a sin that has no end." 30 He said so, because they kept saying, "He is under the spell of a foul spirit."

31 Then His mother and His brothers came. They were standing outside and sent word to call Him. 32And a crowd was sitting around Him when they told Him, "Your mother and your brothers are outside asking for you."

33 He answered them, "Who are my mother and my brothers?" 34 Then looking around at the people sitting about Him, He said, "Here are my mother and my brothers. 35 Whoever does the will of God is my brother and sister and mother."

4 *Teaching by stories, and why: the story of the sower; He explains it; the story of the secretly growing seed; the story of the mustard seed; He stills the storm*

Then He began again to teach by the seashore. And a crowd gathered around Him so great that He got into a boat and was sitting in it, just off the shore, while all the people were on the land close to the sea. 2 He continued teaching them by many stories. In His teaching He spoke to them as follows:

3 "Listen! A sower went out to sow. 4As he was sowing, some of the seed fell along the path, and the birds came and ate them up. 5 Some fell upon rocky ground, where they did not have much soil, and they sprang up at once, because the soil was not deep; 6 but when the sun came up, they were scorched and withered away, because they had not taken root. 7 Some fell among the thorn seed, and the thorns grew up and choked them out, and they yielded no grain. 8 Some fell in rich soil, and came up and grew and yielded thirty, sixty, even a hundredfold."

9 And He said, "Let him who has ears listen!"

[b] Grk., *blasphemes against the Holy Spirit.*

BECK

19 and Judas, the man from Kerioth, who betrayed Him.

Power over the Devil

20 Then Jesus came home. Again such a crowd gathered that Jesus and those with Him couldn't eat. 21 When His family heard about it, they went to take charge of Him, because they were saying, "He's out of His mind!"

22 The men trained in the Bible who had come down from Jerusalem said, "Beelzebul is in Him," and, "The ruler of the devils helps Him drive out the devils."

23 He called them to Him and pictured it to them in this way: "How can the devil drive out the devil? 24 If one part of a kingdom fights another, that kingdom can't stand. 25And if one part of a home fights against the other, it can never stand. 26And so if the devil rebels and fights against himself, he can't stand, but his end has come.

27 "Nobody can go into a strong man's house and take away his goods without first tying up the strong man. After that he will rob his house.

28 "I tell you the truth: Anything that people do will be forgiven, their sins and their slanders, though they slander ever so much. 29 But anyone who slanders the Holy Spirit will never be forgiven. Yes, he is guilty of an everlasting sin." 30 He said this because they had said, "The Spirit in Him is unclean."

31 His mother and His brothers came. They stood outside and sent someone to Him to ask Him to come out. 32 The crowd sitting around Jesus told Him, "Your mother and Your brothers are outside looking for You."

33 "Who are My mother and My brothers?" He asked them. 34 Then looking around at those who sat in a circle around Him, He said, "Here are My mother and My brothers. 35 If you do what God wants, you are My brother and sister and mother."

The Sower

4 Again Jesus began to teach by the lake. The crowd that gathered around Him was so very big that He stepped into a boat and sat in it on the lake, while all the people were on the shore, facing the lake. 2 Then He used parables to teach them many things.

3 "Listen!" He said as 2 He taught them. 3 "A sower went out to sow. 4As he was sowing, some seed fell along the road, and the birds came and ate it. 5 Some seed fell on rocky ground, where it didn't have much soil. Because the soil wasn't deep, the seed came up quickly. 6 When the sun rose, it was scorched, and because it had not taken root, it withered. 7 Some seed fell among thorns. The thorns grew up and choked it, and it produced no grain. 8 But some seed fell on good ground. It came up, grew, and produced grain, thirty, sixty, and a hundred times as much as was sown." 9 He added, "You have ears to hear; then listen."

K.J.V.

He that hath ears to hear, let him hear. 10And when he was alone, they that were about him with the twelve asked of him the parable. 11And he said unto them, Unto you it is given to know the mystery of the kingdom of God: but unto them that are without, all *these* things are done in parables: 12 That seeing they may see, and not perceive; and hearing they may hear, and not understand; lest at any time they should be converted, and *their* sins should be forgiven them. 13And he said unto them, Know ye not this parable? and how then will ye know all parables?

14 The sower soweth the word. 15And these are they by the way side, where the word is sown; but when they have heard, Satan cometh immediately, and taketh away the word that was sown in their hearts. 16And these are they likewise which are sown on stony ground; who, when they have heard the word, immediately receive it with gladness; 17And have no root in themselves, and so endure but for a time: afterward, when affliction or persecution ariseth for the word's sake, immediately they are offended. 18And these are they which are sown among thorns; such as hear the word, 19And the cares of this world, and the deceitfulness of riches, and the lusts of other things entering in, choke the word, and it becometh unfruitful. 20And these are they which are sown on good ground; such as hear the word, and receive *it,* and bring forth fruit, some thirtyfold, some sixty, and some a hundred.

21 And he said unto them, Is a candle brought to be put under a bushel, or under a bed? and not to be set on a candlestick? 22 For there is nothing hid, which shall not be manifested; neither was any thing kept secret, but that it should come abroad. 23 If any man have ears to hear, let him hear. 24And he said unto them, Take heed what ye hear. With what measure ye mete, it shall be measured to you; and unto you that hear shall more be given. 25 For he that hath, to him shall be given; and he that hath not, from him shall be taken even that which he hath.

26 And he said, So is the kingdom of God, as if a man should cast seed into the ground; 27And should sleep, and rise night and day, and the seed should spring and grow up, he knoweth not how. 28 For the earth bringeth forth fruit of herself; first the blade, then the ear, after that the full corn in the ear. 29 But when the fruit is brought forth, immediately he putteth in the sickle, because the harvest is come.

30 And he said, Whereunto shall we liken the kingdom of God? or with what comparison shall we compare it? 31 *It is* like a grain of mustard seed, which, when it is sown in the earth, is less than all the seeds that be in the earth: 32 But when it is sown, it groweth up, and becometh greater than all herbs, and shooteth out great branches; so that the fowls of the air may lodge under the shadow of it. 33And with many such parables spake he the word unto them, as they were able to hear *it.* 34 But without a parable spake he not unto them: and when they were alone, he expounded all things to his disci-

N.A.S.

10 And as soon as He was alone, His followers, along with the twelve, *began* asking Him *about* the parables. 11And He was saying to them, "To you has been given the mystery of the kingdom of God; but those who are outside get everything in parables; 12 in order that WHILE SEEING, THEY MAY SEE AND NOT PERCEIVE; AND WHILE HEARING, THEY MAY HEAR AND NOT UNDERSTAND; LEST THEY RETURN AGAIN AND BE FORGIVEN." 13And He *said to them, "Do you not understand this parable? And how will you understand all the parables? 14 "The sower sows the word. 15 "And these are the ones who are beside the road where the word is sown; and when they hear, immediately Satan comes and takes away the word which has been sown in them. 16 "And in a similar way these are the ones on whom seed was sown on the rocky *places,* who, when they hear the word, immediately receive it with joy; 17 and they have no *firm* root in themselves, but are *only* temporary; then, when affliction or persecution arises because of the word, immediately they fall away. 18 "And others are the ones on whom seed was sown among the thorns; these are the ones who have heard the word, 19 and the worries of the ᵃworld, and the deceitfulness of riches, and the desires for other things enter in and choke the word, and it becomes unfruitful. 20 "And those are the ones on whom seed was sown on the good ground; and they hear the word and accept it, and bear fruit, thirty, sixty, and a hundredfold."

21 And He was saying to them, "A lamp is not brought to be put under a peck-measure, is it, or under a bed? Is it not *brought* to be put on the lampstand? 22 "For nothing is hidden, except to be revealed; nor has *anything* been secret, but that it should come to light. 23 "If any man has ears to hear, let him hear." 24And He was saying to them, "Take care what you listen to; by your standard of measure it shall be measured to you; and more shall be given you besides. 25 "For whoever has, to him shall *more* be given; and whoever does not have, even what he has shall be taken away from him."

26 And He was saying, "The kingdom of God is like a man who cast seed upon the ground; 27 and goes to bed at night and gets up by day, and the seed sprouts up and grows —how, he himself does not know. 28 "The earth produces crops by itself; first the blade, then the head, then the mature grain in the head. 29 "But when the crop permits, he immediately puts in the sickle, because the harvest has come."

30 And He said, "How shall we ᵇpicture the kingdom of God, or by what parable shall we present it? 31 *"It is* like a mustard seed, which, when sown upon the ground, though it is smaller than all the seeds that are upon the ground, 32 yet when it is sown, grows up and becomes larger than all the garden plants and forms large branches; so that the birds of the ᶜair can nest under its shade."

33 And with many such parables He was speaking the word to them as they were able to hear it; 34 and He was not speaking to them without parables; but He was explaining everything privately to His own disciples.

[a] Or, *age.* [b] Lit., *compare.* [c] Or, *sky.*

WILLIAMS

10 When He was by Himself, those who stayed about Him with the Twelve, began to ask Him about the stories. 11 Then He said to them, "To you the secret of the kingdom of God has been entrusted, but to those who are on the outside everything is presented in stories, so that

12 'They may look and look and yet not see, And listen and listen and yet not understand, Lest, perchance, they should turn and be forgiven.'"

13 Then He said to them:

"If you do not understand this story, how, indeed, can you understand any of my stories? 14 The message is what the sower sows. 15 The ones along the path are those who have the message sown in their hearts, but as soon as it is sown there, Satan comes and carries off the message that has been sown in their hearts. 16 In like manner these are the ones sown on rocky ground; as soon as they hear the truth, they accept it with ecstasy, 17 but it does not take real root in them, and so they last only a little while; then when trouble or persecution comes on account of the truth, they at once fall by the way. 18 A different class are those people sown among the thorns. They are people who listen to the message, 19 but the worries of the times, the deceiving pleasures of being rich, and evil desires for other things, creep in and choke the truth out, and it yields nothing. 20 And the people sown in rich soil are the people who listen to the message and welcome it and yield thirty, sixty, even a hundredfold."

21 Then He put a question to them:

"A lamp is not brought to be put under a peck-measure or under a bed, is it? Is it not rather to be put on the lamp-stand? 22 For nothing is ever hidden by people except for the purpose of having it known, and people do not keep secrets except to tell *a* them. 23 If anyone has ears let him listen!"

24 And He was saying to them:

"Take care what you hear. The measure you give will come back to you, and more besides. 25 For whoever has will have more given to him, but whoever has nothing, even what he has will be taken away."

26 He also was saying:

"The kingdom of God is like a man who scatters seed on the ground, 27 then continues sleeping by night and getting up by day, while the seed sprouts and comes up without his knowing how. 28 The ground of itself produces, first the stalk, then the head; at last there is *b* the matured grain of wheat in the head. 29 But as soon as the crop will permit it, he puts in the sickle, for the reaping time has come."

30 Then He kept on saying:

"How can I further picture the kingdom of God, or by what story can I illustrate it? 31 It is like a mustard seed, which, when it is sown in the ground, is the smallest of all seeds, 32 but when it is properly sown, it comes up and grows to be the largest of all the plants, and produces branches so large that the wild birds can roost under its shade."

33 With many stories like these He kept on telling them the message, as far as they could understand it. 34 He did not tell them anything except by stories, but to His own disciples He kept on privately explaining everything.

BECK

10 When He was alone, the twelve and the others around Him asked Him about the parables.

11 "You are given the privilege of knowing the secret of God's kingdom," He answered them, "but to those on the outside everything comes in parables 12 *that they may see and yet not see, hear and yet not understand, and so may never turn to Me and let Me forgive them.*[6]

13 "You don't understand this parable," He said to them. "Then how will you understand any parables?

14 "The sower sows the Word. 15 And these are the ones along the road where the Word is sown: as soon as they hear it, the devil comes and takes away the Word that was sown into them. 16 It is the same with those in whom the seed falls on rocky ground. As soon as they hear the Word, they welcome it with joy, 17 but it doesn't take root in them. They believe for a while. But when the Word brings them trouble or persecution, they immediately fall away. 18 In others the seed falls among thorns. They hear the Word, 19 but the worries of the world, the deceitful pleasure of riches, and the desires for other things come in and choke the Word, and it can't produce anything. 20 The ones in whom the seed falls on good ground are those who continue to hear the Word, welcome it, and go on producing good things, thirty, sixty, and a hundred times as much as was sown.

21 "Do you get out a lamp," He asked them, "to put it under a bucket or under a bed? Shouldn't it be put on a lampstand? 22 Something is secret only to be told, and hidden only to come to light. 23 If you have ears to hear, listen!

24 "Be careful what you hear!" He told them. "The measure you measure with will be used for you. Yes, you will get even more. 25 If you have something, you will be given more. But if you don't have what you should have, even what you have will be taken away from you."

Growing by Itself

26 "God's kingdom," He said, "is like this: A man will sow seed on the ground. 27 He will sleep through the night and get up for the day, and the seed will come up and grow, he doesn't know how. 28 The ground by itself produces grain, first the green blade, then the head, then the full wheat in the head. 29 When the grain is ready, he *swings the sickle, because it is time to cut the grain.*"[7]

The Mustard Seed

30 "What should we say God's kingdom is like," He asked, "or how should we picture it? 31 It's like a mustard seed, which when sown on the ground is the smallest of all the seeds on earth. 32 But when it's sown, it comes up and becomes the largest of all the garden plants. It grows such large branches that *the birds in the air* can *make nests in its shade.*"[8]

33 He used many parables like these to speak the Word as they were able to hear it. 34 He wouldn't speak to them without a parable. But when He was alone with His disciples, He would explain everything to them.

[a] Grk., *come into the open*. [b] Fol. Ms. B.

[6] Is. 6:9-10
[7] Joel 3:13
[8] Ps. 104:12; Ezek. 17:23; 31:6; Dan. 4:12, 21

K.J.V.

N.A.S.

ples. 35And the same day, when the even was come, he saith unto them, Let us pass over unto the other side. 36And when they had sent away the multitude, they took him even as he was in the ship. And there were also with him other little ships. 37And there arose a great storm of wind, and the waves beat into the ship, so that it was now full. 38And he was in the hinder part of the ship, asleep on a pillow: and they awake him, and say unto him, Master, carest thou not that we perish? 39And he arose, and rebuked the wind, and said unto the sea, Peace, be still. And the wind ceased, and there was a great calm. 40And he said unto them, Why are ye so fearful? how is it that ye have no faith? 41And they feared exceedingly, and said one to another, What manner of man is this, that even the wind and the sea obey him?

35 And on that day, when evening had come, He *said to them, "Let us go over to the other side." 36And leaving the multitude, they *took Him along with them, just as He was, in the boat; and other boats were with Him. 37And there *arose a fierce gale of wind, and the waves were breaking over the boat so much that the boat was already filling up. 38And He Himself was in the stern, asleep on the cushion; and they *awoke Him and *said to Him, "Teacher, do You not care that we are perishing?" 39And being aroused, He rebuked the wind and said to the sea, "Hush, be still." And the wind died down and it became perfectly calm. 40And He said to them, "Why are you so timid? How is it that you have no faith?" 41And they became very much afraid and said to one another, "Who then is this, that even the wind and the sea obey Him?"

5 And they came over unto the other side of the sea, into the country of the Gadarenes. 2And when he was come out of the ship, immediately there met him out of the tombs a man with an unclean spirit, 3 Who had *his* dwelling among the tombs; and no man could bind him, no, not with chains: 4 Because that he had been often bound with fetters and chains, and the chains had been plucked asunder by him, and the fetters broken in pieces: neither could any *man* tame him. 5And always, night and day, he was in the mountains, and in the tombs, crying, and cutting himself with stones. 6 But when he saw Jesus afar off, he ran and worshipped him, 7And cried with a loud voice, and said, What have I to do with thee, Jesus, *thou* Son of the most high God? I adjure thee by God, that thou torment me not. 8 (For he said unto him, Come out of the man, *thou* unclean spirit.) 9And he asked him, What *is* thy name? And he answered, saying, My name *is* Legion: for we are many. 10And he besought him much that he would not send them away out of the country. 11 Now there was there nigh unto the mountains a great herd of swine feeding. 12And all the devils besought him, saying, Send us into the swine, that we may enter into them. 13And forthwith Jesus gave them leave. And the unclean spirits went out, and entered into the swine; and the herd ran violently down a steep place into the sea, (they were about two thousand,) and were choked in the sea. 14And they that fed the swine fled, and told *it* in the city, and in the country. And they went out to see what it was that was done. 15And they come to Jesus, and see him that was possessed with the devil, and had the legion, sitting, and clothed, and in his right mind; and they were afraid. 16And they that saw *it* told them how it befell to him that was possessed with the devil, and *also* concerning the swine. 17And they began to pray him to depart out of

5 And they came to the other side of the sea, into the country of the Gerasenes. 2And when He had come out of the boat, immediately a man from the tombs with an unclean spirit met Him, 3 and he had his dwelling among the tombs; and no one was able to bind him any more, even with a chain; 4 because he had often been bound with shackles and chains, and the chains had been torn apart by him, and the shackles broken in pieces, and no one was strong enough to subdue him. 5And constantly night and day, among the tombs and in the mountains, he was crying out and gashing himself with stones. 6And seeing Jesus from a distance, he ran up and bowed down before Him; 7 and crying out with a loud voice, he *said, "What do I have to do with You, Jesus, Son of the Most High God? I implore You by God, do not torment me!" 8 For He had been saying to him, "Come out of the man, you unclean spirit!" 9And He was asking him, "What is your name?" And he *said to Him, "My name is Legion; for we are many." 10And he *began* to entreat Him earnestly not to send them out of the country. 11 Now there was a big herd of swine feeding there on the mountain side. 12And they entreated Him, saying, "Send us into the swine so that we may enter them." 13And He gave them permission. And coming out, the unclean spirits entered the swine; and the herd rushed down the steep bank into the sea, about two thousand *of them;* and they were drowned in the sea. 14And those who tended them ran away and reported it in the city and *out* in the country. And *the people* came to see what it was that had happened. 15And they *came to Jesus and *observed the man who had been demon-possessed sitting down, clothed and in his right mind, the very man who had had the "legion;" and they became frightened. 16And those who had seen it described to them how it had happened to the demon-possessed man, and *all* about the swine. 17And they began to entreat Him to depart

WILLIAMS

35 That same day when it was evening, He said to them, "Let us go over to the other side."

36 So they left the crowd and took Him in the boat in which he was sitting. And there were other boats with Him.

37 But a furious squall of wind came up, and the waves were dashing over into the boat, so that it was fast filling. 38 He was in the stern, asleep on the cushion. So they woke Him up and said to Him, "Teacher, is it no concern to you that we are going down?"

39 Then He aroused Himself and reproved the wind, and said to the sea, "Hush! Be still." And the wind lulled, and there was a great calm. 40 Then He asked them, "Why are you afraid? Have you no faith yet?"

41 They were very much frightened, and said to one another, "Who can He be that even the wind and the sea obey Him?"

5 *Jesus cures an insane man; cures a woman with a hemorrhage; raises Jairus' daughter to life*

So they landed on the other side of the sea in the region of Gerasa. 2As soon as He got out of the boat, a man under the power of a foul spirit and from the tombs met Him. 3 This man lived among the tombs, and no one could any longer subdue him even with a chain, 4 for he had often been fastened with fetters and chains but had snapped the chains and broken the fetters, and no one was strong enough to overpower[a] him. 5All night and all day he kept screaming among the tombs and on the hills, and kept gashing himself with stones.

6 On catching a glimpse of Jesus from a distance, he ran up and fell down on his knees before Him, 7 and screamed aloud, "What do you want of me, Jesus, Son of the Most High God? In God's name, I beg you, do not torture me."

8 For Jesus was saying to him, "You foul spirit, come out of him." 9 He asked him, "What is your name?"

He answered, "My name is Legion, for we are many." 10And they kept on earnestly begging Him not to send them out of that country.

11 Now there was a large drove of hogs grazing on the hillside. 12And they begged Him, "Send us among the hogs, so that we can get into them." 13 So He let them do so. And the foul spirits came out of the man and got into the hogs, and the drove of about two thousand rushed over the cliff and into the sea and were drowned. 14 Then the hog-feeders fled and spread the news in the town and in the country around; and the people came to see what had taken place. 15 When they came to Jesus and saw the man who had once been insane under the power of many demons, sitting, with his clothes on, and in his right mind, they were frightened. 16And those who had seen it told them how it occurred to the man who had been under the power of the demons, and about the hogs. 17 Then they began to beg Jesus to leave their neighborhood.

BECK

Wind and Water Obey Him

35 In the evening of that day Jesus said to His disciples, "Let us cross over to the other side."

36 Leaving the crowd behind, they took Jesus, just as He was, with them in the boat. There were other boats with Him.

37 Then a violent storm came up, and the waves dashed into the boat so that it was filling up fast. 38 Meanwhile, in the back of the boat, He was sleeping on the cushion.

They woke Him up. "Teacher, we're drowning," they told Him. "Don't You care?"

39 He got up and ordered the wind to stop. "Hush!" He said to the lake. "Be still!" And the wind quieted down, and it became very calm.

40 "Why are you such cowards?" He asked them. "Haven't you learned to trust yet?"

41 Struck with awe, they asked one another, "Who is He? Even the wind and the lake obey Him."

The Gerasenes

5 They went to the country of the Gerasenes on the other side of the lake. 2 Just as He stepped out of the boat, a man with an unclean spirit came out of the burial places and met Him. 3 He lived in these burial places. Nobody could bind him any more, not even with a chain. 4 He had often been bound with chains on hands and feet, but he had torn the handcuffs and ground to pieces the chains on his feet, and nobody was strong enough to control him. 5Always, day and night, he was shrieking in the burial places and in the hills and bruising himself with stones.

6 When he saw Jesus at a distance, he ran, bowed down before Him, 7 and yelled at the top of his voice, "Let me alone, Jesus, Son of the most high God! 8 I tell you by God, don't You torture me." Jesus had told him, "You unclean spirit, get out of the man."

9 "What is your name?" Jesus asked him.

"My name is Six Thousand," he told Him, "because we are many." 10 They begged Him earnestly not to send them out of the country. 11 There was a large herd of hogs feeding on the hillside. 12 "Send us to the hogs," they begged Him; "we want to go into them."

13 He let them do this. The unclean spirits came out and went into the hogs, and the herd, about two thousand hogs, stampeded down the cliff into the lake and was drowned.

14 Those who had taken care of them ran away and told about it in the town and in the country, and the people came to see what had happened. They came to Jesus 15 and looked at the man who had been plagued by a legion of devils, but now was sitting there dressed and in his right mind; and they were frightened. 16 Those who had seen it told them what had happened to the man plagued by devils and about the hogs. 17 Then the people begged Jesus to leave their country.

[a] Grk., *tame.*

K.J.V.

their coasts. 18And when he was come into the ship, he that had been possessed with the devil prayed him that he might be with him. 19 Howbeit Jesus suffered him not, but saith unto him, Go home to thy friends, and tell them how great things the Lord hath done for thee, and hath had compassion on thee. 20And he departed, and began to publish in Decapolis how great things Jesus had done for him: and all *men* did marvel. 21And when Jesus was passed over again by ship unto the other side, much people gathered unto him; and he was nigh unto the sea. 22And, behold, there cometh one of the rulers of the synagogue, Jairus by name; and when he saw him, he fell at his feet, 23And besought him greatly, saying, My little daughter lieth at the point of death: *I pray thee,* come and lay thy hands on her, that she may be healed; and she shall live. 24And *Jesus* went with him; and much people followed him, and thronged him. 25And a certain woman, which had an issue of blood twelve years, 26And had suffered many things of many physicians, and had spent all that she had, and was nothing bettered, but rather grew worse, 27 When she had heard of Jesus, came in the press behind, and touched his garment. 28 For she said, If I may touch but his clothes, I shall be whole. 29And straightway the fountain of her blood was dried up; and she felt in *her* body that she was healed of that plague. 30And Jesus, immediately knowing in himself that virtue had gone out of him, turned him about in the press, and said, Who touched my clothes? 31And his disciples said unto him, Thou seest the multitude thronging thee, and sayest thou, Who touched me? 32And he looked round about to see her that had done this thing. 33 But the woman fearing and trembling, knowing what was done in her, came and fell down before him, and told him all the truth. 34And he said unto her, Daughter, thy faith hath made thee whole; go in peace, and be whole of thy plague. 35 While he yet spake, there came from the ruler of the synagogue's *house certain* which said, Thy daughter is dead; why troublest thou the Master any further? 36As soon as Jesus heard the word that was spoken, he saith unto the ruler of the synagogue, Be not afraid, only believe. 37And he suffered no man to follow him, save Peter, and James, and John the brother of James. 38And he cometh to the house of the ruler of the synagogue, and seeth the tumult, and them that wept and wailed greatly. 39And when he was come in, he saith unto them, Why make ye this ado, and weep? the damsel is not dead, but sleepeth. 40And they laughed him to scorn. But when he had put them all out, he taketh the father and the mother of the damsel, and them that were with him, and entereth in where the damsel was lying. 41And he took the damsel by the hand, and said unto her, Talitha cumi; which is, being interpreted, Damsel, (I say unto thee,) arise. 42And straightway the damsel arose, and walked; for she was *of the age of* twelve years. And they were astonished with a great astonishment. 43And he charged them straitly that no man should know it; and commanded that something should be given her to eat.

N.A.S.

from their region. 18And as He was getting into the boat, the man who had been demon-possessed was entreating Him that he might accompany Him. 19And He did not let him, but He *said to him, "Go home to your people and report to them ª what great things the Lord has done for you, and *how* He had mercy on you." 20And he went off and began to proclaim in Decapolis ªwhat great things Jesus had done for him; and everyone marveled.

21 And when Jesus had crossed over again in the boat to the other side, a great multitude gathered about Him; and He stayed by the seashore. 22And one of the synagogue officials named Jairus *came up, and upon seeing Him, *fell at His feet, 23 and *entreated Him earnestly, saying, "My little daughter is at the point of death; *please* come and lay Your hands on her, that she may get well and live." 24And He went off with him; and a great multitude was following Him and pressing in on Him.

25 And a woman who had had a hemorrhage for twelve years, 26 and had endured much at the hands of many physicians, and had spent all that she had and was not helped at all, but rather had grown worse, 27 after hearing about Jesus, came up in the crowd behind *Him,* and touched His cloak. 28 For she thought, "If I just touch His garments, I shall get well." 29And immediately the flow of her blood was dried up; and she felt in her body that she was healed of her affliction. 30And immediately Jesus, perceiving in Himself that the power *proceeding* from Him had gone forth, turned around in the crowd and said, "Who touched My garments?" 31And His disciples said to Him, "You see the multitude pressing in on You, and You say, 'Who touched Me?'" 32And He looked around to see the woman who had done this. 33 But the woman fearing and trembling, aware of what had happened to her, came and fell down before Him, and told Him the whole truth. 34And He said to her, "Daughter, your faith has made you well; go in peace, and be healed of your affliction."

35 While He was still speaking, they *came from the *house of* the synagogue official, saying, "Your daughter has died; why trouble the Teacher any more?" 36 But Jesus, overhearing what was being spoken, *said to the synagogue official, "Do not be afraid *any longer,* only believe." 37And He allowed no one to follow with Him, except Peter and James and John the brother of James. 38And they *came to the house of the synagogue official; and He *beheld a commotion, and *people* loudly weeping and wailing. 39And entering in, He *said to them, "Why make a commotion and weep? The child has not died, but is asleep." 40And they were laughing at Him. But putting them all out, He *took along the child's father and mother· and His own companions, and *entered the *room* where the child was. 41And taking the child by the hand, He *said to her, "Talitha kum!" (which translated means, "Little girl, I say to you, arise!") 42And immediately the girl got up and *began to walk; for she was twelve years old. And immediately they were completely astounded. 43And He gave them strict orders that no one should know about this; and He said that *something* should be given her to eat.

[a] Or, *everything that.*

WILLIAMS

18 And as He was getting into the boat, the once insane[b] man kept begging Him to let him go with Him. 19 However, He did not let him, but said to him, "Go home to your folks, and tell them how much the Lord has done for you, and has taken pity on you." 20 And so he went away and began to tell everybody in the Ten Cities how much Jesus had done for him; and everybody was dumfounded.

21 When Jesus again had crossed in the boat to the other side, a great crowd gathered about Him, as He was standing on the seashore. 22 And a man named Jairus, a leader of a synagogue, came up, and when he saw Jesus he flung himself at His feet 23 and kept earnestly begging Him, saying, "My dear little daughter is at the point of death. Come, lay your hands on her, so that she may get well and live." 24 So He went off with him, and a great crowd kept following Him, and jostling Him.

25 Then a woman who had had a hemorrhage for twelve years, 26 and had suffered much at the hands of many doctors, and had spent all she had, and yet was not a whit benefited but rather grew worse, 27 heard the reports about Jesus. So she came up in the crowd behind Him and touched His coat, 28 for she kept saying, "If I can only touch His clothes, I shall get well." 29 Her hemorrhage stopped at once, and she felt in her body that she was cured.

30 Jesus at once perceived that power had gone out of Him, and so He turned around in the crowd, and asked, "Who touched my clothes?"

31 But the disciples kept saying to Him, "You see the crowd jostling you, and yet you ask, 'Who touched me?'" 32 Still He kept looking around to see her who had done it. 33 So the woman, as she knew what had taken place for her, though frightened and trembling, came forward and fell on her knees before His feet, and told Him the whole truth.

34 And He said to her, "My daughter, your faith has cured you. Go in peace and be free from your disease."

35 Even while He was saying this, people came from the house of the leader of the synagogue and said, "Your daughter is dead; why trouble the Teacher any longer?"

36 But Jesus paid no attention to what was said, but said to the leader of the synagogue, "Do not be afraid; only keep up[c] your faith."

37 He let no one go with Him but Peter, James, and James's brother John. 38 They came to the home of the leader of the synagogue, and there He saw confusion, and people weeping and wailing without restraint. 39 And He went into the house and said to them, "Why do you continue all this confusion and crying? The little girl is not dead but is sleeping." 40 Then they began to laugh in His face. But He drove them all out, and took the little girl's father and mother and the men with Him, and went into the room where the little girl was. 41 Then He grasped her hand and said to her, "Talitha koum," which means, "Little girl, I tell you, get up!"

42 And the little girl at once got up and started walking around, for she was twelve years old. And instantly they were completely dumfounded. 43 But He strictly charged them to let nobody know about it, and told them to give her something to eat.

BECK

18 As He was stepping into the boat, the man in whom the devils had been begged Jesus to let him go with Him. 19 But Jesus didn't let him. "Go home to your people," He told him, "and tell them how much the Lord has done for you and how merciful He has been to you."

20 So the man left and began to tell publicly in the Ten Towns how much Jesus had done for him. And all were amazed.

The Daughter of Jairus

21 When Jesus had again crossed over in the boat to the other side of the lake, a big crowd gathered around Him by the lake.

22 A synagog leader by the name of Jairus came, and when he saw Jesus, he knelt at His feet and earnestly pleaded with Him: 23 "My little daughter is dying. Come and lay your hands on her so she will get well and live."

24 He went with him. A big crowd followed Him and pressed Him on all sides. 25 There was a woman who had a flow of blood for twelve years. 26 She had suffered much under many doctors and had spent all she had. And she had not been helped at all but had actually gotten worse. 27 Since she heard about Jesus, she came from behind in the crowd and touched His garment. 28 "If I touch His clothes," she said, "I'll get well." 29 Immediately her blood stopped flowing, and she felt in her body her trouble was gone and she was well.

30 At that moment Jesus felt power had gone from Him. Turning around in the crowd, He asked, "Who touched My clothes?"

31 "You see how the crowd is pressing you on all sides," His disciples said to Him, "and You ask, 'Who touched Me?'"

32 But He was looking around to see her who had done this. 33 The woman, trembling with fear because she knew what had been done to her, came, bowed down before Him, and told Him the whole truth.

34 "Daughter," He told her, "your faith made you well. Go in peace, be healthy and rid of your trouble."

35 While He was still talking, some men came from the home of the synagog leader. "Your daughter died," they said. "Why trouble the Teacher any more?"

36 Paying no attention to what they said, Jesus told the synagog leader, "Don't be afraid! Only believe!"

37 He let only Peter, James, and John, the brother of James, go with Him. So they came to the home of the synagog leader. 38 There He saw the noisy crowd, crying and wailing aloud. 39 "Why do you make a noise and cry?" He asked them when He came into the house. "The child isn't dead; she's sleeping."

40 They laughed at Him. But He put them all outside, took the child's father and mother and those who were with Him, and went in where the child was. 41 He took the child's hand and said to her, "Talitha,* koom!" which means, "Little girl, I tell you, wake up!"

42 Immediately the girl got up and walked around. She was twelve years old. Then the others were utterly amazed.

43 He gave them strict orders not to let anyone know about this. And He told them to give her something to eat.

---

[b] Grk., demonized man. [c] Keep on believing.

* Talitha originally meant "lamb."

6 And he went out from thence, and came into his own country; and his disciples follow him. 2And when the sabbath day was come, he began to teach in the synagogue: and many hearing *him* were astonished, saying, From whence hath this *man* these things? and what wisdom *is* this which is given unto him, that even such mighty works are wrought by his hands? 3 Is not this the carpenter, the son of Mary, the brother of James, and Joses, and of Juda, and Simon? and are not his sisters here with us? And they were offended at him. 4 But Jesus said unto them, A prophet is not without honour, but in his own country, and among his own kin, and in his own house. 5And he could there do no mighty work, save that he laid his hands upon a few sick folk, and healed *them.* 6And he marvelled because of their unbelief. And he went round about the villages, teaching.

7 And he called *unto him* the twelve, and began to send them forth by two and two; and gave them power over unclean spirits; 8And commanded them that they should take nothing for *their* journey, save a staff only; no scrip, no bread, no money in *their* purse: 9 But *be* shod with sandals; and not put on two coats. 10And he said unto them, In what place soever ye enter into a house, there abide till ye depart from that place. 11And whosoever shall not receive you, nor hear you, when ye depart thence, shake off the dust under your feet for a testimony against them. Verily I say unto you, It shall be more tolerable for Sodom and Gomorrah in the day of judgment, than for that city. 12And they went out, and preached that men should repent. 13And they cast out many devils, and anointed with oil many that were sick, and healed *them.* 14And king Herod heard *of him;* (for his name was spread abroad;) and he said, That John the Baptist was risen from the dead, and therefore mighty works do shew forth themselves in him. 15 Others said, That it is Elias. And others said, That it is a prophet, or as one of the prophets. 16 But when Herod heard *thereof,* he said, It is John, whom I beheaded: he is risen from the dead. 17 For Herod himself had sent forth and laid hold upon John, and bound him in prison for Herodias' sake, his brother Philip's wife; for he had married her. 18 For John had said unto Herod, It is not lawful for thee to have thy brother's wife. 19 Therefore Herodias had a quarrel against him, and would have killed him; but she could not: 20 For Herod feared John, knowing that he was a just man and a holy, and observed him; and when he heard him, he did many things, and heard him gladly. 21And when a convenient day was come, that Herod on his birthday made a supper to his lords, high captains, and chief *estates* of Galilee; 22And when the daughter of the said Herodias came in, and danced, and pleased Herod and them that sat with him, the king said unto the damsel, Ask of me whatsoever thou wilt, and I will give *it* thee. 23And he sware unto her, Whatsover thou shalt

6 And He went out from there; and He *came into His home town; and His disciples *followed Him. 2And when the Sabbath had come, He began to teach in the synagogue; and the many listeners were astonished, saying, "Where did this man *get* these things, and what is *this* wisdom given to Him, and such miracles as these performed by His hands? 3 "Is not this the carpenter, the son of Mary, and brother of James, and Joses, and Judas, and Simon? Are not His sisters here with us?" And they took offense at Him. 4And Jesus said to them, "A prophet is not without honor except in his home town and among his *own* relatives and in his *own* household." 5And He could do no miracle there except that He laid His hands upon a few sick people and healed them. 6And He wondered at their unbelief. And He was going around the villages teaching.

7 And He *summoned the twelve and began to send them out in pairs; and He was giving them authority over the unclean spirits; 8And He instructed them that they should take nothing for *their* journey, except a mere staff; no bread, no bag, no money in their belt; 9 but *to* wear sandals; and *He added,* "Do not put on two *tunics." 10And He was saying to them, "Wherever you enter a house, stay there until you leave town. 11 "And any place that does not receive you or listen to you, as you go out from there, shake off the dust from the soles of your feet for a testimony against them." 12And they went out and preached that *men* should repent. 13And they were casting out many demons and were anointing with oil many sick people and healing them.

14 And king Herod heard *of it;* for His name had become well known; and *people* were saying, "John the Baptist has risen from the dead, and therefore these miraculous powers are at work in him." 15 But others were saying, *"He is* Elijah." And others were saying, *"He is* a prophet, like one of the prophets *of old."* 16 But when Herod heard *of it,* he kept saying, "John, whom I beheaded, he has risen!" 17 For Herod himself had sent and had John arrested and bound in prison on account of Herodias, the wife of his brother Philip, because he had married her. 18 For John had been saying to Herod, "It is not lawful for you to have your brother's wife." 19And Herodias had a grudge against him and wanted to kill him; and could not *do so;* 20 for Herod was afraid of John, knowing that he was a righteous and holy man, and kept him safe. And when he heard him, he was very perplexed; but he used to enjoy listening to him. 21And a strategic day came when Herod on his birthday gave a banquet for his lords and military commanders and the leading men of Galilee; 22 and when the daughter of Herodias herself came in and danced, she pleased Herod and his dinner-guests; and the king said to the girl, "Ask me for whatever you want and I will give it to you." 23And he

[a] Or, *inner garments.*

WILLIAMS

6 *Jesus teaches in His home town, but is disowned by His fellow-townsmen; sends out the twelve; supposed to be John the Baptist by Governor Antipas; feeds five thousand; walks on water, etc.*

He left there and went back to His home town, and His disciples followed Him. 2 When the sabbath came, He began to teach in the synagogue. And the people were dumfounded when they heard Him, and said, "Where did He get all these things? What sort of wisdom is it that has been given Him? And such mighty deeds are done by Him! 3 Is He not the carpenter, Mary's son, and the brother of James, Joses, Judas, and Simon? And do not His sisters live here among us?" And so they found a cause for stumbling over him.

4 But Jesus said to them, "A prophet never fails to be honored except in his native neighborhood, among his kinsmen, and in his own home." 5 He could not do any mighty deeds there, except that He put His hands on a few ailing people and cured them. 6 And He wondered at their lack of faith in Him.

Then He made a circle of the villages and continued teaching. 7 And He called the Twelve to Him and sent them out two by two, and gave them power over the foul spirits. 8 He ordered them not to take anything for the journey except a staff, no bread, no bag, no money in the purse; 9 they were to go with plain sandals on their feet and not to wear two shirts. 10 And He continued to say to them, "Whenever you put up at a house, stay there until you leave that place. 11 And if any place refuses to welcome you or to listen to you, when you leave there shake off the very dust from the soles of your feet as a warning to them." 12 So they went out and preached that men should repent, 13 and drove out many demons, and cured many sick people by rubbing *a* them with oil.

14 King Herod heard of Him, for His name was now on everybody's lips, and people were saying that John the Baptizer had risen from the dead, and that this was why such mighty powers were working in Him. 15 But others were saying that He was Elijah, and still others that He was a prophet like the prophets of old. 16 But when Herod heard of Him, he said, "John, whom I beheaded, has risen from the dead." 17 For this very Herod had sent and seized John and bound him and put him in prison, just to please Herodias, his brother Philip's wife, because Herod had married her. 18 For John kept saying to Herod, "It is not right for you to be living with your brother's wife."

19 So Herodias had it in for him and wanted to have him killed. But she could not have it done, 20 for Herod stood in awe of John, because he knew that he was an upright and holy man, and so he protected him. When he heard him speak, he was very much disturbed, and yet he liked to hear him.

21 When a holiday came and Herod on his birthday gave a banquet to his state officials, his military officers, and other leading men of Galilee, 22 Herodias' daughter came in and danced for them, and fascinated Herod and his guests.

So the king said to the girl, "Ask me for anything you want, and I will give it to you." 23 And he promised her on oath, "I will give

[a] Grk., *anointing.*

BECK

His Last Visit to Nazareth

6 Leaving that place, Jesus went to His home town, and His disciples went with Him. 2 When the Sabbath came, He taught in the synagog. Many who heard Him were amazed. "Where did He get this?" they asked. "What is this wisdom given to Him?" and "Such miracles His hands are doing! 3 Isn't He the carpenter, Mary's son, and a brother of James, Joseph, Judas, and Simon? And aren't His sisters here with us?" So they turned against Him.

4 But Jesus told them, "A prophet is without honor only in his home town, among his relatives, and in his family." 5 He couldn't do any miracle there except lay His hands on a few sick people and make them well. 6 Their unbelief amazed Him.

Then He went around in the villages and taught.

Jesus Sends Out the Twelve

7 Jesus called the twelve and sent them out by twos, giving them authority over the unclean spirits. 8 He gave them these instructions: "Don't take anything with you on the way except a stick—no bread, no bag, and no copper money in your pocket. 9 But have sandals strapped on your feet. And don't wear two tunics.

10 "Wherever you go into a home," He told them, "stay there till you leave the place. 11 If the people of any place don't welcome you or listen to you, leave that place, and shake the dust off the soles of your feet as a warning to them."

12 They left and preached that people should repent. 13 They also drove out many devils and poured oil on many who were sick and made them well.

Herod Kills John

14 King Herod heard about Jesus, because His name was now well known. "John the Baptizer has risen from the dead," he said, "and that's why these powers are working in Him." 15 Others said, "He is Elijah." Still others, "He is a prophet like one of the other prophets." 16 But when Herod heard about it, he said, "John, whose head I cut off, has risen!"

17 Herod had sent men who arrested John, bound him, and put him in prison, because Herod had married Herodias, the wife of his brother Philip. 18 "It isn't right for you to have your brother's wife," John had told Herod.

19 Herodias had a grudge against John and wanted to kill him, but she couldn't do it. 20 Herod was afraid of John because he knew John was a good and holy man. So he protected him. When he listened to John, he was very much disturbed, and yet he liked to hear him.

21 An opportunity came on Herod's birthday, when he gave a dinner for his noblemen, the tribunes, and the leading men of Galilee. 22 His daughter, that is, the daughter of Herodias, came in and danced, and Herod and his guests were delighted with her. "Ask me for anything you want," the king told the girl, "and I'll give it to you." 23 And he solemnly swore to

K.J.V.

ask of me, I will give *it* thee, unto the half of my kingdom. 24And she went forth, and said unto her mother, What shall I ask? And she said, The head of John the Baptist. 25And she came in straightway with haste unto the king, and asked, saying, I will that thou give me by and by in a charger the head of John the Baptist. 26And the king was exceeding sorry; *yet* for his oath's sake, and for their sakes which sat with him, he would not reject her. 27And immediately the king sent an executioner, and commanded his head to be brought: and he went and beheaded him in the prison, 28And brought his head in a charger, and gave it to the damsel: and the damsel gave it to her mother. 29And when his disciples heard *of it,* they came and took up his corpse, and laid it in a tomb. 30And the apostles gathered themselves together unto Jesus, and told him all things, both what they had done, and what they had taught. 31And he said unto them, Come ye yourselves apart into a desert place, and rest a while: for there were many coming and going, and they had no leisure so much as to eat. 32And they departed into a desert place by ship privately. 33And the people saw them departing, and many knew him, and ran afoot thither out of all cities, and outwent them, and came together unto him. 34And Jesus, when he came out, saw much people, and was moved with compassion toward them, because they were as sheep not having a shepherd: and he began to teach them many things. 35And when the day was now far spent, his disciples came unto him, and said, This is a desert place, and now the time *is* far passed: 36 Send them away, that they may go into the country round about, and into the villages, and buy themselves bread: for they have nothing to eat. 37 He answered and said unto them, Give ye them to eat. And they say unto him, Shall we go and buy two hundred pennyworth of bread, and give them to eat? 38 He saith unto them, How many loaves have ye? go and see. And when they knew, they say, Five, and two fishes. 39And he commanded them to make all sit down by companies upon the green grass. 40And they sat down in ranks, by hundreds, and by fifties. 41And when he had taken the five loaves and the two fishes, he looked up to heaven, and blessed, and brake the loaves, and gave *them* to his disciples to set before them; and the two fishes divided he among them all. 42And they did all eat, and were filled. 43And they took up twelve baskets full of the fragments, and of the fishes. 44And they that did eat of the loaves were about five thousand men. 45And straightway he constrained his disciples to get into the ship, and to go to the other side before unto Bethsaida, while he sent away the people. 46And when he had sent them away, he departed into a mountain to pray. 47And when even was come, the ship was in the midst of the sea, and he alone on the land. 48And he saw them toiling in rowing; for the wind was contrary unto them: and about the fourth watch of the night he cometh unto them, walking upon the sea, and would have passed by them. 49 But

N.A.S.

swore to her, "Whatever you ask of me, I will give it to you; up to half of my kingdom." 24And she went out and said to her mother, "What shall I ask for?" And she said, "The head of John the Baptist." 25And immediately she came in haste before the king and asked, saying, "I want you to give me right away the head of John the Baptist on a platter." 26And although the king was very sorry; *yet* because of his oaths and because of his dinner-guests, he was unwilling to refuse her. 27And immediately the king sent an executioner and commanded *him* to bring *back* his head. And he went and beheaded him in the prison, 28 and brought his head on a platter, and gave it to the girl; and the girl gave it to her mother. 29And when his disciples heard *about this,* they came and took away his body and laid it in a tomb.

30 And the apostles *gathered together with Jesus; and they reported to Him all that they had done and taught. 31And He *said to them, "Come away by yourselves to a lonely place and rest a while." (For there were many *people* coming and going, and they did not even have time to eat.) 32And they went away in the boat to a lonely place by themselves. 33And *the people* saw them going, and many recognized *them,* and they ran there together on foot from all the cities, and got there ahead of them. 34And disembarking, He saw a great multitude, and He felt compassion for them because they were like sheep without a shepherd; and He began to teach them many things. 35And when it was already quite late, His disciples came up to Him and *began* saying, "The place is desolate and it is already quite late; 36 send them away so that they may go into the surrounding countryside and villages and buy themselves something to eat." 37 But He answered and said to them, "You give them something to eat!" And they *said to Him, "Shall we go and spend two hundred ªdenarii on bread and give them something to eat?" 38And He *said to them, "How many loaves do you have? Go look!" And when they found out, they *said, "Five and two fish." 39And He commanded them all to recline by groups on the green grass. 40And they reclined in companies of hundreds, and of fifties. 41And He took the five loaves and the two fish, and looking up toward heaven, He blessed *the food* and broke the loaves and He kept giving *them* to the disciples to set before them; and He divided up the two fish among them all. 42And they all ate and were satisfied. 43And they picked up twelve full baskets of the broken pieces, and also of the fish. 44And there were five thousand men who ate the loaves.

45 And immediately He made His disciples get into the boat and go ahead of *Him* to the other side to Bethsaida, while He Himself was sending the multitude away. 46And after bidding them farewell, He departed to the mountain to pray. 47And when it was evening, the boat was in the midst of the sea, and He *was* alone on the land. 48And seeing them straining at the oars, for the wind was against them, at about the fourth watch of the night, He *came to them, walking on the sea; and He intended to pass by them. 49 But when they saw Him walking on

[a] A denarius represented a day's wages for a common laborer.

WILLIAMS

you anything you ask for, up to half of my kingdom."

24 She left the room and asked her mother, "What shall I ask him for?"

And she answered, "The head of John the Baptizer."

25 Then she rushed at once before the king, and made this request, "I want you this very minute to give me John the Baptist's head on a platter."

26 The king, although exceedingly sorry, yet on account of his oath and his guests, did not like to refuse her, 27 and so at once ordered a soldier of his guard to bring his head. The soldier went off and beheaded John in the prison 28 and brought back his head on a platter, and gave it to the girl, and the girl gave it to her mother. 29 When his disciples heard of it, they came and carried off his corpse and laid it in a tomb.

30 The apostles returned and met Jesus and reported to Him everything, how many things they had done and taught. 31And He said to them, "Come with me by yourselves to a quiet place and rest a little while." For there was an endless stream of people coming and going, and they had no time even to eat. 32 So they got off in their boat to be by themselves in a quiet place. 33 But many people saw them start and knew of it and ran around the lake from all the towns and got there ahead of them. 34 So when He got out of the boat, He saw a great crowd waiting, and His heart was moved with pity at the sight of them, for they were like sheep without a shepherd; and so He proceeded to teach them a number of things.

35 When it grew late, His disciples came to Him and said, "This is a destitute place and it is already late. 36 Send the crowds off to the farms and villages to buy themselves something to eat."

37 But He answered them, "Give them something to eat yourselves."

Then they said to Him, "Shall we go and buy forty dollars' worth of bread and give it to them to eat?"

38 Then He asked them, "How many loaves have you? Go and see."

They found out and told Him, "Five, and two fish."

39 Then He ordered them all to sit down in rows on the green grass. 40And so they tumbled down in groups of hundreds and fifties. 41 Then He took the five loaves and the two fish and looked up to heaven and blessed the loaves and broke them in pieces and gave the pieces to the disciples to pass on to the people. He also divided the two fish among them all. 42And they all ate and had plenty. 43And the pieces they took up from the loaves made twelve basketfuls besides the pieces from the fish. 44 There were five thousand men who ate the loaves.

45 Then He insisted that the disciples at once get into their boat and cross ahead of Him toward Bethsaida, while He was sending the crowd away. 46After He had told them "Goodby," He went up the hill to pray. 47 Now when evening had come, the boat was in the middle of the sea, while He was alone on land. 48And because He saw that they were struggling at the oars, for the wind was against them, a while before daybreak He started toward them walking on the sea, and He meant to go right up beside them. 49 But when they saw Him

BECK

her: "I'll give you anything you ask, up to half of my kingdom." [9]

24 She went out and asked her mother, "What should I ask for?"

"The head of John the Baptizer," her mother told her.

25 She hurried right back to the king. "I want you to give me right now," she demanded, "on a platter the head of John the Baptizer."

26 The king felt very sorry. But he had sworn to do it, and there were the guests—so he didn't want to refuse her. 27 The king quickly sent a guard and ordered him to bring John's head. He went and cut off John's head in prison. 28 Then he brought the head on a platter and gave it to the girl, and the girl gave it to her mother.

29 When John's disciples heard about it, they came and took his body and laid it in a grave.

Jesus Feeds Five Thousand

30 The apostles gathered around Jesus and reported to Him everything they had done and taught. 31 "Now you come away to some deserted place," He told them, "where you can be alone, and rest a little." So many were coming and going there wasn't even time to eat.

32 So they went away in the boat to a deserted place to be alone. 33 But many saw them leave and recognized them. And they ran there from all the towns and got there ahead of them. 34 When Jesus stepped out of the boat, He saw a big crowd and felt sorry for them because they were like sheep without a shepherd. [10] He began to teach them many things.

35 When it was quite late, His disciples came to Him. "This is a deserted place," they said, "and it's late. 36 Send them away to the farms and villages around us to buy themselves something to eat."

37 "You give them something to eat," Jesus answered them.

"Should we go and buy bread for two hundred denarii," they asked Him, "and give it to them to eat?"

38 "How many loaves do you have?" He asked them. "Go and see."

They found out and said, "Five, and two fish."

39 He ordered them all to sit down in groups on the green grass. 40 They sat down in groups of hundreds and fifties.

41 Taking the five loaves and the two fish and looking up to heaven, He blessed them. He broke the loaves and gave them to the disciples to give to the people. He also gave pieces of the two fish to everybody. 42All of them ate and had a hearty meal. 43 They picked up pieces of bread and of the fish—twelve baskets full. 44 There were five thousand men who had eaten the bread.

Jesus Walks on Water

45 He quickly made His disciples get into the boat and cross over to Bethsaida ahead of Him; meanwhile He would send the people away. 46After saying good-by to them, He went up the hill to pray. 47 When it got late, the boat was in the middle of the lake, and He was alone on the land.

48 Jesus saw they were in great trouble as they rowed, because the wind was against them. Toward morning He came to them, walking on the lake. He wanted to pass by them. 49 They saw Him walking on the lake, and think-

[9] Esther 5:3; 7:2
[10] Num. 27:17; 1 Kings 22:17; Ezek. 34:5

113

K.J.V.

when they saw him walking upon the sea, they supposed it had been a spirit, and cried out: 50 For they all saw him, and were troubled. And immediately he walked with them, and saith unto them, Be of good cheer: it is I; be not afraid. 51And he went up unto them into the ship; and the wind ceased: and they were sore amazed in themselves beyond measure, and wondered. 52 For they considered not *the miracle* of the loaves; for their heart was hardened. 53And when they had passed over, they came into the land of Gennesaret, and drew to the shore. 54And when they were come out of the ship, straightway they knew him, 55And ran through that whole region round about, and began to carry about in beds those that were sick, where they heard he was. 56And whithersoever he entered, into villages, or cities, or country, they laid the sick in the streets, and besought him that they might touch if it were but the border of his garment: and as many as touched him were made whole.

7 Then came together unto him the Pharisees, and certain of the scribes, which came from Jerusalem. 2And when they saw some of his disciples eat bread with defiled, that is to say, with unwashen hands, they found fault. 3 For the Pharisees, and all the Jews, except they wash *their* hands oft, eat not, holding the tradition of the elders. 4And *when they come* from the market, except they wash, they eat not. And many other things there be, which they have received to hold, *as* the washing of cups, and pots, brazen vessels, and of tables. 5 Then the Pharisees and scribes asked him, Why walk not thy disciples according to the tradition of the elders, but eat bread with unwashen hands? 6 He answered and said unto them, Well hath Esaias prophesied of you hypocrites, as it is written, This people honoureth me with *their* lips, but their heart is far from me. 7 Howbeit in vain do they worship me, teaching *for* doctrines the commandments of men. 8 For laying aside the commandment of God, ye hold the tradition of men, *as* the washing of pots and cups: and many other such like things ye do. 9And he said unto them, Full well ye reject the commandment of God, that ye may keep your own tradition. 10 For Moses said, Honour thy father and thy mother; and, Whoso curseth father or mother, let him die the death: 11 But ye say, If a man shall say to his father or mother, *It is* Corban, that is to say, a gift, by whatsoever thou mightest be profited by me; *he shall be free.* 12And ye suffer him no more to do aught for his father or his mother; 13 Making the word of God of none effect through your tradition, which ye have delivered: and many such like things do ye.

14 And when he had called all the people unto him, he said unto them, Hearken unto me every one *of you,* and understand: 15 There is nothing from without a man, that entering into him can defile him: but the things which come out of him, those are they that defile the man. 16 If any man have ears to hear, let him hear.

N.A.S.

the sea, they supposed that it was a ghost, and cried out; 50 for they all saw Him and were frightened. But immediately He spoke with them and *said to them, "Take courage; it is I, do not be afraid." 51And He got into the boat with them, and the wind stopped; and they were greatly astonished, 52 for they had not gained any insight from the *incident of* the loaves, but their heart was hardened.

53 And when they had crossed over they came to land at Gennesaret, and moored to the shore. 54And when they had come out of the boat, immediately *the people* recognized Him, 55 and ran about that whole country and began to carry about on their pallets those who were sick, to the place they heard He was. 56And wherever He entered villages, or cities, or countryside, they were laying the sick in the market places, and entreating Him that they might just touch the fringe of His cloak; and as many as touched it were being cured.

7 And the Pharisees and some of the scribes gathered together around Him when they had come from Jerusalem, 2 and had seen that some of His disciples were eating their bread with impure hands, that is, unwashed. 3 (For the Pharisees and all the Jews do not eat unless they carefully wash their hands, *thus* observing the traditions of the elders; 4 and *when they come* from the market place, they do not eat unless they cleanse themselves; and there are many other things which they have received in order to observe, such as the washing of cups and pitchers and copper pots.) 5And the Pharisees and the scribes *asked Him, "Why do Your disciples not walk according to the tradition of the elders, but eat their bread with impure hands?" 6And He said to them, "Rightly did Isaiah prophesy of you hypocrites, as it is written,

'THIS PEOPLE HONORS ME WITH THEIR LIPS,
BUT THEIR HEART IS FAR AWAY FROM ME.
7 'BUT IN VAIN DO THEY WORSHIP ME,
TEACHING AS DOCTRINES THE PRECEPTS OF
MEN.'

8 "Neglecting the commandment of God, you hold to the tradition of men." 9 He was also saying to them, "You nicely set aside the commandment of God in order to keep your tradition. 10 "For Moses said, 'HONOR YOUR FATHER AND YOUR MOTHER;' and, 'HE WHO SPEAKS EVIL OF FATHER OR MOTHER, LET HIM BE PUT TO DEATH;' 11 but you say, 'If a man says to *his* father or *his* mother, anything of mine you might have been helped by is 'Corban (that is to say, *given to God*),' 12 you no longer permit him to do anything for *his* father or *his* mother; 13 *thus* invalidating the word of God by your tradition which you have handed down; and you do many such things like that." 14And summoning the multitude again, He *began* saying to them, "Listen to Me, all of you, and understand: 15 there is nothing outside the man which going into him can defile him; but the things which proceed out of the man are what

WILLIAMS

walking on the sea, they thought that it was a ghost and screamed aloud, 50 for they all saw Him and were terrified. But He at once spoke to them and said, "Keep up courage! It is I; stop being afraid." 51 Then He went up to them and got into the boat, and the wind lulled. They were completely dumfounded, 52 for they did not understand the lesson of the loaves; their minds were dull.[b]

53 They crossed over to the other side and came to Gennesaret and anchored the boat. 54As soon as they got out of the boat, the people recognized Him 55 and hurried all over the countryside and began to bring the sick to Him on their pallets, wherever they heard He was. 56And whatever villages or towns or country places He came to, they would lay the sick in the market-places and beg Him to let them touch just the tassel of His coat, and everybody that touched it was cured.

7   *Jesus teaching what real uncleanness is; cures a heathen mother's daughter and a deaf-mute*

The Pharisees met about Him, and also some scribes who had come from Jerusalem. 2 They had noticed that some of His disciples were in the habit of eating their meals without first giving their hands a ceremonial washing to make them clean. 3 For the Pharisees and all the Jews practice the customs handed down to them from their forefathers, 4 and will never eat until they have carefully washed their hands, and they never eat anything brought from the market until they wash it; and they have many other religious practices which they got from their forefathers, as the washing of cups, pitchers, and pans.

5 And so the Pharisees and the scribes asked Him, "Why is it that your disciples do not practice the customs handed down from our fore-fathers, but eat their meals without purifying their hands?"

6 But He answered them, "Isaiah beautifully prophesied about you hypocrites; as the Scripture says:[a]

" 'This people honor me with their lips,
  But their hearts are far, far away from me;
7 Their worship of me is but an empty show;
  The things they teach are but men's precepts.'

8 "You give up what God has commanded, 9 you cling to what men hand down. You are fine teachers to cancel what God commanded, in order to keep what men have handed down! 10 For Moses said, 'Honor your father and your mother,' and again, 'Whoever curses his father or mother must certainly be put to death,' 11 but you say, 'If a man tells his father or mother, "Everything I have that may be of use to you is Corban,"' that is, consecrated to God, 12 you let him off from doing anything more for his father or mother; 13 and so you set aside what God has said by what you have handed down. You have many other practices like these."

14 Again He called the people to Him and said, "Listen to me, all of you, and understand. 15 Nothing that goes into a man from the outside can make him foul, but the things that come from the inside of a man are the things that make him foul."[b]

[b] Grk., *hearts were hardened.* [a] Grk., *It stands written.* [b] V. 16 in A. V. not in best Mss.

BECK

ing He was a ghost, they cried out, 50 because they had all seen Him and were terrified.

Immediately He talked to them. "Have courage!" He said. "It is I. Don't be afraid." 51 He came into the boat with them, and the wind died down. The disciples were completely dumfounded. 52 They hadn't understood about the loaves. Their minds were dull.

53 They crossed over and came to the shore at Gennesaret and anchored there.

54 As soon as they stepped out of the boat, the people recognized Him. 55 They ran all over that part of the country and started to carry the sick on their beds to any place where they heard He was. 56And wherever He came—to villages, towns, or farms—they would lay down the sick in the public places and beg Him just to let them touch the tassel of His garment. And all who touched it were made well.

Unclean Hands

7   The Pharisees and some Bible scholars who had come from Jerusalem gathered around Jesus. 2 They saw some of His disciples eat with unclean hands, that is, without washing them. 3 (Now the Pharisees, like all other Jews, don't eat without washing their hands up to the wrist —to keep the rules handed down by their fathers. 4 Coming from the marketplace, they don't eat without first washing; and there are many other rules they've learned to keep—baptizing cups, pitchers, copper pans, and couches.)

5 "Why don't Your disciples live according to the rules handed down by our fathers?" the Pharisees and the Bible scholars were asking Him. "They eat with unclean hands!"

6 He told them, "Isaiah was right when he prophesied about you hypocrites as it is written: *These people honor Me with their lips, but their hearts are far away from Me. 7 They worship Me in vain because they teach men's rules.*[11] 8 You give up God's commandment and keep men's rules." 9 He added: "You have a fine way of setting aside God's commandment in order to keep your rules! 10 For example, Moses said, *Honor your father and your mother,* and, *Anyone who curses father or mother must die.*[12] 11 But you say, 'If anyone says to his father or mother, "Anything by which I might help you is Korban" ' " (that is, a gift to God), 12 "then you don't let him do anything for his father or his mother anymore. 13 In this way, by the rules you have taught you set aside what God has said. And you're doing many things like that."

14 Then He called the people again and said to them, "Listen to Me, all of you, and understand this: 15 Nothing that comes from the outside into a person can make him unclean, but what comes out of a person makes him unclean." *

---

* Our two oldest manuscripts do not have v. 16: "If you have ears to hear, listen!" See 4:23.
[11] Is. 29:13
[12] Ex. 20:12; Deut. 5:16; Ex. 21:17; Lev. 20:9

K.J.V.

17And when he was entered into the house from the people, his disciples asked him concerning the parable. 18And he saith unto them, Are ye so without understanding also? Do ye not perceive, that whatsoever thing from without entereth into the man, it cannot defile him; 19 Because it entereth not into his heart, but into the belly, and goeth out into the draught, purging all meats? 20And he said, That which cometh out of the man, that defileth the man. 21 For within, out of the heart of men, proceed evil thoughts, adulteries, fornications, murders, 22 Thefts, covetousness, wickedness, deceit, lasciviousness, an evil eye, blasphemy, pride, foolishness: 23All these evil things come from within, and defile the man.

24 And from thence he arose, and went into the borders of Tyre and Sidon, and entered into a house, and would have no man know it: but he could not be hid. 25 For a certain woman, whose young daughter had an unclean spirit, heard of him, and came and fell at his feet: 26 The woman was a Greek, a Syrophenician by nation; and she besought him that he would cast forth the devil out of her daughter. 27 But Jesus said unto her, Let the children first be filled: for it is not meet to take the children's bread, and to cast it unto the dogs. 28And she answered and said unto him, Yes, Lord: yet the dogs under the table eat of the children's crumbs. 29And he said unto her, For this saying go thy way; the devil is gone out of thy daughter. 30And when she was come to her house, she found the devil gone out, and her daughter laid upon the bed.

31 And again, departing from the coasts of Tyre and Sidon, he came unto the sea of Galilee, through the midst of the coasts of Decapolis. 32And they bring unto him one that was deaf, and had an impediment in his speech; and they beseech him to put his hand upon him. 33And he took him aside from the multitude, and put his fingers into his ears, and he spit, and touched his tongue; 34And looking up to heaven, he sighed, and saith unto him, Ephphatha, that is, Be opened. 35And straightway his ears were opened, and the string of his tongue was loosed, and he spake plain. 36And he charged them that they should tell no man: but the more he charged them, so much the more a great deal they published it; 37And were beyond measure astonished, saying, He hath done all things well: he maketh both the deaf to hear, and the dumb to speak.

8 In those days the multitude being very great and having nothing to eat, Jesus called his disciples unto him, and saith unto them, 2 I have compassion on the multitude, because they

N.A.S.

defile the man." 16 (See footnote a) 17And when leaving the multitude, He had entered the house, His disciples questioned Him about the parable. 18And He *said to them, "Are you too so uncomprehending? Do you not see that whatever goes into the man from outside cannot defile him; 19 because it does not go into his heart, but into his stomach, and is eliminated?" (Thus He declared all foods clean.) 20And He was saying, "That which proceeds out of the man, that is what defiles the man. 21 "For from within, out of the heart of men, proceed the evil thoughts and fornications, thefts, murders, adulteries, 22 deeds of coveting and wickedness, as well as deceit, sensuality, envy, slander, pride and foolishness. 23 "All these evil things proceed from within and defile the man."

24 And from there He arose and went away to the region of Tyreᵇ. And when He had entered a house, He wanted no one to know of it; yet He could not escape notice. 25 But after hearing of Him, a woman whose little daughter had an unclean spirit, immediately came and fell at His feet. 26 Now the woman was a cGentile, of the Syrophoenician race. And she kept asking Him to cast the demon out of her daughter. 27And He was saying to her, "Let the children be satisfied first, for it is not good to take the children's bread and throw it to the dogs." 28 But she answered and *said to Him, "Yes, Lord, but even the dogs under the table feed on the children's crumbs." 29And He said to her, "Because of this answer go your way; the demon has gone out of your daughter." 30And going back to her home, she found the child lying on the bed, the demon having departed.

31 And again He went out from the region of Tyre, and came through Sidon to the sea of Galilee, within the region of Decapolis. 32And they * brought to Him one who *was deaf and spoke with difficulty, and they *entreated Him to lay His hand upon him. 33And He took him aside from the multitude by himself, and put His fingers into his ears, and after spitting, He touched his tongue with the saliva; 34 and looking up to heaven with a deep sigh, He *said to him, "Ephphatha!" that is, "Be opened!" 35And his ears were opened, and the impediment of his tongue was removed, and he began speaking plainly. 36And He gave them orders not to tell anyone; but the more He ordered them, the more widely they continued to proclaim it. 37And they were utterly astonished, saying, "He has done all things well; He makes even the deaf to hear, and the dumb to speak."

8 In those days again, when there was a great multitude and they had nothing to eat, He summoned His disciples and *said to them, 2 "I feel compassion for the multitude because

[a] Later mss. add verse 16: "If any man has ears to hear, let him hear." [b] Some early mss. add: and Sidon. [c] Lit., Greek.

WILLIAMS

17 Now when He had left the crowd and gone home, His disciples were asking Him the meaning of this story. 18And He answered them, "Are you too without understanding yet? Do you not know that nothing from the outside that goes into a man can make him foul, 19 because it does not reach his heart but only his stomach, and then passes off into the waste?" In thus speaking He made all foods clean.

20 He kept on saying, "The thing that comes from the inside of a man is the thing that makes him foul, 21 for from the inside, that is, from the hearts of men, designs for doing evil come, sexual immorality, stealing, murder, 22 adultery, greed, malice, deceit, licentiousness, envy, abusiveness, haughtiness, thoughtlessness. 23All these evils come from the inside of a man and make him foul."

24 Then He left there and went into the neighborhood of Tyre and Sidon. He went into a house and wanted no one to know that He was there. But He could not escape public notice. 25 On the contrary, a woman, whose little daughter had a foul spirit, at once heard about Him and came and flung herself at His feet. 26 She was a heathen who spoke Greek and had been born in Syro-Phenicia. And she kept begging Him to drive the demon out of her daughter.

27 But He was saying to her, "Let the children first eat all they want, for it is not right to take the children's bread and throw it out to the house dogs." 28 But she answered Him, "Yes, Lord, and yet the house dogs under the table usually eat the crumbs the children drop."

29 Then He said to her, "Because you have said this, go home; the demon has gone out of your daughter." 30 She went home and found her daughter lying in bed, and the demon gone out.

31 He left the neighborhood of Tyre and went by way of Sidon through the district of the Ten Cities down to the Sea of Galilee. 32And they brought to Him a man who was deaf and almost dumb, and they begged Him to lay His hand upon him. 33 So He took him off from the crowd by himself and put His fingers in his ears and touched his tongue with saliva.

34 Then He looked up to heaven and sighed, as He said, "Ephphatha," which means, "Be opened." 35And his ears were opened and his tongue was untied, and he began to speak distinctly.

36 Then He charged them not to tell anybody about it; but the more He kept charging them, the more they kept spreading the news. 37 So the people were overwhelmingly dumfounded, and kept saying, "How wonderfully He has done everything! He even makes deaf people hear and dumb people talk."

8 *Jesus feeds four thousand; gives no spectacular sign; warns against the teaching of the Pharisees and the pomp of Herod; owned as Christ by Peter; cures a blind man; foretells His death and resurrection*

In those days when a great crowd again had gathered and they had nothing to eat, He called His disciples to Him, and said, 2 "My heart goes out in pity for these people, for they have been

BECK

17 When He had left the people and gone home, His disciples asked Him about the illustration.

18 "Are you just as dull as the rest?" He asked them. "Don't you know that nothing coming from the outside into a person can make him unclean, 19 because it doesn't go into his heart but into his stomach and so passes away?" (Here Jesus made all foods clean.) 20 He added: "What comes out of a person makes him unclean. 21 Yes, from within, out of men's hearts, come evil thoughts, sexual sins, stealing, murders, adulteries, 22 greed, wickedness, cheating, lust, a jealous eye, slander, pride, foolishness. 23All these evils come from within and make a person unclean."

A Non-Jewish Woman

24 Leaving that place, Jesus went away to the neighborhood of Tyre. He went into a house and didn't want anyone to know it but couldn't keep it secret.

25 There was a woman in whose little daughter there was an unclean spirit. As soon as she heard about Him, she came and bowed down at His feet. 26 The woman wasn't Jewish but was born a Phoenician in Syria. She was asking Him to drive the devil out of her daughter.

27 "First let the children eat all they want," He answered her. "It isn't good to take the children's bread and throw it to the puppies."

28 "You're right, Lord," she answered Him, "but even the puppies under the table eat some of the children's crumbs."

29 "Because you said this, go!" Jesus told her. "The devil has gone out of your daughter."

30 The woman went home and found the little child lying on the bed and the devil gone.

A Deaf and Dumb Man

31 Jesus again left the country of Tyre and went through Sidon and the country of the Ten Towns to the Lake of Galilee.

32 Some people brought Him a man who was deaf and tongue-tied, and they urged Jesus to lay His hand on him. 33 Taking him away from the crowd to be alone with him, He put His fingers into the man's ears. He spit and touched his tongue 34 and looked up to heaven and sighed. Then He said to him, "Ephphatha!" which means, "Open!" 35 His ears were opened, his tongue was set free to speak, and he talked naturally.

36 Jesus ordered the people not to tell anyone. But the more He forbade them, the more widely they spread the news. 37 They were dumfounded. "He has done everything well," they said. "He even makes the deaf hear and the dumb speak."

Jesus Feeds Four Thousand

8 At that time there were again many people who had nothing to eat. So He called the disciples. 2 "I feel sorry for the people," He

K.J.V.

have now been with me three days, and have nothing to eat: 3And if I send them away fasting to their own houses, they will faint by the way: for divers of them came from far. 4And his disciples answered him, From whence can a man satisfy these *men* with bread here in the wilderness? 5And he asked them, How many loaves have ye? And they said, Seven. 6And he commanded the people to sit down on the ground: and he took the seven loaves, and gave thanks, and brake, and gave to his disciples to set before *them;* and they did set *them* before the people. 7And they had a few small fishes: and he blessed, and commanded to set them also before *them.* 8 So they did eat, and were filled: and they took up of the broken *meat* that was left seven baskets. 9And they that had eaten were about four thousand: and he sent them away.

10 And straightway he entered into a ship with his disciples, and came into the parts of Dalmanutha. 11And the Pharisees came forth, and began to question with him, seeking of him a sign from heaven, tempting him. 12And he sighed deeply in his spirit, and saith, Why doth this generation seek after a sign? verily I say unto you, There shall no sign be given unto this generation. 13And he left them, and entering into the ship again departed to the other side.

14 Now *the disciples* had forgotten to take bread, neither had they in the ship with them more than one loaf. 15And he charged them, saying, Take heed, beware of the leaven of the Pharisees, and *of* the leaven of Herod. 16And they reasoned among themselves, saying, *It is* because we have no bread. 17And when Jesus knew *it,* he saith unto them, Why reason ye, because ye have no bread? perceive ye not yet, neither understand? have ye your heart yet hardened? 18 Having eyes, see ye not? and having ears, hear ye not? and do ye not remember? 19When I brake the five loaves among five thousand, how many baskets full of fragments took ye up? They say unto him, Twelve. 20And when the seven among four thousand, how many baskets full of fragments took ye up? And they said, Seven. 21And he said unto them, How is it that ye do not understand?

22 And he cometh to Bethsaida; and they bring a blind man unto him, and besought him to touch him. 23And he took the blind man by the hand, and led him out of the town; and when he had spit on his eyes, and put his hands upon him, he asked him if he saw aught. 24And he looked up, and said, I see men as trees, walking. 25After that he put *his* hands again upon his eyes, and made him look up; and he was restored, and saw every man clearly. 26And he sent him away to his house, saying, Neither go into the town, nor tell *it* to any in the town.

N.A.S.

they have remained with Me now three days, and have nothing to eat; 3 and if I send them away fasting to their home, they will faint on the way; and some of them have come from a distance." 4And His disciples answered Him, "Where will anyone be able to *find enough* to satisfy these men with bread here in the wilderness?" 5And He was asking them, "How many loaves do you have?" And they said, "Seven." 6And He *directed the multitude to sit down on the ground; and taking the seven loaves, He gave thanks and broke them, and *began* giving them to His disciples to serve to them, and they served them to the multitude. 7 They also had a few small fish; and after He had blessed them, He ordered these to be served as well. 8And they ate and were satisfied; and they picked up seven full baskets of what was left over of the broken pieces. 9And about four thousand were *there;* and He sent them away. 10And immediately He entered the boat with His disciples, and came to the district of Dalmanutha.

11 And the Pharisees came out and began to argue with Him, seeking from Him a sign from heaven, to test Him. 12And sighing deeply in His spirit, He *said, "Why does this generation seek for a sign? Truly I say to you, no sign shall be given to this generation." 13And leaving them, He again embarked and went away to the other side.

14 And they had forgotten to take bread; and did not have more than one loaf in the boat with them. 15And He was giving orders to them, saying, "Watch out! Beware of the leaven of the Pharisees and the leaven of Herod." 16And they *began* to discuss with one another *the fact* that they had no bread. 17And Jesus, aware of this, *said to them, "Why do you discuss *the fact* that you have no bread? Do you not yet see or understand? Do you have a hardened heart? 18 "HAVING EYES, DO YOU NOT SEE? AND HAVING EARS, DO YOU NOT HEAR? And do you not remember, 19 when I broke the five loaves for the five thousand, how many large baskets full of broken pieces you picked up?" They *said to Him, "Twelve." 20 "And when *I broke* the seven for the four thousand, how many basketfuls of broken pieces did you pick up?" And they *said to Him, "Seven." 21And He was saying to them, "Do you not yet understand?"

22 And they *came to Bethsaida. And they * brought a blind man to Him, and *entreated Him to touch him. 23And taking the blind man by the hand, He brought him out of the village; and after spitting on his eyes, and laying His hands upon him, He asked him, "Do you see anything?" 24And he looked up and said, "I see men, for I am seeing *them* like trees, walking about." 25 Then again He laid His hands upon his eyes; and he looked intently and was restored, and *began* to see everything clearly. 26And He sent him to his home, saying, "Do not even enter the village."

WILLIAMS

staying with me three days now, and they have nothing left to eat. 3And if I send them home hungry, they will give out on the road, for some of them are a long way from home."

4 But His disciples answered Him, "Where can anyone get bread enough here in this destitute place, to give these people plenty?"

5 Then He asked them, "How many loaves have you?"

They answered, "Seven." 6 So He ordered the crowd to sit down on the ground. Then He took the seven loaves and gave thanks and broke them in pieces and gave them to His disciples to pass, and they passed them to the people. 7And they had a few small fish, and He blessed them and told them to pass these, too, to the people. 8And they ate and had plenty. And they took up the pieces left over, which made seven hamper[a]-basketfuls. 9About four thousand people were there. Then He sent them away. 10And He at once got into the boat and crossed to the district of Dalmanutha.

11 Now the Pharisees came out and began a discussion with Him, and to test Him asked Him to show them a spectacular sign from heaven. 12 But He sighed in spirit and said, "Why do the people of these times ask for a spectacular sign? I solemnly say, no sign at all will be given them." 13And He left them and again got into the boat and crossed to the other side.

14 Now they had forgotten to bring any bread; that is, they had only one loaf with them in the boat. 15 Then He kept warning them by saying, "Look out! Keep on guarding yourselves against the yeast of the Pharisees and the yeast of Herod."

16 So they were discussing with one another the fact that they had no bread. 17And as He noticed it He said to them, "Why are you discussing the fact that you have no bread? Do you not yet know nor understand? Are your minds so dull?[b] 18 Since you have eyes can you not see with them? Since you have ears can you not hear with them? 19 Do you not remember how many basketfuls of pieces you picked up when I broke the five loaves in pieces for the five thousand?"

They said to Him, "Twelve."

20 "And how many hamper-basketfuls of pieces when I broke the seven loaves in pieces for the four thousand?"

They said to Him, "Seven."

21 He said to them, "How is it that you do not understand?"

22 Then they came to Bethsaida. And they brought a blind man to Him and begged Him to touch him. 23 He took him by the hand and led him outside the village, then spit in his eyes, laid His hands upon him, and asked him, "Do you see anything?"

24 He looked up and answered, "I see the people, but they look to me like trees moving around."

25 Then He laid His hands upon his eyes again, and he looked the best he could and was cured, and saw everything distinctly. 26 So He sent him home with the warning, "Do not ever go into the village."

BECK

said to them. "They've been with Me three days now and have nothing to eat. 3 If I let them go home without eating, they will get exhausted on the road. Some of them have come a long way."

4 "Where could anyone get enough bread here in the wilderness to feed these?" His disciples asked Him.

5 "How many loaves do you have?" Jesus asked them.

"Seven," they answered.

6 He ordered the people to sit down on the ground. Then He took the seven loaves, gave thanks, broke them, and gave them to His disciples to hand out, and they handed them to the people. 7 They also had a few small fish. He blessed them and asked that these, too, be handed out. 8 They ate and had a hearty meal. And they picked up the pieces that were left— seven baskets. 9 There were about four thousand.

Then He dismissed the people.

A Proof from Heaven

10 Then Jesus and His disciples got into the boat and came into the neighborhood of Dalmanutha.

11 The Pharisees came and started to argue with Him. To test Him, they asked Him for some wonderful proof from heaven.

12 With a deep sigh from His spirit He asked, "Why do the people of today want a proof? Surely, I tell, you, these people will get no proof!"

13 Then He left them.

The Yeast of the Pharisees

13 He got into the boat again and started to cross to the other side. 14 They forgot to take bread and had only one loaf with them in the boat.

15 Then Jesus definitely warned them: "Beware of the yeast of the Pharisees and of Herod!"

16 Arguing about this with one another, they mentioned that they had no bread.

17 Aware of what was going on, Jesus asked, "Why are you arguing about not having any bread? Don't you know or understand yet? Are your minds closed? 18 You have eyes—don't you see? You have ears—don't you hear? [13] 19And don't you remember? When I broke the five loaves for the five thousand, how many baskets full of pieces did you pick up?"

"Twelve," they told Him.

20 "And the seven loaves for the four thousand—how many baskets full of pieces did you pick up?"

"Seven," they answered Him.

21 "Don't you understand yet?" He asked them.

A Blind Man

22 So they came to Bethsaida. There people brought a blind man to Jesus and begged Him to touch him. 23 He took the blind man's hand and led him out of the village. Then He spit on his eyes and laid His hands on him. "Can you see anything?" He asked him.

24 He looked up. "I see the people," he said. "They look to me like trees walking around."

25 When Jesus again laid His hands on his eyes, he saw distinctly; sight came back, and he saw everything clearly. 26 Jesus sent him home, saying, "But don't go into the village."

---

[a] Very large baskets. [b] Grk., heart hardened yet.   [13] Jer. 5:21; Ezek. 12:2

K.J.V.

27 And Jesus went out, and his disciples, into the towns of Caesarea Philippi: and by the way he asked his disciples, saying unto them, Whom do men say that I am? 28And they answered, John the Baptist: but some *say*, Elias; and others, One of the prophets. 29And he saith unto them, But whom say ye that I am? And Peter answereth and saith unto him, Thou art the Christ. 30And he charged them that they should tell no man of him. 31And he began to teach them, that the Son of man must suffer many things, and be rejected of the elders, and *of* the chief priests, and scribes, and be killed, and after three days rise again. 32And he spake that saying openly. And Peter took him, and began to rebuke him. 33 But when he had turned about and looked on his disciples, he rebuked Peter, saying, Get thee behind me, Satan: for thou savourest not the things that be of God, but the things that be of men.

34 And when he had called the people *unto him* with his disciples also, he said unto them, Whosoever will come after me, let him deny himself, and take up his cross, and follow me. 35 For whosoever will save his life shall lose it; but whosoever shall lose his life for my sake and the gospel's, the same shall save it. 36 For what shall it profit a man, if he shall gain the whole world, and lose his own soul? 37 Or what shall a man give in exchange for his soul? 38 Whosoever therefore shall be ashamed of me and of my words, in this adulterous and sinful generation, of him also shall the Son of man be ashamed, when he cometh in the glory of his Father with the holy angels.

9 And he said unto them, Verily I say unto you, That there be some of them that stand here, which shall not taste of death, till they have seen the kingdom of God come with power.

2 And after six days Jesus taketh *with him* Peter, and James, and John, and leadeth them up into a high mountain apart by themselves: and he was transfigured before them. 3And his raiment became shining, exceeding white as snow; so as no fuller on earth can white them. 4And there appeared unto them Elias with Moses: and they were talking with Jesus. 5And Peter answered and said to Jesus, Master, it is good for us to be here: and let us make three tabernacles; one for thee, and one for Moses, and one for Elias. 6 For he wist not what to say; for they were sore afraid. 7And there was a cloud that overshadowed them: and a voice came out of the cloud, saying, This is my beloved Son: hear him. 8And suddenly, when they had looked round about, they saw no man any more, save Jesus only with themselves. 9And as they came down from the mountain, he charged them that they should tell no man what things they had seen, till the Son of man were risen from the dead. 10And they kept that saying with

N.A.S.

27 And Jesus went out, along with His disciples, to the villages of Caesarea Philippi; and on the way He questioned His disciples, saying to them, "Who do people say that I am?" 28And they told Him, saying, "John the Baptist; and others *say* Elijah; but still others, one of the prophets." 29And He *continued* by questioning them, "But who do you say that I am?" Peter *answered and *said to Him, "Thou art the Christ." 30And He warned them to tell no one about Him.

31 And He began to teach them that the Son of Man must suffer many things and be rejected by the elders and the chief priests and the scribes, and be killed, and after three days rise again. 32And He was stating the matter plainly. And Peter took Him aside and began to rebuke Him. 33 But turning around and seeing His disciples, He rebuked Peter, and *said, "Get behind Me, Satan; for you are not setting your mind on ªGod's interests, but man's." 34And He summoned the multitude with His disciples, and said to them, "If anyone wishes to come after Me, let him deny himself, and take up his cross, and follow Me. 35 "For whoever wishes to save his life shall lose it; and whoever loses his life for My sake and the gospel's shall save it. 36 "For what does it profit a man to gain the whole world, and forfeit his soul? 37 "For what shall a man give in exchange for his soul? 38 "For whoever is ashamed of Me and My words in this adulterous and sinful. generation, the Son of Man will also be ashamed of him when He comes in the glory of His Father with the holy angels."

9 And He was saying to them, "Truly I say to you, there are some of those who are standing here who shall not taste of death until they see the kingdom of God after it has come with power."

2 And six days later, Jesus *took with Him Peter and James and John, and * brought them up to a high mountain by themselves. And He was transfigured before them; 3 and His garments became radiant and exceedingly white, as no launderer on earth can whiten them. 4And Elijah appeared to them along with Moses; and they were conversing with Jesus. 5And Peter *answered and *said to Jesus, "Rabbi, it is good for us to be here; and let us make three tabernacles, one for You, and one for Moses, and one for Elijah." 6 For he did not know what to answer; for they became terrified. 7 Then a cloud formed, overshadowing them, and a voice came out of the cloud, "This is My beloved Son, listen to Ḥim!" 8And all at once they looked around and saw no one with them any more, except Jesus only.

9 And as they were coming down from the mountain, He gave them orders not to relate to anyone what they had seen, until the Son of Man should rise from the dead. 10And they

[a] Lit., *the things of God.*

WILLIAMS

27 Then Jesus and His disciples left Galilee and went to the villages around Caesarea Philippi. On the way there He was asking His disciples, "Who do people say that I am?"
28 They answered Him, "John the Baptist; others say, Elijah, and others that you are one of the prophets."
29 Then He began to ask them, "Who do you yourselves say that I am?"
Peter answered Him, "You are the Christ." 30 But He strictly warned them not to tell this about Him to anybody.
31 Then He instructed them for the first time that the Son of Man had to endure great suffering and be disowned by the elders and the high priests and the scribes, and be killed but rise again after three days. 32And without any reserve He was telling them this fact. So Peter took Him aside and began to reprove Him for it. 33 But He turned and glanced at His disciples and reproved Peter by saying, "Get out of my way, Satan! for this view[c] of yours is not from God but from men."
34 Then He called the people to Him along with His disciples, and said to them, "If anyone wants to be my disciple,[d] he must say, 'No' to self, put the cross on his shoulders, and keep on following me. 35 For whoever wants to save his higher life, will have to give up the lower life, and whoever gives up his lower life for me and for the good news, will save the higher life. 36 For what benefit will it be to a man to gain the whole world and fail to gain the higher life? 37 For what price can a man give to buy back life? 38 For whoever is ashamed of me and my teaching in this unfaithful,[e] sinful age, then the Son of Man will be ashamed of him, when He comes back in His Father's splendor with the holy angels."
9:1 And He said to them, "I solemnly say to you, some of the people standing here will certainly live[f] to see the kingdom of God come in its power."

9 *Jesus is transfigured, and Moses and Elijah talk with Him; cures an epileptic boy; again foretells His death; teaches that service is greatness*

2 Six days after this, Jesus took Peter, James, and John with Him, and led them up on a high mountain, alone by themselves. And in their presence His appearance was changed, 3 and His clothes were shining as white as white could be, yea, whiter than any earthly bleacher could bleach them. 4And Elijah appeared to them, accompanied by Moses, and they were talking with Jesus.
5 Then Peter interrupted and said to Jesus, "Teacher, it is good for us to be here. So let us put up three tents, one for you and one for Moses and one for Elijah." 6For he did not really know what to say, he was so frightened.
7 Then a cloud came and was circling over them, and a voice came out of the cloud, "This is my Son, my Beloved; keep on listening to Him!" 8And as quick as a flash, on looking around, they saw no one with them but Jesus by Himself. 9And while they were going down the mountain, He cautioned them not to tell anyone what they had seen, until the Son of Man should rise from the dead. 10And they held that

[c] Grk., *you are thinking, etc.* [d] Grk., *come after me.* [e] *Adulterous.* [f] Grk., *will not die until, etc.*

BECK

"You Are the Promised Savior"

27 Then Jesus and His disciples went to the villages around Philip's Caesarea. On the way He asked His disciples, "Who do people say I am?"
28 "John the Baptizer," they answered Him. "Others say Elijah, and still others, one of the prophets."
29 "But who do you say I am?" He asked them.
"You are the promised Savior!" Peter answered Him.
30 He warned them not to tell anyone about Him.

"I Will Die and Rise Again"

31 Then He was teaching them: "The Son of Man has to suffer much, be rejected by the elders, the ruling priests, and the Bible scholars, be killed, and then rise on the third day." 32 He was speaking quite frankly.
But Peter took Him aside and started to correct Him. 33 Turning, He looked at His disciples and corrected Peter. "Get behind Me, devil!" He said. "You're not thinking what God thinks but what men think."

Take the Cross

34 He called the people as well as His disciples. "If you want to follow Me," He told them, "deny yourself, take up your cross, and come with Me. 35 If you want to save your life, you will lose it. But if you will lose your life for Me and for the good news, you will save it. 36 What good does it do you to win the whole world and lose your life? 37 Or what would you give to buy back your life? 38 If among the unfaithful and sinful people of today you're ashamed of Me and what I say, then the Son of Man will be ashamed of you when He comes with the holy angels in His Father's glory.

9 "Let Me assure you," He told them, "there are some standing here who will never taste death till they see God has come to rule with power."

Jesus Shows His Glory

2 After five days Jesus took Peter, James, and John with Him and led them up a high mountain to be alone with them.
3 He was changed before them, and his clothes became dazzling white—nobody on earth could bleach them so white. 4 Elijah and Moses appeared to them and were talking with Jesus.
5 "Master," Peter said to Jesus, "it's good for us to be here. Let's put up three shelters, one for You, one for Moses, and one for Elijah." 6 He didn't know what he was saying; they were so terrified.
7 A cloud came and overshadowed them, and a voice came out of the cloud: "This is *My Son* whom I love. *Listen to Him.*" [14]
8 Suddenly, as they looked around, they no longer saw anyone but Jesus with them.
9 On their way down the mountain Jesus ordered them not to tell anyone what they had seen, till the Son of Man had risen from the dead. 10 They kept in mind what He said and

[14] Ps. 2:7; Deut. 18:15

K.J.V.

themselves, questioning one with another what the rising from the dead should mean.

11 And they asked him, saying, Why say the scribes that Elias must first come? 12And he answered and told them, Elias verily cometh first, and restoreth all things; and how it is written of the Son of man, that he must suffer many things, and be set at nought. 13 But I say unto you, That Elias is indeed come, and they have done unto him whatsoever they listed, as it is written of him.

14 And when he came to *his* disciples, he saw a great multitude about them, and the scribes questioning with them. 15And straightway all the people, when they beheld him, were greatly amazed, and running to *him* saluted him. 16And he asked the scribes, What question ye with them? 17And one of the multitude answered and said, Master, I have brought unto thee my son, which hath a dumb spirit; 18And wheresoever he taketh him, he teareth him; and he foameth, and gnasheth with his teeth, and pineth away: and I spake to thy disciples that they should cast him out; and they could not. 19 He answereth him, and saith, O faithless generation, how long shall I be with you? how long shall I suffer you? bring him unto me. 20And they brought him unto him: and when he saw him, straightway the spirit tare him; and he fell on the ground, and wallowed foaming. 21And he asked his father, How long is it ago since this came unto him? And he said, Of a child. 22And ofttimes it hath cast him into the fire, and into the waters, to destroy him: but if thou canst do any thing, have compassion on us, and help us. 23 Jesus said unto him, If thou canst believe, all things *are* possible to him that believeth. 24And straightway the father of the child cried out, and said with tears, Lord, I believe; help thou mine unbelief. 25 When Jesus saw that the people came running together, he rebuked the foul spirit, saying unto him, *Thou* dumb and deaf spirit, I charge thee, come out of him, and enter no more into him. 26And *the spirit* cried, and rent him sore, and came out of him: and he was as one dead; insomuch that many said, He is dead. 27 But Jesus took him by the hand, and lifted him up; and he arose. 28And when he was come into the house, his disciples asked him privately, Why could not we cast him out? 29And he said unto them, This kind can come forth by nothing, but by prayer and fasting.

30 And they departed thence, and passed through Galilee; and he would not that any man should know it. 31 For he taught his disciples, and said unto them, The Son of man is delivered into the hands of men, and they shall kill him; and after that he is killed, he shall rise the third day. 32 But they understood not that saying, and were afraid to ask him.

33 And he came to Capernaum: and being in the house he asked them, What was it that ye disputed among yourselves by the way? 34 But

N.A.S.

seized upon that statement, discussing with one another what rising from the dead might mean. 11And they *began* questioning Him, saying, *"Why is it* that the scribes say that first Elijah must come?" 12And He said to them, "Elijah does first come and restore everything. And *yet* how is it written of the Son of Man that He should suffer many things and be treated with contempt? 13 "But I say to you, that Elijah has indeed come, and they did to him whatever they wished, just as it is written of him."

14 And when they came *back* to the disciples, they saw a large crowd around them, and *some* scribes arguing with them. 15And immediately, when the entire crowd saw Him, they were amazed, and *began* running up to greet Him. 16And He asked them, "What are you discussing with them?" 17And one of the crowd answered Him, "Teacher, I brought You my son, possessed with a spirit which makes him mute; 18 and whenever it seizes him, it dashes him *to the ground* and he foams *at the mouth*, and grinds his teeth, and stiffens out. And I told Your disciples to cast it out, and they could not *do it*." 19And He *answered them and *said, "O unbelieving generation, how long shall I be with you? How long shall I put up with you? Bring him to Me!" 20And they brought the boy to Him. And when he saw Him, immediately the spirit threw him into a convulsion, and falling to the ground, he *began* rolling about and foaming *at the mouth*. 21And He asked his father, "How long has this been happening to him?" And he said, "From childhood. 22 "And it has often thrown him both into the fire and into the water to destroy him. But if You can do anything, take pity on us and help us!" 23And Jesus said to him, " 'If You can!' All things are possible to him who believes." 24 Immediately the boy's father cried out and *began* saying, "I do believe; help *me in* my unbelief." 25And when Jesus saw that a crowd was rapidly gathering, He rebuked the unclean spirit, saying to it, "You deaf and dumb spirit, I command you, come out of him and do not enter him again." 26And after crying out and throwing him into terrible convulsions, it came out; and *the boy* became so much like a corpse that most *of them* said, "He is dead!" 27 But Jesus took him by the hand and raised him; and he got up. 28And when He had come into *the* house, His disciples *began* questioning Him privately, "Why is it that we could not cast it out?" 29And He said to them, "This kind cannot come out by anything but prayer." [a]

30 And from there they went out and *began* to go through Galilee, and He was unwilling for anyone to know *about it*. 31 For He was teaching His disciples and telling them, "The Son of Man is to be [b]delivered up into the hands of men, and they will kill Him; and when He has been killed, He will rise again three days later." 32 But they did not understand *this* statement, and they were afraid to ask Him.

33 And they came to Capernaum; and when He was in the house, He *began* to question them, "What were you discussing on the way?" 34 But they kept silent, for on the way they

---

[a] Many mss. add: *and fasting.* [b] Or, *betrayed.*

WILLIAMS

caution fast in their minds, as they continued to discuss among themselves what rising from the dead meant.

11 Then they asked Him, "Why do the scribes say that Elijah has to come first?"

12 He answered them, "Elijah does come first and gets everything ready, but how is it that the Scripture says about the Son of Man that He will suffer much and be rejected? 13 But I tell you, Elijah has already come, and people treated him just as they pleased, as the Scripture says about him."

14 When they came to the disciples, they saw a great crowd around them and some scribes arguing with them. 15And all the people were utterly amazed when they saw Him, and ran up to Him and greeted Him.

16 Then He asked them, "Why are you arguing with them?"

17 A man from the crowd answered Him, "Teacher, I brought my son to you, for he has a dumb spirit. 18 Wherever it seizes him, it convulses him, and he foams at the mouth and grinds his teeth; and is wasting away. So I asked your disciples to drive it out, but they could not do it."

19 He answered them, "Oh, you unbelieving people of the times! a How long must I be with you! How long must I put up with you! Bring him to me." 20And they brought the boy to Him. As soon as the spirit saw Him, it convulsed the boy, and he fell on the ground and kept rolling over and foaming at the mouth.

21 Then He asked his father, "How long has he been like this?"

He answered, "From his childhood; 22 and many a time it has thrown him into the fire or into the water, to destroy him. But if there is anything you can do for him, do pity us and help us!"

23 Jesus said to him, "If there is anything I can do! Everything is possible for him who has faith!"

24 The boy's father at once cried out and said, "I do have faith; help my lack of faith!"

25 Then Jesus, because He saw that a crowd was rushing up to Him, reproved the foul spirit and said to it, "You deaf and dumb spirit, get out of him, I charge you, and never get into him again." 26 Then it gave a shriek and violently convulsed the boy, and got out of him. And the boy looked b like a corpse, so much so that the people said that he was dead. 27 But Jesus grasped his hand and raised him, and he got up.

28 When Jesus got home and was by Himself, His disciples were asking Him, "Why could not we drive it out?"

29 He answered them, "This sort of thing can be driven out only by prayer." c

30 Then they left there and were making a trip through Galilee, and He did not want anybody to know it; 31 for He was now teaching His disciples, and saying to them, "The Son of Man is to be turned over into men's hands, and they will kill Him, but three days after that He will rise again." 32 But they did not understand what this statement meant, and they were afraid to ask Him.

33 Then they reached Capernaum. When He got home, He asked them, "What were you discussing on the way home?" 34 But they had

BECK

argued with one another, asking, "What is this rising from the dead?" 11 So they asked Him, "Why do those who know the Bible say, 'First Elijah has to come'?"

12 "First *Elijah* does come," He told them, "and *puts* everything *in order again.*15 And what is written about the Son of Man? That He must suffer much and be treated shamefully. 13 Yes, I tell you, Elijah has come, and people treated him as they pleased, as it is written about him."

The Epileptic Boy

14 When they got back to the other disciples, they saw a big crowd around them and some Bible scholars arguing with them. 15 Then the whole crowd was amazed to see Jesus, and they ran and welcomed Him.

16 "What is this argument about?" He asked them.

17 "Teacher," someone in the crowd answered, "I brought You my son. There's a speechless spirit in him. 18 Wherever the spirit takes hold of him, it throws him down; he foams at the mouth and grinds his teeth and gets rigid. I asked Your disciples to drive out the spirit, but they couldn't do it."

19 "O you unbelieving people!" Jesus answered. "How long must I be with you? How long must I put up with you? Bring him to Me."

20 They brought the boy to Him. As soon as the spirit saw Jesus, it threw the boy into convulsions. He fell on the ground and rolled around and foamed at the mouth.

21 Jesus asked his father, "How long has he been like this?"

22 "Since he was a child," he said. "It often threw him into fire or into water to kill him. Oh, if You can do anything, have pity on us and help us."

23 "You say, 'If You can'!" Jesus answered him. "Anything can be done if you believe."

24 Immediately the child's father cried out, "I do believe; help me with my unbelief."

25 When Jesus saw a crowd quickly gather around Him, He talked sharply to the unclean spirit: "You deaf and dumb spirit, I order you, 'Come out of him, and don't go into him again.'"

26 It screamed and wrenched him violently and came out. The boy became like a corpse, so that everybody said, "He's dead."

27 Jesus took his hand, helped him get up, and he stood up.

28 When He went into a house and His disciples were alone with Him, they asked him, "Why couldn't we drive out the spirit?"

29 "This kind can be driven out only by prayer," He told them.

"I Will Die and Rise Again"

30 Leaving that place, they started to go on byways through Galilee. Jesus didn't want anybody to know about it, 31 because He was teaching His disciples and telling them: "The Son of Man is going to be betrayed into the hands of men, and they will kill Him, but on the third day after He's killed He will rise." 32 They didn't understand what He said and were afraid to ask Him.

Who Is the Greatest?

33 They went to Capernaum. When He came home, He asked the disciples, "What were you discussing on the way?" 34 They were silent

[a] *Unbelieving age.* [b] Grk., *became a corpse.*
[c] *and fasting,* in A.V., not in best Mss.

[15] Mal. 4:5-6

they held their peace: for by the way they had disputed among themselves, who *should be* the greatest. 35And he sat down, and called the twelve, and saith unto them, If any man desire to be first, *the same* shall be last of all, and servant of all. 36And he took a child, and set him in the midst of them: and when he had taken him in his arms, he said unto them, 37 Whosoever shall receive one of such children in my name, receiveth me; and whosoever shall receive me, receiveth not me, but him that sent me.

38 And John answered him, saying, Master, we saw one casting out devils in thy name, and he followeth not us; and we forbade him, because he followeth not us. 39 But Jesus said, Forbid him not: for there is no man which shall do a miracle in my name, that can lightly speak evil of me. 40 For he that is not against us is on our part. 41 For whosoever shall give you a cup of water to drink in my name, because ye belong to Christ, verily I say unto you, he shall not lose his reward. 42And whosoever shall offend one of *these* little ones that believe in me, it is better for him that a millstone were hanged about his neck, and he were cast into the sea. 43And if thy hand offend thee, cut it off: it is better for thee to enter into life maimed, than having two hands to go into hell, into the fire that never shall be quenched: 44 Where their worm dieth not, and the fire is not quenched. 45And if thy foot offend thee, cut it off: it is better for thee to enter halt into life, than having two feet to be cast into hell, into the fire that never shall be quenched: 46 Where their worm dieth not, and the fire is not quenched. 47And if thine eye offend thee, pluck it out: it is better for thee to enter into the kingdom of God with one eye, than having two eyes to be cast into hell fire: 48 Where their worm dieth not, and the fire is not quenched. 49 For every one shall be salted with fire, and every sacrifice shall be salted with salt. 50 Salt *is* good: but if the salt have lost his saltness, wherewith will ye season it? Have salt in yourselves, and have peace one with another.

had discussed with one another which *of them was* the greatest. 35And sitting down, He called the twelve and *said to them, "If any one wants to be first, he shall be last of all, and servant of all." 36And taking a child, He stood him in the midst of them; and taking him in His arms, He said to them, 37 "Whoever receives one child like this in My name is receiving Me; and whoever receives Me is not receiving Me, but Him who sent Me."

38 John said to Him, "Teacher, we saw someone casting out demons in Your name, and we tried to hinder him because he was not following us." 39 But Jesus said, "Do not hinder him, for there is no one who shall perform a miracle in My name, and be able soon afterward to speak evil of Me. 40 "For he who is not against us is ᵃfor us. 41 "For whoever gives you a cup of water to drink because of your name as *followers* of Christ, truly I say to you, he shall not lose his reward. 42 "And whoever causes one of these little ones who believe to stumble, it would be better for him if with a heavy millstone hung around his neck, he had been cast into the sea. 43 "And if your hand causes you to stumble, cut it off; it is better for you to enter life crippled, than having your two hands, to go into hell, into the unquenchable fire. 44 (See footnote ᵇ) 45 "And if your foot causes you to stumble, cut it off; it is better for you to enter life lame, than having your two feet, to be cast into hell. 46 (See footnote ᵇ) 47 "And if your eye causes you to stumble, cast it out; it is better for you to enter the kingdom of God with one eye, than having two eyes, to be cast into hell; 48 where THEIR WORM DOES NOT DIE, AND THE FIRE IS NOT QUENCHED. 49 "For everyone will be salted with fire. 50 "Salt is good; but if the salt becomes unsalty, with what will you make it salty *again?* Have salt in yourselves, and be at peace with one another."

10 And he arose from thence, and cometh into the coasts of Judea by the farther side of Jordan: and the people resort unto him again; and, as he was wont, he taught them again.

2 And the Pharisees came to him, and asked him, Is it lawful for a man to put away *his* wife? tempting him. 3And he answered and said unto them, What did Moses command you? 4And they said, Moses suffered to write a bill of divorcement, and to put *her* away. 5And Jesus

10 And rising up, He *went from there to the region of Judea, and beyond the Jordan; and crowds *gathered around Him again, and, according to His custom, He once more *began to teach them.

2 And *some* Pharisees came up to Him, testing Him, and *began* to question Him whether it was lawful for a man to divorce a wife. 3And He answered and said to them, "What did Moses command you?" 4And they said, "Moses permitted *a man* to write a certificate of divorce and send *her* away." 5 But Jesus said to them,

[a] Or, *on our side*. [b] Verses 44 and 46, which are identical with verse 48, are not found in the best ancient mss.

WILLIAMS

nothing to say, for they had discussed with one another which of them was to be greatest.

35 So He sat down and called the Twelve to Him and said, "If anyone wants to be the first, he must be the last of all and the servant of all." 36 Then He took a little child and had him stand in the midst of them; then He took him in His arms, and said to them, 37 "Whoever, as a disciple of mine,[d] welcomes one little child like this, welcomes me, and whoever welcomes me, welcomes not merely me but Him who sent me."

38 John said to Him, "Teacher, we saw a man using[e] your name to drive out demons, and we tried to stop him, for he was not one of our followers."

39 Jesus said, "Do not try to stop him, for there is no one who will use my name to do a mighty deed, and then be able soon to abuse me. 40 For whoever is not against us is for us.

41 "For whoever gives you a cup of water to drink, on the ground that you belong to Christ, I solemnly say to you, he will not fail to get his reward. 42 And whoever leads one of these lowly believers to do wrong, might better have a huge millstone hung around his neck and be thrown into the sea. 43 If your hand makes you do wrong, cut it off. You might better go into life maimed than keep both your hands and go down to the pit, to the fire that is never put out.[f] 45 And if your foot makes you do wrong, cut it off. You might better go into life crippled than keep both your feet and be thrown into the pit. 47 And if your eye makes you do wrong, tear it out. You might better go into the kingdom of God with only one eye than keep both your eyes and be thrown into the pit, 48 where the worm that feeds upon them never dies and the fire is never put out. 49 Everyone must be seasoned with fire. Salt is a good thing, but if salt loses its strength, how can you season it again? 50 You must keep on having salt within you, and keep on living in peace with one another."

BECK

because they had on the way discussed who was the greatest. He sat down and called the twelve.

35 "If anyone wants to be first," He told them, "he will have to be last of all and serve everybody." 36 He took a little child, had him stand in front of them, put His arms around him, and said to them, 37 "If you welcome a child like this in My name, you welcome Me. And if you welcome Me, you welcome not only Me but Him who sent Me."

"He Is for Us"

38 "Teacher," John said to Jesus, "we saw a man drive out devils in Your name, and we tried to stop him because he hasn't been with us."

39 "Don't try to stop him," Jesus said. "Anyone who does a miracle in My name cannot turn around and speak evil of Me. 40 Anyone who isn't against us is for us. 41 I tell you, anyone who gives you a cup of water to drink because you belong to Christ will certainly not lose his reward."

Do I Lead Others to Sin?

42 "If anyone leads into sin one of these little ones who believe in Me, it would be better for him to have a big millstone hung around his neck and be thrown into the lake.

43 "If your hand makes you sin, cut it off. It is better for you to go into life crippled than to have two hands and go to hell, where the fire can't be put out.* 45 If your foot makes you sin, cut it off. It is better for you to go into life with only one foot than to have two feet and be thrown into hell.* 47 If your eye makes you sin, throw it away. It is better for you to go into God's kingdom with one eye than to have two eyes and be thrown into hell, 48 where the worm that consumes them doesn't die and the fire isn't put out.[16]

49 "Everyone has to be salted with fire. 50 Salt is good. But if salt loses its taste, how will you make it taste salty again? Keep salt within you, and so live in peace with one another."

Husband and Wife

10 In Perea He answers questions about divorce; blesses little children; tells of the perils of riches; foretells His death again; refuses James's and John's request; says He came to serve and save; cures Bartimeus

Then He left there and went through the district of Judea and crossed the Jordan, and crowds of people again met around Him, and again He began to teach them, as His custom was. 2 Some Pharisees came up, and to test Him they began to ask Him whether a man should be allowed to divorce his wife. 3 And He answered them by asking, "What has Moses commanded you about it?"

4 They answered, "Moses allowed a man to divorce his wife, if he wrote out a divorce charge."

5 But Jesus said to them, "It was due to your

10 Jesus left that place and went into the country of Judea and on the other side of the Jordan, and again the crowds gathered around Him. And again He taught them as He used to do.

2 Some Pharisees came to Him. "Is it right for a man to divorce his wife?" they asked Him in order to test Him.

3 "What did Moses order you to do?" He asked them.

4 "Moses let a man make out a divorce paper and divorce his wife,"[17] they said.

5 "He wrote this law for you on account of

[d] Grk., in my name; so, as a disciple. [e] Grk., driving out—in your name. [f] Vv. 44, 46 not in best Mss.

* Our two oldest manuscripts do not have vv. 44 and 46: "Where their worm doesn't die and the fire isn't put out." See v. 48.
[16] Is. 66:24
[17] Deut. 24:1

K.J.V.

answered and said unto them, For the hardness of your heart he wrote you this precept. 6 But from the beginning of the creation God made them male and female. 7 For this cause shall a man leave his father and mother, and cleave to his wife; 8 And they twain shall be one flesh: so then they are no more twain, but one flesh. 9 What therefore God hath joined together, let not man put asunder. 10 And in the house his disciples asked him again of the same *matter*. 11 And he saith unto them, Whosoever shall put away his wife, and marry another, committeth adultery against her. 12 And if a woman shall put away her husband, and be married to another, she committeth adultery.

13 And they brought young children to him, that he should touch them; and *his* disciples rebuked those that brought *them*. 14 But when Jesus saw *it*, he was much displeased, and said unto them, Suffer the little children to come unto me, and forbid them not; for of such is the kingdom of God. 15 Verily I say unto you, Whosoever shall not receive the kingdom of God as a little child, he shall not enter therein. 16 And he took them up in his arms, put *his* hands upon them, and blessed them.

17 And when he was gone forth into the way, there came one running, and kneeled to him, and asked him, Good Master, what shall I do that I may inherit eternal life? 18 And Jesus said unto him, Why callest thou me good? *there is* none good but one, *that is,* God. 19 Thou knowest the commandments, Do not commit adultery, Do not kill, Do not steal, Do not bear false witness, Defraud not, Honour thy father and mother. 20 And he answered and said unto him, Master, all these have I observed from my youth. 21 Then Jesus beholding him loved him, and said unto him, One thing thou lackest: go thy way, sell whatsoever thou hast, and give to the poor, and thou shalt have treasure in heaven: and come, take up the cross, and follow me. 22 And he was sad at that saying, and went away grieved: for he had great possessions.

23 And Jesus looked round about, and saith unto his disciples, How hardly shall they that have riches enter into the kingdom of God! 24 And the disciples were astonished at his words. But Jesus answereth again, and saith unto them, Children, how hard is it for them that trust in riches to enter into the kingdom of God! 25 It is easier for a camel to go through the eye of a needle, than for a rich man to enter into the kingdom of God. 26 And they were astonished out of measure, saying among themselves, Who then can be saved? 27 And Jesus looking upon them saith, With men *it is* impossible, but not with God: for with God all things are possible. 28 Then Peter began to say unto him, Lo, we have left all, and have followed thee. 29 And Jesus answered and said, Verily I say unto you, There is no man that hath left house, or brethren, or sisters, or father, or mother, or wife, or children, or lands, for my sake, and the gospel's, 30 But he shall receive a hundredfold now in this time, houses, and brethren, and sisters, and mothers, and children, and lands, with persecutions; and in the world to come eternal life. 31 But many *that are* first shall be last; and the last first.

N.A.S.

"Because of your hardness of heart he wrote you this commandment. 6 "But from the beginning of creation, God MADE THEM MALE AND FEMALE. 7 "FOR THIS CAUSE A MAN SHALL LEAVE HIS FATHER AND MOTHER,[a] 8 AND THE TWO SHALL BECOME ONE FLESH; consequently they are no longer two, but one flesh. 9 "What therefore God has joined together, let no man separate." 10 And *back* in the house again, the disciples *began* questioning Him about this *matter*. 11 And He *said to them, "Whoever divorces his wife and marries another woman commits adultery against her; 12 and if she herself divorces her husband and marries another man, she is committing adultery."

13 And they *began* bringing children to Him, so that He might touch them; and the disciples rebuked them. 14 But when Jesus saw this, He was indignant and said to them, "Permit the children to come to Me; do not hinder them; for the kingdom of God belongs to such as these. 15 "Truly I say to you, whoever does not receive the kingdom of God like a child shall not enter it *at all*." 16 And He took them in His arms and *began* blessing them, laying His hands upon them.

17 And as He was setting out on a journey, a man ran up to Him and knelt before Him, and *began* asking Him, "Good Teacher, what shall I do to inherit eternal life?" 18 And Jesus said to him, "Why do you call Me good? No one is good except God alone. 19 "You know the commandments, 'DO NOT MURDER, DO NOT COMMIT ADULTERY, DO NOT STEAL, DO NOT BEAR FALSE WITNESS, Do not defraud, HONOR YOUR FATHER AND MOTHER.' " 20 And he said to Him, "Teacher, I have kept all these things from my youth up." 21 And looking at him, Jesus felt a love for him, and said to him, "One thing you lack: go and sell all you possess, and give *it* to the poor, and you shall have treasure in heaven; and come, follow Me." 22 But at these words his face fell, and he went away grieved, for he was one who owned much property.

23 And Jesus, looking around, *said to His disciples, "How hard it will be for those who are wealthy to enter the kingdom of God!" 24 And the disciples were amazed at His words. But Jesus *answered again and *said to them, "Children, how hard it is [b]to enter the kingdom of God! 25 "It is easier for a camel to go through the eye of a needle than for a rich man to enter the kingdom of God." 26 And they were even more astonished and said to Him, "Then who can be saved?" 27 Looking upon them, Jesus *said, "With men it is impossible, but not with God; for all things are possible with God." 28 Peter began to say to Him, "Behold, we have left everything and followed You." 29 Jesus said, "Truly I say to you, there is no one who has left house or brothers or sisters or mother or father or children or farms, for My sake and for the gospel's sake, 30 but that he shall receive a hundred times as much now in the present age, houses and brothers and sisters and mothers and children and farms, along with persecutions; and in the [c]world to come, eternal life. 31 "But many *who are* first, will be last; and the last, first."

---

[a] Some mss. add: *and shall cleave to his wife.*
[b] Later mss. insert: *for those who trust in wealth.* [c] Or, *age.*

WILLIAMS

moral perversity ^a that Moses wrote that command in your law. 6 But from the beginning of the creation, 'God made them male and female. 7 Therefore, a man must leave his father and mother, and he and his wife must become one,' so they are no longer two but one. 9 Therefore, what God has joined together man must stop separating."

10 On reaching the house the disciples again asked Him about this. 11 So He said to them, "If any man divorces his wife to marry another woman, he commits adultery against his former wife, 12 and if any woman divorces her husband to marry another man, she commits adultery."

13 And people were bringing little children to Him for Him to touch them, but the disciples reproved them for it. 14 When Jesus saw it, He was indignant, and said to them, "Let the little children come to me, and stop keeping them from it, for to such as these the kingdom of God belongs. 15 I solemnly say to you, whoever does not accept the kingdom of God as a little child does, will never get into it at all." 16 Then He took the little children into His arms, and as He laid His hands upon them one by one, He tenderly^b blessed them.

17 As He was again starting on a journey, a man ran up to Him, and knelt to Him, and was asking Him, "Good Teacher, what must I do to get eternal life?"

18 And Jesus answered him, "Why do you call me perfectly good? No one is perfectly good but God Himself. 19 You know the commandments: Do not murder, Do not commit adultery, Do not steal, Do not bear false witness, Do not defraud, Practice honoring your father and mother."

20 But he said to Him, "Teacher, I have kept all these commandments ever since I was a child."

21 Then Jesus looked at him and loved him, and said to him, "You lack one thing. Go, sell everything you have, and give the money to the poor, and you will have riches in heaven; then come back and follow me." 22 But his countenance fell at that command, and he went away in deep distress, for he owned a great deal of property.

23 Then Jesus looked around and said to His disciples, "How hard it will be for those who have money to get into the kingdom of God!" 24 His disciples were startled at this statement. But Jesus again said to them as He continued the topic, "My children, how hard it is to get into the kingdom of God! 25 It is easier for a camel to go through a needle's eye than for a rich man to get into the kingdom of God."

26 They were perfectly dumfounded, and said to Him, "Then who can be saved?"

27 But Jesus looked at them and said, "This is impossible for men, but everything is possible for God."

28 Then Peter started to say to Him, "We have left everything we had and followed you."

29 Jesus said, "I solemnly say to you, there is no one who has given up home or brothers or sisters or mother or father or children or farm for me and for the good news, 30 who will not receive now in this life a hundred times as much in houses and brothers and sisters and mothers and children and farms, but along with them persecution, and in the world to come eternal life. 31 But many who are first now will be last then, and last now who will be first then."

[a] Grk., *hardness of heart.* [b] So comp. vb. Fol. B and Sin. Mss.

BECK

your closed minds," Jesus told them. 6 "But when God made the world, He in the beginning *made them a male and a female.*¹⁸ 7 *That's why a man will leave his father and mother* 8 *and the two will be one flesh.*¹⁹ And so they are no more two but one flesh. 9 Now, what God has joined together man must not separate."

10 In the house the disciples also asked Him about this. 11 "If anyone divorces his wife," He answered them, "and marries another, he's living in adultery with her. 12 And if a wife divorces her husband and marries another man, she's living in adultery."

Jesus Loves Children

13 Some people brought babies to Jesus to have Him touch them, but the disciples sternly told them not to do it.

14 But when Jesus saw this, He didn't like it at all. "Let the little children come to Me," He told them. "Don't keep them away. God's kingdom belongs to such as these. 15 I tell you the truth, if you don't receive God's kingdom like a little child, you will not get into it."

16 He took them in His arms, laid His hands on them, and blessed them.

The Rich Young Leader

17 As Jesus was coming out to the road, a man came running to Him and knelt before Him. "Good Teacher," he asked Him, "what should I do to get everlasting life?"

18 "Why do you call Me good?" Jesus asked him. "Nobody is good except One—God. 19 You know the commandments: *Don't murder, don't commit adultery, don't steal, don't lie, don't rob, honor your father and mother."* ²⁰

20 "Teacher," he told Him, "I've kept all these since I was a child."

21 Jesus looked at him and loved him. "You lack one thing," Jesus told him. "Go, sell everything you have, and give the money to the poor, and you'll have a treasure in heaven. Then come and follow Me."

22 When he heard that, he looked gloomy and went away sad, because he was very rich.

23 Jesus looked around and said to His disciples, "How hard it is for rich people to get into God's kingdom!"

24 The disciples were surprised that He said that. But Jesus said to them again, "Children, how hard it is to get into God's kingdom! 25 It's easier for a camel to go through a needle's eye than for a rich man to get into God's kingdom."

26 They were more amazed than ever. "Who can be saved?" they asked one another.

27 "Men can't do this," Jesus said as He looked at them. "But God can, because *God can do anything."* ²¹

28 Then Peter spoke up: "Look! We gave up everything and followed You."

29 "Let Me assure you," Jesus said, "everyone who gave up his home, brothers or sisters, mother, father, or children, or fields for Me and for the good news, 30 will certainly get a hundred times as much here in this life: houses, brothers and sisters, mothers and children and fields, with persecutions, and in the coming world everlasting life. 31 But many who are first will be last, and the last first."

[18] Gen. 1:27; 5:2
[19] Gen. 2:24
[20] Ex. 20:12-16; Deut. 5:16-20
[21] Gen. 18:14; Job 42:2; Zech. 8:6

K.J.V.

32 And they were in the way going up to Jerusalem; and Jesus went before them: and they were amazed; and as they followed, they were afraid. And he took again the twelve, and began to tell them what things should happen unto him, 33 *Saying,* Behold, we go up to Jerusalem; and the Son of man shall be delivered unto the chief priests, and unto the scribes; and they shall condemn him to death, and shall deliver him to the Gentiles: 34And they shall mock him, and shall scourge him, and shall spit upon him, and shall kill him; and the third day he shall rise again.

35 And James and John, the sons of Zebedee, come unto him, saying, Master, we would that thou shouldest do for us whatsoever we shall desire. 36And he said unto them, What would ye that I should do for you? 37 They said unto him, Grant unto us that we may sit, one on thy right hand, and the other on thy left hand, in thy glory. 38 But Jesus said unto them, Ye know not what ye ask: can ye drink of the cup that I drink of? and be baptized with the baptism that I am baptized with? 39And they said unto him, We can. And Jesus said unto them, Ye shall indeed drink of the cup that I drink of; and with the baptism that I am baptized withal shall ye be baptized: 40 But to sit on my right hand and on my left hand is not mine to give; but *it shall be given to 'them* for whom it is prepared. 41And when the ten heard *it,* they began to be much displeased with James and John. 42 But Jesus called them *to him,* and saith unto them, Ye know that they which are accounted to rule over the Gentiles exercise lordship over them; and their great ones exercise authority upon them. 43 But so shall it not be among you: but whosoever will be great among you, shall be your minister: 44And whosoever of you will be the chiefest, shall be servant of all. 45 For even the Son of man came not to be ministered unto, but to minister, and to give his life a ransom for many.

46 And they came to Jericho: and as he went out of Jericho with his disciples and a great number of people, blind Bartimeus, the son of Timeus, sat by the highway side begging. 47And when he heard that it was Jesus of Nazareth, he began to cry out, and say, *thou* Son of David, have mercy on me. 48And many charged him that he should hold his peace: but he cried the more a great deal, *Thou* Son of David, have mercy on me. 49And Jesus stood still, and commanded him to be called. And they call the blind man, saying unto him, Be of good comfort, rise; he calleth thee. 50And he, casting away his garment, rose, and came to Jesus. 51And Jesus answered and said unto him, What wilt thou that I should do unto thee? The blind man said unto him, Lord, that I might receive my sight. 52And Jesus said unto him, Go thy way; thy faith hath made thee whole. And immediately he received his sight, and followed Jesus in the way.

N.A.S.

32 And they were on the road, going up to Jerusalem, and Jesus was walking on ahead of them; and they were amazed, and those who followed were fearful. And again He took the twelve aside and began to tell them what was going to happen to Him, 33 *saying,* "Behold, we are going up to Jerusalem, and the Son of Man will be ªdelivered up to the chief priests and the scribes; and they will condemn Him to death, and will deliver Him up to the Gentiles. 34 "And they will mock Him and spit upon Him, and scourge Him, and kill *Him,* and three days later He will rise again."

35 And James and John, the two sons of Zebedee, *came up to Him, saying to Him, "Teacher, we want You to do for us whatever we ask of You." 36And He said to them, "What do you want Me to do for you?" 37And they said to Him, "Grant that we may sit in Your glory, one on Your right, and one on *Your* left." 38 But Jesus said to them, "You do not know what you are asking for. Are you able to drink the cup that I drink, or to be baptized with the baptism with which I am baptized?" 39And they said to Him, "We are able." And Jesus said to them, "The cup that I drink you shall drink; and you shall be baptized with the baptism with which I am baptized. 40 "But to sit on My right or on *My* left, this is not Mine to give; but *it is for those* for whom it has been prepared." 41And hearing this, the ten began to feel indignant toward James and John. 42And calling them to Himself, Jesus *said to them, "You know that those who are recognized as rulers of the Gentiles lord it over them; and their great men exercise authority over them. 43 "But it is not so among you, but whoever wishes to become great among you shall be your servant; 44 and whoever wishes to be first among you shall be slave of all. 45 "For even the Son of Man did not come to be served, but to serve, and to give His life a ransom for many."

46 And they *came to Jericho. And as He was going out from Jericho with His disciples and a great multitude, a blind beggar *named* Bartimaeus, the son of Timaeus, was sitting by the road. 47And when he heard that it was Jesus the Nazarene, he began to cry out and say, "Jesus, Son of David, have mercy on me!" 48And many were sternly telling him to be quiet, but he *began* crying out all the more, "Son of David, have mercy on me!" 49And Jesus stopped and said, "Call him *here.*" And they *called the blind man, saying to him, "Take courage, arise! He is calling for you." 50And casting aside his cloak, he jumped up, and came to Jesus. 51And answering him, Jesus said, "What do you want Me to do for you?" And the blind man said to Him, "ᵇRabboni, I want to regain my sight!" 52And Jesus said to him, "Go your way; your faith has made you well." And immediately he received his sight and *began* following Him on the road.

---

[a] Or, *betrayed.* [b] I.e., *My Master.*

WILLIAMS

32 As they were walking along the road up to Jerusalem, Jesus was going on ahead of them, but they were dazed while those who were still following were afraid. Then again He took the Twelve aside and began to tell them what was going to befall Him. 33 "Listen! We are going up to Jerusalem, and the Son of Man will be turned over to the high priests and scribes, and they will sentence Him to death, and will turn Him over to the heathen, 34 and they will make sport of Him, and spit on Him, and flog Him, and kill Him, but three days after He will rise again."

35 And Zebedee's two sons, James and John, came up to Him and said, "Teacher, we want you to do for us whatever we ask."

36 He asked then, "What do you want me to do for you?"

37 They answered Him, "Grant us to sit, one at your right hand and one at your left, in your splendor."

38 Jesus said to them, "You do not realize what you are asking for. Can you drink the cup that I am drinking, or endure the baptism of agony that I am to endure?"

39 They answered Him, "We can."

Jesus said to them, "Yes, the cup that I am drinking you will have to drink, and the baptism of agony that I am enduring you will have to endure, 40 but seats at my right and at my left are not mine to give, but they will be given to those for whom they have been prepared."

41 When the other ten heard of it, they were at first very indignant at James and John. 42 Then Jesus called them to Him, and said to them, "You know that those who are supposed to rule the heathen lord it over them, and their great men rule as despots over them; 43 but this is not to be the case among you. Whoever wants to be great among you must be your servant, 44 and whoever wants to hold the first positions among you must be everybody's slave. 45 For the Son of Man did not come to be served but to serve, and to give His life a ransom price to set many free."

46 Then they came to Jericho. And as He was leaving Jericho, with His disciples and a great crowd, Timeus' son, Bartimeus, a blind beggar, was sitting on the roadside. 47 When he heard that it was Jesus of Nazareth, he began to shout, "Jesus, you son of David, do pity me!"

48 Many of the people began to rebuke him and to tell him to keep quiet, but all the louder he kept shouting, "You son of David, do pity me!"

49 So Jesus stopped and said, "Tell him to come here."

Then they told the blind man, saying, "Cheer up! Get up! He is calling for you." 50 He threw off his coat and jumped up and went to Jesus.

51 Then Jesus asked him, "What do you want me to do for you?"

The blind man answered, "Good Teacher, I want to see again."

52 Then Jesus said to him, "Go; your faith has cured you." And all at once he could see again, and began to follow Jesus along the road.

BECK

The Cup of Suffering

32 As they were on their way up to Jerusalem, Jesus walked ahead of them. They were amazed, and the others who were following Him were afraid. So once again He took the twelve with Him and told them what was going to happen to Him: 33 "Look, we're going up to Jerusalem, and the Son of Man will be betrayed to the ruling priests and the Bible scholars, who will condemn Him to die and hand Him over to the Gentiles. 34 They'll mock Him and spit on Him, scourge Him and kill Him. But on the third day He will rise."

35 James and John, the sons of Zebedee, came to Him. "Teacher," they said to Him, "we want You to do for us what we ask."

36 "What do you want Me to do for you?" He asked them.

37 "Let one of us sit at Your right," they told Him, "and the other at Your left in Your glory."

38 "You don't know what you're asking," Jesus answered them. "Can you drink the cup I'm drinking or be baptized with the baptism with which I'm being baptized?"

39 "We can," they told Him.

"You'll drink the cup I'm drinking," Jesus told them, "and be baptized with the baptism with which I'm being baptized. 40 But sitting at My right or left is something I can give only to those for whom it is prepared."

41 When the other ten heard about it, they got angry with James and John. 42 Then Jesus called them and told them, "You know that those who are considered rulers of the nations are lords over them, and their great men are tyrants over them. 43 But among you it's different. Anyone who wants to become great among you will have to serve you, 44 and anyone who wants to be first among you will have to be everybody's slave. 45 Why, even the Son of Man didn't come to be served but to serve and give His life as a ransom for all people."

Blind Bartimaeus

46 Then they came to Jericho. As Jesus and His disciples and many people were leaving Jericho, Bartimaeus, the son of Timaeus, a blind beggar, was sitting by the road. 47 When he heard it was Jesus from Nazareth, he began to call, "Son of David, Jesus, have pity on me!"

48 Many were urging him to be quiet. But he called all the louder, "Son of David, have pity on me!"

49 Jesus stopped and said, "Call him!" They called the blind man and told him, "Cheer up! Get up! He's calling you." 50 He laid aside his garment, jumped up, and went to Jesus.

51 "What do you want Me to do for you?" Jesus asked him.

"Master, I want to see again," the blind man told Him.

52 "Go," Jesus told him; "your faith has made you well."

Immediately he could see, and he followed Him on the road.

11 And when they came nigh to Jerusalem, unto Bethphage and Bethany, at the mount of Olives, he sendeth forth two of his disciples, 2And saith unto them, Go your way into the village over against you: and as soon as ye be entered into it, ye shall find a colt tied, whereon never man sat; loose him, and bring *him*. 3And if any man say unto you, Why do ye this? say ye that the Lord hath need of him; and straightway he will send him hither. 4And they went their way, and found the colt tied by the door without in a place where two ways met; and they loose him. 5And certain of them that stood there said unto them, What do ye, loosing the colt? 6And they said unto them even as Jesus had commanded: and they let them go. 7And they brought the colt to Jesus, and cast their garments on him; and he sat upon him. 8And many spread their garments in the way; and others cut down branches off the trees, and strewed *them* in the way. 9And they that went before, and they that followed, cried, saying, Hosanna; Blessed *is* he that cometh in the name of the Lord: 10 Blessed *be* the kingdom of our father David, that cometh in the name of the Lord: Hosanna in the highest. 11And Jesus entered into Jerusalem, and into the temple: and when he had looked round about upon all things, and now the eventide was come, he went out unto Bethany with the twelve.

12 And on the morrow, when they were come from Bethany; he was hungry: 13And seeing a fig tree afar off having leaves, he came, if haply he might find any thing thereon: and when he came to it, he found nothing but leaves; for the time of figs was not *yet*. 14And Jesus answered and said unto it, No man eat fruit of thee hereafter for ever. And his disciples heard *it*.

15 And they come to Jerusalem: and Jesus went into the temple, and began to cast out them that sold and bought in the temple, and overthrew the tables of the money changers, and the seats of them that sold doves; 16And would not suffer that any man should carry *any* vessel through the temple. 17And he taught, saying unto them, Is it not written, My house shall be called of all nations the house of prayer? but ye have made it a den of thieves. 18And the scribes and chief priests heard *it*, and sought how they might destroy him: for they feared him, because all the people was astonished at his doctrine. 19And when even was come, he went out of the city.

20 And in the morning, as they passed by, they saw the fig tree dried up from the roots. 21And Peter calling to remembrance saith unto him, Master, behold, the fig tree which thou cursedst is withered away. 22And Jesus answering saith unto them, Have faith in God. 23 For

11 And as they *approached Jerusalem, at Bethphage and Bethany, near the Mount of Olives, He *sent two of His disciples, 2 and *said to them, "Go into the village opposite you, and immediately as you enter it, you will find a colt tied *there*, on which no one yet has ever sat; untie it and bring it *here*. 3 "And if anyone says to you, 'Why are you doing this?' you say, 'The Lord has need of it;' and immediately he will send it back here." 4And they went away and found a colt tied at the door outside in the street; and they *untied it. 5And some of the bystanders were saying to them, "What are you doing, untying the colt?" 6And they spoke to them just as Jesus had told *them*, and they gave them permission. 7And they * brought the colt to Jesus and put their garments on it; and He sat upon it. 8And many spread their garments in the road, and others *spread* leafy branches which they had cut from the fields. 9And those who went before, and those who followed after, were crying out,

"HOSANNA!
BLESSED IS HE WHO COMES IN THE NAME
    OF THE LORD;
10 "Blessed *is* the coming kingdom of our father David;
HOSANNA in the highest."

11 And He entered Jerusalem *and came* into the temple; and after looking all around, He departed for Bethany with the twelve, since it was already late.

12 And on the next day, when they had departed from Bethany, He became hungry. 13And seeing at a distance a fig tree in leaf, He went *to see* if perhaps He would find anything on it; and when He came to it, He found nothing but leaves, for it was not the season for figs. 14And He answered and said to it, "May no one ever eat fruit from you again!" And His disciples were listening.

15 And they *came to Jerusalem. And He entered the temple and began to cast out those who were buying and selling in the temple, and overturned the tables of the money-changers and the seats of those who were selling doves; 16 and He would not permit anyone to carry goods through the temple. 17And He *began* to teach and say to them, "Is it not written, 'MY HOUSE SHALL BE CALLED A HOUSE OF PRAYER FOR ALL THE NATIONS'? But you have made it a robbers' den." 18And the chief priests and the scribes heard *this*, and *began* seeking how to destroy Him; for they were afraid of Him, for all the multitude was astonished at His teaching.

19 And whenever evening came, they would go out of the city.

20 And as they were passing by in the morning, they saw the fig tree withered from the roots *up*. 21And being reminded, Peter *said to Him, "Rabbi, behold, the fig tree which You cursed has withered." 22And Jesus *answered saying to them, "Have faith in God. 23 "Truly

WILLIAMS

11 *Jesus rides as King into Jerusalem; curses the fig tree; drives the traders out of the temple; tells of faith that moves mountains; questioned by the leaders He floors them with a question*

When they were getting near Jerusalem, that is, were at Bethphage and Bethany in front of the Mount of Olives, He sent two of His disciples on ahead, 2 and said to them, "Go into the village in front of you, and as soon as you get into it, you will find a colt tied which has never been ridden by a man. Untie it and bring it here. 3 And if anyone asks you, 'Why are you doing that?' answer, 'The Lord needs it, and will soon send it back here.' "

4 So off they went and found a colt tied outside a door at a street corner. They untied it, 5 but some bystanders said to them, "What are you doing, untying the colt?" 6 And they answered as Jesus had directed them, and so they let them bring it. 7 They brought the colt to Jesus, and they threw their coats over it, and Jesus mounted it. 8 And many of the people spread their coats in the road, while others scattered layers of leaves cut from the fields. 9 Then those in front and those behind Him shouted:

"Welcome Him!

Blessed be He who comes in the name of the Lord;

10 Blessed be the coming reign of our father David!

Welcome Him from on high!"

11 And so He went into Jerusalem and into the temple. After He had looked everything over, as it was already late, He went out with the Twelve to Bethany.

12 Next day, while they were walking over from Bethany, He felt hungry. 13 Now in the distance He saw a fig tree covered with leaves, and He went up to it to see if He might find some figs on it, but when He got to it, He found nothing but leaves, for it was not the time for figs. 14 So He spoke to it and said, "Never again may anyone eat a fig from you!" And His disciples were listening to it.

15 Then they reached Jerusalem, and He went into the temple and began to drive out of it those who were buying and selling things in it. Then He upset the money-changers' tables and the dove-dealers' counters, 16 and would not let anybody carry a vessel through the temple. 17 And He continued teaching them and saying, "Does not the Scripture say, 'My house shall be called a house of prayer for all the nations'? But you have made it a cave for robbers."

18 Then the high priests and the scribes heard of this, and they kept looking for some way to destroy Him, for they were afraid of Him, for everybody was swept off his feet *a* at what He said. 19 So when evening came, He and His disciples used to go out of the city.

20 In the morning as they were passing along, they noticed that the fig tree was withered, clear down to its roots. 21 And Peter remembered about it, and said to Him, "Look, Teacher! The fig tree which you cursed has withered!"

22 Then Jesus answered them, "Have faith in God! 23 I solemnly say to you, whoever says

[a] Grk., *struck out of themselves.*

BECK

The King Comes to Jerusalem

11 When they were getting near Jerusalem and came to Bethphage and Bethany, at the Mount of Olives, Jesus sent two of His disciples. 2 "Go into the village ahead of you," He told them, "and just as you go into it, you'll find a young donkey tied up that nobody ever sat on. Untie it and bring it to Me. 3 And if anybody asks you, 'Why are you doing that?' say, 'The Lord needs it and will promptly send it back here.' "

4 They went and found the colt tied to the gate, outside in the street, and they started to untie it.

5 "What are you doing, untying the colt?" some of the men standing there asked them. 6 They answered them just as Jesus had told them, and the men let them go.

7 So they brought the colt to Jesus, put their garments on it, and He sat on it. 8 Many spread their garments on the road, and others spread .leafy branches that they cut in the fields. 9 Those who went ahead and those who followed Him were shouting:

"Our Savior!

10 *Blessed is He who is coming in the Lord's name!* [23]

Blessed is the coming kingdom of our father David!

Our Savior—in the highest heavens!"

11 He came into Jerusalem and into the temple and looked around at everything. Since it was late now, He went with the twelve out to Bethany.

Nothing but Leaves

12 The next day when they left Bethany, Jesus was hungry. 13 In the distance He saw a fig tree with leaves, and He went to see if He could find anything on it. When He came to it, He found nothing but leaves, because it wasn't the season for figs. 14 Then He said to the tree, and His disciples heard Him: "May nobody ever eat fruit from you again!"

He Cleanses the Temple Again

15 When they came to Jerusalem, He went into the temple and proceeded to drive out those who were selling and buying in the temple, and He upset the tables of the money changers and the chairs of those who sold pigeons. 16 He would not let anyone carry a vessel across the temple grounds.

17 Then He taught: "Isn't it written, *My house should be called a house of prayer for all the nations?* [23] But you made it *a den of robbers.*" [24]

18 When the ruling priests and Bible scholars heard Him, they tried to find a way to kill Him. They were afraid of Him, because He amazed all the people by His teaching.

19 When evening came, He would leave the city.

The Fig Tree Is Withered

20 When they walked by early in the morning, they saw the fig tree withered from the roots up. 21 Peter, remembering, said to Him, "Master, look! The fig tree You cursed is dried up."

22 "Believe in God!" Jesus answered them. 23 "I tell you the truth: If you will say to this

[22] Ps. 118:25-26
[23] Is. 56:7
[24] Jer. 7:11

K.J.V.

verily I say unto you, That whosoever shall say unto this mountain, Be thou removed, and be thou cast into the sea; and shall not doubt in his heart, but shall believe that those things which he saith shall come to pass; he shall have whatsoever he saith. 24 Therefore I say unto you, What things soever ye desire, when ye pray, believe that ye receive *them*, and ye shall have *them*. 25And when ye stand praying, forgive, if ye have aught against any; that your Father also which is in heaven may forgive you your trespasses. 26 But if ye do not forgive, neither will your Father which is in heaven forgive your trespasses.

27 And they come again to Jerusalem: and as he was walking in the temple, there come to him the chief priests, and the scribes, and the elders, 28And say unto him, By what authority doest thou these things? and who gave thee this authority to do these things? 29And Jesus answered and said unto them, I will also ask of you one question, and answer me, and I will tell you by what authority I do these things. 30 The baptism of John, was *it* from heaven, or of men? answer me. 31And they reasoned with themselves, saying, If we shall say, From heaven; he will say, Why then did ye not believe him? 32 But if we shall say, Of men; they feared the people: for all *men* counted John, that he was a prophet indeed. 33And they answered and said unto Jesus, We cannot tell. And Jesus answering saith unto them, Neither do I tell you by what authority I do these things.

12 And he began to speak unto them by parables. A *certain* man planted a vineyard, and set a hedge about *it*, and digged *a place for* the winefat, and built a tower, and let it out to husbandmen, and went into a far country. 2And at the season he sent to the husbandmen a servant, that he might receive from the husbandmen of the fruit of the vineyard. 3And they caught *him*, and beat him, and sent *him* away empty. 4And again he sent unto them another servant; and at him they cast stones, and wounded *him* in the head, and sent *him* away shamefully handled. 5And again he sent another; and him they killed, and many others; beating some, and killing some. 6 Having yet therefore one son, his well beloved, he sent him also last unto them, saying, They will reverence my son. 7 But those husbandmen said among themselves, This is the heir; come, let us kill him, and the inheritance shall be ours. 8And they took him, and killed *him*, and cast *him* out of the vineyard. 9 What shall therefore the lord of the vineyard do? he will come and destroy the husbandmen, and will give the vineyard unto others. 10And have ye not read this Scripture; The stone which the builders rejected is become the head of the corner: 11 This was the Lord's doing, and it is marvellous in our eyes? 12And they sought to lay hold on him, but feared the people; for they knew that he had spoken the parable against them: and they left him, and went their way.

N.A.S.

I say to you, whoever says to this mountain, 'Be taken up and cast into the sea,' and does not doubt in his heart, but believes that what he says is going to happen; it shall be *granted* him. 24 "Therefore I say to you, all things for which you pray and ask, believe that you have received them, and they shall be *granted* you. 25 "And whenever you stand praying, forgive, if you have anything against anyone; so that your Father also who is in heaven may forgive you your transgressions." 26 (See footnote [a])

27 And they *came again to Jerusalem. And as He was walking in the temple, the chief priests, and scribes, and elders *came to Him, 28 and *began saying to Him, "By what authority are You doing these things, or who gave You this authority to do these things?" 29And Jesus said to them, "I will ask you one question, and you answer Me, and *then* I will tell you by what authority I do these things. 30 "Was the baptism of John from heaven, or from men? Answer Me." 31And they *began* reasoning with one another, saying, "If we say, 'From heaven,' He will say, 'Then why did you not believe him?' 32 "But shall we say, 'From men'?"—they were afraid of the multitude, for all considered John to have been a prophet indeed. 33And answering Jesus, they *said, "We do not know." And Jesus *said to them, "Neither will I tell you by what authority I do these things."

12 And He began to speak to them in parables: "A man PLANTED A VINEYARD, AND PUT A WALL AROUND IT, AND DUG A VAT UNDER THE WINEPRESS, AND BUILT A TOWER, and rented it out to [b]vine-growers and went on a journey. 2 "And at the *harvest* time he sent a slave to the vine-growers, in order to receive *some* of the produce of the vineyard from the vine-growers. 3 "And they took him, and beat him, and sent him away empty-handed. 4 "And again he sent them another slave, and they wounded him in the head, and treated him shamefully. 5 "And he sent another, and that one they killed; and *so with* many others, beating some, and killing others. 6 "He had one more *to send*, a beloved son; he sent him last *of all* to them, saying, 'They will respect my son.' 7 "But those vine-growers said to one another, 'This is the heir; come, let us kill him, and the inheritance will be ours!' 8 "And they took him, and killed him, and threw him out of the vineyard. 9 "What will the owner of the vineyard do? He will come and destroy the vine-growers, and will give the vineyard to others. 10 "Have you not even read this scripture:

'THE STONE WHICH THE BUILDERS REJECTED, THIS BECAME THE CHIEF CORNER *stone*; 11 'THIS CAME ABOUT FROM THE LORD, AND IT IS MARVELOUS IN OUR EYES'?"

12And they were seeking to seize Him; and *yet* they feared the multitude; for they understood that He had spoken the parable against them. And *so* they left Him, and went away.

[a] Later mss. add vs. 26: *"But if you do not forgive, neither will your Father who is in heaven forgive your transgressions."* [b] Here and in verses 2, 7, and 9: or, *tenant farmers.*

WILLIAMS

to this mountain, 'Get up and throw yourself into the sea,' and does not doubt at all in his heart, but has faith that what he says will take place, shall have it. 24 So then I tell you, whenever you pray and ask for anything, have faith that it has been granted you, and you will get it. 25 And whenever you stand and pray, if you have anything against anybody, forgive him, so that your Father in heaven too may forgive you your shortcomings." [b]

27 Then again they went into Jerusalem. And while Jesus was walking about in the temple, the high priests, scribes, and elders came up to Him 28 and said to Him, "What sort of authority have you for doing as you do? Or, who gave you the authority to do as you do?"

29 Jesus said to them, "Let me ask you just one question, and if you answer me, I will tell you what sort of authority I have for doing as I do. 30 Was John's baptism from heaven or from men? Answer me."

31 Then they argued with one another in this way, "If we say, 'It was from heaven,' He will say, 'Then why did you not believe him?' 32 On the other hand, can we say, 'It was from men'?" For they were afraid of the people, because everybody thought that John was really a prophet.

33 So they said to Jesus, "We do not know." Jesus also said to them, "Nor am I going to tell you what sort of authority I have for doing as I do."

12 *Jesus tells the story of the villainous tenants; His opponents ask Him "catch" questions: is it right to pay taxes to Rome? Is there a resurrection? Jesus floors them with a question about David's son being his Lord*

Then He began to speak to them in stories. "A man planted a vineyard and fenced it in and hewed out a wine-vat and built a watchtower; then he rented it to tenant farmers, and went abroad. 2 At the proper time he sent a slave to the tenants to collect his part of the grape crop. 3 But they took him and beat him and sent him back empty-handed. 4 And again he sent another slave to them, and they beat his head and treated him shamefully. 5 Then he sent a third one, and they killed him, and many others, some of whom they beat, some they killed. 6 He had one more to send, his dearly loved son; at last he sent him to them, for he said to himself, 'They will surely respect my son.' 7 But those tenants said among themselves, 'This is his heir; come on, let us kill him, and all that is coming to him will be ours.' 8 So they took him and killed him, and threw his body outside the vineyard. 9 Now what will the owner of the vineyard do? He will come back and destroy those tenants and give the vineyard to others. 10 Have you never read this passage of Scripture:

" 'That stone which the builders threw away Has now become the corner-stone;
11 This is the work of the Lord, And seems wonderful to us'?"

12 Then they were trying to have Him arrested, but they were afraid of the people, for they knew that He aimed this story at them. And so they left Him and went away.

[b] Grk., *fallings, failings, so shortcomings;* v. 26 om. by best Mss.

BECK

mount,* 'Be lifted up and be thrown into the sea,' * and have no doubt in your mind but believe what you say will be done, it will be done for you. 24 That's why I tell you, anything you ask for in prayer, believe that you received it, and you will have it. 25 When you stand and pray, if you have anything against anyone, forgive him, so that your Father in heaven will forgive you your sins." **

From Heaven

27 They came again to Jerusalem. As He was walking in the temple, the ruling priests, the Bible scholars, and the elders came to Him. 28 "By what authority are You doing these things?" they asked Him. "Or who gave You the right to do them?"

29 Jesus answered them, "I will ask you a question. You answer Me, and then I'll tell you by what authority I'm doing these things. 30 John's baptism—was it from heaven or from men? Answer Me."

31 They argued among themselves, "If we say, 'From heaven,' He will ask, 'Then why didn't you believe him?' But should we say, 'From men'?" 32 They were afraid of the people. Everybody thought John certainly was a prophet. 33 So they answered Jesus, "We don't know." Then Jesus told them, "Neither will I tell you by what authority I'm doing these things."

God's Vineyard

12 Then He used stories in talking to them: "A man *planted a vineyard. He put a wall around it, cut a vat into the rock, and built a watchtower.*[25] Then he rented it out to workers and left home.

2 "At the right time he sent a slave to the workers to get from them a share of the products of the vineyard. 3 But they took him, beat him, and sent him back empty-handed. 4 He sent another slave to them. They hit him on the head and treated him shamefully. 5 He sent another, and that one they killed. Then many others. Some of these they beat, and others they killed.

6 "He had one more, a son, whom he loved. Finally he sent him to them saying, 'They will respect my son.'

7 "But those workers said to one another, 'This is the heir. Come, let's kill him, and then we'll get the inheritance.' 8 They took him, killed him, and threw him out of the vineyard.

9 "What will the owner of the vineyard do? He will come and kill the workers and give the vineyard to others. 10 Haven't you read this in your Bible, *The stone the builders rejected has become the cornerstone. 11 The Lord has done it, and we think it is wonderful*"?[26]

12 They wanted to grab Him, because they knew His story was aimed at them, but they were afraid of the crowd. So they let Him alone and went away.

* By this mount He means the Mount of Olives. By the sea He means the Dead Sea, which can be seen from the Mount of Olives.
** Our two oldest manuscripts do not have v. 26: "But if you don't forgive, your Father in heaven will not forgive your sins." See Matt. 6:14-15.
[25] Is. 5:1-2
[26] Ps. 118:22-23

K.J.V.

13 And they send unto him certain of the Pharisees and of the Herodians, to catch him in *his* words. 14And when they were come, they say unto him, Master, we know that thou art true, and carest for no man; for thou regardest not the person of men, but teachest the way of God in truth: Is it lawful to give tribute to Cesar, or not? 15 Shall we give, or shall we not give? But he, knowing their hypocrisy, said unto them, Why tempt ye me? bring me a penny, that I may see *it*. 16And they brought *it*. And he saith unto them, Whose *is* this image and superscription? And they said unto him, Cesar's. 17And Jesus answering said unto them, Render to Cesar the things that are Cesar's, and to God the things that are God's. And they marvelled at him.

18 Then come unto him the Sadducees, which say there is no resurrection; and they asked him, saying, 19 Master, Moses wrote unto us, If a man's brother die, and leave *his* wife *behind him*, and leave no children, that his brother should take his wife, and raise up seed unto his brother. 20 Now there were seven brethren: and the first took a wife, and dying left no seed. 21And the second took her, and died, neither left he any seed: and the third likewise. 22And the seven had her, and left no seed: last of all the woman died also. 23 In the resurrection therefore, when they shall rise, whose wife shall she be of them? for the seven had her to wife. 24And Jesus answering said unto them, Do ye not therefore err, because ye know not the Scriptures, neither the power of God? 25 For when they shall rise from the dead, they neither marry, nor are given in marriage; but are as the angels which are in heaven. 26And as touching the dead, that they rise; have ye not read in the book of Moses, how in the bush God spake unto him, saying, I *am* the God of Abraham, and the God of Isaac, and the God of Jacob? 27 He is not the God of the dead, but the God of the living: ye therefore do greatly err.

28 And one of the scribes came, and having heard them reasoning together, and perceiving that he had answered them well, asked him, Which is the first commandment of all? 29And Jesus answered him, The first of all the commandments *is*, Hear, O Israel; The Lord our God is one Lord: 30And thou shalt love the Lord thy God with all thy heart, and with all thy soul, and with all thy mind, and with all thy strength: this *is* the first commandment. 31And the second *is* like, *namely* this, Thou shalt love thy neighbour as thyself. There is none other commandment greater than these. 32And the scribe said unto him, Well, Master, thou hast said the truth: for there is one God; and there is none other but he: 33And to love him with all the heart, and with all the understanding, and with all the soul, and with all the strength, and to love *his* neighbour as himself, is more than all whole burnt offerings and sacrifices. 34And when Jesus saw that he answered discreetly, he said unto him, Thou art not far from the kingdom of God. And no man after that durst ask him *any question*.

N.A.S.

13 And they *sent some of the Pharisees and Herodians to Him, in order to trap Him in a statement. 14And they *came and *said to Him, "Teacher, we know that You are truthful, and defer to no one; for You are not partial to any, but teach the way of God in truth. Is it lawful to pay a poll-tax to Caesar, or not? 15 "Shall we pay, or shall we not pay?" But He, knowing their hypocrisy, said to them, "Why are you testing Me? Bring Me a ᵃdenarius to look at." 16And they brought *one*. And He *said to them, "Whose likeness and inscription is this?" And they said to Him, "Caesar's." 17And Jesus said to them, "Render to Caesar the things that are Caesar's, and to God the things that are God's." And they were amazed at Him.

18 And *some* Sadducees (who say that there is no resurrection) *came to Him, and *began questioning Him, saying, 19 "Teacher, Moses wrote for us a *law* that IF A MAN'S BROTHER DIES, and leaves behind a wife, AND LEAVES NO CHILD, HIS BROTHER SHOULD TAKE THE WIFE, AND RAISE UP OFFSPRING TO HIS BROTHER. 20 "There were seven brothers; and the first one took a wife, and died, leaving no offspring. 21 "And the second one took her, and died, leaving behind no offspring; and the third likewise; 22 and *so* all seven left no offspring. Last of all the woman died too. 23 "In the resurrection, ᵇwhen they rise again, which one's wife will she be? For all seven had her as wife." 24 Jesus said to them, "Is this not the reason you are mistaken, that you do not understand the Scriptures, or the power of God? 25 "For when they rise from the dead, they neither marry, nor are given in marriage, but are like angels in heaven. 26 "But regarding the fact that the dead rise again, have you not read in the book of Moses, in the *passage about the burning* bush, how God spoke to him, saying, 'I AM THE GOD OF ABRAHAM, AND THE GOD OF ISAAC, AND THE GOD OF JACOB'? 27 "He is not *the* God of *the* dead, but of *the* living; you are greatly mistaken."

28 And one of the scribes came and heard them arguing, and recognizing that He had answered them well, asked Him, "What commandment is the foremost of all?" 29 Jesus answered, "The foremost is, 'HEAR, O ISRAEL; THE LORD OUR GOD IS ONE LORD; 30 AND YOU SHALL LOVE THE LORD YOUR GOD WITH ALL YOUR HEART, AND WITH ALL YOUR SOUL, AND WITH ALL YOUR MIND, AND WITH ALL YOUR STRENGTH.' 31 "The second is this, 'YOU SHALL LOVE YOUR NEIGHBOR AS YOURSELF.' There is no other commandment greater than these." 32And the scribe said to Him, "Right, Teacher, You have truly stated that HE IS ONE; AND THERE IS NO ONE ELSE BESIDES HIM; 33 AND TO LOVE HIM WITH ALL THE HEART AND WITH ALL THE UNDERSTANDING AND WITH ALL THE STRENGTH, AND TO LOVE ONE'S NEIGHBOR AS HIMSELF, is much more than all burnt offerings and sacrifices." 34And when Jesus saw that he had answered intelligently, He said to him, "You are not far from the kingdom of God." And after that, no one would venture to ask Him any more questions.

---

[a] The denarius was worth 18 cents in silver, equivalent to a day's wage. [b] Most ancient mss. omit: *when they rise again*.

WILLIAMS

13 Then they sent some Pharisees and Herodians to Him to trap Him in argument. 14And they came up and said to Him, "We know that you always tell the truth, and pay no personal consideration[a] to anyone, but teach the way of God honestly. Is it right to pay the poll-tax to Caesar, or not? 15 Should we pay it, or should we not?"

Now because He saw their pretense, He said to them, "Why are you testing me so? Bring me a twenty-cent coin to look at." 16And they brought Him one.

Then He asked them, "Whose picture and title is this?"

They answered Him, "Caesar's."

17 So He said, "Pay Caesar what belongs to Caesar, and pay God what belongs to God." And they were utterly dumfounded at Him.

18 Then some Sadducees, who claim that there is no resurrection, came up to Him and asked Him this question, 19 "Teacher, Moses gave us a law that if a man's brother died leaving a wife but no child, the man must marry the widow and raise up a family for his brother. 20 There were once seven brothers. The eldest married a wife and on dying left no child, 21 and the second married her and died leaving no child; and so did the third. 22And not one of the seven left a child. At last the woman died too. 23 Now at the resurrection, which one's wife will she be? For all seven of them married her."

24 Jesus said to them, "Does not this prove that you are wrong in your views,[b] because you do not understand either the Scriptures or the power of God? 25 For when people rise from the dead, men do not marry and women are not married, but continue to live together as the angels in heaven, do. 26 But as to the rising of the dead, did you never read in the book of Moses, in the passage about the bush, how God said to him, 'I am the God of Abraham, the God of Isaac, and the God of Jacob'? 27 He is not the God of dead but of living people! You are entirely wrong in your views."

28 Then one of the scribes, on hearing them arguing, came up, and since he saw that Jesus had answered them properly, he asked Him, "What sort of command is the first of all commands?"

29 Jesus answered, "The first one is, 'Hear, O Israel, the Lord our God is one Lord, 30 and you must love the Lord your God with your whole heart, your whole soul, your whole mind, and your whole strength.' 31And this is the second, 'You must love your neighbor as you do yourself.' No other command is greater than these."

32 Then the scribe said to Him, "Indeed, Teacher, you have properly said that He[c] is one by Himself, and there is no other but Him, 33 and to love Him with one's whole heart, one's whole understanding, and one's whole strength, and to love one's neighbor as one loves himself is far more than all the burnt-offerings and sacrifices."

34 So Jesus said to him, as He saw that he had answered thoughtfully, "You are not far from the kingdom of God." And no one ventured to ask Him any more questions.

BECK

Taxes

13 They sent some Pharisees and some of Herod's men to Him in order to trap Him with a question. 14 When they came to Him, they said, "Teacher, we know you're honest and don't care what others think, because You don't favor any special persons but you really teach God's way. Is it right to pay a tax to Caesar or not? Should we pay it or not?"

15 Seeing through their hypocritical way, Jesus asked them, "Why do you test Me? Bring Me a denarius; I want to see it."

16 They brought it. "Whose head is this and whose inscription?" He asked them.

"Caesar's," they told Him.

17 "Give Caesar what is Caesar's," Jesus told them, "and God what is God's." He amazed them.

The Dead Live

18 The Sadducees, who say the dead don't rise, came to Him with this question: 19 "Teacher, Moses wrote for us, *If anyone dies and leaves a wife but no child, his brother should marry his widow and have children for his brother.*[27] 20 Now, there were seven brothers. The first took a wife, died, and left no children. 21 The second married her, died, and left no children. So did the third. 22 None of the seven left any children. Last of all the woman died too. 23 When the dead rise, whose wife will she be? You know, the seven had her as wife."

24 Jesus asked them, "Aren't you wrong because you don't know your Bible or God's power? 25 When they rise from the dead, men and women don't marry but are like angels in heaven. 26About the dead rising, didn't you read in the book of Moses, in the story of the bush, how God told him, *I am the God of Abraham, the God of Isaac, and the God of Jacob?*[28] 27 He's not the God of the dead but of the living. You're badly mistaken!"

Love God and Your Neighbor

28 One of the men trained in the Bible came to Him. Hearing the others argue with Him and seeing how well Jesus answered them, he asked Him, "Which is the most important of all the commandments?"

29 Jesus answered, "The most important is: *Hear, Israel, the Lord our God is one Lord,* 30 *and love the Lord your God with all your heart, with all your life, with all your mind, and with all your strength.*[29] 31 The next is: *Love your neighbor like yourself.*[30] No other commandment is greater than these."

32 "Right, Teacher!" the Bible scholar said to Him. "You told the truth: *He is one, and there is no other one beside Him,* 33 and *loving Him with all your heart,* with all your understanding, *and with all your strength,*[31] and *loving your neighbor like yourself*[30] is more than all the *burnt offerings and sacrifices.*"[32]

34 When Jesus saw how sensibly he answered, He told him, "You're not far from God's kingdom."

Nobody dared to ask Him another question.

[27] Gen. 38:8; Deut. 25:5-6
[28] Ex. 3:6
[29] Deut. 6:4-5
[30] Lev. 19:18
[31] Deut. 4:35; 6:4-5
[32] 1 Sam. 15:22

[a] Grk., *you have no personal bias for anyone.*
[b] Grk., *is it not on acct. of this, because you do not.* [c] Best Mss. om. the word, *God.*

K.J.V.

35 And Jesus answered and said, while he taught in the temple, How say the scribes that Christ is the son of David? 36 For David himself said by the Holy Ghost, The LORD said to my Lord, Sit thou on my right hand, till I make thine enemies thy footstool. 37 David therefore himself calleth him Lord; and whence is he *then* his son? And the common people heard him gladly.

38 And he said unto them in his doctrine, Beware of the scribes, which love to go in long clothing, and *love* salutations in the market-places, 39 And the chief seats in the synagogues, and the uppermost rooms at feasts: 40 Which devour widows' houses, and for a pretence make long prayers: these shall receive greater damnation.

41 And Jesus sat over against the treasury, and beheld how the people cast money into the treasury: and many that were rich cast in much. 42 And there came a certain poor widow, and she threw in two mites, which make a farthing. 43 And he called *unto him* his disciples, and saith unto them, Verily I say unto you, That this poor widow hath cast more in, than all they which have cast into the treasury: 44 For all *they* did cast in of their abundance; but she of her want did cast in all that she had, *even* all her living.

N.A.S.

35 And Jesus answering *began* to say, as He taught in the temple, "How *is it that* the scribes say that the Christ is the son of David? 36 "David himself said in the Holy Spirit,
'THE LORD SAID TO MY LORD,
"SIT AT MY RIGHT HAND,
UNTIL I PUT THINE ENEMIES BENEATH THY FEET." '
37 "David himself calls Him 'Lord;' and *so* in what sense is He his son?" And the great crowd enjoyed listening to Him.

38 And in His teaching He was saying: "Beware of the scribes who like to walk around in long robes, and *like* respectful greetings in the market places, 39 and chief seats in the synagogues, and places of honor at banquets. 40 "They *are* the ones who devour widows' houses, and for appearances' sake offer long prayers; these will receive greater condemnation."

41 And He sat down opposite the treasury, and *began* observing how the multitude were putting money into the treasury; and many rich people were putting in large sums. 42 And a poor widow came and put in two small copper coins, which amount to a cent. 43 And calling His disciples to Him, He said to them, "Truly I say to you, this poor widow put in more than all the contributors to the treasury; 44 for they all put in out of their surplus, but she, out of her poverty, put in all she owned, all she had to live on."

13 And as he went out of the temple, one of his disciples saith unto him, Master, see what manner of stones and what buildings *are here!* 2 And Jesus answering said unto him, Seest thou these great buildings? there shall not be left one stone upon another, that shall not be thrown down. 3 And as he sat upon the mount of Olives, over against the temple, Peter and James and John and Andrew asked him privately, 4 Tell us, when shall these things be? and what *shall be* the sign when all these things shall be fulfilled? 5 And Jesus answering them began to say, Take heed lest any *man* deceive you: 6 For many shall come in my name, saying, I am *Christ;* and shall deceive many. 7 And when ye shall hear of wars and rumours of wars, be ye not troubled: for *such things* must needs be; but the end *shall* not *be* yet. 8 For nation shall rise against nation, and kingdom against kingdom: and there shall be earthquakes in divers places, and there shall be famines and troubles: these *are* the beginnings of sorrows.

9 But take heed to yourselves: for they shall deliver you up to councils; and in the synagogues ye shall be beaten: and ye shall be brought before rulers and kings for my sake, for

13 And as He was going out of the temple, one of His disciples *said to Him, "Teacher, behold ªwhat wonderful stones and ªwhat wonderful buildings!" 2 And Jesus said to him, "Do you see these great buildings? Not one stone shall be left upon another which will not be torn down."

3 And as He was sitting on the Mount of Olives opposite the temple, Peter and James and John and Andrew were questioning Him privately, 4 "Tell us, when will these things be, and what *will be* the sign when these things are going to be fulfilled?" 5 And Jesus began to say to them, "See to it that no one misleads you. 6 "Many will come in My name, saying, 'I am *He*!' and will mislead many. 7 "And when you hear of wars and rumors of wars, do not be frightened; *those things* must take place; but *that is* not yet the end. 8 "For nation will arise against nation, and kingdom against kingdom; there will be earthquakes in various places; there will *also* be famines. These things are *merely* the beginning of birth pangs.

9 "But be on your guard; for they will deliver you up to *the* courts, and you will be flogged in *the* synagogues, and you will stand before governors and kings for My sake, as a

[a] Lit., *how great.*

WILLIAMS

35 While He was teaching in the temple, He answered them and said, "How can the scribes say that the Christ is the son of David? 36 David himself, under the guidance of the Holy Spirit, said:

'The Lord has said to my Lord, "Sit at my right - hand

Until I make your enemies the footstool of your feet." '

37 David himself called him Lord, so how can He be his son?"

Most of the people liked to hear Him. 38 And in His teaching He continued to say: "Beware of the scribes who like to go about in long robes, to be saluted with honor in public places, 39 to be seated in the front seats in the synagogues, to occupy the places of honor at banquets— 40 men who eat up widows' houses and to cover it up make long prayers. They will get a much heavier sentence!"

41 Then He sat down in front of the collection-box and was watching the people as they dropped their money into it. And many rich people were dropping in large sums. 42 Then a poor widow came and dropped in two little copper coins, which make scarcely a cent. 43 And He called His disciples to Him and said, "I solemnly say to you, this poor widow has put in more than all these others who have been putting money into the collection-box. 44 For all of them put in out of their surplus, but she in her want put in all she had, yes, all she had to live on."

13 *Jesus tells of the destruction of Jerusalem; the final coming of Christ; the stories of the fig tree and the doorkeeper, to urge His followers to watch*

As He was leaving the temple, one of His disciples said to Him, "Look, Teacher! What stupendous stones, what beautiful buildings!" [a]
2 Jesus said to him, "Are you looking in wonder at these great buildings? Not one stone will be left here upon another that will not be torn down."
3 As He was sitting on the Mount of Olives opposite the temple, Peter, James, John, and Andrew, in a private group, [b] were asking Him, 4 "When will all this take place? Tell us. And what will be the sign that it is about to be put into effect?"
5 Jesus began to say to them:
"Look out that no one misleads you about it. 6 Many will come bearing the name of Messiah, and saying, 'I am He,' and they will mislead many. 7 But when you hear of wars and rumors of war, stop getting alarmed. They have to come, but the end is not yet. 8 For one nation will go to war with another, and one kingdom with another. There will be earthquakes in many places; [c] there will be famines. But this is only the beginning of the agonies. 9 So you must be on the lookout for yourselves; they will turn you over to courts, and to synagogues where you will be beaten, and you must appear before governors and kings for my sake, to testify to

[a] Grk., *what stones,* etc.! [b] Grk., *alone.* [c] Lit., *birth pangs.*

BECK

David's Son

35 While Jesus was teaching in the temple, He asked, "How can the Bible scholars say the promised Savior is David's Son? 36 David himself by the Holy Spirit said,

The Lord said to my Lord,
'Sit at My right
Till I put your enemies under Your feet.' [33]

37 David himself calls Him Lord. Then how can He be his Son?"

Beware!

The big crowd liked to hear Him. 38 As He taught, He said, "Beware of the Bible scholars, who like to go around in long robes, be greeted in the marketplaces, 39 sit in the front seats in synagogs, and have the places of honor at dinners. 40 They swallow the houses of widows, and then, to cover up, make long prayers. They will be punished all the more."

A Cent

41 As Jesus sat facing the contribution boxes, He was watching how people put money into them. Many rich people put in much. 42 A poor widow came and dropped in two small coins, worth about a cent.
43 He called His disciples. "I tell you," He said to them, "this poor widow certainly put in more than all the others who put in money. 44 All the others took some of what they had left over and dropped it in, but she put in what she needed herself, all she had—all she had to live on."

Sorrow Ahead!

13 As He was going out of the temple, one of His disciples said to Him, "Teacher, look at those wonderful stones and buildings!"
2 "You see these large buildings?" Jesus asked him. "Not a stone will be left on another here but will be torn down."
3 When He was sitting on the Mount of Olives, facing the temple, Peter, James, John, and Andrew asked Him privately: 4 "Tell us, when will this be, and how can we tell when all this is going to happen?"
5 "Be careful not to let anyone deceive you," Jesus told them. 6 "Many will come using My name and saying, 'I am He,' and will deceive many.
7 "When you hear of wars and rumors of wars, don't get alarmed. It must happen, [34] but that's not the end yet. 8 Nation will fight against nation, and kingdom against kingdom. [35] There will be earthquakes in different places, and famines. These are only the first pains. [*]
9 "Be on your guard! Men will hand you over to their courts and whip you in their synagogs. You will be brought before governors and kings for My sake to tell them the

[*] As in childbirth, sharper pains will follow before the Savior comes in glory.
[33] Ps. 110:1
[34] Dan. 2:28
[35] 2 Chron. 15:6; Is. 19:2

K.J.V.

a testimony against them. 10And the gospel must first be published among all nations. 11 But when they shall lead *you,* and deliver you up, take no thought beforehand what ye shall speak, neither do ye premeditate: but whatsoever shall be given you in that hour, that speak ye: for it is not ye that speak, but the Holy Ghost. 12 Now the brother shall betray the brother to death, and the father the son; and children shall rise up against *their* parents, and shall cause them to be put to death. 13And ye shall be hated of all *men* for my name's sake: but he that shall endure unto the end, the same shall be saved.

14 But when ye shall see the abomination of desolation, spoken of by Daniel the prophet, standing where it ought not, (let him that readeth understand,) then let them that be in Judea flee to the mountains: 15And let him that is on the housetop not go down into the house, neither enter *therein,* to take any thing out of his house: 16And let him that is in the field not turn back again for to take up his garment. 17 But woe to them that are with child, and to them that give suck in those days! 18And pray ye that your flight be not in the winter. 19 For *in* those days shall be affliction, such as was not from the beginning of the creation which God created unto this time, neither shall be. 20And except that the Lord had shortened those days, no flesh should be saved: but for the elect's sake, whom he hath chosen, he hath shortened the days. 21And then if any man shall say to you, Lo, here *is* Christ; or, lo, *he is* there; believe *him* not: 22 For false Christs and false prophets shall rise, and shall shew signs and wonders, to seduce, if *it were* possible, even the elect. 23 But take ye heed: behold, I have foretold you all things.

24 But in those days, after that tribulation, the sun shall be darkened, and the moon shall not give her light, 25And the stars of heaven shall fall, and the powers that are in heaven shall be shaken. 26And then shall they see the Son of man coming in the clouds with great power and glory. 27And then shall he send his angels, and shall gather together his elect from the four winds, from the uttermost part of the earth to the uttermost part of heaven. 28 Now learn a parable of the fig tree: When her branch is yet tender, and putteth forth leaves, ye know that summer is near: 29 So ye in like manner, when ye shall see these things come to pass, know that it is nigh, *even* at the doors. 30 Verily I say unto you, that this generation shall not pass, till all these things be done. 31 Heaven and earth shall pass away: but my words shall not pass away.

32 But of that day and *that* hour knoweth no man, no, not the angels which are in heaven, neither the Son, but the Father. 33 Take ye heed, watch and pray: for ye know not when the time is. 34 *For the Son of man is* as a man taking a far journey, who left his house, and gave authority to his servants, and to every man his work, and commanded the porter to watch. 35 Watch

N.A.S.

testimony to them. 10 "And the gospel must first be preached to all the nations. 11 "And when they arrest you and deliver you up, do not be anxious beforehand about what you are to say, but say whatever is given you in that hour; for it is not you who speak, but *it is* the Holy Spirit. 12 "And brother will deliver up brother to death, and a father *his* child; and children will rise up against parents and cause them to be put to death. 13 "And you will be hated by all on account of My name, but it is the one who has endured to the end who will be saved.

14 "But when you see the 'abomination of desolation' standing where it should not be (let the reader understand), then let those who are in Judea flee to the mountains. 15 "And let him who is on the housetop not go down, or enter in, to get anything out of his house; 16 and let him who is in the field not turn back to get his cloak. 17 "But woe to those who are with child and to those who nurse babes in those days! 18 "But pray that it may not happen in the winter. 19 "For those days will be a *time of* tribulation such as has not occurred since the beginning of the creation which God created, until now, and never shall. 20 "And unless the Lord had shortened *those* days, no life would have been saved; but for the sake of the elect whom He chose, He shortened the days. 21 "And then if anyone says to you, 'Behold, here is the Christ;' or 'Behold, *He is* there;' do not believe *him;* 22 for false Christs and false prophets will arise, and will show signs and wonders, in order, if possible, to lead the elect astray. 23 "But take heed; behold, I have told you everything in advance.

24 "But in those days, after that tribulation,
THE SUN WILL BE DARKENED,
AND THE MOON WILL NOT GIVE ITS LIGHT,
25 AND THE STARS WILL BE FALLING from heaven,
and the POWERS THAT ARE IN THE HEAVENS WILL BE shaken.
26 "AND THEN THEY SHALL SEE THE SON OF MAN COMING IN CLOUDS with great power and glory. 27 "And then He will send forth the angels, and WILL GATHER TOGETHER His elect FROM THE FOUR WINDS, FROM THE FARTHEST END OF the earth, TO THE FARTHEST END OF HEAVEN.

28 "Now learn the parable from the fig tree: when its branch has already become tender, and puts forth its leaves, you know that the summer is near. 29 "Even so you too, when you see these things happening, recognize that He is near, *right* at the door. 30 "Truly I say to you, this ªgeneration will not pass away until all these things take place. 31 "Heaven and earth will pass away, but My words will not pass away. 32 "But of that day or hour no one knows, not even the angels in heaven, nor the Son, but the Father *alone.*

33 "Take heed, keep on the alert; for you do not know when the *appointed* time is. 34 "*It is* like a man, away on a journey, *who* upon leaving his house and putting his slaves in charge, *assigning* to each one his task, also commanded the doorkeeper to stay on the alert. 35 "There-

[a] Or, *race.*

138

WILLIAMS

them. 10 But before the end comes, the good news must be proclaimed to all the heathen. 11 Now when they take you to court for trial, do not be worrying beforehand about what you should say, but say whatever is given you at that time, for it is not you that will be speaking, but the Holy Spirit. 12 One brother will turn another over to death, and a father his child, and children will take a stand against their parents and have them put to death. 13 You will be hated by everybody, because you bear my name. But whoever bears up to the end will be saved.

14 "So when you see the destructive desecration standing where he has no right to stand"— let the reader take notice—"then let those who remain in Judea fly to the hills; 15 let him who is on the roof of his house not go down and go into the house to get anything out of it; 16 let him who is in the field not turn back to get his coat. 17 Alas for the women who are expectant mothers and those who have nursing babies, in those days! 18 And pray that it may not be in winter, 19 for there will be such misery at that time as has never been since the beginning of God's creation, and never will be again. 20 If the Lord had not cut those days short, nobody would have escaped, but for the sake of the people chosen as His own He has cut them short.

21 "If anyone says to you at that time, 'Look! Here is the Christ,' or, 'Look! There He is,' do not believe it. 22 For false Christs and false prophets will announce themselves,[d] and they will do signs and wonders to mislead, if possible, even God's chosen people. 23 So you must be on your guard. I have warned you about it all beforehand.

24 "But in those days, after that misery, the sun will turn dark, the moon will not shed its light, 25 the stars will be falling from the sky, and the powers of the sky will be shaken. 26 And then they will see the Son of Man coming on the clouds in overwhelming power and splendor. 27 Then He will send out His angels, and gather His chosen people from the four points of the compass, from one end of the sky to the other. 28 "Now learn what the story of the fig tree means. Just as soon as its branches grow tender, and put forth leaves, you know that summer is near. 29 So when you see all these things taking place, you will know that He is right at the door. 30 I solemnly say to you, the present generation will not pass away before all this takes place. 31 Earth and sky will pass away, but my words will never pass away. 32 But about that day or hour not a single one knows—not even the angels in heaven, nor the Son; not a single one but the Father. 33 Keep looking, keep alert, for you do not know when the time will be. 34 It will be like a man who leaves his home and goes on a journey, after he has given orders to his slaves, to each his particular task, and has given orders to the watchman to keep watch. 35 So you must keep alert, for you do

BECK

truth. 10 The good news must be preached to all nations before the end comes. 11 When they are taking you away to hand you over to the authorities, don't worry beforehand what you will say. But say whatever is given you to say when the time comes; you see, it isn't you that will be speaking but the Holy Spirit.

12 "A brother will betray his brother to death, and a father his child. *Children will rebel against their parents*[36] and kill them. 13 Everybody will hate you because of My name. But endure to the end, and you'll be saved."

Jerusalem Will Be Destroyed

14 "When you see *the abomination laying waste the land*[37] and standing where it should not be (anyone who reads this should understand it), then if you're in Judea, flee to the hills. 15 If you're on the roof, don't come down and go into your house to get anything. 16 If you're in the field, don't turn back to get your garment.

17 "Woe to the women who in those days are expecting babies or nursing them. 18 Pray that it won't happen in winter. 19 *It will be a time of misery such as never has been from the beginning of the world that God made until now*[38] and never will be. 20 And if the Lord had not cut short that time, nobody would be saved. But to help those whom He has chosen, God has cut short the time."

Jesus Is Coming

21 "If anyone tells you then, 'Look, here is Christ!' or, 'There He is!' don't believe it. 22 False Christs and false *prophets will come and do miracles and wonders*[39] to deceive if possible those whom God has chosen. 23 Be on your guard. You see I've told you everything before it happens.

24 "Now, after the misery of that time *the sun will turn dark, the moon will stop shining,* 25 *and the stars will be falling from the sky.* And *the powers of heaven*[40] will be shaken. 26 Then people will see *the Son of Man coming in the clouds*[41] with great power and glory. 27 And then He will send the angels and *gather* His chosen ones *from the north, south, east, and west, and from one end of the world to the other.*[42]

28 "Learn this lesson from a fig tree: When its branch gets tender and grows leaves, you know summer is near. 29 So also when you see those things happen, you know He is near, at your door.

30 "I tell you the truth: These people will not pass away till all this happens. 31 Heaven and earth will pass away, but what I say will not pass away."

Be Ready!

32 "No one knows about that day or hour, not the angels in heaven, not the Son, only the Father. 33 Be careful and watch, because you don't know when it will happen. 34 It's like a man who went on a trip. As he left home, he put his slaves in charge, assigned work to every one, and ordered the doorkeeper to watch. 35 Watch, then, because you don't know when

[36] Micah 7:6
[37] Dan. 9:27; 11:31; 12:11
[38] Dan. 12:1
[39] Deut. 13:1
[40] Is. 13:10; 34:4
[41] Dan. 7:13
[42] Deut. 30:4; Zech. 2:6

[d] Grk., arise.

139

K.J.V.

ye therefore: for ye know not when the master of the house cometh, at even, or at midnight, or at the cockcrowing, or in the morning: 36 Lest coming suddenly he find you sleeping. 37 And what I say unto you I say unto all, Watch.

14 After two days was *the feast of* the passover, and of unleavened bread: and the chief priests and the scribes sought how they might take him by craft, and put *him* to death. 2 But they said, Not on the feast *day*, lest there be an uproar of the people.

3 And being in Bethany, in the house of Simon the leper, as he sat at meat, there came a woman having an alabaster box of ointment of spikenard very precious; and she brake the box, and poured *it* on his head. 4 And there were some that had indignation within themselves, and said, Why was this waste of the ointment made? 5 For it might have been sold for more than three hundred pence, and have been given to the poor. And they murmured against her. 6 And Jesus said, Let her alone; why trouble ye her? she hath wrought a good work on me. 7 For ye have the poor with you always, and whensoever ye will ye may do them good: but me ye have not always. 8 She hath done what she could: she is come aforehand to anoint my body to the burying. 9 Verily I say unto you, Wheresoever this gospel shall be preached throughout the whole world, *this* also that she hath done shall be spoken of for a memorial of her.

10 And Judas Iscariot, one of the twelve, went unto the chief priests, to betray him unto them. 11 And when they heard *it*, they were glad, and promised to give him money. And he sought how he might conveniently betray him.

12 And the first day of unleavened bread, when they killed the passover, his disciples said unto him, Where wilt thou that we go and prepare that thou mayest eat the passover? 13 And he sendeth forth two of his disciples, and saith unto them, Go ye into the city, and there shall meet you a man bearing a pitcher of water: follow him. 14 And wheresoever he shall go in, say ye to the goodman of the house, The Master saith, Where is the guestchamber, where I shall eat the passover with my disciples? 15 And he will shew you a large upper room furnished *and* prepared: there make ready for us. 16 And his disciples went forth, and came into the city, and found as he had said unto them: and they made ready the passover. 17 And in the evening he cometh with the twelve. 18 And as they sat and did eat, Jesus said, Verily I say unto you, One of you which eateth with me shall betray me.

N.A.S.

fore, be on the alert—for you do not know when the master of the house is coming, whether in the evening, at midnight, at cockcrowing, or in the morning;— 36 lest he come suddenly and find you asleep. 37 "And what I say to you I say to all, 'Be on the alert!'"

14 Now *the feast of* the Passover and Unleavened Bread was two days off; and the chief priests and the scribes were seeking how to seize Him by stealth, and kill *Him;* 2 for they were saying, "Not during the festival, lest there be a riot of the people."

3 And while He was in Bethany at the home of Simon the leper, and reclining *at table*, there came a woman with an alabaster vial of costly perfume of pure nard; *and* she broke the vial and poured it over His head. 4 But some were indignantly *remarking* to one another, "For what purpose has this perfume been wasted? 5 "For this perfume might have been sold for over three hundred [a]denarii, and *the money* given to the poor." And they were scolding her. 6 But Jesus said, "Let her alone; why do you bother her? She has done a good deed to Me. 7 "For the poor you always have with you, and whenever you wish, you can do them good; but you do not always have Me. 8 "She has done what she could; she has anointed My body beforehand for the burial. 9 "And truly I say to you, wherever the gospel is preached in the whole world, that also which this woman has done shall be spoken of in memory of her."

10 And Judas Iscariot, who was one of the twelve, went off to the chief priests, in order to betray Him to them. 11 And they were glad when they heard *this*, and promised to give him money. And he *began* seeking how to betray Him at an opportune time.

12 And on the first day of *the Feast of* Unleavened Bread, when the Passover *lamb* was being sacrificed, His disciples *said to Him, "Where do You want us to go and prepare for You to eat the Passover?" 13 And He *sent two of His disciples, and *said to them, "Go into the city, and a man will meet you carrying a pitcher of water; follow him; 14 and wherever he enters, say to the owner of the house, 'The Teacher says, "Where is My guest room in which I may eat the Passover with My disciples?"' 15 "And he himself will show you a large upper room furnished *and* ready; and prepare for us there." 16 And the disciples went out, and came to the city, and found *it* just as He had told them; and they prepared the Passover.

17 And when it was evening He *came with the twelve. 18 And as they were reclining *at table* and eating, Jesus said, "Truly I say to you that one of you will betray Me,—one who is

[a] The denarius was worth 18 cents in silver, equivalent to a day's wage.

WILLIAMS

not know when the master of the house is coming—in the evening or at midnight or at daybreak or early in the morning—36 so that he may not come unexpectedly and find you asleep. 37 And so what I say to you, I say to everybody, keep alert."

14 *Jesus anointed with costly perfume; Judas drives a bargain to betray Him; Passover supper eaten and memorial supper instituted by Jesus; suffering in Gethsemane, betrayed, arrested, and tried in Jewish court*

Now the feast of the Passover and of Unleavened Bread was two days later. So the high priests and scribes kept looking for some way to arrest Him by stratagem and have Him put to death, 2 for they kept saying, "It must not be at the feast, for there might be a riot."

3 While He was in Bethany, He was a guest in the home of Simon the leper, and as He was sitting at table, a woman came in with an alabaster bottle[a] of pure nard perfume, very costly; she broke the bottle and poured the perfume on His head. 4 But some of the guests were indignantly saying to themselves, "Why was such a waste of the perfume made? 5 It might have been sold for more than sixty dollars, and the money have been given to the poor." So they kept on grumbling at her.

6 But Jesus said, "Let her alone; why do you embarrass her? She has done a good deed to me. 7 For you always have the poor among you, and whenever you please you can do them good, but you will not always have me. 8 She has done all she could; she broke the bottle and perfumed my body for my burial. 9 I solemnly say to you, all over the world wherever this good news is proclaimed, the deed that she has done will also be told, in memory of her."

10 Then Judas Iscariot, one of the Twelve, went to the high priests to betray Him to them. 11 They were delighted to hear it, and promised to pay[b] him for it. So he kept looking for a good opportunity to betray Him to them.

12 On the first day of the feast of Unleavened Bread, the usual time for killing the Passover lamb, Jesus' disciples asked Him, "Where do you want us to go and get the Passover supper ready for you to eat?"

13 So He sent off two of His disciples, and said to them, "Go into the city and you will meet a man carrying a pitcher of water. Follow him, 14 and whatever house he goes into, tell the owner that the Teacher asks, 'Where is my room where I may eat the Passover supper with my disciples?' 15 Then he will show you a large upstairs room, furnished and ready; get everything ready for us there." 16 So off the disciples went; they reached the city, found everything just as He had told them, and they got the Passover supper ready.

17 When evening came, He went with the Twelve. 18 And while they were sitting at table and eating, Jesus said, "I solemnly say to you, one of you, one who is now eating with me, is going to betray me."

[a] A sort of flask, but *bottle* in modern Eng. [b] Grk., *gave him money.*

BECK

the master of the house is coming, whether in the evening, at midnight, or at the time when the rooster crows, or early in the morning. 36 Make sure he doesn't come suddenly and find you asleep. 37 What I tell you, I tell everyone: 'Watch'!"

The Plot

14 It was two days before the festival of the Passover and of bread without yeast. The ruling priests and the Bible scholars were looking for some treacherous way to arrest Jesus and kill Him. 2 They said, "Not in the festival crowd, or there will be a riot among the people."

Mary Anoints Jesus

3 While Jesus was in Bethany in the home of Simon the leper and was lying at the table, a woman came with an alabaster jar of perfume, real nard and very expensive. She broke the jar and poured the perfume on His head.

4 Some who were there felt annoyed and said to one another, "Why was the perfume wasted like this? 5 This perfume could have been sold for more than three hundred denarii and the money given to the poor." And they were grumbling at her.

6 "Let her alone," Jesus said. "Why should you trouble her? She has done a beautiful thing to Me. 7 The poor you always have with you, and you can help them whenever you want to, but you will not always have Me. 8 She has done what she could. She came ahead of time to pour the perfume on My body to prepare it for burial. 9 I tell you, wherever the good news is preached in the whole world, certainly what she has done will also be told in memory of her."

Judas Plans to Betray Jesus

10 Judas, the man from Kerioth, one of the twelve, went to the high priests to betray Jesus to them. 11 They were delighted to hear it and promised to give him money. So he was looking for a chance to betray Him.

The Passover

12 On the first of the Passover days of bread without yeast, when it was customary to kill the Passover lamb, the disciples asked Jesus, "Where do You want us to go and get things ready for You to eat the Passover?"

13 He sent two of His disciples and told them: "Go into the city, and you will meet a man carrying a jar of water. 14 Follow him, and when he goes into a house, tell the owner: 'The Teacher asks, "Where is My room in which I can eat the Passover with My disciples?"' 15 Then he will show you a large room upstairs, furnished and ready. Get the things ready for us there."

16 The disciples left, and went into the city, and found everything as He had told them. 17 And so they got the Passover ready.

In the evening He came there with the twelve.

"Is It I?"

18 While they were still lying down and eating, Jesus said, "I tell you the truth: One of you is going to betray Me, one who is *eating with Me!*" [43]

[43] Ps. 41:9

K.J.V.

19And they began to be sorrowful, and to say unto him one by one, *Is* it I? and another *said, Is* it I? 20And he answered and said unto them, *It is* one of the twelve, that dippeth with me in the dish. 21 The Son of man indeed goeth, as it is written of him: but woe to that man by whom the Son of man is betrayed! good were it for that man if he had never been born.

22 And as they did eat, Jesus took bread, and blessed, and brake *it,* and gave to them, and said, Take, eat; this is my body. 23And he took the cup, and when he had given thanks, he gave *it* to them: and they all drank of it. 24And he said unto them, This is my blood of the new testament, which is shed for many. 25 Verily I say unto you, I will drink no more of the fruit of the vine, until that day that I drink it new in the kingdom of God.

26 And when they had sung a hymn, they went out into the mount of Olives. 27And Jesus saith unto them, All ye shall be offended because of me this night: for it is written, I will smite the Shepherd, and the sheep shall be scattered. 28 But after that I am risen, I will go before you into Galilee. 29 But Peter said unto him, Although all shall be offended, yet *will* not I. 30And Jesus saith unto him, Verily I say unto thee, That this day, *even* in this night, before the cock crow twice, thou shalt deny me thrice. 31 But he spake the more vehemently, If I should die with thee, I will not deny thee in any wise. Likewise also said they all. 32And they came to a place which was named Gethsemane: and he saith to his disciples, Sit ye here, while I shall pray. 33And he taketh with him Peter and James and John, and began to be sore amazed, and to be very heavy; 34And saith unto them, My soul is exceeding sorrowful unto death: tarry ye here, and watch. 35And he went forward a little, and fell on the ground, and prayed that, if it were possible, the hour might pass from him. 36And he said, Abba, Father, all things *are* possible unto thee; take away this cup from me: nevertheless, not what I will, but what thou wilt. 37And he cometh, and findeth them sleeping, and saith unto Peter, Simon, sleepest thou? couldest not thou watch one hour? 38 Watch ye and pray, lest ye enter into temptation. The spirit truly *is* ready, but the flesh *is* weak. 39And again he went away, and prayed, and spake the same words. 40And when he returned, he found them asleep again, (for their eyes were heavy,) neither wist they what to answer him. 41And he cometh the third time, and saith unto them, Sleep on now, and take *your* rest: it is enough, the hour is come; behold, the Son of man is betrayed into the hands of sinners. 42 Rise up, let us go; lo, he that betrayeth me is at hand.

43 And immediately, while he yet spake, cometh Judas, one of the twelve, and with him a great multitude with swords and staves, from

N.A.S.

eating with Me." 19 They began to be grieved and to say to Him one by one, "Surely not I?" 20And He said to them, *"It is* one of the twelve, one who dips with Me in the bowl. 21 "For the Son of Man *is to* go, just as it is written of Him; but woe to that man by whom the Son of Man is betrayed! *It would have been* good for that man if he had not been born."

22 And while they were eating, He took *some* bread, and after a blessing He broke *it;* and gave *it* to them, and said, "Take *it;* this is My body." 23And He took a cup, and when He had given thanks, He gave *it* to them; and they all drank from it. 24And He said to them, "This is My blood of the covenant, which is *to be* shed on behalf of many. 25 "Truly I say to you, I shall never again drink of the fruit of the vine until that day when I drink it new in the kingdom of God."

26 And after singing a hymn, they went out to the Mount of Olives.

27 And Jesus *said to them, "You will all fall away, because it is written, 'I WILL STRIKE DOWN THE SHEPHERD, AND THE SHEEP SHALL BE SCATTERED.' 28 "But after I have been raised, I will go before you to Galilee." 29 But Peter said to Him, *"Even* though all may fall away, yet I will not." 30And Jesus *said to him, "Truly I say to you, that you yourself this very night, before a cock crows twice, shall three times deny Me." 31 But *Peter* kept saying insistently, *"Even* if I have to die with You, I will not deny You!" And they all were saying the same thing, too.

32 And they *came to a place named Gethsemane; and He *said to His disciples, "Sit here until I have prayed." 33And He *took with him Peter and James and John, and began to be very distressed and troubled. 34And He *said to them, "My soul is deeply grieved to the point of death; remain here and keep watch." 35And he went a little beyond *them,* and fell to the ground, and *began* praying that if it were possible, the hour might pass Him by. 36And He was saying, "Abba (Father), all things are possible for Thee; remove this cup from Me; yet not what I will, but what Thou wilt." 37And He *came and *found them sleeping, and *said to Peter, "Simon, are you asleep? Could you not keep watch for one hour? 38 "Keep watching and praying, that you may not come into temptation; the spirit is willing, but the flesh is weak." 39And again He went away and prayed, saying the same words. 40And again He came and found them sleeping, for their eyes were very heavy; and they did not know what to answer Him. 41And He *came the third time, and *said to them, "Are you still sleeping and taking your rest? It is enough; the hour has come; behold, the Son of Man is being betrayed into the hands of sinners. 42 "Arise, let us be going; behold, the one who betrays Me is at hand!"

43 And immediately while He was still speaking, Judas, one of the twelve, *came up, accompanied by a multitude with swords and

WILLIAMS

19 And they began to show that they were hurt[c] and to ask Him one by one, "It cannot be I, can it?"

20 He answered them, "It is one of the Twelve, the one who is dipping his bread in the dish with me. 21 For the Son of Man is going away, as the Scriptures say of Him, but a curse will be on that man by whom He is betrayed. It would have been better for that man, if he had never been born."

22 While they were eating, He took a loaf and blessed it and broke it in pieces and gave it to them, saying, "Take this; it is my body."

23 He also took the cup of wine and gave thanks and gave it to them, and they all drank some of it. 24 Then He said to them, "This is my blood which ratifies the covenant, the blood which is to be poured out for many. 25 I solemnly say to you, I will never again drink the product[d] of the vine till the day when I drink the new wine in the kingdom of God."

26 After singing a hymn they went out of the city and up the Mount of Olives. 27 Then Jesus said to them, "You will all stumble over me, for the Scripture says, 'I will strike the shepherd, and the sheep will be scattered.' 28 But after I am raised from the dead, I will go back to Galilee to meet you." [e]

29 Then Peter said to Him, "Although all the rest of them stumble over you, yet I will never do so myself."

30 Then Jesus said to him, "I solemnly say to you, this very night, before the cock crows twice, you, yes, you, will disown me three times."

31 But Peter kept on emphatically saying, "Even if I have to die with you, I will never disown you." And they all kept saying the same thing.

32 Then they came to the place called Gethsemane, and He said to His disciples, "Sit down here while I pray."

33 And He took Peter, James, and John along with Him, and He began to feel completely dazed and to realize His anguish of heart, 34 and so He said to them, "My heart is breaking, it almost kills me! You must stay here and keep watching."

35 Then He walked on a few steps and threw Himself upon the ground, and kept praying that if it were possible He might escape the hour of agony, 36 and He was saying, "Abba," which means, "Father," "anything is possible for you! Take this cup away from me! Yet, I pray, not what I want but what you want!"

37 And He went back and found them asleep, and He said to Peter, "Simon, are you asleep? Could you not watch a single hour? 38 You must all keep watching and praying that you may not be exposed [f] to temptation. Man's spirit is willing but human nature is weak."

39 He went away again and prayed in the same words. 40 When He went back again, He found them asleep again, for their eyes were so heavy they could hardly hold them open; and they did not know what answer to make Him.

41 He came back the third time and said to them, "Are you still sleeping and resting? No more of that! The hour has come. See! The Son of Man is betrayed into the hands of sinful men. 42 Get up, let us be going. Look! here comes my betrayer!"

43 At that very moment, while He was still speaking, Judas, one of the Twelve, came up, and with him a crowd of men with swords and

BECK

19 They felt hurt and asked Him one after another, "You don't mean me?"

20 "One of the twelve," He told them, "one who is dipping into the bowl with Me. 21 The Son of Man is going away as it is written about Him, but woe to that man who betrays the Son of Man! It would be better for that man if he had never been born."

The Lord's Supper

22 While they were eating, Jesus took bread and blessed it. He broke it and gave it to them, and said, "Take it. This is My body."

23 Then He took a cup, gave thanks, and gave it to them. And they all drank of it. 24 He told them, "This is My *blood of the covenant*,[44] poured out for all.

25 "Surely, I tell you, I will not drink again of the product of the vine until that day when I drink it in a new way in God's kingdom."

26 Then they sang a hymn.*

"You Will Deny Me"

26 They started out for the Mount of Olives.

27 Then Jesus told them, "You will all turn against Me, because it is written: I will *strike down the Shepherd, and the sheep will be scattered.*[45] 28 But after I have risen, I will go ahead of you to Galilee."

29 "Even if they all turn against You," Peter answered Him, "I will not."

30 "I tell you the truth," Jesus told him, "tonight, before the rooster crows twice, you will deny Me three times."

31 But he kept insisting all the more, "If I have to die with You, I'll never deny You." All the others said the same thing.

Gethsemane

32 They came to a place called Gethsemane, and He said to His disciples, "Sit down here while I pray."

33 He took Peter, James, and John with Him, and He started to feel terror and grief. 34 "I am so *full of sorrow*," [46] He told them, "I am almost dying. Stay here and keep awake."

35 Going ahead a little, He bowed down to the ground and prayed that if it were possible He might not have to suffer what was ahead of Him. 36 "My Father," He said, "You can do anything. Take this cup away from Me. But let it not be as I want it but as You want it."

37 He came and found them asleep. "Simon, are you sleeping?" He asked Peter. "So you couldn't keep awake one hour? 38 Stay awake and pray that you may not be tempted. The spirit is willing, but the flesh is weak."

39 He went away again and prayed the same as before. 40 He came again and found them asleep—they couldn't keep their eyes open and didn't know what to say to Him.

41 He came back a third time. "Are you going to sleep on now and rest?" He asked them. "It's enough. The time has come. Now the Son of Man will be betrayed into the hands of sinners. 42 Get up, let us go. Here comes the man to betray Me!"

The Arrest

43 Just then, while Jesus was still talking, Judas, one of the twelve, came with a crowd

* Perhaps Psalms 115-118.
[44] Ex. 24:8; Jer. 31:32; Zech. 9:11
[45] Zech. 13:7
[46] Ps. 42:5; 43:5

[c] Grk., *to be grieved* or *pained*. [d] *Fruit*. [e] Grk., *before you*. [f] Grk., *led into*.

K.J.V.

the chief priests and the scribes and the elders. 44And he that betrayed him had given them a token, saying, Whomsoever I shall kiss, that same is he; take him, and lead *him* away safely. 45And as soon as he was come, he goeth straightway to him, and saith, Master, Master; and kissed him.

46 And they laid their hands on him, and took him. 47And one of them that stood by drew a sword, and smote a servant of the high priest, and cut off his ear. 48And Jesus answered and said unto them, Are ye come out, as against a thief, with swords and *with* staves to take me? 49 I was daily with you in the temple teaching, and ye took me not: but the Scriptures must be fulfilled. 50And they all forsook him, and fled. 51And there followed him a certain young man, having a linen cloth cast about *his* naked *body;* and the young men laid hold on him: 52And he left the linen cloth, and fled from them naked.

53 And they led Jesus away to the high priest: and with him were assembled all the chief priests and the elders and the scribes. 54And Peter followed him afar off, even into the palace of the high priest: and he sat with the servants, and warmed himself at the fire. 55And the chief priests and all the council sought for witness against Jesus to put him to death; and found none. 56 For many bare false witness against him, but their witness agreed not together. 57And there arose certain, and bare false witness against him, saying, 58 We heard him say, I will destroy this temple that is made with hands, and within three days I will build another made without hands. 59 But neither so did their witness agree together. 60And the high priest stood up in the midst, and asked Jesus, saying, Answerest thou nothing? what *is it which* these witness against thee? 61 But he held his peace, and answered nothing. Again the high priest asked him, and said unto him, Art thou the Christ, the Son of the Blessed? 62And Jesus said, I am: and ye shall see the Son of man sitting on the right hand of power, and coming in the clouds of heaven. 63 Then the high priest rent his clothes, and saith, What need we any further witnesses? 64 Ye have heard the blasphemy: what think ye? And they all condemned him to be guilty of death. 65And some began to spit on him, and to cover his face, and to buffet him, and to say unto him, Prophesy: and the servants did strike him with the palms of their hands.

66 And as Peter was beneath in the palace, there cometh one of the maids of the high priest: 67And when she saw Peter warming himself, she looked upon him, and said, And thou also wast with Jesus of Nazareth. 68 But he denied, saying, I know not, neither understand I what thou sayest. And he went out into the porch; and the cock crew. 69And a maid saw him again, and began to say to them that stood by, This is *one* of them. 70And he denied it again. And a little after, they that stood by said again to Peter, Surely thou art *one* of them: for thou art a Galilean, and thy speech agreeth

N.A.S.

clubs, from the chief priests and the scribes and the elders. 44 Now he who was betraying Him had given them a signal, saying, "Whomever I shall kiss, He is the one; seize Him, and lead Him away under guard." 45And after coming, he immediately went up to Him, saying, "Rabbi!" and kissed Him. 46And they laid hands on Him, and seized Him. 47 But a certain one of those who stood by drew his sword, and struck the slave of the high priest, and cut off his ear. 48And Jesus answered and said to them, "Have you come out with swords and clubs to arrest Me, as though I were a robber? 49 "Every day I was with you in the temple teaching, and you did not seize Me; but *this has happened* that the Scriptures might be fulfilled." 50And they all left Him and fled.

51 And a certain young man was following Him, wearing *nothing but* a linen sheet over *his* naked *body;* and they *seized him. 52 But he left the linen sheet behind, and escaped naked.

53 And they led Jesus away to the high priest; and all the chief priests and the elders and the scribes *gathered together. 54And Peter had followed Him at a distance, right into the courtyard of the high priest; and he was sitting with the officers, and warming himself at the fire. 55 Now the chief priests and the whole ᵃCouncil kept trying to obtain testimony against Jesus to put Him to death; and they were finding none. 56 For many were giving false testimony against Him, and *yet* their testimony was not consistent. 57And some stood up and *began* to give false testimony against Him, saying, 58 "We heard Him say, 'I will destroy this temple made with hands, and in three days I will build another made without hands.' " 59And not even in this respect was their testimony consistent. 60And the high priest arose *and came* forward and questioned Jesus, saying, "Do You make no answer to what these men are testifying against You?" 61 But He kept silent, and made no answer. Again the high priest was questioning Him, and saying to Him, "Are You the Christ, the Son of the Blessed *One?"* 62And Jesus said, "I am; and you shall see the SON OF MAN SITTING AT THE RIGHT HAND OF POWER, and COMING WITH THE CLOUDS OF HEAVEN." 63And tearing his clothes, the high priest *said, "What further need do we have of witnesses? 64 "You have heard the blasphemy; how does it seem to you?" And they all condemned Him to be deserving of death. 65And some began to spit at Him, and to blindfold Him, and to beat Him with their fists, and to say to Him, "Prophesy!" And the officers received Him with slaps *in the face.*

66 And as Peter was below in the courtyard, one of the servant-girls of the high priest *came, 67 and seeing Peter warming himself, she looked at him, and *said, "You, too, were with Jesus the Nazarene." 68 But he denied *it,* saying, "I neither know nor understand what you are talking about." And he went out onto the porch.ᵇ 69And the maid saw him, and began once more to say to the bystanders, "This is *one* of them!" 70 But again he was denying it. And after a little while the bystanders were again saying to Peter, "Surely you are *one* of them, for you are a Galilean

[a] Or, *Sanhedrin.* [b] Later mss. add: *and a cock crowed.*

WILLIAMS

clubs, from the high priests, scribes, and elders. 44 Now His betrayer had given them a signal, saying, "The one I kiss is He; seize Him and lead Him safely away." 45 So when he came he went straight up to Jesus, and said, "Rabbi," and with much affection kissed Him.

46 Then they laid hands on Him and arrested Him. 47 But one of the bystanders drew his sword and struck at the high priest's slave and cut his ear off. 48 And Jesus spoke and said to them, "Have you come out with swords and clubs to arrest me, as though I were a robber? 49 Day after day I used to be with you teaching in the temple, and you never laid hands on me. But this is so to fulfill the Scriptures."

50 Then all His disciples forsook Him and made their escape. 51 And a young man was following Him, with only a linen sheet thrown about his body; and they seized him, 52 but he left the linen sheet behind and fled away naked.

53 They took Jesus away to the high priest, and all the high priests, elders, and scribes met there. 54 And Peter followed Him at a distance, as far as the courtyard of the high priest; he was sitting with the attendants and warming himself before the fire.

55 The high priests and the whole council were trying to get evidence against Jesus to put Him to death, but they could find none, 56 for although many men gave false testimony against Him, their testimonies did not agree. 57 Some took the witness stand and gave this false testimony against Him: 58 "We ourselves have heard Him say, 'I will tear down this temple built by men's hands, and in three days I will build another, made without hands.'" 59 But even in this matter their testimony did not agree.

60 Then the high priest arose in the midst and asked Jesus, "Have you no answer to make? What about this testimony they are giving against you?" 61 But He kept silent and made no answer at all.

So the high priest again questioned Him in these words, "Are you the Christ, the Son of the Blessed One?"

62 Jesus said, "Yes, I am, and you will all see the Son of Man seated at the right hand of the Almighty and coming in the clouds of the sky!"

63 Then the high priest tore his clothes and said, "What more evidence do we need now? 64 Did you hear His own blasphemy? What do you think now?" And they all condemned Him as deserving to die. 65 And some of them started to spit on Him and to blindfold Him and to hit Him with their fists, and say to Him, "Now play the prophet!" Even the attendants took charge of Him with slaps at Him.

66 While Peter was down in the courtyard, one of the high priest's waiting-girls came up, 67 and when she saw that Peter was warming himself, she looked at him and said, "You were with Jesus of Nazareth too!"

68 But he denied it, saying, "I do not know or understand what you mean." Then he went out of the courtyard and was in the gateway to it.

69 And the waiting-girl saw him there and began again to tell the bystanders, "This fellow is one of them!" 70 But he denied it again.

And again a few minutes later the bystanders began to say to Peter, "You are surely one of them, for you are a Galilean too."

BECK

of men with swords and clubs from the ruling priests, the Bible scholars, and the elders. 44 The traitor had given them a signal. "The One I kiss is the Man," he said. "Grab Him, take Him away, and don't let Him escape."

45 When he came there, he quickly stepped up to Jesus and said, "Master!" and kissed Him.

46 Then the men took hold of Jesus and arrested Him. 47 One of those who were standing near Him drew his sword, struck the high priest's slave, and cut off his ear.

48 "Did you come out to arrest Me," Jesus asked them, "with swords and clubs as if I were a robber? 49 Day after day I was with you as I taught in the temple, and you didn't arrest Me. But what the Bible says has to come true."

50 Then all the disciples left Him and ran away. 51 One young man who also was following Him had nothing on but a linen cloth. They tried to grab him, 52 but he left the linen cloth and ran away naked.

The First Trial Before the Jewish Court

53 The men took Jesus to the high priest, and all the ruling priests, elders, and Bible scholars were coming together. 54 Peter followed Him at a distance and even went into the high priest's courtyard. And he was sitting with the attendants, warming himself at the fire.

55 The ruling priests and the whole Jewish court tried to get some testimony against Jesus in order to kill Him but couldn't find any. 56 While many gave false testimony against Him, their statements didn't agree.

57 Then some got up and gave this false testimony against Him: 58 "We heard Him say, 'I will tear down this temple, made by human hands, and in three days build another not made by human hands.'" 59 But even on this point their statements didn't agree.

60 Then the high priest stepped forward. "Don't you have anything to say to this?" he asked Jesus. "What are these men testifying against You?"

61 But He was silent and didn't answer.

Again the high priest asked Him, "Are You the promised Savior, the Son of the Blessed?"

62 "I am," Jesus said. "And you will all see *the Son of Man sitting at the right hand of power* and *coming in the clouds of heaven.*" 47

63 Then the high priest tore his clothes, saying, "Why do we need any more witnesses? 64 You've heard the blasphemy. What do you think?"

65 Then all condemned Him, saying He must die. Some of them started to spit at Him. They covered His face, hit Him with their fists, and told Him, "Prophesy!" The attendants also slapped Him when they took charge of Him.

Peter Denies Jesus

66 While Peter was down in the courtyard, one of the high priest's maids came and saw Peter warming himself. 67 "You, too, were with the Man from Nazareth—this Jesus," she said, looking at him.

68 But he denied it: "I don't know Him, and I don't know what you're talking about."

He went out to the entrance. Then a rooster crowed.

69 The maid saw him. "He's one of them," she also told those who were standing around. 70 Again he denied.

After a little while those who stood near him also told Peter, "Sure, you're one of them because you're a Galilean!"

[47] Ps. 110:1; Dan. 7:13

thereto. 71 But he began to curse and to swear, *saying,* I know not this man of whom ye speak. 72And the second time the cock crew. And Peter called to mind the word that Jesus said unto him, Before the cock crow twice, thou shalt deny me thrice. And when he thought thereon, he wept.

15 And straightway in the morning the chief priests held a consultation with the elders and scribes and the whole council, and bound Jesus, and carried *him* away, and delivered *him* to Pilate. 2And Pilate asked him, Art thou the King of the Jews? And he answering said unto him, Thou sayest *it.* 3And the chief priests accused him of many things; but he answered nothing. 4And Pilate asked him again, saying, Answerest thou nothing? behold how many things they witness against thee. 5 But Jesus yet answered nothing; so that Pilate marvelled. 6 Now at *that* feast he released unto them one prisoner, whomsoever they desired. 7And there was *one* named Barabbas, *which lay* bound with them that had made insurrection with him, who had committed murder in the insurrection. 8And the multitude crying aloud began to desire *him to do* as he had ever done unto them. 9 But Pilate answered them, saying, Will ye that I release unto you the King of the Jews? 10 For he knew that the chief priests had delivered him for envy. 11 But the chief priests moved the people, that he should rather release Barabbas unto them. 12And Pilate answered and said again unto them, What will ye then that I shall do *unto him* whom ye call the King of the Jews? 13And they cried out again, Crucify him. 14 Then Pilate said unto them, Why, what evil hath he done? And they cried out the more exceedingly, Crucify him.

15 And *so* Pilate, willing to content the people, released Barabbas unto them, and delivered Jesus, when he had scourged *him,* to be crucified. 16And the soldiers led him away into the hall, called Pretorium; and they call together the whole band. 17And they clothed him with purple, and platted a crown of thorns, and put it about his *head,* 18And began to salute him, Hail, King of the Jews! 19And they smote him on the head with a reed, and did spit upon him, and bowing *their* knees worshipped him. 20And when they had mocked him, they took off the purple from him, and put his own clothes on him, and led him out to crucify him. 21And they compel one Simon a Cyrenian, who passed by, coming out of the country, the father of Alexander and Rufus, to bear his cross. 22And they bring him unto the place Golgotha, which is, being interpreted, The place of a skull. 23And

too." 71 But he began to curse and swear, "I do not know this fellow you are talking about!" 72And immediately a cock crowed a second time. And Peter remembered how Jesus had made the remark to him, "Before a cock crows twice, you will deny Me three times." And he *began* to weep.

15 And early in the morning the chief priests with the elders and scribes, and the whole ªCouncil, immediately held a consultation, and binding Jesus, they led Him away, and delivered Him up to Pilate. 2And Pilate questioned Him, "Are You the King of the Jews?" And answering He *said to him, "It is as* you say." 3And the chief priests *began* to accuse Him harshly. 4And Pilate was questioning Him again, saying, "Do You make no answer? See how many charges they bring against You!" 5 But Jesus made no further answer; so that Pilate was astonished. 6 Now at *the* feast he used to release for them *any* one prisoner whom they requested. 7And the man named Barabbas had been imprisoned with the insurrectionists who had committed murder in the insurrection. 8And the multitude went up and began asking him *to do* as he had been accustomed to do for them. 9And Pilate answered them, saying, "Do you want me to release for you the King of the Jews?" 10 For he was aware that the chief priests had delivered Him up because of envy. 11 But the chief priests stirred up the multitude *to ask* him to release Barabbas for them instead. 12And answering again, Pilate was saying to them, "Then what shall I do to Him whom you call the King of the Jews?" 13And they shouted back, "Crucify Him!" 14But Pilate was saying to them, "Why, what evil has He done?" But they shouted all the more, "Crucify Him!" 15And wishing to satisfy the multitude, Pilate released Barabbas for them, and after having Jesus scourged, he delivered Him over to be crucified.

16 And the soldiers took Him away into the palace (that is, the Praetorium), and they *called together the whole *Roman* ᵇcohort. 17And they *dressed Him up in purple, and after weaving a crown of thorns, they put it on Him; 18 and they began to acclaim Him, "Hail, King of the Jews!" 19And they kept beating His head with a ᶜreed, and spitting at Him, and kneeling and bowing before Him. 20And after they had mocked Him, they took the purple off Him, and put His garments on Him. And they *led Him out to crucify Him.

21 And they *pressed into service a passerby coming from the country, Simon of Cyrene (the father of Alexander and Rufus), that he might bear His cross.

22 And they *brought Him to the place Golgotha, which is translated, Place of a Skull. 23And they tried to give Him wine mixed with

[a] Or, *Sanhedrin.* [b] Or, *battalion.* [c] Or, *staff* (made of a reed).

WILLIAMS

71 Then he commenced cursing and swearing, "I do not know this man that you are talking about."

72 At that moment for the second time a cock crowed. Then Peter remembered how Jesus had said to him, "Before the cock crows twice, you will disown me three times!" And when he remembered that, he burst into tears.

15 *Jesus tried in the Roman court; Barabbas set free; the soldiers making sport of Jesus; crucified on Golgotha; suffering six hours; buried by Joseph in His new tomb*

As soon as it was daylight, the high priests held a consultation with the elders and scribes; and the whole council, after binding Jesus, took Him away and turned Him over to Pilate.

2 Then Pilate asked Him, "Are you the king of the Jews?"

He answered, "Yes."

3 And the high priests kept piling up[a] accusations against Him.

4 Then again Pilate asked Him, "Have you no answer to make? Just see how many charges they are making against you!" 5 But Jesus made no further answer at all, so that Pilate was astonished.

6 Now at the time of the feast Pilate usually set a prisoner free whom the people requested. 7 There was in prison a man named Barabbas, among some revolutionaries who in their uprising had committed murder. 8 So a crowd of people came up and started to request of the governor the usual favor.

9 Then Pilate answered them by asking, "Do you want me to set the king of the Jews free for you?" 10 For he knew that the high priests out of envy had turned Him over to him. 11 But the high priests stirred up the crowd to get him to set Barabbas free for them instead.

12 Then Pilate again said to them, "What then do you want me to do to the man whom you call king of the Jews?"

13 They shouted back, "Crucify Him!"

14 Then Pilate again asked, "Why, what has He done that is wrong?"

But they shouted at the top of their voices, "Crucify Him!" 15 So, as Pilate wanted to satisfy the crowd, he set Barabbas free for them, but after having Jesus flogged, he turned Him over to be crucified.

16 Then the soldiers led Him away to a place inside the court yard, that is, of the governor's palace,[b] and they called the whole battalion together. 17 And they dressed Him in a purple robe and made a crown of thorns and crowned Him with it, 18 and they began to shout at Him, "All hail, you king of the Jews!" 19 And they kept hitting Him on the head with a stick, and kept spitting on Him, and on bending knees they kept doing Him homage. 20 When they had finished making sport of Him, they took off the purple robe and put His own clothes on Him.

Then they led Him out of the city to crucify Him. 21 They forced a certain passer-by, who was coming in from the country, to carry His cross—Simon, a Cyrenian, the father of Alexander and Rufus. 22 And they led Him to Golgotha, which means, the Place of the Skull. 23 They offered Him wine flavored with myrrh,

[a] *Were making many accusations.* [b] Grk., *praetorium.*

BECK

71 Then he started to curse and swear: "I don't know this Man you're talking about." 72 Just then a rooster crowed a second time, and Peter remembered Jesus telling him: "Before the rooster crows twice, you will deny Me three times." And he started to cry.

Before Pilate

15 As soon as it was morning, the ruling priests, the elders, and the Bible scholars, that is, the whole Jewish court, came to a decision. They bound Jesus, took Him away, and handed Him over to Pilate.

2 Pilate asked Him, "Are You the King of the Jews?"

"Yes," Jesus answered him.

3 The ruling priests were accusing Him of many things.

4 "Don't You have anything to say to this?" Pilate asked Him again. "See how many accusations they're bringing against You!"

5 But Jesus didn't answer him any more, so that Pilate was surprised.

Barabbas

6 Now, at every festival Pilate used to free a prisoner whom the people asked for. 7 There was a man by the name of Barabbas. He was in prison with the rebels who in their revolt had committed a murder. 8 And the crowd came up and asked Pilate to do for them as he had done before. 9 Pilate answered them by asking, "Do you want me to free the King of the Jews for you?" 10 He knew the ruling priests had handed Jesus over to him because they were jealous.

11 The ruling priests stirred up the people to get him to free Barabbas for them instead.

12 "Now, what should I do with Him you call the King of the Jews?" Pilate again asked them.

13 Then they yelled, "Crucify Him!"

14 "Why, what wrong has He done?" Pilate asked them.

But they yelled all the louder, "Crucify Him!"

15 Then Pilate, wanting to satisfy the people, freed Barabbas for them, but Jesus he scourged and handed over to be crucified.

16 The soldiers took Him into the courtyard of the governor's palace and called together the whole troop of soldiers. 17 They put a purple cloak on Him, twisted some thorns into a crown and placed it on His head, 18 and started to greet Him: "Hail, King of the Jews!" 19 They hit Him on the head with a stick, spit on Him, knelt, and worshiped Him.

"They Crucified Him"

20 After mocking Him, the soldiers took off the purple cloak and put His own clothes on Him. Then they took Him out to crucify Him. 21 A certain Simon from Cyrene, the father of Alexander and Rufus, was on his way in from the country, and as he was going to pass by, they forced him to carry the cross of Jesus. 22 They took Him to the Golgotha place, which means Skull place. 23 They tried to give

K.J.V.

they gave him to drink wine mingled with myrrh: but he received *it* not. 24And when they had crucified him, they parted his garments, casting lots upon them, what every man should take. 25And it was the third hour, and they crucified him. 26And the superscription of his accusation was written over, THE KING OF THE JEWS. 27And with him they crucify two thieves; the one on his right hand, and the other on his left. 28And the Scripture was fulfilled, which saith, And he was numbered with the transgressors. 29And they that passed by railed on him, wagging their heads, and saying, Ah, thou that destroyest the temple, and buildest *it* in three days, 30 Save thyself, and come down from the cross. 31 Likewise also the chief priests mocking said among themselves with the scribes, He saved others; himself he cannot save. 32 Let Christ the King of Israel descend now from the cross, that we may see and believe. And they that were crucified with him reviled him. 33And when the sixth hour was come, there was darkness over the whole land until the ninth hour. 34And at the ninth hour Jesus cried with a loud voice, saying, Eloi, Eloi, lama sabachthani? which is, being interpreted, My God, my God, why hast thou forsaken me? 35And some of them that stood by, when they heard *it*, said, Behold, he calleth Elias. 36And one ran and filled a sponge full of vinegar, and put *it* on a reed, and gave him to drink, saying, Let alone; let us see whether Elias will come to take him down. 37And Jesus cried with a loud voice, and gave up the ghost. 38And the vail of the temple was rent in twain from the top to the bottom.

39 And when the centurion, which stood over against him, saw that he so cried out, and gave up the ghost, he said, Truly this man was the Son of God. 40 There were also women looking on afar off: among whom was Mary Magdalene, and Mary the mother of James the less and of Joses, and Salome; 41 Who also, when he was in Galilee, followed him, and ministered unto him; and many other women which came up with him unto Jerusalem.

42 And now when the even was come, because it was the preparation, that is, the day before the sabbath, 43 Joseph of Arimathea, an honourable counsellor, which also waited for the kingdom of God, came, and went in boldly unto Pilate, and craved the body of Jesus. 44And Pilate marvelled if he were already dead: and calling *unto him* the centurion, he asked him whether he had been any while dead. 45 And when he knew *it* of the centurion, he gave the body to Joseph. 46And he bought fine linen, and took him down, and wrapped him in the linen, and laid him in a sepulchre which was hewn out of a rock, and rolled a stone unto the door of the sepulchre. 47And Mary Magdalene and Mary *the mother* of Joses beheld where he was laid.

N.A.S.

myrrh; but He did not take it. 24And they *crucified Him, and *DIVIDED UP HIS GARMENTS AMONG THEMSELVES, CASTING LOTS FOR THEM, *to decide* what each should take. 25And it was the *third hour when they crucified Him. 26And the inscription of the charge against Him read, "THE KING OF THE JEWS." 27And they *crucified two robbers with Him; one on the right and one on the left. 28(See footnote ᵇ) 29And those passing by were hurling abuse at Him, WAGGING THEIR HEADS, and saying, "Ha! You who *were going to* destroy the temple and rebuild it in three days, 30 save Yourself, and come down from the cross!" 31 In the same way the chief priests along with the scribes were also mocking *Him* among themselves and saying, "He saved others; He cannot save Himself. 32 "Let *this* Christ, the King of Israel, now come down from the cross, so that we may see and believe!" And those who were crucified with Him were casting the same insult at Him.

33 And when the ᶜsixth hour had come, darkness fell over the whole land until the ᵈninth hour. 34And at the ninth hour Jesus cried out with a loud voice, "ELOI, ELOI, LAMA SABACHTHANI?" which is translated, "MY GOD, MY GOD, WHY HAST THOU FORSAKEN ME?" 35And when some of the bystanders heard it, they *began saying, "Behold, He is calling for Elijah." 36And someone ran and filled a sponge with sour wine, put it on a reed, and gave Him a drink, saying, "Let us see whether Elijah will come to take Him down." 37And Jesus uttered a loud cry, and breathed His last. 38And the curtain of the temple was torn in two from top to bottom. 39And when the centurion, who was standing right in front of Him, saw the way He breathed His last, he said, "Truly this man was a son of God!" 40And there were also *some* women looking on from afar, among whom *were* Mary Magdalene, and Mary the mother of James the Less and Joses, and Salome. 41And when He was in Galilee, they used to follow Him and minister to Him; and *there were* many other women who had come up with Him to Jerusalem.

42 And when evening had already come, because it was the Preparation Day, that is, the day before the Sabbath, 43 Joseph of Arimathea came, a prominent member of the Council, a man who was himself waiting for the kingdom of God; and he gathered up courage and went in before Pilate, and asked for the body of Jesus. 44And Pilate wondered if He was dead by this time, and summoning the centurion, he questioned him as to whether He was already dead. 45And ascertaining this from the centurion, he granted the body to Joseph. 46And *Joseph* bought a linen sheet, took Him down, wrapped Him in the linen sheet, and laid Him in a tomb which had been hewn out in the rock; and he rolled a stone against the entrance of the tomb. 47And Mary Magdalene and Mary the *mother* of Joses were looking on *to see* where he was laid.

[a] I.e., 9 a.m. [b] Later mss. add verse 28: *And the Scripture was fulfilled which says, "And He was reckoned with transgressors."* [c] I.e., noon. [d] I.e., 3 p.m.

148

WILLIAMS

but He would not take it. 24 Then they crucified Him and divided among them His clothes, by drawing lots for them to see which piece each of them should have. 25 It was nine o'clock in the morning when they crucified Him. 26And the notice of the charge against Him read, "The king of the Jews." 27 They crucified two robbers along with Him, one at His right and one at His left.*

29 And the passers-by kept hissing at Him, shaking their heads and saying, "Aha! You are the man who would tear down the temple and build another in three days! 30 Now save yourself by coming down from the cross."

31 The high priests too made sport of Him to one another with the scribes, and kept saying, "He saved others but He cannot save Himself! 32 Let the Christ, the king of Israel, come down now from the cross, so that we may see it and believe!" Even the men who were crucified with Him made sport of Him.

33 At twelve o'clock darkness covered the whole land and lasted until three in the afternoon. 34And at three o'clock Jesus cried with a loud voice, *"Eloi! Eloi! lama sabachthani?"* which means, "My God! my God! why have you forsaken me?"

35 Some of the bystanders when they heard it said, "Listen! He is calling for Elijah!"

36 So one man ran and soaked a sponge in vinegar and put it on a stick and held it up to Him to drink, saying, "Wait, let us see whether Elijah does come to take Him down!"

37 Then Jesus gave a loud cry, and expired. 38And the curtain of the sanctuary was torn in two, from top to bottom. 39And when the captain who stood facing him saw that He expired in this way, he said, "This man was surely God's Son."

40 Now several women were there looking on from a distance, among them Mary of Magdala, Mary the mother of the younger James and of Joses, and Salome, 41 who used to accompany Him when He was in Galilee, besides several other women who had come up to Jerusalem with Him.

42 Although it was now evening, yet since it was the Preparation Day, that is, the day before the sabbath, 43 Joseph of Arimathea, a highly honored member of the council, who was himself looking for the kingdom of God, ventured to go to Pilate and ask for Jesus' body. 44 Pilate wondered whether He was dead yet, and calling the captain to him asked whether He was already dead; 45 but when he found out from the captain that He was, he gave him permission to take His body. 46 So he bought a linen sheet, he took Him down from the cross, wrapped Him in the linen sheet, and laid Him in a tomb that had been hewn out of the rock, and rolled a boulder up to the doorway of the tomb. 47And Mary of Magdala and Mary, Joses' mother, were looking on to see where He was put.

BECK

Him wine mixed with myrrh, but He didn't take it. 24 They crucified Him. And *they divided His clothes among them by throwing lots for them*[48] to see what each one should get. 25 It was nine in the morning when they crucified Him. 26 There was a notice stating why Jesus was being punished; it read: THE KING OF THE JEWS. 27 With Him they crucified two robbers, one at His right hand and the other at His left.*

29 Those who passed by were abusing Him, *shaking their heads*[49] and saying, "Ha! You tear down the temple and build it in three days —30 come down from the cross, and save Yourself!" 31 In the same way the ruling priests and the Bible scholars made fun of Him among themselves and said, "He saved others—He can't save Himself. 32 The promised Savior, the King of Israel, should now come down from the cross. He should let us see that, and we'll believe Him." Those crucified with Him also were insulting Him.

Jesus Dies

33 When twelve o'clock came, darkness came over the whole country and lasted till three in the afternoon. 34At three o'clock Jesus called out aloud, *"Eloi, Eloi, lama sabachthani?"* [50] which means, "My God, My God, why did You forsake Me?"

35 Hearing Him, some of those standing near said, "Listen! He's calling Elijah." 36 Someone ran, soaked a sponge in *sour wine*, put it on a stick, and *gave Him a drink.*[51] "Let's see," he said, "if Elijah comes to take Him down."

37 Then Jesus called out loud and died. 38And the curtain in the temple was torn in two from top to bottom.

39 When the captain who stood facing Jesus saw how He gave up His spirit, he said, "This Man certainly was the Son of God!"

40 There were women watching *from a distance.*[52] Among them were Mary from Magdala and Mary, the mother of James the Less and of Joseph and Salome. 41 While He was in Galilee, they had followed Him and helped Him. There were also many other women who had come up to Jerusalem with Him.

Jesus Is Buried

42 In the evening, since it was the day of preparation, that is, Friday, 43 Joseph from Arimathea, an important member of the Jewish court who also was waiting for God's kingdom, dared to go to Pilate and ask for Jesus' body.

44 Pilate was surprised He was already dead. He called the captain and asked him, "Has he died already?" 45 When the captain told him, Pilate let Joseph have the body.

46 Joseph bought some linen, took the body down, wrapped it in the linen, and laid it in a grave that had been cut in the rock, and rolled a stone against the door of the grave.

47 Mary from Magdala and Mary the mother of Joses watched where He was laid.

* Our oldest manuscripts do not have v. 28: "And what the Bible said came true, *He will be counted among criminals.*" See Luke 22:37.
[48] Ps. 22:18
[49] Ps. 109:25
[50] Ps. 22:1
[51] Ps. 69:21
[52] Ps. 38:11

[c] V. 28 om. from best Mss.

K.J.V.

16 And when the sabbath was past, Mary Magdalene, and Mary the *mother* of James, and Salome, had bought sweet spices, that they might come and anoint him. 2And very early in the morning, the first *day* of the week, they came unto the sepulchre at the rising of the sun. 3And they said among themselves, Who shall roll us away the stone from the door of the sepulchre? 4And when they looked, they saw that the stone was rolled away: for it was very great. 5And entering into the sepulchre, they saw a young man sitting on the right side, clothed in a long white garment; and they were affrighted. 6And he saith unto them, Be not affrighted: ye seek Jesus of Nazareth, which was crucified: he is risen; he is not here: behold the place where they laid him. 7But go your way, tell his disciples and Peter that he goeth before you into Galilee: there shall ye see him, as he said unto you. 8And they went out quickly, and fled from the sepulchre; for they trembled and were amazed: neither said they any thing to any *man;* for they were afraid.

9 Now when *Jesus* was risen early the first *day* of the week, he appeared first to Mary Magdalene, out of whom he had cast seven devils. 10*And* she went and told them that had been with him, as they mourned and wept. 11And they, when they had heard that he was alive, and had been seen of her, believed not.

12 After that he appeared in another form unto two of them, as they walked, and went into the country. 13And they went and told *it* unto the residue: neither believed they them.

14 Afterward he appeared unto the eleven as they sat at meat, and upbraided them with their unbelief and hardness of heart, because they believed not them which had seen him after he was risen. 15And he said unto them, Go ye into all the world, and preach the gospel to every creature. 16He that believeth and is baptized shall be saved; but he that believeth not shall be damned. 17And these signs shall follow them that believe; In my name shall they cast out devils; they shall speak with new tongues; 18 They shall take up serpents; and if they drink any deadly thing, it shall not hurt them; they shall lay hands on the sick, and they shall recover. 19 So then, after the Lord had spoken unto them, he was received up into heaven, and sat on the right hand of God. 20And they went forth, and preached every where, the Lord working with *them,* and confirming the word with signs following. Amen.

N.A.S.

16 And when the Sabbath was over, Mary Magdalene, and Mary the *mother* of James, and Salome, bought spices, that they might come and anoint Him. 2And very early on the first day of the week, they *came to the tomb when the sun had risen. 3And they were saying to one another, "Who will roll away the stone for us from the entrance of the tomb?" 4And looking up, they *saw that the stone had been rolled away, although it was extremely large. 5And entering the tomb, they saw a young man sitting at the right, wearing a white robe; and they were amazed. 6And he *said to them, "Do not be amazed; you are looking for Jesus the Nazarene, who has been crucified. He has risen; He is not here; behold, *here is* the place where they laid Him. 7"But go, tell His disciples and Peter, 'He is going before you into Galilee; there you will see Him, just as He said to you.'" 8And they went out and fled from the tomb, for trembling and astonishment had gripped them; and they said nothing to anyone, for they were afraid.

9 [a Now after He had risen early on the first day of the week, He first appeared to Mary Magdalene, from whom He had cast out seven demons. 10 She went and reported to those who had been with Him, while they were mourning and weeping. 11And when they heard that He was alive, and had been seen by her, they refused to believe it.

12 And after that, He appeared in a different form to two of them, while they were walking along on their way to the country. 13And they went away and reported it to the others, but they did not believe them either.

14 And afterward He appeared to the eleven themselves as they were reclining *at table;* and He reproached them for their unbelief and hardness of heart, because they had not believed those who had seen Him after He had risen. 15And He said to them, "Go into all the world and preach the gospel to all creation. 16 "He who has believed and has been baptized shall be saved; but he who has disbelieved shall be condemned. 17 "And these signs will accompany those who have believed: in My name they will cast out demons, they will speak with new tongues; 18 they will pick up serpents, and if they drink any deadly *poison,* it shall not hurt them; they will lay hands on the sick, and they will recover."

19 So then, when the Lord Jesus had spoken to them, He was received up into heaven, and SAT DOWN AT THE RIGHT HAND OF GOD. 20And they went out and preached everywhere, while the Lord worked with them, and confirmed the word by the signs that followed.]

[a] Some of the oldest mss. omit from verse 9 through 20.

16

Some women see the empty tomb; the angel orders them to tell His disciples; Jesus appears to Mary of Magdala; to two more walking into the country; to the Eleven; gives them His last order; goes up to heaven

When the sabbath had ended, Mary of Magdala, Mary, James's mother, and Salome bought spices to go and anoint Him. 2 It was very early, just after the sun had risen, on the first day of the week, when they went to the tomb. 3 And they kept saying to one another, "Who will roll the boulder back from the doorway of the tomb for us?"

4 Then they looked up and saw that the boulder had already been rolled to one side, for it was a very large one. 5 And when they went into the tomb, they saw a young man dressed in a white robe sitting at the right; and they were utterly astounded.

6 But he said to them, "You must not be so astounded; you are looking for Jesus of Nazareth who was crucified. He has risen; He is not here. See! here is the spot where they laid Him. 7 But you go and tell His disciples and Peter, 'He is going back to Galilee to meet you; you will see Him there, just as He told you.'"

8 Then they left the tomb and fled, for they were trembling and bewildered,[a] and they did not tell anybody a single thing about it, for they were afraid to do so.[b]

9 Now after He had risen, early on the first day of the week, He appeared first to Mary of Magdala, out of whom He had driven seven demons. 10 She went out and told it to His disciples, while they were mourning and weeping. 11 But although they had heard that He was alive and had been seen by her, they would not believe it. 12 After this He showed Himself in a different form to two of them as they were walking along, on their way into the country. 13 Then they went back and told the rest, but they would not believe them either. 14 Later on He appeared to the Eleven themselves while they were at table, and reproved them for their lack of faith and their stubbornness,[c] because they had not believed those who had seen Him after He had been raised from the dead.

15 Then He said to them, "You must go all over the world and preach the good news to all the creation. 16 He who believes it and is baptized will be saved, but he who does not believe it will be condemned. 17 And the following signs will attend those who believe: By using my name they will drive out demons; they will speak in foreign[d] languages; 18 they will take snakes in their hands; even if they drink anything poisonous, it will not hurt them; they will lay their hands on the sick, and they will get well."

19 So the Lord Jesus, after He had spoken to them, was caught up into heaven and took His seat at God's right hand. 20 Then they went out and preached everywhere, while the Lord kept on working with them and confirming their message by the signs that attended it.

Jesus Rises

16

On Saturday evening Mary from Magdala, Mary the mother of James, and Salome bought spices to go and anoint Jesus. 2 On Sunday they were going to the grave very early when the sun was up. 3 "Who is going to roll away the stone for us from the door of the grave?" they asked one another; 4 it was very large. But when they looked up, they saw the stone had been rolled back. 5 As they went into the grave, they saw a young man, dressed in a white robe, sitting at the right. And they were amazed.

6 "Don't be amazed," he told them. "You're looking for Jesus from Nazareth, who was crucified. He has risen. He is not here. See the place were He was laid. 7 But go and tell His disciples and Peter, 'He is going ahead of you to Galilee. There you will see Him, as He told you.'"

8 They went out and hurried away from the grave, because they were trembling and bewildered. They were so frightened they didn't tell anybody anything.

*The Living Savior**

9 After Jesus rose early on Sunday, He showed Himself first to Mary from Magdala, out of whom He had driven seven devils. 10 She went and told the news to those who had been with Him and were now mourning and crying. 11 When they heard He was alive and had been seen by her, they didn't believe it.

12 Later He appeared in a different form to two of them as they were walking into the country. 13 They went back and told the others, but these didn't believe them either.

14 Still later He showed Himself to the eleven while they were lying at the table, and He scolded them because their minds were closed and they didn't believe those who had seen Him after He had risen.

15 Then He told them, "Go everywhere in the world and preach the good news to the whole world. 16 He who believes and is baptized will be saved, but he who doesn't believe will be damned.

17 "The believers will have these proofs: In My name they will drive out devils. They will speak new languages. 18 They will pick up snakes. If they drink any deadly poison, it will not hurt them. They will lay their hands on the sick, and these will get well."

19 After talking with them, the Lord was *taken up to heaven and sat down at the right of God.*[53]

20 They went out and preached everywhere, and the Lord worked with them and confirmed the Word by the wonderful proofs that went with it.

---

[a] Grk., *trembling and bewilderment held them.*
[b] End of Mk. in two best Mss. Later Mss. add vv. 9-20. [c] Grk., *hardness of heart.* [d] Grk., *speak in tongues.*

* The two oldest and best manuscripts do not have Mark 16:9-20 but end Mark's Gospel with verse 8.
[53] 2 Kings 2:11; Ps. 110:1

K.J.V.

THE GOSPEL
ACCORDING TO
SAINT LUKE

1 Forasmuch as many have taken in hand to set forth in order a declaration of those things which are most surely believed among us, 2 Even as they delivered them unto us, which from the beginning were eyewitnesses, and ministers of the word; 3 It seemed good to me also, having had perfect understanding of all things from the very first, to write unto thee in order, most excellent Theophilus, 4 That thou mightest know the certainty of those things, wherein thou hast been instructed.

5 There was in the days of Herod, the king of Judea, a certain priest named Zacharias, of the course of Abia: and his wife was of the daughters of Aaron, and her name was Elisabeth. 6 And they were both righteous before God, walking in all the commandments and ordinances of the Lord blameless. 7 And they had no child, because that Elisabeth was barren; and they both were now well stricken in years. 8 And it came to pass, that, while he executed the priest's office before God in the order of his course, 9 According to the custom of the priest's office, his lot was to burn incense when he went into the temple of the Lord. 10 And the whole multitude of the people were praying without at the time of incense. 11 And there appeared unto him an angel of the Lord standing on the right side of the altar of incense. 12 And when Zacharias saw him, he was troubled, and fear fell upon him. 13 But the angel said unto him, Fear not, Zacharias: for thy prayer is heard; and thy wife Elisabeth shall bear thee a son, and thou shalt call his name John. 14 And thou shalt have joy and gladness; and many shall rejoice at his birth. 15 For he shall be great in the sight of the Lord, and shall drink neither wine nor strong drink; and he shall be filled with the Holy Ghost, even from his mother's womb. 16 And many of the children of Israel shall he turn to the Lord their God. 17 And he shall go before him in the spirit and power of Elias, to turn the hearts of the fathers to the children, and the disobedient to the wisdom of the just; to make ready a people prepared for the Lord. 18 And Zacharias said unto the angel, Whereby shall I know this? for I am an old man, and my wife well stricken in years. 19 And the angel answering said unto him, I am Gabriel, that stand in the presence of God; and am sent to speak unto thee, and to shew thee these glad tidings. 20 And, behold, thou shalt be dumb, and not able to speak, until the day that these things shall be performed, because thou believest not my words, which shall be fulfilled in their season. 21 And the people waited for Zacharias, and marvelled that he tarried so long in the temple. 22 And when he came out, he could

N.A.S.

THE GOSPEL
ACCORDING TO
LUKE

1 Inasmuch as many have undertaken to compile an account of the things accomplished among us, 2 just as those who from the beginning were eyewitnesses and servants of the [a]Word have handed them down to us, 3 it seemed fitting for me as well, having investigated everything carefully from the beginning, to write it out for you in consecutive order, most excellent Theophilus; 4 so that you might know the exact truth about the things you have been taught.

5 In the days of Herod, King of Judea, there was a certain priest named Zacharias, of the division of [b]Abijah; and he had a wife [c]from the daughters of Aaron, and her name was Elizabeth. 6 And they were both righteous in the sight of God, walking blamelessly in all the commandments and requirements of the Lord. 7 And they had no child, because Elizabeth was barren, and they were both advanced in years.

8 Now it came about, while he was performing his priestly service before God in the appointed order of his division, 9 according to the custom of the priestly office, he was chosen by lot to enter the temple of the Lord and burn incense. 10 And the whole multitude of the people were in prayer outside at the hour of the incense offering. 11 And an angel of the Lord appeared to him, standing to the right of the altar of incense. 12 And Zacharias was troubled when he saw him, and fear gripped him. 13 But the angel said to him, "Do not be afraid, Zacharias, for your petition has been heard, and your wife Elizabeth will bear you a son, and you will give him the name John. 14 "And you will have joy and gladness, and many will rejoice at his birth. 15 "For he will be great in the sight of the Lord, and he will drink no wine or liquor; and he will be filled with the Holy Spirit, while yet in his mother's womb. 16 "And he will turn back many of the children of Israel to the Lord their God. 17 "And it is he who will go as a forerunner before Him in the spirit and power of Elijah, TO TURN THE HEARTS OF THE FATHERS BACK TO THE CHILDREN, and the disobedient to the attitude of the righteous; so as to make ready a people prepared for the Lord." 18 And Zacharias said to the angel, "How shall I know this for certain? For I am an old man, and my wife is advanced in years." 19 And the angel answered and said to him, "I am Gabriel, who stand in the presence of God; and I have been sent to speak to you, and to bring you this good news. 20 "And behold, you shall be silent and unable to speak until the day when these things take place, because you did not believe my words, which shall be fulfilled in their proper time." 21 And the people were waiting for Zacharias, and were wondering at his delay in the temple. 22 But when he came out, he was unable to speak to them; and they realized that

[a] I.e., Gospel. [b] Gr., Abia. [c] I.e., of priestly descent.

152

WILLIAMS

BECK

THE GOOD NEWS

AS IT WAS TOLD BY

LUKE

LUKE

1 *The writer's foreword; the Baptist's birth foretold; Mary's visit to Elizabeth; Mary's song of praise; Zechariah's song of praise*

Since many writers have undertaken to compose narratives about the facts established among us, 2 just as the original eyewitnesses who became ministers of the message 3 have handed them down to us, I too, most excellent Theophilus, because I have carefully investigated them all from the start, have felt impressed to write them out in order for you, 4 that you may better know the certainty of those things that you have been taught.

5 In the days when Herod was king of Judea, there was a priest whose name was Zechariah, who belonged to the division of Abijah. His wife was also a descendant of Aaron, and her name was Elizabeth. 6 Now they were both upright in the sight of God, walking without reproach in all the Lord's commands and requirements. 7And they had no child, because Elizabeth was barren, and both of them were far advanced in years.

8 Once when he was acting as priest before God, when his division was on duty, it fell to his lot, 9 in accordance with the priests' custom, to go into the sanctuary of the Lord to burn the incense, 10 while all the throng of people were praying outside at the hour of the incense burning. 11 In the meantime, an angel of the Lord appeared to him, standing at the right of the altar of incense. 12 When Zechariah saw him, he was agitated, even overwhelmed with fear.

13 But the angel said to him, "Do not be afraid, Zechariah, because your prayer has been heard, and your wife Elizabeth will bear you a son, and you must name him John. 14 This will bring you gladness and delight, and many will rejoice over his birth. 15 For he will be great in the sight of the Lord. He must drink no wine nor strong drink, and so he will be filled with the Holy Spirit even from his birth. 16And he will turn many of Israel's descendants to the Lord their God. 17 He will go before Him in the spirit and the power of Elijah to turn the hearts of fathers to their children and the disobedient to the wisdom of the upright, to make ready for the Lord a people perfectly prepared."

18 Then Zechariah said to the angel, "How shall I know that this is so? For I am an old man, and my wife is far advanced in years."

19 The angel answered him, "I am Gabriel; I stand in the very presence of God. I have been sent to talk with you and to tell you this good news. 20 Now you will keep silent and be unable to talk until the day when this takes place, because you did not believe what I told you, for it will be fulfilled at the proper time."

21 Meanwhile the people kept waiting for Zechariah and wondering why he stayed so long in the sanctuary. 22 But when he came out, he could not speak to them, and so they knew that

1 Many have undertaken to plan and write a story of what has been done among us, 2 just as we heard it from those who from the first became eyewitnesses and servants of the Word. 3 For this reason I, too, decided to check everything carefully from the beginning and to write it down in the proper order for you, excellent Theophilus, 4 so that you will be sure what you have heard is true.

An Angel Comes to Zacharias

5 When Herod was king in the country of the Jews, there was a priest by the name of Zacharias. He belonged to the division of priests named after Abijah. His wife was a descendant of Aaron, and her name was Elizabeth. 6 Both were righteous before God as they lived blamelessly according to all the rules and regulations of the Lord.

7 But they had no children, because Elizabeth was barren and both were old.

8 Once Zacharias was on duty with his division and serving as priest before God. 9According to the custom of the priests he was chosen by lot to go into the Lord's temple to burn incense. 10All the people were praying outside while he was burning incense.

11 Then he saw the Lord's angel standing at the right side of the altar of incense. 12 Zacharias was startled to see him and was terrified.

13 *"Don't be afraid,* Zacharias," the angel told him. *"Your prayer has been heard.*[1] *You and your wife* Elizabeth *will have a son, and you must call him*[2] John. 14 He will be your joy and delight, and many will be glad he was born.

15 "He will be a great man before the Lord. *He will drink no wine or liquor.*[3] He will be filled with the Holy Spirit even before he is born. 16And he will bring many in Israel back to the Lord their God. 17 He will go ahead of Him with the spirit and power of *Elijah, to move fathers to love their children,*[4] and the disobedient to think as righteous men—and so to get a people thoroughly prepared for the Lord."

18 "How can I be sure of this?" Zacharias asked the angel. "I'm an old man, and my wife is old."

19 "I am Gabriel!" the angel answered him. "I stand before God and was sent to speak to you and tell you this good news. 20And now, you will be silent and not able to talk till the day this happens, because you didn't believe what I said. But it will come true at the right time."

21 Meanwhile the people were waiting for Zacharias and were surprised he was staying so long in the holy place. 22 When he did come out, he couldn't speak to them. Then they

[1] Dan. 10:12
[2] Gen. 17:19
[3] Num. 6:3; Judges 13:4
[4] Mal. 4:5-6

not speak unto them: and they perceived that he had seen a vision in the temple; for he beckoned unto them, and remained speechless. 23And it came to pass, that, as soon as the days of his ministration were accomplished, he departed to his own house. 24And after those days his wife Elisabeth conceived, and hid herself five months, saying, 25 Thus hath the Lord dealt with me in the days wherein he looked on *me*, to take away my reproach among men. 26And in the sixth month the angel Gabriel was sent from God unto a city of Galilee, named Nazareth, 27 To a virgin espoused to a man whose name was Joseph, of the house of David; and the virgin's name *was* Mary. 28And the angel came in unto her, and said, Hail, *thou that art* highly favoured, the Lord *is* with thee: blessed *art* thou among women. 29And when she saw *him,* she was troubled at his saying, and cast in her mind what manner of salutation this should be. 30And the angel said unto her, Fear not, Mary: for thou hast found favour with God. 31And, behold, thou shalt conceive in thy womb, and bring forth a son, and shalt call his name JESUS. 32 He shall be great, and shall be called the Son of the Highest; and the Lord God shall give unto him the throne of his father David: 33And he shall reign over the house of Jacob for ever; and of his kingdom there shall be no end. 34Then said Mary unto the angel, How shall this be, seeing I know not a man? 35And the angel answered and said unto her, The Holy Ghost shall come upon thee, and the power of the Highest shall overshadow thee: therefore also that holy thing which shall be born of thee shall be called the Son of God. 36And, behold, thy cousin Elisabeth, she hath also conceived a son in her old age; and this is the sixth month with her, who was called barren. 37 For with God nothing shall be impossible. 38And Mary said, Behold the handmaid of the Lord; be it unto me according to thy word. And the angel departed from her. 39And Mary arose in those days, and went into the hill country with haste, into a city of Juda; 40And entered into the house of Zacharias, and saluted Elisabeth. 41And it came to pass, that, when Elisabeth heard the salutation of Mary, the babe leaped in her womb; and Elisabeth was filled with the Holy Ghost: 42And she spake out with a loud voice, and said, Blessed *art* thou among women, and blessed *is* the fruit of thy womb. 43And whence *is* this to me, that the mother of my Lord should come to me? 44 For, lo, as soon as the voice of thy salutation sounded in mine ears, the babe leaped in my womb for joy. 45And blessed *is* she that believed: for there shall be a performance of those things which were told her from the Lord. 46And Mary said, My soul doth magnify the Lord, 47And my spirit hath rejoiced in God my Saviour. 48 For he hath regarded the low estate of his handmaiden: for, behold, from henceforth all generations shall call me blessed. 49 For he that is mighty hath done to me great

he had seen a vision in the temple; and he kept making signs to them, and remained mute. 23And it came about, when the days of his priestly service were ended, that he went back home.

24 And after these days Elizabeth his wife became pregnant; and she kept herself in seclusion for five months, saying, 25 "This is the way the Lord has dealt with me in the days when He looked *with favor* upon *me,* to take away my disgrace among men."

26 Now in the sixth month the angel Gabriel was sent from God to a city in Galilee, called Nazareth, 27 to a virgin engaged to a man whose name was Joseph, of the descendants of David; and the virgin's name was Mary. 28And coming in, he said to her, "Hail, favored one! The Lord *is* with you." ª29 But she was greatly troubled at *this* statement, and kept pondering what kind of salutation this might be. 30And the angel said to her, "Do not be afraid, Mary; for you have found favor with God. 31 "And behold, you will conceive in your womb, and bear a son, and you shall name Him Jesus. 32 "He will be great, and will be called the Son of the Most High; and the Lord God will give Him the throne of His father David; 33 and He will reign over the house of Jacob forever; and His kingdom will have no end." 34And Mary said to the angel, "How can this be, since I am a virgin?" 35And the angel answered and said to her, "The Holy Spirit will come upon you, and the power of the Most High will overshadow you; and for that reason the holy offspring shall be called the Son of God. 36 "And behold, even your relative Elizabeth has also conceived a son in her old age; and she who was called barren is now in her sixth month. 37 "For nothing will be impossible with God." 38And Mary said, "Behold, the ᵇbondslave of the Lord; be it done to me according to your word." And the angel departed from her.

39 Now at this time Mary arose and went with haste to the hill country, to a city of Judah, 40 and entered the house of Zacharias and greeted Elizabeth. 41And it came about that when Elizabeth heard Mary's greeting, the baby leaped in her womb; and Elizabeth was filled with the Holy Spirit. 42And she cried out with a loud voice, and said, "Blessed among women *are* you, and blessed *is* the fruit of your womb! 43 "And how has it *happened* to me, that the mother of my Lord should come to me? 44 "For behold, when the sound of your greeting reached my ears, the baby leaped in my womb for joy. 45 "And blessed *is* she who believed that there would be a fulfillment of what had been spoken to her by the Lord." 46And Mary said:

"My soul exalts the Lord,
47 And my spirit has rejoiced in God my Savior.
48 For He has had regard for the humble state of His bondslave;
For behold, from this time on all generations will count me blessed.
49 For the Mighty One has done great things for me; And holy is His name.

[a] Later mss. add: *you are blessed among women.*
[b] I.e., *female slave.*

WILLIAMS

he had seen a vision in the sanctuary. Meanwhile he kept on making signs to them, and remained dumb. 23 But when the period of his service was over, he went back to his home.

24 So after this his wife Elizabeth became pregnant, and she kept herself in seclusion for five months, saying, 25 "This is what the Lord has done for me when He smiled upon me to take away my disgrace among men."

26 Now in the sixth month the angel Gabriel was sent by God to a town in Galilee called Nazareth, 27 to a maiden there engaged to be married to a man named Joseph, a descendant of David; and the maiden's name was Mary. 28 So the angel came to her home and said, "Congratulations, you highly favored woman! The Lord be with you!"

29 But she was agitated at what he said, and began to ponder what this greeting ' meant. 30 Then the angel said, "Stop being afraid, Mary, for you have found favor with God. 31 Listen! You will become pregnant and bear a son, and you must name Him Jesus. 32 He will be great and will be called the Son of the Most High. The Lord God will give Him the throne of His forefather David, 33 and He will reign over the house of Jacob forever; His reign will have no end."

34 But Mary said to the angel, "How can this be, since I have no husband?"

35 Then the angel answered her, "The Holy Spirit will come upon you, and the power of the Most High will overshadow you, and so your child will be called holy, the Son of God. 36And listen! your relative, Elizabeth, has herself too become pregnant, although she is old, and this is the sixth month with her who was called barren. 37 For nothing is ever impossible for God." 38 Then Mary said, "I am the Lord's slave. May what[a] you say take place with me." Then the angel left her.

39 Now in those days Mary got up and hurried off to the hill country, to a town in Judah, 40 and she went to Zechariah's home and greeted Elizabeth. 41 When Elizabeth heard Mary's greeting, the baby leaped within her. And Elizabeth was filled with the Holy Spirit, 42 and with a loud shout she said:

"Blessed are you among women,
And blessed is your child!
43 Why is this privilege mine,
To have the mother of my Lord come to me?
44 "For as soon as your greeting reached my ears,
The baby leaped for joy within me!
45 Blessed is she who has believed,
For what is promised to her by the Lord will be fulfilled."
46 Then Mary said:
"My soul extols the Lord;
47 My spirit exults in God my Saviour;
48 For He has smiled upon His slave in her lowly station,
For from this day all ages will count me happy!
49 "For the Almighty has done wonders for me,
And holy is His name!

BECK

realized he had seen a vision in the holy place. He kept motioning to them and wasn't able to talk.

23 When the days of his service were over, he went home. 24After this, his wife Elizabeth conceived and for five months she didn't show herself in public. 25 "The Lord did this for me," she said. "I was feeling ashamed among people, but He was kind and helped me, and I don't have to feel ashamed any more."

The Angel Comes to Mary

26 Five months later God sent the angel Gabriel to a town in Galilee called Nazareth, 27 to a virgin engaged to a man by the name of Joseph, a descendant of David. The virgin's name was Mary.

28 Coming into her home, the angel said, "Greetings, you blessed one. The Lord is with you."

29 Startled by what he said, she tried to figure out what such a greeting might mean.

30 "Don't be afraid, Mary," the angel told her. "God is good to you. 31 *You see, you will conceive and have a son, and you will call Him*[5] Jesus. 32 He will be great and will be called *the Son of* the most high *God.* 33And the Lord will give Him *the throne of* His ancestor *David. He will be King over* the people of Jacob *forever, and His kingdom will never end."* [6]

34 "How can this be?" Mary asked the angel. "I'm not living with a husband."

35 "The Holy Spirit will come over you," the angel answered her, "and a power of the most high God will overshadow you. And for that reason the Child will be called holy and God's Son. 36 Now there is also Elizabeth, your relative. She is old, but she, too, conceived. People call her childless, but she's now in her sixth month. 37 *There's nothing that God will not be able to do."* [7]

38 "I am the Lord's servant," Mary answered. "Let it happen to me as you said."

Then the angel left her.

Mary Visits Elizabeth

39 Then Mary hurried away to the hill country to a town of Judah. 40 There she went into the home of Zacharias and greeted Elizabeth.

41 When Elizabeth heard Mary's greeting, the baby leaped in her womb. Then Elizabeth was filled with the Holy Spirit, 42 and she shouted, "Blessed are you among women, and blessed is the Child in your womb. 43 But how does this happen to me that the mother of my Lord comes to me? 44 The moment I heard your greeting, the baby leaped with delight in my womb. 45And you are happy for believing that the Lord will do what He promised you."

46 Mary said:

"My soul is praising *the Lord,*
47 And my spirit *delights in God, my Savior,*[8]
48 Because *He has looked kindly at His humble servant.*[9]
Yes, from now on the people in all the ages will call me blessed.
49 He has done great things to me—
He who is mighty
And *whose name is holy*[10]

1 Chron. 17:12-14
[5] Is. 7:14
[6] 2 Sam. 7:12-14, 16; Is. 9:7; Micah 4:7;
[7] Gen. 18:14
[8] 1 Sam. 2:1; Hab. 3:18
[9] 1 Sam. 1:11
[10] Ps. 111:9; Is. 57:15

[a] Grk., *let it be to me according to your word.*

K.J.V.

things; and holy *is* his name. 50And his mercy *is* on them that fear him from generation to generation. 51 He hath shewed strength with his arm; he hath scattered the proud in the imagination of their hearts. 52 He hath put down the mighty from *their* seats, and exalted them of low degree. 53 He hath filled the hungry with good things; and the rich he hath sent empty away. 54 He hath holpen his servant Israel, in remembrance of *his* mercy; 55As he spake to our fathers, to Abraham, and to his seed for ever. 56And Mary abode with her about three months, and returned to her own house. 57 Now Elisabeth's full time came that she should be delivered; and she brought forth a son. 58And her neighbours and her cousins heard how the Lord had shewed great mercy upon her; and they rejoiced with her. 59And it came to pass, that on the eighth day they came to circumcise the child; and they called him Zacharias, after the name of his father. 60And his mother answered and said, Not *so;* but he shall be called John. 61And they said unto her, There is none of thy kindred that is called by this name. 62And they made signs to his father, how he would have him called. 63And he asked for a writing table, and wrote, saying, His name is John. And they marvelled all. 64And his mouth was opened immediately, and his tongue *loosed,* and he spake, and praised God. 65And fear came on all that dwelt round about them: and all these sayings were noised abroad throughout all the hill country of Judea. 66And all they that heard *them* laid *them* up in their hearts, saying, What manner of child shall this be! And the hand of the Lord was with him. 67And his father Zacharias was filled with the Holy Ghost, and prophesied, saying, 68 Blessed *be* the Lord God of Israel; for he hath visited and redeemed his people, 69And hath raised up a horn of salvation for us in the house of his servant David; 70As he spake by the mouth of his holy prophets, which have been since the world began: 71 That we should be saved from our enemies, and from the hand of all that hate us; 72 To perform the mercy *promised* to our fathers, and to remember his holy covenant, 73 The oath which he sware to our father Abra-

N.A.S.

50 AND HIS MERCY IS UPON GENERATION AFTER GENERATION
TOWARDS THOSE WHO FEAR HIM.
51 He has done mighty deeds with His arm;
He has scattered *those who were* proud in the thoughts of their heart.
52 He has brought down rulers from *their* thrones,
And has exalted those who were humble.
53 HE HAS FILLED THE HUNGRY WITH GOOD THINGS;
And sent away the rich empty-handed.
54 He has given help to Israel His servant,
In remembrance of His mercy,
55 As He spoke to our fathers,
To Abraham and his offspring forever."
56 And Mary stayed with her about three months, and *then* returned to her home.
57 Now the time had come for Elizabeth to give birth, and she brought forth a son. 58And her neighbors and her relatives heard that the Lord had displayed His great mercy toward her; and they were rejoicing with her. 59And it came about that on the eighth day they came to circumcise the child, and they were going to call him Zacharias, after his father. 60And his mother answered and said, "No indeed; but he shall be called John." 61And they said to her, "There is no one among your relatives who is called by that name." 62And they made signs to his father, as to what he wanted him called. 63And he asked for a tablet, and wrote as follows, "His name is John." And they were all astonished. 64And at once his mouth was opened and his tongue *loosed,* and he *began* to speak in praise of God. 65And fear came on all those living around them; and all these matters were being talked about in all the hill country of Judea. 66And all who heard them kept them in mind, saying, "What then will this child *turn out to* be?" For the hand of the Lord was certainly with him.
67 And his father Zacharias was filled with the Holy Spirit, and prophesied, saying:
68 "Blessed *be* the Lord God of Israel,
For He has visited us and accomplished redemption for His people,
69 And has raised up a horn of salvation for us
In the house of David His servant—
70 As He spoke by the mouth of His holy prophets from of old—
71 Salvation FROM OUR ENEMIES,
And FROM THE HAND OF ALL WHO HATE US;
72 To show mercy toward our fathers,
And to remember His holy covenant,
73 The oath which He swore to Abraham our father,

WILLIAMS

50 He shows His mercy from age to age
To those who fear him.
51 "He has done mighty deeds with His arm,
He has scattered those that are proud in the
  purpose of their hearts,
52 He has dethroned monarchs and exalted
  the poor,
53 He has satisfied the hungry with good
  things and sent the rich away with empty
  hands.
54 "He has helped His servant Israel,
So as to remember mercy,
55 As He promised our forefathers,
Abraham and his descendants forever."
56 Now Mary stayed with her about three
months, and then returned home.
57 So it was time for Elizabeth to bear a
child, and she bore a son. 58And her neighbors
and relatives heard that the Lord had shown her
great mercy, and so they were rejoicing with her.
59 On the eighth day they came to circumcise
the child, and they tried to name him Zechariah,
after his father. 60 But his mother said, "Never!
But he must be named John."
61 Then they said to her, "There is no one
among your relatives that bears that name."
62 So they began to make signs to his father to
find out what he might wish him to be named.
63 Then he asked for a writing-tablet, and
wrote, "His name is John."
And they were all astonished. 64 Then the use
of his voice and tongue was at once restored,
and he began to speak, and continued to praise
God. 65And all the neighbors were overwhelmed
with awe, and all over the hill country of Judea
these things were being talked, 66 and all who
heard them kept them in their hearts, and said,
"What then is this child to be?" For the hand
of the Lord was with him.
67 Now his father Zechariah was filled with
the Holy Spirit, and he uttered the following
prophecy:
68 "Blessed be the Lord, the God of Israel,
For He has come and brought His people deliverance;[b]
69 And He has made a mighty Saviour for
  us[c]
In the house of His servant David,
70 "As He promised by the lips of His ancient
  prophets
71 Deliverance from our foes and from the
  hands of all who hate us,
72 To show mercy to our forefathers,
And carry out His sacred covenant,
73 "The oath which He swore to our forefather Abraham,

BECK

50   And who is always merciful to those who
      fear Him.[11]
51 "Mighty are the deeds He has done with
      His arm.
      He has scattered [12] those who feel and think
      so proudly.
52 He has pushed strong rulers down from
      their thrones
      And lifted up lowly people.[13]
53 Those who were hungry He has filled with
      good things,[14]
      And the rich He has sent away empty-
      handed.
54 "He has come to help His servant Israel,[15]
      Because He wants to remember His mercy[16]
55   (as He promised our fathers),
      The mercy He has for Abraham
      and his descendants forever." [17]

56 Mary stayed with Elizabeth about three
months and then went back home.

John Is Born

57 The time came for Elizabeth to give birth,
and she had a baby boy. 58 Her neighbors and
relatives heard how the Lord had been unusually kind to her, and they were happy with
her.
59 On the eighth day they came to circumcise the baby. They were going to call him
Zacharias because that was his father's name.
60 But his mother spoke up. "No!" she said.
"He's going to be called John."
61 "But there's nobody among your relatives
who has that name," they told her.
62 Then they motioned to his father to see
what name he might want him to have. 63 He
asked for a writing tablet and wrote, "His name
is John." They were all surprised.
64 Just then he got his speech back and
could talk again. He began to speak, praising
God.
65 All who lived around them were overawed. And all over the hills of Judea people
kept talking about all these things. 66All who
heard of them kept them in mind. "What is this
child going to be?" they asked. It was clear—
the Lord's hand was with him.
67 His father Zacharias was filled with the
Holy Spirit, and he prophesied:
68 "Praise the Lord, the God of Israel,[18]
      Because He has visited His people
      And prepared a ransom for them.[19]
69 He has given a descendant of His servant
      David
      To be our victorious Savior,[20]
70 As He said long ago through His holy
      prophets
71 That He would save us from our enemies,
      From the power of all who hate[21] us.
72 He wanted to be merciful to our fathers[22]
      And keep in mind His holy covenant,
73   The oath He swore to our father Abra-
      ham

[11] Ps. 103:17
[12] Ps. 89:10
[13] Job 12:19; 5:11; Ezek. 21:26
[14] Ps. 107:9
[15] Is. 41:8-9
[16] Ps. 98:3
[17] Gen. 17:7; Micah 7:20
[18] Ps. 41:13; 72:18; 89:52; 106:48
[19] Ps. 111:9
[20] 1 Sam. 2:10; Ps. 18:2; 132:17
[21] Ps. 106:10
[22] Micah 7:20

[b] Grk., redemption, but in general sense. [c]
Grk., raise up a horn of salvation.

K.J.V.

ham, 74 That he would grant unto us, that we, being delivered out of the hand of our enemies, might serve him without fear, 75 In holiness and righteousness before him, all the days of our life. 76And thou, child, shalt be called the prophet of the Highest: for thou shalt go before the face of the Lord to prepare his ways; 77 To give knowledge of salvation unto his people by the remission of their sins, 78 Through the tender mercy of our God; whereby the dayspring from on high hath visited us, 79 To give light to them that sit in darkness and *in* the shadow of death, to guide our feet into the way of peace. 80And the child grew, and waxed strong in spirit, and was in the deserts till the day of his shewing unto Israel.

2 And it came to pass in those days, that there went out a decree from Cesar Augustus, that all the world should be taxed. 2 (*And* this taxing was first made when Cyrenius was governor of Syria.) 3And all went to be taxed, every one into his own city. 4And Joseph also went up from Galilee, out of the city of Nazareth, into Judea, unto the city of David, which is called Bethlehem, (because he was of the house and lineage of David,) 5 To be taxed with Mary his espoused wife, being great with child. 6And so it was, that, while they were there, the days were accomplished that she should be delivered. 7And she brought forth her firstborn son, and wrapped him in swaddling clothes, and laid him in a manger; because there was no room for them in the inn. 8And there were in the same country shepherds abiding in the field, keeping watch over their flock by night. 9And, lo, the angel of the Lord came upon them, and the glory of the Lord shone round about them; and they were sore afraid. 10And the angel said unto them, Fear not: for, behold, I bring you good tidings of great joy, which shall be to all people. 11 For unto you is born this day in the city of David a Saviour, which is Christ the Lord. 12And this *shall be* a sign unto you; Ye shall find the babe wrapped in swaddling clothes, lying in a manger. 13And suddenly there was with the angel a multitude of the heavenly host praising God, and saying, 14 Glory to God in the highest, and on earth peace, good will toward men. 15And it came to pass, as the angels were gone away from them into heaven, the shepherds said one to another, Let us now go even unto Bethlehem, and see this thing which is come to pass, which the Lord hath made known unto us. 16And they came with haste, and found Mary and Joseph, and the babe lying in a manger. 17And when they had seen *it*, they made known abroad the saying which was told them

N.A.S.

74 To grant us that we being delivered from the hand of our enemies,
Might serve Him without fear,
75 In holiness and righteousness before Him all our days.
76 And you, child, will be called the prophet of the Most High;
For you will go on BEFORE THE LORD TO PREPARE HIS WAYS;
77 To give to His people *the* knowledge of salvation
By the forgiveness of their sins,
78 Because of the tender mercy of our God,
With which the Sunrise from on high shall visit us,
79 TO SHINE UPON THOSE WHO SIT IN DARKNESS AND THE SHADOW OF DEATH,
To guide our feet into the way of peace."
80 And the child continued to grow, and to become strong in spirit, and he lived in the deserts until the day of his public appearance to Israel.

2 Now it came about in those days that a decree went out from Caesar Augustus, that a census should be taken of all *a*the inhabited earth. 2 This was the first census taken while *b*Quirinius was governor of Syria. 3And all were proceeding to register for the census, everyone to his own city. 4And Joseph also went up from Galilee, from the city of Nazareth, to Judea, to the city of David, which is called Bethlehem, because he was of the house and family of David; 5in order to register, along with Mary, who was engaged to him, and was with child. 6And it came about that while they were there, the days were completed for her to give birth. 7And she gave birth to her firstborn son; and she wrapped Him in cloths, and laid Him in a manger, because there was no room for them in the inn.

8 And in the same region there were *some* shepherds staying out in the fields, and keeping watch over their flock by night. 9And an angel of the Lord suddenly stood before them, and the glory of the Lord shone around them; and they were terribly frightened. 10And the angel said to them, "Do not be afraid; for behold, I bring you good news of a great joy which shall be for all the people; 11 for today in the city of David there has been born for you a Savior, who is *c*Christ the Lord. 12 "And this *will be* a sign for you: you will find a baby wrapped in cloths, and lying in a manger." 13And suddenly there appeared with the angel a multitude of the heavenly host praising God, and saying,
14 "Glory to God in the highest,
And on earth peace among men *d*with whom He is pleased."
15And it came about that when the angels had gone away from them into heaven, the shepherds *began* saying to one another, "Let us go straight to Bethlehem then, and see this thing that has happened which the Lord has made known to us." 16And they came in haste, and found their way to Mary and Joseph, and the baby as He lay in the manger. 17And when they had seen this, they made known the statement which had been told them about this Child.

[a] I.e., *the Roman empire.* [b] Gr., *Kyrenios.* [c] I.e., *Messiah.* [d] Lit., *of His good pleasure;* or possibly, *of good will.*

WILLIAMS

74 To grant us deliverance from the dreaded
    hand of our foes,
So that we could serve Him 75 in holiness and
    uprightness
In His own presence all our days.
76 "And you, my child, will be called a
    prophet of the Most High,
For you will go before the Lord to make
    ready His ways,
77 To give His people the knowledge of sal-
    vation
Through the forgiveness of their sins.
78 "Because the heart of our God is merci-
    ful,
And so the day will dawn upon us from on
    high,
79 To shine on those who sit in darkness and
    the shadow of death,
To guide our feet into the way of peace."
80 Now the child continued to grow and to
gain strength in the Spirit, and he lived in the
desert until the day when he announced himself
to Israel.

2   *The birth of Jesus; the song of the*
angels and the visit of the shepherds;
the baby circumcised and named Jesus;
Symeon and Hannah praise God for His
birth; the boy Jesus worships

Now in those days an edict was issued by the
Emperor Augustus that a census of the whole
world should be taken. 2 This, the first census,
was taken while Quirinius was governor of
Syria. 3 So everyone was going to his own town
to register. 4And Joseph too went up from Nazareth, a town in Galilee, to the town of David in
Judea called Bethlehem, because he was a
descendant of the house and family of David,
5 to register with Mary who was engaged to be
married to. him and who was an expectant
mother. 6 While they were there, the time came
for her to give birth, 7 and she bore her firstborn
son; and she wrapped Him up and laid Him in
a manger, for there was no room for them at the
inn.
8 Now there were some shepherds in the
same neighborhood, living in the open fields and
keeping watch over their flock by night. 9 Then
an angel of the Lord stood by them, and the
glory of the Lord shone around them, so that
they were fearfully frightened. 10 But the angel
said to them:
"Stop being afraid, for now I bring you good
tidings of great joy which is to be for all the
people; for today, in the town of David, a
Saviour for you has been born, who is to be
your Messiah and Lord. 12And this is proof for
you: You will find a baby wrapped up and
lying in a manger." 13 Then suddenly there appeared with the angel a throng of the heavenly
host, praising God and saying:
14 "Glory to God in highest heaven!
And peace on earth to men who please him."
15 Then when the angel left them and returned to heaven, the shepherds said to one another,
"Let us now go over to Bethlehem and see
this thing that has taken place, which the Lord
has told us." 16 So they hurried to the place and
found Joseph and Mary; also the baby lying in
the manger. 17 When they saw this, they informed them of the story that had been told

BECK

74 To rescue us from our *enemies*[23]
    And let us serve Him without fear
75   In holiness and righteousness before Him
    all our life.
76 "And you, child, will be called a prophet of
    the most high God.
    You will go *ahead of the Lord to prepare*
    the ways for Him,[24]
77 To tell His people they can be saved
    by the forgiveness of their sins,
78 Because our God is merciful
    And will let a heavenly Sun rise among
    us,
79 *To shine on those who sit in the dark*
    and in the shadow of death.[25]
    And to guide our feet into *the way of*
    peace."[26]

80 The child John grew and became strong in
spirit. He lived in the wilderness till he appeared
publicly before Israel.

Jesus Is Born

2   In those days Emperor Augustus ordered
a census taken of the whole world. 2 This
was the first census, and it was taken while
Quirinius was ruling Syria. 3 Everybody went
to register, each to his own town.
4 Joseph also went up from the town of Nazareth in Galilee to David's town, called Bethlehem, in Judea, because he was one of the descendants of David, 5 to register with Mary,
his bride, who was going to have a child.
6 And while they were there, the time came
for her to have her child. 7 She had her first
Son, and she wrapped Him up and laid Him in
a manger because there was no room for them
in the inn.

The Shepherds

8 There were shepherds not far away, living
in the field and taking turns watching their flock
during the night.
9 Then the Lord's angel stood by them, and
the Lord's glory shone around them. They were
terrified. 10 "Don't be afraid," the angel said to
them. "I have good news for you. A great joy
will come to all the people: 11 The Savior, who
is Christ the Lord, was born for you today in
David's town. 12And this is how you will know
Him: you will find a Baby all wrapped up and
lying in a manger."
13 Suddenly there was with the angel a large
crowd of the angels of heaven, who were praising God and saying: 14 "Glory to God in the
highest heavens, and on earth peace among people who have His good will!"
15 When the angels had left them and gone
to heaven, the shepherds said to one another,
"The Lord has told us what has happened. Let's
go to Bethlehem and see it."
16 They hurried over there and searched until
they found Mary and Joseph, and the Baby
lying in the manger. 17 When they had seen Him,
they told others what they had been told about

[23] Gen. 22:16-17; Lev. 26:42; Ps. 105:8-9; 106:
45
[24] Mal. 3:1
[25] Ps. 107:10; Is. 9:2
[26] Is. 59:8

K.J.V.

concerning this child. 18And all they that heard *it* wondered at those things which were told them by the shepherds. 19 But Mary kept all these things, and pondered *them* in her heart. 20And the shepherds returned, glorifying and praising God for all the things that they had heard and seen, as it was told unto them. 21And when eight days were accomplished for the circumcising of the child, his name was called JESUS, which was so named of the angel before he was conceived in the womb. 22And when the days of her purification according to the law of Moses were accomplished, they brought him to Jerusalem, to present *him* to the Lord; 23 (As it is written in the law of the Lord, Every male that openeth the womb shall be called holy to the Lord;) 24And to offer a sacrifice according to that which is said in the law of the Lord, A pair of turtledoves, or two young pigeons. 25And, behold, there was a man in Jerusalem, whose name *was* Simeon; and the same man *was* just and devout, waiting for the consolation of Israel: and the Holy Ghost was upon him. 26And it was revealed unto him by the Holy Ghost, that he should not see death, before he had seen the Lord's Christ. 27And he came by the Spirit into the temple: and when the parents brought in the child Jesus, to do for him after the custom of the law, 28 Then took he him up in his arms, and blessed God, and said, 29 Lord, now lettest thou thy servant depart in peace, according to thy word: 30 For mine eyes have seen thy salvation, 31 Which thou hast prepared before the face of all people; 32A light to lighten the Gentiles, and the glory of thy people Israel. 33And Joseph and his mother marvelled at those things which were spoken of him. 34And Simeon blessed them, and said unto Mary his mother, Behold, this *child* is set for the fall and rising again of many in Israel; and for a sign which shall be spoken against; 35 (Yea, a sword shall pierce through thy own soul also;) that the thoughts of many hearts may be revealed. 36And there was one Anna, a prophetess, the daughter of Phanuel, of the tribe of Aser: she was of a great age, and had lived with a husband seven years from her virginity; 37And she *was* a widow of about fourscore and four years, which departed not from the temple, but served *God* with fastings and prayers night and day. 38And she coming in that instant gave thanks likewise unto the Lord, and spake of him to all them that looked for redemption in Jerusalem. 39And when they had performed all things according to the law of the Lord, they returned into Galilee, to their own city Nazareth. 40And the child grew, and waxed strong in spirit, filled with wisdom; and the grace of God was upon him. 41 Now his parents went to Jerusalem every year at the feast of the passover. 42And when he was twelve years old, they went up to Jerusalem after the custom of the feast. 43And when they

N.A.S.

18And all who heard it wondered at the things which were told them by the shepherds. 19 But Mary treasured up all these things, pondering them in her heart. 20And the shepherds went back, glorifying and praising God for all that they had heard and seen, just as had been told them.

21 And when eight days were completed before His circumcision, His name was *then* called Jesus, the name given by the angel before He was conceived in the womb.

22 And when the days for their purification according to the law of Moses were completed, they brought Him up to Jerusalem to present Him to the Lord 23 (as it is written in the Law of the Lord, "Every *firstborn* MALE THAT OPENS THE WOMB SHALL BE CALLED HOLY TO THE LORD"), 24 and to offer a sacrifice according to what was said in the Law of the Lord, "A PAIR OF TURTLEDOVES, OR TWO YOUNG PIGEONS." 25And behold, there was a man in Jerusalem whose name was Simeon; and this man was righteous and devout, looking for the consolation of Israel; and the Holy Spirit was upon him. 26And it had been revealed to him by the Holy Spirit that he would not see death before he had seen the Lord's Christ. 27And he came in the Spirit into the temple; and when the parents brought in the child Jesus, to carry out for Him the custom of the Law, 28 then he took Him into his arms, and blessed God, and said,

29 "Now Lord, Thou dost let Thy bond-
    servant depart,
In peace, according to Thy word:
30 For mine eyes have seen Thy salvation,
31 Which Thou hast prepared in the presence
    of all peoples,
32 A LIGHT OF REVELATION TO THE GENTILES,
    And the glory of Thy people Israel."

33And His father and mother were amazed at the things which were being said about Him. 34And Simeon blessed them, and said to Mary His mother, "Behold, this *Child* is appointed for the fall and rise of many in Israel, and for a sign to be opposed—35 and a sword will pierce even your own soul—to the end that thoughts from many hearts may be revealed." 36And there was a prophetess, Anna the daughter of Phanuel, of the tribe of Asher. She was advanced in years, having lived with a husband seven years after her marriage, 37and then as a widow to the age of eighty-four. And she *never* left the temple, serving night and day with fastings and prayers. 38And at that very moment she came up and *began* giving thanks to God, and continued to speak of Him to all those who were looking for the redemption of Jeruaslem.

39 And when they had performed everything according to the Law of the Lord, they returned to Galilee, to their own city of Nazareth. 40And the Child continued to grow and become strong, increasing in wisdom; and the grace of God was upon Him.

41 And His parents used to go to Jerusalem every year at the Feast of the Passover. 42And when He became twelve, they went up *there* according to the custom of the Feast; 43 and as

WILLIAMS

BECK

about this child. 18And all who heard it were astounded at what was told them by the shepherds, 19 but Mary continued to treasure it all up and to ponder it in her heart. 20 Then the shepherds went back continuing to give glory and praise to God for all that they had heard and seen, just as it had been told them.

21 When He was eight days old and it was time to circumcise Him, He was named Jesus, the name given by the angel before Mary had conceived Him.

22 Now when the period of their purification ended, in accordance with the law of Moses, they took Him up to Jerusalem to present Him to the Lord, to do as it is written in the law of the Lord, 23 "Every first-born male shall be counted consecrated to the Lord," 24 and to offer the sacrifice in accordance with what is specified in the law of the Lord, A pair of turtle-doves or two young pigeons."

25 Now there was in Jerusalem a man named Symeon, an upright, devout man; he was expecting to see the consolation of Israel, and he was under the guidance of the Holy Spirit.[a] 26 It had been revealed to him by the Holy Spirit that he should not die without seeing the Lord's Messiah. 27 So under the Spirit's guidance he went into the temple, and when the parents brought the child Jesus there to do for Him as the custom of the law required, 28 Symeon also took Him in his arms and blessed God, and said:

29 "Now, Master, you will let your slave go free
In peace, as you have promised;
30 For my eyes have seen your Salvation,
31 Which you prepared before all peoples,
32 A light of revelation to the heathen,
And a glory to your people Israel."

33 And His father and mother kept wondering at the things spoken by Symeon about Him. 34 Then Symeon gave them his blessing, and said to Mary, the child's mother, "This child is destined to bring the falling and the rising of many in Israel, and to be a sign continuously disputed—35 yea, a sword will pierce your heart —so that the secret purposes of many hearts will be revealed."

36 There was also a prophetess there, Hannah, a daughter of Phanuel, who belonged to the tribe of Asher. 37 She was very old; from girlhood she had lived seven years with a husband, and now had been a widow eighty years. She never left the temple, but continued to worship all day and all night with fastings and prayers. 38 Just at that time she came up and began to give thanks to God and to speak about the child to all who were expecing the deliverance of Jerusalem.

39 Now when they had completed everything that was in accordance with the law of the Lord, they returned to Galilee, to their own town of Nazareth. 40And the child continued to grow and gain in strength; He continued to increase in wisdom, and the spiritual blessing of God was on Him.

41 His parents were in the habit of going to Jerusalem every year at the feast of the Passover. 42And when He was twelve years old, they went up as usual to the feast 43 and stayed

this Child. 18And everybody was surprised to hear the story the shepherds told.

19 But Mary treasured all these things in her heart and kept thinking about them.

20 The shepherds went back, glorifying and praising God for everything they had heard and seen. It was just as they had been told.

In the Temple

21 On the eighth day the time came to circumcise the Child, and He was called Jesus, the name the angel gave Him before He was conceived.

22 When *the time came* for them *to be purified* [27] according to the Law of Moses, Joseph and Mary took Jesus up to Jerusalem to give Him to the Lord 23 (as it is written in the Law of the Lord, 24 *Every firstborn boy should be called the Lord's holy one* [28]) and to offer a sacrifice according to the Law of the Lord, *a pair of turtledoves or two young pigeons.* [29]

25 Now, there was in Jerusalem a man by the name of Simeon. He was a good man, fearing God and waiting for the One who would comfort Israel. The Holy Spirit was on him. 26 The Holy Spirit had told him that before he would die he would see the Savior sent by the Lord.

27 Moved by the Spirit, he went into the temple. When the parents brought in the Child Jesus to do for Him what was customary according to the Law, 28 Simeon took Him in his arms, praised God, and said:

29 "Lord, now You are letting Your servant go in peace as You promised,
30 Because my eyes have *seen Your salvation* [30]
31 That You prepared for all people to see,
32 *A light to shine on the Gentiles*,
And the *glory of* Your people *Israel.*" [31]

33 His father and mother were surprised such things were said about Him. 34 Then Simeon blessed them and said to His mother Mary, "Here is what this Child is appointed for: Many in Israel will fall and rise again because of Him; and He'll be a sign that many will talk against, 35 to show what they're thinking in their hearts. And pain, like a sword, will go through your own soul too."

36 Anna, a prophetess, was also there. She was a daughter of Phanuel, of the tribe of Asher. She was now very old. When she was a girl, she had married a man and lived with him seven years. 37After that she was a widow till she was eighty-four. She never left the temple but worshiped day and night, fasting and praying. 38 She, too, came forward just then, thanked God, and talked about the Child to all who were looking for Jerusalem to be set free.

39 When Joseph and Mary had done everything the Law of the Lord told them to do, they went back to Galilee to their town of Nazareth.

The Boy Jesus

40 The little Child grew big and strong and full of wisdom, and God's love was with him.

41 Every year His parents would go to Jerusalem to celebrate the Passover. 42And so when He was twelve, they went up for the festival as usual.

43 When the festival days were over and they

[27] Lev. 12:6
[28] Ex. 13:12
[29] Lev. 5:7, 11; 12:8; Num. 6:10
[30] Is. 40:5; 52:10
[31] Is. 42:6; 46:13; 49:6

[a] Grk., *the Holy Spirit was upon him.*

K.J.V.

had fulfilled the days, as they returned, the child Jesus tarried behind in Jerusalem; and Joseph and his mother knew not *of it*. 44 But they, supposing him to have been in the company, went a day's journey; and they sought him among *their* kinsfolk and acquaintance. 45And when they found him not, they turned back again to Jerusalem, seeking him. 46And it came to pass, that after three days they found him in the temple, sitting in the midst of the doctors, both hearing them, and asking them questions. 47And all that heard him were astonished at his understanding and answers. 48And when they saw him, they were amazed: and his mother said unto him, Son, why hast thou thus dealt with us? behold, thy father and I have sought thee sorrowing. 49And he said unto them, How is it that ye sought me? wist ye not that I must be about my Father's business? 50And they understood not the saying which he spake unto them. 51And he went down with them, and came to Nazareth, and was subject unto them: but his mother kept all these sayings in her heart. 52And Jesus increased in wisdom and stature, and in favour with God and man.

3 Now in the fifteenth year of the reign of Tiberius Cesar, Pontius Pilate being governor of Judea, and Herod being tetrarch of Galilee, and his brother Philip tetrarch of Iturea and of the region of Trachonitis, and Lysanias the tetrarch of Abilene, 2Annas and Caiaphas being the high priests, the word of God came unto John the son of Zacharias in the wilderness. 3And he came into all the country about Jordan, preaching the baptism of repentance for the remission of sins; 4As it is written in the book of the words of Esaias the prophet, saying, The voice of one crying in the wilderness, Prepare ye the way of the Lord, make his paths straight. 5 Every valley shall be filled, and every mountain and hill shall be brought low; and the crooked shall be made straight, and the rough ways *shall be* made smooth; 6And all flesh shall see the salvation of God. 7 Then said he to the multitude that came forth to be baptized of him, O generation of vipers, who hath warned you to flee from the wrath to come? 8 Bring forth therefore fruits worthy of repentance, and begin not to say within yourselves, We have Abraham to *our* father: for I say unto you, That God is able of these stones to raise up children unto Abraham. 9And now also the axe is laid unto the root of the trees: every tree therefore which bringeth not forth good fruit is hewn down, and cast into the fire. 10And the people asked him, saying,

N.A.S.

they were returning, after spending the full number of days, the boy Jesus stayed behind in Jerusalem. And His parents were unaware of it, 44 but supposed Him to be in the caravan, and went a day's journey; and they *began* looking for Him among their relatives and acquaintances. 45And when they did not find Him, they returned to Jerusalem, looking for Him. 46And it came about that after three days they found Him in the temple, sitting in the midst of the teachers, both listening to them, and asking them questions. 47And all who heard Him were amazed at His understanding and His answers. 48And when they saw Him, they were astonished; and His mother said to Him, "Son, why have You treated us this way? Behold, Your father and I have been anxiously looking for You." 49And He said to them, "Why is it that you were looking for Me? Did you not know that I had to be in My Father's *house?*" 50And they did not understand the statement which He had made to them. 51And He went down with them, and came to Nazareth; and He continued in subjection to them; and His mother treasured all *these* things in her heart.

52 And Jesus kept increasing in wisdom and stature, and in favor with God and men.

3 Now in the fifteenth year of the reign of Tiberius Caesar, when Pontius Pilate was governor of Judea, and Herod was tetrarch of Galilee, and his brother Philip was tetrarch of the region of Ituraea and Trachonitis, and Lysanias was tetrarch of Abilene, 2 in the high priesthood of Annas and Caiaphas, the word of God came to John, the son of Zacharias, in the wilderness. 3And he came into all the district around the Jordan, preaching a baptism of repentance for forgiveness of sins; 4 as it is written in the book of the words of Isaiah the prophet, "The voice of one crying in the wilderness,

'MAKE READY THE WAY OF THE LORD,
MAKE HIS PATHS STRAIGHT.
5 EVERY RAVINE SHALL BE FILLED UP,
AND EVERY MOUNTAIN AND HILL SHALL BE BROUGHT LOW;
AND THE CROOKED SHALL BECOME STRAIGHT,
AND THE ROUGH ROADS SMOOTH;
6 AND ALL FLESH SHALL SEE THE SALVATION OF GOD.' "

7 He therefore *began* saying to the multitudes who were going out to be baptized by him, "You brood of vipers, who warned you to flee from the wrath to come? 8 "Therefore bring forth fruits in keeping with your repentance, and do not begin to say to yourselves, 'We have Abraham for our father,' for I say to you that God is able from these stones to raise up children to Abraham. 9 "And also the axe is already laid at the root of the trees; every tree therefore that does not bear good fruit is cut down and thrown into the fire." 10And the multitudes were questioning him, saying, "Then what shall we

WILLIAMS

the usual time. When they returned, the boy Jesus stayed behind in Jerusalem, but His parents were not aware of it. 44 They supposed that He was somewhere in the caravan, and so they traveled a whole day before they began to make an anxious search for Him among His relatives and acquaintances. 45As they did not find Him, they returned to Jerusalem in anxious search for Him. 46And after three days they finally found Him in the temple sitting among the teachers, listening to them and asking them questions. 47 Now everyone who was listening to Him was showing astonishment at His intelligence and at His answers. 48 When His parents saw Him, they were utterly amazed, and yet His mother said to Him, "My child, why did you treat us so? Just see how your father and I, in agony of mind, have been searching for you!"

49 Then He said to them, "Why is it that you were searching for me? Did you not know that I must be in my Father's house?"

50 But they did not understand what He said to them. 51 So He went back to Nazareth with them and continued to obey them. But His mother continued to treasure up all these sayings in her heart. 52 Meanwhile Jesus grew constantly in wisdom and in body, and in favor with God and man.

3 *John preaches repentance and baptizes those who confess their sins; Jesus is baptized and endorsed by heaven; His legal pedigree*

In the fifteenth year of the reign of the Emperor Tiberius, when Pontius Pilate was governor of Judea, and Herod was governor of Galilee, and his brother Philip was governor of the territory of Iturea and Trachonitis, and Lysanias was governor of Abilene, 2 in the high priesthood of Annas and Caiaphas, the message of God came to John, the son of Zechariah, in the desert. 3And he went all over the Jordan valley, preaching a baptism conditioned on repentance to obtain the forgiveness of sins, 4 as it is written in the sermon-book of the prophet Isaiah:

"Here is a voice of one shouting in the
    desert.
'Get the road ready for the Lord,
Make the paths straight for Him.
5 Every ravine must be filled up,
And very mountain and hill leveled down;
The crooked places must become straight
    roads,
And the rough roads must be made smooth,
6 And all mankind must see the salvation of
    God.'"

7 So he used to say to the crowds that continued to come out there to be baptized by him:

"You brood of vipers! Who warned you to escape from the wrath that is coming? 8 Produce, then, fruit that is consistent with the repentance that you profess, and do not even begin to say within yourselves, 'We have Abraham for our forefather,' for I tell you, God can raise up descendants for Abraham even out of these stones. 9 Now the axe is already lying at the roots of the trees. Every tree, then, that fails to bear good fruit is to be cut down and thrown into the fire."

10 So the crowds were asking him this question, "What then ought we to do?"

BECK

started for home, the boy Jesus stayed behind in Jerusalem. But His parents didn't know about it. 44 They thought He was with the others who were traveling with them. After traveling a day, they started to look for Him among their relatives and friends. 45 When they didn't find Him, they went back to Jerusalem, looking for Him.

46 Two days later they found Him in the temple, sitting among the teachers, listening to them and asking them questions. 47 His understanding and His answers surprised all who heard Him.

48 His parents were amazed to see Him there. "Son, why did You do this to us?" His mother asked Him. "See how anxiously Your father and I have been looking for You!"

49 "Why were you looking for Me?" He asked them. "Didn't you know I must be in My Father's house?" 50 But they didn't understand what He told them.

51 Then He went back with them to Nazareth. And He obeyed them.

His mother kept all these things in her heart. 52And Jesus grew wiser and taller and *won the approval of God and of people.*[32]

John Prepares the Way

3 In the fifteenth year of the rule of Emperor Tiberius, Pontius Pilate was governor of Judea, Herod ruled Galilee, his brother Philip ruled Iturea and Trachonitis, Lysanias ruled Abilene, 2 and Annas and Caiaphas were the high priests. Then God spoke to John, the son of Zacharias, in the wilderness. 3 He went into the whole Jordan valley and preached: Repent and be baptized to have your sins forgiven. 4 This was what the prophet Isaiah had said in his book:

Someone will be calling in the wilderness:
"Prepare the way for the Lord,
Make the paths straight for Him.
5 *Every ravine must be filled,*
    And every mountain and hill must be cut
        down.
    The crooked must be made straight
    And the rough roads smooth.
6 *All people must see how God saves them."*[33]

7 So he would say to the crowds who were coming out to be baptized by him, "Brood of snakes, who warned you to run away from the punishment waiting for you? 8 Do the works that show you have repented. And don't start telling yourselves, 'Abraham is our father.' I tell you, God can raise children for Abraham from these stones. 9 The ax is now ready to strike at the roots of the trees, and any tree that doesn't produce good fruit will be cut down and thrown into the fire."

10 "What should we do?" the crowds asked him.

[32] 1 Sam. 2:26
[33] Is. 40:3-5

163

K.J.V.

What shall we do then? 11 He answereth and saith unto them, He that hath two coats, let him impart to him that hath none; and he that hath meat, let him do likewise. 12 Then came also publicans to be baptized, and said unto him, Master, what shall we do? 13 And he said unto them, Exact no more than that which is appointed you. 14 And the soldiers likewise demanded of him, saying, And what shall we do? And he said unto them, Do violence to no man, neither accuse *any* falsely; and be content with your wages. 15 And as the people were in expectation, and all men mused in their hearts of John, whether he were the Christ, or not; 16 John answered, saying unto *them* all, I indeed baptize you with water; but one mightier than I cometh, the latchet of whose shoes I am not worthy to unloose: he shall baptize you with the Holy Ghost and with fire: 17 Whose fan *is* in his hand, and he will thoroughly purge his floor, and will gather the wheat into his garner; but the chaff he will burn with fire unquenchable. 18 And many other things in his exhortation preached he unto the people. 19 But Herod the tetrarch, being reproved by him for Herodias his brother Philip's wife, and for all the evils which Herod had done, 20 Added yet this above all, that he shut up John in prison. 21 Now when all the people were baptized, it came to pass, that Jesus also being baptized, and praying, the heaven was opened, 22 And the Holy Ghost descended in a bodily shape like a dove upon him, and a voice came from heaven, which said, Thou art my beloved Son; in thee I am well pleased. 23 And Jesus himself began to be about thirty years of age, being (as was supposed) the son of Joseph, which was *the son* of Heli, 24 Which was *the son* of Matthat, which was *the son* of Levi, which was *the son* of Melchi, which was *the son* of Janna, which was *the son* of Joseph, 25 Which was *the son* of Mattathias, which was *the son* of Amos, which was *the son* of Naum, which was *the son* of Esli, which was *the son* of Nagge, 26 Which was *the son* of Maath, which was *the son* of Mattathias, which was *the son* of Semei, which was *the son* of Joseph, which was *the son* of Juda, 27 Which was *the son* of Joanna, which was *the son* of Rhesa, which was *the son* of Zorobabel, which was *the son* of Salathiel, which was *the son* of Neri, 28 Which was *the son* of Melchi, which was *the son* of Addi, which was *the son* of Cosam, which was *the son* of Elmodam, which was *the son* of Er, 29 Which was *the son* of Jose, which was *the son* of Eliezer, which was *the son* of Jorim, which was *the son* of Matthat, which was *the son* of Levi, 30 Which was *the son* of Simeon, which was *the son* of Juda, which was *the son* of Joseph, which was *the son* of Jonan, which was *the son* of Eliakim, 31 Which was *the son* of Melea, which was *the son* of Menan, which was *the son* of Mattatha, which was *the son* of Nathan, which was *the son* of David, 32 Which was *the son* of Jesse, which was *the son* of Obed, which was *the son* of Booz, which was *the son* of Salmon, which was *the son* of Naasson, 33 Which was *the son* of Aminadab, which was *the son* of Aram, which was *the son* of Esrom, which was *the son* of Phares, which was *the son* of Juda, 34 Which was *the son* of Jacob, which was *the son* of Isaac, which was *the son* of Abraham, which was *the son* of Thara, which was *the son* of Nachor, 35 Which was *the son* of Saruch, which was *the son* of Ragau, which was *the son* of Phalec, which was *the son* of Heber, which was *the son* of Sala, 36 Which was *the son* of Cainan, which was *the son* of Arphaxad, which was *the son* of Sem, which was *the son* of Noe, which

N.A.S.

do?" 11 And he would answer and say to them, "Let the man who has two tunics share with him who has none; and let him who has food do likewise." 12 And *some* [a]tax-gatherers also came to be baptized, and they said to him, "Teacher, what shall we do?" 13 And he said to them, "Collect no more than what you have been ordered to." 14 And *some* [b]soldiers were questioning him, saying, "And *what about* us, what shall we do?" And he said to them, "Do not take money from anyone by force, or accuse *anyone* falsely, and be content with your wages."

15 Now while the people were in a state of expectation and all were wondering in their hearts about John, as to whether he might be the Christ; 16 John answered and said to them all, "As for me, I baptize you with water; but He who is mightier than I is coming, and I am not fit to untie the thong of His sandals; He Himself will baptize you in the Holy Spirit and fire. 17 "And His winnowing fork is in His hand to clean out His threshing-floor, and to gather the wheat into His barn; but He will burn up the chaff with unquenchable fire."

18 So with many other exhortations also he preached the gospel to the people. 19 But when Herod the tetrarch was reproved by him on account of Herodias, his brother's wife, and on account of all the wicked things which Herod had done, 20 he added this also to them all, that he locked John up in prison.

21 Now it came about that when all the people were baptized, that Jesus also was baptized, and while He was praying, heaven was opened, 22 and the Holy Spirit descended upon Him in bodily form like a dove, and a voice came out of heaven, "Thou art My beloved Son, in Thee I am well pleased."

23 And when He began His ministry, Jesus Himself was about thirty years of age, being supposedly *the* son of Joseph, the *son* of Eli, 24 the *son* of Matthat, the *son* of Levi, the *son* of Melchi, the *son* of Jannai, the *son* of Joseph, 25 the *son* of Mattathias, the *son* of Amos, the *son* of Nahum, the *son* of Hesli, the *son* of Naggai, 26 the *son* of Maath, the *son* of Mattathias, the *son* of Semein, the *son* of Josech, the *son* of Joda, 27 the *son* of Johanan, the *son* of Resa, the *son* of Zerubbabel, the *son* of Shealtiel, the *son* of Neri, 28 the *son* of Melchi, the *son* of Addi, the *son* of Cosam, the *son* of Elmadam, the *son* of Er, 29 the *son* of Joshua, the *son* of Eliezer, the *son* of Jorim, the *son* of Matthat, the *son* of Levi, 30 the *son* of Simeon, the *son* of Judah, the *son* of Joseph, the *son* of Jonam, the *son* of Eliakim, 31 the *son* of Melea, the *son* of Menna, the *son* of Mattatha, the *son* of Nathan, the *son* of David, 32 the *son* of Jesse, the *son* of Obed, the *son* of Boaz, the *son* of Salmon, the *son* of Nahshon, 33 the *son* of Amminadab, the *son* of Admin, the *son* of Ram, the *son* of Hezron, the *son* of Perez, the *son* of Judah, 34 the *son* of Jacob, the *son* of Isaac, the *son* of Abraham, the *son* of Terah, the *son* of Nahor, 35 the *son* of Serug, the *son* of Reu, the *son* of Peleg, the *son* of Heber, the *son* of Shelah, 36 the *son* of Cainan, the *son* of Arphaxad, the *son* of Shem, the *son* of Noah,

[a] Publicans who collected Roman taxes on commission. [b] Lit., men in active military service.

WILLIAMS

11 He answered them, "The man who has two shirts must share with him who has none, and the man who has food must do the same."

12 Then even the tax-collectors came to be baptized, and said to him, "Teacher, what ought we to do?"

13 So he said to them, "Stop collecting any more than is prescribed for you."

14 Then some soldiers too were asking him, "What ought we too to do?"

So he said to them, "Never extort money from anyone, never make a false accusation, and always be satisfied with your wages."

15 Now while the people were on tiptoe in their expectations, and they were all arguing in their hearts about John whether he was himself the Christ, 16 John expressly answered them all,

"I am baptizing you in water only, but there is coming the One who is stronger than I am, whose shoestrings I am not fit to untie. He will baptize you in the Holy Spirit and in fire; 17 His winnowing-fork is in His hand, and He will clean out His threshing-floor, and store His wheat in His barn; but He will burn up the chaff with fire inextinguishable."

18 So with many and varied exhortations John continued to proclaim the good news to the people. 19 But Herod the governor, because he was repeatedly reproved by him for Herodias his brother's wife, and for all the wicked deeds that Herod had done, 20 added this on top of it all, that he put John in prison.

21 Now when all the people had been baptized, and when Jesus had been baptized and was still praying, heaven opened 22 and the Holy Spirit came down upon Him in bodily form as a dove, and a voice came out of heaven,

"You are my Son, my Beloved! In you I am delighted!"

23 Now Jesus Himself was about thirty years old when He began His work; He was the son, as was supposed, of Joseph, the son of Eli, 24 the son of Matthat, the son of Levi, the son of Melchi, the son of Jannai, the son of Joseph, 25 the son of Mattathias, the son of Amos, the son of Nahum, the son of Esli, the son of Naggai, 26 the son of Maath, the son of Mattathias, the son of Semein, the son of Josech, the son of Joda, 27 the son of Johanan, the son of Resa, the son of Zerubbabel, the son of Salathiel, the son of Neri, 28 the son of Melchi, the son of Addi, the son of Cosam, the son of Elmadam, the son of Er, 29 the son of Jesus, the son of Eliezer, the son of Jorim, the son of Matthat, the son of Levi, 30 the son of Symeon, the son of Judah, the son of Joseph, the son of Jonam, the son of Eliakim, 31 the son of Melea, the son of Menna, the son of Mattatha, the son of Nathan, the son of David, 32 the son of Jesse, the son of Obed, the son of Boaz, the son of Sala, the son of Nahshon, 33 the son of Admin,ᵃ the son of Arni, the son of Hezron, the son of Perez, the son of Judah, 34 the son of Jacob, the son of Isaac, the son of Abraham, the son of Terah, the son of Nahor, 35 the son of Serug, the son of Ragau,ᵇ the son of Peleg, the son of Heber, the son of Shelah, 36 the son of Cainan, the son Arphaxad, the son of Shem, the son of Noah, the son of

BECK

11 "If you have two garments," he answered them, "share them with him who has none, and if you have food, do the same."

12 Some tax collectors also came to be baptized. "Teacher," they asked him, "what should we do?"

13 "Don't collect more money than you're ordered to collect," he told them.

14 Some soldiers also asked him, "And what should we do?"

"Don't use threats or blackmail to get money from anyone," he told them, "but be satisfied with your pay."

15 The people were expecting something and all were wondering if John was perhaps the promised Savior. 16 John answered them all: "I baptize you with water. But the One who is mightier than I is coming. I'm not good enough to untie His shoe straps. He will baptize you with the Holy Spirit and fire. 17 He has the winnowing shovel in His hand to clean up His threshing floor and gather the wheat into His barn, but the chaff He'll burn in a fire that can't be put out."

18 And so with many other challenging words he was telling the people the good news.

In Prison

19 When John was showing Herod, the governor, how wrong he was in regard to his brother's wife Herodias and all the other wicked things Herod did, 20 he, on top of everything, locked John up in prison.

John Baptizes Jesus

21 When all the people were being baptized, Jesus was baptized too. 22 While He was praying, heaven opened, and the Holy Spirit came down on Him in the bodily form of a dove. And a voice from heaven said, "You are My Son whom I love. I am delighted ³⁴ with You."

23 Jesus was about thirty years old when He began His work.

The Son of Man

24 Jesus was a son, as people thought, of Joseph, of Heli, of Matthat, of Levi, of Melchi, of Jannai, of Joseph, 25 of Mattathias, of Amos, of Nahum, of Esli, of Naggai, 26 of Maath, of Mattathias, of Semein, of Josech, of Joda, 27 of Joanan, of Rhesa, of Zerubbabel, of Shealtiel, of Neri, 28 of Melchi, of Addi, of Cosam, of Elmadam, of Er, 29 of Jesus, of Eliezer, of Jorim, of Matthat, of Levi, 30 of Simeon, of Judas, of Joseph, of Jonam, of Eliakim, 31 of Melea, of Menna, of Mattatha, of Nathan, of David, 32 of Jesse, of Obed, of Boaz, of Salmon, of Nahshon, 33 of Amminadab, of Ram, of Admin, of Arni, of Hezron, of Perez, of Judah, 34 of Jacob, of Isaac, of Abraham, of Terah, of Nahor, 35 of Serug, of Reu, of Peleg, of Eber, of Shelah, 36 of Cainan, of Arphaxad, of

---

[a] Or, Aminadab. [b] Or, Reu.   [34] Ps. 2:7; Is. 42:1

K.J.V.

was *the son* of Lamech, 37 Which was *the son* of Mathusala, which was *the son* of Enoch, which was *the son* of Jared, which was *the son* of Maleleel, which was *the son* of Cainan, 38 Which was *the son* of Enos, which was *the son* of Seth, which was *the son* of Adam, which was *the son* of God.

4 And Jesus being full of the Holy Ghost returned from Jordan, and was led by the Spirit into the wilderness, 2 Being forty days tempted of the devil. And in those days he did eat nothing: and when they were ended, he afterward hungered. 3And the devil said unto him, If thou be the Son of God, command this stone that it be made bread. 4And Jesus answered him, saying, It is written, That man shall not live by bread alone, but by every word of God. 5And the devil, taking him up into a high mountain, shewed unto him all the kingdoms of the world in a moment of time. 6And the devil said unto him, All this power will I give thee, and the glory of them: for that is delivered unto me; and to whomsoever I will, I give it. 7 If thou therefore wilt worship me, all shall be thine. 8And Jesus answered and said unto him, Get thee behind me, Satan: for it is written, Thou shalt worship the Lord thy God, and him only shalt thou serve. 9And he brought him to Jerusalem, and set him on a pinnacle of the temple, and said unto him, If thou be the Son of God, cast thyself down from hence: 10 For it is written, He shall give his angels charge over thee, to keep thee: 11And in *their* hands they shall bear thee up, lest at any time thou dash thy foot against a stone. 12And Jesus answering said unto him, It is said, Thou shalt not tempt the Lord thy God. 13And when the devil had ended all the temptation, he departed from him for a season.

14 And Jesus returned in the power of the Spirit into Galilee: and there went out a fame of him through all the region round about. 15And he taught in their synagogues, being glorified of all.

16 And he came to Nazareth, where he had been brought up: and, as his custom was, he went into the synagogue on the sabbath day, and stood up for to read. 17And there was delivered unto him the book of the prophet Esaias. And when he had opened the book, he found the place where it was written, 18 The Spirit of the Lord *is* upon me, because he hath anointed me to preach the gospel to the poor; he hath sent me to heal the brokenhearted, to preach deliverance to the captives, and recovering of sight to the blind, to set at liberty them that are bruised, 19 To preach the acceptable year of the Lord. 20And he closed the book, and he gave *it* again to the minister, and sat down. And the eyes of all them that were in the synagogue were fastened on him. 21And he began to say unto them, This day is this Scripture fulfilled in your ears. 22And all bare him witness, and wondered at the gracious words which proceeded out of his mouth. And they said, Is not this Joseph's son? 23And he said unto them, Ye will surely

N.A.S.

the *son* of Lamech, 37 the *son* of Methuselah, the *son* of Enoch, the *son* of Jared, the *son* of Mahalaleel, the *son* of Cainan, 38 the *son* of Enosh, the *son* of Seth, the *son* of Adam, the *son* of God.

4 And Jesus, full of the Holy Spirit, returned from the Jordan and was led about by the Spirit in the wilderness 2 for forty days, while tempted by the devil. And He ate nothing during those days; and when they had ended, He became hungry. 3And the devil said to Him, "If You are the Son of God, tell this stone to become bread." 4And Jesus answered him, "It is written, 'MAN SHALL NOT LIVE ON BREAD ALONE.' " 5And he led Him up and showed Him all the kingdoms of the world in a moment of time. 6And the devil said to Him, "I will give You all this domain and its glory; for it has been handed over to me, and I give it to whomever I wish. 7 "Therefore if You worship before me, it shall all be Yours." 8And Jesus answered and said to him, "It is written, 'YOU SHALL WORSHIP THE LORD YOUR GOD AND SERVE HIM ONLY.' " 9And he led Him to Jerusalem and set Him on the pinnacle of the temple, and said to Him, "If You are the Son of God, cast Yourself down from here; 10 for it is written, 'HE WILL GIVE HIS ANGELS CHARGE CONCERNING YOU TO GUARD YOU,'

11 and,

'ON THEIR HANDS THEY WILL BEAR YOU UP,
LEST YOU STRIKE YOUR FOOT AGAINST A
STONE.' "

12 And Jesus answered and said to him, "It is said, 'YOU SHALL NOT [a]FORCE A TEST ON THE LORD YOUR GOD.' "

13 And when the devil had finished every temptation, he departed from Him until an opportune time.

14 And Jesus returned to Galilee in the power of the Spirit; and news about Him spread through all the surrounding district. 15And He *began* teaching in their synagogues and was praised by all.

16 And He came to Nazareth, where He had been brought up; and as was His custom, He entered the synagogue on the Sabbath, and stood up to read. 17And the book of the prophet Isaiah was handed to Him. And He opened the book, and found the place where it was written,

18 "THE SPIRIT OF THE LORD IS UPON ME,
BECAUSE HE ANOINTED ME TO PREACH THE
GOSPEL TO THE POOR.
HE HAS SENT ME TO PROCLAIM RELEASE TO
THE CAPTIVES,
AND RECOVERY OF SIGHT TO THE BLIND,
TO SET FREE THOSE WHO ARE DOWNTRODDEN,

19 TO PROCLAIM THE FAVORABLE YEAR OF THE
LORD."

20And He closed the book, and gave it back to the attendant, and sat down; and the eyes of all in the synagogue were fixed upon Him. 21And He began to say to them, "Today this Scripture has been fulfilled in your hearing." 22And all were speaking well of Him, and wondering at the gracious words which were falling from His lips; and they were saying, "Is this not Joseph's son?" 23And He said to them, "No

[a] Or, *tempt.*

Lamech, 37 the son of Methuselah, the son of Enoch, the son of Jared, the son of Maleleel, the son of Cainan, 38 the son of Enosh, the son of Seth, the son of Adam, the son of God.

Shem, of Noah, of Lamech, 37 of Methuselah, of Enoch, of Jared, of Mahalaleel, of Cainan, 38 of Enos, of Seth, of Adam, of God.

4 *Jesus tempted by the devil; He begins His work in Galilee, cures the sick, teaches and preaches the message of the kingdom*

Then Jesus, full of the Holy Spirit, returned from the Jordan, and for forty days He was led about in the desert under the Spirit's guidance, 2 while He was being tempted by the devil. During that time He ate nothing, and so at the end of it He felt hungry. 3 Then the devil said to Him, "If you are God's Son, order this stone to turn to a loaf of bread."

4 But Jesus answered him, "The Scripture says, 'Not on bread alone does man live.'"

5 Then he took Him up and in a second of time he showed Him all the kingdoms of the world. 6 And the devil said to Him, "I will give you all this power and all their splendor, for it has been turned over to me, and I give it to anyone I please. 7 So if you will worship before me just once, it shall all be yours."

8 But Jesus answered him, "The Scripture says, 'You must worship the Lord your God, and serve Him alone.'"

9 Then he took Him to Jerusalem, and had Him stand on the tip-top turret of the temple, and said to Him, "If you are God's Son, throw yourself down from here, 10 for the Scripture says, 'He will give His angels directions about you, to protect[a] you,' 11 and, 'They will bear you up on their hands, so that you will never strike your foot against a stone.'"

12 And Jesus answered him, "It has been said, 'You must not try the Lord your God.'"

13 After the devil had finished every sort of temptation, he left Him till another time.

14 Then Jesus in the power of the Spirit returned to Galilee, and news of Him spread all over the surrounding country. 15 Meanwhile He began to teach in their synagogues, and was continuously receiving praise from all.

16 So He came to Nazareth where He had been brought up, and as His habit was on the sabbath, He went to the synagogue and stood up to read. 17 The roll of the prophet Isaiah was handed to Him, and He unrolled it and found the place where it was written:

18 "The Spirit of the Lord is upon me,
For He has consecrated me to preach the good news to the poor;
He has sent me to announce release to captives and recovery of sight to the blind;
To send the downtrodden away in liberty and
19 To announce the year of favor from the Lord."

20 Then He rolled up the roll and gave it back to the attendant and took His seat. Now the eyes of everyone in the synagogue were gazing at Him. 21 Then He began to speak to them, "Today this Scripture has been fulfilled here in your hearing."

22 So they all began to speak well of Him and to wonder at the gracious words that fell from His lips, and yet they continued to say, "Is He not Joseph's son?"

23 He said to them, "Doubtless you will quote

[a] Grk., *thoroughly to guard you.*

The Devil Tempts Jesus

4 Jesus, full of the Holy Spirit, left the Jordan. For forty days the Spirit led Him in the wilderness 2 while the devil tempted Him. He ate nothing during those days, and when they were over, He got hungry.

3 The devil said to Him, "If You're God's Son, tell this stone to become a loaf of bread."

4 "It is written," Jesus answered him, *"A man doesn't live on bread alone."* [35]

5 The devil took Him up and in a moment showed Him all the kingdoms of the world. 6 "I'll give You all this power and glory," the devil told Him, "because it was given to me and I give it to anyone I please. 7 So, if You'll worship me, all this will be Yours."

8 "It is written," Jesus answered him, "Worship *the Lord, your God, and serve Him*[36] only."

9 The devil took Him into Jerusalem and had Him stand on the edge of the temple. "If You're God's Son," he told Him, "jump down from here. 10 It is written, *He will order His angels to watch carefully over you.* 11 *They will carry you in their hands and never let you stub your foot against a stone."* [37]

12 "It is written," Jesus answered him, *"Don't test the Lord your God."* [38]

13 When the devil had finished every way of tempting Him, he left Him till the right time would come.

Nazareth Rejects Jesus

14 With the power of the Spirit Jesus went back to Galilee. The news about Him spread all over the surrounding country. 15 He taught in their synagogs, and everybody praised Him.

16 Then Jesus came to Nazareth, where He had been raised. On the Sabbath He went into the synagog as He used to do. He got up to read 17 and was given the scroll of the prophet Isaiah. Unrolling the scroll, He found the place where it says:

18 *The Spirit of the Lord is on Me because—*
He anointed Me
To tell the poor the good news.
He sent Me
To announce to prisoners, "You are free,"
to the blind, "You will see again,"
To free those who are broken down,
19 *To announce a season when the Lord welcomes people.*[39]

20 He rolled up the scroll, gave it back to the attendant, and sat down. Everybody in the synagog was watching Him closely 21 as He said, "Today, while you're listening, what is written here has come true."

22 All spoke well of Him and were surprised to hear the beautiful words flowing from His lips. "Isn't this Joseph's son?" they were asking.

23 He answered them: "You will undoubtedly

[35] Deut. 8:3
[36] Deut. 6:13
[37] Ps. 91:11-12
[38] Deut. 6:16
[39] Is. 58:6; 61:1-2

K.J.V.

say unto me this proverb, Physician, heal thyself: whatsoever we have heard done in Capernaum, do also here in thy country. 24And he said, Verily I say unto you, No prophet is accepted in his own country. 25 But I tell you of a truth, many widows were in Israel in the days of Elias, when the heaven was shut up three years and six months, when great famine was throughout all the land; 26 But unto none of them was Elias sent, save unto Sarepta, *a city* of Sidon, unto a woman *that was* a widow. 27And many lepers were in Israel in the time of Eliseus the prophet; and none of them was cleansed, saving Naaman the Syrian. 28And all they in the synagogue, when they heard these things, were filled with wrath, 29And rose up, and thrust him out of the city, and led him unto the brow of the hill whereon their city was built, that they might cast him down headlong. 30 But he, passing through the midst of them, went his way, 31And came down to Capernaum, a city of Galilee, and taught them on the sabbath days. 32And they were astonished at his doctrine: for his word was with power.

33 And in the synagogue there was a man, which had a spirit of an unclean devil, and cried out with a loud voice, 34 Saying, Let *us* alone; what have we to do with thee, *thou* Jesus of Nazareth? art thou come to destroy us? I know thee who thou art; the Holy One of God. 35And Jesus rebuked him, saying, Hold thy peace, and come out of him. And when the devil had thrown him in the midst, he came out of him, and hurt him not. 36And they were all amazed, and spake among themselves, saying, What a word *is* this! for with authority and power he commandeth the unclean spirits, and they come out. 37And the fame of him went out into every place of the country round about.

38 And he arose out of the synagogue, and entered into Simon's house. And Simon's wife's mother was taken with a great fever; and they besought him for her. 39And he stood over her, and rebuked the fever; and it left her: and immediately she arose and ministered unto them.

40 Now when the sun was setting, all they that had any sick with divers diseases brought them unto him; and he laid his hands on every one of them, and healed them. 41And devils also came out of many, crying out, and saying, Thou art Christ the Son of God. And he rebuking *them* suffered them not to speak: for they knew that he was Christ. 42And when it was day, he departed and went into a desert place: and the people sought him, and came unto him, and stayed him, that he should not depart from them. 43And he said unto them, I must preach the kingdom of God to other cities also: for therefore am I sent. 44And he preached in the synagogues of Galilee.

5 And it came to pass, that, as the people pressed upon him to hear the word of God, he stood by the lake of Gennesaret, 2And saw

N.A.S.

doubt you will quote this proverb to Me, 'Physician, heal yourself; whatever we heard was done at Capernaum, do here in your home town as well.' " 24And He said, "Truly I say to you, no prophet is welcome in his home town. 25 "But I say to you in truth, there were many widows in Israel in the days of Elijah, when the sky was shut up for three years and six months, when a great famine came over all the land; 26 and yet Elijah was sent to none of them, but only to Zarephath, in the land of Sidon, to a woman who was a widow. 27 "And there were many lepers in Israel in the time of Elisha the prophet; and none of them was cleansed, but only Naaman the Syrian." 28And all in the synagogue were filled with rage as they heard these things; 29and they rose up and cast Him out of the city, and led Him to the brow of the hill on which their city had been built, in order to throw Him down the cliff. 30 But passing through their midst, He went His way.

31 And He came down to Capernaum, a city of Galilee. And He was teaching on Sabbath days; 32 and they were *continually* amazed at His teaching; for His message was with authority. 33And there was a man in the synagogue possessed by the spirit of an unclean demon, and he cried out with a loud voice, 34 "Ha! What do we have to do with You, Jesus of Nazareth? Have You come to destroy us? I know who You are—the Holy One of God!" 35And Jesus rebuked him, saying, "Be quiet and come out of him!" And when the demon had thrown him down in *their* midst, he went out of him without doing him any harm. 36And amazement came upon them all, and they *began* discussing with one another, and saying, "What is this message? For with authority and power He commands the unclean spirits, and they come out." 37And the report about Him was getting out into every locality in the surrounding district.

38 And He arose and *left* the synagogue, and entered Simon's home. Now Simon's mother-in-law was suffering from a high fever; and they made request of Him on her behalf. 39And standing over her, He rebuked the fever, and it left her; and she immediately arose and *began* to wait on them.

40 And while the sun was setting, all who had any sick with various diseases brought them to Him; and laying His hands on every one of them, He was healing them. 41And demons also were coming out of many, crying out and saying, "You are the Son of God!" And rebuking them, He would not allow them to speak, because they knew Him to be the Christ.

42 And when day came, He departed and went to a lonely place; and the multitudes were searching for Him, and came to Him, and tried to keep Him from going away from them. 43 But He said to them, "I must preach the kingdom of God to the other cities also, for I was sent for this purpose."

44 And He kept on preaching in the synagogues of *Judea.

5 Now it came about that while the multitude were pressing around Him and listening to the word of God, He was standing by the lake of Gennesaret; 2 and He saw two boats lying at

[a] I.e., the country of the Jews (including Galilee); some mss. read, *of Galilee.*

WILLIAMS

this proverb to me, 'Doctor, cure yourself! Do the things here in your home town that we hear you did in Capernaum.' " 24 He added, "I solemnly say to you, no prophet is welcome in his native neighborhood. 25 But in truth I tell you, there were many widows in Israel in Elijah's time, when the heaven was closed for three years and a half, and there was a great famine over all the land, 26 and yet Elijah was not sent to a single one of them except to a widow at Zarephath in Sidon. 27 And there were many lepers in Israel in Elisha's time, and yet not one of them was cured except Naaman the Syrian."

28 Then all the people in the synagogue, on hearing these things, were filled with fury, 29 and they rose up and drove Him out of town and took Him to the brow of the hill on which their town was built, to hurl Him down the cliff. 30 But He Himself passed through the midst of them and went on His way.

31 So He came down to Capernaum, a city in Galilee. And He continued to teach them on the sabbath, 32 and they were completely astounded, because His message was spoken with authority.

33 Now there was a man in the synagogue who was under the power of the spirit of a foul demon, and he screamed with a loud voice, 34 "Ha! What do you want of us, Jesus, you Nazarene? Have you come to destroy us? I know who you are. You are God's Holy One."

35 But Jesus reproved him, saying, "Be quiet! Get out of him at once!"

So the demon threw the man down in the midst of them and came out of him without doing him any harm. 36 Amazement then seized them all and they continued to talk it over among themselves, and to say, "What does this message mean? For with authority and power He gives orders to foul spirits, and they come out." 37 And so news of Him continued to spread to every place in the surrounding region.

38 Then He rose to leave the synagogue, and He went to Simon's house. And Simon's mother-in-law was in the grip of a burning fever; so they asked Him about her. 39 Then He took His stand by her and reproved the fever, and it left her. She got up at once and began to wait on them.

40 As the sun was setting, all who had friends sick with various diseases brought them to Him. Then He continued to lay His hands upon them one by one and cured them. 41 Even demons came out of many people, shrieking and saying, "You are the Son of God!" But He reproved them and would not let them speak, because they knew that He was the Christ.

42 As day broke He left the house and went to a lonely spot, and the crowds continued to look for Him; they overtook Him, and tried to keep Him from leaving them. 43 But He said to them, "To other towns also I must preach the good news of the kingdom of God, for that is what I was sent to do."

44 So He continued to preach in the synagogues of Judea.

5   *Simon called to service; a leper and a paralytic cured; Levi, converted, gives Jesus a banquet; stories about fasting*

Once as the crowd was pressing against Him to hear the message of God, He found Himself standing on the shore of Lake Gennesaret. 2 Then He saw two boats lying up on the shore

BECK

quote to Me the proverb 'Doctor, heal yourself!' and say, 'We've heard about everything You did in Capernaum. Do the same here in Your home town.' 24 I tell you," He added, "it is true no prophet is accepted in his home town.

25 "Let Me tell you this truth: There were many widows in Israel in the days of Elijah, when it didn't rain for three years and six months and there was a big famine all over the country. 26 But Elijah wasn't sent to anyone except *a widow at Zarephath in the territory of Sidon.*[40] 27 And there were lepers in Israel at the time of the prophet Elisha. But no one except *Naaman* from *Syria was made clean.*[41]

28 As they were listening, all in the synagog became furious. 29 They got up, pushed Him out of the town, and took Him to a brow of the hill on which their town was built, to hurl Him down the cliff. 30 But He walked right through them and went away.

Jesus Drives Out a Devil

31 He went down to Capernaum, a town in Galilee, and was teaching people on a Sabbath. 32 His teaching amazed them because He spoke with authority.

33 In the synagog there was a man with a spirit of an unclean devil. He screamed out loud, 34 "Oh, leave us alone, Jesus from Nazareth! You've come to destroy us! I know who You are—God's Holy One."

35 Jesus talked sharply to him: "Be quiet, and come out of him." The devil hurled him into the crowd, then came out of him without doing him any harm.

36 They were all amazed and said to one another, "What kind of speaking is this? With authority and power He gives orders to the unclean spirits, and out they go."

37 So the news about Him spread to every place in the surrounding country.

Peter's Mother-in-Law

38 Leaving the synagog, Jesus went to Simon's home. Simon's mother-in-law was sick with a high fever, and they asked Him to help her. 39 He went to her and, bending over her, ordered the fever to leave, and it left. She got up immediately and waited on them.

40 When the sun was going down, all who had sick ones suffering from various diseases brought them to Him. He laid His hands on each of them and made them well. 41 The devils went out of many, screaming, "You're God's Son." He talked sharply to them and wouldn't let them go on talking, because they knew He was the promised Savior.

42 In the morning He went out to a lonely place. The crowds were looking for Him. When they came to Him, they tried to keep Him from leaving them. 43 But He said to them, "I have to tell the good news of God's kingdom also in other towns. That's what I was sent to do."

44 Then He kept on preaching in the synagogs of the country of the Jews.

Fishers of Men

5   One day Jesus was standing by the Lake of Galilee, and the people were crowding Him as they were listening to God's Word. 2 He

[40] 1 Kings 17:9
[41] 2 Kings 5:14

K.J.V.

two ships standing by the lake: but the fishermen were gone out of them, and were washing *their* nets. 3And he entered into one of the ships, which was Simon's, and prayed him that he would thrust out a little from the land. And he sat down, and taught the people out of the ship. 4 Now when he had left speaking, he said unto Simon, Launch out into the deep, and let down your nets for a draught. 5And Simon answering said unto him, Master, we have toiled all the night, and have taken nothing: nevertheless at thy word I will let down the net. 6And when they had this done, they inclosed a great multitude of fishes: and their net brake. 7And they beckoned unto *their* partners, which were in the other ship, that they should come and help them. And they came, and filled both the ships, so that they began to sink. 8 When Simon Peter saw *it*, he fell down at Jesus' knees, saying, Depart from me; for I am a sinful man, O Lord. 9 For he was astonished, and all that were with him, at the draught of the fishes which they had taken: 10And so *was* also James, and John, the sons of Zebedee, which were partners with Simon. And Jesus said unto Simon, Fear not; from henceforth thou shalt catch men. 11And when they had brought their ships to land, they forsook all, and followed him.

12 And it came to pass, when he was in a certain city, behold a man full of leprosy: who seeing Jesus fell on *his* face, and besought him, saying, Lord, if thou wilt, thou canst make me clean. 13And he put forth *his* hand, and touched him, saying, I will: be thou clean. And immediately the leprosy departed from him. 14And he charged him to tell no man: but go, and shew thyself to the priest, and offer for thy cleansing, according as Moses commanded, for a testimony unto them. 15 But so much the more went there a fame abroad of him: and multitudes came together to hear, and to be healed by him of their infirmities.

16 And he withdrew himself into the wilderness, and prayed. 17And it came to pass on a certain day, as he was teaching, that there were Pharisees and doctors of the law sitting by, which were come out of every town of Galilee, and Judea, and Jerusalem: and the power of the Lord was *present* to heal them. 18 And, behold, men brought in a bed a man which was taken with a palsy: and they sought *means* to bring him in, and to lay *him* before him. 19And when they could not find by what *way* they might bring him in because of the multitude, they went upon the housetop, and let him down through the tiling with *his* couch into the midst before Jesus. 20And when he saw their faith, he said unto him, Man, thy sins are forgiven thee. 21And the scribes and the Pharisees began to reason, saying, Who is this which speaketh blasphemies? Who can forgive sins, but God alone? 22 But when Jesus perceived their thoughts, he answering said unto them, What reason ye in your hearts? 23 Whether is easier, to say, Thy sins be forgiven thee; or to say, Rise up and walk? 24 But that ye may know that the Son of man hath power upon earth to forgive sins, (he said unto the sick of the palsy,) I say unto thee, Arise, and take up thy couch, and go into thine house. 25And immediately he rose

N.A.S.

the edge of the lake; but the fishermen had gotten out of them, and were washing their nets. 3And He got into one of the boats, which was Simon's, and asked him to put out a little way from the land. And He sat down and *began* teaching the multitudes from the boat. 4And when He had finished speaking, He said to Simon, "Put out into the deep water and let down your nets for a catch." 5And Simon answered and said, "Master, we worked hard all night and caught nothing, but at Your bidding I will let down the nets." 6And when they had done this, they enclosed a great quantity of fish; and their nets *began* to break; 7 and they signaled to their partners in the other boat, for them to come and help them. And they came, and filled both of the boats, so that they began to sink. 8 But when Simon Peter saw *that*, he fell down at Jesus' feet, saying, "Depart from me, for I am a sinful man, O Lord!" 9 For amazement had seized him and all his companions because of the catch of fish which they had taken; 10 and so also James and John, sons of Zebedee, who were partners with Simon. And Jesus said to Simon, "Do not fear, from now on you will be catching men." 11And when they had brought their boats to land, they left everything and followed Him.

12 And it came about that while He was in one of the cities, behold, *there was* a man full of leprosy; and when he saw Jesus, he fell on his face and implored Him, saying, "Lord, if You are willing, You can make me clean." 13And He stretched out His hand, and touched him, saying, "I am willing; be cleansed." And *immediately* the leprosy left him. 14And he ordered him to tell no one, "But go and show yourself to the priest, and make an offering for your cleansing, just as Moses commanded, for a testimony to them." 15 But the news about Him was spreading even further, and great multitudes were gathering to hear *Him* and to be healed of their sicknesses. 16 But He Himself would *often* slip away to the wilderness and pray.

17 And it came about one day that He was teaching; and there were *some* Pharisees and teachers of the law sitting *there*, who had come from every village of Galilee and Judea and *from* Jerusalem; and the power of the Lord was *present* for Him to perform healing. 18And behold, *some* men *were* carrying on a bed a man who was paralyzed; and they were trying to bring him in, and to set him down in front of Him. 19And not finding any *way* to bring him in because of the crowd, they went up on the roof and let him down through the tiles with his stretcher, right in the center, in front of Jesus. 20And seeing their faith, He said, "Friend, your sins are forgiven you." 21And the scribes and the Pharisees began to reason, saying, "Who is this *man* who speaks blasphemies? Who can forgive sins, but God alone?" 22 But Jesus, aware of their reasonings, answered and said to them, "Why are you reasoning in your hearts? 23 "Which is easier, to say, 'Your sins have been forgiven you,' or to say, 'Rise and walk'? 24 "But in order that you may know that the Son of Man has authority on earth to forgive sins"— He said to the paralytic, "I say to you, rise, and take up your stretcher and go home." 25And at

WILLIAMS

of the lake, but the fishermen had left them and were washing their nets. 3 So He got into one of the boats, which belonged to Simon, and asked him to push out a little from the shore. Then He sat down and continued to teach the crowds from the boat. 4 When He stopped speaking, He said to Simon, "Push out into deep water, and set[a] your nets for a haul."

5 Simon answered, "We have toiled all night and caught nothing, but since you tell me to do so, I will set the nets again." 6 They did so and caught so vast a shoal of fish that their nets began to break. 7 So they beckoned to their partners in the other boat to come and help them. And they came and filled both boats so full that they began to sink. 8 When Simon Peter saw it, he fell down at Jesus' feet and said, "Leave me, Lord, because I am a sinful man." 9 For at the haul of fish that they had made, bewildering amazement had seized him and all his men, 10 as well as James and John, Zebedee's sons, who were Simon's partners.

Then Jesus said to Simon, "Stop being afraid; from now on you will be catching men." 11 So after they had brought the boats to land, they left everything and followed Him.

12 Now while He was in one of the towns, a man covered with leprosy saw Jesus and fell on his face and begged Him, saying, "Lord, if you choose to, you can cure me."

13 So He reached out His hand and touched him, saying, "I do choose to; be cured." And at once the leprosy left him. 14 Then He warned him not to tell anybody, but rather He said, "Go, show yourself to the priest, and, to prove it to the people, make the offering for your purification, just as Moses prescribed."

15 But the news about Him continued to spread, and great crowds were gathering to hear Him and to be cured of their diseases. 16 But Jesus Himself continued His habit of retiring to lonely spots and praying.

17 One day as He was teaching, there were some Pharisees and teachers of the law sitting by who had come from every village of Galilee and Judea and from Jerusalem. And the power of the Lord was with Him to cure people. 18 Now some men were carrying on a bed a man who was paralyzed, and they were trying to get him in and lay him before Jesus. 19And as they could not find a way because of the crowd, they went up on the roof and let him down with his pallet through the tiles, among the people right in front of Jesus. 20 When He saw their faith, He said, "Friend, your sins are forgiven."

21 But the scribes and the Pharisees began to argue, saying, "Who is this fellow who speaks blasphemy? Who can forgive sins but God alone?"

22 Jesus saw that they were arguing, and answered them: "Why are you arguing so in your hearts? 23 Which is easier, to say 'Your sins are forgiven,' or to say 'Get up and start walking'? 24 But to show you that the Son of Man has authority to forgive sins on earth"— turning to the man who was paralyzed, He said to him, "Get up, pick up your pallet, and go home."

25 Then at once he got up before them all,

BECK

saw two boats on the shore of the lake. The fishermen had stepped out of them and were washing their nets. 3 So Jesus got into one of the boats (it belonged to Simon) and asked him to go out a little way from the shore. Then He sat down and taught the people from the boat.

4 When He had stopped speaking, He told Simon, "Take the boat out where the water is deep, and let down your nets for a catch."

5 "Master," Simon answered, "we've worked hard all night and caught nothing. But if You say so, I'll let down the nets."

6 When the men had done this, they caught a very large number of fish, and their nets started to tear. 7 So they waved to their partners in the other boat to come and help them. They came, and now they filled both boats so that they started to sink.

8 When Simon Peter saw this, he fell down at Jesus' knees. "Leave me, Lord," he said. "I'm a sinful man." 9 He and all who were with him were amazed to see the fish they had caught, 10 and so were James and John, Zebedee's sons, who were Simon's partners.

"Don't be afraid," Jesus told Simon. "From now on you're going to catch men."

11 So when they had brought the boats to the shore, they left everything and followed Him.

Jesus Heals a Leper

12 One day Jesus was in a town where there was a man who had leprosy all over his body. When he saw Jesus, he bowed down to the ground. "Lord," he begged Him, "if You want to, You can make me clean."

13 Jesus stretched out His hand and touched him. "I want to," He said. "Be clean!" Immediately the leprosy left him.

14 "Don't tell anyone," Jesus ordered him, "but go, *let the priest examine*[42] you, and for your cleansing offer the sacrifice Moses ordered, to show them you're well."

15 But the news about Jesus spread all the more, and big crowds were gathering to hear Him and have their diseases healed.

16 And He would go away to lonely places and pray.

Jesus Forgives Sins

17 One day as He was teaching, Pharisees and Bible teachers were sitting there. They had come from every village in Galilee and Judea and from Jerusalem. And Jesus had the Lord's power to heal.

18 Then some men brought a paralyzed man on a bed and tried to take him in and lay him in front of Jesus. 19 But when they couldn't find a way to get him in on account of the crowd, they went up on the roof and through the tiles let him and the bed down among the people, right in front of Jesus.

20 When Jesus saw their faith, He said, "Man, your sins are forgiven." 21 Then the Bible scholars and the Pharisees began to argue, saying, "Who is this fellow, talking such blasphemies? Who but God alone can forgive sins?"

22 Jesus knew what they were thinking. "Why do you have such thoughts in your hearts?" He asked them. 23 "Is it easier to say, 'Your sins are forgiven,' or to say, 'Get up and walk'? 24 I want you to know the Son of Man has power on earth to forgive sins"—then He said to the paralyzed man, "I tell you, get up, take your bed, and go home."

25 Immediately the man got up in front of

---

[a] Grk., *let down*, but *set* is the fisherman's term.

[42] Lev. 13:7, 49

K.J.V.

up before them, and took up that whereon he lay, and departed to his own house, glorifying God. 26And they were all amazed, and they glorified God, and were filled with fear, saying, We have seen strange things to day.

27 And after these things he went forth, and saw a publican, named Levi, sitting at the receipt of custom: and he said unto him, Follow me. 28And he left all, rose up, and followed him. 29And Levi made him a great feast in his own house: and there was a great company of publicans and of others that sat down with them. 30 But their scribes and Pharisees murmured against his disciples, saying, Why do ye eat and drink with publicans and sinners? 31And Jesus answering said unto them, They that are whole need not a physician; but they that are sick. 32 I came not to call the righteous, but sinners to repentance.

33 And they said unto him, Why do the disciples of John fast often, and make prayers, and likewise *the disciples* of the Pharisees; but thine eat and drink? 34And he said unto them, Can ye make the children of the bridechamber fast, while the bridegroom is with them? 35 But the days will come, when the bridegroom shall be taken away from them, and then shall they fast in those days.

36 And he spake also a parable unto them; No man putteth a piece of a new garment upon an old; if otherwise, then both the new maketh a rent, and the piece that was *taken* out of the new agreeth not with the old. 37And no man putteth new wine into old bottles; else the new wine will burst the bottles, and be spilled, and the bottles shall perish. 38 But new wine must be put into new bottles; and both are preserved. 39 No man also having drunk old *wine* straightway desireth new; for he saith, The old is better.

6 And it came to pass on the second sabbath after the first, that he went through the corn fields; and his disciples plucked the ears of corn, and did eat, rubbing *them* in *their* hands. 2And certain of the Pharisees said unto them, Why do ye that which is not lawful to do on the sabbath days? 3And Jesus answering them said, Have ye not read so much as this, what David did, when himself was a hungered, and they which were with him; 4 How he went into the house of God, and did take and eat the shewbread, and gave also to them that were with him; which it is not lawful to eat but for the priests alone? 5And he said unto them, That the Son of man is Lord also of the sabbath. 6And it came to pass also on another sabbath, that he entered into the synagogue and taught: and there was a man whose right hand was withered. 7And the scribes and Pharisees watched him, whether he would heal on the sabbath day; that they might find an accusation against him. 8 But he knew their thoughts, and said to the man which had the withered hand, Rise up, and stand forth in the

N.A.S.

once he rose up before them, and took up what he had been lying on, and went home, glorifying God. 26And they were all seized with astonishment and *began* glorifying God; and they were filled with fear, saying, "We have seen remarkable things today."

27 And after that He went out, and noticed a ᵃtax-gatherer named Levi, sitting in the tax office, and He said to him, "Follow Me." 28And he left everything behind, and rose up and *began* to follow Him.

29 And Levi gave a big reception for Him in his house; and there was a great crowd of tax-gatherers and other *people* who were reclining *at table* with them. 30And the Pharisees and their scribes *began* grumbling at His disciples, saying, "Why do you eat and drink with the tax-gatherers and sinners?" 31And Jesus answered and said to them, *"It is* not those who are well who need a physician, but those who are sick. 32 "I have not come to call righteous men but sinners to repentance."

33 And they said to Him, "The disciples of John often fast and offer prayers; the *disciples* of the Pharisees also do the same; but Yours eat and drink." 34And Jesus said to them, "You cannot make the attendants of the bridegroom fast while the bridegroom is with them, can you? 35 "But *the* days will come; and when the bridegroom is taken away from them, then they will fast in those days." 36And He was also telling them a parable: "No one tears a piece from a new garment and puts it on an old garment; otherwise he will both tear the new, and the piece from the new will not match the old. 37 "And no one puts new wine into old wine-skins; otherwise the new wine will burst the skins, and it will be spilled out, and the skins will be ruined. 38 "But new wine must be put into fresh wine-skins. 39 "And no one, after drinking old *wine* wishes for new; for he says, 'The old is good *enough.'* "

6 Now it came about that on a *certain* Sabbath He was passing through *some* grainfields; and His disciples were picking and eating the heads *of wheat*, rubbing them in their hands. 2 But some of the Pharisees said, "Why do you do what is not lawful on the Sabbath?" 3And Jesus answering them said, "Have you not even read what David did when he was hungry, he and those who were with him, 4 how he entered the house of God, and took and ate the ᵇconsecrated bread which is not lawful for any to eat except the priests alone, and gave it to his companions?" 5And He was saying to them, "The Son of Man is lord of the Sabbath."

6 And it came about on another Sabbath, that He entered the synagogue and was teaching; and there was a man there whose right hand was withered. 7And the scribes and the Pharisees were watching Him closely, *to see* if He healed on the Sabbath; in order that they might find *reason* to accuse Him. 8 But He knew what they were thinking, and He said to the man with the withered hand, "Arise and come forward!" And

[a] Publicans who collected Roman taxes for profit. [b] Or, *showbread*, lit., *loaves of presentation.*

WILLIAMS

BECK

picked up the pallet on which he had been lying, and went off home, giving praise to God. 26 Then an overwhelming wonder seized them all and they began to give praise to God. They were filled with awe and continued to say, "We have seen unthinkable wonders today!"

27 After this He went out and saw a tax-collector named Levi in his seat at the tax-collector's desk, and He said to him, "Follow me." 28 So he left everything behind, got up and followed Him.

29 Then Levi gave a great reception for Him in his house, and there was a large crowd of tax-collectors and others who were at table with them. 30 Now the Pharisees and their scribes were grumbling at His disciples, and were saying, "Why are you eating and drinking with tax-collectors and notorious sinners?"

31 But Jesus answered them, "Not well but sick people have to send for the doctor. 32 It is not upright but sinful people that I have come to invite to repentance."

33 After that they said to Him, "John's disciples rigidly practice fasting and offering up prayers; so do the Pharisees, but your disciples keep right on eating and drinking."

34 But Jesus said to them, "You cannot make the wedding-guests fast while the bridegroom is with them, can you? 35 But a time will come when the bridegroom is taken away from them; at that time they will fast."

36 Then He told them a short story: "No one tears a piece from a new coat and puts it on an old one; or if he does, he will tear the new one too, and the patch from the new coat will not match the old one. 37 So no one puts fresh wine into old wine bottles; or, if he does, the fresh wine will burst the bottles, the wine will run out, and the bottles will be ruined. 38 But fresh wine must be put into new bottles. 39 No one after drinking old wine wants new, for he says, 'The old is good enough.'"

6   *Jesus and His disciples breaking the sabbath laws of the Pharisees; the Twelve chosen and sent out; the address on the plain*

One sabbath He happened to be passing through the wheatfields, and His disciples were pulling and eating the heads of wheat, rubbing them in their hands. 2 And some of the Pharisees said, "Why are you doing what is against the law to do on the sabbath?"

3 Jesus answered them, "Did you never read what David did, when he and his soldiers became hungry? 4 How he went into the house of God and took and ate the sacred loaves, which it was against the law for anyone to eat except the priests, and gave some to his soldiers?" 5 Then He said to them, "The Son of Man is Lord of the sabbath."

6 On another sabbath He found Himself in the synagogue teaching; and there was there a man whose right hand was withered. 7 And the scribes and the Pharisees were closely watching Him to see whether He would cure him on the sabbath, in order to get a charge against Him. 8 But He knew what they were thinking, and He said to the man with the withered hand, "Get up and stand at the front." So he got up and stood there.

them, took the bed he had been lying on, and went home, praising God.

26 All were amazed and praised God. Fearfully they declared, "You wouldn't believe what we've seen today!"

Matthew

27 After that He went out and saw a tax collector by the name of Levi sitting in the tax office. "Come with Me," He told him. 28 He got up, left everything, and went with Him.

29 Then Levi gave a big dinner for Him at his home, and there was a big crowd of tax collectors and others who were eating with them.

30 The Pharisees and their Bible scholars complained to His disciples: "Why do you eat and drink with tax collectors and sinners?"

31 "Those who are healthy don't need a doctor," Jesus answered them, "but the sick. 32 I didn't come to call righteous people, but sinners to repent."

The Bridegroom

33 "John's disciples as well as the disciples of the Pharisees often fast and say prayers," said to Him. "Why do Yours eat and drink?"

34 Jesus asked them, "Can you make the bridegroom's friends fast while the bridegroom is with them? 35 The time will come when the bridegroom will be taken away from them, and in those days they will fast."

36 He pictured it to them in this way: "Nobody tears a piece of cloth from a new garment and sews it on an old garment. If you do, you'll tear the new cloth, and the patch from the new won't match the old. 37 Nobody pours new wine into old wineskins. If you do, the new wine will burst the skins and run out, and the skins will be ruined. 38 New wine has to be poured into fresh skins.

39 "Nobody who has drunk old wine wants the new. 'The old tastes good,' he says."

Lord of the Sabbath

6   While Jesus was walking through grainfields on a Sabbath, His disciples were picking the heads of grain, rubbing them in their hands, and eating them.

2 Some of the Pharisees asked, "Why are you doing something you shouldn't do on a day of rest?"

3 "Haven't you read what David did," Jesus asked them, "when he and his men were hungry— 4 how he went into God's house and took the *loaves laid before God*,[43] and ate them and gave his men some? Only the priests had the right to eat them." 5 Then He added, "The Son of Man is Lord of the Sabbath."

The Shriveled Hand

6 On another Sabbath Jesus went into a synagog and taught. And there was a man whose right hand was shriveled. 7 But the Bible scholars and the Pharisees were watching Jesus to see if He would heal him on a Sabbath. They wanted to find something to accuse Him of.

8 But He knew what they were thinking; so He said to the man with the shriveled hand, "Get up and come forward." The man got up and

[43] Lev. 24:5-8; 1 Sam. 21:6

K.J.V.

midst. And he arose and stood forth. 9 Then said Jesus unto them, I will ask you one thing; Is it lawful on the sabbath days to do good, or to do evil? to save life, or to destroy *it?* 10And looking round about upon them all, he said unto the man, Stretch forth thy hand. And he did so: and his hand was restored whole as the other. 11And they were filled with madness; and communed one with another what they might do to Jesus. 12And it came to pass in those days, that he went out into a mountain to pray, and continued all night in prayer to God.

13 And when it was day, he called *unto him* his disciples: and of them he chose twelve, whom also he named apostles; 14 Simon, (whom he also named Peter,) and Andrew his brother, James and John, Philip and Bartholomew, 15 Matthew and Thomas, James the *son* of Alpheus, and Simon called Zelotes, 16And Judas *the brother* of James, and Judas Iscariot, which also was the traitor.

17 And he came down with them, and stood in the plain, and the company of his disciples, and a great multitude of people out of all Judea and Jerusalem, and from the sea coast of Tyre and Sidon, which came to hear him,.and to be healed of their diseases; 18And they that were vexed with unclean spirits: and they were healed. 19And the whole multitude sought to touch him: for there went virtue out of him, and healed *them* all.

20 And he lifted up his eyes on his disciples, and said, Blessed *be ye* poor: for yours is the kingdom of God. 21 Blessed *are ye* that hunger now: for ye shall be filled. Blessed *are ye* that weep now: for ye shall laugh. 22 Blessed are ye, when men shall hate you, and when they shall separate you *from their company,* and shall reproach you, and cast out your name as evil, for the Son of man's sake. 23 Rejoice ye in that day, and leap for joy: for, behold, your reward *is* great in heaven: for in the like manner did their fathers unto the prophets. 24 But woe unto you that are rich! for ye have received your consolation. 25 Woe unto you that are full! for ye shall hunger. Woe unto you that laugh now! for ye shall mourn and weep. 26 Woe unto you, when all men shall speak well of you! for so did their fathers to the false prophets.

27 But I say unto you which hear, Love your enemies, do good to them which hate you, 28 Bless them that curse you, and pray for them which despitefully use you. 29And unto him that smiteth thee on the *one* cheek offer also the other; and him that taketh away thy cloak forbid not *to take thy* coat also. 30 Give to every man that asketh of thee; and of him that taketh away thy goods ask *them* not again. 31And as ye would that men should do to you, do ye also to them likewise. 32 For if ye love them which love you, what thank have ye? for sinners also love

N.A.S.

he arose and came forward. 9 And Jesus said to them, "I ask you, is it lawful on the Sabbath to do good, or to do evil, to save a life, or to destroy it?" 10And after looking around at them all, He said to him, "Stretch out your hand!" And he did *so;* and his hand was *completely* restored. 11 But they themselves were filled with rage, and discussed together what they might do to Jesus.

12 And it was at this time ·that He went off to the mountain to pray, and He spent the whole night in prayer to God. 13And when day came, He called His disciples to Him; and chose twelve of them, whom He also named as apostles: 14 Simon, whom He also named Peter, and Andrew his brother; James and John; Philip and Bartholomew; 15 Matthew and Thomas; James *the son* of Alphaeus, and Simon who was called the Zealot; 16 Judas *the son* of James, and Judas Iscariot, who became a traitor. 17And He descended with them, and stood on a level place; and *there was* a great multitude of His disciples, and a great throng of people from all Judea and Jerusalem and the coastal region of Tyre and Sidon, 18who had come to hear Him, and to be healed of their diseases; and those who were troubled with unclean spirits were being cured. 19And all the multitude were trying to touch Him, for power was coming from Him and healing *them* all.

20 And turning His gaze on His disciples, He *began* to say, "Blessed *are* you *who are* poor, for yours is the kingdom of God.

21 "Blessed *are* you who hunger now, for you shall be satisfied.

Blessed *are* you who weep now, for you shall laugh.

22 "Blessed are you when men hate you, and ostracize you, and heap insults upon you, and spurn your name as evil, for the sake of the Son of Man. 23 "Be glad in that day, and leap *for joy,* for behold, your reward is great in heaven; for in the same way their fathers used to treat the prophets. 24 "But woe to you who are rich, for you are receiving your comfort in full. 25 "Woe to you who are well-fed now, for you shall be hungry. Woe *to you* who laugh now, for you shall mourn and weep. 26 "Woe *to you* when all men speak well of you, for in the same way their fathers used to treat the false prophets.

27 "But I say to you who hear, love your enemies, do good to those who hate you, 28 bless those who curse you, pray for those who mistreat you. 29 "Whoever hits you on the cheek, offer him the other also; and whoever takes away your coat, do not withhold your shirt from him either. 30 "Give to everyone who asks of you, and whoever takes away what is yours, do not demand it back. 31 "And just as you want men to treat you, treat them in the same way. 32 "And if you lose those who love you, what credit is *that* to you? For even sinners love

WILLIAMS

9 Then Jesus said to them, "Is it right on the sabbath to do people good, or to do them evil, to save life or to take it?" 10 Then He glanced around at them all and said to him, "Put out your hand." And he did so, and his hand was at once completely restored. 11 But they were filled with fury and began to discuss what they could do to Jesus.

12 Now it was in those days that He went up on the mountain to pray, and He spent the whole night in prayer to God. 13 When day came, He called His disciples to Him, and selected from them twelve whom He also named apostles: 14 Simon whom He named Peter, his brother Andrew, James, John, Philip, Bartholomew, 15 Matthew, Thomas, James the son of Alpheus, Simon who was called the Zealot, 16 Judas the son of James, and Judas Iscariot, who afterward turned traitor.

17 Then He came down with them and took His stand on a level place where there was a great throng of His disciples and a vast crowd of people from all over Judea and from Jerusalem and the seacoast district of Tyre and Sidon, who had come to hear Him and to be cured of their diseases. 18 Even those who were troubled by foul spirits were being cured. 19 So all the people were trying to touch Him, because power continued to go forth from Him and to cure them all.

20 Then He fixed His eyes upon His disciples, and began to speak.

"Blessed are you who are poor, for the kingdom of God is yours!

21 "Blessed are you who are hungry now, for you will be completely satisfied!

"Blessed are you who are weeping now, for you will laugh!

22 "Blessed are you when people hate you and exclude you and denounce you, and spurn your name as evil, for the sake of the Son of Man. 23 Burst into joy on that day and leap for ecstasy, for your reward will be rich[a] in heaven; for this is the way your forefathers used to treat the prophets.

24 "But a curse on you who are rich, for you are now receiving your comforts in full.

25 "A curse on you who live in luxury[b] now, for you will be hungry.

"A curse on you who laugh now, for you will mourn and weep.

26 "A curse on you when everyone speaks well of you, for this is the way their forefathers used to treat the false prophets.

27 "But I say to you who listen now to me, practice loving your enemies, practice doing good to those who hate you, 28 continue to bless those who curse you, and continue to pray for those who abuse you. 29 To the man who strikes you on one cheek, offer him the other too; and from the man who takes away your coat, do not keep back your shirt either. 30 Practice giving to everyone who asks of you, and stop demanding back your goods from him who takes them away. 31 Yes, you must practice dealing with others as you would like them to deal with you. 32 Now if you practice loving only those who love you, what credit do you get for that? Why, even notorious sinners practice lov-

BECK

stood there. 9 Then Jesus said to them, "I ask you, is it right on a Sabbath to do good or to do evil, to save a life or to kill?" 10 After looking around at all of them, He told the man, "Stretch out your hand." He did, and his hand was made healthy again.

11 They were furious and began to discuss with one another what they could do to Jesus.

Twelve Apostles

12 In those days Jesus went out to the hill to pray, and He prayed to God all night.

13 When it was day, He called His disciples. He chose twelve of them and called them apostles: 14 Simon, whom He also gave the name Peter, and his brother Andrew; James and John, Philip and Bartholomew, 15 Matthew and Thomas; James, the son of Alphaeus; Simon, called Zealot; 16 Judas, the son of James; and Judas, the man from Kerioth, who became a traitor.

Many Are Healed

17 He went down with them and stood on a level place with a big crowd of His disciples and very many people from the whole country of the Jews, from Jerusalem, and from the seacoast of Tyre and Sidon. They had come to hear Him and have their diseases healed. 18 And those who were plagued by unclean spirits were made well. 19 All the people were trying to touch Him, because power came from Him and made them all well.

Happy and Unhappy

20 Jesus looked at His disciples and said:

"Happy are you who are poor—
you have God's kingdom.
21 Happy are you who are hungry now—
you will be satisfied.
Happy are you who are crying now—
you will laugh.
22 Happy are you when people hate you, exclude you from their company, insult you, reject your name as evil because you believe in the Son of Man. 23 On that day be glad and dance with delight, because you have a great reward in heaven. You see, that's how their fathers treated the prophets. 24 But—
Woe to you who are rich—
you've had your comfort.
25 Woe to you who are well fed now—
you will be hungry.
Woe to you who are laughing now—
you will mourn and cry aloud.
26 Woe to you when everybody speaks well of you—
that is how their fathers treated the false prophets."

Love Your Enemies

27 "But I tell you who are listening, love your enemies, be kind to those who hate you, 28 bless those who curse you, and pray for those who insult you. 29 If anyone hits you on your cheek, offer him the other cheek. If anyone takes your coat, don't stop him from taking your shirt. 30 If anyone asks you for anything, give it to him. And if anyone takes what is yours, don't insist on getting it back.

31 "Treat others just as you want them to treat you.

32 "If you love those who love you, how should anyone be especially pleased with you?

[a] Grk., great. [b] Grk., perfectly full.

K.J.V.

those that love them. 33And if ye do good to them which do good to you, what thank have ye? for sinners also do even the same. 34And if ye lend *to them* of whom ye hope to receive, what thank have ye? for sinners also lend to sinners, to receive as much again. 35 But love ye your enemies, and do good, and lend, hoping for nothing again; and your reward shall be great, and ye shall be the children of the Highest: for he is kind unto the unthankful and *to* the evil. 36 Be ye therefore merciful, as your Father also is merciful. 37 Judge not, and ye shall not be judged: condemn not, and ye shall not be condemned: forgive, and ye shall be forgiven: 38 Give, and it shall be given unto you; good measure, pressed down, and shaken together, and running over, shall men give into your bosom. For with the same measure that ye mete withal it shall be measured to you again.

39 And he spake a parable unto them; Can the blind lead the blind? shall they not both fall into the ditch? 40 The disciple is not above his master: but every one that is perfect shall be as his master. 41And why beholdest thou the mote that is in thy brother's eye, but perceivest not the beam that is in thine own eye? 42 Either how canst thou say to thy brother, Brother, let me pull out the mote that is in thine eye, when thou thyself beholdest not the beam that is in thine own eye? Thou hypocrite, cast out first the beam out of thine own eye, and then shalt thou see clearly to pull out the mote that is in thy brother's eye. 43 For a good tree bringeth not forth corrupt fruit; neither doth a corrupt tree bring forth good fruit. 44 For every tree is known by his own fruit. For of thorns men do not gather figs, nor of a bramble bush gather they grapes. 45A good man out of the good treasure of his heart bringeth forth that which is good; and an evil man out of the evil treasure of his heart bringeth forth that which is evil: for of the abundance of the heart his mouth speaketh.

46 And why call ye me, Lord, Lord, and do not the things which I say? 47 Whosoever cometh to me, and heareth my sayings, and doeth them, I will shew you to whom he is like: 48 He is like a man which built a house, and digged deep, and laid the foundation on a rock: and when the flood arose, the stream beat vehemently upon that house, and could not shake it; for it was founded upon a rock. 49 But he that heareth, and doeth not, is like a man that without a foundation built a house upon the earth; against which the stream did beat vehemently, and immediately it fell; and the ruin of that house was great.

7 Now when he had ended all his sayings in the audience of the people, he entered into Capernaum. 2And a certain centurion's servant,

N.A.S.

those who love them. 33 "And if you do good to those who do good to you, what credit is *that* to you? For even sinners do the same thing. 34 "And if you lend to those from whom you expect to receive, what credit is *that* to you? Even sinners lend to sinners, in order to receive back the same *amount.* 35 "But love your enemies, and do good, and lend, expecting nothing in return; and your reward will be great, and you will be sons of the Most High; for He Himself is kind to ungrateful and evil *men.* 36 "Be merciful, just as your Father is merciful. 37 "And do not pass judgment and you will not be judged; and do not condemn, and you shall not be condemned; pardon, and you will be pardoned. 38 "Give, and it will be given to you; good measure, pressed down, shaken together, running over, they will pour into your lap. For whatever measure you deal out *to others,* it will be dealt to you in return."

39 And He also spoke a parable to them: "A blind man cannot guide a blind man, can he? Will they not both fall into a pit? 40 "A pupil is not above his teacher; but everyone, after he has been fully trained, will be like his teacher. 41 "And why do you look at the speck that is in your brother's eye, but do not notice the log that is in your own eye? 42 "Or how can you say to your brother, 'Brother, let me take out the speck that is in your eye,' when you yourself do not see the log that is in your own eye? You hypocrite, first take the log out of your own eye, and then you will see clearly to take out the speck that is in your brother's eye. 43 "For there is no good tree which produces bad fruit; nor on the other hand, a bad tree which produces good fruit. 44 "For each tree is known by its own fruit. For men do not gather figs from thorns, nor do they pick grapes from a briar bush. 45 "The good man out of the good treasure of his heart brings forth what is good; and the evil *man* out of the evil *treasure* brings forth what is evil; for his mouth speaks from that which fills his heart.

46 "And why do you call Me, 'Lord, Lord,' and do not do what I say? 47 "Everyone who comes to Me, and hears My words, and acts upon them, I will show you whom he is like: 48 he is like a man building a house, who dug deep and laid a foundation upon the rock; and when a flood arose, the river burst against that house and could not shake it, because it had been well built. 49 "But the one who has heard, and has not acted *accordingly,* is like a man who built a house upon the ground without any foundation; and the river burst against it and immediately it collapsed, and the ruin of that house was great."

7 When He had completed all His discourse in the hearing of the people, He went to Capernaum.
2 And a certain centurion's slave, who was

WILLIAMS

ing those who love them. 33 And if you practice doing good only to those who do good to you, what credit do you get for that? Even notorious sinners practice the same. 34 And if you ever lend to people expecting to get it back, what credit do you get for that? Even notorious sinners practice lending to one another, expecting to get it back in full. 35 But you must practice loving your enemies, doing good to them, and lending to them, despairing of nothing; so that your reward will be great, and you will be sons of the Most High, because He is kind to the ungrateful and wicked. 36 Continue to be merciful, just as your Father is merciful. 37 Then stop criticizing others, and you will never be criticized; stop condemning others, and you will never be condemned. 38 Practice forgiving others, and you will be forgiven. Practice giving to others, and they will give*e* to you, good measure, pressed down, shaken together, and running over, people will pour into your lap. For the measure you use with others they in turn will use with you."

39 Then He told them a story: "Can one blind man lead another? Will they not both fall into the ditch? 40 A pupil is not better than his teacher, but everyone when fully trained will be like his teacher. 41 Why do you continue to look at the tiny speck in your brother's eye, but pay no attention to the heavy girder in your own eye? 42 How can you say to your brother, 'Brother, let me get that tiny speck out of your eye,' when you cannot see the girder in your own eye? You hypocrite! First get the girder out of your own eye, and then you will see clearly how to get out the tiny speck in your brother's eye.

43 "For there never is a healthy tree that bears poor fruit, nor a sickly tree that bears good fruit. 44 For every tree is known by its fruit. People do not pick figs from thornbushes, or gather grapes from a bramble-bush. 45 The good man, out of his good inner storehouse,*d* brings forth what is good, the bad man, out of his bad one, what is bad. For a man's mouth usually speaks the things that fill his heart.

46 "So why do you call me 'Lord, Lord,' but do not practice what I tell you? 47 Everyone who comes to me and continues to listen to my words and practices their teaching, I will show you whom he is like. 48 He is like a man who was building a house, who dug deep, and laid its foundation upon the rock; and when a flood came, the torrent burst upon that house but it could not shake it, because it was well built.*e* 49 But the man who merely hears them and does not practice them is like a man who built a house upon the ground without a foundation. The torrent burst upon it, and at once it collapsed, and the wreck of that house was complete."

7 *A Roman captain's slave cured; a widow's son at Nain brought to life; the Baptist in doubt, but Jesus pays Him a high tribute; Jesus anointed by the scarlet woman whose sins He forgives*

When He had finished all these sayings in the hearing of the people, He went into Capernaum.
2 There was a Roman captain*a* who had a

[c] Grk., *it will be given to you.* [d] Grk., *out of the treasury of his heart.* [e] Fol. best Mss. [a] Grk., *centurion; captain,* modern.

BECK

Even sinners love those who love them. 33 If you help those who help you, how should anyone be especially pleased with you? Sinners do that too. 34 If you lend anything to those from whom you expect to get something, how should anyone be especially pleased with you? Sinners also lend to sinners to get back what they lend. 35 No, love your enemies, help them, and lend to them without expecting to get anything back. Then you will have a great reward and will be the sons of the most high God, since He is kind to people who don't thank Him and are wicked. 36 Be merciful as your Father is merciful."

Criticize Yourself

37 "Don't judge, and you will not be judged. Don't condemn, and you will not be condemned. Forgive, and you will be forgiven. 38 Give, and it will be given you. A good measure, pressed together, shaken down, and running over, will be put into your lap. You see, the measure you use will be used for you."
39 He pictured it to them in this way: "Can a blind man lead another blind man? Won't they both fall into a ditch? 40 A pupil is not above his teacher. But anyone who is well trained will be like his teacher.
41 "And why do you look at the speck in your brother's eye and don't notice the log in your own eye? 42 How can you say to your brother, 'Brother, let me take the speck out of your eye,' as long as you don't see the log in your own eye? You hypocrite, first throw the log out of your own eye. Then you'll see clearly enough to take the speck out of your brother's eye."

Hear and Do!

43 "A good tree doesn't bear bad fruit, or a bad tree good fruit. 44 Every tree is known by its fruit. You don't pick figs from thornbushes, or grapes from brambles. 45 A good man produces good things from the good stored in his heart, and an evil man produces evil from his evil stored there. What you say flows from your heart.
46 "Why do you call Me Lord, Lord, but don't do what I tell you?
47 "I will show you what kind of man anyone is who comes to Me and hears and does what I say. 48 He's like a man who built a house. He dug deep and laid the foundation on a rock. When there was a flood, the torrent dashed against that house. But it couldn't move it, because it was built right. 49 Anyone who hears what I say but doesn't do it is like a man who built a house on the ground without a foundation. When the torrent dashed against it, that house immediately collapsed and went down with a big crash."

A Believing Captain

7 When Jesus had finished all He had to say to the people who heard Him, He went to Capernaum. 2 There a certain captain's slave

K.J.V.

who was dear unto him, was sick, and ready to die. 3And when he heard of Jesus, he sent unto him the elders of the Jews, beseeching him that he would come and heal his servant. 4And when they came to Jesus, they besought him instantly, saying, That he was worthy for whom he should do this: 5 For he loveth our nation, and he hath built us a synagogue. 6 Then Jesus went with them. And when he was now not far from the house, the centurion sent friends to him, saying unto him, Lord, trouble not thyself; for I am not worthy that thou shouldest enter under my roof: 7 Wherefore neither thought I myself worthy to come unto thee: but say in a word, and my servant shall be healed. 8 For I also am a man set under authority, having under me soldiers, and I say unto one, Go, and he goeth; and to another, Come, and he cometh; and to my servant, Do this, and he doeth *it*. 9 When Jesus heard these things, he marvelled at him, and turned him about, and said unto the people that followed him, I say unto you, I have not found so great faith, no, not in Israel. 10And they that were sent, returning to the house, found the servant whole that had been sick.

11 And it came to pass the day after, that he went into a city called Nain; and many of his disciples went with him, and much people. 12 Now when he came nigh to the gate of the city, behold, there was a dead man carried out, the only son of his mother, and she was a widow: and much people of the city was with her. 13And when the Lord saw her, he had compassion on her, and said unto her, Weep not. 14And he came and touched the bier: and they that bare *him* stood still. And he said, Young man, I say unto thee, Arise. 15And he that was dead sat up, and began to speak. And he delivered him to his mother. 16And there came a fear on all: and they glorified God, saying, That a great prophet is risen up among us; and, That God hath visited his people. 17And this rumour of him went forth throughout all Judea, and throughout all the region round about. 18And the disciples of John shewed him of all these things.

19 And John calling *unto him* two of his disciples sent *them* to Jesus, saying, Art thou he that should come? or look we for another? 20 When the men were come unto him, they said, John Baptist hath sent us unto thee, saying, Art thou he that should come? or look we for another? 21And in that same hour he cured many of *their* infirmities and plagues, and of evil spirits; and unto many *that were* blind he gave sight. 22 Then Jesus answering said unto them, Go your way, and tell John what things ye have seen and heard; how that the blind see, the lame walk, the lepers are cleansed, the deaf hear, the dead are raised, to the poor the gospel is preached. 23And blessed is *he,* whosoever shall not be offended in me.

24 And when the messengers of John were departed, he began to speak unto the people concerning John, What went ye out into the wilderness for to see? A reed shaken with the wind? 25 But what went ye out for to see? A man clothed in soft raiment? Behold, they which are gorgeously apparelled, and live delicately, are in

N.A.S.

highly regarded by him, was sick and about to die. 3And when he heard about Jesus, he sent some Jewish elders asking Him to come and save the life of his slave. 4And when they had come to Jesus, they earnestly entreated Him, saying, "He is worthy for You to grant this to him; 5 for he loves our nation, and it was he who built us our synagogue." 6 Now Jesus *started* on His way with them; and when He was already not far from the house, the centurion sent friends, saying to Him, "Lord, do not trouble Yourself further, for I am not fit for You to come under my roof; 7 for this reason I did not even consider myself worthy to come to You, but just say the word, and my servant will be healed. 8 "For indeed, I am a man under authority, with soldiers under me; and I say to this one, 'Go!' and he goes; and to another, 'Come!' and he comes; and to my slave, 'Do this!' and he does it." 9And when Jesus heard this, He marveled at him, and turned and said to the multitude that was following Him, "I say to you, not even in Israel have I found such great faith." 10And when those who had been sent returned to the house, they found the slave in good health.

11 And it came about soon afterwards, that He went to a city called Nain; and His disciples were going along with Him, accompanied by a large multitude. 12 Now as He approached the gate of the city, behold, a dead man was being carried out, the only son of his mother, and she was a widow; and a sizeable crowd from the city was with her. 13And when the Lord saw her, He felt compassion for her, and said to her, "Do not weep." 14And He came up and touched the coffin; and the bearers came to a halt. And He said, "Young man, I say to you, arise!" 15And the dead man sat up, and began to speak. And *Jesus* gave him back to his mother. 16And fear gripped them all, and they *began* glorifying God, saying, "A great prophet has arisen among us!" and, "God has visited His people!" 17And this report concerning Him went out all over Judea, and in all the surrounding district.

18 And the disciples of John reported to him about all these things. 19And summoning two of his disciples, John sent them to the Lord, saying, "Are You the One who is coming, or do we look for someone else?" 20And when the men had come to Him, they said, "John the Baptist has sent us to You, saying, 'Are You the One who is coming, or do we look for someone else?'" 21At that very time He cured many *people* of diseases and afflictions and evil spirits; and He granted sight to many *who were* blind. 22And He answered and said to them, "Go and report to John what you have seen and heard: *the* BLIND RECEIVE SIGHT, *the* lame walk, *the* lepers are cleansed, and *the* deaf hear, *the* dead are raised up, *the* POOR HAVE THE GOSPEL PREACHED TO THEM. 23 "And blessed is he who keeps from stumbling over Me."

24 And when the messengers of John had left, He began to speak to the multitudes about John, "What did you go out into the wilderness to look at? A reed shaken by the wind? 25 "But what did you go out to see? A man dressed in soft clothing? Behold, those who are splendidly clothed and live in luxury are *found* in royal palaces. 26 "But what did you go out to see? A

WILLIAMS

slave that was very dear to him, and he was sick and at the point of death. 3 When the captain heard about Jesus, he sent some Jewish elders to Him, to ask Him to come and bring his slave safe through the illness. 4 So they went to Jesus and continued to urge Him earnestly, saying, "He deserves that you do this for him, 5 for he loves our nation, and he is the man who built us our synagogue."

6 Then Jesus started to go with them. But when He was not far from the house, the captain sent friends to say to Him, "My Lord, stop troubling yourself, for I am not worthy to have you come under my roof. 7 And so I did not deem myself worthy even to come to you. But simply speak the word, and let my servant-boy be cured. 8 For I too am under authority of others, and have soldiers under me, and I order one to go, and he goes, another to come, and he comes, my slave to do this, and he does it."

9 When Jesus heard this, He was astounded at him, and turning to the crowd that was following Him He said, "I tell you, I have not found, in a single case among the Jews, so great faith as this!" 10 Then the messengers returned to the house and found the slave well.

11 Soon afterwards He chanced to go to a town called Nain, and His disciples and a great throng of people were going along with Him. 12 As He approached the gate of the town, look! there was being carried out a dead man, his mother's only son, and she was a widow. A considerable crowd of townspeople were with her.

13 Now when the Lord saw her, His heart was moved with pity for her, and so He said to her, "Stop weeping." 14 Then He went up and touched the hearse,[b] and the bearers stopped; and He said, "Young man, I tell you, arise."

15 Then the dead man sat up and began to speak, and Jesus gave him back to his mother. 16 So awe seized them all, and they began to praise God, saying, "A great prophet has appeared among us!" and, "God has visited His people!" 17 This story about Him spread all over Judea and all the surrounding country.

18 Now John's disciples told him about all these things. 19 So John called two of them to him and sent them to the Lord, to ask, "Are you the One who was to come, or should we continue to look for someone else?"

20 So the men went to Him and said, "John the Baptist sent us to you to ask, 'Are you the One who was to come, or should we continue to look for someone else?'"

21 At that very hour He cured many people of diseases and scourges and evil spirits, and graciously granted sight to many blind persons. 22 And so He answered them, "Go and report to John what you have seen and heard: The blind are seeing and the crippled are walking, the lepers are being healed and the deaf are hearing, the dead are being raised and the poor are having the good news preached to them. 23 And happy is the man who finds no cause for stumbling over me."

24 But when John's messengers had gone, He began to speak to the crowds about John: "What did you go out into the desert to gaze at? A reed that is tossed to and fro by the wind? 25 If not, what did you go out there to see? A man dressed in silks and satins? No. People who dress gorgeously and live luxuriously are found

[b] Modern term; so we use it rather than *bier*.

BECK

was sick. He was dear to him and now he was dying. 3 The captain heard about Jesus and sent some Jewish elders to ask Him to come and save his slave's life. 4 They came to Jesus and earnestly pleaded with Him, "He deserves to have You do this for him, 5 because he loves our people and built the synagog for us."

6 So Jesus went with them. He wasn't far from the house when the captain sent friends to tell Him, "Lord, don't bother. I'm not good enough for You to come under my roof. 7 And so I didn't think I was fit to come to You either. But just say a word, and my slave will be made well. 8 I'm only a man who has to obey others, but I have soldiers under me. I tell one, Go, and he goes. And another, Come, and he comes. And my slave, Do this, and he does it."

9 Surprised to hear him say this, Jesus turned to the crowd following Him. "I tell you," He said, "Not even in Israel have I found such faith."

10 When the men who had been sent went back to the house, they found the slave well again.

Jesus Raises a Widow's Son

11 Soon after this, Jesus went to a town called Nain, and His disciples and a large crowd went with Him. 12 As He came near the gate of the town, a dead man was carried out. He was his mother's only son, and she was a widow. A big crowd from the town was with her.

13 When the Lord saw her, He felt sorry for her. "Don't cry," He told her.

14 He went up to the open coffin and touched it, and the men who were carrying it stood still. "Young man," He said, "I tell you, wake up." 15 The dead man sat up and started to talk. And Jesus *gave him to his mother.*[44]

16 They were all overawed and praised God. "A great prophet has risen among us," they said, and, "God has come to help His people." 17 This story about Jesus spread all over the country of the Jews and in all the surrounding territory.

John Sends Two Disciples

18 John's disciples told him about all these things. Then John called two of his disciples 19 and sent them to ask the Lord, "Are You the One who is coming, or should we look for someone else?"

20 The men came to Jesus and said, "John the Baptizer sent us to ask You, 'Are You the One who is coming, or should we look for someone else?'"

21 Just then He had healed many people of their diseases, ailments and evil spirits and had given sight to many who were blind.

22 "Go," Jesus answered, "tell John what you've seen and heard: *The blind see,* the lame walk, lepers are made clean, the *deaf hear,* the dead are raised, and *the poor hear the good news*[45]— 23 and happy is anyone who doesn't turn against Me."

About John

24 When John's messengers had left, Jesus talked to the crowds about John:

"What did you go out into the wilderness to see—a reed shaken by the wind? What, then, did you go out to see—a man dressed in soft robes? 25 Those who wear fine clothes and live in luxury you'll find in the palaces of kings.

[44] 1 Kings 17:23
[45] Is. 29:18; 35:5; 61:1

K.J.V.

kings' courts. 26 But what went ye out for to see? A prophet? Yea, I say unto you, and much more than a prophet. 27 This is *he*, of whom it is written, Behold, I send my messenger before thy face, which shall prepare thy way before thee. 28 For I say unto you, Among those that are born of women there is not a greater prophet than John the Baptist: but he that is least in the kingdom of God is greater than he. 29 And all the people that heard *him*, and the publicans, justified God, being baptized with the baptism of John. 30 But the Pharisees and lawyers rejected the counsel of God against themselves, being not baptized of him.

31 And the Lord said, Whereunto then shall I liken the men of this generation? and to what are they like? 32 They are like unto children sitting in the marketplace, and calling one to another, and saying, We have piped unto you, and ye have not danced; we have mourned to you, and ye have not wept. 33 For John the Baptist came neither eating bread nor drinking wine; and ye say He hath a devil. 34 The Son of man is come eating and drinking; and ye say, Behold a gluttonous man, and a winebibber, a friend of publicans and sinners! 35 But wisdom is justified of all her children.

36 And one of the Pharisees desired him that he would eat with him. And he went into the Pharisee's house, and sat down to meat. 37 And, behold, a woman in the city, which was a sinner, when she knew that *Jesus* sat at meat in the Pharisee's house, brought an alabaster box of ointment, 38 And stood at his feet behind *him* weeping, and began to wash his feet with tears, and did wipe *them* with the hairs of her head, and kissed his feet, and anointed *them* with the ointment. 39 Now when the Pharisee which had bidden him saw *it*, he spake within himself, saying, This man, if he were a prophet, would have known who and what manner of woman *this is* that toucheth him; for she is a sinner. 40 And Jesus answering said unto him, Simon, I have somewhat to say unto thee. And he saith, Master, say on. 41 There was a certain creditor which had two debtors: the one owed five hundred pence, and the other fifty. 42 And when they had nothing to pay, he frankly forgave them both. Tell me therefore, which of them will love him most? 43 Simon answered and said, I suppose that *he*, to whom he forgave most. And he said unto him, Thou hast rightly judged. 44 And he turned to the woman, and said unto Simon, Seest thou this woman? I entered into thine house, thou gavest me no water for my feet: but she hath washed my feet with tears, and wiped *them* with the hairs of her head. 45 Thou gavest me no kiss: but this woman, since the time I came in, hath not ceased to kiss my feet. 46 My head with oil thou didst not anoint: but this woman hath anointed my feet with ointment. 47 Wherefore I say unto thee, Her sins, which are many, are forgiven; for she loved much: but to whom little is forgiven, *the same* loveth little. 48 And he said unto her, Thy sins are forgiven. 49 And they that sat at meat with him began to

N.A.S.

prophet? Yes, I say to you, and one who is more than a prophet. 27 "This is the one about whom it is written,

'BEHOLD, I SEND MY MESSENGER BEFORE YOUR FACE,
WHO WILL PREPARE YOUR WAY BEFORE YOU.'

28 "I say to you, among those born of women, there is no one greater than John; yet he who is least in the kingdom of God is greater than he." 29 And when all the people and the [a]tax-gatherers heard *this*, they acknowledged God's justice, having been baptized with the baptism of John. 30 But the Pharisees and the [b]lawyers rejected God's purpose for themselves, not having been baptized by John. 31 "To what then shall I compare the men of this generation, and what are they like? 32 "They are like children who sit in the market place and call to one another; and they say, 'We played the flute for you, and you did not dance; we sang a dirge, and you did not weep.' 33 "For John the Baptist has come eating no bread and drinking no wine; and you say, 'He has a demon!' 34 "The Son of Man has come eating and drinking; and you say, 'Behold, a gluttonous man, and a drunkard, a friend of tax-gatherers and sinners!' 35 "Yet wisdom is vindicated by all her children."

36 Now one of the Pharisees was requesting Him to dine with him. And He entered the Pharisee's house, and reclined *at table*. 37 And behold, there was a woman in the city who was a sinner; and when she learned that He was reclining *at table* in the Pharisee's house, she brought an alabaster vial of perfume, 38 and standing behind *Him* at His feet, weeping, she began to wet His feet with her tears, and kept wiping them with the hair of her head, and kissing His feet, and anointing them with the perfume. 39 Now when the Pharisee who had invited Him saw this, he said to himself, "If this man were a prophet He would know who and what sort of person this woman is who is touching Him, that she is a sinner." 40 And Jesus answered and said to him, "Simon, I have something to say to you." And he replied, "Say it, Teacher." 41 "A certain money-lender had two debtors: one owed five hundred [c]denarii, and the other fifty. 42 "When they were unable to repay, he graciously forgave them both. Which of them therefore will love him more?" 43 Simon answered and said, "I suppose the one whom he forgave more." And He said to him, "You have judged correctly." 44 And turning toward the woman, He said to Simon, "Do you see this woman? I entered your house; you gave Me no water for My feet, but she has wet My feet with her tears, and wiped them with her hair. 45 "You gave Me no kiss; but she, since the time I came in, has not ceased to kiss My feet. 46 "You did not anoint My head with oil, but she anointed My feet with perfume. 47 "For this reason I say to you, her sins, which are many, have been forgiven, for she loved much; but he who is forgiven little, loves little." 48 And He said to her, "Your sins have been forgiven." 49 And

[a] Publicans who collected Roman taxes on commission. [b] I.e., *experts on the Mosaic Law*. [c] The denarius was worth 18 cents in silver, equivalent to a day's wage.

WILLIAMS

in royal palaces. 26 If not, then what did you go out there to see? A prophet? Yes, I tell you, and one who is far more than a prophet. 27 This is the man of whom the Scripture says:

" 'Attention! I send my messenger on before you,
He will prepare the road ahead of you.'

28 "I tell you, of all men born of women there is not one greater than John; and yet the one who is of least importance in the kingdom of God is greater than he. 29 And all the people, even the tax-collectors, when they heard him, vindicated the righteous requirements of God by submitting to John's baptism, 30 but the Pharisees and experts in the law thwarted God's purpose for themselves by refusing to be baptized by him. 31 So to what can I compare the men of this age, and what are they like? 32 They are like little children sitting in the market-place and calling to their fellows in the game:

" 'We played the wedding march for you, but you did not dance;
We sang the funeral dirge, but you did not mourn.'

33 "For John the Baptist came eating no bread and drinking no wine, and yet you say, 'He has a demon!' 34 The Son of Man has come eating and drinking with others, and yet you say, 'Just look at Him! A glutton and a wine-drinker, an intimate friend of tax-collectors and notorious sinners!' 35 But wisdom is vindicated by all who are truly wise." c

36 Now one of the Pharisees invited Him to take dinner with him. So He came to the Pharisee's house and took His place at the table. 37 There was a woman in the town who was a social outcast,d and when she learned that He was taking dinner at the Pharisee's house, she brought an alabaster bottle of perfume 38 and took her stand behind Him at His feet, continually weeping. Then she began to wet His feet with her tears, but she continued to wipe them off with the hair of her head, and she kept right on kissing His feet with affection and anointing them with the perfume. 39 So when the Pharisee who invited Him saw it, he said to himself, "If He were really a prophet, He would know who and of what character the woman is who is clinging to Him—that she is a social outcast." 40 Then Jesus answered him, "Simon, I have something to say to you."

"Teacher," says he, "go on and say it."

41 "Two men were in debt to a money-lender. One owed him a hundred dollars, the other ten. 42 Since they could not pay him, he graciously canceled the debts for both of them. Now which one of them will love him more?" 43 Simon answered, "The one, I suppose, for whom he canceled most."

Then He said, "You are correct in your judgment." 44 And turning face to face with the woman He said to Simon, "Do you see this woman? I came to your house; you did not give me any water for my feet, but she has wet my feet with tears and wiped them with her hair. 45 You did not give me a kiss, but she, from the moment I came in, has not ceased to kiss my feet with affection. 46 You did not anoint my head with oil, but she anointed my feet with perfume. 47 Therefore, I tell you, her sins, as many as they are, are forgiven, for she has loved me so much. But the one who has little to be forgiven loves me little."

48 And He said to her, "Your sins are forgiven!"

49 The men at the table began to say to them-

[c] Grk., sons; i.e., like wisdom; truly wise. [d] Sinner; i.e., a scarlet woman; prostitute.

BECK

26 "What, then, did you go out to see—a prophet? Let Me assure you, far more than a prophet. 27 This is the one of whom it is written, 'I will send My messenger ahead of You to prepare Your way before46 you.' 28 I tell you, no woman's son is greater than John, and yet the least in God's kingdom is greater than he.

29 "By letting John baptize them, all the people who heard him, even the tax collectors, admitted that God was right. 30 But the Pharisees and the learned men of the Law, by not letting John baptize them, rejected what God had planned for them.

31 "How should I picture the people of this age? What are they like? 32 They're like little children sitting in the marketplace and calling to one another, 'We played a tune on the flute for you, but you didn't dance. We sang a funeral song, but you didn't weep.' 33 John the Baptizer has come; he doesn't eat bread or drink wine, and you say, 'There's a devil in him!' 34 The Son of Man has come; He eats and drinks, and you say, 'Look at the glutton and drunkard, the friend of tax collectors and sinners!' 35 And yet wisdom is shown to be right by all her children."

"She Loved Much"

36 One of the Pharisees invited Jesus to eat with him. He went into the Pharisee's home and lay down for the meal.

37 In the town there was a sinful woman. When she found out He was eating at the Pharisee's home, she brought a flask of perfume 38 and stood behind Him at His feet. She was weeping and started to wet His feet with her tears. Then with the hair of her head she dried His feet, kissed them, and poured perfume on them.

39 The Pharisee who had invited Jesus saw this and said to himself, "If He were a prophet, He would know who is touching Him and what kind of woman she is. She's a sinner."

40 "Simon," Jesus answered him, "I have something to tell you."

"Say it, Teacher," he said.

41 "Two men owed a moneylender some money: One owed him five hundred denarii, and the other fifty. 42 When they couldn't pay it back, he was kind enough to cancel the debt for both of them. Now, which of them will love him more?"

43 "I suppose," Simon answered, "the one who had the bigger debt canceled."

44 "You're right," Jesus told him. Then, turning to the woman, He said to Simon, "You see this woman? I came into your home, and you gave Me no water for my feet, but she wet My feet with her tears and dried them with her hair. 45 You gave Me no kiss, but ever since I came in, she hasn't stopped kissing My feet. 46 You poured no oil on My head, but she poured perfume on My feet. 47 That's why I tell you her sins are forgiven, many as they are. You see, she has loved much. Of course, he to whom little is forgiven loves only a little."

48 Then He said to her, "Your sins are forgiven." 49 His fellow guests began to ask among

[46] Ex. 23:20; Mal. 3:1

K.J.V.

say within themselves, Who is this that forgiveth sins also? 50And he said to the woman, Thy faith hath saved thee; go in peace.

8 And it came to pass afterward, that he went throughout every city and village, preaching and shewing the glad tidings of the kingdom of God: and the twelve *were* with him, 2And certain women, which had been healed of evil spirits and infirmities, Mary called Magdalene, out of whom went seven devils, 3And Joanna the wife of Chuza Herod's steward, and Susanna, and many others, which ministered unto him of their substance.

4 And when much people were gathered together, and were come to him out of every city, he spake by a parable: 5A sower went out to sow his seed: and as he sowed, some fell by the way side; and it was trodden down, and the fowls of the air devoured it. 6And some fell upon a rock; and as soon as it was sprung up, it withered away, because it lacked moisture. 7And some fell among thorns; and the thorns sprang up with it, and choked it. 8And other fell on good ground, and sprang up, and bare fruit a hundredfold. And when he had said these things, he cried, He that hath ears to hear, let him hear. 9And his disciples asked him, saying, What might this parable be? 10And he said, Unto you it is given to know the mysteries of the kingdom of God: but to others in parables; that seeing they might not see, and hearing they might not understand. 11 Now the parable is this: The seed is the word of God. 12 Those by the way side are they that hear; then cometh the devil, and taketh away the word out of their hearts, lest they should believe and be saved. 13 They on the rock *are they,* which, when they hear, receive the word with joy; and these have no root, which for a while believe, and in time of temptation fall away. 14And that which fell among thorns are they, which, when they have heard, go forth, and are choked with cares and riches and pleasures of *this* life, and bring no fruit to perfection. 15 But that on the good ground are they, which in an honest and good heart, having heard the word, keep *it,* and bring forth fruit with patience.

16 No man, when he hath lighted a candle, covereth it with a vessel, or putteth *it* under a bed; but setteth *it* on a candlestick, that they which enter in may see the light. 17 For nothing is secret, that shall not be made manifest; neither *any thing* hid, that shall not be known and come abroad. 18 Take heed therefore how ye hear: for whosoever hath, to him shall be

N.A.S.

those who were reclining *at table* with Him began to say to themselves, "Who is this *man* who even forgives sins?" 50And He said to the woman, "Your faith has saved you; go in peace."

8 And it came about soon afterwards, that He *began* going about from one city and village to another, proclaiming and preaching the kingdom of God; and the twelve were with Him, 2 and *also* some women who had been healed of evil spirits and sicknesses: Mary who was called Magdalene, from whom seven demons had gone out, 3 and Joanna the wife of Chuza, Herod's steward, and Susanna, and many others who were contributing to their support out of their private means.

4 And when a great multitude were coming together, and those from the various cities were journeying to Him, He spoke by way of a parable: 5 "The sower went out to sow his seed; and as he sowed, some fell beside the road; and it was trampled under foot, and the birds of the air devoured it. 6 "And other *seed* fell on rocky *soil,* and as soon as it grew up, it withered away, because it had no moisture. 7 "And other *seed* fell among the thorns; and the thorns grew up with it, and choked it out. 8 "And other *seed* fell into the good ground, and grew up, and produced a crop a hundred times as great." As He said these things, He would call out, "He who has ears to hear, let him hear."

9 And His disciples *began* questioning Him as to what this parable might be. 10And He said, "To you it is granted to know the mysteries of the kingdom of God, but to the rest in parables; in order that SEEING THEY MAY NOT SEE, AND HEARING THEY MAY NOT UNDERSTAND. 11 "Now the parable is this: the seed is the word of God. 12 "And those beside the road are those who have heard; then the devil comes and takes away the word from their heart, so that they may not believe and be saved. 13 "And those on the rocky *soil are* those who, when they hear, receive the word with joy; and these have no *firm* root; they believe for a while, and in time of temptation fall away. 14 "And the *seed* which fell among the thorns, these are the ones who have heard, and as they go on their way they are choked with worries and riches and pleasures of *this* life, and bring no fruit to maturity. 15 "And the *seed* in the good ground, these are the ones who have heard the word in an honest and good heart, and hold it fast, and bear fruit with perseverance.

16 "Now no one after lighting a lamp covers it over with a container, or puts it under a bed; but he puts it on a lampstand, in order that those who come in may see the light. 17 "For nothing is hidden that shall not become evident, nor *anything* secret that shall not be known and come to light. 18 "Therefore take care how you listen; for whoever has, to

WILLIAMS

selves, "Who is this man, who even forgives sins?"

50 But He said to the woman, "It is your faith that has saved you; go on in peace."

8 *Touring in Galilee; the story of the sower; stilling the storm; curing an insane man; curing a woman with a hemorrhage; raising Jairus' daughter*

Soon afterwards He chanced to be making a tour of Galilee from town to town and from village to village preaching and telling the good news of the kingdom of God. The Twelve went with Him, 2 and some women who had been cured of evil spirits and diseases: Mary, who was called Mary of Magdala, out of whom seven demons had gone, 3 and Joanna, the wife of Chuza, Herod's household manager, and Susanna, and many other women, who continued to contribute to their needs out of their personal means.

4 Now as a great crowd was coming together and people were coming to Him from one town after another, He said by way of a story:[a]

5 "A sower went out to sow his seed. As he was sowing, some of the seed fell along the path, and were trodden down, and the wild birds ate them up. 6Another portion of them fell upon the rock, and as soon as they sprang up, they withered, because they had no moisture. 7 Still another portion fell among the thorns, and the thorns grew up with them and choked them out. 8And another portion fell in rich soil and grew and yielded a crop of a hundredfold."

As He said this, He exclaimed, "Let him who has ears to hear with, listen!"

9 His disciples were asking Him what this story meant. 10 So He said, "You are granted the privilege of knowing the secrets of the kingdom of God, but to others they are told in stories, so that they may look and not see, may hear and not understand. 11 This is what the story means: The seed is God's message. 12 Those along the path illustrate those who hear it, but then the devil comes and carries off the message from their hearts, so that they may not believe it and be saved. 13 The portion of them on the rock illustrates those who accept the message, bubbling over with joy when they first hear it, but it takes no real root. They believe for awhile, but in the time of testing they fall away. 14And the portion of them falling among the thorns illustrates those who hear it, but as soon as they pass on they are choked out by the worries and wealth and pleasures of life, and thus yield no mature fruit. 15 But the portion in rich soil illustrates those who listen to the message, keep it in good and honest hearts, and in patience yield fruit.

16 "Nobody lights a lamp and then covers it with a pot[b] or puts it under a bed, but puts it on a lampstand, so that those who come in may see the light. 17 For there is nothing hidden which shall not come out into the open, and nothing kept secret which shall not be known and come to light. 18 So take care how you listen; for whoever gets more will have more given to him, and whoever does not get more

BECK

themselves, "Who is This that He should even forgive sins?"

50 Jesus said to the woman, "Your faith saved you. Go in peace!"

Through Galilee

8 After this Jesus traveled from one town and village to another, preaching and telling the good news of God's kingdom. The twelve were with Him. 2 Also some women who had been healed of evil spirits and diseases: Mary, also called the woman from Magdala (seven devils had gone out of her); 3 Johanna, the wife of Herod's manager Chusa; Susanna; and many other women. They supported Jesus and His disciples with their property.

The Sower

4 When a big crowd was gathering and people were coming to Him from every town, He told them a parable:

5 "A sower went out to sow his seed. As he was sowing, some seed fell along the road and was trampled on, and the birds in the air ate it. 6 Some fell on a rock. It came up and withered because it had no moisture. 7 Some seed fell among thorns, and the thorns grew up with it and choked it. 8 But some seed fell on good ground, and it came up and produced a hundred times as much as was sown."

When He had said this, He called out, "You have ears to hear. Then listen!"

9 His disciples asked Him what this parable meant. 10 "You are given the privilege to know the secrets of God's kingdom," He answered, "but to the others they come in parables that *they may see and yet not see, and hear and yet not understand.*[47]

11 "This is what the parable means: The seed is God's Word. 12 The people along the road are those who hear it. Then the devil comes and takes the Word out of their hearts to keep them from believing and being saved. 13 In others it falls on a rock. As soon as they hear it, they welcome the Word with joy, but it doesn't take root in them. They believe for a while, but when they're tempted, they desert. 14 In others the seed falls among thorns. They hear the Word, but as they go along, worries, riches, and pleasures of life choke them, and they don't produce anything good. 15 But in others the seed falls on good ground. They are the ones who hear the Word and keep it in a good and honest heart and go on faithfully producing good things.

16 "Nobody lights a lamp and hides it under a jar or puts it under a bed. No, you put it on a lampstand so that those who come in will see the light. 17 Everything hidden will be uncovered, and every secret will be known and come to the light.

18 "Be careful, then, how you listen! If you have something, you'll be given more. But if you

[a] Grk., *parable;* here a story from the fields.
[b] Grk., *vessel;* likely a pot or a pan.

[47] Is. 6:9

K.J.V.

given; and whosoever hath not, from him shall be taken even that which he seemeth to have.

19 Then came to him *his* mother and his brethren, and could not come at him for the press. 20And it was told him *by certain* which said, Thy mother and thy brethren stand without, desiring to see thee. 21And he answered and said unto them, My mother and my brethren are these which hear the word of God, and do it.

22 Now it came to pass on a certain day, that he went into a ship with his disciples: and he said unto them, Let us go over unto the other side of the lake. And they launched forth. 23 But as they sailed, he fell asleep: and there came down a storm of wind on the lake; and they were filled *with water*, and were in jeopardy. 24Aլd they came to him, and awoke him, saying, Master, Master, we perish. Then he arose, and rebuked the wind and the raging of the water: and they ceased, and there was a calm. 25And he said unto them, Where is your faith? And they being afraid wondered, saying one to another, What manner of man is this! for he commandeth even the winds and water, and they obey him.

26 And they arrived at the country of the Gadarenes, which is over against Galilee. 27And when he went forth to land, there met him out of the city a certain man, which had devils long time, and ware no clothes, neither abode in *any* house, but in the tombs. 28 When he saw Jesus, he cried out, and fell down before him, and with a loud voice said, What have I to do with thee, Jesus, *thou* Son of God most high? I beseech thee, torment me not. 29 (For he had commanded the unclean spirit to come out of the man. For oftentimes it had caught him: and he was kept bound with chains and in fetters; and he brake the bands, and was driven of the devil into the wilderness.) 30And Jesus asked him, saying, What is thy name? And he said, Legion: because many devils were entered into him. 31And they besought him that he would not command them to go out into the deep. 32And there was there a herd of many swine feeding on the mountain: and they besought him that he would suffer them to enter into them. And he suffered them. 33 Then went the devils out of the man, and entered into the swine: and the herd ran violently down a steep place into the lake, and were choked. 34 When they that fed *them* saw what was done, they fled, and went and told *it* in the city and in the country. 35 Then they went out to see what was done; and came to Jesus, and found the man, out of whom the devils were departed, sitting at the feet of Jesus, clothed, and in his right mind: and they were afraid. 36 They also which saw *it* told them by what means he that was possessed of the devils was healed.

37 Then the whole multitude of the country of the Gadarenes round about besought him to depart from them; for they were taken with great fear: and he went up into the ship, and returned back again. 38 Now the man, out of whom the devils were departed, besought him that he might be with him: but Jesus sent him away, saying, 39 Return to thine own house, and shew how great things God hath done unto thee. And he went his way, and published throughout the whole city how great things Je-

N.A.S.

him shall *more* be given; and whoever does not have, even what he thinks he has shall be taken away from him."

19 And His mother came to Him and *His* brothers *also,* and they were unable to get to Him because of the crowd. 20And it was reported to Him, "Your mother and Your brothers are standing outside, wishing to see You." 21 But He answered and said to them, "My mother and My brothers are these who hear the word of God and do it."

22 Now it came about on one of *those* days, that He got into a boat, He and His disciples, and said to them, "Let us go over to the other side of the lake." And they launched out. 23 But as they were sailing along He fell asleep; and a fierce gale of wind descended upon the lake, and they *began* to be swamped and to be in danger. 24And they came to Him, and woke Him up, saying, "Master, Master, we are perishing!" And being aroused, He rebuked the wind and the surging waves, and they stopped, and it became calm. 25And He said to them, "Where is your faith?" And they were fearful and amazed, saying to one another, "Who then is this, that He commands even the winds and the water, and they obey Him?"

26 And they sailed to the country of the Gerasenes, which is opposite Galilee. 27And when He had come out onto the land, a certain man from the city met Him who was possessed with demons; and who had not put on any clothing for a long time, and was not living in a house, but in the tombs. 28And seeing Jesus, he cried out and fell down before Him, and said in a loud voice, "What do I have to do with You, Jesus, Son of the Most High God? I beg You, do not torment me." 29 For He had been commanding the unclean spirit to come out of the man. For it had seized him many times; and he was bound with chains and shackles and kept under guard; and *yet* he would burst his fetters and be driven by the demon into the deserts. 30And Jesus asked him, "What is your name?" And he said, "Legion"; for many demons had entered him. 31And they were entreating Him not to command them to depart into the abyss. 32 Now there was a herd of many swine feeding there on the mountain; and *the demons* entreated Him to permit them to enter the swine. And He gave them permission. 33And the demons came out from the man and entered the swine; and the herd rushed down the steep bank into the lake, and were drowned. 34And when those who tended them saw what had happened, they ran away and reported it in the city and *out* in the country. 35And *the people* went out to see what had happened; and they came to Jesus, and found the man from whom the demons had gone out, sitting down at the feet of Jesus, clothed and in his right mind; and they became frightened. 36And those who had seen it reported to them how the man who was demon-possessed had been made well. 37And all the people of the country of the Gerasenes and the surrounding district asked Him to depart from them; for they were gripped with great fear; and He got into a boat, and returned. 38 But the man from whom the demons had gone out was begging Him that he might accompany Him; but He sent him away, saying, 39 "Return to your house and describe what great things God has done for you." And he departed, proclaiming throughout the whole city what great things Jesus had done for him.

WILLIAMS

will have even what he thinks he has taken away from him."

19 His mother and His brothers came to see Him, but they could not get in touch with Him, on account of the crowd. 20 So it was reported to Him, "Your mother and your brothers are standing outside; they want to see you."

21 Then He answered them, "My mother and my brothers are those who listen to God's message and practice it."

22 One day He got into a boat with His disciples, and He said to them, "Let us cross to the other side of the lake."

So they set sail. 23 Now as they were sailing along, He fell off to sleep. But a furious squall of wind rushed down upon the lake, and they were filling up and were in impending peril. 24 So they came to Him and woke Him up, and said, "Master, Master, we are perishing!" Then He aroused Himself and reproved the wind and the surge of the water, and they stopped at once, and instantly there came a calm.

25 Then He said to them, "Where is your faith?"

But they were frightened and astounded, and continued to say to one another, "Who can He be? For He gives orders even to the winds and the water, and they obey Him."

26 They landed in the neighborhood of Gerasa, which is just across the lake from Galilee. 27 As soon as He stepped out upon the shore, there met Him a man from town, who was under the power of demons; and for a long time he had worn no clothes, and did not stay in a house but in tombs. 28 When he saw Jesus, he screamed and flung himself down before Him, and said in a loud voice, "What do you want of me, Jesus, Son of the Most High God? I beg you not to torture me!" 29 For He was commanding the foul spirit to get out of the man. For on many occasions it had seized him, and repeatedly he had been fastened with chains and fetters under constant guard, and yet he would snap his bonds, and the demon would drive him into desert places.

30 So Jesus asked him, "What is your name?" And he answered, "Legion!" For many demons had gone into him. 31 Then they continued to beg Him not to order them to go off to the bottomless pit.[c] 32 Now there was a large drove of hogs feeding there on the hillside. So they begged Him to let them go into those hogs. And He let them do so. 33 Then the demons came out of the man and went into the hogs, and the drove rushed over the cliff into the lake and were drowned. 34 When the men who fed them saw what had taken place, they fled and spread the news in the town and in the country around. 35 So the people went out to see what had taken place, and they went to Jesus and found the man out of whom the demons had gone sitting at the feet of Jesus, with his clothes on and in his right mind; and they were frightened. 36 Then they who had seen it told them how the man who had been under the power of demons was cured. 37 Then all the inhabitants of the country around Gerasa asked Him to go away from them, because they were terribly frightened. So He got into a boat and went back.

38 The man out of whom the demons had gone begged Him to let him go with Him, but Jesus sent him away and said, 39 "Go back to your home, and continue to tell what great things God has done for you." But he went off and told all over the town what great things Jesus had done for him.

BECK

don't have what you should have, even what you think you have will be taken away from you."

The Mother and Brothers of Jesus

19 His mother and His brothers came to Him but couldn't get near Him on account of the crowd. 20 Jesus was told, "Your mother and Your brothers are standing outside and want to see You."

21 "My mother and My brothers are these," He answered them, "who hear and do what God says."

Wind and Water Obey Him

22 One day He and His disciples stepped into a boat. "Let us cross over to the other side of the lake," He said to them. 23 They started out. And as they were sailing along, He fell asleep.

A violent storm hit the lake, the boat was filling with water, and they were in danger. 24 So they went to Him and woke Him up. "Master, Master!" they called, "we're drowning."

He got up and ordered the winds and the waves to stop. They stopped and it became calm. 25 "Where is your trust?" He asked them.

Frightened and amazed, they asked one another, "Who is He? He orders even the winds and the water, and they obey Him!"

The Gerasenes

26 They landed in the country of the Gerasenes, which is opposite Galilee. 27 When He stepped out on the shore, a man from the town who had devils in him met Him. He had worn no clothes for a long time. He wouldn't stay in a house but in the burial places. 28 When he saw Jesus, he screamed and bowed down before Him. "Let me alone, Jesus, Son of the most high God," he shouted. "I beg you, don't torture me." 29 Jesus had been ordering the unclean spirit to come out of the man. For a long time it had a firm hold on him. He had been bound with chains on hands and feet and had been kept under guard, but he would tear the chains and be driven by the devil into lonely places.

30 "What is your name?" Jesus asked him.

"Six thousand," he answered, because many devils had gone into him. 31 They begged Him not to order them to go into the bottomless pit.

32 There was a herd of many hogs feeding on the hillside. So they begged Him to let them go into these. He let them. 33 The devils came out of the man and went into the hogs, and the herd stampeded down the cliff into the lake and was drowned.

34 But when those who had taken care of the hogs saw what had happened, they ran away and told about it in the town and in the country. 35 The people went out to see what had happened. They came to Jesus and found the man from whom the devils had gone out, now sitting dressed and in his right mind at Jesus' feet; and they were frightened. 36 Those who had seen it told them how the man plagued by devils had been made well.

37 Then all the people of the surrounding country of the Gerasenes asked Jesus to leave them, because terror had gripped them.

He got into a boat and started back. 38 Now, the man from whom the devils had gone out begged Jesus to let him be with Him. But He sent him away and told him, 39 "Go home and tell how much God has done for you." So the man left and preached all over the town how much Jesus had done for him.

[c] *Abyss* in Grk.

K.J.V.

sus had done unto him. 40And it came to pass, that, when Jesus was returned, the people *gladly* received him: for they were all waiting for him. 41 And, behold, there came a man named Jairus, and he was a ruler of the synagogue; and he fell down at Jesus' feet, and besought him that he would come into his house: 42 For he had one only daughter, about twelve years of age, and she lay a dying. But as he went the people thronged him. 43 And a woman having an issue of blood twelve years, which had spent all her living upon physicians, neither could be healed of any, 44 Came behind *him,* and touched the border of his garment: and immediately her issue of blood stanched. 45And Jesus said, Who touched me? When all denied, Peter and they that were with him said, Master, the multitude throng thee and press *thee,* and sayest thou, Who touched me? 46And Jesus said, Somebody hath touched me: for I perceive that virtue is gone out of me. 47And when the woman saw that she was not hid, she came trembling, and falling down before him, she declared unto him before all the people for what cause she had touched him, and how she was healed immediately. 48And he said unto her, Daughter, be of good comfort: thy faith hath made thee whole; go in peace.

49 While he yet spake, there cometh one from the ruler of the synagogue's *house,* saying to him, Thy daughter is dead; trouble not the Master. 50 But when Jesus heard *it,* he answered him, saying, Fear not: believe only, and she shall be made whole. 51And when he came into the house, he suffered no man to go in, save Peter, and James, and John, and the father and the mother of the maiden. 52And all wept, and bewailed her: but he said, Weep not; she is not dead, but sleepeth. 53And they laughed him to scorn, knowing that she was dead. 54And he put them all out, and took her by the hand, and called, saying, Maid, arise. 55And her spirit came again, and she arose straightway: and he commanded to give her meat. 56And her parents were astonished: but he charged them that they should tell no man what was done.

9 Then he called his twelve disciples together, and gave them power and authority over all devils, and to cure diseases. 2And he sent them to preach the kingdom of God, and to heal the sick. 3And he said unto them, Take nothing for *your* journey, neither staves, nor scrip, neither bread, neither money; neither have two coats apiece. 4And whatsoever house ye enter into, there abide, and thence depart. 5And whosoever will not receive you, when ye go out of that city, shake off the very dust from your feet for a testimony against them. 6And they departed, and went through the towns, preaching the gospel, and healing every where.

7 Now Herod the tetrarch heard of all that was done by him: and he was perplexed, because that it was said of some, that John was risen from the dead; 8And of some, that Elias had appeared; and of others, that one of the old

N.A.S.

40 And as Jesus returned, the multitude welcomed Him, for they had all been waiting for Him. 41And behold, there came a man named Jairus, and he was an official of the synagogue; and he fell at Jesus' feet, and *began* to entreat Him to come to his house; 42 for he had an only daughter, about twelve years old, and she was dying. But as He went, the multitudes were pressing against Him.

43 And a woman who had a hemorrhage for twelve years, ªand could not be healed by anyone, 44 came up behind Him, and touched the fringe of His cloak; and immediately her hemorrhage stopped. 45And Jesus said, "Who is the one who touched Me?" And while they were all denying it, Peter said, "Master, the multitudes are crowding and pressing upon You." 46 But Jesus said, "Someone did touch Me, for I was aware that power had gone out of Me." 47And when the woman saw that she had not escaped notice, she came trembling and fell down before Him, and declared in the presence of all the people the reason why she had touched Him, and how she had been immediately healed. 48And He said to her, "Daughter, your faith has made you well; go in peace."

49 While He was still speaking, someone *came from *the house of* the synagogue official, saying, "Your daughter has died; do not trouble the Teacher any more." 50 But when Jesus heard *this,* He answered him, "Do not be afraid *any longer;* only believe, and she shall be made well." 51And when He had come to the house, He did not allow anyone to enter with Him, except Peter, John and James, and the girl's father and mother. 52 Now they were all weeping and lamenting for her; but He said, "Stop weeping, for she has not died, but is asleep." 53And they *began* laughing at Him, knowing that she had died. 54 He, however, took her by the hand and called, saying, "Child, arise!" 55And her spirit returned, and she rose up immediately; and He gave orders for *something* to be given her to eat. 56And her parents were amazed; but He instructed them to tell no one what had happened.

9 And He called the twelve together, and gave them power and authority over all the demons, and to heal diseases. 2And He sent them out to proclaim the kingdom of God, and to perform healing. 3And He said to them, "Take nothing for *your* journey, neither a staff, nor a bag, nor bread, nor money; and do not *even* have two tunics apiece. 4 "And whatever house you enter, stay there, and take your leave from there. 5 "And as for those who do not receive you, when you depart from that city, shake off the dust from your feet as a testimony against them." 6And departing, they *began* going about among the villages, preaching the gospel, and healing everywhere.

7 Now Herod the tetrarch heard of all that was happening; and he was greatly perplexed, because it was said by some that John had risen from the dead, 8 and by some that Elijah had appeared, and by others, that one of the

[a] Some mss. add, *who had spent all her living upon physicians.*

WILLIAMS

40 Now as Jesus was returning, the crowd welcomed Him, for they were all expecting Him. 41 Just then a man named Jairus came up, who had long been leader of the synagogue. He fell down at Jesus' feet and persisted in begging Him to come to his house, 42 because his only daughter, about twelve years old, was dying. While He was going, the crowds of people continued to press upon Him. 43 Then a woman who had had a hemorrhage for twelve years, who could not be cured by anybody, 44 came up behind Him and touched the tassel on His coat, and the hemorrhage stopped at once. 45 Then Jesus said, "Who was it that touched me?"

But as all were denying that they had done so, Peter said, "Master, the crowds are jamming you and jostling you."

46 Still Jesus said, "Somebody touched me, for I felt it when the power passed from me."

47 When the woman saw that she had not escaped His notice, she came forward trembling, and falling down before Him she told in the presence of all the people why she had touched Him and how she had been cured at once. 48 So He said to her, "My daughter, it is your faith that has cured you; go on in peace."

49 While He was still speaking, someone came from the house of the leader of the synagogue and said, "Your daughter is dead; stop troubling the Teacher any more." [d]

50 But Jesus heard it and said to him, "Do not be afraid; just have faith, and she will get well."

51 When He reached the house, He let no one go in with Him but Peter, James, and John, and the child's father and mother. 52 Now they were all weeping and wailing over her. But He said, "Stop weeping! For she is not dead but asleep." 53 Then they began to laugh in His face, for they knew that she was dead. 54 But He grasped her hand and called out, "My child, get up!" 55 So her spirit returned and she got up at once, and He directed that something be given her to eat. 56 And her parents were astounded, but He ordered them not to tell anyone what had taken place.

9 The Twelve touring Galilee; Governor Antipas in dread of Jesus; Peter confesses Jesus as the Christ; how to save the higher life; Jesus transfigured; an epileptic boy cured, etc.

Then He called the Twelve together and gave them power and authority over all the demons, and to cure diseases, 2 and then He sent them out to preach the kingdom of God and to cure the sick. 3 So He said to them, "Take nothing with you for your journey, no staff, no bag, no bread, no money, nor even have two shirts. 4 Into whatever house you go, stay there and continue to go out from it as headquarters. 5 And when you leave that city, shake off the very dust from your feet as a protest against all the people who do not welcome you." 6 And so they set out and went from village to village, telling the good news and curing people everywhere.

7 Now Herod the governor heard of all that was taking place, and he continued to be puzzled over the reports—by some that John had risen from the dead, 8 by others that Elijah had appeared, and by still others that one of the

[d] Fol. WH text and Vat., Sin. Mss.

BECK

The Daughter of Jairus

40 When Jesus came back, the people welcomed Him, because they were all expecting Him.

41 A synagog leader by the name of Jairus came and, kneeling at Jesus' feet, begged Him to come to his home, 42 because his only daughter, about twelve years old, was dying. As he went, the crowd almost crushed Him.

43 There was a woman who had a flow of blood for twelve years. Nobody could cure her. 44 She came to Him from behind and touched the tassel of His garment, and immediately her blood stopped flowing.

45 "Who touched Me?" Jesus asked.

When everybody denied having touched Him, Peter said, "Master, the people are crowding You and pressing against You."

46 "Somebody did touch Me," Jesus said. "I noticed that power went from Me."

47 When the woman saw she was discovered, she came trembling, bowed down before Him, and in front of all the people told why she touched Him and how she was made well immediately.

48 "Daughter," He told her, "your faith made you well. Go in peace!"

49 While He was still speaking, someone came from the synagog leader. "Your daughter is dead," he said. "Don't trouble the Teacher any more."

50 Hearing this, Jesus told him, "Don't be afraid! Only believe, and she'll get well."

51 Coming into the house, He let only Peter, John, James, and the child's father and mother go in with him. 52 Everybody was crying and beating the breast, mourning her. "Don't cry," He said. "She isn't dead; she's sleeping."

53 They laughed at Him, because they knew she had died. 54 He took her hand and called, "Girl, wake up!" 55 Her spirit returned, and she got up immediately. Jesus ordered that she be given something to eat. 56 And her parents were amazed. But He ordered them not to tell anyone what had happened.

Jesus Sends Out the Twelve

9 Jesus called the twelve together and gave them power and authority over all devils and to heal diseases. 2 He sent them to preach God's kingdom and heal the sick.

3 "Don't take anything with you on the way," He told them, "no stick or bag or bread or money. Don't take two tunics. 4 When you go into a home, stay there, and from there go out. 5 If people don't welcome you, leave that town, and shake the dust off your feet as a warning to them."

6 They left and went from village to village, telling the good news everywhere and healing the sick.

Has John Come Back?

7 Herod, the governor, heard about everything Jesus was doing and didn't know what to make of it, because some people said, "John has risen from the dead"; 8 others, "Elijah has appeared"; still others, "One of the old prophets has risen."

K.J.V.

prophets was risen again. 9And Herod said, John have I beheaded; but who is this, of whom I hear such things? And he desired to see him.

10 And the apostles, when they were returned, told him all that they had done. And he took them, and went aside privately into a desert place belonging to the city called Bethsaida. 11And the people, when they knew it, followed him: and he received them, and spake unto them of the kingdom of God, and healed them that had need of healing. 12And when the day began to wear away, then came the twelve, and said unto him, Send the multitude away, that they may go into the towns and country round about, and lodge, and get victuals: for we are here in a desert place. 13 But he said unto them, Give ye them to eat. And they said, We have no more but five loaves and two fishes; except we should go and buy meat for all this people. 14 For they were about five thousand men. And he said to his disciples, Make them sit down by fifties in a company. 15And they did so, and made them all sit down. 16 Then he took the five loaves and the two fishes, and looking up to heaven, he blessed them, and brake, and gave to the disciples to set before the multitude. 17And they did eat, and were all filled: and there was taken up of fragments that remained to them twelve baskets.

18 And it came to pass, as he was alone praying, his disciples were with him; and he asked them, saying, Whom say the people that I am? 19 They answering said, John the Baptist; but some say, Elias; and others say, that one of the old prophets is risen again. 20 He said unto them, But whom say ye that I am? Peter answering said, The Christ of God. 21And he straitly charged them, and commanded them to tell no man that thing; 22 Saying, The Son of man must suffer many things, and be rejected of the elders and chief priests and scribes, and be slain, and be raised the third day.

23 And he said to them all, If any man will come after me, let him deny himself, and take up his cross daily, and follow me. 24 For whosoever will save his life shall lose it: but whosoever will lose his life for my sake, the same shall save it. 25 For what is a man advantaged, if he gain the whole world, and lose himself, or be cast away? 26 For whosoever shall be ashamed of me and of my words, of him shall the Son of man be ashamed, when he shall come in his own glory, and in his Father's, and of the holy angels. 27 But I tell you of a truth, there be some standing here, which shall not taste of death, till they see the kingdom of God.

28 And it came to pass about an eight days after these sayings, he took Peter and John and James, and went up into a mountain to pray. 29And as he prayed, the fashion of his countenance was altered, and his raiment was white and glistering. 30And, behold, there talked with him two men, which were Moses and Elias: 31 Who appeared in glory, and spake of his decease which he should accomplish at Jeru-

N.A.S.

prophets of old had risen again. 9And Herod said, "I myself had John beheaded; but who is this man about whom I hear such things?" And he kept trying to see Him.

10 And when the apostles returned, they gave an account to Him of all that they had done. And taking them with Him, He withdrew privately to a city called Bethsaida. 11 But the multitudes were aware of this and followed Him; and welcoming them, He began speaking to them about the kingdom of God and curing those who had need of healing. 12And the day began to decline, and the twelve came and said to Him, "Send the multitude away, that they may go into the surrounding villages and countryside and find lodging and get something to eat; for here we are in a desolate place." 13 But He said to them, "You give them something to eat!" And they said, "We have no more than five loaves and two fish, unless perhaps we go and buy food for all these people." 14 (For there were about five thousand men). And He said to His disciples, "Have them recline to eat in groups of about fifty each." 15And they did so, and had them all recline. 16And He took the five loaves and the two fish, and looking up to heaven, He blessed them, and broke them, and kept giving them to the disciples to set before the multitude. 17And they all ate and were satisfied; and that which was left over to them of the broken pieces was picked up, twelve baskets full.

18 And it came about that while He was praying alone, the disciples were with Him, and He questioned them, saying, "Who do the multitudes say that I am?" 19And they answered and said, "John the Baptist; but others say, Elijah; and others, that one of the prophets of old has risen again." 20And He said to them, "But who do you say that I am?" And Peter answered and said, "The Christ of God." 21 But He warned them, and instructed them not to tell this to anyone, 22 saying, "The Son of Man must suffer many things, and be rejected by the elders and chief priests and scribes, and be killed, and be raised up on the third day." 23And He was saying to them all, "If anyone wishes to come after Me, let him deny himself, and take up his cross daily, and follow Me. 24 "For whoever wishes to save his life shall lose it, but whoever loses his life for My sake, he is the one who will save it. 25 "For what is a man profited if he gains the whole world, and loses or forfeits himself? 26 "For whoever is ashamed of Me and My words, of him will the Son of Man be ashamed when He comes in His glory, and the glory of the Father and of the holy angels. 27 "But I tell you truly, there are some of those standing here who shall not taste death until they see the kingdom of God."

28 And some eight days after these sayings, it came about that He took along Peter and John and James, and went up to the mountain to pray. 29And while He was praying, the appearance of His face became different, and His clothing became white and gleaming. 30And behold, two men were talking with Him; and they were Moses and Elijah, 31 who, appearing in glory, were speaking of His departure which He was about to accomplish at Jerusalem.

WILLIAMS

ancient prophets had come back to life. 9 So Herod said, "John I beheaded, but who can this be about whom I hear such reports?" So he was trying to see Him.

10 Now the apostles returned and told Jesus all that they had done. Then He took them and privately retired to a town called Bethsaida. 11 But the crowds learned of it, and followed Him; and He welcomed them and began to speak to them about the kingdom of God and to cure the people who needed to be cured. 12 As the day began to decline, the Twelve came up and said to Him, "Send the crowd off to the villages and farms around, to get lodging and to find food there, for we are in a destitute place here."

13 But He said to them, "Give them something to eat yourselves."

Then they said, "We have only five loaves and two fish, unless we go ourselves and buy food for all these people." 14 For there were about five thousand men.

So He said to His disciples, "Have them sit down in reclining groups of about fifty each." 15 And they did so, and made all the people sit down and recline. 16 Then He took the five loaves and two fish and looked up to heaven and blessed them, and He broke them in pieces and gave them to the disciples to pass on to the people. 17 And they all ate and had a plenty, and what they had left over was taken up, twelve baskets of broken pieces.

18 One day while He was praying in solitude, His disciples were near by, and He asked them, "Who do people say that I am?"

19 They answered, "John the Baptist; though others say Elijah, and still others that one of the ancient prophets has come back to life."

20 So He said to them, "But who do you, yourselves, say that I am?"

Peter answered, "The Christ of God!"

21 But He particularly warned, yea, even commanded, them not to tell this to anybody, 22 as He said, "The Son of Man has to endure great suffering and be disowned by the elders, the high priests, and the scribes, and be put to death but be raised to life on the third day."

23 Then He said to them all, "If anyone chooses to be my disciple, he must say 'No' to self, put the cross on his shoulders daily, and continue to follow me. 24 For whoever chooses to save his lower life will lose his higher life, but whoever gives up his lower life for my sake will save his higher life. 25 For what benefit will it be to a man to gain the whole world and lose or forfeit himself? 26 For whoever is ashamed of me and my teaching, the Son of Man will be ashamed of him, when He comes back in all the splendor of His Father and of the holy angels. 27 I solemnly say to you, some of you who stand here will certainly live[a] to see the kingdom of God."

28 Now about eight days after Jesus said this, He took Peter, John, and James, and went up on the mountain to pray. 29 And while He was praying, the look on His face changed, and His clothes turned dazzling white. 30 And two men were talking with Him. They were Moses and Elijah, 31 who appeared in splendor and were speaking of His departure which He was about to accomplish at Jerusalem.

BECK

9 "I cut off John's head," Herod said. "Now who is this about whom I hear such things?" And he wanted to see Jesus.

Jesus Feeds Five Thousand

10 The apostles came back and told Jesus all they had done. He took them away with Him near a town called Bethsaida in order to be alone. 11 But the crowds found out about it and followed Him. He welcomed them, talked to them about God's kingdom, and healed those who needed healing.

12 Toward the end of the day the twelve came to Him and told Him, "Send the crowd away to the villages and farms around us to get shelter and find food. We're here in a deserted place."

13 "You give them something to eat," He told them.

"All we have is five loaves and two fish," they answered, "unless perhaps we go and buy food for all these people." 14 There were about five thousand men.

Then He told His disciples, "Have them sit down in groups of about fifty." 15 They did this and got them all seated.

16 He took the five loaves and the two fish, looked up to heaven, blessed them and broke them, and gave them to the disciples to give to the people. 17 All of them ate and had a hearty meal. And they picked up the pieces that were left—twelve baskets full.

"You Are the Promised Savior"

18 Once when He was praying and only His disciples were with Him, He asked them, "Who do people say I am?"

19 "John the Baptizer," they answered Him; "others say Elijah, and still others that one of the old prophets has come back to life."

20 "And you," He asked them, "who do you say I am?"

"The Savior whom God has sent," Peter answered.

21 But he gave them strict orders not to tell anyone about this.

Take the Cross

22 "The Son of Man has to suffer much," He said, "be rejected by the elders, ruling priests, and Bible scholars, be killed, and then rise on the third day."

23 And He told all of them, "If you want to follow Me, deny yourself, take up your cross every day, and come with Me. 24 If you want to save your life, you will lose it. But if you will lose your life for Me, you will save it. 25 What good does it do you to win the whole world and destroy or lose yourself? 26 If you're ashamed of Me and what I say, then the Son of Man will be ashamed of you when He comes in His glory and the glory of the Father and the holy angels.

27 "Let me assure you, there are some standing here who will never taste death till they see God's kingdom."

Jesus Shows His Glory

28 About a week after He said this, Jesus took Peter, James, and John with Him and went up the mountain to pray. 29 While He was praying, His face changed and looked different, and His clothes got dazzling white. 30 And there were two men talking with Him; they were Moses and Elijah. 31 They appeared in glory and were talking about His leaving this world, which was to happen at Jerusalem.

[a] Grk., *will not taste of death, until,* etc.

K.J.V.

salem. 32 But Peter and they that were with him were heavy with sleep: and when they were awake, they saw his glory, and the two men that stood with him. 33And it came to pass, as they departed from him, Peter said unto Jesus, Master, it is good for us to be here: and let us make three tabernacles; one for thee, and one for Moses, and one for Elias: not knowing what he said. 34 While he thus spake, there came a cloud, and overshadowed them: and they feared as they entered into the cloud. 35And there came a voice out of the cloud, saying, This is my beloved Son: hear him. 36And when the voice was past, Jesus was found alone. And they kept *it* close, and told no man in those days any of those things which they had seen.

37 And it came to pass, that on the next day, when they were come down from the hill, much people met him. 38And, behold, a man of the company cried out, saying, Master, I beseech thee, look upon my son; for he is mine only child. 39And, lo, a spirit taketh him, and he suddenly crieth out; and it teareth him that he foameth again, and bruising him, hardly departeth from him. 40And I besought thy disciples to cast him out; and they could not. 41And Jesus answering said, O faithless and perverse generation, how long shall I be with you, and suffer you? Bring thy son hither. 42And as he was yet a coming, the devil threw him down, and tare *him*. And Jesus rebuked the unclean spirit, and healed the child, and delivered him again to his father.

43 And they were all amazed at the mighty power of God. But while they wondered every one at all things which Jesus did, he said unto his disciples, 44 Let these sayings sink down into your ears: for the Son of man shall be delivered into the hands of men. 45 But they understood not this saying, and it was hid from them, that they perceived it not: and they feared to ask him of that saying.

46 Then there arose a reasoning among them, which of them should be greatest. 47And Jesus, perceiving the thought of their heart, took a child, and set him by him, 48And said unto them, Whosoever shall receive this child in my name receiveth me; and whosoever shall receive me, receiveth him that sent me: for he that is least among you all, the same shall be great.

49 And John answered and said, Master, we saw one casting out devils in thy name; and we forbade him, because he followeth not with us. 50And Jesus said unto him, Forbid *him* not: for he that is not against us is for us.

51 And it came to pass, when the time was come that he should be received up, he steadfastly set his face to go to Jerusalem, 52And sent messengers before his face: and they went, and entered into a village of the Samaritans, to make ready for him. 53And they did not receive him,

N.A.S.

32 Now Peter and his companions had been overcome with sleep; but when they were fully awake, they saw His glory and the two men standing with Him. 33And it came about, as these were parting from Him, Peter said to Jesus, "Master, it is good for us to be here; and let us make three tabernacles: one for You, and one for Moses, and one for Elijah"— not realizing what he was saying. 34And while he was saying this, a cloud formed and *began* to overshadow them; and they were afraid as they entered the cloud. 35And a voice came out of the cloud, saying, "This is My Son, *My Chosen One;* listen to Him!" 36And when the voice had spoken, Jesus was found alone. And they kept silent, and reported to no one in those days any of the things which they had seen.

37 And it came about on the next day, that when they had come down from the mountain, a great multitude met Him. 38And behold, a man from the multitude shouted out, saying, "Teacher, I beg You to look at my son, for he is my only *boy,* 39 and behold, a spirit seizes him, and he suddenly screams, and it throws him into a convulsion with foaming *at the mouth,* and as it mauls him, it scarcely leaves him. 40 And I begged Your disciples to cast it out, and they could not." 41And Jesus answered and said, "O unbelieving and perverted generation, how long shall I be with you, and put up with you? Bring your son here." 42And while he was still approaching, the demon dashed him *to the ground,* and threw him into a violent convulsion. But Jesus rebuked the unclean spirit, and healed the boy, and gave him back to his father. 43And they were all amazed at the greatness of God.

But while everyone was marveling at all that He was doing, He said to His disciples, 44 "Let these words sink into your ears; for the Son of Man is going to be delivered into the hands of men." 45 But they did not understand this statement, and it was concealed from them so that they might not perceive it; and they were afraid to ask Him about this statement.

46 And an argument arose among them as to which of them might be the greatest. 47 But Jesus, knowing what they were thinking in their heart, took a child and stood him by His side, 48 and said to them, "Whoever receives this child in My name receives Me; and whoever receives Me receives Him who sent Me; for he who is least among you, this is the one who is great."

49 And John answered and said, "Master, we saw someone casting out demons in Your name; and we tried to hinder him because he does not follow along with us." 50 But Jesus said to him, "Do not hinder *him;* for he who is not against you is for you."

51 And it came about, when the days were approaching for His ascension, that He resolutely set His face to go to Jerusalem; 52 and He sent messengers on ahead of Him. And they went, and entered a village of the Samaritans, to make arrangements for Him. 53And they did

WILLIAMS

32 Now Peter and his companions had been overcome by sleep, but all at once they became wide awake and saw His splendor and the two men who were standing with Him. 33 And just as they were starting to leave Him, Peter said to Jesus, "Master, it is good for us to be here. Let us put up three tents, one for you, one for Moses, and one for Elijah"—although he did not know what he was saying. 34 But as he was saying this, a cloud came and was circling over them, and they were frightened as the two visitors entered into the cloud.

35 Then a voice came out of the cloud and said, "This is my Son, my Chosen One; continue to listen to Him!"

36 When the voice had ceased, Jesus was found to be alone. And they kept silence and told no one anything that they had seen at that time.

37 The next day, when they had come down from the mountain, a great crowd met Him. 38 Then a man in the crowd at once shouted, "Teacher, I beg you to look at my son, because he is my only child; 39 all at once a spirit seizes him, and he suddenly screams, and convulses him until he foams at the mouth, and in a struggle it bruises him and then leaves him. 40 I begged your disciples to drive it out, but they could not."

41 Then Jesus answered, "O you unbelieving, stubborn people of the times! How long must I be with you and put up with you? Bring him here to me." 42 Even while the boy was coming to Him, the demon dashed him down and convulsed him, but Jesus reproved the foul spirit and cured the boy and gave him back to his father. 43 So they all continued to be utterly astounded at the greatness of God.

Now while everybody was wondering at all that He was doing, He said to His disciples, 44 "You must store away in your memories these words, for the Son of Man is going to be turned over to the hands of men!" 45 But they remained ignorant of what this meant; indeed, it had been hidden from them, so that they did not grasp it, and they were afraid to ask Him about this statement.

46 Now a controversy sprang up among them as to which of them might be the greatest. 47 But Jesus, as He knew that the controversy was going on in their hearts, took a little child and had it stand by His side. 48 Then He said to them, "Whoever welcomes this little child on my account is welcoming me, and whoever welcomes me is welcoming Him who sent me; for the one who is lowliest among you all is really great."

49 Then John answered, "Master, we saw a man driving out demons by the use[b] of your name, and we tried to stop him, because he does not belong to our followers."

50 Jesus said to him, "Stop hindering him, for the man who is not against you is for you."

51 Now as the time was coming to a head[c] when He should be taken up to heaven, He firmly set His face to continue His journey to Jerusalem; 52 so He sent messengers before Him. Then they went on and entered into a Samaritan town, to make preparations for Him. 53 But

BECK

32 But Peter and the men with him had been overcome by sleep. Waking up, they saw His glory and the two men standing with Him. 33 When these were leaving Him, Peter said to Jesus, "Master, it's good for us to be here. Let's put up three shelters, one for You, one for Moses, and one for Elijah." He didn't know what he was saying.

34 While he was saying this, a cloud came and overshadowed them. They were frightened as they went into the cloud. 35 Then a voice came out of the cloud: "This is *My Son whom I have chosen. Listen to Him.*"[48] 36 When the voice had spoken, they saw Jesus was alone.

They kept silent and in those days told nobody anything of what they had seen.

The Epileptic Boy

37 The next day, when they had come down from the mountain, He met a large crowd. 38 Then a man in the crowd called, "Teacher, I beg you, look at my son, he is my only child. 39 A spirit takes hold of him, and suddenly he shrieks. It throws him into convulsions, and he foams at the mouth. It will hardly stop mistreating him. 40 I asked Your disciples to drive out the spirit, but they couldn't do it."

41 "O you unbelieving and perverted people!" Jesus answered. "How long must I be with you and put up with you! Bring your son here."

42 While the boy was coming, the devil dashed him on the ground and threw him into convulsions.

Jesus talked sharply to the unclean spirit, made the boy well, and gave him back to his father. 43 All were amazed to see God's wonderful power.

"I Will Die and Rise Again"

43 While everybody thought how wonderful everything was that Jesus was doing, He said to His disciples, 44 "Listen carefully to what I say. The Son of Man is going to be betrayed into the hands of men."

45 But they didn't know what He meant. It was hidden from them so that they didn't understand it. And they were afraid to ask Him about it.

Who Is the Greatest?

46 A discussion got started among them as to which of them was the greatest. 47 But Jesus knew what they were thinking. He took a little child, had him stand by Him, 48 and said to them, "If you welcome this little child in My name, you welcome Me. And if you welcome Me, you welcome Him who sent Me. You see, if anyone is the least of all of you, he is great."

"He Is for Us"

49 "Master," John said, "we saw a man driving out devils in Your name, and we tried to stop him, because he's not one of us."

50 "Don't stop him," Jesus told him; "anyone who is not against you is for you."

To Jerusalem

51 As the time was coming nearer for Him to be taken up to heaven, He showed He was determined to go to Jerusalem. 52 He sent messengers ahead of Him. They went and stopped in a village of the Samaritans to arrange a place for Him to stay. 53 But the people didn't wel-

[b] Lit., *in or on your name.* [c] Grk., *the days were being completed,* etc.

[48] Ps. 2:7; Is. 42:1; Deut. 18:15

K.J.V.

because his face was as though he would go to Jerusalem. 54And when his disciples James and John saw *this*, they said, Lord, wilt thou that we command fire to come down from heaven, and consume them, even as Elias did? 55 But he turned, and rebuked them, and said, Ye know not what manner of spirit ye are of. 56 For the Son of man is not come to destroy men's lives, but to save *them*. And they went to another village.

57 And it came to pass, that, as they went in the way, a certain *man* said unto him, Lord, I will follow thee whithersoever thou goest. 58And Jesus said unto him, Foxes have holes, and birds of the air *have* nests; but the Son of man hath not where to lay *his* head. 59And he said unto another, Follow me. But he said, Lord, suffer me first to go and bury my father. 60 Jesus said unto him, Let the dead bury their dead: but go thou and preach the kingdom of God. 61And another also said, Lord, I will follow thee; but let me first go bid them farewell, which are at home at my house. 62And Jesus said unto him, No man, having put his hand to the plough, and looking back, is fit for the kingdom of God.

10 After these things the Lord appointed other seventy also, and sent them two and two before his face into every city and place, whither he himself would come. 2 Therefore said he unto them, The harvest truly *is* great, but the labourers *are* few: pray ye therefore the Lord of the harvest, that he would send forth labourers into his harvest. 3 Go your ways: behold, I send you forth as lambs among wolves. 4 Carry neither purse, nor scrip, nor shoes: and salute no man by the way. 5And into whatsoever house ye enter, first say, Peace *be* to this house. 6And if ·the son of peace be there, your peace shall rest upon it: if not, it shall turn to you again. 7And in the same house remain, eating and drinking such things as they give: for the labourer is worthy of his hire. Go not from house to house. 8And into whatsoever city ye enter, and they receive you, eat such things as are set before you: 9And heal the sick that are therein, and say unto them, The kingdom of God is come nigh unto you. 10 But into whatsoever city ye enter, and they receive you not, go your ways out into the streets of the same, and say, 11 Even the very dust of your city, which cleaveth on us, we do wipe off against you: notwithstanding, be ye sure of this, that the kingdom of God is come nigh unto you. 12 But I say unto you, that it shall be more tolerable in that day for Sodom, than for that city. 13 Woe unto thee, Chorazin! woe unto thee, Bethsaida! for if the mighty works had been done in Tyre and Sidon, which have been done in you, they had a great while ago repented, sitting in sackcloth and ashes. 14 But it shall be more tolerable for Tyre

N.A.S.

not receive Him, because He was journeying with His face toward Jerusalem. 54And when His disciples James and John saw *this*, they said, "Lord, do You want us to command fire to come down from heaven and consume them?" 55 But He turned and rebuked them.* 56And they went on to another village.

57 And as they were going along the road, someone said to Him, "I will follow You wherever You go." 58And Jesus said to him, "The foxes have holes, and the birds of the air *have* nests, but the Son of Man has nowhere to lay His head." 59And He said to another, "Follow Me." But he said, "ᵇPermit me first to go and bury my father." 60 But He said to him, "Allow the dead to bury their own dead; but as for you, go and proclaim everywhere the kingdom of God." 61And another also said, "I will follow You, Lord; but first permit me to say good-bye to those at home." 62 But Jesus said to him, "No one, after putting his hand to the plow and looking back, is fit for the kingdom of God."

10 Now after this the Lord appointed seventy others, and sent them two and two ahead of Him to every city and place where He Himself was going to come. 2And He was saying to them, "The harvest is plentiful, but the laborers are few; therefore beseech the Lord of the harvest to send out laborers into His harvest. 3 "Go your ways; behold, I send you out as lambs in the midst of wolves. 4 "Carry no purse, no bag, no shoes; and greet no one on the way. 5 "And whatever house you enter, first say, 'Peace *be* to this house.' 6 "And if a man of peace is there, your peace will rest upon him; but if not, it will return to you. 7 "And stay in that house, eating and drinking what they give you; for the laborer is worthy of his wages. Do not keep moving from house to house. 8 "And whatever city you enter, and they receive you, eat what is set before you; 9 and heal those in it who are sick, and say to them, 'The kingdom of God has come near to you.' 10 "But whatever city you enter and they do not receive you, go out into its streets and say, 11 'Even the dust of your city which clings to our feet, we wipe off *in protest* against you; yet be sure of this, that the kingdom of God has come near.' 12 "I say to you, it will be more tolerable in that day for Sodom, than for that city. 13 "Woe to you, Chorazin! Woe to you, Bethsaida! For if the miracles had been performed in Tyre and Sidon which occurred in you, they would have repented long ago, sitting in sackcloth and ashes. 14 "But it will be more tolerable for Tyre and Sidon in the judgment, than for you.

[a] Later mss. add, *and said, "You do not know what kind of spirit you are of.* 56 *"For the Son of Man did not come to destroy men's lives, but to save them."* [b] Some mss. add, *Lord.*

WILLIAMS

they would not receive Him, because He was facing in the direction[d] of Jerusalem. 54 When the disciples, James and John, saw this, they said, "Lord, do you want us to bid fire come down from heaven and consume them?" 55 But He turned at once and reproved them. 56 Then they went on to a different village.

57 While they were going along the road, a man said to Him, "I will follow you wherever you go."

58 But Jesus said to him, "Foxes have holes, even wild birds have roosts, but the Son of Man has nowhere to lay His head." 59 He said to another man, "Follow me."

But he said, "Let me first go back and bury my father."

60 Then He answered him, "Leave the dead to bury their own dead; but you go on and continue to spread the good news of the kingdom of God."

61 Still another man said, "I will follow you, Lord, but let me first say 'Good-by' to the homefolks."

62 Jesus said to him, "No one who puts his hand to the plough, and then continues to look back, is fitted for service in the kingdom of God."

10 *The seventy sent out; Jesus rejoices over their report and the Father's gracious plan; to show who is a good neighbor He tells the story of the Good Samaritan; He stays in the Bethany home*

After this the Lord appointed seventy others and sent them on before Him, two by two, to every town or place which He was going to visit. 2 So He was saying to them:

"The harvest is plentiful, but the reapers are scarce. So pray the Lord of the harvest to send out reapers to His harvest-field. 3 Go on. Listen! I am sending you out as lambs surrounded by wolves. 4 Do not carry a purse, a bag, or shoes, and do not stop to say 'Good morning' to anybody on the road. 5 Whenever you go to a house for headquarters, first say, 'Peace to this household.' 6 And if anyone there loves peace, your peace will come upon him; but if not, it will come back to you. 7 Stay on at the same house, eating and drinking what they provide, for the workman deserves his support.[a] Do not keep moving about from house to house. 8 And if you go into any town and they welcome you, continue to eat what is offered you, 9 to cure the sick there, and to say, 'The kingdom of God is close upon you.' 10 But if you go into any town and they do not welcome you, go out into the streets and say, 11 'We are wiping off against you the very dust from your town that has stuck to our feet. But understand this, the kingdom of God is close by.' 12 I tell you, on that day the punishment will be lighter[b] for Sodom than for that town. 13 A curse on you, Chorazin! A curse on you, Bethsaida! For if the wonder-works done in you had been done in Tyre and Sidon, long ago they would have repented, sitting in sackcloth and ashes. 14 But at the judgment the punishment will be lighter for Tyre and Sidon

BECK

come Him, because He was going to Jerusalem. 54 When His disciples James and John saw this, they asked, "Lord, do you want us to order *fire to come down from heaven and burn*[49] them up?"

55 But He turned and sternly corrected them. 56 So they went on to another village.

"I Will Follow, but—"

57 As they were walking along the road, a man said to Him, "I will follow You anywhere You go."

58 "Foxes have holes," Jesus told him, "and birds in the air have nests, but the Son of Man doesn't have a place to lay His head."

59 He told another man, "Follow Me."

"Lord, first let me go and bury my father," he asked.

60 But Jesus told him, "Let the dead bury their dead. But you go and tell about God's kingdom."

61 "I will follow You, Lord," said another, "but first let me say good-by to my people at home."

62 "Anyone who lays his hand on a plow," Jesus answered him, "and keeps looking back isn't fit for God's kingdom."

Seventy-Two Missionaries

10 After this the Lord appointed seventy-two others and sent them out by twos to go ahead of Him to every town and place where He intended to go.

2 "There's much grain to be cut, but there are only a few workers," He told them. "Ask the Owner of the crop to send out workers to bring in His grain. 3 Go! I'm sending you like lambs among wolves. 4 Don't carry a purse, a bag, or shoes, and don't stop to greet anyone on the way. 5 When you go into a house, say first, 'May there be peace in this house.' 6 If a man of peace lives there, your peace will rest on him; but if not, it will come back to you. 7 Stay in that house and eat and drink whatever they have, since a worker earns his pay. Don't move from one house to another. 8 When you go into any town and the people welcome you, eat what they serve you. 9 Heal the sick that are there, and tell the people, 'God's kingdom has come close to you!'

10 "But if you go into a town and they don't welcome you, go out on its streets and say, 11 'The dust of your town has clung to our feet—we're wiping it off in protest against you! But realize this: God's kingdom has come near you!' 12 I tell you, on that Day it will be easier for Sodom than for that town.

13 "Woe to you, Chorazin! Woe to you, Bethsaida! If the miracles done in you had been done in Tyre and Sidon, they would long ago have repented, sitting in sackcloth and ashes. 14 In the Judgment it will be easier for Tyre

---

[d] Grk., *His face was going to.* [a] Grk., *worthy of his wages.* [b] Lit., *it will be more bearable,* etc.

[49] 2 Kings 1:10, 12

K.J.V.

and Sidon at the judgment, than for you. 15And thou, Capernaum, which art exalted to heaven, shalt be thrust down to hell. 16 He that heareth you heareth me; and he that despiseth you despiseth me; and he that despiseth me despiseth him that sent me.

17 And the seventy returned again with joy, saying, Lord, even the devils are subject unto us through thy name. 18And he said unto them, I beheld Satan as lightning fall from heaven. 19 Behold, I give unto you power to tread on serpents and scorpions, and over all the power of the enemy; and nothing shall by any means hurt you. 20 Notwithstanding, in this rejoice not, that the spirits are subject unto you; but rather rejoice, because your names are written in heaven.

21 In that hour Jesus rejoiced in spirit, and said, I thank thee, O Father, Lord of heaven and earth, that thou hast hid these things from the wise and prudent, and hast revealed them unto babes: even so, Father; for so it seemed good in thy sight. 22All things are delivered to me of my Father: and no man knoweth who the Son is, but the Father; and who the Father is, but the Son, and he to whom the Son will reveal him.

23 And he turned him unto his disciples, and said privately, Blessed are the eyes which see the things that ye see: 24 For I tell you, that many prophets and kings have desired to see those things which ye see, and have not seen them; and to hear those things which ye hear, and have not heard them.

25 And, behold, a certain lawyer stood up, and tempted him, saying, Master, what shall I do to inherit eternal life? 26 He said unto him, What is written in the law? how readest thou? 27And he answering said, Thou shalt love the Lord thy God with all thy heart, and with all thy soul, and with all thy strength, and with all thy mind; and thy neighbour as thyself. 28And he said unto him, Thou hast answered right: this do, and thou shalt live. 29 But he, willing to justify himself, said unto Jesus, And who is my neighbour? 30And Jesus answering said, A certain man went down from Jerusalem to Jericho, and fell among thieves, which stripped him of his raiment, and wounded him, and departed, leaving him half dead. 31And by chance there came down a certain priest that way; and when he saw him, he passed by on the other side. 32And likewise a Levite, when he was at the place, came and looked on him, and passed by on the other side. 33 But a certain Samaritan, as he journeyed, came where he was; and when he saw him, he had compassion on him, 34And went to him, and bound up his wounds, pouring in oil and wine, and set him on his own beast, and brought him to an inn, and took care of him. 35And on the morrow when he departed, he took out two pence, and gave them to the host, and said unto him, Take care of him: and whatsoever thou spendest more, when I come again, I will repay thee. 36 Which now of these three, thinkest thou, was neighbour unto him that fell among the thieves? 37And he said, He that shewed mercy on him. Then said Jesus unto him, Go, and do thou likewise.

N.A.S.

15 "And you, Capernaum, will not be exalted to heaven, will you? You will be brought down to Hades! 16 "The one who listens to you listens to Me, and the one who rejects you rejects Me, and he who rejects Me rejects the One who sent Me."

17 And the seventy returned with joy, saying, "Lord, even the demons are subject to us in Your name." 18And He said to them, "I was watching Satan fall from heaven like lightning. 19 "Behold, I have given you authority to tread upon serpents and scorpions, and over all the power of the enemy, and nothing shall injure you. 20 "Nevertheless do not rejoice in this, that the spirits are subject to you, but rejoice that your names are recorded in heaven."

21 At that very time He rejoiced greatly in the Holy Spirit, and said, "I praise Thee, O Father, Lord of heaven and earth, that Thou didst hide these things from the wise and intelligent and didst reveal them to babes. Yes, Father, for thus it was well-pleasing in Thy sight. 22 "All things have been handed over to Me by My Father, and no one knows who the Son is except the Father, and who the Father is except the Son, and anyone to whom the Son wills to reveal Him." 23And turning to the disciples, He said privately, "Blessed are the eyes which see the things you see, 24 for I say to you, that many prophets and kings wished to see the things which you see, and did not see them, and to hear the things which you hear, and did not hear them."

25 And behold, a certain lawyer stood up and put Him to the test, saying, "Teacher, what shall I do to inherit eternal life?" 26And He said to him, "What is written in the Law? How does it read to you?" 27And he answered and said, "YOU SHALL LOVE THE LORD YOUR GOD WITH ALL YOUR HEART, AND WITH ALL YOUR SOUL, AND WITH ALL YOUR STRENGTH, AND WITH ALL YOUR MIND; AND YOUR NEIGHBOR AS YOURSELF." 28And He said to him, "You have answered correctly; DO THIS, AND YOU WILL LIVE." 29 But wishing to justify himself, he said to Jesus, "And who is my neighbor?" 30 Jesus replied and said, "A certain man was going down from Jerusalem to Jericho; and he fell among robbers, and they stripped him and beat him, and went off leaving him half dead. 31 "And by chance a certain priest was going down on that road, and when he saw him, he passed by on the other side. 32 "And likewise a Levite also, when he came to the place and saw him, passed by on the other side. 33 "But a certain Samaritan, who was on a journey, came upon him; and when he saw him, he felt compassion, 34 and came to him, and bandaged up his wounds, pouring oil and wine on them; and he put him on his own beast, and brought him to an inn, and took care of him. 35 "And on the next day he took out two ªdenarii and gave them to the innkeeper and said, 'Take care of him; and whatever more you spend, when I return, I will repay you.' 36 "Which of these three do you think proved to be a neighbor to the man who fell into the robbers' hands?" 37And he said, "The one who showed mercy toward him." And Jesus said to him, "Go and do the same."

[a] The denarius was worth 18 cents in silver, equivalent to a day's wage.

WILLIAMS

than for you. 15And you, Capernaum, are you to be exalted to heaven? No, you are to go down to the regions of the dead.*c* 16Whoever listens to you listens to me, and whoever pays no attention to you pays no attention to me, and whoever pays no attention to me pays no attention to Him who sent me."

17 Now the seventy returned and joyously reported, "Lord, even the demons are submitting to us in your name."

18 He said to them, "I was looking at Satan falling like a flash of lightning from heaven. 19 Listen! I have given you power to tread on snakes and scorpions, and to trample on all the power of the enemy, and nothing at all will ever harm you. 20 However, you must stop rejoicing over the fact that the spirits are submitting to you, but continue to rejoice that your names are enrolled in heaven."

21 At that very moment, by the power of the Holy Spirit, He exulted and said, "I thank you, Father, Lord of heaven and earth, for concealing these matters from wise and learned men, and for revealing them to little children. Yes, Father, I thank you that your good pleasure made it so. 22All things have been entrusted to me by my Father, and no one knows who the Son is but the Father, and who the Father is but the Son, and anyone to whom the Son chooses to make Him known."

23 Then He turned to His disciples when they were alone, and said, "Blessed are the eyes that see what you are seeing. 24 For I tell you, many prophets and kings have wished to see what you are seeing, but they did not, and to hear what you are hearing, but they did not."

25 Just then an expert in the law got up to test Him by asking, "Teacher, what shall I do to get possession of eternal life?"

26 And He answered him, "What is written in the law? How does it read?"

27 Then he answered, "You must love the Lord your God with your whole heart, your whole soul, your whole strength, and your whole mind, and your neighbor as you do yourself."

28 He said to him, "You have answered correctly. Continue to do this, and you will live."

29 But he, as he wished to justify his question,*d* said, "But who is my neighbor?"

30 Jesus answered:

"A man was on his way down from Jerusalem to Jericho, and he fell into the hands of robbers, who both stripped him and beat him till he was half dead, and then went off and left him. 31 Now a priest happened to be going that way, but when he saw him, he went by on the other side of the road. 32 So a Levite likewise came down to the place, but when he saw him, he went by on the other side. 33 But a Samaritan, while on a journey, came down to him, and when he saw him, his heart was moved with pity for him. 34 So he went to him and dressed his wounds by pouring oil and wine upon them, and then he put him on his donkey and brought him to an inn and took care of him. 35 The next day he took out a half dollar and handed it to the inn-keeper, and said, 'Take care of him, and on my way back I will repay you.' 36 Which one of these three do you think proved himself a real neighbor to the man who fell into the robbers' hands?"

37 He said, "The one who took pity on him." Jesus said to him, "Go and practice it yourself."

BECK

and Sidon than for you. 15And you, Capernaum, will you be *lifted up to heaven? You will go down to hell.*[50]

16 Anyone who hears you hears Me, and anyone who rejects you rejects Me. But anyone who rejects Me rejects Him who sent Me."

17 The seventy-two came back delighted. "Lord," they said, "even the devils do what we tell them in Your name."

18 "I watched the devil fall from heaven like lightning," He told them. 19 "You know, I've given you the power to *step on snakes*[51] and scorpions and to trample on all the enemy's power, and nothing will hurt you. 20 Only don't be glad that the spirits obey you but that your names are written in heaven."

21 In that hour the Holy Spirit filled Jesus with joy. "I praise You, Father, Lord of heaven and earth," He said, "for hiding these things from wise and intelligent people and revealing them to little children. Yes, Father, I praise You for wanting it to be that way.

22 "My Father has put everything in My hands. Only the Father knows the Son. And only the Son—and anyone to whom the Son wants to reveal Him—knows the Father."

23 Turning to His disciples, He said to them alone, "Happy are the eyes that see what you see. 24 I tell you, many prophets and kings longed to see what you see but didn't see it, and hear what you hear but didn't hear it."

The Good Samaritan

25 Then an expert in the Law came forward to test Jesus. "Teacher," he asked, "what do I do to get everlasting life?"

26 "What is written in the Law?" Jesus asked him. "What do you read there?"

27 *"Love the Lord your God with all your heart,"* he answered, *"and with all your life and with all your strength*[52] and with all your mind, and *your neighbor like yourself."* [53]

28 "You're right," Jesus told him. *"Do that and you will live."* [54]

29 But he wanted to justify himself. So he asked Jesus, "And who is my neighbor?"

30 Jesus went into the matter and said:

"A man going from Jerusalem down to Jericho fell into the hands of robbers. They stripped him, struck him blow after blow, and went away leaving him half dead.

31 "Just at that time a priest happened to go along that road, but when he saw him, he passed by on the other side. 32 So did also a Levite who came to the place: he looked at him and passed by on the other side.

33 "Then a Samaritan, as he was traveling, came near him, and when he saw him, he felt sorry for him. He went to him and bandaged his wounds, pouring on oil and wine. 34 Then he put him on his own animal, brought him to an inn, and took care of him. 35 The next day he took out two denarii and gave them to the innkeeper. 'Take care of him,' he said, 'and anything else you spend on him I'll repay you when I come back.'

36 "Which of those three, do you think, was a neighbor to the man who had fallen into the hands of the robbers?"

37 "The one who was kind enough to help him," he said.

"Go and do as he did," Jesus told him.

[50] Is. 14:13, 15
[51] Ps. 91:13
[52] Deut. 6:5
[53] Lev. 19:18
[54] Lev. 18:5

[c] That is, to Hades. [d] Grk., *to justify himself.*

K.J.V.

38 Now it came to pass, as they went, that he entered into a certain village: and a certain woman named Martha received him into her house. 39And she had a sister called Mary, which also sat at Jesus' feet, and heard his word. 40 But Martha was cumbered about much serving, and came to him, and said, Lord, dost thou not care that my sister hath left me to serve alone? bid her therefore that she help me. 41And Jesus answered and said unto her, Martha, Martha, thou art careful and troubled about many things: 42 But one thing is needful; and Mary hath chosen that good part, which shall not be taken away from her.

11 And it came to pass, that, as he was praying in a certain place, when he ceased, one of his disciples said unto him, Lord, teach us to pray, as John also taught his disciples. 2And he said unto them, When ye pray, say, Our Father which art in heaven, Hallowed by thy name. Thy kingdom come. Thy will be done, as in heaven, so in earth. 3 Give us day by day our daily bread. 4And forgive us our sins; for we also forgive every one that is indebted to us. And lead us not into temptation; but deliver us from evil. 5And he said unto them, Which of you shall have a friend, and shall go unto him at midnight, and say unto him, Friend, lend me three loaves; 6 For a friend of mine in his journey is come to me, and I have nothing to set before him? 7And he from within shall answer and say, Trouble me not: the door is now shut, and my children are with me in bed; I cannot rise and give thee. 8 I say unto you, Though he will not rise and give him, because he is his friend, yet because of his importunity he will rise and give him as many as he needeth. 9And I say unto you, Ask, and it shall be given you; seek, and ye shall find; knock, and it shall be opened unto you. 10 For every one that asketh receiveth; and he that seeketh findeth; and to him that knocketh it shall be opened. 11 If a son shall ask bread of any of you that is a father, will he give him a stone? or if *he ask* a fish, will he for a fish give him a serpent? 12 Or if he shall ask an egg, will he offer him a scorpion? 13 If ye then, being evil, know how to give good gifts unto your children; how much more shall *your* heavenly Father give the Holy Spirit to them that ask him?

14 And he was casting out a devil, and it was dumb. And it came to pass, when the devil was gone out, the dumb spake; and the people wondered. 15 But some of them said, He casteth out devils through Beelzebub the chief of the devils. 16And others, tempting *him,* sought of him a

N.A.S.

38 Now as they were traveling along, He entered a certain village; and a woman named Martha welcomed Him into her home. 39And she had a sister called Mary, who moreover was listening to the Lord's word, seated at His feet. 40 But Martha was distracted with all her preparations; and she came up *to Him,* and said, "Lord, do You not care that my sister has left me to do all the serving alone? Then tell her to help me." 41 But the Lord answered and said to her, "Martha, Martha, you are worried and bothered about *so* many things; 42 but *only* a few things are necessary, really *only* one: for Mary has chosen the good part, which shall not be taken away from her."

11 And it came about that while He was praying in a certain place, after He had finished, one of His disciples said to Him, "Lord, teach us to pray just as John also taught his disciples."
2 And He said to them, "When you pray, say:
"Father, hallowed be Thy name.
Thy Kingdom come.
3 Give us each day our daily bread.
4 And forgive us our sins,
For we ourselves also forgive everyone who is indebted to us.
And lead us not into temptation.' "
5 And He said to them, "Suppose one of you shall have a friend, and shall go to him at midnight, and say to him, 'Friend, lend me three loaves; 6 for a friend of mine has come to me from a journey, and I have nothing to set before him'; 7 and from inside he shall answer and say, 'Do not bother me; the door has already been shut and my children and I are in bed; I cannot get up and give you *anything.*' 8 "I tell you, even though he will not get up and give him *anything* because he is his friend, yet because of his persistence he will get up and give him as much as he needs. 9 "And I say to you, ask, and it shall be given to you; seek, and you shall find; knock, and it shall be opened to you. 10 "For everyone who asks receives; and he who seeks finds; and to him who knocks it shall be opened. 11 "Now suppose one of you fathers is asked by his son for a fish; he will not give him a snake instead of a fish, will he? 12 "Or *if* he is asked for an egg, he will not give him a scorpion, will he? 13 "If you then, being evil, know how to give good gifts to your children, how much more shall *your* Heavenly Father give the Holy Spirit to those who ask Him?"

14 And He was casting out a demon, *and it was* dumb; and it came about that when the demon had gone out, the dumb man spoke; and the multitudes marveled. 15 But some of them said, "He casts out demons by Beelzebul, the ruler of the demons." 16And others, to test *Him,* were demanding of Him a sign from

[a] Some mss. insert phrases from Matt. 6:9-13 to make the two passages closely similar.

<table>
<tr><th>WILLIAMS</th><th>BECK</th></tr>
</table>

WILLIAMS

38 Now as they were journeying on, He came to a certain village where a woman named Martha welcomed Him to her house. 39 She had a sister named Mary who took her seat at the Lord's feet, and remained listening to His message. 40 But Martha was getting worried about having to wait on them so much, so she came up suddenly and said, "Lord, do you not care that my sister has left me to do all the housework alone? Then tell her to take hold and help me."

41 The Lord answered her, "Martha, Martha, you are worried and vexed about many things. 42 But there is actual need of few things, really of only one thing. For Mary has chosen the good portion which must not be taken away from her."

11 *The model prayer and a story on prayer; Jesus accused of being in league with demons; His defense; denounces the wickedness of those times, especially the hypocrisy of the Pharisees*

Once He was praying in a certain place, and when He ceased, one of His disciples said to Him, "Lord, teach us to pray, as John taught his disciples."

2 So He said to them, "Whenever you pray, say:
Father,
Your name be revered,
Your Kingdom come;
3 Continue giving us day by day our daily bread,
4 And forgive us our sins, for we ourselves forgive everyone who does us wrong,
And do not let us be subjected to temptation."

5 Then He said to them: "Suppose one of you has a friend, and you go to him in the middle of the night and say to him, 'Friend, lend me three loaves; 6 for a friend of mine has just come to my house on a journey, and I have nothing to set before him to eat.' 7 And suppose he answers from inside, 'Stop bothering me; the door is now locked, and my children are packed about me in bed; I cannot get up and give you any.' 8 I tell you, although he will not get up and give you any because he is your friend, yet because of your persistence he will get up and give you all your needs. 9 So I tell you, keep on asking, and the gift will be given you; keep on seeking, and you will find; keep on knocking, and the door will open to you. 10 For everyone who keeps on asking, receives; and the one who keeps on seeking, finds; and to the one who keeps on knocking, the door will open. 11 Now is there a father among you who, if his son asks him for a fish, will give him a snake instead? 12 Or, if he asks for an egg, will give him a scorpion? 13 So if you, in spite of your being bad, know how to give your children what is good, how much more surely will your Father in heaven give the Holy Spirit to those who continue to ask Him?"

14 Now He was driving a dumb demon out of a man, and when the demon went out of him, the dumb man spoke. The crowds were astonished. 15 But some of them said, "It is with the help of Beelzebub, the prince of demons, that He is driving the demons out." 16 But others, to test Him, were demanding from Him a spectacular sign from heaven.

BECK

Mary Listens to Jesus

38 As they were walking along, Jesus came to a village where a woman by the name of Martha welcomed Him to her home. 39 She had a sister by the name of Mary. She sat down at Jesus' feet and listened to what He said.

40 But Martha was worried about all she had to do for them. So she came and asked, "Lord, don't You care that my sister has left me and I have to do the work alone? Now tell her to help me."

41 "Martha, Martha," the Lord answered her, "you worry and fuss about a lot of things. 42 But there's only one thing you need. Mary has made the right choice, and it must not be taken away from her."

The Lord's Prayer

11 Once Jesus was praying in a certain place. When He stopped, one of His disciples asked Him, "Lord, teach us to pray as John taught His disciples."

2 He told them, "When you pray, say:
'Father, may Your name be kept holy,
Your kingdom come,
3 Your will be done on earth as it is in heaven.
Give us every day our daily bread.
4 Forgive us our sins, as we, too, forgive everyone who sins against us.
And don't bring us into temptation.'"

Pray!

5 "Suppose one of you has a friend," Jesus said to His disciples, "and you go to him at midnight and ask him, 'Friend, lend me three loaves. 6 A friend of mine on a trip has dropped in on me, and I have nothing to serve him.' 7 Will he answer from within, 'Don't bother me. The door is already locked, and my children are with me in bed. I can't get up and give you anything'? 8 I tell you, although he won't get up and give you anything even though he's your friend, yet because you persist, he'll get up and give you anything you need.

9 "So I tell you: Ask and it will be given to you. Search and you will find. Knock and the door will be opened for you. 10 Anyone who asks receives; anyone who searches finds; and anyone who knocks, the door will be opened for him.

11 "If your son asks you, his father, for a fish, will any of you give him a snake instead of a fish? 12 Or if he asks for an egg, will you give him a scorpion? 13 Now if you, bad as you are, know enough to give your children good gifts, how much more will your Father in heaven give the Holy Spirit to those who ask Him?"

Power over the Devil

14 He was driving out a devil who was speechless. When the devil had gone out, the speechless man spoke.

15 The people were amazed. But some of them said, "He drives out the devils with the help of Beelzebul, who rules over the devils." 16 Others, meaning to test Him, demanded that He show them some wonderful proof from heaven.

K.J.V.

sign from heaven. 17 But he, knowing their thoughts, said unto them, Every kingdom divided against itself is brought to desolation; and a house *divided* against a house falleth. 18 If Satan also be divided against himself, how shall his kingdom stand? because ye say that I cast out devils through Beelzebub. 19And if I by Beelzebub cast out devils, by whom do your sons cast *them* out? therefore shall they be your judges. 20 But if I with the finger of God cast out devils, no doubt the kingdom of God is come upon you. 21 When a strong man armed keepeth his palace, his goods are in peace: 22 But when a stronger than he shall come upon him, and overcome him, he taketh from him all his armour wherein he trusted, and divideth his spoils. 23 He that is not with me is against me; and he that gathereth not with me scattereth. 24 When the unclean spirit is gone out of a man, he walketh through dry places, seeking rest; and finding none, he saith, I will return unto my house whence I came out. 25And when he cometh, he findeth *it* swept and garnished. 26 Then goeth he, and taketh *to him* seven other spirits more wicked than himself; and they enter in, and dwell there: and the last *state* of that man is worse than the first.

27 And it came to pass, as he spake these things, a certain woman of the company lifted up her voice, and said unto him, Blessed *is* the womb that bare thee, and the paps which thou hast sucked. 28 But he said, Yea, rather, blessed *are* they that hear the word of God, and keep it.

29 And when the people were gathered thick together, he began to say, This is an evil generation: they seek a sign; and there shall no sign be given it, but the sign of Jonas the prophet. 30 For as Jonas was a sign unto the Ninevites, so shall also the Son of man be to this generation. 31 The queen of the south shall rise up in the judgment with the men of this generation, and condemn them: for she came from the utmost parts of the earth to hear the wisdom of Solomon; and, behold, a greater than Solomon *is* here. 32 The men of Nineveh shall rise up in the judgment with this generation, and shall condemn it: for they repented at the preaching of Jonas; and, behold, a greater than Jonas *is* here. 33 No man, when he hath lighted a candle, putteth *it* in a secret place, neither under a bushel, but on a candlestick, that they which come in may see the light. 34 The light of the body is the eye: therefore when thine eye is single, thy whole body also is full of light; but when *thine eye* is evil, thy body also *is* full of darkness. 35 Take heed therefore, that the light which is in thee be not darkness. 36 If thy whole body therefore *be* full of light, having no part dark, the whole shall be full of light, as when the bright shining of a candle doth give thee light.

37 And as he spake, a certain Pharisee besought him to dine with him: and he went in, and sat down to meat. 38And when the Pharisee saw *it*, he marvelled that he had not first washed before dinner. 39And the Lord said unto him, Now do ye Pharisees make clean the outside of the cup and the platter; but your inward part is full of ravening and wickedness. 40 *Ye* fools, did not he, that made that which is without, make that which is within also? 41 But rather give alms of such things as ye have; and, behold,

N.A.S.

heaven. 17 But He knew their thoughts, and said to them, "Any kingdom divided against itself is laid waste; and a house divided against itself falls. 18 "And if Satan also is divided against himself, how shall his kingdom stand? For you say that I cast out demons by Beelzebul. 19 "And if I by Beelzebul cast out demons, by whom do your sons cast them out? Consequently they shall be your judges. 20 "But if I cast out demons by the finger of God, then the kingdom of God has come upon you. 21 "When a strong *man* fully armed guards his own homestead, his possessions are undisturbed; 22 but when someone stronger than he attacks him and overpowers him, he takes away from him all his armor on which he had relied, and distributes his plunder. 23 "He who is not with Me is against Me; and he who does not gather with Me, scatters. 24 "When the unclean spirit goes out of a man, it passes through waterless places seeking rest, and not finding any, it says, 'I will return to my house from which I came.' 25 "And when it comes, it finds it swept and put in order. 26 "Then it goes and takes *along* seven other spirits more evil than itself, and they go in and live there; and the last state of that man becomes worse than the first."

27 And it came about while He said these things, one of the women in the crowd raised her voice, and said to Him, "Blessed is the womb that bore You, and the breasts at which You nursed." 28 But He said, "On the contrary, blessed are those who hear the word of God, and observe it."

29 And as the crowds were increasing, He began to say, "This generation is a wicked generation; it seeks for a sign, and *yet* no sign shall be given to it but the sign of Jonah. 30 "For just as Jonah became a sign to the Ninevites, so shall the Son of Man be to this generation. 31 "The Queen of the South shall rise up with the men of this generation at the judgment and condemn them, because she came from the ends of the earth to hear the wisdom of Solomon; and behold, something greater than Solomon is here. 32 "The men of Nineveh shall stand up with this generation at the judgment and condemn it, because they repented at the preaching of Jonah; and behold, something greater than Jonah is here.

33 "No one, after lighting a lamp, puts it away in a cellar, nor under a peck-measure, but on the lampstand, in order that those who enter may see the light. 34 "The lamp of your body is your eye; when your eye is clear, your whole body also is full of light; but when it is bad, your body also is full of darkness. 35 "Then watch out that the light in you may not be darkness. 36 "If therefore your whole body is full of light, with no dark part in it, it shall be wholly illumined, as when the lamp illumines you with its rays."

37 Now when He had spoken, a Pharisee *asked Him to have lunch with him; and He went in, and reclined *at table*. 38And when the Pharisee saw it, he was surprised that He had not first ceremonially washed before the meal. 39 But the Lord said to him, "Now you Pharisees clean the outside of the cup and of the platter; but inside of you, you are full of robbery and wickedness. 40 "You foolish ones, did not He who made the outside make the inside also? 41 "But give that which is within as charity, and then all things are clean for you.

WILLIAMS

17 But He knew what they were thinking, and so said to them, "Any kingdom that is not united is in the process of destruction, and one house falls after another. 18And if Satan is really disunited, how can his kingdom last? Yet you say that I am driving the demons out with Beelzebub's help. 19 Now if I with Beelzebub's help am driving the demons out, with whose help do your sons drive them out? 20 But if I by the finger of God am driving the demons out, then the kingdom of God has come to you. 21 When a strong man well armed keeps guard over his dwelling, his property is secure. 22 But when a man stronger than he attacks him and overcomes him, he strips him of all his arms on which he relied, and distributes his goods as spoils. 23 Whoever is not in partnership with me is against me, and whoever does not gather in partnership with me, scatters.

24 "When the foul spirit goes out of a man, it wanders about in deserts in search for rest, and since it finds none, it says, 'I will go back to my house which I left.' 25And it goes and finds it unoccupied, swept, and ready for use. 26 Then it goes and gets seven other spirits more wicked than itself, and they go in and make their home there, and so the end of that man is worse than the beginning."

27 Just as He was saying this, a woman in the crowd lifted her voice and said, "Blessed is the mother who bore you and nursed you!"

28 But He said, "Yes, but better still, blessed are those who listen to God's message and practice it!"

29 Now as the crowds continued to throng upon Him, He began to say: "This is a wicked age. It is looking for a spectacular sign, but none will be given it but the sign of Jonah. 30 For just as Jonah became a sign to the people of Nineveh, so the Son of Man will be a sign to this age. 31 The queen of the south will rise at the judgment with the men of this age and will condemn them; for she came from the very ends of the earth to listen to Solomon's wisdom; and yet, One who is more than Solomon is here. 32 The men of Nineveh will rise at the judgment with the men of this age and will condemn them, for they turned to the message preached by Jonah, and yet One who is more than Jonah is here. 33 No one lights a lamp and puts it in a cellar or under a peck-measure, but he puts it on the lampstand, that the people who come in may enjoy the light. 34 Your eye is the very lamp of your body. When your eye is sound, your whole body is full of light. But if your eye is unsound, your body is full of darkness. 35 So be on your guard that the very source of light in you is not darkness. 36 If then your whole body is full of light with no part of it in darkness, it will all be as light for you as it is when a lamp makes it light for you by its shining."

37 When He had said this, a Pharisee asked Him to lunch at his house, and He went in and took His place at table. 38 The Pharisee noticed that He did not first wash before lunch, and was surprised. 39 But the Lord said to him, "Now you Pharisees have the habit of cleaning the outside of your cups and dishes, but inside you yourselves are full of greed and wickedness. 40 You fools! Did not the One who made the outside make the inside too? 41 But dedicate once for all your inner self, and at once you will have

BECK

17 Knowing what they were thinking, He said to them, "If one part of any kingdom fights against another part, it loses its people, and one house falls on another. 18 If the devil fights against himself, how can his kingdom stand? I say this because you say Beelzebul helps Me drive out the devils. 19 But if Beelzebul helps Me drive out the devils, who helps your sons drive them out? That's why they'll be your judges. 20 But if God's finger helps Me drive out the devils, then God's kingdom has come to you. 21 "When a strong man, completely armed, guards his palace, his property is not disturbed. 22 But when someone stronger than he attacks him and defeats him, he'll take away his whole armor, in which he trusted, and divide the plunder.

23 "Anyone who is not with Me is against Me, and anyone who doesn't help Me gather scatters.

24 "When an unclean spirit comes out of a man, he goes through dry places looking for rest but doesn't find any. Then he says, 'I'll go back to the home I left.' 25 He comes and finds it swept and decorated. 26 Then he goes and takes home with him seven other spirits worse than himself, and they go in and live there. In the end that man is worse than he was before."

Hear Him!

27 When Jesus said this, a woman in the crowd called loud to Him, "Happy is the mother who bore You and nursed You."

28 "Yes," He said, "but happy are those who listen to God's Word and keep it."

29 As the people were crowding around Him, He said, "These people of our time are wicked. They're looking for a proof, but the only proof they'll get is Jonah. 30 As Jonah became a proof to the people of Nineveh, so the Son of Man will be a proof to these people. 31 The queen of the south will rise up in the Judgment with the men of today and condemn them, because she came from the ends of the earth to hear Solomon's wisdom; and here you see more than Solomon. 32 The men of Nineveh will rise up in the Judgment with the people of today and condemn them, because they repented when Jonah preached; and here you see more than Jonah."

Your Light

33 "You don't light a lamp and put it in a cellar or under the peck measure but on the lampstand so that those who come in will see it shine.

34 "Your eye is the lamp of your body. When your eye is healthy, you have light for your whole body. But when your eye is bad, your body is dark! 35 Then see to it that the light in you isn't dark. 36 Now if you have light for your whole body and no part of it is dark, it will all have light just as when a lamp shines brightly on you."

Warnings

37 Jesus had been speaking, when a Pharisee invited Him to eat at his home. So He went in and lay down to eat. 38 But the Pharisee was surprised to see He didn't wash before the meal.

39 The Lord said to him, "You Pharisees keep cleaning the outside of the cup and of the dish, but inside you're full of greed and wickedness. 40 You fools, didn't He who made the outside make the inside too? 41 Just give your heart in helping the poor, and you'll find everything clean.

K.J.V.

all things are clean unto you. 42 But woe unto you, Pharisees! for ye tithe mint and rue and all manner of herbs, and pass over judgment and the love of God: these ought ye to have done, and not to leave the other undone. 43 Woe unto you, Pharisees! for ye love the uppermost seats in the synagogues, and greetings in the markets. 44 Woe unto you, scribes and Pharisees, hypocrites! for ye are as graves which appear not, and the men that walk over *them* are not aware *of them*.

45 Then answered one of the lawyers, and said unto him, Master, thus saying thou reproachest us also. 46 And he said, Woe unto you also, ye lawyers! for ye lade men with burdens grievous to be borne, and ye yourselves touch not the burdens with one of your fingers. 47 Woe unto you! for ye build the sepulchres of the prophets, and your fathers killed them. 48 Truly ye bear witness that ye allow the deeds of your fathers: for they indeed killed them, and ye build their sepulchres. 49 Therefore also said the wisdom of God, I will send them prophets and apostles, and *some* of them they shall slay and persecute: 50 That the blood of all the prophets, which was shed from the foundation of the world, may be required of this generation; 51 From the blood of Abel unto the blood of Zacharias, which perished between the altar and the temple: verily I say unto you, It shall be required of this generation. 52 Woe unto you, lawyers! for ye have taken away the key of knowledge: ye entered not in yourselves, and them that were entering in ye hindered. 53 And as he said these things unto them, the scribes and the Pharisees began to urge *him* vehemently, and to provoke him to speak of many things: 54 Laying wait for him, and seeking to catch something out of his mouth, that they might accuse him.

12 In the mean time, when there were gathered together an innumerable multitude of people, insomuch that they trode one upon another, he began to say unto his disciples first of all, Beware ye of the leaven of the Pharisees, which is hypocrisy. 2 For there is nothing covered, that shall not be revealed; neither hid, that shall not be known. 3 Therefore, whatsoever ye have spoken in darkness shall be heard in the light; and that which ye have spoken in the ear in closets shall be proclaimed upon the housetops. 4 And I say unto you my friends, Be not afraid of them that kill the body, and after that have no more that they can do. 5 But I will forewarn you whom ye shall fear: Fear him, which after he hath killed hath power to cast into hell; yea, I say unto you, Fear him. 6 Are not five sparrows sold for two farthings, and not one of them is forgotten before God? 7 But even the very hairs of your head are all numbered. Fear not therefore: ye are of more value than many sparrows. 8 Also I say unto you, Whosoever shall confess me before men, him shall the Son of man also confess before the angels of

N.A.S.

42 "But woe to you Pharisees! For you pay tithe of mint and rue and every *kind of* garden herb, and *yet* disregard justice and the love of God; but these are the things you should have done without neglecting the others. 43 "Woe to you Pharisees! For you love the front seats in the synagogues, and the respectful greetings in the market places. 44 "Woe to you! For you are like concealed tombs, and the people who walk over *them* are unaware *of it*."

45 And one of the [a]lawyers *said to Him in reply, "Teacher, when You say this, You insult us too." 46 But He said, "Woe to you lawyers as well! For you weigh men down with burdens hard to bear, while you yourselves will not even touch the burdens with one of your fingers. 47 "Woe to you! For you build the tombs of the prophets, and *it was* your fathers *who* killed them. 48 "Consequently, you are witnesses and approve the deeds of your fathers; because it was they who killed them, and you build *their tombs*. 49 "For this reason also the Wisdom of God said, 'I will send to them prophets and apostles, and *some* of them they will kill and *some* they will persecute, 50 in order that the blood of all the prophets, shed since the foundation of the world, may be charged against this generation, 51 from the blood of Abel to the blood of Zechariah, who perished between the altar and the House *of God*, yes, I tell you, it shall be charged against this generation.' 52 "Woe to you lawyers! For you have taken away the key of knowledge; you did not enter in yourselves, and those who were entering in you hindered."

53 And when He left there, the scribes and the Pharisees began to be very hostile and to question Him closely on many subjects, 54 plotting against Him, to catch *Him* in something He might say.

12 Under these circumstances, after so many thousands of the multitude had gathered together that they were stepping on one another, He began saying to His disciples first *of all*, "Beware of the leaven of the Pharisees, which is hypocrisy. 2 "But there is nothing covered up that will not be revealed, and hidden that will not be known. 3 "Accordingly whatever you have said in the dark shall be heard in the light, and what you have whispered in the inner rooms shall be proclaimed upon the housetops. 4 "And I say to you my friends, do not be afraid of those who killed the body, and after that have no more that they can do. 5 "But I will warn you whom to fear: Fear the One who after He has killed has authority to cast into hell; yes, I tell you, fear Him! 6 "Are not five sparrows sold for two cents? And *yet* not one of them is forgotten before God. 7 "Indeed the very hairs of your head are all numbered. Do not fear; you are of more value than many sparrows. 8 "And I say to you, everyone who confesses Me before men, the Son of Man shall confess him also before the

[a] I.e., *experts in the Mosaic law*.

WILLIAMS

everything clean. 42 But a curse on you Pharisees, because you pay tithes on mint, rue, and every tiny garden herb, but neglect justice and the love of God! These latter especially you ought to have done, but ought not to have neglected the former. 43 A curse on you Pharisees, because you like to have the front seats in synagogues, and to be greeted with honor in public places! 44 A curse on you, because you are like unmarked graves which men walk over without knowing it!"

45 Then an expert in the law interrupted Him and said, "Teacher, in saying this you are insulting us, too."

46 He said, "Yes, a curse on you experts in the law, too, because you load people down with loads too heavy to carry, and yet you do not touch the loads yourselves with one of your fingers! 47 A curse on you, because you build monuments for the prophets, whom your forefathers killed! 48 So you testify to what your forefathers did and approve it, because they killed them and you build monuments for them. 49 This is why the Wisdom of God said, 'I will send to them prophets and apostles, and some of them they will kill, and some they will persecute'; 50 so that the blood of all the prophets that has been shed from the creation of the world may be charged against the men of this age—51 from the blood of Abel to the blood of Zechariah who perished between the altar and the sanctuary. Yes, I tell you, it will be charged against the men of this age. 52 A curse on you experts in the law, because you have taken away the key to the door of knowledge! You did not go in yourselves, and you kept out those who tried to get in."

53 After He left the house, the scribes and the Pharisees began to be violently enraged against Him and to try to draw Him out on many subjects, 54 plotting, as if in ambush, to entrap Him in something that might fall from His lips.

12 *Jesus warns against hypocrisy; tells the story of the foolish farmer to warn against covetousness; commends trustfulness and alertness; tells the story of the good manager to illustrate alertness*

Meanwhile as the people had gathered in tens of thousands, so that they were trampling upon one another, He began to say, first of all, to His disciples:

"Beware of the yeast of the Pharisees, that is, hypocrisy. 2 There is nothing covered up that will not be uncovered, nor secret that will not be made known; 3 because what you have spoken in darkness will be heard in the light, and what you have whispered in people's ears, behind closed doors, will be proclaimed from the housetops. 4 So I tell you, my friends, never be afraid of those who kill the body but after that have nothing more that they can do. 5 But I will show you whom to fear. Fear Him who, after killing you, has power to hurl you down to the pit;* yes, I tell you, fear Him. 6 Are not sparrows sold five for two cents? And yet not one of them is forgotten by God. 7 Yes, the very hairs on your heads have all been counted by God! Stop being afraid; you are worth more than many sparrows. 8 I tell you, everyone who owns me before men the Son of Man will own

[a] *Gehenna.*

BECK

42 "But woe to you Pharisees! You give a tenth of mint, rue, and every vegetable, and you fail to be just and to love God. You should have done these without neglecting the others.

43 "And woe to you Pharisees! You like to have the seats of honor in the synagogs and to be greeted in the marketplaces. 44 Woe to you! You're like the unmarked graves people walk over without knowing what they are."

45 "Teacher," one of the men of the Law said to Him, "when You say that, You insult us too."

46 "Woe also to you experts in the Law!" He said. "You load people with burdens they can hardly carry, but not with one finger will you touch these burdens yourselves. 47 Woe to you! You build monuments for the prophets your fathers murdered. 48 So you are witnesses and approve of what your fathers did. They murdered them, and you just build something. 49 That's why God's wisdom has said: I will send them prophets and apostles, and they will murder or persecute some of them 50 so that the people of today may be punished for the blood of all the prophets poured out since the world was made, 51 from the blood of Abel to the blood of Zechariah, who was killed between the altar and the temple. Yes, I tell you, the people of today will be punished for it.

52 "Woe to you experts in the Law! You've taken away the key to knowledge. You didn't go in yourselves and kept out those who tried to go in."

53 When Jesus went outside, the Bible scholars and the Pharisees fiercely opposed Him and cross-examined Him about many things, 54 watching Him closely to trap Him in something He might say.

Don't Be Afraid of Men

12 When so many thousands of people came together that they trampled on one another, Jesus began to speak first to His disciples: "Beware of the yeast of the Pharisees—I mean, their hypocrisy. 2 Everything that's covered will be uncovered, and every secret will be known. 3 Everything you said in the dark will be heard in the light, and what you whispered in the ear in the inner rooms will be announced from the roofs. 4 But I tell you, My friends, don't be afraid of those who kill the body and then can't do any more. 5 I will point out the One you must fear. Fear Him who after killing you has the power to throw you into hell. Yes, I tell you, fear Him!

6 "Aren't five sparrows sold for two cents? And God doesn't forget any one of them. 7 Why, even the hairs on your heads are all counted! Don't be afraid—you're worth more than many sparrows! 8 I tell you, whoever will confess Me before other people, him the Son of Man will

K.J.V.

God: 9 But he that denieth me before men shall be denied before the angels of God. 10And whosoever shall speak a word against the Son of man, it shall be forgiven him: but unto him that blasphemeth against the Holy Ghost it shall not be forgiven. 11And when they bring you unto the synagogues, and *unto* magistrates, and powers, take ye no thought how or what thing ye shall answer, or what ye shall say: 12 For the Holy Ghost shall teach you in the same hour what ye ought to say.

13 And one of the company said unto him, Master, speak to my brother, that he divide the inheritance with me. 14And he said unto him, Man, who made me a judge or a divider over you? 15And he said unto them, Take heed, and beware of covetousness: for a man's life consisteth not in the abundance of the things which he possesseth. 16And he spake a parable unto them, saying, The ground of a certain rich man brought forth plentifully: 17And he thought within himself, saying, What shall I do, because I have no room where to bestow my fruits? 18And he said, This will I do: I will pull down my barns, and build greater; and there will I bestow all my fruits and my goods. 19And I will say to my soul, Soul, thou hast much goods laid up for many years; take thine ease, eat, drink, *and* be merry. 20 But God said unto him, *Thou* fool, this night thy soul shall be required of thee: then whose shall those things be, which thou hast provided? 21 So *is* he that layeth up treasure for himself, and is not rich toward God.

22 And he said unto his disciples, Therefore I say unto you, Take no thought for your life, what ye shall eat; neither for the body, what ye shall put on. 23 The life is more than meat, and the body *is more* than raiment. 24 Consider the ravens: for they neither sow nor reap; which neither have storehouse nor barn; and God feedeth them: how much more are ye better than the fowls? 25And which of you with taking thought can add to his stature one cubit? 26 If ye then be not able to do that thing which is least, why take ye thought for the rest? 27 Consider the lilies how they grow: they toil not, they spin not; and yet I say unto you, that Solomon in all his glory was not arrayed like one of these. 28 If then God so clothe the grass, which is to day in the field, and to morrow is cast into the oven; how much more *will he clothe* you, O ye of little faith? 29And seek not ye what ye shall eat, or what ye shall drink, neither be ye of doubtful mind. 30 For all these things do the nations of the world seek after: and your Father knoweth that ye have need of these things.

31 But rather seek ye the kingdom of God; and all these things shall be added unto you. 32 Fear not, little flock; for it is your Father's good pleasure to give you the kingdom. 33 Sell that ye have, and give alms; provide yourselves bags which wax not old, a treasure in the heavens that faileth not, where no thief approacheth, neither moth corrupteth. 34 For where your treasure is, there will your heart be also. 35 Let your loins be girded about, and *your* lights burning; 36And ye yourselves like unto men that wait for their lord, when he will return from the wedding; that, when he cometh and knocketh, they may open unto him immediately. 37 Blessed *are* those servants, whom the lord when he cometh shall find watching: verily I say

N.A.S.

angels of God; 9 but he who denies Me before men shall be denied before the angels of God. 10 "And everyone who will speak a word against the Son of Man, it shall be forgiven him; but he who blasphemes against the Holy Spirit, it shall not be forgiven him. 11 "And when they bring you before the synagogues and the rulers and the authorities, do not become anxious about how or what you should speak in your defense, or what you should say; 12 for the Holy Spirit will teach you in that very hour what you ought to say."

13 And someone in the crowd said to Him, "Teacher, tell my brother to divide the *family* inheritance with me." 14 But He said to him, "Man, who appointed Me a judge or arbiter over you?" 15And He said to them, "Beware, and be on your guard against every form of greed; for not *even* when one has an abundance does his life consist of his possessions." 16And He told them a parable, saying, "The land of a certain rich man was very productive. 17 "And he began reasoning to himself, saying, 'What shall I do, since I have no place to store my crops?' 18 "And he said, 'This is what I will do: I will tear down my barns and build larger ones, and there I will store all my grain and my goods. 19 'And I will say to my soul, "Soul, you have many goods laid up for many years *to come;* take your ease, eat, drink *and* be merry." ' 20 "But God said to him, 'You fool! This *very* night your soul is required of you; and *now* who will own what you have prepared?' 21 "So is the man who lays up treasure for himself, and is not rich toward God."

22 And He said to His disciples, "For this reason I say to you, do not be anxious for *your* life, *as to* what you shall eat; nor for your body, *as to* what you shall put on. 23 "For life is more than food, and the body than clothing. 24 "Consider the ravens, for they neither sow nor reap; and they have no storeroom nor barn; and *yet* God feeds them; how much more valuable you are than the birds! 25 "And which of you by being anxious can add a *single* [a]cubit to his [b]life's span? 26 "If then you cannot do even a very little thing, why are you anxious about other matters? 27 "Consider the lilies, how they grow; they neither toil nor spin; but I tell you, even Solomon in all his glory did not clothe himself like one of these. 28 "But if God so *arrays* the grass in the field, which is *alive* today and tomorrow is thrown into the furnace, how much more *will He clothe* you, O men of little faith! 29 "And do not seek what you shall eat, and what you shall drink, and do not keep worrying. 30 "For all these things the nations of the world eagerly seek; but your Father knows that you need these things. 31 "But seek for His kingdom, and these things shall be added to you. 32 "Do not be afraid, little flock, for your Father has chosen gladly to give you the kingdom. 33 "Sell your possessions and give to charity; make yourselves purses which do not wear out, an unfailing treasure in heaven, where no thief comes near, nor moth destroys. 34 "For where your treasure is, there will your heart be also.

35 "Be dressed in readiness, and *keep* your lamps alight. 36 "And be like men who are waiting for their master when he returns from the wedding feast, so that they may immediately open *the door* to him when he comes and knocks. 37 "Blessed are those slaves whom the master shall find on the alert when he comes;

[a] I.e., 18 inches. [b] Or, *height.*

WILLIAMS

before the angels of God; 9 but anyone who disowns me before men will be disowned before the angels of God. 10And anyone who speaks a word against the Son of Man will be forgiven; but no one who speaks abusively about the Holy Spirit will be forgiven. 11 Now when they are bringing you before the synagogues or the magistrates or the authorities, never worry about how to defend yourselves, or what to say, 12 for at that very moment the Holy Spirit will teach you what you ought to say."

13 Just then a man in the crowd said to Him, "Tell my brother to share with me our inheritance."

14 But He said to him, "Man, who made me a judge or umpire in your affairs?" 15And then He said to them, "Be ever on the alert and always on your guard against every form of greed, because a man's life does not consist in his possessions, even though they are abundant."

16 Then He told them a story, as follows: "A certain rich man's lands yielded bountifully. 17 So he began to argue with himself, What am I to do, because I have nowhere to store my crops? 18 Then he said, This is what I will do: I will tear down my barns and build larger ones, and in them I will store all my grains and my goods. 19 Then I will say to my soul, 'Soul, you have plenty of good things laid up for many years. Go on taking your ease; continue to eat, drink, and enjoy yourself.' 20 But God said to him, 'You fool! This very night your soul is to be demanded of you. Then who will have all that you have prepared?' 21 So it is with the man who continues to pile up possessions for himself, and is not rich in God."

22 Then He said to His disciples: "Stop worrying, then, about life, as to what you will have to eat, or about your body, as to what you will have to wear. 23 Your life is worth more than food, and your body more than clothes. 24 Just think of the ravens! For they neither sow nor reap, they have no storehouses nor barns, and yet God continues to feed them. How much more are you worth than the birds! 25 Which of you by worrying can add a single minute to his life? 26 So if you cannot do this very little thing, why should you worry about the rest? 27 Just think of how the lilies grow! They do not toil nor spin. But, I tell you, not even Solomon, in all his splendor, was ever dressed like one of them. 28 Now if God so gorgeously dresses the wild grass which today is green but tomorrow is tossed into the furnace, how much more surely will He clothe you, O you with little faith? 29 So you must stop seeking what to eat and what to drink, and must stop being in suspense about these things. 30 For all these are the very things the nations of the world are greedily trying to get, and surely your Father well knows that you need them. 31 But continue to seek His will,[b] and these things will be yours besides. 32 Stop being afraid, my little flock, for your Father has gladly chosen to give you the kingdom. 33 Sell your property and give to charity. Provide for yourselves purses that will never wear out, riches that never fail in heaven, where a thief cannot come near nor a moth destroy. 34 For wherever your treasure is, there too your heart will be.

35 "You must keep your belts tight and your lamps burning, 36 and be like men waiting for their master when he comes home from the wedding, that when he comes and knocks, they at once may open the door for him. 37 Happy are those slaves whom the master, when he

[b] Grk., seek His kingdom; so will.

BECK

confess before God's angels. 9Anyone who denies Me before other people will be denied before God's angels. 10Anyone who will speak against the Son of Man will be forgiven. But he who slanders the Holy Spirit will not be forgiven.

11 "When they bring you before synagogs, rulers, and authorities, don't worry how you will defend yourselves or what you will say. 12 When that time comes, the Holy Spirit will teach you what to say."

Don't Be Greedy

13 "Teacher," someone in the crowd said to Him, "tell my brother to give me my share of the property our father left us."

14 "Man," He asked him, "who appointed Me to be your judge or to divide your property?"

15 "Be careful," He told the people. "Guard against every kind of greed. Even if you have more than enough, your property doesn't give you life."

16 Then He told them a story: "A rich man had good crops on his land. 17 'What am I going to do?' he said to himself. 'I have no place to store my crops.' 18 Finally he said, 'This is what I'll do: I'll tear down my barns and build bigger ones and store all my grain and goods in them. 19 Then I'll say to myself, You have a lot of good things stored up for many years. Take life easy, eat, drink, and enjoy yourself.'

20 "But God said to him, 'You fool, tonight you die. And what you've prepared—who will get it?' 21 That's how it is when you store up goods for yourself and aren't rich in God.

22 "That is why I tell you," He said to His disciples: "Don't worry about what you'll eat to keep alive or what you'll wear on your bodies. 23 Life is more than food, and the body more than clothes. 24 Look at the crows. They don't sow or cut grain, they have no storeroom or barn; and yet God feeds them. You're worth much more than birds. 25And can any of you by worrying add anything to your life? 26 If you can't do even the smallest thing, why worry about the rest? 27 See how the flowers grow. They don't work or spin. Yet I tell you, even Solomon in all his glory didn't dress like one of them. 28 If that's how God dresses the grass, which lives in the field today and tomorrow is thrown into a stove, how much more certainly will he put clothes on you—who trust Him so little? 29 So don't just think of what you'll eat or drink, and don't worry. 30 The people in the world run after all these things, but your Father knows you need them. 31 Only be eager to have Him as your King, and you'll get these things too. 32 Don't be afraid, little flock. Your Father has decided to give you the kingdom.

33 "Sell what you have and give the money to the poor. Make yourselves purses that don't wear out and a treasure that will never be used up—in heaven, where no thief gets near it and no moth destroys it. 34 Where your treasure is, there your heart will be."

Be Ready

35 "Be ready for action with belts fastened and lamps burning, 36 like men waiting for their master when he comes back from a wedding, so they can open the door for him the moment he comes and knocks. 37 Happy are those slaves whom the master finds watching

K.J.V.

unto you, that he shall gird himself, and make them to sit down to meat, and will come forth and serve them. 38And if he shall come in the second watch, or come in the third watch, and find *them* so, blessed are those servants. 39And this know, that if the goodman of the house had known what hour the thief would come, he would have watched, and not have suffered his house to be broken through. 40 Be ye therefore ready also: for the Son of man cometh at an hour when ye think not.

41 Then Peter said unto him, Lord, speakest thou this parable unto us, or even to all? 42And the Lord said, Who then is that faithful and wise steward, whom *his* lord shall make ruler over his household, to give *them their* portion of meat in due season? 43 Blessed *is* that servant, whom his lord when he cometh shall find so doing. 44 Of a truth I say unto you, that he will make him ruler over all that he hath. 45 But and if that servant say in his heart, My lord delayeth his coming; and shall begin to beat the men-servants and maidens, and to eat and drink, and to be drunken; 46 The lord of that servant will come in a day when he looketh not for *him,* and at an hour when he is not aware, and will cut him in sunder, and will appoint him his portion with the unbelievers. 47And that servant, which knew his lord's will, and prepared not *himself,* neither did according to his will, shall be beaten with many *stripes.* 48 But he that knew not, and did commit things worthy of stripes, shall be beaten with few *stripes.* For unto whomsoever much is given, of him shall be much required; and to whom men have committed much, of him they will ask the more.

49 I am come to send fire on the earth: and what will I, if it be already kindled? 50 But I have a baptism to be baptized with; and how am I straitened till it be accomplished! 51 Suppose ye that I am come to give peace on earth? I tell you, Nay; but rather division: 52 For from henceforth there shall be five in one house divided, three against two, and two against three. 53 The father shall be divided against the son, and the son against the father; the mother against the daughter, and the daughter against the mother; the mother in law against her daughter in law, and the daughter in law against her mother in law.

54 And he said also to the people, When ye see a cloud rise out of the west, straightway ye say, There cometh a shower; and so it is. 55And when *ye see* the south wind blow, ye say, There will be heat; and it cometh to pass. 56 *Ye* hypocrites, ye can discern the face of the sky and of the earth; but how is it that ye do not discern this time? 57 Yea, and why even of yourselves judge ye not what is right?

58 When thou goest with thine adversary to the magistrate, *as thou art* in the way, give diligence that thou mayest be delivered from him; lest he hale thee to the judge, and the judge deliver thee to the officer, and the officer cast thee into prison. 59 I tell thee, thou shalt not depart thence, till thou hast paid the very last mite.

N.A.S.

truly I say to you, that he will gird himself *to serve,* and have them recline *at table,* and will come up and wait on them. 38 "Whether he comes in the ᵃsecond watch, or even in the ᵇthird, and finds *them* so, blessed are those *slaves.* 39 "And be sure of this, that if the head of the house had known at what hour the thief was coming, he would not have allowed his house to be broken into. 40 "You too, be ready; for the Son of Man is coming at an hour that you do not expect."

41 And Peter said, "Lord, are You addressing this parable to us, or to everyone *else* as well?" 42And the Lord said, "Who then is the faithful and sensible steward, whom his master will put in charge of his servants, to give them their rations at the proper time? 43 "Blessed is that slave whom his master finds so doing when he comes. 44 "Truly I say to you, that he will put him in charge of all his possessions. 45 "But if that slave says in his heart, 'My master will be a long time in coming,' and begins to beat the slaves, *both* men and women, and to eat and drink and get drunk; 46 the master of that slave will come on a day when he does not expect *him,* and at an hour he does not know, and will cut him in pieces, and assign him a place with the unbelievers. 47 "And that slave who knew his master's will and did not get ready or act in accord with his will, shall receive many *lashes,* 48 but the one who did not know *it,* and committed deeds worthy of a flogging, will receive but few. And from everyone who has been given much shall much be required; and to whom they entrusted much, of him they will ask all the more.

49 "I have come to cast fire upon the earth; and how I wish it were already kindled! 50 "But I have a baptism to undergo, and how distressed I am until it is accomplished! 51 "Do you suppose that I came to grant peace on earth? I tell you, no, but rather division; 52 for from now on five *members* in one household will be divided, three against two, and two against three. 53 "They will be divided, father against son, and son against father; mother against daughter, and daughter against mother; mother-in-law against daughter-in-law, and daughter-in-law against mother-in-law."

54 And He was also saying to the multitudes, "When you see a cloud rising in the west, immediately you say, 'A shower is coming,' and so it turns out. 55 "And when *you see* a south wind blowing, you say, 'It will be a hot day,' and it turns out *that way.* 56 "You hypocrites! You know how to analyze the appearance of the earth and the sky, but why do you not analyze this present time? 57 "And why do you not even on your own initiative judge what is right? 58 "For while you are going with your opponent to appear before the magistrate, on *your* way *there* make an effort to settle with him, in order that he may not drag you before the judge, and the judge turn you over to the constable, and the constable throw you into prison. 59 "I say to you, you shall not get out of there until you have paid the very last cent."

[a] I.e., 9 p.m. to midnight. [b] I.e., Midnight to 3 a.m.

WILLIAMS

comes, will find on the watch for him. I solemnly say to you, he will tighten his belt and have them sit at table, and he will go around and wait on them. 38 Whether he comes before or after midnight, if he finds them so, happy are they. 39 But be sure of this, that if the master of the house had known what time the thief was coming, he would not have let his house be broken into. 40 So you, too, must always be ready, for at an hour that you are not expecting, the Son of Man will come."

41 Peter said to Him, "Lord, do you mean this story for us, or is it for everybody?"

42 And the Lord said, "Who then is the faithful, thoughtful manager whom his master will put in charge of his household, to give out the supplies at the proper time? 43 Happy is that slave whom his master, when he comes, will find so doing. 44 I tell you truly, he will put him in charge of all his property. 45 But if that slave says to himself, my Master is not coming back for a long time, and begins to beat the men and women slaves, and to eat and drink and get drunk, 46 his master will come back some day when he is not expecting him, and at an hour of which he is not aware, and will cut him in two, and give him his share with the unfaithful. 47 That slave who knows his master's wishes and does not get ready or act upon them will be severely punished.c 48 But the one who does wrong without knowing it will be lightly punished. Much will be demanded from anyone to whom much has been given; yea, people will demand much more from anyone to whom they have entrusted much.

49 "It is fire that I have come to bring upon the earth, and how I wish it were already kindled! 50 I have a baptism to be baptized with, and how I am pressed with anguish till it is accomplished! 51 Do you think that I came to give peace on earth? I tell you, not so at all, but rather discord. 52 For from now on, five in a house will be divided, three against two, and two against three. 53 Father will be against son and son against father, mother against daughter and daughter against mother, mother-in-law against daughter-in-law and daughter-in-law against mother-in-law."

54 And He said to the crowds, "When you see a cloud rising in the west, at once you say, 'It is going to rain,' and it does. 55 And when you see a south wind blowing, you say, 'It is going to be very hot,' and so it is. 56 You hypocrites! You know how to interpret day by day the look of earth and sky. Then how is it that you do not know how to interpret the present crisis? 57 Why do you not of yourselves decide what is right? 58 For instance, when you are on the way to court with your opponent, take the utmost pains on the way to get entirely rid of him, so that he may not rush you before the judge, and the judge turn you over to the sheriff,d and the sheriff put you in prison. 59 I tell you, you will never get out of it until you have paid the last penny!"

BECK

when he comes. I tell you he'll certainly fasten his belt, have them lie down for a meal, and come and serve them. 38 Even if he comes in the middle of the night or toward morning and finds them that way, happy are they.

39 "You know if the owner of a house had known just when the burglar was coming, he would not have let anyone break into his house. 40 You, too, get ready, because the Son of Man is coming when you don't expect Him."

41 "Lord," Peter asked, "by this illustration do you mean to warn us—or everybody else too?"

42 The Lord asked, "Who do you suppose is the manager that can be trusted and has good sense whom the master will put in charge of his servants to give them their share of food at the right time? 43 Happy is that slave whom his master will find doing just this when he comes. 44 I tell you he certainly will make him manager of all his property. 45 But if that slave says to himself, 'My master isn't coming back for some time,' and starts to beat the other slaves, men and women, and eats, drinks, and gets drunk, 46 the master of that slave will come one day when he's not expecting him and at a time he doesn't know and will cut him in pieces and put him with the unfaithful.

47 "That slave who knew what his master wanted and didn't prepare himself or do what he wanted will get many blows. 48 But he who didn't know and did things for which he deserved to be beaten will get few blows. If you were given much, much will be expected of you, and if much was entrusted to you, all the more will be demanded of you."

Sorrow Ahead

49 "I have come to bring fire on earth, and how glad I would be if it were already started! 50 I must be baptized with a baptism, and how I am troubled till it is done!

51 "Do you think I came to bring peace on earth? No, I tell you—to bring division. 52 From now on five in one family will be divided, three against two and two against three. 53 A father will be against a son and *a son against a father*, a mother against a daughter and *a daughter against her mother*, a mother-in-law against her daughter-in-law and *a daughter-in-law against her mother-in-law*." 55

This Is Your Opportunity

54 "When you see a cloud coming up in the west," Jesus said to the people, "you immediately say, 'There's going to be a heavy rain,' and so it rains. 55 And when you see a wind blowing from the south, you say, 'It's going to be hot,' and so it is. 56 You hypocrites! You can tell what the appearance of the earth and of the sky means. How is it that you can't interpret this present time? 57 Why don't you yourselves decide what is right?

58 "When you go with your opponent to be tried before a ruler, do your best to settle with him on the way, or he may drag you before the judge, and the judge will hand you over to the officer, and the officer will put you in prison. 59 I tell you, you will never get out till you pay the last cent."

---

[c] Grk., *beaten with many lashes*. [d] Modern term almost equivalent to the ancient officer.

[55] Micah 7:6

K.J.V.

13 There were present at that season some that told him of the Galileans, whose blood Pilate had mingled with their sacrifices. 2And Jesus answering said unto them, Suppose ye that these Galileans were sinners above all the Galileans, because they suffered such things? 3 I tell you, Nay: but, except ye repent, ye shall all likewise perish. 4 Or those eighteen, upon whom the tower in Siloam fell, and slew them, think ye that they were sinners above all men that dwelt in Jerusalem? 5 I tell you, Nay: but, except ye repent, ye shall all likewise perish.

6 He spake also this parable; A certain *man* had a fig tree planted in his vineyard; and he came and sought fruit thereon, and found none. 7 Then said he unto the dresser of his vineyard, Behold, these three years I come seeking fruit on this fig tree, and find none: cut it down; why cumbereth it the ground? 8And he answering said unto him, Lord, let it alone this year also, till I shall dig about it, and dung *it:* 9And if it bear fruit, *well:* and if not, *then* after that thou shalt cut it down.

10 And he was teaching in one of the synagogues on the sabbath. 11And, behold, there was a woman which had a spirit of infirmity eighteen years, and was bowed together, and could in no wise lift up *herself.* 12And when Jesus saw her, he called *her to him,* and said unto her, Woman, thou art loosed from thine infirmity. 13And he laid *his* hands on her: and immediately she was made straight, and glorified God. 14And the ruler of the synagogue answered with indignation, because that Jesus had healed on the sabbath day, and said unto the people, There are six days in which men ought to work: in them therefore come and be healed, and not on the sabbath day. 15 The Lord then answered him, and said, *Thou* hypocrite, doth not each one of you on the sabbath loose his ox or *his* ass from the stall, and lead *him* away to watering? 16And ought not this woman, being a daughter of Abraham, whom Satan hath bound, lo, these eighteen years, be loosed from this bond on the sabbath day? 17And when he had said these things, all his adversaries were ashamed: and all the people rejoiced for all the glorious things that were done by him.

18 Then said he, Unto what is the kingdom of God like? and whereunto shall I resemble it? 19 It is like a grain of mustard seed, which a man took, and cast into his garden; and it grew, and waxed a great tree; and the fowls of the air lodged in the branches of it. 20And again he said, Whereunto shall I liken the kingdom of God? 21 It is like leaven, which a woman took and hid in three measures of meal, till the whole was leavened. 22And he went through the cities and villages, teaching, and journeying toward Jerusalem. 23 Then said one unto him, Lord, are there few that be saved? And he said unto them, 24 Strive to enter in at the strait gate: for

N.A.S.

13 Now on the same occasion there were some present who reported to Him about the Galileans, whose blood Pilate had mingled with their sacrifices. 2And He answered and said to them, "Do you suppose that these Galileans were *greater* sinners than all *other* Galileans, because they suffered this *fate?* 3 "I tell you, no, but, unless you repent, you will all likewise perish. 4 "Or do you suppose that those eighteen on whom the tower in Siloam fell and killed them, were *worse* culprits than all the men who live in Jerusalem? 5 "I tell you, no, but, unless you repent, you will all likewise perish."

6 And He *began* telling this parable: "A certain man had a fig tree which had been planted in his vineyard; and he came looking for fruit on it, and did not find any. 7 "And he said to the vineyard-keeper, 'Behold, for three years I have come looking for fruit on this fig tree without finding any. Cut it down! Why does it even use up the ground?' 8 "And he answered and said to him, 'Let it alone, sir, for this year too, until I dig around it and put in fertilizer; 9 and if it bears fruit next year, *fine;* but if not, cut it down.'"

10 And He was teaching in one of the synagogues on the Sabbath. 11And behold, there was a woman who for eighteen years had had a sickness caused by a spirit; and she was bent double, and could not straighten up at all. 12And when Jesus saw her, He called her over and said to her, "Woman, you are freed from your sickness." 13And He laid His hands upon her; and immediately she was made erect again, and *began* glorifying God. 14And the synagogue official, indignant because Jesus had healed on the Sabbath, *began* saying to the multitude in response, "There are six days in which work should be done; therefore come during them and get healed, and not on the Sabbath day." 15 But the Lord answered him and said, "You hypocrites, does not each of you on the Sabbath untie his ox or his donkey from the stall, and lead him away to water *him?* 16 "And this woman, a daughter of Abraham as she is, whom Satan has bound for eighteen long years, should she not have been released from this bond on the Sabbath day?" 17And as He said this, all his opponents were being humiliated; and the entire multitude was rejoicing over all the glorious things being done by Him.

18 Therefore He was saying, "What is the kingdom of God like, and to what shall I compare it? 19 "It is like a mustard seed, which a man took and threw into his own garden; and it grew and became a tree; and the birds of the air nested in its branches."

20 And again He said, "To what shall I compare the kingdom of God? 21 "It is like leaven, which a woman took and hid in three pecks of meal, until it was all leavened."

22 And He was passing through from one city and village to another, teaching, and proceeding on His way to Jerusalem. 23And someone said to Him, "Lord, are there *just* a few who are being saved?" And He said to them, 24 "Strive to enter by the narrow door; for

WILLIAMS

13 *Repentance emphasized by examples and story; a woman bent double by rheumatism cured on the sabbath; the stories of the mustard seed and yeast; Governor Antipas reproved; Jerusalem lamented*

Just at that time some people came up to tell Him about the Galileans whose blood Pilate mingled with that of their sacrifices. 2 Then He answered them, "Do you think, because these Galileans suffered like this, that they were worse sinners than all the rest of the Galileans? 3 By no means, I tell you; but unless you repent, you will all perish as they did. 4 Or those eighteen people at Siloam on whom the tower fell and whom it crushed to death, do you think that they were offenders worse than all the rest of the people who live in Jerusalem? 5 By no means, I tell you; but unless you repent, you will all perish as they did."
6 Then He told them this story: "A man had a fig tree planted by his vineyard, and he kept going and looking for figs on it, but did not find any. 7 So he said to the vinedresser, 'Look here! for three years I have been coming to look for figs on this fig tree, and have not found any. Cut it down. Why waste the ground with it?' 8 But he answered, 'Leave it, sir, just one more year, till I dig around it and manure it. 9 If it bears figs in the future, well; but if not, you will have to cut it down.' "
10 One sabbath He was teaching in one of the synagogues, 11 and there was a woman there who for eighteen years had had a disease caused by a spirit. She was bent double and could not straighten herself up at all. 12 As soon as Jesus saw her, He called her to Him and said to her, "Woman, you are freed from your disease!" 13 Then He laid His hands on her, and at once she straightened herself up and burst into praising God.
14 But the leader of the synagogue, indignant because Jesus had cured her on the sabbath, answered the crowd, "There are six days on which people must work; so come on these and be cured, but not on the sabbath."
15 Then the Lord answered him, "You hypocrites! Does not everyone of you on the sabbath untie his ox or donkey and lead him out of the stable to water him? 16 And so was it not right for this woman, a descendant of Abraham, whom Satan has for eighteen years kept bound, to be freed from this bond on the sabbath?"
17 Even while He was saying this, His opponents were blushing with shame, but all the people were rejoicing over all the glorious things that were being done by Him.
18 So He went on to say, "What is the kingdom of God like? To what may I compare it? 19 It is like a mustard seed which a man took and dropped in his garden, and it grew and became a tree, and the wild birds roosted in its branches."
20 And again He said, "To what may I compare the kingdom of God? 21 It is like yeast which a woman took and hid *a* in a bushel of flour until it all had risen."
22 Then He was traveling from town to town and from village to village, teaching and making His way toward Jerusalem. 23 And someone asked Him, "Lord, are only a few to be saved?"
And He said to them, 24 "You must struggle on to get in through the narrow door, for I

[a] In connection with kneading.

BECK

Repent

13 At that time some men were there to tell Him about the Galileans whose blood Pilate had mixed with their sacrifices. 2 Jesus asked them, "Do you think, because this happened to them, those Galileans must have been worse sinners than all the other Galileans? 3 I tell you, no. And if you don't repent, you will all perish as they did. 4 Or those eighteen the tower at Siloam fell on and killed—do you think they must have been worse transgressors than all the other people living in Jerusalem? 5 I tell you, no. And if you don't repent, you will all perish as they did."

Another Year

6 He told them this story:
"A man had a fig tree growing in his vineyard. He came looking for fruit on it but didn't find any. 7 So he said to the man who worked the vineyard, 'Look here! For the last three years I've come looking for figs on this fig tree and haven't found any. Cut it down. Why should it waste the ground?'
8 " 'Master,' he answered him, 'let it stand one more year, and I'll dig around it and fertilize it; 9 it may have figs next year. If not, cut it down.' "

Sick for Eighteen Years

10 Jesus was teaching in one of the synagogs on a Sabbath, 11 and there was a woman whom a spirit had crippled for eighteen years. She was bent over and couldn't stand up straight. 12 When Jesus saw her, He called her and said, "Woman, you're rid of your trouble." 13 He laid His hands on her, and immediately she stood up straight and praised God.
14 But the synagog leader was annoyed with Jesus for healing on a Sabbath. "There are six days to do your work," he told the people. "Come on those days and get healed, but not on the day of rest."
15 "You hypocrites!" the Lord answered him. "Doesn't every one of you on a Saturday untie his ox or donkey from the manger and take it out to water? 16 And this woman, a daughter of Abraham, whom the devil has bound these eighteen years, shouldn't she on the day of rest be freed from what bound her?"
17 As He said this, all His enemies had to feel ashamed, but all the common people were happy over the wonderful things He was doing.

Mustard Seed and Yeast

18 "What is God's kingdom like," He asked, "and what will I compare it with? 19 It's like a mustard seed a man took and planted in his garden. It grew to be a tree, and the *birds in the air nested in its branches.*[56]
20 "With what should I compare God's kingdom?" He asked again. 21 "It's like yeast a woman mixed into a bushel of flour till it was all fermented."

The Narrow Door

22 Then Jesus went and taught in one town and village after another on His way to Jerusalem.
23 Someone asked Him, "Lord, are only a few people saved?"
24 "Struggle to get in through the narrow

[56] Ps. 104:12; 31:6; Ezek. 17:23; Dan. 4:12, 21

K.J.V.

many, I say unto you, will seek to enter in, and shall not be able. 25 When once the master of the house is risen up, and hath shut to the door, and ye begin to stand without, and to knock at the door, saying, Lord, Lord, open unto us; and he shall answer and say unto you, I know you not whence ye are: 26 Then shall ye begin to say, We have eaten and drunk in thy presence, and thou hast taught in our streets. 27 But he shall say, I tell you, I know you not whence ye are; depart from me, all *ye* workers of iniquity. 28 There shall be weeping and gnashing of teeth, when ye shall see Abraham, and Isaac, and Jacob, and all the prophets, in the kingdom of God, and you *yourselves* thrust out. 29And they shall come from the east, and *from* the west, and from the north, and *from* the south, and shall sit down in the kingdom of God. 30And, behold, there are last which shall be first; and there are first which shall be last.

31 The same day there came certain of the Pharisees, saying unto him, Get thee out, and depart hence; for Herod will kill thee. 32And he said unto them, Go ye, and tell that fox, Behold, I cast out devils, and I do cures to day and to morrow, and the third *day* I shall be perfected. 33 Nevertheless I must walk to day, and to morrow, and the *day* following: for it cannot be that a prophet perish out of Jerusalem. 34 O Jerusalem, Jerusalem, which killest the prophets, and stonest them that are sent unto thee; how often would I have gathered thy children together, as a hen *doth gather* her brood under *her* wings, and ye would not! 35 Behold, your house is left unto you desolate: and verily I say unto you, Ye shall not see me, until *the time* come when ye shall say, Blessed *is* he that cometh in the name of the Lord.

14 And it came to pass, as he went into the house of one of the chief Pharisees to eat bread on the sabbath day, that they watched him. 2And, behold, there was a certain man before him which had the dropsy. 3And Jesus answering spake unto the lawyers and Pharisees, saying, Is it lawful to heal on the sabbath day? 4And they held their peace. And he took *him*, and healed him, and let him go; 5And answered them, saying, Which of you shall have an ass or an ox fallen into a pit, and will not straightway pull him out on the sabbath day? 6And they could not answer him again to these things.

7 And he put forth a parable to those which were bidden, when he marked how they chose out the chief rooms; saying unto them, 8 When thou art bidden of any *man* to a wedding, sit not down in the highest room; lest a more honourable man than thou be bidden of him; 9And he that bade thee and him come and say to thee, Give this man place; and thou begin with shame to take the lowest room. 10 But when thou art bidden, go and sit down in the lowest room; that when he that bade thee cometh, he may say unto thee, Friend, go up higher: then shalt thou have worship in the presence of them that sit at meat with thee. 11 For whosoever exalteth himself shall be abased; and he that humbleth himself shall be exalted.

N.A.S.

many, I tell you, will seek to enter and will not be able. 25 "Once the head of the house gets up and shuts the door, and you begin to stand outside and knock on the door, saying, 'Lord, open up to us'! then He will answer and say to you, 'I do not know where you are from.' 26 "Then you will begin to say, 'We ate and drank in Your presence, and You taught in our streets'; 27 and He will say, 'I tell you, I do not know where you are from; DEPART FROM ME, ALL YOU EVIL-DOERS.' 28 "There will be weeping and gnashing of teeth there when you see Abraham and Isaac and Jacob and all the prophets in the kingdom of God, and yourselves being cast out. 29 "And they will come from east and west, and from north and south, and will recline *at table* in the kingdom of God. 30 "And behold, *some* are last who will be first, and *some* are first who will be last."

31 Just at that time some Pharisees came up, saying to Him, "Go away and depart from here, for Herod wants to kill You." 32And He said to them, "Go and tell that fox, 'Behold, I cast out demons and perform cures today and tomorrow, and the third *day* I reach My goal.' 33 "Nevertheless I must journey on today and tomorrow and the next *day;* for it cannot be that a prophet should perish outside of Jerusalem. 34 "O Jerusalem, Jerusalem, *the city* that kills the prophets and stones those sent to her! How often I wanted to gather your children together, just as a hen *gathers* her brood under her wings, and you would not *have it!* 35 "Behold, your house is left to you *desolate;* and I say to you, you shall not see Me until *the time* comes when you say, 'Blessed *is* He who comes in the name of the Lord!' "

14 And it came about that when He went into the house of one of the leaders of the Pharisees on *the* Sabbath to eat bread, that they were watching Him closely. 2And there, in front of Him was a certain man suffering from dropsy. 3And Jesus answered and spoke to the lawyers and Pharisees, saying, "Is it lawful to heal on the Sabbath, or not?" 4 But they kept silent. And He took hold of him, and healed him, and sent him away. 5And He said to them, "Which one of you shall have a son or an ox fall into a well, and will not immediately pull him out on a Sabbath day?" 6And they could make no reply to this.

7 And He *began* speaking a parable to the invited guests when He noticed how they had been picking out the places of honor *at the table;* saying to them, 8 "When you are invited by someone to a wedding feast, do not take the place of honor, lest someone more distinguished than you may have been invited by him, 9 and he who invited you both shall come and say to you, 'Give place to this man', and then in disgrace you proceed to occupy the last place. 10 "But when you are invited, go and recline at the last place, so that when the one who has invited you comes, he may say to you, 'Friend, move up higher'; then you will have honor in the sight of all who are at the table with you. 11 "For everyone who exalts himself shall be humbled, and he who humbles himself shall be exalted."

WILLIAMS / BECK

WILLIAMS

tell you, many will try to get in, but will not succeed, 25 when once the master of the house gets up and shuts the door, and you begin to stand on the outside and to knock on the door again and again, and say, 'Lord, open it for us'; but He will answer, 'I do not know where you come from.' 26 Then you will begin to say, 'We ate and drank with you, and you taught in our streets.' 27 But He will say to you, 'I do not know where you come from. Go away from me, all you wrongdoers!' 28 There you will weep and grind your teeth, when you see Abraham and Isaac and Jacob and all the prophets in the kingdom of God, and you yourselves being driven away on the outside. 29 People will come from east and west, from north and south, and take their seats at the feast in the kingdom of God. 30And so there are those now last who will be first then, and there are those now first who will then be last."

31 Just at that time some Pharisees came up and said to Him, "Get out at once! Get away from here, for Herod wants to kill you!"

32 But He said to them: "Go and tell that fox, 'Here I am, driving out demons and performing cures, today and tomorrow, and on the third day I will finish these tasks. 33 But I must continue on my way, for it is not possible for a prophet to perish outside Jerusalem.'

34 "O Jerusalem! Jerusalem! the city that continues to murder the prophets, and to stone those who are sent to her, how often I have yearned to gather your children around me, as a hen gathers her brood under her wings. But you refused! 35 Now your house is abandoned to its fate! And I tell you, you will never see me again until you say, 'Blessed be He who comes in the name of the Lord!' "

14 *Jesus dines with a Pharisee; cures a man with dropsy; tells three stories about banquets; tells two more stories about counting the cost*

One sabbath, when He went to take a meal at the house of a Pharisee who was a member of the council, they continued to watch Him closely. 2 Just in front of Him was a man who was suffering from dropsy. 3 So He answered the experts in the law and the Pharisees by asking, "Is it right to cure people on the sabbath or not?" 4 But they made no answer. So He took hold of the man and cured him and sent him away. 5 Then He said to them, "Which of you, if his son or ox falls into a well, will not at once pull him out on the sabbath?" 6 But they could make no reply to this.

7 When He noticed how the guests were picking out the best places, He told them the following story:

8 "When you are invited by anyone to a wedding supper, never take the best place, for someone of greater distinction than you may have been invited, 9 so that your host may not come and say to you, 'Make room for this man'; and then in embarrassment you will proceed to take and keep the lowest place. 10 But when you are invited anywhere, go and take the lowest place, so that when your host comes in, he may say to you, 'My friend, come up to a better place.' Then you will be honored in the presence of all your fellow-guests. 11 For everyone who exalts himself will be humbled, but whoever humbles himself will be exalted."

BECK

door," He told them. "I tell you, many will try to get in and not succeed. 25After the Owner of the house gets up and closes the door, you'll be standing outside and knocking at the door. 'Lord, open up for us!' you'll say. But He'll answer you, 'I don't know where you're from.' 26 Then you'll say, 'We ate and drank with You, and You taught in our streets.' 27 But He'll tell you, 'I don't know where you're from. *Get away from Me, all you who do wrong.*' [57] 28 Then you will cry and grind your teeth when you see Abraham, Isaac, Jacob, and all the prophets in God's kingdom but yourselves thrown out. 29 People will come *from the east and the west,*[58] the north and the south, and will eat in God's kingdom. 30 You see, some who are last will be first, and some who are first will be last."

Jesus Warns Jerusalem

31 Just then some Pharisees came and told Him, "Leave and get away from here; Herod wants to kill you."

32 "Go," He answered them, "and tell that fox, 'Listen, today and tomorrow I will drive out devils and do healings, and on the third day I will finish.' 33 But I must be on My way today, tomorrow, and the next day, because a prophet just can't be killed outside Jerusalem.

34 "Jerusalem, Jerusalem, you murder the prophets and stone those sent to you! How often I wanted to gather your children the way a hen gathers her chicks under her wings, but you didn't want to! 35 Look, now your *house is left*[59] to you. I tell you, you will not see Me till you say, '*Blessed is He who is coming in the Lord's name.*' " [60]

Dinner Is Ready!

14 Once on a Saturday Jesus went to the home of a leader of the Pharisees to eat a meal, and they were watching Him carefully. 2 In front of Him was a man who had dropsy. 3 This led Jesus to ask the experts in the Law and the Pharisees, "Is it right to heal on a day of rest or not?" But they didn't say anything. 4 So Jesus took hold of the man, made him well, and sent him away. 5 "If your son or your ox falls into a well," he asked them, "won't anyone of you pull him out immediately on a Sabbath?" 6 They couldn't answer this.

7 He noticed how the guests were trying to get the places of honor, and so He used the scene to teach them: 8 "When anyone invites you to a wedding, don't take the place of honor. He may have invited somebody more important than you. 9And he who invited you and him will come and tell you, 'Give this man your place,' and then you'll feel ashamed when you have to take the lowest place. 10 No, when you're invited, go and take the lowest place, so that when your host comes he'll tell you, 'Friend, move up higher.' Then all your fellow guests will see how you're honored. 11 If you honor yourself, you'll be humbled, but if you humble yourself, you'll be honored."

[57] Ps. 6:8
[58] Mal. 1:11
[59] Jer. 12:7; 22:5
[60] Ps. 118:26

K.J.V.

12 Then said he also to him that bade him, When thou makest a dinner or a supper, call not thy friends, nor thy brethren, neither thy kinsmen, nor *thy* rich neighbours; lest they also bid thee again, and a recompense be made thee. 13 But when thou makest a feast, call the poor, the maimed, the lame, the blind: 14And thou shalt be blessed; for they cannot recompense thee: for thou shalt be recompensed at the resurrection of the just.

15 And when one of them that sat at meat with him heard these things, he said unto him, Blessed *is* he that shall eat bread in the kingdom of God. 16 Then said he unto him, A certain man made a great supper, and bade many: 17And sent his servant at supper time to say to them that were bidden, Come; for all things are now ready. 18And they all with one *consent* began to make excuse. The first said unto him, I have bought a piece of ground, and I must needs go and see it: I pray thee have me excused. 19And another said, I have bought five yoke of oxen, and I go to prove them: I pray thee have me excused. 20And another said, I have married a wife, and therefore I cannot come. 21 So that servant came, and shewed his lord these things. Then the master of the house being angry said to his servant, Go out quickly into the streets and lanes of the city, and bring in hither the poor, and the maimed, and the halt, and the blind. 22And the servant said, Lord, it is done as thou hast commanded, and yet there is room. 23And the lord said unto the servant, Go out into the highways and hedges, and compel *them* to come in, that my house may be filled. 24 For I say unto you, That none of those men which were bidden shall taste of my supper.

25 And there went great multitudes with him: and he turned, and said unto them, 26 If any *man* come to me, and hate not his father, and mother, and wife, and children, and brethren, and sisters, yea, and his own life also, he cannot be my disciple. 27And whosoever doth not bear his cross, and come after me, cannot be my disciple. 28 For which of you, intending to build a tower, sitteth not down first, and counteth the cost, whether he have *sufficient* to finish *it?* 29 Lest haply, after he hath laid the foundation, and is not able to finish *it,* all that behold *it* begin to mock him, 30 Saying, This man began to build, and was not able to finish. 31 Or what king, going to make war against another king, sitteth not down first, and consulteth whether he be able with ten thousand to meet him that cometh against him with twenty thousand? 32 Or else, while the other is yet a great way off, he sendeth an ambassage, and desireth conditions of peace. 33 So likewise, whosoever he be of you that forsaketh not all that he hath, he cannot be my disciple.

34 Salt *is* good: but if the salt have lost his savour, wherewith shall it be seasoned? 35 It is neither fit for the land, nor yet for the dunghill; *but* men cast it out. He that hath ears to hear, let him hear.

N.A.S.

12 And He also went on to say to the one who had invited Him, "When you give a luncheon or a dinner, do not invite your friends or your brothers or your relatives or rich neighbors, lest they also invite you in return, and repayment come to you. 13 "But when you give a reception, invite *the* poor, *the* crippled, *the* lame, *the* blind, 14 and you will be blessed, since they do not have *the means* to repay you; for you will be repaid at the resurrection of the righteous."

15 And when one of those who were reclining *at table* with Him heard this, he said to Him, "Blessed is everyone who shall eat bread in the kingdom of God!" 16 But He said to him, "A certain man was giving a big dinner, and he invited many; 17 and at the dinner hour he sent his slave to say to those who had been invited, 'Come; for everything is ready now.' 18 "But they all alike began to make excuses. The first one said to him, 'I have bought a piece of land and I need to go out and look at it; please consider me excused.' 19 "And another one said, 'I have bought five yoke of oxen, and I am going to try them out; please consider me excused.' 20 "And another one said, 'I have married a wife, and for that reason I cannot come.' 21 "And the slave came *back* and reported this to his master. Then the head of the household became angry and said to his slave, 'Go out at once into the streets and lanes of the city and bring in here the poor and crippled and blind and lame.' 22 "And the slave said, 'Master, what you commanded has been done, and still there is room.' 23 "And the master said to the slave, 'Go out into the highways and along the hedges, and compel *them* to come in, that my house may be filled. 24 'For I tell you, none of those men who were invited shall taste of my dinner.'"

25 Now great multitudes were going along with Him; and He turned and said to them, 26 "If anyone comes to Me, and does not [a]hate his own father and mother and wife and children and brothers and sisters, yes, and even his own life, he cannot be My disciple. 27 "Whoever does not carry his own cross and come after Me cannot be My disciple. 28 "For which one of you, when he wants to build a tower, does not first sit down and calculate the cost, to see if he has enough to complete it? 29 "Otherwise, when he has laid a foundation, and is not able to finish, all who observe it begin to ridicule him, 30 saying, 'This man began to build and was not able to finish.' 31 "Or what king, when he sets out to meet another king in battle, will not first sit down and take counsel whether he is strong enough with ten thousand *men* to encounter the one coming against him with twenty thousand? 32 "Or else, while the other is still far away, he sends a delegation and asks terms of peace. 33 "So therefore, no one of you can be My disciple who does not give up all his own possessions. 34 "Therefore, salt is good; but if even salt has become tasteless, with what will it be seasoned? 35 "It is useless either for the soil or for the manure pile; it is thrown out. He who has ears to hear, let him hear."

[a] I.e., by comparison of his love for Me.

210

WILLIAMS

12 Then He proceeded to say to the man who invited Him:

"When you give a luncheon or a dinner, stop the social custom of inviting your friends or your brothers or your relatives or your rich neighbors, for they may invite you in return and so you will be repaid. 13 But when you give a reception, make it your habit to invite people that are poor, maimed, crippled, or blind. 14 Then you will be happy, because they cannot repay you; you will be repaid at the resurrection of the upright."

15 But one of the fellow-guests heard this, and said to Him, "Happy will be the man who is fortunate enough to be at the feast in the kingdom of God."

16 Then Jesus said to him:

"Once a man was giving a great dinner and invited many people to it. 17 And at the dinner hour he sent his slave to say to the invited guests, 'Come, for it is now ready.' 18 But they all in the same attitude began to excuse themselves. The first one said, 'I have just bought a piece of land and I must go and look it over. Please excuse me.' 19 Another said, 'I have just bought five yoke of oxen, and I am on my way to try them. Please excuse me.' 20 Another said, 'I have just gotten married, and so I cannot come.' 21 So the slave returned and reported these answers to his master. Then the master of the house became angry and said to his slave, 'Hurry out into the streets and lanes of the city and bring in here the poor, the maimed, the crippled, and the blind.' 22 Then the slave said, 'Sir, what you ordered has been done, and still there is room.'

23 "Then the master said to his slave, 'Go out on the roads and by the hedges and make the people come in, so that my house may be filled. 24 For I tell you, not one of those people who were invited shall get a taste of my dinner!' "

25 Now great crowds were going along with Him, and all at once He turned and said to them:

26 "If anyone comes to me and does not hate his own father and mother and wife and children and brothers and sisters, and still more, his own life too, he cannot be a disciple of mine. 27 Whoever does not persevere in carrying his own cross and thus follow after me, cannot be a disciple of mine.

28 "What man among you, if he wishes to build a tower, does not first sit down and calculate the cost, to see whether he has money enough to complete it? 29 Lest, perchance, after he has laid the foundation but cannot complete the building, all who see it begin to make sport of him, 30 and say, 'This fellow started to erect a building but could not complete it!'

31 "Or what king, when he is going to make an attack on another king, does not first sit down and deliberate whether he is able with ten thousand soldiers to meet the other king who is coming against him with twenty thousand? 32 And if he cannot, while the other is still far away, he sends envoys and asks for terms of peace.

33 "Just so, no one of you who does not forsake everything that he has, can be a disciple of mine. 34 Salt is good; but if salt itself loses its strength, how can that strength be restored? 35 It is fit for neither soil nor manure. People throw it away. Let him who has ears to hear with give heed!"

BECK

12 Then He told the man who had invited Him, "When you give a dinner or a supper, don't invite your friends, your brothers, your relatives, or rich neighbors. Otherwise they'll invite you too and pay you back. 13 No, when you give a banquet, invite the poor, crippled, lame, and blind. 14 Then you'll be happy because they can't pay you back. You'll be paid back when the righteous rise from the dead."

15 When one of those eating with Him heard this, he said to Jesus, "Happy is he who will eat bread in God's kingdom."

16 Jesus said to him:

"A man once gave a big dinner and invited many. 17 When it was time for the dinner, he sent his slave to tell those who were invited, 'Come, it's ready now!'

18 "Then they all alike began to excuse themselves. 'I bought a field,' the first told him, 'and I've got to go out and see it. Please excuse me.' 19 Another said, 'I bought five teams of oxen, and I'm on my way to try them out. Please excuse me.' 20 And another said, 'I just got married, and that's why I can't come.'

21 "The slave went back and reported this to his master. Then the master of the house got angry. 'Go out quickly into the streets and alleys of the city,' he told his slave, 'and bring in here the poor, crippled, blind, and lame.'

22 "And the slave said, 'Master, it's done as you ordered, and there's still room.'

23 "Then the master told the slave, 'Go out to the roads and stone fences, and make them come in! I want my house to be full. 24 I tell you, none of those men who were invited will taste my dinner.' "

Leave Everything

25 Large crowds were going with Jesus. 26 Turning to them, He said, "If you come to Me and don't hate your father, mother, wife, children, brothers, and sisters and even your own life, you can't be My disciple. 27 Whoever doesn't carry his cross and follow Me can't be My disciple.

28 "If anyone of you wants to build a tower, won't you first sit down and figure out what it costs, to see if you have enough to finish it? 29 Otherwise, when you've laid a foundation but can't finish the building, all who watch you will make fun of you 30 and say, 'This fellow started to build but couldn't finish it.'

31 "Or suppose a king is going into battle against another king. Won't he first sit down and consider if with ten thousand men he can oppose the other coming against him with twenty thousand? 32 If he can't, then, while the other is still far away, he sends ambassadors to ask for terms of peace. 33 Just so, anyone of you who doesn't say good-by to everything he has can't be My disciple.

34 "Now, salt is good. But if the salt loses its taste, how will it be made salty again? 35 It is no good for the ground or for the manure pile. People throw it away.

"If you have ears to hear, listen!"

15 Then drew near unto him all the publicans and sinners for to hear him. 2And the Pharisees and scribes murmured, saying, This man receiveth sinners, and eateth with them.

3 And he spake this parable unto them, saying, 4 What man of you, having a hundred sheep, if he lose one of them, doth not leave the ninety and nine in the wilderness, and go after that which is lost, until he find it? 5And when he hath found it, he layeth it on his shoulders, rejoicing. 6And when he cometh home, he calleth together his friends and neighbours, saying unto them, Rejoice with me; for I have found my sheep which was lost. 7 I say unto you, that likewise joy shall be in heaven over one sinner that repenteth, more than over ninety and nine just persons, which need no repentance.

8 Either what woman having ten pieces of silver, if she lose one piece, doth not light a candle, and sweep the house, and seek diligently till she find it? 9And when she hath found it, she calleth her friends and her neighbours together, saying, Rejoice with me; for I have found the piece which I had lost. 10 Likewise, I say unto you, there is joy in the presence of the angels of God over one sinner that repenteth.

11 And he said, A certain man had two sons: 12And the younger of them said to his father, Father, give me the portion of goods that falleth to me. And he divided unto them his living. 13And not many days after the younger son gathered all together, and took his journey into a far country, and there wasted his substance with riotous living. 14And when he had spent all, there arose a mighty famine in that land; and he began to be in want. 15And he went and joined himself to a citizen of that country; and he sent him into his fields to feed swine. 16And he would fain have filled his belly with the husks that the swine did eat: and no man gave unto him. 17And when he came to himself, he said, How many hired servants of my father's have bread enough and to spare, and I perish with hunger! 18 I will arise and go to my father, and will say unto him, Father, I have sinned against heaven, and before thee, 19And am no more worthy to be called thy son: make me as one of thy hired servants. 20And he arose, and came to his father. But when he was yet a great way off, his father saw him, and had compassion, and ran, and fell on his neck, and kissed him. 21And the son said unto him, Father, I have sinned against heaven, and in thy sight, and am no more worthy to be called thy son. 22 But the father said to his servants, Bring forth the best robe, and put it on him; and put a ring on his hand, and shoes on his feet: 23And bring hither the fatted calf, and kill it; and let us eat, and be merry: 24 For this my son was dead, and is alive again; he was lost, and is found. And they began to be merry. 25 Now his elder son was in the field: and as he came and drew nigh to the house, he heard music and dancing. 26And he called one of the servants, and asked what these things meant. 27And he said unto him, Thy

15 Now all the tax-gatherers and the sinners were coming near Him to listen to Him. 2And both the Pharisees and the scribes began to grumble, saying, "This man receives sinners and eats with them."

3 And He told them this parable, saying, 4 "What man among you, if he has a hundred sheep and has lost one of them, does not leave the ninety-nine in the open pasture, and go after the one which is lost, until he finds it? 5 "And when he has found it, he lays it on his shoulders, rejoicing. 6 "And when he comes home, he calls together his friends and his neighbors, saying to them, 'Rejoice with me, for I have found my sheep which was lost!' 7 "I tell you that in the same way, there will be more joy in heaven over one sinner who repents, than over ninety-nine righteous persons who need no repentance.

8 "Or what woman, if she has ten silver coins and loses one coin, does not light a lamp and sweep the house and search carefully until she finds it? 9 "And when she has found it, she calls together her friends and neighbors, saying, 'Rejoice with me, for I have found the coin which I had lost!' 10 "In the same way, I tell you, there is joy in the presence of the angels of God over one sinner who repents."

11 And He said, "A certain man had two sons; 12 and the younger of them said to his father, 'Father, give me the share of the estate that falls to me.' And he divided his wealth between them. 13 "And not many days later, the younger son gathered everything together and went on a journey into a distant country, and there he squandered his estate with loose living. 14 "Now when he had spent everything, a severe famine occurred in that country, and he began to be in need. 15 "And he went and attached himself to one of the citizens of that country, and he sent him into his fields to feed swine. 16 "And he was longing to fill his stomach with the pods that the swine were eating, and no one was giving anything to him. 17 "But when he came to his senses, he said, 'How many of my father's hired men have more than enough bread, but I am dying here with hunger! 18 'I will get up and go to my father, and will say to him, "Father, I have sinned against heaven, and in your sight; 19 "I am no longer worthy to be called your son; make me as one of your hired men."' 20 "And he got up and came to his father. But while he was still a long way off, his father saw him, and felt compassion for him, and ran and embraced him, and kissed him. 21 "And the son said to him, 'Father, I have sinned against heaven and in your sight; I am no longer worthy to be called your son.' 22 "But the father said to his slaves, 'Quickly bring out the best robe and put it on him, and put a ring on his hand and sandals on his feet; 23 and bring the fattened calf, kill it, and let us eat and be merry; 24 for this son of mine was dead, and has come to life again; he was lost, and has been found.' And they began to be merry. 25 "Now his older son was in the field, and when he came and approached the house, he heard music and dancing. 26 "And he summoned one of the servants and began inquiring what these things might be. 27 "And he said

WILLIAMS

BECK

15 *Jesus tells three stories to defend His friendship to notorious sinners: the lost sheep, the lost coin, the lost boy*

Now all the tax-collectors and notorious sinners were crowding around Him to listen to Him. 2And so the Pharisees and scribes continually grumbled, and said, "This fellow is welcoming notorious sinners, and even eating with them."

3 So He told them the following story:

4 "What man among you, if he has a hundred sheep, and if he loses one of them, does not leave the ninety-nine in the desert and continue to look for the lost one until he finds it? 5And when he finds it, with joy he puts it on his shoulders, 6 and when he reaches home he calls in his friends and neighbors, and says to them, 'Rejoice with me, because I have found my lost sheep!' 7 Just so, I tell you, there will be more joy in heaven over one sinful person who repents than over ninety-nine upright people who do not need any repentance.

8 "Or what woman, if she has ten silver coins and loses one of them, does not light a lamp and sweep the house, and look carefully until she finds it? 9And when she finds it, she calls in her friends and neighbors, and says, 'Rejoice with me, because I have found the coin which I lost!' 10 Just so, I tell you, there is joy among the angels of God over one sinful person who repents!"

11 Then He said:

"There was a man who had two sons. 12 The younger of them said to his father, 'Father, give me the share of the property that falls to me.' So he divided his property between them. 13 Not many days after that, the younger son got together all he had and went away to a distant country, and there he squandered all his property by living in dissipation. 14After he had spent it all, a severe famine struck that country, and he began to suffer want. 15 So he went and hired himself out to a citizen of that country, and he sent him to his fields to feed hogs. 16And often he craved to fill himself with the carobpods which the hogs were eating, and nobody gave him a bite. 17 Then he came to himself and said, 'How many of my father's hired men have more to eat than they need, and here I am dying of hunger! 18 I will get up and go to my father, and say to him, "Father, I have sinned against heaven and in your opinion; I no longer deserve to be called your son; just treat me like one of your hired men."' 20 So he got up and went to his father. But, while he was still a long way off, his father saw him, and his heart was moved with pity for him, and he ran and fell on his neck, and kissed him affectionately. 21His son said to him, 'Father, I have sinned against heaven and in your opinion; I no longer deserve to be called your son; just treat me like one of your hired men.' 22 But his father said to his slaves, 'Bring out at once a robe, yes, the finest one,ᵃ and put it on him, and put a ring on his hand and shoes on his feet; 23 take the fattening calf and kill it, and let us feast and celebrate, 24because this son of mine was dead and has come to life, was lost and has been found!' So they began to celebrate.

25 "Now his elder son was in the field. So, on coming in, as he came near the house, he heard music and dancing. 26 Then he called one of the servant-boys and asked him what this meant. 27 He said to him, 'Your brother has

[a] Fol. two best Mss.

Lost—a Sheep

15 All the tax collectors and sinners were coming to Jesus to hear Him. 2 But the Pharisees and the Bible scholars grumbled and said, "This man welcomes sinners and eats with them."

3 So He told them this story:

4 "If anyone of you has a hundred sheep and loses one of them, don't you leave the ninety-nine in the wilderness and go after the lost one till you find it? 5 When you find it, you lay it on your shoulders and are glad. 6 You go home and call your friends and neighbors together and say to them, 'Be happy with me. I found my lost sheep!' 7 So, I tell you, there will be more joy in heaven over one sinner who repents than over ninety-nine good people who don't need to repent."

Lost—a Coin

8 "Or suppose a woman has ten coins and loses one. Won't she light a lamp and sweep the house and look for it carefully till she finds it? 9 When she finds it, she calls her women friends and neighbors together and says, 'Be happy with me. I found the coin I lost.' 10 So, I tell you, God's angels will be happy over one sinner who repents."

Lost—a Son

11 Then Jesus said: "A man had two sons. 12 The younger of them said to his father, 'Father, give me my share of the property.' So he divided his property between them.

13 "A few days later the younger son cashed in all he had, left home for a distant country, and there squandered his property by wild living. 14 When he had spent it all, a bad famine came over that country, and he started to be in need. 15 So he went and hired himself out to a citizen of that country, who sent him to his fields to feed hogs. 16And he would have been glad to fill up on the pods the hogs were eating. And nobody would give him anything.

17 "Then he came to his senses and said, 'How many of my father's hired men have more food than they can eat, and here I'm starving to death. 18 I'll start out and go to my father and tell him, "Father, I've sinned against heaven and against you. 19 I don't deserve to be called your son anymore. Make me one of your hired men."'

20 "So he started out and went to his father. While he was still far away, his father saw him and felt sorry for him. He ran and put his arms around him and kissed him. 21 'Father,' the son told him, 'I've sinned against heaven and against you. I don't deserve to be called your son anymore. Make me one of your hired men.'

22 "'Quick,' the father told his slaves, 'bring out a robe—the best—and put it on him, put a ring on his finger and shoes on his feet. 23And bring the fattened calf, kill it, and let's eat and celebrate. 24 This son of mine was dead and is alive. He was lost and is found.' And they started to celebrate.

25 "Now, his older son was out in the field. As he was coming in, he got near the house—he heard music and dancing! 26 Calling one of the servants, he asked, 'What's going on here?'

27 "'Your brother's home,' he was told, 'and

K.J.V.

brother is come; and thy father hath killed the fatted calf, because he hath received him safe and sound. 28And he was angry, and would not go in: therefore came his father out, and entreated him. 29And he answering said to *his* father, Lo, these many years do I serve thee, neither transgressed I at any time thy commandment; and yet thou never gavest me a kid, that I might make merry with my friends: 30 But as soon as this thy son was come, which hath devoured thy living with harlots, thou hast killed for him the fatted calf. 31And he said unto him, Son, thou art ever with me, and all that I have is thine. 32 It was meet that we should make merry, and be glad: for this thy brother was dead, and is alive again; and was lost, and is found.

16 And he said also unto his disciples, There was a certain rich man, which had a steward; and the same was accused unto him that he had wasted his goods. 2And he called him, and said unto him, How is it that I hear this of thee? give an account of thy stewardship; for thou mayest be no longer steward. 3 Then the steward said within himself, What shall I do? for my lord taketh away from me the stewardship: I cannot dig; to beg I am ashamed. 4I am resolved what to do, that, when I am put out of the stewardship, they may receive me into their houses. 5 So he called every one of his lord's debtors *unto him*, and said unto the first, How much owest thou unto my lord? 6And he said, A hundred measures of oil. And he said unto him, Take thy bill, and sit down quickly, and write fifty. 7 Then said he to another, And how much owest thou? And he said, A hundred measures of wheat. And he said unto him, Take thy bill, and write fourscore. 8And the lord commended the unjust steward, because he had done wisely: for the children of this world are in their generation wiser than the children of light. 9And I say unto you, Make to yourselves friends of the mammon of unrighteousness; that, when ye fail, they may receive you into everlasting habitations. 10 He that is faithful in that which is least is faithful also in much: and he that is unjust in the least is unjust also in much. 11 If therefore ye have not been faithful in the unrighteous mammon, who will commit to your trust the true *riches?* 12And if ye have not been faithful in that which is another man's, who shall give you that which is your own? 13 No servant can serve two masters: for either he will hate the one, and love the other; or else he will hold to the one, and despise the other. Ye cannot serve God and mammon. 14And the Pharisees also, who were covetous, heard all these things: and they derided him. 15And he said unto them, Ye are they which

N.A.S.

to him, 'Your brother has come, and your father has killed the fattened calf, because he has received him back safe and sound.' 28 "But he became angry, and was not willing to go in; and his father came out and *began* entreating him. 29 "But he answered and said to his father, 'Look! For so many years I have been serving you, and I have never neglected a command of yours; and *yet* you have never given me a kid, that I might be merry with my friends; 30 but when this son of yours came, who has devoured your wealth with harlots, you killed the fattened calf for him.' 31 "And he said to him, '*My* child, you have always been with me, and all that is mine is yours. 32 'But we had to be merry and rejoice, for this brother of yours was dead and *has begun* to live, and *was* lost and has been found.' "

16 Now He was also saying to the disciples, "There was a certain rich man who had a steward, and this *steward* was reported to him as squandering his possessions. 2 "And he called him and said to him, 'What is this I hear about you? Give an account of your stewardship, for you can no longer be steward.' 3 "And the steward·said to himself, 'What shall I do, since my master is taking the stewardship away from me? I am not strong enough to dig; I am ashamed to beg. 4 'I know what I shall do, so that when I am removed from the stewardship, they will receive me into their homes.' 5 "And he summoned each one of his master's debtors, and he *began* saying to the first, 'How much do you owe my master?' 6 "And he said, 'A hundred measures of oil.' And he said to him, 'Take your bill, and sit down quickly and write fifty.' 7 "Then he said to another, 'And how much do you owe?' And he said, 'A hundred measures of wheat.' He *said to him, 'Take your bill, and write eighty.' 8 "And his master praised the unrighteous steward because he had acted shrewdly; for the sons of this age are more shrewd in relation to their own kind than the sons of light. 9 "And I say to you, make friends for yourselves by means of the ªMammon of unrighteousness; that when it fails, they may receive you into the eternal dwellings. 10 "He who is faithful in a very little thing is faithful also in much; and he who is unrighteous in a very little thing is unrighteous also in much. 11 "If therefore you have not been faithful in the *use of* unrighteous Mammon, who will entrust the true *riches* to you? 12 "And if you have not been faithful in *the use of* that which is another's, who will give you that which is your own? 13 "No servant can serve two masters; for either he will hate the one, and love the other, or else he will hold to one, and despise the other. You cannot serve God and Mammon."

14 Now the Pharisees, who were lovers of money, were listening to all these things, and they were scoffing at Him. 15And He said to

[a] Or, *riches.*

WILLIAMS

come back, and your father has killed the fattening calf, because he has gotten him back safe and sound.' 28 So he became angry and would not go into the house. Then his father came out and began to plead with him. 29 But he answered his father, 'See! I have served you all these years and have never disobeyed a command of yours, but you have never given me even a kid, so that I could celebrate with my friends. 30 But when this son of yours arrives, who has eaten up your property with immoral women, you have killed for him the fattening calf.' 31 Then he said to him, 'My child, you have been with me all the time, and all I have is yours. 32 But we just had to celebrate and rejoice, because this brother of yours was dead and has come to life, was lost and has been found.' "

16 *The story of the dishonest manager; the Pharisees reproved for being lovers of money; the story of the rich man and Lazarus*

Now He was saying to the disciples:

"Once there was a rich man who had a household manager, and he was accused to his master of squandering the latter's property. 2 So he called the manager to him and said, 'What is this that I am hearing about you? Balance your accounts and show how you are conducting my affairs, for you cannot be manager any longer.' 3 Then the manager said to himself, What shall I do, because my master is going to take my position away from me? I am not strong enough to dig; I am ashamed to beg. 4 I know what I will do—I will ask*a* them*b* to take me into their homes when I am removed from my position. 5 So he called in each of his master's debtors, and asked the first one, 'How much do you owe my master?' 6 He answered, 'Nine hundred gallons of oil.' Then he said to him, 'Take your bill and sit right down and write four hundred and fifty.' 7 Then he asked another, 'And how much do you owe?' He answered, 'Twelve hundred bushels of wheat.' He said to him, 'Take your bill and write nine hundred and sixty.' 8And his master praised the dishonest manager, because he acted with shrewd business sense. For the men of the world act with more business sense toward their fellows than the men who enjoy spiritual light. 9 So I tell you, make friends by the right use of your money, which so easily tends to wrongdoing, so that when it fails, your friends may welcome you to the eternal dwellings. 10 The man who is dependable in a very small matter is dependable also in a large deal, the man who is dishonest in a very small matter is dishonest also in a large deal. 11 So if you have not proved dependable in handling your ill-gotten riches, who will trust you with the true riches? 12And if you have not proved dependable in what belongs to someone else, who will trust you with what belongs to you? 13 No house-servant can be a slave to two masters, for either he will hate one and love the other, or he will be devoted to one and despise the other. You cannot serve God and money.*c*

14 Now the Pharisees, who were lovers of money, had been listening to all this, and they began to ridicule Him. 15 Then He said to them,

[a] Implied before the conj. *that.* [b] "My master's debtors," implied. [c] Grk., *Mammon,* the god of money.

BECK

your father has killed the fattened calf because he got him back safe and sound.'

28 "Then he got angry and wouldn't go in. So his father came out and begged him. 29 But he answered his father, 'All these years I've been working like a slave for you and have never disobeyed your order, and you never gave me even a little goat to celebrate with my friends. 30 But as soon as this son of yours came back, who devoured your property with prostitutes, you killed the fattened calf for him.'

31 " 'Son,' the father said to him, 'you're always with me, and everything I have is yours. 32 But we had to celebrate and be glad. This brother of yours was dead and is alive. He was lost and is found.' "

The Dishonest Manager

16 Then Jesus said to His disciples: "There was a rich man whose manager was accused of squandering the man's property. 2 He called the manager. 'What's this I hear about you?' he asked him. 'Give an account of your management, because you can't manage my property any longer.'

3 " 'What'll I do?' the manager said to himself. 'My master is taking my job away from me. I'm not strong enough to dig; I'm ashamed to beg. 4 I know what I'll do so that when I've lost my job people will welcome me into their homes.'

5 "So he called everyone who owed his master anything. 'How much do you owe my master?' he asked the first.

6 " 'Eight hundred gallons of oil,' he answered.

" 'Take your note,' he said, 'sit down quick and write "four hundred." '

7 "Then he asked another, 'How much do you owe?'

" 'A thousand bushels of wheat,' he answered.

" 'Take your note,' he told him, 'and write "eight hundred." '

8 "And the master praised the dishonest manager for acting so shrewdly.

"In dealing with their own kind of people the men of this world are shrewder than those who are in the light.

9 "And I tell you, with the money that's often used in wrong ways win friends for yourselves so that when it's gone you'll be welcomed into the everlasting homes. 10 If you can be trusted with very little, you can be trusted with much. And if you're dishonest with very little, you're dishonest with much. 11 If you couldn't be trusted with wicked money, who will trust you with that which is really good? 12And if you couldn't be trusted with someone else's things, who will give you your own?

13 "No servant can be the slave of two masters. Either he will hate the one and love the other, or he'll be loyal to the one and despise the other. You can't serve God and money."

14 The money-loving Pharisees heard all this and turned up their noses at Him. 15 Then He

K.J.V.

justify yourselves before men; but God knoweth your hearts: for that which is highly esteemed among men is abomination in the sight of God. 16 The law and the prophets *were* until John: since that time the kingdom of God is preached, and every man presseth into it. 17And it is easier for heaven and earth to pass, than one tittle of the law to fail. 18 Whosoever putteth away his wife, and marrieth another, committeth adultery: and whosoever marrieth her that is put away from *her* husband committeth adultery.

19 There was a certain rich man, which was clothed in purple and fine linen, and fared sumptuously every day: 20And there was a certain beggar named Lazarus, which was laid at his gate, full of sores, 21And desiring to be fed with the crumbs which fell from the rich man's table: moreover the dogs came and licked his sores. 22And it came to pass, that the beggar died, and was carried by the angels into Abraham's bosom: the rich man also died, and was buried; 23And in hell he lifted up his eyes, being in torments, and seeth Abraham afar off, and Lazarus in his bosom. 24And he cried and said, Father Abraham, have mercy on me, and send Lazarus, that he may dip the tip of his finger in water, and cool my tongue; for I am tormented in this flame. 25 But Abraham said, Son, remember that thou in thy lifetime receivedst thy good things, and likewise Lazarus evil things: but now he is comforted, and thou art tormented. 26And beside all this, between us and you there is a great gulf fixed: so that they which would pass from hence to you cannot; neither can they pass to us, that *would come* from thence. 27 Then he said, I pray thee therefore, father, that thou wouldest send him to my father's house: 28 For I have five brethren; that he may testify unto them, lest they also come into this place of torment. 29Abraham saith unto him, They have Moses and the prophets; let them hear them. 30And he said, Nay, father Abraham: but if one went unto them from the dead, they will repent. 31And he said unto him, If they hear not Moses and the prophets, neither will they be persuaded, though one rose from the dead.

N.A.S.

them, "You are those who justify yourselves in the sight of men, but God knows your hearts; for that which is highly esteemed among men is detestable in the sight of God. 16 "The Law and the Prophets *were* proclaimed until John; since then the gospel of the kingdom of God is preached, and every one is forcing his way into it. 17 "But it is easier for heaven and earth to pass away than for one stroke of a letter of the Law to fail. 18 "Every one who divorces his wife and marries another commits adultery; and he who marries one who is divorced from a husband commits adultery.

19 "Now there was a certain rich man, and he habitually dressed in purple and fine linen, gaily living in splendor every day. 20 "And a certain poor man named Lazarus was laid at his gate, covered with sores, 21 and longing to be fed with the *crumbs* which were falling from the rich man's table; besides, even the dogs were coming and licking his sores. 22 "Now it came about that the poor man died and he was carried away by the angels to Abraham's bosom; and the rich man also died and was buried. 23 "And in Hades he lifted up his eyes, being in torments, and *saw Abraham far away, and Lazarus in his bosom. 24 "And he cried out and said, 'Father Abraham, have mercy on me, and send Lazarus, that he may dip the tip of his finger in water and cool off my tongue; for I am in agony in this flame.' 25 "But Abraham said, 'Child, remember that during your life you received your good things, and likewise Lazarus bad things; but now he is being comforted here, and you are in agony. 26 'And besides all this, between us and you there is a great chasm fixed, in order that those who wish to come over from here to you may not be able, and *that* none may cross over from there to us.' 27 "And he said, 'Then I beg you, Father, that you send him to my father's house—28 for I have five brothers—that he may warn them, lest they also come to this place of torment.' 29 "But Abraham *said, 'They have Moses and the Prophets; let them hear them.' 30 "But he said, 'No, Father Abraham, but if someone goes to them from the dead, they will repent!' 31 "But he said to him, 'If they do not listen to Moses and the Prophets, neither will they be persuaded if someone rises from the dead.' "

17 Then said he unto the disciples, It is impossible but that offences will come: but woe *unto him,* through whom they come! 2 It were better for him that a millstone were hanged about his neck, and he cast into the sea, than that he should offend one of these little ones. 3 Take heed to yourselves: If thy brother trespass against thee, rebuke him; and if he repent, forgive him. 4And if he trespass against thee

17 And He said to His disciples, "It is inevitable that stumbling-blocks should come, but woe to him through whom they come! 2 "It would be better for him if a millstone were hung around his neck and he were thrown into the sea, than that he should cause one of these little ones to stumble. 3 "Be on your guard! If your brother sins, rebuke him; and if he repents, forgive him. 4 "And if

WILLIAMS

"You are the men who exhibit your uprightness before the public; but God knows your hearts. For what stands high in the sight of men is detestable in the sight of God. 16 It was the law and the prophets until John, but ever since that time the good news of the kingdom of God has been proclaimed, and everybody has been taking it by storm. 17 It is easier for heaven and earth to pass away than for one dotting of an 'i' in the law to fail. 18 Any man who divorces his wife to marry another woman commits adultery, and the man who marries the woman divorced from her husband commits adultery.

19 "Once there was a rich man who used to dress in purple and fine linen and live in dazzling luxury every day. 20 And a beggar named Lazarus, covered with sores, had been laid at his gate, 21 and he was always craving to get a square meal from the scraps that fell from the rich man's table. Yes, the very dogs used to come and lick his sores. 22 One day the beggar died and was carried away by the angels to be Abraham's bosom companion,[d] and the rich man too died and was buried. 23 And in hades[e] he looked up, in constant tortures as he was, and saw Abraham far away and Lazarus his bosom companion. 24 So he called and said, 'Father Abraham, take pity on me and send Lazarus to dip the tip of his finger in water to cool off my tongue, because I am ceaselessly tortured in this flame.' 25 But Abraham said, 'My child, remember that you received in full your blessings in your lifetime, and Lazarus his hardships in his; but now he is continuously comforted here, while you are continuously tortured there. 26 Besides all this, between you and us there stands fixed a great chasm, so that those who want to cross from this side to you cannot, nor can they cross from your side to us.' 27 Then he said, 'For this reason, I beg you, father, to send him to my father's house 28 (for I have five brothers) to warn them, that they too may not come to this place of torture.' 29 But Abraham said, 'They have Moses and the prophets; let them listen to them.' 30 But he pleaded, 'No, father Abraham, but if someone went to them from the dead, they would repent.' 31 Then he answered, 'If they do not listen to Moses and the prophets, they will not be convinced, even if someone rises from the dead.' "

BECK

said to them, "You try to make people think you're good, but God knows your hearts. What people consider great is detested by God.

16 "The Law and the prophets were until John. Since then the good news of God's kingdom is told, and everybody tries to force his way into it. 17 It is easier for heaven and earth to disappear than for the Law to drop one dot of an *i*.

18 "Anyone who divorces his wife and marries another is living in adultery. And the man who marries a woman divorced from her husband is living in adultery."

The Rich Man and Lazarus

19 "There was a rich man who used to dress in purple and fine linen and live in luxury every day. 20 A beggar by the name of Lazarus was laid at his gate. He was covered with sores 21 and longed to satisfy his hunger with anything that might fall from the rich man's table. And the dogs would even come and lick his sores.

22 "One day the beggar died, and the angels carried him to Abraham's bosom. The rich man also died and was buried. 23 Being tormented in hell, he looked up, and though far away, he saw Abraham, and Lazarus at his bosom. 24 'Father Abraham,' he called, 'have pity on me and send Lazarus to dip the tip of his finger in water and cool off my tongue, because I'm suffering in this fire.'

25 "But Abraham said, 'Remember, son, you had your good things in your life, while Lazarus had his misery. Now he is comforted here, while you're suffering. 26 In all these things there's a wide chasm fixed between us and you, so that those who might want to cross from here over to you can't do it, nor do any from there come over to us.'

27 " 'Then I ask you, father,' he said, 'send him to my father's home— 28 I have five brothers—to warn them not to get into this place of torture.'

29 " 'They have Moses and the prophets,' Abraham said. 'They should listen to them.'

30 " 'No, Father Abraham,' he said, 'but if someone comes to them from the dead, they'll repent.'

31 " 'If they don't listen to Moses and the prophets,' he answered him, 'they won't be convinced even if somebody rose from the dead.' "

When Others Sin

17 "Temptations to sin are sure to come," Jesus told His disciples, "but woe to him through whom they come. 2 It would be better for him to have a big millstone hung around his neck and to be thrown into the lake than to lead one of these little ones into sin. 3 Watch yourselves.

"If your brother sins, correct him; and if he's sorry, forgive him. 4 Even if he sins against you

17 *Four great sayings on laying snares for others, forgiving others, triumphant faith, and the story of an unprofitable slave; ten lepers cured; the coming of the kingdom and of the Son of Man*

Now He said to His disciples: "It is inevitable that snares to evil will come, but a curse be on the man through whom they come! 2 It would be better for him to have a millstone hung around his neck, and he be hurled into the sea, than for him to ensnare one of these lowly ones. 3 "Be always looking out for one another. If your brother ever sins, reprove him, and if he repents, forgive him. 4 Even if he sins against

[d] Grk., *to Abraham's bosom.* [e] *Underworld.*

K.J.V.

seven times in a day, and seven times in a day turn again to thee, saying, I repent; thou shalt forgive him. 5And the apostles said unto the Lord, Increase our faith. 6And the Lord said, If ye had faith as a grain of mustard seed, ye might say unto this sycamine tree, Be thou plucked up by the root, and be thou planted in the sea; and it should obey you. 7 But which of you, having a servant ploughing or feeding cattle, will say unto him by and by, when he is come from the field, Go and sit down to meat? 8And will not rather say unto him, Make ready wherewith I may sup, and gird thyself, and serve me, till I have eaten and drunken; and afterward thou shalt eat and drink? 9 Doth he thank that servant because he did the things that were commanded him? I trow not. 10 So likewise ye, when ye shall have done all those things which are commanded you, say, We are unprofitable servants: we have done that which was our duty to do.

11 And it came to pass, as he went to Jerusalem, that he passed through the midst of Samaria and Galilee. 12And as he entered into a certain village, there met him ten men that were lepers, which stood afar off: 13And they lifted up *their* voices, and said, Jesus, Master, have mercy on us. 14And when he saw *them*, he said unto them, Go shew yourselves unto the priests. And it came to pass, that, as they went, they were cleansed. 15And one of them, when he saw that he was healed, turned back, and with a loud voice glorified God, 16And fell down on *his* face at his feet, giving him thanks: and he was a Samaritan. 17And Jesus answering said, Were there not ten cleansed? but where *are* the nine? 18 There are not found that returned to give glory to God, save this stranger. 19And he said unto him, Arise, go thy· way: thy faith hath made thee whole.

20 And when he was demanded of the Pharisees, when the kingdom of God should come, he answered them and said, The kingdom of God cometh not with observation: 21 Neither shall they say, Lo here! or, lo there! for, behold, the kingdom of God is within you. 22And he said unto the disciples, The days will come, when ye shall desire to see one of the days of the Son of man, and ye shall not see *it*. 23And they shall say to you, See here; or, see there: go not after *them*, nor follow *them*. 24 For as the lightning, that lighteneth out of the one *part* under heaven, shineth unto the other *part* under heaven; so shall also the Son of man be in his day. 25 But first must he suffer many things, and be rejected of this generation. 26And as it was in the days of Noe, so shall it be also in the days of the Son of man. 27 They did eat, they drank, they married wives, they were given in marriage, until the day that Noe entered into the ark, and the flood came, and destroyed them all. 28 Likewise also as it was in the days of Lot; they did eat, they drank, they bought, they sold, they planted, they builded; 29 But the same day that Lot went out of Sodom it rained fire and brimstone from heaven, and destroyed *them* all. 30 Even thus shall it be in the day when the Son of man is revealed. 31 In that day, he which shall be upon

N.A.S.

he sins against you seven times a day, and returns to you seven times, saying, 'I repent,' forgive him."

5 And the apostles said to the Lord, "Increase our faith!" 6And the Lord said, "If you had faith like a mustard seed, you would say to this mulberry tree, 'Be uprooted and be planted in the sea'; and it would obey you. 7 "But which of you, having a slave plowing or tending sheep, will say to him when he has come in from the field, 'Come immediately and sit down to eat'? 8 "But will he not say to him, 'Prepare something for me to eat, and *properly* clothe yourself and serve me until I have eaten and drunk; and afterward you will eat and drink'? 9 "He does not thank the slave because he did the things which were commanded, does he? 10 "So you too, when you do all the things which are commanded you, say, 'We are unworthy slaves; we have done *only* that which we ought to have done.'"

11 And it came about while He was on the way to Jerusalem, that He was passing between Samaria and Galilee. 12And as He entered a certain village, there met Him ten leprous men, who stood at a distance; 13 and they raised their voices, saying, "Jesus, Master, have mercy on us!" 14And when He saw them, He said to them, "Go and show yourselves to the priests." And it came about that as they were going, they were cleansed. 15 Now one of them, when he saw that he had been healed, turned back, glorifying God with a loud voice, 16 and he fell on his face at His feet, giving thanks to Him. And he was a Samaritan. 17And Jesus answered and said, "Were there not ten cleansed? But the nine—where are they? 18 "Were there none found who turned back to give glory to God, except this foreigner?" 19And He said to him, "Rise, and go your way; your faith [a]has made you well."

20 Now having been questioned by the Pharisees as to when the kingdom of God was coming, He answered them and said, "The kingdom of God is not coming with signs to be observed; 21 nor will they say, 'Look, here *it is!*' or, 'There *it is!*' For behold, the kingdom of God is in your midst."

22 And He said to the disciples, "The days shall come when you will long to see one of the days of the Son of Man, and you will not see it. 23 "And they will say to you, 'Look there! Look here!' Do not go away, and do not run after *them*. 24 "For just as the lightning, when it flashes out of one part of the sky, shines to the other part of the sky, so will the Son of Man be in His day. 25 "But first He must suffer many things and be rejected by this generation. 26 "And just as it happened in the days of Noah, so it shall be also in the days of the Son of Man: 27 they were eating, they were drinking, they were marrying, they were being given in marriage, until the day that Noah entered the ark, and the flood came and destroyed them all. 28 "It was the same as happened in the days of Lot: they were eating, they were drinking, they were buying, they were selling, they were planting, they were building; 29 but on the day that Lot went out from Sodom it rained fire and brimstone from heaven and destroyed them all. 30 "It will be just the same on the day that the Son of Man is revealed. 31 "On that day, let not the one

[a] Lit., *has saved you.*

WILLIAMS

you seven times in a day and seven times turns to you and says, 'I am sorry,' you must forgive him."

5 Then the apostles said to the Lord, "Give us more faith."

6 Then the Lord said to them, "If you had faith that grows like a mustard seed, you might have been saying to this mulberry tree, 'Pull yourself up by the roots and plant yourself in the sea,' and it would have obeyed you!

7 "What man among you, if he has a slave ploughing or tending sheep, will say to him when he comes in from the field, 'Come at once and take your seat at the table,' 8 but will not rather say to him, 'Get my supper ready, and dress yourself and wait on me until I eat and drink, and you yourself can eat and drink afterward'? 9 Does he praise the slave for doing what he was ordered to do? 10 So you too, when you do all that you are ordered to do, say, 'We are worthless slaves; we have done only what we ought to have done.' "

11 As He was going on to Jerusalem, He chanced to pass through Samaria and Galilee. 12 And as He was going into one village, ten lepers met Him, who got up at some distance from Him, 13 and raised their voices and said, "Jesus, Master, do take pity on us!"

14 So as soon as He saw them, He said to them, "Go at once and show yourselves to the priests." And while they were going they were cured. 15 But one of them, when he saw that he was cured, came back, praising God with a loud voice, 16 and fell on his face at Jesus' feet, and continued to thank Him. Now he was a Samaritan.

17 And Jesus said, "Were not ten cured? Where are the other nine? 18 Were none found to return and give praise to God except this foreigner?" 19 Then He said to him, "Get up and go on your way. Your faith has cured you."

20 Now, when He was asked by the Pharisees when the kingdom of God would come, He answered them, "The kingdom of God is not coming with visible display, 21 and so people will not say, 'Look! Here it is,' nor, 'There it is,' for the kingdom of God is within you."

22 Then He said to His disciples, "The time will come when you will long to see one of the days of the Son of Man, but you will not see it. 23 And men will say to you, 'Look! There he is!' or, 'Look! Here He is!' Do not start in pursuit of Him, 24 for just as when the lightning flashes, it shines from one end of the sky to the other, so will the Son of Man be when He comes. 25 But first He has to endure much suffering, and be disowned by this age. 26 And just as it was in the time of Noah, so it will be in the time of the Son of Man. 27 People continued to eat, drink, marry, and be married, right up to the day when Noah went into the ark, and the Flood came and destroyed them all. 28 It was so in the time of Lot; people continued to eat, drink, buy, sell, plant, and build; 29 and the very day Lot went out of Sodom, it rained fire and brimstone from heaven and destroyed them all. 30 It will be so on the day when the Son of Man appears. 31 The man who is on the roof of his

BECK

seven times in one day and seven times comes back to you and says, 'I'm sorry,' forgive him."

Faith and Duty

5 Then the apostles said to the Lord, "Give us more faith."

6 "If you have a faith like a mustard seed," the Lord said, "you could say to this mulberry tree, 'Be pulled up by the roots, and be planted in the lake,' and it would obey you.

7 "If your slave is plowing or watching sheep and comes in from the field, will any of you say to him, 'Come quickly and eat'? 8 Or won't you rather tell him, 'Prepare something for me to eat, fasten your belt, and serve me while I eat and drink, and afterwards you eat and drink'? 9 You won't thank the slave for doing what he was ordered to do, will you? 10 So you, too, when you've done all you were ordered to do, say, 'We are slaves who claim no credit. We've only done our duty.' "

Only One Thanks God

11 On His way to Jerusalem, Jesus traveled along the border between Samaria and Galilee. 12 As He came to a village, ten lepers came toward Him. They stopped at a distance 13 and called out, "Jesus, Master, have pity on us!"

14 When He saw them, He told them, "Go and *let the priests examine*[42] you."

And here's what happened: As they went, they were cleansed of their leprosy. 15 One of them, seeing he was healed, turned back and loudly praised God. 16 He bowed to the ground at Jesus' feet and thanked Him. And he was a Samaritan.

17 "Weren't there ten cleansed?" Jesus asked. "But the nine—where are they? 18 Weren't there any who came back to give God glory except this foreigner?"

19 And He told him, "Get up and go! Your faith made you well."

Where Is God's Kingdom?

20 "When will God's kingdom come?" the Pharisees asked Jesus.

"People can't see the coming of God's kingdom," He answered them. 21 "They will not say, 'Look, here it is!' or, 'There it is!' You see, God's kingdom is now among you."

Jesus Is Coming

22 "The time will come," He told the disciples, "when you will long to see one of the days of the Son of Man and will not see it. 23 People will say, 'Look, there He is!' or, 'Here He is!' Don't go off and run after them.

24 "The Son of Man will be like the lightning that flashes and lights up the sky from one end to the other. 25 But first He must suffer much and be rejected by these people.

26 "When the Son of Man comes, it will be like the time of Noah: 27 They were eating and drinking, and men and women were marrying till the day *Noah went into the ark*, and *the flood came*[61] and destroyed them all.

28 "Or like the time of Lot: They were eating and drinking, buying and selling, planting and building. 29 But the day Lot left Sodom, *fire and sulfur rained from heaven and destroyed*[62] them all. 30 That is how it will be on the day the Son of Man is revealed.

31 "On that day, if you're on the roof and

[61] Gen. 7:6-7
[62] Gen. 19:24-25

K.J.V.

the housetop, and his stuff in the house, let him not come down to take it away: and he that is in the field, let him likewise not return back. 32 Remember Lot's wife. 33 Whosoever shall seek to save his life shall lose it; and whosoever shall lose his life shall preserve it. 34 I tell you, in that night there shall be two *men* in one bed; the one shall be taken, and the other shall be left. 35 Two *women* shall be grinding together; the one shall be taken, and the other left. 36 Two *men* shall be in the field; the one shall be taken, and the other left. 37And they answered and said unto him, Where, Lord? And he said unto them, Wheresoever the body *is*, thither will the eagles be gathered together.

18 And he spake a parable unto them *to this end,* that men ought always to pray, and not to faint; 2 Saying, There was in a city a judge, which feared not God, neither regarded man: 3And there was a widow in that city; and she came unto him, saying, Avenge me of mine adversary. 4And he would not for a while: but afterward he said within himself, Though I fear not God, nor regard man; 5 Yet because this widow troubleth me, I will avenge her, lest by her continual coming she weary me. 6And the Lord said, Hear what the unjust judge saith. 7 And shall not God avenge his own elect, which cry day and night unto him, though he bear long with them? 8 I tell you that he will avenge them speedily. Nevertheless, when the Son of man cometh, shall he find faith on the earth? 9And he spake this parable unto certain which trusted in themselves that they were righteous, and despised others: 10 Two men went up into the temple to pray; the one a Pharisee, and the other a publican. 11 The Pharisee stood and prayed thus with himself, God, I thank thee, that I am not as other men *are,* extortioners, unjust, adulterers, or even as this publican. 12 I fast twice in the week, I give tithes of all that I possess. 13And the publican, standing afar off, would not lift up so much as *his* eyes unto heaven, but smote upon his breast, saying, God be merciful to me a sinner. 14 I tell you, this man went down to his house justified *rather* than the other: for every one that exalteth himself shall be abased; and he that humbleth himself shall be exalted. 15And they brought unto him also infants, that he would touch them: but when *his* disciples saw *it,* they rebuked them. 16 But Jesus called them *unto him,* and said, Suffer little children to come unto me, and forbid them not: for of such is the kingdom of God. 17 Verily I say unto you, Whosoever shall

N.A.S.

who is on the housetop and whose goods are in the house go down to take them away; and likewise let not the one who is in the field turn back. 32 "Remember Lot's wife. 33 "Whoever seeks to keep his life shall lose it, and whoever loses *his life* shall preserve it alive. 34 "I tell you, on that night there will be two men in one bed; one will be taken, and the other will be left. 35 "There will be two women grinding at the same place; one will be taken, and the other will be left." 36 (See footnote *ᵃ*) 37And answering they *said to Him, "Where, Lord?" And He said to them, "Where the body *is*, there also will the vultures be gathered."

18 Now He was telling them a parable to show that at all times they ought to pray and not to lose heart, 2 saying, "There was in a certain city a judge who did not fear God, and did not respect man. 3 "And there was a widow in that city, and she kept coming to him, saying, 'Give me legal protection from my opponent.' 4 "And for a while he was unwilling; but afterward he said to himself, 'Even though I do not fear God nor respect man, 5 yet because this widow bothers me, I will give her legal protection, lest by continually coming she wear me out.' " 6And the Lord said, "Hear what the unrighteous judge *said; 7 now shall not God bring about justice for His elect, who cry to Him day and night, and will He delay long over them? 8 "I tell you that He will bring about justice for them speedily. However, when the Son of Man comes, will He find faith on the earth?"

9 And He also told this parable to certain ones who trusted in themselves that they were righteous, and viewed others with contempt: 10 "Two men went up into the temple to pray, one a Pharisee, and the other a tax-gatherer. 11 "The Pharisee stood and was praying thus to himself, 'God, I thank Thee that I am not like other people, swindlers, unjust, adulterers, or even like this tax-gatherer. 12 'I fast twice a week; I pay tithes of all that I get.' 13 "But the tax-gatherer, standing some distance away, was even unwilling to lift up his eyes to heaven, but was beating his breast, saying, 'God, be merciful to me, the sinner!' 14 "I tell you, this man went down to his house justified rather than the other; for every one who exalts himself shall be humbled, but he who humbles himself shall be exalted."

15 And they were bringing even their babies to Him, in order that He might touch them, but when the disciples saw it, they *began re-buking them. 16 But Jesus called for them, saying, "Permit the children to come to Me, and stop hindering them, for the kingdom of God belongs to such as these. 17 "Truly I say

[a] Some mss. add verse 36, *Two men will be in the field; one will be taken and the other will be left.* cf. Matt. 24:40.

WILLIAMS

house that day, and his goods in the house, must not come down to carry them out; and the man in the field, too, must not turn back. 32 Remember Lot's wife! 33 Whoever tries to preserve his life will lose it, but whoever loses it will preserve it. 34 I tell you, two men will be in the same bed that night; one will be taken, the other left. 35 Two women will be grinding together; one will be taken, the other left." a

37 Then they asked Him, "Where, Lord, will this be?"

And He said to them, "Wherever there is carrion b the vultures will flock."

18 *The story of the godless judge; of the Pharisee and the tax-collector; little children to be allowed to come to Jesus; the rich young ruler's refusal shows it is hard for the rich to be saved; blind Bartimeus cured*

Now He told them the following story to show how necessary it is for people always to pray and never to give up:

2 "Once there was in a city a judge who had no reverence for God nor respect for men. 3 And in that city there was a widow who continued to come to him and say, 'Give me justice and protection from my opponent.' 4 And he would not for a time, but afterward he said to himself, Though I have no reverence for God nor respect for men, 5 yet because this widow continues to bother me, I will give her justice and protection, so that she may not finally wear me out by her continual coming."

6 Then the Lord added, "Listen to what the unrighteous judge says! 7 And will not God give justice and protection to His chosen people who continue to cry to Him day and night, since He is so patient with them? 8 I tell you, He will give them justice and protection, and that without delay. But when the Son of Man comes, will He find faith on earth?"

9 To some people who were confident that they themselves were upright, but who scorned everybody else, He told the following story:

10 "Two men went up to the temple to pray, one a Pharisee, the other a tax-collector. 11 The Pharisee stood and said this self-centered prayer, 'O God, I thank you that I am not like the rest of men, robbers, rogues, adulterers, or even like this tax-collector. 12 I fast two days in the week. I pay a tithe on everything I get.' 13 But the tax-collector stood at a distance and would not even lift his eyes to heaven, but continued to beat his breast and say, 'O God, have mercy on me, a sinner!' 14 I tell you, this man, and not the other, went back home forgiven and accepted a by God. For everyone who exalts himself will be humbled; but whoever humbles himself will be exalted."

15 Now some people were bringing even their babies to Him to have Him touch them, but the disciples, when they saw it, reproved them for it.

16 But Jesus called them to Him and said, "Let the little children come to me, and stop preventing them from it, for to such as these the kingdom of God belongs. 17 I solemnly say

BECK

have your goods in the house, don't go down to get them. If you're in the field, don't *turn back.* 32 Remember *Lot's wife!* 63 33 If you try to save your life, you'll lose it, but if you'll lose it, you'll save it.

34 "I tell you, that night there will be two men in one bed. One will be taken and the other left. 35 Two women will be grinding together. One will be taken and the other left." *

37 They asked Him, "Where, Lord?"

"Where there's a dead body," He told them, "there the vultures will gather."

God Hears

18 Jesus told them a story to show that they should always pray and not get tired of it:

2 "In a town there was a judge who didn't fear God or care what people thought. 3 In that town there was also a widow who kept coming to him and saying, 'Get me justice and defend me against my enemy!'

4 "For a while he refused to do anything, but then he said to himself, 'Even though I don't fear God or care what people think, 5 this widow keeps bothering me, I'll have to see that she gets justice, or she'll keep coming till she wears me out.'"

6 The Lord added, "Listen to what the unjust judge says. 7 And won't God get justice for His chosen ones who cry to Him day and night? Is He slow to help them? 8 I tell you, He will quickly get justice for them. But when the Son of Man comes, will He find faith on earth?"

The Pharisee and the Tax Collector

9 Jesus told this story to some who were sure they were righteous and so looked down on everybody else:

10 "Two men went up to the temple to pray. One was a Pharisee and the other a tax collector. 11 The Pharisee stood and prayed by himself: 'God, I thank You I'm not like the other people: robbers, wrongdoers, adulterers, or even like that tax collector. 12 I fast twice a week and give a tenth of all my income.'

13 "But the tax collector, standing a distance away, wouldn't even look up to heaven but was beating his breast and saying, 'God, forgive me, a sinner!'

14 "I tell you, this man, and not the other, went home righteous. Everyone who honors himself will be humbled; but if you humble yourself, you will be honored."

Jesus Loves Children

15 Some people brought babies to Jesus to have Him touch them. When the disciples saw them, they sternly told them not to do it.

16 But Jesus called the children to Him and said, "Let the little children come to Me, and don't keep them away. God's kingdom belongs to such as these. 17 I tell you the truth, if you

[a] V. 36 om. by best Mss. [b] Lk. fol. Homer in use of *soma* for *carcass*. [a] Grk., *justified.*

* Our three oldest manuscripts, including Papyrus 75, do not have v. 36: "Two will be in a field. One will be taken and the other left." See Matt. 24:40.
[63] Gen. 19:17, 26

K.J.V.

not receive the kingdom of God as a little child shall in no wise enter therein. 18And a certain ruler asked him, saying, Good Master, what shall I do to inherit eternal life? 19And Jesus said unto him, Why callest thou me good? none *is* good, save one, *that is,* God. 20 Thou knowest the commandments, Do not commit adultery, Do not kill, Do not steal, Do not bear false witness, Honour thy father and thy mother. 21And he said, All these have I kept from my youth up. 22 Now when Jesus heard these things, he said unto him, Yet lackest thou one thing: sell all that thou hast, and distribute unto the poor, and thou shalt have treasure in heaven: and come, follow me. 23And when he heard this, he was very sorrowful: for he was very rich. 24And when Jesus saw that he was very sorrowful, he said, How hardly shall they that have riches enter into the kingdom of God! 25 For it is easier for a camel to go through a needle's eye, than for a rich man to enter into the kingdom of God. 26And they that heard *it* said, Who then can be saved? 27And he said, The things which are impossible with men are possible with God. 28 Then Peter said, Lo, we have left all, and· followed thee. 29And he said unto them, Verily I say unto you, There is no man that hath left house, or parents, or brethren, or wife, or children, for the kingdom of God's sake, 30 Who shall not receive manifold more in this present time, and in the world to come life everlasting.

31 Then he took *unto him* the twelve, and said unto them, Behold, we go up to Jerusalem, and all things that are written by the prophets concerning the Son of man shall be accomplished. 32 For he shall be delivered unto the Gentiles, and shall be mocked, and spitefully entreated, and spitted on: 33 And they shall scourge *him,* and put him to death; and the third day he shall rise again. 34And they understood none of these things: and this saying was hid from them, neither knew they the things which were spoken.

35 And it came to pass, that as he was come nigh unto Jericho, a certain blind man sat by the way side begging: 36And hearing the multitude pass by, he asked what it meant. 37And they told him, that Jesus of Nazareth passeth by. 38And he cried, saying, Jesus, *thou* Son of David, have mercy on me. 39And they which went before rebuked him, that he should hold his peace: but he cried so much the more, *Thou* Son of David, have mercy on me. 40And Jesus stood, and commanded him to be brought unto him: and when he was come near, he asked him, 41 Saying, What wilt thou that I shall do unto thee? And he said, Lord, that I may receive my sight. 42And Jesus said unto him, Receive thy sight: thy faith hath saved thee. 43 And immediately he received his sight, and followed him, glorifying God: and all the people, when they saw *it,* gave praise unto God.

N.A.S.

to you, whoever does not receive the kingdom of God like a child shall not enter it *at all."*

18 And a certain ruler questioned Him, saying, "Good Teacher, what shall I do to obtain eternal life?" 19And Jesus said to him, "Why do you call Me good? No one is good except God alone. 20 "You know the commandments, 'DO NOT COMMIT ADULTERY, DO NOT MURDER, DO NOT STEAL, DO NOT BEAR FALSE WITNESS, HONOR YOUR FATHER AND MOTHER.'" 21And he said, "All these things I have kept from *my* youth." 22And when Jesus heard *this,* He said to him, "One thing you still lack; sell all that you possess, and distribute it to the poor, and you shall have treasure in heaven; and come, follow Me." 23 But when he had heard these things, he became very sad; for he was extremely rich. 24And Jesus looked at him and said, "How hard it is for those who are wealthy to enter the kingdom of God! 25 "For it is easier for a camel to go through the eye of a needle, than for a rich man to enter the kingdom of God." 26And they who heard it said, "Then who can be saved?" 27 But He said, "The things impossible with men are possible with God." 28And Peter said, "Behold, we have left our own *homes,* and followed You." 29And He said to them, "Truly I say to you, there is no one who has left house or wife or brothers or parents or children, for the sake of the kingdom of God, 30 who shall not receive many times as much at this time and in the age to come, eternal life."

31 And He took the twelve aside and said to them, "Behold, we are going up to Jerusalem, and all things which are written through the prophets about the Son of Man will be accomplished. 32 "For He will be delivered up to the Gentiles, and will be mocked and mistreated and spit upon, 33 and after they have scourged Him, they will kill Him; and the third day He will rise again." 34And they understood none of these things, and this saying was hidden from them, and they did not comprehend the things that were said.

35 And it came about that as He was approaching Jericho, a certain blind man was sitting by the road, begging. 36 Now hearing a multitude going by, he *began* to inquire what this might be. 37And they told him that Jesus of Nazareth was passing by. 38And he called out, saying, "Jesus, Son of David, have mercy on me!" 39And those who led the way were sternly telling him to be quiet; but he kept crying out all the more, "Son of David, have mercy on me!" 40And Jesus stopped and commanded that he be brought to Him; and when he had come near, He questioned him, 41 "What do you want Me to do for you?" And he said, "Lord, I *want* to receive my sight!" 42And Jesus said to him, "Receive your sight; your faith has made you well." 43And immediately he received his sight, and *began* following Him, glorifying God; and when all the people saw it, they gave praise to God.

WILLIAMS

to you, whoever does not accept the kingdom of God as a little child does, will never get into it at all."

18 Then a certain member of the council asked Him, "Good Teacher, what must I do to get possession of eternal life?"

19 Jesus said to him, "Why do you call me perfectly good? No one is perfectly good but God Himself. 20 You know the commandments: 'Do not commit adultery, Do not murder, Do not steal, Do not bear false witness, Practice honoring your father and mother.'"

21 But he said, "I have kept all these commandments ever since I was a child."

22 When Jesus heard this, He said to him, "One thing you still lack. Sell everything you have, and distribute the money among the poor, and you will have riches in heaven; then come back and follow me." 23 But when he heard that, he was very sad, for he was surpassingly rich.

24 So when Jesus saw it, He said, "How hard it is for those who have money to get into the kingdom of God! 25 For it is easier for a camel to go through a needle's eye than for a rich man to get into the kingdom of God."

26 But those who heard it said, "Then who can be saved?"

27 So He said, "The things impossible for men are possible for God."

28 Then Peter said to Him, "We have left our very own, homes and all, and have followed you."

29 So He said to them, "I solemnly say to you, there is no one who has given up home or wife or brothers or parents or children for the kingdom of God, 30 who will not receive in return many times more in this world, and in the next eternal life."

31 Now He took the Twelve aside and said to them, "Listen! We are going up to Jerusalem, and everything written by the prophets about the Son of Man will be fulfilled. 32 For He will be turned over to the heathen and sport made of Him, He will be insulted and spit upon, 33 and then they will flog Him and kill Him, but on the third day He will rise again." 34 But they did not understand about these things, and this statment was an insoluble riddle[b] to them; they did not even begin to grasp what He meant.

35 As He was approaching Jericho, a blind man chanced to be sitting by the roadside begging. 36 As he heard a crowd going by, he asked what it meant. 37 They told him that Jesus of Nazareth was coming by. 38 Then he cried out, "Jesus, you Son of David, do pity me!" 39 But those who were marching in front reproved him and told him to keep quiet, but he cried out all the louder, "O Son of David, do pity me!"

40 Then Jesus stopped and ordered him to be brought to Him. And when he approached Jesus, He said to him, 41 "What do you want me to do for you?"

He answered, "Lord, I want to see again!"

42 Then Jesus said to him, "See again! Your faith has cured you." 43 So at once he saw again, and began to follow Him, giving thanks to God. And all the people saw it and gave praise to God.

BECK

don't receive God's kingdom like a little child, you will not get into it."

The Rich Young Leader

18 An official asked Him, "Good Teacher, what do I do to get everlasting life?"

19 "Why do you call Me good?" Jesus asked him. "Nobody is good except One—God. 20 You know the commandments: *Don't commit adultery, don't murder, don't steal, don't lie, honor your father and mother.*" [64]

21 "I've kept all these since I was a child," he said.

22 When Jesus heard this, He told him, "You still lack one thing: Sell everything you have, distribute the money among the poor, and you'll have a treasure in heaven. Then come and follow Me."

23 When he heard this, he got very sad, because he was very rich. 24 Jesus watched him and said, "How hard it is for rich people to get into God's kingdom! 25 It's easier for a camel to go through a needle's eye than for a rich man to get into God's kingdom."

26 Those who heard Him asked, "Who can be saved?"

27 "What men can't do God can do," He answered.

28 Then Peter said, "Look, we've left our things and followed You."

29 "Let Me assure you," He answered them, "everyone who gave up his home or wife, brothers, parents, or children for God's kingdom 30 will certainly get a hundred times as much in this life, and in the coming world everlasting life."

The Shadow of the Cross

31 He took the twelve aside and said to them: "Look, we're going up to Jerusalem, and everything the prophets wrote for the Son of Man will be done: 32 He'll be handed over to the non-Jews. They'll mock and insult Him, spit on Him, 33 scourge and kill Him. And on the third day He'll rise."

34 But they understood none of this. It was a mystery to them, and they didn't know what He meant.

A Blind Man

35 As He came near Jericho, there was a blind man sitting by the road, begging. 36 Hearing a crowd go by, he tried to find out what it was all about.

37 "Jesus from Nazareth is passing by," they told him.

38 He called, "Jesus, Son of David, have pity on me!" 39 Those who went ahead were urging him to be quiet. But he called all the louder, "Son of David, have pity on me!"

40 Jesus stopped and ordered the man brought to Him. When he came near, Jesus asked him, 41 "What do you want Me to do for you?"

"Lord, I want to see," he said.

42 "See!" Jesus told him. "Your faith has made you well." 43 Immediately he could see, and he followed Jesus, praising God. And all the people praised God for what they had seen.

---

[b] Grk., *hidden from* (them).   [64] Ex. 20:12-16; Deut. 5:16-20

K.J.V.

N.A.S.

19 And *Jesus* entered and passed through Jericho. 2And, behold, *there was* a man named Zaccheus, which was the chief among the publicans, and he was rich. 3And he sought to see Jesus who he was; and could not for the press, because he was little of stature. 4And he ran before, and climbed up into a sycamore tree to see him; for he was to pass that *way.* 5And when Jesus came to the place, he looked up, and saw him, and said unto him, Zaccheus, make haste, and come down; for to day I must abide at thy house. 6And he made haste, and came down, and received him joyfully. 7And when they saw *it,* they all murmured, saying, That he was gone to be guest with a man that is a sinner. 8And Zaccheus stood, and said unto the Lord; Behold, Lord, the half of my goods I give to the poor; and if I have taken any thing from any man by false accusation, I restore *him* fourfold. 9And Jesus said unto him, This day is salvation come to this house, forasmuch as he also is a son of Abraham. 10 For the Son of man is come to seek and to save that which was lost. 11And as they heard these things, he added and spake a parable, because he was nigh to Jerusalem, and because they thought that the kingdom of God should immediately appear. 12 He said therefore, A certain nobleman went into a far country to receive for himself a kingdom, and to return. 13And he called his ten servants, and delivered them ten pounds, and said unto them, Occupy till I come. 14 But his citizens hated him, and sent a message after him, saying, We will not have this *man* to reign over us. 15And it came to pass, that when he was returned, having received the kingdom, then he commanded these servants to be called unto him, to whom he had given the money, that he might know how much every man had gained by trading. 16 Then came the first, saying, Lord, thy pound hath gained ten pounds. 17And he said unto him, Well, thou good servant: because thou hast been faithful in a very little, have thou authority over ten cities. 18And the second came, saying, Lord, thy pound hath gained five pounds. 19And he said likewise to him, Be thou also over five cities. 20And another came, saying, Lord, behold, *here is* thy pound, which I have kept laid up in a napkin: 21 For I feared thee, because thou art an austere man: thou takest up that thou layedst not down, and reapest that thou didst not sow. 22And he saith unto him, Out of thine own mouth will I judge thee, *thou* wicked servant. Thou knewest that I was an austere man, taking up that I laid not down, and reaping that I did not sow: 23 Wherefore then gavest not thou my money into the bank, that at my coming I might have required mine own with usury? 24And he said unto them that stood by, Take from him the pound, and give *it* to him that hath ten pounds. 25 (And they said unto him, Lord, he hath ten pounds.)

19 And He entered and was passing through Jericho. 2And behold, there was a man called by the name of Zaccheus; and he was a chief tax-gatherer, and he was rich. 3And he was trying to see who Jesus was, and he was unable because of the crowd, for he was small in stature. 4And he ran on ahead and climbed up into a sycamore tree in order to see Him, for He was about to pass through that way. 5And when Jesus came to the place, He looked up and said to him, "Zaccheus, hurry and come down, for today I must stay at your house." 6And he hurried and came down, and received Him gladly. 7And when they saw it, they all *began* to grumble, saying, "He has gone to be the guest of a man who is a sinner." 8And Zaccheus stopped and said to the Lord, "Behold, Lord, half of my possessions I will give to the poor, and if I have defrauded anyone of anything, I will give back four times as much." 9And Jesus said to him, "Today salvation has come to this house, because he, too, is a son of Abraham. 10 "For the Son of Man has come to seek and to save that which was lost."

11 And while they were listening to these things, He went on to tell a parable, because He was near Jerusalem, and they supposed that the kingdom of God was going to appear immediately. 12 He said therefore, "A certain nobleman went to a distant country to receive a kingdom for himself, and *then* return. 13 "And he called ten of his slaves, and gave them ten *ªminas, and said to them, 'Do business *with this* until I come *back.'* 14 "But his citizens hated him, and sent a delegation after him, saying, 'We do not want this man to reign over us.' 15 "And it came about that when he returned, after receiving the kingdom, he ordered that these slaves, to whom he had given the money, be called to him in order that he might know what business they had done. 16 "And the first appeared, saying, 'Master, your mina has made ten minas more.' 17 "And he said to him, 'Well done, good slave, because you have been faithful in a very little thing, be in authority over ten cities.' 18 "And the second came, saying, 'Your mina, master, has made five minas.' 19 "And he said to him also, 'And you are to be over five cities.' 20 "And the other came, saying, 'Master, behold your mina, which I kept put away in a handkerchief; 21 for I was afraid of you, because you are an exacting man; you take up what you did not lay down, and reap what you did not sow.' 22 "He *said to him, 'By your own words I will judge you, you worthless slave. Did you know that I am an exacting man, taking up what I did not lay down, and reaping what I did not sow? 23 'Then why did you not put the money in the bank, and having come, I would have collected it with interest?' 24 "And he said to the bystanders, 'Take the mina away from him, and give it to the one who has the ten minas.' 25 "And they said to him, 'Master, he has ten

[a] A mina is equal to about 100 days' wages or nearly $20.

BECK

Zaccheus

19 *Rich Zaccheus entertains Jesus; Jesus blesses him and his home; Jesus tells the story of the pounds; He rides into Jerusalem as king; weeps over the city; drives the traders out*

Then He went into Jericho and was passing through it. 2 Here there was a man named Zaccheus, who was tax-commissioner of the district, and he was a rich man too. 3 Now he was trying to see Jesus to find out who He was, but he could not because of the crowd, as he was so small in stature. 4 So he ran on ahead and climbed up in a mulberry tree, just to get a glimpse of Him, for Jesus was coming through on that street.

5 And as Jesus came to the place, He looked up and said to him, "Zaccheus, come down quickly! for today I must stop at your house." 6 So in haste he came down, and with gladness welcomed Him.

7 And when they all saw it, they began to grumble and say, "He has gone in to lodge with a notorious sinner!"

8 Then Zaccheus got up and said to the Lord, "Listen, Lord! I now give to the poor half of my property, and if I have defrauded anyone of anything, I will pay him back four times as much."

9 Then Jesus said to him, "Today salvation has come to this home, for he too is a real descendant of Abraham. 10 For the Son of Man has come to seek and to save the people that are lost."

11 As they were listening to these things, He told them another story, because He was near Jerusalem and because they supposed that the kingdom of God was going to appear at once. 12 So He said:

"Once upon a time a man of noble birth went off to a distant country to get for himself a kingdom and then return. 13 He called in ten of his slaves and gave them twenty dollars apiece and told them to do business with his money while he was gone. 14 But his citizens continued to hate him, and sent a delegation after him to say, 'We do not want this man to become king over us.' 15 Then after he had gotten the appointment as king, he returned and ordered those slaves to whom he had given his money to be called in, that he might find out what business they had done. 16 Now the first one came in and said, 'Your twenty dollars, sir, has made two hundred more.' 17 So he said to him, 'Well done, my good slave! Because you have proven dependable in a very small business, be governor of ten cities!' 18 The second one came in and said, 'Your twenty dollars, sir, has made a hundred!' 19 So he said to him too, 'Be governor of five cities!' 20 But another one came in and said, 'Here is your twenty dollars, sir, which I kept laid away in a handkerchief. 21 For I lived in constant dread of you, because you are a stern man, you pick up what you did not put down, you reap what you did not sow.' 22 He said to him, 'On the ground of what you say I will sentence you, you wicked slave! You knew that I was a stern man, that I picked up what I did not put down, and reaped what I did not sow. 23 So why did you not put my money into the bank? In that case, when I came back I could have gotten interest on my principal.' 24 So he said to the bystanders, 'Take the twenty dollars away from him and give it to the man who has the two hundred.' 25 And they said, 'Sir, he has two hundred already.'

Zaccheus

19 He went into Jericho and was passing through it. 2 Here there was a man by the name of Zacchaeus. He was an overseer of tax collectors and was rich. 3 He was trying to see what kind of person Jesus was, but, being a small man, he couldn't see Him on account of the crowd. 4 So he ran ahead and climbed up a fig-mulberry tree to see Him, because Jesus was coming that way.

5 When Jesus came to the place, He looked up. "Zacchaeus, hurry down," He told him. "Today I must stay at your home."

6 He hurried down and was happy to welcome Him. 7 But all who saw them started to grumble: "He went to be the guest of a sinful man."

8 Zacchaeus stood there and said to the Lord, "Look, Lord, half of my property I'm giving to the poor, and if I've cheated anybody, I'm paying him back four times as much."

9 "Today salvation has come to this home," Jesus told him, "since he, too, is a son of Abraham. 10 The Son of Man came to *look for* and save *the lost*." 65

Use God's Gifts

11 While they were listening to this, Jesus went on to tell them a story, because He was near Jerusalem and they thought God's kingdom was to appear immediately.

12 "A nobleman," He said, "went to a distant country to be made a king and then came back. 13 He called ten of his slaves, gave them a thousand denarii* and told them, 'Trade with these till I come.'

14 "But the men of his own country hated him and sent representatives after him to say, 'We don't want this man to be our king.'

15 "But he was made king. When he came back, he said, 'Call those slaves whom I gave the money. I want to see what each one has made by his trading.'

16 "The first came and said, 'Master, your hundred denarii have made a thousand more denarii.'

17 " 'Well done, my good slave!' he told him. 'You proved you could be trusted in a very small matter. Take charge of ten cities.'

18 "The second came and said, 'Your hundred denarii, master, made five hundred denarii.'

19 " 'You be in charge of five cities,' he told this one.

20 "Then the one who was different came and said, 'Master, here are your hundred denarii. I put them away in a cloth and kept them there. 21 I was afraid of you. You're a hard man. You take what you didn't deposit, and you get grain you didn't sow.'

22 " 'I'll judge you by what you say, you wicked slave!' he told him. 'You knew I'm a hard man, taking what I didn't deposit and getting grain I didn't sow? 23 Why didn't you put my money in the bank? Then, when I came back, I could have collected it with interest.' 24 So he told his men, 'Take his hundred denarii away and give it to the man who has a thousand.'

25 " 'Master,' they answered him, 'He has a thousand denarii.'

---

* One denarius was a day's pay.
[65] Ezek. 34:16

K.J.V.

26 For I say unto you, That unto every one which hath shall be given; and from him that hath not, even that he hath shall be taken away from him. 27 But those mine enemies, which would not that I should reign over them, bring hither, and slay *them* before me.

28 And when he had thus spoken, he went before, ascending up to Jerusalem. 29And it came to pass, when he was come nigh to Bethphage and Bethany, at the mount called *the mount* of Olives, he sent twc of his disciples, 30 Saying, Go ye into the village over against *you;* in the which at your entering ye shall find a colt tied, whereon yet never man sat: loose him, and bring *him hither.* 31And if any man ask you, Why do ye loose *him?* thus shall ye say unto him, Because the Lord hath need of him. 32And they that were sent went their way, and found even as he had said unto them. 33And as they were loosing the colt, the owners thereof said unto them, Why loose ye the colt? 34And they said, The Lord hath need of him. 35And they brought him to Jesus: and they cast their garments upon the colt, and they set Jesus thereon. 36And as he went, they spread their clothes in the way. 37And when he was come nigh, even now at the descent of the mount of Olives, the whole multitude of the disciples began to rejoice and praise God with a loud voice for all the mighty works that they had seen; 38 Saying, Blessed *be* the King that cometh in the name of the Lord: peace in heaven, and glory in the highest. 39And some of the Pharisees from among the multitude said unto him, Master, rebuke thy disciples. 40And he answered and said unto them, I tell you that, if these should hold their peace, the stones would immediately cry out.

41 And when he was come near, he beheld the city, and wept over it, 42 Saying, if thou hadst known, even thou, at least in this thy day, the things *which belong* unto thy peace! but now they are hid from thine eyes. 43 For the days shall come upon thee, that thine enemies shall cast a trench about thee, and compass thee round, and keep thee in on every side, 44And shall lay thee even with the ground, and thy children within thee; and they shall not leave in thee one stone upon another; because thou knewest not the time of thy visitation. 45And he went into the temple, and began to cast out them that sold therein, and them that bought; 46 Saying unto them, It is written, My house is the house of prayer; but ye have made it a den of thieves. 47And he taught daily in the temple. But the chief priests and the scribes and the chief of the people sought to destroy him, 48And could not find what they might do: for all the people were very attentive to hear him.

N.A.S.

minas *already*.' 26 "I tell you, that to everyone who has shall *more* be given, but from the one who does not have, even what he does have shall be taken away. 27 'But these enemies of mine, who did not want me to reign over them, bring them here, and slay them in my presence.' "

28 And after He had said these things, He was going on ahead, ascending to Jerusalem.

29 And it came about that when He approached Bethphage and Bethany, near the mount that is called Olivet, He sent two of the disciples, 30 saying, "Go into the village opposite *you,* in which as you enter you will find a colt tied, on which no one yet has ever sat; untie it, and bring it *here.* 31 "And if anyone asks you, 'Why are you untying it?' thus shall you speak, 'The Lord has need of it.' " 32And those who were sent away and found it just as He had told them. 33And as they were untying the colt, its owners said to them, "Why are you untying the colt?" 34And they said, "The Lord has need of it." 35And they brought it to Jesus, and they threw their garments on the colt, and put Jesus *on it.* 36And as He was going, they were spreading their garments in the road. 37And as He was now approaching, near the descent of the Mount of Olives, the whole multitude of the disciples began to praise God joyfully with a loud voice for all the miracles which they had seen, 38 saying,

"BLESSED IS THE KING WHO COMES IN THE NAME OF THE LORD;

Peace in heaven and glory in the highest!" 39And some of the Pharisees in the multitude said to Him, "Teacher, rebuke Your disciples." 40And He answered and said, "I tell you, if these become silent, the stones will cry out!"

41 And when He approached, He saw the city and wept over it, 42 saying, "If you had known in this day, even you, the things which make for peace! But now they have been hidden from your eyes. 43 "For the days shall come upon you when your enemies will throw up a bank before you, and surround you, and hem you in on every side, 44 and will level you to the ground and your children within you, and they will not leave in you one stone upon another, because you did not recognize the time of your visitation."

45 And He entered the temple and began to cast out those who were selling, 46 saying to them, "It is written, 'AND MY HOUSE SHALL BE A HOUSE OF PRAYER,' but you have made it a robbers' den."

47 And He was teaching daily in the temple; but the chief priests and the scribes and the leading men among the people were trying to destroy Him, 48 and they could not find anything that they might do, for all the people were hanging upon His words.

WILLIAMS

26 'I tell you, the man who gets will have more given to him, but the man who does not get will have even what he has taken away from him! 27 But bring those enemies of mine here who did not want me to become king over them and slay them in my presence!' "

28 After saying these things, He went on ahead of them, on His way to Jerusalem.

29 When He approached Bethphage and Bethany by the hill called the Mount of Olives, He sent on two of His disciples, and 30 said, "Go on to the village in front of you, in which, just as you enter, you will find a colt tied, which no man has ever yet ridden. Untie it and bring it here to me. 31And if anyone asks you why you are untying it, you are to answer, 'The Lord needs it.' "

32 So off the two messengers went and found it just as He had told them. 33And while they were untying the colt, its owners said to them, "Why are you untying the colt?"

34 And they answered, "The Lord needs it." 35 So they brought it to Jesus. 36 Then they threw their coats upon it and mounted Jesus upon it. As He was going on, the people continued to spread their coats under Him on the road. 37 Just as He was approaching the city, going down the Mount of Olives, the whole throng of the disciples began to praise God exultantly and loudly for all the wonder-works that they had seen, 38 and said:

"Blessed is the King who comes in the name of the Lord;

Peace in heaven and praise on high!"

39 Then some Pharisees in the crowd said to Him, "Teacher, reprove your disciples."

40 But He answered, "I tell you, if they keep silent, the stones will cry out!"

41 As He approached it, just as soon as He saw the city, He burst into tears over it, 42 and said: "If today you yourself had only known the conditions of peace! But now they are hidden from you. 43 For a time is coming upon you when your enemies will throw up earthworks around you and surround you and hem you in on all sides, 44 and they will throw you and your children within you to the ground, and they will not leave one stone upon another in you, because you did not know when God visited you."

45 Then He went into the temple and began to drive out those who were selling things in it, 46 and He said to them, "The Scripture says, 'And my house shall be a house of prayer,' but you have made it a cave for robbers."

47 So He was teaching daily in the temple, and the high priests and the scribes and the leading men of the people were trying to destroy Him, 48 but they could not find, as hard as they tried, what to do with Him, for all the people continued to hang on His words.

BECK

26 " 'I tell you, everyone who has something will be given more, and anyone who doesn't have what he should have, even what he has will be taken away. 27 But those enemies of mine who didn't want me to be their king—bring them here and kill them in front of me.' "

28 After Jesus had said this, He continued on His way up to Jerusalem.

The King Is Coming

29 When He came near Bethphage and Bethany at the Mount of Olives, as it was called, He sent two of His disciples. 30 "Go into the village ahead of you," He said, "and as you go in, you'll find a colt tied up that nobody ever sat on. Untie it and bring it to Me. 31And if anybody asks you, 'Why are you untying it?' say, 'The Lord needs it.' "

32 The men whom He sent went and found it as He had told them. 33 While they were untying the colt, its owners asked them, "Why are you untying the colt?"

34 "The Lord needs it," they said.

35 So they brought it to Jesus, put their garments on the colt, and set Jesus on it. 36As He was riding along, people spread their garments on the road. 37And as He was coming near the place where the road goes down the Mount of Olives, the whole crowd of the disciples began to praise God joyfully and loudly for all the miracles they had seen. 38 They said,

"Blessed is the King who is coming in the Lord's name! [66]

In heaven peace, and glory in the highest heavens."

39 Some of the Pharisees in the crowd said to Him, "Teacher, urge Your disciples to be quiet."

40 "I tell you," He answered them, "if these are quiet, the stones will cry out."

41 When He came near and saw the city, He wept loud over it 42 and said, "If today you only knew—yes, you—the way to peace! 43 But now it's hidden so that you can't see it. The time will come for you when your enemies will put up ramparts against you and surround you and press against you from every side. 44 They'll dash you and your children to the ground [67] and not leave one stone on another in you, because you didn't know the time your help came to you."

He Cleanses the Temple

45 Jesus went into the temple and proceeded to drive out the men who were selling things there. 46 He said to them, "It is written, My house should be a house of prayer, [68] but you have made it a den of robbers." [69]

47 Every day He was teaching in the temple. The ruling priests, the Bible scholars, and the leaders of the people were trying to kill Him, 48 but they couldn't find a way to do it, because the people were all eager to hear Him.

[66] Ps. 118:26
[67] Ps. 137:9
[68] Is. 56:7
[69] Jer. 7:11

20 And it came to pass, *that* on one of those days, as he taught the people in the temple, and preached the gospel, the chief priests and the scribes came upon *him* with the elders, 2And spake unto him, saying, Tell us, by what authority doest thou these things? or who is he that gave thee this authority? 3And he answered and said unto them, I will also ask you one thing; and answer me: 4 The baptism of John, was it from heaven, or of men? 5And they reasoned with themselves, saying, If we shall say, From heaven; he will say, Why then believed ye him not? 6 But and if ye say, Of men; all the people will stone us: for they be persuaded that John was a prophet. 7And they answered, that they could not tell whence *it was.* 8And Jesus said unto them, Neither tell I you by what authority I do these things. 9 Then began he to speak to the people this parable; A certain man planted a vineyard, and let it forth to husbandmen, and went into a far country for a long time. 10And at the season he sent a servant to the husbandmen, that they should give him of the fruit of the vineyard: but the husbandmen beat him, and sent *him* away empty. 11And again he sent another servant: and they beat him also, and entreated *him* shamefully, and sent *him* away empty. 12And again he sent a third: and they wounded him also, and cast *him* out. 13 Then said the lord of the vineyard, What shall I do? I will send my beloved son: it may be they will reverence *him* when they see him. 14 But when the husbandmen saw him, they reasoned among themselves, saying, This is the heir: come, let us kill him, that the inheritance may be ours. 15 So they cast him out of the vineyard, and killed *him.* What therefore shall the lord of the vineyard do unto them? 16 He shall come and destroy these husbandmen, and shall give the vineyard to others. And when they heard *it,* they said, God forbid. 17And he beheld them, and said, What is this then that is written, The stone which the builders rejected, the same is become the head of the corner? 18 Whosoever shall fall upon that stone shall be broken; but on whomsoever it shall fall, it will grind him to powder.

19 And the chief priests and the scribes the same hour sought to lay hands on him; and they feared the people: for they perceived that he had spoken this parable against them. 20And they watched *him,* and sent forth spies, which should feign themselves just men, that they might take hold of his words, that so they might deliver him unto the power and authority of the governor. 21And they asked him, saying, Master, we know that thou sayest and teachest rightly, neither acceptest thou the person *of any,* but teachest the way of God truly: 22 Is it lawful for us to give tribute unto Cesar, or no? 23 But he perceived their craftiness, and said unto them, Why tempt ye me? 24 Shew me a penny. Whose image and superscription hath it? They answered and said, Cesar's. 25And he said unto them, Render therefore unto Cesar the things which be Cesar's, and unto God the things which be

20 And it came about on one of the days while He was teaching the people in the temple and preaching the gospel, that the chief priests and the scribes with the elders confronted *Him,* 2 and they spoke, saying to Him, "Tell us by what authority You are doing these things, or who is the one who gave You this authority?" 3And He answered and said to them, "I shall also ask you a question, and you tell Me: 4 "Was the baptism of John from heaven or from men?" 5And they reasoned among themselves, saying, "If we say, 'From heaven,' He will say, 'Why did you not believe him?' 6 "But if we say, 'From men,' all the people will stone us to death, for they are convinced that John was a prophet." 7And they answered that they did not know where *it came* from. 8And Jesus said to them, "Neither will I tell you by what authority I am doing these things."

9 And He began to tell the people this parable: "A man planted a vineyard and rented it out to vine-growers, and went on a journey for a long time. 10 "And at the *harvest* time he sent a slave to the vine-growers, in order that they might give him *some* of the produce of the vineyard; but the vine-growers beat him and sent him away empty-handed. 11 "And he proceeded to send another slave; and they beat him also and treated him shamefully, and sent him away empty-handed. 12 "And he proceeded to send a third; and this one also they wounded and cast out. 13 "And the owner of the vineyard said, 'What shall I do? I will send my beloved son; perhaps they will respect him.' 14 "But when the vine-growers saw him, they reasoned with one another, saying, 'This is the heir; let us kill him that the inheritance may be ours.' 15 "And they cast him out of the vineyard and killed him. What, therefore, will the owner of the vineyard do to them? 16 "He will come and destroy these vine-growers and will give the vineyard to others." And when they heard it, they said, "May it never be!" 17 But He looked at them and said, "What then is this that is written,

The STONE WHICH THE BUILDERS REJECTED, THIS BECAME THE CHIEF CORNER *stone'?*
18 "Every one who falls on that stone will be broken to pieces; but on whomever it falls, it will scatter him like dust."

19 And the scribes and the chief priests tried to lay hands on Him that very hour, and they feared the people; for they understood that He spoke this parable against them. 20And they watched Him, and sent spies who pretended to be righteous, in order that they might catch Him in some statement, so as to deliver Him up to the rule and the authority of the governor. 21And they questioned Him, saying, "Teacher, we know that You speak and teach correctly, and You are not partial to any, but teach the way of God in truth. 22 "Is it lawful for us to pay taxes to Caesar, or not?" 23 But He detected their trickery and said to them, 24 "Show Me a ᵉdenarius. Whose head and inscription does it have?" And they said, "Caesar's." 25And He said to them, "Then render to Caesar the things that are Caesar's, and to God the things

[a] The denarius was worth 18 cents in silver, equivalent to one day's wages.

WILLIAMS

BECK

From Heaven

WILLIAMS

20 *Jesus' authority challenged; He aims at His challengers the story of the villainous tenants; they ask Him two "catch" questions: Is it right to pay taxes to Rome? Is there a resurrection? He routs them with a question*

One day while He was teaching the people in the temple and preaching the good news, the high priests and the scribes, together with the elders, took a stand against Him, 2 and said to Him, "Tell us what sort of authority you have for doing as you do, or who is it that gave you such authority?"
3 Then He answered them, "I will ask you a question too. Tell me, 4 was John's baptism from heaven or from men?"
5 And they argued with one another, and said, "If we say, 'From heaven,' He will say, 'Why did you not believe him?' 6 But if we say, 'From men,' all the people will stone us to death, for they are convinced that John was a prophet." 7 So they answered and said that they did not know where it was from.
8 Then Jesus said to them, "Nor am I going to tell you what sort of authority I have for doing as I do."
9 Then He went on to tell the people the following story:
"Once upon a time a man planted a vineyard and leased it to tenant farmers, and then went abroad for a long stay. 10 So at the proper time He sent a slave to the tenants, that they might pay him his part of the grape-crop, but the tenants beat him and sent him back empty-handed. 11 Then again he sent another slave, and they beat him and insulted him, and sent him back empty-handed. 12And again he sent a third slave, and they wounded him and threw him out of the vineyard. 13 Then the owner of the vineyard said, 'What shall I do? I will send my dearly loved son. They will, I should think, respect him.' 14 But when the tenants saw him, they argued among themselves, 'This is the heir, let us kill him, so that what he inherits may be ours.' 15 So they drove him out of the vineyard and killed him. What then will the owner of the vineyard do to them? 16 He will come and put those tenants to death and give the vineyard to others."
When they heard this, they said, "May it never be so!"
17 But He glanced at them and said, "Then what does this Scripture mean:
'That stone which the builders threw away
Has now become the cornerstone'?
18 Everyone who falls upon that stone will be shattered, and he on whom it falls will be crushed to dust."
19 Then the scribes and the high priests tried to arrest Him at that very hour, but they were afraid of the people; for they knew that He meant this story for them. 20 So they closely watched and sent spies who pretended to be upright men, to catch Him in His conversation, so as to turn Him over to the power and authority of the governor. 21 They asked Him, "Teacher, we know that you speak and teach what is right, and show no favors to anyone, but teach the way of God honestly. 22 Is it right for us to pay taxes to Caesar, or not?"
23 But He detected their cunning, and said to them, 24 "Show me a twenty-cent coin. Whose picture and title does it bear?"
They answered, "Caesar's."
25 He said to them, "Then pay Caesar what belongs to Caesar, and pay God what belongs

BECK

From Heaven

20 One day, as He was teaching the people in the temple and telling them the good news, the ruling priests, Bible scholars, and elders came to Him. 2 "Tell us," they asked Him, "by what authority are You doing these things? Or who gives You the right to do them?"
3 Jesus answered them, "I will ask you a question. Tell Me, 4 John's baptism—was it from heaven or from men?"
5 They argued among themselves, "If we say, 'From heaven,' He will ask, 'Why didn't you believe him?' 6 But if we say, 'From men,' all the people will stone us. They're convinced John was a prophet." 7 So they answered they didn't know where it was from.
8 Then Jesus told them, "Neither will I tell you by what authority I'm doing these things."

God's Vineyard

9 Then He told the people this story:
"A man *planted a vineyard,*[70] rented it out to workers, and left to be gone a long time.
10 "At the right time he sent a slave to the workers to get from them a share of the products of the vineyard. But the workers beat him and sent him back empty-handed. 11 He sent another slave; they beat him, too, treated him shamefully, and sent him back empty-handed. 12 Then he sent a third; they wounded him and threw him out.
13 "Then the owner of the vineyard said, 'What should I do? I'll send my son whom I love. Maybe they'll respect him.'
14 "When the workers saw him, they talked it over among themselves, saying, 'This is the heir. Let's kill him and get the inheritance.' 15 So they threw him out of the vineyard and killed him.
16 "Now, what will the owner of the vineyard do to them? He will come and kill those workers and give the vineyard to others."
"That must never happen!" said those who heard Him.
17 Jesus looked at them and asked, "What does this mean in your Bible: *The stone the builders rejected has become the cornerstone?*[71] 18 Everyone who falls on that Stone will be dashed in pieces, and if that Stone falls on anyone, it will scatter him like dust."
19 The Bible scholars and the ruling priests wanted to grab Him then and there, because they knew He had aimed this story at them, but they were afraid of the people.

Taxes

20 They watched for an opportunity and sent spies to act holy in order to catch Him in what He would say. They wanted to hand Him over to the governor's control and authority. 21 They had a question for Him. "Teacher," they said, "we know You're right in what You say and teach, and You don't favor any special persons but really teach God's way. 22 Is it right for us to pay a tax to Caesar or not?"
23 Seeing through their tricky way, He told them, 24 "Show Me a denarius. Whose head is on it and whose inscription?"
"Caesar's," they answered.
25 "Well, then, give Caesar what is Caesar's," He told them, "and God what is God's."

[70] Is. 5:2
[71] Ps. 118:22

K.J.V.

God's. 26And they could not take hold of his words before the people: and they marvelled at his answer, and held their peace.

27 Then came to *him* certain of the Sadducees, which deny that there is any resurrection; and they asked him, 28 Saying, Master, Moses wrote unto us, If any man's brother die, having a wife, and he die without children, that his brother should take his wife, and raise up seed unto his brother. 29 There were therefore seven brethren: and the first took a wife, and died without children. 30And the second took her to wife, and he died childless. 31And the third took her; and in like manner the seven also: and they left no children, and died. 32 Last of all the woman died also. 33 Therefore in the resurrection whose wife of them is she? for seven had her to wife. 34And Jesus answering said unto them, The children of this world marry, and are given in marriage: 35 But they which shall be accounted worthy to obtain that world, and the resurrection from the dead, neither marry, nor are given in marriage: 36 Neither can they die any more: for they are equal unto the angels; and are the children of God, being the children of the resurrection. 37 Now that the dead are raised, even Moses shewed at the bush, when he calleth the Lord the God of Abraham, and the God of Isaac, and the God of Jacob. 38 For he is not a god of the dead, but of the living: for all live unto him.

39 Then certain of the scribes answering said, Master, thou hast well said. 40And after that they durst not ask him any *question at all.* 41And he said unto them, How say they that Christ is David's son? 42And David himself saith in the book of Psalms, The Lord said unto my Lord, Sit thou on my right hand, 43 Till I make thine enemies thy footstool. 44 David therefore calleth him Lord, how is he then his son?

45 Then in the audience of all the people he said unto his disciples, 46 Beware of the scribes, which desire to walk in long robes, and love greetings in the markets, and the highest seats in the synagogues, and the chief rooms at feasts; 47 Which devour widows' houses, and for a shew make long prayers: the same shall receive greater damnation.

N.A.S.

that are God's." 26And they were unable to catch Him in a saying in the presence of the people; and marveling at His answer, they became silent.

27 Now there came to Him some of the Sadducees (who say that there is no resurrection), 28 and they questioned Him, saying, "Teacher, Moses wrote us that IF A MAN'S BROTHER DIES, having a wife, AND HE IS CHILD-LESS, HIS BROTHER SHOULD TAKE THE WIFE AND RAISE UP OFFSPRING TO HIS BROTHER. 29 "Now there were seven brothers; and the first took a wife, and died childless; 30 and the second 31 and the third took her; and in the same way the seven also died, leaving no children. 32 "Finally the woman died also. 33 "In the resurrection therefore, which one's wife will the woman be? For the seven had her as wife." 34And Jesus said to them, "The sons of this age marry and are given in marriage, 35 but those who are considered worthy to attain to that age and the resurrection from the dead, neither marry, nor are given in marriage; 36 for neither can they die any more, for they are like angels, and are sons of God, being sons of the resurrection. 37 "But that the dead are raised, even Moses showed, in the *passage about the burning* bush, where he calls the Lord THE GOD OF ABRAHAM, AND THE GOD OF ISAAC, AND THE GOD OF JACOB. 38 "Now He is not the God of the dead, but of the living; for all live to Him." 39And some of the scribes answered and said, "Teacher, You have spoken well." 40 For they did not have courage to question Him any longer about anything.

41 And He said to them, "How *is it that* they say "the Christ is David's son? 42 For David himself says in the book of Psalms,
'THE LORD SAID TO MY LORD,
"SIT AT MY RIGHT HAND,
43 UNTIL I MAKE THINE ENEMIES A FOOTSTOOL
FOR THY FEET." '
44 "David therefore calls Him 'Lord,' and how is He his son?"

45 And while all the people were listening, He said to the disciples, 46 "Beware of the scribes, who like to walk around in long robes, and love respectful greetings in the market places, and chief seats in the synagogues, and places of honor at banquets, 47 who devour widows' houses, and for appearances' sake offer long prayers; these will receive greater condemnation."

21 And he looked up, and saw the rich men casting their gifts into the treasury. 2And he saw also a certain poor widow casting in thither two mites. 3And he said, Of a truth I say unto you, that this poor widow hath cast

21 And He looked up and saw the rich putting their gifts into the treasury. 2And He saw a certain poor widow putting in two small copper coins. 3And He said, "Truly I say to you, this poor widow put in more than

[a] I.e., *the Messiah.*

230

WILLIAMS

to God!" 26 So they could not use^a what he said before the people, and in astonishment at His answer they said no more.

27 Then some of the Sadducees, who say that there is no resurrection, came up and asked Him, 28 "Teacher, Moses wrote for us a law that, if a man's brother dies and leaves a wife but no child, the man should take the widow and raise up a family for his brother. 29 Now there were seven brothers. And the first brother married a wife and died childless. 30 Then the second, 31 and the third, married her; as also the seven did who died but left no child. 32 Last of all, the woman died. 33 Now at the resurrection which one's wife will the woman be? For the seven married her."

34 Jesus said to them, "The people of this world marry and are married, 35 but those who are considered worthy to attain that other world and the resurrection from the dead, neither marry nor are married. 36 For they cannot die again. They are like the angels, and since they are reborn in the resurrection,^b are children of God. 37 But that the dead are raised, even Moses at the bush has demonstrated, when he calls the Lord 'the God of Abraham, the God of Isaac, and the God of Jacob.' 38 He is not the God of dead but of living people, for all live to Him."

39 Then some of the scribes answered Him, "Teacher, you have given a fine answer." 40 For they did not dare to ask Him any more questions.

41 Then He said to them, "How do people say that the Christ is David's Son? 42 For David himself in the Book of Psalms says:
'The Lord has said to my Lord, "Sit at my right hand,
43 Until I make your enemies the footstool of your feet." '
44 So David calls Him Lord, then how can He be his Son?"

45 While all the people were listening, He said to His disciples, 46 "Beware of the scribes who like to go about in long robes and love to be saluted with honor in public places, to be seated in the front seats in the synagogues, and to occupy the places of honor at banquets— 47 men who eat up widows' houses and to cover it up make long prayers! They will receive a much heavier sentence."

21 *The widow's one-cent contribution commended by Jesus; the destruction of Jerusalem and His second coming foretold; His warning against persecution and suffering*

Now He looked up and saw the rich people dropping their gifts into the treasury. 2 Then He saw a poor widow drop in two little coins which make scarcely a cent. 3 And He said, "I tell you the truth, this poor widow has dropped

[a] Grk., *take hold of His saying*—to twist it.
[b] Grk., *being sons of the resurrection.*

BECK

26 So they couldn't catch Him before the people in anything He said. His answer surprised them so much they didn't say anything.

The Dead Live

27 Some of the Sadducees, who say the dead don't rise, came to Him with this question: 28 "Teacher, Moses wrote for us, *If any married man dies and has no children, his brother should marry the widow and have children for his brother.*⁷² 29 Now, there were seven brothers. The first married and died childless. 30 Then the second brother 31 married the widow, and so did the third. In the same way all seven died and left no children. 32 Finally the woman died too. 33 Now, when they rise from the dead, whose wife will she be? You know, the seven had her as wife."

34 "In this world men and women marry," Jesus told them; 35 "but those who are considered worthy to rise from the dead and live in the other world don't marry. 36 Nor can they die anymore, because they're like the angels. They're God's children and share in the resurrection.

37 "That the dead rise, Moses showed in the story about the bush when he called the Lord *the God of Abraham, the God of Isaac, and the God of Jacob.*⁷³ 38 He's not the God of dead but of the living. All who are with Him are alive."

39 "Teacher," some Bible scholars told Him, "You have told the truth." 40 Nobody dared to ask Him another question.

David's Son

41 "How can people say the promised Savior is David's Son?" He asked them. 42 "David himself says in the book of Psalms,

The Lord said to my Lord,
43 *'Sit at My right*
*Till I make Your enemies Your footstool.'*⁷⁴

44 So David calls Him Lord. Then how can He be his Son?"

Beware!

45 While all the people were listening, He said to the disciples: 46 "Beware of the Bible scholars. They like to go around in long robes and love to be greeted in the marketplaces, to sit in the front seats in the synagogs, and to have the places of honor at dinners. 47 They swallow the widows' houses and then, to cover up, make long prayers. They'll be punished all the more."

A Cent

21 Looking up, He saw rich people dropping their gifts into the contribution boxes. 2 And He saw a poor widow drop in two small coins. 3 He said, "I tell you, this poor widow

[72] Gen. 38:8; Deut. 25:26
[73] Ex. 3:6
[74] Ps. 110:1

K.J.V.

in more than they all: 4 For all these have of their abundance cast in unto the offerings of God: but she of her penury hath cast in all the living that she had.

5 And as some spake of the temple, how it was adorned with goodly stones and gifts, he said, 6 *As for* these things which ye behold, the days will come, in the which there shall not be left one stone upon another, that shall not be thrown down. 7 And they asked him, saying, Master, but when shall these things be? and what sign *will there be* when these things shall come to pass? 8 And he said, Take heed that ye be not deceived: for many shall come in my name, saying, I am *Christ;* and the time draweth near: go ye not therefore after them. 9 But when ye shall hear of wars and commotions, be not terrified: for these things must first come to pass; but the end *is* not by and by. 10 Then said he unto them, Nation shall rise against nation, and kingdom against kingdom: 11 And great earthquakes shall be in divers places, and famines, and pestilences; and fearful sights and great signs shall there be from heaven. 12 But before all these, they shall lay their hands on you, and persecute *you,* delivering *you* up to the synagogues, and into prisons, being brought before kings and rulers for my name's sake. 13 And it shall turn to you for a testimony. 14 Settle *it* therefore in your hearts, not to meditate before what ye shall answer: 15 For I will give you a mouth and wisdom, which all your adversaries shall not be able to gainsay nor resist. 16 And ye shall be betrayed both by parents, and brethren, and kinsfolks, and friends; and *some* of you shall they cause to be put to death. 17 And ye shall be hated of all *men* for my name's sake. 18 But there shall not a hair of your head perish. 19 In your patience possess ye your souls. 20 And when ye shall see Jerusalem compassed with armies, then know that the desolation thereof is nigh. 21 Then let them which are in Judea flee to the mountains; and let them which are in the midst of it depart out; and let not them that are in the countries enter thereinto. 22 For these be the days of vengeance, that all things which are written may be fulfilled. 23 But woe unto them that are with child, and to them that give suck, in those days! for there shall be great distress in the land, and wrath upon this people. 24 And they shall fall by the edge of the sword, and shall be led away captive into all nations: and Jerusalem shall be trodden down of the Gentiles, until the times of the Gentiles be fulfilled.

25 And there shall be signs in the sun, and in the moon, and in the stars; and upon the earth distress of nations, with perplexity; the sea and the waves roaring; 26 Men's hearts failing them for fear, and for looking after those things which are coming on the earth: for the powers of heaven shall be shaken.

N.A.S.

all *of them;* 4 for they all out of their surplus put into the offering; but she out of her poverty put in all that she had to live on."

5 And while some were talking about the temple, that it was adorned with beautiful stones and votive gifts, He said, 6 "*As for* these things which you are looking at, the days will come in which there will not be left one stone upon another which will not be torn down." 7 And they questioned Him, saying, "Teacher, when therefore will these things be? And what *will be* the sign when these things are about to take place?" 8 And He said, "Take heed that you be not misled; for many will come in My name, saying, 'I am *He,*' and, 'The time is at hand'; do not go after them. 9 "And when you hear of wars and disturbances, do not be terrified; for these things must take place first, but the end *does* not *follow* immediately."

10 Then He continued by saying to them, "Nation will rise against nation, and kingdom against kingdom, 11 and there will be great earthquakes, and in various places plagues and famines; and there will be terrors and great signs from heaven. 12 "But before all these things, they will lay their hands on you and will persecute you, delivering you to the synagogues and prisons, bringing you before kings and governors for My name's sake. 13 "It will lead to an opportunity for your testimony. 14 "So make up your minds not to prepare beforehand to defend yourselves; 15 for I will give you utterance and wisdom which none of your opponents will be able to resist or refute. 16 "But you will be betrayed even by parents and brothers and relatives and friends, and they will put *some* of you to death, 17 and you will be hated by all on account of My name. 18 "Yet not a hair of your head will perish. 19 "By your perseverance you will win your souls.

20 "But when you see Jerusalem surrounded by armies, then recognize that her desolation is at hand. 21 "Then let those who are in Judea flee to the mountains, and let those who are in the midst of the city depart, and let not those who are in the country enter the city; 22 because these are days of vengeance, in order that all things which are written may be fulfilled. 23 "Woe to those who are with child and to those who nurse babes in those days; for there will be great distress upon the land, and wrath to this people, 24 and they will fall by the edge of the sword, and will be led captive into all the nations; and Jerusalem will be trampled underfoot by the Gentiles until the times of the Gentiles be fulfilled.

25 "And there will be signs in sun and moon and stars, and upon the earth dismay among nations, in perplexity at the roaring of the sea and the waves, 26 men fainting from fear and the expectation of the things which are coming upon the world; for the powers of the

in more than all of them; 4 for all the rest of them made their contributions out of their surplus, but she out of her want dropped in all that she had to live on."

5 Now while some people were talking about the temple, how it was decorated with beautiful stones and votive-offerings, He said,

6 "As for all this that you are admiring, the time is coming when not one stone will be left upon another, that will not be torn down."

7 Then they asked Him, "Teacher, when will this be? And what is the sign that it is about to take place?"

8 So He said, "You must take care not to be misled about it! For many will come bearing the name of Messiah, and saying, 'I am He,' and, 'The time is near.' Do not go after them. 9 And when you hear of wars and tumults, never be panic-stricken. For this has to take place first, but the end will not come all at once."

10 Then He continued to say to them, "One nation will go to war with another, and one kingdom with another. 11 There will be great earthquakes and pestilences and famines in various places, and there will be dreadful portents and awful signs in the sky. 12 But before all this takes place, people will arrest you and persecute you, and turn you over to synagogues and prisons, and you will be brought before kings and governors for my name's sake. 13 It will furnish you an opportunity to testify. 14 So you must purpose in your hearts not to prepare beforehand how to make your defense, 15 for I will give you such wisdom of speech as all your opponents combined will not be able to resist and refute. 16 Yes, you will be betrayed even by parents and brothers and kinsmen and friends, and they will put some of you to death, 17 and you will be continuously hated by everyone, because you bear my name. 18 And yet not a single hair on your head will perish. 19 By your endurance you will win your souls.

20 "When you see Jerusalem being surrounded by armies, then understand that her devastation is near. 21 Then let those in Judea begin to fly to the mountains, and those within the city begin to get out of it, 22 for these are the days of vengeance when all that is written in the Scriptures will be fulfilled. 23 Alas for the women who are pregnant and those who have nursing babies in those days! For there will be great misery in the land and wrath on this people. 24 They will fall by the edge of the sword and will be carried off as captives among all the nations, and Jerusalem will be trampled under the feet of the heathen, until the times of the heathen come to full measure. 25 And there will be signs in sun and moon and stars, and on earth despair of nations in bewilderment at the roaring of the sea and its waves, 26 men fainting with fear and apprehension of the things that are to come upon the world, for the powers of

certainly put in more than all the others. 4 All the others took some of what they had left over and dropped it in among the gifts. But she put in what she needed for herself, all she had to live on."

Sorrow Ahead!

5 Some were saying about the temple, "It is beautifully constructed with fine stones and gifts."

6 "About these things that you see," He said, "the time will come when not a stone will be left on another here but will be torn down."

7 "Teacher," they asked Him, "when will this be, and how can we tell when this will happen?"

8 "Be careful not to let anyone deceive you," Jesus said. "Many will come using My name and saying, 'I am He!' and, 'The time has come.' Don't follow them.

9 "When you hear of wars and revolutions, don't get alarmed. These things *must happen*[75] first, but the end won't come right away."

10 Then He told them, "*Nation will fight against nation, and kingdom against kingdom.*[76] 11 There will be great earthquakes and famines and plagues in different places, terrible sights and great signs coming from heaven.

12 "Before all these things happen, men will arrest you and persecute you, hand you over to church councils, and put you in prisons. They'll bring you before kings and governors on account of My name. 13 It will be your chance to tell them the truth. 14 So make up your minds not to worry beforehand how you'll defend yourselves. 15 I'll give you such speech and wisdom none of your enemies will be able to oppose it or talk against it.

16 "Even parents, brothers, relatives, and friends will betray you and kill some of you, 17 and everybody will hate you because of My name. 18 But not a hair on your head will be lost. 19 Endure patiently, and you'll win your lives."

Jerusalem Will Be Destroyed

20 "When you see Jerusalem surrounded by an army, then know the time has come for her to be destroyed. 21 Then if you're in Judea, flee to the hills. If you're in Jerusalem, leave it. If you're in the country, don't go into the city. 22 Those will be *days of vengeance*[77] when everything must happen as it is written.

23 "Woe to the women who in those days are expecting babies or nursing them. There will be great distress in this country, and God will punish this nation. 24 The sword will cut them down, they'll be taken away as prisoners among all nations, and *the Gentiles will trample on Jerusalem*[78] till the time for the Gentiles has passed."

Jesus Is Coming

25 "There will be signs in the sun, the moon, and the stars, and on the earth *nations* will be in distress, not knowing which way to turn from *the roaring and tossing of the sea.*[79] 26 People will faint as they fearfully wait for what will happen to the world. *The powers of the heavens*[80] will be shaken.

[75] Dan. 2:28
[76] Is. 19:2; 2 Chron. 15:6
[77] Deut. 32:35; Hos. 9:7
[78] Is. 63:18; Zech. 12:3
[79] Ps. 65:7
[80] Is. 34:4

K.J.V.

27And then shall they see the Son of man coming in a cloud with power and great glory. 28And when these things begin to come to pass, then look up, and lift up your heads; for your redemption draweth nigh. 29And he spake to them a parable; Behold the fig tree, and all the trees; 30 When they now shoot forth, ye see and know of your own selves that summer is now nigh at hand. 31 So likewise ye, when ye see these things come to pass, know ye that the kingdom of God is nigh at hand. 32 Verily I say unto you, This generation shall not pass away, till all be fulfilled. 33 Heaven and earth shall pass away; but my words shall not pass away.

34 And take heed to yourselves, lest at any time your hearts be overcharged with surfeiting, and drunkenness, and cares of this life, and so that day come upon you unawares. 35 For as a snare shall it come on all them that dwell on the face of the whole earth. 36 Watch ye therefore, and pray always, that ye may be accounted worthy to escape all these things that shall come to pass, and to stand before the Son of man. 37And in the daytime he was teaching in the temple; and at night he went out, and abode in the mount that is called *the mount* of Olives. 38And all the people came early in the morning to him in the temple, for to hear him.

22 Now the feast of unleavened bread drew nigh, which is called the passover. 2And the chief priests and scribes sought how they might kill him; for they feared the people. 3 Then entered Satan into Judas surnamed Iscariot, being of the number of the twelve. 4And he went his way, and communed with the chief priests and captains, how he might betray him unto them. 5And they were glad, and covenanted to give him money. 6And he promised, and sought opportunity to betray him unto them in the absence of the multitude.

7 Then came the day of unleavened bread, when the passover must be killed. 8And he sent Peter and John, saying, Go and prepare us the passover, that we may eat. 9And they said unto him, Where wilt thou that we prepare? 10And he said unto them, Behold, when ye are entered into the city, there shall a man meet you, bearing a pitcher of water; follow him into the house where he entereth in. 11And ye shall say unto the goodman of the house, The Master saith unto thee, Where is the guestchamber, where I shall eat the passover with my disciples? 12And he shall shew you a large upper room furnished: there make ready. 13And they went, and found as he had said unto them: and they made ready the passover. 14And when the hour was come, he sat down, and the

N.A.S.

heavens will be shaken. 27 "And then will they see THE SON OF MAN COMING IN A CLOUD with power and great glory. 28 "But when these things begin to take place, straighten up and lift up your heads, because your redemption is drawing near."

29 And He told them a parable: "Behold the fig tree, and all the trees; 30 as soon as they put forth *leaves,* you see it and know for yourselves that the summer is now near. 31 "Even so you too, when you see these things happening, recognize that the kingdom of God is near. 32 "Truly I say to you, this generation will not pass away until all things take place. 33 "Heaven and earth will pass away, but My words will not pass away.

34 "Be on guard, that your hearts may not be weighted down with dissipation and drunkenness and the worries of life, and that day come on you suddenly like a trap; 35 for it will come upon all those who dwell on the face of all the earth. 36 "But keep on the alert at all times, praying in order that you may have strength to escape all these things that are about to take place, and to stand before the Son of Man."

37 Now during the day He was teaching in the temple, but at evening He would go out and spend the night on the mount that is called Olivet. 38And all the people would get up early in the morning *to come* to Him in the temple to listen to Him.

22 Now the Feast of Unleavened Bread, which is called the Passover, was approaching. 2And the chief priests and the scribes were seeking how they might put Him to death; for they were afraid of the people. 3 And Satan entered into Judas who was called Iscariot, belonging to the number of the twelve. 4And he went away and discussed with the chief priests and officers how he might betray Him to them. 5And they were delighted, and agreed to give him money. 6And he consented, and *began* seeking a good opportunity to betray Him to them apart from the multitude.

7 Then came the day of Unleavened Bread on which the Passover *lamb* had to be sacrificed. 8And He sent Peter and John, saying, "Go and prepare the Passover for us, that we may eat it." 9And they said to Him, "Where do You want us to prepare it?" 10And He said to them, "Behold, when you have entered the city, a man will meet you carrying a pitcher of water; follow him into the house that he enters. 11 "And you shall say to the owner of the house, 'The Teacher says to you, "Where is the guest room in which I may eat the Passover with My disciples?"' 12 "And he will show you a large, furnished, upper room; prepare it there." 13And they departed and found *everything* just as He had told them; and they prepared the Passover.

14 And when the hour had come He reclined

WILLIAMS

the sky will be shaken. 27 Then they will see the Son of Man coming on a cloud in overwhelming power and splendor. 28 When these things begin to take place, look up and lift your heads, for your deliverance is drawing near."

29 Then He told them a story. "Look at the fig tree and all the trees. 30 When you see them shooting forth their buds, you know of yourselves that summer now is near. 31 So when you see these things taking place, you must understand that the kingdom of God is near.

32 "I solemnly say to you, this generation will not pass away before all this takes place. 33 Sky and earth will pass away, but my words will never pass away. 34 But ever be on your guard, so that your hearts may not be loaded down with self-indulgence, drunkenness, and worldly worries, and that day, like a trap, catch you unawares. 35 For it will come upon all who are living anywhere on the face of the earth. 36 But ever be watching and always praying, so that you may have strength to escape all this that is going to take place, and so you may take your stand in the presence of the Son of Man."

37 Now during the days He continued to teach in the temple, but He would go out and spend the nights on the hill called the Mount of Olives; 38 while all the people would rise early in the mornings and come to listen to Him in the temple.

22 *Judas bargains to betray Him; Jesus institutes the memorial supper; defines true greatness; warns Peter that Satan will sift him; warns all of approaching perils; in Gethsemane suffering, betrayed, arrested; tried in the Jewish court*

Now the feast of Unleavened Bread, which is called the Passover, was drawing near. 2 So the high priests and the scribes continued to seek how they might put Him to death, for they were afraid of the people. 3 But Satan entered into Judas, who is called Iscariot, who belonged to the circle of the Twelve. 4 So he went off and discussed with the high priests and captains of the temple how he could betray Him to them. 5 They were delighted and made a bargain to pay him for it. 6 He in turn accepted their offer and began to seek a favorable opportunity to betray Him to them without exciting an uprising.

7 Then the day of Unleavened Bread came, on which the Passover lamb had to be sacrificed. 8 So He sent Peter and John, saying to them, "Go and make preparations for us to eat the Passover meal."

9 They asked Him, "Where do you wish us to prepare it?"

10 He answered them, "Just after you enter the city, a man with a pitcher of water will meet you. Follow him into the house which he enters 11 and say to the owner of the house, 'Our Teacher says to you, "Where is the room in which I am to eat the Passover supper with my disciples?"' 12 Then he will show you a large room upstairs already furnished. There make the preparations." 13 So they went off and found it just as He had said, and they prepared the Passover supper.

14 Now when the hour came, He took His place at the table, with the apostles about Him.

BECK

27 "Then they will see *the Son of Man coming in a cloud* [81] with power and great glory.
28 "When these things begin to happen, stand ready and look forward cheerfully because you will soon be set free."

29 Then He pictured it this way: "Look at a fig tree, or any of the trees. 30 As soon as leaves grow on it, you see and know without being told that summer is near. 31 So also when you see those things happen, you know God's kingdom is near.

32 "I tell you the truth: These people will not pass away till everything happens. 33 Heaven and earth will pass away, but what I say will not pass away.

34 "Be careful never to get your hearts burdened with drunkenness and its nausea and with worries about this life, or that day will take you by surprise like *a trap*. 35 It will surprise all people wherever they *live on the earth*. [82] 36 But always watch and pray to be considered worthy to escape all these things that are going to happen and to stand before the Son of Man."

37 During the day He would teach in the temple, but at night He would go out to the Mount of Olives, as it was called, and stay there for the night. 38 All the people used to get up early to go to Him in the temple and hear Him.

The Plot

22 The festival of bread without yeast, called the Passover, was near. 2 Then the ruling priests and the Bible scholars were looking for a way to kill Him. They were afraid of the people.

3 The devil went into Judas, called the man from Kerioth, one of the twelve. 4 He went to the high priests and the captains of the temple and discussed with them how he might betray Jesus to them. 5 They were delighted and agreed to give him some money. 6 He promised to do it and so was looking for a chance to betray Him when He was away from the crowd.

The Passover

7 Then came the day of the festival of bread without yeast, when the Passover lamb had to be killed. 8 Jesus sent Peter and John, saying, "Go, get the Passover ready for us to eat."

9 "Where do You want us to get it ready?" they asked Him.

10 "Go into the city," He told them, "and you'll meet a man carrying a jar of water. 11 Follow him into the house he enters, and tell the owner of the house: 'The Teacher asks you, "Where is the room in which I can eat the Passover with My disciples?"' 12 He will show you a large furnished room upstairs. Get things ready there."

13 They went and found it as He had told them, and they got the Passover ready.

14 When the hour had come, He and the

[81] Dan. 7:13
[82] Is. 24:17

K.J.V.

twelve apostles with him. 15And he said unto them, With desire I have desired to eat this passover with you before I suffer: 16 For I say unto you, I will not any more eat thereof, until it be fulfilled in the kingdom of God. 17And he took the cup, and gave thanks, and said, Take this, and divide *it* among yourselves: 18 For I say unto you, I will not drink of the fruit of the vine, until the kingdom of God shall come.

19 And he took bread, and gave thanks, and brake *it*, and gave unto them, saying, This is my body which is given for you: this do in remembrance of me. 20 Likewise also the cup after supper, saying, This cup *is* the new testament in my blood, which is shed for you.

21 But, behold, the hand of him that betrayeth me *is* with me on the table. 22And truly the Son of man goeth, as it was determined: but woe unto that man by whom he is betrayed! 23And they began to inquire among themselves, which of them it was that should do this thing.

24 And there was also a strife among them, which of them should be accounted the greatest. 25And he said unto them, The kings of the Gentiles exercise lordship over them; and they that exercise authority upon them are called benefactors. 26 But ye *shall* not *be* so: but he that is greatest among you, let him be as the younger; and he that is chief, as he that doth serve. 27 For whether *is* greater, he that sitteth at meat, or he that serveth? *is* not he that sitteth at meat? but I am among you as he that serveth. 28 Ye are they which have continued with me in my temptations. 29And I appoint unto you a kingdom, as my Father hath appointed unto me; 30 That ye may eat and drink at my table in my kingdom, and sit on thrones judging the twelve tribes of Israel.

31 And the Lord said, Simon, Simon, behold, Satan hath desired *to have* you, that he may sift *you* as wheat: 32 But I have prayed for thee, that thy faith fail not: and when thou art converted, strengthen thy brethren. 33And he said unto him, Lord, I am ready to go with thee, both into prison, and to death. 34And he said, I tell thee, Peter, the cock shall not crow this day, before that thou shalt thrice deny that thou knowest me. 35And he said unto them, When I sent you without purse, and scrip, and shoes, lacked ye any thing? And they said, Nothing. 36 Then said he unto them, But now, he that hath a purse, let him take *it*, and likewise *his* scrip: and he that hath no sword, let him sell his garment, and buy one. 37 For I say unto you, that this that is written must yet be accomplished in me, And he was reckoned among the transgressors: for the things concerning me have an end. 38And they said, Lord, behold, here *are* two swords. And he said unto them, It is enough.

N.A.S.

at table, and the apostles with Him. 15And He said to them, "I have earnestly desired to eat this Passover with you before I suffer; 16 for I say to you, I shall never again eat it until it is fulfilled in the kingdom of God." 17And having taken a cup, when He had given thanks, He said, "Take this and share it among yourselves; 18 for I say to you, I will not drink of the fruit of the vine from now on until the kingdom of God comes." 19And having taken *some* bread, when He had given thanks, He broke *it*, and gave *it* to them, saying, "This is My body "which is given for you; do this in remembrance of Me." 20And in the same way *He took* the cup after they had eaten, saying, "This cup which is poured out for you is the new covenant in My blood. 21 "But behold, the hand of the one betraying Me is with Me on the table. 22 "For indeed, the Son of Man is going as it has been determined; but woe to that man through whom He is betrayed!" 23And they began to discuss among themselves which one of them it might be who was going to do this thing.

24 And there arose also a dispute among them *as to* which one of them was regarded to be greatest. 25And He said to them, "The kings of the Gentiles lord it over them; and those who have authority over them are called 'Benefactors.' 26 "But not so with you, but let him who is the greatest among you become as the youngest, and the leader as the servant. 27 "For who is greater, the one who reclines *at table,* or the one who serves? Is it not the one who reclines *at table?* But I am among you as the one who serves. 28 "And you are those who have stood by Me in My trials; 29 and just as My Father has granted Me a kingdom, I grant you 30 that you may eat and drink at My table in My kingdom, and you will sit on thrones judging the twelve tribes of Israel.

31 "Simon, Simon, behold, Satan has demanded *permission* to sift you like wheat; 32 but I have prayed for you, that your faith may not fail; and you, when once you have turned again, strengthen your brothers." 33And he said to Him, "Lord, with You I am ready to go both to prison and to death!" 34And He said, "I tell you, Peter, the cock will not crow today until you have denied three times that you know Me."

35 And He said to them, "When I sent you out without purse and bag and sandals, you did not lack anything, did you?" And they said, *"No,* nothing." 36And He said to them, "But now, let him who has a purse take it along, likewise also a bag, and let him who has no sword sell his robe and buy one. 37 "For I tell you, that this which is written must be fulfilled in Me, 'AND HE WAS CLASSED AMONG CRIMINALS'; for that which refers to Me has *its* fulfillment." 38And they said, "Lord, look, here are two swords." And He said to them, "It is enough."

[a] Some ancient mss. omit the remainder of verse 19 and all of verse 20.

WILLIAMS

15And He said to them, "I have heartily desired to eat this Passover supper with you before I suffer. 16 For I tell you, I shall never again eat one until it finds its full fruition in the kingdom of God."

17 Then He received a cup of wine, gave thanks, and said, "Take this and share it among you, 18 for I tell you, I shall not after today drink the product of the vine until the kingdom of God comes."

19 Then He took a loaf, gave thanks, and broke it in pieces, and gave it to them, and said, "This is my body which is to be given for you. Do this as a memorial to me."

20 In like manner after supper He took a cup of wine, and said, "This cup of wine is the new covenant to be ratified by my blood,a which is to be poured out for you. 21 Yet look! The hand of the man who is betraying me is with me on the table! 22 For the Son of Man is going away, as it has been divinely decreed, but a curse will be on that man by whom He is betrayed!"

23 Then they began to discuss among themselves which one it was who was going to do this. 24 There arose also among them a contention as to which one of them should rank as greatest. 25 But He said to them, "The kings of the heathen lord it over them and those who exercise authority over them are given the title of 'Benefactor.' 26 But you are not to do so. On the contrary, the greatest among you must be like the youngest and the leader as the servant. 27 Which one, indeed, is the greater, the guest at the table or the servant who waits on him? Is it not the guest at the table? But I am among you as the servant who waits on you. 28 Yet you have continued to stand by me in my trials; 29 and as my Father has conferred on me a kingdom, 30 so I confer on you the privilege of eating and drinking at my table in my kingdom and of sitting on thrones and judging the twelve tribes of Israel.

31 "Simon, Simon, listen! Satan has asked permission to sift all of you like wheat, 32 but I have prayed especially for you that your own faith may not utterly fail. And you yourself, after you have turned, must strengthen your brothers."

33 But Peter said to Him, "Lord, I am ready to go even to prison and to death with you!" 34 But He said, "I tell you, Peter, the cock will not crow today before you deny three times that you know me!"

35 Then He said to them, "When I sent you out without purse or bag or shoes, you did not need anything, did you?"

They answered, "Nothing at all."

36 Then He said to them, "But now the man who has a purse must take it, and a bag too. And the man who does not have a sword must sell his coat and buy one. 37 For I tell you, what has been written about me must be fulfilled: 'He was classed with the outlaws.' Yes, that saying about me has its fulfillment."

38 So they said, "Lord, look! here are two swords!"

And He answered them, "Enough!"

BECK

apostles lay down for the meal. 15 "I have very much longed to eat this Passover with you before I suffer," He said to them. 16 "I tell you, I will not eat it again till it comes true in God's kingdom." Then He was handed a cup, and He gave thanks. 17 "Take this," He said, "and share it."

The Lord's Supper

18 "I tell you, from now on I will not drink of the product of the vine till God's kingdom comes."

19 Jesus took bread, gave thanks, broke it, and gave it to them, saying, "This is My body which is given for you. Do this to remember Me."

20 He did the same with the cup when the supper was over, saying, "This cup is the new covenant in My blood,83 poured out for you."

"Is It I?"

21 "Look, the hand of him who is betraying Me is with Me on the table. 22 The Son of Man is going as it is decreed, but woe to that man who is betraying Him."

23 They started to discuss with one another which of them was going to do this.

"Who Is the Greatest?"

24 Then the disciples started to quarrel among themselves as to which of them was considered the greatest.

25 "The kings of the nations lord it over them," He told them, "and their rulers call themselves benefactors. 26 With you it's different. The greatest among you should become like the youngest, and one who leads should be like one who serves. 27 Who is greater, the one who lies down to eat or the one who serves? Isn't it the one who lies down to eat? But I am among you as one who serves.

28 "You have stood by Me in the troubles that have tested Me. 29As My Father has appointed Me to be King, so I appoint you 30 to eat and drink at My table in My kingdom and to sit on thrones and rule the twelve tribes of Israel."

You Will Be Tested

31 "Simon, Simon," said the Lord, "you know the devil has begged to have all of you to sift you like wheat. 32 But I prayed for you, Simon, that your faith will not die. And when you come back, strengthen your fellow disciples."

33 "Lord," he told Him, "I'm ready to go to prison and to die with You."

34 "I tell you, Peter," He said, "the rooster will not crow tonight till you deny three times that you know Me."

35 Then He asked them, "When I sent you out without purse, bag, or shoes, you didn't lack anything, did you?"

"Not a thing!" they answered.

36 "But now," He told them, "if you have a purse, take it, and also a bag. And if you don't have a sword, sell your garment and buy one. 37 It is written, He will be counted among criminals,84 and I tell you, that must happen to Me. Whatever is written about Me must happen!"

38 "Lord, look, here are two swords!" they said.

"Enough of that!" He told them.

[83] Ex. 24:8; Jer. 31:32; Zech. 9:11
[84] Is. 53:12

[a] Grk., in my blood.

K.J.V.

39 And he came out, and went, as he was wont, to the mount of Olives; and his disciples also followed him. 40And when he was at the place, he said unto them, Pray that ye enter not into temptation. 41And he was withdrawn from them about a stone's cast, and kneeled down, and prayed, 42 Saying, Father, if thou be willing, remove this cup from me: nevertheless, not my will, but thine, be done. 43And there appeared an angel unto him from heaven, strengthening him. 44And being in an agony he prayed more earnestly: and his sweat was as it were great drops of blood falling down to the ground. 45And when he rose up from prayer, and was come to his disciples, he found them sleeping for sorrow, 46And said unto them, Why sleep ye? rise and pray, lest ye enter into temptation.

47 And while he yet spake, behold a multitude, and he that was called Judas, one of the twelve, went before them, and drew near unto Jesus to kiss him. 48 But Jesus said unto him, Judas, betrayest thou the Son of man with a kiss? 49 When they which were about him saw what would follow, they said unto him, Lord, shall we smite with the sword?

50 And one of them smote the servant of the high priest, and cut off his right ear. 51And Jesus answered and said, Suffer ye thus far. And he touched his ear, and healed him. 52 Then Jesus said unto the chief priests, and captains of the temple, and the elders, which were come to him, Be ye come out, as against a thief, with swords and staves? 53 When I was daily with you in the temple, ye stretched forth no hands against me: but this is your hour, and the power of darkness.

54 Then took they him, and led him, and brought him into the high priest's house. And Peter followed afar off. 55And when they had kindled a fire in the midst of the hall, and were set down together, Peter sat down among them. 56 But a certain maid beheld him as he sat by the fire, and earnestly looked upon him, and said, This man was also with him. 57And he denied him, saying, Woman, I know him not. 58And after a little while another saw him, and said, Thou art also of them. And Peter said, Man, I am not. 59And about the space of one hour after another confidently affirmed, saying, Of a truth this fellow also was with him; for he is a Galilean. 60And Peter said, Man, I know not what thou sayest. And immediately, while he yet spake, the cock crew. 61And the Lord turned, and looked upon Peter. And Peter remembered the word of the Lord, how he had said unto him, Before the cock crow, thou shalt deny me thrice. 62And Peter went out, and wept bitterly.

63 And the men that held Jesus mocked him, and smote him. 64And when they had blindfolded him, they struck him on the face, and asked him, saying, Prophesy, who is it that

N.A.S.

39 And He came out and proceeded as was His custom to the Mount of Olives; and the disciples also followed Him. 40And when He arrived at the place, He said to them, "Pray that you may not enter into temptation." 41And He withdrew from them about a stone's throw, and He knelt down and began to pray, 42 saying, "Father, if Thou art willing, remove this cup from Me; yet not My will, but Thine be done." 43 Now an angel from heaven appeared to Him, strengthening Him. 44And being in agony He was praying very fervently; and His sweat became like drops of blood, falling down upon the ground. 45And when He rose from prayer, He came to His disciples and found them sleeping from sorrow, 46 and said to them, "Why are you sleeping? Rise and pray that you may not enter into temptation."

47 While He was still speaking, behold, a multitude came, and the one called Judas, one of the twelve, was preceding them; and he approached Jesus to kiss Him. 48 But Jesus said to him, "Judas, are you betraying the Son of Man with a kiss?" 49And when those who were around Him saw what was going to happen, they said, "Lord, shall we strike with the sword?" 50And a certain one of them struck the slave of the high priest and cut off his right ear. 51 But Jesus answered and said, "Stop! No more of this." And He touched his ear and healed him. 52And Jesus said to the chief priests and officers of the temple and elders who had come against Him, "Have you come out with swords and clubs as against a robber? 53 "While I was with you daily in the temple, you did not lay hands on Me; but this hour and the power of darkness are yours."

54 And having arrested Him, they led Him away, and brought Him to the house of the high priest; but Peter was following at a distance. 55And after they had kindled a fire in the middle of the courtyard and had sat down together, Peter was sitting among them. 56And a certain servant-girl, seeing him as he sat in the firelight, and looking intently at him, said, "This man was with Him too." 57 But he denied it, saying, "Woman, I do not know Him." 58And a little later, another saw him and said, "You are one of them too!" But Peter said, "Man, I am not!" 59And after about an hour had passed, another man began to insist, saying, "Certainly this man also was with Him, for he is a Galilean too." 60 But Peter said, "Man, I do not know what you are talking about." And immediately, while he was still speaking, a cock crowed. 61And the Lord turned and looked at Peter. And Peter remembered the word of the Lord, how He had told him, "Before a cock crows today, you will deny Me three times." 62And he went outside and wept bitterly.

63 And the men who were holding Jesus in custody were mocking Him, and beating Him, 64 and they blindfolded Him and were asking Him, saying, "Prophesy, who is the one who

WILLIAMS

39 Then He went out of the city and up the Mount of Olives, as He was in the habit of doing; and His disciples, too, followed Him there. 40 Now when He reached the spot, He said to them, "Continue to pray that you may not be subjected [b] to temptation."

41 And He Himself withdrew about a stone's throw from them, and after kneeling down He continued to pray, 42 "Father, if you are willing, take this cup away from me. Yet, not my will but always yours be done!" [c]

45 When He rose from His prayer, He went to the disciples and found them asleep from sorrow. 46 Then He said to them, "Why are you sleeping? Get up and keep praying that you may not be subjected to temptation."

47 While He was still speaking, look! a crowd had come up, and Judas, one of the Twelve, was their guide; and he stepped up to Jesus to kiss Him. 48 Then Jesus said to him, "Judas, will you betray the Son of Man with a kiss?"

49 Those who were about Him saw what was about to take place, and said, "Lord, shall we use our swords now?" 50 Then one of them struck the high priest's slave and cut off his right ear.

51 But Jesus said, "Permit me to go as far as this!" So He touched his ear and healed him. 52 Then Jesus said to the high priests, captains of the temple, and elders, who had come to take Him, "Have you come out with swords and clubs as though I were a robber? 53 While I was among you day after day in the temple, you never laid a hand on me! But this is your opportunity, even the power which darkness gives you!"

54 Then they arrested Him and led Him away and brought Him to the house of the high priest. Peter was following at a distance. 55 And when they had kindled a fire in the middle of the courtyard and had taken their seats together, Peter, too, was sitting among them. 56 A servant-girl saw him sitting by the fire and fixed her eyes on him and said, "This fellow was with Him too."

57 But he denied it and said, "I do not know Him, woman."

58 A little later a man looked at him and said, "You are one of them too."

But Peter said, "Man, I am not." 59 About an hour later another man emphatically asserted, "He certainly was with Him, for he is a Galilean!"

60 But Peter said, "Man, I do not know what you mean." And all at once, while he was still speaking, a cock crowed. 61 Then the Lord turned and looked at Peter, and Peter was reminded of the word that the Lord had spoken to him, "Before a cock crows today, you will disown me three times." 62 And he went outside and burst into bitter tears.

63 Then the men who held Him in custody flogged Him and made sport of Him, 64 and after blindfolding Him they asked Him, "Play the prophet and tell us who it is that struck you!"

BECK

Gethsemane

39 Jesus went out and as usual came to the Mount of Olives. The disciples went with Him. 40 When He came to the place, He told them, "Pray that you may not be tempted."

41 He withdrew from them about as far as you'd throw a stone, knelt, and prayed, 42 "Father, if You wish, take this cup away from Me; but let it not be as I want it but as You want it."

43 An angel from heaven appeared to Him and gave Him strength. 44 And as He began to struggle inwardly, He prayed more earnestly, and His sweat became like thick drops of blood falling on the ground.*

45 After praying, He got up, went to the disciples, and found them sleeping because they were feeling sad. 46 "Why are you sleeping?" He asked them. "Get up and pray that you may not be tempted."

The Arrest

47 While He was still talking, the crowd came. The one called Judas, one of the twelve, was leading them, and he came close to Jesus to kiss Him.

48 "Judas," Jesus asked him, "are you betraying the Son of Man with a kiss?"

49 The men around Jesus, seeing what was going to happen, asked, "Lord, should we strike with our swords?" 50 And one of them struck the high priest's slave and cut off his right ear.

51 Then Jesus said, "Let them do it. No more of this!" And, touching the ear, He healed him.

52 Then Jesus said to the ruling priests, captains of the temple, and elders who had come for Him, "You came out for Me with swords and clubs as if I were a robber! 53 Day after day I was with you in the temple, and you laid no hands on Me. But this is your time when darkness rules."

54 They arrested Him, led Him away, and took Him to the high priest's palace.

Peter Denies Jesus

54 Peter followed at a distance.

55 The men had lit a fire in the middle of the courtyard, and as they sat together, Peter sat among them. 56 A maid saw him sitting in the light of the fire, and looking straight at him, she said, "He, too, was with Him."

57 But he denied and said, "I don't know Him, woman."

58 A little later someone else looked at him and said, "You're one of them."

"Man, I'm not!" Peter said.

59 About an hour later another insisted: "Certainly he was with Him. Why, he's a Galilean!"

60 "Man, I don't know what you're talking about," Peter said.

Just then, while he was still speaking, a rooster crowed. 61 Then the Lord turned and looked at Peter, and Peter remembered the Lord telling him, "Before the rooster crows today, you will deny Me three times." 62 So he went outside and cried bitterly.

The Jewish Court Condemns Jesus

63 The men who were holding Him were making fun of Him as they struck Him. 64 They covered His face and kept asking Him: "Proph-

[b] Grk., *not to enter at all into.* [c] Vv. 43 and 44 om. in best Mss.

* Papyrus 75 and other old manuscripts omit verses 43-44.

K.J.V.

smote thee? 65And many other things blasphemously spake they against him.

66 And as soon as it was day, the elders of the people and the chief priests and the scribes came together, and led him into their council, saying, 67Art thou the Christ? tell us. And he said unto them, If I tell you, ye will not believe: 68And if I also ask *you*, ye will not answer me, nor let *me* go. 69Hereafter shall the Son of man sit on the right hand of the power of God. 70Then said they all, Art thou then the Son of God? And he said unto them, Ye say that I am. 71And they said, What need we any further witness? for we ourselves have heard of his own mouth.

23 And the whole multitude of them arose, and led him unto Pilate. 2And they began to accuse him, saying, We found this *fellow* perverting the nation, and forbidding to give tribute to Cesar, saying that he himself is Christ a king. 3And Pilate asked him, saying, Art thou the King of the Jews? And he answered him and said, Thou sayest *it*. 4Then said Pilate to the chief priests and *to* the people, I find no fault in this man. 5And they were the more fierce, saying, He stirreth up the people, teaching throughout all Jewry, beginning from Galilee to this place. 6When Pilate heard of Galilee he asked whether the man were a Galilean. 7And as soon as he knew that he belonged unto Herod's jurisdiction, he sent him to Herod, who himself also was at Jerusalem at that time.

8 And when Herod saw Jesus, he was exceeding glad: for he was desirous to see him of a long *season*, because he had heard many things of him; and he hoped to have seen some miracle done by him. 9Then he questioned with him in many words; but he answered him nothing. 10And the chief priests and scribes stood and vehemently accused him. 11And Herod with his men of war set him at nought, and mocked *him*, and arrayed him in a gorgeous robe, and sent him again to Pilate.

12 And the same day Pilate and Herod were made friends together; for before they were at enmity between themselves.

13 And Pilate, when he had called together the chief priests and the rulers and the people, 14Said unto them, Ye have brought this man unto me, as one that perverteth the people; and, behold, I, having examined *him* before you, have found no fault in this man touching those things whereof ye accuse him: 15No, nor yet Herod: for I sent you to him; and, lo, nothing worthy of death is done unto him. 16I will therefore chastise him, and release *him*. 17(For of necessity he must release one unto them at

N.A.S.

hit You?" 65And they were saying many other things against Him, blaspheming.

66 And when it was day, the ªCouncil of Elders of the people assembled, both chief priests and scribes, and they led Him away to their council *chamber*, saying, 67"If You are the Christ, tell us." But He said to them, "If I tell you, you will not believe; 68and if I ask a question, you will not answer. 69"But from now on THE SON OF MAN WILL BE SEATED AT THE RIGHT HAND of the power OF GOD." 70And they all said, "Are You the Son of God, then?" And He said to them, "Yes, I am." 71And they said, "What further need do we have of testimony? For we have heard it ourselves from His own mouth."

23 Then the whole body of them arose and brought Him before Pilate. 2And they began to accuse Him, saying, "We found this man misleading our nation and forbidding to pay taxes to Caesar, and saying that He Himself is Christ, a King." 3And Pilate asked Him, saying, "Are You the King of the Jews?" And He answered him and said, *"It is as* you say." 4And Pilate said to the chief priests and the multitudes, "I find no guilt in this man." 5But they kept on insisting, saying, "He stirs up the people, teaching all over Judea, starting from Galilee, even as far as this place." 6But when Pilate heard it, he asked whether the man were a Galilean. 7And when he learned that He belonged to Herod's jurisdiction, he sent Him to Herod, who himself also was in Jerusalem at that time.

8 Now Herod was very glad when he saw Jesus; for he had wanted to see Him for a long time, because he had been hearing about Him and was hoping to see some sign performed by Him. 9And he questioned Him at some length; but He answered him nothing. 10And the chief priests and the scribes were standing there, accusing Him vehemently. 11And Herod with his soldiers, after treating Him with contempt and mocking Him, dressed Him in a gorgeous robe and sent Him back to Pilate. 12Now Herod and Pilate became friends with one another that very day; for before they had been at enmity with each other.

13 And Pilate summoned the chief priests and the rulers and the people, 14and said to them, "You brought this man to me as one who incites the people to rebellion, and behold, having examined Him before you, I have found no guilt in this man regarding the charges which you make against Him. 15"No, nor has Herod, for he sent Him back to us; and behold, nothing deserving death has been done by Him. 16"I will therefore punish Him and

[a] Or, *Sanhedrin.*

240

WILLIAMS

65And they continued to say many other abusive[d] things to Him.

66 As soon as day came, the elders of the people, the high priests, and the scribes assembled, and brought Him back before their council, and said, 67 "Tell us, if you are the Christ."

But He said to them, "If I tell you, you will not believe me, 68 and if I ask you a question, you will not answer me. 69 But from today the Son of Man will be seated at the right hand of the mighty God."

70 Then they all asked, "Are you then the Son of God?"

And He answered, "Yes, I am."

71 Then they said, "What more evidence do we need? For we have heard it ourselves from His own mouth!"

23 *Jesus stands at the Roman bar; Antipas makes sport of Him; Pilate declares Him innocent, but lets them crucify Him; six hours of suffering on Calvary; a penitent robber promised paradise; Joseph buries Jesus*

Then the whole body of them arose and brought Him to Pilate. 2 Here they began to make the following charges against Him:

"We have found this fellow corrupting our nation and forbidding to pay taxes to Caesar and claiming to be a king himself."

3 Then Pilate asked Him, "Are you the king of the Jews?"

And He answered him, "Yes, I am."

4 Then Pilate said to the high priests and crowds, "I do not find anything blameworthy in this man."

5 But they continued emphatically insisting, "He is exciting the people by teaching all over Judea. He started in Galilee and now He is here."

6 When Pilate heard this, He asked if the man were a Galilean. 7 So when he learned with certainty that he belonged to Herod's jurisdiction, He sent Him up to Herod, for he was in Jerusalem at that time. 8 Now Herod was very glad to see Jesus, for he had been wanting to see Him for a long time on account of what he had heard about Him; also he was hoping to see some spectacular performance done by Him. 9 So he continued to question Him for a long time, but Jesus gave him no answer at all. 10 Meanwhile the high priests and the scribes stood by and continued vehemently to accuse Him. 11 Then Herod and his body-guard treated Him with contempt and made sport of Him and put a gorgeous robe on Him and sent Him back to Pilate. 12 So Herod and Pilate became personal friends that very day; they had been at enmity before.

13 Then Pilate called a meeting of the high priests, the leaders of the council, and the people, 14 and said to them, "You brought this man to me on a charge of turning the people from allegiance, and here in your presence I have examined Him and do not find Him guilty of the charges you make against Him. 15 No; nor does Herod, for he has sent Him back to us. Indeed, He has done nothing to deserve the death penalty. 16 So I will flog Him and let Him go." [a]

[d] Grk., *in blaspheming they were saying many other things*, etc. [a] V. 17 om. by most ancient Mss.

BECK

esy! Who hit You?" 65And so they went on insulting Him in many other ways.

66 In the morning all the elders of the people, ruling priests, and Bible scholars had a meeting. They brought Jesus before their court and asked, 67 "Are You the promised Savior? Tell us." "If I tell you, you won't believe Me," He said to them. 68 "And if I ask you a question, you won't answer. 69 But from now on *the Son of Man*[85] will be *sitting at the right of God's*[86] power."

70 "Are You, then, the Son of God?" all of them asked.

He answered them, "As you say: I am He."

71 "Why do we need any more testimony?" they asked. "We've heard Him say it ourselves."

23 Then the whole crowd of them got up and took Him to Pilate.

Before Pilate

2 Then they started to accuse Him: "We found that He makes our people disloyal, keeps them from paying taxes to the emperor, and says He is Christ, a king."

3 Pilate asked Him, "Are You the King of the Jews?"

"Yes," He answered him.

4 Pilate told the ruling priests and the crowd, "I don't find this Man guilty of anything."

Before Herod

5 The priests and the crowd kept urging him: "He stirs up the people by teaching all over the country of the Jews, beginning in Galilee and coming here."

6 When Pilate heard that, he asked, "Is the Man from Galilee?" 7And when he found out Jesus came from the country governed by Herod, he sent Him to Herod, who also was in Jerusalem at that time.

8 Herod was very glad to see Jesus. For a long time he had wanted to see Him, because he had heard about Him, and He expected to see Jesus do some miracle. 9 He asked Him a lot of questions, but Jesus didn't answer him. 10 The ruling priests and the Bible scholars were standing there and accusing Him vehemently.

11 So Herod and his soldiers treated Him with contempt and made fun of Him. They put a splendid garment on Him and then sent Him back to Pilate. 12 On that day Herod and Pilate became friends. Before this they had been enemies.

13 Then Pilate called the ruling priests, the other leaders, and the people together. 14 "You brought me this man as one who turns the people against the government," he told them. "And now look, I've examined this Man before you and found Him innocent of the things you accuse Him of. 15And Herod did, too, because he sent Him back to us. You see, He hasn't done anything to deserve death. 16 So I'm going to teach Him a lesson and let Him go." *

* Our oldest papyrus, P[75], and our oldest parchment, Codex Vaticanus, do not have v. 17: "At every festival he had to set someone free for them." See Matt. 27:15; Mark 15:6; John 18:39.
[85] Dan. 7:13
[86] Ps. 110:1

K.J.V.

the feast.) 18And they cried out all at once, saying, Away with this *man*, and release unto us Barabbas: 19 (Who for a certain sedition made in the city, and for murder, was cast into prison.) 20 Pilate therefore, willing to release Jesus, spake again to them. 21 But they cried, saying, Crucify *him*, crucify him. 22And he said unto them the third time, Why, what evil hath he done? I have found no cause of death in him: I will therefore chastise him, and let *him* go. 23And they were instant with loud voices, requiring that he might be crucified: and the voices of them and of the chief priests prevailed. 24And Pilate gave sentence that it should be as they required. 25And he released unto them him that for sedition and murder was cast into prison, whom they had desired; but he delivered Jesus to their will. 26And as they led him away, they laid hold upon one Simon, a Cyrenian, coming out of the country, and on him they laid the cross, that he might bear *it* after Jesus.

27 And there followed him a great company of people, and of women, which also bewailed and lamented him. 28 But Jesus turning unto them said, Daughters of Jerusalem, weep not for me, but weep for yourselves, and for your children. 29 For, behold, the days are coming, in the which they shall say, Blessed *are* the barren, and the wombs that never bare, and the paps which never gave suck. 30 Then shall they begin to say to the mountains, Fall on us; and to the hills, Cover us. 31 For if they do these things in a green tree, what shall be done in the dry? 32And there were also two others, malefactors, led with him to be put to death. 33And when they were come to the place, which is called Calvary, there they crucified him, and the malefactors, one on the right hand, and the other on the left.

34 Then said Jesus, Father, forgive them; for they know not what they do. And they parted his raiment, and cast lots. 35And the people stood beholding. And the rulers also with them derided *him*, saying, He saved others; let him save himself, if he be Christ, the chosen of God. 36And the soldiers also mocked him, coming to him, and offering him vinegar, 37And saying, If thou be the King of the Jews, save thyself. 38And a superscription also was written over him in letters of Greek, and Latin, and Hebrew, THIS IS THE KING OF THE JEWS.

39 And one of the malefactors which were hanged railed on him, saying, If thou be Christ,

N.A.S.

release Him." 17 (See footnote *ᵃ*) 18 But they cried out all together, saying, "Away with this man, and release for us Barabbas!" 19 (He was one who had been thrown in prison for a certain insurrection made in the city, and for murder.) 20And Pilate, wanting to release Jesus, addressed them again, 21 but they kept on calling out, saying, "Crucify, crucify Him!" 22And he said to them the third time, "Why, what evil has this man done? I have found in Him no guilt *demanding* death; I will therefore punish Him and release Him." 23 But they were insistent, with loud voices asking that He be crucified. And their voices *began* to prevail. 24And Pilate pronounced sentence that their demand should be granted. 25And he released the man they were asking for who had been thrown into prison for insurrection and murder, but he turned Jesus over to their will.

26 And when they led Him away, they laid hold of one Simon, a Cyrenian, coming in from the country, and placed on him the cross to carry behind Jesus.

27 And there were following Him a great multitude of the people, and of women who were mourning and lamenting Him. 28 But Jesus turning to them said, "Daughters of Jerusalem, stop weeping for Me, but weep for yourselves and for your children. 29 "For behold, the days are coming when they will say, 'Blessed are the barren, and the wombs that never bore, and the breasts that never nursed.' 30 "Then they will begin TO SAY TO THE MOUNTAINS, 'FALL ON US,' AND TO THE HILLS, 'COVER US.' 31 "For if they do these things in the green tree, what will happen in the dry?"

32 And two others also, who were criminals, were being led away to be put to death with Him.

33 And when they came to the place called The Skull, there they crucified Him and the criminals, one on the right and the other on the left. 34 But Jesus was saying, "Father forgive them; for they do not know what they are doing." AND THEY CAST LOTS, DIVIDING UP HIS GARMENTS AMONG THEMSELVES. 35And the people stood by, looking on. And even the rulers were sneering at Him, saying, "He saved others; let Him save Himself if this is the Christ of God, His Chosen One." 36And the soldiers also mocked Him, coming up to Him, offering Him sour wine, 37 and saying, "If You are the King of the Jews, save Yourself!" 38 Now there was also an inscription above Him, "THIS IS THE KING OF THE JEWS."

39 And one of the criminals who were hanged *there* was hurling abuse at Him, saying, "Are You not the Christ? Save Yourself

[a] Some mss. insert verse 17, *Now he was obliged to release to them at the feast one* prisoner.

WILLIAMS

18 But they all together began to shout, "Away with this fellow, but let us have Barabbas released! 19 (He was a man who had been put in prison for a riot that had occurred in the city and for murder.) 20 Then Pilate again appealed to them, for He wanted to let Jesus go. 21 But they continued to shout at him, "Crucify Him, crucify Him!"

22 Then a third time he spoke to them, "Why, what wrong has He done? I have found nothing in Him deserving the death penalty. So I will flog Him and let Him go."

23 But they continued to press him with loud voices in their ceaseless demands that He be crucified, and their shouts began to prevail. 24 Then Pilate pronounced his sentence that their demand be carried out. 25 So he released the man who had been put in prison for riot and murder, whom they continued to demand, but turned Jesus over to their will.

26 Now as they led Him away, they seized a man named Simon, from Cyrene, as he was coming in from the country, and put the cross on his shoulders, for him to carry as he walked behind Jesus. 27 There was following Him also a vast throng of the people and of women who were beating their breasts and lamenting Him.

28 But Jesus turned to the women and said, "Women of Jerusalem, stop weeping for me, but continue to weep for yourselves and for your children. 29 For a time is coming when people will say, 'Happy are the women who are childless, and the women who have never borne and nursed babies!' 30 Then people will begin to say to the mountains, 'Fall upon us!' and to the hills, 'Cover us up!' 31 For if they do this when the wood is green, what will they do when it is dry?"

32 Two others, criminals, were also led out to be executed with Him.

33 When they reached the place called "The Skull," they crucified Him there; also the criminals, one at His right and one at His left. 34 b They drew lots to divide His clothes among them. 35 Meanwhile the people stood looking on. Even the members of the council were scoffing at Him and saying, "He saved others, let Him now save Himself, if He really is the Christ of God, His Chosen One!"

36 The soldiers also made sport of Him as they continued to come up and offer Him vinegar, 37 and to say, "If you are the king of the Jews, save yourself!" 38 Yes, there was a placard above His head: THIS IS THE KING OF THE JEWS."

39 Now one of the criminals who were hanging from their crosses kept abusing Him, saying, "Are you not the Christ? Then save yourself and us too!"

BECK

Barabbas

18 Then the whole crowd yelled: "Away with Him. Free Barabbas for us." 19 He had been put in prison for a revolt that had taken place in the city and for murder.

20 But Pilate wanted to let Jesus go, so he called to them again.

21 But they kept yelling: "Crucify, crucify Him!"

22 And Pilate spoke to them a third time: "Why, what wrong has He done? I haven't found anything in Him that deserves death. So I will teach Him a lesson and let Him go."

23 But they kept pressing him with loud shouts, demanding He be crucified, and their shouts were overpowering Pilate. 24 Then Pilate decided what they demanded should be done: 25 he let them have Barabbas, who had been put in prison for revolt and murder, but whom they were asking for, and he let them have their way with Jesus.

On the Way

26 As they led Jesus away, they took hold of Simon, a man from Cyrene, who was coming in from the country, and they laid the cross on him, to carry it behind Jesus.

27 A large crowd of the people followed Him. The women in the crowd were beating their breasts and weeping over Him. 28 Turning to them, Jesus said, "Daughters of Jerusalem, don't cry over Me, but cry over yourselves and your children, 29 because the time is coming when people will say:

'Happy are—
The women who couldn't have children,
The wombs that didn't bear,
And the breasts that didn't nurse.'

30 Then people will say—
To the mountains: 'Fall on us!'
And to the hills: 'Cover us!' 87

31 If this is done to the green tree, what will be done to a dry one?"

32 Two others, who were criminals, were also taken away to be killed with Him.

"They Crucified Him"

33 When they came to the place called Skull, they crucified Him there with the criminals, one at His right and the other at His left.

34 Then Jesus said, "Father, forgive them; they don't know what they are doing." *

*They divided His clothes among them by throwing lots*88 *for them.*

35 The people stood there *watching.* The rulers were *sneering,*89 "He saved others. He should save Himself if He's the Savior whom God has chosen." 36 The soldiers also made fun of Him by going up to Him and *offering Him sour wine.*90 37 "If You're the King of the Jews," they said, "save Yourself."

38 There was a notice placed above Him: THIS IS THE KING OF THE JEWS.

A Robber Turns to Jesus

39 One of the crucified criminals was mocking Him, "Aren't You the promised Savior? Save Yourself and us!"

* Papyrus 75 and some other old manuscripts omit this first word from the cross.
[87] Hos. 10:8
[88] Ps. 22:18
[89] Ps. 22:7
[90] Ps. 69:21

[b] Oldest and best Mss. omit "And Jesus said . . . what they do."

K.J.V.

save thyself and us. 40 But the other answering rebuked him, saying, Dost not thou fear God, seeing thou art in the same condemnation? 41And we indeed justly; for we receive the due reward of our deeds: but this man hath done nothing amiss. 42And he said unto Jesus, Lord, remember me when thou comest into thy kingdom. 43And Jesus said unto him, Verily I say unto thee, To day shalt thou be with me in paradise. 44And it was about the sixth hour, and there was a darkness over all the earth until the ninth hour. 45And the sun was darkened, and the vail of the temple was rent in the midst.

46 And when Jesus had cried with a loud voice, he said, Father, into thy hands I commend my spirit: and having said thus, he gave up the ghost. 47 Now when the centurion saw what was done, he glorified God, saying, Certainly this was a righteous man. 48And all the people that came together to that sight, beholding the things which were done, smote their breasts, and returned. 49And all his acquaintance, and the women that followed him from Galilee, stood afar off, beholding these things.

50 And, behold, *there was* a man named Joseph, a counsellor; *and he was* a good man, and a just: 51 (The same had not consented to the counsel and deed of them:) *he was* of Arimathea, a city of the Jews; who also himself waited for the kingdom of God. 52 This *man* went unto Pilate, and begged the body of Jesus. 53And he took it down, and wrapped it in linen, and laid it in a sepulchre that was hewn in stone, wherein never man before was laid. 54And that day was the preparation, and the sabbath drew on. 55And the women also, which came with him from Galilee, followed after, and beheld the sepulchre, and how his body was laid. 56And they returned, and prepared spices and ointments; and rested the sabbath day according to the commandment.

24 Now upon the first *day* of the week, very early in the morning, they came unto the sepulchre, bringing the spices which they had prepared, and certain *others* with them. 2And they found the stone rolled away from the sepulchre. 3And they entered in, and found not the body of the Lord Jesus. 4And it came to pass, as they were much perplexed thereabout, behold, two men stood by them in shining garments: 5And as they were afraid, and bowed down *their* faces to the earth, they said unto them, Why seek ye the living among the dead?

N.A.S.

and us!" 40 But the other answered, and rebuking him said, "Do you not even fear God, since you are under the same sentence of condemnation? 41 "And we indeed justly, for we are receiving what we deserve for our deeds; but this man has done nothing wrong." 42And he was saying, "Jesus, remember me when You come in Your kingdom!" 43And He said to him, "Truly I say to you, today you shall be with Me in Paradise."

44 And it was now about °the sixth hour, and darkness fell over the whole land until ᵇthe ninth hour, 45 the sun being obscured; and the curtain of the temple was torn in two. 46And Jesus, crying out with a loud voice, said, "Father, into Thy hands I commit My spirit." And having said this, He breathed His last. 47 Now when the centurion saw what had happened, he *began* praising God, saying, "Certainly this man was innocent." 48And all the multitudes who came together for this spectacle, when they observed what had happened, *began* to return, beating their breasts. 49And all His acquaintances and the women who accompanied Him from Galilee, were standing at a distance, seeing these things.

50 And behold, a man named Joseph, who was a member of the Council, a good and righteous man, 51 (he had not consented to their plan and action) *a man* from Arimathea, a city of the Jews, who was waiting for the kingdom of God, 52 this man went to Pilate and asked for the body of Jesus. 53And he took it down and wrapped it in a linen cloth, and laid Him in a tomb cut into the rock, where no one had ever lain. 54And it was the Preparation Day, and the Sabbath was about to begin. 55 Now the women who had come with Him out of Galilee followed after, and saw the tomb and how His body was laid. 56And they returned and prepared spices and perfumes.

And on the Sabbath they rested according to the commandment.

24 But on the first day of the week, at early dawn, they came to the tomb, bringing the spices which they had prepared. 2And they found the stone rolled away from the tomb, 3 but when they entered, they did not find the body of the Lord Jesus. 4And it happened that while they were perplexed about this, behold, two men suddenly stood near them in dazzling apparel; 5 and as *the women* were terrified and bowed their faces to the ground, *the men* said to them, "Why do you seek the

[a] I.e., 12 noon. [b] I.e., 3 p.m.

WILLIAMS

40 But the other one reproved him and said, "Do you not fear even God when you are suffering the same penalty? 41And we are suffering it justly, for we are getting our deserts for what we have done, but this man has done nothing wrong." 42 Then he went on to say, "Jesus, remember me when you come in your kingdom!"

43 So He said to him, "I solemnly say to you, this very day you will be in paradise with me."

44 It was already about noon, and darkness covered the whole country, and lasted until three o'clock, 45 for the sun had failed to shine. And the curtain before the sanctuary was torn in two.

46 Then Jesus uttered a loud cry, and said, "Father, I now commit my spirit to your care." As He said this He breathed His last.

47 When the captain saw what had taken place, he praised God and said, "He certainly was an innocent[c] man!"

48 And all the crowds who had come together for this sight, when they had seen what took place, returned to the city but continued to beat their breasts in grief. 49 But all His acquaintances, and the women who used to follow Him from Galilee in a group, were standing at a distance looking on.

50 Now there was a man named Joseph, a member of the council, a good and upright man, 51 who had not voted for the plan and action of the council. He came from a Jewish town, Arimathea, and he was waiting for the kingdom of God. 52 He went to Pilate and asked for Jesus' body. 53 Then he took it down from the cross and wrapped it in a linen sheet and laid it in a tomb hewn out of rock, where no one had yet been laid. 54 It was the Preparation Day, and the sabbath was just beginning. 55 So the women, who had come with Jesus from Galilee, followed closely after Joseph and saw the tomb and how His body was laid there. 56 Then they went back home, and prepared spices and perfumes.

24 *The tomb found empty by the women; the story of Jesus' making Himself known to two disciples at Emmaus; He appears to Peter, then to a group of disciples in Jerusalem; He gives His farewell message; ascends to heaven*

Now on the sabbath they rested, in accordance with the commandment, but on the first day of the week at early dawn they went to the tomb, taking the spices which they had prepared. 2 But they found the boulder rolled back from the tomb, 3 and yet on going inside they did not find the body.[a]

4 And as they were being perplexed about this, two men in dazzling robes suddenly took their stand beside them. 5 Because the women were so frightened and were turning their faces to the ground, they said to them, "Why are you looking among the dead for Him who is

[c] Grk., *righteous.* [a] Phrase, *of the Lord Jesus,* om. by WH.

BECK

40 But the other warned him. "Aren't you afraid of God?" he asked him. "You're condemned just as He is. 41 Our punishment is just. We're getting what we deserve for what we've done. But this One has done nothing wrong."

42 Then he said, "Jesus, remember me when You come to Your kingdom."

43 "I tell you the truth," Jesus said to him, "today you will be with Me in Paradise."

Jesus Dies

44 It was about twelve o'clock when darkness came over the whole country, 45 because the sun stopped shining, and the darkness lasted till three in the afternoon. 44 The curtain in the temple was torn in two.

46 Then Jesus called out loud, "Father, *into Your hands I entrust My Spirit.*"[91] After He said this, He died.

47 When the captain saw what had happened, he praised God and said, "This Man certainly was righteous." 48 When all the people, who had come there to see this, saw what happened, they beat their breasts and turned back. 49 All *His friends were standing at a distance,*[92] also the women who had followed Him from Galilee and now were watching these things.

Jesus Is Buried

50 There was a man by the name of Joseph, a member of the Jewish court, a good and righteous man 51 who had not voted for their plan and action. He was from Arimathea, a Jewish town, and was looking forward to God's kingdom.

52 He went to Pilate and asked for Jesus' body. 53 He took it down, wrapped it in some linen, and laid it in a grave cut in the rock, in which no one had yet been laid. 54 It was the day of preparation, and the day of rest was just starting.

55 The women who had come with Him from Galilee, following close behind, saw the grave and how His body was laid. 56 Then they went back and prepared spices and perfumes. But on Saturday they rested according to the commandment.

Jesus Rises

24 Very early on Sunday morning the women came to the grave bringing the spices they had prepared. 2 They found the stone rolled back from the grave, 3 but when they went in, they didn't find the body of the Lord Jesus. 4 While they were troubled about this, suddenly two men stood beside them in clothes that flashed like lightning. 5 The women were terrified, and they bowed down to the ground. "Why do you look among the dead for Him

[91] Ps. 31:5
[92] Ps. 38:11

K.J.V.

6 He is not here, but is risen: remember how he spake unto you when he was yet in Galilee, 7 Saying, The Son of man must be delivered into the hands of sinful men, and be crucified, and the third day rise again. 8And they remembered his words, 9And returned from the sepulchre, and told all these things unto the eleven, and to all the rest. 10 It was Mary Magdalene, and Joanna, and Mary *the mother* of James, and other *women that were* with them, which told these things unto the apostles. 11And their words seemed to them as idle tales, and they believed them not. 12 Then arose Peter, and ran unto the sepulchre; and stooping down, he beheld the linen clothes laid by themselves, and departed, wondering in himself at that which was come to pass.

13 And, behold, two of them went that same day to a village called Emmaus, which was from Jerusalem *about* threescore furlongs. 14And they talked together of all these things which had happened. 15And it came to pass, that, while they communed *together* and reasoned, Jesus himself drew near, and went with them. 16 But their eyes were holden that they should not know him. 17And he said unto them, What manner of communications *are* these that ye have one to another, as ye walk, and are sad? 18And the one of them, whose name was Cleopas, answering said unto him, Art thou only a stranger in Jerusalem, and hast not known the things which are come to pass there in these days? 19And he said unto them, What things? And they said unto him, Concerning Jesus of Nazareth, which was a prophet mighty in deed and word before God and all the people: 20And how the chief priests and our rulers delivered him to be condemned to death, and have crucified him. 21 But we trusted that it had been he which should have redeemed Israel: and beside all this, to day is the third day since these things were done. 22 Yea, and certain women also of our company made us astonished, which were early at the sepulchre; 23And when they found not his body, they came, saying, that they had also seen a vision of angels, which said that he was alive. 24And certain of them which were with us went to the sepulchre, and found *it* even so as the women had said: but him they saw not. 25 Then he said unto them, O fools, and slow of heart to believe all that the prophets have spoken: 26 Ought not Christ to have suffered these things, and to enter into his glory? 27And beginning at Moses and all the prophets, he expounded unto them in all the Scriptures the things concerning himself. 28And they drew nigh unto the village, whither they went: and he made as though he would have gone further. 29 But they constrained him, saying, Abide with us; for it is toward evening, and the day is far spent. And he went in to tarry with them. 30And it came to pass, as he sat at meat with them, he took bread, and blessed *it,* and brake, and gave to them. 31And their eyes were opened, and they knew him; and he vanished out of their sight. 32And they said one to another, Did not our heart burn within us, while he talked with us by the way, and while he opened to us the Scriptures? 33And they rose up the same hour, and returned to Jerusalem, and found the eleven gathered together, and them that were with them, 34 Saying, The Lord is risen indeed, and

N.A.S.

living One among the dead? 6 "He is not here, but He has risen. Remember how He spoke to you while He was still in Galilee, 7 saying that the Son of Man must be delivered into the hands of sinful men, and be crucified, and the third day rise again." 8And they remembered His words, 9 and returned from the tomb and reported all these things to the eleven and to all the rest. 10 Now they were Mary Magdalene and Joanna and Mary the *mother* of James; also the other women with them were telling these things to the apostles. 11And these words appeared to them as nonsense, and they would not believe them. 12 [ªBut Peter arose and ran to the tomb; and stooping and looking in, he *saw the linen wrappings only; and he went away to his home, marveling at that which had happened.]

13 And behold, two of them were going that very day to a village named Emmaus, which was ᵇabout seven miles from Jerusalem. 14And they were conversing with each other about all these things which had taken place. 15And it came about that while they were conversing and discussing, Jesus Himself approached, and *began* traveling with them. 16 But their eyes were prevented from recognizing Him. 17And He said to them, "What are these words that you are exchanging with one another as you are walking?" And they stood still, looking sad. 18And one of them, named Cleopas, answered and said to Him, "Are You the only one visiting Jerusalem and unaware of the things which have happened here in these days?" 19And He said to them, "What things?" And they said to Him, "The things about Jesus the Nazarene, who was a prophet mighty in deed and word in the sight of God and all the people, 20 and how the chief priests and our rulers delivered Him up to the sentence of death, and crucified Him. 21 "But we were hoping that it was He who was going to redeem Israel. Indeed, besides all this, it is the third day since these things happened. 22 "But also some women among us amazed us. When they were at the tomb early in the morning, 23 and did not find His body, they came, saying that they had also seen a vision of angels, who said that He was alive. 24 "And some of those who were with us went to the tomb and found it just exactly as the women also had said; but Him they did not see." 25And He said to them, "O foolish men and slow of heart to believe in all that the prophets have spoken! 26 "Was it not necessary for the Christ to suffer these things and to enter into His glory?" 27And beginning with Moses and with all the prophets, He explained to them the things concerning Himself in all the Scriptures. 28And they approached the village where they were going, and He acted as though He would go farther. 29And they urged Him, saying, "Stay with us, for it is *getting* toward evening, and the day is now nearly over." And He went in to stay with them. 30And it came about that when He had reclined *at table* with them, He took the bread and blessed *it,* and breaking *it,* He *began* giving *it* to them. 31And their eyes were opened and they recognized Him; and He vanished from their sight. 32And they said to one another, "Were not our hearts burning within us while He was speaking to us on the road, while He was explaining the Scriptures to us?" 33And they arose that very hour and returned to Jerusalem, and found gathered together the eleven and those who were with them, 34 saying, "The Lord has really risen, and has ap-

[a] Some ancient mss. omit verse 12. [b] Lit., 60 stadia, one stadion equals 600 feet.

WILLIAMS

alive? 6 [He is not here but has risen.] Remember what He told you while He was still in Galilee, when 7 He said that the Son of Man had to be turned over to wicked men and crucified, but was to rise again on the third day."

8 Then they recalled His words 9 and returned from the tomb and reported all these things to the Eleven and all the rest. 10 They were Mary of Magdala and Joanna, and Mary, James's mother, who, with the other women, reported these things to the apostles. 11 But the report seemed to them to be nonsense, and so they continued to disbelieve the women. 12 [Peter, however, got up and ran to the tomb, and stooped down and saw the linen clothes but nothing else. Then he went home wondering at what had taken place.]

13 On that very day, strange to say, two of them were on their way to a village called Emmaus, about seven miles from Jerusalem, 14 and were talking together about all these things that had taken place. 15 And as they were talking, and discussing these things, Jesus Himself came up near to them and continued to walk with them, 16 but their eyes were in such a state as to keep them from recognizing Him. 17 Then He said to them, "What is this that you are discussing together as you walk?"

So they stopped and stood still with puzzled countenances. 18 Finally one of them, whose name was Cleopas, answered Him, "Are you the only visitor to Jerusalem who has not heard of the things that have taken place there in these last days?"

19 And He said to them, "What sort of things?"

They answered Him, "The things about Jesus of Nazareth, who in the sight of God and of all the people became a prophet mighty in deed and word, 20 and how the high priests and leading men turned Him over to be sentenced to death, and had Him crucified. 21 But we kept hoping that He was the One who was coming to set Israel free. Moreover, besides all this, it is now the third day since these things occurred. 22 Yes, indeed, some women of our number have astounded us! They went to the tomb early this morning 23 and could not find His body, but came and told us that they had actually had a vision of angels who said He was alive. 24 Then some of our company went to the tomb and found it just as the women had said, but they did not see Him."

25 Then He said to them, "O men sluggish in mind and slow in heart to believe all that the prophets have said! 26 Did not the Christ have to suffer these things and thus to enter into His glory?" 27 Then He began with Moses and went through all the prophets and explained to them all the passages in the Scriptures about Himself.

28 Then they approached the village to which they were going, and He acted as though He were going on farther, 29 but they earnestly urged Him, and said, "Stop and stay with us, for it is getting toward evening and the day is nearly spent."

So He went in to stay with them. 30 And after He had taken His place at table with them, He took the loaf and blessed it and broke it in pieces and handed it to them. 31 Then their eyes were instantly opened and they recognized Him, and at once He vanished from them.

32 Then they said to each other, "Did not our hearts keep burning in our bosoms as He was talking to us on the road, as He went on explaining the Scriptures to us?" 33 So at once they got up and went back to Jerusalem and found the Eleven and their company all together, 34 who told them that the Lord had really risen

BECK

who is alive?" they asked the women. 6 "He is not here; He has risen! Remember what He told you while He was still in Galilee, 7 'The Son of Man must be handed over to sinful men, be crucified, and rise on the third day.'"

8 They remembered what He had said. 9 They left the grave, went back, and reported all this to the eleven and all the others. 10 The women who told the apostles about it were Mary from Magdala and Johanna and Mary, the mother of James, and the others.

11 The apostles thought it was nonsense and wouldn't believe them.

12 But Peter started out and ran to the grave. He bent down and saw only the linen cloths. Then he went home, amazed at what had happened.

On the Way to Emmaus

13 On the same day, two of them were going to a village called Emmaus, about seven miles from Jerusalem. 14 They were talking about everything that had happened.

15 While they were talking and discussing, Jesus Himself joined them and walked with them. 16 They saw Him but were kept from knowing who He was.

17 "What are you discussing as you're walking along?" He asked them.

They stood still and looked gloomy. 18 "Are you the only stranger living in Jerusalem," the one by the name of Cleopas asked Him, "who doesn't know what happened there these days?"

19 "What do you mean?" He asked.

"All about Jesus from Nazareth," they told Him, "who was a prophet, mighty in what He did and said before God and all the people, 20 and how our high priests and rulers handed Him over to be condemned to death and crucified Him. 21 But we were hoping He would be the One to free Israel. What is more, this is now the third day since it happened. 22 And now some of our women startled us. They went to the grave early this morning 23 and didn't find His body. They came and told us they had even seen a vision of angels who said He is alive. 24 Some of our men went to the grave and found it as the women had said; and they didn't see Him."

25 "How foolish you are," He told them, "and how slow to believe everything the prophets said! 26 Didn't the promised Savior have to suffer this and so go to His glory?" 27 Then He explained to them, starting with Moses and all the prophets, what they said about Him in all their writings.

28 And so they came near the village where they were going, and He acted as if He were going farther. 29 "Stay with us," they urged Him. "It's getting late, and the day is almost gone." So He went in to stay with them.

30 While He was at the table with them, He took the bread, blessed and broke it, and gave it to them. 31 Then their eyes were opened, and they knew who He was. But He vanished from them.

32 "Didn't our hearts glow," they said to each other, "as He was talking to us on the way and explaining the Bible to us?"

33 That same hour they started out, went back to Jerusalem, and found the eleven and those who were with them all together. 34 These said, "The Lord really did rise, and Simon saw Him."

K.J.V.

hath appeared to Simon. 35And they told what things *were done* in the way, and how he was known of them in breaking of bread.

36 And as they thus spake, Jesus himself stood in the midst of them, and saith unto them, Peace *be* unto you. 37 But they were terrified and affrighted, and supposed that they had seen a spirit. 38And he said unto them, Why are ye troubled? and why do thoughts arise in your hearts? 39 Behold my hands and my feet, that it is I myself: handle me, and see; for a spirit hath not flesh and bones, as ye see me have. 40And when he had thus spoken, he shewed them *his* hands and *his* feet. 41And while they yet believed not for joy, and wondered, he said unto them, Have ye here any meat? 42And they gave him a piece of a broiled fish, and of a honeycomb. 43And he took *it,* and did eat before them. 44And he said unto them, These *are* the words which I spake unto you, while I was yet with you, that all things must be fulfilled, which were written in the law of Moses, and *in* the prophets, and *in* the psalms, concerning me. 45 Then opened he their understanding, that they might understand the Scriptures, 46And said unto them, Thus it is written, and thus it behooved Christ to suffer, and to rise from the dead the third day: 47And that repentance and remission of sins should be preached in his name among all nations, beginning at Jerusalem. 48And ye are witnesses of these things.

49 And, behold, I send the promise of my Father upon you: but tarry ye in the city of Jerusalem, until ye be endued with power from on high.

50 And he led them out as far as to Bethany, and he lifted up his hands, and blessed them. 51And it came to pass, while he blessed them, he was parted from them, and carried up into heaven. 52And they worshipped him, and returned to Jerusalem with great joy: 53And were continually in the temple, praising and blessing God. Amen.

N.A.S.

peared to Simon." 35And they *began* to relate their experiences on the road and how He was recognized by them in the breaking of the bread.

36 And while they were telling these things, He Himself stood in their midst.[a] 37 But they were startled and frightened and thought that they were seeing a spirit. 38And He said to them, "Why are you troubled, and why do doubts arise in your hearts? 39 "See My hands and My feet, that it is I Myself; touch Me and see, for a spirit does not have flesh and bones as you see that I have." 40 (See footnote [b]) 41And while they still could not believe *it* for joy and were marveling, He said to them, "Have you anything here to eat?" 42And they gave Him a piece of a broiled fish; 43 and He took it and ate *it* in their sight.

44 Now He said to them, "These are My words which I spoke to you while I was still with you, that all things which are written about Me in the Law of Moses and the Prophets and the Psalms must be fulfilled." 45 Then He opened their minds to understand the Scriptures, 46 and He said to them, "Thus it is written, that the Christ should suffer and rise again from the dead the third day; 47 and that repentance for forgiveness of sins should be proclaimed in His name to all the nations— beginning from Jerusalem. 48 "You are witnesses of these things. 49 "And behold, I am sending forth the promise of My Father upon you; but you are to stay in the city until you are clothed with power from on high."

50 And He led them out as far as Bethany, and He lifted up His hands and blessed them. 51And it came about that while He was blessing them, He parted from them.[c] 52And they[d] returned to Jerusalem with great joy, 53 and were continually in the temple, praising God.

[a] Some ancient mss. insert, *And He says to them, "Peace be to you."* [b] Some mss. add verse 40, *And when He had said this, He showed them His hands and His feet.* [c] Some mss. add, *and was carried up into heaven.* [d] Some mss. insert, *worshiped Him, and . . .*

WILLIAMS

and had been seen by Simon. 35 Then they themselves began to tell what had occurred on the road, and how He was recognized by them when He broke the loaf in pieces.

36 Even while they were talking about these things, He took His stand among them Himself, [and said to them, "Peace to you!"] *b* 37 and they were so startled and terror-stricken that they were beginning to think that they saw a ghost.

38 But He said to them, "Why are you so disturbed and why are doubts arising in your hearts? 39 Look at my hands and my feet, for it is I, myself. Feel of me and see for yourselves, for a ghost does not have flesh and bones, as you see I have." 40 [After He had said this He showed them His hands and His feet.] *b*

41 So while they were still disbelieving for sheer joy and still wondering about it, He asked them, "Have you anything here to eat?" 42 Then they gave Him a piece of broiled fish, 43 and He took it and ate it before their eyes.

44 Then He said to them, "This is what I told you while I was still with you, that everything which is written about me in the law of Moses, in the prophets, and in the Psalms, had to be fulfilled."

45 Then He opened their minds so that they might continue to understand the Scriptures, 46 and said to them, "The Scriptures said that the Christ should suffer as He has suffered, should rise from the dead on the third day, 47 and that in His name repentance as the condition*c* for the forgiveness of sins should be preached to all the nations. Beginning at Jerusalem 48 you are to continue as witnesses to these things. 49 And I will send down upon you what my Father has promised. But you, on your part, must stay right here in the city until you are clothed with power from on high."

50 Then He led them out as far as Bethany, and lifted up His hands and blessed them. 51 And while He was blessing them, He parted from them, and was taken up to heaven.*d* 52 And with great joy they went back to Jerusalem; 53 and they were continually in the temple, praising God.

BECK

35 Then the two men told what had happened on the way and how they had recognized Him while He was breaking the bread.

Behind Locked Doors

36 While they were talking about what had happened, Jesus stood among them. "Peace to you!" He said to them. 37 They were startled and terrified and thought they were seeing a ghost. 38 "Why are you troubled?" He asked them. "And why do doubts come into your minds? 39 Look at My hands and My feet: it is I Myself. Feel Me and see. A ghost doesn't have any flesh and bones as you see Me have." 40 As He said this, He showed them His hands and His feet.

41 They were so happy—they thought it was too good to be true—and they were surprised. "Do you have anything here to eat?" He asked them. 42 They gave Him a piece of broiled fish. 43 He took it and ate it while they watched Him.

44 "While I was still with you," He said to them, "I told you that everything written about Me in the Law of Moses, the prophets, and the Psalms must come true." 45 Then He opened their minds to understand the Bible. 46 "This," He told them, "is what is written: The promised Savior will suffer, rise from the dead on the third day, 47 and in His name you will preach to all people, beginning at Jerusalem, that they repent of their sins so that they will be forgiven. 48 You will testify of these things."

Jesus Goes Up to Heaven

49 "I am sending you Him whom My Father promised. Wait here in the city till you are armed with power from above."

50 He took them out to a place where Bethany lay ahead of them. Then He raised His hands and blessed them. 51 While He was blessing them, He parted from them and was taken up to heaven.

52 They knelt and worshiped Jesus. And then they went back to Jerusalem very happy. 53 And they were always in the temple praising God.

---

[b] So in WH, though found in some ancient Mss.
[c] Grk., *repentance with a view to forgiveness*, etc.
[d] Fol. B. the best Ms.

K.J.V.

THE GOSPEL

ACCORDING TO

SAINT JOHN

N.A.S.

THE GOSPEL

ACCORDING TO

JOHN

1 In the beginning was the Word, and the Word was with God, and the Word was God. 2 The same was in the beginning with God. 3 All things were made by him; and without him was not any thing made that was made. 4 In him was life; and the life was the light of men. 5 And the light shineth in darkness; and the darkness comprehended it not.

6 There was a man sent from God, whose name *was* John. 7 The same came for a witness, to bear witness of the Light, that all *men* through him might believe. 8 He was not that Light, but *was sent* to bear witness of that Light. 9 *That* was the true Light, which lighteth every man that cometh into the world. 10 He was in the world, and the world was made by him, and the world knew him not. 11 He came unto his own, and his own received him not. 12 But as many as received him, to them gave he power to become the sons of God, *even* to them that believe on his name: 13 Which were born, not of blood, nor of the will of the flesh, nor of the will of man, but of God. 14 And the Word was made flesh, and dwelt among us, (and we beheld his glory, the glory as of the only begotten of the Father,) full of grace and truth.

15 John bare witness of him, and cried, saying, This was he of whom I spake, He that cometh after me is preferred before me; for he was before me. 16 And of his fulness have all we received, and grace for grace. 17 For the law was given by Moses, *but* grace and truth came by Jesus Christ. 18 No man hath seen God at any time; the only begotten Son, which is in the bosom of the Father, he hath declared *him*.

19 And this is the record of John, when the Jews sent priests and Levites from Jerusalem to ask him, Who art thou? 20 And he confessed, and denied not; but confessed, I am not the Christ. 21 And they asked him, What then? Art thou Elias? And he saith, I am not. Art thou that Prophet? And he answered, No. 22 Then said they unto him, Who art thou? that we may give an answer to them that sent us. What sayest thou of thyself? 23 He said, I *am* the voice of one crying in the wilderness, Make straight the way of the Lord, as said the prophet Esaias.

1 In the beginning was the Word, and the Word was with God, and the Word was God. 2 He was in the beginning with God. 3 All things came into being through Him; and apart from Him nothing came into being that has come into being. 4 In Him was life; and the life was the light of men. 5 And the light shines in the darkness; and the darkness did not [a]comprehend it.

6 There [b]came a man, sent from God, whose name was John. 7 He came for a witness, that he might bear witness of the light, that all might believe through him. 8 He was not the light, but *came* that he might bear witness of the light.

9 There was the true light [c]which, coming into the world, enlightens every man. 10 He was in the world, and the world was made through Him, and the world did not know Him. 11 He came to His [d]own, and those who were His own did not receive Him. 12 But as many as received Him, to them He gave the right to become children of God, *even* to those who believe in His name: 13 who were born not of blood, nor of the will of the flesh, nor of the will of man, but of God.

14 And the Word became flesh, and dwelt among us, and we beheld His glory, glory as of the Only Begotten from the Father, full of grace and truth. 15 John *bore witness of Him, and cried out, saying, "This was He of whom I said, 'He who comes after me has a higher rank than I, for He existed before me.'" 16 For of His fullness we have all received, and grace upon grace. 17 For the law was given through Moses; grace and truth were realized through Jesus Christ. 18 No man has seen God at any time; the only begotten [e]God, who is in the bosom of the Father, He has explained *Him*.

19 And this is the witness of John, when the Jews sent to him priests and Levites from Jerusalem to ask him, "Who are you?" 20 And he confessed, and did not deny, and he confessed, "I am not the Christ." 21 And they asked him, "What then? Are you Elijah?" And he *said, "I am not." "Are you the Prophet?" And he answered, "No." 22 They said then to him, "Who are you, so that we may give an answer to those who sent us? What do you say about yourself?" 23 He said, "I am a voice of one crying in the wilderness, 'MAKE STRAIGHT THE WAY OF THE LORD,' as Isaiah the prophet said."

[a] Or, *overpower.* [b] Or, *came into being.* [c] Or, *which enlightens every man coming into the world.* [d] Gr., *His own things, possessions, domain.* [e] Some later mss. read, *Son.*

THE GOOD NEWS
AS IT WAS TOLD BY

JOHN

JOHN

1 *The eternal Word became human, to make God known to men, to make men God's children; the Baptist's testimony to Jesus; Jesus' first disciples*

In the beginning the Word existed; and the Word was face to face with God; yea, the Word was God Himself. 2 He is the One who was face to face with God in the beginning. 3 It was through Him that everything came into existence, and apart from Him not a single thing came into existence. 4 It was by Him that life began to exist, and that life was the light of mankind. 5 So the light continues to shine in the darkness, for the darkness has never overpowered it.

6 There appeared a man named John, sent from God. 7 He came for the purpose of testifying, to testify to the light, so that everyone through him might come to believe. 8 He was not the light; he came to testify to the light. 9 The real light, which sheds light upon everyone, was just coming into the world. 10 He came into the world, and though*a* the world through Him began to exist, it did not recognize Him. 11 He came into His own world, but His own people did not welcome Him. 12 But to all who did accept Him, and trust in His name, He gave the right to become the children of God, 13 who were born of God and not of natural blood nor of physical or human impulse.*b*

14 So the Word became human and lived a little while among us, and we actually saw His glory, the glory of One who is an only Son from His Father, and He was full of spiritual blessing and truth. 15 John testified to Him and cried out, for this was the one who said, "The One who is coming after me has been put before me, because He existed before me."

16 For from His bounty we have all received spiritual blessing after spiritual blessing.*c* 17 For while the law was given through Moses, spiritual blessing and truth have come through Jesus Christ. 18 No one has ever seen God; the only son, Deity Himself, who lies upon His Father's breast, has made him known.*d*

19 Now this is the testimony which John gave when the Jews sent priests and Levites to him from Jerusalem, to ask him, "Who are you?"

20 He frankly admitted, and did not try at all to deny it; yes, he frankly admitted, "I am not the Christ."

21 So they asked him again, "What are you then? Elijah?"

And he answered, "Of course, I am not."

"Are you the prophet?"

He answered, "No."

22 Then they said to him, "Who are you? Tell us, so that we can have an answer to give to those who sent us. What have you to say for yourself?"

23 He said, "I am a voice of one shouting in the desert, 'Make the road straight for the Lord,' as the prophet Isaiah said."

[a] Implied. [b] Lit., *nor of the will of flesh or man.* [c] Lit., *grace for grace.* [d] Grk., *interpreted Him.*

1 In the beginning was the Word, and the Word was with God, and the Word was God. 2 He was in the beginning with God.

3 Everything was made by Him, and not one thing that was made was made without Him. 4 In Him was life, and the Life was the Light of men. 5 The Light is shining in the dark, and the darkness has not put it out.

6 A man came—God sent him—his name was John. 7 He came to tell the truth about the Light to help everyone believe. 8 He was not the Light but came to tell the truth about the Light.

9 The true Light that gives light to everyone was coming into the world. 10 He was in the world, and He made the world, and the world didn't know Him. 11 He came to His own, and His own people didn't welcome Him. 12 But to all who welcomed Him, who believe in His name, He gave the power to become God's children. 13 They have been born, not of the blood of parents or of a sexual desire or of a man's desire but of God.

14 And the Word became flesh and lived among us as in the tabernacle, and we saw His glory, a glory of the only Son from His Father, full of love and truth.

15 John told the truth about Him when he called: "This is the One of whom I said, He who is coming after me is ahead of me because He was before me."

16 All of us have taken from all that is in Him—gift after gift of His love. 17 The Law was given through Moses, but Jesus Christ brought love and truth. 18 Nobody has ever seen God. The only Son who is God and close to the Father's heart has told us about Him.

The Lamb of God

19 When the Jews in Jerusalem sent priests and Levites to John to ask him, "Who are you?" this was John's testimony. 20 He confessed and didn't deny. He confessed: "I'm not the promised Savior."

21 "What are you then?" they asked him. "Are you Elijah?"

"I am not," he said.

"Are you the prophet?"

"No," he answered.

22 Then they asked him, "Who are you? We want to bring an answer to those who sent us. What do you say about yourself?"

23 He said: "I am *someone calling in the wilderness, 'Make straight the way for the Lord,'* [1] as the prophet Isaiah said."

[1] Is. 40:3

K.J.V.

24And they which were sent were of the Pharisees. 25And they asked him, and said unto him, Why baptizest thou then, if thou be not that Christ, nor Elias, neither that Prophet? 26 John answered them, saying, I baptize with water: but there standeth one among you, whom ye know not; 27 He it is, who coming after me is preferred before me, whose shoe's latchet I am not worthy to unloose. 28 These things were done in Bethabara beyond Jordan, where John was baptizing.

29 The next day John seeth Jesus coming unto him, and saith, Behold the Lamb of God, which taketh away the sin of the world! 30 This is he of whom I said, After me cometh a man which is preferred before me; for he was before me. 31And I knew him not: but that he should be made manifest to Israel, therefore am I come baptizing with water. 32And John bare record, saying, I saw the Spirit descending from heaven like a dove, and it abode upon him. 33And I knew him not: but he that sent me to baptize with water, the same said unto me, Upon whom thou shalt see the Spirit descending, and remaining on him, the same is he which baptizeth with the Holy Ghost. 34And I saw, and bare record that this is the Son of God.

35 Again the next day after, John stood, and two of his disciples; 36And looking upon Jesus as he walked, he saith, Behold the Lamb of God! 37And the two disciples heard him speak, and they followed Jesus. 38 Then Jesus turned, and saw them following, and saith unto them, What seek ye? They said unto him, Rabbi, (which is to say, being interpreted, Master,) where dwellest thou? 39 He saith unto them, Come and see. They came and saw where he dwelt, and abode with him that day: for it was about the tenth hour. 40 One of the two which heard John *speak*, and followed him, was Andrew, Simon Peter's brother. 41 He first findeth his own brother Simon, and saith unto him, We have found the Messias, which is, being interpreted, the Christ. 42And he brought him to Jesus. And when Jesus beheld him, he said, Thou art Simon the son of Jona: thou shalt be called Cephas, which is by interpretation, A stone.

43 The day following Jesus would go forth into Galilee, and findeth Philip, and saith unto him, Follow me. 44 Now Philip was of Bethsaida, the city of Andrew and Peter. 45 Philip findeth Nathanael, and saith unto him, We have found him, of whom Moses in the law, and the prophets, did write, Jesus of Nazareth, the son of Joseph. 46And Nathanael said unto him, Can there any good thing come out of Nazareth? Philip saith unto him, Come and see. 47 Jesus saw Nathanael coming to him, and saith of him, Behold an Israelite indeed, in whom is no guile! 48 Nathanael saith unto him, Whence knowest thou me? Jesus answered and said unto him, Before that Philip called thee, when thou wast under the fig tree, I saw thee. 49 Nathanael answered and saith unto him, Rabbi, thou art the Son of God; thou art the King of Israel. 50 Jesus answered and said unto thee, Because I said unto thee, I saw thee under the fig tree, believest thou? thou shalt see greater things than these. 51And he saith unto him, Verily, verily, I

N.A.S.

24 Now they had been sent from the Pharisees. 25And they asked him, and said to him, "Why then are you baptizing, if you are not the Christ, nor Elijah, nor the Prophet?" 26 John answered them saying, "I baptize ªin water, *but* among you stands One whom you do not know. 27 "*It is* He who comes after me, the thong of whose sandal I am not worthy to untie." 28 These things took place in Bethany beyond the Jordan, where John was baptizing.

29 The next day he *saw Jesus coming to him, and *said, "Behold, the Lamb of God who takes away the sin of the world! 30 "This is He on behalf of whom I said, 'After me comes a Man who has a higher rank than I, for He existed before me.' 31 "And I did not recognize Him, but in order that He might be manifested to Israel, I came baptizing ªin water." 32And John bore witness saying, "I have beheld the Spirit descending as a dove out of heaven; and He remained upon Him. 33 "And I did not recognize Him, but He who sent me to baptize ªin water said to me, 'He upon whom you see the Spirit descending and remaining upon Him, this is the one who baptizes ªin the Holy Spirit.' 34 "And I have seen, and have borne witness that this is the Son of God."

35 Again the next day John was standing, and two of his disciples; 36 and he looked upon Jesus as He walked, and *said, "Behold, the Lamb of God!" 37And the two disciples heard him speak, and they followed Jesus. 38And Jesus turned, and beheld them following, and *said to them, "What do you seek?" And they said to Him, "Rabbi (which translated means Teacher), where are You staying?" 39 He *said to them, "Come, and you will see." They came therefore and saw where He was staying; and they stayed with Him that day, for it was about the ᵇtenth hour. 40 One of the two who heard John *speak*, and followed Him, was Andrew, Simon Peter's brother. 41 He *found first his own brother Simon, and *said to him, "We have found the Messiah" (which translated means Christ). 42 He brought him to Jesus. Jesus looked at him, and said, "You are Simon the son of John; you shall be called Cephas" (which translated means Peter).

43 The next day *He* purposed to go forth into Galilee, and He *found Philip, and Jesus *said to him, "Follow Me." 44 Now Philip was from Bethsaida, of the city of Andrew and Peter. 45 Philip *found Nathanael, and *said to him, "We have found Him, of whom Moses in the Law, and the Prophets, wrote, Jesus of Nazareth, the son of Joseph." 46And Nathanael *said to him, "Can any good thing come out of Nazareth?" Philip *said to him, "Come and see." 47 Jesus saw Nathanael coming to Him, and *said of him, "Behold, an Israelite indeed, in whom is no guile!" 48 Nathanael *said to Him, "How do You know me?" Jesus answered and said to him, "Before Philip called you, when you were under the fig tree, I saw you." 49 Nathanael answered Him, "Rabbi, You are the Son of God; You are the King of Israel." 50 Jesus answered and said to him, "Because I said to you that I saw you under the fig tree, do you believe? You shall see greater things than these." 51And He *said to him, "Truly, truly, I

[a] The Greek here can be translated *in, with,* or *by*. [b] I.e., 4 p.m.

WILLIAMS

24 Now the messengers belonged to the party of the Pharisees; 25 so they asked him, "Why are you baptizing then, if you are not the Christ, nor Elijah, nor the prophet?"

26 John answered them, "I am baptizing only in water. There is standing among you One with whom you are not acquainted. 27 He is to become my successor, because He has been put before me, and I am not fit to untie His shoe-strings." 28 This took place at Bethany on the farther side of the Jordan, where John was baptizing.

29 The next day John saw Jesus coming toward him, and he said, "Look! He is the Lamb of God who is to take away the world's sin. 30 This is the One about whom I said, 'After me there is coming a man who has already been put before me, because He existed before me.' 31 I did not know Him myself, but I came baptizing in water, that He might be made known to Israel."

32 Then John gave this testimony: "I saw the Spirit coming down from heaven like a dove, and it remained on Him. 33 I did not know Him myself, but the very One, who sent me to baptize in water said to me, 'The One on whom you see the Spirit coming down and remaining, is the One who is to baptize in the Holy Spirit.' 34 I did see it, and my testimony is that He is the Son of God."

35 Again the next day John was standing with two of his disciples, 36 and as he saw Jesus passing by he said, "Look! He is the Lamb of God!"

37 The two disciples heard him say this, and so they followed Jesus. 38 Now Jesus turned, and as He saw them following Him, He said, "What are you looking for?"

They said to Him, "Rabbi," (which means Teacher), "where are you staying?"

39 He said to them, "Come and you will see." So they went and saw where He was staying, and they spent the rest of the day with Him; it was about four in the afternoon.

40 Andrew, Simon Peter's brother, was one of the two who heard John and followed Jesus. 41 He first found his brother Simon and said to him, "We have found the Messiah" (which means, the Christ). 42 Then he took him to Jesus.

Jesus looked him over and said, "You are Simon, son of John. From now on your name shall be Cephas" (which means Peter, or Rock).

43 The next day Jesus decided to leave for Galilee. So He sought out Philip and said to him, "Follow me."

44 Now Philip was from Bethsaida, the town of Andrew and Peter. 45 Philip sought out Nathaniel and said to him, "We have found the One about whom Moses wrote in the law and the One about whom the prophets wrote; it is Jesus, the son of Joseph, who comes from Nazareth."

46 Then Nathaniel said to him, "Can anything good come out of Nazareth?"

Philip said to him, "Come and see."

47 Jesus saw Nathaniel coming toward Him, and said of him, "Here is a genuine Israelite with no deceit in him!"

48 Nathaniel said to Him, "How do you know me?"

Jesus answered him, "While you were still under the fig tree, before Philip called you, I saw you."

49 Nathaniel answered Him, "Teacher, you are the Son of God, you are the king of Israel!"

50 Jesus answered him, "Do you believe in me because I told you that I saw you under the fig tree? You will see greater things than this." 51 Then He said to him, "I most solemnly say

BECK

24 Some who had been sent belonged to the Pharisees. 25 They asked him, "Why, then, do you baptize if you're not the promised Savior or Elijah or the prophet?"

26 "I baptize with water," John answered them. "There is standing among you Someone you don't know, 27 the One who is coming after me. I'm not good enough to untie His shoe strap."

28 This happened at Bethany on the other side of the Jordan, where John was baptizing.

29 The next day John sees Jesus coming toward him. And he says, "Look at the Lamb of God who takes away the sin of the world. 30 He is the One I meant when I said, 'A Man is coming after me but is ahead of me, because He was before me.' 31 Even I didn't know who He was, but I came and baptized with water to show Him to Israel."

32 John testified: "I saw the Spirit come down from heaven as a dove and stay on Him. 33 I didn't know who He was, but He who sent me to baptize with water told me, 'When you see the Spirit come down on Someone and stay on Him, He is the One who baptizes with the Holy Spirit.' 34 I saw it and testified, 'This is the Son of God.' "

The First Disciples

35 The next day, while John was again standing with two of his disciples, 36 he saw Jesus passing by. "Look at the Lamb of God!" he said. 37 When the two disciples heard him say this, they followed Jesus.

38 Jesus turned around and saw them following. "What are you looking for?" He asked them.

"Rabbi" (which means Teacher), "where are You staying?" they asked Him.

39 "Come and you'll see," He told them. So they came and saw where He was staying, and they stayed with Him that day. It was about ten in the forenoon.

40 One of the two who heard John and then followed Jesus was Andrew, Simon Peter's brother. 41 He first found his own brother Simon and told him, "We have found the promised Savior." (The Greek word for Him is Christ.) 42 He brought him to Jesus.

Looking at him, Jesus said, "You are Simon, John's son. Your name will be Cephas" * (which means Peter*).

43 The next day Jesus wanted to go to Galilee. He found Philip. "Follow Me!" Jesus told him. 44 Philip was from Bethsaida, the home town of Andrew and Peter.

45 Philip found Nathanael and told him, "The One Moses wrote about in the Law, and the prophets too—we've found Him, Jesus, Joseph's Son from Nazareth."

46 "Nazareth—can anything good come from there?" Nathanael asked him.

"Come and see!" Philip told him.

47 Jesus saw Nathanael coming toward Him. "Here's a real Israelite in whom there is no deceit," He said of him.

48 "Where did You get to know me?" Nathanael asked Him.

"Before Philip called you," Jesus answered him, "when you were under the fig tree, I saw you."

49 "Master," Nathanael answered Him, "You are God's Son! You are Israel's King!"

50 "You believe because I told you I saw you under the fig tree," Jesus answered him. 51 "You

* Cephas in Aramaic and Peter in Greek both mean "rock."

253

say unto you, Hereafter ye shall see heaven open, and the angels of God ascending and descending upon the Son of man.

say to you, you shall see the heaven opened, and the angels of God ascending and descending upon the Son of Man."

2 And the third day there was a marriage in Cana of Galilee; and the mother of Jesus was there: 2And both Jesus was called, and his disciples, to the marriage. 3And when they wanted wine, the mother of Jesus saith unto him, They have no wine. 4 Jesus saith unto her, Woman, what have I to do with thee? mine hour is not yet come. 5 His mother saith unto the servants, Whatsoever he saith unto you, do *it*. 6And there were set there six waterpots of stone, after the manner of the purifying of the Jews, containing two or three firkins apiece. 7 Jesus saith unto them, Fill the waterpots with water. And they filled them up to the brim. 8And he saith unto them, Draw out now, and bear unto the governor of the feast. And they bare *it*. 9 When the ruler of the feast had tasted the water that was made wine, and knew not whence it was, (but the servants which drew the water knew,) the governor of the feast called the bridegroom, 10And saith unto him, Every man at the beginning doth set forth good wine; and when men have well drunk, then that which is worse: *but* thou hast kept the good wine until now. 11 This beginning of miracles did Jesus in Cana of Galilee, and manifested forth his glory; and his disciples believed on him.

12 After this he went down to Capernaum, he, and his mother, and his brethren, and his disciples; and they continued there not many days.

13 And the Jews' passover was at hand, and Jesus went up to Jerusalem, 14And found in the temple those that sold oxen and sheep and doves, and the changers of money sitting: 15And when he had made a scourge of small cords, he drove them all of the temple, and the sheep, and the oxen; and poured out the changers' money, and overthrew the tables; 16And said unto them that sold doves, Take these things hence; make not my Father's house a house of merchandise. 17And his disciples remembered that it was written, The zeal of thine house hath eaten me up.

18 Then answered the Jews and said unto him, What sign shewest thou unto us, seeing that thou doest these things? 19 Jesus answered and said unto them, Destroy this temple, and in three days I will raise it up. 20 Then said the Jews, Forty and six years was this temple in building, and wilt thou rear it up in three days? 21 But he spake of the temple of his body. 22 When therefore he was risen from the dead, his disciples remembered that he had said this unto them; and they believed the Scripture, and the word which Jesus had said.

2 And on the third day there was a wedding in Cana of Galilee; and the mother of Jesus was there; 2 and Jesus also was invited, and His disciples, to the wedding. 3And when the wine gave out, the mother of Jesus *said to Him, "They have no wine." 4And Jesus *said to her, "Woman, what do I have to do with you? My hour has not yet come." 5 His mother *said to the servants, "Whatever He says to you, do it." 6 Now there were six stone waterpots set there for the Jewish custom of purification, containing twenty or thirty gallons each. 7 Jesus *said to them, "Fill the waterpots with water." And they filled them up to the brim. 8And He *said to them, "Draw *some* out now, and take it to the °headwaiter." And they took it *to him*. 9And when the headwaiter tasted the water which had become wine, and did not know where it came from (but the servants who had drawn the water knew), the headwaiter *called the bridegroom, 10 and *said to him, "Every man serves the good wine first, and when *men* have drunk freely, *then* that which is poorer; you have kept the good wine until now." 11 This beginning of *His* signs Jesus did in Cana of Galilee, and manifested His Glory, and His disciples believed in Him.

12 After this He went down to Capernaum, He and His mother, and *His* brothers, and His disciples; and there they stayed a few days.

13 And the Passover of the Jews was at hand, and Jesus went up to Jerusalem. 14And He found in the temple those who were selling oxen and sheep and doves, and the money-changers seated. 15And He made a scourge of cords, and drove *them* all out of the temple, with the sheep and the oxen; and He poured out the coins of the money-changers, and overturned their tables; 16 and to those who were selling the doves He said, "Take these things away; stop making My Father's house a house of merchandise." 17 His disciples remembered that it was written, "ZEAL FOR THY HOUSE WILL CONSUME ME." 18 The Jews therefore answered and said to Him, "What sign do You show to us, seeing that You do these things?" 19 Jesus answered and said to them, "Destroy this temple, and in three days I will raise it up." 20 The Jews therefore said, "It took forty-six years to build this temple, and will You raise it up in three days?" 21 But He was speaking of the temple of His body. 22 When therefore He was raised from the dead, His disciples remembered that He said this; and they believed the Scripture, and the word which Jesus had spoken.

[a] Or, *steward*.

WILLIAMS   ## BECK

to you all, you will see heaven opened and the angels of God going up, and coming down upon the Son of Man!"

will see greater things than that." And He said to him, "I tell you people the truth, you will see *heaven opened and God's angels going up and coming down*[2] on the Son of Man."

2 *Jesus performing His first wonder-work, turning water into wine; driving the traders out of the temple court*

Two days later there was a wedding at Cana in Galilee, and Jesus' mother was there. 2 Jesus and His disciples, too, were invited to the wedding. 3 When the wine was all gone, Jesus' mother said to Him, "They have no wine!" 4 Jesus said to her, "Woman, what have you to do with me? My time to act has not yet come." 5 His mother said to the servants, "Do whatever He tells you." 6 Now in accordance with the custom of purification practiced by the Jews, six stone water jars were standing there, each holding from twenty to thirty gallons. 7 Jesus said to them, "Fill these jars with water." So they filled them up to the brim. 8 Then He said to them, "Now draw some out and take it to the manager[a] of the feast." So they took him some. 9 As soon as the manager tasted the water just turned into wine, without knowing where it came from, although the servants who had drawn the water did know, He called the bridegroom 10 and said to him, "Everybody, as a rule, serves his good wine first, and his poorer wine after people have drunk freely; you have kept the good wine till now." 11 Jesus performed this, the first of His wonder-works, at Cana in Galilee. By it He showed His glorious power, and so His disciples believed in Him. 12 After this Jesus went home to Capernaum, with His mother and brothers and disciples, and stayed there for a few days. 13 Now the Jewish Passover was approaching; so Jesus went up to Jerusalem. 14 And in the temple court He found the dealers in cattle, sheep, and pigeons; the money-changers, too, seated at their tables. 15 So He made a lash out of cords, and drove them all, together with the sheep and cattle, out of the temple court, scattered the money-changers' coins and upset their tables. 16 Then He said to the pigeon-dealers, "Take these things out of here! Stop using my Father's house as a market place!" 17 His disciples recalled that the Scriptures say, "My zeal for your house will consume me!" 18 Then the Jews addressed Him and asked, "What sign can you show us that you have authority to act in this way?" 19 Jesus answered them, "Destroy this sanctuary, and I will raise it in three days." 20 Then the Jews retorted, "It took forty-six years to build this sanctuary, and you are going to raise it in three days!" 21 But He meant the sanctuary of His body. 22 So after He had risen from the dead, His disciples recalled that He had said this, and so believed the Scripture and the statement that He had made.

Jesus Changes Water to Wine

2 Two days later there was a wedding in Cana in Galilee, and Jesus' mother was there. 2 Jesus and His disciples had also been invited to the wedding. 3 When the people were out of wine, Jesus' mother said to Him, "They don't have any wine." 4 "Will you leave that to Me, woman?" Jesus asked her. "It isn't the right time yet." 5 His mother told the waiters, *"Do anything He tells you."*[3] 6 Six stone water jars were standing there for the religious washings of the Jews. Each jar held eighteen to twenty-seven gallons. 7 "Fill the jars with water," Jesus told them. And they filled them to the top. 8 "Now take some of it," He told them, "and bring it to the manager of the dinner." So they brought it to him. 9 When the manager tasted the water that had been changed to wine, he didn't know where it was from; only the waiters who had dipped the water knew. So the manager called the groom. 10 "Everybody serves his good wine first," he told him, "and when people have drunk much, then the poorer wine. You've kept the good wine till now." 11 Jesus did this, the first of His miracles, in Cana in Galilee. He showed His glory, and His disciples believed in Him. 12 After this He, His mother, His brothers, and His disciples went down to Capernaum and stayed there a few days.

Jesus Cleans the Temple

13 The Jewish Passover was near, so Jesus went up to Jerusalem. 14 In the temple He found men selling cattle, sheep, and pigeons, and the money changers were sitting there. 15 So He made a whip of small ropes and with their sheep and cattle drove them all out of the temple. He scattered the coins of the money changers and upset their tables. 16 "Take these away!" He told those who sold pigeons. "Don't make My Father's house a place for business." 17 His disciples had to think of what the Bible said: *The zeal for Your house will consume Me.*[4] 18 Then the Jews came back at Him by asking, "By what miracle can You prove to us You may do this?" 19 "Tear down this temple," Jesus answered them, "and I will raise it in three days." 20 "It took forty-six years to build this temple," said the Jews, "and You'll raise it in three days?" 21 But the temple He spoke of was His own body. 22 After He rose from the dead, His disciples remembered He had said this, and they believed the Bible and what Jesus had said.

[2] Gen. 28:12
[3] Gen. 41:55
[4] Ps. 69:9

[a] Lit., *ruler;* our *manager,* or *toastmaster.*

255

K.J.V.

23 Now when he was in Jerusalem at the passover, in the feast *day*, many believed in his name, when they saw the miracles which he did. 24 But Jesus did not commit himself unto them, because he knew all *men*, 25 And needed not that any should testify of man: for he knew what was in man.

3 There was a man of the Pharisees, named Nicodemus, a ruler of the Jews: 2 The same came to Jesus by night, and said unto him, Rabbi, we know that thou art a teacher come from God: for no man can do these miracles that thou doest, except God be with him. 3 Jesus answered and said unto him, Verily, verily, I say unto thee, Except a man be born again, he cannot see the kingdom of God. 4 Nicodemus saith unto him How can a man be born when he is old? can he enter the second time into his mother's womb, and be born? 5 Jesus answered, Verily, verily, I say unto thee, Except a man be born of water and *of* the Spirit, he cannot enter into the kingdom of God. 6 That which is born of the flesh is flesh; and that which is born of the Spirit is spirit. 7 Marvel not that I said unto thee, Ye must be born again. 8 The wind bloweth where it listeth, and thou hearest the sound thereof, but canst not tell whence it cometh, and whither it goeth: so is every one that is born of the Spirit. 9 Nicodemus answered and said unto him, How can these things be? 10 Jesus answered and said unto him, Art thou a master of Israel, and knowest not these things? 11 Verily, verily, I say unto thee, We speak that we do know, and testify that we have seen; and ye receive not our witness. 12 If I have told you earthly things and ye believe not, how shall ye believe, if I tell you *of* heavenly things? 13 And no man hath ascended up to heaven, but he that came down from heaven, *even* the Son of man which is in heaven.

14 And as Moses lifted up the serpent in the wilderness, even so must the Son of man be lifted up: 15 That whosoever believeth in him should not perish, but have eternal life.

16 For God so loved the world, that he gave his only begotten Son, that whosoever believeth in him should not perish, but have everlasting life. 17 For God sent not his Son into the world to condemn the world; but that the world through him might be saved.

18 He that believeth on him is not condemned: but he that believeth not is condemned already, because he hath not believed in the name of the only begotten Son of God. 19 And this is the condemnation, that light is come into the world, and men loved darkness rather than light, because their deeds were evil. 20 For every one that doeth evil hateth the light, neither cometh to the light, lest his deeds should be reproved. 21 But he that doeth truth cometh to the light, that his deeds may be made manifest, that they are wrought in God.

N.A.S.

23 Now when He was in Jerusalem at the Passover, during the feast, many believed in His name, beholding His signs which He was doing. 24 But Jesus, on His part, was not entrusting Himself to them, for He knew all men, 25 and because He did not need any one to bear witness concerning man for He Himself knew what was in Man.

3 Now there was a man of the Pharisees, named Nicodemus, a ruler of the Jews; 2 this man came to Him by night, and said to Him, "Rabbi, we know that You have come from God *as* a teacher; for no one can do these signs that You do unless God is with him." 3 Jesus answered and said to him, "Truly, truly, I say to you, unless one is born again, he cannot see the kingdom of God." 4 Nicodemus *said to Him, "How can a man be born when he is old? He cannot enter a second time into his mother's womb, and be born, can he?" 5 Jesus answered, "Truly, truly, I say to you, unless one is born of water and the Spirit, he cannot enter into the kingdom of God. 6 "That which is born of the flesh is flesh; and that which is born of the Spirit is spirit. 7 "Do not marvel that I said to you, 'You must be born again.' 8 "The wind blows where it wishes and you hear the sound of it, but do not know where it comes from and where it is going; so is every one who is born of the Spirit." 9 Nicodemus answered and said to Him, "How can these things be?" 10 Jesus answered and said to him, "Are you the teacher of Israel, and do not understand these things? 11 "Truly, truly, I say to you, we speak that which we know, and bear witness of that which we have seen; and you do not receive our witness. 12 "If I told you earthly things and you do not believe, how shall you believe if I tell you heavenly things? 13 "And no one has ascended into heaven, but He who descended from heaven, *even* the Son of Man. 14 "And as Moses lifted up the serpent in the wilderness, even so must the Son of Man be lifted up; 15 that whoever °believes may in Him have eternal life.

16 "For God so loved the world, that He gave His only begotten Son, that whoever believes in Him should not perish, but have eternal life. 17 "For God did not send the Son into the world to judge the world; but that the world should be saved through Him. 18 "He who believes in Him is not judged; he who does not believe has been judged already, because he has not believed in the name of the only begotten Son of God. 19 "And this is the judgment, that the light is come into the world, and men loved the darkness rather than the light; for their deeds were evil. 20 "For everyone who does evil hates the light, and does not come to the light, lest his deeds should be exposed. 21 "But he who practices the truth comes to the light, that his deeds may be manifested as having been wrought in God."

[a] Some mss. read, *believes in Him may have eternal life.*

WILLIAMS

BECK

Nicodemus

23 Now while He was in Jerusalem at the Passover Feast, many people, because they saw the wonder-works which He was performing, trusted in Him as the Christ. 24 But He would not trust Himself to them, because He knew all men 25 and needed no testimony from anyone about them, for He well knew what was in human nature.

23 Now, while He was in the crowd at the Passover in Jerusalem, many believed in His name when they saw the miracles He was doing. 24 Jesus, however, wouldn't trust them, because He knew everybody. 25 He didn't need to be told about anyone, because He knew what was in him.

3 *Jesus tells Nicodemus about the new birth; God's love and His Son's mission to the world; John further testifies to Jesus*

Now there was a man named Nicodemus, who belonged to the party of the Pharisees and was a leader among the Jews. 2 He came to Jesus one night and said to Him, "Teacher, we know that you have come from God, for no one can perform the wonder-works that you are doing, unless God is with him."

3 Jesus answered him, "I most solemnly say to you, no one can ever see the kingdom of God, unless he is born from above."

4 Nicodemus said to Him, "How can a man be born when he is old? He cannot again enter his mother's womb and be born, can he?"

5 Jesus answered, "I most solemnly say to you, no one can ever get into the kingdom of God, unless he is born of. water and the Spirit. 6 Whatever is born of the physical is physical, and whatever is born of the Spirit is spiritual. 7 Never wonder at my telling you that you must all be born from above. 8 The wind blows where it pleases, and you hear the sound of it, but you do not know where it comes from or where it goes. That is just the way it is with everyone who is born of the Spirit."

9 Then Nicodemus answered by asking, "How can this be?"

10 Jesus answered him, "Are you a teacher of Israel and do not know this? 11 I most solemnly say to you, we know what we are talking about and we have seen what we are testifying to, yet you are all rejecting our testimony. 12 If you do not believe the earthly things I tell you, how can you believe the heavenly things, if I tell you about them? 13 And yet no one has gone up into heaven except the Son of Man who came down out of heaven. 14 And just as Moses in the desert lifted the serpent on the pole, the Son of Man must be lifted up, 15 so that everyone who trusts in Him may have eternal life.

16 "For God loved the world so much that He gave His Only Son, so that anyone who trusts in Him may never perish but have eternal life. 17 For God sent His Son into the world, not to pass sentence on it, but that the world through Him might be saved. 18 Whoever trusts in Him is never to come up for judgment; but whoever does not trust in Him has already received his sentence, because he has not trusted in the name of God's only Son. 19 And the ground for the sentence is this, that the light has come into the world, and yet, because their actions were evil, men have loved darkness more than the light. 20 For anyone who is in the habit of doing wrong hates the light, and to keep his actions from being reproved, he does not come out into the daylight. 21 But whoever is in the habit of living the truth will come out in the daylight, that his actions may be shown to be performed with God's help."

3 Now, there was a Pharisee by the name of Nicodemus, a member of the Jewish court. 2 He came to Jesus one night. "Master," he said to Him, "we know You're a teacher who has come from God. Nobody can do these miracles You do unless God is with him."

3 "I tell you the truth," Jesus answered him, "if anyone isn't born from above, he can't see God's kingdom."

4 "How can anyone be born when he's old?" Nicodemus asked Him. "He can't go back into his mother's womb and be born again, can he?"

5 "I tell you the truth," Jesus answered him, "if anyone isn't born of water and the Spirit, he can't get into God's kingdom. 6 Anything born of the flesh is flesh, but anything born of the Spirit is spirit. 7 Don't be surprised when I tell you you must all be born from above. 8 The wind blows where it pleases and you hear the sound of it, but you don't know where it's coming from or where it's going. So it is with everyone born of the Spirit."

9 "How can that be?" Nicodemus asked Him.

10 "You are the teacher in Israel," Jesus said to him, "and don't know this? 11 I assure you, We tell what We know, and We testify to what We have seen. But you people don't accept Our testimony. 12 If you don't believe the earthly things I told you, how will you believe Me if I tell you heavenly things? 13 No one has gone up to heaven except the One who came down from heaven—the Son of Man.

14 "As Moses lifted up the snake in the desert, so the Son of Man must be lifted up 15 so that everyone who believes in Him has everlasting life. 16 God so loved the world that He gave His only Son so that everyone who believes in Him doesn't perish but has everlasting life. 17 You see, God didn't send His Son into the world to condemn the world but to save the world through Him. 18 If you believe in Him, you're not condemned. But if you don't believe, you're already condemned because you don't believe in the name of God's only Son. 19 This is why people are condemned: The Light came into the world, but people have loved darkness instead of the Light because they have been doing wrong. 20 Everyone who does wrong hates the Light and will not come to the Light—he doesn't want his works to be seen in the light. 21 But anyone who lives in the truth comes to the Light so that his works may be seen to have been done in God."

K.J.V.

22 After these things came Jesus and his disciples into the land of Judea; and there he tarried with them, and baptized.

23 And John also was baptizing in Enon near to Salim, because there was much water there: and they came, and were baptized. 24 For John was not yet cast into prison.

25 Then there arose a question between *some* of John's disciples and the Jews about purifying. 26And they came unto John, and said unto him, Rabbi, he that was with thee beyond Jordan, to whom thou barest witness, behold, the same baptizeth, and all *men* come to him. 27 John answered and said, A man can receive nothing, except it be given him from heaven. 28 Ye yourselves bear me witness, that I said, I am not the Christ, but that I am sent before him. 29 He that hath the bride is the bridegroom: but the friend of the bridegroom, which standeth and heareth him, rejoiceth greatly because of the bridegroom's voice: this my joy therefore is fulfilled. 30 He must increase, but I *must* decrease. 31 He that cometh from above is above all: he that is of the earth is earthly, and speaketh of the earth: he that cometh from heaven is above all. 32And what he hath seen and heard, that he testifieth; and no man receiveth his testimony. 33 He that hath received his testimony hath set to his seal that God is true. 34 For he whom God hath sent speaketh the words of God: for God giveth not the Spirit by measure *unto him*. 35 The Father loveth the Son, and hath given all things into his hand. 36 He that believeth on the Son hath everlasting life: but he that believeth not the Son shall not see life; but the wrath of God abideth on him.

4 When therefore the Lord knew how the Pharisees had heard that Jesus made and baptized more disciples than John, 2 (Though Jesus himself baptized not, but his disciples,) 3 He left Judea, and departed again into Galilee. 4And he must needs go through Samaria. 5 Then cometh he to a city of Samaria, which is called Sychar, near to the parcel of ground that Jacob gave to his son Joseph. 6 Now Jacob's well was there. Jesus therefore, being wearied with *his* journey, sat thus on the well: *and* it was about the sixth hour. 7 There cometh a woman of Samaria to draw water: Jesus saith unto her, Give me to drink. 8 (For his disciples were gone away unto the city to buy meat.) 9 Then saith the woman of Samaria unto him, How is it that thou, being a Jew, askest drink of me, which am a woman of Samaria? for the Jews have no dealings with the Samaritans. 10 Jesus answered and said unto her, If thou knewest the gift of God, and who it is that saith to thee, Give me to drink; thou wouldest have asked of him, and he would have given thee living water. 11 The woman saith unto him, Sir, thou hast nothing to draw with, and the well is deep: from whence

N.A.S.

22 After these things Jesus came, and His disciples, into the land of Judea; and there He was spending time with them, and baptizing. 23And John also was baptizing in Aenon near Salim, because there was much water there; and they were coming, and were being baptized. 24 For John had not yet been thrown into prison. 25 There arose therefore a discussion on the part of John's disciples with a Jew about purification. 26And they came to John, and said to him, "Rabbi, He who was with you beyond the Jordan, to whom you have borne witness, behold, He is baptizing, and all are coming to Him." 27 John answered and said, "A man can receive nothing, unless it has been given him from heaven. 28 "You yourselves bear me witness, that I said, 'I am not the Christ', but, 'I have been sent before Him.' 29 "He who has the bride is the bridegroom; but the friend of the bridegroom, who stands and hears him, rejoices greatly because of the bridegroom's voice. And so this joy of mine has been made full. 30 "He must increase, but I must decrease.

31 "He who comes from above is above all, he who is of the earth is from the earth and speaks of the earth. He who comes from heaven is above all. 32 "What He has seen and heard, of that He bears witness; and no man receives His witness. 33 "He who has received His witness has set his seal to *this*, that God is true. 34 "For He whom God has sent speaks the words of God; for He gives the Spirit without measure. 35 "The Father loves the Son, and has given all things into His hand. 36 "He who believes in the Son has eternal life; but he who does not obey the Son shall not see life, but the wrath of God abides on him."

4 When therefore the Lord knew that the Pharisees had heard that Jesus was making and baptizing more disciples than John 2 (although Jesus Himself was not baptizing, but His disciples were), 3 He left Judea, and departed again into Galilee. 4And He had to pass through Samaria. 5 So He *came to a city of Samaria, called Sychar, near the parcel of ground that Jacob gave to his son Joseph; 6 and Jacob's well was there. Jesus therefore, being wearied from His journey, was sitting thus by the well. It was about the *sixth hour. 7 There *came a woman of Samaria to draw water. Jesus *said to her, "Give Me a drink." 8 For His disciples had gone away into the city to buy food. 9 The Samaritan woman therefore *said to Him, "How is it that You, being a Jew, ask me for a drink since I am a Samaritan woman?" (For Jews have no dealings with Samaritans.) 10 Jesus answered and said to her, "If you knew the gift of God, and who it is who says to you, 'Give Me a drink;' you would have asked Him, and He would have given you living water." 11 She *said to Him, "Sir, You have nothing to draw with and the well is deep; where then do You get that

[a] I.e., noon.

WILLIAMS

22 After this, Jesus and His disciples went into Judea, and for some time He stayed there with them and kept baptizing people. 23 But John too was baptizing people at Aenon, near Salim, for there was plenty of water there, and so the people were coming and being baptized. 24 (For John had not yet been put in prison.) 25 Then a discussion came up between John's disciples and a Jew about purification. 26 And they went to John and said to him, "Teacher, the man who was with you on the other side of the Jordan, to whom you bore testimony yourself, is baptizing people and everybody is going to Him."

27 John answered, "A man cannot get anything, unless it is given to him from heaven. 28 You can bear testimony to me yourselves that I said, 'I am not the Christ, but I have been sent as His announcer.' 29 It is the bridegroom who has the bride, but the bridegroom's friend, who stands outside and listens to him, is very happy to hear the bridegroom's voice. So this happiness of mine is running over. 30 He must grow greater and greater, but I less and less."

31 He who comes from above is far above all others. He who springs from earth belongs to the earth and speaks of earth. He who comes from heaven is far above all others. 32 He continues to bear testimony to what He has actually seen and heard, and yet no one accepts His testimony. 33 Whoever does accept His testimony has certified with a seal that God is true. 34 For He whom God has sent continues to speak the words of God, for God continues to give Him the Spirit without measure. 35 The Father loves His Son and has put everything in His hands. 36 Whoever trusts in the Son possesses eternal life, but whoever refuses to trust in the Son will not see life, but the wrath of God continues to remain on him.

BECK

John Is Happy in Jesus

22 After this, Jesus and His disciples went into the country of Judea, and there He spent some time with them and baptized.

23 John, too, was baptizing in Aenon, near Salim, because there was much water there. So people came and were baptized. 24 John had not yet been put in prison.

25 John's disciples started a discussion with a Jew about religious cleansing, 26 and they came to John. "Teacher," they told him, "He who was with you on the other side of the Jordan and to whom you gave your testimony —He's here. He's baptizing, and everybody's going to Him."

27 "A man can get only what Heaven has given him," John answered. 28 "You yourselves are witnesses that I said I'm not the promised Savior but am sent ahead of Him.

29 "The One who has the bride is the Bridegroom. The Bridegroom's friend stands and listens to Him. And when the Bridegroom speaks, he makes His friend very happy. Now, this is my happiness, and it's complete. 30 He must grow while I must become less. 31 The One who comes from above is above all others.

"Anyone who comes from the earth is earthly and talks about earthly things. The One who comes from heaven is above all others. 32 He tells the truth of what He has seen and heard, and nobody accepts the truth He tells. 33 But anyone who has accepted the truth He tells has stamped with his seal of approval that God tells the truth. 34 The One whom God has sent says what God says because God gives Him His Spirit without a limit. 35 The Father loves the Son and has put everything in His hands. 36 Anyone who believes in the Son has everlasting life. But anyone who will not listen to the Son will not see life, but God will always be angry with him."

---

4 Jesus leaves Judea for Galilee; talks with the woman of Samaria and tells her He is the teaching Messiah; the men of Sychar hear Him and proclaim Him the Saviour of the world

Now when the Lord learned that the Pharisees had heard that He was winning and baptizing more disciples than John—2 though Jesus Himself was not baptizing, it was His disciples—3 He left Judea and went back again to Galilee. 4 And He had to go through Samaria. 5 So He came to a town in Samaria called Sychar, near the field which Jacob gave to his son Joseph; 6 and Jacob's spring was there. So Jesus, tired from His journey, was sitting by the spring just as He was. It was about noon. 7 A woman of Samaria came to draw water. Jesus said to her, "Give me a drink." 8 For His disciples had gone into the town to buy some food.

9 So the Samaritan woman said to Him, "How is it that a Jew like you asks a Samaritan woman like me for a drink?" For Jews have nothing to do with Samaritans.

10 Jesus answered her, "If you just knew what God has to give and who it is that said to you, 'Give me a drink,' you would have been the one to ask Him, and He would have given you living water."

11 She said to Him, "You have nothing to draw with, sir, and the well is deep. Where do

The Samaritan Woman

4 The Lord found out that the Pharisees had heard, "Jesus is making and baptizing more disciples than John," 2 although it wasn't really Jesus but His disciples who baptized. 3 Then He left Judea and started back on the way to Galilee, 4 and He had to go through Samaria. 5 He came to a town in Samaria by the name of Sychar, near the piece of land Jacob gave his son Joseph. 6 Jacob's Well was there. So Jesus, tired as He was from traveling, sat down by the well. It was about six in the evening.

7 A woman of Samaria came to draw water. "Give me a drink," Jesus said to her. 8 His disciples had gone into the town to buy food.

9 The Samaritan woman asked Him: "How can You, a Jew, ask me, a Samaritan woman, for a drink?" Jews, you see, don't drink from the same jar with Samaritans.

10 "If you knew what God is giving," Jesus answered her, "and who it is that says to you, 'Give Me a drink,' you would have asked Him, and He would have given you living water."

11 "Sir, you have nothing to draw water with," she told Him, "and the well is deep. Where can You get living water from a spring?

K.J.V.

then hast thou that living water? 12 Art thou greater than our father Jacob, which gave us the well, and drank thereof himself, and his children, and his cattle? 13 Jesus answered and said unto her, Whosoever drinketh of this water shall thirst again: 14 But whosoever drinketh of the water that I shall give him shall never thirst; but the water that I shall give him shall be in him a well of water springing up into everlasting life. 15 The woman saith unto him, Sir, give me this water, that I thirst not, neither come hither to draw. 16 Jesus saith unto her, Go, call thy husband, and come hither. 17 The woman answered and said, I have no husband. Jesus said unto her, Thou hast well said, I have no husband: 18 For thou hast had five husbands; and he whom thou now hast is not thy husband: in that saidst thou truly. 19 The woman saith unto him, Sir, I perceive that thou art a prophet. 20 Our fathers worshipped in this mountain; and ye say, that in Jerusalem is the place where men ought to worship. 21 Jesus saith unto her, Woman, believe me, the hour cometh, when ye shall neither in this mountain, nor yet at Jerusalem, worship the Father. 22 Ye worship ye know not what: we know what we worship; for salvation is of the Jews. 23 But the hour cometh, and now is, when the true worshippers shall worship the Father in spirit and in truth: for the Father seeketh such to worship him. 24 God is a Spirit: and they that worship him must worship him in spirit and in truth. 25 The woman saith unto him, I know that Messias cometh, which is called Christ: when he is come, he will tell us all things. 26 Jesus saith unto her, I that speak unto thee am he.

27 And upon this came his disciples, and marvelled that he talked with the woman: yet no man said, What seekest thou? or, Why talkest thou with her? 28 The woman then left her waterpot, and went her way into the city, and saith to the men, 29 Come, see a man, which told me all things that ever I did: is not this the Christ? 30 Then they went out of the city, and came unto him.

31 In the mean while his disciples prayed him, saying, Master, eat. 32 But he said unto them, I have meat to eat that ye know not of. 33 Therefore said the disciples one to another, Hath any man brought him aught to eat? 34 Jesus saith unto them, My meat is to do the will of him that sent me, and to finish his work. 35 Say not ye, There are yet four months, and then cometh harvest? behold, I say unto you, Lift up your eyes, and look on the fields; for they are white already to harvest. 36 And he that reapeth receiveth wages, and gathereth fruit unto life eternal: that both he that soweth and he that reapeth may rejoice together. 37 And herein is that saying true, One soweth, and another reapeth. 38 I sent you to reap that whereon ye bestowed no labour: other men laboured, and ye are entered into their labours.

39 And many of the Samaritans of that city believed on him for the saying of the woman, which testified, He told me all that ever I did. 40 So when the Samaritans were come unto him,

N.A.S.

living water? 12 "You are not greater than our father Jacob, are You, who gave us the well, and drank of it himself, and his sons, and his cattle?" 13 Jesus answered and said to her, "Everyone who drinks of this water shall thirst again; 14 but whoever drinks of the water that I shall give him shall never thirst; but the water that I shall give him shall become in him a well of water springing up to eternal life." 15 The woman *said to Him, "Sir, give me this water, so I will not be thirsty, nor come all the way here to draw." 16 He *said to her, "Go, call your husband, and come here." 17 The woman answered and said, "I have no husband." Jesus *said to her, "You have well said, 'I have no husband;' 18 for you have had five husbands; and the one whom you now have is not your husband; this you have said truly." 19 The woman *said to Him, "Sir, I perceive that You are a prophet. 20 "Our fathers worshiped in this mountain; and you people say that in Jerusalem is the place where men ought to worship." 21 Jesus *said to her, "Woman, believe Me, an hour is coming when neither in this mountain, nor in Jerusalem, shall you worship the Father. 22 "You worship that which you do not know; we worship that which we know; for salvation is from the Jews. 23 "But an hour is coming, and now is, when the true worshipers shall worship the Father in spirit and truth; for such people the Father seeks to be His worshipers. 24 "God is spirit; and those who worship Him must worship in spirit and truth." 25 The woman *said to Him, "I know that Messiah is coming (He who is called Christ); when that One comes, He will declare all things to us." 26 Jesus *said to her, "I who speak to you am He."

27 And at this point His disciples came, and they marveled that He had been speaking with a woman; yet no one said, "What do You seek?" or, "Why do You speak with her?" 28 So the woman left her waterpot, and went into the city, and *said to the men, 29 "Come, see a man who told me all the things that I have done; this is not the Christ, is it?" 30 They went out of the city, and were coming to Him. 31 In the meanwhile the disciples were requesting Him, saying, "Rabbi, eat." 32 But He said to them, "I have food to eat that you do not know about." 33 The disciples therefore were saying to one another, "No one brought Him anything to eat, did he?" 34 Jesus *said to them, "My food is to do the will of Him who sent Me, and to accomplish His work. 35 "Do you not say, 'There are yet four months, and then comes the harvest'? Behold, I say to you, lift up your eyes, and look on the fields, that they are white for harvest. 36 "Already he who reaps is receiving wages, and is gathering fruit for life eternal; that he who sows and he who reaps may rejoice together. 37 "For in this case the saying is true, 'One sows, and another reaps.' 38 "I sent you to reap that for which you have not labored; others have labored, and you have entered into their labor."

39 And from that city many of the Samaritans believed in Him because of the word of the woman who testified, "He told me all the things that I have done." 40 So when the Samaritans

WILLIAMS

you get your living water? 12 You are not greater than our forefather Jacob, are you, who gave us this well, and drank from it himself, with all his sons and flocks?"

13 Jesus answered her, "Anyone who drinks this water will get thirsty again; 14 but whoever drinks the water that I will give him will never, no never, be thirsty again, for the water that I will give him will become a spring of water that keeps on bubbling up within him for eternal life."

15 The woman said to Him, "Give me this water at once, sir, so I may never get thirsty again, nor have to come so far to draw water."

16 He said to her, "Go and call your husband and come back here."

17 The woman answered, "I have no husband."

Jesus said to her, "You were right in saying, 'I have no husband,' 18 for you have had five husbands, and the man you now have is not your husband. What you have said is true."

19 The woman said to Him, "I see that you are a prophet. 20 Our forefathers worshiped on this mountain, but you Jews say that Jerusalem is the place where people ought to worship Him."

21 Jesus said to her, "Believe me, woman, the time is coming when you will worship the Father neither on this mountain nor in Jerusalem. 22 You Samaritans do not know what you are worshiping; we Jews do know what we are worshiping, for salvation comes from the Jews. 23 But a time is coming—indeed, it is already here—when the real worshipers will worship the Father in spirit and reality, for the Father is looking for just such worshipers. 24 God is a spiritual Being, and his worshipers must worship Him in spirit and reality."

25 The woman said to Him, "I know that the Messiah is coming, the One who is called the Christ. When He comes, He will tell us everything."

26 Jesus said to her, "I, the very one who is talking to you, am He!"

27 Just then His disciples came up, and they were surprised to find Him talking with a woman, yet not one of them asked Him, "What do you want?" or "Why are you talking with her?"

28 The woman then left her pitcher and went back to town and said to the people, 29 "Come, see a man who has told me everything I ever did. He is not the Christ, is He?" 30 So the people left town and rushed out to see Him.

31 Meanwhile the disciples were asking Him, and saying, "Teacher, eat something."

32 But He said to them, "I have food to eat of which you do not know."

33 So the disciples began to say to one another, "Nobody has brought Him anything to eat, has he?"

34 Jesus said to them, "My food is to do the will of Him who sent me, and to finish His work. 35 Are you not saying, 'In four months more the harvest comes'? Look! I tell you, lift up your eyes and scan the fields, for they are already white for harvesting. 36 Now the reaper is already getting pay, for he is gathering a crop for eternal life, so that the sower and the reaper may rejoice together. 37 For in this matter the adage is true, 'One sows, another reaps.' 38 I have sent you to reap a harvest which you have not labored to make. Other men have labored, but you have reaped the results of their labors."

39 Many of the Samaritans in that town believed in Him because of the woman's testimony, when she said, "He has told me everything I ever did." 40 So when the Samaritans

BECK

12 Are you greater than Jacob, our ancestor, who gave us the well? He himself drank from it, and also his sons and his animals."

13 "Everyone who drinks this water," Jesus answered her, "will get thirsty again. 14 Anyone who drinks the water I'll give him will never get thirsty again. But the water I'll give him will be in him a spring of water bubbling up to everlasting life."

15 "Sir, give me this water," the woman told Him. "Then I won't get thirsty or have to come out here to draw water."

16 "Go, call your husband," Jesus told her, "and come back here."

17 "I don't have any husband," the woman answered Him.

"You're right when you say, 'I don't have any husband,'" Jesus told her. 18 "You've had five husbands, and the man you have now isn't your husband. You've told the truth!"

19 "Sir," the woman said to Him, "I see You're a prophet! 20 Our ancestors worshiped on this mountain, but you say, 'The place where people must worship is in Jerusalem.'"

21 "Believe Me, woman," Jesus told her, "the time is coming when you will not be worshiping the Father on this mountain or in Jerusalem. 22 You don't know what you're worshiping. We know what we're worshiping, because salvation comes from the Jews. 23 But the time is coming, and it is here now, when real worshipers will worship the Father in spirit and in truth. You see, the Father is looking for such people to worship Him. 24 God is a spirit, and those who worship Him must worship in spirit and in truth."

25 The woman said to Him, "I know that the promised Savior" (who is called Christ) "is coming. When He comes, He'll tell us everything."

26 "I am He—I who am talking to you," Jesus told her.

27 Just then His disciples came and were surprised to find Him talking to a woman. But none of them asked, "What do you want?" or, "Why are You talking to her?"

28 Then the woman left her water jar and went back into the town. 29 "Come," she told the people, "see a Man who told me everything I've done. Could He be the promised Savior?" 30 They left the town and were coming to Him.

31 Meanwhile the disciples were urging Him, "Master, eat."

32 He told them, "I have food to eat which you don't know about."

33 "Could anyone have brought Him something to eat?" the disciples asked one another.

34 "My food is to do what He wants who sent Me," Jesus told them, "and to finish His work. 35 "Don't you say, 'Four more months and we'll cut the grain'? I tell you, look and see how the fields are white and ready to be cut. 36 Already the reaper is getting paid and is gathering grain for everlasting life, so that the sower is happy with the reaper. 37 Here the saying is true, 'One man sows, and another cuts the grain.' 38 I sent you to cut grain where you had not worked before. Others have done the hard work, and you have succeeded them in their work."

39 Many Samaritans in that town believed in Him because the woman had declared, "He told me everything I've done." 40 When the Samari-

K.J.V.

they besought him that he would tarry with them: and he abode there two days. 41And many more believed because of his own word; 42And said unto the woman, Now we believe, not because of thy saying: for we have heard *him* ourselves, and know that this is indeed the Christ, the Saviour of the world.

43 Now after two days he departed thence, and went into Galilee. 44 For Jesus himself testified, that a prophet hath no honour in his own country. 45 Then when he was come into Galilee, the Galileans received him, having seen all the things that he did at Jerusalem at the feast: for they also went unto the feast. 46 So Jesus came again into Cana of Galilee, where he made the water wine. And there was a certain nobleman, whose son was sick at Capernaum. 47 When he heard that Jesus was come out of Judea into Galilee, he went unto him, and besought him that he would come down, and heal his son: for he was at the point of death. 48 Then said Jesus unto him, Except ye see signs and wonders, ye will not believe. 49 The nobleman saith unto him, Sir, come down ere my child die. 50 Jesus saith unto him, Go thy way; thy son liveth. And the man believed the word that Jesus had spoken unto him, and he went his way. 51And as he was now going down, his servants met him, and told *him*, saying, Thy son liveth. 52 Then inquired he of them the hour when he began to amend. And they said unto him, Yesterday at the seventh hour the fever left him. 53 So the father knew that *it was* at the same hour, in the which Jesus said unto him, Thy son liveth: and himself believed, and his whole house. 54 This *is* again the second miracle *that* Jesus did, when he was come out of Judea into Galilee.

5 After this there was a feast of the Jews; and Jesus went up to Jerusalem. 2 Now there is at Jerusalem by the sheep *market* a pool, which is called in the Hebrew tongue Bethesda, having five porches. 3 In these lay a great multitude of impotent folk, of blind, halt, withered, waiting for the moving of the water. 4 For an angel went down at a certain season into the pool, and troubled the water: whosoever then first after the troubling of the water stepped in was made whole of whatsoever disease he had. 5And a certain man was there, which had an infirmity thirty and eight years. 6 When Jesus saw him lie, and knew that he had been now a long time *in that case*, he saith unto him, Wilt thou be made whole? 7 The impotent man answered him, Sir, I have no man, when the water is troubled, to put me into the pool: but while I am coming, another stepteth down before me. 8 Jesus saith unto him, Rise, take up thy bed, and walk. 9And immediately the man was made whole, and took up his bed, and walked: and on the same day was the sabbath.

10 The Jews therefore said unto him that was cured, It is the sabbath day: it is not lawful for thee to carry *thy* bed. 11 He answered them, He that made me whole, the same said unto me,

N.A.S.

came to Him, they were asking Him to stay with them; and He stayed there two days. 41And many more believed because of His word; 42 and they were saying to the woman, "It is no longer because of what you said that we believe, for we have heard for ourselves and know that this One is indeed the Savior of the world."

43 And after the two days He went forth from there into Galilee. 44 For Jesus Himself testified that a prophet has no honor in his own country. 45 So when He came to Galilee, the Galileans received Him, having seen all the things that He did in Jerusalem at the feast; for they themselves also went to the feast.

46 He came therefore again to Cana of Galilee where He had made the water wine. And there was a certain royal official, whose son was sick at Capernaum. 47 When he heard that Jesus had come out of Judea into Galilee, he went to Him, and was requesting *Him* to come down and heal his son; for he was at the point of death. 48 Jesus therefore said to him, "Unless you *people* see signs and wonders, you *simply* will not believe." 49 The royal official *said to Him, "Sir, come down before my child dies." 50 Jesus *said to him, "Go your way; your son lives." The man believed the word that Jesus spoke to him, and he started off. 51And as he was now going down, *his* slaves met him, saying that his son was living. 52 So he inquired of them the hour when he began to get better. They said therefore to him, "Yesterday at the ªseventh hour the fever left him." 53 So the father knew that *it was* at that hour in which Jesus said to him, "Your son lives;" and he himself believed, and his whole household. 54 This is again a second sign that Jesus performed, when He had come out of Judea into Galilee.

5 After these things there was ᵇa feast of the Jews; and Jesus went up to Jerusalem. 2 Now there is in Jerusalem by the sheep *gate* a pool, which is called in Hebrew Bethesda, having five porticoes. 3 In these lay a multitude of those who were sick, blind, lame, withered. 4 (See footnote ᶜ) 5And a certain man was there, who had been thirty-eight years in his sickness. 6 When Jesus saw him lying there, and knew that he had already been a long time *in that condition*, He *said to him, "Do you wish to get well?" 7 The sick man answered Him, "Sir, I have no man to put me into the pool when the water is stirred up, but while I am coming, another steps down before me." 8 Jesus *said to him, "Arise, take up your pallet, and walk." 9And immediately the man became well, and took up his pallet and *began* to walk.

Now it was the Sabbath on that day. 10 Therefore the Jews were saying to him who was cured, "It is the Sabbath, and it is not permissible for you to carry your pallet." 11 But he answered them, "He who made me well was the one who said to me, 'Take up your pallet

[a] I.e., 1 p.m. [b] Many good mss. read, *the feast*, i.e., the Passover. [c] Many authorities insert, wholly or in part, *waiting for the moving of the waters*; V. 4 *for an angel of the Lord went down at certain seasons into the pool, and stirred up the water: whoever then first after the stirring up of the water stepped in was made well from whatever disease with which he was afflicted.*

WILLIAMS

came to Jesus, they kept on urging Him to stay with them; so He did stay there two days. 41 Then a much larger number believed in Him because of what He said Himself, 42 and they were saying to the woman, "It is not merely because of what you said that we now believe, for we have heard Him ourselves, and we know that He is really the Saviour of the world."

43 After the two days were over, Jesus left there and went on to Galilee, 44 for He Himself declared that a prophet had no honor in his own country. 45 So when He reached Galilee, the Galileans welcomed Him, for they had seen everything that He had done at the feast in Jerusalem, for they too had attended the feast.

46 So He came back to Cana in Galilee where He had turned the water into wine. Now there was at Capernaum an officer of the king's court whose son was sick. 47 When he heard that Jesus had come back from Judea to Galilee, he went to Him and began to beg Him to come down and cure his son, for he was at the point of death. 48 Then Jesus said to him, "Unless you see signs and wonders, you will never believe."

49 The king's officer pleaded with Him, "Sir, come down at once before my child is dead!"

50 Jesus said to him, "You may go; your son is going to live."

The man believed what Jesus said to him and started home. 51 While he was still coming down, his slaves met him and told him, "Your boy is going to live." 52 So he asked them at what hour he began to get better, and they said to him, "Yesterday at one o'clock the fever left him."

53 Then the father knew that that was the very hour when Jesus had said to him, "Your son is going to live." So he and his whole household believed in Jesus. 54 This is the second wonder-work that Jesus performed after He had come back from Judea to Galilee.

5   *A crippled man cured; the Pharisees raise a controversy because He was cured on the sabbath; Jesus announces He is the resurrection life*

After this there was a feast of the Jews, and so Jesus went up to Jerusalem. 2 Now in Jerusalem near the sheep-gate there is a pool called in Hebrew Bethzatha, which has five porticoes, 3 and in these there used to lie a great crowd of sick people, blind, crippled, paralyzed.ᵃ 5 And there was one man there who had been an invalid for thirty-eight years. 6 Jesus saw him lying there, and when He found out that he had been in that condition for a long time, He asked him, "Do you want to get well?"

7 The sick man answered, "Sir, I have no one to put me into the pool when the water is moved, but while I am trying to get down, somebody else steps down ahead of me."

8 Jesus said to him, "Get up, pick up your pallet, and go to walking." 9 And at once the man was well, and picked up his pallet, and went to walking.

Now it was the sabbath. 10 So the Jews began to say to the man who had been cured, "It is the sabbath, and it is against the law for you to carry your pallet."

11 He answered them, "The man who cured me said to me, 'Pick up your pallet and go to walking.' "

[a] V. 4 not in best Mss.

BECK

tans came to Him, they asked Him to stay with them. And He stayed there two days. 41 Then many more believed because of what He said. 42 "We no longer believe on account of what you said," they told the woman. "Now we heard Him ourselves and know He certainly is the Savior of the world."

43 After two days He left and went to Galilee.

An Officer's Son

44 Jesus Himself declared a prophet is not honored in his own country. 45 Now, when He came to Galilee, the people in Galilee welcomed Him. They had seen all He did at the festival in Jerusalem, since they, too, had gone to the festival.

46 Then Jesus went again to Cana in Galilee, where He had changed water to wine.

One of the king's officers lived at Capernaum. Now, his son was sick. 47 When he heard Jesus had come from Judea to Galilee, he went to Him and asked Him to come down and heal his son, who was dying.

48 "If you don't see wonderful proofs and miracles," Jesus told him, "you won't believe."

49 "Lord, come down," the officer asked Him, "before my little boy dies."

50 "Go," Jesus told him, "your boy is well." The man believed what Jesus told him and left.

51 On his way back his slaves met him and told him his boy was well. 52 So he asked them what time he got better. They told him, "Yesterday at seven in the evening the fever left him." 53 Then the father knew it was the same hour when Jesus had told him, "Your boy is well." And he and everybody at his house believed.

54 This was the second miracle Jesus did after He had come from Judea to Galilee.

Sick for 38 Years

5   After this there was a Jewish festival, and Jesus went up to Jerusalem.

2 Near the Sheep Gate in Jerusalem there's a pool that the Jews call Bethesda. It has five porches. 3 In them there used to lie a crowd of people who were sick, blind, lame, and paralyzed.* 5 One man who was there had been sick thirty-eight years. 6 Jesus saw him lying there and found out he had been sick a long time. "Would you like to get well?" He asked him.

7 "Lord," the sick man answered Him, "I don't have anybody to put me into the pool when the water is stirred. And while I'm trying to get there, somebody else steps in ahead of me."

8 "Get up," Jesus told him, "pick up your bed, and walk." 9 Immediately the man got well, picked up his bed, and walked.

10 That day was a Sabbath. "Today is the day of rest," the Jews told the man who had been healed. "It's wrong for you to carry your bed."

11 He answered them, "The One who made me well told me, 'Pick up your bed and walk.' "

* Our oldest manuscripts, including Papyrus 75 and Papyrus 66, do not have vv. 3b-4: "waiting for the water to be stirred. At a certain time the Lord's angel would come down into the pool and stir the water. After the stirring of the water, the first to step in got well, whatever disease he was suffering from."

K.J.V.

Take up thy bed, and walk. 12 Then asked they him, What man is that which said unto thee, Take up thy bed, and walk? 13And he that was healed wist not who it was: for Jesus had conveyed himself away, a multitude being in *that* place. 14Afterward Jesus findeth him in the temple, and said unto him, Behold, thou art made whole: sin no more, lest a worse thing come unto thee. 15 The man departed, and told the Jews that it was Jesus, which had made him whole. 16And therefore did the Jews persecute Jesus, and sought to slay him, because he had done these things on the sabbath day.

17 But Jesus answered them, My Father worketh hitherto, and I work. 18 Therefore the Jews sought the more to kill him, because he not only had broken the sabbath, but said also that God was his Father, making himself equal with God. 19 Then answered Jesus and said unto them, Verily, verily, I say unto you, The Son can do nothing of himself, but what he seeth the Father do: for what things soever he doeth, these also doeth the Son likewise. 20 For the Father loveth the Son, and sheweth him all things that himself doeth: and he will shew him greater works than these, that ye may marvel. 21 For as the Father raiseth up the dead, and quickeneth *them;* even so the Son quickeneth whom he will. 22 For the Father judgeth no man, but hath committed all judgment unto the Son: 23 That all *men* should honour the Son, even as they honour the Father. He that honoureth not the Son honoureth not the Father which hath sent him. 24 Verily, verily, I say unto you, He that heareth my word, and believeth on him that sent me, hath everlasting life, and shall not come into condemnation; but is passed from death unto life. 25 Verily, verily, I say unto you, The hour is coming, and now is, when the dead shall hear the voice of the Son of God: and they that hear shall live. 26 For as the Father hath life in himself; so hath he given to the Son to have life in himself; 27 And hath given him authority to execute judgment also, because he is the Son of man. 28 Marvel not at this: for the hour is coming, in the which all that are in the graves shall hear his voice, 29And shall come forth; they that have done good, unto the resurrection of life; and they that have done evil, unto the resurrection of damnation. 30 I can of mine own self do nothing: as I hear, I judge: and my judgment is just; because I seek not mine own will, but the will of the Father which hath sent me. 31 If I bear witness of myself, my witness is not true.

32 There is another that beareth witness of me; and I know that the witness which he witnesseth of me is true. 33 Ye sent unto John, and he bare witness unto the truth. 34 But I receive not testimony from man: but these things I say, that ye might be saved. 35 He was a burning and a shining light: and ye were willing for a season to rejoice in his light.

36 But I have greater witness than *that* of John: for the works which the Father hath given me to finish, the same works that I do, bear witness of me, that the Father hath sent me. 37And the Father himself, which hath sent me, hath borne witness of me. Ye have neither heard his voice at any time, nor seen his shape. 38And ye have not his word abiding in you: for whom he hath sent, him ye believe not.

N.A.S.

and walk.' " 12 They asked him, "Who is the man who said to you, 'Take up *your* pallet, and walk'?" 13 But he who was healed did not know who it was; for Jesus had slipped away while there was a crowd in *that* place. 14Afterward Jesus *found him in the temple, and said to him, "Behold, you have become well; do not sin any more, so that nothing worse may befall you." 15 The man went away, and told the Jews that it was Jesus who had made him well. 16And for this reason the Jews were persecuting Jesus, because He was doing these things on the Sabbath. 17 But He answered them, "My Father is working until now, and I Myself am working." 18 For this cause therefore the Jews were seeking all the more to kill Him, because He not only was breaking the Sabbath, but also was calling God His own Father, making Himself equal with God.

19 Jesus therefore answered and was saying to them, "Truly, truly, I say to you, the Son can do nothing of Himself, unless *it is* something He sees the Father doing; for whatever *the Father* does, these things the Son also does in like manner. 20 "For the Father loves the Son, and shows Him all things that He himself is doing; and greater works than these will He show Him, that you may marvel. 21 "For just as the Father raises the dead and gives them life, even so the Son also gives life to whom He wishes. 22 "For not even the Father judges any one, but He has given all judgment to the Son, 23 in order that all may honor the Son, even as they honor the Father. He who does not honor the Son does not honor the Father who sent Him. 24 "Truly, truly, I say to you, he who hears My word, and believes Him who sent Me, has eternal life, and does not come into judgment, but has passed out of death into life. 25 "Truly, truly, I say to you, an hour is coming and now is, when the dead shall hear the voice of the Son of God; and those who hear shall live. 26 "For just as the Father has life in Himself, even so He gave to the Son also to have life in Himself; 27 and He gave Him authority to execute judgment, because He is *the* Son of Man. 28 "Do not marvel at this; for an hour is coming, in which all who are in the tombs shall hear His voice, 29 and shall come forth; those who did the good *deeds,* to a resurrection of life, those who committed the evil *deeds* to a resurrection of judgment.

30 "I can do nothing on My own initiative, as I hear, I judge; and My judgment is just; because I do not seek My own will, but the will of Him who sent Me. 31 "If I *alone* bear witness of Myself, My testimony is not true. 32 "There is another who bears witness of Me; and I know that the testimony which He bears of Me is true. 33 "You have sent to John, and he has borne witness to the truth. 34 "But the witness which I receive is not from man; but I say these things, that you may be saved. 35 "He was the lamp that was burning and was shining and you were willing to rejoice for a while in his light. 36 "But the witness which I have is greater than *that* of John; for the works which the Father has given Me to accomplish, the very works that I do, bear witness of Me, that the Father has sent Me. 37 "And the Father who sent Me, He has borne witness of Me. You have neither heard His voice at any time, nor seen His form. 38 "And you do not have His word abiding in you, for you do not believe

WILLIAMS

12 They asked him, "Who is the man that said to you, 'Pick up your pallet and go to walking'?" 13 The man who had been cured did not know who He was, for since there was a crowd at the place, Jesus had slipped away.

14 Afterward Jesus found him in the temple court, and said to him, "See! You are now well. Stop sinning or something worse may befall you." 15 The man went back and told the Jews that it was Jesus who had cured him. 16 This is why the Jews were persecuting Jesus, because He persisted in doing such things on the sabbath.

17 Then He answered them, "My Father is still working, and so am I." 18 It was on account of this that the Jews tried all the harder to put Him to death, because He not only persisted in breaking the sabbath, but also kept on saying that God was His Father, and so was making Himself equal to God.

19 So Jesus answered them:

"I most solemnly say to you, the Son can do nothing by Himself, except as He sees the Father doing it, for whatever the Father is in the habit of doing the Son also persists in doing. 20 For the Father loves the Son and shows Him everything that He Himself is doing, and He will show Him greater deeds than these, so that you will keep on wondering. 21 For just as the Father raises the dead and makes them live on, so the Son too makes alive any whom He chooses to. 22 For the Father passes sentence on no one, but He has committed all judgment to the Son, 23 that all men may honor the Son as they do the Father. Whoever does not honor the Son does not honor the Father who sent Him.

24 "I most solemnly say to you, whoever listens to me and believes Him who has sent me possesses eternal life, and will never come under condemnation, but has already passed out of death into life. 25 I most solemnly say to you, a time is coming—indeed, it is already here—when the dead will listen to the voice of the Son of God, and those who listen to it will live. 26 For just as the Father has life in Himself, so He has granted to the Son to have life in Himself. 27 He has also granted to Him authority to act as Judge,[b] because He is the Son of Man. 28 Stop being surprised at this, for the time is coming when all that are in the graves will listen to His voice, 29 and those who have done good will come out for a resurrection to life, but those who have done evil for a resurrection to condemnation. 30 I cannot do anything by myself. As I get orders, so I judge, and my judgment is a just one, for I am not trying to do my own will but the will of Him who has sent me.

31 "If I bear witness to myself, my testimony is of no force.[c] 32 There is someone else who testifies to me, and I know that the testimony which He gives to me is of force. 33 You yourselves sent to John, and he has testified to the truth. 34 However, I do not accept mere human testimony, but I am saying this that you may be saved. 35 John was the lamp that kept on burning and shining, and you decided for a time to delight yourselves in his light. 36 But I have testimony that is higher[d] than John's, for the works which my Father has committed to me to finish, the very works that I am doing, testify to me that the Father has sent me; 37 yes, the Father who has sent me has testified to me Himself. You have never heard His voice nor seen His form; 38 and you do not keep His message living in you, because you do not believe in the messenger whom He has sent.

[b] Lit., do justice, judgment. [c] Grk., not true. [d] Grk., greater (in quality).

BECK

12 They asked him, "Who is the man that told you, 'Pick it up and walk'?" 13 But the man who had been healed didn't know who He was, because Jesus had disappeared in the crowd that was there.

14 Later Jesus found him in the temple and said to him, "Look, you're well now. Don't sin any more, or something worse may happen to you."

15 The man went back and told the Jews it was Jesus who made him well.

God's Son

16 Because Jesus was doing such things on a Sabbath, the Jews started to persecute Him.

17 But Jesus answered them, "My Father has been working until now, and so I am working."

18 Then the Jews were all the more eager to kill Him, because He wasn't only abolishing the Sabbath but even calling God His own Father, making Himself equal to God.

19 "I tell you the truth," Jesus answered them, "the Son can do nothing by Himself but only what He sees the Father doing. You see, the Son does exactly what the Father does. 20 The Father loves the Son and shows Him everything He is doing. And He will show Him even greater works than these so that you'll be surprised. 21 As the Father wakes up the dead and makes them live, so the Son makes alive whom He wants to make alive.

22 "The Father doesn't judge anyone but has entrusted the judgment entirely to the Son 23 so that all should honor the Son as they honor the Father. Anyone who doesn't honor the Son doesn't honor the Father who sent Him. 24 I tell you the truth: If you listen to what I say and believe Him who sent Me, you have everlasting life, and you will not be judged, but you have come from death to life.

25 "Let me assure you, the hour is coming and is here now when the dead will hear God's Son calling them, and those who hear Him will live. 26 As the Father has life in Himself, so He has given the Son the power of having life in Himself.

27 "He has also given Him power to judge because He is the Son of Man. 28 This should not surprise you, because the hour is coming when all who are in their graves will hear Him calling and will come out. 29 Those who have done good will rise to live; those who have done evil will rise to be condemned. 30 I can do nothing by Myself. I judge only as I'm told to do, and so My judgment is just, because I'm not trying to do what I want but what He wants who sent Me.

31 "If I alone testify about Myself, My testimony isn't dependable.

32 There's Someone else testifying about Me, and I know what He testifies about Me is true. 33 You sent to John, and he testified to the Truth. 34 Not that I get My testimony from a man, but I say this to save you. 35 John was a lighted lamp that shone, and for a while you wanted to enjoy his light.

36 But I have a greater testimony than John had. The works the Father gave Me to finish, these works that I do testify the Father sent Me. 37 The Father who sent Me—He testified about Me. You never heard His voice or saw His form. 38 You don't keep His Word within you because you don't believe Him whom He sent.

K.J.V.

39 Search the Scriptures; for in them ye think ye have eternal life: and they are they which testify of me. 40And ye will not come to me, that ye might have life. 41 I receive not honour from men. 42 But I know you, that ye have not the love of God in you. 43 I am come in my Father's name, and ye receive me not: if another shall come in his own name, him ye will receive. 44 How can ye believe, which receive honour one of another, and seek not the honour that *cometh* from God only? 45 Do not think that I will accuse you to the Father: there is *one* that accuseth you, *even* Moses, in whom ye trust. 46 For had ye believed Moses, ye would have believed me: for he wrote of me. 47 But if ye believe not his writings, how shall ye believe my words?

6 After these things Jesus went over the sea of Galilee, which is *the sea* of Tiberias. 2And a great multitude followed him, because they saw his miracles which he did on them that were diseased. 3And Jesus went up into a mountain, and there he sat with his disciples. 4And the passover, a feast of the Jews, was nigh.

5 When Jesus then lifted up *his* eyes, and saw a great company come unto him, he saith unto Philip, Whence shall we buy bread, that these may eat? 6And this he said to prove him: for he himself knew what he would do. 7 Philip answered him, Two hundred pennyworth of bread is not sufficient for them, that every one of them may take a little. 8 One of his disciples, Andrew, Simon Peter's brother, saith unto him, 9 There is a lad here, which hath five barley loaves, and two small fishes: but what are they among so many? 10And Jesus said, Make the men sit down. Now there was much grass in the place. So the men sat down, in number about five thousand. 11And Jesus took the loaves; and when he had given thanks, he distributed to the disciples, and the disciples to them that were set down; and likewise of the fishes as much as they would. 12 When they were filled, he said unto his disciples, Gather up the fragments that remain, that nothing be lost. 13 Therefore they gathered *them* together, and filled twelve baskets with the fragments of the five barley loaves, which remained over and above unto them that had eaten. 14 Then those men, when they had seen the miracle that Jesus did, said, This is of a truth that Prophet that should come into the world.

15 When Jesus therefore perceived that they would come and take him by force, to make him a king, he departed again into a mountain himself alone. 16And when even was *now* come, his disciples went down unto the sea, 17And entered into a ship, and went over the sea toward Capernaum. And it was now dark, and Jesus was not come to them. 18And the sea arose by reason of a great wind that blew. 19 So when they had

N.A.S.

Him whom He sent. 39 [a] "You search the Scriptures, because you think that in them you have eternal life; and it is these that bear witness of Me; 40 and you are unwilling to come to Me, that you may have life. 41 "I do not receive glory from men; 42 but I know you, that you do not have the love of God in yourselves. 43 "I have come in My Father's name, and you do not receive Me; if another shall come in his own name, you will receive him. 44 "How can you believe, when you receive glory from one another, and you do not seek the glory that is from the *one and* only God? 45 "Do not think that I will accuse you before the Father; the one who accuses you is Moses, in whom you have set your hope. 46 "For if you believed Moses, you would believe Me; for he wrote of Me. 47 "But if you do not believe his writings, how will you believe My words?"

6 After these things Jesus went away to the other side of the sea of Galilee, (or Tiberias). 2And a great multitude was following Him, because they were seeing the signs which He was performing on those who were sick. 3And Jesus went up on the mountain, and there He sat with His disciples. 4 Now the Passover, the feast of the Jews, was at hand. 5 Jesus therefore lifting up His eyes, and seeing that a great multitude was coming to Him, *said to Philip, "Where are we to buy bread, that these may eat?" 6And this He was saying to test him; for He Himself knew what He was intending to do. 7 Philip answered Him, "Two hundred [b]denarii worth of bread is not sufficient for them, for every one to receive a little." 8 One of his disciples, Andrew, Simon Peter's brother, *said to Him, 9 "There is a lad here, who has five barley loaves, and two fish; but what are these for so many people?" 10 Jesus said, "Have the people sit down." Now there was much grass in the place. So the men sat down, in number about five thousand. 11 Jesus therefore took the loaves; and having given thanks, He distributed to those who were seated; likewise also of the fish as much as they wanted. 12And when they were filled, He *said to His disciples, "Gather up the left-over fragments that nothing may be lost." 13And so they gathered them up, and filled twelve baskets with fragments from the five barley loaves, which were left over by those who had eaten. 14 When therefore the people saw the sign which He had performed, they said, "This is of a truth the Prophet who is to come into the world."

15 Jesus therefore perceiving that they were intending to come and take Him by force, to make Him king, withdrew again to the mountain by Himself alone.

16 Now when evening came, His disciples went down to the sea, 17 and after getting into a boat, they *started to* cross the sea to Capernaum. And it had already become dark, and Jesus had not yet come to them. 18And the sea *began* to be stirred up because a strong wind was blowing. 19 When therefore they had

[a] Or, (a command) *Search the Scriptures!* [b] A denarius represented a day's wages for a common laborer.

WILLIAMS

39 "You keep on searching the Scriptures, for you yourselves suppose that you will get possession of eternal life through them; and yet they are witnesses that testify to me, 40 but you refuse to come to me to get possession of life. 41 I do not accept any honor from men, 42 but I am sure that you do not have the love of God in your hearts. 43 I have come in my Father's name, but you refuse to accept me. If anyone else should come in his own name, you would accept him. 44 How can you believe, you who are always accepting honor from one another, but never seek the honor that comes from the one God? 45 Do not be thinking that I am going to accuse you to the Father. You have your accuser; it is Moses on whom you have set your hopes! 46 For if you really believed Moses, you would believe me, for he wrote about me. 47 But if you do not believe what he wrote, how will you ever believe what I say?"

6 *Jesus feeds the five thousand; they try to crown Him king, but He retires to pray; walking on the water of the sea of Galilee; He tells them He is the bread from heaven; many forsake Him; the Twelve stand by Him*

After this Jesus went to the other side of the sea of Galilee, or Tiberias. 2 And a vast crowd continued to follow Him, for they pressed on to view the wonder-works which He performed for the sick people. 3 And so Jesus went up on the hill and was sitting there with His disciples. 4 Now the Passover, the Jewish feast, was approaching. 5 So Jesus looked up and saw that a vast crowd was coming toward Him, and said to Philip, "Where can we buy bread for these people to eat?" 6 He was saying this to test him, for He knew Himself what He was going to do.

7 Philip answered Him, "Forty dollars' worth of bread is not enough to give them all even a scanty meal apiece."

8 Another of His disciples, Andrew, Simon Peter's brother, said to Him, 9 "There is a little boy here who has five barley loaves and a couple of fish, but what are they among so many?"

10 Jesus said, "Make the people sit down." Now there was plenty of grass at the spot; so the men, about five thousand, threw themselves down. 11 Then Jesus took the loaves and gave thanks, and distributed them among the people who were sitting on the ground; so too with the fish as much as they wanted. 12 When they had a plenty, He said to His disciples, "Pick up the pieces that are left, that nothing be wasted." 13 So they picked them up and filled twelve baskets with the pieces that were left from the five barley loaves, which were more than the eaters wanted.

14 When the people, therefore, saw the wonder-works that He performed, they began to say, "This is surely the prophet who was to come into the world." 15 So when Jesus learned that they were going to come and carry Him off by force to crown Him king, He again retired to the hill by Himself.

16 When evening came, His disciples went down to the sea 17 and got into a boat and started across the sea to Capernaum. Now it was already dark, and Jesus had not come to them. 18 The sea was getting rough, because a strong wind was blowing. 19 When they had

BECK

39 You search the Scriptures because you think you have everlasting life in them; and yet they testify about Me! 40 But you don't want to come to Me to have life.

41 "I don't get glory from men. 42 But I know in your hearts you don't love God. 43 I have come in My Father's name, and you don't accept Me. If someone else comes in his own name, you'll accept him. 44 How can you believe while you accept honor from one another but are not eager to have the honor that comes from the only God?

45 "Don't think that I will accuse you before the Father. There is already one who accuses you—Moses, whom you trust. 46 If you really believe Moses, you would believe Me, because he wrote about Me. 47 But if you don't believe what he wrote, how will you believe what I say?"

Jesus Feeds Five Thousand

6 Some time later Jesus crossed over to the other side of the Lake of Galilee, which is the Lake of Tiberias. 2 A large crowd was following Him because they saw the miracles He did on the sick. 3 Jesus went up the hill and sat down there with His disciples. 4 The Jewish festival of the Passover was near.

5 As Jesus looked up, He saw a large crowd coming to Him. He turned to Philip: "Where should we buy bread for these people to eat?" 6 He asked this only to test him, since He knew what He was going to do.

7 "Two hundred denarii,*" Philip answered, "wouldn't buy enough bread for each of them to get just a little."

8 One of His disciples, Andrew, Simon Peter's brother, told Him, 9 "There's a boy here who has five barley loaves and two fish. But what is that among so many?"

10 "Have the people sit down," Jesus said. There was much grass at the place. So they sat down. There were about five thousand men.

11 Then Jesus took the loaves, gave thanks, and distributed them to the people who were sitting down, and in the same way as much of the fish as they wanted.

12 When they had enough, He told His disciples, "Gather the pieces that are left so that nothing will be wasted." 13 They gathered them and filled twelve baskets with pieces of the five barley loaves left by those who had eaten.

14 Seeing the miracle He did, the people said, "This certainly is the Prophet who is coming into the world."

Jesus Walks on Water

15 When Jesus learned that the people meant to come and take Him by force and make Him king, He went back again to the hill by Himself. 16 Meanwhile, as it got late, His disciples went down to the lake, 17 stepped into a boat, and were on their way across the lake to Capernaum. By this time it was dark, and Jesus hadn't come to them yet. 18 A strong wind started to blow and stir up the lake.

19 After they had rowed three or four miles,

* A denarius was a day's pay.

K.J.V.

rowed about five and twenty or thirty furlongs, they see Jesus walking on the sea, and drawing nigh unto the ship: and they were afraid. 20 But he saith unto them, It is I; be not afraid. 21 Then they willingly received him into the ship: and immediately the ship was at the land whither they went.

22 The day following, when the people, which stood on the other side of the sea, saw that there was none other boat there, save that one whereinto his disciples were entered, and that Jesus went not with his disciples into the boat, but *that* his disciples were gone away alone; 23 Howbeit there came other boats from Tiberias nigh unto the place where they did eat bread, after that the Lord had given thanks: 24 When the people therefore saw that Jesus was not there, neither his disciples, they also took shipping, and came to Capernaum, seeking for Jesus. 25 And when they had found him on the other side of the sea, they said unto him, Rabbi, when camest thou hither? 26 Jesus answered them and said, Verily, verily, I say unto you, Ye seek me, not because ye saw the miracles, but because ye did eat of the loaves, and were filled. 27 Labour not for the meat which perisheth, but for that meat which endureth unto everlasting life, which the Son of man shall give unto you: for him hath God the Father sealed. 28 Then said they unto him, What shall we do, that we might work the works of God? 29 Jesus answered and said unto them, This is the work of God, that ye believe on him whom he hath sent. 30 They said therefore unto him, What sign shewest thou then, that we may see, and believe thee? what dost thou work? 31 Our fathers did eat manna in the desert; as it is written, He gave them bread from heaven to eat. 32 Then Jesus said unto them, Verily, verily, I say unto you, Moses gave you not that bread from heaven; but my Father giveth you the true bread from heaven. 33 For the bread of God is he which cometh down from heaven, and giveth life unto the world. 34 Then said they unto him, Lord, evermore give us this bread. 35 And Jesus said unto them, I am the bread of life: he that cometh to me shall never hunger; and he that believeth on me shall never thirst. 36 But I said unto you, That ye also have seen me, and believe not. 37 All that the Father giveth me shall come to me; and him that cometh to me I will in no wise cast out. 38 For I came down from heaven, not to do mine own will, but the will of him that sent me. 39 And this is the Father's will which hath sent me, that of all which he hath given me I should lose nothing, but should raise it up again at the last day. 40 And this is the will of him that sent me, that every one which seeth the Son, and believeth on him, may have everlasting life: and I will raise him up at the last day. 41 The Jews then murmured at him, because he said, I am the bread which came down from heaven. 42 And they said, Is not this Jesus, the son of Joseph, whose father and mother we know? how is it then that he saith, I came down from heaven? 43 Jesus therefore answered and said unto them, Murmur not among yourselves. 44 No man can come to me, except the Father which hath sent me draw him: and I will raise him up at the last day. 45 It is written in the prophets, And they shall be all taught of God. Every man therefore that hath heard, and hath learned of the Father, cometh unto me. 46 Not that any man hath seen

N.A.S.

rowed about three or four miles, they *beheld Jesus walking on the sea, and drawing near to the boat; and they were frightened. 20 But He *said to them, "It is I; do not be afraid." 21 They were willing therefore to receive Him into the boat; and immediately the boat was at the land to which they were going.

22 The next day the multitude that stood on the other side of the sea saw that there was no other small boat there, except one, and that Jesus had not entered with His disciples into the boat, but *that* His disciples had gone away alone. 23 There came other small boats from Tiberias near to the place where they ate the bread after the Lord had given thanks. 24 When the multitude therefore saw that Jesus was not there, nor His disciples, they themselves got into the small boats, and came to Capernaum, seeking Jesus. 25 And when they found Him on the other side of the sea, they said to Him, "Rabbi, when did You get here?" 26 Jesus answered them and said, "Truly, truly, I say to you, you seek Me, not because you saw signs, but because you ate of the loaves, and were filled. 27 "Do not work for the food which perishes, but for the food which endures to eternal life, which the Son of Man shall give to you, for on Him the Father, *even* God, has set His seal." 28 They said therefore to Him, "What shall we do, that we may work the works of God?" 29 Jesus answered and said to them, "This is the work of God, that you believe in Him whom He has sent." 30 They said therefore to Him, "What then do You do for a sign, that we may see, and believe You? What work do You perform? 31 "Our fathers ate the manna in the wilderness; as it is written, 'HE GAVE THEM BREAD OUT OF HEAVEN TO EAT'." 32 Jesus therefore said to them, "Truly, truly, I say to you, it is not Moses who has given you the bread out of heaven, but it is My Father who gives you the true bread out of heaven. 33 "For the bread of God is ᵃthat which comes down out of heaven, and gives life to the world." 34 They said therefore to Him, "Lord, evermore give us this bread." 35 Jesus said to them, "I am the bread of life; he who comes to Me shall not hunger, and he who believes in Me shall never thirst. 36 "But I said to you, that you have seen Me, and yet do not believe. 37 "All that the Father gives Me shall come to Me; and the one who comes to Me I will certainly not cast out. 38 "For I have come down from heaven, not to do My own will, but the will of Him who sent Me. 39 "And this is the will of Him who sent Me, that of all that He has given Me I lose nothing, but raise it up on the last day. 40 "For this is the will of My Father, that every one who beholds the Son, and believes in Him, may have eternal life; and I Myself will raise him up on the last day."

41 The Jews therefore were grumbling about Him, because He said, "I am the bread that came down out of heaven." 42 And they were saying, "Is not this Jesus, the son of Joseph, whose father and mother we know? How does He now say, 'I have come down out of heaven'?" 43 Jesus answered and said to them, "Do not grumble among yourselves. 44 "No one can come to Me, unless the Father who sent Me draws him; and I will raise him up on the last day. 45 "It is written in the prophets, 'AND THEY SHALL ALL BE TAUGHT OF GOD.' Every one who has heard and learned from the Father, comes to Me. 46 "Not that any man has seen

[a] Or, *He who comes.*

WILLIAMS

rowed about three or four miles, they saw Jesus walking on the sea and coming near the boat, and they were terror-stricken. 20 But He said to them, "It is I; stop being afraid!" 21 Then they were willing to take Him on board, and at once the boat came to the shore it was making for.

22 Next day the people who had stayed on the other side of the sea saw that there was only one boat there, and that Jesus had not gotten into it with His disciples, but that His disciples had gone away by themselves. 23 Other boats from Tiberias had landed near the place where the people ate the bread after the Lord had given thanks. 24 So when the crowd saw that neither Jesus nor His disciples were there, they got into boats themselves and went to Capernaum to look for Jesus.

25 So when they had crossed the sea and found Him, they asked Him, "Teacher, when did you get here?"

26 Jesus answered them, "I most solemnly say to you, you are looking for me, not because of the wonder-works you saw, but because you ate the loaves and had plenty. 27 Stop toiling for the food that perishes, but toil for the food that lasts for eternal life, which the Son of Man will give you, for God the Father has given Him authority[a] to do so."

28 Then they asked Him, "What must we do to perform the works that God demands?"

29 Jesus answered them, "The work that God demands of you is this, to believe in the messenger whom He has sent."

30 So they asked Him, "What wonder-work then are you going to perform for us to see and so believe in you? What work are you going to do? 31 Our forefathers in the desert ate the manna, as the Scripture says, 'He gave them out of heaven bread to eat.'"

32 Then Jesus said to them, "I most solemnly say to you, it was not Moses who gave you the real bread out of heaven, but it is my Father who gives you the real bread out of heaven, 33 for the bread that God gives is what comes down out of heaven and gives life to the world."

34 Then they said to Him, "Give us that bread always, sir!"

35 Jesus said to them, "I am the bread that gives life. Whoever comes to me will never get hungry, and whoever believes in me will never get thirsty. 36 But I have told you that, although you have seen me, yet you do not believe in me. 37 All that my Father gives to me will come to me, and I will never, no, never reject anyone who comes to me, 38 because I have come down from heaven, not to do my own will but the will of Him who sent me. 39 Now the will of Him who sent me is this, that I should lose none of all that He has given me, but should raise them to life on the last day. 40 For it is my Father's will that everyone who sees the Son and believes in Him shall have eternal life, and that I shall raise him to life on the last day."

41 Then the Jews began to grumble about His saying, "I am the bread that came down out of heaven." 42 And they said, "Is He not Jesus, Joseph's son, whose father and mother we know? So how can He say, 'I have come down out of heaven'?"

43 Jesus answered them, "Stop grumbling to one another. 44 No one can come to me unless the Father who sent me draws him to me; then I myself will raise him to life on the last day. 45 In the prophets it is written, 'And all men will be taught by God.' Everyone who ever listens to the Father and learns from Him will come to me. 46 Not that anyone has ever seen the Father,

BECK

they saw Jesus walking on the lake and coming near the boat, and they were terrified.

20 "It is I," He told them. "Don't be afraid."

21 They wanted to take Him into the boat. And in a moment the boat came to the shore where they were going.

Bread from Heaven

22 The next day the people were still lingering on the other side of the lake. They had noticed only one boat was there and Jesus had not stepped into that boat with His disciples but they had gone away without Him. 23 Other boats came from Tiberias near the place where they had eaten the bread after the Lord gave thanks. 24 When the people saw that neither Jesus nor His disciples were there, they stepped into these boats and came to Capernaum, looking for Jesus. 25 They found Him on the other side of the lake and asked Him, "Master, when did You get here?"

26 "Surely, I tell you," Jesus answered them, "you're not looking for Me because you've seen miracles but because you've eaten some of the bread and been well fed. 27 Don't work for the food that spoils but for the food that keeps for everlasting life, which the Son of Man will give you because God the Father has sealed in Him the power to give it."

28 "What are the works God wants us to do?" they asked Him.

29 "What God wants you to do," Jesus answered them, "is to believe in Him whom He sent."

30 "What miracle can you do?" they asked Him. "Let us see it, and we'll believe You. What can You do? 31 Our fathers ate the manna in the desert, as it is written: *He gave them bread from heaven to eat.*" [5]

32 "I tell you the truth," Jesus said to them, "Moses didn't give you the bread from heaven, but My Father gives you the real bread from heaven. 33 God's bread is coming down from heaven and giving life to the world."

34 "Lord," they said to Him, "always give us this bread."

35 "I am the Bread of Life," Jesus told them. "Come to Me, and you will never be hungry. Believe in Me, and you will never be thirsty. 36 But I have told you, 'You have seen Me, and you don't believe!' 37 Everything the Father gives Me will come to Me, and anyone who comes to Me I will never turn away, 38 because I came down from heaven, not to do what I want but what He wants who sent Me; 39 and He who sent Me doesn't want Me to lose any of those He gave Me but to raise them on the last day. 40 Yes, My Father wants everyone who sees the Son and believes in Him to have everlasting life, and He wants Me to raise him on the last day."

41 Then the Jews grumbled because He said, "I am the Bread that came down from heaven." 42 "Isn't this Jesus, Joseph's son," they asked, "whose father and mother we know? Then how can He say, 'I came down from heaven'?"

43 "Don't grumble among yourselves," Jesus answered them. 44 "A person can come to Me only if the Father who sent Me draws him. Then I will raise him on the last day. 45 The prophets wrote, *God will teach everyone.*[6] Everyone who listens to the Father and learns from Him comes to Me. 46 Not that anyone has seen the

[a] Grk., *sealed, so certified with authority.*

[5] Ex. 16:4, 15; Ps. 78:24
[6] Is. 54:13

the Father, save he which is of God, he hath seen the Father. 47 Verily, verily, I say unto you, He that believeth on me hath everlasting life. 48 I am that bread of life. 49 Your fathers did eat manna in the wilderness, and are dead. 50 This is the bread which cometh down from heaven, that a man may eat thereof, and not die. 51 I am the living bread which came down from heaven: if any man eat of this bread, he shall live for ever: and the bread that I will give is my flesh, which I will give for the life of the world. 52 The Jews therefore strove among themselves, saying, How can this man give us *his* flesh to eat? 53 Then Jesus said unto them, Verily, verily, I say unto you, Except ye eat the flesh of the Son of man, and drink his blood, ye have no life in you. 54 Whoso eateth my flesh, and drinketh my blood, hath eternal life; and I will raise him up at the last day. 55 For my flesh is meat indeed, and my blood is drink indeed. 56 He that eateth my flesh, and drinketh my blood, dwelleth in me, and I in him. 57As the living Father hath sent me, and I live by the Father; so he that eateth me, even he shall live by me. 58 This is that bread which came down from heaven: not as your fathers did eat manna, and are dead: he that eateth of this bread shall live for ever. 59 These things said he in the synagogue, as he taught in Capernaum. 60 Many therefore of his disciples, when they had heard *this,* said, This is a hard saying; who can hear it? 61 When Jesus knew in himself that his disciples murmured at it, he said unto them, Doth this offend you? 62 *What* and if ye shall see the Son of man ascend up where he was before? 63 It is the Spirit that quickeneth; the flesh profiteth nothing: the words that I speak unto you, *they* are spirit, and *they* are life. 64 But there are some of you that believe not. For Jesus knew from the beginning who they were that believed not, and who should betray him. 65And he said, Therefore said I unto you, that no man can come unto me, except it were given unto him of my Father.

66 From that *time* many of his disciples went back, and walked no more with him. 67 Then said Jesus unto the twelve, Will ye also go away? 68 Then Simon Peter answered him, Lord, to whom shall we go? thou hast the words of eternal life. 69And we believe and are sure that thou art that Christ, the Son of the living God. 70 Jesus answered them, Have not I chosen you twelve, and one of you is a devil? 71 He spake of Judas Iscariot *the son* of Simon: for he it was that should betray him, being one of the twelve.

7 After these things Jesus walked in Galilee: for he would not walk in Jewry, because the Jews sought to kill him. 2 Now the Jews' feast

the Father, except the One who is from God, He has seen the Father. 47 "Truly, truly, I say to you, he who believes has eternal life. 48 "I am the bread of life. 49 "Your fathers ate the manna in the wilderness, and they died. 50 "This is the bread which comes down out of heaven, so that one may eat of it and not die. 51 "I am the living bread that came down out of heaven; if any one eats of this bread, he shall live forever; and the bread also which I shall give for the life of the world is My flesh."

52 The Jews therefore *began* to argue with one another, saying, "How can this man give us *His* flesh to eat?" 53 Jesus therefore said to them, "Truly, truly, I say to you, unless you eat the flesh of the Son of Man and drink His blood, you have no life in yourselves. 54 "He who eats My flesh and drinks My blood has eternal life; and I will raise him up on the last day. 55 "For My flesh is true food, and My blood is true drink. 56 "He who eats My flesh and drinks My blood abides in Me, and I in him. 57 "As the living Father sent Me, and I live because of the Father; so he who eats Me, he also shall live because of Me. 58 "This is the bread which came down out of heaven; not as the fathers ate, and died; he who eats this bread shall live forever." 59 These things He said in the synagogue, as He taught in Capernaum.

60 Many therefore of His disciples, when they heard *this* said, "This is a difficult statement; who can listen to it?" 61 But Jesus, conscious that His disciples grumbled at this, said to them, "Does this cause you to stumble? 62 "*What* then if you should behold the Son of Man ascending where He was before? 63 "It is the Spirit who gives life; the flesh profits nothing; the words that I have spoken to you are spirit and are life. 64 "But there are some of you who do not believe." For Jesus knew from the beginning who they were who did not believe, and who it was that would betray Him. 65And He was saying, "For this reason I have said to you, that no one can come to Me, unless it has been granted him from the Father."

66 As a result of this many of His disciples withdrew, and were not walking with Him any more. 67 Jesus said therefore to the twelve, "You do not want to go away also, do you?" 68 Simon Peter answered Him, "Lord, to whom shall we go? You have words of eternal life. 69 "And we have believed and have come to know that You are the Holy One of God." 70 Jesus answered them, "Did I Myself not choose you, the twelve, and *yet* one of you is a devil?" 71 Now He meant Judas *the son* of Simon Iscariot, for he, one of the twelve, was going to betray Him.

7 And after these things Jesus was walking in Galilee; for He was unwilling to walk in Judea, because the Jews were seeking to kill Him. 2 Now the feast of the Jews, the Feast

WILLIAMS

except Him who is from God; of course, He has seen the Father. 47 I most solemnly say to you, whoever believes in me possesses eternal life. 48 I am the bread that gives life. 49 Your forefathers in the desert ate the manna, and yet they died. 50 But here is the bread that comes down out of heaven, so that anyone may eat it and never die. 51 I am this living bread that has come down out of heaven. If anyone eats this bread, he will live forever, and the bread that I will give for the life of the world is my own flesh."

52 But the Jews kept on wrangling with one another and saying, "How can He give us His flesh to eat?"

53 Then Jesus said to them, "I most solemnly say to you, unless you eat the flesh of the Son of Man and drink His blood, you do not have life in you. 54 Whoever continues to eat my flesh and drink my blood already possesses eternal life, and I will raise him to life on the last day. 55 For my flesh is real food and my blood is real drink. 56 Whoever continues to eat my flesh and drink my blood continues to live[b] in union[c] with me and I in union with him. 57 Just as the living Father has sent me and I live because of the Father, so whoever keeps on eating me will live because of me. 58 This is the bread that has come down out of heaven; not as your forefathers ate the manna, and yet died. Whoever continues to eat this bread will live forever."

59 He said this as He taught in the synagogue at Capernaum.

60 So many of His disciples, when they heard it, said, "This teaching is hard to take in. Who can listen to it?"

61 But as Jesus naturally knew that His disciples were grumbling about this, He said to them, "Is this shocking to you? 62 Suppose you were to see the Son of Man going back where He was before? 63 The Spirit is what gives life; the flesh does not help at all. The truths[d] that I have told you are spirit and life. 64 But there are some of you who do not trust in me." For Jesus knew from the start who they were that did not trust in Him, and who it was that was going to betray Him. 65 So He continued, "This is why I told you that no one can come to me, unless it is granted to him by my Father."

66 As a result of this many of His disciples turned their backs on Him and stopped accompanying Him. 67 So Jesus said to the Twelve, "You too do not want to go back, do you?"

68 Simon Peter answered Him, "To whom can we go, Lord? You have the message that gives eternal life, 69 and we have come to believe, yes more, we know by experience, that you are the Holy One of God."

70 Jesus answered them, "Did I not myself select you as the Twelve? And yet one of you is a devil." 71 He was referring to Judas, Simon Iscariot's son, for he was going to betray Him, although he was one of the Twelve.

7 *Jesus' brothers do not accept Him as the Christ; He claims to have come from God; the people and leaders are startled; at the feast of tents He offers rivers of living water*

After this, Jesus went on moving about in Galilee; He would not do so in Judea, because the Jews were trying to kill Him. 2 Now the [b] Lit., *abide.* [c] Grk., *in me.* [d] Grk., *the things* or *words.*

BECK

Father; 47 only He who comes from God has seen the Father. I tell you the truth, if you believe, you have everlasting life.

48 "I am the Bread of Life. 49 Your fathers ate the manna in the desert, and they died. 50 But this' is the Bread coming down from heaven so that anyone may eat it and not die. 51 I am the living Bread that came down from heaven. If anyone eats this Bread, he will live forever. The bread I'll give to bring life to the world is My flesh."

52 Then the Jews argued with one another: "How can He give us His flesh to eat?"

53 "I tell you the truth," Jesus answered them, "unless you eat the flesh of the Son of Man and drink His blood, you don't have any life in you. 54 If you eat My flesh and drink My blood, you have everlasting life, and I will raise you on the last day. 55 My flesh is a real food, and my blood is a real drink. 56 If you eat My flesh and drink My blood, you stay in Me and I in you. 57 As the living Father sent Me and I live because of the Father, so if you eat Me, you will live because of Me. 58 This is the Bread that came down from heaven. It isn't like the bread the fathers ate. They died. Eat this Bread, and you will live forever."

59 He said this while He was teaching in a synagog in Capernaum. 60 When they heard it, many of His disciples said, "This is hard to take. Who can listen to Him?"

61 Inwardly aware that His disciples were complaining about this, Jesus asked them, "Does this upset you? 62 What if you see the Son of Man go up where He was before? 63 The Spirit makes alive; the flesh doesn't help. The words I spoke to you are Spirit, and they are life. But some of you don't believe." 64 Jesus knew from the beginning who wouldn't believe and who would betray Him. 65 So He added, "That is why I told you a person can come to Me only if the Father gives him the power."

66 As a result many of His disciples went back to their old life and wouldn't go with Him anymore. 67 Then Jesus asked the twelve, "Do you want to leave Me too?"

68 "Lord, to whom should we go?" Simon Peter answered Him. "You have words of everlasting life. 69 And we have come to believe and know You are God's Holy One."

70 "Didn't I choose the twelve of you," Jesus asked, "and one of you is a devil?" 71 He meant Judas, the son of Simon, the man from Kerioth. He was going to betray Him—one of the twelve.

To Jerusalem

7 Later Jesus went around in Galilee. He didn't want to travel in Judea because the Jews were trying to kill Him.

2 The Jewish festival of Booths was near.

K.J.V.

of tabernacles was at hand. 3 His brethren therefore said unto him, Depart hence, and go into Judea, that thy disciples also may see the works that thou doest. 4 For *there is* no man *that* doeth any thing in secret, and he himself seeketh to be known openly. If thou do these things, shew thyself to the world. 5 For neither did his brethren believe in him. 6 Then Jesus said unto them, My time is not yet come: but your time is always ready. 7 The world cannot hate you; but me it hateth, because I testify of it, that the works thereof are evil. 8 Go ye up unto this feast: I go not up yet unto this feast; for my time is not yet full come. 9 When he had said these words unto them, he abode *still* in Galilee.

10 But when his brethren were gone up, then went he also up unto the feast, not openly, but as it were in secret. 11 Then the Jews sought him at the feast, and said, Where is he? 12 And there was much murmuring among the people concerning him: for some said, He is a good man: others said, Nay; but he deceiveth the people. 13 Howbeit no man spake openly of him for fear of the Jews.

14 Now about the midst of the feast Jesus went up into the temple, and taught. 15 And the Jews marvelled, saying, How knoweth this man letters, having never learned? 16 Jesus answered them, and said, My doctrine is not mine, but his that sent me. 17 If any man will do his will, he shall know of the doctrine, whether it be of God, or *whether* I speak of myself. 18 He that speaketh of himself seeketh his own glory: but he that seeketh his glory that sent him, the same is true, and no unrighteousness is in him. 19 Did not Moses give you the law, and *yet* none of you keepeth the law? Why go ye about to kill me? 20 The people answered and said, Thou hast a devil: who goeth about to kill thee? 21 Jesus answered and said unto them, I have done one work, and ye all marvel. 22 Moses therefore gave unto you circumcision; (not because it is of Moses, but of the fathers;) and ye on the sabbath day circumcise a man. 23 If a man on the sabbath day receive circumcision, that the law of Moses should not be broken; are ye angry at me, because I have made a man every whit whole on the sabbath day? 24 Judge not according to the appearance, but judge righteous judgment. 25 Then said some of them of Jerusalem, Is not this he, whom they seek to kill? 26 But, lo, he speaketh boldly, and they say nothing unto him. Do the rulers know indeed that this is the very Christ? 27 Howbeit we know this man whence he is: but when Christ cometh, no man knoweth whence he is. 28 Then cried Jesus in the temple as he taught, saying, Ye both know me, and ye know whence I am: and I am not come of myself, but he that sent me is true, whom ye know not. 29 But I know him; for I am from him, and he hath sent me. 30 Then they sought to take him: but no man laid hands on him, because his hour was not yet come. 31 And many of the people believed on him, and said, When Christ cometh, will he do more miracles than these which this *man* hath done?

N.A.S.

of Tabernacles, was at hand. 3 His brothers therefore said to Him, "Depart from here, and go into Judea, that Your disciples also may behold Your works which You are doing. 4 "For no one does anything in secret, when he himself seeks to be *known* publicly. If You do these things, show Yourself to the world." 5 For not even His brothers were believing in Him. 6 Jesus therefore *said to them, "My time is not yet at hand; but your time is always opportune. 7 "The world cannot hate you; but it hates Me, because I testify of it, that its deeds are evil. 8 "Go up to the feast yourselves; I do not go up to this feast; because My time has not yet fully come." 9 And having said these things to them, He stayed in Galilee.

10 But when His brothers had gone up to the feast, then He Himself also went up, not publicly, but as it were, in secret. 11 The Jews therefore were seeking Him at the feast, and were saying, "Where is He?" 12 And there was much grumbling among the multitudes concerning Him; some were saying, "He is a good man"; others were saying, "No, on the contrary, He leads the multitude astray." 13 Yet no one was speaking openly of Him for fear of the Jews.

14 But when it was now the midst of the feast Jesus went up into the temple, and *began to* teach. 15 The Jews therefore were marveling, saying, "How has this man become learned, having never been educated?" 16 Jesus therefore answered them, and said, "My teaching is not Mine, but His who sent Me. 17 "If any man is willing to do His will, he shall know of the teaching, whether it is of God, or *whether* I speak from Myself. 18 "He who speaks from himself seeks his own glory; but He who is seeking the glory of the one who sent Him, He is true, and there is no unrighteousness in Him. 19 "Did not Moses give you the law, and *yet* none of you carries out the law? Why do you seek to kill Me?" 20 The multitude answered, "You have a demon! Who seeks to kill You?" 21 Jesus answered and said to them, "I did one deed, and you all marvel. 22 "On this account Moses has given you circumcision (not because it is from Moses, but from the fathers); and on *the* Sabbath you circumcise a man. 23 "If a man receives circumcision on *the* Sabbath that the Law of Moses may not be broken, are you angry with Me because I made an entire man well on *the* Sabbath? 24 "Do not judge according to appearance, but judge with righteous judgment."

25 Therefore some of the people of Jerusalem were saying, "Is this not the man whom they are seeking to kill? 26 "And look, He is speaking publicly, and they are saying nothing to Him. The rulers do not really know that this is the Christ, do they? 27 "However we know where this man is from; but whenever the Christ may come, no one knows where He is from." 28 Jesus therefore cried out in the temple, teaching and saying, "You both know Me, and know where I am from; and I have not come of Myself, but He who sent Me is true, whom you do not know. 29 "I know Him; because I am from Him, and He sent Me." 30 They were seeking therefore to seize Him; and no man laid his hand on Him, because His hour had not yet come. 31 But many of the multitude believed in Him; and they were saying, "When the Christ shall come, He will not perform more signs than those which this man

WILLIAMS

Jewish feast of Dwelling in Tents was approaching. 3 So His brothers said to Him, "You must leave here and go to Judea, to let your disciples also see the works that you are doing; 4 for no one does anything in secret when he is trying to be known to the public. If you are going to do this, show yourself publicly to the world." 5 For even His brothers did not believe in Him.

6 Then Jesus said to them, "It is not yet time for me to do so, but any time is suitable for you. 7 It is impossible for the world to hate you; it is I whom it hates, because I continue to testify that its works are wicked. 8 Go up to the feast yourselves; I am not going up to it yet, for it is not quite time for me to go." 9 He told them this and stayed on in Galilee.

10 But after His brothers had gone up to the feast, then He went up too, not publicly but, as it were, privately. 11 Now the Jews at the feast were looking for Him and kept asking, "Where is He?" 12And there was a great deal of grumbling about Him among the crowds, some saying that He was a good man, and others that He was not, but was misleading the masses. 13And yet, for fear of the Jews, nobody dared to speak in public about Him.

14 Now when the feast was already half over, Jesus went up to the temple and began to teach. 15 The Jews were dumfounded and said, "How can this uneducated man know the Scriptures?" 16 Jesus answered them, "My teaching is not my own, but it comes from Him who sent me. 17 If anyone is willing to keep on doing God's will, he will know whether my teaching comes from God, or merely expresses my own ideas. 18 Whoever utters merely his own ideas is seeking his own honor, but whoever seeks the honor of him who sent him is sincere, and there is no dishonesty[a] in him. 19 Did not Moses give you the law? And yet not one of you is keeping that law. If so, why are you trying to kill me?"

20 The crowd answered, "You are certainly under the power of a demon! Who is trying to kill you?"

21 Jesus answered them, "I have done just one deed, and yet you are all dumfounded! 22 Then Moses gave you the rite of circumcision —not that it had its origin with Moses but with your earlier forefathers—and you circumcise a male child even on the sabbath. 23 Well, if a male child undergoes circumcision on the sabbath, to keep the law of Moses from being broken, are you angry with me for making a man perfectly well on the sabbath? 24 Stop judging superficially,[b] you must judge fairly."

25 Then some of the people of Jerusalem said, "Is not this the man they are trying to kill? 26 Just look! He is talking in public, and yet they do not say a word to Him! It cannot be that the authorities have really learned that He is the Christ, can it? 27 But we know where this man is from; when the Christ comes, however, no one will know where He is from."

28 So Jesus, as He was teaching in the temple, cried out, "Yes, you do know me and you do know where I come from, and I have not come on my own authority, but the One who has sent me exists as the Real One, whom you do not know. 29 I know Him myself, because I have come from Him, and He has sent me."

30 Then they kept on trying to arrest Him, and yet no one laid a hand on Him, for the time had not yet come. 31 But many of the crowd believed in Him, and said, "When the Christ comes, He will not perform greater wonder-works than He did, will He?"

[a] Grk., no unrighteousness. [b] Grk., by external appearances.

BECK

3 So His brothers told Jesus, "Leave this place, go to Judea, and there let Your disciples see the works You're doing. 4 Nobody goes on doing things secretly when he wants to be known publicly. If You do these things, let the world see You." 5 Not even His brothers believed in Him.

6 "It isn't the right time for Me yet," Jesus told them, "but any time is right for you. 7 The world can't hate you, but it hates Me because I tell the truth about it that it is doing wrong. 8 You go up to the festival. I'm not going up to this festival right now, because it isn't the right time for Me yet."

9 After telling them this, He did stay in Galilee.

10 But after His brothers had gone up to the festival, He went up too, not publicly but without being seen.

At the Festival of Booths

11 So the Jews were looking for Jesus in the crowd at the festival. "Where is He?" they kept asking. 12And there was much whispering about Him in the crowds. "He's a good man," some said; but others, "No, He deceives the people." 13 Yet nobody would talk about Him in public because everybody was afraid of the Jews.

14 But when the festival was already half over, Jesus went up to the temple and started to teach. 15 The Jews were surprised. "How can He know so much," they asked, "when He hasn't been in the schools?"

16 "What I teach doesn't come from Me," Jesus answered them, "but from Him who sent Me. 17 If anyone wants to do His will, he'll know whether My teaching is from God or I speak My own thoughts. 18 Anyone who speaks his own thoughts tries to glorify himself. But He who wants to glorify the One who sent Him tells the truth, and there's nothing wrong in Him. 19 Didn't Moses give you the Law? Yet none of you does what the Law tells you. Why do you want to kill Me?"

20 "There's a devil in You," the crowd answered. "Who wants to kill You?"

21 "I did one thing," Jesus answered them, "and you're all surprised about it. 22 Moses gave you circumcision (not that it came from Moses but from our ancestors), and you circumcise a person on a Sabbath. 23 If a child is circumcised on a day of rest to keep the Law of Moses, do you feel bitter toward Me because I made all of a man well on a Sabbath? 24 Don't judge by what you see, but be fair when you judge."

25 Then some of the men from Jerusalem said, "Isn't He the man they want to kill? 26 But here He speaks in public, and they don't say a thing to Him! Surely the rulers haven't found out He's the promised Savior, have they? 27 Now, we know where this One comes from. But when the promised Savior comes, nobody knows where He's from."

28 "You know Me," Jesus called aloud as He was teaching in the temple, "and you know where I come from. I didn't by Myself decide to come, but there's One who is real who sent me. You don't know Him. 29 but I know Him because I come from Him and He sent Me."

30 Then they tried to arrest Him, but nobody laid a hand on Him, because the right time hadn't come yet for Him.

31 But many in the crowd believed in Him. "When the promised Savior comes," they asked, "will He do more miracles than this One has done?"

273

K.J.V.

32 The Pharisees heard that the people murmured such things concerning him; and the Pharisees and the chief priests sent officers to take him. 33 Then said Jesus unto them, Yet a little while am I with you, and *then* I go unto him that sent me. 34 Ye shall seek me, and shall not find *me:* and where I am, *thither* ye cannot come. 35 Then said the Jews among themselves, Whither will he go, that we shall not find him? will he go unto the dispersed among the Gentiles, and teach the Gentiles? 36 What *manner of* saying is this that he said, Ye shall seek me, and shall not find *me:* and where I am, *thither* ye cannot come? 37 In the last day, that great *day* of the feast, Jesus stood and cried, saying, If any man thirst, let him come unto me, and drink. 38 He that believeth on me, as the Scripture hath said, out of his belly shall flow rivers of living water. 39 (But this spake he of the Spirit, which they that believe on him should receive: for the Holy Ghost was not yet *given;* because that Jesus was not yet glorified.)

40 Many of the people therefore, when they heard this saying, said, Of a truth this is the Prophet. 41 Others said, This is the Christ. But some said, Shall Christ come out of Galilee? 42 Hath not the Scripture said, That Christ cometh of the seed of David, and out of the town of Bethlehem, where David was? 43 So there was a division among the people because of him. 44 And some of them would have taken him; but no man laid hands on him.

45 Then came the officers to the chief priests and Pharisees; and they said unto them, Why have ye not brought him? 46 The officers answered, Never man spake like this man. 47 Then answered them the Pharisees, Are ye also deceived? 48 Have any of the rulers or of the Pharisees believed on him? 49 But this people who knoweth not the law are cursed. 50 Nicodemus saith unto them, (he that came to Jesus by night, being one of them,) 51 Doth our law judge *any* man, before it hear him, and know what he doeth? 52 They answered and said unto him, Art thou also of Galilee? Search, and look: for out of Galilee ariseth no prophet.

53 And every man went unto his own house.

8 Jesus went unto the mount of Olives. 2 And early in the morning he came again into the temple, and all the people came unto him; and he sat down, and taught them. 3 And the scribes and Pharisees brought unto him a woman taken in adultery; and when they had set her in the midst, 4 They say unto him, Master, this woman was taken in adultery, in the very act. 5 Now Moses in the law commanded us, that such should be stoned: but what sayest thou? 6 This they said, tempting him, that they might have to accuse him. But Jesus stooped down, and with *his* finger wrote on the ground, *as though he*

N.A.S.

has, will He?" 32 The Pharisees heard the multitude muttering these things about Him; and the chief priests and the Pharisees sent officers to seize Him. 33 Jesus therefore said, "For a little while longer I am with you, then I go to Him who sent Me. 34 "You shall seek Me, and shall not find Me; and where I am, you cannot come." 35 The Jews therefore said to one another, "Where does this man intend to go that we shall not find Him? He is not intending to go to the Dispersion among the Greeks, and teach the Greeks, is He? 36 "What is this statement that He said, 'You will seek Me, and will not find Me; and where I am, you cannot come'?"

37 Now on the last day, the great *day* of the feast, Jesus stood and cried out, saying, "If any man is thirsty, let him come to Me and drink. 38 "He who believes in Me, as the Scripture said, 'From his innermost being shall flow rivers of living water.'" 39 But this He spoke of the Spirit, whom those who believed in Him were to receive; for the Spirit was not yet *given,* because Jesus was not yet glorified. 40 *Some* of the multitude therefore, when they heard these words, were saying, "This certainly is the Prophet." 41 Others were saying, "This is the Christ." Still others were saying, "Surely the Christ is not going to come from Galilee, is He? 42 "Has not the Scripture said that THE CHRIST COMES FROM THE OFFSPRING OF DAVID, AND FROM BETHLEHEM, the village where David was?" 43 So there arose a division in the multitude because of Him. 44 And some of them wanted to seize Him, but no one laid hands on Him.

45 The officers therefore came to the chief priests and Pharisees, and they said to them, "Why did you not bring Him?" 46 The officers answered, "Never did a man speak the way this man speaks." 47 The Pharisees therefore answered them, "You have not also been led astray, have you? 48 "No one of the rulers or Pharisees has believed in Him, has he? 49 "But this multitude which does not know the Law is accursed." 50 Nicodemus *said to them (he who came to Him before, being one of them), 51 "Our Law does not judge a man, unless it first hears from him and knows what he is doing, does it?" 52 They answered and said to him, "You are not also from Galilee, are you? Search, and see that no prophet arises out of Galilee." 53 a[And everyone went to his home;

8 But Jesus went to the Mount of Olives. 2 And early in the morning He came again into the temple, and all the people were coming to Him; and He sat down and *began* to teach them. 3 And the scribes and the Pharisees *brought a woman caught in adultery, and having set her in the midst, 4 they *said to Him, "Teacher, this woman has been caught in adultery, in the very act. 5 "Now in the law Moses commanded us to stone such women; what then do You say?" 6 And they were saying this, testing Him, in order that they might have grounds for accusing Him. But Jesus stooped down, and with His finger wrote on the ground.

[a] Most of the ancient authorities omit John 7:53-8:11. Those which contain it vary much from each other.

WILLIAMS

32 The Pharisees heard the people whispering this about Him, and so the high priests and Pharisees sent some officers to arrest Him. 33 Then Jesus said to them, "Just a little while longer I am to be with you, and then I am going back to Him who has sent me. 34 You will then look for me, but you will not find me, and you cannot come where I am going."

35 The Jews then said to one another, "Where is He about to go that we shall not find Him? He is not going to our people scattered among the Greeks, and going to teach the Greeks, is He? 36 What does He mean by saying, 'You will look for me and will not find me, and you cannot come where I am going'?"

37 On the last day, the great day, of the feast, Jesus stood and cried aloud, "If anyone is thirsty, let him come to me and drink. 38 Whoever continues to believe in me will have, as the Scripture says, rivers of living water continuously flowing from within him." 39 By this He referred to the Spirit that those believing in Him were going to receive—for the Spirit had not yet come, because Jesus had not yet been glorified.

40 So some of the people, when they heard this, said, "This is surely the prophet."

41 Others said, "This is the Christ." But still others said, "The Christ does not come from Galilee, does He? 42 Do not the Scriptures say that the Christ is to spring[c] from David and to come from the village of Bethlehem where David lived?"

43 So the people were divided because of Him, 44 and some of them wanted to arrest Him, but no one ventured to lay a hand upon Him.

45 So the officers went back to the high priests and Pharisees. The latter asked the officers, "Why have you not brought Him?"

46 The officers answered, "No man ever talked as He does!"

47 Then the Pharisees answered, "You are not swept off your feet[d] too, are you? 48 None of the authorities or of the Pharisees have believed in Him, have they? 49 But this mob, which knows nothing about the law, is bound to be accursed!"

50 One of them, Nicodemus, who had formerly gone to Jesus, said to them, 51 "Our law does not condemn a man before it hears what he has to say and finds out what he is doing, does it?"

52 Then they answered him, "You are not from Galilee, too, are you? Search the record and see that no prophet has ever come from Galilee." [e]

BECK

32 The Pharisees heard the people muttering such things about Him. So the ruling priests as well as the Pharisees sent their men to arrest Him.

33 "I'll be with you just a little longer," said Jesus; "then I go to Him who sent Me. 34 You'll be looking for Me and won't find Me; and where I am, you can't come."

35 The Jews asked one another, "Where's He intending to go, saying we won't find Him? He doesn't intend to go to our people scattered among the non-Jews and teach the non-Jews, does He? 36 What does He mean by saying, 'You'll be looking for Me and won't find Me,' and, 'Where I am, you can't come'?"

37 On the last day, the great day of the festival, as Jesus was standing there, He called out loud, "If you're thirsty, come to Me and drink. 38 If You believe in Me, streams of living water will flow from you, as the Bible has said." 39 By this He meant the Spirit whom those who believed in Him were to receive. The Spirit hadn't come yet, because Jesus hadn't been glorified yet.

40 After they heard Him say this, some of the people said, "This is certainly the Prophet." 41 Others said, "This is the promised Savior." Still others asked, "What! Does the promised Savior come from Galilee? 42 Doesn't the Bible say, 'The promised Savior *will come from the descendants of David* and *from* the little town of *Bethlehem*,[7] where David lived'?" 43 So the people were divided over Him. 44 Some of them wanted to arrest Him, but nobody laid hands on Him.

45 When the men who had been sent went back to the ruling priests and Pharisees, these asked them, "Why didn't you bring Him?"

46 "Nobody ever spoke like this Man," the men answered.

47 "You haven't been deceived too, have you?" the Pharisees asked them. 48 "No ruler or Pharisee has believed in Him, has he? 49 But this crowd, which doesn't know the Bible, is cursed."

50 One of them, Nicodemus, who had once come to Jesus, asked them, 51 "Does our Law condemn anyone without first hearing what he has to say and finding out what he's doing?"

52 "Are you from Galilee too?" they asked him. "Search and see; the Prophet doesn't come from Galilee."

8 *The Father testifies to Jesus as Son; Jesus tells the Jews He is soon to go away; that they are not God's children but are slaves of sin; they accuse Him of being under the power of a demon*

The Adulteress*

8 Then everyone went home. But Jesus went to the Mount of Olives. 2 Early in the morning He came back into the temple. All the people came to Him, and He sat down and taught them.

3 The Bible scholars and the Pharisees brought to Him a woman who had been caught in adultery and had her stand in the middle. 4 "Teacher," they told Him, "this woman was caught in the act of adultery. 5 In the Law, Moses ordered us to stone such women. Now, what do You say?" 6 They asked this to test Him. They wanted to find something to accuse Him of.

Jesus bent down and with His finger wrote

* Our best manuscripts, including the two oldest papyri (P[06] and P[75], dated about A. D. 200), omit this story. It is most likely a true story in the life of Jesus but not a part of the Gospel that John wrote.
[7] 2 Sam. 7:12; Micah 5:2

[c] Grk., *is from David's seed*. [d] Lit., *deceived*.
[e] V. 53 not in best Mss.

K.J.V.

heard them not. 7 So when they continued asking him, he lifted up himself, and said unto them, He that is without sin among you, let him first cast a stone at her. 8And again he stooped down, and wrote on the ground. 9And they which heard *it*, being convicted by *their own* conscience, went out one by one, beginning at the eldest, *even* unto the last: and Jesus was left alone, and the woman standing in the midst. 10 When Jesus had lifted up himself, and saw none but the woman, he said unto her, Woman, where are those thine accusers? hath no man condemned thee? 11 She said, No man, Lord. And Jesus said unto her, Neither do I condemn thee: go, and sin no more.

12 Then spake Jesus again unto them, saying, I am the light of the world: he that followeth me shall not walk in darkness, but shall have the light of life. 13 The Pharisees therefore said unto him, Thou bearest record of thyself; thy record is not true. 14 Jesus answered and said unto them, Though I bear record of myself, *yet* my record is true: for I know whence I came, and whither I go; but ye cannot tell whence I come, and whither I go. 15 Ye judge after the flesh; I judge no man. 16And yet if I judge, my judgment is true: for I am not alone, but I and the Father that sent me. 17 It is also written in your law, that the testimony of two men is true. 18 I am one that bear witness of myself, and the Father that sent me beareth witness of me. 19 Then said they unto him, Where is thy Father? Jesus answered, Ye neither know me, nor my Father: if ye had known me, ye should have known my Father also. 20 These words spake Jesus in the treasury, as he taught in the temple: and no man laid hands on him; for his hour was not yet come. 21 Then said Jesus again unto them, I go my way, and ye shall seek me, and shall die in your sins: whither I go, ye cannot come. 22 Then said the Jews, Will he kill himself? because he saith, Whither I go, ye cannot come. 23 And he said unto them, Ye are from beneath; I am from above: ye are of this world; I am not of this world. 24 I said therefore unto you, that ye shall die in your sins: for if ye believe not that I am *he,* ye shall die in your sins. 25 Then said they unto him, Who art thou? And Jesus saith unto them, Even *the same* that I said unto you from the beginning. 26 I have many things to say and to judge of you: but he that sent me is true; and I speak to the world those things which I have heard of him. 27 They understood not that he spake to them of the Father. 28 Then said Jesus unto them, When ye have lifted up the Son of man, then shall ye know that I am *he,* and *that* I do nothing of myself; but as my Father hath taught me, I speak these things. 29And he that sent me is with me: the Father hath not left me alone; for

N.A.S.

7 But when they persisted in asking Him, He straightened up, and said to them, "He who is without sin among you, let him *be the* first to throw a stone at her." 8And again He stooped down, and wrote on the ground. 9And when they heard it, they *began* to go out one by one, beginning with the older ones, and He was left alone, and the woman, *where she had been,* in the midst. 10And straightening up, Jesus said to her, "Woman, where are they? Did no one condemn you?" 11And she said, "No one, Lord." And Jesus said, "Neither do I condemn you; go your way; from now on sin no more."]

12 Again therefore Jesus spoke to them, saying, "I am the light of the world; he who follows Me shall not walk in the darkness, but shall have the light of life." 13 The Pharisees therefore said to Him, "You are bearing witness of Yourself; Your witness is not true." 14 Jesus answered and said to them, "Even if I bear witness of Myself, My witness is true; for I know where I came from, and where I am going; but you do not know where I come from, or where I am going. 15 "You people judge according to the flesh; I am not judging any one. 16 "But even if I do judge, My judgment is true; for I am not alone *in it,* but I and ªHe who sent Me. 17 "Even in your law it has been written, that the testimony of two men is true. 18 "I am He who bears witness of Myself, and the Father who sent Me bears witness of Me." 19And so they were saying to Him, "Where is Your Father?" Jesus answered, "You know neither Me, nor My Father; if you knew Me, you would know My Father also." 20 These words He spoke in the treasury, as He taught in the temple; and no one seized Him, because His hour had not yet come.

21 He said therefore again to them, "I go away, and you shall seek Me, and shall die in your sin; where I am going, you cannot come." 22 Therefore the Jews were saying, "Surely He will not kill Himself, will He, since He says, 'Where I am going, you cannot come'?" 23And He was saying to them, "You are from below, I am from above; you are of this world; I am not of this world. 24 "I said therefore to you, that you shall die in your sins; for unless you believe that I am *He,* you shall die in your sins." 25And so they were saying to Him, "Who are You?" Jesus said to them, "What have I been saying to you *from* the beginning? 26 "I have many things to speak and to judge concerning you, but He who sent Me is true; and the things which I heard from Him, these I speak to the world." 27 They did not realize that He had been speaking to them about the Father. 28 Jesus therefore said, "When you lift up the Son of Man, then you will know that I am *He,* and I do nothing on My own initiative, but I speak these things as the Father taught Me. 29 "And He who sent Me is with Me; He has not left Me alone, for I always do the

[a] Many ancient mss. read, *the Father who sent Me.*

WILLIAMS

BECK

on the ground. 7 But when they kept on asking Him, He got up. "Anyone that's without sin among you," He said, "should be the first to throw a stone at her." 8 Then He bent down again and wrote on the ground.

9 Convicted by their conscience as they heard Him, they went out one by one, beginning with the older men, till all had gone and Jesus was left alone with the woman in the middle of the place. 10 Jesus got up. "Woman, where are they?" He asked her. "Didn't anyone condemn you?"

"No one, Lord," she said.

11 "I don't condemn you either," Jesus said. "Go, from now on don't sin anymore."

Jesus Argues with the Jews

12 Jesus spoke to them again, "I am the Light of the World. Follow Me, and you will never wander in the dark but will have the Light of Life."

13 "You testify about Yourself," the Pharisees said to Him. "We can't depend on Your testimony."

14 "Even if I testify about Myself," Jesus answered them, "you can depend on My testimony, because I know where I came from and where I'm going; but you don't know where I came from or where I'm going. 15 You judge in a human way, a way in which I don't judge anybody. 16 But whenever I judge, you can depend on My judgment because I am not alone, but I'm with the Father who sent Me. 17 In your own Law it is written the testimony of two men is valid. 18 I testify about Myself, and the Father who sent Me testifies about Me."

19 "Where is Your Father?" they asked Him.

"You don't know Me or My Father," Jesus answered. "If you knew Me, you would know My Father."

20 He said this in the room of the treasury while He was teaching in the temple; nobody arrested Him, because the right time hadn't come yet for Him.

21 "I'm going away," He said to them again, "and you'll be looking for Me, but you will die in your sin. Where I'm going, you can't come."

22 "Is He going to kill Himself?" the Jews asked. "Is that what He means when He says, 'Where I'm going, you can't come'?"

23 "You're from below," He told them. "I'm from above. Your home is in this world. My home is not in this world. 24 That's why I told you, 'You will die in your sins'; if you don't believe I'm the One, you will die in your sins."

25 "Who are You?" they asked Him.

"What should I tell you first?" Jesus asked them. 26 "I have much to say about you and to condemn. But I tell the world only what I heard from Him who sent Me, and He tells the truth." 27 They didn't understand He was talking to them about the Father.

28 So Jesus told them, "When you have lifted up the Son of Man, you will know I am the One and I do nothing by Myself, but I speak as My Father taught me. 29 And He who sent Me is with Me and has not left Me alone, because I always do what pleases Him."

12 * Then Jesus again addressed them and said, "I am the light of the world. Whoever continues to follow me need never walk in darkness, but he will enjoy[b] the light that means life."

13 The Pharisees then said to Him, "You are testifying to yourself; your testimony is not true."

14 Jesus answered them, "Even if I do testify to myself, my testimony is true, because I know where I have come from and where I am going. But you do not know where I come from or where I am going. 15 You are judging in accordance with external standards, but I judge nobody. 16 Even if I should judge, my decision is fair, because I am not alone, but there are two of us, I and the Father who has sent me. 17 Even in your own law it is written, 'The testimony of two persons is true.' 18 I do testify to myself, and the Father who has sent me testifies to me."

19 Then they began to say to Him, "Where is your Father?"

Jesus answered, "You do not know either me or my Father. If you knew me, you would know my Father too."

20 He said these things in the treasury as He was teaching in the temple, and yet no one ventured to arrest Him, because the time had not yet come for Him.

21 Then Jesus again said to them, "I am going away, and you will look for me, but you will die under the curse of your sins; for where I am going you can never come."

22 Then the Jews began to say, "He is not going to kill Himself, is He? Is that why He said, 'Where I am going you can never come'?"

23 He continued, "You are from below; I am from above. You belong to this present world; I do not belong to this present world. 24 So I have told you that you would die under the curse of your sins, for unless you believe that I am the Christ, you will die under the curse of your sins."

25 Then they asked Him, "Who are you anyway?"

Jesus answered them, "Why do I even talk to you at all? 26 I have much to say about you and much to condemn in you; but He who sent me is truthful, and I am telling the world only what I have learned from Him." 27 They did not understand that He was speaking to them about the Father. 28 So Jesus said to them, "When you lift the Son of Man [on the cross], you will know that I am the Christ, and that I do nothing on my own authority, but that I say exactly what my Father has instructed me to say. 29 Yes, He who sent me is ever with me; I am not alone, because I always practice what

[a] Vv. 1-11 not in best Mss. [b] Lit., have.

K.J.V.

I do always those things that please him. 30As he spake these words, many believed on him. 31 Then said Jesus to those Jews which believed on him, If ye continue in my word, *then* are ye my disciples indeed; 32And ye shall know the truth, and the truth shall make you free.

33 They answered him, We be Abraham's seed, and were never in bondage to any man: how sayest thou, Ye shall be made free? 34 Jesus answered them, Verily, verily, I say unto you, Whosoever committeth sin is the servant of sin. 35And the servant abideth not in the house for ever: *but* the Son abideth ever. 36 If the Son therefore shall make you free, ye shall be free indeed. 37 I know that ye are Abraham's seed; but ye seek to kill me, because my word hath no place in you. 38 I speak that which I have seen with my Father: and ye do that which ye have seen with your father. 39 They answered and said unto him, Abraham is our father. Jesus saith unto them, If ye were Abraham's children, ye would do the works of Abraham. 40 But now ye seek to kill me, a man that hath told you the truth, which I have heard of God: this did not Abraham. 41 Ye do the deeds of your father. Then said they to him, We be not born of fornication; we have one Father, *even* God. 42 Jesus said unto them, If God were your Father, ye would love me: for I proceeded forth and came from God; neither came I of myself, but he sent me. 43 Why do ye not understand my speech? *even* because ye cannot hear my word. 44 Ye are of *your* father the devil, and the lusts of your father ye will do: he was a murderer from the beginning, and abode not in the truth, because there is no truth in him. When he speaketh a lie, he speaketh of his own: for he is a liar, and the father of it. 45And because I tell *you* the truth, ye believe me not. 46 Which of you convicteth me of sin? And if I say the truth, why do ye not believe me? 47 He that is of God heareth God's words: ye therefore hear *them* not, because ye are not of God. 48 Then answered the Jews, and said unto him, Say we not well that thou art a Samaritan, and hast a devil? 49 Jesus answered, I have not a devil; but I honour my Father, and ye do dishonour me. 50And I seek not mine own glory: there is one that seeketh and judgeth. 51 Verily, verily, I say unto you, If a man keep my saying, he shall never see death. 52 Then said the Jews unto him, Now we know that thou hast a devil. Abraham is dead, and the prophets; and thou sayest, If a man keep my saying, he shall never taste of death. 53Art thou greater than our father Abraham, which is dead? and the prophets are dead: whom makest thou thyself? 54 Jesus answered, If I honour myself, my honour is nothing: it is my Father that

N.A.S.

things that are pleasing to Him." 30As He spoke these things, many came to believe in Him.

31 Jesus therefore was saying to those Jews who had believed Him, "If you abide in My word, *then* you are truly disciples of Mine; 32 and you shall know the truth, and the truth shall make you free." 33 They answered Him, "We are Abraham's offspring, and have never yet been enslaved to any one; how is it that You say, 'You shall become free'?" 34 Jesus answered them, "Truly, truly, I say to you, every one who commits sin is the slave of sin. 35 "And the slave does not remain in the house forever; the son does remain forever. 36 "If therefore the Son shall make you free, you shall be free indeed. 37 "I know that you are Abraham's offspring; yet you seek to kill Me, because My word has no place in you. 38 "I speak the things which I have seen with *My* Father; therefore you also do the things which you heard from *your* father." 39 They answered and said to Him, "Abraham is our father." Jesus *said to them, "If you are Abraham's children, do the deeds of Abraham. 40 "But as it is, you are seeking to kill Me, a man who has told you the truth, which I heard from God; this Abraham did not do. 41 "You are doing the deeds of your father." They said to Him, "We were not born of fornication; we have one Father, *even* God." 42 Jesus said to them, "If God were your Father, you would love Me; for I proceeded forth and have come from God, for I have not even come on My own initiative, but He sent Me. 43 "Why do you not understand what I am saying? *It is* because you cannot hear My word. 44 "You are of *your* father the devil, and you want to do the desires of your father. He was a murderer from the beginning, and does not stand in the truth, because there is no truth in him. Whenever he speaks a lie, he speaks from his own *nature;* for he is a liar, and the father of lies. 45 "But because I speak the truth, you do not believe Me. 46 "Which one of you convicts Me of sin? If I speak truth, why do you not believe Me? 47 "He who is of God hears the words of God; for this reason you do not hear *them*, because you are not of God."

48 The Jews answered and said to Him, "Do we not say rightly that You are a Samaritan and have a demon?" 49 Jesus answered, "I do not have a demon; but I honor My Father, and you dishonor Me. 50 "But I do not seek My glory; there is One who seeks and judges. 51 "Truly, truly, I say to you, if anyone keeps My word he shall never see death." 52 The Jews said to Him, "Now we know that You have a demon. Abraham died, and the prophets *also;* and You say, 'If anyone keeps My word, he shall never taste of death.' 53 "Surely You are not greater than our father Abraham, who died? The prophets died too; whom do You make Yourself out *to be?*" 54 Jesus answered, "If I glorify Myself, My glory is nothing; it is

WILLIAMS

pleases Him." 30 Even while He was saying this, many believed in Him.

31 So Jesus said to the Jews who believed in Him, "If you live[e] in accordance with what I teach, you are really my disciples, 32 and you will know the truth and the truth will set you free."

33 They answered Him, "We are Abraham's descendants and we never have been anybody's slaves. How can you say to us, 'You will be set free'?"

34 Jesus answered them, "I most solemnly say to you, everyone who lives in sin is a slave of sin. 35 Now a slave does not live permanently in a household, but a son does. 36 So if the Son sets you free, you will be really free. 37 I know that you are Abraham's descendants, and yet you are trying to kill me, because there is no room[d] in you for my teaching. 38 I am telling you what I have seen in my Father's presence, and you are practicing what you have learned from your[e] father."

39 They answered Him, "Our father is Abraham."

Jesus said to them, "If you are Abraham's children, you must be practicing what Abraham did. 40 But right now you are trying to kill me, a man who has told you the truth that He has learned from God. Abraham never did that. 41 You are practicing what your real father does."

They said to Him, "We are not illegitimate children; we have one Father, even God."

42 Then Jesus said to them, "If God were your Father, you would love me, for I came from God and now am here. No, indeed, I have not come on my own authority, but He has sent me. 43 Why is it that you misunderstand what I say? It is because you cannot listen to what I teach. 44 You sprang from the devil, your real father, and you want to practice your father's wishes. He was a murderer from the very start, and he does not stand by the truth, because there is no truth in him. When he tells a lie, he speaks out of his own nature, because he is a liar and the father of lies. 45 But because I tell you the truth, you do not believe me. 46 Who of you can prove me guilty of sin? But if I do tell you the truth, why do you not believe me? 47 Whoever is sprung from God listens to what God says. This is why you do not listen to me: you are not sprung from God."

48 Then the Jews answered Him, "Are we not right in saying that you are a Samaritan and are under the power of a demon?"

49 Jesus answered: "I am not under the power of a demon; on the other hand, I am honoring my Father, but you are dishonoring me. 50 However, I am not seeking honor for myself; there is One who is seeking it for me, and He is judge. 51 I most solemnly say to you, if anyone follows[f] my teaching, he will never experience death."

52 Then the Jews said to Him, "Now we know that you are under the power of a demon. Abraham is dead; the prophets too, and yet you say, 'If anyone follows my teaching, he will never experience death.' 53 You are not greater than our forefather Abraham, are you? He is dead and the prophets are dead. Who do you claim to be?"

54 Jesus answered, "If I glorify myself, such glory amounts to nothing. It is the Father who

BECK

30 As He was saying this, many believed in Him. 31 Then Jesus said to those Jews who believed in Him, "If you live in My Word, you are really My disciples, 32 and you will know the truth, and the truth will free you."

33 "We are Abraham's descendants," they answered Him, "and have never been anybody's slaves. How can You say, 'You'll be freed'?"

34 "I tell you the truth," Jesus answered them, "everyone who lives in sin is a slave to sin. 35 A slave doesn't stay in the home forever. A son stays forever. 36 If, then, the Son frees you, you will really be free. 37 I know you're Abraham's descendants. But you want to kill Me because My Word is not working in you. 38 I'm telling what I've seen, being with My Father, and you do what you've heard from your father."

39 "Abraham is our father," they answered Him.

"If you were Abraham's children," Jesus told them, "you would do what Abraham did. 40 But now you want to kill Me, a Man who told you the truth, which I heard from God. Abraham didn't do that. 41 You're doing what your father does."

"We weren't born outside of marriage," they said. "God alone is our Father."

42 "If God were your Father," Jesus told them, "you would love Me because I came from God, and as such I am here. I did not by Myself decide to come, but He sent Me. 43 Why don't you understand what I say? Because you can't listen to what I tell you. 44 Your father is the devil, and you want to do what your father wants. From the beginning he has been murdering people and hasn't stood in the truth, because there's no truth in him. When he tells a lie, he's telling it from his heart, because he's a liar and the father of lies. 45 Now, because I tell the truth, you don't believe Me. 46 Which of you can prove Me guilty of a sin? If I tell the truth, why don't you believe Me? 47 A child of God listens to what God says. You don't listen to Him because you're not God's children."

48 "Aren't we right," the Jews answered Him, "when we say You're a Samaritan and there's a devil in You?"

49 "There's no devil in Me," Jesus answered. "No, I honor My Father, but you dishonor Me. 50 I'm not trying to get glory for Myself. There's One who wants Me to have it, and He's the Judge. 51 Let me assure you: If you keep My Word, you will never see death."

52 "Now we know there's a devil in You," the Jews told Him. "Abraham died, and so did the prophets, but You say, 'If you keep My Word, you will never taste death.' 53 Are You greater than our father Abraham? He died, and the prophets died. Who do You think You are?"

54 "If I glorify Myself," Jesus said, "My glory is nothing. It is My Father who glorifies

---

[c] Lit., *abide in my word.* [d] Lit., *my word has no place in you.* [e] Om. by WH and best Mss., but implied. [f] Grk., *keeps.*

K.J.V.

honoureth me; of whom ye say, that he is your God: 55 Yet ye have not known him; but I know him: and if I should say, I know him not, I shall be a liar like unto you: but I know him, and keep his saying. 56 Your father Abraham rejoiced to see my day: and he saw *it,* and was glad. 57 Then said the Jews unto him, Thou art not yet fifty years old, and hast thou seen Abraham? 58 Jesus said unto them, Verily, verily, I say unto you, Before Abraham was, I am. 59 Then took they up stones to cast at him: but Jesus hid himself, and went out of the temple, going through the midst of them, and so passed by.

9 And as *Jesus* passed by, he saw a man which was blind from *his* birth. 2 And his disciples asked him, saying, Master, who did sin, this man, or his parents, that he was born blind? 3 Jesus answered, Neither hath this man sinned, nor his parents: but that the works of God should be made manifest in him. 4 I must work the works of him that sent me, while it is day: the night cometh, when no man can work. 5 As long as I am in the world, I am the light of the world. 6 When he had thus spoken, he spat on the ground, and made clay of the spittle, and he anointed the eyes of the blind man with the clay, 7 And said unto him, Go, wash in the pool of Siloam, (which is by interpretation, Sent.) He went his way therefore, and washed, and came seeing.

8 The neighbours therefore, and they which before had seen him that he was blind, said, Is not this he that sat and begged? 9 Some said, This is he: others *said,* He is like him: *but* he said, I am *he.* 10 Therefore said they unto him, How were thine eyes opened? 11 He answered and said, A man that is called Jesus made clay, and anointed mine eyes, and said unto me, Go to the pool of Siloam, and wash: and I went and washed, and I received sight. 12 Then said they unto him, Where is he? He said, I know not.

13 They brought to the Pharisees him that aforetime was blind. 14 And it was the sabbath day when Jesus made the clay, and opened his eyes. 15 Then again the Pharisees also asked him how he had received his sight. He said unto them, He put clay upon mine eyes, and I washed, and do see. 16 Therefore said some of the Pharisees, This man is not of God, because he keepeth not the sabbath day. Others said, How can a man that is a sinner do such miracles? And there was a division among them. 17 They say unto the blind man again, What sayest thou of him, that he hath opened thine eyes?

N.A.S.

My Father who glorifies Me, of whom you say, 'He is our God;' 55 and you have not come to know Him, but I know Him; and if I say that I do not know Him, I shall be a liar like you; but I do know Him, and keep His word. 56 "Your father Abraham rejoiced to see My day; and he saw *it,* and was glad." 57 The Jews therefore said to Him, "You are not yet fifty years old, and have You seen Abraham?" 58 Jesus said to them, "Truly, truly, I say to you, before Abraham was born, I AM." 59 Therefore they picked up stones to throw at Him; but Jesus hid Himself, and went out of the temple.

9 And as He passed by, He saw a man blind from birth. 2 And His disciples asked Him, saying, "Rabbi, who sinned, this man, or his parents, that he should be born blind?" 3 Jesus answered, "*It was* neither *that* this man sinned, nor his parents; but *it was* in order that the works of God might be displayed in him. 4 "We must work the works of Him who sent Me, as long as it is day; night is coming, when no man can work. 5 "While I am in the world, I am the light of the world." 6 When He had said this, He spat on the ground, and made clay of the spittle, and applied the clay to his eyes, 7 and said to him, "Go, wash in the pool of Siloam" (which is translated, Sent). And so he went away and washed, and came *back* seeing. 8 The neighbors therefore, and those who previously saw him as a beggar, were saying, "Is not this the one who used to sit and beg?" 9 Others were saying, "This is he," *still* others were saying, "No, but he is like him." He kept saying, "I am the one." 10 Therefore they were saying to him, "How then were your eyes opened?" 11 He answered, "The man who is called Jesus made clay, and anointed my eyes, and said to me, 'Go to Siloam, and wash'; so I went away and washed, and I received sight." 12 And they said to him, "Where is He?" He *said, "I do not know."

13 They *brought to the Pharisees him who was formerly blind. 14 Now it was a Sabbath on the day when Jesus made the clay, and opened his eyes. 15 Again therefore the Pharisees also were asking him how he received his sight. And he said to them, "He applied clay to my eyes, and I washed, and I see." 16 Therefore some of the Pharisees were saying, "This man is not from God, because he does not keep the Sabbath." But others were saying, "How can a man who is a sinner perform such signs?" And there was a division among them. 17 They *said therefore to the blind man again, "What do you say about Him, since He opened your

WILLIAMS

glorifies me; and you claim that He is your God. 55And yet you have not learned to know Him: but I know Him, and if I say I do not know Him, I will be a liar like you. On the other hand, I do know Him and I do follow His teaching. 56 Your forefather Abraham exulted in the hope of seeing my day. He has seen it and is glad of it."

57 The Jews then said to Him, "You are not yet fifty years old, and have you seen Abraham?" *g*

58 Then Jesus said to them, "I most solemnly say to you, I existed before Abraham was born." 59At this the Jews took up stones to stone Him, but Jesus made His way out of the temple unperceived.

9 *A man born blind is made to see; because it occurred on the sabbath, the Pharisees put the man out of the synagogue; Jesus leads the man to believe in Him, but condemns the Pharisees for being blind*

As He passed along, He saw a man who had been blind from his birth. 2 So His disciples asked Him, "Teacher, for whose sin was this man born blind, his own or that of his parents?"

3 Jesus answered, "It was neither for his own sin nor for that of his parents, but to show what God could do*a* in his case. 4 We must continue to do the works of Him who sent me while it is daylight. Night is coming when no one can do any work. 5 While I am in the world, I am the light of the world."

6 On saying this He spit on the ground and made clay with the saliva, and put it on the man's eyes, 7 and said, "Go and wash them in the pool of Siloam" (which means One who has been sent). So he went and washed them and went home seeing.

8 Now his neighbors and those who saw that he was formerly blind, kept saying, "Is not this the man who used to sit and beg?"

9 Some said, "Yes, it is he." Others said, "No, but it surely does look like him."

He himself said, "I am the man."

10 So they kept on asking him, "How in the world did you come to see?"

11 He answered, "The man called Jesus made some clay and rubbed it on my eyes, and said to me, 'Go to Siloam and wash them.' So when I had gone and washed them I could see."

12 Then they asked him, "Where is He?"

He answered, "I do not know."

13 They took the man who had been blind to the Pharisees. 14 Now it was on the sabbath when Jesus had made the clay and caused the man's eyes to see. 15 So the Pharisees again asked him how he had come to see. He answered them: "He put some clay on my eyes, and I washed them, and so now I can see."

16 Then some of the Pharisees said, "This man does not come from God, for He does not keep the sabbath."

Others said, "How can a sinful man perform such wonder-works?" So there was a difference of opinion among them.

17 Then again they asked the blind man, "What do you say about Him yourself, since He has made your eyes to see?"

BECK

Me, He of whom you say, 'He's our God.' 55 You don't know Him, but I know Him. And if I would say I don't know Him, I'd be a liar like you. But I do know Him, and I obey His word. 56 Your father Abraham was delighted to know of My day; he saw it and was glad."

57 "You're not fifty years old yet," the Jews said to Him, "and Abraham has seen You?"

58 "I tell you the truth," Jesus told them, "I was before Abraham."

59 Then they picked up stones to throw at Him. But Jesus hid Himself and left the temple.

A Blind Man Sees

9 As Jesus was passing by, He saw a man who had been blind from his birth. 2 "Master," His disciples asked Him, "why was he born blind? Did he sin or his parents?"

3 "Neither he nor his parents," Jesus answered. "He is blind to show what God can do with him. 4 We must do the works of Him who sent Me while it is day. The night is coming when nobody can work. 5As long as I'm in the world, I'm the Light of the world."

6 After He said this, He spit on the ground and with the spit made some mud and put the mud on the man's eyes. 7 "Go," He told him, "wash in the pool of Siloam" (the name means "sent"). He went and washed. And as he walked away, he could see.

8 Now, his neighbors and others who used to see him as a beggar asked, "Isn't this the man who used to sit and beg?"

9 "It is he," some said. Others said, "No, but he looks like him." But he himself said, "I'm the one."

10 Then they asked him, "How did you get your sight?"

11 "The man they call Jesus made some mud," he answered, "and put it on my eyes and told me, 'Go to Siloam and wash.' So I went and washed, and then I could see."

12 "Where is He?" they asked him.

"I don't know," he answered.

13 They brought him who had been blind to the Pharisees. 14 Now, it was a Sabbath when Jesus made the mud and gave him his sight. 15 So the Pharisees also asked him how he got his sight.

"He put mud on my eyes," the man told them, "and I washed them, and now I can see."

16 "This Man is not from God," said some of the Pharisees, "because He doesn't rest on a Sabbath." Others asked, "How can a sinful man do such miracles?" So they disagreed.

17 Then they asked the blind man again, "What do you say about Him, since He gave you your sight?"

---

[g] Some Mss. read, *Has A. seen you?* [a] Lit., *that the works of God might be shown.*

K.J.V.

He said, He is a prophet. 18 But the Jews did not believe concerning him, that he had been blind, and received his sight, until they called the parents of him that had received his sight. 19And they asked them, saying, Is this your son, who ye say was born blind? how then doth he now see? 20 His parents answered them and said, We know that this is our son, and that he was born blind: 21 But by what means he now seeth, we know not; or who hath opened his eyes, we know not: he is of age; ask him: he shall speak for himself. 22 These *words* spake his parents, because they feared the Jews: for the Jews had agreed already, that if any man did confess that he was Christ, he should be put out of the synagogue. 23 Therefore said his parents, He is of age; ask him. 24 Then again called they the man that was blind, and said unto him, Give God the praise: we know that this man is a sinner. 25 He answered and said, Whether he be a sinner *or no,* I know not: one thing I know, that, whereas I was blind, now I see. 26 Then said they to him again, What did he to thee? how opened he thine eyes? 27 He answered them, I have told you already, and ye did not hear: wherefore would ye hear *it* again? will ye also be his disciples? 28 Then they reviled him, and said, Thou art his disciple; but we are Moses' disciples. 29 We know that God spake unto Moses: *as for* this *fellow,* we know not from whence he is. 30 The man answered and said unto them, Why herein is a marvellous thing, that ye know not from whence he is, and *yet* he hath opened mine eyes. 31 Now we know that God heareth not sinners: but if any man be a worshipper of God, and doeth his will, him he heareth. 32 Since the world began was it not heard that any man opened the eyes of one that was born blind. 33 If this man were not of God, he could do nothing. 34 They answered and said unto him, Thou wast altogether born in sins, and dost thou teach us? And they cast him out. 35 Jesus heard that they had cast him out; and when he had found him, he said unto him, Dost thou believe on the Son of God? 36 He answered and said, Who is he, Lord, that I might believe on him? 37 And Jesus said unto him, Thou hast both seen him, and it is he that talketh with thee. 38And he said, Lord, I believe. And he worshipped him.

39 And Jesus said, For judgment I am come into this world, that they which see not might see; and that they which see might be made blind. 40And *some* of the Pharisees which were with him heard these words, and said unto him, Are ye blind also? 41 Jesus said unto them, If ye were blind, ye should have no sin: but now ye say, We see; therefore your sin remaineth.

N.A.S.

eyes?" And he said, "He is a prophet." 18 The Jews therefore did not believe *it* of him, that he had been blind, and had received sight, until they called the parents of the very one who had received his sight, 19 and questioned them, saying, "Is this your son, whom you say was born blind? Then how does he now see?" 20 His parents answered then, and said, "We know that this is our son, and that he was born blind; 21 but how he now sees, we do not know; or who opened his eyes, we do not know. Ask him; he is of age, he shall speak for himself." 22 His parents said this because they were afraid of the Jews; for the Jews had already agreed, that if any one should confess Him to be Christ, he should be put out of the synagogue. 23 For this reason his parents said, "He is of age; ask him."

24 So a second time they called the man who had been blind, and said to him, "Give glory to God; we know that this man is a sinner." 25 He therefore answered, "Whether He is a sinner, I do not know; one thing I do know, that, whereas I was blind, now I see." 26 They said therefore to him, "What did He do to you? How did He open your eyes?" 27 He answered them, "I told you already, and you did not listen; why do you want to hear *it* again? You do not want to become His disciples too, do you?" 28And they reviled him, and said, "You are His disciple; but we are disciples of Moses. 29 "We know that God has spoken to Moses; but as for this man, we do not know where He is from." 30 The man answered and said to them, "Well, here is an amazing thing, that you do not know where He is from, and *yet* He opened my eyes. 31 "We know that God does not hear sinners; but if any one is God-fearing, and does His will, He hears him. 32 "Since the beginning of time it has never been heard that any one opened the eyes of a person born blind. 33 "If this man were not from God, He could do nothing." 34 They answered and said to him, "You were born entirely in sins, and are you teaching us?" And they put him out.

35 Jesus heard that they had put him out; and finding him, He said, "Do you believe in the Son of Man?" 36 He answered and said, "And who is He, Lord, that I may believe in Him?" 37 Jesus said to him, "You have both seen Him, and He is the one who is talking with you." 38And he said, "Lord, I believe." And he worshiped Him. 39And Jesus said, "For judgment I came into this world, that those who do not see may see; and that those who see may become blind." 40 Those of the Pharisees who were with Him heard these things, and said to Him, "We are not blind too, are we?" 41 Jesus said to them, "If you were blind, you would have no sin; but now you say, 'We see;' your sin remains.

WILLIAMS

He answered, "He is a prophet."

18 But the Jews did not believe that he had really been blind and that he had come to see again, until they called the parents of the man who saw again, 19 and asked them, "Is this your son, and do you affirm that he was born blind? If so, how is it then that he now can see?"

20 His parents answered, "We know that this is our son, and that he was born blind. 21 But we do not know how it is that he now can see, or who it was that made his eyes to see. Ask him; he is of age; he can speak for himself." 22 His parents said this, because they were afraid of the Jews, for the Jews had already agreed that if anyone owned Jesus as the Christ, he should be shut out of the synagogues. 23 This is why his parents said, "He is of age, ask him."

24 So a second time they called the man who had been blind, and said to him, "Give God the praise; we know this man is a sinner."

25 Then he answered, "I do not know whether He is a sinner. I do know one thing, that once I was blind but now I can see."

26 Again they said to him, "What did He do to you? How did He make your eyes to see again?"

27 He answered them, "I have already told you and you would not listen to me. Why do you want to hear it again? You do not want to become His disciples, do you?"

28 Then they jeered him, and said, "You are a disciple of His yourself, but we are disciples of Moses. 29 We do know that God spoke to Moses, but we do not know where this fellow comes from."

30 The man answered them, "Well, there is something strange about this! You do not know where He comes from! And yet He has made my eyes to see! 31 We know that God does not listen to sinful men; but He does listen to anyone who worships God and lives to do His will.*b* 32 It has never been heard of in this world that anyone ever made the eyes of a man who was born blind to see. 33 If this man had not come from God, He could not have done anything like this."

34 Then they retorted, "You were born in total depravity, and yet you are trying to teach us!" And so they turned *c* him out of the synagogue.

35 Jesus heard that they had turned the man out of the synagogue; so He found him and said to him, "Do you believe in the Son of Man yourself?"

36 He answered, "Who is He, sir? Tell me, so that I may believe in Him."

37 Jesus answered him, "You have seen Him; you are talking to Him right now!"

38 So he said, "Lord, I believe!" Then he worshiped Him.

39 Then Jesus said, "I have come into this world to judge people, so that those who do not may see, and those who do see may become blind."

40 Some of the Pharisees who were with Him heard this, and asked Him, "We are not blind, are we?"

41 Jesus answered them, "If you were blind, you would not be guilty; but now you keep on claiming, 'We can see'; so your sin remains."

BECK

"He's a prophet," he answered.

18 The Jews didn't believe the man had been blind and got his sight till they called the parents of the man who could see now. 19 "Is this your son who you say was born blind?" they asked them. "How does it happen he can see now?"

20 "We know he's our son," his parents answered, "and was born blind. 21 But we don't know how it is he can see now or who gave him his sight. Ask him; he's of age. He'll tell you about himself." 22 His parents said this because they were afraid of the Jews. The Jews had already agreed to put out of the synagog anyone who confessed Jesus was the promised Savior. 23 That is why his parents said, "He's of age; ask him."

24 So once again they called the man who had been blind. "Give glory to God," they told him. "We know this Man is a sinner."

25 "I don't know if He's a sinner," he answered. "I know only one thing—I used to be blind, and now I can see."

26 "What did He do to you?" they asked him. "How did He give you your sight?"

27 "I've already told you," he answered them, "and you heard it. Why do you want to hear it again? You don't want to be His disciples too, do you?"

28 "You're His disciple," they answered him scornfully, "but we're Moses' disciples. 29 We know God spoke to Moses, but this Fellow—we don't know where He's from."

30 "Well, that's strange!" the man answered them. "You don't know where He's from, and yet He gave me my sight. 31 We know that God doesn't hear sinners but hears anyone who worships God and does what He wants. 32 Nobody has ever heard of anyone giving sight to a man born blind. 33 If this One were not from God, He couldn't do anything."

34 "You were altogether born in sins," they answered him, "and are you trying to teach us?" Then they put him out of the synagog.

35 Jesus heard they had put him out. Finding him, He asked him, "Do you believe in the Son of Man?"

36 "Who is He, sir?" he asked. "I want to believe in Him."

37 "You've seen Him," Jesus told him. "It is He who is now talking to you."

38 "I do believe, Lord," he said and bowed down to worship Him.

39 Then Jesus said, "I've come into this world to judge men, so that those who don't see may see and those who see may turn blind."

40 Some Pharisees who were near Him heard this. "We aren't blind, are we?" they asked Him.

41 "If you were blind," Jesus told them, "you wouldn't be sinning. But now you say, 'We see,' and you go on sinning."

---

[b] Lit., *Keeps on doing His will.* [c] Lit., *threw him out.*

K.J.V.

10 Verily, verily, I say unto you, He that entereth not by the door into the sheepfold, but climbeth up some other way, the same is a thief and a robber. 2 But he that entereth in by the door is the shepherd of the sheep. 3 To him the porter openeth; and the sheep hear his voice: and he calleth his own sheep by name, and leadeth them out. 4And when he putteth forth his own sheep, he goeth before them, and the sheep follow him: for they know his voice. 5And a stranger will they not follow, but will flee from him; for they know not the voice of strangers. 6 This parable spake Jesus unto them; but they understood not what things they were which he spake unto them. 7 Then said Jesus unto them again, Verily, verily, I say unto you, I am the door of the sheep. 8All that ever came before me are thieves and robbers: but the sheep did not hear them. 9 I am the door: by me if any man enter in, he shall be saved, and shall go in and out, and find pasture. 10 The thief cometh not, but for to steal, and to kill, and to destroy: I am come that they might have life, and that they might have *it* more abundantly. 11 I am the good shepherd: the good shepherd giveth his life for the sheep. 12 But he that is a hireling, and not the shepherd, whose own the sheep are not, seeth the wolf coming, and leaveth the sheep, and fleeth; and the wolf catcheth them, and scattereth the sheep. 13 The hireling fleeth, because he is a hireling, and careth not for the sheep. 14 I am the good shepherd, and know my *sheep,* and am known of mine. 15As the Father knoweth me, even so know I the Father: and I lay down my life for the sheep. 16And other sheep I have, which are not of this fold: them also I must bring, and they shall hear my voice; and there shall be one fold, *and* one shepherd. 17 Therefore doth my Father love me, because I lay down my life, that I might take it again. 18 No man taketh it from me, but I lay it down of myself. I have power to lay it down, and I have power to take it again. This commandment have I received of my Father.

19 There was a division therefore again among the Jews for these sayings. 20And many of them said, He hath a devil, and is mad; why hear ye him? 21 Others said, These are not the words of him that hath a devil. Can a devil open the eyes of the blind?

22 And it was at Jerusalem the feast of the dedication, and it was winter. 23And Jesus walked in the temple in Solomon's porch. 24 Then came the Jews round about him, and said unto him, How long dost thou make us to doubt? If thou be the Christ, tell us plainly. 25 Jesus answered them, I told you, and ye believed not: the works that I do in my Father's name, they bear witness of me. 26 But ye believe not, because ye are not of my sheep, as I said unto you. 27 My sheep hear my voice, and I know them, and they follow me: 28And I give unto

N.A.S.

10 "Truly, truly, I say to you, He who does not enter by the door into the fold of the sheep, but climbs up some other way, he is a thief and a robber. 2 "But he who enters by the door is a shepherd of the sheep. 3 "To him the doorkeeper opens; and the sheep hear his voice; and he calls his own sheep by name, and leads them out. 4 "When he puts forth all his own, he goes before them, and the sheep follow him; because they know his voice. 5 "And a stranger they simply will not follow, but will flee from him, because they do not know the voice of strangers." 6 This figure of speech Jesus spoke to them, but they did not understand what those things were which He had been saying to them.

7 Jesus therefore said to them again, "Truly, truly, I say to you, I am the door of the sheep. 8 "All who came before Me are thieves and robbers; but the sheep did not hear them. 9 "I am the door; if anyone enters through Me, he shall be saved, and shall go in and out, and find pasture. 10 "The thief comes only to steal, and kill, and destroy; I came that they might have life, and might have *it* abundantly. 11 "I am the good shepherd; the good shepherd lays down His life for the sheep. 12 "He who is a hireling, and not a shepherd, who is not the owner of the sheep, beholds the wolf coming, and leaves the sheep, and flees, and the wolf snatches them, and scatters *them.* 13 *"He flees* because he is a hireling, and is not concerned about the sheep. 14 "I am the good shepherd; and I know My own, and My own know Me, 15 even as the Father knows Me and I know the Father; and I lay down My life for the sheep. 16 "And I have other sheep, which are not of this fold; I must bring them also, and they shall hear My voice; and they shall become one flock *with* one Shepherd. 17 "For this reason the Father loves Me, because I lay down My life that I may take it again. 18 "No one [a]has taken it away from Me, but I lay it down on My own initiative. I have authority to lay it down, and I have authority to take it up again. This commandment I received from My Father."

19 There arose a division again among the Jews because of these words. 20And many of them were saying, "He has a demon, and is insane; why do you listen to Him?" 21 Others were saying, "These are not the sayings of one demon-possessed. A demon cannot open the eyes of the blind, can he?"

22 At that time the Feast of the Dedication took place at Jerusalem; 23 it was winter, and Jesus was walking in the temple in the portico of Solomon. 24 The Jews therefore gathered around Him, and were saying to Him, "How long will You keep us in suspense? If You are the Christ, tell us plainly." 25 Jesus answered them, "I told you, and you do not believe; the works that I do in My Father's name, these bear witness of Me. 26 "But you do not believe, because you are not of My sheep. 27 "My sheep hear My voice, and I know them, and they follow Me; 28 and I give eternal life to

[a] Many Greek mss. read, *takes.*

WILLIAMS

10 *Jesus the door to the sheepfold; the good shepherd too; He guarantees that He and His Father will protect his sheep; the Jews tried to arrest Him for claiming to be one with the Father*

"I most solemnly say to you, whoever does not enter the sheepfold by the door, but climbs over at some other place is a thief and a robber. 2 But the one who enters by the door is the shepherd of the sheep. 3 The doorkeeper opens the door to him, and the sheep obey his voice; and he calls his own sheep by name, and leads them out. 4 So when he gets his sheep all out, he goes on before them, and the sheep come on behind him, because they know his voice. 5 But they will never come on behind a stranger, but will run away from him, because they do not know the voice of strangers."

6 Jesus told them this allegory, but they did not understand what He meant by it. 7 So Jesus said to them again:

"I most solemnly say to you, I am the door to the sheepfold myself. 8 All who came as such before me are thieves and robbers, but the true sheep would not listen to them. 9 I am the door myself. Whoever enters through me will be saved, and will go in and out and find pasture. 10 A thief does not come for any purpose but to steal and kill and destroy; I have come for people to have life and have it till it overflows. 11 I am the good shepherd myself. The good shepherd gives his own life for his sheep. 12 The hired man, who is not a shepherd and does not own the sheep, sees the wolf coming and leaves the sheep and runs away, and the wolf carries off some of the sheep and scatters the flock. 13 This is because he is a hired man and does not care a straw for the sheep. 14 I am the good shepherd myself. I know my sheep and my sheep know me, 15 just as the Father knows me and I know the Father, and I am giving my own life for my sheep. 16 I have other sheep too that do not belong to this fold. I must lead them too, and they will listen to my voice, and all my sheep will become one flock with one shepherd. 17 This is why the Father loves me, because I am giving my own life to take it back again. 18 No one has taken it from me, but I am giving it as a free gift. I have the right to give it and I have the right to take it back. I have gotten this order from my Father."

19 These words again led to difference of opinion among the Jews. 20 Many of them said, "He is under the power of a demon and is going crazy. Why are you listening to Him?" 21 Others said, "These are not the words of a man who is under the power of a demon. A demon cannot make the eyes of the blind see, can he?"

22 At that time came the feast of Rededication at Jerusalem. It was winter 23 and Jesus was walking in Solomon's portico. 24 So the Jews surrounded Him and kept asking Him, "How much longer are you going to keep us in suspense? If you are really the Christ, tell us so plainly."

25 Jesus answered them, "I have already told you so, but you do not believe me. The works which I am doing on my Father's authority are my credentials, 26 but still you do not believe in me, for you do not belong to my sheep. 27 My sheep listen to my voice, and I know them and they follow me, 28 and I give to

BECK

The Good Shepherd

10 "I tell you the truth: The man who doesn't come into the sheepfold through the door but climbs over somewhere else, is a thief and a robber. 2 But the one who comes in through the door is the shepherd of the sheep. 3 The doorkeeper opens the door for him, and the sheep listen to his voice. He calls his own sheep by their names and leads them out. 4 When he has brought out all his own sheep, he walks ahead of them, and the sheep follow him because they know his voice. 5 They will not follow a stranger but will run away from him because they don't know the voice of strangers."

6 This was the illustration Jesus used in talking to them, but they didn't know what He meant. 7 So Jesus spoke again: "I tell you the truth: I am the Door for the sheep. 8 All who came before Me were thieves and robbers, but the sheep didn't listen to them. 9 I am the Door. If anyone comes in through Me, he will be saved and will go in and out and find pasture.

10 "A thief comes only to steal and kill and destroy. I came so that they will have life and have it overflowing in them. 11 I am the Good Shepherd. The Good Shepherd gives his life for the sheep. 12 When a hired man, who isn't a shepherd and doesn't own the sheep, sees a wolf coming, he leaves the sheep and runs away—and the wolf carries them off and scatters them— 13 because he works for money and doesn't care about the sheep. 14 I am the Good Shepherd, and I know My own and My own know Me, 15 as the Father knows Me and I know the Father. And I give My life for the sheep. 16 I have other sheep too, that are not in this fold. I must lead those too, and they will listen to My voice, and so they will become one flock with *One Shepherd*.[8] 17 The Father loves Me because I give My life in order to take it back again. 18 Nobody takes it from Me. No, of My own free will I am giving it. I have the power to give it, and I have the power to take it back again. This is what My Father ordered Me to do."

19 These words again caused a split among the Jews. 20 Many of them said, "There's a devil in Him and He's crazy. Why do you listen to Him?" 21 Others said, "Nobody talks like this when there's a devil in him. Can a devil give sight to the blind?"

"I and the Father Are One"

22 Then came the festival of Dedication in Jerusalem. It was winter, 23 and Jesus was walking in Solomon's porch in the temple. 24 There the Jews surrounded Him. "How long will You keep us in suspense?" they asked Him. "If You're the promised Savior, tell us frankly."

25 "I did tell you," Jesus answered them, "but you don't believe it. The works I do in My Father's name tell the truth about Me. 26 But you don't believe, because you're not My sheep. 27 My sheep listen to My voice, and I know them, and they follow Me, 28 and I give them

[8] Ezek. 34:23

K.J.V.

them eternal life; and they shall never perish, neither shall any *man* pluck them out of my hand. 29 My Father, which gave *them* me, is greater than all; and no *man* is able to pluck *them* out of my Father's hand. 30 I and *my* Father are one. 31 Then the Jews took up stones again to stone him. 32 Jesus answered them, Many good works have I shewed you from my Father; for which of those works do ye stone me? 33 The Jews answered him, saying, For a good work we stone thee not; but for blasphemy; and because that thou, being a man, makest thyself God. 34 Jesus answered them, Is it not written in your law, I said, Ye are gods? 35 If he called them gods, unto whom the word of God came, and the Scripture cannot be broken; 36 Say ye of him, whom the Father hath sanctified, and sent into the world, Thou blasphemest; because I said, I am the Son of God? 37 If I do not the works of my Father, believe me not. 38 But if I do, though ye believe not me, believe the works; that ye may know, and believe, that the Father *is* in me and I in him. 39 Therefore they sought again to take him; but he escaped out of their hand, 40 And went away again beyond Jordan into the place where John at first baptized; and there he abode. 41 And many resorted unto him, and said, John did no miracle: but all things that John spake of this man were true. 42 And many believed on him there.

11 Now a certain *man* was sick, *named* Lazarus, of Bethany, the town of Mary and her sister Martha. 2 (It was *that* Mary which anointed the Lord with ointment, and wiped his feet with her hair, whose brother Lazarus was sick.) 3 Therefore his sisters sent unto him, saying, Lord, behold, he whom thou lovest is sick. 4 When Jesus heard *that*, he said, This sickness is not unto death, but for the glory of God, that the Son of God might be glorified thereby. 5 Now Jesus loved Martha, and her sister, and Lazarus. 6 When he had heard therefore that he was sick, he abode two days still in the same place where he was. 7 Then after that saith he to *his* disciples, Let us go into Judea again. 8 *His* disciples say unto him, Master, the Jews of late sought to stone thee; and goest thou thither again? 9 Jesus answered, Are there not twelve hours in the day? If any man walk in the day, he stumbleth not, because he seeth the light of this world. 10 But if a man walk in the night, he stumbleth, because there is no light in him. 11 These things said he: and after that he saith unto them, Our friend Lazarus sleepeth; but I go, that I may awake him out of sleep. 12 Then said his disciples, Lord, if he sleep, he shall do well. 13 Howbeit Jesus spake of his death: but

N.A.S.

them; and they shall never perish, and no one shall snatch them out of My hand. 29 d "My Father, who has given *them* to Me, is greater than all; and no one is able to snatch *them* out of the Father's hand. 30 "I and the Father are one." 31 The Jews took up stones again to stone Him. 32 Jesus answered them, "I showed you many good works from the Father; for which of them are you stoning Me?" 33 The Jews answered Him, "For a good work we do not stone You, but for blasphemy; and because You, being a man, make Yourself out *to be* God." 34 Jesus answered them, "Has it not been written in your Law, 'I said, you are gods'? 35 "If he called them gods, to whom the word of God came (and the Scripture cannot be broken), 36 do you say of Him, whom the Father sanctified and sent into the world, 'You are blaspheming'; because I said, 'I am the Son of God'? 37 "If I do not do the works of My Father, do not believe Me; 38 but if I do them, though you do not believe Me, believe the works; that you may know and understand that the Father is in Me, and I in the Father." 39 Therefore they were seeking again to seize Him; and He eluded their grasp. 40 And He went away again beyond the Jordan to the place where John was first baptizing; and He was staying there. 41 And many came to Him; and they were saying, "While John performed no sign, yet everything John said about this man was true." 42 And many believed in Him there.

11 Now a certain man was sick, Lazarus of Bethany, of the village of Mary and her sister Martha. 2 And it was the Mary who anointed the Lord with ointment, and wiped His feet with her hair, whose brother Lazarus was sick. 3 The sisters therefore sent to Him, saying, "Lord, behold, he whom You love is sick." 4 But when Jesus heard it, He said, "This sickness is not unto death, but for the glory of God, that the Son of God may be glorified by it." 5 Now Jesus loved Martha, and her sister, and Lazarus. 6 When therefore He heard that he was sick, He stayed then two days *longer* in the place where He was. 7 Then after this He *said to the disciples, "Let us go to Judea again." 8 The disciples *said to Him, "Rabbi, the Jews were just now seeking to stone You; and are You going there again?" 9 Jesus answered, "Are there not twelve hours in the day? If anyone walks in the day, he does not stumble, because he sees the light of this world. 10 "But if anyone walks in the night, he stumbles, because the light is not in him." 11 This He said, and after that He *said to them, "Our friend Lazarus has fallen asleep; but I go, that I may awaken him out of sleep." 12 The disciples therefore said to Him, "Lord, if he has fallen asleep, he will recover." 13 Now

[a] Some early mss. read, *What My Father has given Me is greater than all.*

286

WILLIAMS

them eternal life, and they shall never get lost, and no one shall snatch them out of my hand. 29 My Father who gave them to me is stronger[a] than all, and no one can snatch them out of my Father's hand. 30 The Father and I are one."

31 The Jews again picked up stones to stone Him. 32 Jesus answered them, "I have shown you many good deeds from my Father. For which of them are you going to stone me?"

33 The Jews retorted, "It is not for a good deed but for blasphemy we are going to stone you; namely, because you, although a mere man, claim to be God."

34 Jesus answered them, "Is it not written in your law, 'I said, "You are gods"'? 35 If men to whom God's message came are called gods—and the Scriptures cannot be made null and void—36 do you now say to me whom my Father has set apart to it and sent into the world, 'You are a blasphemer,' because I said, 'I am the Son of God'? 37 If I am not doing the things that my Father is doing, do not believe me. 38 But if I am doing so, even if you will not believe me, believe the deeds, that you may come to know and continue to know that the Father is in union with me and I am in union with the Father."

39 Once more they were trying to arrest Him, but He escaped from their hands. 40 He again crossed the Jordan at the place where John at first used to baptize, and there He stayed. 41 And many people came to Him and kept on saying, "John did not perform any wonder-works, but everything he ever said about this man was true." 42 And so many of them at that place believed in Him.

11 *Lazarus is sick; Martha and Mary, his sisters, send for Jesus; He waits for him to die, then comes and brings him back to life; the council plots to kill Him*

Now a man was sick; it was Lazarus who lived in Bethany, the village of Mary and her sister Martha. 2 It was the Mary who poured the perfume upon the Lord and wiped His feet with her hair, whose brother Lazarus was sick. 3 So the sisters sent this message to Jesus, "Lord, listen! the one you love so well is sick."

4 When Jesus received the message, He said, "The sickness is not to end in death but is to honor God, that the Son of God through it may be honored."

5 Now Jesus held in loving esteem Martha and her sister and Lazarus. 6 But when He heard that Lazarus was sick, He stayed over for two days in the place where He was. 7 After that He said to His disciples, "Let us go back to Judea."

8 The disciples said to Him, "Teacher, the Jews just now were trying to stone you, and are you going back there again?"

9 Jesus answered, "Does not the day have twelve hours? If a man travels in the daytime, he does not stumble, for he can see the light of this world; 10 but if he travels in the nighttime, he does stumble, because he has no light." 11 He said this, and after that He added, "Our friend Lazarus has fallen asleep, but I am going there to wake him."

12 The disciples said to Him, "Lord, if he has merely fallen asleep, he will recover." 13 But

BECK

everlasting life. They will never be lost, and nobody will tear them out of My hand. 29 My Father, who gave them to Me, is greater than all others, and nobody can tear them out of My Father's hand. 30 I and the Father are one."

31 Again the Jews picked up stones to stone Him. 32 Jesus answered them, "I have shown you many good works that come from the Father. For which of these works are you trying to stone Me?"

33 "We're stoning You," the Jews answered Him, "not for a good work but for blasphemy because You, a man, claim to be God."

34 Jesus said to them, "Isn't it written in your Bible, *I said, 'You are gods'?* [9] 35 If it called them gods to whom God's Word came—and the Bible can't be set aside— 36 do you say to Me, whom the Father appointed for His holy purpose and sent into the world, 'You're blaspheming,' because I said, 'I'm God's Son'? 37 If I'm not doing My Father's works, don't trust Me. 38 But if I do them, even if you don't trust Me, trust My works so as to learn and understand the Father is in Me and I am in the Father."

39 Again they tried to arrest Him, but He escaped from their hands. 40 He went back across the Jordan to the place where John had been baptizing earlier, and He stayed there.

41 Many came to Him. "John did no miracle," they said, "but everything John said about this One is true." And many believed in Him there.

Jesus Raises Lazarus

11 Then Lazarus was sick. He was in Bethany, the village where Mary and her sister Martha were living. 2 Mary was the one who poured perfume on the Lord and wiped His feet with her hair. It was her brother Lazarus who was sick.

3 So the sister sent someone to tell Jesus, "Lord, the one You love is sick."

4 When Jesus heard it, He said, "The purpose of this sickness isn't death but to show God's glory; it is to glorify God's Son."

5 Jesus loved Martha and her sister and Lazarus. 6 Now, when He heard Lazarus was sick, He stayed two days where He was. 7 After that He said to His disciples, "Let us go back to Judea."

8 "Master," the disciples said to Him, "the Jews have just been wanting to stone You, and You're going back there?"

9 "Aren't there twelve hours in a day?" Jesus answered. "If you walk during the day, you don't stumble, because you see the light of this world. 10 But if you walk at night, you stumble, because you have no light."

11 After He said this, He told them, "Our friend Lazarus has gone to sleep, but I'm going there to wake him up."

12 "Lord, if he has gone to sleep," His disciples said to Him, "he'll get well."

13 Jesus meant he was dead, but they

K.J.V.

they thought that he had spoken of taking of rest in sleep. 14 Then said Jesus unto them plainly, Lazarus is dead. 15And I am glad for your sakes that I was not there, to the intent ye may believe; nevertheless let us go unto him. 16 Then said Thomas, which is called Didymus, unto his fellow disciples, Let us also go, that we may die with him. 17 Then when Jesus came, he found that he had *lain* in the grave four days already. 18 Now Bethany was nigh unto Jerusalem, about fifteen furlongs off: 19And many of the Jews came to Martha and Mary, to comfort them concerning their brother. 20 Then Martha, as soon as she heard that Jesus was coming, went and met him: but Mary sat *still* in the house. 21 Then said Martha unto Jesus, Lord, if thou hadst been here, my brother had not died. 22 But I know, that even now, whatsoever thou wilt ask of God, God will give *it* thee. 23 Jesus saith unto her, Thy brother shall rise again. 24 Martha saith unto him, I know that he shall rise again in the resurrection at the last day. 25 Jesus said unto her, I am the resurrection, and the life: he that believeth in me, though he were dead, yet shall he live: 26And whosoever liveth and believeth in me shall never die. Believest thou this? 27 She saith unto him, Yea, Lord: I believe that thou art the Christ, the Son of God, which should come into the world. 28And when she had so said, she went her way, and called Mary her sister secretly, saying, The Master is come, and calleth for thee. 29As soon as she heard *that,* she arose quickly, and came unto him. 30 Now Jesus was not yet come into the town, but was in that place where Martha met him. 31 The Jews then which were with her in the house, and comforted her, when they saw Mary, that she rose up hastily and went out, followed her, saying, She goeth unto the grave to weep there. 32 Then when Mary was come where Jesus was, and saw him, she fell down at his feet, saying unto him, Lord, if thou hadst been here, my brother had not died. 33 When Jesus therefore saw her weeping, and the Jews also weeping which came with her, he groaned in the spirit, and was troubled, 34And said, Where have ye laid him? They say unto him, Lord, come and see. 35 Jesus wept. 36 Then said the Jews, Behold how he loved him! 37And some of them said, Could not this man, which opened the eyes of the blind, have caused that even this man should not have died? 38 Jesus therefore again groaning in himself cometh to the grave. It was a cave, and a stone lay upon it. 39 Jesus said, Take ye away the stone. Martha, the sister of him that was dead, saith unto him, Lord, by this time he stinketh: for he hath been *dead* four days. 40 Jesus saith unto her, Said I not unto thee, that, if thou wouldest believe, thou shouldest see the glory of God? 41 Then they took away the stone *from the place* where the dead was laid. And Jesus lifted up *his* eyes, and said, Father, I thank thee that thou hast heard me. 42And I knew that thou hearest me always: but because of the people which stand by I said *it,* that they may believe that thou hast

N.A.S.

Jesus had spoken of his death; but they thought that He was speaking of literal sleep. 14 Then Jesus therefore said to them plainly, "Lazarus is dead. 15 and I am glad for your sakes that I was not there, so that you may believe; but let us go to him." 16 Thomas therefore, who is called Didymus, said to *his* fellow disciples, "Let us also go, that we may die with Him." 17 So when Jesus came, He found that he had already been in the tomb four days. 18 Now Bethany was near Jerusalem, about two miles off; 19 and many of the Jews had come to Martha and Mary, to console them concerning *their* brother. 20 Martha therefore, when she heard that Jesus was coming, went to meet Him; but Mary still sat in the house. 21 Martha therefore said to Jesus, "Lord, if You had been here, my brother would not have died. 22 "Even now I know that whatever You ask of God, God will give You." 23 Jesus *said to her, "Your brother shall rise again." 24 Martha *said to Him, "I know that he will rise again in the resurrection on the last day." 25 Jesus said to her, "I am the resurrection, and the life; he who believes in Me shall live even if he dies, 26 and everyone who lives and believes in Me shall never die. Do you believe this?" 27 She *said to Him, "Yes Lord; I have believed that You are the Christ, the Son of God, *even* He who comes into the world." 28And when she had said this, she went away, and called Mary her sister, saying secretly, "The Teacher is here, and is calling for you." 29And when she heard it, she *arose quickly, and was coming to Him. 30 Now Jesus had not yet come into the village, but was still in the place where Martha met Him. 31 The Jews then who were with her in the house, and consoling her, when they saw that Mary rose up quickly and went out, followed her, supposing that she was going to the tomb to weep there. 32 Therefore, when Mary came where Jesus was, she saw Him, and fell at His feet, saying to Him, "Lord, if You had been here, my brother would not have died." 33 When Jesus therefore saw her weeping, and the Jews who came with her, *also* weeping, He was deeply moved in spirit, and was troubled, 34 and said, "Where have you laid him?" They *said to Him, "Lord, come and see." 35 Jesus wept. 36And so the Jews were saying, "Behold how He loved him!" 37 But some of them said, "Could not this man, who opened the eyes of him who was blind, have kept this man also from dying?" 38 Jesus therefore again being deeply moved within, *came to the tomb. Now it was a cave, and a stone was lying against it. 39 Jesus *said, "Remove the stone." Martha, the sister of the deceased, *said to Him, "Lord, by this time there will be a stench; for he *has been dead* four days." 40 Jesus *said to her, "Did I not say to you, if you believe, you will see the glory of God?" 41And so they removed the stone. And Jesus raised His eyes, and said, "Father, I thank Thee that Thou heardest Me. 42 "And I knew that Thou hearest Me always; but because of the people standing around I said it, that they may believe that Thou didst

WILLIAMS

Jesus had spoken about his death. However, they supposed that He was referring to falling into a natural sleep.

14 So Jesus then told them plainly: "Lazarus is dead, 15 and I am glad for your sake that I was not there so that you may come to have real faith in me. But let us go to him."

16 Then Thomas the Twin said to his fellow-disciples, "Let us go too, and die with Him."

17 When Jesus reached there, He found that Lazarus had been buried for four days. 18 Now Bethany is only about two miles from Jerusalem, 19 and a goodly number of Jews had come out to see Martha and Mary, to sympathize with them over their brother. 20 When Martha heard that Jesus was coming, she went out to meet Him, but Mary stayed at home. 21 Then Martha said to Jesus, "Lord, if you had been here, my brother would not have died. 22 But even now I know that whatever you ask God for He will give you."

23 Jesus said to her, "Your brother will rise again."

24 Martha said to Him, "I know that he will rise at the resurrection, on the last day."

25 Jesus said to her, "I am the resurrection and the life myself. Whoever continues to believe in me will live right on, even though he dies, 26 and no person who continues to live and believe in me will ever die at all. Do you believe this?"

27 She said to Him, "Yes, Lord, I believe that you are the Christ, the Son of God, who was to come into the world."

28 On saying this she went back and called her sister Mary, whispering to her, "The Teacher is here and is asking for you."

29 As soon as she heard it, she jumped up and started to Jesus, 30 for He had not yet come into the village, but He was still at the place where Martha had met Him. 31 So the Jews who were with her in the house sympathizing with her, when they saw Mary jump up and go out, followed her, because they supposed that she was going to the grave to pour out her grief there. 32 When Mary came where Jesus was and saw Him, she threw herself at His feet, and said, "Lord, if you had been here, my brother would not have died."

33 So when Jesus saw her weeping and the Jews who had come with her weeping too, He sighed in sympathy and shook with emotion, 34 and asked, "Where have you laid him?"

They answered, "Lord, come and see." 35 Jesus burst into tears.

36 So the Jews said, "See how tenderly He loved him!" 37 But some of them said, "Could not this man, who made that blind man see, have kept Lazarus from dying?"

38 Now Jesus sighed again and continued to sigh as He went to the grave. It was a cave with a stone lying over the mouth of it.

39 Jesus said, "Slip the stone aside."

The dead man's sister, Martha, said to Him, "Lord, by this time he is offensive, for he has been dead four days."

40 Jesus said to her, "Did I not promise you that if you would believe in me, you should see the glory of God?" 41 So they slipped the stone aside.

And Jesus looked up and said, "Father, I thank you for listening to me; 42 yes, I knew that you always listen to me. But I have said this for the sake of the crowd that is standing by, that they may come to believe that you have

BECK

thought He meant he was only sleeping. 14 Then Jesus told them in plain words, "Lazarus died. 15 And I'm glad I wasn't there; it will help you believe. But let us go to him."

16 Then Thomas, who was called Twin, said to his fellow disciples, "Let us go, too, and die with Him."

17 When Jesus got there, He found that Lazarus had been in the grave four days already.

18 Bethany was near Jerusalem, not quite two miles away, 19 and many Jews had come to Martha and Mary to comfort them about their brother.

20 Now, when Martha heard, "Jesus is coming," she went to meet Him, while Mary stayed at home. 21 "Lord, if You had been here," Martha told Jesus, "my brother wouldn't have died. 22 But even now I know God will give You anything You ask Him."

23 "Your brother will rise again," Jesus told her.

24 "I know he'll rise again," Martha answered Him, "in the resurrection on the last day."

25 "I am the Resurrection and the Life," Jesus said to her. 26 "Anyone who believes in Me will live even if he dies. 26 Yes, anyone who lives and believes in Me will never die. Do you believe that?"

27 "Yes, Lord," she told Him, "I believe You are the promised Savior, God's Son, who is coming into the world."

28 After she said this, she went to call her sister Mary. "The Teacher is here," she whispered, "and is calling for you."

29 When Mary heard it, she got up quickly to go to Him. 30 Jesus hadn't come to the village yet but was still where Martha had met Him. 31 Now, the Jews who were in the house with Mary to comfort her saw her get up quickly and leave. So they followed her, thinking she was going to the grave to weep there. 32 When Mary came where Jesus was and saw Him, she bowed down at His feet and said, "Lord, if You had been here, my brother wouldn't have died."

33 When Jesus saw her weeping, and the Jews weeping who came with her, He groaned deeply and was troubled.

34 "Where did you lay him?" He asked.

"Lord, come and see," they answered Him. 35 Jesus burst into tears. 36 "See how He loved him," the Jews said. 37 But some of them asked, "He gave sight to the blind man—couldn't He have kept this man from dying?"

38 Groaning deeply again, Jesus went to the grave. It was a cave, and a stone was laid against it. 39 "Move the stone away," said Jesus.

Martha, the dead man's sister, told Him, "Lord, he smells already. He's been dead four days."

40 Jesus said to her, "Didn't I tell you, 'If you believe, you will see God's glory'?" 41 So they moved the stone away.

Jesus looked up and said, "Father, I thank You for hearing Me. 42 I knew You always hear Me. But I spoke so that the people standing around Me will believe You sent Me."

K.J.V.

sent me. 43 And when he thus had spoken, he cried with a loud voice, Lazarus, come forth. 44 And he that was dead came forth, bound hand and foot with graveclothes; and his face was bound about with a napkin. Jesus saith unto them, Loose him, and let him go. 45 Then many of the Jews which came to Mary, and had seen the things which Jesus did, believed on him. 46 But some of them went their ways to the Pharisees, and told them what things Jesus had done.

47 Then gathered the chief priests and the Pharisees a council, and said, What do we? for this man doeth many miracles. 48 If we let him thus alone, all *men* will believe on him; and the Romans shall come and take away both our place and nation. 49 And one of them, *named* Caiaphas, being the high priest that same year, said unto them, Ye know nothing at all, 50 Nor consider that it is expedient for us, that one man should die for the people, and that the whole nation perish not. 51 And this spake he not of himself: but being high priest that year, he prophesied that Jesus should die for that nation; 52 And not for that nation only, but that also he should gather together in one the children of God that were scattered abroad. 53 Then from that day forth they took counsel together for to put him to death. 54 Jesus therefore walked no more openly among the Jews; but went thence unto a country near to the wilderness, into a city called Ephraim, and there continued with his disciples.

55 And the Jews' passover was nigh at hand: and many went out of the country up to Jerusalem before the passover, to purify themselves. 56 Then sought they for Jesus, and spake among themselves, as they stood in the temple, What think ye, that he will not come to the feast? 57 Now both the chief priests and the Pharisees had given a commandment, that, if any man knew where he were, he should shew *it*, that they might take him.

12 Then Jesus six days before the passover came to Bethany, where Lazarus was which had been dead, whom he raised from the dead. 2 There they made him a supper; and Martha served: but Lazarus was one of them that sat at the table with him. 3 Then took Mary a pound of ointment of spikenard, very costly, and anointed the feet of Jesus, and wiped his feet with her hair: and the house was filled with the odour of the ointment. 4 Then saith one of his disciples, Judas Iscariot, Simon's *son*, which should betray him, 5 Why was not this ointment sold for three hundred pence, and given to the poor? 6 This he said, not that he cared for the poor; but because he was a thief, and had the bag, and bare what was put therein. 7 Then said

N.A.S.

send Me." 43 And when He had said these things, He cried out with a loud voice, "Lazarus, come forth." 44 He who had died came forth, bound hand and foot with wrappings; and his face was wrapped around with a cloth. Jesus *said to them, "Unbind him, and let him go."

45 Many therefore of the Jews, who had come to Mary and beheld what He had done, believed in Him. 46 But some of them went away to the Pharisees, and told them the things which Jesus had done.

47 Therefore the chief priests and the Pharisees convened a council, and were saying, "What are we doing? For this man is performing many signs. 48 "If we let Him *go on* like this, all men will believe in Him, and the Romans will come and take away both our place and our nation." 49 But a certain one of them, Caiaphas, who was high priest that year, said to them, "You know nothing at all, 50 nor do you take into account that it is expedient for you that one man should die for the people, and that the whole nation should not perish." 51 Now this he did not say on his own initiative; but being high priest that year, he prophesied that Jesus was going to die for the nation; 52 and not for the nation only, but that He might also gather together into one the children of God who are scattered abroad. 53 So from that day on they planned together to kill Him.

54 Jesus therefore no longer continued to walk publicly among the Jews, but went away from there to the country near the wilderness, into a city called Ephraim; and there He stayed with the disciples. 55 Now the Passover of the Jews was at hand, and many went up to Jerusalem out of the country before the Passover, to purify themselves. 56 Therefore they were seeking for Jesus, and were saying to on another, as they stood in the temple, "What do you think; that He will not come to the feast at all?" 57 Now the chief priests and the Pharisees had given orders that if any one knew where He was, he should report it, that they might seize Him.

12 Jesus therefore six days before the Passover came to Bethany, where Lazarus was, whom Jesus had raised from the dead. 2 So they made Him a supper there; and Martha was serving; but Lazarus was one of those reclining *at the table* with Him. 3 Mary therefore took a pound of very costly, genuine spikenard-ointment, and anointed the feet of Jesus, and wiped His feet with her hair; and the house was filled with the fragrance of the ointment. 4 But Judas Iscariot, one of His disciples, who was intending to betray Him, *said, 5 "Why was this ointment not sold for ªthree hundred denarii, and given to poor *people?*" 6 Now he said this, not because he was concerned about the poor, but because he was a thief, and as he had the money box, he used to pilfer what was put into it. 7 Jesus therefore said, "Let her

[a] Monetary value $50, but equal to 11 months wages.

290

WILLIAMS

sent me." 43 On saying this, He shouted aloud, "Lazarus, come out!"

44 Then out came the dead man, his feet and hands tied with wrappings, and his face tied up with a handkerchief. Jesus said to them, "Untie him and let him go."

45 Thus many of the Jews, who came to see Mary and who saw what Jesus had done, believed in Him; 46 but some of them went back to the Pharisees and told them what He had done.

47 So the high priests and the Pharisees called a meeting of the council, and began to say, "What are we to do? For this man is certainly performing many wonder-works. 48 If we let Him go on this way, everybody will believe in Him, and the Romans will come and blot out both our city and nation."

49 But one of them, Caiaphas, who was high priest that year, said to them, "You know nothing about this; 50 you do not take into account that it is for your own welfare that one man should die for the people, and not that the whole nation should be destroyed." 51 Now he did not say this on his own authority, but because he was high priest that year he uttered this prophecy from God, that Jesus was to die for the nation, 52 and not only for the nation, but also to unite the scattered children of God. 53 So from that day they plotted to kill Jesus.

54 It was for this reason that Jesus no more appeared in public among the Jews, but He left that part of the country and went to the district near the desert, to a town called Ephraim, and stayed there with His disciples. 55 Now the Jewish Passover was approaching, and many people from the country went up to Jerusalem, to purify themselves before the Passover. 56 So they kept looking for Jesus and saying to one another, as they stood in the temple, "What do you think? Do you think He will not come to the feast at all?"

57 Now the high priests and the Pharisees had given orders that if anyone should learn where He was, he should let it be known so that they might arrest Him.

12 *Mary pours her costly perfume on Jesus; Jesus rides as king into Jerusalem; Greeks interview Jesus; He teaches that life comes from sacrificial death; opposition increases as He continues to claim God as Father*

Now six days before the Passover, Jesus came to Bethany where Lazarus lived, whom He had raised from the dead. 2 So they gave a dinner there in honor of Jesus, and Martha was waiting on them, but Lazarus was one of the guests with Jesus. 3 Then Mary took a pound of expensive perfume, made of the purest oil, and poured it on Jesus' feet, and wiped them with her hair; and the whole house was filled with the fragrance of the perfume.

4 But Judas Iscariot, one of His disciples, who was going to betray Him, said, 5 "Why was this perfume not sold for sixty dollars and the money given to the poor?" 6 He said this, not because he cared for the poor, but because he was a thief and as the carrier of the purse for the Twelve he was in the habit of taking what was put into it.

7 Then Jesus said, "Let her alone; let her

BECK

43 After He had said this, He called out loud, "Lazarus, come out!"

44 The dead man came out, his feet and hands wrapped in bandages and his face wrapped in a cloth. "Unwrap him," Jesus told them, "and let him go."

45 Then many of the Jews who had come to Mary and had seen what He did believed in Him. 46 But some of them went to the Pharisees and told them what Jesus had done. 47 Then the ruling priests and the Pharisees called a meeting of the council. "What are we doing?" they asked. "This Man is doing many miracles. 48 If we let Him go on like this, everybody will believe in Him, and then the Romans will come and take away our place and our nation."

49 But one of them, Caiaphas, who was high priest that year, told them, "You don't know anything, 50 and you don't consider it is better for you that one man dies instead of the people and the whole nation doesn't perish." 51 He didn't think of this himself, but being high priest that year, he prophesied Jesus was going to die for the nation, 52 and not only for this nation but also to bring God's scattered children together and make them one.

53 From that day on they planned to kill Him. 54 So Jesus no longer walked in public among the Jews but left and went into the country near the wilderness, to a town called Ephraim and stayed there with His disciples.

Mary Anoints Jesus

55 The Jewish Passover was near, and many came from the country to Jerusalem before the Passover to purify themselves. 56 They were looking for Jesus and asking one another as they stood in the temple, "What do you think? He isn't coming to the festival, is He?" 57 The ruling priests and the Pharisees had given orders if anyone found out where He was he should report it so that they might arrest Him.

12 Six days before the Passover, Jesus came to Bethany, where Lazarus was, whom Jesus had raised from the dead. 2 There a dinner was prepared for Him. Martha served, and Lazarus was one of those eating with Him.

3 Then Mary took a pound of perfume, real nard and very expensive, and poured it on Jesus' feet and dried His feet with her hair. The fragrance of the perfume filled the house.

4 Judas (the man from Kerioth, one of His disciples, who was going to betray Him) asked, 5 "Why wasn't this perfume sold for three hundred denarii and the money given to the poor?" 6 He didn't say this because he cared about the poor but because he was a thief and used to steal what was put in the money box he carried.

7 "Let her do it for the day of My burial,"

K.J.V.

Jesus, Let her alone: against the day of my burying hath she kept this. 8 For the poor always ye have with you; but me ye have not always. 9 Much people of the Jews therefore knew that he was there: and they came not for Jesus' sake only, but that they might see Lazarus also, whom he had raised from the dead.

10 But the chief priests consulted that they might put Lazarus also to death; 11 Because that by reason of him many of the Jews went away, and believed on Jesus.

12 On the next day much people that were come to the feast, when they heard that Jesus was coming to Jerusalem, 13 Took branches of palm trees, and went forth to meet him, and cried, Hosanna: blessed *is* the King of Israel that cometh in the name of the Lord. 14 And Jesus, when he had found a young ass, sat thereon; as it is written, 15 Fear not, daughter of Sion: behold, thy King cometh, sitting on an ass's colt. 16 These things understood not his disciples at the first: but when Jesus was glorified, then remembered they that these things were written of him, and *that* they had done these things unto him. 17 The people therefore that was with him when he called Lazarus out of his grave, and raised him from the dead, bare record. 18 For this cause the people also met him, for that they heard that he had done this miracle. 19 The Pharisees therefore said among themselves, Perceive ye how ye prevail nothing? behold, the world is gone after him.

20 And there were certain Greeks among them that came up to worship at the feast: 21 The same came therefore to Philip, which was of Bethsaida of Galilee, and desired him, saying, Sir, we would see Jesus. 22 Philip cometh and telleth Andrew: and again Andrew and Philip tell Jesus.

23 And Jesus answered them, saying, The hour is come, that the Son of man should be glorified. 24 Verily, verily, I say unto you, Except a corn of wheat fall into the ground and die, it abideth alone: but if it die, it bringeth forth much fruit. 25 He that loveth his life shall lose it; and he that hateth his life in this world shall keep it unto life eternal. 26 If any man serve me, let him follow me; and where I am, there shall also my servant be: if any man serve me, him will *my* Father honour. 27 Now is my soul troubled; and what shall I say? Father, save me from this hour: but for this cause came I unto this hour. 28 Father, glorify thy name. Then came there a voice from heaven, *saying,* I have both glorified *it,* and will glorify *it* again. 29 The people therefore that stood by, and heard *it,* said that it thundered: others said, An angel spake to him. 30 Jesus answered and said, This voice came not because of me, but for your sakes. 31 Now is the judgment of this world: now shall the prince of this world be cast out. 32 And I, if I be lifted up from the earth, will draw all *men* unto me. 33 This he said, signifying what death he should die. 34 The people answered him, We have heard out of the law that

N.A.S.

alone, in order that she may keep it for the day of My burial. 8 "For the poor you always have with you; but you do not always have Me."

9 The great multitude therefore of the Jews learned that He was there; and they came, not for Jesus' sake only, but that they might also see Lazarus, whom He raised from the dead. 10 But the chief priests took counsel that they might put Lazarus to death also; 11 because on account of him many of the Jews were going away, and were believing in Jesus.

12 On the next day the great multitude who had come to the feast, when they heard that Jesus was coming to Jerusalem, 13 took the branches of the palm trees, and went out to meet Him, and *began* to cry out, "Hosanna: BLESSED *is* HE WHO COMES IN THE NAME OF THE LORD, even the King of Israel." 14 And Jesus, finding a young donkey, sat on it; as it is written, 15 "FEAR NOT, DAUGHTER OF ZION; BEHOLD, YOUR KING COMES SITTING ON A DONKEY'S COLT." 16 These things His disciples did not understand at the first; but when Jesus was glorified, then they remembered that these things were written of Him, and that they had done these things to Him. 17 And so the multitude who were with Him when He called Lazarus out of the tomb, and raised him from the dead, were bearing Him witness. 18 For this cause also the multitude went and met Him, because they heard that He had performed this sign. 19 The Pharisees therefore said to one another, "You see that you are not doing any good; look, the world has gone after Him."

20 Now there were certain Greeks among those who were going up to worship at the feast; 21 these therefore came to Philip, who was from Bethsaida of Galilee, and *began* to ask him, saying, "Sir, we wish to see Jesus." 22 Philip *came and *told Andrew; Andrew *came, and Philip, and they *told Jesus. 23 And Jesus *answered them, saying, "The hour has come for the Son of Man to be glorified. 24 "Truly, truly, I say to you, unless a grain of wheat falls into the earth and dies, it remains by itself alone; but if it dies, it bears much fruit. 25 "He who loves his life loses it; and he who hates his life in this world shall keep it to life eternal. 26 "If any one serves Me, let him follow Me; and where I am, there shall My servant also be; if any one serves Me, the Father will honor him.

27 "Now My soul has become troubled; and what shall I say? 'Father, save Me from this hour'? But for this purpose I came to this hour. 28 "Father, glorify Thy name." There came therefore a voice out of heaven: "I have both glorified it, and will glorify it again." 29 The multitude therefore, who stood by and heard it, were saying that it had thundered; others were saying, "An angel has spoken to Him." 30 Jesus answered and said, "This voice has not come for My sake, but for your sakes. 31 "Now judgment is upon this world; now the ruler of this world shall be cast out. 32 "And I, if I be lifted up from the earth, will draw all men to Myself." 33 But He was saying this to indicate the kind of death by which He was to die. 34 The multitude therefore answered Him, "We have heard out of the Law that the

[a] I.e., the custom of anointing for burial.

WILLIAMS

keep it for the day of my funeral,ᵃ 8 for you always have the poor among you, but you will not always have me."

9 A goodly number of the Jews learned that He was at Bethany, and so they came there, not only to see Jesus but also to see Lazarus, whom He had raised from the dead. 10 But the high priests planned to kill Lazarus, 11 for on account of him many of the Jews were leaving them and believing in Jesus.

12 The next day the vast crowd that had come to the feast, on hearing that Jesus was coming into Jerusalem, 13 took palm-branches and went out to meet Him, and kept on shouting:

"Blessings on Him! ᵇ
Blessed be He who comes in the name of the Lord;
Blessings on the King of Israel!"

14 Then Jesus found a young donkey and mounted it, doing as the Scripture says:

15 "Cease from fearing, Daughter of Zion;
See, your King is coming mounted on an ass's colt!"

16 His disciples at the time did not understand this, but after Jesus was glorified, they remembered that this had been written about Him and that they had fulfilled it in His case. 17 The crowd that had been with Him when He called Lazarus out of the grave and raised him from the dead, kept on talking about it. 18 This is why the crowd went out to meet Him, because they had heard that He had performed this wonder-work. 19 So the Pharisees said to one another, "You see, you cannot help it at all; the whole world has gone off after Him!"

20 There were some Greeks among those who were coming up to worship at the feast, 21 and they went to Philip who was from Bethsaida in Galilee, and kept making this request of him, "Sir, we want to see Jesus."

22 Philip went and told Andrew; Andrew and Philip both went and told Jesus. 23 Jesus answered them, "The time has come for the Son of Man to be glorified. 24 I most solemnly say to you, unless a grain of wheat falls into the ground and dies, it remains a single grain. But if it does die, it yields a great harvest. 25 Whoever loves his lower life will lose the higher; but whoever hates his lower life in this world preserves the higher for eternal life. 26 If anyone serves me, he must continue to follow me, and my servant also must go wherever I go. If anyone serves me, my Father will show him honor. 27 Now my soul is troubled; what shall I say? Father, save me from this hour of agony! And yet it was for this very purpose that I came to this hour of agony. 28 Father, glorify your name."

Then a voice came out of heaven, "I have already glorified it and I will again glorify it."

29 The crowd of bystanders on hearing it said that it was thunder; others, however, said, "An angel has spoken to Him!"

30 Jesus answered, "This voice did not come for my sake, but for yours. 31 This world is now in process of judgment; the prince of this world is now to be expelled. 32 And if I am lifted up from the earth, I will draw all men to me." 33 He said this to show the kind of death He was going to die.

34 The crowd answered Him, "We have learned from the law that the Christ is to remain here forever, and so how can you say

BECK

Jesus said. 8 "The poor you always have with you, but you don't always have Me."

9 A large crowd of the Jews found out He was there, and they came, not only on account of Jesus but also to see Lazarus, whom He had raised from the dead. 10 But the ruling priests decided to kill Lazarus too, 11 because he was the reason many Jews were going over to Jesus and believing in Him.

The King Comes to Jerusalem

12 The next day the large crowd that had come to the festival and heard, "Jesus is coming to Jerusalem," 13 took branches from the palm trees and went out to meet Him, shouting:

"Our Savior!
Blessed is He who is coming in the Lord's name,¹⁰
The King of Israel!"

14 Jesus found a donkey and sat on it, as it is written:

15 Don't be afraid, daughter of Zion!
Look! Your King is coming, riding on a donkey's colt! ¹¹

16 At that time His disciples didn't know what it meant, but after Jesus was glorified, they remembered this was written about Him and was done to Him.

17 The people who had been with Him when He called Lazarus out of the grave and raised him from the dead were telling what they had seen. 18 Because the crowd heard He had done this miracle, it came to meet Him.

19 Then the Pharisees said to one another, "You see, you're not getting anywhere. Look! The world is running after Him."

Death and Glory

20 Among those who came up to worship at the festival were some Greeks. 21 They went to Philip (who was from Bethsaida in Galilee) and told him, "Sir, we want to see Jesus." 22 Philip went and told Andrew. Andrew and Philip went and told Jesus.

23 Jesus answered them, "The time has come for the Son of Man to be glorified. 24 Surely, I tell you, if a kernel of wheat doesn't fall into the ground and die, it will be just one kernel. But if it dies, it produces much grain. 25 Love your life and lose it, but hate your life in this world, and you will keep it for an everlasting life. 26 If you serve Me, follow Me; and where I am, there My servant will be. If you serve Me, the Father will honor you.

27 "I am deeply troubled¹² now. But what should I say? Father, save Me from what is going to happen? No! I came to suffer this now. 28 Father, glorify Your name."

Then a voice came from heaven: "I have glorified My name and will glorify it again."

29 The crowd, which stood there and heard it, said it had thundered. Others said, "An angel talked to Him." 30 Jesus explained: "That voice did not come for My benefit but for yours.

31 "Now this world is being judged; now the ruler of this world will be thrown out. 32 And once I have been lifted up from the earth, I will draw all people to Me." 33 He said this to indicate how He was going to die.

34 Then the crowd answered Him, "We've heard from the Bible the promised Savior lives forever. How then, can You say the Son of

[a] Lit., *burial.* [b] Lit., *Hosanna.*

[10] Ps. 118:25-26
[11] Is. 40:9; 62:11; Zech. 9:9
[12] Ps. 6:3

K.J.V.

Christ abideth for ever: and how sayest thou, The Son of man must be lifted up? who is this Son of man? 35 Then Jesus said unto them, Yet a little while is the light with you. Walk while ye have the light, lest darkness come upon you: for he that walketh in darkness knoweth not whither he goeth. 36 While ye have light, believe in the light, that ye may be the children of light. These things spake Jesus, and departed, and did hide himself from them.

37 But though he had done so many miracles before them, yet they believed not on him: 38 That the saying of Esaias the prophet might be fulfilled, which he spake, Lord, who hath believed our report? and to whom hath the arm of the Lord been revealed? 39 Therefore they could not believe, because that Esaias said again, 40 He hath blinded their eyes, and hardened their heart; that they should not see with *their* eyes, nor understand with *their* heart, and be converted, and I should heal them. 41 These things said Esaias, when he saw his glory, and spake of him.

42 Nevertheless among the chief rulers also many believed on him; but because of the Pharisees they did not confess *him*, lest they should be put out of the synagogue: 43 For they loved the praise of men more than the praise of God.

44 Jesus cried and said, He that believeth on me, believeth not on me, but on him that sent me. 45 And he that seeth me seeth him that sent me. 46 I am come a light into the world, that whosoever believeth on me should not abide in darkness. 47 And if any man hear my words, and believe not, I judge him not: for I came not to judge the world, but to save the world. 48 He that rejecteth me, and receiveth not my words, hath one that judgeth him: the word that I have spoken, the same shall judge him in the last day. 49 For I have not spoken of myself; but the Father which sent me, he gave me a commandment, what I should say, and what I should speak: 50 And I know that his commandment is life everlasting: whatsoever I speak therefore, even as the Father said unto me, so I speak.

N.A.S.

Christ is to remain forever; and how can You say, 'The Son of Man must be lifted up'? Who is this Son of Man?" 35 Jesus therefore said to them, "For a little while longer the light is among you. Walk while you have the light, that darkness may not overtake you; he who walks in the darkness does not know where he goes. 36 "While you have the light, believe in the light, in order that you may become sons of light."

These things Jesus spoke, and He departed and hid Himself from them. 37 But though He had performed so many signs before them, *yet* they were not believing in Him; 38 that the word of Isaiah the prophet might be fulfilled, which he spoke, "LORD, WHO HAS BELIEVED OUR REPORT? AND TO WHOM HAS THE ARM OF THE LORD BEEN REVEALED?" 39 For this cause they could not believe, for Isaiah said again, 40 "HE HAS BLINDED THEIR EYES, AND HE HARDENED THEIR HEART; LEST THEY SEE WITH THEIR EYES, AND PERCEIVE WITH THEIR HEART, AND BE CONVERTED, AND I HEAL THEM." 41 These things Isaiah said, because he saw His glory, and he spoke of Him. 42 Nevertheless many even of the rulers believed in Him, but because of the Pharisees they were not confessing *Him*, lest they should be put out of the synagogue; 43 for they loved the approval of men rather than the approval of God.

44 And Jesus cried out and said, "He who believes in Me does not believe in Me, but in Him who sent Me. 45 "And he who beholds Me beholds the One who sent Me. 46 "I have come *as* light into the world, that everyone who believes in Me may not remain in darkness. 47 "And if any one hears My sayings, and does not keep them, I do not judge him; for I did not come to judge the world, but to save the world. 48 "He who rejects Me, and does not receive My sayings, has one who judges him; the word I spoke is what will judge him at the last day. 49 "For I did not speak on My own initiative, but the Father Himself who sent Me has given Me commandment, what to say, and what to speak. 50 "And I know that His commandment is eternal life; therefore the things I speak, I speak just as the Father has told Me."

13 Now before the feast of the passover, when Jesus knew that his hour was come that he should depart out of this world unto the Father, having loved his own which were in the world, he loved them unto the end. 2 And supper being ended, the devil having now put into the heart of Judas Iscariot, Simon's *son*, to betray him; 3 Jesus knowing that the Father had given all things into his hands, and that he was come from God, and went to God; 4 He riseth from supper, and laid aside his garments; and took a towel, and girded himself. 5 After that he poureth water into a basin, and began to wash the disci-

13 Now before the feast of the Passover, Jesus knowing that His hour had come that He should depart out of this world to the Father, having loved His own who were in the world, He loved them to the end. 2 And during supper, the devil having already put into the heart of Judas Iscariot, *the son* of Simon, to betray Him, 3 *Jesus*, knowing that the Father had given all things into His hands, and that He had come forth from God, and was going back to God, 4 *rose from supper, and *laid aside His garments; and taking a towel, girded Himself about. 5 Then He *poured water into the basin, and began to wash the disciples'

WILLIAMS

that the Son of Man must be lifted up? Who is this Son of Man?"

35 Jesus said to them, "Only a little while longer you will have the light. Keep on living by it while you have the light, so that darkness may not overtake you, for whoever walks about in the dark does not know where he is going. 36 While you have the light believe in the light, that you may become sons of light." On saying this Jesus went away and hid Himself.

37 Although He had performed so many wonder-works right before their eyes, they did not believe in Him, 38 so that the utterance of the prophet Isaiah was fulfilled:

"Lord, who has believed what they heard from us?
And to whom has the mighty arm of the Lord been shown?"

39 So they could not believe, for Isaiah again has said:

40 "He has blinded their eyes and benumbed their hearts,
So that they cannot see with their eyes and understand with their hearts.
And turn to me to cure them."

41 Isaiah said this, because he saw His glory; yes, he spoke about Him. 42 And yet in spite of all this, even among the leading men many came to believe in Him, but because of the Pharisees they did not own it, for fear of being turned out of the synagogue; 43 for they loved the praise of men instead of the praise of God.

44 But Jesus cried aloud, "Whoever believes in me believes not merely in me but in Him who has sent me; 45 and whoever sees me sees Him who has sent me. 46 I have come as light into the world, so that no one who continues to believe in me can remain in darkness. 47 If anyone hears my words and fails to keep them, it is not I that judge him, for I have not come to judge but to save the world. 48 Whoever persistently rejects me and refuses to accept my teachings has something to judge him; the very message I have spoken will judge him on the last day. 49 This is because I have not spoken on my own authority, but the Father who has sent me has given me orders Himself what to say and what to tell. 50 And I know that His orders mean eternal life. So whatever I speak I am speaking as the Father has told me."

13 *Jesus washes the disciples' feet and by example teaches them that humility and service pave the way to happiness; Judas Iscariot pointed out; Peter warned that he is going to disown Christ*

Before the Passover feast started, Jesus knew that His time had come for Him to leave the world and go to the Father, and as He had loved His own in the world He loved them to the last. 2 So Jesus, while supper was on—although He knew that the devil had suggested *a* to Judas Iscariot, Simon's son, to betray Him—3 because He was sure that the Father had put everything into His hands, and that He had come from God and was going back to God, 4 got up from the table, took off His Outer clothes, and took a towel and tied it around His waist. 5 Then He poured water into a basin and began to wash

[a] Grk., *put into the heart.*

BECK

Man must be lifted up? Who is this Son of Man?"

35 "The Light will be with you just a little longer," Jesus answered them. "Walk while you have the Light, or darkness will overtake you. If you walk in the dark, you don't know where you're going. 36 While you have the Light, believe in the Light in order to become enlightened people."

After Jesus had said this, He went away and hid from them.

37 Although they had seen Him do so many miracles, they wouldn't believe in Him— 38 what the prophet Isaiah said had to come true:

*Lord, who has believed what we preach?
And to whom has the Lord's arm been uncovered?* [13]

39 And so they couldn't believe, because Isaiah also said,

40 *He blinded their eyes
And dulled their minds
So that their eyes don't see,
Their minds don't understand,
And they don't turn and let Me heal them.* [14]

41 Isaiah said this because he saw His glory and spoke of Him. 42 And yet even many of the rulers believed in Him but wouldn't say so publicly, because the Pharisees would have put them out of the synagog. 43 Yes, they loved to be praised by men more than by God.

44 Then Jesus called out, "If you believe in Me, you don't believe only in Me but in Him who sent Me. 45 And if you see Me, you see Him who sent Me. 46 I have come as a light into the world so that anyone who believes in Me will not have to stay in the dark. 47 If anyone hears what I say but doesn't keep it, I don't condemn him, because I didn't come to condemn the world but to save the world. 48 If anyone rejects Me and doesn't take to heart what I say, he has one that is condemning him. The Word that I spoke will condemn him on the last day, 49 because what I said didn't come from Me, but the Father who sent Me ordered Me to say and tell it. 50 I know what He orders is everlasting life. And so, whatever I say, I say it just as the Father told Me."

Jesus Washes the Disciples' Feet

13 Before the Passover festival Jesus knew the time had come for Him to leave this world and go to the Father. He had loved His own who were in the world, and now He loved them to the end.

2 It was during the supper. The devil had already put the idea of betraying Jesus into the mind of Judas, the son of Simon from Kerioth. 3 Jesus knew the Father put everything in His hands and He had come from God and was going back to God. 4 So Jesus rose from supper, laid aside His outer garment, took a towel, and tied it around Him. 5 Then He poured water into a basin and started to wash the disciples' feet and to dry

[13] Is. 53:1
[14] Is. 6:10

K.J.V.

ples' feet, and to wipe *them* with the towel wherewith he was girded. 6 Then cometh he to Simon Peter: and Peter saith unto him, Lord, dost thou wash my feet? 7 Jesus answered and said unto him, What I do thou knowest not now; but thou shalt know hereafter. 8 Peter saith unto him, Thou shalt never wash my feet. Jesus answered him, If I wash thee not, thou hast no part with me. 9 Simon Peter saith unto him, Lord, not my feet only, but also *my* hands and *my* head. 10 Jesus saith to him, He that is washed needeth not save to wash *his* feet, but is clean every whit: and ye are clean, but not all. 11 For he knew who should betray him; therefore said he, Ye are not all clean. 12 So after he had washed their feet, and had taken his garments, and was set down again, he said unto them, Know ye what I have done to you? 13 Ye call me Master and Lord: and ye say well; for *so* I am. 14 If I then, *your* Lord and Master, have washed your feet; ye also ought to wash one another's feet. 15 For I have given you an example, that ye should do as I have done to you. 16 Verily, verily, I say unto you, The servant is not greater than his lord; neither he that is sent greater than he that sent him. 17 If ye know these things, happy are ye if ye do them.

18 I speak not of you all: I know whom I have chosen: but that the Scripture may be fulfilled, He that eateth bread with me hath lifted up his heel against me. 19 Now I tell you before it come, that, when it is come to pass, ye may believe that I am *he*. 20 Verily, verily, I say unto you, He that receiveth whomsoever I send receiveth me; and he that receiveth me receiveth him that sent me. 21 When Jesus had thus said, he was troubled in spirit, and testified, and said, Verily, verily, I say unto you, that one of you shall betray me. 22 Then the disciples looked one on another, doubting of whom he spake. 23 Now there was leaning on Jesus' bosom one of his disciples, whom Jesus loved. 24 Simon Peter therefore beckoned to him, that he should ask who it should be of whom he spake. 25 He then lying on Jesus' breast saith unto him, Lord, who is it? 26 Jesus answered, He it is, to whom I shall give a sop, when I have dipped *it*. And when he had dipped the sop, he gave *it* to Judas Iscariot, *the son* of Simon. 27 And after the sop Satan entered into him. Then said Jesus unto him, That thou doest, do quickly. 28 Now no man at the table knew for what intent he spake this unto him. 29 For some *of them* thought, because Judas had the bag, that Jesus had said unto him, Buy *those things* that we have need of against the feast; or, that he should give something to the poor. 30 He then, having received the sop, went immediately out; and it was night.

31 Therefore, when he was gone out, Jesus said, Now is the Son of man glorified, and God

N.A.S.

feet, and to wipe them with the towel with which He was girded. 6And so He *came to Simon Peter. He *said to Him, "Lord, do You wash my feet?" 7 Jesus answered and said to him, "What I do you do not realize now; but you shall understand hereafter." 8 Peter *said to Him, "Never shall You wash my feet!" Jesus answered him, "If I do not wash you, you have no part with Me." 9 Simon Peter *said to Him, "Lord, not my feet only, but also my hands and my head." 10 Jesus *said to him, "He who has bathed needs only to wash his feet, but is completely clean; and you are clean, but not all *of you*." 11 For He knew the one who was betraying Him; for this reason He said, "Not all of you are clean."

12 And so when He had washed their feet, and taken His garments, and reclined *at table* again, He said to them, "Do you know what I have done to you? 13 "You call Me Teacher, and Lord; and you are right; for *so* I am. 14 "If I then, the Lord and the Teacher, washed your feet, you also ought to wash one another's feet. 15 "For I gave you an example that you also should do as I did to you. 16 "Truly, truly, I say to you, a slave is not greater than his master; neither one who is sent greater than the one who sent him. 17 "If you know these things, you are blessed if you do them. 18 "I do not speak of all of you. I know the ones I have chosen; but *it is* that the Scripture may be fulfilled, 'HE WHO EATS MY BREAD HAS LIFTED UP HIS HEEL AGAINST ME.' 19 "From now on I am telling you before *it* comes to pass, so that when it does occur, you may believe that I am *He*. 20 "Truly, truly, I say to you, he who receives whomever I send receives Me; and he who receives Me receives Him who sent Me."

21 When Jesus had said this, He became troubled in spirit, and testified, and said, "Truly, truly, I say to you, that one of you will betray Me." 22 The disciples *began* looking at one another, at a loss *to know* of which one He was speaking. 23 There was reclining on Jesus' breast one of His disciples, whom Jesus loved. 24 Simon Peter therefore *gestured to him, and *said to him, "Tell *us* who it is of whom He is speaking." 25 He, leaning back thus on Jesus' breast, *said to Him, "Lord, who is it?" 26 Jesus therefore *answered, "That is the one for whom I shall dip the morsel, and give it to him." So when He had dipped the morsel, He *took and *gave it to Judas, *the son* of Simon Iscariot. 27 And after the morsel, Satan then entered into him. Jesus therefore *said to him, "What you do, do quickly." 28 Now no one of those reclining *at table* knew for what purpose He had said this to him. 29 For some were supposing, because Judas had the money box, that Jesus was saying to him, "Buy the things we have need of for the feast"; or else, that he should give something to the poor. 30 And so after receiving the morsel he went out immediately; and it was night.

31 When therefore he had gone out, Jesus *said, "Now is the Son of Man glorified, and

WILLIAMS

the disciples' feet and to wipe them with the towel which was around His waist. 6 Thus He came to Simon Peter. Peter said to Him, "Lord, are you going to wash my feet?"

7 Jesus answered him, "You do not now understand what I am doing, but by-and-by you will learn."

8 Peter said to Him, "You must never wash my feet!"

Jesus answered, "Unless I do wash you, you can have no share with me."

9 Simon Peter said to Him, "Lord, do not stop with my feet, then; but wash my hands and face too!"

10 Jesus said to him, "Anyone who has just taken a bath has no need of washing anything but his feet, but he is clean all over. And you are now clean, though not all of you are." 11 For He knew who was going to betray Him; this is why He said, "You are not all clean."

12 So when He had washed their feet and had put on His clothes and taken His place at the table, He said to them again: "Do you understand what I have done to you? 13 You call me Teacher and Lord, and you are right in calling me so, for that is what I am. 14 If I then, your Lord and Teacher, have washed your feet, you too ought to wash one another's feet. 15 For I have set you an example, in order that you too may practice what I have done to you. 16 I most solemnly say to you, no slave is superior to his master, and no messenger is greater than the man who sends him. 17 If you know all this, happy are you if you practice it. 18 I do not mean all of you. I know whom I have chosen; but I know that the Scriptures must be fulfilled:

'The man who is eating my bread
Has lifted his heel against me.'

19 From now on I will tell you things before they take place, so that when they do take place, you may believe that I am the Christ. 20 I most solemnly say to you, whoever welcomes any messenger I send welcomes me, and whoever welcomes me welcomes Him who has sent me."

21 After saying this Jesus was deeply moved in spirit and solemnly said, "I most solemnly say to you, one of you is going to betray me."

22 The disciples kept looking at one another, but were at a loss to know which one He meant. 23 One of the disciples, whom Jesus specially loved, was sitting very close to Jesus at His right.[b] 24 So Simon Peter nodded to him to ask Him which one it was that He meant. 25 He leaned back on Jesus' breast and said to Him, "Lord, who is it?"

26 Jesus answered, "It is that one to whom I give the piece of bread when I dip it in the dish." So he dipped it into the dish and took it and gave it to Judas, Simon Iscariot's son. 27 As soon as he took the bread, Satan took possession of Judas.

Then Jesus said to him, "Make quick work of what you are to do." 28 But no one else at the table knew what He meant by this, 29 for some of them were thinking, as Judas had the purse, that Jesus meant to say to him, "Buy what we need for the feast," or to give something to the poor. 30 So as soon as he took the piece of bread, he left the room. It was then night.

31 When he had left, Jesus said, "Now the Son of Man has been glorified, and God has

BECK

them with the towel that was tied around Him.

6 And so He came to Simon Peter. "Lord," Peter asked Him, "are You going to wash my feet?"

7 "You don't know now what I'm doing," Jesus answered him. "But later you will understand."

8 "No!" Peter told Him. "You'll never wash my feet."

"If I don't wash you," Jesus answered him, "you have no share in Me."

9 "Lord," Simon Peter told Him, "not only my feet but also my hands and my head."

10 "Anyone who has bathed needs only to have his feet washed," Jesus told him. "He's clean all over. You're clean, but not all of you." 11 He knew who was betraying Him. That's why He said, "Not all of you are clean."

12 After He had washed their feet and put on His garment, He lay down again. 13 "Do you know what I've done to you?" He asked them. "You call Me Teacher and Lord, and you're right because I am that. 14 Now if I, the Lord and the Teacher, have washed your feet, you, too, should wash one another's feet. 15 I've given you an example so that you will do as I did to you. 16 Surely, I tell you, a slave is no greater than his Master, and if you're sent, you're no greater than He who sent you. 17 If you know this, you're happy if you do it.

18 "I'm not talking about all of you. I know whom I've chosen. But what the Bible says has to come true: *He who eats My bread kicks Me.*[15] 19 From now on I'm telling you these things before they happen so that when they happen you believe I am the One.

20 "Let Me assure you, if you receive anyone I send, you receive Me, and if you receive Me, you receive Him who sent Me."

"Is It I?"

21 After saying this, Jesus was deeply troubled. "I tell you the truth," He declared, "one of you is going to betray Me!"

22 The disciples started to look at one another, wondering whom He meant.

23 One of His disciples, the one Jesus loved, was lying close to Jesus' bosom. 24 Simon Peter motioned to him to ask whom He meant.

25 Leaning back, where he was, against Jesus' bosom, he asked Him, "Lord, who is it?"

26 "I'll dip this piece of bread and give it to him," Jesus answered. "He's the one." Then he dipped it and gave it to Judas, the son of Simon from Kerioth.

27 After Judas took the piece of bread, the devil went into him. So Jesus told him, "What you're doing, do quickly." 28 What He meant by telling him this, nobody at the table knew. 29 Some thought, since Judas had the money box Jesus was telling him, "Buy what we need for the festival," or that he should give something to the poor.

30 Right after taking the piece of bread Judas went outside. And it was night.

31 When Judas had gone out, Jesus said, "Now the Son of Man is glorified, and in Him

---

[b] Lit., *reclining on His bosom,* the place of first honor.

[15] Ps. 41:9

K.J.V.

is glorified in him. 32 If God be glorified in him, God shall also glorify him in himself, and shall straightway glorify him. 33 Little children, yet a little while I am with you. Ye shall seek me; and as I said unto the Jews, Whither I go, ye cannot come; so now I say to you. 34A new commandment I give unto you, That ye love one another; as I have loved you, that ye also love one another. 35 By this shall all *men* know that ye are my disciples, if ye have love one to another.

36 Simon Peter said unto him, Lord, whither goest thou? Jesus answered him, Whither I go, thou canst not follow me now; but thou shalt follow me afterwards. 37 Peter said unto him, Lord, why cannot I follow thee now? I will lay down my life for thy sake. 38 Jesus answered him, Wilt thou lay down thy life for my sake? Verily, verily, I say unto thee, The cock shall not crow, till thou hast denied me thrice.

14 Let not your heart be troubled: ye believe in God, believe also in me. 2 In my Father's house are many mansions: if *it were not so,* I would have told you. I go to prepare a place for you. 3And if I go and prepare a place for you, I will come again, and receive you unto myself; that where I am, *there* ye may be also. 4And whither I go ye know, and the way ye know. 5 Thomas saith unto him, Lord, we know not whither thou goest; and how can we know the way? 6 Jesus saith unto him, I am the way, the truth, and the life: no man cometh unto the Father, but by me. 7 If ye had known me, ye should have known my Father also: and from henceforth ye know him, and have seen him. 8 Philip saith unto him, Lord, shew us the Father, and it sufficeth us. 9 Jesus saith unto him, Have I been so long time with you, and yet hast thou not known me, Philip? he that hath seen me hath seen the Father; and how sayest thou *then,* Shew us the Father? 10 Believest thou not that I am in the Father, and the Father in me? the words that I speak unto you I speak not of myself: but the Father that dwelleth in me, he doeth the works. 11 Believe me that I *am* in the Father, and the Father in me: or else believe me for the very works' sake. 12 Verily, verily, I say unto you, He that believeth on me, the works that I do shall he do also; and greater *works* than these shall he do; because I go unto my Father. 13And whatsoever ye shall ask in my name, that will I do, that the Father may be

N.A.S.

God is glorified in Him; 32 if God is glorified in Him, God will also glorify Him in Himself, and will glorify Him immediately. 33 "Little children, I am with you a little while longer. You shall seek Me; and as I said to the Jews, 'Where I am going, you cannot come', now I say to you also. 34 "A new commandment I give to you, that you love one another, even as I have loved you, that you also love one another. 35 "By this all men will know that you are My disciples, if you have love for one another."

36 Simon Peter *said to Him, "Lord, where are You going?" Jesus answered, "Where I go, you cannot follow Me now; but you shall follow later." 37 Peter *said to Him, "Lord, why can I not follow You right now? I will lay down my life for You." 38 Jesus *answered, "Will you lay down your life for Me? Truly, truly, I say to you, a cock shall not crow, until you deny Me three times.

14 "Let not your heart be troubled; ᵃbelieve in God, believe also in Me. 2 "In My Father's house are many dwelling places; if it were not so, I would have told you; for I go to prepare a place for you. 3 "And if I go and prepare a place for you, I will come again, and receive you to Myself; that where I am, *there* you may be also. 4 ᵇ"And you know the way where I am going." 5 Thomas *said to Him, "Lord, we do not know where You are going; how do we know the way?" 6 Jesus *said to him, "I am the way, and the truth, and the life; no one comes to the Father, but through Me. 7 "If you had known Me, you would have known My Father also; from now on you know Him, and have seen Him." 8 Philip *said to Him, "Lord, show us the Father, and it is enough for us." 9 Jesus *said to him, "Have I been so long with you, and yet you have not come to know Me, Philip? He who has seen Me has seen the Father; how do you say, 'Show us the Father'? 10 "Do you not believe that I am in the Father, and the Father is in Me? The words that I say to you I do not speak on My own initiative, but the Father abiding in Me does His works. 11 "Believe Me that I am in the Father, and the Father in Me; otherwise believe on account of the works themselves. 12 "Truly, truly, I say to you, he who believes in Me, the works that I do shall he do also; and greater *works* than these shall he do; because I go to the Father. 13 "And whatever you ask in My name, that will I do, that the Fa-

[a] Or, *you believe in God.* [b] Many ancient authorities read, *And where I go you know, and the way you know.*

WILLIAMS

been glorified in Him, 32 and God will through Himself glorify Him, and He will glorify Him at once. 33 Dear children, I am to be with you only a little while longer. You will look for me, but, as I told the Jews, so I now tell you, you cannot just now go where I am going. 34 I give you a new command, to love one another. Just as I have loved you, you too must love one another. 35 By this everybody will know that you are my disciples, if you keep on showing love for one another."

36 Simon Peter said to Him, "Lord, where are you going?"

Jesus answered, "I am going where you cannot follow me just now, but you will later follow me."

37 Peter said to Him, "Lord, why can I not follow you right now? I will lay down my life for you."

38 Jesus answered, "You will lay down your life for me! I most solemnly say to you, before a cock crows, you will three times disown me!"

14 *Jesus comforts His troubled disciples by telling them He is going to prepare for them dwelling places in heaven; that He will come back to take them there; promises the Spirit to help and guide them till then*

"Stop letting your hearts be troubled; keep on believing in God, and also in me. 2 In my Father's house there are many dwelling places; if there were not, I would have told you, for I am going away to make ready a place for you, 3And if I go and make it ready for you, I will come back and take you to be face to face with me, so that you may always be right where I am. 4And you know the way to the place where I am going."

5 Thomas said to Him, "Lord, we do not know where you are going, and so how can we know the way?"

6 Jesus answered him, "I am the way and the truth and the life. No one can come to the Father except through me. 7 If you knew me, you would know my Father too. From now on you do know Him and you have seen Him."

8 Philip said to Him, "Lord, let us see the Father, and that will satisfy us."

9 Jesus said to him, "Have I been with you disciples so long, and yet you, Philip, have not recognized me? Whoever has seen me has seen the Father. How can you say, 'Let us see the Father'? 10 Do you not believe that I am in union with the Father and that the Father is in union with me? I am not saying these things on my own authority, but the Father who always remains in union with me is doing these things Himself. 11 You must believe me, that I am in union with the Father and that the Father is in union with me, or else you must do so because of the very things that I am doing. 12 I most solemnly say to you, whoever perseveres in believing in me can himself do the things that I am doing; yes, he can do even greater things than I am doing, because I am going to the Father. 13And anything you ask for as bearers of my name[a] I will do for you, so that the Father

[a] Grk., *in my name.*

BECK

God is glorified. 32 God will also glorify Him in Himself; yes, He will glorify Him now."

Jesus Warns Peter

33 "Children," Jesus said, "I'm with you just a little longer. You will look for Me, but as I told the Jews, so I tell you now: Where I'm going, you can't come.

34 "I'm giving you a new order: Love one another! Love one another as I have loved you. 35 By your loving one another everybody will know you're My disciples."

36 "Lord, where are You going?" Simon Peter asked Him.

"Where I'm going you can't follow Me now," Jesus answered him; "but you will follow Me later."

37 "Lord, why can't I follow You now?" Peter asked Him. "I'll give my life for You."

38 "You'll give your life for Me?" Jesus asked. "I tell you the truth: The rooster will not crow till you've denied Me three times."

"I Am Going Away"

14 "Don't feel troubled. Believe in God, and believe in Me. 2 In My Father's house there are many rooms. If it were not so, I would have told you, because I go to prepare a place for you. 3And when I have gone and prepared a place for you, I'll come again and take you home with Me so you'll be where I am. 4 You know the way to the place where I'm going."

5 "Lord, we don't know where You're going," Thomas said to Him. "So how can we know the way?"

6 "I am the Way, the Truth, and the Life," Jesus answered him. "No one comes to the Father except by Me. 7 If you have learned to know Me, you'll know My Father too. From now on you know Him and have seen Him."

8 Philip said to Him, "Lord, show us the Father; that's enough for us."

9 "I've been with all of you so long," Jesus answered him, "and you don't know Me, Philip? If you have seen Me, you have seen the Father. How can you say, 'Show us the Father'? 10 Don't you believe I am in the Father and the Father is in Me? What I tell you doesn't come from Me, but the Father who lives in Me is doing His works. 11 Believe Me, I am in the Father, and the Father is in Me. Or else believe Me on account of My works.

12 "I tell you the truth, if you believe in Me you'll do the works I'm doing, and you'll do greater works than these, because I'm going to the Father, 13 and I will do anything you ask in My name in order that the Son may glorify

K.J.V.

glorified in the Son. 14 If ye shall ask any thing in my name, I will do *it.*

15 If ye love me, keep my commandments. 16 And I will pray the Father, and he shall give you another Comforter, that he may abide with you for ever; 17 *Even* the Spirit of truth; whom the world cannot receive, because it seeth him not, neither knoweth him: but ye know him; for he dwelleth with you, and shall be in you. 18 I will not leave you comfortless: I will come to you. 19 Yet a little while, and the world seeth me no more; but ye see me: because I live, ye shall live also. 20 At that day ye shall know that I *am* in my Father, and ye in me, and I in you. 21 He that hath my commandments, and keepeth them, he it is that loveth me: and he that loveth me shall be loved of my Father, and I will love him, and will manifest myself to him. 22 Judas saith unto him, not Iscariot, Lord, how is it that thou wilt manifest thyself unto us, and not unto the world? 23 Jesus answered and said unto him, If a man love me, he will keep my words: and my Father will love him, and we will come unto him, and make our abode with him. 24 He that loveth me not keepeth not my sayings: and the word which ye hear is not mine, but the Father's which sent me. 25 These things have I spoken unto you, being *yet* present with you. 26 But the Comforter, *which is* the Holy Ghost, whom the Father will send in my name, he shall teach you all things, and bring all things to your remembrance, whatsoever I have said unto you. 27 Peace I leave with you, my peace I give unto you: not as the world giveth, give I unto you. Let not your heart be troubled, neither let it be afraid. 28 Ye have heard how I said unto you, I go away, and come *again* unto you. If ye loved me, ye would rejoice, because I said, I go unto the Father: for my Father is greater than I. 29 And now I have told you before it come to pass, that, when it is come to pass, ye might believe. 30 Hereafter I will not talk much with you: for the prince of this world cometh, and hath nothing in me. 31 But that the world may know that I love the Father; and as the Father gave me commandment, even so I do. Arise, let us go hence.

15 I am the true vine, and my Father is the husbandman. 2 Every branch in me that beareth not fruit he taketh away: and every *branch* that beareth fruit, he purgeth it, that it may bring forth more fruit. 3 Now ye are clean through the word which I have spoken unto you. 4 Abide in me, and I in you. As the branch cannot bear fruit of itself, except it abide in the

N.A.S.

ther may be glorified in the Son. 14 "If you ask Me anything in My name, I will do *it.* 15 "If you love Me, you will keep My commandments. 16 "And I will ask the Father, and He will give you another Helper, that He may be with you forever; 17 *that is* the Spirit of truth, whom the world cannot receive, because it does not behold Him or know Him, *but* you know Him because He abides with you, and will be in you. 18 "I will not leave you as orphans; I will come to you. 19 "After a little while the world will behold Me no more; but you *will* behold Me; because I live, you shall live also. 20 "In that day you shall know that I am in My Father, and you in Me, and I in you. 21 "He who has My commandments, and keeps them, he it is who loves Me; and he who loves Me shall be loved by My Father, and I will love him, and will disclose Myself to him." 22 Judas (not Iscariot) *said to Him, "Lord, what then has happened that You are going to disclose Yourself to us, and not to the world?" 23 Jesus answered and said to him, "If anyone loves Me, he will keep My word; and My Father will love him, and We will come to him, and make Our abode with him. 24 "He who does not love Me does not keep My words; and the word which you hear is not Mine, but the Father's who sent Me.

25 "These things I have spoken to you, while abiding with you. 26 "But the Helper, the Holy Spirit, whom the Father will send in My name, He will teach you all things, and bring to your remembrance all that I said to you. 27 "Peace I leave with you; My peace I give to you; nót as the world gives, do I give to you. Let not your heart be troubled, nor let it be fearful. 28 "You heard that I said to you, 'I go away, and I will come to you.' If you loved Me, you would have rejoiced, because I go to the Father; for the Father is greater than I. 29 "And now I have told you before it comes to pass, that when it comes to pass, you may believe. 30 "I will not speak much more with you, for the ruler of the world is coming, and he has nothing in Me; 31 but that the world may know that I love the Father, and as the Father gave Me commandment, even so I do. Arise, let us go from here.

15 "I am the true vine, and My Father is the vinedresser. 2 "Every branch in Me that does not bear fruit, He takes away; and every *branch* that bears fruit, He *prunes it, that it may bear more fruit. 3 "You are already clean because of the word which I have spoken to you. 4 "Abide in Me, and I in you. As the branch cannot bear fruit of itself, unless it

[a] Lit., *cleanses.*

WILLIAMS

may be glorified through the Son. 14 Yes, I repeat it, anything you ask for as bearers of my name I will do it for you.

15 "If you really love me, you will keep my commands. 16And I will ask the Father and He will give you another Helper, to remain with you to the end of the age; 17 even the Spirit of truth, whom the world cannot accept, because it does not see Him or recognize Him, because He is going to remain with you, and will be within you. 18 I will not leave you helpless orphans. I am coming back to you. 19 In just a little while the world will not see me any more, but you will be seeing me. Because I am to live on, you too will live on. 20At that time you will know that I am in union with my Father and you are in union with me and I am in union with you. 21 Whoever continues to hold and keep my commands is the one who really loves me, and whoever really loves me will be loved by my Father; yes, I will love him myself and will make myself real b to him."

22 Judas (not Judas Iscariot) said to Him, "Why is it, Lord, that you are going to make yourself real to us and not to the world?" 23 Jesus answered him, "If anyone really loves me, he will observe my teaching, and my Father will love him, and both of us will come in face-to-face fellowship with him; yes, we will make our special dwelling place with him. 24 Whoever does not really love me does not observe my teaching; and yet the teaching which you are listening to is not mine but comes from the Father who has sent me.

25 "I have told you this while I am still staying with you. 26 But the Helper, the Holy Spirit, whom the Father will send to represent me, will teach you everything Himself, and cause you to remember everything that I have told you. 27 I now leave you the blessing of peace, I give you the blessing of my own peace. I myself do not give it in the way the world gives it. Stop letting your hearts be troubled or timid. 28 You have heard me say that I am going away and coming back to you; if you really loved me, you would rejoice over my telling you that I am going to the Father, because my Father is greater than I. 29 And now I have told you this before it takes place, that when it does take place you may believe in me.

30 "I shall not talk much more with you, for the evil ruler of this world is coming and he has nothing in common with me, 31 but he is coming that the world may know that I love the Father and am doing what the Father has ordered me to do. Get up and let us go away."

BECK

the Father. 14 If you ask Me for anything in My name, I'll do it.

15 "If you love Me, you will do what I order. 16And I will ask the Father, and He will give you another Comforter to be with you forever. 17 He is the Spirit of truth, whom the world cannot receive, because it doesn't see or know Him. You know Him, because He lives with you and will be in you.

18 "I will not leave you orphans; I'm coming back to you. 19 Only a little while and the world won't see Me any more. But you will see Me, because I live, and you, too, will live. 20 On that day you will know I'm in My Father and you in Me and I in you. 21 If you have My commandments and obey them, you love Me. And if you love Me, My Father will love you, and I will love you and show Myself to you."

22 Judas (not the man from Kerioth) asked Him, "Lord, what has happened that you're going to show yourself to us and not to the world?"

23 Jesus answered him, "If you love Me, you'll do what I say, and My Father will love you, and We will come to you and live with you. 24Anyone who doesn't love Me doesn't do what I say. And you are hearing, not what I say but what the Father says who sent Me.

25 "I've told you this while I'm still with you. 26 But the Comforter, the Holy Spirit, whom the Father will send in My name, will teach you everything and remind you of everything I told you.

27 "I leave peace with you, I give you My peace. I don't give it to you as the world gives it. Don't feel troubled or afraid. 28 You heard Me tell you, 'I'm going away, but I'm coming back to you.' If you loved Me, you'd be glad I'm going to the Father, because the Father is greater than I.

29 "I've told you this now before it happens, so that when it happens, you believe. 30 I won't say much to you any more, because the ruler of the world is coming. He has no claim on Me. 31 But I want the world to know I love the Father and am doing just what the Father ordered Me to do.

"Come, let us go away."

---

15 *The allegory of the vine and its branches; the joy of union with Christ; the world to hate the disciples; the guilt of sinning against the light; the Spirit, the Helper, will testify to Jesus*

"I am the real vine, and my Father is the cultivator. 2 He cuts away any branch on me that stops bearing fruit, and He repeatedly prunes every branch that continues to bear fruit, to make it bear more. 3 You are already pruned because of the teaching that I have given you. 4 You must remain in union with me and I will remain in union with you. Just as no branch by itself can bear fruit unless it remains united

The Vine and the Branch

15 "I am the real Vine, and My Father takes care of the vineyard. 2 He cuts away any branch of Mine that bears no fruit, and He trims any branch that bears fruit to make it bear more fruit.

3 "What I have said to you has already made you clean. Stay in Me, and I will stay in you. 4A branch can't bear any fruit by

[b] Lit., *will appear* or *show Myself*.

301

K.J.V.

vine; no more can ye, except ye abide in me. 5 I am the vine, ye *are* the branches. He that abideth in me, and I in him, the same bringeth forth much fruit; for without me ye can do nothing. 6 If a man abide not in me, he is cast forth as a branch, and is withered; and men gather them, and cast *them* into the fire, and they are burned. 7 If ye abide in me, and my words abide in you, ye shall ask what ye will, and it shall be done unto you. 8 Herein is my Father glorified, that ye bear much fruit; so shall ye be my disciples. 9As the Father hath loved me, so have I loved you: continue ye in my love. 10 If ye keep my commandments, ye shall abide in my love; even as I have kept my Father's commandments, and abide in his love. 11 These things have I spoken unto you, that my joy might remain in you, and *that* your joy might be full. 12 This is my commandment, That ye love one another, as I have loved you. 13 Greater love hath no man than this, that a man lay down his life for his friends. 14 Ye are my friends, if ye do whatsoever I command you. 15 Henceforth I call you not servants; for the servant knoweth not what his lord doeth: but I have called you friends; for all things that I have heard of my Father I have made known unto you. 16 Ye have not chosen me, but I have chosen you, and ordained you, that ye should go and bring forth fruit, and *that* your fruit should remain; that whatsoever ye shall ask of the Father in my name, he may give it you. 17 These things I command you, that ye love one another. 18 If the world hate you, ye know that it hated me before *it hated* you. 19 If ye were of the world, the world would love his own; but because ye are not of the world, but I have chosen you out of the world, therefore the world hateth you. 20 Remember the word that I said unto you, The servant is not greater than his lord. If they have persecuted me, they will also persecute you; if they have kept my saying, they will keep yours also. 21 But all these things will they do unto you for my name's sake, because they know not him that sent me. 22 If I had not come and spoken unto them, they had not had sin; but now they have no cloak for their sin. 23 He that hateth me hateth my Father also. 24 If I had not done among them the works which none other man did, they had not had sin: but now have they both seen and hated both me and my Father. 25 But *this cometh to pass,* that the word might be fulfilled that is written in their law, They hated me without a cause. 26 But when the Comforter is come, whom I will send unto you from the Father, *even* the Spirit of truth, which proceedeth from the Father, he shall testify of me: 27And ye also shall bear witness, because ye have been with me from the beginning.

N.A.S.

abides in the vine, so neither *can* you, unless you abide in Me. 5 "I am the vine, you are the branches; he who abides in Me, and I in him, he bears much fruit; for apart from Me you can do nothing. 6 "If anyone does not abide in Me, he is thrown away as a branch, and dries up; and they gather them, and cast them into the fire, and they are burned. 7 "If you abide in Me, and My words abide in you, ask whatever you wish, and it shall be done for you. 8 "By this is My Father glorified, that you bear much fruit, and *so* prove to be My disciples. 9 "Just as the Father has loved Me, I have also loved you; abide in My love. 10 "If you keep My commandments, you will abide in My love; just as I have kept My Father's commandments, and abide in His love. 11 "These things I have spoken to you, that My joy may be in you, and *that* your joy may be made full. 12 "This is My commandment, that you love one another, just as I have loved you. 13 "Greater love has no one than this, that one lay down his life for his friends. 14 "You are My friends, if you do what I command you. 15 "No longer do I call you slaves; for the slave does not know what his master is doing; but I have called you friends, for all things that I have heard from My Father I have made known to you. 16 "You did not choose Me, but I chose you, and appointed you, that you should go and bear fruit, and *that* your fruit should remain; that whatever you ask of the Father in My name, He may give to you. 17 "This I command you, that you love one another. 18 "If the world hates you, you know that it has hated Me before *it hated* you. 19 "If you were of the world, the world would love its own; but because you are not of the world, but I chose you out of the world, therefore the world hates you. 20 "Remember the word that I said to you, 'A slave is not greater than his master.' If they persecuted Me, they will also persecute you; if they kept My word, they will keep yours also. 21 "But all these things they will do to you for My name's sake, because they do not know the One who sent Me. 22 "If I had not come and spoken to them, they would not have sin; but now they have no excuse for their sin. 23 "He who hates Me hates My Father also. 24 "If I had not done among them the works which no one else did, they would not have sin; but now they have both seen and hated Me and My Father as well. 25 "But *they have done this* in order that the word may be fulfilled that is written in their Law, 'THEY HATED ME WITHOUT A CAUSE.' 26 "When the Helper comes, whom I will send to you from the Father, *that is* the Spirit of truth, who proceeds from the Father, He will bear witness of Me, 27 and you *will* bear witness also, because you have been with Me from the beginning.

WILLIAMS

to the vine, so you cannot unless you remain in union with me. 5 I am the vine, you are the branches. Whoever remains in union with me and I in union with him will bear abundant fruit, because you cannot do anything cut off from union with me. 6 If anyone does not remain in union with me, he is thrown away as a mere branch and is dried up; then it is picked up and thrown into the fire and burned up. 7 If you remain in union with me and my words remain in you, you may ask whatever you please and you shall have it. 8 By your continuously bearing abundant fruit and in this way proving yourselves to be real disciples of mine, my Father is glorified. 9 I have loved you just as the Father has loved me. You must remain in my love. 10 If you continue to keep my commands, you will remain in my love, just as I have kept my Father's commands and remain in His love.

11 "I have told you these things, that the joy which I have had may remain in you and that your joy may be complete. 12 This is my command to you, to keep on loving one another as I have loved you. 13 No one can show greater love than this, the giving of his life for his friends. 14 You are my friends, if you keep on doing what I command you to do. 15 I no longer call you slaves, because the slave does not know what his master is doing; I now call you friends, because I have told you everything that I have learned from my Father. 16 You have not chosen me; I have chosen you, and appointed you to go and bear fruit, that your fruit may remain too, so that the Father may grant you, as bearers of my name, whatever you ask Him for.

17 "What I command you to do is, to keep on loving one another. 18 If the world continues to hate you, remember that it has first hated me. 19 If you belonged to the world, the world would love what is its own. But it is because you do not belong to the world, but I have chosen you out of the world, that the world hates you. 20 Remember what I once told you: No slave is greater than his master. If they have persecuted me, they will persecute you too. If they have observed my teaching, they will observe yours too. 21 They will do all this to you on account of me, because they do not know Him who has sent me.

22 "If I had not come and spoken to them, they would not be guilty of sin. But now the fact is, they have no excuse for their sin. 23 Whoever continues to hate me continues to hate my Father too. 24 If I had not done things among them that no one else has ever done, they would not be guilty of sin. But now the fact is, they have seen and even hated both my Father and me. 25 But this is so that the saying written in their law may be fulfilled, 'They hated me without a cause.'

26 "When the Helper comes whom I will send from the Father to you, the Spirit of truth that comes from the Father, He will testify to me. 27And you too are to bear testimony to me, because you have been with me from the start."

BECK

itself—if it doesn't stay in the vine. Neither can you if you don't stay in Me. 5 I am the Vine, you are the branches. If you stay in Me and I in you, you bear much fruit. Without Me you can't do anything. 6 If anyone doesn't stay in Me, he's thrown away like a branch and dries up. Such branches are gathered, thrown into the fire, and burned. 7 If you stay in Me and what I say stays in you, ask for anything you want, and it will be done for you. 8 You glorify My Father when you bear much fruit and so prove to be My disciples. 9 As the Father has loved Me, so I have loved you. Stay in My love. 10 If you obey My commandments, you'll stay in My love, as I have obeyed My Father's commandments and stay in His love. 11 I told you this so that My joy will be in you and you will be very happy. 12 This is what I order you to do: Love one another as I have loved you. 13 No one has a greater love than he who gives his life for his friends. 14 You're My friends. if you do what I order you to do. 15 I don't call you servants any more, because a servant doesn't know what his master is doing. But I've called you friends because I've told you everything I heard from My Father. 16 You didn't choose Me, but I chose you and appointed you to go and bear fruit that doesn't pass away and to have the Father give you anything you ask Him in My name. 17 This is what I order you to do: Love one another.

18 "If the world hates you, you know it hated Me first. 19 If you belonged to the world, the world would love you as its own. But you don't belong to the world; I took you away from the world; that's why the world hates you. 20 Remember what I told you: a slave is no greater than his Master. If they persecuted Me, they'll persecute you. If they did what I said, they'll do what you say. 21 Now they will do all this to you on account of Me, because they don't know Him who sent Me. 22 If I hadn't come and spoken to them, they wouldn't be sinning, but now they have no excuse for their sin. 23 Anyone who hates Me hates My Father. 24 If I hadn't done among them the works no one else has done, they wouldn't be sinning. But now they have seen and hated Me and My Father. 25 What is written in their Bible has to come true: *They will hate Me without any reason.*[16]

26 "When the Comforter comes, whom I'll send you from the Father, the Spirit of truth, who comes from the Father, He'll tell the truth about Me. 27 And you, too, tell the truth, because you've been with Me from the beginning."

[16] Ps. 35:19; 69:4

K.J.V.

16 These things have I spoken unto you, that ye should not be offended. 2 They shall put you out of the synagogues: yea, the time cometh, that whosoever killeth you will think that he doeth God service. 3And these things will they do unto you, because they have not known the Father, nor me. 4 But these things have I told you, that when the time shall come, ye may remember that I told you of them. And these things I said not unto you at the beginning, because I was with you. 5 But now I go my way to him that sent me; and none of you asketh me, Whither goest thou? 6 But because I have said these things unto you, sorrow hath filled your heart. 7 Nevertheless I tell you the truth; It is expedient for you that I go away: for if I go not away, the Comforter will not come unto you; but if I depart, I will send him unto you. 8And when he is come, he will reprove the world of sin, and of righteousness, and of judgment: 9 Of sin, because they believe not on me; 10 Of righteousness, because I go to my Father, and ye see me no more; 11 Of judgment, because the prince of this world is judged. 12 I have yet many things to say unto you, but ye cannot bear them now. 13 Howbeit when he, the Spirit of truth, is come, he will guide you into all truth: for he shall not speak of himself; but whatsoever he shall hear, *that* shall he speak: and he will shew you things to come. 14 He shall glorify me: for he shall receive of mine, and shall shew *it* unto you. 15All things that the Father hath are mine: therefore said I, that he shall take of mine, and shall shew *it* unto you. 16A little while, and ye shall not see me: and again, a little while, and ye shall see me, because I go to the Father. 17 Then said *some* of his disciples among themselves, What is this that he saith unto us, A little while, and ye shall not see me: and again, a little while, and ye shall see me: and, Because I go to the Father? 18 They said therefore, What is this that he saith, A little while? we cannot tell what he saith. 19 Now Jesus knew that they were desirous to ask him, and said unto them, Do ye inquire among yourselves of that I said, A little while, and ye shall not see me: and again, a little while, and ye shall see me? 20 Verily, verily, I say unto you, That ye shall weep and lament, but the world shall rejoice; and ye shall be sorrowful, but your sorrow shall be turned into joy. 21A woman when she is in travail hath sorrow, because her hour is come: but as soon as she is delivered of the child, she remembereth no more the anguish, for joy that a man is born into the world. 22And ye now therefore have sorrow: but I will see you again, and your heart shall rejoice, and your joy no man taketh from you. 23And in that day ye shall ask me nothing. Verily, verily, I say unto you, What-

N.A.S.

16 "These things I have spoken to you, that you may be kept from stumbling. 2 "They will make you outcasts from the synagogue; but an hour is coming for everyone who kills you to think that he is offering service to God. 3 "And these things they will do, because they have not known the Father, or Me. 4 "But these things I have spoken to you, that when their hour comes, you may remember that I told you of them. And these things I did not say to you at the beginning, because I was with you. 5 "But now I am going to Him who sent Me; and none of you asks Me, 'Where are you going?' 6 "But because I have said these things to you, sorrow has filled your heart. 7 "But I tell you the truth, it is to your advantage that I go away; for if I do not go away, the Helper shall not come to you; but if I go, I will send Him to you. 8 "And He, when He comes, will convict the world concerning sin, and righteousness, and judgment; 9 concerning sin, because they do not believe in Me; 10 and concerning righteousness, because I go to the Father, and you no longer behold Me; 11 and concerning judgment, because the ruler of this world has been judged. 12 "I have many more things to say to you, but you cannot bear *them* now. 13 "But when He, the Spirit of truth, comes, He will guide you into all the truth; for He will not speak on His own initiative, but whatever He hears, He will speak; and He will disclose to you what is to come. 14 "He shall glorify Me; for He shall take of Mine, and shall disclose *it* to you. 15 "All things that the Father has are Mine; therefore I said that He takes of Mine, and will disclose *it* to you. 16 "A little while, and you *will* no longer behold Me; and again a little while, and you will see Me." 17 *Some* of His disciples therefore said to one another, "What is this thing He is telling us, 'A little while, and you *will* not behold Me; and again a little while, and you will see Me'; and, 'Because I go to the Father'?" 18And so they were saying, "What is this that He says, 'A little while'? We do not know what He is talking about." 19 Jesus knew that they wished to question Him, and He said to them, "Are you deliberating together about this, that I said, 'A little while, and you *will* not behold Me, and again a little while, and you *will* see Me'? 20 "Truly, truly, I say to you, that you will weep and lament, but the world will rejoice; you will be sorrowful, but your sorrow will be turned to joy. 21 "Whenever a woman is in travail she has sorrow, because her hour has come; but when she gives birth to the child, she remembers the anguish no more, for joy that a child has been born into the world. 22 "Therefore you, too, now have sorrow; but I will see you again, and your heart will rejoice, and no one takes your joy away from you. 23 "And in that day you will ask Me no question. Truly, truly, I say to you, if you shall ask the

WILLIAMS

16 *Jesus warns of future hardships; if He leaves, the Helper will come to convince the world; He will lead the disciples to know spiritual truths; Jesus cheers their sorrowing hearts*

"I have told you these things to keep you from falling over stumbling blocks. 2 Men will turn you out of their synagogues. Yes, indeed, the time is coming when anyone who kills you will think that he is rendering a religious service to God. 3 They will do this, because they have never come to know God nor me. 4 But I have told you these things that when the time does come, you may remember that I told you. I did not tell you these things at the start, because I was with you. 5 But now I am going away to Him who has sent me, and not one of you is asking me where I am going, 6 but sorrow has taken complete possession of your hearts, because I have told you these things. 7 Yet it is nothing but the truth I now tell you, that it is better for you that I should go away. For if I do not go away, the Helper will not come into close fellowship with you, but if I do go away, I will send Him to be in close fellowship with you.

8 "And when He comes, He will bring conviction to worldly people[a] about sin and uprightness and judgment; 9 about sin, because they do not believe in me; 10 about uprightness, because I go away to the Father so that you can no longer see me; 11 about judgment, because the evil ruler of this world has been condemned.

12 "I have much more to tell you, but you cannot grasp it now. 13 But when the Spirit of truth comes, He will guide you into the whole truth; for He will not speak on His own authority but will tell what is told Him, and will announce to you the things that are to come. 14 He will glorify me, because He will take the things that belong to me and tell them to you. 15 Everything that the Father has is mine; this is why I have told you, 'He will take the things that are mine and tell them to you.'

16 "In just a little while you will not see me any longer; and yet, in just a little while after you will see me again."

17 So some of His disciples said to one another, "What does He mean by telling us, 'In just a little while you will not see me, and yet in just a little while after you will see me again,' and 'Because I am going away to the Father'?" 18 So they kept saying, "What does He mean by saying, 'a little while'? We do not know what He is talking about."

19 Jesus knew that they wanted to ask Him a question, and so He said to them, "Are you inquiring of one another about this saying of mine, 'In just a little while you will not see me, and yet in just a little while after you will see me again'? 20 I most solemnly say to you, you will weep and wail, but the world will be glad; you will grieve but your grief will be turned into gladness. 21 When a woman is in labor, she is in pain, for her time has come, but when the baby is born, she forgets her pain because of her joy that a human being has been born into the world. 22 So you too are now in sorrow; but I am going to see you again, and then your hearts will be happy, and no one can rob you of your happiness. 23 At that time you will ask me no more questions. I most

BECK

Sorrow Will Turn to Joy

16 "I told you this so that nothing will upset your faith. 2 You will be put out of the synagog. Yes, the time will come when anyone who murders you will think he's serving God. 3 Men will do these things because they didn't get to know the Father or Me. 4 But I told you this so that when it happens you'll remember I told you about it. I didn't tell you this at first, because I was with you.

5 "Now I'm going to Him who sent Me, and none of you asks Me, 'Where are You going?' 6 But because I told you this, you feel very sad. 7 But I tell you the truth, it's good for you that I go away. If I don't go away, the Comforter will not come to you. But if I go, I'll send Him to you. 8 He will come and convince the world of sin, righteousness, and judgment: 9 of sin because they don't believe in Me; 10 of righteousness because I'm going to the Father and you won't see Me any more; 11 of judgment because the ruler of this world is judged.

12 "I have much more to tell you, but it would be too much for you now. 13 When the Spirit of truth comes, He will lead you into the whole truth. What He will say will not come from Himself, but He'll speak what He hears and tell you what is coming. 14 He will glorify Me, because He'll take from what is Mine and tell it to you. 15 Everything the Father has is Mine. That is why I said, 'He takes from what is Mine and will tell it to you.'

16 "A little while and you'll not see Me any more; and again a little while and you'll see Me."

17 Then some of His disciples asked one another, "What does He mean when He tells us, 'Just a little while and you'll not see Me; and again only a little while and you'll see Me,' and 'I'm going to the Father'?" 18 So they were asking, "What does He mean when He says, 'A little while'? We don't know what He means."

19 Jesus knew they wanted to ask Him something. "Are you trying to find out from one another," He asked them, "what I meant by saying, 'A little while and you'll not see Me; and again a little while and you'll see Me'? 20 I tell you the truth, you will cry and mourn, but the world will be glad. You will have sorrow, but your sorrow will turn to joy. 21 When a woman is going to have a child, she has pains because her time has come. But after the child is born, she's so happy a child was brought into the world she doesn't remember her pains any more. 22 You, too, are sad now; but I'll see you again, *and then you'll be glad*,[17] and nobody will take your joy away from you. 23 Then you won't ask Me any questions. I tell you the truth,

[a] Grk., *the world*.

[17] Is. 66:14

K.J.V.

soever ye shall ask the Father in my name, he will give *it* you. 24 Hitherto have ye asked nothing in my name: ask, and ye shall receive, that your joy may be full. 25 These things have I spoken unto you in proverbs: but the time cometh, when I shall no more speak unto you in proverbs, but I shall shew you plainly of the Father. 26 At that day ye shall ask in my name: and I say not unto you, that I will pray the Father for you: 27 For the Father himself loveth you, because ye have loved me, and have believed that I came out from God. 28 I came forth from the Father, and am come into the world: again, I leave the world, and go to the Father. 29 His disciples said unto him, Lo, now speakest thou plainly, and speakest no proverb. 30 Now are we sure that thou knowest all things, and needest not that any man should ask thee: by this we believe that thou camest forth from God. 31 Jesus answered them, Do ye now believe? 32 Behold, the hour cometh, yea, is now come, that ye shall be scattered, every man to his own, and shall leave me alone: and yet I am not alone, because the Father is with me. 33 These things I have spoken unto you, that in me ye might have peace. In the world ye shall have tribulation: but be of good cheer; I have overcome the world.

17 These words spake Jesus, and lifted up his eyes to heaven, and said, Father, the hour is come; glorify thy Son, that thy Son also may glorify thee: 2 As thou hast given him power over all flesh, that he should give eternal life to as many as thou hast given him. 3 And this is life eternal, that they might know thee the only true God, and Jesus Christ, whom thou hast sent. 4 I have glorified thee on the earth: I have finished the work which thou gavest me to do. 5 And now, O Father, glorify thou me with thine own self with the glory which I had with thee before the world was. 6 I have manifested thy name unto the men which thou gavest me out of the world: thine they were, and thou gavest them me; and they have kept thy word. 7 Now they have known that all things whatsoever thou hast given me are of thee. 8 For I have given unto them the words which thou gavest me; and they have received *them,* and have known surely that I came out from thee, and they have believed that thou didst send me. 9 I pray for them: I pray not for the world, but for them which thou hast given me; for they are thine. 10 And all mine are thine, and thine are mine; and I am glorified in them. 11 And now I am no more in the world, but these are in the world, and I come to thee. Holy Father, keep through thine own name those whom thou hast given me, that they may be one, as we *are.* 12 While I was with them in

N.A.S.

Father for anything, He will give it to you in My name. 24 "Until now you have asked for nothing in My name; ask, and you will receive, that your joy may be made full.

25 "These things I have spoken to you in figurative language; an hour is coming, when I will speak no more to you in figurative language, but will tell you plainly of the Father. 26 "In that day you will ask in My name; and I do not say to you that I will request the Father on your behalf; 27 for the Father Himself loves you, because you have loved Me, and have believed that I came forth from the Father. 28 "I came forth from the Father, and have come into the world; I am leaving the world again, and going to the Father." 29 His disciples *said, "Lo, now You are speaking plainly, and are not using a figure of speech. 30 "Now we know that You know all things, and have no need for anyone to question You; by this we believe that You came from God." 31 Jesus answered them, "Do you now believe? 32 "Behold, an hour is coming, and has *already* come, for you to be scattered, each to his own *home,* and to leave Me alone; and *yet* I am not alone, because the Father is with Me. 33 "These things I have spoken to you, that in Me you may have peace. In the world you have tribulation, but take courage; I have overcome the world."

17 These things Jesus spoke; and lifting up His eyes to heaven, He said, "Father, the hour has come; glorify Thy Son, that the Son may glorify Thee, 2 even as Thou gavest Him authority over all mankind, that to all whom Thou hast given Him, He may give eternal life. 3 "And this is eternal life, that they may know Thee the only true God, and Jesus Christ whom Thou hast sent. 4 "I glorified Thee on the earth, having accomplished the work which Thou hast given Me to do. 5 "And now, glorify Thou Me together with Thyself, Father, with the glory which I ever had with Thee before the world was. 6 "I manifested Thy name to the men whom Thou gavest Me out of the world; Thine they were, and Thou gavest them to Me, and they have kept Thy word. 7 "Now they have come to know that everything Thou hast given Me is from Thee; 8 for the words which Thou gavest Me I have given to them; and they received *them,* and truly understood that I came forth from Thee, and they believed that Thou didst send Me. 9 "I ask on their behalf; I do not ask on behalf of the world, but of those whom Thou hast given Me; for they are Thine; 10 and all things that are Mine are Thine, and Thine are Mine; and I have been glorified in them. 11 "And I am no more in the world; and *yet* they themselves are in the world, and I come to Thee. Holy Father, keep them in Thy name, *the name* which Thou hast given Me, that they may be one, even as We *are.* 12 "While I was with them, I was

WILLIAMS

solemnly say to you, the Father will give you, as bearers of my name, whatever you ask Him for. 24 Up to this time you have not asked for anything as bearers of my name, but now you must keep on asking, and you will receive, that your cup of joy may be full to the brim.

25 "I have told you these things in allegories, but a time is coming when I shall not do so any longer, but will plainly tell you about the Father. 26At that time you will ask, as bearers of my name, and I do not say that I will ask the Father for you, 27 for the Father tenderly loves you Himself, because you now tenderly love me and now believe that I have come from the Father. 28 I did come from the Father and I have come into the world. Now I am leaving the world and going back to the Father."

29 His disciples said to Him, "Now you are talking plainly and not in allegory at all. 30 Now we know that you know everything and do not need that anyone should ask you questions. For this reason we believe that you have come from God."

31 Jesus answered them, "Do you now really believe? 32 Listen! A time is coming, yea, it is right here, when you will all be scattered to your own homes and will leave me alone. And yet, I am not alone, because the Father is with me. 33 I have told you these things, that you through union with me may have peace. In the world you have trouble; but be courageous! I have conquered the world."

17

Jesus prays for Himself, for His disciples, and all His future followers; He asks that they be preserved, consecrated, unified, and glorified

When Jesus had said all these things, He lifted His eyes to heaven and said: "Father, the time has come. Glorify your Son, that He may glorify you, 2 just as you have given Him authority over all mankind to give eternal life to all whom you have given Him. 3 Now eternal life means knowing you as the only true God and knowing Jesus your messenger as Christ. 4 I have glorified you down here upon the earth by completing the work which you have given me to do. 5 So now, Father, glorify me up there in your presence just as you did [a] before the world existed.

6 "I have made your very self known to the men whom you have given me out of the world. At first they were yours, but now you have given them to me, and they have obeyed your message. 7 Now they have come to know that everything you have given me really comes from you; 8 for I have given them the teachings that you gave me, and they have accepted them, and they have come to know in reality that I did come from you, and so they are convinced that you did send me. 9 I am praying for them. I am not praying for the world now, but only for those whom you have given me, because they are yours—10 really, all that is mine is yours, and all that is yours is mine—and I have been glorified through them. 11And now I am no longer to be in the world, but they are to stay on in the world, while I am going to be with you. Holy Father, keep them by the power which you have given me, so that they may be one just as we are. 12As long as I was with

BECK

if you ask the Father for anything, He will give it to you in My name. 24 So far you haven't asked for anything in My name. Ask and you will receive and be very happy.

25 "I used veiled speech in telling you these things. The time is coming when I won't use veiled speech any more in talking to you, but I'll tell you about the Father in plain words. 26 Then you will ask in My name, and I don't tell you I'll ask the Father for you. 27 The Father Himself loves you because you have loved Me and believe that I came from the Father. 28 I left the Father and came into the world; and now I'm leaving the world again and going to the Father."

29 "Yes, now You're talking in plain words," His disciples said, "and using no veiled speech. 30 Now we know You know everything and don't need to have anyone ask You anything. That's why we believe You've come from God."

31 "Now you believe," Jesus answered them. 32 "The hour is coming, in fact, it's here now, when you'll be scattered, everyone to his home, and you'll leave Me alone. But I'm not alone, because the Father is with Me. 33 I told you this so you will have peace in Me. In the world you have trouble. But have courage; I've conquered the world."

Jesus Prays

17

After saying this, Jesus looked up to heaven and said:

"Father, the time has come. Glorify Your Son so that Your Son will glorify You, 2 since You have given Him power over all men, to give everlasting life to all whom You gave Him. 3 This is everlasting life—to know You, the only true God, and Jesus Christ, whom You sent. 4 I have glorified You on earth by finishing the work You gave Me to do. 5And now, Father, glorify Me at Your side with the glory I had with You before the world began.

6 "I made Your name known to the people You gave Me out of the world. They were Yours, and You gave them to Me, and they have kept Your Word. 7 Now they know everything You gave Me comes from You, 8 because I gave them the message You gave Me. And they have accepted it and learned the truth that I came from You, and have believed You sent Me.

9 "I pray for them. I don't pray for the world but for those You gave Me, because they are Yours. 10All that is Mine is Yours, and what is Yours is Mine. And I am glorified in them. 11 I am no longer in the world, but they are in the world, and I am coming to You. Holy Father, keep them in Your name, which You gave Me, so that they will be one as We are one. 12 While I was with them, I kept them safe

[a] Grk., *with the glory which I had.*

K.J.V.

the world, I kept them in thy name: those that thou gavest me I have kept, and none of them is lost, but the son of perdition; that the Scripture might be fulfilled. 13 And now come I to thee; and these things I speak in the world, that they might have my joy fulfilled in themselves. 14 I have given them thy word; and the world hath hated them, because they are not of the world, even as I am not of the world. 15 I pray not that thou shouldest take them out of the world, but that thou shouldest keep them from the evil. 16 They are not of the world, even as I am not of the world. 17 Sanctify them through thy truth: thy word is truth. 18 As thou hast sent me into the world, even so have I also sent them into the world. 19 And for their sakes I sanctify myself, that they also might be sanctified through the truth. 20 Neither pray I for these alone, but for them also which shall believe on me through their word; 21 That they all may be one; as thou, Father, *art* in me, and I in thee, that they also may be one in us: that the world may believe that thou hast sent me. 22 And the glory which thou gavest me I have given them; that they may be one, even as we are one: 23 I in them, and thou in me, that they may be made perfect in one; and that the world may know that thou hast sent me, and hast loved them, as thou hast loved me. 24 Father, I will that they also, whom thou hast given me, be with me where I am; that they may behold my glory, which thou hast given me: for thou lovedst me before the foundation of the world. 25 O righteous Father, the world hath not known thee: but I have known thee, and these have known that thou hast sent me. 26 And I have declared unto them thy name, and will declare *it;* that the love wherewith thou hast loved me may be in them, and I in them.

N.A.S.

keeping them in Thy name which Thou hast given Me; and I guarded them, and not one of them perished but the son of perdition, that the Scripture might be fulfilled. 13 "But now I come to Thee; and these things I speak in the world, that they may have My joy made full in themselves. 14 "I have given them Thy word; and the world has hated them, because they are not of the world, even as I am not of the world. 15 "I do not ask Thee to take them out of the world, but to keep them from the evil *one*. 16 "They are not of the world, even as I am not of the world. 17 "Sanctify them in the truth; Thy word is truth. 18 "As Thou didst send Me into the world, I also have sent them into the world. 19 "And for their sakes I sanctify Myself, that they themselves also may be sanctified in truth. 20 "I do not ask in behalf of these alone, but for those also who believe in Me through their word; 21 that they may all be one; even as Thou, Father, *art* in Me, and I in Thee, that they also may be in Us; that the world may believe that Thou didst send Me. 22 "And the glory which Thou hast given Me I have given to them; that they may be one, just as We are one; 23 I in them, and Thou in Me, that they may be perfected in unity, that the world may know that Thou didst send Me, and didst love them, even as Thou didst love Me. 24 "Father, I desire that they also whom Thou hast given Me be with Me where I am, in order that they may behold My glory, which Thou hast given Me; for Thou didst love Me before the foundation of the world. 25 "O righteous Father, although the world has not known Thee, yet I have known Thee; and these have known that Thou didst send Me; 26 and I have made Thy name known to them, and will make it known; that the love wherewith Thou didst love Me may be in them, and I in them."

18 When Jesus had spoken these words, he went forth with his disciples over the brook Cedron, where was a garden, into the which he entered, and his disciples. 2 And Judas also, which betrayed him, knew the place: for Jesus ofttimes resorted thither with his disciples. 3 Judas then, having received a band *of men* and officers from the chief priests and Pharisees, cometh thither with lanterns and torches and weapons. 4 Jesus therefore, knowing all things that should come upon him, went forth, and said unto them, Whom seek ye? 5 They answered him, Jesus of Nazareth. Jesus saith unto them, I am *he.* And Judas also, which betrayed him, stood with them. 6 As soon then as he had said unto them, I am *he,* they went backward, and fell to the ground. 7 Then asked he them

18 When Jesus had spoken these words, He went forth with His disciples over the ravine of the Kidron, where there was a garden, into which He Himself entered, and His disciples. 2 Now Judas also, who was betraying Him, knew the place; for Jesus had often met there with His disciples. 3 Judas then, having received the *Roman* Cohort, and officers from the chief priests and the Pharisees, *came there with lanterns and torches and weapons. 4 Jesus therefore, knowing all the things that were coming upon Him, went forth, and *said to them, "Whom do you seek?" 5 They answered Him, "Jesus the Nazarene." He *said to them, "I am *He.*" And Judas also who was betraying Him, was standing with them. 6 When therefore He said to them, "I am *He*", they drew back, and fell to the ground. 7 Again therefore

WILLIAMS

them, I kept them by your power which you gave me, and I protected them, and not one of them was lost, except the one who is now doomed [b] to be lost, so that the Scripture might be fulfilled. 13 And now I am going to be with you, and I am saying these things while still in the world, that the joy which I experience may be fully experienced in their own souls. 14 I have given them your message, and the world has hated them, because they do not belong to the world, just as I do not belong to it. 15 I am not asking you to take them out of the world, but to keep them from the evil in it. 16 They do not belong to the world just as I do not belong to it. 17 Consecrate [c] them by your truth; your message is truth. 18 Just as you have sent me into the world, I have sent them into the world, too. 19 And so for their sake I am consecrating [c] myself, that they too may be consecrated [c] by truth.

20 "I make this petition, not for them only, but for all who ever come to believe in me through their message, 21 for them all to be one, just as you, Father, are in union with me and I in union with you, for them to be in union with us, so that the world may be convinced that you have sent me. 22 I have given them the glory which you gave me, so that they may be one, just as we are, 23 I in union with them and you in union with me, so that they may be perfectly united, and the world may be sure that you sent me and that you have loved them just as you have loved me. 24 Father, I want to have those whom you have given me right where I am, in order that they may see the glory which you have given me, because you loved me before the creation of the world. 25 Righteous Father, although the world did not know you, I did know you, and these men have come to know that you sent me, 26 and I made known to them your very self, and I will make you known still further, so that the love which you have shown to me may be felt in them, and I in union with them."

18 *Judas guides the officers to arrest Jesus; then they take Him before Annas and Caiaphas; Peter disowns Jesus while He is being tried in the Roman court*

On saying these things He went out with His disciples across the Ravine of Cedars to a place where there was a garden, and He went into it with His disciples. 2 Now Judas, too, who betrayed Him, knew the spot, because Jesus had often met with His disciples there. 3 So Judas got together the Roman garrison and some attendants from the high priests and Pharisees, and went there with lanterns and torches and weapons.

4 Then Jesus, as He knew everything that was going to befall Him, came forward and asked them, "Who is it that you are looking for?"

5 They answered Him, "Jesus of Nazareth." He said to them, "I am He." And Judas who betrayed Him was standing among them. 6 So when He said to them, "I am He," they took a lurch backward and fell to the ground. 7 So once more He asked them, "Who is it that you are looking for?"

BECK

in Your name, which You gave Me. I watched over them, and none of them was lost except that lost one—what the Bible says had to come true.

13 "But now I am coming to You, and I say this while I am in the world so that they will feel all My joy in their hearts. 14 I gave them Your Word. But the world has hated them because they don't belong to the world any more than I belong to the world. 15 I'm not asking You to take them out of the world, but to keep them from the evil one. 16 They don't belong to the world any more than I belong to the world.

17 "Make them holy by the truth; Your Word is truth. 18 As You sent Me into the world, I sent them into the world. 19 In this holy way I give Myself for them to make them holy, too, by the truth. 20 I'm not asking for them only but also for those who through their Word believe in Me 21 that they all be one. As You, Father, are in Me and I in You, let them be in Us so that the world may believe You sent Me. 22 I gave them the glory You gave Me to make them one as We are one. 23 I am in them, and You are in Me to make them perfectly one that the world may know You sent Me and loved them as You loved Me.

24 "Father, I want those You gave Me to be with Me where I am and to see My glory that You gave Me because You loved Me before the world was made. 25 Righteous Father, the world didn't know You, but I knew You, and these have learned to know You sent Me. 26 I told them and I am going to tell them Your name, so that the love You have for Me will be in them and I will be in them."

The Arrest

18 After Jesus said this, He took His disciples to the other side of the Kidron valley where there was a garden. He and His disciples went into it.

2 Judas, who was betraying Him, also knew the place because Jesus and His disciples often got together there. 3 So Judas took the troop of soldiers and servants from the ruling priests and Pharisees and came there with lanterns and torches and weapons.

4 Then Jesus went out, knowing exactly what was going to happen to Him. "Whom are you looking for?" He asked them.

5 "Jesus from Nazareth," they answered Him.

"I am He," Jesus told them.

Judas, ready to betray Him, was standing with them. 6 When Jesus told them, "I am He," they went backward and fell to the ground.

7 He asked them again, "Whom are you looking for?"

[b] Grk., *the son of perdition.* [c] I.e., set apart.

K.J.V.

again, Whom seek ye? And they said, Jesus of Nazareth. 8 Jesus answered, I have told you that I am *he:* if therefore ye seek me, let these go their way: 9 That the saying might be fulfilled, which he spake, Of them which thou gavest me have I lost none. 10 Then Simon Peter having a sword drew it, and smote the high priest's servant, and cut off his right ear. The servant's name was Malchus. 11 Then said Jesus unto Peter, Put up thy sword into the sheath: the cup which my Father hath given me, shall I not drink it? 12 Then the band and the captain and officers of the Jews took Jesus, and bound him, 13 And led him away to Annas first; for he was father in law to·Caiaphas, which was the high priest that same year. 14 Now Caiaphas was he, which gave counsel to the Jews, that it was expedient that one man should die for the people.

15 And Simon Peter followed Jesus, and *so did* another disciple: that disciple was known unto the high priest, and went in with Jesus into the palace of the high priest. 16 But Peter stood at the door without. Then went out that other disciple, which was known unto the high priest, and spake unto her that kept the door, and brought in Peter. 17 Then saith the damsel that kept the door unto Peter, Art not thou also *one* of this man's disciples? He saith, I am not. 18 And the servants and officers stood there, who had made a fire of coals, for it was cold; and they warmed themselves: and Peter stood with them, and warmed himself.

19 The high priest then asked Jesus of his disciples, and of his doctrine. 20 Jesus answered him, I spake openly to the world; I ever taught in the synagogue, and in the temple, whither the Jews always resort; and in secret have I said nothing. 21 Why askest thou me? ask them which heard me, what I have said unto them: behold, they know what I said. 22 And when he had thus spoken, one of the officers which stood by struck Jesus with the palm of his hand, saying, Answerest thou the high priest so? 23 Jesus answered him, if I have spoken evil, bear witness of the evil: but if well, why smitest thou me? 24 Now Annas had sent him bound unto Caiaphas the high priest. 25 And Simon Peter stood and warmed himself. They said therefore unto him, Art not thou also *one* of his disciples? He denied *it,* and said, I am not. 26 One of the servants of the high priest, being *his* kinsman whose ear Peter cut off, saith, Did not I see thee in the garden with him? 27 Peter then denied again; and immediately the cock crew.

28 Then led they Jesus from Caiaphas unto the hall of judgment: and it was early; and they themselves went not into the judgment hall, lest they should be defiled; but that they might eat the passover. 29 Pilate then went out unto them,

N.A.S.

He asked them, "Whom do you seek?" And they said, "Jesus the Nazarene." 8 Jesus answered, "I told you that I am *He;* if therefore you seek Me, let these go their way," 9 that the word might be fulfilled which He spoke, "Of those whom Thou hast given Me I lost not one." 10 Simon Peter therefore having a sword, drew it, and struck the high priest's slave, and cut off his right ear; and the slave's name was Malchus. 11 Jesus therefore said to Peter, "Put the sword into the sheath; the cup which the Father has given Me, shall I not drink it?"

12 So the *Roman* Cohort and the commander, and the officers of the Jews, arrested Jesus and bound Him, 13 and led Him to Annas first; for he was father-in-law of Caiaphas, who was high priest that year. 14 Now Caiaphas was the one who had advised the Jews that it was expedient for one man to die on behalf of the people.

15 And Simon Peter was following Jesus, and *so was* another disciple. Now that disciple was known to the high priest, and entered with Jesus into the court of the high priest, 16 but Peter was standing at the door outside. So the other disciple, who was known to the high priest, went out and spoke to the doorkeeper, and brought in Peter. 17 The slave-girl therefore who kept the door *said to Peter, "You are not also *one* of this man's disciples, are you?" He *said, "I am not." 18 Now the slaves and the officers were standing *there,* having made a charcoal fire, for it was cold and they were warming themselves; and Peter also was with them, standing and warming himself.

19 The high priest therefore questioned Jesus about His disciples, and about His teaching. 20 Jesus answered him, "I have spoken openly to the world; I always taught in synagogues, and in the temple, where all the Jews come together; and I spoke nothing in secret. 21 "Why do you question Me? Question those who have heard what I spoke to them; behold, these know what I said." 22 And when He had said this, one of the officers standing by gave Jesus a blow, saying, "Is that the way You answer the high priest?" 23 Jesus answered him, "If I have spoken wrongly, bear witness of the wrong; but if rightly, why do you strike Me?" 24 Annas therefore sent Him bound to Caiaphas the high priest.

25 Now Simon Peter was standing and warming himself. They said therefore to him, "You are not also *one* of His disciples, are you?" He denied *it,* and said, "I am not." 26 One of the slaves of the high priest, being a relative of the one whose ear Peter cut off, *said, "Did I not see you in the garden with Him?" 27 Peter therefore denied *it* again; and immediately a cock crowed.

28 They *led Jesus therefore from Caiaphas into the ªPraetorium; and it was early; and they themselves did not enter into the ªPraetorium in order that they might not be defiled, but might eat the Passover. 29 Pilate therefore went out

[a] Or, *governor's official residence.*

310

WILLIAMS

They said, "Jesus of Nazareth."

8 Jesus answered, "I have already told you that I am He; so if you are really looking for me, let these men go." 9 He said this that the statement He had just made might be fulfilled, "I have not lost one of those whom you have given me." 10 So Simon Peter, who had a sword, drew it and struck the high priest's slave and cut off his right ear. The slave's name was Malchus.

11 Then Jesus said to Peter, "Put your sword back into the sheath. Must I not drink the cup which the Father has handed me?"

12 So the garrison and its commander and the attendants of the Jews arrested Jesus and put handcuffs on Him, 13 and took Him first to Annas. For he was father-in-law of Caiaphas who was high priest that year. 14 Now it was Caiaphas who had advised the Jews that it was for their welfare that one should die for the people.

15 Simon Peter and another disciple followed on after Jesus. And that other disciple was acquainted with the high priest, and so went on with Jesus into the high priest's courtyard, 16 but Peter stood outside before the door. So this other disciple, who was acquainted with the high priest, stepped out and spoke to the woman doorkeeper and brought Peter in. 17 Then the servant-girl at the door said to Peter, "You too are not one of this man's disciples, are you?"

He answered, "No, I am not." 18 Because it was cold, the slaves and attendants had made a charcoal fire and were standing about it warming themselves; so Peter too was standing among them warming himself.

19 Then the high priest questioned Jesus about His disciples and His teaching. 20 Jesus answered him, "I have spoken publicly to the world; I have always taught in the synagogues and in the temple where all the Jews are in the habit of meeting, and I have not spoken anything in secret. 21 So why are you questioning me? Ask those who heard what I told them. Of course, they know what I said."

22 After He had said this, one of the attendants standing by slapped Jesus in the face, and said, "Is this the way you answer the high priest?"

23 Jesus answered him, "If I have said anything wrong, on oath tell what it is; but if what I have said is true, why do you slap me?" 24 So Annas sent Him over, still in handcuffs, to Caiaphas the high priest.

25 But Simon Peter still stood warming himself. So they said to him, "You too are not one of His disciples, are you?"

He denied it and said, "No, I am not."

26 One of the high priest's slaves, who was a kinsman of the one whose ear Peter had cut off, said, "Did I not see you in the garden with Him?"

27 Then Peter again denied it, and at that moment a cock crowed.

28 Then they took Jesus from Caiaphas to the governor's palace. It was early in the morning, and they would not go into the governor's palace themselves, in order not to be defiled, so as to be unfit to eat the Passover supper. 29 So Pilate

BECK

"Jesus from Nazareth," they said.

8 "I told you I am He," Jesus answered. "So if I'm the One you want, let these others go." 9 This was to make good what He had said: "I lost none of those You gave Me." *

10 Then Simon Peter, who had a sword, drew it, struck the high priest's slave, and cut off his right ear. The slave's name was Malchus.

11 "Put your sword into its scabbard," Jesus told Peter. "The cup My Father gave Me—shouldn't I drink it?"

12 So the troop of soldiers, the tribune, and the attendants of the Jews arrested Jesus, bound Him, 13 and took Him first to Annas, because he was the father-in-law of Caiaphas, who was high priest that year. 14 It was Caiaphas who advised the Jews, "It is better that one man dies instead of the people."

Peter Denies Jesus

15 Now, Simon Peter and another disciple were following Jesus. The other disciple was known to the high priest and went with Jesus into the high priest's courtyard. But Peter was standing outside the door. 16 So the other disciple, whom the high priest knew, went out and talked to the girl watching the door and brought Peter in.

17 This doorkeeper asked Peter, "You aren't one of this Man's disciples too, are you?"

"I'm not," he answered.

18 The slaves and the attendants were standing around and had made a heap of burning coals because it was cold. As they warmed themselves, Peter was standing with them warming himself.

Before Annas

19 Then the high priest asked Jesus about His disciples and His teaching.

20 "I have spoken publicly to the world," Jesus answered him. "I have always taught in a synagog or in the temple, where all the Jews gather, and I haven't said anything in secret. 21 Why do you ask Me? Ask those who heard Me what I said to them; they know what I said."

22 When He said this, one of the attendants standing near Jesus slapped His face. "Is that how You answer the high priest?" he asked.

23 "If I said anything wrong," Jesus answered him, "tell us what was wrong. But if I told the truth, why do you hit Me?"

24 Then Annas sent Him, still bound, to Caiaphas, the high priest.

Peter Denies Again

25 Simon Peter continued to stand and warm himself. So the men asked him, "You aren't one of His disciples too, are you?"

He denied, saying, "I'm not!"

26 One of the high priest's slaves, a relative of the man whose ear Peter had cut off, asked, "Didn't I see you with Him in the garden?"

27 Again, Peter denied, and just then a rooster crowed.

Before Pilate

28 The Jews took Jesus from Caiaphas to the governor's palace. It was early in the morning. To keep from getting unclean (they wanted to celebrate the Passover), the Jews themselves didn't go into the governor's palace. 29 So Pilate

* John 6:39; 17:12

311

K.J.V.

and said, What accusation bring ye against this man? 30 They answered and said unto him, If he were not a malefactor, we would not have delivered him up unto thee. 31 Then said Pilate unto them, Take ye him, and judge him according to your law. The Jews therefore said unto him, It is not lawful for us to put any man to death: 32 That the saying of Jesus might be fulfilled, which he spake, signifying what death he should die. 33 Then Pilate entered into the judgment hall again, and called Jesus, and said unto him, Art thou the King of the Jews? 34 Jesus answered him, Sayest thou this thing of thyself, or did others tell it thee of me? 35 Pilate answered, Am I a Jew? Thine own nation and the chief priests have delivered thee unto me: what hast thou done? 36 Jesus answered, My kingdom is not of this world: if my kingdom were of this world, then would my servants fight, that I should not be delivered to the Jews: but now is my kingdom not from hence. 37 Pilate therefore said unto him, Art thou a king then? Jesus answered, Thou sayest that I am a king. To this end was I born, and for this cause came I into the world, that I should bear witness unto the truth. Every one that is of the truth heareth my voice. 38 Pilate saith unto him, What is truth? And when he had said this, he went out again unto the Jews, and saith unto them, I find in him no fault *at all*. 39 But ye have a custom, that I should release unto you one at the passover: will ye therefore that I release unto you the King of the Jews? 40 Then cried they all again, saying, Not this man, but Barabbas. Now Barabbas was a robber.

19 Then Pilate therefore took Jesus, and scourged *him*. 2 And the soldiers platted a crown of thorns, and put *it* on his head, and they put on him a purple robe, 3 And said, Hail, King of the Jews! and they smote him with their hands. 4 Pilate therefore went forth again, and saith unto them, Behold, I bring him forth to you, that ye may know that I find no fault in him. 5 Then came Jesus forth, wearing the crown of thorns, and the purple robe. And *Pilate* saith unto them, Behold the man! 6 When the chief priests therefore and officers saw him, they cried out, saying, Crucify *him*, crucify *him*. Pilate saith unto them, Take ye him, and crucify *him*: for I find no fault in him. 7 The Jews answered

N.A.S.

to them, and *said, "What accusation do you bring against this Man?" 30 They answered and said to him, "If this Man were not an evil-doer, we would not have delivered Him up to you." 31 Pilate therefore said to them, "Take Him yourselves, and judge Him according to your law." The Jews said to him, "We are not permitted to put any one to death;" 32 that the word of Jesus might be fulfilled, which He spoke, signifying by what kind of death He was about to die.

33 Pilate therefore entered again into the *a*Praetorium, and summoned Jesus, and said to Him, "You are the King of the Jews?" 34 Jesus answered, "Are you saying this on your own initiative, or did others tell you about Me?" 35 Pilate answered, "I am not a Jew, am I? Your own nation and the chief priests delivered You up to me; what have You done?" 36 Jesus answered, "My kingdom is not of this world. If My kingdom were of this world, then My servants would be fighting, that I might not be delivered up to the Jews; but as it is, My kingdom is not *b*of this realm." 37 Pilate therefore said to Him, "So You are a king?" Jesus answered, "You say *correctly* that I am a king. For this I have been born, and for this I have come into the world, to bear witness to the truth. Every one who is of the truth hears My voice." 38 Pilate *said to Him, "What is truth?"

And when he had said this, he went out again to the Jews, and *said to them, "I find no guilt in Him. 39 "But you have a custom, that I should release someone for you at the Passover; do you wish then that I release for you the King of the Jews?" 40 Therefore they cried out again, saying, "Not this Man, but Barabbas." Now Barabbas was a robber.

19 Then Pilate therefore took Jesus, and scourged Him. 2 And the soldiers wove a crown of thorns and put it on His head, and arrayed Him in a purple robe; 3 and they *began* to come up to Him, and say, "Hail, King of the Jews!" and to give Him blows in the face. 4 And Pilate came out again, and *said to them, "Behold, I am bringing Him out to you, that you may know that I find no guilt in Him." 5 Jesus therefore came out, wearing the crown of thorns and the purple robe. And *Pilate* *said to them, "Behold, the Man!" 6 When therefore the chief priests and the officers saw Him, they cried out, saying, "Crucify, crucify!" Pilate *said to them, "Take Him yourselves, and crucify Him, for I find no guilt in Him." 7 The Jews answered

[a] Or, *governor's official residence.* [b] Lit., *from here.*

WILLIAMS

came outside and asked, "What is the charge you bring against this man?"

30 They retorted, "If He were not a criminal, we would not have turned Him over to you."

31 Pilate said to them, "Take Him yourselves, and try Him in accordance with your own law."

Then the Jews said to him, "It is not lawful for us to execute the death penalty on anyone." 32 This made it possible for the word of Jesus to be fulfilled which He spoke to indicate what sort of death He was to die.

33 So Pilate went back into the governor's palace and called Jesus and asked Him, "Are you the king of the Jews?"

34 Jesus answered him, "Do you ask me this on your own initiative, or have others suggested it to you about me?"

35 Pilate answered, "I am not a Jew, am I? Your own people and their high priests have turned you over to me. What have you done?"

36 Jesus answered, "My kingdom does not belong to this world. If my kingdom did belong to this world, my attendants would have been fighting to keep me from being turned over to the Jews. But as a matter of fact, my kingdom does not come from such a source."

37 Then Pilate said to Him, "So you are a king then?"

Jesus answered, "Certainly I am a king. For this very purpose I was born, for this very purpose I have come into the world, to testify for truth. Everybody who is a friend of truth listens to my voice."

38 Pilate asked Him, "What is truth?"

On saying this he went outside again to the Jews, and said to them, "As far as I can see, I can find no ground for a charge against Him. 39 Now you have a custom to have me set one man free at your Passover time. So do you wish me to set the king of the Jews free?"

40 Then they all shouted back, "No! Not Him, but Barabbas!" Now Barabbas was a robber.

19 *Pilate orders Jesus flogged; then sentences Him to death; the soldiers crucify Him and take His clothes; He commits His mother to John; He expires; His side is pierced by a soldier's lance; buried by Joseph and Nicodemus*

So then Pilate took Jesus and had Him flogged. 2 And the soldiers made a crown out of thorns and put it on His head, and put a purple coat on Him, 3 and kept marching up to Him and saying, "All hail, you king of the Jews!" each one slapping Him on the face.

4 And Pilate went outside again and said to the Jews, "Listen! I am going to bring Him out to you, for you to see that I can find no ground for a charge against Him." 5 So Jesus came outside still wearing the crown of thorns and the purple coat. Then Pilate said to them, "Here is the man!"

6 When the high priests and attendants saw Him, they shouted, "Crucify Him! Crucify Him!"

Pilate said to them, "Take Him yourselves and crucify Him, for I can find no ground for a charge against Him."

7 The Jews answered him, "We have a law,

BECK

came out to them. "What accusation are you bringing against this Man?" he asked.

30 "If He weren't a criminal," they answered him, "we wouldn't have handed Him over to you."

31 "Take Him yourselves," Pilate therefore told them, "and judge Him according to your law."

"We're not allowed to kill anyone," the Jews answered him. 32 And so what Jesus said when He predicted how He would die was to come true.

33 Pilate went back into the palace and called for Jesus. "Are You the King of the Jews?" he asked Him.

34 "Did you think of that yourself," Jesus asked, "or did others tell you about Me?"

35 "Am I a Jew?" Pilate asked. "Your own people and the ruling priests handed You over to me. What did You do?"

36 "My kingdom is not of this world," Jesus answered. "If My kingdom were of this world, My servants would fight to keep Me from being handed over to the Jews. But now My kingdom is not of this world."

37 "Then You are a king?" Pilate asked Him.

"Yes, I am a king!" Jesus answered. "I was born and came into the world to testify to the truth. Everyone who lives in the truth listens to Me."

38 Pilate said to Him, "What is truth?" After saying that, he went to the Jews again and told them, "I don't find this Man guilty of anything.

39 "You have a custom that I set someone free for you at the Passover. So would you like me to set the King of the Jews free for you?"

40 Then they yelled: "Not this One but Barabbas!" Now, Barabbas was a robber.

"Look at the Man!"

19 Then Pilate took Jesus and had Him scourged. 2 The soldiers twisted some thorns into a crown and placed it on His head and put a purple garment on Him. 3 They went up to Him and said, "Hail, King of the Jews!" and slapped His face.

4 Pilate went outside again. "I'm bringing Him out to you," he told them, "to let you know I don't find Him guilty of anything." 5 Jesus came outside, wearing the crown of thorns and the purple cloak. "Look at the Man!" Pilate said to them.

6 When the ruling priests and the servants saw Him, they shouted, "Crucify, crucify Him!"

"Take Him yourselves," Pilate told them, "and crucify Him. I don't find Him guilty of anything."

7 "We have a law," the Jews answered Him,

K.J.V.

him. We have a law, and by our law he ought to die, because he made himself the Son of God.

8 When Pilate therefore heard that saying, he was the more afraid; 9And went again into the judgment hall, and saith unto Jesus, Whence art thou? But Jesus gave him no answer. 10 Then saith Pilate unto him, Speakest thou not unto me? knowest thou not that I have power to crucify thee, and have power to release thee? 11 Jesus answered, Thou couldest have no power *at all* against me, except it were given thee from above: therefore he that delivered me unto thee hath the greater sin. 12And from thenceforth Pilate sought to release him: but the Jews cried out, saying, If thou let this man go, thou art not Cesar's friend: whosoever maketh himself a king speaketh against Cesar.

13 When Pilate therefore heard that saying, he brought Jesus forth, and sat down in the judgment seat in a place that is called the Pavement, but in the Hebrew, Gabbatha. 14And it was the preparation of the passover, and about the sixth hour: and he saith unto the Jews, Behold your King! 15 But they cried out, Away with *him*, away with *him*, crucify him. Pilate saith unto them, Shall I crucify your King? The chief priests answered, We have no king but Cesar. 16 Then delivered he him therefore unto them to be crucified. And they took Jesus, and led *him* away. 17And he bearing his cross went forth into a place called *the place* of a skull, which is called in the Hebrew Golgotha: 18 Where they crucified him, and two others with him, on either side one, and Jesus in the midst.

19 And Pilate wrote a title, and put *it* on the cross. And the writing was, JESUS OF NAZARETH THE KING OF THE JEWS. 20 This title then read many of the Jews; for the place where Jesus was crucified was nigh to the city: and it was written in Hebrew, *and* Greek, *and* Latin. 21 Then said the chief priests of the Jews to Pilate, Write not, The King of the Jews; but that he said, I am King of the Jews. 22 Pilate answered, What I have written I have written.

23 Then the soldiers, when they had crucified Jesus, took his garments, and made four parts, to every soldier a part; and also *his* coat: now the coat was without seam, woven from the top throughout. 24 They said therefore among themselves, Let us not rend it, but cast lots for it, whose it shall be: that the Scripture might be fulfilled, which saith, They parted my raiment among them, and for my vesture they did cast lots. These things therefore the soldiers did.

25 Now there stood by the cross of Jesus his mother, and his mother's sister, Mary the *wife* of Cleophas, and Mary Magdalene. 26 When Jesus therefore saw his mother, and the disciple standing by, whom he loved, he saith unto his mother, Woman, behold thy son! 27 Then saith he to the disciple, Behold thy mother! And from that hour that disciple took her unto his own *home*.

28 After this, Jesus knowing that all things were now accomplished, that the Scripture might

N.A.S.

him, "We have a law, and by that law He ought to die because He made Himself out *to be* the Son of God." 8 When Pilate therefore heard this statement, he was the more afraid; 9 and he entered into the [a]Praetorium again, and *said to Jesus, "Where are You from?" But Jesus gave him no answer. 10 Pilate therefore *said to Him, "You do not speak to me? Do You not know that I have authority to release You, and I have authority to crucify You?" 11 Jesus answered, "You would have no authority over Me, unless it had been given you from above; for this reason he who delivered Me up to you has *the greater sin." 12As a result of this Pilate made efforts to release Him, but the Jews cried out, saying, "If you release this Man, you are no friend of Caesar; every one who makes himself out *to be* a king opposes Caesar." 13 When Pilate therefore heard these words, he brought Jesus out, and sat down on the judgment-seat at a place called The Pavement, but in Hebrew, Gabbatha. 14 Now it was the day of preparation for the Passover; it was about the [b]sixth hour. And he *said to the Jews, "Behold, your King!" 15 They therefore cried out, "Away with *Him*, away with *Him*, crucify Him!" Pilate *said to them, "Shall I crucify your King?" The chief priests answered, "We have no king but Caesar." 16And so he then delivered Him up to them to be crucified.

17 They took Jesus therefore; and He went out, bearing His own cross, to the place called the Place of a Skull, which is called in Hebrew Golgotha; 18 where they crucified Him, and with Him two other men, one on either side, and Jesus in between. 19And Pilate wrote an inscription also, and put it on the cross. And it was written, "JESUS THE NAZARENE, THE KING OF THE JEWS." 20 Therefore this inscription many of the Jews read, for the place where Jesus was crucified was near the city; and it was written in Hebrew, Latin, *and* in Greek. 21And so the chief priests of the Jews were saying to Pilate, "Do not write, 'The King of the Jews'; but that He said, 'I am King of the Jews.'" 22 Pilate answered, "What I have written I have written."

23 The soldiers therefore, when they had crucified Jesus, took His outer garments and made four parts, a part to every soldier and *also* the [c]tunic; now the tunic was seamless, woven in one piece. 24 They said therefore to one another, "Let us not tear it, but cast lots for it, *to decide* whose it shall be;" that the Scripture might be fulfilled, "THEY DIVIDED MY OUTER GARMENTS AMONG THEM, AND FOR MY CLOTHING THEY CAST LOTS." 25 Therefore the soldiers did these things. But there were standing by the cross of Jesus His mother, and His mother's sister, Mary the *wife* of Clopas, and Mary Magdalene. 26 When Jesus therefore saw His mother, and the disciple whom He loved standing nearby, He *said to His mother, "Woman, behold, your son!" 27 Then He *said to the disciple, "Behold, your mother!" And from that hour the disciple took her into his own *household*.

28 After this Jesus, knowing that all things had already been accomplished, in order that the Scripture might be fulfilled, *said, "I am

[a] Or, *governor's offical residence.* [b] I.e., noon. [c] Gr., *khiton,* the garment worn next to the skin.

WILLIAMS

and in accordance with that law He deserves to die, for claiming to be God's Son."

8 As soon as Pilate heard that, he was more awe-stricken than before 9 and went back into the governor's palace and asked Jesus, "Where do you come from?" But Jesus made no answer. 10 Then Pilate said to Him, "Do you refuse to speak to me? Do you not know that I have it in my power to set you free or to crucify you?" 11 Jesus answered him, "You would have no power at all over me, if it had not been given to you from above. So the man who betrayed me to you is more guilty than you."

12 Because of this Pilate kept on trying to set Him free, but the Jews shouted, "If you set Him free, you are no friend to the emperor. Anyone who claims to be a king is uttering treason against the emperor!" 13 On hearing this Pilate had Jesus brought out and had Him sit on the judge's bench at the place called the Stone Platform, or in Hebrew, Gabbatha. 14 It was the day of Preparation for the Passover, and it was about noon. Then Pilate said to the Jews, "There is your king!"

15 But they shouted, "Kill him! Kill Him! Crucify Him!"

Pilate said to them, "Must I crucify your king?"

The high priests answered, "We have no king but the emperor!"

16 So Pilate then turned Him over to them to be crucified.

Then they took Jesus, 17 and He went out carrying the cross by Himself to a spot called The Place of the Skull, or in Hebrew, Golgotha. 18 There they crucified Him, with two others, one on each side, and Jesus in the middle. 19 Pilate had a placard written and had it put over the cross: "JESUS OF NAZARETH, THE KING OF THE JEWS."

20 Many of the Jews read this placard, because the place where Jesus was crucified was near the city, and it was written in Hebrew, Latin, and Greek. 21 So the high priests of the Jews said to Pilate, "You must not write, 'The king of the Jews,' but write, 'He said, I am the king of the Jews.' "

22 Pilate answered, "What I have written, I have written!"

23 When the soldiers had crucified Jesus, they took His clothes and divided them into four parts, one for each soldier, except the coat, which was without a seam, woven in one piece from top to bottom. 24 So they said to one another, "Let us not tear it, but let us draw for it to see who gets it." This was to fulfill the Scripture which says,

"They divided my clothes among them,
And for my clothing they cast lots."
Now this was what the soldiers did.

25 Near Jesus' cross were standing His mother and her sister Mary, the wife of Clopas, and Mary of Magdala. 26 So Jesus, on seeing His mother and the disciple whom He loved standing near, said to his mother, "There is your son."

27 Then He said to His disciple, "There is your mother." And from that very hour His disciple took her to his own home.

28 After this, as Jesus knew that everything was now finished, that the Scripture might be fulfilled, He said, "I am thirsty."

BECK

"and according to the law He must die. He has claimed to be God's Son."

8 When Pilate heard them say that, he was frightened more than ever. 9 He went into the palace again. "Where are You from?" he asked Jesus. But Jesus didn't answer him.

10 "Don't You speak to me?" Pilate then asked Him. "Don't You know I have the power to free You or to crucify You?"

11 "You wouldn't have any power over Me," Jesus answered him, "if it hadn't been given to you from above. That is why the man who handed Me over to you is guilty of a greater sin."

12 This made Pilate anxious to let Him go, but the Jews shouted, "If you let Him go, you're no friend of Caesar. Anyone who makes himself a king is against Caesar."

13 When Pilate heard this, he brought Jesus outside and sat in the judge's seat at a place called Stone Pavement, or Gabbatha in the Jewish language. 14 It was the Friday of the Passover and about six o'clock.

"Look at your King!" he said to the Jews.

15 Then they shouted, "Away with Him! Kill him! Crucify Him!"

"Should I crucify your King?" Pilate asked them.

"We don't have any king but Caesar," the ruling priests answered.

16 Then Pilate handed Jesus over to them to be crucified.

"They Crucified Him"

16 So they took Jesus, 17 and He, carrying His cross, went out to what was called Skull Place, which the Jews call Golgotha. 18 There they crucified Him with two others, one on each side and Jesus in the middle.

19 Pilate also wrote a notice and put it on the cross. It read: JESUS FROM NAZARETH, THE KING OF THE JEWS. 20 Many Jews read this notice, because the place where Jesus was crucified was near the city, and it was written in Aramaic, Latin, and Greek.

21 Then the high priests of the Jews told Pilate, "Don't write, 'The King of the Jews,' but, 'He said, "I am the King of the Jews." ' "

22 Pilate answered, "What I've written I've written."

23 When the soldiers had crucified Jesus, they took His clothes and divided them into four parts, one for each soldier, and the tunic was left over. The tunic was without a seam, woven in one piece from top to bottom. 24 "Let's not tear it," they said to one another, "but let's throw lots and see who gets it"—what the Bible said had to come true: *They divided My clothes among them, and for My garment they threw lots.*[18] So that's what the soldiers did.

Mary

25 Now, His mother and her sister, Mary the wife of Clopas, and Mary from Magdala were standing near Jesus' cross.

26 Jesus saw His mother and the disciple He loved standing near. "Woman," He said to His mother, "there is your son!" Then He said to the disciple, "There is your mother!"

27 The disciple took her and from that time on had her in his home.

Jesus Dies

28 After that, knowing everything had now been done, and to have the words of the Bible come true, Jesus said, *"I am thirsty."*

[18] Ps. 22:18

K.J.V.

be fulfilled, saith, I thirst. 29 Now there was set a vessel full of vinegar: and they filled a sponge with vinegar, and put it upon hyssop, and put it to his mouth. 30 When Jesus therefore had received the vinegar, he said, It is finished: and he bowed his head, and gave up the ghost. 31 The Jews therefore, because it was the preparation, that the bodies should not remain upon the cross on the sabbath day, (for that sabbath day was a high day,) besought Pilate that their legs might be broken, and that they might be taken away. 32 Then came the soldiers, and brake the legs of the first, and of the other which was crucified with him. 33 But when they came to Jesus, and saw that he was dead already, they brake not his legs: 34 But one of the soldiers with a spear pierced his side, and forthwith came there out blood and water. 35And he that saw it bare record, and his record is true; and he knoweth that he saith true, that ye might believe. 36 For these things were done, that the Scripture should be fulfilled, A bone of him shall not be broken. 37And again another Scripture saith, They shall look on him whom they pierced.

38 And after this Joseph of Arimathea, being a disciple of Jesus, but secretly for fear of the Jews, besought Pilate that he might take away the body of Jesus: and Pilate gave him leave. He came therefore, and took the body of Jesus. 39And there came also Nicodemus, (which at the first came to Jesus by night,) and brought a mixture of myrrh and aloes, about a hundred pound weight. 40 Then took they the body of Jesus, and wound it in linen clothes with the spices, as the manner of the Jews is to bury. 41 Now in the place where he was crucified there was a garden; and in the garden a new sepulchre, wherein was never man yet laid. 42 There laid they Jesus therefore because of the Jews' preparation day; for the sepulchre was nigh at hand.

20 The first day of the week cometh Mary Magdalene early, when it was yet dark, unto the sepulchre, and seeth the stone taken away from the sepulchre. 2 Then she runneth, and cometh to Simon Peter, and to the other disciple, whom Jesus loved, and saith unto them, They have taken away the Lord out of the sepulchre, and we know not where they have laid him. 3 Peter therefore went forth, and that other disciple, and came to the sepulchre. 4 So they ran both together: and the other disciple did outrun Peter, and came first to the sepulchre. 5And he stooping down, and looking in, saw the linen clothes lying; yet went he not in. 6 Then cometh Simon Peter following him, and went

N.A.S.

thirsty." 29A jar full of sour wine was standing there; so they put a sponge full of the sour wine upon a branch of hyssop, and brought it up to His mouth. 30 When Jesus therefore had received the sour wine, He said, "It is finished!" And He bowed His head, and gave up His spirit.

31 The Jews therefore, because it was the day of preparation, so that the bodies should not remain on the cross on the Sabbath (for that Sabbath was a high day), asked Pilate that their legs might be broken, and that they might be taken away. 32 The soldiers therefore came, and broke the legs of the first man, and of the other man who was crucified with Him; 33 but coming to Jesus, when they saw that He was already dead, they did not break His legs; 34 but one of the soldiers pierced His side with a spear, and immediately there came out blood and water. 35And he who has seen has borne witness, and his witness is true; and he knows that he is telling the truth, so that you also may believe. 36 For these things came to pass, that the Scripture might be fulfilled, "NOT A BONE OF HIM SHALL BE BROKEN." 37And again another Scripture says, "THEY SHALL LOOK ON HIM WHOM THEY PIERCED."

38 And after these things Joseph of Arimathea, being a disciple of Jesus, but a secret one, for fear of the Jews, asked Pilate that he might take away the body of Jesus; and Pilate granted permission. He came therefore, and took away His body. 39And Nicodemus came also, who had first come to Him by night; bringing a mixture of myrrh and aloes, about a hundred pounds weight. 40And so they took the body of Jesus and bound it in linen wrappings with the spices, as is the burial custom of the Jews. 41 Now in the place where He was crucified there was a garden; and in the garden a new tomb, in which no one had yet been laid. 42 Therefore on account of the Jewish day of preparation, because the tomb was nearby, they laid Jesus there.

20 Now on the first day of the week Mary Magdalene *came early to the tomb, while it *was still dark, and *saw the stone already taken away from the tomb. 2And so she *ran and *came to Simon Peter, and to the other disciple whom Jesus loved, and *said to them, "They have taken away the Lord out of the tomb, and we do not know where they have laid Him." 3 Peter therefore went forth, and the other disciple, and they were going to the tomb. 4And the two were running together; and the other disciple ran ahead faster than Peter, and came to the tomb first; 5 and stooping and looking in, he *saw the linen wrappings lying there; but he did not go in. 6 Simon Peter therefore also *came, following him, and entered the

WILLIAMS

29 A bowl full of sour wine was sitting there. So they put a sponge soaked in sour wine on a stick[a] and put it to His lips.

30 As soon as Jesus took the sour wine, He said, "It is finished!" Then He bowed His head and gave up His spirit.

31 As it was the day of Preparation for the Passover, that the bodies might not remain on the crosses during the sabbath, for that sabbath was a very important one, the Jews requested Pilate to have their legs broken and their bodies taken down. 32 So the soldiers went and broke the legs of the first man and of the other one who had been crucified with Him. 33 But when they came to Jesus, as they saw that He was already dead, they did not break His legs, 34 but one of the soldiers thrust a lance into His side and blood and water at once flowed out. 35 The man who saw it has testified to it—and his testimony is true, and he knows that he is telling the truth—in order that you too may come to believe it. 36 For this took place that this Scripture might be fulfilled, "Not a bone of His will be broken." 37 And again another Scripture says, "They shall look at Him whom they pierced."

38 After this, Joseph of Arimathea, who was a disciple of Jesus, but a secret one because of his fear of the Jews, asked permission of Pilate to remove the body of Jesus, and Pilate granted it. So he went and removed His body. 39 Now Nicodemus also, who had formerly come to Jesus at night, went and took a mixture of myrrh and aloes that weighed about one hundred pounds. 40 So they took the body of Jesus and wrapped it in bandages with the spices, in accordance with the Jewish custom of preparing a body for burial. 41 There was a garden at the place where Jesus had been crucified, and in the garden there was a new tomb in which no one had yet been laid. 42 So, because it was the Jewish Preparation day and because the tomb was near by, they laid Him there.

20   *The tomb found empty by Mary, Peter, and John; Jesus appears to Mary, the ten, and the eleven (especially to Thomas); John's aim in writing*

On the first day of the week, very early in the morning while it was still dark, Mary of Magdala went to the tomb, and she saw that the stone had been removed from the tomb. 2 So she ran away and went to Simon Peter and the other disciple whom Jesus tenderly loved, and said to them, "They have taken away the Lord from the tomb, and we do not know where they have put Him."

3 So Peter and the other disciple left the city and started for the tomb. 4 And they both kept running, but the other disciple outran Peter and got to the tomb first. 5 And he stooped down and peered in and saw the bandages lying on the ground, but he did not go in. 6 Then Simon Peter came running up behind him, and he went in-

[a] Lit., *hyssop;* stick of hyssop plant.

BECK

29 A jar full of *sour wine*[19] was standing there. So they put a sponge soaked in the wine on a hyssop stem and held it to His mouth.

30 When Jesus had taken the wine, He said, *"It is finished."* [20]

Then He bowed His head and gave up His spirit.

No Bone Broken

31 Since it was Friday and the Jews didn't want the bodies to stay on the crosses on Saturday, because that Sabbath was an important day, they asked Pilate to have the legs of the men broken and the bodies taken away. 32 So the soldiers came and broke the legs of the first man and then of the other who had been crucified with him.

33 But when they came to Jesus and saw He was dead already, they didn't break His legs, 34 but one of the soldiers stuck a spear into His side, and immediately blood and water came out. 35 He who saw it has testified about it, and his testimony is true, and he knows he is telling the truth so that you, too, will believe.

36 In this way what the Bible said had to come true: *None of His bones will be broken.*[21] 37 And it says in another place, *They will look at Him whom they pierced.*[22]

Jesus Is Buried

38 Later Joseph from Arimathea—who was a disciple of Jesus, but secretly because he was afraid of the Jews—asked Pilate to let him take Jesus' body away. Pilate let him have it. So he came and took His body away. 39 Then came also Nicodemus, who had first come to Jesus at night. He brought a mixture of myrrh and aloes, about seventy-five pounds.

40 They took Jesus' body and wrapped it with the spices in linen according to the Jewish custom of burying the dead.

41 There was a garden at the place where Jesus was crucified, and in the garden was a new grave, in which no one had yet been laid. 42 Here, then—because it was Friday (when the Jews got ready for the Sabbath) and the grave was near—they laid Jesus.

Peter and John

20   Early on Sunday morning while it was still dark Mary from Magdala went to the grave and saw the stone had been taken away from the grave. 2 So she ran and came to Simon Peter and the other disciple, whom Jesus loved. "They've taken the Lord out of the grave," she told them, "and we don't know where they laid Him."

3 So Peter and the other disciple started out for the grave. 4 The two were running side by side, but the other disciple ran faster than Peter and got to the grave first. 5 He looked in and saw the linen wrappings lying there but didn't go in.

6 When Simon Peter got there after him, he

[19] Ps. 69:21
[20] Ps. 22:31
[21] Ex. 12:46; Num. 9:12; Ps. 34:20
[22] Zech. 12:10

K.J.V.

into the sepulchre, and seeth the linen clothes lie, 7And the napkin, that was about his head, not lying with the linen clothes, but wrapped together in a place by itself. 8 Then went in also that other disciple, which came first to the sepulchre, and he saw, and believed. 9 For as yet they knew not the Scripture, that he must rise again from the dead. 10 Then the disciples went away again unto their own home.

11 But Mary stood without at the sepulchre weeping: and as she wept, she stooped down, *and looked* into the sepulchre, 12And seeth two angels in white sitting, the one at the head, and the other at the feet, where the body of Jesus had lain. 13And they say unto her, Woman, why weepest thou? She saith unto them, Because they have taken away my Lord, and I know not where they have laid him. 14And when she had thus said, she turned herself back, and saw Jesus standing, and knew not that it was Jesus. 15 Jesus saith unto her, Woman, why weepest thou? whom seekest thou? She, supposing him to be the gardener, saith unto him, Sir, if thou have borne him hence, tell me where thou hast laid him, and I will take him away. 16 Jesus saith unto her, Mary. She turned herself, and saith unto him, Rabboni; which is to say, Master. 17 Jesus saith unto her, Touch me not; for I am not yet ascended to my Father: but go to my brethren, and say unto them, I ascend unto my Father, and your Father; and *to* my God, and your God. 18 Mary Magdalene came and told the disciples that she had seen the Lord, and *that* he had spoken these things unto her.

19 Then the same day at evening, being the first *day* of the week, when the doors were shut where the disciples were assembled for fear of the Jews, came Jesus and stood in the midst, and saith unto them, Peace *be* unto you. 20And when he had so said, he shewed unto them *his* hands and his side. Then were the disciples glad, when they saw the Lord. 21 Then said Jesus to them again, Peace *be* unto you: as *my* Father hath sent me, even so send I you. 22And when he had said this, he breathed on *them,* and saith unto them, Receive ye the Holy Ghost: 23 Whosesoever sins ye remit, they are remitted unto them; *and* whosesoever *sins* ye retain, they are retained.

24 But Thomas, one of the twelve, called Didymus, was not with them when Jesus came. 25 The other disciples therefore said unto him, We have seen the Lord. But he said unto them, Except I shall see in his hands the print of the nails, and put my finger into the print of the nails, and thrust my hand into his side, I will not believe.

26 And after eight days again his disciples were within, and Thomas with them: *then* came Jesus, the doors being shut, and stood in the midst, and said, Peace *be* unto you. 27 Then saith he to Thomas, Reach hither thy finger, and behold my hands; and reach hither thy hand, and thrust *it* into my side; and be not faithless, but believing. 28 And Thomas answered and said unto him, My Lord and my God. 29 Jesus saith

N.A.S.

tomb; and he * beheld the linen wrappings lying *there,* 7 and the face-cloth, which had been on His head, not lying with the linen wrappings, but rolled up in a place by itself. 8 Then entered in therefore the other disciple also, who had first come to the tomb, and he saw, and believed. 9 For as yet they did not understand the Scripture, that He must rise again from the dead. 10 So the disciples went away again to their own homes.

11 But Mary was standing outside the tomb weeping; and so, as she wept, she stooped and looked into the tomb; 12 and she *beheld two angels in white sitting, one at the head, and one at the feet, where the body of Jesus had been lying. 13And they *said to her, "Woman, why are you weeping?" She *said to them, "Because they have taken away my Lord, and I do not know where they have laid Him." 14 When she had said this, she turned around and *beheld Jesus standing *there,* and did not know it was Jesus. 15 Jesus *said to her, "Woman, why are you weeping? Whom are you seeking?" Supposing Him to be the gardener, she *said to Him, "Sir, if you have carried Him away, tell me where you have laid Him, and I will take Him away." 16 Jesus *said to her, "Mary!" She *turned and *said to Him in Hebrew, "Rabboni," (which means, Teacher). 17 Jesus *said to her, "Stop clinging to Me; for I have not yet ascended to the Father; but go to My brethren, and say to them, 'I ascend to My Father and your Father, and My God and your God.' " 18 Mary Magdalene *came, announcing to the disciples, "I have seen the Lord;" and *that* He had said these things to her.

19 When therefore it was evening, on that day, the first *day* of the week, and when the doors were shut where the disciples were, for fear of the Jews, Jesus came and stood in their midst, and *said to them, "Peace *be* with you." 20And when He had said this, He showed them both His hands and His side. The disciples therefore rejoiced when they saw the Lord. 21 Jesus therefore said to them again, "Peace *be* with you; as the Father has sent Me, I also send you." 22And when He had said this, He breathed on them, and *said to them, "Receive the Holy Spirit. 23 "If you forgive the sins of any, *their sins* have been forgiven them; if you retain the *sins* of any, they have been retained."

24 But Thomas, one of the twelve, called Didymus, was not with them when Jesus came. 25 The other disciples therefore were saying to him, "We have seen the Lord!" But he said to them, "Unless I shall see in His hands the imprint of the nails, and put my finger into the place of the nails, and put my hand into His side, I will not believe."

26 And after eight days again His disciples were inside, and Thomas with them. Jesus *came, the doors having been shut, and stood in their midst, and said, "Peace *be* with you." 27 Then He *said to Thomas, "Reach here your finger, and see My hands; and reach here your hand, and put it into My side; and be not unbelieving, but believing." 28 Thomas answered and said to Him, "My Lord and my God!" 29 Jesus *said to him, "Because you have seen

WILLIAMS

BECK

side, and saw the bandages lying on the ground, 7 but the handkerchief which had been over His face was not lying with the bandages, but was folded up by itself in another place. 8 So then the other disciple, who had reached the tomb first, went inside and saw, and he came to believe it. 9 For they had not previously understood the Scripture which said that He must rise from the dead. 10 So the disciples went home again.

11 But Mary stood just outside the tomb and kept weeping. So, as she was weeping, she stooped down and peered into the tomb 12and saw seated there two angels in white robes, one at the head, one at the feet, where Jesus' body had lain. 13And they said to her, "Woman, why are you weeping?"

She said to them, "They have taken away my Lord, and I do not know where they have put him." 14 On saying this she turned around and saw Jesus standing there, but she did not know that it was Jesus.

15 Jesus said to her, "Woman, why are you weeping? Whom are you looking for?"

Because she supposed it was the gardener, she said to Him, "If it was you, sir, who carried Him away, tell me where you put Him, and I will remove Him."

16 Jesus said to her, "Mary!"

At once she turned and said to Him in Hebrew, "Rabboni!" which means Teacher.

17 Jesus said to her, "Stop clinging to me so, for I have not yet gone up to my Father; but go to my brothers and tell them that I am going up to my Father and your Father, to my God and your God."

18 Mary of Magdala went and announced to the disciples that she had seen the Lord and that He had told her this.

19 In the evening of that same first day of the week, even with the doors of the room bolted where the disciples had met for fear of the Jews, Jesus went in and stood among them and said to them, "Peace be with you!" 20 On saying this, He showed them His hands and His side, and the disciples were thrilled with joy over seeing their Lord.

21 Jesus again said to them, "Peace be with you! Just as my Father has sent me forth, so I am now sending you."

22 On saying this, He breathed upon them, and said, "Receive the Holy Spirit! 23 If you get[a] forgiveness for people's sins, they are forgiven them; if you let people's sins fasten upon them, they will remain fastened upon them."

24 Now Thomas, one of the Twelve, who was called the Twin, was not with them when Jesus came in. 25 So the rest of the disciples kept saying to him, "We have seen the Lord!"

But he said to them, "Unless I see the nailprints in His hands, and put my finger into them, and put my hand into His side, I will never believe it!"

26 Just a week later the disciples were in the room again and Thomas was with them. Although the doors were bolted, Jesus came in and stood among them, and said, "Peace be with you!"

27 Then He said to Thomas, "Put your finger here and look at my hands, and take your hand and put it in my side, and stop being an unbeliever, but be a believer!"

28 Thomas answered Him, "My Lord and my God!"

29 Jesus said to him, "Is it because you have

went into the grave. He saw the linen wrappings lying there, 7 also the cloth that had been on Jesus' head, not lying with the linen wrappings but rolled up in a place by itself. 8 Then the other disciple, who got to the grave first, also went in, saw it, and believed. 9 They didn't know yet what the Bible meant when it said He had to rise from the dead.

10 So the disciples went home again.

"Mary!"

11 Mary stood outside, facing the grave and crying. 12As she cried, she looked into the grave and saw two angels in white clothes sitting where Jesus' body had been lying, one at the head and the other at the feet. 13 "Woman, why are you crying?" they asked her.

"They've taken my Lord away," she told them, "and I don't know where they laid Him."

14 After she said this, she turned around and saw Jesus standing there but didn't know it was Jesus. 15 "Woman, why are you crying?" Jesus asked her. "Whom are you looking for?"

"Sir," she said to Him, thinking He was the gardener, "if you carried Him away, tell me where you laid Him, and I will take Him away."

16 Jesus said to her, "Mary!"

She turned. "Rabboni!" she said to Him in the Jewish language. (The word means "Teacher.")

17 "Don't hold on to Me," Jesus told her. "I didn't go up to the Father yet. But go to My brothers and tell them, 'I am going up to My Father and your Father, to My God and your God.' "

18 Mary from Magdala went and told the disciples, "I saw the Lord," and that He said this to her.

Behind Locked Doors

19 That Sunday evening the doors were locked where the disciples were, because they were afraid of the Jews. Then Jesus came and stood among them and said to them "Peace to you!" 20 When He said this, He showed them His hands and His side. Then the disciples were delighted to see the Lord.

21 "Peace to you!" Jesus said to them again. "As the Father sent Me, so I send you." When He had said this, He breathed on them and said, 23 "Receive the Holy Spirit. If you forgive sins, they are forgiven; if you don't forgive sins, they're not forgiven."

Thomas Sees Jesus

24 But Thomas, one of the twelve, who was called Twin, was not with them when Jesus came. 25 So the other disciples told him, "We saw the Lord."

"Unless I see the marks of the nails in His hands," he told them, "and put my finger in the marks of the nails and put my hand in His side, I won't believe it."

26 A week later His disciples were again in the house, and Thomas was with them. The doors were locked, but Jesus came and stood among them. "Peace to you!" He said. 27 Then He told Thomas, "Put your finger here, and look at My hands—and take your hand and put it in My side. And don't doubt but believe."

28 "My Lord and my God!" Thomas answered Him.

29 "Do you believe because you've seen Me?"

---

[a] Lit., *if you forgive;* but He is emphasizing their winning others; hence our tr. inserting *get.*

K.J.V.

unto him, Thomas, because thou hast seen me, thou hast believed: blessed *are* they that have not seen, and *yet* have believed.

30 And many other signs truly did Jesus in the presence of his disciples, which are not written in this book: 31 But these are written, that ye might believe that Jesus is the Christ, the Son of God; and that believing ye might have life through his name.

21 After these things Jesus shewed himself again to the disciples at the sea of Tiberias; and on this wise shewed he *himself*. 2 There were together Simon Peter, and Thomas called Didymus, and Nathanael of Cana in Galilee, and the *sons* of Zebedee, and two other of his disciples. 3 Simon Peter saith unto them, I go a fishing. They say unto him, We also go with thee. They went forth, and entered into a ship immediately; and that night they caught nothing. 4 But when the morning was now come, Jesus stood on the shore; but the disciples knew not that it was Jesus. 5 Then Jesus saith unto them, Children, have ye any meat? They answered him, No. 6And he said unto them, Cast the net on the right side of the ship, and ye shall find. They cast therefore, and now they were not able to draw it for the multitude of fishes. 7 Therefore that disciple whom Jesus loved saith unto Peter, It is the Lord. Now when Simon Peter heard that it was the Lord, he girt *his* fisher's coat *unto him,* (for he was naked,) and did cast himself into the sea. 8And the other disciples came in a little ship, (for they were not far from land, but as it were two hundred cubits,) dragging the net with fishes. 9As soon then as they were come to land, they saw a fire of coals there, and fish laid thereon, and bread. 10 Jesus saith unto them, Bring of the fish which ye have now caught. 11 Simon Peter went up, and drew the net to land full of great fishes, a hundred and fifty and three: and for all there were so many, yet was not the net broken. 12 Jesus saith unto them, Come *and* dine. And none of the disciples durst ask him, Who art thou? knowing that it was the Lord. 13 Jesus then cometh, and taketh bread, and giveth them, and fish likewise. 14 This is now the third time that Jesus shewed himself to his disciples, after that he was risen from the dead.

15 So when they had dined, Jesus saith to Simon Peter, Simon, *son* of Jonas, lovest thou me more than these? He saith unto him, Yea, Lord; thou knowest that I love thee. He saith unto him, Feed my lambs. 16 He saith to him again the second time, Simon, *son* of Jonas, lovest thou me? He saith unto him, Yea, Lord; thou knowest that I love thee. He saith unto him,

N.A.S.

Me, have you believed? Blessed *are* they who did not see, and *yet* believed."

30 Many other signs therefore Jesus also performed in the presence of the disciples, which are not written in this book; 31 but these have been written that you may believe that Jesus is the Christ, the Son of God; and that believing you may have life in His name.

21 After these things Jesus manifested Himself again to the disciples at the sea of Tiberias; and He manifested *Himself* in this way. 2 There were together Simon Peter, and Thomas called Didymus, and Nathanael of Cana in Galilee, and the *sons* of Zebedee, and two others of His disciples. 3 Simon Peter *said to them, "I am going fishing." They *said to him, "We will also come with you." They went out, and got into the boat; and that night they caught nothing. 4 But when the day was now breaking, Jesus stood on the beach; yet the disciples did not know that it was Jesus. 5 Jesus therefore *said to them, "Children, you do not have any fish, do you?" They answered Him, "No." 6And He said to them, "Cast the net on the right-hand side of the boat, and you will find *a catch.*" They cast therefore, and then they were not able to haul it in because of the great number of fish. 7 That disciple therefore whom Jesus loved *said to Peter, "It is the Lord." And so when Simon Peter heard that it was the Lord, he put his outer garment on (for he was stripped *for work*), and threw himself into the sea. 8 But the other disciples came in the little boat, for they were not far from the land, but about one hundred yards away, dragging the net *full* of fish. 9And so when they got out upon the land, they *saw a charcoal fire *already* laid, and fish placed on it, and bread. 10 Jesus *said to them, "Bring some of the fish which you have now caught." 11 Simon Peter went up, and drew the net to land, full of large fish, a hundred and fifty-three; and although there were so many, the net was not torn. 12 Jesus *said to them, "Come *and* have breakfast." None of the disciples ventured to question Him, "Who are You?" knowing that it was the Lord. 13 Jesus *came and *took the bread, and *gave them, and the fish likewise. 14 This is now the third time that Jesus was manifested to the disciples, after He was raised from the dead.

15 So when they had finished breakfast, Jesus *said to Simon Peter, "Simon, *son* of John, do you love Me more than these?" He *said to Him, "Yes, Lord; You know that I love You." He *said to him, "Tend My lambs." 16 He *said to him again a second time, "Simon, *son* of John, do you love Me?" He *said to Him, "Yes, Lord; You know that I love You." He

WILLIAMS

seen me, Thomas, that you believe? Blessed be those who believe, even though they have not seen me!"

30 Now there are many other wonder-works which Jesus performed in the disciples' presence which are not recorded in this book. 31 But these have been recorded, in order that you may believe that Jesus is the Christ, the Son of God, and that through believing you may have life, as bearers of His name.

21 *Jesus appears to seven disciples in a great catch of fish; He prepares and eats breakfast with them; tests Peter's love*

After this Jesus again showed Himself to the disciples at the sea of Tiberias, and this is the way He showed Himself.
2 Simon Peter, Thomas called the Twin, Nathaniel of Cana in Galilee, the sons of Zebedee, and two other disciples of Jesus, were all together. 3 Simon Peter said to them, "I am going fishing."
They said to him, "We are going with you too." They went out and got into the boat, but that night they caught nothing.

4 Now just as day was breaking, Jesus took His stand on the shore, though the disciples did not know that it was Jesus. 5 So Jesus said to them, "Lads, you have no fish, have you?"
They answered, "No."
6 Then He said to them, "Set your net on the right side of the boat, and you will catch them."
They did so, and they could not drag it in for the big catch of fish. 7 So that disciple whom Jesus used to love tenderly said to Peter, "It is the Lord!"
When Simon Peter heard that it was the Lord, he belted on his fisherman's coat, for he had taken it off, and plunged into the sea. 8 The rest of the disciples followed in the little boat, for they were not far from shore—only about a hundred yards—dragging in the net full of fish.
9 When they landed, they saw a charcoal fire all made and a fish lying on it; also some bread. 10 Jesus said to them, "Fetch some of the fish you have just caught." 11 So Simon Peter got into the boat, and pulled the net ashore, full of big fish, a hundred and fifty-three; and though there were so many, the net was not torn. 12 Jesus said to them, "Come and have breakfast."
None of the disciples dared to ask Him, "Who are you?" because they knew it was the Lord. 13 Jesus went and took the bread and gave it to them, and the fish too. 14 This was now the third time that Jesus showed Himself to His disciples, after He had risen from the dead.
15 After they had finished breakfast, Jesus said to Simon Peter, "Simon, son of John, are you more devoted to me than you are to these things?"
Peter answered Him, "Yes, Lord, you know that I tenderly love you."
Jesus said to him, "Then feed my lambs."
16 Jesus again said to him a second time, "Simon, son of John, are you really devoted to me?"
He said to Him, "Yes, Lord, you know that I tenderly love you."
Jesus said to him, "Then be a shepherd to my sheep."

BECK

Jesus asked him. "Blessed are those who didn't see Me and still believed."

Much More

30 His disciples saw Jesus do many other miracles that are not written in this book. 31 But these things are written so that you believe Jesus is the promised Savior, God's Son, and by believing have life in His name.

Breakfast with Jesus

21 After that, Jesus showed Himself again to the disciples at the Lake of Galilee. This is how He showed Himself.
2 Simon Peter, Thomas (called Twin), Nathanael from Cana in Galilee, Zebedee's sons, and two other disciples of Jesus were together. 3 Simon Peter said to the others, "I'm going fishing."
"We're going with you," they told him.
They went out and got into the boat. But that night they caught nothing. 4 When morning came, Jesus stood on the shore. But the disciples didn't know it was Jesus.
5 "Boys, you don't have any fish, do you?" Jesus asked them.
They answered Him, "No."
6 "Drop the net on the right side of the boat," He told them, "and you will find some." So they dropped it. And now they couldn't pull it in, there were so many fish.
7 The disciple whom Jesus loved said to Peter, "It is the Lord." When Simon Peter heard him say, "It is the Lord," he put on the coat he had taken off, fastened it with his belt, and jumped into the lake. 8 But the other disciples, who were not far from the shore, only about a hundred yards, came in the small boat, dragging the net full of fish.
9 As they stepped out on the shore, they saw burning coals there with fish lying on them, and bread.
10 "Bring some of the fish you just caught," Jesus told them. 11 Simon Peter got into the small boat and pulled the net on the shore. It was filled with a hundred and fifty-three big fish. Although there were so many, the net wasn't torn.
12 "Come, have breakfast," Jesus told them. None of the disciples dared to ask Him, "Who are You?" They knew it was the Lord. 13 Jesus came, took the bread, and gave it to them, and also the fish.
14 This was the third time Jesus showed Himself to the disciples after He rose from the dead.

"Do You Love Me?"

15 When they had eaten breakfast, Jesus asked Simon Peter, "Simon, son of John, do you love Me more than these do?"
"Yes, Lord," he answered Him, "You know I love You."
"Feed My lambs," Jesus told him.
16 "Simon, son of John," He asked him a second time, "do you love Me?"
"Yes, Lord," he answered Him, "You know I love You."
"Be a shepherd of My sheep," Jesus told him.

321

K.J.V.

Feed my sheep. 17 He saith unto him the third time, Simon, *son* of Jonas, lovest thou me? Peter was grieved because he said unto him the third time, Lovest thou me? And he said unto him, Lord, thou knowest all things; thou knowest that I love thee. Jesus saith unto him, Feed my sheep. 18 Verily, verily, I say unto thee, When thou wast young, thou girdedst thyself, and walkedst whither thou wouldest: but when thou shalt be old, thou shalt stretch forth thy hands, and another shall gird thee, and carry *thee* whither thou wouldest not. 19 This spake he, signifying by what death he should glorify God. And when he had spoken this, he saith unto him, Follow me. 20 Then Peter, turning about, seeth the disciple whom Jesus loved following; which also leaned on his breast at supper, and said, Lord, which is he that betrayeth thee? 21 Peter seeing him saith to Jesus, Lord, and what *shall* this man *do?* 22 Jesus saith unto him, If I will that he tarry till I come, what *is that* to thee? follow thou me. 23 Then went this saying abroad among the brethren, that that disciple should not die: yet Jesus said not unto him, He shall not die; but, If I will that he tarry till I come, what *is that* to thee? 24 This is the disciple which testifieth of these things, and wrote these things: and we know that his testimony is true. 25 And there are also many other things which Jesus did, the which, if they should be written every one, I suppose that even the world itself could not contain the books that should be written. Amen.

N.A.S.

*said to him, "Shepherd My sheep." 17 He *said to him the third time, "Simon, *son* of John, do you love Me?" Peter was grieved because He said to him the third time, "Do you love Me?" And he said to Him, "Lord, You know all things; You know that I love You." Jesus *said to him, "Tend My sheep. 18 "Truly, truly, I say to you, when you were younger, you used to gird yourself, and walk wherever you wished; but when you grow old, you will stretch out your hands, and someone else will gird you, and bring you where you do not wish to *go*." 19 Now this He said, signifying by what kind of death he would glorify God. And when He had spoken this, He *said to him, "Follow Me!" 20 Peter, turning around, *saw the disciple whom Jesus loved following *them;* the one who also had leaned back on His breast at the supper, and said, "Lord, who is the one who betrays You?" 21 Peter therefore seeing him *said to Jesus, "Lord, and what about this man?" 22 Jesus *said to him, "If I want him to remain until I come, what *is that* to you? You follow Me!" 23 This saying therefore went out among the brethren that that disciple would not die; yet Jesus did not say to him that he would not die; but *only*, "If I want him to remain until I come, what *is that* to you?"

24 This is the disciple who bears witness of these things, and wrote these things; and we know that his witness is true.

25 And there are also many other things which Jesus did, which if they *were written in detail, I suppose that even the world itself *would not contain the books which *were written.

WILLIAMS

17 For the third time Jesus asked him, "Simon, son of John, do you really tenderly love me?"

Peter was hurt because Jesus the third time asked him, "Do you really tenderly love me?" So he answered Him, "Lord, you know everything; you know that I do tenderly love you."

Jesus said to him, "Then feed my sheep. 18 I most solemnly say to you, when you were young, you used to put on your own belt and go where you pleased, but when you grow old, you will stretch out your hands and someone else will put a belt on you and you will go where you do not please to go." 19 He said this to point out the sort of death by which Peter was to glorify God. So after He had said this, He said to Peter, "Keep on following me!"

20 Peter turned and saw following them the disciple whom Jesus specially loved, who at the supper leaned back upon Jesus' breast and asked, "Lord, who is it that is going to betray you?" 21 So when Peter saw him, he said to Jesus, "But, Lord, what about him?"

22 Jesus answered him, "If I wish him to wait until I come, what is that to you? You must keep on following me."

23 So the report got out among the brothers that this disciple was not going to die. But Jesus did not tell him that he was not going to die; He said only, "If I wish him to wait until I come, what is that to you?"

24 This is the disciple who testifies to these things and who wrote them down, and we know that his testimony is true.

25 There are many other things that Jesus did, which, if they were all written down in detail, I do not suppose that the world itself could hold the books that would have to be written.

BECK

17 "Simon, son of John," He asked him a third time, "do you love Me?"

Peter felt sad because He asked him a third time, "Do you love Me?" "Lord, You know everything," he answered Him, "You know I love You."

18 "Feed My sheep," Jesus told him. "I tell you the truth: When you were younger, you used to fasten your belt and go where you wanted to. But when you're old, you'll stretch out your hands, and someone else will tie you and take you where you don't want to go." 19 He said this to show by what kind of death Peter would glorify God. After saying this, He told him, "Follow Me."

20 Peter turned and saw the disciple whom Jesus loved following them. He was the one who at the supper leaned against Jesus' breast and asked, "Lord, who is going to betray You?" 21 When Peter saw him, he asked Jesus, "Lord, what about him?"

22 "If I want him to stay till I come," Jesus asked him, "what is that to you? You follow Me." 23 And so it was said among the Christians, "That disciple will not die." But Jesus didn't say, "He will not die," but, "If I want him to stay till I come, what is that to you?"

24 This is the disciple who testified about these things and wrote this. And we know what he testifies is true.

Much More

25 Jesus also did many other things. If every one of these were written, I suppose the world would not have room for the books that would be written.

THE ACTS OF THE

APOSTLES

THE ACTS

1 The former treatise have I made, O Theophilus, of all that Jesus began both to do and teach, 2 Until the day in which he was taken up, after that he through the Holy Ghost had given commandments unto the apostles whom he had chosen: 3 To whom also he shewed himself alive after his passion by many infallible proofs, being seen of them forty days, and speaking of the things pertaining to the kingdom of God: 4And, being assembled together with *them,* commanded them that they should not depart from Jerusalem, but wait for the promise of the Father, which, *saith he,* ye have heard of me. 5 For John truly baptized with water; but ye shall be baptized with the Holy Ghost not many days hence. 6 When they therefore were come together, they asked of him, saying, Lord, wilt thou at this time restore again the kingdom to Israel? 7 And he said unto them, It is not for you to know the times or the seasons, which the Father hath put in his own power. 8 But ye shall receive power, after that the Holy Ghost is come upon you: and ye shall be witnesses unto me both in Jerusalem, and in all Judea, and in Samaria, and unto the uttermost part of the earth. 9And when he had spoken these things, while they beheld, he was taken up; and a cloud received him out of their sight. 10And while they looked steadfastly toward heaven as he went up, behold, two men stood by them in white apparel; 11 Which also said, Ye men of Galilee, why stand ye gazing up into heaven? this same Jesus, which is taken up from you into heaven, shall so come in like manner as ye have seen him go into heaven. 12 Then returned they unto Jerusalem from the mount called Olivet, which is from Jerusalem a sabbath day's journey. 13And when they were come in, they went up into an upper room, where abode both Peter, and James, and John, and Andrew, Philip, and Thomas, Bartholomew, and Matthew, James *the son* of Alpheus and Simon Zelotes, and Judas *the brother* of James. 14 These all continued with one accord in prayer and supplication, with the women, and Mary the mother of Jesus, and with his brethren. 15 And in those days Peter stood up in the midst of the disciples, and said, (the number of names together were about a hundred and twenty,) 16 Men *and* brethren, this Scripture must needs have been fulfilled, which the Holy Ghost by the mouth of David spake before concerning Judas, which was guide to them that took Jesus. 17 For he was numbered with us, and had obtained part of this ministry. 18 Now this man purchased a field with the reward of iniquity; and falling headlong, he burst asunder in the midst, and all his bowels gushed out. 19And it was known unto all the dwellers at

1 The first account I composed, Theophilus, about all that Jesus began to do and teach, 2 until the day when He was taken up, after He had by the Holy Spirit given orders to the apostles whom He had chosen. 3 To these He also presented Himself alive, after His suffering, by many convincing proofs, appearing to them over *a period of* forty days, and speaking of the things concerning the kingdom of God. 4And gathering them together, He commanded them not to leave Jerusalem, but to wait for what the Father had promised, "Which," *He said,* "you heard of from Me; 5 for John baptized with water, but you shall be baptized with the Holy Spirit not many days from now." 6 And so when they had come together, they were asking Him, saying, "Lord, is it at this time You are restoring the kingdom to Israel?" 7 He said to them, "It is not for you to know times or epochs which the Father has fixed by His own authority; 8 but you shall receive power when the Holy Spirit has come upon you; and you shall be My witnesses both in Jerusalem, and in all Judea and Samaria, and even to the remotest part of the earth." 9And after He had said these things, He was lifted up while they were looking on, and a cloud received Him out of their sight. 10And as they were gazing intently into the sky while He was departing, behold, two men in white clothing stood beside them; 11 and they also said, "Men of Galilee, why do you stand looking into the sky? This Jesus, who has been taken up from you into heaven, will come in just the same way as you have watched Him go into heaven." 12 Then they returned to Jerusalem from the mount called Olivet, which is near Jerusalem, a Sabbath day's journey away. 13And when they had entered, they went up to the upper room, where they were staying; that is, Peter and John and James and Andrew, Philip and Thomas, Bartholomew and Matthew, James *the son* of Alphaeus, and Simon the Zealot, and Judas *the son* of James. 14 These all with one mind were continually devoting themselves to prayer, along with *the* women, and Mary the mother of Jesus, and with His brothers. 15 And at this time Peter stood up in the midst of the brethren (a gathering of about one hundred and twenty persons was there together), and said, 16 "Brethren, the Scripture had to be fulfilled, which the Holy Spirit foretold by the mouth of David concerning Judas, who became a guide to those who arrested Jesus. 17 "For he was counted among us, and received his portion in this ministry." 18 (Now this man acquired a field with the price of his wickedness; and falling headlong, he burst open in the middle and all his bowels gushed out. 19And it

THE ACTS OF THE APOSTLES

THE ACTS

1 *The risen Jesus gives convincing proofs that He is alive, gives final orders; goes back to heaven; the apostles and others meet to pray; Peter suggests the choosing of Judas' successor; Matthias chosen*

I wrote my first volume, Theophilus, about all that Jesus did and taught from the beginning 2 up to the day when through the Holy Spirit He gave the Apostles whom He had chosen their orders, and then was taken up to heaven. 3 After He had suffered, He had shown Himself alive to them, by many convincing proofs, appearing to them through a period of forty days, and telling them the things about the kingdom of God. 4And once while He was eating with them, He charged them not to leave Jerusalem but to wait for what the Father had promised.

"You have heard me speak of it," He said, 5 "for John baptized people in water, but in a few days you will be baptized in the Holy Spirit."

6 So those who were present began to ask Him, "Lord, is this the time when you are going to set up the kingdom again for Israel?"

7 He answered them, "It is not your business to learn times and dates which the Father has a right to fix, 8 but you are going to receive power when the Holy Spirit comes upon you, and you must be witnesses for me in Jerusalem and all over Judea and Samaria, and to the very ends of the earth."

9 After saying this, He was taken up while they were looking at Him, and a cloud swept under Him and carried Him out of their sight. 10And while they were gazing after Him into heaven, two men dressed in white suddenly stood beside them, 11 and said to them, "Men of Galilee, why do you stand looking up into heaven? This very Jesus who has been taken up from you into heaven will come back in just the way you have seen Him go up into heaven."

12 Then they returned to Jerusalem from the hill called The Mount of Olives, which is near Jerusalem, only half a mile away. 13 When they reached the city, they went to the room upstairs where they had been staying; they were Peter and John, James and Andrew, Philip and Thomas, Bartholomew and Matthew, James the son of Alpheus, Simon the Zealot, and Judas the son of James. 14 With one mind they were all continuing to devote themselves to prayer, with the women and Mary and His brothers.

15 At that time Peter got up among the brothers*a* (there were about a hundred and twenty present) and said, 16 "Brothers, that Scripture had to be fulfilled which the Holy Spirit uttered by the mouth of David in the former times about Judas who became the guide to those who arrested Jesus; 17 for he was one of our number,*b* and he received a share in this ministry of ours. 18 (This man bought a piece of land with the money which he took for his treachery, and he fell there face downward and his body broke in two, and all his intestines poured out. 19 It became known to all the resi-

1 In my first book, Theophilus, I wrote about everything Jesus did and taught 2 till the day He was taken up to heaven after giving orders by the Holy Spirit to the apostles He had chosen.

Jesus Goes Up to Heaven

3 After His suffering Jesus in many convincing ways proved to the apostles He was alive as He showed Himself to them during forty days and talked about God's kingdom.

4 When He met with them, He ordered them not to leave Jerusalem but to wait for what the Father had promised: "You heard Me tell about Him: 5 John baptized with water, but in a few days you will be baptized with the Holy Spirit."

6 When they came together, they asked Him, "Lord, are You now going to make Israel an independent kingdom again?"

7 "It isn't for you to know," He told them, "what times or periods the Father has set by His own authority. 8 But when the Holy Spirit comes on you, you will receive power and will testify of Me in Jerusalem, in all Judea and Samaria, and to the farthest parts of the world."

9 When He had said this and while they were watching Him, He was lifted up, and a cloud took Him away so they couldn't see Him anymore.

10 As He was going and they were gazing up into the sky, two men in white clothes were standing right beside them. 11 "Men of Galilee," they asked, "why are you standing here looking up to heaven? This Jesus, who was taken away from you to heaven, will come back the same way you saw Him go to heaven."

12 Then they went back to Jerusalem from the Mount of Olives, as it was called (it's near Jerusalem, only half a mile away).

There Must Be Twelve

13 When they came into the city, they went to the second-floor room where they were staying—Peter, John, James, and Andrew; Philip and Thomas; Bartholomew and Matthew; James, the son of Alphaeus, Simon the Zealot, and Judas, the son of James. 14 With one mind these all kept praying together. With them were the women, including Jesus' mother Mary, and His brothers.

15 In those days Peter got up among the disciples (a crowd of them was there, about a hundred and twenty), and he said, 16 "Brothers, long ago the Holy Spirit spoke through David about Judas, who led the men that arrested Jesus. And what He wrote had to come true. 17 Judas was one of us twelve and was given a share in the work we're doing. 18 With the money he got for his crime he bought a piece of land; and falling on his face, he burst in the middle, and all his intestines poured out. 19 Everybody living in Jerusalem heard about

[a] Fol. two best Mss. [b] *Numbered with us.*

K.J.V.

Jerusalem; insomuch as that field is called, in their proper tongue, Aceldama, that is to say, The field of blood. 20 For it is written in the book of Psalms, Let his habitation be desolate, and let no man dwell therein: and, His bishoprick let another take. 21 Wherefore of these men which have companied with us all the time that the Lord Jesus went in and out among us, 22 Beginning from the baptism of John, unto that same day that he was taken up from us, must one be ordained to be a witness with us of his resurrection. 23 And they appointed two, Joseph called Barsabas, who was surnamed Justus, and Matthias. 24 And they prayed, and said, Thou, Lord, which knowest the hearts of all *men,* shew whether of these two thou hast chosen, 25 That he may take part of this ministry and apostleship, from which Judas by transgression fell, that he might go to his own place. 26 And they gave forth their lots; and the lot fell upon Matthias; and he was numbered with the eleven apostles.

2 And when the day of Pentecost was fully come, they were all with one accord in one place. 2 And suddenly there came a sound from heaven as of a rushing mighty wind, and it filled all the house where they were sitting. 3 And there appeared unto them cloven tongues like as of fire, and it sat upon each of them. 4 And they were all filled with the Holy Ghost, and began to speak with other tongues, as the Spirit gave them utterance. 5 And there were dwelling at Jerusalem Jews, devout men, out of every nation under heaven. 6 Now when this was noised abroad, the multitude came together, and were confounded, because that every man heard them speak in his own language. 7 And they were all amazed and marvelled, saying one to another, Behold, are not all these which speak Galileans? 8 And how hear we every man in our own tongue, wherein we were born? 9 Parthians, and Medes, and Elamites, and the dwellers in Mesopotamia, and in Judea, and Cappadocia, in Pontus, and Asia, 10 Phrygia, and Pamphylia, in Egypt, and in the parts of Libya about Cyrene, and strangers of Rome, Jews and proselytes, 11 Cretes and Arabians, we do hear them speak in our tongues the wonderful works of God. 12 And they were all amazed, and were in doubt, saying one to another, What meaneth this? 13 Others mocking said, These men are full of new wine.

14 But Peter, standing up with the eleven, lifted up his voice, and said unto them, Ye men of Judea, and all ye that dwell at Jerusalem, be this known unto you, and hearken to my words: 15 For these are not drunken, as ye suppose, seeing it is *but* the third hour of the day. 16 But this is that which was spoken by the prophet

N.A.S.

became known to all who were living in Jerusalem; so that in their own language that field was called Hakeldama, that is, Field of Blood). 20 "For it is written in the book of Psalms,
'LET HIS HOMESTEAD BE MADE DESOLATE,
AND LET NO MAN DWELL IN IT;'
and,
'HIS OFFICE LET ANOTHER MAN TAKE.'
21 "It is therefore necessary that of the men who have accompanied us all the time that the Lord Jesus went in and out among us— 22 beginning with the baptism of John, until the day that He was taken up from us—one of these should become a witness with us of His resurrection." 23 And they put forward two men, Joseph called Barsabbas (who was also called Justus), and Matthias. 24 And they prayed, and said, "Thou, Lord, who knowest the hearts of all men, show which one of these two Thou hast chosen 25 to occupy this ministry and apostleship from which Judas turned aside to go to his own place." 26 And they drew lots for them, and the lot fell to Matthias; and he was numbered with the eleven apostles.

2 And when the day of Pentecost had come, they were all together in one place. 2 And suddenly there came from heaven a noise like a violent, rushing wind, and it filled the whole house where they were sitting. 3 And there appeared to them tongues as of fire distributing themselves, and they rested on each one of them. 4 And they were all filled with the Holy Spirit and began to speak with other tongues, as the Spirit was giving them utterance.
5 Now there were Jews living in Jerusalem, devout men, from every nation under heaven. 6 And when this sound occurred, the multitude came together, and were bewildered, because they were each one hearing them speak in his own language. 7 And they *began* to be amazed and to marvel, saying, "Why, are not all these who are speaking Galileans? 8 "And how is it that we each hear *them* in our own language to which we were born? 9 "Parthians and Medes and Elamites, and residents of Mesopotamia, Judea and Cappadocia, Pontus and Asia, 10 Phrygia and Pamphylia, Egypt and the districts of Libya around Cyrene, and visitors from Rome, both Jews and "proselytes, 11 Cretans and Arabs—we hear them in our *own* tongues speaking of the mighty deeds of God." 12 And they continued in amazement and great perplexity, saying to one another, "What does this mean?" 13 But others were mocking and saying, "They are full of sweet wine."
14 But Peter, taking his stand with the eleven, raised his voice and declared to them: "Men of Judea, and all you who live in Jerusalem, let this be known to you, and give heed to my words. 15 "For these men are not drunk, as you suppose, for it is *only* the ᵇthird hour of the day; 16 but this is what was spoken of through the prophet Joel:

[a] I.e., Gentile converts to Judaism. [b] I.e., 9 a.m.

WILLIAMS

dents of Jerusalem, so that this piece of land was called in their language Akeldamach, that is, The Field of Blood.) 20 For in the Book of Psalms it is written:

'Let his estate be desolate,
And let no one live on it,'

and

'Let someone else take his position.'

21 "So one of these men who have been associated with us all the time the Lord Jesus came and went among us, 22 from the time of His baptism by John down to the day when He was taken up from us, must be added to our number as a witness to His resurrection."

23 Then they nominated two men, Joseph called Barsabbas, who was also called Justus, and Matthias. 24And they prayed, saying, "Lord, you who know the hearts of all, show us which one of these two men you have chosen 25 to take a share in this service as an apostle,° from which Judas fell away to go to his own place."

26 They then drew lots for them, and the lot fell on Matthias, and he was added to the eleven apostles.

2 *The Spirit comes at Pentecost; Peter explains the startling effects of the Spirit on the disciples; shows that Jesus is the Messiah, His death being a part of God's program to save the world; three thousand repent and are baptized; the church an influential brotherhood*

When the day of Pentecost had now come, they were all meeting in one mind, 2 when suddenly there came from heaven a sound like a terrific blast of wind, and it filled the whole house where they were sitting. 3And they saw tongues like flames of fire separating and resting on their heads, one to each of them, 4 and they were all filled with the Holy Spirit, and began to speak in foreign languages as the Spirit granted them to utter divine things.

5 Now there were devout Jews from every part of the world living in Jerusalem. 6And when this sound was heard, the crowd rushed together in great excitement, because each one heard them speaking in his own language. 7 They were perfectly astounded, and in bewilderment they continued to say, "Are not all these men who are speaking Galileans? 8 So how is it that each of us hears them speaking in his own native tongue? 9 Parthians, Medes, Elamites, residents of Mesopotamia, of Judea and Cappadocia, of Pontus and Asia, 10 of Phrygia and Pamphylia, of Egypt and the district of Lybia around Cyrene, transient dwellers from Rome, Jews and proselytes, 11 Cretans and Arabs—we hear them all alike telling in our own tongues the great wonders of God." 12And thus they all continued to be astounded and bewildered, and continued to say to each other, "What can this mean?"

13 But others in derision were saying, "They are running over with new wine."

14 Then Peter stood with the Eleven around him, and raising his voice he addressed them, "Men of Judea and all you residents of Jerusalem, let me explain this to you, and give close attention to my words. 15 These men are not drunk as you suppose, for it is only nine o'clock in the morning. 16 But this is what was spoken by the prophet Joel:

BECK

it. And so that piece of land is called Akeldama" in their language; the word means place of blood. 20 "It is written in the book of Psalms: *His home should be deserted, and nobody should live there.[1] And somebody else should take over his office.[2]* 22 Then someone should be added to our number as a witness of His resurrection. 21 He should be one of these men who went with us all the time the Lord Jesus went in and out among us, 22 from John's baptism to the day He was taken up from us."

23 The disciples named two: Joseph (called Barsabbas; he was also called Justus) and Matthias. 24 Then they prayed, "Lord, You know the hearts of all. Show us which of these two You have chosen 25 to serve in this office of apostle, which Judas left to go where he belonged."

26 They provided lots for them, and so Matthias was chosen and added to the eleven apostles.

The Holy Spirit Comes

2 The day of Pentecost* came, and they were all together in one place. 2 Suddenly a sound like a violent blast of wind came from heaven and filled the whole house where they were sitting. 3 They saw tongues like flames that separated, and one rested on each of them. 4 They were all filled with the Holy Spirit and started to speak in other languages as the Spirit gave them the ability to speak.

5 Jews who feared God had come from every nation under heaven to live in Jerusalem. 6 When that sound came, the crowd gathered and was dumfounded because each one heard the disciples speak his own language. 7Amazed and wondering, they asked, "Don't all these who are speaking come from Galilee? 8And how does every one of us hear his own language he was born in—9 Parthians, Medes, Elamites, and people living in Mesopotamia, Judea and Cappadocia, Pontus and the province of Asia, 10 Phrygia and Pamphilia, Egypt and the country near Cyrene in Libya, the visitors from Rome, 11 Jews and those who have accepted the Jewish religion, people from Crete and Arabia? In our own languages we hear them tell about God's wonderful things." 12 They were all amazed and puzzled. "What can this mean?" they asked one another. 13 Others sneered: "They're full of new wine."

Peter's Pentecost Sermon

14 Then Peter got up with the eleven, raised his voice, and addressed them:

"Jews and all you who live in Jerusalem, understand this, and listen to what I say. 15 These men are not drunk, as you suppose. Why, it's only nine in the morning. 16 No, this

* A festival on the 50th day after the Passover.
[1] Ps. 69:25
[2] Ps. 109:8

[c] Grk., *service and apostleship.*

K.J.V.

Joel; 17And it shall come to pass in the last days, saith God, I will pour out of my Spirit upon all flesh: and your sons and your daughters shall prophesy, and your young men shall see visions, and your old men shall dream dreams: 18And on my servants and on my handmaidens I will pour out in those days of my Spirit; and they shall prophesy: 19And I will shew wonders in heaven above, and signs in the earth beneath; blood, and fire, and vapour of smoke: 20 The sun shall be turned into darkness, and the moon into blood, before that great and notable day of the Lord come: 21And it shall come to pass, *that* whosoever shall call on the name of the Lord .shall be saved. 22 Ye men of Israel, hear these words; Jesus of Nazareth, a man approved of God among you by miracles and wonders and signs, which God did by him in the midst of you, as ye yourselves also know: 23 Him, being delivered by the determinate counsel and foreknowledge of God, ye have taken, and by wicked hands have crucified and slain: 24 Whom God hath raised up, having loosed the pains of death: because it was not possible that he should be holden of it. 25 For David speaketh concerning him, I foresaw the Lord always before my face; for he is on my right hand, that I should not be moved: 26 Therefore did my heart rejoice, and my tongue was glad; moreover also my flesh shall rest in hope: 27 Because thou wilt not leave my soul in hell, neither wilt thou suffer thine Holy One to see corruption. 28 Thou hast made known to me the ways of life; thou shalt make me full of joy with thy countenance. 29 Men *and* brethren, let me freely speak unto you of the patriarch David, that he is both dead and buried, and his sepulchre is with us unto this day. 30 Therefore being a prophet, and knowing that God had sworn with an oath to him, that of the fruit of his loins, according to the flesh, he would raise up Christ to sit on his throne; 31 He, seeing this before, spake of the resurrection of Christ, that his soul was not left in hell, neither his flesh did see corruption. 32 This Jesus hath God raised up, whereof we all are witnesses. 33 Therefore being by the right hand of God exalted, and having received of the Father the promise of the Holy Ghost, he hath shed forth this, which ye now see and hear. 34 For David is not ascended into the heavens: but he saith himself, The Lord said unto my Lord, Sit thou on my right hand, 35 Until I make thy foes thy footstool. 36 Therefore let all the house of Israel know assuredly, that God hath made that same Jesus, whom ye have crucified, both Lord and Christ.

37 Now when they heard *this,* they were

N.A.S.

17 'AND IT SHALL BE IN THE LAST DAYS, GOD SAYS,
THAT I WILL POUR FORTH OF MY SPIRIT UPON ALL MANKIND;
AND YOUR SONS AND YOUR DAUGHTERS SHALL PROPHESY,
AND YOUR YOUNG MEN SHALL SEE VISIONS,
AND YOUR OLD MEN SHALL DREAM DREAMS;
18 'EVEN UPON MY BONDSLAVES, BOTH MEN AND WOMEN,
I WILL IN THOSE DAYS POUR FORTH OF MY SPIRIT
And they shall prophesy.
19 'AND I WILL GRANT WONDERS IN THE SKY ABOVE,
AND SIGNS ON THE EARTH BENEATH,
BLOOD, AND FIRE, AND VAPOR OF SMOKE.
20 'THE SUN SHALL BE TURNED INTO DARKNESS,
AND THE MOON INTO BLOOD,
BEFORE THE GREAT GLORIOUS DAY OF THE LORD SHALL COME.
21 'AND IT SHALL BE, THAT EVERY ONE WHO CALLS ON THE NAME OF THE LORD SHALL BE SAVED.'

22 "Men of Israel, listen to these words: Jesus the Nazarene, a man attested to you by God with miracles and wonders and signs which God performed through Him in your midst, just as you yourselves know— 23 this *Man,* delivered up by the predetermined plan and foreknowledge of God, you nailed to a cross by the hands of godless men and put *Him* to death. 24 "And God raised Him up again, putting an end to the agony of death, since it was impossible for Him to be held in its power. 25 "For David says of Him,
'I WAS ALWAYS BEHOLDING THE LORD IN MY PRESENCE;
FOR HE IS AT MY RIGHT HAND, THAT I MAY NOT BE SHAKEN.
26 'THEREFORE MY HEART WAS GLAD AND MY TONGUE EXULTED;
MOREOVER MY FLESH ALSO WILL ABIDE IN HOPE;
27 'BECAUSE THOU WILT NOT ABANDON MY SOUL TO HADES,
NOR ALLOW THY HOLY ONE TO UNDERGO DECAY.
28 'THOU HAST MADE KNOWN TO ME THE WAYS OF LIFE;
THOU WILT MAKE ME FULL OF GLADNESS WITH THY PRESENCE.'

29 "Brethren, I may confidently say to you regarding the patriarch David that he both died and was buried, and his tomb is with us to this day. 30 "And so, because he was a prophet, and knew that God had sworn to him with an oath to seat *one* of his descendants upon his throne, 31 he looked ahead and spoke of the resurrection of *the Christ, that He was neither abandoned to Hades, nor did His flesh suffer decay. 32 "This Jesus God raised up again, to which we are all witnesses. 33 "Therefore having been exalted to the right hand of God, and having received from the Father the promise of the Holy Spirit, He has poured forth this which you both see and hear. 34 "For it was not David who ascended into heaven, but he himself says:
'THE LORD SAID TO MY LORD,
"SIT AT MY RIGHT HAND,
35 UNTIL I MAKE THINE ENEMIES A FOOTSTOOL FOR THY FEET." '
36 "Therefore let all the house of Israel know for certain that God has made Him both Lord and Christ—this Jesus whom you crucified."

37 Now when they heard *this,* they were

[a] I.e., *the Messiah.*

WILLIAMS

17 'It will occur in the last days, says God,
That I will pour out my Spirit upon all man-
    kind;
Your sons and daughters will prophesy,
Your young men will have visions,
Your old men will have dreams.
18 Even on my slaves, both men and women,
I will pour out my Spirit in those days,
And they will become prophets.
19 I will show wonders in the sky above
And signs upon the earth below,
Yes, blood and fire and smoky mist.
20 The sun will turn to darkness,
And the moon to blood,
Before the coming of the great and glorious
    day of the Lord.
21 Then everyone who calls upon the name
    of the Lord will be saved.'
22 "Fellow Israelites, listen to what I say.
Jesus of Nazareth, as you yourselves well know,
a man accredited to you by God through mighty
deeds and wonders and wonder-works which
God performed through Him right here among
you, 23 this very Jesus, I say, after He was betrayed, in accordance with the predetermined
plan and foreknowledge of God, you had wicked
men kill by nailing Him to a cross; 24 but God
raised Him up by loosing Him from the pangs
of death, since it was impossible for Him to be
held by the power of death. 25 For David says
of Him:

'I always kept my eyes upon the Lord,
For He is at my right hand, so that I may not
    be removed.
26 So my heart is glad and my tongue exults
And my body still lives in hope.
27 For you will not forsake my soul to hades,
Nor will you let your Holy One experience
    decay.
28 You have made known to me the ways of
    life,
And you will fill me with delight in your pres-
    ence.'
29 "Brothers, I may confidently say to you
about the patriarch David, that he died and was
buried, and that his grave is here among us to
this very day. 30 So, as he was a prophet and
knew that God with an oath had promised to
put one of his descendants on his throne, 31 he
foresaw the resurrection of the Christ and told
of it, for He was not forsaken to Hades, and His
body did not undergo decay. 32 I mean Jesus
whom God raised from the dead, to which fact
we are all witnesses. 33 So He has been exalted
to God's right hand and has received from His
Father, as promised, and has poured out upon us
the Holy Spirit, as you see and hear. 34 For
David did not go up to heaven, but he himself
says:

'The Lord said to my Lord, "Sit at my right
    hand,
35 Until I make your enemies the footstool
    of your feet." '
36 "Therefore, let all the descendants of Israel
understand beyond a doubt that God has made
this Jesus whom you crucified both Lord and
Christ."
37 When they heard this, they were stabbed

BECK

is what the prophet Joel spoke about: 17 'In
the last days,' God says, 'I will pour out My
Spirit on all people. Then your sons and your
daughters will speak God's Word, your young
men will have visions, and your old men will
have dreams. 18 In those days I will pour
out My Spirit on My servants, both men and
women, and they will speak God's Word. 19 I
will give you startling wonders in the sky above
and marvelous signs on the earth below:
20 Blood and fire and a cloud of smoke; the
sun will turn dark and the moon to blood
before the coming of the Lord's great and
splendid day. 21 Then everyone who calls on the
Lord's name will be saved.' [3]
22 "Men of Israel, listen to what I have to
say: Jesus from Nazareth—God showed you
who the Man is by doing miracles, startling
wonders, and signs through Him among you,
as you know. 23 God definitely planned and
intended to have Him betrayed, and so you
had wicked men nail Him to a cross, and you
killed Him. 24 But God set aside the pains of
death and raised Him—death could not hold
Him.
25 "David says of Him, 'I always see the
Lord before Me. He is at My right side so
that I will not be shaken. 26 And so My heart
is glad, and My tongue rejoices, yes, even My
body will rest hopefully, 27 Because You will
not leave Me in the grave or let Your Loved
One experience decay. 28 You show Me ways
of life. You will fill Me with joy by being with
Me.' [4]
29 "Fellow Jews, I can tell you frankly our
ancestor David died and was buried, and his
grave is here to this day. 30 He was a prophet
and knew God had sworn to him to put one
of his descendants on his throne. [5] 31 David
saw what was ahead and said the promised
Savior would rise again: He was not deserted
when He was dead, and His body did not
experience decay. [6] 32 God has raised this Jesus—we're all witnesses of that. 33 Lifted up
to God's right side and receiving from the
Father the promised Holy Spirit, He has poured
out what you see and hear. 34 David didn't go
up to heaven, but he says, 'The Lord says to my
Lord, "Sit at My right 35 till I make Your
enemies Your footstool." ' [7]
36 "Then all the people of Israel should
know it's true that God made Him Lord and
Christ—this Jesus whom you crucified."
37 When the people heard this, they felt

[3] Joel 2:28-32
[4] Ps. 16:8-11
[5] Ps. 89:3-4; 132:11
[6] Ps. 16:10
[7] Ps. 110:1

329

K.J.V.

pricked in their heart, and said unto Peter and to the rest of the apostles, Men *and* brethren, what shall we do? 38 Then Peter said unto them, Repent, and be baptized every one of you in the name of Jesus Christ for the remission of sins, and ye shall receive the gift of the Holy Ghost. 39 For the promise is unto you, and to your children, and to all that are afar off, *even* as many as the Lord our God shall call. 40And with many other words did he testify and exhort, saying, Save yourselves from this untoward generation.

41 Then they that gladly received his word were baptized: and the same day there were added *unto them* about three thousand souls. 42And they continued steadfastly in the apostles' doctrine and fellowship, and in breaking of bread, and in prayers. 43And fear came upon every soul: and many wonders and signs were done by the apostles. 44And all that believed were together, and had all things common; 45And sold their possessions and goods, and parted them to all *men*, as every man had need. 46And they, continuing daily with one accord in the temple, and breaking bread from house to house, did eat their meat with gladness and singleness of heart, 47 Praising God, and having favour with all the people. And the Lord added to the church daily such as should be saved.

3 Now Peter and John went up together into the temple at the hour of prayer, *being* the ninth *hour*. 2And a certain man lame from his mother's womb was carried, whom they laid daily at the gate of the temple which is called Beautiful, to ask alms of them that entered into the temple; 3 Who, seeing Peter and John about to go into the temple, asked an alms. 4And Peter, fastening his eyes upon him with John, said, Look on us. 5And he gave heed unto them, expecting to receive something of them. 6 Then Peter said, Silver and gold have I none; but such as I have give I thee: In the name of Jesus Christ of Nazareth rise up and walk. 7And he took him by the right hand, and lifted *him* up: and immediately his feet and ankle bones received strength. 8And he leaping up stood, and walked, and entered with them into the temple, walking and leaping, and praising God. 9And all the people saw him walking and praising God: 10And they knew that it was he which sat for alms at the Beautiful gate of the temple: and they were filled with wonder and amazement at that which had happened unto him. 11And as the lame man which was healed held Peter and John, all the people ran together unto them in the porch that is called Solomon's, greatly wondering.

12 And when Peter saw *it*, he answered unto the people, Ye men of Israel, why marvel ye at this? or why look ye so earnestly on us, as though by our own power or holiness we had made this man to walk? 13 The God of Abraham, and of Isaac, and of Jacob, the God of our fathers, hath glorified his Son Jesus; whom ye

N.A.S.

pierced to the heart, and said to Peter and the rest of the apostles, "Brethren, what shall we do?" 38And Peter *said* to them, "Repent, and let each of you be baptized in the name of Jesus Christ for the forgiveness of your sins; and you shall receive the gift of the Holy Spirit. 39 "For the promise is for you and your children, and for all who are far off, as many as the Lord our God shall call to Himself." 40And with many other words he solemnly testified and kept on exhorting them, saying, "Be saved from this perverse generation!" 41 So then, those who had received his word were baptized; and there were added that day about three thousand ᵃsouls. 42And they were continually devoting themselves to the apostles' teaching and to fellowship, to the breaking of bread and to prayer.

43 And everyone kept feeling a sense of awe; and many wonders and signs were taking place through the apostlesᵇ. 44And all those who had believed ᶜwere together, and had all things in common; 45 and they *began* selling their property and possessions, and were sharing them with all, as anyone might have need. 46And day by day continuing with one mind in the temple, and breaking bread from house to house, they were taking their meals together with gladness and sincerity of heart, 47 praising God, and having favor with all the people. And the Lord was adding to their number day by day those who were being saved.

3 Now Peter and John were going up to the temple at the ᵈninth *hour*, the hour of prayer. 2And a certain man who had been lame from his mother's womb was being carried along, whom they used to set down every day at the gate of the temple which is called Beautiful, in order to beg ᵉalms of those who were entering the temple. 3And when he saw Peter and John about to go into the temple, he *began* asking to receive alms. 4And Peter, along with John, fixed his gaze upon him and said, "Look at us!" 5And he *began* to give them his attention, expecting to receive something from them. 6 But Peter said, "I do not possess silver and gold, but what I do have I give to you: In the name of Jesus Christ the Nazarene—walk!" 7And seizing him by the right hand, he raised him up; and immediately his feet and his ankles were strengthened. 8And with a leap, he stood upright and *began* to walk; and he entered the temple with them, walking and leaping and praising God. 9And all the people saw him walking and praising God; 10 and they were taking note of him as being the one who used to sit at the Beautiful Gate of the temple to *beg* alms, and they were filled with wonder and amazement at what had happened to him.

11 And while he was clinging to Peter and John, all the people ran together to them at the so-called portico of Solomon, full of amazement. 12 But when Peter saw *this*, he replied to the people, "Men of Israel, why do you marvel at this, or why do you gaze at us, as if by our own power or piety we had made him walk? 13 "The God of Abraham, Isaac, and Jacob, the God of our fathers, has glorified His Servant

[a] I.e., *persons*. [b] Some ancient mss. add, *in Jerusalem; and great fear was upon all*. [c] Some ancient mss. omit, *were*. [d] I.e., 3 p.m. [e] Or, *a gift of charity*.

WILLIAMS

to the heart, and said to Peter and the rest of the apostles, "Brothers, what shall we do?"

38 Peter said to them, "You must repent— and, as an expression of it,[a] let everyone of you be baptized in the name of Jesus Christ— that you may have your sins forgiven; and then you will receive the gift of the Holy Spirit, 39 for the promise belongs to you and your children, as well as to all those who are far away whom the Lord our God may call to Him."

40 With many more words he continued to testify and to plead with them to save themselves from that crooked age. 41 So they accepted his message and were baptized, and about three thousand persons united with them on that day. 42 And they devoted themselves to the teaching of the apostles and to fellowship with one another, to the breaking of bread and to prayer.

43 A sense of reverence seized everyone, and many wonders and wonder-works were done by the apostles. 44And all the believers lived together and held all they had as common goods to be shared by one another. 45And so they continued to sell their property and goods and to distribute the money to all, as anyone had special need. 46 Day after day they regularly attended the temple; they practiced breaking their bread together in their homes, and eating their food with glad and simple hearts, 47 constantly praising God and always having the favor of all the people. And every day the Lord continued to add to them the people who were being saved.

3 *A crippled beggar cured by Peter and John; the cure is credited to Jesus; the people urged to repent and believe in Jesus*

Peter and John were on their way up to the temple at the three o'clock hour of prayer, 2 when a man crippled from his birth was being carried by, who used to be laid every day at what was called The Beautiful Gate of the temple, to beg from people on their way into the temple. 3 So when he saw Peter and John about to go into the temple, he asked them to give him something. 4 Peter looked him straight in the eye, and so did John, and said, "Look at us."

5 The beggar looked at them, supposing that he was going to get something from them. 6 But Peter said, "No silver or gold have I, but what I do have I will give you. In the name of Jesus of Nazareth start walking." 7 Then he took him by the right hand and lifted him, and his feet and ankles instantly grew strong, 8 and at once he leaped to his feet and started walking; then he went into the temple with them, walking, leaping, and praising God. 9 When all the people saw him walking about and praising God, 10 and recognized him as the very man who used to sit at The Beautiful Gate of the temple to beg, they were completely astounded and bewildered at what occurred to him.

11 While he was still clinging to Peter and John, all the people in utter amazement crowded around them in what was called Solomon's portico. 12 When Peter saw this, he said to the people, "Fellow Israelites, why are you so surprised at this? Why do you keep staring at us, as though we had by our own power or piety made this man walk? 13 The God of Abraham, Isaac, and Jacob, the God of our forefathers,

[a] These five words implied from context and usage in the Early Church.

BECK

crushed. They asked Peter and the other apostles, "Fellow Jews, what should we do?"

38 Peter answered them, "Repent and be baptized, every one of you, in the name of Jesus Christ so that your sins will be forgiven, and you will be given the Holy Spirit. 39 What is promised belongs to you, to your children, and to all *who are far away*,[8] all *whom the Lord our God will call*." [9]

40 He said much more to warn them. "Let yourselves be saved from these crooked people." he urged them.

41 Those who accepted what he said were baptized, and that day about three thousand persons were added.

How Christians Lived

42 They were loyal to what the apostles taught, in their fellowship, in eating together, and in praying. 43Awe came on everybody—the apostles were doing many wonders and miracles. 44All who believed were together and shared everything with one another. 45 They would sell their lands and other property and distribute the money to anyone as he needed it. 46All were one at heart as they went to the temple regularly every day. They had their meals in their homes and ate their food with glad and simple hearts, 47 praising God and having the good will of all the people. And every day the Lord added to their number those who were being saved.

The Cripple

3 Peter and John were going up to the temple for the hour of prayer at three in the afternoon. 2 Now there was a man who had been a cripple from his birth. Men would carry him and lay him every day at the temple gate called Beautiful so he could beg the people for gifts as they went into the temple. 3 When he saw Peter and John were going into the temple, he asked them for a gift.

4 Peter and John looked at him. "Look at us!" Peter said. 5 He looked at them, expecting to get something from them. 6 "I don't have any silver or gold," Peter said, "but I'll give you what I have. In the name of Jesus Christ from Nazareth, walk!" 7 He took hold of his right hand and raised him up. Immediately his feet and ankles were made strong. 8 He jumped up, stood, and started to walk. And he went with them into the temple, walking, jumping, and praising God.

9 When all the people saw him walking and praising God, 10 they knew he was the man who used to sit and beg at the Beautiful gate of the temple, and they were very much surprised and amazed to see what had happened to him. 11As he clung to Peter and John, all the people came running together to them in Solomon's Porch, as it was called. They were dumfounded.

12 When Peter saw the people, he said to them, "Men of Israel, why are you wondering about this, or why are you staring at us as if by our own power or piety we had made him walk? 13 *The God of Abraham, Isaac, and Jacob*,[10] the God of our fathers, has *glorified*

[8] Is. 57:19
[9] Joel 2:32
[10] Ex. 3:6

K.J.V.

delivered up, and denied him in the presence of Pilate, when he was determined to let *him* go. 14 But ye denied the Holy One and the Just, and desired a murderer to be granted unto you; 15And killed the Prince of life, whom God hath raised from the dead; whereof we are witnesses. 16And his name, through faith in his name, hath made this man strong, whom ye see and know: yea, the faith which is by him hath given him this perfect soundness in the presence of you all. 17And now, brethren, I wot that through ignorance ye did *it*, as *did* also your rulers. 18 But those things, which God before had shewed by the mouth of all his prophets, that Christ should suffer, he hath so fulfilled.

19 Repent ye therefore, and be converted, that your sins may be blotted out, when the times of refreshing shall come from the presence of the Lord; 20And he shall send Jesus Christ, which before was preached unto you: 21 Whom the heaven must receive until the times of restitution of all things, which God hath spoken by the mouth of all his holy prophets since the world began. 22 For Moses truly said unto the fathers, A Prophet shall the Lord your God raise up unto you of your brethren, like unto me; him shall ye hear in all things whatsoever he shall say unto you. 23And it shall come to pass, *that* every soul, which will not hear that Prophet, shall be destroyed from among the people. 24 Yea, and all the prophets from Samuel and those that follow after, as many as have spoken, have likewise foretold of these days. 25 Ye are the children of the prophets, and of the covenant which God made with our fathers, saying unto Abraham, And in thy seed shall all the kindreds of the earth be blessed. 26 Unto you first God, having raised up his Son Jesus, sent him to bless you, in turning away every one of you from his iniquities.

4 And as they spake unto the people, the priests, and the captain of the temple, and the Sadducees, came upon them, 2 Being grieved that they taught the people, and preached through Jesus the resurrection from the dead. 3And they laid hands on them, and put *them* in hold unto the next day: for it was now eventide. 4 Howbeit many of them which heard the word believed; and the number of the men was about five thousand.

5 And it came to pass on the morrow that their rulers, and elders, and scribes, 6And Annas the high priest, and Caiaphas, and John, and Alexander, and as many as were of the kindred of the high priest, were gathered together at Jerusalem. 7And when they had set them in the midst, they asked, By what power, or by what name, have ye done this? 8 Then Peter, filled with the Holy Ghost, said unto them, Ye rulers of the people, and elders of Israel, 9 If we this day be examined of the good deed done to the impotent man, by what means he is made whole; 10 Be it known unto you all, and to all the peo-

N.A.S.

Jesus, *the one* whom you delivered up, and disowned in the presence of Pilate, when he had decided to release Him. 14 "But you disowned the Holy and Righteous One, and asked for a murderer to be granted to you, 15 but put to death the Prince of life, *the one* whom God raised from the dead,—*a fact* to which we are witnesses. 16 "And on the basis of faith in His name, *it is* the name of Jesus which has strengthened this man whom you see and know; and the faith which *comes* through Him has given him this perfect health in the presence of you all. 17 "And now, brethren, I know that you acted in ignorance, just as your rulers did also. 18 "But the things which God announced beforehand by the mouth of all the prophets, that His Christ should suffer, He has thus fulfilled. 19 "Repent therefore and return, that your sins may be wiped away, in order that times of refreshing may come from the presence of the Lord; 20 and that He may send Jesus, the Christ appointed for you, 21 whom heaven must receive until *the* period of restoration of all things, about which God spoke by the mouth of His holy prophets from ancient time. 22 "Moses said, 'THE LORD GOD SHALL RAISE UP FOR YOU A PROPHET LIKE ME FROM YOUR BRETHREN; TO HIM YOU SHALL GIVE HEED IN EVERYTHING HE SAYS to you. 23 'AND IT SHALL BE THAT EVERY SOUL THAT DOES NOT HEED THAT PROPHET SHALL BE UTTERLY DESTROYED FROM AMONG THE PEOPLE.' 24 "And likewise, all the prophets who have spoken, from Samuel and *his* successors onward, also announced these days. 25 "It is you who are the sons of the prophets, and of the covenant which God made with your fathers, saying to Abraham, 'AND IN YOUR SEED ALL THE FAMILIES OF THE EARTH SHALL BE BLESSED.' 26 "For you first, God raised up His Servant, and sent Him to bless you by turning every one *of you* from your wicked ways."

4 And as they were speaking to the people, the priests and the captain of the temple *guard,* and the Sadducees, came upon them, 2 being greatly disturbed because they were teaching the people, and proclaiming in Jesus the resurrection from the dead. 3And they laid hands on them, and put them in jail until the next day, for it was already evening. 4 But many of those who had heard the message believed; and the number of the men came to be about five thousand.

5 And it came about on the next day, that their rulers and elders and scribes were gathered together in Jerusalem; 6 and Annas the high priest *was there,* and Caiaphas and John and Alexander, and all who were of high-priestly descent. 7And when they had placed them in the center, they *began to* inquire, "By what power, or in what name, have you done this?" 8 Then Peter, filled with the Holy Spirit, said to them, "Rulers and elders of the people, 9 if we are on trial today for a benefit done to a sick man, as to how this man has been made well, 10 let it be known to all of you, and to all

WILLIAMS

has glorified His Servant Jesus, whom you yourselves betrayed and disowned before Pilate, although he had decided to set Him free. 14 Yes, you disowned the Holy and Righteous One and asked a murderer to be pardoned as a favor to you, 15 and you killed the Prince of life; but God raised Him from the dead, to which fact we are witnesses. 16 It is His name, that is, on condition of faith in His name, that has made strong again this man whom you see and recognize—yes, faith inspired by Him has given this man the perfect health you all see.

17 "And yet, I know, brothers, that you did not realize what you were doing, any more than your leaders did. 18 But in this way God fulfilled what He by the lips of all the prophets foretold, that the Christ should suffer. 19 So now repent and turn to Him, to have your sins wiped out, that times of revival may come from the presence of the Lord, 20 and He may send back Jesus, the Christ who long ago was appointed for you. 21 Yet heaven must retain[a] Him till the time for the universal restoration of which God in the early ages spoke through the lips of His holy prophets. 22 Moses, indeed, said:

'The Lord God will raise up a prophet for you from among your brothers, as He did me. You must attentively listen to everything that He tells you. 23 The result will be, that any person who will not listen to that prophet will be utterly destroyed from among the people.' 24 Yes, all the prophets who have spoken, from Samuel down, have also foretold these days. 25 And you are the descendants of the prophets and the heirs of the sacred compact which God made with your forefathers, when He said to Abraham: 'All the families of the earth are to be blessed through your posterity.' 26 It was to you first that He sent His Servant, after raising Him from the dead, to bless you by causing every one of you to turn from his wicked ways."

4 *Peter and John arrested and put into prison; tried and set free; the church prays for courage to be loyal under persecution; they practice brotherly love by holding their goods in common*

While they were talking to the people, the high priests, the military commander of the temple, and the Sadducees came down upon them, 2 because they were very much disturbed over their continuing to teach the people and to declare in the case of Jesus the resurrection from the dead. 3 So they arrested them and put them into prison until next morning, for it was already evening. 4 But many of those who heard their message believed, and the number of the men grew to about five thousand.

5 On the next day the leading members of the council, the elders, and the scribes, 6 met in Jerusalem, including Annas the high priest, Caiaphas, John, Alexander, and all that were members of the high priest's family.

7 They had the men stand before them and repeatedly inquired of them, "By what sort of power and authority have you done this?"

8 Then Peter, because he was filled with the Holy Spirit, said to them, "Leaders and elders of the people, 9 if it is for a good deed to a helpless man, or to learn how he was cured, that we are today being tried, 10 you and all the peo-

BECK

His Servant[11] Jesus, whom you delivered and denied before Pilate when he had decided to let Him go. 14 You denied the holy and righteous One and asked to have a murderer given to you. 15 You killed the Lord and Giver of life. But God raised Him from the dead—we're witnesses of that. 16 His name, because we believe in it, made this man strong whom you see and know. The faith that Jesus works has given him this perfect health right in front of all of you.

17 "And now, fellow Jews, I know that like your rulers you didn't know what you were doing, 18 but in this way God did what He predicted by all the prophets—His Christ had to suffer. 19 Repent then, and turn, to have your sins wiped out 20 that a time may come when the Lord refreshes you and sends Jesus, whom He appointed to be your Savior 21 and whom heaven had to receive until the time when everything will be restored, as God said long ago by His holy prophets.

22 "Moses said, *The Lord our God will raise one of your people to be a Prophet to you like me. Listen to everything He tells*[12] you. 23 *And destroy anyone among the people who will not listen to that Prophet.*[13] 24 Samuel and all the other prophets after him, as many as have spoken, told about these days. 25 You are the heirs of the prophets and of the covenant God made with our fathers when He said to Abraham, *And in your Descendant all the people on earth will be blessed.*[14] 26 Now that God has given His Servant, He sent Him first to you to bless you by turning every one of you from your wicked ways."

In Court

4 While they were talking to the people, the priests, the captain of the temple, and the Sadducees stepped up to them, 2 much annoyed because they were teaching the people and preaching that in Jesus the dead rise. 3 They arrested them, and since it was already evening, they put them in prison till the next day.

4 But many of those who had heard the Word believed, and the number of the men grew to about five thousand.

5 The next day their rulers, elders, and Bible scholars met in Jerusalem 6 with Annas the high priest, Caiaphas, John, Alexander, and all the others of the high priest's family. 7 And they had the two men stand before them. "By what power or name did you do this?" they asked.

8 Then Peter was filled with the Holy Spirit. "Rulers of the people and elders," he said to them, 9 "if we're questioned today about helping a cripple, how he was made well, 10 all of

[a] Grk., *receive—retain* implied.

[11] Is. 52:13
[12] Deut. 18:15, 18-19
[13] Lev. 23:29; Deut. 18:19
[14] Gen. 12:3; 18:18; 22:18; 26:4; 28:14

K.J.V.

ple of Israel, that by the name of Jesus Christ of Nazareth, whom ye crucified, whom God raised from the dead, *even* by him doth this man stand here before you whole. 11 This is the stone which was set at nought of you builders, which is become the head of the corner. 12 Neither is there salvation in any other: for there is none other name under heaven given among men, whereby we must be saved.

13 Now when they saw the boldness of Peter and John, and perceived that they were unlearned and ignorant men, they marvelled; and they took knowledge of them, that they had been with Jesus. 14And beholding the man which was healed standing with them, they could say nothing against it. 15 But when they had commanded them to go aside out of the council, they conferred among themselves, 16 Saying, What shall we do to these men? for that indeed a notable miracle hath been done by them *is* manifest to all them that dwell in Jerusalem; and we cannot deny *it*. 17 But that it spread no further among the people, let us straitly threaten them, that they speak henceforth to no man in this name. 18And they called them, and commanded them not to speak at all nor teach in the name of Jesus. 19 But Peter and John answered and said unto them, Whether it be right in the sight of God to hearken unto you more than unto God, judge ye. 20 For we cannot but speak the things which we have seen and heard. 21 So when they had further threatened them, they let them go, finding nothing how they might punish them, because of the people: for all *men* glorified God for that which was done. 22 For the man was above forty years old, on whom this miracle of healing was shewed.

23 And being let go, they went to their own company, and reported all that the chief priests and elders had said unto them. 24And when they heard that, they lifted up their voice to God with one accord, and said, Lord, thou *art* God, which hast made heaven, and earth, and the sea, and all that in them is; 25 Who by the mouth of thy servant David hast said, Why did the heathen rage, and the people imagine vain things? 26 The kings of the earth stood up, and the rulers were gathered together against the Lord, and against his Christ. 27 For of a truth against thy holy child Jesus, whom thou hast anointed, both Herod, and Pontius Pilate, with the Gentiles, and the people of Israel, were gathered together, 28 For to do whatsoever thy hand and thy counsel determined before to be done. 29And now, Lord, behold their threatenings: and grant unto thy servants, that with all boldness they may speak thy word, 30 By stretching forth thine hand to heal; and that signs and wonders may be done by the name of thy holy child Jesus. 31 And when they had prayed, the place was shaken where they were assembled together; and they were all filled with the Holy Ghost, and they spake the word of God with boldness. 32And the multitude of them that believed were of one heart and of one soul: neither said any *of them* that aught of the things which he possessed was his own; but they had all things common. 33And with great power gave the apostles

N.A.S.

the people of Israel, that by the name of Jesus Christ the Nazarene, whom you crucified, whom God raised from the dead,—by this *name* this man stands here before you in good health. 11 "He is the STONE WHICH WAS REJECTED by you, THE BUILDERS, *but* WHICH BECAME THE VERY CORNER *stone*. 12 "And there is salvation in no one else; for there is no other name under heaven that has been given among men, by which we must be saved."

13 Now as they observed the confidence of Peter and John, and understood that they were uneducated and untrained men, they were marveling, and *began* to recognize them as having been with Jesus. 14And seeing the man who had been healed standing with them, they had nothing to say in reply. 15 But when they had ordered them to go aside out of the Council, they *began* to confer with one another, 16 saying, "What shall we do with these men? For the fact that a noteworthy miracle has taken place through them is apparent to all who live in Jerusalem, and we cannot deny it. 17 "But in order that it may not spread any further among the people, let us warn them to speak no more to any man in this name." 18And when they had summoned them, they commanded them not to speak or teach at all in the name of Jesus. 19 But Peter and John answered and said to them, "Whether it is right in the sight of God to give heed to you rather than to God, you be the judge; 20 for we cannot stop speaking what we have seen and heard." 21And when they had threatened them further, they let them go (finding no basis on which they might punish them) on account of the people, because they were all glorifying God for what had happened; 22 for the man was more than forty years old on whom this miracle of healing had been performed.

23 And when they had been released, they went to their own *companions,* and reported all that the chief priests and the elders had said to them. 24And when they heard *this,* they lifted their voice to God with one accord and said, "O Lord, it is Thou who DIDST MAKE THE HEAVEN AND THE EARTH AND THE SEA, AND ALL THAT IS IN THEM, 25 who by the Holy Spirit, *through* the mouth of our father David Thy servant, didst say,
'WHY DID THE ᵃGENTILES RAGE,
AND THE PEOPLES DEVISE FUTILE THINGS?
26 'THE KINGS OF THE EARTH TOOK THEIR STAND,
AND THE RULERS WERE GATHERED TOGETHER,
AGAINST THE LORD, AND AGAINST HIS CHRIST.'
27 "For truly in this city there were gathered together against Thy holy Servant Jesus, whom Thou didst anoint, both Herod and Pontius Pilate, along with the ᵃGentiles and the peoples of Israel, 28 to do whatever Thy hand and Thy purpose predestined to occur. 29 "And now, Lord, take note of their threats, and grant that Thy bond-servants may speak Thy word with all confidence, 30 while Thou dost extend Thy hand to heal, and signs and wonders take place through the name of Thy holy Servant Jesus." 31And when they had prayed, the place where they had gathered together was shaken, and they were all filled with the Holy Spirit, and *began* to speak the word of God with boldness.

32 And the congregation of those who believed were of one heart and soul; and not one *of them* claimed that anything belonging to him was his own; but all things were common property to them. 33And with great power the

[a] Or, *Nations.*

WILLIAMS

ple of Israel must know that it is by the authority of Jesus Christ of Nazareth, whom you crucified but whom God raised from the dead—yes, I repeat it, it is by His authority that this man stands here before you well. 11 He is the stone that was thrown away by you builders, which has become the cornerstone. 12 There is no salvation by anyone else, for no one else in all the wide world *a* has been appointed among men as our only medium by which to be saved.

13 They were surprised to see the courage shown by Peter and John and to find that they were uneducated men, and especially untrained in the schools; but they recognized the fact that they had been companions of Jesus, 14 and since they saw the man who had been cured standing with them, they had nothing to say in reply. 15 But they ordered the prisoners to step outside the council, and they conferred together 16 and repeated, "What shall we do with these men? For it is evident to everybody living in Jerusalem that an unmistakable wonder-work has been done by them; and we cannot deny it. 17 But to keep it from spreading farther among the people, let us severely threaten them not to say anything at all to anyone else about this person."

18 So they called them in and ordered them not to speak or teach at all about the name of Jesus. 19 But Peter and John answered them, "You must decide whether it is right in the sight of God to obey you instead of Him, 20 for we cannot keep from telling what we have seen and heard."

21 So, after further threatening them, they turned them loose, because they could not find any way to punish them, on account of the people, because they all continued to praise God for what had taken place; 22 for the man on whom the wonderful cure had been performed was more than forty years old.

23 When they were turned loose, the apostles went back to their companions and told them what the high priests and elders had said to them. 24 When they heard this, with one united prayer to God they said:

"O Lord, you are the Maker of heaven, earth, and sea, and everything that is in them, and the One 25 who spoke thus through the Holy Spirit by the lips of our forefather David, your servant:

'Why did the heathen rage,
And the peoples make vain designs?
26 The kings of the earth took their stand,
The rulers met
Against the Lord, and too, against His Christ.'

27 For in this city they actually met against your holy Servant Jesus, whom you had consecrated—Herod and Pontius Pilate, with the heathen and the peoples of Israel, 28 to do all that your hand and will had predetermined to take place. 29 And now, Lord, give attention to their threats and help your slaves with perfect courage to continue to speak your message, 30 by stretching out your hand to cure people and to perform signs and wonders by the authority of your holy Servant Jesus."

31 When they had prayed, the place where they were meeting was shaken, and they were all filled with the Holy Spirit, and continued courageously to speak God's message.

32 Now there was but one heart and soul in the vast number of those who had become believers, and not one of them claimed that anything that he had was his own, but they shared everything that they had as common property. 33 So with great power the apostles continued to

BECK

you and all the people of Israel should know this man stands healthy before you by the name of Jesus Christ from Nazareth, whom you crucified but God raised from the dead. 11 He is *the Stone rejected* by you *builders and has become the Cornerstone.*[15] 12 No one else can save us, because in all the world there is only one name given us by which we must be saved."

13 When they found out Peter and John had no education or training, they were surprised to see how boldly they spoke. Then they realized these men had been with Jesus. 14 And seeing the healed man standing with them, they couldn't say anything against them. 15 So they ordered them to leave the court and talked the matter over among themselves: 16 "What should we do with these men? They've done a miracle; everybody living in Jerusalem can see it clearly, and we can't deny it. 17 But to keep this from spreading any more among the people, let's warn them never again to speak to anyone in this name."

18 They called Peter and John and ordered them not to say or teach anything in the name of Jesus.

19 Peter and John answered them, "Does God consider it right to listen to you and not to God? Judge for yourselves. 20 We can't stop telling what we've seen and heard."

21 Once more they threatened them and then let them go. They couldn't find any way to punish them, because all the people were praising God for what had happened; 22 the man who had been healed by this miracle was over forty years old.

The Church Prays

23 When Peter and John were free again, they went to their friends and told them everything the high priests and elders had said. 24 When they heard it they all raised their voices together to God and said, "Lord, You *made heaven and earth, the sea, and everything in them.*[16] 25 You said by the Holy Spirit through our ancestor, Your servant David:

*Why do the nations rage
And the people plan in vain?
26 The kings of the earth stand ready,
And the rulers get together
Against the Lord and His Anointed.*[17]

27 "Herod and Pontius Pilate *certainly got together* with *non-Jews and the people* of Israel in this city against Your holy Servant Jesus, *whom You anointed,*[17] 28 to do everything You by Your will and power long ago decided should be done.

29 "And now, Lord, see how they're threatening, and grant that Your servants speak Your Word very boldly 30 as You stretch out Your hand to heal and do miracles and wonders by the name of Your holy Servant Jesus."

31 When they had prayed, the place where they were meeting was shaken, and they were all filled with the Holy Spirit and boldly spoke God's Word.

Sharing

32 The whole group of believers was one in heart and soul. And nobody called anything he had his own, but they shared everything.

33 With great power the apostles told the

[15] Ps. 118:22
[16] Ex. 20:11; Ps. 146:6; Neh. 9:6
[17] Ps. 2:1-2

[a] Lit., *under heaven.*

335

K.J.V.

witness of the resurrection of the Lord Jesus: and great grace was upon them all. 34 Neither was there any among them that lacked: for as many as were possessors of lands or houses sold them, and brought the prices of the things that were sold, 35And laid *them* down at the apostles' feet: and distribution was made unto every man according as he had need. 36And Joses, who by the apostles was surnamed Barnabas, (which is, being interpreted, The son of consolation,) a Levite, *and* of the country of Cyprus, 37 Having land, sold *it*, and brought the money, and laid *it* at the apostles' feet.

5 But a certain man named Ananias, with Sapphira his wife, sold a possession, 2And kept back *part* of the price, his wife also being privy *to it,* and brought a certain part, and laid *it* at the apostles' feet. 3 But Peter said, Ananias, why hath Satan filled thine heart to lie to the Holy Ghost, and to keep back *part* of the price of the land? 4 While it remained, was it not thine own? and after it was sold, was it not in thine own power? why hast thou conceived this thing in thine heart? thou hast not lied unto men, but unto God. 5And Ananias hearing these words fell down, and gave up the ghost: and great fear came on all them that heard these things. 6And the young men arose, wound him up, and carried *him* out, and buried *him.* 7And it was about the space of three hours after, when his wife, not knowing what was done, came in. 8And Peter answered unto her, Tell me whether ye sold the land for so much? And she said, Yea, for so much. 9 Then Peter said unto her, How is it that ye have agreed together to tempt the Spirit of the Lord? behold, the feet of them which have buried thy husband *are* at the door, and shall carry thee out. 10 Then fell she down straightway at his feet, and yielded up the ghost: and the young men came in, and found her dead, and, carrying *her* forth, buried *her* by her husband. 11And great fear came upon all the church, and upon as many as heard these things.

12 And by the hands of the apostles were many signs and wonders wrought among the people; (and they were all with one accord in Solomon's porch. 13And of the rest durst no man join himself to them: but the people magnified them. 14And believers were the more added to the Lord, multitudes both of men and women;) 15 Insomuch that they brought forth the sick into the streets, and laid *them* on beds and couches, that at the least the shadow of Peter passing by might overshadow some of them. 16 There came also a multitude *out* of the cities round about unto Jerusalem, bringing sick folks, and them which were vexed with unclean spirits: and they were healed every one.

N.A.S.

apostles were giving witness to the resurrection of the Lord Jesus, and abundant grace was upon them all. 34 For there was not a needy person among them, for all who were owners of lands or houses would sell them and bring the proceeds of the sales, 35 and lay them at the apostles' feet; and they would be distributed to each, as any had need.

36 And Joseph, a Levite of Cyprian birth, who was also called Barnabas by the apostles (which translated means, Son of Encouragement), 37 and who owned a tract of land, sold it and brought the money and laid it at the apostles' feet.

5 But a certain man named Ananias, with his wife Sapphira, sold a piece of property, 2 and kept back *some* of the price for himself, with his wife's full knowledge, and bringing a portion of it, he laid it at the apostles' feet. 3 But Peter said, "Ananias, why has Satan filled your heart to lie to the Holy Spirit, and to keep back *some* of the price of the land? 4 "While it remained *unsold*, did it not remain your own? And after it was sold, was it not under your control? Why is it that you have conceived this deed in your heart? You have not lied to men, but to God." 5And as he heard these words, Ananias fell down and breathed his last; and great fear came upon all who heard of it. 6And the young men arose and covered him up, and after carrying him out, they buried him.

7 Now there elapsed an interval of about three hours, and his wife came in, not knowing what had happened. 8And Peter responded to her, "Tell me whether you sold the land for such and such a price?" And she said, "Yes, that was the price." 9 Then Peter *said* to her, "Why is it that you have agreed together to put the Spirit of the Lord to the test? Behold, the feet of those who have buried your husband are at the door, and they shall carry you out *as well.*" 10And she fell immediately at his feet, and breathed her last; and the young men came in and found her dead, and they carried her out and buried her beside her husband. 11And great fear came upon the whole church, and upon all who heard of these things.

12 And at the hands of the apostles many signs and wonders were taking place among the people; and they were all with one accord in Solomon's portico. 13 But none of the rest dared to associate with them; however, the people held them in high esteem. 14And all the more believers in the Lord, multitudes of men and women, were constantly added to *their number;* 15 to such an extent that they even carried the sick out into the streets, and laid them on cots and pallets, so that when Peter came by, at least his shadow might fall on any one of them. 16And also the people from the cities in the vicinity of Jerusalem were coming together, bringing people who were sick °or afflicted with unclean spirits; and they were all being healed.

[a] Lit., *and.*

WILLIAMS

give their testimony to the resurrection of the Lord Jesus, and God's favor rested richly on them all. 34 For none of them was in want, for as many of them as were owners of farms or houses proceeded to sell them, one by one, and continued to bring the money received for the things sold 35 and to put it at the disposal of the apostles; then distribution was continuously made to everyone in proportion to his need.

36 Now Joseph, a Levite, a native of Cyprus, who by the apostles was named Barnabas, which means Son of Encouragement, 37 sold the farm he had and brought the money and put it at the disposal of the apostles.

5   *Ananias and Sapphira, hypocrites, punished with death; the apostles perform many wonders but are put into prison; delivered by the Lord, they continue to preach as before; Gamaliel, council member, pleads for caution*

But a man named Ananias, in partnership with his wife Sapphira, sold a piece of property, 2 and with his wife's full knowledge of it kept back for themselves a part of the money and brought only a part of it and put it at the disposal of the apostles.

3 And Peter said, "Ananias, why has Satan so completely possessed your heart that you have lied to the Holy Spirit and kept back for yourselves a part of the money received for the land? 4 As long as it was unsold, was it not yours, and when it was sold, was not the money at your disposal?[a] How could you have the heart to do such a thing! You did not lie to men but to God!"

5 When Ananias heard these words, he fell dead, and a strange awe seized everybody who heard it. 6 The younger men, however, got up, wrapped up his body, carried it out, and buried it.

7 About three hours later, his wife came in, without having learned what had taken place. 8 Peter said to her, "Tell me, did you sell the land for such and such a sum?"

She answered, "Yes, that is it."

9 Peter said to her, "How could both of you agree in such a way to test the Spirit of the Lord? Listen! The feet of the men who buried your husband are at the door; they will carry you out, too."

10 She instantly fell dead at his feet. When the young men came in, they found her dead, and they carried her out and buried her beside her husband. 11 So a strange awe seized the whole church and everybody who heard it.

12 Many signs and wonders were continuously performed by the apostles among the people. And by common consent they all used to meet in Solomon's portico. 13 Not one of those on the outside dared to associate with them, although the people continued to hold them in high regard; 14 but still a vast number of people, both men and women, who believed in the Lord, continued to join them, 15 so that they kept bringing out into the streets their sick ones and putting them on little couches or pallets, that at least the shadow of Peter, as he went by, might fall on some of them. 16 Even from the towns around Jerusalem crowds continued coming in to bring their sick ones and those troubled with foul spirits, and they were all cured.

[a] Grk., *in your authority.*

BECK

truth that the Lord Jesus had risen, and much good will rested on all of them.

34 None of them was in need, because all who had land or houses would sell them and bring the money they got for them 35 and lay it at the apostles' feet. Then it was distributed to each one as he needed it. 36 There was Joseph, for example, a descendant of Levi, born on Cyprus. The apostles called him Barnabas, which means "a man of comfort." 37 He had some land and sold it and brought the money and laid it at the apostles' feet.

Ananias and Sapphira

5   But a man by the name of Ananias and his wife Sapphira sold some property; 2 he kept some of the money for himself—and his wife knew about it—and some of it he brought and laid at the apostles' feet.

3 "Ananias," Peter asked, "why did the devil fill your heart so that you should lie to the Holy Spirit and keep back some of the money you got for the land? 4 While you had the land, wasn't it your own? And after it was sold, couldn't you have done as you pleased with the money? How could you think of doing such a thing? You didn't lie to men but to God!"

5 When Ananias heard him say this, he fell down and died. And all who heard of it were terrified. 6 The young men got up, wrapped him up, carried him out, and buried him.

7 About three hours later his wife came in. She didn't know what had happened. 8 "Tell me," Peter asked her, "did you sell the land for that price?"

"Yes, that was the price," she answered.

9 "Why did you two agree to put the Lord's Spirit to a test?" Peter asked her. "There at the door are the feet of those who buried your husband, and they'll carry you out."

10 Immediately she fell down at his feet and died. When the young men came in, they found her dead and carried her out and buried her beside her husband. 11 The whole church and all others who heard about it were terrified.

Many Miracles

12 Many miracles and startling wonders were done among the people by the apostles' hands. 13 And they were all together in Solomon's Porch. None of the others dared to come too near them. But the people thought very highly of them, 14 and still more believers, a large number of men and women, were added to the Lord. 15 As a result people carried their sick out into the streets and laid them down on cots and mats, to have at least Peter's shadow fall on someone of them when he went by. 16 Even from the towns around Jerusalem crowds would gather, bringing their sick and those who were troubled by unclean spirits, and they were all made well.

K.J.V.

17 Then the high priest rose up, and all they that were with him, (which is the sect of the Sadducees,) and were filled with indignation, 18And laid their hands on the apostles, and put them in the common prison. 19 But the angel of the Lord by night opened the prison doors, and brought them forth, and said, 20 Go, stand and speak in the temple to the people all the words of this life. 21And when they heard *that,* they entered into the temple early in the morning, and taught. But the high priest came, and they that were with him, and called the council together, and all the senate of the children of Israel, and sent to the prison to have them brought. 22 But when the officers came, and found them not in the prison, they returned, and told, 23 Saying, The prison truly found we shut with all safety, and the keepers standing without before the doors: but when we had opened, we found no man within. 24 Now when the high priest and the captain of the temple and the chief priests heard these things, they doubted of them whereunto this would grow. 25 Then came one and told them, saying, Behold, the men whom ye put in prison are standing in the temple, and teaching the people. 26 Then went the captain with the officers, and brought them without violence: for they feared the people, lest they should have been stoned. 27And when they had brought them, they set *them* before the council: and the high priest asked them, 28 Saying, Did not we straitly command you that ye should not teach in this name? and, behold, ye have filled Jerusalem with your doctrine, and intend to bring this man's blood upon us.

29 Then Peter and the *other* apostles answered and said, We ought to obey God rather than men. 30 The God of our fathers raised up Jesus, whom ye slew and hanged on a tree. 31 Him hath God exalted with his right hand *to be* a Prince and a Saviour, for to give repentance to Israel, and forgiveness of sins. 32And we are his witnesses of these things; and *so is* also the Holy Ghost, whom God hath given to them that obey him.

33 When they heard *that,* they were cut *to the heart,* and took counsel to slay them. 34 Then stood there up one in the council, a Pharisee, named Gamaliel, a doctor of the law, had in reputation among all the people, and commanded to put the apostles forth a little space; 35And said unto them, Ye men of Israel, take heed to yourselves what ye intend to do as touching these men. 36 For before these days rose up Theudas, boasting himself to be somebody; to whom a number of men, about four hundred, joined themselves: who was slain; and all, as many as obeyed him, were scattered, and brought to nought. 37After this man rose up Judas of Galilee in the days of the taxing, and drew away much people after him: he also perished; and all, *even* as many as obeyed him, were dispersed. 38And now I say unto you, Refrain from these men, and let them alone: for if this counsel or this work be of men, it will come to nought: 39 But if it be of God, ye cannot overthrow it; lest haply ye be found even to fight against God. 40And to him they agreed: and when they had called the apostles, and beaten *them,* they commanded that they should not speak in the name of Jesus, and let them go.

41 And they departed from the presence of the council, rejoicing that they were counted worthy to suffer shame for his name. 42And daily in the temple, and in every house, they ceased not to teach and preach Jesus Christ.

N.A.S.

17 But the high priest rose up, along with all his associates (that is the sect of the Sadducees), and they were filled with jealousy; 18 and they laid hands on the apostles, and put them in a public jail. 19 But an angel of the Lord during the night opened the gates of the prison, and taking them out he said, 20 "Go your way, stand and speak to the people in the temple the whole message of this Life." 21And upon hearing *this,* they entered into the temple about daybreak, and *began* to teach. Now when the high priest and his associates had come, they called the Council together, and all the Senate of the Children of Israel, and sent *orders* to the prison-house for them to be brought. 22 But the officers who came did not find them in the prison; and they returned, and reported back, 23 saying, "We found the prison-house locked quite securely and the guards standing at the doors; but when we had opened up, we found no one inside." 24 Now when the captain of the temple *guard* and the chief priests heard these words, they were greatly perplexed about them as to what would come of this. 25 But someone came and reported to them, "Behold, the men whom you put in prison are standing in the temple and teaching the people!" 26 Then the captain went along with the officers and *proceeded* to bring them *back* without violence; (for they were afraid of the people, lest they should be stoned). 27And when they had brought them, they stood them before the Council. And the high priest questioned them, 28 saying, "We gave you strict orders not to continue teaching in this name, and behold, you have filled Jerusalem with your teaching, and intend to bring this man's blood upon us." 29 But Peter and the apostles answered and said, "We must obey God rather than men. 30 "The God of our fathers raised up Jesus, whom you had put to death by hanging Him on a cross. 31 "He is the one whom God exalted to His right hand as a Prince and a Savior, to grant repentance to Israel, and forgiveness of sins. 32 "And we are witnesses*a* of these things; and *so is* the Holy Spirit, whom God has given to those who obey Him."

33 But when they heard this, they were cut to the quick and were intending to slay them. 34 But a certain Pharisee named Gamaliel, a teacher of the Law, respected by all the people, stood up in the Council and gave orders to put the men outside for a short time. 35And he said to them, "Men of Israel, take care what you propose to do with these men. 36 "For sometime ago Theudas rose up, claiming to be somebody; and a group of about four hundred men joined up with him. And he was slain; and all who followed him were dispersed and came to nothing. 37 "After this man Judas of Galilee rose up in the days of the census, and drew away *some* people after him; he too perished, and all those who followed him were scattered. 38 "And so in the present case, I say to you, stay away from these men and let them alone, for if this plan or action should be of men, it will be overthrown; 39 but if it is of God, you will not be able to overthrow them; or else you may even be found fighting against God." 40And they took his advice; and after calling the apostles in, they flogged them and ordered them to speak no more in the name of Jesus, and *then* released them. 41 So they went on their way from the presence of the Council, rejoicing that they had been considered worthy to suffer shame for *His* name. 42And every day, in the temple and from house to house, they kept right on teaching and preaching Jesus *as* the Christ.

[a] Some mss. add, *in Him,* or, *of Him.*

WILLIAMS

17 Now the high priest took a stand, and all his friends, the party of the Sadducees; and being filled with jealousy, 18 they had the apostles arrested and put into the common jail.

19 But in the night the angel of the Lord threw open the jail doors and let them out, and said to them, 20 "Go and take your stand in the temple square and continue to tell the people the message of this new life." 21 So they obeyed, and about the break of day they went into the temple square and began to teach.

The high priest and his party arrived and called a meeting of the council and the whole senate of the sons of Israel, and sent to the prison to have the men brought in. 22 But the attendants who went for them could not find them in the jail, and so came back and 23 reported, "We found the prison safely locked and the keepers on duty at the doors, but on opening the doors we found no one on the inside." 24 When the military commander of the temple square and the high priest heard this, they were utterly at a loss to know how this might turn out.

25 But somebody came by and reported to them, "The men that you put in jail are standing right here in the temple square, teaching the people." 26 Then the military commander went with his attendants and brought them back, but without any violence, for they were afraid of being pelted with stones by the people. 27 So they brought them and had them stand before the council.

And the high priest asked them, 28 "Did we not positively forbid you to teach any more on this authority, and yet you have filled Jerusalem with your teaching, and now want to bring on us the people's vengeance for this man's death!"

29 Peter and the apostles answered, "We must obey God rather than men. 30 The God of our forefathers raised Jesus to life after you had hanged Him on a cross and killed Him. 31 God has exalted to His right hand this very One as our Leader and Saviour, in order to give repentance and forgiveness of sins to Israel. 32 We and the Holy Spirit that God has given to those who practice obedience to Him are witnesses to these things."

33 When they heard this, they were furious, and wanted to kill them. 34 But a Pharisee named Gamaliel, a teacher of the law, highly respected by all the people, got up in the council and gave orders to put the men out of the council a little while; 35 then he said to them:

"Fellow Israelites, take care as to what you are about to do to these men. 36 For in the days gone by Theudas appeared, claiming that he was a man of importance, and a considerable number of men, about four hundred, espoused his cause, but he was slain and all his followers were dispersed and as a party annihilated. 37 After him, at the time of the enrollment for the Roman tax, Judas the Galilean appeared and influenced people to desert and follow him; but he too perished and all his followers were scattered. 38 So in the present case, I warn you, stay away from these men, let them alone. For, if this program or movement has its origin in men, it will go to pieces, 39 but if it has its origin in God, you can never stop it. It is to be feared that you may find yourselves fighting God."

40 They were convinced by him, and after calling the apostles in and having them flogged, they charged them to stop speaking on the authority of Jesus, and then turned them loose. 41 So they went out from the presence of the council, rejoicing that they had been considered worthy to suffer disgrace for Jesus' name; 42 and not for a single day did they stop teaching in the temple square and in private houses the good news of Jesus the Christ.

BECK

In Court

17 The high priest and all who were with him, that is, the party of the Sadducees, got very jealous. They went 18 and arrested the apostles and put them in the public prison.

19 But at night the Lord's angel opened the prison doors and brought them out. 20 "Go," he said, "stand in the temple, and keep on telling the people everything about this life." 21 After they had heard him, they went into the temple early in the morning and started to teach.

The high priest and those who were with him came and called the council and all the elders of Israel together and sent men to the prison to get the apostles. 22 But when the men got there, they didn't find them in prison. 23 They came back and reported, "We found the prison very securely locked and the guards standing at the doors, but when we opened them, we found nobody inside." 24 When the captain of the temple and the high priests heard this, they were puzzled as to what could have happened to them.

25 Then somebody came and told them, "The men you put in prison are standing in the temple teaching the people."

26 Then the captain and his men went and got them, but without using force, because they were afraid the people would stone them. 27 They brought them and had them stand before the council.

The high priest questioned them and said, 28 "We gave you strict orders not to teach in this name, and here you have filled Jerusalem with your teaching. And you want to get us punished for killing this Man."

29 Peter and the other apostles answered, "We must obey God rather than men. 30 *You hanged* Jesus *on a cross*[18] and murdered Him. But the God of our fathers raised Him 31 and took Him up to His right side as Leader and Savior in order to have the people of Israel repent and to forgive their sins. 32 We are witnesses of these things—we and the Holy Spirit, whom God has given those who obey Him."

33 When they heard this, they got furious and wanted to kill them. 34 But a Pharisee in the court by the name of Gamaliel, a teacher of the Law, highly respected by all the people, got up and ordered the men taken outside a little while.

35 "Men of Israel," he said to them, "consider carefully what you're going to do with these men. 36 Sometime ago Theudas appeared, claiming to be somebody, and about four hundred men joined him. He was killed, and all who followed him were scattered, and they disappeared.

37 "After him, at the time of the census, came Judas from Galilee and got people to follow him in a revolt. He perished too, and all who followed him were scattered.

38 "And now I tell you, keep away from these men and let them alone. If it's only men planning or doing this, it will break down, 39 but if it's God, you won't be able to stop them. You may even be fighting against God."

They took his advice. 40 They called the apostles, beat them, ordered them not to speak in the name of Jesus, and let them go. 41 The apostles left the court, happy to have been thought worthy to suffer shame for Jesus. 42 And every day, in the temple and from house to house, they kept right on teaching and telling the good news: Jesus is the promised Savior.

[18] Deut. 21:22

| K.J.V. | N.A.S. |

6 And in those days, when the number of the disciples was multiplied, there arose a murmuring of the Grecians against the Hebrews, because their widows were neglected in the daily ministration. 2 Then the twelve called the multitude of the disciples *unto them,* and said, It is not reason that we should leave the word of God, and serve tables. 3 Wherefore, brethren, look ye out among you seven men of honest report, full of the Holy Ghost and wisdom, whom we may appoint over this business. 4 But we will give ourselves continually to prayer, and to the ministry of the word.

5 And the saying pleased the whole multitude: and they chose Stephen, a man full of faith and of the Holy Ghost, and Philip, and Prochorus, and Nicanor, and Timon, and Parmenas, and Nicolas a proselyte of Antioch; 6 Whom they set before the apostles: and when they had prayed, they laid *their* hands on them. 7 And the word of God increased; and the number of the disciples multiplied in Jerusalem greatly; and a great company of the priests were obedient to the faith. 8 And Stephen, full of faith and power, did great wonders and miracles among the people.

9 Then there arose certain of the synagogue, which is called *the synagogue* of the Libertines, and Cyrenians, and Alexandrians, and of them of Cilicia and of Asia, disputing with Stephen. 10 And they were not able to resist the wisdom and the spirit by which he spake. 11 Then they suborned men, which said, We have heard him speak blasphemous words against Moses, and *against* God. 12 And they stirred up the people, and the elders, and the scribes, and came upon *him,* and caught him, and brought *him* to the council, 13 And set up false witnesses, which said, This man ceaseth not to speak blasphemous words against this holy place, and the law: 14 For we have heard him say, that this Jesus of Nazareth shall destroy this place, and shall change the customs which Moses delivered us. 15 And all that sat in the council, looking steadfastly on him, saw his face as it had been the face of an angel.

6 Now at this time while the disciples were increasing *in number,* a complaint arose on the part of the [a]Hellenistic *Jews* against the *native* Hebrews, because their widows were being overlooked in the daily serving *of food.* 2 And the Twelve summoned the congregation of the disciples and said, "It is not desirable for us to neglect the word of God in order to serve tables. 3 "But select from among you, brethren, seven men of good reputation, full of the Spirit and of wisdom, whom we may put in charge of this task. 4 "But we will devote ourselves to prayer, and to the ministry of the word." 5 And the statement found approval with the whole congregation; and they chose Stephen, a man full of faith and of the Holy Spirit, and Philip, Prochorus, Nicanor, Timon, Parmenas and Nicolas, a [b]proselyte from Antioch. 6 And these they brought before the apostles; and after praying, they laid their hands on them.

7 And the word of God kept on spreading; and the number of the disciples continued to increase greatly in Jerusalem, and a great many of the priests were becoming obedient to the faith.

8 And Stephen, full of grace and power, was performing great wonders and signs among the people. 9 But some men from what was called the Synagogue of the Freedmen, *including* both Cyrenians and Alexandrians, and some from Cilicia and Asia, rose up and argued with Stephen. 10 And *yet* they were unable to cope with the wisdom and the Spirit with which he was speaking. 11 Then they secretly induced men to say, "We have heard him speak blasphemous words against Moses and *against* God." 12 And they stirred up the people, the elders and the scribes, and they came upon him and dragged him away, and brought him before the Council. 13 And they put forward false witnesses who said, "This man incessantly speaks against this holy place, and the Law; 14 for we have heard him say that this Nazarene, Jesus, will destroy this place and alter the customs which Moses handed down to us." 15 And fixing their gaze on him, all who were sitting in the Council saw his face like the face of an angel.

7 Then said the high priest, Are these things so? 2 And he said, Men, brethren, and fathers, hearken; The God of glory appeared unto our father Abraham, when he was in Mesopotamia, before he dwelt in Charran, 3 And said unto him, Get thee out of thy country, and from thy kindred, and come into the land which I shall shew thee. 4 Then came he out of the land of the Chaldeans, and dwelt in Charran: and from thence, when his father was dead, he removed him into this land, wherein ye now dwell. 5 And he gave him none inheritance in it, no, not *so much as* to set his foot on: yet he promised that he would give it to him for a possession, and to

7 And the high priest said, "Are these things so?"

2 And he said, "Hear me, brethren and fathers! The God of glory appeared to our father Abraham when he was in Mesopotamia, before he lived in Haran, 3 AND SAID TO HIM, 'DEPART FROM YOUR COUNTRY AND YOUR RELATIVES, AND COME INTO THE LAND THAT I WILL SHOW YOU.' 4 "Then he departed from the land of the Chaldeans, and settled in Haran. And from there, after his father died, God removed him into this country in which you are now living. 5 "And He gave him no inheritance in it, not even a foot of ground; and *yet,* even when he had no child, He promised that HE WOULD GIVE

[a] I.e., non-Palestinian Jews who normally spoke Greek. [b] I.e., a former convert to Judaism.

Seven Helpers

6 *Seven new officers selected by the church to serve the needy; Stephen arrested for championing the new faith*

In those days, as the number of the disciples was increasing, complaint was made by the Greek-speaking Jews against the native Jews that their widows were being neglected in the daily distribution of food. 2 So the Twelve called together the whole body of the disciples, and said, "It is not desirable that we should leave off preaching the word of God to wait on tables. 3 So, brothers, you must select from your number seven men of good standing, full of the Spirit, and of good practical sense, and we will assign them to this business, 4 while we will go on devoting ourselves to prayer and the word of God."
5 This suggestion was approved by the whole body, and so they selected Stephen, a man full of faith and of the Holy Spirit, Philip, Procorus, Nikanor, Timon, Parmenas, and Nicholas of Antioch, who was a convert to Judaism. 6 They presented these men to the apostles, and after they had prayed they laid their hands upon them.
7 So God's message continued to spread, and the number of the disciples in Jerusalem continued to grow rapidly; a large number even of priests continued to surrender[a] to the faith.
8 Now Stephen, full of grace and power, went on performing great signs and wonders among the people. 9 But members of the synagogue known as that of the Libyans, Cyreneans, and Alexandrians, and men from Cilicia and Asia, got to debating with Stephen, 10 but they could not cope with his good practical sense and the spiritual power with which he usually spoke. 11 So they instigated men to say, "We have heard him speaking abusive words against Moses and God."
12 By this means they excited the people, the elders, and the scribes, and so they rushed upon him, seized him, and brought him before the council. 13 Then they put up false witnesses who said, "This man never stops saying things against this holy place and against the law, 14 for we have heard him say that Jesus of Nazareth will tear this place down, and change the customs which Moses handed down to us."
15 Then all who were seated in the council fixed their eyes upon him and saw that his face was like that of an angel.

6 In those days, as the number of the disciples grew larger and larger, a complaint was brought against those 'who spoke Aramaic by those who spoke Greek that every day, when the food was handed out, their widows were being neglected.
2 The twelve called the whole group of disciples together and said, "Nobody likes it if we give up teaching God's Word and serve at tables. 3 Now, fellow disciples, appoint seven men among you whom people speak well of, who are full of the Spirit and wisdom, and we'll put them in charge of this work. 4 Then we'll devote ourselves to praying and to serving by speaking the Word."
5 The whole group liked the idea. So they chose Stephen, a man full of faith and of the Holy Spirit, Philip, Prochorus, Nicanor, Timon, Parmenas, and Nicolaus (who had become a Jew in Antioch). 6 They had these men stand before the apostles, who prayed and laid their hands on them.
7 God's Word kept on spreading, and the number of disciples in Jerusalem was getting very large. Even a large crowd of the priests came to believe and obey the Word.

Stephen Is Arrested

8 Stephen, full of God's gifts and power, was doing great wonders and miracles among the people. 9 Some men of the Synagog of the Freedmen, as it was called, and of men from Cyrene and Alexandria, and men from Cilicia and Asia got up to argue with Stephen. 10 But they couldn't resist the wisdom and the Spirit by whom he spoke.
11 Then they secretly got some men to say, "We heard him slander Moses and God." 12 They stirred up the people, the elders, and the men of the Law, and rushing at him, took him by force and brought him before the court. 13 There they had witnesses stand up and lie, "This man won't stop talking against the holy place and the Law. 14 We heard him say, 'This Jesus from Nazareth will tear this place down and change the customs Moses gave us.' "
15 All who sat in the court stared at him and saw his face—it was like an angel's face.

7 *Stephen speaks in his own defense but still is stoned to death; he prays for his enemies while heaven opens to give him a vision of Jesus exalted in glory*

The high priest asked, "Are these statements true?"
2 He answered:
"Listen, brothers and fathers. The glorious God appeared to our forefather Abraham while he was in Mesopotamia before he ever made his home in Haran, 3 and said to him, 'Leave your country and your kinsmen and come to whatever country I may show you.' 4 So he left the country of the Chaldeans and for a time made his home in Haran. Then after the death of his father, God had him move to this country in which you now live. 5 He gave him no property in it, not even a foot of land, and yet He promised to give it to him and his descendants

Stephen Defends Himself

7 Then the high priest asked, "Is this so?"
2 He answered, "Fellow Jews and fathers, listen. *The God of glory*[19] appeared to our father Abraham while he was in Mesopotamia before he lived in Haran. 3 *'Leave your country and your relatives,'* God told him, *'and come to the country I will show you.'* [20]
4 "Then Abraham left the country of the Chaldeans and lived in Haran. After his father died, God had him move from there to this country where you live now. 5 He *gave* him nothing to call his own, *not even enough to set his foot on,*[21] but promised *to give it to him*

[a] Lit., *obey*.

[19] Ps. 29:3
[20] Gen. 12:1
[21] Deut. 2:5

K.J.V.

his seed after him, when *as yet* he had no child. 6And God spake on this wise, That his seed should sojourn in a strange land; and that they should bring them into bondage, and entreat *them* evil four hundred years. 7And the nation to whom they shall be in bondage will I judge, said God: and after that shall they come forth, and serve me in this place. 8And he gave him the covenant of circumcision: and so *Abraham* begat Isaac, and circumcised him the eighth day; and Isaac *begat* Jacob; and Jacob *begat* the twelve patriarchs. 9And the patriarchs, moved with envy, sold Joseph into Egypt: but God was with him, 10And delivered him out of all his afflictions, and gave him favour and wisdom in the sight of Pharaoh king of Egypt; and he made him governor over Egypt and all his house. 11 Now there came a dearth over all the land of Egypt and Chanaan, and great affliction: and our fathers found no sustenance. 12 But when Jacob heard that there was corn in Egypt, he sent out our fathers first. 13And at the second *time* Joseph was made known to his brethren; and Joseph's kindred was made known unto Pharaoh. 14 Then sent Joseph, and called his father Jacob to *him,* and all his kindred, three-score and fifteen souls. 15 So Jacob went down into Egypt, and died, he, and our fathers, 16 And were carried over into Sychem, and laid in the sepulchre that Abraham bought for a sum of money of the sons of Emmor, *the father* of Sychem. 17 But when the time of the promise drew nigh, which God had sworn to Abraham, the people grew and multiplied in Egypt, 18 Till another king arose, which knew not Joseph. 19 The same dealt subtilely with our kindred, and evil entreated our fathers, so that they cast out their young children, to the end they might not live. 20 In which time Moses was born, and was exceeding fair, and nourished up in his father's house three months: 21And when he was cast out, Pharaoh's daughter took him up, and nourished him for her own son. 22And Moses was learned in all the wisdom of the Egyptians, and was mighty in words and in deeds. 23And when he was full forty years old, it came into his heart to visit his brethren the children of Israel. 24And seeing one *of them* suffer wrong, he defended *him,* and avenged him that was oppressed, and smote the Egyptian: 25 For he supposed his brethren would have understood how that God by his hand would deliver them; but they understood not. 26And the next day he shewed himself unto them as they strove, and would have set them at one again, saying, Sirs, ye are brethren; why do ye wrong one to another? 27 But he that did his neighbour wrong

N.A.S.

IT TO HIM AS A POSSESSION, AND TO HIS OFF-SPRING AFTER HIM. 6 "But God spoke to this effect, that HIS OFFSPRING WOULD BE ALIENS IN A FOREIGN LAND, AND THAT THEY WOULD BE EN-SLAVED AND MISTREATED FOR FOUR HUNDRED YEARS. 7 "'AND WHATEVER NATION TO WHICH THEY SHALL BE IN BONDAGE I MYSELF WILL JUDGE,' said God, 'AND AFTER THAT THEY WILL COME OUT AND "SERVE ME IN THIS PLACE.' 8 "And He gave him the covenant of circumcision; and so *Abraham* became the father of Isaac, and circumcised him on the eighth day; and Isaac *became the father of* Jacob, and Jacob *of* the twelve patriarchs. 9 "And the patriarchs BECAME JEALOUS OF JOSEPH AND SOLD HIM INTO EGYPT. And *yet* GOD WAS WITH HIM, 10 and rescued him from all his afflictions, and GRANTED HIM FAVOR and wisdom IN THE SIGHT OF PHARAOH, KING OF EGYPT; AND HE MADE HIM GOVERNOR OVER EGYPT AND ALL HIS HOUSEHOLD. 11 "Now A FAMINE CAME OVER ALL EGYPT AND CANAAN, and great affliction; and our fathers could find no food. 12 "But WHEN JACOB HEARD THAT THERE WAS GRAIN IN EGYPT, he sent our fathers *there* the first time. 13 "And on the second *visit* Joseph made himself known to his brothers, and Joseph's family was disclosed to Pharaoh. 14 "And Joseph sent *word* and invited Jacob his father and all his relatives to come to him, seventy-five persons *in all.* 15 "And Jacob WENT DOWN TO EGYPT AND *there* PASSED AWAY, he and our fathers. 16 "And *from there* they were removed to Shechem, and laid in the tomb which Abraham had purchased for a sum of money from the sons of Hamor in Shechem. 17 "But as the time of the promise was approaching which God had assured to Abraham, the people increased and multiplied in Egypt, 18 until THERE AROSE ANOTHER KING OVER EGYPT WHO KNEW NOTHING ABOUT JOSEPH. 19 "It was he who took shrewd advantage of our race, and mistreated our fathers so that they would expose their infants and they would not survive. 20 "And it was at this time that Moses was born; and he was lovely in the sight of God; and he was nurtured three months in his father's home. 21 "And after he had been exposed, Pharaoh's daughter took him away, and nurtured him as her own son. 22 "And Moses was educated in all the learning of the Egyptians, and he was a man of power in words and deeds. 23 "But when he was approaching the age of forty, it entered his mind to visit his brethren, the children of Israel. 24 "And when he saw one *of them* being treated unjustly, he defended him and took vengeance for the oppressed by striking down the Egyptian. 25 "And he supposed that his brethren understood that God was granting them deliverance through him; but they did not understand. 26 "And on the following day he appeared to them as they were fighting together, and he tried to reconcile them in peace, saying, 'Men, you are brethren, why do you injure one another?' 27 'BUT THE ONE WHO WAS INJURING HIS NEIGH-

[a] Or, *worship.*

342

WILLIAMS

after him, as a permanent possession, although he had no child at that time. 6 This is what God promised: 'His descendants will be strangers living in a foreign land, and its people will enslave and oppress them for four hundred years.' 7 But God further promised: 'I will pass sentence on the nation that enslaves them, and after that they will leave that country and worship me on this very spot.' 8 And with Abraham He made the sacred compact of circumcision, and he became the father of Isaac and circumcised him on the eighth day, and Isaac became the father of Jacob, and Jacob of the twelve patriarchs. 9 And the patriarchs became jealous of Joseph and sold ·him as a slave into Egypt. But God was with him 10 and delivered him from all his troubles, and allowed him to win favor and to show wisdom before Pharaoh, king of Egypt, and so he appointed Joseph governor of Egypt and of his whole household. 11 Then a famine spread all over Egypt and Canaan, and with it great suffering, and our forefathers could not find the simplest food. 12 But Jacob heard that there was food in Egypt and sent our forefathers on their first visit down there. 13 On their second visit Joseph made himself known to his brothers, and thus Joseph's race*a* was revealed to Pharaoh. 14 Then Joseph sent and invited his father Jacob and all his kinsmen, seventy-five in all; 15 and Jacob came down to Egypt. There he and our forefathers died 16 and were carried back to Shechem and laid in the tomb which Abraham had bought with a sum of money from the sons of Hamor in Shechem. 17 As the time approached for realizing the promise which God had made to Abraham, the people multiplied and became more numerous in Egypt, 18 until another king, who knew nothing about Joseph, ascended the throne. 19 By taking a cunning advantage of our race he oppressed our forefathers by forcing them to expose their infants so that they should not live. 20 At this time Moses was born. He was a divinely beautiful child. For three months he was cared for in his father's house. 21 When he was exposed,*b* Pharaoh's daughter adopted him and brought him up as her own son. Thus 22 Moses was educated in all the culture of the Egyptians, and was a mighty man in speech and action. 23 As he was rounding out his fortieth year, it occurred to him to visit his brothers, the descendants of Israel. 24 Because he saw one of them being mistreated, he defended and avenged the man who was suffering ill-treatment by striking down the Egyptian. 25 He supposed that his brothers would understand that God through his instrumentality was going to deliver them, but they did not. 26 The next day he showed himself to two of them engaged in a fight, and he tried to get them to make friends, saying, 'You are brothers, why should you harm each other?' 27 But the man who was harming

BECK

as his own and to his descendants after him,[22] although he had no child. 6 This is what God said: *His descendants would be strangers in a foreign country, and its people would make slaves of them and mistreat them four hundred years.* 7 'But I will punish the people whom they will serve,' God said, 'and after that they will leave[23] and worship Me in this[24] place.' 8 He gave him a *covenant of circumcision.*[25] And so, when his son Isaac was born, *he circumcised him on the eighth day.*[26] Isaac did the same to his son Jacob, and Jacob to his twelve sons, the ancestors of our tribes.

9 "These ancestors *were jealous of Joseph and sold him into Egypt,*[27] but *God was with him.*[28] 10 He rescued him from all his troubles *and gave him the good will*[29] *of Pharaoh the king of Egypt, and wisdom as he stood before him*[30] *—Pharaoh made him ruler of Egypt and of his whole palace.*[31] 11 But a *famine* with much misery came *over* all Egypt and *Canaan,*[32] and our ancestors couldn't find any food. 12 When *Jacob heard there was grain in Egypt,*[33] he sent our ancestors on their first trip. 13 On the second, *Joseph told his brothers who he was,*[34] and Pharaoh learned about the family from which Joseph came. 14 Joseph sent and had his father Jacob come to him, and all his relatives— *seventy-five persons.* 15 And so *Jacob went down to Egypt.*[35] Then he and our ancestors died 16 and *were brought* to *Shechem* and *laid in the* tomb *Abraham bought* for a sum of money *from Hamor's sons at Shechem.*[36]

17 "When the time that God set in His promise to Abraham had almost come, the people *had grown and their number had become very large* in Egypt. 18 And now *a different king who knew nothing of Joseph became ruler of Egypt.* 19 He *was shrewd in scheming against* our people, and he *mistreated*[37] our fathers. He wanted to put away their babies so they wouldn't live.

20 "At that time Moses was born, and he was a *beautiful* child before God. For *three months*[38] he was cared for in his father's home. 21 When he was set out, *Pharaoh's daughter took him up* and raised him *as her son.*[39] 22 Moses was educated in all the wisdom of the Egyptians and became a great man in what he said and did. 23 When he was forty years old, he thought he would *visit his own people, the Israelites.* 24 There he saw a man wronged and defended him. He avenged the man who was mistreated, by *striking down the Egyptian.* 25 He thought his own people would understand he was the one by whom God was freeing them, but they didn't understand. 26 *The next day he came* to them *as they were fighting,*[40] and he tried to make peace between them. 'Men, you are brothers,' he said. 'Why are you doing wrong to one another?'

27 "But *the man who was doing wrong to*

[22] Gen. 12:7; 13:15; 17:8; 48:4
[23] Gen. 15:13-14; Ex. 2:22; 12:40
[24] Ex. 3:12
[25] Gen. 17:10
[26] Gen. 21:4
[27] Gen. 37:11, 28; 45:4
[28] Gen. 39:2-3, 21
[29] Gen. 39:21
[30] Gen. 41:46
[31] Gen. 41:40-41, 43; Ps. 105:21
[32] Gen. 41:54; 42:5
[33] Gen. 42:2
[34] Gen. 45:1
[35] Gen. 46:6, 27; Ex. 1:5; Deut. 10:22
[36] Gen. 50:13; Joshua 24:32
[37] Ex. 1:7-8, 10-11
[38] Ex. 2:2
[39] Ex. 2:5, 10
[40] Ex. 2:11-12

[a] Word means *origin, family, race.* [b] *Put out to die.*

K.J.V.

thrust him away, saying, Who made thee a ruler and a judge over us? 28 Wilt thou kill me, as thou didst the Egyptian yesterday? 29 Then fled Moses at this saying, and was a stranger in the land of Madian, where he begat two sons. 30 And when forty years were expired, there appeared to him in the wilderness of mount Sina an angel of the Lord in a flame of fire in a bush. 31 When Moses saw it, he wondered at the sight: and as he drew near to behold it, the voice of the Lord came unto him, 32 Saying, I am the God of thy fathers, the God of Abraham, and the God of Isaac, and the God of Jacob. Then Moses trembled, and durst not behold. 33 Then said the Lord to him, Put off thy shoes from thy feet: for the place where thou standest is holy ground. 34 I have seen, I have seen the affliction of my people which is in Egypt, and I have heard their groaning, and am come down to deliver them. And now come, I will send thee into Egypt. 35 This Moses whom they refused, saying, Who made thee a ruler and a judge? the same did God send to be a ruler and a deliverer by the hand of the angel which appeared to him in the bush. 36 He brought them out, after that he had shewed wonders and signs in the land of Egypt, and in the Red sea, and in the wilderness forty years.

37 This is that Moses, which said unto the children of Israel, A Prophet shall the Lord your God raise up unto you of your brethren, like unto me; him shall ye hear. 38 This is he, that was in the church in the wilderness with the angel which spake to him in the mount Sina, and with our fathers: who received the lively oracles to give unto us: 39 To whom our fathers would not obey, but thrust him from them, and in their hearts turned back again into Egypt, 40 Saying unto Aaron, Make us gods to go before us: for as for this Moses, which brought us out of the land of Egypt, we wot not what is become of him. 41 And they made a calf in those days, and offered sacrifice unto the idol, and rejoiced in the works of their own hands. 42 Then God turned, and gave them up to worship the host of heaven; as it is written in the book of the prophets, O ye house of Israel, have ye offered to me slain beasts and sacrifices by the space of forty years in the wilderness? 43 Yea, ye took up the tabernacle of Moloch, and the star of your god Remphan, figures which ye made to worship them: and I will carry you away beyond Babylon. 44 Our fathers had the tabernacle of witness in the wilderness, as he had appointed, speaking unto Moses, that he should make it according to the fashion that he had seen. 45 Which also our fathers that came after brought in with Jesus into the possession of the Gentiles, whom God drave out before the face of our fathers, unto the days of David; 46 Who found favour before God, and desired to find a tabernacle for the God of Jacob. 47 But Solomon built him a house. 48 Howbeit the Most High dwelleth not in temples made with hands; as saith the prophet, 49 Heaven is my throne, and earth is my footstool: what house will ye build me? saith the

N.A.S.

BOR pushed him away, saying, 'WHO MADE YOU A RULER AND JUDGE OVER US? 28 'YOU DO NOT MEAN TO KILL ME AS YOU KILLED THE EGYPTIAN YESTERDAY, DO YOU?' 29 "AND AT THIS REMARK MOSES FLED, AND BECAME AN ALIEN IN THE LAND OF MIDIAN, where he became the father of two sons. 30 "And after forty years had passed, AN ANGEL APPEARED TO HIM IN THE WILDERNESS OF MOUNT Sinai, IN THE FLAME OF A BURNING THORN-BUSH. 31 "And when Moses saw it, he began to marvel at the sight; and as he approached to look more closely, there came the voice of the Lord: 32 'I AM THE GOD OF YOUR FATHERS, THE GOD OF ABRAHAM AND ISAAC AND JACOB.' And Moses shook with fear and would not venture to look. 33 "BUT THE LORD SAID TO HIM, 'TAKE OFF THE SANDALS FROM YOUR FEET, FOR THE PLACE ON WHICH YOU ARE STANDING IS HOLY GROUND. 34 'I HAVE CERTAINLY SEEN THE OPPRESSION OF MY PEOPLE IN EGYPT, AND HAVE HEARD THEIR GROANS, AND I HAVE COME DOWN TO DELIVER THEM; COME NOW, AND I WILL SEND YOU TO EGYPT.' 35 "This Moses whom they disowned, saying, 'WHO MADE YOU A RULER AND A JUDGE?' is the one whom God sent to be both a ruler and a deliverer with the help of the angel who appeared to him in the thorn-bush. 36 "This man led them out, performing wonders and signs in the land of Egypt and in the Red Sea and in the wilderness for forty years. 37 "This is the Moses who said to the children of Israel, 'GOD SHALL RAISE UP FOR YOU A PROPHET LIKE ME FROM YOUR BRETHREN.' 38 "This is the one who was in the congregation in the wilderness together with the angel who was speaking to him in Mount Sinai, and who was with our fathers; and he received living oracles to pass on to you. 39 "And our fathers were unwilling to be obedient to him, but repudiated him and in their hearts turned back to Egypt, 40 SAYING TO AARON, 'MAKE FOR US GODS WHO WILL GO BEFORE US; FOR THIS MOSES WHO LED US OUT OF THE LAND OF EGYPT—WE DO NOT KNOW WHAT HAPPENED TO HIM.' 41 "And at that time they made a calf and brought a sacrifice to the idol, and were rejoicing in the works of their hands. 42 "But God turned away and delivered them up to serve the host of heaven; as it is written in the book of the prophets, 'IT WAS NOT TO ME THAT YOU OFFERED VICTIMS AND SACRIFICES FORTY YEARS IN THE WILDERNESS, WAS IT, O HOUSE OF ISRAEL? 43 'YOU ALSO TOOK ALONG THE TABERNACLE OF MOLOCH AND THE STAR OF THE GOD ROMPHA, THE IMAGES WHICH YOU MADE TO WORSHIP THEM. I ALSO WILL REMOVE YOU BEYOND BABYLON.' 44 "Our fathers had the tabernacle of testimony in the wilderness, just as He who spoke to Moses directed him to make it according to the pattern which he had seen. 45 "And having received it in their turn, our fathers brought it in with Joshua upon dispossessing the nations whom God drove out before our fathers, until the time of David. 46 "And David found favor in God's sight, and asked that he might find a dwelling place for the °God of Jacob. 47 "But it was Solomon who built a house for Him. 48 "However, the Most High does not dwell in houses made by human hands; as the prophet says:

49 'HEAVEN IS MY THRONE,
AND EARTH IS THE FOOTSTOOL OF MY FEET;
WHAT KIND OF HOUSE WILL YOU BUILD FOR
   ME? says the LORD;
OR WHAT PLACE IS THERE FOR MY REPOSE?

[a] The earliest mss. read house instead of God; the Septuagint reads, God.

344

WILLIAMS

his brother pushed him aside, saying, 'Who made you our ruler and referee? 28 Do you want to kill me as you did the Egyptian yesterday?' 29 At this statement Moses fled, and went and lived in the land of Midian, and became the father of two sons. 30 When forty years had passed, an angel appeared to him in the desert of Mount Sinai, in the flame of a burning bush. 31 When Moses saw it, he wondered at the sight, and when he went up to look at it, the voice of the Lord said to him, 32 'I am the God of your forefathers, the God of Abraham, Isaac, and Jacob.' Moses was so terrified that he did not dare to look at the bush.c 33 Then the Lord said to him, 'Take your shoes off your feet, for the place where you are standing is sacred ground. 34 Because I have seen the oppression of my people in Egypt and heard their groans, I have come down to deliver them. So come! I will send you back to Egypt as my messenger.' 35 That very Moses whom they refused, saying, 'Who made you our ruler and referee?' was the man whom God sent to be both their ruler and deliverer, by the help of the angel who had appeared to him in the bush. 36 It was he who brought them out of Egypt by performing wonders and signs there and at the Red Sea—as he did also in the desert for forty years. 37 It was this Moses who said to the descendants of Israel, 'God will raise up a prophet for you from among you, just as He did me.' 38 This is the one who in the congregation in the desert went between the angel, who spoke to him on Mount Sinai, and our forefathers, who also received, to be handed down to you, utterances that still live. 39 But our forefathers would not listen to him, but pushed him aside, and in their hearts they hankered after Egypt; 40 and they said to Aaron, 'Make us gods to march in front of us, for as for this Moses, who brought us out of the land of Egypt, we do not know what has become of him!' 41 In those days they even made a calf, and offered sacrifice to their idol, and held a celebration over the works of their own hands. 42 So God turned away from them and gave them over to worship the starry host, as it is written in the Book of the Prophets:

'Did you really offer me victims and sacrifices
Those forty years in the desert, O house of Israel?
43 No, you offered me the tent of Moloch
And the star of your god Rompha,
The images you had made to worship!
So I will now remove you beyond Babylon.'
44 "In the desert our forefathers had the tent of the testimony, like the model Moses had seen, as God who spoke to him ordered him to make it. 45 This tent our forefathers brought in and passed on when under Joshua they dispossessed the nations which God drove out before them, and it remained until the time of David. 46 He found favor with God and begged to design a dwelling for the God of Jacob, 47 but it was Solomon who came to build a house for Him. 48 But the Most High does not live in buildings built by human hands. As the prophet says:
49 ' "Heaven is my throne,
And earth a footstool for my feet.
What house can you build for me?" says the Lord;
"Or what place is there in which I can rest?

BECK

his neighbor pushed Moses away. 'Who made you ruler and judge over us?' he asked. 28 'Do you want to kill me as you killed the Egyptian yesterday?' 29 When he said that, Moses fled and became a stranger in the land of Midian. There he had two sons.41
30 "And so forty years passed. Then an Angel appeared to him in the wilderness of Mount Sinai in the flames of a burning thornbush. 31 Moses was surprised to see this. As he went closer to examine it, the Lord said, 32 'I am the God of your fathers, the God of Abraham, Isaac, and Jacob.' Moses started to tremble and didn't dare to look. 33 The Lord told him, 'Take your shoes off; the place where you're standing is holy ground. 34 I have seen how My people are mistreated in Egypt, I have heard their groaning and have come down to rescue them. And now come, I will send you to Egypt.' 42
35 "This Moses whom they rejected by saying, 'Who made you ruler and judge?' 43 this one God sent to rule and free them with the help of the Angel he saw in the thornbush. 36 He led them out, doing startling wonders and miracles in Egypt, at the Red Sea, and for forty years in the desert.44 37 It was this Moses who told the Israelites, God will raise one of your people to be a Prophet to you like me.45 38 Moses was in the congregation in the wilderness with the Angel who spoke to him on Mount Sinai and with our fathers. He received living truths to give you, 39 but our fathers refused to obey him. Yes, they rejected him, and their hearts turned away to Egypt.46 40 'Make gods for us who will lead us,' they told Aaron. 'This Moses who took us out of Egypt—we don't know what happened to him.' 41 That was the time they made a calf, brought a sacrifice to the idol, and delighted 47 in what their hands had made.
42 "So God perverted and abandoned them to worship the sun, the moon, and the stars,48 as it is written in the book of the prophets: People of Israel, you didn't offer Me slaughtered animals and sacrifices during the forty years in the desert, did you? 43 You even took along the tent of Moloch, the star of the god Rompha, and the images you made in order to worship them. And so I will send you away to live on the other side49 of Babylon.
44 "In the desert our fathers had the tabernacle in which God spoke to His people.50 It was built like the model Moses had seen, just as He who spoke to Moses had ordered him to make51 it. 45 From him our fathers received it, and they brought it here under Joshua when they took the country from the nations God drove out before our fathers, and here it was till the time of David. 46 He found God was kind to him and asked that he might find a home for the God of Jacob.52 47 And Solomon built Him a temple.53
48 "But the Most High God doesn't live in anything made by human hands, as the prophet says, 'Heaven is My throne, and the earth My footstool. 49 What kind of temple will you build Me, the Lord asks, or what place is there where

[41] Ex. 2:13-15, 22; 18:3
[42] Ex. 2:24; 3:1-8, 10; 4:19
[43] Ex. 2:14
[44] Ex. 7:3; Num. 14:33
[45] Deut. 18:15, 18
[46] Num. 14:3-4
[47] Ex. 32:1, 23, 4, 6
[48] Jer. 7:18; 19:13
[49] Amos 5:25-27
[50] Ex. 27:21
[51] Ex. 25:1, 40
[52] Ps. 132:5
[53] 1 Kings 6:1

[c] Implied.

K.J.V.

Lord: or what *is* the place of my rest? 50 Hath not my hand made all these things?

51 Ye stiffnecked and uncircumcised in heart and ears, ye do always resist the Holy Ghost: as your fathers *did,* so *do* ye. 52 Which of the prophets have not your fathers persecuted? and they have slain them which shewed before of the coming of the Just One; of whom ye have been now the betrayers and murderers: 53 Who have received the law by the disposition of angels, and have not kept *it.*

54 When they heard these things, they were cut to the heart, and they gnashed on him with *their* teeth. 55 But he, being full of the Holy Ghost, looked up steadfastly into heaven, and saw the glory of God, and Jesus standing on the right hand of God, 56And said, Behold, I see the heavens opened, and the Son of man standing on the right hand of God. 57 Then they cried out with a loud voice, and stopped their ears, and ran upon him with one accord, 58And cast *him* out of the city, and stoned *him:* and the witnesses laid down their clothes at a young man's feet, whose name was Saul. 59And they stoned Stephen, calling upon *God,* and saying, Lord Jesus, receive my spirit. 60And he kneeled down, and cried with a loud voice, Lord, lay not this sin to their charge. And when he had said this, he fell asleep.

8 And Saul was consenting unto his death. And at that time there was a great persecution against the church which was at Jerusalem; and they were all scattered abroad throughout the regions of Judea and Samaria, except the apostles. 2And devout men carried Stephen *to his burial,* and made great lamentation over him. 3As for Saul, he made havoc of the church, entering into every house, and haling men and women committed *them* to prison. 4 Therefore they that were scattered abroad went every where preaching the word. 5 Then Philip went down to the city of Samaria, and preached Christ unto them. 6And the people with one accord gave heed unto those things which Philip spake, hearing and seeing the miracles which he did. 7 For unclean spirits, crying with loud voice, came out of many that were possessed *with them:* and many taken with palsies, and that were lame, were healed. 8And there was great joy in that city. 9 But there was a certain man, called Simon, which beforetime in the same city used sorcery, and bewitched the people of Samaria, giving out that himself was some great one: 10 To whom they all gave heed, from the least to the greatest, saying, This man is the great power of God. 11And to him they had regard, because that of long time he had bewitched them with sorceries. 12 But when they believed Philip preaching the things concerning the kingdom of God, and the name of Jesus Christ, they were baptized, both men and women. 13 Then

N.A.S.

50 'WAS IT NOT MY HAND WHICH MADE ALL THESE THINGS?'

51 "You men who are stiffnecked and uncircumcised in heart and ears are always resisting the Holy Spirit; you are doing just as your fathers did. 52 "Which one of the prophets did your fathers not persecute? And they killed those who had previously announced the coming of the Righteous One, whose betrayers and murderers you have now become; 53 you who received the law as ordained by angels, and *yet* did not keep it."

54 Now when they heard this, they were cut to the quick, and they *began* gnashing their teeth at him. 55 But being full of the Holy Spirit, he gazed intently into heaven and saw the glory of God, and Jesus standing at the right hand of God; 56 and he said, "Behold, I see the heavens opened up and the Son of Man standing at the right hand of God." 57 But they cried out with a loud voice, and covered their ears, and they rushed upon him with one impulse. 58And when they had driven him out of the city, they *began* stoning *him,* and the witnesses laid aside their robes at the feet of a young man named Saul. 59And they went on stoning Stephen as he called upon *the Lord* and said, "Lord Jesus, receive my spirit!" 60And falling on his knees, he cried out with a loud voice, "Lord, do not hold this sin against them!" And having said this, he fell asleep.

8 And Saul was in hearty agreement with putting him to death.

And on that day a great persecution arose against the church in Jerusalem; and they were all scattered throughout the regions of Judea and Samaria, except the apostles. 2And *some* devout men buried Stephen, and made loud lamentation over him. 3 But Saul *began* ravaging the church, entering house after house and dragging off men and women, he would put them in prison.

4 Therefore, those who had been scattered went about preaching the word. 5And Philip went down to the city of Samaria and *began* proclaiming Christ to them. 6And the multitudes with one accord were giving attention to what was said by Philip, as they heard and saw the signs which he was performing. 7 For *in the case of* many who had unclean spirits, they were coming out *of them* shouting with a loud voice; and many who had been paralyzed and lame were healed. 8And there was much rejoicing in that city.

9 Now there was a certain man named Simon, who formerly was practicing magic in the city, and astonishing the people of Samaria, claiming to be someone great; 10 and they all, from smallest to greatest, were giving attention to him, saying, "This man is what is called the Great Power of God." 11And they were giving him attention because he had for a long time astonished them with his magic arts. 12 But when they believed Philip preaching the good news about the kingdom of God and the name of Jesus Christ, they were being baptized, men and women alike. 13And even Simon himself

| WILLIAMS | BECK |

WILLIAMS

50 Was it not my hand that made them all?" '

51 "You people, stubborn in will, heathenish in hearts and ears, you are always resisting the Holy Spirit, as your forefathers did, too. 52 Which of the prophets did your forefathers fail to persecute? They killed the prophets who foretold the coming of the Righteous One, and now you have betrayed and murdered Him, 53 you who received the law by order of the angels, and yet you did not obey it!"

54 As they continued to listen to this address, they were becoming infuriated and began to grind their teeth at him. 55 But since he was full of the Holy Spirit, he looked right into heaven and saw the glory of God and Jesus standing at God's right hand. 56 So he said, "Look! I see heaven open, and the Son of Man standing at God's right hand."

57 But they raised a great shout and held their ears, and all together rushed upon him, 58 and dragged him out of the city and continued stoning him. The witnesses, in the meantime, laid their clothes at the feet of a young man named Saul. 59 They continued stoning Stephen as he continued praying, "Lord Jesus, receive my spirit!"

60 Then he fell on his knees and cried out, "Lord, do not charge this sin on the book against them!" On saying this he fell asleep in death.

8 *Stephen is buried; Christians persecuted but preaching the good news wherever they flee; Philip preaches it in Samaria; believers there receive the Spirit; Philip preaches to an Ethiopian state treasurer*

Saul heartily approved of his being put to death. So on that day a severe persecution broke out against the church in Jerusalem, and all of them, except the apostles, were scattered over Judea and Samaria. 2 Some devout men buried Stephen and made loud lamentation for him. 3 But Saul continued to harass the church, and by going from house to house and dragging off men and women he continued to put them into prison.

4 Now those who were scattered went from place to place preaching the good news of the message. 5 So Philip went down to the city of Samaria and began to preach the Christ to the Samaritans. 6 As the crowds continued to listen to his message and continued to see his wonderworks which he was performing, as with one mind they became interested in what was said by Philip. 7 For many of those under the power of foul spirits cried out and the spirits came out of them, and many paralyzed and crippled people were cured. 8 So there was great rejoicing in that city.

9 There was a man named Simon in the city, who had kept the Samaritan people thrilled by practicing magic there and by claiming to be a great man. 10 Everybody, high and low,ᵃ kept running after him, saying, "He is certainly what is known as the Great Power of God!" 11 They kept running after him, because for a long time he had thrilled them with his magical performances. 12 But when the people came to believe the good news proclaimed by Philip about the kingdom of God and the name of Jesus Christ, both men and women were constantly baptized. 13 So Simon himself came to believe too, and

[a] *Small and great.*

BECK

I can rest? 50 Didn't *My hand make all this?'* ⁵⁴

51 *"How stubborn you are and pagan at heart and deaf to the truth!* ⁵⁵ You're always *opposing the Holy Spirit.*⁵⁶ Your fathers did it, and so do you! 52 Was there ever a prophet your fathers didn't persecute? They killed those who announced, 'The Righteous One will come!' and now you betrayed and murdered Him. 53 Angels were ordered to give you the Law, but you didn't keep it!"

Stoning Stephen

54 While they were listening, the men of the court got furious and ground their teeth at him. 55 But he, full of the Holy Spirit, gazed up to heaven and saw God's glory and Jesus standing at God's right side. 56 "Look!" he said, "I see heaven opened and the Son of Man standing at God's right side."

57 But they yelled at the top of their voices, held their ears shut, and all together rushed at him. 58 They threw him out of the city and started to stone him. The witnesses had laid their outer clothes at the feet of a young man —his name was Saul.

59 While they were stoning Stephen, he called, "Lord Jesus, receive my spirit." 60 Then, kneeling, he called out loud, "Lord, don't hold this sin against them." When he had said this, he fell asleep.

8 And Saul also approved of their killing him.

That day a great persecution broke out against the church in Jerusalem, and all except the apostles were scattered over the open country of Judea and Samaria.

2 God-fearing men buried Stephen and mourned loud for him.

The Samaritans Believe

3 Saul was trying to destroy the church. Going into one house after another and dragging off men and women, he put them in prison.

4 So the people who were scattered went from place to place telling the good news. 5 Philip went down to the city of Samaria and preached Christ to the people. 6 When they heard him, all listened eagerly to what Philip had to say, especially when they saw the miracles he did. 7 There were those who were plagued by unclean spirits; many came screaming out of them. And many who were paralyzed and lame were made well. 8 So there was great joy in that city.

9 There was in the city a man by the name of Simon who was practicing witchcraft and amazing the people of Samaria, claiming to be a great man. 10 Everybody from the least to the greatest listened eagerly to him, saying, "He's God's power; people call it great." 11 They were so interested in him because he had for a long time amazed them by his witchcraft. 12 But when Philip told the good news of God's kingdom and of the name of Jesus Christ, men and women believed him and were baptized. 13 Even

[54] Is. 66: 1-2
[55] Ex. 33:3, 5; Lev. 26:41; Jer. 9:26; 6:10
[56] Num. 27:14; Is. 63:10

K.J.V.

Simon himself believed also: and when he was baptized, he continued with Philip, and wondered, beholding the miracles and signs which were done. 14 Now when the apostles which were at Jerusalem heard that Samaria had received the word of God, they sent unto them Peter and John: 15 Who, when they were come down, prayed for them, that they might receive the Holy Ghost: 16 (For as yet he was fallen upon none of them: only they were baptized in the name of the Lord Jesus.) 17 Then laid they *their* hands on them, and they received the Holy Ghost. 18 And when Simon saw that through laying on of the apostles' hands the Holy Ghost was given, he offered them money, 19 Saying, Give me also this power, that on whomsoever I lay hands, he may receive the Holy Ghost. 20 But Peter said unto him, Thy money perish with thee, because thou hast thought that the gift of God may be purchased with money. 21 Thou hast neither part nor lot in this matter: for thy heart is not right in the sight of God. 22 Repent therefore of this thy wickedness, and pray God, if perhaps the thought of thine heart may be forgiven thee. 23 For I perceive that thou art in the gall of bitterness, and *in* the bond of iniquity. 24 Then answered Simon, and said, Pray ye to the Lord for me, that none of these things which ye have spoken come upon me. 25 And they, when they had testified and preached the word of the Lord, returned to Jerusalem, and preached the gospel in many villages of the Samaritans. 26 And the angel of the Lord spake unto Philip, saying, Arise, and go toward the south, unto the way that goeth down from Jerusalem unto Gaza, which is desert. 27 And he arose and went: and, behold, a man of Ethiopia, a eunuch of great authority under Candace queen of the Ethiopians, who had the charge of all her treasure, and had come to Jerusalem for to worship, 28 Was returning, and sitting in his chariot read Esaias the prophet. 29 Then the Spirit said unto Philip, Go near, and join thyself to this chariot. 30 And Philip ran thither to *him,* and heard him read the prophet Esaias, and said, Understandest thou what thou readest? 31 And he said, How can I, except some man should guide me? And he desired Philip that he would come up and sit with him. 32 The place of the Scripture which he read was this, He was led as a sheep to the slaughter; and like a lamb dumb before his shearer, so opened he not his mouth: 33 In his humiliation his judgment was taken away: and who shall declare his generation? for his life is taken from the earth. 34 And the eunuch answered Philip, and said, I pray thee, of whom speaketh the prophet this? of himself, or of some other man? 35 Then Philip opened his mouth, and began at the same Scripture, and preached unto him Jesus. 36 And as they went on *their* way, they came unto a certain water: and the eunuch said, See, *here is* water; what doth hinder me to be baptized? 37 And Philip said, If thou believest with all thine heart, thou mayest. And he answered and said, I believe that Jesus Christ is the Son of God.

N.A.S.

believed; and after being baptized, he continued on with Philip; and as he observed signs and great miracles taking place, he was constantly amazed.

14 Now when the apostles in Jerusalem heard that Samaria had received the word of God, they sent them Peter and John, 15 who came down and prayed for them, that they might receive the Holy Spirit. 16 For He had not yet fallen upon any of them; they had simply been baptized in the name of the Lord Jesus. 17 Then they *began* laying their hands on them, and they were receiving the Holy Spirit. 18 Now when Simon saw that the Spirit was bestowed through the laying on of the apostles' hands, he offered them money, 19 saying, "Give this authority to me as well, so that every one on whom I lay my hands may receive the Holy Spirit." 20 But Peter said to him, "May your silver perish with you, because you thought you could obtain the gift of God with money! 21 "You have no part or portion in this matter, for your heart is not right before God. 22 "Therefore repent of this wickedness of yours, and pray the Lord that if possible, the intention of your heart may be forgiven you. 23 "For I see that you are in the gall of bitterness and in the bondage of iniquity." 24 But Simon answered and said, "Pray to the Lord for me yourselves, so that nothing of what you have said may come upon me."

25 And so, when they had solemnly testified and spoken the word of the Lord, they started back to Jerusalem, and were preaching the gospel to many villages of the Samaritans.

26 But an angel of the Lord spoke to Philip saying, "Arise and go south to the road that descends from Jerusalem to Gaza." (This is a desert *road.*) 27 And he arose and went; and behold, there was an Ethiopian eunuch, a court official of Candace, queen of the Ethiopians, who was in charge of all her treasure; and he had come to Jerusalem to worship. 28 And he was returning and sitting in his chariot, and was reading the prophet Isaiah. 29 And the Spirit said to Philip, "Go up and join this chariot." 30 And when Philip had run up, he heard him reading Isaiah the prophet, and said, "Do you understand what you are reading?" 31 And he said, "Well, how could I, unless someone guides me?" And he invited Philip to come up and sit with him. 32 Now the passage of Scripture which he was reading was this:

"HE WAS LED AS A SHEEP TO SLAUGHTER;
AND AS A LAMB BEFORE ITS SHEARER IS SILENT,
SO HE DOES NOT OPEN HIS MOUTH.
33 "IN HUMILIATION HIS JUDGMENT WAS TAKEN AWAY;
WHO SHALL RELATE HIS GENERATION?
FOR HIS LIFE IS REMOVED FROM THE EARTH."
34 And the eunuch answered Philip and said, "Please *tell me,* of whom does the prophet say this? Of himself, or of someone else?" 35 And Philip opened his mouth, and beginning from this Scripture he preached Jesus to him. 36 And as they went along the road they came to some water; and the eunuch *said, "Look! Water! What prevents me from being baptized?"

WILLIAMS

after he was baptized he continued to be devoted to Philip, and he was always thrilled at seeing such great signs and wonder-works continuously performed.

14 When the apostles at Jerusalem heard that Samaria had accepted God's message, they sent Peter and John there. 15 They came and prayed for them that they might receive the Holy Spirit, 16 for as yet He had not come upon any of them, but they had been baptized merely in the name of the Lord Jesus. 17 Then they laid their hands upon them, and one by one they received the Holy Spirit. 18 So when Simon saw that the Holy Spirit was conferred by the laying on of the apostles' hands, he offered them money, 19 and said, "Give me this power too, that when I lay my hands on anyone he may receive the Holy Spirit."

20 But Peter said to him, "Your money go to perdition with you for even dreaming you could buy the gift of God with money! 21 You have no share or part in this matter, for your heart is not sincere in the sight of God. 22 So repent of this wickedness of yours, and pray to the Lord, to see if this thought of your heart may be forgiven you. 23 For I see that you are a bitter weed and a bundle of crookedness!"

24 So Simon answered, "Both of you beg the Lord for me that none of the things you have said may befall me!"

25 So after they had given their testimony and spoken the Lord's message, they started back to Jerusalem, and on the way continued to tell the good news in many Samaritan villages.

26 Now an angel of the Lord said to Philip, "Get up and go south by the road that leads from Jerusalem to Gaza; this is the desert road." 27 So he got up and went.

Now there was an Ethiopian official,[b] a member of the court of Candace, queen of the Ethiopians, her chief treasurer, who had come to Jerusalem to worship, 28 and now was on his way home. He was seated in his chariot, reading the prophet Isaiah. 29 So the Spirit said to Philip, "Go up and join him in his chariot."

30 Then Philip ran up and listened to him reading the prophet Isaiah, and he asked, "Do you understand what you are reading?" 31 He answered, "How in the world could I, unless someone teaches me?" And he begged him to get up and sit with him. 32 Now this was the passage of Scripture that he was reading:
"Like a sheep He was led away to be slaughtered,
And just as a lamb is dumb before its shearer, So He does not open His mouth.
33 Justice was denied Him in His humiliation. Who can tell of His times?[c]
For His life is removed from the earth."

34 "Tell me, I pray, of whom is the prophet speaking," asked the official of Philip, "of himself or of someone else?" 35 Then Philip opened his mouth, and starting from this passage, he told him the good news about Jesus.

36 As they continued down the road, they came to some water, and the official said, "Look! here is some water! What is there to keep me

BECK

Simon believed, and when he was baptized, he stayed with Philip. He was amazed to see the miracles and wonderful works that were done.

14 When the apostles in Jerusalem heard Samaria had accepted God's Word, they sent Peter and John to them. 15 These two went down and prayed that the people would receive the Holy Spirit. 16 He had not come on any of them yet; but they had only been baptized into the name of the Lord Jesus. 17 Then Peter and John laid their hands on them, and they received the Holy Spirit.

18 Simon saw the Spirit was given when the apostles laid their hands on anyone. So he offered them money. 19 "Give me this power," he said, "that anyone I lay my hands on receives the Holy Spirit."

20 "Your money perish with you," Peter told him, "because you meant to buy God's gift with money. 21 You have no part or share in this because your *heart isn't right with God.*[57] 22 Now repent of this wickedness of yours, and ask the Lord if He will perhaps forgive you for thinking such a thing. 23 I see you're turning to *bitter poison*[58] and being *chained by wickedness.*"[59]

24 "You ask the Lord for me," Simon answered, "that none of the things you said may happen to me."

25 After they had testified and spoken the Lord's Word, they also brought the good news to many Samaritan villages on their way back to Jerusalem.

The Treasurer from Ethiopia

26 The Lord's angel said to Philip, "Get up and go south to the road going from Jerusalem down to Gaza." It is a deserted road.

27 He got up and went. Here there was a man from Ethiopia, a eunuch and high official of Candace, queen of the Ethiopians, in charge of all her treasures. He had come to Jerusalem to worship 28 and was on his way home, sitting in his chariot and reading the prophet Isaiah.

29 The Spirit said to Philip, "Go over to that chariot and keep close to it."

30 Philip ran up to it and there heard him reading the prophet Isaiah. "Do you really understand what you're reading?" he asked.

31 "Why, how can I without somebody to guide me?" he asked, and he urged Philip to come up and sit with him.

32 This was the part of the Bible he was reading:

He will be led away like a sheep to be slaughtered,
And as a lamb is dumb before the man who cut off her wool,
So He will not open His mouth.
33 When He humbles Himself, His condemnation will be taken away.
Who will describe the people of His time? His life will be cut off from the earth.[60]

34 "I ask you," the eunuch said to Philip, "whom is the prophet talking about—himself or somebody else?"

35 Then Philip spoke. Starting with this statement of the Bible, he told him the good news of Jesus. 36 As they were going along the road, they came to some water. "Here is water," the eunuch said. "What keeps me from being baptized?" *

* Our oldest manuscripts do not have v. 37: " 'If you believe with all your heart,' Philip said, 'you may.' He answered, 'I believe Jesus Christ is God's Son.' "
[57] Ps. 78:37
[58] Deut. 29:18
[59] Is. 58:6
[60] Is. 53: 7-8

[b] Lit., *eunich,* but he was an official; most attendants at court were made eunuchs in those days.
[c] Grk., *generation.*

K.J.V.

38And he commanded the chariot to stand still: and they went down both into the water, both Philip and the eunuch; and he baptized him. 39And when they were come up out of the water, the Spirit of the Lord caught away Philip, that the eunuch saw him no more: and he went on his way rejoicing. 40 But Philip was found at Azotus: and passing through he preached in all the cities, till he came to Cesarea.

9 And Saul, yet breathing out threatenings and slaughter against the disciples of the Lord, went unto the high priest, 2And desired of him letters to Damascus to the synagogues, that if he found any of this way, whether they were men or women, he might bring them bound unto Jerusalem. 3And as he journeyed, he came near Damascus: and suddenly there shined round about him a light from heaven: 4And he fell to the earth, and heard a voice saying unto him, Saul, Saul, why persecutest thou me? 5And he said, Who art thou, Lord? And the Lord said, I am Jesus whom thou persecutest: *it is* hard for thee to kick against the pricks. 6And he trembling and astonished said, Lord, what wilt thou have me to do? And the Lord *said* unto him, Arise, and go into the city, and it shall be told thee what thou must do. 7And the men which journeyed with him stood speechless, hearing a voice, but seeing no man. 8And Saul arose from the earth; and when his eyes were opened, he saw no man: but they led him by the hand, and brought *him* into Damascus. 9And he was three days without sight, and neither did eat nor drink.

10 And there was a certain disciple at Damascus, named Ananias; and to him said the Lord in a vision, Ananias. And he said, Behold, I *am here,* Lord. 11And the Lord *said* unto him, Arise, and go into the street which is called Straight, and inquire in the house of Judas for *one* called Saul, of Tarsus: for, behold, he prayeth, 12And hath seen in a vision a man named Ananias coming in, and putting *his* hand on him, that he might receive his sight. 13 Then Ananias answered, Lord, I have heard by many of this man, how much evil he hath done to thy saints at Jerusalem: 14And here he hath authority from the chief priests to bind all that call on thy name. 15 But the Lord said unto him, Go thy way: for he is a chosen vessel unto me, to bear my name before the Gentiles, and kings, and the children of Israel: 16 For I will shew him how great things he must suffer for my name's sake. 17And Ananias went his way, and entered into the house; and putting his hands on him said, Brother Saul, the Lord, *even* Jesus, that appeared unto thee in the way as thou camest, hath sent me, that thou mightest receive thy sight, and be filled with the Holy Ghost. 18And immediately there fell from his eyes as it had been scales: and he received sight forthwith,

N.A.S.

37 (See footnote *) 38And he ordered the chariot to stop; and they both went down into the water, Philip as well as the eunuch; and he baptized him. 39And when they came up out of the water, the Spirit of the Lord snatched Philip away; and the eunuch saw him no more, but went on his way rejoicing. 40 But Philip found himself at Azotus; and as he passed through he kept preaching the gospel to all the cities, until he came to Caesarea.

9 Now Saul, still breathing threats and murder against the disciples of the Lord, went to the high priest, 2 and asked for letters from him to the synagogues at Damascus, so that if he found any belonging to the Way, both men and women, he might bring them bound to Jerusalem. 3And it came about that as he journeyed, he was approaching Damascus, and suddenly a light from heaven flashed around him; 4 and he fell to the ground, and heard a voice saying to him, "Saul, Saul, why are you persecuting Me?" 5And he said, "Who art Thou, Lord?" And He *said,* "I am Jesus whom you are persecuting, 6 but rise, and enter the city, and it shall be told you what you must do." 7And the men who traveled with him stood speechless, hearing the voice, but seeing no one. 8And Saul got up from the ground, and though his eyes were open, he could see nothing; and leading him by the hand, they brought him into Damascus. 9And he was three days without sight, and neither ate nor drank.

10 Now there was a certain disciple at Damascus, named Ananias; and the Lord said to him in a vision, "Ananias." And he said, "Behold, *here am* I, Lord." 11And the Lord *said* to him, "Arise and go to the street called Straight, and inquire at the house of Judas for a man from Tarsus named Saul, for behold, he is praying, 12 and he has seen ᵇin a vision a man named Ananias come in and lay his hands on him, so that he might regain his sight." 13 But Ananias answered, "Lord, I have heard from many about this man, how much harm he did to Thy saints at Jerusalem; 14 and here he has authority from the chief priests to bind all who call upon Thy name." 15 But the Lord said to him, "Go, for he is a chosen ᶜinstrument of Mine, to bear My name before the Gentiles and kings and the children of Israel; 16 for I will show him how much he must suffer for My name's sake." 17And Ananias departed and entered the house, and after laying his hands on him said, "Brother Saul, the Lord Jesus, who appeared to you on the road by which you were coming, has sent me so that you may regain your sight, and be filled with the Holy Spirit." 18And immediately there fell from his eyes something like scales, and he regained his sight, and he arose and

[a] Late mss. insert verse 37: *And Philip said, "If you believe with all your heart, you may." And he answered and said, "I believe that Jesus Christ is the Son of God."* [b] Some mss. omit, *in a vision.* [c] Or, *vessel.*

WILLIAMS

from being baptized?" [d] 38 So he ordered the chariot to stop, and Philip and the official both went down into the water, and Philip baptized him. 39 When they came up out of the water, the Spirit of the Lord suddenly took Philip away; the official saw him no more, for he went on home rejoicing; 40 but Philip was found at Ashdod, and he went on telling the good news in all the towns until he reached Caesarea.

9 *Saul converted; preaches at Damascus that Jesus is the Christ; Jews plot to kill Him; Christians rescue Him in a basket; at Jerusalem Jews try to kill Him; escapes to Tarsus; Peter preaches; raises Dorcas to life*

Now Saul, as he was still breathing threats of murder against the disciples of the Lord, went to the high priest 2 and asked him for letters to the synagogues in Damascus, that if he found any men or women belonging to The Way he might bring them in chains to Jerusalem. 3 As he traveled on he finally approached Damascus, and suddenly a light from heaven flashed around him.

4 He dropped to the ground; then he heard a voice saying to him, "Saul, Saul, why are you persecuting me?"

5 He asked, "Who are you, sir?"

And He said, "I am Jesus whom you are persecuting. 6 But get up and go into the city, and there it will be told you what you ought to do." [a]

7 His fellow-travelers stood speechless, for they heard the voice but could not see anyone. 8 Then Saul got up off the ground, but he could not see anything, although his eyes were wide open. So they took him by the hand and led him into Damascus, 9 and for three days he could not see, and he did not eat or drink anything.

10 Now there was in Damascus a disciple named Ananias, and the Lord said to him in a vision, "Ananias!"

And he answered, "Yes, Lord, I am here."

11 And the Lord said to him, "Get up and go to the street called 'The Straight Street,' and ask at the house of Judas for one named Saul, from Tarsus, for he is now praying there. 12 He has seen in a vision a man named Ananias come in and lay his hands on him, to restore his sight."

13 But Ananias answered, "Lord, I have heard many people tell of this man, especially the great sufferings he has brought on your people[b] in Jerusalem. 14 Now he is here and has authority from the high priests to put in chains all who call upon your name."

15 But the Lord said to him, "Go, for he is a chosen instrument of mine to carry my name to the heathen and their kings, and to the descendants of Israel. 16 For I am going to show him how great are the sufferings he must endure for my name's sake."

17 So Ananias left and went to that house, and there he laid his hands upon Saul, and said, "Saul, my brother, the Lord Jesus, who appeared to you on the road on which you were coming here, has sent me that you may regain your sight and be filled with the Holy Spirit." 18 And all at once something like scales fell from his eyes, he regained his sight, got up and was bap-

BECK

38 He ordered the chariot to stop, and both Philip and the eunuch stepped down into the water, and Philip baptized him. 39 When they had stepped out of the water, the Lord's Spirit suddenly took Philip away, and the eunuch, happily going his way, didn't see him again.

40 But Philip found himself in Ashdod. He went through all the towns, bringing them the good news, till he came to Caesarea.

Jesus Changes Paul

9 And Saul, still breathing threats and murder against the Lord's disciples, went to the high priest 2 and asked him for letters to the synagogs in Damascus, in order to bring any of Jesus' followers he might find there, men or women, back to Jerusalem in chains.

3 On his way, as he was coming near Damascus, suddenly a light from heaven flashed around him. 4 He fell to the ground and heard a voice saying to him, "Saul! Saul! Why are you persecuting Me?"

5 "Who are You, Lord?" he asked.

"I am Jesus," He said, "whom you are persecuting. 6 But get up, go into the city, and you will be told what you should do."

7 Meanwhile the men traveling with him were standing speechless. They heard the voice but didn't see anyone.

8 Saul got up from the ground. When he opened his eyes, he couldn't see anything. So they took him by the hand and led him into Damascus. 9 For three days he couldn't see and didn't eat or drink.

Ananias Comes to Saul

10 In Damascus there was a disciple by the name of Ananias. The Lord said to him in a vision: "Ananias!"

"Yes, Lord," he answered.

11 "Get up," the Lord told him, "go to the street called Straight, and in the home of Judas look for a man from Tarsus by the name of Saul. You see, he's praying. 12 And in a vision he has seen a man by the name of Ananias come in and lay his hands on him so he will see again."

13 "Lord," Ananias answered, "I've heard many tell how much wrong this man has done to Your holy people in Jerusalem, 14 and he's here with authority from the high priests to put in chains all who call on Your name."

15 "Go," the Lord told him, "he's an instrument I have chosen to bring My name before the Gentiles, before kings, and the people of Israel. 16 I will show him how much he has to suffer for Me."

17 Ananias went. When he came into the house, he laid his hands on Saul. "Brother Saul," he said, "the Lord sent me—Jesus, whom you saw on your way here—so that you will see again and be filled with the Holy Spirit."

18 Immediately something like scales fell from his eyes, and he saw again. He got up and was

[d] V. 37 not in best Mss. [a] The rest of vv. 5 and 6 not in best Mss. [b] Grk., *your saints.*

351

K.J.V.

and arose, and was baptized. 19And when he had received meat, he was strengthened. Then was Saul certain days with the disciples which were at Damascus. 20And straightway he preached Christ in the synagogues, that he is the Son of God. 21 But all that heard *him* were amazed, and said; Is not this he that destroyed them which called on this name in Jerusalem, and came hither for that intent, that he might bring them bound unto the chief priests? 22 But Saul increased the more in strength, and confounded the Jews which dwelt at Damascus, proving that this is very Christ.

23 And after that many days were fulfilled, the Jews took counsel to kill him: 24 But their laying wait was known of Saul. And they watched the gates day and night to kill him. 25 Then the disciples took him by night, and let *him* down by the wall in a basket. 26And when Saul was come to Jerusalem he assayed to join himself to the disciples: but they were all afraid of him, and believed not that he was a disciple. 27 But Barnabas took him, and brought *him* to the apostles, and declared unto them how he had seen the Lord in the way, and that he had spoken to him, and how he had preached boldly at Damascus in the name of Jesus. 28And he was with them coming in and going out at Jerusalem. 29And he spake boldly in the name of the Lord Jesus, and disputed against the Grecians: but they went about to slay him. 30 *Which* when the brethren knew, they brought him down to Cesarea, and sent him forth to Tarsus. 31 Then had the churches rest throughout all Judea and Galilee and Samaria, and were edified; and walking in the fear of the Lord, and in the comfort of the Holy Ghost, were multiplied.

32 And it came to pass, as Peter passed throughout all *quarters*, he came down also to the saints which dwelt at Lydda. 33And there he found a certain man named Eneas, which had kept his bed eight years, and was sick of the palsy. 34And Peter said unto him, Eneas, Jesus Christ maketh thee whole: arise, and make thy bed. And he arose immediately. 35And all that dwelt at Lydda and Saron saw him, and turned to the Lord.

36 Now there was at Joppa a certain disciple named Tabitha, which by interpretation is called Dorcas: this woman was full of good works and almsdeeds which she did. 37And it came to pass in those days, that she was sick, and died: whom when they had washed, they laid *her* in an upper chamber. 38And forasmuch as Lydda was nigh to Joppa, and the disciples had heard that Peter was there, they sent unto him two men, desiring *him* that he would not delay to come to them. 39 Then Peter arose and went with them. When he was come, they brought him into the upper chamber: and all the widows stood by him weeping, and shewing the coats and garments which Dorcas made, while she was with them. 40 But Peter put them all forth, and kneeled down, and prayed; and turning *him* to the body said, Tabitha, arise. And she opened her eyes: and when she saw Peter, she sat up. 41And he gave her *his* hand, and lifted her up; and when he had called the saints and widows, he pre-

N.A.S.

was baptized; 19 and he took food and was strengthened.

Now for several days he was with the disciples who were at Damascus, 20 and immediately he *began* to proclaim Jesus in the synagogues, saying, "He is the Son of God." 21And all those hearing him continued to be amazed, and were saying, "Is this not he who in Jerusalem destroyed those who called on this name, and *who* had come here for the purpose of bringing them bound over before the chief priests?" 22 But Saul kept increasing in strength and confounding the Jews who lived at Damascus by proving that this *Jesus* is the Christ.

23 And when many days had elapsed, the Jews plotted together to do away with him, 24 but their plot became known to Saul. And they were also watching the gates day and night so that they might put him to death; 25 but his disciples took him by night, and let him down through *an opening in* the wall, lowering him in a basket.

26 And when he had come to Jerusalem, he was trying to associate with the disciples; and they were all afraid of him, not believing that he was a disciple. 27 But Barnabas took hold of him and brought him to the apostles and described to them how he had seen the Lord on the road, and that He had talked to him, and how at Damascus he had spoken out boldly in the name of Jesus. 28And he was with them moving about freely in Jerusalem, speaking out boldly in the name of the Lord. 29And he was talking and arguing with the Hellenistic *Jews;* but they were attempting to put him to death. 30 But when the brethren learned *of it,* they brought him down to Caesarea and sent him away to Tarsus.

31 So the church throughout all Judea and Galilee and Samaria enjoyed peace, being built up; and, going on in the fear of the Lord and in the comfort of the Holy Spirit, it continued to increase.

32 Now it came about that as Peter was traveling through all *those parts,* he came down also to the saints who lived at Lydda. 33And there he found a certain man named Aeneas, who had been bedridden eight years, for he was paralyzed. 34And Peter said to him, "Aeneas, Jesus Christ heals you; arise, and make your bed." And immediately he arose. 35And all who lived at Lydda and Sharon saw him, and they turned to the Lord.

36 Now in Joppa there was a certain disciple named Tabitha (which translated *in Greek* is called Dorcas); this woman was abounding with deeds of kindness and charity, which she continually did. 37And it came about at that time that she fell sick and died; and when they had washed her body, they laid it in an upper room. 38And since Lydda was near Joppa, the disciples, having heard that Peter was there, sent two men to him, entreating him, "Do not delay to come to us." 39And Peter arose and went with them. And when he had come, they brought him into the upper room; and all the widows stood beside him weeping, and showing all the *tunics and garments that Dorcas used to make while she was with them. 40 But Peter sent them all out and knelt down and prayed, and turning to the body, he said, "Tabitha, arise." And she opened her eyes, and when she saw Peter, she sat up. 41And he gave her his hand and raised her up; and calling the saints and widows, he pre-

[a] Or, *inner garments.*

WILLIAMS

tized, 19 and after taking some food he felt strong again.

For several days he stayed with the disciples at Damascus, 20 and at once he began to preach in their synagogues that Jesus is the Son of God. 21And all who heard him were astounded and said, "Is not this the man who harassed those who called upon this name in Jerusalem, and has come here expressly for the purpose of putting them in chains and taking them back to the high priests?" 22 But Saul grew stronger and stronger and continued to put to utter confusion the Jews who lived in Damascus, by proving that Jesus is the Christ.

23 After several days had gone by, the Jews laid a plot to murder him, 24 but their plot was found out by Saul. Day and night they kept guarding the city gates, to murder him, 25 but his disciples took him one night and let him down through the city-wall, by lowering him in a hamper-basket.

26 Now when Saul arrived at Jerusalem, he tried to join the disciples there, but they were all afraid of him, because they did not believe that he was really a disciple. 27 Barnabas, however, took him up and presented him to the apostles, and he told them how on the road he had seen the Lord, and how the Lord had spoken to him, and how courageously he had spoken in the name of Jesus at Damascus. 28 So he was one of them, going in and out constantly at Jerusalem, 29 and he continued to speak courageously in the name of the Lord, and to speak and debate with the Greek-speaking Jews. But they kept trying to murder him. 30 So when the brothers found this out, they took him down to Caesarea, and from there sent him back to Tarsus.

31 So the church all over Judea, Galilee, and Samaria enjoyed peace, and as it continued to be built up spiritually and to live in reverence for the Lord, it continued to increase in numbers through the encouragement that the Holy Spirit gave.

32 Now, as Peter was going here and there among them all, he finally went down to God's people who lived at Lydda. 33 There he found a man named Aeneas, who had been bedridden for eight years as a paralytic. 34 So Peter said to him, "Aeneas, Jesus Christ now cures you! Get up and make your bed!" And at once he got up. 35 Then all the people who lived at Lydda and Sharon saw him, and so they turned to the Lord.

36 At Joppa there was a woman, a disciple, whose name was Tabitha, which in Greek means Dorcas, that is, Gazelle. She had filled her life with good deeds and works of charity, which she was always doing. 37 Just at that time it happened that she had been taken ill and had died. They washed her body and laid her out in a room upstairs. 38 As Joppa was near Lydda, the disciples heard that Peter was there, and sent two men to him, begging him to come to them without delay. 39 So Peter at once got up and went with them. When he reached there, they took him to the room upstairs, and all the widows took their stand around him, crying and showing him the shirts and coats that Dorcas had made while she was still with them.

40 Then Peter put them all out of the room, knelt down and prayed, and, turning to the body, said, "Tabitha, get up!" Then she opened her eyes, and when she saw Peter, she sat up. 41 He gave her his hand and lifted her to her feet, and calling in the Lord's people and the widows, he

BECK

baptized. 19 Then he had something to eat and was strengthened.

Paul Preaches Jesus

20 While Saul was with the disciples in Damascus several days, he immediately started to preach in the synagogs: "Jesus is God's Son." 21All who heard him were amazed. "Isn't this the man," they asked, "who in Jerusalem destroyed those who call on this name, and didn't he come here to bring them in chains to the high priests?"

22 But Saul grew more and more powerful and bewildered the Jews living in Damascus by proving "He is the promised Savior." 23 After some time the Jews plotted to murder him, but Saul was told about their plot. 24 When they were even watching the gates day and night to murder him, 25 his disciples took him one night and let him down through an opening in the wall by lowering him in a basket.

26 He went to Jerusalem and there tried to join the disciples. But they were all afraid of him because they wouldn't believe he was a disciple. 27 Then Barnabas took him, brought him to the apostles, and told them how Saul saw the Lord on the road and the Lord spoke to him and how in Damascus Saul boldly preached in Jesus' name. 28 Then he went in and out among them in Jerusalem, preaching boldly in the Lord's name. 29 He was talking and arguing with the Greek-speaking Jews. But they were trying to kill him. 30As soon as the other disciples found out about it, they took him down to Caesarea and sent him away to Tarsus.

31 So the church all over Judea, Galilee, and Samaria had peace and was built up. Living in the fear of the Lord and in the comfort of the Holy Spirit, it grew larger and larger.

Aeneas—Tabitha

32 Now when Peter was going around among all the disciples, he also came down to the holy people living in Lydda. 33 There he found a man by the name of Aeneas who was paralyzed and had been lying on a mat for eight years. 34 "Aeneas," Peter said to him, "Jesus Christ makes you well. Get up and make your bed." And immediately he got up.

35 All who lived in Lydda and Sharon saw him and turned to the Lord.

36 In Joppa there was a disciple by the name of Tabitha,* which in Greek is Dorcas.* She was always doing good works and giving things to the poor. 37 Just at that time she got sick and died; so she was washed and laid in a room upstairs.

38 Lydda is near Joppa. When the disciples heard Peter was in Lydda, they sent two men to him and urged him: "Come to us without delay!"

39 Peter went with them. When he came there, they took him upstairs. There all the widows stood around him; they were crying and showing all the inner and outer garments Dorcas made while she was still with them.

40 But Peter made them all leave the room. He knelt and prayed. Then, turning toward the body, he said, "Tabitha, get up!"

She opened her eyes, and seeing Peter, she sat up. 41 He gave her his hand and helped her stand up. Then he called the holy people, and especially the widows, and gave her back to them alive.

* Both names mean gazelle.

sented her alive. 42And it was known through-out all Joppa; and many believed in the Lord. 43And it came to pass, that he tarried many days in Joppa with one Simon a tanner.

10 There was a certain man in Cesarea called Cornelius, a centurion of the band called the Italian *band*, 2*A* devout *man*, and one that feared God with all his house, which gave much alms to the people, and prayed to God always. 3 He saw in a vision evidently, about the ninth hour of the day, an angel of God coming in to him, and saying unto him, Cornelius. 4And when he looked on him, he was afraid, and said, What is it, Lord? And he said unto him, Thy prayers and thine alms are come up for a memorial be-fore God. 5And now send men to Joppa, and call for *one* Simon, whose surname is Peter: 6 He lodgeth with one Simon a tanner, whose house is by the sea side: he shall tell thee what thou oughtest to do. 7And when the angel which spake unto Cornelius was departed, he called two of his household servants, and a devout soldier of them that waited on him continually; 8And when he had declared all *these* things unto them, he sent them to Joppa.

9 On the morrow, as they went on their jour-ney, and drew nigh unto the city, Peter went up upon the housetop to pray about the sixth hour: 10And he became very hungry, and would have eaten: but while they made ready, he fell into a trance, 11And saw heaven opened, and a certain vessel descending unto him, as it had been a great sheet knit at the four corners, and let down to the earth: 12 Wherein were all manner of fourfooted beasts of the earth, and wild beasts, and creeping things, and fowls of the air. 13And there came a voice to him, Rise, Peter; kill, and eat. 14 But Peter said, Not so, Lord; for I have never eaten any thing that is common or un-clean. 15And the voice *spake* unto him again the second time, What God hath cleansed, *that* call not thou common. 16 This was done thrice: and the vessel was received up again into heaven. 17 Now while Peter doubted in himself what this vision which he had seen should mean, behold, the men which were sent from Cornelius had made inquiry for Simon's house, and stood be-fore the gate, 18And called, and asked whether Simon, which was surnamed Peter, were lodged there.

19 While Peter thought on the vision, the Spirit said unto him, Behold, three men seek thee. 20Arise therefore, and get thee down, and go with them, doubting nothing: for I have sent them. 21 Then Peter went down to the men which were sent unto him from Cornelius; and said, Behold, I am he whom ye seek: what *is* the cause wherefore ye are come? 22 And they said, Cornelius the centurion, a just man, and one that feareth God, and of good report among all the nation of the Jews, was warned from God by a holy angel to send for thee into his house,

sented her alive. 42And it became known all over Joppa, and many believed in the Lord. 43And it came about that he stayed many days in Joppa with a certain tanner, Simon.

10 Now *there was* a certain man at Caesarea named Cornelius, a centurion of what was called the Italian ªCohort. 2 a devout man, and one who feared God with all his household, and gave many ᵇalms to the *Jewish* people, and prayed to God continually. 3About the ᶜninth hour of the day he clearly saw in a vision an angel of God who had *just* come in to him, and said to him, "Cornelius!" 4And fixing his gaze upon him and being much alarmed, he said, "What is it, Lord?" And he said to him, "Your prayers and ᵈalms have ascended as a memorial before God. 5 "And now dispatch *some* men to Joppa, and send for a man *named* Simon, who is also called Peter; 6 he is staying with a certain tanner *named* Simon, whose house is by the sea." 7And when the angel who was speaking to him had departed, he sum-moned two of his servants and a devout soldier of those who were in constant attendance upon him, 8 and after he had explained everything to them, he sent them to Joppa.

9 And on the next day, as they were on their way, and approaching the city, Peter went up on the housetop about the ᵉsixth hour to pray. 10And he became hungry, and was desiring to eat; but while they were making preparations, he fell into a trance; 11 and he *beheld the sky opened up, and a certain ᶠobject like a great sheet coming down, lowered by four corners to the ground, 12 and there were in it all *kinds of* four-footed animals and ᵍcrawling creatures of the earth and birds of the air. 13And a voice came to him, "Arise, Peter, kill and eat!" 14 But Peter said, "By no means, Lord, for I have never eaten anything unholy and unclean." 15And again a voice *came* to him a second time, "What God has cleansed, no *longer* con-sider unholy." 16And this happened three times; and immediately the ᶠobject was taken up into the sky.

17 Now while Peter was greatly perplexed in mind as to what the vision which he had seen might be, behold, the men who had been sent by Cornelius, having asked directions for Si-mon's house, appeared at the gate; 18 and call-ing out, they were asking whether Simon, who was also called Peter, was staying there. 19And while Peter was reflecting on the vision, the Spirit said to him, "Behold, three men are look-ing for you. 20 "But arise, go downstairs, and accompany them without misgivings; for I have sent them Myself." 21And Peter went down to the men and said, "Behold, I am the one you are looking for; what is the reason for which you have come?" 22And they said, "Cornelius a centurion, a righteous and God-fearing man well spoken of by the entire nation of the Jews, was *divinely* directed by a holy angel to send for you *to come* to his house and hear a mes-

[a] Or, *Battalion*. [b] Or, *gifts of charity*. [c] I.e., 3 p.m. [d] Or, *deeds of charity*. [e] I.e., noon. [f] Or, *vessel*. [g] Or possibly, *reptiles*.

WILLIAMS

gave her back to them alive. 42 This became known all over Joppa, and many came to believe in the Lord. 43 So it came about that Peter stayed in Joppa several days, at the house of a tanner named Simon.

10 Colonel Cornelius and friends in Caesarea converted as Peter preaches to them, prepared by a vision thus to do; these heathen believers receive the Holy Spirit as the church in Jerusalem did at Pentecost

Now at Caesarea there was a man named Cornelius, a colonel in what was known as the Italian regiment, 2 a religious man, too, who revered God with all his household, who was always liberal in his many deeds of charity to the people, and who had the habit of praying to God. 3 One afternoon about three o'clock he had a vision and clearly saw an angel of God come to him and say, "Cornelius!"

4 He stared at him and in terror asked, "What is it, sir?"

The angel answered him, "Your prayers and your deeds of charity have gone up and been remembered before God. 5 So now send men to Joppa and invite over a man named Simon, who is also called Peter. 6 He is a guest of a tanner named Simon, whose house is close by the sea."

7 After the angel who had spoken to him had gone, Cornelius called two of his household servants, and a religious soldier who was one of his devoted attendants, 8 and after telling them the whole story, sent them to Joppa.

9 The next day, while those men were traveling on and not far from the town, Peter went up on the housetop about noon to pray. 10 But he got very hungry and wanted something to eat. While they were getting it ready, he fell into a trance 11 and saw the sky opened, and something like a great sheet coming down, lowered to the earth by the four corners, 12 which contained all kinds of four-footed animals, reptiles, and wild birds. 13 A voice came to him, "Get up, Peter, kill something and eat it."

14 But Peter said, "Never by any means, sir, for I have never eaten anything common, or not ceremonially cleansed."

15 A second time the voice came to him, "The things that God has cleansed you must not call unclean." 16 This took place three times; then all at once the thing was taken up into the sky.

17 Now while Peter was still at a loss to know what the vision he had seen could mean, the men who had been sent by Cornelius had asked for the way to Simon's house and had stopped at the gate; 18 and they called and inquired if Simon who was called Peter was staying there. 19 While Peter was meditating on the vision, the Spirit said to him, "There are two men looking for you. 20 Get up and go down, and without hesitation go on with them, for I have sent them."

21 So Peter went down and said to the men, "I am the man you are looking for. What is the purpose of your coming?"

22 They answered, "Cornelius, a colonel in the army, an upright man and one who reveres God, and a man of high reputation with the whole Jewish nation, was instructed by a holy angel to send for you to come to his house and

BECK

42 The news spread all over Joppa, and many believed in the Lord.

Cornelius Sees a Vision

43 Peter stayed for some time with Simon, a tanner, in Joppa.

10 Now, there was a man in Caesarea by the name of Cornelius, a captain in the troop called Italian. 2 He was a religious man, who with all those in his home feared God. He gave much to the poor among the people and was always praying to God.

3 One day about three in the afternoon he had a vision in which he clearly saw God's angel come to him and say to him, "Cornelius!"

4 He stared at the angel and was terrified, "What is it, Lord?" he asked him.

"Your prayers and your gifts to the poor," the angel answered him, "have come up before God as an offering He remembers. 5 And now send men to Joppa, and get Simon, who is also called Peter. 6 He is a guest of Simon, a tanner, whose house is by the sea."

7 When the angel who was speaking to him had left, he called two of his slaves and a God-fearing soldier, one of those who served him regularly. 8 After telling them everything he sent them to Joppa.

Peter Sees a Vision

9 The next day about noon, while they were on their way and getting near the town, Peter went up on the roof to pray. 10 But he got hungry and wanted to eat. While the food was being prepared, he fell into a trance. 11 He saw heaven opened and something like a large linen sheet coming down, being let down by its four corners to the ground. 12 In it were all kinds of animals, four-footed ones and those that creep on the ground, and birds of the air.

13 "Get up, Peter," a voice told him, "kill and eat."

14 "Oh no, Lord!" Peter answered, "I've never eaten anything common or unclean."

15 A voice spoke to him a second time: "Don't make unclean what God has made clean."

16 This happened three times, then the sheet was quickly taken up to the sky.

17 While Peter was still puzzling over the meaning of the vision he had seen, the men sent by Cornelius asked for Simon's house and came to the gate. 18 They called and asked, "Is Simon, who is called Peter, staying here?" 19 Peter was still thinking about the vision when the Spirit said, "There are three men looking for you. 20 Now come, go down, and go with them. Don't treat them as different people, because I sent them."

21 So Peter went down to the men. "I'm the man you're looking for," he said. "What brings you here?"

22 They answered, "Cornelius is a captain, a righteous man who fears God, and all the Jewish people speak well of him. A holy angel told him to bring you to his home and hear what you have to say."

K.J.V.

and to hear words of thee. 23 Then called he them in, and lodged *them*. And on the morrow Peter went away with them, and certain brethren from Joppa accompanied him. 24And the morrow after they entered into Cesarea. And Cornelius waited for them, and had called together his kinsmen and near friends. 25And as Peter was coming in, Cornelius met him, and fell down at his feet, and worshipped *him*. 26 But Peter took him up, saying, Stand up; I myself also am a man. 27And as he talked with him, he went in, and found many that were come together. 28And he said unto them, Ye know how that it is an unlawful thing for a man that is a Jew to keep company, or come unto one of another nation; but God hath shewed me that I should not call any man common or unclean. 29 Therefore came I *unto you* without gainsaying, as soon as I was sent for: I ask therefore for what intent ye have sent for me? 30And Cornelius said, Four days ago I was fasting until this hour; and at the ninth hour I prayed in my house, and, behold, a man stood before me in bright clothing, 31And said, Cornelius, thy prayer is heard, and thine alms are had in remembrance in the sight of God. 32 Send therefore to Joppa, and call hither Simon, whose surname is Peter; he is lodged in the house of *one* Simon a tanner by the sea side: who, when he cometh, shall speak unto thee. 33 Immediately therefore I sent to thee; and thou hast well done that thou art come. Now therefore are we all here present before God, to hear all things that are commanded thee of God.

34 Then Peter opened *his* mouth, and said, Of a truth I perceive that God is no respecter of persons: 35 But in every nation he that feareth him, and worketh righteousness, is accepted with him. 36 The word which *God* sent unto the children of Israel, preaching peace by Jesus Christ: (he is Lord of all:) 37 That word, *I say,* ye know, which was published throughout all Judea, and began from Galilee, after the baptism which John preached; 38 How God anointed Jesus of Nazareth with the Holy Ghost and with power: who went about doing good, and healing all that were oppressed of the devil; for God was with him. 39And we are witnesses of all things which he did both in the land of the Jews, and in Jerusalem; whom they slew and hanged on a tree: 40 Him God raised up the third day, and shewed him openly; 41 Not to all the people, but unto witnesses chosen before of God, *even* to us, who did eat and drink with him after he rose from the dead. 42And he commanded us to preach unto the people, and to testify that it is he which was ordained of God *to be* the Judge of quick and dead. 43 To him give all the prophets witness, that through his name whosoever believeth in him shall receive remission of sins.

44 While Peter yet spake these words, the Holy Ghost fell on all them which heard the word. 45And they of the circumcision which believed were astonished, as many as came with Peter, because that on the Gentiles also was poured out the gift of the Holy Ghost. 46 For they heard them speak with tongues, and magnify God. Then answered Peter, 47 Can any man forbid water, that these should not be baptized, which have received the Holy Ghost as well as we? 48And he commanded them to be baptized in the name of the Lord. Then prayed they him to tarry certain days.

N.A.S.

sage from you." 23And so he invited them in and gave them lodging.

And on the next day he arose and went away with them, and some of the brethren from Joppa accompanied him. 24And on the following day he entered Caesarea. Now Cornelius was waiting for them, and had called together his relatives and close friends. 25And when it came about that Peter entered, Cornelius met him, and fell at his feet and worshiped *him*. 26 But Peter raised him up, saying, "Stand up; I too am *just* a man." 27And as he talked with him, he entered, and found many people assembled. 28And he said to them, "You yourselves know how unlawful it is for a man who is a Jew to associate with a foreigner or to visit him; and *yet* God has shown me that I should not call any man unholy or unclean. 29 "That is why I came without even raising any objection when I was sent for. And so I ask for what reason you have sent for me." 30And Cornelius said, "Four days ago to this hour, I was praying in my house during the ⁿninth hour; and behold, a man stood before me in shining garments, 31 and he *said, 'Cornelius, your prayer has been heard and your alms have been remembered before God. 32 'Send therefore to Joppa and invite Simon, who is also called Peter, to come to you; he is staying at the house of Simon *the* tanner by the sea.' 33 "And so I sent to you immediately, and you have been kind enough to come. Now then, we are all here present before God to hear all that you have been commanded by the Lord." 34And opening his mouth, Peter said:

"I most certainly understand *now* that God is not one to show partiality, 35 but in every nation the man who fears Him and does what is right, is welcome to Him. 36 "The word which He sent to the children of Israel, preaching peace through Jesus Christ (He is Lord of all)— 37 you yourselves know the thing which took place throughout all Judea, starting from Galilee, after the baptism which John proclaimed. 38 *"You know of* Jesus of Nazareth, how God anointed Him with the Holy Spirit and with power, and *how* He went about doing good, and healing all who were oppressed by the devil; for God was with Him. 39 "And we are witnesses of all the things He did both in the land of the Jews and in Jerusalem. And they also put Him to death by hanging Him on a cross. 40 "God raised Him up on the third day, and granted that He should become visible, 41 not to all the people, but to witnesses who were chosen beforehand by God, *that is,* to us, who ate and drank with Him after He arose from the dead. 42 "And He ordered us to preach to the people, and solemnly to testify that this is the One who has been appointed by God as Judge of the living and the dead. 43 "Of Him all the prophets bear witness that through His name every one who believes in Him has received forgiveness of sins."

44 While Peter was still speaking these words, the Holy Spirit fell upon all those who were listening to the message. 45And all the circumcised believers who had come with Peter were amazed, because the gift of the Holy Spirit had been poured out upon the Gentiles also. 46 For they were hearing them speaking with tongues and exalting God. Then Peter answered, 47 "Surely no one can refuse the water for these to be baptized who have received the Holy Spirit just as we *did,* can he?" 48And he ordered them to be baptized in the name of Jesus Christ. Then they asked him to stay on for a few days.

[a] I.e., 3 to 4 p.m.

WILLIAMS

to listen to a message you would bring." 23 So Peter invited them in and entertained them.

24 The next day he started off with them, and some of the brothers in Joppa went along with him. The day after that they reached Caesarea. Cornelius was waiting for him, as he had invited in his kinsmen and close friends. 25 When Peter went into the house, Cornelius met him and fell at his feet and did homage to him. 26 But Peter lifted him to his feet, saying, "Get up, I too am just a man myself."

27 As he continued to talk with him he went into the house and found a great crowd had gathered, 28 and he said to him, "You know that it is against the law for a Jew to associate with a foreigner or to visit one; but God has taught me not to call any man vulgar or ceremonially unclean; 29 so I have come, since I was sent for, without any hesitation."

30 Then Cornelius said, "Four days ago, about this hour, three o'clock in the afternoon, I was praying in my house, and all at once a man in dazzling clothing stood before me, 31 and said, 'Cornelius, your prayer has been heard and your deeds of charity have been remembered by God. 32 So send to Joppa and invite Simon, who is called Peter, to come over. He is being entertained at the house of a tanner named Simon, by the seashore.' 33 So at once I sent for you, and you have been kind enough to come. So now we are all here in God's presence to listen to anything that the Lord has commanded you to say."

34 Then Peter opened his mouth and said, "Now I really see that God shows no partiality, 35 but in every nation the man who reveres God and practices doing right is acceptable to Him. 36 He has sent His message to the descendants of Israel, by telling them the good news of peace through Jesus Christ. He is Lord of all. 37 You know the story yourselves that spread all over Judea, beginning from Galilee after the baptism that John preached, 38 how God consecrated Jesus of Nazareth with the Holy Spirit and power, and then He went about doing good and curing all who were overpowered by the devil, because God was with Him. 39 We are witnesses of everything that He did in the country of the Jews and in Jerusalem. Yet they murdered Him by hanging Him upon a tree. 40 But God raised Him to life on the third day, and permitted Him to be clearly seen, 41 not by all the people but by witnesses whom God had beforehand appointed, namely, but us who ate and drank with Him after His resurrection from the dead. 42 He also ordered us to proclaim to the people and solemnly to testify that this is the One whom God has appointed to be the Judge of the living and the dead. 43 To this very One all the prophets bear witness that everyone who believes in Him is to receive the forgiveness of sins through His name."

44 While Peter was still speaking these truths, the Holy Spirit fell upon all who were listening to the message. 45 Then the Jewish believers who had gone along with Peter were astounded because the gift of the Holy Spirit had been showered upon the heathen too, 46 for they heard them speaking in foreign languages and telling of the greatness of God. Then Peter asked, 47 "No one can refuse the use of water, can he, for these to be baptized, since they have received the Holy Spirit just as we did ourselves?" 48 So he ordered them to be baptized in the name of Jesus Christ.

Then they begged him to stay on there a few days.

BECK

23 Peter asked them to come in, and they were his guests.

Peter and Cornelius

23 The next day he left with them, and some fellow disciples from Joppa went along. 24 The following day he came to Caesarea. Cornelius was expecting them and had called his relatives and close friends together.

25 When Peter was about to go in, Cornelius met him, bowed down at his feet, and worshiped him. 26 But Peter made him stand up. "Get up," he said. "I'm only a man."

27 Talking with him, he went in and found many people had gathered. 28 "You understand," he said to them, "how wrong it is for a Jew to live with or visit anyone who's not a Jew. But God has taught me not to call anyone common or unclean. 29 That's why I didn't object to coming here when you sent for me. Now I want to know: Why did you send for me?"

30 "Three days ago," Cornelius answered, "I was at home praying till this hour, at three in the afternoon, when a man in shining clothes stood in front of me. 31 'Cornelius,' he said, 'God has heard your prayer and remembers your gifts to the poor. 32 Now send to Joppa and ask Simon, who is called Peter, to come to you. He's a guest in the home of Simon, a tanner, by the sea.' 33 So I sent to you immediately, and it was good of you to come. We're all here before God now, ready to hear everything the Lord has ordered you to say."

34 Then Peter spoke: "Now I really understand that *God doesn't prefer one person to another.*[61] 35 It doesn't matter what people you belong to; if you fear Him and do what's right, He accepts you. 36 *He sent His Word*[62] to the people of Israel to *bring the news of peace*[63] in Jesus Christ—He is Lord of all! 37 You know what happened in the whole country of the Jews, how after the baptism that John preached, 38 *God anointed* Jesus from Nazareth *with the Holy Spirit*[64] and power, and Jesus, beginning in Galilee, went around doing good and healing all who were under the tyranny of the devil, because God was with Him. 39 We have seen everything He did in the land of the Jews and in Jerusalem, and we can tell about it. Men *hanged Him on a cross*[65] and killed Him. 40 But God raised Him on the third day and showed Him to us—41 not to all our people but to us whom God had chosen to be witnesses and who ate and drank with Him after He rose from the dead. 42 He ordered us to preach to the people and warn them that 43 God has appointed Him to judge the living and the dead. All the prophets declare that through His name everyone who believes in Him has his sins forgiven."

44 While Peter was still speaking, the Holy Spirit came down on all who heard the Word. 45 All the Jewish believers who had come with Peter were surprised the gift of the Holy Spirit had been poured out also on people who were not Jews. 46 They heard them speaking in other languages and praising God.

47 Then Peter asked, "Can anyone keep the water from baptizing these people? They have received the Holy Spirit just as we did." 48 And he ordered them baptized in the name of Jesus Christ.

Then they asked him to stay several days.

[61] Deut. 10:17
[62] Ps. 107:20; 147:18
[63] Is. 52:7; Nah. 1:15
[64] Is. 61:1
[65] Deut. 21:22-23

K.J.V.

11 And the apostles and brethren that were in Judea heard that the Gentiles had also received the word of God. 2And when Peter was come up to Jerusalem, they that were of the circumcision contended with him, 3 Saying, Thou wentest in to men uncircumcised, and didst eat with them. 4 But Peter rehearsed *the matter* from the beginning, and expounded *it* by order unto them, saying, 5 I was in the city of Joppa praying: and in a trance I saw a vision, A certain vessel descend, as it had been a great sheet, let down from heaven by four corners; and it came even to me: 6 Upon the which when I had fastened mine eyes, I considered, and saw four-footed beasts of the earth, and wild beasts, and creeping things, and fowls of the air. 7And I heard a voice saying unto me, Arise, Peter; slay and eat. 8 But I said, Not so, Lord: for nothing common or unclean hath at any time entered into my mouth. 9 But the voice answered me again from heaven, What God hath cleansed, *that* call not thou common. 10And this was done three times: and all were drawn up again into heaven. 11And, behold, immediately there were three men already come unto the house where I was, sent from Cesarea unto me. 12And the Spirit bade me go with them, nothing doubting. Moreover these six brethren accompanied me, and we entered into the man's house: 13And he shewed us how he had seen an angel in his house, which stood and said unto him, Send men to Joppa, and call for Simon, whose surname is Peter; 14 Who shall tell thee words, whereby thou and all thy house shall be saved. 15And as I began to speak, the Holy Ghost fell on them, as on us at the beginning. 16 Then remembered I the word of the Lord, how that he said, John indeed baptized with water; but ye shall be baptized with the Holy Ghost. 17 Forasmuch then as God gave them the like gift as *he did* unto us, who believed on the Lord Jesus Christ, what was I, that I could withstand God? 18 When they heard these things, they held their peace, and glorified God, saying, Then hath God also to the Gentiles granted repentance unto life.

19 Now they which were scattered abroad upon the persecution that arose about Stephen travelled as far as Phenice, and Cyprus, and Antioch, preaching the word to none but unto the Jews only. 20And some of them were men of Cyprus and Cyrene, which, when they were come to Antioch, spake unto the Grecians, preaching the Lord Jesus. 21And the hand of the Lord was with them: and a great number believed, and turned unto the Lord.

22 Then tidings of these things came unto the ears of the church which was in Jerusalem: and they sent forth Barnabas, that he should go as far as Antioch. 23 Who, when he came, and had seen the grace of God, was glad, and exhorted them all, that with purpose of heart they would cleave unto the Lord. 24 For he was a good man,

N.A.S.

11 Now the apostles and the brethren who were throughout Judea heard that the Gentiles also had received the word of God. 2And when Peter came up to Jerusalem, those who were circumcised took issue with him, 3 saying, "You went to uncircumcised men and ate with them." 4 But Peter began *speaking* and *proceeded* to explain to them in orderly sequence, saying, 5 "I was in the city of Joppa praying; and in a trance I saw a vision, a certain object coming down like a great sheet lowered by four corners from the sky; and it came right down to me, 6 and when I had fixed my gaze upon it and was observing it, I saw the four-footed animals of the earth and the wild beasts and the ªcrawling creatures and the birds of the air. 7 "And I also heard a voice saying to me, 'Arise, Peter; kill and eat.' 8 "But I said, 'By no means, Lord, for nothing unholy or unclean has ever entered my mouth.' 9 "But a voice from heaven answered a second time, 'What God has cleansed, no longer consider unholy.' 10 "And this happened three times, and everything was drawn back up into the sky. 11 "And behold, at that moment three men appeared before the house in which we were *staying*, having been sent to me from Caesarea. 12 "And the Spirit told me to go with them without misgivings. And these six brethren also went with me, and we entered the man's house. 13 "And he reported to us how he had seen the angel standing in his house, and saying, 'Send to Joppa, and have Simon, who is also called Peter, brought here; 14 and he shall speak words to you by which you will be saved, you and all your household.' 15 "And as I began to speak, the Holy Spirit fell upon them, just as *He did* upon us at the beginning. 16 "And I remembered the word of the Lord, how He used to say, 'John baptized with water, but you shall be baptized with the Holy Spirit.' 17 "If God therefore gave to them the same gift as *He gave* to us also after believing in the Lord Jesus Christ, who was I that I could stand in God's way?" 18And when they heard this, they quieted down, and glorified God, saying, "Well then, God has granted to the Gentiles also the repentance *that leads* to life."

19 So then those who were scattered because of the persecution that arose in connection with Stephen made their way to Phoenicia and Cyprus and Antioch, speaking the word to no one except to Jews alone. 20 But there were some of them, men of Cyprus and Cyrene, who came to Antioch and *began* speaking to the ᵇGreeks also, preaching the Lord Jesus. 21And the hand of the Lord was with them, and a large number who believed turned to the Lord. 22And the news about them reached the ears of the church at Jerusalem, and they sent Barnabas off to Antioch. 23 Then when he had come and witnessed the grace of God, he rejoiced and *began* to encourage them all with resolute heart to remain *true* to the Lord; 24 for he was a good man, and full of the Holy

---

[a] Or possibly, *reptiles.* [b] Some mss. read, *Greek-speaking Jews.*

WILLIAMS

11 Peter defends himself before the church in Jerusalem for eating with the heathen; the first church on heathen soil organized at Antioch; Barnabas and Saul conduct a great revival there; they take a contribution from Antioch Christians to suffering Jewish Christians

Now the apostles and the brothers all over Judea heard that the heathen too had accepted God's message. 2 So when Peter returned to Jerusalem, the champions of circumcision began to bring charges against him 3 for having visited and eaten with men who were not Jews.*

4 Then Peter explained the whole matter to them from beginning to end. He said, 5 "I was praying in the town of Joppa, and while I was praying I fell in a trance and had a vision. I saw something like a great sheet coming down out of the sky, lowered by the four corners; and it came right down to me. 6 With fixed eyes I kept looking at it and saw all kinds of four-footed animals, wild beasts, reptiles, and wild birds. 7 And I heard a voice say to me, 'Get up, Peter, kill something and eat it!' 8 But I answered, 'Never by any means, sir, for nothing common or not ceremonially cleansed has ever passed my lips.' 9 Then the voice from heaven answered again, 'The things that God has cleansed you must not call unclean.' 10 This took place three times; then all at once the whole thing was drawn back into the sky. 11 Just at that moment three men, who had been sent from Caesarea for me, stopped at the house where we were staying. 12 And the Spirit told me to go with them without any hesitation at all. These six brothers, too, went with me, and we all went into the man's house. 13 Then he told us how he had seen the angel stand in his house and say to him, 'Send to Joppa and invite Simon, who is called Peter, to come over; 14 he will tell you truths through which you and your whole household will be saved.' 15 When I began to speak, the Holy Spirit fell upon them as He did upon us at the beginning, 16 and I remembered the saying of the Lord, 'John baptized in water, but you will be baptized in the Holy Spirit.' 17 So if God had given them the same gift that He gave us when we believed upon the Lord Jesus Christ, who was I to try—and how could I if I tried—to thwart God?"

18 When they heard this, they had no answer to make, but gave God the glory, saying, "So God has given even the heathen the repentance that leads to life."

19 Now the fugitives from the persecution that started over Stephen went all the way to Phoenicia, Cyprus, and Antioch, telling the message to none but Jews. 20 But there were some of them, men from Cyprus and Cyrene, who on reaching Antioch began to speak to the Greeks too, and proceeded to tell them the good news about the Lord Jesus. 21 And the hand of the Lord was with them, and a large number of people believed and turned to the Lord. 22 Now the news about them came to the ears of the church at Jerusalem, and so they sent Barnabas all the way to Antioch. 23 When he reached there and saw the spiritual blessing God had given them,*b* he was delighted, and continuously encouraged them all with hearty purpose to continue to be devoted to the Lord; 24 for he

BECK

Peter Defends Himself

11 The apostles and other disciples in all Judea heard: "The non-Jewish people, too, have accepted God's Word." 2 But when Peter went up to Jerusalem, those who still believed in circumcision disagreed with him. 3 "You went to visit uncircumcised men," they said, "and you ate with them."

4 Then Peter explained to them point by point what had happened. 5 "I was in the town of Joppa praying," he said, "when in a trance I saw a vision: Something like a large linen sheet was coming down. It was lowered by its four corners from the sky, and came down to me. 6 Looking in, I examined it and saw four-footed animals of the earth, wild animals, reptiles, and birds of the air. 7 I also heard a voice telling me, 'Get up, Peter, kill and eat.'

8 "But I answered, 'Oh no, Lord. Nothing common or unclean has ever come into my mouth.'

9 "A voice spoke from heaven a second time, 'Don't make unclean what God has made clean.' 10 This happened three times. Then all of it was pulled up to the sky again.

11 "At that moment three men, sent to me from Caesarea, came to the house we were in. 12 The Spirit told me to go with them and not treat them as different people. These six fellow disciples went with me, and we came into the man's home.

13 "He told us how he had seen the angel standing in his home and saying, 'Send to Joppa and get Simon, who is called Peter. 14 What he will tell you will save you and everybody in your home.'

15 "While I was speaking, the Holy Spirit came down on these people as He originally came on us, 16 and I had to think of what the Lord had said: 'John baptized with water, but you will be baptized with the Holy Spirit.' 17 Now if God gave them the same gift He gave us when we began to believe in the Lord Jesus Christ, who was I—could I stop God?"

18 When the others heard this, they kept quiet. And they praised God, saying, "Then God has given repentance also to the non-Jewish people so that they will live."

The New Church in Antioch

19 The people scattered by the persecution that broke out over Stephen went as far as Phoenicia, Cyprus, and Antioch, and they spoke the Word only to the Jews. 20 But among them were some men from Cyprus and Cyrene who came to Antioch and started talking also to the non-Jews, telling them the good news of the Lord Jesus. 21 The Lord's hand was with them, and a large number believed and turned to the Lord.

22 The church in Jerusalem heard the news about them, and they sent Barnabas to Antioch. 23 When he came there, he was delighted to see what God's love had done, and he urged them all with a hearty determination to be faithful to the Lord. 24 He was a good man, full of the

---

[a] Lit., *not circumcised.* [b] Grk., *the grace or favor of God.*

K.J.V.

and full of the Holy Ghost and of faith: and much people was added unto the Lord. 25 Then departed Barnabas to Tarsus, for to seek Saul: 26And when he had found him, he brought him unto Antioch. And it came to pass, that a whole year they assembled themselves with the church, and taught much people. And the disciples were called Christians first in Antioch.

27 And in these days came prophets from Jerusalem unto Antioch. 28And there stood up one of them named Agabus, and signified by the Spirit that there should be great dearth throughout all the world: which came to pass in the days of Claudius Cesar. 29 Then the disciples, every man according to his ability, determined to send relief unto the brethren which dwelt in Judea: 30 Which also they did, and sent it to the elders by the hands of Barnabas and Saul.

12 Now about that time Herod the king stretched forth *his* hands to vex certain of the church. 2And he killed James the brother of John with the sword. 3And because he saw it pleased the Jews, he proceeded further to take Peter also. (Then were the days of unleavened bread.) 4And when he had apprehended him, he put *him* in prison, and delivered *him* to four quaternions of soldiers to keep him; intending after Easter to bring him forth to the people. 5 Peter therefore was kept in prison: but prayer was made without ceasing of the church unto God for him. 6And when Herod would have brought him forth, the same night Peter was sleeping between two soldiers, bound with two chains: and the keepers before the door kept the prison. 7And, behold, the angel of the Lord came upon *him*, and a light shined in the prison: and he smote Peter on the side, and raised him up, saying, Arise up quickly. And his chains fell off from *his* hands. 8And the angel said unto him, Gird thyself, and bind on thy sandals: and so he did. And he saith unto him, Cast thy garment about thee, and follow me. 9And he went out, and followed him; and wist not that it was true which was done by the angel; but thought he saw a vision. 10 When they were past the first and the second ward, they came unto the iron gate that leadeth unto the city; which opened to them of his own accord: and they went out, and passed on through one street; and forthwith the angel departed from him. 11And when Peter was come to himself, he said, Now I know of a surety, that the Lord hath sent his angel, and hath delivered me out of the hand of Herod, and *from* all the expectation of the people of the Jews. 12And when he had considered *the thing*, he came to the house of Mary the mother of John, whose surname was Mark; where many were gathered together praying. 13And as Peter knocked at the door of the gate, a damsel came to hearken, named Rhoda. 14And when she knew Peter's voice, she opened not the gate for gladness, but ran in, and told how Peter

N.A.S.

Spirit and of faith. And considerable numbers were brought to the Lord. 25And he left for Tarsus to look for Saul; 26 and when he had found him, he brought him to Antioch. And it came about that for an entire year they met with the church, and taught considerable numbers; and the disciples were first called Christians in Antioch.

27 Now at this time some prophets came down from Jerusalem to Antioch. 28And one of them named Agabus stood up and *began* to indicate by the Spirit that there would certainly be a great famine all over the world. And this took place in the *reign* of Claudius. 29And in the proportion that any of the disciples had means, each of them determined to send *a contribution* for the relief of the brethren living in Judea. 30And this they did, sending it in charge of Barnabas and Saul to the elders.

12 Now about that time Herod the king laid hands on some who belonged to the church, in order to mistreat them. 2And he had James the brother of John put to death with the sword. 3And when he saw that it pleased the Jews, he proceeded to arrest Peter also. Now it was during the days of *the Feast of* Unleavened Bread. 4And when he had seized him, he put him in prison, delivering him to four squads of soldiers to guard him, intending after the Passover to bring him out before the people. 5 So Peter was kept in the prison, but prayer for him was being made fervently by the church to God. 6And on the very night when Herod was about to bring him forward, Peter was sleeping between two soldiers, bound with two chains; and guards in front of the door were watching over the prison. 7And behold, an angel of the Lord suddenly appeared, and a light shone in the cell; and he struck Peter's side and roused him, saying, "Get up quickly." And his chains fell off his hands. 8And the angel said to him, "Gird yourself and put on your sandals." And he did so. And he *said to him, "Wrap your cloak around you and follow me." 9And he went out and continued to follow, and he did not know that what was being done by the angel was real, but thought he was seeing a vision. 10And when they had passed the first and second guard, they came to the iron gate that leads into the city, which opened for them by itself; and they went out and went along one street; and immediately the angel departed from him. 11And when Peter came to himself, he said, "Now I know for sure that the Lord has sent forth His angel and rescued me from the hand of Herod and from all that the Jewish people were expecting." 12And when he realized *this*, he went to the house of Mary, the mother of John who was also called Mark, where many were gathered together and were praying. 13And when he knocked at the door of the gate, a servant-girl named Rhoda came to answer. 14And when she recognized Peter's voice, because of her joy she did not open the gate, but ran in and announced that Peter was standing in front of

WILLIAMS

was a good man, and full of the Holy Spirit and faith. So a large number of people were united to the Lord. 25 Then Barnabas went over to Tarsus to search out Saul, 26 and after he had found him, he brought him to Antioch.

Now for a whole year their meeting with the church lasted, and they taught large numbers of people. It was at Antioch too that the disciples first came to be known as "Christians."

27 At that time some prophets from Jerusalem came down to Antioch, 28 and one of them named Agabus got up and, through the Holy Spirit, foretold that there was going to be a great famine all over the world, which occurred in the reign of Claudius. 29 So the disciples decided to send a contribution, each in proportion to his prosperity, to help the brothers who lived in Judea. 30 And this they did and sent it to the elders by Barnabas and Saul.

12 *James beheaded, Peter put into prison; the church prays for Peter's release; an angel releases him; the guardsmen killed for letting him get out; Herod Agrippa meets a tragic death for accepting praise as a God.*

About that time Herod arrested some who belonged to the church, in order to do them violence. 2 He had James the brother of John murdered with a sword, 3 and when he saw that this was agreeable to the Jews, he proceeded to arrest Peter too—it was at the time of the feast of Unleavened Bread. 4 He had him seized and put into prison, and turned him over to four squads of soldiers to guard him, planning after the Passover to bring him out again to the people. 5 So Peter was being kept in prison, but earnest prayer to God for him was persistently made by the church.

6 Now just as Herod was going to bring him out, that is, the very night before, Peter was fastened with two chains and was sleeping between two soldiers, and the guards were at the door guarding the prison. 7 And suddenly an angel of the Lord stood by him, and a light shone in his cell, and by striking Peter on the side the angel woke him, and said, "Get up quickly!" At once the chains fell off his hands.

8 Then the angel said to him, "Tighten your belt and put on your shoes!" He did so.

Then the angel said to him, "Put on your coat and follow me!"

9 So he kept following him out, but he was not conscious that what was being done by the angel was real; he thought he was dreaming it. 10 They passed the first guard, then the second, and at last came to the iron gate which led into the city. The gate of itself opened to them, and they passed out and proceeded one block, when all at once the angel left him.

11 Then Peter came to himself and said, "Now I really know that the Lord has sent His angel and rescued me from the power of Herod and from all that the Jewish people were expecting to do to me."

12 When he became conscious of his situation, he went to the house of Mary, the mother of John who was also called Mark, where a large number of people had met and were praying. 13 When he knocked at the outer door, a servant-girl named Rhoda came to answer it, 14 and on recognizing Peter's voice, in her joy she failed to open the door but ran and told them that Peter was standing at the door.

BECK

Holy Spirit and faith. And a large crowd was brought to the Lord.

25 Then Barnabas left for Tarsus to look for Saul. 26 He found him and brought him to Antioch. And they were guests of the church for a whole year and taught a large crowd.— It was in Antioch the disciples were first called Christians.

27 At that time some prophets came from Jerusalem down to Antioch. 28 One of them by the name of Agabus got up and by the Spirit predicted there would be a big famine all over the world (it came while Claudius was emperor). 29 Every one of the disciples decided, as he was able, to send relief to the fellow Christians living in Judea. 30 They did this by sending Barnabas and Saul to bring it to the elders.

An Angel Frees Peter

12 At that time King Herod arrested some members of the church in order to mistreat them. 2 He killed John's brother James with a sword. When he saw how the Jews liked that, he arrested Peter too. 3 It happened during the Passover days of bread without yeast. 4 When he arrested Peter, he put him in prison and had sixteen soldiers in squads of four guard him. He wanted to bring him before the people after the Passover. 5 So Peter was kept in prison.

But the church was earnestly praying to God for him. 6 The night before Herod was going to bring him before the people, Peter, bound with two chains, was sleeping between two soldiers, and guards in front of the door were watching the prison.

7 Suddenly the Lord's angel stood near him, and a light shone in his cell. He struck Peter on his side, woke him, and said, "Get up! Quick!" Peter's chains dropped from his wrists.

8 "Fasten your belt," the angel told him, "and tie on your sandals!" He did this. "Put on your garment," the angel told him, "and follow me."

9 Peter followed him outside, not realizing the angel was actually doing this. He thought he was seeing a vision. 10 They passed through the first guards and the second guards and came to the iron gate leading into the city. It opened by itself before them, and they went outside and up the street. There the angel suddenly left him.

11 "Now I'm sure the Lord sent His angel," Peter said when he was himself again, "and He rescued me from Herod and from everything the Jewish people were expecting."

Peter Comes to His Friends

12 When he realized what had happened, He went to the home of Mary (the mother of John —the one called Mark), where many had gathered and were praying. 13 He knocked at the entrance gate, and a maid by the name of Rose came to answer. 14 Recognizing Peter's voice, she was so happy she didn't open the gate but ran in and announced, "Peter is standing at the gate!"

K.J.V.

stood before the gate. 15And they said unto her, Thou art mad. But she constantly affirmed that it was even so. Then said they, It is his angel. 16 But Peter continued knocking: and when they had opened *the door,* and saw him, they were astonished. 17 But he, beckoning unto them with the hand to hold their peace, declared unto them how the Lord had brought him out of the prison. And he said, Go shew these things unto James, and to the brethren. And he departed, and went into another place. 18 Now as soon as it was day, there was no small stir among the soldiers, what was become of Peter. 19And when Herod had sought for him, and found him not, he examined the keepers, and commanded that *they* should be put to death. And he went down from Judea to Cesarea, and *there* abode.

20 And Herod was highly displeased with them of Tyre and Sidon: but they came with one accord to him, and, having made Blastus the king's chamberlain their friend, desired peace; because their country was nourished by the king's. *country.* 21And upon a set day Herod, arrayed in royal apparel, sat upon his throne, and made an oration unto them. 22And the people gave a shout, *saying, It is* the voice of a god, and not of a man. 23And immediately the angel of the Lord smote him, because he gave not God the glory: and he was eaten of worms, and gave up the ghost.

24 But the word of God grew and multiplied. 25And Barnabas and Saul returned from Jerusalem, when they had fulfilled *their* ministry, and took with them John, whose surname was Mark.

N.A.S.

the gate. 15And they said to her, "You are out of your mind!" But she kept insisting that it was so. And they kept saying, "It is his angel." 16 But Peter continued knocking; and when they had opened, they saw him and were amazed. 17 But motioning to them with his hand to be silent, he described to them how the Lord had led him out of the prison. And he said, "Report these things to James and the brethren." And he departed and went to another place.

18 Now when day came, there was no small disturbance among the soldiers *as to* what could have become of Peter. 19And when Herod had searched for him and had not found him, he examined the guards and ordered that they be led away *to execution.* And he went down from Judea to Caesarea and was spending time there.

20 Now he was very angry with the people of Tyre and Sidon; and with one accord they came to him, and having won over Blastus the king's chamberlain, they were asking for peace, because their country was fed by the king's country. 21And on an appointed day Herod, having put on his royal apparel, took his seat on the rostrum and *began* delivering an address to them. 22And the people kept crying out, "The voice of a god and not of a man!" 23And immediately an angel of the Lord struck him because he did not give God the glory, and he was eaten by worms and died.

24 But the word of the Lord continued to grow and to be multiplied.

25 And Barnabas and Saul returned from Jerusalem when they had fulfilled their mission, taking along with *them* John, who was also called Mark.

13 Now there were in the church that was at Antioch certain prophets and teachers; as Barnabas, and Simeon that was called Niger, and Lucius of Cyrene, and Manaen, which had been brought up with Herod the tetrarch, and Saul. 2As they ministered to the Lord, and fasted, the Holy Ghost said, Separate me Barnabas and Saul for the work whereunto I have called them. 3And when they had fasted and prayed, and laid *their* hands on them, they sent *them* away.

4 So they, being sent forth by the Holy Ghost, departed unto Seleucia; and from thence they sailed to Cyprus. 5And when they were at Salamis, they preached the word of God in the synagogues of the Jews: and they had also John to *their* minister. 6And when they had gone through the isle unto Paphos, they found a certain sorcerer, a false prophet, a Jew, whose name *was* Bar-jesus: 7 Which was with the deputy of the country, Sergius Paulus, a prudent man; who called for Barnabas and Saul, and desired to hear the word of God. 8 But Elymas the

13 Now there were at Antioch, in the church that was *there,* prophets and teachers: Barnabas, and Simeon who was called Niger, and Lucius of Cyrene, and Manaen who had been brought up with Herod the tetrarch, and Saul. 2And while they were ministering to the Lord and fasting, the Holy Spirit said, "Set apart for me Barnabas and Saul for the work to which I have called them." 3 Then, when they had fasted and prayed and laid their hands on them, they sent them away.

4 So, being sent out by the Holy Spirit, they went down to Seleucia and from there they sailed to Cyprus. 5And when they reached Salamis, they *began* to proclaim the word of God in the synagogues of the Jews; and they also had John as their helper. 6And when they had gone through the whole island as far as Paphos, they found a certain magician, a Jewish false prophet whose name was Bar-Jesus, 7 who was with the proconsul, Sergius Paulus, a man of intelligence. This man summoned Barnabas and Saul and sought to hear the word of God. 8 But Elymas the magician (for

WILLIAMS

15 They said to her, "You are crazy!" But she persistently insisted that it was so. Then they said, "It is his guardian angel!" *

16 But Peter, meanwhile, kept on knocking. So they opened the door, and when they saw him, they were astounded. 17 With his hand he motioned to them to be quiet, and then he told them how the Lord had brought him out of the prison. He added, "Tell all these things to James and the brothers." Then he left them and went somewhere else.

18 When morning came, there was no little commotion among the soldiers as to what had become of Peter. 19 Herod had search made for him, and when he could not find him, he examined the guards and ordered them to be put to death. Then he left Judea for Caesarea, and stayed there.

20 Now Herod cherished a bitter grudge against the people of Tyre and Sidon. So in a united body they came to meet him, and after winning the favor of Blastus, the king's chamberlain, they asked for peace, because their country depended for its food-supply upon the king's country. 21 So, on a day appointed, Herod, dressed in his royal robes, took his seat on his throne, and made them a popular address, 22 and the people shouted, "It is a god's voice, not a man's!"

23 But the angel of the Lord at once struck him down, because he did not give the glory to God; he was eaten by worms, and so died. 24 But the message of the Lord continued to grow and spread.

25 When Barnabas and Saul had finished their helpful service, they returned from Jerusalem, and took along with them John who was called Mark.

13 *Barnabas and Saul the world's first foreign missionaries; sent out by the Spirit through the church at Antioch; visit Cyprus, Pisidian Antioch, Iconium, Lystra, and Derbe, making many converts and founding churches*

Now in the church at Antioch there were prophets and teachers, Barnabas, Simeon who is called Niger, Lucius the Cyrenian, Manaen who was an intimate friend* of the governor, and Saul. 2 While they were worshiping the Lord and fasting, the Holy Spirit said, "Set apart for me Barnabas and Saul, for the work to which I have called them." 3 So after fasting and praying, they laid their hands upon them and let them go.

4 So, as they were sent out by the Holy Spirit, they went down to Seleucia, and from that port sailed away to Cyprus. 5 When they reached Salamis, they began to preach God's message in the Jewish synagogues. They had John with them as their assistant.

6 Then they went through the whole island as far as Paphos, and there they found a Jewish magician and false prophet whose name was Barjesus. 7 He was an intimate friend of the governor, Sergius Paulus, who was an intelligent man. The governor sent for Barnabas and Saul and in this way tried to hear God's message. 8 But Elymas the magician—for this is the mean-

BECK

15 "You're crazy!" they told her. But she insisted it was so. "It's his angel," they said.

16 But Peter kept on knocking. When they opened the gate, they were surprised to see him. 17 He waved his hand to quiet them down and told them how the Lord had taken him out of the prison. "Tell James and the other Christians about this," he said. Then he left and went to another place.

18 In the morning the soldiers were very much upset as they asked, "What happened to Peter?" 19 Herod searched for him but didn't find him. So he examined the guards and ordered them executed.

Herod Dies

19 Then Herod left Judea, went down to Caesarea, and stayed there awhile.

20 He had a violent quarrel with the people of Tyre and Sidon. So they came to him in a body. After they had won over Blastus, who took care of the king's bedroom, they asked for peace because the king's country provided food for their country.

21 On a day that was set, Herod put on his royal robe, sat on the platform, and made a speech to them. 22 The people shouted, "It's a god speaking, not a man!"

23 Immediately the Lord's angel struck him because he didn't give glory to God. He was eaten by worms, and he died.

24 But God's Word continued to spread and win many followers.

On Cyprus

25 After Barnabas and Saul had delivered the offering for relief, they came back from Jerusalem, bringing with them John, also called Mark.

13 The following were prophets and teachers in the church at Antioch: Barnabas, Symeon, called Black, Lucius from Cyrene, Manaen, who had been raised with Herod the governor, and Saul.

2 While the Christians were worshiping the Lord and fasting, the Holy Spirit said, "Set Barnabas and Saul apart for Me to do the work I called them for."

3 Then they fasted and prayed, laid their hands on them, and let them go. 4 And so they, sent by the Holy Spirit, went down to Seleucia and from there sailed to Cyprus. 5 They came to Salamis and there started to preach God's Word in the synagogs of the Jews. They also had John to help them. 6 They went through the whole island as far as Paphos. There they found a Jewish sorcerer and false prophet by the name of Barjesus, 7 who was with the proconsul Sergius Paulus, an intelligent man. He sent for Barnabas and Saul and wanted to hear God's Word. 8 But Elymas, the sorcerer (that was

[a] Lit., *his angel,* guardian implied.
[a] So in inscriptions (Deissmann).

363

K.J.V.

sorcerer (for so is his name by interpretation) withstood them, seeking to turn away the deputy from the faith. 9 Then Saul, (who also *is called* Paul,) filled with the Holy Ghost, set his eyes on him, 10And said, O full of all subtilty and all mischief, *thou* child of the devil, *thou* enemy of all righteousness, wilt thou not cease to pervert the right ways of the Lord? 11And now, behold, the hand of the Lord *is* upon thee, and thou shalt be blind, not seeing the sun for a season. And immediately there fell on him a mist and a darkness; and he went about seeking some to lead him by the hand. 12 Then the deputy, when he saw what was done, believed, being astonished at the doctrine of the Lord. 13 Now when Paul and his company loosed from Paphos, they came to Perga in Pamphylia: and John departing from them returned to Jerusalem.

14 But when they departed from Perga, they came to Antioch in Pisidia, and went into the synagogue on the sabbath day, and sat down. 15And after the reading of the law and the prophets, the rulers of the synagogue sent unto them, saying, *Ye* men *and* brethren, if ye have any word of exhortation for the people, say on. 16 Then Paul stood up, and beckoning with *his* hand said, Men of Israel, and ye that fear God, give audience. 17 The God of this people of Israel chose our fathers, and exalted the people when they dwelt as strangers in the land of Egypt, and with a high arm brought he them out of it. 18And about the time of forty years suffered he their manners in the wilderness. 19And when he had destroyed seven nations in the land of Chanaan, he divided their land to them by lot. 20And after that he gave *unto them* judges about the space of four hundred and fifty years, until Samuel the prophet. 21And afterward they desired a king; and God gave unto them Saul the son of Cis, a man of the tribe of Benjamin, by the space of forty years. 22And when he had removed him, he raised up unto them David to be their king; to whom also he gave testimony, and said, I have found David the *son* of Jesse, a man after mine own heart, which shall fulfil all my will. 23 Of this man's seed hath God, according to *his* promise, raised unto Israel a Saviour, Jesus: 24 When John had first preached before his coming the baptism of repentance to all the people of Israel. 25And as John fulfilled his course, he said, Whom think ye that I am? I am not *he*. But, behold, there cometh one after me, whose shoes of *his* feet I am not worthy to loose. 26 Men *and* brethren, children of the stock of Abraham, and whosoever among you feareth God, to you is the word of this salvation sent. 27 For they that dwell at Jerusalem, and their rulers, because they knew him not, nor yet the voices of the prophets which are read every sabbath day, they have fulfilled *them* in condemning *him*. 28And though they found no cause of death *in him*, yet desired they Pilate that he should be slain. 29And when they had fulfilled all that was written of him, they took *him* down from the tree, and laid *him* in a sepulchre. 30 But God raised him from the dead: 31And he

N.A.S.

thus his name is translated) was opposing them, seeking to turn the proconsul away from the faith. 9 But Saul, who was also *known as* Paul, filled with the Holy Spirit, fixed his gaze upon him, 10 and said, "You who are full of all deceit and fraud, you son of the devil, you enemy of all righteousness, will you not cease to make crooked the straight ways of the Lord? 11 "And now, behold, the hand of the Lord is upon you, and you will be blind and not see the sun for a time." And immediately a mist and a darkness fell upon him, and he went about seeking those who would lead him by the hand. 12 Then the proconsul believed when he saw what had happened, being amazed at the teaching of the Lord.

13 Now Paul and his companions put out to sea from Paphos and came to Perga in Pamphylia; and John left them and returned to Jerusalem. 14 But going on from Perga, they arrived at Pisidian Antioch, and on the Sabbath day they went into the synagogue and sat down. 15And after the reading of the Law and the Prophets the synagogue officials sent to them, saying, "Brethren, if you have any word of exhortation for the people, say it." 16And Paul stood up, and motioning with his hand, he said,

"Men of Israel, and you who fear God, listen: 17 "The God of this people Israel chose our fathers, and made the people great during their stay in the land of Egypt, and with an uplifted arm He led them out from it. 18 "And for about a period of forty years He put up with them in the wilderness. 19 "And when He had destroyed seven nations in the land of Canaan, He distributed their land as an inheritance—*all of which took* about four hundred and fifty years. 20 "And after these things He gave *them* judges until Samuel the prophet. 21 "And then they asked for a king, and God gave them Saul the son of Kish, a man of the tribe of Benjamin, for forty years. 22 "And after He had removed him, He raised up David to be their king, concerning whom He also testified and said, 'I have found David the son of Jesse, a man after My heart, who will do all My will.' 23 "From the offspring of this man according to promise God has brought to Israel a Savior, Jesus, 24 after John had proclaimed before His coming a baptism of repentance to all the people of Israel. 25 "And while John was completing his course, he kept saying, 'What do you suppose that I am? I am not *He*. But behold, one is coming after me the sandals of whose feet I am not worthy to untie.' 26 "Brethren, children of Abraham's family, and those among you who fear God, to us the word of this salvation is sent out. 27 "For those who live in Jerusalem, and their rulers, recognizing neither Him nor the utterances of the prophets which are read every Sabbath, fulfilled *these* by condemning *Him*. 28 "And though they found no ground for *putting Him to* death, they asked Pilate that He be executed. 29 "And when they had carried out all that was written concerning Him, they took Him down from the cross and laid Him in a tomb. 30 "But God raised Him from the dead; 31 and for many days He appeared to

WILLIAMS

ing of his name—continued to oppose them by trying to keep the governor from accepting the faith.

9 Then Saul, who was also called Paul, because he was full of the Holy Spirit, looked him straight in the eye 10 and said, "You expert in every form of deception and sleight-of-hand, you son of the devil, you enemy of all that is right, will you never stop trying to make the Lord's straight paths crooked! 11 Right now the hand of the Lord is upon you, and you will be so blind that you cannot see the sun for a time." And suddenly a dark mist fell upon him, and he kept groping about begging people to lead him by the hand. 12 Then the governor, because he saw what had occurred, was thunderstruck at the Lord's teaching, and so came to believe.

13 Then Paul and his party set sail from Paphos and crossed over to Perga in Pamphylia. Here John quit[b] them and returned to Jerusalem, 14 but they went on from Perga and arrived at Antioch in Pisidia. On the sabbath they went to the synagogue and took seats. 15 After the reading of the law and the prophets, the leaders of the synagogue worship sent to them and said, "Brothers, if you have any message of encouragement for the people, you may speak."

16 Then Paul got up and motioned with his hand and said:

"Fellow Israelites, and you who reverence God, listen! 17 The God of this people Israel chose our forefathers, and made this people important during their stay in Egypt, and then with an uplifted arm He led them out of it. 18 Then after He had fed them forty years in the desert, 19 He destroyed seven nations in Canaan 20 and gave them their land as an inheritance for about four hundred and fifty years. And after that He gave them judges until the time of Samuel the prophet. 21 Then they demanded a king, and for forty years God gave them Saul, the son of Kish, a man of the tribe of Benjamin. 22 Then He deposed him and raised up for them David to be king, to whom He bore this testimony, 'I have found in David, the son of Jesse, a man after my own heart, who will do all that my will requires.' 23 It is from this man's descendants that God, as He promised, has brought to Israel a Saviour in the person of Jesus, 24 as John, before His coming, had already preached baptism as an expression of repentance, for all the people of Israel. 25 As John was closing his career, he said, 'What do you take me to be? I am not the Christ; no, but He is coming after me, and I am not fit to untie the shoes on His feet.' 26 Brothers, descendants of the race of Abraham, and all among you who reverence God, it is to us that the message of this salvation has been sent. 27 For the people of Jerusalem and their leaders, because they were ignorant of Him, by condemning Him have actually fulfilled the utterances of the prophets which are read every sabbath, 28 and although they could not find Him guilty of a capital offense,[c] they begged Pilate to have Him put to death. 29 When they had carried out everything that had been written in the Scriptures about Him, they took Him down from the cross and laid Him in a tomb. 30 But God raised Him from the dead, 31 and for many days He ap-

BECK

what his name meant), opposed them and tried to turn the proconsul away from the faith.

9 But Saul (who was Paul), filled with the Holy Spirit, looked steadily at him 10 and said, "O you who are full of every treachery and villainy, you son of the devil, enemy of all that is right! Won't you stop twisting *the Lord's right ways?*[66] 11 And now the Lord's hand is on you: You'll be blind and not see the sun for a while."

At that moment a mist and a darkness came over him, and he went around looking for people to take his hand and lead him. 12 When the proconsul saw what had happened, he believed. The Lord's teaching amazed him.

At Antioch near Pisidia

13 Paul and his men took a ship from Paphos and came to Perga in Pamphylia. There John* left them and went back to Jerusalem. 14 But they went on from Perga and came to Antioch near Pisidia. On Saturday they went into the synagog and sat down.

15 After the reading of the Law and the prophets, the synagog leaders had a man go and tell them, "Fellow Jews, if you have anything to say to encourage the people, speak."

16 Paul got up and motioned with his hand. "Men of Israel," he said, "and you others who fear God, listen to me. 17 The God of this people Israel chose our fathers and made them a great people while they lived as strangers in Egypt, and *with an uplifted arm He led them out of it.*[67] 18 About forty years *He put up with them in the desert.*[68] 19 Then *He destroyed seven nations in Canaan and gave* their *country* to His people *as an inheritance.*[69] 20 He did all this in about 450 years. After that He gave them judges till the time of the prophet Samuel.

21 "Then the people demanded a king, and God gave them Saul for forty years. He was a son of Kish, a man of the tribe of Benjamin. 22 But God took the throne away from him again and made David their king. In regard to him he declared, '*I found David,* Jesse's son, *to be a man after My own heart,*[70] who *will do everything I want him to do.*'[71]

23 "As He had promised, God had a Savior —Jesus—come from David's descendants to Israel. 24 When He came into the world, John went ahead of Him as herald to tell all the people of Israel to repent and be baptized. 25 As John was finishing his work, he said, 'Who do you think I am? I'm not the One. No, there's Someone coming after me, and I don't deserve to untie the shoes on His feet.'

26 "Fellow Jews, Abraham's descendants, and you others who fear God, *the message* of this salvation *was sent*[72] to us. 27 Not knowing who Jesus was or what the prophets meant that are read every Saturday, the people in Jerusalem and their rulers by condemning Jesus did what their prophets predicted. 28 Although they found no good reason to kill Him, they asked Pilate to have Him killed. 29 When they had done everything that was written about Him, they took Him down from the cross and laid Him in a grave. 30 But God raised Him from the dead, 31 and for many days He was seen

* Mark
[66] Hosea 14:9
[67] Ex. 6:1, 6; 14:8
[68] Deut. 1:31
[69] Deut. 7:1; Joshua 14:1
[70] 1 Sam. 13:14; Ps. 89:20
[71] Is. 44:28
[72] Ps. 107:20

[b] Grk., *separated from.* [c] Lit., *no cause of death, not worthy of death.*

K.J.V.

was seen many days of them which came up with him from Galilee to Jerusalem, who are his witnesses unto the people. 32 And we declare unto you glad tidings, how that the promise which was made unto the fathers, 33 God hath fulfilled the same unto us their children, in that he hath raised up Jesus again; as it is also written in the second psalm, Thou art my Son, this day have I begotten thee. 34 And as concerning that he raised him up from the dead, *now* no more to return to corruption, he said on this wise, I will give you the sure mercies of David. 35 Wherefore he saith also in another *psalm,* Thou shalt not suffer thine Holy One to see corruption. 36 For David, after he had served his own generation by the will of God, fell on sleep, and was laid unto his fathers, and saw corruption: 37 But he, whom God raised again, saw no corruption.

38 Be it known unto you therefore, men *and* brethren, that through this man is preached unto you the forgiveness of sins: 39 And by him all that believe are justified from all things, from which ye could not be justified by the law of Moses. 40 Beware therefore, lest that come upon you, which is spoken of in the prophets; 41 Behold, ye despisers, and wonder, and perish: for I work a work in your days, a work which ye shall in no wise believe, though a man declare it unto you. 42 And when the Jews were gone out of the synagogue, the Gentiles besought that these words might be preached to them the next sabbath. 43 Now when the congregation was broken up, many of the Jews and religious proselytes followed Paul and Barnabas; who, speaking to them, persuaded them to continue in the grace of God.

44 And the next sabbath day came almost the whole city together to hear the word of God. 45 But when the Jews saw the multitudes, they were filled with envy, and spake against those things which were spoken by Paul, contradicting and blaspheming. 46 Then Paul and Barnabas waxed bold, and said, It was necessary that the word of God should first have been spoken to you: but seeing ye put it from you, and judge yourselves unworthy of everlasting life, lo, we turn to the Gentiles. 47 For so hath the Lord commanded us, *saying,* I have set thee to be a light of the Gentiles, that thou shouldest be for salvation unto the ends of the earth. 48 And when the Gentiles heard this, they were glad, and glorified the word of the Lord: and as many as were ordained to eternal life believed. 49 And the word of the Lord was published throughout all the region. 50 But the Jews stirred up the devout and honourable women, and the chief men of the city, and raised persecution against Paul and Barnabas, and expelled them out of their coasts. 51 But they shook off the dust of their feet against them, and came unto Iconium. 52 And the disciples were filled with joy, and with the Holy Ghost.

N.A.S.

those who came up with Him from Galilee to Jerusalem, the very ones who are now His witnesses to the people. 32 "And we preach to you the good news of the promise made to the fathers, 33 that God has fulfilled this *promise* to our children in that He raised up Jesus, as it is also written in the second Psalm, 'THOU ART MY SON; TODAY I HAVE BEGOTTEN THEE.' 34 "*And as for the fact* that He raised Him up from the dead, no more to return to decay, He has spoken in this way: 'I WILL GIVE YOU THE HOLY AND SURE *blessings* OF DAVID.' 35 "Therefore He also says in another *Psalm,* 'THOU WILT NOT ALLOW THY HOLY ONE TO UNDERGO DECAY.' 36 "For David, after he had served the purpose of God in his own generation, fell asleep, and was laid among his fathers, and underwent decay; 37 but He whom God raised did not undergo decay. 38 "Therefore let it be known to you, brethren, that through Him forgiveness of sins is proclaimed to you, 39 and through Him everyone who believes is freed from all things, from which you could not be freed through the Law of Moses. 40 "Take heed therefore, so that the thing spoken of in the Prophets may not come upon *you:*

> 41 'BEHOLD, YOU SCOFFERS, AND MARVEL, AND PERISH;
> FOR I AM ACCOMPLISHING A WORK IN YOUR DAYS,
> A WORK WHICH YOU WILL NEVER BELIEVE, THOUGH SOMEONE SHOULD DESCRIBE IT TO YOU.' "

42 And as Paul and Barnabas were going out, the people kept begging that these things might be spoken to them the next Sabbath. 43 Now when *the meeting of* the synagogue had broken up, many of the Jews and of the God-fearing proselytes followed Paul and Barnabas, who, speaking to them, were urging them to continue in the grace of God.

44 And the next Sabbath nearly the whole city assembled to hear the word of God. 45 But when the Jews saw the crowds, they were filled with jealousy, and *began* contradicting the things spoken by Paul, and were blaspheming. 46 And Paul and Barnabas spoke out boldly and said, "It was necessary that the word of God should be spoken to you first; since you repudiate it, and judge yourselves unworthy of eternal life, behold, we are turning to the Gentiles. 47 "For thus the Lord has commanded us,

> 'I HAVE PLACED YOU AS A LIGHT FOR THE GENTILES,
> THAT YOU SHOULD BRING SALVATION TO THE END OF THE EARTH.' "

48 And when the Gentiles heard this, they *began* rejoicing and glorifying the word of the Lord; and as many as had been appointed to eternal life believed. 49 And the word of the Lord was being spread through the whole region. 50 But the Jews aroused the devout women of prominence and the leading men of the city, and instigated a persecution against Paul and Barnabas, and drove them out of their district. 51 But they shook off the dust of their feet *in protest* against them and went to Iconium. 52 And the disciples were continually filled with joy and with the Holy Spirit.

WILLIAMS

peared to those who had come up with Him from Galilee to Jerusalem, and they are now witnesses for Him to the people. 32 So now we are bringing you the good news about the promise that was made to our forefathers, 33 that God has fulfilled it to us their children, by raising Jesus to life, just as the Scripture says in the Second Psalm, 'You are my Son, today I have become your Father.' *d* 34 Now as a proof that He has raised Him from the dead, no more to return to decay, He has spoken this, 'I will fulfill to you the holy promises made to David.' 35 Because in another psalm he says, 'You will not let your Holy One experience decay.' 36 For David, after having served God's purpose in his own generation, fell asleep and was laid among his forefathers, and so he did experience decay, 37 but He whom God raised to life did not experience it. 38 So, my brothers, you must understand that through Him the forgiveness of your sins is now proclaimed to you, 39 and that through union with Him every one of you who believes is given right standing with God and freed from every charge from which you could not be freed by the law of Moses. 40 So take care that what is said in the prophets does not come upon you:

41 'Look, you scoffers! Then wonder and vanish away,
For I am doing a work in your times
Which you will not at all believe though one may tell you in detail.' "

42 As they were leaving the synagogue,*e* the people kept begging that all this be repeated to them the next sabbath, 43 and after the congregation had broken up, many Jews and devout converts to Judaism allied themselves with Paul and Barnabas, and they kept talking to them and urging them to continue to rely on the unmerited favor of God.

44 The next sabbath almost the whole town turned out to hear God's message. 45 But when the Jews saw the crowds, they were completely overcome by their jealousy and began to contradict the statements made by Paul, and even to abuse him.

46 Then Paul and Barnabas courageously spoke out, "God's message had to be spoken to you Jews first, but since you continue to thrust it from you and since you show yourselves unworthy to receive eternal life, now and here we turn to the heathen. 47 For here are the orders that the Lord has given us:

'I have made you a light to the heathen,
To be the means of salvation to the very ends of the earth.' "

48 The heathen kept on listening and rejoicing and giving the glory to God's message, and all who had been destined to eternal life believed, 49 and so the message of the Lord spread all over the country.

50 But the Jews stirred up the devout women of high rank and the men of first rank in town, and so started a persecution against Paul and Barnabas, and drove them out of their district. 51 But they shook off the dust from their feet as a protest against them, and went to Iconium; 52 and the disciples continued to be full of joy and the Holy Spirit.

BECK

by those who had come with Him from Galilee up to Jerusalem. They are now telling the people the truth about Him. 32 And we are bringing you the good news: 33 What God promised the fathers He did for our children by raising Jesus, as it is written in the second Psalm:

You are My Son,
Today I am Your Father.[73]

34 "He raised Him from the dead, never to suffer *decay*, as He said, 'I will give *you what I gave David—mercies You can trust.*' [74] 35 Another Psalm says, '*You will not let Your Loved One experience decay.*' [75] 36 When *David* had served the people of his time, he by God's will *went to his rest* and was laid away *with his fathers.*[76] His body decayed, 37 but the body of Him whom God raised did not decay.

38 "And so you should know, my fellow men —we are announcing to you this Jesus forgives your sins and 39 makes everyone who believes righteous and free 38 from everything from which Moses' Law couldn't free you.

40 "Now be careful, or what the prophets said will happen to you: 41 *Look, you scorners, then wonder and perish, because I'm doing something in your days that you would never believe if anyone told you.*" [77]

42 As Paul and Barnabas were going out, the people urged them to tell them the same things the next Saturday. 43 When the meeting of the synagog broke up, many Jews and others who had come to fear God followed Paul and Barnabas, who talked to them and urged them to stay in God's love.

44 The next Saturday almost the whole town was there to hear God's Word. 45 When the Jews saw the crowds, they got very jealous. They contradicted what Paul said and abused him.

46 Paul and Barnabas boldly declared: "We had to speak God's Word to you first, but since you reject it and judge yourselves unworthy of everlasting life, we are now turning to the non-Jews. 47 That is what the Lord has ordered us to do: '*I have made you a light for the non-Jews, to save people all over the earth.*' " [78]

48 The non-Jews were delighted to hear what the Lord had said and praised Him for it, and all who had been appointed for everlasting life believed. 49 The Lord's Word spread all over the country. 50 But the Jews stirred up the noble women who worshiped with them, and the leaders of the town. These started a persecution against Paul and Barnabas and drove them out of their territory.

51 In protest against them Paul and Barnabas shook the dust off their feet and went to Iconium. 52 Meanwhile the disciples continued to be full of joy and of the Holy Spirit.

---

[d] Grk., *I have begotten you.* [e] Not in best Mss. but implied.

[73] Ps. 2:7
[74] Is. 55:3
[75] Ps. 16:10
[76] 1 Kings 2:10
[77] Hab. 1:5
[78] Is. 49:6

K.J.V.

14 And it came to pass in Iconium, that they went both together into the synagogue of the Jews, and so spake, that a great multitude both of the Jews and also of the Greeks believed. 2 But the unbelieving Jews stirred up the Gentiles, and made their minds evil affected against the brethren. 3 Long time therefore abode they speaking boldly in the Lord, which gave testimony unto the word of his grace, and granted signs and wonders to be done by their hands. 4 But the multitude of the city was divided: and part held with the Jews, and part with the apostles. 5And when there was an assault made both of the Gentiles, and also of the Jews with their rulers, to use *them* despitefully, and to stone them, 6 They were ware of *it*, and fled unto Lystra and Derbe, cities of Lycaonia, and unto the region that lieth round about: 7And there they preached the gospel.

8 And there sat a certain man at Lystra, impotent in his feet, being a cripple from his mother's womb, who never had walked: 9 The same heard Paul speak: who steadfastly beholding him, and perceiving that he had faith to be healed, 10 Said with a loud voice, Stand upright on thy feet. And he leaped and walked. 11And when the people saw what Paul had done, they lifted up their voices, saying in the speech of Lycaonia, The gods are come down to us in the likeness of men. 12And they called Barnabas, Jupiter; and Paul, Mercurius, because he was the chief speaker. 13 Then the priest of Jupiter, which was before their city, brought oxen and garlands unto the gates, and would have done sacrifice with the people. 14 *Which* when the apostles, Barnabas and Paul, heard *of*, they rent their clothes, and ran in among the people, crying out, 15And saying, Sirs, why do ye these things? We also are men of like passions with you, and preach unto you that ye should turn from these vanities unto the living God, which made heaven, and earth, and the sea, and all things that are therein: 16 Who in times past suffered all nations to walk in their own ways. 17 Nevertheless he left not himself without witness, in that he did good, and gave us rain from heaven, and fruitful seasons, filling our hearts with food and gladness. 18And with these sayings scarce restrained they the people, that they had not done sacrifice unto them.

19 And there came thither *certain* Jews from Antioch and Iconium, who persuaded the people, and, having stoned Paul, drew *him* out of the city, supposing he had been dead. 20 Howbeit, as the disciples stood round about him, he rose up, and came into the city: and the next day he departed with Barnabas to Derbe. 21And when they had preached the gospel to that city, and had taught many, they returned again to Lystra, and *to* Iconium, and Antioch, 22 Confirming the souls of the disciples, *and* exhorting them to continue in the faith, and that we must through much tribulation enter into the king-

N.A.S.

14 And it came about that in Iconium they entered the synagogue of the Jews together, and spoke in such a manner that a great multitude believed, both of Jews and of Greeks. 2 But the Jews who disbelieved stirred up the minds of the Gentiles, and embittered them against the brethren. 3 Therefore they spent a long time *there* speaking boldly *with reliance* upon the Lord, who was bearing witness to the word of His grace, granting that signs and wonders be done by their hands. 4 But the multitude of the city was divided; and some sided with the Jews, and some with the apostles. 5And when an attempt was made by both the Gentiles and the Jews with their rulers, to mistreat and to stone them, 6 they became aware of it and fled to the cities of Lycaonia, Lystra and Derbe, and the surrounding region; 7 and there they continued to preach the gospel.

8 And at Lystra there was sitting a certain man, without strength in his feet, lame from his mother's womb, who had never walked. 9 This man was listening to Paul as he spoke, who, when he had fixed his gaze upon him, and had seen that he had faith to be made well, 10 said with a loud voice, "Stand upright on your feet." And he leaped up and *began* to walk. 11And when the multitudes saw what Paul had done, they raised their voice, saying in the Lycaonian language, "The gods have become like men and have come down to us." 12And they *began* calling Barnabas, Zeus, and Paul, Hermes, because he was the chief speaker. 13And the priest of Zeus, whose *temple* was just outside the city, brought oxen and garlands to the gates, and wanted to offer sacrifice with the crowds. 14 But when the apostles, Barnabas and Paul, heard of it, they tore their robes and rushed out into the crowd, crying out 15 and saying, "Men, why are you doing these things? We are also men of the same nature as you, and preach the gospel to you in order that you should turn from these ªvain things to a living God, WHO MADE THE HEAVEN AND THE EARTH AND THE SEA, AND ALL THAT IS IN THEM. 16 "And in the generations gone by He permitted all the nations to go their own ways; 17 and yet He did not leave Himself without witness, in that He did good and gave you rains from heaven and fruitful seasons, satisfying your hearts with food and gladness." 18And *even* saying these things, they with difficulty restrained the crowds from offering sacrifice to them.

19 But Jews came from Antioch and Iconium, and having won over the multitudes, they stoned Paul and dragged him out of the city, supposing him to be dead. 20 But while the disciples stood around him, he arose and entered the city. And the next day he went away with Barnabas to Derbe. 21And after they had preached the gospel to that city and had made many disciples, they returned to Lystra and to Iconium and to Antioch, 22 strengthening the souls of the disciples, encouraging them to continue in the faith, and *saying*, "Through many tribulations we must

[a] I.e., *idols*.

14 *Persecuted in Iconium they flee to Lystra; worshiped by the Lystrans for curing a crippled man; Paul stoned almost to death; escapes to Derbe; retracing their steps, they organize churches; report to home base*

At Iconium too they went to the Jewish synagogue and spoke in such a way that a great number of both Jews and Greeks came to believe. 2 But the Jews who refused to accept their message aroused and exasperated the minds of the heathen against the brothers. 3 In spite of this, however, they stayed there a considerable time and continued to speak with courage from the Lord, who continued to bear testimony to His gracious message and kept on granting signs and wonders to be done by them. 4 But the masses of the town were divided; some sided with the Jews and some with the apostles. 5 And so when there was a movement on the part of both the heathen and the Jews, along with their authorities, to insult and stone them, 6 they became aware of it and fled to the Lycaonian towns of Lystra and Derbe, and the surrounding country, 7 and there they continued to tell the good news.

8 Now in the streets of Lystra a man used to sit who had no strength in his feet, who had been crippled from his birth, and had never walked. 9 He continued listening to Paul as he spoke, and as Paul by looking straight at him observed that he had faith that he would be cured, 10 he shouted aloud to him, "Get on your feet and stand erect!" Then up he leaped and began to walk.

11 So the crowds, because they saw what Paul had done, shouted in the Lycaonian language, "The gods in human form[a] have come down to us!" 12 They called Barnabas Zeus and Paul, because he was the principal speaker, Hermes. 13 The priest of the temple of Zeus, which stood at the entrance to the town, came with crowds of people to the gates, bringing bulls and garlands; he meant to offer sacrifices to them.

14 But the apostles, Barnabas and Paul, when they heard it, tore their clothes and rushed into the crowd, 15 and shouted. "Men, why are you doing this? We are merely men with natures like your own, who are telling you the good news, so that you may turn from these foolish things to the living God, who made heaven and earth and sea and all that they contain. 16 In ages past He let all the heathen go on in their own ways; 17 though He did not fail to furnish evidences about Himself, in constantly showing His kindness to you, in sending you rain from heaven and fruit-producing seasons, in giving you food and happiness to your heart's content." 18 Even by saying this it was all that they could do to keep the crowds from offering sacrifices to them.

19 But some Jews came from Antioch and Iconium, and won the crowds by persuasion, and they stoned Paul, and dragged him outside the town, supposing he was dead. 20 But the disciples formed a circle about him, and he got up and went back to town. The next day he went on with Barnabas to Derbe. 21 They told the good news in that town, and after winning many disciples there, they returned to Lystra, Iconium, and Antioch, 22 strengthening the hearts of the disciples and encouraging them to continue in the faith, and warning them that it is through enduring many hardships that we must get into the kingdom of God.

[a] Lit., *making themselves like men.*

In Iconium

14 The same thing happened in Iconium. Paul and Barnabas went into the synagog of the Jews and spoke in such a way that a big crowd of Jews and non-Jews believed. 2 But the Jews who refused to believe stirred up the non-Jews and poisoned their minds against the Christians. 3 For a long time Paul and Barnabas continued to speak boldly, trusting in the Lord, who gave His approval to the words of His love by letting their hands do miracles and wonders. 4 But the people of the town were divided— some were with the Jews, others with the apostles.

5 But when non-Jews and Jews with their rulers planned to mistreat and stone them, 6 they found out about it and escaped to Lystra and Derbe, towns of Lycaonia, and to the surrounding territory. 7 There they kept on telling the good news.

In Lystra

8 In Lystra there was a man sitting who couldn't use his feet. He had been lame from his birth and had never walked. 9 He was listening to Paul as he spoke. Paul watched him, and when he saw the man believed he would be made well, 10 he called out loud, *"Stand up straight on your feet."* [79] The man jumped up and walked around.

11 The people who saw what Paul had done shouted in the language of Lycaonia, "The gods have become like men and have come down to us." 12 And they called Barnabas Zeus, and Paul Hermes, because he was the main speaker. 13 The priest of the temple of Zeus in front of the town brought bulls and garlands to the gates. He and the crowd wanted to sacrifice.

14 When the apostles Barnabas and Paul heard of it, they tore their clothes and rushed out into the crowd. 15 "You men, why are you doing this?" they shouted. "We're just human beings too, with experiences like yours and are telling you the good news to turn from these empty things to the living God, *who made heaven and earth, the sea, and everything in them.* [80] 16 In the ages that have gone by He let all people go their own ways; 17 yet He didn't fail to give evidence of Himself by doing good, giving you rains from heaven and crops in their seasons, filling you with food, and making you happy."

18 Even by saying this they could hardly keep the crowd from sacrificing to them.

19 But then some Jews came from Antioch and Iconium and won the people over. So they stoned Paul and dragged him out of the town, thinking he was dead. 20 But when the disciples came and stood around him, he got up and went into the town.

Derbe and Back Home

21 The next day he and Barnabas left for Derbe. As they were telling the good news in that town, they won many disciples. Then they went back to Lystra, Iconium, and Antioch, 22 strengthening the disciples and encouraging them to be loyal to the faith, saying, "We must suffer much to go into God's kingdom."

[79] Ezek. 2:1-2
[80] Ex. 20:11

K.J.V.

dom of God. 23And when they had ordained them elders in every church, and had prayed with fasting, they commended them to the Lord, on whom they believed. 24And after they had passed throughout Pisidia, they came to Pamphylia. 25And when they had preached the word in Perga, they went down into Attalia: 26And thence sailed to Antioch, from whence they had been recommended to the grace of God for the work which they fulfilled. 27And when they were come, and had gathered the church together, they rehearsed all that God had done with them, and how he had opened the door of faith unto the Gentiles. 28And there they abode long time with the disciples.

15 And certain men which came down from Judea taught the brethren, *and said,* Except ye be circumcised after the manner of Moses, ye cannot be saved. 2 When therefore Paul and Barnabas had no small dissension and disputation with them, they determined that Paul and Barnabas, and certain other of them, should go up to Jerusalem unto the apostles and elders about this question. 3And being brought on their way by the church, they passed through Phenice and Samaria, declaring the conversion of the Gentiles: and they caused great joy unto all the brethren. 4And when they were come to Jerusalem, they were received of the church, and *of* the apostles and elders, and they declared all things that God had done with them. 5 But there rose up certain of the sect of the Pharisees which believed, saying, That it was needful to circumcise them, and to command *them* to keep the law of Moses.

6 And the apostles and elders came together for to consider of this matter. 7And when there had been much disputing, Peter rose up, and said unto them, Men *and* brethren, ye know how that a good while ago God made choice among us, that the Gentiles by my mouth should hear the word of the gospel, and believe. 8And God, which knoweth the hearts, bare them witness, giving them the Holy Ghost, even as *he did* unto us; 9And put no difference between us and them, purifying their hearts by faith. 10 Now therefore why tempt ye God, to put a yoke upon the neck of the disciples, which neither our fathers nor we were able to bear? 11 But we believe that through the grace of the Lord Jesus Christ we shall be saved, even as they.
12 Then all the multitude kept silence, and gave audience to Barnabas and Paul, declaring what miracles and wonders God had wrought among the Gentiles by them.
13 And after they had held their peace, James answered, saying, Men *and* brethren, hearken unto me: 14 Simeon hath declared how God at the first did visit the Gentiles, to take out of them a people for his name. 15And to this agree the words of the prophets; as it is written, 16After this I will return, and will build again the tabernacle of David, which is fallen down; and I will build again the ruins thereof, and I

N.A.S.

enter the kingdom of God." 23And when they had appointed elders for them in every church, having prayed with fasting, they commended them to the Lord in whom they had believed. 24And they passed through Pisidia and came into Pamphylia. 25And when they had spoken the word in Perga, they went down to Attalia; 26 and from there they sailed to Antioch, from which they had been commended to the grace of God for the work that they had accomplished. 27And when they had arrived and gathered the church together, they *began* to report all things that God had done with them and how He had opened a door of faith to the Gentiles. 28And they spent a long time with the disciples.

15 And some men came down from Judea and *began* teaching the brethren, "Unless you are circumcised according to the custom of Moses, you cannot be saved." 2And when Paul and Barnabas had great dissension and debate with them, *the brethren* determined that Paul and Barnabas and certain others of them, should go up to Jerusalem to the apostles and elders concerning this issue. 3 Therefore, being sent on their way by the church, they were passing through both Phoenicia and Samaria, describing in detail the conversion of the Gentiles, and were bringing great joy to all the brethren. 4And when they arrived at Jerusalem, they were received by the church and the apostles and the elders, and they reported all that God had done with them. 5 But certain ones of the sect of the Pharisees who had believed, stood up, saying, "It is necessary to circumcise them, and to direct them to observe the Law of Moses."

6 And the apostles and the elders came together to look into this matter. 7And after there had been much debate, Peter stood up and said to them, "Brethren, you know that in the early days God made a choice among you, that by my mouth the Gentiles should hear the word of the gospel and believe. 8 "And God, who knows the heart, bore witness to them, giving them the Holy Spirit, just as He also did to us; 9 and He made no distinction between us and them, cleansing their hearts by faith. 10 "Now therefore why do you put God to the test by placing upon the neck of the disciples a yoke which neither our fathers nor we have been able to bear? 11 "But we believe that we are saved through the grace of the Lord Jesus, in the same way as they also are."
12 And all the multitude kept silent, and they were listening to Barnabas and Paul as they were relating what signs and wonders God had done through them among the Gentiles. 13And after they had stopped speaking, James answered, saying, "Brethren, listen to me. 14 "Simeon has related how God first concerned Himself about taking from among the Gentiles a people for His name. 15 "And with this the words of the Prophets agree, just as it is written,

16 'AFTER THESE THINGS I WILL RETURN,
AND I WILL REBUILD THE TABERNACLE OF
  DAVID WHICH HAS FALLEN,
AND I WILL REBUILD ITS RUINS,
AND I WILL RESTORE IT,

23 They helped them select elders in each church, and after praying and fasting they committed them to the Lord in whom they had believed. 24 Then they passed through Pisidia and went down to Pamphylia, 25 and after telling their message in Perga, they went on to Attalia, 26 and from there they sailed back to Antioch, where they had first been committed to God's favor for the work which they had finished. 27 On arriving there they called the church together, and in detail reported to them all that God had done through them as instruments, and how He had opened to the heathen the door of faith. 28 And there they stayed a long time with the disciples.

15 *Jewish fanatics teach in Antioch that circumcision is essential to salvation; the church sends Paul and Barnabas to confer with the apostles about it; result, Christianity is freed from Judaism*

Some people came down from Judea and began to teach the brothers, "Unless you are circumcised in accordance with the custom that Moses handed down, you cannot be saved."
2 So, as a dire disturbance and a serious discussion had been created between Paul and Barnabas and them, they decided that Paul and Barnabas and some others from their number should go up to Jerusalem to confer with the apostles and elders about this question. 3 So they were endorsed and sent on by the church, and as they passed through Phoenicia and Samaria, they told of the conversion of the heathen and brought great rejoicing to all the brothers.
4 When they arrived at Jerusalem, they were welcomed by the church, the apostles, and the elders, and they reported what God had done through them as instruments. 5 But some members of the Pharisaic party, who had become believers, arose and said that such converts must be circumcised and told to keep the law of Moses.
6 Now the apostles and elders met to consider this matter. 7 After a lengthy discussion Peter got up and said to them, "Brothers, you know that in the early days God chose among you that through me the heathen should hear the message of the good news and believe it. 8 And God who knows men's hearts testifies for them by giving them the Holy Spirit, as He did us, 9 and in this way He put no difference between us and them, because He cleansed their hearts by faith. 10 Then why do you now try to test God by putting on these disciples' necks a yoke which neither our forefathers nor we could bear? 11 In fact, we believe that it is through the favor of the Lord Jesus that we are saved, just as they are."
12 By this he quieted the whole congregation, and they listened to Barnabas and Paul tell of the signs and wonders which God had done through them among the heathen.
13 When they finished, James responded as follows: "Brothers, listen to me. 14 Symeon has told how God at first graciously visited the heathen to take from among them a people to bear His name. 15 The words of the prophets are in accord with this, as it is written:
16 'After this I will return and rebuild David's fallen dwelling;
I will rebuild its ruins and set it up again,

Must Non-Jews Be Circumcised?

15 Some men came down from Judea and started to teach the Christians: "If you're not circumcised according to the custom taught by Moses, you can't be saved." 2 When Paul and Barnabas had no little conflict and argument with them, Paul and Barnabas and some of the others were appointed to go up to Jerusalem and see the apostles and elders about this question.
3 The church sent them on their way. As they were going through Phoenicia and Samaria, they told the whole story how the non-Jews were turning to God, and they made all the Christians very happy.
4 When they came to Jerusalem, they were welcomed by the church, the apostles, and the elders and told everything God had done with them. 5 But some believers of the party of the Pharisees got up and said, "We must circumcise people and order them to keep the Law of Moses."
6 The apostles and elders met to look into this matter. 7 After much discussion Peter got up. "Fellow Christians," he said to the others, "you know in the early days God chose me to be the one among you to tell the good news to the non-Jews so that they would hear it and believe. 8 And God, who knows our hearts, showed them He approved by giving them the Holy Spirit as He gave Him to us. 9 And by cleansing their hearts by faith He has declared we are not different from them. 10 Now then, why do you test God by putting on the disciples' neck a yoke neither our fathers nor we could bear? 11 No, by the love of the Lord Jesus we believe in order to be saved; and so do they."
12 The whole crowd was silent. Then they heard Barnabas and Paul tell about all the miracles and wonders God had done among the non-Jews through them.
13 After they finished speaking, James said, "Fellow Christians, listen to me. 14 Simon has explained how God first came to the non-Jews to get a people for Himself. 15 This agrees with what the prophets said. It is wrtiten: 16 'Afterwards I will come back[81] and build again David's hut that has fallen down. And its ruins I will

K.J.V.

will set it up: 17 That the residue of men might seek after the Lord, and all the Gentiles, upon whom my name is called, saith the Lord, who doeth all these things. 18 Known unto God are all his works from the beginning of the world. 19 Wherefore my sentence is, that we trouble not them, which from among the Gentiles are turned to God: 20 But that we write unto them, that they abstain from pollutions of idols, and *from* fornication, and *from* things strangled, and *from* blood. 21 For Moses of old time hath in every city them that preach him, being read in the synagogues every sabbath day. 22 Then pleased it the apostles and elders, with the whole church, to send chosen men of their own company to Antioch with Paul and Barnabas; *namely,* Judas surnamed Barsabas, and Silas, chief men among the brethren: 23 And they wrote *letters* by them after this manner; The apostles and elders and brethren *send* greeting unto the brethren which are of the Gentiles in Antioch and Syria and Cilicia: 24 Forasmuch as we have heard, that certain which went out from us have troubled you with words, subverting your souls, saying, Ye *must* be circumcised, and keep the law; to whom we gave no *such* commandment: 25 It seemed good unto us, being assembled with one accord, to send chosen men unto you with our beloved Barnabas and Paul, 26 Men that have hazarded their lives for the name of our Lord Jesus Christ. 27 We have sent therefore Judas and Silas, who shall also tell *you* the same things by mouth. 28 For it seemed good to the Holy Ghost, and to us, to lay upon you no greater burden than these necessary things; 29 That ye abstain from meats offered to idols, and from blood, and from things strangled, and from fornication: from which if ye keep yourselves, ye shall do well. Fare ye well. 30 So when they were dismissed, they came to Antioch: and when they had gathered the multitude together, they delivered the epistle: 31 *Which* when they had read, they rejoiced for the consolation. 32 And Judas and Silas, being prophets also themselves, exhorted the brethren with many words, and confirmed *them.* 33 And after they had tarried *there* a space, they were let go in peace from the brethren unto the apostles. 34 Notwithstanding it pleased Silas to abide there still. 35 Paul also and Barnabas continued in Antioch, teaching and preaching the word of the Lord, with many others also.

36 And some days after, Paul said unto Barnabas, Let us go again and visit our brethren in every city where we have preached the word of the Lord, *and see* how they do. 37 And Barnabas determined to take with them John, whose surname was Mark. 38 But Paul thought not good to take him with them, who departed from them from Pamphylia, and went not with them to the work. 39 And the contention was so sharp between them, that they departed asunder one from the other: and so Barnabas took Mark, and sailed unto Cyprus; 40 And Paul chose Silas, and departed, being recommended by the brethren unto the grace of God. 41 And he went through Syria and Cilicia, confirming the churches.

N.A.S.

17 'IN ORDER THAT THE REST OF MANKIND MAY SEEK THE LORD,
AND ALL THE GENTILES WHO ARE CALLED BY MY NAME,
18 'SAYS THE LORD, WHO MAKES THESE THINGS KNOWN FROM OF OLD.'
19 "Therefore it is my judgment that we do not trouble those who are turning to God from among the Gentiles, 20 but that we write to them that they abstain from things contaminated by idols and from fornication and from what is strangled and from blood. 21 "For Moses from ancient generations has in every city those who preach him, since he is read in the synagogues every Sabbath."
22 Then it seemed good to the apostles and the elders, with the whole church, to choose men from among them to send to Antioch with Paul and Barnabas—Judas called Barsabbas, and Silas, leading men among the brethren, 23 and they sent this letter by them,
"The apostles and the brethren who are elders, to the brethren in Antioch and Syria and Cilicia who are from the Gentiles, greetings.
24 "Since we have heard that some of our number to whom we gave no instruction have disturbed you with *their* words, unsettling your souls,
25 it seemed good to us, having become of one mind, to select men to send to you with our beloved Barnabas and Paul,
26 men who have risked their lives for the name of our Lord Jesus Christ.
27 "Therefore we have sent Judas and Silas, who themselves will also report the same things by word *of mouth.*
28 "For it seemed good to the Holy Spirit and to us to lay upon you no greater burden than these essentials:
29 that you abstain from things sacrificed to idols and from blood and from things strangled and from fornication; if you keep yourselves free from such things, you will do well. Farewell."
30 So, when they were sent away, they went down to Antioch; and having gathered the congregation together, they delivered the letter. 31 And when they had read it, they rejoiced because of its encouragement. 32 And Judas and Silas, also being prophets themselves, encouraged and strengthened the brethren with a lengthy message. 33 And after they had spent time *there,* they were sent away from the brethren in peace to those who had sent them out. 34 (See footnote [a]) 35 But Paul and Barnabas stayed in Antioch, teaching and preaching with many others also the word of the Lord.
36 And after some days Paul said to Barnabas, "Let us return and visit the brethren in every city in which we proclaimed the word of the Lord, *and see* how they are." 37 And Barnabas was desirous of taking John, called Mark, along with them also. 38 But Paul kept insisting that they should not take him along who had deserted them in Pamphylia and had not gone with them to the work. 39 And there arose such a sharp disagreement that they separated from one another, and Barnabas took Mark with him and sailed away to Cyprus. 40 But Paul chose Silas and departed, being committed by the brethren to the grace of the Lord. 41 And he was traveling through Syria and Cilicia, strengthening the churches.

[a] Some mss. add verse 34, *But it seemed good to Silas to remain there.*

WILLIAMS

17 So that the rest of mankind may earnestly
   seek the Lord,
Yes, all the heathen who are called by my
   name,
Says the Lord, 18 who has been making this
   known from ages past.'
19 So I give it as my opinion, we ought not
to put difficulties in the way of the heathen who
turn to God, 20 but we should write them to
abstain from everything that is contaminated by
idols, from sexual immorality, from the meat of
strangled animals, and from tasting blood. 21 For
Moses from the ancient generations has had his
preachers in every town, and on every sabbath
has been read aloud in the synagogues."
   22 Then the apostles and elders in co-operation with the whole church passed a resolution
to select and send some men of their number
with Paul and Barnabas to Antioch. These were
Judas, who was called Barsabbas, and Silas,
leading men among the brothers. 23 They sent
this letter by them:
   "The apostles and elders as brothers send
greeting to the brothers from among the heathen
in Antioch, Syria, and Cilicia. 24 As we have
heard that some of our number have disturbed
you by their teaching, by continuing to unsettle
your minds, 25 we have passed a unanimous resolution to select and send messengers to you with
our beloved brothers Barnabas and Paul, 26 who
have risked their lives for the sake of our Lord
Jesus Christ. 27 So we send Judas and Silas to
you, to bring you the same message by word of
mouth. 28 For the Holy Spirit and we have decided not to lay upon you any burden but these
essential requirements, 29 that you abstain from
everything that is offered to idols, from tasting
blood, from the meat of animals that have been
strangled, and from sexual immorality. If you
keep yourselves free from these things, you will
prosper. Good-by."
   30 So the messengers were sent out, and they
went down to Antioch, called a meeting of the
congregation, and delivered the letter. 31 When
they had read it, they were delighted with the
encouragement it brought them. 32 Now Judas
and Silas, as they were prophets themselves, in
a lengthy talk encouraged and strengthened the
brothers. 33 After spending some time there, they
were sent back with a greeting[a] to those who
sent them.[b] 35 But Paul and Barnabas stayed on
at Antioch, and with many others continued to
teach the Lord's message and to tell the good
news.
   36 Some days after this Paul said to Barnabas,
"Let us go back and visit the brothers in every
town where we preached the Lord's message, to
see how they are." 37 But Barnabas persisted in
wanting to take along John who was called
Mark. 38 Paul, however, did not consider such a
man fit to take along with them, the man who
deserted them in Pamphylia and did not go on
with them to the work. 39 The disagreement was
so sharp that they separated, and Barnabas took
Mark and sailed for Cyprus. 40 But Paul selected
Silas and set out, after the brothers had committed him to the favor of the Lord. 41 He
journeyed on through Syria and Cilicia and continued to strengthen the churches.

BECK

build and set up again, 17 so that the rest of
the people, yes, all the nations who are called
by My name, may search for the Lord. 18 The
Lord says this and does this which was known
long ago.' [82] 19 So it is my judgment that we
should not trouble these non-Jews who are
turning to God 20 but write them to keep away
from the unclean things of idols and from sexual
sin and not eat anything strangled or any blood.
21 Ever since the earliest days there are in each
town those who preach Moses when he is read
in the synagogs every Saturday."
   22 Then the apostles, the elders, and the
whole church decided to choose some of their
men and send them with Paul and Barnabas to
Antioch: Judas, called Barsabas, and Silas—
leaders among the Christians. 23 And they wrote
this letter for them to deliver:
   "The apostles and elders, Christians, send
greetings to their non-Jewish fellow Christians
in Antioch, Syria, and Cilicia.
   24 "Since we heard that some men, coming
from us without instructions from us, have said
things to trouble you, and they continue to upset
you, 25 we have unanimously decided to choose
men and send them to you with our dear Barnabas and Paul, 26 who are living only for our
Lord Jesus Christ. 27 So we are sending Judas
and Silas to talk to you and tell you the same
things.
   28 "The Holy Spirit and we have decided
not to burden you more than is necessary:
29 Keep away from food sacrificed to idols,
from blood, from the meat of strangled animals,
and from sexual sin. Be careful to avoid these
and you will be doing right. Farewell!"
   30 So they were sent on their way and came
to Antioch, where they got the church together
and delivered the letter. 31 The people read it
and were delighted with the encouragement it
brought them. 32 And Judas and Silas, who also
were prophets, said much to encourage and
strengthen the Christians.
   33 After they had stayed for some time, the
Christians let Judas and Silas go back with a
friendly greeting to those who had sent them.
*35 But Paul and Barnabas stayed in Antioch
and with the help of many others taught and
told the Lord's good news.

Paul Takes Silas with Him

   36 After a while Paul said to Barnabas, "Let's
go back and visit our fellow Christians in every
town where we told them the Lord's Word, and
let's see how they are."
   37 Barnabas wanted to take along John, who
was called Mark. 38 But Paul thought it best
not to take the man who had deserted them in
Pamphylia and had not gone with them into the
work. 39 They disagreed so sharply they separated, and Barnabas, taking Mark along, sailed
away to Cyprus. 40 But Paul chose Silas and
started out, his fellow Christians entrusting him
to the Lord's love.

Timothy Joins Paul in Lystra

   41 He went through Syria and Cilicia,
strengthening the churches.

[a] Lit., with peace. [b] V. 34 not in the best Mss.

* Our two oldest manuscripts do not have v. 34:
"But Silas decided to stay there, and Judas left
alone."
[82] Amos 9:11-12; Is. 45:21

K.J.V.

16 Then came he to Derbe and Lystra: and, behold, a certain disciple was there, named Timotheus, the son of a certain woman, which was a Jewess, and believed; but his father *was* a Greek: 2 Which was well reported of by the brethren that were at Lystra and Iconium. 3 Him would Paul have to go forth with him; and took and circumcised him because of the Jews which were in those quarters: for they knew all that his father was a Greek. 4And as they went through the cities, they delivered them the decrees for to keep, that were ordained of the apostles and elders which were at Jerusalem. 5And so were the churches established in the faith, and increased in number daily. 6 Now when they had gone throughout Phrygia and the region of Galatia, and were forbidden of the Holy Ghost to preach the word in Asia, 7 After they were come to Mysia, they assayed to go into Bithynia: but the Spirit suffered them not. 8And they passing by Mysia came down to Troas. 9And a vision appeared to Paul in the night; There stood a man of Macedonia, and prayed him, saying, Come over into Macedonia, and help us. 10And after he had seen the vision, immediately we endeavoured to go into Macedonia, assuredly gathering that the Lord had called us for to preach the gospel unto them. 11 Therefore loosing from Troas, we came with a straight course to Samothracia, and the next *day* to Neapolis; 12And from thence to Philippi, which is the chief city of that part of Macedonia, *and* a colony: and we were in that city abiding certain days. 13And on the sabbath we went out of the city by a river side, where prayer was wont to be made; and we sat down, and spake unto the women which resorted *thither*.

14 And a certain woman named Lydia, a seller of purple, of the city of Thyatira, which worshipped God, heard *us:* whose heart the Lord opened, that she attended unto the things which were spoken of Paul. 15And when she was baptized, and her household, she besought *us,* saying, If ye have judged me to be faithful to the Lord, come into my house, and abide *there.* And she constrained us.

16 And it came to pass, as we went to prayer, a certain damsel possessed with a spirit of divination met us, which brought her masters much gain by soothsaying: 17 The same followed Paul and us, and cried, saying, These men are the servants of the most high God, which shew unto us the way of salvation. 18And this did she many days. But Paul, being grieved, turned and said to the spirit, I command thee in the name of Jesus Christ to come out of her. And he came out the same hour.

19 And when her masters saw that the hope of their gains was gone, they caught Paul and Silas, and drew *them* into the marketplace unto the rulers, 20And brought them to the magistrates, saying, These men, being Jews, do ex-

N.A.S.

16 And he came also to Derbe and to Lystra. And behold, a certain disciple was there, named Timothy, the son of a Jewish woman who was a believer, but his father was a Greek, 2 and he was well spoken of by the brethren who were in Lystra and Iconium. 3 Paul wanted this man to go with him; and he took him and circumcised him because of the Jews who were in those parts, for they all knew that his father was a Greek. 4 Now while they were passing through the cities, they were delivering the decrees, which had been decided upon by the apostles and elders who were in Jerusalem, for them to observe. 5 So the churches were being strengthened in the faith, and were increasing in number daily.

6 And they passed through the Phrygian and Galatian region, having been forbidden by the Holy Spirit to speak the word in Asia; 7 and when they had come to Mysia, they were trying to go into Bithynia, and the Spirit of Jesus did not permit them; 8 and passing by Mysia, they came down to Troas. 9And a vision appeared to Paul in the night: A certain man of Macedonia was standing and appealing to him, and saying, "Come over to Macedonia and help us." 10And when he had seen the vision, immediately we sought to go into Macedonia, concluding that God had called us to preach the gospel to them.

11 Therefore putting out to sea from Troas, we ran a straight course to Samothrace, and on the day following to Neapolis; 12 and from there to Philippi, which is a leading city of the district of Macedonia, a *Roman* colony; and we were staying in this city for some days. 13And on the Sabbath day we went outside the gate to a river side, where we were supposing that there would be a place of prayer; and we sat down and began speaking to the women who had assembled. 14And a certain woman named Lydia, from the city of Thyatira, a seller of purple fabrics, a worshiper of God, was listening; and the Lord opened her heart to respond to the things spoken by Paul. 15And when she and her household had been baptized, she urged us, saying, "If you have judged me to be faithful to the Lord, come into my house and stay." And she prevailed upon us.

16 And it happened that as we were going to the place of prayer, a certain slave-girl having a spirit of divination met us, who was bringing her masters much profit by fortune-telling. 17 Following after Paul and us, she kept crying out, saying, "These men are bondservants of the Most High God, who are proclaiming to you the way of salvation." 18And she continued doing this for many days. But Paul was greatly annoyed, and turned and said to the spirit, "I command you in the name of Jesus Christ to come out of her!" And it came out at that very moment.

19 But when her masters saw that their hope of profit was gone, they seized Paul and Silas and dragged them into the market place before the authorities, 20 and when they had brought them to the chief magistrates, they said, "These men are throwing our city into confusion, being

WILLIAMS

16 *Timothy becomes a missionary partner of Paul; they go down to historic Troy, then cross to Europe; Philippi honored by having the first Christians and the first church in Europe; Lydia the first convert there*

Now he went to Derbe and Lystra too. At Lystra there was a disciple named Timothy, whose mother was a Christian Jewess, but his father was a Greek. 2 He had a high reputation among the brothers in Lystra and Iconium. 3 Paul wanted this man to join him in his journey; so on account of the Jews in that district he took him and had him circumcised, for everybody knew that his father was a Greek. 4 As they journeyed on from town to town, they delivered to the brothers to keep the decisions reached by the apostles and elders at Jerusalem. 5 So the churches through faith continued to grow in strength and to increase in numbers from day to day.

6 Then they crossed Phrygia and Galatia. But because they were prevented by the Holy Spirit from speaking the message in Asia, 7 they went on to Mysia and tried to get into Bithynia, but the Spirit of Jesus would not permit them. 8 So they passed by Mysia and went down to Troas. 9 There Paul had a vision one night: a man from Macedonia kept standing and pleading with him in these words, "Come over to Macedonia and help us!"

10 As soon as he had this vision, we laid our plans to get off to Macedonia, because we confidently concluded that God had called us to tell them the good news.

11 So we sailed away from Troy and struck a bee line for Samothrace, and the next day on to Neapolis. 12 From there we went on to Philippi, a Roman colony, the leading town in that part of Macedonia.

In this town we stayed some days. 13 On the sabbath we went outside the gate, to the bank of the river, where we supposed there was a place of prayer, and we sat down and began to talk with the women who had met there. 14 Among them was a woman named Lydia, a dealer in purple goods from the town of Thyatira, and she stayed to listen to us. She was already a worshiper of God, and the Lord so moved upon her heart that she accepted the message spoken by Paul. 15 When she and her household were baptized, she begged us by continuing to say, "If you have made up your mind that I am a real believer in the Lord, come and stay at my house." And she continued to insist that we do so.

16 Once as we were on our way to the place of prayer, a slave-girl met us who had the gift*a* of magical fortune-telling, and continued to make great profits for her owners by fortune-telling. 17 This girl kept following Paul and the rest of us, shrieking, "These men are slaves of the Most High God, and they are proclaiming to you a way of salvation." 18 She kept this up for a number of days.

Because Paul was so much annoyed by her, he turned and said to the spirit in her, "In the name of Jesus Christ I order you to come out of her." And that very moment it came out.

19 But as the owners saw that the hope of their profit-making was gone, they seized Paul and Silas and dragged them to the public square,*b* before the authorities, 20 and brought them to the chiefs of the police court. They said, "These men are Jews; they continue to

[a] Grk., *had the spirit.* [b] Grk., *market place, our public square.*

BECK

16 He came down to Derbe, then to Lystra. Here there was a disciple by the name of Timothy. His mother was a Jewish Christian, but his father was a Greek. 2 The Christians in Lystra and Iconium spoke well of him. 3 Paul wanted him to go with him, so he took him and circumcised him on account of the Jews who were in those places, because everybody knew his father was a Greek.

4 As they went through the towns, they delivered the decisions the apostles and elders in Jerusalem had made and the people were to keep. 5 So the churches were strengthened in the faith and grew in number more and more every day.

The Call to Europe

6 They went through the region of Phrygia and Galatia because the Holy Spirit kept them from speaking the Word in the province of Asia. 7 They came as far as Mysia and tried to get into Bithynia, but the Spirit of Jesus did not let them. 8 So they passed through Mysia and went down to Troas.

9 One night Paul saw a vision—a man from Macedonia was standing there and urging him, "Come over to Macedonia and help us!"

10 As soon as he had seen the vision, we looked for a way to get to Macedonia since we concluded God had called us to tell them the good news.

At Philippi

11 Sailing from Troas, we went straight to Samothrace, the next day to Neapolis, 12 and from there to Philippi, a leading city in that part of Macedonia and a colony of Rome. We stayed in that city for some days.

13 On Saturday we went out of the gate and along the river, where we thought there was a place for prayer. We sat down and started to talk to the women gathered there. 14 There was a woman by the name of Lydia, a dealer in purple goods, who came from the town of Thyatira. She worshiped God. As she listened, the Lord opened her heart to be interested in what Paul said. 15 When she and her family were baptized, she urged us, "If you're convinced I believe in the Lord, come and stay at my home." And she made us come.

16 One day when we were going to the place of prayer, we met a slave girl with a spirit of fortune-telling in her; she made much money for her owners by telling the unknown. 17 She would follow Paul and us and shout, "These men are servants of the most high God and are telling you how to be saved." 18 She kept on doing this for many days until Paul, very much annoyed, turned to the spirit and said, "In the name of Jesus Christ I order you to go out of her!"

19 Then and there the spirit went out of her, and with it, as her owners realized, went their chance of making money. So they grabbed Paul and Silas, dragged them before the officers in the marketplace, 20 and brought them before the highest Roman officials. "These men are stirring up a lot of trouble in our city," they said.

ceedingly trouble our city, 21And teach customs, which are not lawful for us to receive, neither to observe, being Romans. 22And the multitude rose up together against them; and the magistrates rent off their clothes, and commanded to beat *them*. 23And when they had laid many stripes upon them, they cast *them* into prison, charging the jailer to keep them safely: 24 Who, having received such a charge, thrust them into the inner prison, and made their feet fast in the stocks.

25 And at midnight Paul and Silas prayed, and sang praises unto God: and the prisoners heard them. 26And suddenly there was a great earthquake, so that the foundations of the prison were shaken: and immediately all the doors were opened, and every one's bands were loosed. 27And the keeper of the prison awaking out of his sleep, and seeing the prison doors open, he drew out his sword, and would have killed himself, supposing that the prisoners had been fled. 28 But Paul cried with a loud voice, saying, Do thyself no harm: for we are all here. 29 Then he called for a light, and sprang in, and came trembling, and fell down before Paul and Silas, 30And brought them out, and said, Sirs, what must I do to be saved? 31And they said, Believe on the Lord Jesus Christ, and thou shalt be saved, and thy house. 32And they spake unto him the word of the Lord, and to all that were in his house. 33And he took them the same hour of the night, and washed *their* stripes; and was baptized, he and all his, straightway. 34And when he had brought them into his house, he set meat before them, and rejoiced, believing in God with all his house. 35And when it was day, the magistrates sent the serjeants, saying, Let those men go. 36And the keeper of the prison told this saying to Paul, The magistrates have sent to let you go: now therefore depart, and go in peace. 37 But Paul said unto them, They have beaten us openly uncondemned, being Romans, and have cast *us* into prison; and now do they thrust us out privily? nay verily; but let them come themselves and fetch us out. 38And the serjeants told these words unto the magistrates: and they feared, when they heard that they were Romans. 39And they came and besought them, and brought *them* out, and desired *them* to depart out of the city. 40And they went out of the prison, and entered into *the house of* Lydia: and when they had seen the brethren, they comforted them, and departed.

17 Now when they had passed through Amphipolis and Apollonia, they came to Thessalonica, where was a synagogue of the Jews: 2And Paul, as his manner was, went in unto them, and three sabbath days reasoned with them out of the Scriptures, 3 Opening and alleging, that Christ must needs have suffered, and

Jews, 21 and are proclaiming customs which it is not lawful for us to accept or to observe, being Romans." 22And the crowd rose up together against them, and the chief magistrates tore their robes off them, and proceeded to order *them* to be beaten with rods. 23And when they had inflicted many blows upon them, they threw them into prison, commanding the jailer to guard them securely; 24 and he, having received such a command, threw them into the inner prison, and fastened their feet in the stocks. 25 But about midnight Paul and Silas were praying and singing hymns of praise to God, and the prisoners were listening to them; 26 and suddenly there came a great earthquake, so that the foundations of the prison-house were shaken; and immediately all the doors were opened, and everyone's chains were unfastened. 27And when the jailer had been roused out of sleep and had seen the prison doors opened, he drew his sword and was about to kill himself, supposing that the prisoners had escaped. 28 But Paul cried out with a loud voice, saying, "Do yourself no harm, for we are all here!" 29And he called for lights and rushed in and trembling with fear, he fell down before Paul and Silas, 30 and after he brought them out, he said, "Sirs, what must I do to be saved?" 31And they said, "Believe in the Lord Jesus, and you shall be saved, you and your household." 32And they spoke the word of the Lord to him together with all who were in his house. 33And he took them that *very* hour of the night and washed their wounds, and immediately he was baptized, he and all his *household*. 34And he brought them into his house and set food before them, and rejoiced greatly, having believed in God with his whole household.

35 Now when day came, the chief magistrates sent their policemen, saying, "Release those men." 36And the jailer reported these words to Paul, *saying*, "The chief magistrates have sent to release you. Now therefore come out and go in peace." 37 But Paul said to them, "They have beaten us in public without trial, men who are Romans, and have thrown us into prison; and now are they sending us away secretly? No indeed! But let them come themselves and bring us out." 38And the policemen reported these words to the chief magistrates. And they were afraid when they heard that they were Romans, 39 and they came and appealed to them, and when they had brought them out, they kept begging them to leave the city. 40And they went out of the prison and entered *the house of* Lydia, and when they saw the brethren, they encouraged them and departed.

17 Now when they had traveled through Amphipolis and Apollonia, they came to Thessalonica, where there was a synagogue of the Jews. 2And according to Paul's custom, he went to them, and for three Sabbaths reasoned with them from the Scriptures, 3 explaining and giving evidence that the Christ had to suffer and

WILLIAMS

BECK

make great disturbance in our town 21 and to advocate practices which it is against the law for us Romans to accept or observe."

22 The crowd also joined in the attack upon them, and the chiefs of the police court had them stripped and flogged. 23 After flogging them severely, they put them into jail, and gave the jailer orders to keep close watch on them. 24 Because he had such strict orders, he put them into the inner cell and fastened their feet in the stocks.

25 But about midnight, while Paul and Silas were praying and singing hymns of praise to God, and the prisoners were listening to them, 26 suddenly there was an earthquake so great that it shook the very foundations of the jail, the doors all flew open, and every prisoner's chains were unfastened. 27 When the jailer awoke and saw that the jail-doors were open, he drew his sword and was on the point of killing himself, because he thought that the prisoners had escaped.

28 But Paul at once shouted out to him, "Do yourself no harm, for we are all here!"

29 Then the jailer called for lights and rushed in and fell trembling at the feet of Paul and Silas. 30 After leading them out of the jail, he said, "Sirs, what must I do to be saved?"

31 They answered, "Believe on the Lord Jesus, and you and your household will be saved." 32 Then they told God's message to him and to all the members of his household. 33 Even at that time of the night he took them and washed their wounds, and he and all the members of his household at once were baptized. 34 Then he took them up to his house and gave them food, and he and all the members of his household were happy in their faith in God.

35 When day broke, the chiefs of the police court sent policemen with the message to let the men go. 36 The jailer reported this message to Paul, saying, "The chiefs of the police court have sent orders to let you go. So now you may come out and go in peace."

37 But Paul said to them, "They beat us in public and that without a trial, and put us in jail although we are Roman citizens! Let them come here themselves and take us out!"

38 The policemen reported this message to the chiefs of the police court, and they became alarmed when they heard that they were Roman citizens, 39 and came and pleaded with them, and took them out and begged them to leave town. 40 After getting out of jail, they went to Lydia's house; they saw the brothers and encouraged them, and then left town.

"They're Jews, 21 and they're teaching religious ways that we as Romans aren't allowed to adopt or practice."

22 The crowd also joined in attacking them. Then the officials tore the clothes off Paul and Silas and ordered them beaten with rods. 23 After striking them many times, the men put them in prison and ordered the jailer to watch them and not let them escape. 24 He did as he was ordered and put them in the inner cell and fastened their feet in the stocks.

25 About midnight Paul and Silas were praying and singing to God, and the other prisoners were listening to them. 26 Suddenly the earth quaked so violently the foundations of the prison were shaken, all the doors flew open, and everybody's chains were unfastened.

27 The jailer woke up and saw the prison doors open. Thinking the prisoners had escaped, he drew his sword and was going to kill himself. 28 But Paul called out loud, "Don't harm yourself! We're all here!"

29 The jailer asked for lights, rushed in, and fell down trembling before Paul and Silas. 30 Then he took them outside and asked, "Sirs, what do I have to do to be saved?"

31 "Believe in the Lord Jesus," they answered, "and you and your family will be saved." 32 They spoke the Lord's Word to him and everyone in his home.

33 At that hour of the night he took them with him and washed their wounds. And he and all who were with him were baptized immediately. 34 He took them up into his home and gave them a meal. He and everyone in his home were very happy to have found faith in God.

35 In the morning the officials sent attendants and said, "Let those men go."

36 The jailer reported the message to Paul. "The officials sent word to let you go," he said. "Come out now, and go in peace." 83

37 But Paul told them, "They have beaten us publicly without trying and condemning us, although we're Roman citizens, and have put us in prison. And now they're trying to put us out secretly? I should say not! They should come themselves and take us out."

38 The attendants reported to the officials what Paul said. Hearing that Paul and Silas were Roman citizens, they were frightened. 39 So they came and pleaded with them, took them out, and asked them to leave the city.

40 Leaving the prison, they went to Lydia, saw and encouraged the Christians there, and then left.

---

17 *They make many converts at Thessalonica; run out of town by a riot, they go to Berea; here the people read the Scriptures; driven from Berea, Paul goes to Athens; he preaches in its famous auditorium but is heckled by the philosophers*

Now they traveled on through Amphipolis and Apollonia until they reached Thessalonica. Here there was a Jewish synagogue. 2 So Paul, as he usually did, went to the synagogue, and for three sabbaths discussed with them the Scriptures, 3 explaining them and proving that the Christ had to suffer and rise from the dead, and

In Thessalonica

17 Paul and Silas traveled through Amphipolis and Apollonia and came to Thessalonica. Here the Jews had a synagog. 2 Paul went in as usual and on three Saturdays had Bible discussions with them. 3 He explained and showed them: "The promised Savior had to

[83] Judges 18:6

377

K.J.V.

risen again from the dead; and that this Jesus, whom I preach unto you, is Christ. 4And some of them believed, and consorted with Paul and Silas; and of the devout Greeks a great multitude, and of the chief women not a few.

5 But the Jews which believed not, moved with envy, took unto them certain lewd fellows of the baser sort, and gathered a company, and set all the city on an uproar, and assaulted the house of Jason, and sought to bring them out to the people. 6And when they found them not, they drew Jason and certain brethren unto the rulers of the city, crying, These that have turned the world upside down are come hither also; 7 Whom Jason hath received: and these all do contrary to the decrees of Cesar, saying that there is another king, *one* Jesus. 8And they troubled the people and the rulers of the city, when they heard these things. 9And when they had taken security of Jason, and of the others, they let them go.

10 And the brethren immediately sent away Paul and Silas by night unto Berea: who coming *thither* went into the synagogue of the Jews. 11 These were more noble than those in Thessalonica, in that they received the word with all readiness of mind, and searched the Scriptures daily, whether those things were so. 12 Therefore many of them believed; also of honourable women which were Greeks, and of men, not a few. 13 But when the Jews of Thessalonica had knowledge that the word of God was preached of Paul at Berea, they came thither also, and stirred up the people. 14And then immediately the brethren sent away Paul to go as it were to the sea: but Silas and Timotheus abode there still. 15And they that conducted Paul brought him unto Athens: and receiving a commandment unto Silas and Timotheus for to come to him with all speed, they departed.

16 Now while Paul waited for them at Athens, his spirit was stirred in him, when he saw the city wholly given to idolatry. 17 Therefore disputed he in the synagogue with the Jews, and with the devout persons, and in the market daily with them that met with him. 18 Then certain philosophers of the Epicureans, and of the Stoics, encountered him. And some said, What will this babbler say? other some, He seemeth to be a setter forth of strange gods: because he preached unto them Jesus, and the resurrection. 19And they took him, and brought him unto Areopagus, saying, May we know what this new doctrine, whereof thou speakest, *is*? 20 For thou bringest certain strange things to our ears: we would know therefore what these things mean. 21 (For all the Athenians, and strangers which were there, spent their time in nothing else, but either to tell or to hear some new thing.)

22 Then Paul stood in the midst of Mars' hill, and said, *Ye* men of Athens, I perceive that in all things ye are too superstitious. 23 For as I passed by, and beheld your devotions, I found an altar with this inscription, TO THE UNKNOWN GOD. Whom therefore ye ignorantly worship, him declare I unto you. 24 God that made the world and all things therein, seeing that he is Lord of heaven and earth, dwelleth

N.A.S.

rise again from the dead, and *saying*, "This Jesus whom I am proclaiming to you is the Christ." 4And some of them were persuaded and joined Paul and Silas, along with a great multitude of the God-fearing Greeks and a number of the leading women. 5 But the Jews, becoming jealous and taking along some wicked men from the market place, formed a mob and set the city in an uproar; and coming upon the house of Jason, they were seeking to bring them out to the people. 6And when they did not find them, they *began* dragging Jason and some brethren before the city authorities, shouting, "These men who have upset *ª*the world have come here also; 7 and Jason has welcomed them, and they all act contrary to the decrees of Caesar, saying that there is another king, Jesus." 8And they stirred up the crowd and the city authorities who heard these things. 9And when they had received a pledge from Jason and the others, they released them.

10 And the brethren immediately sent Paul and Silas away by night to Berea; and when they arrived, they went into the synagogue of the Jews. 11 Now these were more noble-minded than those in Thessalonica, for they received the word with great eagerness, examining the Scriptures daily, *to see* whether these things were so. 12 Many of them therefore believed, along with a number of prominent Greek women and men. 13 But when the Jews of Thessalonica found out that the word of God had been proclaimed by Paul in Berea also, they came there likewise, agitating and stirring up the crowds. 14And then immediately the brethren sent Paul out to go as far as the sea; and Silas and Timothy remained there. 15 Now those who conducted Paul brought him as far as Athens; and receiving a command for Silas and Timothy to come to him as soon as possible, they departed.

16 Now while Paul was waiting for them at Athens, his spirit was being provoked within him as he was beholding the city full of idols. 17 So he was reasoning in the synagogue with the Jews and the God-fearing *Gentiles,* and in the market place every day with those who happened to be present. 18And also some of the Epicurean and Stoic philosophers were conversing with him. And some were saying, "What would this idle babbler wish to say?" Others, "He seems to be a proclaimer of strange deities,"—because he was preaching Jesus and the resurrection. 19And they took him and brought him to the Areopagus, saying, "May we know what this new teaching is which you are proclaiming? 20 "For you are bringing some strange things to our ears; we want to know therefore what these things mean." 21 (Now all the Athenians and the strangers visiting there used to spend their time in nothing other than telling or hearing something new.) 22And Paul stood in the midst of the Areopagus and said, "Men of Athens, I observe that you are very religious in all respects. 23 "For while I was passing through and examining the objects of your worship, I also found an altar with this inscription, 'TO AN UNKNOWN GOD.' What therefore you worship in ignorance, this I proclaim to you. 24 "The God who made the world and all things in it, since He is Lord of heaven and earth, does not dwell in temples

---

[a] Lit., *the inhabited earth.*

WILLIAMS

said, "This very Jesus whom I proclaim to you is the Christ."

4 So some of them were convinced, and they joined Paul and Silas; also quite a number of devout Greeks and not a few women of the first rank. 5 But this enraged the Jews; so they got together some wicked loafers about the public square, formed a mob, and set the town in an uproar. 6 They stopped at Jason's house and tried to bring them out to the people. So, as they could not find them, they dragged Jason and some of the brothers before the town magistrates, shouting, "These fellows, who have turned the world topsy-turvy, have come here too, 7 and Jason has welcomed them. They are all acting contrary to the Emperor's decrees, because they claim there is another king, Jesus."

8 Thus they wrought up to great excitement the crowd and the town magistrates, on their hearing this, 9 and they made Jason and the other brothers give bond, and then turned them loose.

10 That night at once the brothers sent Paul and Silas away to Berea, and on arriving there they went to the Jewish synagogue. 11 The Jews there were better disposed than those in Thessalonica, for they welcomed the message with all eagerness and carried on a daily study of the Scriptures to see if Paul's message was true. 12 Many of them came to believe, and not a few distinguished Greek women and men. 13 But when the Jews at Thessalonica learned that God's message had been proclaimed at Berea by Paul, they came there too to excite the masses and stir up a riot. 14 Then the brothers at once sent Paul off to the coast, while Silas and Timothy stayed on there. 15 The men who acted as Paul's bodyguard took him all the way to Athens, and then went back with orders for Silas and Timothy to come to him as soon as possible.

16 While Paul was waiting for them at Athens, his spirit was stirred to its depths to see the city completely steeped in idolatry. 17 So he kept up his discussions in the synagogue with the Jews and the pagans[a] who were worshiping there, and also day by day in the public square with any who chanced to be there.

18 Some of the Epicurean and the Stoic philosophers began to debate with him; and some said, "What is this scraps-of-truth-picker trying to say?"

Others said, "He seems to be a preacher of foreign deities." They said so because he was telling the good news of Jesus and the resurrection.

19 So they took him and brought him to the city auditorium[b] and said, "May we know what this new teaching of yours is? 20 For some of the things you bring sound startling to us; so we want to know just what they mean." 21 (Now all the Athenians and foreign visitors in Athens used to spend their time in nothing else than telling or listening to the latest new thing out.)

22 So Paul stood up in the center of the auditorium and said:

"Men of Athens, at every turn I make I see that you are very religious. 23 For as I was going here and there and looking at the things you worship, I even found an altar with this inscription, 'TO AN UNKNOWN GOD.' So it is about the Being whom you are in ignorance already worshiping that I am telling you. 24 The God who made the world and all that it contains, since He is Lord of heaven and earth, does not

[a] Grk., *those worshiping there*, pagan converts to Judaism. [b] *Mars' Hill*.

BECK

suffer and rise from the dead, and this Savior is the Jesus I'm telling you about."

4 He convinced some of the Jews, and they joined Paul and Silas, and also a large crowd of the Greeks who worshiped God, and many of the wives of the leaders.*

5 Then the Jews got jealous, took some wicked men in the marketplace, formed a mob, and started a riot in the city. They attacked Jason's home and searched for Paul and Silas to bring them out to the people. 6 When they didn't find them, they dragged Jason and some other Christians before the city officials, shouting, "Those men who have made trouble all over the world are here now 7 and are Jason's guests. They're all going against the emperor's decrees by saying there's another king—Jesus!"

8 Hearing this, the crowd and the officials were upset. 9 But after they had taken security from Jason and the others, they let them go.

10 That same night the Christians sent Paul and Silas away to Berea.

At Berea

When they came there, they went into the synagog of the Jews. 11 These people were nobler than those at Thessalonica—they were very eager to get the Word and every day studied the Bible to see if those things were so. 12 And many of them believed, also many noble Greeks, women as well as men.

13 But when the Jews at Thessalonica found out Paul had now preached God's Word also in Berea, they came there to stir up trouble among the people. 14 Immediately the Christians sent Paul away to the sea, but Silas and Timothy stayed there.

In Athens

15 Those who escorted Paul took him all the way to Athens. When they left, they took instructions to Silas and Timothy to come to him as soon as possible.

16 While Paul was waiting for them in Athens, he was inwardly stirred up when he saw how many idols there were in the city. 17 Then he had discussions in the synagog with Jews and others who feared God, and every day in the marketplace with those who happened to be there. 18 Some Epicurean and Stoic philosophers also debated with him, but some asked, "What is this fellow with his scraps of learning trying to say?" Others said, "He seems to be telling about foreign gods"—because he was telling the good news of Jesus and the resurrection.

19 Then they took him and brought him before the court of Mars' Hill and asked, "Could we know, what is this new thing you teach? 20 You bring some things that sound strange to us, and we want to know what they mean."

21 Now everybody in Athens, also the visitors staying there, used their time only to tell or hear the latest news.

22 Paul stood before the court of Mars' Hill and said, "Men of Athens, I see how very religious you are in every way. 23 As I went through your city and saw the things you worship, I found an altar with the inscription TO AN UNKNOWN GOD. Now I'm telling you about what you don't know and yet worship. 24 *The God who made* the world and everything in it is the Lord of *heaven and earth* and doesn't

* About this time Timothy came to Paul, bringing money and food from Philippi. Paul says, "Even while I was in Thessalonica, you more than once sent help for my needs." (Phil. 4:16; cp. v. 15; 1 Thess. 1:1; 2 Thess. 1:1).

K.J.V.

not in temples made with hands; 25 Neither is worshipped with men's hands, as though he needed any thing, seeing he giveth to all life, and breath, and all things; 26And hath made of one blood all nations of men for to dwell on all the face of the earth, and hath determined the times before appointed, and the bounds of their habitation; 27 That they should seek the Lord, if haply they might feel after him, and find him, though he be not far from every one of us: 28 For in him we live, and move, and have our being; as certain also of your own poets have said, For we are also his offspring. 29 Forasmuch then as we are the offspring of God, we ought not to think that the Godhead is like unto gold, or silver, or stone, graven by art and man's device. 30And the times of this ignorance God winked at; but now commandeth all men every where to repent: 31 Because he hath appointed a day, in the which he will judge the world in righteousness by *that* man whom he hath ordained; *whereof* he hath given assurance unto all *men*, in that he hath raised him from the dead.

32 And when they heard of the resurrection of the dead, some mocked: and others said, We will hear thee again of this *matter*. 33 So Paul departed from among them. 34 Howbeit certain men clave unto him, and believed: among the which *was* Dionysius the Areopagite, and a woman named Damaris, and others with them.

18 After these things Paul departed from Athens, and came to Corinth; 2And found a certain Jew named Aquila, born in Pontus, lately come from Italy, with his wife Priscilla, (because that Claudius had commanded all Jews to depart from Rome,) and came unto them. 3And because he was of the same craft, he abode with them, and wrought: (for by their occupation they were tentmakers.) 4And he reasoned in the synagogue every sabbath, and persuaded the Jews and the Greeks. 5And when Silas and Timotheus were come from Macedonia, Paul was pressed in the spirit, and testified to the Jews *that* Jesus *was* Christ. 6And when they opposed themselves, and blasphemed, he shook *his* raiment, and said unto them, Your blood *be* upon your own heads; I *am* clean: from henceforth I will go unto the Gentiles.

7 And he departed thence, and entered into a certain *man's* house, named Justus, *one* that worshipped God, whose house joined hard to the synagogue. 8And Crispus, the chief ruler of the synagogue, believed on the Lord with all his house; and many of the Corinthians hearing believed, and were baptized. 9 Then spake the Lord to Paul in the night by a vision, Be not afraid, but speak, and hold not thy peace: 10 For I am with thee, and no man shall set on thee to hurt thee: for I have much people in this city. 11And he continued *there* a year and six months, teaching the word of God among them.

N.A.S.

made with hands; 25 neither is He served by human hands, as though He needed anything, since He Himself gives to all life and breath and all things; 26 and He made from *one every nation of mankind to live on all the face of the earth, having determined *their* appointed times, and the boundaries of their habitation, 27 that they should seek God, if perhaps they might grope for Him and find Him, though He is not far from each one of us; 28 for in Him we live and move and exist, as even some of your own poets have said, 'For we also are His offspring.' 29 "Being then the offspring of God, we ought not to think that the Divine Nature is like gold or silver or stone, an image formed by the art and thought of man. 30 "Therefore having overlooked the times of ignorance, God is now declaring to men that all everywhere should repent, 31 because He has fixed a day in which He will judge the world in righteousness through a Man whom He has appointed, having furnished proof to all men by raising Him from the dead."

32 Now when they heard of the resurrection of the dead, some *began* to sneer, but others said, "We shall hear you again concerning this." 33 So Paul went out of their midst. 34 But some men joined him and believed, among whom also was Dionysius the Areopagite and a woman named Damaris and others with them.

18 After these things he left Athens and went to Corinth. 2And he found a certain Jew named Aquila, a native of Pontus, having recently come from Italy with his wife Priscilla, because Claudius had commanded all the Jews to leave Rome. He came to them, 3 and because he was of the same trade, he stayed with them and they were working; for by trade they were tentmakers. 4And he was reasoning in the synagogue every Sabbath and trying to persuade Jews and Greeks.

5 But when Silas and Timothy came down from Macedonia, Paul *began* devoting himself completely to the word, solemnly testifying to the Jews that Jesus was the Christ. 6And when they resisted and blasphemed, he shook out his garments and said to them, "Your blood *be* upon your own heads, I am clean; from now on I shall go to the Gentiles." 7And he departed from there and went to the house of a certain man named Titius Justus, a worshiper of God, whose house was next to the synagogue. 8And Crispus, the leader of the synagogue, believed in the Lord with all his household, and many of the Corinthians when they heard were believing and being baptized. 9And the Lord said to Paul in the night by a vision, "Do not be afraid *any longer*, but go on speaking and do not be silent; 10 for I am with you, and no man will attack you in order to harm you, for I have many people in this city." 11And he settled *there* a year and six months, teaching the word of God among them.

[a] Some later mss. read, *one blood.*

WILLIAMS

dwell in temples made by human hands, 25 nor is He served by human hands as though He were in need of anything, for He Himself gives all men life and breath and everything else. 26 From one forefather He made every nation of mankind, for living all over the face of the earth, fixing their appointed times and the limits of their lands, 27 so that they might search for God, possibly they might grope for Him, and find Him, though He is really not far from any of us. 28 For it is through union with Him that we live and move and exist, as some of your own poets have said,

" 'For we are His offspring too.' 29 Since then we are God's offspring, we ought not to suppose that His nature is like gold or silver or stone or anything carved by man's art and thought. 30 Though God overlooked those times of ignorance, He now commands all men everywhere to repent, 31 since He has set a day on which He will justly judge the world through a man whom He has appointed. He has made this credible to all by raising Him from the dead."

32 But when they heard of the resurrection of the dead, some sneered, but others said, "We will hear you again on this subject."

33 So Paul left the auditorium. 34 Some men, however, joined him and came to believe, among them Dionysius, a member of the city council; also a woman named Damaris, and some others.

18 *In Corinth Paul stays with Aquila and Priscilla, Jewish refugees from Rome; Silas and Timothy come and tell of the Thessalonians; Paul before Judge Gallio who dismisses the case; Apollos taught by Priscilla*

After this he left Athens and went to Corinth. 2 There he found a Jew named Aquila, a native of Pontus, who had recently come from Italy with his wife Priscilla, because Claudius had issued an edict for all Jews to leave Rome. So Paul paid them a visit, 3 and as they all had the same trade, they proceeded to work together. 4 Every sabbath it was Paul's habit to preach in the synagogue and to persuade both Jews and Greeks.

5 By the time Silas and Timothy arrived from Macedonia, Paul was wholly absorbed in preaching the message and was enthusiastically assuring[a] the Jews that Jesus is the Christ. 6 But as they opposed and abused him, he shook out his clothes in protest and said to them, "Your blood be upon your own heads! I am not to blame for it myself. Hereafter I am going to the heathen."

7 So he moved into the house of a pagan named Titus Justus, who worshiped the true God; his house was next to the synagogue. 8 But Crispus, the leader of the synagogue, became a believer in the Lord, and so did all his family, and from time to time many of the Corinthians heard, believed, and were baptized.

9 One night in a vision the Lord said to Paul, "Stop being afraid, go on speaking, never give up; 10 because I am with you, and no one is going to attack you so as to injure you, because I have many people in this city." 11 So for a year and a half he settled down among them and went on teaching God's message.

[a] Lit., *thoroughly testifying to.*

BECK

live in temples made by human hands, 25 and He isn't served by human hands as if He needed anything. He Himself *gives* everyone life and *breath*[84] and everything. 26 From one man He made every nation to have the people live all over the earth, setting the times allotted to them and the boundaries they live in, 27 that they should look for God and perhaps feel their way to Him and find Him. He is never far from any one of us, 28 because we live and move and are in Him; as some of your poets* have said, 'You see, we are His children.' 29 Now, if we're God's children, we shouldn't think God is like gold, silver, or stone, carved by man's art and imagination.

30 "While God overlooked the times when people were ignorant, He now tells all of them everywhere to be sorry for their sins, 31 because He has set a day when *He is going to* have a Man *judge the world with justice.*[85] He has appointed Him for this. And by raising Him from the dead has given everyone a good reason to believe."

32 When they heard about a resurrection of the dead, some started to mock, while others said, "We'll hear you again about this."

33 And so Paul left the meeting. 34 Some men joined him and believed. Among them were Dionysius, a member of the court, and a woman by the name of Damaris, and some others with them.

In Corinth

18 After that he left Athens and came to Corinth. 2 There he found a Jew by the name of Aquila, born in Pontus, and his wife Priscilla. They had recently come from Italy because Claudius had ordered all Jews to leave Rome. Paul went to them, 3 and because they made tents for a living just as he did, he stayed with them, and they worked together.

4 Every Saturday he would argue in the synagog and try to win Jews and Greeks. 5 But when Silas and Timothy came down from Macedonia, Paul devoted himself entirely to teaching the Word as he solemnly assured the Jews, "Jesus is the promised Savior!" 6 But they opposed him and abused him. In protest he shook the dust from his clothes and told them, "Your blood be on your own heads. I am innocent. From now on I'll go to the non-Jews."

7 Then he left the place and went to the home of a man by the name of Titius Justus, who worshiped God. His house was right beside the synagog. 8 Now Crispus, the synagog leader, and all who were in his home believed in the Lord. And many other people in Corinth who heard Paul believed and were baptized.

9 One night the Lord spoke to Paul in a vision, *"Don't be afraid!* But speak, and don't be silent—10 *I am with you,*[86] and nobody will attack you so as to harm you, because I have many people in this city."

11 He stayed there a year and six months and taught God's Word among them.**

* Aratus and Cleanthes wrote this about 270 B. C.
** In the year 50 Paul wrote the two letters to the Thessalonians.
[84] Is. 42:5
[85] Ps. 9:8; 96:13; 98:9
[86] Ex. 3:12; Joshua 1:5; Is. 41:10; 43:5; Jer. 1:8

K.J.V.

12 And when Gallio was the deputy of Achaia, the Jews made insurrection with one accord against Paul, and brought him to the judgment seat, 13 Saying, This *fellow* persuadeth men to worship God contrary to the law. 14And when Paul was now about to open *his* mouth, Gallio said unto the Jews, If it were a matter of wrong or wicked lewdness, O *ye* Jews, reason would that I should bear with you: 15 But if it be a question of words and names, and *of* your law, look ye *to it;* for I will be no judge of such *matters.* 16And he drave them from the judgment seat. 17 Then all the Greeks took Sosthenes, the chief ruler of the synagogue, and beat *him* before the judgment seat. And Gallio cared for none of those things.

18 And Paul *after this* tarried *there* yet a good while, and then took his leave of the brethren, and sailed thence into Syria, and with him Priscilla and Aquila; having shorn *his* head in Cenchrea: for he had a vow. 19And he came to Ephesus, and left them there: but he himself entered into the synagogue, and reasoned with the Jews. 20 When they desired *him* to tarry longer time with them, he consented not; 21 But bade them farewell, saying, I must by all means keep this feast that cometh in Jerusalem: but I will return again unto you, if God will. And he sailed from Ephesus. 22And when he had landed at Cesarea, and gone up, and saluted the church, he went down to Antioch. 23And after he had spent some time *there,* he departed, and went over *all* the country of Galatia and Phrygia in order, strengthening all the disciples.

24 And a certain Jew named Apollos, born at Alexandria, an eloquent man, *and* mighty in the Scriptures, came to Ephesus. 25 This man was instructed in the way of the Lord; and being fervent in the spirit, he spake and taught diligently the things of the Lord, knowing only the baptism of John. 26And he began to speak boldly in the synagogue: whom when Aquila and Priscilla had heard, they took him unto *them,* and expounded him the way of God more perfectly. 27And when he was disposed to pass into Achaia, the brethren wrote, exhorting the disciples to receive him: who, when he was come, helped them much which had believed through grace: 28 For he mightily convinced the Jews, *and that* publicly, shewing by the Scriptures that Jesus was Christ.

N.A.S.

12 But while Gallio was proconsul of Achaia, the Jews with one accord rose up against Paul and brought him before the judgment-seat, 13 saying, "This man persuades men to worship God contrary to the law." 14 But when Paul was about to open his mouth, Gallio said to the Jews, "If it were a matter of wrong or of vicious crime, O Jews, it would be reasonable for me to put up with you; 15 but if there are questions about words and names and your own Law, look after it yourselves; I am unwilling to be a judge of these matters." 16And he drove them away from the judgment-seat. 17And they all took hold of Sosthenes, the leader of the synagogue, and *began* beating him in front of the judgment-seat. And Gallio was not concerned about any of these things.

18 And Paul, having remained many days longer, took leave of the brethren and put out to sea for Syria, and with him were Priscilla and Aquila. In Cenchrea he had his hair cut, for he was keeping a vow. 19And they came to Ephesus, and he left them there. Now he himself entered the synagogue and reasoned with the Jews. 20And when they asked him to stay for a longer time, he did not consent, 21 but taking leave of them and saying, "I will return to you again if God wills," he set sail from Ephesus.

22 And when he had landed at Caesarea, he went up and greeted the church, and went down to Antioch. 23And having spent some time *there,* he departed and passed successively through the Galatian region and Phrygia, strengthening all the disciples.

24 Now a certain Jew named Apollos, an Alexandrian by birth, an eloquent man, came to Ephesus; and he was mighty in the Scriptures. 25 This man had been instructed in the way of the Lord; and being fervent in spirit, he was speaking and teaching accurately the things concerning Jesus, being acquainted only with the baptism of John; 26 and he began to speak out boldly in the synagogue. But when Priscilla and Aquila heard him, they took him aside and explained to him the way of God more accurately. 27And when he wanted to go across to Achaia, the brethren encouraged him and wrote to the disciples to welcome him; and when he had arrived, he helped greatly those who had believed through grace; 28 for he powerfully refuted the Jews in public, demonstrating by the Scriptures that Jesus was the Christ.

19 And it came to pass, that, while Apollos was at Corinth, Paul having passed through the upper coasts came to Ephesus; and finding certain disciples, 2 He said unto them, Have ye received the Holy Ghost since ye believed? And they said unto him, We have not so much as

19 And it came about that while Apollos was at Corinth, Paul having passed through the upper country came to Ephesus, and found some disciples, 2 and he said to them, "Did you receive the Holy Spirit when you believed?" And they *said* to him, "No, we have not even

WILLIAMS

12 While Gallio was governor of Greece, the Jews unanimously attacked Paul and one day brought him before the court, 13 and said, "This fellow is inducing people to worship God in ways that violate our laws."
14 As Paul was about to open his mouth, Gallio said to the Jews, "If it were some misdemeanor or underhanded rascality, O Jews, I would in reason listen to you; 15 but as it is questions about words and titles and your own law, you will have to see to it yourselves. I refuse to act as judge in these matters." 16 So he drove them away from the court. 17 Then they all seized Sosthenes, the leader of the synagogue, and kept beating him right in front of the court; but Gallio paid no attention to it.
18 Now Paul stayed a considerable time longer in Corinth, and then bade the brothers good-by and set sail for Syria, accompanied by Aquila and Priscilla. At Cenchreae he had his hair cut, for he was under a vow. 19 Then they came to Ephesus, and Paul left them there. He went into the synagogue and had a discussion with the Jews. 20 They asked him to stay longer, but he would not consent. 21 But as he bade them good-by, he promised, "I will come back to you again, if it is God's will." Then he set sail from Ephesus. 22 When he reached Caesarea, he went up to Jerusalem and greeted the church there; then he went down to Antioch.
23 After spending some time there, he started out again, and by a definite schedule traveled all over Galatia and Phrygia, imparting new strength to all the disciples.
24 Meanwhile, a Jew named Apollos came to Ephesus. He was a native of Alexandria, a learned man, and skillful in the use of the Scriptures. 25 He had been instructed about the way of the Lord, and with spiritual fervor he was speaking and was accurately teaching some details about Jesus, although he knew of no baptism but John's. 26 He started speaking courageously in the synagogue, but when Priscilla and Aquila heard him, they took him home with them and more accurately explained the way of God to him. 27 Because he wished to cross to Greece, the brothers wrote and urged the disciples there to welcome him. On his arrival he rendered great service to those who through God's favor had believed, 28 for he successfully refuted the Jews in public and proved by the Scriptures that Jesus was the Christ.

BECK

12 But when Gallio was proconsul of Greece, the Jews united in an attack on Paul and brought him before Gallio as judge. 13 "This man," they said, "is persuading people to worship God in ways that are against the Law."
14 Just as Paul was going to answer, Gallio said to the Jews, "If this were a crime or vicious wrong, it would be only fair that I listen to you Jews. 15 But since we have questions here about words, names, and your own Law, see to it yourselves. I don't want to be a judge of those things." 16 And he drove them away from his platform.
17 Then all of them took Sosthenes, the synagog leader, and beat him in front of the judge's platform. But Gallio paid no attention to it.

Home

18 After staying there quite a while longer, Paul said good-by to the Christians. Priscilla and Aquila went with him. At Cenchrea he had his hair cut, since he had been under a vow. They took a boat for Syria 19 and came to Ephesus, where Paul left Priscilla and Aquila. There he went into the synagog and had a discussion with the Jews. 20 They asked him to stay longer, but he refused. 21 As he said good-by to them, he told them, "I will come back to you if God wants me to."
22 He sailed from Ephesus and landed at Caesarea. He went up, greeted the church, and then went down to Antioch.

Apollos

23 After staying there for some time, Paul left and went from place to place through the Galatian country and through Phrygia, strengthening all the disciples.
24 A Jew by the name of Apollos, who was born in Alexandria, came to Ephesus. He was a learned man and mighty in the Bible. 25 After he had been instructed in the Lord's way, he spoke with a glowing enthusiasm and taught correctly about Jesus but knew only John's baptism. 26 He started to speak boldly in the synagog. When Priscilla and Aquila heard him, they took him with them and explained God's way to him more accurately.
27 As he wanted to cross over to Greece, the Christians wrote to the disciples there urging them to welcome him. When he got there, he gave much help to those who by God's love were now believers. 28 Publicly and vigorously he proved the Jews were wrong as he showed from the Bible that Jesus is the promised Savior.

19 *Paul in Ephesus, headquarters for his work in Roman Asia (province); He works miracles; Sceva's seven sons reproved for imitating Him; Demetrius sets the city in an uproar; Paul rescued by Roman officers*

It was while Apollos was in Corinth that Paul, by passing through the inland districts, came to Ephesus. He found a few disciples there 2 and asked them, "Did you receive the Holy Spirit when you believed?"
They answered him, "So far from that, we never even heard that there is a Holy Spirit."

Paul in Ephesus

19 While Apollos was in Corinth, Paul traveled over the hills to get to Ephesus. Meeting some disciples there, 2 he asked them, "Did you receive the Holy Spirit when you became believers?"
"No," they answered him, "we haven't even heard there is a Holy Spirit."

K.J.V.

heard whether there be any Holy Ghost. 3And he said unto them, Unto what then were ye baptized? And they said, Unto John's baptism. 4 Then said Paul, John verily baptized with the baptism of repentance, saying unto the people, that they should believe on him which should come after him, that is, on Christ Jesus. 5 When they heard *this,* they were baptized in the name of the Lord Jesus. 6And when Paul had laid *his* hands upon them, the Holy Ghost came on them; and they spake with tongues, and prophesied. 7And all the men were about twelve. 8And he went into the synagogue, and spake boldly for the space of three months, disputing and persuading the things concerning the kingdom of God. 9 But when divers were hardened, and believed not, but spake evil of that way before the multitude, he departed from them, and separated the disciples, disputing daily in the school of one Tyrannus. 10And this continued by the space of two years; so that all they which dwelt in Asia heard the word of the Lord Jesus, both Jews and Greeks. 11And God wrought special miracles by the hands of Paul: 12 So that from his body were brought unto the sick handkerchiefs or aprons, and the diseases departed from them, and the evil spirits went out of them.

13 Then certain of the vagabond Jews, exorcists, took upon them to call over them which had evil spirits the name of the Lord Jesus, saying, We adjure you by Jesus whom Paul preacheth. 14And there were seven sons of *one* Sceva, a Jew, *and* chief of the priests, which did so. 15And the evil spirit answered and said, Jesus I know, and Paul I know; but who are ye? 16And the man in whom the evil spirit was leaped on them, and overcame them, and prevailed against them, so that they fled out of that house naked and wounded. 17And this was known to all the Jews and Greeks also dwelling at Ephesus; and fear fell on them all, and the name of the Lord Jesus was magnified. 18And many that believed came, and confessed, and shewed their deeds. 19 Many of them also which used curious arts brought their books together, and burned them before all *men:* and they counted the price of them, and found *it* fifty thousand *pieces* of silver. 20 So mightily grew the word of God and prevailed.

21 After these things were ended, Paul purposed in the spirit, when he had passed through Macedonia and Achaia, to go to Jerusalem, saying, After I have been there, I must also see Rome. 22 So he sent into Macedonia two of them that ministered unto him, Timotheus and Erastus; but he himself stayed in Asia for a season. 23And the same time there arose no small stir about that way. 24 For a certain *man* named Demetrius, a silversmith, which made silver shrines for Diana, brought no small gain unto the craftsmen; 25 Whom he called together with the workmen of like occupation, and said, Sirs, ye know that by this craft we have our wealth. 26 Moreover ye see and hear, that not alone at Ephesus, but almost throughout all Asia, this Paul hath persuaded and turned away much people, saying that they be no gods, which

N.A.S.

heard whether there is a Holy Spirit." 3And he said, "Into what then were you baptized?" And they said, "Into John's baptism." 4And Paul said, "John baptized with the baptism of repentance, telling the people to believe in Him who was coming after him, that is, in Jesus." 5And when they heard this, they were baptized in the name of the Lord Jesus. 6And when Paul had laid his hands upon them, the Holy Spirit came on them, and they *began* speaking with tongues and prophesying. 7And there were in all about twelve men.

8 And he entered the synagogue and continued speaking out boldly for three months, reasoning and persuading *them* about the kingdom of God. 9 But when some were becoming hardened and disobedient, speaking evil of the Way before the multitude, he withdrew from them and took away the disciples, reasoning daily in the school of Tyrannus. 10And this took place for two years, so that all who lived in Asia heard the word of the Lord, both Jews and Greeks. 11And God was performing extraordinary miracles by the hands of Paul, 12 so that handkerchiefs or aprons were even carried from his body to the sick, and the diseases left them and the evil spirits went out. 13 But also some of the Jewish exorcists, who went from place to place, attempted to name over those who had the evil spirits the name of the Lord Jesus, saying, "I adjure you by Jesus whom Paul preaches." 14And seven sons of one Sceva, a Jewish chief priest, were doing this. 15And the evil spirit answered and said to them, "I recognize Jesus, and I know about Paul, but who are you?" 16And the man in whom was the evil spirit leaped on them and subdued both of them and overpowered them, so that they fled out of that house naked and wounded. 17And this became known to all, both Jews and Greeks, who lived in Ephesus; and fear fell upon them all and the name of the Lord Jesus was being magnified. 18 Many also of those who had believed kept coming, confessing and disclosing their practices. 19And many of those who practiced magic brought their books together and *began* burning them in the sight of all; and they counted up the price of them and found it fifty thousand pieces of silver. 20 So the word of the Lord was growing mightily and prevailing.

21 Now after these things were finished, Paul purposed in the spirit to go to Jerusalem after he had passed through Macedonia and Achaia, saying, "After I have been there, I must also see Rome." 22And having sent into Macedonia two of those who ministered to him, Timothy and Erastus, he himself stayed in Asia for a while.

23 And about that time there arose no small disturbance concerning the Way. 24 For a certain man named Demetrius, a silversmith, who made silver shrines of Artemis, was bringing no little business to the craftsmen; 25 these he gathered together with the workmen of similar *trades,* and said, "Men, you know that our prosperity depends upon this business. 26 "And you see and hear that not only in Ephesus, but in almost all of Asia, this Paul has persuaded and turned away a considerable number of people, saying that gods made with hands are

WILLIAMS

3 He then asked, "With what sort of baptism then were you baptized?"

They answered, "With John's baptism."

4 Then Paul said, "John baptized with a baptism that was an expression of repentance, telling the people to believe in Him who was to come after him; that is, in Jesus." 5 On hearing this they were baptized in the name of the Lord Jesus, 6 and when Paul laid his hands upon them, the Holy Spirit came upon them, and they began to speak in foreign tongues and to prophesy. 7 In all there were about twelve men.

8 He went to the synagogue there and for three months courageously spoke, keeping up his discussions and continuing to persuade them about the kingdom of God. 9 But as some of them grew harder and harder and refused to believe, actually criticizing the Way before the people, he left them, withdrew his disciples, and continued his discussions in the lecture-hall of Tyrannus. 10 This went on for two years, so that everybody living in the province of Asia, Greeks as well as Jews, heard the Lord's message.

11 God also continued to do such wonder-works through Paul 12 as an instrument that the people carried off to the sick, towels or aprons used by him, and at their touch they were cured of their diseases, and the evil spirits went out of them. 13 But some wandering Jews who claimed to be driving out the evil spirits tried to use the name of the Lord Jesus on those who had evil spirits in them, saying, "I command you by that Jesus whom Paul preaches!"

14 Sceva, a Jewish high priest, had seven sons who were doing this. 15 But on one occasion the evil spirit answered, "Jesus I know and Paul I know about, but who are you?"

16 So the man in whom the evil spirit was, leaped upon them and so violently overpowered two of them that they ran out of the house stripped of their clothes and wounded. 17 This at once became known to everybody living in Ephesus, Greeks as well as Jews, and awe fell upon them all, and the name of the Lord Jesus began to be held in high honor. 18 And many who became believers kept coming and confessing and uncovering their former practices. 19 Many people who had practiced magic brought their books together and burned them up before the public gaze. They estimated the price of them and found it to be ten thousand dollars. 20 In a way of just such power as this the Lord's message kept on spreading and prevailing.

21 After these events had been brought to a close, Paul under the guidance of the Spirit decided to pass through Macedonia and Greece on his way to Jerusalem, saying, "After I have gone there I must see Rome too." 22 So he sent off to Macedonia two of his assistants, Timothy and Erastus, while he stayed on for a while in Asia.

23 Now just about that time a great commotion arose about the Way. 24 A silversmith named Demetrius, by manufacturing silver shrines of Artemis, was bringing in great profits to his workmen. 25 He called together his workmen, and others engaged in similar trades, and said to them:

"Men, you well know that our prosperity depends on this business of ours, 26 and you see and hear that, not only in Ephesus but all over the province of Asia, this man Paul has led away a vast number of people by persuading them, telling them that gods made by human hands

BECK

3 "Into what then were you baptized?" he asked them.

"Into John's baptism," they answered.

4 Paul said, "John baptized those who were sorry for their sins and told the people to believe in the One coming after him, that is Jesus."

5 When they heard this, they were baptized into the name of the Lord Jesus. 6 And as Paul laid his hands on them, the Holy Spirit came on them, and they started to talk in other languages and to speak God's Word. 7 There were about twelve men in the group.

8 He went into the synagog and spoke there boldly for three months, discussing and trying to convince people about God's kingdom. 9 When some got stubborn, refused to believe, and slandered the Christian religion before the crowd, he left them, took his disciples away from them, and had daily discussions in the lecture hall of Tyrannus. 10 This went on for two years so that all who lived in the province of Asia, Jews and Greeks, heard the Lord's Word.

11 God did extraordinary miracles by Paul's hands. 12 When handkerchiefs and aprons that had touched his skin were taken to the sick, their sicknesses left them, and the evil spirits went out of them.

13 Some Jews who made it their business to go around and drive out evil spirits tried to use the name of the Lord Jesus over those having the evil spirits. "I order you by that Jesus whom Paul preaches," they said. 14 Seven sons of Sceva, a Jewish ruling priest, were doing this. 15 But the evil spirit answered them, "I know Jesus, and I know Paul, but who are you?" 16 Then the man with the evil spirit jumped on them, got the better of them, and overpowered them all so that they ran naked and bruised out of that house.

17 All the Jews and Greeks living in Ephesus heard about it. They were all frightened and started to think very highly of the name of the Lord Jesus. 18 Many believers came to confess and tell about their magic spells. 19 Many of those who had practiced magic gathered their books and burned them in front of everybody. They added up the cost of these books and found they were worth fifty thousand denarii.* 20 In that way the Lord's Word grew mightily and triumphed.**

21 After all these things had happened, Paul decided to go through Macedonia and Greece and then to Jerusalem. "When I get there," he said, "I must also see Rome." 22 But he sent two of his helpers, Timothy and Erastus, to Macedonia, while he himself stayed in the province of Asia a while longer.

The Riot

23 During that time there was a big disturbance over the Christian religion.

24 A silversmith by the name of Demetrius provided a big income for the skilled workers by making silver shrines of Artemis. 25 He called a meeting of these and others who did similar work. "Men," he said, "you know we're getting a fine income from this business, 26 and you see and hear how this Paul has won and taken away a large crowd not only in Ephesus but almost all over the province of Asia by telling them, 'Gods made by human hands are

* A denarius was one day's pay.
** From Ephesus, during the time of A. D. 54-55, Paul wrote his first letter to the Corinthians. There are good reasons to believe that here he also wrote the letters to the Philippians, Philemon, Colossians, and Ephesians.

K.J.V.

are made with hands: 27 So that not only this our craft is in danger to be set at nought; but also that the temple of the great goddess Diana should be despised, and her magnificence should be destroyed, whom all Asia and the world worshippeth. 28And when they heard *these sayings,* they were full of wrath, and cried out, saying, Great *is* Diana of the Ephesians. 29And the whole city was filled with confusion: and having caught Gaius and Aristarchus, men of Macedonia, Paul's companions in travel, they rushed with one accord into the theatre. 30And when Paul would have entered in unto the people, the disciples suffered him not. 31And certain of the chief of Asia, which were his friends, sent unto him, desiring *him* that he would not adventure himself into the theatre. 32 Some therefore cried one thing, and some another: for the assembly was confused; and the more part knew not wherefore they were come together. 33And they drew Alexander out of the multitude, the Jews putting him forward. And Alexander beckoned with the hand, and would have made his defence unto the people. 34 But when they knew that he was a Jew, all with one voice about the space of two hours cried out, Great *is* Diana of the Ephesians. 35And when the townclerk had appeased the people, he said, *Ye* men of Ephesus, what man is there that knoweth not how that the city of the Ephesians is a worshipper of the great goddess Diana, and of the *image* which fell down from Jupiter? 36 Seeing then that these things cannot be spoken against, ye ought to be quiet, and to do nothing rashly. 37 For ye have brought hither these men, which are neither robbers of churches, nor yet blasphemers of your goddess. 38 Wherefore if Demetrius, and the craftsmen which are with him, have a matter against any man, the law is open, and there are deputies: let them implead one another. 39 But if ye inquire any thing concerning other matters, it shall be determined in a lawful assembly. 40 For we are in danger to be called in question for this day's uproar, there being no cause whereby we may give an account of this concourse. 41And when he had thus spoken, he dismissed the assembly.

20 And after the uproar was ceased, Paul called unto *him* the disciples, and embraced *them,* and departed for to go into Macedonia. 2And when he had gone over those parts, and had given them much exhortation, he came into Greece, 3And *there* abode three months. And when the Jews laid wait for him, as he was about to sail into Syria, he purposed to return through Macedonia. 4And there accompanied him into Asia Sopater of Berea; and of the Thessalonians, Aristarchus and Secundus; and Gaius of Derbe, and Timotheus; and of Asia, Tychicus and Trophimus. 5 These going before tarried for us at Troas. 6And we sailed away from Philippi after the days of unleavened bread, and came unto them to Troas in five

N.A.S.

no gods *at all.* 27 "And not only is there danger that this trade of ours fall into disrepute, but also that the temple of the great goddess Artemis be regarded as worthless and that she whom all of Asia and the world worship should even be dethroned from her magnificence." 28And when they heard *this* and were filled with rage, they *began* crying out, saying, "Great is Artemis of the Ephesians!" 29And the city was filled with the confusion, and they rushed with one accord into the theater, dragging along Gaius and Aristarchus, Paul's traveling companions from Macedonia. 30And when Paul wanted to go in to the assembly, the disciples would not let him. 31And also some of the °Asiarchs who were friends of his sent to him and repeatedly urged him not to venture into the theater. 32 So then, some were shouting one thing and some another, for the assembly was in confusion, and the majority did not know for what cause they had come together. 33And some of the crowd concluded *it was* Alexander, since the Jews had put him forward; and having motioned with his hand, Alexander was intending to make a defense to the assembly. 34 But when they recognized that he was a Jew, a single outcry arose from them all as they shouted for about two hours, "Great is Artemis of the Ephesians!" 35And after quieting the multitude the townclerk *said, "Men of Ephesus, what man is there after all who does not know that the city of the Ephesians is guardian of the temple of the great Artemis, and of the *image* which fell down from heaven? 36 "Since then these are undeniable facts, you ought to keep calm and to do nothing rash. 37 "For you have brought these men *here* who are neither robbers of temples nor blasphemers of our goddess. 38 "So then, if Demetrius and the craftsmen who are with him have a complaint against any man, the courts are in session and proconsuls are *available;* let them bring charges against one another. 39 "But if you want anything beyond this, it shall be settled in the lawful assembly. 40 "For indeed we are in danger of being accused of a riot in connection with today's affair, since there is no *real* cause *for it;* and in this connection we shall be unable to account for this disorderly gathering." 41And after saying this he dismissed the assembly.

20 And after the uproar had ceased, Paul sent for the disciples and when he had exhorted them and taken his leave of them, he departed to go to Macedonia. 2And when he had gone through those districts and had given them much exhortation, he came to Greece. 3And *there* he spent three months, and when a plot was formed against him by the Jews as he was about to set sail for Syria, he determined to return through Macedonia. 4And he was accompanied by Sopater of Berea, *the son* of Pyrrhus; and by Aristarchus and Secundus of the Thessalonians; and Gaius of Derbe, and Timothy; and Tychicus and Trophimus of Asia. 5 But these had gone on ahead and were waiting for us at Troas. 6And we sailed from Philippi after the days of Unleavened Bread, and came to them at Troas within five days; and there we stayed seven days.

[a] I.e., political or religious officials of the province of Asia.

WILLIAMS

are not gods at all. 27 Now the danger facing us is, not only that our business will lose its reputation but also that the temple of the great goddess Artemis will be brought into contempt and that she whom all Asia and all the world now worship will soon be dethroned from her majestic glory!"

28 When they heard this, they became furious and kept on shouting, "Great Artemis of Ephesus!" 29 So the whole city was thrown into confusion and with one impulse the people rushed into the theatre and dragged with them two Macedonians, Gaius and Aristarchus, Paul's traveling companions. 30 Paul wanted to go into the assembly and address the people, but the disciples would not let him. 31 Some of the public officials in Asia, who were friendly to him, also sent word to him, begging him not to risk himself in the theatre. 32 So they kept on shouting, some one thing, some another, for the assembly was in confusion, and the majority of them did not know why they had met. 33 Some of the crowd concluded that it was Alexander, since the Jews had pushed him to the front, and since Alexander had made a gesture of the hand as though he would make a defense before the people. 34 But as soon as they saw that he was a Jew, a shout went up from them all as the shout of one man, lasting for two hours:

"Great Artemis of Ephesus!"

35 At last the city recorder quieted the mob and said:

"Men of Ephesus, who in the world does not know that the city of Ephesus is the guardian of the temple of the great Artemis and of the image that fell down from heaven? 36 So, as this cannot be denied, you must be quiet and do nothing rash. 37 For you have brought these men here, although they are not guilty of sacrilege or of abusive speech against our goddess. 38 So then, if Demetrius and his fellow-workmen have a charge against anybody, there are the courts and the judges; let them go to law. 39 But if you require anything beyond this, it must be settled in the regular assembly. 40 For we are in danger of being charged with rioting for today's assembly, as there is not a single reason we can give for it." 41 With these words he dismissed the assembly.

20 *Paul goes to Macedonia, Greece, and Troy; at Troy he speaks till midnight; youthful Eutychus falls dead from a third story window; Paul raises him to life; at Miletus he makes a farewell speech to the Ephesian elders*

When the uproar had ceased, Paul sent for the disciples and encouraged them. Then he bade them good-by and started off for Macedonia. 2 He passed through those districts and by continuing to talk to them encouraged the people. He then went on to Greece 3 where he stayed three months. Just as he was about to sail for Syria, he changed his mind and returned by way of Macedonia, because a plot against him had been laid by the Jews. 4 He had as companions Sopater, the son of Pyrrhus, from Berea, Aristarchus and Secundus from Thessalonica, Gaius from Derbe, Timothy, and Tychicus and Trophimus from the province of Asia. 5 They went on to Troas and waited for us, 6 while we, after the feast of Unleavened Bread, sailed from Philippi, and five days after joined them at Troas, where we spent a week.

BECK

no gods.' 27 There is a danger people will not only reject our line of business but will also think nothing of the temple of the great goddess Artemis, and then she whom all Asia and the world worship will be robbed of her glory."

28 When they heard this, they got furious and shouted, "Great is Artemis of the Ephesians!" 29 The confusion spread all over the city. And they all rushed into the theater together, dragging with them Gaius and Aristarchus, Paul's fellow travelers from Macedonia.

30 Paul wanted to go into the crowd, but the disciples wouldn't let him. 31 Even some officials of the province of Asia who were his friends sent men to him and urged him not to risk going into the theater.

32 Some were shouting one thing, some another. The crowd was confused, and most of them didn't know why they were meeting. 33 Then the Jews pushed Alexander to the front, and some of the crowd told him what to do. Alexander waved his hand to quiet them and wanted to make a defense before the people. 34 But when they found out he was a Jew, they all started to shout in unison and kept it up for about two hours, "Great is Artemis of the Ephesians!"

35 Then the city secretary quieted the crowd. "Men of Ephesus," he said, "who in the world doesn't know that this city of the Ephesians is the keeper of the temple of the great Artemis and of the statue that fell down from Zeus? 36 Since nobody can deny this, you must be quiet and not do anything reckless. 37 The men you brought here don't rob temples or insult our goddess. 38 Now if Demetrius and his workers have something against anyone, we have special days and proconsuls to hold court; there they should accuse one another. 39 And if you want anything else, it must be settled in a legal meeting. 40 We're in danger of being accused of a riot today for which there is no good reason. We'll not be able to explain this mob." 41 After saying this, he dismissed the meeting.

20 When the uproar had died down, Paul sent for the disciples, encouraged them, and saying good-by to them, left to go to Macedonia.* 2 He went through those parts of the country and spoke much to encourage the people and then went to Greece 3 and stayed there three months.**

At Troas

3 Just as Paul was going to sail for Syria, the Jews plotted against him, so he decided to go back through Macedonia. 4 Sopater from Berea, the son of Pyrrhus, went with him; also Aristarchus and Secundus from Thessalonica, and Gaius from Derbe, and Timothy, but Tychicus and Trophimus were from the province of Asia; 5 they came and were waiting for us in Troas. 6 After the Passover days of bread without yeast we sailed from Philippi and in five days came to them in Troas and stayed there seven days.

* From Macedonia in A. D. 55 Paul wrote his second letter to the Corinthians.
** From Corinth in A. D. 56 Paul wrote his letter to the Romans.

K.J.V.

days; where we abode seven days. 7And upon the first *day* of the week, when the disciples came together to break bread, Paul preached unto them, ready to depart on the morrow; and continued his speech until midnight. 8And there were many lights in the upper chamber, where they were gathered together. 9And there sat in a window a certain young man named Eutychus, being fallen into a deep sleep: and as Paul was long preaching, he sunk down with sleep, and fell down from the third loft, and was taken up dead. 10And Paul went down, and fell on him, and embracing *him* said, Trouble not yourselves; for his life is in him. 11When he therefore was come up again, and had broken bread, and eaten, and talked a long while, even till break of day, so he departed. 12And they brought the young man alive, and were not a little comforted.

13 And we went before to ship, and sailed unto Assos, there intending to take in Paul: for so had he appointed, minding himself to go afoot. 14And when he met with us at Assos, we took him in, and came to Mitylene. 15And we sailed thence, and came the next *day* over against Chios; and the next *day* we arrived at Samos, and tarried at Trogyllium; and the next *day* we came to Miletus. 16 For Paul had determined to sail by Ephesus, because he would not spend the time in Asia: for he hasted, if it were possible for him, to be at Jerusalem the day of Pentecost.

17 And from Miletus he sent to Ephesus, and called the elders of the church. 18And when they were come to him, he said unto them, Ye know, from the first day that I came into Asia, after what manner I have been with you at all seasons, 19 Serving the Lord with all humility of mind, and with many tears, and temptations, which befell me by the lying in wait of the Jews: 20*And* how I kept back nothing that was profitable *unto you,* but have shewed you, and have taught you publicly, and from house to house, 21 Testifying both to the Jews, and also to the Greeks, repentance toward God, and faith toward our Lord Jesus Christ. 22And now, behold, I go bound in the spirit unto Jerusalem, not knowing the things that shall befall me there: 23 Save that the Holy Ghost witnesseth in every city, saying that bonds and afflictions abide me. 24 But none of these things move me, neither count I my life dear unto myself, so that I might finish my course with joy, and the ministry, which I have received of the Lord Jesus, to testify the gospel of the grace of God. 25And now, behold, I know that ye all among whom I have gone preaching the kingdom of God, shall see my face no more. 26 Wherefore I take you to record this day, that I *am* pure from the blood of all *men.* 27 For I have not shunned to declare unto you all the counsel of God.

28 Take heed therefore unto yourselves, and to all the flock, over the which the Holy Ghost hath made you overseers, to feed the church of God, which he hath purchased with his own blood. 29 For I know this, that after my departing shall grievous wolves enter in among you, not sparing the flock. 30Also of your own selves shall men arise, speaking perverse things, to draw away disciples after them. 31 Therefore watch, and remember, that by the space of three years I ceased not to warn every one night and day with tears. 32And now, brethren, I commend you to God, and to the word of his grace, which is able to build you up, and to give you an inheritance among all them which are sanctified. 33 I have coveted no man's silver, or gold, or

N.A.S.

7 And on the first day of the week, when we were gathered together to break bread, Paul *began* talking to them, intending to depart the next day, and he prolonged his message until midnight. 8And there were many lamps in the upper room where we were gathered together. 9And there was a certain young man named Eutychus sitting on the window-sill, sinking into a deep sleep; and as Paul kept on talking, he was overcome by sleep and fell down from the third floor, and was picked up dead. 10 But Paul went down and fell upon him and after embracing him, he said, "Do not be troubled, for his life is in him." 11And when he had gone *back* up, and had broken the bread and eaten, he talked with them a long while, until daybreak, and so departed. 12And they took away the boy alive, and were greatly comforted.

13 But we, going ahead to the ship, set sail for Assos, intending from there to take Paul on board; for thus he had arranged it, intending himself to go by land. 14And when he met us at Assos, we took him on board and came to Mitylene. 15And sailing from there, we arrived the following day opposite Chios; and the next day we crossed over to Samos; and the day following we came to Miletus. 16 For Paul had decided to sail past Ephesus in order that he might not have to spend time in Asia; for he was hurrying to be in Jerusalem, if possible, on the day of Pentecost.

17 And from Miletus he sent to Ephesus and called to him the elders of the church. 18And when they had come to him, he said to them. "You yourselves know, from the first day that I set foot in Asia, how I was with you the whole time, 19 serving the Lord with all humility and with tears and with trials which came upon me through the plots of the Jews; 20 how I did not shrink from declaring to you anything that was profitable, and teaching you publicly and from house to house, 21 solemnly testifying to both Jews and Greeks of repentance toward God and faith in our Lord Jesus Christ. 22 "And now, behold, bound in spirit, I am on my way to Jerusalem, not knowing what will happen to me there, 23 except that the Holy Spirit solemnly testifies to me in every city, saying that bonds and afflictions await me. 24 "But I do not consider my life of any account as dear to myself, in order that I may finish my course, and the ministry which I received from the Lord Jesus, to testify solemnly of the gospel of the grace of God. 25 "And now, behold, I know that you all, among whom I went about preaching the kingdom, will see my face no more. 26 "Therefore I testify to you this day, that I am innocent of the blood of all men. 27 "For I did not shrink from declaring to you the whole purpose of God. 28 "Be on guard for yourselves and for all the flock, among which the Holy Spirit has made you overseers, to shepherd the church of God which He purchased with His own blood. 29 "I know that after my departure savage wolves will come in among you, not sparing the flock; 30 and from among your own selves men will arise, speaking perverse things, to draw away the disciples after them. 31 "Therefore be on the alert, remembering that night and day for a period of three years I did not cease to admonish each one with tears. 32 "And now I commend you to God and to the word of His grace, which is able to build *you* up and to give *you* the inheritance among all those who are sanctified. 33 "I have coveted no one's silver

WILLIAMS

7 On the first day of the week when we had met to break bread, Paul addressed them, since he was leaving the next day, and prolonged his speech till midnight. 8 There were many lamps in the room upstairs where we met, 9 and a young man named Eutychus, who was sitting by the window, was gradually overcome by heavy drowsiness, as Paul kept speaking longer and longer, and at last he went fast asleep and fell from the third story to the ground and was picked up dead.
10 But Paul went down and fell on him and embraced him, and said, "Stop being alarmed, his life is still in him." 11 So he went back upstairs, and broke the bread and ate with them, and after talking with them extendedly, even till daylight, he left them. 12 Then they took the boy home alive, and were greatly comforted.
13 We had already gone on board the ship and set sail for Assos, where we were to take Paul on board; for it had been so arranged by him, as he intended to travel there on foot. 14 So when he met us as Assos, we took him on board and sailed on to Mitylene. 15 On the next day we sailed from there and arrived off Chios. On the next day we crossed to Samos, and the next we reached Miletus. 16 For Paul's plan was to sail past Ephesus, so as not to lose any time in the province of Asia; for he was eager, if possible, to reach Jerusalem by Pentecost.
17 From Miletus he sent to Ephesus for the elders of the church. 18 When they arrived, he said to them:
"You know how I lived among you all the time from the day I first set foot in the province of Asia, and how I continued 19 to serve the Lord with all humility and in tears, through the trials that befell me because of the plots of the Jews. 20 I never shrank from telling you anything that was for your good, nor from teaching you in public and in private, 21 but constantly and earnestly I urged Greeks as well as Jews to turn with repentance to God and to have faith in our Lord Jesus. 22 And I am here now on my way to Jerusalem, because I am impelled by the Spirit to do so, though I am not aware what will befall me there, 23 except that in town after town the Holy Spirit emphatically assures me that imprisonment and sufferings are awaiting me. 24 But now I count as nothing the sacrifice of my life, if only I can finish my race and render the service entrusted to me by the Lord Jesus, of faithfully telling the good news of God's favor. 25 And now I know that none of you among whom I went about preaching the kingdom will ever see my face again. 26 I therefore protest to you today that I am not responsible for the blood of any of you, 27 for I never shrank from telling you God's whole plan. 28 Take care of yourselves and of the whole flock, of which the Holy Spirit has made you overseers, so as to continue to be shepherds of the church of God,ᵃ which He bought with His own blood. 29 Because I know that after I have gone violent wolves will break in among you and will not spare the flock. 30 Even from your own number men will appear who will try, by speaking perversions of truth, to draw away the disciples after them. 31 So ever be on your guard and always remember that for three years, night and day, I never ceased warning you one by one, and that with tears. 32 And now I commit you to the Lord, and to the message of His favor, which is able to build you up and to give you your proper possessionᵇ among all God's consecrated people. 33 I have never coveted any man's

BECK

7 On Sunday, when we met for a meal, Paul spoke to the people. Since he intended to leave the next day, he went on talking till midnight. 8 There were many lamps in the upstairs room where we were meeting.
9 A young man by the name of Eutychus, sitting in the window, was dropping off into a deep sleep as Paul talked on and on. Finally, overcome by sleep, he fell down from the third story and was picked up dead. 10 But Paul went down, lay on him, and took him into his arms. "Don't get excited," he said. "He's alive!" 11 Then he went upstairs again, broke the bread, and ate. And after a long talk that lasted till the sun rose, he left.
12 The people took the boy away alive and were very much comforted.

From Troas to Miletus

13 We went ahead to the boat and sailed to Assos. There we were going to take Paul into the boat; he had arranged it that way, planning himself to go there on foot. 14 When we met him in Assos, we took him on board and went on to Mitylene. 15 We sailed from there and on the following day came opposite Chios. The next day we crossed over to Samos and on the next came to Miletus. 16 Paul had decided to sail past Ephesus to avoid spending time in the province of Asia; he was in a hurry to get to Jerusalem for the day of Pentecost if possible.

With the Pastors of Ephesus

17 From Miletus he sent men to Ephesus to get the pastors of the church. 18 When they came to him, he said to them: "You know how I lived with you all the time from the first day I came into the province of Asia; 19 how I served the Lord very humbly, with tears, and in trials I endured as the Jews plotted against me; 20 how I didn't shrink from telling you anything that would help you or from teaching you publicly and from house to house; 21 and how I earnestly warned Jews and non-Jews to turn from sin to God and believe in our Lord Jesus. 22 And now, you see, the Spirit compels me to go to Jerusalem. 23 I don't know what will happen to me there, except that the Holy Spirit keeps warning me from town to town that chains and troubles are waiting for me. 24 I don't count my life worth anything. I just want to finish running my race and doing the work the Lord Jesus entrusted to me, declaring the good news of God's love.
25 "I went around among you preaching the Kingdom, and now I know none of you will see me again. 26 That is why I declare to you today I am innocent of the blood of any of you, 27 because I didn't shrink from telling you God's whole plan.
28 "Take care of yourselves and the whole flock in which the Holy Spirit has made you overseers to be shepherds of God's church that He bought⁸⁷ with His own blood. 29 I know when I'm gone fierce wolves will come among you and not spare the flock. 30 And even some of you men will start to tell perversions of the truth to get the disciples to leave and follow you. 31 So watch and remember how for three years, day and night, I didn't stop warning everyone with tears. 32 And now I entrust you to God and to the Word of His love, which can build you up and give you the salvation to be shared by all who are made holy.⁸⁸
33 "I didn't want anyone's silver or gold or

[a] Some good Mss. read, the church of the Lord.
[b] Grk., inheritance.

[87] Ps. 74:1-2
[88] Deut. 33:3-4

389

K.J.V.

apparel. 34 Yea, ye yourselves know, that these hands have ministered unto my necessities, and to them that were with me. 35 I have shewed you all things, how that so labouring ye ought to support the weak, and to remember the words of the Lord Jesus, how he said, It is more blessed to give than to receive.

36 And when he had thus spoken, he kneeled down, and prayed with them all. 37And they all wept sore, and fell on Paul's neck, and kissed him, 38 Sorrowing most of all for the words which he spake, that they should see his face no more. And they accompanied him unto the ship.

21 And it came to pass, that after we were gotten from them, and had launched, we came with a straight course unto Coos, and the *day* following unto Rhodes, and from thence unto Patara: 2And finding a ship sailing over unto Phenicia, we went aboard, and set forth. 3 Now when we had discovered Cyprus, we left it on the left hand, and sailed into Syria, and landed at Tyre: for there the ship was to unlade her burden. 4And finding disciples, we tarried there seven days: who said to Paul through the Spirit, that he should not go up to Jerusalem. 5And when we had accomplished those days, we departed and went our way; and they all brought us on our way, with wives and children, till *we were* out of the city: and we kneeled down on the shore, and prayed. 6And when we had taken our leave one of another, we took ship; and they returned home again. 7And when we had finished *our* course from Tyre, we came to Ptolemais, and saluted the brethren, and abode with them one day. 8And the next *day* we that were of Paul's company departed, and came unto Cesarea; and we entered into the house of Philip the evangelist, which was *one* of the seven; and abode with him. 9And the same man had four daughters, virgins, which did prophesy. 10And as we tarried *there* many days, there came down from Judea a certain prophet, named Agabus. 11And when he was come unto us, he took Paul's girdle, and bound his own hands and feet, and said, Thus saith the Holy Ghost, So shall the Jews at Jerusalem bind the man that owneth this girdle, and shall deliver *him* into the hands of the Gentiles. 12And when we heard these things, both we, and they of that place, besought him not to go up to Jerusalem. 13 Then Paul answered, What mean ye to weep and to break mine heart? for I am ready not to be bound only, but also to die at Jerusalem for the name of the Lord Jesus. 14And when he would not be persuaded, we ceased, saying, The will of the Lord be done. 15And after those days we took up our carriages, and went up to Jerusalem. 16 There went with us also *certain* of the disciples of Cesarea, and brought with them one Mnason of Cyprus, an old disciple, with whom we should lodge. 17And when we were come to Jerusalem, the brethren received us gladly. 18And the *day* following Paul went in with us unto James; and all the elders were present. 19And when he had saluted them, he declared .particularly what things God had wrought

N.A.S.

or gold or clothes. 34 "You yourselves know that these hands ministered to my *own* needs and to the men who were with me. 35 "In every thing I showed you that by working hard in this manner you must help the weak and remember the words of the Lord Jesus, that He Himself said, 'It is more blessed to give than to receive.' "

36 And when he had said these things, he knelt down and prayed with them all. 37And they *began* to weep aloud and embraced Paul, and repeatedly kissed him, 38 grieving especially over the word which he had spoken, that they should see his face no more. And they were accompanying him to the ship.

21 And when it came about that we had parted from them and had set sail, we ran a straight course to Cos and the next day to Rhodes and from there to Patara; 2 and having found a ship crossing over to Phoenicia, we went aboard and set sail. 3And when we had come in sight of Cyprus, leaving it on the left, we kept sailing to Syria and landed at Tyre; for there the ship was to unload its cargo. 4And after looking up the disciples, we stayed there seven days; and they kept telling Paul through the Spirit not to set foot in Jerusalem. 5And when it came about that our days there were ended, we departed and started on our journey, while they all, with wives and children, escorted us until *we were* out of the city. And after kneeling down on the beach and praying, we said farewell to one another. 6 Then we went on board the ship, and they returned home again.

7 And when we had finished the voyage from Tyre, we arrived at Ptolemais; and after greeting the brethren, we stayed with them for a day. 8And on the next day we departed and came to Caesarea; and entering the house of Philip the evangelist, who was one of the seven, we stayed with him. 9 Now this man had four virgin daughters who were prophetesses. 10And as we were staying there for some days, a certain prophet named Agabus came down from Judea. 11And coming to us, he took Paul's belt and bound his own feet and hands, and said, "This is what the Holy Spirit says: 'In this way the Jews at Jerusalem will bind the man who owns this belt and deliver him into the hands of the Gentiles.' " 12And when we had heard this, we as well as the local residents *began* begging him not to go up to Jerusalem. 13 Then Paul answered, "What are you doing, weeping and breaking my heart? For I am ready not only to be bound, but even to die at Jerusalem for the name of the Lord Jesus." 14And since he would not be persuaded, we fell silent, remarking, "The will of the Lord be done!"

15 And after these days we got ready and started on our way up to Jerusalem. 16And *some* of the disciples from Caesarea also came with us, taking us to Mnason of Cyprus, a disciple of long standing with whom we were to lodge.

17 And when we had come to Jerusalem, the brethren received us gladly. 18And now the following day Paul went in with us to James, and all the elders were present. 19And after he had greeted them, he *began* to relate one by one the things which God had done among the

WILLIAMS

silver or gold or clothes. 34 You know yourselves that these hands of mine provided for my own needs and for my companions. 35 In everything I showed you that by working hard like this we must help those who are weak, and remember the words of the Lord Jesus, that He said, 'It makes one happier to give than to get.' "

36 After he had finished this speech, he fell on his knees with them all and prayed. 37 There was loud weeping by them all, as they threw their arms around Paul's neck and kept on kissing him with affection, because they were especially pained at his saying that they would never see his face again. Then they went down to the ship with him.

21 *Paul goes on to Jerusalem; stops with Philip at Caesarea; warned by prophet Agabus of imprisonment but not deterred; reaches Jerusalem, interviews Pastor James, tries to win the Jewish Christians; seized by a mob but rescued by the Roman colonel*

When we had torn ourselves away from them, we struck a bee line for Cos, and the next day on to Rhodes, and from there to Patara. 2 There we found a ship bound for Phoenicia, and so we went aboard and sailed away. 3 After sighting Cyprus and leaving it on our left, we sailed on for Syria, and put in at Tyre, for the ship was to unload her cargo there. 4 So we looked up the disciples there and stayed a week with them. Because of impressions made by the Spirit they kept on warning Paul not to set foot in Jerusalem. 5 But when our time was up, we left there and went on, and all of them with their wives and children accompanied us out of town. There we knelt down on the beach and prayed; 6 there we bade one another good-by, and we went aboard the ship, while they went back.

7 On finishing the sail from Tyre we landed at Ptolemais. Here we greeted the brothers and spent a day with them. 8 The next day we left there and went on to Caesarea, where we went to the house of Philip the evangelist, who was one of the Seven, and stayed with him. 9 He had four unmarried daughters who were prophetesses. 10 While we were spending some days here, a prophet named Agabus came down from Judea. 11 He came to see us and took Paul's belt and with it bound his own hands and feet, and said, "This is what the Holy Spirit says, 'The Jews at Jerusalem will bind the man who owns this belt like this, and then will turn him over to the heathen.' "

12 When we heard this, we and all the people there begged him not to go up to Jerusalem. 13 Then Paul answered, "What do you mean by crying and breaking my heart? Why, I am ready not only to be bound at Jerusalem but to die there for the sake of the Lord Jesus."

14 So, since he would not yield to our appeal, we stopped begging him, and said, "The Lord's will be done!"

15 After this we got ready and started up to Jerusalem. 16 Some of the disciples from Caesarea went with us and took us to the house of Mnason, a man from Cyprus, one of the early disciples, to spend the night. 17 When we reached Jerusalem, the brothers there gave us a hearty welcome. 18 On the next day we went with Paul to see James, and all the elders of the church came too. 19 Paul first greeted them and then gave them a detailed account of what God had done among the heathen through his service.

BECK

clothes. 34 You know these hands worked for what I needed and for the men with me. 35 In every way I showed you that by working hard as I do we should help the weak and remember what the Lord Jesus said: "We are happier when we give than when we get something."

36 When he had said this, he knelt down with all of them and prayed. 37 They wept very much, put their arms around Paul, and kissed him, 38 It hurt them most of all that he had said they wouldn't see him again. Then they took him to the ship.

At Tyre

21 When we had broken away from them, we sailed and followed a straight course to Cos and the next day to Rhodes and from there to Patara. 2 We found a ship going across to Phoenicia, went on board, and sailed. 3 We came in sight of Cyprus, and leaving it on our left, sailed on to Syria and landed at Tyre because the ship was to unload its cargo there.

4 We looked up the disciples and stayed there seven days. By the Spirit they told Paul not to go up to Jerusalem. 5 When our time was up, we started on our way. All of them with their wives and children accompanied us out of the city. There we knelt on the beach and prayed and said good-by to one another. 6 Then we went on board the ship, and they went back home.

At Caesarea

7 We continued our sailing, going from Tyre to Ptolemais. There we greeted our fellow Christians and spent a day with them. 8 The next day we left and came to Caesarea. We went into the home of Philip the evangelist, one of the seven, and stayed with him. 9 He had four unmarried daughters who spoke God's Word.

10 While we were staying there longer than we had expected, a prophet by the name of Agabus came down from Judea. 11 He came to us, took Paul's belt, tied his own feet and hands, and said, "The Holy Spirit says, 'This is how the Jews in Jerusalem will tie the man this belt belongs to and hand him over to the non-Jews.' "

12 When we heard this, we and those living there urged him not to go up to Jerusalem. 13 Then Paul answered, "What are you doing—crying and making me weak in my purpose? I'm ready not only to be bound but even to die in Jerusalem for the name of the Lord Jesus."

14 When he would not be persuaded, we were silent and could only say, "The Lord's will be done."

In Jerusalem

15 After those days we got ready and started for Jerusalem. 16 Some of the disciples from Caesarea came with us and took us to the home of Mnason to be his guests. He was from Cyprus and was one of the first disciples. 17 When we came to Jerusalem, our fellow Christians eagerly welcomed us.

18 The next day we went with Paul to James, and all the elders came there too. 19 After greeting them, Paul told them everything God had done through his work among the non-Jews.

among the Gentiles by his ministry. 20And when they heard *it*, they glorified the Lord, and said unto him, Thou seest, brother, how many thousands of Jews there are which believe; and they are all zealous of the law: 21And they are informed of thee, that thou teachest all the Jews which are among the Gentiles to forsake Moses, saying that they ought not to circumcise *their* children, neither to walk after the customs. 22 What is it therefore? the multitude must needs come together: for they will hear that thou art come. 23 Do therefore this that we say to thee: We have four men which have a vow on them; 24 Them take, and purify thyself with them, and be at charges with them, that they may shave *their* heads: and all may know that those things, whereof they were informed concerning thee, are nothing; but *that* thou thyself also walkest orderly, and keepest the law. 25As touching the Gentiles which believe, we have written *and* concluded that they observe no such thing, save only that they keep themselves from *things* offered to idols, and from blood, and from strangled, and from fornication. 26 Then Paul took the men, and the next day purifying himself with them entered into the temple, to signify the accomplishment of the days of purification, until that an offering should be offered for every one of them. 27And when the seven days were almost ended, the Jews which were of Asia, when they saw him in the temple, stirred up all the people, and laid hands on him, 28 Crying out, Men of Israel, help: This is the man, that teacheth all *men* every where against the people, and the law, and this place: and further brought Greeks also into the temple, and hath polluted this holy place. 29 (For they had seen before with him in the city Trophimus an Ephesian, whom they supposed that Paul had brought into the temple.) 30And all the city was moved, and the people ran together: and they took Paul, and drew him out of the temple: and forthwith the doors were shut. 31And as they went about to kill him, tidings came unto the chief captain of the band, that all Jerusalem was in an uproar: 32 Who immediately took soldiers and centurions, and ran down unto them: and when they saw the chief captain and the soldiers, they left beating of Paul. 33 Then the chief captain came near, and took him, and commanded *him* to be bound with two chains; and demanded who he was, and what he had done. 34And some cried one thing, some another, among the multitude: and when he could not know the certainty for the tumult, he commanded him to be carried into the castle. 35And when he came upon the stairs, so it was, that he was borne of the soldiers for the violence of the people. 36 For the multitude of the people followed after, crying, Away with him. 37And as Paul was to be led into the castle, he said unto the chief captain, May I speak unto thee? Who said, Canst thou speak Greek? 38Art not thou that Egyptian, which before these days madest an uproar, and leddest out into the wilderness four thousand men that were murderers? 39 But Paul said, I am a man *which am* a Jew of Tarsus, *a city* in Cilicia, a citizen of no mean city: and, I beseech thee, suffer me to speak unto the people. 40And when he had given him license, Paul stood on the stairs, and beckoned with the hand unto the people. And when there was made a great silence, he spake unto *them* in the Hebrew tongue, saying,

Gentiles through his ministry. 20And when they heard it they *began* glorifying God; and they said to him, "You see, brother, how many thousands there are among the Jews of those who have believed, and they are all zealous for the Law; 21 and they have been told about you, that you are teaching all the Jews who are among the Gentiles to forsake Moses, telling them not to circumcise their children nor to walk according to the customs. 22 "What, then, is *to be done?* They will certainly hear that you have come. 23 "Therefore do this that we tell you: We have four men who are under a vow; 24 take them and purify yourself along with them, and pay their expenses in order that they may shave their heads; and all will know that there is nothing to the things which they have been told about you, but that you yourself also walk orderly, keeping the Law. 25 "But concerning the Gentiles who have believed, we wrote, having decided that they should abstain from meat sacrificed to idols and from blood and from what is strangled and from fornication." 26 Then Paul took the men, and the next day purifying himself along with them went into the temple, giving notice of the completion of the days of purification, until the sacrifice was offered for each one of them.

27 And when the seven days were almost over, the Jews from Asia, upon seeing him in the temple, *began* to stir up all the multitude and laid hands on him, 28 crying out, "Men of Israel, come to our aid! This is the man who preaches to all men everywhere against our people, and the Law, and this place; and besides he has even brought Greeks into the temple and has defiled this holy place." 29 For they had previously seen Trophimus the Ephesian in the city with him, and they supposed that Paul had brought him into the temple. 30And all the city was aroused, and the people rushed together; and taking hold of Paul, they dragged him out of the temple; and immediately the doors were shut. 31And while they were seeking to kill him, a report came up to the *ªcommander of the Roman Cohort that all Jerusalem was in confusion. 32And at once he took along *some* soldiers and centurions, and ran down to them; and when they saw the commander and the soldiers, they stopped beating Paul. 33 Then the commander came up and took hold of him, and ordered him to be bound with two chains; and he *began* asking who he was and what he had done. 34 But among the crowd some were shouting one thing *and* some another, and when he could not find out the facts on account of the uproar, he ordered him to be brought into the barracks. 35And when he got to the stairs, it so happened that he was carried by the soldiers because of the violence of the mob; 36 for the multitude of the people kept following behind, crying out, "Away with him!"

37 And as Paul was about to be brought into the barracks, he said to the commander, "May I say something to you?" And he *said, "Do you know Greek? 38 "Then you are not the Egyptian who some time ago stirred up a revolt and led the four thousand men of the Assassins out into the wilderness?" 39 But Paul said, "I am a Jew of Tarsus in Cilicia, a citizen of no insignificant city; and I beg you, allow me to speak to the people." 40And when he had given him permission, Paul, standing on the stairs, motioned to the people with his hand; and when there was a great hush, he spoke to them in the Hebrew dialect, saying,

[a] Lit., *chiliarch*, in command of one thousand troops.

WILLIAMS

20 They gave the glory to God, when they heard it, and said to him, "You see, brother, how many thousand believers there are among the Jews, all of them zealous champions of the law. 21 They have been repeatedly told about you that you continuously teach the Jews who live among the heathen to turn their backs on Moses, and that you continue to tell them to stop circumcising their children, and to stop observing the cherished customs. 22 What is your duty, then? They will certainly hear that you have come. 23 Now you must do just what we tell you. We have here four men who are under a vow. 24 Take them along with you, purify yourself with them, and bear the expense for them of having their heads shaved. Then everybody will know that none of those things they have been told about you are so, but that you yourself are living as a constant observer of the law. 25 As for the heathen who have become believers, we have sent them our resolution that they must avoid anything that is contaminated by idols, the tasting of blood, the meat of strangled animals, and sexual immorality."

26 Then Paul took the men along with him and on the next day went into the temple with them, purified, and announced the time when the purification would be completed, when the sacrifice for each one of them could be offered.

27 As the seven days were drawing to a close, the Jews from Asia caught a glimpse of him in the temple and began to stir up all the crowd, and seized him, 28 as they kept shouting, "Men of Israel, help! help! This is the man who teaches everybody everywhere against our people and the law and this place; yea, more than that, he has actually brought Greeks into the temple and desecrated this sacred place." 29 For they had previously seen Trophimus of Ephesus in the city with him, and so they supposed that Paul had brought him into the temple.

30 The whole city was stirred with excitement, and all at once the people rushed together, and seized Paul and dragged him out of the temple, and its gates at once were shut. 31 Now while they were trying to kill him, news reached the colonel of the regiment that all Jerusalem was in a ferment. 32 So he at once got together some soldiers and captains and hurried down against them, but as soon as they saw the colonel and his soldiers, they stopped beating Paul. 33 Then the colonel came up and seized Paul and ordered him to be bound with two chains; he then asked who he was and what he had done. 34 But they kept shouting in the crowd, some one thing, some another. As he could not with certainty find out about it, because of the tumult, he ordered him to be brought into the barracks. 35 When Paul got to the steps, he was actually borne by the soldiers because of the violence of the mob, 36 for a tremendous crowd of people kept following them and shouting, "Away with him!"

37 As he was about to be taken into the barracks, Paul said to the colonel, "May I say something to you?"

The colonel asked, "Do you know Greek? 38 Are you not the Egyptian who some time ago raised a mob of four thousand cutthroats and led them out into the desert?"

39 Paul answered, "I am a Jew from Tarsus, in Cilicia, a citizen of no insignificant city. Please let me speak to the people." 40 He granted the request, and Paul, as he was standing on the steps, made a gesture to the people, and after everybody had quieted down, he spoke to them in Hebrew as follows:

BECK

20 When they heard about it, they praised God. They told him, "You see, brother, how many tens of thousands among the Jews now believe, and all are zealous for the Law. 21 They've been told you teach all the Jews living among the non-Jews to turn away from Moses and tell them not to circumcise their children or follow the customs. 22 What should we do about it? They will certainly hear you have come. 23 So do what we tell you. We have four men who are under a vow. 24 Take them, purify yourself with them, and pay their expenses so that they may shave their heads. Then everybody will know there's nothing in what they've told about you but you live strictly according to the Law. 25 About the non-Jews who now believe, we wrote in a letter we decided they should keep away from food sacrificed to idols, from blood, from the meat of strangled animals, and from sexual sin."

26 Then Paul took the men and the next day purified himself with them and went to the temple to announce when, with the bringing of the sacrifice for each of them, *the days* of purification *would be over.*[80]

In Chains

27 When the seven days were almost over, the Jews from the province of Asia, seeing him in the temple, stirred up the whole crowd. They grabbed him, yelling, 28 "Men of Israel, help! This is the man who in his teaching everybody everywhere is against our people, the Law, and this place. And now he has even brought non-Jews into the temple and made this holy place unclean." 29 They had seen Trophimus from Ephesus with him in the city and thought Paul had taken him into the temple.

30 The whole city was aroused and the people rushed together. They took Paul, dragged him out of the temple, and immediately the doors were shut.

31 They were trying to kill him when it was reported to the tribune who was in charge of about six hundred soldiers: "All Jerusalem is stirred up!" 32 Immediately he took soldiers and captains and ran down to them. When they saw the tribune and the soldiers, they stopped hitting Paul. 33 Then the tribune went to him, arrested him, and ordered him bound with two chains.

He asked who he was and what he had done. 34 Some in the crowd shouted this and some that. There was such a noisy confusion he couldn't get the facts, so he ordered Paul to be taken to the barracks. 35 When Paul came to the stairs, the crowd was so violent the soldiers had to carry him. 36 The mob was right behind them, yelling, "Kill him!"

Paul Defends Himself

37 Just as he was going to be taken into the barracks, Paul asked the tribune, "May I say something to you?"

38 "Can you talk Greek?" he asked. "Aren't you the Egyptian who sometime ago got four thousand dagger-men to rebel and follow him into the wilderness?"

39 "I'm a Jew," Paul answered, "from Tarsus in Cilicia, a citizen of an important city. Now I'm asking you, let me talk to the people."

40 And he let him. Then Paul, standing on the stairs, waved his hand to quiet the people. When there was a hush all around, he spoke to them in the Jewish language:

[89] Num. 6:13

K.J.V.

22 Men, brethren, and fathers, hear ye my defence *which I make* now unto you. 2 (And when they heard that he spake in the Hebrew tongue to them, they kept the more silence: and he saith,) 3 I am verily a man *which am* a Jew, born in Tarsus, *a city* in Cilicia, yet brought up in this city at the feet of Gamaliel, *and* taught according to the perfect manner of the law of the fathers, and was zealous toward God, as ye all are this day. 4And I persecuted this way unto the death, binding and delivering into prisons both men and women. 5As also the high priest doth bear me witness, and all the estate of the elders: from whom also I received letters unto the brethren, and went to Damascus, to bring them which were there bound unto Jerusalem, for to be punished. 6And it came to pass, that, as I made my journey, and was come nigh unto Damascus about noon, suddenly there shone from heaven a great light round about me. 7And I fell unto the ground, and heard a voice saying unto me, Saul, Saul, why persecutest thou me? 8And I answered, Who art thou, Lord? And he said unto me, I am Jesus of Nazareth, whom thou persecutest. 9And they that were with me saw indeed the light, and were afraid; but they heard not the voice of him that spake to me. 10And I said, What shall I do, Lord? And the Lord said unto me, Arise, and go into Damascus; and there it shall be told thee of all things which are appointed for thee to do. 11And when I could not see for the glory of that light, being led by the hand of them that were with me, I came into Damascus. 12And one Ananias, a devout man according to the law, having a good report of all the Jews which dwelt *there,* 13 Came unto me, and stood, and said unto me, Brother Saul, receive thy sight. And the same hour I looked up upon him. 14And he said, The God of our fathers hath chosen thee, that thou shouldest know his will, and see that Just One, and shouldest hear the voice of his mouth. 15 For thou shalt be his witness unto all men of what thou hast seen and heard. 16And now why tarriest thou? arise, and be baptized, and wash away thy sins, calling on the name of the Lord. 17And it came to pass, that, when I was come again to Jerusalem, even while I prayed in the temple, I was in a trance; 18And saw him saying unto me, Make haste, and get thee quickly out of Jerusalem: for they will not receive thy testimony concerning me. 19And I said, Lord, they know that I imprisoned and beat in every synagogue them that believed on thee: 20And when the blood of thy martyr Stephen was shed, I also was standing by, and consenting unto his death, and kept the raiment of them that slew him. 21And he said unto me, Depart: for I will send thee far hence unto the Gentiles. 22And they gave him audience unto this word, and *then* lifted up their voices, and said, Away with such a *fellow* from the earth: for it is not fit that he should live. 23And as they cried out, and cast off *their* clothes, and threw dust into the air, 24The chief captain commanded him to be brought into the castle, and bade that he should be examined by scourging; that he might know wherefore they cried so against him. 25And as they bound him with thongs, Paul said unto the centurion that stood by, Is it lawful for you to scourge a man that is a Roman, and uncondemned? 26 When the centurion heard *that,* he

N.A.S.

22 "Brethren and fathers, hear my defense which I now *offer* to you." 2 And when they heard that he was addressing them in the Hebrew dialect, they became even more quiet; and he *said, 3 "I am a Jew, born in Tarsus of Cilicia, but brought up in this city, educated under Gamaliel, strictly according to the law of our fathers, being zealous for God, just as you all are today. 4 "And I persecuted this Way to the death, binding and putting both men and women into prisons, 5 as also the high priest and all the Council of the elders can testify. From them I also received letters to the brethren, and started off for Damascus in order to bring even those who were there to Jerusalem as prisoners to be punished. 6 "And it came about that as I was on my way, approaching Damascus about noontime, a very bright light suddenly flashed from heaven all around me, 7 and I fell to the ground and heard a voice saying to me, 'Saul, Saul, why are you persecuting Me?' 8 "And I answered, 'Who art Thou, Lord?' And He said to me, 'I am Jesus the Nazarene, whom you are persecuting.' 9 "And those who were with me beheld the light, to be sure, but did not understand the voice of the One who was speaking to me. 10 "And I said, 'What shall I do, Lord?' And the Lord said to me, 'Arise and go on into Damascus; and there you will be told of all that has been appointed for you to do.' 11 "But since I could not see because of the brightness of that light, I was led by the hand by those who were with me, and came into Damascus. 12 "And a certain Ananias, a man who was devout by the standard of the Law, *and* well spoken of by all the Jews who lived there, 13 came to me, and standing near said to me, 'Brother Saul, receive your sight!' And at that very time I looked up at him. 14 "And he said, 'The God of our fathers has appointed you to know His will, and to see the Righteous One, and to hear an utterance from His mouth. 15 'For you will be a witness for Him to all men of what you have seen and heard. 16 'And now why do you delay? Arise, and be baptized, and wash away your sins, calling on His name.' 17 "And it came about that when I returned to Jerusalem and was praying in the temple, I fell into a trance, 18 and I saw Him saying to me, 'Make haste, and get out of Jerusalem quickly, because they will not accept your testimony about Me.' 19 "And I said, 'Lord, they themselves understand that in one synagogue after another I used to imprison and beat those who believed in Thee. 20 'And when the blood of Thy witness Stephen was being shed, I also was standing by approving, and watching out for the cloaks of those who were slaying him.' 21 "And He said to me, 'Go! For I will send you far away to the Gentiles.' " 22 And they listened to him up to this statement, and *then* they raised their voices and said, "Away with such a fellow from the earth, for he should not be allowed to live!" 23And as they were crying out and throwing off their cloaks and tossing dust into the air, 24 the ᵃcommander ordered him to be brought into the barracks, stating that he should be examined by scourging so that he might find out the reason why they were shouting against him that way. 25And when they had stretched him out with thongs, Paul said to the centurion who was standing by, "Is it lawful for you to scourge a man who is a Roman and uncondemned?" 26And when the centurion heard *this,* he went

[a] Lit., *chiliarch,* in command of one thousand troops.

WILLIAMS

22 *Paul in an address to the Jewish people tells the story of his conversion; then he is arrested and taken before the court*

"Brothers and fathers, listen now to what I have to say in my defense." 2 When they heard him speaking to them in Hebrew, they became even more quiet, and he continued:

3 "I am a Jew, born in Tarsus in Cilicia, but brought up here in this city, and carefully educated under the teaching of Gamaliel in the law of our forefathers. I was zealous for God, as all of you are today. 4 I persecuted this Way even to the death, and kept on binding both men and women and putting them in jail, 5 as the high priest and the whole council will bear me witness. Indeed, I had received letters from them to the brothers in Damascus, and I was on the way there to bind those who were there and bring them back to Jerusalem to be punished. 6 But on my way, just before I reached Damascus, suddenly about noon a blaze of light from heaven flashed around me, 7 and I fell to the ground and heard a voice saying to me, 'Saul! Saul! Why are you persecuting me?' 8 I answered, 'Who are you, Sir?' He said to me, 'I am Jesus of Nazareth whom you are persecuting.' 9 The men who were with me saw the light, but they did not hear the voice of Him who was speaking to me. 10 Then I asked, 'What am I to do, Lord?' And the Lord answered, 'Get up and go into Damascus, and there it will be told you what you are destined to do.' 11 Since I could not see because of the dazzling sheen of that light, I was led by the hand by my companions, and in this way I reached Damascus. 12 There a man named Ananias, a man devout in strict accordance with the law, of good reputation among all the Jews who lived there, 13 came to see me, and standing by my side said to me, 'Saul, my brother, recover your sight!' Then instantly I did recover it and looked at him, 14 and he said, 'The God of our forefathers has appointed you to learn His will and to see the Righteous One and to hear Him speak, 15 because you are to be His witness to all men of what you have seen and heard. 16 And now, why are you waiting? Get up and be baptized and wash your sins away by calling on His name.' 17 After I had come back to Jerusalem, one day while I was praying in the temple, I fell into a trance, 18 and saw Him saying to me, 'Make haste and at once get out of Jerusalem, because they will not accept your testimony about me.' 19 So I said, 'Lord, they know for themselves that from one synagogue to another I used to imprison and flog those who believed in you, 20 and when the blood of your martyr Stephen was being shed, I stood by and approved it, and held the clothes of those who killed him.' 21 Then He said to me, 'Go, because I am to send you out and far away among the heathen.' "

22 They listened to him until he said this, and then all at once they shouted, "Away with such a fellow from the earth! He is certainly not fit to live!"

23 While they were shouting and tossing their clothes about and flinging dust into the air, 24 the colonel ordered Paul to be brought into the barracks, and told them to examine him by flogging, in order that he might find out why they were crying out against him in such a way. 25 But when they had tied him for the flogging, Paul asked the captain who was standing by, "Is it lawful for you to flog a Roman, and one who is uncondemned at that?"

26 When the captain heard that, he went to

BECK

22 "Brothers and fathers, listen as I now defend myself before you."

2 When they heard him call to them in their own language, they quieted down still more.

3 Then he said: "I'm a Jew, born in Tarsus in Cilicia but raised in this city, trained at the feet of Gamaliel in the strict ways of the Law of our fathers, as zealous for God as all of you are today. 4 I hunted to their death men and women who believed as I do now, tying them up and putting them in prisons, 5 as the high priest and the whole council of elders can tell about me. From them I got letters to our fellow Jews in Damascus and was going there to bind those who were there and bring them to Jerusalem to be punished. 6 But as I was on my way and coming near Damascus, suddenly about noon a bright light from heaven flashed around me. 7 I fell to the ground and heard a voice asking me, Saul! Saul! Why are you persecuting Me?'

8 "I asked, 'Who are You, Lord?'

" 'I am Jesus from Nazareth,' He told me, 'whom you are persecuting.' 9 The men who were with me saw the light but didn't understand the voice of Him who was talking to me.

10 "Then I asked, 'What should I do, Lord?'

"The Lord told me, 'Get up, go into Damascus, and there you will be told everything you are ordered to do.'

11 "That light was so bright I couldn't see anything. So the men who were with me took me by the hand and led me into Damascus.

12 "There was Ananias, a man who feared God according to the Law, and all the Jews living there spoke well of him. 13 He came to me and stood by me. 'Brother Saul,' he said to me, 'see again!' Immediately I could see him.

14 "He said, 'The God of our fathers chose you to learn what He wants, to see the Righteous One and hear Him speak to you, 15 because you must be His witness and tell everybody what you've seen and heard. 16 And now, what are you waiting for? Get up, and calling on His name, have yourself baptized and your sins washed away.'

17 "I came back to Jerusalem. While I was praying in the temple, I fell into a trance 18 and saw Him. 'Hurry,' He told me, 'and get out of Jerusalem quickly because they will not accept the truth you tell about Me.'

19 " 'Lord,' I said, 'they know I went from synagog to synagog and put in prison and beat those who believe in You. 20 And when the blood of Your witness Stephen was being poured out, I was standing by, approving, and watching the clothes of those who were murdering him.'

21 " 'Go,' He told me. 'I will send you far away to people who are not Jews.' "

22 They listened to him till he said that. Then they shouted, "Kill him! Rid the world of such a fellow! He's not fit to live!"

23 While they were yelling, tossing their clothes around, and throwing dust in the air, 24 the tribune ordered him taken to the barracks and told his men to get information from Paul by whipping him. He wanted to find out why the people were yelling at him like this. 25 But when his men had stretched him out with the straps, Paul asked the captain standing near, "Is it right for you to whip a Roman citizen who hasn't been condemned?"

26 When the captain heard this, he went and

K.J.V.

N.A.S.

went and told the chief captain, saying, Take heed what thou doest; for this man is a Roman. 27 Then the chief captain came, and said unto him, Tell me, art thou a Roman? He said, Yea. 28And the chief captain answered, With a great sum obtained I this freedom. And Paul said, But I was *free* born. 29 Then straightway they departed from him which should have examined him: and the chief captain also was afraid, after he knew that he was a Roman, and because he had bound him. 30 On the morrow, because he would have known the certainty wherefore he was accused of the Jews, he loosed him from *his* bands, and commanded the chief priests and all their council to appear, and brought Paul down, and set him before them.

to the commander and told him, saying, "What are you about to do? For this man is a Roman." 27And the commander came and said to him, "Tell me, are you a Roman?" And he said, "Yes." 28And the commander answered, "I acquired this citizenship with a large sum of money." And Paul said, "But I was actually born *a citizen.*" 29 Therefore those who were about to examine him immediately let go of him; and the commander also was afraid when he found out that he was a Roman, and because he had put him in chains.

30 But on the next day, wishing to know for certain why he had been accused by the Jews, he released him and ordered the chief priests and all the Council to assemble, and brought Paul down and set him before them.

23 And Paul, earnestly beholding the council, said, Men *and* brethren, I have lived in all good conscience before God until this day. 2And the high priest Ananias commanded them that stood by him to smite him on the mouth. 3 Then said Paul unto him, God shall smite thee, *thou* whited wall: for sittest thou to judge me after the law, and commandest me to be smitten contrary to the law? 4And they that stood by said, Revilest thou God's high priest? 5 Then said Paul, I wist not, brethren, that he was the high priest: for it is written, Thou shalt not speak evil of the ruler of thy people. 6 But when Paul perceived that the one part were Sadducees, and the other Pharisees, he cried out in the council, Men *and* brethren, I am a Pharisee, the son of a Pharisee: of the hope and resurrection of the dead I am called in question. 7And when he had so said, there arose a dissension between the Pharisees and the Sadducees: and the multitude was divided. 8 For the Sadducees say that there is no resurrection, neither angel, nor spirit: but the Pharisees confess both. 9And there arose a great cry: and the scribes *that were* of the Pharisees' part arose, and strove, saying, We find no evil in this man: but if a spirit or an angel hath spoken to him, let us not fight against God. 10And when there arose a great dissension, the chief captain, fearing lest Paul should have been pulled in pieces of them, commanded the soldiers to go down, and to take him by force from among them, and to bring *him* into the castle. 11And the night following the Lord stood by him, and said, Be of good cheer, Paul: for as thou hast testified of me in Jerusalem, so must thou bear witness also at Rome. 12And when it was day, certain of the Jews banded together, and bound themselves under a curse, saying that they would neither eat nor drink till they had killed Paul. 13And they were more than forty which had

23 And Paul, looking intently at the Council, said, "Brethren, I have lived my life with a perfectly good conscience before God up to this day." 2And the high priest Ananias commanded those standing beside him to strike him on the mouth. 3 Then Paul said to him, "God is going to strike you, you white-washed wall! And do you sit to try me according to the Law, and in violation of the Law order me to be struck?" 4 But the bystanders said, "Do you revile God's high priest?" 5And Paul said, "I was not aware, brethren, that he was high priest; for it is written, 'YOU SHALL NOT SPEAK EVIL OF A RULER OF YOUR PEOPLE.'" 6 But perceiving that one party were Sadducees and the other Pharisees, Paul *began* crying out in the Council, "Brethren, I am a Pharisee, a son of Pharisees; I am on trial for the hope and resurrection of the dead!" 7And as he said this, there arose a dissension between the Pharisees and Sadducees; and the assembly was divided. 8 For the Sadducees say that there is no resurrection, nor an angel, nor a spirit; but the Pharisees acknowledge them all. 9And there arose a great uproar; and some of the scribes of the Pharisaic party stood up and *began* to argue heatedly, saying, "We find nothing wrong with this man; suppose a spirit or an angel has spoken to him?" 10And as a great dissension was developing, the ᵃcommander was afraid Paul would be torn to pieces by them and ordered the troops to go down and take him away from them by force, and bring him into the barracks.

11 But on the night *immediately* following, the Lord stood at his side and said, "Take courage; for as you have solemnly witnessed to My cause at Jerusalem, so you must witness at Rome also."

12 And when it was day, the Jews formed a conspiracy and bound themselves under an oath, saying that they would neither eat nor drink until they had killed Paul. 13 And there were

[a] Lit., *chiliarch,* in command of one thousand troops.

WILLIAMS

the colonel and reported it. Then he asked him, "What are you going to do? This man is a Roman citizen."

27 So the colonel came to Paul and asked, "Tell me, are you a Roman citizen?"

He answered, "Yes."

28 Then the colonel said, "I paid a large sum for this citizenship of mine."

Paul said, "But I was born a citizen."

29 So the men who were going to examine him left him at once, and the colonel himself was frightened when he learned that he was a Roman citizen and that he had had him bound.

30 The next day, as he wished to learn the exact reason why the Jews accused him, he had him unbound, and ordered the high priest and the whole council to assemble, and took Paul down and brought him before them.

23 Paul ingeniously divides the court, Pharisees against Sadducees; he protests his innocence; Jesus comforts him; the Jews plot to kill him; the colonel finds out and sends him to Caesarea for safety

Paul fixed his eyes upon the council and said, "Brothers, with a clear conscience I have done my duty to God up to this very day."

2 At this the high priest Ananias ordered the people standing near him to strike him on the mouth.

3 Then Paul said to him, "You white-washed wall, God will strike you! Do you sit as a judge to try me in accordance with the law and yet in violation of the law you order them to strike me?"

4 The people standing near him said, "Do you mean to insult God's high priest?"

5 Paul answered, "I did not know, brothers, that he was high priest, for the Scripture says, 'You must not speak evil against any ruler of your people.'"

6 Because Paul knew that part of them were Sadducees and part of them Pharisees, he began to cry out in the council chamber, "Brothers, I am a Pharisee, a Pharisee's son, and now I am on trial for the hope of the resurrection of the dead."

7 When he said that, an angry dispute arose between the Pharisees and the Sadducees, and the crowded court was divided. 8 For the Sadducees hold that there is no resurrection, and no such thing as an angel or spirit, but the Pharisees believe in all of them.

9 So there was a vociferous yelling until some of the scribes, belonging to the party of the Pharisees, got up and fiercely contended, "We find nothing wrong with this man. Suppose a spirit or angel has really spoken to him!"

10 Since the dispute kept growing hotter and hotter, the colonel became alarmed that Paul might be torn in pieces by them, and so ordered the army to march down and take him out of their hands and bring him back to the barracks.

11 But that same night the Lord stood by Paul's side and said, "Courage! For just as you have testified for me in Jerusalem, you must testify for me in Rome, too."

12 After day had dawned, the Jews formed a conspiracy and took an oath not to eat or drink till they had killed Paul. 13 There were more than forty of them who formed this conspiracy.

BECK

told the tribune about it. "What are you going to do?" he asked. "This man is a Roman citizen."

27 The tribune went and asked Paul, "Tell me, are you a Roman citizen?"

"Yes," he said.

28 The tribune declared, "I had to pay a lot of money to be a citizen."

"But I was born a citizen," Paul said.

29 Immediately those who were going to examine him withdrew from him. When the tribune found out Paul was a Roman citizen, he was frightened because he had tied him up.

Paul Before the Council

30 The next day, since he wanted to find out exactly what the Jews were accusing Paul of, he untied him and ordered the high priests and the whole council to meet. Then he brought Paul down and had him stand before them.

23 Paul looked earnestly at the council and said, "Fellow Jews, I have lived before God with a very good conscience till this day."

2 The high priest Ananias ordered the men standing near him to strike him on the mouth.

3 Then Paul said to him, "God will strike you, you whitewashed wall! Do you sit there to judge me according to the Law and yet break the Law by ordering them to strike me?"

4 The men standing near him asked, "Do you insult God's high priest?"

5 "Fellow Jews," Paul answered, "I didn't know he's the high priest. The Bible does say, *Don't speak evil of a ruler of your people*." [90]

6 When Paul saw that some of them were Sadducees and others Pharisees, he called out in the council, "Fellow Jews, I'm a Pharisee and a son of Pharisees. I'm on trial for my hope that the dead will rise."

7 When he said that, the Pharisees and Sadducees started to quarrel, and the men in the meeting were divided. 8 The Sadducees say the dead don't rise and there is no angel or spirit, while the Pharisees believe in all these things. 9 So there was some loud shouting. Some of the Bible scholars who belonged to the party of the Pharisees got up and argued vehemently: "We find nothing wrong with this man. Suppose a spirit spoke to him, or an angel—."

10 The quarrel was getting violent, and the tribune was afraid they would tear Paul to pieces. So he ordered the soldiers to go down, take him away from them by force, and bring him to the soldiers' quarters.

11 That night the Lord stood near him and said, "Keep up your courage! As you have told the truth about Me in Jerusalem, so you must tell it in Rome."

The Plot to Kill Paul

12 In the morning the Jews banded together and vowed God should punish them if they ate or drank anything before they had killed Paul. 13 There were more than forty who swore to carry out this plot.

[90] Ex. 22:28

K.J.V.

made this conspiracy. 14And they came to the chief priests and elders, and said, We have bound ourselves under a great curse, that we will eat nothing until we have slain Paul. 15 Now therefore ye with the council signify to the chief captain that he bring him down unto you to morrow, as though ye would inquire something more perfectly concerning him: and we, or ever he come near, are ready to kill him. 16And when Paul's sister's son heard of their lying in wait, he went and entered into the castle, and told Paul. 17 Then Paul called one of the centurions unto *him*, and said, Bring this young man unto the chief captain: for he hath a certain thing to tell him. 18 So he took him, and brought *him* to the chief captain, and said, Paul the prisoner called me unto *him*, and prayed me to bring this young man unto thee, who hath something to say unto thee. 19 Then the chief captain took him by the hand, and went *with him* aside privately, and asked *him*, What is that thou hast to tell me? 20And he said, The Jews have agreed to desire thee that thou wouldest bring down Paul to morrow into the council, as though they would inquire somewhat of him more perfectly. 21 But do not thou yield unto them: for there lie in wait for him of them more than forty men, which have bound themselves with an oath, that they will neither eat nor drink till they have killed him: and now are they ready, looking for a promise from thee. 22 So the chief captain *then* let the young man depart, and charged *him*, *See thou* tell no man that thou hast shewed these things to me. 23And he called unto *him* two centurions, saying, Make ready two hundred soldiers to go to Cesarea, and horsemen threescore and ten, and spearmen two hundred, at the third hour of the night; 24And provide *them* beasts, that they may set Paul on, and bring *him* safe unto Felix the governor. 25And he wrote a letter after this manner: 26 Claudius Lysias unto the most excellent governor Felix *sendeth* greeting. 27 This man was taken of the Jews, and should have been killed of them: then came I with an army, and rescued him, having understood that he was a Roman. 28And when I would have known the cause wherefore they accused him, I brought him forth into their council: 29 Whom I perceived to be accused of questions of their law, but to have nothing laid to his charge worthy of death or of bonds. 30And when it was told me how that the Jews laid wait for the man, I sent straightway to thee, and gave commandment to his accusers also to say before thee what *they had* against him. Farewell. 31 Then the soldiers, as it was commanded them, took Paul, and brought *him* by night to Antipatris. 32 On the morrow they left the horsemen to go with him, and returned to the castle: 33 Who, when they came to Cesarea, and delivered the epistle to the governor, presented Paul also before him. 34And when the governor had read *the letter,* he asked of what province he was. And when he understood that *he was* of Cilicia; 35 I will hear thee, said he, when thine accusers are also come. And he commanded him to be kept in Herod's judgment hall.

N.A.S.

more than forty who formed this plot. 14And they came to the chief priests and the elders, and said, "We have bound ourselves under a solemn oath to taste nothing until we have killed Paul. 15 "Now, therefore, you and the Council notify the commander to bring him down to you, as though you were going to determine his case by a more thorough investigation; and we for our part are ready to slay him before he comes near *the place."* 16 But the son of Paul's sister heard of their ambush, and he came and entered the barracks and told Paul. 17And Paul called one of the centurions to him and said, "Lead this young man to the commander, for he has something to report to him." 18 So he took him and led him to the commander and *said, "Paul the prisoner called me to him and asked me to lead this young man to you since he has something to tell you." 19And the commander took him by the hand and stepping aside, *began* to inquire of him privately, "What is it that you have to report to me?" 20And he said, "The Jews have agreed to ask you to bring Paul down tomorrow to the Council, as though you were going to inquire somewhat more thoroughly about him. 21 "So do not listen to them, for more than forty of them are lying in wait for him who have bound themselves under a curse not to eat or drink until they slay him; and now they are ready and waiting for the promise from you." 22 Therefore the commander let the young man go, instructing him, "Tell no one that you have notified me of these things." 23And he called to him two of the centurions, and said, "Get two hundred soldiers ready by ªthe third hour of the night to proceed to Caesarea, with seventy horsemen and two hundred spearmen." 24 *They were* also to provide mounts to put Paul on and bring him safely to Felix the governor. 25And he wrote a letter having this form:

26 "Claudius Lysias, to the most excellent governor Felix, greetings. 27 When this man was arrested by the Jews and was about to be slain by them, I came upon them with the troops and rescued him, having learned that he was a Roman. 28And wanting to ascertain the charge for which they were accusing him, I brought him down to their Council; 29 and I found him to be accused over questions about their Law, but under no accusation deserving death or imprisonment. 30And when I was informed that there would be a plot against the man, I sent him to you at once, also instructing his accusers to bring charges against him before you."

31 So the soldiers, in accordance with their orders, took Paul and brought him by night to Antipatris. 32 But the next day, leaving the horsemen to go on with him, they returned to the barracks. 33And when these had come to Caesarea and delivered the letter to the governor, they also presented Paul to him. 34And when he had read it, he asked from what province he was; and when he learned that he was from Cilicia, 35 he said, "I will give you a hearing after your accusers arrive also," giving orders for him to be kept in Herod's ᵇPraetorium.

[a] I.e., 9 p.m. [b] Or, *governor's official residence.*

WILLIAMS

14 They went to the high priests and elders and said to them, "We have taken a solemn oath not to taste a morsel till we have killed Paul. 15 So you and the council must now notify the colonel to bring him down to you, as though you were going to look into his case more carefully, but before he gets down we will be ready to kill him."

16 But Paul's nephew heard of the plot and came to the barracks and told Paul. 17 So Paul called one of the captains and said, "Take this young man to the colonel, for he has something to tell him."

18 So he took him and brought him to the colonel and said, "The prisoner Paul called me to him and asked me to bring this young man to you, because he has something to tell you."

19 So the colonel took him by the arm, stepped to one side so as to be alone, and asked him, "What is it you have to tell me?"

20 He answered, "The Jews have agreed to ask you to bring Paul down to the council tomorrow, as though you were going to examine his case more carefully. 21 But do not yield to them, for more than forty of them are lying in wait for him; they have taken an oath not to eat or drink till they have killed him. They are all ready now, just waiting for your promise."

22 So the colonel sent the young man away, with strict directions not to tell anybody that he had notified him of this plot. 23 Then he called in two of his captains and said to them, "Get two hundred men ready to march to Caesarea, with seventy mounted soldiers and two hundred armed with spears, to leave at nine o'clock tonight." 24 He further told them to provide horses for Paul to ride, so as to bring him in safety to Felix, the governor, to whom 25 he wrote the following letter:

26 "Claudius Lysias sends greetings to his Excellency Felix, the governor. 27 This man had been seized by the Jews and they were on the point of killing him when I came upon them with the soldiers and rescued him, because I had learned that he was a Roman citizen. 28 As I wanted to know the exact charge they were making against him, I brought him before their council, 29 and found him to be charged with questions about their law, but having no charge against him involving death or imprisonment. 30 Because a plot against the man has been reported to me as brewing, I at once am sending him on to you and have directed his accusers to present their charge against him before you."

31 So the soldiers took Paul, as they had been ordered to do, and brought him by night as far as Antipatris. 32 The next day they returned to the barracks, leaving the mounted men to go on with him; 33 they, on reaching Caesarea, delivered the letter to the governor and turned Paul over to him, too. 34 He read the letter and asked Paul what province he was from, and on learning that he was from Cilicia, 35 he said, "I will carefully hear your case as soon as your accusers arrive."

Then he ordered him to be kept in custody in Herod's palace.

BECK

14 They went to the high priests and elders and said, "We have vowed God should punish us if we taste any food before we have killed Paul. 15 Now then, you and the council tell the tribune to bring him down to you as if you meant to get more exact information about him. We're ready to kill him before he gets to you."

16 But the son of Paul's sister heard about the ambush. He came and got into the barracks and told Paul. 17 Then Paul called one of the captains and told him, "Take this young man to the tribune. He has something to tell him."

18 He took him to the tribune and said, "The prisoner Paul called me and asked me to bring this young man to you. He has something to tell you."

19 The tribune took him by the arm and stepping aside to be alone with him, he asked him, "What have you got to tell me?"

20 "The Jews," he answered, "have agreed to ask you to bring Paul down to the council tomorrow as if they meant to get more exact information about him. 21 Now, don't you listen to them. More than forty of them are ambushing him. They have vowed God should punish them if they eat or drink anything before they have murdered him. They're ready now, just waiting for you to promise them."

22 The tribune dismissed the young man. "Don't tell anybody you reported this to me," he ordered.

23 Then he called two of his captains and said, "Get two hundred soldiers to go to Caesarea, and seventy on horses, and two hundred with spears, and have them ready to start at nine tonight." 24 They were also to provide animals for Paul to ride on and so to take him safely to Governor Felix. 25 The tribune wrote a letter with this message:

26 "Claudius Lysias sends greetings to the excellent Governor Felix.

27 "The Jews had seized this man and were going to murder him, but when I found out he was a Roman citizen, I came with the soldiers and rescued him. 28 I wanted to know what they had against him; so I took him down to their council 29 and found their accusations had to do with questions about their Law, but there was none for which he deserved to die or be in chains. 30 Since I'm informed they're plotting against the man, I'm quickly sending him to you and also ordering his accusers to state before you what they have against him."

31 So the foot soldiers, as they were ordered, took Paul and brought him to Antipatris during the night. 32 The next day they returned to their barracks, letting the men on horses ride on with him. 33 When these came to Caesarea, they delivered the letter to the governor and handed Paul over to him.

34 After he read the letter, he asked which province he was from and found out he was from Cilicia. 35 "I will hear your case," he said, "when your accusers come." And he ordered him kept in Herod's palace.

24 And after five days Ananias the high priest descended with the elders, and *with* a certain orator *named* Tertullus, who informed the governor against Paul. 2And when he was called forth, Tertullus began to accuse *him*, saying, Seeing that by thee we enjoy great quietness, and that very worthy deeds are done unto this nation by thy providence, 3 We accept *it* always, and in all places, most noble Felix, with all thankfulness. 4 Notwithstanding, that I be not further tedious unto thee, I pray thee that thou wouldest hear us of thy clemency a few words. 5 For we have found this man *a* pestilent *fellow*, and a mover of sedition among all the Jews throughout the world, and a ringleader of the sect of the Nazarenes: 6 Who also hath gone about to profane the temple: whom we took, and would have judged according to our law. 7 But the chief captain Lysias came *upon us*, and with great violence took *him* away out of our hands, 8 Commanding his accusers to come unto thee: by examining of whom thyself mayest take knowledge of all these things, whereof we accuse him. 9And the Jews also assented, saying that these things were so. 10 Then Paul, after that the governor had beckoned unto him to speak, answered, Forasmuch as I know that thou hast been of many years a judge unto this nation, I do the more cheerfully answer for myself: 11 Because that thou mayest understand, that there are yet but twelve days since I went up to Jerusalem for to worship. 12And they neither found me in the temple disputing with any man, neither raising up the people, neither in the synagogues, nor in the city: 13 Neither can they prove the things whereof they now accuse me. 14 But this I confess unto thee, that after the way which they call heresy, so worship I the God of my fathers, believing all things which are written in the law and in the prophets: 15And have hope toward God, which they themselves also allow, that there shall be a resurrection of the dead, both of the just and unjust. 16And herein do I exercise myself, to have always a conscience void of offence toward God, and *toward* men. 17 Now after many years I came to bring alms to my nation, and offerings. 18 Whereupon certain Jews from Asia found me purified in the temple, neither with multitude, nor with tumult. 19 Who ought to have been here before thee, and object, if they had aught against me. 20 Or else let these same *here* say, if they have found any evil doing in me, while I stood before the council, 21 Except it be for this one voice, that I cried standing among them, Touching the resurrection of the dead I am called in question by you this day. 22And when Felix heard these things, having more perfect knowledge of *that* way, he deferred them, and said, When Lysias the chief captain shall come down, I will know the uttermost of your matter. 23And he commanded a centurion to keep Paul, and to let *him* have liberty, and that he should forbid none of his acquaintance to minister or come unto him. 24And after certain days, when Felix came with his wife Drusilla, which was a Jewess, he sent for Paul, and heard him concerning the faith in Christ. 25And as he

24 And after five days the high priest Ananias came down with some elders, and a certain attorney *named* Tertullus; and they brought charges to the governor against Paul. 2And after *Paul* had been summoned, Tertullus began to accuse him, saying *to the governor*,
"Since we have through you attained much peace, and since by your providence reforms are being carried out for this nation, 3 we acknowledge *this* in every way and everywhere, most excellent Felix, with all thankfulness. 4 "But, that I may not weary you any further, I beg you to grant us, by your kindness, a brief hearing. 5 "For we have found this man a real pest and a fellow who stirs up dissension among all the Jews throughout *a*the world, and a ringleader of the sect of the Nazarenes. 6 "And he even tried to desecrate the temple; and then we arrested him. 7(See footnote *b*) 8 "And by examining him yourself concerning all these matters, you will be able to ascertain the things of which we accuse him." 9And the Jews also joined in the attack, asserting that these things were so.
10 And when the governor had nodded for him to speak, Paul responded:
"Knowing that for many years you have been a judge to this nation, I cheerfully make my defense, 11 since you can take note of the fact that no more than twelve days ago I went up to Jerusalem to worship. 12 "And neither in the temple, nor in the synagogues, nor in the city *itself* did they find me carrying on a discussion with anyone or causing a riot. 13 "Nor can they prove to you the charges of which they now accuse me. 14 "But this I admit to you, that according to the Way which they call a sect I do serve the God of our fathers, believing everything that is in accordance with the Law, and that is written in the Prophets; 15 having a hope in God, which these men cherish themselves, that there shall certainly be a resurrection of both the righteous and the wicked. 16 "In view of this, I also do my best to maintain always a blameless conscience *both* before God and before men. 17 "Now after several years I came to bring *c*alms to my nation and to present offerings; 18 in which they found me *occupied* in the temple, having been purified, without *any* crowd or uproar. But *there were* certain Jews from Asia—19 who ought to have been present before you, and to make accusation, if they should have anything against me. 20 "Or else let these men themselves tell what misdeed they found when I stood before the Council, 21 other than for this one statement which I shouted out while standing among them, 'For the resurrection of the dead I am on trial before you today.' "
22 But Felix, having a more exact knowledge about the Way, put them off, saying, "When Lysias the *d*commander comes down, I will decide your case." 23And he gave orders to the centurion for him to be kept in custody and *yet* have *some* freedom, and not to prevent any of his friends from ministering to him.
24 But some days later, Felix arrived with Drusilla, his wife who was a Jewess, and sent for Paul, and heard him *speak* about faith in Christ Jesus. 25And as he was discussing

[a] Lit., *the inhabited earth.* [b] Some later mss. add, [*And we wanted to judge him according to our own Law.* 7 "But Lysias the commander came along, and with much violence took him out of our hands, 8 ordering his accusers to come before you.] [c] Or, *gifts to charity.* [d] Lit., *chiliarch,* in command of one thousand troops.

WILLIAMS

24 *Paul on trial before the Roman judge Felix; Tertullus, a brilliant orator, prosecutes him; Paul maintains his innocence; though uncondemned, still left in prison in Caesarea*

Five days later, the high priest Ananias came down with some elders and a prosecuting attorney, Tertullus, and through him they presented their case against Paul before the governor. 2 When Paul was called, Tertullus opened the prosecution by saying:

"Your Excellency, Felix, since we are enjoying perfect peace through you and since reforms for this nation are being brought about through your foresight, 3 we always and everywhere acknowledge it with profound gratitude. 4 But, not to detain you too long, I beg you in your kindness to give us a brief hearing. 5 For we have found this man a perfect pest and a disturber of the peace among the Jews throughout the world. He is a ringleader in the sect of the Nazarenes; 6 once he tried to desecrate the temple, but we arrested him,*a* 8 and now, by examining him for yourself, you can find out exactly what charges we bring against him."

9 The Jews also joined in the charges and maintained that they were true. 10At the governor's signal to Paul, he answered:

"Since I know that you for many years have acted as judge for this nation, I cheerfully make my defense, 11 for you can verify the fact that not more than twelve days ago I went up to Jerusalem to worship, 12 and they have never found me debating with anybody in the temple nor making a disturbance in the synagogues or about the city, 13 and they cannot prove the charges they have just made against me. 14 But I certainly admit this as a fact that in accordance with the Way—that they call heresy—I continue to worship the God of my forefathers, and I still believe in everything taught in the law and written in the prophets, 15 and I have the same hope in God that they cherish for themselves, that there is to be a resurrection of the upright and the wicked. 16 So I am always striving to have a conscience that is clear before God and men. 17After several years' absence I came to bring contributions of charity for my nation, and to offer sacrifices. 18 While I was performing these duties they found me just as I had completed the rites of my purification in the temple; however, there was no crowd with me and no disturbance at all. 19 But there were some Jews from Asia who ought to be here before you and to present their charges, if they have any, against me. 20 Or let these men themselves tell what wrong they found in me when I appeared before the council—21 unless it is for one thing that I shouted out as I stood among them, 'It is for the resurrection of the dead that I am here on trial before you today.'"

22 Then Felix, who had a fairly clear conception of the principles involved in the Way, adjourned the trial, saying to the Jews, "When Lysias, the colonel, comes down here, I will carefully look into your case." 23 He ordered the captain to keep Paul in custody but to let him have freedom and not to prevent his friends from showing him kindness.

24 Some days later, Felix came with his wife Drusilla, who was a Jewess, and sent for Paul and heard him talk about faith in Christ Jesus. 25 But as he continued to talk about uprightness,

[a] V. 7 not in oldest Mss.

BECK

Before Felix

24 Five days later the high priest Ananias came down with some elders and Tertullus, an attorney, and they reported to the governor what they had against Paul.

2 When Paul had been called, Tertullus started to accuse him, saying, "Excellent Felix, you have brought us much peace, and your foresight has given these people reforms 3 in every way and in every place. We appreciate them and thank you very much. 4 Not to keep you too long—I ask you to listen in your kindly way to what we briefly have to say. 5 We have found this man a pest who starts quarrels among all the Jews in the world, and he is a ringleader of the sect of the Nazarenes. 6 He even tried to pollute the temple, and so we arrested him.* 8 When you examine him yourself, you will be able to find out from him everything of which we accuse him."

9 The Jews supported his attack by declaring these things were so.

10 The governor nodded to Paul to speak, and he answered, "For many years you have been a judge of this nation. Knowing that, I'm glad to defend myself. 11 Only eleven days ago, as you can find out for yourself, I went up to Jerusalem to worship. 12 They didn't find me arguing with anyone in the temple or stirring up a crowd in the synagogs or in the city; 13 and they can't prove to you the things they're now accusing me of. 14 But I confess to you that according to the way they call a sect I worship the God of our fathers. I believe everything written in the Law and the prophets 15 and trust God for the same thing they're looking for, that the dead will rise, the righteous and the wicked. 16 That's why I'm doing my best always to have a clear conscience before God and men. 17After seven years I came to my people to bring gifts for the poor and offerings. 18 They found me busy with these and purified in the temple, but there was no crowd or noisy mob. 19 There were some Jews from the province of Asia, who should be here before you to accuse me if they have anything against me. 20 Or these men should tell what wrong they found in me as I stood before their court, 21 unless it's the one thing I shouted when I stood among them: 'I'm on trial before you today in regard to the resurrection of the dead.'"

22 But Felix, who knew the Christian religion rather well, told them to wait for a decision. "When Tribune Lysias comes down," he said, "I will decide your case." 23 He ordered the captain to guard him but to let him have some liberty and not keep any of his friends from helping him.

24 Some days later Felix came again. His wife Drusilla, who was a Jew, was with him. He sent for Paul and heard him tell about faith in Christ Jesus. 25As he spoke of righteous-

* Our oldest manuscripts do not have vv. 6b-8a: "And we wanted to try him under our Law. But Tribune Lysias came along and with much force took him out of our hands, ordering his accusers to come before you."

K.J.V.

reasoned of righteousness, temperance, and judgment to come, Felix trembled, and answered, Go thy way for this time; when I have a convenient season, I will call for thee. 26 He hoped also that money should have been given him of Paul, that he might loose him: wherefore he sent for him the oftener, and communed with him. 27 But after two years Porcius Festus came into Felix' room: and Felix, willing to shew the Jews a pleasure, left Paul bound.

25 Now when Festus was come into the province, after three days he ascended from Cesarea to Jerusalem. 2 Then the high priest and the chief of the Jews informed him against Paul, and besought him, 3 And desired favour against him, that he would send for him to Jerusalem, laying wait in the way to kill him. 4 But Festus answered, that Paul should be kept at Cesarea, and that he himself would depart shortly *thither.* 5 Let them therefore, said he, which among you are able, go down with *me,* and accuse this man, if there be any wickedness in him. 6 And when he had tarried among them more than ten days, he went down unto Cesarea; and the next day sitting on the judgment seat commanded Paul to be brought. 7 And when he was come, the Jews which came down from Jerusalem stood round about, and laid many and grievous complaints against Paul, which they could not prove. 8 While he answered for himself, Neither against the law of the Jews, neither against the temple, nor yet against Cesar, have I offended any thing at all. 9 But Festus, willing to do the Jews a pleasure, answered Paul, and said, Wilt thou go up to Jerusalem, and there be judged of these things before me? 10 Then said Paul, I stand at Cesar's judgment seat, where I ought to be judged: to the Jews have I done no wrong, as thou very well knowest. 11 For if I be an offender, or have committed any thing worthy of death, I refuse not to die: but if there be none of these things whereof these accuse me, no man may deliver me unto them. I appeal unto Cesar. 12 Then Festus, when he had conferred with the council, answered, Hast thou appealed unto Cesar? unto Cesar shalt thou go. 13 And after certain days king Agrippa and Bernice came unto Cesarea to salute Festus. 14 And when they had been there many days, Festus declared Paul's cause unto the king, saying, There is a certain man left in bonds by Felix: 15 About whom, when I was at Jerusalem, the chief priests and the elders of the Jews informed *me,* desiring *to have* judgment against him. 16 To whom I answered, It is not the manner of the Romans to deliver any man to die, before that he which is accused have the accusers face to face, and have license to answer for himself concerning the crime laid against him. 17 Therefore, when they were come hither, without any delay on the morrow I sat on the judgment seat, and commanded the man to be brought forth. 18 Against whom when the accusers stood up, they brought none accusation of such things as I supposed: 19 But had certain questions against him of their

N.A.S.

righteousness, self-control and the judgment to come, Felix became frightened and said, "Go away for the present, and when I find time, I will summon you." 26 At the same time too, he was hoping that money would be given him by Paul; therefore he also used to send for him quite often and converse with him. 27 But after two years had passed. Felix was succeeded by Porcius Festus; and wishing to do the Jews a favor, Felix left Paul imprisoned.

25 Festus therefore, having arrived in the province, three days later went up to Jerusalem from Caesarea. 2 And the chief priests and the leading men of the Jews brought charges against Paul; and they were urging him, 3 requesting a concession against Paul, that he might have him brought to Jerusalem, (*at the same time,* setting an ambush to kill him on the way). 4 Festus then answered that Paul was being kept in custody at Caesarea and that he himself was about to leave shortly. 5 "Therefore," he *said, "let the influential men among you go there with me, and if there is anything wrong about the man, let them prosecute him." 6 And after he had spent not more than eight or ten days among them, he went down to Caesarea; and on the next day he took his seat on the tribunal and ordered Paul to be brought. 7 And after he had arrived, the Jews who had come down from Jerusalem stood around him, bringing many and serious charges against him which they could not prove; 8 while Paul said in his own defense, "I have committed no offense either against the Law of the Jews or against the temple or against Caesar." 9 But Festus, wishing to do the Jews a favor, answered Paul and said, "Are you willing to go up to Jerusalem and stand trial before me on these charges?" 10 But Paul said, "I am standing before Caesar's tribunal, where I ought to be tried. I have done no wrong to *the* Jews, as you also very well know. 11 "If then I am a wrongdoer, and have committed anything worthy of death, I do not refuse to die; but if none of those things is *true* of which these men accuse me, no one can hand me over to them. I appeal to Caesar." 12 Then when Festus had conferred with his council, he answered, "You have appealed to Caesar, to Caesar you shall go."

13 Now when several days had elapsed, King Agrippa and Bernice arrived at Caesarea, and paid their respects to Festus. 14 And while they were spending many days there, Festus laid Paul's case before the king, saying, "There is a certain man left a prisoner by Felix; 15 and when I was at Jerusalem, the chief priests and the elders of the Jews brought charges against him, asking for a sentence of condemnation upon him. 16 "And I answered them that it is not the custom of the Romans to hand over any man before the accused meets his accusers face to face, and has an opportunity to make his defense against the charges. 17 "And so after they had assembled here, I made no delay, but on the next day took my seat on the tribunal, and ordered the man to be brought. 18 "And when the accusers stood up, they *began* bringing charges against him not of such crimes as I was expecting; 19 but they *simply* had some points of disagreement with him about

WILLIAMS

self-control, and the coming judgment, Felix became alarmed, and said, "For the present you may go, but when I find a good opportunity, I will send for you." 26 At the same time he was hoping to get money from Paul, and so he kept on sending for him and talking with him.

27 But at the close of two whole years Felix was succeeded by Porcius Festus, and as he wanted to gratify the Jews, Felix left Paul still in prison.

25 *Before Festus, Paul again pleads not guilty; he appeals to the emperor; Festus tells Agrippa II about Paul; Agrippa hears Paul*

Now three days after his arrival Festus went up from Caesarea to Jerusalem, 2 and the high priests and the Jewish elders presented their charges against Paul, 3 and begged the governor as a favor to have Paul come to Jerusalem, because they were plotting an ambush to kill him on the way. 4 Festus answered that Paul was being kept in custody in Caesarea, and that he himself was going there soon.

5 "So have your influential men go down with me," said he, "and present charges against the man, if there is anything wrong with him."

6 After staying there not more than eight or ten days, he went down to Caesarea, and the next day, after taking his seat on the judge's bench, he ordered Paul brought in. 7 When he arrived, the Jews who had come down from Jerusalem surrounded him, and continued to bring a number of serious charges against him, none of which they could prove. 8 Paul continued to maintain, in his defense, "I have committed no offense against the Jewish law or temple or against the emperor."

9 Then Festus, as he wanted to ingratiate himself with the Jews, said to Paul, "Will you go up to Jerusalem and be tried on these charges before me there?"

10 But Paul said, "I now am standing before the emperor's court where I ought to be tried. I have done the Jews no wrong, as you very well know. 11 If I am guilty and have done anything that deserves death, I am not begging to keep from dying; but if there is nothing in the charges which these men make against me, no one can give me up as a favor to them. I appeal to the emperor."

12 Then Festus, after conferring with the council, answered, "To the emperor you have appealed, to the emperor you shall go!"

13 After the passing of a few days, King Agrippa and Bernice came to Caesarea to pay official respects to Festus, 14 and as they stayed for several days, Festus laid Paul's case before the king. He said, "There is a man here who was left in prison by Felix, 15 and when I was in Jerusalem, the Jewish high priests and elders presented their case against him, and continued to ask for a judgment against him. 16 I answered them that it was not the Roman custom to give up anyone for punishment until the accused met his accusers face to face and had an opportunity to defend himself against their accusations. 17 So they came back here with me, and I made no delay to take my seat on the judge's bench, and ordered the man to be brought in. 18 But when his accusers appeared before me, they did not charge him with the crimes of which I had been suspecting him. 19 They merely had a quarrel with him about their own religion and

BECK

ness, self-control, and the coming judgment, Felix was frightened and answered, "Go now. When I get a chance, I'll send for you." 26 At the same time he expected Paul to give him money. And so he used to send for him often and talk with him.

27 Two whole years passed. Then Porcius Festus succeeded Felix. Since Felix wanted the Jews to remember him for a kindness, he left Paul in prison.

Paul Appeals to the Emperor

25 Three days after Festus took over his duties in the province of Judea he went from Caesarea up to Jerusalem. 2 The high priests and the leaders of the Jews reported to Festus what they had against Paul. They urged 3 and begged him to do them a favor and have Paul brought to Jerusalem. They were laying an ambush to kill him on the way.

4 But Festus answered that Paul would be kept in Caesarea and he himself would be going there soon. 5 "Those of you who have the authority," he said, "come down with me, and if the man has done anything wrong, accuse him."

6 He stayed with them no more than eight or ten days and then went down to Caesarea. The next day he sat on the judge's chair and ordered Paul brought in.

7 When Paul came in, the Jews who had come down from Jerusalem surrounded him and were accusing him of many serious wrongs that they couldn't prove. 8 Paul defended himself: "I have in no way sinned against the Law of the Jews or the temple or the emperor."

9 But Festus wanted the Jews to remember him for a kindness. So he asked Paul, "Do you want to go up to Jerusalem to be tried there before me in regard to these things?"

10 "I'm standing before the emperor's judgment seat," Paul said, "and there I must be tried. I haven't done the Jews any wrong, as you, too, know very well. 11 Now if I'm guilty and have done something to deserve to die, I don't refuse to die. But if their accusations are nothing, nobody can hand me over to them. I appeal to the emperor!"

12 Festus talked it over with his council and then answered, "You appealed to the emperor; you will go to the emperor!"

13 Some time later King Agrippa and Bernice came down to Caesarea to welcome Festus. 14 When they stayed there a number of days, Festus laid Paul's case before the king.

"There's a man here whom Felix left in prison," he said. 15 "When I went up to Jerusalem, the high priests and elders of the Jews informed me about him and asked me to condemn him.

16 "I answered them, 'It isn't customary for Romans to hand over a man before he has faced his accusers and had a chance to defend himself against their accusation.'

17 "They came here with me, and the next day without any delay I sat down in the judge's chair and ordered the man to be brought. 18 When his accusers got up, they didn't accuse him of the crimes I was suspecting. 19 But they disagreed with him about their own religion and

K.J.V.

own superstition, and of one Jesus, which was dead, whom Paul affirmed to be alive. 20And because I doubted of such manner of questions, I asked *him* whether he would go to Jerusalem, and there be judged of these matters. 21 But when Paul had appealed to be reserved unto the hearing of Augustus, I commanded him to be kept till I might send him to Cesar. 22 Then Agrippa said unto Festus, I would also hear the man myself. To morrow, said he, thou shalt hear him. 23And on the morrow, when Agrippa was come, and Bernice, with great pomp, and was entered into the place of hearing, with the chief captains, and principal men of the city, at Festus' commandment Paul was brought forth. 24And Festus said, King Agrippa, and all men which are here present with us, ye see this man, about whom all the multitude of the Jews have dealt with me, both at Jerusalem, and *also* here, crying that he ought not to live any longer. 25 But when I found that he had committed nothing worthy of death, and that he himself hath appealed to Augustus, I have determined to send him. 26 Of whom I have no certain thing to write unto my lord. Wherefore I have brought him forth before you, and specially before thee, O king Agrippa, that, after examination had, I might have somewhat to write. 27 For it seemeth to me unreasonable to send a prisoner, and not withal to signify the crimes *laid* against him.

26 Then Agrippa said unto Paul, Thou art permitted to speak for thyself. Then Paul stretched forth the hand, and answered for himself: 2 I think myself happy, king Agrippa, because I shall answer for myself this day before thee touching all the things whereof I am accused of the Jews: 3 Especially *because I know* thee to be expert in all customs and questions which are among the Jews: wherefore I beseech thee to hear me patiently. 4 My manner of life from my youth, which was at the first among mine own nation at Jerusalem, know all the Jews; 5 Which knew me from the beginning, if they would testify, that after the most straitest sect of our religion I lived a Pharisee. 6And now I stand and am judged for the hope of the promise made of God unto our fathers: 7 Unto which *promise* our twelve tribes, instantly serving *God* day and night, hope to come. For which hope's sake, king Agrippa, I am accused of the Jews. 8 Why should it be thought a thing incredible with you, that God should raise the dead? 9 I verily thought with myself, that I ought to do many things contrary to the name of Jesus of Nazareth. 10 Which thing I also did in Jerusalem: and many of the saints did I shut up in prison, having received authority from the chief priests; and when they were put to death, I gave my voice against *them*. 11And I punished them oft in every synagogue, and compelled *them* to blaspheme; and being exceedingly mad against them, I persecuted *them* even unto strange cities. 12 Whereupon as I went to Damascus with authority and commission from the chief priests, 13At midday, O king, I saw in the way a light

N.A.S.

their own religion and about a certain dead man, Jesus, whom Paul asserted to be alive. 20 "And being at a loss how to investigate such matters, I asked whether he was willing to go to Jerusalem and there stand trial on these matters. 21 "But when Paul appealed to be held in custody for ᵉthe Emperor's decision, I ordered him to be kept in custody until I send him to Caesar." 22And Agrippa *said* to Festus, "I also would like to hear the man myself." "Tomorrow," he *said, you shall hear him."

23 And so, on the next day when Agrippa had come together with Bernice, amid great pomp, and had entered the auditorium ᵇaccompanied by the commanders and the prominent men of the city, at the command of Festus, Paul was brought in. 24And Festus *said, "King Agrippa, and all you gentlemen here present with us, you behold this man about whom all the people of the Jews appealed to me, both at Jerusalem and here, loudly declaring that he ought not to live any longer. 25 "But I found that he had committed nothing worthy of death; since he himself appealed to the Emperor, I decided to send him. 26 "Yet I have nothing definite about him to write to my lord. Therefore I have brought him before you all and especially before you, King Agrippa, so that after the investigation has taken place, I may have something to write. 27 "For it seems absurd to me in sending a prisoner, not to indicate also the charges against him."

26 And Agrippa said to Paul, "You are permitted to speak for yourself." Then Paul stretched out his hand and *proceeded* to make his defense:
2 "In regard to all the things of which I am accused by the Jews, I consider myself fortunate, King Agrippa, that I am about to make my defense before you today; 3 especially because you are an expert in all customs and questions among *the* Jews; therefore I beg you to listen to me patiently. 4 "So then, all Jews know my manner of life from my youth up, which from the beginning was spent among my *own* nation and at Jerusalem; 5 since they have known about me for a long time previously, if they are willing to testify, that I lived *as* a Pharisee according to the strictest sect of our religion. 6 "And now I am standing trial for the hope of the promise made by God to our fathers; 7 *the promise* to which our twelve tribes hope to attain, as they earnestly serve *God* night and day. And for this hope, O king, I am being accused by Jews. 8 "Why is it considered incredible among you *people* if God does raise the dead? 9 "So then, I thought to myself that I had to do many things hostile to the name of Jesus of Nazareth. 10 "And this is just what I did in Jerusalem; not only did I lock up many of the saints in prisons, having received authority from the chief priests, but also when they were being put to death I cast my vote against them. 11 "And as I punished them often in all the synagogues, I tried to force them to blaspheme; and being furiously enraged at them, I kept pursuing them even to foreign cities. 12 "While thus engaged as I was journeying to Damascus with the authority and commission of the chief priests, 13 at midday, O King, I saw on the way

[a] Lit., *the Augustus* (in this case Nero). [b] Lit., *and with.*

WILLIAMS

about a certain Jesus who had died, but who Paul kept saying was still alive. 20 I was at a loss how to investigate such matters and so asked Paul if he would go to Jerusalem and there stand trial on these matters. 21 But as Paul appealed to have his case kept for his Majesty's decision, I ordered him kept in custody until I could send him up to the emperor."

22 "I should like to hear the man myself," said Agrippa to Festus.

"Tomorrow you shall hear him," said Festus.

23 So the next day, Agrippa and Bernice came with splendid pomp and went into the audience-room, attended by the colonels and the leading citizens of the town, and at the command of Festus, Paul was brought in. 24 Then Festus said:

"King Agrippa and all who are present with us, you now see this man about whom the whole Jewish nation made suit to me, both in Jerusalem and here, continuously clamoring that he ought not to live any longer. 25 But I found that he had not done anything for which he deserved to die; however, as he has himself appealed to his Majesty, I have decided to send him up. 26 Yet, I have nothing definite to write our Sovereign about him. So I have brought him before all of you, especially before you, King Agrippa, to get from your examination something to put in writing. 27 For it seems to me absurd to send a prisoner up, without specifying the charges against him."

26 *Paul's address before King Agrippa II; he tells the story of his life; Festus pronounces him crazy; Agrippa pronounces him innocent*

Then Agrippa said to Paul, "You have permission to speak in defense of yourself."

So Paul with outstretched arm began to make his defense.

2 "I count myself fortunate, King Agrippa," said he, "that it is before you that I can defend myself today against all the charges which the Jews have preferred against me, 3 especially because you are familiar with all the Jewish customs and questions. I beg you, therefore, to hear me with patience.

4 "The kind of life I have lived from my youth up, as spent in my early days among my own nation and in Jerusalem, is well known to all Jews, 5 for they have known all along from the first, if they would but testify to it, that I as a Pharisee have lived by the standard of the strictest sect of our religion. 6 And now it is for the hope of the promise made by God to our forefathers that I stand here on trial, 7 which promise our twelve tribes, by devotedly worshiping day and night, hope to see fulfilled for them. It is for this hope, your Majesty, that I am accused by some Jews. 8 Why is it considered incredible by all of you that God should raise the dead? 9 I myself, indeed, once thought it my duty to take extreme measures in hostility to the name of Jesus of Nazareth. 10 That was what I did at Jerusalem; yes, I received authority from the high priests and shut behind the prison bars many of God's people. Yes, when they were put to death, I cast my vote against them, and often in all the synagogues 11 I had them punished and tried to force them to use abusive language; in my extreme fury against them I continued to pursue them even into distant towns. 12 While in this business I once was on my way to Damascus with authority based on a commission from the high priests, 13 and

BECK

about a certain Jesus who died; Paul claimed He is alive. 20 I was puzzled how I should look into this and asked if he would like to go to Jerusalem and be tried there in regard to these things. 21 But Paul appealed. He wanted to be held and have Augustus* decide his case. So I ordered him to be kept in prison till I send him to the emperor."

22 Agrippa told Festus, "I myself would like to hear the man."

"Tomorrow," he answered, "you will hear him."

Before Agrippa

23 The next day Agrippa and Bernice came with great pomp and went with the tribunes and leading men of the city into the hall. Then Festus gave the order, and Paul was brought in.

24 "King Agrippa and all you men here with us," Festus said, "you see this man about whom all the Jewish people in Jerusalem and here have appealed to me, shouting he mustn't live any longer. 25 I found he hasn't done anything to deserve to die, but when he appealed to Augustus, I decided to send him. 26 I don't have anything reliable to write our lord about him. So I have brought him before you, and especially before you, King Agrippa, so we could examine him and I'll have something to write. 27 It makes no sense to me to send a prisoner without reporting what he's accused of."

26 Agrippa said to Paul, "You may speak for yourself."

Then Paul, stretching out his hand, began to defend himself:

2 "King Agrippa, I think I'm fortunate I'm going to defend myself today before you in regard to everything the Jews accuse me of, 3 because you are so very familiar with all the Jewish customs and problems. So I ask you to listen to me patiently.

4 "The Jews all know how I lived from my youth, from my earliest days, among my people in Jerusalem. 5 They have known long ago, if they want to tell the truth, that I lived the life of a Pharisee, the strictest party of our religion.

6 "And now I'm on trial here because I trust the promise God made to our fathers. 7 Our twelve tribes, worshiping zealously day and night, expect to see this promise come true. This is the hope, King, in regard to which some Jews accuse me. 8 Why do you think it incredible that God raises the dead?

9 "Once I believed I had to work hard against the name of Jesus from Nazareth. 10 I did that in Jerusalem. By the power I got from the high priests I locked up many of the holy people in prison, and when they were to be killed, I voted against them. 11 And many a time in every synagog I would punish them to make them blaspheme, and raging furiously against them, I hunted them down even to foreign cities.

12 "That is how I came to be traveling to Damascus, authorized and appointed by the high priests, 13 when on the way, King, at

* Another title for Nero.

405

K.J.V.

from heaven, above the brightness of the sun, shining round about me and them which journeyed with me. 14And when we were all fallen to the earth, I heard a voice speaking unto me, and saying in the Hebrew tongue, Saul, Saul, why persecutest thou me? *it is* hard for thee to kick against the pricks. 15And I said, Who art thou, Lord? And he said, I am Jesus whom thou persecutest. 16 But rise, and stand upon thy feet: for I have appeared unto thee for this purpose, to make thee a minister and a witness both of these things which thou hast seen, and of those things in the which I will appear unto thee; 17 Delivering thee from the people, and *from* the Gentiles, unto whom now I send thee, 18 To open their eyes, *and* to turn *them* from darkness to light, and *from* the power of Satan unto God, that they may receive forgiveness of sins, and inheritance among them which are sanctified by faith that is in me. 19 Whereupon, O king Agrippa, I was not disobedient unto the heavenly vision: 20 But shewed first unto them of Damascus, and at Jerusalem, and throughout all the coasts of Judea, and *then* to the Gentiles, that they should repent and turn to God, and do works meet for repentance. 21 For these causes the Jews caught me in the temple, and went about to kill *me*. 22 Having therefore obtained help of God, I continue unto this day, witnessing both to small and great, saying none other things than those which the prophets and Moses did say should come: 23 That Christ should suffer, *and* that he should be the first that should rise from the dead, and should shew light unto the people, and to the Gentiles. 24And as he thus spake for himself, Festus said with a loud voice, Paul, thou art beside thyself; much learning doth make thee mad. 25 But he said, I am not mad, most noble Festus; but speak forth the words of truth and soberness. 26 For the king knoweth of these things, before whom also I speak freely: for I am persuaded that none of these things are hidden from him; for this thing was not done in a corner. 27 King Agrippa, believest thou the prophets? I know that thou believest. 28 Then Agrippa said unto Paul, Almost thou persuadest me to be a Christian. 29And Paul said, I would to God, that not only thou, but also all that hear me this day, were both almost, and altogether such as I am, except these bonds. 30And when he had thus spoken, the king rose up, and the governor, and Bernice, and they that sat with them: 31And when they were gone aside, they talked between themselves, saying, This man doeth nothing worthy of death or of bonds. 32 Then said Agrippa unto Festus, This man might have been set at liberty, if he had not appealed unto Cesar.

27 And when it was determined that we should sail into Italy, they delivered Paul and certain other prisoners unto *one* named Julius, a centurion of Augustus' band. 2And entering into a ship of Adramyttium, we launched, meaning to sail by the coasts of Asia; *one* Aristarchus, a Macedonian of Thessalonica, being

N.A.S.

a light from heaven, brighter than the sun, shining all around me and those who were journeying with me. 14 "And when we had all fallen to the ground, I heard a voice saying to me in the Hebrew dialect, 'Saul, Saul, why are you persecuting Me? It is hard for you to kick against the goads.' 15 "And I said, 'Who art Thou, Lord?' And the Lord said, 'I am Jesus whom you are persecuting. 16 'But arise, and stand on your feet; for this purpose I have appeared to you, to appoint you a minister and a witness not only to the things which you have seen, but also to the things in which I will appear to you; 17 delivering you from the *Jewish* people and from the Gentiles, to whom I am sending you, 18 to open their eyes so that they may turn from darkness to light and from the dominion of Satan to God, in order that they may receive forgiveness of sins and an inheritance among those who have been sanctified by faith in Me.' 19 "Consequently, King Agrippa, I did not prove disobedient to the heavenly vision, 20 but *kept* declaring both to those of Damascus first, and *also* at Jerusalem and *then* throughout all the region of Judea, and *even* to the Gentiles, that they should repent and turn to God, performing deeds appropriate to repentance. 21 "For this reason *some* Jews seized me in the temple and tried to put me to death. 22 "And so, having obtained help from God, I stand to this day testifying both to small and great, stating nothing but what the Prophets and Moses said was going to take place; 23 that the Christ was to suffer, *and* that by reason of *His* resurrection from the dead He should be the first to proclaim light both to the *Jewish* people and to the Gentiles."

24 And while *Paul* was saying this in his defense, Festus *said in a loud voice, "Paul, you are out of your mind! *Your* great learning is driving you mad." 25 But Paul *said, "I am not out of my mind, most excellent Festus, but I utter words of sober truth. 26 "For the king knows about these matters, and I speak to him also with confidence, since I am persuaded that none of these things escape his notice; for this has not been done in a corner. 27 "King Agrippa, do you believe the Prophets? I know that you do." 28 And Agrippa *replied* to Paul, "In a short time you will persuade me to become a Christian." 29And Paul *said, "I would to God, that whether in a short or long time, not only you, but also all who hear me this day, might become such as I am, except for these chains."

30 And the king arose and the governor and Bernice, and those who were sitting with them, 31 and when they had drawn aside, they *began* talking to one another, saying, "This man is not doing anything worthy of death or imprisonment." 32And Agrippa said to Festus, "This man might have been set free if he had not appealed to Caesar."

27 And when it was decided that we should sail for Italy, they proceeded to deliver Paul and some other prisoners to a centurion of the Augustan a Cohort named Julius. 2And embarking in an Adramyttian ship, which was about to sail to the regions along the coast of Asia, we put out to sea, accompanied by Aris-

[a] Or, *Battalion.*

on the road at noon, your Majesty, I saw a light from heaven, brighter than the sun, flash around me and my fellow-travelers. 14 We all fell to the ground, and I heard a voice say to me in Hebrew, 'Saul! Saul! Why do you continue to persecute me? It is hurting you to keep on kicking against the goad.' 15 'Who are you Sir?' said I. 'I am Jesus,' the Lord said, 'whom you are persecuting. 16 But get up and stand on your feet, for I have appeared to you for the very purpose of appointing you my servant and a witness to me of the things which you have seen and those which I shall yet enable you to see. 17 I will continue to rescue you from the Jewish people and from the heathen to whom I am going to send you, 18 to open their eyes and turn them from darkness to light and from Satan's power to God, so as to have their sins forgiven and have a possession among those that are consecrated by faith in me.' 19 Therefore, King Agrippa, I could not disobey that heavenly vision, 20 but I began to preach first to the people of Damascus and Jerusalem, and all over Judea, and then to the heathen, to repent and turn to God, and to live lives consistent with such repentance. 21 For these very things the Jews arrested me in the temple and kept on trying to kill me. 22 As I have gotten help from God clear down to this very day, I stand here to testify to high and low alike, without adding a syllable to what Moses and the prophets said should take place, 23 if the Christ should suffer, and by being the first to rise from the dead was to proclaim the light to the Jewish people and to the heathen."

24 As Paul continued to make his defense, Festus shouted aloud, "You are going crazy, Paul! That great learning of yours is driving you crazy!"

25 Paul answered, "I am not going crazy, your Excellency, Festus, but I am telling the straight truth. 26 The king, indeed, knows about this and I can speak to him with freedom. I do not believe that any of this escaped his notice, for it did not occur in a corner! 27 King Agrippa, do you believe the prophets? I know that you do."

28 Then Agrippa answered Paul, "In brief you are trying to persuade me and make a Christian of me!" 29 Paul answered, "In brief or at length, I would to God that not only you but all my hearers today were what I am—excepting these chains!"

30 Then the king rose, with the governor and Bernice and those who had been seated with them, 31 and after leaving the room, as they continued to talk the matter over together, they said, "This man has done nothing to deserve death or imprisonment."

32 Agrippa said to Festus, "He might have been set at liberty, if he had not appealed to the emperor."

27 The voyage to Rome; Paul under Roman guard; Colonel Julius kind to him; a furious storm threatens ship and all on board; Paul cheers them by saying none shall be lost; ship stranded on Malta; every life saved

When it was decided that we should sail for Italy, they turned over Paul and some other prisoners to a colonel of the imperial regiment, named Julius. 2 After going on board an Adramyttian ship bound for the ports of Asia, we set sail. On board with us was Aristarchus,

---

noon I saw a light brighter than the sun, flashing from heaven around me and those who were going with me. 14 All of us fell to the ground, and I heard a voice asking me in the Jewish language, 'Saul, Saul! Why are you persecuting Me? You're only hurting yourself by kicking against the goads.'

15 "I asked, 'Who are you, Lord?'

" 'I am Jesus,' the Lord answered, 'whom you are persecuting. 16 But get up and *stand on your feet.*[91] I showed Myself to you to appoint you to serve Me and tell the truth of what you have seen and what you will see whenever I appear to you. 17 *I will rescue you* from your people and *from the non-Jews to whom I'm sending you,*[92] 18 *to open their eyes* and turn them *from darkness to light*[93] and from the devil's control to God to have their sins forgiven and get a share of what the people enjoy who are made holy by believing in Me.'

19 "And so, King Agrippa, I didn't disobey what I saw from heaven, 20 but first I told the people in Damascus and Jerusalem, then the whole country of the Jews, and the other nations to turn from sin to God and do the works that show they have repented. 21 For this the Jews grabbed me in the temple and tried to murder me.

22 "God has helped me to this day, and so I have been standing and telling the truth to high and low, stating only what the prophets and Moses said would happen, 23 that Christ had to suffer and by being the first to rise from the dead would announce light to our people and the other nations."

24 As he was defending himself in this way, Festus shouted, "You're crazy, Paul! Your great learning is driving you crazy!"

25 "I'm not crazy, excellent Festus," Paul said, "but I'm telling the sober truth. 26 The king knows about these things, and I'm talking boldly to him. I'm sure he hasn't missed any of them, since this wasn't done in a corner. 27 King Agrippa, do you believe the prophets? I know you believe them!"

28 "You're trying to persuade me," Agrippa said to Paul, "that with a little effort you've made me a Christian!"

29 "I wish to God," Paul said, "that with little or much effort not only you but all who hear me today would become what I am—except for these chains!"

30 The king, the governor, Bernice, and those who sat with them got up 31 and left and said to one another, "This man isn't doing anything to deserve to die or be in chains."

32 "This man could be free," Agrippa told Festus, "if he hadn't appealed to the emperor."

Paul Sails for Rome

27 When it was decided we should sail to Italy, Paul and some other prisoners were turned over to a captain by the name of Julius, of the troop of Augustus. 2 We boarded a ship from Adramyttium that was going to sail to the ports on the coast of the province of Asia, and we started out. Aristarchus, a Macedonian from Thessalonica, went with us.

[91] Ezek. 2:1-2
[92] 1 Chron. 16:35; Jer. 1:7-8
[93] Is. 35:5; 42:7, 16

K.J.V.

with us. 3And the next *day* we touched at Sidon. And Julius courteously entreated Paul, and gave *him* liberty to go unto his friends to refresh himself. 4And when we had launched from thence, we sailed under Cyprus, because the winds were contrary. 5And when we had sailed over the sea of Cilicia and Pamphylia, we came to Myra, *a city* of Lycia. 6And there the centurion found a ship of Alexandria sailing into Italy; and he put us therein. 7And when we had sailed slowly many days, and scarce were come over against Cnidus, the wind not suffering us, we sailed under Crete, over against Salmone; 8And, hardly passing it, came unto a place which is called the Fair Havens; nigh whereunto was the city *of* Lasea. 9 Now when much time was spent, and when sailing was now dangerous, because the fast was now already past, Paul admonished *them,* 10And said unto them, Sirs, I perceive that this voyage will be with hurt and much damage, not only of the lading and ship, but also of our lives. 11 Nevertheless the centurion believed the master and the owner of the ship, more than those things which were spoken by Paul. 12And because the haven was not commodious to winter in, the more part advised to depart thence also, if by any means they might attain to Phenice, *and there* to winter; *which is* a haven of Crete, and lieth toward the southwest and northwest. 13And when the south wind blew softly, supposing that they had obtained *their* purpose, loosing *thence,* they sailed close by Crete. 14 But not long after there arose against it a tempestuous wind, called Euroclydon. 15And when the ship was caught, and could not bear up into the wind, we let *her* drive. 16And running under a certain island which is called Clauda, we had much work to come by the boat: 17 Which when they had taken up, they used helps, undergirding the ship; and, fearing they should fall into the quicksands, strike sail, and so were driven. 18And we being exceedingly tossed with a tempest, the next *day* they lightened the ship; 19And the third *day* we cast out with our own hands the tackling of the ship. 20And when neither sun nor stars in many days appeared, and no small tempest lay on *us,* all hope that we should be saved was then taken away. 21 But after long abstinence, Paul stood forth in the midst of them, and said, Sirs, ye should have hearkened unto me, and not have loosed from Crete, and to have gained this harm and loss. 22And now I exhort you to be of good cheer: for there shall be no loss of *any man's* life among you, but of the ship. 23 For there stood by me this night the angel of God, whose I am, and whom I serve, 24 Saying, Fear not, Paul; thou must be brought before Cesar: and, lo, God hath given thee all them that sail with thee. 25 Wherefore, sirs, be of good cheer: for I believe God, that it shall be even as it was told me. 26 Howbeit we must be cast upon a certain island. 27 But when the fourteenth night was come, as we were driven up and down in Adria, about midnight the shipmen deemed that they drew near to some country; 28And sounded, and found *it* twenty fathoms: and when they

N.A.S.

tarchus, a Macedonian of Thessalonica. 3And the next day we put in at Sidon; and Julius treated Paul with consideration and allowed him to go to his friends and receive care. 4And from there we put out to sea and sailed under the shelter of Cyprus because the winds were contrary. 5And when we had sailed through the sea along the coast of Cilicia and Pamphylia, we landed at Myra in Lycia. 6And there the centurion found an Alexandrian ship sailing for Italy, and he put us aboard it. 7And when we had sailed slowly for a good many days, and with difficulty had arrived off Cnidus, since the wind did not permit us *to go* farther, we sailed under the shelter of Crete, off Salmone; 8 and with difficulty sailing past it we came to a certain place called Fair Havens, near which was the city of Lasea.

9 And when considerable time had passed and the voyage was now dangerous, since even the *ª*Fast was already over, Paul *began* to admonish them, 10 and said to them, "Men, I perceive that the voyage will certainly be *attended* with damage and great loss, not only of the cargo and the ship, but also of our lives." 11 But the centurion was more persuaded by the pilot and the captain of the ship, than by what was being said by Paul. 12And because the harbor was not suitable for wintering, the majority reached a decision to put out to sea from there, if somehow they could reach Phoenix, a harbor of Crete, facing northeast and southeast, and spend the winter *there.* 13And when a moderate south wind came up, supposing that they had gained their purpose, they weighed anchor and *began* sailing along Crete, close *inshore.* 14 But before very long there rushed down from the land a violent wind, called *ᵇ*Euraquilo; 15 and when the ship was caught *in it,* and could not face the wind, we gave way *to it,* and let ourselves be driven along. 16And running under the shelter of a small island called Clauda, we were scarcely able to get the *ship's* boat under control. 17And after they had hoisted it up, they used supporting cables in undergirding the ship; and fearing that they might run aground on *the shallows* of Syrtis, they let down the sea anchor, and so let themselves be driven along. 18 The next day as we were being violently storm-tossed, they began to jettison the cargo; 19 and on the third day they threw the ship's tackle overboard with their own hands. 20And since neither sun nor stars appeared for many days, and no small storm was assailing *us,* from then on all hope of our being saved was gradually abandoned. 21 And when they had gone a long time without food, then Paul stood up in their midst and said, "Men, you ought to have followed my advice and not to have set sail from Crete, and incurred this damage and loss. 22 "And *yet* now I urge you to keep up your courage, for there shall be no loss of life among you, but *only* of the ship. 23 "For this very night an angel of the God to whom I belong and whom I serve stood before me, 24 saying, 'Do not be afraid, Paul; you must stand before Caesar; and behold, God has granted you all those who are sailing with you.' 25 "Therefore, keep up your courage, men, for I believe God, that it will turn out exactly as I have been told. 26 "But we must run aground on a certain island."

27 But when the fourteenth night had come, as we were being driven about in the Adriatic Sea, about midnight the sailors *began* to surmise that they were approaching some land. 28And they took soundings, and found *it to be* twenty fathoms; and a little farther on they

[a] I.e., the Day of Atonement in October. [b] I.e., a northeaster.

WILLIAMS

a Macedonian from Thessalonica. 3 The next day we landed at Sidon, and Julius kindly permitted Paul to visit his friends and enjoy their attentions. 4After setting sail from there, we sailed under the lee of Cyprus, because the wind was against us, 5 and after sailing the whole length of the sea off Cilicia and Pamphylia, we reached Myra in Lycia. 6 There the colonel found an Alexandrian ship bound for Italy, and put us on board her. 7 For a number of days we sailed on slowly and with difficulty arrived off Cnidus. Then, because the wind did not permit us to go on, we sailed under the lee off Cape Salmone, 8 and with difficulty coasted along it and finally reached a place called Fair Havens, near the town of Lasea.

9 After considerable time had gone by, and navigation had become dangerous, and the fast was now over, Paul began to warn them 10 by saying, "Men, I see that this voyage is likely to be attended by disaster and heavy loss, not only to the cargo and the ship, but also to our lives." 11 But the colonel was influenced by the pilot and the captain of the ship rather than by what Paul said. 12And as the harbor was not fit to winter in, the majority favored the plan to set sail from there and see if they could reach Phoenix and winter there, this being a harbor in Crete facing west-southwest and west-northwest. 13 When a light breeze from the south began to blow, thinking their purpose was about to be realized, they weighed anchor and coasted along by Crete, hugging the shore. 14 But it was not long before a violent wind, which is called a Northeaster, swept down from it. 15 The ship was snatched along by it and since she could not face the wind, we gave up and let her drive. 16As we passed under the lee of a small island called Cauda, with great difficulty we were able to secure the ship's boat. 17 After hoisting it on board, they used ropes to brace the ship, and since they were afraid of being stranded on the Syrtis quicksands, they lowered the sail and let her drift. 18 The next day, because we were so violently beaten by the storm, they began to throw the cargo overboard, 19 and on the next day with their own hands they threw the ship's tackle overboard. 20 For a number of days neither the sun nor the stars were to be seen, and the storm continued to rage, until at last all hope of being saved was now vanishing. 21After they had gone a long time without any food, then Paul got up among them and said:

"Men, you ought to have listened to me and not to have sailed from Crete, and you would have escaped this disaster and loss. 22 Even now I beg you to keep up your courage, for there will be no loss of life, but only of the ship. 23 For just last night an angel of God, to whom I belong and whom I serve, stood by my side 24 and said, 'Stop being afraid, Paul. You must stand before the Emperor; and listen! God has graciously given to you the lives of all who are sailing with you.' 25 So keep up your courage, men, for I have confidence in my God that it will all come out just as I was told. 26And yet we must be stranded on some island."

27 It was now the fourteenth night and we were drifting on the Adriatic sea, when at midnight the sailors suspected that land was near. 28 On taking soundings they found a depth of

BECK

3 The next day we landed at Sidon, where Julius treated Paul kindly and let him go to his friends to get any care he needed. 4 Leaving Sidon, we sailed on the sheltered side of Cyprus because the winds were against us. 5 We crossed the sea off Cilicia and Pamphylia and landed at Myra in Lycia. 6 There the captain of the soldiers found a ship from Alexandria sailing to Italy and put us on it. 7 We were sailing slowly for a number of days and had some difficulty getting near Cnidus. The wind wouldn't let us go on, and so, starting at Cape Salmone, we sailed on the sheltered side of Crete. 8 Hugging the coast, we struggled on to a place called Fair Havens, near the town of Lasea.

9 We had lost a lot of time, even the day of fasting* had already gone by, and sailing was now dangerous. 10 So Paul advised them: "Men, I see that in this sailing we're going to suffer hardship and a heavy loss not only of the cargo and ship but also of our lives." 11 But the captain of the soldiers listened to the pilot and the captain of the ship and not to what Paul said. 12 Since that harbor was not a good place to spend the winter, the majority decided to sail away, hoping they could somehow reach Phoenix to spend the winter there. It is a harbor of Crete facing southwest and northwest. 13 When a gentle breeze blew from the south, they felt they could easily make it. They took up the anchor and sailed close to the shore of Crete.

14 But after a little while a hurricane, called the Northeastern, dashed down from Crete. 15 It caught the ship so that it couldn't face the wind, and we gave up and were swept along. 16As we ran into the shelter of a small island called Clauda, we managed with a struggle to get hold of the small boat. 17 They pulled it up on deck. Then they passed ropes around the ship to reinforce it. Fearing they would run on the great sandbank near Africa, they lowered the sail and so drifted along. 18 We continued to be tossed by the storm so violently that the next day the men started to throw the cargo overboard, 19 and on the third with their own hands they threw the ship's equipment overboard. 20 For a number of days we couldn't see any sun or stars and were in a great storm until at last we were giving up all hope of coming through alive. 21 Since hardly anybody wanted to eat, Paul stepped before them and said, "Men, you should have listened to me and not have sailed from Crete. You would have avoided this hardship and damage. 22 But now I urge you to cheer up because you will lose no lives but only the ship. 23 I am God's own and serve Him. Last night His angel stood by me. 24 'Don't be afraid, Paul!' he said. 'You must stand before the emperor, and now God has given you all who are sailing with you.' 25 So, cheer up, men, because I trust God it will be just as He told me. 26 But we must run on some island."

The Shipwreck

27 It was the fourteenth night and we were drifting through the Adriatic Sea** when about midnight the sailors suspected land was coming closer. 28 They dropped the lead and found the water 120 feet deep. A little farther they

---

* The Day of Atonement, September 15, in the year 58.
** At that time the "Adriatic" Sea included the present Adriatic plus a large part of the Mediterranean Sea south of it.

K.J.V.

had gone a little further, they sounded again, and found it fifteen fathoms. 29 Then fearing lest we should have fallen upon rocks, they cast four anchors out of the stern, and wished for the day. 30 And as the shipmen were about to flee out of the ship, when they had let down the boat into the sea, under colour as though they would have cast anchors out of the foreship, 31 Paul said to the centurion and to the soldiers, Except these abide in the ship, ye cannot be saved. 32 Then the soldiers cut off the ropes of the boat, and let her fall off. 33 And while the day was coming on, Paul besought them all to take meat, saying, This day is the fourteenth day that ye have tarried and continued fasting, having taken nothing. 34 Wherefore I pray you to take some meat; for this is for your health: for there shall not a hair fall from the head of any of you. 35 And when he had thus spoken, he took bread, and gave thanks to God in presence of them all; and when he had broken it, he began to eat. 36 Then were they all of good cheer, and they also took some meat. 37 And we were in all in the ship two hundred threescore and sixteen souls. 38 And when they had eaten enough, they lightened the ship, and cast out the wheat into the sea. 39 And when it was day, they knew not the land: but they discovered a certain creek with a shore, into the which they were minded, if it were possible, to thrust in the ship. 40 And when they had taken up the anchors, they committed themselves unto the sea, and loosed the rudder bands, and hoised up the mainsail to the wind, and made toward shore. 41 And falling into a place where two seas met, they ran the ship aground; and the forepart stuck fast, and remained unmoveable, but the hinder part was broken with the violence of the waves. 42 And the soldiers' counsel was to kill the prisoners, lest any of them should swim out, and escape. 43 But the centurion, willing to save Paul, kept them from their purpose; and commanded that they which could swim should cast themselves first into the sea, and get to land: 44 And the rest, some on boards, and some on broken pieces of the ship. And so it came to pass, that they escaped all safe to land.

28 And when they were escaped, then they knew that the island was called Melita. 2 And the barbarous people shewed us no little kindness: for they kindled a fire, and received us every one, because of the present rain, and because of the cold. 3 And when Paul had gathered a bundle of sticks, and laid them on the fire, there came a viper out of the heat, and fastened on his hand. 4 And when the barbarians saw the venomous beast hang on his hand, they said among themselves, No doubt this man is a murderer, whom, though he hath escaped the sea, yet vengeance suffereth not to live. 5 And he shook off the beast into the fire, and felt no harm. 6 Howbeit they looked when he should

N.A.S.

took another sounding and found it to be fifteen fathoms. 29 And fearing that we might run aground somewhere on the rocks, they cast four anchors from the stern and wished for daybreak. 30 And as the sailors were trying to escape from the ship, and had let down the ship's boat into the sea, on the pretense of intending to lay out anchors from the bow, 31 Paul said to the centurion and to the soldiers, "Unless these men remain in the ship, you yourselves cannot be saved." 32 Then the soldiers cut away the ropes of the ship's boat, and let it fall away. 33 And until the day was about to dawn, Paul was encouraging them all to take some food, saying, "Today is the fourteenth day that you have been constantly watching and going without eating, having taken nothing. 34 "Therefore I encourage you to take some food, for this is for your preservation; for not a hair from the head of any of you shall perish." 35 And having said this, he took bread and gave thanks to God in the presence of all; and he broke it and began to eat. 36 And all of them were encouraged, and they themselves also took food. 37 And all of us in the ship were two hundred and seventy-six persons. 38 And when they had eaten enough, they began to lighten the ship by throwing out the wheat into the sea. 39 And when day came, they could not recognize the land; but they did observe a certain bay with a beach, and they resolved to ᵃdrive the ship onto it if they could. 40 And casting off the anchors, they left them in the sea while at the same time they were loosening the ropes of the rudders, and hoisting the foresail to the wind, they were heading for the beach. 41 But striking a reef where two seas met, they ran the vessel aground; and the prow stuck fast and remained immovable, but the stern began to be broken up by the force of the waves. 42 And the soldiers' plan was to kill the prisoners, that none of them should swim away and escape; 43 but the centurion, wanting to bring Paul safely through, kept them from their intention, and commanded that those who could swim should jump overboard first and get to land, 44 and the rest should follow, some on planks, and others on various things from the ship. And thus it happened that they all were brought safely to land.

28 And when they had been brought safely through, then we found out that the island was called Malta. 2 And the natives showed us extraordinary kindness; for because of the rain that had set in and because of the cold, they kindled a fire and received us all. 3 But when Paul had gathered a bundle of sticks and laid them on the fire, a viper came out because of the heat, and fastened on his hand. 4 And when the natives saw the creature hanging from his hand, they began saying to one another, "Undoubtedly this man is a murderer, and though he has been saved from the sea, Justice has not allowed him to live." 5 However he shook the creature off into the fire and suffered no harm. 6 But they were expecting that he was

[a] Some ancient mss. read, bring the ship safely ashore.

410

WILLIAMS

twenty fathoms; and a little later again taking soundings, they found it was fifteen. 29 Since they were afraid of our going on the rocks, they dropped four anchors from the stern, and kept wishing for daylight to come. 30Although the sailors were trying to escape from the ship and had actually lowered the boat into the sea, pretending that they were going to run out anchors from the bow, 31 Paul said to the colonel and his soldiers, "Unless these sailors remain on the ship, you cannot be saved." 32 Then the soldiers cut the ropes that held the boat and let it drift away.

33 Until day was about to break Paul kept begging them all to take something to eat. He said, "For fourteen days today you have been constantly waiting and going without food, not even taking a bite. 34 So I beg you to eat something, for it is necessary for your safety. For not a hair will be lost from the head of a single one of you."

35 After saying this he took some bread and thanked God for it before them all; then he broke it in pieces and began to eat it. 36 Then they all were cheered and took something to eat themselves. 37 There were about seventy-six of us on the ship. 38 When they had eaten enough, they began to lighten the ship by throwing the wheat into the sea. 39 When day broke, they could not recognize the land, but they spied a bay that had a beach, and determined, if possible, to run the ship ashore. 40 So they cast off the anchors and left them in the sea; at the same time they undid the ropes of the rudders, and hoisting the foresail to the breeze they headed for the beach. 41 But they struck a shoal and ran the ship aground; the bow stuck and remained unmoved, while the stern began to break to pieces under the beating of the waves. 42 The soldiers planned to kill the prisoners, to keep any of them from swimming ashore and escaping, 43 but the colonel wanted to save Paul, and so he prevented them from carrying out this plan, and ordered all who could swim to jump overboard first and get to land, and the rest to follow, 44 some on planks and others on various bits of the ship. And thus they all got safely to land.

28 *Wintering on the island of Malta; Paul not poisoned by a viper bite; cures the father of Governor Publius and others; loaded down by gifts of islanders, Paul goes on to Rome; welcomed by Christians; treated kindly by Roman officials; as a prisoner, allowed to live in private home*

After we had been rescued, we learned that the island was called Malta. 2 Now the natives showed us remarkable kindness, for they made us a fire and welcomed us to it because of the downpouring rain and the cold. 3 Paul, too, gathered a bundle of sticks, and as he put them on the fire, because of the heat, a viper crawled out of them and fastened itself upon his hand. 4 When the natives saw the reptile hanging from his hand, they said to one another, "Beyond a doubt this man is a murderer, for though he has been rescued from the sea, justice will not let him live." 5 But he simply shook the reptile off into the fire and suffered no harm. 6 The natives kept on looking for him

BECK

dropped it again and found it was 90 feet. 29 Fearing we might run on rocks, they dropped four anchors from the back of the ship and prayed for morning to come.

30 Then the sailors tried to escape from the ship. They let the boat down into the sea, pretending they were going to take out the anchors from the front of the ship and let them down. 31 But Paul told the captain of the soldiers and his men, "If these don't stay on the ship, you can't be rescued." 32 Then the soldiers cut the ropes that held the boat and let it drift away.

33 Just before daybreak Paul was urging them all to eat something. "This is the fourteenth day you've waited and gone hungry and not eaten a thing. 34 So I urge you to eat something. It will help you come through this safely. None of you will lose a hair of his head." 35After saying this, he took some bread, thanked God in front of everybody, broke it, and started to eat. 36 They were all cheered up, and they too, had something to eat. 37 There were 276 of us in the ship. 38After they had eaten all they wanted, they lightened the ship by dumping the wheat into the sea.

39 In the morning they couldn't tell what land it was but gradually could see a bay with a beach on which they planned if possible to run the ship ashore. 40 They cut off the anchors and left them in the sea. At the same time they untied the ropes that held up the steering oars, spread out the foresail to catch the wind, and steered the ship to the shore. 41 They struck a bank in the water and ran the ship aground. The front of the ship stuck and couldn't be moved, while the back was being pounded to pieces by the sea.

42 To keep any of the prisoners from swimming away and escaping, the soldiers planned to kill them, 43 but the captain of the soldiers wanted to save Paul, so he kept them from doing this. He ordered those who could swim to jump out first and get to the shore, 44 and the rest to follow, some on planks and some on other pieces from the ship. In this way all of them came safely to the shore.

Safe on Malta

28 Once we were safe on the shore, we recognized that it was called Malta. 2 The natives were unusually kind to us. It had started to rain and was cold, and so they made a fire and welcomed all of us around it.

3 Paul gathered an armful of dry branches and put them on the fire. The heat made a viper come out, and it bit his hand. 4 When the natives saw the snake hanging from his hand, they said to one another, "This man certainly is a murderer! He did escape from the sea, but Justice didn't let him live."

5 So he shook the snake into the fire and suffered no harm. 6 They were waiting for him to

K.J.V.

have swollen, or fallen down dead suddenly: but after they had looked a great while, and saw no harm come to him, they changed their minds, and said that he was a god. 7 In the same quarters were possessions of the chief man of the island, whose name was Publius; who received us, and lodged us three days courteously. 8And it came to pass, that the father of Publius lay sick of a fever and of a bloody flux: to whom Paul entered in, and prayed, and laid his hands on him, and healed him. 9 So when this was done, others also, which had diseases in the island, came, and were healed: 10 Who also honoured us with many honours; and when we departed, they laded us with such things as were necessary. 11And after three months we departed in a ship of Alexandria, which had wintered in the isle, whose sign was Castor and Pollux. 12And landing at Syracuse, we tarried *there* three days. 13And from thence we fetched a compass, and came to Rhegium: and after one day the south wind blew, and we came the next day to Puteoli: 14 Where we found brethren, and were desired to tarry with them seven days: and so we went toward Rome. 15And from thence, when the brethren heard of us, they came to meet us as far as Appii Forum, and the Three Taverns; whom when Paul saw, he thanked God, and took courage. 16And when we came to Rome, the centurion delivered the prisoners to the captain of the guard: but Paul was suffered to dwell by himself with a soldier that kept him. 17And it came to pass, that after three days Paul called the chief of the Jews together: and when they were come together, he said unto them, Men *and* brethren, though I have committed nothing against the people, or customs of our fathers, yet was I delivered prisoner from Jerusalem into the hands of the Romans: 18 Who, when they had examined me, would have let *me* go, because there was no cause of death in me. 19 But when the Jews spake against *it,* I was constrained to appeal unto Cesar; not that I had aught to accuse my nation of. 20 For this cause therefore have I called for you, to see *you,* and to speak with *you:* because that for the hope of Israel I am bound with this chain. 21And they said unto him, We neither received letters out of Judea concerning thee, neither any of the brethren that came shewed or spake any harm of thee. 22 But we desire to hear of thee what thou thinkest: for as concerning this sect, we know that every where it is spoken against. 23And when they had appointed him a day, there came many to him into *his* lodging; to whom he expounded and testified the kingdom of God, persuading them concerning Jesus, both out of the law of Moses, and *out of* the prophets, from morning till evening. 24And some believed the things which were spoken, and some believed not. 25And when they agreed not among themselves, they departed, after that Paul had spoken one word, Well spake the Holy Ghost by Esaias the prophet unto our fathers, 26 Saying, Go unto this people, and say, Hearing ye shall hear, and shall not understand; and seeing ye shall see,

N.A.S.

about to swell up or suddenly fall down dead. But after they had waited a long time and had seen nothing unusual happen to him, they changed their minds and *began* to say that he was a god. 7 Now in the neighborhood of that place were lands belonging to the leading man of the island, named Publius, who welcomed us and entertained us courteously three days. 8And it came about that the father of Publius was lying *in bed* afflicted with *recurrent* fever and dysentery; and Paul went in *to see* him and after he had prayed, he laid his hands on him and healed him. 9And after this had happened, the rest of the people on the island who had diseases were coming to him and getting cured. 10And they also honored us with many marks of respect; and when we were setting sail, they supplied *us* with all we needed.

11 And at the end of three months we set sail on an Alexandrian ship which had wintered at the island, and which had the Twin Brothers for its figurehead. 12And after we put in at Syracuse, we stayed there for three days. 13And from there we sailed around and arrived at Rhegium, and a day later a south wind sprang up, and on the second day we came to Puteoli. 14 There we found *some* brethren, and were invited to stay with them for seven days; and thus we came to Rome. 15And the brethren, when they heard about us, came from there as far as the Market of Appius and Three Inns to meet us; and when Paul saw them, he thanked God and took courage.

16 And when we entered Rome, Paul was allowed to stay by himself, with the soldier who was guarding him.

17 And it happened that after three days he called together those who were the leading men of the Jews, and when they had come together, he *began* saying to them, "Brethren, though I had done nothing against our people, or the customs of our fathers, yet I was delivered prisoner from Jerusalem into the hands of the Romans. 18 "And when they had examined me, they were willing to release me because there was no ground for putting me to death. 19 "But when the Jews objected, I was forced to appeal to Caesar; not that I had any accusation against my nation. 20 "For this reason therefore I requested to see you and to speak with you, for I am wearing this chain for the sake of the hope of Israel." 21And they said to him, "We have neither received letters from Judea concerning you, nor have any of the brethren come here and reported or spoken anything bad about you. 22 "But we desire to hear from you what your views are; for concerning this sect, it is known to us that it is spoken against everywhere."

23 And when they had set a day for him, they came to him at his lodging in large numbers; and he was explaining to them by solemnly testifying about the kingdom of God, and trying to persuade them concerning Jesus, from both the Law of Moses and from the Prophets, from morning until evening. 24And some were being persuaded by the things spoken, but others would not believe. 25And when they did not agree with one another, they *began* leaving after Paul had spoken one parting word, "The Holy Spirit rightly spoke through Isaiah the prophet to your fathers, 26 saying,

'GO TO THIS PEOPLE AND SAY,

"YOU WILL KEEP ON HEARING, BUT WILL NOT
    UNDERSTAND;

AND YOU WILL KEEP ON SEEING, BUT WILL
    NOT PERCEIVE;

to swell up or suddenly drop dead, but after waiting a long time and seeing nothing unusual take place on him, they changed their minds and said that he was a god.

7 The governor of the island, whose name was Publius, owned estates in that part of the island, and he welcomed us and entertained us with hearty hospitality for three days. 8 Publius' father chanced to be sick in bed with fever and dysentery, and Paul went to see him and after praying laid his hands upon him and cured him. 9 Because this cure was performed, the rest of the sick people on the island kept coming to him and by degrees were cured. 10 They also honored us with many presents, and when we set sail, they supplied us with everything that we needed.

11 Three months later, we set sail in an Alexandrian ship named The Twin Brothers, which had wintered at the island. 12 We landed at Syracuse and stayed there three days. 13 After weighing anchor and leaving there, we arrived at Rhegium. The next day, a south wind began to blow, and the following day we got to Puteoli. 14 There we found some brothers, and they begged us to spend a week with them. In this way we finally reached Rome. 15 Because the brothers at Rome had heard of our coming, they came as far as Appius' Market and the Three Taverns to meet us, and as soon as Paul caught sight of them, he thanked God and took courage.

16 When we did arrive at Rome, Paul was granted permission to live by himself—excepting a soldier to guard him.

17 Three days later, he invited the leading men of the Jews to come to see him, and when they came, he said to them, "Brothers, I have done nothing against our people or the customs of our forefathers; yet at Jerusalem I was turned over to the Romans as a prisoner. 18 After examining me the Romans wanted to set me free, because I was innocent of any crime that deserved the death penalty. 19 But the Jews objected, so I was forced to appeal to the Emperor; yet it was not because I had any charge to make against my own nation. 20 Now it is for this reason that I invited you to come, namely, to see you and speak with you, for it is on account of Israel's hope that I am wearing this chain."

21 They answered him, "We have not received any letters from Judea about you, and not one of our Jewish brothers has come and reported or stated anything wicked about you. 22 But we think it fitting to let you tell us what your views are, for as to this sect it is known by all of us that it is everywhere denounced."

23 So they set a day for him, and came in large numbers to see him at the place where he was lodging, and from morning till night he continued to explain to them the kingdom of God, at the same time giving them his own testimony and trying from the law of Moses and the prophets to convince them about Jesus. 24 Some of them were convinced by what he said, but others would not believe. 25 Because they could not agree among themselves, they started to leave, when Paul had spoken one word more:

"The Holy Spirit beautifully expressed it in speaking to your forefathers through the prophet Isaiah:

26 'Go to this people and say to them,
"You will listen, and listen, and never understand,
And you will look, and look, and never see!

swell up or suddenly fall down dead. But they waited long and saw nothing unusual happen to him. Then they changed their minds and said he was a god.

7 The governor of the island, whose name was Publius, had land around that place. He welcomed us and treated us kindly while we were his guests for three days. 8 The father of Publius happened to be sick in bed with fever and dysentery. Paul went to him, prayed, and laid his hands on him, and made him well.

9 After that had happened, the other sick people on the island also came to him and were made well. 10 They honored us in many ways, and when we were going to sail, they put on board whatever we needed.

From Malta to Rome

11 After three months we sailed on a ship from Alexandria that had stopped at the island for the winter. It had in front a figure of the Twin Sons of Zeus.* 12 We stopped at Syracuse and stayed there three days. 13 From there we sailed around and came to Rhegium. After a day a south wind started blowing, and on the second day we came to Puteoli. 14 There we found fellow Christians who urged us to stay seven days with them.

15 And so we came to Rome. The fellow Christians in Rome, who had heard about us, came as far as the Market Town of Appius and the Three Shops to meet us. When Paul saw them, he thanked God and felt encouraged.

In Rome

16 When we came into Rome, Paul was allowed to live by himself with the soldier guarding him. 17 After three days he called the leaders of the Jews together. When they came, he said to them, "Fellow Jews, although I haven't done anything against our people or the customs of our fathers, I'm a prisoner from Jerusalem who was handed over to the Romans. 18 They examined me and wanted to let me go because I had done no wrong to deserve to die. 19 But the Jews objected and forced me to appeal to the emperor—not that I'm accusing my people of anything. 20 That's why I asked to see you and talk to you, since it is for the hope of Israel I wear this chain."

21 "We have had no letters from Judea about you," they told him, "and no Jew coming here has reported or said anything bad about you. 22 We would like to hear from you what you think, because we know that everywhere people are talking against this sect."

23 They set a day to meet with him, and more of them came to him where he was staying. From morning till evening he explained the matter to them, earnestly telling the truth about God's kingdom and trying to convince them about Jesus from the Law of Moses and the prophets. 24 Some of them were convinced by what he said, but others wouldn't believe.

25 They disagreed with one another as they were leaving, and Paul added a statement: "The Holy Spirit spoke the truth to your fathers through the prophet Isaiah 26 when he said, *Go to these people and say.*

*You will hear and never understand,
look and never see,*

---

* Castor and Pollux, the guardian gods of sailors.

K.J.V.

and not perceive: 27 For the heart of this people is waxed gross, and their ears are dull of hearing, and their eyes have they closed; lest they should see with *their* eyes, and hear with *their* ears, and understand with *their* heart, and should be converted, and I should heal them. 28 Be it known therefore unto you, that the salvation of God is sent unto the Gentiles, and *that* they will hear it. 29And when he had said these words, the Jews departed, and had great reasoning among themselves. 30And Paul dwelt two whole years in his own hired house, and received all that came in unto him, 31 Preaching the kingdom of God, and teaching those things which concern the Lord Jesus Christ, with all confidence, no man forbidding him.

N.A.S.

27 FOR THE HEART OF THIS PEOPLE HAS BE-
  COME DULL,
AND WITH THEIR EARS THEY SCARCELY HEAR,
AND THEY HAVE CLOSED THEIR EYES;
LEST THEY SHOULD SEE WITH THEIR EYES,
AND HEAR WITH THEIR EARS,
AND UNDERSTAND WITH THEIR HEART AND
  TURN AGAIN,
AND I SHOULD HEAL THEM." '
28 "Let it be known to you therefore, that this salvation of God has been sent to the Gentiles; they will also listen." 29 (See footnote ª)

30 And he stayed two full years in his own rented quarters, and was welcoming all who came to him, 31 preaching the kingdom of God, and teaching concerning the Lord Jesus Christ with all openness, unhindered.

[a] Some mss. add vs. 29, *And when he had spoken these words, the Jews departed, having a great dispute among themselves.*

WILLIAMS

27 For this people's soul has grown dull,
And they scarcely hear with their ears,
And they have shut tight their eyes,
So that they may never see with their eyes,
And understand with their souls,
And turn to me,
That I may cure them." '
28 "So you must understand that this message of God's salvation has been sent to the heathen; and they will listen to it!"[a]
30 So Paul for two whole years lived in a rented house of his own; he continued to welcome everybody who came to see him; 31 yes, he continued to preach to them the kingdom of God, and to teach them about the Lord Jesus Christ, and that with perfect, unfettered freedom of speech.

BECK

27 *Because these people have become dull at heart*
and hard of hearing
and have shut their eyes,
So that their eyes don't see,
their ears don't hear,
their minds don't understand,
And they don't turn to Me and let Me heal them.[94]

28 "You should know that *God's salvation* has been sent *to the non-Jews,*[95] and they will listen." *
30 For two whole years he lived in his own rented place and welcomed all who came to him. 31 He preached God's kingdom and very boldly taught the truth about the Lord Jesus Christ, and nobody stopped him.

* Our oldest manuscripts do not have v. 29: "And after he said this, the Jews left, arguing vigorously among themselves."
[94] Is. 6:9-10
[95] Ps. 67:2; 98:2-3

[a] V. 29 not in best Mss.

THE EPISTLE OF

PAUL THE APOSTLE

TO THE

ROMANS

1 Paul, a servant of Jesus Christ, called *to be* an apostle, separated unto the gospel of God, 2 (Which he had promised afore by his prophets in the holy Scriptures,) 3 Concerning his Son Jesus Christ our Lord, which was made of the seed of David according to the flesh; 4 And declared *to be* the Son of God with power, according to the Spirit of holiness, by the resurrection from the dead: 5 By whom we have received grace and apostleship, for obedience to the faith among all nations, for his name: 6 Among whom are ye also the called of Jesus Christ: 7 To all that be in Rome, beloved of God, called *to be* saints: Grace to you, and peace, from God our Father and the Lord Jesus Christ. 8 First, I thank my God through Jesus Christ for you all, that your faith is spoken of throughout the whole world. 9 For God is my witness, whom I serve with my spirit in the gospel of his Son, that without ceasing I make mention of you always in my prayers; 10 Making request, if by any means now at length I might have a prosperous journey by the will of God to come unto you. 11 For I long to see you, that I may impart unto you some spiritual gift, to the end ye may be established; 12 That is, that I may be comforted together with you by the mutual faith both of you and me. 13 Now I would not have you ignorant, brethren, that oftentimes I purposed to come unto you, (but was let hitherto,) that I might have some fruit among you also, even as among other Gentiles. 14 I am debtor both to the Greeks, and to the Barbarians; both to the wise, and to the unwise. 15 So, as much as in me is, I am ready to preach the gospel to you that are at Rome also. 16 For I am not ashamed of the gospel of Christ: for it is the power of God unto salvation to every one that believeth; to the Jew first, and also to the Greek. 17 For therein is the righteousness of God revealed from faith to faith: as it is written, The just shall live by faith. 18 For the wrath of God is revealed from heaven against all ungodliness and unrighteousness of men, who hold the truth in unrighteousness; 19 Because that which may be known of God is manifest in them; for God hath shewed *it* unto them. 20 For the invisible

THE EPISTLE OF PAUL

TO THE

ROMANS

1 Paul, a bond-servant of Christ Jesus, called *as* an apostle, set apart for the gospel of God, 2 which He promised beforehand through His prophets in the holy Scriptures, 3 concerning His Son, who was born of the seed of David according to the flesh, 4 who was declared *a*with power *to be* the Son of God by the resurrection from the dead, according to the Spirit of holiness, Jesus Christ our Lord, 5 through whom we have received grace and apostleship to bring about *the* obedience of faith among all the Gentiles, for His name's sake, 6 among whom you also are the called of Jesus Christ; 7 to all who are beloved of God in Rome, called *as* saints: Grace to you and peace from God our Father and the Lord Jesus Christ. 8 First, I thank my God through Jesus Christ for you all, because your faith is being proclaimed throughout the whole world. 9 For God, whom I serve in my spirit in the *preaching of the* gospel of His Son, is my witness *as to* how unceasingly I make mention of you, 10 always in my prayers making request, if perhaps now at last by the will of God I may succeed in coming to you. 11 For I long to see you in order that I may impart some spiritual gift to you, that you may be established; 12 that is, that I may be encouraged together with you *while* among you, each of us by the other's faith, both yours and mine. 13 And I do not want you to be unaware, brethren, that often I have planned to come to you (and have been prevented thus far) in order that I might obtain some fruit among you also, even as among the rest of the Gentiles. 14 I am *b*under obligation both to Greeks and to Barbarians, both to the wise and to the foolish. 15 Thus, for my part, I am eager to preach the gospel to you also who are in Rome.

16 For I am not ashamed of the gospel, for it is the power of God for salvation to every one who believes, to the Jew first and also to the Greek. 17 For in it *the* righteousness of God is revealed from faith to faith; as it is written, "BUT THE RIGHTEOUS *man* SHALL LIVE BY FAITH."

18 For the wrath of God is revealed from heaven against all ungodliness and unrighteousness of men, who suppress the truth in unrighteousness, 19 because that which is known about God is evident within them; for God made it evident to them. 20 For since the creation of

---

[a] Or, *in an act of power.* [a] Lit., *debtor.*

ROMANS

PAUL

WRITES TO THE

ROMANS

1 *Greets the Roman Christians; tells of his relations to them; states his theme, saved through faith; lists twenty-one sins of the heathen*

Paul, a slave of Jesus Christ, called as an apostle, set apart to preach God's good news, 2 which long ago He promised through His prophets in the holy Scriptures, 3 about His Son, who on the physical*a* side became a descendant of David, and on the holy spiritual side*b* 4 proved to be God's Son in power by the resurrection from the dead—I mean, Jesus Christ our Lord, 5 through whom we have received God's favor and a commission as an apostle in His name to urge upon all the heathen obedience inspired by faith, 6 among whom you too as called ones belong to Jesus Christ—7 to all those in Rome who are God's loved ones, called to be His people: spiritual blessing*c* and peace be yours from God our Father and from our Lord Jesus Christ.

8 First, through Jesus Christ I thank my God for you all, because the report of your faith is spreading all over the world. 9 Indeed, my witness is God, whom I serve in my spirit by telling the good news about His Son, that I never fail to mention you every time I pray, 10 always entreating God that somehow by His will I may some day at last succeed in getting to see you. 11 For I am longing to see you, to impart to you some spiritual gift, that you may be strengthened; 12 in other words, that we may be mutually encouraged, while I am with you, by one another's faith, yours and mine. 13 Furthermore, I want you to know, brothers, that I have often planned to come to see you (though until now I have been prevented), in order that I may gather some fruit among you too, as I have among the rest of the heathen. 14 To Greeks and to all the other nations, to cultured and to uncultured people alike, I owe a duty. 15 So, as far as I can, I am eager to preach the good news to you at Rome, too.

16 For I am not ashamed of the good news, for it is God's power for the salvation of everyone who trusts, of the Jew first and then of the Greek. 17 For in the good news God's Way of man's right standing with him*d* is uncovered, the Way of faith that leads to greater faith, just as the Scripture says, "The upright man must live by faith."

18 For God's anger from heaven is being uncovered against all the impiety and wickedness of the men who in their wickedness are suppressing the truth; 19 because what can be known of God is clear to their inner moral sense; for in this way God Himself has shown it to them. 20 For ever since the creation of the

1 Paul, servant of Jesus Christ, called to be an apostle and appointed to tell God's good news—

2 He promised it long ago through His prophets in the Holy Bible. 3 It is about His Son, who was born a descendant of David according to His flesh 4 but according to His spirit of holiness was by a rising of the dead declared to be the mighty Son of God. And He is our Lord Jesus Christ, 5 who loved us and made us apostles so that people will believe and obey and so glorify Him among all nations. 6 This includes you who have been called to belong to Jesus Christ

7 —to all in Rome whom God loves and has called to be His holy people: May God our Father and the Lord Jesus Christ continue to love you and give you peace!

I Want to See You

8 First, I thank my God through Jesus Christ for all of you because the news of your faith is spreading all over the world. 9 God, whom I serve in my spirit by telling the good news of His Son, knows how I never fail to mention you 10 whenever I pray and to ask that somehow by God's will I will now at last succeed in coming to you. 11 I long to see you, to share a spiritual gift with you to strengthen you. 12 I mean when I'm with you I'll be encouraged by your faith and you by mine. 13 I want you to know, fellow Christians, so far I have been kept from coming to you, but I often planned to come in order to enjoy some results of working among you as I do among the other non-Jewish people. 14 I must help Greeks and non-Greeks, the wise and the foolish. 15 So I'm eager to bring the good news also to you in Rome.

16 I am not ashamed of the good news. It is God's power to save everyone who believes it, the Jew first and also the Greek. 17 It reveals God's righteousness as being by faith and for faith, as the Bible says, *By faith you are righteous and you will live.*[1]

God Is Angry

18 God in heaven shows He is angry at all the ungodliness and wickedness of people who by their wickedness hold back the truth. 19 What can be known about God is clear to them because God has made it clear to them. 20 Ever

---

[a] Lit., *according to the flesh.* [b] Grk., *according to the spirit of holiness.* [c] Grk., *favor, grace.* [d] Grk., *God's righteousness.*

[1] Hab. 2:4

K.J.V.

things of him from the creation of the world are clearly seen, being understood by the things that are made, *even* his eternal power and Godhead; so that they are without excuse: 21 Because that, when they knew God, they glorified *him* not as God, neither were thankful; but became vain in their imaginations, and their foolish heart was darkened. 22 Professing themselves to be wise, they became fools, 23 And changed the glory of the uncorruptible God into an image made like to corruptible man, and to birds, and fourfooted beasts, and creeping things. 24 Wherefore God also gave them up to uncleanness, through the lusts of their own hearts, to dishonour their own bodies between themselves: 25 Who changed the truth of God into a lie, and worshipped and served the creature more than the Creator, who is blessed for ever. Amen. 26 For this cause God gave them up unto vile affections: for even their women did change the natural use into that which is against nature: 27 And likewise also the men, leaving the natural use of the woman, burned in their lust one toward another; men with men working that which is unseemly, and receiving in themselves that recompence of their error which was meet. 28 And even as they did not like to retain God in *their* knowledge, God gave them over to a reprobate mind, to do those things which are not convenient; 29 Being filled with all unrighteousness, fornication, wickedness, covetousness, maliciousness; full of envy, murder, debate, deceit, malignity; whisperers, 30 Backbiters, haters of God, despiteful, proud, boasters, inventors of evil things, disobedient to parents, 31 Without understanding, covenant-breakers, without natural affection, implacable, unmerciful: 32 Who, knowing the judgment of God, that they which commit such things are worthy of death, not only do the same, but have pleasure in them that do them.

2 Therefore thou art inexcusable, O man, whosoever thou art that judgest: for wherein thou judgest another, thou condemnest thyself; for thou that judgest doest the same things. 2 But we are sure that the judgment of God is according to truth against them which commit such things. 3 And thinkest thou this, O man, that judgest them which do such things, and doest the same, that thou shalt escape the judgment of God? 4 Or despisest thou the riches of his goodness and forbearance and long suffering; not knowing that the goodness of God leadeth thee to repentance? 5 But, after thy hardness and impenitent heart, treasurest up unto thyself wrath against the day of wrath and revelation of the righteous judgment of God; 6 Who will render to every man according to his deeds: 7 To them who by patient continuance in well doing seek for glory and honour and immortality, eternal life: 8 But unto them that are contentious, and do not obey the truth, but obey unrighteousness, indignation and wrath, 9 Tribula-

N.A.S.

the world His invisible attributes, His eternal power and divine nature, have been clearly seen, being understood through what has been made, so that they are without excuse. 21 For even though they knew God, they did not ªhonor Him as God, or give thanks; but they became futile in their speculations, and their foolish heart was darkened. 22 Professing to be wise, they became fools, 23 and exchanged the glory of the incorruptible God for an image in the form of corruptible man and of birds and four-footed animals and ᵇcrawling creatures.

24 Therefore God gave them over in the lusts of their hearts to impurity, that their bodies might be dishonored among them. 25 For they exchanged the truth of God for a lie, and worshiped and served the creature rather than the Creator, who is blessed forever. Amen.

26 For this reason God gave them over to degrading passions; for their women exchanged the natural function for that which is unnatural, 27 and in the same way also the men abandoned the natural function of the woman and burned in their desire towards one another, men with men committing indecent acts and receiving in their own persons the due penalty of their error.

28 And just as they did not see fit to acknowledge God any longer, God gave them over to a depraved mind, to do those things which are not proper, 29 being filled with all unrighteousness, wickedness, greed, malice; full of envy, murder, strife, deceit, malice; *they are* gossips, 30 slanderers, haters of God, insolent, arrogant, boastful, inventors of evil, disobedient to parents, 31 without understanding, untrustworthy, unloving, unmerciful, 32 and, although they know the ordinance of God, that those who practice such things are worthy of death, they not only do the same, but also give hearty approval to those who practice them.

2 Therefore you are without excuse, every man *of you* who passes judgment, for in that you judge another, you condemn yourself; for you who judge practice the same things. 2 And we know that the judgment of God rightly falls upon those who practice such things. 3 And do you suppose this, O man, when you pass judgment upon those who practice such things and do the same *yourself*, that you will escape the judgment of God? 4 Or do you think lightly of the riches of His kindness and forbearance and patience, not knowing that the kindness of God leads you to repentance? 5 But because of your stubbornness and unrepentant heart you are storing up wrath for yourself in the day of wrath and revelation of the righteous judgment of God; 6 who WILL RENDER TO EVERY MAN ACCORDING TO HIS DEEDS: 7 to those who by perseverance in doing good seek for glory and honor and immortality, eternal life; 8 but to those who are selfishly ambitious and do not obey the truth, but obey unrighteousness, wrath and indignation. 9 *There will be* tribulation and

[a] Lit., *glorify.* [b] Or possibly, *reptiles.*

WILLIAMS

world, His invisible characteristics—His eternal power and divine nature—have been made intelligible and clearly visible by His works. So they are without excuse, 21 because, although they once knew God, they did not honor Him as God, or give Him thanks, but became silly in their senseless speculations, and so their insensible hearts have been shrouded in darkness. 22 Though claiming to be wise, they made fools of themselves, 23 and have transformed the splendor of the immortal God into images in the form of mortal man, birds, beasts, and reptiles.

24 So God has given them up to sexual impurity, in the evil trend of their heart's desires, so that they degrade their own bodies with one another, 25 for they had utterly transformed the reality of God into what was unreal, and worshiped and served the creature rather than the Creator, who is blessed forever! Amen. 26 This is why God has given them up to degrading passions. For their females have exchanged their natural function for one that is unnatural, 27 and males too have forsaken the natural function of females and been consumed by flaming passion for one another, males practicing shameful vice with other males, and continuing to suffer in their persons the inevitable penalty for doing what is improper. 28 And so, as they did not approve of fully recognizing God any longer, God gave them up to minds that He did not approve, to practices that were improper; 29 because they overflow with every sort of evil-doing, wickedness, greed, and malice; they are full of envy, murder, quarreling, deceit, ill-will; 30 they are secret backbiters, open slanderers, hateful to God, insolent, haughty, boastful; inventors of new forms of evil, undutiful to parents, 31 conscienceless, treacherous, with no human love or pity. 32 Although they know full well God's sentence that those who practice such things deserve to die, yet they not only practice them but even applaud others who do them.

2 *All, Jews and heathen, sinners; God's judgment impartial; Jews have greater light, greater punishment; genuine Israelites such in heart, not blood*

Therefore, you have no excuse, whoever you are, who pose as a judge of others, for when you pass judgment on another, you condemn yourself, for you who pose as a judge are practicing the very same sins yourself. 2 Now we know that God's judgment justly falls on those who practice such sins as these. 3 And you, who pose as a judge of those who practice such sins and yet continue doing the same yourself, do you for once suppose that you are going to escape the judgment of God? 4 Do you think so little of the riches of God's kindness, forbearance, and patience, not conscious that His kindness is meant to lead you to repentance? 5 But in your stubbornness and impenitence of heart you are storing up wrath for yourself on the day of wrath, when the justice of God's judgments will be uncovered. 6 For when He finally judges, He will pay everyone with exactness for what he has done, 7 eternal life to those who patiently continue doing good and striving for glory, honor, and immortality; 8 but wrath and fury, crushing suffering and awful anguish, to the self-willed who are always resisting the right and yielding to the wrong, 9 to every human soul who prac-

BECK

since He made the world, they have seen the unseen things of God—from the things He made they can tell He has everlasting power and is God. Then they have no excuse. 21 They knew God and didn't honor Him as God or thank Him, but their thoughts turned to worthless things, 22 and their ignorant hearts were darkened. Claiming to be wise, they showed how silly they are 23 when *for the glory* of God, who cannot die, *they substituted images*[2] of man, who dies, and of birds, four-footed animals, and reptiles. 24 And so God, letting them follow the lusts of their hearts, gave them up to live immorally and dishonor their bodies 25 because they traded the true God for a lie, worshiped and served what the Creator made instead of the Creator, who is blessed forever. Amen! 26 That is why God gave them up to shameful lusts. Women have changed their natural way to an unnatural one. 27 And men likewise have given up the natural relation with a woman and burned with lust for one another, men doing the shameful act with men and for their error getting punished in themselves as they must. 28 As they refused to know God any longer, God gave them up so that their minds were degraded and they lived immorally. 29 Their lives are full of all kinds of wrongdoing, wickedness, greed, malice. They are full of envy, murder, quarreling, treachery, viciousness. They gossip 30 and slander. They hate God. They are insulting, proud, boasting. They invent new sins. They disobey parents. 31 They are foolish. They break their promises. They have no love or mercy. 32 Knowing God's righteous decree that those who do such things deserve to die, they not only do them but approve when others do them.

God Will Judge the Jews

2 So, whoever you are, if you condemn anyone, you have no excuse. What you condemn in anyone else you condemn in yourself, since you, the judge, are doing the same things. 2 We know God is right when He condemns people for doing such things. 3 When you condemn people for doing such things but do them yourself, do you think you will escape being condemned by God? 4 Or do you think lightly of God, who is very kind to you, patiently puts up with you, and waits so long before He punishes you? Can't you see God is kind to you to get you to feel sorry for your sins?

5 But you stubbornly refuse to turn from sin, and so you make God more and more angry with you till the day of His anger, when God will show how righteous He is in judging you. 6 *He will give everyone according to what he has done.*[3] 7 everlasting life to those who by patiently doing good look for glory, honor, and immortality, 8 but anger and fury to those who, because they are selfish and refuse to listen to the truth, follow wickedness. 9 There will be

[2] Ps. 106:20
[3] Ps. 62:12; Prov. 24:12

419

K.J.V.

tion and anguish, upon every soul of man that doeth evil; of the Jew first, and also of the Gentile; 10 But glory, honour, and peace, to every man that worketh good; to the Jew first, and also to the Gentile: 11 For there is no respect of persons with God. 12 For as many as have sinned without law shall also perish without law; and as many as have sinned in the law shall be judged by the law; 13 (For not the hearers of the law *are* just before God, but the doers of the law shall be justified. 14 For when the Gentiles, which have not the law, do by nature the things contained in the law, these, having not the law, are a law unto themselves: 15 Which shew the work of the law written in their hearts, their conscience also bearing witness, and *their* thoughts the mean while accusing or else excusing one another;) 16 In the day when God shall judge the secrets of men by Jesus Christ according to my gospel. 17 Behold, thou art called a Jew, and restest in the law, and makest thy boast of God, 18And knowest *his* will, and approvest the things that are more excellent, being instructed out of the law; 19And art confident that thou thyself art a guide of the blind, a light of them which are in darkness, 20An instructor of the foolish, a teacher of babes, which hast the form of knowledge and of the truth in the law. 21 Thou therefore which teachest another, teachest thou not thyself? thou that preachest a man should not steal, dost thou steal? 22 Thou that sayest a man should not commit adultery, dost thou commit adultery? thou that abhorrest idols, dost thou commit sacrilege? 23 Thou that makest thy boast of the law, through breaking the law dishonourest thou God? 24 For the name of God is blasphemed among the Gentiles through you, as it is written. 25 For circumcision verily profiteth, if thou keep the law: but if thou be a breaker of the law, thy circumcision is made uncircumcision. 26 Therefore, if the uncircumcision keep the righteousness of the law, shall not his uncircumcision be counted for circumcision? 27And shall not uncircumcision which is by nature, if it fulfil the law, judge thee, who by the letter and circumcision dost transgress the law? 28 For he is not a Jew, which is one outwardly; neither *is that* circumcision, which is outward in the flesh: 29 But he *is* a Jew, which is one inwardly; and circumcision *is that* of the heart, in the spirit, *and* not in the letter; whose praise *is* not of men, but of God.

3 What advantage then hath the Jew? or what profit *is there* of circumcision? 2 Much every way: chiefly, because that unto them were committed the oracles of God. 3 For what if some did not believe? shall their unbelief make the faith of God without effect? 4 God forbid: yea, let God be true, but every man a liar; as it is written, That thou mightest be justified in thy

N.A.S.

distress for every soul of man who does evil, of the Jew first and also of the Greek, 10 but glory and honor and peace to every man who does good, to the Jew first and also to the Greek. 11 For there is no partiality with God. 12 For all who have sinned without the Law will also perish without the Law; and all who have sinned under the Law will be judged by the Law; 13 for not the hearers of the Law are just before God, but the doers of the Law will be justified. 14 For when Gentiles who do not have the Law do instinctively the things of the Law, these, not having the Law, are a law to themselves, 15 in that they show the work of the Law written in their hearts, their conscience bearing witness, and their thoughts alternately accusing or else defending themselves, 16 on the day when, according to my gospel, God will judge the secrets of men through Christ Jesus.

17 But if you bear the name "Jew," and rely upon the Law, and boast in God, 18 and know *His* will, and approve the things that are essential, being instructed out of the Law, 19 and are confident that you yourself are a guide to the blind, a light to those who are in darkness, 20 a corrector of the foolish, a teacher of the immature, having in the Law the embodiment of knowledge and of the truth; 21 you therefore who teach another, do you not teach yourself? You who preach that one should not steal, do you steal? 22 You who say that one should not commit adultery, do you commit adultery? You who abhor idols, do you rob temples? 23 You who boast in the Law, through your breaking the Law, do you dishonor God? 24 For "THE NAME OF GOD IS BLASPHEMED AMONG THE GENTILES BECAUSE OF YOU," just as it is written. 25 For indeed circumcision is of value, if you practice the Law; but if you are a transgressor of the Law, your circumcision has become uncircumcision. 26 If therefore the uncircumcised man keep the requirements of the Law, will not his uncircumcision be regarded as circumcision? 27And will not he who is physically uncircumcised, if he keeps the Law, will he not judge you who though having the letter *of the Law* and circumcision are a transgressor of the Law? 28 For he is not a Jew who is one outwardly; neither is circumcision that which is outward in the flesh; 29 but he is a Jew who is one inwardly; and circumcision is that which is of the heart, by the Spirit, not by the letter; and his praise is not from men, but from God.

3 Then what advantage has the Jew? Or what is the benefit of circumcision? 2 Great in every respect. First of all, that they were entrusted with the oracles of God. 3 What then? If some did not believe, their unbelief will not nullify the faithfulness of God, will it? 4 May it never be! Rather, let God be found true, though every man *be found* a liar, as it is written,

"THAT THOU MIGHTEST BE JUSTIFIED IN THY WORDS,

WILLIAMS

tices doing evil, the Jew first and then the Greek. 10 But glory, honor, and peace will come to everyone who practices doing good, the Jew first and then the Greek; 11 for there is no partiality in God's dealings.

12 All who sin without having the law will also perish apart from the law, and all who sin under the law will be judged by the law. 13 For merely hearing the law read does not make men upright with God; but men who practice the law will be recognized as upright. 14 Indeed, when heathen people who have no law instinctively do what the law demands, although they have no law they are a law to themselves, 15 for they show that the deeds the law demands are written on their hearts, because their consciences will testify for them, and their inner thoughts will either accuse or defend them, 16 on the day when God through Jesus Christ, in accordance with the good news I preach, will judge the secrets people have kept.

17 Now if you call yourself a Jew, and rely on law, and boast about God, 18 and understand His will, and by being instructed in the law can know the things that excel, 19 and if you are sure that you are a guide to the blind, a light to those in darkness, 20 a tutor of the foolish, a teacher of the young, since you have a knowledge of the truth as formulated in the law— 21 you who teach others, do you not teach yourself too? You who preach that men should not steal, do you steal yourself? 22 You who warn men to stop committing adultery, do you practice it yourself? You who shrink in horror from idols, do you rob their temples? 23 You who boast about the law, do you by breaking it dishonor God? 24 For, as the Scripture says, the name of God is abused among the heathen because of you.

25 Now circumcision benefits you only if you practice the law; but if you break the law, your circumcision is no better than uncircumcision. 26 So if the uncircumcised heathen man observes the just demands of the law, will he not be counted as though he were a Jew? 27 And shall not the heathen man who is physically uncircumcised, and yet observes the law, condemn you who have the letter of the law and are physically circumcised, and yet break the law? 28 For the real Jew is not the man who is a Jew on the outside, and real circumcision is not outward physical circumcision. 29 The real Jew is the man who is a Jew on the inside, and real circumcision is heart-circumcision, a spiritual, not a literal, affair. This man's praise originates, not with men, but with God.

3 *He replies to Jewish objections to his conclusions that all, Jews and heathen alike, are sinners; quotes their Scriptures to prove it; sets forth God's way of forgiveness by faith in Christ*

What special privilege, then, has a Jew? Or, what benefit does circumcision confer? 2 They are great from every point of view. In the first place, the Jews are entrusted with the utterances of God. 3 What then, if some of them have proved unfaithful? Can their unfaithfulness make null and void God's faithfulness? 4 Not at all. Let God prove true, though every man be false! As the Scripture says,

"That you may prove yourself upright in words you speak,

BECK

sorrow and anguish for every human being doing wrong, for the Jew first and also the Greek; 10 but glory, honor, and peace for everyone doing good, for the Jew first and also the Greek. 11 God doesn't prefer one to another.

12 All who sin without having the Law will perish without the Law. And all who sin having the Law will be judged by the Law. 13 We aren't righteous before God if we only hear the Law, but if we do what the Law says, we'll be righteous.* 14 When people who are not Jews and don't have the Law do by nature what the Law says, they who don't have the Law are a law to themselves. 15 They show that what the Law wants them to do is written in their hearts. Their conscience tells the same truth, and their thoughts between themselves accuse them or defend them, 16 as we'll see on the day when God through Christ Jesus judges the secrets of people according to the good news I tell.

Who Is a Jew?

17 Suppose you call yourself a Jew, rest comfortably in your Law, feel proud of your God, 18 know what He wants, and approve of the better things, being instructed in the Law, 19 and feel sure you're a guide to the blind and a light to those in the dark, 20 that you can train the foolish and teach children because you have in the Law the body of knowledge and truth. 21 You teach someone else—won't you teach yourself? You preach, "Don't steal"—are you stealing? 22 You say, "Don't commit adultery" —are you doing it yourself? You are disgusted with idols—are you robbing their temples? 23 You feel proud of the Law—are you breaking the Law and so dishonoring God? 24 *You make the non-Jews slander God's name,*[4] as the Bible says.

25 Circumcision helps you only if you do what the Law says. If you are breaking the Law, you have lost your circumcision. 26 If an uncircumcised man does what the Law demands, will he not be considered circumcised? 27 If a man who has never been circumcised really does what the Law says, he will condemn you with your written Law and circumcision for breaking the Law. 28 He is no Jew who is one only outwardly, nor is that circumcision which is only outward and physical. 29 But he is a Jew who is one inwardly, and a man is circumcised in his heart by the Spirit, not just by doing what the words say. Such a person will not be praised by men but by God.

3 What is the advantage then of being a Jew? Or what good is there in being circumcised? 2 Much in every way! The most important advantage is that God entrusted His Word to the Jews.

God Is Faithful

3 What if some were unfaithful? Will their unfaithfulness make God unfaithful? 4 Never! God must be true and *any man a liar,*[5] as the Bible says,

That You may be right when You speak

---

* See note at 3:20.
[4] Is. 52:5
[5] Ps. 116:11

K.J.V.

sayings, and mightest overcome when thou art judged. 5 But if our unrighteousness commend the righteousness of God, what shall we say? *Is* God unrighteous who taketh vengeance? (I speak as a man) 6 God forbid: for then how shall God judge the world? 7 For if the truth of God hath more abounded through my lie unto his glory; why yet am I also judged as a sinner? 8 And not *rather,* (as we be slanderously reported, and as some affirm that we say,) Let us do evil, that good may come? whose damnation is just. 9 What then? are we better *than they?* No, in no wise: for we have before proved both Jews and Gentiles, that they are all under sin; 10 As it is written, There is none righteous, no, not one: 11 There is none that understandeth, there is none that seeketh after God. 12 They are all gone out of the way, they are together become unprofitable; there is none that doeth good, no, not one. 13 Their throat *is* an open sepulchre; with their tongues they have used deceit; the poison of asps *is* under their lips: 14 Whose mouth *is* full of cursing and bitterness: 15 Their feet *are* swift to shed blood: 16 Destruction and misery *are* in their ways: 17 And the way of peace have they not known: 18 There is no fear of God before their eyes. 19 Now we know that what things soever the law saith, it saith to them who are under the law: that every mouth may be stopped, and all the world may become guilty before God. 20 Therefore by the deeds of the law there shall no flesh be justified in his sight: for by the law *is* the knowledge of sin. 21 But now the righteousness of God without the law is manifested, being witnessed by the law and the prophets; 22 Even the righteousness of God *which is* by faith of Jesus Christ unto all and upon all them that believe; for there is no difference: 23 For all have sinned, and come short of the glory of God; 24 Being justified freely by his grace through the redemption that is in Christ Jesus: 25 Whom God hath set forth *to be* a propitiation through faith in his blood, to declare his righteousness for the remission of sins that are past, through the forbearance of God; 26 To declare, *I say,* at this time his righteousness: that he might be just, and the justifier of him which believeth in Jesus. 27 Where *is* boasting then? It is excluded. By what law? of works? Nay; but by the law of faith. 28 Therefore we conclude that a man is justified by faith without the deeds of the law. 29 *Is he* the God of the Jews only? *is he* not also of the Gentiles? Yes, of the Gentiles also: 30 Seeing *it is* one God, which shall justify the circumcision by faith, and uncircumcision

N.A.S.

AND MIGHTEST PREVAIL WHEN THOU ART JUDGED." 5 But if our unrighteousness demonstrates the righteousness of God, what shall we say? The God who inflicts wrath is not unrighteous, is He? (I am speaking in human terms.) 6 May it never be! For otherwise how will God judge the world? 7 But if through my lie the truth of God abounded to His glory, why am I also still being judged as a sinner? 8 And why not say (as we are slanderously reported and as some affirm that we say), "Let us do evil that good may come"? Their condemnation is just.

9 What then? Are we better than they? Not at all; for we have already charged that both Jews and Greeks are all under sin; 10 as it is written,
"THERE IS NONE RIGHTEOUS, NOT EVEN ONE;
11 THERE IS NONE WHO UNDERSTANDS,
THERE IS NONE WHO SEEKS FOR GOD;
12 ALL HAVE TURNED ASIDE, TOGETHER THEY
HAVE BECOME USELESS;
THERE IS NONE WHO DOES GOOD,
THERE IS NOT EVEN ONE."
13 "THEIR THROAT IS AN OPEN GRAVE,
WITH THEIR TONGUES THEY KEPT DECEIVING,"
"THE POISON OF ASPS IS UNDER THEIR LIPS;"
14 "WHOSE MOUTH IS FULL OF CURSING AND
BITTERNESS;"
15 "THEIR FEET ARE SWIFT TO SHED BLOOD,
16 DESTRUCTION AND MISERY ARE IN THEIR
PATHS,
17 AND THE PATH OF PEACE HAVE THEY NOT
KNOWN."
18 "THERE IS NO FEAR OF GOD BEFORE THEIR
EYES."
19 Now we know that whatever the Law says, it speaks to those who are under the Law, that every mouth may be closed, and all the world may become accountable to God; 20 because by the works of the Law no flesh will be justified in His sight; for through the Law *comes* the knowledge of sin.

21 But now apart from the Law *the* righteousness of God has been manifested, being witnessed by the Law and the Prophets; 22 even *the* righteousness of God through faith in Jesus Christ for all those who believe; for there is no distinction; 23 for all have sinned and fall short of the glory of God, 24 being justified as a gift by His grace through the redemption which is in Christ Jesus; 25 whom God displayed publicly as a propitiation in His blood through faith. *This was* to demonstrate His righteousness, because in the forbearance of God He passed over the sins previously committed; 26 for the demonstration, *I say,* of His righteousness at the present time, that He might be just and the justifier of the one who has faith in Jesus. 27 Where then is boasting? It is excluded. By what kind of law? Of works? No, but by a law of faith. 28 For we maintain that a man is justified by faith apart from works of the Law. 29 Or is God *the God* of Jews only? Is He not *the God* of Gentiles also? Yes, of Gentiles also—30 if indeed God is one—and He will justify the circumcised by faith and the uncircumcised through faith.

WILLIAMS

And win your case when you go into court."
5 But if our wrongdoing brings to light the uprightness of God, what shall we infer? Is it wrong (I am using everyday human terms) for God to inflict punishment? 6 Not at all! If that were so, how could He judge the world? 7 But, as you say, if the truthfulness of God has redounded to His glory because of my falsehood, why am I still condemned as a sinner? 8 Why should we not say, as people abusively say of us, and charge us with actually saying, "Let us do evil that good may come from it"? Their condemnation is just.

9 What is our conclusion then? Is it that we Jews are better than they? Not at all! For we have already charged that Jews and Greeks alike are all under the sway of sin, 10 as the Scriptures say:

"Not a single human creature is upright,
11 No one understands, no one is searching for God;
12 They all have turned aside, all have become corrupt,
No one does good, not even one!
13 Their throats are just like open graves,
With their tongues they have spoken treachery;
The poison of asps is under their lips.
14 Their mouths are full of bitter cursing.
15 Their feet are swift for shedding blood,
16 Ruin and wretchedness are on their paths,
17 They do not know the way of peace.
18 There is no reverence for God before their eyes."

19 Now we know that everything the law says is spoken to those who are under its authority, that every mouth may be stopped and the whole world be held responsible to God. 20 Because no human creature can be brought into right standing with God by observing the law. For all the law can do is to make men conscious of sin.

21 But now God's way of giving men right standing with Himself[a] has come to light; a way without connection with the law, and yet a way to which the law and the prophets testify. 22 God's own way of giving men right standing with Himself is through faith in Jesus Christ. It is for everybody who has faith, for no distinction at all is made. 23 For everybody has sinned and everybody continues to come short of God's glory, 24 but anybody may have right standing with God as a free gift of His undeserved favor, through the ransom provided in Christ Jesus. 25 For God once publicly offered Him in His death as a sacrifice of reconciliation through faith, to demonstrate His own justice (for in His forbearance God has passed over men's former sins); 26 yes, to demonstrate His justice at the present time, to prove that He is right Himself, and that He considers right with Himself the man who has faith in Jesus.

27 So where has human boasting gone? It was completely shut out. On what principle? On that of doing something? No, but on the principle of faith. 28 For we hold that a man is brought into right standing with God by faith, that observance of the law has no connection with it. 29 Or is He the God of Jews alone? Is He not the God of heathen peoples too? Of course, He is the God of heathen peoples too, 30 since there is but one God, who will consider the Jews in right standing with Himself, only on condition of their faith, and the heathen peo-

BECK

And prove You are superior when You judge.[6]

5 But if our wrong shows how right God is, what'll we say? Is God wrong (I'm talking like a man) when He's angry and He punishes? 6 Never! Otherwise how could God judge the world? 7 But if my lie honors God by showing how much truth there's in Him, why am I still condemned as a sinner? 8 And "shouldn't we do evil that good may come of it?" Some slander us and claim we say that. They are condemned as they deserve.

All Are Sinners

9 What then? Do we have any advantage? Not at all. We have already accused everybody, Jews and Greeks, that they are under sin, 10 as the Bible says: *No one is righteous, no, not one.* 11 *No one understands. No one is searching for God.* 12 *All have turned away and have one and all become worthless. No one is doing anything good, not a single one.*[7] 13 *Their throats are an open grave. They have spoken to deceive.*[8] *Their lips hide the poison of snakes.*[9] 14 *Their mouths are full of cursing and bitterness.*[10] 15 *Their feet run fast to pour out blood.* 16 *Wherever they go, there is destruction and misery.* 17 *They have not learned the way of peace.*[11] 18 *God does not terrify them.*[12]

19 We know that everything the Law says it says to those who are under the Law so that nobody can say anything and the whole world must let God judge it. 20 What *anyone* does to keep the Law *will not make him righteous** *before God,*[13] because the Law shows us our sin.

God Makes Us Righteous

21 But now God has shown us His righteousness; the Law and the prophets tell about it, but it is without the Law. 22 God's righteousness comes to all who believe, just by their believing in Jesus Christ.

23 There is no difference. All have sinned and are without God's glory. 24 They become righteous* by a gift of His love, by the ransom Christ Jesus paid to free them. 25 God set Him up publicly to pour out His blood before God to take away sins through faith, to show His righteousness even though He had patiently passed by the sins done in the past. 26 Now He wanted to show His righteousness, to be righteous Himself and make righteous* anyone who believes in Jesus.

27 What then becomes of our pride? It is excluded. How? By the way of works? No, by the way of faith. 28 We are convinced anyone is righteous* by faith without doing what the Law says.

29 Or is God only the God of the Jews? Isn't He also the God of the non-Jews? Certainly also of the non-Jews. 30 There is only one God, and He will make the circumcised man righteous* on the basis of faith and the uncircumcised by the same faith.

* "Righteous" is a court term. God, who gives us the righteousness of Christ (3:23-24; 4:5; Phil. 3:9), as a judge declares us righteous and by His creative verdict makes us righteous.

[6] Ps. 51:4
[7] Ps. 14:1-3; 53:1-3; Eccl. 7:20
[8] Ps. 5:9
[9] Ps. 140:3
[10] Ps. 10:7
[11] Is. 59:7-8
[12] Ps. 36:1
[13] Ps. 143:2

[a] Lit., *God's righteousness.*

K.J.V.

through faith. 31 Do we then make void the law through faith? God forbid: yea, we establish the law.

4 What shall we say then that Abraham our father, as pertaining to the flesh, hath found? 2 For if Abraham were justified by works, he hath *whereof* to glory; but not before God. 3 For what saith the Scripture? Abraham believed God, and it was counted unto him for righteousness. 4 Now to him that worketh is the reward not reckoned of grace, but of debt. 5 But to him that worketh not, but believeth on him that justifieth the ungodly, his faith is counted for righteousness. 6 Even as David also describeth the blessedness of the man, unto whom God imputeth righteousness without works, 7 *Saying,* Blessed *are* they whose iniquities are forgiven, and whose sins are covered. 8 Blessed *is* the man to whom the Lord will not impute sin. 9 *Cometh* this blessedness then upon the circumcision *only,* or upon the uncircumcision also? for we say that faith was reckoned to Abraham for righteousness. 10 How was it then reckoned? when he was in circumcision, or in uncircumcision? Not in circumcision, but in uncircumcision. 11And he received the sign of circumcision, a seal of the righteousness of the faith which *he had yet* being uncircumcised: that he might be the father of all them that believe, though they be not circumcised; that righteousness might be imputed unto them also: 12And the father of circumcision to them who are not of the circumcision only, but who also walk in the steps of that faith of our father Abraham, which *he had* being *yet* uncircumcised. 13 For the promise, that he should be the heir of the world, *was* not to Abraham, or to his seed, through the law, but through the righteousness of faith. 14 For if they which are of the law be heirs, faith is made void, and the promise made of none effect: 15 Because the law worketh wrath: for where no law is, *there is* no transgression. 16 Therefore *it is* of faith, that *it might be* by grace; to the end the promise might be sure to all the seed; not to that only which is of the law, but to that also which is of the faith of Abraham; who is the father of us all, 17 (As it is written, I have made thee a father of many nations,) before him whom he believed, *even* God, who quickeneth the dead, and calleth those things which be not as though they were:

N.A.S.

31 Do we then nullify the Law through faith? May it never be! On the contrary, we establish the Law.

4 What then shall we say that Abraham, our forefather according to the flesh, has found? 2 For if Abraham was justified by works, he has something to boast about; but not before God. 3 For what does the Scripture say? "AND ABRAHAM BELIEVED GOD, AND IT WAS RECKONED TO HIM AS RIGHTEOUSNESS." 4 Now to the one who works, his wage is not reckoned as a favor but as what is due. 5 But to the one who does not work, but believes in Him who justifies the ungodly, his faith is reckoned as righteousness. 6 Just as David also speaks of the blessing upon the man to whom God reckons righteousness apart from works:

7 "BLESSED ARE THOSE WHOSE LAWLESS DEEDS HAVE BEEN FORGIVEN,
AND WHOSE SINS HAVE BEEN COVERED.
8 "BLESSED IS THE MAN WHOSE SIN THE LORD WILL NOT TAKE INTO ACCOUNT."

9 Is this blessing then upon the circumcised, or upon the uncircumcised also? For we say, "FAITH WAS RECKONED TO ABRAHAM AS RIGHTEOUSNESS." 10 How then was it reckoned? While he was circumcised, or uncircumcised? Not while circumcised, but while uncircumcised; 11 and he received the sign of circumcision, a seal of the righteousness of the faith which he had while uncircumcised, that he might be the father of all who believe without being circumcised, that righteousness might be reckoned to them, 12 and the father of circumcision to those who not only are of the circumcision, but who also follow in the steps of the faith of our father Abraham which he had while uncircumcised. 13 For the promise to Abraham or to his descendants that he would be heir of the world was not through the Law, but through the righteousness of faith. 14 For if those who are of the Law are heirs, faith is made void and the promise is nullified; 15 for the Law brings about wrath, but where there is no law, neither is there violation. 16 For this reason *it is* by faith, that *it might be* in accordance with grace, in order that the promise may be certain to all the descendants, not only to those who are of the Law, but also to those who are of the faith of Abraham, who is the father of us all, 17 (as it is written, "A FATHER OF MANY NATIONS HAVE I MADE YOU") in the sight of Him whom he believed, *even* God, who gives life to the dead and calls into being that which does not exist.

WILLIAMS

ples on the same condition. 31 Do we then through faith make null and void the law? Not at all; instead, we confirm it.

4 *Abraham had right standing with God by faith, not by circumcision; it was only a seal of his right standing; so He is Father of all who believe; resurrection faith, like Abraham's, brings right standing with God*

Then what are we to say about our forefather Abraham? 2 For if he was considered in right standing with God on the condition of what he did, he has something to boast of; but not before God. 3 For what does the Scripture say? "Abraham put his faith in God, and it was credited to him as right standing with God." 4 Now when a workman gets his pay, it is not considered from the point of view of a favor but of an obligation; 5 but the man who does no work, but simply puts his faith in Him who brings the ungodly into right standing with Himself, has his faith credited to him as right standing. 6 So David, too, describes the happiness of the man to whom God credits right standing with Himself, without the things he does having anything to do with it:[a]
7 "Happy are they whose transgressions have been forgiven,
Whose sins were covered up;
8 Happy the man whose sin the Lord does not charge against him!"
9 Now does this happiness come to the Jews alone, or to the heathen peoples too? For we say, "Abraham's faith was credited to him as right standing." 10 Under what circumstances was it credited to him as right standing? Was it after he was circumcised, or before? Not after but before he was circumcised. 11 Afterward he received the mark of circumcision as God's seal of his right standing with Him on condition of faith which he had before he was circumcised, that he might be the forefather of all who have faith while still uncircumcised, that they might have their faith credited to them as right standing with God; 12 and the forefather of those Jews who not only belong to the circumcision but also follow in the footsteps of our forefather Abraham in the faith he had before he was circumcised.
13 For the promise made to Abraham and his descendants, that he should own the world, was not conditioned on the law, but on the right standing he had with God through faith. 14 For if the law party is to possess the world, then faith has been nullified and the promise has been made null and void. 15 For the law results[b] in wrath alone; but where there is no law, there can be no violation of it. 16 So it is conditioned on faith, that it might be in accordance with God's unmerited favor, so that the promise might be in force for all the descendants of Abraham, not only for those who belong to the law party but also for those who belong to the faith group of Abraham. He is the father of us all, 17 as the Scripture says, "I have made you the father of many nations." That is, the promise is in force in the sight of God in whom he put his faith, the God who can bring the dead to life and can call to Himself the things that

[a] Grk., *apart from works.* [b] Lit., *produces, effects.*

BECK

31 Do we then by faith cancel the Law? Never! We uphold the Law.

If We Believe, We're Righteous

4 What should we say Abraham, our natural ancestor, found? 2 If he got to be righteous* by what he did, he had something to be proud of. But he couldn't feel proud before God. 3 What does the Bible say? *Abraham believed God and so he was counted righteous.*[14]
4 If you work, your pay isn't considered a gift but a debt. 5 But if instead of working you believe in Him who makes the ungodly righteous, your faith is counted as righteousness. 6 So David calls the man happy whom God counts righteous apart from what he does: 7 *Happy are you if your wrongs are forgiven and your sins are covered.* 8 *Happy are you if the Lord doesn't count sins against you.*[15]
9 Can only a circumcised person be happy in this way or also an uncircumcised person? We say, *Abraham's faith was counted as his righteousness.*[14] 10 How was it counted? Was he circumcised then, or not? He wasn't circumcised but uncircumcised. 11 And he received *circumcision as a mark* to confirm the righteousness he got by believing *before he was circumcised.*[16] He was to be the father of all who without being circumcised believe *and so are counted righteous*[14] 12 as well as the father of the Jews who are not only circumcised but also walk in the footsteps of our father Abraham by believing as he did before he was circumcised.
13 It wasn't by the Law that Abraham or his descendants got the promise that the world should be theirs but by the righteousness of faith. 14 If the Law is the way to get it, then faith can't get anything and the promise can't give anything. 15 No, the Law brings God's anger on us, and only where there is no Law there is no breaking of the Law. 16 God promises to those who believe, in order to bring them a gift of His love. And the promise should hold for all descendants, not only those who cling to the Law but also those who only believe as Abraham did. He is the father of all of us, 17 as it is written, *I have made you a father of many nations.*[17] Standing before God, Abraham believed God makes the dead live and calls into being that which doesn't exist.

* See note at 3:20
[14] Gen. 15:6
[15] Ps. 32:1-2
[16] Gen. 17:11
[17] Gen. 17:5

K.J.V.

18 Who against hope believed in hope, that he might become the father of many nations, according to that which was spoken, So shall thy seed be. 19And being not weak in faith, he considered not his own body now dead, when he was about a hundred years old, neither yet the deadness of Sarah's womb: 20 He staggered not at the promise of God through unbelief; but was strong in faith, giving glory to God; 21And being fully persuaded, that what he had promised, he was able also to perform. 22And therefore it was imputed to him for righteousness. 23 Now it was not written for his sake alone, that it was imputed to him; 24 But for us also, to whom it shall be imputed, if we believe on him that raised up Jesus our Lord from the dead; 25 Who was delivered for our offences, and was raised again for our justification.

5 Therefore being justified by faith, we have peace with God through our Lord Jesus Christ: 2 By whom also we have access by faith into this grace wherein we stand, and rejoice in hope of the glory of God. 3And not only *so*, but we glory in tribulations also; knowing that tribulation worketh patience; 4And patience, experience; and experience, hope: 5And hope maketh not ashamed; because the love of God is shed abroad in our hearts by the Holy Ghost which is given unto us. 6 For when we were yet without strength, in due time Christ died for the ungodly. 7 For scarcely for a righteous man will one die: yet peradventure for a good man some would even dare to die. 8 But God commendeth his love toward us, in that, while we were yet sinners, Christ died for us. 9 Much more then, being now justified by his blood, we shall be saved from wrath through him. 10 For if, when we were enemies, we were reconciled to God by the death of his Son; much more, being reconciled, we shall be saved by his life. 11And not only *so*, but we also joy in God through our Lord Jesus Christ, by whom we have now received the atonement. 12 Wherefore, as by one man sin entered into the world, and death by sin; and so death passed upon all men, for that all have sinned: 13 (For until the law sin was in the world: but sin is not imputed when there is no law. 14 Nevertheless death reigned from

N.A.S.

18 In hope against hope he believed, in order that he might become a father of many nations, according to that which had been spoken, "SO SHALL YOUR DESCENDANTS BE." 19And without becoming weak in faith he contemplated his own body, now as good as dead since he was about a hundred years old, and the deadness of Sarah's womb; 20 yet, with respect to the promise of God, he did not waver in unbelief, but grew strong in faith, giving glory to God, 21 and being fully assured that what He had promised, He was able also to perform. 22 Therefore also IT WAS RECKONED TO HIM AS RIGHTEOUSNESS. 23 Now not for his sake only was it written, that "IT WAS RECKONED TO HIM," 24 but for our sake also, to whom it will be reckoned, as those who believe in Him who raised Jesus our Lord from the dead, 25 Him who was delivered up because of our transgressions, and was raised because of our justification.

5 Therefore having been justified by faith, we have peace with God through our Lord Jesus Christ, 2 through whom also we have obtained our introduction by faith into this grace in which we stand; and we exult in hope of the glory of God. 3And not only this, but we also exult in our tribulations; knowing that tribulation brings about perseverance; 4 and perseverance, proven character; and proven character, hope; 5 and hope does not disappoint; because the love of God has been poured out within our hearts through the Holy Spirit who was given to us. 6 For while we were still helpless, at the right time Christ died for the ungodly. 7 For one will hardly die for a righteous man; though perhaps for the good man someone would dare even to die. 8 But God demonstrates His own love toward us, in that while we were yet sinners, Christ died for us. 9 Much more then, having now been justified by His blood, we shall be saved from the wrath *of God* through Him. 10 For if while we are enemies, we were reconciled to God through the death of His Son, much more, having been reconciled, we shall be saved by His life. 11And not only this, but we also exult in God through our Lord Jesus Christ, through whom we have now received the reconciliation.

12 Therefore, just as through one man sin entered into the world, and death through sin, and so death spread to all men, because all sinned—13 for until the Law sin was in the world; but sin is not imputed when there is no law. 14 Nevertheless death reigned from

WILLIAMS

do not exist as though they did. 18Abraham, building on hope in spite of hopeless circumstances, had faith, and so he actually became the father of many nations, just as it had been told him, "So numberless shall your descendants be." 19 Because he never weakened in faith, he calmly contemplated his own vital powers as worn out (for he was about one hundred years old) and the inability of Sarah to bear a child, 20 and yet he never staggered in doubt at the promise of God but grew powerful in faith, because he gave the glory to God 21 in full assurance that He was able to do what He had promised. 22 Therefore, his faith was credited to him as right standing with God.

23 It was not for his sake alone that it was written, "It was credited to him"; 24 it was for our sakes too, for it is going to be credited to us who put our faith in God who raised from the dead our Lord Jesus, 25 who was given up to death because of our short-comings and was raised again to give us right standing with God.

5 *The happy state of the person in right standing with God; God proved His love for sinful men by letting His Son die for them; sin and death through Adam, right standing with God and life through Christ*

Since we have been given right standing with God through faith, then let us continue enjoying peace with God through our Lord Jesus Christ, 2 by whom we have an introduction through faith into this state of God's favor, in which we safely stand; and let us continue exulting in the hope of enjoying the glorious presence of God. 3And not only that, but this too: let us continue exulting in our sufferings, for we know that suffering produces endurance, 4 and endurance, tested character, and tested character, hope, 5 and hope never disappoints^a us; for through the Holy Spirit that has been given us, God's love has flooded our hearts.

6 For when we were still helpless, Christ at the proper time died for us ungodly men. 7 Now a man will scarcely ever give his life for an upright person, though once in a while a man is brave enough to die for a generous friend.^b 8 But God proves His love for us by the fact that Christ died for us while we were still sinners. 9 So if we have already been brought into right standing with God by Christ's death, it is much more certain that by Him we shall be saved from God's wrath. 10 For if while we were God's enemies, we were reconciled to Him through the death of His Son, it is much more certain that since we have been reconciled we shall finally be saved through His new life. 11And not only that, but this too: we shall continue exulting in God through our Lord Jesus Christ, through whom we have obtained our reconciliation.

12 So here is the comparison: As through one man sin came into the world, and death as the consequence of sin, and death spread to all men, because all men sinned. 13 Certainly sin was in the world before the law was given, but it is not charged to men's account where there is no law. 14And yet death reigned from Adam

[a] Grk., *puts to shame.* [b] Grk., *a good man,* but qualities of unselfish generosity included.

BECK

18 Hoping contrary to what he could expect, he had the faith to become *a father of many nations,*[17] as he had been told, *So many descendants you will have.*[18] 19 He didn't get weak in faith, although he realized that, being about a hundred years old, he couldn't have children any more, and Sarah couldn't have any either. 20 There was no unbelief to make him doubt what God promised, but by faith he got strong and gave glory to God. 21 He was fully convinced God could do what He promised. 22 That is why *he was counted righteous.* 23 But the words *he was counted righteous* were written not only for him 24 but also for us. We are to be *counted righteous* if we *believe*[14] in Him who raised from the dead our Lord Jesus, 25 who was *handed over to die*[19] for our sins and was raised to make us righteous.

Our Hope

5 Now that we who believe are righteous,* we have peace with God through our Lord Jesus Christ, 2 who gave us the way to come to God's love in which we stand. And we feel proud as we hope for God's glory.

3 More than that, we also feel proud of our sufferings. We know suffering stirs up the power to endure, 4 and if we endure, we prove our strength, and if we prove our strength, we have hope. 5 In this *hope we're not disappointed,*[20] because the Holy Spirit, who has been given to us, poured God's love into our hearts.

6 At the right time, while we were still helpless, Christ died for the ungodly. 7A man will hardly die for a righteous person; oh, for a kind person somebody may dare to die. 8 But God shows how He loves us by this, that while we were still sinners Christ died for us.

9 Now that His blood has made us righteous,* we are all the more certain He will save us from God's anger. 10 If while we were His enemies we were made God's friends by the death of His Son, now that we are His friends we are all the more certain He will save us by His life. 11 More than that, we rejoice in God through our Lord Jesus Christ, who has now given us this friendship.

Adam and Christ

12 One man brought sin into the world, and his sin brought death. And so because all have sinned, death spread to all people. 13 There was sin in the world before the Law was given, but where there is no Law, sin isn't counted. 14 Still death ruled from Adam to Moses even

* See note at 3:20.
[17] Gen. 17:5
[18] Gen. 15:5
[19] Is. 53:12
[20] Ps. 22:5; 25:3, 20

K.J.V.

Adam to Moses, even over them that had not sinned after the similitude of Adam's transgression, who is the figure of him that was to come. 15 But not as the offence, so also *is* the free gift: for if through the offence of one many be dead, much more the grace of God, and the gift by grace, *which is* by one man, Jesus Christ, hath abounded unto many. 16 And not as *it was* by one that sinned, *so is* the gift: for the judgment *was* by one to condemnation, but the free gift *is* of many offences unto justification. 17 For if by one man's offence death reigned by one; much more they which receive abundance of grace and of the gift of righteousness shall reign in life by one, Jesus Christ.) 18 Therefore, as by the offence of one *judgment came* upon all men to condemnation; even so by the righteousness of one *the free gift came* upon all men unto justification of life. 19 For as by one man's disobedience many were made sinners, so by the obedience of one shall many be made righteous. 20 Moreover the law entered, that the offence might abound. But where sin abounded, grace did much more abound: 21 That as sin hath reigned unto death, even so might grace reign through righteousness unto eternal life by Jesus Christ our Lord.

6 What shall we say then? Shall we continue in sin, that grace may abound? 2 God forbid. How shall we, that are dead to sin, live any longer therein? 3 Know ye not, that so many of us as were baptized into Jesus Christ were baptized into his death? 4 Therefore we are buried with him by baptism into death: that like as Christ was raised up from the dead by the glory of the Father, even so we also should walk in newness of life. 5 For if we have been planted together in the likeness of his death, we shall be also *in the likeness of his* resurrection: 6 Knowing this, that our old man is crucified with *him,* that the body of sin might be destroyed, that henceforth we should not serve sin. 7 For he that is dead is freed from sin. 8 Now if we be dead with Christ, we believe that we shall also live with him: 9 Knowing that Christ being raised from the dead dieth no more; death hath no more dominion over him. 10 For in that he died, he died unto sin once: but in that he liveth, he liveth unto God. 11 Likewise reckon ye also yourselves to be dead indeed unto sin, but alive unto God through Jesus Christ our Lord. 12 Let not sin therefore reign in your mortal body,

N.A.S.

Adam until Moses, even over those who had not sinned in the likeness of Adam's offense, who is a [a]type of Him who was to come. 15 But the free gift is not like the transgression. For if by the transgression of the one the many died, much more did the grace of God and the gift by the grace of the one man, Jesus Christ, abound to the many. 16 And the gift is not like *that which came* through the one who sinned; for on the one hand the judgment *arose* from one *transgression* resulting in condemnation, but on the other hand the free gift *arose* from many transgressions resulting in justification. 17 For if by the transgression of the one, death reigned through the one, much more those who receive the abundance of grace and of the gift of righteousness will reign in life through the one, Jesus Christ. 18 So then as through one transgression there resulted condemnation to all men; even so through one act of righteousness there resulted justification of life to all men. 19 For as through the one man's disobedience the many were made sinners, even so through the obedience of the one the many will be made righteous. 20 And the Law came in that the transgression might increase; but where sin increased, grace abounded all the more, 21 that, as sin reigned in death, even so grace might reign through righteousness to eternal life through Jesus Christ our Lord.

6 What shall we say then? Are we to continue in sin that grace might increase? 2 May it never be! How shall we who died to sin still live in it? 3 Or do you not know that all of us who have been baptized into Christ Jesus have been baptized into His death? 4 Therefore we have been buried with Him through baptism into death, in order that as Christ was raised from the dead through the glory of the Father, so we too might walk in newness of life. 5 For if we have become united with *Him* in the likeness of His death, certainly we shall be also *in the likeness* of His resurrection, 6 knowing this, that our old self was crucified with *Him,* that our body of sin might be done away with, that we should no longer be slaves to sin; 7 for he who has died is freed from sin. 8 Now if we have died with Christ, we believe that we shall also live with Him, 9 knowing that Christ, having been raised from the dead, is never to die again; death no longer is master over Him. 10 For the death that He died, He died to sin, once for all; but the life that He lives, He lives to God. 11 Even so consider yourselves to be dead to sin, but alive to God in Christ Jesus.
12 Therefore do not let sin reign in your

[a] Or, *foreshadowing.*

WILLIAMS

to Moses, even over those who had not sinned in the way Adam had, against a positive command. For Adam was a figure of Him who was to come. 15 But God's free gift is not at all to be compared with the offense. For if by one man's offense the whole race of men have died, to a much greater degree God's favor and His gift imparted by His favor through the one man Jesus Christ, has overflowed for the whole race of men. 16And the gift is not at all to be compared with the results of that one man's sin. For that sentence resulted from the offense of one man, and it meant condemnation; but the free gift resulted from the offenses of many, and it meant right standing. 17 For if by one man's offense death reigned through that one, to a much greater degree will those who continue to receive the overflow of His unmerited favor and His gift of right standing with Himself, reign in real life through One, Jesus Christ.

18 So, as through one offense there resulted condemnation for all men, just so through one act of uprightness there resulted right standing involving life for all men. 19 For just as by that man's disobedience the whole race of men were constituted sinners, so by this One's obedience the whole race of men may be brought into right standing with God. 20 Then law crept in to multiply the offense. Though sin has multiplied, yet God's favor has surpassed it and overflowed, 21 so that just as sin had reigned by death, so His favor too might reign in right standing with God which issues in eternal life through Jesus Christ our Lord.

6 *Right living results from right standing with God; union with Christ kills sin; baptism pictures our union with Christ's death and resurrection life; no longer slaves to sin, believers freed to serve God and right*

What is our conclusion then? Are we to continue to sin for His unmerited favor to multiply? 2 Not at all! Since we have ended our relation[a] to sin, how can we live in it any longer? 3 Or, do you not know that all of us who have been baptized into union with Christ Jesus have been baptized into His death? 4 So through baptism we have been buried with Him in death, so that just as Christ was raised from the dead by the Father's glorious power, so we too should live an entirely new life. 5 For if we have grown into fellowship with Him by sharing[b] a death like His, surely we shall share a resurrection life like His, 6 for we know that our former self was crucified with Him, to make our body that is liable to sin inactive,[c] so that we might not a moment longer continue to be slaves to sin. 7 For when a man is dead, he is freed from the claims of sin. 8 So if we died with Christ, we believe that we shall also live with Him, 9 for we know that Christ, who once was raised from the dead, will never die again; death has no more power over Him. 10 For by the death He died He once for all ended His relation to sin, and by the life He now is living He lives in unbroken relation to God. 11 So you too must consider yourselves as having ended your relation to sin but living in unbroken relation to God.

12 Accordingly sin must not continue to reign

[a] Lit., *died to sin.* [b] Grk., *by the likeness of His death.* [c] Lit., *dead.*

BECK

over those who when they sinned didn't break a law as Adam did.

He was a picture of Him who was to come. 15 But the gift is more than the sin. If one man's sin brought death to all people, we are all the more certain God's love and the free gift of His love in one Man, Jesus Christ, have been richly poured out on all people. 16 The gift also does more than that one man's sin. The sentence, due to one man, condemns us, but the gift, following many sins, makes us righteous. 17 If one man by his sin made death a king, we, on whom God has poured His love and His gift of righteousness, are all the more certain the one Jesus Christ makes us live and be kings.

18 Now then, as by one sin all people were condemned, so by one righteous work all people were judged to be righteous and alive. 19 When one man disobeyed, all were made sinners. So when One obeyed, all will be made righteous. 20 The Law came to multiply sin, but where there was much sin, God's gift of love was so much greater 21 that, as sin ruled in its deadly way, so His love is to rule, giving a righteousness by which we live forever through our Lord Jesus Christ.

Live for God

6 What does it mean? Should we go on sinning so that God may love us all the more? Certainly not! 2 We died to sin. How can we live in it any longer?

3 Or don't you know that all of us who were baptized into Christ Jesus by our baptism share in His death? 4 Sharing in His death by our baptism, we were buried with Him so that as the Father's glory raised Christ from the dead we, too, will live a new life. 5 If we were united with Him to die as He did, then we'll also rise as He did. 6 We know our old self was nailed with Him to the cross to stop our sinful body and keep us from serving sin any longer. 7 When we're dead, we're free from sin. 8 But if we died with Christ, we believe we'll also live with Him 9 because we know that Christ, risen from the dead, will not die again. Death has no hold on Him any more. 10 When He died, He died to sin once, never to die again, and the life He lives He lives for God. 11 So you, too, because you are in Christ Jesus, think of yourselves as dead to sin and living for God.

12 Then sin should no longer rule in your

K.J.V.

that ye should obey it in the lusts thereof. 13 Neither yield ye your members *as* instruments of unrighteousness unto sin: but yield yourselves unto God, as those that are alive from the dead, and your members *as* instruments of righteousness unto God. 14 For sin shall not have dominion over you: for ye are not under the law, but under grace. 15 What then? shall we sin, because we are not under the law, but under grace? God forbid. 16 Know ye not, that to whom ye yield yourselves servants to obey, his servants ye are to whom ye obey; whether of sin unto death, or of obedience unto righteousness? 17 But God be thanked, that ye were the servants of sin, but ye have obeyed from the heart that form of doctrine which was delivered you. 18 Being then made free from sin, ye became the servants of righteousness. 19 I speak after the manner of men because of the infirmity of your flesh: for as ye have yielded your members servants to uncleanness and to iniquity unto iniquity; even so now yield your members servants to righteousness unto holiness. 20 For when ye were the servants of sin, ye were free from righteousness. 21 What fruit had ye then in those things whereof ye are now ashamed? for the end of those things *is* death. 22 But now being made free from sin, and become servants to God, ye have your fruit unto holiness, and the end everlasting life. 23 For the wages of sin *is* death; but the gift of God *is* eternal life through Jesus Christ our Lord.

7 Know ye not, brethren, (for I speak to them that know the law,) how that the law hath dominion over a man as long as he liveth? 2 For the woman which hath a husband is bound by the law to *her* husband so long as he liveth; but if the husband be dead, she is loosed from the law of *her* husband. 3 So then if, while *her* husband liveth, she be married to another man, she shall be called an adulteress: but if her husband be dead, she is free from that law; so that she is no adulteress, though she be married to another man. 4 Wherefore, my brethren, ye also are become dead to the law by the body of Christ; that ye should be married to another, *even* to him who is raised from the dead, that we should bring forth fruit unto God. 5 For when we were in the flesh, the motions of sins, which were by the law, did work in our members to bring forth fruit unto death. 6 But now we are delivered from the law, that being dead

N.A.S.

mortal body that you should obey its lusts, 13 and do not go on presenting the members of your body to sin *as* instruments of unrighteousness; but present yourselves to God as those alive from the dead, and your members *as* instruments of righteousness to God. 14 For sin shall not be master over you, for you are not under law, but under grace.

15 What then? Shall we sin because we are not under law but under grace? May it never be! 16 Do you not know that when you present yourselves to someone *as* slaves for obedience, you are slaves of the one whom you obey, either of sin resulting in death, or of obedience resulting in righteousness? 17 But thanks be to God that though you were slaves of sin, you became obedient from the heart to that form of teaching to which you were committed. 18 and having been freed from sin, you became slaves of righteousness. 19 I am speaking in human terms because of the weakness of your flesh. For just as you presented your members *as* slaves to impurity and to lawlessness, resulting in *further* lawlessness, so now present your members *as* slaves to righteousness, resulting in sanctification. 20 For when you were slaves of sin, you were free in regard to righteousness. 21 Therefore what benefit were you then deriving from the things of which you are now ashamed? For the outcome of those things is death. 22 But now having been freed from sin and enslaved to God, you derive your benefit, resulting in sanctification, and the outcome, eternal life. 23 For the wages of sin is death, but the free gift of God is eternal life in Christ Jesus our Lord.

7 Or do you not know, brethren (for I am speaking to those who know the law), that the law has jurisdiction over a person as long as he lives? 2 For the married woman is bound by law to her husband while he is living; but if her husband dies, she is released from the law concerning the husband. 3 So then if, while her husband is living, she is joined to another man, she shall be called an adulteress; but if her husband dies, she is free from the law, so that she is not an adulteress, though she is joined to another man. 4 Therefore, my brethren, you also were made to die to the Law through the body of Christ, that you might be joined to another, to Him who was raised from the dead, that we might bear fruit for God. 5 For while we were in the flesh, the sinful passions, which were *aroused* by the Law, were at work in the members of our body to bear fruit for death. 6 But now we have been released from the Law, having died to that by which we were bound, so that we serve in new-

WILLIAMS

over your mortal bodies, so as to make you continue to obey their evil desires, 13 and you must stop offering to sin the parts of your bodies as instruments for wrongdoing, but you must once for all offer yourselves to God as persons raised from the dead to live on perpetually, and once for all offer the parts of your bodies to God as instruments for right-doing. 14 For sin must not any longer exert its mastery over you, for now you are not living as slaves to law but as subjects to God's favor.

15 What are we to conclude? Are we to keep on sinning, because we are not living as slaves to law but as subjects to God's favor? Never! 16 Do you not know that when you habitually offer yourselves to anyone for obedience to him, you are slaves to that one whom you are in the habit of obeying, whether it is the slavery to sin whose end is death or to obedience whose end is right-doing? 17 But, thank God! that though you once were slaves of sin, you became obedient from your hearts to that form of teaching in which you have been instructed, 18 and since you have been freed from sin, you have become the slaves of right-doing. 19 I am speaking in familiar human terms because of the frailty of your nature. For just as you formerly offered the parts of your bodies in slavery to impurity and to ever increasing lawlessness, so now you must once for all offer them in slavery to right-doing, which leads to consecration. 20 For when you were slaves of sin, you were free so far as doing right was concerned. 21 What benefit did you then derive from doing the things of which you are now ashamed? None, for they end in death. 22 But now, since you have been freed from sin and have become the slaves of God, the immediate result is consecration, and the final destiny is eternal life. 23 For the wages paid by sin is death, but the gracious gift of God is eternal life through union with Christ Jesus our Lord.

7 *Believers freed from sin but married to Christ as in a second marriage; the function of the law to awaken the sinner to feel his need of Christ; the lower nature dominated by sin, the higher struggles against it*

Do you not know, brothers—for I speak to those who are acquainted with the law—that the law can press its claim over a man only so long as he lives? 2 For a married woman is bound by law to her husband while he lives, but if her husband dies, she is freed from the marriage bond. 3 So if she marries another man while her husband is living, she is called an adulteress; but if he dies, she is free from that marriage bond, so that she will not be an adulteress though later married to another man. 4 So, my brothers, you too in the body of Christ have ended your relation to the law, so that you may be married to another husband, to Him who was raised from the dead, in order that we might bear fruit for God. 5 For when we were living in accordance with our lower nature, the sinful passions that were aroused by the law were operating in the parts of our bodies to make us bear fruit that leads to death. 6 But now we have been freed from our relation to the law; we have ended our relation to that by which we once were held in bonds,

BECK

dying bodies and make you do what they wish. 13 Don't let sin keep on using your organs as tools for doing wrong. But as people who have come back from the dead and live, give yourselves to God, and let God use your organs as tools for doing what is right. 14 Sin will never rule over you, because you are not under the Law but under God's love.

15 What then? Are we going to sin because we are not under the Law but under God's love? Certainly not! 16 Don't you know if you give yourselves to anyone to obey him as slaves, you are his slaves? Either you are the slaves of sin and will die, or you obey God and become righteous. 17 But thank God! Although you once were the slaves of sin, you have heartily obeyed the pattern of teaching to which you were entrusted. 18 Freed from sin, you were made the servants of righteousness. I talk in a human way because you are naturally weak. 19 But just as you once let uncleanness and wickedness use your organs as slaves to do wrong, so now let righteousness use your organs as slaves in order to live holy. 20 When you were slaves of sin, you weren't free to serve righteousness as your master. 21 What was your advantage then in doing the things that make you blush now? Why, they end in death. 22 But now that you've been made free from sin and servants of God, your advantage is that you live holy and finally have everlasting life. 23 Sin pays off with death, but God gives everlasting life in Christ Jesus, our Lord.

7 Or don't you know, my fellow Christians— I'm speaking to people who know the Law —that you have to obey the Law only as long as you live? 2 The Law, for example, binds a married woman to her husband while he is living, but if her husband dies, the Law doesn't bind her to her husband any more. 3 So, while her husband is living, she will be called an adulteress if she lives with another man. But if her husband dies, she is free and no longer bound by the Law, and so she's no adulteress if she marries another man.

4 So you too, my fellow Christians, have through Christ's body died to the Law to marry Another—Him who rose from the dead so that we will produce good things for God. 5 While we were living in the flesh, the Law stirred the sinful lusts in our organs into action to produce fruit for Death. 6 But now that we have died to the Law which bound us, we are freed from it,

431

K.J.V.

wherein we were held; that we should serve in newness of spirit, and not *in* the oldness of the letter. 7 What shall we say then? *Is* the law sin? God forbid. Nay, I had not known sin, but by the law: for I had not known lust, except the law had said, Thou shalt not covet. 8 But sin, taking occasion by the commandment, wrought in me all manner of concupiscence. For without the law sin *was* dead. 9 For I was alive without the law once: but when the commandment came, sin revived, and I died. 10 And the commandment, which *was ordained* to life, I found *to be* unto death. 11 For sin, taking occasion by the commandment, deceived me, and by it slew *me*. 12 Wherefore the law *is* holy, and the commandment holy, and just, and good. 13 Was then that which is good made death unto me? God forbid. But sin, that it might appear sin, working death in me by that which is good; that sin by the commandment might become exceeding sinful. 14 For we know that the law is spiritual: but I am carnal, sold under sin. 15 For that which I do, I allow not: for what I would, that do I not; but what I hate, that do I. 16 If then I do that which I would not, ·I consent unto the law that *it is* good. 17 Now then it is no more I that do it, but sin that dwelleth in me. 18 For I know that in me (that is, in my flesh,) dwelleth no good thing: for to will is present with me; but *how* to perform that which is good I find not. 19 For the good that I would, I do not: but the evil which I would not, that I do. 20 Now if I do that I would not, it is no more I that do it, but sin that dwelleth in me. 21 I find then a law, that, when I would do good, evil is present with me. 22 For I delight in the law of God after the inward man: 23 But I see another law in my members, warring against the law of my mind, and bringing me into captivity to the law of sin which is in my members. 24 O wretched man that I am! who shall deliver me from the body of this death? 25 I thank God through Jesus Christ our Lord. So then with the mind I myself serve the law of God; but with the flesh the law of sin.

N.A.S.

ness of the [a]Spirit and not in oldness of the letter.
7 What shall we say then? Is the Law sin? May it never be! On the contrary, I would not have come to know sin except through the Law; for I would not have known about coveting if the Law had not said, "YOU SHALL NOT COVET." 8 But sin, taking opportunity through the commandment, produced in me coveting of every kind; for apart from the Law sin *is* dead. 9 And I was once alive apart from the Law; but when the commandment came, sin became alive, and I died; 10 and this commandment, which was to result in life, proved to result in death for me; 11 for sin, taking opportunity through the commandment, deceived me, and through it killed me. 12 So then, the Law is holy, and the commandment is holy and righteous and good. 13 Therefore did that which is good become *a cause of* death for me? May it never be! Rather it was sin, in order that it might be shown to be sin by effecting my death through that which is good, that through the commandment sin might become utterly sinful. 14 For we know that the Law is spiritual; but I am of flesh, sold into bondage to sin. 15 For that which I am doing, I do not understand; for I am not practicing what I *would* like to *do*, but I am doing the very thing I hate. 16 But if I do the very thing I do not wish *to do*, I agree with the Law, *confessing* that it is good. 17 So now, no longer am I the one doing it, but sin which indwells me. 18 For I know that nothing good dwells in me, that is, in my flesh; for the wishing is present in me, but the doing of the good *is* not. 19 For the good that I wish, I do not do; but I practice the very evil that I do not wish. 20 But if I am doing the very thing I do not wish, I am no longer the one doing it, but sin which dwells in me. 21 I find then the principle that evil is present in me, the one who wishes to do good. 22 For I joyfully concur with the law of God in the inner man, 23 but I see a different law in the members of my body, waging war against the law of my mind, and making me a prisoner of the law of sin which is in my members. 24 Wretched man that I am! Who will set me free from the body of this death? 25 Thanks be to God through Jesus Christ our Lord! So then, on the one hand I myself with my mind am serving the law of God, but on the other, with my flesh the law of sin.

8 *There is* therefore now no condemnation to them which are in Christ Jesus, who walk not after the flesh, but after the Spirit. 2 For the law of the Spirit of life in Christ Jesus hath made me free from the law of sin and death. 3 For what the law could not do, in that it was weak through the flesh, God sending his own Son in the likeness of sinful flesh, and for sin,

8 There is therefore now no condemnation for those who are in Christ Jesus. 2 For the law of the Spirit of life in Christ Jesus has set [b]you free from the law of sin and of death. 3 For what the Law could not do, weak as it was through the flesh, God *did:* sending His own Son in the likeness of sinful flesh and *as an offering* for sin, He condemned sin in the flesh,

[a] Or, *spirit.* [b] Some ancient mss. read, *me.*

WILLIAMS

so that we may serve in a new spiritual way and not in the old literalistic way.

7 What are we then to conclude? Is the law sin? Of course not! Yet, if it had not been for the law, I should not have learned what sin was, for I should not have known what an evil desire was, if the law had not said, "You must not have an evil desire." 8 Sin found its rallying point in that command and stirred within me every sort of evil desire, for without law sin is lifeless. 9 I was once alive when I had no connection with the law, but when the command came, sin revived, and then I died; 10 and so, in my case, the command which should have meant life turned out to mean death. 11 For sin found its rallying point in that command and through it deceived me and killed me. 12 So the law itself is holy, and its specific commands are holy, right, and good.

13 Did that which is good, then, result in death to me? Of course not! It was sin that did it, so that it might show itself as sin, for by means of that good thing it brought about my death, so that through the command sin might appear surpassingly sinful. 14 For we know that the law is spiritual, but I am made of flesh that is frail, sold into slavery to sin. 15 Indeed, I do not understand what I do, for I do not practice what I want to do, but I am always doing what I hate. 16 But if I am always doing what I do not want to do, I agree that the law is right. 17 Now really it is not I that am doing these things, but it is sin which has its home within me. 18 For I know that nothing good has its home in me; that is, in my lower self; I have the will but not the power to do what is right. 19 Indeed, I do not do the good things that I want to do, but I do practice the evil things that I do not want to do. 20 But if I do the things that I do not want to do, it is really not I that am doing these things, but it is sin which has its home within me. 21 So I find this law: When I want to do right, the wrong is always in my way. 22 For in accordance with my better inner nature I approve God's law, 23 but I see another power operating in my lower nature in conflict with the power operated by my reason,[a] which makes me a prisoner to the power of sin which is operating in my lower nature. 24 Wretched man that I am! Who can save me from this deadly lower nature? 25 Thank God! it has been done through Jesus Christ our Lord! So in my higher nature I am a slave to the law of God, but in my lower nature, to the law of sin.

8 *In union with Christ the Spirit sets us free; he helps God's children live holy lives; sufferings strew their path to glory but polish their characters; the Spirit helps and keeps them through God's unchangeable love*

So then there is no condemnation at all for those who are in union with Christ Jesus. 2 For the life-giving power of the Spirit through union with Christ Jesus has set us free from the power of sin and death. 3 For though the law could not do it, because it was made helpless through our lower nature, yet God, by sending His own Son in a body similar to that of our lower nature, and as a sacrifice for sin, passed

BECK

not to serve in the old way under the Law but in the new way of the Spirit.

The Law Shows What Sin Is

7 What does it mean? Is the Law sin? Certainly not! But only by the Law did I learn what sin is. For example, only when the Law said, *Don't lust,*[21] did I know how wrong it is to lust. 8 Taking the commandment as a challenge, sin worked in me every kind of wrong desire. Without the Law sin is dead. 9 Once I was alive without the Law, but when the commandment came, sin became alive, 10 and I died. And the commandment which is to bring life actually brought me death. 11 Taking the commandment as a challenge, sin seduced me and with the commandment killed me.

12 So the Law itself is holy, and the commandment is holy, right, and good. 13 Now, did this good thing kill me? Certainly not! But sin, to be sin, clearly used this good thing to kill me so that sin would by the commandment become extremely sinful.

Struggling with Sin

14 We know the Law is spiritual, but I am flesh, sold to be a slave of sin. 15 I am doing something strange, because I don't do what I like but what I hate. 16 But if I do what I don't like, I agree that the Law is right. 17 It is really no longer I doing it, but sin living in me. 18 I know that nothing good lives in me, that is, in my flesh. 19 I'm willing, but I'm not doing what is right. I don't do the good things I like, but I do the evil I don't like. 20 Now if I do what I don't like, it is no longer I doing it but sin living in me.

21 So I find it a rule: When I want to do what is right, evil is there with me. 22 In my inner being I delight in God's Law, 23 but all through my body I see another law fighting against the Law in my mind and making me a prisoner to the sin ruling my body. 24 What a miserable man I am! Who will rescue me from the body that brings me to this death? 25 Thank God—He does it through our Lord Jesus Christ! So I serve the Law of God with my mind but with my flesh the law of sin.

The Spirit Gives Life

8 Now those who are in Christ Jesus cannot be condemned. 2 The rule of the Spirit, who gives life, has in Christ Jesus freed you from the rule of sin that kills. 3 What the Law, weakened by the flesh, could not do God has done by sending His Son to be like sinful flesh and to be a sacrifice for sin. He condemned sin

[a] Grk., *mind, reason, higher nature.*

[21] Ex. 20:17; Deut. 5:21

K.J.V.

condemned sin in the flesh: 4 That the right- eousness of the law might be fulfilled in us, who walk not after the flesh, but after the Spirit. 5 For they that are after the flesh do mind the things of the flesh; but they that are after the Spirit, the things of the Spirit. 6 For to be carnally minded *is* death; but to be spiritually minded *is* life and peace. 7 Because the carnal mind *is* enmity against God: for it is not subject to the law of God, neither indeed can be. 8 So then they that are in the flesh cannot please God. 9 But ye are not in the flesh, but in the Spirit, if so be that the Spirit of God dwell in you. Now if any man have not the Spirit of Christ, he is none of his. 10 And if Christ *be* in you, the body *is* dead because of sin; but the Spirit *is* life because of righteousness. 11 But if the Spirit of him that raised up Jesus from the dead dwell in you, he that raised up Christ from the dead shall also quicken your mortal bodies by his Spirit that dwelleth in you. 12 Therefore, brethren, we are debtors, not to the flesh, to live after the flesh. 13 For if ye live after the flesh, ye shall die: but if ye through the Spirit do mortify the deeds of the body, ye shall live. 14 For as many as are led by the Spirit of God, they are the sons of God. 15 For ye have not re- ceived the spirit of bondage again to fear; but ye have received the Spirit of adoption, whereby we cry, Abba, Father. 16 The Spirit itself beareth witness with our spirit, that we are the children of God: 17 And if children, then heirs; heirs of God, and joint heirs with Christ; if so be that we suffer with *him*, that we may be also glorified together. 18 For I reckon that the sufferings of this present time *are* not worthy *to be com- pared* with the glory which shall be revealed in us. 19 For the earnest expectation of the creature waiteth for the manifestation of the sons of God. 20 For the creature was made subject to vanity, not willingly, but by reason of him who hath subjected *the same* in hope; 21 Because the creature itself also shall be delivered from the bondage of corruption into the glorious liberty of the children of God. 22 For we know that the whole creation groaneth and travaileth in pain together until now. 23 And not only *they,* but ourselves also, which have the firstfruits of the Spirit, even we ourselves groan within ourselves, waiting for the adoption, *to wit,* the redemption of our body. 24 For we are saved by hope: but hope that is seen is not hope: for what a man seeth, why doth he yet hope for? 25 But if we hope for that we see not, *then* do we with pa- tience wait for *it.* 26 Likewise the Spirit also helpeth our infirmities: for we know not what we should pray for as we ought: but the Spirit itself maketh intercession for us with groanings which cannot be uttered. 27 And he that search- eth the hearts knoweth what *is* the mind of the Spirit, because he maketh intercession for the saints according to *the will of* God. 28 And we

N.A.S.

4 in order that the requirement of the Law might be fulfilled in us, who do not walk ac- cording to the flesh, but according to the Spirit. 5 For those who are according to the flesh set their minds on the things of the flesh, but those who are according to the Spirit, the things of the Spirit. 6 For the mind set on the flesh is death, but the mind set on the Spirit is life and peace; 7 because the mind set on the flesh is hostile toward God; for it does not subject itself to the Law of God, for it is not even able *to do so;* 8 and those who are in the flesh cannot please God. 9 However you are not in the flesh but in the Spirit, if indeed the Spirit of God dwells in you. But if anyone does not have the Spirit of Christ, he does not belong to Him. 10 And if Christ is in you, though the body is dead because of sin, yet the spirit is alive because of righteousness. 11 But if the Spirit of Him who raised Jesus from the dead dwells in you, He who raised Christ Jesus from the dead will also give life to your mortal bodies *a* through His Spirit who indwells you.

12 So then, brethren, we are under obligation, not to the flesh, to live according to the flesh— 13 for if you are living according to the flesh, you must die; but if by the Spirit you are putting to death the deeds of the body, you will live. 14 For all who are being led by the Spirit of God, these are sons of God. 15 For you have not received a spirit of slavery leading to fear again, but you have received a spirit of adop- tion as sons by which we cry out, "Abba! Fa- ther!" 16 The Spirit Himself bears witness with our spirit that we are children of God, 17 and if children, heirs also, heirs of God and fellow- heirs with Christ, if indeed we suffer with *Him* in order that we may also be glorified with *Him.*

18 For I consider that the sufferings of this present time are not worthy to be compared with the glory that is to be revealed to us. 19 For the anxious longing of the creation waits eagerly for the revealing of the sons of God. 20 For the creation was subjected to futility, not of its own will, but because of Him who sub- jected it, *b* in hope 21 that the creation itself also will be set free from its slavery to corruption into the freedom of the glory of the children of God. 22 For we know that the whole crea- tion groans and suffers the pains of child-birth together until now. 23 And not only this, but also we ourselves, having the first-fruits of the Spirit, even we ourselves groan within ourselves, wait- ing eagerly for *our* adoptions as sons, the re- demption of our body. 24 For in hope we have been saved, but hope that is seen is not hope; for *c* why does one also hope for what he sees? 25 But if we hope for what we do not see, with perseverance we wait eagerly for it.

26 And in the same way the Spirit also helps our weakness; for we do not know how to pray as we should, but the Spirit Himself intercedes for *us* with groanings too deep for words; 27 and He who searches the hearts knows what the mind of the Spirit is, because He intercedes for the saints according to *the will of* God. 28 And we know that *d* God causes all things to work to-

WILLIAMS

sentence upon sin through His body, 4 so that the requirement of the law might be fully met in us who do not live by the standard set by our lower nature, but by the standard set by the Spirit. 5 For people who live by the standard set by their lower nature are usually thinking the things suggested by that nature, and people who live by the standard set by the Spirit are usually thinking the things suggested by the Spirit. 6 For to be thinking the things suggested by the lower nature means death, but to be thinking the things suggested by the Spirit means life and peace. 7 Because one's thinking the things suggested by the lower nature means enmity to God, for it does not subject itself to God's law, nor indeed can it. 8 The people who live on the plane of the lower nature cannot please God. 9 But you are not living on the plane of the lower nature, but on the spiritual plane, if the Spirit of God has His home within you. Unless a man has the Spirit of Christ, he does not belong to Him. 10 But if Christ lives in you, although your bodies must die because of sin, your spirits are now enjoying life because of right standing with God. 11 If the Spirit of Him who raised Jesus from the dead has His home within you, He who raised Christ Jesus from the dead will also give your mortal bodies life through His Spirit that has His home within you.

12 So, brothers, we are under obligations, but not to our lower nature to live by the standard set by it; 13 for if you live by such a standard, you are going to die, but if by the Spirit you put a stop[a] to the doings of your lower nature, you will live. 14 For all who are guided by God's Spirit are God's sons. 15 For you do not have a sense of servitude to fill you with dread again, but the consciousness of adopted sons by which we cry, "Abba," that is, "Father." 16 The Spirit Himself bears witness with our spirits that we are God's children; 17 and if children, then also heirs, heirs of God and fellow-heirs with Christ—if in reality we share His sufferings, so that we may share His glory too.

18 For I consider all that we suffer in this present life is nothing to be compared with the glory which by-and-by is to be uncovered for us. 19 For all nature[b] is expectantly waiting for the unveiling of the sons of God. 20 For nature did not of its own accord give up to failure; it was for the sake of Him who let it thus be given up, in the hope, 21 that even nature itself might finally be set free from its bondage to decay, so as to share the glorious freedom of God's children. 22 Yes, we know that all nature has gone on groaning in agony together till the present moment. 23 Not only that but this too, we ourselves who enjoy the Spirit as a foretaste of the future, even we ourselves, keep up our inner groanings while we wait to enter upon our adoption as God's sons at the redemption of our bodies. 24 For we were saved in such a hope. 25 But a hope that is seen is not real hope, for who hopes for what he actually sees? But if we hope for something we do not see, we keep on patiently waiting for it.

26 In the same way the Spirit, too, is helping us in our weakness, for we do not know how to pray as we should, but the Spirit Himself pleads for us with unspeakable yearnings, 27 and He who searches our hearts knows what the Spirit thinks, for He pleads for His people in accordance with God's will. 28 Yes, we know that all things go on working together for the

[a] Lit., put to death. [b] Lit., creation.

BECK

in the flesh 4 so that we who don't follow the flesh but the Spirit will be as righteous as the Law demands. 5 Those who follow the flesh have their minds on the things of the flesh, but those who follow the Spirit have their minds on the things of the Spirit. 6 What the flesh thinks kills; what the Spirit thinks gives life and peace. 7 This is so because the fleshly mind hates God. It refuses to obey God's Law because it can't obey it. 8 Those who are in the flesh can't please God. 9 You are not in the flesh but in the Spirit if God's Spirit lives in you. But anyone who doesn't have the Spirit of Christ doesn't belong to Him. 10 But if Christ is in you, even though your bodies are dead because you were sinful, your spirits are alive because you are righteous. 11 And if the Spirit of Him who raised Jesus from the dead lives in you, He who raised Christ Jesus from the dead will also make your dying bodies alive by His Spirit living in you.

12 And so, fellow Christians, we don't owe it to the flesh to live according to the flesh. 13 If you live according to the flesh, you will die. But if by the Spirit you kill the activities of the body, you will live. 14 All who are moved by God's Spirit are God's children. 15 You didn't receive the spirit of slaves to make you feel afraid again, but you received the Spirit who makes us God's children and moves us to call "Father!" 16 This Spirit assures our spirit we are God's children, 17 and if children, then heirs, God's heirs, who share Christ's inheritance with Him—if we really suffer with Him in order to be glorified with Him.

We Want to Be Free

18 I think what we suffer now isn't important when I compare it with the glory to be revealed to us. 19 Nature is waiting on tiptoe to see the unveiling of God's family. 20 Nature must waste away, not because it wants to but because its Master would have it so, but nature hopes 21 it, too, will be freed from the slavery that destroys it, to share the freedom of God's family in glory. 22 We know that all nature has been groaning with the pains of childbirth until now.

23 More than that. Since the Spirit whom we have is our first taste of heaven, we, too, groan inwardly as we look ahead to have our bodies freed and so to be His family. 24 We are saved, hoping for this. But if we hope for something we see, we really don't hope. Why should we hope for what we can see? 25 But if we hope for what we can't see, we wait for it patiently.

26 In the same way the Spirit helps us in our weakness, because we don't know how we should pray, but the Spirit Himself pleads for us with yearnings that can't find any words. 27 He who searches our hearts knows what the Spirit means to do, that in God's own way He's pleading for the holy people.

God Gives Us Glory

28 We know that God helps us in every way to have what is good, us who love Him and

K.J.V.

know that all things work together for good to them that love God, to them who are the called according to *his* purpose. 29 For whom he did foreknow, he also did predestinate *to be* conformed to the image of his Son, that he might be the firstborn among many brethren. 30 Moreover, whom he did predestinate, them he also called: and whom he called, them he also justified: and whom he justified, them he also glorified. 31 What shall we then say to these things? If God *be* for us, who *can be* against us? 32 He that spared not his own Son, but delivered him up for us all, how shall he not with him also freely give us all things? 33 Who shall lay any thing to the charge of God's elect? *It is* God that justifieth. 34 Who *is* he that condemneth? *It is* Christ that died, yea rather, that is risen again, who is even at the right hand of God, who also maketh intercession for us. 35 Who shall separate us from the love of Christ? *shall* tribulation, or distress, or persecution, or famine, or nakedness, or peril, or sword? 36 As it is written, For thy sake we are killed all the day long; we are accounted as sheep for the slaughter. 37 Nay, in all these things we are more than conquerors through him that loved us. 38 For I am persuaded, that neither death, nor life, nor angels, nor principalities, nor powers, nor things present, nor things to come, 39 Nor height, nor depth, nor any other creature, shall be able to separate us from the love of God, which is in Christ Jesus our Lord.

9 I say the truth in Christ, I lie not, my conscience also bearing me witness in the Holy Ghost, 2 That I have great heaviness and continual sorrow in my heart. 3 For I could wish that myself were accursed from Christ for my brethren, my kinsmen according to the flesh: 4 Who are Israelites; to whom *pertaineth* the adoption, and the glory, and the covenants, and the giving of the law, and the service *of God,* and the promises; 5 Whose *are* the fathers, and of whom as concerning the flesh Christ *came,* who is over all, God blessed for ever. Amen. 6 Not as though the word of God hath taken none effect. For they *are* not all Israel, which are of Israel: 7 Neither, because they are the seed of Abraham, *are they* all children: but, In Isaac shall thy seed be called. 8 That is, They which are the children of the flesh, these *are* not the children of God: but the children of the promise are counted for the seed. 9 For this *is* the word of promise, At this time will I come, and Sarah shall have a son. 10 And not only *this;* but when Rebecca also had conceived by one, *even* by our father Isaac, 11 (For *the children* being not yet born, neither having done any good or evil, that the purpose of God according to election might stand, not of works, but

N.A.S.

gether for good to those who love God, to those who are called according to *His* purpose. 29 For whom He foreknew, He also predestined *to become* conformed to the image of His Son, that He might be the first-born among many brethren; 30 and whom He predestined, these He also called; and whom He called, these He also justified; and whom He justified, these He also glorified.

31 What then shall we say to these things? If God *is* for us, who *is* against us? 32 He who did not spare His own Son, but delivered Him up for us all, how will He not also with Him freely give us all things? 33 Who will bring a charge against God's elect? God is the one who justifies; 34 who is the one who condemns? Christ Jesus is He who died, yes, rather who was ᵃraised, who is at the right hand of God, who also intercedes for us. 35 Who shall separate us from the love of ᵇChrist? Shall tribulation, or distress, or persecution, or famine, or nakedness, or peril, or sword? 36 Just as it is written,

"FOR THY SAKE WE ARE BEING PUT TO DEATH ALL DAY LONG;
WE WERE CONSIDERED AS SHEEP TO BE SLAUGHTERED."

37 But in all these things we overwhelmingly conquer through Him who loved us. 38 For I am convinced that neither death, nor life, nor angels, nor principalities, nor things present, nor things to come, nor powers, 39 nor height, nor depth, nor any other created thing, shall be able to separate us from the love of God, which is in Christ Jesus our Lord.

9 I am telling the truth in Christ, I am not lying, my conscience bearing me witness in the Holy Spirit, 2 that I have great sorrow and unceasing grief in my heart. 3 For I could wish that I myself were accursed, *separated* from Christ for the sake of my brethren, my kinsmen according to the flesh, 4 who are Israelites, to whom belongs the adoption as sons and the glory and the covenants and the giving of the Law and the *temple* service and the promises, 5 whose are the fathers, and from whom is the Christ according to the flesh, who is over all, God blessed forever. Amen.

6 But *it is* not as though the word of God has failed. For they are not all Israel who are *descended* from Israel; 7 neither are they all children because they are Abraham's descendants, but: "THROUGH ISAAC YOUR DESCENDANTS WILL BE NAMED." 8 That is, it is not the children of the flesh who are children of God, but the children of the promise are regarded as descendants. 9 For this is a word of promise: "AT THIS TIME I WILL COME, AND SARAH SHALL HAVE A SON." 10 And not only this, but there was Rebekah also, when she had conceived *twins* by one man, our father Isaac; 11 for though *the twins* were not yet born, and had not done anything good or bad, in order that God's purpose according to *His* choice might stand, not because of works, but because of Him who calls,

[a] Some ancient mss. read, *raised from the dead.*
[b] Some ancient mss. read, *God.*

WILLIAMS

good of those who keep on loving God, who are called in accordance with God's purpose. 29 For those on whom He set His heart beforehand He marked off as His own to be made like His Son, that He might be the eldest of many brothers; 30 and those whom He marked off as His own He also calls; and those whom He calls He brings into right standing with Himself; those whom He brings into right standing with Himself He also glorifies.

31 What are we then to say to facts like these? If God is for us, who can be against us? 32 Since He did not spare His own Son but gave Him up for us all, will He not with Him graciously give us everything else? 33 Who can bring any charge against those whom God has chosen? It is God who declared them in right standing; 34 who can condemn them? Christ Jesus who died, or rather, who was raised from the dead, is now at God's right hand, and is actually pleading for us. 35 Who can separate us from Christ's love? Can suffering or misfortune or persecution or hunger or destitution or danger or the sword? 36As the Scripture says:

"For your sake we are being put to death the livelong day;
We are treated like sheep to be slaughtered."
37And yet in all these things we keep on gloriously conquering through Him who loved us. 38 For I have full assurance that neither death nor life nor angels nor principalities nor the present nor the future 39 nor evil forces above or beneath, nor anything else in all creation, will be able to separate us from the love of God as shown in Christ Jesus our Lord.

9 *Paul's grief over God's rejecting Israel for their unbelief in Jesus; God is right though He acts as a sovereign in saving men, as a potter does in making pots; so heathen are included in God's choice*

I am telling the truth as a Christian man, I am telling no lie, because my conscience enlightened by the Holy Spirit is bearing me witness to this fact, 2 that I have deep grief and constant anguish in my heart; 3 for I could wish myself accursed, even cut off from Christ, for the sake of my brothers, my natural kinsmen. 4 For they are Israelites; to them belong the privileges of sonship, God's glorious presence, the special covenants, the giving of the law, the temple service, the promises, 5 the patriarchs, and from them by natural descent the Christ has come, who is exalted over all, God blessed forever. Amen!

6 But it is not that God's word has failed. For not everybody that is descended from Israel really belongs to Israel, 7 nor are they all children of Abraham, because they are his descendants, but the promise was "In the line of Isaac your descendants will be counted." 8 That is, it is not Abraham's natural descendants who are God's children, but those who are made children by the promise are counted his true descendants. 9 For this is the language of the promise, "About this time next year I will come back, and Sarah will have a son." 10 Not only that but this too: there was Rebecca who was impregnated by our forefather Isaac. 11 For even before the twin sons were born, and though they had done nothing either good or bad, that God's purpose in accordance with His choice might continue to stand, conditioned not on men's actions but on God's calling them,

BECK

are called according to His plan. 29 Those whom He chose from the first He also appointed long ago to be thoroughly like His Son so He would be the firstborn among many brothers. 30 Those whom He appointed long ago He called. Those whom He called He made righteous. And those whom He made righteous* He glorified.

31 What does this mean? If God is for us, who can be against us? 32 He didn't spare His own Son but gave Him up for all of us—He will certainly with Him give us everything. 33 Who will accuse those whom God has chosen? It is God *who makes us righteous.* * 34 *Who will condemn?* 22 Christ died, more than that, He rose, He is at the right of God, and He prays for us. 35 Who will separate us from God's love? Will sorrow, hardship or persecution, hunger or nakedness, danger or a sword? 36 So it is written, *For you we are being killed all day long. We are considered sheep to be slaughtered.* 23 37 But in all this He who loved us helps us win an overwhelming victory. 38 I'm convinced that no death or life, no angels or their rulers, nothing now or in the future, no powers, 39 nothing above or below, or any other creature can ever separate us from God, who loves us in Christ Jesus, our Lord.

God's People

9 I'm telling the truth in Christ, I'm not lying, as my conscience by the Holy Spirit assures me, 2 when I say I have a great sorrow and in my heart a pain that never leaves me. 3 I could wish myself cut off from Christ and damned for my fellow Jews, my own flesh and blood. 4 They are the people of Israel. They were made God's family. They have the glory, the covenant, the Law, the worship, and the promises. 5 They have the ancestors, and from them according to His body came Christ, who is God over everything, blessed forever. Amen.

6 It doesn't mean God failed to do what He said. Not all who are descended from Israel are the real Israel, 7 and not all who are descended from Abraham are for that reason his real children. No, *Isaac's children will be called your descendants.* 24 8 This means children born in a natural way are not God's children. Only the children he had because God promished them are counted his descendants.

God's Right to Choose

9 God promised, *I will come back at the right time, and Sarah will have a son.* 25 10 The same thing happened to Rebekah. She was going to bear children for our ancestor Isaac. 11 They had not been born yet or done anything good or bad. Even then—in order that God may carry out His purpose according to His choice,

---

* See note at 3:20.
[22] Is. 50:8
[23] Ps. 44:22
[24] Gen. 21:12
[25] Gen. 18:10, 14

K.J.V.

of him that calleth;) 12 It was said unto her, The elder shall serve the younger. 13 As it is written, Jacob have I loved, but Esau have I hated. 14 What shall we say then? *Is there* unrighteousness with God? God forbid. 15 For he saith to Moses, I will have mercy on whom I will have mercy, and I will have compassion on whom I will have compassion. 16 So then *it is* not of him that willeth, nor of him that runneth, but of God that sheweth mercy. 17 For the Scripture saith unto Pharaoh, Even for this same purpose have I raised thee up, that I might shew my power in thee, and that my name might be declared throughout all the earth. 18 Therefore hath he mercy on whom he will *have mercy,* and whom he will he hardeneth. 19 Thou wilt say then unto me, Why doth he yet find fault? For who hath resisted his will? 20 Nay but, O man, who art thou that repliest against God? Shall the thing formed say to him that formed *it,* Why hast thou made me thus? 21 Hath not the potter power over the clay, of the same lump to make one vessel unto honour, and another unto dishonour? 22 *What* if God, willing to shew *his* wrath, and to make his power known, endured with much longsuffering the vessels of wrath fitted to destruction: 23 And that he might make known the riches of his glory on the vessels of mercy, which he had afore prepared unto glory, 24 Even us, whom he hath called, not of the Jews only, but also of the Gentiles? 25 As he saith also in Osee, I will call them my people, which were not my people; and her beloved, which was not beloved. 26 And it shall come to pass, *that* in the place where it was said unto them, Ye *are* not my people; there shall they be called the children of the living God. 27 Esaias also crieth concerning Israel, Though the number of the children of Israel be as the sand of the sea, a remnant shall be saved: 28 For he will finish the work, and cut *it* short in righteousness: because a short work will the Lord make upon the earth. 29 And as Esaias said before, Except the Lord of Sabaoth had left us a seed, we had been as Sodoma, and been made like unto Gomorrah. 30 What shall we say then? That the Gentiles, which followed not after righteousness, have attained to righteousness, even the righteousness which is of faith. 31 But Israel, which followed after the law of righteousness, hath not attained to the law of righteousness. 32 Wherefore? Because *they* sought *it* not by faith, but as it were by the works of the law. For they stumbled at that stumblingstone; 33 As it is written, Behold, I lay in Sion a stumblingstone and rock of offence: and whosoever believeth on him shall not be ashamed.

N.A.S.

12 it was said to her, "THE OLDER WILL SERVE THE YOUNGER." 13 Just as it is written, "JACOB I LOVED, BUT ESAU I HATED."

14 What shall we say then? There is no injustice with God, is there? May it never be! 15 For He says to Moses, "I WILL HAVE MERCY ON WHOM I HAVE MERCY, AND I WILL HAVE COMPASSION ON WHOM I HAVE COMPASSION." 16 So then it *does* not *depend* on the man who wills or the man who runs, but on God who has mercy. 17 For the Scripture says to Pharaoh, "FOR THIS VERY PURPOSE I RAISED YOU UP, TO DEMONSTRATE MY POWER IN YOU, AND THAT MY NAME MIGHT BE PROCLAIMED THROUGHOUT THE WHOLE EARTH." 18 So then He has mercy on whom He desires, and He hardens whom He desires.

19 You will say to me then, "Why does He still find fault? For who resists His will?" 20 On the contrary, who are you, O man, who answers back to God? The thing molded will not say to the molder, "Why did you make me like this," will it? 21 Or does not the potter have a right over the clay, to make from the same lump one vessel for honorable use, and another for common use? 22 What if God, although willing to demonstrate His wrath and to make His power known, endured with much patience vessels of wrath prepared for destruction? 23 And *He did so* in order that He might make known the riches of His glory upon vessels of mercy, which He prepared beforehand for glory, 24 *even* us, whom He also called, not from among Jews only, but also from among Gentiles. 25 As He says also in Hosea,

"I WILL CALL THOSE WHO WERE NOT MY
    PEOPLE, 'MY PEOPLE,'
AND HER WHO WAS NOT BELOVED, 'BELOVED.' "
26 "AND IT SHALL BE THAT IN THE PLACE
    WHERE IT WAS SAID TO THEM, 'YOU ARE
    NOT MY PEOPLE,'
THERE THEY SHALL BE CALLED SONS OF THE
    LIVING GOD."

27 And Isaiah cries out concerning Israel, "THOUGH THE NUMBER OF THE CHILDREN OF ISRAEL BE AS THE SAND OF THE SEA, IT IS THE REMNANT THAT WILL BE SAVED; 28 FOR THE LORD WILL EXECUTE HIS WORD UPON THE EARTH, THOROUGHLY AND QUICKLY." 29 And just as Isaiah foretold,

"EXCEPT THE LORD OF SABAOTH HAD LEFT TO
    US A POSTERITY,
WE WOULD HAVE BECOME AS SODOM, AND
    WOULD HAVE RESEMBLED GOMORRAH."

30 What shall we say then? That Gentiles, who did not pursue righteousness, attained righteousness, even the righteousness which is by faith; 31 but Israel, pursuing a law of righteousness, did not arrive at *that* law. 32 Why? Because *they* did not *pursue it* by faith, but as though *it were* by works. They stumbled over THE STUMBLING-STONE, 33 just as it is written,

"BEHOLD, I LAY IN ZION A STONE OF STUM-
    BLING AND A ROCK OF OFFENSE,
AND HE WHO BELIEVES IN HIM WILL NOT BE
    DISAPPOINTED."

WILLIAMS

12 she was told, "The elder will be a slave to the younger." 13 As the Scripture says, "Jacob I have loved, but Esau I have hated."

14 What are we then to conclude? It is not that there is injustice in God, is it? Of course not! 15 For He says to Moses, "I will have mercy on any man that I choose to have mercy on, and take pity on any man that I choose to take pity on." 16 So one's destiny does not depend on his own willing or strenuous actions but on God's having mercy on him. 17 For the Scripture says to Pharaoh, "I have raised you to your position for this very purpose of displaying my power in dealing with you, of announcing my name all over the earth." 18 So He has mercy on any man that He chooses to, and He hardens any man that He chooses to harden.

19 So you will ask me, "Why does He still find fault? For who can resist His will?" 20 On the contrary, friend, who are you anyway that you would answer back to God? Can the clay that is molded ask the man who molds it, "Why did you make me like this?" 21 Has not the potter the right with his clay to make of the same lump one vessel for ornamental purposes, another for degrading service? 22 And what if God, though wishing to display His anger and make known His power, yet has most patiently borne with the objects of His anger, already ripe for destruction, 23 so as to make known the riches of His glory for the objects of His mercy, whom He prepared in ages past to share His glory—24 even us whom He has called, not only from among the Jews but from among the heathen too? 25 Just as He says in Hosea:

"I will call a people that was not mine, my people,

And her who was not beloved, my beloved,

26 And in the place where it was said, 'You are no people of mine,'

They shall be called sons of the living God."

27 And Isaiah cries out about Israel, "Although the sons of Israel are as numberless as the sands of the sea, only a remnant of them will be saved, 28 for the Lord will completely and quickly execute His sentence on the earth." 29 As Isaiah again has foretold,

"Unless the Lord of hosts had left us some descendants, we would have fared as Sodom did and would have been like Gomorrah."

30 What are we then to conclude? That heathen peoples who were not in search for right standing with God have obtained it, and that a right standing conditioned on faith; 31 while Israel, though ever in pursuit of a law that would bring right standing, did not attain to it. 32 Why? Because they did not try through faith but through what they could do. They have stumbled over the stone that causes people to stumble, 33 as the Scripture says:

"See, I put on Zion a stone for causing people to stumble, a rock to trip them on,

But no one who puts his faith in it will ever be put to shame."

BECK

12 which doesn't depend on anything we do but on Him who calls us—she was told, *The older will serve the younger.*[26] 13 And so the Bible says, *I loved Jacob, but I hated Esau.*[27]

14 Does this mean God is unjust? Never! 15 He says to Moses, *I will be merciful to whom I want to be merciful; I will pity whom I want to pity.*[28] 16 Then it doesn't depend on anyone wanting it or trying hard but on God being merciful. 17 The Bible says to Pharaoh, *I raised you to the throne to demonstrate My power on you and to spread the news of Me all over the earth.*[29] 18 So He pities whom He wants to pity and *makes stubborn*[30] whom He wants to make stubborn.

19 You will ask me, "Why does He still find fault with anyone? Who can resist His will?" 20 But now, who are you, man, to talk back to God? *Will anything shaped by a man say to him,*[31] "Why did you make me like this?" 21 Doesn't *a potter* have the right over *his clay*[32] to make out of the same mud one thing for a noble purpose and another for a lowly purpose?

22 God wanted to show people His anger and let them know His power, but He waited very patiently before He would *punish those who deserved it* and had prepared themselves *for destruction,*[33] 23 so as to show the riches of glory He has in store for those He's merciful to and long ago prepared for glory—24 I mean us whom He called not only from the Jews but also from the non-Jews.

God Chooses Non-Jews

25 So He says in Hosea, *Those who are not My people I will call My people, and those who are not loved I will call My loved ones,* 26 *and where they were told, "You are not My people," they will be called sons of the living God.*[34] 27 Isaiah exclaims in regard to Israel, *Though the people of Israel are as many as the sand by the sea, only a remnant will be saved.* 28 *The Lord will completely and decisively execute His sentence on the country.*[35] 29 So Isaiah said long ago, *If the Lord of armies hadn't left us some survivors, we would have become like Sodom and ended like Gomorrah.*[36]

30 What does it mean? Non-Jewish people who didn't search for righteousness found a righteousness we get by believing, 31 while Israel, pursuing a Law with its righteousness, didn't find it. Why? 32 They didn't try to get it by faith but thought they could get it by works. They stumbled over *the stumbling block,* 33 as the Bible says, *I'm putting in Zion a stone they will stumble over and a rock they will fall over. But if you believe in Him, you will not be disappointed.*[37]

[26] Gen. 25:23
[27] Mal. 1:2-3
[28] Ex. 33:19
[29] Ex. 9:16
[30] Ex. 4:21; 7:3; 9:12; 14:4, 17
[31] Is. 29:16; 45:9
[32] Jer. 18:6
[33] Is. 13:5; Jer. 50:25
[34] Hos. 2:1, 23; 1:10
[35] Is. 10:22-23; 28:22
[36] Is. 1:9
[37] Is. 8:14; 28:16

10 Brethren, my heart's desire and prayer to God for Israel is, that they might be saved. 2 For I bear them record that they have a zeal of God, but not according to knowledge. 3 For they, being ignorant of God's righteousness, and going about to establish their own righteousness, have not submitted themselves unto the righteousness of God. 4 For Christ *is* the end of the law for righteousness to every one that believeth. 5 For Moses describeth the righteousness which is of the law, That the man which doeth those things shall live by them. 6 But the righteousness which is of faith speaketh on this wise, Say not in thine heart, Who shall ascend into heaven? (that is, to bring Christ down *from above:*) 7 Or, Who shall descend into the deep? (that is, to bring up Christ again from the dead.) 8 But what saith it? The word is nigh thee, *even* in thy mouth, and in thy heart: that is, the word of faith, which we preach; 9 That if thou shalt confess with thy mouth the Lord Jesus, and shalt believe in thine heart that God hath raised him from the dead, thou shalt be saved. 10 For with the heart man believeth unto righteousness; and with the mouth confession is made unto salvation. 11 For the Scripture saith, Whosoever believeth on him shall not be ashamed. 12 For there is no difference between the Jew and the Greek: for the same Lord over all is rich unto all that call upon him. 13 For whosoever shall call upon the name of the Lord shall be saved. 14 How then shall they call on him in whom they have not believed? and how shall they believe in him of whom they have not heard? and how shall they hear without a preacher? 15And how shall they preach, except they be sent? as it is written, How beautiful are the feet of them that preach the gospel of peace, and bring glad tidings of good things! 16 But they have not all obeyed the gospel. For Esaias saith, Lord, who hath believed our report? 17 So then faith *cometh* by hearing, and hearing by the word of God. 18 But I say, Have they not heard? Yes verily, their sound went into all the earth, and their words unto the ends of the world. 19 But I say, Did not Israel know? First Moses saith, I will provoke you to jealousy by *them that are* no people, *and* by a foolish nation I will anger you. 20 But Esaias is very bold, and saith, I was found of them that sought me not; I was made manifest unto them that asked not after me. 21 But to Israel he saith, All day long I have stretched forth my hands unto a disobedient and gainsaying people.

10 Brethren, my heart's desire and my prayer to God for them is for *their* salvation. 2 For I bear them witness that they have a zeal for God, but not in accordance with knowledge. 3 For not knowing about God's righteousness, and seeking to establish their own, they did not subject themselves to the righteousness of God. 4 For Christ is the end of the law for righteousness to everyone who believes. 5 For Moses writes that the man who practices the righteousness which is based on law shall live by that righteousness. 6 But the righteousness based on faith speaks thus,

"DO NOT SAY IN YOUR HEART, 'WHO WILL ASCEND INTO HEAVEN?' (that is, to bring Christ down),

7 or 'WHO WILL DESCEND INTO THE ABYSS?' (that is, to bring Christ up from the dead)." 8 But what does it say? "THE WORD IS NEAR YOU, IN YOUR MOUTH AND IN YOUR HEART"—that is, the word of faith which we are preaching, 9 that if you confess with your mouth Jesus *as* Lord, and believe in your heart that God raised Him from the dead, you shall be saved; 10 for with the heart man believes, resulting in righteousness, and with the mouth he confesses, resulting in salvation. 11 For the Scripture says, "WHOEVER BELIEVES IN HIM WILL NOT BE DISAPPOINTED." 12 For there is no distinction between Jew and Greek; for the same *Lord* is Lord of all, abounding in riches for all who call upon Him; 13 for "WHOEVER WILL CALL UPON THE NAME OF THE LORD WILL BE SAVED." 14 How then shall they call upon Him in whom they have not believed? And how shall they believe in Him whom they have not heard? And how shall they hear without a preacher? 15And how shall they preach unless they are sent? Just as it is written, "HOW BEAUTIFUL ARE THE FEET OF THOSE WHO BRING GLAD TIDINGS OF GOOD THINGS!"

16 However, they did not all heed the glad tidings; for Isaiah says, "LORD, WHO HAS BELIEVED OUR REPORT?" 17 So faith *comes* from hearing, and hearing by the word of Christ. 18 But I say, surely they have never heard, have they? Indeed they have:

"THEIR VOICE HAS GONE OUT INTO ALL THE EARTH,

AND THEIR WORDS TO THE ENDS OF THE WORLD."

19 But I say, surely Israel did not know, did they? At the first Moses says,

"I WILL MAKE YOU JEALOUS BY THAT WHICH IS NOT A NATION,

BY A NATION WITHOUT UNDERSTANDING WILL I ANGER YOU."

20And Isaiah is very bold and says,

"I WAS FOUND BY THOSE WHO SOUGHT ME NOT,

I BECAME MANIFEST TO THOSE WHO DID NOT ASK FOR ME."

21 But as for Israel he says, "ALL THE DAY LONG I HAVE STRETCHED OUT MY HANDS TO A DISOBEDIENT AND OBSTINATE PEOPLE."

WILLIAMS

BECK

10 *The faith method of right standing with God intended for all; so the good news must be proclaimed to all*

Brothers, my heart's good will goes out for them, and my prayer to God is that they may be saved. 2 For I can testify that they are zealous for God, but they are not intelligently so. 3 For they were ignorant of God's way of right standing and were trying to set up one of their own, and so would not surrender to God's way of right standing. 4 For Christ has put an end to law*a* as a way to right standing for everyone who puts his trust in Him. 5 For Moses says of the law-way to right standing with God that whoever can perform the law will live by it. 6 But here is what the faith-way to right standing*b* says, "Do not say to yourself, 'Who will go up to heaven?'" that is, to bring Christ down; 7 or "'Who will go down into the depths?'" that is, to bring Christ up from the dead. 8 But what does it say? "God's message is close to you, on your very lips and in your heart"; that is, the message about faith which we preach. 9 For if with your lips you acknowledge the fact that Jesus is Lord, and in your hearts you believe that God raised Him from the dead, you will be saved. 10 For in their hearts people exercise the faith that leads to right standing, and with their lips they make the acknowledgment which means*c* salvation. 11 For the Scripture says, "No one who puts his faith in Him will ever be put to shame." 12 But there is no distinction between Jew and Greek, for the same Lord is over them all, because He is infinitely kind to all who call upon Him. 13 For everyone who calls upon the name of the Lord will be saved.

14 But how can people call upon One in whom they have not believed? And how can they believe in One about whom they have not heard? And how can people hear without someone to preach to them? 15 And how can men preach unless they are sent to do so? As the Scripture says, "How beautiful are the feet of men who bring the glad news of His good things!"

16 However, they have not all given heed to the good news, for Isaiah says, "Lord, who has put faith in what we told?" 17 So faith comes from hearing what is told, and hearing through the message about Christ. 18 But may I ask, They had no chance to hear, did they? Yes, indeed:

"All over the earth their voices have gone,
To the ends of the world their words."

19 But again I ask, Israel did not understand, did they? For in the first place Moses says:

"I will make you jealous of a nation that is
    no nation;
I will provoke you to anger at a senseless
    nation."

20 Then Isaiah was bold enough to say:

"I have been found by a people who were
    not searching for me,
I have made known myself to people who
    were not asking to know me."

21 But of Israel he said:

"All day long I have held out my hands to a
    people that is disobedient and obsti-
    nate."

[a] Grk., *is the end of the law.* [b] Lit., *the right standing conditioned on faith.* [c] Grk., *unto salvation.*

10 Fellow Christians, my heart's desire and my prayer to God is to save the Israelites. 2 I can testify they are zealous for God but don't understand. 3 Not knowing the righteousness God gives, and trying to set up their own, they haven't submitted to God's righteousness. 4 You see, Christ is the end of the Law to give righteousness to everyone who believes.

5 Moses writes, *if you have done* the righteous things demanded by the Law, *you will find life in them.*[38] 6 But the righteousness you get by faith says this: *Don't ask yourself,*[39] *Who will go up to heaven?* which means, bring Christ down, 7 or, Who will *go down into the depths?* which means, bring Christ up from the dead. 8 But what does it say? *The word is near you, in your mouth and in your heart.*[40] This is the word of faith that we preach. 9 If with your mouth you confess, "Jesus is the Lord," and in your heart you believe "God raised Him from the dead," you will be saved. 10 With your heart you believe and become righteous; with your mouth you confess and are saved. 11 *Anyone who believes in Him,* the Bible says, *will not be disappointed.*[41] 12 There is no difference between Jew and Greek, because they all have the same Lord, who gives His riches to all who call on Him. 13 *Everyone who calls on the Lord's name will be saved.*[42]

14 But how can they call on Him if they haven't believed in Him? And how can they believe in Him if they haven't heard Him? How can they hear if nobody preaches? 15 How can men preach if they're not sent? Just as the Bible says, *How beautiful is the coming of those who bring good news!*[43]

16 But not all have obeyed the good news. Isaiah asks, *Lord, who has believed what we told them?*[44] 17 So when we tell people, they believe, and we tell them by letting Christ speak.

18 But I ask, didn't they hear it? Of course they did.

*Their voices have gone all over the earth
And their words to the farthest parts of the
    world.*[45]

19 Again I ask, didn't Israel know? Moses was the first to say,

*I will make you jealous of those who are not
    a nation,
I will make you angry with a people who
    don't understand.*[46]

20 Then Isaiah boldly says,

*I will let those who don't look for Me find
    Me.
I will let those who don't ask for Me know
    Me.*

21 And He says about Israel, *All day long I have stretched out My hands to a people who disobey Me and oppose Me.*[47]

[38] Lev. 18:5
[39] Deut. 9:4
[40] Deut. 30:12, 14; (Ps. 107:26)
[41] Is. 28:16
[42] Joel 2:32
[43] Is. 52:7
[44] Is. 53:1
[45] Ps. 19:4
[46] Deut. 32:21
[47] Is. 65:1-2

K.J.V.

11 I say then, Hath God cast away his people? God forbid. For I also am an Israelite, of the seed of Abraham, *of* the tribe of Benjamin. 2 God hath not cast away his people which he foreknew. Wot ye not what the Scripture saith of Elias? how he maketh intercession to God against Israel, saying, 3 Lord, they have killed thy prophets, and digged down thine altars; and I am left alone, and they seek my life. 4 But what saith the answer of God unto him? I have reserved to myself seven thousand men, who have not bowed the knee to *the image of* Baal. 5 Even so then at this present time also there is a remnant according to the election of grace. 6 And if by grace, then *is it* no more of works: otherwise grace is no more grace. But if *it be* of works, then is it no more grace: otherwise work is no more work. 7 What then? Israel hath not obtained that which he seeketh for; but the election hath obtained it, and the rest were blinded 8 (According as it is written, God hath given them the spirit of slumber, eyes that they should not see, and ears that they should not hear;) unto this day. 9 And David saith, Let their table be made a snare, and a trap, and a stumblingblock, and a recompense unto them: 10 Let their eyes be darkened, that they may not see, and bow down their back alway. 11 I say then, Have they stumbled that they should fall? God forbid: but *rather* through their fall salvation *is come* unto the Gentiles, for to provoke them to jealousy. 12 Now if the fall of them *be* the riches of the world, and the diminishing of them the riches of the Gentiles; how much more their fulness? 13 For I speak to you Gentiles, inasmuch as I am the apostle of the Gentiles, I magnify mine office: 14 If by any means I may provoke to emulation *them which are* my flesh, and might save some of them. 15 For if the casting away of them *be* the reconciling of the world, what *shall* the receiving *of them be,* but life from the dead? 16 For if the firstfruit *be* holy, the lump *is* also *holy:* and if the root *be* holy, so *are* the branches. 17 And if some of the branches be broken off, and thou, being a wild olive tree, wert graffed in among them, and with them partakest of the root and fatness of the olive tree; 18 Boast not against the branches. But if thou boast, thou bearest not the root, but the root thee. 19 Thou wilt say then, The branches were broken off, that I might be graffed in. 20 Well; because of unbelief they were broken off, and thou standest by faith. Be

N.A.S.

11 I say then, God has not rejected His people, has He? May it never be! For I too am an Israelite, a descendant of Abraham, of the tribe of Benjamin. 2 God has not rejected His people whom He foreknew. Or do you not know what the Scripture says in *the passage about* Elijah, how he pleads with God against Israel? 3 "LORD, THEY HAVE KILLED THY PROPHETS, THEY HAVE TORN DOWN THINE ALTARS, AND I ALONE AM LEFT, AND THEY ARE SEEKING MY LIFE." 4 But what is the divine response to him? "I HAVE KEPT FOR MYSELF SEVEN THOUSAND MEN WHO HAVE NOT BOWED THE KNEE TO BAAL." 5 In the same way then, there has also come to be at the present time a remnant according to *God's* gracious choice. 6 But if it is by grace, it is no longer on the basis of works, otherwise grace is no longer grace. 7 What then? That which Israel is seeking for, it has not obtained, but those who were chosen obtained it, and the rest were hardened; 8 just as it is written,

"GOD GAVE THEM A SPIRIT OF STUPOR,
EYES TO SEE NOT AND EARS TO HEAR NOT,
DOWN TO THIS VERY DAY."

9 And David says,
"LET THEIR TABLE BECOME A SNARE and a trap,
AND A STUMBLING-BLOCK AND A RETRIBUTION TO THEM,
10 LET THEIR EYES BE DARKENED TO SEE NOT,
AND BEND THEIR BACKS FOREVER."

11 I say then, they did not stumble so as to fall, did they? May it never be! But by their transgression salvation *has come* to the Gentiles, to make them jealous. 12 Now if their transgression be riches for the world and their failure be riches for the Gentiles, how much more will their fulfillment be! 13 But I am speaking to you who are Gentiles. Inasmuch then as I am an apostle of Gentiles, I magnify my ministry, 14 if somehow I might move to jealousy my fellow-countrymen and save some of them. 15 For if their rejection be the reconciliation of the world, what will *their* acceptance be but life from the dead? 16 And if the first piece *of dough* be holy, the lump is also; and if the root be holy, the branches are too. 17 But if some of the branches were broken off, and you, being a wild olive, were grafted in among them and became partaker with them of the rich root of the olive tree, 18 do not be arrogant toward the branches; but if you are arrogant, *remember that* it is not you who supports the root, but the root *supports* you. 19 You will say then, "Branches were broken off so that I might be grafted in." 20 Quite right, they were broken off for their unbelief, and you stand *only* by your

WILLIAMS

11 *Only a remnant of Jews now saved; as most of them are rejected, heathen peoples are saved; God's severity and goodness, man's fear and humility; God's universal mercy and inexhaustible resources in wisdom and knowledge*

I say then, God has not disowned His people, has He? Of course not! Why, I am an Israelite myself, a descendant of Abraham, a member of the tribe of Benjamin. 2 No, God has not disowned His people, on whom He set His heart beforehand. Do you know what the Scripture says in Elijah's case, how he pleaded with God against Israel? 3 "Lord, they have killed your prophets, they have demolished your altars; I alone have been left, and they are trying to kill me." 4 But how did God reply to him? "I have reserved for myself seven thousand men who have never bent their knees to Baal." 5 So it is at the present time; a remnant remains, in accordance with God's unmerited favor. 6 But if it is by His unmerited favor, it is not at all conditioned on what they have done. If that were so, His favor would not be favor at all. 7 What are we then to conclude? Israel has failed to obtain what it is still in search for, but His chosen ones have obtained it. The rest have become insensible to it, 8 as the Scripture says, "God has given them over to an attitude of insensibility, so that their eyes cannot see and their ears cannot hear, down to this very day." 9 And David said:
"Let their food become a snare and a trap to them,
Their pitfall and retribution;
10 Let their eyes be darkened, so they cannot see,
And forever bend their backs beneath the load."
11 I say then, they did not stumble so as to fall in utter ruin, did they? Of course not! On the contrary, because of their stumbling, salvation has come to heathen peoples, to make the Israelites jealous. 12 But if their stumbling has resulted in the enrichment of the world, and their overthrow becomes the enrichment of heathen peoples, how much richer the result will be when the full quota of Jews comes in! 13 Yes, I now am speaking to you who are a part of the heathen peoples. As I am an apostle to the heathen peoples, I am making the most of my ministry to them, to see 14 if I can make my fellow-countrymen jealous, and so save some of them. 15 For if the rejection of them has resulted in the reconciling of the world, what will the result be of the final reception of them but life from the dead? 16 If the first handful of dough is consecrated, so is the whole mass; if the tree's root is consecrated, so are the branches. 17 If some of the branches have been broken off, and yet you, although you were wild olive suckers, have been grafted in among the native branches, and been made to share the rich sap of the native olive's root, 18 you must not be boasting against the natural branches. And if you do, just consider, you do not support the root, but the root supports you. 19 Then you will say, "Branches have been broken off for us to be grafted in." 20 Very well; but it was for lack of faith that they were broken off, and it is through your faith that you now stand where you are. Stop your haughty thinking; rather

BECK

The Remnant

11 So I ask, "Has *God rejected His people?*" Certainly not—I'm an Israelite myself, a descendant of Abraham and of the tribe of Benjamin. 2 *God has not rejected His people*[48] whom He chose long ago. Or don't you know what the Bible says in the story of Elijah when he pleads with God against Israel: 3 *Lord, they have killed Your prophets, they have torn down Your altars, I am the only one left, and they are trying to kill me?* 4 *But* what did *God answer him? I have kept for Myself seven thousand men who have not knelt to Baal.*[49] 5 So there is right now, too, a remnant God has chosen by His love. 6 But if He was moved only by His love, it couldn't have been due to what they have done; otherwise it wouldn't be His unearned love anymore.

7 What does it mean? Israel didn't get what it wanted, but those whom God chose did get it.

God's Way of Winning Jews

8 And the minds of the others were dulled, as the Bible says,

> God has given them a spirit of deep sleep,
> eyes that should not see,
> and ears that should not hear,
> And so it has been until this day.[50]

9 And David says,

> Let their table be a snare and a trap,
> To make them fall and get what they deserve.
> 10 Let their eyes turn dark so they cannot see,
> And bend their backs forever.[51]

11 Did they stumble, I ask, to be lost altogether? Certainly not! By their error salvation has come to the non-Jews *to make the Jews jealous.*[46] 12 And if their error made the world rich and their loss made the non-Jews rich, how much more certainly will that happen when their full number comes in! 13 Now, I am speaking to you non-Jews. As I am sent to the non-Jews, I glorify my work. 14 Perhaps I can *make* my fellow Jews *jealous*[46] and save some of them. 15 When God rejects them, the world is reconciled to God; when God accepts them, what can it mean but that the dead will live?

16 If the first handful of dough is holy, so is the whole dough. If the root is holy, so are the branches. 17 But if some of the branches have been broken off, and you, a wild olive, have been grafted in among them, and the rich sap from the root of the olive tree nourishes you too, 18 don't brag of being more than the other branches. If you brag, remember you don't support the root, but the root supports you. 19 "Branches were cut off," you will say, "to graft me in." 20 Right! They were broken off because they didn't believe, but you stand by

[48] 1 Sam. 12:22; Ps. 94:14
[49] 1 Kings 19:10, 14, 15, 18
[50] Deut. 29:4; Is. 29:10
[51] Ps. 69:22-23

K.J.V.

not highminded, but fear: 21 For if God spared not the natural branches, *take heed* lest he also spare not thee. 22 Behold therefore the goodness and severity of God: on them which fell, severity; but toward thee, goodness, if thou continue in *his* goodness: otherwise thou also shalt be cut off. 23And they also, if they abide not still in unbelief, shall be graffed in: for God is able to graff them in again. 24 For if thou wert cut out of the olive tree which is wild by nature, and wert graffed contrary to nature into a good olive tree; how much more shall these, which be the natural *branches,* be graffed into their own olive tree? 25 For I would not, brethren, that ye should be ignorant of this mystery, lest ye should be wise in your own conceits, that blindness in part is happened to Israel, until the fulness of the Gentiles be come in. 26And so all Israel shall be saved: as it is written, There shall come out of Sion the Deliverer, and shall turn away ungodliness from Jacob: 27 For this *is* my covenant unto them, when I shall take away their sins. 28As concerning the gospel, *they are* enemies for your sakes: but as touching the election, *they are* beloved for the fathers' sakes. 29 For the gifts and calling of God *are* without repentance. 30 For as ye in times past have not believed God, yet have now obtained mercy through their unbelief: 31 Even so have these also now not believed, that through your mercy they also may obtain mercy. 32 For God hath concluded them all in unbelief, that he might have mercy upon all. 33 O the depth of the riches both of the wisdom and knowledge of God! how unsearchable *are* his judgments, and his ways past finding out! 34 For who hath known the mind of the Lord? or who hath been his counsellor? 35 Or who hath first given to him, and it shall be recompensed unto him again? 36 For of him, 'and through him, and to him, *are* all things: to whom *be* glory for ever. Amen.

12 I beseech you therefore, brethren, by the mercies of God, that ye present your bodies a living sacrifice, holy, acceptable unto God, *which is* your reasonable service. 2And be not conformed to this world: but be ye transformed by the renewing of your mind, that ye may prove what *is* that good, and acceptable, and perfect will of God. 3 For I say, through the grace given unto me, to every man that is among you, not to think *of himself* more highly than he ought to think; but to think soberly, according as God hath dealt to every man the

N.A.S.

faith. Do not be conceited, but fear; 21 for if God did not spare the natural branches, neither will He spare you. 22 Behold then the kindness and severity of God; to those who fell, severity, but to you, God's kindness, if you continue in His kindness; otherwise you also will be cut off. 23And they also, if they do not continue in their unbelief, will be grafted in; for God is able to graft them in again. 24 For if you were cut off from what is by nature a wild olive tree, and were grafted contrary to nature into a cultivated olive tree, how much more shall these who are the natural *branches* be grafted into their own olive tree?

25 For I do not want you, brethren, to be uninformed of this mystery, lest you be wise in your own estimation, that a partial hardening has happened to Israel until the fulness of the Gentiles has come in; 26 and thus all Israel will be saved; just as it is written,

"The Deliverer will come from Zion,
He will remove ungodliness from Jacob."
27 "And this is My covenant with them,
When I take away their sins."

28 From the standpoint of the gospel they are enemies for your sake, but from the standpoint of *God's* choice they are beloved for the sake of the fathers; 29 for the gifts and the calling of God are irrevocable. 30 For just as you once were disobedient to God but now have been shown mercy because of their disobedience, 31 so these also now have been disobedient, in order that because of the mercy shown to you they also may now be shown mercy. 32 For God has shut up all in disobedience that He might show mercy to all.

33 Oh the depth of the riches both of the wisdom and knowledge of God! How unsearchable are His judgments and unfathomable His ways! 34 For who has known the mind of the Lord, or who became His counselor? 35 Or who has first given to Him that it might be paid back to Him again? 36 For from Him and through Him and to Him are all things. To Him *be* the glory forever. Amen.

12 I urge you therefore, brethren, by the mercies of God, to present your bodies a living and holy sacrifice, acceptable to God, *which is* your spiritual service of worship. 2And do not be conformed to this world, but be transformed by the renewing of your mind, that you may prove what the will of God is, that which is good and acceptable and perfect.

3 For through the grace given to me I say to every man among you not to think more highly of himself than he ought to think; but to think so as to have sound judgment, as God has al-

WILLIAMS

continue to be reverent, 21 for if God did not spare the natural branches, certainly He will not spare you. 22 So take a look at the goodness and the severity of God; severity to those who have fallen, but goodness to you, on condition that you continue to live by His goodness; otherwise, you too will be pruned away. 23 And they too, if they do not continue to live by their unbelief, will be grafted in, for God is amply able to graft them in. 24 For if you were cut off from an olive wild by nature, and contrary to nature were grafted on to a fine olive stock, how much easier will it be for the natural branches to be grafted on to their own olive stock?

25 For to keep you from being self-conceited, brothers, I do not want to have a misunderstanding of this uncovered secret, that only temporary insensibility has come upon Israel until the full quota of the heathen peoples comes in, 26 and so in that way all Israel will be saved, just as the Scripture says:

"From Zion the Deliverer will come;
He will remove ungodliness from Jacob;
27 And this my covenant I make with them,
When I shall take away their sins."

28 As measured by the good news the Jews are God's enemies for your sakes, but as measured by God's choice they are His beloved because of their forefathers, 29 for the gracious gifts and call of God are never taken back. 30 For just as you once disobeyed God, but now have had mercy shown you because of their disobedience, 31 so they too are now disobedient because of the mercy shown you, that they too may now have mercy shown them. 32 For God has locked up all mankind in the prison of disobedience so as to have mercy on them all.

33 How fathomless the depths of God's resources, wisdom, and knowledge! How unsearchable His decisions, and how mysterious[a] His methods! 34 For who has ever understood the thoughts of the Lord, or has ever been His adviser? 35 Or who has ever advanced God anything to have Him pay him back? 36 For from Him everything comes, through Him everything lives, and for Him everything exists. Glory to Him forever! Amen.

12 *God's mercy the ground of social service, which is rooted in personal consecration; through union with Christ we are His body each with fitting functions; love, sympathy, humility, kindness, forgiveness, and similar social graces*

I beg you, therefore, brothers, through these mercies God has shown you, to make a decisive[a] dedication of your bodies as a living sacrifice, devoted and well-pleasing to God, which is your reasonable service. 2 Stop living in accordance with the customs of this world, but by the new ideals that mold your minds continue to transform yourselves, so as to find and follow God's will; that is, what is good, well-pleasing to Him, and perfect.

3 Now through the unmerited favor God has shown me I would say to every one of you not to estimate himself above his real value, but to make a sober rating of himself, in accordance with the degree of faith which God has appor-

BECK

believing. Don't feel proud but be afraid. 21 If God didn't spare the natural branches, He will not spare you. 22 Now see how kind and how severe God can be—severe to those who fell but kind to you if you cling to His kindness; otherwise you, too, will be cut off.

23 And if the others will no more refuse to believe, they will be grafted in, because God can graft them in again. 24 You have been cut from an olive tree that grows wild and have been unnaturally grafted into a cultivated olive; how much more likely it is that these natural branches will be grafted back into their own olive tree!

25 To keep you from thinking too well of yourselves, my fellow Christians, I want you to know this secret truth: The minds of a part of the Jews were dulled until the full number of the non-Jews comes in. 26 And in this way all Israel will be saved, as the Bible says, *The Savior will come from Zion. He will get rid of ungodliness in Jacob. 27 And this will be My covenant with them when I take away their sins.*[52]

28 God's rule in telling the good news is to treat them as His enemies to help you. But He chose them, and so He loves them on account of their fathers. 29 God never changes His mind when He gives anything or calls anyone. Once you disobeyed God, 30 but now that the Jews have disobeyed, He has been merciful to you. 31 So they also have disobeyed now that when you enjoy His mercy, they may have it too. 32 You see, God has put all people in a prison of disobedience in order to be merciful to all.

33 How deep are God's riches, wisdom, and knowledge, how impossible it is to find out His decisions and trace His ways! 34 *Who has found out how the Lord thinks? Or who has become His adviser?*[53] 35 *Or who has first given Him something for which he must be paid back?*[54] 36 Everything is from Him, by Him, and for Him. To Him be glory forever. Amen.

Live for God

12 I appeal to you, fellow Christians, by the mercies of God, to give your bodies as a living sacrifice, holy and pleasing to God, and so worship Him as thinking beings. 2 Don't live like this world, but let yourselves be transformed by a renewing of your minds so you can test and be sure what God wants, what is good and pleasing and perfect.

3 As God gave me His gift of love for every one of you, I tell you, don't think too highly of yourselves, but take a sane view of yourselves, everyone according to the amount of faith God

---

[a] Grk. literally means *untraceable*.
[a] *Once for all offer.*

[52] Is. 59:20-21; 27:9
[53] Is. 40:13
[54] Job 35:7; 41:11

K.J.V.

measure of faith. 4 For as we have many members in one body, and all members have not the same office: 5 So we, *being* many, are one body in Christ, and every one members one of another. 6 Having then gifts differing according to the grace that is given to us, whether prophecy, *let us prophesy* according to the proportion of faith; 7 Or ministry, *let us wait* on *our* ministering; or he that teacheth, on teaching; 8 Or he that exhorteth, on exhortation: he that giveth, *let him do it* with simplicity; he that ruleth, with diligence; he that sheweth mercy, with cheerfulness. 9 *Let* love be without dissimulation. Abhor that which is evil; cleave to that which is good. 10 *Be* kindly affectioned one to another with brotherly love; in honour preferring one another; 11 Not slothful in business; fervent in spirit; serving the Lord; 12 Rejoicing in hope; patient in tribulation; continuing instant in prayer; 13 Distributing to the necessity of saints; given to hospitality. 14 Bless them which persecute you: bless, and curse not. 15 Rejoice with them that do rejoice, and weep with them that weep. 16 *Be* of the same mind one toward another. Mind not high things, but condescend to men of low estate. Be not wise in your own conceits. 17 Recompense to no man evil for evil. Provide things honest in the sight of all men. 18 If it be possible, as much as lieth in you, live peaceably with all men. 19 Dearly beloved, avenge not yourselves, but *rather* give place unto wrath: for it is written, Vengeance *is* mine; I will repay, saith the Lord. 20 Therefore if thine enemy hunger, feed him; if he thirst, give him drink: for in so doing thou shalt heap coals of fire on his head. 21 Be not overcome of evil, but overcome evil with good.

13 Let every soul be subject unto the higher powers. For there is no power but of God: the powers that be are ordained of God. 2 Whosoever therefore resisteth the power, resisteth the ordinance of God: and they that resist shall receive to themselves damnation. 3 For rulers are not a terror to good works, but to the evil. Wilt thou then not be afraid of the power? do that which is good, and thou shalt have praise of the same: 4 For he is the minister of God to thee for good. But if thou do that which is evil, be afraid; for he beareth not the sword in vain: for he is the minister of God, a revenger to *execute* wrath upon him that doeth evil. 5 Wherefore *ye* must needs be subject, not only for wrath, but also for conscience' sake. 6 For, for this cause pay ye tribute also: for they are God's ministers, attending continually upon this very thing. 7 Render therefore to all their dues: tribute to whom tribute *is due;* custom to whom

N.A.S.

lotted to each a measure of faith. 4 For just as we have many members in one body and all the members do not have the same function, 5 so we, who are many, are one body in Christ, and individually members one of another. 6 And since we have gifts that differ according to the grace given to us, *let each exercise them accordingly:* if prophecy, according to the proportion of his faith; 7 if service, in his serving; or he who teaches, in his teaching; 8 or he who exhorts, in his exhortation; he who gives, with [a]liberality; he who leads, with diligence; he who shows mercy, with cheerfulness.

9 Let love be without hypocrisy. Abhor what is evil; cleave to what is good. 10 Be devoted to one another in brotherly love; give preference to one another in honor; 11 not lagging behind in diligence, fervent in spirit, serving the Lord; 12 rejoicing in hope, persevering in tribulation, devoted to prayer, 13 contributing to the needs of the saints, practicing hospitality. 14 Bless those who persecute [b]you; bless and curse not. 15 Rejoice with those who rejoice, and weep with those who weep. 16 Be of the same mind toward one another; do not be haughty in mind, but associate with the lowly. Do not be wise in your own estimation. 17 Never pay back evil for evil to anyone. Respect what is right in the sight of all men. 18 If possible, so far as it depends on you, be at peace with all men. 19 Never take your own revenge, beloved, but leave room for the wrath *of God,* for it is written, "VENGEANCE IS MINE, I WILL REPAY, SAYS THE LORD." 20 "BUT IF YOUR ENEMY IS HUNGRY, FEED HIM, AND IF HE IS THIRSTY, GIVE HIM A DRINK; FOR IN SO DOING YOU WILL HEAP BURNING COALS UPON HIS HEAD." 21 Do not be overcome by evil, but overcome evil with good.

13 Let every person be in subjection to the governing authorities. For there is no authority except from God, and those which exist are established by God. 2 Therefore he who resists authority has opposed the ordinance of God; and they who have opposed will receive condemnation upon themselves. 3 For rulers are not a cause of fear for good behavior, but for evil. Do you want to have no fear of authority? Do what is good, and you will have praise from the same; 4 for it is a minister of God to you for good. But if you do what is evil, be afraid; for it does not bear the sword for nothing; for it is a minister of God, an avenger who brings wrath upon the one who practices evil. 5 Wherefore it is necessary to be in subjection, not only because of wrath, but also for conscience's sake. 6 For because of this you also pay taxes, for *rulers* are servants of God, devoting themselves to this very thing. 7 Render to all what is due them: tax to whom tax *is due;* custom to whom

[a] Or, *simplicity.* [b] Some ancient mss. omit, *you.*

WILLIAMS   ## BECK

tioned to him. 4 For just as we have many parts united in our physical bodies, and the parts do not all have the same function, 5 so we, though many, are united in one body through union with Christ, and we are individually parts of one another. 6 As we have gifts that differ in accordance with the favor God has shown us, if it is that of preaching, let it be done in proportion to our faith; 7 or of practical service, in the field of service; or of a teacher, in the field of teaching; 8 or of one who encourages others, in the field of encouragement; or one who gives his money, with liberality; or one who leads others, with earnestness; or one who does deeds of charity, with cheerfulness.

9 Your love must be true. You must always turn in horror from what is wrong, but keep on holding to what is right. 10 In brotherly love be affectionate to one another, in personal honors put one another to the fore, 11 never slack in earnestness, always on fire with the Spirit, always serving the Lord, 12 ever happy in hope, always patient in suffering, ever persistent in prayer, 13 always supplying the needs of God's people, ever practicing hospitality. 14 Keep on blessing your persecutors; keep on blessing and stop cursing them. 15 Practice rejoicing with people who rejoice, and weeping with people who weep. 16 Keep on thinking in harmony with one another. Stop being high-minded but keep on associating with lowly people. Stop being conceited. 17 Stop returning evil for evil to anyone. Always see to it that your affairs are right in the sight of everybody. 18 If possible, so far as it depends on you, live in peace with everybody. 19 Stop taking revenge on one another, beloved, but leave a place for God's anger, for the Scripture says, "Vengeance belongs to me; I will pay them back, says the Lord." 20 Do the opposite. If your enemy is hungry, give him something to eat. If he is thirsty, give him something to drink. For if you act in this way, you will heap burning coals upon his head! 21 Stop being conquered by evil, but keep on conquering evil with good.

13 *The state a divine institution; duties of Christian citizens; true love obeys God's commands; Christ's second coming a motive to higher living*

Everybody must obey the civil authorities that are over him, for no authority exists except by God's permission; the existing authorities have been established by Him, 2 so that anyone who resists the authorities sets himself against what God has established, and those who set themselves against Him will get the penalty due them. 3 For civil authorities are not a terror to the man who does right, but they are to the man who does wrong. Do you want to have no dread of the civil authorities? Then practice doing right and you will be commended for it. 4 For the civil authorities are God's servants to do you good. But if you practice doing wrong, you should dread them, for they do not wield the sword for nothing. Indeed, they are God's servants to inflict punishment upon people who do wrong. 5 Therefore, you must obey them, not only for the sake of escaping punishment, but also for conscience' sake; 6 for this is the reason why you pay your taxes, for the civil authorities are God's official servants faithfully devoting themselves to this very end. 7 Pay all of them what is due them—tribute to the officer

gave you. 4 We have many parts in one body, and these parts don't all do the same thing. 5 In the same way, many as we are, we are one body in Christ and individually parts of one another. 6 We have gifts that are different according to what His love gave us. If you can speak God's Word, do it according to the faith you have. 7 If you can serve, then serve. If you can teach, teach. 8 If you can encourage, encourage. If you share, be generous. If you manage anything, do it eagerly. If you help people in need, do it cheerfully.

Love

9 Love sincerely. Hate evil; cling to what is good. 10 Love one another tenderly as fellow Christians. Outdo one another in showing respect. 11 Don't be backward in zeal. Glow with the Spirit. Serve the Lord. 12 Be happy in your hope, patient in trouble, and keep busy praying. 13 Share what you have with the holy people who need it. Eagerly welcome strangers as guests.

14 Bless those who persecute you, bless, and don't curse them. 15 Be happy with those who are happy, weep with those who weep. 16 Live in harmony with one another. Don't be too ambitious, but go along with the humble ways of others. *Don't think you are wise.*[55]

17 Don't pay back evil for evil. *Be concerned with things that everybody considers noble.*[56] 18 As much as you can, live in peace with everybody. 19 Don't take revenge, dear friends, but let God punish, because the Bible says, *I alone have the right to avenge. I will pay back,*[57] says the Lord. 20 No, *if your enemy is hungry, feed him. If he is thirsty, give him a drink. If you do this, you'll heap burning coals on his head.*[58] 21 Don't let evil conquer you, but conquer evil with good.

Obey Your Government

13 Everyone should obey the government that is over him, because there is no government except that which is put there by God. God has ordered our government to be over us. 2 Then anyone who is against the government opposes what God has ordered, and those who oppose will be condemned.

3 If you do right, you don't have to be afraid of those who rule, but only if you do wrong. Would you like to live without being afraid of your government? Do what is right, and it will praise you. 4 It is God's servant to help you. If you do wrong, you should be afraid, because the government doesn't carry a sword without a purpose. It is God's servant, an avenger, who must punish anyone doing wrong. 5 You must obey, then, not only because God punishes wrong but also because your conscience tells you to obey.

6 That is why you also pay taxes. Men in the government serve God and are busy doing their work. 7 Pay to all whatever you owe them. If you owe anyone tribute, pay tribute;

[55] Prov. 3:7
[56] Prov. 3:4, Greek
[57] Deut. 32:35
[58] Prov. 25:21-22

K.J.V.

custom; fear to whom fear; honour to whom honour. 8 Owe no man any thing, but to love one another: for he that loveth another hath fulfilled the law. 9 For this, Thou shalt not commit adultery, Thou shalt not kill, Thou shalt not steal, Thou shalt not bear false witness, Thou shalt not covet; and if *there be* any other commandment, it is briefly comprehended in this saying, namely, Thou shalt love thy neighbour as thyself. 10 Love worketh no ill to his neighbour: therefore love *is* the fulfilling of the law. 11 And that, knowing the time, that now *it is* high time to awake out of sleep: for now *is* our salvation nearer than when we believed. 12 The night is far spent, the day is at hand: let us therefore cast off the works of darkness, and let us put on the armour of light. 13 Let us walk honestly, as in the day; not in rioting and drunkenness, not in chambering and wantonness, not in strife and envying: 14 But put ye on the Lord Jesus Christ, and make not provision for the flesh, to *fulfil* the lusts *thereof.*

14 Him that is weak in the faith receive ye, *but* not to doubtful disputations. 2 For one believeth that he may eat all things: another, who is weak, eateth herbs. 3 Let not him that eateth despise him that eateth not; and let not him which eateth not judge him that eateth: for God hath received him. 4 Who art thou that judgest another man's servant? to his own master he standeth or falleth; yea, he shall be holden up: for God is able to make him stand. 5 One man esteemeth one day above another: another esteemeth every day *alike.* Let every man be fully persuaded in his own mind. 6 He that regardeth the day, regardeth *it* unto the Lord; and he that regardeth not the day, to the Lord he doth not regard *it.* He that eateth, eateth to the Lord, for he giveth God thanks; and he that eateth not, to the Lord he eateth not, and giveth God thanks. 7 For none of us liveth to himself, and no man dieth to himself. 8 For whether we live, we live unto the Lord; and whether we die, we die unto the Lord: whether we live therefore, or die, we are the Lord's. 9 For to this end Christ both died, and rose, and revived, that he might be Lord both of the dead and living. 10 But why dost thou judge thy brother? or why dost thou set at nought thy brother? for we shall all stand before the judgment seat of Christ. 11 For it is written, *As I* live, saith the Lord, every knee shall bow to me, and every tongue shall confess to God. 12 So then every one of us shall give account of himself to God. 13 Let us not therefore judge

N.A.S.

custom; fear to whom fear; honor to whom honor.

8 Owe nothing to anyone except to love one another; for he who loves his neighbor has fulfilled *the* law. 9 For this, "YOU SHALL NOT COMMIT ADULTERY, YOU SHALL NOT MURDER, YOU SHALL NOT STEAL, YOU SHALL NOT COVET," and if there is any other commandment, it is summed up in this saying, "YOU SHALL LOVE YOUR NEIGHBOR AS YOURSELF." 10 Love does no wrong to a neighbor; love therefore is the fulfillment of *the* law.

11 And this *do,* knowing the time, that it is already the hour for you to awaken from sleep; for now [a]salvation is nearer to us than when we believed. 12 The night is almost gone, and the day is at hand. Let us therefore lay aside the deeds of darkness and put on the armor of light. 13 Let us behave properly as in the day, not in carousing and drunkenness, not in sexual promiscuity and sensuality, not in strife and jealousy. 14 But put on the Lord Jesus Christ, and make no provision for the flesh in regard to *its* lusts.

14 Now accept the one who is weak in faith, *but* not for *the purpose of* passing judgment on his opinions. 2 One man has faith that he may eat all things, but he who is weak eats vegetables *only.* 3 Let not him who eats regard with contempt him who does not eat, and let not him who does not eat judge him who eats, for God has accepted him. 4 Who are you to judge the servant of another? To his own master he stands or falls; and stand he will, for the Lord is able to make him stand. 5 One man regards one day above another, another regards every day *alike.* Let each man be fully convinced in his own mind. 6 He who observes the day, observes it for the Lord, and he who eats, does so for the Lord, for he gives thanks to God; and he who eats not, for the Lord he does not eat, and gives thanks to God. 7 For not one of us lives for himself, and not one dies for himself; 8 for if we live, we live for the Lord, or if we die, we die for the Lord; therefore whether we live or die, we are the Lord's. 9 For to this end Christ died and lived *again,* that He might be Lord both of the dead and of the living. 10 But you, why do you judge your brother? Or you again, why do you regard your brother with contempt? For we shall all stand before the judgment-seat of God. 11 For it is written,
"AS I LIVE, SAYS THE LORD, EVERY KNEE
    SHALL BOW TO ME,
AND EVERY TONGUE SHALL GIVE PRAISE TO
    GOD."
12 So then each one of us shall give account of himself to God.

13 Therefore let us not judge one another any

[a] Or, *our salvation is nearer than when . . .*

WILLIAMS

to receive it, taxes to the officer to receive them, respect to the man entitled to it, and honor to the man entitled to it.

8 Stop owing anybody anything, except the obligation to love one another, for whoever practices loving others has perfectly satisfied the law. 9 For the commandments, "You must not commit adultery, You must not murder, You must not steal, You must not have an evil desire," and any other commandment if there is any, are summed up in this command, "You must love your neighbor as you do yourself." 10 Love never does a wrong to one's neighbor; so love is the perfect satisfaction of the law.

11 Do this in particular because you know the present crisis, that it is high time for you to wake up out of your sleep, for our salvation is now nearer to us than when we first believed. 12 The night has almost passed; the day is at hand. So let us put aside the deeds of darkness, and put on the weapons of light. 13 Let us live becomingly for people who are in the light of day, not in carousing and drunkenness, nor in sexual immorality and licentiousness, nor in quarreling and jealousy. 14 Instead, put on the Lord Jesus Christ, and put a stop to gratifying the evil desires that lurk in your lower nature.

14 *As we have conscientious differences of opinion on minor matters, we must put the law of brotherly love above our personal freedom and refrain from doing many things, not wrong in themselves, if they hurt others*

Make it your practice to receive into full Christian fellowship people who are overscrupulous, but not to criticize their views. 2 One man believes that he can eat anything, another who is overscrupulous eats nothing but vegetables. 3 The man who eats anything must not look down on the man who does not do so, nor must the man who does not do so condemn the man who does, for God has fully accepted him. 4 Who are you to criticize another man's servant? It is his own master's business whether he stands or falls, and he will stand, for the Lord has power to make him stand. 5 One man rates one day above another, another rates them all alike. Let every man be fully convinced in his own mind. 6 The man who keeps a certain day keeps it for the Lord. The man who eats anything does it for the Lord too, for he gives God thanks. The man who refuses to eat anything does it for the Lord too, and gives God thanks.

7 For none of us can live alone by himself, and none of us can die alone by himself; 8 indeed, if we live, we always live in relation to the Lord, and if we die, we always die in relation to the Lord. So whether we live or die we belong to the Lord. 9 For Christ died and lived again for the very purpose of being Lord of both the dead and the living. 10 Then why should you criticize your brother? Or, why should you look down on your brother? Surely, we shall all stand before God to be judged, 11 for the Scripture says:

    " 'As surely as I live,' says the Lord, 'every
        knee shall bend before me,
    And every tongue shall make acknowledgment
        to God.' "

12 So each of us must give an account of himself to God.

13 Then let us stop criticizing one another;

BECK

if taxes, then taxes; if respect, then respect; if honor, then honor.

Love One Another

8 Don't owe anybody anything but to love one another. If you love the other person, you have kept the Law. 9 The commandments— *don't commit adultery, don't kill, don't steal, don't be greedy*[59]—and any others are summed up in this: *Love your neighbor like yourself.*[60] 10 Love does no wrong to another person. So by love you keep the Law in every way.

11 Do this especially since you know the time we're living in. It's time now for you to wake up from sleep because we are now nearer being rescued than when we first believed. 12 The night is almost over, and the day is dawning. Then let us put away the works of darkness and put on the armor of light. 13 Let us live nobly as in the daytime, not carousing or getting drunk, not sinning sexually or living wild, not quarreling or being jealous. 14 But put on the Lord Jesus Christ, and don't plan to have your fleshly desires aroused.

Weak Christians

14 Welcome a man who is weak in his faith and not just to argue about different opinions. 2 One person believes he can eat anything, but a weak Christian eats only vegetables. 3 If you eat, don't despise anyone who doesn't eat, and if you don't eat, don't criticize anyone who eats, because God has accepted him. 4 Who are you to criticize Someone else's servant? He belongs to the Lord, who is concerned whether he succeeds or fails. And he will succeed, because the Lord can make him succeed.

5 One man thinks one day is better than the other; another thinks they're all alike. Everyone should be thoroughly convinced in his own mind. 6 He who has a special day means to honor the Lord. He who eats does it for the Lord since he thanks God. And he who keeps from eating does it for the Lord, and he thanks God. 7 None of us lives for himself, and none dies for himself. 8 If we live, we live for the Lord; and if we die, we die for the Lord. So whether we live or die, we belong to the Lord. 9 Christ died and became alive again to be Lord of the dead and the living.

10 I ask one of you, "Why do you criticize your fellow Christian?" Or another, "Why do you despise your fellow Christian?" We must all stand before God to be judged. 11 It is written, *"As sure as I live,"* says the Lord,[61] *"everyone will kneel to Me, and every tongue will praise God."* [62] 12 So each of us will have to give an account of himself to God.

13 Then let us stop criticizing one another.

[59] Ex. 20:13-15, 17; Deut. 5:17-19, 21
[60] Lev. 19:18
[61] Is. 49:18
[62] Is. 45:23-24

K.J.V.

one another any more: but judge this rather, that no man put a stumblingblock or an occasion to fall in *his* brother's way. 14 I know, and am persuaded by the Lord Jesus, that *there is* nothing unclean of itself: but to him that esteemeth any thing to be unclean, to him *it is* unclean. 15 But if thy brother be grieved with *thy* meat, now walkest thou not charitably. Destroy not him with thy meat, for whom Christ died. 16 Let not then your good be evil spoken of: 17 For the kingdom of God is not meat and drink; but righteousness, and peace, and joy in the Holy Ghost. 18 For he that in these things serveth Christ *is* acceptable to God, and approved of men. 19 Let us therefore follow after the things which make for peace, and things wherewith one may edify another. 20 For meat destroy not the work of God. All things indeed *are* pure; but *it is* evil for that man who eateth with offence. 21 *It is* good neither to eat flesh, nor to drink wine, nor *any thing* whereby thy brother stumbleth, or is offended, or is made weak. 22 Hast thou faith? have *it* to thyself before God. Happy *is* he that condemneth not himself in that thing which he alloweth. 23And he that doubteth is damned if he eat, because *he eateth* not of faith: for whatsoever *is* not of faith is sin.

15 We then that are strong ought to bear the infirmities of the weak, and not to please ourselves. 2 Let every one of us please *his* neighbour for *his* good to edification. 3 For even Christ pleased not himself; but, as it is written, The reproaches of them that reproached thee fell on me. 4 For whatsoever things were written aforetime were written for our learning, that we through patience and comfort of the Scriptures might have hope. 5 Now the God of patience and consolation grant you to be likeminded one toward another according to Christ Jesus: 6 That ye may with one mind *and* one mouth glorify God, even the Father of our Lord Jesus Christ. 7 Wherefore receive ye one another, as Christ also received us, to the glory of God. 8 Now I say that Jesus Christ was a minister of the circumcision for the truth of God, to confirm the promises *made* unto the fathers: 9And that the Gentiles might glorify God for *his* mercy; as it is written, For this cause I will confess to thee among the Gentiles, and sing unto thy name. 10And again he saith, Rejoice, ye Gentiles, with his people. 11And

N.A.S.

more, but rather determine this—not to put an obstacle or a stumbling-block in a brother's way. 14 I know and am convinced in the Lord Jesus that nothing is unclean in itself; but to him who thinks anything to be unclean, to him it is unclean. 15 For if because of food your brother is hurt, you are no longer walking according to love. Do not destroy with your food him for whom Christ died. 16 Therefore do not let what is for you a good thing be spoken of as evil; 17 for the kingdom of God is not eating and drinking, but righteousness and peace and joy in the Holy Spirit. 18 For he who in this *way* serves Christ is acceptable to God and approved by men. 19 So then ª let us pursue the things which make for peace and the building up of one another. 20 Do not tear down the work of God for the sake of food. All things indeed are clean, but they are evil for the man who eats and gives offense. 21 It is good not to eat meat or to drink wine, or *to do anything* by which your brother stumbles. 22 The faith which you have, have as your own conviction before God. Happy is he who does not condemn himself in what he approves. 23 But he who doubts is condemned if he eats, because *his eating is* not from faith; and whatever is not from faith is sin.

15 Now we who are strong ought to bear the weaknesses of those without strength and not *just* please ourselves. 2 Let each of us please his neighbor for his good, to his edification. 3 For even Christ did not please Himself; but as it is written, "THE REPROACHES OF THOSE WHO REPROACHED THEE FELL UPON ME." 4 For whatever was written in earlier times was written for our instruction, that through perseverance and the encouragement of the Scriptures we might have hope. 5 Now may the God who gives perseverance and encouragement grant you to be of the same mind with one another according to Christ Jesus; 6 that with one accord you may with one voice glorify the God and Father of our Lord Jesus Christ.

7 Wherefore, accept one another, just as Christ also accepted us to the glory of God. 8 For I say that Christ has become a servant to the circumcision on behalf of the truth of God to confirm the promises *given* to the fathers, 9 and for the Gentiles to glorify God for His mercy; as it is written,

"THEREFORE I WILL GIVE PRAISE TO THEE
　AMONG THE GENTILES,
AND I WILL SING TO THY NAME."
10And again he says,
"REJOICE, O GENTILES, WITH HIS PEOPLE."
11And again,

[a] Many ancient mss. read, *we pursue.*

WILLIAMS

instead, do this, determine to stop putting stumbling blocks or hindrances in your brother's way. 14 I know, and through my union with the Lord Jesus I have a clear conviction, that nothing is unclean in itself; that a thing is unclean only to the person who thinks it unclean. 15 For if your brother is hurt because of the food you eat, you are not living by the standard of love. Stop ruining, by what you eat, the man for whom Christ died. 16 Then stop abusing your rights. 17 For the kingdom of God does not consist in what we eat and drink, but in doing right, in peace and joy through the Holy Spirit; 18 whoever in this way continues serving Christ is well-pleasing to God and approved by men. 19 So let us keep on pursuing the things that make for peace and our mutual upbuilding. 20 Stop undoing the work of God just for the sake of food. Everything is clean, but it is wrong for a man to eat anything when it makes another stumble. 21 The right thing to do is not to eat meat, or drink wine, or do anything else, that makes your brother stumble. 22 On your part, you must exercise your faith by the standard of yourself in the sight of God. Happy is the man who need not condemn himself for doing the thing that he approves. 23 But the man who has misgivings about eating, if he then eats, has already condemned himself by so doing, because he did not follow his faith, and any action that does not follow one's faith is a sin.

15 *The strong to bear with the weaknesses of the weak; to please others as Christ did; Christ welcomes Hebrews and heathen alike; to pray for joy, peace, and hope; personal matters and requests*

It is the duty of us who are strong to bear with the weaknesses of those who are not strong, and not merely to please ourselves. 2 Each one of us must practice pleasing his neighbor, to help in his immediate upbuilding for his eternal good. 3 Christ certainly did not please Himself; instead, as the Scripture says, "The reproaches of those who reproach you have fallen upon me." 4 For everything that was written in the earlier times was written for our instruction, so that by our patient endurance and through the encouragement the Scriptures bring we might continuously cherish our hope. 5 May God, who gives men patient endurance and encouragement, grant you such harmony with one another, in accordance with the standard which Christ Jesus sets, 6 that with united hearts and lips you may praise the God and Father of our Lord Jesus Christ.

7 Therefore, practice receiving one another into full Christian fellowship, just as Christ has so received you to Himself. 8 Yes, I mean that Christ has become a servant to Israel to prove God's truthfulness, to make valid His promises to our forefathers, 9 and for the heathen peoples to praise God for His mercy, as the Scripture says:
"For this I will give thanks to you among
    the heathen,
And will sing praises to your name."
10 And again:
"Rejoice, you heathen peoples, with His
    people!"
11 And again:

BECK

But instead decide not to lay any stumbling block or trap in the way of a fellow Christian. 14 I know and am convinced in the Lord Jesus nothing is unclean in itself. Anything is unclean only to him who thinks it is unclean. 15 But if what you eat hurts your fellow Christian, you're not living according to love anymore. By what you eat don't ruin him for whom Christ died. 16 You have something good that nobody should say anything bad about. 17 God's kingdom is not eating and drinking but righteousness, peace, and joy in the Holy Spirit. 18 If you serve Christ in this way, God is pleased with you, and people approve of you.

19 So we eagerly go after the things which mean peace and by which we help one another grow. 20 Don't ruin God's work just for food. Everything is clean, but it's wrong for you to eat if it makes someone stumble. 21 It is good not to eat meat, drink wine, or do anything else that makes your fellow Christian stumble, sin, or be weak in faith. 22 The faith you have, have it between yourself and God. Happy are you if you never have to condemn yourself in regard to anything you approve. 23 If anyone doubts and still eats, he is condemned because he doesn't go by what he believes. Anything that is not an act of faith is sin.

15 But we who are strong must be patient with the weaknesses of the weak and not just please ourselves. 2 Every one of us should please his neighbor for his good, to help him grow. 3 Even Christ didn't please Himself, but it happened to Him as it is written, *Those who insult You insult Me.*[63]

Jews and Non-Jews

4 All that was written long ago was written to teach us by the endurance and encouragement we get from the Bible to have hope. 5 May God, who helps you to endure and encourages you, give you such harmony with one another as you follow Christ Jesus 6 that together with one voice you praise the God and Father of our Lord Jesus Christ.

7 Then, as Christ has welcomed you, welcome one another in order to glorify God. 8 I tell you Christ became a servant to the Jews to do what God promised the fathers—showing that He tells the truth— 9 and to have the other nations praise God for His mercy, as it is written,

*For this I will praise You among the nations
And sing to honor Your name.*[64]

10 And again,

*Be happy, you other nations, with His own
    people!*[65]

11 And again,

[63] Ps. 69:9
[64] 2 Sam. 22:50; Ps. 18:49
[65] Deut. 32:43

K.J.V.

again, Praise the Lord, all ye Gentiles; and laud him, all ye people. 12And again, Esaias saith, There shall be a root of Jesse, and he that shall rise to reign over the Gentiles; in him shall the Gentiles trust. 13 Now the God of hope fill you with all joy and peace in believing, that ye may abound in hope, through the power of the Holy Ghost. 14And I myself also am persuaded of you, my brethren, that ye also are full of goodness, filled with all knowledge, able also to admonish one another. 15 Nevertheless, brethren, I have written the more boldly unto you in some sort, as putting you in mind, because of the grace that is given to me of God, 16 That I should be the minister of Jesus Christ to the Gentiles, ministering the gospel of God, that the offering up of the Gentiles might be acceptable, being sanctified by the Holy Ghost. 17 I have therefore whereof I may glory through Jesus Christ in those things which pertain to God. 18 For I will not dare to speak of any of those things which Christ hath not wrought by me, to make the Gentiles obedient, by word and deed, 19 Through mighty signs and wonders, by the power of the Spirit of God; so that from Jerusalem, and round about unto Illyricum, I have fully preached the gospel of Christ. 20 Yea, so have I strived to preach the gospel, not where Christ was named, lest I should build upon another man's foundation: 21 But as it is written, To whom he was not spoken of, they shall see: and they that have not heard shall understand. 22 For which cause also I have been much hindered from coming to you. 23 But now having no more place in these parts, and having a great desire these many years to come unto you; 24 Whensoever I take my journey into Spain, I will come to you: for I trust to see you in my journey, and to be brought on my way thitherward by you, if first I be somewhat filled with your *company*. 25 But now I go unto Jerusalem to minister unto the saints. 26 For it hath pleased them of Macedonia and Achaia to make a certain contribution for the poor saints which are at Jerusalem. 27 It hath pleased them verily; and their debtors they are. For if the Gentiles have been made partakers of their spiritual things, their duty is also to minister unto them in carnal things. 28 When therefore I have performed this, and have sealed to them this fruit, I will come by you into Spain. 29And I am sure that, when I come unto you, I shall come in the fullness of the blessing of the gospel of Christ. 30 Now I beseech you, brethren, for the Lord Jesus Christ's sake, and for the love of the Spirit, that ye strive together with me in *your* prayers to God for me; 31 That I may be delivered from them that do not believe in Judea; and that my service which *I have* for Jerusalem may be accepted of the saints; 32 That I may come unto you with joy by the will of God, and may with you be refreshed. 33 Now the God of peace *be* with you all Amen.

N.A.S.

"PRAISE THE LORD ALL YOU GENTILES,
AND LET ALL THE PEOPLES PRAISE HIM."
12And again Isaiah says,
"THERE SHALL COME THE ROOT OF JESSE,
AND HE WHO ARISES TO RULE OVER THE GENTILES;
IN HIM SHALL THE GENTILES HOPE."
13 Now may the God of hope fill you with all joy and peace in believing, that you may abound in hope by the power of the Holy Spirit.

14 And concerning you, my brethren, I myself also am convinced that you yourselves are full of goodness, filled with all knowledge, and able also to admonish one another. 15 But I have written very boldly to you on some points, so as to remind you again, because of the grace that was given me from God, 16 to be a minister of Christ Jesus to the Gentiles, ministering as a priest the gospel of God, that *my* offering of the Gentiles might become acceptable, sanctified by the Holy Spirit. 17 Therefore in Christ Jesus I have found reason for boasting in things pertaining to God. 18 For I will not presume to speak of anything except what Christ has accomplished through me, resulting in the obedience of the Gentiles by word and deed, 19 in the power of signs and wonders, in the power of the Spirit; so that from Jerusalem and round about as far as Illyricum I have fully preached the gospel of Christ. 20And thus I aspired to preach the gospel, not where Christ was *already* named, that I might not build upon another man's foundation; 21 but as it is written,

"THEY WHO HAD NO NEWS OF HIM SHALL SEE,
AND THEY WHO HAVE NOT HEARD SHALL UNDERSTAND."

22 For this reason I have often been hindered from coming to you; 23 but now, with no further place for me in these regions, and since I have had for many years a longing to come to you 24 whenever I go to Spain—for I hope to see you in passing, and to be helped on my way there by you, when I have first enjoyed your company for awhile— 25 but now, I am going to Jerusalem serving the saints. 26 For Macedonia and Achaia have been pleased to make a contribution for the poor among the saints in Jerusalem. 27 Yes, they were pleased *to do so,* and they are indebted to them. For if the Gentiles have shared in their spiritual things, they are indebted to minister to them also in material things. 28 Therefore, when I have finished this, and have put my seal on this fruit of theirs, I will go on by way of you to Spain. 29And I know that when I come to you, I will come in the fulness of the blessing of Christ.

30 Now I urge you, brethren, by our Lord Jesus Christ and by the love of the Spirit to strive together with me in your prayers to God for me, 31 that I may be delivered from those who are disobedient in Judea, and *that* my service for Jerusalem may prove acceptable to the saints; 32 so that I may come to you in joy by the will of God and find *refreshing* rest in your company. 33 Now the God of peace be with you all. Amen.

WILLIAMS

"All you heathen peoples, praise the Lord,
Yea, let all peoples sing His praise."
12 And again Isaiah says:
"The noted Son of Jesse will come,
Even He who rises to rule the heathen;
On Him the heathen will set their hope."
13 May the hope-inspiring God so fill you with
perfect joy and peace through your continuing
faith, that you may bubble over with hope by
the power of the Holy Spirit.

14 As far as I am concerned about you, my
brothers, I am convinced that you especially are
abounding in the highest goodness, richly supplied with perfect knowledge and competent to
counsel one another. 15 And yet, to refresh your
memories, I have written you rather freely on
some details, because of the unmerited favor
shown me by God 16 in making me a minister
of Christ Jesus to the heathen peoples, to have
me act as a sacrificing minister of the good news,
in order that my offering of the heathen peoples
to God may be acceptable, consecrated by the
Holy Spirit. 17 So, as a Christian, I am proud [a]
of the things that I have done for God. 18 For
I would venture to mention only what Christ
has accomplished through me in bringing the
heathen peoples to obedience, by word and by
work, 19 by the power of signs and wonders, by
the power of the Holy Spirit. So I have completed the telling of the good news of Christ all
the way from Jerusalem around to Illyricum.
20 In this matter it has ever been my ambition
to tell the good news where Christ's name had
never been mentioned, so as not to build upon
foundations laid by other men, 21 but, as the
Scripture says:
"They will see who were never told of Him,
And they will understand who have not
heard."
22 This is the reason why I have so often
been prevented from coming to see you. 23 But
now, as there are no more places for me to
occupy in this part of the world, and as I have
for many years been longing to come to see
you, 24 when I make my trip to Spain, I certainly hope to see you on my way there and to
be helped forward by you, after I have enjoyed
being with you awhile. 25 But just now I am
on my way to Jerusalem to help God's people.
26 For Macedonia and Greece were delighted to
make a contribution to the poor among God's
people in Jerusalem. 27 They certainly were delighted to do it, and they really are under obligation to them, for if the heathen peoples have
shared in their spiritual blessings, they ought to
serve them in material blessings. 28 So, after I
have finished this matter and made sure of the
results of this contribution for them, I shall come
by you on my way to Spain. 29 And I feel sure
that when I do come to you, I shall come with
Christ's abundant blessing on me.

30 Now I beg you, brothers, for the sake of
our Lord Jesus Christ and by the love that the
Spirit inspires, to wrestle with me in prayers
to God on my behalf, 31 that I may be delivered
from those in Judea who are disobedient, and
that the help which I am taking to Jerusalem
may be well received by God's people there, 32 so
that, if it is God's will, I may come with a
happy heart to see you and have a refreshing
rest while with you. 33 The peace-giving God be
with you all! Amen.

BECK

All you nations, praise the Lord,
And all the people should praise Him.[66]

12 Again, Isaiah says,

Jesse will have the Descendant
Who will rise to rule the nations,
And He will be the hope of the nations.[67]

13 The God of hope fill you with perfect
happiness and peace as you believe, to make
you overflow with hope by the power of the
Holy Spirit.

New Fields

14 I am convinced, my fellow Christians,
you are full of kindness, fully equipped with
every kind of knowledge, and able to correct
one another. 15 Just to remind you, I have
written you a letter, part of which is rather bold
because God has by a special gift of His love
16 made me a servant of Christ Jesus among
the non-Jewish nations, to work for God's good
news as a priest and to bring the nations as an
offering made holy by the Holy Spirit and
accepted by God. 17 So I can in Christ Jesus
be proud of what I'm doing before God 18 because I'll dare to tell only what Christ has done
through me to make the nations obedient, by
my speaking and working, 19 by the power to
do miracles and wonders, by the power of God's
Spirit, so that I have finished telling the good
news of Christ all the way from Jerusalem as
far around as Illyricum.
20 But I was ambitious to tell the good news
only where Christ's name wasn't known, so as
not to build on any foundation others had laid,
21 but as it is written,

Those who were never told about Him will
see,
And those who never heard will understand.[68]

I Hope to See You

22 That is why I have so often been kept
from coming to you. 23 But now there is in
this territory no more opportunity for me to
work, and for many years I have longed to
come to you 24 on my way to Spain. I hope to
see you when I pass through and after I have
enjoyed being with you for a while to have you
send me on my way there.
25 Right now I am going to Jerusalem to
bring help to the holy people there. 26 You see,
Macedonia and Greece decided to share their
goods with the poor among the holy people in
Jerusalem. 27 So they decided, and they really
owe something to the Jews. If the Jews have
shared their spiritual goods with the non-Jews,
the non-Jews owe it to them to serve them with
their earthly goods. 28 When that is done and
I've brought them this contribution with my
seal on it, I will come to you on my way to
Spain. 29 I know when I come to you I'll bring
a full blessing of Christ.
30 By our Lord Jesus Christ and the love
we have from the Spirit I urge you to join
me in my struggle by praying for me to God
31 to rescue me from those in Judea who refuse to believe and to have the holy people in
Jerusalem welcome the help I bring 32 so that
by God's will I'll come to you with joy and be
refreshed with you.
33 The God of peace be with you all. Amen.

[66] Ps. 117:1
[67] Is. 11:1, 10
[68] Is. 52:15

[a] Lit., I am boasting in Christ.

K.J.V.

16 I commend unto you Phebe our sister, which is a servant of the church which is at Cenchrea: 2 That ye receive her in the Lord, as becometh saints, and that ye assist her in whatsoever business she hath need of you: for she hath been a succourer of many, and of myself also. 3 Greet Priscilla and Aquila, my helpers in Christ Jesus: 4 Who have for my life laid down their own necks: unto whom not only I give thanks, but also all the churches of the Gentiles. 5 Likewise *greet* the church that is in their house. Salute my well beloved Epenetus, who is the firstfruits of Achaia unto Christ. 6 Greet Mary, who bestowed much labour on us. 7 Salute Andronicus and Junia, my kinsmen, and my fellow prisoners, who are of note among the apostles, who also were in Christ before me. 8 Greet Amplias, my beloved in the Lord. 9 Salute Urbane, our helper in Christ, and Stachys my beloved. 10 Salute Apelles approved in Christ. Salute them which are of Aristobulus' *household.* 11 Salute Herodion my kinsman. Greet them that be of the *household* of Narcissus, which are in the Lord. 12 Salute Tryphena and Tryphosa, who labour in the Lord. Salute the beloved Persis, which laboured much in the Lord. 13 Salute Rufus chosen in the Lord, and his mother and mine. 14 Salute Asyncritus, Phlegon, Hermas, Patrobas, Hermes, and the brethren which are with them. 15 Salute Philologus, and Julia, Nereus, and his sister, and Olympas, and all the saints which are with them. 16 Salute one another with a holy kiss. The churches of Christ salute you. 17 Now I beseech you, brethren, mark them which cause divisions and offences contrary to the doctrine which ye have learned; and avoid them. 18 For they that are such serve not our Lord Jesus Christ, but their own belly; and by good words and fair speeches deceive the hearts of the simple. 19 For your obedience is come abroad unto all *men.* I am glad therefore on your behalf: but yet I would have you wise unto that which is good, and simple concerning evil. 20 And the God of peace shall bruise Satan under your feet shortly. The grace of our Lord Jesus Christ *be* with you. Amen. 21 Timotheus my workfellow, and Lucius, and Jason, and Sosipater, my kinsmen, salute you. 22 I Tertius, who wrote *this* epistle, salute you in the Lord. 23 Gaius mine host, and of the whole church, saluteth you. Erastus the chamberlain of the city saluteth you, and Quartus a brother. 24 The grace of our Lord

N.A.S.

16 I commend to you our sister Phoebe, who is a servant of the church which is at Cenchrea; 2 that you receive her in the Lord in a manner worthy of the saints, and that you help her in whatever matter she may have need of you; for she herself has also been a helper of many, and of myself as well.

3 Greet Prisca and Aquila my fellow-workers in Christ Jesus, 4 who for my life risked their own necks, to whom not only do I give thanks, but also all the churches of the Gentiles; 5 also *greet* the church that is in their house. Greet Epaenetus my beloved, who is the first convert to Christ from Asia. 6 Greet Mary, who has worked hard for you. 7 Greet Andronicus and Junias, my kinsmen, and my fellow-prisoners, who are outstanding among the apostles, who also were in Christ before me. 8 Greet Ampliatus my beloved in the Lord. 9 Greet Urbanus our fellow-worker in Christ, and Stachys my beloved. 10 Greet Apelles the approved in Christ. Greet those who are of the *household* of Aristobulus. 11 Greet Herodion my kinsman. Greet those of the *household* of Narcissus, who are in the Lord. 12 Greet Tryphaena and Tryphosa, workers in the Lord. Greet Persis the beloved, who has worked hard in the Lord. 13 Greet Rufus, a choice man in the Lord, also his mother and mine. 14 Greet Asyncritus, Phlegon, Hermas, Patrobas, Hermes and the brethren with them. 15 Greet Philologus and Julia, Nereus and his sister, and Olympas, and all the saints who are with them. 16 Greet one another with a holy kiss. All the churches of Christ greet you.

17 Now I urge you, brethren, keep your eye on those who cause dissensions and hindrances contrary to the teaching which you learned, and turn away from them. 18 For such men are slaves not of our Lord Christ but of their own appetites; and by their smooth and flattering speech they deceive the hearts of the unsuspecting. 19 For the report of your obedience has reached to all; therefore I am rejoicing over you, but I want you to be wise in what is good, and innocent in what is evil. 20 And the God of peace will soon crush Satan under your feet.

The grace of our Lord Jesus be with you.

21 Timothy my fellow-worker greets you; and *so do* Lucius and Jason and Sosipater, my kinsmen. 22 I, Tertius, who write this letter, greet you in the Lord. 23 Gaius, host to me and to the whole church, greets you. Erastus, the city-treasurer greets you, and Quartus, the brother. 24 (See footnote [a])

[a] Some ancient mss. add vs. 24, *The grace of our Lord Jesus Christ be with you all. Amen.*

WILLIAMS   BECK

16 *Phoebe the bearer of the letter introduced; Paul asks to be remembered to friends in Rome; his friends also wish to be remembered to them; he warns against troublemakers in the church, gives praise to God*

Now I introduce[a] to you our sister Phoebe, who is a deaconess in the church at Cenchreae, 2 that you may give her a Christian welcome in a manner becoming God's people, and give her whatever help she needs from you, for she herself has given protection to many, including myself.

3 Remember me to Prisca and Aquila, my fellow-workers in the work of Christ Jesus, 4 who once risked their very necks for my life. I am so thankful to them; not only I but also all the churches among the heathen thank them. 5 Remember me to the church too, that meets at their house. Remember me to my dear Epaenetus, who was the first convert[b] to Christ in the province of Asia. 6 Remember me to Mary, who has toiled so hard for you. 7 Remember me to Andronicus and Junias, my fellow-countrymen, who also served in prison with me; they are held in high esteem among the apostles, and became Christians before I did. 8 Remember me to Ampliatus, my dear Christian friend. 9 Remember me to Urbanus, my fellow-worker in the work of Christ, and to my dear friend Stachys. 10 Remember me to Apelles, that most venerated Christian. Remember me to the members of Aristobulus' family. 11 Remember me to Herodion, my fellow-countryman. Remember me to the Christian members of Narcissus' family. 12 Remember me to Tryphaena and Tryphosa, who continued to toil in the work of the Lord. Remember me to my dear friend Persis, who toiled so hard in the work of the Lord. 13 Remember me to Rufus, that choicest Christian, and to his mother, who has been a mother to me too. 14 Remember me to Asyncritus, Phlegon, Hermes, Patrobas, Hermas, and the brothers who are associated with them. 15 Remember me to Philologus and Julia, to Nereus and his sister, and to Olympas, and all God's people who are associated with them. 16 Greet one another with a consecrated kiss. All the churches of Christ wish to be remembered to you.

17 But I beg you, brothers, to keep on the lookout for those who stir up divisions and put hindrances in your way, in opposition to the instruction that you had, and always avoid them. 18 For such men are really not serving our Lord Christ but their own base appetites, and by their fair and flattering talk they are deceiving the hearts of unsuspecting people. 19 Yes, your obedience has been told to everybody; so I am delighted about you, but I want you to be wise about what is good and innocent about what is bad. 20 Now the peace-giving God will soon crush Satan under your feet. The spiritual blessing of our Lord Jesus be with you.

21 Timothy, my fellow-worker, wishes to be remembered to you; so do Lucius, Jason, and Sosipater too, my fellow-countrymen. 22 I, Tertius, who write this letter, wish to be remembered to you as a fellow-Christian. 23 Gaius, my host, and host of the whole church here, wishes to be remembered to you. Erastus, the treasurer of the city, wishes to be remembered to you, and so does our brother Quartus.[c]

[a] Grk., *commend.* [b] Lit., *first fruits.* [c] V. 24 not in best Mss.

16 I'm introducing Phoebe, our fellow Christian, to you. She is a worker in the church in Cenchreae. 2 Welcome her in the Lord as holy people should, and give her any help she may need from you, because she has become a protector of many, including me.

3 Greet Prisca and Aquila, my fellow workers in Christ Jesus, 4 who risked their necks to save my life. Not only I but all the churches among the non-Jews are thanking them. 5 Greet also the church that meets at their home.

Greet my dear Epaenetus, who was the first in the province of Asia to turn to Christ. 6 Greet Mary, who has worked very hard for you. 7 Greet Andronicus and Junias, my fellow Jews, who went to prison with me. They are outstanding among the apostles. They also came to Christ before I did. 8 Greet Ampliatus, who is dear to me in the Lord. 9 Greet Urban, our fellow worker in Christ, and my dear Stachys. 10 Greet Apelles, a veteran in Christ.

Greet those who belong to the family of Aristobulus. 11 Greet Herodian, my fellow Jew.

Greet those in the family of Narcissus who are in the Lord. 12 Greet Tryphaena and Tryphosa, who have worked hard for the Lord.

Greet dear Persis, who has worked very hard for the Lord. 13 Greet Rufus, the chosen one in the Lord, and his mother—who has been a mother to me too. 14 Greet Asyncritus, Phlegon, Hermes, Patrobas, Hermas, and the fellow Christians who are with them. 15 Greet Philologus, Julia, Nereus, and his sister, and Olympas, and all the holy people who are with them.

16 Greet one another with a holy kiss. All the churches of Christ greet you.

17 I urge you, fellow Christians, to watch those who cause disagreements and make people fall by going against the teaching you learned. Turn away from them. 18 Such men are not serving Christ, our Lord, but their own bellies and by their fine and flattering talk are deceiving innocent people. 19 Everybody has heard how you obey, and so I'm happy about you. I want you to be wise for anything good, and too innocent for anything bad.—20 The God of peace will soon crush the devil under your feet.

The love of our Lord Jesus be with you!

21 Timothy, my fellow worker, greets you; so do Lucius, Jason, and Sosipater, my fellow Jews.

22 I, Tertius, who wrote this letter, greet you in the Lord.

23 Gaius, my host and the host of the whole church, greets you. Erastus, the city treasurer, greets you, and Quartus, our fellow Christian.*

* Our oldest manuscripts, including Papyrus 46, do not have v. 24: "The love of our Lord Jesus (Christ) be with you all. Amen." They have most of these words at the end of v. 20.

K.J.V.

Jesus Christ *be* with you all. Amen. 25 Now to him that is of power to stablish you according to my gospel, and the preaching of Jesus Christ, according to the revelation of the mystery, which was kept secret since the world began, 26 But now is made manifest, and by the Scriptures of the prophets, according to the commandment of the everlasting God, made known to all nations for the obedience of faith: 27 To God only wise, *be* glory through Jesus Christ for ever. Amen.

Written to the Romans from Corinthus, *and sent* by Phebe servant of the church at Cenchrea.

N.A.S.

25 Now to Him who is able to establish you according to my gospel and the preaching of Jesus Christ, according to the revelation of the mystery which has been kept secret for long ages past, 26 but now is manifested, and by the Scriptures of the prophets, according to the commandment of the eternal God, has been made known to all the nations, *leading* to obedience of faith; 27 to the only wise God, through Jesus Christ, to whom be the glory forever. Amen.

WILLIAMS

25 To Him who can make you strong in accordance with the good news I bring and in accordance with the message preached about Jesus Christ, in accordance with the uncovering of the secret which for ages past had not been told, 26 but now has been fully brought to light by means of the prophetic Scriptures, and in accordance with the command of the eternal God has been made known to all the heathen, to win them to obedience inspired by faith—27 to the one wise God be glory forever through Jesus Christ. Amen.

BECK

25 Now, to Him—
who can make you strong by the good news I bring and the preaching of Jesus Christ, by unveiling the mystery veiled in silence for long ages 26 but now brought to light and by the writings of the prophets, as the everlasting God ordered them, shown to all the nations to get them to believe and obey
27—to the only wise God through Jesus Christ be glory forever. Amen.

| K.J.V. | N.A.S. |

THE FIRST EPISTLE OF PAUL THE APOSTLE TO THE CORINTHIANS

THE FIRST EPISTLE OF PAUL TO THE CORINTHIANS

1 Paul, called *to be* an apostle of Jesus Christ through the will of God, and Sosthenes *our* brother, 2 Unto the church of God which is at Corinth, to them that are sanctified in Christ Jesus, called *to be* saints, with all that in every place call upon the name of Jesus Christ our Lord, both theirs and ours: 3 Grace *be* unto you, and peace, from God our Father, and *from* the Lord Jesus Christ. 4 I thank my God always on your behalf, for the grace of God which is given you by Jesus Christ; 5 That in every thing ye are enriched by him, in all utterance, and *in* all knowledge; 6 Even as the testimony of Christ was confirmed in you: 7 So that ye come behind in no gift; waiting for the coming of our Lord Jesus Christ: 8 Who shall also confirm you unto the end, *that he may be* blameless in the day of our Lord Jesus Christ. 9 God *is* faithful, by whom ye were called unto the fellowship of his Son Jesus Christ our Lord. 10 Now I beseech you, brethren, by the name of our Lord Jesus Christ, that ye all speak the same thing, and *that* there be no divisions among you; but *that* ye be perfectly joined together in the same mind and in the same judgment. 11 For it hath been declared unto me of you, my brethren, by them *which are of the house* of Chloe, that there are contentions among you. 12 Now this I say, that every one of you saith, I am of Paul; and I of Apollos; and I of Cephas; and I of Christ. 13 Is Christ divided? was Paul crucified for you? or were ye baptized in the name of Paul? 14 I thank God that I baptized none of you, but Crispus and Gaius; 15 Lest any should say that I had baptized in mine own name. 16 And I baptized also the household of Stephanas: besides, I know not whether I baptized any other. 17 For Christ sent me not to baptize, but to preach the gospel: not with wisdom of words, lest the cross of Christ should be made of none effect. 18 For the preaching of the cross is to them that perish, foolishness; but unto us which are saved, it is the power of God. 19 For it is written, I will

1 Paul, called *as* an apostle of Jesus Christ by the will of God, and Sosthenes our brother, 2 to the church of God which is at Corinth, to those who have been sanctified in Christ Jesus, saints by calling, with all who in every place call upon the name of our Lord Jesus Christ, their *Lord* and ours: 3 Grace to you and peace from God our Father and the Lord Jesus Christ. 4 I thank [a]my God always concerning you, for the grace of God which was given you in Christ Jesus, 5 that in everything you were enriched in Him, in all speech and all knowledge, 6 even as the testimony concerning Christ was confirmed in you, 7 so that you are not lacking in any gift, awaiting eagerly the revelation of our Lord Jesus Christ, 8 who shall also confirm you to the end, blameless in the day of our Lord Jesus Christ. 9 God is faithful, through whom you were called into fellowship with His Son, Jesus Christ our Lord. 10 Now I exhort you, brethren, by the name of our Lord Jesus Christ, that you all agree, and there be no divisions among you, but you be made complete in the same mind and in the same judgment. 11 For I have been informed concerning you, my brethren, by Chloe's *people*, that there are quarrels among you. 12 Now I mean this, that each one of you is saying, "I am of Paul," and "I of Apollos," and "I of Cephas," and "I of Christ." 13 Has Christ been divided? Paul was not crucified for you, was he? Or were you baptized in the name of Paul? 14 [b]I thank God that I baptized none of you, except Crispus and Gaius, 15 that no man should say you were baptized in my name. 16 Now I did baptize also the household of Stephanas; beyond that, I do not know whether I baptized any other. 17 For Christ did not send me to baptize, but to preach the gospel, not in cleverness of speech, that the cross of Christ should not be made void. 18 For the word of the cross is to those who are perishing foolishness, but to us who are being saved it is the power of God. 19 For it is written,

[a] Some ancient mss. omit *my*. [b] Some ancient mss. read, *I give thanks that*.

WILLIAMS

FIRST CORINTHIANS

1 *He greets them; thanks God for their spiritual gifts; pleads for unity in the church; tells how the message of the cross affects the perishing and the saved, Jews and Greeks; tells of their lowly social status*

Paul, by the will of God called as an apostle of Jesus Christ, and our brother Sosthenes, 2 to the church of God at Corinth, to those who are consecrated by union with Christ Jesus, and called to be God's people, in fellowship with those who anywhere call upon the name of Jesus Christ, their Lord and ours: 3 spiritual blessing and peace to you from God our Father and from our Lord Jesus Christ.

4 I am always thanking God for you, for the spiritual blessing given you by God through union with Christ Jesus; 5 because you have in everything been richly blessed through union with Him, with perfect expression and fullness of knowledge. 6 In this way my testimony to Christ has been confirmed in your experience, 7 so that there is no spiritual gift in which you consciously come short, while you are waiting for the unveiling of our Lord Jesus Christ, 8 and to the very end He will guarantee that you are vindicated at the day of our Lord Jesus Christ. 9 God is entirely trustworthy, and it is He through whom you have been called into this fellowship with His Son, Jesus Christ our Lord.

10 Now I beg you all, brothers, for the sake of our Lord Jesus Christ, to be harmonious in what you say and not to have factions among you, but to be perfectly harmonious in your minds and judgments. 11 For I have been informed about you, my brothers, by Chloe's people, that there are wranglings among you. 12 I mean this, that one of you says, "I belong to Paul's party," another, "And I belong to Apollos' party," another, "And I belong to Cephas' party," another, "And I belong to Christ's party." 13 Christ has been parceled out by you! It was not Paul who was crucified for you, was it? You were not baptized in Paul's name, were you? 14 I am thankful that I baptized none of you but Crispus and Gaius, 15 so as to keep anyone from saying that you were baptized in my name. 16 Yes, I did baptize the family of Stephanas, too; I do not now recall that I baptized anyone else. 17 For Christ did not send me to baptize, but to preach the good news—but not by means of wisdom and rhetoric, so that the cross of Christ may not be emptied of its power.

18 For the message of the cross is nonsense to those who are in the process of being destroyed, but it is the power of God to those who are in the process of being saved. 19 For the Scripture says:

BECK

PAUL WRITES THE FIRST LETTER TO THE CORINTHIANS

1 Paul, apostle of Christ Jesus, called by God's will, and Sosthenes, my fellow worker, 2 to God's church in Corinth, made holy by Christ Jesus and called to be holy, with all who anywhere call on the name of our Lord Jesus Christ, their Lord and ours— 3 may God our Father and the Lord Jesus Christ love you and give you peace.

4 I am always thanking God for you, because He has loved you in Christ Jesus 5 and in Him made you rich in every way, in speech and knowledge of every kind, 6 as the truth of Christ we spoke was confirmed in you. 7 And so you don't lack any gift as you eagerly look for our Lord Jesus Christ to appear again. 8 He will strengthen you to the end so that nobody can accuse you of anything on the day of our Lord Jesus Christ. 9 You can depend on God, who called you to the fellowship of His Son Jesus Christ, our Lord.

Everyone for Christ

10 Fellow Christians, by the name of our Lord Jesus Christ I urge you all to agree and not be divided but perfectly united in your understanding and judgment. 11 Chloe's people told me you are quarreling, my fellow Christians. 12 I mean that each of you says, "I belong to Paul," or, "I belong to Apollos," or, "I belong to Peter," or, "I belong to Christ." 13 Is Christ divided? Was Paul crucified for you? Or were you baptized into Paul's name? 14 I thank God I didn't baptize any of you except Crispus and Gaius. 15 Then nobody can say you were baptized into my name. 16 I also baptized the family of Stephanas. I don't know if I baptized anyone else. 17 Christ didn't send me to baptize but to tell the good news; nor to be a clever speaker, or the cross of Christ would lose its power.

God's Foolish Things

18 The story of the cross is something foolish to those who perish, but it is God's power to us who are saved. 19 The Bible says, *I will destroy*

K.J.V.

destroy the wisdom of the wise, and will bring to nothing the understanding of the prudent. 20 Where *is* the wise? where *is* the scribe? where *is* the disputer of this world? hath not God made foolish the wisdom of this world? 21 For after that in the wisdom of God the world by wisdom knew not God, it pleased God by the foolishness of preaching to save them that believe. 22 For the Jews require a sign, and the Greeks seek after wisdom: 23 But we preach Christ crucified, unto the Jews a stumblingblock, and unto the Greeks foolishness; 24 But unto them which are called, both Jews and Greeks, Christ the power of God, and the wisdom of God. 25 Because the foolishness of God is wiser than men; and the weakness of God is stronger than men. 26 For ye see your calling, brethren, how that not many wise men after the flesh, not many mighty, not many noble, *are called:* 27 But God hath chosen the foolish things of the world to confound the wise; and God hath chosen the weak things of the world to confound the things which are mighty; 28 And base things of the world, and things which are despised, hath God chosen, *yea,* and things which are not, to bring to nought things that are: 29 That no flesh should glory in his presence. 30 But of him are ye in Christ Jesus, who of God is made unto us wisdom, and righteousness, and sanctification, and redemption: 31 That, according as it is written, He that glorieth, let him glory in the Lord.

N.A.S.

"I WILL DESTROY THE WISDOM OF THE WISE, AND THE CLEVERNESS OF THE CLEVER I WILL SET ASIDE."

20 Where is the wise man? Where is the scribe? Where is the debater of this age? Has not God made foolish the wisdom of the world? 21 For since in the wisdom of God, the world through its wisdom did not *come to* know God, God was well pleased through the foolishness of the message preached to save those who believe. 22 For indeed Jews ask for signs, and Greeks search for wisdom; 23 but we preach ªChrist crucified, to Jews a stumbling-block, and to Gentiles foolishness, 24 but to those who are the called, both Jews and Greeks, Christ the power of God and the wisdom of God. 25 Because the foolishness of God is wiser than men, and the weakness of God is stronger than men.

26 For consider your call, brethren, that there were not many wise according to the flesh, not many mighty, not many noble; 27 but God has chosen the foolish things of the world to shame the wise, and God has chosen the weak things of the world to shame the things which are strong, 28 and the base things of the world and the despised, God has chosen, the things that are not, that He might nullify the things that are, 29 that no man should boast before God. 30 But by His doing you are in Christ Jesus, who became to us wisdom from God, and righteousness and sanctification, and redemption, 31 that, just as it is written, "LET HIM WHO BOASTS, BOAST IN THE LORD."

2 And I, brethren, when I came to you, came not with excellency of speech or of wisdom, declaring unto you the testimony of God. 2 For I determined not to know any thing among you, save Jesus Christ, and him crucified. 3 And I was with you in weakness, and in fear, and in much trembling. 4 And my speech and my preaching *was* not with enticing words of man's wisdom, but in demonstration of the Spirit and of power: 5 That your faith should not stand in the wisdom of men, but in the power of God. 6 Howbeit we speak wisdom among them that are perfect: yet not the wisdom of this world, nor of the princes of this world, that come to nought: 7 But we speak the wisdom of God in a mystery, *even* the hidden *wisdom,* which God ordained before the world unto our glory; 8 Which none of the princes of this world knew: for had they known *it,* they would not have crucified the Lord of glory. 9 But as it is written, Eye hath not seen, nor ear heard, neither have entered into the

2 And when I came to you, brethren, I did not come with superiority of speech or of wisdom, proclaiming to you the ᵇtestimony of God. 2 For I determined to know nothing among you except Jesus Christ, and Him crucified. 3 And I was with you in weakness and in fear and in much trembling. 4 And my message and my preaching were not in persuasive words of wisdom, but in demonstration of the Spirit and of power, 5 that your faith should not rest on the wisdom of men, but on the power of God.

6 Yet we do speak wisdom among those who are mature; a wisdom, however, not of this age, nor of the rulers of this age, who are passing away; 7 but we speak God's wisdom in a mystery, the hidden *wisdom,* which God predestined before the ages to our glory; 8 *the wisdom* which none of the rulers of this age has understood; for if they had understood it, they would not have crucified the Lord of glory; 9 but just as it is written,

"THINGS WHICH EYE HAS NOT SEEN AND EAR HAS NOT HEARD,

[a] I.e., *Messiah.* [b] Some ancient mss. read, *mystery.*

WILLIAMS

"I will destroy the wisdom of the wise,
And I will set aside the learning of the
learned."
20 So where is your philosopher? Where is
your man of letters? Where is your logician of
this age? Has not God shown up the nonsense
of the world's wisdom? 21 For since in accordance with the wisdom of God the world had
never in reality,*a* by means of its wisdom, come
to know God, God chose through the nonsense
of the message proclaimed, to save the people
who put their faith in Him. 22 While Jews are
demanding spectacular signs and Greeks are
searching for philosophy, 23 we are preaching the
Christ who was crucified—a message that is a
trap-stick*b* to the Jews and nonsense to the
Greeks, 24 but to those whom God has called,
both Jews and Greeks alike, the Christ who is
God's power and God's wisdom. 25 It is so,
because God's nonsense is wiser than men's
wisdom, and God's weakness is mightier than
men's might.
26 For consider, brothers, the way God called
you; that not many of you, in accordance with
human standards, were wise, not many influential, not many of high birth. 27 Just the opposite: God chose what the world calls foolish
to put the wise to shame, what the world calls
weak to put the strong to shame, 28 what the
world calls of low degree, yea, what it counts as
nothing and what it thinks does not exist, God
chose to put a stop to what it thinks exists, 29 so
that no mortal man might ever boast in the
presence of God. 30 So you owe it all to Him
through union with Christ Jesus, whom God
has made our wisdom, our means of right standing, our consecration, and our redemption, 31 so
that, as the Scripture says, "Let him who boasts
boast in the Lord."

2 *Paul's simple style of preaching; the
good news, God's wisdom not man's;
only God's Spirit can uncover this spiritual wisdom to men*

Now when I came to you, brothers, I did not
come and tell you God's uncovered secret in
rhetorical language or human philosophy, 2 for
I determined, while among you, to be uncon-
scious of everything but Jesus Christ and Him
as crucified. 3 Yes, as for myself, it was in weakness and fear and great trembling that I came
to you, 4 and my language and the message I
preached were not adorned with pleasing words
of worldly wisdom,*a* but they were attended
with proof and power given by the Spirit, 5 so
that your faith might not be in men's wisdom,
but in God's power.
6 Yet, when among mature believers we do
set forth a wisdom, but a wisdom that does not
belong to this world or to the leaders of this
world who are passing away; 7 rather, we are
setting forth a wisdom that came from God,
once a covered secret but now uncovered, which
God marked off as His plan for bringing us to
glory. 8 Not one of this world's leaders understands it, for if they had, they would never have
crucified our glorious Lord. 9 But, as the Scripture says, they are:
"Things which eye has never seen and ear has
never heard,

[a] Grk., *had never known by experience.* [b] *The
stick that throws the trap to catch the bird;* so the
cross has thrown the trap to catch the Jew.
[a] Lit., *persuasive words of wisdom.*

BECK

the wisdom of the wise and defeat the intelligence of the intelligent.[1] 20 *Where is the wise
man? Where is the Bible scholar?*[2] Where is the
debater of our time? Hasn't God *made foolish
the wisdom*[3] of the world? 21 Since by God's
wisdom the world by its wisdom didn't get to
know God, God decided to use our foolish
preaching to save those who believe it. 22 Now
that Jews ask for wonderful proofs and Greeks
look for wisdom, 23 we preach a crucified
Christ. The Jews stumble over Him, the Greeks
think He's something foolish, 24 but to those
who are called, both Jews and Greeks, He is
Christ, God's power and God's wisdom. 25 The
foolish thing God does is wiser than men, and
the weak thing God does is stronger than men.
26 You see what happened, fellow Christians,
when God called you. Not many of you are
wise as the world judges, not many in positions
of power, not many born of noble parents.
27 No, God chose the foolish things in the world
to make wise men feel ashamed. God chose the
weak things in the world to make strong men
feel ashamed. 28 God chose the low things in
the world, what it despises, what is nothing, to
make what is something nothing— 29 and to
keep anybody from bragging before God. 30 He
gave you your life in Christ Jesus, whom God
made our wisdom, righteousness, holiness, and
ransom from sin, 31 so that it may be as the
Bible says, *If you feel proud, feel proud of the
Lord.*[4]

2 When I came to you, fellow Christians, I
didn't come to tell you God's truth with any
extra-fine speech or wisdom. 2 While I was with
you, I was determined to know only Jesus Christ
and Him nailed to a cross. 3 I came to you weak
and afraid and with much trembling. 4 When I
spoke and preached, I didn't use clever talk to
persuade you, but I let the Spirit and His power
prove the truth to you 5 so that your faith will
not depend on men's wisdom but on God's
power.
6 But we do speak a wisdom to those who
are ripe for it, a wisdom unknown to the world
today and to its rulers who pass away. 7 Yes,
we tell about God's secret wisdom that was
kept hidden but that God before the world began planned for our glory. 8 None of those who
rule this world knew it. 9 If they had known it,
they would not have crucified the Lord of glory.
But it is as the Bible says:

No eye has seen,
No ear has heard,
And no mind has thought of

[1] Is. 29:14; Ps. 33:10
[2] Is. 19:12; 33:18
[3] Is. 44:25
[4] Jer. 9:24

K.J.V.

heart of man, the things which God hath prepared for them that love him. 10 But God hath revealed *them* unto us by his Spirit: for the Spirit searcheth all things, yea, the deep things of God. 11 For what man knoweth the things of a man, save the spirit of man which is in him? even so the things of God knoweth no man, but the Spirit of God. 12 Now we have received, not the spirit of the world, but the Spirit which is of God; that we might know the things that are freely given to us of God. 13 Which things also we speak, not in the words which man's wisdom teacheth, but which the Holy Ghost teacheth; comparing spiritual things with spiritual. 14 But the natural man receiveth not the things of the Spirit of God: for they are foolishness unto him: neither can he know *them,* because they are spiritually discerned. 15 But he that is spiritual judgeth all things, yet he himself is judged of no man. 16 For who hath known the mind of the Lord, that he may instruct him? But we have the mind of Christ.

3 And I, brethren, could not speak unto you as unto spiritual, but as unto carnal, *even* as unto babes in Christ. 2 I have fed you with milk, and not with meat: for hitherto ye were not able *to bear it,* neither yet now are ye able. 3 For ye are yet carnal: for whereas *there is* among you envying, and strife, and divisions, are ye not carnal, and walk as men? 4 For while one saith, I am of Paul; and another, I *am* of Apollos; are ye not carnal? 5 Who then is Paul, and who *is* Apollos, but ministers by whom ye believed, even as the Lord gave to every man? 6 I have planted, Apollos watered; but God gave the increase. 7 So then neither is he that planteth any thing, neither he that watereth; but God that giveth the increase. 8 Now he that planteth and he that watereth are one: and every man shall receive his own reward according to his own labour. 9 For we are labourers together with God: ye are God's husbandry, *ye are* God's building. 10 According to the grace of God which is given unto me, as a wise masterbuilder, I have laid the foundation, and another buildeth thereon. But let every man take heed how he buildeth thereupon. 11 For other foundation can no man lay than that is laid, which is Jesus Christ. 12 Now if any man build upon this foundation gold, silver, precious stones, wood, hay, stubble; 13 Every man's work shall be made manifest: for the day shall declare it, because it shall be revealed by fire; and the fire shall try every man's work of what sort it is. 14 If any man's work abide which he hath built

N.A.S.

AND *which* HAVE NOT ENTERED THE HEART OF MAN,

ALL THAT GOD HAS PREPARED FOR THOSE WHO LOVE HIM."

10 "For to us God revealed *them* through the Spirit; for the Spirit searches all things, even the depths of God. 11 For who among men knows the *thoughts* of a man except the spirit of the man, which is in him? Even so the *thoughts* of God no one knows except the Spirit of God. 12 Now we have received, not the spirit of the world, but the Spirit who is from God, that we might know the things freely given to us by God, 13 which things we also speak, not in words taught by human wisdom, but in those taught by the Spirit, combining spiritual *thoughts* with spiritual *words.* 14 But a natural man does not accept the things of the Spirit of God; for they are foolishness to him, and he cannot understand them, because they are spiritually appraised. 15 But he who is spiritual appraises all things, yet he himself is appraised by no man. 16 FOR WHO HAS KNOWN THE MIND OF THE LORD, THAT HE SHOULD INSTRUCT HIM? But we have the mind of Christ.

3 And I, brethren, could not speak to you as to spiritual men, but as to men of flesh, as to babes in Christ. 2 I gave you milk to drink, not solid food; for you were not yet able *to receive it.* Indeed, even now you are not yet able, 3 for you are still fleshly. For since there is jealousy and strife among you, are you not fleshly, and are you not walking like mere men? 4 For when one says, "I am of Paul," and another, "I am of Apollos," are you not *mere* men? 5 What then is Apollos? And what is Paul? Servants through whom you believed, even as the Lord gave *opportunity* to each one. 6 I planted, Apollos watered, but God was causing the growth. 7 So then neither the one who plants nor the one who waters is anything, but God who causes the growth. 8 Now he who plants and he who waters are one; but each will receive his own reward according to his own labor. 9 For we are God's fellow-workers; you are God's field, God's building.

10 According to the grace of God which was given to me, as a wise masterbuilder I laid a foundation, and another is building upon it. But let each man be careful how he builds upon it. 11 For no man can lay a foundation other than the one which is laid, which is Jesus Christ. 12 Now if any man builds upon the foundation with gold, silver, precious stones, wood, hay, straw, 13 each man's work will become evident; for the day will show it, because it is *to be* revealed with fire; and the fire itself will test the quality of each man's work. 14 If any man's

[a] Some ancient mss. use, *But.*

WILLIAMS

And never have occurred to human hearts,
Which God prepared for those who love
Him."
10 For God unveiled them to us through
His Spirit, for the Spirit by searching discovers
everything, even the deepest truths about God.
11 For what man can understand his own inner
thoughts except by his own spirit within him?
Just so no one but the Spirit of God can
understand the thoughts of God. 12 Now we
have not received the spirit that belongs to the
world but the Spirit that comes from God,
that we may get an insight into the blessings
God has graciously given us. 13 These truths
we are setting forth, not in words that man's
wisdom teaches but in words that the Spirit
teaches, in this way fitting spiritual words to
spiritual truths. 14 An unspiritual man does not
accept the things that the Spirit of God
teaches, for they are nonsense to him; and
he cannot understand them, because they are
appreciated by spiritual insight. 15 But the
spiritual man appreciates everything, and yet
he himself is not really appreciated by anybody.
16 For who has ever known the Lord's
thoughts, so that he can instruct Him? But we
now possess Christ's thoughts.

3 *Factious Christians unspiritual; spiritual
teachers God's fellow-workers; such
teachers responsible to build into God's
temple enduring materials, and not to
spoil it with perishing materials*

So I myself, brothers, could not deal with
you as spiritual persons, but as creatures of
human clay, as merely baby Christians. 2 I
fed you with milk, not solid food, for you
could not take it. Why, you cannot take it
even now, 3 for you are still unspiritual.[a] For
when there are still jealousy and wrangling
among you, are you not still unspiritual and
living by a human standard? 4 For when one
says, "I belong to Paul's party," and another,
"I belong to Apollos' party," are you not acting as mere human creatures?
5 Then what is Apollos? Or what is Paul?
Mere servants through whom you came to believe, as the Lord gave each of us his task.
6 I did the planting, Apollos did the watering,
but it was God who kept the plants growing.
7 So neither the planter nor the waterer counts
for much, but God is everything in keeping the
plants growing. 8 The planter and the waterer
are one in aim, and yet each of us will get his
own pay in accordance with his own work,
9 for we belong to God as His fellow-workers;
you belong to God as His field to be tilled, as
His building to be built.
10 As a skilled architect, in accordance with
God's unmerited favor given to me, I laid a
foundation, and now another is building upon
it. But every builder must be careful how he
builds upon it; 11 for no one can lay any other
foundation than the one that is laid, that is,
Jesus Christ Himself. 12 And whether one puts
into the building on the foundation gold or
silver or costly stones, or wood or hay or
straw, 13 the character of each one's work will
come to light, for the judgment day will show
it up. This is so, because that day will show
itself in fire, and the fire will test the character
of each one's work. 14 If the structure which

BECK

What God has prepared *for those who* love
Him.[5]

10 God has revealed it to us by His Spirit.
The Spirit finds out everything, even the deep
things of God. 11 Who knows what a man thinks
except his own inner spirit? In the same way
only God's Spirit knows what God thinks.
12 Now we were not given the spirit of the
world but the Spirit who comes from God so
that we know the good things God gave us.
13 And we tell about them in words not taught by
human wisdom but taught by the Spirit as we
explain the things of the Spirit to those who
have the Spirit.
14 But a natural man doesn't welcome the
things of God's Spirit. He thinks they are foolish
and can't understand them, because you must
have the Spirit to see their real value. 15 If you
have the Spirit, you can find out the real value
of everything, but nobody can know your real
value. 16 *Who has known the mind of the Lord
so as to teach Him?*[6] And we have the mind of
Christ.

We Plant and Build

3 Fellow Christians, I couldn't talk to you as
spiritual people but had to treat you as living in your weak flesh, as babies in Christ. 2 I
gave you milk to drink, not solid food, because
you weren't ready for it. 3 Why, you aren't
ready for it even now yet, because you still live
in your weak flesh.
When you are jealous, quarreling, and forming different parties, aren't you following your
flesh and acting like other people? 4 When one
of you says, "I belong to Paul," and another,
"I belong to Apollos," aren't you just ordinary
people? 5 What is Apollos anyhow? Or what is
Paul? Men by whose help you came to believe,
and each helped only as the Lord gave him the
ability. 6 I planted, Apollos watered, but God
made it grow. 7 Now then, the one who plants
isn't anything, or the one who waters, but God,
who makes it grow. 8 The man who plants and
the one who waters are together, but each of us
will get paid for his own work. 9 We are God's
men, working together. You are God's field.
You are God's building. 10 In His love God
gave me a work to do, and so as an expert
master builder I laid a foundation, and somebody else is building on it. Everyone should be
careful how he builds on it. 11 Nobody can lay
any other foundation than the one that is already laid, and that is Jesus Christ. 12 If on
this foundation you build anything of gold,
silver, fine stones, wood, hay, or straw, 13 what
each one does will be known. That day will show
what it is because the fire will reveal it and test
it to show what kind of work everyone has done.
14 If what you built on the foundation stands the

---

[a] Grk., *fleshly,* opposite of *spiritual.*

[5] Is. 64:4
[6] Is. 40:13

K.J.V.

thereupon, he shall receive a reward. 15 If any man's work shall be burned, he shall suffer loss: but he himself shall be saved; yet so as by fire. 16 Know ye not that ye are the temple of God, and *that* the Spirit of God dwelleth in you? 17 If any man defile the temple of God, him shall God destroy; for the temple of God is holy, which *temple* ye are. 18 Let no man deceive himself. If any man among you seemeth to be wise in this world, let him become a fool, that he may be wise. 19 For the wisdom of this world is foolishness with God: for it is written, He taketh the wise in their own craftiness. 20And again, The Lord knoweth the thoughts of the wise, that they are vain. 21 Therefore let no man glory in men: for all things are yours; 22 Whether Paul, or Apollos, or Cephas, or the world, or life, or death, or things present, or things to come; all are yours; 23And ye are Christ's; and Christ *is* God's.

4 Let a man so account of us, as of the ministers of Christ, and stewards of the mysteries of God. 2 Moreover it is required in stewards, that a man be found faithful. 3 But with me it is a very small thing that I should be judged of you, or of man's judgment: yea, I judge not mine own self. 4 For I know nothing by myself; yet am I not hereby justified: but he that judgeth me is the Lord. 5 Therefore judge nothing before the time, until the Lord come, who both will bring to light the hidden things of darkness, and will make manifest the counsels of the hearts: and then shall every man have praise of God. 6And these things, brethren, I have in a figure transferred to myself and *to* Apollos for your sakes; that ye might learn in us not to think *of men* above that which is written, that no one of you be puffed up for one against another. 7 For who maketh thee to differ *from another?* and what hast thou that thou didst not receive? now if thou didst receive *it,* why dost thou glory, as if thou hadst not received *it?* 8 Now ye are full, now ye are rich, ye have reigned as kings without us: and I would to God ye did reign, that we also might reign with you. 9 For I think that God hath set forth us the apostles last, as it were appointed to death: for we are made a spectacle unto the world, and to angels, and to men. 10 We *are* fools for Christ's sake, but ye *are* wise in Christ; we *are* weak, but ye *are* strong; ye *are* honourable, but we *are* despised. 11 Even unto this present hour we both hunger, and thirst, and are naked, and are buffeted, and

N.A.S.

work which he has built upon it remains, he shall receive a reward. 15 If any man's work is burned up, he shall suffer loss; but he himself shall be saved, yet so as through fire. 16 Do you not know that you are a temple of God, and *that* the Spirit of God dwells in you? 17 If any man destroys the temple of God, God will destroy him, for the temple of God is holy, and that is what you are. 18 Let no man deceive himself. If any man among you thinks that he is wise in this age, let him become foolish that he may become wise. 19 For the wisdom of this world is foolishness before God. For it is written, "He is THE ONE WHO CATCHES THE WISE IN THEIR CRAFTINESS"; 20 and again, "THE LORD KNOWS THE REASONINGS of the wise, THAT THEY ARE USELESS." 21 So then let no one boast in men. For all things belong to you, 22 whether Paul or Apollos or Cephas or the world or life or death or things present or things to come, all things belong to you, 23 and you belong to Christ; and Christ belongs to God.

4 Let a man regard us in this manner, as servants of Christ, and stewards of the mysteries of God. 2 In this case, moreover, it is required of stewards that one be found trustworthy. 3 But to me it is a very small thing that I should be examined by you, or by *any* human court; in fact, I do not even examine myself. 4 I am conscious of nothing against myself, yet I am not by this acquitted; but the one who examines me is the Lord. 5 Therefore do not go on passing judgment before *the time, but wait* until the Lord comes who will both bring to light the things hidden in the darkness and disclose the motives of *men's* hearts; and then each man's praise will come to him from God. 6 Now these things, brethren, I have figuratively applied to myself and Apollos for your sakes, that in us you might learn not to exceed what is written, in order that no one of you might become arrogant in behalf of one against the other. 7 For who regards you as superior? And what do you have that you did not receive? But if you did receive it, why do you boast as if you had not received it? 8 You are already filled, you have already become rich, you have become kings without us; and would indeed that you had become kings so that we also might reign with you. 9 For, I think, God has exhibited us apostles last of all, as men condemned to death; because we have become a spectacle to the world, both to angels and to men. 10 We are fools for Christ's sake, but you are prudent in Christ; we are weak, but you are strong; you are distinguished, but we are without honor. 11 To this present hour we are both hungry and thirsty, and are poorly clothed, and

[a] I.e., the appointed time of judgment.

WILLIAMS

one builds upon stands the test,[b] he will get his pay. 15 If the structure which one builds is burned up, he will get no pay;[c] and yet he himself will be saved; but just as one who goes through a fire.

16 Are you not conscious that you are God's temple, and that the Spirit of God has His permanent home in you? 17 If anyone destroys God's temple, God will destroy him. For God's temple is sacred to Him, and you are that temple.

18 Let no one deceive himself. If any one of you supposes that he is wise in this world's wisdom, as compared with the rest of you, to become really wise he must become a fool. 19 For this world's wisdom is mere nonsense to God. For the Scripture says, "He who catches the wise with their own cunning," 20 and again, "The Lord knows that the arguings of the wise are useless." 21 So let no one boast in men. For everything belongs to you—Paul, Apollos, Cephas, the world, life, death, the present, the future—they all belong to you. 22 Yes, you belong to Christ, and Christ belongs to God.

4 *Ministers, trustees of God's truth; the apostle cuts with keenest irony; then counsels them as a loving father; though conscious of his authority, he prefers to lead by love*

As for us apostles, men ought to think of us as ministers of Christ and trustees to handle God's uncovered truths. 2 Now in this matter of trustees the first and final requirement is that they should prove to be trustworthy. 3 As for me, myself, it is of very little concern to me to be examined by you or any human court; in fact, I do not even examine myself. 4 For although my conscience does not accuse me, yet I am not entirely vindicated by that. It is the Lord Himself who must examine me. 5 So you must stop forming any premature judgments, but wait until the Lord shall come again; for He will bring to light the secrets hidden in the dark and will make known the motives of men's hearts, and the proper praise will be awarded each of us.

6 Now, brothers, for your sakes I have applied all this to Apollos and myself, that from us as illustrations you might learn the lesson, "Never go beyond what is written," so that you might stop boasting in favor of one teacher against another. 7 For who makes you superior? And what do you have that you did not get from someone? But if you got it from someone, why do you boast as though you had not? 8 Are you satisfied already? Have you grown rich already? Have you ascended your thrones without us to join you? Yes, I could wish that you had ascended your thrones, that we too might join you on them! 9 For it seems to me that God has put us apostles on exhibition at the disgraced end of the procession, as they do with men who are doomed to die in the arena. 10 For we have become a spectacle to the universe, to angels as well as men. For Christ's sake we are held as fools, while you through union with Christ are men of wisdom. We are weak; you are strong. You are held in honor; we in dishonor. 11 To this very hour we have gone hungry, thirsty, poorly clad; we have been roughly

[b] Grk., *remains*. [c] Lit., *suffer loss* (of pay).

BECK

test, you will get paid. 15 If your work is burned, you will lose something, but you will be saved, though it will be like going through a fire.

16 Don't you know you are God's temple and God's Spirit lives in you? 17 If anybody destroys God's temple, God will destroy him, because God's temple is holy. And you are that temple.

18 Don't deceive yourself. If any one of you imagines he is wise in the ways of this world, he should become a fool to become really wise. 19 God considers this world's wisdom to be foolish, as the Bible says, *He catches the wise with their own trickery*,[7] 20 and again, *The Lord knows that the planning of the wise is useless*.[8] 21 So don't feel proud of men. You see, everything is yours— 22 Paul, Apollos, Peter, the world, life or death, present or future things— everything is yours, 23 but you belong to Christ, and Christ to God.

We Are Managers

4 Think of us as servants of Christ and managers who distribute God's hidden truths. 2 Now then, you demand of any manager that he can be trusted.

3 It means very little to me that you or any human judges should examine me. I don't even examine myself. 4 I don't know of anything that is against me, but that doesn't make me righteous.* It is the Lord who examines me. 5 So, don't judge anything too early. Wait till the Lord comes. He will let the light shine on what is hidden in the dark and bring to the light the plans people have in their hearts. And then everyone will get his praise from God.

6 Fellow Christians, in a special way of speaking I have referred only to myself and Apollos, but I want you to learn from us not to get away from the Bible and not to brag about one man at the expense of another.

Not a King but a Father

7 Does anyone see anything special in you? What do you have that wasn't given to you? And if it was given to you, why do you brag as if it hadn't been given to you?

8 So you're already satisfied! You've already become rich! You've become kings without us! I only wish you had become kings—we would like to be kings with you.

9 I think God has had us apostles come last in the procession like men condemned to die because we have become a big show for the world, for angels and people to see. 10 We are fools for Christ's sake, but you are wise in Christ. We are weak, but you are strong. You are honored, but we are despised. 11 Up to this hour we are hungry, thirsty, poorly dressed,

* See note at Rom. 3:20.
[7] Job 5:13
[8] Ps. 94:11

465

K.J.V.

have no certain dwellingplace; 12And labour, working with our own hands: being reviled, we bless; being persecuted, we suffer it: 13 Being defamed, we entreat: we are made as the filth of the world, *and are* the offscouring of all things unto this day. 14 I write not these things to shame you, but as my beloved sons I warn *you.* 15 For though ye have ten thousand instructors in Christ, yet *have ye* not many fathers: for in Christ Jesus I have begotten you through the gospel. 16 Wherefore I beseech you, be ye followers of me. 17 For this cause have I sent unto you Timotheus, who is my beloved son, and faithful in the Lord, who shall bring you into remembrance of my ways which be in Christ, as I teach every where in every church. 13 Now some are puffed up, as though I would not come to you. 19 But I will come to you shortly, if the Lord will, and will know, not the speech of them which are puffed up, but the power. 20 For the kingdom of God *is* not in word, but in power. 21 What will ye? shall I come unto you with a rod, or in love, and *in* the spirit of meekness?

5 It is reported commonly *that there is* fornication among you, and such fornication as is not so much as named among the Gentiles, that one should have his father's wife. 2And ye are puffed up, and have not rather mourned, that he that hath done this deed might be taken away from among you. 3 For I verily, as absent in body, but present in spirit, have judged already, as though I were present, *concerning* him that hath so done this deed, 4 In the name of our Lord Jesus Christ, when ye are gathered together, and my spirit, with the power of our Lord Jesus Christ, 5 To deliver such a one unto Satan for the destruction of the flesh, that the spirit may be saved in the day of the Lord Jesus. 6 Your glorying *is* not good. Know ye not that a little leaven leaveneth the whole lump? 7 Purge out therefore the old leaven, that ye may be a new lump, as ye are unleavened. For even Christ our passover is sacrificed for us: 8 Therefore let us keep the feast, not with old leaven, neither with the leaven of malice and wickedness; but with the unleavened *bread* of sincerity and truth. 9 I wrote unto you in an epistle not to company with fornicators: 10 Yet not altogether with the fornicators of this world, or with the covetous, or extortioners, or with idolaters; for then must ye needs go out of the world. 11 But now I have written unto you not to keep company, if any man that is called a brother be a fornicator, or covetous, or an idolater, or a railer, or a drunkard, or an extortioner; with such a one no not to eat. 12 For what have I to do to judge them also that are without? do not ye judge them

N.A.S.

are roughly treated, and are homeless; 12 and we toil, working with our own hands; when we are reviled, we bless; when we are persecuted, we endure; 13 when we are slandered, we try to conciliate; we have become as the scum of the world, the dregs of all things, *even* until now.

14 I do not write these things to shame you, but to admonish you as my beloved children. 15 For if you were to have countless tutors in Christ, yet *you would* not *have* many fathers; for in Christ Jesus I became your father through the gospel. 16 I exhort you therefore, be imitators of me. 17 For this reason I have sent to you Timothy, who is my beloved and faithful child in the Lord, and he will remind you of my ways which are in Christ, just as I teach everywhere in every church. 18 Now some have become arrogant, as though I were not coming to you. 19 But I will come to you soon, if the Lord wills, and I shall find out, not the words of those who are arrogant, but their power. 20 For the kingdom of God does not consist in words, but in power. 21 What do you desire? Shall I come to you with a rod or with love and a spirit of gentleness?

5 It is actually reported that there is immorality among you, and immorality of such a kind as does not exist even among the Gentiles, that someone has his father's wife. 2And you have become arrogant, and have not mourned instead, in order that the one who had done this deed might be removed from your midst. 3 For I, on my part, though absent in body but present in spirit, have already judged him who has so committed this, as though I were present. 4 In the name of our Lord Jesus, when you are assembled, and I with you in spirit, with the power of our Lord Jesus, 5 *I have decided* to deliver such a one to Satan for the destruction of his flesh, that his spirit may be saved in the day of the Lord [a]Jesus. 6 Your boasting is not good. Do you not know that a little leaven leavens the whole lump *of dough?* 7 Clean out the old leaven, that you may be a new lump, just as you are *in fact* unleavened. For Christ our Passover also has been sacrificed. 8 Let us therefore celebrate the feast, not with old leaven, nor with the leaven of malice and wickedness, but with the unleavened bread of sincerity and truth.

9 I wrote you in my letter not to associate with immoral people; 10 I *did* not at all *mean* with the immoral people of this world, or with the covetous and swindlers, or with idolaters; for then you would have to go out of the world. 11 But actually, I wrote to you not to associate with any so-called brother if he should be an immoral person, or covetous, or an idolater, or a reviler, or a drunkard, or a swindler—not even to eat with such a one. 12 For what have I to do with judging outsiders? Do you not

[a] Some ancient mss. omit, *Jesus.*

WILLIAMS

knocked around, we have had no home, 12 we have worked hard with our own hands for a living. When abused by people we bless them, when persecuted we patiently bear it, 13 when we are slandered by them we try to conciliate them. To this very hour we have been made the filth of the world, the scum of the universe!

14 I do not write this to make you blush with shame but to give you counsel as my dear children. 15 For though you have ten thousand teachers in the Christian life, you certainly could not have many fathers. For it was I myself who became your father through your union with Christ Jesus, which resulted from my telling you the good news. 16 So I beg you, make it your habit to follow my example. 17 This is why I have sent Timothy to you. He is a dear child of mine and trustworthy in the Lord's work; he will call to your minds my methods in the work of Christ Jesus, just as I teach them everywhere in every church.

18 But some of you have become conceited over the thought that I am not coming to see you. 19 But I am coming, and coming soon, if the Lord is willing, and then I will find out, not only what those conceited fellows say but what they can do, 20 for the kingdom of God does not consist in talking but in doing. 21 Which do you prefer? My coming to you with a club, or in a gentle, loving spirit?

5 *He rebukes the church for tolerating a case of grossest indecency; the church had disregarded his previous warning*

A case of immorality is reported as actually existing among you, an immorality unheard of even among the heathen—that a man co-habits with his father's wife. 2 And yet, you are proud of it, instead of being sorry for it, and seeing to it that the man who has done this be removed from your membership! 3 For my part, though I have been absent from you in person, I have been present with you in spirit, and so as really present, by the authority of our Lord Jesus, I have already passed judgment upon the man who has done this—4 for when you met I too met with you in spirit by the power of our Lord Jesus—5 to turn such a man as this over to Satan for the destruction of his lower nature, in order that his spirit may be saved on the day of the Lord. 6 Your ground for boasting about such a case is not good. Are you not aware that a little yeast will change the whole lump of dough? 7 You must clean out the old yeast, that you may be a fresh lump, as you are to be free from the old yeast. For our Passover Lamb, Christ, has already been sacrificed. 8 So let us keep our feast, not with old yeast nor with the yeast of vice and wickedness, but with the bread of purity and truth without the yeast.

9 I wrote you in my letter to stop associating with sexually immoral people—10 not that you are to stop all dealings with sexually immoral people of this world, any more than with its greedy graspers, or its idolaters, for then you would have to get clear out of the world. 11 Now what I really meant was for you to stop associating with any so-called brother, if he is sexually immoral, a greedy grasper, an idolater, a slanderer, a drunkard, or a swindler—with such a person you must even stop eating. 12 For what right have I to judge outsiders? Is it not for you to judge those who are inside the

BECK

beaten, homeless, 12 and we wear ourselves out working with our hands. When we're insulted, we bless. When we're persecuted, we put up with it. 13 When slandered, we talk kindly. We have come to be the filth of the world, the scum of the earth, and we are that to this day.

14 I'm not writing this to make you feel ashamed, but I'm warning you as my dear children. 15 You may have ten thousand to guide you in Christ, but not many fathers, because in Christ Jesus I became your father by telling you the good news. 16 So I urge you to become like me. 17 That is why I sent you Timothy, who is my dear and dependable son in the Lord. He will help you keep in mind my ways in Christ Jesus, just as I teach them everywhere in every church.

18 Some of you are puffed up as though I were not coming to you. 19 But I'll come to you soon if the Lord wants me to, and then I will find out, not what these puffed-up fellows say but what they can do. 20 God's kingdom isn't just talk but power.

21 Which would you like? Should I come to you with a stick or with love and a gentle spirit?

Put Out the Wicked Man

5 We actually hear there is sexual sin among you, and such as isn't found even among the people of the world, that a man has his father's wife. And you feel proud of yourselves! 2 Shouldn't you rather have wept and put away from you the man who did this? 3 Although I'm away from you, I am with you in spirit, and being with you, I have already decided in regard to the man who did this. 4 Call a meeting. My spirit and the power of our Lord Jesus will be with you. Then in the name of our Lord Jesus 5 hand such a person over to the devil, to destroy his sinful ways in order to save his spirit on the Lord's day.

6 It isn't good for you to feel proud. Don't you know a little yeast makes the whole dough sour? 7 Get rid of the old yeast in order to be a new dough, as you are really free from the old yeast, because our *Passover Lamb* was *sacrificed;*° it is Christ. 8 Let us, then, celebrate our festival, not with old yeast, not with any yeast of vice and wickedness, but with the sweet bread of purity and truth.

9 In my letter I wrote you not to mix with those who live in sexual sin. 10 I didn't mean you should altogether keep away from people who live in sexual sin in this world, from those who are greedy, who rob, or worship idols; then you would have to get out of this world. 11 But now I write you: Don't mix with anyone who calls himself a Christian but lives in sexual sin or is greedy, worships idols, slanders, gets drunk, or robs. Don't even eat with such a person.

12 Is it my business to judge those who are

[9] Ex. 12:21

467

that are within? 13 But them that are without God judgeth. Therefore put away from among yourselves that wicked person.

6 Dare any of you, having a matter against another, go to law before the unjust, and not before the saints? 2 Do ye not know that the saints shall judge the world? and if the world shall be judged by you, are ye unworthy to judge the smallest matters? 3 Know ye not that we shall judge angels? how much more things that pertain to this life? 4 If then ye have judgments of things pertaining to this life, set them to judge who are least esteemed in the church. 5 I speak to your shame. Is it so, that there is not a wise man among you? no, not one that shall be able to judge between his brethren? 6 But brother goeth to law with brother, and that before the unbelievers? 7 Now therefore there is utterly a fault among you, because ye go to law one with another. Why do ye not rather take wrong? Why do ye not rather *suffer yourselves to* be defrauded? 8 Nay, ye do wrong, and defraud, and that *your* brethren. 9 Know ye not that the unrighteous shall nor inherit the kingdom of God? Be not deceived: neither fornicators, nor idolaters, nor adulterers, nor effeminate, nor abusers of themselves with mankind, 10 Nor thieves, nor covetous, nor drunkards, nor revilers, nor extortioners, shall inherit the kingdom of God. 11And such were some of you: but ye are washed, but ye are sanctified, but ye are justified in the name of the Lord Jesus, and by the Spirit of our God. 12All things are lawful unto me, but all things are not expedient: all things are lawful for me, but I will not be brought under the power of any. 13 Meats for the belly, and the belly for meats: but God shall destroy both it and them. Now the body *is* not for fornication, but for the Lord; and the Lord for the body. 14And God hath both raised up the Lord, and will also raise up us by his own power. 15 Know ye not that your bodies are the members of Christ? shall I then take the members of Christ, and make *them* the members of a harlot? God forbid. 16 What! know ye not that he which is joined to a harlot is one body? for two, saith he, shall be one flesh. 17 But he that is joined unto the Lord is one spirit. 18 Flee fornication. Every sin that a man doeth is without the body; but he that committeth fornication sinneth against his own body. 19 What! know ye not that your body is the temple of

judge those who are within *the church?* 13 But those who are outside God judges. Remove the wicked man from among yourselves.

6 Does any one of you, when he has a case against his neighbor, dare to go to law before the unrighteous, and not before the saints? 2 Or do you not know that the saints will judge the world? And if the world is judged by you, are you not competent *to constitute* the smallest law courts? 3 Do you not know that we shall judge angels? How much more, matters of this life? 4 If then you have law courts dealing with matters of this life, do you appoint them as judges who are of no account in the church? 5 I say *this* to your shame. *Is it* so, *that* there is not among you one wise man who will be able to decide between his brethren, 6 but brother goes to law with brother, and that before unbelievers? 7Actually, then, it is already a defeat for you, that you have lawsuits with one another. Why not rather be wronged? Why not rather be defrauded? 8 On the contrary, you yourselves wrong and defraud, and that *your* brethren. 9 Or do you not know that the un-righteous shall not inherit the kingdom of God? Do not be deceived; neither fornicators, nor idolaters, nor adulterers, nor [a]effeminate, nor homosexuals, 10 nor thieves, nor covetous, nor drunkards, nor revilers, nor swindlers, shall in-herit the kingdom of God. 11And such were some of you; but you were washed, but you were sanctified, but you were justified in the name of the Lord Jesus Christ, and in the Spirit of our God.

12 All things are lawful for me, but not all things are profitable. All things are lawful for me, but I will not be mastered by anything. 13 Food is for the stomach, and the stomach is for food; but God will do away with both of them. Yet the body is not for immorality, but for the Lord; and the Lord is for the body. 14 Now God has not only raised the Lord, but will also raise us up through His power. 15 Do you not know that your bodies are members of Christ? Shall I then take away the members of Christ and make them members of a harlot? May it never be! 16 Or do you not know that the one who joins himself to a harlot is one body *with her?* For He says, "THE TWO WILL BECOME ONE FLESH." 17 But the one who joins himself to the Lord is one spirit *with Him.* 18 Flee immorality. Every *other* sin that a man commits is outside the body, but the immoral man sins against his own body. 19 Or do you not know that your body is a temple of the

[a] I.e., effeminate, by perversion.

WILLIAMS

church, 13 but for God to judge those who are outside? You must expel that wicked person from your membership.

6 *Christians not to go to law in heathen courts; urged not to go to law with one another; pagan vices inconsistent with Christian living; our freedom no excuse for sensuality; Christian reasons for personal purity*

When one of you has a grievance against his neighbor, does he dare to go to law before a heathen court, instead of laying the case before God's people? 2 Do you not know that God's people are to judge the world? And if the world is to be judged before you, are you unfit to try such petty cases? 3 Do you not know that we Christians are to sit in judgment on angels, to say nothing of the ordinary cases of life? 4 So if you have the ordinary cases of life for settlement, do you set up as judges the very men in the church who have no standing? 5 I ask this to make you blush with shame. Has it come to this, that there is not a single wise man among you who could settle a grievance of one brother against another, 6 but one brother has to go to law with another, and that before unbelieving judges? 7 To say no more, it is a mark of moral failure among you to have lawsuits at all with one another. Why not rather suffer being wronged? Why not suffer being robbed? 8 On the contrary, you practice wronging and robbing others, and that your brothers.

9 Do you not know that wrongdoers will not have a share in the kingdom of God? Stop being misled; people who are sexually immoral or idolaters or adulterers or sensual or guilty of unnatural sexual vice 10 or thieves or greedy graspers for more or drunkards or slanderers or swindlers will not have a share in the kingdom of God. 11And these are just the characters some of you used to be. But now you have washed yourselves clean, you have been consecrated, you are now in right standing with God, by the name of our Lord Jesus Christ and by the Spirit of God.

12 Everything is permissible for me, but not everything is good for me. Everything is permissible for me, but I will not become a slave to anything. 13 Foods are intended for the stomach, and the stomach for foods, but God will finally put a stop to both of them. The body is not intended for sexual immorality but for the service of the Lord, and the Lord is for the body to serve. 14And as God by His power raised the Lord to life, so He will raise us too.

15 Do you not know that your bodies are parts of Christ Himself? Then may I take away parts of Christ and make them parts of a prostitute? Never! Never! 16 Or, are you not aware that a man who has to do with a prostitute makes his body one with hers? For God says, "The two shall be physically one." 17 But the man who is in union with the Lord is spiritually one with Him. 18 Keep on running from sexual immorality! Any other sin that a man commits is one outside his body, but the man who commits the sexual sin is sinning against his own body. 19 Or, are you not conscious that your body is a temple of the Holy Spirit that is in you, whom you have as a gift

BECK

outside the church? 13 God judges those who are outside. Shouldn't you judge those who are inside the church? *Put the wicked man away from you.*[10]

Don't Sue One Another

6 When one of you has a case against another, do you dare to bring it before a court of unrighteous men and not before the holy people? 2 Or don't you know these holy people will judge the world? And if you judge the world, aren't you able to judge trifles? 3 Don't you know we'll judge angels? Shouldn't we then judge things of this life? 4 If then you are having things of this life decided, will you let men who count nothing in the church be your judges? 5 I say this to make you feel ashamed. Really, isn't any one of you wise enough to decide a matter between one Christian and another? 6 No, one Christian sues another—and before unbelievers!

7 Without going any further, suing one another means you have utterly failed. Why don't you rather suffer wrong? Why don't you rather let yourselves be robbed? 8 No, you do wrong, and you rob, and you do it to your own fellow Christians.

You Are God's Temple

9 Or don't you know wicked people will have no share in God's kingdom? Don't be mistaken about this: Nobody who lives in sexual sin or worships idols, no adulterers or men who sin sexually with other men, 10 who steal, are greedy, get drunk, slander, rob will have a share in God's kingdom. 11 Some of you used to do these things. But you have washed, you've been made holy and righteous* by the name of the Lord Jesus Christ and by the Spirit of our God.

12 I'm allowed to do anything, but not everything is good for us. I'm allowed to do anything, but I'll not be a slave of anything. 13 Food is for the stomach, and the stomach for food, but God will put an end to both of them. The body is not made for sexual sin but for the Lord; and the Lord is for the body. 14And God, who raised the Lord, will also raise us by His power.

15 Don't you know your bodies are members of Christ? Now, should I take the members of Christ and make them members of a prostitute? Never! 16 Or don't you know he who gives himself to a prostitute is one body with her? The Bible says, *The two will be one flesh.*[11] 17 But if you give yourself to the Lord, you are one spirit with Him.

18 Flee from sexual sin. Every other sin a man may do is outside his body. But if he sins sexually, he sins against his own body. 19 Or don't you know your body is a temple of the

* See note at Rom. 3:20.
[10] Deut. 17:7; 19:19; 22:21, 24; 24:7
[11] Gen. 2:24

469

the Holy Ghost *which is* in you, which ye have of God, and ye are not your own? 20 For ye are bought with a price: therefore glorify God in your body, and in your spirit, which are God's.

Holy Spirit who is in you, whom you have from God, and that you are not your own? 20 For you have been bought with a price; therefore glorify God in your body.

7 Now concerning the things whereof ye wrote me: *It is* good for a man not to touch a woman. 2 Nevertheless, *to avoid* fornication, let every man have his own wife, and let every woman have her own husband. 3 Let the husband render unto the wife due benevolence: and likewise also the wife unto the husband. 4 The wife hath not power of her own body, but the husband: and likewise also the husband hath not power of his own body, but the wife. 5 Defraud ye not one the other, except *it be* with consent for a time, that ye may give yourselves to fasting and prayer; and come together again, that Satan tempt you not for your incontinency. 6 But I speak this by permission, *and* not of commandment. 7 For I would that all men were even as I myself. But every man hath his proper gift of God, one after this manner, and another after that. 8 I say therefore to the unmarried and widows, It is good for them if they abide even as I. 9 But if they cannot contain, let them marry: for it is better to marry than to burn. 10 And unto the married I command, *yet* not I, but the Lord, Let not the wife depart from *her* husband: 11 But and if she depart, let her remain unmarried, or be reconciled to *her* husband: and let not the husband put away *his* wife. 12 But to the rest speak I, not the Lord: If any brother hath a wife that believeth not, and she be pleased to dwell with him, let him not put her away. 13 And the woman which hath a husband that believeth not, and if he be pleased to dwell with her, let her not leave him. 14 For the unbelieving husband is sanctified by the wife, and the unbelieving wife is sanctified by the husband: else were your children unclean; but now are they holy. 15 But if the unbelieving depart, let him depart. A brother or a sister is not under bondage in such *cases:* but God hath called us to peace. 16 For what knowest thou, O wife, whether thou shalt save *thy* husband? or how knowest thou, O man, whether thou shalt save *thy* wife? 17 But as God hath distributed to every man, as the Lord hath called every one, so let him walk. And so ordain I in all churches. 18 Is any man called being circumcised? let him not become uncircumcised. Is any called in uncircumcision? let him not be circum-

7 Now concerning the things about which you wrote, it is good for a man not to touch a woman. 2 But because of immoralities, let each man have his own wife, and let each woman have her own husband. 3 Let the husband fulfill his duty to his wife, and likewise also the wife to her husband. 4 The wife does not have authority over her own body, but the husband *does;* and likewise also the husband does not have authority over his own body, but the wife *does.* 5 Stop depriving one another, except by agreement for a time that you may devote yourselves to prayer, and come together again lest Satan tempt you because of your lack of self-control. 6 But this I say by way of concession, not of command. 7 *[a]*Yet I wish that all men were even as I myself am. However, each man has his own gift from God, one in this manner, and another in that. 8 But I say to the unmarried and to widows that it is good for them if they remain even as I. 9 But if they do not have self-control, let them marry; for it is better to marry than to burn. 10 But to the married I give instructions, not I, but the Lord, that the wife should not leave her husband 11 (but if she does leave, let her remain unmarried, or else be reconciled to her husband), and that the husband should not send his wife away. 12 But to the rest I say, not the Lord, that if any brother has a wife who is an unbeliever, and she consents to live with him, let him not send her away. 13 And a woman who has an unbelieving husband, and he consents to live with her, let him not send her husband away. 14 For the unbelieving husband is sanctified through his wife, and the unbelieving wife is sanctified through her believing husband; for otherwise your children are unclean, but now they are holy. 15 Yet if the unbelieving one leaves, let him leave; the brother or the sister is not under bondage in such *cases,* but God has called *[b]*us to peace. 16 For how do you know, O wife, whether you will save your husband? Or how do you know, O husband, whether you will save your wife?

17 Only, as the Lord has assigned to each one, as God has called each, in this manner let him walk. And thus I direct in all the churches. 18 Was any man called *already* circumcised? Let him not become uncircumcised. Has anyone been called in uncircumcision? Let him not be

[a] Some ancient mss. read, *For.* [b] Some ancient mss. read, *you.*

WILLIAMS

from God? Furthermore, you are not your own, 20 for you have been bought and actually paid for. So you must honor God with your bodies.

7 *Single or married state, which? Husbands and wives urged not to separate; Christians to remain in present social conditions; earthly life fleeting; a father's duty to his single daughter; widows may marry again*

Now I take up the matters about which you wrote me. It may be a good thing for a man to remain unmarried; 2 but because of so much sexual immorality every man should have a wife of his own, and every woman a husband of her own. 3 The husband must always give his wife what is due her, and the wife too must do so for her husband. 4 The wife does not have the right to do as she pleases with her own body; the husband has his right to it. In the same way the husband does not have the right to do as he pleases with his own body; the wife has her right to it. 5 You husbands and wives must stop refusing each other what is due, unless you agree to do so just for awhile, so as to have plenty of time for prayer, and then to be together again, so as to keep Satan from tempting you because of your lack of self-control. 6 But I say this by way of concession, not by way of command. 7 However, I should like for everyone to be just as I am myself, yet each of us has his own special gift from God, one for one way, another for another.

8 To unmarried people and to widows I would say this: It would be a fine thing for them to remain single, as I am. 9 But if they do not practice self-control, let them marry. For it is better to marry than to be burning in the fire of passion. 10 To the people already married I give this instruction—no, not I but the Lord—that a wife is not to leave her husband. 11 But if she does leave him, she must remain single, or better, be reconciled to her husband. I instruct the husband too not to divorce his wife.

12 To the rest of the people I myself would say—though the Lord Himself has said nothing about it—if a Christian has a wife that is not a believer and she consents to live with him, he must not divorce her; 13 and a woman who has a husband that is not a believer, but he consents to live with her, must not divorce her husband. 14 For the unbelieving husband is consecrated by union with his wife and the unbelieving wife by union with her Christian husband; for otherwise your children would be unblessed, but in this way they are consecrated. 15 But if the unbelieving consort actually leaves, let the separation stand. In such cases the Christian husband or wife is not morally bound; God has called us to live in peace. 16 For how do you know, wife, whether you will save your husband? Or, how do you know, husband, whether you will save your wife?

17 Only, everybody must continue to live in the station which the Lord assigned to him, in that in which God called him. These are my orders in all the churches. 18 Has a man been called after he was circumcised? He must not try to change it. Has a man been called without being circumcised? He must not be cir-

BECK

Holy Spirit, whom God gives you and who is in you? You don't belong to yourselves, 20 because you were bought for a price. Then glorify God with your bodies.

If You Are Married

7 Now about the things you wrote—it is good for a man not to have sex relations with a woman. 2 But to avoid sexual sins, every man should have his own wife, and every woman her own husband.

3 A husband should do for his wife what he owes her, and a wife should do the same for her husband. 4 A wife can't do as she likes with her body; her husband has a right to it. In the same way a husband can't do as he likes with his body; his wife has a right to it. 5 Don't deprive one another, unless you agree to do so for a while to take time to pray. And come together again, or the devil will tempt you because you cannot control yourselves. 6 But as I say this, I'm yielding to you, not ordering you.

7 I would like everybody to be like myself, but each one has only the gift God gave him, one this and another that. 8 To those who aren't married and to widows I say, It is good for you to stay single like myself, 9 but if you can't control yourselves, get married; it is better to marry than to burn with desire.

10 If you are married, I—that is, not I, but the Lord—order a wife not to leave her husband. 11 If she does leave him, she should stay single or make up with her husband. And a husband should not divorce his wife.

If You're Married to an Unchristian

12 To the rest I say (not the Lord), if a Christian has a wife who doesn't believe and she agrees to live with him, he should not divorce her. 13 And if a wife has a husband who doesn't believe and he agrees to live with her, she should not divorce her husband. 14 An unbelieving man married to such a woman serves a holy purpose, and an unbelieving wife married to a Christian serves a holy purpose. Otherwise your children would be unclean, but now they are holy. 15 But if the unbelieving person leaves, let him go. In such a case a Christian man or woman is not bound. But God called us to live in peace. 16 You wife, what do you know—you may save your husband. Or you husband, what do you know—you may save your wife.

Stay as God Called You

17 But everyone should live the life the Lord assigned to him just as God called him. This is the rule I lay down in all the churches.

18 Were you circumcised when you were called? Don't try to get rid of your circumcision. Were you uncircumcised when you were called?

K.J.V.

cised. 19 Circumcision is nothing, and uncircumcision is nothing, but the keeping of the commandments of God. 20 Let every man abide in the same calling wherein he was called. 21 Art thou called *being* a servant? care not for it: but if thou mayest be made free, use *it* rather. 22 For he that is called in the Lord, *being* a servant, is the Lord's freeman: likewise also he that is called, *being* free, is Christ's servant. 23 Ye are bought with a price; be not ye the servants of men. 24 Brethren, let every man, wherein he is called, therein abide with God. 25 Now concerning virgins I have no commandment of the Lord: yet I give my judgment, as one that hath obtained mercy of the Lord to be faithful. 26 I suppose therefore that this is good for the present distress, *I say*, that *it is* good for a man so to be. 27 Art thou bound unto a wife? seek not to be loosed. Art thou loosed from a wife? seek not a wife. 28 But and if thou marry, thou hast not sinned; and if a virgin marry, she hath not sinned. Nevertheless such shall have trouble in the flesh: but I spare you. 29 But this I say, brethren, the time *is* short: it remaineth, that both they that have wives be as though they had none; 30 And they that weep, as though they wept not; and they that rejoice, as though they rejoiced not; and they that buy, as though they possessed not; 31 And they that use this world, as not abusing *it:* for the fashion of this world passeth away. 32 But I would have you without carefulness. He that is unmarried careth for the things that belong to the Lord, how he may please the Lord: 33 But he that is married careth for the things that are of the world, how he may please *his* wife. 34 There is difference *also* between a wife and a virgin. The unmarried woman careth for the things of the Lord, that she may be holy both in body and in spirit: but she that is married careth for the things of the world, how she may please *her* husband. 35 And this I speak for your own profit; not that I may cast a snare upon you, but for that which is comely, and that ye may attend upon the Lord without distraction. 36 But if any man think that he behaveth himself uncomely toward his virgin, if she pass the flower of *her* age, and need so require, let him do what he will, he sinneth not: let them marry. 37 Nevertheless he that standeth steadfast in his heart, having no necessity, but hath power over his own will, and hath so decreed in his heart that he will keep his virgin, doeth well. 38 So then he that giveth *her* in marriage doeth well; but he that giveth *her* not in marriage doeth better. 39 The wife is bound by the law as long as her husband liveth; but if her husband be dead, she is at liberty to be married to whom she will; only in the Lord. 40 But she is happier if she so abide, after my judgment: and I think also that I have the Spirit of God.

N.A.S.

circumcised. 19 Circumcision is nothing, and uncircumcision is nothing, but *what matters is* the keeping of the commandments of God. 20 Let each man remain in that condition in which he was called. 21 Were you called while a slave? Do not worry about it; but if you are able also to become free, rather do that. 22 For he who was called in the Lord while a slave, is the Lord's freedman; likewise he who was called while free, is Christ's slave. 23 You were bought with a price; do not become slaves of men. 24 Brethren, let each man remain with God in that *condition* in which he was called.

25 Now concerning virgins I have no command of the Lord, but I give an opinion as one who by the mercy of the Lord is trustworthy. 26 I think then that this is good in view of the present distress, that it is good for a man to remain as he is. 27 Are you bound to a wife? Do not seek to be released. Are you released from a wife? Do not seek a wife. 28 But if you should marry, you have not sinned; and if a virgin should marry, she has not sinned. Yet such will have trouble in this life, and I am trying to spare you. 29 But this I say, brethren, the time has been shortened, so that from now on both those who have wives should be as though they had none; 30 and those who weep, as though they did not weep; and those who rejoice, as though they did not rejoice; and those who buy, as though they did not possess; 31 and those who use the world, as though they did not make full use of it; for the form of this world is passing away. 32 But I want you to be free from concern. One who is unmarried is concerned about the things of the Lord, how he may please the Lord; 33 but one who is married is concerned about the things of the world, how he may please his [a]wife, 34 and *his interest* are divided. And the woman who is unmarried, and the virgin, is concerned about the things of the Lord, that she may be holy both in body and spirit; but one who is married is concerned about the things of the world, how she may please her husband. 35 And this I say for your own benefit; not to put a restraint upon you, but to promote what is seemly, and *to secure* undistracted devotion to the Lord.

36 But if any man thinks that he is acting unbecomingly toward his virgin *daughter*, if she should be of full age, and if it must be so, let him do what he wishes, he does not sin; let them marry. 37 But he who stands firm in his heart, being under no constraint, but has authority over his own will, and has decided this in his own heart, to keep his own virgin *daughter*, he will do well. 38 So then both he who gives his own virgin *daughter* in marriage does well, and he who does not give her in marriage will do better.

39 A wife is bound as long as her husband lives; but if her husband is dead, she is free to be married to whom she wishes, only in the Lord. 40 But in my opinion she is happier if she remains as she is; and I think that I also have the Spirit of God.

[a] Some mss. read, *wife. And there is a difference also between the wife and the virgin. One who is unmarried is concerned* . . .

WILLIAMS

cumcised. 19 Being circumcised or not being circumcised has no value, but keeping God's commands is important. 20 Everybody must remain in the station in which he was called. 21 Were you called while a slave? Stop letting that annoy you. Yet, if you can win your freedom, take advantage of such an opportunity. 22 For the slave who has been called to union with the Lord is the Lord's freedman; in the same way the freeman who has been called is a slave of Christ. 23 You have been bought and actually paid for; stop becoming slaves to men. 24 Brothers, each one must continue close to God in the very station in which he was called.

25 About unmarried women I have no command from the Lord, but I will give you my opinion as of one who is trustworthy, since I have had mercy shown me by the Lord. 26 Now this is my opinion in the light of the present distress: That it is a good thing for a man to remain as he is. 27 Are you married? Stop trying to get a divorce. Are you unmarried? Stop looking for a wife. 28 But if you do get married, you have not sinned in doing so. And if a girl gets married, she has not sinned in doing so. But those who do will have trouble in their earthly life, and I am trying to spare you this. 29 I mean this, brothers. The time has been cut short. For the future, men who have wives should live as though they had none, 30 and those that mourn as though they did not mourn, and those who are glad as though they were not glad, and those who buy as though they did not own a thing, 31 and those who are enjoying the world as though they were not entirely absorbed in it. For the outward order of this world is passing away. 32 I want you to be free from worldly worries. An unmarried man is concerned about the affairs of the Lord. 33 A married man is concerned about the affairs of the world, and how he can please his wife, and so his devotion is divided. 34 An unmarried woman or a girl is concerned about the affairs of the Lord, so as to be consecrated in body and spirit, but a married woman is concerned about the affairs of the world, and how she can please her husband. 35 It is for your welfare that I am saying this, not to put restraint on you, but to foster good order and to help you to an undivided devotion to the Lord.

36 Now if a father thinks that he is not doing the proper thing regarding his single daughter, if she is past the bloom of her youth, and she ought to do so, let him do what she desires; he commits no sin. Let the daughter and her suitor marry. 37 But the father who stands firm in his purpose, without having any necessity for doing so, and he has made the decision in his own heart to keep her single, will do what is right. 38 And so the man who gives his daughter in marriage does what is right, and yet the man who does not do so does even better.

39 A wife is bound to her husband as long as he lives. If her husband dies, she is free to marry anyone she pleases, except that he must be a Christian. 40 But in my opinion she will be happier, if she remains as she is, and I think too that I have God's Spirit.

BECK

Don't be circumcised. 19 Circumcision is nothing, and the lack of it is nothing, but doing what God orders is everything. 20 Everyone should stay as he was called. 21 Were you a slave when you were called? Don't let that trouble you. Of course, if you have a chance to get free, take it. 22 If you are a slave when you are called in the Lord, you are the Lord's free man. In the same way, if you are free when you are called, you are Christ's slave. 23 You were bought for a price; don't become slaves of men. 24 My fellow Christians, everyone should stay with God just as he was when he was called.

To Marry or Not to Marry

25 For the unmarried girls I have no order from the Lord, but the Lord's mercy made me one you can trust, and I'll tell you what I think. 26 On account of the troubles we're in I believe it is good for anyone to stay as he is. 27 Are you married? Don't look for a divorce. Are you separated from a wife? Don't look for a wife. 28 But if you get married, it's no sin, and if a girl gets married, it's no sin. But if you do, you'll have trouble in your life, and I'm trying to spare you.

29 I mean, my fellow Christians, the time has been shortened. While it lasts, if you have a wife, live as if you had none. 30 If you weep, as if you weren't weeping. If you're happy, as if you weren't happy. If you buy anything, act as if you didn't have it. 31 While you use the world, don't try to get out of it all you can, since this world in its present form is passing away.

32 I don't want you to worry. An unmarried man is concerned about the Lord's things, how he can please the Lord. 33 But once he's married, he worries about earthly things, how he can please his wife. 34 He's interested in two different things. An unmarried woman or girl is concerned about the Lord's things, to be holy in body and in spirit. But once she's married, she worries about earthly things, how she can please her husband. 35 I'm saying this to help you, not to hold you by a rope but to show you how to live nobly for the Lord without being troubled about other things.

36 If a man thinks he's not acting properly toward his girl, if his passion is too strong and it must be so, he should do what he wants to—it's no sin—they should be married. 37 But suppose a man has a strong character and the will power and feels no necessity but has made up his mind to keep his girl as she is, he'll be doing right. 38 If, then, he marries his girl, he's doing right. But if he doesn't marry her, he'll be doing better.

39 A wife is bound to her husband as long as he lives. If her husband dies, she's free to marry anyone she wants to, but it should be in the Lord. But she'll be happier if she stays as she is. 40 That is my judgment, and I think I, too, have God's Spirit.

8 Now as touching things offered unto idols, we know that we all have knowledge. Knowledge puffeth up, but charity edifieth. 2And if any man think that he knoweth any thing, he knoweth nothing yet as he ought to know. 3 But if any man love God, the same is known of him. 4As concerning therefore the eating of those things that are offered in sacrifice unto idols, we know that an idol *is* nothing in the world, and that *there is* none other God but one. 5 For though there be that are called gods, whether in heaven or in earth, (as there be gods many, and lords many,) 6 But to us *there is but* one God, the Father, of whom *are* all things, and we in him; and one Lord Jesus Christ, by whom *are* all things, and we by him. 7 Howbeit *there is* not in every man that knowledge: for some with conscience of the idol unto this hour eat *it* as a thing offered unto an idol; and their conscience being weak is defiled. 8 But meat commendeth us not to God: for neither, if we eat, are we the better; neither, if we eat not, are we the worse. 9 But take heed lest by any means this liberty of yours become a stumblingblock to them that are weak. 10 For if any man see thee which hast knowledge sit at meat in the idol's temple, shall not the conscience of him which is weak be emboldened to eat those things which are offered to idols; 11And through thy knowledge shall the weak brother perish, for whom Christ died? 12 But when ye sin so against the brethren, and wound their weak conscience, ye sin against Christ. 13 Wherefore, if meat make my brother to offend, I will eat no flesh while the world standeth, lest I make my brother to offend.

9 Am I not an apostle? am I not free? have I not seen Jesus Christ our Lord? are not ye my work in the Lord? 2 If I be not an apostle unto others, yet doubtless I am to you: for the seal of mine apostleship are ye in the Lord. 3 Mine answer to them that do examine me is this: 4 Have we not power to eat and to drink? 5 Have we not power to lead about a sister, a wife, as well as other apostles, and *as* the brethren of the Lord, and Cephas? 6 Or I only and Barnabas, have not we power to forbear working? 7 Who goeth a warfare any time at his own charges? who planteth a vineyard, and eateth not of the fruit thereof? or who feedeth a flock,

8 Now concerning things sacrificed to idols, we know that we all have knowledge. Knowledge makes arrogant, but love edifies. 2 If any one supposes that he knows anything, he has not yet known as he ought to know; 3 but if any one loves God, he is known by Him. 4 Therefore concerning the eating of things sacrificed to idols, we know that *there is no such thing as an idol in the world, and that there is no God but one. 5 For even if there are so-called gods whether in heaven or on earth, as indeed there are many gods and many lords, 6 yet for us there is *but* one God, the Father, from whom are all things, and we *exist* for Him; and one Lord, Jesus Christ, through whom are all things, and we *exist* through Him.

7 However not all men have this knowledge; but some, being accustomed to the idol until now, eat food as if it were sacrificed to an idol; and their conscience being weak is defiled. 8 But food will not commend us to God; we are neither the worse if we do not eat, nor the better if we do eat. 9 But take care lest this liberty of yours somehow become a stumblingblock to the weak. 10 For if someone sees you who have knowledge dining in an idol's temple, will not his conscience, if he is weak, be strengthened to eat things sacrificed to idols? 11 For through your knowledge he who is weak is ruined, the brother for whose sake Christ died. 12And thus, by sinning against the brethren and wounding their conscience when it is weak, you sin against Christ. 13 Therefore, if food causes my brother to stumble, I will never eat meat again, that I might not cause my brother to stumble.

9 Am I not free? Am I not an apostle? Have I not seen Jesus our Lord? Are you not my work in the Lord? 2 If to others I am not an apostle, at least I am to you; for you are the seal of my apostleship in the Lord. 3 My defense to those who examine me is this: 4 Do we not have a right to eat and drink? 5 Do we not have a right to take along a believing wife, even as the rest of the apostles, and the brothers of the Lord, and Cephas? 6 Or do only Barnabas and I not have a right to refrain from working? 7 Who at any time serves as a soldier at his own expense? Who plants a vineyard, and does not eat the fruit of it? Or who tends a flock and does not use

[a] i.e., has no real existence.

WILLIAMS

8 *May Christians eat food once sacrificed to idols? Brotherly love solves this problem*

Now about the foods that have been sacrificed to idols: We know that every one of us has some knowledge of the matter. Knowledge puffs up, but love builds up. 2 If a man supposes that he has already gotten some true knowledge, as yet he has not learned it as he ought to know it. 3 But if a man loves God, God is known by him. 4 So, as to eating things that have been sacrificed to idols, we are sure that an idol is nothing in the world, and that there is no God but One. 5 For even if there are so-called gods in heaven or on earth—as there are, indeed, a vast number of gods and lords—6 yet for us there is but one God, the Father, who is the source of all things and the goal of our living, and but one Lord, Jesus Christ, through whom everything was made and through whom we live.

7 But it is not in all of you that such knowledge is found. Some, because of their past habits with idols, even down to the present moment, still eat such food as was really sacrificed to an idol, and so their consciences, because they are overscrupulous, are contaminated. 8 Food will never bring us near to God. We are no worse if we do not eat it; we are no better if we do. 9 But you must see to it that this right of yours does not become a stumbling block to overscrupulous people. 10 For if somebody sees you, who have an intelligent view of this matter, partaking of a meal in an idol's temple, will he not be emboldened, with his overscrupulous conscience, to eat the food which has been sacrificed to an idol? 11 Yes, the overscrupulous brother, for whom Christ died, is ruined by your so-called knowledge. 12 Now if in such a way you sin against your brothers and wound their overscrupulous consciences, you are actually sinning against Christ. 13 So then, if food can make my brother fall, I will never, no, never, eat meat again, in order to keep my brother from falling.

9 *The Church in Corinth proof of Paul's apostleship; his right to marry and his right to be supported as a minister; his motives to win others to Christ; the wreath that never withers*

Am I not free? Am I not an apostle? Have I not seen Jesus our Lord? Are you not the product of my work for the Lord? 2 If I am not an apostle to other people, I certainly am one to you, for you yourselves, by virtue of your union with the Lord, are the proof of my apostleship.

3 My vindication of myself to those who are investigating me is this: 4 It cannot be that we have no right to our food and drink, can it? 5 It cannot be that we have no right to take a Christian wife about with us, can it, as well as the rest of the apostles and the Lord's brothers, and Cephas? 6 Or is it Barnabas and I alone who have no right to refrain from working for a living? 7 What soldier ever goes to war at his own expense? Who plants a vineyard and does not eat any of its grapes? Who shepherds a flock and does not drink any of the milk the

BECK

Meat Sacrificed to Idols

8 About the meat sacrificed to idols. We know that all of us have some knowledge. Knowledge puffs up, but love builds up. 2 If anybody thinks he knows something, he still has something to learn. 3 But if he loves God, God knows him.

4 Now about eating meat that was sacrificed to idols, we know there is no real idol in the world and there is only one God. 5 Even if there are so-called gods in heaven or on earth (as there are many gods and many lords), 6 yet we have one God, the Father: From Him comes everything, and we live for Him. And one Lord, Jesus Christ: He made everything, and we live by Him.

7 But not everybody knows this. Some are still so used to an idol they think of the meat they eat as sacrificed to the idol, and their conscience, being weak, is stained with guilt.

8 Food will not bring us closer to God. We lose nothing by not eating and gain nothing by eating. 9 But be careful, or weak Christians may fall into sin because you do as you please. 10 If anybody sees you who knows better lying down to eat in the temple of an idol, won't you be encouraging him who has a weak conscience to eat the meat sacrificed to idols? 11 Then your knowledge is ruining the weak fellow Christian for whom Christ died. 12 But when you sin against your fellow Christians in this way and wound their weak consciences, you sin against Christ.

13 So if food makes my fellow Christian sin, I will never eat meat—I don't want to give him a reason for sinning.

A Pastor's Pay

9 Am I not free? Am I not an apostle? Didn't I see Jesus, our Lord? Aren't you my work in the Lord? 2 If I'm not an apostle to others, I certainly am one to you. You are the Lord's seal that proves I'm an apostle. 3 That's how I defend myself before those who examine me. 4 Don't we have the right to eat and drink? 5 Don't we have the right to take a Christian wife with us like the other apostles, the Lord's brothers, and Peter? 6 Or do only I and Barnabas have no right to stop working for a living?

7 Does a soldier ever pay his own expenses? Does anyone plant a vineyard and not eat its grapes? Or does anyone take care of a flock and

K.J.V.

and eateth not of the milk of the flock? 8 Say I these things as a man? or saith not the law the same also? 9 For it is written in the law of Moses, Thou shalt not muzzle the mouth of the ox that treadeth out the corn. Doth God take care for oxen? 10 Or saith he *it* altogether for our sakes? For our sakes, no doubt, *this* is written: that he that plougheth should plough in hope; and that he that thresheth in hope should be partaker of his hope. 11 If we have sown unto you spiritual things, *is it* a great thing if we shall reap your carnal things? 12 If others be partakers of *this* power over you, *are* not we rather? Nevertheless we have not used this power; but suffer all things, lest we should hinder the gospel of Christ. 13 Do ye not know that they which minister about holy things live *of the things* of the temple? and they which wait at the altar are partakers with the altar? 14 Even so hath the Lord ordained that they which preach the gospel should live of the gospel. 15 But I have used none of these things: neither have I written these things, that it should be so done unto me: for *it were* better for me to die, than that any man should make my glorying void. 16 For though I preach the gospel, I have nothing to glory of: for necessity is laid upon me; yea, woe is unto me, if I preach not the gospel! 17 For if I do this thing willingly, I have a reward: but if against my will, a dispensation *of the gospel* is committed unto me. 18 What is my reward then? *Verily* that, when I preach the gospel, I may make the gospel of Christ without charge, that I abuse not my power in the gospel. 19 For though I be free from all *men*, yet have I made myself servant unto all, that I might gain the more. 20 And unto the Jews I became as a Jew, that I might gain the Jews; to them that are under the law, as under the law, that I might gain them that are under the law; 21 To them that are without law, as without law, (being not without law to God, but under the law to Christ,) that I might gain them that are without law. 22 To the weak became I as weak, that I might gain the weak: I am made all things to all *men*, that I might by all means save some. 23 And this I do for the gospel's sake, that I might be partaker thereof with *you*. 24 Know ye not that they which run in a race run all, but one receiveth the prize? So run, that ye may obtain. 25 And every man that striveth for the mastery is temperate in all things. Now they *do it* to obtain a corruptible crown; but we an incorruptible. 26 I therefore so run, not as uncertainly; so fight I, not as one that beateth the air: 27 But I keep under my body, and bring *it* into subjection: lest that by any means, when I have preached to others, I myself should be a castaway.

N.A.S.

the milk of the flock? 8 I am not speaking these things according to human judgment, am I? Or does not the Law also say these things? 9 For it is written in the Law of Moses, "YOU SHALL NOT MUZZLE THE OX WHILE HE IS THRESHING." God is not concerned about oxen, is He? 10 Or is He speaking altogether for our sake? Yes, for our sake it was written, because the plowman ought to plow in hope, and the thresher *to thresh* in hope of sharing *the crops.* 11 If we sowed spiritual things in you, is it too much if we should reap material things from you? 12 If others share the right over you, do we not more? Nevertheless, we did not use this right, but we endure all things, that we may cause no hindrance to the gospel of Christ. 13 Do you not know that those who perform sacred services eat the *food* of the temple, *and* those who attend regularly to the altar have their share with the altar? 14 So also the Lord directed those who proclaim the gospel to get their living from the gospel. 15 But I have used none of these things. And I am not writing these things that it may be done so in my case; for it would be better for me to die than have any man make my boast an empty one. 16 For if I preach the gospel, I have nothing to boast of, for I am under compulsion; for woe is me if I do not preach the gospel. 17 For if I do this voluntarily, I have a reward; but if against my will, I have a stewardship entrusted to me. 18 What then is my reward? That, when I preach the gospel, I may offer the gospel without charge, so as not to make full use of my right in the gospel.

19 For though I am free from all *men*, I have made myself a slave to all, that I might win the more. 20 And to the Jews I became as a Jew, that I might win Jews; to those who are under the Law, as under the Law, though not being myself under the Law, that I might win those who are under the Law; 21 to those who are without law, as without law, though not being without the law of God but under the law of Christ, that I might win those who are without law. 22 To the weak I became weak, that I might win the weak; I have become all things to all men, that I may by all means save some. 23 And I do all things for the sake of the gospel, that I may become a fellow-partaker of it.

24 Do you not know that those who run in a race all run, but *only* one receives the prize? Run in such a way that you may win. 25 And everyone who competes in the games exercises self-control in all things. They then *do it* to receive a perishable wreath, but we an imperishable. 26 Therefore I run in such a way, as not without aim; I box in such a way, as not beating the air; 27 but I buffet my body and make it my slave, lest possibly, after I have preached to others, I myself should be disqualified.

WILLIAMS

flock produces? 8 I am not saying this only by way of human illustrations, am I? Does not the law say so too? 9 For in the law of Moses it is written, "You must not muzzle an ox that is treading out your grain." Is it that God is concerned about oxen only? 10 Is He not really speaking on our behalf? Yes, indeed, this law was written on our behalf, because the plowman ought to plow and the thresher ought to thresh, in the hope of sharing in the crop. 11 If we have sown the spiritual seed for you, is it too great for us to reap a material support from you? 12 If others share this right with you, have we not a stronger claim? Yet, we have never used this right; no, we keep on bearing everything, to keep from hindering the progress of the good news of Christ. 13 Do you not know that those who do the work about the temple get their living from the temple, and those who constantly attend on the altar share its offerings? 14 Just so the Lord has issued orders that those who preach the good news shall get their living out of it. 15 But I myself have never used any of these rights. And I am not writing this just to make it so in my case, for I had rather die than do that. No one shall rob me of this ground of boasting. 16 For if I do preach the good news, I have no ground for boasting of it, for I cannot help doing it. Yes, indeed, I. am accursed if I do not preach the good news. 17 For if I do it of my own accord, I get my pay; but if I am unwilling to do it, I still am entrusted with trusteeship.ᵃ 18 Then what is the pay that I am getting? To be able to preach the good news without expense to anybody, and so never to make full use of my rights in preaching the good news.

19 Yes, indeed, though I am free from any human power, I have made myself a slave to everybody, to win as many as possible. 20 To the Jews I have become like a Jew for the winning of Jews; to men under the law, like one under the law, though I am not under the law myself, to win the men under the law; 21 to men who have no written law, like one without any law, though I am not without God's law but specially under Christ's law, to win the men who have no written law. 22 To the overscrupulous I have become overscrupulous, to win the overscrupulous; yes, I have become everything to everybody, in order by all means to save some of them. 23 And I do it all for the sake of the good news, so as to share with others in its blessings.

24 Do you not know that in a race the runners all run, but only one can get the prize? You must run in such a way that you can get the prize. 25 Any man who enters an athletic contest practices rigid self-control in training, only to win a wreath that withers, but we are in to win a wreath that never withers. 26 So that is the way I run, with no uncertainty as to winning. That is the way I box, not like one that punches the air. 27 But I keep on beating and bruising my body and making it my slave, so that I, after I have summoned others to the race, may not myself become unfit to run.ᵇ

BECK

not drink any milk from it? 8 Am I stating only a human rule? Doesn't the Law say the same thing? 9 The Law of Moses says, *Don't muzzle an ox when he's treading out grain.*¹² Is God here interested in oxen? 10 Surely He has us in mind. This was written to show us when we plow or thresh we should expect to get a share of the crop. 11 If we have sown the spiritual life in you, is it too much if we'll reap your earthly goods? 12 If others enjoy this right over you, don't we have a better claim? But we haven't made use of this right. No, we put up with anything in order not to hinder the preaching of Christ.

13 Don't you know that the men who work at the temple get their food from the temple? That those who help at the altar get their share of what is on the altar? 14 In the same way the Lord has ordered that those who tell the good news should get their living from the good news.

15 But I haven't used any of these rights. And I'm not writing this to get such things done for me. I'd rather die than let anyone take away my boast. 16 If I tell the good news, I have nothing to boast about. I must tell it. Woe to me if I don't tell the good news! 17 If I do it because I want to, I get a reward. But if I don't want to do it, I still have this work entrusted to me.

18 What then is my reward? Just this: When I tell the good news, I won't let it cost anybody anything, and so I won't take advantage of my right in telling the good news.

Everything to Everybody

19 Although I am free from all people, I made myself a slave of all of them to win more of them. 20 To the Jews I became like a Jew to win Jews; to those under the Law I became like a man under the Law—although I'm not under the Law—to win those under the Law. 21 To those who don't have the Law I became like a man without the Law—although I'm not outside the Law of God but under the law of Christ —to win those who don't have the Law. 22 To weak persons I became weak to win the weak. I've been everything to everybody to be sure to save some of them.

23 I'm doing everything for the good news in order to have a share of what it gives. 24 Don't you know that all who are in a race run but only one wins the prize? Like them, run to win! 25 Anyone who enters a contest goes into strict training. Now, they do it to win a wreath that withers, but we to win one that never withers. 26 So I run with a clear goal ahead of me. I fight and don't just hit the air. 27 No, I beat my body and make it my slave so that, when I've called others to run the race, I myself will not somehow be disqualified.

---

[a] Lit., *stewardship.* [b] Lit., *rejected, disqualified.*   [12] Deut. 25:4

K.J.V.

10 Moreover, brethren, I would not that ye should be ignorant, how that all our fathers were under the cloud, and all passed through the sea; 2And were all baptized unto Moses in the cloud and in the sea; 3And did all eat the same spiritual meat; 4And did all drink the same spiritual drink; for they drank of that spiritual Rock that followed them: and that Rock was Christ. 5 But with many of them God was not well pleased: for they were overthrown in the wilderness. 6 Now these things were our examples, to the intent we should not lust after evil things, as they also lusted. 7 Neither be ye idolaters, as *were* some of them; as it is written, The people sat down to eat and drink, and rose up to play. 8 Neither let us commit fornication, as some of them committed, and fell in one day three and twenty thousand. 9 Neither let us tempt Christ, as some of them also tempted, and were destroyed of serpents. 10 Neither murmur ye, as some of them also murmured, and were destroyed of the destroyer. 11 Now all these things happened unto them for ensamples: and they are written for our admonition, upon whom the ends of the world are come. 12 Wherefore let him that thinketh he standeth take heed lest he fall. 13 There hath no temptation taken you but such as is common to man: but God *is* faithful, who will not suffer you to be tempted above that ye are able; but will with the temptation also make a way to escape, that ye may be able to bear *it*. 14 Wherefore, my dearly beloved, flee from idolatry. 15 I speak as to wise men; judge ye what I say. 16 The cup of blessing which we bless, is it not the communion of the blood of Christ? The bread which we break, is it not the communion of the body of Christ? 17 For we *being* many are one bread, *and* one body: for we are all partakers of that one bread. 18 Behold Israel after the flesh: are not they which eat of the sacrifices partakers of the altar? 19 What say I then? that the idol is any thing, or that which is offered in sacrifice to idols is any thing? 20 But *I say*, that the things which the Gentiles sacrifice, they sacrifice to devils, and not to God: and I would not that ye should have fellowship with devils. 21 Ye cannot drink the cup of the Lord, and the cup of devils: ye cannot be partakers of the Lord's table, and of the table of devils. 22 Do we provoke the Lord to jealousy? are we stronger than he? 23 All things are lawful for me, but all things are not expedient: all things are lawful for me, but all things edify not. 24 Let no man seek his own, but every man another's *wealth*. 25 Whatsoever

N.A.S.

10 For I do not want you to be unaware, brethren, that our fathers were all under the cloud, and all passed through the sea; 2 and all *were baptized into Moses in the cloud and in the sea; 3 and all ate the same spiritual food; 4 and all drank the same spiritual drink, for they were drinking from a spiritual rock which followed them; and the rock was Christ. 5 Nevertheless, with most of them God was not well pleased; for they were laid low in the wilderness. 6 Now these things happened as examples for us, that we should not crave evil things, as they also craved. 7And do not be idolaters, as some of them were; as it is written, "The people sat down to eat and drink, and stood up to play." 8 Nor let us act immorally, as some of them did, and twenty-three thousand fell in one day. 9 Nor let us try the Lord, as some of them did, and were destroyed by the serpents. 10 Nor grumble, as some of them did, and were destroyed by the destroyer. 11 Now these things happened to them as an example, and they were written for our instruction, upon whom the ends of the ages have come. 12 Therefore let him who thinks he stands take heed lest he fall. 13 No temptation has overtaken you but such as is common to man; and God is faithful, who will not allow you to be tempted beyond what you are able; but with the temptation will provide the way of escape also, that you may be able to endure it.

14 Therefore, my beloved, flee from idolatry. 15 I speak as to wise men; you judge what I say. 16 Is not the cup of blessing which we bless a sharing in the blood of Christ? Is not the bread which we break a sharing in the body of Christ? 17 Since there is one bread, we who are many are one body; for we all partake of the one bread. 18 Look at the nation Israel; are not those who eat the sacrifices sharers in the altar? 19 What do I mean then? That a thing sacrificed to idols is anything, or that an idol is anything? 20 No; but *I say* that the things which the Gentiles sacrifice, they sacrifice to demons, and not to God; and I do not want you to become sharers in demons. 21 You cannot drink the cup of the Lord, and the cup of demons; you cannot partake of the table of the Lord, and the table of demons. 22 Or do we provoke the Lord to jealousy? We are not stronger than He, are we?

23 All things are lawful, but not all things are profitable. All things are lawful, but not all things edify. 24 Let no one seek his own *good*, but that of his neighbor. 25 Eat anything that

[a] Some ancient mss. read, *received baptism.*

478

WILLIAMS

BECK

10 *Israelites in the desert, lacking self-control, missed the prize; every temptation may be overcome; warns against idolatry; brotherly love limits personal freedom*

For I would not have you, brothers, to be ignorant of the fact that though our forefathers were all made safe by the cloud, and all went securely through the sea, and in the cloud and the sea 2 they all allowed themselves to be baptized as followers of Moses, 3 and all ate the same spiritual food, 4 and all drank the same spiritual drink—for they continued to drink the water from the spiritual Rock which accompanied them, and that Rock was the Christ— 5 still with the most of them God was not at all satisfied, for He allowed them to be laid low in the desert.

6 Now all these things occurred as warnings[a] to us, to keep us from hankering after what is evil, in the ways they did. 7 Now stop being idolaters, as some of them were, for the Scripture says, "The people sat down to eat and drink and got up to dance." 8 Let us stop practicing immorality, as some of them did, and on one day twenty-three thousand fell dead. 9 Let us stop trying the Lord's patience, as some of them did, and for it were destroyed by the snakes. 10 You must stop grumbling, as some of them did, and for it were destroyed by the destroying angel. 11 These things continued to befall them as warnings to others, and they were written down for the purpose of instructing us, in whose lives the climax of the ages has been reached.

12 So the man who thinks he stands securely must be on the lookout not to fall. 13 No temptation has taken hold of you but what is common to human nature. And God is to be trusted not to let you be tempted beyond your strength, but when temptation comes, to make a way out of it, so that you can bear up under it.

14 So then, my dearly beloved, keep on running from idolatry. 15 I am speaking to sensible men; decide for yourselves about what I say. 16 Is not the consecrated cup which we consecrate a sign of our sharing in the blood of Christ? Is not the loaf which we break a sign of our sharing in the body of Christ? 17 Because there is only one loaf, so we, though many, are only one body, for we all partake of one loaf. 18 Look at the Israelites in their practices. Are not those who eat the sacrifices in spiritual fellowship with the altar? 19 Then what do I mean? That the sacrifice to an idol is a reality, or that an idol itself is a reality? Of course not! 20 I mean that what the heathen sacrifice they sacrifice to demons, not to God, and I do not want you to be in fellowship with demons. 21 You cannot drink the cup of the Lord and the cup of demons. You cannot eat at the table of the Lord and at the table of demons. 22 Or, are we trying to incite the Lord to jealousy? We are not stronger than He, are we?

23 Everything is permissible for people, but not everything is good for them. Everything is permissible for people, but not everything builds up their personality. 24 No one should always be looking after his own welfare, but also that of his neighbor.

25 As a rule eat anything that is sold in the

[a] Lit., *types.*

A Warning

10 I want you to know, fellow Christians, our fathers were all under the cloud and all went through the sea, 2 and by baptism in the cloud and in the sea all were united with Moses, 3 all ate the same food of the Spirit, 4 and all drank the same water of the Spirit, because they drank from the spiritual Rock that went with them, and that Rock was Christ. 5 Yet God wasn't pleased with most of them—*they were killed in the desert.*[13]

6 Now, this happened in order to warn us not to long for[14] what is evil as they did. 7 Don't worship idols as some of them did, as the Bible says, *The people sat down to eat and drink and got up to play.*[15] 8 Let us not sin sexually as some of them did—23,000 died on one day. 9 Let us not go too far in testing the Lord's patience as some of them did—the snakes killed them. 10 Don't complain as some of them did—the angel of death killed them. 11 These things happened to them to make them a lesson to others and were written down to warn us who are living when the world is coming to an end. 12 So if you think you can stand, be careful you don't fall.

13 You haven't been tempted more than you could expect. And you can trust God He will not let you be tested more than you can stand. But when you are tested, He will also make a way out so that you can bear it.

Meat Sacrificed to Idols

14 And so, my dear friends, keep away from the worship of idols.

15 I'm talking to sensible people. Judge for yourselves what I say. 16 When we drink the blessed cup that we bless, don't we share the blood of Christ? When we eat the bread that we break, don't we share the body of Christ? 17 All of us are one body, because there is one bread and all of us share that one bread.

18 See how the Jews do it. Don't those who eat the sacrifices share the altar? 19 What do I mean by this? That a sacrifice made to an idol is something or that an idol really is something? 20 No, these *sacrifices* of the non-Jews *are made to devils and not to God.*[16] I don't want you to be partners of devils. 21 You can't drink the Lord's cup and the cup of devils. You can't share the *Lord's table*[17] and the table of devils. 22 Or are we *trying to make the Lord jealous?*[18] Are we stronger than He?

23 We are allowed to do anything, but not everything is good for others. We are allowed to do anything, but not everything helps them grow. 24 Nobody should look for his own good, but everybody for the good of the other person. 25 Eat anything sold in the market, and don't

[13] Num. 14:16
[14] Num. 11:4, 34
[15] Ex. 32:6
[16] Deut. 32:17; Ps. 106:37
[17] Mal. 1:7, 12
[18] Deut. 32:21

is sold in the shambles, *that* eat, asking no question for conscience' sake: 26 For the earth *is* the Lord's, and the fulness thereof. 27 If any of them that believe not bid you *to a feast,* and ye be disposed to go; whatsoever is set before you, eat, asking no question for conscience' sake. 28 But if any man say unto you, This is offered in sacrifice unto idols, eat not for his sake that shewed it, and for conscience' sake: for the earth *is* the Lord's, and the fulness thereof: 29 Conscience, I say, not thine own, but of the other: for why is my liberty judged of another *man's* conscience? 30 For if I by grace be a partaker, why am I evil spoken of for that for which I give thanks? 31 Whether therefore ye eat, or drink, or whatsoever ye do, do all to the glory of God. 32 Give none offence, neither to the Jews, nor to the Gentiles, nor to the church of God: 33 Even as I please all *men* in all *things,* not seeking mine own profit, but the *profit* of many, that they may be saved.

11 Be ye followers of me, even as I also *am* of Christ. 2 Now I praise you, brethren, that ye remember me in all things, and keep the ordinances, as I delivered *them* to you. 3 But I would have you know, that the head of every man is Christ; and the head of the woman *is* the man; and the head of Christ *is* God. 4 Every man praying or prophesying, having *his* head covered, dishonoureth his head. 5 But every woman that prayeth or prophesieth with *her* head uncovered dishonoureth her head: for that is even all one as if she were shaven. 6 For if the woman be not covered, let her also be shorn: but if it be a shame for a woman to be shorn or shaven, let her be covered. 7 For a man indeed ought not to cover *his* head, forasmuch as he is the image and glory of God: but the woman is the glory of the man. 8 For the man is not of the woman; but the woman of the man. 9 Neither was the man created for the woman; but the woman for the man. 10 For this cause ought the woman to have power on *her* head because of the angels. 11 Nevertheless neither is the man without the woman, neither the woman without the man, in the Lord. 12 For as the woman *is* of the man, even so *is* the man also by the woman; but all things of God. 13 Judge in yourselves: is it comely that a woman pray unto God uncovered? 14 Doth not even nature itself teach you, that, if a man have long hair, it is a shame unto him? 15 But if a woman have long hair, it is a glory to her: for *her* hair is given her for a covering. 16 But if any man seem to be contentious, we have no such custom, neither the churches of God. 17 Now in this that I declare *unto you* I praise *you* not, that ye come together not for the better, but for the worse. 18 For first of all, when ye come together

is sold in the meat market, without asking questions for conscience' sake; 26 FOR THE EARTH IS THE LORD'S, AND ALL IT CONTAINS. 27 If one of the unbelievers invites you, and you wish to go, eat anything that is set before you, without asking questions for conscience' sake. 28 But if anyone should say to you, "This is meat sacrificed to idols," do not eat *it,* for the sake of the one who informed *you,* and for conscience' sake; 29 I mean not your own conscience, but the other *man's;* for why is my freedom judged by another's conscience? 30 If I partake with thankfulness, why am I slandered concerning that for which I give thanks? 31 Whether, then, you eat or drink or whatever you do, do all to the glory of God. 32 Give no offense either to Jews or to Greeks or to the church of God; 33 just as I also please all men in all things, not seeking my own profit, but the *profit* of the many, that they may be saved.

11 Be imitators of me, just as I also am of Christ. 2 Now I praise you because you remember me in everything, and hold firmly to the traditions, just as I delivered them to you. 3 But I want you to understand that Christ is the head of every man, and the man is the head of a woman, and God is the head of Christ. 4 Every man who has *something* on his head while praying or prophesying, disgraces his head. 5 But every woman who has her head uncovered while praying or prophesying, disgraces her head; for she is one and the same with her whose head is shaved. 6 For if a woman does not cover her head, let her also have her hair cut off; but if it is disgraceful for a woman to have her hair cut off or her head shaved, let her cover her head. 7 For a man ought not to have his head covered, since he is the image and glory of God; but the woman is the glory of man. 8 For man does not originate from woman, but woman from man; 9 for indeed man was not created for the woman's sake, but woman for the man's sake. 10 Therefore the woman ought to have *a symbol of* authority on her head, because of the angels. 11 However, in the Lord, neither is woman independent of man, nor is man independent of woman. 12 For as the woman originates from the man, so also the man has his birth through the woman; and all things originate from God. 13 Judge for yourselves: is it proper for a woman to pray to God *with head* uncovered? 14 Does not even nature itself teach you that if a man has long hair, it is a dishonor to him, 15 but if a woman has long hair, it is a glory to her? For her hair is given to her for a covering. 16 But if one is inclined to be contentious, we have no other practice, nor have the churches of God. 17 But in giving this instruction, I do not praise you, because you come together not for the better but for the worse. 18 For, in the first

WILLIAMS

meat market without raising any question about it for conscience' sake, 26 for the earth and everything that it contains belong to the Lord. 27 If some unbelieving heathen invites you to his house, and you wish to go, eat whatever is set before you without raising any question for conscience' sake. 28 But if someone says to you, "This meat has been offered as a heathen sacrifice," make it your rule not to eat it, for the sake of the man who warned you and for conscience' sake; 29 I mean his conscience, not yours. Why then should my personal freedom be limited by another's conscience? 30 If I give thanks and thus partake of food, why am I to be blamed for that for which I give thanks?

31 So if you eat or drink or do anything else, do everything to honor God. 32 Stop being stumbling blocks to Jews or Greeks or to the church of God, 33 just as I myself am in the habit of pleasing everybody in everything, not aiming at my own welfare but at that of as many people as possible, in order that they may be saved. 11:1 You must follow my example, just as I myself am following Christ's.

11 *Woman's status and service in the church; cliques in church meetings; disorders in observing the Lord's Supper; origin and sacred significance of the Lord's Supper*

2 I prize and praise you for always remembering me and for firmly standing by the teachings as I passed them on to you. 3 But I want you to realize the fact that Christ is the Head of every man, that the husband is the head of the wife, and that God is the Head of Christ. 4 Any man who prays or preaches*a* with anything on his head dishonors his head, 5 and any woman who prays or prophesies bareheaded dishonors her head, for it is one and the same thing with having her head shaved. 6 For if a woman will not wear a veil, let her have her hair cut off too. Now if it is a dishonor for a woman to have her hair cut off, or her head shaved, let her wear a veil. 7 For a man ought not to wear anything on his head, because he is the image and reflected glory of God, but woman is man's reflected glory. 8 For man did not originate from woman, but woman did from man, 9 and man was not created for woman's sake, but woman was for man's sake. 10 This is why woman ought to wear upon her head a symbol of man's authority, especially out of respect to the angels. 11 But from the Lord's point of view woman is not independent of man nor man of woman. 12 For just as woman originated from man, so man is born of woman, and both, with everything else, originated from God. 13 You must judge for yourselves in this matter. Is it proper for a woman to pray to God with nothing on her head? 14 Does not nature itself teach you that it is degrading*b* for a man to wear long hair, 15 but that it is a woman's glory to do so? For her hair is given her for a covering. 16 But if anyone is inclined to be contentious about it, I for my part prescribe no other practice than this, and neither do the churches of God.

17 But as I am giving you these instructions I cannot approve of your meetings, because they do not turn out for the better but for the worse. 18 For, in the first place, when you meet

[a] Lit., *prophesies*. [b] Grk., *dishonoring*.

BECK

ask any questions or let your conscience trouble you, 26 because *the earth and everything in it belong to the Lord.*[19] 27 If any of the unbelievers invites you and you want to go, eat anything they serve you, and don't ask any questions or let your conscience trouble you. 28 But if somebody tells you, "This was sacrificed," don't eat it, keeping in mind him who told you, 29 and conscience—I don't mean yours but the other one's conscience. What good is there in doing what I please if someone else's conscience condemns it? 30 If I give thanks for what I eat, why should I let myself be denounced for eating what I thank God for? 31 So, whether you eat or drink or do anything else, do everything to glorify God. 32 Don't be the reason for others to sin, whether they are Jews, Greeks, or God's church. 33 So I try to please everybody in every way and don't look for my advantage but for that of many people so that they may be saved.

11 Imitate me as I imitate Christ.

Long Hair and Hats

2 I praise you for thinking of me in every way and for keeping the truths as I delivered them to you. 3 I want you to know that the head of every man is Christ, the head of a woman is her husband, and the head of Christ is God. 4 Any man who keeps his head covered when he prays or speaks God's Word dishonors his head. 5 But any woman who prays or speaks God's Word with nothing on her head dishonors her head. She's exactly like the woman whose head is shaved. 6 If a woman wears nothing on her head, she should also get her hair cut. But if it is a disgrace for a woman to get her hair cut or shaved off, she should keep her head covered. 7 A man shouldn't cover his head, because he is *God's image*[20] and glory; but a woman is a man's glory. 8 The man wasn't made from the woman but the woman from the man, 9 and the man wasn't made for the woman but the woman for the man. 10 That's why a woman should wear something on her head to show she is under authority, out of respect for the angels. 11 Yet in the Lord a woman needs a man, and a man needs a woman. 12 As the woman was made from the man, so a man is born of a woman, and it all comes from God.

13 Judge for yourselves. Is it proper for a woman to pray to God with nothing on her head? 14 Doesn't nature itself teach you it's disgraceful for a man to have long hair 15 but that it's a woman's glory to wear her hair long? Her hair is given her as a covering. 16 But if anybody means to argue about it—we don't have such a custom, nor do God's churches.

How to Go to the Lord's Supper

17 While I'm giving these instructions, I'm not praising you for doing harm instead of good at your meetings. 18 In the first place, I hear

[19] Ps. 24:1
[20] Gen. 1:27

481

K.J.V.

in the church, I hear that there be divisions among you; and I partly believe it. 19 For there must be also heresies among you, that they which are approved may be made manifest among you. 20 When ye come together therefore into one place, *this* is not to eat the Lord's supper. 21 For in eating every one taketh before *other* his own supper: and one is hungry, and another is drunken. 22 What! have ye not houses to eat and to drink in? or despise ye the church of God, and shame them that have not? What shall I say to you? shall I praise you in this? I praise *you* not. 23 For I have received of the Lord that which also I delivered unto you, That the Lord Jesus, the *same* night in which he was betrayed, took bread: 24 And when he had given thanks, he brake *it*, and said, Take, eat; this is my body, which is broken for you: this do in remembrance of me. 25 After the same manner also *he took* the cup, when he had supped, saying, This cup is the new testament in my blood: this do ye, as oft as ye drink *it*, in remembrance of me. 26 For as often as ye eat this bread, and drink this cup, ye do shew the Lord's death till he come. 27 Wherefore whosoever shall eat this bread, and drink *this* cup of the Lord, unworthily, shall be guilty of the body and blood of the Lord. 28 But let a man examine himself, and so let him eat of *that* bread, and drink of *that* cup. 29 For he that eateth and drinketh unworthily, eateth and drinketh damnation to himself, not discerning the Lord's body. 30 For this cause many *are* weak and sickly among you, and many sleep. 31 For if we would judge ourselves, we should not be judged. 32 But when we are judged, we are chastened of the Lord, that we should not be condemned with the world. 33 Wherefore, my brethren, when ye come together to eat, tarry one for another. 34 And if any man hunger, let him eat at home; that ye come not together unto condemnation. And the rest will I set in order when I come.

N.A.S.

place, when you come together as a church, I hear that divisions exist among you; and in part, I believe it. 19 For there must also be factions among you, in order that those who are approved may become evident among you. 20 Therefore when you meet together, it is not to eat the Lord's Supper, 21 for in your eating each one takes his own supper first; and one is hungry and another is drunk. 22 What! Do you not have houses in which to eat and drink? Or do you despise the church of God, and shame those who have nothing? What shall I say to you? Shall I praise you? In this I will not praise you. 23 For I received from the Lord that which I also delivered to you, that the Lord Jesus in the night in which He was betrayed took bread; 24 and when He had given thanks, He broke it, and said, "This is My body, which °is for you; do this in remembrance of Me." 25 In the same way the cup also, after supper, saying, "This cup is the new covenant in My blood; do this, as often as you drink *it*, in remembrance of Me." 26 For as often as you eat this bread and drink the cup, you proclaim the Lord's death until He comes. 27 Therefore whoever eats the bread or drinks the cup of the Lord in an unworthy manner, shall be guilty of the body and the blood of the Lord. 28 But let a man examine himself, and so let him eat of the bread and drink of the cup. 29 For he who eats and drinks, eats and drinks judgment to himself, if he does not judge the body rightly. 30 For this reason many among you are weak and sick, and a number sleep. 31 But if we judged ourselves rightly, we should not be judged. 32 But when we are judged, we are disciplined by the Lord in order that we may not be condemned along with the world. 33 So then, my brethren, when you come together to eat, wait for one another. 34 If anyone is hungry, let him eat at home, so that you may not come together for judgment. And the remaining matters I shall arrange when I come.

---

12 Now concerning spiritual *gifts*, brethren, I would not have you ignorant. 2 Ye know that ye were Gentiles, carried away unto these dumb idols, even as ye were led. 3 Wherefore I give you to understand, that no man speaking by the Spirit of God calleth Jesus accursed: and *that* no man can say that Jesus is the Lord, but by the Holy Ghost. 4 Now there are diversities of gifts, but the same Spirit. 5 And there are differences of administrations, but the same Lord. 6 And there are diversities of operations, but it is the same God which worketh all in all. 7 But the manifestation of the Spirit is given to every man to profit withal. 8 For to one is given by

12 Now concerning spiritual *gifts*, brethren, I do not want you to be unaware. 2 You know that when you were pagans, *you were* led astray to the dumb idols, however you were led. 3 Therefore I make known to you, that no one speaking by the Spirit of God says, "Jesus is accursed"; and no one can say, "Jesus is Lord," except by the Holy Spirit. 4 Now there are varieties of gifts, but the same Spirit. 5 And there are varieties of ministries, and the same Lord. 6 And there are varieties of effects, but the same God who works all things in all *persons*. 7 But to each one is given the manifestation of the Spirit for the common good. 8 For to one is given the word

[a] Some ancient mss. read, *is broken*.

WILLIAMS

as a congregation, I hear that there are cliques[c] among you, and I partly believe it. 19 Yes, indeed, there must be parties among you, in order that people of approved fitness may come to the front among you.

20 So when you hold your meetings, it is not to eat the Lord's Supper, 21 for each of you is in a rush to eat his own supper, and one goes hungry while another gets drunk. 22 It is not that you have no houses to eat and drink in, is it? Or, are you trying to show your contempt for the church of God and trying to humiliate those who have no houses? What shall I say to you? Shall I praise you? No, I cannot praise you for this. 23 For the account that I passed on to you I myself received from the Lord Himself, that the Lord Jesus on the night He was betrayed took a loaf of bread 24 and gave thanks for it and broke it and said, "This is my body which is given for you. Do this in memory of me." 25 In the same way, after supper, He took the cup of wine, saying, "This cup is the new covenant ratified by my blood. Whenever you drink it, do so in memory of me."

26 For every time you eat this bread and drink from this cup, you proclaim the Lord's death until He comes again, 27 So whoever eats the bread and drinks from the Lord's cup in an unworthy way is guilty of sinning against the Lord's body and blood. 28 A man, then, must examine himself, and only in this way should he eat any of the bread and drink from the cup. 29 For whoever eats and drinks without recognizing His body, eats and drinks a judgment on himself. 30 This is why many of you are sick and feeble, and a considerable number are falling asleep. 31 But if we properly saw ourselves, we would not bring down upon us this judgment. 32 But since we do bring down upon us this judgment, we are being disciplined by the Lord, so that finally we may not be condemned along with the world. 33 So, my brothers, when you meet to eat, wait for one another. 34 If anyone is hungry, let him eat at home, so that your meetings may not bring on you judgment. I will settle in detail the matters that remain, when I come.

12 *Spiritual gifts; spiritual insight needed; these gifts vary; Christians constitute an organic unit, Christ's body; as in the natural body, all parts of His body essential for strength and efficiency*

About spiritual gifts, brothers, I do not want you to be without information. 2 You know that when you were heathen you were in the habit of going off, wherever you might be led, after idols that could not speak. 3 So I want to inform you that no one speaking under the power of the Spirit of God can say, "Jesus is accursed!" and no one except one under the power of the Holy Spirit can really say, "Jesus is Lord!"

4 There are varieties of gifts, but the Spirit is the same in all; 5 there are varieties of service, but the Lord to be served is the same; 6 there are varieties of activities, but it is the same God who does all things by putting energy in us all. 7 To each of us is given a special spiritual illumination[a] for the common good. 8 To one,

BECK

that when you meet as a church you are divided, and some of it I believe is true. 19 Of course there must be divisions among you to show clearly which of you can stand the test.

20 When you meet, you can't be eating the Lord's Supper. 21 Everyone eats his own supper ahead of the others, and then one is hungry and another gets drunk. 22 Don't you have homes where you can eat and drink? Or do you despise God's church and humiliate those who don't have anything? What should I say to you? Should I praise you? I won't praise you for this.

23 The Lord gave me what I taught you, that the night He was betrayed the Lord Jesus took bread. 24 He gave thanks, broke it, and said, "This is My Body, which is for you. Do this to remember Me." 25 He did the same with the cup after the supper. He said, "This cup is the new *covenant* in My *blood*.[21] Every time you drink it, do it to remember Me."

26 Every time you eat this bread and drink the cup, you are telling how the Lord died, till He comes. 27 Then anyone who eats the bread or drinks the Lord's cup in an unworthy way is sinning against the Lord's body and blood. 28 Examine yourself and then eat some of the bread and drink from the cup. 29 Anyone who eats and drinks without seeing that the body is there is condemned for his eating and drinking.

30 That is why many of you are sick and ailing and a number are dead. 31 If we would look at ourselves critically, we would not be judged. 32 But if the Lord judges us, He corrects us to keep us from being condemned with the world.

33 So then, my fellow Christians, when you get together to eat, wait for one another. 34 If you are hungry, eat at home, so you will not meet just to be condemned.

About the other things I'll give directions when I come.

The Spirit's Gifts

12 Fellow Christians, I want you to know about the gifts of the Spirit. 2 You know that when you were people of the world, you were led away to the idols, that can't talk, as you felt yourselves moved. 3 So I tell you, if you are moved by God's Spirit, you don't say, "Jesus is cursed," and only if you are moved by the Holy Spirit can you say, "Jesus is the Lord."

4 Now gifts are given to different persons but by the same Spirit. 5 Ways of serving are assigned to them but by the same Lord. 6 Powers are given to them, but the same God works everything in all people. 7 Now, the Spirit shows Himself to each one to make him useful. 8 The

[c] Lit., *schisms*. [a] Grk., *manifestation*.   [21] Ex. 24:8; Zech. 9:11

K.J.V.

the Spirit the word of wisdom; to another the word of knowledge by the same Spirit; 9 To another faith by the same Spirit; to another the gifts of healing by the same Spirit; 10 To another the working of miracles; to another prophecy; to another discerning of spirits; to another *divers* kinds of tongues; to another the interpretation of tongues: 11 But all these worketh that one and the selfsame Spirit, dividing to every man severally as he will. 12 For as the body is one, and hath many members, and all the members of that one body, being many, are one body: so also *is* Christ. 13 For by one Spirit are we all baptized into one body, whether *we be* Jews or Gentiles, whether *we be* bond or free; and have been all made to drink into one Spirit. 14 For the body is not one member, but many. 15 If the foot shall say, Because I am not the hand, I am not of the body; is it therefore not of the body? 16And if the ear shall say, Because I am not the eye, I am not of the body; is it therefore not of the body? 17 If the whole body *were* an eye, where *were* the hearing? If the whole *were* hearing, where *were* the smelling? 18 But now hath God set the members every one of them in the body, as it hath pleased him. 19And if they were all one member, where *were* the body? 20 But now *are they* many members, yet but one body. 21And the eye cannot say unto the hand, I have no need of thee: nor again the head to the feet, I have no need of you. 22 Nay, much more those members of the body, which seem to be more feeble, are necessary: 23And those *members* of the body, which we think to be less honourable, upon these we bestow more abundant honour; and our uncomely *parts* have more abundant comeliness. 24 For our comely *parts* have no need: but God hath tempered the body together, having given more abundant honour to that *part* which lacked: 25 That there should be no schism in the body; but *that* the members should have the same care one for another. 26And whether one member suffer, all the members suffer with it; or one member be honoured, all the members rejoice with it. 27 Now ye are the body of Christ, and members in particular. 28And God hath set some in the church, first apostles, secondarily prophets, thirdly teachers, after that miracles, then gifts of healings, helps, governments, diversities of tongues. 29*Are* all apostles? *are* all prophets? *are* all teachers? *are* all workers of miracles? 30 Have all the gifts of healing? do all speak with tongues? do all interpret? 31 But covet earnestly the best gifts: and yet shew I unto you a more excellent way.

N.A.S.

of wisdom through the Spirit, and to another the word of knowledge according to the same Spirit; 9 to another faith by the same Spirit, and to another gifts of healing by the one Spirit, 10 and to another the effecting of miracles, and to another prophecy, and to another the distinguishing of spirits, to another *various* kinds of tongues, and to another the interpretation of tongues. 11 But one and the same Spirit works all these things, distributing to each one individually just as He wills.

12 For even as the body is one and *yet* has many members, and all the members of the body, though they are many, are one body, so also is Christ. 13 For by one Spirit we were all baptized into one body, whether Jews or Greeks, whether slaves or free, and we were all made to drink of one Spirit. 14 For the body is not one member, but many. 15 If the foot should say, "Because I am not a hand, I am not *a part* of the body," it is not for this reason any the less *a part* of the body. 16And if the ear should say, "Because I am not an eye, I am not *a part* of the body," it is not for this reason any the less *a part* of the body. 17 If the whole body were an eye, where would the hearing be? If the whole were hearing, where would the sense of smell be? 18 But now God has placed the members, each one of them, in the body, just as He desired. 19 And if they were all one member, where would the body be? 20 But now there are many members, but one body. 21And the eye cannot say to the hand, "I have no need of you"; or again the head to the feet, "I have no need of you." 22 On the contrary, it is much truer that the members of the body which seem to be weaker are necessary; 23 and those *members* of the body, which we deem less honorable, on these we bestow more abundant honor, and our unseemly *members come to* have more abundant seemliness, 24 whereas our seemly *members* have no need *of it*. But God has *so* composed the body, giving more abundant honor to that *member* which lacked, 25 that there should be no division in the body, but *that* the members should have the same care for one another. 26And if one member suffers, all the members suffer with it; if *one* member is honored, all the members rejoice with it. 27 Now you are Christ's body, and individually members of it. 28And God has appointed in the church, first apostles, second prophets, third teachers, then miracles, then gifts of healings, helps, administrations, *various* kinds of tongues. 29All are not apostles, are they? All are not prophets, are they? All are not teachers, are they? All are not *workers of* miracles, are they? 30All do not have gifts of healings, do they? All do not speak with tongues, do they? All do not interpret, do they? 31 But earnestly desire the greater gifts.

And I show you a still more excellent way.

13 Though I speak with the tongues of men and of angels, and have not charity, I am become *as* sounding brass, or a tinkling cymbal. 2And though I have *the gift of* prophecy, and

13 If I speak with the tongues of men and of angels, but do not have love, I have become a noisy gong or a clanging cymbal. 2And

WILLIAMS

wise speech is given by the Spirit; to another, by the same Spirit, intelligent speech is given; 9 to another, through union with the same Spirit, faith; to another, by one and the same Spirit, power to cure the sick; 10 to another, power for working wonders; to another, prophetic insight; to another, the power to discriminate between the true Spirit and false spirits; to another, various ecstatic utterances; and to another, the power to explain them. 11 But the one and same Spirit accomplishes all these achievements, and apportions power to each of us as He chooses.

12 For just as the human body is one and yet has many parts, and all the parts of the body, many as they are, constitute but one body, so it is with Christ. 13 For by one Spirit all of us, Jews or Greeks, slaves or free men, have been baptized into one body, and were all imbued with one Spirit. 14 For the body does not consist of one part but of many. 15 If the foot says, "Since I am not a hand, I am not a part of the body," that does not make it any less a part of the body. 16 If the ear says, "Since I am not an eye, I am not a part of the body," that does not make it any less a part of the body. 17 If all the body were an eye, how could we hear? If all the body were an ear, how could we smell? 18 But as it now is, God has placed the parts, every one of them, in the body just as He wanted them to be. 19 If they were all one part, how could it be a body? 20 But as it now is, there are many parts, but one body. 21 The eye cannot say to the hand, "I do not need you," or the hand to the feet, "I do not need you." 22 No, on the contrary, even those parts of the body that seem to be most delicate are indispensable, 23 and the parts of it we deem devoid of honor we dress with special honor, and our ill-shaped parts receive more careful attention, 24 while our well-shaped parts do not want for anything. Yes, God has perfectly adjusted the body, giving great honor to its apparently inferior parts, 25 so that there is no disharmony in the body, but all the parts have a common care for one another. 26 If one part suffers, all the parts suffer with it. If one part receives an honor, all the parts can share its joy.

27 So you are Christ's body, and individually parts of it. 28 And God has placed people in the church, first as apostles, second as prophets, third as teachers, then wonder-workers; then people with power to cure the sick, helpers, managers, ecstatic speakers. 29 Not all are apostles, are they? Not all are prophets, are they? Not all are teachers, are they? Not all are wonder-workers, are they? 30 Not all are people with power to cure the sick, are they? Not all are ecstatic speakers, are they? Not all can explain ecstatic speaking, can they? 31 But you must earnestly continue to cultivate your higher spiritual gifts.

BECK

Spirit gives one person the ability to speak of wisdom. 9 To another the same Spirit gives the ability to speak intelligently. To another the same Spirit gives faith. To another that same Spirit gives the ability to heal. 10 Another can work miracles. Another can speak God's Word. Another can tell the true Spirit from evil spirits. Another can talk strange languages. Another can tell the meaning of languages. 11 One and the same Spirit works all these things and gives as He wishes to each in his own way.

12 As the body is one and yet has many parts, and all the parts of the body, many as they are, form one body, so is Christ. 13 By one Spirit all of us—Jews or Greeks, slaves or free—were baptized to form one body, and that one Spirit was poured out for all of us to drink.

14 Not one part but many make up the body. 15 Suppose a foot says, "I'm not a hand, and so I'm not a part of the body"; it is still a part of the body. 16 Or suppose an ear says, "I'm not an eye, and so I'm not a part of the body"; it is still a part of the body. 17 If the whole body were an eye, how could we hear? If it were all hearing, how could we smell? 18 As it is, God arranged the parts, each of them into the body as He wanted it to be. 19 If all of it were one part, how could there be a body? 20 As it is, there are many parts and one body.

21 The eye cannot say to the hand, "I don't need you," or the head to the feet, "I don't need you." 22 No, we really can't do without the parts of the body that we think are weaker. 23 And the parts of the body that we think less honorable we dress with special honor so that our shameful parts have a special nobility, 24 which our noble parts don't need. But God has put the body together and given special honor to the part that lacks it, 25 to keep the body from dividing and have the parts feel the same concern for one another. 26 If one member suffers, all the others suffer with it. If one is honored, all the others are happy with it.

27 Now, you are the body of Christ, and everyone has his place in it. 28 God has appointed in the church first apostles, next preachers, third teachers, then miracle workers, then healers, helpers, managers, and those who can talk strange languages. 29 Are all apostles? Are all preachers? Are all teachers? Can all do miracles? 30 Can all heal? Can all talk strange languages? Can all tell what they mean? No, 31 but try to have the better gifts.

Love

And now I'll show you the best way of all.

13 *A poem on love; love gives quality to all other gifts; love achieves the greatest wonders; love endures forever*

12:31 And yet I will show you a way that is better by far:
If I could speak the languages of men, of angels too,
And have no love,
I am only a rattling pan or a clashing cymbal. 2 If I should have the gift of prophecy,

13 If I speak the languages of men and of angels but don't have any love, I've become a loud gong or a clashing cymbal. 2 Even

K.J.V.

understand all mysteries, and all knowledge; and though I have all faith, so that I could remove mountains, and have not charity, I am nothing. 3 And though I bestow all my goods to feed *the poor,* and though I give my body to be burned, and have not charity, it profiteth me nothing. 4 Charity suffereth long, *and* is kind; charity envieth not; charity vaunteth not itself, is not puffed up, 5 Doth not behave itself unseemly, seeketh not her own, is not easily provoked, thinketh no evil; 6 Rejoiceth not in iniquity, but rejoiceth in the truth; 7 Beareth all things, believeth all things, hopeth all things, endureth all things. 8 Charity never faileth: but whether *there be* prophecies, they shall fail; whether *there be* tongues, they shall cease; whether *there be* knowledge, it shall vanish away. 9 For we know in part, and we prophesy in part. 10 But when that which is perfect is come, then that which is in part shall be done away. 11 When I was a child, I spake as a child, I understood as a child, I thought as a child: but when I became a man, I put away childish things. 12 For now we see through a glass, darkly; but then face to face: now I know in part; but then shall I know even as also I am known. 13 And now abideth faith, hope, charity, these three; but the greatest of these *is* charity.

14 Follow after charity, and desire spiritual *gifts,* but rather that ye may prophesy. 2 For he that speaketh in an *unknown* tongue speaketh not unto men, but unto God: for no man understandeth *him;* howbeit in the spirit he speaketh mysteries. 3 But he that prophesieth speaketh unto men *to* edification, and exhortation, and comfort. 4 He that speaketh in an *unknown* tongue edifieth himself; but he that prophesieth edifieth the church. 5 I would that ye all spake with tongues, but rather that ye prophesied: for greater *is* he that prophesieth than he that speaketh with tongues, except he interpret, that the church may receive edifying. 6 Now, brethren, if I come unto you speaking with tongues, what shall I profit you, except I shall speak to you either by revelation, or by knowledge, or by prophesying, or by doctrine? 7 And even things without life giving sound, whether pipe or harp, except they give a dis-

N.A.S.

if I have *the gift of* prophecy, and know all mysteries and all knowledge; and if I have all faith, so as to remove mountains, but do not have love, I am nothing. 3 And if I give all my possessions to feed *the poor,* and if I deliver my body ᵃto be burned, but do not have love, it profits me nothing. 4 Love is patient, love is kind, *and* is not jealous; love does not brag *and* is not arrogant, 5 does not act unbecomingly; it does not seek its own, is not provoked, does not take into account a wrong *suffered,* 6 does not rejoice in unrighteousness, but rejoices with the truth; 7 bears all things, believes all things, hopes all things, endures all things. 8 Love never fails; but if *there are gifts of* prophecy, they will be done away; if *there are* tongues, they will cease; if *there is* knowledge, it will be done away. 9 For we know in part, and we prophesy in part; 10 but when the perfect comes, the partial will be done away. 11 When I was a child, I used to speak as a child, think as a child, reason as a child; when I became a man, I did away with childish things. 12 For now we see in a mirror dimly, but then face to face; now I know in part, but then I shall know fully just as I also have been fully known. 13 But now abide faith, hope, love, these three; but the greatest of these is love.

14 Pursue love, yet especially that you may prophesy. 2 For one who speaks in a tongue does not speak to men, but to God; for no one understands, but in *his* spirit he speaks mysteries. 3 But one who prophesies speaks to men for edification and exhortation and consolation. 4 One who speaks in a tongue edifies himself; but one who prophesies edifies the church. 5 Now I wish that you all spoke in tongues, but *even* more that you would prophesy; and greater is one who prophesies than one who speaks in tongues, unless he interprets, so that the church may receive edifying. 6 But now, brethren, if I come to you speaking in tongues, what shall I profit you, unless I speak to you either by way of revelation or of knowledge or of prophecy or of teaching? 7 Yet *even* lifeless things, either flute or harp, in producing a sound, if they do not produce a distinction in the tones, how will

[a] Some ancient mss. read, *that I may boast.*

WILLIAMS

And know all secret truths, and knowledge in
its every form,
And have such perfect faith that I could move
mountains,
But have no love, I am nothing.
3 If I should dole out everything I have for
charity,
And give my body up to torture in mere boasting pride,
But have no love, I get from it no good at all.
4 Love is so patient and so kind;
Love never boils with jealousy;
It never boasts, is never puffed with pride;
5 It does not act with rudeness, or insist upon
its rights;
It never gets provoked, it never harbors evil
thoughts;
6 Is never glad when wrong is done,
But always glad when truth prevails;
7 It bears up under anything,
It exercises faith in everything,
It keeps up hope in everything,
It gives us power to endure in anything.
8 Love never fails;
If there are prophecies, they will be set aside;
If now exist ecstatic speakings, they will cease;
If there is knowledge, it will soon be set aside;
9 For what we know is incomplete and what we
prophesy is incomplete.
10 But when perfection comes, what is imperfect will be set aside.
11 When I was a child, I talked like a child,
I thought like a child, I reasoned like a child.
When I became a man, I laid aside my childish
ways.
12 For now we see a dim reflection in a look-
ing-glass,
But then we shall see face to face;
Now what I know is imperfect,
But then I shall know perfectly, as God knows
me.
13 And so these three, faith, hope, and love endure,
But the greatest of them is love.

14 *Prophecy superior to ecstatic speaking;
good order to be observed in exercis-
ing spiritual gifts; woman's place in
public worship; the apostle's authority
to speak on this matter*

Keep on pursuing love, but still keep cultivating your spiritual gifts, especially the gift of
prophesying. 2 For whoever speaks in ecstasy is
speaking not to men but to God, for no one
understands him, and yet by the Spirit he is
speaking secret truths. 3 But whoever prophesies is speaking to men for their upbuilding, encouragement, and comfort. 4 Whoever speaks in
ecstasy builds up himself alone, but whoever
prophesies builds up the congregation too. 5 I
would like for all of you to speak in ecstasy,
but I would rather that you prophesy. The man
who speaks with real prophetic insight renders
greater service than the man who speaks in
ecstasy, unless the latter explains it, so the congregation may receive an uplift.
6 But as it now is, brothers, if I do come
back to you speaking in ecstasy, what good
shall I do you, unless my speech contains a
revelation or new knowledge or a prophetic
message or some teaching? 7 Even inanimate
things, like the flute or the harp, may give out
sounds, but if there is no difference in the

BECK

if I speak God's Word and know every kind of
hidden truth and have every kind of knowledge,
even if I have all the faith to move mountains
but don't have any love, I'm nothing. 3 Even if
I give away all I have to feed the hungry and
give up my body but only to boast and don't
have any love, it doesn't help me.
4 Love is patient. Love is kind. Love isn't
jealous. It doesn't brag or get conceited. 5 It isn't
indecent. It isn't selfish. It doesn't get angry.
It *doesn't plan to hurt anyone.*[22] 6 It doesn't
delight in evil but is happy with the truth. 7 It
bears everything, believes everything, hopes for
everything, endures everything.
8 Love never dies. If there are prophecies,
they will come to an end. Or strange languages,
they will stop. Or knowledge, it will vanish.
9 We learn only a part of anything and prophesy only a part. 10 But when that which is
perfect comes, what is only a part will vanish.
11 When I was a child, I used to talk like a
child, think like a child, plan like a child. Now
that I'm a man, I've given up the ways of a
child. 12 Now we see by a mirror and are puzzled, but then we'll see face to face. Now I
learn only a part of anything, but then I'll know
as He has known me.
13 And now these three, faith, hope, and love,
go on, but the most important of these is love.

Speak to Be Understood

14 Pursue love, be eager to have the gifts of
the Spirit, and especially to speak God's
Word. 2 When a man talks a strange language,
he doesn't talk to people but to God, because
nobody understands him; his spirit is talking
mysteries. 3 But when you speak God's Word,
you talk to people to help them grow, to encourage and comfort them. 4 When you talk a
strange language, you encourage yourself. But
when you speak God's Word, you help the
church grow. 5 I want you all to talk strange
languages, but I would rather have you speak
God's Word. It is more important to speak
God's Word than strange languages, unless you
explain what you say in order to help the church
grow. 6 Now, my fellow Christians, if I come to
you and talk strange languages, how can I help
you unless I tell you what God has told me and
bring it as His Word or as something I know
and teach?
7 Lifeless instruments such as a flute or a
lyre produce sounds, but if there's no differ-

[22] Zech. 7:10; 8:17

K.J.V.

tinction in the sounds, how shall it be known what is piped or harped? 8 For if the trumpet give an uncertain sound, who shall prepare himself to the battle? 9 So likewise ye, except ye utter by the tongue words easy to be understood, how shall it be known what is spoken? for ye shall speak into the air. 10 There are, it may be, so many kinds of voices in the world, and none of them *is* without signification. 11 Therefore if I know not the meaning of the voice, I shall be unto him that speaketh a barbarian, and he that speaketh *shall be* a barbarian unto me. 12 Even so ye, forasmuch as ye are zealous of spiritual *gifts,* seek that ye may excel to the edifying of the church. 13 Wherefore let him that speaketh in an *unknown* tongue pray that he may interpret. 14 For if I pray in an *unknown* tongue, my spirit prayeth, but my understanding is unfruitful. 15 What is it then? I will pray with the spirit, and I will pray with the understanding also: I will sing with the spirit, and I will sing with the understanding also. 16 Else, when thou shalt bless with the spirit, how shall he that occupieth the room of the unlearned say Amen at thy giving of thanks, seeing he understandeth not what thou sayest? 17 For thou verily givest thanks well, but the other is not edified. 18 I thank my God, I speak with tongues more than ye all: 19 Yet in the church I had rather speak five words with my understanding, that *by my voice* I might teach others also, than ten thousand words in an *unknown* tongue. 20 Brethren, be not children in understanding: howbeit in malice be ye children, but in understanding be men. 21 In the law it is written, With *men of* other tongues and other lips will I speak unto this people; and yet for all that will they not hear me, saith the Lord. 22 Wherefore tongues are for a sign, not to them that believe, but to them that believe not: but prophesying *serveth* not for them that believe not, but for them which believe. 23 If therefore the whole church be come together into one place, and all speak with tongues, and there come in *those that are* unlearned, or unbelievers, will they not say that ye are mad? 24 But if all prophesy, and there come in one that believeth not, or *one* unlearned, he is convinced of all, he is judged of all: 25 And thus are the secrets of his heart made manifest; and so falling down on *his* face he will worship God, and report that God is in you of a truth. 26 How is it then, brethren? when ye come together, every one of you hath a psalm, hath a doctrine, hath a tongue, hath a revelation, hath an interpretation. Let all things be done unto edifying. 27 If any man speak in an *unknown* tongue, *let it be* by two, or at the most *by* three, and *that* by course; and let one interpret. 28 But if there be no interpreter, let him keep silence in the church; and let him speak to himself, and to God. 29 Let the prophets speak two or three, and let the other judge. 30 If *any thing* be revealed to another that sitteth by, let the first hold his peace. 31 For ye may all prophesy one by one, that all may learn, and all may be comforted. 32 And the spirits of the prophets are subject to the prophets. 33 For God is not *the author* of confusion, but of peace, as in all churches of the saints. 34 Let your

N.A.S.

it be known what is played on the flute or on the harp? 8 For if the bugle produces an indistinct sound, who will prepare himself for battle? 9 So also you, unless you utter by the tongue speech that is clear, how will it be known what is spoken? For you will be speaking into the air. 10 There are, perhaps, a great many kinds of languages in the world, and no *kind* is without meaning. 11 If then I do not know the meaning of the language, I shall be to the one who speaks a barbarian, and the one who speaks will be a barbarian to me. 12 So also you, since you are zealous of spiritual *gifts,* seek to abound for the edification of the church. 13 Therefore let one who speaks in a tongue pray that he may interpret. 14 For if I pray in a tongue, my spirit prays, but my mind is unfruitful. 15 What is *the outcome* then? I shall pray with the spirit and I shall pray with the mind also; I shall sing with the spirit and I shall sing with the mind also. 16 Otherwise if you bless in the spirit *only,* how will the one who fills the place of the ungifted say the "Amen" at your giving of thanks, since he does not know what you are saying? 17 For you are giving thanks well enough, but the other man is not edified. 18 I thank God, I speak in tongues more than you all; 19 however, in the church I desire to speak five words with my mind, that I may instruct others also, rather than ten thousand words in a tongue.

20 Brethren, do not be children in your thinking; yet in evil be babes, but in your thinking be mature. 21 In the Law it is written, "BY MEN OF STRANGE TONGUES AND BY THE LIPS OF STRANGERS I WILL SPEAK TO THIS PEOPLE, AND EVEN SO THEY WILL NOT LISTEN TO ME," says the Lord. 22 So then tongues are for a sign, not to those who believe, but to unbelievers; but prophecy *is for a sign,* not to unbelievers, but to those who believe. 23 If therefore the whole church should assemble together and all speak in tongues, and ungifted men or unbelievers enter, will they not say that you are mad? 24 But if all prophesy, and an unbeliever or an ungifted man enters, he is convicted by all, he is called to account by all; 25 the secrets of his heart are disclosed; and so he will fall on his face and worship God, declaring that God is certainly among you.

26 What is *the outcome* then, brethren? When you assemble, each one has a psalm, has a teaching, has a revelation, has a tongue, has an interpretation. Let all things be done for edification. 27 If any one speaks in a tongue, *it should be* by two or at the most three, and *each* in turn, and let one interpret; 28 but if there is no interpreter, let him keep silent in the church; and let him speak to himself and to God. 29 And let two or three prophets speak, and let the others pass judgment. 30 But if a revelation is made to another who is seated, let the first keep silent. 31 For you can all prophesy one by one, so that all may learn and all may be exhorted; 32 and the spirits of prophets are subject to prophets; 33 for God is not *a God* of confusion but of peace, as in all the churches of the saints.

34 Let the women keep silent in the churches;

WILLIAMS

notes, how can the tune that is played on the flute or the harp be told? 8 Again, indeed, if the bugle does not sound a call distinct and clear, who will prepare for battle? 9 So it is with you; unless in your ecstatic speaking you speak a message that is clearly intelligible, how can the message spoken by you be understood? You might just as well be talking to the air! 10 There are, supposedly, ever so many languages in the world, and not one is without its own meaning. 11 So if I do not know the meaning of the language, I should be a foreigner to the man who speaks it, and he would be a foreigner to me. 12 So, as you are ambitious for spiritual gifts, you must keep trying to excel for the upbuilding of the church. 13 Therefore, the man who speaks in ecstasy must pray for power to explain what he says. 14 For if I pray in ecstasy, my spirit is praying, but my mind produces no results for anyone. 15 What is my conclusion then? I will certainly pray with my spirit, but I will pray with my mind in action too. I will certainly sing with my spirit, but I will sing with my mind in action too. For if you give thanks with your spirit only, 16 how is the man who occupies the place of the illiterate to say "Amen" to your thanksgiving? For he does not know what you are saying. 17 You are, indeed, doing right to give thanks, but your neighbor[a] is not built up. 18 Thank God, I speak in ecstasy more than any of you. 19 But in the public congregation I would rather speak five words with my mind in action, in order to instruct the people too, than ten thousand words in ecstasy.

20 Brothers, stop being children in intelligence,[b] but as to evil keep on being babies; and yet as to intelligence be men of maturity. 21 In the law it is written, "By men of foreign languages and by the lips of foreigners I will speak to this people, but even then they will not listen to me, says the Lord." 22 So speaking in ecstasy is meant as a sign, not for believers but for unbelievers, while prophecy is meant, not for unbelievers but for believers. 23 Hence, if the whole church has met and everybody speaks in ecstasy, and illiterate people or unbelievers come in, will they not say that you are crazy? 24 But if everybody prophesies, and some unbeliever or illiterate man comes in, he is convinced of his sins by all, he is closely questioned by all, 25 the secrets of his heart are laid bare, he falls upon his face and worships God, declaring, "God is really among you."

26 Then what is our conclusion, brothers? When you meet together, everybody has a song, something to teach, a revelation, an ecstatic utterance, or an explanation of one. It must all be for the upbuilding of all. 27 If anybody speaks in ecstasy, there must be only two, or three at most, and let one speak at a time, and someone explain what he says. 28 But if there is no one to explain it, let him keep quiet in the church and speak to himself and God alone. 29 Let two or three prophets speak, and the rest consider carefully what is said; 30 and if anything is revealed to another who is seated, let the speaker stop. 31 For in this way you can all, one after another, speak your prophetic message, so that all may learn and be encouraged, 32 for the spirits of prophets yield to prophets; 33 for God is not a God of disorder but of order, as it is in all the churches of God's people.

34 Women must keep quiet in the churches,

BECK

ence in the sounds, how can you tell what is played on a flute or a lyre? 8 And if the trumpet doesn't sound a clear call, who will get ready for battle? 9 In the same way, if you don't talk with a clear meaning, how will anyone know what you're saying? You'll be talking into the air. 10 There are, I suppose, ever so many different languages in the world, and none is without meaning. 11 Now if I don't know what a language means, I'll be a foreigner to him who speaks it, and he'll be a foreigner to me. 12 So you, too, since you are eager to have the Spirit's gifts, try to be rich in them so as to build up the church. 13 If then you talk a strange language, pray to be able to explain it.

14 If I pray in a strange language, my spirit prays, but my mind isn't helping anyone. 15 What then? I will pray in my spirit but also pray so as to be understood. I will sing praise in my spirit but also sing so as to be understood. 16 Otherwise, if you praise God only with your spirit, how can an ordinary person who is there say "Amen" to your prayer of thanks? He doesn't know what you mean. 17 It is good that you give thanks, but it doesn't help the other person. 18 I thank God I talk more in strange languages than any of you, 19 but in a church I would rather say five words that can be understood, in order to teach others, than ten thousand words in a language nobody understands.

20 Fellow Christians, don't be childish in your understanding. In evil be babies, but grow up in your thinking. 21 It is written in the Bible, "In strange languages and by the mouth of foreigners I will speak to these people, but even then they will not listen[23] to Me," says the Lord. 22 Then strange languages are not meant to warn believers but unbelievers, while God's Word isn't meant for unbelievers but for believers. 23 Now if the whole congregation meets and all talk strange languages and then some ordinary people or unbelievers come in, won't they say you're crazy? 24 But if all speak God's Word and some unbeliever or ordinary person comes in, all convince him of his sin and all examine him. 25 The secrets of his heart are shown, and so he bows down with his face on the ground, worships God, and declares, "God is certainly here among you."[24]

Keep Order in Your Meetings

26 What should you do, then, my fellow Christians? When you meet, everyone is ready with a song, something to teach, some truth from God, a strange language, or an explanation. Do it all to help one another grow. 27 If you talk a strange language, only two should talk, or three at the most, and one at a time, and somebody should explain. 28 If there's nobody to explain what you say, you shouldn't say anything in church but only talk to yourself and to God.

29 Two or three should speak God's Word, and the others should decide whether they are telling it right or not. 30 If God gives a truth to another person who is seated, the first speaker should stop talking. 31 You can all speak God's Word one after another so that everybody learns something and is encouraged. 32 Men who speak God's Word control their own spirits. 33 You see, God is not a God of disorder but of peace.

As in all the churches of the holy people, 34 the women should be silent in church be-

---

[a] Grk., the other man. [b] Grk., in minds.

[23] Is. 28:11-12
[24] Is. 45:14

K.J.V.

women keep silence in the churches: for it is not permitted unto them to speak; but *they are commanded* to be under obedience, as also saith the law. 35And if they will learn any thing, let them ask their husbands at home: for it is a shame for women to speak in the church. 36What! came the word of God out from you? or came it unto you only? 37If any man think himself to be a prophet, or spiritual, let him acknowledge that the things that I write unto you are the commandments of the Lord. 38But if any man be ignorant, let him be ignorant. 39Wherefore, brethren, covet to prophesy, and forbid not to speak with tongues. 40Let all things be done decently and in order.

15 Moreover, brethren, I declare unto you the gospel which I preached unto you, which also ye have received, and wherein ye stand; 2By which also ye are saved, if ye keep in memory what I preached unto you, unless ye have believed in vain. 3For I delivered unto you first of all that which I also received, how that Christ died for our sins according to the Scriptures: 4And that he was buried, and that he rose again the third day according to the Scriptures: 5And that he was seen of Cephas, then of the twelve: 6After that, he was seen of above five hundred brethren at once; of whom the greater part remain unto this present, but some are fallen asleep. 7After that, he was seen of James; then of all the apostles. 8And last of all he was seen of me also, as of one born out of due time. 9For I am the least of the apostles, that am not meet to be called an apostle, because I persecuted the church of God. 10But by the grace of God I am what I am: and his grace which *was bestowed* upon me was not in vain; but I laboured more abundantly than they all: yet not I, but the grace of God which was with me. 11Therefore whether *it were* I or they, so we preach, and so ye believed. 12Now if Christ be preached that he rose from the dead, how say some among you that there is no resurrection of the dead? 13But if there be no resurrection of the dead, then is Christ not risen: 14And if Christ be not risen, then *is* our preaching vain, and your faith *is* also vain. 15Yea, and we are found false witnesses of God; because we have testified of God that he raised up Christ: whom he raised not up, if so be that the dead rise not. 16For if the dead rise not, then is not Christ raised: 17And if Christ be not raised, your faith *is* vain; ye are yet in your sins. 18Then they also which are fallen asleep in Christ are perished. 19If in this life only we have hope in

N.A.S.

for they are not permitted to speak, but let them subject themselves, just as the Law also says. 35And if they desire to learn anything, let them ask their own husbands at home; for it is improper for a woman to speak in church. 36Was it from you that the word of God *first* went forth? Or has it come to you only?

37If any one thinks he is a prophet or spiritual, let him recognize that the things which I write to you are the Lord's commandments. 38But if any one ªdoes not recognize *this,* he is not recognized.

39Therefore, my brethren, desire earnestly to prophesy, and do not forbid to speak in tongues. 40But let all things be done properly and in an orderly manner.

15 Now I make known to you, brethren, the gospel which I preached to you, which also you received, in which also you stand, 2by which also you are saved, if you hold fast the word which I preached to you, unless you believed in vain. 3For I delivered to you as of first importance what I also received, that Christ died for our sins according to the Scriptures, 4and that He was buried, and that He was raised on the third day according to the Scriptures, 5and that He appeared to Cephas, then to the twelve. 6After that He appeared to more than five hundred brethren at one time, most of whom remain until now, but some have fallen asleep; 7then He appeared to James, then to all the apostles; 8and last of all, as it were to one untimely born, He appeared to me also. 9For I am the least of the apostles, who am not fit to be called an apostle, because I persecuted the church of God. 10But by the grace of God I am what I am, and His grace toward me did not prove vain; but I labored even more than all of them, yet not I, but the grace of God with me. 11Whether then *it was* I or they, so we preach and so you believed.

12Now if Christ is preached, that He has been raised from the dead, how do some among you say that there is no resurrection of the dead? 13But if there is no resurrection of the dead, not even Christ has been raised; 14and if Christ has not been raised, then our preaching is vain, your faith also is vain. 15Moreover we are even found *to be* false witnesses of God, because we witnessed against God that He raised ᵇChrist, whom He did not raise, if in fact the dead are not raised. 16For if the dead are not raised, not even Christ has been raised; 17and if Christ has not been raised, your faith is worthless; you are still in your sins. 18Then those also who have fallen asleep in Christ have perished. 19If we have only hoped in Christ in this life, we are of all men most to be pitied.

[a] Some ancient mss. read, *is ignorant, let him be ignorant.* [b] I.e., *the Messiah.*

WILLIAMS

for no permission is given them to speak. On the contrary, they must take a subordinate place, just as the law says. 35 If they want to find out about something, they should ask their own husbands at home, for it is disgraceful for a woman to speak in church. 36 Did the message of God begin with you Corinthians? Or, are you the only people it has reached?

37 If anyone claims to have the prophetic spirit, or any other spiritual gift, let him recognize that what I now am writing is the Lord's command. 38 If anyone ignores it, let him ignore it. 39 So, my brothers, cultivate the gift of prophetic speaking, but stop preventing others from speaking in ecstasy. 40 Everything must always be done in a proper and orderly way.

15 *The resurrection of Jesus a first principle in the good news; proved a fact by His appearances; the Greeks, doubting any resurrection, answered; because Jesus rose, Christians will rise with spiritual, immortal bodies*

Now let me remind you, brothers, of the essence of the good news which I proclaimed to you, which you accepted, on which you now are standing, 2 and through which you are to be saved, unless your faith at first was spurious. 3 For I passed on to you, among the primary principles of the good news, what I had received, that Christ died for our sins, in accordance with the Scriptures, 4 that He was buried, that on the third day He was raised from the dead, in accordance with the Scriptures, 5 and that He was seen by Cephas, and then by the Twelve. 6 After that, at one time He was seen by more than five hundred brothers, most of whom are still living, though some of them have fallen asleep. 7 Then He was seen by James, then by all the apostles, and finally 8 He was seen by me, too, as though I were born out of time. 9 For I belong to the lowest rank of the apostles, and am not fit to bear the title apostle, because I once persecuted the church of God. 10 But by God's unmerited favor I have become what I am, and His unmerited favor shown to me was not bestowed for nothing; for I have toiled more extensively than any of them, and yet it was not I but God's unmerited favor working with me. 11 But whether it was I or they, this is what we preach, and this is what you believed.

12 Now if we preach that Christ has been raised from the dead, how is it that some of you are saying that there is no such thing as a resurrection of the dead? 13 If there is no resurrection of the dead, then Christ has not been raised, 14 and if Christ was not raised, the message which we preach has nothing in it; there is nothing in our faith either, 15 and we are found guilty of lying about God, for we have testified that He raised Christ, whom He did not raise, if indeed the dead are never raised. 16 For if the dead are never raised, Christ has not been raised; 17 and if Christ has not been raised, your faith is a mere delusion; you are still under the penalty of your sins. 18 Yes, even those who have fallen asleep, though in union with Christ, have perished. 19 If for this life only we Christians have set our hopes on Christ, we are the most pitiable people in the world.

BECK

cause they are not allowed to speak. They should submit, as the Law says. 35 If there is something they want to know, they should ask their husbands at home. It is a disgrace for a woman to speak in church.

36 Did God's Word first come from you? Or were you the only ones to whom it came? 37 If anyone thinks he speaks for God or has the Spirit, he should know that what I write you is what the Lord orders. 38 But if anyone ignores this, he should be ignored.

39 So, my fellow Christians, be eager to speak God's Word, and don't try to keep anyone from talking strange languages. 40 But everything should be done in a fine and orderly way.

Jesus Rose

15 My fellow Christians, I am telling you the good news I brought you and you accepted. You stand in it 2 and are saved by it if you cling to the words I used in telling it to you—unless you were trifling when you believed. 3 I brought you what I received—something very important—that Christ died for our sins as the Bible said He would, 4 He was buried, and He rose on the third day as the Bible said He would. 5 Peter saw Him, then the twelve, 6 then more than five hundred Christians at one time; most of these are still living, but some have gone to their rest. 7 Then James saw Him, then all the apostles. 8 Last of all I saw Him, I who am like an abortion, 9 since I am the least of the apostles and not fit to be called an apostle because I persecuted God's church. 10 God's love made me what I am, and His love wasn't wasted on me. But I did far more work than all the others—not I but God's love that was with me. 11 Now, whether I did it or they, this is what we preach, and this is what you believed.

We'll Rise

12 If we preach that Christ rose from the dead, how can some of you say, "The dead don't rise"? 13 If the dead don't rise, Christ didn't rise. 14 And if Christ didn't rise, our preaching means nothing, and your faith means nothing. 15 And we stand there as men who lied about God, because we testified against God that He raised Christ, whom He didn't raise if it is true that the dead don't rise. 16 You see, if the dead don't rise, Christ didn't rise. 17 But if Christ didn't rise, your faith can't help you, and you are still in your sins. 18 Then also those who have gone to their rest in Christ have perished. 19 If Christ is our hope only for this life, we should be pitied more than any other people.

K.J.V.

Christ, we are of all men most miserable. 20 But now is Christ risen from the dead, *and* become the firstfruits of them that slept. 21 For since by man *came* death, by man *came* also the resurrection of the dead. 22 For as in Adam all die, even so in Christ shall all be made alive. 23 But every man in his own order: Christ the firstfruits; afterward they that are Christ's at his coming. 24 Then *cometh* the end, when he shall have delivered up the kingdom to God, even the Father; when he shall have put down all rule, and all authority and power. 25 For he must reign, till he hath put all enemies under his feet. 26 The last enemy *that* shall be destroyed *is* death. 27 For he hath put all things under his feet. But when he saith, All things are put under *him, it is* manifest that he is excepted, which did put all things under him. 28And when all things shall be subdued unto him, then shall the Son also himself be subject unto him that put all things under him, that God may be all in all. 29 Else what shall they do which are baptized for the dead, if the dead rise not at all? why are they then baptized for the dead? 30And why stand we in jeopardy every hour? 31 I protest by your rejoicing which I have in Christ Jesus our Lord, I die daily. 32 If after the manner of men I have fought with beasts at Ephesus, what advantageth it me, if the dead rise not? let us eat and drink; for to morrow we die. 33 Be not deceived: evil communications corrupt good manners. 34Awake to righteousness, and sin not; for some have not the knowledge of God: I speak *this* to your shame. 35 But some *man* will say, How are the dead raised up? and with what body do they come? 26 *Thou* fool, that which thou sowest is not quickened, except it die: 37And that which thou sowest, thou sowest not that body that shall be, but bare grain, it may chance of wheat, or of some other *grain:* 38 But God giveth it a body as it hath pleased him, and to every seed his own body. 39All flesh *is* not the same flesh: but *there is* one *kind of* flesh of men, another flesh of beasts, another of fishes, *and* another of birds. 40 *There are* also celestial bodies, and bodies terrestrial: but the glory of the celestial *is* one, and the *glory* of the terrestrial *is* another. 41 *There is* one glory of the sun, and another glory of the moon, and another glory of the stars; for *one* star differeth from *another* star in glory. 42 So also *is* the resurrection of the dead. It is sown in corruption, it is raised in incorruption: 43 It is sown in dishonour, it is raised in glory: it is sown in weakness, it is raised in power: 44 It is sown a natural body, it is raised a spiritual body. There is a natural body, and there is a spiritual body. 45And so it is written, The first man Adam was made a living soul; the last Adam *was made* a quickening spirit. 46 Howbeit that *was* not first which is spiritual, but that which is natural; and afterward that which is spiritual. 47 The first man *is* of the earth, earthy: the second man *is* the Lord

N.A.S.

20 But now Christ has been raised from the dead, the first fruits of those who are asleep. 21 For since by a man *came* death, by a man also *came* the resurrection of the dead. 22 For as in Adam all die, so also in Christ all shall be made alive. 23 But each in his own order: Christ the first fruits, after that those who are Christ's at His coming, 24 then *comes* the end, when He delivers up the kingdom to the God and Father, when He has abolished all rule and all authority and power. 25 For He must reign until He has put all His enemies under His feet. 26 The last enemy that will be abolished is death. 27 For HE HAS PUT ALL THINGS IN SUBJECTION UNDER HIS FEET. But when He says, "All things are put in subjection," it is evident that He is excepted who put all things in subjection to Him. 28And when all things are subjected to Him, then the Son Himself also will be subjected to the one who subjected all things to Him, that God may be all in all.

29 Otherwise, what will those do who are baptized for the dead? If the dead are not raised at all, why then are they baptized for them? 30 Why are we also in danger every hour? 31 I protest, brethren, by the boasting in you, which I have in Christ Jesus our Lord, I die daily. 32 If from human motives I fought with wild beasts at Ephesus, what does it profit me? If the dead are not raised, LET US EAT AND DRINK, FOR TOMORROW WE DIE. 33 Do not be deceived: "Bad company corrupts good morals." 34 Become soberminded as you ought, and stop sinning; for some have no knowledge of God. I speak *this* to your shame.

35 But some one will say, "How are the dead raised? And with what kind of body do they come?" 36 You fool! That which you sow does not come to life unless it dies; 37 and that which you sow, you do not sow the body which is to be, but a bare grain, perhaps of wheat or of something else. 38 But God gives it a body just as He wished, and to each of the seeds a body of its own. 39All flesh is not the same flesh, but there is *one flesh* of men, and another flesh of beasts, and another flesh of birds, and another of fish. 40 There are also heavenly bodies and earthly bodies, but the glory of the heavenly is one, and the *glory* of the earthly is another. 41 There is one glory of the sun, and another glory of the moon, and another glory of the stars; for star differs from star in glory. 42 So also is the resurrection of the dead. It is sown a perishable *body,* it is raised an imperishable *body;* 43 it is sown in dishonor, it is raised in glory; it is sown in weakness, it is raised in power; 44 it is sown a natural body, it is raised a spiritual body. If there is a natural body, there is also a spiritual *body.* 45 So also it is written, "The first MAN, Adam, BECAME A LIVING SOUL." The last Adam *became* a lifegiving spirit. 46 However, the spiritual is not first, but the natural; then the spiritual. 47 The first man is from the earth, earthy; the second

WILLIAMS

20 But in reality Christ has been raised from the dead, the first[a] to be raised of those who have fallen asleep. 21 For since it was through a man that death resulted, it was also through a man that the resurrection of the dead resulted. 22 For just as all men die by virtue of their descent from Adam, so all such as are in union with Christ will be made to live again. 23 But each in his proper order; Christ first, then at His coming those who belong to Christ. 24 After that comes the end, when He will turn the kingdom over to God His Father, when He will put an end to all other government, authority, and power; 25 for He must continue to be king until He puts all His enemies under His feet. 26 Death is the last enemy to be stopped, 27 for He has put everything in subjection under His feet. But when He says that everything has been put in subjection to Him, He Himself is evidently excepted who put it all in subjection to Him. 28 And when everything has been put in subjection to Him, then the Son Himself will also become subject to Him who has put everything in subjection to Him, so that God may be everything to everybody.

29 Otherwise, what do those people mean who submit to being baptized on behalf of their dead? If the dead are never raised at all, why do they submit to being baptized on their behalf? 30 Why too do we ourselves run such risks every hour? 31 I protest, by the boasting which I do about you, my brothers, through our union with Christ Jesus our Lord, I myself run the risk of dying every single day! 32 If from merely human motives I have fought wild beasts in Ephesus, what profit will it be to me? If the dead are never raised at all, "Let us eat and drink, for tomorrow we shall be dead." 33 Do not be so misled: "Evil companionships corrupt good character." 34 Sober up, as is right, and stop sinning, for some of you—to your shame I say so—are without any true knowledge of God.

35 But someone will ask, "How can the dead rise? With what kind of body do they come back?" 36 You foolish man! the seed that you sow never comes to life unless it dies first; 37 and what you sow does not have the body that it is going to have, but is a naked grain, of wheat (it may be) or something else; 38 but God gives it just the body He sees fit, even each kind of seed its own body. 39 Every kind of flesh is different. One kind belongs to men, another to cattle, another to birds, another to fish. 40 There are heavenly bodies, and earthly bodies, but the splendor of the heavenly bodies is of one kind, and the splendor of the earthly bodies is of another. 41 One kind of splendor belongs to the sun, another to the moon, and another to the stars; yes, one star differs from another in splendor. 42 It is just like this with the resurrection of the dead. 43 The body is sown in decay, it is raised without decay; it is sown in humiliation, it is raised in splendor; it is sown in weakness, it is raised in strength; 44 it is sown a physical body, it is raised a spiritual body. If there is a physical body, there is a spiritual body too. 45 This is the way the Scripture puts it too, "The first man Adam became a living creature." The last Adam has become a life-giving Spirit. 46 But it is not the spiritual that comes first; it is the physical, and then the spiritual. 47 The first man was made of the dust of the earth; the second Man is from

BECK

20 But now Christ did rise from the dead, the first in the harvest of those who are sleeping in their graves. 21 Since a man brought death, a Man also brought the resurrection of the dead. 22 As in Adam all die, so in Christ all will be made alive. 23 But everyone in his own group: first Christ, then, when He comes, those who belong to Christ.

24 Then the end will come when He hands over the kingdom to God the Father after He has put an end to every other government, authority, and power, 25 since He must rule as King till *He puts all enemies under His feet.*[25] 26 The last enemy He will get rid of is death. 27 You see, *He puts everything under His feet.* When He says, *Everything is put under Him,* this clearly doesn't include Him who *puts everything under Him.* 28 But when *everything has been put under Him,* then the Son also will put Himself under Him who *put everything under*[26] the Son so that God will be everything in everything.

29 Otherwise, what will they do who are baptized for the dead?* Why are they baptized for them if the dead don't actually rise?

30 And why are we in danger every hour? 31 As I'm proud of you, my fellow Christians, in Christ Jesus, our Lord, I assure you I'm facing death every day. 32 If like other men I have fought with wild animals in Ephesus, what good is it to me? If the dead don't rise, *let us eat and drink—tomorrow we die!*[27] 33 Don't let anybody deceive you. "Bad company ruins good habits."** 34 Come back to a sober and righteous life, and don't sin any more. Some people don't know God. I say this to make you feel ashamed.

Our Glorified Bodies

35 But somebody will ask, "How do the dead rise? And what kind of body will they have when they come back?"

36 Just think a little! The seed you sow has to die before it is made alive. 37 And the seed you sow is not the body that it will be, but a bare kernel, maybe wheat or something else. 38 But God gives it the body He wanted it to have, and to each kind of seed its own body. 39 Not all flesh is the same. Human beings have one kind of flesh, animals have another, birds have another, and fish have another kind of flesh. 40 And so there are heavenly bodies and earthly bodies. But the splendor of the heavenly bodies is different from that of the earthly bodies. 41 The shining of the sun is different from the shining of the moon, and the shining of the stars is different again. Even one star shines brighter than another.

42 That is how it will be when the dead rise. When the body is sown, it decays; when it rises, it can't decay. 43 When it is sown, it isn't wonderful; when it rises, it is wonderful. It is sown weak; it rises strong. 44 It is sown a natural body; it rises a body of the Spirit. Just as there is a natural body, so there is a body of the Spirit.

45 That is what the Bible says: *Adam, the first man, was made a natural living being;* the last Adam became a Spirit who makes alive. 46 That which has the Spirit doesn't come first, but the natural; then that which has the Spirit. 47 The first *man is made of the soil of the*

* The relative of a Christian who had died may wish to be baptized in order to see this Christian again in heaven. Or he may want to express the hope that a Christian friend who has died will rise.
** Menander.
[25] Ps. 110:1
[26] Ps. 8:6
[27] Is. 22:13

[a] Lit., *first fruits.*

493

K.J.V.

from heaven. 48As *is* the earthy, such *are* they also that are earthy: and as *is* the heavenly, such *are* they also that are heavenly. 49And as we have borne the image of the earthy, we shall also bear the image of the heavenly. 50 Now this I say, brethren, that flesh and blood cannot inherit the kingdom of God; neither doth corruption inherit incorruption. 51 Behold, I shew you a mystery; We shall not all sleep, but we shall all be changed, 52 In a moment, in the twinkling of an eye, at the last trump: for the trumpet shall sound, and the dead shall be raised incorruptible, and we shall be changed. 53 For this corruptible must put on incorruption, and this mortal *must* put on immortality. 54 So when this corruptible shall have put on incorruption, and this mortal shall have put on immortality, then shall be brought to pass the saying that is written, Death is swallowed up in victory. 55 O death, where *is* thy sting? O grave, where *is* thy victory? 56 The sting of death *is* sin; and the strength of sin *is* the law. 57 But thanks *be* to God, which giveth us the victory through our Lord Jesus Christ. 58 Therefore, my beloved brethren, be ye steadfast, unmoveable, always abounding in the work of the Lord, forasmuch as ye know that your labour is not in vain in the Lord.

16 Now concerning the collection for the saints, as I have given order to the churches of Galatia, even so do ye. 2 Upon the first *day* of the week let every one of you lay by him in store, as *God* hath prospered him, that there be no gatherings when I come. 3 And when I come, whomsoever ye shall approve by *your* letters, them will I send to bring your liberality unto Jerusalem. 4 And if it be meet that I go also, they shall go with me. 5 Now I will come unto you, when I shall pass through Macedonia: for I do pass through Macedonia. 6 And it may be that I will abide, yea, and winter with you, that ye may bring me on my journey whithersoever I go. 7 For I will not see you now by the way; but I trust to tarry a while with you, if the Lord permit. 8 But I will tarry at Ephesus until Pentecost. 9 For a great door and effectual is opened unto me, and *there are* many adversaries. 10 Now if Timotheus come, see that he may be with you without fear: for he worketh the work of the Lord, as I also *do*. 11 Let no man therefore despise him: but conduct him forth in peace, that he may come unto me: for I look for him with the brethren. 12 As touching *our* brother Apollos, I greatly desired him to come

N.A.S.

man is from heaven. 48As is the earthy, so also are those who are earthy; and as is the heavenly, so also are those who are heavenly. 49And just as we have borne the image of the earthy, *a*we shall also bear the image of the heavenly. 50 Now I say this, brethren, that flesh and blood cannot inherit the kingdom of God; nor does the perishable inherit the imperishable. 51 Behold, I tell you a mystery; we shall not all sleep, but we shall all be changed, 52 in a moment, in the twinkling of an eye, at the last trumpet; for the trumpet will sound, and the dead will be raised imperishable, and we shall be changed. 53 For this perishable must put on the imperishable, and this mortal must put on immortality. 54 But when this perishable will have put on the imperishable, and this mortal will have put on immortality, then will come about the saying that is written, "DEATH IS SWALLOWED UP IN VICTORY. 55 "O DEATH, WHERE IS YOUR VICTORY? O DEATH, WHERE IS YOUR STING?" 56 The sting of death is sin, and the power of sin is the law; 57 but thanks be to God, who gives us the victory through our Lord Jesus Christ. 58 Therefore, my beloved brethren, be steadfast, immovable, always abounding in the work of the Lord, knowing that your toil is not *in* vain in the Lord.

16 Now concerning the collection for the saints, as I directed the churches of Galatia, so do you also. 2 On the first day of every week let each one of you put aside and save, as he may prosper, that no collections be made when I come. 3 And when I arrive, whomever you may approve, I shall send them with letters to carry your gift to Jerusalem; 4 and if it is fitting for me to go also, they will go with me. 5 But I shall come to you after I go through Macedonia, for I am going through Macedonia; 6 and perhaps I shall stay with you, or even spend the winter, that you may send me on my way wherever I may go. 7 For I do not wish to see you now *just* in passing; for I hope to remain with you for some time, if the Lord permits. 8 But I shall remain in Ephesus until Pentecost; 9 for a wide door for effective *service* has opened to me, and there are many adversaries.

10 Now if Timothy comes, see that he is with you without cause to be afraid; for he is doing the Lord's work, as I also am. 11 Let no one therefore despise him. But send him on his way in peace, so that he may come to me; for I expect him with the brethren. 12 But concerning Apollos our brother, I encouraged him greatly to come to you with the brethren; and

[a] Some ancient mss. read, *let us also*.

WILLIAMS

heaven. 48 Now those who are made of the dust are just like him who was first made of dust, and those who are heavenly are like Him who is from heaven, 49 and as we have reflected the likeness of him who was made of dust, let us also reflect the likeness of the Man from heaven.

50 But this I tell you, brothers: Our physical bodies cannot take part in the kingdom of God; what is decaying will never take part in what is immortal. 51 Let me tell you a secret. We shall not all fall asleep, but we shall all be changed, 52 in a moment, in the twinkling of an eye, at the sound of the last trumpet. For the trumpet will sound, and the dead will be raised with bodies not subject to decay, and we shall be changed. 53 For this decaying part of us must put on the body that can never decay, and this part once capable of dying must put on the body that can never die. 54 And when this part once capable of dying puts on the body that can never die, then what the Scripture says will come true, "Death has been swallowed up in victory. 55 O Death, where is your victory now? O Death, where is your sting?" 56 Now sin gives death its sting, and the law gives sin its power. 57 But thank God! He gives us victory through our Lord Jesus Christ. 58 So, my dear brothers, continue to be firm, incapable of being moved, always letting the cup run over in the work of the Lord, because you know that your labor in the service of the Lord is never thrown away.[b]

16 *The contribution for the famine-stricken in Judea; principles of giving; Timothy and Apollos to visit Corinth, as well as Paul; Paul cheered by report of Stephanas' committee from Corinth; greets them*

Now about the contribution for God's people. I want you to do as I directed the churches of Galatia to do. 2 On the first day of every week each of you must put aside and store up something in proportion as he is prospered, so that no contributions need be made when I come back. 3 When I get there, I will send on, with credentials, the persons whom you approve, to carry your gift of charity to Jerusalem. 4 And if it seems proper for me to go too, they shall go as my companions.

5 I will come to see you after I pass through Macedonia—for I am to pass through Macedonia—6 and I shall likely stay over with you some time, or may be, spend the winter with you, so that you may help me on to whatever points I may visit. 7 I do not want to see you right now in a mere stop-over visit, for later I hope to spend some time with you, if the Lord permits me. 8 But I shall stay on in Ephesus until the time of Harvest Feast. 9 For I have an opportunity here that is great and calls for work, and it has many opponents.

10 If Timothy gets there, see that he is at ease among you, for he is devotedly doing the work of the Lord, just as I am. 11 So no one must slight him at all. But send him on with your good-by, that he may come back to me, for I am expecting him with the other brothers.

12 As for our brother Apollos, I have earnestly urged him to go to see you, but he is not

[b] Lit., *in vain*, to no purpose.

BECK

ground;[28] the Second Man is from heaven. 48 The people of the ground are like the man from the ground; the people of heaven are like the Man from heaven. 49 Just as we have been like the man from the ground, let us be like the Man from heaven. 50 I tell you, fellow Christians, flesh and blood can't have a share in God's kingdom, or decay have what doesn't decay.

51 Now I'll tell you a secret. We're not all going to die, but we're all going to be changed—52 in a moment, in the twinkling of an eye when the last trumpet sounds. It will sound, and the dead will rise immortal, and we'll be changed. 53 This decaying body must be made one that can't decay, and this dying body must be made one that can't die. 54 When this decaying body is made one that can't decay and this dying body is made one that can't die, then will happen what is written: *Death is destroyed in victory!* [29]

> 55 *Where, Death, is your victory?*
> *Where, Death, is your sting?* [30]

56 Sin gives death its sting, and the Law gives sin its power. 57 But thank God! He gives us the victory through our Lord Jesus Christ.

58 Stand firm, then, my dear fellow Christians, and let nothing move you. Always keep on doing a great work for the Lord since you know in the Lord your hard work isn't wasted.

The Collection

16 About the collection for the holy people —do just as I ordered the churches in Galatia to do. 2 Every Sunday each of you should at home lay aside some money he makes and save it so that none will have to be collected when I come. 3 But when I come, I will send the men whom you approve with letters to take your gift to Jerusalem. 4 If it is worthwhile for me to go, too, I'll go with them.

I Am Coming

5 I will come to you when I go through Macedonia. I am going through Macedonia, 6 and probably will stay with you or even spend the winter with you so that you will send me on my way wherever I'm going. 7 I don't want to see you now just in passing, because I hope to stay with you for some time if the Lord will let me. 8 But I'll be staying in Ephesus till Pentecost, 9 because a door has opened wide for me to do effective work, and many are opposing me.

Timothy, Apollos, and Others

10 If Timothy comes, see to it he's not afraid when he's with you. He's doing the Lord's work just as I am. 11 Nobody should despise him. Send him on his way in peace so he will come to me, because I'm expecting him with the other Christians.

12 As for Apollos, our fellow worker—I tried hard to get him to go to you with the other

[28] Gen. 2:7
[29] Is. 25:8
[30] Hos. 13:14

K.J.V.

unto you with the brethren: but his will was not at all to come at this time; but he will come when he shall have convenient time. 13 Watch ye, stand fast in the faith, quit you like men, be strong. 14 Let all your things be done with charity. 15 I beseech you, brethren, (ye know the house of Stephanas, that it is the firstfruits of Achaia, and *that* they have addicted themselves to the ministry of the saints,) 16 That ye submit yourselves unto such, and to every one that helpeth with *us*, and laboureth. 17 I am glad of the coming of Stephanas and Fortunatus and Achaicus: for that which was lacking on your part they have supplied. 18 For they have refreshed my spirit and yours: therefore acknowledge ye them that are such. 19 The churches of Asia salute you. Aquila and Priscilla salute you much in the Lord, with the church that is in their house. 20 All the brethren greet you. Greet ye one another with a holy kiss. 21 The salutation of *me* Paul with mine own hand. 22 If any man love not the Lord Jesus Christ, let him be Anathema, Maran atha. 23 The grace of our Lord Jesus Christ *be* with you. 24 My love *be* with you all in Christ Jesus. Amen.

The first *epistle* to the Corinthians was written from Philippi by Stephanas, and Fortunatus, and Achaicus, and Timotheus.

N.A.S.

it was not at all *his* desire to come now, but he will come when he has opportunity. 13 Be on the alert, stand firm in the faith, act like men, be strong. 14 Let all that you do be done in love.

15 Now I urge you, brethren (you know the household of Stephanas, that they were the firstfruits of Achaia, and that they have devoted themselves for ministry to the saints), 16 that you also be in subjection to such men and to everyone who helps in the work and labors. 17 And I rejoice over the coming of Stephanas and Fortunatus and Achaicus; because they have supplied what was lacking on your part. 18 For they have refreshed my spirit and yours. Therefore acknowledge such men.

19 The churches of Asia greet you. Aquila and Prisca greet you heartily in the Lord, with the church that is in their house. 20 All the brethren greet you. Greet one another with a holy kiss.

21 The greeting is in my own hand—Paul. 22 If any one does not love the Lord, let him be accursed. Marana tha. 23 The grace of the Lord Jesus be with you. 24 My love be with you all in Christ Jesus. Amen.

WILLIAMS

at all inclined to come just now; yet he is coming when he has a good opportunity.

13 Be always on your guard; stand firm in your faith; keep on acting like men; continue to grow in strength; 14 let everything be done in love.

15 Now I beg you, brothers—you know that the family of Stephanas were the first converts in Greece, and that they have devoted themselves to the service of God's people—16 I beg you to put yourselves under leaders like these, and under anyone who co-operates with you, and labors hard. 17 And I am glad that Stephanas, Fortunatus, and Achaicus have come to see me, because they have supplied what you lacked. 18 Yes, they have cheered my spirit, and yours too. You must deeply appreciate such men.

19 The churches of Asia wish to be remembered to you. Aquila and Prisca, with the church that meets at their house, send you their cordial Christian greetings. 20 All the brothers wish to be remembered to you. Greet one another with a sacred kiss.

21 The final greeting is mine—Paul's—with my own hand. 22 A curse upon anyone who does not love the Lord! Our Lord is coming. 23 The spiritual blessing of the Lord Jesus be with you! 24 My love be with you all in union with Christ Jesus.

BECK

Christians, but God didn't at all want him to go now. He will come when the time is right.

13 Watch, stand firm in your faith, *be men, be strong.*[31] 14 Do everything with love.

15 You know that the family of Stephanas was the first to be won in Greece, and they gave themselves to the service of the holy people. I urge you, my fellow Christians, 16 let such people and anyone else who works hard with you lead you. 17 I'm glad Stephanas, Fortunatus, and Achaicus came here, because they have made up for your absence: 18 They have refreshed me—and you too. You should appreciate men like that.

Greetings

19 The churches in the province of Asia greet you. Aquila and Prisca and the church at their home send you hearty greetings in the Lord. 20 All the Christians greet you. Greet one another with a holy kiss. 21 Here is the greeting that I, Paul, write with my own hand.

22 If anyone doesn't love the Lord, a curse on him! Our Lord, come!

23 May the Lord Jesus love you! 24 My love be with you all in Christ Jesus. Amen.

K.J.V.

THE SECOND EPISTLE OF PAUL THE APOSTLE TO THE

CORINTHIANS

1 Paul, an apostle of Jesus Christ by the will of God, and Timothy *our* brother, unto the church of God which is at Corinth, with all the saints which are in all Achaia: 2 Grace *be* to you, and peace, from God our Father, and *from* the Lord Jesus Christ. 3 Blessed *be* God, even the Father of our Lord Jesus Christ, the Father of mercies, and the God of all comfort; 4 Who comforteth us in all our tribulation, that we may be able to comfort them which are in any trouble, by the comfort wherewith we ourselves are comforted of God. 5 For as the sufferings of Christ abound in us, so our consolation also aboundeth by Christ. 6 And whether we be afflicted, *it is* for your consolation and salvation, which is effectual in the enduring of the same sufferings which we also suffer: or whether we be comforted, *it is* for your consolation and salvation. 7 And our hope of you *is* steadfast, knowing, that as ye are partakers of the sufferings, so *shall ye be* also of the consolation. 8 For we would not, brethren, have you ignorant of our trouble which came to us in Asia, that we were pressed out of measure, above strength, insomuch that we despaired even of life: 9 But we had the sentence of death in ourselves, that we should not trust in ourselves, but in God which raiseth the dead: 10 Who delivered us from so great a death, and doth deliver: in whom we trust that he will yet deliver *us;* 11 Ye also helping together by prayer for us, that for the gift *bestowed* upon us by the means of many persons thanks may be given by many on our behalf. 12 For our rejoicing is this, the testimony of our conscience, that in simplicity and godly sincerity, not with fleshly wisdom, but by the grace of God, we have had our conversation in the world, and more abundantly to youward. 13 For we write none other things unto you, than what ye read or acknowledge; and I trust ye shall acknowledge even to the end; 14 As also ye have acknowledged us in part, that we are your rejoicing, even as ye also *are* ours in the day of the Lord Jesus. 15 And in this confidence I was minded to come unto you before, that ye might have a second benefit; 16 And to pass by you into Macedonia, and to come again out of Macedonia unto you, and of you to be brought on my way toward Judea. 17 When I therefore was thus minded, did I use lightness? or the things that I purpose, do I purpose ac-

N.A.S.

THE SECOND EPISTLE OF PAUL TO THE

CORINTHIANS

1 Paul, an apostle of Christ Jesus by the will of God, and Timothy *our* brother, to the church of God which is at Corinth with all the saints who are throughout Achaia: 2 Grace to you and peace from God our Father and the Lord Jesus Christ. 3 Blessed *be* the God and Father of our Lord Jesus Christ, the Father of mercies and God of all comfort; 4 who comforts us in all our affliction so that we may be able to comfort those who are in any affliction with the comfort with which we ourselves are comforted by God. 5 For just as the sufferings of Christ are ours in abundance, so also our comfort is abundant through Christ. 6 But if we are afflicted, it is for your comfort and salvation; or if we are comforted, it is for your comfort, which is effective in the patient enduring of the same sufferings which we also suffer; 7 and our hope for you is firmly grounded, knowing that as you are sharers of our sufferings, so also you are *sharers* of our comfort. 8 For we do not want you to be unaware, brethren, of our affliction which came *to us* in Asia, that we were burdened excessively, beyond our strength, so that we despaired even of life; 9 indeed, we had the sentence of death within ourselves in order that we should not trust in ourselves, but in God who raises the dead; 10 who delivered us from so great a *peril of* death, and will deliver *us*, He on whom we have set our hope. And He will yet deliver us, 11 you also joining in helping us through your prayers, that thanks may be given by many persons on our behalf for the favor bestowed upon us through *the prayers of* many. 12 For our proud confidence is this, the testimony of our conscience that in holiness and godly sincerity, not in fleshly wisdom but in the grace of God, we have conducted ourselves in the world, and especially toward you. 13 For we write nothing else to you than what you read and understand, and I hope you will understand until the end; 14 just as you also partially did understand us, that we are your reason to be proud as you also are ours, in the day of our Lord Jesus. 15 And in this confidence I intended at first to come to you, that you might twice receive a blessing; 16 that is, to pass your way into Macedonia, and again from Macedonia to come to you, and by you to be helped on my journey to Judea. 17 Therefore, I was not vacillating when I intended to do this, was I? Or that which I purpose, do I purpose according

PAUL

WRITES THE SECOND

LETTER TO THE

SECOND CORINTHIANS

CORINTHIANS

1 *He greets them; gives thanks to God for comforting him; tells of his motives as pure, and why he postpones his visit to Corinth*

Paul, by the will of God an apostle of Christ Jesus, and Timothy our brother, to the church of God that is at Corinth, with all God's people all over Greece: 2 spiritual blessing and peace to you from God our Father and the Lord Jesus Christ.

3 Blessed be the God and Father of our Lord Jesus Christ, the merciful Father and the all-comforting God, 4 who comforts me in every sorrow I have, so that I can comfort people who are in sorrow with the comfort with which I am comforted by. God. 5 For just as my sufferings for Christ are running over the cup, so through Christ my comfort is running over too. 6 If I am in sorrow, it is on behalf of your comfort and salvation; if I am comforted, it is for the comfort that is experienced by you in your patient endurance of the same sort of sufferings that I am enduring too. 7 My hope for you is well founded; because I know that just as you, brothers, are sharers of my sufferings, so you will be sharers of my comfort too. 8 For I do not want you to be uninformed about the sorrow that I suffered in Asia, because I was so crushed beyond any power to endure that I was in dire despair of life itself. 9 Yes, I felt within my very self the sentence of death, to keep me from depending on myself instead of God who raises the dead. 10 He saved me from a death so horrible, and He will save me again! He it is on whom I have set my hope that He will still save me, 11 because you are helping me by your prayers for me, so that thanks to God will be given by many on my behalf for God's gracious gift to me in answer to the prayers of many.

12 For my boast is this, to which my conscience testifies, that before the world, but especially before you, I have acted from pure motives and in sincerity before God, not depending on worldly wisdom but on God's unmerited favor. 13 For what I am writing you is nothing more than what you can read and understand, and I hope that you will understand it perfectly, just as some of you have come to understand me partially; 14 that is, to understand that you have grounds for boasting of me just as I have for boasting of you, on the day of our Lord Jesus.

15 It was because of this confidence that first I planned to visit you, to give you a double delight; 16 that is, to go by you on my way to Macedonia, and then to come back to you from Macedonia, and have you send me on to Judea. 17 Now I did not resort to fickleness, did I, in planning that? Or, do I make my plans in ac-

1 Paul, apostle of Christ Jesus by God's will, and Timothy, our fellow worker, to God's church in Corinth and to all the holy people everywhere in Greece— 2 may God our Father and the Lord Jesus Christ love you and give you peace!

God Comforts and Rescues Us

3 Let us praise the God and Father of our Lord Jesus Christ, the Father of mercy and the God of every comfort. 4 He comforts us in all our suffering to make us able to comfort others in all their suffering with the same comfort with which God comforts us. 5 As Christ's sufferings overflow to us, so Christ makes our comfort overflow. 6 If we suffer, it helps us to comfort and save you. If we are comforted, it helps us to comfort you effectively when you endure the same sufferings as we do. 7 Our hope for you is unshaken because we know as you share our sufferings you share our comfort.

8 Fellow Christians, we want you to know our suffering in the province of Asia was so extreme, so much more than we could stand, we even despaired of living. 9 Yes, we felt sentenced to death. We were not to trust ourselves but God, who raises the dead. 10 He rescued us from such a death, and He who is our hope will rescue us again. He will continue to rescue us 11 if you, too, will help us by praying—and have many people look up to God and thank Him for what He gave us.

We Were Sincere

12 This is what we're proud of. Our conscience tells us that with God's holiness and sincerity, without human cleverness but with God's love, we have lived in the world and especially with you. 13 We are writing you only what you can read and understand. And I hope you will understand till the end, 14 As you have to some extent understood us, that you can be proud of us as also we of you on the day of our Lord Jesus.

15 Feeling sure of this, I wanted you to have the benefit of a double visit. I planned to come to you first, 16 go from you to Macedonia, then come back again from Macedonia to you and let you send me on to Judea.

17 When I wanted to do this, was I trifling? Or do I go on making my plans any way I please

K.J.V.

cording to the flesh, that with me there should be yea, yea, and nay, nay? 18 But *as* God *is* true, our word toward you was not yea and nay. 19 For the Son of God, Jesus Christ, who was preached among you by us, *even* by me and Silvanus and Timotheus, was not yea and nay, but in him was yea. 20 For all the promises of God in him *are* yea, and in him Amen, unto the glory of God by us. 21 Now he which stablisheth us with you in Christ, and hath anointed us, *is* God; 22 Who hath also sealed us, and given the earnest of the Spirit in our hearts. 23 Moreover I call God for a record upon my soul, that to spare you I came not as yet unto Corinth. 24 Not for that we have dominion over your faith, but are helpers of your joy: for by faith ye stand.

2 But I determined this with myself, that I would not come again to you in heaviness. 2 For if I make you sorry, who is he then that maketh me glad, but the same which is made sorry by me? 3 And I wrote this same unto you, lest, when I came, I should have sorrow from them of whom I ought to rejoice; having confidence in you all, that my joy is *the joy* of you all. 4 For out of much affliction and anguish of heart I wrote unto you with many tears; not that ye should be grieved, but that ye might know the love which I have more abundantly unto you. 5 But if any have caused grief, he hath not grieved me, but in part: that I may not overcharge you all. 6 Sufficient to such a man *is* this punishment, which *was inflicted* of many. 7 So that contrariwise ye *ought* rather to forgive *him*, and comfort *him*, lest perhaps such a one should be swallowed up with overmuch sorrow. 8 Wherefore I beseech you that ye would confirm *your* love toward him. 9 For to this end also did I write, that I might know the proof of you, whether ye be obedient in all things. 10 To whom ye forgive any thing, I *forgive* also: for if I forgave any thing, to whom I forgave *it*, for your sakes *forgave I it* in the person of Christ; 11 Lest Satan should get an advantage of us: for we are not ignorant of his devices. 12 Furthermore, when I came to Troas to *preach* Christ's gospel, and a door was opened unto me of the Lord, 13 I had no rest in my spirit, because I found not Titus my brother; but taking my leave of them, I went from thence into Macedonia. 14 Now thanks *be* unto God, which always causeth us to triumph in Christ, and maketh manifest the savour of his knowledge by us in every place. 15 For we are unto God a sweet savour of Christ, in them that are saved, and in them that perish: 16 To the one *we are* the savour of death unto death; and to the other the savour of life unto life. And who *is* sufficient for these things? 17 For we are not as many, which corrupt the word of God; but as of sin-

N.A.S.

to the flesh, that with me there should be yes, yes and no, no *at the same time?* 18 But as God is faithful, our word to you is not yes and no. 19 For the Son of God, Christ Jesus, who was preached among you by us,—by me and Silvanus and Timothy—was not yes and no, but is yes in Him. 20 For as many as may be the promises of God, in Him they are yes; wherefore also by Him is our Amen to the glory of God through us. . 21 Now He who establishes us with you in Christ and anointed us is God, 22 who also sealed us and gave *us* the Spirit in our hearts as a pledge.

23 But I call God as witness to my soul, that to spare you I came no more to Corinth. 24 Not that we lord it over your faith, but are workers with you for your joy; for in your faith you are standing firm.

2 But I determined this for my own sake, that I would not come to you in sorrow again. 2 For if I cause you sorrow, who then makes me glad but the one whom I made sorrowful? 3 And this is the very thing I wrote you, lest, when I came, I should have sorrow from those who ought to make me rejoice; having confidence in you all, that my joy would be *the joy* of you all. 4 For out of much affliction and anguish of heart I wrote to you with many tears; not that you should be made sorrowful, but that you might know the love which I have especially for you.

5 But if any has caused sorrow, he has caused sorrow not to me, but in some degree —in order not to say too much—to all of you. 6 Sufficient for such a one is this punishment which was *inflicted by* the majority, 7 so that on the contrary you should rather forgive and comfort *him*, lest somehow such a one be overwhelmed by excessive sorrow. 8 Wherefore I urge you to reaffirm *your* love for him. 9 For to this end also I wrote that I might put you to the test, whether you are obedient in all things. 10 But whom you forgive anything, I *forgive* also; for indeed what I have forgiven, if I have forgiven anything, I *did it* for your sakes in the presence of Christ, 11 in order that no advantage be taken of us by Satan; for we are not ignorant of his schemes.

12 Now when I came to Troas for the gospel of Christ and when a door was opened for me in the Lord, 13 I had no rest for my spirit, not finding Titus my brother; but taking my leave of them, I went on to Macedonia.

14 But thanks be to God, who always leads us in His triumph in Christ, and manifests through us the sweet aroma of the knowledge of Him in every place. 15 For we are a fragrance of Christ to God among those who are being saved and among those who are perishing; 16 to the one an aroma from death to death, to the other an aroma from life to life. And who is adequate for these things? 17 For we are not like many, [a]peddling the word of

[a] Or, *corrupting.*

WILLIAMS

cordance with worldly notions, to have my "Yes" mean "No," if I want it so? 18 As certainly as God is to be trusted, my message to you has not been a "Yes" that might mean "No." 19 For God's Son, Christ Jesus, who was preached among you by us, Silvanus, Timothy, and me, did not become a "Yes" that might mean "No." 20 But with Him it is always "Yes," for, as many as the promises of God may be, through Him they are always "Yes." This is why our "Amen" through Him is for the glory of God when spoken by us. 21 But it is God who makes us as well as you secure through union with Christ, and has anointed us, 22 and put His seal upon us, and given us His Spirit in our hearts as a first installment of future rewards.

23 But upon my soul I call God to witness that it was to spare you pain that I gave up my visit to Corinth. 24 Not that we are trying to lord it over your faith, but we are workers with you to promote your joy, for in your faith you are standing firm.

2 *He writes in love; begs the church to forgive the penitent offender; tells of his sorrow and his success*

For I have definitely decided not to pay you another painful visit. 2 For if I make you sad, who is there to make me glad but the very man who has been made sad by me? 3 This is the very thing I wrote you, that when I did come I might not be made sad by the very people who ought to make me glad, for I had confidence in you all that my gladness would be gladness to you all. 4 For out of great sorrow and distress of heart, yes, while shedding many tears, I wrote you, not to make you sad but to make you realize that my love for you continues running over.

5 But if anyone has made anyone sad, it is not I, but you that he has made sad, at least, some of you, not to be severe on all of you. 6 To a man like that, this censure by the majority has been sufficient punishment, 7 so you must do the opposite, freely forgive and comfort him, to keep him from being overwhelmed by his excessive sadness. 8 So I beg you in your love to reinstate him entirely. 9 For this is why I wrote you, to see if you would stand the test, to see if you would be obedient in everything. 10 The man that you forgive I too forgive. For if I have forgiven him anything, it is what I have forgiven him in the very presence of Christ for your sake, 11 to keep us from being worsted by Satan, for we know what his intentions are.

12 When I went to Troas to preach the good news of Christ, although I had an opportunity in the service of the Lord, 13 I had no rest of spirit, because I did not find my brother Titus there. So I said good-by to them and left for Macedonia. 14 But thanks be to God, for He always leads me in His triumphal train, through union with Christ, and everywhere through me keeps spreading the perfume of the knowledge of Him. 15 Indeed, I am the fragrance of Christ to God, alike for those who are being saved and for those who are perishing; 16 to the one a deadly perfume that leads to death, to the other a living perfume that leads to life. 17 Now who is qualified for such a task? I am, for I am not a peddler of God's message, like the

BECK

so that I can say "Yes, yes" and "No, no"? 18 You can trust God that what we tell you isn't yes and no. 19 God's Son Jesus Christ, whom I, Silas, and Timothy preached to you, wasn't yes and no, but in Him there has come and is a yes. 20 For all God's promises He is the Yes that makes them come true. And so He makes it possible for us to give glory to God by saying, "It is true."

21 It is God who makes us and you firm in the anointed Savior and also has anointed us. 22 He has put His seal on us and given us the Spirit as a guarantee in our hearts.

I Don't Want to Hurt You

23 I call on God as a witness against me that I stayed away from Corinth in order not to hurt you. 24 I don't mean we're lords of your faith, but we're working with you to make you happy. You stand on your own feet in your faith.

2 I made up my mind not to come if I had to bring you grief again. 2 If I make you sad, who should make me happy but the person I'm making sad? 3 This is what I said in my letter. I didn't want to come and be made sad by those who should have made me happy. Feeling sure about all of you that what makes me happy makes all of you happy too. 4 I was deeply troubled and in anguish when I wrote you with much weeping, not to make you sad but to have you realize how very much I love you.

Forgive the Man Who Did Wrong

5 If someone caused grief, he didn't do it to me but to some extent (not to make it too strong) to all of you. 6 Most of you have punished him; that's enough for such a person. 7 Now you should turn around, forgive and comfort him, or too much grief may overwhelm such a person. 8 So I urge you to assure him of your love. 9 I wrote you to see if you would stand the test and obey in every way.

10 When you forgive anyone, I do too. If I forgave anything, I did it in the presence of Christ to help you 11 and to keep the devil from getting the best of us. We know what he has in mind.

An Odor of Life

12 I went to Troas to tell the good news of Christ, and there a door to do the Lord's work stood wide open for me, 13 but my spirit couldn't get any relief because I didn't find Titus, my fellow worker. So I said good-by to the people and went to Macedonia.

14 But thank God! He always leads us on triumphantly in Christ and everywhere through us spreads the fragrance of knowing Him. 15 Yes, we are a fragrance of Christ to God among those who are saved and among those who perish— 16 to some an odor of death that kills, to others an odor of life that gives life.

17 And who is qualified for this?—At least we don't peddle an impure Word of God like

K.J.V.

cerity, but as of God, in the sight of God speak we in Christ.

3 Do we begin again to commend ourselves? or need we, as some *others,* epistles of commendation to you, or *letters* of commendation from you? 2 Ye are our epistle written in our hearts, known and read of all men: 3 *Forasmuch as ye are* manifestly declared to be the epistle of Christ ministered by us, written not with ink, but with the Spirit of the living God; not in tables of stone, but in fleshly tables of the heart. 4And such trust have we through Christ to God-ward: 5 Not that we are sufficient of ourselves to think any thing as of ourselves; but our sufficiency *is* of God; 6 Who also hath made us able ministers of the new testament; not of the letter, but of the spirit: for the letter killeth, but the spirit giveth life. 7 But if the ministration of death, written *and* engraven in stones, was glorious, so that the children of Israel could not steadfastly behold the face of Moses for the glory of his countenance; which *glory* was to be done away; 8 How shall not the ministration of the spirit be rather glorious? 9 For if the ministration of condemnation *be* glory, much more doth the ministration of righteousness exceed in glory. 10 For even that which was made glorious had no glory in this respect, by reason of the glory that excelleth. 11 For if that which is done away *was* glorious, much more that which remaineth *is* glorious. 12 Seeing then that we have such hope, we use great plainness of speech: 13And not as Moses, *which* put a vail over his face, that the children of Israel could not steadfastly look to the end of that which is abolished: 14 But their minds were blinded: for until this day remaineth the same vail untaken away in the reading of the old testament; which *vail* is done away in Christ. 15 But even unto this day, when Moses is read, the vail is upon their heart. 16 Nevertheless, when it shall turn to the Lord, the vail shall be taken away. 17 Now the Lord is that Spirit: and where the Spirit of the Lord *is,* there *is* liberty. 18 But we all, with open face beholding as in a glass the glory of the Lord, are changed into the same image from glory to glory, *even* as by the Spirit of the Lord.

N.A.S.

God, but as from sincerity, but as from God, we speak in Christ in the sight of God.

3 Are we beginning to commend ourselves again? Or do we need, as some, letters of commendation to you or from you? 2 You are our letter, written in our hearts, known and read by all men; 3 being manifested that you are a letter of Christ, cared for by us, written not with ink, but with the Spirit of the living God, not on tablets of stone, but on tablets of human hearts. 4And such confidence we have through Christ toward God. 5 Not that we are adequate in ourselves to consider anything as *coming* from ourselves, but our adequacy is from God, 6 who also made us adequate *as* servants of a new covenant, not of the letter, but of the Spirit; for the letter kills, but the Spirit gives life. 7 But if the ministry of death, in letters engraved on stones, came with glory, so that the children of Israel could not look intently at the face of Moses because of the glory of his face, fading *as* it was, 8 how shall the ministry of the Spirit fail to be even more with glory? 9 For if the ministry of condemnation has glory, much more does the ministry of righteousness abound in glory. 10 For indeed what had glory, in this case has no glory on account of the glory that surpasses *it.* 11 For if that which fades away *was* with glory, much more that which remains *is* in glory.

12 Having therefore such a hope, we use great boldness in *our* speech, 13 and *are* not as Moses, *who* used to put a veil over his face that the children of Israel might not look intently at the end of what was fading away. 14 But their minds were hardened; for until this very day at the reading of the old covenant the same veil remains unlifted, because it is removed in Christ. 15 But to this day whenever Moses is read, a veil lies over their heart; 16 BUT WHENEVER A MAN TURNS TO THE LORD, THE VEIL IS TAKEN AWAY. 17 Now the Lord is the Spirit; and where the Spirit of the Lord is, *there* is liberty. 18 But we all, with unveiled face beholding as in a mirror the glory of the Lord, are being transformed into the same image from glory to glory, just as from the Lord, the Spirit.

WILLIAMS

BECK

most of them, but like a man of sincerity, like a man that is sent from God and living in His presence, in union with Christ I speak His message.

3 *His converts at Corinth proof that God called him to be an apostle; tells of the surpassing glory of this spiritual ministry*

Am I beginning to recommend myself again? I do not, like some people, do I, need letters of recommendation to you or from you? 2 You are my letter of recommendation, written on my heart, read and understood by everybody, 3 for you are always showing that you are a letter of Christ, produced by my service, written not in ink but by the Spirit of the living God, not on tablets of stone, but on human hearts.

4 Such is the confidence I have through Christ in the presence of God. 5 Not that I am myself qualified to consider anything as coming from me myself. No; my qualification comes from God, for 6 He has qualified even me as a minister of the new covenant, which is not a written but a spiritual covenant. For the letter kills, but the Spirit gives life.

7 Now if the old religious service which resulted in death, although its law was carved in letters of stone, was introduced with a splendor so great that the Israelites could not keep their eyes fixed on Moses' face because of the splendor that was fading from it, 8 why should not this spiritual service be attended with much greater splendor? 9 For if the service connected with condemnation had such splendor, the service resulting in right standing with God will surely far surpass it in splendor. 10 For on account of its surpassing splendor, what was once so splendid has now no splendor at all. 11 For if what passed away was introduced with splendor, with how much greater splendor must what is permanent be attended?

12 So, as I have such a hope, I speak with the greatest boldness, 13 not as Moses did, who used to wear a veil over his face, to keep the Israelites from gazing at the end of what was passing away. 14 Besides, their minds were made dull; for to this day that same veil remains unlifted, whenever they read the Old Covenant; because it is only through union with Christ that it is removed. 15 Indeed, to this very day, whenever Moses is read, a veil hangs over their hearts, 16 but whenever anybody turns to the Lord, the veil is removed. 17 Now the Lord means the Spirit, and wherever the Spirit of the Lord is, there is freedom. 18 And all of us, with faces uncovered, because we continue to reflect like mirrors the splendor of the Lord, are being transformed into likeness to Him, from one degree of splendor to another, since it comes from the Lord who is the Spirit.

many others, but in Christ we talk sincerely as men who come from God and stand before God.

3 Are we again recommending ourselves? Or do we, like some people, need letters of recommendation to you or from you? 2 You are our letter, written in our hearts, known and read by everybody. 3 Anyone can see you are Christ's letter, prepared by us, not written with ink but with the Spirit *of* the living *God,* not *on stone plates* but *on human hearts.*[1]

4 That is how Christ gives us confidence in God. 5 We can't do anything by ourselves and so claim to produce it ourselves, but God gives us our ability. 6 He has made us able servants of a new covenant, not of a written Law but of the Spirit, because the written Law kills, but the Spirit makes alive.

The Glory of the New Covenant

7 Now if that service, engraved in stone and bringing death, came with such glory the people of Israel couldn't look at *Moses' face* because it *shone with the glory* that was fading, 8 how much more certainly will the service of the Spirit have *glory?* 9 If the service that condemns has *glory,* the service that gives righteousness much more certainly overflows with *glory.* 10 That which had *glory* lost it because the other *glory* outshone it. 11 If that which fades away had its *glory,* that which is permanent much more certainly has *glory.*

12 Because we expect this, we are very bold 13 and not like *Moses,* who *wore a veil over his face* to keep the people of Israel from seeing the last rays of the fading *glory.* 14 But their minds have been closed. To this day the same *veil* is still there on the reading of the old covenant and isn't taken away, because it is put away only in Christ. 15 Yes, to this day, when they read Moses, a *veil* lies on their hearts. 16 But *whenever anyone turns to the Lord, the veil is taken away.*[2]

17 The Lord is the Spirit, and where the Spirit of the Lord is, there is liberty. 18 And all of us, reflecting *the Lord's glory*[3] in our unveiled faces, are changed from glory to glory to be like Him, as we expect it from the Lord, who is the Spirit.

[1] Ex. 24:12; 31:18; Prov. 3:3; Ezek. 11:19; 36:26
[2] Ex. 34:29-30, 33-35
[3] Ex. 16:7, 10; 24:17

4 Therefore, seeing we have this ministry, as we have received mercy, we faint not; 2 But have renounced the hidden things of dishonesty, not walking in craftiness, nor handling the word of God deceitfully; but, by manifestation of the truth, commending ourselves to every man's conscience in the sight of God. 3 But if our gospel be hid, it is hid to them that are lost: 4 In whom the god of this world hath blinded the minds of them which believe not, lest the light of the glorious gospel of Christ, who is the image of God, should shine unto them. 5 For we preach not ourselves, but Christ Jesus the Lord; and ourselves your servants for Jesus' sake. 6 For God, who commanded the light to shine out of darkness, hath shined in our hearts, to *give* the light of the knowledge of the glory of God in the face of Jesus Christ. 7 But we have this treasure in earthen vessels, that the excellency of the power may be of God, and not of us. 8 *We are* troubled on every side, yet not distressed; *we are* perplexed, but not in despair; 9 Persecuted, but not forsaken; cast down, but not destroyed; 10 Always bearing about in the body the dying of the Lord Jesus, that the life also of Jesus might be made manifest in our body. 11 For we which live are alway delivered unto death for Jesus' sake, that the life also of Jesus might be made manifest in our mortal flesh. 12 So then death worketh in us, but life in you. 13 We having the same spirit of faith, according as it is written, I believed, and therefore have I spoken; we also believe, and therefore speak; 14 Knowing that he which raised up the Lord Jesus shall raise up us also by Jesus, and shall *present us* with you. 15 For all things *are* for your sakes, that the abundant grace might through the thanksgiving of many redound to the glory of God. 16 For which cause we faint not; but though our outward man perish, yet the inward *man* is renewed day by day. 17 For our light affliction, which is but for a moment, worketh for us a far more exceeding *and* eternal weight of glory; 18 While we look not at the things which are seen, but at the things which are not seen: for the things which are seen *are* temporal; but the things which are not seen *are* eternal.

4 Therefore since we have this ministry, as we received mercy, we do not lose heart, 2 but we have renounced the things hidden because of shame, not walking in craftiness or adulterating the word of God, but by the manifestation of truth commending ourselves to every man's conscience in the sight of God. 3 And even if our gospel is veiled, it is veiled to those who are perishing. 4 in whose case the god of this world has blinded the minds of the unbelieving, that they might not see the light of the gospel of the glory of Christ, who is the image of God. 5 For we do not preach ourselves but Christ Jesus as Lord, and ourselves as your bond-servants for Jesus' sake. 6 For God, who said, "Light shall shine out of darkness," is the One who has shone in our hearts to give the light of the knowledge of the glory of God in the face of Christ.

7 But we have this treasure in earthen vessels, that the surpassing greatness of the power may be of God and not from ourselves; 8 *we are* afflicted in every way, but not crushed; perplexed, but not despairing; 9 persecuted, but not forsaken; struck down, but not destroyed; 10 always carrying about in the body the dying of Jesus, that the life of Jesus also may be manifested in our body. 11 For we who live are constantly being delivered over to death for Jesus' sake, that the life of Jesus also may be manifested in our mortal flesh. 12 So death works in us, but life in you. 13 But having the same spirit of faith, according to what is written, "I BELIEVED, THEREFORE I SPOKE," we also believe, therefore also we speak; 14 knowing that He who raised the Lord Jesus will raise us also with Jesus and will present us with you. 15 For all things *are* for your sakes, that the grace which is spreading to more and more people may cause the giving of thanks to abound to the glory of God.

16 Therefore we do not lose heart, but though our outer man is decaying, yet our inner man is being renewed day by day. 17 For momentary, light affliction is producing for us an eternal weight of glory far beyond all comparison, 18 while we do not look at the things which are seen, but at the things which are not seen; for the things which are seen are temporal, but the things which are not seen are eternal.

WILLIAMS

4 *Paul faithfully preaches the good news; God gives him strength to bear his sorrows; he hopes for his body to be raised and his sorrows to increase his future glories*

So, because I hold a place[a] in this ministry and that because I have had God's mercy shown me, I never give up. 2 On the other hand, I have renounced all underhanded, disgraceful methods; I neither practice cunning nor do I tamper with God's message, but by clear and candid statements of truth I try to commend myself to every human conscience in God's sight. 3 If the meaning of the good news I preach is covered up at all, it is so only in the case of those who are on the way to destruction. 4 In their case, the god of this world has blinded the eyes of the unbelievers, to keep the glorious light of the good news of Christ, who is the likeness of God, from dawning upon them. 5 For I am not proclaiming myself but Christ Jesus as Lord, and myself a slave of yours for Jesus' sake. 6 For God who said, "Let light shine out of darkness," is the One who has shone in my heart, to give me the light of the knowledge of God's glory, reflected on the face of Christ.

7 But I am keeping this jewel[b] in an earthen jar, to prove that its surpassing power is God's, not mine. 8 On every side I am ever hard-pressed, but never hemmed in; always perplexed, but never to the point of despair; 9 always being persecuted, but not deserted; always getting a knockdown, but never a knock-out;[c] 10 always being exposed to death as Jesus was, so that in my body the life of Jesus may be clearly shown. 11 For all the time I continue to live I am being given up to death for Jesus' sake, so that in my mortal lower nature the life of Jesus may be clearly shown. 12 So it is death that works in me, but it is life that works in you.

13 Now since I have the same spirit of faith as he who said in the Scriptures, "I believed, and so I spoke," I too believe, and so I speak, 14 because I know that He who raised the Lord Jesus from the dead will raise me too in fellowship with you. 15 For everything is for your sakes, in order that His favor by multiplying the thanksgiving of many may make the cup run over to the praise of God.

16 So I never give up; instead, although my outer nature is wasting away, my inner nature is constantly renewed from day to day. 17 For this slight and momentary sorrow continues to accumulate for me a solid and eternal glory far beyond any comparison, 18 because I do not keep my eyes on things that are seen but things that are unseen. For things that are seen are temporary, but things that are unseen are eternal.

BECK

Treasure in Clay Jars

4 And so we who by God's mercy have this service don't get discouraged. 2 But we have renounced the secret ways that anybody should feel ashamed of. We don't use trickery or falsify God's Word. But by clearly telling the truth we recommend ourselves to everyone's conscience before God.

3 If the good news we tell is veiled, it is veiled to those who perish, 4 whose minds the god of this world has blinded—they don't believe—to keep them from seeing the light of the good news of the glory of Christ, who is God's image.

5 You see, we don't preach ourselves but Jesus Christ as the Lord, and we are your servants for Jesus' sake. 6 God, who said, "*Let light shine*[4] out of the dark," has shone in our hearts to bring you the light of knowing God's glory in the face of Jesus Christ.

7 We have this treasure in clay jars to show that its extraordinary power comes from God and not from us. 8 In every way we are hard pressed but not crushed, in doubt but not in despair; 9 hunted but not forsaken; struck down but not destroyed. 10 We are in our bodies always being killed with Jesus so that you can see in our bodies the life of Jesus. 11 While we're living, we're always being given up to die for Jesus so that you can see in our dying bodies the life of Jesus. 12 So death is working in us, but life is working in you.

13 It is written, *I believed and so I spoke.*[5] Having the same spirit of faith, we also believe and so we speak, 14 because we know that He who raised the Lord Jesus will also raise us with Jesus and bring us with you before Him.

15 All this is to help you so that God's love, as it spreads will move more and more people to overflow with thanks to God's glory. 16 That is why we are not discouraged. No, even if we outwardly perish, inwardly we're renewed from day to day. 17 The light trouble of this moment is preparing for us an everlasting weight of glory, greater than anything we can imagine. 18 We don't look at the things that are seen but at the things that are not seen. What we see lasts only a while, but what we don't see lasts forever.

---

[a] Lit., *I hold or have this ministry.* [b] Lit., *treasure—the ministry of the good news.* [c] Lit., *never destroyed.*

[4] Gen. 1:3
[5] Ps. 116:10

5 For we know that, if our earthly house of this tabernacle were dissolved, we have a building of God, a house not made with hands, eternal in the heavens. 2 For in this we groan, earnestly desiring to be clothed upon with our house which is from heaven: 3 If so be that being clothed we shall not be found naked. 4 For we that are in this tabernacle do groan, being burdened: not for that we would be unclothed, but clothed upon, that mortality might be swallowed up of life. 5 Now he that hath wrought us for the selfsame thing is God, who also hath given unto us the earnest of the Spirit. 6 Therefore we are always confident, knowing that, whilst we are at home in the body, we are absent from the Lord: 7 (For we walk by faith, not by sight:) 8 We are confident, I say, and willing rather to be absent from the body, and to be present with the Lord. 9 Wherefore we labour, that, whether present or absent, we may be accepted of him. 10 For we must all appear before the judgment seat of Christ; that every one may receive the things done in his body, according to that he hath done, whether it be good or bad. 11 Knowing therefore the terror of the Lord, we persuade men; but we are made manifest unto God; and I trust also are made manifest in your consciences. 12 For we commend not ourselves again unto you, but give you occasion to glory on our behalf, that ye may have somewhat to answer them which glory in appearance, and not in heart. 13 For whether we be beside ourselves, it is to God: or whether we be sober, it is for your cause. 14 For the love of Christ constraineth us; because we thus judge, that if one died for all, then were all dead: 15And that he died for all, that they which live should not henceforth live unto themselves, but unto him which died for them, and rose again. 16 Wherefore henceforth know we no man after the flesh: yea, though we have known Christ after the flesh, yet now henceforth know we him no more. 17 Therefore if any man be in Christ, he is a new creature: old things are passed away; behold, all things are become new. 18And all things are of God, who hath reconciled us to himself by Jesus Christ, and hath given to us the ministry of reconciliation; 19 To wit, that God was in Christ, reconciling the world unto himself, not imputing their trespasses unto them; and hath committed unto us the word of reconciliation. 20 Now then we are ambassadors for Christ, as though God did beseech you by us: we pray you in Christ's stead, be ye reconciled to God. 21 For he hath made him to be sin for us, who knew no sin; that we might be made the righteousness of God in him.

5 For we know that if the earthly tent which is our house is torn down, we have a building from God, a house not made with hands, eternal in the heavens. 2 For indeed in this house we groan, longing to be clothed with our dwelling from heaven; 3 inasmuch as we, having put it on, shall not be found naked. 4 For indeed while we are in this tent, we groan, being burdened, because we do not want to be unclothed, but to be clothed, in order that what is mortal may be swallowed up by life. 5 Now He who prepared us for this very purpose is God, who gave to us the Spirit as a pledge. 6 Therefore, being always of good courage, and knowing that while we are at home in the body we are absent from the Lord—7 for we walk by faith, not by sight— 8 we are of good courage, I say, and prefer rather to be absent from the body and to be at home with the Lord. 9 Therefore also we have as our ambition, whether at home or absent, to be pleasing to Him. 10 For we must all appear before the judgment-seat of Christ, that each one may be recompensed for his deeds in the body, according to what he has done, whether good or bad. 11 Therefore knowing the fear of the Lord, we persuade men, but we are made manifest to God; and I hope that we are made manifest also in your consciences. 12 We are not again commending ourselves to you but are giving you an occasion to be proud of us, that you may have an answer for those who take pride in appearance, and not in heart. 13 For if we are beside ourselves, it is for God; if we are of sound mind, it is for you. 14 For the love of Christ controls us, having concluded this, that one died for all, therefore all died; 15 and He died for all, that they who live should no longer live for themselves, but for Him who died and rose again on their behalf. 16 Therefore from now on we recognize no man according to the flesh; even though we have known Christ according to the flesh, yet now we know Him thus no longer. 17 Therefore if any man is in Christ, he is a new creature; the old things passed away; behold, new things have come. 18 Now all these things are from God, who reconciled us to Himself through Christ, and gave us the ministry of reconciliation, 19 namely, that God was in Christ reconciling the world to Himself, not counting their trespasses against them, and He has committed to us the word of reconciliation. 20 Therefore, we are ambassadors for Christ, as though God were entreating through us; we beg you on behalf of Christ, be reconciled to God. 21 He made Him who knew no sin to be sin on our behalf, that we might become the righteousness of God in Him.

WILLIAMS

5 On leaving his physical body, Paul hopes to move into a spiritual body, to be the home of his spirit forever; is inspired by fear, but especially by love, to live the higher life of service

For I know that if this earthly tent in which I live is taken down, I have a building in heaven which comes from God, a house not built by human hands but eternal. 2 For in this one I am sighing, because I long to put on, like a robe, my heavenly body, my future home, 3 and if I do put it on, I shall not find myself to be disembodied. 4 For I who am still in my tent am sighing beneath my burdens, because I do not want it to be put off but to put on the other over it, so that my dying body may be absorbed in life. 5 Now it is God Himself who has put the finishing touches on me for this change, because He has given me the Spirit as the first installment of future bliss.

6 So I am always cheerful and confident, although I know that as long as I am at home in the body I am away from home and the Lord 7 (for here I live by what I believe and not by what I see), 8 and yet I am cheerful and confident, but really I prefer to be away from home in the body and to be at home with the Lord. 9 So whether I am at home or away from home, it is my constant ambition to please Him. 10 For we must all appear before the judgment-bar of Christ, that each may get his pay for what he has done, whether it be good or bad.

11 So, since I know what the fear of God can do, I am trying to win men. My inner self is perfectly known to God, and I hope, to your consciences too. 12 I am not trying to recommend myself to you again. I am giving you ground for speaking well of me, that you may have something to say to those who are constantly prating about external privileges and not concerned about the state of the heart. 13 For if I did go crazy, it was for God's glory; and if I am keeping my head cool, it is for your good. 14 For the love of Christ continuously constrains me, because I am convinced that as One died for all, all have died, 15 and He died for all, that those who live might live no longer for themselves, but for Him who died for them and rose again.

16 So from this moment on, I do not estimate anybody by the standard of outward appearances. Although I once did estimate Christ by this standard, I do not do so any longer. 17 For if anybody is in union with Christ, he is the work of a new creation; the old condition[a] has passed away, a new condition has come. 18 This has all originated with God, for He through Christ has reconciled me to Himself and has given me the ministry of reconciliation. 19 For it was through Christ that God was reconciling the world to Himself instead of debiting men's offenses against them, and He has committed to me the message of this reconciliation.

20 So I am an envoy to represent Christ, because it is through me that God is making His appeal. As one representing Christ I beg you, be reconciled to God. 21 He made Him who personally knew nothing of sin to be a sin-offering for us, so that through union with Him we might come into right standing with God.

BECK

We Long for a Heavenly Body

5 If the earthly tent we live in is torn down, we know we'll get one from God, not made by human hands but lasting forever in heaven. 2 In this body we sigh as we long to put on and live in the body we get from heaven. 3 Of course, if we put that on, we'll not be found without a body. 4 So while we are in this tent, we sigh, feeling oppressed because we don't want to put off this body but put on the other and have life swallow up our death. 5 It is God who has prepared us for this and given us His Spirit as a guarantee.

6 And so we always feel confident. We know that as long as we are living in this body we are living away from the Lord. 7 We live by trusting Him, without seeing Him. 8 We feel bold and prefer to move out of this body and move in with the Lord. 9 Now, whether we live here or move out, we try hard to please Him. 10 We must all appear before the judgment seat of Christ each to get paid for what he has done with his body, good or bad.

Christ Compels Us

11 Since we know the terror of the Lord, we're trying to win the confidence of people. God already knows what we really are, and I hope you, too, are clearly conscious of it. 12 We are not recommending ourselves to you again but giving you a reason to be proud of us so that you can answer those who boast about outward things but nothing in the heart. 13 If we were crazy, it was for God. If we're sane, it is for you. 14 The love of Christ compels us because we're convinced One died for all and so all have died. 15 He died for all that those who live should no longer live for themselves but for Him who died and rose for them.

16 And so from now on we don't think of anyone only as a human being. Once we thought of Christ only as a man, but not now anymore. 17 So if anyone is in Christ, he is a new being. The old things have passed away. They have become new.

Be God's Friends

18 But God has done it all. When we were His enemies, through Christ He made us His friends and gave us the work of making friends of enemies. 19 In Christ, God was getting rid of the enmity between Himself and the people of the world by not counting their sins against them, and He has put into our hands the message how God and men are made friends again. 20 Since God is pleading through us, we are ambassadors for Christ. We ask you for Christ, "Come and be God's friends." 21 God made Him who did not know sin to be sin for us to make us God's righteousness in Him.

[a] The old things.

507

K.J.V.

6 We then, *as* workers together *with him*, beseech *you* also that ye receive not the grace of God in vain. 2 (For he saith, I have heard thee in a time accepted, and in the day of salvation have I succoured thee: behold, now *is* the accepted time; behold, now *is* the day of salvation.) 3 Giving no offence in any thing, that the ministry be not blamed: 4 But in all *things* approving ourselves as the ministers of God, in much patience, in afflictions, in necessities, in distresses, 5 In stripes, in imprisonments, in tumults, in labours, in watchings, in fastings; 6 By pureness, by knowledge, by longsuffering, by kindness, by the Holy Ghost, by love unfeigned, 7 By the word of truth, by the power of God, by the armour of righteousness on the right hand and on the left, 8 By honour and dishonour, by evil report and good report: as deceivers, and *yet* true; 9As unknown, and *yet* well known; as dying, and, behold, we live; as chastened, and not killed; 10As sorrowful, yet alway rejoicing; as poor, yet making many rich; as having nothing, and *yet* possessing all things. 11 O *ye* Corinthians, our mouth is open unto you, our heart is enlarged. 12 Ye are not straitened in us, but ye are straitened in your own bowels. 13 Now for a recompense in the same, (I speak as unto *my* children,) be ye also enlarged. 14 Be ye not unequally yoked together with unbelievers: for what fellowship hath righteousness with unrighteousness? and what communion hath light with darkness? 15And what concord hath Christ with Belial? or what part hath he that believeth with an infidel? 16And what agreement hath the temple of God with idols? for ye are the temple of the living God; as God hath said, I will dwell in them, and walk in *them;* and I will be their God, and they shall be my people. 17 Wherefore come out from among them, and be ye' separate, saith the Lord, and touch not the unclean *thing;* and I will receive you, 18And will be a Father unto you, and ye shall be my sons and daughters, saith the Lord Almighty.

N.A.S.

6 And working together *with Him,* we also urge you not to receive the grace of God in vain;—2 for he says,

"AT THE ACCEPTABLE TIME I LISTENED TO YOU,

AND ON THE DAY OF SALVATION I HELPED YOU";

behold, now is "THE ACCEPTABLE TIME," behold, now is "THE DAY OF SALVATION";—3 giving no cause for offense in anything, in order that the ministry be not discredited, 4 but in everything commending ourselves as servants of God, in much endurance, in afflictions, in hardships, in distresses, 5 in beatings, in imprisonments, in tumults, in labors, in sleeplessness, in hunger, 6 in purity, in knowledge, in patience, in kindness, in the Holy Spirit, in genuine love, 7 in the word of truth, in the power of God; by the weapons of righteousness for the right hand and the left, 8 by glory and dishonor, by evil report and good report; *regarded* as deceivers and yet true; 9 as unknown yet well-known, as dying yet behold, we live; as punished yet not put to death, 10 as sorrowful yet always rejoicing, as poor yet making many rich, as having nothing yet possessing all things.

11 Our mouth has spoken freely to you, O Corinthians, our heart is opened wide. 12 You are not restrained by us, but you are restrained in your own affections. 13 Now in a like exchange—I speak as to children,—open wide *to us* also.

14 Do not be bound together with unbelievers; for what partnership have righteousness and lawlessness, or what fellowship has light with darkness? 15 Or what harmony has Christ with Belial, or what has a believer in common with an unbeliever? 16 Or what agreement has the temple of God with idols? For we are the temple of the living God; just as God said,

"I WILL DWELL IN THEM AND WALK AMONG THEM;

AND I WILL BE THEIR GOD, AND THEY SHALL BE MY PEOPLE.

17 "Therefore, COME OUT FROM THEIR MIDST AND BE SEPARATE, says the Lord,

AND DO NOT TOUCH WHAT IS UNCLEAN;

AND I WILL WELCOME YOU,

18 AND I WILL BE A FATHER TO YOU,

AND YOU SHALL BE SONS and daughters TO ME,

SAYS THE LORD ALMIGHTY."

WILLIAMS

6 *As Christ's envoy, Paul pleads with them to realize this reconciliation; gives his credentials and affection; warns them not to walk with unbelievers*

As God's fellow-worker I beg you too not to accept God's favor and throw it away. 2 For He says:

"At a welcome time I have listened to you,
And on a day of salvation I have helped you."

Right now the time of welcome is here; right now it is the day of salvation. 3 To keep my ministry from being found fault with, I am trying not to put a single hindrance in anybody's way. 4 On the contrary, I am trying in everything to prove of people that I am a true servant of God: by my tremendous endurance in sorrows, distresses, difficulties; 5 in floggings, imprisonments, riots, labors, sleepless nights, and hunger; 6 through my personal purity, my knowledge, my patience, my kindness; through the Holy Spirit, my genuine love, 7 my message of truth, and the power of God; with the weapons of right-doing in my right hand and my left; 8 in honor or dishonor, in slander or praise; considered a deceiver and yet true, 9 obscure and yet well-known, on the point of dying and yet I go on living, punished and yet not put to death, 10 sad but always glad, poor but making many people rich, penniless but really possessing everything.

11 O Corinthians, my tongue is telling you everything; my heart is stretched with love for you. 12 You are not squeezed into a tiny corner in my heart, but you are in your own affections. 13 To pay me back, I tell you, my children, you too must stretch your hearts with love for me.

14 Stop forming intimate and inconsistent relations with unbelievers. What partnership can right-doing have with law-breaking, or how can light participate with darkness? 15 What harmony exists between Christ and Belial, o~ what is common between a believer and an unbeliever? 16 And what agreement can a temple of God make with idols? For we are the temple of the living God, just as God said:

"I will live in them and walk in them,
And I will be their God and they will be my people."

17 Therefore:

" 'Come out of company with them,
And separate from them,' the Lord has said,
'And stop touching what is unclean;
Then I will welcome you,
18 I will be a Father to you,
And you will be sons and daughters of mine,'
The Lord Almighty said."

7:1 So, since we have such promises as these, dearly beloved, let us cleanse ourselves from everything that defiles our bodies and spirits, and in reverence to God carry on our consecration to completeness.

BECK

6 As men who are working with God we plead with you: Don't let God's love be wasted on you. 2 He says,

When the time comes to be kind, I will answer you,
And when the time comes to save, I will help you.

You know

Now is *the time when He welcomes* us,
Now is *the time when He saves*[6] us.

So We Endure

3 We're not in any way giving people a reason to turn away, to keep them from finding fault with our work. 4 Instead we're in everything showing we're God's good workers by great endurance in suffering, in need, and in hardships; 5 when we're beaten or put in prison; in riots; when we're overworked and go without sleep and food; 6 by being pure, by knowledge, by patience and kindness; by the Holy Spirit; by sincere love; 7 by telling the truth; by God's power; with the weapons of righteousness in the right hand and the left; 8 when we're honored or dishonored, blamed or praised. Treated as deceivers, we are honest; 9 as unknown, we are well known; as *dying,* and you see, we go on *living;* as *corrected but not killed;*[7] 10 as sad, we're always glad; as beggars, we're making many rich; as having nothing, we really have everything.

11 We have talked frankly to you Corinthians. Our *hearts are wide open.*[8] 12 There's plenty of room in them for you, but you're narrow in your feelings toward us. 13 I ask you as my children: Treat me as I treat you, and open your hearts wide, too.

Don't Touch Anything Unclean

14 Don't be yoked with unbelievers. How can right and wrong be partners? Or how can light have anything to do with darkness? 15 How can Christ agree with the devil? Or what does a believer have in common with an unbeliever? 16 How can God's temple agree with idols? Now, we are the temple of the living God, as God said, *I will live and walk among them, and I will be their God, and they will be My people.* 17 So, *come out of them, and separate from them,* says the Lord, *and don't touch anything unclean. Then I will welcome you,* 18 *and I will be* your *Father, and you will be My sons* and daughters, says *the Almighty Lord.*[9]

---

[6] Is. 49:8
[7] Ps. 118:17-18
[8] Ps. 119:32
[9] Lev. 26:11-12; 2 Sam. 7:7, 14; Is. 52:11; Jer. 32:38; 51:45; Ezek. 20:34, 41; 37:27; Amos 4:13

K.J.V.

7 Having therefore these promises, dearly beloved, let us cleanse ourselves from all filthiness of the flesh and spirit, perfecting holiness in the fear of God. 2 Receive us; we have wronged no man, we have corrupted no man, we have defrauded no man. 3 I speak not *this* to condemn *you:* for I have said before, that ye are in our hearts to die and live with *you.* 4 Great *is* my boldness of speech toward you, great *is* my glorying of you: I am filled with comfort, I am exceeding joyful in all our tribulation. 5 For, when we were come into Macedonia, our flesh had no rest, but we were troubled on every side; without *were* fightings, within *were* fears. 6 Nevertheless God, that comforteth those that are cast down, comforted us by the coming of Titus; 7 And not by his coming only, but by the consolation wherewith he was comforted in you, when he told us your earnest desire, your mourning, your fervent mind toward me; so that I rejoiced the more. 8 For though I made you sorry with a letter, I do not repent, though I did repent: for I perceive that the same epistle hath made you sorry, though *it were* but for a season. 9 Now I rejoice, not that ye were made sorry, but that ye sorrowed to repentance: for ye were made sorry after a godly manner, that ye might receive damage by us in nothing. 10 For godly sorrow worketh repentance to salvation not to be repented of: but the sorrow of the world worketh death. 11 For behold this selfsame thing, that ye sorrowed after a godly sort, what carefulness it wrought in you, yea, *what* clearing of yourselves, yea, *what* indignation, yea, *what* fear, yea, *what* vehement desire, yea, *what* zeal, yea, *what* revenge! In all *things* ye have approved yourselves to be clear in this matter. 12 Wherefore, though I wrote unto you, *I did it* not for his cause that had done the wrong, nor for his cause that suffered wrong, but that our care for you in the sight of God might appear unto you. 13 Therefore we were comforted in your comfort: yea, and exceedingly the more joyed we for the joy of Titus, because his spirit was refreshed by you all. 14 For if I have boasted any thing to him of you, I am not ashamed; but as we spake all things to you in truth, even so our boasting, which *I made* before Titus, is found a truth. 15 And his inward affection is more abundant toward you, whilst he remembereth the obedience of you all, how with fear and trembling ye received him. 16 I rejoice therefore that I have confidence in you in all *things.*

8 Moreover, brethren, we do you to wit of the grace of God bestowed on the churches of Macedonia; 2 How that in a great trial of

N.A.S.

7 Therefore, having these promises, beloved, let us cleanse ourselves from all defilement of flesh and spirit, perfecting holiness in the fear of God.
2 Make room for us *in your hearts;* we wronged no one, we corrupted no one, we took advantage of no one. 3 I do not speak to condemn you; for I have said before that you are in our hearts to die together and to live together. 4 Great is my confidence in you, great is my boasting on your behalf; I am filled with comfort, I am overflowing with joy in all our affliction.
5 For even when we came into Macedonia our flesh had no rest, but we were afflicted on every side; conflicts without, fears within. 6 But God, who comforts the depressed, comforted us by the coming of Titus; 7 and not only by his coming, but also by the comfort with which he was comforted in you, as he reported to us your longing, your mourning, your zeal for me; so that I rejoiced even more. 8 For though I caused you sorrow by my letter, I do not regret it; though I did regret it,—*for I* see that that letter caused you sorrow, though only for a while— 9 I now rejoice, not that you were made sorrowful, but that you were made sorrowful to *the point of* repentance; for you were made sorrowful according to *the will of* God, in order that you might not suffer loss in anything through us. 10 For the sorrow that is according to *the will of* God produces a repentance without regret, *leading* to salvation; but the sorrow of the world produces death. 11 For behold what earnestness this very thing, this godly sorrow, has produced in you, what vindication of yourselves, what indignation, what fear, what longing, what zeal, what avenging of wrong! In everything you demonstrated yourselves to be innocent in the matter. 12 So although I wrote to you *it was* not for the sake of the offender, nor for the sake of the one offended, but that your earnestness on our behalf might be made known to you in the sight of God. 13 For this reason we have been comforted.
And besides our comfort, we rejoiced even much more for the joy of Titus, because his spirit has been refreshed by you all. 14 For if in anything I have boasted to him about you, I was not put to shame; but as we spoke all things to you in truth, so also our boasting before Titus proved to be *the* truth. 15 And his affection abounds all the more toward you, as he remembers the obedience of you all, how you received him with fear and trembling. 16 I rejoice that in everything I have confidence in you.

8 Now, brethren, we *wish* to make known to you the grace of God which has been given in the churches of Macedonia, 2 that in a great

WILLIAMS

7 *Continues to tell of his love for the Corinthians; Titus reports true repentance at Corinth; Paul's hope realized, and his cup of joy runs over*

2 Make room for me in your hearts. I have not wronged or harmed or taken advantage of a single one of you. 3 I do not mean this for your condemnation, because, as I have said before, you have such a place in my heart that I would live with you or die with you. 4 I have the greatest confidence in you; I speak most highly of you. I am fully comforted; in the face of all my sorrow my cup is running over with joy.

5 For even after I had gotten to Macedonia, my frail, human nature could find no relief; I was crushed with sorrow at every turn—fightings without and fears within. 6 But God, who comforts the downhearted, comforted me by the coming of Titus, 7 and not only by his coming but by the comfort he had gotten from you, because he kept on telling me how you were longing to see me, how sorry you were, and how loyal you were to me, so that I was gladder still.

8 For, although I did cause you sorrow by that letter, I do not now regret it; although I did regret it then. I see that the letter caused you sorrow only for a time. 9 I am glad of it now, not because you had such sorrow, but because your sorrow led you to repentance, for you took your sorrow in accordance with the will of God, so that you should not suffer any loss at all from me. 10 For the sorrow that comes in accordance with the will of God results in repentance that leads to salvation and leaves no regrets; but the sorrow the world produces results in death. 11 For see what this very sorrow, suffered in accordance with the will of God, has done for you! How earnest it has made you, how concerned to clear yourselves, how indignant, how alarmed, how much it made you long to see me, how loyal to me, how determined to punish the offender! At every point you have cleared yourselves in the matter. 12 So, although I did write to you, it was not for the offender's sake, nor for the offended party's sake, but in the sight of God for the sake of having your enthusiasm for me made perfectly clear to you. This is why I am so comforted.

13 In addition to my own comfort, I was made so glad that my cup ran over at the gladness Titus felt, because his spirit has been set at rest by you. 14 Indeed, if I have been doing some boasting of you to him, I have never been ashamed of it; but just as all I said to him was true, so now my boasting before Titus has been shown to be true. 15 Yes, his heart is running over toward you, as he continues recalling how you all obeyed him, with what reverence and trembling you welcomed him. 16 I am glad that I have perfect confidence in you now.

8 *Examples of generous giving; churches in Macedonia give beyond their ability; Jesus gave Himself, so did they; Titus and another round up the contribution*

Now I am going to tell you, brothers, of God's spiritual blessing which was given in the churches of Macedonia, 2 because in spite of a

BECK

7 Since we have such promises, dear friends, let us cleanse ourselves from everything that soils body and spirit as we try to be perfectly holy in the fear of God.

You Encouraged Us

2 Make room in your hearts for us. We haven't wronged anyone, ruined anyone, gotten the best of anyone. 3 I'm not saying this to condemn you. I've told you before, you are in our hearts to die together and to live together. 4 I have much confidence in you. I'm very proud of you. I'm very much encouraged. I'm overjoyed in all our troubles.

5 Even when we came to Macedonia, our bodies got no rest. We were in every kind of trouble, outwardly fighting and inwardly afraid. 6 But *God, who comforts those who feel miserable, comforted* [10] us by the coming of Titus, 7 and not only by his coming but also by the way you encouraged him. He told us how you long for me, how sorry you are, and how eager to take my side, and this made me happier still.

8 I'm not sorry if my letter made you sad. Even if I did feel sorry when I saw that letter make you sad, though only for a while, 9 I'm glad now, not that you were sad but that your sadness led you to feel sorry for sin. You were sad in God's way. And so we haven't done you any harm. 10 Being sad in God's way makes you feel sorry for sin so as to save you—you can't regret that. But the sorrow of the world brings death. 11 See how eager God's sorrow has made you, how ready to clear yourselves, how disgusted with wrong, how alarmed you were, what longing and zeal you felt, and how ready you were to punish! In every way you've shown you're innocent in this matter. 12 Although I wrote you, I didn't have in mind the man who did wrong or him who was wronged, but I wanted to show you before God how zealous you are for us. 13 This is what encouraged us.

While we were encouraged, we were much more delighted to see how happy Titus was because all of you had cheered him up. 14 If I boasted to him about you, you didn't disappoint me. But just as everything we told you was true, so what we had proudly told Titus proved to be true. 15 And his heart goes out to you, all the more as he recalls how ready all of you were to do what he asked and how you welcomed him with respect and trembling. 16 I'm glad I can in every way feel confident about you.

Finish Your Collection

8 Fellow Christians, we want you to know what God's gift of love has done in the churches of Macedonia. 2 While they were

[10] Is. 49:13

K.J.V.

affliction, the abundance of their joy and their deep poverty abounded unto the riches of their liberality. 3 For to *their* power, I bear record, yea, and beyond *their* power *they were* willing of themselves; 4 Praying us with much entreaty that we would receive the gift, and *take upon us* the fellowship of the ministering to the saints. 5And *this they did*, not as we hoped, but first gave their own selves to the Lord, and unto us by the will of God. 6 Insomuch that we desired Titus, that as he had begun, so he would also finish in you the same grace also. 7 Therefore, as ye abound in every *thing, in* faith, and utterance, and knowledge, and *in* all diligence, and *in* your love to us, *see* that ye abound in this grace also. 8 I speak not by commandment, but by occasion of the forwardness of others, and to prove the sincerity of your love. 9 For ye know the grace of our Lord Jesus Christ, that, though he was rich, yet for your sakes he became poor, that ye through his poverty might be rich. 10And herein I give *my* advice: for this is expedient for you, who have begun before, not only to do, but also to be forward a year ago. 11 Now therefore perform the doing *of it; that* as *there was* a readiness to will, so *there may be* a performance also out of that which ye have. 12 For if there be first a willing mind, *it is* accepted according to that a man hath, *and* not according to that he hath not. 13 For *I mean* not that other men be eased, and ye burdened: 14 But by an equality, *that* now at this time your abundance *may be a supply* for their want, that their abundance also may be *a supply* for your want; that there may be equality: 15As it is written, He that *had gathered* much had nothing over; and he that *had gathered* little had no lack. 16 But thanks *be* to God, which put the same earnest care into the heart of Titus for you. 17 For indeed he accepted the exhortation; but being more forward, of his own accord he went unto you. 18And we have sent with him the brother, whose praise *is* in the gospel throughout all the churches; 19And not *that* only, but who was also chosen of the churches to travel with us with this grace, which is administered by us to the glory of the same Lord, and *declaration of* your ready mind: 20Avoiding this, that no man should blame us in this abundance which is administered by us: 21 Providing for honest things, not only in the sight of the Lord, but also in the sight of men. 22And we have sent with them our brother, whom we have oftentimes proved diligent in many things, but now much more diligent, upon the great confidence which *I have* in you. 23 Whether *any do inquire* of Titus, *he is* my partner and fellow helper concerning you: or our brethren *be inquired of, they are* the messengers of the churches, *and* the glory of Christ. 24 Wherefore shew ye to them, and before the churches, the proof of your love, and of our boasting on your behalf.

N.A.S.

ordeal of affliction their abundance of joy and their deep poverty overflowed in the wealth of their liberality. 3 For I testify that according to their ability, and beyond their ability *they gave* of their own accord, 4 begging us with much entreaty for the favor of participation in the support of the saints, 5 and *this,* not as we had expected, but they first gave themselves to the Lord and to us by the will of God. 6 Consequently we urged Titus that as he had previously made a beginning, so he would also complete in you this gracious work as well. 7 But just as you abound in everything, in faith and utterance and knowledge and in all earnestness and in the ᵃlove we inspired in you, *see* that you abound in this gracious work also. 8 I am not speaking *this* as a command, but as proving through the earnestness of others the sincerity of your love also. 9 For you know the grace of our Lord Jesus Christ, that though He was rich, yet for your sake He became poor, that you through His poverty might become rich. 10And I give *my* opinion in this matter, for this is to your advantage, who were the first to begin a year ago not only to do *this,* but also to desire *to do it.* 11 But now finish doing it also; that just as *there was* the readiness to desire it, so *there may be* also the completion of it by your ability. 12 For if the readiness is present, it is acceptable according to what *a man* has, not according to what he does not have. 13 For *this* is not for the ease of others *and* for your affliction, but by way of equality—14 at ˙this present time your abundance *being a supply* for their want, that their abundance also may become *a supply* for your want, that there may be equality; 15 as it is written, "He who *gathered* MUCH DID NOT HAVE TOO MUCH, AND HE WHO *gathered* LITTLE HAD NO LACK."

16 But thanks be to God, who puts the same earnestness on your behalf in the heart of Titus. 17 For he not only accepted our appeal, but being himself very earnest, he has gone to you of his own accord. 18And we have sent along with him the brother whose fame in *the things of* the gospel *has spread* through all the churches; 19 and not only *this,* but he has also been appointed by the churches to travel with us in this gracious work, which is being administered by us for the glory of the Lord Himself, and *to show* our readiness, 20 taking precaution that no one should discredit us in our administration of this generous gift; 21 for we have regard for what is honorable, not only in the sight of the Lord, but also in the sight of men. 22And we have sent with them our brother, whom we have often tested and found diligent in many things, but now even more diligent, because of *his* great confidence in you. 23As for Titus, *he is* my partner and fellow-worker among you; as for our brethren, *they are* messengers of the churches, a glory to Christ. 24 Therefore openly before the churches show them the proof of your love and of our reason for boasting about you.

---

[a] Lit., *love from us in you;* some ancient mss. read, *your love for us.*

512

WILLIAMS

terrible test of trouble, the mighty flood of their gladness mingling with the depths of their poverty has overflowed and resulted in the abundance of their liberality. 3 For they have given, I can testify, to the utmost of their ability, and even beyond their ability. Of their own accord, 4 with earnest entreaty, they kept on begging me for the favor of sharing in this service that is being rendered to God's people. 5 They did not do as I expected but even more; they first by God's will gave themselves to the Lord, and then to me; 6 so that I insisted that Titus, as he had formerly commenced it, should bring to completion this gracious contribution among you too. 7 Yes, just as you are growing rich[a] in everything else, in faith, expression, knowledge, perfect enthusiasm, and the love inspired in you by us, you must see to it that you grow rich in this gracious contribution too.

8 I am not saying this in the spirit of a command, but I am simply trying to test the genuineness of your love by the enthusiasm of others. 9 For by experience you know the unmerited favor shown by our Lord Jesus Christ; that although He was rich, yet for your sakes He became poor, in order that by His poverty you might become rich. 10 Now I will give you my opinion on this matter. For this is for your interest, because you were not only the first to do anything about it, but the first to want to do so; you started it a year ago. 11 Now finish doing it too, so that your readiness to finish it may be just like your readiness to start it, in accordance with what you have. 12 If a man is ready and willing to give, his gift is acceptable in accordance with what he has, not with what he does not have. 13 For I do not want it to be a relief for others and a burden on you, 14 but through an equalizing of matters in the present crisis I do want your abundance to relieve their need, that some day their abundance may relieve your need, so that equality may exist—15 just as the Scripture says, "The man who gathered much did not have too much, and the man who gathered little did not have too little."

16 But thanks be to God, who kindles in the heart of Titus the same enthusiasm for you that I have; 17 because he has acceded to my request, or rather, because he is so enthusiastic for you, of his own accord he is off to visit you. 18 I am sending with him the well-known brother whose praise for spreading the good news is ringing through all the churches. 19 Not only that, but he has been selected by the churches to travel with me for this gracious contribution which is being raised by me, so that it may turn out for the glory of the Lord and a proof of my readiness to serve. 20 I am arranging it so that no one can blame me in the matter of this munificent fund that is being handled by me. 21 For I am taking the precaution to do what is right, not only in the sight of the Lord but also in the eyes of men. 22 I send with them another brother of ours, whom I have often in many ways tested and found to be enthusiastic, but now he is more enthusiastic than ever, because of his great confidence in you.

23 As for Titus, he is my partner and comrade in the work for you, while these brothers of ours, the representatives of the churches, will bring glory to Christ. 24 So you must furnish them, before all the churches, proof of your love and ground for my praising you so highly.

[a] Grk., *abounding, overflowing.*

BECK

severely tested by trouble, their overflowing joy and their deep poverty have yielded a richly overflowing generosity. 3 I assure you they have given all they could, yes, more than they could give, 4 of their own free will, and with much pleading they begged us for the privilege of sharing in the help given the holy people. 5 They did more than we expected: they gave themselves to the Lord first and then to us, doing just what God wanted.

6 This led us to urge Titus, as he had started it, to finish in you, too, this work of love. 7 As you are rich in everything, in faith, speech, knowledge, every kind of zeal, and in the love we stirred up in you, we want you also to be rich in this work of kindness.

8 I'm not ordering you but testing you by the zeal of others to see how real your love is. 9 You know the love of our Lord Jesus Christ —He was rich, but became poor for you to make you rich by His poverty.

10 I'm telling you what I think you should do about this, because it is best for you. Last year you were the first not only to do something but to want to do something. 11 Now finish the job—you were eager to undertake it— in the same way finish it as well as you can. 12 If you're eager to give, God accepts you according to what you have, not according to what you don't have.

13 We don't mean to bring relief to others and hardship to you but to be fair. 14 Right now what you don't need should relieve their need so that what they will not need will relieve your need, and so it will be fair, 15 as it is written: *Anyone who got much didn't have too much, and anyone who got little didn't have too little.*[11]

16 We thank God for making Titus just as eager to help you as I am. 17 He welcomed my request. He's very eager and is by his own choice coming to you.

18 We're sending with him the fellow Christian whom all the churches praise for his telling the good news. 19 More than that, the churches appointed him to travel with us in this work of love we're doing to honor the Lord and show we're willing to help.

20 We're trying to avoid any criticism of the way we're handling this great gift. 21 We *intend to do what's right not only before the Lord but also before other people.*[12]

22 We are also sending with them our fellow Christian whom we have often tested in many ways and found zealous and now more eager than ever because he has so much confidence in you.

23 As for Titus, he is my partner and fellow worker among you. And our fellow Christians, the messengers of the churches, are the glory of Christ. 24 Show the churches how you love them and how right we were when we boasted to them about you.

[11] Ex. 16:18
[12] Prov. 3:4

K.J.V.

9 For as touching the ministering to the saints, it is superfluous for me to write to you: 2 For I know the forwardness of your mind, for which I boast of you to them of Macedonia, that Achaia was ready a year ago; and your zeal hath provoked very many. 3 Yet have I sent the brethren, lest our boasting of you should be in vain in this behalf; that, as I said, ye may be ready: 4 Lest haply if they of Macedonia come with me, and find you unprepared, we (that we say not, ye) should be ashamed in this same confident boasting. 5 Therefore I thought it necessary to exhort the brethren, that they would go before unto you, and make up beforehand your bounty, whereof ye had notice before, that the same might be ready, as *a matter of* bounty, and not as *of* covetousness. 6 But this *I say,* He which soweth sparingly shall reap also sparingly; and he which soweth bountifully shall reap also bountifully. 7 Every man according as he purposeth in his heart, *so let him give;* not grudgingly, or of necessity: for God loveth a cheerful giver. 8 And God *is* able to make all grace abound toward you; that ye, always having all sufficiency in all *things,* may abound to every good work: 9 (As it is written, He hath dispersed abroad; he hath given to the poor: his righteousness remaineth for ever. 10 Now he that ministereth seed to the sower both minister bread for *your* food, and multiply your seed sown, and increase the fruits of your righteousness:) 11 Being enriched in every thing to all bountifulness, which causeth through us thanksgiving to God. 12 For the administration of this service not only supplieth the want of the saints, but is abundant also by many thanksgivings unto God; 13 While by the experiment of this ministration they glorify God for your professed subjection unto the gospel of Christ, and for *your* liberal distribution unto them, and unto all *men;* 14 And by their prayer for you, which long after you for the exceeding grace of God in you. 15 Thanks *be* unto God for his unspeakable gift.

10 Now I Paul myself beseech you by the meekness and gentleness of Christ, who in presence *am* base among you, but being absent am bold toward you: 2 But I beseech *you,* that I may not be bold when I am present with that confidence, wherewith I think to be bold against some, which think of us as if we walked according to the flesh. 3 For though we walk in the

N.A.S.

9 For it is superfluous for me to write to you about this ministry to the saints; 2 for I know your readiness, of which I boast about you to the Macedonians, *namely,* that Achaia has been prepared since last year, and your zeal has stirred up most of them. 3 But I have sent the brethren, that our boasting about you may not be made empty in this case, that, as I was saying, you may be prepared; 4 lest if any Macedonians come with me and find you unprepared, we (not to speak of you) should be put to shame by this confidence. 5 So I thought it necessary to urge the brethren that they would go on ahead to you and arrange beforehand your previously promised bountiful gift, that the same might be ready as a bountiful gift, and not affected by covetousness.

6 Now this *I say,* he who sows sparingly shall also reap sparingly; and he who sows bountifully shall also reap bountifully. 7 Let each one *do* just as he has purposed in his heart; not grudgingly or under compulsion; for God loves a cheerful giver. 8 And God is able to make all grace abound to you, that always having all sufficiency in everything, you may have an abundance for every good deed; 9 as it is written,

"HE SCATTERED ABROAD, HE GAVE TO THE POOR,

HIS RIGHTEOUSNESS ABIDES FOREVER."

10 Now He who supplies seed to the sower and bread for food, will supply and multiply your seed for sowing and increase the harvest of your righteousness; 11 you will be enriched in everything for all liberality, which through us is producing thanksgiving to God. 12 For the ministry of this service is not only fully supplying the needs of the saints, but is also overflowing through many thanksgivings to God. 13 Because of the proof given by this ministry they will glorify God for *your* obedience to your confession of the gospel of Christ, and for the liberality of your contribution to them and to all, 14 while they also, by prayer on your behalf, yearn for you because of the surpassing grace of God in you. 15 Thanks be to God for His indescribable gift!

10 Now I Paul myself urge you by the meekness and gentleness of Christ,—I who am meek when face to face with you, but bold toward you when absent!—2 I ask that when I am present I may not be bold with the confidence with which I propose to be courageous against some, who regard us as if we walked according to the flesh. 3 For

WILLIAMS

9 *The contribution to be ready when Paul arrives; the way to give; gracious blessings on generous giving*

It is really superfluous for me to write to you about this service which is being rendered to God's people, 2 for I know your readiness to help in it. I am boasting of you about it to the Macedonians, reminding them that Greece has been ready since last year, and your enthusiasm has stimulated the most of them. 3 But I send the brothers that in this matter my boasting of you may not turn out to be an idle boasting, that you all may be ready, as I have told them you will be, 4 to keep me—not to mention you—from being humiliated for having such confidence in you, if some Macedonians come with me and find that you are not ready. 5 So I have thought it necessary to urge these brothers to visit you ahead of me and get your promised love-offering ready beforehand, so as to have it ready as a real love-offering, not as one grasped and grudgingly given.

6 Now this is the way it is: Whoever sows sparingly will reap sparingly too, but whoever sows bountifully will reap bountifully too. 7 Each must give what he has purposed in his heart to give, not sorrowfully or under compulsion, for it is the happy giver that God loves. 8 And God is able to make your every spiritual blessing overflow for you, so that you will always have in every situation an entire sufficiency and so overflow for every good cause; 9 as the Scripture says:

"He has generously given to the poor,
His deeds of charity go on forever."

10 He who always supplies the sower with seed and the eater with bread will supply you with seed and multiply it and enlarge the harvest which your deeds of charity yield. 11 In every way you will grow richer and richer so as to give with perfect liberality, which will through me result in thanksgiving to God for it. 12 Because the service rendered by this sacred offering is not only fully supplying the needs of God's people, but it is also running over with many thanks to God for it. 13 For through the test you get by doing this service you will continue praising God for your fidelity to your confession of the good news of Christ, and for the liberality of your contributions to them and all others; 14 and so in their prayers for you they will continue longing for you, because of God's surpassing favor shown you. 15 Thank God for His unspeakable gift!

10 *Paul proves that he is an apostle; answers charges against his personal appearance and speech; Corinth belongs to his apostolic commission*

Now I appeal to you in person, by the gentleness and fairness of Christ, I, Paul, who am so "condescending when face to face with you, but so courageous toward you when far away!" 2 I beg you not to make me too courageous in that confidence in which I think to take a daring stand against some people who try to think that I am acting from the lowest human motives. 3 For though I do still live the life of a physical human creature, I am not

BECK

How to Give

9 I really don't need to write you about helping the holy people, 2 because I know how eager you are. That's what I'm telling the people in Macedonia in boasting about you, "Greece has been ready since last year," and your enthusiasm has stirred up most of them. 3 Now I'm sending my fellow workers so that we may not have been wrong in boasting about you on this point but that you may be ready as I said. 4 Otherwise, if any Macedonians come with me and find you aren't ready, you would make us (to say nothing of yourselves) feel ashamed of being so confident. 5 So I thought it necessary to urge these fellow workers to go to you ahead of me, arrange in advance the gift you promised and have it ready as money that was gladly given and not forced out of you.

6 Remember this: *If you sow little, you* won't *get* much *grain.* But *if you sow* generously, *you will get* much *grain.* 7 Everyone should do what he has made up his mind to do, not with regret or being forced, because *God* loves *anyone who gives gladly.*[13]

God Blesses You

8 God can pour out every gift of His love on you so you will always in every way have all you need and plenty to do any good work. 9 The Bible says of such a person, *He scatters his gifts to the poor. His righteousness goes on forever.*[14] 10 He who gives *seed to the sower and bread to eat,*[15] will give you seed and multiply it and make *your righteous grain*[16] grow. 11 You will get rich in everything so you can give generously in every way; through us this will make people thank God. 12 This work you do in serving others doesn't only supply the needs of the holy people; it makes them pour out many thanks to God. 13 As you prove by this service what you are, they praise God that you submit to the good news of Christ which you confess and that you freely share with them and with everybody. 14 While they pray for you, they long for you because they see what an extraordinary gift God's love has brought you. 15 Thanks be to God for His gift that is more than we can tell.

I Am Bold

10 I myself, Paul, plead with you with the gentleness and kindliness of Christ—I who am humble when I'm face to face with you but get bold toward you when I'm away! 2 I beg you that when I come I don't have to be as confident and bold as I think I'll dare to be against some men who think we're living according to the flesh. 3 Of course, we're living in the flesh,

[13] Prov. 22:8
[14] Ps. 112:9
[15] Is. 55:10
[16] Hos. 10:12

K.J.V.

flesh, we do not war after the flesh: 4 (For the weapons of our warfare *are* not carnal, but mighty through God to the pulling down of strong holds;) 5 Casting down imaginations, and every high thing that exalteth itself against the knowledge of God, and bringing into captivity every thought to the obedience of Christ; 6And having in a readiness to revenge all disobedience, when your obedience is fulfilled. 7 Do ye look on things after the outward appearance? If any man trust to himself that he is Christ's, let him of himself think this again, that, as he *is* Christ's, even so *are* we Christ's. 8 For though I should boast somewhat more of our authority, which the Lord hath given us for edification, and not for your destruction, I should not be ashamed: 9 That I may not seem as if I would terrify you by letters. 10 For *his* letters, say they, *are* weighty and powerful; but *his* bodily presence *is* weak, and *his* speech contemptible. 11 Let such a one think this, that, such as we are in word by letters when we are absent, such *will we* be also in deed when we are present. 12 For we dare not make ourselves of the number, or compare ourselves with some that commend themselves: but they, measuring themselves by themselves, and comparing themselves among themselves, are not wise. 13 But we will not boast of things without *our* measure, but according to the measure of the rule which God hath distributed to us, a measure to reach even unto you. 14 For we stretch not ourselves beyond *our measure*, as though we reached not unto you; for we are come as far as to you also in *preaching* the gospel of Christ: 15 Not boasting of things without *our* measure, *that is,* of other men's labours; but having hope, when your faith is increased, that we shall be enlarged by you according to our rule abundantly, 16 To preach the gospel in the *regions* beyond you, *and* not to boast in another man's line of things made ready to our hand. 17 But he that glorieth, let him glory in the Lord. 18 For not he that commendeth himself is approved, but whom the Lord commendeth.

N.A.S.

though we walk in the flesh, we do not war according to the flesh, 4 for the weapons of our warfare are not of the flesh, but divinely powerful for the destruction of fortresses. 5 *We are* destroying speculations and every lofty thing raised up against the knowledge of God, and *we are* taking every thought captive to the obedience of Christ, 6 and we are ready to punish all disobedience, whenever your obedience is complete. 7 You are looking at things as they are outwardly. If any one is confident in himself that he is Christ's, let him consider this again within himself, that just as he is Christ's, so also are we. 8 For even if I should boast somewhat further about our authority, which the Lord gave for building you up and not for destroying you, I shall not be put to shame, 9 for I do not wish to seem as if I would terrify you by my letters. 10 For they say, "His letters are weighty and strong, but his personal presence is unimpressive, and his speech contemptible." 11 Let such a person consider this, that what we are in word by letters when absent, such persons *are* also in deed when present. 12 For we are not bold to class or compare ourselves with some of those who commend themselves; but when they measure themselves by themselves, and compare themselves with themselves, they are without understanding. 13 But we will not boast beyond *our* measure, but within the measure of the sphere which God apportioned to us as a measure, to reach even as far as you. 14 For we are not overextending ourselves, as if we did not reach to you, for we were the first to come even as far as you in the gospel of Christ; 15 not boasting beyond *our* measure, *that is,* in other men's labors, but with the hope that as your faith grows, we shall be, within our sphere, enlarged even more by you, 16 so as to preach the gospel even to the regions beyond you, *and* not to boast in what has been accomplished in the sphere of another. 17 But HE WHO BOASTS, LET HIM BOAST IN THE LORD. 18 For not he who commends himself is approved, but whom the Lord commends.

11 Would to God ye could bear with me a little in *my* folly: and indeed bear with me. 2 For I am jealous over you with godly jealousy: for I have espoused you to one husband, that I may present *you as* a chaste virgin to Christ. 3 But I fear, lest by any means, as the serpent beguiled Eve through his subtilty, so your minds should be corrupted from the simplicity that is in Christ. 4 For if he that cometh preacheth another Jesus, whom we have not preached, or *if* ye receive another spirit, which ye have not re-

11 I wish that you would bear with me in a little foolishness; but indeed you are bearing with me. 2 For I am jealous for you with a godly jealousy; for I betrothed you to one husband, that to Christ I might present you *as* a pure virgin. 3 But I am afraid, lest as the serpent deceived Eve by his craftiness, your minds should be led astray from the simplicity and purity *of devotion* to Christ. 4 For if one comes and preaches another Jesus whom we have not preached, or you receive a different spirit which you have not received,

WILLIAMS

waging this war in accordance with physical human standards, 4 for the weapons used in my warfare are not mere human ones, but through my God are mighty for demolishing fortresses. 5 For I am demolishing arguments and every barrier that is raised against the genuine knowledge of God, taking captive every thought to make it obedient to Christ, 6 and am prepared to punish any disobedience, when your obedience is made complete.

7 You look at me and measure me by outward appearances. If anyone is confident in himself that he belongs to Christ, let him have another thought about himself, that just as he belongs to Christ, so do I. 8 For if I do boast a little too much about my authority, which the Lord gave me for building you up and not for tearing you down, I shall never have to blush for doing so. 9 I do not want to seem to be frightening you with my letters. 10 For they say, "His letters are impressive and forceful, but his physical personality is unimpressive, and his delivery is perfectly contemptible." 11 Such people should consider this: When I arrive for action I shall do exactly what I said I would in my letters when far away.

12 Indeed, I do not dare to count or compare myself with certain men who are always recommending themselves. But they do not show good sense, because they do continue measuring themselves with one another and comparing themselves with one another. 13 But I shall never go too far in my boasting; no, I shall stay within the limits of the sphere which God apportioned me, so as to reach even you. 14 For I am not overstepping my authority, as though I should not reach you, for I was the very first to reach as far as you with the good news of Christ. 15 I am not going too far in my boasting, and actually boasting of other men's labors, but I am cherishing the hope that your faith may so continue to grow that through you my work within my sphere may be so enlarged as to run over, 16 so that I can preach the good news in the regions beyond you, without boasting in another man's sphere of work already done by him. 17 "But the man who boasts must boast in the Lord." 18 For it is not the man who keeps on recommending himself who is really approved, but it is the man whom the Lord recommends.

BECK

but we're not fighting in a fleshly way. 4 The weapons we fight with are not those of the flesh but have the power before God to tear down fortresses. With them we tear down arguments 5 and everything raising its proud head against the knowledge of God and make every opposing thought a prisoner and have it obey Christ. 6 We're ready to punish every disobedience when you are completely obedient.

7 You see things as they are outwardly. If anyone feels sure he belongs to Christ, he should remind himself that we belong to Christ just as as does. 8 If I boast a little too much about our authority, which the Lord gave us to build you up and not to tear you down, I will not have to feel ashamed. 9 I don't want to seem to scare you with my letters.

10 "His letters are impressive and strong," somebody says, "but when he's with us, he's weak, and people despise what he says." 11 Such a person should understand: When we come, we'll act exactly the way we express ourselves in letters when we're away.

We Are Proud of Our Work

12 We don't dare to put ourselves in a class or compare ourselves with some of those who speak highly of themselves, but when they measure themselves by their own yardstick and compare themselves with themselves, they don't show good sense.

13 Now we'll limit our boasting. Our limit is the field of work to which God has bound us. This includes coming to you. 14 It is not as though we were not coming to you and so we are reaching beyond our limit. We were the first to reach you with the good news of Christ. 15 We are not going beyond our limit and boasting of work done by others, but we expect your faith to grow so as to enlarge the work in our field in your area till it goes beyond you, 16 and so we'll tell the good news in the countries beyond you without boasting of work already done in another man's field.

17 But *if anyone feels proud, he should feel proud of the Lord.*[17] 18 Not the man who approves of himself is really approved but he of whom the Lord approves.

---

11 *Love moves Paul to defend his authority; tells why he gives up his right to support; calls his critics sham apostles; ironically defends his sanity; claims his sufferings are his credentials to apostleship*

I wish you would now listen to a little folly of mine. Please do listen to me! 2 For I feel a divine jealousy for you, as I betrothed you to Christ, to present you as a pure bride to her one husband. 3 But I am apprehensive that, somehow or other, as the serpent by his cunning deceived Eve, your thoughts may be turned aside[a] from single-hearted devotion to Christ. 4 For if anybody comes along and preaches another Jesus than the one I preached, or you receive another spirit different from the one you did receive or a glad message different

I Am Jealous

11 I wish you would put up with a little foolishness of mine. Yes, do put up with me. 2 I am jealous of you with God's own jealousy. I promised you in marriage, to bring you as a pure bride to one husband—to Christ. 3 But I'm afraid that as *the snake* by its trickery *seduced*[18] Eve, your minds may somehow be corrupted and you may lose your simple and pure loyalty to Christ. 4 When somebody comes along and preaches a different Jesus whom we didn't preach or gives you a different spirit you didn't get before or a different gospel you didn't re-

---

[a] Lit., *corrupted.*

[17] Jer. 9:24
[18] Gen. 3:4, 13

K.J.V.

ceived, or another gospel, which ye have not accepted, ye might well bear with *him*. 5 For I suppose I was not a whit behind the very chiefest apostles. 6 But though *I be* rude in speech, yet not in knowledge; but we have been thoroughly made manifest among you in all things. 7 Have I committed an offence in abasing myself that ye might be exalted, because I have preached to you the gospel of God freely? 8 I robbed other churches, taking wages *of them,* to do you service. 9 And when I was present with you, and wanted, I was chargeable to no man: for that which was lacking to me the brethren which came from Macedonia supplied: and in all *things* I have kept myself from being burdensome unto you, and *so* will I keep *myself.* 10 As the truth of Christ is in me, no man shall stop me of this boasting in the regions of Achaia. 11 Wherefore? because I love you not? God knoweth. 12 But what I do, that I will do, that I may cut off occasion from them which desire occasion; that wherein they glory, they may be found even as we. 13 For such *are* false apostles, deceitful workers, transforming themselves into the apostles of Christ. 14 And no marvel; for Satan himself is transformed into an angel of light. 15 Therefore *it is* no great thing if his ministers also be transformed as the ministers of righteousness; whose end shall be according to their works. 16 I say again, Let no man think me a fool; if otherwise, yet as a fool receive me, that I may boast myself a little. 17 That which I speak, I speak *it* not after the Lord, but as it were foolishly, in this confidence of boasting. 18 Seeing that many glory after the flesh, I will glory also. 19 For ye suffer fools gladly, seeing ye *yourselves* are wise. 20 For ye suffer, if a man bring you into bondage, if a man devour *you,* if a man take *of you,* if a man exalt himself, if a man smite you on the face. 21 I speak as concerning reproach, as though we had been weak. Howbeit, whereinsoever any is bold, (I speak foolishly,) I am bold also. 22 Are they Hebrews? so *am* I. Are they Israelites? so *am* I. Are they the seed of Abraham? so *am* I. 23 Are they ministers of Christ? (I speak as a fool,) I *am* more; in labours more abundant, in stripes above measure, in prisons more frequent, in deaths oft. 24 Of the Jews five times received I forty *stripes* save one. 25 Thrice was I beaten with rods, once was I stoned, thrice I suffered shipwreck, a night and a day I have been in the deep; 26 *In* journeyings often, *in* perils of waters, *in* perils of robbers, *in* perils by *mine own* countrymen, *in* perils by the heathen, *in* perils in the city, *in* perils in the wilderness, *in* perils in the sea, *in* perils among false brethren; 27 In weariness and painfulness, in watchings often, in hunger and thirst, in fastings often, in cold and nakedness. 28 Beside those things that are without, that which cometh upon me daily, the care of all the

N.A.S.

or a different gospel which you have not accepted, you bear *this* beautifully. 5 For I consider myself not in the least inferior to the most eminent apostles. 6 But even if I am unskilled in speech, yet I am not *so* in knowledge; in fact, in every way we have made *this* evident to you in all things. 7 Or did I commit a sin in humbling myself that you might be exalted, because I preached the gospel of God to you without charge? 8 I robbed other churches, taking wages *from them* to serve you; 9 and when I was present with you and was in need, I was not a burden to anyone; for when the brethren came from Macedonia, they fully supplied my need, and in everything I kept myself from being a burden to you, and will continue to do so. 10 As the truth of Christ is in me, this boasting of mine will not be stopped in the regions of Achaia. 11 Why? Because I do not love you? God knows *I do!* 12 But what I am doing, I will continue to do, that I may cut off opportunity from those who desire an opportunity to be regarded just as we are in the matter about which they are boasting. 13 For such men are false apostles, deceitful workers, disguising themselves as apostles of Christ. 14 And no wonder, for even Satan disguises himself as an angel of light. 15 Therefore it is not surprising if his servants also disguise themselves as servants of righteousness; whose end shall be according to their deeds.

16 Again I say, let no one think me foolish; but if *you do,* receive me even as foolish, that I also may boast a little. 17 That which I am speaking, I am not speaking as the Lord would, but as in foolishness, in this confidence of boasting. 18 Since many boast according to the flesh, I will boast also. 19 For you, being *so* wise, bear with the foolish gladly. 20 For you bear with anyone if he enslaves you, if he devours you, if he takes advantage of you, if he exalts himself, if he hits you in the face. 21 To *my* shame I *must* say that we have been weak *by comparison.* But in whatever respect anyone *else* is bold (I speak in foolishness), I am just as bold myself. 22 Are they Hebrews? So am I. Are they Israelites? So am I. Are they descendants of Abraham? So am I. 23 Are they servants of Christ? (I speak as if insane) I more so; in far more labors, in far more imprisonments, beaten times without number, often in danger of death. 24 Five times I received from the Jews thirty-nine *lashes.* 25 Three times I was beaten with rods, once I was stoned, three times I was shipwrecked, a night and a day I have spent in the deep. 26 *I have been* on frequent journeys, in dangers from rivers, dangers from robbers, dangers from *my* countrymen, dangers from the Gentiles, dangers in the city, dangers in the wilderness, dangers on the sea, dangers among false brethren; 27 *I have been* in labor and hardship, through many sleepless nights, in hunger and thirst, often without food, in cold and exposure. 28 Apart from *such* external things, there is the daily pressure upon me *of* con-

from the one you did accept, you listen to it all right! 5 For I consider myself not a single bit inferior to those surpassingly superior apostles of yours! 6 Although I am untrained as an orator, yet I am not so in the field of knowledge. Surely, I have always made that perfectly clear to you.

7 Did I do wrong in taking a lowly place to let you have an exalted one, in that I preached the good news about God to you without accepting any pay? 8 I sponged[b] on other churches by taking pay from them to render service to you, 9 and when I was with you and needed money, I never burdened a single one of you a cent, for the brothers came from Macedonia and supplied what I needed. And so I kept myself, as I shall always do, from being a burden to you in any way. 10 By the truth of Christ in me, this boasting of mine shall never be stopped in the boundaries of Greece. 11 Why? Because I do not love you? God knows I do.

12 And I shall keep on doing as I am, in order to cut the ground from under the feet of those who want an opportunity to show themselves on a level with me in the matters of which they boast. 13 For such men are sham[c] apostles, dishonest workmen, masquerading as apostles of Christ. 14 And no wonder, for even Satan himself masquerades as an angel of light. 15 So it is no surprise if his servants also masquerade as ministers for doing right, whose doom shall be in accordance with what they do.

16 Let me say again that no one must think that I am a fool; but if you do, please treat me like a fool and let me do a little boasting too, as other fools do. 17 But when I talk in this boastful confidence, I am not talking in accordance with the way the Lord talked, but just as a fool talks. 18 Since many boast in accordance with their human nature, I will do it too. 19 For you who are so wise yourselves are glad to listen to fools! 20 For you listen to a man, if he makes you his slave, or spends your money for his living, or cheats you, or puts on airs, or slaps you in the face.

21 I am ashamed to say that I was, as it were, so weak in the matter. And yet in whatever respect anyone else is daring to boast—I am talking like a fool—I too will dare to boast. 22 Are they Hebrews? So am I. Are they Israelites? So am I. Are they descendants of Abraham? So am I. 23 Are they ministers of Christ? So am I. I am talking like a man that has gone crazy—as such I am superior!—serving Him with labors greater by far, with far more imprisonments, with floggings vastly worse, and often at the point of death. 24 Five times I have taken thirty-nine lashes from the Jews, 25 three times I have been beaten by the Romans, once I was pelted with stones; three times I have been shipwrecked, and once I have spent a day and a night adrift at sea. 26 I have served Him on frequent journeys, in dangers from rivers, dangers from robbers, dangers from my own people, dangers from the heathen, dangers in the city, dangers in the desert, dangers at sea, dangers from false brothers, 27 through toil and hardship, through many a sleepless night, through hunger and thirst, through many a fasting season, poorly clad and exposed to cold. 28 Besides all other things, there is my concern for all the

ceive before, you put up with it well enough. 5 I don't think I'm in any way less than your "super" apostles. 6 Even if I'm no trained speaker, I know what I'm talking about. In every way we have shown you this before everybody.

7 Did I do wrong when I humbled myself so you would be lifted up, when I charged you nothing for bringing you God's good news? 8 I robbed other churches, taking pay from them in order to serve you. 9 When I was with you and needed anything, I didn't bother anyone to help me, because our fellow workers* who came from Macedonia supplied all I needed. I kept myself from being a burden to you in any way, and I'll continue to do so. 10 As the truth of Christ is in me, this boast of mine will not be silenced anywhere in Greece. 11 Why? Because I don't love you? God knows I do. 12 And I will go on doing as I do, to take away the opportunity of those who want it to get others to think they are like us in the work they're boasting about. 13 Such men are false apostles, deceitful workers masquerading as apostles of Christ. 14 And no wonder, when the devil himself masquerades as an angel of light. 15 So it isn't surprising if his servants also masquerade as servants of righteousness. In the end they'll get what they deserve for what they're doing.

I Will Boast

16 Again I say nobody should think I'm a fool. But if you do, then let me come to you as a fool and also boast a little. 17 What I say when I boast so confidently is not the Lord's way of speaking but a fool's. 18 Since many brag in a human way, I will, too, 19 because you, being wise, like to put up with fools. 20 You put up with anyone who makes you his slaves or devours what you have or traps you or lords it over you or slaps your face. 21 I'm ashamed to admit it: As you say, we have been too weak.

But what anyone else dares to claim—I'm talking like a fool—I can claim too. 22 Are they Jews? So am I! Do they belong to the people of Israel? So do I! Are they descended from Abraham? So am I! 23 Are they servants of Christ? I'm mad to talk like this, but I'm a better one! I've done much more hard work, been in prison much more, been beaten very much more, and often faced death. 24 Five times the Jews gave me thirty-nine lashes, three times I was beaten with a stick, once I was stoned, 25 three times I was in a shipwreck, a night and a day I drifted in the water. 26 I've traveled much and faced dangers of flooded streams and of robbers, dangers from Jews and non-Jews, dangers in the city, in the wilderness, and on the sea, dangers from false friends. 27 I have toiled and struggled, often sleepless, hungry and thirsty, often starving, cold, and naked. 28 Besides everything else, I have a daily burden—I'm anxiously con-

---

[b] Grk., *taking money without working for it.*
[c] Grk., *false.*

* Silas and Timothy. (Acts 18:5; 2 Cor. 1:19).

K.J.V.

churches. 29 Who is weak, and I am not weak? who is offended, and I burn not? 30 If I must needs glory, I will glory of the things which concern mine infirmities. 31 The God and Father of our Lord Jesus Christ, which is blessed for evermore, knoweth that I lie not. 32 In Damascus the governor under Aretas the king kept the city of the Damascenes with a garrison, desirous to apprehend me: 33 And through a window in a basket was I let down by the wall, and escaped his hands.

12 It is not expedient for me doubtless to glory. I will come to visions and revelations of the Lord. 2 I knew a man in Christ above fourteen years ago, (whether in the body, I cannot tell; or whether out of the body, I cannot tell: God knoweth;) such a one caught up to the third heaven. 3 And I knew such a man, (whether in the body, or out of the body, I cannot tell: God knoweth;) 4 How that he was caught up into paradise, and heard unspeakable words, which it is not lawful for a man to utter. 5 Of such a one will I glory: yet of myself I will not glory, but in mine infirmities. 6 For though I would desire to glory, I shall not be a fool; for I will say the truth: but now I forbear, lest any man should think of me above that which he seeth me to be, or that he heareth of me. 7 And lest I should be exalted above measure through the abundance of the revelations, there was given to me a thorn in the flesh, the messenger of Satan to buffet me, lest I should be exalted above measure. 8 For this thing I besought the Lord thrice, that it might depart from me. 9 And he said unto me, My grace is sufficient for thee: for my strength is made perfect in weakness. Most gladly therefore will I rather glory in my infirmities, that the power of Christ may rest upon me. 10 Therefore I take pleasure in infirmities, in reproaches, in necessities, in persecutions, in distresses for Christ's sake: for when I am weak, then am I strong. 11 I am become a fool in glorying; ye have compelled me: for I ought to have been commended of you: for in nothing am I behind the very chiefest apostles, though I be nothing. 12 Truly the signs of an apostle were wrought among you in all patience, in signs, and wonders, and mighty deeds. 13 For what is it wherein ye were inferior to other churches, except it be that I myself was not burdensome to you? forgive me this wrong. 14 Behold, the third time I am ready to come to you;

N.A.S.

cern for all the churches. 29 Who is weak without my being weak? Who is led into sin without my intense concern? 30 If I have to boast, I will boast of what pertains to my weakness. 31 The God and Father of the Lord Jesus, He who is blessed forever, knows that I am not lying. 32 In Damascus the ethnarch under Aretas the king was guarding the city of the Damascenes in order to seize me, 33 and I was let down in a basket through a window in the wall, and so escaped his hands.

12 Boasting is necessary, though it is not profitable; but I will go on to visions and revelations of the Lord. 2 I know a man in Christ who fourteen years ago—whether in the body I do not know, or out of the body I do not know, God knows—such a man was caught up to the third heaven. 3 And I know how such a man—whether in the body or apart from the body I do not know, God knows—4 was caught up into Paradise, and heard inexpressible words, which a man is not permitted to speak. 5 On behalf of such a man will I boast; but on my own behalf I will not boast, except in regard to my weaknesses. 6 For if I do wish to boast I shall not be foolish, for I shall be speaking the truth; but I refrain from this, so that no one may credit me with more than he sees in me or hears from me. 7 And because of the surpassing greatness of the revelations, for this reason, to keep me from exalting myself, there was given me a thorn in the flesh, a messenger of Satan to buffet me—to keep me from exalting myself! 8 Concerning this I entreated the Lord three times that it might depart from me. 9 And He has said to me, "My grace is sufficient for you, for apower is perfected in weakness." Most gladly, therefore, I will rather boast about my weaknesses, that the power of Christ may dwell in me. 10 Therefore I am well content with weaknesses, with insults, with distresses, with persecutions, with difficulties, for Christ's sake; for when I am weak, then I am strong.

11 I have become foolish; you yourselves compelled me. Actually I should have been commended by you, for in no respect was I inferior to the most eminent apostles, even though I am a nobody. 12 The signs of a true apostle were performed among you with all perseverance, by signs and wonders and miracles. 13 For in what respect were you treated as inferior to the rest of the churches, except that I myself did not become a burden to you? Forgive me this wrong!

14 Here for this third time I am ready to come to you, and I will not be a burden to

[a] Later mss. read, My power.

WILLIAMS

churches. 29 Who is weak without my being weak too? Who is caused to fall without my being fired with indignation? 30 If I must boast, I will boast of the things that show my weakness! 31 The God and Father of the Lord Jesus, who is blessed forever, knows that I am telling the truth. 32At Damascus the governor under King Aretas kept guards watching the city gates to capture me, 33 but through a hole in the wall I was lowered in a basket, and so escaped from his clutches.

12 *Though Paul's visions are sublime, his sufferings are more valuable as credentials; he has given the real signs of a true apostle; asserts his motives are unselfish, yet uneasy as to expected visit*

I have to keep on boasting. There is no good to be gotten from it, but I will go on to visions and revelations which the Lord has given me. 2 I know a man in union with Christ fourteen years ago—whether in the body or out of it, I do not know, but God knows—who was caught up to the third heaven. 3 Yes, I know that this man—whether in or out of the body, I do not know, but God knows—4 was actually caught up into paradise, and heard things that must not be told, which no man has a right even to mention. 5 On behalf of this man with such an experience I will boast, but on behalf of myself personally I will boast only about my weaknesses. 6 However, if I want to boast, I will not play the fool, for it will be nothing but the truth that I will tell. But I refrain from doing so, to keep anybody, on account of the superiority of the revelations, from giving me a higher rating than my actions and teachings deserve. 7 So, to keep me from being overelated, there was sent upon me a physical disease, sharp as a piercing stake, a messenger of Satan, to continue afflicting me, and so to keep me, I repeat, from being overelated. 8 Three times I begged the Lord about this to make it go away and leave me, 9 but He said to me, "My spiritual strength*a* is sufficient, for it is only by means of conscious weakness that perfect power is developed."

10 So I most happily boast about my weaknesses, so that the strength of Christ may overshadow me. That is why I take such pleasure in weaknesses, insults, distresses, persecution, and difficulties, which I endure for Christ's sake, for it is when I am consciously weak that I am really strong.

11 I have made a fool of myself, but you have forced me to do it, for I am the man who ought to have been constantly approved by you. For I am not a single bit inferior to your surpassingly superior apostles, though really I am "nobody." 12 The marks that signify the genuine apostle were exhibited among you in my perfect patience, in signs, wonders, and wonder-works. 13 In what respect, then, were you inferior to the rest of the churches, except for the fact that I, and I only, never received from you any financial support? Please forgive me this wrong.

14 It is now the third time that I have been ready to come to see you, and I will never ask you for financial support, for it is not your

[a] Lit., *favor, grace.*

BECK

cerned about all the churches. 29 When anyone is weak, am I not weak too? When anyone is led into sin, don't I feel a burning shame? 30 If I have to boast, I'll boast of the things that show how weak I am. 31 The God and Father of the Lord Jesus, who is blessed forever, knows I'm not lying. 32 In Damascus the governor under King Aretas had the city of Damascus watched to catch me, 33 but through an opening in the wall I was let down in a basket, and I escaped.

Caught Up to Paradise

12 I have to boast. It doesn't do any good, but I'll go on with what the Lord has shown and told me. 2 I know a man in Christ; fourteen years ago—whether in his body or outside it, I don't know, God knows—that man was caught up to the third heaven. 3 I know that such a man—whether in his body or outside it, I don't know, God knows— 4 was caught up to Paradise and heard what no human being can or may tell. 5About such a man I will boast, but as to myself, I will boast only of my weaknesses.

6 But if I would want to boast, I wouldn't be a fool, because I'd be telling the truth. But I'm not going to do it, in order to keep anyone from thinking more of me than he judges me to be by seeing me or hearing me.

7 To keep me from feeling proud because such wonderful things were revealed to me, a thorn was put into my flesh, the devil's messenger to plague me and keep me from getting proud. 8 Three times I begged the Lord to have him leave me alone, 9 but He told me, "My love is enough for you. When you are weak, My power is doing its best work." So I'll delight rather to feel proud of my weaknesses in order to have Christ's power rest on me. 10 That's why I'm glad to be weak and mistreated, to suffer hardships, to be persecuted and hard pressed for Christ. You see, when I'm weak, then I'm strong.

I Will Be No Burden

11 I've become a fool. You forced me to it. Really, you should have spoken well of me. Even if I'm nothing, I wasn't in any way inferior to your "super" apostles. 12 The miracles that prove I'm an apostle were very patiently done among you—miracles, wonders, and works of power.

13 How were you treated worse than the other churches except that I didn't burden you? Forgive me this wrong! 14 Here I'm ready to come to you a third time, and I'm not going

and I will not be burdensome to you: for I seek not yours, but you: for the children ought not to lay up for the parents, but the parents for the children. 15And I will very gladly spend and be spent for you; though the more abundantly I love you, the less I be loved. 16 But be it so, I did not burden you: nevertheless, being crafty, I caught you with guile. 17 Did I make a gain of you by any of them whom I sent unto you? 18 I desired Titus, and with *him* I sent a brother. Did Titus make a gain of you? walked we not in the same spirit? *walked we* not in the same steps? 19Again, think ye that we excuse ourselves unto you? we speak before God in Christ: but *we do* all things, dearly beloved, for your edifying. 20 For I fear, lest, when I come, I shall not find you such as I would, and *that* I shall be found unto you such as ye would not: lest *there be* debates, envyings, wraths, strifes, backbitings, whisperings, swellings, tumults: 21*And* lest, when I come again, my God will humble me among you, and *that* I shall bewail many which have sinned already, and have not repented of the uncleanness and fornication and lasciviousness which they have committed.

you; for I do not seek what is yours, but you; for children are not responsible to save up for *their* parents, but parents for *their* children. 15And I will most gladly spend and be expended for your souls. If I love you the more, am I to be loved the less? 16 But be that as it may, I did not burden you myself; nevertheless, crafty fellow that I am, I took you in by deceit. 17 Certainly I have not taken advantage of you through any of those whom I have sent to you, have I? 18 I urged Titus *to go*, and sent the brother with him. Titus did not take any advantage of you, did he? Did we not conduct ourselves in the same spirit *and walk* in the same steps?

19 All this time you have been thinking that we are defending ourselves to you. *Actually,* it is in the sight of God that we have been speaking in Christ; and all for your upbuilding, beloved. 20 For I am afraid that perhaps when I come I may find you to be not what I wish and may be found by you to be not what you wish; that perhaps *there may be* strife, jealousy, angry tempers, disputes, slanders, gossip, arrogance, disturbances; 21 I am afraid that when I come again my God may humiliate me before you, and I may mourn over many of those who have sinned in the past and not repented of the impurity, immorality and sensuality which they have practiced.

13 This *is* the third *time* I am coming to you. In the mouth of two or three witnesses shall every word be established. 2 I told you before, and foretell you, as if I were present, the second time; and being absent now I write to them which heretofore have sinned, and to all other, that, if I come again, I will not spare: 3 Since ye seek a proof of Christ speaking in me, which to you-ward is not weak, but is mighty in you. 4 For though he was crucified through weakness, yet he liveth by the power of God. For we also are weak in him, but we shall live with him by the power of God toward you. 5 Examine yourselves, whether ye be in the faith; prove your own selves. Know ye not your own selves, how that Jesus Christ is in you, except ye be reprobates? 6 But I trust that ye shall know that we are not reprobates. 7 Now I pray to God that ye do no evil; not that we should appear approved, but that ye should do that which is honest, though we be as reprobates. 8 For we can do nothing against the truth, but for the truth. 9 For we are glad, when we are weak, and ye are strong: and this also we wish, *even* your perfection. 10 Therefore I write these things being absent, lest being present I should use sharp-

13 This is the third time I am coming to you. EVERY FACT IS TO BE CONFIRMED BY THE TESTIMONY OF TWO OR THREE WITNESSES. 2 I have previously said when present the second time, and though now absent I say in advance to those who have sinned in the past and to all the rest as well, that if I come again, I will not spare *anyone*,—3 since you are seeking for proof of the Christ who speaks in me, and who is not weak toward you, but mighty in you. 4 For indeed He was crucified because of weakness, yet He lives because of the power of God. For we also are weak *a*in Him, yet we shall live with Him because of the power of God *directed* toward you. 5 Test yourselves *to see* if you are in the faith; examine yourselves! Or do you not recognize this about yourselves, that Jesus Christ is in you—unless indeed you fail the test? 6 But I trust that you will realize that we ourselves do not fail the test. 7 Now we pray to God that you do no wrong; not that we ourselves may appear approved, but that you may do what is right, even though we should appear unapproved. 8 For we can do nothing against the truth, but *only* for the truth. 9 For we rejoice when we ourselves are weak but you are strong; this we also pray for, that you be made complete. 10 For this reason I am writing these things while absent, in order that when present I may not use severity in accordance with the author-

[a] Some early mss. read, *with Him.*

WILLIAMS

money but you yourselves that I want; for children are not by duty bound to lay up money for their parents, but parents for their children. 15 So in my own case, I will most happily spend my money and myself for your sakes. If I love you much more than I love others, am I to be loved less by you? 16 But let it be granted, you say, that I never received from you financial support, yet, you say, by being a trickster I cheated you by my cunning. 17 I did not make any money out of you through anybody that I sent to you, did I? 18 I actually begged Titus to go, and sent the well-known brother with him. Titus did not make any money out of you, did he? Did not he and I act in the same spirit, and take the very same steps?

19 Are you thinking all this time that I am defending myself to you? It is in the very presence of God and as one who is in union with Christ that I am speaking. And it is all for building you up, beloved, for I am apprehensive that, somehow or other, when I come I shall find you not as I want to find you, and that you may find me not as you want to find me. 20 I repeat it, I am apprehensive that, somehow or other, there may be quarreling, jealousy, anger, rivalries, slanders, gossiping, haughty pride, and disorders, 21 and that when I come back my God may humiliate me before you, and I may have to mourn over some of those who formerly have committed shocking sins, and have not repented for them—their impurity, sexual immorality, and sensuality, which once they practiced.

13 *He asks that offenders be examined and, if guilty, punished; gives his farewell warnings; sends greetings*

This is my third visit to you. Any charge preferred must be sustained by the evidence of two or three witnesses. 2 I have already warned those who formerly committed shocking sins, and all the rest, and though so far away I warn them now, as I did on my second visit, that if I come back I will not spare them, 3 since you demand a proof that Christ is speaking through me. For Christ is not exhibiting weakness toward you but power in you. 4 For though He was crucified in weakness, yet by the power of God He goes on living. We too, indeed, show weakness through our union with Him, yet by the power of God we too shall be alive toward you through fellowship with Him. 5 You yourselves must continue testing yourselves to see whether you are continuing in the faith. You must continue standing the test. Do you not know by a growing experience that Jesus Christ is in you?—provided you stand the test.

6 Now I hope that you will learn that I am standing the test. 7 But I am praying God that you may never do anything wrong, not to show that I am standing the test, but that you should continue doing right, though I should fail to stand the test. 8 For I cannot do anything against the truth, but only for it. 9 I am glad to be consciously weak, if you are really strong. This is my continual prayer, the perfecting of your characters. 10 This is why I am writing this while far away from you, that when I do come, I may not have to deal harshly with you in accordance with the authority

BECK

to be a burden, because I don't want your things but you. Children shouldn't save up for their parents but parents for their children. 15 And I'll be very glad to spend what I have and myself, too, to help you. Do you love me less because I love you so much?

16 But granting I was no burden to you, was I a clever fellow who trapped you with some trick? 17 Did I take advantage of you through any of the men I sent you? 18 I urged Titus to go to you, and I sent the fellow worker with him. Titus didn't take advantage of you, did he? Didn't both of us act in the same spirit? And do exactly the same things?

19 Have you been thinking all along we're only defending ourselves before you? We are speaking before God in Christ, and everything, dear friends, is meant to help you.

Will There Be Trouble?

20 I'm afraid I may come and find you different from what I want you to be, and you may find me different from what you want me to be. And there may be quarreling, jealousy, angry feelings, selfishness, slander, gossip, proud and disorderly behavior. 21 When I come, my God may again humble me before you, and I may have to weep over many who formerly lived in sin and haven't felt sorry for the unclean, sexual, and lustful things they did.

13 This will be the third time I'm coming to you.
Everything must be proved by two or three witnesses.[19] 2 When I was with you the second time as well as now when I'm not with you, I warned and I still warn you who formerly lived in sin and all you others: When I come again, I won't spare you— 3 seeing that you want proof that Christ is speaking through me. He's not weak in dealing with you but powerful in you. 4 He died on a cross in weakness, but He lives by God's power. We, too, are weak in Him, but with Him we'll live by God's power as it comes to you.

5 Examine yourselves to see if you really believe. Test yourselves. Don't you know Jesus Christ is in you—unless you fail in your test? 6 I hope you'll see we haven't failed in our test. 7 We pray God you will do no wrong—not to show we haven't failed, but we want you to do what is right even if we may seem to have failed. 8 We can't do anything against the truth but only work for it. 9 We are glad when we're weak and you're strong. And we're praying that you may grow to be perfect.

10 Here's the reason I'm writing this while I'm not with you: When I come, I don't want to be

[19] Deut. 19:15

K.J.V.

ness, according to the power which the Lord hath given me to edification, and not to destruction. 11 Finally, brethren, farewell. Be perfect, be of good comfort, be of one mind, live in peace; and the God of love and peace shall be with you. 12 Greet one another with a holy kiss. 13 All the saints salute you. 14 The grace of the Lord Jesus Christ, and the love of God, and the communion of the Holy Ghost, *be* with you all. Amen.

The second *epistle* to the Corinthians was written from Philippi, *a city* of Macedonia, by Titus and Lucas.

N.A.S.

ity which the Lord gave me for building up and not for tearing down.

11 Finally, brethren, rejoice, be made complete, be comforted, be like-minded, live in peace; and the God of love and peace shall be with you. 12 Greet one another with a holy kiss. 13 All the saints greet you.

14 The grace of the Lord Jesus Christ, and the love of God, and the fellowship of the Holy Spirit, be with you all.

WILLIAMS

which the Lord has given me, for building you up, not for tearing you down.

11 Finally, brothers, good-by! Practice the perfecting of your characters, keep listening to my appeals, continue thinking in harmony and living in peace, and the loving, peace-giving God will be with you. 12 Greet one another with a sacred kiss. 13 All God's people wish to be remembered to you.

14 The spiritual blessing of the Lord Jesus Christ, the love of God, and the common sharing of the Holy Spirit be with you all.

BECK

sharp in using the authority the Lord gave me to build you up and not to tear you down.

Farewell

11 Finally, fellow Christians, farewell! Keep on growing to be perfect. Take encouragement from me. Agree with one another, live in peace, and the God of love and peace will be with you. 12 Greet one another with a holy kiss. All the holy people greet you.

13 The grace of the Lord Jesus Christ, the love of God, and the Holy Spirit as you share Him be with you all!

THE EPISTLE OF
PAUL THE APOSTLE
TO THE
GALATIANS

1 Paul, an apostle, (not of men, neither by man, but by Jesus Christ, and God the Father, who raised him from the dead;) 2And all the brethren which are with me, unto the churches of Galatia: 3 Grace *be* to you, and peace, from God the Father, and *from* our Lord Jesus Christ, 4 Who gave himself for our sins, that he might deliver us from this present evil world, according to the will of God and our Father: 5 To whom *be* glory for ever and ever. Amen. 6 I marvel that ye are so soon removed from him that called you into the grace of Christ unto another gospel: 7 Which is not another; but there be some that trouble you, and would pervert the gospel of Christ. 8 But though we, or an angel from heaven, preach any other gospel unto you than that which we have preached unto you, let him be accursed. 9As we said before, so say I now again, If any *man* preach any other gospel unto you than that ye have received, let him be accursed. 10 For do I now persuade men, or God? or do I seek to please men? for if I yet pleased men, I should not be the servant of Christ. 11 But I certify you, brethren, that the gospel which was preached of me is not after man. 12 For I neither received it of man, neither was I taught *it,* but by the revelation of Jesus Christ. 13 For ye have heard of my conversation in time past in the Jews' religion, how that beyond measure I persecuted the church of God, and wasted it: 14And profited in the Jews' religion above many my equals in mine own nation, being more exceedingly zealous of the traditions of my fathers. 15 But when it pleased God, who separated me from my mother's womb, and called *me* by his grace, 16 To reveal his Son in me, that I might preach him among the heathen; immediately I conferred not with flesh and blood: 17 Neither went I up to Jerusalem to them which were apostles before me; but I went into Arabia, and returned again unto Damascus. 18 Then after three years I went up to Jerusalem to see Peter, and abode with him fifteen days. 19 But other of the apostles saw I none, save James the Lord's brother. 20 Now the things which I write unto you, be-

THE EPISTLE OF PAUL
TO THE
GALATIANS

1 Paul, an apostle (not *sent* from men, nor through the agency of man, but through Jesus Christ, and God the Father, who raised Him from the dead), 2 and all the brethren who are with me, to the churches of Galatia: 3 Grace to you and peace from God our Father, and the Lord Jesus Christ, 4 who gave Himself for our sins, that He might deliver us out of this present evil age, according to the will of our God and Father, 5 to whom *be* the glory forevermore. Amen.
6 I am amazed that you are so quickly deserting Him who called you by the grace of Christ, for a different gospel; 7 which is *really* not another; only there are some who are disturbing you, and want to distort the gospel of Christ. 8 But even though we, or an angel from heaven, should preach to you a gospel contrary to that which we have preached to you, let him be accursed. 9As we have said before, so I say again now, if any man is preaching to you a gospel contrary to that which you received, let him be accursed. 10 For am I now seeking the favor of men, or of God? Or am I striving to please men? If I were still trying to please men, I would not be a bond-servant of Christ.
11 For I would have you know, brethren, that the gospel which was preached by me is not according to man. 12 For I neither received it from man, nor was I taught it, but *I received it* through a revelation of Jesus Christ. 13 For you have heard of my former manner of life in Judaism, how I used to persecute the church of God beyond measure, and tried to destroy it; 14 and I was advancing in Judaism beyond many of my contemporaries among my countrymen, being more extremely zealous for my ancestral traditions. 15 But when He who had set me apart, *even* from my mother's womb, and called me through His grace, was pleased 16 to reveal His Son in me, that I might preach Him among the Gentiles, I did not immediately consult with flesh and blood, 17 nor did I go up to Jerusalem to those who were apostles before me; but I went away to Arabia, and returned once more to Damascus.
18 Then three years later I went up to Jerusalem to become acquainted with Cephas, and stayed with him fifteen days. 19 But I did not see any other of the apostles except James the Lord's brother. 20 (Now in what I am writing

GALATIANS

1 *In greeting them he tells of his commission from the Lord; proves that his
apostleship and message are from Christ
the Lord; is astonished that they are
turning from this message*

Paul, an apostle sent not from men nor by
any man, but by Jesus Christ and God the
Father who raised Him from the dead—2 and
all the brothers who are here with me—to the
churches of Galatia: 3 spiritual blessing and
peace to you from God the Father and the
Lord Jesus Christ, 4 who gave Himself for our
sins, to save us from the present wicked world
in accordance with the will of our God and
Father; 5 to Him be glory forever and ever.
Amen.

6 I am astonished that you are beginning so
soon to turn away from Him who called you
by the favor of Christ, to a different good
news, 7 which is not really another one; only
there are certain people who are trying to unsettle you and want to turn the good news of
Christ upside down. 8 But even if I or an angel from heaven preach a good news that is
contrary to the one which I have already
preached to you, a curse upon him! 9 As I have
said it before, so now I say it again, if anybody is preaching to you a good news that is
contrary to the one which you have already
received, a curse upon him!

10 Am I now trying to win men's favor, or
God's? Or, am I trying to be pleasing to men?
If I were still trying to be pleasing to men, I
would not be a slave of Christ at all. 11 For I
tell you, brothers, the good news which was
preached by me is not a human message, 12 for
I did not get it from any man; I was not
taught it, but I got it through a revelation
given by Jesus Christ.

13 You have heard, indeed, of my former
conduct as an adherent of the Jewish religion,
how I kept on furiously persecuting the church
of God, and tried to destroy it, 14 and how I
outstripped many of my own age among my
people in my devotion to the Jewish religion,
because I surpassed all others in my zeal for
the traditions handed down by my forefathers.
15 But when God, who had already set me
apart from my birth, and had called me by His
unmerited favor, 16 chose to unveil His Son
in me, so that I might preach the good news
about Him among the heathen, at once, before
I conferred with any human creatures, 17 and
before I went up to Jerusalem to see those
who had been apostles before me, I retired to
Arabia, and afterwards returned to Damascus.
18 Then three years later I went up to
Jerusalem to get acquainted with Cephas, but
I spent only two weeks with him; 19 and not
another single one of the apostles did I see,
except James, the Lord's brother. 20 In writing
you this, I swear before God, I am telling you

PAUL
WRITES TO THE
GALATIANS

1 Paul, an apostle not sent from men or by
any man but by Jesus Christ and by God the
Father, who raised Him from the dead, 2 and
all the Christians who are with me, to the
churches in Galatia—3 love and peace to you
from God the Father and our Lord Jesus Christ,
4 who gave Himself for our sins to save us
from this present wicked world according to the
will of our God and Father. 5 To Him be glory
forever! Amen.

You Are Turning Away

6 I am surprised you are so soon leaving Him
who called you by the love of Christ and are
turning to another kind of good news, 7 which
really is not another. But there are some men
who are troubling you and want to change the
good news of Christ. 8 But even if we or an
angel from heaven would bring you any other
good news than what we brought you, a curse
be on him! 9 I say again what we said before:
If anyone brings you any other good news than
the one you received, a curse be on him!
10 Do I say this now to get the approval of
men—or of God? Or am I trying to please men?
If I were still trying to please men, I wouldn't
be a servant of Christ.

Jesus Gave Me the Good News

11 I tell you, my fellow Christians, the good
news I told is not a human idea, 12 because no
man gave it or taught it to me, but Jesus Christ
revealed it to me.
13 You have heard what I used to do when
I still lived according to the Jewish religion,
how violently I persecuted God's church and
tried to destroy it 14 and how in this Jewish
religion I was ahead of many of my own age
among my people, so extremely zealous was I
for the traditions of my ancestors.
15 But God *had appointed me before I was
born,*[1] and in His love He called me. 16 And
when He kindly decided to show me His Son
so that I would tell the good news of Him
among the Gentiles, I didn't talk it over with
other men 17 or go up to Jerusalem to see those
who were apostles before me, but I went immediately to Arabia and then came back to
Damascus.
18 After three years I went up to Jerusalem to get to know Peter, and I stayed
with him fifteen days. 19 But I didn't see any
of the other apostles, only James, the Lord's
brother. 20 (And I declare before God I'm writ-

[1] Is. 49:1

527

hold, before God, I lie not. 21Afterwards I came into the regions of Syria and Cilicia; 22And was unknown by face unto the churches of Judea which were in Christ: 23 But they had heard only, That he which persecuted us in times past now preacheth the faith which once he destroyed. 24And they glorified God in me.

2 Then fourteen years after I went up again to Jerusalem with Barnabas, and took Titus with *me* also. 2And I went up by revelation, and communicated unto them that gospel which I preach among the Gentiles, but privately to them which were of reputation, lest by any means I should run, or had run, in vain. 3 But neither Titus, who was with me, being a Greek, was compelled to be circumcised: 4And that because of false brethren unawares brought in, who came in privily to spy out our liberty which we have in Christ Jesus, that they might bring us into bondage: 5 To whom we gave place by subjection, no, not for an hour; that.the truth of the gospel might continue with you. 6 But of those who seemed to be somewhat, whatsoever they were, it maketh no matter to me: God accepteth no man's person: for they who seemed *to be somewhat* in conference added nothing to me: 7 But contrariwise, when they saw that the gospel of the uncircumcision was committed unto me, as *the gospel* of the circumcision *was* unto Peter; 8(For he that wrought effectually in Peter to the apostleship of the circumcision, the same was mighty in me toward the Gentiles;) 9And when James, Cephas, and John, who seemed to be pillars, perceived the grace that was given unto me, they gave to me and Barnabas the right hands of fellowship; that we *should* go unto the heathen, and they unto the circumcision. 10 Only *they would* that we should remember the poor; the same which I also was forward to do. 11 But when Peter was come to Antioch, I withstood him to the face, because he was to be blamed. 12 For before that certain came from James, he did eat with the Gentiles: but when they were come, he withdrew and separated himself, fearing them which were of the circumcision. 13And the other Jews dissembled likewise with him; insomuch that Barnabas also was carried away with their dissimulation. 14 But when I saw that they walked not uprightly according to the truth of the gospel, I said unto Peter before *them* all, If thou, being a Jew, livest after the manner of Gentiles, and not as do the Jews, why compellest thou the Gentiles to live as do the Jews? 15 We *who are* Jews by nature, and not sinners of the Gentiles, 16 Knowing that a man is not justified by the works of the law, but by the faith of Jesus Christ, even

to you, I assure you before God *that* I am not lying.) 21 Then I went into the regions of Syria and Cilicia. 22And I was *still* unknown by sight to the churches of Judea which were in Christ; 23 but only, they kept hearing, "He who once persecuted us is now preaching the faith which he once *tried to* destroy." 24And they were glorifying God because of me.

2 Then after an interval of fourteen years I went up again to Jerusalem with Barnabas, taking Titus along also. 2And it was because of a revelation that I went up; and I submitted to them the gospel which I preach among the Gentiles, but I did so in private to those who were of reputation, for fear that I might be running, or had run, in vain. 3 But not even Titus who was with me, though he was a Greek, was compelled to be circumcised. 4 But *it was* because of the false brethren who had sneaked in to spy out our liberty which we have in Christ Jesus, in order to bring us into bondage. 5 But we did not yield in subjection to them for even an hour, so that the truth of the gospel might remain with you. 6 But from those who were of high reputation (what they were makes no difference to me; God shows no partiality)—well, those who were of reputation contributed nothing to me. 7 But on the contrary, seeing that I had been entrusted with the gospel to the uncircumcised, just as Peter with *the gospel* to the circumcised 8 (for He who effectually worked for Peter in *his* apostleship to the circumcised effectually worked for me also to the Gentiles), 9 and recognizing the grace that had been given to me, James and Cephas and John, who were reputed to be pillars, gave to me and Barnabas the right hand of fellowship, that we might go to the Gentiles, and they to the circumcised. 10 *They* only *asked* us to remember the poor— the very thing I also was eager to do.
    11 But when Cephas came to Antioch, I opposed him to his face, because he stood condemned. 12 For prior to the coming of certain men from James, he used to eat with the Gentiles; but when they came, he *began* to withdraw and hold himself aloof, fearing the party of the circumcision. 13 And the rest of the Jews joined him in hypocrisy, with the result that even Barnabas was carried away by their hypocrisy. 14 But when I saw that they were not straightforward about the truth of the gospel, I said to Cephas in the presence of all, "If you, being a Jew, live like the Gentiles and not like the Jews, how *is it that* you compel the Gentiles to live like Jews? 15 "We *are* Jews by nature, and not sinners from among the Gentiles; 16 nevertheless knowing that a man is not justified by the works of the Law but through faith in Christ Jesus, even we have

WILLIAMS

the solemn truth. 21After that I went into the districts of Syria and Cilicia. 22 But I was personally unknown to the Christian churches in Judea; 23 only they kept hearing people say, "Our former persecutor is now preaching as good news the faith which once he tried to destroy," 24 and they kept on praising God for me.

2 *His interview with the apostles at Jerusalem conference proves his point; Paul later teaches Peter instead of Peter teaching Paul; again emphasizes right standing with God by trust in Christ*

Then, fourteen years later, I again went up to Jerusalem, with Barnabas, and took Titus with me too. 2 I went up under the guidance of a divine revelation. Now I laid before them the good news that I was in the habit of preaching among the heathen, but first I did so privately before the leaders, for fear that my course might be or might have been to no purpose. 3 But they did not even try to compel my companion, Titus, although he was a Greek, to be circumcised—4 they did not try it even for the sake of the false brothers who had been smuggled in, who stole in to spy out the freedom we enjoy in Christ Jesus, so as to make us slaves again. 5 But we did not for a moment yield them submission, in order that the truth of the good news might prevail for you. 6 Those who were looked upon as leaders —what they were makes no difference to me— God pays no attention to outward appearances —these leaders added nothing new to me. 7 On the contrary, because they saw that I had been entrusted with the good news for the heathen,[a] just as Peter had been entrusted with it for the Jews—[a] 8 for He who had been at work in Peter for his apostleship to the Jews had been at work in me too for the apostleship to the heathen—9 and because they recognized the favor God had shown me, James, Cephas, and John, the so-called pillar apostles, gave Barnabas and me the right hand of fellowship, with the understanding that we should go to the heathen and they to the Jews. 10 Only they wanted us to remember the poor, the very thing that I was eager to do.
11 Now when Cephas came to Antioch, I opposed him to his face, because he stood condemned. 12 For before the coming of certain people from James, he was in the habit of eating with heathen Christians, but after they came, he began to draw back and hold aloof from them, because he was afraid of the circumcision party. 13 The rest of the Jewish Christians, too, joined him in this pretense, so that even Barnabas was influenced to join them in their pretense. 14 But when I saw that they were not living up to the truth of the good news, I said to Cephas, and that before them all, "if you are living like a heathen and not like a Jew, although you are a Jew yourself, why do you try to make the heathen live like Jews?"
15 We ourselves are Jews by birth and not heathen sinners, and yet, 16 because we know that a man does not come into right standing with God by doing what the law commands,

BECK

ing you no lie.) 21 Then I went to the regions of Syria and Cilicia. 22 In Judea the churches of Christ didn't know me personally. 23 They only heard people say: "The man who used to persecute us is now preaching the faith he once tried to destroy," 24 and they praised God for what they saw in me.

Fellowship with the Apostles

2 Fourteen years later I went up to Jerusalem again, this time with Barnabas, and I also took Titus with me. 2 (God had told me to go.) Then I laid before the Christians, and privately before the leaders, the good news I preach among the non-Jewish people. I didn't in any way want to run or to have run in vain.
3 Titus was with me, and he's a Greek. But nobody forced him to be circumcised 4 to please the false Christians who had come in secretly. They sneaked in to spy out the liberty we have in Christ Jesus and to make us slaves. 5 Not for a moment did we let them dictate to us, so that you will always have the real good news.
6 I don't care what those leaders once were —*God doesn't prefer one to another.*[a] Those leaders didn't teach me anything new. 7 On the contrary, they saw I had been entrusted with bringing the good news to the non-Jews as Peter was to bring it to the Jews. 8 He who had worked in Peter to make him an apostle to the Jews had worked in me to make me an apostle to the non-Jews. 9 When James, Peter, and John, who were considered pillars, saw what God's love had given me, they gave me and Barnabas the right hand of fellowship with the understanding that we work among the non-Jews and they among the Jews. 10 All they asked was that we remember the poor, and that I was eager to do.

I Criticized Peter

11 But when Peter came to Antioch, I opposed him to his face because he had shown how wrong he was. 12 He had been eating with the non-Jews before certain men came from James. But when they came, he held back and kept away from non-Jews because he was afraid of those who believed in circumcision. 13 And the other Jews acted just as insincerely as he did, so much so even Barnabas was carried away to be a hypocrite with them.
14 But when I saw they were not doing right according to the truth of the good news, I told Peter before everybody: "If you, a Jew, don't live like a Jew but like a non-Jew, how can you insist the non-Jews must live like Jews?
15 "We were born Jews and not Gentile sinners; 16 yet we know a person cannot become righteous* by doing what the Law says, but only by believing in Jesus Christ. Even

[a] Lit., *uncircumcision . . . circumcision* (abstract for concrete).

* See note at Rom. 3:20.
[2] Deut. 10:17

we have believed in Jesus Christ, that we might be justified by the faith of Christ, and not by the works of the law: for by the works of the law shall no flesh be justified. 17 But if, while we seek to be justified by Christ, we ourselves also are found sinners, *is* therefore Christ the minister of sin? God forbid. 18 For if I build again the things which I destroyed, I make myself a transgressor. 19 For I through the law am dead to the law, that I might live unto God. 20 I am crucified with Christ: nevertheless I live; yet not I, but Christ liveth in me: and the life which I now live in the flesh I live by the faith of the Son of God, who loved me, and gave himself for me. 21 I do not frustrate the grace of God: for if righteousness *come* by the law, then Christ is dead in vain.

3 O foolish Galatians, who hath bewitched you, that ye should not obey the truth, before whose eyes Jesus Christ hath been evidently set forth, crucified among you? 2 This only would I learn of you, Received ye the Spirit by the works of the law, or by the hearing of faith? 3 Are ye so foolish? having begun in the Spirit, are ye now made perfect by the flesh? 4 Have ye suffered so many things in vain? if *it be* yet in vain. 5 He therefore that ministereth to you the Spirit, and worketh miracles among you, *doeth he it* by the works of the law, or by the hearing of faith? 6 Even as Abraham believed God, and it was accounted to him for righteousness. 7 Know ye therefore that they which are of faith, the same are the children of Abraham. 8 And the Scripture, foreseeing that God would justify the heathen through faith, preached before the gospel unto Abraham, *saying,* In thee shall all nations be blessed. 9 So then they which be of faith are blessed with faithful Abraham. 10 For as many as are of the works of the law are under the curse: for it is written, Cursed *is* every one that continueth not in all things which are written in the book of the law to do them. 11 But that no man is justified by the law in the sight of God, *it is* evident: for, The just shall live by faith. 12 And the law is not of faith: but, The man that doeth them shall live in them. 13 Christ hath redeemed us from the curse of the law, being made a curse for us: for it is written, Cursed *is* every one that hangeth on a tree: 14 That the blessing of Abraham might come on the Gentiles through Jesus Christ; that

believed in Christ Jesus, that we may be justified by faith in Christ, and not by the works of the Law; since by the works of the Law shall no flesh be justified. 17 "But if, while seeking to be justified in Christ, we ourselves have also been found sinners, is Christ then a minister of sin? May it never be! 18 "For if I rebuild what I have *once* destroyed, I prove myself to be a transgressor. 19 "For through the Law I died to the Law, that I might live to God. 20 "I have been crucified with Christ; and it is no longer I who live, but Christ lives in me; and the *life* which I now live in the flesh I live by faith in the Son of God, who loved me, and delivered Himself up for me. 21 "I do not nullify the grace of God; for if righteousness *comes* through the Law, then Christ died needlessly."

3 You foolish Galatians, who has bewitched you, before whose eyes Jesus Christ was publicly portrayed *as* crucified? 2 This is the only thing I want to find out from you: Did you receive the Spirit by the works of the Law, or by hearing with faith? 3 Are you so foolish? Having begun by the Spirit, are you now being perfected by the flesh? 4 Did you suffer so many things in vain—if indeed it was in vain? 5 Does He then who provides you with the Spirit and works miracles among you, do it by the works of the Law, or by hearing with faith? 6 Even so Abraham BELIEVED GOD, AND IT WAS RECKONED TO HIM AS RIGHTEOUSNESS. 7 Therefore, be sure that it is those who are of faith that are sons of Abraham. 8 And the Scripture, foreseeing that God would justify the Gentiles by faith, preached the gospel beforehand to Abraham, *saying,* "ALL THE NATIONS SHALL BE BLESSED IN YOU." 9 So then those who are of faith are blessed with Abraham, the believer. 10 For as many as are of the works of the Law are under a curse; for it is written, "CURSED IS EVERY ONE WHO DOES NOT ABIDE BY ALL THINGS WRITTEN IN THE BOOK OF THE LAW, TO PERFORM THEM." 11 Now that no one is justified by the Law before God is evident; for, "THE RIGHTEOUS MAN SHALL LIVE BY FAITH." 12 However, the Law is not of faith; on the contrary, "HE WHO PRACTICES THEM SHALL LIVE BY THEM." 13 Christ redeemed us from the curse of the Law, having become a curse for us—for it is written, "CURSED IS EVERY ONE WHO HANGS ON A TREE"— 14 in order that in Christ Jesus the blessing of Abraham might come to the Gen-

WILLIAMS

but by simple trust in Christ, we too have trusted in Christ Jesus, in order to come into right standing with God by simple trust in Christ and not by doing what the law commands, because by doing what the law commands no man can come into right standing with God. 17 Now if, in our efforts to come into right standing with God through union with Christ, we have proved ourselves to be sinners like the heathen themselves, does that make Christ a party to our sin? Of course not. 18 For if I try to build again what I tore down, I really prove myself to be a wrongdoer. 19 For through the law I myself have become dead to the law, so that I may live for God. 20 I have been crucified with Christ, and I myself no longer live, but Christ is living in me; the life I now live as a mortal man I live by faith in the Son of God who loved me and gave Himself for me. 21 I never can nullify the unmerited favor of God. For if right standing with God could come through law, then Christ died for nothing.

3 *The readers' experience proves that right standing with God comes by faith in Christ; believers, genuine sons of Abraham; Christ ransomed us from the law's curse; law not against the promise but leads us to Christ*

O senseless Galatians! Who has bewitched you, before whose very eyes Jesus Christ was pictured as the crucified One? 2 I want to ask you only this one thing: Did you receive the Spirit by doing what the law commands, or by believing the message you heard? 3 Are you so senseless? Did you begin by the Spirit, but are now approaching perfection by fleshly means? 4 Have you suffered so much for nothing? If it really is for nothing. 5 Now when He supplies you with the Spirit and performs His wonderworks among you, does He do it because you do what the law commands, or because you believe the message that you heard— 6 just as "Abraham put his faith in God, and it was credited to him as right standing with God"?

7 So you see, it is the men of faith who are the real descendants of Abraham. 8 Because the Scripture foresaw that God would bring the heathen into right standing with Himself on condition of faith, He beforehand proclaimed the good news to Abraham in the promise, "It is through you that all the heathen will be blessed." 9 So the men of faith are blessed as partners with trusting Abraham.

10 For those who depend on what the law commands are under a curse, for the Scripture says, "Cursed be everyone who does not continue in all the commands that are written in the book of the law, to do them." 11 Now it is evident that through the law no man is brought into right standing with God, for "The man in right standing with God will live by faith," 12 and the law has nothing to do with faith, but it says, "It is the man who does these things that will live by doing them." 13 Christ ransomed us from the curse of the law by becoming a curse for us—for the Scripture says, "Cursed be everyone who is hanged on a tree"—14 that the blessing promised to Abraham might through Jesus Christ come

BECK

we came to believe in Jesus Christ to become righteous* by believing in Christ and not by doing what the Law says, because *no one will become righteous** * by doing what the Law says.

17 "Now if we who want to be righteous in Christ are found to be sinners like the non-Jews, does Christ encourage us to sin? Never! 18 But if I build up again what I've torn down, I make myself a sinner. 19 By the Law I died to the Law, to live for God.** 20 I was crucified with Christ, and I don't live any more, but Christ lives in me. The life I now live in my body I live by believing in the God and Christ who loved me and gave Himself for me. 21 I don't reject God's gift of love. You see, if we could get righteousness through the Law, then Christ died for nothing."

The Believer is Blessed

3 You foolish Galatians! Who has bewitched you—you who saw Jesus Christ publicly pictured as crucified? 2 I want you to tell me just one thing: Did you get the Spirit by doing what the Law says or by the truth you heard and believed? 3 Are you so foolish? You started with the Spirit; are you now going to finish with the flesh? 4 Did you experience so much for nothing? Perhaps it really was for nothing! 5 Does God give you the Spirit and make such powers active in you by your doing what the Law says or by the truth you hear and believe?

6 It was the same way with *Abraham*. He *believed God, and so he was counted righteous.*[4] 7 You see, then, that those who believe are Abraham's real descendants. 8 The Bible foresaw that God would make the nations righteous* by faith, and long ago He told Abraham the good news, *Through you all nations will be blessed.*[5] 9 So those who believe are blessed with Abraham, who believed.

10 There is a curse on all who depend on doing what the Law says, because it is written, *Cursed is everyone who doesn't follow and do everything written in the book of the Law.*[6] 11 It is clear the Law makes no one righteous* before God, because *if you believe, you are righteous* and you will live.*[7] 12 But the Law is not based on faith; no, it says. *If you do these things, you will find life in them.*[8] 13 Christ paid the price to free us from the curse of the Law when He was cursed for us (it is written, *Cursed is everyone who hangs on a cross*[9]) 14 so that in Jesus Christ Abraham's blessing would come

* See note at Rom. 3:20.
** The meaning of verses 17-19 is this: When we don't try to be righteous by doing what the Law demands, we "tear down" the Law, and the Jews may think we are just non-Jewish sinners. If to please the Jews, we try again to do what the Law demands and so "build it up," the Law only condemns us as sinners. The Law condemned Jesus for our sins and killed Him, and us with Him. Now the Law can't demand any more from us than from a dead person.
[3] Ps. 143:2
[4] Gen. 15:6
[5] Gen. 12:3; 18:18; 22:18; 26:4; 28:14
[6] Deut. 27:26
[7] Hab. 2:4
[8] Lev. 18:5
[9] Deut. 21:23

K.J.V.

we might receive the promise of the Spirit through faith. 15 Brethren, I speak after the manner of men; Though it be but a man's covenant, yet if it be confirmed, no man disannulleth, or addeth thereto. 16 Now to Abraham and his seed were the promises made. He saith not, And to seeds, as of many; but as of one, And to thy seed, which is Christ. 17And this I say, that the covenant, that was confirmed before of God in Christ, the law, which was four hundred and thirty years after, cannot disannul, that it should make the promise of none effect. 18 For if the inheritance be of the law, it is no more of promise: but God gave it to Abraham by promise. 19 Wherefore then serveth the law? It was added because of transgressions, till the seed should come to whom the promise was made; and it was ordained by angels in the hand of a mediator. 20 Now a mediator is not a mediator of one, but God is one. 21 Is the law then against the promises of God? God forbid: for if there had been a law given which could have given life, verily righteousness should have been by the law. 22 But the Scripture hath concluded all under sin, that the promise by faith of Jesus Christ might be given to them that believe. 23 But before faith came, we were kept under the law, shut up unto the faith which should afterwards be revealed. 24 Wherefore the law was our schoolmaster to bring us unto Christ, that we might be justified by faith. 25 But after that faith is come, we are no longer under a schoolmaster. 26 For ye are all the children of God by faith in Christ Jesus. 27 For as many of you as have been baptized into Christ have put on Christ. 28 There is neither Jew nor Greek, there is neither bond nor free, there is neither male nor female: for ye are all one in Christ Jesus. 29And if ye be Christ's, then are ye Abraham's seed, and heirs according to the promise.

4 Now I say, That the heir, as long as he is a child, differeth nothing from a servant, though he be lord of all; 2 But is under tutors and governors until the time appointed of the father. 3 Even so we, when we were children, were in bondage under the elements of the world: 4 But when the fulness of the time was come, God sent forth his Son, made of a woman, made under the law, 5 To redeem them that were under the law, that we might receive the adoption of sons. 6And because ye are sons, God hath sent forth the Spirit of his Son into your hearts, crying, Abba, Father. 7 Wherefore thou art no more a servant, but a son; and if a son,

N.A.S.

tiles, so that we might receive the promise of the Spirit through faith. 15 Brethren, I speak in terms of human relations: even though it is only a man's covenant, yet when it has been ratified, no one sets it aside or adds conditions to it. 16 Now the promises were spoken to Abraham and to his seed. He does not say, "AND TO SEEDS," as referring to many, but rather to one, "AND TO YOUR SEED," that is, Christ. 17 What I am saying is this: the Law, which came four hundred and thirty years later, does not invalidate a covenant previously ratified by God, so as to nullify the promise. 18 For if the inheritance is based on law, it is no longer based on a promise; but God has granted it to Abraham by means of a promise. 19 Why the Law then? It was added because of transgressions, having been ordained through angels by the agency of a mediator, until the seed should come to whom the promise had been made. 20 Now a mediator is not for one party only; whereas God is only one. 21 Is the Law then contrary to the promises of God? May it never be! For if a law had been given which was able to impart life, then righteousness would indeed have been based on law. 22 But the Scripture has shut up all men under sin, that the promise by faith in Jesus Christ might be given to those who believe.

23 But before faith came, we were kept in custody under the law, being shut up to the faith which was later to be revealed. 24 Therefore the Law has become our tutor to lead us to Christ, that we may be justified by faith. 25 But now that faith has come, we are no longer under a tutor. 26 For you are all sons of God through faith in Christ Jesus. 27 For all of you who were baptized into Christ have clothed yourselves with Christ. 28 There is neither Jew nor Greek, there is neither slave nor free man, there is neither male nor female; for you are all one in Christ Jesus. 29And if you belong to Christ, then you are Abraham's offspring, heirs according to promise.

4 Now I say, as long as the heir is a child, he does not differ at all from a slave although he is owner of everything, 2 but he is under guardians and managers until the date set by the father. 3 So also we, while we were children, were held in bondage under the elemental things of the world. 4 But when the fulness of the time came, God sent forth His Son, born of a woman, born under the Law, 5 in order that He might redeem those who were under the Law, that we might receive the adoption as sons. 6And because you are sons, God has sent forth the Spirit of His Son into our hearts, crying, "Abba! Father!" 7 Therefore you are no longer a slave, but a son; and if a son, then an heir through God.

WILLIAMS

to the heathen, so that through faith we might receive the promised Spirit.

15 Brothers, I am going to use a human illustration: Even a human contract, once it has been ratified, no one can annul or change. 16 Now the promises were made to Abraham and his descendant. It does not say, "and to your descendants," in the plural, but in the singular, "and to your descendant," that is, Christ. 17 I mean this: The law which was given four hundred and thirty years later could not annul the contract which had already been ratified by God, so as to cancel the promise. 18 For if our inheritance depends on the law, it can no longer depend on the promise. But it was by promise that God so graciously bestowed it upon Abraham.

19 Then what about the law? It was added later on to increase transgressions, until the descendant to whom the promise was made should come, enacted through the agency of angels in the person of an intermediary. 20 Though an intermediary implies more than one party, yet God is only one. 21 Is the law then contrary to God's promises? Of course not. For if a law had been given that was able to impart life, surely, then, right standing would have come through law. 22 But the Scripture pictures all mankind as prisoners of sin, so that the promised blessing through faith in Christ might be given to those who have faith.

23 But before this faith came, we were kept locked up under the law, in preparation for the faith which was to be unveiled. 24 So the law has been our attendant to lead us to Christ, so that we might through faith obtain right standing with God. 25 But now that this faith has come, we are no longer in charge of the attendant. 26 For all of you are sons of God through faith in Christ Jesus. 27 For all of you who have been baptized into union with Christ have clothed yourselves with Christ. 28 There is no room for Jew or Greek, no room for slave or freeman, no room for male or female, for you are all one through union with Christ Jesus. 29 And if you belong to Christ, then you are real descendants of Abraham, and heirs in accordance with the promise made to him.

4 *Believers in Christ, God's sons; outward rites of no avail; the apostle anxious though conscious of the readers' former affection for him; allegory of Ishmael and Isaac illustrates the law and the faith systems*

I mean this: As long as the heir is under age he is not a whit better off than a slave, although he is heir of all the property, 2 but he is under guardians and trustees until the time fixed by the father. 3 So when we were spiritually under age, we were slaves to the world's crude notions, 4 but when the proper time had come, God sent His Son, born of a woman, born subject to law, 5 to ransom those who were subject to law, so that we might be adopted as sons. 6 And because you are sons, God has sent the Spirit of His Son into your hearts, crying, "Abba," that is, "Father." 7 So you are no longer a slave, but a son; and if a son, then an heir by God's own act.

BECK

to the nations and we by believing would get the promised Spirit.

The Promise Was First

15 My fellow Christians, let me use an example from daily life. Once a will is ratified, even if it's only a man's will, nobody sets it aside or adds to it. 16 Now the promises were made to Abraham and to his descendant. He doesn't say, "and, by the descendants," in the plural, but in the singular, and *by your Descendant*,[10] which is Christ. 17 Now, I say this: First God confirmed His covenant; and the Law, which came 430 years later, doesn't set aside and cancel its promise. 18 If we get the inheritance by the Law, we don't get it by a promise; but God gave it to Abraham by a promise.

Our Guardian

19 Why, then, was the Law given? It was added to arouse transgressions* until the Descendant would come to whom the promise was made. And it was given through angels in the hands of a mediator. 20 A mediator deals with more than one, but God is one.**

21 Is the Law, then, opposed to God's promises? Never! If a law had been given that could make us alive, it certainly would have given us righteousness. 22 But the Bible has condemned all people as sinners so that believers by believing in Jesus Christ would get the promised blessing. 23 Before faith came, we were under the Law, guarded in prison for the faith that was to be revealed. 24 Then the Law has been our guardian so that we would come to Christ and become righteous by faith. 25 But now that faith has come, we are no longer under a guardian. 26 You are all God's children by believing in Christ Jesus, 27 because all of you who were baptized into Christ have put on Christ. 28 There is no Jew or Greek, no slave or free person, no man or woman—you're all one in Christ Jesus. 29 If you belong to Christ, then you are Abraham's descendants and heirs of the blessing God promised.

God's Sons

4 Now, I say that as long as the heir is a child, he is no better than a slave, although he owns everything. 2 He is under guardians and managers till the day set by his father. 3 So it is with us. When we were children, we were slaves under the elementary ways of the world. 4 But when the right time came, God sent His Son, born of a woman, born under the Law, 5 to free those under the Law and make us His sons. 6 And because you are sons, God sent into our hearts the Spirit of His Son, who cries, "Father!" 7 So you are no longer a slave but a son. And if you are His son, God has made you His heir.

---

* The Law was like a stick with which a trainer stirs up a sleeping wild animal to show how terrible it is.
** God gave the Law to Moses, who brought it to the people, but God gave His promise directly to Abraham.
[10] Gen. 22:18; 26:4

K.J.V.

then an heir of God through Christ. 8 Howbeit then, when ye knew not God, ye did service unto them which by nature are no gods. 9 But now, after that ye have known God, or rather are known of God, how turn ye again to the weak and beggarly elements, whereunto ye desire again to be in bondage? 10 Ye observe days, and months, and times, and years. 11 I am afraid of you, lest I have bestowed upon you labour in vain. 12 Brethren, I beseech you, be as I *am;* for I *am* as ye *are:* ye have not injured me at all. 13 Ye know how through infirmity of the flesh I preached the gospel unto you at the first. 14And my temptation which was in my flesh ye despised not, nor rejected; but received me as an angel of God, *even* as Christ Jesus. 15 Where is then the blessedness ye spake of? for I bear you record, that, if *it had been* possible, ye would have plucked out your own eyes, and have given them to me. 16Am I therefore become your enemy, because I tell you the truth? 17 They zealously affect you, *but* not well; yea, they would exclude you, that ye might affect them. 18 But *it is* good to be zealously affected always in *a* good *thing,* and not only when I am present with you. 19 My little children, of whom I travail in birth again until Christ be formed in you, 20 I desire to be present with you now, and to change my voice; for I stand in doubt of you. 21 Tell me, ye that desire to be under the law, do ye not hear the law? 22 For it is written, that Abraham had two sons, the one by a bondmaid, the other by a free woman. 23 But he *who was* of the bondwoman was born after the flesh; but he of the free woman *was* by promise. 24 Which things are an allegory: for these are the two covenants; the one from the mount Sinai, which gendereth to bondage, which is Agar. 25 For this Agar is mount Sinai in Arabia, and answereth to Jerusalem which now is, and is in bondage with her children. 26 But Jerusalem which is above is free, which is the mother of us all. 27 For it is written, Rejoice, thou barren that bearest not; break forth and cry, thou that travailest not: for the desolate hath many more children than she which hath a husband. 28 Now we, brethren, as Isaac was, are the children of promise. 29 But as then he that was born after the flesh persecuted him *that was born* after the Spirit, even so *it is* now. 30 Nevertheless what saith the Scripture? Cast out the bondwoman and her son: for the son of the bondwoman shall not be heir with the son of the free woman. 31 So then, brethren, we are not children of the bondwoman, but of the free.

N.A.S.

8 However at that time, when you did not know God, you were slaves to those which by nature are no gods. 9 But now that you have come to know God, or rather to be known by God, how is it that you turn back again to the weak and worthless elemental things, to which you desire to be enslaved all over again? 10 You observe days and months and seasons and years. 11 I fear for you, that perhaps I have labored over you in vain.

12 I beg of you, brethren, become as *I am,* for I also *have become* as you *are.* You have done me no wrong; 13 but you know that it was because of a bodily illness that I preached the gospel to you the first time; 14 and that which was a trial to you in my bodily condition you did not despise or loathe, but you received me as an angel of God, as Christ Jesus *Himself.* 15 Where then is that sense of blessing you had? For I bear you witness, that if possible, you would have plucked out your eyes and given them to me. 16 Have I therefore become your enemy by telling you the truth? 17 They eagerly seek you, not commendably, but they wish to shut you out, in order that you may seek them. 18 But it is good always to be eagerly sought in a commendable manner, and not only when I am present with you. 19 My children, with whom I am again in labor until Christ is formed in you— 20 but I could wish to be present with you now and to change my tone, for I am perplexed about you.

21 Tell me, you who want to be under law, do you not listen to the law? 22 For it is written that Abraham had two sons, one by the bondwoman and one by the free woman. 23 But the son by the bondwoman was born according to the flesh, and the son by the free woman through the promise. 24 This contains an allegory: for these *women* are two covenants, one *proceeding* from Mount Sinai bearing children who are to be slaves; she is Hagar. 25 Now this Hagar is Mount Sinai in Arabia, and corresponds to the present Jerusalem, for she is in slavery with her children. 26 But the Jerusalem above is free; she is our mother. 27 For it is written,

"REJOICE, BARREN WOMAN WHO DOES NOT
      BEAR;
BREAK FORTH AND SHOUT, YOU WHO ARE NOT
      IN LABOR;
FOR MORE ARE THE CHILDREN OF THE DESO-
      LATE
THAN OF THE ONE WHO HAS A HUSBAND."

28And you brethren, like Isaac, are children of promise. 29 But as at that time he who was born according to the flesh persecuted him *who was born* according to the Spirit, so it is now also. 30 But what does the Scripture say?

"CAST OUT THE BONDWOMAN AND HER SON,
FOR THE SON OF THE BONDWOMAN SHALL NOT
      BE AN HEIR WITH THE SON OF THE FREE
      WOMAN."

31 So then, brethren, we are not children of a bondwoman, but of the free woman.

WILLIAMS

8 But at that former time, as you did not know the true God, you were slaves to gods that do not really exist, 9 but now, since you have come to know God, or rather have come to be known by Him, how can you turn back to your own crude notions, so weak and worthless, and wish to become slaves to them again? 10 You are observing days, months, seasons, years. 11 I am beginning to fear that I have bestowed my labors on you for nothing.

12 I beg you, brothers, take my point of view, just as I took yours. You did me no injustice then. 13 And yet you know that it was because of an illness of mine that I preached the good news to you the first time, 14 but still you did not scorn the test my illness made of you, nor did you spurn me for it; on the contrary, you welcomed me as an angel of God, as Christ Jesus Himself. 15 Where is your self-congratulation? For I can testify that you would have torn out your very eyes, if you could, and have given them to me. 16 Have I then turned into an enemy to you, because I tell you the truth?

17 These men are paying you special attention, but not sincerely. They want to shut you off from me, so that you may keep on paying them special attention. 18 Now it is a fine thing to have special attention paid you, if it is done sincerely and unceasingly, and not only when I am with you. 19 O my dear children, I am suffering a mother's birth pangs for you again, until Christ is formed in you. 20 I wish I could be with you right now and change the tone of my speech, for I do not know which way to turn in your case.

21 Tell me, you who want to be subject to law, will you not listen to what the law says? 22 For the Scripture says that Abraham had two sons, one by a slave-girl, the other by a free woman. 23 But the child of the slave-girl was born in the ordinary course of nature, while the child of the free woman was born to fulfill the promise. 24 This is spoken as an allegory. For these women are two covenants, one coming from Mount Sinai, bearing children that are to be slaves; 25 that is, Hagar (and Hagar means Mount Sinai, in Arabia) and corresponds to the present Jerusalem, for Jerusalem is in slavery with her children. 26 But the Jerusalem that is above is free, and she is our mother. 27 For the Scripture says:
"Rejoice, you childless woman, who never bore a child;
Break forth into shouting, you who feel no birth pangs;
For the desolate woman has many children, Even more than the married one."
28 Now we, brothers, like Isaac, are children born to fulfill the promise. 29 But just as then the child born in the ordinary course of nature persecuted the one born by the power of the Spirit, so it is today. 30 But what does the Scripture say? "Drive off the slave-girl and her son, for the slave-girl's son shall never share the inheritance with the son of the free woman." 31 So, brothers, we are children, not of a slave-girl but of a free woman.

BECK

8 But when you didn't know God, you were slaves to gods who really don't exist. 9 Now that you know God—or rather, God knows you—how can you turn back to those elementary ways, so weak and beggarly, and want to be slaves to them again? 10 You keep days, months, seasons, and years! 11 I'm afraid the work I did on you may have been wasted.

You Welcomed Me

12 I beg you, my fellow Christians, become like me, since I became like you. You did me no wrong. 13 You know I brought you the good news the first time because I was sick.* 14 Though my sick body was a test to you, you didn't despise or scorn me, but you welcomed me as if I were God's angel or Christ Jesus Himself. 15 You thought you were happy— what has become of that? I tell you, if possible, you would have torn out your eyes and given them to me. 16 Can it be I have become your enemy by telling you the truth?

17 Those men are making much of you without meaning well. They want to exclude you,** so that you will have to make much of them. 18 It is fine if somebody, meaning well, is always making much of you, not just while I'm with you.

19 My children, I'm suffering birth pains for you again till Christ is formed in you. 20 I could wish I were with you right now and could talk in a different tone of voice because I'm puzzled about you.

We Are like Isaac

21 Tell me, you who want to be under the Law, will you not listen to what the Law says? 22 It is written: Abraham had two sons; one was the son of the slave and the other the son of the free woman. 23 Now, the son of the slave was born like other children, but the son of the free woman by being promised.

24 This has a special meaning. The women are two covenants. The children of the covenant given on Mount Sinai are born to be slaves; this is Hagar. 25 "Hagar" in Arabia means Mount Sinai. She is like Jerusalem today, because she and her children are slaves. 26 But the Jerusalem that is above is free; and she is our mother. 27 It is written:

Be glad, barren woman, you who don't have any children;
Break into shouting, you who feel no pains of childbirth,
Because the deserted woman has many more children
Than the one who has the husband.[11]

28 Now you, my fellow Christians, like Isaac, are children born by a promise.

29 At that time the son born like other children persecuted the son born by the Spirit. And so it is now. 30 But what does the Bible say? Put away the slave and her son, because the son of the slave must not get any of the inheritance of the son[12] of the free woman. 31 Now, then, fellow Christians, we are not children of a slave but of a free woman.

* It may have been malaria which forced Paul to leave the swampy country of Pamphylia and to go up into the mountains, 3,600 feet above sea level, and so to come to the Galatians. (Acts 13: 13-14)
** Perhaps from Paul, who was anxious to win the non-Jews, and from happiness in Christ.
[11] Is. 54:1
[12] Gen. 21:10

K.J.V.

5 Stand fast therefore in the liberty where-with Christ hath made us free, and be not entangled again with the yoke of bondage. 2 Behold, I Paul say unto you, that if ye be circumcised, Christ shall profit you nothing. 3 For I testify again to every man that is circumcised, that he is a debtor to do the whole law. 4 Christ is become of no effect unto you, whosoever of you are justified by the law; ye are fallen from grace. 5 For we through the Spirit wait for the hope of righteousness by faith. 6 For in Jesus Christ neither circumcision availeth any thing, nor uncircumcision; but faith which worketh by love. 7 Yé did run well; who did hinder you that ye should not obey the truth? 8 This persuasion *cometh* not of him that calleth you. 9 A little leaven leaveneth the whole lump. 10 I have confidence in you through the Lord, that ye will be none otherwise minded: but he that troubleth you shall bear his judgment, whosoever he be. 11And I, brethren, if I yet preach circumcision, why do I yet suffer persecution? then is the offence of the cross ceased. 12 I would they were even cut off which trouble you. 13 For, brethren, ye have been called unto liberty; only *use* not liberty for an occasion to the flesh, but by love serve one another. 14 For all the law is fulfilled in one word, *even* in this; Thou shalt love thy neighbour as thyself. 15 But if ye bite and devour one another, take heed that ye be not consumed one of another. 16 *This* I say then, Walk in the Spirit, and ye shall not fulfil the lust of the flesh. 17 For the flesh lusteth against the Spirit, and the Spirit against the flesh: and these are contrary the one to the other; so that ye cannot do the things that ye would. 18 But if ye be led of the Spirit, ye are not under the law. 19 Now the works of the flesh are manifest, which are *these*, Adultery, fornication, uncleanness, lasciviousness, 20 Idolatry, witchcraft, hatred, variance, emulations, wrath, strife, seditions, heresies, 21 Envyings, murders, drunkenness, revellings, and such like: of the which I tell you before, as I have also told *you* in time past, that they which do such things shall not inherit the kingdom of God. 22 But the fruit of the Spirit is love, joy, peace, longsuffering, gentleness, goodness, faith, 23 Meekness, temperance: against such there is no law. 24And they that are Christ's have crucified the flesh with the affections and

N.A.S.

5 It was for freedom that Christ set us free: therefore keep standing firm and do not be subject again to a yoke of slavery. 2 Behold I, Paul, say to you that if you receive circumcision, Christ will be of no benefit to you. 3And I testify again to every man who receives circumcision, that he is under oblgiation to keep the whole Law. 4 You have been severed from Christ, you who are seeking to be justified by law; you have fallen from grace. 5 For we through the Spirit, by faith, are waiting for the hope of righteousness. 6 For in Christ Jesus neither circumcision nor uncircumcision means anything, but faith working through love. 7 You were running well; who hindered you from obeying the truth? 8 This persuasion *did* not *come* from Him who calls you. 9A little leaven leavens the whole lump *of dough*. 10 I have confidence in you in the Lord, that you will adopt no other view; but the one who is disturbing you shall bear his judgment, whoever he is. 11 But I, brethren, if I still preach circumcision, why am I still persecuted? Then the stumbling-block of the cross has been abolished. 12 Would that those who are troubling you would even mutilate themselves.

13 For you were called to freedom, brethren; only *do* not *turn* your freedom into an opportunity for the flesh, but through love serve one another. 14 For the whole Law is fulfilled in one word, in the *statement*, "YOU SHALL LOVE YOUR NEIGHBOR AS YOURSELF." 15 But if you bite and devour one another, take care lest you be consumed by one another.

16 But I say, walk by the Spirit, and you will not carry out the desire of the flesh. 17 For the flesh sets its desire against the Spirit, and the Spirit against the flesh; for these are in opposition to one another, so that you may not do the things that you please. 18 But if you are led by the Spirit, you are not under the Law. 19 Now the deeds of the flesh are evident, which are: immorality, impurity, sensuality, 20 idolatry, sorcery, enmities, strife, jealousy, outbursts of anger, disputes, dissentions, factions, 21 envyings, drunkenness, carousings, and things like these, of which I forewarn you just as I have forewarned you that those who practice such things shall not inherit the kingdom of God. 22 But the fruit of the Spirit is love, joy, peace, patience, kindness, goodness, faithfulness, 23 gentleness, self-control; against such things there is no law. 24 Now those who belong to Christ Jesus have crucified the flesh with its passions and desires.

WILLIAMS

BECK

WILLIAMS

5 *The legal way shuts out the faith way; the apostle's protest; love, the law of those not subject to the law; the struggle between the lower nature and the Spirit of God*

This is the freedom with which Christ has made us free. So keep on standing in it, and stop letting your necks be fastened in the yoke of slavery again.
2 Here is what I am saying to you: if you let yourselves be circumcised, Christ can do you no good. 3 I again insist that if any man lets himself be circumcised, he is under obligation to obey the whole law. 4 You people, whoever you are among you, who try to get into right standing with God through law have cut yourselves off from Christ, you have missed the way of God's favor.ᵃ 5 For we, by the Spirit, are awaiting the hoped-for blessing which our right standing with God will bring us. 6 For in union with Christ Jesus neither circumcision nor the lack of it counts for anything; but only faith that is spurred on to action by love.
7 You were running beautifully! Who was it that cut into your way and kept you from obeying the truth? 8 Such persuasion never came from Him who called you. 9 A little yeast will transform the whole dough. 10 By our union with the Lord I have confidence in you that you will take no other view of the matter. The man who is unsettling you will certainly pay the penalty for it, no matter who it turns out to be. 11 As for me, myself, brothers, if I am still preaching circumcision, why am I still being persecuted? In such a case the hindrance done by the cross has presumably ceased! 12 I almost wish that these men who are upsetting you would go all the way, and have themselves mutilated.
13 For you, brothers, were called to freedom; only you must not let your freedom be an excuse for the gratification of your lower nature, but in love be slaves to one another. 14 For the whole law is summed up in one saying, "You must love your neighbor as you do yourself." 15 But if you continue to bite and eat one another, beware lest you are destroyed by one another.
16 I mean this: Practice living by the Spirit and then by no means will you gratify the cravings of your lower nature. 17 For the cravings of the lower nature are just the opposite to those of the Spirit, and the cravings of the Spirit are just the opposite of those of the lower nature; these two are opposed to each other, so that you cannot do anything you please. 18 But if you are guided by the Spirit, you are not subject to the law. 19 Now the practices of the lower nature are clear enough: Sexual immorality, impurity, sensuality, 20 idolatry, sorcery, enmity, quarreling, jealousy, anger, intrigues, dissensions, party-spirit, 21 envy, drunkenness, carousing, and the like. I now warn you, as I have done before, that those who practice such things shall not be heirs of the kingdom of God. 22 But the product of the Spirit is love, joy, peace, patience, kindness, goodness, faithfulness, 23 gentleness, self-control. There is no law against such things. 24 And those who belong to Jesus the Christ have crucified the lower nature with its passions and evil cravings.

BECK

Christ Freed Us

5 Christ has freed us so that we'll be free. Stand firm, then, and don't get caught again under a yoke of slavery.
2 I, Paul, tell you, if you get circumcised, Christ will do you no good. 3 And again I warn everyone who gets circumcised he must do everything the Law says. 4 You who try to become righteous by the Law have cut yourselves off from Christ and lost God's love. 5 But we who believe by the Spirit eagerly wait for the hope of the righteous. 6 In Christ Jesus no circumcision or the lack of it can do anything but only faith that is active in love.
7 You were running well. Who has kept you from obeying the truth? 8 You were not persuaded by Him who called you. 9 A little yeast makes the whole dough sour. 10 I'm convinced in the Lord you'll think as I do, but anyone who troubles you will have to take his punishment, whoever he may be. 11 My fellow Christians, if I'm "still preaching that people have to be circumcised," why am I still persecuted? If I were preaching that, the Jews would have no reason to oppose the Cross. 12 I could wish the men who upset you would castrate themselves.
13 You were called to be free, my fellow Christians. Only don't use your freedom as a chance to sin as you like, but in love serve one another. 14 You keep the whole Law when you do one thing—*love your neighbor like yourself.*¹³ 15 But if you bite and eat one another, be careful, or you'll be devoured by one another.
16 I say, follow the Spirit, and you will not do what the flesh wants. 17 What the flesh wants is against the Spirit, and what the Spirit wants is against the flesh, because they are opposed to each other and so keep you from doing what you want to do. 18 But if the Spirit leads you, you are not under the Law.
19 Now, you know the works of the flesh. They are: sexual sin, uncleanness, wild living, 20 worshiping of idols, witchcraft, hate, wrangling, jealousy, anger, selfishness, quarreling, divisions, 21 envy, drunkenness, carousing, and the like. I warn you, as I did before, those who do such things will have no share in God's kingdom.
22 But the Spirit produces love, joy, peace. He makes us patient, kindly, good, faithful, 23 gentle, and gives us self-control. There's no law against such things. 24 But if we belong to Christ Jesus, we have crucified the flesh with

---

[a] Lit., *fallen out of the grace* (way).

[13] Lev. 19:18

K.J.V.

lusts. 25 If we live in the Spirit, let us also walk in the Spirit. 26 Let us not be desirous of vainglory, provoking one another, envying one another.

6 Brethren, if a man be overtaken in a fault, ye which are spiritual, restore such a one in the spirit of meekness; considering thyself, lest thou also be tempted. 2 Bear ye one another's burdens, and so fulfil the law of Christ. 3 For if a man think himself to be something, when he is nothing, he deceiveth himself. 4 But let every man prove his own work, and then shall he have rejoicing in himself alone, and not in another. 5 For every man shall bear his own burden. 6 Let him that is taught in the word communicate unto him that teacheth in all good things. 7 Be not deceived; God is not mocked: for whatsoever a man soweth, that shall he also reap. 8 For he that soweth to his flesh shall of the flesh reap corruption; but he that soweth to the Spirit shall of the Spirit reap life everlasting. 9 And let us not be weary in well doing: for in due season we shall reap, if we faint not. 10 As we have therefore opportunity, let us do good unto all men, especially unto them who are of the household of faith. 11 Ye see how large a letter I have written unto you with mine own hand. 12 As many as desire to make a fair shew in the flesh, they constrain you to be circumcised; only lest they should suffer persecution for the cross of Christ. 13 For neither they themselves who are circumcised keep the law; but desire to have you circumcised, that they may glory in your flesh. 14 But God forbid that I should glory, save in the cross of our Lord Jesus Christ, by whom the world is crucified unto me, and I unto the world. 15 For in Christ Jesus neither circumcision availeth any thing, nor uncircumcision, but a new creature. 16 And as many as walk according to this rule, peace *be* on them, and mercy, and upon the Israel of God. 17 From henceforth let no man trouble me: for I bear in my body the marks of the Lord Jesus. 18 Brethren, the grace of our Lord Jesus Christ *be* with your spirit. Amen.

Unto the Galatians written from Rome.

N.A.S.

25 If we live by the Spirit, let us also walk by the Spirit. 26 Let us not become boastful, challenging one another, envying one another.

6 Brethren, even if a man is caught in any trespass, you who are spiritual, restore such a one in a spirit of gentleness; looking to yourself, lest you too be tempted. 2 Bear one another's burdens, and thus fulfill the law of Christ. 3 For if anyone thinks he is something when he is nothing, he deceives himself. 4 But let each one examine his own work, and then he will have *reason for* boasting in regard to himself alone, and not in regard to another. 5 For each one shall bear his own load.

6 And let the one who is taught the word share all good things with him who teaches. 7 Do not be deceived, God is not mocked; for whatever a man sows, this he will also reap. 8 For the one who sows to his own flesh shall from the flesh reap corruption, but the one who sows to the Spirit shall from the Spirit reap eternal life. 9 And let us not lose heart in doing good, for in due time we shall reap if we do not grow weary. 10 So then, while we have opportunity, let us do good to all men, and especially to those who are of the household of the faith.

11 See with what large letters I am writing to you with my own hand. 12 Those who desire to make a good showing in the flesh try to compel you to be circumcised, simply that they may not be persecuted for the cross of Christ. 13 For those who "are circumcised do not even keep the Law themselves, but they desire to have you circumcised, that they may boast in your flesh. 14 But may it never be that I should boast, except in the cross of our Lord Jesus Christ, through which the world has been crucified to me, and I to the world. 15 For neither is circumcision anything, nor uncircumcision, but a new creation. 16 And those who will walk by this rule, peace and mercy *be* upon them, and upon the Israel of God.

17 From now on let no one cause trouble for me, for I bear on my body the brand-marks of Jesus.

18 The grace of our Lord Jesus Christ be with your spirit, brethren. Amen.

[a] Some ancient mss. read, *have been.*

WILLIAMS

25 If we live by the Spirit, let us also walk where the Spirit leads. 26 Let us stop being ambitious for honors, so challenging one another, envying one another.

6 *Sympathy to be shown the falling Christian; we reap what we sow; writer's own handwriting; boasts in the cross alone; says good-by*

Brothers, if anybody is caught in the very act of doing wrong, you who are spiritual, in the spirit of gentleness, must set him right; each of you continuing to think of yourself, for you may be tempted too. 2 Practice bearing one another's burdens, and in this way carry out the law of Christ. 3 For if anybody thinks he is somebody when really he is nobody, he deceives himself. 4 Everyone should test his own work until it stands the test, and then he will have ground for boasting with reference to himself alone, and not with reference to someone else. 5 For everyone must carry his own load.

6 Those who are taught the truth should share all their goods with the man who teaches them. 7 Do not be deceived any more; God is not to be scoffed at. A person will reap just what he sows, whatever it is. 8 The person who sows to gratify his lower nature will reap destruction from that lower nature, and the person who sows to gratify his higher nature will reap eternal life from the Spirit. 9 Let us stop getting tired of doing good, for at the proper time we shall reap if we do not give up. 10 So then whenever we have an opportunity, let us practice doing good to everybody, but especially to the members of the family of faith.

11 See what large letters I make, when I write to you with my own hand! 12 These men who are trying to force you to let yourselves be circumcised simply want to make a fine outward show, only to keep you from being persecuted for the cross of our Lord Jesus Christ. 13 Indeed, the very men who let themselves be circumcised do not themselves observe the law. But they simply want you to let yourselves be circumcised, so that they can boast of you as members of their party. 14 But may it never be mine to boast of anything but the cross of our Lord Jesus Christ, by which the world has been crucified to me and I to the world! 15 For neither circumcision nor the lack of it has any value, but only a new creation. 16 Now peace and mercy be on all who walk by this rule; that is, on the true Israel of God.

17 Let nobody trouble me after this, for I carry on my body the scars that mark me as Jesus' slave.

18 The spiritual blessing of our Lord Jesus Christ be with your spirit, brothers. Amen.

BECK

its passions and desires. 25 If we live by the Spirit, let us also follow the Spirit. 26 Let us not get conceited, challenge one another and get jealous of one another.

When Anyone Sins

6 My fellow Christians, if you find anyone doing wrong, you who have the Spirit should set him right. But be gentle and keep an eye on yourself; you may be tempted too. 2 Help one another carry these loads, and so do everything the Law of Christ demands.

3 If anyone thinks he's something when he's nothing, he's cheating himself. 4 Everyone should examine his own work. Then he will have something in himself that deserves praise, without comparing himself with anyone else. 5 Everyone will have to carry his own load.

We Reap What We Sow

6 If someone teaches you the Word, share all your good things with your teacher. 7 Don't make a mistake; you can't fool God. Whatever you sow you'll reap. 8 If you sow to please your own flesh, you will from your flesh reap destruction. If you sow to please the Spirit, you will from the Spirit reap everlasting life. 9 Let us not get tired of doing good. At the right time we'll reap if we don't give up. 10 So whenever we have a chance, let us do good to everybody but especially to our family of believers.

The World Is Crucified to Me

11 See what big letters I make when I write to you with my own hand.

12 These men who want to be popular in a worldly way are insisting you must be circumcised only to keep themselves from being persecuted for the Cross of Christ. 13 Why, these who are circumcised don't keep the Law themselves, but they want you to be circumcised so they can boast of that physical fact about you. 14 May I never boast of anything but the Cross of our Lord Jesus Christ, by whom the world is crucified to me and I to the world. 15 No circumcision or the lack of it is anything, but only the new life that is created. 16 *Peace* and mercy on all who follow this rule, that is, *on God's Israel.*[14]

17 From now on nobody should make trouble for me, because I have on my body the scars of a slave of Jesus.

18 The love of our Lord Jesus Christ be with your spirit, my fellow Christians. Amen.

[14] Ps. 125:5; 128:6

THE EPISTLE OF
PAUL THE APOSTLE
TO THE
EPHESIANS

THE EPISTLE OF PAUL
TO THE
EPHESIANS

1 Paul, an apostle of Jesus Christ by the will of God, to the saints which are at Ephesus, and to the faithful in Christ Jesus: 2 Grace *be* to you, and peace, from God our Father, and *from* the Lord Jesus Christ. 3 Blessed *be* the God and Father of our Lord Jesus Christ, who hath blessed us with all spiritual blessings in heavenly *places* in Christ: 4According as he hath chosen us in him before the foundation of the world, that we should be holy and without blame before him in love: 5 Having predestinated us unto the adoption of children by Jesus Christ to himself, according to the good pleasure of his will, 6 To the praise of the glory of his grace, wherein he hath made us accepted in the beloved: 7 In whom we have redemption through his blood, the forgiveness of sins, according to the riches of his grace; 8 Wherein he hath abounded toward us in all wisdom and prudence; 9 Having made known unto us the mystery of his will, according to his good pleasure which he hath purposed in himself: 10 That in the dispensation of the fulness of times he might gather together in one all things in Christ, both which are in heaven, and which are on earth; *even* in him: 11 In whom also we have obtained an inheritance, being predestinated according to the purpose of him who worketh all things after the counsel of his own will: 12 That we should be to the praise of his glory, who first trusted in Christ. 13 In whom ye also *trusted,* after that ye heard the word of truth, the gospel of your salvation: in whom also, after that ye believed, ye were sealed with that Holy Spirit of promise, 14 Which is the earnest of our inheritance until the redemption of the purchased possession, unto the praise of his glory. 15 Wherefore I also, after I heard of your faith in the Lord Jesus, and love unto all the saints, 16 Cease not to give thanks for you, making mention of you in my prayers; 17 That the God of our Lord Jesus Christ, the Father of glory, may give unto you the spirit of wisdom and revelation in the knowledge of him: 18 The eyes of your understanding being enlightened; that ye may know what is

1 Paul, an apostle of Christ Jesus by the will of God, to the saints who are *at Ephesus, and *who are* faithful in Christ Jesus: 2 Grace to you and peace from God our Father and the Lord Jesus Christ.
3 Blessed *be* the God and Father of our Lord Jesus Christ, who has blessed us with every spiritual blessing in the heavenly *places* in Christ, 4 just as He chose us in Him before the foundation of the world, that we should be holy and blameless before *b Him. In love 5 He predestined us to adoption as sons through Jesus Christ to Himself, according to the kind intention of His will, 6 to the praise of the glory of His grace, which He freely bestowed on us in the Beloved. 7 In Him we have redemption through His blood, the forgiveness of our trespasses, according to the riches of His grace, 8 which He lavished upon us. In all wisdom and insight 9 He made known to us the mystery of His will, according to His kind intention which He purposed in Him 10 with a view to an administration suitable to the fulness of the times, *that is,* the summing up of all things in Christ, things in the heavens and things upon the earth. In Him 11 also we have obtained an inheritance, having been predestined according to His purpose who works all things after the counsel of His will, 12 to the end that we who were the first to hope in *Christ should be to the praise of His glory. 13 In Him, you also, after listening to the message of truth, the gospel of your salvation—having also believed, you were sealed in Him with the Holy Spirit of promise, 14 who is given as a pledge of our inheritance, with a view to the redemption of *God's own* possession, to the praise of His glory.
15 For this reason I too, having heard of the faith in the Lord Jesus which *exists* among you, and *your love for all the saints, 16 do not cease giving thanks for you, while making mention *of you* in my prayers; 17 that the God of our Lord Jesus Christ, the Father of glory, may give to you a spirit of wisdom and of revelation in the knowledge of Him. 18 *I pray that* the eyes of your heart may be enlightened, so that you may know what is the hope of His

[a] Some ancient mss. omit, *at Ephesus.* [b] Or, *Him, in love.* [c] I.e., *the Messiah.* [d] Many ancient mss. omit, *your love.*

WILLIAMS   BECK

EPHESIANS

PAUL

WRITES TO THE

EPHESIANS

1 *He greets them; tells of God's eternal purpose of love; universal ransom by Christ; tells that the Spirit stamps believers as God's own; he prays his first prayer for them to realize their hope and God's power*

Paul, by God's will an apostle of Christ Jesus, to God's people[a] who are faithful in Christ Jesus; 2 spiritual blessing and peace to you from God our Father and the Lord Jesus Christ.

3 Blessed be the God and Father of our Lord Jesus Christ, who through Christ has blessed us with every spiritual blessing in the heavenly realm. 4 Through Him He picked us out[b] before the creation of the world, to be consecrated and above reproach in His sight in love. 5 He foreordained us to become His sons by adoption through Christ Jesus, to carry out the happy choice of His will, 6 so that we might praise the splendid favor which He has shown us in His beloved Son. 7 It is through union with Him that we have redemption by His blood and the forgiveness of our shortcomings, in accordance with the generosity of His unmerited favor 8 which He lavished upon us. Through perfect wisdom and spiritual insight 9 He has made known to us the secret of His will, which is in accordance with His purpose which He planned in Christ, 10 so that, at the coming of the climax of the ages, everything in heaven and on earth should be unified through Christ, 11 in union with whom we were made God's portion, since we had been foreordained in accordance with the purpose of Him who in everything carries out the plan of His will, 12 that we who had first put our hope in Christ might praise His glory. 13 You too, as you have heard the message of the truth, the good news that means your salvation, and as you have trusted in Him too, have been stamped with the seal of the promised Holy Spirit, 14 who is the first installment of our inheritance, so that we may finally come into full possession of the prize of redemption, and praise His glory for it.

15 This is why I myself, since I have heard of your faith in the Lord Jesus and in all His people, 16 never cease to thank God for you when I mention you in my prayers, 17 that the God of our Lord Jesus Christ, the glorious Father, may grant you the Spirit to give wisdom and revelation which come through a growing knowledge of Him, 18 by having the eyes of your hearts enlightened, so that you may know what the hope is to which He calls

1 Paul, apostle of Christ Jesus by God's will, to the people who are holy and faithful in Christ Jesus: 2 May God our Father and the Lord Jesus Christ love you and give you peace.

What God Has Done

3 Let us praise the God and Father of our Lord Jesus Christ, who in Christ has blessed us with every spiritual blessing in heaven.

5 He has done what in His kindness He planned to do: 4 Before He made the world, He who loved us 5 appointed us to be made His sons by Jesus Christ. 4 In Him He chose us to be holy and blameless before Him 6 in order to praise the glory of the love 7 He gave us in His dear Son, who bought us with His blood to forgive our sins and set us free. So 8 He poured out the riches of His love on us, giving us every kind of wisdom and understanding 9 as He told us the hidden meaning of His will.

It was His kindly purpose in Christ 10 to manage everything in heaven and on earth in such a way that when the right time would come it would all be organized under Christ as its Head.

11 He who accomplishes everything just as He wants to plan it long ago appointed us in Christ and chose us according to His purpose 12 that we, the first to find our hope in Christ, should live to praise His glory. 13 When you heard the message of the truth, the good news that you were saved, and you believed in Him, you, too, were sealed in Him by the Holy Spirit—whom He promised 14 and who is now the Guarantee of our inheritance—that He might free you to be His people and to praise His glory.

I'm Praying for You

15 That is why, since I heard how you believe in the Lord Jesus and love all the holy people, 16 I never stop thanking God for you as I remember you in my prayers. 17 I ask the God of our Lord Jesus Christ, the Father of glory, to give you His Spirit to make you wise and reveal the truth to you as you learn to know Him better 18 and to enlighten the eyes of your minds so that you know the hope He

[a] Om. *In Eph.*, on evidence of best Mss. [b] Exact meaning of Grk. vb., *to elect.*

K.J.V.

the hope of his calling, and what the riches of the glory of his inheritance in the saints, 19And what *is* the exceeding greatness of his power to us-ward who believe, according to the working of his mighty power, 20 Which he wrought in Christ, when he raised him from the dead, and set *him* at his own right hand in the heavenly *places,* 21 Far above all principality, and power, and might, and dominion, and every name that is named, not only in this world, but also in that which is to come: 22And hath put all *things* under his feet, and gave him *to be* the head over all *things* to the church, 23 Which is his body, the fulness of him that filleth all in all.

2 And you *hath he quickened,* who were dead in trespasses and sins; 2 Wherein in time past ye walked according to the course of this world, according to the prince of the power of the air, the spirit that now worketh in the children of disobedience: 3Among whom also we all had our conversation in times past in the lusts of our flesh, fulfilling the desires of the flesh and of the mind; and were by nature the children of wrath, even as others. 4 But God, who is rich in mercy, for his great love wherewith he loved us, 5 Even when we were dead in sins, hath quickened us together with Christ, (by grace ye are saved;) 6And hath raised *us* up together, and made *us* sit together in heavenly *places* in Christ Jesus: 7 That in the ages to come he might shew the exceeding riches of his grace, in *his* kindness toward us, through Christ Jesus. 8 For by grace are ye saved through faith; and that not of yourselves: *it is* the gift of God: 9 Not of works, lest any man should boast. 10 For we are his workmanship, created in Christ Jesus unto good works, which God hath before ordained that we should walk in them. 11 Wherefore remember, that ye *being* in time past Gentiles in the flesh, who are called Uncircumcision by that which is called the Circumcision in the flesh made by hands; 12 That at that time ye were without Christ, being aliens from the commonwealth of Israel, and strangers from the covenants of promise, having no hope, and without God in the world: 13 But now, in Christ Jesus, ye who sometime were far off are made nigh by the blood of Christ. 14 For he is our peace, who hath made both one, and hath broken down the middle wall of partition *between us;* 15 Having abolished in his flesh the enmity, *even* the law of commandments *contained* in ordinances; for to make in himself of twain one new man, *so* making peace; 16And that he might reconcile both unto God in one body by the cross, having slain the enmity thereby: 17And came and preached peace to you which were afar off, and to them

N.A.S.

calling, what are the riches of the glory of His inheritance in the saints, 19 and what is the surpassing greatness of His power toward us who believe. *These are* in accordance with the working of the strength of His might 20 which He brought about in Christ, when He raised Him from the dead, and seated Him at His right hand in the heavenly *places,* 21 far above all rule and authority and power and dominion, and every name that is named, not only in this age, but also in the one to come. 22And He put all things in subjection under His feet, and gave Him as head over all things to the church, 23 which is His body, the fulness of Him who fills all in all.

2 And you were dead in your trespasses and sins, 2 in which you formerly walked according to the course of this world, according to the prince of the power of the air, of the spirit that is now working in the sons of disobedience. 3Among them we too all formerly lived in the lusts of our flesh, indulging the desires of the flesh and of the mind, and were by nature children of wrath, even as the rest. 4 But God, being rich in mercy, because of His great love with which He loved us, 5 even when we were dead in our transgressions, made us alive together ªwith Christ (by grace you have been saved), 6 and raised us up with Him, and seated us with Him in the heavenly *places,* in Christ Jesus, 7 in order that in the ages to come He might show the surpassing riches of His grace in kindness toward us in Christ Jesus. 8 For by grace you have been saved through faith; and that not of yourselves, *it is* the gift of God; 9 not as a result of works, that no one should boast. 10 For we are His workmanship, created in Christ Jesus for good works, which God prepared beforehand, that we should walk in them.

11 Therefore remember, that formerly you, the Gentiles in the flesh, who are called "Uncircumcision" by the so-called "Circumcision," *which is* performed in the flesh by human hands— 12 *remember* that you were at that time separate from Christ, excluded from the commonwealth of Israel, and strangers to the covenants of promise, having no hope and without God in the world. 13 But now in Christ Jesus you who formerly were far off have been brought near by the blood of Christ. 14 For He Himself is our peace, who made both *groups into* one, and broke down the barrier of the dividing wall, 15 by abolishing in His flesh the enmity, *which is* the Law of commandments *contained* in ordinances, that in Himself He might make the two into one new man, *thus* establishing peace, 16 and might reconcile them both in one body to God through the cross, by it having put to death the enmity. 17AND HE CAME AND PREACHED PEACE TO YOU WHO WERE FAR AWAY, AND PEACE TO THOSE WHO WERE

---

[a] Some ancient mss. read, *in Christ.*

WILLIAMS

you, how gloriously rich God's portion in His people is, 19 and how surpassingly great is His power for us who believe, measured by His tremendously mighty power 20 when He raised Christ from the dead, and seated Him at His right hand in heaven, 21 far above every other government, authority, power, and dominion, yea, far above every other title that can be conferred, not only in this world but in the world to come. 22And so He has put all things under His feet and made Him the supreme Head of the church, 23 which is His body, that is being filled by Him who fills everything everywhere.

2 *Jews and heathen, lost in sin, saved by God's unmerited favor through faith in Christ; Christ the bond of international peace*

You too were dead because of the shortcomings and sins 2 in which you once lived in accordance with the spirit of this present world, and the mighty prince of the air, who is always at work in the disobedient, among whom all of us, we Jews as well as you heathen, 3 once lived while gratifying the cravings of our lower nature, as we continued to carry out the impulses of our lower nature and its thoughts, and by nature we were exposed to God's wrath, as the rest of mankind. 4 But God, who is so rich in mercy on account of the great love He has for us, 5 has made us, though dead because of our shortcomings, live again in fellowship with Christ—it is by His unmerited favor that you have been saved. 6And He raised us with Him and through union with Christ Jesus He made us sit down with Him in the heavenly realm, 7 to show, throughout the coming ages, the boundless generosity of His unmerited favor shown us in His goodness to us through Christ Jesus. 8 For it is by His unmerited favor through faith that you have been saved; it is not by anything that you have done, it is the gift of God. 9 It is not the result of what anyone can do, so that no one can boast of it. 10 For He has made us what we are, because He has created us through our union with Christ Jesus for doing good deeds which He beforehand planned for us to do. 11 So remember that you were once heathen in a physical sense, called the uncircumcised by those who call themselves the circumcised—though only in a physical sense, by human hands. 12At that time you were without any connection with Christ; you were aliens to the commonwealth of Israel, strangers to the sacred compacts made by God's promise, with no hope, and no God in the world. 13 But now through your union with Christ Jesus you who were once far away have through the blood of Christ been brought near. 14 For He Himself is our peace, He is the one who has made us both into one body and has broken down the barrier that kept us apart; 15 through His human nature He has put a stop to the hostility between us, namely, the law with its commands and decrees, in order to create one new humanity out of the two parties and so make peace through union with Himself, and in one body 16 to reconcile them both to God with His cross after He had killed the hostility through it. 17 When He came, He brought the good news of peace for you who were far away

BECK

called you to, the riches of the glory of the *inheritance* He gives to *His holy people*,[1] 19 and the vast resources of His power working in us who believe. It is the same mighty power 20 with which He worked in Christ, raised Him from the dead, and *made Him sit at His right*[2] in heaven, 21 above all rulers, authorities, powers, lords, and any name that can be mentioned, not only in this world but also in the next. 22And *He put everything under His feet*,[3] and gave Him as the Head of everything to the church, 23 which is His body, having all that is in Him who fills everything in every way.

God's Love Saved You

2 You, too, were dead in your transgressions and sins, 2 in which you once followed the ways of this present world and the ruler whose power is in the air, the spirit who is now working in the people who disobey. 3Among them all of us once lived in our fleshly lusts, doing what our flesh and mind wanted to do, and by nature we, like the others, were people with whom God was angry.

4 But God, who is rich in mercy, loved us with such a great love 5 He made us who were dead in sins alive with Christ. (You are saved by a gift of His love.) 6And since we are in Christ Jesus, He raised us with Him and had us sit with Him in heaven 7 to show in the coming ages the immeasurable riches of His love by being kind to us in Christ Jesus. 8 You are saved by a gift of love you get by faith. You didn't do it. It is God's gift. 9 It isn't because of anything you have done, or you might boast. 10 He has made us what we are, creating us in Christ Jesus to do good works, which God long ago planned for us to live in.

Jews and Non-Jews

11 Remember, then, physically you once were Gentiles, and those who call themselves "circumcised" (which is physical and done by human hands) called you "uncircumcised." 12 You were then without Christ, excluded from being citizens of Israel and strangers to the covenants that had the promise. You had no hope or God in the world. 13 Once you were *far away*, but now in Christ Jesus the blood of Christ has brought you *near*. 14 He is our *Peace*:[4] In His flesh He has made the Jew and the non-Jew one by breaking down the wall of enmity that kept them apart 15 and by putting away the Law with its rules and regulations, in order to make the Jew and the non-Jew in Himself one new man (so making peace) 16 and to make both in one body friends with God by His cross, on which He killed the enmity. 17And He came with *the good news of peace*[5] *to you who were far away and to us who were near*,[4]

[1] Deut. 33:3-4
[2] Ps. 110:1
[3] Ps. 8:6
[4] Is. 57:19
[5] Is. 52:7

K.J.V.

that were nigh. 18 For through him we both have access by one Spirit unto the Father. 19 Now therefore ye are no more strangers and foreigners, but fellow citizens with the saints, and of the household of God; 20And are built upon the foundation of the apostles and prophets, Jesus Christ himself being the chief corner *stone;* 21 In whom all the building fitly framed together groweth unto a holy temple in the Lord: 22 In whom ye also are builded together for a habitation of God through the Spirit.

3 For this cause I Paul, the prisoner of Jesus Christ for you Gentiles, 2 If ye have heard of the dispensation of the grace of God which is given me to you-ward: 3 How that by revelation he made known unto me the mystery; (as I wrote afore in few words; 4 Whereby, when ye read, ye may understand my knowledge in the mystery of Christ,) 5 Which in other ages was not made known unto the sons of men, as it is now revealed unto his holy apostles and prophets by the Spirit; 6 That the Gentiles should be fellow heirs, and of the same body, and partakers of his promise in Christ by the gospel: 7 Whereof I was made a minister, according to the gift of the grace of God given unto me by the effectual working of his power. 8 Unto me, who am less than the least of all saints, is this grace given, that I should preach among the Gentiles the unsearchable riches of Christ; 9And to make all *men* see what *is* the fellowship of the mystery, which from the beginning of the world hath been hid in God, who created all things by Jesus Christ: 10 To the intent that now unto the principalities and powers in heavenly *places* might be known by the church the manifold wisdom of God, 11According to the eternal purpose which he purposed in Christ Jesus our Lord: 12 In whom we have boldness and access with confidence by the faith of him. 13 Wherefore I desire that ye faint not at my tribulations for you, which is your glory. 14 For this cause I bow my knees unto the Father of our Lord Jesus Christ, 15 Of whom the whole family in heaven and earth is named, 16 That he would grant you, according to the riches of his glory, to be strengthened with might by his Spirit in the inner man; 17 That Christ may dwell in your hearts by faith; that ye, being rooted and grounded in love, 18 May be able to comprehend with all saints what *is* the breadth, and length, and depth, and height; 19 And to know the love of Christ, which passeth knowledge, that ye might be filled with all the fulness of God. 20 Now unto him that is able to do exceeding

N.A.S.

NEAR; 18 for through Him we both have our access in one Spirit to the Father. 19 So then you are no longer strangers and aliens, but you are fellow-citizens with the saints, and are of God's household, 20 having been built upon the foundation of the apostles and prophets, Christ Jesus Himself being the cornerstone, 21 in whom the whole building, being fitted together is growing into a holy temple in the Lord; 22 in whom you also are being built together into a dwelling of God in the Spirit.

3 For this reason I, Paul, the prisoner of Christ Jesus for the sake of you Gentiles— 2 if indeed you have heard of the stewardship of God's grace which was given to me for you; 3 that by revelation there was made known to me the mystery, as I wrote before in brief. 4And by referring to this, when you read you can understand my insight into the mystery of Christ, 5 which in other generations was not made known to the sons of men, as it has now been revealed to His holy apostles and prophets in the Spirit; 6 *to be specific,* that the Gentiles are fellow-heirs and fellow-members of the body, and fellow-partakers of the promise in Christ Jesus through the gospel, 7 of which I was made a minister, according to the gift of God's grace which was given to me according to the working of His power. 8 To me, the very least of all saints, this grace was given, to preach to the Gentiles the unfathomable riches of Christ, 9 and to bring to light what is the administration of the mystery which for ages has been hidden in God, who created all things; 10 in order that the manifold wisdom of God might now be made known through the church to the rulers and the authorities in the heavenly *places.* 11 *This was* in accordance with the eternal purpose which He carried out in Christ Jesus our Lord, 12 in whom we have boldness and confident access through faith in Him. 13 Therefore I ask you not to lose heart at my tribulations on your behalf, for they are your glory.

14 For this reason, I bow my knees before the Father, 15 from whom every family in heaven and on earth derives its name, 16 that He would grant you, according to the riches of His glory, to be strengthened with power through His Spirit in the inner man; 17 so that Christ may dwell in your hearts through faith; *and* that you, being rooted and grounded in love, 18 may be able to comprehend with all the saints what is the breadth and length and height and depth, 19 and to know the love of Christ which surpasses knowledge, that you may be filled up to all the fulness of God.

20 Now to Him who is able to do exceeding

WILLIAMS

and for you who were near; 18 for it is by Him through one Spirit that both of us now have an introduction to the Father. 19 So you are no longer foreigners and strangers, but you are fellow-citizens of God's people and members of His family; 20 for you are built upon the foundation of the apostles and prophets, with Christ Jesus Himself the cornerstone. 21 In union with Him the whole building is harmoniously fitted together and continues to grow into a temple, sacred through its union with the Lord, 22 and you yourselves, in union with Him, in fellowship with one another, are being built up into a dwelling for God through the Spirit.

3 *Paul is entrusted with the secret of universal peace; again he prays for his readers to have spiritual strength, to have Christ in their hearts, and to know Christ's boundless love*

This is why I, Paul, a prisoner of Christ Jesus for the sake of the heathen—2 that is, if you have heard how God's favor has been entrusted to me for you, 3 and how by revelation the secret was made known to me, as I have briefly written before. 4 By reading this you will be able to understand my insight into the secret about the Christ—5 which in the earlier ages, so different from the present, was not made known to mankind as fully as now, but through the Spirit it has been revealed to His holy apostles and prophets—6 that the heathen through union with Christ Jesus are fellow-heirs with the Jews, are members with them of the same body, and sharers with them of the promise through the good news, 7 for which I was called to serve in accordance with the gift of God's unmerited favor which was bestowed on me by the exercise of His power—8 yes, on me, the very least of all His people, this unmerited favor was bestowed—that I might preach as good news to the heathen the boundless riches of Christ, 9 and to make clear how is to be carried out the trusteeship of this secret which has for ages been hidden away in God, the Creator of all things, 10 so that the many phases of God's wisdom may now through the church be made known to the rulers and authorities in heaven, 11 in accordance with the eternal purpose which God executed in the gift of Christ Jesus our Lord. 12 By union with Him and through faith in Him we have a free and confidential introduction to God. 13 So I beg you not to lose heart over the sorrows that I am suffering for your sake, for they bring you honor. 14 For this reason I kneel before the Father, 15 from whom every family in heaven and on earth derives its name, 16 and beg Him to grant you, in accordance with the riches of His perfect character, to be mightily strengthened by His Spirit in your inmost being, 17 and that Christ in His love, through your faith, may make His permanent home in your hearts. You must be deeply rooted, your foundations must be strong, 18 so that you with all God's people may be strong enough to grasp the idea of the breadth and length, the height and depth, 19 yes, to come at last to know the love of Christ, although it far surpasses human understanding, so that you may be filled with the perfect fullness of God. 20 To Him who by

BECK

18 since by one Spirit He enables both to come to the Father.

19 Then you are no longer foreigners or strangers but fellow citizens, a part of God's holy people and members of His family. 20 You are built on the *foundation* of the apostles and prophets, and Christ Jesus Himself is the *Cornerstone*.[6] 21 In Him the whole building is fitted together and grows to be a holy temple in the Lord. 22 In Him you, too, are built up with the others to be God's home in the Spirit.

God's Purpose in Me

3 For this reason I, Paul, whom Christ Jesus made a prisoner for you who are not Jews—* 2 surely you've heard how God gave me gifts of His love to bring you 3 and how He revealed to me the hidden truth, as I have briefly written. 4 When you read this, you can see I understand the hidden truth of Christ. 5 The people of other times weren't told about it as the Spirit now has revealed it to His holy apostles and prophets, 6 that in Christ Jesus the people who are not Jews have the same inheritance, belong to the same body, and have the same promise through the good news.

7 I was made a servant of it by the gift of love God gave me by the working of His power. 8 To me, the least of all His holy people, He gave this gift of His love: to bring the news of the unsearchable riches of Christ to the non-Jews 9 and let everybody see clearly what God planned to do according to the truth hidden from the beginning in God, who created everything, 10 so that through the church God's many-sided wisdom would now be shown to the rulers and authorities in heaven. 11 He planned it through the ages and then did it in Christ Jesus, our Lord. 12 In Him, by believing in Him, we have confidence and can boldly come to God. 13 So I ask you not to get discouraged by what I suffer for you. It is an honor to you.

How Christ Loves Me

14 For this reason I kneel before the "Father," 15 from whom every group in heaven and on earth gets the name of "family," ** 16 and ask Him, as He is rich in glory, to give you this: that His Spirit will inwardly strengthen you with power, 17 Christ will live in your hearts by faith, and you will be firmly rooted and built up in love 18 so that you and all the holy people can grasp how broad and long and high and deep love is, 19 and know how Christ loves us—more than we can know—and so you will be filled with all that is in God.

20 Now to Him who by the power working

---

* Here Paul breaks off and doesn't take up the thought again until v. 14.
** "Family" (= clan) in Greek is the same word as "Father" with a special ending.
[6] Is. 28:16

K.J.V.

abundantly above all that we ask or think, according to the power that worketh in us, 21 Unto him *be* glory in the church by Christ Jesus throughout all ages, world without end. Amen.

4 I therefore, the prisoner of the Lord, beseech you that ye walk worthy of the vocation wherewith ye are called, 2 With all lowliness and meekness, with longsuffering, forbearing one another in love; 3 Endeavouring to keep the unity of the Spirit in the bond of peace. 4 *There is* one body, and one Spirit, even as ye are called in one hope of your calling; 5 One Lord, one faith, one baptism, 6 One God and Father of all, who *is* above all, and through all, and in you all. 7 But unto every one of us is given grace according to the measure of the gift of Christ. 8 Wherefore he saith, When he ascended up on high, he led captivity captive, and gave gifts unto men. 9 (Now that he ascended, what is it but that he also descended first into the lower parts of the earth? 10 He that descended is the same also that ascended up far above all heavens, that he might fill all things.) 11 And he gave some, apostles; and some, prophets; and some, evangelists; and some, pastors and teachers; 12 For the perfecting of the saints, for the work of the ministry, for the edifying of the body of Christ: 13 Till we all come in the unity of the faith, and of the knowledge of the Son of God, unto a perfect man, unto the measure of the stature of the fulness of Christ: 14 That we *henceforth* be no more children, tossed to and fro, and carried about with every wind of doctrine, by the sleight of men, *and* cunning craftiness, whereby they lie in wait to deceive; 15 But speaking the truth in love, may grow up into him in all things, which is the head, *even* Christ: 16 From whom the whole body fitly joined together and compacted by that which every joint supplieth, according to the effectual working in the measure of every part, maketh increase of the body unto the edifying of itself in love. 17 This I say therefore, and testify in the Lord, that ye henceforth walk not as other Gentiles walk, in the vanity of their mind, 18 Having the understanding darkened, being alienated from the life of God through the ignorance that is in them, because of the blindness of their heart: 19 Who being past feeling have given themselves over unto lasciviousness, to work all uncleanness with greediness. 20 But ye have not so learned Christ; 21 If so be that ye have heard him, and have been taught by him, as the truth is in Jesus:

N.A.S.

abundantly beyond all that we ask or think, according to the power that works within us, 21 to Him *be* the glory in the church and in Christ Jesus to all generations forever and ever. Amen.

4 I therefore, the prisoner of the Lord, entreat you to walk in a manner worthy of the calling with which you have been called, 2 with all humility and gentleness, with patience, showing forbearance to one another in love, 3 being diligent to preserve the unity of the Spirit in the bond of peace. 4 *There is* one body and one Spirit, just as also you were called in one hope of your calling; 5 one Lord, one faith, one baptism, 6 one God and Father of all who is over all and through all and in all. 7 But to each one of us grace was given according to the measure of Christ's gift. 8 Therefore it says,
"WHEN HE ASCENDED ON HIGH,
HE LED CAPTIVE A HOST OF CAPTIVES,
AND HE GAVE GIFTS TO MEN."
9 (Now this *expression,* "He ascended," what does it mean except that He also had descended into the lower parts of the earth? 10 He who descended is Himself also He who ascended far above all the heavens, that He might fill all things.) 11 And He gave some *as* apostles, and some *as* prophets, and some *as* evangelists, and some *as* pastors and teachers, 12 for the equipping of the saints for the work of service, to the building up of the body of Christ; 13 until we all attain to the unity of the faith, and of the knowledge of the Son of God, to a mature man, to the measure of the stature which belongs to the fulness of Christ. 14 As a result, we are no longer to be children, tossed here and there by waves, and carried about by every wind of doctrine, by the trickery of men, by craftiness in deceitful scheming; 15 but speaking the truth in love, we are to grow up in all *aspects* into Him, who is the head, *even* Christ, 16 from whom the whole body, being fitted and held together by that which every joint supplies, according to the proper working of each individual part, causes the growth of the body for the building up of itself in love.

17 This I say therefore, and affirm together with the Lord, that you walk no longer just as the Gentiles also walk, in the futility of their mind, 18 being darkened in their understanding, excluded from the life of God, because of the ignorance that is in them, because of the hardness of their heart; 19 and they, having become callous, have given themselves over to sensuality, for the practice of every kind of impurity with greediness. 20 But you did not learn Christ in this way, 21 if indeed you have heard Him and have been taught in Him, just as truth is in

WILLIAMS

His power that is at work within us can do surpassingly more than all we ask or imagine, 21 be glory in the church and through Christ Jesus to all generations for ever and ever. Amen.

4 *The moral and spiritual life: to be fostered through unity and service rendered by all with varying gifts; vices to be laid aside, virtues cultivated*

So I, a prisoner for the Lord's sake, entreat you to live lives worthy of the call you have received, 2 with perfect humility and gentleness, with patience, lovingly bearing with one another, 3 continuing with eager earnestness to maintain the unity of the Spirit through the tie of peace. 4 There is but one body and one Spirit, just as there is but one hope resulting from the call you have received; 5 there is but one Lord, one faith, one baptism, 6 one God and Father of all, who is over us all, who pervades us all, and who is within us all.

7 In accordance with the measure of Christ's gift, His favor has been bestowed upon each one of us. 8 Concerning this the Scripture says:

"He led a host of captives, when He went up on high,
And granted gifts to men."

9 What does "He went up" mean, except that He had first gone down into the lower regions of the earth? 10 The very One that went down has gone up, too, far above all the heavens, to fill the universe.[a] 11 And He has given some men to be apostles, some to be prophets, some to be evangelists, some to be pastors and teachers, 12 for the immediate equipment of God's people for the work of service, for the ultimate building up of the body of Christ, 13 until we all attain to unity in faith and to perfect knowledge of the Son of God, namely, to a mature manhood and to a perfect measure of Christ's moral stature; 14 so that we may not be babies any longer, or like sailors tossed about and driven around by every wind of doctrine, by the trickery of men through their cunning in inventing new methods of error. 15 But, on the other hand, we shall go on holding to the truth and in love growing up into perfect union with Him, that is, Christ Himself who is the Head. 16 For it is under His direction that the whole body is perfectly adjusted and united by every joint that furnishes its supplies; and by the proper functioning of each particular part there is brought about the growing of the body for its building up in love.

17 So I mean this and now testify to it in the name of the Lord: You must now stop living as the heathen usually do, in the frivolity of their minds, 18 with darkened understanding, estranged from the life of God because of the ignorance that exists among them and because of the stubbornness of their hearts; 19 for in their recklessness they have abandoned themselves to sensuality which leads to excessive practices of all sorts of immorality. 20 But this is not the way you have learned what Christ means, 21 if, as I take it, you have heard Him and in union with Him have been taught the truth as it is seen in Jesus,

BECK

in us can do far, far more than anything we ask or imagine, 21 to Him be glory in the church and in Christ Jesus to all ages forever. Amen.

We Are One

4 So I, a prisoner in the Lord, urge you to live as people whom God has called should live. 2 Be humble and gentle in every way, be patient, and lovingly bear with one another. 3 Do your best to keep the oneness of the Spirit by living together in peace: 4 one body and one Spirit—even as you have been called to share one hope— 5 one Lord, one faith, one baptism, 6 one God and Father of all, who rules over us all, works through us all, and lives in us all.

7 But each of us has been given the gift measured out by Christ who gave it. 8 So it says: He *went up on high, took prisoners,* and gave *gifts to people.*[7] 9 Now what can "He went up" mean but that He had gone down to the lower parts of the earth? 10 He who went down also "went up" above all the heavens to fill everything. 11 And He gave us some men to be apostles, some to speak the Word, some to tell the good news, some to be pastors and teachers, 12 in order to get His holy people ready to serve as workers and build the body of Christ 13 till all of us get to be one as we believe and know God's Son, reach a mature manhood, and grow to the full height of Christ. 14 We shouldn't be babies any longer, tossed and driven by every windy thing that is taught, by the trickery of men and their clever scheming in error. 15 Let us tell the truth with love and in every way grow up into Him who is the Head—Christ. 16 He makes the whole body fit together, unites it by every contact with its support, and to the extent that each part is working He makes the body grow and builds it up in love.

A New Life

17 So I tell you and call on you in the Lord not to live any more like the people of the world. Their minds are set on worthless things. 18 Their understanding is darkened. Their ignorance and their closed minds have made them strangers to the life God gives. 19 Having lost their sense of right and wrong, they've given themselves up to a life of lust to practice every kind of vice with greed.

20 But that is not what you learned when you got to know Christ, 21 if you have heard Him and in Him have been taught the truth

[a] Lit., *the all things,* so universe.

[7] Ps. 68:18

K.J.V.

22 That ye put off concerning the former conversation the old man, which is corrupt according to the deceitful lusts; 23And be renewed in the spirit of your mind; 24And that ye put on the new man, which after God is created in righteousness and true holiness. 25 Wherefore putting away lying, speak every man truth with his neighbour: for we are members one of another. 26 Be ye angry, and sin not: let not the sun go down upon your wrath: 27 Neither give place to the devil. 28 Let him that stole steal no more: but rather let him labour, working with *his* hands the thing which is good, that he may have to give to him that needeth. 29 Let no corrupt communication proceed out of your mouth, but that which is good to the use of edifying, that it may minister grace unto the hearers. 30And grieve not the Holy Spirit of God, whereby ye are sealed unto the day of redemption. 31 Let all bitterness, and wrath, and anger, and clamour, and evil speaking, be put away from you, with all malice: 32And be ye kind one to another, tenderhearted, forgiving one another, even as God for Christ's sake hath forgiven you.

5 Be ye therefore followers of God, as dear children; 2And walk in love, as Christ also hath loved us, and hath given himself for us an offering and a sacrifice to God for a sweet-smelling savour. 3 But fornication, and all uncleanness, or covetousness, let it not be once named among you, as becometh saints; 4 Neither filthiness, nor foolish talking, nor jesting, which are not convenient: but rather giving of thanks. 5 For this ye know, that no whoremonger, nor unclean person, nor covetous man, who is an idolater, hath any inheritance in the kingdom of Christ and of God. 6 Let no man deceive you with vain words: for because of these things cometh the wrath of God upon the children of disobedience. 7 Be not ye therefore partakers with them. 8 For ye were sometime darkness, but now *are ye* light in the Lord: walk as children of light; 9 (For the fruit of the Spirit *is* in all goodness and righteousness and truth;) 10 Proving what is acceptable unto the Lord. 11And have no fellowship with the unfruitful works of darkness, but rather reprove *them*. 12 For it is a shame even to speak of those things which are done of them in secret. 13 But all things that are reproved are made manifest by the light: for whatsoever doth make manifest is light. 14 Wherefore he saith, Awake thou that sleepest, and arise from the dead, and Christ

N.A.S.

Jesus, 22 that, in reference to your former manner of life, you lay aside the old self, which is being corrupted in accordance with the lusts of deceit, 23 and that you be renewed in the spirit of your mind, 24 and put on the new self, which in *the likeness of* God has been created in righteousness and holiness of the truth.

25 Therefore, laying aside falsehood, SPEAK TRUTH, EACH ONE *of* you, WITH HIS NEIGHBOR, for we are members of one another. 26 BE ANGRY, AND *yet* DO NOT SIN; do not let the sun go down on your anger, 27 and do not give the devil an opportunity. 28 Let him who steals steal no longer; but rather let him labor, performing with his own hands what is good, in order that he may have *something* to share with him who has need. 29 Let no unwholesome word proceed from your mouth, but only such *a word* as is good for edification according to the need *of the moment*, that it may give grace to those who hear. 30And do not grieve the Holy Spirit of God, by whom you were sealed for the day of redemption. 31 Let all bitterness and wrath and anger and clamor and slander be put away from you, along with all malice. 32And be kind to one another, tender-hearted, forgiving each other, just as God in Christ also has forgiven ªyou.

5 Therefore be imitators of God, as beloved children; 2 and walk in love, just as Christ also loved ªyou, and gave Himself up for us, an offering and a sacrifice to God as a fragrant aroma.
3 But do not let immorality or any impurity or greed even be named among you, as is proper among saints; 4 and *there must be no* filthiness and silly talk, or coarse jesting, which are not fitting, but rather giving of thanks. 5 For this you know with certainty, that no immoral or impure person or covetous man, who is an idolater, has an inheritance in the kingdom of Christ and God. 6 Let no one deceive you with empty words, for because of these things the wrath of God comes upon the sons of disobedience. 7 Therefore do not be partakers with them; 8 for you were formerly darkness, but now you are light in the Lord; walk as children of light 9 (for the fruit of the light *consists* in all goodness and righteousness and truth), 10 trying to learn what is pleasing to the Lord. 11And do not participate in the unfruitful deeds of darkness, but instead even expose them; 12 for it is disgraceful even to speak of the things which are done by them in secret. 13 But all things become visible when they are exposed by the light, for everything that becomes visible is light. 14 For this reason it says,
"AWAKE, SLEEPER,
AND ARISE FROM THE DEAD,
AND CHRIST WILL SHINE ON YOU."

[a] Some ancient mss. read, *us.*

WILLIAMS

22 to lay aside, with your former way of living, your old self which is on the way to destruction in accordance with its deceptive impulses; 23 and to have a new attitude of mind 24 and put on the new self which has been created in the likeness of God, which fruits in right and holy living inspired by the truth.

25 So you must lay aside falsehood and each of you practice telling the truth to his neighbor, for we are parts of one another. 26 If you do get angry, you must stop sinning in your anger. Do not ever let the sun go down on your anger; 27 stop giving the devil a chance. 28 The man who used to steal must now stop stealing; rather, he must keep on working and toiling with his own hands at some honest vocation, so as to have something to contribute to the needy. 29 You must stop letting any bad word pass your lips, but only words that are good for building up as the occasion demands, so that they will result in spiritual blessing to the hearers. 30 You must stop offending the Holy Spirit of God by whom you have been stamped for the day of redemption. 31 You must remove all bitterness, rage, anger, loud threats, and insults, with all malice. 32 You must practice being kind to one another, tender-hearted, forgiving one another, just as God through Christ has graciously forgiven you.

5   *Again warns them against living in vices; must live in the light, be alert, spiritual, ever singing; tells duties of husbands and wives*

So you must keep on following God's example, as dearly loved children of His, 2 and practice living in love, just as Christ loved you too and gave Himself for you as a fragrant offering and sacrifice to God.

3 But sexual vice and any form of immorality or sensual greed must not so much as be mentioned among you, as that is the only course becoming in God's people; 4 there must be no indecency, silly talk or suggestive jesting, for they are unbecoming. There should be thanksgiving instead. 5 For you may be absolutely sure that no one who is sexually impure, immoral or greedy for gain (for that is idolatry) can have a part in the kingdom of Christ and God.

6 Stop letting anyone deceive you with groundless arguments about these things, for it is because of these very sins that God's anger comes down upon the disobedient. 7 So you must stop having anything to do with them. 8 For at one time you were darkness itself, but now in union with the Lord you are light itself. You must live like children of light, 9 for the product of light consists in practicing everything that is good and right and true; 10 you must approve what is pleasing to the Lord. 11 Stop having anything to do with the profitless doings of darkness; instead you must continue to expose them. 12 For it is disgraceful even to mention the vices practiced in secret by them; 13 and yet anything that is exposed by the light is made clear to them, for anything that is made clear is light. 14 So it is said:

"Wake up, sleeper,
Get up from the dead,
And Christ will make day dawn on you."

BECK

as it is in Jesus: 22 Strip off your old self, which follows your former ways of living and ruins you as it follows the desires that deceive you. 23 Become new in the spirit of your minds, 24 and put on the new self, which is created to be like God, righteous and holy in the truth.

25 So don't lie any more, but *tell one another the truth,*[8] because we are members of one another. 26 *Be angry but don't sin.*[9] Don't let the sun go down on your anger. 27 Don't give the devil a chance to work.

28 Anyone who has been stealing should not steal any more, but instead work hard, doing something good with his own hands so that he has something to share with anyone in need. 29 Don't say anything bad but only what is good, so that you help where there's a need and benefit those who hear it.

30 And don't grieve God's Holy Spirit, by whom you were sealed for the day when you will be set free.

31 Get rid of all bitter feelings, temper, anger, yelling, slander, and every way of hurting one another. 32 Be kind to one another and tenderhearted, and forgive one another as God in Christ has forgiven you.

You Are a Light

5   As God's dear children try to be like Him 2 and live in love as Christ loved us and gave Himself for us as a *fragrant*[10] offering and *sacrifice*[11] to God.

3 Sexual sins, anything unclean, or greed shouldn't even be mentioned among you. This is the right attitude for holy people. 4 No shameful things, foolish talk, or coarse jokes! These aren't proper. Instead give thanks. 5 Be sure of this, that nobody who is immoral, unclean, or greedy (a greedy person worships an idol) has any share in the kingdom of Christ and God. 6 Don't let anybody fool you with meaningless words. These things bring God's anger and punishment on those who don't obey the truth. 7 So don't share their ways.

8 Once you were darkness, but now you are light in the Lord. Live as children of light, 9 since light produces everything good and righteous and true. 10 And test things to see if they please the Lord. 11 Don't have anything to do with the works of darkness, from which no good can come. Instead show that they are wrong. 12 We're ashamed even to mention what such people do secretly. 13 When you show that anything is wrong, it is seen in the light; anything you can see is as clear as light. 14 So it says: "Wake up, sleeper! Rise from the dead, and Christ will shine on you."

[8] Zech. 8:16
[9] Ps. 4:4
[10] Ezek. 20:41
[11] Ps. 40:6

K.J.V.

shall give thee light. 15 See then that ye walk circumspectly, not as fools, but as wise, 16 Redeeming the time, because the days are evil. 17 Wherefore be ye not unwise, but understanding what the will of the Lord *is*. 18 And be not drunk with wine, wherein is excess; but be filled with the Spirit; 19 Speaking to yourselves in psalms and hymns and spiritual songs, singing and making melody in your heart to the Lord; 20 Giving thanks always for all things unto God and the Father in the name of our Lord Jesus Christ; 21 Submitting yourselves one to another in the fear of God. 22 Wives, submit yourselves unto your own husbands, as unto the Lord. 23 For the husband is the head of the wife, even as Christ is the head of the church: and he is the Saviour of the body. 24 Therefore as the church is subject unto Christ, so *let* the wives *be* to their own husbands in every thing. 25 Husbands, love your wives, even as Christ also loved the church, and gave himself for it; 26 That he might sanctify and cleanse it with the washing of water by the word, 27 That he might present it to himself a glorious church, not having spot, or wrinkle, or any such thing; but that it should be holy and without blemish. 28 So ought men to love their wives as their own bodies. He that loveth his wife loveth himself. 29 For no man ever yet hated his own flesh; but nourisheth and cherisheth it, even as the Lord the church: 30 For we are members of his body, of his flesh, and of his bones. 31 For this cause shall a man leave his father and mother, and shall be joined unto his wife, and they two shall be one flesh. 32 This is a great mystery: but I speak concerning Christ and the church. 33 Nevertheless, let every one of you in particular so love his wife even as himself; and the wife *see* that she reverence *her* husband.

6 Children, obey your parents in the Lord: for this is right. 2 Honour thy father and mother; which is the first commandment with promise; 3 That it may be well with thee, and thou mayest live long on the earth. 4 And, ye fathers, provoke not your children to wrath: but bring them up in the nurture and admonition of the Lord. 5 Servants, be obedient to them that are *your* masters according to the flesh, with fear and trembling, in singleness of your heart, as unto Christ; 6 Not with eyeservice, as menpleasers; but as the servants of Christ, doing the will of God from the heart; 7 With good will doing service, as to the Lord, and not to men: 8 Knowing that whatsoever good thing any man doeth, the same shall he receive of the Lord, whether *he be* bond or free. 9 And, ye masters, do the same things unto them, forbearing threatening: knowing that your Master also is in heaven; neither is there respect of persons with

N.A.S.

15 Therefore be careful how you walk, not as unwise men, but as wise, 16 making the most of your time, because the days are evil. 17 So then do not be foolish, but understand what the will of the Lord is. 18 And do not get drunk with wine, for that is dissipation, but be filled with the Spirit, 19 speaking to one another in psalms and hymns and spiritual songs, singing and making melody with your heart to the Lord; 20 always giving thanks for all things in the name of our Lord Jesus Christ to God, even the Father; 21 and be subject to one another in the fear of Christ.

22 Wives, *be subject* to your own husbands, as to the Lord. 23 For the husband is the head of the wife, as Christ also is the head of the church, He Himself *being* the Savior of the body. 24 But as the church is subject to Christ, so also the wives *ought to be* to their husbands in everything. 25 Husbands, love your wives, just as Christ also loved the church and gave Himself up for her; 26 that He might sanctify her, having cleansed her by the washing of water with the word, 27 that He might present to Himself the church in all her glory, having no spot or wrinkle or any such thing; but that she should be holy and blameless. 28 So husbands ought also to love their own wives as their own bodies. He who loves his own wife loves himself; 29 for no one ever hated his own flesh, but nourishes and cherishes it, just as Christ also *does* the church, 30 because we are members of His body. 31 FOR THIS CAUSE A MAN SHALL LEAVE HIS FATHER AND MOTHER, AND SHALL CLEAVE TO HIS WIFE; AND THE TWO SHALL BECOME ONE FLESH. 32 This mystery is great; but I am speaking with reference to Christ and the church. 33 Nevertheless let each individual among you also love his own wife even as himself; and *let* the wife *see to it* that she respect her husband.

6 Children, obey your parents in the Lord, for this is right. 2 HONOR YOUR FATHER AND MOTHER (which is the first commandment with a promise), 3 THAT IT MAY BE WELL WITH YOU, AND THAT YOU MAY LIVE LONG ON THE EARTH. 4 And, fathers, do not provoke your children to anger; but bring them up in the discipline and instruction of the Lord.

5 Slaves, be obedient to those who are your masters according to the flesh, with fear and trembling, in the sincerity of your heart, as to Christ; 6 not by way of eyeservice, as menpleasers, but as slaves of Christ, doing the will of God from the heart. 7 With good will render service, as to the Lord, and not to men, 8 knowing that whatever good thing each one does, this he will receive back from the Lord, whether slave or free. 9 And, masters, do the same things to them, and give up threatening, knowing that both their Master and yours is in heaven, and there is no partiality with Him.

WILLIAMS

15 So you must be very careful how you live, not thoughtlessly but thoughtfully, 16 and continue to make the most of your opportunities, for the times are evil. 17 So stop becoming senseless, but understand what the Lord's will is. 18 Stop getting drunk on wine, for that means profligacy, but ever be filled with the Spirit, 19 and always be speaking to one another in psalms, hymns, and spiritual songs. Keep on praying and praising the Lord with all your heart; 20 continue giving thanks for everything to God our Father; 21 keep on living in subordination to one another out of reverence to Christ.

22 You married women must continue to live in subordination to your husbands, as you do to the Lord, 23 for a husband is the head of his wife, just as Christ is the Head of the church, His body, and Saviour of it. 24 Just as the church is subject to Christ, so the married women in everything must be subject to their husbands. 25 You married men must love your wives, just as Christ loved the church and gave Himself for her, 26 to consecrate her, after cleansing her through His word, as pictured in the water bath, 27 that He might present the church to Himself as a splendid bride without a blot or wrinkle or anything like it, but to be consecrated and faultless. 28 This is the way married men ought to love their wives, as they do their own bodies. The married man who loves his wife is really loving himself, 29 for no one ever hates his own physical person, but he feeds and fosters it, just as Christ does the church; 30 because we are parts of His body. 31 Therefore, a man must leave his father and mother and so perfectly unite himself to his wife that the two shall be one. 32 This is a great secret; I mean this about Christ and the church. 33 But each one of you married men must love his wife as he loves himself, and the married woman, too, must respect her husband.

6 *Duties of children and parents; of slaves and masters; spiritual weapons for meeting spiritual foes; Tychicus to report Paul's condition; farewell*

Children, obey your parents, for this is right. 2 "You must honor your father and mother"—this is the first commandment, with a promise to make it good—ᵃ 3 "so that you may prosper and live a long life on earth." 4 You parents,ᵇ too, must stop exasperating your children, but continue to bring them up with the sort of education and counsel the Lord approves.

5 You slaves must practice obedience to your earthly masters, with reverence and awe, with sincerity of heart, as you would obey Christ, 6 not serving them as though they were watching you, but as true slaves of Christ, trying to carry out the will of God. 7 Heartily and cheerfully keep on working as slaves, as though it were for the Lord and not for men, 8 for you know that everyone, slave or free, will get his reward from the Lord for anything good he has done. 9 You slaveowners, too, must maintain the same attitude toward your slaves, and stop threatening them, for you know that their real Lord and yours is in heaven, and that He never shows partiality.

[a] Last phrase implied. [b] Lit., *fathers*; often used for both parents.

BECK

15 Be very careful, then, how you live. Don't be unwise but wise. 16 And make the most of your opportunities because these are evil days. 17 So don't be foolish, but understand what the Lord wants. 18 *Don't get drunk on wine,*¹² which means wild living. But let the Spirit fill you 19 as you speak psalms, hymns, and songs to one another, and with your hearts sing and play music to the Lord, 20 always thanking God the Father for everything in the name of our Lord Jesus Christ.

Husband and Wife

21 As you respect Christ, submit to one another. 22 You married women, obey your husbands as you obey the Lord, 23 because a husband is the head of his wife as Christ is the Head of the church, which is His body that He saves. 24 Yes, as the church obeys Christ, so wives should obey their husbands in everything.

25 You husbands, love your wives, as Christ loved the church and gave Himself for it 26 to make it holy by washing it clean with water by the Word, 27 to have the church stand before Him as something wonderful, without a spot or a wrinkle or anything like that; yes, it should be holy and without a fault. 28 This is how husbands should love their wives, like their own bodies. A man who loves his wife is loving himself. 29 Nobody ever hated his own body. Everybody feeds it and treats it tenderly, as Christ does the church 30 because we are parts of His body. 31 *This is why a man will leave his father and mother and live with his wife, and the two will be one flesh.*¹³ 32 There's a great truth hidden here—I mean that of Christ and the church. 33 But every one of you, too, love your wife as you love yourself. And a wife should respect her husband.

Children and Parents

6 Children, obey your parents in the Lord, because it is right. 2 *Honor your father and mother*—this is an important commandment with a promise: 3 *it will be well with you and you will live long on the earth.*¹⁴ 4 And you fathers, don't make your children angry, but raise them by letting *the Lord train*¹⁵ and correct them.

Slaves and Masters

5 You slaves, obey those who are your masters in this world, with respect and trembling and as sincerely as you obey Christ, 6 working not only while you are being watched, as if you merely wanted to please men, but as slaves of Christ who are glad to do what God wants them to do. 7 Serve eagerly as you would serve the Lord and not merely men. 8 You know that if you do a good thing, the Lord will pay you back whether you are a slave or a free man.

9 You masters, treat your slaves in the same way, and stop threatening them. You know that they and you have one Master in heaven, and He doesn't prefer one to another.

[12] Prov. 23:31
[13] Gen. 2:24
[14] Ex. 20:12
[15] Prov. 3:11

K.J.V.

him. 10 Finally, my brethren, be strong in the Lord, and in the power of his might. 11 Put on the whole armour of God, that ye may be able to stand against the wiles of the devil. 12 For we wrestle not against flesh and blood, but against principalities, against powers, against the rulers of the darkness of this world, against spiritual wickedness in high *places*. 13 Wherefore take unto you the whole armour of God, that ye may be able to withstand in the evil day, and having done all, to stand. 14 Stand therefore, having your loins girt about with truth, and having on the breastplate of righteousness; 15And your feet shod with the preparation of the gospel of peace; 16Above all, taking the shield of faith, wherewith ye shall be able to quench all the fiery darts of the wicked. 17And take the helmet of salvation, and the sword of the Spirit, which is the word of God: 18 Praying always with all prayer and supplication in the Spirit, and watching thereunto with all perseverance and supplication for all saints; 19And for me, that utterance may be given unto me, that I may open my mouth boldly, to make known the mystery of the gospel, 20 For which I am an ambassador in bonds; that therein I may speak boldly, as I ought to speak. 21 But that ye also may know my affairs, *and* how I do, Tychicus, a beloved brother and faithful minister in the Lord, shall make known to you all things: 22 Whom I have sent unto you for the same purpose, that ye might know our affairs, and *that* he might comfort your hearts. 23 Peace *be* to the brethren, and love with faith, from God the Father and the Lord Jesus Christ. 24 Grace *be* with all them that love our Lord Jesus Christ in sincerity. Amen.

Written from Rome unto the Ephesians by Tychicus.

N.A.S.

10 Finally, be strong in the Lord, and in the strength of His might. 11 Put on the full armor of God, that you may be able to stand firm against the schemes of the devil. 12 For our struggle is not against flesh and blood, but against the rulers, against the powers, against the world-forces of this darkness, against the spiritual *forces* of wickedness in the heavenly *places*. 13 Therefore take up the full armor of God, that you may be able to resist in the evil day, and having done everything, to stand firm. 14 Stand firm therefore, HAVING GIRDED your LOINS WITH TRUTH, and HAVING PUT ON THE BREASTPLATE OF RIGHTEOUSNESS, 15 and having shod YOUR FEET WITH THE PREPARATION OF THE GOSPEL OF PEACE; 16 in addition to all, taking up the shield of faith with which you will be able to extinguish all the flaming missiles of the evil *one*. 17And take the helmet of salvation, and the sword of the Spirit, which is the word of God. 18 With all prayer and petition pray at all times in the Spirit, and with this is view, be on the alert with all perseverance and petition for all the saints, 19 and *pray* on my behalf, that utterance may be given to me in the opening of my mouth, to make known with boldness the mystery of the gospel, 20 for which I am an ambassador in chains; that °in *proclaiming* it I may speak boldly, as I ought to speak.

21 But that you also may know about my circumstances, how I am doing, Tychicus, the beloved brother and faithful minister in the Lord, will make everything known to you. 22And I have sent him to you for this very purpose, so that you may know about us, and' that he may comfort your hearts.

23 Peace be to the brethren, and love with faith, from God the Father and the Lord Jesus Christ. 24 Grace be with all those who love our Lord Jesus Christ with *a love* incorruptible.

[a] Some ancient mss. read, *I may speak it boldly.*

WILLIAMS

10 From now on you must grow stronger through union with the Lord and through His mighty power. 11 You must put on God's full armor, so as to be able to stand up against the devil's stratagems. 12 For our contest[c] is not with human foes alone, but with the rulers, authorities, and cosmic powers of this dark world; that is, with the spirit-forces of evil challenging us in the heavenly contest. 13 So you must take on God's full armor, so as to be able to take a stand in the day when evil attacks you, and, after having completely finished the contest, to hold your own. 14 Hold your position, then, with your waist encircled with the belt of truth, put on right-doing as a coat of mail, 15 and put on your feet the preparation the good news of peace supplies. 16 Besides all these, take on the shield which faith provides, for with it you will be able to put out all the fire-tipped arrows shot by the evil one, 17 take the helmet salvation provides, and take the sword the Spirit wields, which is the word of God. 18 Keep on praying in the Spirit, with every kind of prayer and entreaty, at every opportunity, be ever on the alert with perfect devotion and entreaty for all God's people, 19 and for me that a message may be given me when I open my lips, so that I may boldly make known the open secret of the good news, 20 for the sake of which I am an envoy in prison; so that, when I tell it, I may speak as courageously as I ought.

21 That you may also know how I am, Tychicus, our dearly loved brother and a faithful minister in the Lord's service, will give you all the information; 22 that is the very reason I am sending him, to let you know how I am and to cheer your hearts.

23 Peace to the brothers and love with faith, from God our Father and the Lord Jesus Christ 24 Spiritual blessing be with all who have an undying love for our Lord Jesus Christ.

BECK

Put on the Whole Armor

10 Finally, let the Lord and His mighty power make you strong. 11 Put on God's whole armor, and you will be able to stand against the devil's tricky ways. 12 You're not fighting against flesh and blood but against the rulers, authorities, and lords of this dark world, against the evil spirits that are above. 13 This is why you should take God's whole armor; then you can resist when things are at their worst and having done everything, you can hold your ground. 14 Stand, then, *with truth as a belt fastened around* your *waist,*[16] *with righteousness covering you as a breastplate.*[17] 15 and with shoes on your *feet,* ready to *bring the good news of peace.*[18] 16 Besides all these, take faith as the shield with which you can put out all the flaming arrows of the evil one. 17 And take *salvation as your helmet,*[17] and the Spirit's *sword,*[19] which is God's Word.

18 Pray at all times in the Spirit, using every kind of prayer. Be alert and keep at it continually as you pray for all the holy people. 19 For me, too, that when I start to talk I'll be told what to say and will boldly tell the hidden truth of the good news 20 (for which I'm an ambassador in chains) just as boldly as I must tell it.

Farewell

21 You should know what is happening to me and how I'm getting along. And so Tychicus, our dear fellow Christian and loyal helper in the Lord, will tell you everything. 22 I'm sending him to you to let you know about us and to encourage you.

23 May God the Father and the Lord Jesus Christ give our fellow Christians peace and love with faith! 24 His love be with all who have an undying love for our Lord Jesus Christ.

[16] Is. 11:5
[17] Is. 59:17
[18] Is. 52:7
[19] Is. 49:2

[c] Lit., *wrestling.*

K.J.V.

THE EPISTLE OF

PAUL THE APOSTLE

TO THE

PHILIPPIANS

N.A.S.

THE EPISTLE OF PAUL

TO THE

PHILIPPIANS

1 Paul and Timotheus, the servants of Jesus Christ, to all the saints in Christ Jesus which are at Philippi, with the bishops and deacons: 2 Grace *be* unto you, and peace, from God our Father and *from* the Lord Jesus Christ. 3 I thank my God upon every remembrance of you, 4 Always in every prayer of mine for you all making request with joy, 5 For your fellowship in the gospel from the first day until now; 6 Being confident of this very thing, that he which hath begun a good work in you will perform *it* until the day of Jesus Christ: 7 Even as it is meet for me to think this of you all, because I have you in my heart; inasmuch as both in my bonds, and in the defence and confirmation of the gospel, ye all are partakers of my grace. 8 For God is my record, how greatly I long after you all in the bowels of Jesus Christ. 9 And this I pray, that your love may abound yet more and more in knowledge and *in* all judgment; 10 That ye may approve things that are excellent; that ye may be sincere and without offence till the day of Christ; 11 Being filled with the fruits of righteousness, which are by Jesus Christ, unto the glory and praise of God. 12 But I would ye should understand, brethren, that the things *which happened* unto me have fallen out rather unto the furtherance of the gospel; 13 So that my bonds in Christ are manifest in all the palace, and in all other *places;* 14 And many of the brethren in the Lord, waxing confident by my bonds, are much more bold to speak the word without fear. 15 Some indeed preach Christ even of envy and strife; and some also of good will: 16 The one preach Christ of contention, not sincerely, supposing to add affliction to my bonds: 17 But the other of love, knowing that I am set for the defence of the gospel. 18 What then? notwithstanding, every way, whether in pretence, or in truth, Christ is preached; and I therein do rejoice, yea, and will rejoice. 19 For I know that this shall turn to my salvation through your prayer, and the supply of the Spirit of Jesus

1 Paul and Timothy, bond-servants of Christ Jesus, to all the saints in Christ Jesus who are in Philippi, including the overseers and deacons: 2 Grace to you and peace from God our Father and the Lord Jesus Christ.

3 I thank my God in all my remembrance of you, 4 always offering prayer with joy in my every prayer for you all, 5 in view of your participation in the gospel from the first day until now. 6 *For I am* confident of this very thing, that He who began a good work in you will perfect it until the day of Christ Jesus. 7 For it is only right for me to feel this way about you all, because I have you in my heart, since both in my imprisonment and in the defense and confirmation of the gospel, you all are partakers of grace with me. 8 For God is my witness, how I long for you all with the affection of Christ Jesus. 9 And this I pray, that your love may abound still more and more in real knowledge and all discernment, 10 so that you may approve the things that are excellent, in order to be sincere and blameless until the day of Christ; 11 having been filled with the fruit of righteousness which *comes* through Jesus Christ, to the glory and praise of God.

12 Now I want you to know, brethren, that my circumstances have turned out for the greater progress of the gospel, 13 so that my imprisonment in *the cause of* Christ has become well-known throughout the whole ªpraetorian guard and to everyone else, 14 and that most of the brethren, trusting in the Lord because of my imprisonment, have far more courage to speak the word of God without fear. 15 Some, to be sure, are preaching Christ even from envy and strife, but some also from good will; 16 ᵇthe latter *do it* out of love, knowing that I am appointed for the defense of the gospel; 17 the former proclaim Christ out of selfish ambition, rather than from pure motives, thinking to cause me distress in my imprisonment. 18 What then? Only that in every way, whether in pretense or in truth, Christ is proclaimed; and in this I rejoice, yes, and I will rejoice. 19 For I know that this shall turn out for my deliverance through your prayers and the pro-

---

[a] Or, *governor's palace.* [b] Some later mss. reverse the order of vss. 16 and 17.

PHILIPPIANS

PAUL
WRITES TO THE
PHILIPPIANS

1 *He greets them and prays for them; rejoices over their co-operation and that Christ is being preached; weighs which is better: to live or to die; points to life of self-sacrifice*

Paul and Timothy, slaves of Christ Jesus, to all God's people in union with Christ Jesus who are at Philippi, with the overseers and assistants:[a] 2 spiritual blessing and peace to you from God our Father and the Lord Jesus Christ.

3 Every time I remember you I thank my God, 4 and always do it with joy in every entreaty I make for all of you, 5 for your co-operation in spreading the good news, from the first day you heard it until now. 6 For I am certain of this very thing, that He who began the good work in you will go on until the day of Jesus Christ to complete it. 7 And I have a right to think this way about you, because I always have you in my heart, whether shut up in prison or out defending and vindicating the good news, for you are sharers with me of God's favor. 8 For God is my witness how I never stop yearning for all of you with the affection Christ Jesus inspires.

9 And it is my prayer that your love may overflow still more and more, directed by fuller knowledge and keener insight, 10 so that you may always approve the better things, and be men of transparent character and blameless life, 11 men that are abounding in the fruits of right-doing with the help of Jesus Christ, to the honor and praise of God.

12 Now I want you to rest assured, brothers, that those things which have befallen me have actually resulted in the progress of the good news; 13 in this way it has become well known throughout the Imperial Guard and to all the rest here that I am a prisoner in the service of Christ, 14 and that most of the Christian brothers have grown confident enough, because of my imprisonment, to dare to tell God's message without being afraid.

15 Some, indeed, are actually preaching Christ because they are moved by jealousy and partisanship, but others are doing so from the motive of good-will; 16 the latter, indeed, are doing so from love to me, for they know that I am providentially put here to defend the good news; 17 the former are preaching Christ from the motive of rivalry, not in sincerity, supposing that this is making it harder for me to bear my imprisonment.

18 What difference then does it make? In one way or another, whether in pretense or in sincerity, Christ is being preached, and that is the thing that makes me glad; yes, more too, I will continue to be glad of it, 19 for I know that through your prayers and a bountiful supply of the Spirit of Jesus Christ this will

[a] Lit., *servants,* deacons.

1 Paul and Timothy, servants of Christ Jesus, to all who are holy in Christ Jesus in Philippi, especially to the pastors and helpers: 2 May God our Father and the Lord Jesus Christ love you and give you peace.

You Are in My Heart

3 Every time I think of you, I thank my God. 4 Every time I pray for all of you, I always do it with joy 5 because you have shared in telling the good news from the first day till now. 6 I'm sure that He who started a good work in you will go on to finish it till the day of Christ Jesus. 7 And it is right for me to feel like this about all of you. Whether I'm in my chains or defending and confirming the good news, you're all in my heart as sharing God's love with me. 8 God knows how I long for you all with the tenderness of Christ Jesus.

9 And I pray your love will still grow more and more in knowledge and in every kind of understanding 10 so that you approve the better things and are pure, harming nobody, till the day of Christ, 11 as Jesus Christ has filled your life with righteous works by which you glorify and praise God.

If Only Christ Is Preached

12 I want you to know, my fellow Christians, that what happened to me actually helped spread the good news 13 so that the governor's whole palace and all the others have found out I'm in chains for Christ. 14 And so my chains have given most of our friends the confidence in the Lord to speak God's Word more boldly and fearlessly than ever.

15 Some men are moved by jealousy and rivalry to preach Christ, but others by good will. 16 Those who love to preach Him know I'm appointed to defend the good news. 17 But the others preach Christ selfishly, without a pure motive, and mean to stir up trouble for me even while I am in chains. 18 But what does it mean? Only this, that in one way or another, whether their motive is false or real, they preach Christ—and I'm glad of that.

Live or Die?

19 Yes, and I'm also going to be happy because I know that your prayer and the help of the Spirit of Jesus Christ will make *this turn*

K.J.V.

Christ, 20According to my earnest expectation and *my* hope, that in nothing I shall be ashamed, but *that* with all boldness, as always, *so* now also Christ shall be magnified in my body, whether *it be* by life, or by death. 21 For to me to live *is* Christ, and to die *is* gain. 22 But if I live in the flesh, this *is* the fruit of my labour: yet what I shall choose I wot not. 23 For I am in a strait betwixt two, having a desire to depart, and to be with Christ; which is far better: 24 Nevertheless to abide in the flesh *is* more needful for you. 25And having this confidence, I know that I shall abide and continue with you all for your furtherance and joy of faith; 26 That your rejoicing may be more abundant in Jesus Christ for me by my coming to you again. 27 Only let your conversation be as it becometh the gospel of Christ: that whether I come and see you, or else be absent, I may hear of your affairs, that ye stand fast in one spirit, with one mind striving together for the faith of the gospel; 28And in nothing terrified by your adversaries: which is to them an evident token of perdition, but to you of salvation, and that of God. 29 For unto you it is given in the behalf of Christ, not only to believe on him, but also to suffer for his sake; 30 Having the same conflict which ye saw in me, and now hear *to be* in me.

2 If *there be* therefore any consolation in Christ, if any comfort of love, if any fellowship of the Spirit, if any bowels and mercies, 2 Fulfil ye my joy, that ye be likeminded, having the same love, *being* of one accord, of one mind. 3 *Let* nothing *be done* through strife or vainglory; but in lowliness of mind let each esteem other better than themselves. 4 Look not every man on his own things, but every man also on the things of others. 5 Let this mind be in you, which was also in Christ Jesus: 6 Who, being in the form of God, thought it not robbery to be equal with God: 7 But made himself of no reputation, and took upon him the form of a servant, and was made in the likeness of men: 8 And being found in fashion as a man, he humbled himself, and became obedient unto death, even the death of the cross. 9 Wherefore God also hath highly exalted him, and given him a name which is above every name: 10 That at the name of Jesus every knee should bow, of *things* in heaven, and *things* in earth, and *things* under the earth;

N.A.S.

vision of the Spirit of Jesus Christ, 20 according to my earnest expectation and hope, that I shall not be put to shame in anything, but *that* with all boldness, Christ shall even now, as always, be exalted in my body, whether by life or by death. 21 For to me, to live is Christ, and to die is gain. 22 But if *I am* to live *on* in the flesh, this *will mean* fruitful labor for me; and I do not know which to choose. 23 But I am hard pressed from both *directions,* having the desire to depart and be with Christ, for *that* is very much better; 24 yet to remain on in the flesh is more necessary for your sake. 25And convinced of this, I know that I shall remain and continue with you all for your progress and joy in the faith, 26 so that your proud confidence in me may abound in Christ Jesus through my coming to you again.

27 Only conduct yourselves in a manner worthy of the gospel of Christ; so that whether I come and see you or remain absent, I may hear of you that you are standing firm in one spirit, with one mind striving together for the faith of the gospel; 28 in no way alarmed by *your* opponents—which is a sign of destruction for them, but of salvation for you, and that *too,* from God. 29 For to you it has been granted for Christ's sake, not only to believe in Him, but also to suffer for His sake, 30 experiencing the same conflict which you saw in me, and now hear *to be* in me.

2 If therefore there is any encouragement in Christ, if there is any consolation of love, if there is any fellowship of the Spirit, if any affection and compassion, 2 make my joy complete by being of the same mind, maintaining the same love, united in spirit, intent on one purpose. 3 Do nothing from selfishness or empty conceit, but with humility of mind let each of you regard one another as more important than himself; 4 do not *merely* look out for your own personal interests, but also for the interests of others. 5 Have this attitude in yourselves which was also in Christ Jesus, 6 who, although He existed in the form of God, did not regard equality with God a thing to be grasped, 7 but *emptied Himself, taking the form of a bondservant, *and* being made in the likeness of men. 8And being found in appearance as a man, He humbled Himself by becoming obedient to the point of death, even death on a cross. 9 Therefore also God highly exalted Him, and bestowed on Him the name which is above every name, 10 that at the name of Jesus every knee should bow, of those who are in heaven, and on earth,

[a] I.e., *laid aside His privileges.*

WILLIAMS

turn out for my spiritual welfare, 20 in accordance with my eager expectation and hope that I shall never disgrace myself, but that now as always hitherto, by my all-conquering courage, whether by living or dying, Christ will be honored in me.

21 For to me living means Christ and dying brings gain. 22 But if to keep on living here means fruit from my labor, I cannot tell which to choose. 23 I am hesitating between two desires, for I long to depart and to be with Christ, for that is far, far better. 24And yet for your sakes it is very necessary for me to stay on here. 25 Now since I am certain of this, I know that I shall stay on and stay by you all to promote the progress of your faith 26 which will result in your joy; so that, through union with Christ Jesus, you may have more than sufficient ground for boasting about me, through my being with you again.

27 Only you must practice living lives that are worthy of the good news, so that whether I come and see you or stay away, I may hear of you that you are standing firm in one spirit, and that with one purpose you are continuing to co-operate in the fight for faith in the good news. 28 Never in the slightest degree be frightened by your opponents, for such fearlessness will be strong evidence to them of their impending destruction, but to you a sure sign, and that from God, of your salvation. 29 For it has been graciously granted to you for Christ's sake, not only to trust in Him but also to suffer for Him, 30 since you are having the same struggle that you once saw me have and which you hear that I am still having.

2 *He appeals for brotherly love; urges Christ's example of humility and self-sacrifice; tells of salvation as a process toward a finishing point; Timothy sent to them; Epaphroditus to be sent back*

So, if there is any appeal in our union with Christ, if there is any persuasive power in love, if we have any common share in the Spirit, if you have any tenderheartedness and sympathy, 2 fill up my cup of joy by living in harmony, by fostering the same disposition of love, your hearts beating in unison, your minds set on one purpose. 3 Stop acting from motives of selfish strife or petty ambition, but in humility practice treating one another as your superiors. 4 Stop looking after your own interests only but practice looking out for the interests of others too.

5 Keep on fostering the same disposition that Christ Jesus had.[a] 6 Though He was existing in the nature of God, He did not think His being on an equality with God a thing to be selfishly grasped, 7 but He laid it aside[b] as He took on the nature of a slave and became like other men. 8 Because He was recognized as a man, in reality as well as in outward form, He finally humiliated Himself in obedience[c] so as to die, even to die on a cross. 9 This is why God has highly exalted Him, and given Him the name that is above every other name, 10 so that in the name of Jesus everyone should kneel, in heaven, on earth, and in the under-

BECK

out victoriously for me[1] 20 as I eagerly hope there will be nothing for me to be ashamed of. But by speaking very boldly I will now as always glorify Christ in my body by living or by dying 21 since for me to live is Christ, and to die is gain. 22 If I live here in my body, I'll enjoy the results of my work. And which would I like best? I don't know. 23 I find it hard to choose between the two. 24 I want to leave and be with Christ; that is much better. But when I think of you, I feel a greater need to stay in my body. 25And since I feel convinced of this, I know I'll live and be with all of you to help you grow and be happy in your faith. 26And so by coming to you again I want to give you all the more reason to glory in Christ Jesus.

Fighting for the Faith

27 But live as citizens worthy of the good news of Christ so that, whether I come and see you or stay away, I will hear you are standing firm, one in spirit, and fighting side by side like one man for the faith in the good news. 28 Don't let your enemeis frighten you in any way. This is how you prove to them they will be destroyed and you will be saved, and this proof is from God. 29 It is given to you to be for Christ, not only to believe in Him but also to suffer for Him 30 as you have the same struggle you once saw me have and now hear that I have.

Live in Harmony

2 Now if you are encouraged in Christ, moved by comforting words of love, if you and we have the same Spirit, if you are tender and sympathetic, 2 make me very happy—be one in thought and in love, live in harmony, keep one purpose in mind. 3 Don't be selfish or proud, but humbly treat others as better than yourselves. 4 Each of you, be interested not only in your own things but also in those of others.

Be like Jesus

5 Think just as Christ Jesus thought: 6 Although He was God, He decided not to take advantage of His being equal with God as though it were stolen goods, 7 but He emptied Himself, made Himself a slave, became like other human beings, and was seen to have the ways of a man. 8 He became obedient and humbled Himself till He died, yes, died on a cross. 9 That is why God also raised Him up on high and gave Him the name above every other name 10 that at the name of JESUS *everyone* in heaven and on earth and under the earth *should*

[a] Grk., *have the mind that was in Christ Jesus.*
[b] Lit., *emptied Himself.* [c] Grk. says, *by becoming obedient,* etc.

[1] Job 13:16

K.J.V.

11And *that* every tongue should confess that Jesus Christ *is* Lord, to the glory of God the Father. 12 Wherefore, my beloved, as ye have always obeyed, not as in my presence only, but now much more in my absence, work out your own salvation with fear and trembling: 13 For it is God which worketh in you both to will and to do of *his* good pleasure. 14 Do all things without murmurings and disputings: 15 That ye may be blameless and harmless, the sons of God, without rebuke, in the midst of a crooked and perverse nation, among whom ye shine as lights in the world; 16 Holding forth the word of life; that I may rejoice in the day of Christ, that I have not run in vain, neither laboured in vain. 17 Yea, and if I be offered upon the sacrifice and service of your faith, I joy, and rejoice with you all. 18 For the same cause also do ye joy, and rejoice with me. 19 But I trust in the Lord Jesus to send Timotheus shortly unto you, that I also may be of good comfort, when I know your state. 20 For I have no man likeminded, who will naturally care for your state. 21 For all seek their own, not the things which are Jesus Christ's. 22 But ye know the proof of him, that, as a son with the father, he hath served with me in the gospel. 23 Him therefore I hope to send presently, so soon as I shall see how it will go with me. 24 But I trust in the Lord that I also myself shall come shortly. 25 Yet I supposed it necessary to send to you Epaphroditus, my brother, and companion in labour, and fellow soldier, but your messenger, and he that ministered to my wants. 26 For he longed after you all, and was full of heaviness, because that ye had heard that he had been sick. 27 For indeed he was sick nigh unto death: but God had mercy on him; and not on him only, but on me also, lest I should have sorrow upon sorrow. 28 I sent him therefore the more carefully, that, when ye see him again, ye may rejoice, and that I may be the less sorrowful. 29 Receive him therefore in the Lord with all gladness; and hold such in reputation: 30 Because for the work of Christ he was nigh unto death, not regarding his life, to supply your lack of service toward me.

3 Finally, my brethren, rejoice in the Lord. To write the same things to you, to me indeed *is* not grievous, but for you *it is* safe. 2 Beware of dogs, beware of evil workers, beware of the concision. 3 For we are the circumcision, which worship God in the spirit, and rejoice in Christ Jesus, and have no confidence in the flesh. 4 Though I might also have confidence in the

N.A.S.

and under the earth, 11 and that every tongue should confess that Jesus Christ is Lord, to the glory of God the Father.

12 So then, my beloved, just as you have always obeyed, not as in my presence only, but now much more in my absence, work out your salvation with fear and trembling; 13 for it is God who is at work in you, both to will and to work for *His* good pleasure. 14 Do all things without grumbling or disputing; 15 that you may prove yourselves to be blameless and innocent, children of God above reproach in the midst of a crooked and perverse generation, among whom you appear as lights in the world, 16 holding fast the word of life, so that in the day of Christ I may have cause to glory because I did not run in vain nor toil in vain. 17 But even if I am being poured out as a drink-offering upon the sacrifice and service of your faith, I rejoice and share my joy with you all. 18And you too, *I urge you,* rejoice in the same way and share your joy with me.

19 But I hope in the Lord Jesus to send Timothy to you shortly, so that I also may be encouraged when I learn of your condition. 20 For I have no one *else* of kindred spirit who will genuinely be concerned for your welfare. 21 For they all seek after their own interests, not those of Christ Jesus. 22 But you know of his proven worth that he served with me in the furtherance of the gospel like a child *serving* his father. 23 Therefore I hope to send him immediately, as soon as I see how things *go* with me; 24 and I trust in the Lord that I myself also shall be coming shortly. 25 But I thought it necessary to send to you Epaphroditus, my brother and fellow-worker and fellow-soldier, who is also your messenger and minister to my need; 26 because he was longing ªfor you all and was distressed because you had heard that he was sick. 27 For indeed he was sick to the point of death, but God had mercy on him, and not on him only but also on me, lest I should have sorrow upon sorrow. 28 Therefore I have sent him all the more eagerly in order that when you see him again you may rejoice and I may be less concerned *about you.* 29 Therefore receive him in the Lord with all joy, and hold men like him in high regard; 30 because he came close to death for the work of Christ, risking his life to complete what was deficient in your service to me.

3 Finally, my brethren, rejoice in the Lord. To write the same things *again* is no trouble to me, and it is a safeguard for you. 2 Beware of the dogs, beware of the evil workers, beware of the false circumcision; 3 for we are the *true* circumcision, who worship in the Spirit of God and glory in Christ Jesus and put no confidence in the flesh, 4 although I myself might have confidence even in the flesh. If anyone else has a mind to put confidence in the flesh, I far

[a] Some ancient mss. read, *to see you all.*

WILLIAMS

world, 11 and everyone should confess that Jesus Christ is Lord, to the praise of God the Father.

12 So, my dearly loved friends, as you have always been obedient, so now with reverence and awe keep on working clear down to the finishing point of your salvation, not only as though I were with you but much more because I am away; 13 for it is God Himself who is at work in you to help you desire it as well as do it. 14 Practice doing everything without grumbling and disputing, 15 so that you may prove to be blameless and spotless, faultless children of God in a crooked and perverted age, in which you shine as light-bearers in the world as you continue 16 to hold up the message of life. That will give me ground for boasting on the day of Christ, because neither my career nor my labor has been a failure. 17 Yes, even if I am pouring out my life as a libation on the sacrifice and service your faith is rendering, I am glad to do so and congratulate you upon it; 18 you too must do likewise, be glad of it, and congratulate me.

19 I hope, with the approval of the Lord Jesus, soon to send Timothy to you, so that I too may be cheered on getting the news about you. 20 For I have no one else with a heart like his who would take such genuine interest in you, 21 for most people are looking out for their own interests, not for the interests of Jesus Christ. 22 But you know his tested character, how like a son in fellowship with his father he has toiled with me like a slave in preaching the good news. 23 So I hope to send him to you just as soon as I can see how my case is going to turn out. 24 Really, I am trusting that by the help of the Lord I soon shall come myself.

25 But I think it proper now to send back to you Epaphroditus, my brother, fellow-laborer, and fellow-soldier, but your messenger to minister to my needs, 26 for he has been longing to see you and has been homesick because you have heard that he was sick. 27 For he was so sick that he was on the point of dying, but God took pity on him, and not only on him but on me too, to keep me from having one sorrow after another. 28 I very eagerly send him, so that when you see him you may be glad of it, and I may be less sorrowful. 29 So give him a hearty Christian welcome and hold in honor men like him, 30 because he came near dying for the sake of the Lord's work and risked his life to make up for your lack of opportunity to minister to me.

3 Outward privileges worthless as means of right standing with God; Paul counts his privileges but refuse compared with personal experience in trusting Jesus; aspires to Christ-likeness

Finally, my brothers, continue to be glad that you are in union with the Lord. I am not tired of writing you the same things over and over: it means your safety.

2 Look out for those dogs, those mischief-makers, those self-mutilators! 3 For we are the true circumcision, who by the Spirit of God worship Him, who take pride in Christ Jesus only, and do not rely on outward privileges, 4 though I too might rely on these. If anyone

BECK

kneel 11 and *everyone should confess,* "JESUS CHRIST IS *LORD!*" and so *glorify God* [2] the Father.

Work Out Your Salvation

12 My dear friends, you have always obeyed, not only when I was with you but even more now that I'm away. And so work out your salvation with fear and trembling 13 since it is God who makes you willing and gives you the energy to do what He wants.

14 Do everything without complaining or arguing, 15 so that you will be blameless and innocent, *God's children with whom nobody can find a fault in the middle of a crooked and perverted people,* [3] among whom you shine like stars in the world 16 as you cling to the Word of Life. Then I can boast on the day of Christ I didn't run in vain or *work in vain.* [4] 17 But even if my life is poured out while I bring your faith as a sacrifice and service to God, I'm glad, and I'm happy with all of you. 18 You, too, be glad and be happy with me.

Timothy and Epaphroditus

19 I hope in the Lord Jesus to send Timothy to you soon to get news about you that will cheer me up too. 20 You see, I don't have anybody who will take such a real interest in your welfare as he will. 21 All look after their own interests, not after those of Jesus Christ. 22 But you know how he has stood the test, how like a son helping his father he worked hard with me to tell the good news. 23 So I expect to send him as soon as I see what's going to happen to me. 24 And I trust the Lord that I'll be coming soon too.

25 I feel I must send you Epaphroditus, my fellow Christian, fellow worker, and fellow soldier, whom you sent to help me in my needs, 26 since he has been longing to see all of you and is feeling troubled because you heard he was sick. 27 He was sick and almost died, but God had pity on him and helped him; not only him but me, to keep me from having one sorrow after another. 28 So I'm especially eager to send him and give you the joy of seeing him again and to feel more relief myself. 29 So give him a very happy welcome in the Lord, 30 and value men like him. For the work of Christ he risked his life and almost died, to make up for the service you couldn't give me.

Only Christ

3 Now, then, my fellow Christians, be happy in the Lord. It is no trouble to write the same things to you, and it is necessary for your safety. 2 Look out for those dogs, look out for those who do wrong, look out for the men who circumcise only their bodies. 3 We are really the circumcised people, we who worship by God's Spirit, are proud of Christ Jesus, and don't trust anything human, 4 though I, too, have

[2] Is. 45:23-24
[3] Deut. 32:5
[4] Is. 49:4; 65:23

K.J.V.

flesh. If any other man thinketh that he hath whereof he might trust in the flesh, I more: 5 Circumcised the eighth day, of the stock of Israel, *of* the tribe of Benjamin, a Hebrew of the Hebrews; as touching the law, a Pharisee; 6 Concerning zeal, persecuting the church; touching the righteousness which is in the law, blameless. 7 But what things were gain to me, those I counted loss for Christ. 8 Yea doubtless, and I count all things *but* loss for the excellency of the knowledge of Christ Jesus my Lord: for whom I have suffered the loss of all things, and do count them *but* dung, that I may win Christ, 9 And be found in him, not having mine own righteousness, which is of the law, but that which is through the faith of Christ, the righteousness which is of God by faith: 10 That I may know him, and the power of his resurrection, and the fellowship of his sufferings, being made conformable unto his death; 11 If by any means I might attain unto the resurrection of the dead. 12 Not as though I had already attained, either were already perfect: but I follow after, if that I may apprehend that for which also I am apprehended of Christ Jesus. 13 Brethren, I count not myself to have apprehended: but *this* one thing *I do,* forgetting those things which are behind, and reaching forth unto those things which are before, 14 I press toward the mark for the prize of the high calling of God in Christ Jesus. 15 Let us therefore, as many as be perfect, be thus minded: and if in any thing ye be otherwise minded, God shall reveal even this unto you. 16 Nevertheless, whereto we have already attained, let us walk by the same rule, let us mind the same thing. 17 Brethren, be followers together of me, and mark them which walk so as ye have us for an ensample. 18 (For many walk, of whom I have told you often, and now tell you even weeping, *that they are* the enemies of the cross of Christ: 19 Whose end *is* destruction, whose God *is their* belly, and *whose* glory *is* in their shame, who mind earthly things.) 20 For our conversation is in heaven; from whence also we look for the Saviour, the Lord Jesus Christ: 21 Who shall change our vile body, that it may be fashioned like unto his glorious body, according to the working whereby he is able even to subdue all things unto himself.

4 Therefore, my brethren dearly beloved and longed for, my joy and crown, so stand fast in the Lord, *my* dearly beloved. 2 I beseech Euodias, and beseech Syntyche, that they be of the same mind in the Lord. 3 And I entreat thee also, true yokefellow, help those women which laboured with me in the gospel, with Clement

N.A.S.

more: 5 circumcised the eighth day, of the nation of Israel, of the tribe of Benjamin, a Hebrew of Hebrews; as to the Law, a Pharisee; 6 as to zeal, persecuting the church; as to the righteousness which is in the Law, found blameless. 7 But whatever things were gain to me, those things I have counted as loss for the sake of Christ. 8 More than that, I count all things to be loss in view of the surpassing value of knowing Christ Jesus my Lord, for whom I have suffered the loss of all things, and count them but rubbish in order that I may gain Christ, 9 and may be found in Him, not having a righteousness of my own derived from *the* Law, but that which is through faith in Christ, the righteousness which *comes* from God on the basis of faith, 10 that I may know Him, and the power of His resurrection and the fellowship of His sufferings, being conformed to His death; 11 in order that I may attain to the resurrection from the dead. 12 Not that I have already obtained *it,* or have already become perfect, but I press on in order that I may lay hold of that for which also I was laid hold of by Christ Jesus. 13 Brethren, I do not regard myself as having laid hold of *it* yet; but one thing *I do:* forgetting what *lies* behind and reaching forward to what *lies* ahead, 14 I press on toward the goal for the prize of the upward call of God in Christ Jesus. 15 Let us therefore, as many as are perfect, have this attitude; and if in anything you have a different attitude, God will reveal that also to you; 16 however, let us keep living by that same *standard* to which we have attained.

17 Brethren, join in following my example, and observe those who walk according to the pattern you have in us. 18 For many walk, of whom I often told you, and now tell you even weeping, *that they are* enemies of the cross of Christ, 19 whose end is destruction, whose god is *their* appetite, and *whose* glory is in their shame, who set their minds on earthly things. 20 For our citizenship is in heaven, from which also we eagerly wait for a Savior, the Lord Jesus Christ; 21 who will transform the body of our humble state into conformity with the body of His glory, by the exertion of the power that He has even to subject all things to Himself.

4 Therefore, my beloved brethren whom I long *to see,* my joy and crown, so stand firm in the Lord, my beloved.
2 I urge Euodia and I urge Syntyche to live in harmony in the Lord. 3 Indeed, true comrade, I ask you also to help these women who have shared my struggle in *the cause of* the gospel,

WILLIAMS   ## BECK

thinks that he can rely on outward privileges, far more might I do so: 5 circumcised when I was a week old; a descendant of Israel; a member of the tribe of Benjamin; a Hebrew, a son of Hebrews. Measured by the standard set by the law, I was a Pharisee; 6 by the standard set by zeal, I was a persecutor of the church, and measured by the uprightness reached by keeping the law, I was faultless. 7 But for Christ's sake I have counted all that was gained to me as loss. 8 Yes, indeed, I certainly do count everything as loss compared with the priceless privilege*a* of knowing Christ Jesus my Lord. For His sake I have lost everything, and value it all as mere refuse, in order to gain Christ 9 and be actually*b* in union with Him, not having a supposed right standing with God which depends on my doing what the law commands, but one that comes through faith in Christ, the real right standing with God which originates from Him and rests on faith. 10 Yes, I long to come to know Him; that is, the power of His resurrection and so to share with Him His sufferings as to be continuously transformed by His death, 11 in the hope of attaining, in some measure, the resurrection that lifts me out from among the dead. 12 It is not a fact that I have already secured it or already reached perfection, but I am pressing on to see if I can capture it, the ideal for which I was captured by Christ Jesus. 13 Brothers, I do not think that I have captured it yet, but here is my one aspiration, so forgetting what is behind me and reaching out for what is ahead of me, 14 I am pressing onward toward the goal, to win the prize to which God through Jesus Christ is calling us upward. 15 So let us all who are mature have this attitude. If you have a different attitude, God will make it clear to you. 16 However, we must continue to live up to that degree of success that we have already reached.

17 Follow my example, brothers, and keep your eyes on those who practice living by the pattern we have set you. 18 For there are many, of whom I have often told you, and now tell you in tears, who practice living as the enemies of the cross of Christ. 19 Their doom is destruction, their stomach is their god, their glory is in their shame, and their minds are feeding on earthly things. 20 But we are citizens of the republic in heaven, from which we are eagerly waiting for our Saviour, the Lord Jesus Christ. 21 He will so change the outward appearance of our lowly bodies that they will be like His glorious body, by the exertion of the power He has to subject everything to Himself.

something human to trust. If anybody else thinks he has anything human to trust, I have more. 5 I was circumcised on the eighth day, a descendant of Israel of the tribe of Benjamin, a Hebrew son of Hebrew parents; in regard to the Law, a Pharisee, 6 so zealous I persecuted the church and according to the Law so righteous nobody could find any fault with me.

7 But any advantages I had I considered a loss for Christ. 8 Yes, I think it is all a loss because it is so much better to know Christ Jesus, my Lord. For Him I have lost everything and consider it garbage in order to win Christ 9 and find myself in Him, not having my own righteousness based on the Law but the righteousness that depends on faith, that God gives those who believe in Christ. 10 I want to know Him and the power of His resurrection, to share His sufferings and be like Him in His death 11 if somehow I will get to be one of those who rise from the dead.

12 I don't mean I have already reached this or am already at the goal, but I eagerly go after it to make it mine because Christ Jesus made me His own. 13 Fellow Christians, I don't think I have it in my hands. But one thing I do: I forget what is behind, reach for what is ahead, 14 and with my eyes on the mark I go after the heavenly prize to which God has called us in Christ Jesus. 15 Let us all who are mature think this way. But if you think differently about anything, God will reveal this to you too. 16 Only be guided by what we have learned so far.

Citizens of Heaven

17 My fellow Christians, all together imitate me more and more, and watch those who live according to the example we're giving you. 18 As I have often told you and now tell you with tears, many live as the enemies of the cross of Christ. 19 In the end they will be destroyed. Their god is their belly, they glory in their shame, and their mind is on earthly things. 20 But we are citizens of heaven and look for the Lord Jesus Christ to come from heaven as the Savior, 21 who will change our humble bodies and make them like His glorified body by the power by which He can make everything serve Him.

4 *He calls them his crown of reward; begs Euodia and Syntyche to agree; inspires them to "beautiful thoughts and noble lives"; thanks them for many gifts to him; sends farewell greetings*

So, my dearly loved brothers, whom I long to see, my joy and crown, by the help of the Lord keep on standing firm, dearly loved friends. 2 I beg Euodia and I beg Syntyche to live in harmony by the help of the Lord. 3 And I solemnly beg you, my true comrade, keep on co-operating with those two women, because

4 And so, my fellow Christians, whom I love and long for, my joy and crown, stand firm in the Lord, dear friends.

Two Women

2 I urge Euodia and Syntyche to agree in the Lord. 3 And I beg you, my true fellow worker, help them. They fought side by side with me in telling the good news, and with Clement and

[a] Lit., *the surpassing excellence of the knowledge*, etc. [b] *Found in Him.*

K.J.V.

also, and *with* other my fellow labourers, whose names *are* in the book of life. 4 Rejoice in the Lord always: *and* again I say, Rejoice. 5 Let your moderation be known unto all men. The Lord *is* at hand. 6 Be careful for nothing; but in every thing by prayer and supplication with thanksgiving let your requests be made known unto God. 7 And the peace of God, which passeth all understanding, shall keep your hearts and minds through Christ Jesus. 8 Finally, brethren, whatsoever things are true, whatsoever things *are* honest, whatsoever things *are* just, whatsoever things *are* pure, whatsoever things *are* lovely, whatsoever things *are* of good report; if *there be* any virtue, and if *there be* any praise, think on these things. 9 Those things, which ye have both learned, and received, and heard, and seen in me, do: and the God of peace shall be with you. 10 But I rejoiced in the Lord greatly, that now at the last your care of me hath flourished again; wherein ye were also careful, but ye lacked opportunity. 11 Not that I speak in respect of want: for I have learned, in whatsoever state I am, *therewith* to be content. 12 I know both how to be abased, and I know how to abound: every where and in all things I am instructed both to be full and to be hungry, both to abound and to suffer need. 13 I can do all things through Christ which strengtheneth me. 14 Notwithstanding, ye have well done, that ye did communicate with my affliction. 15 Now ye Philippians know also, that in the beginning of the gospel, when I departed from Macedonia, no church communicated with me as concerning giving and receiving, but ye only. 16 For even in Thessalonica ye sent once and again unto my necessity. 17 Not because I desire a gift: but I desire fruit that may abound to your account. 18 But I have all, and abound: I am full, having received of Epaphroditus the things *which were sent* from you, an odour of a sweet smell, a sacrifice acceptable, well pleasing to God. 19 But my God shall supply all your need according to his riches in glory by Christ Jesus. 20 Now unto God and our Father *be* glory for ever and ever. Amen. 21 Salute every saint in Christ Jesus. The brethren which are with me greet you. 22 All the saints salute you, chiefly they that are of Cesar's household. 23 The grace of our Lord Jesus Christ *be* with you all. Amen.

It was written to the Philippians from Rome by Epaphroditus.

N.A.S.

together with Clement also, and the rest of my fellow-workers, whose names are in the book of life.

4 Rejoice in the Lord always; again I will say, rejoice! 5 Let your forbearing *spirit* be known to all men. The Lord is near. 6 Be anxious for nothing, but in everything by prayer and supplication with thanksgiving let your requests be made known to God. 7 And the peace of God, which surpasses all comprehension, shall guard your hearts and your minds in Christ Jesus.

8 Finally, brethren, whatever is true, whatever is honorable, whatever is right, whatever is pure, whatever is lovely, whatever is of good repute, if there is any excellence and if anything worthy of praise, let your mind dwell on these things. 9 The things you have learned and received and heard and seen in me, practice these things; and the God of peace shall be with you.

10 But I rejoiced in the Lord greatly, that now at last you have revived your concern for me; indeed, you were concerned *before*, but you lacked opportunity. 11 Not that I speak from want; for I have learned to be content in whatever circumstances I am. 12 I know how to get along with humble means, and I also know how to live in prosperity; in any and every circumstance I have learned the secret of being filled and going hungry, both of having abundance and suffering need. 13 I can do all things through Him who strengthens me. 14 Nevertheless, you have done well to share *with me* in my affliction. 15 And you yourselves also know, Philippians, that at the first preaching of the gospel, after I departed from Macedonia, no church shared with me in the matter of giving and receiving but you alone; 16 for even in Thessalonica you sent *a gift* more than once for my needs. 17 Not that I seek the gift itself, but I seek for the profit which increases to your account. 18 But I have received everything in full, and have an abundance; I am amply supplied, having received from Epaphroditus what you have sent, a fragrant aroma, an acceptable sacrifice, wellpleasing to God. 19 And my God shall supply all your needs according to His riches in glory in Christ Jesus. 20 Now to our God and Father *be* the glory forever and ever. Amen.

21 Greet every saint in Christ Jesus. The brethren who are with me greet you. 22 All the saints greet you, especially those of Caesar's household.

23 The grace of the Lord Jesus Christ be with your spirit.

WILLIAMS

BECK

WILLIAMS

they shared with me the struggle in spreading the good news, together with Clement and the rest of my fellow-workers, whose names are in the book of life.

4 By the help of the Lord always keep up the glad spirit; yes, I will repeat it, keep up the glad spirit. 5 Let your forbearing spirit be known to everybody. The Lord is near. 6 Stop being worried about anything, but always,ᵃ in prayer and entreaty, and with thanksgiving, keep on making your wants known to God. 7 Then, through your union with Christ Jesus, the peace of God, that surpasses all human thought, will keep guard over your hearts and thoughts.

8 Now, brothers, practice thinking on what is true, what is honorable, what is right, what is pure, what is lovable, what is high-toned, yes, on everything that is excellent or praiseworthy. 9 Practice the things you learned, received, and heard from me, things that you saw me do, and then the God who gives us peace will be with you.

10 I was made very happy as a Christianᵇ to have your interest in my welfare revived again after so long; because you have always had the interest but not the opportunity to show it. 11 Not that I refer to any personal want, for I have learned to be contented in whatever circumstances I am. 12 I know how to live in lowly circumstances and I know how to live in plenty. I have learned the secret, in all circumstances, of either getting a full meal or of going hungry, of living in plenty or being in want. 13 I can do anythingᶜ through Him who gives me strength. 14 But you did me a kindness to share my sorrow with me. 15And you Philippians yourselves know that immediately after the good news was first preached to you, when I left Macedonia, no church but yours went into partnership with me to open an account of credits and debits. 16 Even while I was at Thessalonica you sent money more than once for my needs. 17 It is not your gift that I want, but I do want the profits to pile up to your credit. 18 I have received your payment in full, and more too. I am amply supplied after getting the things you sent by Epaphroditus; they are like sweet incense, the kind of sacrifice that God accepts and approves. 19 My God will amply supply your every need, through Christ Jesus, from His riches in glory. 20 Glory to our God and Father forever and ever. Amen.

21 Remember me to every one of God's people in union with Christ Jesus. The brothers who are with me wish to be remembered to you. 22All God's people wish to be remembered to you, but more especially the members of the Emperor's household.

23 The spiritual blessing of our Lord Jesus Christ be with your spirits.

BECK

the rest of my fellow workers, whose names are in *the book of life.*⁵

Be Happy

4 Be happy in the Lord always! I'll say it again: Be happy! 5 Everybody should know how gentle you can be. The Lord is near. 6 Don't worry about anything, but in everything go to God, and pray to let Him know what you want, and give thanks. 7 Then God's peace, better than all our thinking, will guard your hearts and minds in Christ Jesus.

8 Finally, my fellow Christians, keep your minds on all that is true or noble, right or pure, lovely or appealing, on anything that is excellent or that deserves praise. 9 Do what you have learned, received, and heard from me and what you saw me do. Then the God of peace will be with you.

Your Gift

10 It made me very happy in the Lord that now again you showed a fresh interest in me. You were interested but didn't have a chance to show it. 11 I'm not saying I need anything. I've learned to have enough whatever my condition. 12 I know how to live with too little or too much. In every way of life I've learned the secret of eating heartily and of being hungry, of having too much and too little. 13 I can do everything through Him who gives me the strength.

14 But it was kind of you to share my trouble. 15 You people at Philippi know, too, that when I first told you the good news and then left Macedonia, you were the only church to share with me by an account of gifts and receipts. 16 Even while I was in Thessalonica, you more than once sent help for my needs. 17 It isn't the gift I want but to see the profits growing and credited to you. 18 You have paid me in full, and I have more than enough. I am fully supplied, now that I received from Epaphroditus what you sent. It is *a sweet odor,*⁶ a sacrifice that God accepts and is pleased with. 19And my God will give you all you need according to His riches, in His glory, and in Christ Jesus. 20 To our God and Father be glory forever. Amen.

21 Greet everyone who is holy in Christ Jesus. The Christians who are with me greet you. 22All the holy people greet you, especially those of the emperor's household. 23 The love of our Lord Jesus Christ be with your spirits. Amen.

[a] Lit., *in everything.* [b] Lit., *greatly rejoiced in Christ.* [c] Lit., *I have power for all things through Him who puts a dynamo in me.*

[5] Ps. 69:28
[6] Ezek. 20:41

THE EPISTLE OF
PAUL THE APOSTLE
TO THE
COLOSSIANS

1 Paul, an apostle of Jesus Christ by the will of God, and Timotheus *our* brother, 2 To the saints and faithful brethren in Christ which are at Colosse: Grace *be* unto you, and peace, from God our Father and the Lord Jesus Christ. 3 We give thanks to God and the Father of our Lord Jesus Christ, praying always for you, 4 Since we heard of your faith in Christ Jesus, and of the love *which ye have* to all the saints, 5 For the hope which is laid up for you in heaven, whereof ye heard before in the word of the truth of the gospel; 6 Which is come unto you, as *it is* in all the world; and bringeth forth fruit, as *it doth* also in you, since the day ye heard *of it,* and knew the grace of God in truth: 7 As ye also learned of Epaphras our dear fellow servant, who is for you a faithful minister of Christ; 8 Who also declared unto us your love in the Spirit. 9 For this cause we also, since the day we heard *it,* do not cease to pray for you, and to desire that ye might be filled with the knowledge of his will in all wisdom and spiritual understanding; 10 That ye might walk worthy of the Lord unto all pleasing, being fruitful in every good work, and increasing in the knowledge of God; 11 Strengthened with all might, according to his glorious power, unto all patience and longsuffering with joyfulness; 12 Giving thanks unto the Father, which hath made us meet to be partakers of the inheritance of the saints in light: 13 Who hath delivered us from the power of darkness, and hath translated *us* into the kingdom of his dear Son: 14 In whom we have redemption through his blood, *even* the forgiveness of sins: 15 Who is the image of the invisible God, the firstborn of every creature: 16 For by him were all things created, that are in heaven, and that are in earth, visible and invisible, whether *they be* thrones, or dominions, or principalities, or powers: all things were created by him, and for him: 17 And he is before all things, and by him all things consist: 18 And he is the head of the body, the church: who is the beginning, the firstborn from the dead; that in all things he might have the preeminence. 19 For it pleased *the Father* that in him should all fulness dwell; 20 And, having made peace through the blood of his cross, by him to reconcile all things unto himself; by him, *I say,* whether *they be*

THE EPISTLE OF PAUL
TO THE
COLOSSIANS

1 Paul, an apostle of Jesus Christ by the will of God and Timothy our brother, 2 to the saints and faithful brethren in Christ *who are* at Colossae: Grace to you and peace from God our Father. 3 We give thanks to God, the Father of our Lord Jesus Christ, praying always for you, 4 since we heard of your faith in Christ Jesus and the love which you have for all the saints; 5 because of the hope laid up for you in heaven, of which you previously heard in the word of truth, the gospel, 6 which has come to you, just as in all the world also it is constantly bearing fruit and increasing, even as *it has been doing* in you also since the day you heard *of it* and understood the grace of God in truth; 7 just as you learned *it* from Epaphras, our beloved fellow bond-servant, who is a faithful servant of Christ on ªour behalf, 8 and he also informed us of your love in the Spirit. 9 For this reason also, since the day we heard *of it,* we have not ceased to pray for you and to ask that you may be filled with the knowledge of His will in all spiritual wisdom and understanding, 10 so that you may walk in a manner worthy of the Lord, to please *Him* in all respects, bearing fruit in every good work and increasing in the knowledge of God; 11 strengthened with all power, according to His glorious might, for the attaining of all steadfastness and patience, joyously 12 giving thanks to the Father, who has qualified us to share in the inheritance of the saints in light. 13 For He delivered us from the domain of darkness, and transferred us to the kingdom of His beloved Son, 14 in whom we have redemption, the forgiveness of sins. 15 And He is the image of the invisible God, the first-born of all creation. 16 For in Him all things were created, *both* in the heavens and on earth, visible and invisible, whether thrones or dominions or rulers or authorities—all things have been created through Him and for Him. 17 And He is before all things, and in Him all things hold together. 18 He is also head of the body, the church; and He is the beginning, the first-born from the dead; so that He Himself might come to have first place in everything. 19 For it was the *Father's* good pleasure for all the fulness to dwell in Him, 20 and through Him to reconcile all things to Himself, having made peace through the blood of His cross; through Him, *I say,* whether things

[a] Some later mss. read, *your.*

COLOSSIANS

1 *He greets them; tells of his gratitude for them; prays for their growing knowledge of God and strength to bear fruit; tells of Christ's person and works, divine and majestic; of his sufferings in telling the good news*

Paul, by God's will an apostle of Christ Jesus, and our brother Timothy, 2 to the consecrated and faithful brothers at Colossae who are in union with Christ: spiritual blessing and peace to you from God our Father.

3 Every time we pray for you we thank God the Father of our Lord Jesus Christ, 4 because we have heard of your faith in Christ Jesus and of your love for all God's people, 5 because of your hope of what is laid up for you in heaven. Long ago you heard of this hope through the message of the good news 6 which reached you, and since it is bearing fruit and growing among you, just as it is all over the world, from the day you first heard of God's favor and in reality came to know it, 7 as you learned it from Epaphras, our dearly loved fellow-slave. As a faithful minister of Christ for me 8 he is the very one who told me of the love awakened in you by the Spirit.

9 This is why, ever since I heard of it, I have never ceased praying for you and asking God to fill you, through full wisdom and spiritual insight, with a clear knowledge of His will, 10 so that you may lead lives worthy of the Lord to His full satisfaction, by perennially bearing fruit in every good enterprise and by a steady growth in fuller knowledge of God; 11 then you will be perfectly empowered by His glorious might for every sort of joyous endurance and forbearance, 12 and you will always be thanking the Father who has qualified you to share the lot of His people in the realm of light.

13 It is God who has delivered us out of the dominion of darkness and has transferred us into the kingdom of His dearly loved Son, 14 by whom we possess the ransom from captivity, which means the forgiveness of our sins. 15 Yes, He is the exact likeness of the unseen God, His first-born Son who existed before any created thing, 16 for it was through Him that everything was created in heaven and on earth, the seen and the unseen, thrones, dominions, principalities, authorities; all things have been created through Him and for Him. 17 So He existed before all things, and through Him all things are held together. 18 Yes, He is the Head of the church as His body. For He is the beginning, the first-born among the dead, so that He alone should stand first in everything. 19 It is so because it was the divine choice that all the divine fullness should dwell in Him, 20 and that through Him He might reconcile to Himself all things on earth or in heaven, making this peace through the blood He shed on His cross.

PAUL

WRITES TO THE

COLOSSIANS

1 Paul, apostle of Christ Jesus by God's will, and our fellow worker Timothy, 2 to the holy and faithful fellow believers in Christ at Colossae: May God our Father love you and give you peace.

We're Praying for You

3 In our prayers for you we are always thanking God, the Father of our Lord Jesus Christ, 4 because we have heard how you believe in Christ Jesus and love all the holy people 5 and what you hope for is stored up for you in heaven. You heard of it before when you were told the truth of the good news 6 that has come to you. As it is producing fruit and growing all over the world, so it did among you since the day you heard it and got to know what it really means to have God love you, 7 as you learned it from Epaphras, our dear fellow servant, who is loyally serving Christ in our place. 8 And he's the one who told us about your love in the Spirit.

9 That is why, since the day we heard of it, we haven't stopped praying for you and asking God to fill you with a clear knowledge of His will by giving you every kind of spiritual wisdom and understanding 10 so that you live worthy of the Lord, aiming to please Him in every way as you produce every kind of good work and grow by knowing your God better. 11 We ask Him according to His wonderful might to strengthen you with all the power you need to endure patiently whatever comes 12 as you joyfully thank the Father, who made you fit to share everything the holy people have in the light.

God's Son Brought Peace

13 He rescued us from the tyranny of darkness and transferred us into the kingdom of the Son He loves, 14 who paid the ransom to forgive our sins and set us free. 15 He is the image of the invisible God, born before and above everything created, 16 since in Him was created everything you can see and cannot see in heaven and on earth—thrones, lords, rulers, or powers—everything was created by Him and for Him. 17 He was before everything, and He holds everything together. 18 He is the Head of the church, which is His body. He is the Beginning, the first among the dead to become alive that He may be first in everything. 19 God decided to have His whole being live in Him 20 and by Him to reconcile to Himself * everything on earth and in heaven in a peace made by the blood on His cross.

* God and the world, who are enemies, become friends in Christ.

K.J.V.

things in earth, or things in heaven. 21And you, that were sometime alienated and enemies in *your* mind by wicked works, yet now hath he reconciled 22 In the body of his flesh through death, to present you holy and unblameable and unreproveable in his sight: 23 If ye continue in the faith grounded and settled, and *be* not moved away from the hope of the gospel, which ye have heard, *and* which was preached to every creature which is under heaven; whereof I Paul am made a minister; 24 Who now rejoice in my sufferings for you, and fill up that which is behind of the afflictions of Christ in my flesh for his body's sake, which is the church: 25 Whereof I am made a minister, according to the dispensation of God which is given to me for you, to fulfil the word of God; 26 *Even* the mystery which hath been hid from ages and from generations, but now is made manifest to his saints: 27 To whom God would make known what *is* the riches of the glory of this mystery among the Gentiles; which is Christ in you, the hope of glory: 28 Whom we preach, warning every man, and teaching every man in all wisdom; that we may present every man perfect in Christ Jesus: 29 Whereunto I also labour, striving according to his working, which worketh in me mightily.

2 For I would that ye knew what great conflict I have for you, and *for* them at Laodicea, and *for* as many as have not seen my face in the flesh; 2 That their hearts might be comforted, being knit together in love, and unto all riches of the full assurance of understanding, to the acknowledgment of the mystery of God, and of the Father, and of Christ; 3 In whom are hid all the treasures of wisdom and knowledge. 4And this I say, lest any man should beguile you with enticing words. 5 For though I be absent in the flesh, yet am I with you in the spirit, joying and beholding your order, and the steadfastness of your faith in Christ. 6As ye have therefore received Christ Jesus the Lord, *so* walk ye in him: 7 Rooted and built up in him, and stablished in the faith, as ye have been taught, abounding therein with thanksgiving. 8 Beware lest any man spoil you through philosophy and vain deceit, after the tradition of men, after the rudiments of the world, and not after Christ. 9 For in him dwelleth all the fulness of the Godhead bodily. 10And ye are complete in him, which is the head of all principality and power: 11 In whom also ye are circumcised with the circumcision made without hands, in putting off the body of the sins of the flesh by the circumcision of Christ: 12 Buried with him in baptism, wherein also ye are risen with *him* through the faith of the operation of God, who hath raised

N.A.S.

on earth or things in heaven. 21And although you were formerly alienated and hostile in mind, *engaged* in evil deeds, 22 yet He has now reconciled you in His fleshly body through death, in order to present you before Him holy and blameless and beyond reproach— 23 if indeed you continue in the faith firmly established and steadfast, and not moved away from the hope of the gospel that you have heard, which was proclaimed in all creation under heaven, and of which I, Paul, was made a minister.

24 Now I rejoice in my sufferings for your sake, and in my flesh I do my share on behalf of His body (which is the church) in filling up that which is lacking in Christ's afflictions. 25 Of *this church* I was made a minister according to the stewardship from God bestowed on me for your benefit, that I might fully carry out the *preaching of* the word of God, 26 *that is,* the mystery which has been hidden from the *past* ages and generations; but has now been manifested to His saints, 27 to whom God willed to make known what is the riches of the glory of this mystery among the Gentiles, which is Christ in you, the hope of glory. 28And we proclaim Him, admonishing every man and teaching every man with all wisdom, that we may present every man complete in Christ. 29And for this purpose also I labor, striving according to His power, which mightily works within me.

2 For I want you to know how great a struggle I have on your behalf, and for those who are at Laodicea, and for all those who have not personally seen my face, 2 that their hearts may be encouraged, having been knit together in love, and *attaining* to all the wealth that comes from the full assurance of understanding, *resulting* in a true knowledge of God's mystery, *that is,* Christ *Himself,* 3 in whom are hidden all the treasures of wisdom and knowledge. 4 I say this in order that no one may delude you with persuasive argument. 5 For even though I am absent in body, nevertheless I am with you in spirit, rejoicing to see your good discipline and the stability of your faith in Christ.

6 As you therefore have received Christ Jesus the Lord, *so* walk in Him, 7 having been firmly rooted *and now* being built up in Him and established [a]in your faith, just as you were instructed, *and* overflowing with gratitude.

8 See to it that no one take you captive through philosophy and empty deception, according to the tradition of men, according to the elementary principles of the world, rather than according to Christ. 9 For in Him all the fulness of deity dwells in bodily form, 10 and in Him you have been made complete, and He is the head over all rule and authority; 11 and in Him you were also circumcised with a circumcision made without hands, in the removal of the body of the flesh by the circumcision of Christ; 12 having been buried with Him in baptism, in which you were also raised up with Him through faith in the working of God, who

[a] Or, *by.*

WILLIAMS

21 So you, who were once estranged from Him, and hostile in disposition as shown by your wrongdoings, He has now reconciled 22 by His death in His human body, so as to present you consecrated, faultless, and blameless in His presence, 23 if indeed you continue well grounded and firm in faith and never shift from the hope inspired by the good news you heard, which has been preached all over the world, and of which I, Paul, have been made a minister.

24 I am now glad to be suffering for you, and in my own person I am filling in what is lacking in Christ's sufferings for His body, that is, the church. 25 In it I have been made a minister in accordance with the trusteeship God entrusted to me for you, that I might prove among you the universal message of God, 26 the open secret, covered up from the people of former ages and generations, but now uncovered to God's people, 27 to whom God has chosen to make known how glorious are the riches of this open secret among the heathen, namely, Christ in you the hope of your glorification. 28 We are proclaiming Him, warning everyone and teaching everyone with ample wisdom, in order to present to God everyone mature through union with Christ. 29 For this I am toiling and struggling by His active energy which is mightily working in me.

2 *In pain he warns against the gnostics; begs them to live in conscious union with Christ; reasserts the full divinity of Christ and His ransoming us through His death; angels cannot mediate; asceticism worthless*

I want you to know what a battle I am fighting for you and for those in Laodicea, yes, for all who have never known me personally, 2 that their hearts may be encouraged, by having been knit together in love and by having attained to the full assurance of understanding, so that they may finally reach the fullest knowledge of the open secret, Christ Himself, 3 in whom all the treasures of wisdom and knowledge are stored up. 4 I am saying this to keep anyone from misleading you by persuasive arguments. 5 For though I am far away in person, still I am with you in spirit, and I am glad to note your fine order and the firmness of your faith in Christ.

6 So, just as you once accepted Christ Jesus as your Lord, you must continue living in vital union with Him, 7 with your roots deeply planted in Him, being continuously built up in Him, and growing stronger in faith, just as you were taught to do, overflowing through it in your gratitude.

8 Take care that nobody captures you by the idle fancies of his so-called philosophy, following human tradition and the world's crude notions instead of Christ. 9 For it is in Him that all the fullness of Deity continues to live embodied, 10 and through union with Him you too are filled with it. He is the Head of all principalities and dominions. 11 And through your union with Him you once received, not a hand-performed circumcision but one performed by Christ, in stripping you of your lower nature, 12 for you were buried with Him in baptism and raised to life with Him through your faith in the power of God who raised Him

BECK

Our Work Among You

21 Once you were strangers to God and in your hearts His enemies, doing wicked things, 22 but now by dying in His human body He has made of you enemies friends 23 in order to have you stand before Him without sin or fault or blame if, of course, you continue in your faith to stand firm on the foundation and are not moved from the hope of the good news you heard. This has been preached to every creature under heaven, and I, Paul, was made its servant.

24 I delight to suffer for you now and in my body am enduring what still needs' to be endured of Christ's sorrows for His body, which is the church. 25 God made me its servant when He gave me this work among you in order to do everything God meant to do by His Word. 26 This was a mystery hidden from the people of all the ages but now shown to His holy people, 27 whom God wanted to tell how rich among the non-Jews is the glory of this hidden truth: Christ, the Hope of glory, is in you.

28 Him we preach, warning everyone and teaching everyone, using every kind of wisdom, in order to present everyone perfect in Christ. 29 This is what I'm working for, struggling like an athlete by His power that is working mightily in me.

2 I want you to know how much I'm struggling for you and the people of Laodicea and all who haven't seen me face to face, 2 to encourage you, as you're bound together by love, to be ever so richly convinced in your understanding and to know well God's hidden truth, that is Christ, 3 in whom are hidden all the treasures of wisdom and knowledge. 4 I say this so that nobody will mislead you by fine-sounding arguments. 5 Although I'm away from you, I'm with you in spirit and delight to see how orderly and firm you are in your faith in Christ.

You Live in Christ

6 Just as you accepted Christ Jesus as your Lord, so live in Him. 7 In Him be rooted, built up, and strengthened in your faith, as you were taught, and overflow with thanksgiving.

8 Be careful or somebody will capture you by his philosophy, tricking you with meaningless words, as he follows the traditions of men and the elements of the world but not Christ.

9 God's whole being lives in Christ, that is, in His body. 10 And in Him, who is the Lord of all rulers and powers, you have a full life. 11 In Him you also were circumcised, not by human hands but by putting away the sinful body by the circumcision of Christ 12 since in baptism you were buried with Him and raised with Him by believing in the power of God, who raised Him from the dead.

K.J.V.

him from the dead. 13And you, being dead in your sins and the uncircumcision of your flesh, hath he quickened together with him, having forgiven you all trespasses; 14 Blotting out the handwriting of ordinances that was against us, which was contrary to us, and took it out of the way, nailing it to his cross; 15*And* having spoiled principalities and powers, he made a shew of them openly, triumphing over them in it. 16 Let no man therefore judge you in meat, or in drink, or in respect of a holyday, or of the new moon, or of the sabbath *days:* 17 Which are a shadow of things to come; but the body *is* of Christ. 18 Let no man beguile you of your reward in a voluntary humility and worshipping of angels, intruding into those things which he hath not seen, vainly puffed up by his fleshly mind, 19And not holding the Head, from which all the body by joints and bands having nourishment ministered, and knit together, increaseth with the increase of God. 20 Wherefore if ye be dead with Christ from the rudiments of the world, why, as though living in the world, are ye subject to ordinances, 21 (Touch not; taste not; handle not; 22 Which all are to perish with the using;) after the commandments and doctrines of men? 23 Which things have indeed a shew of wisdom in willworship, and humility, and neglecting of the body; not in any honour to the satisfying of the flesh.

3 If ye then be risen with Christ, seek those things which are above, where Christ sitteth on the right hand of God. 2 Set your affection on things above, not on things on the earth. 3 For ye are dead, and your life is hid with Christ in God. 4 When Christ, *who is* our life, shall appear, then shall ye also appear with him in glory. 5 Mortify therefore your members which are upon the earth; fornication, uncleanness, inordinate affection, evil concupiscence, and covetousness, which is idolatry: 6 For which things' sake the wrath of God cometh on the children of disobedience: 7 In the which ye also walked sometime, when ye lived in them. 8 But now ye also put off all these; anger, wrath, malice, blasphemy, filthy communication out of your mouth. 9 Lie not one to another, seeing that ye have put off the old man with his deeds; 10And have put on the new *man,* which is renewed in knowledge after the image of him that created him: 11 Where there is neither Greek nor Jew, circumcision nor uncircumcision, Barbarian, Scythian,

N.A.S.

raised Him from the dead. 13And when you were dead in your transgressions and the uncircumcision of your flesh, He made you alive together with Him, having forgiven us all our transgressions, 14 having cancelled out the certificate of debt consisting of decrees against us *and* which was hostile to us; and He has taken it out of the way, having nailed it to the cross. 15 When He had disarmed the rulers and authorities, He made a public display of them, having triumphed over them through Him.

16 Therefore let no one act as your judge in regard to food or drink or in respect to a festival or a new moon or a Sabbath day— 17 things which are a *mere* shadow of what is to come; but the substance belongs to Christ. 18 Let no one keep defrauding you of your prize by delighting in self-abasement and the worship of the angels, taking his stand on *visions* he has seen, inflated without cause by his fleshly mind, 19 and not holding fast to the Head, from whom the entire body, being supplied and held together by the joints and ligaments, grows with a growth which is from God.

20 If you have died with Christ to the elementary principles of the world, why, as if you were living in the world, do you submit yourself to decrees, such as, 21 "Do not handle, do not taste, do not touch!" 22 (which all *refer to* things destined to perish with the using)—in accordance with the commandments and teachings of men? 23 These are matters which have, to be sure, the appearance of wisdom in selfmade religion and self-abasement and severe treatment of the body, *but are* of no value against fleshly indulgence.

3 If then you have been raised up with Christ, keep seeking the things above, where Christ is, seated at the right hand of God. 2 Set your mind on the things above, not on the things that are on earth. 3 For you have died and your life is hidden with Christ in God. 4 When Christ, who is our life, is revealed, then you also will be revealed with Him in glory. 5 Therefore consider the members of your earthly body as dead to immorality, impurity, passion, evil desire, and greed, which amounts to idolatry. 6 For it is on account of these things that the wrath of God will come[a], 7 and in them you also once walked, when you were living in them. 8 But now you also, put them all aside: anger, wrath, malice, slander, *and* abusive speech from your mouth. 9 Do not lie to one another, since you laid aside the old self with its *evil* practices, 10 and have put on the new self who is being renewed to a true knowledge according to the image of the One who created him, 11 —a *renewal* in which there is no *distinction between* Greek and Jew, circumcised and uncircumcised, barbarian, Scythian, slave and freeman, but Christ is all, and in all.

[a] Some early mss. add, *upon the sons of disobedience.*

WILLIAMS

from the dead. 13 Yes, although you were dead through your shortcomings and were physically uncircumcised, God made you live again through fellowship with Christ. He graciously forgave us all our shortcomings, 14 canceled the note*a* that stood against us, with its requirements, and has put it out of our way by nailing it to the cross. 15 He thus stripped the principalities and dominions of power and made a public display of them, triumphing over them by the cross.

16 Stop letting anyone pass judgment on you in matters of eating and drinking, or in the matter of annual or monthly feasts or sabbaths. 17 These were but the shadow of what was coming; the reality belongs to Christ. 18 Stop letting anyone, in gratuitious humility and worship of angels, defraud you as an umpire, for such a one is taking his stand on the mere visions he has seen, and is groundlessly conceited over his sensuous mind. 19 Such a person is not continuing in connection with the Head, from which the whole body, when supplied and united through its joints and sinews, grows with a growth that God produces.

20 If once through fellowship with Christ you died and· were separated from the world's crude notions, why do you live as though you belonged to the world? Why submit to rules such as, 21 "You must not handle," "You must not taste," "You must not touch," 22 which refer to things that perish in the using, in accordance with human rules and teachings? 23 Such practices have the outward expression of wisdom, with their self-imposed devotions, their self-humiliation, their torturings of the body, but they are of no value; they really satisfy the lower nature.

3   *Results of union with Christ: evil habits given up, the finer virtues put on like new clothes; duties of husbands and wives, of children and parents, of slaves and their owners*

So if you have been raised to life in fellowship with Christ, keep on seeking the things above, where Christ is seated at the right hand of God. 2 Practice occupying your minds with the things above, not with the things on earth; 3 for you have died, and your life is now hidden in God through your fellowship with Christ. 4 When Christ, who is our life, appears, you too will appear to be glorified in fellowship with Him.

5 So once for all put to death your lower, earthly nature with respect to sexual immorality, impurity, passion, evil desire, and greed, which is real idolatry. 6 It is on account of these very sins that God's anger is coming. 7 You too used to practice these sins, when you used to live that sort of life. 8 But now you too must once for all put them all aside—anger, rage, malice, and abusive, filthy talk from your lips. 9 Stop lying to one another, for you have stripped off the old self with its practices, 10 and have put on the new self which is in the process of being made new in the likeness of its Creator, so that you may attain a perfect knowledge of Him. 11 In this new relation there is no Greek and Jew, no circumcised and uncircumcised, no barbarian, Scythian, slave and freeman, but Christ is everything and in us all.

[a] Lit., *handwriting*, so note or bond.

BECK

13 Yes, you who were dead in sins and in your uncircumcised bodies He has made alive with Him when He forgave us all our sins, 14 wiped out the Law's demands that were against us and took them out of the way by nailing them to the cross. 15 He stripped rulers and powers of their armor and made a public show of them as He triumphed over them in Christ.

Man-made Rules

16 Then nobody should say you are wrong in what you eat or drink or do on a festival, on the first of the month, or on a Sabbath. 17 These have been a shadow of the coming things, but the real things are in Christ. 18 Nobody who likes to be humble and worship angels should condemn you. Such a person goes on searching his visions and without a reason is puffed up by his fleshly mind. 19 He doesn't cling to the Head, who by being in touch with the whole body nourishes it and by its ligaments binds it together to make it grow as God gives it growth.

20 With Christ you have died to the elements of the world. Then why, as though you were living with the world, do you let others dictate to you: 21 "Don't take hold, don't taste, and don't touch"? 22 These are rules about all such things as are meant to be used up and pass away. You are doing *what men order and teach;*[1] 23 this looks like wisdom, with its self-imposed worship, humble way, and harsh treatment of the body. But it lacks honor—it serves the full enjoyment of the flesh.

In Christ We Put Away Sin

3   Now if you were raised with Christ, be eager for the things that are above, where Christ is *sitting at the right of God.*[2] 2 Keep your mind on things above, not on earthly things. 3 You see, you have died, and your life is hidden with Christ in God. 4 When Christ, your Life, appears, then you, too, will appear with Him in glory.

5 Kill, then, what is earthly in you: sexual sin, uncleanness, passion, evil lust, and greed, which is idol worship; 6 these are bringing down God's anger. 7 Once you also practiced them when you lived in them. 8 But now also get rid of all such things as anger, rage, malice, slander, and dirty talk. 9 Don't lie to one another, seeing that you have put away your old self and its ways 10 and have put on the new self, which is continually renewed in knowledge *to be like Him who made him.*[3] 11 Here there is no Greek or Jew, circumcised or uncircumcised, barbarian, Scythian, slave or free, but Christ is everything and in everything.

[1] Is. 29:13
[2] Ps. 110:1
[3] Gen. 1:26-27

K.J.V.

bond *nor* free: but Christ *is* all, and in all. 12 Put on therefore, as the elect of God, holy and beloved, bowels of mercies, kindness, humbleness of mind, meekness, longsuffering; 13 Forbearing one another, and forgiving one another, if any man have a quarrel against any: even as Christ forgave you, so also *do* ye. 14And above all these things *put on* charity, which is the bond of perfectness. 15And let the peace of God rule in your hearts, to the which also ye are called in one body; and be ye thankful. 16 Let the word of Christ dwell in you richly in all wisdom; teaching and admonishing one another in psalms and hymns and spiritual songs, singing with grace in your hearts to the Lord. 17And whatsoever ye do in word or deed, *do* all in the name of the Lord Jesus, giving thanks to God and the Father by him. 18 Wives, submit yourselves unto your own husbands, as it is fit in the Lord. 19 Husbands, love *your* wives, and be not bitter against them. 20 Children, obey *your* parents in all things: for this is well pleasing unto the Lord. 21 Fathers, provoke not your children *to anger,* lest they be discouraged. 22 Servants, obey in all things *your* masters according to the flesh; not with eyeservice, as menpleasers; but in singleness of heart, fearing God: 23And whatsoever ye do, do *it* heartily, as to the Lord, and not unto men; 24 Knowing that of the Lord ye shall receive the reward of the inheritance: for ye serve the Lord Christ. 25 But he that doeth wrong shall receive for the wrong which he hath done: and there is no respect of persons.

4 Masters, give unto *your* servants that which is just and equal; knowing that ye also have a Master in heaven. 2 Continue in prayer, and watch in the same with thanksgiving; 3 Withal praying also for us, that God would open unto us a door of utterance, to speak the mystery of Christ, for which I am also in bonds: 4 That I may make it manifest, as I ought to speak. 5 Walk in wisdom toward them that are without, redeeming the time. 6 Let your speech *be* always with grace, seasoned with salt, that ye may know how ye ought to answer every man. 7All my state shall Tychicus declare unto you, *who is* a beloved brother, and a faithful minister and fellow servant in the Lord: 8 Whom I have sent unto you for the same purpose, that he might know your estate, and comfort your hearts; 9 With Onesimus, a faithful and beloved brother, who is *one* of you. They shall make known unto you all

N.A.S.

12 And so, as those who have been chosen of God, holy and beloved, put on a heart of compassion, kindness, humility, gentleness and patience; 13 bearing with one another, and forgiving each other, whoever has a complaint against any one; just as the Lord forgave you, so also should you. 14And beyond all these things *put on* love, which is the perfect bond of unity. 15And let the peace of Christ rule in your hearts, to which indeed you were called in one body; and be thankful. 16 Let the word of *a*Christ richly dwell within you; with all wisdom teaching and admonishing one another with psalms *and* hymns *and* spiritual songs, singing with thankfulness in your hearts to God. 17And whatever you do in word or deed, *do* all in the name of the Lord Jesus, giving thanks through Him to God the Father.

18 Wives, be subject to your husbands, as is fitting in the Lord. 19 Husbands, love your wives, and do not be embittered against them. 20 Children, be obedient to your parents in all things, for this is well pleasing to the Lord. 21 Fathers, do not *b*exasperate your children, that they may not lose heart. 22 Slaves, in all things obey those who are your masters on earth, not with external service, as those who *merely* please men, but with sincerity of heart, fearing the Lord. 23 Whatever you do, do your work heartily, as for the Lord rather than for men; 24 knowing that from the Lord you will receive the reward of the inheritance. It is the Lord Christ whom you serve. 25 For he who does wrong will receive the consequences of the wrong which he has done, and that without partiality.

4 Masters, grant to your slaves justice and fairness, knowing that you too have a Master in heaven.

2 Devote yourselves to prayer, keeping alert in it with *an attitude of* thanksgiving; 3 praying at the same time for us as well, that God may open up to us a door for the word, so that we may speak forth the mystery of Christ, for which I have also been imprisoned; 4 in order that I may make it clear in the way I ought to speak. 5 Conduct yourselves with wisdom toward outsiders, making the most of your time. 6 Let your speech always be with grace, seasoned, *as it were,* with salt, so that you may know how you should respond to each person.

7 As to all my affairs, Tychicus, *our* beloved brother and faithful servant and fellow-bondslave in the Lord, will bring you information. 8 For I have sent him to you for this very purpose, that you may know *about* our circumstances and that he may encourage your hearts; 9 and with him Onesimus, *our* faithful and beloved brother, who is one of your *number.* They will inform you about the whole situation here.

[a] Some mss. read, *the Lord;* others read, *God.*
[b] Some early mss. read, *provoke to anger.*

WILLIAMS

12 So as God's own chosen people, consecrated and dearly loved, you must once for all clothe yourselves with tenderheartedness, kindness, humility, gentleness, patience; you must keep on 13 forbearing one another and freely forgiving one another, if anyone has a complaint against another; just as the Lord has freely forgiven you, so must you also do. 14And over all these qualities put on love, which is the tie of perfection that binds us together. 15 Let the peace that Christ can give keep on acting as umpire in your hearts, for you were called to this state as members of one body. And practice being thankful. 16 Let the message of Christ continue to live in you in all its wealth of wisdom; keep on teaching it to one another and training one another in it with thankfulness, in your hearts singing praise to God with psalms, hymns, and spiritual songs. 17And whatever you say or do, let it all be done with reference to the Lord Jesus, and through Him continue to give thanks to God the Father.

18 You married women must continue to live in subordination to your husbands, for this is your Christian duty. 19 You husbands must continue to love your wives and stop being harsh with them. 20 Children, practice obedience to your parents in everything, for this is acceptable in Christians. 21 Fathers, stop exasperating your children, so as to keep them from losing heart. 22 Slaves, practice obedience to your earthly masters in everything, not as though they were watching you and as though you were merely pleasing men, but with sincerity of heart, because you fear the Lord. 23 Whatever you do, do it with all your heart, as work for the Lord and not for men, 24 for you know that it is from the Lord that you are going to get your pay in the form of an inheritance; so keep on serving Christ the Lord. 25 For the man who wrongs another will be paid back the wrong he has done; and there are no exceptions. 4:1 Masters, you must practice doing the right and square things by your slaves, for you know that you have a Master in heaven.

4 *He urges them to be prayerful and prudent; sends Tychicus and Onesimus; sends greetings from his many friends; instructions concerning his letters*

2 You must persevere in prayer and by this means stay wide awake when you give thanks. 3 At the same time keep on praying for me too, that God may open the door of opportunity for the message, so that I may tell the open secret about Christ, for the sake of which I am held a prisoner, 4 in order to make it evident why I have to tell it. 5 Practice living prudently in your relations with outsiders, making the most of your opportunities. 6 Always let your conversation be seasoned with salt, that is, with winsomeness, so that you may know how to make a fitting answer to everyone.

7 My dearly loved Tychicus, a faithful minister and my fellow-servant in the Lord's work, will tell you all about me. 8 I am sending him to you for the express purpose of letting you know my circumstances, and of cheering your hearts; 9 he is accompanied by Onesimus, a faithful and dearly loved brother, who is one of your own number. They will tell you everything that is going on here.

BECK

Live as God's People

12 Then, as holy people whom God has chosen and loved, be tenderhearted, kind, humble, gentle, patient; 13 bear with one another and forgive one another if you have a complaint against anyone. Forgive as the Lord forgave you. 14 With all this have love, which binds it all together to make it perfect.

15 Let the peace of Christ, to which you were called as one body, be in your hearts to decide things for you. And be thankful. 16 Let Christ's Word live richly in you as you teach and warn one another, using every kind of wisdom. With thankful hearts sing psalms, hymns, and spiritual songs to God. 17 And everything you say or do, do it in the name of the Lord Jesus, and by Him give thanks to God the Father.

Parents, Children, and Slaves

18 You married women, submit to your husbands as it is right in the Lord. 19 You husbands, love your wives, and don't be harsh with them.

20 You children, obey your parents in everything. This is pleasant when it is done in the Lord. 21 Parents, don't irritate your children, or they will get discouraged.

22 You slaves, obey your earthly masters in everything. Don't serve them only when they are watching you, as if you meant only to please them, but sincerely because you respect the Lord. 23 Whatever you do, work heartily as for the Lord and not for men, 24 because you know the Lord will give you the inheritance as your reward. Serve the Lord Christ. 25 The man who does wrong will get paid for the wrong he has done, and there will be no exceptions.

4 You masters, be just and fair to your slaves because you know you, too, have a Master in heaven.

Winning the Others

2 Keep on praying, watch as you pray, and give thanks. 3 At the same time also pray for us that God will open a door for the Word and let us tell the hidden truth of Christ, for which I am in chains, 4 that I may make it as well known as I should.

5 Be wise in the way you live with those who are outside, and make the most of your opportunities. 6 Always talk pleasantly, season your talk with salt so you will know how you should answer everyone.

Tychicus and Onesimus

7 Tychicus, a dear fellow Christian, loyal helper and fellow servant in the Lord, will tell you all about me. 8 I'm sending him to you to bring you the news about us and encourage you. 9 Onesimus, our loyal and dear fellow Christian who is one of you, is with him. They will tell you about everything that is happening here.

K.J.V.

things which *are done* here. 10Aristarchus my fellow prisoner saluteth you, and Marcus, sister's son to Barnabas, (touching whom ye received commandments: if he come unto you, receive him;) 11And Jesus, which is called Justus, who are of the circumcision. These only *are my* fellow workers unto the kingdom of God, which have been a comfort unto me. 12 Epaphras, who is *one* of you, a servant of Christ, saluteth you, always labouring fervently for you in prayers, that ye may stand perfect and complete in all the will of God. 13 For I bear him record, that he hath a great zeal for you, and them *that are* in Laodicea, and them in Hierapolis. 14 Luke, the beloved physician, and Demas, greet you. 15 Salute the brethren which are in Laodicea, and Nymphas, and the church which is in his house. 16And when this epistle is read among you, cause that it be read also in the church of the Laodiceans; and that ye likewise read the *epistle* from Laodicea. 17And say to Archippus, Take heed to the ministry which thou hast received in the Lord, that thou fulfil it. 18 The salutation by the hand of me Paul. Remember my bonds. Grace *be* with you. Amen.

Written from Rome to the Colossians by Tychicus and Onesimus.

N.A.S.

10 Aristarchus, my fellow prisoner, sends you his greetings; and *also* Barnabas' cousin Mark (about whom you received instructions: if he comes to you, welcome him); 11 and *also* Jesus who is called Justus; these are the only fellow-workers for the kingdom of God who are from the circumcision; and they have proved to be an encouragement to me. 12 Epaphras, who is one of your number, a bondslave of Jesus Christ, sends you his greetings, always laboring earnestly for you in his prayers, that you may stand perfect and fully assured in all the will of God. 13 For I bear him witness that he has a deep concern for you and for those who are in Laodicea and Hierapolis. 14 Luke, the beloved physician, sends you his greetings, and *also* Demas. 15 Greet the brethren who are in Laodicea and also aNympha and the church that is in her house. 16And when this letter is read among you, have it also read in the church of the Loadiceans; and you for your part read my letter *that is coming* from Laodicea. 17And say to Archippus, "Take heed to the ministry which you have received in the Lord, that you may fulfill it."

18 I, Paul, write this greeting with my own hand. Remember my imprisonment. Grace be with you.

[a] Or, *Nymphas* (masc.)

WILLIAMS

10 Aristarchus, my fellow-prisoner, wishes to be remembered to you; and so does Mark, the cousin of Barnabas; if he comes to see you, give him a hearty welcome. 11 So does Jesus who is called Justus. These are the only converts from Judaism that are fellow-workers with me here for the kingdom of God, who have proved a real comfort to me. 12 Epaphras, one of your own number, a slave of Christ Jesus, wishes to be remembered to you. He is always earnestly pleading for you in his prayers that you may stand fast as men mature and of firm convictions in everything required by the will of God. 13 For I can testify how great his toiling for you is and for the brothers in Laodicea and Hierapolis. 14 Our dearly loved Luke, the physician, and Demas, wish to be remembered to you. 15 Remember me to the brothers in Laodicea and to Nympha and the church that meets at her house. 16 When this letter has been read to you, have it read to the church at Laodicea too, and see to it that you too read the one that is coming from Laodicea. 17 And tell Archippus, "See to it that you continue until you fill full your ministry which you received in the Lord's work."

18 This farewell greeting is in my own hand, from Paul. Remember that I am still a prisoner. Spiritual blessing be with you.

BECK

Greetings

10 Aristarchus, my fellow prisoner, sends greetings. So does Mark, the cousin of Barnabas. You received directions about him. If he comes to you, welcome him. 11 Jesus, called Justus, also greets you. They are the only Jews working with me for God's kingdom. They've been a comfort to me. 12 Epaphras, one of your men, a servant of Christ Jesus, greets you. He is always wrestling in prayer for you that you will stand mature and convinced in everything God wants. 13 I assure you he works hard for you and the people in Laodicea and Hierapolis. 14 Luke, the doctor and dear friend, and Demas greet you. 15 Greet the fellow Christians in Laodicea, and Nympha and the church that meets at her home.

16 When this letter has been read to you, have it read also in the church at Laodicea, and see that you also read the letter from Laodicea.

17 Tell Archippus, "See that you do all the work you were given to do as the Lord's servant."

18 I, Paul, am writing this greeting with my own hand. Remember I'm in chains. May the Lord love you!

THE FIRST EPISTLE

OF PAUL THE APOSTLE

TO THE

THESSALONIANS

THE FIRST EPISTLE

OF PAUL TO THE

THESSALONIANS

K.J.V.

1 Paul, and Silvanus, and Timotheus, unto the church of the Thessalonians *which is* in God the Father, and *in* the Lord Jesus Christ: Grace *be* unto you, and peace, from God our Father, and the Lord Jesus Christ. 2 We give thanks to God always for you all, making mention of you in our prayers; 3 Remembering without ceasing your work of faith, and labour of love, and patience of hope in our Lord Jesus Christ, in the sight of God and our Father; 4 Knowing, brethren beloved, your election of God. 5 For our gospel came not unto you in word only, but also in power, and in the Holy Ghost, and in much assurance; as ye know what manner of men we were among you for your sake. 6 And ye became followers of us, and of the Lord, having received the word in much affliction, with joy of the Holy Ghost: 7 So that ye were ensamples to all that believe in Macedonia and Achaia. 8 For from you sounded out the word of the Lord not only in Macedonia and Achaia, but also in every place your faith to God-ward is spread abroad; so that we need not to speak any thing. 9 For they themselves shew of us what manner of entering in we had unto you, and how ye turned to God from idols to serve the living and true God; 10 And to wait for his Son from heaven, whom he raised from the dead, *even* Jesus, which delivered us from the wrath to come.

N.A.S.

1 Paul and Silvanus and Timothy to the church of the Thessalonians in God the Father and the Lord Jesus Christ: Grace to you and peace.
2 We give thanks to God always for all of you, making mention *of you* in our prayers; 3 constantly bearing in mind your work of faith and labor of love and steadfastness of hope in our Lord Jesus Christ in the presence of our God and Father; 4 knowing, brethren beloved by God, *His* choice of you, 5 for our gospel did not come to you in word only, but also in power and in the Holy Spirit and with full conviction; just as you know what kind of men we proved to be among you for your sake. 6 You also became imitators of us and of the Lord, having received the word in much tribulation with the joy of the Holy Spirit, 7 so that you became an example to all the believers in Macedonia and in Achaia. 8 For the word of the Lord has sounded forth from you, not only in Macedonia and Achaia, but also in every place your faith toward God has gone forth, so that we have no need to say anything. 9 For they themselves report about us what kind of a reception we had with you, and how you turned to God from idols to serve a living and true God, 10 and to wait for His Son from heaven, whom He raised from the dead, *that is* Jesus, who delivers us from the wrath to come.

2 For yourselves, brethren, know our entrance in unto you, that it was not in vain: 2 But even after that we had suffered before, and were shamefully entreated, as ye know, at Philippi, we were bold in our God to speak unto you the gospel of God with much contention. 3 For our exhortation *was* not of deceit, nor of uncleanness, nor in guile: 4 But as we were allowed of God to be put in trust with the gospel, even so we speak; not as pleasing men, but God, which trieth our hearts. 5 For neither at any time used

2 For you yourselves know, brethren, that our coming to you was not in vain, 2 but after we had already suffered and been mistreated in Philippi, as you know, we had the boldness in our God to speak to you the gospel of God amid much opposition. 3 For our exhortation does not *come* from error or impurity or by way of deceit; 4 but just as we have been approved by God to be entrusted with the gospel, so we speak, not as pleasing men but God, who examines our hearts. 5 For we never

FIRST THESSALONIANS

THESSALONIANS

1 *He greets them; thanks God for their faith, devotion, and hope; they had be-become an example to other believers everywhere*

Paul, Silvanus, and Timothy to the Thessalonian church in union with God the Father and the Lord Jesus Christ: spiritual blessing and peace be to you.

2 We always thank God for you all as we continually mention you in our prayers, 3 for we can never for a moment before our God forget your energizing faith,[a] your toiling love, and your enduring hope in our Lord Jesus Christ. 4 For we know, brothers so beloved by God, that He has chosen you, 5 for our preaching of the good news came to you not entirely in words but with power and with the Holy Spirit and with absolute certainty (for you know the kind of men we were among you for your own sakes). 6And you followed the example set by us and by the Lord, because you welcomed our message with a joy inspired by the Holy Spirit, in spite of the painful persecutions it brought you, 7 so that you became examples to all the believers in Macedonia and Greece. For the message of the Lord has rung out from you, not only in Macedonia and Greece, but everywhere the report of your faith in God has been told, so that we need never mention it. 8 For the people themselves tell us what a welcome you gave us, and how you turned from idols to the true God, to serve the God who lives on and is real, 9 and to wait for the coming from heaven of His Son, whom He raised from the dead, Jesus who delivers us from the wrath to come.

2 *Reminds them how he told them the good news; how he lived among them; thanks God for their endurance in persecution; longs to see them*

For you know yourselves, brothers, that our visit to you was by no means a failure. 2 But, although we had just suffered and been insulted, as you remember, at Philippi, we again summoned courage by the help of God, in spite of the terrific strain, to tell you God's good news. 3 For our appeal did not originate from a delusion or an impure motive; it was not made in fraud; 4 for since we have been so approved by God as to be entrusted with the good news, we are now telling it, not to please men but God, who proves and finds approved our hearts.

5 Indeed, we never resorted to flattery, as

[a] Lit., *your work of faith,* etc.

1 Paul, Silas, and Timothy to the church of the Thessalonians which is in God the Father and the Lord Jesus Christ: Love to you and peace!

The Good News

2 We always thank God for all of you and mention you in our prayers, 3 never forgetting before our God and Father how your faith is working, your love is toiling, and your hope in our Lord Jesus Christ is enduring. 4 We know, fellow Christians, whom God has loved, that He has chosen you, 5 because the good news we told wasn't just words to you, 6 but it had power, the Holy Spirit, and a strong conviction; you know this is the kind of men we proved to be among you for your good. And you became just like us and like the Lord as you welcomed the Word, which brought you much suffering, with such joy in the Holy Spirit 7 that you became a model for all the believers in Macedonia and Greece. 8 Not only has the Lord's Word spread from you through Macedonia and Greece, but everywhere people have heard of your faith in God so that we don't need to say anything. 9 They tell how we came to you and you turned from the idols to God, to serve a God who lives and is real 10 and to wait for His Son to come from heaven—whom He raised from the dead—Jesus, who saves us from the punishment that is coming.

2 You know, my fellow Christians, our coming to you wasn't in vain. 2 We had suffered and been shamefully mistreated in Philippi, as you know. But then we took courage in our God to tell you God's good news though it meant a hard struggle.

3 Our appeal isn't based on error or an unclean desire, and we aren't tricking you. 4 No, we have God's approval to be entrusted with the good news. And so we tell it, not to please people but God, *who tests our hearts.*[1] 5 We never flattered, as you know, or found

[1] Jer. 11:20

575

K.J.V.

we flattering words, as ye know, nor a cloak of covetousness; God *is* witness: 6 Nor of men sought we glory, neither of you, nor *yet* of others, when we might have been burdensome, as the apostles of Christ. 7 But we were gentle among you, even as a nurse cherisheth her children: 8 So being affectionately desirous of you, we were willing to have imparted unto you, not the gospel of God only, but also our own souls, because ye were dear unto us. 9 For ye remember, brethren, our labour and travail: for labouring night and day, because we would not be chargeable unto any of you, we preached unto you the gospel of God. 10 Ye *are* witnesses, and God *also*, how holily and justly and unblameably we behaved ourselves among you that believe: 11 As ye know how we exhorted and comforted and charged every one of you, as a father *doth* his children, 12 That ye would walk worthy of God, who hath called you unto his kingdom and glory. 13 For this cause also thank we God without ceasing, because, when ye received the word of God which ye heard of us, ye received *it* not *as* the word of men, but, as it is in truth, the word of God, which effectually worketh also in you that believe. 14 For ye, brethren, became followers of the churches of God which in Judea are in Christ Jesus: for ye also have suffered like things of your own countrymen, even as they *have* of the Jews: 15 Who both killed the Lord Jesus, and their own prophets, and have persecuted us; and they please not God, and are contrary to all men: 16 Forbidding us to speak to the Gentiles that they might be saved, to fill up their sins always: for the wrath is come upon them to the uttermost. 17 But we, brethren, being taken from you for a short time in presence, not in heart, endeavoured the more abundantly to see your face with great desire. 18 Wherefore we would have come unto you, even I Paul, once and again; but Satan hindered us. 19 For what *is* our hope, or joy, or crown of rejoicing? *Are* not even ye in the presence of our Lord Jesus Christ at his coming? 20 For ye are our glory and joy.

3 Wherefore when we could no longer forbear, we thought it good to be left at Athens alone; 2 And sent Timotheus, our brother, and minister of God, and our fellow labourer in the gospel of Christ, to establish you, and to comfort you concerning your faith: 3 That no man should be moved by these afflictions: for yourselves know that we are appointed thereunto. 4 For verily, when we were with you, we told you before that we should suffer tribulation; even as it came to pass, and ye know. 5 For this cause, when I could no longer forbear, I sent to know your faith, lest by some means the tempter have tempted you, and our labour be in vain. 6 But now when Timotheus came from you unto us, and brought us good tidings of your faith and charity, and that ye have good remembrance

N.A.S.

came with flattering speech, as you know, nor with a pretext for greed—God is witness— 6 nor did we seek glory from men, either from you or from others, even though as apostles of Christ we might have asserted our authority. 7 But we proved to be [a]gentle among you, as a nursing *mother* tenderly cares for her own children. 8 Having thus a fond affection for you, we were well pleased to impart to you not only the gospel but also our own lives, because you had become very dear to us. 9 For you recall, brethren, our labor and hardship, *how* working night and day so as not to be a burden to any of you, we proclaimed to you the gospel of God. 10 You are witnesses, and *so is* God, how devoutly and uprightly and blamelessly we behaved toward you believers; 11 just as you know how we *were* exhorting and encouraging and imploring each one of you as a father *would* his own children, 12 so that you may walk in a manner worthy of the God who calls you into His own kingdom and glory.

13 And for this reason we also constantly thank God that when you received from us the word of God's message, you accepted *it* not *as* the word of men, but *for* what it really is, the word of God, which also performs its work in you who believe. 14 For you, brethren, became imitators of the churches of God in Christ Jesus that are in Judea, for you also endured the same sufferings at the hands of your own countrymen, even as they *did* from the Jews, 15 who both killed the Lord Jesus and the prophets, and drove us out; they are not pleasing to God, but hostile to all men, 16 hindering us from speaking to the Gentiles that they might be saved; with the result that they always fill up the measure of their sins. But wrath has come upon them [b]to the utmost.

17 But we, brethren, having been bereft of you for a short while—in person, not in spirit— were all the more eager with great desire to see your face. 18 For we wanted to come to you—I, Paul, more than once—and *yet* Satan thwarted us. 19 For who is our hope or joy or crown of exultation? Is it not even you, in the presence of our Lord Jesus at His coming? 20 For you are our glory and joy.

3 Therefore when we could endure *it* no longer, we thought it best to be left behind at Athens alone; 2 and we sent Timothy, our brother and God's fellow-worker in the gospel of Christ, to strengthen and encourage you as to your faith; 3 so that no man may be disturbed by these afflictions; for you yourselves know that we have been destined for this. 4 For indeed when we were with you, we *kept* telling you in advance that we were going to suffer affliction; and so it came to pass, as you know. 5 For this reason, when I could endure *it* no longer, I also sent to find out about your faith, for fear that the tempter might have tempted you, and our labor should be in vain. 6 But now that Timothy has come to us from you, and has brought us good news of your faith and love, and that you always think kindly of us,

[a] Some ancient mss. read, *babes.* [b] Or, *forever; or, altogether.*

WILLIAMS

you are well aware, nor to any pretext for making money; God is our witness. 6 We never sought praise from men, neither from you or from anyone else; although as apostles we could have stood on our official dignity. 7 Instead we were little children among you; we were like a mother nursing her children. 8 Because we were yearning for you so tenderly, we were willing, not only to share with you God's good news, but to lay down our very lives too for you, all because you were so dearly loved by us. 9 You remember, brothers, our hard labor and toil. We kept up our habit of working night and day, in order not to be a burden to any of you when we preached to you. 10 You can testify, and God too, with what pure, upright, and irreproachable motives I dealt with you who believed; 11 for you know how, as a father deals with his children, we used to encourage you, cheer you on, and charge each of you 12 to live lives worthy of God who calls you into His kingdom and His glory.

13 For another reason too, we, as far as we are concerned, are constantly giving thanks to God; that is, when you received the message you heard from us, you welcomed it not as the message of men but as the message of God, as it really is, which keeps on working in you who believe. 14 For you, brothers, followed the example of God's churches in Judea that are in union with Christ Jesus, for you too have suffered the same sort of ill-treatment at the hands of your fellow-countrymen as they did at the hands of the Jews, 15 who killed the Lord Jesus and persecuted the prophets and us; and who continue to displease God and show themselves in opposition to all mankind, 16 by trying to keep us from speaking to the heathen, so that they may be saved, so as always to fill to the brim the cup of their sins. But at last God's wrath has come upon them.

17 Now we, brothers, on our part, when we were separated from you for a little while—in person but not in heart—were extremely eager and intensely longing to see you. 18 Because we did want to come to see you; I mean, that I myself, Paul, wanted again and again to come, but Satan prevented it. 19 For what is our hope or happiness or crown of boasting, except you, in the presence of our Lord Jesus Christ when He comes? 20 You, indeed, are our glory and our joy.

3 *He sends Timothy to cheer them; he is grateful for the good tidings that Timothy brought; he prays for their growth in love and purity*

So when I could not bear it any longer, I decided to be left behind in Athens alone, 2 and so I sent my brother Timothy, God's minister in the preaching of the good news of Christ, to strengthen and encourage you in your faith, 3 so that none of you might be deceived amid these difficulties. For you knew yourselves that this is our appointed lot, 4 for when we were with you, we told you beforehand that we were going to be pressed with difficulties, and it took place, as you know. 5 That was why, when I could bear it no longer, I sent to learn about your faith, for I was afraid that the tempter had tempted you and our labor might be lost.

6 But now, since Timothy has just come back to me from you, and brought me good tidings of your faith and love, and told me how kindly

BECK

excuses to make money, as God knows, 6 nor did we try to get you or other people to praise us, 7 although we can claim respect as apostles of Christ.

You Are Dear to Us

But we became children when we were with you—and like a mother tenderly caring for her children. 8 So we longed for you and were determined to share with you not only God's good news but our own lives, so dear had you become to us. 9 You remember, my fellow Christians, how hard we worked and struggled. Night and day working for our living, not to burden any of you, we preached God's good news to you. 10 You are witnesses and God too, how holy, righteous, and blameless we proved to be to you who believe. 11 As you know, like a father urging his children we used to urge, 12 encourage, and warn every one of you to live worthy of God, who is calling you into His kingdom and glory.

13 We continually thank God also for this, that when you accepted God's Word, which you heard from us, you didn't accept it as the word of men but as the Word of God, which it really is. And it is working in you who believe.

14 You, our fellow Christians, became just like God's churches in Christ Jesus that are in Judea, since you suffered the same things from your own people as they did from the Jews. 15 These killed the Lord Jesus and the prophets and drove us out. They don't please God, are opposed to everybody, 16 and try to keep us from talking to the non-Jews to save them, and so they always *fill up the cup of* their *sins.*[2] Now God is angry with them forever.

17 My fellow Christians, when we were torn from you like orphans for a little while—you were out of sight but not out of mind—we were all the more eagerly and intensely longing to see you. 18 We wanted to come to you—I, Paul, wanted to again and again—but the devil stopped us.

19 After all, who is our hope or joy or crown of glory before our Lord Jesus when He comes? Aren't you that? 20 Why, you are our glory and joy!

We Long to See You

3 When we couldn't stand it any longer, we thought it best to be left alone in Athens, 2 and we sent Timothy, our fellow Christian who works with God in telling the good news of Christ, to strengthen you and encourage you in your faith, 3 so that these troubles will not disturb anyone, because you know they are planned for us. 4 When we were with you, we warned you, "We're going to suffer." And so it happened, as you know. 5 That's why I couldn't stand it any longer, and I sent to find out about your faith. I was afraid the Tempter had in some way tempted you and our work was wasted.

6 But now Timothy came back to us from you and told us the good news of your faith and love, also that you always think kindly of us

[2] Gen. 15:16

577

K.J.V.

of us always, desiring greatly to see us, as we also *to see* you: 7 Therefore, brethren, we were comforted over *you* in all our affliction and distress by your faith: 8 For now we live, if ye stand fast in the Lord. 9 For what thanks can we render to God again for you, for all the joy wherewith we joy for your sakes before our God; 10 Night and day praying exceedingly that we might see your face, and might perfect that which is lacking in your faith? 11 Now God himself and our Father, and our Lord Jesus Christ, direct our way unto you. 12 And the Lord make you to increase and abound in love one toward another, and toward all *men,* even as we *do* toward you: 13 To the end he may stablish your hearts unblameable in holiness before God, even our Father, at the coming of our Lord Jesus Christ with all his saints.

4 Furthermore then we beseech you, brethren, and exhort you by the Lord Jesus, that as ye have received of us how ye ought to walk and to please God, *so* ye would abound more and more. 2 For ye know what commandments we gave you by the Lord Jesus. 3 For this is the will of God, *even* your sanctification, that ye should abstain from fornication; 4 That every one of you should know how to possess his vessel in sanctification and honour; 5 Not in the lust of concupiscence, even as the Gentiles which know not God: 6 That no *man* go beyond and defraud his brother in *any* matter: because that the Lord *is* the avenger of all such, as we also have forewarned you and testified. 7 For God hath not called us unto uncleanness, but unto holiness. 8 He therefore that despiseth, despiseth not man, but God, who hath also given unto us his Holy Spirit. 9 But as touching brotherly love ye need not that I write unto you: for ye yourselves are taught of God to love one another. 10 And indeed ye do it toward all the brethren which are in all Macedonia: but we beseech you, brethren, that ye increase more and more; 11 And that ye study to be quiet, and to do your own business, and to work with your own hands, as we commanded you; 12 That ye may walk honestly toward them that are without, and *that* ye may have lack of nothing. 13 But I would not have you to be ignorant, brethren, concerning them which are asleep, that ye sorrow not, even as others which have no hope. 14 For if we believe that Jesus died and rose again, even so them also which sleep in Jesus will God bring with him. 15 For this we say unto you by the word of the Lord, that we which are alive *and* remain unto the coming of the Lord shall not

N.A.S.

longing to see us just as we also long to see you, 7 for this reason, brethren, in all our distress and affliction we were comforted about you through your faith; 8 for now we *really* live, if you stand firm in the Lord. 9 For what thanks can we render to God for you in return for all the joy with which we rejoice before our God on your account, 10 as we night and day keep praying most earnestly that we may see your face, and may complete what is lacking in your faith?

11 Now may our God and Father Himself and Jesus our Lord direct our way to you; 12 and may the Lord cause you to increase and abound in love for one another, and for all men, just as we also *do* for you; 13 so that He may establish your hearts unblameable in holiness before our God and Father at the coming of our Lord Jesus with all His saints.

4 Finally then, brethren, we request and exhort you in the Lord Jesus that, as you received from us *instruction* as to how you ought to walk and please God (just as you actually do [a]walk), that you may excel still more. 2 For you know what commandments we gave you [b]by *the authority of* the Lord Jesus. 3 For this is the will of God, your sanctification; *that is,* that you abstain from sexual immorality; 4 that each of you know how to possess his own [c]vessel in sanctification and honor, 5 not in lustful passion, like the Gentiles who do not know God; 6 *and* that no man transgress and defraud his brother in the matter because the Lord is *the* avenger in all these things, just as we also told you before and solemnly warned *you.* 7 For God has not called us for the purpose of impurity, but in sanctification. 8 Consequently, he who rejects *this* is not rejecting man but the God who gives His Holy Spirit to you.

9 Now as to the love of the brethren, you have no need for *any one* to write to you, for you yourselves are taught by God to love one another; 10 for indeed you do practice it toward all the brethren who are in all Macedonia. But we urge you, brethren, to excel still more, 11 and to make it your ambition to lead a quiet life and attend to your own business and work with your hands, just as we commanded you; 12 so that you may behave properly toward outsiders and not be in any need.

13 But we do not want you to be uninformed, brethren, about those who are asleep, that you may not grieve, as do the rest who have no hope. 14 For if we believe that Jesus died and rose again, even so God will bring with Him those who have fallen asleep in Jesus. 15 For this we say to you by the word of the Lord, that we who are alive, and remain until the coming of the Lord, shall not precede those

[a] Or, *conduct yourselves.* [b] Lit., *through the Lord.* [c] I.e., *body,* or possibly, *wife.*

WILLIAMS

BECK

you remembered me and that you are longing to see me as much as I am to see you, 7 this is the very reason, namely, through your faith, brothers, that I have been encouraged about you, in spite of all my distresses and crushing difficulties, 8 for now I am really living, since you are standing firm in the Lord. 9 For how can I render God enough thanks for you, for all the joy I have on account of you in the presence of our God, 10 as night and day I continue to pray with deepest earnestness and keenest eagerness that I may see your faces and round out to completeness what is lacking in your faith?

11 Now may our God and Father Himself and our Lord Jesus guide my way to you! 12 May the Lord make you increase and overflow in love for one another and for all men, as my love for you does, 13 so that He may strengthen your hearts to be faultless in purity in the sight of God, when our Lord Jesus comes back with all His consecrated ones.

4 *He urges them to personal purity, brotherly love, and honest toil; assures and comforts them that when Jesus comes back their dead loved ones will rise to meet the Lord before the living see Him*

Now, brothers, we ask and beg you, in the face of our union with the Lord Jesus, as you once received from us how you ought to live so as to please God—as indeed you are living—to continue to live this life better and better. 2 For you are aware of the instructions which we gave you by the authority of the Lord Jesus.

3 For it is God's will that you should keep pure in person, that you should practice abstinence from sexual immorality, 4 that each man among you should learn to take his own wife out of pure and honorable motives, 5 not out of evil passions*a* as the heathen do who do not know God; 6 that no one should do wrong and defraud his brother in this matter, because the Lord takes vengeance for all such things, as we told you before and solemnly warned you. 7 For God did not call us to a life of immorality, but to one of personal purity. 8 So whoever rejects this teaching is rejecting not man but God who continues to put His Spirit in you.

9 Now as to brotherly love, you have no need of anyone's writing you, for you have yourselves been taught by God to love one another, 10 as you are practicing it toward all the brothers all over Macedonia.

We beg you, brothers, to continue to live better and better; 11 also keep up your ambition to live quietly, to practice attending to your own business and to work with your own hands, as we directed you, 12 so that you may live influentially with the outsiders, and not be dependent on anybody.

13 Also we do not want you to have any misunderstanding, brothers, about those who are falling asleep, so as to keep you from grieving over them as others do who have no hope. 14 For if we believe that Jesus died and rose again, then through Jesus, God will bring back with Him those who have fallen asleep. 15 For on the Lord's own authority we say that those of us who may be left behind and are still living when the Lord comes back, will have no advantage at all over those who have

and long to see us as we long to see you. 7 So you, fellow Christians, by your faith have encouraged us in all our distress and trouble. 8 Now we live if you stand firm in the Lord.

9 How can we thank God for all the joy you give us before our God 10 as day and night we are most ardently praying to see you face to face and to supply whatever is lacking in your faith? 11 May our God and Father Himself and the Lord Jesus lead us to you.

12 The Lord make you grow in love and overflow with it for one another and for everybody, just as we love you, 13 and so may He give you inward strength to be holy and without a fault before our God and Father when our Lord Jesus comes with all His holy ones! Amen.

Live to Please God

4 And now, my fellow Christians, this is what we ask and urge you to do in the Lord Jesus. You learned from us how you must live and please God, and that is how you are living. But now do so more and more. 2 You know what instructions we gave you by the Lord Jesus. 3 God wants you to be holy and keep away from sexual sin. 4 Every one of you should know how to get a wife in a holy and honorable way 5 and not in the way of passionate lust like *the people of the world who don't know God.*[3] 6 Nobody should wrong and cheat his fellow Christian in business, because *the Lord avenges*[4] all these things, as we told you and warned you before. 7 God didn't call us to be unclean but holy. 8 Now, if anyone rejects this, he doesn't reject a man but God, *who gives you His* Holy *Spirit.*[5]

9 You don't need anyone to write you about brotherly love, because God has taught you to love one another, 10 and you are practicing it toward all the Christians all over Macedonia. But we urge you, my fellow Christians, grow more and more, 11 do your best to live quietly, mind your own business, and work with your hands, as we ordered you to do, 12 so that you live nobly with those who are not Christians—without needing anything.

Your Dead Will Rise

13 We want you to know about those who go to their rest, my fellow Christians, so you don't grieve like the others, who have no hope. 14 We believe that Jesus died and rose again; then God will in the same way through Jesus bring with Him those who went to their rest. 15 We tell you only what the Lord has told us: We who are left behind and are still living when the Lord comes will not get ahead of

[a] Lit., *with personal purity and honor, not in lustful passions.*

[3] Ps. 79:6; Jer. 10:25
[4] Ps. 94:1
[5] Ezek. 36:27; 37:14

K.J.V.

prevent them which are asleep. 16 For the Lord himself shall descend from heaven with a shout, with the voice of the archangel, and with the trump of God: and the dead in Christ shall rise first: 17 Then we which are alive *and* remain shall be caught up together with them in the clouds, to meet the Lord in the air: and so shall we ever be with the Lord. 18 Wherefore comfort one another with these words.

5 But of the times and the seasons, brethren, ye have no need that I write unto you. 2 For yourselves know perfectly that the day of the Lord so cometh as a thief in the night. 3 For when they shall say, Peace and safety; then sudden destruction cometh upon them, as travail upon a woman with child; and they shall not escape. 4 But ye, brethren, are not in darkness, that that day should overtake you as a thief. 5 Ye are all the children of light, and the children of the day: we are not of the night, nor of darkness. 6 Therefore let us not sleep, as *do* others; but let us watch and be sober. 7 For they that sleep sleep in the night; and they that be drunken are drunken in the night. 8 But let us, who are of the day, be sober, putting on the breastplate of faith and love; and for a helmet, the hope of salvation. 9 For God hath not appointed us to wrath, but to obtain salvation by our Lord Jesus Christ, 10 Who died for us, that, whether we wake or sleep, we should live together with him. 11 Wherefore comfort yourselves together, and edify one another, even as also ye do. 12 And we beseech you, brethren, to know them which labour among you, and are over you in the Lord, and admonish you; 13 And to esteem them very highly in love for their work's sake. *And* be at peace among yourselves. 14 Now we exhort you, brethren, warn them that are unruly, comfort the feebleminded, support the weak, be patient toward all *men.* 15 See that none render evil for evil unto any *man;* but ever follow that which is good, both among yourselves, and to all *men.* 16 Rejoice evermore. 17 Pray without ceasing. 18 In every thing give thanks: for this is the will of God in Christ Jesus concerning you. 19 Quench not the Spirit. 20 Despise not prophesyings. 21 Prove all things; hold fast that which is good. 22 Abstain from all appearance of evil. 23 And the very God of peace sanctify you wholly; and *I pray God* your whole spirit and soul and body be preserved blameless unto the coming of our Lord Jesus Christ. 24 Faithful *is* he that calleth you, who also will do*, it. 25 Brethren, pray for us. 26 Greet all the brethren with a holy kiss. 27 I charge you by the Lord, that this epistle be read unto all the holy brethren. 28 The grace of our Lord Jesus Christ *be* with you. Amen.

The first, *epistle* unto the Thessalonians was written from Athens.

N.A.S.

who have fallen asleep. 16 For the Lord Himself will descend from heaven with a shout, with the voice of *the* archangel, and with the trumpet of God; and the dead in Christ shall rise first. 17 Then we who are alive and remain shall be caught up together with them in the clouds to meet the Lord in the air, and thus we shall always be with the Lord. 18 Therefore comfort one another with these words.

5 Now as to the times and the epochs, brethren, you have no need of anything to be written to you. 2 For you yourselves know full well that the day of the Lord will come just like a thief in the night. 3 While they are saying, "Peace and safety!" then destruction will come upon them suddenly like birth pangs upon a woman with child; and they shall not escape. 4 But you, brethren, are not in darkness, that the day should overtake you like a thief; 5 for you are all sons of light and sons of day. We are not of night nor of darkness; 6 so then let us not sleep as others do, but let us be alert and ᵃsober. 7 For those who sleep do their sleeping at night, and those who get drunk, get drunk at night. 8 But since we are of *the* day, let us be ᵃsober, having put on the breastplate of faith and love, and as a helmet, the hope of salvation. 9 For God has not destined us for wrath, but for obtaining salvation through our Lord Jesus Christ, 10 who died for us, that whether we are awake or asleep, we may live together with Him. 11 Therefore encourage one another, and build up one another, just as you also are doing.

12 But we request of you, brethren, that you appreciate those who diligently labor among you, and have charge over you in the Lord and give you instruction, 13 and that you esteem them very highly in love because of their work. Live in peace with one another. 14 And we urge you, brethren, admonish the unruly, encourage the fainthearted, help the weak, be patient with all men. 15 See that no one repays another with evil for evil, but always seek after that which is good for one another and for all men. 16 Rejoice always; 17 pray without ceasing; 18 in everything give thanks; for this is God's will for you in Christ Jesus. 19 Do not quench the Spirit; 20 do not despise prophetic ᵇutterances. 21 But examine everything *carefully;* hold fast to that which is good; 22 abstain from every ᶜform of evil.

23 Now may the God of peace Himself sanctify you entirely; and may your spirit and soul and body be preserved complete, without blame at the coming of our Lord Jesus Christ. 24 Faithful is He who calls you, and He also will bring it to pass.

25 Brethren, pray for usᵈ.

26 Greet all the brethren with a holy kiss. 27 I adjure you by the Lord to have this letter read to all the brethren.

28 The grace of our Lord Jesus Christ be with you.

[a] Or, *self-controlled.* ᵃ[b] Or, *gifts.* [c] Or, *appearance.* [d] Some mss. add. *also.*

WILLIAMS

fallen asleep. 16 For the Lord himself, at the summons sounded by the archangel's call and by God's trumpet, will come down from heaven, and first of all the dead in union with Christ will rise, 17 then those of us who are still living will be caught up along with them on clouds in the air to meet the Lord, and so we shall be with the Lord forever. 18 So continue encouraging one another with this truth.

5 *When Christ is to come unknown; so watch and wait; hints on daily living; full publicity for this letter*

But as to times and dates, brothers, you have no need of anyone's writing you, 2 for you yourselves know perfectly well that the day of the Lord is coming like a thief in the night. 3 When people say, "Such peace and security!" then suddenly destruction falls upon them, like birth pains upon a woman who is about to become a mother, but they shall not escape, no, not at all. 4 But you, brothers, are not in darkness, so that that day, like a thief, should take you by surprise; 5 for you are all sons of the light and sons of the day. We do not belong to the night or the darkness. 6 So let us stop sleeping as others do, but let us stay awake and keep sober. 7 For those who sleep sleep at night and those who get drunk are drunken at night, 8 but let us who belong to the day keep sober, clothed with faith and love for a coat of mail and with the hope of salvation for a helmet. 9 For God appointed us not to reap His wrath but to gain salvation through our Lord Jesus Christ, 10 who died for us, so that whether we still live or sleep[a] we may live in fellowship with Him. 11 So continue encouraging one another and helping one another in character building.

12 We beg you, brothers, to practice showing respect to those who labor among you, who are your leaders in the Lord's work, and who advise you; 13 continue to hold them in the highest esteem for the sake of the work they do. Practice living at peace with one another. 14 We beg you, brothers, continue to warn the shirkers, to cheer the faint-hearted, to hold up the weak, and to be patient with everybody. 15 Take care that none of you ever pays back evil for evil, but always keep looking for ways to show kindness to one another and everybody. 16 Always be joyful. 17 Never stop praying. 18 Make it a habit to give thanks for everything, for this is God's will for you through Christ Jesus. 19 Stop stifling the Spirit. 20 Stop treating the messages of prophecy with contempt, 21 but continue to prove all things until you can approve them, and then hold on to what is good. 22 Continue to abstain from every sort of evil.

23 May God Himself, who gave you peace, consecrate your whole being. May you be safely kept, spirit, soul, and body, so as to be blameless when our Lord Jesus Christ comes back. 24 He who calls you is trustworthy and He will do this. 25 Brothers, pray for us. 26 Greet all the brothers with a sacred kiss. 27 I solemnly charge you before the Lord to have this letter read to all the brothers.

28 The spiritual blessing of our Lord Jesus Christ be with you.

[a] Still live or die.

BECK

those who went to their rest. 16 When the order is given and the archangel calls and God's trumpet sounds, the Lord Himself will come down from heaven, and the dead who are in Christ will rise first. 17 Then we who are still living and left behind will be caught up with them in the clouds to meet the Lord in the air, and so we'll always be with the Lord. 18 Now, then, comfort one another with what I have told you.

Watch!

5 You don't need anyone to write and tell you exactly when things will happen, my fellow Christians, 2 because you know very well the Lord's day will come just like a thief in the night. 3 When people say, "All's well and safe!" then destruction will come on them suddenly like pains on a woman who is going to have a baby, and they will not escape. 4 But you, my fellow Christians, are not in the dark that you should let that day take you by surprise like a thief. 5 You are all the children of light and of the day. We have nothing to do with night and darkness. 6 Let us not sleep, then, like the others, but be awake and sober. 7 People sleep at night and get drunk at night. 8 But let us who live in the daylight be sober and *put on* faith and love *as a breastplate* and the hope of *salvation as a helmet.*[6] 9 God didn't appoint us to be punished by His anger but to be saved by our Lord Jesus Christ, 10 who died for us so that, awake or asleep, we may live with Him. 11 Then encourage one another and strengthen one another just as you are doing.

Some Last Words

12 We ask you, fellow Christians, to appreciate the men who work with you and lead you in the Lord and warn you. 13 Love them and think very highly of them on account of the work they're doing. Live in peace with one another.

14 We urge you, fellow Christians, warn those who are disorderly, cheer up those who are discouraged, help the weak, be patient with everybody. 15 Don't let anyone pay back wrong for wrong, but always be eager to help one another and everybody.

16 Always be happy. 17 Never stop praying. 18 Whatever happens, thank God, because that is what God in Christ Jesus wants you to do.

19 Don't put out the fire of the Spirit. 20 Don't despise God's Word when anyone speaks it. 21 But test everything and cling to what is good. 22 *Keep away from every* kind of *evil.*[7]

23 The God of peace make you holy in every way and keep your spirit and life and body sound and without a fault when our Lord Jesus Christ comes. 24 You can depend on Him who calls you—He will do it.

25 My fellow Christians, pray for us.

26 Greet all the Christians with a holy kiss.

27 I order you by the Lord to read this letter to all the Christians.

28 The love of our Lord Jesus Christ be with you. Amen.

[6] Is. 59:17
[7] Job 1:1, 8; 2:3

K.J.V.

THE SECOND EPISTLE
OF PAUL THE APOSTLE
TO THE
THESSALONIANS

1 Paul, and Silvanus, and Timotheus, unto the church of the Thessalonians in God our Father and the Lord Jesus Christ: 2 Grace unto you, and peace, from God our Father and the Lord Jesus Christ. 3 We are bound to thank God always for you, brethren, as it is meet, because that your faith groweth exceedingly, and the charity of every one of you all toward each other aboundeth; 4 So that we ourselves glory in you in the churches of God, for your patience and faith in all your persecutions and tribulations that ye endure: 5 *Which is* a manifest token of the righteous judgment of God, that ye may be counted worthy of the kingdom of God, for which ye also suffer: 6 Seeing *it is* a righteous thing with God to recompense tribulation to them that trouble you; 7 And to you who are troubled rest with us, when the Lord Jesus shall be revealed from heaven with his mighty angels, 8 In flaming fire taking vengeance on them that know not God, and that obey not the gospel of our Lord Jesus Christ: 9 Who shall be punished with everlasting destruction from the presence of the Lord, and from the glory of his power; 10 When he shall come to be glorified in his saints, and to be admired in all them that believe (because our testimony among you was believed) in that day. 11 Wherefore also we pray always for you, that our God would count you worthy of *this* calling, and fulfil all the good pleasure of *his* goodness, and the work of faith with power: 12 That the name of our Lord Jesus Christ may be glorified in you, and ye in him, according to the grace of our God and the Lord Jesus Christ.

2 Now we beseech you, brethren, by the coming of our Lord Jesus Christ, and *by* our gathering together unto him, 2 That ye be not

N.A.S.

THE SECOND EPISTLE
OF PAUL TO THE
THESSALONIANS

1 Paul and Silvanus and Timothy to the church of the Thessalonians in God our Father and the Lord Jesus Christ: 2 Grace to you and peace from God the Father and the Lord Jesus Christ.
3 We ought always to give thanks to God for you, brethren, as is *only* fitting, because your faith is greatly enlarged, and the love of each one of you all toward one another grows *ever* greater; 4 therefore, we ourselves speak proudly of you among the churches of God for your perseverance and faith in the midst of all your persecutions and afflictions which you endure. 5 *This is* a plain indication of God's righteous judgment so that you may be considered worthy of the kingdom of God, for which indeed you are suffering. 6 For after all it is *only* just for God to repay with affliction those who afflict you, 7 and *to give* relief to you who are afflicted and to us as well when the Lord Jesus shall be revealed from heaven with His mighty angels in flaming fire, 8 dealing out retribution to those who do not know God and to those who do not obey the gospel of our Lord Jesus. 9 And these will pay the penalty of eternal destruction, away from the presence of the Lord and from the glory of His power, 10 when He comes to be glorified in His saints on that day, and to be marveled at among all who have believed—for our testimony to you was believed. 11 To this end also we pray for you always that our God may count you worthy of your calling, and fulfill every desire for goodness and the work of faith with power; 12 in order that the name of our Lord Jesus may be glorified in you, and you in Him, according to the grace of our God and the Lord Jesus Christ.

2 Now we request you, brethren, with regard to the coming of our Lord Jesus Christ, and our gathering together to Him, 2 that you

PAUL

WRITES THE SECOND

LETTER TO THE

SECOND

THESSALONIANS

THESSALONIANS

1 *He greets them; thanks God for their faith, love, endurance; tells them that the Lord will vindicate their sufferings when He comes; prays continually for them*

Paul, Silvanus, and Timothy to the Thessalonian church in union with God our Father and the Lord Jesus Christ: 2 spiritual blessing and peace be to you.

3 We always ought to be thanking God for you, brothers, as it is right to do so, because your faith is growing so much and the love of every one of you for one another is increasing 4 so that we are always boasting of you among the churches of God for your patient endurance and faith, in spite of your persecutions and crushing sorrows which you are enduring. 5 This is a proof of God's righteous judgment, His aim being to let you show yourselves worthy of His kingdom, for which you are suffering; since, 6 indeed, it is right for God to repay with crushing sorrows those who cause you these crushing sorrows, 7 and to give rest to you who are being crushed with sorrows, along with us, at the unveiling of our Lord Jesus Christ from heaven, with His mighty angels 8 in a flame of fire, who will take vengeance on those who do not know God, that is, those who will not listen to the good news of our Lord Jesus. 9 These will receive the punishment of eternal destruction as exiles from the presence of the Lord and His glorious might, 10 when on that day He comes to be glorified in His consecrated ones and to be admired by all who believe in Him—because our testimony has been confidently accepted among you.

11 With this in view we are always praying for you too, that our God may make you worthy of His call, and by His power fully satisfy your every desire for goodness, and complete every activity of your faith, 12 so that the name of our Lord Jesus may be glorified in you and you through union with Him, in accordance with the favor of our God and the Lord Jesus Christ.

2 *Some events to precede the Lord's return, so it is not to be at once; he again thanks God for them, pleads with them, prays for them*

As to the coming of our Lord Jesus Christ and our final muster before Him, we beg you, brothers, 2 not to let your minds be easily un-

1 Paul, Silas, and Timothy to the church of the Thessalonians in God our Father and the Lord Jesus Christ: 2 Love to you and peace from God our Father and the Lord Jesus Christ.

Look to God in Suffering

3 We always have to thank God for you, my fellow Christians. It is the right thing to do because your faith is growing wonderfully and the love of every one of you for one another is increasing, 4 so much so that we're boasting about you in God's churches how you endure and trust no matter how much you're persecuted and made to suffer. 5 It shows how God judges righteously: He means to make you worthy of His kingdom, for which you are suffering; 6 it really is just for God to pay back with suffering those who make you suffer 7 and to give relief to you who suffer and to us when the Lord Jesus will be revealed from heaven with His mighty angels 8 *in a blaze of fire, to take vengeance*[1] *on those who don't know God*[2] *and on those who will not obey*[3] the good news of our Lord Jesus. 9 They will be punished by being taken *away from the Lord and from the glory of His power*[4] to be destroyed eternally 10 when He comes on that Day[5] to *be glorified in His holy people*[6] and *admired*[7] by all who believed (you did believe the truth we told you). 11 With this in mind we're always praying for you that our God will make you worthy of His calling and by His power accomplish every good thing you decide to do and every work of faith, 12 *so as to glorify the name of our Lord*[8] Jesus among you, and you in Him, according to the love of our God and Lord Jesus Christ.

The Man of Sin

2 Our Lord Jesus Christ is coming, and we'll be gathered to meet Him. But we ask you, fellow Christians, 2 not to lose your heads so

[1] Is. 66:15
[2] Ps. 79:6; Jer. 10:25
[3] Is. 66:4
[4] Is. 2:10, 19, 21
[5] Is. 2:11, 17
[6] Ps. 88:7; Is. 49:3
[7] Ps. 68:35
[8] Is. 66:5

K.J.V.

soon shaken in mind, or be troubled, neither by spirit, nor by word, nor by letter as from us, as that the day of Christ is at hand. 3 Let no man deceive you by any means: for *that day shall not come,* except there come a falling away first, and that man of sin be revealed, the son of perdition; 4 Who opposeth and exalteth himself above all that is called God, or that is worshipped; so that he as God sitteth in the temple of God, shewing himself that he is God. 5 Remember ye not, that, when I was yet with you, I told you these things? 6 And now ye know what withholdeth that he might be revealed in his time. 7 For the mystery of iniquity doth already work: only he who now letteth *will let,* until he be taken out of the way. 8 And then shall that Wicked be revealed, whom the Lord shall consume with the spirit of his mouth, and shall destroy with the brightness of his coming: 9 *Even him,* whose coming is after the working of Satan with all power and signs and lying wonders, 10 And with all deceivableness of unrighteousness in them that perish; because they received not the love of the truth, that they might be saved. 11 And for this cause God shall send them strong delusion, that they should believe a lie: 12 That they all might be damned who believed not the truth, but had pleasure in unrighteousness. 13 But we are bound to give thanks always to God for you, brethren beloved of the Lord, because God hath from the beginning chosen you to salvation through sanctification of the Spirit and belief of the truth: 14 Whereunto he called you by our gospel, to the obtaining of the glory of our Lord Jesus Christ. 15 Therefore, brethren, stand fast, and hold the traditions which ye have been taught, whether by word, or our epistle. 16 Now our Lord Jesus Christ himself, and God, even our Father, which hath loved us, and hath given *us* everlasting consolation and good hope through grace, 17 Comfort your hearts, and stablish you in every good word and work.

3 Finally, brethren, pray for us, that the word of the Lord may have *free* course, and be glorified, even as *it is* with you: 2 And that we may be delivered from unreasonable and wicked men: for all *men* have not faith. 3 But the Lord is faithful, who shall stablish you, and keep *you* from evil. 4 And we have confidence in the Lord touching you, that ye both do and will do the things which we command you. 5 And the Lord direct your hearts into the love of God, and

N.A.S.

may not be quickly shaken from your composure or be disturbed either by a spirit or a message or a letter as if from us, to the effect that the day of the Lord has come. 3 Let no one in any way deceive you, for *it will not come* unless the ªapostasy come first, and the man of lawlessness is revealed, the son of destruction, 4 who opposes and exalts himself above every so-called god or object of worship, so that he takes his seat in the temple of God, displaying himself as being God. 5 Do you not remember that while I was still with you, I was telling you these things? 6 And you know what restrains him now, so that in his time he may be revealed. 7 For the mystery of lawlessness is already at work; only he who now restrains *will do so* until he is taken out of the way. 8 And then that lawless one will be revealed whom the Lord will slay with the breath of His mouth and bring to an end by the appearance of His coming; 9 *that is,* the one whose coming is in accord with the activity of Satan, with all power and signs and false wonders, 10 and with all the deception of wickedness for those who perish, because they did not receive the love of the truth so as to be saved. 11 And for this reason God will send upon them a deluding influence so that they might believe what is false, 12 in order that they all may be judged who did not believe the truth, but took pleasure in wickedness.

13 But we should always give thanks to God for you, brethren beloved by the Lord, because God has chosen you ᵇfrom the beginning for salvation through sanctification by the Spirit and faith in the truth. 14 And it was for this He called you through our gospel, that you may gain the glory of our Lord Jesus Christ. 15 So then, brethren, stand firm and hold to the traditions which you were taught, whether by word *of mouth* or by letter from us.

16 Now may our Lord Jesus Christ Himself and God our Father, who has loved us and given us eternal comfort and good hope by grace, 17 comfort and strengthen your hearts in every good work and word.

3 Finally, brethren, pray for us that the word of the Lord may spread rapidly and be glorified, just as *it did* also with you; 2 and that we may be delivered from perverse and evil men; for not all have faith. 3 But the Lord is faithful, and He will strengthen and protect you from the evil *one.* 4 And we have confidence in the Lord concerning you, that you are doing and will continue to do what we command. 5 And may the Lord direct your hearts into the love of God and into the steadfastness of Christ.

[a] Or, *falling away* from the faith. [b] Some ancient mss. read, *first fruits.*

WILLIAMS

settled or even be excited, whether by some message by the Spirit or by some saying or letter that is claimed as coming from me, saying that the day of the Lord is already here. 3 Do not let anybody at all deceive you about this, because that cannot take place until the great revolt[a] occurs and the representative of lawlessness is uncovered, the one who is doomed to destruction, 4 the one who keeps up his opposition and so far exalts himself above every so-called god or object of worship, that he actually takes his seat in the sanctuary of God, proclaiming himself to be God. 5 Do you not remember that while I was with you I used to tell you this? 6 So now you know the power[b] that is holding him back, that he is to be unveiled at His own appointed time. 7 For the secret power of lawlessness is already at work, but only until he who is holding it back has been gotten out of the way. 8 Then the representative of lawlessness will be uncovered, and the Lord Jesus will destroy him with the breath of His mouth and put a stop to his operations by His appearance and coming; 9 that is, the representative of lawlessness, whose coming is in accordance with the working of Satan, with his plenitude of power and pretended signs and wonders, 10 and with a completely wicked deception for men who are on the way to destruction, because they refused to love the truth so as to be saved. 11 This is why God sends them a misleading influence till they actually believe what is false, 12 so that all who have refused to believe the truth but have chosen unrighteousness instead might be condemned.

13 We ought always to be thanking God for you, brothers dearly loved by the Lord, because God chose you from the beginning for salvation through the Spirit's consecration of you and through your faith in the truth, 14 and to this end He called you by our preaching of the good news, so that you may obtain the glory of our Lord Jesus Christ.

15 So then, brothers, continue to stand firm and keep a tight grip on the teachings you have received from us, whether by word of mouth or by letter. 16 May our Lord Jesus Christ Himself and God our Father, who has loved us and graciously given us encouragement that is eternal, and a hope that is well-founded, 17 encourage your hearts and strengthen you in every good thing you do or say.

3 *He asks them to pray for him; he prays for them; urges them to follow his example in honest toil, to hold aloof from shirkers; how to identify his letters; sends blessing*

Finally, brothers, pray for us, that the message of the Lord may continue to spread and prove its glorious power as it did among you, 2 and that we may be delivered from unprincipled and wicked men; for not all men have faith.

3 But the Lord is to be trusted, and He will give you strength and guard you from the evil one. 4 We have confidence in you through the Lord that you are now practicing the directions which we give you and that you will continue to do so. 5 May the Lord guide you into a realization of God's love for you and into a patient endurance like Christ's.

[a] *Apostasy.* [b] *The thing that,* etc.

BECK

quickly or get alarmed either by a "spirit" message or by any word or letter that seemed to come from us, saying "The day of the Lord has already come!" 3 Don't let anybody deceive you in any way. First there must be a revolt, and the man of sin must be revealed, who is doomed to destruction, 4 who opposes and *sets himself above anyone* who is called *God*[9] or anything we worship, so that *he sits in God's temple* and proclaims *he is God.*[10]

5 Don't you remember I told you this when I was still with you? 6 And now you know what's holding him back so that he will be revealed when his time comes. 7 This wicked thing is already working secretly, but only till he who is now holding it back gets out of the way. 8 Then the wicked one will be revealed, and the Lord Jesus *will destroy him with the breath of His mouth*[11] and wipe him out by coming and showing Himself. 9 The coming of this wicked one is the work of the devil who uses every kind of false power, miracle, and wonder, 10 and every wicked way to deceive those who are perishing because they refused to love the truth and be saved. 11 That is why God sends them a power to deceive them so they will believe the lie 12 and all will be condemned who did not believe the truth but delighted in wrong.

God Has Chosen You

13 But we always have to thank God for you, my fellow Christians, whom *the Lord loves,*[12] because in the beginning God chose you to be made holy by the Spirit, to believe the truth, and so to be saved. 14 For this purpose He called you by the good news we tell; He wants you to have the glory of our Lord Jesus Christ.

15 Stand then, fellow Christians, and cling to the instructions we gave you when we spoke to you or wrote to you.

16 Now our Lord Jesus Christ Himself and God our Father, who loved us and by His love gave us an everlasting comfort and a good hope, 17 inwardly comfort and strengthen you to do and say everything that is good.

Pray for Us

3 Finally, my fellow Christians, pray for us that the Lord's Word will run well and win glory as it did among you 2 and we'll be rescued from wrong-minded and wicked people. Not everybody has faith.

3 But the Lord is faithful. He will strengthen you and protect you against the evil one. 4 We are certain in the Lord you are doing and will be doing what we order you to do. 5 And may the Lord lead you to realize how God loves you and how patiently Christ suffered.

[9] Dan. 11:36
[10] Ezek. 28:2
[11] Job 4:9; Is. 11:4
[12] Deut. 33:12

K.J.V.

into the patient waiting for Christ. 6 Now we command you, brethren, in the name of our Lord Jesus Christ, that ye withdraw yourselves from every brother that walketh disorderly, and not after the tradition which he received of us. 7 For yourselves know how ye ought to follow us: for we behaved not ourselves disorderly among you; 8 Neither did we eat any man's bread for nought; but wrought with labour and travail night and day, that we might not be chargeable to any of you: 9 Not because we have not power, but to make ourselves an ensample unto you to follow us. 10 For even when we were with you, this we commanded you, that if any would not work, neither should he eat. 11 For we hear that there are some which walk among you disorderly, working not at all, but are busybodies. 12 Now them that are such we command and exhort by our Lord Jesus Christ, that with quietness they work, and eat their own bread. 13 But ye, brethren, be not weary in well doing. 14And if any man obey not our word by this epistle, note that man, and have no company with him, that he may be ashamed. 15 Yet count *him* not as an enemy, but admonish *him* as a brother. 16 Now the Lord of peace himself give you peace always by all means. The Lord *be* with you all. 17 The salutation of Paul with mine own hand, which is the token in every epistle: so I write. 18 The grace of our Lord Jesus Christ *be* with you all. Amen.

The second *epistle* to the Thessalonians was written from Athens.

N.A.S.

6 Now we command you, brethren, in the name of our Lord Jesus Christ, that you keep aloof from every brother who leads an unruly life and not according to the tradition which you received from us. 7 For you yourselves know how you ought to follow our example; because we did not act in an undisciplined manner among you, 8 nor did we eat anyone's bread without paying for it, but with labor and hardship we *kept* working night and day so that we might not be a burden to any of you; 9 not because we do not have the right *to this*, but in order to offer ourselves as a model for you, that you might follow our example. 10 For even when we were with you, we used to give you this order: If anyone will not work, neither let him eat. 11 For we hear that some among you are leading an undisciplined life, doing no work at all, but acting like busybodies. 12 Now such persons we command and exhort in the Lord Jesus Christ to work in quiet fashion and eat their own bread. 13 But as for you, brethren, do not grow weary of doing good. 14And if anyone does not obey our instruction in this letter, take special note of that man and do not associate with him, so that he may be put to shame. 15And *yet* do not regard him as an enemy, but admonish him as a brother.

16 Now may the Lord of peace Himself continually grant you peace in every circumstance. The Lord be with you all!

17 I, Paul, write this greeting with my own hand, and this is a distinguishing mark in every letter: this is the way I write. 18 The grace of our Lord Jesus Christ be with you all.

WILLIAMS

6 Now we charge you, brothers, on the authority of the Lord Jesus Christ, to hold yourselves aloof from any brother who is living as a shirker instead of following the teachings you received from us. 7 You know yourselves how you ought to follow my example; for I was not a shirker when I was with you; 8 I did not eat any man's bread without paying for it, but with toil and hard labor I worked night and day, in order not to be a burden to any of you. 9 Not that I have no right to be supported, but to make myself an example for you to follow. 10 For when I was with you, I gave you this direction, "If a person refuses to work, he must not be allowed to eat." 11 But we are informed that some among you are living as shirkers, mere busybodies, instead of busy at work. 12 Now on the authority of the Lord Jesus Christ we charge and exhort such persons to do their own work with quiet and eat their own bread. 13 But you, brothers, must never grow tired of doing right. 14 If anyone refuses to obey what we have said in this letter, mark that person and stop having anything to do with him, so that he will feel ashamed of it. 15 You must not regard him as an enemy but warn him as a brother. 16 And may the Lord who gives us peace give you peace in whatever circumstances you may be. The Lord be with you all.

17 This greeting is in my own hand, Paul's; it is the mark in every letter of mine. This is my handwriting. 18 The spiritual blessing of our Lord Jesus Christ be with you all.

BECK

Work

6 Now we order you, fellow Christians, in the name of our Lord Jesus Christ to keep away from any Christian who refuses to live and work as we instructed you. 7 You know how you should imitate us. 8 We were not idle when we were with you and took no free meals from anyone but worked hard and struggled day and night in order not to burden any of you. 9 Not as though we didn't have a right to get support. No, we wanted to give you an example to imitate. 10 And while we were with you, we gave you the order, "If anyone doesn't want to work, he shouldn't eat."

11 We hear that some of you are living a lazy life, not doing any work, but being busybodies. 12 Such people we order and encourage by the Lord Jesus Christ to work quietly and eat their own bread. 13 And you, fellow Christians, don't get tired of doing good.

14 If anyone will not listen to what we say in this letter, mark him, and don't have anything to do with him, so he will feel ashamed. 15 Don't treat him like an enemy, but warn him like a brother.

Farewell

16 The Lord of peace always give you peace in every way. The Lord be with you all.

17 I'm writing this greeting with my own—that is, Paul's—hand. By this you can recognize every letter: This is my handwriting.

18 The love of our Lord Jesus Christ be with you all!

THE FIRST EPISTLE
OF PAUL THE APOSTLE
TO
TIMOTHY

THE FIRST EPISTLE
OF PAUL TO
TIMOTHY

1 Paul, an apostle of Jesus Christ by the commandment of God our Saviour, and Lord Jesus Christ, *which is* our hope; 2 Unto Timothy, *my* own son in the faith: Grace, mercy, *and* peace, from God our Father, and Jesus Christ our Lord. 3As I besought thee to abide still at Ephesus, when I went into Macedonia, that thou mightest charge some that they teach no other doctrine, 4 Neither give heed to fables and endless genealogies, which minister questions, rather than godly edifying which is in faith: *so do.* 5 Now the end of the commandment is charity out of a pure heart, and *of* a good conscience, and *of* faith unfeigned: 6 From which some having swerved have turned aside unto vain jangling; 7 Desiring to be teachers of the law; understanding neither what they say, nor whereof they affirm. 8 But we know that the law *is* good, if a man use it lawfully; 9 Knowing this, that the law is not made for a righteous man, but for the lawless and disobedient, for the ungodly and for sinners, for unholy and profane, for murderers of fathers and murderers of mothers, for manslayers, 10 For whoremongers, for them that defile themselves with mankind, for menstealers, for liars, for perjured persons, and if there be any other thing that is contrary to sound doctrine; 11According to the glorious gospel of the blessed God, which was committed to my trust. 12And I thank Christ Jesus our Lord, who hath enabled me, for that he counted me faithful, putting me into the ministry; 13 Who was before a blasphemer, and a persecutor, and injurious: but I obtained mercy, because I did *it* ignorantly in unbelief. 14And the grace of our Lord was exceeding abundant with faith and love which is in Christ Jesus. 15 This *is* a faithful saying, and worthy of all acceptation, that Christ Jesus came into the world to save sinners; of whom I am chief. 16 Howbeit for this cause I obtained mercy, that in me first Jesus Christ might shew forth all longsuffering, for a pattern to them which should hereafter believe on him to life everlasting. 17 Now unto the King eternal, immortal, invisi-

1 Paul, an apostle of Christ Jesus according to the commandment of God our Savior, and of Christ Jesus, *who is* our hope; 2 to Timothy, *my* true child in *the* faith: Grace, mercy *and* peace from God the Father and Christ Jesus our Lord.
3 As I urged you upon my departure for Macedonia, remain on at Ephesus, in order that you may instruct certain men not to teach strange doctrines, 4 nor to pay attention to myths and endless genealogies, which give rise to mere speculation rather than *furthering* the administration of God which is by faith. 5 But the goal of our instruction is love from a pure heart and a good conscience and a sincere faith. 6 For some men, straying from these things, have turned aside to fruitless discussion, 7 wanting to be teachers of the Law, even though they do not understand either what they are saying or the matters about which they make confident assertions. 8 But we know that the Law is good, if one uses it lawfully, 9 realizing the fact that law is not made for a righteous man, but for those who are lawless and rebellious, for the ungodly and sinners, for the unholy and profane, for those who kill their fathers or mothers, for murderers 10 and immoral men and homosexuals and kidnappers and liars and perjurers, and whatever else is contrary to sound teaching, 11 according to the glorious gospel of the blessed God, with which I have been entrusted.
12 I thank Christ Jesus our Lord, who has strengthened me, because He considered me faithful, putting me into service; 13 even though I was formerly a blasphemer and a persecutor and a violent aggressor. And yet I was shown mercy, because I acted ignorantly in unbelief; 14 and the grace of our Lord was more than abundant, with the faith and love which are *found* in Christ Jesus. 15 It is a trustworthy statement, deserving full acceptance, that Christ Jesus came into the world to save sinners, among whom I am foremost *of all.* 16And yet for this reason I found mercy, in order that in me as the foremost Jesus Christ might demonstrate His perfect patience, as an example for those who would believe in Him for eternal life. 17 Now

FIRST
TIMOTHY

TIMOTHY

1 *He greets Timothy; urges him to warn the false teachers; tells of the practical aim of the law; thanks God for saving him though once a persecutor of the church; urges Timothy to continue the good fight*

Paul, an apostle of Christ Jesus by command of God our Saviour and of Christ Jesus our hope, 2 to Timothy my genuine child in faith: spiritual blessing, mercy, and peace be with you from God our Father and Christ Jesus our Lord.
3 As I begged you to do when I was on my way to Macedonia, I still beg you to stay on in Ephesus to warn certain teachers to 4 stop devoting themselves to myths and never-ending pedigrees, for such things lead to controversies rather than stimulate our trusteeship to God through faith. 5 But the aim of your instruction is to be love that flows out of a pure heart, a good conscience, and a sincere faith. 6 Some people have stepped aside from these things and turned to fruitless talking. 7 They want to be teachers of the law, although they do not understand the words they use or the things about which they make such confident assertions.
8 Indeed, I know that the law is an excellent thing, if a man makes a lawful use of it; 9 that is, if he understands that law is not enacted for upright people but for the lawless and disorderly, the godless and sinful, the ignorant and profane, people who kill their fathers or mothers, murderers, 10 the immoral, men who practice sodomy, men who make other men their slaves, liars, perjurers, or anything else that is contrary to sound teaching, 11 as measured by the glorious good news of the blessed God, with which I have been entrusted.
12 I am always thanking Christ Jesus our Lord who has given me strength for it, for thinking me trustworthy and putting me into the ministry, 13 though I once used to abuse, persecute, and insult Him. But mercy was shown me by Him, because I did it in ignorance and unbelief, 14 and the spiritual blessing of our Lord in increasing floods[a] has come upon me, accompanied by faith and love inspired by union with Christ Jesus. 15 It is a saying to be trusted and deserves our fullest acceptance, that Christ Jesus came into the world to save sinners; and I am the foremost of them. 16 Yet, mercy was shown me for the very purpose that in my case as the foremost of sinners Jesus might display His perfect patience, to make me an example to those who in the future might believe on Him to obtain eternal life. 17 To the King eternal, immortal,

1 Paul, apostle of Christ Jesus by the order of God, our Savior, and Christ Jesus, our Hope, 2 to Timothy, my real son by faith: Love, mercy, and peace from God the Father and Christ Jesus, our Lord.

Teaching the Law

3 When I was going to Macedonia, I urged you to stay in Ephesus. I wanted you to order certain men not to teach anything different 4 and not to busy themselves with stories and endless records of ancestors, that provide speculations but no divine training in faith.
5 The goal of our instruction is love flowing from a pure heart, from a good conscience, and from a sincere faith. 6 Certain people have failed to find this and have turned to silly talk. 7 They want to be teachers of the Law but don't understand what they say or the things they so confidently express.
8 But we know the Law is good if it is used as it was meant to be used, 9 if we keep in mind that the Law is not meant for a righteous man but for those who break the Law and rebel against it, the ungodly and sinners, those who live unholy lives and insult holy things, those who kill their fathers or mothers, murderers, 10 men who sin sexually with women or with other men, slave dealers, those who lie or swear to lies—and anything else that is contrary to sound teaching. 11 This is according to the good news of the glory of God, the Blessed, that was entrusted to me.

God Was Merciful to Me

12 I thank Christ Jesus, our Lord, whose power has been in me. He thought I could be trusted and appointed me to do His work 13 although I used to slander, persecute, and shamefully mistreat Him. But He was merciful to me because, when I didn't believe, I didn't know what I was doing. 14 Our Lord poured His undeserved kindness on me, bringing faith and love in Christ Jesus.
15 We can trust this statement and accept it absolutely: Christ Jesus came into the world to save sinners. I am the worst of them, 16 but God was merciful to me so that Jesus Christ would first show in me all His long-suffering and make me an example to those who are going to believe in Him and live forever. 17 To

[a] Lit., *flowed superabundantly.*

589

K.J.V.

ble, the only wise God, *be* honour and glory for ever and ever. Amen. 18 This charge I commit unto thee, son Timothy, according to the prophecies which went before on thee, that thou by them mightest war a good warfare; 19 Holding faith, and a good conscience; which some having put away, concerning faith have made shipwreck: 20 Of whom is Hymeneus and Alexander; whom I have delivered unto Satan, that they may learn not to blaspheme.

2 I exhort therefore, that, first of all, supplications, prayers, intercessions, *and* giving of thanks, be made for all men; 2 For kings, and *for* all that are in authority; that we may lead a quiet and peaceable life in all godliness and honesty. 3 For this *is* good and acceptable in the sight of God our Saviour; 4 Who will have all men to be saved, and to come unto the knowledge of the truth. 5 For *there is* one God, and one mediator between God and men, the man Christ Jesus; 6 Who gave himself a ransom for all, to be testified in due time. 7 Whereunto I am ordained a preacher, and an apostle, (I speak the truth in Christ, *and* lie not,) a teacher of the Gentiles in faith and verity. 8 I will therefore that men pray every where, lifting up holy hands, without wrath and doubting. 9 In like manner also, that women adorn themselves in modest apparel, with shamefacedness and sobriety; not with braided hair, or gold, or pearls, or costly array; 10 But (which becometh women professing godliness) with good works. 11 Let the woman learn in silence with all subjection. 12 But I suffer not a woman to teach, nor to usurp authority over the man, but to be in silence. 13 For Adam was first formed, then Eve. 14And Adam was not deceived, but the woman being deceived was in the transgression. 15 Notwithstanding she shall be saved in childbearing, if they continue in faith and charity and holiness with sobriety.

3 This *is* a true saying, If a man desire the office of a bishop, he desireth a good work. 2A bishop then must be blameless, the husband of one wife, vigilant, sober, of good behaviour, given to hospitality, apt to teach; 3 Not given to wine, no striker, not greedy of filthy lucre; but patient, not a brawler, not covetous; 4 One that ruleth well his own house, having his children in subjection with all gravity; 5 (For if a

N.A.S.

to the King eternal, immortal, invisible, the only God, *be* honor and glory forever and ever. Amen.

18 This command I entrust to you, Timothy, my son, in accordance with the prophecies previously made concerning you, that by them you may fight the good fight, 19 keeping faith and a good conscience, which some have rejected and suffered shipwreck in regard to their faith. 20Among these are Hymenaeus and Alexander, whom I have delivered over to Satan, so that they may be taught not to blaspheme.

2 First of all, then, I urge that entreaties *and* prayers, petitions *and* thanksgivings, be made on behalf of all men, 2 for kings and all who are in authority, in order that we may lead a tranquil and quiet life in all godliness and dignity. 3 This is good and acceptable in the sight of God our Savior, 4 who desires all men to be saved and to come to the knowledge of the truth. 5 For there is one God, *and* one mediator also between God and men, *the* man Christ Jesus, 6 who gave Himself a ransom for all, the testimony *borne* at the proper time. 7And for this I was appointed a preacher and an apostle (I am telling the truth, I am not lying) as a teacher of the Gentiles in faith and truth.

8 Therefore I want the men in every place to pray, lifting up holy hands, without wrath and dissension. 9 Likewise, *I want* women to adorn themselves with proper clothing, modestly and discreetly, not with braided hair and gold or pearls or costly garments; 10 but rather by means of good works, as befits women making a claim to godliness. 11 Let a woman quietly receive instruction with entire submissiveness. 12 But I do not allow a woman to teach or exercise authority over a man, but to remain quiet. 13 For it was Adam who was first created, *and* then Eve. 14And *it was* not Adam *who* was deceived, but the woman being quite deceived, fell into transgression. 15 But women shall be preserved through the bearing of children if *they* continue in faith and love and sanctity with self restraint.

3 It is a trustworthy statement; if any man aspires to the office of overseer, it is a fine work he desires *to do.* 2An overseer, then, must be above reproach, the husband of one wife, temperate, prudent, respectable, hospitable, able to teach, 3 not addicted to wine or pugnacious, but gentle, uncontentious, free from the love of money. 4 *He must be* one who manages his own household well, keeping his children under control with all dignity 5 (but if a man does not

WILLIAMS

BECK

invisible, the only God, be honor and glory forever and ever! Amen.

18 This is the instruction which I entrust to you, my son Timothy, which is in accordance with the prophetic utterances formerly made about you, that you may, aided by them, continue to fight the good fight, 19 by keeping your hold on faith and a good conscience; for some have thrust the latter aside and so have made shipwreck of their faith. 20Among these are Hymenaeus and Alexander, whom I have turned over to Satan to be so disciplined that they will stop their abusive speech.

the everlasting King, the immortal, invisible, and only God, be honor and glory forever. Amen.

Fight and Pray

18 I'm giving you these instructions, my son Timothy, according to the prophecies made earlier about you. In the spirit of those prophecies fight a good fight 19 with faith and a good conscience. Some refused to listen to their conscience and suffered shipwreck in their faith. 20Among them are Hymenaeus and Alexander, whom I turned over to the devil to teach them not to slander holy things.

2 Christians must pray for all, especially for civil officers; men must lead the public prayers; women must dress modestly, be subordinate to men

First of all, then, I urge that entreaties, prayers, and thanksgiving be offered for all men, 2 for kings and all who are in authority, so that we may lead peaceful, quiet lives in perfect piety and seriousness. 3 This is the right thing to do and it pleases God our Saviour, 4 who is ever willing for all mankind to be saved and to come to an increasing knowledge of the truth. 5 For there is but one God and one intermediary between God and men, the man Christ Jesus 6 who gave Himself as a ransom for all, a fact that was testified to at the proper time, 7 and for which purpose I was appointed a preacher and an apostle—I am telling the truth, I am not lying,—a teacher of the heathen in the realm of faith and truth.

8 So I want the men everywhere to offer prayer, lifting to heaven holy hands which are kept unstained by anger and dissensions. 9 I want the women, on their part, to dress becomingly, that is, modestly and sensibly, not adorning themselves with braided hair and gold or pearls or expensive dresses, 10 but with good deeds; for this is appropriate for women who profess to be pious.

11 A married woman must learn in quiet and in perfect submission. 12 I do not permit a married woman to practice teaching or domineering over a husband; she must keep quiet. 13 For Adam was formed first, and then Eve; 14 and it was not Adam who was deceived, but it was the woman who was utterly deceived and fell into transgression. 15 But women will be saved through motherhood, if they continue to live in faith, love, and purity, blended with good sense.

2 I urge you, as most important of all, to ask, pray, plead, and give thanks for all people, 2 for kings and all who are over us, so that we may live quietly and peacefully and be godly and noble in every way. 3 This is good and pleases God our Savior, 4 who wants all people to be saved and to come to know the truth.

5 There is one God, and One who brings God and men together, the Man Christ Jesus, 6 who gave Himself as a ransom to free all people, and this was announced at the right times. 7 For this purpose I was appointed a preacher and an apostle (I'm telling the truth and not lying) to teach the non-Jews to believe the truth.

8 So I want the men to pray everywhere, lifting up holy hands, not in a mood of anger or argument.

Women

9 Women should dress in decent clothes, modestly and properly, without braiding their hair, without gold, pearls, or expensive dresses 10 but as it is proper for women who promise to worship God with good works.

11 A woman should learn in silence, completely submitting herself. 12 I don't let a woman teach and have authority over a man; she should keep silent. 13 The reason is that Adam was formed first, then Eve. 14And Adam wasn't deceived; the woman was deceived and so fell into sin. 15 But women, having children, will be saved if they live in faith, love, and holiness, and use good judgment.

3 The qualifications of pastors, deacons, and deaconesses; the church, the pillar and foundation of truth

This is a saying to be trusted: "Whoever aspires to the office of pastor desires an excellent work." 2 So the pastor must be a man above reproach, must have only one wife, must be temperate, sensible, well-behaved, hospitable, skillful in teaching; 3 not addicted to strong drink, not pugnacious, gentle and not contentious, not avaricious, 4 managing his own house well, with perfect seriousness keeping his children under control 5 (if a man does not know

Church Workers

3 You can depend on this: If anyone sets his heart on being a pastor, he wants to do a noble kind of work. 2 Now, a pastor must be blameless, the husband of one wife, not drinking too much wine, a man of good judgment and fine behavior, kind to guests, able to teach, 3 no drunkard, not violent but gentle, not quarrelsome, not one who loves money. 4 He should manage his own family well and have his children obey him as he treats them very seriously. 5 If anyone doesn't know how to manage

K.J.V.

man know not how to rule his own house, how shall he take care of the church of God?) 6 Not a novice, lest being lifted up with pride he fall into the condemnation of the devil. 7 Moreover he must have a good report of them which are without; lest he fall into reproach and the snare of the devil. 8 Likewise *must* the deacons *be* grave, not double-tongued, not given to much wine, not greedy of filthy lucre; 9 Holding the mystery of the faith in a pure conscience. 10And let these also first be proved; then let them use the office of a deacon, being *found* blameless. 11 Even so *must their* wives *be* grave, not slanderers, sober, faithful in all things. 12 Let the deacons be the husbands of one wife, ruling their children and their own houses well. 13 For they that have used the office of a deacon well purchase to themselves a good degree, and great boldness in the faith which is in Christ Jesus. 14 These things write I unto thee, hoping to come unto thee shortly: 15 But if I tarry long, that thou mayest know how thou oughtest to behave thyself .in the house of God, which is the church of the living God, the pillar and ground of the truth. 16And without controversy great is the mystery of godliness: God was manifest in the flesh, justified in the Spirit, seen of angels, preached unto the Gentiles, believed on in the world, received up into glory.

4 Now the Spirit speaketh expressly, that in the latter times some shall depart from the faith, giving heed to seducing spirits, and doctrines of devils; 2 Speaking lies in hypocrisy; having their conscience seared with a hot iron; 3 Forbidding to marry, *and commanding* to abstain from meats, which God hath created to be received with thanksgiving of them which believe and know the truth. 4 For every creature of God *is* good, and nothing to be refused, if it be received with thanksgiving: 5 For it is sanctified by the word of God and prayer. 6 If thou put the brethren in remembrance of these things, thou shalt be a good minister of Jesus Christ, nourished up in the words of faith and of good doctrine, whereunto thou hast attained. 7 But refuse profane and old wives' fables, and exercise thyself *rather* unto godliness. 8 For bodily exercise profiteth little: but godliness is profitable unto all things, having promise of the life that now is, and of that which is to come. 9 This *is* a faithful saying, and worthy of all acceptation. 10 For therefore we both labour and suffer reproach, because we trust in the living God, who is the Saviour of all men, specially of those that

N.A.S.

know how to manage his own household, how will he take care of the church of God?); 6 *and* not a new convert, lest he become conceited and fall into the condemnation incurred by the devil. 7And he must have a good reputation with those outside *the church*, so that he may not fall into reproach and the snare of the devil. 8 Deacons likewise *must be* men of dignity, not double-tongued, or addicted to much wine or fond of sordid gain, 9 *but* holding to the mystery of the faith with a clear conscience. 10And let these also first be tested; then let them serve as deacons if they are beyond reproach. 11 Women *must* likewise *be* dignified, not malicious gossips, but temperate, faithful in all things. 12 Let deacons be husbands of *only* one wife, *and* good managers of *their* children and their own households. 13 For those who have served well as deacons obtain for themselves a high standing and great confidence in the faith that is in Christ Jesus.

14 I am writing these things to you, hoping to come to you before long; 15 but in case I am delayed, *I write* so that you may know how one ought to conduct himself in the household of God, which is the church of the living God, the pillar and support of the truth. 16And by common confession great is the mystery of godliness:

*He who was revealed in the flesh,
Was vindicated in the Spirit,
Beheld by angels,
Proclaimed among the nations,
Believed on in the world,
Taken up in glory.*

4 But the Spirit explicitly says that in later times some will fall away from the faith, paying attention to deceitful spirits and doctrines of demons, 2 by means of the hypocrisy of liars seared in their own conscience as with a branding iron, 3 *men* who forbid marriage *and advocate* abstaining from foods, which God has created to be gratefully shared in by those who believe and know the truth. 4 For everything created by God is good, and nothing is to be rejected, if it is received with gratitude; 5 for it is sanctified by means of the word of God and prayer.

6 In pointing out these things to the brethren, you will be a good servant of Christ Jesus, *constantly* nourished on the words of the faith and of the sound doctrine which you have been following. 7 But have nothing to do with worldly fables fit only for old women. On the other hand, discipline yourself for the purpose of godliness; 8 for bodily discipline is only of little profit, but godliness is profitable for all things, since it holds promise for the present life and *also* for the *life* to come. 9 It is a trustworthy statement deserving full acceptance. 10 For it is for this we labor and strive, because we have fixed our hope on the living God, who is the Savior of all

[a] Some later mss. read, *God.*

WILLIAMS

how to manage his own house, how can he take care of a church of God?). 6 He must not be a new convert, or else becoming conceited he may incur the doom the devil met. 7 He must also have a good reputation with outsiders, or else he may incur reproach and fall into the devil's trap.

8 Deacons, too, must be serious, sincere in their talk,[a] not addicted to strong drink or dishonest gain, 9 but they must continue to hold the open secret of faith with a clear conscience. 10 They, too, should first be tested till approved, and then, if they are found above reproach, they should serve as deacons. 11 The deaconesses too must be serious, not gossips; they must be temperate and perfectly trustworthy. 12 A deacon too must have only one wife, and manage his children and household well. 13 For those who render good service win a good standing for themselves in their faith in Christ Jesus.

14 Though I hope to come to you soon, I am writing you this, 15 so that, if I am detained, you may know how people ought to conduct themselves in the house of God, which is the church of the living God, the pillar and foundation of the truth. 16 Undoubtedly the mystery of our religion is a great wonder:
"He was made visible in human form,
He was vindicated by the Spirit,
He was seen by angels,
He was proclaimed among the heathen,
He was trusted in throughout the world,
He was taken up to glory."

4 *Teachers teach falsely about marriage and foods; Timothy to rebuke them and train himself in pure living, spiritual exercises, and patient teaching*

Now the Spirit distinctly declares that in later times some will turn away from the faith, because they continuously give their attention to deceiving spirits and the things that demons teach 2 through the pretensions of false teachers, men with seared consciences, 3 who forbid people to marry and teach them to abstain from certain sorts of food which God created for the grateful enjoyment of those who have faith and a clear knowledge of the truth. 4 For everything in God's creation is good, and nothing is to be refused, provided it is accepted with thanksgiving; 5 for in this way it is consecrated by the word of God and prayer.

6 If you continue to put these things before the brothers, you will be a good minister of Christ Jesus, ever feeding your own soul on the truths of the faith and of the fine teaching which you have followed. 7 But make it your habit to let worldly and old women's stories alone. Continue training yourself for the religious life. 8 Physical training, indeed, is of some service, but religion[a] is of service for everything, for it contains a promise for the present life as well as the future. 9 This is a saying to be trusted and deserves to be accepted by all. 10 To this end we are toiling and struggling, because we have fixed our hope on the living God, who is the Saviour of all mankind, especially of believers.

[a] *Not double-worded.*
[a] *Lit., godliness, or worshiping well.*

BECK

his own family, how can he take care of God's church? 6 He should not be a person who has just been won, or he may feel proud and so be condemned with the devil. 7 The people outside the church must speak well of him, or he may fall into disgrace and the devil's snare.

8 In the same way the helpers in the church should be serious, sincere in speech, not drinking a lot of wine, not greedy. 9 With a clear conscience they should keep the hidden truth they believe. 10 They, too, should first be tested; then if no fault is found in them, they should serve. 11 In the same way the wives should be serious, not slandering, not drinking too much wine, but trustworthy in every way. 12 A church worker should be the husband of one wife and should manage his children and his home well. 13 When they have served well, they get a good standing and can talk very confidently of their faith in Christ Jesus.

We Bring the Truth

14 I hope to come to you soon but am writing you this 15 so that if I'm delayed you know how people should behave in God's family, which is the church of the living God, a pillar and support of the truth.

16 It must be admitted the hidden truth of our religion is great—

He appeared in flesh,
Became righteous in spirit,
Was seen by angels,
Was preached among nations,
Was believed in the world,
Was taken up in glory.

Danger Ahead

4 The Spirit says clearly that in later times some will turn away from the faith as they listen to spirits who deceive and to what devils teach 2 and are taken in by the hypocrisy of liars branded in their consciences as the devil's slaves, 3 who order people not to marry and to keep away from foods that God created to be eaten with thanks by those who believe and know the truth. 4 Everything God created is good. We shouldn't reject any of it but take it and thank God for it, 5 because the Word of God and prayer make it holy.

How to Serve Christ

6 Point these things out to our fellow Christians, and you will be a good servant of Christ Jesus, nourished by the words of the faith and of the sound teaching you have followed. 7 Don't have anything to do with unholy stories such as old women tell. Train yourself for a godly life. 8 Training the body helps a little, but godliness helps in every way, having a promise of life here and hereafter 9 (you can trust His Word and accept it absolutely); 10 that is what we work and struggle for, because our hope is in the living God, who is the Savior of all people, especially of those who believe.

593

K.J.V.

believe. 11 These things command and teach. 12 Let no man despise thy youth; but be thou an example of the believers, in word, in conversation, in charity, in spirit, in faith, in purity. 13 Till I come, give attendance to reading, to exhortation, to doctrine. 14 Neglect not the gift that is in thee, which was given thee by prophecy, with the laying on of the hands of the presbytery. 15 Meditate upon these things; give thyself wholly to them; that thy profiting may appear to all. 16 Take heed unto thyself, and unto the doctrine; continue in them: for in doing this thou shalt both save thyself, and them that hear thee.

5 Rebuke not an elder, but entreat *him* as a father; *and* the younger men as brethren; 2 The elder women as mothers; the younger as sisters, with all purity. 3 Honour widows that are widows indeed. 4 But if any widow have children or nephews, let them learn first to shew piety at home, and to requite their parents: for that is good and acceptable before God. 5 Now she that is a widow indeed, and desolate, trusteth in God, and continueth in supplications and prayers night and day. 6 But she that liveth in pleasure is dead while she liveth. 7 And these things give in charge, that they may be blameless. 8 But if any provide not for his own, and specially for those of his own house, he hath denied the faith, and is worse than an infidel. 9 Let not a widow be taken into the number under threescore years old, having been the wife of one man, 10 Well reported of for good works; if she have brought up children, if she have lodged strangers, if she have washed the saints' feet, if she have relieved the afflicted, if she have diligently followed every good work. 11 But the younger widows refuse: for when they have begun to wax wanton against Christ, they will marry; 12 Having damnation, because they have cast off their first faith. 13 And withal they learn *to be* idle, wandering about from house to house; and not only idle, but tattlers also and busybodies, speaking things which they ought not. 14 I will therefore that the younger women marry, bear children, guide the house, give none occasion to the adversary to speak reproachfully. 15 For some are already turned aside after Satan. 16 If any man or woman that believeth have widows, let them relieve them, and let not the church be charged; that it may relieve them that are widows indeed. 17 Let the elders that rule well be counted worthy of double honour, especially they who labour in the word and doctrine. 18 For the Scripture saith, Thou shalt not muzzle the ox that treadeth out the corn. And, The labourer *is* worthy of his reward. 19 Against an elder receive not an accusation, but before two or three witnesses. 20 Them that sin rebuke

N.A.S.

men, especially of believers. 11 Prescribe and teach these things. 12 Let no one look down on your youthfulness, but *rather* in speech, conduct, love, faith *and* purity, show yourself an example of those who believe. 13 Until I come, give attention to the *public* reading of *Scripture*, to exhortation and teaching. 14 Do not neglect the spiritual gift within you, which was bestowed upon you through prophetic utterance with the laying on of hands by the presbytery. 15 Take pains with these things; be *absorbed* in them, so that your progress may be evident to all. 16 Pay close attention to yourself and to your teaching; persevere in these things; for as you do this you will insure salvation both for yourself and for those who hear you.

5 Do not sharply rebuke an older man, *but rather* appeal to him as a father; the younger men as brothers, 2 the older women as mothers, *and* the younger women as sisters, in all purity. 3 Honor widows who are widows indeed; 4 but if any widow has children or grandchildren, let them first learn to practice piety in regard to their own family, and to make some return to their parents; for this is acceptable in the sight of God. 5 Now she who is a widow indeed and who has been left alone has fixed her hope on God, and continues in entreaties and prayers night and day. 6 But she who gives herself to wanton pleasure is dead even while she lives. 7 Prescribe these things as well, so that they may be above reproach. 8 But if any one does not provide for his own, and especially for those of his household, he has denied the faith, and is worse than an unbeliever. 9 Let a widow be put on the list only if she is not less than sixty years old, *having been* the wife of one man, 10 having a reputation for good works; *and if* she has brought up children, if she has shown hospitality to strangers, if she has washed the saints' feet, if she has assisted those in distress, *and* if she has devoted herself to every good work. 11 But refuse *to put* younger widows *on the list*, for when they feel sensual desires in disregard of Christ, they want to get married, 12 *thus* incurring condemnation, because they have set aside their previous pledge. 13 And at the same time they also learn *to be* idle, as they go around from house to house; and not merely idle, but also gossips and busybodies, talking about things not proper *to mention*. 14 Therefore, I want younger *widows* to get married, bear children, keep house, *and* give the enemy no occasion for reproach; 15 for some have already turned aside to follow Satan. 16 If any woman who is a believer has *dependent* widows, let her assist them, and let not the church be burdened, so that it may assist those who are widows indeed.

17 Let the elders who rule well be considered worthy of double honor, especially those who work hard at preaching and teaching. 18 For the Scripture says, "YOU SHALL NOT MUZZLE THE OX WHILE HE IS THRESHING," and "The laborer is worthy of his wages." 19 Do not receive an accusation against an elder except on the basis of two or three witnesses. 20 Those who continue in sin, rebuke in the presence of all, so that the

WILLIAMS

11 Continue to give these orders and to teach these truths. 12 Let no one think little of you because you are young, but always set an example for believers, in speech, conduct, love, faith, and purity. 13 Until I come, devote yourself to the public reading of the Scriptures, and to preaching and teaching. 14 Stop neglecting the gift you received, which was given you through prophetic utterance when the elders laid their hands upon you. 15 Continue cultivating these things; be devoted to them, so that everybody will see your progress. 16 Make it your habit to pay close attention to yourself and your teaching. Persevere in these things, for if you do you will save both yourself and those who listen to you.

5 *Tells Timothy how to treat the old and the young, especially widows; how to select and treat the officers of the churches*

Never reprove an older man, but always appeal to him as a father. Treat younger men like brothers, 2 older women like mothers, younger women like sisters, with perfect purity. 3 Always care for widows who are really dependent. 4 But if a widow has children or grandchildren, they must first learn to practice piety in the treatment of their own families, and to pay the debt they owe their parents or grandparents, for this is acceptable to God. 5 But a woman who is really a widow and lives alone has fixed her hope on God, and night and day devotes herself to prayers and entreaties, 6 while a widow who gives herself up to luxury is really dead though still alive. 7 Continue to give these directions so that the people may be without reproach. 8 Whoever fails to provide for his own relatives, and especially for those of his immediate family, has disowned the faith and is worse than an unbeliever. 9 No widow under sixty years of age should be put on this roll. A widow must have had but one husband, 10 must have a reputation for doing good deeds, as bringing up children, being hospitable to strangers, washing the feet of God's people, helping people in distress, or devoting herself to any sort of doing good. 11 Keep the young widows off this roll, for when they get to indulging their lower nature in opposition to Christ, they want to marry, 12 and so deserve censure for breaking their previous pledge. 13 Besides, as they get the habit of gadding about from house to house, they learn to be idle, and not only idle but gossips and busybodies, talking of things they ought not to mention. 14 So I would have the younger women marry, have children, and keep house, so as not to give our opponents any occasion for slander. 15 For some widows have already turned aside to follow Satan. 16 If a Christian woman has widowed relatives, she should help them, and let the church be free from the burden, so that it can help the widows who are really dependent.

17 Elders who do their duties well should be considered as deserving twice the salary they get, especially those who keep on toiling in preaching and teaching. 18 For the Scripture says, "You must not muzzle an ox when he is treading out the grain," and, "The workman deserves his pay." 19 Make it a rule not to consider a charge preferred against an elder, unless it is supported by two or three witnesses. 20 Those who are guilty reprove in public, so

BECK

11 Order them to do these things, and keep on teaching.
12 Don't let anyone look down on you because you're young, but be an example to those who believe, in speech, behavior, love, faith, and purity. 13 Till I come, take care of the public reading, encouragement, and teaching. 14 Don't neglect the gift you have which was given you by prophecy when the elders laid their hands on you. 15 Practice these things, continue in them, so that everybody can see your progress. 16 Watch yourself and your teaching. Keep right on in these things. If you do that, you will save yourself and those who hear you.

5 Don't be harsh with an older man, but encourage him like a father, young men like brothers, 2 older women like mothers, younger women like sisters, keeping yourself altogether pure.

Take Care of Widows

3 Treat with respect widows who are all alone. 4 If any widow has children or grandchildren, these should learn as their first duty to respect their own family and repay their parents, because that pleases God. 5 A widow who is all alone and forsaken trusts the Lord and keeps on praying day and night. 6 But one who lives for pleasure is dead while she lives.
7 Order them to do these things so that they can't be criticized. 8 If anyone doesn't take care of his own relatives, especially his family, he has denied the faith and is worse than an unbeliever. 9 Put a widow on your list if she isn't under sixty, if she was faithful to her husband, 10 if people tell about the good she has done, if she raised children, welcomed strangers, washed the feet of holy people, helped the suffering, and was busy doing every kind of good work. 11 But don't put younger widows on the list. When they feel vigorous and turn against Christ, they want to marry 12 and so are guilty of breaking the pledge they made in the beginning. 13 At the same time they learn to be idle and go around in the homes. And they're not only idle but gossiping and meddling, saying things they shouldn't say.
14 So I want younger women to marry, have children, manage their homes, and give the enemy no chance to slander them. 15 Some have already left us to follow the devil. 16 If any believing woman has widows, she should help them and not let them be a burden to the church, so that the church may help those widows who are all alone.
17 Pastors who lead well should be considered worthy of double honor, especially if their work is preaching and teaching, 18 because the Bible says, *When an ox is treading out the grain, don't muzzle him,*[1] and "a worker deserves his pay." *
19 Don't accept an accusation against a pastor unless *it is supported by two or three witnesses.*[2] 20 Those who keep on sinning, correct before everybody in order to make the others afraid.

* Matt. 10:10.
[1] Deut. 25:4.
[2] Deut. 19:15

K.J.V.

before all, that others also may fear. 21 I charge *thee* before God, and the Lord Jesus Christ, and the elect angels, that thou observe these things without preferring one before another, doing nothing by partiality. 22 Lay hands suddenly on no man, neither be partaker of other men's sins: keep thyself pure. 23 Drink no longer water, but use a little wine for thy stomach's sake and thine often infirmities. 24 Some men's sins are open beforehand, going before to judgment; and some *men* they follow after. 25 Likewise also the good works *of some* are manifest beforehand; and they that are otherwise cannot be hid.

6 Let as many servants as are under the yoke count their own masters worthy of all honour, that the name of God and *his* doctrine be not blasphemed. 2And they that have believing masters, let them not despise *them,* because they are brethren; but rather do *them* service, because they are faithful and beloved, partakers of the benefit. These things teach and exhort. 3 If any man teach otherwise, and consent not to wholesome words, *even* the words of our Lord Jesus Christ, and to the doctrine which is according to godliness; 4 He is proud, knowing nothing, but doting about questions and strifes of words, whereof cometh envy, strife, railings, evil surmisings, 5 Perverse disputings of men of corrupt minds, and destitute of the truth, supposing that gain is godliness: from such withdraw thyself. 6 But godliness with contentment is great gain. 7 For we brought nothing into *this* world, *and it is* certain we can carry nothing out. 8And having food and raiment, let us be therewith content. 9 But they that will be rich fall into temptation and a snare, and *into* many foolish and hurtful lusts, which drown men in destruction and perdition. 10 For the love of money is the root of all evil· which while some coveted after, they have erred from the faith, and pierced themselves through with many sorrows. 11 But thou, O man of God, flee these things; and follow after righteousness, godliness, faith, love, patience, meekness. 12 Fight the good fight of faith, lay hold on eternal life, whereunto thou art also called, and hast professed a good profession before many witnesses. 13 I give thee charge in the sight of God, who quickeneth all things, and *before* Christ Jesus, who before Pontius Pilate witnessed a good confession; 14 That thou keep *this* commandment without spot, unrebukeable, until the appearing of our Lord Jesus Christ: 15 Which in his times he shall shew, *who is* the blessed and only Potentate, the King of kings, and Lord of lords; 16 Who only hath immortality, dwelling in the light which no man can approach unto; whom no man hath seen, nor can see: to whom *be* honour and

N.A.S.

rest also may be fearful *of sinning.* 21 I solemnly charge you in the presence of God and of Christ Jesus and of *His* chosen angels, to maintain these *principles* without bias, doing nothing in *a spirit of* partiality. 22 Do not lay hands upon any one *too* hastily and thus share *responsibility for* the sins of others; keep yourself free from sin. 23 No longer drink water *exclusively,* but use a little wine for the sake of your stomach and your frequent ailments. 24 The sins of some men are quite evident, going before them to judgment; for others, their *sins* follow after. 25 Likewise also, deeds that are good are quite evident, and those which are otherwise cannot be concealed.

6 Let all who are under the yoke as slaves regard their own masters as worthy of all honor so that the name of God and *our* doctrine may not be spoken against. 2And let those who have believers as their masters not be disrespectful to them because they are brethren, but let them serve them all the more, because those who partake of the benefit are believers and beloved. Teach and preach these *principles.* 3 If any one advocates a different doctrine, and does not agree with sound words, those of our Lord Jesus Christ, and with the doctrine conforming to godliness, 4 he is conceited *and* understands nothing; but he has a morbid interest in controversial questions and disputes about words, out of which arise envy, strife, abusive language, evil suspicions, 5 and constant friction between men of depraved mind and deprived of the truth, who suppose that godliness is a means of gain. 6 But godliness *actually* is a means of great gain, when accompanied by contentment. 7 For we have brought nothing into the world, *so we cannot take anything out of it either. 8 And if we have food and covering, with these we shall be content. 9 But those who want to get rich fall into temptation and a snare and many foolish and harmful desires which plunge men into ruin and destruction. 10 For the love of money is a root of all sorts of evil, and some by longing for it have wandered away from the faith, and pierced themselves with many a pang.

11 But flee from these things, you man of God; and pursue after righteousness, godliness, faith, love, perseverance *and* gentleness. 12 Fight the good fight of faith; take hold of the eternal life to which you were called, and you made the good confession in the presence of many witnesses. 13 I charge you in the presence of God, who gives life to all things, and of Christ Jesus, who testified the good confession before Pontius Pilate; 14 that you keep the commandment without stain or reproach, until the appearing of our Lord Jesus Christ, 15 which He will bring about at the proper time—He who is the blessed and only Sovereign, the King of kings and Lord of lords; 16 who alone possesses immortality and dwells in unapproachable light; whom no man has seen or can see. To Him *be* honor and eternal dominion! Amen.

[a] Later mss. read, *it is clear that.*

WILLIAMS

that others may be warned. 21 I solemnly charge you before God and Christ Jesus and the chosen angels, to carry out these instructions without prejudice and with perfect impartiality. 22 Make it a rule not to ordain anyone in haste, and not to be responsible for the sins of others; keep yourself pure. 23 Stop drinking water only, but take a little wine to strengthen your stomach and relieve its frequent attacks. 24 Some men's sins are very evident and clearly lead them on to judgment, but the sins of others lag behind. 25 Good deeds, too, are usually very evident, and if they are not, they cannot be completely concealed.

6 *Slaves must render willing service; he warns against false teaching and greed; Timothy solemnly charged, especially to urge the rich to do good with their money; he warns again; says farewell*

All who are under the yoke of slavery must esteem their masters to be deserving the highest respect, so that the name of God and our teaching may not be abused. 2 Those who have Christian masters must not pay them less respect because they are brothers; they must serve them all the better, because those who get the benefit of their service are believers and so are dear to them.

These are the things that you must continue to teach and urge them to do. 3 If anyone teaches different doctrines and refuses to agree with the wholesome messages of our Lord Jesus Christ, the teaching that is in accordance with true religion, 4 he is a conceited ignoramus with a morbid appetite for discussions and controversies which lead to envy, quarreling, abuse, base suspicions, 5 and perpetual friction between people who are depraved in mind and deprived of truth, who imagine that religion is only a means of gain. 6 Now the fact is, religion with contentment is a means of great gain. 7 For we bring nothing into the world and surely we can take nothing out of it. 8 If we have food and clothes we will be satisfied. 9 But men who keep planning to get rich fall into temptations and snares and many foolish, hurtful desires which plunge people into destruction and ruin. 10 For the love of money is the root of all sorts of evil, and some men in reaching after riches have wandered from the faith and pierced their hearts with many a pang. 11 But you, as a man of God, must be fleeing always from these things; you must constantly strive for uprightness, godliness, faith, love, steadfastness, gentleness. 12 Keep up the good fight for the faith. Keep your hold on eternal life, to which God called you, when before many witnesses you made the good profession of faith. 13 Before God who preserves the life of all His creatures and before Christ Jesus who in testifying before Pontius Pilate made His good profession, I solemnly charge you 14 to keep His command stainless and irreproachable until the appearance of our Lord Jesus Christ, 15 which will be brought about in His own time by the blessed, only Sovereign, the King of kings, the Lord of lords, 16 who alone possesses immortality and dwells in unapproachable light, whom no man has ever seen or can see. To Him be honor and eternal dominion. Amen.

BECK

21 I solemnly call on you before God and Christ Jesus and the chosen angels to keep these things without a prejudice and without a preference for anyone in anything you do. 22 Don't be in a hurry to ordain anyone. Don't share in the sins of others. Keep yourself pure. 23 Don't drink water only, but use a little wine for your stomach because you are often sick. 24 Anybody can see the sins of some people as these sins go ahead of them to judgment, but the sins of others follow them there. 25 And so anybody can also see good works, and even when they can't be seen, they can't stay hidden.

Slaves and Masters

6 All who are under the yoke of slavery should think of their masters as men who deserve every respect, so that God's name and what we teach isn't slandered. 2 If you have masters who believe, don't think less of them because they are fellow Christians, but serve them all the better because those who get the benefit of your work are believers and dear to you.

Religion and Contentment

3 Teach and urge them to do these things. If anyone teaches anything else and will not agree with the sound words of our Lord Jesus Christ and godly teaching, 4 he is proud and doesn't know anything; he has a morbid craving for debates and arguments, which produce jealousy, quarreling, insults, evil suspicions, 5 continued wrangling of people whose minds are corrupt, who have lost the truth and think religion is a way to make money. 6 Of course, there's a big profit in religion if we're satisfied. 7 We didn't bring anything into the world, and we can't take anything out. 8 If we have food and clothing, we'll be satisfied. 9 But people who want to get rich fall into temptation and a snare and many foolish and harmful desires that drown them in destruction and ruin. 10 Love of money is a root of all evils, and some people, eager to get rich, have wandered away from the faith and pierced themselves with much pain.

Fight the Good Fight

11 But you, man of God, flee from these things. Be eager to be righteous, godly, full of faith and love, able to endure, gentle. 12 Fight the good fight of faith, take hold of the everlasting life to which you were called when you made a good confession before many witnesses. 13 I order you before God, from whom comes all life, and before Christ Jesus, who testified before Pontius Pilate and made a good confession, 14 that you do what you are ordered, without spot or blame, till our Lord Jesus Christ appears. 15 At His own right time God will show Him to us—He, the blessed and only Ruler, the King of kings and Lord of lords, 16 who alone cannot die, who lives in a light to which no one can come near, whom no one has ever seen or can see. To Him be honor and power forever. Amen.

K.J.V.

power everlasting. Amen. 17 Charge them that are rich in this world, that they be not high-minded, nor trust in uncertain riches, but in the living God, who giveth us richly all things to enjoy; 18 That they do good, that they be rich in good works, ready to distribute, willing to communicate; 19 Laying up in store for themselves a good foundation against the time to come, that they may lay hold on eternal life. 20 O Timothy, keep that which is committed to thy trust, avoiding profane *and* vain babblings, and oppositions of science falsely so called: 21 Which some professing have erred concerning the faith. Grace *be* with thee. Amen.

The first to Timothy was written from Laodicea, which is the chiefest city of Phrygia Pacatiana.

N.A.S.

17 Instruct those who are rich in this present world not to be conceited or to fix their hope on the uncertainty of riches, but on God, who richly supplies us with all things to enjoy. 18 *Instruct them* to do good, to be rich in good works, to be generous and ready to share, 19 storing up for themselves the treasure of a good foundation for the future, so that they may take hold of that which is life indeed.
20 O Timothy, guard what has been entrusted to you, avoiding worldly *and* empty chatter *and* the opposing arguments of what is falsely called "knowledge"— 21 which some have professed and thus gone astray from the faith.
Grace be with you.

WILLIAMS

17 Continue charging the rich of this world to stop being haughty and not to fix their hope on a thing so uncertain as riches, but on God who richly and ceaselessly provides us with everything for our enjoyment; 18 charge them to continue doing good and being rich in good deeds, open-handed and generous-hearted, 19 in this way amassing for themselves the riches that forever endure in the life to come, so that at last they may grasp the life that is life indeed.

20 Timothy, guard what has been entrusted to you; continue to turn away from the worldly, futile phrases and contradictions of what is falsely called "knowledge," 21 by professing which some individuals have failed in the faith. Spiritual blessing be with you all.

BECK

17 Tell those who are rich in this world not to feel proud and not to trust anything as uncertain as riches but to trust God, who richly gives us everything to enjoy. 18 Tell them to do good, to be rich in good works, to be glad to give and share, 19 and so to store up for themselves a treasure, a good foundation for the future, and to take hold of the life that is real.

20 Timothy, guard what has been entrusted to you. Turn away from empty, unholy talk and contradictory statements of what is falsely called knowledge. 21 Some claim to have it and have lost their faith.

God's love be with you all!

K.J.V.

THE SECOND EPISTLE

OF PAUL THE APOSTLE

TO

TIMOTHY

N.A.S.

THE SECOND EPISTLE

OF PAUL TO

TIMOTHY

1 Paul, an apostle of Jesus Christ by the will of God, according to the promise of life which is in Christ Jesus, 2 To Timothy, *my* dearly beloved son: Grace, mercy, *and* peace, from God the Father and Christ Jesus our Lord. 3 I thank God, whom I serve from *my* forefathers with pure conscience, that without ceasing I have remembrance of thee in my prayers night and day; 4 Greatly desiring to see thee, being mindful of thy tears, that I may be filled with joy; 5 When I call to remembrance the unfeigned faith that is in thee, which dwelt first in thy grandmother Lois, and thy mother Eunice; and I am persuaded that in thee also. 6 Wherefore I put thee in remembrance, that thou stir up the gift of God, which is in thee by the putting on of my hands. 7 For God hath not given us the spirit of fear; but of power, and of love, and of a sound mind. 8 Be not thou therefore ashamed of the testimony of our Lord, nor of me his prisoner: but be thou partaker of the afflictions of the gospel according to the power of God; 9 Who hath saved us, and called *us* with a holy calling, not according to our works, but according to his own purpose and grace, which was given us in Christ Jesus before the world began; 10 But is now made manifest by the appearing of our Saviour Jesus Christ, who hath abolished death, and hath brought life and immortality to light through the gospel: 11 Whereunto I am appointed a preacher, and an apostle, and a teacher of the Gentiles. 12 For the which cause I also suffer these things: nevertheless I am not ashamed; for I know whom I have believed, and am persuaded that he is able to keep that which I have committed unto him against that day. 13 Hold fast the form of sound words, which thou hast heard of me, in faith and love which is in Christ Jesus. 14 That good thing which was committed unto thee keep by the Holy Ghost which dwelleth in us. 15 This thou knowest, that all they which are in Asia be turned away from me; of whom are Phygellus and Hermogenes. 16 The Lord give mercy unto the house of Onesiphorus; for he oft refreshed me, and was not ashamed of my chain: 17 But, when he was in Rome, he sought me out very diligently, and found *me*. 18 The Lord grant unto him that he may find mercy of the Lord in that

1 Paul, an apostle of Christ Jesus by the will of God, according to the promise of life in Christ Jesus, 2 to Timothy, my beloved son: Grace, mercy *and* peace from God the Father and Christ Jesus our Lord. 3 I thank God, whom I serve with a clear conscience the way my forefathers did, as I constantly remember you in my prayers night and day, 4 longing to see you, even as I recall your tears, so that I may be filled with joy. 5 For I am mindful of the sincere faith within you, which first dwelt in your grandmother Lois, and your mother Eunice, and I am sure that *it is* in you as well. 6 And for this reason I remind you to kindle afresh the gift of God which is in you through the laying on of my hands. 7 For God has not given us a spirit of timidity, but of power and love and discipline. 8 Therefore do not be ashamed of the testimony of our Lord, or of me His prisoner; but join with *me* in suffering for the gospel according to the power of God; 9 who has saved us, and called us with a holy calling, not according to our works, but according to His own purpose and grace which was granted us in Christ Jesus from all eternity, 10 but now has been revealed by the appearing of our Savior Christ Jesus, who abolished death, and brought life and immortality to light through the gospel, 11 for which I was appointed a preacher and an apostle and a teacher. 12 For this reason I also suffer these things, but I am not ashamed; for I know whom I have believed and I am convinced that He is able to guard what I have entrusted to Him until that day. 13 Retain the standard of sound words which you have heard from me, in the faith and love which are in Christ Jesus. 14 Guard through the Holy Spirit who dwells in us, the treasure which has been entrusted to *you*.

15 You are aware of the fact that all who are in Asia turned away from me, among whom are Phygelus and Hermogenes. 16 The Lord grant mercy to the house of Onesiphorus for he often refreshed me, and was not ashamed of my chains; 17 but when he was in Rome, he eagerly searched for me, and found me— 18 the Lord grant to him to find mercy from the Lord on

PAUL

WRITES THE SECOND

LETTER TO

SECOND TIMOTHY

TIMOTHY

1 *Greets Timothy; thanks God for his early religious training; urges him to be courageous; two traitors exposed; a hero exhibited*

Paul, an apostle of Christ Jesus by the will of God, in accordance with the promise of the life that comes through union with Christ Jesus, 2 to my dearly loved child Timothy: spiritual blessing, mercy, and peace be with you from God our Father and Christ Jesus our Lord.

3 I thank God, whom I worship, as my fore-fathers did, with a clear conscience, as I ceaselessly remember you in my prayers. Because I remember the tears you shed for me, I am always longing night and day 4 to see you again, that I may feel the fullest joy 5 on being reminded of your genuine faith, a faith that first found a home[a] in the heart of your grandmother Lois, then in the heart of your mother Eunice, and now in yours too, I am sure.

6 For this reason I now remind you to re-kindle and keep burning the fire of the divine gift which came upon you when I laid my hands upon you. 7 For the Spirit that God has given us does not impart timidity but power and love and self-control. 8 So you must never be ashamed of me His prisoner, but suffer for the good news in fellowship with me and by the power of God. 9 For He saved us and called us with a holy call, not in accordance with anything that we had done, but in accordance with His own purpose and unmerited favor which was shown us through union with Christ Jesus eternal ages ago, 10 but has only recently been made known through the appearance of our Savior Christ Jesus, who through the good news has put a stop to the power of death, and brought life and immortality to light. 11 Of this good news I have been appointed a preacher, an apostle, and a teacher. 12 This is why I am suffering so, but I am not ashamed of it, for I know whom I have trusted and I am absolutely sure that He is able to guard what I have entrusted to Him until that day. 13 Continue to be an example in wholesome instructions which you learned from me, in the faith and love that come through union with Christ Jesus. 14 Guard this fine deposit of truth by the aid of the Holy Spirit who has His home in our hearts.

15 You know that everyone here who belongs to the Roman province of Asia has deserted me, including Phygelus and Hermogenes. 16 May the Lord show mercy to the family of Onesiphorus, because he often cheered me and was not ashamed of the chains I wore. 17 Yes, when he got to Rome he took pains to look me up and finally found me. 18 The Lord grant that he may find mercy at His hands on that

[a] *To dwell permanently.*

1 Paul, apostle of Christ Jesus by God's will because God promised life in Christ Jesus, 2 to Timothy, my dear son—God the Father and Christ Jesus, our Lord, give you love, mercy, and peace!

3 I thank God—whom I, like my fathers, serve with a clear conscience—when I remember you in my prayers, as I never fail to do day and night. 4 Remembering your tears, I long to see you and so to be perfectly happy. 5 I recall how sincere your faith was; just as it lived in your grandmother Lois and your mother Eunice before you, so I am convinced it is in you too.

Stir Up God's Gift

6 That is why I remind you to stir into a flame God's gift that is in you through the laying on of my hands. 7 God didn't give us a cowardly Spirit but a Spirit of power and love and good judgment. 8 So don't be ashamed to tell about our Lord, and don't be ashamed of me, His prisoner, but with God's power to back us, join me in suffering for the good news. 9 He saved us and called us to be holy, not because we did anything, but because He planned a gift of His love and gave it to us in Christ Jesus before the world began; 10 it has now come to light by the coming of our Savior Christ Jesus. He took away the power of death and by the good news brought into the light the life that can't be destroyed. 11 To tell about it, I was appointed a preacher, apostle, and teacher.

12 That is why I suffer as I do, but I'm not ashamed, because I know Him whom I trust, and I'm sure He can keep for that day what I have entrusted to Him.

13 With a faith and a love in Christ Jesus keep what you heard me say as an example of sound teaching. 14 With the help of the Holy Spirit living in us, guard the good thing entrusted to you.

Onesiphorus

15 You know how everybody in the province of Asia deserted me, including Phygelus and Hermogenes.

16 The Lord be merciful to the family of Onesiphorus because he often cheered me up. 17 He didn't feel ashamed of my being a prisoner, but coming to Rome, he searched hard for me and found me. 18 May the Lord let him find mercy from the Lord on that day.

K.J.V.

day: and in how many things he ministered unto me at Ephesus, thou knowest very well.

2 Thou therefore, my son, be strong in the grace that is in Christ Jesus. 2And the things that thou hast heard of me among many witnesses, the same commit thou to faithful men, who shall be able to teach others also. 3 Thou therefore endure hardness, as a good soldier of Jesus Christ. 4 No man that warreth entangleth himself with the affairs of *this* life; that he may please him who hath chosen him to be a soldier. 5And if a man also strive for masteries, *yet* is he not crowned, except he strive lawfully. 6 The husbandman that laboureth must be first partaker of the fruits. 7 Consider what I say; and the Lord give thee understanding in all things. 8 Remember that Jesus Christ of the seed of David was raised from the dead, according to my gospel: 9 Wherein I suffer trouble, as an evil doer, *even* unto bonds; but the word of God is not bound. 10 Therefore I endure all things for the elect's sake, that they may also obtain the salvation which is in Christ Jesus with eternal glory. 11 *It is* a faithful saying: For if we be dead with *him,* we shall also live with *him:* 12 If we suffer, we shall also reign with *him:* if we deny *him,* he also will deny us: 13 If we believe not, *yet* he abideth faithful: he cannot deny himself. 14 Of these things put *them* in remembrance, charging *them* before the Lord that they strive not about words to no profit, *but* to the subverting of the hearers. 15 Study to shew thyself approved unto God, a workman that needeth not to be ashamed, rightly dividing the word of truth. 16 But shun profane *and* vain babblings: for they will increase unto more ungodliness. 17And their word will eat as doth a canker: of whom is Hymeneus and Philetus; 18 Who concerning the truth have erred, saying that the resurrection is past already; and overthrow the faith of some. 19 Nevertheless the foundation of God standeth sure, having this seal, The Lord knoweth them that are his. And, Let every one that nameth the name of Christ depart from iniquity. 20 But in a great house there are not only vessels of gold and of silver, but also of wood and of earth; and some to honour, and some to dishonour. 21 If a man therefore purge himself from these, he shall be a vessel unto honour, sanctified, and meet for the master's use, *and* prepared unto every good work. 22 Flee also youthful lusts: but follow righteousness, faith, charity, peace, with them that call on the Lord out of a pure heart. 23 But foolish and unlearned questions avoid, knowing that they do gender strifes. 24And the servant

N.A.S.

that day—and you know very well what services he rendered at Ephesus.

2 You therefore, my son, be strong in the grace that is in Christ Jesus. 2 And the things which you have heard from me in the presence of many witnesses, these entrust to faithful men, who will be able to teach others also. 3 Suffer hardship with *me,* as a good soldier of Christ Jesus. 4 No soldier in active service entangles himself in the affairs of everyday life, so that he may please the one who enlisted him as a soldier. 5 And also if any one competes as an athlete, he does not win the prize unless he competes according to the rules. 6 The hardworking farmer ought to be the first to receive his share of the crops. 7 Consider what I say, for the Lord will give you understanding in everything. 8 Remember Jesus Christ, risen from the dead, descendant of David, according to my gospel; 9 for which I suffer hardship even to imprisonment as a criminal, but the word of God is not imprisoned. 10 For this reason I endure all things for the sake of those who are chosen, that they also may obtain the salvation which is in Christ Jesus *and* with *it* eternal glory. 11 It is a trustworthy statement:

For if we died with Him, we shall also live with Him;
12 If we endure, we shall also reign with Him; If we deny Him, He also will deny us;
13 If we are faithless, He remains faithful; for He cannot deny Himself.

14 Remind *them* of these things, and solemnly charge *them* in the presence of God not to wrangle about words, which is useless, *and leads* to the ruin of the hearers. 15 Be diligent to present yourself approved to God as a workman who does not need to be ashamed, handling accurately the word of truth. 16 But avoid worldly *and* empty chatter, for it will lead to further ungodliness, 17 and their talk will spread like ªgangrene, among whom are Hymenaeus and Philetus, 18 *men* who have gone astray from the truth saying that the resurrection has already taken place, and thus they upset the faith of some. 19 Nevertheless, the firm foundation of God stands, having this seal, "The Lord knows those who are His," and, "Let every one who names the name of the Lord abstain from wickedness." 20 Now in a large house there are not only gold and silver vessels, but also vessels of wood and of earthenware, and some to honor and some to dishonor. 21 Therefore, if a man cleanses himself from these *things,* he will be a vessel for honor, sanctified, useful to the Master, prepared for every good work. 22 Now flee from youthful lusts, and pursue after righteousness, faith, love *and* peace, with those who call on the Lord from a pure heart. 23 But refuse foolish and ignorant speculations, knowing that they produce quarrels. 24 And the Lord's bond-

[a] Or, *cancer.*

WILLIAMS

day. And you very well know yourself how great were the services he rendered me at Ephesus.

2 Timothy urged to be diligent in teaching, patient and courageous in suffering; to discourage petty debating; tells of two sorts of Christians; Timothy warned of some personal perils

So you, my son, must keep renewing your strength in the spiritual blessing that comes through union with Christ Jesus. 2 The things you learned from me before many witnesses you must commit to trustworthy men who will be competent to teach others too. 3 Take your share of hardships like a good soldier of Christ Jesus. 4 No soldier ever allows himself to be involved in the business affairs of life, so that he may please the officer who enlisted him. 5 No contestant in the games is crowned, unless he competes according to the rules. 6 The toiling farmer ought to be the first to share the crop. 7 Keep on thinking about what I am saying, for the Lord will grant you understanding of it in all its phases. 8 Continue to remember Jesus Christ as risen from the dead, and descended from David, in accordance with the good news that I preach, 9 for the sake of which I am suffering hardships even to the extent of wearing chains as though I were a criminal. But God's message is not in chains. 10 For this reason I am bearing anything for the sake of His chosen people, so that they too may obtain the salvation that comes through Christ Jesus and with it eternal glory. 11 This message is to be trusted: "If we indeed have died with Him, we will live with Him too. 12 If we patiently endure, we will reign with Him too. If we disown Him, He will disown us too. 13 If we are unfaithful, He remains faithful, for He cannot prove false to Himself."

14 Keep on reminding men of these things. Solemnly charge them before God to stop petty debating, which does no good at all but brings destruction on those who hear it. 15 Do your best to present yourself to God an approved workman who has nothing to be ashamed of, who properly presents the message of truth. 16 Continue shunning worldly, futile phrases, for they lead on to greater depths of godlessness, 17 and their message will spread like a cancer; men like Hymenaeus and Philetus, 18 who have missed the truth by saying that the resurrection has already taken place, are undermining some people's faith. 19 But God's foundation stands unshaken, with these inscriptions: "The Lord knows the people who belong to Him" and "Everyone who bears the name of the Lord must abstain from evil."

20 In any great house there are not only gold and silver articles but also wooden utensils, some for honorable uses and some for lowly uses. 21 So if a man will cleanse himself from these things, he will be an instrument for honorable uses, consecrated, useful for the Master, and ready for any good service. 22 You must keep on fleeing from the evil impulses of youth, but ever strive for uprightness, faith, love, and peace, in association with those who call upon the Lord with pure hearts. 23 Always avoid foolish discussions with ignorant men, for you know that they breed quarrels, 24 and a slave of the Lord must not quarrel but must be gentle to everybody; he must

BECK

And you know very well all he did to help me in Ephesus.

Be a Good Soldier

2 You, my son, let God's love in Christ Jesus make you strong, 2 and what you heard me say before many witnesses entrust to faithful people who will be able to teach others.

3 Share hardships with me like a good soldier of Christ Jesus. 4 If you're in the army, you don't get tangled up with the ways of making a living; you want to please him who made you a soldier. 5 If you enter a contest, you win a prize only if you compete according to the rules. 6 If you work the ground, you should be the first to get what grows on it. 7 Try to understand what I say, because the Lord will give you understanding in everything.

8 Keep in mind Jesus Christ risen from the dead, a descendant of David—this is the good news I tell. 9 For this I'm suffering and am even chained like a criminal. But God's Word isn't chained. 10 That's why I can endure anything for the chosen people to have them get salvation in Christ Jesus and everlasting glory. 11 You can depend on this: If we have died with Him, we'll live with Him. If we endure, we'll rule with Him. 12 If we disown Him, He'll disown us. 13 If we're disloyal, he stays loyal because He cannot be untrue to Himself.

14 Remind them of these things and warn them before the Lord not to fight about words; it doesn't do any good but only ruins those who are listening.

15 Do your best to come before God as one whom He approves, a worker who doesn't have to feel ashamed as he teaches the Word of truth in the right way. 16 Keep away from empty, unholy talk, because such people get to be more and more ungodly, 17 and their talk will spread like a cancer. Among them are Hymenaeus and Philetus, 18 who have lost the truth by saying the resurrection has already taken place. They're upsetting some people's faith.

19 But there stands God's solid foundation, and it has this seal: *The Lord has chosen those who belong to Him,*[1] and: "Everyone who *calls on the Lord's name,*[2] must give up doing wrong."

20 In a big house there are not only things of gold and silver but also of wood and clay. Some are used in a noble way and some are not. 21 Now if anyone will cleanse himself from bad ways, he'll be ready for a noble purpose, purified, useful to the owner, and prepared to do any good work.

22 Flee from the lusts of young people, try to be righteous, faithful, loving, peaceful with people who with pure hearts call on the Lord. 23 Don't have anything to do with foolish and unintelligent arguments; you know they breed quarrels. 24 A Lord's servant must not quarrel

[1] Num. 16:5
[2] Is. 26:13

603

K.J.V.

of the Lord must not strive; but be gentle unto all *men*, apt to teach, patient; 25 In meekness instructing those that oppose themselves; if God peradventure will give them repentance to the acknowledging of the truth; 26And *that* they may recover themselves out of the snare of the devil, who are taken captive by him at his will.

3 This know also, that in the last days perilous times shall come. 2 For men shall be lovers of their own selves, covetous, boasters, proud, blasphemers, disobedient to parents, unthankful, unholy, 3 Without natural affection, trucebreakers, false accusers, incontinent, fierce, despisers of those that are good, 4 Traitors, heady, highminded, lovers of pleasures more than lovers of God; 5 Having a form of godliness, but denying the power thereof: from such turn away. 6 For of this sort are they which creep into houses, and lead captive silly women laden with sins, led away with divers lusts, 7 Ever learning, and never able to come to the knowledge of the truth. 8 Now as Jannes and Jambres withstood Moses, so do these also resist the truth: men of corrupt minds, reprobate concerning the faith. 9 But they shall proceed no further: for their folly shall be manifest unto all *men*, as theirs also was. 10 But thou hast fully known my doctrine, manner of life, purpose, faith, long-suffering, charity, patience, 11 Persecutions, afflictions, which came unto me at Antioch, at Iconium, at Lystra; what persecutions I endured: but out of *them* all the Lord delivered me. 12 Yea, and all that will live godly in Christ Jesus shall suffer persecution. 13 But evil men and seducers shall wax worse and worse, deceiving, and being deceived. 14 But continue thou in the things which thou hast learned and hast been assured of, knowing of whom thou hast learned *them;* 15And that from a child thou hast known the holy Scriptures, which are able to make thee wise unto salvation through faith which is in Christ Jesus. 16All Scripture is given by inspiration of God, and *is* profitable for doctrine, for reproof, for correction, for instruction in righteousness: 17 That the man of God may be perfect, thoroughly furnished unto all good works.

4 I charge *thee* therefore before God, and the Lord Jesus Christ, who shall judge the quick and the dead at his appearing and his kingdom; 2 Preach the word; be instant in season, out of season; reprove, rebuke, exhort with all long-

N.A.S.

servant must not be quarrelsome, but be kind to all, able to teach, patient when wronged, 25 with gentleness correcting those who are in opposition; if perhaps God may grant them repentance leading to the knowledge of the truth, 26 and they may come to their senses *and escape* from the snare of the devil, having been held captive by him to do his will.

3 But realize this, that in the last days difficult times will come. 2 For men will be lovers of self, lovers of money, boastful, arrogant, revilers, disobedient to parents, ungrateful, unholy, 3 unloving, irreconcilable, malicious gossips, without self-control, brutal, haters of good, 4 treacherous, reckless, conceited, lovers of pleasure rather than lovers of God; 5 holding to a form of godliness, although they have denied its power; and avoid such men as these. 6 For among them are those who enter into households and captivate weak women weighed down with sins, led on by various impulses, 7 always learning and never able to come to the knowledge of the truth. 8 And just as Jannes and Jambres opposed Moses, so these *men* also oppose the truth, men of depraved mind, rejected as regards the faith. 9 But they will not make further progress; for their folly will be obvious to all, as also that of those *two* came to be. 10 But you followed my teaching, conduct, purpose, faith, patience, love, perseverance, 11 persecutions, sufferings, such as happened to me at Antioch, at Iconium *and* at Lystra; what persecutions I endured, and out of them all the Lord delivered me! 12 And indeed, all who desire to live godly in Christ Jesus will be persecuted. 13 But evil men and imposters will proceed *from bad* to worse, deceiving and being deceived. 14 You, however, continue in the things you have learned and become convinced of, knowing from whom you have learned *them;* 15 and that from childhood you have known the sacred writings which are able to give you the wisdom that leads to salvation through faith which is in Christ Jesus. 16 ªAll Scripture is inspired by God and profitable for teaching, for reproof, for correction, for training in righteousness; 17 that the man of God may be adequate, equipped for every good work.

4 I solemnly charge *you* in the presence of God and of Christ Jesus, who is to judge the living and the dead, and by His appearing and His kingdom: 2 preach the word; be ready in season *and* out of season; reprove, rebuke,

[a] Or possibly, *Every Scripture inspired by God is also* . . .

WILLIAMS

be a skillful teacher, and not resentful under injuries. 25 With gentleness he must correct his opponents, for God might grant them repentance that would lead them to a full knowledge of the truth, 26 and they might recover their senses and escape from the devil's trap in which they have been caught by him to do his will.

3 *Last days terrible in crimes and false teachings; false teachers like Jannes and Jambres of old; Timothy urged to be faithful to his training*

Now you must know that in the last days there are going to be hard times. 2 For people will be selfish, avaricious, boastful, haughty, abusive, disobedient to parents, ungrateful, irreverent, 3 lacking in love for kinsmen, irreconcilable, slanderers, having no self-control, savage, lacking in love for the good, 4 treacherous, reckless, conceited, loving pleasure more than God, 5 keeping up the forms of religion but not giving expression to its power. Avoid such people. 6 For some of them practice going into people's houses and capturing weak and silly women who are overwhelmed with the weight of their sins, who are easily led about by all sorts of evil impulses, 7 who are always trying to learn but never able to come to a full knowledge of the truth. 8 Just as Jannes and Jambres resisted Moses, these people resist the truth, for they are depraved in mind and so counterfeits in the faith. 9 But they will not make any more progress, for their folly will be evident to everybody, as theirs was. 10 But you, on your part, have faithfully followed my teaching, my conduct, my aim, my faith, my patience, my love, my steadfastness, 11 my persecutions, my sufferings, such as befell me at Antioch, Iconium, and Lystra, such as I endured—but the Lord delivered me out of them all. 12 Yes, indeed, everyone who wants to live a godly life as a follower of Christ Jesus will be persecuted. 13 But bad men and impostors will go on from bad to worse, misleading others and misled themselves. 14 But you, on your part, must continue to abide by what you have learned and been led to rely upon, because you know from whom you learned it 15 and that from childhood you have known the sacred Scriptures which can give you wisdom that leads to salvation through the faith that leans on Christ Jesus. 16All Scripture is inspired by God, and useful for teaching, for reproof, for correction, for training in doing what is right, 17 so that the man of God may be perfectly fit, thoroughly equipped for every good enterprise.

4 *Timothy urged to be zealous and to control himself; Paul optimistic as he faces his beheading; yet lonely, so he sends for Mark, his coat, and his books; still absolutely trustful in the Lord, he says farewell*

I solemnly charge you, before God and Christ Jesus who is to judge the living and the dead, and by His appearing and His kingdom, 2 preach the message, stay at it in season and out of season; convince, reprove, exhort people

BECK

but be kind to everyone. He should be a good teacher, ready to suffer wrong, 25 and gentle in correcting those who oppose him. Perhaps God will change their hearts and lead them to know the truth. 26 Then they'll escape the snare of the devil, who trapped them to do what he wants, and they'll come to their senses.

The Last Days

3 Understand this, that in the last days there will come times of trouble. 2 People will love themselves and money. They'll brag and be proud. They'll blaspheme. They'll disobey parents. They'll be ungrateful and unholy, 3 without love, never forgiving an enemy, slandering. They'll be without control, wild, with no love for what is good. 4 They'll be treacherous, reckless, proud. They'll love pleasure and not God. 5 They'll have the essence of godliness but refuse to let it be a power. Keep away from such people. 6 Some of them get into homes and captivate weak women, loaded with sins, driven by all kinds of desires, 7 always learning and never able to understand the truth. 8 Just as Jannes and Jambres opposed Moses, so they oppose the truth. Their minds are corrupt, and their faith is no good. 9 But they won't get very far; like Jannes and Jambres, they will be seen by everybody to be the plain fools they are.

Teach the Truth

10 But you have followed closely my teaching, way of living, and purpose, my faith, patience, love, and endurance, 11 my persecutions and sufferings, the things that happened to me in Antioch, Iconium, and Lystra, the persecutions I endured. The Lord rescued me from everything. 12All who want to live a godly life in Christ Jesus will be persecuted.

13 But bad men and swindlers will get worse as they cheat and are cheated. 14 But you stay with what you've learned and found to be true. You know from whom you learned it 15 and how since you were a little child you have known the Holy Scriptures, which can make you wise and save you if you believe in Christ Jesus. 16All Scripture is inspired by God and helps us to teach, to show what is wrong, to improve and train in right living 17 so that a man of God is ready and equipped for every good work.

4 Before God and Christ Jesus, who is going to judge the living and the dead, I solemnly call on you—in view of His coming and ruling over us— 2 preach the Word, keep at it at the right time and the wrong time, correct, rebuke, encourage, being very patient and thorough in your teaching.

K.J.V.

suffering and doctrine. 3 For the time will come when they will not endure sound doctrine; but after their own lusts shall they heap to themselves teachers, having itching ears; 4And they shall turn away *their* ears from the truth, and shall be turned unto fables. 5 But watch thou in all things, endure afflictions, do the work of an evangelist, make full proof of thy ministry. 6 For I am now ready to be offered, and the time of my departure is at hand. 7 I have fought a good fight, I have finished *my* course, I have kept the faith: 8 Henceforth there is laid up for me a crown of righteousness, which the Lord, the righteous judge, shall give me at that day: and not to me only, but unto all them also that love his appearing. 9 Do thy diligence to come shortly unto me: 10 For Demas hath forsaken me, having loved this present world, and is departed unto Thessalonica; Crescens to Galatia, Titus unto Dalmatia. 11 Only Luke is with me. Take Mark, and bring him with thee: for he is profitable to me for the ministry. 12And Tychicus have I sent to Ephesus. 13 The cloak that I left at Troas with Carpus, when thou comest, bring *with thee,* and the books, *but* especially the parchments. 14Alexander the coppersmith did me much evil: the Lord reward him according to his works: 15 Of whom be thou ware also; for he hath greatly withstood our words. 16At my first answer no man stood with me, but all *men* forsook me: *I pray God* that it may not be laid to their charge. 17 Notwithstanding the Lord stood with me, and strengthened me; that by me the preaching might be fully known, and *that* all the Gentiles might hear: and I was delivered out of the mouth of the lion. 18And the Lord shall deliver me from every evil work, and will preserve *me* unto his heavenly kingdom: to whom *be* glory for ever and ever. Amen. 19 Salute Prisca and Aquila, and the household of Onesiphorus. 20 Erastus abode at Corinth: but Trophimus have I left at Miletum sick. 21 Do thy diligence to come before winter. Eubulus greeteth thee, and Pudens, and Linus, and Claudia, and all the brethren. 22 The Lord Jesus Christ *be* with thy spirit. Grace *be* with you. Amen.

The second *epistle* unto Timotheus, ordained the first bishop of the church of the Ephesians, was written from Rome, when Paul was brought before Nero the second time.

N.A.S.

exhort, with great patience and instruction. 3 For the time will come when they will not endure sound doctrine; but *wanting* to have their ears tickled, they will accumulate for themselves teachers in accordance to their own desires; 4 and will turn away their ears from the truth, and will turn aside to myths. 5 But you, be sober in all things, endure hardship, do the work of an evangelist, fulfill your ministry. 6 For I am already being poured out as a drink-offering, and the time of my departure has come. 7 I have fought the good fight, I have finished the course, I have kept the faith; 8 in the future there is laid up for me the crown of righteousness, which the Lord, the righteous Judge, will award to me on that day; and not only to me, but also to all who have loved His appearing.

9 Make every effort to come to me soon; 10 for Demas, having loved this present world, has deserted me and gone to Thessalonica; Crescens *has gone* to Galatia, Titus to Dalmatia. 11 Only Luke is with me. Pick up Mark and bring him with you, for he is useful to me for service. 12 But Tychicus I have sent to Ephesus. 13 When you come bring the cloak which I left at Troas with Carpus, and the books, especially the parchments. 14 Alexander the coppersmith did me much harm; the Lord will repay him according to his deeds. 15 Be on guard against him yourself, for he vigorously opposed our teaching. 16 At my first defense no one supported me, but all deserted me; may it not be counted against them. 17 But the Lord stood with me, and strengthened me, in order that through me the proclamation might be fully accomplished, and that all the Gentiles might hear; and I was delivered out of the lion's mouth. 18 The Lord will deliver me from every evil deed, and will bring me safely to His heavenly kingdom; to Him *be* the glory forever and ever. Amen.

19 Greet Prisca and Aquila, and the household of Onesiphorus. 20 Erastus remained at Corinth; but Trophimus I left sick at Miletus. 21 Make every effort to come before winter. Eubulus greets you, also Pudens and Linus and Claudia and all the brethren.

22 The Lord be with your spirit. Grace be with you.

WILLIAMS

with perfect patience as a teacher.[a] 3 For a time will come when they will not listen to wholesome teaching, but to gratify their own evil desires will surround themselves with teachers who teach to gratify their own evil desires, because their ears are itching so to be tickled, 4 and they will cease to listen to the truth and will turn to listen to myths. 5 But you, on your part, must always keep your head cool, suffer hardship, do your work as a herald of the good news, and so fill your ministry to the brim.

6 My life, indeed, is already ebbing out, and the time has come for me to sail away. 7 I have fought the fight for the good, I have run my race, I have kept the faith. 8 Now the crown for doing right awaits me, which the Lord, the righteous Judge, will award me on that day, and not only me but also all who have loved His appearing.

9 Do your best to come to me soon, 10 for Demas has forsaken me because he loved the present world, and has gone to Thessalonica; Crescens has gone to Galatia, Titus to Dalmatia; 11 Luke is the only one who is now with me. Pick up Mark and bring him with you, for he is of great service to me, 12 and I have sent Tychicus off to Ephesus. 13 When you come, bring the coat which I left with Carpus at Troas; bring the books, too, especially the parchments. 14 Alexander, a worker in metal, did me ever so much harm. The Lord will repay him for what he did. 15 You too must be on your guard against him, for he has vigorously opposed my teaching.

16 When I first defended myself at court, nobody came to help me, but everybody deserted me. May it never be charged to their account. 17 But the Lord stood by me and gave me strength, so that the message preached by me might have its full effect and all the heathen might hear it. So I was rescued from the lion's jaws.[b] 18 The Lord will rescue me from every wicked work and save me to His heavenly kingdom. To Him be glory for ever and ever. Amen.

19 Remember me to Prisca and Aquila, and to the family of Onesiphorus. 20 Erastus stayed in Corinth; I left Trophimus sick at Miletus. 21 Do your best to get here before winter. Eubulus wishes to be remembered to you, and so do Pudens, Linus, Claudia, and all the brothers.

22 The Lord be with your spirit. Spiritual blessing be with you all.

BECK

3 A time will come when people will not listen to sound teaching but, craving to hear something different, will get more and more teachers whom they like. 4 They will refuse to listen to the truth and will turn to fictions.

5 But you, keep a clear head in everything, endure hardship, do your work of telling the good news, and everything else you should do as a pastor.

The Lord Will Deliver Me

6 I'm now being sacrificed, and it's time for me to leave. 7 I fought the good fight, I ran the race, I kept the faith. 8 Now there is waiting for me the crown of righteousness which the Lord, the righteous Judge, will give me on that day, and not only me but all who love to see Him come again.

9 Do your best to come to me soon. 10 Demas fell in love with this world, deserted me, and went to Thessalonica. Crescens went to Galatia, Titus to Dalmatia. 11 Only Luke is with me. Get Mark and bring him with you, because he's a good help to me in my work. 12 I sent Tychicus to Ephesus.

13 When you come, bring the warm coat I left with Carpus in Troas, and the scrolls, especially the parchments.

14 Alexander the metalworker did me a lot of wrong. *The Lord will pay him back for what he did.*[3] 15 Be on your guard against him, because he was very much opposed to what we said.

16 The first time I had to defend myself nobody came to help me, but everybody deserted me—may it not be held against them. 17 But the Lord stood by me and gave me the strength to finish my preaching so that all the non-Jews would hear it. *I was rescued from the lion's mouth.*[4] 18 The Lord will rescue me from all the evil that is done and will save me and take me to His heavenly kingdom. To Him be glory forever. Amen.

Greetings

19 Greet Prisca and Aquila and the family of Onesiphorus. 20 Erastus stayed in Corinth. I left Trophimus sick in Miletus. 21 Do your best to get here before the winter. Eubulus and Pudens and Linus and Claudia and all the fellow Christians greet you.

22 The Lord Jesus Christ be with your spirit! God's love be with you all!

---

[a] Grk., *with all patience and teaching.* [b] Lit., *the lion's mouth*—referring to Nero.

[3] Ps. 62:12; Prov. 24:12
[4] Ps. 22:21; Dan. 6:20, 27

K.J.V.

THE

EPISTLE OF PAUL

TO

TITUS

N.A.S.

THE EPISTLE OF PAUL

TO

TITUS

1 Paul, a servant of God, and an apostle of Jesus Christ, according to the faith of God's elect, and the acknowledging of the truth which is after godliness; 2 In hope of eternal life, which God, that cannot lie, promised before the world began; 3 But hath in due times manifested his word through preaching, which is committed unto me according to the commandment of God our Saviour; 4 To Titus, mine own son after the common faith: Grace, mercy, and peace, from God the Father and the Lord Jesus Christ our Saviour. 5 For this cause left I thee in Crete, that thou shouldest set in order the things that are wanting, and ordain elders in every city, as I had appointed thee: 6 If any be blameless, the husband of one wife, having faithful children not accused of riot or unruly. 7 For a bishop must be blameless, as the steward of God; not selfwilled, not soon angry, not given to wine, no striker, not given to filthy lucre; 8 But a lover of hospitality, a lover of good men, sober, just, holy, temperate; 9 Holding fast the faithful word as he hath been taught, that he may be able by sound doctrine both to exhort and to convince the gainsayers. 10 For there are many unruly and vain talkers and deceivers, especially they of the circumcision; 11 Whose mouths must be stopped, who subvert whole houses, teaching things which they ought not, for filthy lucre's sake. 12 One of themselves, even a prophet of their own, said, The Cretians are always liars, evil beasts, slow bellies. 13 This witness is true. Wherefore rebuke them sharply, that they may be sound in the faith; 14 Not giving heed to Jewish fables, and commandments of men, that turn from the truth. 15 Unto the pure all things are pure: but unto them that are defiled and unbelieving is nothing pure; but even their mind and conscience is defiled. 16 They profess that they know God; but in works they deny him, being abominable, and disobedient, and unto every good work reprobate.

1 Paul, a bondservant of God, and an apostle of Jesus Christ, for the faith of those chosen of God and the knowledge of the truth which is according to godliness, 2 in the hope of eternal life, which God, who cannot lie, promised long ages ago, 3 but at the proper time manifested, even His word, in the proclamation with which I was entrusted according to the commandment of God our Savior; 4 to Titus, my true child in a common faith: Grace and peace from God the Father and Christ Jesus our Savior.

5 For this reason I left you in Crete, that you might set in order what remains, and appoint elders in every city as I directed you, 6 namely, if any man be above reproach, the husband of one wife, having children who believe, not accused of dissipation or rebellion. 7 For the overseer must be above reproach as God's steward, not self-willed, not quick-tempered, not addicted to wine, not pugnacious, not fond of sordid gain, 8 but hospitable, loving what is good, sensible, just, devout, self-controlled, 9 holding fast the faithful word which is in accordance with the teaching, that he may be able both to exhort in sound doctrine and to refute those who contradict.

10 For there are many rebellious men, empty talkers and deceivers, especially those of the circumcision, 11 who must be silenced because they are upsetting whole families, teaching things they should not teach, for the sake of sordid gain. 12 "One of themselves, a prophet of their own, said, "Cretans are always liars, evil beasts, lazy gluttons." 13 This testimony is true. For this cause reprove them severely that they may be sound in the faith, 14 not paying attention to Jewish myths and commandments of men who turn away from the truth. 15 To the pure, all things are pure; but to those who are defiled and unbelieving, nothing is pure, but both their mind and their conscience are defiled. 16 They profess to know God, but by their deeds they deny Him, being detestable and disobedient, and worthless for any good deed.

[a] Comp. Acts 17:28. The Gr. hexameter is said to be taken from a work by the Cretan poet Epimenides.

PAUL

WRITES TO

TITUS

TITUS

1 He greets Titus; states the qualifications of pastors; Titus urged to denounce false teachings; the immoral practices of the Cretans

Paul, a slave of God, and an apostle of Jesus Christ, to stimulate faith in God's chosen people and to lead them on to a full knowledge of religious truth, 2 in the hope of eternal life which God, who never lies, promised ages ago 3 but at the proper time made known as His message through the message that I preach with which I have been entrusted by the command of God our Saviour; 4 to Titus, my genuine child in our common faith: be spiritual blessing and peace from God our Father and Christ Jesus our Saviour.

5 I left you in Crete for this express purpose, to set in order the things that are lacking, and to appoint elders in each town, as I directed you—6 each elder must be above reproach, have only one wife, and his children must not be liable to the charge of profligacy or disobedience. 7 For as God's trustee a pastor must be above reproach, not stubborn or quick-tempered or addicted to strong drink or pugnacious or addicted to dishonest gain, 8 but hospitable, a lover of goodness, sensible, upright, of pure life, self-controlled, 9 and a man who continues to cling to the trustworthy message as he was taught it, so that he may be competent to encourage others with wholesome teaching and to convict those who oppose him.

10 For there are many insubordinate people, mere talkers with nothing to say, but deceivers of their own minds, especially those of the circumcision party, 11 whose mouths must be stopped, for they upset whole families by teaching things they ought not to think, for the sake of dishonest gain. 12 One of them, a prophet of their own countrymen, has said, "Cretans are always liars, wicked brutes, lazy bellies." 13 Now this tendency is true. So continue correcting them severely, that they may be healthy in faith, 14 by ceasing to give attention to Jewish myths and to the commands of men who turn their backs on the truth. 15 To the pure everything is pure, but to the impure and unbelieving nothing is pure, but their very minds and consciences are impure. 16 They profess to know God, but by their actions they disown Him; they are detestable, disobedient, and useless for anything good.

1 Paul, servant of God and apostle of Jesus Christ—

sent to help God's chosen people to believe and know the truth which promotes godliness, 2 hoping, as we do, for everlasting life, which God, who never lies, promised ages ago 3 and at His own right times revealed in His Word by the preaching entrusted to me by an order of God our Savior

4 —to Titus, my real son by the faith we share: May God the Father and Christ Jesus our Savior love you and give you peace!

Appoint Good Pastors

5 I left you behind in Crete to make the improvements still needed and to appoint pastors in every town as I directed you— 6 someone who is blameless, who has one wife, and believing children not accused of wild living or disobedient. 7 As a manager appointed by God, a pastor should be blameless. He shouldn't do as he pleases, get angry easily, drink too much, be quick to strike anyone, or be greedy. 8 He should welcome guests, love anything good, use good judgment, live right and holy. He should control himself. 9 He should cling to the Word, which he can depend on, just as he was taught, so that by sound teaching he can encourage people and correct those who oppose him.

Correct Your Opponents

10 There are many who can't be controlled, who talk foolishly and deceive, especially the Jews. 11 They must be silenced. They are ruining whole families by teaching what they must not teach, only to make money in such a shameful way.

12 One of their own men, their own prophet, said, "Men of Crete are always liars, savage animals, lazy bellies." * 13 That statement is true. For that reason correct them sharply so that they may be sound in their faith 14 instead of listening to Jewish myths or orders given by men who reject the truth. 15 Everything is pure to those who are pure. But nothing is pure to the evilminded who don't believe—their minds and consciences are unclean. They openly claim to know God but deny Him by what they do. 16 They're abominable, disobedient, and not fit to do anything good.

* This may have been said by Epimenides about 500 B. C.

K.J.V.

2 But speak thou the things which become sound doctrine: 2 That the aged men be sober, grave, temperate, sound in faith, in charity, in patience. 3 The aged women likewise, that *they be* in behaviour as becometh holiness, not false accusers, not given to much wine, teachers of good things; 4 That they may teach the young women to be sober, to love their husbands, to love their children, 5 *To be* discreet, chaste, keepers at home, good, obedient to their own husbands, that the word of God be not blasphemed. 6 Young men likewise exhort to be soberminded. 7 In all things shewing thyself a pattern of good works: in doctrine *shewing* uncorruptness, gravity, sincerity, 8 Sound speech, that cannot be condemned; that he that is of the contrary part may be ashamed, having no evil thing to say of you. 9 *Exhort* servants to be obedient unto their own masters, *and* to please *them* well in all things; not answering again; 10 Not purloining, but shewing all good fidelity; that they may adorn the doctrine of God our Saviour in all things. 11 For the grace of God that bringeth salvation hath appeared to all men, 12 Teaching us that, denying ungodliness and worldly lusts, we should live soberly, righteously, and godly, in this present world; 13 Looking for that blessed hope, and the glorious appearing of the great God and our Saviour Jesus Christ; 14 Who gave himself for us, that he might redeem us from all iniquity, and purify unto himself a peculiar people, zealous of good works. 15 These things speak, and exhort, and rebuke with all authority. Let no man despise thee.

3 Put them in mind to be subject to principalities and powers, to obey magistrates, to be ready to every good work, 2 To speak evil of no man, to be no brawlers, *but* gentle, shewing all meekness unto all men. 3 For we ourselves also were sometimes foolish, disobedient, deceived, serving divers lusts and pleasures, living in malice and envy, hateful, *and* hating one another. 4 But after that the kindness and love of God our Saviour toward man appeared, 5 Not by works of righteousness which we have done, but according to his mercy he saved us, by the washing of regeneration, and renewing of the Holy Ghost; 6 Which he shed on us abundantly through Jesus Christ our Saviour; 7 That being justified by his grace, we should be made heirs according to the hope of eternal life. 8 *This is* a faithful saying, and these things I will that thou affirm constantly, that they which have believed in God might be careful to maintain good works. These things are good and profitable unto men. 9 But avoid foolish questions, and genealogies, and contentions, and strivings about

N.A.S.

2 But as for you, speak the things which are fitting for sound doctrine. 2 Older men are to be temperate, dignified, sensible, sound in faith, in love, in perseverance. 3 Older women likewise are to be reverent in their behavior, not malicious gossips, nor enslaved to much wine, teaching what is good, 4 that they may encourage the young women to love their husbands, to love their children, 5 *to be* sensible, pure, workers at home, kind, being subject to their own husbands, that the word of God may not be dishonored. 6 Likewise urge the young men to be sensible; 7 in all things show yourself to be an example of good deeds, *with* purity in doctrine, dignified, 8 sound *in* speech which is beyond reproach, in order that the opponent may be put to shame, having nothing bad to say about us. 9 Urge bond-slaves to be subject to their own masters in everything, to be well pleasing, not argumentative, 10 not pilfering, but showing all good faith that they may adorn the doctrine of God our Savior in every respect. 11 For the grace of God has appeared, bringing salvation to all men, 12 instructing us to deny ungodliness and worldly desires and to live sensibly, righteously and godly in the present age, 13 looking for the blessed hope and the appearing of the glory of our great God and Savior, Christ Jesus; 14 who gave Himself for us, that HE MIGHT REDEEM US FROM EVERY LAWLESS DEED AND PURIFY FOR HIMSELF A PEOPLE FOR HIS OWN POSSESSION, zealous for good deeds. 15 These things speak and exhort and reprove with all authority. Let no one disregard you.

3 Remind them to be subject to rulers, to authorities, to be obedient, to be ready for every good deed, 2 to malign no one, to be uncontentious, gentle, showing every consideration for all men. 3 For we also once were foolish ourselves, disobedient, deceived, enslaved to various lusts and pleasures, spending our life in malice and envy, hateful, hating one another. 4 But when the kindness of God our Savior and *His* love for mankind appeared, 5 He saved us, not on the basis of deeds which we have done in righteousness, but according to His mercy, by the washing of regeneration and renewing by the Holy Spirit, 6 whom He poured out upon us richly through Jesus Christ our Savior, 7 that being justified by His grace we might be made heirs according to *the* hope of eternal life. 8 This is a trustworthy statement, and concerning these things I want you to speak confidently, so that those who have believed God may be careful to engage in good deeds. These things are good and profitable for men. 9 But shun foolish controversies and genealogies and strife and disputes about the Law; for they are unprofitable and

WILLIAMS

BECK

WILLIAMS

2 *He states the duties of the aged, of the young, and of slaves; he demands pure living of those ransomed by Christ*

You must continue telling the people what is proper for wholesome teaching: 2 the older men to be temperate, serious, and sensible, healthy in faith, in love, and in steadfastness; 3 the older women, too, to be reverent in their deportment, and not to be slanderers or slaves to heavy drinking, but to be teachers of what is right, 4 so as to train the younger women to be affectionate wives and mothers, 5 to be serious, pure, homekeepers, kind, and subordinate to their husbands, so as not to cause God's message to suffer reproach. 6 Keep urging the younger men to be sensible. 7 In everything you yourself continue to set them a worthy example of doing good; be sincere and serious in your teaching, 8 let your message be wholesome and unobjectionable, so that our opponent may be put to shame at having nothing evil to say about us. 9 Continue urging slaves to practice perfect submission to their masters and to give them perfect satisfaction, 10 to stop resisting them and stealing from them, but to show such perfect fidelity as to adorn, in everything they do, the teaching of God our Saviour.

11 For God's favor has appeared with its offer of salvation to all mankind, 12 training us to give up godless ways and worldly cravings and live serious, upright, and godly lives in this world, 13 while we are waiting for the realization of our blessed hope at the glorious appearing of our great God and Saviour Christ Jesus, 14 who gave Himself for us to ransom us from all iniquity and purify for Himself a people to be His very own, zealous of good works.

15 You must continue teaching this, and continue exhorting and reproving people, with full authority. Let no one belittle you.

3 *Christians must be law-abiding, social-minded citizens; good examples to be set; controversies to be avoided; makes requests; says farewell*

Constantly remind people to submit to and obey the rulers who have authority over them, so as to be ready for any good enterprise, 2 to stop abusing anyone, to be peaceable, fair-minded, showing perfect gentleness to everybody.

3 For once we too were without understanding, disobedient, misled, habitual slaves to all sorts of passions and pleasures, spending our lives in malice and envy. 4 But when the goodness and lovingkindness of God our Saviour were brought to light, 5 He saved us, not for upright deeds that we had done, but in accordance with His mercy, through the bath of regeneration and renewal of the Holy Spirit, 6 which He abundantly poured out upon us through Jesus Christ our Saviour, 7 so that we might come into right standing with God through His unmerited favor and become heirs of eternal life in accordance with our hope.

8 It is a message to be trusted, and I want you to be emphatic about these things, so that those who believe in God may be careful to take the lead in doing good. These things are right and render service to mankind. 9 But hold yourself aloof from foolish controversies, pedigrees, strife, and wrangles about the law, for

BECK

Special Instructions

2 But you tell people what is right according to sound teaching.

2 Tell older men: Be sober, serious, sensible, and sound in faith, love, and endurance.

3 In the same way tell older women: Behave as holy women should behave. Don't slander. Don't be slaves to much wine. Teach what is good, 4 in order to train young women to love their husbands and their children, 5 to use good judgment and be pure, to keep house, to be good, to submit to their husbands, so that people don't slander God's Word.

6 In the same way urge the young men to use good judgment. 7 In everything be an example of good works. Don't let anything corrupt your teaching. But be noble, 8 and give a sound message that can't be condemned so that anyone who opposes us will feel foolish because he can't say anything bad about us.

9 Tell slaves: Obey your masters in everything, please them, 10 and don't talk back. Don't steal, but show you can be trusted in every way, so that in everything you show the beauty of the teaching of God, who saves us.

Jesus Is Coming

11 God has shown His love. It brings salvation to all people 12 and trains us to say no to ungodliness and worldly lusts, to use good judgment, and to live right and godly in this world 13 as we look for the blessed One who is our hope, for our great God and Savior Christ Jesus to show Himself in glory. 14 He gave Himself as *a payment* for us *to free* us *from all wickedness*[1] and cleanse us *to be His own people*,[2] eager to do good works.

15 Talk and urge these things, and correct with full authority—nobody should ignore you.

3 Remind people to submit to governments and authorities, to obey, to be ready to do any good work, 2 not to insult anyone or fight, but to yield and show themselves perfectly gentle to everyone.

What God Did for Us

3 Once we, too, were foolish, disobedient, led astray, slaves to many kinds of passions and pleasures. We lived in wickedness and jealousy, being hated and hating one another.

4 But when God our Savior showed how kind He is and how He loves us, 5 He saved us, not because of any good works we did but because He was merciful. He saved us by the washing in which the Holy Spirit gives us a new birth and a new life. 6 He poured a rich measure of this Spirit on us through Jesus Christ our Savior, 7 to make us righteous by a gift of His love and, as we hope, heirs of everlasting life. 8 You can depend on this statement.

And I want you to insist on these things so that those who believe in God have their minds on being busy with good works. This is good, and it helps other people.

9 But keep away from foolish arguments, lists of ancestors, quarreling, and fighting about the Law. These help nobody and are worthless.

[1] Ps. 130:8
[2] Ex. 19:5; Deut. 14:2

K.J.V.

the law; for they are unprofitable and vain. 10A man that is a heretic, after the first and second admonition, reject; 11 Knowing that he that is such is subverted, and sinneth, being condemned of himself. 12 When I shall send Artemas unto thee, or Tychicus, be diligent to come unto me to Nicopolis: for I have determined there to winter. 13 Bring Zenas the lawyer and Apollos on their journey diligently, that nothing be wanting unto them. 14And let ours also learn to maintain good works for necessary uses, that they be not unfruitful. 15All that are with me salute thee. Greet them that love us in the faith. Grace *be* with you all. Amen.

It was written to Titus, ordained the first bishop of the church of the Cretians, from Nicopolis of Macedonia.

N.A.S.

worthless. 10 Reject a factious man after a first and second warning, 11 knowing that such a man is perverted and is sinning, being self-condemned.

12 When I send Artemas or Tychicus to you, make every effort to come to me at Nicopolis, for I have decided to spend the winter there. 13 Diligently help Zenas the lawyer and Apollos on their way so that nothing is lacking for them. 14And let our *people* also learn to engage in good deeds to meet pressing needs, that they may not be unfruitful.

15 All who are with me greet you. Greet those who love us in *the* faith.

Grace be with you all.

WILLIAMS

these are fruitless and futile. 10After one or two warnings to a man who is factious, stop having anything to do with him, 11 for you may be sure that such a man is crooked and sinful, even self-condemned.

12 When I send Artemas or Tychicus to you, do your best to come to me at Nicopolis, for I have decided to spend the winter there.

13 Give a hearty send-off to Zenas the lawyer, and Apollos, so that they may want for nothing. 14 Our people too must set examples of doing good, so as to meet the necessary demands and not to live unfruitful lives.

15 All who are with me wish to be remembered to you. Remember me to all who love me as Christians. Spiritual blessing be with you all.

BECK

10A man who chooses to be different in his teaching warn once and a second time, and then don't have anything more to do with him 11 because you know such a man is set in his wrong way and is a sinner who condemns himself.

Farewell

12 When I send Artemas or Tychicus to you, hurry to come to me at Nicopolis; I've decided to stay there for the winter. 13 Do your best to help Zenas the lawyer and Apollos to get on their way; they should have everything they need.

14 Our people should learn to be busy with good works to help real needs and not waste their lives.

15 All who are here with me send greetings. Greet those who love us as fellow believers.

God's love be with you all!

THE

EPISTLE OF PAUL

TO

PHILEMON

THE EPISTLE OF PAUL

TO

PHILEMON

Paul, a prisoner of Jesus Christ, and Timothy *our* brother, unto Philemon our dearly beloved, and fellow labourer, 2And to *our* beloved Apphia, and Archippus our fellow soldier, and to the church in thy house: 3 Grace to you, and peace, from God our Father and the Lord Jesus Christ. 4 I thank my God, making mention of thee always in my prayers, 5 Hearing of thy love and faith, which thou hast toward the Lord Jesus, and toward all saints; 6 That the communication of thy faith may become effectual by the acknowledging of every good thing which is in you in Christ Jesus. 7 For we have great joy and consolation in thy love, because the bowels of the saints are refreshed by thee, brother. 8 Wherefore, though I might be much bold in Christ to enjoin thee that which is convenient, 9 Yet for love's sake I rather beseech *thee*, being such a one as Paul the aged, and now also a prisoner of Jesus Christ. 10 I beseech thee for my son Onesimus, whom I have begotten in my bonds: 11 Which in time past was to thee unprofitable, but now profitable to thee and to me: 12 Whom I have sent again: thou therefore receive him, that is, mine own bowels: 13 Whom I would have retained with me, that in thy stead he might have ministered unto me in the bonds of the gospel: 14 But without thy mind would I do nothing; that thy benefit should not be as it were of necessity, but willingly. 15 For perhaps he therefore departed for a season, that thou shouldest receive him for ever; 16 Not now as a servant, but above a servant, a brother beloved, specially to me, but how much more unto thee, both in the flesh, and in the Lord? 17 If thou count me therefore a partner, receive him as myself. 18 If he hath wronged thee, or oweth *thee* aught, put that on mine account; 19 I Paul have written *it* with mine own hand, I will repay *it*: albeit I do not say to thee how thou owest unto me even thine own self besides. 20 Yea, brother, let me have joy of thee in the Lord: refresh my bowels in the Lord. 21 Having confidence in thy obedience I wrote unto thee, knowing that thou wilt also do more than I say. 22 But withal prepare me also a lodging: for I trust that through your prayers I shall be given unto you. 23 There salute thee Epaphras, my fellow prisoner in Christ Jesus; 24 Marcus, Aristarchus, Demas, Lucas, my fellow labourers. 25 The grace of our Lord Jesus Christ *be* with your spirit. Amen.

Written from Rome to Philemon, by Onesimus a servant.

Paul, a prisoner of Christ Jesus, and Timothy our brother, to Philemon our beloved *brother* and fellow-worker, 2 and to Apphia our sister, and to Archippus our fellow-soldier, and to the church in your[a] house: 3 Grace to you and peace from God our Father and the Lord Jesus Christ. 4 I thank my God always, making mention of you[a] in my prayers, 5 because I hear of your love, and of the faith which you have toward the Lord Jesus, and toward all the saints; 6 *and I pray* that the fellowship of your faith may become effective [a]through the knowledge of every good thing which is in [b]you for Christ's sake. 7 For I have come to have much joy and comfort in your[a] love, because the hearts of the saints have been refreshed through you, brother. 8 Therefore, though I have enough confidence in Christ to order you *to do* that which is proper, 9 yet for love's sake I rather appeal *to* you—since I am such a person as Paul the aged, and now also a prisoner of Christ Jesus—10 I appeal to you for my child, whom I have begotten in my imprisonment, [c]Onesimus, 11 who formerly was useless to you, but now is useful both to you and to me. 12 And I have sent him back to you in person, that is, *sending* my very heart; 13 whom I wished to keep with me, that in your behalf he might minister to me in my imprisonment for the gospel; 14 but without your consent I did not want to do anything, that your goodness should not be as it were by compulsion, but of your own free will. 15 For perhaps he was for this reason parted *from you* for a while, that you should have him back forever, 16 no longer as a slave, but more than a slave, a beloved brother, especially to me, but how much more to you, both in the flesh and in the Lord. 17 If then you regard me a partner, accept him as *you would* me. 18 But if he has wronged you in any way, or owes you anything, charge that to my account; 19 I, Paul, am writing this with my own hand, I will repay it (lest I should mention to you that you owe to me even your own self as well). 20 Yes, brother, let me benefit from you in the Lord; refresh my heart in Christ. 21 Having confidence in your obedience, I write to you, since I know that you will do even more than I say. 22 And at the same time also prepare me a lodging; for I hope that through your[p1] prayers I shall be given to you. 23 Epaphras, my fellow-prisoner in Christ Jesus, greets you[a]; 24 *as do* Mark, Aristarchus, Demas, Luke, my fellow-workers. 25 The grace of the Lord Jesus Christ be with your[p1] spirit.[a]

---

[a] Or, *in*. [b] Some ancient mss. read, *us*. [c] I.e., *Useful*. [a] Some ancient mss. add, *Amen*.

PAUL

WRITES TO

PHILEMON

PHILEMON

He greets Philemon; his slave, Onesimus, converted under Paul's preaching, is now being returned; Paul speaks for a room at Philemon's

Paul, a prisoner for Christ Jesus, and my brother Timothy, to our dearly loved fellow-worker Philemon, 2 to our sister Apphia, to our fellow-soldier Archippus, and to the church that meets at your house: 3 spiritual blessing be with you and peace from God our Father and the Lord Jesus Christ.

4 I always thank my God every time I mention you in my prayers, 5 because I continue to hear of the love and faith you have in the Lord Jesus and all His people, 6 and I pray that their sharing of your faith may result in their recognition in us of everything that is right with reference to Christ. 7 Yes, I have felt great joy and encouragement over your love, because the hearts of God's people have been refreshed by you, my brother.

8 So, although through union with Christ I have full freedom to order you to do your duty, 9 yet I prefer to appeal to you for love's sake, although I am such as I am, Paul an envoy of Christ Jesus but now a prisoner for Him too; 10 yes, I appeal to you for my child Onesimus, whose father I have become while wearing these chains. 11 Once he proved to be useless, but now he is useful to you and me; 12 I am sending him back to you, which is all the same as sending my very heart. 13 I would have liked to keep him with me, to wait on me in your stead while I wear these chains for the good news, 14 but I would not do a single thing about it without your consent, so that this kindness of yours to me might not seem to come by compulsion but voluntarily. 15 For perhaps it was for this reason that he was parted from you for a while, that you might have him back forever, 16 not as a slave any longer but more than a slave, a dearly loved brother, especially to me and much more to you, both as a servant and as a Christian. 17 So, if you consider me a comrade, take him to your bosom as you would me. 18 And if he has done you any wrong and owes you anything, charge it to my account. 19 I, Paul, write it with my own hand, I will pay it in full—not to mention the fact that you owe me your very self besides. 20 Yes, brother, I would like some return myself from you in the Lord's work. Through Christ refresh my heart.

21 I write you in perfect confidence in your compliance with my wish, because I am sure that you will do even more than I ask. 22 And have a guest-room ready for me, too, for I hope that through your prayers I shall have the gracious privilege of coming to you.

23 Epaphras, my fellow-prisoner in the cause of Christ Jesus, wishes to be remembered to you. 24 So do Mark, Aristarchus, Demas, and Luke, my fellow-workers.

25 The spiritual blessing of the Lord Jesus Christ be with your spirit.

Paul, a prisoner of Christ Jesus, and Timothy, my fellow worker, to Philemon, our dear fellow worker, 2 Apphia, our fellow Christian, Archippus, our fellow soldier, and to the church that meets at your home: 3 May God our Father and the Lord Jesus Christ love you and give you peace!

4 I'm always thanking my God when I mention you in my prayers, 5 because I hear how you believe in the Lord Jesus and love Him and all the holy people, 6 so that, knowing every good thing you have in Christ, you vigorously share your faith. 7 Your love delighted and encouraged me very much because you, my fellow Christian, have refreshed the hearts of our holy people.

8 For that reason, although I feel bold enough in Christ to order you to do what is right, 9 I am moved by love just to urge you. As Paul, an old man and now a prisoner of Christ Jesus, 10 I appeal to you for my son Onesimus,* who became my son while I have been in chains. 11 Once he was useless* to you, but now he's quite useful * to you and me.

12 I'm sending him back to you—and my heart goes with him. 13 I would have liked to keep him with me and have him serve me in your place while I'm in chains for the good news, 14 but I don't want to do anything without your approval. I don't want you to be kind because you must but because you want to be. 15 Perhaps Onesimus left you for a while only to be yours again forever, 16 no longer a slave but more than a slave, a dear fellow Christian, especially to me, but how much more to you, as a man and as a Christian.

17 Now if you can think of me as your partner, welcome him as you would welcome me. 18 If he cheated you or owes you anything, charge it to me. 19 I, Paul, am writing this with my own hand—I'll pay it back. I don't want to mention that you owe me more than that—your own self. 20 Yes, my fellow Christian, I want you to be useful to me in the Lord. Refresh my heart in Christ. 21 As I write you, I'm sure you'll do this. I know you'll do even more than I ask.

22 One thing more: Have a guest room ready for me, because I hope by the prayers of all of you to be given back to you.

23 Greetings to you from Epaphras, my fellow prisoner in Christ Jesus, 24 and from my fellow workers: Mark, Aristarchus, Demas, Luke.

25 The love of the Lord Jesus Christ be with your spirits. Amen.

* Onesimus means "useful."

K.J.V.

THE EPISTLE
OF PAUL THE APOSTLE
TO THE
HEBREWS

1 God, who at sundry times and in divers manners spake in time past unto the fathers by the prophets, 2 Hath in these last days spoken unto us by *his* Son, whom he hath appointed heir of all things, by whom also he made the worlds; 3 Who being the brightness of *his* glory, and the express image of his person, and upholding all things by the word of his power, when he had by himself purged our sins, sat down on the right hand of the Majesty on high; 4 Being made so much better than the angels, as he hath by inheritance obtained a more excellent name than they. 5 For unto which of the angels said he at any time, Thou art my Son, this day have I begotten thee? And again, I will be to him a Father, and he shall be to me a Son? 6 And again, when he bringeth in the firstbegotten into the world, he saith, And let all the angels of God worship him. 7 And of the angels he saith, Who maketh his angels spirits, and his ministers a flame of fire. 8 But unto the Son *he saith,* Thy throne, O God, *is* for ever and ever: a sceptre of righteousness *is* the sceptre of thy kingdom. 9 Thou hast loved righteousness, and hated iniquity; therefore God, *even* thy God, hath anointed thee with the oil of gladness above thy fellows. 10 And, Thou, Lord, in the beginning hast laid the foundation of the earth; and the heavens are the works of thine hands. 11 They shall perish, but thou remainest: and they all shall wax old as doth a garment; 12 And as a vesture shalt thou fold them up, and they shall be changed: but thou art the same, and thy years shall not fail. 13 But to which of the angels said he at any time, Sit on my right hand, until I make thine enemies thy footstool? 14 Are they not all ministering spirits, sent forth to minister for them who shall be heirs of salvation?

N.A.S.

THE EPISTLE TO THE
HEBREWS

1 God, after He spoke long ago to the fathers in the prophets in many portions and in many ways, 2 in these last days has spoken to us in *His* Son, whom He appointed heir of all things, through whom also He made the world. 3 And He is the radiance of His glory and the exact representation of His nature, and upholds all things by the word of His power. When He had made purification of sins, He sat down at the right hand of the Majesty on high; 4 having become as much better than the angels, as He has inherited a more excellent name than they. 5 For to which of the angels did He ever say,

"THOU ART MY SON,
TODAY I HAVE BEGOTTEN THEE"?

And again,

"I WILL BE A FATHER TO HIM,
AND HE SHALL BE A SON TO ME"?

6 And when He again brings the firstborn into the world, He says,

"AND LET ALL THE ANGELS OF GOD WORSHIP HIM."

7 And of the angels He says,

"WHO MAKES HIS ANGELS WINDS,
AND HIS MINISTERS A FLAME OF FIRE."

8 But of the Son *He says,*

"THY THRONE, O GOD, IS FOREVER AND EVER,
AND THE RIGHTEOUS SCEPTER IS THE SCEPTER OF [a]HIS KINGDOM.

9 "THOU HAST LOVED RIGHTEOUSNESS AND HATED LAWLESSNESS;
THEREFORE GOD, THY GOD, HATH ANOINTED THEE
WITH THE OIL OF GLADNESS ABOVE THY COMPANIONS."

10 And,

"THOU, LORD, IN THE BEGINNING DIDST LAY THE FOUNDATION OF THE EARTH,
AND THE HEAVENS ARE THE WORKS OF THY HANDS;

11 THEY WILL PERISH, BUT THOU REMAINEST;
AND THEY ALL WILL BECOME OLD AS A GARMENT,

12 AND AS A MANTLE THOU WILT ROLL THEM UP;
AS A GARMENT THEY WILL ALSO BE CHANGED.
BUT THOU ART THE SAME,
AND THY YEARS WILL NOT COME TO AN END."

13 But to which of the angels has He ever said,

"SIT AT MY RIGHT HAND,
UNTIL I MAKE THINE ENEMIES
A FOOTSTOOL FOR THY FEET"?

14 Are they not all ministering spirits, sent out to render service for the sake of those who will inherit salvation?

[a] Some mss. read, *Thy.*

WILLIAMS   BECK

HEBREWS

THE LETTER TO THE

HEBREWS

1 *He shows the Son to be superior to prophets and angels; Christ is the Son, but angels only servants who worship Him*

It was bit by bit and in many different ways that God in olden times spoke to our forefathers through the prophets, 2 but in these latter days He has spoken to us through a Son, whom He had appointed lawful owner of everything, and through whom He had made the worlds. 3 He is the reflection of God's glory and the perfectᵃ representation of His being, and continues to uphold the universe by His mighty word. After He had procured man's purification from sins, He took His seat at the right hand of God's majesty, 4 thus proving Himself to be as much superior to angels as the title He has inherited is superior to theirs. 5 For to what angel did God ever say, "You are my Son, today I have become your Father"?

6 Or again, "I will become His Father, and He shall become my Son"?

But when He brings again His first-born Son into the world, He says, "And let all the angels worship Him."

7 However, regarding the angels He says:
"He turns His angels into winds
And His attendants into flames of fire."
8 But regarding the Son He says:
"Your throne, O God, will stand forever and ever;
A righteous scepter is the scepter of His kingdom.
9 You loved the right and hated wrong;
So God, your God, anointed you
With oil of exultation beyond all your companions."
10 And:
"You, Lord, in the beginning founded the earth,
And the heavens are the works of your hands.
11 They will perish, but you always remain;
They all will grow old like a coat,
12 And you will fold them up just like a robe,
And they will be changed like the changing of one's coat,
But you are the same, and your years will never cease."
13 But to what angel did He ever say:
"Just keep your seat at my right hand,
Until I make your foes a footstool for your feet"?
14 Are not the angels all attending spirits sent forth to serve for the sake of those who are going to be unceasing possessors of salvation?

1 Long ago God spoke to our fathers in many different ways by the prophets, 2 but in these last days He has spoken to us by His Son, whom He made the heir of everything and by whom He made the world. 3 He who shines with God's glory and is the copy of His being carries everything by His mighty Word. He made a cleansing from sins, *sat down at the right*¹ of the Majesty in heaven, 4 and became as much greater than angels as the name He has is better than theirs.
5 To which of the angels did God ever say,

You are My Son,
Today I am Your Father? ²

Or again,

I will be His Father,
And He will be My Son? ³

6And when He again will bring the firstborn Son into the world, He says,

*All of God's angels should worship Him,*⁴

7 He says of the angels,

He makes His angels winds
*And His servants fiery flames.*⁵

8 But to the Son He says,

Your throne, O God, is forever,
And You rule Your kingdom with a scepter of righteousness.
9 *You have loved right and hated wrong.*
*That is why God, Your God, has put You above your companions by anointing You with the oil of joy.*⁶

10And,

Lord, in the beginning You laid the foundation of the earth,
And Your hands made the heavens!
11 *They will perish,*
But You continue.
They will all get old like a garment,
12 *And like a garment they will be changed.*
But You are the same,
*And Your years will never end.*⁷

13 To which of the angels did He ever say, *Sit at My right till I make Your enemies a footstool for Your feet?* ⁸ 14Aren't all angels spirits that serve Him and are sent to help those who are going to be saved?

[1] Ps. 110:1
[2] Ps. 2:7
[3] 2 Sam. 7:14
[4] Deut. 32:43; Ps. 97:7
[5] Ps. 104:4
[6] Ps. 45:6-7
[7] Ps. 102:25-27; Is. 50:9; 51:6
[8] Ps. 110:1

[a] Grk., *exact imprint.*

2 Therefore we ought to give the more earnest heed to the things which we have heard, lest at any time we should let *them* slip. 2 For if the word spoken by angels was steadfast, and every transgression and disobedience received a just recompense of reward; 3 How shall we escape, if we neglect so great salvation; which at the first began to be spoken by the Lord, and was confirmed unto us by them that heard *him;* 4 God also bearing *them* witness, both with signs and wonders, and with divers miracles, and gifts of the Holy Ghost, according to his own will? 5 For unto the angels hath he not put in subjection the world to come, whereof we speak. 6 But one in a certain place testified, saying, What is man, that thou art mindful of him? or the son of man, that thou visitest him? 7 Thou madest him a little lower than the angels; thou crownedst him with glory and honour, and didst set him over the works of thy hands: 8 Thou hast put all things in subjection under his feet. For in that he put all in subjection under him, he left nothing *that is* not put under him. But now we see not yet all things put under him. 9 But we see Jesus, who was made a little lower than the angels for the suffering of death, crowned with glory and honour; that he by the grace of God should taste death for every man. 10 For it became him, for whom *are* all things, and by whom *are* all things, in bringing many sons unto glory, to make the captain of their salvation perfect through sufferings. 11 For both he that sanctifieth and they who are sanctified *are* all of one: for which cause he is not ashamed to call them brethren, 12 Saying, I will declare thy name unto my brethren, in the midst of the church will I sing praise unto thee. 13 And again, I will put my trust in him. And again, Behold I and the children which God hath given me. 14 Forasmuch then as the children are partakers of flesh and blood, he also himself likewise took part of the same; that through death he might destroy him that had the power of death, that is, the devil; 15 And deliver them, who through fear of death were all their lifetime subject to bondage. 16 For verily he took not on *him the nature of* angels; but he took on *him the seed* of Abraham. 17 Wherefore in all things it behooved him to be made like unto *his* brethren, that he might be a merciful and faithful high priest in things *pertaining* to God, to make reconciliation for the sins of the people. 18 For in that he himself hath suffered being tempted, he is able to succour them that are tempted.

2 For this reason we must pay much closer attention to what we have heard, lest we drift away *from it.* 2 For if the word spoken through angels proved unalterable, and every transgression and disobedience received a just recompense, 3 how shall we escape if we neglect so great a salvation? After it was at the first spoken through the Lord, it was confirmed to us by those who heard, 4 God also bearing witness with them, both by signs and wonders and by various miracles and by gifts of the Holy Spirit according to His own will.

5 For He did not subject to angels the world to come, concerning which we are speaking. 6 But one has testified somewhere, saying,

"WHAT IS MAN, THAT THOU REMEMBEREST HIM?

OR THE SON OF MAN, THAT THOU ART CONCERNED ABOUT HIM?

7 "THOU HAST MADE HIM FOR A LITTLE WHILE LOWER THAN THE ANGELS;

THOU HAST CROWNED HIM WITH GLORY AND HONOR,

*a*AND HAST APPOINTED HIM OVER THE WORKS OF THY HANDS;

8 THOU HAST PUT ALL THINGS IN SUBJECTION UNDER HIS FEET."

For in subjecting all things to him, He left nothing that is not subject to him. But now we do not yet see all things subjected to him. 9 But we do see Him who has been made for a little while lower than the angels, *namely,* Jesus, because of the suffering of death crowned with glory and honor, that by the grace of God He might taste death for every one. 10 For it was fitting for Him, for whom are all things, and through whom are all things, in bringing many sons to glory, to perfect the author of their salvation through sufferings. 11 For both He who sanctifies and those who are sanctified are all from one *Father;* for which reason He is not ashamed to call them brethren, 12 saying,

"I WILL PROCLAIM THY NAME TO MY BRETHREN,

IN THE MIDST OF THE CONGREGATION I WILL SING THY PRAISE."

13 And again,

"I WILL PUT MY TRUST IN HIM."

And again,

"BEHOLD, I AND THE CHILDREN WHOM GOD HAS GIVEN ME."

14 Since then the children share in flesh and blood, He Himself likewise also partook of the same, that through death He might render powerless him who had the power of death, that is, the devil; 15 and might deliver those who through fear of death were subject to slavery all their lives. 16 For assuredly He does not give help to angels, but He gives help to the seed of Abraham. 17 Therefore, He had to be made like His brethren in all things, that He might become a merciful and faithful high priest in things pertaining to God, to make propitiation for the sins of the people. 18 For since He Himself was tempted in that which He has suffered, He is able to come to the aid of those who are tempted.

[*a*] Some ancient mss. omit, And . . . hands.

WILLIAMS

2 *Dangerous to disobey the Son; Jesus the Son crowned with glory because He died for all; Jesus made perfect through suffering*

This is why we must pay much closer attention to the message once heard, to keep from drifting to one side. 2 For if the message spoken through angels proved to be valid, and every violation and infraction of it had its adequate penalty, 3 how can we escape, if we pay no attention at all to a salvation that is so great? This is so because it was first proclaimed by the Lord Himself, and then it was proved to us to be valid by the very men who heard Him themselves, 4 while God continued to confirm their testimony with signs, marvels, and various sorts of wonder-works, and with gifts of the Holy Spirit distributed in accordance with His will.

5 For it was not to angels that He gave authority over that world to be, of which we are speaking. 6 For someone somewhere has solemnly said:
"What is man that you should think of him, Or the Son of Man that you should care for Him?
7 You made Him inferior to angels for a little while,
Yet you have crowned Him with glory and honor,
You have set Him over the works of your hands,
8 You have put all things under His feet!"
Now when He gave Him authority over everything, He did not leave a single thing that was not put under His authority. But as yet we do not see everything actually under His authority, 9 but we do see Jesus, who was made inferior to the angels for a little while, crowned with glory and honor because He suffered death, so that by God's favor He might experience death for every human being. 10 For it was appropriate for Him, who is the Final Goal and the First Cause of the universe, in bringing many children to glory, to make the Leader in their salvation perfect through the process of sufferings. 11 For both He who is purifying them and those who are being purified all spring from one Father; so He is not ashamed to call them brothers, 12 when He says:
"I will announce your name to my brothers; In the midst of the congregation I will sing your praise";
13 and again,
"I too will put my trust in God";
and again,
"Here I am and the children God has given me."
14 Since then the children mentioned share our mortal nature, He too took on Himself a full share of the same, in order that He by His death might put a stop to the power of him who has the power of death, that is, the devil, 15 and set at liberty those who all their lifetime had been subject to slavery because of their dread of death. 16 For of course it is not angels but descendants of Abraham that He is to help. 17 Therefore He had to be made like His brothers, so that He could be a sympathetic High Priest, as well as a faithful one, in things relating to God, in order to atone for the people's sins. 18 For inasmuch as He has suffered Himself by being tempted, He is able to give immediate help to any that are tempted.

BECK

Don't Neglect Your Salvation

2 That is why we should listen all the more carefully to what we have been told, or we may drift away. 2 If what God said through angels was valid, and every transgression and disobedience got a just punishment, 3 how can we escape if we neglect a salvation as great as this? First the Lord spoke of it, and then those who heard Him guaranteed its truth to us, 4 while God added His testimony by supernatural proofs, wonders, different kinds of miracles, and by giving the Holy Spirit as He wanted to give Him.

Lord of Everything

5 He didn't put the coming world that we're talking about under the controls of angels. 6 But somewhere someone has declared,

What is man that You should think of him? Or a son of man that You should come to help him?
You make Him lower than the angels for a little while,
7 Then crown Him with glory and honor And make Him Ruler over what Your hands have made
And put everything under His feet.

8 Now when *He put everything under His feet*, He left nothing outside His control.

Jesus Died for Us

9 As it is, we do not yet see *everything put under Him.* But we do see Jesus, who *for a little while was made lower than the angels, now crowned with glory and honor*[9] because He suffered death in order by God's love to taste death for everyone. 10 It fitted Him well for whom and by whom everything exists that in bringing many sons to glory He should make the One who gives them salvation perfect through suffering.

11 He who makes men holy and those who are made holy all have one Father. That is why He is not ashamed to call them *brothers.* 12 He says,

I will tell My brothers Your name, In the congregation I will sing Your praise.[10]

13 And again, *I will trust Him.*[11] And again, *Here am I and the children God has given Me.*[12]

14 Now since all these *children* have flesh and blood, He in the same way took on flesh and blood in order to die and so take away all the powers of him who had the power of death, that is, the devil, 15 and to free those who, terrified by death, had to be slaves all their lives. 16 It is clear He didn't *come to help* angels but *Abraham's descendants.*[13] 17 And so in every way He had to become like His brothers to be merciful and faithful as high priest before God and pay for the sins* of the people. 18 Because He Himself suffered when He was tested, He can help others when they're tested.

---

* He wipes out our sins by His blood and so changes God's anger to love.
[9] Ps. 8:4-6
[10] Ps. 22:22
[11] Ps. 18:2; 2 Sam. 22:3; Is. 8:17
[12] Is. 8:18
[13] Is. 41:8-9

K.J.V.

3 Wherefore, holy brethren, partakers of the heavenly calling, consider the Apostle and High Priest of our profession, Christ Jesus; 2 Who was faithful to him that appointed him, as also Moses *was faithful* in all his house. 3 For this *man* was counted worthy of more glory than Moses, inasmuch as he who hath builded the house hath more honour than the house. 4 For every house is builded by some *man;* but he that built all things *is* God. 5And Moses verily *was* faithful in all his house as a servant, for a testimony of those things which were to be spoken after; 6 But Christ as a son over his own house; whose house are we, if we hold fast the confidence and the rejoicing of the hope firm unto the end. 7 Wherefore as the Holy Ghost saith, To day if ye will hear his voice, 8 Harden not your hearts, as in the provocation, in the day of temptation in the wilderness; 9 When your fathers tempted me, proved me, and saw my works forty years. 10 Wherefore I was grieved with that generation, and said, They do always err in *their* heart; and they have not known my ways. 11 So I sware in my wrath, They shall not enter into my rest. 12 Take heed, brethren, lest there be in any of you an evil heart of unbelief, in departing from the living God. 13 But exhort one another daily, while it is called To day; lest any of you be hardened through the deceitfulness of sin. 14 For we are made partakers of Christ, if we hold the beginning of our confidence steadfast unto the end; 15 While it is said, To day if ye will hear his voice, harden not your hearts, as in the provocation. 16 For some, when they had heard, did provoke: howbeit not all that came out of Egypt by Moses. 17 But with whom was he grieved forty years? *was it* not with them that had sinned, whose carcasses fell in the wilderness? 18And to whom sware he that they should not enter into his rest, but to them that believed not? 19 So we see that they could not enter in because of unbelief.

4 Let us therefore fear, lest, a promise being left *us* of entering into his rest, any of you should seem to come short of it. 2 For unto us was the gospel preached, as well as unto them: but the word preached did not profit them, not being mixed with faith in them that heard *it*. 3 For we which have believed do enter into rest, as he said, As I have sworn in my wrath, if they

N.A.S.

3 Therefore, holy brethren, partakers of a heavenly calling, consider Jesus, the Apostle and High Priest of our confession. 2 He was faithful to Him who appointed Him, as Moses also was in all His house. 3 For He has been counted worthy of more glory than Moses, by just so much as the builder of the house has more honor than the house. 4 For every house is built by someone, but the builder of all things is God. 5 Now Moses was faithful in all His house as a servant, for a testimony of those things which were to be spoken later; 6 but Christ *was faithful* as a Son over His house whose house we are, if we hold fast our confidence and the boast of our hope firm until the end. 7 Therefore, just as the Holy Spirit says,

"TODAY IF YOU HEAR HIS VOICE,
8 DO NOT HARDEN YOUR HEARTS AS WHEN THEY PROVOKED ME,
AS IN THE DAY OF TRIAL IN THE WILDERNESS,
9 WHERE YOUR FATHERS TRIED *Me* BY TESTING *Me*,
AND SAW MY WORKS FOR FORTY YEARS.
10 "THEREFORE I WAS ANGRY WITH THIS GENERATION,
AND SAID, 'THEY ALWAYS GO ASTRAY IN THEIR HEART;
AND THEY DID NOT KNOW MY WAYS';
11 AS I SWORE IN MY WRATH,
'THEY SHALL NOT ENTER MY REST.'"

12 Take care, brethren, lest there should be in any one of you an evil, unbelieving heart, in falling away from the living God. 13 But encourage one another day after day, as long as it is *still* called "Today," lest any one of you be hardened by the deceitfulness of sin. 14 For we have become partakers of Christ, if we hold fast the beginning of our assurance firm until the end; 15 while it is said,

"TODAY IF YOU HEAR HIS VOICE,
DO NOT HARDEN YOUR HEARTS, AS WHEN THEY PROVOKED ME."

16 For who provoked *Him* when they had heard? Indeed, did not all those who came out of Egypt *led* by Moses? 17And with whom was He angry for forty years? Was it not with those who sinned, whose bodies fell in the wilderness? 18And to whom did He swear that they should not enter His rest, but to those who were disobedient? 19And *so* we see that they were not able to enter because of unbelief.

4 Therefore, let us fear lest, while a promise remains of entering His rest, any one of you should seem to have come short of it. 2 For indeed we have had good news preached to us, just as they also; but the word they heard did not profit them, because it was not united by faith in those who heard. 3 [a]For we who have believed enter that rest; just as He has said,

"AS I SWORE IN MY WRATH,

[a] Some ancient mss. read, *Therefore.*

620

3 *Jesus superior to Moses; the writer warns against unbelief and its consequences*

Therefore, my Christian[a] brothers, fix your thoughts on Jesus, the Messenger and High Priest whom we profess to follow, 2 to see how faithful He was to God who appointed Him, just as Moses was in all the house of God. 3 For just as the man who builds a house has greater glory than the house, by just so much is Jesus judged to be worthy of greater glory than Moses. 4 For every house is built by somebody, but the builder and furnisher of the universe is God. 5 Now Moses was faithful in all the house of God, yet only as a servant to bear witness to the message that should be spoken, 6 but Christ as a Son set over the house of God was faithful; and we are that house, if we keep up our courage and the joy that hope inspires to the very end. 7 Therefore, as the Holy Spirit says:

"If you but hear His voice today,
8 You must not harden your hearts as they did in provoking me,
As on the day in the desert they tested me,
9 Where your forefathers found I stood their test,
Because they saw my works for forty years.
10 So I was indignant with that generation,
And I said, 'Their hearts are always going astray,
And they have never come to know my ways.'
11 So in my anger I took oath,
'They shall not be admitted to my rest!' "

12 See to it, my brothers, that no wicked, unbelieving heart is found in any of you, as shown by your turning away from the ever-living God, 13 but day by day, as long as "Today" shall last, continue to encourage one another, so that not one of you may be hardened by sin's deceiving ways. 14 For we have become real sharers in Christ, if we keep firm to the end the faith we had at first, 15 and yet the warning continues to be spoken:

"If you but hear His voice,
You must not harden your hearts as they did in provoking me."

16 For who was it that heard and yet provoked Him? Was it not all who came out of Egypt led by Moses? 17 With whom was He disgusted forty years? Was it not with those who had sinned, whose carcasses fell in the desert? 18 To whom did He take oath that they should not be admitted to His rest, if it was not to those who disobeyed Him? So we see that it was because of their unbelief that they could not be admitted to it.

4 *He continues warning; then makes an earnest appeal; Jesus, the Son, our High Priest, sympathizes with us*

So let us fear that when the promise for us to be admitted to His rest is still remaining valid some one of you may be found to have missed it. 2 For we have had the good news told to us as well as they, but the message heard did them no good, because they were not by faith made one with those who heeded it. 3 For we who have believed are being admitted to that rest, just as He has said:

[a] Grk., *holy brothers; set apart to Christ.*

Greater than Moses

3 And so, fellow Christians—you're holy, and heaven called you as it called us—look at Jesus, the Apostle and High Priest whom we confess, 2 being *faithful* to Him who appointed Him, just as *Moses was faithful in God's whole family.* 3 He deserves greater glory than Moses, as the builder of a house is honored more than the house. 4 Every house is built by someone, but He who built everything is God.

5 Now, *Moses was faithful in God's whole family* as *a servant* who was to testify of what would be said later, 6 but Christ was faithful as the Son in charge of *God's family.*[14] We are His family if to the end we continue unshaken in our courage and in feeling proud of our hope.

Don't Close Your Minds

7 And so, as the Holy Spirit says, *Today, if you hear Him speak,* 8 *don't close your minds as it happened when the people provoked Me at the time they tested Me in the desert,* 9 *where your fathers put Me to a test* 10 *when for forty years they saw what I could do.* That was why *I was angry with those people, and I said,* "In *their hearts they always wander around and never have learned My paths."* 11 *So because I was angry I swore they will never come to My place of rest!*

12 See to it, fellow Christians, that none of you has a wicked, unbelieving heart that turns away from the living God. 13 Yes, encourage one another every day, as long as you can say *today,* to keep sin from deceiving anyone of you with its pleasure and *closing your mind* to the truth. 14 We share in Christ if we only keep our first confidence unshaken to the end.

15 When it says, *Today, if you hear Him speak, don't close your minds as it happened when the people provoked Me—* 16 who were those that heard Him and yet *provoked* Him? Were they not all those Moses led out of Egypt? 17 With whom was He *angry for forty years?*[15] Was it not with those who sinned and whose *bodies dropped dead in the desert?* 18 To whom did He *swear they would not come to His place of rest*[15] if not to those who disobeyed? 19 So we see that they couldn't come there because they didn't believe.

4 We should be fearful then. While we still have the promise of coming to His place of rest, someone of you may be judged to have missed it. 2 The good news came to us as it came to them, but the message they heard didn't help them because those who heard it didn't believe it and let it influence them.

There Is a Rest for Us

3 We who have believed *go to a rest,* since He has said, *So I swore in My anger they will*

[14] Num. 12:7
[15] Num. 14:22; Ps. 95:7-11
[16] Num. 14:29

K.J.V.

shall enter into my rest: although the works were finished from the foundation of the world. 4 For he spake in a certain place of the seventh *day* on this wise, And God did rest the seventh day from all his works. 5And in this *place* again, If they shall enter into my rest. 6 Seeing therefore it remaineth that some must enter therein, and they to whom it was first preached entered not in because of unbelief: 7Again, he limited a certain day, saying in David, To day, after so long a time; as it is said, To day if ye will hear his voice, harden not your hearts. 8 For if Jesus had given them rest, then would he not afterward have spoken of another day. 9 There remaineth therefore a rest to the people of God. 10 For he that is entered into his rest, he also hath ceased from his own works, as God *did* from his. 11 Let us labour therefore to enter into that rest, lest any man fall after the same example of unbelief. 12 For the word of God *is* quick, and powerful, and sharper than any twoedged sword, piercing even to the dividing asunder of soul and spirit, and of the joints and marrow, and *is* a discerner of the thoughts and intents of the heart. 13 Neither is there any creature that is not manifest in his sight: but all things *are* naked and opened unto the eyes of him with whom we have to do. 14 Seeing then that we have a great high priest, that is passed into the heavens, Jesus the Son of God, let us hold fast *our* profession. 15 For we have not a high priest which cannot be touched with the feeling of our infirmities; but was in all points tempted like as *we are, yet* without sin. 16 Let us therefore come boldly unto the throne of grace, that we may obtain mercy, and find grace to help in time of need.

5 For every high priest taken from among men is ordained for men in things *pertaining* to God, that he may offer both gifts and sacrifices for sins: 2 Who can have compassion on the ignorant, and on them that are out of the way; for that he himself also is compassed with infirmity. 3And by reason hereof he ought, as for the people, so also for himself, to offer for sins. 4And no man taketh this honour unto himself, but he that is called of God, as *was* Aaron. 5 So also Christ glorified not himself to be made a high priest; but he that said unto him, Thou art my Son, to day have I begotten thee. 6As he saith also in another *place,* Thou *art* a priest for ever after the order of Melchisedec. 7 Who in the days of his flesh, when he had offered up prayers and supplications with strong crying and tears unto him that was able to save him from death, and was heard in that he feared;

N.A.S.

THEY SHALL NOT ENTER MY REST," although His works were finished from the foundation of the world. 4 For He has thus said somewhere concerning the seventh *day,* "AND GOD RESTED ON THE SEVENTH DAY FROM ALL HIS WORKS"; 5 and again in this *passage,* "THEY SHALL NOT ENTER MY REST." 6 Since therefore it remains for some to enter it, and those who formerly had good news preached to them failed to enter because of disobedience, 7 He again fixes a certain day, "Today," saying through David after so long a time just as has been said before,

"TODAY IF YOU HEAR HIS VOICE,
DO NOT HARDEN YOUR HEARTS."

8 For if Joshua had given them rest, He would not have spoken of another day after that. 9 There remains therefore a Sabbath rest for the people of God. 10 For the one who has entered His rest has himself also rested from his works, as God did from His. 11 Let us therefore be diligent to enter that rest, lest anyone fall through *following* the same example of disobedience. 12 For the word of God is living and active and sharper than any two-edged sword, and piercing as far as the division of soul and spirit, of both joints and marrow, and able to judge the thoughts and intentions of the heart. 13And there is no creature hidden from His sight, but all things are open and laid bare to the eyes of Him with whom we have to do.

14 Since then we have a great high priest who has passed through the heavens, Jesus the Son of God, let us hold fast our confession. 15 For we do not have a high priest who cannot sympathize with our weaknesses, but one who has been tempted in all things as *we are, yet* without sin. 16 Let us therefore draw near with confidence to the throne of grace, that we may receive mercy and may find grace to help in time of need.

5 For every high priest taken from among men is appointed on behalf of men in things pertaining to God in order to offer both gifts and sacrifices for sins; 2 he can deal gently with the ignorant and misguided, since he himself also is beset with weakness; 3 and because of it he is obligated to offer *sacrifices* for sins, as for the people, so also for himself. 4And no one takes the honor to himself, but *receives it* when he is called by God, even as Aaron was. 5 So also Christ did not glorify Himself so as to become a high priest, but He who said to Him,

"THOU ART MY SON,
TODAY I HAVE BEGOTTEN THEE";

6 just as He says also in another *passage,*

"THOU ART A PRIEST FOREVER
ACCORDING TO THE ORDER OF MELCHIZEDEK."

7 In the days of His flesh, when He offered up both prayers and supplications with loud crying and tears to Him who was able to save Him from death, and who was heard because of His

WILLIAMS

"As in my anger I took oath,
They shall not be admitted to my rest,"
although God's works had been completed at
the creation of the world. 4 For somewhere He
speaks of the seventh day:
"On the seventh day God rested from all His
works";
5 while in this passage again He says:
"They shall not be admitted to my rest."
6 Since then it still remains that some are
being admitted to it and that those who first
had the good news told to them were not admitted because of disobedience, 7 He again fixes
a definite day, saying long afterward through
David, as has been quoted:
"If you but hear His voice,
You must not harden your hearts."
8 For if Joshua had really given them rest, He
would not afterward have been speaking of another day. 9 So a sabbath of rest is still awaiting
God's people. 10 For whoever is admitted into
God's rest himself has rested from his works,
just as God did.
11 So let us do our best to be admitted to
that rest, so that not one of us may fail through
the same sort of disobedience. 12 For God's
message is alive and full of power in action,
sharper than any double-edged sword, piercing
even to the depths of soul and spirit, to the
dividing of joints and marrow, and passing
judgment on the thoughts and purposes of the
heart. 13 No creature of His can escape God's
sight, but everything is bare and exposed to the
eyes of Him to whom we have to give account.
14 Since then we have in Jesus, the Son of
God, a great High Priest who has gone right up
to heaven itself, let us continue to keep a firm
hold on our profession of faith in Him. 15 For
we do not have a High Priest who is incapable
of sympathizing with us in our weaknesses, but
we have One who was tempted in every respect as we are, and yet without committing
any sin. 16 So let us continue coming with
courage to the throne of God's unmerited favor
to obtain His mercy and to find His spiritual
strength to help us when we need it.

5 *As High Priest, Jesus, both divine and
human, must have an appointment from
God; once He agonized in prayer in the
garden; the readers so dull in spiritual
things they need to be warned*

For every high priest who is taken from men
is appointed to officiate on behalf of men in
matters relating to God, that is, to offer gifts
and sin-offerings. 2 Such a one is capable of
dealing tenderly with the ignorant and erring
ones, since he himself is subject to weakness,
3 and so is obliged to offer sin-offerings, not
only for the people but for himself as well.
4And no one takes this honor upon himself but
is called to it by God, as Aaron was. 5 So
Christ too did not take upon Himself the glory
of being appointed High Priest, but it was
God who said:
"You are my Son;
I have today become your Father,"
6 as also in another passage He says:
"You are a priest forever,
Belonging to the rank of Melchizedek."
7 For during His human life He offered up
prayers and entreaties, crying aloud with tears
to Him who was always able to save Him out
of death, and because of His beautiful spirit of

BECK

never come to My place of rest.[15] And yet God
finished His work when He made the world,
4 because in one place He said about the seventh
day, *On the seventh day God rested from all
He had done.*[17] 5And here, too, He says, *They
will never come to My place of rest.* 6 Now, it
is still true that some *will go to His rest,* and
those who once heard the good news didn't *go
to it* because they disobeyed; 7 so He sets another day—*today*—when long afterwards He
says in David's words, already quoted, *Today if
you hear Him speak, don't close your minds.*
8 If Joshua had given them rest, God wouldn't
later have spoken of another day. 9 So there is
still a sabbath of rest for God's people, 10 since
anyone who *goes to his rest*[15] *finds rest after his
work* as *God* did *after His.*[17]
11 Let us then do our best to *come to* that
rest[15] so that no one may disobey and fall like
those people.

The Living Word

12 God's Word lives and is active. It cuts
better than any two-edged sword. It pierces till
it divides soul and spirit, joints and marrow.
And it can judge thoughts and purposes of the
heart. 13 No creature can hide from Him. Everything is naked and helpless before the eyes of
Him to whom we must give account.

Our High Priest

14 Now that we have a great High Priest who
has gone through the heavens, Jesus, God's Son,
let us cling to what we confess. 15 We have a
High Priest who can sympathize with our weaknesses. He was tempted in every way just as we
are, only without sin. 16 So let us come boldly
to God's throne of love to get mercy and find
love to help us when we need it.

5 Any high priest selected from men is appointed to represent them before God and
to bring gifts and sacrifices for sins. 2 He can
be gentle with ignorant and erring people because he, too, is troubled with weakness 3 and
for that reason must bring sacrifices for sins for
himself just as he does for the people.
4 No one takes the honor of this office, but
God calls a man as He called Aaron. 5 So Christ
didn't take the glory of being a high priest but
was given it by Him who said to Him,

You are My Son,
Today I am Your Father.[18]

6And so He said in another place, *You are like
Melchizedek a priest forever.*[19]
7 In His humble life on earth Jesus came to
Him who could save Him from death and
prayed and pleaded, crying loud with tears, and

[17] Gen. 2:2
[18] Ps. 2:7
[19] Ps. 110:4

K.J.V.

8 Though he were a Son, yet learned he obedience by the things which he suffered; 9And being made perfect, he became the author of eternal salvation unto all them that obey him; 10 Called of God a high priest after the order of Melchisedec. 11 Of whom we have many things to say, and hard to be uttered, seeing ye are dull of hearing. 12 For when for the time ye ought to be teachers, ye have need that one teach you again which *be* the first principles of the oracles of God; and are become such as have need of milk, and not of strong meat. 13 For every one that useth milk *is* unskilful in the word of righteousness: for he is a babe. 14 But strong meat belongeth to them that are of full age, *even* those who by reason of use have their senses exercised to discern both good and evil.

6 Therefore leaving the principles of the doctrine of Christ, let us go on unto perfection; not laying again the foundation of repentance from dead works, and of faith toward God, 2 Of the doctrine of baptisms, and of laying on of hands, and of resurrection of the dead, and of eternal judgment. 3And this will we do, if God permit. 4 For *it is* impossible for those who were once enlightened, and have tasted of the heavenly gift, and were made partakers of the Holy Ghost, 5And have tasted the good word of God, and the powers of the world to come, 6 If they shall fall away, to renew them again unto repentance; seeing they crucify to themselves the Son of God afresh, and put *him* to an open shame. 7 For the earth which drinketh in the rain that cometh oft upon it, and bringeth forth herbs meet for them by whom it is dressed, receiveth blessing from God: 8 But that which beareth thorns and briers *is* rejected, and *is* nigh unto cursing; whose end *is* to be burned. 9 But, beloved, we are persuaded better things of you, and things that accompany salvation, though we thus speak. 10 For God *is* not unrighteous to forget your work and labour of love, which ye have shewed toward his name, in that ye have ministered to the saints, and do minister. 11And we desire that every one of you do shew the same diligence to the full assurance of hope unto the end: 12 That ye be not slothful, but followers of them who through faith and patience inherit the promises. 13 For when God made promise to Abraham, because he could swear by no greater, he sware by himself, 14 Saying, Surely blessing I will bless thee, and multiplying I will multiply

N.A.S.

piety, 8 although He was a Son, He learned obedience from the things which He suffered; 9 and having been made perfect, He became to all those who obey Him the source of eternal salvation; 10 being designated by God as a high priest according to the order of Melchizedek.

11 Concerning him we have much to say, and *it is* hard to explain, since you have become dull of hearing. 12 For though by this time you ought to be teachers, you have need again for some one to teach you the elementary principles of the oracles of God, and you have come to need milk and not solid food. 13 For every one who partakes *only* of milk is not accustomed to the word of righteousness, for he is a babe. 14 But solid food is for the mature, who because of practice have their senses trained to discern good and evil.

6 Therefore leaving the elementary teaching about the Christ, let us press on to maturity, not laying again a foundation of repentance from dead works and of faith toward God, 2 of instruction about washings, and laying on of hands, and the resurrection of the dead, and eternal judgment. 3And this we shall do, if God permits. 4 For in the case of those who have once been enlightened and have tasted of the heavenly gift and have been made partakers of the Holy Spirit, 5 and have tasted the good word of God and the powers of the age to come, 6 and *then* have fallen away, it is impossible to renew them again to repentance, since they again crucify to themselves the Son of God, and put Him to open shame. 7 For ground that drinks the rain which often falls upon it and brings forth vegetation useful to those for whose sake it is also tilled, receives a blessing from God; 8 but if it yields thorns and thistles, it is worthless and close to being cursed, and it ends up being burned.

9 But, beloved, we are convinced of better things concerning you, and things that accompany salvation, though we are speaking in this way. 10 For God is not unjust so as to forget your work and the love which you have shown toward His name, in having ministered and in still ministering to the saints. 11And we desire that each one of you show the same diligence so as to realize the full assurance of hope until the end, 12 that you may not be sluggish, but imitators of those who through faith and patience inherit the promises. 13 For when God made the promise to Abraham, since He could swear by no one greater, He swore by Himself, 14 saying, "I WILL SURELY

WILLIAMS

worship His prayer was heard. 8Although He was a Son, He learned from what He suffered how to obey, 9 and because He was perfectly qualified for it He became the author of endless salvation for all who obey Him, 10 since He had received from God the title of a High Priest with the rank of Melchizedek.

11 I have much to say to you about Him, but it is difficult to make it clear to you, since you have become so dull in your spiritual senses. 12 For although you ought to be teachers of others because you have been Christians so long, you actually need someone to teach you over and over again the very elements of the truths that God has given us, and you have gotten into such a state that you are in constant need of milk instead of solid food. 13 For everyone who uses milk alone is inexperienced in the message of right-doing; he is only an infant. 14 But solid food belongs to full-grown men who on account of constant use have their faculties trained to distinguish good and evil.

6 *He appeals to them for heroic progress; he hopes for better things for them; such hope, inspired by God's promises, is the anchor to the soul*

So then let us once for all quit the elementary teaching about Christ and continue progressing toward maturity; let us stop relaying a foundation of repentance from works that mean only death,[a] and of faith in God, 2 of teaching about ceremonial washings and the laying on of hands, the resurrection of the dead and final judgment. 3 And we will progress, if God permits. 4 For it is impossible for those who have once for all been enlightened and have experienced the gift from heaven, who have been made sharers of the Holy Spirit 5 and have experienced how good God's message is and the mighty powers of the age to come, 6 and then have fallen by the wayside—it is impossible, I say, to keep on restoring them to their first[b] repentance, since they continue to crucify the Son of God to their detriment and hold Him up to contempt. 7 For a piece of ground that drinks in the rains so frequently falling on it, and continues yielding vegetation useful to those for whose sakes it is cultivated, receives from God His blessings. 8 But if it continues to yield thorns and thistles, it is considered worthless and in danger of being cursed, and its final fate is burning.

9 But in your case, my dearly loved friends, even though we speak in such a tone, we are sure of better things, yea, things that point to salvation. 10 For God is not so unjust as to forget the work you have done and the love you have shown His name in the service you have rendered for your fellow-Christians, and still are doing. 11 And we desire each one of you to continue to show the same earnestness to the very end, that you may enjoy your hope to the fullest, 12 so that you may not grow careless,[c] but may follow the example of those who through their faith and patient endurance are now possessors of the blessings promised. 13 For when God made His promise to Abraham, He took an oath by Himself, since He had no one greater by whom He could take it, 14 saying:

"I will certainly bless you over and over

[a] Lit., *dead works*. [b] Lit., *renew them to repentance* (first step in Chn. life; so EGT). [c] Lit., *dull, sluggish*.

BECK

because He feared God, He was heard. 8 Although Jesus is the Son, He found out from what He suffered what it means to obey. 9 And when He was finished, He became One who gives *everlasting salvation*[20] to all who obey Him, 10 being proclaimed by God a high *priest like Melchizedek.*[19]

More than ABC

11 We have much to say about this, but it's difficult to explain because you have become too dull to understand. 12 At a time when you should be teachers you need someone to teach you the ABC of God's Word again. It has come to this that you need milk again instead of solid food. 13 Anyone who lives on milk, being a baby, doesn't have enough experience to talk of what is right. 14 But solid food is for grown-up people, whose senses are trained by practice to tell good from bad.

6 Let us leave behind the ABC of Christ and not lay again a foundation of repentance from dead works, faith in God, 2 teaching about baptisms, laying on hands, raising the dead, and everlasting judgment. 3 But let us go on to be mature. We will do this if God lets us. 4 When those who once had the light and tasted the gift from heaven, who had the Holy Spirit just as others did 5 and tasted how good God's Word is and the powers of the coming world— 6 when those fall away, it is impossible to bring them back to a new repentance because they to their own undoing again crucify God's Son and hold Him up for mockery. 7 When *ground* drinks the rain that often falls on it and *produces plants*[21] that can be used by those for whom it is worked, it is blessed by God. 8 But if *it produces thorns and thistles,* it is worthless. A *curse*[22] hangs over it, and finally it will be burned.

9 Although we say this, we are convinced that for you, dear friends, there are better things that mean salvation. 10 God is righteous to remember your work and the love you showed for Him as you helped His holy people and still help them. 11 But we want every one of you to show the same zeal to make certain of your hope till the end, 12 and not get lazy but be like those who by believing and being patient are getting what is promised.

13 God promised Abraham, and since He had no one greater to swear by, He *swore by Himself* 14 and said, *I will certainly bless you and*

[20] Is. 45:17
[21] Gen. 1:11-12
[22] Gen. 3:17-18

K.J.V.

thee. 15And so, after he had patiently endured, he obtained the promise. 16 For men verily swear by the greater: and an oath for confirmation *is* to them an end of all strife. 17 Wherein God, willing more abundantly to shew unto the heirs of promise the immutability of his counsel, confirmed *it* by an oath: 18 That by two immutable things, in which *it was* impossible for God to lie, we might have a strong consolation, who have fled for refuge to lay hold upon the hope set before us: 19 Which *hope* we have as an anchor of the soul, both sure and steadfast, and which entereth into that within the vail; 20 Whither the forerunner is for us entered, *even* Jesus, made a high priest for ever after the order of Melchisedec.

7 For this Melchisedec, king of Salem, priest of the most high God, who met Abraham returning from the slaughter of the kings, and blessed him; 2 To whom also Abraham gave a tenth part of all; first being by interpretation King of righteousness, and after that also King of Salem, which is, King of peace; 3 Without father, without mother, without descent, having neither beginning of days, nor end of life; but made like unto the Son of God; abideth a priest continually. 4 Now consider how great this man *was,* unto whom even the patriarch Abraham gave the tenth of the spoils. 5And verily they that are of the sons of Levi, who receive the office of the priesthood, have a commandment to take tithes of the people according to the law, that is, of their brethren, though they come out of the loins of Abraham: 6 But he whose descent is not counted from them received tithes of Abraham, and blessed him that had the promises. 7And without all contradiction the less is blessed of the better. 8And here men that die receive tithes; but there he *receiveth them,* of whom it is witnessed that he liveth. 9And as I may so say, Levi also, who receiveth tithes, paid tithes in Abraham. 10 For he was yet in the loins of his father, when Melchisedec met him. 11 If therefore perfection were by the Levitical priesthood, (for under it the people received the law,) what further need *was there* that another priest should rise after the order of Melchisedec, and not be called after the order of Aaron? 12 For the priesthood being changed, there is made of necessity a change also of the law. 13 For he of whom these things are spoken pertaineth to another tribe, of which no man gave attendance at the altar. 14 For *it is* evident that our Lord sprang out of Juda; of which tribe Moses spake nothing concerning priesthood. 15And it is yet far more evident: for that after the similitude of Melchisedec there ariseth another priest, 16 Who is made, not after the law

N.A.S.

BLESS YOU, AND I WILL SURELY MULTIPLY YOU." 15And thus, having patiently waited, he obtained the promise. 16 For men swear by one greater *than themselves,* and with them an oath *given* as confirmation is an end of every dispute. 17 In the same way God, desiring even more to show to the heirs of the promise the unchangeableness of His purpose, interposed with an oath, 18 in order that by two unchangeable things, in which it is impossible for God to lie, we may have strong encouragement, we who have fled for refuge in laying hold of the hope set before us. 19 This hope we have as an anchor of the soul, a *hope* both sure and steadfast and one which enters within the veil, 20 where Jesus has entered as a forerunner for us, having become a high priest forever according to the order of Melchizedek.

7 For this Melchizedek, king of Salem, priest of the Most High God, who met Abraham as he was returning from the slaughter of the kings and blessed him, 2 to whom also Abraham apportioned a tenth part of all *the spoils,* was first of all, by the translation *of his name,* king of righteousness, and then also king of Salem, which is king of peace. 3 Without father, without mother, without genealogy, having neither beginning of days nor end of life, but made like the Son of God, he abides a priest perpetually.

4 Now observe how great this man was to whom Abraham, the patriarch, gave a tenth of the choicest spoils. 5And those indeed of the sons of Levi who receive the priest's office have commandment in the Law to collect a tenth from the people, that is, from their brethren, although these are descended from Abraham. 6 But the one whose genealogy is not traced from them collected a tenth from Abraham, and blessed the one who had the promise. 7 But without any dispute the lesser is blessed by the greater. 8And in this case mortal men receive tithes, but in that case one *receives them,* of whom it is witnessed that he lives on. 9And, so to speak, through Abraham even Levi, who received tithes, paid tithes, 10 for he was still in the loins of his father when Melchizedek met him.

11 Now if perfection was through the Levitical priesthood (for on the basis of it the people received the Law), what further need *was there* for another priest to arise according to the order of Melchizedek, and not be designated according to the order of Aaron? 12 For when the priesthood is changed, of necessity there takes place a change of law also. 13 For the one concerning whom these things are spoken belongs to another tribe, from which no one has officiated at the altar. 14 For it is evident that our Lord was descended from Judah, a tribe with reference to which Moses spoke nothing concerning priests. 15And this is clearer still, if another priest arises according to the likeness of Melchizedek, 16 who has become *such* not on the basis of a law of physical requirement, but

WILLIAMS

again, I will extensively increase your numbers."
15 And so by patiently waiting he obtained what
God had promised him. 16 For it is a custom
among men to take oath by something greater
than themselves, and an oath taken for confirmation settles any dispute among them. 17 Therefore, because God wanted to make the strongest
demonstration of the unchangeable character of
His purpose, He interposed with an oath, 18 so
that by these two unchangeable things in which
it is impossible for God to prove false, we who
have taken refuge with Him may have encouragement strong enough to make us seize upon
the hope that lies ahead of us. 19 This hope we
have as an anchor for our souls, secure and safe,
which reaches up behind the heavenly veil, where
Jesus has blazed the way for us and became a
High Priest with the rank of Melchizedek.

7 *Melchizedek's high priesthood suggests
Christ's perpetual high priesthood; his
superiority to Abraham, so to Levi, and
so to Levitical high priests; their priesthood imperfect, so superseded by
Christ's*

For this man Melchizedek, king of Salem
and priest of the Most High God, who met
Abraham as he was coming back from the
defeat of the kings, and put his blessing on
him, 2 to whom Abraham contributed a tenth
of all his spoils, who first of all, in accordance
with the meaning of his name, is king of
righteousness, and then king of Salem, which
means king of peace; 3 with no father, no
mother, no ancestry; no beginning to his days,
no end to his life, but, like the Son of God,
as priest continues on and on with no successor.
4 Now see how great this man must have
been that even the patriarch Abraham gave
him a tenth of his spoils. 5 And those of the
descendants of Levi who accept the priesthood
are authorized by the law to collect a tenth
from the people; that is, from their own
brothers, though they have sprung from Abraham. 6 But in this case, the man whose ancestry
is not traced from them collected a tenth from
Abraham, and put his blessing on the man who
had the promises from God. 7 Now beyond any
contradiction, it is always the inferior that is
blessed by the superior. 8 In the one case, mortal
men collect the tenth, in the other, one who, as
the witness states, lives on. 9 And I might almost
say, Levi too, who now collects the tenth,
through Abraham paid the tenth, 10 for he
was a vital part of his forefather though yet
unborn, when Melchizedek met him.
11 Now if perfection had been reached
through the Levitical priesthood—for on it as a
basis even the law was enacted for the people—
what further need would there have been of
appointing a different priest, with the rank of
Melchizedek, instead of designating one with
the rank of Aaron? 12 For when a change in
the priesthood takes place, a change in its law
necessarily takes place. 13 For He of whom this
is said became a member of a different tribe
no member of which ever officiated at the altar.
14 For it is very clear that our Lord sprang from
Judah, a tribe about which Moses said nothing
as to priests. 15 And it is still more overwhelmingly clear, since a different priest in the likeness
of Melchizedek is appointed, 16 who is appointed
not on the basis of a physical qualification but

BECK

make you many people.[23] 15 And so, after waiting patiently, Abraham got what God promised.
16 People swear by Someone greater to guarantee what they say and to silence anyone who
opposes them. 17 So God, wanting to make it perfectly clear, to those who would get His promise,
that He can't change His plan, bound Himself
with an oath 18 so that we who have fled to
Him would have two unchangeable things, in
which God cannot lie, to give us a strong encouragement to take hold of the hope set before
us. 19 We have this hope like an anchor for our
lives, sure and strong and *reaching behind the
curtain,*[24] 20 where Jesus has gone for us, ahead
of us, having become *like Melchizedek a high
priest forever.*[19]

A Priest Forever

7 This *Melchizedek, king of Salem* and *priest
of the most high God met Abraham coming
back from defeating the kings, and he blessed
Abraham.* 2 *And Abraham gave him a tenth of
everything.* His name, in the first place, means
king of righteousness, but then he is also *king
of Salem,* that is, *king of peace.*[25] 3 He is without father, mother, or line of ancestors. His life
has no beginning or end. Like God's Son he
continues *a priest forever.*[19]
4 See how great he was! *Abraham,* the father
of the people, *gave him a tenth* from the best of
the spoils. 5 And the Law orders those descendants of Levi who become priests to take a tenth
from the people, that is, from other Israelites,
although they, too, have descended from Abraham. 6 But this man, who was outside their line
of descent, took *a tenth* from *Abraham* and
blessed him who had the promises. 7 Nobody
can deny the higher one blesses the lower.
8 And here those who take a tenth are people
who die, but there we are assured it is one who
lives. 9 And we may say that Levi, who takes a
tenth, in *Abraham gave a tenth,* 10 since he was
in the body of his ancestor when *Melchizedek*[25]
met him.
11 Levi's descendants were the priests; on this
basis the people got the Law. Now, if the priests
who descended from Levi could have given us
something perfect, why did another *priest* still
need to come who is *like Melchizedek* and said
to be different from Aaron? 12 When a different
person is made priest, the Law also has to be
changed. 13 The One here spoken of belongs to
a different tribe, which never had a priest serving at the altar. 14 Everybody knows our Lord
came from Judah, but Moses said nothing about
priests in this tribe. 15 That point is much clearer
still when we see a different *Priest* coming *like
Melchizedek,* 16 not appointed according to a
Law that says he must be someone's descendant

[23] Gen. 22:16-17
[24] Lev. 16:2, 12
[25] Gen. 14:17-20

K.J.V.

of a carnal commandment, but after the power of an endless life. 17 For he testifieth, Thou *art* a priest for ever after the order of Melchisedec. 18 For there is verily a disannulling of the commandment going before for the weakness and unprofitableness thereof. 19 For the law made nothing perfect, but the bringing in of a better hope *did;* by the which we draw nigh unto God. 20And inasmuch as not without an oath *he was made priest:* 21 (For those priests were made without an oath; but this with an oath by him that said unto him, The Lord sware and will not repent, Thou *art* a priest for ever after the order of Melchisedec:) 22 By so much was Jesus made a surety of a better testament. 23And they truly were many priests, because they were not suffered to continue by reason of death: 24 But this *man,* because he continueth ever, hath an unchangeable priesthood. 25 Wherefore he is able also to save them to the uttermost that come unto God by him, seeing he ever liveth to make intercession for them. 26 For such a high priest became us, *who is* holy, harmless, undefiled, separate from sinners, and made higher than the heavens; 27 Who needeth not daily, as those high priests, to offer up sacrifice, first for his own sins, and then for the people's: for this he did once, when he offered up himself. 28 For the law maketh men high priests which have infirmity; but the word of the oath, which was since the law, *maketh* the Son, who is consecrated for evermore.

8 Now of the things which we have spoken *this is* the sum: We have such a high priest, who is set on the right hand of the throne of the Majesty in the heavens; 2A minister of the sanctuary, and of the true tabernacle, which the Lord pitched, and not man. 3 For every high priest is ordained to offer gifts and sacrifices: wherefore *it is* of necessity that this man have somewhat also to offer. 4 For if he were on earth, he should not be a priest, seeing that there are priests that offer gifts according to the law: 5 Who serve unto the example and shadow of heavenly things, as Moses was admonished of God when he was about to make the tabernacle: for, See, saith he, *that* thou make all things according to the pattern shewed to thee in the mount. 6 But now hath he obtained a more excellent ministry, by how much also he is the mediator of a better covenant, which was established upon better promises. 7 For if that first *covenant* had been faultless, then should no place have been sought for the second. 8 For finding fault with them, he saith, Behold, the days come, saith the Lord, when I will make a new covenant with the house of Israel and with

N.A.S.

according to the power of an indestructible life. 17 For it is witnessed *of Him,*

"THOU ART A PRIEST FOREVER ACCORDING TO THE ORDER OF MELCHIZEDEK." 18 For, on the one hand, there is a setting aside of a former commandment because of its weakness and uselessness 19 (for the Law made nothing perfect), and on the other hand there is a bringing in of a better hope, through which we draw near to God. 20And inasmuch as *it was* not without an oath 21 (for they indeed became priests without an oath, but he with an oath through the one who said to Him,

"THE LORD HAS SWORN AND WILL NOT CHANGE HIS MIND, 'THOU ART A PRIEST FOREVER' ");

22 so much the more also Jesus has become the guarantee of a better covenant. 23And the *former* priests, on the one hand, existed in greater numbers, because they were prevented by death from continuing, 24 but He, on the other hand, because He abides forever, holds His priesthood permanently. 25 Hence also He is able to save forever those who draw near to God through Him, since He always lives to make intercession for them.

26 For it was fitting that we should have such a high priest, holy, innocent, undefiled, separated from sinners and exalted above the heavens; 27 who does not need daily, like those high priests, to offer up sacrifices, first for His own sins, and then for the *sins* of the people, because this He did once for all when He offered up Himself. 28 For the Law appoints men as high priests who are weak, but the word of the oath, which came after the Law, *appoints* a Son, made perfect forever.

8 Now the main point in what has been said is this: we have such a high priest, who sat down at the right hand of the throne of the Majesty in the heavens, 2 a minister in the sanctuary, and in the true tabernacle, which the Lord pitched, not man. 3 For every high priest is appointed to offer both gifts and sacrifices; hence it is necessary that this *high priest* also have something to offer. 4 Now if He were on earth, He would not be a priest at all, since there are those who offer the gifts according to the Law; 5 who serve a copy and shadow of the heavenly things, just as Moses is warned *by God* when he was about to erect the tabernacle; for, "SEE," He says, "THAT YOU MAKE ALL THINGS ACCORDING TO THE PATTERN WHICH WAS SHOWN YOU ON THE MOUNTAIN." 6 But now He has obtained a more excellent ministry, by as much as He is also the mediator of a better covenant, which has been enacted on better promises. 7 For if that first *covenant* had been faultless, there would have been no occasion sought for a second. 8 For finding fault with them, He says,

"BEHOLD, DAYS ARE COMING, SAYS THE LORD, WHEN I WILL EFFECT A NEW COVENANT WITH THE HOUSE OF ISRAEL AND WITH THE HOUSE OF JUDAH;

WILLIAMS

on the basis of a power flowing from a life that cannot end. 17 For the Scripture bears witness: "You are a priest forever, with the rank of Melchizedek."

18 Indeed, the rescinding of a previous regulation takes place, because it was weak and ineffective—19 for the law had never made anything perfect—and so a better hope is brought to us, through which we have approach to God.

20 And by so much as He was not appointed without God's taking an oath—21 for the Levitical priests were appointed without His taking an oath, but He with His oath, when He said to Him:

"The Lord took oath and will not change, You are a priest forever"—

22 so much the more Jesus has become the guarantee of a better covenant. 23 And the Levitical priests, on the one hand, have become numerous, because they have been prevented by death from continuing in office, 24 but He, on the other hand, because He Himself lives on forever, enjoys the only priesthood that has no successors in office. 25 Therefore, because He Himself lives always to intercede for them always, He is able to save completely any and all who come to God through Him.

26 For we needed such a High Priest, holy, innocent, unstained, far removed from sinful men, and elevated far above the very heavens, 27 who does not need, as did the Levitical priests, to offer sacrifices, first for his own sins and then for those of the people; this latter is just what He did once for all when He offered up Himself. 28 For the law appoints imperfect men as high priests, but the assertion about the taking of an oath, which was spoken after the time of the law, appoints a Son who is perfectly qualified to be High Priest forever.

8 *Christ officiates in heaven itself; the earthly sanctuary, the mere shadow of the heavenly; the new and better covenant*

Now the main point in what I am saying is this: We have such a High Priest as this, one who has taken His seat at the right hand of God's majestic throne in heaven 2 as officiating Priest in that sanctuary, which is also the true tent of worship, which the Lord and not man set up.

3 For every high priest is appointed to offer gifts and sacrifices; so this High Priest too must have some sacrifice to offer. 4 However, if He were still on earth, He would not be a priest at all, because there are those who officiate in accordance with the law in offering the gifts; 5 and yet they officiate in a sanctuary that is a mere copy and shadow of the heavenly one, as Moses, when he was about to make the tent of worship, was warned, for, said He, "See to it that you make it all just like the pattern shown you on the mountain." 6 But, as the case with Him now stands, He has entered upon a priestly service as much superior to theirs as the covenant of which He is the Mediator is superior to theirs, superior because it has been enacted upon superior promises.

7 For if the first covenant had been faultless, there could have been no room for a second one. 8 For, because He was dissatisfied with His people, He said:

" 'See; the time is coming,' says the Lord, 'When I will make a new covenant With the house of Israel and the house of Judah,

BECK

but by the power of a life that can't be destroyed. We are assured, 17 *You are like Melchizedek a Priest forever.* 18 The earlier rule is canceled because it is weak and can't help us. 19 The Law made nothing perfect, but the coming of a better hope did—it brings us close to God.

20 When those men were made priests, there was no oath. 21 But when Jesus was appointed, God swore as He said to Him (*The Lord has sworn and will not change His mind*): *You are a Priest forever.* Swearing to it 22 made the agreement Jesus guarantees so much the better.

23 Once many were made priests because death didn't let them continue as priests. 24 But because Jesus lives forever, He will *always* be the *Priest.* 25 And so He can forever save those who come to God by Him, because He always lives to pray for them.

26 Here is the High Priest we needed—holy, innocent, spotless, separated from sinners, and risen higher than the heavens, 27 who doesn't need to bring sacrifices every day like those high priests, first for His own sins, then for the sins of the people. He did this only once when He sacrificed Himself. 28 The Law appointed weak men to be high priests, but when God speaks with *an oath* later than the Law, He appoints the *Son,*[26] who was made perfect *forever.*[19]

A Better Covenant

8 Now, this is my main point. We have such a High Priest, and He *sat down at the right*[27] of the throne of the Majesty in heaven 2 to serve as priest in the holy place and in the real *tabernacle set up by the Lord*[28] and not by men. 3 As every high priest is appointed to offer gifts and sacrifices, this One, too, had to bring some sacrifice.

4 If he were on earth, He wouldn't even be a priest, because there are priests who offer the gifts demanded by the Law. 5 They serve a copy and a shadow of what is in heaven, as God told Moses when he was going to make the tabernacle: *"Be careful to make all of it like the pattern you were shown on the mountain."*[29]

6 Now, the priestly work that Jesus was given to do is as much better as the covenant of which He is the Mediator is a better one because God has based it on better promises. 7 If that first covenant had been without a fault, nobody would have wanted a second one. 8 But God is finding fault with them when He says, *"See! The time is coming,"* says the Lord, *"when I will set up a new covenant with the people of*

[26] Ps. 2:7
[27] Ps. 110:1
[28] Num. 24:6
[29] Ex. 25:40; 25:9, 40; 26:30; 27:8

K.J.V.

the house of Judah; 9 Not according to the covenant that I made with their fathers, in the day when I took them by the hand to lead them out of the land of Egypt; because they continued not in my covenant, and I regarded them not, saith the Lord. 10 For this *is* the covenant that I will make with the house of Israel after those days, saith the Lord; I will put my laws into their mind, and write them in their hearts: and I will be to them a God, and they shall be to me a people: 11And they shall not teach every man his neighbour, and every man his brother, saying, Know the Lord: for all shall know me, from the least to the greatest. 12 For I will be merciful to their unrighteousness, and their sins and their iniquities will I remember no more. 13 In that he saith, A new *covenant*, he hath made the first old. Now that which decayeth and waxeth old *is* ready to vanish away.

9 Then verily the first *covenant* had also ordinances of divine service, and a worldly sanctuary. 2 For there was a tabernacle made; the first, wherein *was* the candlestick, and the table, and the shewbread; which is called the sanctuary. 3And after the second vail, the tabernacle which is called the holiest of all; 4 Which had the golden censer, and the ark of the covenant overlaid round about with gold, wherein *was* the golden pot that had manna, and Aaron's rod that budded, and the tables of the covenant; 5And over it the cherubim of glory shadowing the mercy seat; of which we cannot now speak particularly. 6 Now when these things were thus ordained, the priests went always into the first tabernacle, accomplishing the service *of God.* 7 But into the second *went* the high priest alone once every year, not without blood, which he offered for himself, and *for* the errors of the people: 8 The Holy Ghost this signifying, that the way into the holiest of all was not yet made manifest, while as the first tabernacle was yet standing: 9 Which *was* a figure for the time then present, in which were offered both gifts and sacrifices, that could not make him that did the service perfect, as pertaining to the conscience; 10 *Which stood* only in meats and drinks, and divers washings, and carnal ordinances, imposed *on them* until the time of reformation. 11 But Christ being come a high priest of good things

N.A.S.

9 NOT LIKE THE COVENANT WHICH I MADE WITH THEIR FATHERS
ON THE DAY WHEN I TOOK THEM BY THE HAND
TO LEAD THEM OUT OF THE LAND OF EGYPT;
FOR THEY DID NOT CONTINUE IN MY COVENANT,
AND I DID NOT CARE FOR THEM, SAYS THE LORD.
10 "FOR THIS IS THE COVENANT THAT I WILL MAKE WITH THE HOUSE OF ISRAEL
AFTER THOSE DAYS, SAYS THE LORD:
I WILL PUT MY LAWS INTO THEIR MINDS,
AND I WILL WRITE THEM UPON THEIR HEARTS.
AND I WILL BE THEIR GOD,
AND THEY SHALL BE MY PEOPLE.
11 "AND THEY SHALL NOT TEACH EVERY ONE HIS FELLOW-CITIZEN,
AND EVERY ONE HIS BROTHER, SAYING, 'KNOW THE LORD.'
FOR ALL SHALL KNOW ME,
FROM THE LEAST TO THE GREATEST OF THEM.
12 "FOR I WILL BE MERCIFUL TO THEIR INIQUITIES,
AND I WILL REMEMBER THEIR SINS NO MORE."
13 When He said, "A new *covenant,*" He has made the first obsolete. But whatever is becoming obsolete and growing old is ready to disappear.

9 Now even the first *covenant* had regulations of divine worship and the earthly sanctuary. 2 For there was a tabernacle prepared, the outer one, in which *were* the lampstand and the table and the sacred bread; this is called the holy place. 3And behind the second veil, there was a tabernacle which is called the Holy of Holies, 4 having a golden altar of incense and the ark of the covenant covered on all sides with gold, in which *was* a golden jar holding the manna, and Aaron's rod which budded, and the tables of the covenant. 5And above it *were* the cherubim of glory overshadowing the mercyseat; but of these things we cannot now speak in detail. 6 Now when these things have been thus prepared, the priests are continually entering the outer tabernacle, performing the divine worship, 7 but into the second only the high priest *enters,* once a year, not without *taking* blood, which he offers for himself and for the sins of the people committed in ignorance. 8 The Holy Spirit *is* signifying this, that the way into the holy place has not yet been disclosed, while the outer tabernacle is still standing; 9 which *is* a symbol for the time *then* present, according to which both gifts and sacrifices are offered which cannot make the worshiper perfect in conscience, 10 since they *relate* only to food and drink and various washings, regulations for the body imposed until a time of reformation.
11 But when Christ appeared *as* a high priest of the good things [a]to come, *He entered* through

[a] Some ancient mss. read, *that have come.*

WILLIAMS	BECK

WILLIAMS

9 Unlike the one that I made with their
   forefathers
The day I took them by the hand
To lead them out from the land of Egypt,
For they did not abide by their covenant with
   me,
So I did not care for them,' says the Lord.
10 'For this is the covenant that I will make
   with the house of Israel
In those days,' says the Lord;
'I will put my laws into their minds,
And write them on their hearts,
And I will be their God,
And they will be my people.
And nevermore will each one need to teach
   his fellow-citizen,
11 And each one teach his brother, saying,
   "Know the Lord,"
For all will know me,
From the lowest to the highest.
12 For I will be merciful to their deeds of
   wrong,
And never, never any more will I recall their
   sins.' "
13 In speaking of a new covenant He makes
the first one obsolete; and whatever is obsolete
and antiquated is on the verge of vanishing.

BECK

Israel and the people of Judah, 9 *not like the
covenant I made with their fathers when I took
them by the hand to lead them out of Egypt,
because they have not been loyal to My covenant. And so I turned away from them," says
the Lord.* 10 *"The covenant I will make with the
people of Israel after those days," says the Lord,
"is this: I will put My laws into their minds and
write them on their hearts, and I will be their
God, and they will be My people.* 11 *No more
will anyone teach his* fellow citizen *or his brother
and say, 'Know the Lord!' They will all know
Me from the least to the greatest of them,* 12 *because I will forgive their wrongs and not remember their sins any more."* [30] 13 *By saying a
new covenant He made the first one old. When
He treats it as old and it is getting old, it is
ready to vanish.*

9 *He describes the earthly sanctuary; its
equipment; the real sanctuary of God's
presence not opened till Christ opened
it by offering His own blood; the new
covenant validated by sacrificing Himself, so taking away sin*

So indeed the first covenant had its regulations for worship and its earthly sanctuary.
2 For the first or outer part of the tent, which is
called the holy place, was equipped with the
lamp and table and the presentation bread.
3 But behind the second curtain is the tent that
is called the holy of holies, 4 with its golden
incense-altar and the chest for the covenant,
completely covered with gold, and in it a
golden jar which held the manna, Aaron's staff
that budded, and the tablets on which the
covenant was written; 5 and above the chest
were the winged creatures,[a] the symbols of
God's glorious presence, overshadowing the
mercy seat, of which I cannot now speak in
detail.
6 With these arrangements completed in this
way, the priests in conducting their official
services regularly go into the outer part of the
tent of worship; 7 but into the second or inner
part nobody but the high priest may go, and
he only once a year, and never without blood
which he offers for himself and for the sins
committed in ignorance by the people. 8 By this
the Holy Spirit was showing that there was as
yet no access to the real sanctuary while the
outer tent was still in existence, 9 for it is
merely a symbol of the present time in connection with which gifts and sacrifices are repeatedly
offered though they cannot make the conscience
of the worshiper perfect, 10 since they deal only
with food and drink and various washings, that
is, with mere material regulations which are in
force only until the time of setting things
straight.
11 But when Christ came as the High Priest
of good things that have already taken place,

The Tabernacle

9 The first covenant had its regulations for
   worship and the earthly holy place. 2 A
tabernacle was set up. In the first part were the
lampstand, the table, and the bread laid before
God; this is called the holy place. 3 Behind the
second curtain was the part of the tabernacle
called the most holy place 4 with the golden
altar of incense and the ark of the covenant,
completely covered with gold. In the ark were
the golden jar containing the manna, Aaron's
rod that had budded, and the tablets on which
the covenant was written. 5 Above it were the
angels of glory overshadowing the cover on
which the blood was sprinkled.—I can't tell
about these in detail now.
6 But that is how it was arranged. The priests
are always going into the first part of the tabernacle to serve God, 7 but only the high priest
goes into the second part once a year with blood
he offers for himself and for the sins the people
have done in ignorance. 8 And so the Holy Spirit
clearly tells us that the way into the real holy
place had not yet been shown as long as the
outer part of the tabernacle was still standing.
9 This is a picture of our time: Gifts and
sacrifices are brought which can't make the
worshiper feel perfect in his conscience 10 but
deal only with gifts of food and drink and various baptisms, which are regulations for the body
imposed till the time when things would be set
right.

Jesus' Blood

11 But Christ came as a High Priest of the
good things that have come and went through

[a] *Cherubim,* the symbol of glory.

[30] Jer. 31:31-34

K.J.V.

to come, by a greater and more perfect tabernacle, not made with hands, that is to say, not of this building; 12 Neither by the blood of goats and calves, but by his own blood he entered in once into the holy place, having obtained eternal redemption *for us.* 13 For if the blood of bulls and of goats, and the ashes of a heifer sprinkling the unclean, sanctifieth to the purifying of the flesh; 14 How much more shall the blood of Christ, who through the eternal Spirit offered himself without spot to God, purge your conscience from dead works to serve the living God? 15And for this cause he is the mediator of the new testament, that by means of death, for the redemption of the transgressions *that were* under the first testament, they which are called might receive the promise of eternal inheritance. 16 For where a testament *is,* there must also of necessity be the death of the testator. 17 For a testament *is* of force after men are dead: otherwise it is of no strength at all while the testator liveth. 18 Whereupon neither the first *testament* was dedicated without blood. 19 For when Moses had spoken every precept to all the people according to the law, he took the blood of calves and of goats, with water, and scarlet wool, and hyssop, and sprinkled both the book and all the people, 20 Saying, This *is* the blood of the testament which God hath enjoined unto you. 21 Moreover he sprinkled likewise with blood both the tabernacle, and all the vessels of the ministry. 22And almost all things are by the law purged with blood; and without shedding of blood is no remission. 23 *It was* therefore necessary that the patterns of things in the heavens should be purified with these; but the heavenly things themselves with better sacrifices than these. 24 For Christ is not entered into the holy places made with hands, *which are* the figures of the true; but into heaven itself, now to appear in the presence of God for us: 25 Nor yet that he should offer himself often, as the high priest entereth into the holy place every year with blood of others; 26 For then must he often have suffered since the foundation of the world: but now once in the end of the world hath he appeared to put away sin by the sacrifice of himself. 27And as it is appointed unto men once to die, but after this the judgment: 28 So Christ was once offered to bear the sins of many; and unto them that look for him shall he appear the second time without sin unto salvation.

10 For the law having a shadow of good things to come, *and* not the very image of the things, can never with those sacrifices, which

N.A.S.

the greater and more perfect tabernacle, not made with hands, that is to say, not of this creation; 12 and not through the blood of goats and calves, but through His own blood, He entered the holy place once for all, having obtained eternal redemption. 13 For if the blood of goats and bulls and the ashes of a heifer sprinkling those who have been defiled, sanctify for the cleansing of the flesh, 14 how much more will the blood of Christ, who through the eternal Spirit offered Himself without blemish to God, cleanse your conscience from dead works to serve the living God? 15And for this reason He is the mediator of a new covenant, in order that since a death has taken place for the redemption of the transgressions that were *committed* under the first covenant, those who have been called may receive the promise of the eternal inheritance. 16 For where a covenant is, there must of necessity be the death of the one who made it. 17 For a covenant is valid *only* when men are dead, *a*for it is never in force while the one who made it lives. 18 Therefore even the first *covenant* was not inaugurated without blood. 19 For when every commandment had been spoken by Moses to all the people according to the Law, he took the blood of the calves and the goats, with water and scarlet wool and hyssop, and sprinkled both the book itself and all the people, 20 saying, "THIS IS THE BLOOD OF THE COVENANT WHICH GOD COMMANDED YOU." 21And in the same way he sprinkled both the tabernacle and all the vessels of the ministry with the blood. 22And according to the Law, *one may* almost *say,* all things are cleansed with blood, and without shedding of blood there is no forgiveness. 23 Therefore it was necessary for the copies of the things in the heavens to be cleansed with these, but the heavenly things themselves with better sacrifices than these. 24 For Christ did not enter a holy place made with hands, a *mere* copy of the true one, but into heaven itself, now to appear in the presence of God for us; 25 nor was it that He should offer Himself often, as the high priest enters the holy place year by year with blood not his own. 26 Otherwise, He would have needed to suffer often since the foundation of the world; but now once at the consummation He has been manifested to put away sin by the sacrifice of Himself. 27And inasmuch as it is appointed for men to die once, and after this *comes* judgment; 28 so Christ also, having been offered once to bear the sins of many, shall appear a second time, not to bear sin, to those who eagerly await Him, for salvation.

10 For the Law, since it has *only* a shadow of the good things to come *and* not the very form of things, *b*can never by the same sacrifices year by year, which they offer con-

[a] Some ancient mss. read, *for is it then . . . lives?* [b] Some ancient mss. read, *they can.*

WILLIAMS

He went by way of that greater and more perfect tent of worship, not made by human hands, that is, not belonging to this material creation, 12 and not with blood of goats and calves, but with His own blood He once for all went into the real sanctuary and secured our eternal redemption. 13 For if the blood of bulls and goats and a heifer's ashes sprinkling those who are ceremonially unclean purifies them with physical cleansing, 14 how much more surely will the blood of Christ, who with an eternal Spirit[b] gave Himself a spotless offering to God, purify your consciences from works that mean mere death, to serve the ever living God?

15 And this is why He is the Mediator of a new covenant, in order that, after He had suffered death for securing redemption from the offenses committed under the first covenant, those who had been invited to share it might obtain the eternal inheritance promised them. 16 For when a will is made, it is necessary that the death of him who makes it be proved. 17 For a will is valid only after a man is dead, since it has no force whatever while the one who made it is alive. 18 So not even the first covenant was ratified without the use of blood. 19 For after every regulation in the law had been spoken by Moses to all the people, he took the blood of calves and goats, with water, crimson wool, and a bunch of hyssop, and sprinkled the book containing the law and all the people, 20 saying, "This is the blood that ratifies the covenant which God commanded me to make with you." 21 In the same way he sprinkled with blood the tent and all the utensils of the priestly service. 22 In fact, under the law, almost everything is purified with blood, and without the shedding of blood no forgiveness is granted.

23 So, on the one hand, the copies of the original things in heaven had to be purified with such sacrifices; but on the other hand, the original things themselves in heaven with better sacrifices than these. 24 For it was not a sanctuary made by human hands, a mere copy of the true one, that Christ entered, but it was into heaven itself that He went, in order now to appear for us in the very presence of God. 25 And He does not enter to offer Himself over and over again, as the high priest enters the sanctuary year after year with blood that is not his own; 26 for, if that had been the case, He would have had to suffer over and over again, ever since the creation of the world. But, as it is, once at the close of the ages He has appeared, to put away sin by His sacrifice. 27 Indeed, just as men must die but once and after that be judged, 28 so Christ was offered once for all to take away the sins of many, but again He will appear, without having anything to do with sin, to save those who are eagerly waiting for Him to bring them final salvation.

10 *The sacrifices under the law unable to take away sins; Christ's one sacrifice has taken away sins, because it was made in accordance with God's will; to show that it is effective He sits at God's right hand*

For since the law cast only a shadow of the blessings to come and did not possess the reality itself of those blessings, the priests with the

[b] The Son's pre-existent Spirit.

BECK

that greater and more perfect tabernacle not made by human hands (that is, not a part of our created world). 12 And He didn't use the blood of goats and calves but His own blood to go only once into the holy place and pay a price that frees us forever. 13 Now, sprinkling the blood of goats and bulls and the ashes of a calf on unclean people makes them outwardly holy and clean. 14 How much more will the blood of Christ, who by His everlasting spirit offered Himself without a spot to God, wash our consciences clean from dead works to worship the living God?

15 And He is the Mediator of a new covenant. By dying He paid the ransom to free people from the sins under the first covenant, and those who are called are to get the everlasting inheritance promised them. 16 Where there is a will, it must be shown that the one who made it died, 17 since a will takes effect only when a person is dead. It is not in force as long as the one who made it is still living. 18 That is why the first covenant was also dedicated with blood. 19 When *Moses* had told all the people every commandment of the Law, he *took the blood* of calves and goats and some water, scarlet wool, and hyssop *and sprinkled* the scroll and *all the people.* 20 *"This is the blood of the covenant,"* he said, *"that God has ordered you*[31] *to keep."* 21 In the same way he sprinkled blood on the tabernacle and on everything used in the worship. 22 According to the Law almost everything is cleansed by blood, and if no blood is poured out, no sins are forgiven.

One Perfect Sacrifice

23 Now, the copies of the things in heaven had to be cleansed by these sacrifices, but the heavenly things themselves needed better sacrifices. 24 Christ didn't go into a holy place made by human hands and just a copy of the real thing but into heaven itself, now to appear before God for us. 25 And not to sacrifice Himself over and over again like that high priest going every year into the holy place with blood that is not his own. 26 Otherwise He would have had to suffer many times since the world was made. But as it is, He appeared only once at the end of the ages to get rid of sin by His sacrifice. 27 And as people are appointed to die once and after that to be judged, 28 so Christ also was sacrificed once to *take away the sins of many people,*[32] but those who eagerly look for Him will see Him again, without sin, when He comes to save them.

10 The Law, having only a dim outline of the good things in the future and not their substance, can never by the same sacrifices, re-

[31] Ex. 24:8
[32] Is. 53:12

K.J.V.

they offered year by year continually, make the comers thereunto perfect. 2 For then would they not have ceased to be offered? because that the worshippers once purged should have had no more conscience of sins. 3 But in those *sacrifices there is* a remembrance again *made* of sins every year. 4 For *it is* not possible that the blood of bulls and of goats should take away sins. 5 Wherefore, when he cometh into the world, he saith, Sacrifice and offering thou wouldest not, but a body hast thou prepared me: 6 In burnt offerings and *sacrifices* for sin thou hast had no pleasure. 7 Then said I, Lo, I come (in the volume of the book it is written of me) to do thy will, O God. 8 Above when he said, Sacrifice and offering and burnt offerings and *offering* for sin thou wouldest not, neither hadst pleasure *therein;* which are offered by the law; 9 Then said he, Lo, I come to do thy will, O God. He taketh away the first, that he may establish the second. 10 By the which will we are sanctified through the offering of the body of Jesus Christ once *for all.* 11 And every priest standeth daily ministering and offering oftentimes the same sacrifices, which can never take away sins: 12 But this man, after he had offered one sacrifice for sins for ever, sat down on the right hand of God; 13 From henceforth expecting till his enemies be made his footstool. 14 For by one offering he hath perfected for ever them that are sanctified. 15 *Whereof* the Holy Ghost also is a witness to us: for after that he had said before, 16 This *is* the covenant that I will make with them after those days, saith the Lord; I will put my laws into their hearts, and in their minds will I write them; 17 And their sins and iniquities will I remember no more. 18 Now where remission of these *is, there is* no more offering for sin. 19 Having therefore, brethren, boldness to enter into the holiest by the blood of Jesus, 20 By a new and living way, which he hath consecrated for us, through the vail, that is to say, his flesh; 21 And *having* a high priest over the house of God; 22 Let us draw near with a true heart in full assurance of faith, having our hearts sprinkled from an evil conscience, and our bodies washed with pure water. 23 Let us hold fast the profession of *our* faith without wavering; for he *is* faithful that promised; 24 And let us consider one another to provoke unto love and to good works: 25 Not forsaking the assembling of ourselves together, as the manner of some *is;* but exhorting *one another:* and so much the more, as ye see the day approaching. 26 For if we sin wilfully after that we have received the knowledge of the truth, there remaineth no more sacrifice for sins, 27 But a certain fearful looking for of judgment and fiery indignation, which shall devour the adversaries. 28 He that despised Moses' law died without mercy under two or three witnesses: 29 Of how much sorer punishment, suppose ye, shall he be thought worthy, who hath trodden under foot the Son of God, and hath counted the blood of the covenant,

N.A.S.

tinually, make perfect those who draw near. 2 Otherwise, would they not have ceased to be offered, because the worshipers, having once been cleansed, would no longer have had consciousness of sins? 3 But in those *sacrifices* there is a reminder of sins year by year. 4 For it is impossible for the blood of bulls and goats to take away sins. 5 Therefore, when He comes into the world, He says,

"SACRIFICE AND OFFERING THOU HAST NOT DESIRED,

BUT A BODY THOU HAST PREPARED FOR ME;

6 IN WHOLE BURNT OFFERINGS AND *sacrifices* FOR SIN THOU HAST TAKEN NO PLEASURE.

7 "THEN I SAID, 'BEHOLD, I HAVE COME

(IN THE ROLL OF THE BOOK IT IS WRITTEN OF ME)

TO DO THY WILL, O GOD.' "

8 After saying above, "SACRIFICES AND OFFERINGS AND WHOLE BURNT OFFERINGS AND *sacrifices* FOR SIN THOU HAST NOT DESIRED, NOR HAST THOU TAKEN PLEASURE *in them*" (which are offered according to the Law), 9 then He said, "BEHOLD, I HAVE COME TO DO THY WILL." He takes away the first in order to establish the second. 10 By this will we have been sanctified through the offering of the body of Jesus Christ once for all. 11 And every priest stands daily ministering and offering time after time the same sacrifices, which can never take away sins; 12 but He, having offered one sacrifice for sins for all time, sat down at the right hand of God, 13 waiting from that time onward UNTIL HIS ENEMIES BE MADE A FOOTSTOOL FOR HIS FEET. 14 For by one offering He has perfected for all time those who are sanctified. 15 And the Holy Spirit also bears witness to us; for after saying,

16 "THIS IS THE COVENANT THAT I WILL MAKE WITH THEM

AFTER THOSE DAYS, SAYS THE LORD:

I WILL PUT MY LAWS UPON THEIR HEART,

AND UPON THEIR MIND I WILL WRITE THEM,"

He then says, 17 "AND THEIR SINS AND THEIR LAWLESS DEEDS I WILL REMEMBER NO MORE." 18 Now where there is forgiveness of these things, there is no longer *any* offering for sin.

19 Since therefore, brethren, we have confidence to enter the holy place by the blood of Jesus, 20 by a new and living way which He inaugurated for us through the veil, that is, His flesh, 21 and since *we have* a great priest over the house of God, 22 let us draw near with a sincere heart in full assurance of faith, having our hearts sprinkled *clean* from an evil conscience, and our body washed with pure water. 23 Let us hold fast the confession of our hope without wavering, for He who promised is faithful; 24 and let us consider how to stimulate one another to love and good deeds, 25 not forsaking our own assembling together, as is the habit of some, but encouraging *one another;* and all the more, as you see the day drawing near.

26 For if we go on sinning willfully after receiving the knowledge of the truth, there no longer remains a sacrifice for sins, 27 but a certain terrifying expectation of judgment, and THE FURY OF A FIRE WHICH WILL CONSUME THE ADVERSARIES. 28 Anyone who has set aside the Law of Moses dies without mercy on *the testimony* of two or three witnesses. 29 How much severer punishment do you think he will deserve who has trampled under foot the Son of God, and

WILLIAMS

same sacrifices that are perpetually offered year after year cannot make perfect those who come to worship. 2 Otherwise, would they not have ceased offering them, because those who offered them, having once been purified, would have had no further consciousness of sins? 3 On the other hand, through these sacrifices there is given a real reminder of their sins, 4 for the blood of bulls and goats is unable to take away sins. 5 So, when Christ was coming into the world, He said:

6 "Sacrifice and offering you did not wish,
But a body you have prepared for me;
In burnt-offerings and sin-offerings you never took delight.
7 Then I said, 'See, I have come, just as the Scripture writes about me in the book, O God, to do your will.' "

8 Although at first He said, "You never wished or took delight in sacrifices and offerings, burnt-offerings and sin-offerings"—all of which are repeatedly offered in accordance with the law— 9 He afterward said, "See, I have come to do your will." He is taking away the first to let the second take its place. 10 It is by this will of God that we are consecrated through the offering of Jesus' body once for all. 11 Every other priest stands officiating day after day and over and over again offering the same sacrifices, although they are unable to take away our sins. 12 But this One offered up once for all and for all time one sacrifice for sins, and once for all took His seat at God's right hand, 13 from that time waiting till His enemies should be made the footstool of His feet. 14 For by that one sacrifice He has made perfect for all time those who are consecrated to Him. 15 Now the Holy Spirit, too, gives us the testimony, for after saying:

16 " 'This is the covenant that I will make with them
In those last days,' says the Lord:
'I will put my laws into their hearts,
And write them on their minds,' "

17 He continues to say:

"I will never, never any more recall their sins and deeds of wrong." 18 For when these are forgiven, there is no more need of an offering for sin.

19 Since then, my brothers, we have free access to the real sanctuary through the blood of Jesus, 20 the new and living way which He opened for us, through the curtain, that is, His physical nature, 21 and since in Him we have a Great Priest over the house of God, 22 let us continue to draw near to God with sincere hearts and perfect faith; with our hearts cleansed from the sense of sin, and our bodies bathed in clean water; 23 let us, without ever wavering, keep on holding to the hope that we profess, for He is to be trusted who has made the promise. 24 Let us continue so to consider one another as to stimulate one another to love and good deeds. 25 Let us stop neglecting our meeting together, as some do, but let us continue to encourage one another, and all the more because you see that the great day is drawing near.

26 For if we go willfully sinning after we have received full knowledge of the truth, there is no sacrifice left to be offered for our sins, 27 but only a terrifying prospect of judgment and that fiery indignation which is going to devour God's enemies. 28 Anyone who breaks the law of Moses pays the death penalty without any show of pity, on the evidence of two or three witnesses only. 29 How much severer punishment do you suppose that one deserves who tramples the Son of God underfoot, and counts as a

BECK

peated endlessly year after year, make perfect those who come. 2 Otherwise wouldn't they have stopped bringing sacrifices? Once cleansed, the worshipers would no longer be aware of any sins. 3 No, year after year these sacrifices reminded people of their sins. 4 The blood of bulls and goats can't take away sins.

5 That is why He says when He comes into the world, *You didn't like sacrifice and offering, but prepared a body for Me.* 6 *Burnt offerings and sacrifices for sin didn't please You.* 7 *Then I said, "I have come (the writing in the scroll of the book tells about Me). I'm here to do what You want, O God."* 8 First He says, *You didn't like and weren't pleased with sacrifices, offerings, burnt offerings, and sacrifices for sin* which are offered according to the Law. 9 Then He says, *I have come and am here to do what You want.* He takes away the first to set up the second. 10 *Doing God's will,* Jesus Christ sacrificed His body[33] only once and so made us holy.

11 Every other priest stands and serves day after day, and over and over again brings the same sacrifices, which can never take away sins. 12 But He made one sacrifice for sins, good forever, *sat down at the right of God,* 13 and since then is waiting *for His enemies to be made a footstool for His feet.*[34] 14 By one sacrifice He forever made perfect those who are made holy.

15 The Holy Spirit assures us of this. First He says, 16 *"This is the covenant I will make with them after those days," says the Lord: "I will put My laws on their hearts and write them on their minds."* 17 Then *"I will not remember their sins and their wrongs any more."*[35] 18 Now, where sins are forgiven, there is no more sacrificing for sin.

19 Fellow Christians, with the blood of Jesus we can now boldly go into the holy place 20 by the new, living way He opened for us through the curtain, the way of His body, 21 and we have a *great Priest* in charge of *God's family.*[36] 22 Let us then come near God, sincere in our hearts and convinced in our faith, because our hearts were sprinkled to take away our guilty feelings, and our bodies were washed with clean water. 23 Let us cling to the confession of our hope and not waver in it. We can trust Him who gave us His promise.

Give Up Sin

24 And let us consider how we can stimulate one another to love and to do good works. 25 Let us not stay away from our meetings, as some are regularly doing, but let us encourage one another, all the more because you see the day coming nearer.

26 If we choose to go on sinning after we have learned the truth, there is no more sacrifice for our sins, 27 only a terrible waiting for judgment and *a fire that will be eager to devour the enemies.*[37] 28 Anyone who violates the Law of Moses *dies* without pity *on the testimony of two or three witnesses.*[38] 29 How much worse a punishment do you think he will deserve who tram-

[33] Ps. 40:6-8
[34] Ps. 110:1
[35] Jer. 31:33-34
[36] Zech. 6:11-13
[37] Is. 26:11
[38] Deut. 17:6

K.J.V.

wherewith he was sanctified, an unholy thing, and hath done despite unto the Spirit of grace? 30 For we know him that hath said, Vengeance *belongeth* unto me, I will recompense, saith the Lord. And again, The Lord shall judge his people. 31 *It is* a fearful thing to fall into the hands of the living God. 32 But call to remembrance the former days, in which, after ye were illuminated, ye endured a great fight of afflictions; 33 Partly, whilst ye were made a gazingstock both by reproaches and afflictions; and partly, whilst ye became companions of them that were so used. 34 For ye had compassion of me in my bonds, and took joyfully the spoiling of your goods, knowing in yourselves that ye have in heaven a better and an enduring substance. 35 Cast not away therefore your confidence, which hath great recompense of reward. 36 For ye have need of patience, that, after ye have done the will of God, ye might receive the promise. 37 For yet a little while, and he that shall come will come, and will not tarry. 38 Now the just shall live by faith: but if *any man* draw back, my soul shall have no pleasure in him. 39 But we are not of them who draw back unto perdition; but of them that believe to the saving of the soul.

11 Now faith is the substance of things hoped for, the evidence of things not seen. 2 For by it the elders obtained a good report. 3 Through faith we understand that the worlds were framed by the word of God, so that things which are seen were not made of things which do appear. 4 By faith Abel offered unto God a more excellent sacrifice than Cain, by which he obtained witness that he was righteous, God testifying of his gifts: and by it he being dead yet speaketh. 5 By faith Enoch was translated that he should not see death; and was not found, because God had translated him: for before his translation he had this testimony, that he pleased God. 6 But without faith *it is* impossible to please *him:* for he that cometh to God must believe that he is, and *that* he is a rewarder of them that diligently seek him. 7 By faith Noah, being warned of God of things not seen as yet, moved with fear, prepared an ark to the saving of his house; by the which he condemned the world, and became heir of the righteousness which is by faith. 8 By faith Abraham, when he was called to go out into a place which he should after receive for an inheritance, obeyed; and he went out, not knowing whither he went. 9 By faith he sojourned in the land of promise, as *in* a strange country, dwelling in tabernacles with

N.A.S.

has regarded as unclean the blood of the covenant by which he was sanctified, and has insulted the Spirit of grace? 30 For we know Him who said, "VENGEANCE IS MINE, I WILL REPAY." And again, "THE LORD WILL JUDGE HIS PEOPLE." 31 It is a terrifying thing to fall into the hands of the living God.

32 But remember the former days, when, after being enlightened, you endured a great conflict of sufferings, 33 partly, by being made a public spectacle through reproaches and tribulations, and partly by becoming sharers with those who were so treated. 34 For you showed sympathy to the prisoners, and accepted joyfully the seizure of your property, knowing that you have for yourselves a better possession and an abiding one. 35 Therefore, do not throw away your confidence, which has a great reward. 36 For you have need of endurance, so that when you have done the will of God, you may receive what was promised.

37 FOR YET IN A VERY LITTLE WHILE,
HE WHO IS COMING WILL COME, AND WILL
    NOT DELAY.
38 BUT MY RIGHTEOUS ONE SHALL LIVE BY
    FAITH;
AND IF HE SHRINKS BACK, MY SOUL HAS NO
    PLEASURE IN HIM.

39 But we are not of those who shrink back to destruction, but of those who have faith to the preserving of the soul.

11 Now faith is the assurance of *things* hoped for, the conviction of things not seen. 2 For by it the men of old gained approval. 3 By faith we understand that the worlds were prepared by the word of God, so that what is seen was not made out of things which are visible. 4 By faith Abel offered to God a better sacrifice than Cain, through which he obtained the testimony that he was righteous, God testifying about his gifts, and through faith, though he is dead, he still speaks. 5 By faith Enoch was taken up so that he should not see death; and he was not found because God took him up; for he obtained the witness that before his being taken up he was pleasing to God. 6 And without faith it is impossible to please *Him*, for he who comes to God must believe that He is, and *that* He is a rewarder of those who seek Him. 7 By faith Noah, being warned *by God* about things not yet seen, in reverence prepared an ark for the salvation of his household, by which he condemned the world, and became an heir of the righteousness which is according to faith. 8 By faith Abraham, when he was called, obeyed by going out to a place which he was to receive for an inheritance; and he went out, not knowing where he was going. 9 By faith he lived as an alien in the land of promise, as in

WILLIAMS

common thing the blood of the covenant by which he was consecrated, and has insulted the Spirit that grants God's unmerited favor? 30 For we know who it was that said, "Vengeance belongs to me, I will pay back!" and again, "The Lord will be His people's judge." 31 It is a terrifying thing to fall into the hands of the ever living God!

32 But you must continue to remember those earlier days when first you received the light and then endured so great a struggle with persecution, 33 partly by being exposed as a public spectacle to insults and violent sufferings, and partly by showing yourselves ready to share with those who were living in this condition. 34 For you showed sympathy with those who were in prison and cheerfully submitted to the violent seizure of your property, for you knew that you had in yourselves and in heaven one that was lasting. 35 So you must never give up your confident courage, for it holds a rich reward for you. 36 Indeed, to carry out the will of God and to receive the blessing He has promised, you need endurance, for:

37 "In just a very little while

The Coming One will come and not delay;

38 Meantime my righteous servant will live on by faith.

But if a man draws back, my soul has no delight in him."

39 But we are not of a disposition to draw back so as to perish, but we have faith that leads to the saving of the soul.

11 *He calls the roll of the heroes of faith —from Abel, Enoch, Noah, Abraham, Moses, down to the prophets and Maccabean conquerors and sufferers; Christian faith-conquerors needed to complete the roll*

Now faith is the assurance of the things we hope for, the proof of the reality of the things we cannot see. 2 For by it the men of old won God's approval. 3 By faith we understand that the worlds were created, beautifully co-ordinated, and now exist, at God's command; so the things that we see did not develop out of mere matter. 4 By faith Abel offered a sacrifice more acceptable to God than Cain did, for by it he was approved as an upright man, since God approved him for the offering he made; and by it he still continues to speak, though dead. 5 By faith Enoch was transplanted from earth, so that he did not experience dying; and he could not be found, because God had transplanted him from earth. For before he was transplanted from earth evidence was given him that he pleased God; 6 but without faith it is impossible to please Him, for anyone who approaches God must believe that there is a God and that He gives rewards to all who earnestly try to find Him. 7 By faith Noah, on being divinely warned about things not seen as yet, in reverence prepared an ark for saving his family, and by his faith condemned the world and became possessor of the uprightness that results from faith.

8 By faith Abraham, on being called, obeyed in starting off for a country which he was to receive as his own, and he did it in spite of the fact that he did not know where he was going. 9 By faith he made his temporary home in the land that God had promised him, although a land inhabited by others, living merely in

BECK

ples on God's Son, treats as an unholy thing *the blood of the covenant*[39] that made him holy, and insults the Spirit of love? 30 We know Him who said, *I have the right to punish; I will pay back*, and again, *The Lord will judge His people.*[40] 31 It is terrible to fall into the hands of the living God.

Endure

32 Remember those early days, how after you received the light you successfully came through a hard and painful struggle. 33 Mocked and mistreated, you were made a public show, or you shared the life of those who were treated that way. 34 You sympathized with the prisoners, and when you were robbed of your property, you took it cheerfully because you knew you have something better that is permanent.

35 Then don't lose your courage. There's a great reward for it. 36 You need endurance to do what God wants and so to get what He promised. 37 *Soon, very soon,*[41] *He who is coming will come and will not delay,* 38 *and by faith My righteous one will live. If he shrinks back, I will not be pleased with him.* 39 Now, we're not those who *shrink back* and so are lost, but we have *faith*[42] and so are saved.

Faith

11 Faith is being sure of the things we hope for, being convinced of the things we can't see. 2 The men of long ago won approval for their faith.

3 By faith we know God made the world by His Word so that what we see wasn't made of what can be seen.

4 By faith *Abel brought* to God a better sacrifice than Cain and was declared to be righteous. *God* approved *his offerings.*[43] He died, but by his faith he is still speaking to us.

5 By faith *Enoch* was taken away without dying *and couldn't be found, because God had taken him.* We are assured *he pleased God* before he was taken. But you can't *please*[44] God without faith. 6 If you come to God, you must believe He exists and will always reward those who search for Him.

7 By faith Noah, when he was warned about the things nobody could foresee, respected God and built an ark to save his family, and by such a faith he condemned the world and got the righteousness that is to be had by faith.

8 By faith *Abraham* obeyed when he was called to *leave* home and go to a place he would get as his own, and he *left* without knowing where he was going. 9 By faith he *lived as a stranger*[45] in the promised land, as though it belonged to someone else, and lived in tents with

[39] Ex. 24:8
[40] Deut. 32:35-36; Ps. 135:14
[41] Is. 26:20
[42] Hab. 2:3-4
[43] Gen. 4:4
[44] Gen. 5:24
[45] Gen. 12:1, 4; 23:4; 47:9

K.J.V.

Isaac and Jacob, the heirs with him of the same promise: 10 For he looked for a city which hath foundations, whose builder and maker *is* God. 11 Through faith also Sarah herself received strength to conceive seed, and was delivered of a child when she was past age, because she judged him faithful who had promised. 12 Therefore sprang there even of one, and him as good as dead, *so many* as the stars of the sky in multitude, and as the sand which is by the sea shore innumerable. 13 These all died in faith, not having received the promises, but having seen them afar off, and were persuaded of *them,* and embraced *them,* and confessed that they were strangers and pilgrims on the earth. 14 For they that say such things declare plainly that they seek a country. 15 And truly, if they had been mindful of that *country* from whence they came out, they might have had opportunity to have returned. 16 But now they desire a better *country,* that is, a heavenly: wherefore God is not ashamed to be called their God: for he hath prepared for them a city. 17 By faith Abraham, when he was tried, offered up Isaac: and he that had received the promises offered up his only begotten *son,* 18 Of whom it was said, That in Isaac shall thy seed be called: 19 Accounting that God *was* able to raise *him* up, even from the dead; from whence also he received him in a figure. 20 By faith Isaac blessed Jacob and Esau concerning things to come. 21 By faith Jacob, when he was a dying, blessed both the sons of Joseph; and worshipped, *leaning* upon the top of his staff. 22 By faith Joseph, when he died, made mention of the departing of the children of Israel; and gave commandment concerning his bones. 23 By faith Moses, when he was born, was hid three months of his parents, because they saw *he was* a proper child; and they were not afraid of the king's commandment. 24 By faith Moses, when he was come to years, refused to be called the son of Pharaoh's daughter; 25 Choosing rather to suffer affliction with the people of God, than to enjoy the pleasures of sin for a season; 26 Esteeming the reproach of Christ greater riches than the treasures in Egypt: for he had respect unto the recompense of the reward. 27 By faith he forsook Egypt, not fearing the wrath of the king: for he endured, as seeing him who is invisible. 28 Through faith he kept the passover, and the sprinkling of blood, lest he that destroyed the firstborn should touch them. 29 By faith they passed through the Red sea as by dry *land:* which the Egyptians assaying to do were drowned. 30 By faith the walls of Jericho fell down, after they were compassed about seven days. 31 By faith the harlot Rahab perished not with them that believed not, when she had received the spies with peace. 32 And what shall I more say? for the time would fail me to tell of Gideon, and *of* Barak, and *of* Samson, and *of* Jephthah; *of* David also, and Samuel, and *of* the prophets: 33 Who through faith subdued kingdoms, wrought righteousness, obtained promises, stopped the mouths of lions, 34 Quenched the violence of fire, escaped the edge of the sword, out of weakness were made strong, waxed valiant in fight, turned to flight the armies of the aliens. 35 Women received their

N.A.S.

a foreign *land,* dwelling in tents with Isaac and Jacob, fellow-heirs of the same promise; 10 for he was looking for the city which has foundations, whose architect and builder is God. 11 By faith even Sarah herself received ability to conceive, even beyond the proper time of life, since she considered Him faithful who had promised; 12 therefore also there was born of one man, and him as good as dead at that, *as many descendants* AS THE STARS OF HEAVEN IN NUMBER, AND INNUMERABLE AS THE SAND WHICH IS BY THE SEASHORE.

13 All these died in faith, without receiving the promises, but having seen them and having welcomed them from a distance, and having confessed that they were strangers and exiles on the earth. 14 For those who say such things make it clear that they are seeking a country of their own. 15 And indeed if they had been thinking of that *country* from which they went out, they would have had opportunity to return. 16 But as it is, they desire a better *country,* that is a heavenly one. Therefore God is not ashamed to be called their God; for He has prepared a city for them.

17 By faith Abraham, when he was tested, offered up Isaac; and he who had received the promises was offering up his only begotten *son;* 18 *it was he* to whom it was said, "IN ISAAC YOUR SEED SHALL BE CALLED." 19 He considered that God is able to raise *men* even from the dead; from which he also received him back as a type. 20 By faith Isaac blessed Jacob and Esau, even regarding things to come. 21 By faith Jacob, as he was dying, blessed each of the sons of Joseph, and worshiped, *leaning* on the top of his staff. 22 By faith Joseph, when he was dying, made mention of the exodus of the children of Israel, and gave orders concerning his bones. 23 By faith Moses, when he was born, was hidden for three months by his parents, because they saw he was a beautiful child; and they were not afraid of the king's edict. 24 By faith Moses, when he had grown up, refused to be called the son of Pharaoh's daughter; 25 choosing rather to endure ill-treatment with the people of God, than to enjoy the passing pleasures of sin; 26 considering the reproach of Christ greater riches than the treasures of Egypt; for he was looking to the reward. 27 By faith he left Egypt, not fearing the wrath of the king; for he endured, as seeing Him who is unseen. 28 By faith he kept the Passover and the sprinkling of the blood, so that he who destroyed the firstborn might not touch them. 29 By faith they passed through the Red Sea as though *they were passing* through dry land; and the Egyptians, when they attempted it, were drowned. 30 By faith the walls of Jericho fell down, after they had been encircled for seven days. 31 By faith Rahab the harlot did not perish along with those who were disobedient, after she had welcomed the spies in peace.

32 And what more shall I say? For time will fail me if I tell of Gideon, Barak, Samson, Jephthah; of David and Samuel and the prophets; 33 who by faith conquered kingdoms, performed *acts of* righteousness, obtained promises, shut the mouths of lions, 34 quenched the power of fire, escaped the edge of the sword, from weakness were made strong, became mighty in war, put foreign armies to flight. 35 Women received *back* their dead by resur-

WILLIAMS

tents with Isaac and Jacob, who were to share the promise with him. 10 For he was confidently looking forward to that city with the solid foundations, whose architect and builder is God. 11 By faith Sarah received strength to become pregnant, and actually gave birth to a child, although she was past the time of life for it, because she thought that He who made her the promise was to be trusted. 12 And so there sprang from one man, and that dead as to any prospects for offspring, a people as numberless as the stars in the sky and as the sands beside the seashore.

13 These people all died victoriously as a result of their faith, although they did not receive the blessings promised; that is, because they really saw them in the far-off future and welcomed them, and so professed to be only foreigners and strangers here on earth. 14 For people who make such a profession as this show that they are in search of a country of their own. 15 And if they had been cherishing the memory of the country they had left, they would have had an opportunity to go back. 16 But in reality they were aspiring for a better country, I mean, a heavenly one. This is why God is not ashamed to be called their God, for He has prepared a city for them.

17 By faith Abraham, when he was put to the test, offered Isaac as a sacrifice; that is, he who had received the promise was starting to offer as a sacrifice his only son, 18 of whom it had been said, "Through Isaac your offspring must be traced." 19 For he considered the fact that God was able to raise people from the dead; and so from the dead, in a figure, he did receive him back.

20 By faith Isaac put his blessings for the future on Jacob and Esau. 21 By faith Jacob, when about to die, put his blessing on each of Joseph's sons, and worshiped, leaning on the top of his staff. 22 By faith Joseph, at the closing of his life, made mention of the future migration of the Israelites, and gave directions what to do with his body. 23 By faith, Moses, at his birth was hidden three months by his parents, because they saw that he was a beautiful child, and they were not afraid of the king's decree. 24 By faith Moses, when he had grown up, refused to be known as a son of Pharaoh's daughter, 25 because he preferred to suffer hardships with the people of God than to have the passing enjoyment that results from sin, 26 and thought the reproach endured for the Christ was greater wealth than all the treasures in Egypt, for he kept his eye upon the reward. 27 By faith he left Egypt, because he was not afraid of the king's anger, for he persevered as though he were actually seeing Him who is unseen. 28 By faith he instituted the Passover and the pouring of blood upon the doorposts, so that the destroyer of the first-born might not touch them. 29 By faith they crossed the Red Sea as though it were dry land, while the Egyptians, in attempting it, were drowned. 30 By faith the walls of Jericho collapsed, after being surrounded each of seven days. 31 By faith Rahab the prostitute did not perish with those who disobeyed God, because she had welcomed the scouts as friends.

32 And why should I continue to mention more? For time would fail me to tell of Gideon, Barak, Samson, Jephthah, David, Samuel, and the prophets, 33 who by their faith conquered kingdoms, administered justice, received new promises, shut the mouths of lions, 34 stopped the force of fire, escaped from dying by the sword, out of weakness found great strength, grew mighty in war, put foreign armies to flight. 35 Women by a resurrection received their dead

BECK

Isaac and Jacob, who had the same promise he had. 10 He was looking for the city with foundations, the one God built and made. 11 By faith Sarah, even though she was too old, got the strength to have a child because she believed she could trust Him who had promised. 12 And so, although he was as good as dead, one man had *many* descendants, *like the stars in the sky and the sand on the seashore that nobody can count.*[46]

13 All these died in faith without getting what was promised. But they saw it far ahead and welcomed it, and they confessed they were *strangers who had no permanent home*[45] on earth. 14 Those who talk that way show they're looking for a country of their own. 15 If their hearts had been in the country they left, they could have found an opportunity to go back. 16 Instead, they were longing for a better country—I mean heaven. That is why God is not ashamed to be called their God, because He has prepared a city for them.

17 By faith *Abraham,* when he was *tested, offered Isaac.*[47] Yes, this man, who received the promises 18 and was told, *Isaac's children will be called your descendants,*[48] was sacrificing *his only son,*[47] 19 thinking, "God can even raise him from the dead." And in a way he did get him back from the dead.

20 By faith Isaac blessed Jacob and Esau in regard to their future. 21 By faith a dying Jacob blessed each of Joseph's sons and *worshiped leaning on the top of his staff.*[49] 22 By faith Joseph, when his end was near, remembered how the Israelites would leave Egypt and gave directions for his burial.

23 By faith, when Moses was born, his parents *hid him three months* because *they saw he was a fine baby*[50] and were not afraid of the king's order. 24 By faith *Moses, when he grew up,*[51] refused to be called a son of Pharaoh's daughter 25 and preferred being mistreated with God's people to enjoying the short-lived pleasures of sin. 26 He considered the *abuse suffered by Christ*[52] greater riches than the treasures of Egypt, because he was looking ahead to the reward.

27 By faith he left Egypt without fearing the king's anger. He persisted as one who was constantly seeing Him who can't be seen. 28 By faith he celebrated the *Passover* and put the *blood* on the doorposts to keep him who *destroyed*[53] the firstborn from touching his people. 29 By faith they went through the Red Sea as if it were dry land. The Egyptains tried it, too, but were drowned.

30 By faith the walls of Jericho fell when the people marched around them seven days. 31 By faith the prostitute Rahab welcomed the spies as friends and didn't perish with her disobedient people.

32 And what more should I say? There will not be time enough for me to tell about Gideon, Barak, Samson, Jephthah, David, Samuel, and the prophets, 33 who by faith conquered kingdoms, did righteous works, got what was promised, shut the mouths of lions, 34 put out raging fires, escaped death by the sword, found strength when weak, proved to be mighty in battle, put foreign armies to flight. 35 Women got their dead

[46] Gen. 15:5; 22:17; 32:12
[47] Gen. 22:1-2, 10, 12
[48] Gen. 21:12
[49] Gen. 47:31
[50] Ex. 2:2
[51] Ex. 2:11
[52] Ps. 69:9; 89:50-51
[53] Ex. 12:12-13

K.J.V.

dead raised to life again: and others were tortured, not accepting deliverance; that they might obtain a better resurrection: 36And others had trial of *cruel* mockings and scourgings, yea, moreover of bonds and imprisonment. 37 They were stoned, they were sawn asunder, were tempted, were slain with the sword: they wandered about in sheepskins and goatskins; being destitute, afflicted, tormented; 38 Of whom the world was not worthy: they wandered in deserts, and *in* mountains, and *in* dens and caves of the earth. 39And these all, having obtained a good report through faith, received not the promise: 40 God having provided some better thing for us, that they without us should not be made perfect.

12 Wherefore, seeing we also are compassed about with so great a cloud of witnesses, let us lay aside every weight, and the sin which doth so easily beset *us,* and let us run with patience the race that is set before us, 2 Looking unto Jesus the author and finisher of *our* faith; who for the joy that was set before him endured the cross, despising the shame, and is set down at the right hand of the throne of God. 3 For consider him that endured such contradiction of sinners against himself, lest ye be wearied and faint in your minds. 4 Ye have not yet resisted unto blood, striving against sin. 5And ye have forgotten the exhortation which speaketh unto you as unto children, My son, despise not thou the chastening of the Lord, nor faint when thou art rebuked of him: 6 For whom the Lord loveth he chasteneth, and scourgeth every son whom he receiveth. 7 If ye endure chastening, God dealeth with you as with sons; for what son is he whom the father chasteneth not? 8 But if ye be without chastisement, whereof all are partakers, then are ye bastards, and not sons. 9 Furthermore, we have had fathers of our flesh which corrected *us,* and we gave *them* reverence: shall we not much rather be in subjection unto the Father of spirits, and live? 10 For they verily for a few days chastened *us* after their own pleasure; but he for *our* profit, that *we* might be partakers of his holiness. 11 Now no chastening for the present seemeth to be joyous, but grievous: nevertheless, afterward it yieldeth the peaceable fruit of righteousness unto them which are exercised thereby. 12 Wherefore lift up the hands which hang down, and the feeble knees; 13And make straight paths for your feet, lest that which is lame be turned out of the way; but let it rather be healed. 14 Follow peace with all *men,* and holiness, without which no man shall see the Lord: 15 Looking diligently lest any man fail of the grace of God; lest any root of bitter-

N.A.S.

rection; and others were tortured, not accepting their release, in order that they might obtain a better resurrection; 36 and others experienced mockings and scourgings, yes, also chains and imprisonment. 37 They were stoned, they were sawn in two, [a]they were tempted, they were put to death with the sword; they went about in sheepskins, in goatskins; being destitute, afflicted, ill-treated 38 (*men* of whom the world was not worthy), wandering in deserts and mountains and caves and holes in the ground. 39And all these, having gained approval through their faith, did not receive what was promised, 40 because God had provided something better for us, so that apart from us they should not be made perfect.

12 Therefore, since we have so great a cloud of witnesses surrounding us, let us also lay aside every encumbrance, and the sin which so easily entangles us, and let us run with endurance the race that is set before us, 2 fixing our eyes on Jesus the author and perfecter of faith, who for the joy set before Him endured the cross, despising the shame, and has sat down at the right hand of the throne of God. 3 For consider Him who has endured such hostility by sinners against Himself, so that you may not grow weary and lose heart. 4 You have not yet resisted to the point of shedding blood, in your striving against sin; 5 and you have forgotten the exhortation which is addressed to you as sons,

"MY SON, DO NOT REGARD LIGHTLY THE DISCIPLINE OF THE LORD,
NOR FAINT WHEN YOU ARE REPROVED BY HIM;
6 FOR THOSE WHOM THE LORD LOVES HE DISCIPLINES,
AND HE SCOURGES EVERY SON WHOM HE RECEIVES."

7 It is for discipline that you endure; God deals with you as with sons; for what son is there whom *his* father does not discipline? 8 But if you are without discipline, of which all have become partakers, then you are illegitimate children and not sons. 9 Furthermore, we had earthly fathers to discipline us, and we respected them; shall we not much rather be subject to the Father of spirits, and live? 10 For they disciplined us for a short time as seemed best to them, but He disciplines us for *our* good, that we may share His holiness. 11All discipline for the moment seems not to be joyful, but sorrowful; yet to those who have been trained by it, afterwards it yields the peaceful fruit of righteousness. 12 Therefore, strengthen the hands that are weak and the knees that are feeble, 13 and make straight paths for your feet, so that *the limb* which is lame may not be put out of joint, but rather be healed.

14 Pursue after peace with all men, and after the sanctification without which no one will see the Lord. 15 See to it that no one comes short of the grace of God; that no root of bitterness

[a] Some mss. omit, *they were tempted.*

WILLIAMS

again; others endured tortures, because they would not accept release, that they might rise to a better life. 36 Still others stood the test of taunts and tortures, and even chains and prisons. 37 They were stoned to death, they were tortured to death, they were sawn in two, they were killed with the sword. With nothing on their bodies but skins of sheep or goats they wandered here and there, destitute, oppressed, mistreated— 38 men of whom the world was not worthy, though wandering in deserts, mountains, caves, and holes in the ground.

39 Though all these people by their faith won God's approval, yet none of them received what He had promised, 40 for God had provided something still better for us, that they, apart from us might not attain perfection.

12 *Jesus our model hero of faith; His sufferings far greater than ours; our Father letting us suffer to discipline and refine our souls; so be cheerful, consecrated, cautious; Sinai and Mt. Zion contrasted*

Therefore, as we have so vast a crowd of spectators in the grandstands, let us throw off every impediment and the sin that easily entangles our feet, and run with endurance the race for which we are entered, 2 keeping our eyes on Jesus, the perfect leader and example of faith, who, instead of the joy which lay before Him, endured the cross with no regard for its shame, and since has taken His seat at the right hand of the throne of God.

3 Yes, to keep from growing weary and fainthearted, just think of the examples set by Him who has endured so great opposition aimed at Him by sinful men! 4 You have not yet, as you have struggled on against sin, resisted to the point of pouring out your blood, 5 and you have forgotten the encouragement which is addressed to you as sons:

"My son, refrain from thinking lightly of the discipline the Lord inflicts,
And giving up when you are corrected by Him.
6 For He disciplines everyone He loves,
And chastises every son whom He heartily receives."

7 You must submit to discipline. God is dealing with you as His sons. For who is the son that his father never disciplines? 8 Now if you are without any discipline, in which all true sons share, you are only illegitimate children and not true sons. 9 Furthermore, we had earthly fathers who disciplined us, and we used to treat them with respect; how much more cheerfully should we submit to the Father of our spirits, and live! 10 For they disciplined us only a short time, as it seemed proper to them; but He does it for our good, in order that we may share His holy character. 11 Now for the time being no discipline seems to be pleasant; it is painful; later on, however, to those who are trained by it, it yields the fruit of peace which grows from upright character. 12 So tighten the grip of your slipping hands; stiffen the stand of your knocking knees; 13 and keep your feet in straight paths, so that limbs may not be dislocated, but instead be cured.

14 Continue to live in peace with everybody and strive for that consecration without which no one can see the Lord. 15 Continue to look after one another, that no one fails to gain

BECK

back alive. Some were tortured; they refused to be freed, in order to rise to a better life. 36 Others suffered mocking and scourging and were even put in chains and in prison. 37 They were stoned, tempted, sawed in two, murdered with a sword. They went around in sheepskins and goatskins, needy, oppressed, mistreated. 38 The world wasn't worthy of them as they wandered around in deserts and in the hills, in caves and holes in the ground.

39 By faith all these won approval but didn't get what was promised. 40 God provided something better for us in order to have them reach their goal with us.

Run the Race

12 Now then, with all these witnesses around us like a cloud, let us get rid of every burden and the sin we easily fall into and with endurance run the race laid out before us, 2 looking to Jesus, who gives us our faith from start to finish. For the joy that was set before Him He endured the cross, thinking nothing of its shame, and *sat down at the right*[54a] of God's throne.

3 Think of how sinners opposed Him and He endured it. It will help you not to get tired and give up. 4 In your struggle against sin you haven't yet resisted till blood has flowed. 5 And you have forgotten the encouragement spoken to you as sons:

My son, don't think lightly of the Lord's training
Or give up when He corrects you.
6 *The Lord corrects whom He loves,*
And He whips everyone He accepts as His son.

7 What you endure is to *correct* you. God is treating you *as His sons.* Is there a *son* whom his father doesn't *correct?* 8 All sons are corrected; if you're not *corrected,* you're *no sons*[54a] but bastards. 9 Furthermore, our natural fathers used to correct us, and we respected them. Shouldn't we much more submit to the Father of spirits and live? 10 They corrected us for a short time as it seemed best to them. But He corrects us for our good, to have us share His holiness. 11 While we're being corrected, it always seems unpleasant and painful. But after we've been trained, correction gives us the peaceful fruit of righteousness.

12 And so, *if your hands are letting go, take a firm hold; if you feel weak in your knees, stand firm;*[55] and *march on without wavering.*[56] 13 Then a cripple will not be turned away but be made well.

14 *Try hard to live in peace*[57] with everybody and to be holy. Without holiness nobody will see the Lord. 15 See to it that no one loses God's

[54] Prov. 3:11-12; Job 5:17
[55] Is. 35:3
[56] Prov. 4:26
[57] Ps. 34:14

K.J.V.

ness springing up trouble *you,* and thereby many be defiled; 16 Lest there *be* any fornicator, or profane person, as Esau, who for one morsel of meat sold his birthright. 17 For ye know how that afterward, when he would have inherited the blessing, he was rejected: for he found no place of repentance, though he sought it carefully with tears. 18 For ye are not come unto the mount that might be touched, and that burned with fire, nor unto blackness, and darkness, and tempest, 19And the sound of a trumpet, and the voice of words; which *voice* they that heard entreated that the word should not be spoken to them any more: 20 (For they could not endure that which was commanded, And if so much as a beast touch the mountain, it shall be stoned, or thrust through with a dart: 21And so terrible was the sight, *that* Moses said, I exceedingly fear and quake:) 22 But ye are come unto mount Sion, and unto the city of the living God, the heavenly Jerusalem, and to an innumerable company of angels, 23 To the general assembly and church of the firstborn, which are written in heaven, and to God the Judge of all, and to the spirits of just men made perfect, 24And to Jesus the mediator of the new convenant, and to the blood of sprinkling, that speaketh better things than *that of* Abel. 25 See that ye refuse not him that speaketh: for if they escaped not who refused him that spake on earth, much more *shall not* we *escape,* if we turn away from him that *speaketh* from heaven: 26 Whose voice then shook the earth: but now he hath promised, saying, Yet once more I shake not the earth only, but also heaven. 27And this *word,* Yet once more, signifieth the removing of those things that are shaken, as of things that are made, that those things which cannot be shaken may remain. 28 Wherefore we receiving a kingdom which cannot be moved, let us have grace, whereby we may serve God acceptably with reverence and godly fear: 29 For our God *is* a consuming fire.

13 Let brotherly love continue. 2 Be not forgetful to entertain strangers: for thereby some have entertained angels unawares. 3 Remember them that are in bonds, as bound with them; *and* them which suffer adversity, as being yourselves also in the body. 4 Marriage *is* honourable in all, and the bed undefiled: but whoremongers and adulterers God will judge. 5 *Let your* conversation *be* without covetousness; *and be* content with such things as ye have: for he hath said, I will never leave thee, nor forsake thee. 6 So that we may boldly say, The Lord *is* my helper, and I will not fear what man shall do unto me. 7 Remember them which have the rule over you, who have spoken unto you the word of God: whose faith follow, considering

N.A.S.

springing up cause trouble, and by it many be defiled; 16 that *there be* no immoral or godless person like Esau, who sold his own birthright for a single meal. 17 For you know that even afterwards, when he desired to inherit the blessing, he was rejected, for he found no place for repentance, though he sought for it with tears. 18 For you have not come to *a mountain* that may be touched and to a blazing fire, and to darkness and gloom and whirlwind, 19 and to the blast of a trumpet and the sound of words, which *sound was such that* those who heard begged that no further word should be spoken to them. 20 For they could not bear the command, "IF EVEN A BEAST TOUCHES THE MOUNTAIN, IT WILL BE STONED." 21And so terrible was the sight, *that* Moses said, "I AM FULL OF FEAR AND TREMBLING." 22 But you have come to Mount Zion and to the city of the living God, the heavenly Jerusalem, and to myriads of angels, 23 to the general assembly and church of the first-born who are enrolled in heaven, and to God the Judge of all, and to the spirits of righteous men made perfect, 24 and to Jesus the mediator of a new covenant and to the sprinkled blood, which speaks better than *the blood* of Abel. 25 See to it that you do not refuse him who is speaking. For if those did not escape when they refused him who warned *them* on earth, much less *shall* we *escape* who turn away from Him who *warns* from heaven. 26And His voice shook the earth then, but now He has promised, saying, "YET ONCE MORE I WILL SHAKE NOT ONLY THE EARTH, BUT ALSO THE HEAVEN." 27And this *expression,* "Yet once more," denotes the removing of those things which can be shaken, as of created things, in order that those things which cannot be shaken may remain. 28 Therefore, since we receive a kingdom which cannot be shaken, let us show gratitude, by which we may offer to God an acceptable service with reverence and awe; 29 for our God is a consuming fire.

13 Let love of the brethren continue. 2 Do not neglect to show hospitality to strangers, for by this some have entertained angels without knowing it. 3 Remember the prisoners, as though in prison with them; and those who are ill-treated, since you yourselves also are in the body. 4 *Let* marriage *be held* in honor among all, and let the *marriage* bed *be* undefiled; for fornicators and adulterers God will judge. 5 Let your way of life be free from the love of money, being content with what you have; for He Himself has said, "I WILL NEVER DESERT YOU, NOR WILL I EVER FORSAKE YOU," 6 so that we confidently say, "THE LORD IS MY HELPER, I WILL NOT BE AFRAID. WHAT SHALL MAN DO TO ME?" 7 Remember those who led you, who spoke the word of God to you; and considering the outcome of their way of life, imitate their faith.

WILLIAMS

God's spiritual blessing; or some evil like a bitter root may spring up and trouble you, and many of you be contaminated by it— 16 some immoral or godless person like Esau, who sold his own birthright for a single meal. 17 For you know that, when later he wanted to get possession of the blessing, he was rejected, for he could find no opportunity to repent, although with tears he tried to get the blessing.

18 For you have not come to a blazing fire that can be touched, to gloom and darkness, storm 19 and trumpet-blast, and a voice whose words made the hearers beg that not a word more should be added; 20 for they did not try to bear the order, "Even if a wild animal touches the mountain, it must be stoned to death," 21 and so terrifying was the sight that Moses said, "I am terrified and terror-stricken!" 22 But you have come to Mount Zion, even to the city of the living God, the heavenly Jerusalem, and to countless hosts of angels, 23 to the festal gathering and assembly of God's first-born sons enrolled as citizens in heaven, to a Judge who is the God of all, to the spirits of upright men who have attained perfection, 24 to Jesus the Mediator of the new covenant, and to the sprinkled blood which speaks a better message than even Abel's did.

25 See to it that you do not refuse to listen to Him who is speaking to you. For if they did not escape, because they refused to listen to him who warned them here on earth, how much less can we, if we reject Him who is from heaven? 26 Then His voice shook the earth, 27 but now His promise is, "Once more I will make not only the earth but heaven itself to tremble." Now that expression, "Once more," signifies the final removal of the things that can be shaken, to let remain the things that cannot be shaken. 28 Let us, therefore, be thankful for receiving a kingdom that cannot be shaken, and in this way continue to serve God acceptably in reverence and fear; 29 for our God, indeed, is a consuming fire.

13 *He urges them to practice brotherly love, purity, contentment; Christ and Christian truth unchangeable; He tells of the Christian's true sacrifice and home land; gives parting directions and greetings*

You must let your brotherly love continue. 2 Do not remain neglectful of hospitality to strangers, for by it some have entertained angels without knowing it. 3 Continue to remember those who are in prison, as though you were in prison with them, and those who are being ill-treated, since you, too, are liable to similar physical punishment. 4 Marriage must be held in honor by all, and the marriage relations kept sacred. Persons who are sexually vicious and immoral God will punish. 5 You must have a turn of mind that is free from avarice; you must be content with what you have, for God Himself has said, "I will never fail you, I will never forsake you." 6 So we can confidently say:
"The Lord is my helper; I will not be afraid. What can men do to me?"
7 You must not forget your former leaders, for it was they who brought you the message of God. Consider how they closed their lives; imi-

BECK

love, *that no root with bitter fruit grows up to trouble you*[58] and so defiles all of you, 16 that nobody lives in sexual sin or is unholy like *Esau*, who for one meal, *sold his rights as the first-born.*[59] 17 You know that later, when he wanted to get the blessing, he was rejected. He had no chance to change his mind although he begged for it with tears.

You Have Come to God

18 *You didn't come to anything you could touch,* to *a blazing fire, darkness, gloom, a storm,* 19 *the blast of a trumpet,* or the speaking of *a voice.* 20 Those who heard that begged to be told no more, because they couldn't endure the order that was given, *Even an animal, if it touches the mountain, must be stoned.*[60] 21 And the sight was so terrible Moses said, "*I am terrified* [61] and trembling."

22 No, you have come to Mount Zion, the city of the living God, the heavenly Jerusalem. Here are tens of thousands of angels, the whole festival gathering 23 and church of God's first-born people with their names written in heaven. Here is the Judge and God of all. Here are the spirits of the righteous who have been perfected. 24 And here is Jesus, who gave us a new covenant with God, and the sprinkled blood that has better things to tell than Abel.

25 See that you don't refuse to listen to Him who is speaking. If the others didn't escape when they refused to listen to Him warning them on earth, much less will we if we turn away from Him who warns us from heaven. 26 Then His voice shook the earth. But now He has promised, *Once more I will shake* not only *the earth* but also *heaven.* 27 The words *once more* show clearly He will take away what is *shaken,* seeing He made it, leaving what isn't *shaken* as permanent. 28 Since we have received a kingdom that can't be *shaken,*[62] let us thank God and so worship in a way that pleases Him, with fear and awe, 29 because our *God is a consuming fire.*[63]

Live as Christians

13 Christians, keep on loving one another. 2 Don't neglect to welcome guests. This is how some without knowing it had angels as their guests. 3 Remember those in prison as if you were in chains with them, and those who are mistreated as if you could feel it.

4 Everybody should think highly of marriage and keep married life pure, because God will judge those who sin sexually whether single or married.

5 Don't be greedy. Be satisfied with what you have, because He said, *I will never leave you or desert you.*[64] 6 And so we have the courage to say, *The Lord is my Help. I will not be afraid. What can man do to me?* [65]

Follow Your Teachers

7 Remember your leaders who told you God's Word. Consider how their lives ended, and imitate their faith.

[58] Deut. 29:18
[59] Gen. 25:33-34
[60] Ex. 19:12-13, 16; Deut. 4:11
[61] Deut. 9:19
[62] Hag. 2:6
[63] Deut. 4:24; 9:3
[64] Deut. 31:6, 8; Joshua 1:5; 1 Chron. 28:20
[65] Ps. 56:4, 11; 118:6

K.J.V.

the end of *their* conversation. 8 Jesus Christ the same yesterday, and to day, and for ever. 9 Be not carried about with divers and strange doctrines: for *it is* a good thing that the heart be established with grace; not with meats, which have not profited them that have been occupied therein. 10 We have an altar, whereof they have no right to eat which serve the tabernacle. 11 For the bodies of those beasts, whose blood is brought into the sanctuary by the high priest for sin, are burned without the camp. 12 Wherefore Jesus also, that he might sanctify the people with his own blood, suffered without the gate. 13 Let us go forth therefore unto him without the camp, bearing his reproach. 14 For here have we no continuing city, but we seek one to come. 15 By him therefore let us offer the sacrifice of praise to God continually, that is, the fruit of *our* lips, giving thanks to his name. 16 But to do good and to communicate forget not: for with such sacrifices God is well pleased. 17 Obey them that have the rule over you, and submit yourselves: for they watch for your souls, as they that must give account, that they may do it with joy, and not with grief: for that *is* unprofitable for you. 18 Pray for us: for we trust we have a good conscience, in all things willing to live honestly. 19 But I beseech *you* the rather to do this, that I may be restored to you the sooner. 20 Now the God of peace, that brought again from the dead our Lord Jesus, that great Shepherd of the sheep, through the blood of the everlasting covenant, 21 Make you perfect in every good work to do his will, working in you that which is well pleasing in his sight, through Jesus Christ; to whom *be* glory for ever and ever. Amen. 22 And I beseech you, brethren, suffer the word of exhortation: for I have written a letter unto you in few words. 23 Know ye that *our* brother Timothy is set at liberty; with whom, if he come shortly, I will see you. 24 Salute all them that have the rule over you, and all the saints. They of Italy salute you. 25 Grace *be* with you all. Amen.

Written to the Hebrews from Italy by Timothy.

N.A.S.

8 Jesus Christ *is* the same yesterday and today, *yes* and forever. 9 Do not be carried away by varied and strange teachings; for it is good for the heart to be strengthened by grace, not by foods, through which those who were thus occupied were not benefited. 10 We have an altar, from which those who serve the tabernacle have no right to eat. 11 For the bodies of those animals whose blood is brought into the holy place by the high priest *as an offering* for sin, are burned outside the camp. 12 Therefore Jesus also, that He might sanctify the people through His own blood, suffered outside the gate. 13 Hence, let us go out to Him outside the camp, bearing His reproach. 14 For here we do not have a lasting city, but we are seeking *the city* which is to come. 15 Through Him then let us continually offer up a sacrifice of praise to God, that is, the fruit of lips that give thanks to His name. 16 And do not neglect doing good and sharing; for with such sacrifices God is pleased. 17 Obey your leaders, and submit *to them;* for they keep watch over your souls, as those who will give an account. Let them do this with joy and not with grief, for this would be unprofitable for you.

18 Pray for us, for we are sure that we have a good conscience, desiring to conduct ourselves honorably in all things. 19 And I urge *you* all the more to do this, that I may be restored to you the sooner.

20 Now the God of peace, who brought up from the dead the great Shepherd of the sheep through the blood of the eternal covenant, *even* Jesus our Lord, 21 equip you in every good thing to do His will, working in us that which is pleasing in His sight, through Jesus Christ; to whom *be* the glory forever and ever. Amen.

22 But I urge you, brethren, bear with this word of exhortation, for I have written to you briefly. 23 Take notice that our brother Timothy has been released; with whom, if he comes soon, I shall see you. 24 Greet all of your leaders and all the saints. Those from Italy greet you.

25 Grace be with you all.

WILLIAMS

tate their faith. 8 Jesus Christ is the same yesterday and today, yes, forever. 9 You must stop
being carried away with varied and strange
teachings. For it is a good thing for the heart
to be strengthened by God's spiritual strength,
not by special kinds of food, from which those
adhering to them have gotten no good.

10 We Christians have an altar at which the
ministers of the Jewish tent of worship have
no right to eat. 11 For the bodies of those animals, whose blood is taken into the sanctuary
by the priest as a sin-offering, are burned outside the camp. 12 So Jesus, too, in order to
purify the people by His own blood, suffered
outside the gate. 13 Let us, therefore, go to Him
outside the camp, enduring the reproach that
He endured; 14 for we have no permanent city
here, but we are searching for that city which
is to be ours. 15 So then, through Christ, let
us always offer God the sacrifice of praise;
that is, the speech*a* of lips that glorify the
name of God. 16 And stop neglecting to do
good and to be generous, for God is highly
pleased with just such sacrifices as these.

17 Continue to obey and to be submissive
to your leaders, for they are ever watching in
defense of your souls, as men who will have to
give account of their trust. Treat them in this
way, so that they may work with joy and not
with grief.

18 Pray for me, for I am sure that I have a
clear conscience, and in everything I want to
live a noble life. 19 And more especially do I
beg you to do so, that I may very soon be
brought back to you.

20 May God, who gives us peace, who
brought back from the dead our Lord Jesus,
who through the blood by which He ratified
the everlasting covenant, is now the Great
Shepherd of the sheep, 21 perfectly fit you to
do His will, He Himself, through Jesus Christ,
accomplishing through you what is pleasing to
Him. To Him be glory forever and ever. Amen.

22 I beg you, brothers, to listen patiently
to this message, for I have written you only a
short letter. 23 You must know that our brother
Timothy has been released from prison. If he
comes soon, he and I will see you together.
24 Remember us to all your leaders and to all
the Christians.*b* The Christians from Italy wish
to be remembered to you.

25 God's spiritual blessings be with you all.
Amen.

BECK

8 Jesus Christ is the same yesterday, today,
and forever.

9 Don't get carried away with different kinds
of strange teachings. It is good to be inwardly
strengthened by God's love, not by foods, which
haven't helped those who make so much of them
in their lives. 10 We have an altar, and those who
still worship at the Jewish tabernacle have no
right to eat from this altar.

11 The high priest *brings the blood* of animals
into the holy place for sin, but the bodies of
those animals are *burned outside the camp.*
12 And so Jesus suffered outside the gate to make
the people holy by His own blood. 13 Then let
us go out to join Him *outside the camp*[66] and
bear the abuse He suffered. 14 You see, we don't
have a permanent city here but look for the
one that's coming. 15 Through Jesus let us always *bring to God a sacrifice of praise,*[67] that is,
the fruit of our lips,[68] praising His name. 16 And
don't forget to do good and to share; such sacrifices please God.

17 Your leaders, who have to give an account,
watch over you. Obey them and submit to them
so that they may be happy in their work and
not groaning, because that isn't good for you.

18 Pray for us as we're sure we have a good
conscience and want to live right in every way.
19 I urge you the more earnestly to do this that
I may be brought back to you sooner.

Farewell

20 The God of peace *brought back* from the
dead our Lord Jesus, who by His *blood made
an everlasting covenant* to become the great
Shepherd of the sheep[69]—21 may He give you
every good thing you need, to do what He
wants you to do, working in us through Jesus
Christ what pleases Him. To Him be glory forever. Amen.

22 I urge you, fellow Christians, listen patiently to what I say to encourage you, because
I've written you a short letter. 23 You should
know that Timothy, our fellow worker, is free
again. If he comes here soon, he and I will see
you.

24 Greet all your leaders and all the holy
people. The Christians from Italy greet you.

25 God's love be with all of you.

---

[a] Lit., *fruit of lips that confess,* etc. [b] Gr.., *to all the saints.*

[66] Ex. 29:14; Lev. 4:12, 21; 8:17; 9:11; 16:27;
Num. 19:3, 5
[67] Ps. 50:14, 23
[68] Hos. 14:2
[69] Is. 55:3; 63:11-12; Jer. 32:40; 50:5; Ezek.
16:60; 37:26; Zech. 9:11

K.J.V.

THE
GENERAL EPISTLE
OF
JAMES

1 James, a servant of God and of the Lord Jesus Christ, to the twelve tribes which are scattered abroad, greeting. 2 My brethren, count it all joy when ye fall into divers temptations; 3 Knowing *this,* that the trying of your faith worketh patience. 4 But let patience have *her* perfect work, that ye may be perfect and entire, wanting nothing. 5 If any of you lack wisdom, let him ask of God, that giveth to all *men* liberally, and upbraideth not; and it shall be given him. 6 But let him ask in faith, nothing wavering: for he that wavereth is like a wave of the sea driven with the wind and tossed. 7 For let not that man think that he shall receive any thing of the Lord. 8 A double minded man *is* unstable in all his ways. 9 Let the brother of low degree rejoice in that he is exalted: 10 But the rich, in that he is made low: because as the flower of the grass he shall pass away. 11 For the sun is no sooner risen with a burning heat, but it withereth the grass, and the flower thereof falleth, and the grace of the fashion of it perisheth: so also shall the rich man fade away in his ways. 12 Blessed *is* the man that endureth temptation: for when he is tried, he shall receive the crown of life, which the Lord hath promised to them that love him. 13 Let no man say when he is tempted, I am tempted of God: for God cannot be tempted with evil, neither tempteth he any man: 14 But every man is tempted, when he is drawn away of his own lust, and enticed. 15 Then when lust hath conceived, it bringeth forth sin; and sin, when it is finished, bringeth forth death. 16 Do not err, my beloved brethren. 17 Every good gift and every perfect gift is from above, and cometh down from the Father of lights, with whom is no variableness, neither shadow of turning. 18 Of his own will begat he us with the word of truth, that we should be a kind of firstfruits of his creatures. 19 Wherefore, my beloved brethren, let every man be swift to hear, slow to speak, slow to wrath: 20 For the wrath of man worketh not the righteousness of God. 21 Wherefore lay apart all filthiness and

N.A.S.

THE EPISTLE OF
JAMES

1 James, a bondservant of God and of the Lord Jesus Christ, to the twelve tribes who are dispersed abroad, greetings.
2 Consider it all joy, my brethren, when you encounter various trials; 3 knowing that the testing of your faith produces endurance. 4 And let endurance have *its* perfect result, that you may be perfect and complete, lacking in nothing.
5 But if any of you lacks wisdom, let him ask of God, who gives to all men generously and without reproach, and it will be given to him. 6 But let him ask in faith without any doubting, for the one who doubts is like the surf of the sea driven and tossed by the wind. 7 For let not that man expect that he will receive anything from the Lord, 8 *being* a double-minded man, unstable in all his ways.
9 But let the brother of humble circumstances glory in his high position; 10 and *let* the rich man *glory* in his humiliaton, because like flowering grass he will pass away. 11 For the sun rises with a scorching wind, and withers the grass; and its flower falls off, and the beauty of its appearance is destroyed; so too the rich man in the midst of his pursuits will fade away.
12 Blessed is a man who perseveres under trial; for once he has been approved, he will receive the crown of life, which *the Lord* has promised to those who love Him. 13 Let no one say when he is tempted, "I am being tempted by God"; for God cannot be tempted by evil, and He Himself does not tempt any one. 14 But each one is tempted when he is carried away and enticed by his own lust. 15 Then when lust has conceived, it gives birth to sin; and when sin is accomplished, it brings forth death. 16 Do not be deceived, my beloved brethren. 17 Every good thing bestowed and every perfect gift is from above, coming down from the Father of lights, with whom there is no variation, or shifting shadow. 18 In the exercise of His will He brought us forth by the word of truth, so that we might be as it were the first-fruits among His creatures.
19 [a]*This* you know, my beloved brethren. But let every one be quick to hear, slow to speak *and* slow to anger; 20 for the anger of man does not achieve the righteousness of God. 21 Therefore putting aside all filthiness and *all*

[a] Or, *Know* this.

WILLIAMS   BECK

THE LETTER OF

JAMES

JAMES

1 *He greets them; shows that trials, through prayer and patience, lead to perfection; that Christian faith is democratic; conquering temptation brings the crown of life; God gives all good; temper and tongue must be controlled; we are to be charitable and unstained*

James, a slave of God and of the Lord Jesus Christ, sends greetings to the twelve tribes that are scattered over the world.

2 You must consider it the purest joy, my brothers, when you are involved in various trials, 3 for you surely know that what is genuine in your faith produces the patient mind that endures; 4 but you must let your endurance come to its perfect product, so that you may be fully developed and perfectly equipped, without any defects. 5 But if any one of you is deficient in wisdom, let him ask God who generously gives to everyone and never reproaches one with his lack, and it will be given to him. 6 But he must ask in faith, without a doubt, for the man who doubts is like a wave of the sea that is whirled and swayed by the wind. 7-8 Such a man, indeed, a person with two minds, unreliable in every step he takes, must not expect to get anything from the Lord.

9 Let the poor brother of lowly station rejoice in his exalted station as a Christian, 10 and the rich brother rejoice in his being on a level with the poor, because the rich will fade away like the flower of the grass. 11 For the sun comes up with its scorching heat and dries up the grass, and its flowers wither, and its beauty fades away; so will rich men fade away in their pursuits.

12 Blessed is the person who endures trial, for when he stands the test, he will receive the crown of life, which God has promised to those who love Him. 13 No one must say, when he is tempted to do evil, "I have a temptation from God to do evil," for God cannot be tempted to do evil, and He never tempts anyone to do so. 14 But anyone is tempted to do evil when he is allured by his own evil desire and enticed by a bait. 15 Then evil desire conceives and gives birth to sin, and when sin is completed, it brings forth death.

16 You must avoid being misled, my dearly loved brothers. 17 Every good gift and every perfect boon is from above, and comes down from the Father of lights, in whom there is no variation or changing shadow. 18 In accordance with His will He made us His children by the message of truth, that we might be a kind of first fruits among His creatures.

19 You must understand this, my dearly loved brothers. Everyone must be quick to hear, slow to speak, slow to get angry; 20 for a man's anger does not produce the uprightness that God requires. 21 So strip yourselves of every-

1 James, servant of God and the Lord Jesus Christ, to the twelve tribes living scattered in the world: Greetings.

Cheer Up

2 When you're tested in different ways, my fellow Christians, consider it a pure joy 3 because you know the testing of your faith stirs up your power to endure. 4 Then let endurance finish its work so that you may be perfect and complete, lacking nothing.

5 If you lack wisdom, ask God, who gives to everyone with an open hand and doesn't scold, and He will give it to you. 6 You should ask with faith and have no doubts. Anyone who doubts is like a wave of the sea, driven and tossed by the wind. 7 Such a man should not expect to get anything from the Lord. 8 He's half-hearted—wavering in everything he does.

9 A lowly Christian should feel proud of his high position, 10 and a rich man of his lowliness, because he will pass away *like a flower in the grass.* 11 The sun comes up with a burning heat and *dries up the grass; the flower in it drops off,*[1] and its beauty is gone. That's how the rich man will fade away in what he undertakes.

Our Desires Tempt Us

12 *Blessed is* the man *who endures patiently* when he is tested. 13 When he passes the test, *he will get the crown of life*[2] God promised those who love Him. When you're tempted, don't say, "God is tempting me." God can't be tempted to do wrong, and He doesn't tempt anyone. 14 Everyone's own desire tempts him, draws him away, and tries to trap him. 15 When desire conceives, it gives birth to sin, and when sin grows up, it gives birth to death.

God's Children

16 Don't make a mistake, my dear Christian friends. 17 Every gift is good, and everything given is perfect—it comes down from above, from the Father of lights, who doesn't, like the sun and the moon, move or by changing cast a shadow.

18 As He wanted it, He gave birth to us by the Word of truth so we would be the first and best of His creatures.

19 My dear fellow Christians, you should know this. Everyone should be quick to listen, slow to talk, slow to get angry. 20 An angry man doesn't do what's right before God. 21 So

[1] Is. 40:6-8
[2] Dan. 12:12; Zech. 6:14

K.J.V.

superfluity of naughtiness, and receive with meekness the engrafted word, which is able to save your souls. 22 But be ye doers of the word, and not hearers only, deceiving your own selves. 23 For if any be a hearer of the word, and not a doer, he is like unto a man beholding his natural face in a glass: 24 For he beholdeth himself, and goeth his way, and straightway forgetteth what manner of man he was. 25 But whoso looketh into the perfect law of liberty, and continueth *therein*, he being not a forgetful hearer, but a doer of the work, this man shall be blessed in his deed. 26 If any man among you seem to be religious, and bridleth not his tongue, but deceiveth his own heart, this man's religion *is* vain. 27 Pure religion and undefiled before God and the Father is this, To visit the fatherless and widows in their affliction, *and* to keep himself unspotted from the world.

2 My brethren, have not the faith of our Lord Jesus Christ, *the Lord* of glory, with respect of persons. 2 For if there come unto your assembly a man with a gold ring, in goodly apparel, and there come in also a poor man in vile raiment; 3 And ye have respect to him that weareth the gay clothing, and say unto him, Sit thou here in a good place; and say to the poor, Stand thou there, or sit here under my footstool: 4 Are ye not then partial in yourselves, and are become judges of evil thoughts? 5 Hearken, my beloved brethren, Hath not God chosen the poor of this world rich in faith, and heirs of the kingdom which he hath promised to them that love him? 6 But ye have despised the poor. Do not rich men oppress you, and draw you before the judgment seats? 7 Do not they blaspheme that worthy name by the which ye are called? 8 If ye fulfil the royal law according to the Scripture, Thou shalt love thy neighbour as thyself, ye do well: 9 But if ye have respect to persons, ye commit sin, and are convinced of the law as transgressors. 10 For whosoever shall keep the whole law, and yet offend in one *point*, he is guilty of all. 11 For he that said, Do not commit adultery, said also, Do not kill. Now if thou commit no adultery, yet if thou kill, thou art become a transgressor of the law. 12 So speak ye, and so do, as they that shall be judged by the law of liberty. 13 For he shall have judgment without mercy, that hath shewed no mercy; and mercy rejoiceth against judgment. 14 What *doth it* profit, my brethren, though a man say he hath faith, and have not works? can faith save him? 15 If a brother or sister be naked, and destitute of daily food, 16 And one of you say unto them, Depart in peace, be *ye* warmed and filled; notwithstanding ye give them not those things which are needful to the body; what *doth it* profit? 17 Even so faith, if it hath not works, is dead,

N.A.S.

that remains of wickedness, in humility receive the word implanted, which is able to save your souls. 22 But prove yourselves doers of the word, and not merely hearers who delude themselves. 23 For if any one is a hearer of the word and not a doer, he is like a man who looks at his natural face in a mirror; 24 for *once* he has looked at himself and gone away, he has immediately forgotten what kind of person he was. 25 But one who looks intently at the perfect law, the *law* of liberty, and abides by it, not having become a forgetful hearer but an effectual doer, this man shall be blessed in what he does. 26 If any one thinks himself to be religious, and yet does not bridle his tongue but deceives his *own* heart, this man's religion is worthless. 27 This is pure and undefiled religion in the sight of *our* God and Father, to visit orphans and widows in their distress, *and* to keep oneself unstained by the world.

2 My brethren, do not hold your faith in our glorious Lord Jesus Christ with *an attitude of* personal favoritism. 2 For if a man comes into your assembly with a gold ring and dressed in fine clothes, and there also comes in a poor man in dirty clothes, 3 and you pay special attention to the one who is wearing the fine clothes, and say, "You sit here in a good place," and you say to the poor man, "You stand over there, or sit down by my footstool"; 4 have you not made distinctions among yourselves, and become judges with evil motives? 5 Listen, my beloved brethren: did not God choose the poor of this world *to be* rich in faith, and heirs of the kingdom which He promised to those who love Him? 6 But you have dishonored the poor man. Is it not the rich who oppress you and personally drag you into court? 7 Do they not blaspheme the fair name by which you have been called? 8 If, however, you are fulfilling the royal law, according to the Scripture, "YOU SHALL LOVE YOUR NEIGHBOR AS YOURSELF," you are doing well. 9 But if you show partiality, you are committing sin *and* are convicted by the law as transgressors. 10 For whoever keeps the whole law and yet stumbles in one *point*, he has become guilty of all. 11 For He who said, "DO NOT COMMIT ADULTERY," also said, "DO NOT COMMIT MURDER." Now if you do not commit adultery, but do commit murder, you have become a transgressor of the law. 12 So speak and so act, as those who are to be judged by *the* law of liberty. 13 For judgment *will be* merciless to one who has shown no mercy; mercy triumphs over judgment.

14 What use is it, my brethren, if a man says he has faith, but he has no works? Can that faith save him? 15 If a brother or sister is without clothing and in need of daily food, 16 and one of you says to them, "Go in peace, be warmed and be filled"; and yet you do not give them what is necessary for *their* body; what use is that? 17 Even so faith, if it has no

WILLIAMS

thing impure and all the evils prevailing around you, and in humble spirit welcome the message which when rooted in your hearts is able to save your souls. 22 Keep on obeying this message; do not merely listen to it, and so deceive yourselves. 23 Because if anyone merely listens to the message without obeying it, he is like a man who looks in a mirror at his own face, 24 for he looks and then goes off and at once forgets how he looked. 25 But the man who looks at the flawless law that makes men free, and keeps on looking, proving himself to be, not a forgetful hearer but an actual doer of what it requires, will be blessed in what he does. 26 If anyone thinks he is religious, and does not bridle his tongue, but deceives himself, his religious worship is worthless. 27 A religious worship that is pure and stainless in the sight of God the Father is this: To look after orphans and widows in their trouble, and to keep one's own self unstained by the world.

2 *Christians not to practice partiality; dead and living faith contrasted; Christians urged to show their faith by doing good*

My brothers, stop trying to maintain your faith in our Lord Jesus Christ, the glorious presence of God on earth, along with acts of partiality to certain ones. 2 For if a man with a gold ring, dressed in fine clothes, comes to your meeting, and at the same time a poor man clad in dirty clothes, 3 and you pay special attention to the man who wears the fine clothes, and say to him, "Sit here in this fine place," and say to the poor man, "Stand up, or sit there on the floor at my feet," 4 do you not make improper distinctions among yourselves and prove to be critics with evil motives? 5 Listen, my dearly loved brothers. Has not God chosen the poor of the world to be rich in faith and to possess the kingdom which He promised to those who love Him? 6 But you, in contrast, have humiliated the poor man. Are not the rich men those who oppress you and drag you to court? 7 Are not they the ones who scoff at the beautiful name you bear? 8 But if you really observe the law of the King in accordance with the Scripture, "You must love your neighbor as you do yourself," you are doing right; 9 but if you show partiality, you are committing sin, because you are convicted by the law as lawbreakers. 10 For whoever obeys the whole law, except to slip in a single instance, is guilty of breaking it all. 11 For He who said, "You must not commit adultery," also said, "You must not commit murder." Now if you do not commit adultery but you do commit murder, you are just the same a lawbreaker. 12 You must continue talking and acting like people who are to be judged by the law that treats them as free. 13 For merciless judgment will be the portion of the merciless man; yet mercy will triumph over judgment. 14 My brothers, what good is there in a man's saying that he has faith, if he has no good deeds to prove it? Such faith cannot save him, can it? 15 If some brother or sister is thinly clad and has no food for the day, 16 and one of you says to him, "Blessings on you, keep warm, eat until you have a plenty," without giving him the things that are needed for the body, what good does it do? 17 So faith by itself, if it has no deeds to back it up, is dead.

BECK

get rid of everything filthy and every breaking out of wickedness, and with a gentle spirit welcome the Word that's planted in you and can save your souls.

22 Always do what the Word says; don't merely listen to it and so deceive yourselves. 23 If anyone listens to the Word but doesn't do what it says, he's like a man who in a mirror sees the face he was born with. 24 He looks at himself, goes away, and immediately forgets what he looked like. 25 But if you look into God's perfect Word, which makes us free, and are loyal to it, if you don't merely listen and forget but do what it says, you'll be happy as you do it. 26 Someone may think he's religious, but if he doesn't control his tongue, he's deceiving himself—his religion is worthless. 27 Your way of worshiping is pure and stainless before God the Father if you look after orphans and widows in their troubles and keep yourself unspotted by the world.

Don't Prefer the Rich

2 My fellow Christians, believing as you do in Jesus Christ, our Lord of glory, don't prefer one person to another. 2 If a man wearing gold rings and fine clothes comes into your meeting and a poor man in dirty clothes also comes in 3 and you give special attention to the one wearing fine clothes and say, "Please take this seat," but you say to the poor man, "Stand there," or "Sit here by my footstool"—4 haven't you contradicted yourselves and become men who are wrong in their judgment? 5 Listen, my dear fellow Christians, didn't God choose those who are poor in the world to be rich in faith and inherit the kingdom He promised those who love Him? 6 But you have insulted the poor man. Don't the rich oppress you and drag you into court? 7 Don't they slander the beautiful name by which you were called the Lord's own? 8 If you really do everything the royal law demands, as it is written, *Love your neighbor like yourself*,[3] you're doing right. 9 But if you prefer one to another, you're sinning, and the Law convicts you of sin.

Keep the Whole Law

10 If you keep the whole Law but fail in one point, you're guilty of breaking all of it. 11 The One who said, *Don't commit adultery*, also said, *Don't kill*. If you *don't commit adultery* but you *kill*,[4] you're a lawbreaker. 12 Talk and act as people who are going to be judged by the Law that brings liberty. 13 Anyone who shows no mercy will be judged without mercy. Mercy triumphs over judgment.

Faith Is Active

14 What good does it do, my fellow Christians, if you say you have faith but don't have any works? Can such a faith save you? 15 If a Christian man or woman doesn't have clothes or daily food 16 and one of you tells them, "Good-by, keep warm, and eat heartily," but you don't give them what the body needs, what good does it do? 17 So faith by itself, if it doesn't have any works, is dead.

[3] Lev. 19:18
[4] Ex. 20:13-14; Deut. 5:17-18

K.J.V.

being alone. 18 Yea, a man may say, Thou hast faith, and I have works: shew me thy faith without thy works, and I will shew thee my faith by my works. 19 Thou believest that there is one God; thou doest well: the devils also believe, and tremble. 20 But wilt thou know, O vain man, that faith without works is dead? 21 Was not Abraham our father justified by works, when he had offered Isaac his son upon the altar? 22 Seest thou how faith wrought with his works, and by works was faith made perfect? 23 And the Scripture was fulfilled which saith, Abraham believed God, and it was imputed unto him for righteousness: and he was called the Friend of God. 24 Ye see then how that by works a man is justified, and not by faith only. 25 Likewise also was not Rahab the harlot justified by works, when she had received the messengers, and had sent *them* out another way? 26 For as the body without the spirit is dead, so faith without works is dead also.

3 My brethren, be not many masters, knowing that we shall receive the greater condemnation. 2 For in many things we offend all. If any man offend not in word, the same *is* a perfect man, *and* able also to bridle the whole body. 3 Behold, we put bits in the horses' mouths, that they may obey us; and we turn about their whole body. 4 Behold also the ships, which though *they be* so great, and *are* driven of fierce winds, yet are they turned about with a very small helm, whithersoever the governor listeth. 5 Even so the tongue is a little memoer, and boasteth great things. Behold, how great a matter a little fire kindleth! 6 And the tongue *is* a fire, a world of iniquity: so is the tongue among our members, that it defileth the whole body, and setteth on fire the course of nature; and it is set on fire of hell. 7 For every kind of beasts, and of birds, and of serpents, and of things in the sea, is tamed, and hath been tamed of mankind: 8 But the tongue can no man tame; *it is* an unruly evil, full of deadly poison. 9 Therewith bless we God, even the Father; and therewith curse we men, which are made after the similitude of God. 10 Out of the same mouth proceedeth blessing and cursing. My brethren, these things ought not so to be. 11 Doth a fountain send forth at the same place sweet *water* and bitter? 12 Can the fig tree, my brethren, bear olive berries? either a vine, figs? so *can* no fountain both yield salt water and fresh. 13 Who *is* a wise man and endued with knowledge among you? let him shew out of a good conversation his works with meekness of wisdom. 14 But if ye have bitter envying and strife in your hearts, glory not, and lie not against the truth. 15 This wisdom descendeth not from above, but *is* earthly, sensual, devilish. 16 For where envying and strife *is*, there *is* confusion and every evil work. 17 But the wisdom that is from above is first pure, then peaceable, gentle, *and* easy to be entreated, full of mercy and good fruits, without

N.A.S.

works, is dead, *being* by itself. 18 But some one may *well* say, "You have faith, and I have works; show me your faith without the works, and I will show you my faith by my works." 19 You believe that *a*God is one. You do well; the demons also believe, and shudder. 20 But are you willing to recognize, you foolish fellow, that faith without works is useless? 21 Was not Abraham our father justified by works, when he offered up Isaac his son on the altar? 22 You see that faith was working with his works, and as a result of the works, faith was perfected; 23 and the Scripture was fulfilled which says, "AND ABRAHAM BELIEVED GOD, AND IT WAS RECKONED TO HIM AS RIGHTEOUSNESS," and he was called the friend of God. 24 You see that a man is justified by works, and not by faith alone. 25 And in the same way was not Rahab the harlot also justified by works, when she received the messengers and sent them out by another way? 26 For just as the body without *the* spirit is dead, so also faith without works is dead.

3 Let not many *of you* become teachers, my brethren, knowing that as such we shall incur a stricter judgment. 2 For we all stumble in many *ways*. If any one does not stumble in what he says, he is a perfect man, able to bridle the whole body as well. 3 Now if we put the bits into the horses' mouths so that they may obey us, we direct their entire body as well. 4 Behold, the ships also, though they are so great and are driven by strong winds, are still directed by a very small rudder, wherever the inclination of the pilot desires. 5 So also the tongue is a small part of the body, and *yet* it boasts of great things. Behold, how great a forest is set aflame by such a small fire! 6 And the tongue is a fire, the *very* world of iniquity; the tongue is set among our members as that which defiles the entire body, and sets on fire the course of *our* life, and is set on fire by hell. 7 For every species of beasts and birds, of reptiles and creatures of the sea, is tamed, and has been tamed by the human race. 8 But no one can tame the tongue; *it is* a restless evil *and* full of deadly poison. 9 With it we bless *our* Lord and Father; and with it we curse men, who have been made in the likeness of God; 10 from the same mouth come *both* blessing and cursing. My brethren, these things ought not to be this way. 11 Does a fountain send out from the same opening *both* fresh and bitter *water*? 12 Can a fig tree, my brethren, produce olives, or a vine produce figs? Neither *can* salt water produce fresh.

13 Who among you is wise and understanding? Let him show by his good behavior his deeds in the gentleness of wisdom. 14 But if you have bitter jealousy and selfish ambition in your heart, do not be arrogant and *so* lie against the truth. 15 This wisdom is not that which comes down from above, but is earthly, natural, demonic. 16 For where jealousy and selfish ambition exist, there is disorder and every evil thing. 17 But the wisdom from above is first pure, then peaceable, gentle, reasonable, full of mercy and good fruits, unwavering,

[a] Or, *there is one God.*

WILLIAMS

18 But someone may say, "You have faith, and I have good deeds. Show me your faith without any good deeds, but I will show you mine by my good deeds." 19 Do you believe in one God? Very well; the demons, too, believe that, and shudder. 20 But, O senseless man, are you willing to learn that faith without good deeds is worthless? 21 Was not our forefather Abraham shown to be upright[a] by his good deeds, namely, by offering Isaac his son upon the altar? 22 You see that faith co-operated with his good deeds, and by his good deeds faith was made complete; 23 and so the Scripture was fulfilled which says, "Abraham put his faith in God, and it was credited to him for uprightness, and he was called God's friend." 24 You see that a man is shown to be upright by his good deeds, and not merely by his faith. 25 Was not even Rahab the prostitute shown to be upright by her good deeds, namely, by entertaining the scouts and sending them off by a different road? 26 Just as the body without the spirit is dead, so faith without good deeds is dead.

3 The need of bridling the tongue; true wisdom shows itself in noble character and living

Many of you, my brothers, should avoid becoming teachers, because you know that we teachers are going to be judged with stricter judgment than other people. 2 For we all make many a slip. If anyone never slips in speech, he is a man of maturity; he can control his whole body too. 3 If we put bridles into horses' mouths to make them obey us, we can guide their whole bodies, too. 4 Look at ships, too; though great and driven by violent winds, they are steered with a tiny rudder wherever the pilot pleases. 5 So the tongue, too, is a little organ but can boast of great achievements. See how a spark, ever so tiny can set a vast forest on fire! 6 And the tongue is a fire, and takes its place among the parts of our bodies as a world of evil; it soils the whole body and sets on fire the circle[a] of man's nature, and itself is set on fire by hell. 7 For every kind of beasts and birds, of reptiles and sea animals, can be, or have been, tamed by man; 8 but the tongue no human being can tame. It is an evil incapable of being quieted, full of deadly poison. 9 With it we bless the Lord and Father, and with it we curse men who are made in God's likeness. 10 Out of the same mouth flow blessing and cursing! It ought not to be like this, my brothers. 11 A fountain cannot pour from the same opening fresh and brackish water, can it? 12 A fig tree, my brothers, cannot bear olives, or a grape vine figs, can it? And a salt spring cannot furnish fresh water.

13 Who among you is wise and intelligent? Let him show by his noble living that his good deeds are done in humility, which wisdom prompts. 14 But if you cherish bitter jealousy and rivalry in your hearts, stop being proud of it and stop being false to the standard of truth. 15 This is not the kind of wisdom that comes down from above; no, it is earthly, human, demoniacal. 16 For wherever jealousy and rivalry exist, there will be confusion and all sorts of evil practices. 17 The wisdom that is from above is first pure, then peaceable, gentle, willing to yield, full of compassion and good

[a] Grk., justified.
[a] Grk., wheel.

BECK

18 But somebody will say, "You have faith, and I have works." Prove to me you have faith without any works, and by my works I'll prove to you I have faith. You believe there is one God.[5] That's fine! 19 The devils believe it too— and shudder.

20 Do you want proof, you foolish fellow, that faith without works is dead? 21 Didn't our father Abraham get to be righteous* on the basis of works when he offered his son Isaac on the altar?[6] 22 You see his faith was active with works and by works reached its goal. 23 And what is written came true: Abraham believed God and so was counted righteous[7] and was called God's friend.[8] 24 You see a man gets to be righteous* on the basis of his works and not by faith alone. 25 The same is true of the prostitute Rahab. Didn't she get to be righteous* on the basis of works when she welcomed the messengers and sent them away on a different road? 26 Just as the body without the spirit is dead, so faith without works is dead.

Control Your Tongue

3 Not many of you should become teachers, my fellow Christians, because you know we who teach will be judged more severely.

2 All of us sin much. If anyone doesn't sin in what he says, he's a perfect man who can control his whole body. 3 If we put bits into the mouths of horses to make them obey us, we direct their whole bodies. 4 Look at the ships —so big and driven by strong winds; but a very small rudder steers a ship anywhere the pilot wants it to go. 5 So the tongue is a small organ but can boast of big things.

6 You know how just a spark will set a large forest on fire. The tongue is a fire, a world of wrong! Set among the parts of our body, the tongue soils the whole body and enflames the course of life as it gets its fire from hell. 7 A human being can tame and has tamed all kinds of animals, birds, reptiles, and creatures in the sea. 8 But nobody can tame the tongue—a restless evil, full of deadly poison.

9 We praise the Lord and Father with our tongue and with it curse other people, who once were made like God.[9] 10 Praise and cursing come from the same mouth. We mustn't do that, my fellow Christians. 11 Does a spring from the same opening pour fresh and bitter water? 12 My fellow Christians, can a fig tree produce olives? Or a grapevine figs? Neither can a salt spring produce fresh water.

Wisdom from Above

13 Is anyone of you wise and intelligent? In a gentle spirit of wisdom show by a good life what you can do. 14 But if you feel a bitter jealousy and a selfish ambition in your hearts, don't brag and lie against the truth. 15 Such wisdom doesn't come from above, but from this earth, from this life, and from the devil. 16 Where there is such jealousy and selfishness, there is confusion and every kind of evil.

17 The wisdom that comes from above is first of all pure, then peaceful, gentle, willing to obey, full of mercy and good works, without doubts or

* See note at Rom. 3:20.
[5] Deut. 6:4; Zech. 14:9; Mal. 2:10
[6] Gen. 22:2, 9
[7] Gen. 15:6
[8] Is. 41:8; 2 Chron. 20:7
[9] Gen. 1:27; 5:1

K.J.V.

partiality, and without hypocrisy. 18And the fruit of righteousness is sown in peace of them that make peace.

4 From whence *come* wars and fightings among you? *come they* not hence, *even* of your lusts that war in your members? 2 Ye lust, and have not: ye kill, and desire to have, and cannot obtain: ye fight and war, yet ye have not, because ye ask not. 3 Ye ask, and receive not, because ye ask amiss, that ye may consume *it* upon your lusts. 4 Ye adulterers and adulteresses, know ye not that the friendship of the world is enmity with God? whosoever therefore will be a friend of the world is the enemy of God. 5 Do ye think that the Scripture saith in vain, The spirit that dwelleth in us lusteth to envy? 6 But he giveth more grace. Wherefore he saith, God resisteth the proud, but giveth grace unto the humble. 7 Submit yourselves therefore to God. Resist the devil, and he will flee from you. 8 Draw nigh to God, and he will draw nigh to you. Cleanse *your* hands, *ye* sinners; and purify *your* hearts, ye doubleminded. 9 Be afflicted, and mourn, and weep: let your laughter be turned to mourning, and *your* joy to heaviness. 10 Humble yourselves in the sight of the Lord, and he shall lift you up. 11 Speak not evil one of another, brethren. He that speaketh evil of *his* brother, and judgeth his brother, speaketh evil of the law, and judgeth the law: but if thou judge the law, thou art not a doer of the law, but a judge. 12 There is one lawgiver, who is able to save and to destroy: who art thou that judgest another? 13 Go to now, ye that say, To day or to morrow we will go into such a city, and continue there a year, and buy and sell, and get gain: 14 Whereas ye know not what *shall be* on the morrow. For what *is* your life? It is even a vapour, that appeareth for a little time, and then vanisheth away. 15 For that ye *ought* to say, If the Lord will, we shall live, and do this, or that. 16 But now ye rejoice in your boastings: all such rejoicing is evil. 17 Therefore to him that knoweth to do good, and doeth *it* not, to him it is sin.

5 Go to now, *ye* rich men, weep and howl for your miseries that shall come upon *you*. 2 Your riches are corrupted, and your garments

N.A.S.

without hypocrisy. 18And the seed whose fruit is righteousness is sown in peace by those who make peace.

4 What is the source of quarrels and conflicts among you? Is not the source your pleasures that wage war in your members? 2 You lust and do not have; *so* you commit murder. And you are envious and cannot obtain; *so* you fight and quarrel. You do not have because you do not ask. 3 You ask and do not receive, because you ask with wrong motives, so that you may spend *it* on your pleasures. 4 You adulteresses, do you not know that friendship with the world is hostility toward God? Therefore whoever wishes to be a friend of the world makes himself an enemy of God. 5 Or do you think that the Scripture speaks to no purpose: "[a]He jealously desires the spirit which He has made to dwell in us"? 6 But He gives a greater grace. Therefore *it* says, "GOD IS OPPOSED TO THE PROUD, BUT GIVES GRACE TO THE HUMBLE." 7 Submit therefore to God. Resist the devil and he will flee from you. 8 Draw near to God and He will draw near to you. Cleanse your hands, you sinners; and purify your hearts, you doubleminded. 9 Be miserable and mourn and weep: let your laughter be turned into mourning, and your joy to gloom. 10 Humble yourselves in the presence of the Lord, and He will exalt you.

11 Do not speak against one another, brethren. He who speaks against a brother, or judges his brother, speaks against the law, and judges the law; but if you judge the law, you are not a doer of the law, but a judge *of it*. 12 There is *only* one Lawgiver and Judge, the One who is able to save and to destroy; but who are you who judges your neighbor?

13 Come now, you who say, "Today or tomorrow, we shall go to such and such a city, and spend a year there and engage in business and make a profit." 14 Yet you do not know what your life will be like tomorrow. You are *just* a vapor that appears for a little while and then vanishes away. 15 Instead, *you ought* to say, "If the Lord wills, we shall live and also do this or that." 16 But as it is, you boast in your arrogance; all such boasting is evil. 17 Therefore, to one who knows *the* right thing to do, and does not do it, to him it is sin.

5 Come now, you rich, weep and howl for your miseries which are coming upon you. 2 Your riches have rotted and your garments

[a] Or, *The Spirit which He has made to dwell in us jealously desires* us.

WILLIAMS

deeds, free from doubts and insincerity. 18 The harvest of uprightness is grown from the seed of peace by those who are peacemakers.

4 *Evil desires the real cause of strife and war; the friendship of the world means enmity with God; evil-speaking to be stopped; life uncertain*

What causes wars and quarrels among you? Is it not your different desires which are ever at war within your bodies? [a] You desire things and cannot have them, and so you commit murder. 2 You covet things, but cannot acquire them, and so you quarrel and fight. You do not have them, because you do not ask for them. 3 You ask and fail to get them, because you ask with evil, selfish motives, to spend them on your pleasures.

4 You faithless wives! Do you not know that the friendship of the world means enmity with God? So whoever wants to be a friend to the world puts himself down as an enemy to God. 5 Or, do you think that the Scripture means nothing when it says, "He jealously yearns for the Spirit that He causes to dwell in your hearts"? 6 But He gives a greater spiritual blessing. He says, "God opposes haughty people but blesses humble people." 7 So then, submit to God. Resist the devil and he will fly from you. 8 Draw near to God and He will draw near to you. Get your hands clean, you sinners. Get your hearts purified, you double-minded. 9 Be miserable, mourn, and weep aloud. Let your laughter be turned to grief and your joy to gloom. 10 Humble yourselves before the Lord, and He will lift you high.

11 Stop talking against one another, brothers. Whoever is in the habit of talking against a brother or of criticizing his brother is criticizing and condemning the law. But if you are in the habit of criticizing the law, you are not a practicer but a critic of the law. 12 There is but one Lawgiver and Judge, the One who has the power to save and to destroy; then who are you that you presume to judge your brother? 13 Come now, you who say, "Today or tomorrow we are going to such and such a city and stay a year, go into business and make money," 14 although you do not have the slightest knowledge of tomorrow. What is the nature of your life? It is really nothing but a mist which appears for a little while and then disappears. 15 Instead, you ought to say, "If the Lord is willing, we shall live and do this or that." 16 But, as it is, you boast of your proud pretensions. All such boasting is wicked. 17 So when a man knows what is right but does not do it, he is guilty of sin.

5 *Tainted money a curse; the Lord's return should inspire to the patience of the prophets, the endurance of Job; telling the truth without an oath; prayer, praise, confession; the happy soul-winner*

Come now, you rich people, weep aloud and howl over the miseries that are sure to overtake you. 2 Your wealth has rotted, your clothes are

BECK

hypocrisy. 18 When we work for peace, we sow in peace a seed that produces righteousness.

Don't Love the World

4 Why is there fighting and quarreling among you? Isn't it because your cravings for pleasure are fighting in your bodies? 2 You want something but don't get it, and so you kill. And you try to get something but you can't lay your hands on it, and so you quarrel and fight. You don't get things because you don't ask for them. 3 Or you ask for something but don't get it because you want it for a wrong purpose—to spend it on your pleasures.

4 Adulterous people, don't you know that to love the world is to hate God? If you want to be a friend of the world, you make yourself an enemy of God. 5 Or do you think the statement means nothing: "The Spirit whom He caused to live in us yearns for us even with jealousy"? 6 But *He gives a* greater *blessing.* And so it says, *God opposes the proud but gives a blessing to the humble.*[10] 7 Then submit to God. Resist the devil and he will run away from you. 8 Come close to God, and He will come close to you. Wash your hands, you sinners, and purify your hearts, you doubters. 9 Be miserable, mourn, and cry. Turn your laughter into mourning and your joy into gloom. 10 Humble yourselves before the Lord, and He will honor you.

Don't Talk Against One Another

11 Stop talking against one another, my fellow Christians. Anyone who talks against his fellow Christian or condemns him talks against the Law and condemns the Law. If you condemn the Law, you're not doing what it says but you're being its judge. 12 There's only one Lawgiver and Judge. He can save and destroy. And who are you to judge your neighbor?

"If the Lord Is Willing"

13 Come now, you who say, "Today or tomorrow we'll go into this city, stay there a year, do business, and make money." 14 You don't know about tomorrow. What is your life? You're a mist, seen for a little while, then vanishing. 15 You should say: "If the Lord is willing, we'll live and do this or that." 16 But instead you brag and boast. All such boasting is wrong.

17 If you know what's right but don't do it, you're sinning.

Woe to the Rich

5 Come now, you rich people, cry and howl over the miseries that are coming to you. 2 Your riches are rotten, your clothes are eaten

[a] Lit., *in your members, parts.*   [10] Prov. 3:34

K.J.V.

are motheaten. 3 Your gold and silver is cankered; and the rust of them shall be a witness against you, and shall eat your flesh as it were fire. Ye have heaped treasure together for the last days. 4 Behold, the hire of the labourers who have reaped down your fields, which is of you kept back by fraud, crieth: and the cries of them which have reaped are entered into the ears of the Lord of Sabaoth. 5 Ye have lived in pleasure on the earth, and been wanton; ye have nourished your hearts, as in a day of slaughter. 6 Ye have condemned *and* killed the just; *and* he doth not resist you. 7 Be patient therefore, brethren, unto the coming of the Lord. Behold, the husbandman waiteth for the precious fruit of the earth, and hath long patience for it, until he receive the early and latter rain. 8 Be ye also patient; stablish your hearts: for the coming of the Lord draweth nigh. 9 Grudge not one against another, brethren, lest ye be condemned: behold, the judge standeth before the door. 10 Take, my brethren, the prophets, who have spoken in the name of the Lord, for an example of suffering affliction, and of patience. 11 Behold, we count them happy which endure. Ye have heard of the patience of Job, and have seen the end of the Lord; that the Lord is very pitiful, and of tender mercy. 12 But above all things, my brethren, swear not, neither by heaven, neither by the earth, neither by any other oath: but let your yea be yea; and *your* nay, nay; lest ye fall into condemnation. 13 Is any among you afflicted? let him pray. Is any merry? let him sing psalms. 14 Is any sick among you? let him call for the elders of the church; and let them pray over him, anointing him with oil in the name of the Lord: 15 And the prayer of faith shall save the sick, and the Lord shall raise him up; and if he have committed sins, they shall be forgiven him. 16 Confess *your* faults one to another, and pray one for another, that ye may be healed. The effectual fervent prayer of a righteous man availeth much. 17 Elias was a man subject to like passions as we are, and he prayed earnestly that it might not rain: and it rained not on the earth by the space of three years and six months. 18 And he prayed again, and the heaven gave rain, and the earth brought forth her fruit. 19 Brethren, if any of you do err from the truth, and one convert him; 20 Let him know, that he which converteth the sinner from the error of his way shall save a soul from death, and shall hide a multitude of sins.

N.A.S.

have become moth-eaten. 3 Your gold and your silver have rusted; and their rust will be a witness against you and will consume your flesh like fire. It is in the Last Days that you have stored up your treasure! 4 Behold, the pay of the laborers who mowed your fields, *and* which has been withheld by you, cries out *against you;* and the outcry of those who did the harvesting has reached the ears of the Lord of Sabaoth. 5 You have lived luxuriously on the earth and led a life of wanton pleasure; you have fattened your hearts in a day of slaughter. 6 You have condemned and put to death the righteous *man;* he does not resist you.

7 Be patient, therefore, brethren, until the coming of the Lord. Behold, the farmer waits for the precious produce of the soil, being patient about it, until it gets the early and late rains. 8 You too be patient; strengthen your hearts, for the coming of the Lord is at hand. 9 Do not complain, brethren, against one another, that you yourselves may not be judged; behold, the Judge is standing right at the door. 10 As an example, brethren, of suffering and patience, take the prophets who spoke in the name of the Lord. 11 Behold, we count those blessed who endured. You have heard of the endurance of Job and have seen the outcome of the Lord's dealings, that the Lord is full of compassion and *is* merciful.

12 But above all, my brethren, do not swear, either by heaven or by earth or with any other oath; but let your yes be yes, and your no, no; so that you may not fall under judgment.

13 Is anyone among you suffering? Let him pray. Is anyone cheerful? Let him sing praises. 14 Is anyone among you sick? Let him call for the elders of the church, and let them pray over him, anointing him with oil in the name of the Lord; 15 and the prayer offered in faith will ªrestore the one who is sick, and the Lord will raise him up, and if he has committed sins, they will be forgiven him. 16 Therefore, confess your sins to one another, and pray for one another, so that you may be healed. The effective prayer of a righteous man can accomplish much. 17 Elijah was a man with a nature like ours, and he prayed earnestly that it might not rain; and it did not rain on the earth for three years and six months. 18 And he prayed again, and the sky poured rain, and the earth produced its fruit.

19 My brethren, if any among you strays from the truth, and one turns him back; 20 let him know that he who turns a sinner from the error of his way will save his soul from death, and will cover a multitude of sins.

[a] Or, *save.*

WILLIAMS

moth-eaten, 3 your gold and silver have rusted, and their rust will testify against you and devour your flesh like fire. You have stored up these things for the last days. 4 See! the wages that you have kept back from the laborers who reaped your fields are crying aloud, and the cries of the reapers have reached the ears of the Lord of hosts. 5 Here on earth you have lived in luxury and self-indulgence; you have fattened your hearts for the day of slaughter. 6 You have condemned and murdered the upright man; he offers no resistance.

7 So be patient, brothers, until the coming of the Lord. See how the farmer keeps on waiting and waiting for the precious crop from his land; how he keeps up his patience over it until he gets the early and the late rains. 8 You must be patient, too; you must put iron into your hearts, because the coming of the Lord is close at hand. 9 Stop muttering against one another, brothers, so as to keep from being judged yourselves. The Judge is standing at the very door. 10 As an example of ill-treatment and patience, brothers, take the prophets, who spoke in the name of the Lord. 11 See how we call those who thus endured happy! You have heard how patiently Job endured and have seen how the Lord finally blessed him, because the Lord is tenderhearted and merciful.

12 Above all, my brothers, stop swearing, either by heaven or by the earth, or by anything else. Let your "Yes" mean Yes, and your "No," No, so as to keep from falling under condemnation.

13 Is any one of you suffering ill-treatment? He should keep on praying. Is anyone in a happy mood? He should keep on singing praise to God. 14 Is anyone sick among you? He should call in the elders of the church, and they should pray over him, and anoint him with oil in the name of the Lord, 15 and the prayer that is offered in faith will save the sick man; the Lord will raise him to health, and if he has committed sins, he will be forgiven. 16 So practice confessing your sins to one another, and praying for one another, that you may be cured. An upright man's prayer, when it keeps at work, is very powerful. 17 Elijah was a man with feelings just like ours, and yet he earnestly prayed for it not to rain, and it did not rain on the land for three years and six months. 18 Then again he prayed, and the heavens yielded rain and the earth produced its crops.

19 My brothers, if any one of you has wandered away from the truth, and someone brings him back, 20 you may be sure that whoever brings a sinner back from his evil ways will save the man's soul from death, and cover up a multitude of sins.

BECK

by moths, 3 your gold and silver are tarnished, and their tarnish will be evidence against you and will *eat* your flesh like *fire*. You have *piled up treasures*[11] in these last days. 4 But now *the wages you never paid the men*[12] who reaped your fields cry out. And the *groans* of those who cut the grain *have come to the ears of the Lord of armies*.[13] 5 You have lived here on earth in luxuries and pleasures. You have fattened yourselves for *the day of slaughter*.[14] 6 You have condemned and murdered the righteous man— he doesn't resist you.

Be Patient

7 Be patient, fellow Christians, till the Lord comes. See how the farmer looks for the precious crop on the ground and waits patiently for it to get *the fall and the spring rains*.[15] 8 You, too, be patient, and keep your courage because the Lord will soon be here. 9 Don't blame your troubles on one another, fellow Christians, or you will be judged. You know, the Judge is standing at the door.

10 As your example of patiently suffering wrong, fellow Christians, take the prophets who spoke in the Lord's name. 11 Remember, *we call those happy who endured*.[16] You heard how Job endured, and you saw how the Lord finally treated him because *the Lord is tenderhearted and merciful*.[17]

Don't Swear

12 Above all things, my fellow Christians, don't swear by heaven or by the earth or any other oath, but let your yes be just yes and your no be no, or you will be condemned for it.

The Power of Prayer

13 Is anyone of you suffering? Pray! Are you happy? Sing a song of praise! 14 Is anyone of you sick? Call the elders of the church to pray over you, pouring on oil in the Lord's name. 15 And if you believe, your prayer will make the sick person well. The Lord will make him healthy, and if he feels guilty of sins, he will be forgiven. 16 Confess your sins to one another, and pray for one another to be healed.

A good man can do much by praying vigorously. 17 Elijah was a man just like us, and he prayed earnestly there should be no rain, and no rain fell on the ground for three years and six months. 18 Then he prayed again, and heaven sent rain, and the ground produced its crops.

Bring Back the Lost

19 My fellow Christians, if one of you wanders away from the truth and someone brings him back, 20 you should know that whoever brings a sinner back from his wrong way will save his soul from death and *cover many sins*.[18]

[11] Ps. 21:9; Prov. 16:27
[12] Mal. 3:5
[13] Ex. 2:23; 3:9; Lev. 19:13; Ps. 18:6; 2 Sam. 22:7; Is. 5:9
[14] Jer. 12:3
[15] Deut. 11:14
[16] Dan. 12:12
[17] Ex. 34:6; Ps. 86:15; 103:8; 111:4; 112:4; 145:8; Joel 2:13; Jonah 4:2; Neh. 9:17, 31; 2 Chron. 30:9
[18] Prov. 10:12

K.J.V.

THE FIRST
EPISTLE GENERAL
OF
PETER

1 Peter, an apostle of Jesus Christ, to the strangers scattered throughout Pontus, Galatia, Cappadocia, Asia, and Bithynia, 2 Elect according to the foreknowledge of God the Father, through sanctification of the Spirit, unto obedience and sprinkling of the blood of Jesus Christ: Grace unto you, and peace, be multiplied. 3 Blessed *be* the God and Father of our Lord Jesus Christ, which according to his abundant mercy hath begotten us again unto a lively hope by the resurrection of Jesus Christ from the dead, 4 To an inheritance incorruptible, and undefiled. and that fadeth not away, reserved in heaven for you, 5 Who are kept by the power of God through faith unto salvation ready to be revealed in the last time. 6 Wherein ye greatly rejoice, though now for a season, if need be, ye are in heaviness through manifold temptations: 7 That the trial of your faith, being much more precious than of gold that perisheth, though it be tried with fire, might be found unto praise and honour and glory at the appearing of Jesus Christ: 8 Whom having not seen, ye love; in whom, though now ye see *him* not, yet believing, ye rejoice with joy unspeakable and full of glory: 9 Receiving the end of your faith, *even* the salvation of *your* souls. 10 Of which salvation the prophets have inquired and searched diligently, who prophesied of the grace *that should come* unto you: 11 Searching what, or what manner of time the Spirit of Christ which was in them did signify, when it testified beforehand the sufferings of Christ, and the glory that should follow. 12 Unto whom it was revealed, that not unto themselves, but unto us they did minister the things, which are now reported unto you by them that have preached the gospel unto you with the Holy Ghost sent down from heaven; which things the angels desire to look into. 13 Wherefore gird up the loins of your mind, be sober, and hope to the end for the grace that is to be brought unto you at the revelation of Jesus Christ; 14 As obedient children, not fashioning yourselves according to the former lusts in your ignorance: 15 But as he

N.A.S.

THE FIRST EPISTLE OF
PETER

1 Peter, an apostle of Jesus Christ, to those who reside as aliens, scattered throughout Pontus, Galatia, Cappadocia, Asia, and Bithynia, who are chosen 2 according to the foreknowledge of God the Father, by the sanctifying work of the Spirit, that you may obey Jesus Christ and be sprinkled with His blood: May grace and peace be multiplied to you. 3 Blessed be the God and Father of our Lord Jesus Christ, who according to His great mercy has caused us to be born again to a living hope through the resurrection of Jesus Christ from the dead, 4 to *obtain* an inheritance *which is* imperishable and undefiled and will not fade away, reserved in heaven for you, 5 who are protected by the power of God through faith for a salvation ready to be revealed in the last time. 6 In this you greatly rejoice, even though now for a little while, if necessary, you have been distressed by various trials, 7 that the proof of your faith, *being* more precious than gold which is perishable, even though tested by fire, may be found to result in praise and glory and honor at the revelation of Jesus Christ; 8 and though you have not seen Him, you love Him, and though you do not see Him now, but believe in Him, you greatly rejoice with joy inexpressible and full of glory, 9 obtaining as the outcome of your faith the salvation of "your souls. 10 As to this salvation, the prophets who prophesied of the grace that *would come* to you made careful search and inquiry, 11 seeking to know what person or time the Spirit of Christ within them was indicating as He predicted the sufferings of Christ and the glories to follow. 12 It was revealed to them that they were not serving themselves but you in these things which now have been announced to you through those who preached the gospel to you by the Holy Spirit sent from heaven,—things into which angels long to look. 13 Therefore, gird your minds for action, keep sober *in spirit,* fix your hope completely on the grace to be brought to you at the revelation of Jesus Christ. 14 As obedient children, do not be conformed to the former lusts *which were yours* in your ignorance, 15 but like

---

[a] Some ancient mss. omit, *your.*

FIRST PETER

THE FIRST LETTER OF

PETER

1 *He greets them; gives thanks for the hope of tomorrow, rejoices in the trials of today; prophets and angels interested in this salvation; as redeemed ones, we must live pure, obedient, consecrated lives and love one another*

Peter, an apostle of Jesus Christ, to the foreign-born[a] Jews who are scattered over Pontus, Galatia, Cappadocia, Asia, and Bithynia, 2 the people chosen in accordance with the foreknowledge of God the Father, by the consecration of the Spirit, to obey Jesus Christ and to be sprinkled with His blood: spiritual blessing and peace to you in increasing abundance.
3 Blessed be the God and Father of our Lord Jesus Christ! In accordance with His great mercy He has begotten us anew to an ever living hope through the resurrection of Jesus Christ from the dead; 4 yes, to an inheritance that is imperishable, unsullied, and unfading, which is kept in heaven for you 5 who are always guarded by the power of God through faith, in order that you may receive that final salvation which will be ready to be uncovered for you at the last time. 6 In such a hope keep on rejoicing, although for a little while you must be sorrow-stricken with various trials, 7 so that the genuineness of your faith, which is more precious than gold that perishes even after it is shown by the test of fire to be genuine, may result in your praise and glory and honor at the unveiling of Jesus Christ. 8 You must continue to love Him, although you have never seen Him, but because you do believe in Him, although you do not now see Him, you must continue to rejoice with an unutterable and triumphant joy, 9 because you will receive the goal of your faith, the ultimate salvation of your souls.
10 Even the prophets, who prophesied about the spiritual blessing meant for you, made careful investigations and persistent research about this salvation, 11 earnestly trying to find out the time, and the nature of the times, which the Spirit of the Christ within them pointed to, in foretelling the sufferings of the Christ and the glory that should follow them. 12 It was made known to them that they were serving not themselves but you, in their searching for these things that have already been told to you by those who through the Holy Spirit sent from heaven brought you the good news. The angels long to take a peep into these things.
13 Therefore, as a means of spiritual preparation, tighten up the belt about your minds, keep perfectly calm, keep your hope on the spiritual blessing to be conferred upon you at the unveiling of Jesus Christ. 14 As obedient children, stop molding your character by the evil desires you used to cherish when you did not know any better, 15 but in accordance with the

1 Peter, apostle of Jesus Christ, to the chosen people living scattered as strangers in Pontus, Galatia, Cappadocia, the province of Asia, and Bithynia, 2 chosen long ago by God the Father to be made holy by the Spirit, to obey Jesus Christ and be *sprinkled with His blood:*[1] God give *you more and more* love and *peace!*[2]

Christ Saves You

3 Let us praise the God and Father of our Lord Jesus Christ, who by raising Jesus Christ from the dead has in His great mercy given us a new birth so that we live and hope 4 for an inheritance that isn't destroyed or defiled and never fades away, as it is kept for you in heaven. 5 And you by believing are protected by God's power till you come to the salvation that is waiting to be revealed at the end of time. 6 This delights you, although now for a little while you may have had to suffer various trials. 7 Gold is tested by fire, and your faith, when it is tested, should be found to be much more precious than gold, which perishes. This is how you will have praise and glory and honor when Jesus Christ appears again.
8 You never saw Him, but you love Him. You don't see Him now, but you believe in Him. And a joy, unspeakable and wonderful, fills you with delight 9 as you get what by faith you're looking for—your salvation.
10 The prophets, who long ago wrote about what God's love would do for you, made a thorough search to learn all about this salvation. 11 They tried to find out whom and what time the Spirit of Christ in them was pointing out when He exactly predicted the sufferings of Christ and the glories that would follow. 12 God told them they were not serving themselves but you in these things. And now the Holy Spirit, sent from heaven, had men, telling you the good news, announce to you these things the angels long to look into.

Be Holy

13 Now, then, get mentally ready for action, keep a clear head, and feel perfectly sure of what God's love will give you when Jesus Christ appears. 14 Being children who know how to obey, don't live according to your lusts as you once did when you didn't know any better. 15 But get to be holy in all your ways, like the

[a] *The dispersion*—Jews scattered in other lands.

[1] Ex. 24:6, 8; Lev. 16:14-15
[2] Dan. 3:31; 6:26

K.J.V.

which hath called you is holy, so be ye holy in all manner of conversation; 16 Because it is written, Be ye holy; for I am holy. 17And if ye call on the Father, who without respect of persons judgeth according to every man's work, pass the time of your sojourning *here* in fear: 18 Forasmuch as ye know that ye were not redeemed with corruptible things, *as* silver and gold, from your vain conversation *received* by tradition from your fathers; 19 But with the precious blood of Christ, as of a lamb without blemish and without spot: 20 Who verily was foreordained before the foundation of the world, but was manifest in these last times for you, 21 Who by him do believe in God, that raised him up from the dead, and gave him glory; that your faith and hope might be in God. 22 Seeing ye have purified your souls in obeying the truth through the Spirit unto unfeigned love of the brethren, *see that ye* love one another with a pure heart fervently: 23 Being born again, not of corruptible seed, but of incorruptible, by the word of God, which liveth and abideth for ever. 24 For all flesh *is* as grass, and all the glory of man as the flower of grass. The grass withereth, and the flower thereof falleth away: 25 But the word of the Lord endureth for ever. And this is the word which by the gospel is preached unto you.

2 Wherefore laying aside all malice, and all guile, and hypocrisies, and envies, and all evil speakings, 2As newborn babes, desire the sincere milk of the word, that ye may grow thereby: 3 If so be ye have tasted that the Lord *is* gracious. 4 To whom coming, *as unto* a living stone, disallowed indeed of men, but chosen of God, *and* precious, 5 Ye also, as lively stones, are built up a spiritual house, a holy priesthood, to offer up spiritual sacrifices, acceptable to God by Jesus Christ. 6 Wherefore also it is contained in the Scripture, Behold, I lay in Sion a chief corner stone, elect, precious: and he that believeth on him shall not be confounded. 7 Unto you therefore which believe *he is* precious: but unto them which be disobedient, the stone which the builders disallowed, the same is made the head of the corner, 8And a stone of stumbling, and a rock of offence, *even to them* which stumble at the word, being disobedient: whereunto also they were appointed. 9 But ye *are* a chosen generation, a royal priesthood, a holy nation, a peculiar people; that ye should shew forth the praises of him who hath called you out of dark-

N.A.S.

the Holy One who called you, be holy yourselves also in all *your* behavior; 16 because it is written, "YOU SHALL BE HOLY, FOR I AM HOLY." 17And if you address as Father the One who impartially judges according to each man's work, conduct yourselves in fear during the time of your stay *upon earth;* 18 knowing that you were not redeemed with perishable things like silver or gold from your futile way of life inherited from your forefathers, 19 but with precious blood, as of a lamb unblemished and spotless, *the blood* of Christ. 20 For He was foreknown before the foundation of the world, but has appeared in these last times for the sake of you 21 who through Him are believers in God, who raised Him from the dead and gave Him glory, so that your faith and hope are in God.

22 Since you have in obedience to the truth purified your souls for a sincere love of the brethren, fervently love one another from [a]the heart, 23 for you have been born again not of seed which is perishable but imperishable, *that is,* through the living and abiding word of God. 24 For,

"ALL FLESH IS LIKE GRASS,
AND ALL ITS GLORY LIKE THE FLOWER OF GRASS.
THE GRASS WITHERS,
AND THE FLOWER FALLS OFF,
25 BUT THE WORD OF THE LORD ABIDES FOREVER."
And this is the word which was preached to you.

2 Therefore, putting aside all malice and all guile and hypocrisy and envy and all slander, 2 like newborn babes, long for the pure milk of the word, that by it you may grow in respect to salvation, 3 if you have tasted the kindness of the Lord. 4And coming to Him as to a living stone, rejected by men, but choice and precious in the sight of God, 5 you also, as living stones, are being built up as a spiritual house for a holy priesthood, to offer up spiritual sacrifices acceptable to God through Jesus Christ. 6 For *this* is contained in Scripture:

"BEHOLD I LAY IN ZION A CHOICE STONE, A PRECIOUS CORNER *stone,*
AND HE WHO BELIEVES IN HIM SHALL NOT BE DISAPPOINTED."
7 This precious value, then, is for you who believe, but for those who disbelieve,
"THE STONE WHICH THE BUILDERS REJECTED,
THIS BECAME THE VERY CORNER *stone,*
8 and,
"A STONE OF STUMBLING AND A ROCK OF OFFENSE";
for they stumble because they are disobedient to the word, and to this *doom* they were also appointed. 9 But you are A CHOSEN RACE, A ROYAL PRIESTHOOD, A HOLY NATION, A PEOPLE FOR *God's* OWN POSSESSION, that you may proclaim the excellencies of Him who has called you out of darkness into His marvelous light;

[a] Some mss. read, *a clean heart.*

WILLIAMS

Holy Being who has called you, you must prove to be holy too, 16 for the Scripture says:
"You ought to be holy,
Because I am holy."
17 And if you address as Father, Him who judges everyone impartially in accordance with what he does, you must live reverently all your fleeting stay on earth, 18 because you know that you have not been ransomed with things that perish as silver or gold, from the futile way of living taught by your fathers, 19 but with the precious blood of Christ, like that of a lamb without a blemish or a blot, 20 who was foreordained [b] for it before the foundation of the world but was brought out to public view at the end of the ages, for the sake of you 21 who through Him trust in God, who raised Him from the dead and gave Him glory; so that your faith and hope may rest in God.
22 Since you have purified your souls by obeying the truth, in sincere love for the brotherhood you must love one another heartily and fervently, 23 because you have been born anew, not from a germ that perishes but from one that does not perish, by the word of the living and everlasting God. 24 For:
"All human life is just like grass
And all its glory like the flower of grass.
The grass dries up,
The flowers drop off,
25 But the word of the Lord lives on forever";
that is, the message of the good news which has been brought to you.

2 *Loving Christians living stones in the spiritual temple built on Christ; living right silences foes; civic duties; servants to be faithful even to cruel masters; Christ our example of suffering*

So once for all get rid of all malice, deceit, hypocrisy, envy, and all sorts of slander, 2 and like new-born babies thirst for pure spiritual milk, so that by it you may grow up to final salvation, 3 since you have learned by experience that the Lord is kind. 4 Keep on coming to Him, as to a living stone, rejected by men but chosen by God and precious in His sight, 5 and keep on building yourselves up, as living stones, into a spiritual house for a consecrated priesthood, to offer up, through Jesus Christ, spiritual sacrifices that will be acceptable to God. 6 It must be so, because the Scriptures say:
"Here now I lay in Zion a chosen stone, a costly cornerstone,
And not a single one who puts his trust in Him will ever be put to shame."
7 So to you who put your trust in Him the honor belongs, but to those who fail to trust Him:
"That stone which then the builders threw away
Has now become the cornerstone,"
8 and:
"A stone for them to stumble over and a rock to trip them up."
They keep on stumbling over the message, because they are disobedient to it, and this is their appointed doom. 9 But you are the chosen race, the royal priesthood, the consecrated nation, the people to be His very own, to proclaim the perfections of Him who called you out of

[b] Lit., *foreknown*.

BECK

Holy One who called you. 16 It is written: *Be holy, because I am holy.*[3] 17 And if you *call on Him* as your *Father,*[4] who judges each one according to what he has done, without preferring one to another, live reverently as long as you are strangers here, 18 knowing *you* were *freed* from the worthless life you inherited from your fathers, *not by a payment of silver*[5] *or gold,* which perish, 19 but by the precious blood of Christ, the Lamb without a fault or a spot. 20 Appointed before the world was made, He was revealed in the last period of time to help you. 21 And through Him you believe God, who raised Him from the dead and gave Him glory; and so your faith and hope rest in God.

The Living Word

22 Now that by obeying the truth you purified yourselves to love sincerely as brothers, love one another with a pure heart and intensely. 23 You were born again, not by a seed that perishes but one that cannot perish, *God's ever-living*[6] Word.

24 *All people are like grass,*
    And all their glory like the flower in the grass.
    The grass withers,
    And the flower drops off,
25 *But the Lord's Word lives forever.*

This *Word* is the *good news* you have been *told.*[7]

2 Then get rid of every kind of wickedness and deceit, hypocrisy, jealousy, and every kind of slander, 2 and like new-born babies, thirst for the pure milk of the Word so that you'll grow till you're saved. 3 Surely *you have tasted that the Lord is good.*[8]

The Living Stone

4 Come to Him. He is the living *Stone* whom men rejected but God *selected* as *precious.* And let yourselves be built as living stones into a spiritual temple, 5 to be holy priests who bring spiritual sacrifices that God gladly accepts through Jesus Christ.
6 The Bible says, *I am laying in Zion a Cornerstone, chosen and precious, and if you believe in Him, you'll never be disappointed.*[9] 7 He is *precious*[9] to you who believe, but to those who do not believe *He is the Stone which, rejected by the builders, has become the Cornerstone.*[10] 8 *a Stone they stumble over and a Rock they fall over.*[11] When they disobey the Word, they stumble over it; that's the end appointed for them.

God's People

9 But you are *a chosen people, priests of a King, a holy nation, a people saved to be His own and to tell of the wonderful deeds*[12] of Him who called you out of darkness into His

[3] Lev. 11:44-45; 19:2; 20:7, 26
[4] Ps. 89:26
[5] Is. 52:3
[6] Dan. 6:27; 12:7
[7] Is. 40:6-9
[8] Ps. 34:8
[9] Is. 28:16
[10] Ps. 118:22
[11] Is. 8:14
[12] Ex. 19:5-6; 23:22; Is. 42:12; 43:20-21; Dan. 7:6; 14:2

K.J.V.

ness into his marvellous light: 10 Which in time past *were* not a people, but *are* now the people of God: which had not obtained mercy, but now have obtained mercy. 11 Dearly beloved, I beseech *you* as strangers and pilgrims, abstain from fleshly lusts, which war against the soul; 12 Having your conversation honest among the Gentiles: that, whereas they speak against you as evil doers, they may by *your* good works, which they shall behold, glorify God in the day of visitation. 13 Submit yourselves to every ordinance of man for the Lord's sake: whether it be to the king, as supreme; 14 Or unto governors, as unto them that are sent by him for the punishment of evil doers, and for the praise of them that do well. 15 For so is the will of God, that with well doing ye may put to silence the ignorance of foolish men: 16As free, and not using *your* liberty for a cloak of maliciousness, but as the servants of God. 17 Honour all *men.* Love the brotherhood. Fear God. Honour the king. 18 Servants, *be* subject to *your* masters with all fear; not only to the good and gentle, but also to the froward. 19 For this *is* thankworthy, if a man for conscience toward God endure grief, suffering wrongfully. 20 For what glory *is it,* if, when ye be buffeted for your faults, ye shall take it patiently? but if, when ye do well, and suffer *for it,* ye take it patiently, this *is* acceptable with God. 21 For even hereunto were ye called: because Christ also suffered for us, leaving us an example, that ye should follow his steps: 22 Who did no sin, neither was guile found in his mouth: 23 Who, when he was reviled, reviled not again; when he suffered, he threatened not; but committed *himself* to him that judgeth righteously: 24 Who his own self bare our sins in his own body on the tree, that we, being dead to sins, should live unto righteousness: by whose stripes ye were healed. 25 For ye were as sheep going astray; but are now returned unto the Shepherd and Bishop of your souls.

3 Likewise, ye wives, *be* in subjection to your own husbands; that, if any obey not the word, they also may without the word be won by the conversation of the wives; 2 While they behold your chaste conversation *coupled* with fear. 3 Whose adorning, let it not be that outward *adorning* of plaiting the hair, and of wearing of gold, or of putting on of apparel; 4 But *let it be* the hidden man of the heart, in that which is not corruptible, *even the ornament* of a meek and quiet spirit, which is in the sight of God of great price. 5 For after this manner in the old time the holy women also, who trusted in God, adorned themselves, being in subjection unto their own husbands: 6 Even as Sarah obeyed Abraham, calling him lord: whose daughters ye

N.A.S.

10 for you once were NOT A PEOPLE, but now you are THE PEOPLE OF GOD; you had NOT RECEIVED MERCY, but now you have RECEIVED MERCY. 11 Beloved, I urge you as aliens and strangers to abstain from fleshly lusts, which wage war against the soul. 12 Keep your behavior excellent among the Gentiles, so that in the thing in which they slander you as evil-doers, they may on account of your good deeds, as they observe *them,* glorify God in the day of *a*visitation. 13 Submit yourselves for the Lord's sake to every human institution: whether to a king as the one in authority; 14 or to governors, as sent by him for the punishment of evil-doers and the praise of those who do right. 15 For such is the will of God that by doing right you may silence the ignorance of foolish men. 16*Act* as free men, and do not use your freedom as a covering for evil, but *use it* as bond-slaves of God. 17 Honor all men; love the brotherhood, fear God, honor the king. 18 Servants, be submissive to your masters with all respect, not only to those who are good and gentle, but also to those who are unreasonable. 19 For this *finds* favor, if for the sake of conscience toward God a man bears up under sorrows when suffering unjustly. 20 For what credit is there if, when you sin and are harshly treated, you endure it with patience? But if when you do what is right and suffer *for it* you patiently endure it, this *finds* favor with God. 21 For you have been called for this purpose, since Christ also suffered for you, leaving you an example for you to follow in His steps, 22 WHO COMMITTED NO SIN, NOR WAS ANY DECEIT FOUND IN HIS MOUTH; 23 and while being reviled, He did not revile in return; while suffering, He uttered no threats, but kept entrusting *Himself* to Him who judges righteously; 24 and He Himself bore our sins in His body on the cross, that we might die to sin and live to righteousness; for by His wounds you were healed. 25 For you were continually straying like sheep, but now you have returned to the Shepherd and Guardian of your souls.

3 In the same way, you wives, be submissive to your own husbands so that even if any *of them* are disobedient to the word they may be won without a word by the behavior of their wives, 2 as they observe your chaste and respectful behavior. 3And let not your adornment be external *only*—braiding the hair, and wearing gold jewelry, and putting on dresses; 4 but *let it be* the hidden person of the heart, with the imperishable quality of a gentle and quiet spirit, which is precious in the sight of God. 5 For in this way in former times the holy women also, who hoped in God, used to adorn themselves, being submissive to their own husbands. 6 Thus Sarah obeyed Abraham, calling him lord, and you have become her children

---

[a] I.e., *Christ's coming again in judgment.*

WILLIAMS

darkness into His wonderful light. 10 Once you were not a people, but now you are the people of God; once His mercy had not been shown you, but now it has.

11 Dearly beloved, I beg you as aliens and exiles to keep on abstaining from the evil desires of your lower nature, because they are always at war with the soul. 12 Keep on living upright lives among the heathen, so that, when they slander you as evildoers, by what they see of your good deeds they may come to praise God on the judgment day.

13 For the Lord's sake submit to all human authority; to the emperor as supreme, 14 and to governors as sent by Him to punish those who do evil and to reward those who do right. 15 For it is God's will that by doing right you should silence the ignorant talk of foolish people. 16 Live like free men, only do not make your freedom a pretext for doing evil, but live like slaves of God. 17 Show honor to everyone. Practice love for the brotherhood; practice reverence to God and honor to the Emperor.

18 You house-servants must be submissive to your masters and show them perfect respect, not only to those who are kind and fair but also to those who are cruel. 19 For it is pleasing in the sight of God for one to bear his sorrows though suffering innocently. 20 For what credit is it to bear it patiently, if you do wrong and are beaten for it? But if you do right and patiently suffer for it, it is pleasing in the sight of God. 21 Indeed, it was to this kind of living that you were called, because Christ also suffered for you, leaving you an example that you might follow His footsteps. 22 He never committed a sin, and deceit was never found on His lips. 23 Although He was abused, He never retorted; although He continued to suffer, He never threatened, but committed His case to Him who judges justly. 24 He bore our sins in His own body on the cross, that we might die to sin and live to uprightness. By His wounds you have been healed, 25 for once you were going astray like sheep, but now you have returned to the Shepherd and Overseer of your souls.

3 *Married women to live in chastity and to dress in simplicity; married men to defer to their wives; all urged to live in brotherhood; to win the wicked by suffering for being good; Christ our example of suffering*

You married women, in the same way, must be submissive to your husbands, so that, if any of them do not believe the message, they may be won over without a word through the living of the wives, 2 when they see how chaste and respectful you are. 3 Your adornments must be not of an external nature, with braids of hair or ornaments of gold, or changes of dress, 4 but they must be of an internal nature, the character concealed in the heart, in the imperishable quality of a quiet and gentle spirit, which is of great value in the sight of God. 5 For this is the way the pious women of olden times, who set their hope on God, used to adorn themselves. 6 They were submissive to their husbands, as Sarah, for example, obeyed Abraham and called him master. You have

BECK

marvelous light. 10 Once you were *no people,* but now you are *God's people.* Once you had *received no mercy,* but now you have *received mercy.*[13]

11 Dear friends, I urge you, as *guests and strangers*[14] in this world: Refuse to do what the body wants, because its appetites fight against the soul. 12 Live a noble life among the people of the world, that instead of accusing you of doing wrong, they may see the good you do and glorify God *when He visits them.*[15]

Submit to Authorities

13 Submit to every human authority to please the Lord: 14 To the emperor as one who is over you, or to governors as men whom he sent to punish those who do wrong and to praise those who do right. 15 God wants you to silence ignorant and foolish people by doing right. 16 Act as free men, and don't use your freedom as an excuse to do wrong, but be God's slaves. 17 Honor everyone, love your fellow Christians. *Fear God;* honor the *emperor.*[16]

18 Servants, submit to your masters, showing every respect, not only when they're good and kind but also when they're unfair.

Suffer Patiently

19 It is a fine thing if, moved by your conscience to please God, you suffer patiently when wronged. 20 What credit is it to you if you sin and patiently take a beating for it? But if you suffer for doing good and take it patiently, God is pleased with you.

21 This is what you were called for, seeing that Christ also suffered for you and left you an example so that you'll follow in His steps. 22 *He never sinned or was found to be deceiving when He spoke.*[17] 23 When others abused Him, He didn't abuse them; when He suffered, He didn't threaten but left it in the hands of Him who judges fairly. 24 *He carried our sins*[18] in His body to the cross so that we'll die to sin and live for righteousness. *His wounds have healed you.* 25 You were *like lost sheep,*[19] but now you've come back to the Shepherd who takes care of you.

Wives and Husbands

3 Similarly, you married women, submit to your husbands. Then even if some of them refuse to listen to the Word, you will win them, without talking about it, by the way you wives live, 2 when they see how you fear God and are pure in your lives.

3 Your beauty should not be anything outward—braiding the hair, putting on gold ornaments and dresses— 4 but the person you are in your heart, with the imperishable quality of a gentle and quiet spirit; this is very precious to God. 5 And this is how long ago the holy women who trusted God used to make themselves beautiful: They submitted to their husbands, 6 like *Sarah,* who obeyed Abraham and

[13] Hos. 1:6, 8-10; 2:1, 23
[14] Gen. 23:4; Lev. 25:23; Ps. 39:12; 1 Chron. 29:15
[15] Is. 10:3
[16] Prov. 24:21
[17] Ps. 32:2; Is. 53:9; Zeph. 3:13
[18] Is. 53:4, 12
[19] Is. 53:5-6; Ezek. 34:5

K.J.V.

are, as long as ye do well, and are not afraid with any amazement. 7 Likewise, ye husbands, dwell with *them* according to knowledge, giving honour unto the wife, as unto the weaker vessel, and as being heirs together of the grace of life; that your prayers be not hindered. 8 Finally, *be ye* all of one mind, having compassion one of another; love as brethren, *be* pitiful, *be* courteous: 9 Not rendering evil for evil, or railing for railing: but contrariwise blessing; knowing that ye are thereunto called, that ye should inherit a blessing. 10 For he that will love life, and see good days, let him refrain his tongue from evil, and his lips that they speak no guile: 11 Let him eschew evil, and do good; let him seek peace, and ensue it. 12 For the eyes of the Lord *are* over the righteous, and his ears *are* open unto their prayers: but the face of the Lord *is* against them that do evil. 13 And who *is* he that will harm you, if ye be followers of that which is good? 14 But and if ye suffer for righteousness' sake, happy *are ye:* and be not afraid of their terror, neither be troubled; 15 But sanctify the Lord God in your hearts: and *be* ready always to *give* an answer to every man that asketh you a reason of the hope that is in you, with meekness and fear: 16 Having a good conscience; that, whereas they speak evil of you, as of evil doers, they may be ashamed that falsely accuse your good conversation in Christ. 17 For *it is* better, if the will of God be so, that ye suffer for well doing, than for evil doing. 18 For Christ also hath once suffered for sins, the just for the unjust, that he might bring us to God, being put to death in the flesh, but quickened by the Spirit: 19 By which also he went and preached unto the spirits in prison; 20 Which sometime were disobedient, when once the longsuffering of God waited in the days of Noah, while the ark was a preparing, wherein few, that is, eight souls were saved by water. 21 The like figure whereunto *even* baptism doth also now save us, (not the putting away of the filth of the flesh, but the answer of a good conscience toward God,) by the resurrection of Jesus Christ: 22 Who is gone into heaven, and is on the right hand of God; angels and authorities and powers being made subject unto him.

4 Forasmuch then as Christ hath suffered for us in the flesh, arm yourselves likewise with the same mind: for he that hath suffered in the flesh hath ceased from sin; 2 That he no longer should live the rest of *his* time in the flesh to the lusts of men, but to the will of God. 3 For the time past of *our* life may suffice us to have wrought the will of the Gentiles, when we walked in lasciviousness, lusts, excess of wine, revellings, banquetings, and abominable idola-

N.A.S.

if you do what is right without being frightened by any fear. 7 You husbands likewise, live with your wives in an understanding way, as with a weaker vessel, since she is a woman; and grant her honor as a fellow-heir of the grace of life, so that your prayers may not be hindered.

8 To sum up, let all be harmonious, sympathetic, brotherly, kind-hearted, and humble in spirit; 9 not returning evil for evil, or insult for insult, but giving a blessing instead; for you were called for the very purpose that you might inherit a blessing. 10 For

"LET HIM WHO MEANS TO LOVE LIFE AND SEE GOOD DAYS

REFRAIN HIS TONGUE FROM EVIL AND HIS LIPS FROM SPEAKING GUILE.

11 "AND LET HIM TURN AWAY FROM EVIL AND DO GOOD;

LET HIM SEEK PEACE AND PURSUE IT.

12 "FOR THE EYES OF THE LORD ARE UPON THE RIGHTEOUS,

AND HIS EARS ATTEND TO THEIR PRAYER,

BUT THE FACE OF THE LORD IS AGAINST THOSE WHO DO EVIL."

13 And who is there to harm you if you prove zealous for what is good? 14 But even if you should suffer for the sake of righteousness, *you are* blessed. AND DO NOT FEAR THEIR INTIMIDATION, AND DO NOT BE TROUBLED, 15 but [a]SANCTIFY Christ as Lord in your hearts, always *being* ready to make a defense to every one who asks you to give an account for the hope that is in you, yet with gentleness and reverence; 16 and keep a good conscience so that in the thing in which you are slandered, those who revile your good behavior in Christ may be put to shame. 17 For it is better, if God should will it so, that you suffer for doing what is right rather than for doing what is wrong. 18 For Christ also died for sins once for all, *the* just for *the* unjust, in order that He might bring us to God, having been put to death in the flesh, but made alive in the spirit; 19 in which also He went and made proclamation to the spirits *now* in prison, 20 who once were disobedient, when the patience of God kept waiting in the days of Noah, during the construction of the ark, in which a few, that is, eight persons, were brought safely through *the* water. 21 And corresponding to that, baptism now saves you—not the removal of dirt from the flesh, but an appeal to God for a good conscience—through the resurrection of Jesus Christ, 22 who is at the right hand of God, having gone into heaven, after angels and authorities and powers had been subjected to Him.

4 Therefore, since Christ has [b]suffered in the flesh, arm yourselves also with the same purpose, because he who has suffered in the flesh has ceased from sin, 2 so as to live the rest of the time in the flesh no longer for the lusts of men, but for the will of God. 3 For the time already past is sufficient *for you* to have carried out the desire of the Gentiles, having pursued a course of sensuality, lusts, drunkenness, carousals, drinking parties and

---

[a] I.e., *set apart*. [b] I.e., *suffered death*.

WILLIAMS

become true daughters of hers, if you practice doing right and cease from every fear.

7 You married men, in the same way, must live with your wives in an intelligent consideration of them; you must show them deference, too, as the weaker sex, as they share with you the gracious gift of life, so that your prayers may not be hindered.

8 Finally, you must all live in harmony, be sympathetic, loving as brothers, tenderhearted, humble, 9 never returning evil for evil or abuse for abuse, but blessing instead, because it was for this that you were called, to obtain the blessing of heirs. 10 For:

"Whoever wants to enjoy life
And see delightful days
Must keep his tongue from evil
And his lips from speaking deceit.
11 He must turn, too, away from evil and do right;
He must seek peace and follow it,
12 Because the eyes of the Lord are on upright men,
And His ears listen to their pleading cries,
But His face is against them that do wrong."

13 And who is it that will harm you if you are enthusiastic to do right? 14 Instead, you are happy, even if you should suffer for doing right. Never be afraid of their threats, and never be disturbed, 15 but in your hearts be consecrated to Christ as Lord, and always be ready to make your defense to anyone who asks a reason for the hope you have. But you must do it in gentleness and reverence, 16 and keep your conscience clear, so that those who bitterly abuse your excellent conduct as Christians may be ashamed of slandering you.

17 For it is better, if the will of God should plan it so, to suffer for doing right than for doing wrong. 18 For Christ Himself, once for all, died for our sins, the Innocent for the guilty[a] to bring us to God, being put to death in physical form but made alive in the Spirit, 19 in which He went and preached to the spirits in prison, 20 who had once been disobedient, while God's patience was awaiting in the days when Noah was preparing an ark, in which a few people—eight, to be exact—were brought safely through the water. 21 Baptism, which corresponds to this figure, now saves you, too— I do not mean the mere removal of physical stains, but the craving for a clear conscience toward God—through the resurrection of Jesus Christ, 22 who has gone to heaven and is now at God's right hand, with angels, heavenly authorities and powers made subject to Him.

4 *Inspired by Christ's example to be courageous and pure; as time is short, live to love your fellows, to glorify God, to suffer for Christ*

So then, since Christ has suffered in our physical form, you too must arm yourselves with the same determination. For whoever suffers in his physical form has done with sin, 2 so that he no longer can spend the rest of his earthly life in harmony with human desires but in accordance with God's will. 3 For the time that is past is enough for you to have accomplished what the heathen like to do, leading lives that are steeped in sensuality, lustful desires, drunkenness, carousing, revelry, dissipation, and idolatry that leads to lawless-

[a] Lit., *the Righteous for the unrighteous.*

BECK

called him *lord.*[20] You are her daughters if you do good and *let nothing terrify you.*[21]

7 In the same way, you husbands, live with your wives with understanding; they are weaker than you are. Honor them as sharing the gift of life with you—so that nothing will interfere with your prayers.

When You Are Wronged

8 Finally, all of you, live in harmony, be sympathetic, love your fellow Christians, be tenderhearted and humble. 9 Don't pay back evil for evil, insult for insult, but bless others instead. That is what you were called to do to get a blessing.

10 *If you want to love life*
And enjoy happy days,
Stop speaking evil
Or saying anything to deceive.
11 *Turn away from wrong and do good.*
Be eager for peace and go after it.
12 *The Lord watches the righteous*
And hears their prayer,
But the Lord is against those who do wrong.[22]

13 Who will harm you if you're eager to do good? 14 But even if you suffer because you're righteous, you are happy. *Never let others terrify or trouble you.* 15 *But make* Christ *the holy Lord*[23] in your hearts. And always be ready to answer anyone who asks you to explain the hope you have, 16 but be gentle and respectful. Keep a good conscience so that those who slander your good life in Christ will feel ashamed of their slander. 17 It is better, if God wants it that way, to suffer for doing right than for doing wrong.

The Righteous One Died

18 Christ died once for our sins, the Righteous One for the guilty, to bring us to God. He was killed in His body but made alive in His spirit. 19 In this spirit He also went and preached to the spirits kept in prison 20 who disobeyed long ago in the days of Noah when God waited patiently while the ark was being built, in which a few, that is, eight persons, were saved by water. 21 In the same way now the water saves you in baptism—not by washing dirt from the body but by asking God for a good conscience —by the resurrection of Jesus Christ, 22 who has gone to heaven and is at the right of God, where angels, rulers, and powers have been put under Him.

You Have Given Up Sin

4 Now since Christ has suffered for us in His body, you, too, arm yourselves with the same way of thinking, that if you have suffered in your body, you have given up sin 2 and don't follow human desires anymore but do what God wants as long as you live in this world. 3 You spent enough time in the past doing what the world likes to do, when you lived in unbridled immorality, lusts, drunkenness, wild celebrations, drinking parties, and the abominable worship of

[20] Gen. 18:12
[21] Prov. 3:25
[22] Ps. 34:12-16
[23] Is. 8:12-13

K.J.V.

tries: 4 Wherein they think it strange that ye run not with *them* to the same excess of riot, speaking evil of *you:* 5 Who shall give account to him that is ready to judge the quick and the dead. 6 For, for this cause was the gospel preached also to them that are dead, that they might be judged according to men in the flesh, but live according to God in the spirit. 7 But the end of all things is at hand: be ye therefore sober, and watch unto prayer. 8 And above all things have fervent charity among yourselves: for charity shall cover the multitude of sins. 9 Use hospitality one to another without grudging. 10 As every man hath received the gift, *even so* minister the same one to another, as good stewards of the manifold grace of God. 11 If any man speak, *let him speak* as the oracles of God; if any man minister, *let him do it* as of the ability which God giveth; that God in all things may be glorified through Jesus Christ: to whom be praise and dominion for ever and ever. Amen. 12 Beloved, think it not strange concerning the fiery trial which is to try you, as though some strange thing happened unto you: 13 But rejoice, inasmuch as ye are partakers of Christ's sufferings; that, when his glory shall be revealed, ye may be glad also with exceeding joy. 14 If ye be reproached for the name of Christ, happy *are ye;* for the Spirit of glory and of God resteth upon you: on their part he is evil spoken of, but on your part he is glorified. 15 But let none of you suffer as a murderer, or *as* a thief, or *as* an evil doer, or as a busybody in other men's matters. 16 Yet if *any man suffer* as a Christian, let him not be ashamed; but let him glorify God on this behalf. 17 For the time *is come* that judgment must begin at the house of God: and if *it* first *begin* at us, what shall the end *be* of them that obey not the gospel of God? 18 And if the righteous scarcely be saved, where shall the ungodly and the sinner appear? 19 Wherefore, let them that suffer according to the will of God commit the keeping of their souls *to him* in well doing, as unto a faithful Creator.

5 The elders which are among you I exhort, who am also an elder, and a witness of the sufferings of Christ, and also a partaker of the glory that shall be revealed: 2 Feed the flock of God which is among you, taking the oversight *thereof,* not by constraint, but willingly; not for filthy lucre, but of a ready mind; 3 Neither as being lords over *God's* heritage, but being ensamples to the flock. 4 And when the chief Shepherd shall appear, ye shall receive a crown of glory that fadeth not away. 5 Likewise, ye younger, submit yourselves unto the elder. Yea, all *of you* be subject one to another, and be clothed with humility: for God resisteth the proud, and giveth grace to the humble. 6 Hum-

N.A.S.

abominable idolatries. 4 And in *all* this, they are surprised that you do not run with *them* into the same excess of dissipation, and they malign *you;* 5 but they shall give account to Him who is ready to judge the living and the dead. 6 For the gospel has for this purpose been preached even to those who are dead, that though they are judged in the flesh as men, they may live in the spirit according to *the will of* God.

7 The end of all things is at hand; therefore, be of sound judgment and sober *spirit* for the purpose of prayer. 8 Above all, keep fervent in your love for one another, because love covers a multitude of sins. 9 Be hospitable to one another without complaint. 10 As each one has received a *special* gift, employ it in serving one another, as good stewards of the manifold grace of God. 11 Whoever speaks, *let him speak,* as it were, the utterances of God; whoever serves, *let him do so* as by the strength which God supplies; so that in all things God may be glorified through Jesus Christ, to whom belongs the glory and dominion forever and ever. Amen.

12 Beloved, do not be surprised at the fiery ordeal among you, which comes upon you for your testing, as though some strange thing were happening to you; 13 but to the degree that you share the sufferings of Christ, keep on rejoicing; so that also at the revelation of His glory, you may rejoice with exultation. 14 If you are reviled for the name of Christ, you are blessed, because the Spirit of glory and of God rests upon you. 15 By no means let any of you suffer as a murderer, or thief, or evil-doer, or a troublesome meddler; 16 but if *anyone suffers* as a Christian, let him not feel ashamed, but in that name let him glorify God. 17 For *it is* time for judgment to begin with the household of God; and if *it begins* with us first, what *will be* the outcome for those who do not obey the gospel of God? 18 AND IF IT IS WITH DIFFICULTY THAT THE RIGHTEOUS IS SAVED, WHAT WILL BECOME OF THE GODLESS MAN AND THE SINNER? 19 Therefore, let those also who suffer according to the will of God entrust their souls to a faithful Creator in doing what is right.

5 Therefore, I exhort the elders among you, as *your* fellow-elder and witness of the sufferings of Christ, and a partaker also of the glory that is to be revealed, 2 shepherd the flock of God among you, not under compulsion, but voluntarily, according to *the will of* God; and not for sordid gain, but with eagerness; 3 nor yet as lording it over those allotted to your charge, but proving to be examples to the flock. 4 And when the Chief Shepherd appears, you will receive the unfading crown of glory. 5 You younger men, likewise, be subject to your elders; and all of you, clothe yourselves with humility toward one another, for GOD IS OPPOSED TO THE PROUD, BUT GIVES GRACE TO THE HUMBLE.

6 Humble yourselves, therefore, under the

WILLIAMS

ness. 4 They are astonished that you are not still rushing hand in hand with them into the same excesses of profligate living, and they abuse you for it; 5 but they will have to give account for it to Him who is ready to judge living and dead. 6 This is why the good news was preached to the dead too, that they may be judged in their physical nature as men are, but live in the Spirit as God does.

7 But the end of everything on earth is near. So be serious and soberminded, that you may give yourselves to prayer. 8 Above everything else keep your love for one another fervent, because love covers up a multitude of sins. 9 Be ungrudgingly hospitable to one another. 10 As all of you have received your spiritual talents, you must keep on using them in serving one another, as good trustees of God's many-sided favor. 11 If anyone is preaching, let him do it as one who utters the oracles of God; if anyone is rendering any service to others, let him do it with all the strength that God supplies, so that in everything God may be glorified through Jesus Christ. To Him be glory and dominion forever and ever. Amen.

12 Dearly beloved, do not be astonished that a test by fire is coming upon you, as though something strange were happening to you, 13 but so far as you are sharing Christ's sufferings, keep on rejoicing, so that at the uncovering of His glory you may rejoice triumphantly. 14 If you are suffering abuse because you bear the name of Christ, you are happy, because the glorious Spirit of God is resting upon you. 15 For not one of you should suffer as a murderer or as a thief or any sort of criminal, or as a meddler in other people's business, 16 but if anyone suffers for being a Christian, he must not be ashamed of it, but should keep on praising God for bearing that name. 17 Because the time has come for judgment to begin at the household of God, and if it begins with us, what will the end be of those who are rejecting God's good news? 18 And if it is hard for the upright man to be saved, what will become of the godless and sinful? 19 Therefore, those who suffer in accordance with God's will must also, in doing right, entrust their souls to the Creator who is faithful.

5 *Pastors to live as examples to their flocks; as the tempter prowls about like a lion, Christians must be alert; sends farewell greeting*

So, as a joint-elder with them, a witness of the suffering borne by Christ, and a sharer of the glory that is to be uncovered, I beg the elders among you, 2 be shepherds of the flock of God that is among you, not as though you had to but of your own free will, not from the motive of personal profit but freely, 3 and not as domineering over those in your charge but proving yourselves models for the flock to imitate; 4 and when the Chief Shepherd appears, you will receive the glorious crown that never fades. 5 You younger men, on your part, must be submissive to the elders. And you must all put on the servant's apron of humility to one another, because God opposes the haughty but bestows His unmerited favor on the humble. 6 Therefore humbly submit to

BECK

idols. 4 They're surprised now you don't plunge into the same flood of wild living with them, and they slander you. 5 They will have to give an account to Him who is ready to judge the living and the dead. 6 The dead also once heard the good news, so that they will be judged as human beings in their earthly life, but then will live like God by the Spirit.

Love Fervently

7 The end of everything is near. So be sensible and keep your heads clear for your prayers. 8 Above all, continue to love one another fervently, because *love covers many sins.*[24] 9 Welcome one another as guests without grumbling. 10 Serve one another, each with the gift he received, as good managers of the various gifts of God. 11 If you speak, say what God says. If you serve, do it with the strength God gives you so that in every way you glorify God through Jesus Christ. His is the glory and the power forever! Amen.

You Share Christ's Sufferings

12 Dear friends, don't be surprised that you're being tested by a fiery trial as though something strange were happening to you. 13 But as you share Christ's sufferings, be happy so that you will also enjoy the delights when His glory will be revealed. 14 If you're insulted now for the name of Christ, you're happy because the Spirit of glory and power, *the Spirit of God, is resting*[25] on you.

15 Of course, none of you should suffer as a murderer, a thief, a criminal, or one who meddles in the affairs of others. 16 But if you suffer for being a Christian, don't feel ashamed, but praise God with that name. 17 It is time for the judgment to *start in God's temple.*[26] But if it is starting with us, how will it end for those who refuse to listen to God's good news?

18 *If it is hard for a righteous person to be saved,*
What will happen to the ungodly and the sinner?[27]

19 So you, too, who suffer as God wants you to suffer, entrust yourselves to Him—you can trust Him who created you—and keep on doing good.

To the Pastors

5 I appeal to you pastors, I who also am a pastor. I saw Christ suffer, and I share in the glory that is to be revealed. 2 Be shepherds of God's flock that is with you, watching over it, not because you must but willingly, as God would have you do it; 3 not greedily but eagerly; not lording it over the people entrusted to you but being examples to the flock. 4 And when the Head Shepherd appears, you will win the unfading garland of glory.

Humble Yourselves

5 In a similar way, you young people, submit to those who are older.

All of you, put on the apron of humility before one another, because *God opposes the proud but is kind to the humble.*[28] 6 Humble

[24] Prov. 10:12
[25] Is. 11:2
[26] Ezek. 9:6
[27] Prov. 11:31
[28] Prov. 3:34

K.J.V.

ble yourselves therefore under the mighty hand of God, that he may exalt you in due time: 7 Casting all your care upon him; for he careth for you. 8 Be sober, be vigilant; because your adversary the devil, as a roaring lion, walketh about, seeking whom he may devour: 9 Whom resist steadfast in the faith, knowing that the same afflictions are accomplished in your brethren that are in the world. 10 But the God of all grace, who hath called us unto his eternal glory by Christ Jesus, after that ye have suffered a while, make you perfect, stablish, strengthen, settle *you*. 11 To him *be* glory and dominion for ever and ever. Amen. 12 By Silvanus, a faithful brother unto you, as I suppose, I have written briefly, exhorting, and testifying that this is the true grace of God wherein ye stand. 13 The *church that is* at Babylon, elected together with *you*, saluteth you; and *so doth* Marcus my son. 14 Greet ye one another with a kiss of charity. Peace *be* with you all that are in Christ Jesus. Amen.

N.A.S.

mighty hand of God, that He may exalt you at the proper time, 7 casting all your anxiety upon Him, because He cares for you. 8 Be of sober *spirit*, be on the alert. Your adversary, the devil, prowls about like a roaring lion, seeking someone to devour. 9 But resist him, firm in *your* faith, knowing that the same experiences of suffering are being accomplished by your brethren who are in the world. 10And after you have suffered for a little, the God of all grace, who called you to His eternal glory in Christ, will Himself perfect, confirm, strengthen *and* ªestablish you. 11 To Him *be* dominion forever and ever. Amen.

12 Through Silvanus, our faithful brother (for so I regard *him*), I have written to you briefly, exhorting and testifying that this is the true grace of God. Stand firm in it! 13 ᵇShe who is in Babylon, chosen together with you, sends you greetings, and *so does* my son, Mark. 14 Greet one another with a kiss of love.

Peace be to you all who are in Christ.

[a] Omitted by some ancient mss. [b] Some mss. read, *The church which.*

WILLIAMS

God's strong hand, so that at the proper time He may exalt you. 7 Cast every worry you have upon Him, because He cares for you.

8 Be calm and alert. Your opponent the devil is always prowling about like a roaring lion, trying to devour you. 9 Resist him and be strong in faith, because you know that your brotherhood all over the world is experiencing the same sort of sufferings. 10And God, the giver of every spiritual blessing, who through your union with Christ has called you to His eternal glory, after you have suffered a little while, will Himself make you perfect, firm, and strong. 11 To Him be dominion forever. Amen.

12 By Silvanus, our faithful brother, as I regard him, I have written you this short letter, to encourage you and to testify that this is the true, unmerited favor of God. Stand firm in it. 13 Your sister-church in Babylon, chosen along with you, and Mark my son, wish to be remembered to you. 14 Greet one another with a kiss of love. Peace to all of you that are in union with Christ.

BECK

yourselves, then, under God's mighty hand so that He may honor you when His time comes.

Watch

7 *Throw all your worry on Him* because *He* takes care of *you.*[20] 8 Keep a clear head and watch! Your enemy, the devil, is prowling around like a roaring lion, looking for someone to devour. 9 Be strong in your faith and resist him, knowing that your fellow Christians in the world are paying the same price of suffering. 10After you have suffered a little while, the God of all love, who called you in Christ Jesus to His everlasting glory, will make you perfect, firm, and strong. 11 He has the power forever. Amen.

Farewell!

12 With the help of Silas, whom I consider a faithful fellow Christian, I'm writing you this short letter to encourage you and testify this is God's true love. Stand firm in it.

13 Your sister church in Babylon,* chosen by God, greets you; and so does Mark, my son. Greet one another with a kiss of love. 14 Peace to all of you who are in Christ!

---

* By "Babylon" Peter seems to mean Rome.
[29] Ps. 55:22

K.J.V.

THE SECOND EPISTLE GENERAL OF

PETER

1 Simon Peter, a servant and an apostle of Jesus Christ, to them that have obtained like precious faith with us through the righteousness of God and our Saviour Jesus Christ: 2 Grace and peace be multiplied unto you through the knowledge of God, and of Jesus our Lord, 3 According as his divine power hath given unto us all things that *pertain* unto life and godliness, through the knowledge of him that hath called us to glory and virtue: 4 Whereby are given unto us exceeding great and precious promises; that by these ye might be partakers of the divine nature, having escaped the corruption that is in the world through lust. 5And besides this, giving all diligence, add to your faith virtue; and to virtue, knowledge; 6And to knowledge, temperance; and to temperance, patience; and to patience, godliness; 7And to godliness, brotherly kindness; and to brotherly kindness, charity. 8 For if these things be in you, and abound, they make *you that ye shall* neither *be* barren nor unfruitful in the knowledge of our Lord Jesus Christ. 9 But he that lacketh these things is blind, and cannot see afar off, and hath forgotten that he was purged from his old sins. 10 Wherefore the rather, brethren, give diligence to make your calling and election sure: for if ye do these things, ye shall never fall: 11 For so an entrance shall be ministered unto you abundantly into the everlasting kingdom of our Lord and Saviour Jesus Christ. 12 Wherefore I will not be negligent to put you always in remembrance of these things, though ye know *them*, and be established in the present truth. 13 Yea, I think it meet, as long as I am in this tabernacle, to stir you up by putting *you* in remembrance; 14 Knowing that shortly I must put off *this* my tabernacle, even as our Lord Jesus Christ hath shewed me. 15 Moreover I will endeavour that ye may be able after my decease to have these things always in remembrance. 16 For we have not followed cunningly devised fables, when we made known unto you the power and coming of our Lord Jesus Christ, but were eyewitnesses of his majesty. 17 For he received from God the Father honour and glory, when there came such a voice to him from the excellent glory, This is my beloved Son, in whom I am well pleased. 18And this voice which came from heaven we heard, when we were with him in the holy mount. 19 We have also a more sure word of prophecy; whereunto ye do well that ye take heed, as unto

N.A.S.

THE SECOND EPISTLE OF

PETER

[a]Simon Peter, a bondservant and apostle of Jesus Christ, to those who have received a faith of the same kind as ours, by the righteousness of our God and Savior, Jesus Christ: 2 Grace and peace be multiplied to you in the knowledge of God and of Jesus our Lord; 3 seeing that His divine power has granted to us everything pertaining to life and godliness, through the true knowledge of Him who called us by His own glory and excellence. 4 For by these He has granted to us His precious and magnificent promises, in order that by them you might become partakers of *the* divine nature, having escaped the corruption that is in the world by lust. 5 Now for this very reason also, applying all diligence, in your faith supply moral excellence, and in *your* moral excellence, knowledge; 6 and in *your* knowledge, self-control, and in *your* self-control, perseverance, and in *your* perseverance, godliness; 7 and in *your* godliness, brotherly kindness, and in *your* brotherly kindness, *Christian* love. 8 For if these *qualities* are yours and are increasing, they render you neither useless nor unfruitful in the true knowledge of our Lord Jesus Christ. 9 For he who lacks these *qualities* is blind *or* shortsighted, having forgotten *his* purification from his former sins. 10 Therefore, brethren, be all the more diligent to make certain about His calling and choosing you; for as long as you practice these things, you will never stumble; 11 for in this way the entrance into the eternal kingdom of our Lord and Savior Jesus Christ will be abundantly supplied to you.
12 Therefore, I shall always be ready to remind you of these things, even though you *already* know *them,* and have been established in the truth which is present with *you.* 13And I consider it right, as long as I am in this *earthly* dwelling, to stir you up by way of reminder, 14 knowing that the laying aside of my *earthly* dwelling is imminent, as also our Lord Jesus Christ has made clear to me. 15And I will also be diligent that at any time after my departure you may be able to call these things to mind. 16 For we did not follow cleverly devised tales when we made known to you the power and coming of our Lord Jesus Christ, but we were eyewitnesses of His majesty. 17 For when He received honor and glory from God the Father, such an utterance as this was made to Him by the Majestic Glory, "This is My beloved Son with whom I am well pleased,"— 18 and we ourselves heard this utterance made from heaven when we were with Him on the holy mountain. 19And *so* we have the prophetic word *made* more sure, to

[a] Most early mss. read, *Simeon.*

SECOND PETER

1 *He greets them; relying on God's promises, we are to keep growing like Christ; the apostle inspired to zeal by his impending death; Christ's transfiguration suggests His second coming; Old Testament implies it*

Simon Peter, a slave and apostle of Jesus Christ, to those who through the righteousness of our God and Saviour Jesus Christ have obtained the same precious faith that we have: 2 spiritual blessing and peace be to you in increasing abundance through a full knowledge of God and of Jesus our Lord; 3 because His divine power has given us everything that is needful for life and piety, through our full knowledge of Him who through His glory and excellence has called us to Him. 4 It is through these that He has given us His precious and glorious promises, so that through them, after you have escaped from the corruption that is in the world because of evil desires, you may come to share in the divine nature. 5 Now for this very reason you must do your level best to supplement your faith with moral character, moral character with knowledge, 6 knowledge with self-control, self-control with patient endurance, patient endurance with piety, 7 piety with brotherly affection, brotherly affection with universal love. 8 For if you have these qualities and they continue to increase in you, they will make you neither idle nor unproductive in attaining a full knowledge of our Lord Jesus Christ. 9 For whoever lacks these qualities is blind—or short-sighted—and forgetful of the cleansing that he has received from his former sins. 10 Therefore, brothers, be all the more in earnest to make certain to yourselves God's call and choice of you. For if you cultivate these qualities, you will never slip, 11 for it is in this way that to you will be generously granted a triumphant admittance into the eternal kingdom of our Lord and Saviour Jesus Christ.

12 Therefore, I will always remind you of these things, although you know them and are firmly grounded in the truth that you already have. 13 Yet I think it right, as long as I live in this bodily tent, to arouse you by a reminder, 14 because I know that the removal of my bodily tent is to be very soon, as our Lord Jesus Christ has shown me. 15 Yes, I will be in earnest, so that every time you have occasion, after I have gone away, you may call these things to mind. 16 For it was not mere stories of fancy that we followed when we told you of the power and coming of our Lord Jesus Christ, but we had been eyewitnesses of His majesty. 17 For when He received such honor and glory from God the Father, when from the majestic glory there was borne to Him a voice like this, "This is my Son, my Beloved, in whom I take delight," 18 we heard this voice ourselves borne from heaven while we were with Him on that sacred mountain. 19 So we have the message of the prophets more certainly

THE SECOND LETTER OF

PETER

1 Simon Peter, servant and apostle of Jesus Christ, to the people who by the righteousness of our God and Savior Jesus Christ were given a faith as precious as ours: 2 As you know God and our Lord Jesus, *may you enjoy more and more* of His love and *peace.*[1]

Grow

3 By His glory and might 4 He once gave us very great and precious promises 3 and now has called us. When we got to know Him, His divine power gave us everything for life and godliness 4 to help you escape the corruption that lust brought into the world and to share the divine nature.

5 In view of that, try very hard to add to your faith moral power, to moral power knowledge, 6 to knowledge self-control, to self-control endurance, to endurance godliness, 7 to godliness brotherly kindness, to brotherly kindness love. 8 If you have these and they grow more and more, they keep you from being useless and unproductive in the knowledge of our Lord Jesus Christ. 9 But if anyone doesn't have these, he's blind, shortsighted, and has forgotten that his old sins were washed away.

10 Be all the more eager, then, fellow Christians, to make sure you're God's called and chosen ones. If you do this, you will never fail. 11 Then with rich gifts you will be welcomed into the everlasting kingdom of our Lord and Savior Jesus Christ.

12 And so I'm always going to remind you of this, although you already know it and are well grounded in the truth you have. 13 I think it's right, as long as I'm in the tent of this body, to refresh your memory 14 because I know I'm soon going to lay aside my tent; our Lord Jesus Christ has told me. 15 And I'll do my best to make it possible for you to remember these things at any time after I'm gone.

God's Word

16 We didn't follow any clever myths when we told you about the power of our Lord Jesus Christ and His coming. No, with our own eyes we saw His majesty. 17 God the Father gave Him honor and glory when from His wonderful glory He said to Him: *"This is My Son* whom I love and *am delighted with."*[2] 18 We heard that voice speak to Him from heaven when we were with Him on the holy mountain.

19 And so we have God's Word that is all the more certain. Please look to it as to a light

[1] Dan. 3:31; 6:26
[2] Ps. 2:7; 2 Sam. 7:14; Is. 42:1

K.J.V.

a light that shineth in a dark place, until the day dawn, and the daystar arise in your hearts: 20 Knowing this first, that no prophecy of the Scripture is of any private interpretation. 21 For the prophecy came not in old time by the will of man: but holy men of God spake *as they were* moved by the Holy Ghost.

2 But there were false prophets also among the people, even as there shall be false teachers among you, who privily shall bring in damnable heresies, even denying the Lord that bought them, and bring upon themselves swift destruction. 2 And many shall follow their pernicious ways; by reason of whom the way of truth shall be evil spoken of. 3 And through covetousness shall they with feigned words make merchandise of you: whose judgment now of a long time lingereth not, and their damnation slumbereth not. 4 For if God spared not the angels that sinned, but cast *them* down to hell, and delivered *them* into chains of darkness, to be reserved unto judgment; 5 And spared not the old world, but saved Noah the eighth *person*, a preacher of righteousness, bringing in the flood upon the world of the ungodly; 6 And turning the cities of Sodom and Gomorrah into ashes condemned *them* with an overthrow, making *them* an ensample unto those that after should live ungodly; 7 And delivered just Lot, vexed with the filthy conversation of the wicked: 8 (For that righteous man dwelling among them, in seeing and hearing, vexed *his* righteous soul from day to day with *their* unlawful deeds:) 9 The Lord knoweth how to deliver the godly out of temptation, and to reserve the unjust unto the day of judgment to be punished: 10 But chiefly them that walk after the flesh in the lust of uncleanness, and despise government. Presumptuous *are they*, selfwilled, they are not afraid to speak evil of dignities. 11 Whereas angels, which are greater in power and might, bring not railing accusation against them before the Lord. 12 But these, as natural brute beasts made to be taken and destroyed, speak evil of the things that they understand not; and shall utterly perish in their own corruption; 13 And shall receive the reward of unrighteousness, *as* they that count it pleasure to riot in the daytime. Spots *they are* and blemishes, sporting themselves with their own deceivings while they feast with you; 14 Having eyes full of adultery, and that cannot cease from sin; beguiling unstable souls: a heart they have exercised with covetous practices; cursed children: 15 Which have forsaken the right way, and are gone astray, following the way of Balaam *the son* of Bosor, who loved the wages of unrighteousness; 16 But was rebuked for his iniquity: the dumb ass speaking with man's voice

N.A.S.

which you do well to pay attention as to a lamp shining in a dark place, until the day dawns and the morning star arises in your hearts. 20 But know this first of all, that no prophecy of Scripture is *a matter* of one's own interpretation, 21 for no prophecy was ever made by an act of human will, but men moved by the Holy Spirit spoke from God.

2 But false prophets also arose among the people, just as there will also be false teachers among you, who will secretly introduce destructive heresies, even denying the Master who bought them, bringing swift destruction upon themselves. 2 And many will follow their sensuality, and because of them the way of the truth will be maligned; 3 and in *their* greed they will exploit you with false words; their judgment from long ago is not idle, and their destruction is not asleep. 4 For if God did not spare angels when they sinned, but cast them into hell and committed them to pits of darkness, reserved for judgment; 5 and did not spare the ancient world, but preserved Noah, a preacher of righteousness, with seven others, when He brought a flood upon the world of the ungodly; 6 and *if* He condemned the cities of Sodom and Gomorrah to destruction by reducing *them* to ashes, having made them an example to those who would live ungodly thereafter; 7 and if He rescued righteous Lot, oppressed by the sensual conduct of unprincipled men 8 (for by what he saw and heard *that* righteous man, while living among them, felt *his* righteous soul tormented day after day with *their* lawless deeds), 9 *then* the Lord knows how to rescue the godly from temptation, and to keep the unrighteous under punishment for the day of judgment, 10 and especially those who indulge the flesh in *its* corrupt desires and despise authority. Daring, self-willed, they do not tremble when they revile angelic majesties, 11 whereas angels who are greater in might and power do not bring a reviling judgment against them before the Lord. 12 But these, like unreasoning animals, born as creatures of instinct to be captured and killed, reviling where they have no knowledge, will in the destruction of those creatures also be destroyed, 13 suffering wrong as the wages of doing wrong. They count it a pleasure to revel in the daytime. They are stains and blemishes, revelling in their ªdeceptions, as they carouse with you; 14 having eyes full of adultery and that never cease from sin; enticing unstable souls, having a heart trained in greed, accursed children; 15 forsaking the right way they have gone astray, having followed the way of Balaam, the *son* of Beor, who loved the wages of unrighteousness, 16 but he received a rebuke for his own transgression; *for* a dumb donkey, speaking with a voice of a man, restrained the madness of the prophet.

[a] Some ancient mss. read, *love-feasts*, cf. Jude 12.

guaranteed. Please pay attention to this message as to a lamp that is shining in a dismal place, until the day dawns and the morning star rises in your hearts; 20 because you recognize this truth above all else, that no prophecy in Scripture is to be interpreted by one's own mind, 21 for no prophecy has ever yet originated in man's will, but men who were led by the Holy Spirit spoke from God.

2

False teachers foretold and foredoomed; examples of God's punishing the wicked but preserving the righteous; false teachers described; their influence in degrading backsliders

Now there were false prophets among the people, just as there will be false teachers among you too, who will insidiously introduce destructive heresies and deny the Master who has bought them, thus bringing on themselves swift destruction. 2 Many people will follow their immoral ways, and because of them the true Way will be abused. 3 In their greed they will exploit you with messages manufactured by themselves. From of old their condemnation has not been idle and their destruction has not been slumbering.

4 For if God did not spare angels when they sinned, but hurled them down to Tartarus[a] and committed them to dark dungeons to await their doom, 5 and if He did not spare the ancient world, but preserved Noah, a preacher of righteousness, and seven others when He brought the flood upon the world of godless people; 6 and if He condemned, by burning them to ashes, the cities of Sodom and Gomorrah, making them an example to godless people of what was coming to them, 7 and saved the upright Lot who was constantly distressed by the immoral conduct of lawless men—8 for as long as that upright man was living among them, his upright soul, day and night, was always being tortured by what he saw and heard in their lawless actions—9 surely, then, the Lord knows how to rescue godly people from trial and to keep wrongdoers under punishment for the day of judgment, 10 especially those who satisfy their lower nature by indulging in its evil passions which defile them, and who despise authority. Daring, headstrong men! They do not tremble when they abuse persons of majesty, 11 whereas angels who are far superior in strength and power to these beings bring no abusive accusation against them before the Lord. 12 These men, like irrational animals, mere creatures of instinct created to be caught and killed, abuse the things that they do not understand, and so by their corruption they will be destroyed, suffering wrong as punishment for their wrongdoing. 13 They think their daily luxurious living real pleasure; they are spots and blots, deceitfully living in luxurious pleasure while they continue their religious feasting with you. 14 They have eyes full of adultery and insatiable by sin. They practice enticing unsteady souls. They have trained their hearts in greed. They are doomed to a curse![b] 15 They have left the straight road and gone astray. They have followed the road that Balaam, the son of Beor, trod, who fell in love with the profits of wrongdoing 16 but was reproved for his offense; a dumb animal spoke with a human voice and stopped the prophet's madness.

[a] That is, *hell.* [b] Lit., *children of a curse.*

shining in a gloomy place till the day dawns and the *morning star rises*[3] in your hearts. 20 Understand this first, that no one can explain any written Word of God as he likes, 21 because it never was the will of a human being that brought us God's Word, but the Holy Spirit moved holy men to say what God told them.

Men Who Teach Lies

2

But there were also men who preached lies among the people, just as there will also be among you those who teach lies. They will secretly bring in their own destructive teachings. Denying the Lord who has bought them, they quickly destroy themselves. 2 And many will follow their immoral ways and *cause* people *to slander*[4] the way of truth. 3 In their greed they will talk dishonestly to you to make a profit. A just punishment has long been getting ready for them, and destruction has been watching for them.

4 God didn't spare angels who sinned but put them into the gloomy dungeons of hell to be kept for judgment. 5 And He didn't spare the ancient world but protected Noah, who preached righteousness, and seven others when He brought a flood on a world of ungodly people. 6 And He condemned the towns of Sodom and Gomorrah, destroyed them by burning them to ashes, and made them a warning to those who are going to be ungodly, 7 but He rescued righteous Lot, whom the wicked people vexed with their immoral life. 8 (Seeing and hearing the wicked things they did, this righteous man tortured his righteous soul day after day as he lived among them.) 9 The Lord knows how to rescue godly people when they are tested and to keep the wicked under punishment for the day of judgment, 10 especially those who go lusting after sinful flesh to defile themselves and who despise the Lord.

Bold and headstrong men, without trembling they slander beings of glory, 11 whom even angels, although they're greater in strength and power, don't condemn and abuse before the Lord. 12 But like unthinking animals that are born to be physical, to be caught and killed, they slander what they don't understand, and like animals they will be destroyed— 13 and so lose what they hoped to gain by their wrongdoing.

Their idea of pleasure is to carouse in broad daylight. They are spots and faults! They enjoy deceiving you while they feast with you. 14 They have eyes only for an adulterous woman and are restlessly looking for sin. They try to trap weak souls.

Their hearts are trained to be greedy. Cursed people! 15 Leaving the right way, they've gone wrong. They've gone the way of Balaam, Beor's son, who loved the reward he would get for doing wrong. 16 But he was shown how wrong he was: A speechless donkey spoke with a human voice and didn't let the prophet go on in his crazy way.

[3] Is. 14:12
[4] Is. 52:5

K.J.V.

forbade the madness of the prophet. 17 These are wells without water, clouds that are carried with a tempest; to whom the mist of darkness is reserved for ever. 18 For when they speak great swelling *words* of vanity, they allure through the lusts of the flesh, *through much* wantonness, those that were clean escaped from them who live in error. 19 While they promise them liberty, they themselves are the servants of corruption: for of whom a man is overcome, of the same is he brought in bondage. 20 For if after they have escaped the pollutions of the world through the knowledge of the Lord and Saviour Jesus Christ, they are again entangled therein, and overcome, the latter end is worse with them than the beginning. 21 For it had been better for them not to have known the way of righteousness, than, after they have known *it,* to turn from the holy commandment delivered unto them. 22 But it is happened unto them according to the true proverb, The dog *is* turned to his own vomit again; and, The sow that was washed to her wallowing in the mire.

3 This second epistle, beloved, I now write unto you; in *both* which I stir up your pure minds by way of remembrance: 2 That ye may be mindful of the words which were spoken before by the holy prophets, and of the commandment of us the apostles of the Lord and Saviour: 3 Knowing this first, that there shall come in the last days scoffers, walking after their own lusts, 4 And saying, Where is the promise of his coming? for since the fathers fell asleep, all things continue as *they were* from the beginning of the creation. 5 For this they willingly are ignorant of, that by the word of God the heavens were of old, and the earth standing out of the water and in the water: 6 Whereby the world that then was, being overflowed with water, perished: 7 But the heavens and the earth, which are now, by the same word are kept in store, reserved unto fire against the day of judgment and perdition of ungodly men. 8 But, beloved, be not ignorant of this one thing, that one day *is* with the Lord as a thousand years, and a thousand years as one day. 9 The Lord is not slack concerning his promise, as some men count slackness; but is longsuffering to us-ward, not willing that any should perish, but that all should come to repentance. 10 But the day of the Lord will come as a thief in the night; in the which the heavens shall pass away with a great noise, and the elements shall melt with fervent heat, the earth also and the works that are therein shall be burned up. 11 *Seeing* then *that* all these things shall be dissolved, what manner *of persons* ought ye to be in *all* holy conversation and godliness, 12 Looking for and hasting unto the coming of the day of God, wherein the heavens being on fire shall be dissolved, and the elements shall melt with fervent heat? 13 Nevertheless we, according to his prom-

N.A.S.

17 These are springs without water, and mists driven by a storm, for whom the black darkness has been reserved. 18 For speaking out arrogant *words* of vanity they entice by fleshly desires, by sensuality those who barely escape from the ones who live in error, 19 promising them freedom while they themselves are slaves of corruption; for by what a man is overcome, by this he is enslaved. 20 For if after they have escaped the defilements of the world by the knowledge of the Lord and Savior Jesus Christ, they are again entangled in them and are overcome, the last state has become worse for them than the first. 21 For it would be better for them not to have known the way of righteousness, than having known it, to turn away from the holy commandment delivered to them. 22 It has happened to them according to the true proverb, "A DOG RETURNS TO ITS OWN VOMIT," and, "A sow, after washing, *returns* to wallowing in the mire."

3 This is now, beloved, the second letter I am writing to you in which I am stirring up your sincere mind by way of reminder, 2 that you should remember the words spoken beforehand by the holy prophets and the commandment of the Lord and Savior *spoken* by your apostles. 3 Know this first of all, that in the last days mockers will come with *their* mocking, following after their own lusts, 4 and saying, "Where is the promise of His coming? For *ever* since the fathers fell asleep, all continues just as it was from the beginning of creation." 5 For when they maintain this, it escapes their notice that by the word of God *the* heavens existed long ago and *the* earth was formed out of water and by water, 6 through which the world at that time was destroyed, being flooded with water. 7 But the present heavens and earth by His word are being reserved for fire, kept for the day of judgment and destruction of ungodly men.

8 But do not let this one *fact* escape your notice, beloved, that with the Lord one day is as a thousand years, and a thousand years as one day. 9 The Lord is not slow about His promise, as some count slowness, but is patient toward you, not wishing for any to perish but for all to come to repentance. 10 But the day of the Lord will come like a thief, in which the heavens will pass away with a roar and the elements will be destroyed with intense heat, and the earth and its works will be ᵃburned up. 11 Since all these things are to be destroyed in this way, what sort of people ought you to be in holy conduct and godliness, 12 looking for and hastening the coming of the day of God, on account of which the heavens will be destroyed by burning, and the elements will melt with intense heat. 13 But according to His promise we are looking for new heavens

---

[a] Some ancient mss. read, *discovered.*

WILLIAMS

17 Such men are dried-up springs, clouds driven by the storm, and they are doomed to densest darkness. 18 For by uttering arrogant nonsense, through base desires of the lower nature, they entice into immorality men who are just escaping from those who live in error, 19 promising them freedom, though they are slaves of destruction themselves; for a man is the slave of anything that conquers him.

20 For if, after men have escaped the corrupting ways of the world through a full knowledge of the Lord and Saviour Jesus Christ, they again become entangled in them and are conquered by them, then their last condition is worse than their former one. 21 For it would have been better for them never to have known the way of uprightness than to have known it and then to turn their backs on the sacred command committed to their trust. 22 In them is verified the truth of the proverb, "A dog turns back to what he has vomited"; and of that other proverb, "A sow that has washed herself goes back to wallow in the mire."

3 *Why the author writes; he warns them as to false teachers who ridicule the delayed return of Christ; yet this return is certain though sudden; in the light of that great day he urges them to better living*

This is the second letter, dearly beloved, that I have already written to you, in both of which I am trying by reminders to stir up your unsullied minds 2 to remember the things foretold by the holy prophets, and the command of the Lord and Saviour through your apostles.

3 First of all, you must understand this, that in the last days mockers will come with their mockeries, living in accordance with their evil passions, 4 and saying, "Where is His promised coming? For ever since our forefathers fell asleep everything has remained exactly as it was from the beginning of creation!" 5 For they willfully ignore the fact that long ago the heavens existed and the earth that had been formed by God's command out of water and through water, 6 by which also the world, through being deluged with water, was destroyed. 7 But by the same command the present heavens and earth are stored up for fire and are kept for the day when godless men are to be doomed and destroyed.

8 But you must avoid forgetting this one fact, dearly beloved, that with the Lord a single day is like a thousand years and a thousand years are like a single day. 9 The Lord is not slow about His promise, in the sense in which some think of slowness, but He is really dealing patiently with you, because He is not willing for any to perish but for all to have an opportunity to repent. 10 The day of the Lord will come like a thief; on that day the heavens will pass away with a roar, the heavenly bodies will be destroyed by being burned up, and the earth with all its works will melt away. 11 If all these things are to be dissolved in this way, what men you ought to be! What holy and pious lives you ought to lead, 12 since you are awaiting and hastening the coming of the day of God, which will cause the heavens to blaze and dissolve and the heavenly bodies to burn up and melt away! 13 In accordance with His promise we are expecting new heavens

BECK

17 They are dried-up springs, fogs driven by a storm. Dark gloom is reserved for them. 18 By talking high-sounding nonsense and using physical cravings they set traps baited with lusts for the people who are just escaping from those who live in error. 19 Promising them freedom, they are themselves slaves of corruption—anyone is a slave of that which defeated him.

20 If by knowing the Lord and Savior Jesus Christ they escaped the world's corruptions but are again entangled and conquered by them, these people are worse off in the end than they were before. 21 It would have been better for them never to have known the right way than to learn it and then turn their backs on the holy commandment that was given them. 22 The proverb is true that tells what happened to them: *A dog goes back to what he has vomited up,*[5] and a sow that has washed goes back to roll in the mud.

The World Will Be Destroyed

3 Dear friends, this is now the second letter I'm writing you. In both of them I stir up your pure minds by reminding you 2 to think of what the holy prophets predicted and what the Lord and Savior ordered through your apostles.

3 First of all you should know that in the last days mockers, following their own impulses, will come mocking: 4 "He promised to come. What has happened? From the time the fathers went to their rest everything has stayed as it was since the world was first created."

5 When they insist on this, they forget that long ago God's Word made the sky and formed the earth out of water and with water. 6 Then this water also flooded the world and destroyed it. 7 And the same Word has preserved the present heavens and the earth for the fire and keeps them for the day when the ungodly will be judged and destroyed.

8 Don't forget, dear friends, with the Lord one day is like a thousand years, and *a thousand years are like one day.*[6] 9 The Lord isn't slow to do what He promised, as some people think. He is patient with you and doesn't want any to perish but wants them all to turn from sin to Him.

10 The Lord's day will come like a thief. On that day the heavens will pass away with a roar, the elements will be destroyed by heat—with the earth; and what was done on it will be shown.

11 Since all these things will be destroyed in this way, think how holy and godly you should live, 12 waiting for and speeding the coming of God's day that will destroy the heavens with fire and melt the elements with heat. 13 But according to His promise we expect *new heavens*

[5] Prov. 26:11
[6] Ps. 90:4

K.J.V.

ise, look for new heavens and a new earth, wherein dwelleth righteousness. 14 Wherefore, beloved, seeing that ye look for such things, be diligent that ye may be found of him in peace, without spot, and blameless. 15 And account *that* the longsuffering of our Lord *is* salvation; even as our beloved brother Paul also according to the wisdom given unto him hath written unto you; 16 As also in all *his* epistles, speaking in them of these things; in which are some things hard to be understood, which they that are unlearned and unstable wrest, as *they do* also the other Scriptures, unto their own destruction. 17 Ye therefore, beloved, seeing ye know *these things* before, beware lest ye also, being led away with the error of the wicked, fall from your own steadfastness. 18 But grow in grace, and *in* the knowledge of our Lord and Saviour Jesus Christ. To him *be* glory both now and for ever. Amen.

N.A.S.

and a new earth, in which righteousness dwells. 14 Therefore, beloved, since you look for these things, be diligent to be found by Him in peace, spotless and blameless, 15 and regard the patience of our Lord *to be* salvation; just as also our beloved brother Paul, according to the wisdom given him, wrote to you, 16 as also in all *his* letters, speaking in them of these things, in which are some things hard to understand, which the untaught and unstable distort, as *they do* also the rest of the Scriptures, to their own destruction. 17 You therefore, beloved, knowing this beforehand, be on your guard lest, being carried away by the error of unprincipled men, you fall from your own steadfastness, 18 but grow in the grace and knowledge of our Lord and Savior Jesus Christ. To Him *be* the glory, both now and to the day of eternity. Amen.

and a new earth, in which uprightness will have its permanent home.

14 Therefore, dearly beloved, since you are expecting this, be in earnest to be found by Him without a blot, without reproach, and at peace. 15Always think of our Lord's patience as salvation, just as our dearly beloved brother Paul, with the wisdom granted him, wrote you to do, 16 speaking of it as he does in all his letters. In them are some things hard to understand, which the ignorant and unsteady twist to their ruin, as they do the rest of the Scriptures.

17 So, dearly beloved, since you have been forewarned, you must always be on your guard against being led astray by the errors of lawless men, and so against falling away from your present firmness; 18 but instead, you must continue to grow in the spiritual strength and knowledge of our Lord and Saviour Jesus Christ. To Him be glory now and forever!

and a new earth[7] where righteousness lives. 14 With this to look forward to, dear friends, do your best to have Him find you without a spot or a fault and at peace.

15 Believe that our Lord's patience means salvation, just as our dear brother Paul wrote you according to the wisdom given him. 16 He talks about this in all his letters. Some things in them are hard to understand, and those who are ignorant and not well grounded misinterpret them as they do the rest of the Bible, and so they destroy themselves.

17 Now you, dear friends, are warned. Be on your guard, and don't let men without principles sweep you off your feet by their error. 18 But grow in God's love and in knowing our Lord and Savior Jesus Christ. To Him be glory now and forever. Amen.

THE FIRST
EPISTLE GENERAL
OF
JOHN

1 That which was from the beginning, which we have heard, which we have seen with our eyes, which we have looked upon, and our hands have handled, of the Word of life; 2 (For the life was manifested, and we have seen *it*, and bear witness, and shew unto you that eternal life, which was with the Father, and was manifested unto us;) 3 That which we have seen and heard declare we unto you, that ye also may have fellowship with us: and truly our fellowship *is* with the Father, and with his Son Jesus Christ. 4And these things write we unto you, that your joy may be full. 5 This then is the message which we have heard of him, and declare unto you, that God is light, and in him is no darkness at all. 6 If we say that we have fellowship with him, and walk in darkness, we lie, and do not the truth: 7 But if we walk in the light, as he is in the light, we have fellowship one with another, and the blood of Jesus Christ his Son cleanseth us from all sin. 8 If we say that we have no sin, we deceive ourselves, and the truth is not in us. 9 If we confess our sins, he is faithful and just to forgive us *our* sins, and to cleanse us from all unrighteousness. 10 If we say that we have not sinned, we make him a liar, and his word is not in us.

2 My little children, these things write I unto you, that ye sin not. And if any man sin, we have an advocate with the Father, Jesus Christ the righteous: 2And he is the propitiation for our sins: and not for ours only, but also for *the sins of* the whole world. 3And hereby we do know that we know him, if we keep his commandments. 4 He that saith, I know him, and keepeth not his commandments, is a liar, and the truth is not in him. 5 But whoso keepeth his word, in him verily is the love of God perfected: hereby know we that we are in him. 6 He that

THE FIRST EPISTLE OF
JOHN

1 What was from the beginning, what we have heard, what we have seen with our eyes, what we beheld and our hands handled, concerning the Word of life—2 and the life was manifested, and we have seen and bear witness and proclaim to you the eternal life, which was with the Father and was manifested to us—3 what we have seen and heard we proclaim to you also, that you also may have fellowship with us; and indeed our fellowship is with the Father, and with His Son Jesus Christ. 4And these things we write, so that our joy may be made complete.

5 And this is the message which we have heard from Him and announced to you, that God is light, and in Him there is no darkness at all. 6 If we say that we have fellowship with Him and *yet* walk in the darkness, we lie and do not practice the truth; 7 but if we walk in the light as He Himself is in the light, we have fellowship with one another, and the blood of Jesus His Son cleanses us from all sin. 8 If we say that we have no sin, we are deceiving ourselves, and the truth is not in us. 9 If we confess our sins, He is faithful and righteous to forgive us our sins and to cleanse us from all unrighteousness. 10 If we say that we have not sinned, we make Him a liar, and His word is not in us.

2 My little children, I am writing these things to you that you may not sin. And if anyone sins, we have an ªAdvocate with the Father, Jesus Christ the righteous; 2 and He Himself is the propitiation for our sins; and not for ours only, but also for *those of* the whole world. 3And by this we know that we have come to know Him, if we keep His commandments. 4 The one who says, "I have come to know Him," and does not keep His commandments, is a liar, and the truth is not in him; 5 but whoever keeps His word, in him the love of God has truly been perfected. By this we know that we are in Him: 6 the one who says he

[a] Gr., *Paracletos*, equals one called alongside to help.

FIRST JOHN

1 *Eternal life has been brought to us through Jesus as a real man; since God is light we are to live pure lives, kept so by Jesus' blood but are not to claim to be sinless*

It is what existed from the beginning, what we have heard, what we have seen with our own eyes, what we have beheld, what our own hands have touched, about the very message of life— 2 and that life has been unveiled to us, and we have seen it and now testify to it and we now announce it to you, yea, the eternal life that was with the Father and has been unveiled to us. 3 I repeat, it is what we have seen and heard that we now announce to you, so that you too may share this fellowship with us, for this fellowship that we have is with the Father and with His Son Jesus Christ; 4 and now we write these things to you to make our joy complete.

5 And this is the message that we have heard from Him and now announce to you: God is light, and there is no darkness at all in Him.

6 If we say "We have fellowship with Him," and yet live in darkness, we are lying and not practicing the truth. 7 But if we continue to live in the light, just as He is in the light, we have unbroken fellowship with one another, and the blood of Jesus His Son continues to cleanse us from every sin. 8 If we claim "We are already free from sin," we are deceiving ourselves and the truth is not in our hearts. 9 If we confess our sins, He is to be depended on, since He is just, to forgive us our sins and to cleanse us from every wrong. 10 If we claim "We have not sinned," we are making Him a liar, and His message is not in our hearts.

2 *To keep His commands gives assurance that He is our Saviour; to love one another means to live in the light; tells why He writes; we cannot love God and the world too; warns against backsliding*

My dear children, I am writing you this so that you may not sin; yet if anyone ever sins, we have One who pleads our case with the Father, Jesus Christ, One who is righteous. 2 And He is Himself the atoning sacrifice for our sins; and not for ours alone, but also for the whole world. 3 By this we can be sure that we know Him—if we practice obedience to His commands. 4 Whoever says, "I know Him," but does not practice obedience to His commands is a liar, and there is no truth in his heart; 5 but whoever practices obedience to His message really has a perfect love of God in his heart. By this we can be sure that we are in union with Him: 6 Whoever claims, "I am

THE FIRST LETTER OF

JOHN

1 It was there from the beginning, we heard It, we saw It with our eyes, we looked at It, and our hands touched It—we're writing about the Word of Life. 2 That Life showed itself and we saw It, and now we testify and tell you about the everlasting Life that was with the Father and showed itself to us. 3 We saw and heard It, and we tell you about It so that you, too, will have It in fellowship with us. 4 Our fellowship is with the Father and with His Son Jesus Christ. We're writing this so that our joy may be complete.

5 This is what we heard Him tell us and we're telling you: God is Light, and there is nothing dark in Him. 6 If we say we share what He has but live in the dark, we're lying and not living the truth.

Jesus' Blood

7 If we live in the light as He is in the light, we have it in fellowship with one another, and the blood of Jesus, His Son, washes us clean from every sin. 8 If we say we don't have any sin, we deceive ourselves, and the truth isn't in us. 9 If we confess our sins, we can depend on Him to do what is right—He will forgive our sins and wash away every wrong. 10 If we say we haven't sinned, we make Him a liar, and His Word is not in us.

2 My children, I'm writing this to you to keep you from sinning. If anyone sins, we have One to plead for us with the Father— Jesus Christ, who is righteous. 2 He has paid for our sins,* and not for ours only but for the whole world.

Live and Love

3 We're sure we know Him if we do what He orders us to do. 4 Anyone who says, "I know Him," but doesn't do what He orders is a liar and doesn't have the truth. 5 But if you do what He says, God's love has in you really accomplished what He wants. 6 That's how we know

---

* His sacrifice wipes out our sins and changes God's anger to love.

K.J.V.

saith he abideth in him ought himself also so to walk, even as he walked. 7 Brethren, I write no new commandment unto you, but an old commandment which ye had from the beginning. The old commandment is the word which ye have heard from the beginning. 8Again, a new commandment I write unto you, which thing is true in him and in you: because the darkness is past, and the true light now shineth. 9 He that saith he is in the light, and hateth his brother, is in darkness even until now. 10 He that loveth his brother abideth in the light, and there is none occasion of stumbling in him. 11 But he that hateth his brother is in darkness, and walketh in darkness, and knoweth not whither he goeth, because that darkness hath blinded his eyes. 12 I write unto you, little children, because your sins are forgiven you for his name's sake. 13 I write unto you, fathers, because ye have known him *that is* from the beginning. I write unto you, young men, because ye have overcome the wicked one. I write unto you, little children, because ye have known the Father. 14 I have written unto you, fathers, because ye have known him *that is* from the beginning. I have written unto you, young men, because ye are strong, and the word of God abideth in you, and ye have overcome the wicked one. 15 Love not the world, neither the things *that are* in the world. If any man love the world, the love of the Father is not in him. 16 For all that *is* in the world, the lust of the flesh, and the lust of the eyes, and the pride of life, is not of the Father, but is of the world. 17And the world passeth away, and the lust thereof: but he that doeth the will of God abideth for ever. 18 Little children, it is the last time: and as ye have heard that antichrist shall come, even now are there many antichrists; whereby we know that it is the last time. 19 They went out from us, but they were not of us; for if they had been of us, they would *no doubt* have continued with us: but *they went out,* that they might be made manifest that they were not all of us. 20 But ye have an unction from the Holy One, and ye know all things. 21 I have not written unto you because ye know not the truth, but because ye know it, and that no lie is of the truth. 22 Who is a liar but he that denieth that Jesus is the Christ? He is antichrist, that denieth the Father and the Son. 23 Whosoever denieth the Son, the same hath not the Father: [*but*] *he that acknowledgeth the Son hath the Father also.* 24 Let that therefore abide in you, which ye have heard from the beginning. If that which ye have heard from the beginning shall remain in you, ye also shall continue in the Son, and in the Father. 25And this is the promise that he hath promised us, *even* eternal life. 26 These things have I written unto you concerning them that seduce you. 27 But the anointing which ye have received of him abideth in you, and ye need not that any man teach you: but as the same anointing teacheth you of all things, and is truth, and is no lie, and even as it hath taught you, ye shall abide in him. 28And now, little children, abide in him; that, when he shall appear, we may have confidence, and not be ashamed before him at his coming. 29 If ye know that he is righteous, ye know that every one that doeth righteousness is born of him.

N.A.S.

abides in Him ought himself to walk in the same manner as He walked.
7 Beloved, I am not writing a new commandment to you, but an old commandment which you have had from the beginning; the old commandment is the word which you have heard. 8 On the other hand, I am writing a new commandment to you, which is true in Him and in you, because the darkness is passing away, and the true light is already shining. 9 The one who says he is in the light and *yet* hates his brother is in the darkness until now. 10 The one who loves his brother abides in the light and there is no cause for stumbling in him. 11 But the one who hates his brother is in the darkness and walks in the darkness, and does not know where he is going because the darkness has blinded his eyes.
12 I am writing to you, little children, because your sins are forgiven you for His name's sake. 13 I am writing to you, fathers, because you know Him who has been from the beginning. I am writing to you, young men, because you have overcome the evil one. I have written to you, children, because you know the Father. 14 I have written to you, fathers, because you know Him who has been from the beginning. I have written to you, young men, because you are strong, and the word of God abides in you, and you have overcome the evil one. 15 Do not love the world, nor the things in the world. If any one loves the world, the love of the Father is not in him. 16 For all that is in the world, the lust of the flesh and the lust of the eyes and the boastful pride of life, is not from the Father, but is from the world. 17And the world is passing away, and *also* its lusts; but the one who does the will of God abides forever.
18 Children, it is the last hour; and just as you heard that antichrist is coming, even now many antichrists have arisen; from this we know that it is the last hour. 19 They went out from us, but they were not *really* of us; for if they had been of us, they would have remained with us; but *they went out,* in order that it might be shown that they all are not of us. 20 But you have an anointing from the Holy One, and you all know. 21 I have not written to you because you do not know the truth, but because you do know it, and because no lie is of the truth. 22 Who is the liar but the one who denies that Jesus is the Christ? This is the antichrist, the one who denies the Father and the Son. 23 Whoever denies the Son does not have the Father; the one who confesses the Son has the Father also. 24As for you, let that abide in you which you heard from the beginning. If what you heard from the beginning abides in you, you also will abide in the Son and in the Father. 25And this is the promise which He Himself made to us, the eternal life. 26 These things I have written to you concerning those who are trying to deceive you. 27And as for you, the anointing which you received from Him abides in you, and you have no need for any one to teach you; but as His anointing teaches you about all things, and is true and is not a lie, and just as it has taught you, you abide in Him. 28And now, little children, abide in Him, so that if He should appear, we may have confidence and not shrink away from Him in shame at His coming. 29 If you know that He is righteous, you know that every one also who practices righteousness is born of Him.

WILLIAMS

always in union with Him," ought to live as He lived.

7 Dearly beloved, I am not writing you a new command, but an old one that you have had from the beginning. That old command is the message that you have heard. 8 Yet it is a new command that I am writing you; it is true in Him and in you, because the darkness is passing away and the true light is already shining.

9 Whoever claims to be in the light, and yet continues to hate his brother is still in darkness. 10 Whoever continues to love his brother is always in the light, and he is no hindrance to others. 11 But whoever continues to hate his brother is in darkness and is living in darkness, and he does not know where he is going, because the darkness has blinded his eyes.

12 I am writing to you, dear children, because for His sake your sins have been forgiven. 13 I am writing to you, fathers, because you know Him who has existed from the beginning. I am writing to you, young men, because you have conquered the evil one. I write to you, little children, because you know the Father. 14 I write to you, fathers, because you know Him who has existed from the beginning. I write to you, young men, because you are strong, and God's message is always in your hearts, and you have conquered the evil one.

15 Stop loving the world, or the things that are in the world. If anyone persists in loving the world, there is no love for the Father in his heart, 16 because everything that is in the world, the things that our lower nature and eyes are longing for, and the proud pretensions of life, do not come from the Father, but from the world; 17 and the world is passing away and with it the evil longings it incites, but whoever perseveres in doing God's will lives on forever.

18 Little children, it is the last hour, just as you have heard that Antichrist is coming, and already many Antichrists have appeared; so we may be sure that it is the last hour. 19 They have gone out from our own number, but they did not really belong to us; for if they had, they would have stayed with us. It was to show that none of those who went out really belonged to us. 20 But you have been anointed by the Holy One. You all know the truth; 21 I do not write to you because you do not know it, but because you do know it.

22 Who is the notorious liar, if it is not the man who denies that Jesus is the Christ? He is the real Antichrist, the man who disowns the Father and the Son. 23 No one who disowns the Son can have the Father. Whoever owns the Son has the Father too. 24 Let what you have heard from the beginning continue to live in your hearts; if you do, you will always remain in union with the Son and the Father. 25 And the very thing that He Himself has promised us is eternal life.

26 I write you this with reference to those who are trying to lead you astray. 27 The anointing of the Spirit which you received still remains in your hearts, and so you have no need that anyone should teach you. But just as that anointing of His teaches you about everything, and as it is true and no falsehood, and as it has taught you to do so, you must continue to live in union with Him. 28 And now, dear children, I repeat, you must continue to live in union with Him, so that if He is unveiled, we may have unshaken confidence and not shrink away from Him in shame when He comes. 29 If you know that He is upright, you must know that everyone who practices uprightness is born of Him.

BECK

we're in Him. If you say, "I live in Him," you should live just as He lived.

7 Dear friends, I'm not writing you a new commandment but an old one that you had from the beginning. This old commandment is the Word you've heard. 8 On the other hand, I'm writing you a new commandment, one that is real in Him and in you. I know this because the darkness is passing away and the real light is already shining.

9 Anyone who says, "I am in the light," but hates his brother is still in the dark. 10 If you love your brother, you live in the light, and there's nothing in you to offend anyone. 11 Anyone who hates his brother is in the dark and walks in the dark and doesn't know where he's going, because the darkness has blinded his eyes.

Don't Love the World

12 I'm writing you, children, because your sins are forgiven for His sake. 13 I'm writing you, fathers, because you know Him who has been from the beginning. I'm writing you, young men, because you have conquered the evil one. 14 I'm writing you, children, because you know the Father. I'm writing you, fathers, because you know Him who has been from the beginning. I'm writing you, young men, because you're strong, God's Word lives in you, and you conquered the evil one.

15 Don't love the world or anything in the world. If anyone loves the world, he doesn't love the Father, 16 because everything in the world—the lust of the flesh, the lust of the eyes, and the vain display of property—doesn't come from the Father but from the world. 17 And the world with its lust is passing away. But if you do what God wants, you live forever.

18 Children, it is the last hour. You heard an antichrist is coming, and now many antichrists have come. That is how we know it is the last hour. 19 They left us, but they never really belonged to us. If they had been a part of us, they would have stayed with us. But they left, to show that not all belong to us.

You Have the Son

20 The Holy One has anointed you, and now all of you know. 21 I'm writing you, not as though you don't know the truth but because you know it and no lie comes from the truth.

22 Who is such a liar as he who denies Jesus is the promised Savior? He is the antichrist because he denies the Father and the Son. 23 Anyone who denies the Son doesn't have the Father. If you confess the Son, you also have the Father. 24 Keep in you what you have heard from the beginning. If what you have heard from the beginning stays in you, you will live in the Son and in the Father. 25 And this is what He promised us—everlasting life!

26 I'm writing you about those who are trying to lead you astray. 27 He anointed you, and that anointing stays in you, and you don't need anyone to teach you. But as His anointing teaches you everything—and it is real and no lie—as He has taught you, live in Him.

28 And now, children, live in Him so that when He appears we may be bold and not shrink from Him in shame when He comes.

God's Children

29 If you know He is righteous, you know that everyone who does right is His child.

K.J.V.

3 Behold, what manner of love the Father hath bestowed upon us, that we should be called the sons of God: therefore the world knoweth us not, because it knew him not. 2 Beloved, now are we the sons of God, and it doth not yet appear what we shall be: but we know that, when he shall appear, we shall be like him; for we shall see him as he is. 3And every man that hath this hope in him purifieth himself, even as he is pure. 4 Whosoever committeth sin transgresseth also the law: for sin is the transgression of the law. 5And ye know that he was manifested to take away our sins; and in him is no sin. 6 Whosoever abideth in him sinneth not: whosoever sinneth hath not seen him, neither known him. 7 Little children, let no man deceive you: he that doeth righteousness is righteous, even as he is righteous. 8 He that committeth sin is of the devil; for the devil sinneth from the beginning. For this purpose the Son of God was manifested, that he might destroy the works of the devil. 9 Whosoever is born of God doth not commit sin; for his seed remaineth in him: and he cannot sin, because he is born of God. 10 In this the children of God are manifest, and the children of the devil: whosoever doeth not righteousness is not of God, neither he that loveth not his brother. 11 For this is the message that ye heard from the beginning, that we should love one another. 12 Not as Cain, *who* was of that wicked one, and slew his brother. And wherefore slew he him? Because his own works were evil, and his brother's righteous. 13 Marvel not, my brethren, if the world hate you. 14 We know that we have passed from death unto life, because we love the brethren. He that loveth not *his* brother abideth in death. 15 Whosoever hateth his brother is a murderer: and ye know that no murderer hath eternal life abiding in him. 16 Hereby perceive we the love *of God,* because he laid down his life for us: and we ought to lay down *our* lives for the brethren. 17 But whoso hath this world's good, and seeth his brother have need, and shutteth up his bowels *of compassion* from him, how dwelleth the love of God in him? 18 My little children, let us not love in word, neither in tongue; but in deed and in truth. 19And hereby we know that we are of the truth, and shall assure our hearts before him. 20 For if our heart condemn us, God is greater than our heart, and knoweth all things. 21 Beloved, if our heart condemn us not, *then* have we confidence toward God. 22And whatsoever we ask, we receive of him, because we keep his commandments, and do those things that are pleasing in his sight. 23And this is his commandment, That we should believe on the name of his Son Jesus Christ, and love one another, as he gave us commandment. 24And he that keepeth his commandments dwelleth in him, and he in him. And hereby we

N.A.S.

3 See how great a love the Father has bestowed upon us, that we should be called children of God; and *such* we are. For this reason the world does not know us, because it did not know Him. 2 Beloved, now we are children of God, and it has not appeared as yet what we shall be. We know that, if He should appear, we shall be like Him, because we shall see Him just as He is. 3And every one who has this hope *fixed* on Him purifies himself, just as He is pure. 4 Every one who practices sin also practices lawlessness; and sin is lawlessness. 5And you know that He appeared in order to take away sins; and in Him there is no sin. 6 No one who abides in Him sins; no one who sins has seen Him or knows Him. 7 Little children, let no one deceive you; the one who practices righteousness is righteous, just as He is righteous; 8 the one who practices sin is of the devil; for the devil has sinned from the beginning. The Son of God appeared for this purpose, that He might destroy the works of the devil. 9 No one who is born of God practices sin, because His seed abides in him; and he cannot sin, because he is born of God. 10 By this the children of God and the children of the devil are obvious; any one who does not practice righteousness is not of God, nor the one who does not love his brother. 11 For this is the message which you have heard from the beginning, that we should love one another; 12 not as Cain *who* was of the evil one, and slew his brother. And for what reason did he slay him? Because his deeds were evil, and his brother's were righteous.

13 Do not marvel, brethren, if the world hates you. 14 We know that we have passed out of death into life, because we love the brethren. He who does not love abides in death. 15 Every one who hates his brother is a murderer; and you know that no murderer has eternal life abiding in him. 16 We know love by this, that He laid down His life for us; and we ought to lay down our lives for the brethren. 17 But whoever has the world's goods, and beholds his brother in need and closes his heart against him, how does the love of God abide in him? 18 Little children, let us not love with word or with tongue, but in deed and truth. 19 We shall know by this that we are of the truth, and shall assure our heart before Him, 20 in whatever our heart condemns us; for God is greater than our heart, and knows all things. 21 Beloved, if our heart does not condemn us, we have confidence before God; 22 and whatever we ask we receive from Him, because we keep His commandments and do the things that are pleasing in His sight. 23And this is His commandment, that we believe in the name of His Son Jesus Christ, and love one another, just as He commanded us. 24And the one who keeps His commandments abides in Him, and

WILLIAMS

3 *God's wonderful love has made us His children and now inspires us to be pure, for as such we cannot practice sinning; true love a proof that we are God's children; God answers the prayers of His obedient children*

See what wonderful love the Father has bestowed on us in letting us be called God's children, and that is what we are! This is why the world does not know what we are, because it has never come to know Him. 2 Dearly beloved, we are now God's children, but what we are going to be has not been unveiled. We know that if it is unveiled, we shall be like Him, because we shall see Him as He is. 3 And everyone who has this hope in him tries to make himself as pure as He is.

4 Everyone who commits sin commits lawlessness; sin is lawlessness. 5 You know that He appeared to take our sins away, and that there is no sin in Him. 6 No one who continues to live in union with Him practices sin. No one who practices sin has ever seen Him or come to know Him. 7 Dear children, avoid letting anyone lead you astray. Whoever practices doing right is upright, just as He is upright. 8 Whoever practices sin belongs to the devil, because the devil has practiced sin from the beginning. This is why the Son of God appeared, to undo the devil's works.

9 No one who is born of God makes a practice of sinning, because the God-given life-principle[a] continues to live in him, and so he cannot practice sinning, because he is born of God. 10 This is the way to distinguish God's children from the devil's. No one who fails to do right is God's child, and no one who fails to love his brother. 11 It is so because the message that you have heard from the beginning is this: We should love one another. 12 We must not be like Cain who belonged to the evil one and butchered his brother. And why did he butcher him? Because his own actions were wicked and his brother's upright.

13 You must not be surprised, brothers, if the world hates you. 14 We know that we have passed out of death into life, because we love our brothers. Whoever does not continue to love continues still in death. 15 Anyone who keeps on hating his brother is a murderer, and you know that no murderer can have eternal life remaining in him.

16 We know what love is from the fact that He laid down His life for us; and so we ought to lay down our lives for our brothers. 17 But if anyone has the world's means of supporting life and sees his brother in need and closes his heart against him, how can love to God remain in him? 18 Dear children, let us stop loving with words or lips alone, but let us love with actions and in truth.

19 In this way we shall know by experience that we are on the side of the truth, and satisfy our consciences in God's sight, 20 because if our consciences do condemn us, God is greater than our consciences, and He knows everything. 21 Dearly beloved, if our consciences do not condemn us, we come with perfect confidence to God, 22 and we obtain from Him whatever we ask for, because we practice obedience to His commands and do what pleases Him. 23 His command is this, that we should believe in the name of His Son Jesus Christ and practice loving one another, just as He commanded us to do. 24 Whoever practices obedience to His commands remains in union with Him and He

[a] Grk., *seed;* so *the life-principle.*

BECK

3 See how the Father has loved us—we are called God's children, and that's what we are. The world doesn't know us because it didn't get to know Him. 2 Dear friends, we are now God's children, but it hasn't yet been shown what we're going to be. We know that when it will be shown, we'll be like Him because we'll see Him as He is. 3 And everyone who trusts Him for this purifies himself as He is pure.

4 Everyone who sins breaks the Law. Sin is breaking the Law. 5 And you know He appeared in order to take away our sins. There is no sin in Him. 6 Anyone who stays in Him doesn't sin. Anyone who sins hasn't seen or known Him. 7 Children, don't let anybody deceive you. Whoever does right is righteous as He is righteous.

8 Anyone who lives in sin is the devil's child because the devil has been sinning from the beginning. God's Son appeared in order to undo the devil's works. 9 Everyone who is God's child refuses to sin because God's new life is in him, and he cannot sin because he is God's child. 10 You can see who are God's children and who are the devil's children: Anyone who doesn't do right or love his brother isn't God's child.

Love One Another

11 This is the message you have heard from the beginning: Love one another. 12 Don't be like Cain. He was a son of the evil one and murdered his brother. And why did he murder him? Because he did wrong and his brother did right. 13 Don't be surprised, fellow Christians, if the world hates you.

14 We know we have come from death into life, because we love our fellow Christians. Anyone who doesn't love stays dead. 15 Everyone who hates his brother is a murderer, and you know no murderer keeps everlasting life in him.

16 This is how we learned what love is: He gave His life for us. We, too, should give our lives for our fellow Christians. 17 If anyone has this world's goods and sees his fellow Christian is in need but shuts his heart against him, how can he still be loving God? 18 Children, let us not love only in words or in talk, but let us put our love into action and make it real.

19 This is how we'll know we're born of the truth and will reassure ourselves before Him: 20 Whenever our conscience condemns us, God is greater than our conscience and knows everything. 21 Dear friends, if our conscience doesn't condemn us, we can talk boldly to God 22 and get from Him anything we ask because we obey His orders and do what pleases Him. 23 He orders us to believe in the name of His Son Jesus Christ and to love one another as He has ordered us to do. 24 Anyone who does what He orders lives in God and God in him. And this

K.J.V.

know that he abideth in us, by the Spirit which he hath given us.

4 Beloved, believe not every spirit, but try the spirits whether they are of God: because many false prophets are gone out into the world. 2 Hereby know ye the Spirit of God: Every spirit that confesseth that Jesus Christ is come in the flesh is of God: 3 And every spirit that confesseth not that Jesus Christ is come in the flesh is not of God: and this is that *spirit* of antichrist, whereof ye have heard that it should come; and even now already is it in the world. 4 Ye are of God, little children, and have overcome them: because greater is he that is in you, than he that is in the world. 5 They are of the world: therefore speak they of the world, and the world heareth them. 6 We are of God: he that knoweth God heareth us; he that is not of God heareth not us. Hereby know we the spirit of truth, and the spirit of error. 7 Beloved, let us love one another: for love is of God; and every one that loveth is born of God, and knoweth God. 8 He that loveth not, knoweth not God; for God is love. 9 In this was manifested the love of God toward us, because that God sent his only begotten Son into the world, that we might live through him. 10 Herein is love, not that we loved God, but that he loved us, and sent his Son *to be* the propitiation for our sins. 11 Beloved, if God so loved us, we ought also to love one another. 12 No man hath seen God at any time. If we love one another, God dwelleth in us, and his love is perfected in us. 13 Hereby know we that we dwell in him, and he in us, because he hath given us of his Spirit. 14 And we have seen and do testify that the Father sent the Son *to be* the Saviour of the world. 15 Whosoever shall confess that Jesus is the Son of God, God dwelleth in him, and he in God. 16 And we have known and believed the love that God hath to us. God is love; and he that dwelleth in love dwelleth in God, and God in him. 17 Herein is our love made perfect, that we may have boldness in the day of judgment: because as he is, so are we in this world. 18 There is no fear in love; but perfect love casteth out fear: because fear hath torment. He that feareth is not made perfect in love. 19 We love him, because he first loved us. 20 If a man say, I love God, and hateth his brother, he is a liar: for he that loveth not his brother whom he hath seen, how can he love God whom he hath not seen? 21 And this commandment have we from him, That he who loveth God love his brother also.

N.A.S.

He in him. And we know by this that He abides in us, by the Spirit which He has given us.

4 Beloved, do not believe every spirit, but test the spirits to see whether they are from God; because many false prophets have gone out into the world. 2 By this you know the Spirit of God: every spirit that confesses that Jesus Christ has come in the flesh is from God; 3 and every spirit that does not confess Jesus is not from God; and this is the *spirit* of the antichrist, of which you have heard that it is coming, and now it is already in the world. 4 You are from God, little children, and have overcome them; because greater is He who is in you than he who is in the world. 5 They are from the world; therefore they speak *as* from the world, and the world listens to them. 6 We are from God; he who knows God listens to us; he who is not from God does not listen to us. By this we know the spirit of truth and the spirit of error. 7 Beloved, let us love one another, for love is from God; and every one who loves is born of God and knows God. 8 The one who does not love does not know God, for God is love. 9 By this the love of God was manifested in us, that God has sent His only begotten Son into the world so that we might live through Him. 10 In this is love, not that we loved God, but that He loved us and sent His Son *to be* the propitiation for our sins. 11 Beloved, if God so loved us, we also ought to love one another. 12 No one has beheld God at any time; if we love one another, God abides in us, and His love is perfected in us. 13 By this we know that we abide in Him and He in us, because He has given us of His Spirit. 14 And we have beheld and bear witness that the Father has sent the Son *to be* the Savior of the world. 15 Whoever confesses that Jesus is the Son of God, God abides in him, and he in God. 16 And we have come to know and have believed the love which God has for us. God is love, and the one who abides in love abides in God, and God abides in him. 17 By this love is perfected with us, that we may have confidence in the day of judgment; because as He is, so also are we in this world. 18 There is no fear in love; but perfect love casts out fear, because fear involves punishment, and the one who fears is not perfected in love. 19 We love, because He first loved us. 20 If some one says, "I love God," and hates his brother, he is a liar; for the one who does not love his brother whom he has seen, cannot love God whom he has not seen. 21 And this commandment we have from Him, that the one who loves God should love his brother also.

WILLIAMS

in union with him; and in this way we know that He remains in union with us, by the Spirit that He has given us.

4 *How to distinguish true teaching from false; another way, God's Spirit helps us to know the true; love to one another marks us as God's children; His love to us inspires us to trust and love Him*

Dearly beloved, stop believing every so-called spiritual utterance, but keep testing them to see whether they come from God, because many false prophets have gone out into the world. 2 In this way you can recognize the Spirit of God: Every spiritual utterance which owns that Jesus Christ has come in human form comes from God, 3 and no spiritual utterance which disowns Jesus can come from God; it is the utterance of Antichrist. You have heard that it is coming, and right now it is already in the world.

4 You are children of God, dear children, and you have conquered these men, because He who is in our hearts is greater than he who is in the world. 5 They are children of the world; this is why they speak what the world inspires, and why the world listens to them. 6 We are children of God. Whoever knows God by experience listens to us; whoever is not a child of God does not listen to us. This is the way to distinguish a true spiritual utterance from one that is false.

7 Dearly beloved, let us practice loving one another, because love originates with God, and everyone who practices loving is a child of God and knows God by experience. 8 Whoever does not love has never come to know God by experience, because God is love. 9 This is the way God's love for us has been shown, namely, God has sent His only Son into the world that we through Him might have life. 10 In this way is seen the true love, not that we loved God but that He loved us and sent His Son to be the atoning sacrifice for our sins.

11 Dearly beloved, if God has loved us so, we ought to love one another too. 12 No one has ever seen God; yet if we practice loving one another, God remains in union with us, and our love for Him attains perfection in our hearts. 13 By the fact that He has given us a portion of His Spirit we can be sure that we remain in union with Him and He in union with us. 14 We have seen and now testify that the Father has sent His Son to be the Saviour of the world. 15 Whoever owns that Jesus is the Son of God, God remains in union with him and he in union with God. 16 So we know by experience and trust the love that God has for us.

God is love, and whoever continues to love continues in union with God and God in union with him. 17 Our love attains perfection through our having perfect confidence about the day of judgment, because here in this world we are living as He did. 18 There is no fear in love, and perfect love drives out fear, because fear pertains to punishment, and no one who is subject to fear has attained perfection in love. 19 We love, because He loved us first. 20 If anyone says, "I love God," and yet habitually hates his brother, he is a liar; for whoever does not love his brother whom he has seen cannot love God whom he has not seen. 21 This is the command that we get from Him, that whoever loves God loves his brother too.

BECK

is how we know He lives in us: by the Spirit whom He has given us.

False Prophets

4 Dear friends, don't believe every spirit, but test the spirits to see if they are from God. Many false prophets have gone out into the world. 2 This is how you can recognize God's Spirit: Every spirit who confesses that Jesus Christ has come in the flesh is from God. 3 And any spirit who doesn't confess this Jesus isn't from God. This is the spirit of the antichrist which you heard is coming, and here it is already in the world.

4 Children, you are God's family, and you have won a victory over these men because He who is in you is greater than he who is in the world. 5 These men belong to the world. That is why they speak the thoughts of the world, and the world listens to them. 6 We are God's children. Anyone who knows God listens to us. Anyone who is not God's child will not listen to us. In this way we can tell what is the spirit of truth and what is the spirit of error.

God's Love in Us

7 Dear friends, let us love one another because love comes from God and everyone who loves is God's child and knows God. 8 He who doesn't love hasn't learned to know God, because God is Love. 9 God has shown us His love by sending His only Son into the world for us to live through Him. 10 This is love, not that we loved God but that He loved us and sent His Son to pay for our sins.* 11 Dear friends, if that's how God loved us, then we should love one another. 12 Nobody has ever seen God. If we love one another, God lives in us, and His love has accomplished in us what He wants. 13 This is how we know we live in Him and He in us: He has given us some of His Spirit.

14 We have seen and can tell the truth that the Father sent His Son to save the world. 15 If you confess Jesus is God's Son, God lives in you and you in God. 16 And we have come to know and believe the love God has for us. God is Love, and if you live in love, you live in God, and God lives in you.

17 His love has accomplished what He wants when we can look ahead confidently to the day of judgment because we are what He is in this world. Such love isn't terrified, 18 but the finest love throws out terror. We are terrified by punishment, and if we're terrified, our love isn't at its best.

19 We love because He first loved us. 20 If anyone says, "I love God," but hates his brother, he's a liar. If anyone doesn't love his brother whom he has seen, he can't love God whom he hasn't seen. 21 And this is the order He gave us: If you love God, love your brother.

* His sacrifice wipes out our sins and changes God's anger to love.

K.J.V.

5 Whosoever believeth that Jesus is the Christ is born of God: and every one that loveth him that begat loveth him also that is begotten of him. 2 By this we know that we love the children of God, when we love God, and keep his commandments. 3 For this is the love of God, that we keep his commandments: and his commandments are not grievous. 4 For whatsoever is born of God overcometh the world: and this is the victory that overcometh the world, *even* our faith. 5 Who is he that overcometh the world, but he that believeth that Jesus is the Son of God? 6 This is he that came by water and blood, *even* Jesus Christ; not by water only, but by water and blood. And it is the Spirit that beareth witness, because the Spirit is truth. 7 For there are three that bear record in heaven, the Father, the Word, and the Holy Ghost: and these three are one. 8 And there are three that bear witness in earth, the spirit, and the water, and the blood: and these three agree in one. 9 If we receive the witness of men, the witness of God is greater: for this is the witness of God which he hath testified of his Son. 10 He that believeth on the Son of God hath the witness in himself: he that believeth not God hath made him a liar; because he believeth not the record that God gave of his Son. 11 And this is the record, that God hath given to us eternal life, and this life is in his Son. 12 He that hath the Son hath life; *and* he that hath not the Son of God hath not life. 13 These things have I written unto you that believe on the name of the Son of God; that ye may know that ye have eternal life, and that ye may believe on the name of the Son of God. 14 And this is the confidence that we have in him, that, if we ask any thing according to his will, he heareth us: 15 And if we know that he hear us, whatsoever we ask, we know that we have the petitions that we desired of him. 16 If any man see his brother sin a sin *which is* not unto death, he shall ask, and he shall give him life for them that sin not unto death. There is a sin unto death: I do not say that he shall pray for it. 17 All unrighteousness is sin: and there is a sin not unto death. 18 We know that whosoever is born of God sinneth not; but he that is begotten of God keepeth himself, and that wicked one toucheth him not. 19 *And* we know that we are of God, and the whole world lieth in wickedness. 20 And we know that the Son of God is come, and hath given us an understanding, that we may know him that is true; and we are in him that is true, *even* in his Son Jesus Christ. This is the true God, and eternal life. 21 Little children, keep yourselves from idols. Amen.

N.A.S.

5 Whoever believes that Jesus is the [a]Christ is born of God; and whoever loves the Father loves the *child* born of Him. 2 By this we know that we love the children of God, when we love God and observe His commandments. 3 For this is the love of God, that we keep His commandments; and His commandments are not burdensome. 4 For whatever is born of God overcomes the world; and this is the victory that has overcome the world—our faith. 5 And who is the one who overcomes the world, but he who believes that Jesus is the Son of God? 6 This is the one who came by water and blood, Jesus Christ; not with the water only, but with the water and with the blood. 7 And it is the Spirit who bears witness, because the Spirit is the truth. 8 For there are three that bear witness, the Spirit and the water and the blood; and the three are in agreement. 9 If we receive the witness of men, the witness of God is greater; for the witness of God is this, that He has borne witness concerning His Son. 10 The one who believes in the Son of God has the witness in himself; the one who does not believe God has made Him a liar, because he has not believed in the witness that God has borne concerning His Son. 11 And the witness is this, that God has given us eternal life, and this life is in His Son. 12 He who has the Son has the life; he who does not have the Son of God does not have the life.

13 These things I have written to you who believe in the name of the Son of God, in order that you may know that you have eternal life. 14 And this is the confidence which we have before Him, that, if we ask anything according to His will, He hears us. 15 And if we know that He hears us *in* whatever we ask, we know that we have the requests which we have asked from Him. 16 If any one sees his brother committing a sin not *leading* to death, he shall ask and *God* will for him give life to those who commit sin not *leading* to death. There is a sin *leading* to death; I do not say that he should make request for this. 17 All unrighteousness is sin, and there is a sin not *leading* to death.

18 We know that no one who is born of God sins; but He who was born of God keeps him and the evil one does not touch him. 19 We know that we are of God, and the whole world lies in *the power of* the evil one. 20 And we know that the Son of God has come, and has given us understanding, in order that we might know Him who is true, and we are in Him who is true, in His Son Jesus Christ. This is the true God and eternal life. 21 Little children, guard yourselves from idols.

[a] I.e., *Messiah.*

WILLIAMS

5 *Victorious faith proves that we are God's children; three witnesses that God's Son came in human form; certain of eternal life, of answered prayer*

Everyone who believes that Jesus is the Christ is born of God, and everyone who loves the Father loves His child. 2 This is how we can be sure that we love the children of God, by continuing to love God and to obey His commands. 3 For love to God means this, to practice obedience to His commands, and His commands are not burdensome, 4 for every child of God continues to conquer the world. Our faith is the victory that has conquered the world. 5 Now who is it that continues to conquer the world, if it is not the person who believes that Jesus is the Son of God? 6 He is the One who came through water and blood—Jesus Christ; not through water only but through water and blood. The Spirit also testifies to this, because the Spirit is truth.[a] 8 Because there are three that testify to it, the Spirit, the water, and the blood, and the three agree. 9 If we accept the testimony of men, the testimony of God is stronger still; because this is the testimony that God has borne to His Son. 10 Whoever believes in the Son of God has this testimony in his own heart. Whoever does not believe God has made Him a liar, because he has not believed the testimony that God has borne to His Son. 11And this testimony is that God has given us eternal life, and this life is given through union with His Son. 12 Whoever has the Son has life; whoever does not have the Son does not have life.

13 I have written this to you who believe in the person of the Son of God, so that you may know that you already have eternal life. 14And this is the confidence that we have in Him, that if we ask for anything that is in accordance with His will, He will listen to us. 15And if we know that He listens to us in whatever we ask Him for, we know that we get from Him the things that we have asked Him for. 16 If anyone sees his brother committing a sin that does not lead to death, he will ask and God will grant him life; yea, He will grant it to any who do not commit a sin that leads to death. There is a sin that leads to death; I do not say that one should pray for that. 17Any wrongdoing is sin; and there are sins that do not lead to death. 18 We know that no one who is born of God makes a practice of sinning, but the Son who was born of God continues to keep him, and the evil one cannot touch him. 19 We know that we are children of God, and that the whole world is under the power of the evil one. 20And we know that the Son of God has come, and has given us insight to recognize the True One; and we are in union with the True One through His Son, Jesus Christ. He is the true God and eternal life.

21 Dear children, once for all put yourselves beyond the reach of idols.

BECK

5 Everyone who believes Jesus is the promised Savior is God's child. And everyone who loves the Father loves the Father's child. 2 We know we love God's children when we love God and do what He orders us to do. 3 Loving God means we do what He orders. And what He orders is no burden.

God's Life in Us

4 Every child of God conquers the world. Our faith is the victory over the world. 5 Who conquers the world but he who believes Jesus is God's Son?

6 This is He who came by water and blood—Jesus Christ. Not by water only but by water and blood. And the Spirit is telling the truth because the Spirit is the truth. 7 There are three who bring us the truth:[*] 8 the Spirit, the water, and the blood, and these three have one purpose.

9 If we accept the testimony of men, God's testimony is greater because God's testimony is the truth He told about His Son. 10 If you believe in God's Son, you have in you the testimony of the truth. Anyone who will not believe God has made Him a liar because he hasn't believed the truth God told about His Son.

11 He told us this truth that God has given us everlasting life and this life is in His Son. 12 If you have the Son, you have life. If you don't have God's Son, you don't have life. 13 I'm writing you this so that you who believe in the name of God's Son will know you have everlasting life.

14 We feel sure of Him that if we ask for anything according to His will, He listens to us. 15And if we know He listens to us whatever we ask, we know we get what we ask Him for. If anyone sees His brother sinning but the sin isn't deadly, 16 he should pray, and God will give him life for those who sin if the sin isn't deadly. There is a sin that's deadly; I don't tell you to pray for it. 17 Every kind of wrong is sin, but there is a sin that isn't deadly.

18 We know that no child of God goes on sinning, but God's Son protects him, and the evil one doesn't touch him. 19 We know we're God's children, and the whole world is in the power of the evil one.

20 We know God's Son came and gave us the understanding to know Him who is real, and we are in Him who is real, in His Son Jesus Christ. He is the true God and everlasting life. 21 Children, keep away from idols.

* Our oldest manuscripts do not have vv. 7b-8a: "in heaven: the Father, the Word, and the Holy Spirit, and these three are one. And there are three testifying on earth." Early in the 16th century an editor translated these words from Latin manuscripts and inserted them in his Greek New Testament. Erasmus took them from this Greek New Testament and inserted them in the third edition (1522) of his Greek New Testament. Luther used the text prepared by Erasmus. But even though the inserted words taught the Trinity, Luther ruled them out and never had them in his translation. In 1550 Bugenhagen objected to these words "on account of the truth." In 1574 Feyerabend, a printer, added them to Luther's text, and in 1596 they appeared in the Wittenberg copies. They were not in Tyndale's or Coverdale's Bible or in the Great Bible.

[a] V. 7 in A. V. not in best Mss.

K.J.V.

THE
SECOND EPISTLE
OF
JOHN

The elder unto the elect lady and her children, whom I love in the truth; and not I only, but also all they that have known the truth; 2 For the truth's sake, which dwelleth in us, and shall be with us for ever. 3 Grace be with you, mercy, *and* peace, from God the Father, and from the Lord Jesus Christ, the Son of the Father, in truth and love. 4 I rejoiced greatly that I found of thy children walking in truth, as we have received a commandment from the Father. 5 And now I beseech thee, lady, not as though I wrote a new commandment unto thee, but that which we had from the beginning, that we love one another. 6 And this is love, that we walk after his commandments. This is the commandment, That, as ye have heard from the beginning, ye should walk in it. 7 For many deceivers are entered into the world, who confess not that Jesus Christ is come in the flesh. This is a deceiver and an antichrist. 8 Look to yourselves, that we lose not those things which we have wrought, but that we receive a full reward. 9 Whosoever transgresseth, and abideth not in the doctrine of Christ, hath not God. He that abideth in the doctrine of Christ, he hath both the Father and the Son. 10 If there come any unto you, and bring not this doctrine, receive him not into *your* house, neither bid him God speed: 11 For he that biddeth him God speed is partaker of his evil deeds. 12 Having many things to write unto you, I would not *write* with paper and ink: but I trust to come unto you, and speak face to face, that our joy may be full. 13 The children of thy elect sister greet thee. Amen.

N.A.S.

THE SECOND EPISTLE OF
JOHN

The elder to the chosen lady and her children, whom I love in truth; and not only I, but also all who know the truth, 2 for the sake of the truth which abides in us and will be with us forever: 3 Grace, mercy *and* peace will be with us, from God the Father and from Jesus Christ, the Son of the Father, in truth and love. 4 I was very glad to find *some* of your children walking in truth, just as we have received commandment *to do* from the Father. 5 And now I ask you, lady, not as writing to you a new commandment, but the one which we have had from the beginning, that we love one another. 6 And this is love, that we walk according to His commandments. This is the commandment, just as you have heard from the beginning, that you should walk in it. 7 For many deceivers have gone out into the world, those who do not acknowledge Jesus Christ *as* coming in the flesh. This is the deceiver and the antichrist. 8 Watch yourselves, that you might not lose what we have accomplished, but that you may receive a full reward. 9 Any one who goes too far and does not abide in the teaching of Christ, does not have God; the one who abides in the teaching, he has both the Father and the Son. 10 If any one comes to you and does not bring this teaching, do not receive him into *your* house, and do not give him a greeting; 11 for the one who gives him a greeting participates in his evil deeds.
12 Having many things to write to you, I do not want to *do so* with paper and ink; but I hope to come to you and speak face to face, that your joy may be made full. 13 The children of your chosen sister greet you.

THE SECOND LETTER OF

SECOND JOHN

JOHN

He greets them; rejoices in their loyalty but warns them against the false teachers; shows the need of such loyalty to the truth; could talk about much more

The Elder to the chosen lady and her children, whom I truly love, and not only I but all who know the truth, 2 because of the truth that lives on in our hearts and will be with us forever: 3 spiritual blessing, mercy, and peace will be with us from God the Father and Jesus Christ, the Father's Son, in truth and love.

4 I am happy to find that some of your children are living by the truth, just as we had been commanded from the Father to do. 5 And now I beg you, my lady, not as though I were writing you a new command, but one which we had from the beginning, that we continue to love one another. 6 Now love means this, that we keep on living in accordance with His commands. The command is this, that we continue to live in love. 7 For many impostors have gone out into the world, men who do not own that Jesus Christ continues to come in human form. A person like this is the impostor and the Antichrist. 8 Look out for yourselves, so as not to lose what we have worked for, but so as to get your full reward. 9 No one has God, who goes too far and fails to stay by the teaching of Christ. Whoever stays by this teaching has the Father and the Son. 10 If anyone continuously comes to see you without bringing this teaching, you must stop welcoming him to your house and stop bidding him good morning. 11 For whoever keeps on bidding him good morning is sharing in his wicked works.

12 Though I have much to write you, I do not choose to do so with paper and ink, but I hope to come to see you and talk with you face to face, so that your happiness may be complete. 13 The children of your chosen sister wish to be remembered to you.

The pastor to the chosen lady and her children, whom I love in the truth, and not I alone but all who know the truth, 2 because the truth lives in us and will be with us forever— 3 God the Father and Jesus Christ, the Father's Son, will give us love, mercy, and peace as we are in the truth and in love.

4 I was very happy to find some of your children living in the truth as the Father has ordered us. 5 And now I ask you, lady (I'm not writing you a new commandment but one we've had from the beginning): Let us love one another. 6 Love means that we live according to His commandments. The commandment as you have heard it from the beginning is: Live in love.

7 Many deceivers have gone out into the world. They don't confess Jesus Christ as One who comes in the flesh. That is the mark of the deceiver and the antichrist. 8 Watch yourselves so you will not lose what you worked for but will get your full reward.

9 Anyone who goes too far and doesn't stay with what Christ has taught doesn't have God. If you stay with what He taught, you have the Father and the Son. 10 If anyone comes to you and doesn't teach this, don't take him into your home or greet him. 11 If you greet him, you share the wicked things he does.

12 While I have much to write you, I don't want to do it with paper and ink, but I hope to come to you and tell you face to face so that you may be very happy.

13 The children of your sister, whom God has chosen, greet you.

K.J.V.   N.A.S.

THE

THIRD EPISTLE

OF

JOHN

THE THIRD EPISTLE OF

JOHN

The elder unto the well beloved Gaius, whom I love in the truth. 2 Beloved, I wish above all things that thou mayest prosper and be in health, even as thy soul prospereth. 3 For I rejoiced greatly, when the brethren came and testified of the truth that is in thee, even as thou walkest in the truth. 4 I have no greater joy than to hear that my children walk in truth. 5 Beloved, thou doest faithfully whatsoever thou doest to the brethren, and to strangers; 6 Which have borne witness of thy charity before the church: whom if thou bring forward on their journey after a godly sort, thou shalt do well: 7 Because that for his name's sake they went forth, taking nothing of the Gentiles. 8 We therefore ought to receive such, that we might be fellow helpers to the truth. 9 I wrote unto the church: but Diotrephes, who loveth to have the preeminence among them, receiveth us not. 10 Wherefore, if I come, I will remember his deeds which he doeth, prating against us with malicious words: and not content therewith, neither doth he himself receive the brethren, and forbiddeth them that would, and casteth *them* out of the church. 11 Beloved, follow not that which is evil, but that which is good. He that doeth good is of God: but he that doeth evil hath not seen God. 12 Demetrius hath good report of all *men*, and of the truth itself: yea, and we *also* bear record; and ye know that our record is true. 13 I had many things to write, but I will not with ink and pen write unto thee: 14 But I trust I shall shortly see thee, and we shall speak face to face. Peace *be* to thee. *Our* friends salute thee. Greet the friends by name.

The elder to the beloved Gaius, whom I love in truth.

2 Beloved, I pray that in all respects you may prosper and be in good health, just as your soul prospers. 3 For I was very glad when brethren came and bore witness to your truth, *that is,* how you are walking in truth. 4 I have no greater joy than this, to hear of my children walking in the truth.

5 Beloved, you are acting faithfully in whatever you accomplish for the brethren, and especially *when they are* strangers; 6 and they bear witness to your love before the church; and you will do well to send them on their way in a manner worthy of God. 7 For they went out for the sake of the Name, accepting nothing from the Gentiles. 8 Therefore we ought to support such men, that we may be fellow-workers with the truth.

9 I wrote something to the church; but Diotrephes, who loves to be first among them, does not accept what we say. 10 For this reason, if I come, I will call attention to his deeds which he does, unjustly accusing us with wicked words; and not satisfied with this, neither does he himself receive the brethren, and he forbids those who desire *to do so,* and puts *them* out of the church. 11 Beloved, do not imitate what is evil, but what is good. The one who does good is of God; the one who does evil has not seen God. 12 Demetrius has received a good testimony from every one, and from the truth itself; and we also bear witness, and you know that our witness is true.

13 I had many things to write to you, but I am not willing to write *them* to you with pen and ink; 14 but I hope to see you shortly, and we shall speak face to face. Peace *be* to you. The friends greet you. Greet the friends by name.

THIRD JOHN

He greets and commends Gaius; reminds the church of Diotrephes' ambitions; tells of Demetrius' good reputation; concludes

The Elder to the dearly beloved Gaius, whom I truly love.
2 Dearly beloved, I am praying for you to continue to prosper in everything, and to keep well, just as your soul is prospering. 3 For I am happy to have some brothers come and testify to the truth that is in you, since you are living by the truth. 4 I have no greater spiritual blessing than this, to hear that my children are living by the truth.
5 Dearly beloved, you are acting faithfully in doing what you can for the brothers, especially as they are strangers. 6 They have testified before the church to your love. You will please send them off on their journey in a way befitting the service of God. 7 For they have started out for His name's sake and so accept nothing from the heathen. 8 So we ought to show hospitality to such men, to prove that we co-operate with them for the truth.
9 I have written briefly to the church, but Diotrephes, who likes to be first among them, refuses to listen to me. 10 So, if I come, I will remind you of what he is doing, how with malicious insinuations he is talking about me. Not content with that, he refuses to welcome the brothers himself, he interferes with those who want to do so, and tries to put them out of the church.
11 Dearly beloved, do not follow bad examples but good ones. Whoever practices doing right is God's child; whoever practices doing wrong has never seen God. 12 Demetrius has a good testimony from everybody and from truth itself; yea, from me too, and you know that my testimony to him is true.
13 I have much to say to you, but I do not want to write it with pen and ink. 14 I hope to see you very soon and will talk it over face to face. Good-by. Our friends wish to be remembered to you. Remember me to our friends individually.

THE THIRD LETTER OF

JOHN

The pastor to my dear Gaius, whom I love in truth.
2 Dear friend, I pray that you're doing well in every way and are also healthy, just as your soul is doing well. 3 I was delighted when some Christians came and told me about the truth you have—how you live in it. 4 Nothing gives me greater joy than to hear that my children live in the truth.
5 Dear friend, you're loyal in whatever you do for the fellow Christians even though they're strangers. 6 They have publicly told the church about your love. Please help them on their way as it is right before God, 7 because they went out for Jesus, taking nothing from the people of the world. 8 We should help such people in order to work with them for the truth.
9 I wrote something to the church, but Diotrephes, who likes to be their leader, won't listen to us. 10 So, if I come, I'll bring up what he's doing when he talks such wicked nonsense about us. Not satisfied with that, he also will not welcome the fellow Christians as guests and stops those who want to welcome them and tries to put them out of the church.
11 Dear friend, don't imitate what is wrong but what is right. If you do right, you're God's child. Anyone who does wrong hasn't seen God.
12 Everybody speaks well of Demetrius, and so does the truth itself. We also speak well of him, and you know we tell the truth.
13 I have much to write you, but I don't want to do it with pen and ink. 14 I hope to see you very soon and talk to you face to face.
15 Peace to you! The friends here send you their greetings. Greet each of our friends by name.

K.J.V.

THE

GENERAL EPISTLE

OF

JUDE

N.A.S.

THE EPISTLE OF

JUDE

Jude, the servant of Jesus Christ, and brother of James, to them that are sanctified by God the Father, and preserved in Jesus Christ, *and* called: 2 Mercy unto you, and peace, and love, be multiplied. 3 Beloved, when I gave all diligence to write unto you of the common salvation, it was needful for me to write unto you, and exhort *you* that ye should earnestly contend for the faith which was once delivered unto the saints. 4 For there are certain men crept in unawares, who were before of old ordained to this condemnation, ungodly men, turning the grace of our God into lasciviousness, and denying the only Lord God, and our Lord Jesus Christ. 5 I will therefore put you in remembrance, though ye once knew this, how that the Lord, having saved the people out of the land of Egypt, afterward destroyed them that believed not. 6 And the angels which kept not their first estate, but left their own habitation, he hath reserved in everlasting chains under darkness unto the judgment of the great day. 7 Even as Sodom and Gomorrha, and the cities about them in like manner, giving themselves over to fornication, and going after strange flesh, are set forth for an example, suffering the vengeance of eternal fire. 8 Likewise also these *filthy* dreamers defile the flesh, despise dominion, and speak evil of dignities. 9 Yet Michael the archangel, when contending with the devil he disputed about the body of Moses, durst not bring against him a railing accusation, but said, The Lord rebuke thee. 10 But these speak evil of those things which they know not: but what they know naturally, as brute beasts, in those things they corrupt themselves. 11 Woe unto them! for they have gone in the way of Cain, and ran greedily after the error of Balaam for reward, and perished in the gainsaying of Core. 12 These are spots in your feasts of charity, when they feast with you, feeding themselves without fear: clouds *they are* without water, carried about of winds; trees whose fruit withereth, without fruit, twice dead, plucked up by the roots; 13 Raging waves of the sea, foaming out their own shame; wandering stars, to whom is reserved the blackness of darkness for ever. 14 And Enoch also, the seventh from Adam, prophesied of these, saying, Behold, the Lord cometh with ten thousands of his saints, 15 To execute judgment upon all, and to convince all that are ungodly among them of all their ungodly deeds which they have ungodly committed, and of all their hard *speeches* which ungodly sinners have spoken against him. 16 These are murmurers, complainers, walking after their own lusts; and their mouth speaketh great swelling *words,* having men's persons in admiration because of advan-

Jude, a bondservant of Jesus Christ, and brother of James, to those who are the called, beloved in God the Father, and kept for Jesus Christ: 2 May mercy and peace and love be multiplied to you.

3 Beloved, while I was making every effort to write you about our common salvation, I felt the necessity to write to you appealing that you contend earnestly for the faith which was once for all delivered to the saints. 4 For certain persons have crept in unnoticed, those who were long beforehand marked out for this condemnation, ungodly persons who turn the grace of our God into licentiousness and deny our only Master and Lord, Jesus Christ.

5 Now I desire to remind you, though you know all things once for all, that [a]the Lord, after saving a people out of the land of Egypt, subsequently destroyed those who did not believe. 6 And angels who did not keep their own domain, but abandoned their proper abode, He has kept in eternal bonds under darkness for the judgment of the great day. 7 Just as Sodom and Gomorrah and the cities around them, since they in the same way as these indulged in gross immorality and went after strange flesh, are exhibited as an example, in undergoing the punishment of eternal fire. 8 Yet in the same manner these men also by dreaming defile the flesh, and reject authority, and revile angelic majesties. 9 But Michael the archangel, when he disputed with the devil and argued about the body of Moses did not dare pronounce against him a railing judgment, but said, "THE LORD REBUKE YOU." 10 But these men revile the things which they do not understand; and the things which they know by instinct, like unreasoning animals, by these things they are destroyed. 11 Woe to them! For they have gone the way of Cain, and for pay they have rushed headlong into the error of Balaam, and perished in the rebellion of Korah. 12 These men are those who are hidden reefs in your love-feasts when they feast with you without fear, caring for themselves; clouds without water, carried along by winds; autumn trees without fruit, doubly dead, uprooted; 13 wild waves of the sea, casting up their own shame like foam; wandering stars, for whom the black darkness has been reserved forever. 14 And about these also Enoch, *in* the seventh *generation* from Adam, prophesied, saying, "Behold, the Lord came with many thousands of His holy ones, 15 to execute judgment upon all, and to convict all the ungodly of all their ungodly deeds which they have done in an ungodly way, and of all the harsh things which ungodly sinners have spoken against Him." 16 These are grumblers, finding fault, following after their *own* lusts, they speak arrogantly, flattering people for the sake of *gaining an* advantage.

[a] Some ancient mss. read, *Jesus.*

JUDE

He greets them; He urges them to defend the teaching of the apostles; gives examples of judgment on the godless; describes the disgraceful lives of the false teachers; tells how to live with such men

Jude, a slave of Jesus Christ, and a brother of James, to those who have been called, who are beloved by God the Father and have been kept through union with Jesus Christ: 2 may mercy, peace, and love in abundance be given you.

3 Dearly beloved, while I was doing my best to begin writing you about our common salvation, I found it necessary to write and urge you to carry on a vigorous defense of the faith that was once for all entrusted to God's people. 4 For certain persons have sneaked in—their doom was written down long ago—godless persons, who turn the favor of our God into an excuse for licentiousness, and disown our only Master and Lord, Jesus Christ.

5 Now I want to remind you, though you know it all already, that although the Lord had saved a people out of the land of Egypt, He afterward destroyed those who did not believe. 6 And angels, who did not preserve their original rank but left their proper home, He has kept in everlasting chains under darkness, for the day of judgment, 7 just as Sodom and Gomorrah and the neighboring towns which like them indulged in grossest immorality and unnatural vice, stand as a perpetual warning, in suffering the punishment of eternal fire.

8 In just the same way these dreamers defile the body, discard authority, and deride the majesties. 9 But the archangel Michael himself, when he disputed and argued with the devil about Moses' body, did not dare to bring against him a charge of blasphemy, but merely said, "May the Lord rebuke you!" 10 But these persons abuse everything they do not understand, and they are going to be destroyed by the very things they know by instinct, like the irrational animals. 11 Alas for them, because they have trod the road that Cain did; for gain they have rushed into Balaam's error and have perished in rebellion like that of Korah! 12 They are blots on your love feasts while they feast with you, daringly caring for no one but themselves; rainless clouds swept along by winds; leafless trees that bear no fruit, doubly dead, uprooted; 13 wild waves of the sea foaming up their own shame; wandering stars that are forever doomed to utter darkness.

14 It was about such men also that Enoch, the seventh generation from Adam, prophesied when he said: "See! The Lord comes with myriads of His people 15 to execute judgment upon all, to convict all the godless of their godless deeds which in their godlessness they have committed, and of all the harsh things that godless sinners have said against Him."

16 These persons are grumblers, ever complaining about their lot. They live to satisfy their evil passions, their lips boast arrogant things, and they flatter others for personal gain.

THE LETTER OF
JUDE

Jude, servant of Jesus Christ and brother of James, to you who have been called, who are loved in God the Father and kept for Jesus Christ: 2 *May more and more* mercy, *peace*, and love *be yours.*[1]

Fight for the Faith

3 While I've been very eager to write you, dear friends, about the salvation we share, it's now necessary that I write you and urge you to fight for the faith once entrusted to the holy people.

4 There have sneaked in among you some men—some time ago it was written they must be condemned this way—ungodly persons who turn the love our God has for us into unbridled lust and disown our only Master and Lord Jesus Christ.

5 You already know it all, but I want to remind you how the Lord saved His people from Egypt but afterwards destroyed those who didn't believe. 6 And the angels who didn't keep their position of authority but left their home He put in everlasting chains and gloom to be kept for the judgment of the great day—7 just like Sodom and Gomorrah and the towns around them, who for their sexual sins and unnatural vice have suffered their punishment and lie before us as a warning of everlasting fire.

8 Yet in the same way these men with their dreams defile the body, reject the Lord, and slander beings of glory. 9 When *the archangel Michael*[2] was debating with the devil and arguing about Moses' body, he didn't dare to condemn and abuse him but said, *"The Lord rebuke you!"*[3] 10 But whatever beings these men don't understand they slander, and whatever they know by instinct like unthinking animals they use to destroy themselves. 11 Woe to them! They've gone the way of Cain. For a profit they've rushed into the error of Balaam. They've rebelled like Korah and perished.

12 They're a blot on your love meals, where they banquet together without fear. They're shepherds who take care of themselves; clouds driven along by the winds without giving rain; trees that in late fall have no fruit but are torn up by the roots and so are twice dead; 13 wild waves of the sea, foaming out their own shame; wandering stars for whom dark gloom is reserved forever.

14 Enoch, the sixth after Adam, prophesied about them. "The Lord has come with ten thousands of His holy ones," he said, 15 "to bring judgment on all of them and to convict all the ungodly of all the ungodliness they've done and of all the defiant things ungodly sinners have said against Him."

16 They grumble, complain about their lot, follow their lusts, brag, and flatter people to take advantage of them.

[1] Dan. 3:31; 6:26
[2] Dan. 10:13, 21; 12:1
[3] Zech. 3:2

K.J.V.

tage. 17 But, beloved, remember ye the words which were spoken before of the apostles of our Lord Jesus Christ; 18 How that they told you there should be mockers in the last time, who should walk after their own ungodly lusts. 19 These be they who separate themselves, sensual, having not the Spirit. 20 But ye, beloved, building up yourselves on your most holy faith, praying in the Holy Ghost, 21 Keep yourselves in the love of God, looking for the mercy of our Lord Jesus Christ unto eternal life. 22 And of some have compassion, making a difference: 23 And others save with fear, pulling *them* out of the fire; hating even the garment spotted by the flesh. 24 Now unto him that is able to keep you from falling, and to present *you* faultless before the presence of his glory with exceeding joy, 25 To the only wise God our Saviour, *be* glory and majesty, dominion and power, both now and ever. Amen.

N.A.S.

17 But you, beloved, ought to remember the words that were spoken beforehand by the apostles of our Lord Jesus Christ; 18 that they were saying to you, "In the last time there shall be mockers, following after their own ungodly lusts." 19 These are the ones who cause divisions, worldly-minded, devoid of the Spirit. 20 But you, beloved, building yourselves up on your most holy faith; praying in the Holy Spirit; 21 keep yourselves in the love of God, waiting anxiously for the mercy of our Lord Jesus Christ to eternal life. 22 And have mercy on some, who are doubting; 23 save others, snatching them out of the fire; and on some have mercy with fear, hating even the garment polluted by the flesh.

24 Now to Him who is able to keep you from stumbling, and to make you stand in the presence of His glory blameless with great joy, 25 to the only God our Savior, through Jesus Christ our Lord, *be* glory, majesty, dominion and authority, before all time and now and forever. Amen.

WILLIAMS

17 But you, dearly beloved, must remember the words that have already been spoken by the apostles of our Lord Jesus Christ, 18 because they said to you, "In the last times there will be mockers who will live to satisfy their own godless passions." 19 These are men who cause divisions; mere animals, destitute of any spiritual nature.

20 But you, dearly beloved, must continue to build yourselves up on the groundwork of your most holy faith and to pray in the Holy Spirit; 21 you must keep yourselves in the love of God and continue to wait for the mercy of our Lord Jesus Christ, to bring you to eternal life. 22 Some people, who continue to waver through doubts, you must pity 23 and save, snatching them out of the fire; and others you must pity with dread, loathing even the clothes that are soiled by their lower nature.

24 Now to Him who is able to keep you from stumbling and to make you stand in His glorious presence faultless and full of triumphant joy, 25 to the only God our Saviour, through Jesus Christ our Lord, be glory, majesty, might, and authority, as it was before all time, both now and forever and ever. Amen.

BECK

17 But you, dear friends, remember what the apostles of our Lord Jesus Christ predicted. 18 "In the last time," they told you, "there will be scoffers, following their own ungodly lusts." 19 Thy're causing divisions. They're worldly because they don't have the Spirit.

Build Yourselves Up

20 But you, dear friends, building yourselves up on your most holy faith and praying in the Holy Spirit, 21 keep yourselves in God's love, as you look for the mercy of our Lord Jesus Christ to give you everlasting life.

22 Some people are in doubt—pity them, *snatch them from the fire,*[3] and save them. 23 Pity others with fear as you hate even their clothes spotted by their flesh.

24 To Him who is able to keep you from falling and have you stand without a fault and with great joy before His glory, 25 to the only God, who saves us through Jesus Christ our Lord—to Him be glory, majesty, power, and authority—as it was from everlasting, so be it now and forever. Amen.

THE REVELATION OF

St. JOHN the Divine

THE REVELATION OF

JOHN

1 The Revelation of Jesus Christ, which God gave unto him, to shew unto his servants things which must shortly come to pass; and he sent and signified *it* by his angel unto his servant John: 2 Who bare record of the word of God, and of the testimony of Jesus Christ, and of all things that he saw. 3 Blessed *is* he that readeth, and they that hear the words of this prophecy, and keep those things which are written therein: for the time *is* at hand.

4 John to the seven churches which are in Asia: Grace *be* unto you, and peace, from him which is, and which was, and which is to come; and from the seven Spirits which are before his throne; 5 And from Jesus Christ, *who is* the faithful witness, *and* the first-begotten of the dead, and the prince of the kings of the earth. Unto him that loved us, and washed us from our sins in his own blood, 6And hath made us kings and priests unto God and his Father; to him *be* glory and dominion for ever and ever. Amen. 7 Behold, he cometh with clouds; and every eye shall see him, and they *also* which pierced him: and all kindreds of the earth shall wail because of him. Even so, Amen. 8 I am Alpha and Omega, the beginning and the ending, saith the Lord, which is, and which was, and which is to come, the Almighty. 9 I John, who also am your brother, and companion in tribulation, and in the kingdom and patience of Jesus Christ, was in the isle that is called Patmos, for the word of God, and for the testimony of Jesus Christ. 10 I was in the Spirit on the Lord's day, and heard behind me a great voice, as of a trumpet, 11 Saying, I am Alpha and Omega, the first and the last: and, What thou seest, write in a book, and send *it* unto the seven churches which are in Asia; unto Ephesus, and unto Smyrna, and unto Pergamos, and unto Thyatira, and unto Sardis, and unto Philadelphia, and unto Laodicea. 12And I turned to see the voice that spake with me. And being turned, I saw seven golden candlesticks; 13And in the midst of the seven candlesticks *one* like unto the Son of man, clothed with a garment down to the foot, and girt about the paps with a golden girdle. 14 His head and *his* hairs *were* white like wool, as white as snow; and his eyes *were* as a flame of fire; 15And his feet like unto fine brass, as if they burned in a furnace; and his voice as the sound of many waters. 16And he had in his

1 The Revelation of Jesus Christ, which God gave Him to show to His bondservants, the things which must shortly take place; and He sent and communicated *it* by His angel to His bondservant John; 2 who bore witness to the word of God and to the testimony of Jesus Christ, *even* to all that he saw. 3 Blessed is he who reads and those who hear the words of the prophecy, and heed the things which are written in it; for the time is near.

4 John to the seven churches that are in Asia: Grace to you and peace, from Him who is and who was and who is to come; and from the seven Spirits who are before His throne; 5 and from Jesus Christ, the faithful witness, the first-born of the dead, and the ruler of the kings of the earth. To Him who loves us, and released us from our sins by His blood, 6 and He has made us *to be* a kingdom, priests to His God and Father; to Him *be* the glory and the dominion forever and ever. Amen. 7 Behold, He is coming with the clouds, and every eye will see Him, even those who pierced Him; and all the tribes of the earth will mourn over Him. Even so. Amen.

8 "I am the Alpha and the Omega," says the Lord God, "who is and who was and who is to come, the Almighty."

9 I, John, your brother and fellow-partaker in the tribulation and kingdom and perseverance *which are* in Jesus, was on the island called Patmos, because of the word of God and the testimony of Jesus. 10 I was *a*in the Spirit on the Lord's day, and I heard behind me a loud voice like *the sound* of a trumpet, 11 saying, "Write in a book what you see, and send *it* to the seven churches: to Ephesus and to Smyrna and to Pergamum and to Thyatira and to Sardis and to Philadelphia and to Laodicea." 12And I turned to see the voice that was speaking with me. And having turned I saw seven golden lampstands; 13 and in the middle of the lampstands one like *b*a son of man, clothed in a robe reaching to the feet, and girded across His breasts with a golden girdle. 14And His head and His hair were white like white wool, like snow; and His eyes were like a flame of fire; 15 and His feet *were* like burnished bronze, when it has been caused to glow in a furnace, and His voice *was* like the sound of many waters. 16And in His

[a] Or, *in spirit.* [b] Or, *the Son of Man.*

THE REVELATION

JOHN WRITES REVELATION

1 *What the book is; the writer; he greets the seven churches; praises the Lamb who loosed us from sin; where and how the message came; has a vision of the glorified Redeemer who speaks to encourage*

A revelation given by Jesus Christ which God gave to Him, to make known to His slaves what must very soon take place. He sent and communicated it through His angel to His slave John, 2 who testifies to what he saw, the message of God and the testimony of Jesus Christ. 3 Blessed be the man who reads them and the people who hear the messages of this prophecy read, and heed what is written in it, for the time is near.

4 John to the seven churches in Asia: spiritual blessing and peace to you from Him who is and was and is to come, and from the seven spirits that are before His throne, 5 and from Jesus Christ the trustworthy witness, the First-born of the dead, and the Sovereign of the kings of the earth. To Him who ever loves us and once for all released us from our sins by His blood, 6 and has made us a kingdom of priests for His God and Father: to Him be glory forever. Amen. 7 See! He is coming on the clouds, and every eye will see Him, even the men who pierced Him, and all the tribes of the earth will lament over Him. Even so. Amen.

8 "I am the Alpha and the Omega," says the Lord God, who is and was and is to come, the Almighty.

9 I, John, your brother and companion with you in the trouble, the kingdom, and the patient endurance which Jesus gives, found myself on the island called Patmos, for preaching God's message and testifying to Jesus. 10 On the Lord's day I was in the Spirit's power,[a] and I heard a voice like a trumpet behind me say:

11 "Write what you see in a book and send it to the seven churches, to Ephesus, Smyrna, Pergamum, Thyatira, Sardis, Philadelphia, and Laodicea."

12 I turned to see who it was that was speaking to me, and as I turned I saw seven golden lampstands, 13 and among the lampstands One resembling the Son of Man, wearing a robe that reached to His feet, and with a belt of gold around His breast. 14 His head and hair were as white as white wool, as white as snow. His eyes were like coals of fire; 15 His feet were like bronze refined to white heat in a furnace, and His voice was like the roar of many waters. 16 In His right hand He was hold-

1 This is a revelation by Jesus Christ that God gave Him to show His servants *what must happen*[1] soon. He sent His angel to show His servant John, 2 and he tells the truth about everything he saw, what God said and Jesus Christ testified. 3 Happy are you who read and you who hear this prophecy as you keep what is written here—because the time is near.

To the Seven Churches

4 John to the seven churches in the province of Asia: Love and peace to you from Him *who is*[2] and was and *is coming*,[3] from the seven spirits who are before His throne, 5 and from Jesus Christ, *the Witness whom we can trust*,[4] *the First* of the dead *to live* again, and *the One who rules over the kings of the world*.[5]

To Him who loves us and by His blood has *freed* us *from* our *sins*[6] 6 and has made us *a kingdom* and *priests*[7] serving His God and Father—to Him be glory and power forever. Amen. 7 *Look, He is coming in the clouds*,[8] and every eye *will see Him, even the men who pierced Him, and all the people on earth will mourn over Him*.[9] So it will be. Amen. 8 "*I am*[2] the A and the Z," *says the Lord God*,[10] *who is*[2] and was and *is coming*,[3] *the Almighty*.[10]

9 I, John, your fellow Christian, who in Jesus share with you suffering and ruling and enduring, was on the island called Patmos for speaking God's Word and the truth told by Jesus. 10 I came under the Spirit's power on the Lord's Day, and I heard behind me a loud voice like a trumpet saying, 11 "What you see write on a scroll and send it to the seven churches in Ephesus, Smyrna, Pergamum, Thyatira, Sardis, Philadelphia, and Laodicea."

12 I turned to see who was talking to me. And when I turned, *I saw* seven golden lampstands 13 and among the lampstands *Someone like the Son of Man*. He wore a robe reaching down to his feet, with a golden belt around His breast. 14 *His head and hair were white like white wool, like snow, His eyes like flames of fire*, 15 *His feet like* white-*glowing bronze* refined in a furnace, *and His voice like the sound of many waters*.[11] 16 In His right hand He held

[1] Is. 48:6; Dan. 2:28-30, 45
[2] Ex. 3:14
[3] Ps. 40:8; 118:26; Is. 40:10; Hab. 2:3; Zech. 14:10; Mal. 3:1; Dan. 7:13; 9:26
[4] Ps. 89:37; Jer. 42:5
[5] Ps. 89:27
[6] Is. 40:2
[7] Ex. 19:6; Is. 61:6; Dan. 7:18, 22, 27
[8] Dan. 7:13
[9] Zech. 12:10, 12, 14
[10] The Septuagint, the ancient Greek translation of the Old Testament, translates "the Lord of armies" with "the Lord Almighty" exactly 100 times.
[11] Ezek. 1:24; 9:2, 3, 11; 43:2; Dan. 7:9, 13; 10:5-6

[a] Grk., *in the Spirit.*

K.J.V.

right hand seven stars: and out of his mouth went a sharp twoedged sword: and his countenance *was* as the sun shineth in his strength. 17And when I saw him, I fell at his feet as dead. And he laid his right hand upon me, saying unto me, Fear not; I am the first and the last: 18 I *am* he that liveth, and was dead; and, behold, I am alive for evermore. Amen; and have the keys of hell and of death. 19 Write the things which thou hast seen, and the things which are, and the things which shall be hereafter; 20 The mystery of the seven stars which thou sawest in my right hand, and the seven golden candlesticks. The seven stars are the angels of the seven churches: and the seven candlesticks which thou sawest are the seven churches.

2 Unto the angel of the church of Ephesus write; These things saith he that holdeth the seven stars in his right hand, who walketh in the midst of the seven golden candlesticks; 2 I know thy works, and thy labour, and thy patience, and how thou canst not bear them which are evil: and thou hast tried them which say they are apostles, and are not, and hast found them liars: 3And hast borne, and hast patience, and for my name's sake hast laboured, and hast not fainted. 4 Nevertheless I have *somewhat* against thee, because thou hast left thy first love. 5 Remember therefore from whence thou art fallen, and repent, and do the first works; or else I will come unto thee quickly, and will remove thy candlestick out of his place, except thou repent. 6 But this thou hast, that thou hatest the deeds of the Nicolaitans, which I also hate. 7 He that hath an ear, let him hear what the Spirit saith unto the churches; To him that overcometh will I give to eat of the tree of life, which is in the midst of the paradise of God. 8And unto the angel of the church in Smyrna write: These things saith the first and the last, which was dead, and is alive; 9 I know thy works, and tribulation, and poverty, (but thou art rich) and *I know* the blasphemy of them which say they are Jews, and are not, but *are* the synagogue of Satan. 10 Fear none of those things which thou shalt suffer: behold, the devil shall cast *some* of you into prison, that ye may be tried; and ye shall have tribulation ten days: be thou faithful unto death, and I will give thee a crown of life. 11 He that hath an ear, let him hear what the Spirit saith unto the churches; He that overcometh shall not be hurt of the second death. 12And to the angel of the church in Pergamos write; These things saith he which hath the sharp sword with two edges; 13 I know thy works, and where thou dwellest, *even* where Satan's seat *is:* and thou holdest fast my name, and hast not denied my faith, even in those days wherein Antipas *was* my faithful martyr, who was slain among you, where Satan dwelleth. 14 But I have a few things against thee, because thou hast there them that hold the doctrine of Balaam, who taught Balak to cast a stumblingblock before the children of Israel, to eat things sacrificed unto idols, and to commit fornication.

N.A.S.

right hand He held seven stars; and out of His mouth came a sharp two-edged sword; and His face was like the sun shining in its strength. 17And when I saw Him, I fell at His feet as a dead man. And He laid His right hand upon me, saying, "Do not be afraid; I am the first and the last, 18 and the living One; and I was dead, and behold, I am alive forevermore, and I have the keys of death and of Hades. 19 "Write therefore the things which you have seen, and the things which are, and the things which shall take place after these things. 20 "As for the mystery of the seven stars which you saw in My right hand, and the seven golden lampstands, the seven stars are the angels of the seven churches, and the seven lampstands are the seven churches.

2 "To the angel of the church in Ephesus write:
'The One who holds the seven stars in His right hand, the One who walks among the seven golden lampstands, says this: 2 'I know your deeds and your toil and perseverance, and that you cannot endure evil men, and you put to the test those who call themselves apostles, and they are not, and you found them *to be* false; 3 and you have perseverance and have endured for My name's sake, and have not grown weary. 4 'But I have *this* against you, that you have left your first love. 5 'Remember therefore from where you have fallen, and repent and do the deeds you did at first; or else I am coming to you, and will remove your lampstand out of its place—unless you repent. 6 'Yet this you do have, that you hate the deeds of the Nicolaitans, which I also hate. 7 'He who has an ear, let him hear what the Spirit says to the churches. To him who overcomes, I will grant to eat of the tree of life, which is in the Paradise of God.'
8 "And to the angel of the church in Smyrna write:
'The first and the last, who was dead, and has come to life, says this: 9 'I know your tribulation and your poverty (but you are rich), and the blasphemy by those who say they are Jews and are not, but are a synagogue of Satan. 10 'Do not fear what you are about to suffer. Behold, the devil is about to cast some of you into prison, that you may be tested, and you will have tribulation ten days. Be faithful until death, and I will give you the crown of life. 11 'He who has an ear, let him hear what the Spirit says to the churches. He who overcomes shall not be hurt by the second death.'
12 "And to the angel of the church in Pergamum write:
'The One who has the sharp two-edged sword says this: 13 'I know where you dwell, where Satan's throne is; and you hold fast My name, and did not deny My faith, even in the days of Antipas My witness, My faithful one, who was killed among you, where Satan dwells. 14 'But I have a few things against you, because you have there some who hold the teaching of Balaam, who kept teaching Balak to put a stumbling-block before the children of Israel, to eat things sacrificed to idols, and to commit

WILLIAMS

BECK

ing seven stars, and a sharp, double-edged sword was coming out of His mouth, and His face was shining like the sun at midday. 17 So when I saw Him, I fell at His feet like a dead man. But He laid His right hand upon me and said: "Do not be afraid any more. I am the First and the Last; 18 yea, the ever-living One. I once was dead, but now I live forever and ever. I carry the keys of death and the underworld.[b] 19 So write what you have seen, what is and what is to take place hereafter. 20 The open secret of the seven stars that you have seen in my right hand, and of the seven golden lampstands, is this: The seven stars are the messengers of the seven churches, and the seven lampstands are the seven churches.

2 *The letters to the churches at Ephesus, Smyrna, Pergamum, and Thyatira*

"To the messenger of the church in Ephesus write:

" 'The One who is holding the seven stars in His right hand and is walking among the golden lampstands speaks as follows: 2 "I know what you have done; your hard work and patient endurance; that you cannot tolerate wicked persons; that you have tested those who claimed to be apostles although they were not, and have found them to be impostors. 3 You are showing patient endurance, and you have borne it for my sake, and have not grown weary. 4 But I hold it against you that you do not love me as you did at first. 5 So remember the heights from which you have fallen, and repent and do as you did at first, or else I will surely come and move your lampstand from its place—if you do not repent. 6 But you have it to your credit that you hate what the Nicolaitans are doing, as I do too. 7 Let everyone who has ears listen to what the Spirit says to the churches. I will give to him who conquers the privilege of eating the fruit of the tree of life that stands in the paradise of God." '

8 "To the messenger of the church in Smyrna write:

" 'The First and the Last, who once was dead but came to life again, speaks as follows: 9 "I know your pressing trouble and poverty, but still you are rich; I know how you are abused by those who claim to be Jews although they are not, but are only a synagogue of Satan. 10 Do not be so afraid of what you are to suffer. See! The devil is going to throw some of you into prison to be tested there and for ten days to suffer pressing troubles. Each one of you must prove to be faithful, even if you have to die, and I will give you the crown of life. 11 Let everyone who has ears listen to what the Spirit says to the churches. Whoever conquers will not be hurt at all by the second death." '

12 "To the messenger of the church in Pergamum write:

" 'The One who is wielding the sharp, double-edged sword speaks as follows: 13 "I know where you live, where Satan has his throne. Yet you are clinging to my name and have never renounced your faith in me, even in the days of Antipas, my faithful martyred witness, who was put to death among you, right where Satan lives. 14 Yet I hold it somewhat against you that you have among you some who are clinging to the teaching of Balaam, who taught Balak to set a trap for the children of Israel, to entice them to eat the meat that had been sacrificed to idols and to commit immoral practices.

[b] *Hades*, the underworld.

seven stars, and out of His mouth came a sharp, double-edged sword, and His face was *like the sun* when it shines *very brightly*.[12]

17 When I saw Him, I fell down at His feet like a dead man. Then He laid His right hand on me. *"Don't be afraid,"* He said, *"I am the First and the Last,*[13] and the One who is living. 18 I died, but now you see I am living forever and have the keys of death and hell. 19 Write what you have seen, what is now, and *what is going to happen later*. 20 *The hidden meaning*[l] of the seven stars you saw in My right hand and of the seven golden lampstands is this: The seven stars are the angels of the seven churches, and the seven lampstands are the seven churches.

2 "Write to the angel of the church in Ephesus:

" 'He who holds the seven stars in His right hand and walks among the seven golden lampstands says:

2 " 'I know what you have done, how hard you have worked, how you have endured, and that you can't tolerate wicked people, and you have tested those who call themselves apostles but are none and found them to be liars. 3 You have endurance, you have borne trouble for Me and aren't tired out.

4 " 'But I hold it against you that your love isn't what it was at first. 5 Remember from what you have fallen, and be sorry, and do as you did at first, or else if you aren't sorry, I will come to you and take your lampstand from its place.

6 " 'But you have one thing. You hate what the Nicolaitans are doing, and I hate it too.

7 " 'You have ears; then listen to what the Spirit says to the churches. Be victorious, and I will let you eat from *the tree of life that stands in* God's *Paradise*.' [14]

8 "And write to the angel of the church in Smyrna:

" 'The First and the Last,*[13] who died and became alive, says:

9 " 'I know how you have to suffer and how poor you are (but you're rich!) and the slander of those who say they are Jews when they're not but are the devil's synagog. 10 Don't be afraid of what you're going to suffer. You see, the devil is going to put some of you in prison. This is to *test* you, and you will have to suffer for *ten days*.[15] Be faithful till you die, and I will give you the crown of life.

11 " 'You have ears; then listen to what the Spirit says to the churches. Be victorious, and the second death will not hurt you.'

12 "And write to the angel of the church in Pergamum:

" 'He who holds the sharp, double-edged sword says:

13 " 'I know where you live. The devil is there on his throne. But you cling to My name and didn't deny your faith in Me even in the days of Antipas, My loyal witness, who was killed among you—you have the devil living there!

14 " 'But I have a few things against you because you have men there who hold what *Balaam* taught. He taught Balak how to trap *the people of Israel* to get them *to eat food*

[12] Judges 5:31
[13] Is. 44:2, 6; 48:12
[14] Gen. 2:9; 3:22, 24; Ezek. 31:8
[15] Dan. 1:12, 14

K.J.V.

15 So hast thou also them that hold the doctrine of the Nicolaitans, which thing I hate. 16 Repent; or else I will come unto thee quickly, and will fight against them with the sword of my mouth. 17 He that hath an ear, let him hear what the Spirit saith unto the churches; To him that overcometh will I give to eat of the hidden manna, and will give him a white stone, and in the stone a new name written, which no man knoweth saving he that receiveth it. 18 And unto the angel of the church in Thyatira write; These things saith the Son of God, who hath his eyes like unto a flame of fire, and his feet *are* like fine brass; 19 I know thy works, and charity, and service, and faith, and thy patience, and thy works; and the last *to be* more than the first. 20 Notwithstanding I have a few things against thee, because thou sufferest that woman Jezebel, which calleth herself a prophetess, to teach and to seduce my servants to commit fornication, and to eat things sacrificed unto idols. 21 And I gave her space to repent of her fornication; and she repented not. 22 Behold, I will cast her into a bed, and them that commit adultery with her into great tribulation, except they repent of their deeds. 23 And I will kill her children with death; and all the churches shall know that I am he which searcheth the reins and hearts: and I will give unto every one of you according to your works. 24 But unto you I say, and unto the rest in Thyatira, as many as have not this doctrine, and which have not known the depths of Satan, as they speak; I will put upon you none other burden. 25 But that which ye have *already,* hold fast till I come. 26 And he that overcometh, and keepeth my works unto the end, to him will I give power over the nations: 27 And he shall rule them with a rod of iron; as the vessels of a potter shall they be broken to shivers: even as I received of my Father. 28 And I will give him the morning star. 29 He that hath an ear, let him hear what the Spirit saith unto the churches.

3 And unto the angel of the church in Sardis write; These things saith he that hath the seven Spirits of God, and the seven stars; I know thy works, that thou hast a name that thou livest, and art dead. 2 Be watchful, and strengthen the things which remain, that are ready to die: for I have not found thy works perfect before God. 3 Remember therefore how thou hast received and heard, and hold fast, and repent. If therefore thou shalt not watch, I will come on thee as a thief, and thou shalt not know what hour I will come upon thee. 4 Thou hast a few names even in Sardis which have not defiled their garments; and they shall walk with me in white: for they are worthy. 5 He that overcometh, the same shall be clothed in white raiment; and I will not blot out his name out of the book of life, but I will confess his name before my Father, and before his angels. 6 He that hath an ear, let him hear what the Spirit saith unto

N.A.S.

acts of immorality. 15 'Thus you also have some who in the same way hold the teaching of the Nicolaitans. 16 'Repent therefore; or else I am coming to you quickly, and I will make war against them with the sword of My mouth. 17 'He who has an ear, let him hear what the Spirit says to the churches. To him who overcomes, to him I will give *some* of the hidden manna, and I will give him a white stone, and a new name written on the stone which no one knows but he who receives it.'

18 "And to the angel of the church in Thyatira write:

'The Son of God, who has eyes like a flame of fire, and His feet are like burnished bronze, says this: 19 'I know your deeds, and your love and faith and service and perseverance, and that your deeds of late are greater than at first. 20 'But I have *this* against you, that you tolerate the woman Jezebel, who calls herself a prophetess, and she teaches and leads my bond-servants astray, so that they commit *acts of* immorality and eat things sacrificed to idols. 21 'And I gave her time to repent; and she does not want to repent of her immorality. 22 'Behold, I will cast her upon a bed *of sickness,* and those who commit adultery with her into great tribulation, unless they repent of ᵃher deeds. 23 'And I will kill her children with pestilence; and all the churches will know that I am He who searches the minds and hearts; and I will give to each one of you according to your deeds. 24 'But I say to you, the rest who are in Thyatira, who do not hold this teaching, who have not known the deep things of Satan, as they call them—I place no other burden on you. 25 'Nevertheless what you have, hold fast until I come. 26 'And he who overcomes, and he who keeps My deeds until the end, TO HIM I WILL GIVE AUTHORITY OVER THE NATIONS; 27 AND HE SHALL RULE THEM WITH A ROD OF IRON, AS THE VESSELS OF THE POTTER ARE BROKEN TO PIECES, as I also have received *authority* from My Father; 28 and I will give him the morning star. 29 'He who has an ear, let him hear what the Spirit says to the churches.'

3 "And to the angel of the church in Sardis write:

'He who has the seven Spirits of God, and the seven stars, says this: I know your deeds, that you have a name that you are alive, and you are dead. 2 'Wake up, and strengthen the things that remain, which were about to die; for I have not found your deeds completed in the sight of My God. 3 'Remember therefore what you have received and heard; and keep *it,* and repent. If therefore you will not wake up, I will come like a thief, and you will not know at what hour I will come upon you. 4 'But you have a few people in Sardis who have not soiled their garments; and they will walk with Me in white; for they are worthy. 5 'He who overcomes shall thus be clothed in white garments; and I will not erase his name from the book of life, and I will confess his name before My Father, and before His angels. 6 'He who has an ear, let him hear what the Spirit says to the churches.'

[a] Some mss. read, *their.*

15And you also have among you some who are clinging to the teaching of the Nicolaitans. 16 So repent, or else I will quickly come and make war upon them with the sword that comes from my mouth. 17 Let everyone who has ears listen to what the Spirit says to the churches. I will give to him who conquers some of the hidden manna, and I will give him a white stone with a new name written on it which no one knows except the man who receives it."'

18 "To the messenger of the church in Thyatira write:

" 'The Son of God, whose eyes are like coals of fire, and whose feet are like bronze refined to white heat, speaks as follows: 19 "I know what you are doing, I know your love and faithfulness, your service and patient endurance, and I know that you are now working harder than you did at first. 20 But I hold it against you that you are tolerating that Jezebel of a woman who claims to be a prophetess, and by her teaching is misleading my slaves to practice immorality and to eat meat that has been sacrificed to idols. 21 I have given her time to repent, but she refuses to repent of her immorality. 22 See! I am going to lay her on a bed of sickness, and bring down to great and pressing sorrow those who practice immorality with her, unless they repent of their practices; 23 and I will surely strike her children dead. So all the churches will know that I am He who searches men's inmost hearts, and that I will repay each of you for exactly what you have done. 24 But to the rest of you at Thyatira, who do not hold this teaching and have not learned the 'deep things' of Satan—as they speak of them—to you I say, I have no extra burden to lay on you, 25 but keep your hold on what you have until I come. 26 To him who conquers and continues to the very end to do the works that please me, I will give authority over the heathen; 27 he will govern them with a scepter of iron and shatter them like earthen jars—just such authority as I have received from my Father—28 and I will give him the morning star. 29 Let everyone who has ears listen to what the Spirit says to the churches."'

3 The letters to the churches at Sardis, Philadelphia, and Laodicea

"To the messenger of the church at Sardis write:

" 'The One who holds the seven spirits of God and the seven stars speaks as follows: "I know what you are doing; you have the reputation of being alive, but in reality you are dead. 2 Wake up, and strengthen what is left, although it is on the very point of dying, for I have not found a thing that you have done complete in the sight of God. 3 So remember what you have received and heard, and continue to obey it, and repent. If you do not wake up, I will come like a thief, and you will never know the hour when I come upon you. 4 Yet you have in Sardis a few who have not soiled their clothes. They will walk with me in white, for they deserve to do so. 5 Whoever conquers will be clothed this way—in white clothes—and I will never blot his name out of the book of life, but I will own him as mine in the presence of my Father and His angels. 6 Let everyone who has ears listen to what the Spirit says to the churches."'

sacrificed to idols and sin sexually.[16] 15 So you, too, have some who hold what the Nicolaitans teach. 16 Be sorry then, or else I will come to you quickly and fight them with the sword in My mouth.

17 " 'You have ears; then listen to what the Spirit says to the churches. Be victorious, and I will give you some of the hidden manna, and I will give you a white stone, and on the white stone is written a new name[17] that is known only to him who gets it.'

18 "And write to the angel of the church at Thyatira:

" 'God's Son, whose eyes are like flames of fire and whose feet are like white-glowing bronze,[18] says:

19 " 'I know what you're doing and your love and faith and service and endurance and that lately you've done more than at first.

20 " 'But I hold it against you that you let the woman Jezebel, who calls herself a prophet, teach My servants and mislead them to sin sexually and to eat food sacrificed to idols.[16] 21And I gave her time to change, but she refuses to turn from her sexual sins. 22 Now I'm throwing her on a bed and will make those who live in sexual sin with her suffer much if they will not turn away from what she's doing. 23And I will kill her children. Then all the churches will know I am the One who searches minds and hearts,[19] and I will give each of you according to what you have done.[20]

24 " 'But I say to the rest of you in Thyatira, all who don't hold this teaching and haven't learned "the devil's deep things," as they call them: I'm putting no other burden on you. 25 Only cling to what you have till I come.

26 " 'Be victorious and continue to do My works till the end, and I will give you power over the nations, 28 just as I received it from My Father, 27 and you will rule them with an iron rod, shattering them like pottery.[21] 28And I will give you the morning star.

29 " 'You have ears; then listen to what the Spirit says to the churches.'

3 "And write to the angel of the church in Sardis:

" 'He who has God's seven spirits and the seven stars says:

" 'I know what you're doing, that people say you're living—but you're dead. 2 Wake up and strengthen the rest that are dying. I have found that your works are not finished before My God. 3 So remember how you once accepted and listened to the truth. Take it to heart and repent. If you don't wake up, I will come like a thief, and you will not know when I'm coming to you.

4 " 'But you have a few people in Sardis who have not soiled their clothes, and they will walk with me in white garments because they deserve it. 5 Be victorious and that's how you will be dressed—in white garments—and I will not erase your name from the book of life[22] but will confess your name before My Father and before His angels.

6 " 'You have ears; then listen to what the Spirit says to the churches.'

[16] Num. 25:1-2; 31:16
[17] Is. 56:5; 62:2; 65:15
[18] Dan. 10:6
[19] Ps. 7:9; 26:2; Jer. 11:20; 17:10; 20:12
[20] Ps. 62:12; Prov. 24:12
[21] Ps. 2:8-9
[22] Ex. 32:32-33; Ps. 69:28

K.J.V.

the churches. 7And to the angel of the church in Philadelphia write; These things saith he that is holy, he that is true, he that hath the key of David, he that openeth, and no man shutteth; and shutteth, and no man openeth; 8 I know thy works: behold, I have set before thee an open door, and no man can shut it: for thou hast a little strength, and hast kept my word, and hast not denied my name. 9 Behold, I will make them of the synagogue of Satan, which say they are Jews, and are not, but do lie; behold, I will make them to come and worship before thy feet, and to know that I have loved thee. 10 Because thou hast kept the word of my patience, I also will keep thee from the hour of temptation, which shall come upon all the world, to try them that dwell upon the earth. 11 Behold, I come quickly: hold that fast which thou hast, that no man take thy crown. 12 Him that overcometh will I make a pillar in the temple of my God, and he shall go no more out: and I will write upon him the name of my God, and the name of the city of my God, *which is* new Jerusalem, which cometh down out of heaven from my God: and *I will write upon him* my new name. 13 He that hath an ear, let him hear what the Spirit saith unto the churches. 14And unto the angel of the church of the Laodiceans write; These things saith the Amen, the faithful and true witness, the beginning of the creation of God; 15 I know thy works, that thou art neither cold nor hot: I would thou wert cold or hot. 16 So then because thou art lukewarm, and neither cold nor hot, I will spew thee out of my mouth. 17 Because thou sayest, I am rich, and increased with goods, and have need of nothing; and knowest not that thou art wretched, and miserable, and poor, and blind, and naked: 18 I counsel thee to buy of me gold tried in the fire, that thou mayest be rich; and white raiment, that thou mayest be clothed, and *that* the shame of thy nakedness do not appear; and anoint thine eyes with eyesalve, that thou mayest see. 19As many as I love, I rebuke and chasten: be zealous therefore, and repent. 20 Behold, I stand at the door, and knock: if any man hear my voice, and open the door, I will come in to him, and will sup with him, and he with me. 21 To him that overcometh will I grant to sit with me in my throne, even as I also overcame, and am set down with my Father in his throne. 22 He that hath an ear, let him hear what the Spirit saith unto the churches.

4 After this I looked, and, behold, a door *was* opened in heaven: and the first voice which I heard *was* as it were of a trumpet talking with me; which said, Come up hither, and I will shew thee things which must be hereafter. 2And immediately I was in the Spirit: and, behold, a throne was set in heaven, and *one* sat on the throne. 3And he that sat was to look upon

N.A.S.

7 "And to the angel of the church in Philadelphia write:

'He who is holy, who is true, who has the key of David, who opens and no one will shut, and who shuts and no one opens, says this: 8 'I know your ᵃdeeds. Behold, I have put before you an open door which no one can shut, because you have a little power, and have kept My word, and have not denied My name. 9 'Behold, I will cause *those* of the synagogue of Satan, who say that they are Jews, and are not, but lie—behold, I will make them to come and bow down at your feet, and to know that I have loved you. 10 'Because you have kept the word of My perseverance, I also will keep you from the hour of testing, that *hour* which is about to come upon the whole world, to test those who dwell upon the earth. 11 'I am coming quickly; hold fast what you have, in order that no one take your crown. 12 'He who overcomes, I will make him a pillar in the temple of My God, and he will not go out from it any more; and I will write upon him the name of My God, and the name of the city of My God, the new Jerusalem, which comes down out of heaven from My God, and My new name. 13 'He who has an ear, let him hear what the Spirit says to the churches.'

14 "And to the angel of the church in Laodicea write:

'The Amen, the faithful and true Witness, the ᵇBeginning of the creation of God, says this: 15 'I know your deeds, that you are neither cold nor hot; I would that you were cold or hot. 16 'So because you are lukewarm, and neither hot nor cold, I will spit you out of My mouth. 17 'Because you say, "I am rich, and have become wealthy, and have need of nothing," and you do not know that you are wretched and miserable and poor and blind and naked. 18 'I advise you to buy from Me gold refined by fire, that you may become rich, and white garments, that you may clothe yourself, and *that* the shame of your nakedness may not be revealed, and eyesalve to anoint your eyes, that you may see. 19 'Those whom I love, I reprove and discipline; be zealous therefore, and repent. 20 'Behold, I stand at the door and knock; if any one hears My voice and opens the door, I will come in to him, and will dine with him, and he with Me. 21 'He who overcomes, I will grant to him to sit down with Me on My throne, as I also overcame, and sat down with My Father on His throne. 22 'He who has an ear, let him hear what the Spirit says to the churches.' ''

4 After these things I looked, and behold, a door *standing* open in heaven, and the first voice which I had heard, like *the sound* of a trumpet speaking with me, said, "Come up here, and I will show you what must take place after these things." 2 Immediately I was ᶜin the Spirit; and behold, a throne was standing in heaven, and One sitting on the throne. 3And He who

---

[a]. Or, *deeds* (*behold . . . shut*), *that you.* [b] I.e., origin or source. [c] Or, *in spirit.*

WILLIAMS

7 "To the messenger of the church in Philadelphia write:

" 'The Holy and True One, who carries the keys of David, who opens and no one can shut, who shuts and no one can open, speaks as follows: 8 "I know what you are doing. See! I have put before you an open door that no one can shut. I know that you have but little strength, and yet you have obeyed my message and you have not disowned my name. 9 I will make some, who claim to be Jews although they are not, but are lying—I will make them come and fall at your feet and find out that I have loved you. 10 Because you have kept my message with the patient endurance that I give you, I also will keep you from the time of testing that is about to come upon the whole world, to test the inhabitants of the earth. 11 I am coming soon. Hold on to what you have, so that no one may take away your crown. 12 I will make him who conquers a pillar in the temple of my God, and he shall never again go out of it. I will write on him the name of my God and the name of the city of my God, the new Jerusalem, which is coming down out of heaven from my God, and my own new name. 13 Let everyone who has ears listen to what the Spirit says to the churches." '

14 "To the messenger of the church in Laodicea write:

" 'The Amen, the true and faithful witness, the origin[a] of God's creation, speaks as follows: 15 "I know what you are doing, and that you are neither cold nor hot. I wish you were cold or hot. 16 As it is, because you are lukewarm and neither hot nor cold, I am going to vomit you out of my mouth. 17 Because you say, 'I am rich, I have already become rich, I need nothing,' and you do not know that you are the very one that is wretched, pitiable, poor, blind, and naked; 18 I advise you to buy of me gold that has been refined in the fire, so that you may become rich, and white clothes to put on, to hide your shameful nakedness, and salve to put on your eyes, to make you see. 19 The people whom I dearly love, I always reprove and discipline. So keep on being earnest and once for all repent. 20 I am now standing at the door and knocking. If anyone listens to my voice and opens the door, I will be his guest and feast with him, and he with me. 21 I will give to him who conquers the privilege of taking his seat with me on my throne, just as I have conquered and taken my seat with my Father on His throne. 22 Let everyone who has ears listen to what the Spirit says to the churches." ' "

4 He sees the majesty of God; the splendor around the throne; the majesty of God Himself

After this I had another vision: A door was standing open in heaven, and the first voice, like a trumpet, that I had heard speaking with me, said, "Come up here, and I will show you what must take place."

2 Immediately I was under the Spirit's power, and I saw a throne in heaven with One seated on it. 3 The One who was seated on it looked

BECK

7 "And write to the angel of the church in Philadelphia:

" 'This is He who is holy and true, who has the key of David. When He opens a door, nobody will shut it; when He shuts a door, nobody will open it.[23] He says: 8 'I know what you're doing. See, I have opened before you a door nobody can shut. Although you have only a little strength, you have kept My Word and not denied Me.

9 " 'There are those of the devil's synagog who say they're Jews when they're not but are lying. I'll make them come and bow down at your[24] feet and learn that I have loved you.[25] 10 Because you have waited patiently for Me as you were told, I will keep you safe when the time of testing comes for the whole world, to test those living on the earth. 11 I am coming soon. Cling to what you have and don't let anybody take your crown.

12 " 'Be victorious, and I will make you a pillar in the temple of My God, and you will never leave it again. I will write on you the name of My God and the name of the city[26] of My God—the new Jerusalem coming down from My God in heaven—and My new name.[27]

13 " 'You have ears; then listen to what the Spirit says to the churches.'

14 "And write to the angel of the church in Laodicea:

" 'The Amen, the Witness who is faithful [a] and true, the Origin of God's creation,[27] says:

15 " 'I know what you're doing, that you aren't cold or hot. I wish you were cold or hot. 16 But now that you are lukewarm and not hot or cold, I'm going to spit you out of My mouth.

17 " 'You say, "I am rich and wealthy[28] and don't need anything," and you don't know you're miserable, pitiful, poor, blind, and naked. 18 So I advise you to buy from Me—gold, purified in fire, to make you rich; white clothes to put on, to keep your shameful nakedness from showing; salve to put on your eyes to help you see. 19 I correct and discipline all whom I love.[29] Be eagerly concerned then, and repent.

20 " 'See, I'm standing at the door and knocking. If you will listen to My voice and open[30] the door, I will come in to you and eat with you, and you with Me.

21 " 'Be victorious, and I will have you sit with Me on My throne, as I have won the victory and have sat down with My Father on His throne.

22 " 'You have ears; then listen to what the Spirit says to the churches.' "

Around the Throne

4 After this I saw a door opened in heaven, and there was the voice I had heard at first speaking to me like a trumpet. It said, "Come up[31] here, and I will show you what must happen[1] after this."

2 Just then I came under the Spirit's power. I saw a throne standing in heaven and Someone sitting on the throne. 3 The One who sat[32]

[23] Job 12:14; Is. 22:22
[24] Ps. 22:27; 86:9; Is. 45:14; 49:23; 60:14; 66: 23; Jer. 16:19
[25] Is. 43:4
[26] Ezek. 48:35
[27] Prov. 8:22-23
[28] Hos. 12:8
[29] Prov. 3:12
[30] Song of Sol. 5:2
[31] Ex. 19:16, 24
[32] 1 Kings 22:19; Ps. 47:9; Is. 6:1; 2 Chron. 18:18

[a] Grk., beginning.

K.J.V.

like a jasper and a sardine stone: and *there was* a rainbow round about the throne, in sight like unto an emerald. 4And round about the throne *were* four and twenty seats: and upon the seats I saw four and twenty elders sitting, clothed in white raiment; and they had on their heads crowns of gold. 5And out of the throne proceeded lightnings and thunderings and voices: and *there were* seven lamps of fire burning before the throne, which are the seven Spirits of God. 6And before the throne *there was* a sea of glass like unto crystal: and in the midst of the throne, and round about the throne, *were* four beasts full of eyes before and behind. 7And the first beast *was* like a lion, and the second beast like a calf, and the third beast had a face as a man, and the fourth beast *was* like a flying eagle. 8And the four beasts had each of them six wings about *him;* and *they were* full of eyes within: and they rest not day and night, saying, Holy, holy, holy, Lord God Almighty, which was, and is, and is to come. 9And when those beasts give glory and honour and thanks to him that sat on the throne, who liveth for ever and ever, 10 The four and twenty elders fall down before him that sat on the throne, and worship him that liveth for ever and ever, and cast their crowns before the throne, saying, 11 Thou art worthy, O Lord, to receive glory and honour and power: for thou hast created all things, and for thy pleasure they are and were created.

5 And I saw in the right hand of him that sat on the throne a book written within and on the back side, sealed with seven seals. 2And I saw a strong angel proclaiming with a loud voice, Who is worthy to open the book, and to loose the seals thereof? 3And no man in heaven, nor in earth, neither under the earth, was able to open the book, neither to look thereon. 4And I wept much, because no man was found worthy to open and to read the book, neither to look thereon. 5And one of the elders saith unto me, Weep not: behold, the Lion of the tribe of Juda, the Root of David, hath prevailed to open the book, and to loose the seven seals thereof. 6And I beheld, and, lo, in the midst of the throne and of the four beasts, and in the midst of the elders, stood a Lamb, as it had been slain, having seven horns and seven eyes, which are the seven Spirits of God sent forth into all the earth. 7And he came and took the book out of the right hand of him that sat upon the throne. 8And when he had taken the book, the four beasts and four *and* twenty elders fell down before the Lamb, having every one of them harps, and golden vials full of odours, which are the prayers of saints.

N.A.S.

was sitting *was* like a jasper stone and a sardius in appearance; and *there was* a rainbow around the throne, like an emerald in appearance. 4And around the throne *were* twenty-four thrones; and upon the thrones *I saw* twenty-four elders sitting, clothed in white garments, and golden crowns on their heads. 5And from the throne proceed flashes of lightning and sounds and peals of thunder. And *there were* seven lamps of fire burning before the throne, which are the seven Spirits of God; 6 and before the throne *there was*, as it were, a sea of glass like crystal; and in the center and around the throne, four living creatures full of eyes in front and behind. 7And the first creature *was* like a lion, and the second creature like a calf, and the third creature had a face like that of a man, and the fourth creature *was* like a flying eagle. 8And the four living creatures, each one of them having six wings, are full of eyes around and within; and day and night they do not cease to say,

"HOLY, HOLY, HOLY, *is* THE LORD GOD, THE ALMIGHTY,

who was and who is and who is to come." 9And when the living creatures give glory and honor and thanks to Him who sits on the throne, to Him who lives forever and ever, 10 the twenty-four elders will fall down before Him who sits on the throne, and will worship Him who lives forever and ever, and will cast their crowns before the throne, saying, 11 "Worthy art Thou, our Lord and our God, to receive glory and honor and power; for Thou didst create all things, and because of Thy will they existed, and were created."

5 And I saw in the right hand of Him who sat on the throne a book written inside and on the back, sealed up with seven seals. 2And I saw a strong angel proclaiming with a loud voice, "Who is worthy to open the book and to break its seals?" 3And no one in heaven, or on the earth, or under the earth, was able to open the book, or to look into it. 4And I *began* to weep greatly, because no one was found worthy to open the book, or to look into it; 5 and one of the elders *said to me, "Stop weeping; behold, the Lion that is from the tribe of Judah, the Root of David, has overcome so as to open the book and its seven seals." 6And I saw ᵃbetween the throne (with the four living creatures) and the elders a Lamb standing, as if slain, having seven horns and seven eyes, which are the seven Spirits of God, sent out into all the earth. 7And He came, and He took *it* out of the right hand of Him who sat on the throne. 8And when He had taken the book, the four living creatures and the twenty-four elders fell down before the Lamb, having each one a harp, and golden bowls full of incense,

[a] Lit., *in the middle of the throne and of the four living creatures, and in the middle of the elders.*

WILLIAMS

like jasper or sardius, and around the throne there was a rainbow that looked like an emerald. 4Around the throne there were twenty-four thrones, with twenty-four elders seated on them, clothed in white and with crowns of gold on their heads.

5 Out from the throne came flashes of lightning, rumblings and peals of thunder, while in front of it seven flaming lamps were burning; they were the seven spirits of God. 6Also in front of the throne there was something like a sea of glass as clear as crystal. Around the throne, at the middle of each side were four living creatures dotted with eyes in front and behind. 7 The first living creature was like a lion, the second was like an ox, the third had a face like a man's, and the fourth was like an eagle flying. 8And the four living creatures have each of them six wings, and they are dotted with eyes all around and beneath the wings. And day and night they never cease saying:
"Holy, holy, holy is the Lord God, the Almighty, who was and is and is to come."
9 And whenever the living creatures offer glory, honor, and thanksgiving to Him who is seated on the throne, to Him who lives forever and ever, 10 the twenty-four elders fall down before Him who is seated on the throne, and worship Him who lives forever and ever, and they throw their crowns in front of the throne, and say:
11 "You are worthy, our Lord and God,
To have ascribed to you the glory, honor, and power;
For you created everything,
And since you willed it so, they came into existence and were created."

5 *He sees the book of the future; none could open it but the Lion of Judah; sees the Lamb of God, and thousands, angels and others, praising Him*

Then I saw in the right hand of Him who was seated on the throne a book with writing on both sides, sealed with seven seals.

2 And I saw a mighty angel announcing in a loud voice, "Who deserves to open the book and break its seals?" 3 But no one in heaven or on earth or underneath the earth could open the book or look into it. 4 Then I began to weep bitterly because no one could be found deserving to open the book or look into it.

5 But one of the elders said to me, "Stop weaping! See! The Lion who sprang from the tribe of Judah, who belongs to the line of David, has conquered, so that He can open the book and break its seven seals."

6 Then I saw, midway between the throne and the four living creatures, standing among the elders, a Lamb that looked as though He had been slaughtered. He had seven horns and seven eyes; the latter are the seven spirits of God which are sent on duty to every portion of the earth. 7 He came and took the book from the right hand of Him who was seated on the throne. 8 When He took it, the four living creatures and the twenty-four elders fell down before the Lamb, each with a harp, and golden bowls that were full of incense, which represent the prayers of God's people.

BECK

there looked like jasper and carnelian, and *a rainbow around* [33] the throne looked like an emerald. 4Around the throne I saw twenty-four other thrones, and on these thrones sat twenty-four elders dressed in white clothes, with golden crowns on their heads. 5 From the throne *came flashes of lightning, rumblings,* [34] and peals of thunder. Seven flaming torches were burning in front of the throne; these are God's seven spirits. 6 In front of the throne there was also something like a sea of glass, like crystal. Around the throne, *in the middle* of each side of the throne, *were four living beings. They had eyes everywhere,* [35] in front and behind. 7 *The first living being was like a lion, the second like a young bull, the third had a human face, and the fourth was like a flying eagle.* [36] 8And *each* of the four living beings *had six wings,* and *everywhere, all around* and under, *they had eyes.* And day and night without stopping they were saying: *Holy, holy, holy is the Lord God Almighty,* [37] *Who* was and *is* [a] and *is coming.* [a] 9And whenever the living beings *give glory* [38] and honor and thanks to *Him who is sitting on the throne* [32] and *living forever,* [38] 10 the twenty-four elders *bow down before Him* [24] who is *sitting on the throne* [32] and *worship Him* [24] *who lives forever,* [38] throwing down their crowns before the throne and saying, 11 "Our Lord and God, You deserve to receive glory and honor and power because You created everything and Your will caused them to be created and to be."

The Scroll with Seven Seals

5 In the right hand of *Him who sat on the throne* [32] I saw *a scroll, written on both sides and sealed* [39] with seven seals. 2And I saw a mighty angel, calling out loud, "Who can open the scroll and break the seals on it?"

3 But no one in heaven, on earth, or under the earth could open the scroll and look into it. 4And I cried bitterly because no one was found who could open the scroll and look into it.

5 Then one of the elders said to me, "Don't cry! You see, the *Lion* from the tribe of *Judah,* [40] *the Descendant of David,* [41] has won a victory, and He can open the scroll and its seven seals."

6 Between the throne (with the four living beings) and the elders I saw a *Lamb* standing as though it had been *slaughtered.* [42] He had seven horns and *seven eyes,* which are God's seven spirits that are sent *all over the world.* [43] 7 He went and took the scroll from the right hand of Him who sat *on the throne.* [32] 8 When He had taken the scroll, the four living beings and the twenty-four elders bowed down before the Lamb, each holding a lyre and golden bowls full of *incense* [44] (which are the *prayers* of the

[33] Ezek. 1:26-28
[34] Ex. 19:16; Ezek. 1:13
[35] Ezek. 1:5, 18; 10:12
[36] Ezek. 1:10; 10:24
[37] Is. 6:2-3; Ezek. 1:18; 10:12. See No. 10
[38] Dan. 4:34; 6:26; 12:7
[39] Is. 29:11; Ezek. 2:9-10
[40] Gen. 49:9-10
[41] Is. 11:1, 10; Jer. 23:5
[42] Is. 53:7
[43] Zech. 4:10
[44] Ps. 141:2

K.J.V.

9And they sung a new song, saying, Thou art worthy to take the book, and to open the seals thereof: for thou wast slain, and hast redeemed us to God by thy blood out of every kindred, and tongue, and people, and nation; 10And hast made us unto our God kings and priests: and we shall reign on the earth. 11And I beheld, and I heard the voice of many angels round about the throne, and the beasts, and the elders: and the number of them was ten thousand times ten thousand, and thousands of thousands; 12 Saying with a loud voice, Worthy is the Lamb that was slain to receive power, and riches, and wisdom, and strength, and honour, and glory, and blessing. 13And every creature which is in heaven, and on the earth, and under the earth, and such as are in the sea, and all that are in them, heard I saying, Blessing, and honour, and glory, and power, *be* unto him that sitteth upon the throne, and unto the Lamb for ever and ever. 14And the four *and* twenty elders fell down and worshipped him that liveth for ever and ever.

6 And I saw when the Lamb opened one of the seals, and I heard, as it were the noise of thunder, one of the four beasts saying, Come and see. 2And I saw, and behold a white horse: and he that sat on him had a bow; and a crown was given unto him: and he went forth conquering, and to conquer. 3And when he had opened the second seal, I heard the second beast say, Come and see. 4And there went out another horse *that was* red: and *power* was given to him that sat thereon to take peace from the earth, and that they should kill one another: and there was given unto him a great sword. 5And when he had opened the third seal, I heard the third beast say, Come and see. And I beheld, and lo a black horse; and he that sat on him had a pair of balances in his hand. 6And I heard a voice in the midst of the four beasts say, A measure of wheat for a penny, and three measures of barley for a penny; and *see* thou hurt not the oil and the wine. 7And when he had opened the fourth seal, I heard the voice of the fourth beast say, Come and see. 8And I looked, and behold a pale horse: and his name that sat on him was Death, and Hell followed with him. And power was given unto them over the fourth part of the earth, to kill with sword, and with hunger, and with death, and with the beasts of the earth. 9And when he had opened the fifth seal, I saw under the altar the souls of them that were slain for the word of God, and for the testimony which they held: 10And they cried with a loud voice, saying, How long, O Lord, holy and true, dost thou not judge and avenge our blood on them that dwell on the earth? 11And white robes were given unto every one of them; and it was said unto them, that they should rest yet for a little season, until their fellow servants also and their brethren, that should be killed as they

N.A.S.

which are the prayers of the saints. 9And they *sang a new song, saying,
"Worthy art Thou to take the book, and to break its seals; for Thou wast slain, and didst purchase for God with Thy blood *men* from every tribe and tongue and people and nation.
10 "And Thou has made them *to be* a kingdom and priests to our God; and they will reign upon the earth."
11And I looked, and I heard the voice of many angels around the throne and the living creatures and the elders; and the number of them was myriads of myriads, and thousands of thousands; 12 saying with a loud voice,
"Worthy is the Lamb that was slain to receive power and riches and wisdom and might and honor and glory and blessing."
13And every created thing which is in heaven and on the earth and under the earth and on the sea, and all things in them, I heard saying,
"To Him who sits on the throne, and to the Lamb, *be* blessing and honor and glory and dominion forever and ever."
14And the four living creatures kept saying, "Amen." And the elders fell down and worshiped.

6 And I saw when the Lamb broke one of the seven seals, and I heard one of the four living creatures saying as with a voice of thunder, "Come." 2And I looked, and behold, a white horse, and he who sat on it had a bow; and a crown was given to him; and he went out conquering, and to conquer.
3 And when He broke the second seal, I heard the second living creature saying, "Come." 4And another, a red horse, went out; and to him who sat on it, it was granted to take peace from the earth, and that *men* should slay one another; and a great sword was given to him.
5 And when He broke the third seal, I heard the third living creature saying, "Come." And I looked, and behold, a black horse; and he who sat on it had a pair of scales in his hand. 6And I heard as it were a voice in the center of the four living creatures saying, "A aquart of wheat for a bdenarius, and three quarts of barley for a denarius; and do not harm the oil and the wine."
7 And when He broke the fourth seal, I heard the voice of the fourth living creature saying, "Come." 8And I looked, and behold, an ashen horse; and he who sat on it had the name "Death"; and Hades was following with him. And authority was given to them over a fourth of the earth, TO KILL WITH SWORD AND WITH FAMINE AND WITH PESTILENCE AND BY THE WILD BEASTS OF THE EARTH.
9 And when He broke the fifth seal, I saw underneath the altar the souls of those who had been slain because of the word of God, and because of the testimony which they had maintained; 10 and they cried out with a loud voice, saying, "How long, O Lord, holy and true, wilt Thou refrain from judging and avenging our blood on those who dwell on the earth?" 11And there was given to each of them a white robe; and they were told that they should rest for a little while longer, until *the number of* their fellow-servants and their brethren who were to be killed even as they had been, should be completed also.

[a] Lit., *choenix;* a dry measure almost equal to a quart. [b] A denarius was worth about 18 cents in silver, equal to a day's wage.

9 Then they sang a new song: "You deserve to take the book and break its seals, because you have been slaughtered, and with your blood have brought men from every tribe, tongue, people, and nation, 10 and have made them a kingdom of priests for our God; and they will rule over the earth."

11 Then I looked and heard the voices of many angels surrounding the throne, the living creatures, and the elders. Their number was myriads of myriads and thousands of thousands, 12 saying in a loud voice:

"The Lamb that was slaughtered deserves to receive power, riches, wisdom, might, honor, glory, and blessing." 13 Then I heard every creature in heaven, on earth, underneath the earth, and on the sea, and all that they contain, say:

"Blessing, honor, glory, and power be to Him who is seated on the throne and to the Lamb forever."

14 Then the four living creatures said, "Amen!" And the elders fell down and worshiped.

6 *The first, second, third, fourth, fifth, and sixth seals broken*

And when the Lamb broke the first of the seven seals, I looked and heard one of the four living creatures say with a voice like thunder, "Come!"

2 Then I looked, and a white horse appeared, and his rider was carrying a bow. A crown was given to him, and he rode forth conquering and to conquer.

3 When He broke the second seal, I heard the second living creature say, "Come!"

4 And another horse came forth, as red as fire, and power was given to its rider to take peace away from the earth, and to make men slaughter one another; a great sword was given to him.

5 When He broke the third seal, I heard the third living creature say, "Come!"

I looked, and a black horse appeared, and its rider was carrying a pair of scales in his hands, 6 and I heard what seemed to be a voice from the midst of the four living creatures say:

"Wheat fifty cents a quart, barley fifty cents for three quarts! But you must not injure the oil and wine."

7 When He broke the fourth seal, I heard the voice of the fourth living creature say, "Come!"

8 I looked, and a pale horse appeared, and its rider's name was Death, and Hades followed him. Power was given to them over one quarter of the earth, to kill the people with sword, famine, death,[a] and the wild animals of the earth.

9 When He broke the fifth seal, I saw underneath the altar the souls of those who had been slaughtered for being faithful to God's message and for the testimony they bore to it. 10 Then in a loud voice they cried out, "Holy and true Master, how long will you refrain from charging and avenging our blood upon the inhabitants of the earth?"

11 Then a white robe was given to each of them, and they were told to keep quiet a little while longer, until the number of their fellow-slaves and brothers, who were killed as they had been, was complete.

[a] Hebrew, *pestilence*.

holy people). 9 And they *sang a new song:*[45] "You are qualified to take the scroll and open the seals on it because You were sacrificed and with Your blood You bought them from every *tribe, language, people, and nation*[46] to be God's own 10 and made them a *kingdom* and *priests* of our God, and they will rule as *kings over the earth."* [47]

11 As I saw this, I heard around the throne (with the four living beings and the elders) the voices of many angels, numbering *ten thousands of ten thousands and thousands of thousands,*[48] 12 who called out loud, "The *Lamb* who was *sacrificed* [42] deserves to get power and wealth, wisdom and strength, honor, glory, and praise."

13 Then I heard every creature in heaven, on earth, under the earth, and on the sea, and all that are in them saying, "To *Him who sits on the throne*[32] and to the Lamb be praise and honor, glory and might forever!"

14 The four living beings said, "Amen!" And the elders *bowed down and worshiped.*[24]

6 I saw when the Lamb opened the first of the seven seals, and I heard one of the four living beings call with a voice like thunder: "Come!" 2 And there *I saw a white horse,* and its rider had a bow. He was given a crown and rode off as a conqueror to conquer.

3 When He opened the second seal, I heard the second living being call, "Come!" 4 And another *horse* came out, fiery *red,* and its rider was given the power to take away peace from the earth and to have people slaughter one another, and he was given a big sword.

5 When He opened the third seal, I heard the third living being call, "Come!" And there I saw a *black horse,*[49] and its rider had a scale in his hand. 6 I heard a voice that seemed to come from the middle of the four living beings saying, "A quart of wheat for a day's pay, and three quarts of barley for a day's pay, but don't damage the oil and the wine."

7 When He opened the fourth seal, I heard the fourth living being call, "Come!" 8 And there I saw a pale-green horse, and its rider's name was *Death,* and *Hell* came close behind, and they were given power over a fourth of the earth, to *kill* people *with sword, famine,* and *plague,* and by the *animals*[50] on the earth.

9 When He opened the fifth seal, I saw under the altar the souls of those who had been killed for God's Word and the truth they were telling. 10 They called out loud, *"Master,* holy and true, *how long*[51] will You wait before You judge the people on the earth and *punish* them *for killing*[52] us?" 11 Then each of them was given a white robe, and they were told to wait quietly a little longer till all their fellow servants and fellow Christians were present who were to be killed as they had been.

[45] Ps. 33:3
[46] Dan. 3:4; 7:14
[47] Ex. 19:6; Is. 61:6
[48] Dan. 7:10
[49] Zech. 6:1, 3
[50] Jer. 14:12; 15:2; 21:7; Ezek. 5:12; 14:21; Hos. 13:14
[51] Ps. 79:5
[52] Deut. 32:43; 2 Kings 9:7

K.J.V.

were, should be fulfilled. 12And I beheld when he had opened the sixth seal, and, lo, there was a great earthquake; and the sun became black as sackcloth of hair, and the moon became as blood. 13And the stars of heaven fell unto the earth, even as a fig tree casteth her untimely figs, when she is shaken of a mighty wind. 14And the heaven departed as a scroll when it is rolled together; and every mountain and island were moved out of their places. 15And the kings of the earth, and the great men, and the rich men, and the chief captains, and the mighty men, and every bond man, and every free man, hid themselves in the dens and in the rocks of the mountains; 16And said to the mountains and rocks, Fall on us, and hide us from the face of him that sitteth on the throne, and from the wrath of the Lamb: 17For the great day of his wrath is come; and who shall be able to stand?

7 And after these things I saw four angels standing on the four corners of the earth, holding the four winds of the earth, that the wind should not blow on the earth, nor on the sea, nor on any tree. 2And I saw another angel ascending from the east, having the seal of the living God: and he cried with a loud voice to the four angels, to whom it was given to hurt the earth and the sea, 3 Saying, Hurt not the earth, neither the sea, nor the trees, till we have sealed the servants of our God in their foreheads. 4And I heard the number of them which were sealed: and there were sealed a hundred and forty and four thousand of all the tribes of the children of Israel. 5 Of the tribe of Juda were sealed twelve thousand. Of the tribe of Reuben were sealed twelve thousand. Of the tribe of Gad were sealed twelve thousand. 6 Of the tribe of Aser were sealed twelve thousand. Of the tribe of Nephthalim were sealed twelve thousand. Of the tribe of Manasses were sealed twelve thousand. 7 Of the tribe of Simeon were sealed twelve thousand. Of the tribe of Levi were sealed twelve thousand. Of the tribe of Issachar were sealed twelve thousand. 8 Of the tribe of Zabulon were sealed twelve thousand. Of the tribe of Joseph were sealed twelve thousand. Of the tribe of Benjamin were sealed twelve thousand. 9After this I beheld, and, lo, a great multitude, which no man could number, of all nations, and kindreds, and people, and tongues, stood before the throne, and before the Lamb, clothed with white robes, and palms in their hands; 10And cried with a loud voice, saying, Salvation to our God which sitteth upon the throne, and unto the Lamb. 11And all the angels stood round about the throne, and about the elders and the four beasts, and fell before the throne on their faces, and worshipped God, 12 Saying, Amen: Blessing, and glory, and wisdom, and thanksgiving, and honour, and power, and might, be unto our God for ever and ever. Amen. 13And one of the elders answered, saying unto me, What are these which are arrayed in white robes? and whence came they? 14And I said unto him, Sir, thou knowest. And he said to me, These are they which came out of great tribulation, and have washed their robes, and made

N.A.S.

12 And I looked when He broke the sixth seal, and there was a great earthquake; and the sun became black as sackcloth made of hair, and the whole moon became like blood; 13 and the stars of the sky fell to the earth, as a fig tree casts its unripe figs when shaken by a great wind. 14And the sky was split apart like a scroll when it is rolled up; and every mountain and island were moved out of their places. 15And the kings of the earth and the great men and the *commanders and the rich and the strong and every slave and free man, hid themselves in the caves and among the rocks of the mountains; 16 and they *said to the mountains and to the rocks, "Fall on us and hide us from the presence of Him who sits on the throne, and from the wrath of the Lamb; 17 for the great day of their wrath has come; and who is able to stand?"

7 After this I saw four angels standing at the four corners of the earth, holding back the four winds of the earth, so that no wind should blow on the earth or on the sea or on any tree. 2And I saw another angel ascending from the rising of the sun, having the seal of the living God; and he cried out with a loud voice to the four angels to whom it was granted to harm the earth and the sea, 3 saying, "Do not harm the earth or the sea or the trees, until we have sealed the bondservants of our God on their foreheads." 4And I heard the number of those who were sealed, one hundred and forty-four thousand sealed from every tribe of the children of Israel: 5 from the tribe of Judah, twelve thousand were sealed, from the tribe of Reuben twelve thousand, from the tribe of Gad twelve thousand, 6 from the tribe of Asher twelve thousand, from the tribe of Naphtali twelve thousand, from the tribe of Manasseh twelve thousand, 7from the tribe of Simeon twelve thousand, from the tribe of Levi twelve thousand, from the tribe of Issachar twelve thousand, 8 from the tribe of Zebulun twelve thousand, from the tribe of Joseph twelve thousand, from the tribe of Benjamin, twelve thousand were sealed.
9 After these things I looked, and behold, a great multitude, which no one could count, from every nation and all tribes and peoples and tongues, standing before the throne and before the Lamb, clothed in white robes, and palm branches were in their hands; 10 and they cry out with a loud voice, saying,
"Salvation to our God who sits on the throne, and to the Lamb." 11And all the angels were standing around the throne and around the elders and the four living creatures; and they fell on their faces before the throne and worshiped God, 12 saying,
"Amen, blessing and glory and wisdom and thanksgiving and honor and power and might, be to our God forever and ever. Amen." 13And one of the elders answered, saying to me, "These who are clothed in the white robes, who are they, and from where have they come?" 14And I said to him, "My lord, you know." And he said to me, "These are the ones who come out of the great tribulation, and they have washed their robes and made them white in the blood of

[a] Lit., chiliarch, in command of one thousand troops.

WILLIAMS

12 When He broke the sixth seal, I looked, and there was a great earthquake, and the sun turned black as sackcloth, and the full moon became like blood, 13 and the stars of the sky fell to the earth, just as a fig tree, when shaken by a violent wind, drops its unripe figs. 14 The sky was swept away just like a scroll that is rolled up; and every mountain and island moved out of its place. 15 The kings of the earth, the great men, the military leaders, the rich, the mighty—everybody, whether slaves or free—hid themselves in the caves and among the rocks of the mountains. 16And they said to the mountains and the rocks:

"Fall on us and conceal us from the sight of Him who is seated on the throne, and from the anger of the Lamb, 17 because the great day of their anger has come, and who can stand it?"

7 *God's people preserved in disasters; though having to suffer, saved through the Lamb; a countless throng before the throne*

After this I saw four angels standing at the four corners of the earth holding back the four winds of the earth, so that no wind should blow on the earth, the sea, or any tree. 2 Then I saw another angel coming up from the east with the seal of the living God, and he cried out to the four angels who had the power to injure the earth and the sea:

3 "Do not injure the earth, the sea, or the trees, until we mark the slaves of our God with His seal on their foreheads." 4And I heard the number of those who were marked with the seal, one hundred and forty-four thousand. Those that were marked with the seal were from every tribe of the children of Israel: 5 twelve thousand from the tribe of Judah; twelve thousand from the tribe of Reuben; twelve thousand from the tribe of Gad; 6 twelve thousand from the tribe of Asher; twelve thousand from the tribe of Naphtali; twelve thousand from the tribe of Manasseh; 7 twelve thousand from the tribe of Simeon; twelve thousand from the tribe of Levi; twelve thousand from the tribe of Issachar; 8 twelve thousand from the tribe of Zebulon; twelve thousand from the tribe of Joseph; twelve thousand from the tribe of Benjamin.

9 After this I looked, and there was a vast throng that no one could count from every nation, tribe, people, and tongue, standing before the throne and before the Lamb, clothed in white robes, with palm branches in their hands, 10 and they cried in a loud voice:

"Our salvation is due to our God, who is seated on the throne, and to the Lamb." 11 Then all the angels stood around the throne, the elders, and the four living creatures, and fell on their faces before the throne and worshiped God, 12 saying:

"Amen! Blessing, glory, wisdom, thanksgiving, honor, power, and strength be to our God forever and ever. Amen!"

13 Then one of the elders addressed me and said, "Who are these people clothed in white robes, and where did they come from?"

14 I answered him, "You know, my lord."

He said to me: "These are the people who are coming through the great persecution, who have washed their robes and made them white

BECK

12 When He opened the sixth seal, I saw a great earthquake, and the *sun turned black* like coarse cloth of hair, *the* full *moon became* like *blood,* 13 *the stars fell from the sky* to the earth like figs dropping from *a fig tree* shaken by a strong wind, 14 *the sky* vanished *like a scroll being rolled up,*[53] and every mountain and island was moved from its place. 15 *The kings of the earth,*[54] the great men, the tribunes, the rich, the powerful, and every slave and free man *hid in the caves and among the rocks* of the mountains, 16 *calling to the mountains and rocks, "Fall on us and hide us from*[55] *Him who sits on the throne*[32] and from the anger of the Lamb, 17 because *the great day of* their *anger has come, and who can stand before it?"*[56]

Saved!

7 After that I saw four angels standing at the *four corners* of the earth, holding back the *four winds of the earth*[57] to keep any of them from blowing on land or sea or against any tree.

2 Then I saw another angel coming up from the east with the seal of the living God, and he called out loud to the four angels who had been given power to damage land and sea. 3 "Don't damage land, sea, or trees," he said, "till we have put the *seal on the foreheads*[58] of the servants of our God." 4And I heard the number of those who were sealed: "144,000." They were from every tribe of the people of Israel. 5 There were sealed—

12,000 from the tribe of Judah,
12,000 from the tribe of Reuben,
12,000 from the tribe of Gad,
6 12,000 from the tribe of Asher,
12,000 from the tribe of Naphtali,
12,000 from the tribe of Manasseh,
7 12,000 from the tribe of Simeon,
12,000 from the tribe of Levi,
12,000 from the tribe of Issachar,
8 12,000 from the tribe of Zebulun,
12,000 from the tribe of Joseph,
12,000 from the tribe of Benjamin.

9 After that I saw a large crowd that nobody could count, from every *nation, tribe, people, and language*[46] standing before the throne and before the Lamb, wearing white robes, with palms in their hands. 10And they called out loud, "We are saved by our *God who sits on the throne*[32] and by the Lamb!"

11 All the angels stood around the throne, around the elders and the four living beings, and *bowed down* before the throne, with their faces on the ground, *worshiped God,*[34] 12 and said, "Amen! Praise, glory, wisdom, thanks, honor, power, strength be to our God forever! Amen."

13 Then one of the elders turned to me and asked, "These people dressed in white robes—who are they and where did they come from?"

14 And I answered him, "My lord, you know."

Then he told me, "They are the people who have come through great suffering who have *washed* their *robes* and made them white in

[53] Is. 13:10; 34:4; Ezek. 32:7-8; Joel 2:30-31
[54] Ps. 2:2
[55] Is. 2:10, 19, 21; Jer. 4:29; Hos. 10:8
[56] Ps. 76:8; Joel 2; 11, 31; Nah. 1:6; Zeph. 1:14-15; Mal. 3:2; 4:5
[57] Jer. 49:36; Ezek. 7:2; 37:9; Dan. 7:2; Zech. 6:5
[58] Ezek. 9:4, 6

K.J.V.

them white in the blood of the Lamb. 15 Therefore are they before the throne of God, and serve him day and night in his temple: and he that sitteth on the throne shall dwell among them. 16 They shall hunger no more, neither thirst any more; neither shall the sun light on them, nor any heat. 17 For the Lamb which is in the midst of the throne shall feed them, and shall lead them unto living fountains of waters: and God shall wipe away all tears from their eyes.

8 And when he had opened the seventh seal, there was silence in heaven about the space of half an hour. 2And I saw the seven angels which stood before God; and to them were given seven trumpets. 3And another angel came and stood at the altar, having a golden censer; and there was given unto him much incense, that he should offer *it* with the prayers of all saints upon the golden altar which was before the throne. 4And the smoke of the incense, *which came* with the prayers of the saints, ascended up before God out of the angel's hand. 5And the angel took the censer, and filled it with fire of the altar, and cast *it* into the earth: and there were voices, and thunderings, and lightnings, and an earthquake. 6And the seven angels which had the seven trumpets prepared themselves to sound. 7 The first angel sounded, and there followed hail and fire mingled with blood, and they were cast upon the earth: and the third part of trees was burnt up, and all green grass was burnt up. 8And the second angel sounded, and as it were a great mountain burning with fire was cast into the sea: and the third part of the sea became blood; 9And the third part of the creatures which were in the sea, and had life, died; and the third part of the ships were destroyed. 10And the third angel sounded, and there fell a great star from heaven, burning as it were a lamp, and it fell upon the third part of the rivers, and upon the fountains of waters; 11And the name of the star is called Wormwood: and the third part of the waters became wormwood; and many men died of the waters, because they were made bitter. 12And the fourth angel sounded, and the third part of the sun was smitten, and the third part of the moon, and the third part of the stars; so as the third part of them was darkened, and the day shone not for a third part of it, and the night likewise. 13And I beheld, and heard an angel flying through the midst of heaven, saying with a loud voice, Woe, woe, woe, to the inhabiters of the earth by reason of the other voices of the trumpet of the three angels, which are yet to sound!

N.A.S.

the Lamb. 15 "For this reason, they are before the throne of God; and they serve Him day and night in His temple; and He who sits on the throne shall spread His tabernacle over them. 16 "They shall hunger no more, neither thirst any more; neither shall the sun beat down on them, nor any heat; 17 for the Lamb in the center of the throne shall be their shepherd, and shall guide them to springs of the water of life; and God shall wipe every tear from their eyes "

8 And when He broke the seventh seal, there was silence in heaven for about half an hour. 2And I saw the seven angels who stand before God; and seven trumpets were given to them.
3 And another angel came and stood at the altar, holding a golden censer; and much incense was given to him, that he might add it to the prayers of all the saints upon the golden altar which was before the throne. 4And the smoke of the incense, with the prayers of the saints, went up before God out of the angel's hand. 5And the angel took the censer; and he filled it with the fire of the altar and threw it to the earth; and there followed peals of thunder and sounds and flashes of lightning and an earthquake.
6 And the seven angels who had the seven trumpets prepared themselves to sound them.
7 And the first sounded, and there came hail and fire, mixed with blood, and they were thrown to the earth; and a third of the earth was burnt up, and a third of the trees were burnt up, and all the green grass was burnt up.
8 And the second angel sounded, and *something* like a great mountain burning with fire was thrown into the sea; and a third of the sea became blood; 9 and a third of the creatures, which were in the sea and had life, died; and a third of the ships were destroyed.
10 And the third angel sounded, and a great star fell from heaven, burning like a torch, and it fell on a third of the rivers and on the springs of waters; 11 and the name of the star is called Wormwood; and a third of the waters became wormwood; and many men died from the waters, because they were made bitter.
12 And the fourth angel sounded, and a third of the sun and a third of the moon and a third of the stars were smitten, so that a third of them might be darkened and the day might not shine for a third of it, and the night in the same way.
13 And I looked, and I heard an eagle flying in midheaven, saying with a loud voice, "Woe, woe, woe, to those who dwell on the earth; because of the remaining blasts of the trumpet of the three angels who are about to sound!"

WILLIAMS

in the blood of the Lamb. 15 This is why they are before the throne of God, and day and night serve Him in His temple, and He who is seated on His throne will shelter them in His tent. 16 They will never again be hungry or thirsty, and never again will the sun strike them, or any scorching heat, 17 because the Lamb who is in the center of the throne will be their Shepherd, and God will wipe every tear from their eyes."

8 *The seventh seal is broken; the prayers of God's people represented by rising incense, the punishment of their enemies by the flinging of fire to the earth; four trumpets are blown to show God's curses*

When He broke the seventh seal, there was silence in heaven for about half an hour. 2 Then I saw the seven angels who stand before God, and seven trumpets were given to them. 3 Then another angel with a censer of gold came and stood at the altar, and a great quantity of incense was given to him to mingle with the prayers of all God's people, on the altar of gold that stood before the throne. 4 So the smoke of the incense went up from the angel's hand to the presence of God for the prayers of His people. 5 Then the angel took the censer, filled it with fire from the altar, and flung it to the earth, and there followed peals of thunder with its rumblings, flashes of lightning, and an earthquake. 6 And the seven angels with the seven trumpets prepared to blow them.

7 The first one blew his trumpet, and there was a shower of hail and fire mixed with blood as it hurled itself upon the earth, and one-third of the earth was burned up, and all the green grass was burned up.

8 Then the second angel blew his trumpet, and what seemed to be a great mountain all ablaze with fire hurled itself into the sea, and one-third of the sea was turned into blood, 9 and one-third of all the living creatures in the sea perished, and one-third of the ships were destroyed.

10 Then the third angel blew his trumpet, and there fell from the sky a great star blazing like a torch, and it fell upon one-third of the rivers and the springs of water. 11 The star is called Absinthus, that is, Wormwood. So one-third of the waters turned to wormwood, and great numbers of people died of the waters, because they had turned bitter.

12 Then the fourth angel blew his trumpet, and one-third of the sun was cursed with a plague, and one-third of the moon, and one-third of the stars, so that one-third of them were darkened, and there was no light for one-third of the day and for one-third of the night.

13 Then I looked, and I heard an eagle flying in mid-air say in a loud voice, "Alas! Alas! Alas for the inhabitants of the earth because of the remaining blasts of the three angels who are going to blow their trumpets!"

BECK

the blood of the Lamb.[59] 15 That is why they are before the throne of God and serve Him day and night in His temple, and *He who sits on the throne*[32] will spread His tent over them. 16 *They will never be hungry or thirsty again,* and *the sun or any heat will never burn them,* 17 because the Lamb before the throne *will be their Shepherd and will lead them to springs of the water of life.*[60] And *God will wipe every tear from their eyes."* [61]

Prayer like Incense

8 When He opened the seventh seal, there was silence in heaven for about half an hour.

2 And I saw the seven angels standing before God, and they were given seven trumpets.

3 Another angel, with a golden censer, came and *stood at the altar,*[62] and He was given much *incense* to add to the *prayers* of all the holy people as he put it on the golden altar in front of the throne. 4 From the angel's hand the smoke of the *incense* went up before God with the *prayers*[44] of the holy people.

Fire and Death

5 Then the angel took *the censer* and *filled it with fire from the altar*[63] and poured it on the earth, and there came peals of thunder, *rumblings, flashes of lightning,*[64] and an earthquake.

6 The seven angels who had the seven trumpets got ready to blow them.

7 The first blew his trumpet, and there came *hail and fire* mixed with blood which were poured *on the earth.*[65] And a third of the earth was burned up, a third of the trees, and all the green grass.

8 The second angel blew his trumpet, and something like a big *burning mountain*[66] was thrown into the sea, and a third of the sea *turned to blood,*[67] 9 a third of the creatures living in the sea died, and a third of the ships were destroyed.

10 Then the third angel blew his trumpet, and a big *star,* flaming like a torch, *fell from the sky,*[68] and it fell on a third of the rivers and on the springs of water. 11 That star was called Wormwood. Then a third of the waters turned to wormwood, and many people died from the water because it had turned bitter.

12 Then the fourth angel blew his trumpet, and a third of the sun was struck, a third of the moon, and a third of the stars, so that a third of them turned dark, and there was no light for a third of the day and for a third of the night.

13 Then I saw and heard an eagle flying in the middle of the sky. He called out loud, "Woe, woe, woe to those living on earth, because the other three angels are still going to blow their trumpets."

[59] Gen. 49:11; Ex. 12:5, 7
[60] Ps. 23:2; 121:6; Is. 49:10; Jer. 2:13; Ezek. 34:23
[61] Is. 25:8
[62] Amos 9:1
[63] Lev. 16:12
[64] Ex. 19:16
[65] Ex. 9:23-24; Ezek. 38:22
[66] Jer. 51:25
[67] Ex. 7:20-21
[68] Is. 14:12; Dan. 8:10

K.J.V.

9 And the fifth angel sounded, and I saw a star fall from heaven unto the earth: and to him was given the key of the bottomless pit. 2And he opened the bottomless pit; and there arose a smoke out of the pit, as the smoke of a great furnace; and the sun and the air were darkened by reason of the smoke of the pit. 3And there came out of the smoke locusts upon the earth: and unto them was given power, as the scorpions of the earth have power. 4And it was commanded them that they should not hurt the grass of the earth, neither any green thing, neither any tree; but only those men which have not the seal of God in their foreheads. 5And to them it was given that they should not kill them, but that they should be tormented five months: and their torment *was* as the torment of a scorpion, when he striketh a man. 6And in those days shall men seek death, and shall not find it; and shall desire to die, and death shall flee from them. 7And the shapes of the locusts *were* like unto horses prepared unto battle; and on their heads *were* as it were crowns like gold, and their faces *were* as the faces of men. 8And they had hair as the hair of women, and their teeth were as *the teeth* of lions. 9And they had breastplates, as it were breastplates of iron; and the sound of their wings *was* as the sound of chariots of many horses running to battle. 10And they had tails like unto scorpions, and there were stings in their tails: and their power *was* to hurt men five months. 11And they had a king over them, *which is* the angel of the bottomless pit, whose name in the Hebrew tongue *is* Abaddon, but in the Greek tongue hath *his* name Apollyon. 12 One woe is past; *and,* behold, there come two woes more hereafter. 13And the sixth angel sounded, and I heard a voice from the four horns of the golden altar which is before God, 14 Saying to the sixth angel which had the trumpet, Loose the four angels which are bound in the great river Euphrates. 15And the four angels were loosed, which were prepared for an hour, and a day, and a month, and a year, for to slay the third part of men. 16And the number of the army of the horsemen *were* two hundred thousand thousand: and I heard the number of them. 17And thus I saw the horses in the vision, and them that sat on them, having breastplates of fire, and of jacinth, and brimstone: and the heads of the horses *were* as the heads of lions; and out of their mouths issued fire and smoke and brimstone. 18 By these three was the third part of men killed, by the fire, and by the smoke, and by the brimstone, which issued out of their mouths. 19 For their power is in their mouth, and in their tails: for their tails *were* like unto serpents, and had heads, and with them they do hurt. 20And the rest of the men which were not killed by these plagues yet repented not of the works of their hands, that they should not worship devils, and idols of gold, and silver, and brass, and stone, and of wood; which neither can see, nor hear, nor walk: 21 Neither repented they of their murders, nor of their sorceries, nor of their fornication, nor of their thefts.

N.A.S.

9 And the fifth angel sounded, and I saw a star from heaven which had fallen to the earth; and the key of the bottomless pit was given to him. 2And he opened the bottomless pit; and smoke went up out of the pit, like the smoke of a great furnace; and the sun and the air were darkened by the smoke of the pit. 3And out of the smoke came forth locusts upon the earth; and power was given them, as the scorpions of the earth have power. 4And they were told that they should not hurt the grass of the earth, nor any green thing, nor any tree, but only the men who do not have the seal of God on their foreheads. 5And they were not permitted to kill anyone, but to torment for five months; and their torment was like the torment of a scorpion when it stings a man. 6And in those days men will seek death and will not find it; and they will long to die and death flees from them. 7And the appearance of the locusts was like horses prepared for battle; and on their heads, as it were, crowns like gold, and their faces were like the faces of men. 8And they had hair like the hair of women, and their teeth were like *the teeth* of lions. 9And they had breastplates like breastplates of iron; and the sound of their wings was like the sound of chariots, of many horses rushing to battle. 10And they have tails like scorpions, and stings; and in their tails is their power to hurt men for five months. 11 They have as king over them, the angel of the abyss; his name in Hebrew is ᵃAbaddon, and in the Greek he has the name Apollyon.

12 The first Woe is past; behold, two Woes are still coming after these things.

13 And the sixth angel sounded, and I heard a voice from the ᵇfour horns of the golden altar which is before God, 14 one saying to the sixth angel who had the trumpet, "Release the four angels who are bound at the great river Euphrates." 15And the four angels, who had been prepared for the hour and day and month and year, were released, so that they might kill a third of mankind. 16And the number of the armies of the horsemen was two hundred million; I heard the number of them. 17And this is how I saw in the vision the horses and those who sat on them: *the riders* had breastplates *the color* of fire and of hyacinth and of brimstone; and the heads of the horses are like the heads of lions; and out of their mouths proceed fire and smoke and brimstone. 18A third of mankind was killed by these three plagues, by the fire and the smoke and the brimstone, which proceeded out of their mouths. 19 For the power of the horses is in their mouth and in their tails; for their tails are like serpents and have heads; and with them they do harm. 20And the rest of mankind, who were not killed by these plagues, did not repent of THE WORKS OF THEIR HANDS, SO as not to worship DEMONS, AND THE IDOLS OF GOLD AND OF SILVER AND OF BRASS AND STONE AND OF WOOD, WHICH CAN NIETHER SEE NOR HEAR NOR WALK; 21 and they did not repent of their murders nor of their sorceries nor of their immorality nor of their thefts.

[a] Or, *Destruction.* [b] Some ancient mss. omit, *four.*

WILLIAMS

9 *The fifth trumpet is blown, and monstrous locusts torture mankind; the sixth is blown, and numberless horsemen ride forth to kill*

Then the fifth angel blew his trumpet, and I saw a star that had fallen from the sky upon the earth. To this angel the key to the pit of the abyss was given, 2 and he opened the pit of the abyss, and smoke like the smoke of a huge furnace puffed up out of the pit, and the sun and the air were darkened by the smoke from the pit. 3 Out of the smoke came locusts upon the earth, but the power that was given to them was like the power of earthly scorpions. 4 They were told not to injure the grass of the earth or any plant or tree, but only the people who did not have the mark of God's seal on their foreheads. 5 They were not permitted to kill them, but only to torture them for five months, and the torture they inflicted was like the torture of a scorpion when it stings a man. 6 In those days people will look for death but will not find it, they will long to die but death will flee from them. 7 The locusts look like horses armed for battle; on their heads were what appeared to be crowns of gold; their faces were like human faces; 8 they had hair that looked like women's hair; their teeth were like lions' teeth; 9 they had breastplates that seemed to be made of steel; the noise of their wings was like the noise of vast numbers of chariots and horses rushing into battle; 10 they had tails like scorpions with stings in them, so in their tails their power lay to injure men for five months. 11 They had over them as king the angel of the abyss; in Hebrew he is called Abaddon, in Greek, Apollyon.[a]

12 The first woe is past. See! Two other woes are yet to come.

13 Then the sixth angel blew his trumpet, and I heard a voice from the corners of the altar of gold that was before God 14 say to the sixth angel who had the trumpet:

"Turn loose the four angels that are bound at the river Euphrates." 15 Then the four angels that were kept in readiness for that hour and day and month and year were turned loose to kill one-third of mankind. 16 The number of the armies of the horsemen was two hundred million; I heard their number. 17 In my vision the horses and the horsemen looked like this: Their breastplates were red, blue, and yellow; the horses' heads were like lions' heads, and fire, smoke, and sulphur kept pouring out of their mouths. 18 One-third of mankind was killed by these three plagues: the fire, smoke, and sulphur that kept pouring out of their mouths. 19 For the power of the horses lay in their mouths and their tails; their tails were like snakes, and they had heads with which they injured people. 20 But the rest of mankind, who were not killed by these plagues, did not repent of the works their hands had done, so as to give up worshiping demons and idols of gold, silver, bronze, stone, and wood, which cannot either see or hear or move; 21 and they never did repent of their murders, their practices in magic, their immorality, or their thefts.

BECK

The First Woe

9 Then the fifth angel blew his trumpet, and I saw *a star that had fallen from the sky to the earth.*[69] He was given the key to the shaft of the abyss. 2 He opened the shaft of the abyss, and *smoke went up from the shaft like the smoke from a big furnace,*[60] and it *darkened the sun*[70] and the air.

3 Out of the smoke *came grasshoppers on the earth,*[71] and they were given power like the power of earthly scorpions. 4 But they were told not to harm the grass on the earth or any green plant or tree, only the people who don't have God's *seal on their foreheads.*[58] 5 They were not allowed to kill these, only to torture them for five months, and the torture was like that of a scorpion when it stings a person. 6 In those days people will *look for death and not find it;*[72] they will long to die, and death will flee from them. 7 The grasshoppers were *like horses* armed *for battle.* On their heads there seemed to be crowns that looked like gold. Their faces were like human faces. 8 They had hair like women and *teeth like lions.* 9 Their breasts were like iron breastplates, and the noise of their wings was *like the roar of chariots* with many horses *rushing into battle.*[73] 10 They had tails like scorpions, with stings, and their tails had the power to hurt people for five months. 11 The king who was over them was the angel of the abyss. The Jews call him Abaddon,* but in Greek he is called Apollyon.*

12 The first woe is past. There are two more woes still coming.

The Second Woe

13 The sixth angel blew his trumpet, and I heard a voice from the four horns of the golden altar before God 14 say to the sixth angel who had the trumpet, "Free the four angels who are held bound at *the big river Euphrates.*" [74] 15 And the four angels who had been held ready for that hour, day, month, and year were set free to kill a third of the people.

16 I heard how many soldiers there were on horses; there were two hundred million. 17 In my vision I saw how the horses and their riders looked. Their breastplates were red like fire, blue like bluebells, and yellow like sulfur. The horses had heads like lions, and out of their mouths came fire, smoke, and sulfur. 18 These three plagues—the fire, smoke, and sulfur coming out of their mouths—killed a third of the people. 19 The power of the horses was in their mouths and in their tails. Their tails were like snakes, having heads with which they wounded people.

20 But the rest of the people, whom these plagues hadn't killed, weren't sorry and didn't turn from *what their hands had made* or give up worshiping devils and *idols of gold, silver, copper, stone, and wood, that can't see or hear*[75] or walk. 21 And they were not sorry for their murders, their *magic arts,* their *sexual vice,*[76] and their stealing.

---

* The Destroyer.
[69] Gen. 19:28; Ex. 19:18
[70] Joel 2:10
[71] Ex. 10:12
[72] Job 3:21
[73] Joel 2:4-5; 1:6
[74] Gen. 15:18; Deut. 1:7; 11:24; Joshua 1:4
[75] Deut. 4:28; Ps. 115:4; 135:15-17; Is. 2:8, 20; 17:8; Jer. 1:16; Dan. 5:4, 23
[76] 2 Kings 9:22

---

[a] Both names mean, *the Destroyer.*

10 And I saw another mighty angel come down from heaven, clothed with a cloud: and a rainbow *was* upon his head, and his face *was* as it were the sun, and his feet as pillars of fire: 2And he had in his hand a little book open: and he set his right foot upon the sea, and *his* left *foot* on the earth, 3And cried with a loud voice, as *when* a lion roareth: and when he had cried, seven thunders uttered their voices. 4And when the seven thunders had uttered their voices, I was about to write: and I heard a voice from heaven saying unto me, Seal up those things which the seven thunders uttered, and write them not. 5And the angel which I saw stand upon the sea and upon the earth lifted up his hand to heaven, 6And sware by him that liveth for ever and ever, who created heaven, and the things that therein are, and the earth, and the things that therein are, and the sea, and the things which are therein, that there should be time no longer: 7 But in the days of the voice of the seventh angel, when he shall begin to sound, the mystery of God should be finished, as he hath declared to his servants the prophets. 8And the voice which I heard from heaven spake unto me again, and said, Go *and* take the little book which is open in the hand of the angel which standeth upon the sea and upon the earth. 9And I went unto the angel, and said unto him, Give me the little book. And he said unto me, Take *it,* and eat it up; and it shall make thy belly bitter, but it shall be in thy mouth sweet as honey. 10And I took the little book out of the angel's hand, and ate it up; and it was in my mouth sweet as honey: and as soon as I had eaten it, my belly was bitter. 11And he said unto me, Thou must prophesy again before many peoples, and nations, and tongues, and kings.

11 And there was given me a reed like unto a rod: and the angel stood, saying, Rise, and measure the temple of God, and the altar, and them that worship therein. 2 But the court which is without the temple leave out, and measure it not; for it is given unto the Gentiles: and the holy city shall they tread under foot forty *and* two months. 3And I will give *power* unto my two witnesses, and they shall prophesy a thousand two hundred *and* threescore days, clothed in sackcloth. 4 These are the two olive trees, and the two candlesticks standing before the God of the earth. 5And if any man will hurt them, fire proceedeth out of their mouth, and devoureth their enemies: and if any man will hurt them, he must in this manner be killed. 6 These have power to shut heaven, that it rain not in the days

10 And I saw another strong angel coming down out of heaven, clothed with a cloud; and the rainbow was upon his head, and his face was like the sun, and his feet like pillars of fire; 2 and he had in his hand a little book which was open. And he placed his right foot on the sea and his left on the land; 3 and he cried out with a loud voice, as when a lion roars; and when he had cried out, the seven peals of thunder uttered their voices. 4And when the seven peals of thunder had spoken, I was about to write; and I heard a voice from heaven saying, "Seal up the things which the seven peals of thunder have spoken, and do not write them." 5And the angel whom I saw standing on the sea and on the land LIFTED UP HIS RIGHT HAND TO HEAVEN, 6 AND SWORE BY HIM WHO LIVES FOREVER AND EVER, WHO CREATED HEAVEN AND THE THINGS IN IT, AND THE EARTH AND THE THINGS IN IT, AND THE SEA AND THE THINGS IN IT, that there shall be delay no longer, 7 but in the days of the voice of the seventh angel, when he is about to sound, then the mystery of God is finished, as He preached to His servants the prophets. 8And the voice which I heard from heaven, *I heard* again speaking with me, and saying, "Go, take the book which is open in the hand of the angel who stands on the sea and on the land." 9And I went to the angel, telling him to give me the little book. And he *said to me, "Take it, and eat it; and it will make your stomach bitter, but in your mouth it will be sweet as honey." 10And I took the little book out of the angel's hand and ate it, and it was in my mouth sweet as honey; and when I had eaten it, my stomach was made bitter. 11And they *said to me, "You must prophesy again concerning many peoples and nations and tongues and kings."

11 And there was given me a measuring rod like a staff; and someone said, "Rise and measure the temple of God, and the altar, and those who worship in it. 2 "And leave out the court which is outside the temple, and do not measure it; for it has been given to the nations; and they will tread under foot the holy city for forty-two months. 3 "And I will grant *authority* to my two witnesses, and they will prophesy for twelve hundred and sixty days, clothed in sackcloth." 4 These are the two olive trees and the two lampstands that stand before the Lord of the earth. 5And if any one desires to harm them, fire proceeds out of their mouth and devours their enemies; and if any one would desire to harm them, in this manner he must be killed. 6 These have the power to shut up the sky, in order that rain may not fall during the days of their prophesying; and they have power

WILLIAMS

10 *The mighty angel and the seven peals of thunder; God's purposes soon to be accomplished; the seer then eats the angel's little book*

Then I saw another mighty angel coming down from heaven. He was clothed in a cloud, with a rainbow over his head; his face was like the sun, his legs were like pillars of fire, 2 and he had a little book open in his hand. He set his right foot on the sea and his left foot on the land, 3 and in a loud voice he shouted like the roaring of a lion; and when he had shouted, the seven thunders rumbled. 4 When the seven thunders had rumbled, I was going to write it down, but I heard a voice from heaven say:

"Seal up what the seven thunders have said, and do not write it down!"

5 Then the angel, whom I had seen standing on the sea and on the land, raised his right hand to heaven, 6 and swore by Him who lives forever and ever, who created the heavens and all that they contain, the earth and all that it contains, and the sea and all that it contains, that there should be no more delay, 7 but in the days when the seventh angel speaks, when he is about to blow his trumpet, then God's mysterious message, in accordance with the good news He gave to His slaves, the prophets, would be accomplished.

8 Then the voice that I heard from heaven spoke to me again, and said, "Go and take the little book that is open in the hand of the angel who is standing on the sea and on the land."

9 So I went up to the angel and asked him to give me the little book. And he said to me, "Take it and eat it; it will make your stomach bitter, but in your mouth it will taste as sweet as honey." 10 So I took the little book from the angel's hand and ate it all, and in my mouth it did taste as sweet as honey, but when I had eaten it all, it made my stomach bitter.

11 Then they said to me, "You must prophesy again about many peoples, nations, languages, and kings."

11 *He measures the temple—a sign of how God takes care of His own; the two witnesses are vested with peculiar power but finally are murdered and ascend to heaven; the seventh trumpet is blown*

Then a measuring rod like a staff was given to me, and I was told:

"Rise and measure the temple of God and the altar, counting those who worship there, 2 but leave off the court outside the temple; do not measure it, because it has been given over to the heathen, and for forty-two months they will trample the city under foot. 3 And I will permit my two witnesses, clothed in sackcloth, to prophesy for one thousand, two hundred and sixty days."

4 They are the two olive trees and the two lampstands that stand before the Lord of the earth. 5 If anyone wants to injure them, fire comes out of their mouths and consumes their enemies; if anyone wants to injure them, he must himself be killed in that way. 6 They have the power to shut up the sky, so that no rain will fall upon the earth as long as they prophesy,

BECK

The Scroll

10 I saw another mighty angel come down from heaven. He was robed in a cloud, and there was a rainbow over his head. His face was like the sun, and his feet were like pillars of fire. 2 In his hand he held a little scroll unrolled. He set his right foot on the sea, and his left on the land. 3 Then he shouted loud like a lion roaring. When he shouted, the seven thunders spoke with voices of their own. 4 When the seven thunders had spoken, I was going to write it down. But I heard someone say from heaven, *"Keep secret*[77] what the seven thunders have said, and don't write it down."

5 Then the angel whom I saw standing on the sea and on the land *raised his right hand to heaven* 6 *and swore by Him who lives forever, who created heaven* and what's in it, *the earth and what's in it, and the sea and what's in it.*[78] "There will be no more delay, 7 but the time comes for the seventh angel to blow his trumpet, and *God's secret* purpose *as He told it to His servants, the prophets,*[79] is carried out."

8 Then he who had spoken to me from heaven spoke to me again. "Go," he said, "take the scroll that lies unrolled in the hand of the angel standing on the sea and on the land."

9 I went to the angel and told him, "Give me the little scroll."

"Take it," *he said to me,* "and *eat* all of *it,* and it will be bitter *in your stomach,* but in your mouth it will be *sweet as honey."*

10 *I* took the little scroll from the angel's hand and *ate it, and it was sweet as honey in my mouth. But when I had eaten it,* it was bitter *in my stomach.*[80]

11 Then they told me, "You must prophesy again about many *peoples, nations, languages,*[46] and kings."

Two Preachers

11 Then I was given a measuring stick like a rod. "Go," he said, "and measure God's temple and the altar, and count those who worship there. 2 Omit the court outside the temple, and don't measure it, because it is given to *the non-Jewish people,* who will *trample on the holy*[81] city for forty-two months. 3 I will let my two witnesses, dressed in sackcloth, speak God's Word for 1,260 days.

4 *"These are the two olive trees and the two* lampstands *standing before the Lord of the earth.*[82] 5 And if anyone wants to hurt them, *fire* comes *out of their mouths* and *consumes* their *enemies;*[83] that is how anyone who wants to hurt them must be killed. 6 They have the power to shut up the sky and keep *rain* from falling during the days when they are speaking God's Word and the power over *waters to turn*

[77] Dan. 8:26; 12:4, 9
[78] Gen. 14:19; Ex. 20:11; Deut. 32:40; Ps. 146: 6; Dan. 4:34; 6:26; 12:7; Neh. 9:6
[79] Deut. 29:27; Amos 3:7; Zech. 1:6
[80] Ezek. 2:8-9; 3:1-3
[81] Is. 63:18; Zech. 12:3
[82] Zech. 4:3, 11-12, 14
[83] 2 Sam. 22:9; 2 Kings 1:10, 12; Is. 26:11; Jer. 5:14

K.J.V.

of their prophecy: and have power over waters to turn them to blood, and to smite the earth with all plagues, as often as they will. 7And when they shall have finished their testimony, the beast that ascendeth out of the bottomless pit shall make war against them, and shall overcome them, and kill them. 8And their dead bodies *shall lie* in the street of the great city, which spiritually is called Sodom and Egypt, where also our Lord was crucified. 9And they of the people and kindreds and tongues and nations shall see their dead bodies three days and a half, and shall not suffer their dead bodies to be put in graves. 10And they that dwell upon the earth shall rejoice over them, and make merry, and shall send gifts one to another; because these two prophets tormented them that dwelt on the earth. 11And after three days and a half the Spirit of life from God entered into them, and they stood upon their feet; and great fear fell upon them which saw them. 12And they heard a great voice from heaven saying unto them, Come up hither. And they ascended up to heaven in a cloud; and their enemies beheld them. 13And the same hour was there a great earthquake, and the tenth part of the city fell, and in the earthquake were slain of men seven thousand: and the remnant were affrighted, and gave glory to the God of heaven. 14 The second woe is past; *and,* behold, the third woe cometh quickly. 15And the seventh angel sounded; and there were great voices in heaven, saying, The kingdoms of this world are become *the kingdoms* of our Lord, and of his Christ; and he shall reign for ever and ever. 16And the four and twenty elders, which sat before God on their seats, fell upon their faces, and worshipped God, 17Saying, We give thee thanks, O Lord God Almighty, which art, and wast, and art to come; because thou hast taken to thee thy great power, and hast reigned. 18And the nations were angry, and thy wrath is come, and the time of the dead, that they should be judged, and that thou shouldest give reward unto thy servants the prophets, and to the saints, and them that fear thy name, small and great; and shouldest destroy them which destroy the earth. 19And the temple of God was opened in heaven, and there was seen in his temple the ark of his testament: and there were lightnings, and voices, and thunderings, and an earthquake, and great hail.

12 And there appeared a great wonder in heaven; a woman clothed with the sun, and the moon under her feet, and upon her head a crown of twelve stars: 2And she being with child cried, travailing in birth, and pained to be delivered. 3And there appeared another wonder

N.A.S.

over the waters to turn them into blood, and to smite the earth with every plague, as often as they desire. 7And when they have finished their testimony, the beast that comes up out of the abyss will make war with them, and overcome them and kill them. 8And their dead [a]bodies *will lie* in the street of the great city, which [b]mystically is called Sodom and Egypt, where also their Lord was crucified. 9And those from the peoples and tribes and tongues and nations *will* look at their dead [c]bodies for three days and a half, and will not permit their dead bodies to be laid in a tomb. 10And those who dwell on the earth *will* rejoice over them and make merry; and they will send gifts to one another, because these two prophets tormented those who dwell on the earth. 11And after the three days and a half the breath of life from God came into them, and they stood on their feet; and great fear fell upon those who were beholding them. 12And they heard a loud voice from heaven saying to them, "Come up here." And they went up into heaven in the cloud, and their enemies beheld them. 13And in that hour there was a great earthquake, and a tenth of the city fell; and seven thousand people were killed in the earthquake, and the rest were terrified and gave glory to the God of heaven.

14 The second Woe is past; behold, the third Woe is coming quickly.

15 And the seventh angel sounded; and there arose loud voices in heaven, saying,

"The kingdom of the world has become *the kingdom* of our Lord, and of His [d]Christ; and He will reign forever and ever." 16And the twenty-four elders, who sit on their thrones before God, fell on their faces and worshiped God, 17 saying,

"We give Thee thanks, O Lord God, the Almighty, who art and who wast, because Thou hast taken Thy great power and hast begun to reign. 18 "And the nations were enraged, and Thy wrath came, and the time *came* for the dead to be judged, and *the time* to give their reward to Thy bond-servants the prophets and to the saints and to those who fear Thy name, the small and the great, and to destroy those who destroy the earth."

19 And the temple of God which is in heaven was opened; and the ark of His covenant appeared in His temple, and there were flashes of lightning and sounds and peals of thunder and an earthquake and a great hailstorm.

12 And a great sign appeared in heaven: a woman clothed with the sun, and the moon under her feet, and on her head a crown of twelve stars; 2 and she was with child; and she *cried out, being in labor and in pain to give birth. 3And another sign appeared in heaven:

[a] Some ancient mss. read, *body.* [b] Lit., *spiritually.* [c] Lit., *body.* [d] I.e., *Messiah.*

WILLIAMS

and they have power over the waters to turn them into blood, and to smite the earth with any plague as often as they please. 7 Then, when they have finished testifying, the wild beast that is coming up out of the abyss will make war on them and conquer them and kill them, 8 and their lifeless bodies will lie on the streets of the great city that is figuratively called Sodom and Egypt, where their Lord also was crucified. 9 For three days and a half men of all peoples, tribes, languages, and nations will look upon their lifeless bodies, and will not let them be buried. 10 The inhabitants of the earth will gloat over them and celebrate with feasts and the sending of gifts to one another, because these two prophets had tormented the inhabitants of the earth.

11 After three days and a half the breath of life from God came into them again, and they stood on their feet, and consternation seized those who saw them.

12 And they heard a loud voice from heaven say to them, "Come up here." And they went up to heaven in a cloud, and their enemies looked on as spectators. 13 At that very hour there was a great earthquake, and one-tenth of the city went down. Seven thousand people were killed in the earthquake, and the rest were stricken with awe, and gave glory to the God of heaven.

14 The second woe is past. See! The third woe is soon to come.

15 Then the seventh angel blew his trumpet, and loud voices were heard in heaven, saying, "The sovereignty of the world has come into the possession of our Lord and His Christ, and He will reign forever and ever."

16 Then the twenty-four elders who were seated on their thrones before God fell on their faces and worshiped God, 17 saying:

"We give you thanks, Lord God Almighty, who are and were, because you have assumed your great power and begun to reign. 18 The heathen were enraged, but now your anger has come, and the time for the dead to be judged, and for you to reward your slaves the prophets and your people, great and small, who revere your name, and to destroy the destroyers of the earth."

19 Then the doors of God's temple in heaven were thrown open, and inside the temple was seen the chest containing God's covenant, and there followed flashes of lightning, rumblings, peals of thunder, an earthquake and heavy hail.

12 *He sees the seven symbols: the sunclad woman; the dragon who is hurled down to earth; Christ triumphs though the dragon persecutes the woman*

Then a great symbol was seen in heaven—a woman clothed in the sun with the moon under her feet, and on her head a crown of twelve stars. 2 She was about to become a mother, and she cried out in anguish in giving birth to a child.

3 Another symbol was seen in heaven—there

BECK

them into blood and to *strike* the earth *with any plague*[84] as often as they want to.

7 "When they finish testifying, *the animal coming up* out of the abyss *will fight with* them, *conquer them,*[85] and kill them. 8 And their dead bodies will lie on the street of the great city, which is called Sodom and Egypt, to show what kind of city it is. 9 Here their Lord also was crucified. And some of the *peoples, tribes, languages,* and *nations*[46] will look at their dead bodies for three and a half days and not let anybody bury them. 10 The people living on the earth will be delighted over them and will celebrate and send gifts to one another because these two prophets tormented the people living on the earth.

11 "After three and a half days a *breath of life* from God *went into them, and they got up on their feet,*[86] and those who watched them *were terrified.*[87] 12 They heard someone calling loud to them from heaven, 'Come up here.' And they went up to heaven in a cloud while their enemies watched them. 13 *Just then there was a big earthquake,* a tenth of the city *fell,*[88] and seven thousand people were killed by the earthquake. The rest were terrified and gave glory to *the God of heaven.*" [139]

14 The second woe is past. The third woe will soon be here.

The Third Woe

15 The seventh angel blew his trumpet. Then there were loud voices in heaven, saying, "The kingdom of the world has become *the kingdom of* our *Lord and of His Christ, and He will be King forever.*" [89]

16 Then the twenty-four elders who were sitting on their thrones before God *bowed down* on their faces *and worshiped God,*[24] 17 Saying, "*Lord God Almighty,*[10] *You are*[2] now, and You were. We thank You for taking Your great power and *becoming King.* 18 *The nations got angry,*[90] but Your anger has come, and so has the time to judge the dead, to reward *Your servants, the prophets,*[91] and the holy people, *little and great, who fear*[92] Your name, and to destroy those who are destroying the earth."

19 Then God's temple in heaven was opened, and *the ark of His covenant* was seen in His *temple,*[93] and there were *flashes of lightning, rumblings,* peals of thunder, an earthquake, and *heavy hail.*[94]

The Woman's Son and the Dragon

12 A great sign was seen in the sky: a woman with the sun for her garment, the moon under her feet, and a crown of twelve stars on her head. 2 She was going to have a Child, and she cried out *in pain* and agony *to give birth.*[95]

3 Another sign was seen in the sky: There

[84] Ex. 7:17, 21; 1 Sam. 4:8; 1 Kings 17:1
[85] Dan. 7:3, 21
[86] Ezek. 37:5, 10
[87] Gen. 15:12
[88] Ezek. 38: 19-20
[89] Ex. 15:18; Ps. 2:2; 10:16; 22:28; 1 Sam. 12:3; Ob. 21; Micah 4:7; Dan. 2:44
[90] Ps. 99:1
[91] Amos 3:7; Zech. 1:6; Dan. 9:6, 10
[92] Ps. 115:13
[93] 1 Kings 8:1, 6
[94] Ex. 9:23; 19:16
[95] Is. 66:7; Micah 4:10

K.J.V.

in heaven; and behold a great red dragon, having seven heads and ten horns, and seven crowns upon his heads. 4And his tail drew the third part of the stars of heaven, and did cast them to the earth: and the dragon stood before the woman which was ready to be delivered, for to devour her child as soon as it was born. 5And she brought forth a man child, who was to rule all nations with a rod of iron: and her child was caught up unto God, and to his throne. 6And the woman fled into the wilderness, where she hath a place prepared of God, that they should feed her there a thousand two hundred and threescore days. 7And there was war in heaven: Michael and his angels fought against the dragon; and the dragon fought and his angels, 8And prevailed not; neither was their place found any more in heaven. 9And the great dragon was cast out, that old serpent, called the Devil, and Satan, which deceiveth the whole world: he was cast out into the earth, and his angels were cast out with him. 10And I heard a loud voice saying in heaven, Now is come salvation, and strength, and the kingdom of our God, and the power of his Christ: for the accuser of our brethren is cast down, which accused them before our God day and night. 11And they overcame him by the blood of the Lamb, and by the word of their testimony; and they loved not their lives unto the death. 12 Therefore rejoice, ye heavens, and ye that dwell in them. Woe to the inhabiters of the earth and of the sea! for the devil is come down unto you, having great wrath, because he knoweth that he hath but a short time. 13And when the dragon saw that he was cast unto the earth, he persecuted the woman which brought forth the man child. 14And to the woman were given two wings of a great eagle, that she might fly into the wilderness, into her place, where she is nourished for a time, and times, and half a time, from the face of the serpent. 15And the serpent cast out of his mouth water as a flood after the woman, that he might cause her to be carried away of the flood. 16And the earth helped the woman; and the earth opened her mouth, and swallowed up the flood which the dragon cast out of his mouth. 17And the dragon was wroth with the woman, and went to make war with the remnant of her seed, which keep the commandments of God, and have the testimony of Jesus Christ.

13 And I stood upon the sand of the sea, and saw a beast rise up out of the sea, having seven heads and ten horns, and upon his horns ten crowns, and upon his heads the name of blasphemy. 2And the beast which I saw was like unto a leopard, and his feet were as the feet of a bear, and his mouth as the mouth of a lion: and the dragon gave him his power, and his seat, and great authority. 3And I saw one of his heads as it were wounded to death; and his

N.A.S.

and behold, a great red dragon having seven heads and ten horns, and on his heads were seven diadems. 4And his tail *swept away a third of the stars of heaven, and threw them to the earth. And the dragon stood before the woman who was about to give birth, so that when she gave birth he might devour her child. 5And she gave birth to a son, a male child, who is to rule all the nations with a rod of iron; and her child was caught up to God and to His throne. 6And the woman fled into the wilderness where she *had a place prepared by God, so that there she might be nourished for one thousand two hundred and sixty days.

7 And there was war in heaven, Michael and his angels waging war with the dragon. And the dragon and his angels waged war, 8 and they were not strong enough, and there was no longer a place found for them in heaven. 9And the great dragon was thrown down, the serpent of old who is called the Devil and Satan, who deceives the whole world; he was thrown down to the earth, and his angels were thrown down with him. 10And I heard a loud voice in heaven, saying,

"Now the salvation, and the power, and the kingdom of our God and the authority of His Christ have come, for the accuser of our brethren has been thrown down, who accuses them before our God day and night. 11"And they overcame him because of the blood of the Lamb and because of the word of their testimony, and they did not love their life even to death. 12 "For this reason, rejoice, O heavens and you who dwell in them. Woe to the earth and the sea; because the devil has come down to you, having great wrath, knowing that he has only a short time."

13 And when the dragon saw that he was thrown down to the earth, he persecuted the woman who gave birth to the male child. 14And the two wings of the great eagle were given to the woman, in order that she might fly into the wilderness to her place, where she *was nourished for a time and times and half a time, from the presence of the serpent. 15And the serpent poured water like a river out of his mouth after the woman, so that he might cause her to be swept away with the flood. 16And the earth helped the woman, and the earth opened its mouth and drank up the river which the dragon poured out of his mouth. 17And the dragon was enraged with the woman, and went off to make war with the rest of her offspring, who keep the commandments of God and hold to the testimony of Jesus.

13 And he stood on the sand of the seashore. And I saw a beast coming up out of the sea, having ten horns and seven heads, and on his horns were ten diadems, and on his heads were blasphemous names. 2And the beast which I saw was like a leopard, and his feet were like those of a bear, and his mouth like the mouth of a lion. And the dragon gave him his power and his throne and great authority. 3And I saw one of his heads as if it had been slain, and his

WILLIAMS

was a huge dragon, red as fire, with seven heads and ten horns, with seven diadems on his heads. 4 His tail was dragging after it a third part of the stars of heaven and dashed them down upon the earth. The dragon stood in front of the woman who was about to give birth to a child, in order to devour her child as soon as it was born. 5 She gave birth to a son, a male child who is going to rule all the nations with a scepter of iron; and the child was caught up to God, to His throne. 6 Then the woman fled into the desert, where she had a place of safety made ready by God, so that she might be cared for one thousand, two hundred and sixty days.

7 Then war broke out in heaven: Michael and his angels going to war with the dragon. The dragon and his angels fought, 8 but they were defeated, and there was no room for them in heaven any longer. 9 So the huge dragon, the ancient serpent, called the devil and Satan, who deceives the whole world, was hurled down to the earth, and his angels were hurled down with him.

10 Then I heard a loud voice in heaven say: "The salvation, power, and kingdom of our God, and the sovereignty of His Christ, have already come, because the accuser of our brothers, who always day and night accuses them before our God, has been hurled down. 11 But they have conquered him because of the blood of the Lamb and because of the message to which they bore testimony, because they did not cling to life but courted death. 12 So celebrate your triumph, you heavens and you who live in them! Alas for the earth and the sea, because the devil has come down to you in a great rage, since he knows that his time is short!"

13 When the dragon saw that he had been hurled down to the earth, he started persecuting the woman who had given birth to the male child. 14 But the two wings of a great eagle were given to the woman, so that she could fly to her place in the desert, where she could be taken care of for a time, times, and a half-time, safe from the presence of the serpent. 15 Then the serpent made water, like a river, spout from his mouth after the woman, to sweep her away with its torrent. 16 But the earth helped the woman, for it opened its mouth and swallowed the river which the dragon made to spout from his mouth. 17 So the dragon was enraged against the woman, and he went off to make war with the rest of her descendants, who continue to keep God's commands and to bear testimony to Jesus.

13 *He sees other symbols: the first wild beast; certain retribution for the persecutors; the second wild beast*

Then I stood on the sand of the seashore, and I saw a wild beast coming up out of the sea with ten horns and seven heads, with ten diadems on his horns, and blasphemous titles on his heads. 2 The wild beast which I saw was like a leopard, but his feet were like a bear's, and his mouth was like a lion's mouth. To him the dragon gave his own power and throne with great authority. 3 I saw that one of his heads seemed to have been mortally wounded, but its mortal wound had been healed.

BECK

was a large fiery dragon *with* seven heads and *ten horns*[96] and with seven crowns on his heads. 4 His tail swept away a third of *the stars in the sky* and *hurled them to the earth.*[97] Then the dragon stood in front of the woman who was going to have a Child, to devour her Child as soon as it was born.

5 She *gave birth to a Son, a Boy,*[98] *who is to rule* all *the nations with an iron rod.*[21] Her Child was snatched away and brought to God and to His throne. 6 The woman fled into the desert, where God has prepared a place for her and she is to be fed for 1,260 days.

7 Then war broke out in heaven: Michael and his angels fought with the dragon. And the dragon and his angels fought, 8 but they couldn't win, and *couldn't be found anywhere in heaven anymore.*[99] 9 So the great dragon was thrown out. The old *snake,* called *Devil* and *Satan,* who *deceives*[100] the whole world, was hurled to the earth, and his angels were hurled down with him.

10 Then I heard someone calling out loud in heaven: "Now has come the salvation, power, and kingdom of our God and the rule of His Christ, because he who accused our fellow Christians day and night before our God has been thrown out. 11 But they conquered him on account of *the blood of the Lamb*[101] and the truth they spoke and didn't love their life but were willing to die. 12 For this *be glad, you heavens,*[102] and you who live in them. Woe to the earth and the sea—the devil has come down to you and is very angry because he knows he has only a little time left."

The Devil and the Church

13 When the dragon saw he had been hurled to the earth, he persecuted the woman who had given birth to the Boy. 14 The woman was given two wings of the big eagle to fly to her place in the desert, away from the snake, where she is fed for *three and a half years.*[103] 15 Then the snake poured from his mouth a stream of water after the woman to sweep her away. 16 But the earth helped the woman; it opened its mouth and swallowed the stream that the dragon poured from his mouth.

17 The dragon was angry with the woman and went away to fight with her other children, those who do what God has ordered and keep on speaking the truth told by Jesus. He stopped on the sandy shore of the sea.

13 Then I saw *an animal coming up out of the sea.* He had *ten horns*[104] and seven heads, and on his horns were ten crowns, and on his heads were blasphemous names. 2 The animal I saw was *like a leopard* and had feet *like a bear* and a mouth *like a lion.*[105] The dragon gave him his power, his throne, and great authority. 3 One of his heads seemed to have received a deadly wound, but his deadly wound had been healed.

[96] Dan. 7:7, 20, 24
[97] Dan. 8:10
[98] Is. 66:7; Jer. 20:15
[99] Dan. 2:35
[100] Gen. 3:13; Zech. 3:1
[101] Ex. 12:5, 7
[102] Is. 44:23; 49:13
[103] Dan. 7:25; 12:7
[104] Dan. 7:3, 7, 20, 24
[105] Dan. 7:4-6

deadly wound was healed: and all the world wondered after the beast. 4And they worshipped the dragon which gave power unto the beast: and they worshipped the beast, saying, Who *is* like unto the beast? who is able to make war with him? 5And there was given unto him a mouth speaking great things and blasphemies; and power was given unto him to continue forty *and* two months. 6And he opened his mouth in blasphemy against God, to blaspheme his name, and his tabernacle, and them that dwell in heaven. 7And it was given unto him to make war with the saints, and to overcome them: and power was given him over all kindreds, and tongues, and nations. 8And all that dwell upon the earth shall worship him, whose names are not written in the book of life of the Lamb slain from the foundation of the world. 9 If any man have an ear, let him hear. 10 He that leadeth into captivity shall go into captivity: he that killeth with the sword must be killed with the sword. Here is the patience and the faith of the saints. 11And I beheld another beast coming up out of the earth; and he had two horns like a lamb, and he spake as a dragon. 12And he exerciseth all the power of the first beast before him, and causeth the earth and them which dwell therein to worship the first beast, whose deadly wound was healed. 13And he doeth great wonders, so that he maketh fire come down from heaven on the earth in the sight of men, 14And deceiveth them that dwell on the earth by *the means of* those miracles which he had power to do in the sight of the beast; saying to them that dwell on the earth, that they should make an image to the beast, which had the wound by a sword, and did live. 15And he had power to give life unto the image of the beast, that the image of the beast should both speak, and cause that as many as would not worship the image of the beast should be killed. 16And he causeth all, both small and great, rich and poor, free and bond, to receive a mark in their right hand, or in their foreheads: 17And that no man might buy or sell, save he that had the mark, or the name of the beast, or the number of his name. 18 Here is wisdom. Let him that hath understanding count the number of the beast: for it is the number of a man; and his number *is* Six hundred threescore *and* six.

fatal wound was healed. And the whole earth was amazed *and followed* after the beast; 4 and they worshiped the dragon, because he gave his authority to the beast; and they worshiped the beast, saying, "Who is like the beast, and who is able to wage war with him?" 5And there was given to him a mouth speaking arrogant words and blasphemies; and authority to act for forty-two months was given to him. 6And he opened his mouth in blasphemies against God, to blaspheme His name and His tabernacle, *that is,* those who dwell in heaven. 7And it was given to him to make war with the saints and to overcome them; and authority over every tribe and people and tongue and nation was given to him. 8And all who dwell on the earth will worship him, *every one* whose name has not been ªwritten from the foundation of the world in the book of life of the Lamb who has been slain. 9 If any one has an ear, let him hear. 10 If any one ᵇ*is destined* for captivity, to captivity he goes; if any one kills with the sword, with the sword he must be killed. Here is the perseverance and the faith of the saints.

11 And I saw another beast coming up out of the earth; and he had two horns like a lamb, and he spoke as a dragon. 12And he exercises all the authority of the first beast in his presence. And he makes the earth and those who dwell in it to worship the first beast, whose fatal wound was healed. 13And he performs great signs, so that he even makes fire come down out of heaven to the earth in the presence of men. 14And he deceives those who dwell on the earth because of the signs which it was given him to perform in the presence of the beast, telling those who dwell on the earth to make an image to the beast who *had the wound of the sword and has come to life. 15And there was given to him to give breath to the image of the beast, that the image of the beast might even ᶜspeak and cause as many as do not worship the image of the beast to be killed. 16And he causes all, the small and the great, and the rich and the poor, and the free men and the slaves, to be given a mark on their right hand, or on their forehead, 17 and *he provides* that no one should be able to buy or to sell, except the one who has the mark, *either* the name of the beast or the number of his name. 18 Here is wisdom. Let him who has understanding calculate the number of the beast, for the number is that of a man; and his number is ᵈsix hundred and sixty-six.

14 And I looked, and, lo, a Lamb stood on the mount Sion, and with him a hundred forty *and* four thousand, having his Father's name written in their foreheads. 2And I heard a voice from heaven, as the voice of many waters, and as the voice of a great thunder: and I heard the voice of harpers harping with their harps: 3And they sung as it were a new song before the throne, and before the four beasts, and the elders: and no man could learn that

14 And I looked, and behold, the Lamb *was* standing on Mount Zion, and with Him one hundred and forty-four thousand, having His name and the name of His Father written on their foreheads. 2And I heard a voice from heaven, like the sound of many waters and like the sound of loud thunder, and the voice which I heard *was* like *the sound* of harpists playing on their harps. 3And they *sang a new song before the throne and before the four living creatures and the elders; and no one could

[a] Or, *written in the book . . . slain from the foundation of the world.* [b] Or, *leads into captivity.* [c] Some ancient mss. read, *speak, and he will cause.* [d] Some mss. read, 616.

WILLIAMS

And the whole world was so amazed that they followed the wild beast, 4 and worshiped the dragon for giving the wild beast his authority; they also worshiped the wild beast, and said, "Who is there like the wild beast? Who is there to make war on him?"

5 Then there was given to the wild beast a mouth that uttered boastful, blasphemous words, and permission to wield his authority for forty-two months. 6 Then he opened his mouth to blaspheme against God, His name, and His dwelling place; that is, against those who live in heaven. 7 Permission was given to him to make war on God's people and to conquer them; authority was given to him over every tribe, people, language, and nation. 8All the inhabitants of the earth whose names, from the foundation of the world, have not been written in the slaughtered Lamb's book of life, will worship him.

9 If anyone has ears let him listen. 10 Whoever leads others into captivity will go into captivity himself. Whoever kills with the sword must be killed with the sword himself. In this way will be shown the patient endurance and the fidelity of God's people.

11 Then I saw another wild beast coming up out of the land. He had two horns like a lamb, but he spoke like a dragon. 12 He exercises the full authority of the first wild beast in his presence; he makes the earth and its inhabitants worship the first wild beast, whose mortal wound had been healed. 13 He performs great wonders; even makes fire come down out of heaven to earth before men's eyes. 14 He leads the inhabitants of the earth astray because of the wonders he is permitted to perform in the presence of the wild beast, telling the inhabitants of the earth to erect a statue*a* to the wild beast that bears the sword-thrust and yet has lived. 15 Permission has also been given him to impart life to the statue of the wild beast so that it can speak, and to have all who do not worship the statue of the wild beast killed. 16And he makes all, great and small, rich and poor, freemen and slaves, have a mark stamped on their right hands or on their foreheads, 17 and he permits no one to buy or sell anything unless he bears the mark; that is, the name of the wild beast or the number that represents the name.

18 Here is scope for wisdom! Let anyone who has the mental keenness calculate the number of the wild beast, for it is the number of a certain man; his number is six hundred and sixty-six.

14 *He hears the new song the redeemed are singing; hears four angels speak; sees the judgment sickle in the hand of the Son of Man*

Then I looked, and there the Lamb was standing on Mount Zion, and with Him one hundred and forty-four thousand people who had His name and the name of His Father written on their foreheads. 2And I heard a sound from heaven like the roar of great waters and the rumbling of loud thunders. The sound that I heard was like that of harpists playing on their harps. 3 They were singing a new song before the throne, the four living creatures, and

BECK

The whole world was amazed as it followed the animal 4 and worshiped the dragon because he had given power to the animal, and it worshiped the animal. "Is there anyone like the animal?" they asked. "And is there anyone who can fight with him?"

5 He was allowed *to talk big* and blasphemous *things* and was given authority to *act* for forty-two months. 6 He opened his mouth to slander God, His name, His home, and those who live in it in heaven. 7 He was allowed *to fight with the holy people and to conquer them*[106] and was given authority over every *tribe, people, language,* and *nation.*[46] 8 Everybody who lives on earth will worship him—everybody whose name *isn't written in the book of life*[107] of the *Lamb* that was *sacrificed*[108] since the world was made.

9 You have ears; then listen. 10 *If anyone is to be taken prisoner, he'll be taken prisoner.*[109] If anyone kills with a sword, he must be killed by a sword. Here is where the holy people will need to endure and trust.

11 Then I saw another animal come up out of the ground, and he had two horns like a lamb but talked like a dragon. 12 He is acting for the first animal with all his authority. He makes the earth and those living on it worship the first animal, whose deadly wound has been healed. 13 He also does great miracles, even makes fire come down from the sky to the ground before people. 14 He deceives those who live on the earth because of the wonders he is allowed to do for the animal, and he tells those who live on the earth to make a statue for the animal that was wounded by a sword and yet lived. 15 He was allowed to put a spirit into the animal's statue so that the animal's statue could talk, and to have *all who would not worship the* animal's *statue*[110] killed. 16 He forces all, great and small, rich and poor, free and slave to be branded on their right hands or on their foreheads, 17 and only he who has the brand—the animal's name or the number of its name—can buy or sell.

18 Here we need to be wise. If you can understand, figure out the animal's number, because it is a man's number. His number is 666.

The New Song

14 Then I saw the Lamb standing on Mount Zion and with Him 144,000 people who had His name and His Father's name written on their foreheads.

2 And I heard a *sound* from heaven *like the noise of many waters*[111] and of loud thunder. The sound I heard was also like the singing of musicians playing on their lyres. 3 They were *singing a new song*[112] before the throne, before the four living beings and the elders. And only

[106] Dan. 7:8, 21; 11:36
[107] Ex. 32:32-33; Ps. 69:28; 139:16; Is. 4:3; Mal. 3:16; Dan. 12:1
[108] Ex. 12:6, 21; Lev. 1:11; Is. 53:7; Jer. 11:19
[109] Jer. 15:2
[110] Dan 3:5-6
[111] Ezek. 1:24; 43:2
[112] Ps. 33:3; 40:3; 96:1; 98:1; 144:9; 149:1; Is. 42:10

[a] Lit., *make an image.*

K.J.V.

song but the hundred *and* forty *and* four thousand, which were redeemed from the earth. 4 These are they which were not defiled with women; for they are virgins. These are they which follow the Lamb whithersoever he goeth. These were redeemed from among men, *being* the firstfruits unto God and to the Lamb. 5And in their mouth was found no guile: for they are without fault before the throne of God. 6And I saw another angel fly in the midst of heaven, having the everlasting gospel to preach unto them that dwell on the earth, and to every nation, and kindred, and tongue, and people, 7 Saying with a loud voice, Fear God, and give glory to him; for the hour of his judgment is come: and worship him that made heaven, and earth, and the sea, and the fountains of waters. 8And there followed another angel, saying, Babylon is fallen, is fallen, that great city, because she made all nations drink of the wine of the wrath of her fornication. 9And the third angel followed them, saying with a loud voice, If any man worship the beast and his image and receive *his* mark in his forehead, or in his hand, 10 The same shall drink of the wine of the wrath of God, which is poured out without mixture into the cup of his indignation; and he shall be tormented with fire and brimstone in the presence of the holy angels, and in the presence of the Lamb: 11And the smoke of their torment ascendeth up for ever and ever: and they have no rest day nor night, who worship the beast and his image, and whosoever receiveth the mark of his name. 12 Here is the patience of the saints: here *are* they that keep the commandments of God, and the faith of Jesus. 13And I heard a voice from heaven saying unto me, Write, Blessed *are* the dead which die in the Lord from henceforth: Yea, saith the Spirit, that they may rest from their labours; and their works do follow them. 14And I looked, and behold a white cloud, and upon the cloud *one* sat like unto the Son of man, having on his head a golden crown, and in his hand a sharp sickle. 15And another angel came out of the temple, crying with a loud voice to him that sat on the cloud, Thrust in thy sickle, and reap: for the time is come for thee to reap; for the harvest of the earth is ripe. 16And he that sat on the cloud thrust in his sickle on the earth; and the earth was reaped. 17And another angel came out of the temple which is in heaven, he also having a sharp sickle. 18And another angel came out from the altar, which had power over fire; and cried with a loud cry to him that had the sharp sickle, saying, Thrust in thy sharp sickle, and gather the clusters of the vine of the earth; for her grapes are fully ripe. 19And the angel thrust in his sickle into the earth, and gathered the vine of the earth, and cast *it* into the great winepress of the wrath of God. 20And the winepress

N.A.S.

learn the song except the one hundred and forty-four thousand who had been purchased from the earth. 4 These are the ones who have not been defiled with women, for they are ᵃcelibates. These *are* the ones who follow the Lamb wherever He goes. These have been purchased from among men as firstfruits to God and to the Lamb. 5And no lie was found in their mouth; they are blameless. 6 And I saw another angel flying in midheaven, having an eternal gospel to preach to those who live on the earth, and to every nation and tribe and tongue and people; 7 and He said with a loud voice, "Fear God, and give Him glory, because the hour of His judgment has come; and worship Him who made the heaven and the earth and sea and springs of waters." 8 And another angel, a second one, followed, saying, "Fallen, fallen is Babylon the great, she who has made all the nations drink of the wine of the passion of her immorality." 9 And another angel, a third one, followed them, saying with a loud voice, "If any one worships the beast and his image, and receives a mark on his forehead or upon his hand, 10 he also will drink of the wine of the wrath of God, which is mixed in full strength in the cup of His anger; and he will be tormented with fire and brimstone in the presence of the holy angels and in the presence of the Lamb. 11 "And the smoke of their torment goes up forever and ever; and they have no rest day and night, those who worship the beast and his image, and whoever receives the mark of his name." 12 Here is the perseverance of the saints who keep the commandments of God and their faith in Jesus. 13 And I heard a voice from heaven, saying, "Write, 'Blessed are the dead who die in the Lord from now on!' " "Yes," says the Spirit, "that they may rest from their labors, for their deeds follow with them." 14 And I looked, and behold, a white cloud, and sitting on the cloud *was* one like ᵇa son of man, having a golden crown on His head, and a sharp sickle in His hand. 15And another angel came out of the temple, crying out with a loud voice to Him who sat on the cloud, "Put in your sickle and reap, because the hour to reap has come, because the harvest of the earth is ripe." 16And He who sat on the cloud swung His sickle over the earth; and the earth was reaped. 17 And another angel came out of the temple which is in heaven, and he also had a sharp sickle. 18And another angel, the one who has power over fire, came out from the altar; and he called with a loud voice to him who had the sharp sickle, saying, "Put in your sharp sickle, and gather the clusters from the vine of the earth, because her grapes are ripe." 19And the angel swung his sickle to the earth, and gathered *the clusters from* the vine of the earth, and threw them into the great wine press of the wrath of God. 20And the wine press was trodden

[a] Or, *chaste men*, lit., *virgins*. [b] Or, *the Son of Man.*

WILLIAMS

the elders, and no one could learn the song except the hundred and forty-four thousand who had been redeemed from the earth. 4 These are the men who have not been defiled by relations with women, for they are as pure as virgins. These are the men who follow the Lamb wherever He goes. These have been redeemed from among men as the first fruits for God and the Lamb, 5 and they have never been known to tell a lie with their lips; they are blameless.

6 Then I saw another angel flying in mid-air, with eternal good news to tell to the inhabitants of the earth, to every nation, tribe, language, and people.

7 He cried in a loud voice, "Fear God and give Him glory, because the hour of His judgment has come. Worship Him who made heaven and earth and sea and the springs of water."

8 Then a second angel followed, saying: "She has fallen! Mighty Babylon has fallen, who made all the nations drink the wine of vengeance due her immorality!"

9 Then a third angel followed them, saying in a loud voice: "Whoever worships the wild beast and his statue and lets his mark be stamped on his forehead or on his hand, 10 himself will have to drink the wine of God's vengeance, poured unmixed into the cup of His wrath, and be tortured with fire and brimstone before the eyes of the holy angels and the Lamb. 11 The smoke of their torture will go up forever and ever, and they will have no rest day or night—those who worship the wild beast and his statue, and anyone who bears the mark of his name." 12 In this way is shown the patient endurance of God's people, who always cling to God's commands and their faith in Jesus.

13 Then I heard a voice from heaven say, "Write, 'Blessed are the dead who from this time die as Christians.' " [a]

"Yes," says the Spirit, "let them rest from their toils, for the things they have done are going with them."

14 Then I looked, and there was a bright cloud with one seated on it like the Son of man, with a crown of gold on His head and a sharp sickle in His hand.

15 Then another angel came out of the temple and cried in a loud voice to Him who was seated on the cloud, "Put forth your sickle and reap, for the time to reap has come, because the earth's harvest is ripe." 16 So He who was seated on the cloud swung His sickle over the earth, and the earth was reaped.

17 Then another angel came out of the temple in heaven, and he too had a sharp sickle. 18 And another angel came from the altar, who had power over the fire, and he called in a loud voice to him who had the sharp sickle, "Put forth your sharp sickle, and gather the bunches of grapes from the earth's vine, because its grapes are fully ripe."

19 So the angel swung his sickle over the earth and gathered the grapes of the earth's vine, and flung them into the wine press of God's wrath. 20 The grapes in the wine press

BECK

the 144,000 who had been bought from the earth could learn the song.

4 These are the men who have not soiled themselves with women; they are pure. They follow the Lamb wherever He goes. They were bought as the first ones among men to belong to God and the Lamb. 5 *They've never been known to tell a lie.*[113] They're without a fault.

The Angel with the Good News

6 I saw another angel flying high in midair with everlasting good news to tell those living on the earth, every *nation, tribe, language,* and *people.*[46] 7 "Fear God and give Him glory," he called out loud; "the time has come for Him to judge. And worship Him *who made heaven, the earth, the sea,*[114] and springs of water."

Babylon Has Fallen

8 A second angel followed him. *"She has fallen!"* he said. *"The great Babylon has fallen* —she who made all *the nations drink of the wine of her*[115] immoral passion."

9 A third angel followed them. "If *anyone worships the* animal and his *statue,"*[110] he called out loud, "and is branded on his forehead or on his hand, 10 he must also *drink of the wine of God's anger,* poured out *unmixed into the cup* of *His punishment,*[116] and must be tortured by *fire and sulfur* before the holy angels and before the Lamb. 11 *The smoke of* their torture *goes up forever.* There's no rest *day and night*[117] for *those who worship the* animal and his *statue*[110] and for anyone branded with his name."

12 Here the holy people need to stand their ground as they keep on doing what God orders and trusting in Jesus.

13 Then I heard someone say from heaven: "Write, happy are the dead who are dying in the Lord!"

"Certainly," says the Spirit, "let them rest from their hard work; what they have done goes along with them."

Swing the Sickle

14 Then I saw a white cloud, and *on the cloud sat One who was like the Son of Man,*[118] with a golden crown on His head and a sharp sickle in His hand. 15 And another angel came out of the temple, calling out loud to Him who sat on the cloud: *"Swing Your Sickle*[119] and reap because *the time has come to cut the grain.*[120] *The crop* on the earth *is very ripe."* 16 And the One who sat on the cloud *swung His sickle* over the earth, and its grain was cut.

17 Another angel came out of the temple in heaven, and he, too, had a sharp sickle. 18 And another angel came from the altar with power over fire. He called out loud to the one with the sharp sickle: *"Swing your* sharp *sickle* and gather the bunches of grapes from the vine of the earth, because the grapes on it are ripe."

19 The angel *swung his sickle*[119] on the earth and gathered the grapes from the vine of the earth and threw them into the great winepress of *God's anger.* 20 *The grapes were trodden in*

[113] Ps. 32:2; Is. 53:9; Zeph. 3:13
[114] Gen. 14:19, 22; Ex. 20:11; Ps. 146:6; Neh. 9:6
[115] Is. 21:9; Jer. 25:15; 50:2; 51:7-8; Dan. 4:30
[116] Ps. 75:8; Is. 51:17; Jer. 25:15
[117] Gen. 19:24; Is. 34:10
[118] Dan. 7:13
[119] Joel 3:13
[120] Jer. 51:33

[a] Lit., *die in the Lord.*

K.J.V.

was trodden without the city, and blood came out of the winepress, even unto the horse bridles, by the space of a thousand *and* six hundred furlongs.

15 And I saw another sign in heaven, great and marvellous, seven angels having the seven last plagues; for in them is filled up the wrath of God. 2And I saw as it were a sea of glass mingled with fire: and them that had gotten the victory over the beast, and over his image, and over his mark, *and* over the number of his name, stand on the sea of glass, having the harps of God. 3And they sing the song of Moses the servant of God, and the song of the Lamb, saying, Great and marvellous *are thy* works, Lord God Almighty; just and true *are* thy ways, thou King of saints. 4 Who shall not fear thee, O Lord, and glorify thy name? for *thou* only *art* holy: for all nations shall come and worship before thee; for thy judgments are made manifest. 5And after that I looked, and, behold, the temple of the tabernacle of the testimony in heaven was opened: 6And the seven angels came out of the temple, having the seven plagues, clothed in pure and white linen, and having their breasts girded with golden girdles. 7And one of the four beasts gave unto the seven angels seven golden vials full of the wrath of God, who liveth for ever and ever. 8And the temple was filled with smoke from the glory of God, and from his power; and no man was able to enter into the temple, till the seven plagues of the seven angels were fulfilled.

16 And I heard a great voice out of the temple saying to the seven angels, Go your ways, and pour out the vials of the wrath of God upon the earth. 2And the first went, and poured out his vial upon the earth; and there fell a noisome and grievous sore upon the men which had the mark of the beast, and *upon* them which worshipped his image. 3And the second angel poured out his vial upon the sea; and it became as the blood of a dead *man:* and every living soul died in the sea. 4And the third angel poured out his vial upon the rivers and fountains of waters; and they became blood.

N.A.S.

outside the city, and blood came out from the wine press, up to the horses' bridles, for a distance of *a*two hundred miles.

15 And I saw another sign in heaven, great and marvelous, seven angels who had seven plagues, *which are* the last, because in them the wrath of God is finished.

2 And I saw, as it were, a sea of glass mixed with fire, and those who had come off victorious from the beast and from his image and from the number of his name, standing on the sea of glass, holding harps of God. 3And they *sang the song of Moses the bond-servant of God and the song of the Lamb, saying,

"Great and marvelous are Thy works,
O Lord God, the Almighty;
Righteous and true are Thy ways,
Thou King of the *bnations.
4 "Who will not fear, O Lord, and glorify
Thy name?
For Thou alone art holy;
For all the nations will come and wor-
ship before Thee,
For Thy righteous acts have been revealed."

5 After these things I looked, and the temple of the tabernacle of testimony in heaven was opened, 6 and the seven angels who had seven plagues came out of the temple, clothed in *clinen, clean *and* bright, and girded around their breasts with golden girdles. 7And one of the four living creatures gave to the seven angels seven golden bowls full of the wrath of God, who lives forever and ever. 8And the temple was filled with smoke from the glory of God and from His power; and no one was able to enter the temple until the seven plagues of the seven angels were finished.

16 And I heard a loud voice from the temple, saying to the seven angels, "Go and pour out the seven bowls of the wrath of God into the earth."

2 And the first *angel* went and poured out his bowl into the earth; and it became a loathsome and malignant sore upon the men who had the mark of the beast and who worshiped his image.

3 And the second *angel* poured out his bowl into the sea, and it became blood like *that* of a dead man; and every living *dthing in the sea died.

4 And the third *angel* poured out his bowl into the rivers and the springs of waters; and

[a] Lit., *sixteen hundred stadia.* A stadion was about six hundred feet. [b] Some ancient mss. read, *ages.* [c] Some mss. read, *stone.* [d] Lit., *soul.* Some ancient mss. read, *thing, the things in the sea.*

WILLIAMS

were trodden outside the city, and blood streamed from the wine press until it reached the horses' bridles for a distance of two hundred miles.

15 *He sees seven angels bringing seven plagues; hears the redeemed sing a song of triumph; the plagues are sent from heaven*

Then I saw another symbol in heaven, great and wonderful: seven angels bringing seven plagues which are to be the last, because with them God's wrath is completely expressed. 2 Then I saw something that looked like a sea of glass mixed with fire, and standing upon the sea of glass were those who had conquered the wild beast, his statue, and the number representing his name; and they had harps that God had given them. 3 And they were singing the song of Moses, the slave of God, and the song of the Lamb:

"Great and wonderful are your works,
Lord God, Almighty One;
Upright and true your ways,
O King of the ages.
4 Who will not fear and glorify your name,
O Lord?
For you alone are holy.
All the nations will come and worship you,
Because the justice of your sentences has now
been shown."

5 After this I looked, and the sanctuary of the tent of testimony was thrown open in heaven, 6 and the seven angels bringing the seven plagues came out of the sanctuary. They were clothed in clean, brilliant linen and had belts of gold around their breasts. 7 Then one of the four living creatures gave the seven angels seven bowls of gold, full of the wrath of God who lives for ever and ever, 8 and the sanctuary was filled with smoke from the glory and power of God, and no one could go into the sanctuary until the seven plagues of the seven angels were at an end.

16 *He sees the seven plagues take place: men afflicted with sores, sea turned into blood, waters too, sun scorching men, throne of the wild beast cursed, Euphrates dried up, and foul spirits seize kings; thunders, earthquakes, curses*

Then I heard a loud voice from the sanctuary say to the seven angels:
"Go and empty the seven bowls of God's
wrath upon the earth."
2 So the first angel went and emptied his bowl upon the earth, and horrible, painful sores broke out on the men who bore the mark of the wild beast and worshiped his statue. 3 Then the second angel emptied his bowl into the sea, and it turned into blood like a dead man's, and every living thing that was in the sea died. 4 Then the third angel emptied his bowl into the rivers and the springs of water, and they turned into blood.

BECK

the winepress[121] outside the city, and the blood flowed from the winepress till for two hundred miles it came up to the horse's bridles.

Seven Plagues

15 Then I saw in heaven another sign, great and wonderful: seven angels with *seven plagues;*[122] the last plagues, since with them God in His anger has finished what He intends to do.
2 And I saw what looked like a sea of glass mixed with fire, and standing on the glassy sea were those who had come away victorious from the animal, its statue, and the number of its name. They were holding God's lyres 3 and singing *the song of Moses, God's servant,*[123] and the song of the Lamb:

Great and wonderful are Your works,[124]
Lord God Almighty.[10]
Righteous and true are Your ways,[125] King
of the ages.
4 Is there anyone, Lord, who will not fear
and glorify Your name? [126]
You alone are holy.
All the nations will come and worship
You[127]
Because they have seen Your righteous
acts.

5 After this I saw the temple of *the tabernacle containing God's Word* [128] in heaven opened, 6 and the seven angels with the *seven plagues*[122] came out of the temple. They wore clean, shining linen and golden belts fastened around their breasts. 7 Then one of the four living beings gave to the seven angels seven golden bowls full of the anger of *God, who lives forever.*[38] 8 *God's glory* and power *filled the temple with smoke,* and nobody *could go into*[129] the temple till the *seven plagues*[122] of the seven angels were over.

16 Then I heard *someone from the temple*[130] call out loud to the seven angels, "Go, *pour out* the seven bowls of *God's anger on the earth."* [131]
2 The first went and poured out his bowl on the earth, and bad and *painful sores came on the people*[132] who had the brand of the animal and *worshiped its statue.*[110]
3 The second poured out his bowl into the sea, and *it turned to blood* like that of a dead man, and every living thing in the sea *died.*
4 The third poured out his bowl into the *rivers* and the springs of water, and *they turned to blood.*[133]

[121] Is. 63:2-3
[122] Lev. 26:21
[123] Ex. 15:1; Joshua 14:7
[124] Ex. 34:10; Deut. 32:4; Ps. 111:2; 139:14
[125] Deut. 32:4; Ps. 145:17
[126] Jer. 10:7; Mal. 1:11
[127] Ps. 22:27; 86:9; Is. 66:23
[128] Ex. 38:21; Num. 1:50, 53; 9:15; 10:11; 17:7,
8; 18:2; 2 Chron. 24:6
[129] Ex. 40:34-35; 1 Kings 8:10-11; Is. 6:1, 4;
Ezek. 44:4
[130] Is. 66:6
[131] Ps. 69:24; Jer. 10:25; Zeph. 3:8
[132] Ex. 9:10; Deut. 28:35
[133] Ex. 7:17, 19-21; Ps. 78:44

K.J.V.

5And I heard the angel of the waters say, Thou art righteous, O Lord, which art, and wast, and shalt be, because thou hast judged thus. 6 For they have shed the blood of saints and prophets, and thou hast given them blood to drink; for they are worthy. 7And I heard another out of the altar say, Even so, Lord God Almighty, true and righteous *are* thy judgments. 8And the fourth angel poured out his vial upon the sun; and power was given unto him to scorch men with fire. 9And men were scorched with great heat, and blasphemed the name of God, which hath power over these plagues: and they repented not to give him glory. 10And the fifth angel poured out his vial upon the seat of the beast; and his kingdom was full of darkness; and they gnawed their tongues for pain, 11And blasphemed the God of heaven because of their pains and their sores, and repented not of their deeds. 12And the sixth angel poured out his vial upon the great river Euphrates; and the water thereof was dried up, that the way of the kings of the east might be prepared. 13And I saw three unclean spirits like frogs *come* out of the mouth of the dragon, and out of the mouth of the beast, and out of the mouth of the false prophet. 14For they are the spirits of devils, working miracles, *which* go forth unto the kings of the earth and of the whole world, to gather them to the battle of that great day of God Almighty. 15Behold, I come as a thief. Blessed *is* he that watcheth, and keepeth his garments, lest he walk naked, and they see his shame. 16And he gathered them together into a place called in the Hebrew tongue Armageddon. 17And the seventh angel poured out his vial into the air; and there came a great voice out of the temple of heaven, from the throne, saying, It is done. 18And there were voices, and thunders, and lightnings; and there was a great earthquake, such as was not since men were upon the earth, so mighty an earthquake, *and* so great. 19And the great city was divided into three parts, and the cities of the nations fell: and great Babylon came in remembrance before God, to give unto her the cup of the wine of the fierceness of his wrath. 20And every island fled away, and the mountains were not found. 21And there fell upon men a great hail out of heaven, *every stone* about the weight of a talent: and men blasphemed God because of the plague of the hail; for the plague thereof was exceeding great.

17 And there came one of the seven angels which had the seven vials, and talked with me, saying unto me, Come hither; I will shew unto thee the judgment of the great whore that sitteth upon many waters; 2With whom the

N.A.S.

[a]they became blood. 5And I heard the angel of the waters saying, "Righteous art Thou, who art and who wast, O Holy One, because Thou didst judge these things; 6 for they poured out the blood of saints and prophets, and Thou hast given them blood to drink. They deserve it." 7And I heard the altar saying, "Yes, O Lord God, the Almighty, true and righteous are Thy judgments."

8 And the fourth *angel* poured out his bowl upon the sun; and it was given to it to scorch men with fire. 9And men were scorched with fierce heat; and they blasphemed the name of God who has the power over these plagues; and they did not repent, so as to give Him glory.

10 And the fifth *angel* poured out his bowl upon the throne of the beast; and his kingdom became darkened; and they gnawed their tongues because of pain, 11 and they blasphemed the God of heaven because of their pains and their sores; and they did not repent of their deeds.

12 And the sixth *angel* poured out his bowl upon the great river, the Euphrates; and its water was dried up, that the way might be prepared for the kings from the east. 13And I saw *coming* out of the mouth of the dragon and out of the mouth of the beast and out of the mouth of the false prophet, three unclean spirits like frogs; 14 for they are spirits of demons, performing signs, which go out to the kings of the whole world, to gather them together for the war of the great day of God, the Almighty. 15 (Behold, I am coming like a thief. Blessed is the one who stays awake and keeps his garments, lest he walk about naked and men see his shame.) 16And they gathered them together to the place which in Hebrew is called [b]Har-Magedon.

17 And the seventh *angel* poured out his bowl upon the air; and a loud voice came out of the temple from the throne, saying, "It is done." 18And there were flashes of lightning and sounds and peals of thunder; and there was a great earthquake, such as there had not been since man came to be upon the earth, so great an earthquake *was it, and* so mighty. 19And the great city was split into three parts, and the cities of the nations fell. And Babylon the great was remembered before God, to give her the cup of the wine of His fierce wrath. 20And every island fled away, and the mountains were not found. 21And huge hailstones, about [c]one hundred pounds each, *came down from heaven upon men; and men blasphemed God because of the plague of the hail, because its plague *was extremely severe.

17 And one of the seven angels who had the seven bowls came and spoke with me, saying, "Come here, I shall show you the judgment of the great harlot who sits on many waters, 2 with whom the kings of the earth

---

[a] Some ancient mss. read, *it became.* [b] Some editors read, *Armageddon.* [c] Lit., *the weight of a talent.*

WILLIAMS

5 Then I heard the angel of the waters say: "You are just in passing such a sentence, you who are and were, you the Holy One. 6 Because they have shed the blood of your people and prophets, you have given them blood to drink; they deserve it."

7 And I heard the altar say, "Yes, Lord God Almighty! Your sentences are true and just."

8 Then the fourth angel emptied his bowl upon the sun, and permission was given it to scorch mankind with its fiery heat, 9 so that men were severely scorched, but they only cursed the name of God who had authority over these plagues, and would not repent and give Him glory.

10 Then the fifth angel emptied his bowl upon the throne of the wild beast, and his kingdom was shrouded in darkness, and men in agony gnawed their tongues, 11 and cursed the God of heaven because of their sufferings and sores, but they would not repent of what they had done.

12 Then the sixth angel emptied his bowl upon the great river Euphrates, and its waters were dried up to prepare the way for the kings from the east. 13 Then I saw three foul spirits leap like frogs from the mouth of the dragon, from the mouth of the wild beast, and from the mouth of the false prophet. 14 They are the spirits of demons that perform wonders, and they go forth to the kings of the whole world, to muster them for battle on the great day of the Almighty God. 15 (See! I am coming like a thief! Blessed is he who stays awake and keeps his clothes ready, so that he may not go naked and people see his shame.) 16 So they mustered the kings at the place called in Hebrew, Armageddon.

17 Then the seventh angel emptied his bowl into the air, and a loud voice came out of the sanctuary from the throne, saying, "It is done."

18 Then there were flashes of lightning, rumblings, and peals of thunder; then there was a great earthquake, an earthquake so great that none like it had ever been since man first existed on the earth. 19 The great city was broken into three parts; the cities of the heathen fell, and God remembered to give mighty Babylon the cup of the wine of His raging wrath. 20 Every island vanished; not a mountain could be seen; 21 huge hailstones as heavy as talents fell on men from heaven, and men cursed God for the plague of hail, because the torture of it was severe.

BECK

5 I heard the angel of the waters say, "O *holy One, You are*[2] and You were. *You are just in judging*[134] this way; 6 *they have poured out the blood* [135] of holy people and prophets, and You gave *them blood to drink*[136] as they deserve."

7 I heard the altar answer, "Yes, *Lord God Almighty,*[10] *Your judgments are true and just."* [137]

8 The fourth poured out his bowl on the sun, and it was allowed to burn people. 9 When they were badly burned, they blasphemed the name of God, who controlled these plagues, and their hearts didn't turn to give Him glory.

10 The fifth poured out his bowl on the animal's throne, and its kingdom *turned dark.*[138] 11 People gnawed their tongues in anguish, cursed *the God of heaven*[139] for their pains and their sores but weren't sorry for what they had done.

12 The sixth poured out his bowl on *the big Euphrates river.*[73] Then *the water in it dried up,*[140] to prepare the road for the kings *from the east.*[141]

13 Then I saw three unclean spirits, like frogs come out of the dragon's mouth, the animal's mouth, and the false prophet's* mouth. They were spirits of devils, doing miracles. 14 They went out to the kings of the whole world to gather them for war on the great day of the Almighty God.—

15 "See, I am coming like a thief. Happy is he who stays awake and keeps his clothes, so he will not have to go naked and let others see his shameful parts."—

16 The spirits gathered the kings at the place the Jews call Armageddon.

17 Then the seventh poured out his bowl over the air, and someone *called* out loud *from* the throne in *the temple*[130]: "It is done!" 18 *There were flashes of lightning, rumblings,*[64] and peals of thunder, and a big earthquake. *There never was such* an earthquake *since there were* people *on earth.*[142] 19 The great city split into three parts, and the other cities of the nations fell. And God remembered to give *the great Babylon the cup of the wine of His* fierce *anger.*[115, 116] 20 Every island vanished, and the mountains couldn't be seen any more. 21 *Huge hailstones* weighing about a hundred pounds fell from the sky on people, and they blasphemed God for the plague of hail, so *terrible*[143] was that plague.

17

He sees a woman in purple and scarlet; He hears what the symbol of the woman means

Then one of the seven angels with the seven bowls came and spoke to me, saying: "Come, I will show you the doom of the noted prostitute who is seated on many waters, 2 in whose

---

The Woman and the Animal

17

One of the seven angels who held the seven bowls came and told me, "Come, I will show you how the great prostitute who sits *by many waters*[144] is judged. 2 *The kings of the*

* The second animal, 13:11-18; 19:20; 20:10.

[134] Ps. 119:137; 145:17
[135] Ps. 79:3
[136] Is. 49:26
[137] Ps. 19:9
[138] Ex. 10:22
[139] Dan. 2:19
[140] Is. 44:27; Jer. 50:38
[141] Is. 41:2, 25
[142] Dan. 12:1
[143] Ex. 9:24
[144] Jer. 51:13

kings of the earth have committed fornication, and the inhabitants of the earth have been made drunk with the wine of her fornication. 3 So he carried me away in the spirit into the wilderness: and I saw a woman sit upon a scarlet coloured beast, full of names of blasphemy, having seven heads and ten horns. 4And the woman was arrayed in purple and scarlet colour, and decked with gold and precious stones and pearls, having a golden cup in her hand full of abominations and filthiness of her fornication: 5And upon her forehead *was* a name written, MYSTERY, BABYLON THE GREAT, THE MOTHER OF HARLOTS AND ABOMINATIONS OF THE EARTH. 6And I saw the woman drunken with the blood of the saints, and with the blood of the martyrs of Jesus: and when I saw her, I wondered with great admiration. 7And the angel said unto me, Wherefore didst thou marvel? I will tell thee the mystery of the woman, and of the beast that carrieth her, which hath the seven heads and ten horns. 8 The beast that thou sawest was, and is not; and shall ascend out of the bottomless pit, and go into perdition: and they that dwell on the earth shall wonder, whose names were not written in the book of life from the foundation of the world, when they behold the beast that was, and is not, and yet is. 9And here *is* the mind which hath wisdom. The seven heads are seven mountains, on which the woman sitteth. 10And there are seven kings: five are fallen, and one is, *and* the other is not yet come; and when he cometh, he must continue a short space. 11And the beast that was, and is not, even he is the eighth, and is of the seven, and goeth into perdition. 12And the ten horns which thou sawest are ten kings, which have received no kingdom as yet; but receive power as kings one hour with the beast. 13 These have one mind, and shall give their power and strength unto the beast. 14 These shall make war with the Lamb, and the Lamb shall overcome them: for he is Lord of lords, and King of kings: and they that are with him *are* called, and chosen, and faithful. 15And he saith unto me, The waters which thou sawest, where the whore sitteth, are peoples, and multitudes, and nations, and tongues. 16And the ten horns which thou sawest upon the beast, these shall hate the whore, and shall make her desolate and naked, and shall eat her flesh, and burn her with fire. 17 For God hath put in their hearts to fulfil his will, and to agree, and give their kingdom unto the beast, until the words of God shall be fulfilled. 18And the woman which thou sawest is that great city, which reigneth over the kings of the earth.

committed *acts of* immorality, and those who dwell on the earth were made drunk with the wine of her immorality." 3And he carried me away ᵃin the Spirit into a wilderness; and I saw a woman sitting on a scarlet beast, full of blasphemous names, having seven heads and ten horns. 4And the woman was clothed in purple and scarlet, and adorned with gold and precious stones and pearls, having in her hand a gold cup full of abominations and of the unclean things of her immorality, 5 and upon her forehead a name *was* written, a mystery, "BABYLON THE GREAT, THE MOTHER OF HARLOTS AND OF THE ABOMINATIONS OF THE EARTH." 6And I saw the woman drunk with the blood of the saints, and with the blood of the witnesses of Jesus. And when I saw her, I wondered greatly. 7And the angel said to me, "Why do you wonder? I shall tell you the mystery of the woman and of the beast that carries her, which has the seven heads and the ten horns. 8 "The beast that you saw was and is not, and is about to come up out of the abyss and ᵇto go to destruction. And those who dwell on the earth will wonder, whose name has not been written in the book of life from the foundation of the world, when they see the beast, that he was and is not and will come. 9 "Here is the mind which has wisdom. The seven heads are seven mountains on which the woman sits, 10 and they are seven kings; five have fallen, one is, the other has not yet come; and when he comes, he must remain a little while. 11 "And the beast which was and is not, is himself also an eighth, and is *one* of the seven, and he goes to destruction. 12 "And the ten horns which you saw are ten kings, who have not yet received a kingdom, but they receive authority as kings with the beast for one hour. 13 "These have one purpose and they give their power and authority to the beast. 14 "These will wage war against the Lamb, and the Lamb will overcome them, because He is Lord of lords and King of kings, and those who are with Him *are the* called and chosen and faithful." 15And he *said to me, "The waters which you saw where the harlot sits, are peoples and multitudes and nations and tongues. 16 "And the ten horns which you saw, and the beast, these will hate the harlot and will make her desolate and naked, and will eat her flesh and will burn her up with fire. 17 "For God has put it in their hearts to execute His purpose by having a common purpose, and by giving their kingdom to the beast, until the words of God should be fulfilled. 18 "And the woman whom you saw is the great city, which reigns over the kings of the earth."

18 And after these things I saw another angel come down from heaven, having great power; and the earth was lightened with his glory. 2And he cried mightily with a strong voice, saying, Babylon the great is fallen, is fallen, and is become the habitation of devils, and the hold of every foul spirit, and a cage of

18 After these things I saw another angel coming down from heaven, having great authority; and the earth was illumined with his glory. 2And he cried out with a mighty voice, saying, "Fallen, fallen is Babylon the great! And she has become a dwelling place of demons and a prison of every unclean spirit, and a

[a] Or, *in spirit*. [b] Some ancient mss. read, *he goes.*

WILLIAMS	BECK

prostitution the kings of the earth have joined, and with the wine of whose prostitution the inhabitants of the earth have been intoxicated."

3 So he carried me away in spiritual rapture to a desert, and I saw a woman seated on a scarlet wild beast, covered with blasphemous titles; he had seven heads and ten horns. 4 The woman was dressed in purple and scarlet, decorated in gold and precious stones and pearls, and she had in her hand a cup of gold, full of abominations and the impurities of her immorality. 5 On her forehead was written a name with a symbolical meaning, "Mighty Babylon, the mother of prostitutes and of earth's abominations." 6 I saw the woman drinking herself drunk with the blood of God's people and the blood of the martyred witnesses to Jesus.

When I saw her I was utterly astonished, 7 but the angel said to me: "Why are you astonished? I will tell you the symbolical meaning of the woman, and the wild beast with seven heads and ten horns, that carries her. 8 The wild beast that you saw, once was but now is no more; he is going to come up out of the abyss, but he is going to be destroyed. The inhabitants of the earth, whose names from the foundation of the world have not been written in the book of life, will be astonished when they see that the wild beast once was but now is no more, and yet is to come. 9 Here is scope for a mind that is packed with wisdom. The seven heads are the seven hills on which the woman is seated. 10 There are also seven kings; five have fallen, one is on the throne, the other has not yet come, and when he does he must stay but a little while. 11 So it is with the wild beast that once was but is no more; he is the eighth, and yet is one of the seven, and he is going to be destroyed. 12 The ten horns that you saw are ten kings, who have not yet become kings, but for a single hour they accept authority as kings allied with the wild beast. 13 They have one common policy. They give their power and authority to the wild beast. 14 They will make war upon the Lamb, but the Lamb will conquer them, and His chosen, elect, and faithful followers will conquer with Him, too, because He is Lord of lords and King of kings."

15 He also said to me: "The waters that you saw, on which the prostitute was seated, are peoples, multitudes, nations, and languages. 16 The ten horns that you saw and the wild beast will be the very ones to hate the prostitute, to make her desolate and naked, to eat up her flesh, and burn her up with fire. 17 For God has put it into their hearts to carry out His purpose by giving up their authority to the wild beast until God's words are carried out. 18 And the woman whom you saw is the great city that has dominion over the kings of the earth."

18 *He hears that mighty Babylon (Rome) has fallen; friends in grief, God's people escape, heaven rejoices; a hurled stone symbolizes her complete ruin.*

After this I saw another angel coming down from heaven. He had great authority and the earth was lighted up with his splendor.

2 He shouted with a mighty voice: "She has fallen! Mighty Babylon has fallen! She has become a den for demons, a dungeon for every foul spirit and every unclean and loathsome

earth lived in sexual sin[145] with her, and *the people on earth got drunk on the wine of her*[146] sexual vice."

3 He took me in spirit to a desert. There I saw a woman sitting on a scarlet *animal* covered with blasphemous names, and it *had* seven heads and *ten horns.*[147] 4 The woman wore purple and scarlet and ornaments of gold, jewels, and pearls. In her hand she held *a golden cup*[146] full of the abominations and the unclean things of her sexual vice, 5 and on her forehead was written a name with a hidden meaning: *THE GREAT BABYLON,*[148] THE MOTHER OF PROSTITUTES AND OF THE ABOMINATIONS OF THE EARTH. 6 I saw the woman was drunk with the blood of the holy people and the blood of the witnesses of Jesus. And I was very much surprised to see her.

7 "Why are you surprised?" the angel asked me. "I'll tell you the hidden meaning of the woman and of the *animal* she rides *that has* the seven heads and the *ten horns.*[147] 8 *The animal* you saw once was but is no more, and it will *come up from*[149] the abyss and go to its destruction. And the people living on the earth whose names since the world was made have not been *written in the book of life*[107] will be surprised to see the animal—it was and is no more and will come again.

9 "Here is something for an intelligent person to think about. The seven heads are seven hills on which the woman is sitting. 10 They are also seven kings: five have fallen, one is ruling now, the other hasn't come yet, and when he comes, he must stay a little while. 11 The animal that was and is no more is the eighth king; he comes from the seven and goes to his destruction.

12 *"The ten horns you saw are ten kings*[147] who have not yet started to rule but for an hour get authority as kings with the animal. 13 They have one purpose and give their power and authority to the animal. 14 They will go to war against the Lamb, but the Lamb, and the called, chosen, and faithful people with Him, will conquer them because He is *the Lord of lords and the King of kings.*[150]

15 "The waters you saw where the prostitute was sitting," he told me, "are *peoples,* crowds, *nations,* and *languages.*[46] 16 *The ten horns*[147] you saw and the animal will hate the prostitute, lay her waste, strip her, devour her flesh, and burn her with fire. 17 God has put it into their hearts to do what He has decided, to carry out one purpose, and to give their kingdom to the animal till what God has said is carried out. 18 The woman you saw is the great city that rules over *the kings of the earth.*" [151]

Babylon Has Fallen

18 After that I saw another angel come down from heaven. He had great power, and his glory lit up the earth. 2 He called out with a loud voice: *"She has fallen, the great Babylon has fallen*[115] *and has become a home for devils,* a dungeon for every unclean spirit and for every

[145] Is. 23:17
[146] Jer. 51:7
[147] Dan. 7:7, 20, 24
[148] Dan. 4:30
[149] Dan. 7:3
[150] Deut. 10:17; Dan. 2:47
[151] Ps. 2:2; 89:27

K.J.V.

every unclean and hateful bird. 3 For all nations have drunk of the wine of the wrath of her fornication, and the kings of the earth have committed fornication with her, and the merchants of the earth are waxed rich through the abundance of her delicacies. 4 And I heard another voice from heaven, saying, Come out of her, my people, that ye be not partakers of her sins, and that ye receive not of her plagues. 5 For her sins have reached unto heaven, and God hath remembered her iniquities. 6 Reward her even as she rewarded you, and double unto her double according to her works: in the cup which she hath filled, fill to her double. 7 How much she hath glorified herself, and lived deliciously, so much torment and sorrow give her: for she saith in her heart, I sit a queen, and am no widow, and shall see no sorrow. 8 Therefore shall her plagues come in one day, death, and mourning, and famine; and she shall be utterly burned with fire: for strong *is* the Lord God who judgeth her. 9 And the kings of the earth, who have committed fornication and lived deliciously with her, shall bewail her, and lament for her, when they shall see the smoke of her burning, 10 Standing afar off for the fear of her torment, saying, Alas, alas, that great city Babylon, that mighty city! for in one hour is thy judgment come. 11 And the merchants of the earth shall weep and mourn over her; for no man buyeth their merchandise any more: 12 The merchandise of gold, and silver, and precious stones, and of pearls, and fine linen, and purple, and silk, and scarlet, and all thyine wood, and all manner vessels of ivory, and all manner vessels of most precious wood, and of brass, and iron, and marble. 13 And cinnamon, and odours, and ointments, and frankincense, and wine, and oil, and fine flour, and wheat, and beasts, and sheep, and horses, and chariots, and slaves, and souls of men. 14 And the fruits that thy soul lusted after are departed from thee, and all things which were dainty and goodly are departed from thee, and thou shalt find them no more at all. 15 The merchants of these things, which were made rich by her, shall stand afar off for the fear of her torment, weeping and wailing, 16 And saying, Alas, alas, that great city, that was clothed in fine linen, and purple, and scarlet, and decked with gold, and precious stones, and pearls! 17 For in one hour so great riches is come to nought. And every shipmaster, and all the company in ships, and sailors, and as many as trade by sea, stood afar off, 18 And cried when they saw the smoke of her burning, saying, What *city is* like unto this great city! 19 And they cast dust on their heads, and cried, weeping and wailing, saying, Alas, alas, that great city, wherein were made rich all that had ships in the sea by reason of her costliness! for

N.A.S.

prison of every unclean and hateful bird. 3 "For all the nations [a]have drunk of the wine of the passion of her immorality, and the kings of the earth have committed *acts of* immorality with her, and the merchants of the earth have become rich by the wealth of her sensuality."

4 And I heard another voice from heaven, saying, "Come out of her, my people, that you may not participate in her sins and that you may not receive of her plagues; 5 for her sins have piled up as high as heaven, and God has remembered her iniquities. 6 "Pay her back even as she has paid, and give back *to her* double according to her deeds; in the cup which she has mixed, mix twice as much for her. 7 "To the degree that she glorified herself and lived sensuously, to the same degree give her torment and mourning; for she says in her heart, 'I sit *as* a queen and I am not a widow, and will never see mourning.' 8 "For this reason in one day her plagues will come, pestilence and mourning and famine, and she will be burned up with fire; for the Lord God who judges her is strong. 9 "And the kings of the earth, who committed *acts of* immorality and lived sensuously with her, will weep and lament over her when they see the smoke of her burning, 10 standing at a distance because of the fear of her torment, saying, 'Woe, woe, the great city, Babylon, the strong city! For in one hour your judgment has come.' 11 "And the merchants of the earth weep and mourn over her, because no one buys their cargoes any more; 12 cargoes of gold and silver and precious stones and pearls and fine linen and purple and silk and scarlet, and every *kind of* citron wood and every article of ivory and every article *made* from very costly wood and bronze and iron and marble, 13 and cinnamon and spice and incense and perfume and frankincense and wine and olive oil and fine flour and wheat and cattle and sheep, and *cargoes* of horses and chariots and slaves, and human lives. 14 "And the fruit you long for has gone from you, and all things that were luxurious and splendid have passed away from you and *men* will no longer find them. 15 "The merchants of these things, who became rich from her, will stand at a distance because of the fear of her torment, weeping and mourning, 16 saying, 'Woe, woe, the great city, she who was clothed in fine linen and purple and scarlet, and adorned with gold and precious stones and pearls; 17 for in one hour such great wealth has been laid waste.' And every shipmaster and every passenger and sailor, and as many as make their living by the sea, stood at a distance, 18 and were crying out as they saw the smoke of her burning, saying, 'What *city* is like the great city?' 19 "And they threw dust on their heads and were crying out, weeping and mourning, saying, 'Woe, woe, the great city, in which all who had ships at sea became rich by her wealth, for in one hour she has been laid waste.'

[a] Many ancient mss. read, *have fallen by.*

WILLIAMS

bird, 3 because all the nations have fallen by drinking the raging wine of her immorality; the kings of the earth have joined her in her immorality, and the businessmen of the earth have grown rich from the wealth[a] of her luxury."

4 Then I heard another voice from heaven say:

"Come out of her, my people, so that you may not share in her sins and suffer from her plagues. 5 For her sins are piled clear up to heaven, and God has remembered the wrongs which she has done. 6 Pay her back in her own coin; give her double for what she has done. In the cup that she has mixed, mix twice as much for her. 7 To the same degree in which she has lived in splendor and luxury, give her torture and tears. Because she is always boasting in her heart, 'I sit enthroned as queen; I am not a widow, I shall never experience any sorrow'—8 for this very reason her plagues will overtake her in a single day, death, grief, and famine, and she will be burned up with fire; because the Lord who has judged her is mighty. 9 The kings of the earth who have joined her in her immorality and luxury will weep and lament over her when they see the smoke from her burning. 10 They will stand a long way off for fear of her torture, saying, 'Alas! alas for the great city, for Babylon the mighty city, because in a single day your judgment has overtaken you!' 11 The businessmen of the earth will weep and mourn over her, because no one can buy their cargoes any more—12 cargoes of gold, silver, precious stones, fine linen, silk, and scarlet, all kinds of citron wood, all kinds of goods in ivory and costly woods, bronze, iron, and marble, 13 cinnamon, spices, incense, perfume, frankincense, wine, oil, fine flour, wheat, cattle, sheep, horses, carriages, slaves, and the lives of human beings. 14 The ripe fruit of your soul's desire has gone from you, all your luxury and splendor have perished from your hands, and people will never find them again. 15 The businessmen who dealt in these things, who had grown rich from their business with her, will stand a long way off for fear of her torture, weeping and mourning, 16 and saying, 'Alas! alas for the great city that was dressed in fine linen, purple, and scarlet, that was decorated in gold, precious stones, and pearls, 17 because in a single hour a wealth so vast has been destroyed!' All ship pilots and all who travel by sea, sailors and seafaring men, stood a long way off 18 and cried out when they saw the smoke from her burning, 'What city was like the great city?' 19 They threw dust on their heads and wept and mourned, crying out, 'Alas! alas for the great city where all who had ships on the sea grew rich from her great wealth! For in a single

BECK

foul *bird* [152] we loathe. 3 All *the nations* fell by *the wine of her*[115] immoral passion. *The kings of the earth have lived in sexual sin*[145] with her. And the wealth of her luxury has made the merchants of the earth rich."

4 Then I heard Someone else call from heaven:

Come out of her, My people,[153]
So you will not share her sins
Or suffer from any of her plagues.
5 Her sins *have reached up to heaven*.[154]
And God has remembered her crimes.
6 *Pay her back in her own coin*,[155]
And give her double *for what she has done*.[156]
Mix a double drink for her in the cup she mixed for others.
7 Give her as much torture and misery
As she gave glory to herself and *lived in luxury*,
Because *she thinks*, "I'm a queen on a throne,
I'm no widow, *and I'll never feel miserable*."

8 For that reason her plagues—death and misery and hunger—*will come on one day*,[157] and she will be *burned with fire*, because the Lord God, *who has judged* her, is *mighty*.[158]
9 *The kings of the earth who lived in sexual vice*[145] and luxury with her will weep and mourn over her when they see the smoke rise where she burns. 10 Frightened by her torture, they will stand far off and say: "Woe, woe to the great city, *the mighty city of Babylon!*[159] In one hour judgment has come on you."
11 And the merchants of the earth weep and mourn over her because nobody buys their loads of goods any more, 12 their loads of gold, silver, jewels, pearls, fine linen, purple, silk, and scarlet cloth, all kinds of citrus wood, all kinds of ivory goods, and all kinds of articles made of very costly wood, of copper, iron, and marble; 13 and cinnamon, ointment, incense, perfume, frankincense, wine, olive oil, fine wheat flour, wheat, cattle, sheep, horses, wagons, slaves—even *human beings*.[160] 14 The fruit you longed for is gone, all your fat and your splendor have perished, and nobody will ever find them again. 15 The people who traded in those things and whom she has made rich, frightened by her torture, will stand far off, weeping and mourning. 16 They will say, "Woe, woe to the great city that wore fine linen and purple and scarlet and ornaments of gold, jewels, and pearls. 17 In one hour all this wealth has been laid waste."
18 Every pilot and all who go anywhere in a ship, *sailors* and all others whose work is on the sea, *stood* far off *and shouted* when they saw the smoke rise where she was burning. "Was there ever a city as great as this?" they asked. 19 *They threw dust on their heads,* and *weeping and mourning,* they called:

Woe, woe to the great city,
Whose treasures have made everyone *rich*[161]
Who had a ship on the sea.
In one hour she's been laid waste.

[152] Is. 13:20-21; 34:11, 14
[153] Gen. 19:14; Is. 48:20; 52:11; Jer. 50:8; 51:6, 45
[154] Jer. 51:9
[155] Ps. 137:8
[156] Jer. 50:29
[157] Is. 47:8-9
[158] Jer. 50:32, 34
[159] Ezek. 26:17
[160] Ezek. 27:13
[161] Ezek. 27:29-33

[a] Lit., *power*.

K.J.V.

in one hour is she made desolate. 20 Rejoice over her, *thou* heaven, and *ye* holy apostles and prophets; for God hath avenged you on her. 21And a mighty angel took up a stone like a great millstone, and cast *it* into the sea, saying, Thus with violence shall that great city Babylon be thrown down, and shall be found no more at all. 22And the voice of harpers, and musicians, and of pipers, and trumpeters, shall be heard no more at all in thee; and no craftsman, of whatsoever craft *he be*, shall be found any more in thee; and the sound of a millstone shall be heard no more at all in thee; 23And the light of a candle shall shine no more at all in thee; and the voice of the bridegroom and of the bride shall be heard no more at all in thee: for thy merchants were the great men of the earth; for by thy sorceries were all nations deceived. 24And in her was found the blood of prophets, and of saints, and of all that were slain upon the earth.

19 And after these things I heard a great voice of much people in heaven, saying, Alleluia; Salvation, and glory, and honour, and power, unto the Lord our God: 2 For true and righteous *are* his judgments; for he hath judged the great whore, which did corrupt the earth with her fornication, and hath avenged the blood of his servants at her hand. 3And again they said, Alleluia. And her smoke rose up for ever and ever. 4And the four and twenty elders and the four beasts fell down and worshipped God that sat on the throne, saying, Amen; Alleluia. 5And a voice came out of the throne, saying, Praise our God, all ye his servants, and ye that fear him, both small and great. 6And I heard as it were the voice of a great multitude, and as the voice of many waters, and as the voice of mighty thunderings, saying, Alleluia: for the Lord God omnipotent reigneth. 7 Let us be glad and rejoice, and give honour to him: for the marriage of the Lamb is come, and his wife hath made herself ready. 8And to her was granted that she should be arrayed in fine linen, clean and white: for the fine linen is the righteousness of saints. 9And he saith unto me, Write, Blessed *are* they which are called unto the marriage supper of the Lamb. And he saith unto me, These are the true sayings of God. 10And I fell at his feet to worship him. And he said unto me, See *thou do it* not: I am thy fellow servant, and of thy brethren that have the testimony of Jesus: worship God: for the testimony of Jesus is the

N.A.S.

20 "Rejoice over her, O heaven, and you saints and apostles and prophets, because God has pronounced judgment for you against her." 21 And a strong angel took up a stone like a great millstone and threw it into the sea, saying, "Thus will Babylon, the great city, be thrown down with violence, and will not be found any longer. 22 "And the sound of harpists and musicians and flute-players and trumpeters will not be heard in you any longer; and no craftsman of any craft will be found in you any longer; and the sound of a mill will not be heard in you any longer; 23 and the light of a lamp will not shine in you any longer; and the voice of the bridegroom and bride will not be heard in you any longer; for your merchants were the great men of the earth, because all the nations were deceived by your sorcery. 24 "And in her was found the blood of prophets and of saints and of all who have been slain on the earth."

19 After these things I heard, as it were, a loud voice of a great multitude in heaven, saying,

"Hallelujah! Salvation and glory and power belong to our God; 2 BECAUSE HIS JUDGMENTS ARE TRUE AND RIGHTEOUS; for He has judged the great harlot who was corrupting the earth with her immorality, and HE HAS AVENGED THE BLOOD OF HIS BOND-SERVANTS ON HER." 3And a second time they said, "HALLELUJAH! HER SMOKE RISES UP FOREVER AND EVER." 4And the twenty-four elders and the four living creatures fell down and worshiped God who sits on the throne, saying, "Amen. Hallelujah!" 5And a voice came from the throne, saying,

"GIVE PRAISE TO OUR GOD, ALL YOU HIS BOND-SERVANTS, YOU WHO FEAR HIM, THE SMALL AND THE GREAT." 6And I heard, as it were, the voice of a great multitude and as the sound of many waters and as the sound of mighty peals of thunder, saying,

"Hallelujah! For the Lord our God, the Almighty, reigns. 7 "Let us rejoice and be glad and give the glory to Him, for the marriage of the Lamb has come and His bride has made herself ready." 8And it was given to her to clothe herself in fine linen, bright *and* clean; for the fine linen is the righteous acts of the saints. 9And he *said to me, "Write, 'Blessed are those who are invited to the marriage supper of the Lamb.'" And he *said to me, "These are true words of God." 10And I fell at his feet to worship him. And he *said to me, "Do not do that; I am a fellow-servant of yours and your brethren who hold the testimony of Jesus; worship God. For the testimony of Jesus is the spirit of prophecy."

hour she has been destroyed.' 20 Celebrate over her, O heaven, you saints, apostles, and prophets too, because God has taken vengeance on her for you."

21 Then a mighty angel picked up a stone like a huge millstone and hurled it into the sea, saying: "With violence like this, Babylon the great city will be hurled to ruin, and it will never be found again. 22 The sound of harpists, musicians, flute-players, and trumpeters will never be heard in you again. No craftsmen of any kind will ever be found in you again, and the sound of the grinding mill will never be heard in you again; 23 the light of the lamp will never shine in you again; the voice of bride and bridegroom will never be heard in you again. For your businessmen were the great men of the earth; by your magic all the nations have been led astray; 24 in her has been found the blood of prophets, saints, and all who have been slaughtered on the earth."

19 *He hears all heaven praising the Lord that the kingdom and feast of the Lord has come; sees Jesus riding a white horse as King of kings and Lord of lords; sees his foes utterly destroyed*

After this I heard something like the loud shout of a great multitude in heaven, saying: "Praise the Lord! Salvation, glory, and power belong to our God, 2 because His judgments are true and just. Because He has passed judgment on the notorious prostitute who corrupted the earth with her immorality, and for the blood of His slaves He has taken vengeance upon her!"

3 A second time they shouted, "Praise the Lord! For the smoke from her continues to go up forever and ever."

4 Then the twenty-four elders and the four living creatures fell down and worshiped God who was seated on the throne, saying, "Amen! Praise the Lord!"

5 And there came a voice from the throne, saying, "Praise our God, all you slaves of His who fear Him, great and small."

6 Then I heard something like the shout of a great multitude and the roar of many waters and the peal of mighty thunders, saying:

"Praise the Lord! For the Lord, our Almighty God, has now begun to reign! 7 Let us be glad and shout for joy and give Him glory, because the marriage of the Lamb has come, and His bride has made herself ready. 8 Permission has been granted her to dress in clean, brilliant linen, for linen signifies the upright deeds of God's people."

9 Then he said to me, "Write, 'Blessed are they who are invited to the marriage supper of the Lamb.' These," he said to me, "are the true words of God."

10 Then I fell before his feet to worship him, but he said to me, "You must take care not to do that. I am only a fellow-slave of yours and of your brothers who hold to the testimony borne by Jesus. Worship God. For the testimony borne by Jesus is the inspiring spirit of prophecy."

20 *Be happy* over her, *heaven,*
Holy *people,*[162] apostles and prophets,
Because God has punished her for you.

21 Then a mighty angel lifted up *a stone* like a large millstone, *threw it into* the sea, and said: "With *such* violence *will Babylon, the great* city, *be hurled down* and never be found again. 22 Singing with lyres and the *playing of musical instruments,* of flutes and trumpets, *will never be heard in you again.*[163] No skilled worker will ever be found in you again. The sound of a millstone will never be heard in you again. 23 *The light of a lamp* will never shine in you again. *The voices of a groom and a bride*[164] will never be heard in you again. Your *merchants were the great men of the world,*[165] but your magic deceived all the nations, 24 and there was found in you the blood of prophets and holy ones, of all who had been slaughtered on the earth.

Praise the Lord!

19 After that I heard what sounded like a large crowd in heaven calling out: "*Praise the Lord!*[166] Salvation, glory, and power belong to our God 2 because *His judgments are true and just*[167] and He has sentenced the great prostitute who corrupted the world with her sexual vice and *has punished* her *for the blood of His servants.*"[168]

3 Again they called: "*Praise the Lord!*[166] *The smoke goes up from her forever.*"[169]

4 And the twenty-four elders and the four living beings *bowed down and worshiped God,*[24] *sitting on the throne.*[32] They answered, *"So be it! Praise the Lord!"*[170]

5 Then a voice came from the throne and said, *"Praise our God, all His servants, you who fear Him, small and great."*[171]

The Lamb's Wedding

6 Then I heard what sounded *like the voices of a* large *crowd*[172] and *the noise of many waters*[173] and loud peals of thunder, saying, "*Praise the Lord! The Lord our God, the Almighty, is King.*[10, 174] 7 *Let us rejoice and be delighted*[175] and give Him glory because the marriage of the Lamb has come, and His bride has prepared herself. 8 She has been permitted to put on dazzling and pure linen. Her fine linen is the righteous living of the holy people."

9 Then he said to me: "Write: Happy are those who are invited to the Lamb's wedding dinner. These," he told me, "are God's true words."

10 I *bowed down at his feet to worship him.*[24] "Be careful! Don't do that!" he told me. "I'm a fellow servant of yours and of your fellow Christians who are speaking the truth told by Jesus. Worship God. The truth Jesus told is the Spirit's Word."

[162] Deut. 32:43; Is. 44:23; Jer. 51:48
[163] Jer. 51:63-64; Ezek. 26:12-13; Dan. 4:30
[164] Jer. 7:34; 16:9; 25:10
[165] Is. 23:8
[166] Ps. 104:35
[167] Ps. 19:9; 119:137
[168] Deut. 32:43; 2 Kings 9:7
[169] Is. 34:10
[170] Ps. 106:48
[171] Ps. 22:23; 115:13; 134:1; 135:1
[172] Dan. 10:5-6
[173] Ezek. 1:24; 43:2; Ps. 93:4
[174] Ps. 93:1; 97:1; 99:1
[175] Ps. 118:24

K.J.V.

spirit of prophecy. 11And I saw heaven opened, and behold a white horse; and he that sat upon him *was* called Faithful and True, and in righteousness he doth judge and make war. 12 His eyes *were* as a flame of fire, and on his head *were* many crowns; and he had a name written, that no man knew, but he himself. 13And he *was* clothed with a vesture dipped in blood: and his name is called The Word of God. 14And the armies *which were* in heaven followed him upon white horses, clothed in fine linen, white and clean. 15And out of his mouth goeth a sharp sword, that with it he should smite the nations; and he shall rule them with a rod of iron: and he treadeth the winepress of the fierceness and wrath of Almighty God. 16And he hath on *his* vesture and on his thigh a name written, KING OF KINGS, AND LORD OF LORDS. 17And I saw an angel standing in the sun; and he cried with a loud voice, saying to all the fowls that fly in the midst of heaven, Come and gather yourselves together unto the supper of the great God; 18 That ye may eat the flesh of kings, and the flesh of captains, and the flesh of mighty men, and the flesh of horses, and of them that sit on them, and the flesh of all *men, both* free and bond, both small and great. 19And I saw the beast, and the kings of the earth, and their armies, gathered together to make war against him that sat on the horse, and against his army. 20And the beast was taken, and with him the false prophet that wrought miracles before him, with which he deceived them that had received the mark of the beast, and them that worshipped his image. These both were cast alive into a lake of fire burning with brimstone. 21And the remnant were slain with the sword of him that sat upon the horse, which *sword* proceeded out of his mouth: and all the fowls were filled with their flesh.

20 And I saw an angel come down from heaven, having the key of the bottomless pit and a great chain in his hand. 2And he laid hold on the dragon, that old serpent, which is the Devil, and Satan, and bound him a thousand years, 3And cast him into the bottomless pit, and shut him up, and set a seal upon him, that he should deceive the nations no more, till the thousand years should be fulfilled: and after that he must be loosed a little season. 4And I saw thrones, and they sat upon them, and judgment was given unto them: and *I saw* the souls of them that were beheaded for the witness of Jesus, and for the word of God, and which had not worshipped the beast, neither his image, neither had received *his* mark upon their foreheads, or in their hands; and they lived and reigned with Christ a thousand years. 5 But the rest of the dead lived not again until the thousand years were finished. This *is* the first resurrection. 6 Blessed and holy *is* he that hath part in the first resurrection: on such the second death hath no power, but they shall be priests of God and of Christ, and shall reign with him a thousand

N.A.S.

11 And I saw heaven opened; and behold, a white horse, and He who sat upon it *is* called Faithful and True; and in righteousness He judges and wages war. 12And his eyes *are* a flame of fire, and upon His head *are* many diadems; and He has a name written *upon Him* which no one knows except Himself. 13And *He is* clothed with a robe dipped in blood; and His name is called The Word of God. 14And the armies which are in heaven, clothed in fine linen, white *and* clean, were following Him on white horses. 15And from His mouth comes a sharp sword, so that with it He may smite the nations; and He will rule them with a rod of iron; and He treads the wine press of the fierce wrath of God, the Almighty. 16And on His robe and on His thigh He has a name written, "KING OF KINGS, AND LORD OF LORDS."

17 And I saw an angel standing in the sun; and he cried out with a loud voice, saying to all the birds which fly in midheaven, "Come, assemble for the great supper of God; 18 in order that you may eat the flesh of kings and the flesh of [a]commanders and the flesh of mighty men and the flesh of horses and of those who sit on them and the flesh of all men, both free men and slaves, and small and great."

19 And I saw the beast and the kings of the earth and their armies, assembled to make war against Him who sat upon the horse, and against His army. 20And the beast was seized, and with him the false prophet who performed the signs in his presence, by which he deceived those who had received the mark of the beast and those who worshiped his image; these two were thrown alive into the lake of fire which burns with brimstone. 21And the rest were killed with the sword which came from the mouth of Him who sat upon the horse, and all the birds were filled with their flesh.

20 And I saw an angel coming down from heaven, having the key of the abyss and a great chain in his hand. 2And he laid hold of the dragon, the serpent of old, who is the Devil and Satan, and bound him for a thousand years, 3 and threw him into the abyss, and shut *it* and sealed *it* over him, so that he should not deceive the nations any longer, until the thousand years were completed; after these things he must be released for a short time.

4 And I saw thrones, and they sat upon them, and judgment was given to them. And I *saw* the souls of those who had been beheaded because of the testimony of Jesus and because of the word of God, and those who had not worshiped the beast or his image, and had not received the mark upon their forehead and upon their hand; and they came to life and reigned with Christ for a thousand years. 5 The rest of the dead did not come to life until the thousand years were completed. This is the first resurrection. 6 Blessed and holy is the one who has a part in the first resurrection; over these the second death has no power, but they will be priests of God and of Christ and will reign with Him for a thousand years.

[a] Lit., *chiliarchs,* in command of one thousand troops.

WILLIAMS

11 Then I saw heaven thrown open and a white horse appeared. His rider was called Faithful and True, and in justice He passes judgment and wages war. 12 His eyes were like coals of fire. On His head were many diadems, and on Him a name was written which no one knew but Himself. 13 He wore · a garment dipped in blood, and His name was the Word of God. 14 The armies of heaven, wearing pure white linen, followed Him on white horses. 15 From His mouth shot a sharp sword, so that He could smite the nations with it. He will rule them with a scepter of iron, and will tread the wine press of the raging wrath of the Almighty God. 16 On His garment and on His thigh He has this title written: King of kings and Lord of lords.

17 Then I saw an angel standing on the sun, and in a loud voice shouting to all the birds that fly in mid-air: "Come! Gather for God's great banquet, 18 to feast on the flesh of kings, generals, heroes, of horses and their riders; yes, the flesh of all men, freemen and slaves, great and small."

19 Then I saw the wild beast, the kings of the earth, and their armies gather to go to war with the Rider of the horse and His army. 20 Then the wild beast was captured and with him the false prophet who performed wonders in his presence, by which he led astray those who let the mark of the wild beast be put on them and worshiped his statue. Both of them were hurled alive into the fiery lake that burns with brimstone. 21 The rest were killed with the sword that shot from the mouth of the horse's Rider, and all the birds were gorged with their flesh.

20 *The devil is put into prison; the martyrs are enthroned in a new life; then the devil is let loose a little while; the resurrection and the judgment*

Then I saw an angel coming down from heaven with the key of the abyss and a great chain in his hand. 2 He seized the dragon, the ancient serpent, who is the devil and Satan, and bound him for a thousand years. 3 Then he hurled him into the abyss, closed it, and sealed it over him, to keep him from leading the nations astray any more, until the thousand years are at an end; after that he must be let loose a little while.

4 Then I saw thrones and those who were seated on them, and permission was granted them to pass judgment, even those who had been beheaded for bearing testimony to Jesus and for preaching the word of God, who refused to worship the wild beast and his statue, and would not let his mark be stamped upon their foreheads and upon thir hands. They lived and reigned with Christ a thousand years. 5 The rest of the dead did not live again until the thousand years had ended. This is the first resurrection. 6 Blessed and holy is the man who shares in the first resurrection! Over such the second death will have no power, but they will be priests of God and Christ, and reign with Him the thousand years.

BECK

The King of Kings

11 Then *I saw heaven opened,*[176] and there was a white horse, and its Rider is called Faithful and True. *He is righteous when He judges*[177] and goes to battle. 12 *His eyes are flames of fire,*[178] on His head are many crowns, and there's a name written on Him, but only He knows what it is. 13 He wears a garment dipped in blood and is called the Word of God. 14 Heaven's armies, dressed in pure, white linen, have been following Him on white horses. 15 A sharp sword comes *out of His mouth to strike down*[179] the nations, and He *will rule them with an iron rod* [21] and will *tread the winepress of* the fierce *anger*[180] *of Almighty God.*[10] 16 On His garment and on His thigh He has a name written:

KING OF KINGS AND LORD OF LORDS! [181]

17 Then I saw an angel standing in the sun, and he called out loud *to all the birds flying* in midair, *"Come together for* God's great banquet, 18 *to eat the bodies of* kings, generals, *warriors, of horses and their riders, of all people,*[182] free and slave, small and great."

19 Then I saw the animal and the *kings of the earth* with their armies *gathered* [183] to fight against the Rider on the horse and His army. 20 And the animal was captured and with it the false prophet who for it had done the miracles by which he deceived those who had received the animal's brand and *worshiped its statue.*[110] Both were thrown into the fiery lake of *burning sulfur.*[184] 21 And the sword that came out of the mouth of the Rider on the horse killed the rest, and all the birds gorged themselves on their bodies.

The Devil's Last Battle

20 Then I saw an angel coming down from heaven with the key to the abyss in his hand, and a big chain. 2 He took the dragon, the old *snake,*[185] that is, the *devil* or Satan,[186] bound him for a thousand years, 3 threw him into the abyss, and locked and sealed it over him so to keep him from deceiving the nations any more till the thousand years are over. After that he must be set free for a little while.

4 Then *I saw thrones,* and those who sat on them were *given authority to judge.*[187] I also saw the souls of those who had been beheaded for speaking the truth told by Jesus and God's Word. They had not *worshiped the* animal and its *statue*[110] and were not branded on their foreheads and hands. *They lived* and *ruled*[187] with Christ a thousand years. 5 The rest of the dead didn't live until the thousand years were over. This is the first resurrection. 6 Happy and holy are those who share in the first resurrection; the second death has no power over them, but they will be *priests of God* [188] and of Christ and will rule with Him during the thousand years.

[176] Ezek. 1:1
[177] Ps. 96:13; Is. 11:4-5
[178] Dan. 10:6
[179] Is. 11:4
[180] Joel 3:13; Is. 63:2-3; Lam. 1:15
[181] Deut. 10:17; Dan. 2:47
[182] Ezek. 39:4, 17-20
[183] Ps. 2:2
[184] Is. 30:33
[185] Gen. 3:1, 13
[186] Zech. 3:1
[187] Dan. 7:9, 22, 27
[188] Is. 61:6

K.J.V.

years. 7And when the thousand years are expired, Satan shall be loosed out of his prison, 8And shall go out to deceive the nations which are in the four quarters of the earth, Gog and Magog, to gather them together to battle: the number of whom *is* as the sand of the sea. 9And they went up on the breadth of the earth, and compassed the camp of the saints about, and the beloved city: and fire came down from God out of heaven, and devoured them. 10And the devil that deceived them was cast into the lake of fire and brimstone, where the beast and the false prophet *are*, and shall be tormented day and night for ever and ever. 11And I saw a great white throne, and him that sat on it, from whose face the earth and the heaven fled away; and there was found no place for them. 12And I saw the dead, small and great, stand before God; and the books were opened: and another book was opened, which is *the book* of life: and the dead were judged out of those things which were written in the books, according to their works. 13And the sea gave up the dead which were in it; and death and hell delivered up the dead which were in them: and they were judged every man according to their works. 14And death and hell were cast into the lake of fire. This is the second death. 15And whosoever was not found written in the book of life was cast into the lake of fire.

21 And I saw a new heaven and a new earth: for the first heaven and the first earth were passed away; and there was no more sea. 2And I John saw the holy city, new Jerusalem, coming down from God out of heaven, prepared as a bride adorned for her husband. 3And I heard a great voice out of heaven saying, Behold, the tabernacle of God *is* with men, and he will dwell with them, and they shall be his people, and God himself shall be with them, *and be* their God. 4And God shall wipe away all tears from their eyes; and there shall be no more death, neither sorrow, nor crying, neither shall there be any more pain: for the former things are passed away. 5And he that sat upon the throne said, Behold, I make all things new. And he said unto me, Write: for these words are true and faithful. 6And he said unto me, It is done. I am Alpha and Omega, the beginning and the end. I will give unto him that is athirst of the fountain of the water of life freely. 7 He that overcometh shall inherit all things; and I will be his God, and he shall be my son. 8 But the fearful, and unbelieving, and the abominable, and murderers, and whoremongers, and sorcerers,

N.A.S.

7 And when the thousand years are completed, Satan will be released from his prison, 8 and will come out to deceive the nations which are in the four corners of the earth, Gog and Magog, to gather them together for the war; the number of them is like the sand of the seashore. 9And they came up on the broad plain of the earth and surrounded the camp of the saints and the beloved city, and fire came down from heaven and devoured them. 10And the devil who deceived them was thrown into the lake of fire and brimstone, where the beast and the false prophet are also; and they will be tormented day and night forever and ever. 11 And I saw a great white throne and Him who sat upon it, from whose presence earth and heaven fled away, and no place was found for them. 12And I saw the dead, the great and the small, standing before the throne, and books were opened; and another book was opened, which is *the book* of life; and the dead were judged from the things which were written in the books, according to their deeds. 13And the sea gave up the dead which were in it, and death and Hades gave up the dead which were in them; and they were judged, every one *of them* according to their deeds. 14And death and Hades were thrown into the lake of fire. This is the second death, the lake of fire. 15And if anyone's name was not found written in the book of life, he was thrown into the lake of fire.

21 And I saw a new heaven and a new earth; for the first heaven and the first earth passed away, and there is no longer *any* sea. 2And I saw the holy city, new Jerusalem, coming down out of heaven from God, made ready as a bride adorned for her husband. 3And I heard a loud voice from the throne, saying, "Behold, the tabernacle of God is among men, and He shall dwell among them, and they shall be His peoples, and God Himself shall be among them,[a] 4 and He shall wipe away every tear from their eyes; and there shall no longer be *any* death; there shall no longer be *any* mourning, or crying, or pain; the first things have passed away." 5And He who sits on the throne said, "Behold, I am making all things new." And He *said*, "Write, for these words are faithful and true." 6And He said to me, "It is done. I am the Alpha and the Omega, the beginning and the end. I will give to the one who thirsts from the spring of the water of life without cost. 7 "He who overcomes shall inherit these things, and I will be his God and he will be My son. 8 "But for the cowardly and unbelieving and abominable and murderers and immoral persons and sorcerers and idolaters and all liars, their part *will be* in the lake

---

[a] Some ancient mss. add, *and be their God.*

WILLIAMS

7 When the thousand years have ended,
Satan will be let loose from his prison. 8 He will
go forth to lead astray the nations that are in
the four corners of the earth, Gog and Magog,
and to muster them for battle, and their number will be like the sands of the seashore.
9 They came up on the broad plain of the
earth and surrounded the camp of God's people, and the beloved city. Then fire came down
from heaven and consumed them. 10 Then the
devil who led them astray was hurled into the
fiery lake of burning brimstone, where the wild
beast and false prophet were, and there they
are to be tortured day and night forever and
ever.
11 Then I saw a great white throne and Him
who was seated on it, from whose presence
earth and sky fled away, no more to be found.
12 I saw the dead, great and small, standing
before the throne, and books were opened.
Then another book was opened; it was the
book of. life. And the dead were judged by
what was written in the books in accordance
with what they had done. 13 The sea gave up
the dead that were in it, and death and the
underworld[a] gave up the dead that were in
them, and they were all judged in accordance
with what they had done. 14 Then death and
the underworld were hurled into the fiery lake.
This is the second death—the fiery lake. 15 If
anyone's name was not found written in the
book of life, he was hurled into the fiery lake.

<h3 style="text-align:center">21</h3>

21 *He sees the new Jerusalem; the earth
becomes a new creation; the splendors
of the new Jerusalem, its precious
stones, its sanctuary, its sun*

Then I saw a new heaven and a new earth,
for the first heaven and the first earth had
passed away, and there was no longer any sea.
2 And I saw the new Jerusalem, the holy city,
coming down out of heaven from God, made
ready like a bride to join her husband.
3 Then I heard a loud voice from the throne
say: "See! God's dwelling place is with men,
and He will live with them, 4 and He will wipe
every tear from their eyes. There will be no
death any longer, no sorrow, no crying, no
pain. The first order of things has passed
away."
5 Then He who was seated on the throne
said, "See! I am making everything new." He
continued, "Write this, for these words are
trustworthy and true." 6 He further said to me:
"They have come true. I am the Alpha and the
Omega, the beginning and the end. I myself,
without cost, will give to anyone who is thirsty
water from the springs of living water. 7 Whoever conquers will come into possession of these
things, and I will be his God and he will be my
son. 8 But the cowards, the unfaithful, the
polluted, the murderers, the sexually immoral,
the practicers of magic, the worshipers of
idols, and all liars will have their portion in the

[a] *Hades*, the unseen world where all the dead
are.

BECK

7 When the thousand years are over, the
devil will be freed from his prison 8 and will
come out to deceive the nations in all parts of
the world—that is, *Gog and Magog*[189]—to
gather them for battle; they will be as many
as the sand by the sea.
9 So they came up, *spreading over the
earth,*[190] and surrounded the camp of the holy
people and the city He loves. But *fire came
down from heaven and consumed them.*[83] 10 And
the devil who deceived them was thrown into
the lake of *fire and sulfur,*[191] where the animal
and the false prophet are, and they will be
tortured day and night forever.

The Judgment

11 Then *I saw a* great white *throne* and *Him
sitting on it*[82] *from whom the earth*[192] *and the
sky* fled so far *they couldn't be found anywhere.*[99] 12 Then I saw the dead, great and small,
standing before the throne, and *books were
opened.*[193] Another book also was opened—it
was *the book of life.*[107] And the dead were judged
according to what they had done as it was written in the books. 13 The sea gave up the dead
that were in it, and death and the grave gave
up the dead that were in them, and each one
was judged *according to what he had done.*[194]
14 Then death and the grave were thrown into
the fiery lake. The fiery lake is the second death.
15 And if anyone wasn't found *written in the
book of life,*[107] he was thrown into the fiery lake.

The New Jerusalem

21 Then I saw *a new heaven and a new
earth,*[195] because the first heaven and the
first earth had passed away. And there was no
longer any sea. 2 And I saw *the holy city,* a new
Jerusalem,*[196] coming down from God in heaven,
dressed as a bride,*[197] ready to meet her husband.
3 And I heard a loud voice from the throne
say: "Look! *God's home is among the people,
and He will live with them. They will be His
people,*[198] *and God Himself will be with them.*[199]
4 *He will wipe* every *tear from their eyes.* There
will be *no* more *death,*[61] and there will be no
more grief or crying or pain, because the first
things have passed away."
5 "Look! *I am making* everything *new,*"[200]
said *He who sat on the throne.*[8] And He added,
"Write this because these words are true and
you can trust them." 6 Then He said to me,
"It is done! I am A and Z, the Beginning and
the End. *To anyone who is thirsty* I will give
water, that costs nothing,[201] from the spring of
the *water of life.*[202] 7 Be victorious, and you
will have these things, and *I will be your God,
and you will be My son.*[203]
8 "But cowardly, untrustworthy, and abominable people, and those who murder, sin sexually, practice witchcraft, and worship idols, and

[189] Ezek. 38:2
[190] Hab. 1:6
[191] Gen. 19:24
[192] Ps. 114:7
[193] Dan. 7:10
[194] Ps. 28:4; 62:12
[195] Is. 65:17; 66:22
[196] Is. 52:1
[197] Is. 61:10
[198] Ezek. 37:27; Zech. 2:10
[199] Is. 7:14; 8:8, 10
[200] Is. 43:19
[201] Is. 55:1
[202] Zech. 14:8
[203] 2 Sam. 7:14; Ps. 69:26-27; Zech. 8:8

K.J.V.

and idolaters, and all liars, shall have their part in the lake which burneth with fire and brimstone: which is the second death. 9And there came unto me one of the seven angels which had the seven vials full of the seven last plagues, and talked with me, saying, Come hither, I will shew thee the bride, the Lamb's wife. 10And he carried me away in the spirit to a great and high mountain, and shewed me that great city, the holy Jerusalem, descending out of heaven from God, 11 Having the glory of God: and her light *was* like unto a stone most precious, even like a jasper stone, clear as crystal; 12And had a wall great and high, *and* had twelve gates, and at the gates twelve angels, and names written thereon, which are *the names* of the twelve tribes of the children of Israel: 13 On the east three gates; on the north three gates; on the south three gates; and on the west three gates. 14And the wall of the city had twelve foundations, and in them the names of the twelve apostles of the Lamb. 15And .he that talked with me had a golden reed to measure the city, and the gates thereof, and the wall thereof. 16And the city lieth foursquare, and the length is as large as the breadth: and he measured the city with the reed, twelve thousand furlongs. The length and the breadth and the height of it are equal. 17And he measured the wall thereof, a hundred *and* forty *and* four cubits, *according to* the measure of a man, that is, of the angel. 18And the building of the wall of it was *of* jasper: and the city *was* pure gold, like unto clear glass. 19And the foundations of the wall of the city *were* garnished with all manner of precious stones. The first foundation *was* jasper; the second, sapphire; the third, a chalcedony; the fourth, an emerald; 20 The fifth, sardonyx; the sixth, sardius; the seventh, chrysolite; the eighth, beryl; the ninth, a topaz; the tenth, a chrysoprasus; the eleventh, a jacinth; the twelfth, an amethyst. 21And the twelve gates *were* twelve pearls; every several gate was of one pearl: and the street of the city *was* pure gold, as it were transparent glass. 22And I saw no temple therein: for the Lord God Almighty and the Lamb are the temple of it. 23And the city had no need of the sun, neither of the moon, to shine in it: for the glory of God did lighten it, and the Lamb *is* the light thereof. 24And the nations of them which are saved shall walk in the light of it: and the kings of the earth do bring their glory and honour into it. 25And the gates of it shall not be shut at all by day: for there shall be no night there. 26And they shall bring the glory and honour of the nations into it. 27And there shall in no wise enter into it any thing that defileth, neither *whatsoever* worketh abomination, or *maketh* a lie: but they which are written in the Lamb's book of life.

22 And he shewed me a pure river of water of life, clear as crystal, proceeding out of the throne of God and of the Lamb. 2 In the

N.A.S.

that burns with fire and brimstone, which is the second death."

9 And one of the seven angels who had the seven bowls full of the seven last plagues, came and spoke with me, saying, "Come here, I shall show you the bride, the wife of the Lamb." 10And he carried me away *a*in the Spirit to a great and high mountain, and showed me the holy city, Jerusalem, coming down out of heaven from God, 11 having the glory of God. Her brilliance was like a very costly stone, as a stone of crystal-clear jasper. 12 It had a great and high wall, with twelve gates, and at the gates twelve angels; and names *were* written on them, which are *those* of the twelve tribes of the children of Israel. 13 *There were* three gates on the east and three gates on the north and three gates on the south and three gates on the west. 14And the wall of the city had twelve foundation stones, and on them *were* the twelve names of the twelve apostles of the Lamb. 15And the one who spoke with me had a gold measuring rod to measure the city, and its gates and its wall. 16And the city is laid out as a square, and its length is as great as the width; and he measured the city with the rod, *b*fifteen hundred miles; its length and width and height are equal. 17And he measured its wall, *c*seventy-two yards, *according to* human measurements, which are *also* angelic *measurements*. 18And the material of the wall was jasper; and the city was pure gold, like clear glass. 19 The foundation stones of the city wall were adorned with every kind of precious stone. The first foundation stone was jasper; the second, sapphire; the third, chalcedony; the fourth, emerald; 20 the fifth, sardonyx; the sixth, sardius; the seventh, chrysolite; the eighth, beryl; the ninth, topaz; the tenth, chrysoprase; the eleventh, jacinth; the twelfth, amethyst. 21And the twelve gates were twelve pearls; each one of the gates was a single pearl. And the street of the city was pure gold, like transparent glass. 22And I saw no temple in it, for the Lord God, the Almighty, and the Lamb, are its temple. 23And the city has no need of the sun or of the moon to shine upon it, for the glory of God has illumined it, and its lamp *is* the Lamb. 24And the nations shall walk by its light, and the kings of the earth shall bring their glory into it. 25And in the daytime (for there shall be no night there) its gates shall never be closed; 26 and they shall bring the glory and the honor of the nations into it; 27 and nothing unclean and no one who practices abomination and lying, shall ever come into it, but only those whose names are written in the Lamb's book of life.

22 And he showed me a river of the water of life, clear as crystal, coming from the throne of God and of *d*the Lamb, 2 in the mid-

[a] Or, *in spirit.* [b] Lit., *twelve thousand stadia;* a stadion was about 600 ft. [c] Lit., *one hundred forty-four cubits.* [d] Or, *the Lamb. In the middle of its street, and on either side of the river, was.*

WILLIAMS

lake that keeps on burning with fire and brimstone. This is the second death."

9 Then one of the seven angels who had the seven bowls that were full of the seven plagues came and talked with me, and said, "Come; I will show you the bride, the wife of the Lamb."

10 So he carried me off under the power of the Spirit to a great, high mountain and showed me Jerusalem, the holy city, coming down out of heaven from God; 11 and it continued to retain the glory of God. The luster of it was like a very precious stone, like jasper, clear as crystal. 12 It had a great, high wall, with twelve huge gates, and twelve angels in charge of the gates, which had inscribed upon them the names of the twelve tribes of Israel. 13 There were three gates on the east, three gates on the north, three gates on the south, and three gates on the west. 14 The wall of the city had twelve foundation stones, and on them were the twelve names of the Lamb's twelve apostles. 15 The angel who was talking with me had a measuring rod of gold, to measure the city, its gates and wall. 16 The city lies in a square, its length the same as its breadth. He measured the city with his rod, and it was one thousand, five hundred miles. Its length, breadth, and height were the same. 17 He measured its wall, two hundred and sixteen feet as a man measures, which is the way the angel measured.

18 The material of its wall was jasper, but the city itself was pure gold, as transparent as glass. 19 The foundation stones of the city's wall were ornamented with all sorts of precious stones. The first foundation stone was jasper, the second sapphire, the third chalcedony, the fourth emerald, 20 the fifth sardonyx, the sixth sardius, the seventh chrysolite, the eighth beryl, the ninth topaz, the tenth chrysoprase, the eleventh jacinth, the twelfth amethyst. 21 The twelve gates were twelve pearls, each gate built of a single pearl. The Broadway of the city was pure gold, as transparent as glass.

22 I saw no temple in it, for the Lord God Almighty Himself and the Lamb Himself are its temple. 23 The city does not need the sun or moon to shine in it, for the glory of God has lighted it, and the Lamb is its lamp. 24 The nations will walk by its light; the kings of the earth will bring their splendor into it. 25 Its gates will never be closed by day—for there will be no night there—26 and they will bring the splendor and honor of the nations into it. 27 Nothing unclean will ever enter it, nor anyone who practices abominable living and lying, but only those who are written in the Lamb's book of life.

BECK

all liars will find themselves in the lake *burning with fire and sulfur;*[204] this is the second death."

9 Then came one of those seven angels with the seven bowls full of the *seven* last *plagues.*[205] "Come," He said to me, "I will show you the bride, the Lamb's wife."

10 He carried me in spirit *on a* large and *high mountain* and showed me *the holy city of Jerusalem*[206] coming down from God in heaven. 11 *It has God's glory*[207] and a brilliance like a very precious stone, like jasper that is clear as crystal. 12 It has a large, high wall with *twelve gates,* and at the gates twelve angels, and on the gates *are written the names of the twelve tribes of Israel.* 13 There are *three gates on the east side, three gates on the north, three gates on the south, and three gates on the west.*[208] 14 And the wall of the city has twelve foundation stones, and on them are the twelve names of the twelve apostles of the Lamb.

15 The angel who was talking to me had a golden *measuring rod*[209] to measure the city, its gates, and its wall. 16 The city is *square*[210]— it is as wide as it is long. He measured the city with the rod—it is fifteen hundred miles.* Its length, breadth, and height are the same. 17 Then he measured its wall; it is seventy-two yards as people measure—and angels too.

18 Its wall is made of jasper, but the city is of gold as pure as clear glass. 19 *The foundations* of the city wall are made beautiful with all kinds of precious stones: the first foundation stone is jasper, the second *sapphire,*[211] the third agate, the fourth emerald, 20 the fifth sardonyx, the sixth carnelian, the seventh chrysolite, the eighth beryl, the ninth topaz, the tenth chrysoprase, the eleventh jacinth, the twelfth amethyst. 21 The twelve gates are twelve pearls; each gate is made of one pearl. The street of the city is of gold as pure as clear glass.

22 But I didn't see any temple in it, because the *Lord God, the Almighty,*[10] and the Lamb are its temple. 23 And the city doesn't need *any sun or moon to give it light,* because *God's glory is its light,*[212] and the Lamb is its lamp. 24 *The nations will walk by its light, and the kings* of the earth *will bring* their glory into it. 25 Its *gates will never be shut any day,*[213] because *there will be no night*[214] there. 26 People will bring the glory and wealth of the nations into it. 27 But *nothing unclean will ever come into it,*[215] or anyone who does anything abominable or tells lies, only those who are *written in the Lamb's book of life.*[107]

---

22 *He sees the river of life and the tree of life; is assured that what he sees will certainly come to pass; the Lord is coming soon; he makes a last, loving invitation; that book not to be tampered with*

Then he showed me a river of living water, clear as crystal, which continued to flow from the throne of God and of the Lamb 2 down the

22 Then he showed me a river of the *water of life,* bright as crystal, *flowing from*[216] the throne of God and of the Lamb 2 and down

* This seems to be the length of one side.
[204] Is. 30:33
[205] Lev. 26:21
[206] Is. 52:1; Ezek. 40:2
[207] Is. 58:8; 60:1-2, 19
[208] Ex. 28:21; Ezek. 48:31-35
[209] Ezek. 40:3, 5
[210] Ezek. 43:16
[211] Is. 54:11
[212] Is. 60:19
[213] Is. 60:3, 5, 11
[214] Zech. 14:7
[215] Is. 52:1
[216] Ezek. 47:1, 12; Joel 3:18; Zech. 14:8

[a] *12,000 stadia equal 1,500 miles.*

K.J.V.

midst of the street of it, and on either side of the river, *was there* the tree of life, which bare twelve *manner of* fruits, *and* yielded her fruit every month: and the leaves of the tree *were* for the healing of the nations. 3And there shall be no more curse: but the throne of God and of the Lamb shall be in it; and his servants shall serve him: 4And they shall see his face; and his name *shall be* in their foreheads. 5And there shall be no light there; and they need no candle, neither light of the sun; for the Lord God giveth them light: and they shall reign for ever and ever. 6And he said unto me, These sayings *are* faithful and true: and the Lord God of the holy prophets sent his angel to shew unto his servants the things which must shortly be done. 7 Behold, I come quickly: blessed *is* he that keepeth the sayings of the prophecy of this book. 8And I John saw these things, and heard *them*. And when I had heard and seen, I fell down to worship before the feet of the angel which shewed me these things. 9 Then saith he unto me, See *thou do it* not: for I am thy fellow servant, and of thy brethren the prophets, and of them which keep the sayings of this book: worship God. 10And he saith unto me, Seal not the sayings of the prophecy of this book: for the time is at hand. 11 He that is unjust, let him be unjust still: and he which is filthy, let him be filthy still: and he that is righteous, let him be righteous still: and he that is holy, let him be holy still. 12And, behold, I come quickly; and my reward *is* with me, to give every man according as his work shall be. 13 I am Alpha and Omega, the beginning and the end, the first and the last. 14 Blessed *are* they that do his commandments, that they may have right to the tree of life, and may enter in through the gates into the city. 15 For without *are* dogs, and sorcerers, and whoremongers, and murderers, and idolaters, and whosoever loveth and maketh a lie. 16 I Jesus have sent mine angel to testify unto you these things in the churches. I am the root and the offspring of David, *and* the bright and morning star. 17And the Spirit and the bride say, Come. And let him that heareth say, Come. And let him that is athirst come. And whosoever will, let him take the water of life freely. 18 For I testify unto every man that heareth the words of the prophecy of this book, If any man shall add unto these things, God shall add unto him the plagues that are written in this book: 19And if any man shall take away from the words of the book of this prophecy, God shall take away his part out of the book of life, and out of the holy city, and *from* the things which are written in this book. 20 He which testifieth these things saith, Surely I come quickly: Amen. Even so, come, Lord Jesus. 21 The grace of our Lord Jesus Christ *be* with you all. Amen.

N.A.S.

dle of its street. And on either side of the river was the tree of life, bearing twelve *kinds of* fruit, yielding its fruit every month; and the leaves of the tree were for the healing of the nations. 3And there shall no longer be any curse; and the throne of God and of the Lamb shall be in it, and His bond-servants shall serve Him; 4 and they shall see His face, and His name *shall be* on their foreheads. 5And there shall no longer be *any* night; and they shall not have need of the light of a lamp nor the light of the sun, because the Lord God shall illumine them; and they shall reign forever and ever.

6 And he said to me, "These words are faithful and true"; and the Lord, the God of the spirits of the prophets, sent His angel to show to His bond-servants the things which must shortly take place. 7 "And behold, I am coming quickly. Blessed is he who heeds the words of the prophecy of this book."

8 And I, John, am the one who heard and saw these things. And when I heard and saw, I fell down to worship at the feet of the angel who showed me these things. 9And he *said to me, "Do not do that; I am a fellow-servant of yours and of your brethren the prophets and of those who heed the words of this book; worship God."

10 And he *said to me, "Do not seal up the words of the prophecy of this book, for the time is near. 11 "Let the one who does wrong, still do wrong; and let the one who is filthy, still be filthy; and let the one who is righteous, still practice righteousness; and let the one who is holy, still keep himself holy. 12 "Behold, I am coming quickly, and My reward is with Me, to render to every man according to what he has done. 13 "I am the Alpha and the Omega, the first and the last, the beginning and the end." 14 Blessed are those who wash their robes, that they may have the right to the tree of life, and may enter by the gates into the city. 15 Outside are the dogs and the sorcerers and the immoral persons and the murderers and the idolaters, and everyone who loves and practices lying.

16 "I, Jesus, have sent My angel to testify to you these things for the churches. I am the root and the offspring of David, the bright morning star."

17 And the Spirit and the bride say, "Come." And let the one who hears say, "Come." And let the one who is thirsty come; let the one who wishes take the water of life without cost.

18 I testify to everyone who hears the words of the prophecy of this book: if anyone adds to them, God shall add to him the plagues which are written in this book; 19 and if anyone takes away from the words of the book of this prophecy, God shall take away his part from the tree of life and from the holy city, which are written in this book.

20 He who testifies to these things says, "Yes, I am coming quickly." Amen. Come, Lord Jesus.

21 The grace of the Lord Jesus be with *all. Amen.

[a] Or, crops of *fruit.* [b] Some ancient mss. read *the saints.*

WILLIAMS

middle of the city's Broadway. On both sides of the river grew the tree of life, which bore twelve kinds of fruit, yielding a different kind each month, and its leaves contained the remedy to cure the nations. 3 No longer will there be anything that has a curse on it. The throne of God and of the Lamb will be in the city, and His slaves will worship Him. 4 They will see His face, and His name will be on their foreheads. 5 There will be no night any longer; so they will need no lamplight nor sunlight, for the Lord God will give them light, and they will rule forever and ever.

6 Then he said to me: "These words are trustworthy and true; the Lord, the God of the spirits of the prophets, sent His angel to show His slaves what must soon take place. 7 See! I am coming soon! Blessed is he who practices the truths of prophecy contained in this book."

8 It is I, John, who heard and saw these things. When I heard and saw them, I fell at the feet of the angel who was showing them to me, to worship him. 9 But he said to me: "You must be careful not to do that; I am only a fellow-slave of yours, of your brothers the prophets, and of the people who practice the truths contained in this book. Worship God."

10 Then he said to me: "Do not seal up the words of prophecy contained in this book, for the time of their coming true is near. 11 Let the person who is doing evil do evil still; let the filthy person be filthy still; let the upright person still do right; let the consecrated person still be consecrated.

12 "See! I am coming soon, and my rewards are with me, to repay each one just as his work has been. 13 I am the Alpha and the Omega, the first and the last, the beginning and the end. 14 Blessed are those who wash their robes, so as to have a right to the tree of life and to enter the gates of the city. 15 The dogs, that is, those who practice magic and immorality, murderers, idolaters, and who love and practice lying, are on the outside.

16 "I, Jesus, sent my angel to bear this testimony to you for the churches. I belong to the line and family of David; I am the bright morning star."

17 The Spirit and the bride say, "Come." Let everyone who hears this say, "Come." Let everyone who is thirsty come. Let everyone who wishes come and take the living water without any cost.

18 I warn everyone who hears the words of prophecy contained in this book that if anyone adds anything to it, God will add to him the plagues that are described in this book; 19 and if anyone subtracts from it some of the words of this prophetic book, God will subtract from him his share in the tree of life and the holy city which are described in this book.

20 He who testifies to this says, "Yes, I am coming soon!"

Amen! Come, Lord Jesus!

21 The spiritual blessing of the Lord Jesus be with His people.

BECK

the middle of the street of the city. *On each side of the river is a tree of life, producing twelve kinds of fruit, for each month its own fruit; and the leaves of the tree are to heal* [217] the nations. 3 *There will no longer be anything that is cursed.*[218]

The throne of God and of the Lamb will be in the city. His servants will worship Him 4 and *see Him,*[219] and His name will be on their foreheads. 5 *There will be no more night,*[214] and they will not need any light of a lamp or of *the sun* because *the Lord God will shine*[220] on them, and *they will be kings forever.*[221]

I Am Coming Soon

6 "You can trust these words," he told me; "they are true. And the Lord, the God of the spirits of the prophets, has sent His angel to show His servants *what must happen*[1] soon. 7 Remember, *I am coming*[222] soon! Happy is he who keeps what the prophecy of this book tells him."

8 I, John, heard and saw these things, and when I had heard and seen them, I *bowed down to worship*[24] at the feet of the angel who showed them to me.

9 "Be careful! Don't do that!" he told me. "I'm a fellow servant of yours and of the other Christians, the prophets, and those who keep what this book says. Worship God.

10 "*Don't keep secret* what the prophecy of *this book* tells you," he said to me, "because the *time*[223] is near when it will come true. 11 Let *the wrongdoer still do wrong,*[224] the filthy one still be filthy, and let the righteous one still do right and the holy one still be holy."

12 "Yes, *I am coming*[222] soon and *will have my reward with me* to *pay everyone according to what he has done.*[225] 13 I am A and Z, *the first and the last,*[18] the Beginning and the End. 14 Happy are those who *wash their robes*[226] so that they have the right to *the tree of life*[227] and go through the gates into the city. 15 Outside are the dogs and people who do witchcraft, sin sexually, murder, worship idols, and everyone who loves lies and sins.

16 "I, Jesus, have sent my angel to tell you these truths for the churches. I am *David's Descendant*[41] and the bright morning Star."

17 "Come!" say the Spirit and the bride. If you hear this, say, "Come!" *If you are thirsty, come.* If you want it, take *the water of life—it costs nothing.*[228]

18 I warn everyone who hears what the prophecy of this book tells him: If you *add anything to this,* God will *add to you* the plagues *written in this book.* 19 And if you *take away* any words in this book of prophecy, *God will take away*[229] your share in *the tree of life*[227] and in the holy city that are described in this book.

20 He who spoke these truths says: "Yes, *I am coming*[222] soon!"

Certainly! Come, Lord Jesus!

The love of the Lord Jesus be with all the holy people. Amen.

[217] Gen. 2:9; 3:22, 24; Ezek. 47:7, 12
[218] Zech. 14:11
[219] Ps. 17:15; 42:2
[220] Is. 60:19
[221] Dan. 7:18, 22, 27
[222] Dan. 8:26; 12:4
[223] Dan. 8:26; 12:4
[224] Dan. 12:10
[225] Ps. 28:4; 62:12; Is. 40:10
[226] Gen. 49:11
[227] Gen. 2:9; 3:22, 24
[228] Is. 55:1; Zech. 14:8
[229] Deut. 4:2; 13:1; 29:19-20